PAN BOOKS ED

Cassell's Compact
German - English
English - German
Dictionary

The emphasis of the dictionary is on straightforward
contemporary German, while including some of the most
common literary and poetical terms.

The needs of the traveller and tourist, the reader of
contemporary literature and of newspapers and magazines,
and the student of science and technology have
also been kept in mind.

Phonetic pronunciation, using the symbols of the
International Phonetic Association, is given in brackets
after each word with a key to pronunciation at the front
of the book.

There is detailed advice to the user, tables of German and
English irregular verbs, a list of abbreviations and
numerical tables are also included.

'These excellent foreign-language dictionaries.'
American Publishers' Weekly

PAN BOOKS EDITION OF

Cassell's Compact German-English

English-German Dictionary

Compiled by

H.-C. Sasse
MA(Adel.), M Litt(Cantab.), Lecturer in German
in the University of Newcastle upon Tyne

Dr J. Horne
Lecturer in German in the University
of Birmingham

Dr Charlotte Dixon

Pan Books London and Sydney

Cassell's Compact German-English, English-German Dictionary
First published 1925
Fifth edition (revised and enlarged) 1936
Twentieth edition 1964
Cassell's New Compact
German-English, English-German Dictionary
First published 1966
Second edition first published 1966 by Cassell & Co Ltd
This edition published 1970 by Pan Books Ltd,
Cavaye Place, London SW10 9PG
7th printing 1979
© Cassell & Co Ltd 1966
ISBN 0 330 02536 8
Printed in Great Britain by Cox & Wyman Ltd,
London, Reading and Fakenham

Contents

Preface   vi

Advice to the User   viii

Zur Benutzung

des Wörterbuches   ix

Key to Pronunciation   xiv

List of Abbreviations   xvi

German-English Dictionary   1

English-German Dictionary   301

German Irregular Verbs   520

English Irregular Verbs   534

Numerical Tables   541

Preface

Among the difficulties that arise in the compilation of a Compact Dictionary that of the selection of words is undoubtedly the most formidable one. The decision as to what to include and, much more difficult, what to exclude, must to a considerable extent depend on the type of student of a foreign language who is most likely to use it. Primarily a dictionary of this kind is intended for the student in the earlier stages of learning German, whether at school or university. As the study of German, even at an early stage, is likely to include the reading of literary texts from the eighteenth century onwards, it was felt that some attention at least must be paid to the inclusion of words no longer in common use today but frequently found in the prescribed texts, whether poetry, drama or prose. That in this respect severe limitations are imposed by the very concept of a 'Compact' Dictionary is of course obvious, but an attempt has been made to include at least some of the most common literary and poetical terms. However, the main emphasis throughout must of course be on straightforward contemporary German. In addition to the needs of the student, those of the traveller and the tourist, of the reader of contemporary literature and of newspapers and magazines, have been kept in mind. It is hoped that the student of science and technology too will find the dictionary useful, though in his case additional reference must of course be made to one of the growing number of specialized works dealing with the technical vocabulary of his particular discipline.

The aim of a Compact Dictionary must be to achieve some kind of viable compromise between conciseness on the one hand and completeness on the other. To make the dictionary as helpful as possible—given only a limited amount of space—certain economies were called for. Omissions were inevitable. What is similarly inevitable is that, except in the most obvious cases, no two experts are likely

to agree as to what may safely be omitted unless (as was attempted here) one makes frequency of usage and general usefulness the main criteria.

It should be remembered, lastly, that this is a concise dictionary which cannot remotely hope to do justice to all the finer meanings and nuances of two highly developed and complex languages. But it is hoped that the student and reader of German, especially in the earlier stages of learning the language, will find here all the help he needs.

For more detailed reference the user will find Cassell's New German Dictionary (ed. Dr. H. T. Betteridge) of considerable help, while the Duden works of reference on German are regarded as the authoritative last word on matters of controversy. In the final analysis there will always be areas of doubt and dispute. That is the prerogative of a living and developing language.

Finally, thanks are due on behalf of the publishers to Prof. W. E. Collinson, late of the University of Liverpool, who acted in a consultative capacity.

H.-C. Sasse

Advice to the User

As a guide to the nature of words which have inevitably been omitted from a dictionary of this size, it may be helpful to state that, when a German *Fremdwort* is identical with the corresponding English term and possesses no grammatical peculiarities, it appears only in the English–German section. For example, it was felt that the word *Atom* (and *a fortiori* derivative compounds such as *Atomphysik*) was unlikely to perplex any English reader and it has therefore been omitted from the German–English, but included in the English–German, section. For the same reason, a somewhat similar plan has been followed with regard to the names of countries. These have mostly been given in German–English only, whereas the corresponding nouns and adjectives of nationality or race are given in English–German only.

Arrangement of Entries

Strict alphabetical order seemed to be most helpful in a dictionary intended primarily for readers in the earlier stages of acquiring a knowledge of German. Within the entries themselves literal meanings and frequency of usage determine the sequence of definitions. Admittedly the second criterion is to a considerable extent a matter of personal linguistic judgment, indeed of *Sprachgefühl*, but it is hoped that in most cases the reader will thereby more readily discover the meaning of any particular word. It can generally be assumed that definitions separated by commas have much the same meaning, whereas differences in meaning or usage are marked by semicolons. Where it was thought desirable and feasible to include idiomatic phrases, relative frequency of usage appeared a more helpful criterion than strict alphabetic sequence.

Words which are spelt alike but are etymologically distinct

Zur Benutzung des Wörterbuches

Ein Hinweis auf die Art der Wörter, auf die in einem Taschenwörterbuch unweigerlich verzichtet werden muss, wird dem Leser die Anwendung dieses Nachschalwerkes gewiss erleichtern: Ein deutsches Fremdwort, das mit dem entsprechenden englischen Ausdruck identisch ist und keine grammatikalischen Besonderheiten aufweist, erscheint als Stichwort nicht in beiden Sprachen, sondern wird nur im englisch–deutschen Teil aufgeführt. Man darf wohl annehmen, dass ein Wort wie z.B. *Atom* (und *a fortiori* abgeleitete Zusammensetzungen wie *Atomphysik*) einen englischen Leser kaum verwirren wird, weshalb es denn auch im deutsch–englischen Teil weggelassen, indessen im englisch–deutschen Teil berücksichtigt wurde. Aus dem gleichen Grunde wurde bei den Namen von Ländern ein ähnliches Prinzip beachtet. Diese wurden in der Regel nur im deutsch–englischen Teil aufgeführt, während die entsprechenden Substantive und Adjektive der Nationalität oder Rasse nur im englisch–deutschen Teil erscheinen.

Anordnung der Stichwörter

Die strikte alphabetische Reihenfolge schien vorteilhaft für ein Nachschlagwerk, das in erster Linie für Lernende gedacht ist, die die deutsche Sprache noch nicht völlig beherrschen. Bei den gegebenen Übersetzungen eines Stichwortes bestimmen die wörtliche Übertragung sowie die Häufigkeit des Gebrauches die Folge der Definitionen. Gewiss ist das zweite Kriterium weitgehend eine Angelegenheit der persönlichen linguistischen Beurteilung, in der Tat des Sprachgefühls. Doch ist zu hoffen, dass der Leser in den meisten Fällen gerade dadurch der Bedeutung eines Begriffes näher kommt. Allgemein gilt, dass durch ein Komma getrennte Wörter eine annähernd gleiche Bedeutung haben, während Unterschiede in Bedeutung oder Anwendung

have been given separate, numbered entries for the sake of clarity.

A word should be added on the subject of compounds. Most students of German come to realize before long that the notoriously long German nouns, far from complicating the understanding of the language, are merely a matter of syntactical and grammatical convenience, a device for structural conciseness within a given sentence construction. In a 'Compact' Dictionary only such compounds can be given which have a meaning which can be arrived at only with difficulty or not at all. Where a compound is not given, the constituent parts of the word should be looked up. The meaning should then become self-evident.

Grammar

Parts of Speech. These are indicated by abbreviations in italics (*adj.*, *v.a.* etc.), the meaning of which will be found in the List of Abbreviations. It has not been felt necessary to indicate the nature of English proper names.

Genders. In the German-English section nouns are denoted by their gender (*m.*, *f.* or *n.*). In the English-German section gender is shown by the definite article preceding the noun; in a series of nouns the gender is sometimes omitted when it is the same as that of the preceding noun or nouns.

Declension. The Genitive singular and Nominative plural of German nouns are given in parentheses after the gender. The plurals of English nouns are not given, except for certain very irregular forms. The cases governed by prepositions have been included.

Verbs. In both German and English the indication *irr.* refers the user to the tables of Irregular Verbs. Where a compound irregular verb is not given, its forms are identical with those of the simple irregular verb in the table. "To" is omitted from English infinitives throughout. German inseparable verbs are described as such only when there is any possibility of doubt, *e.g.* in the case of prepositional prefixes. Where prefixes are axiomatically always part of an

Zur Benutzung des Wörterbuches

durch ein Semikolon markiert sind. Wo es als notwendig und durchführbar erachtet wurde, idiomatische Redewendungen zu zitieren, schien die relative Häufigkeit der Anwendung ein nützlicheres Kriterium als die strenge alphabetische Folge. Orthographisch gleiche Wörter, die sich durch ihre etymologische Herkunft unterscheiden, wurden um der Klarheit willen als einzelne Stichwörter aufgeführt und mit Ziffern versehen. Noch ein Wort zum Thema der Wortzusammensetzungen: Die meisten Deutschlernenden werden bald erkennen, dass die berüchtigt langen deutschen Substantive das Verständnis der Sprache keineswegs erschweren. Sie sind lediglich eine Sache syntaktischer und grammatikalischer Vereinfachung, ein Hilfsmittel zu struktureller Kürze und Prägnanz innerhalb einer gegebenen Satzbildung. In einem Taschenwörterbuch können allein solche Wortverbindungen berücksichtigt werden, die nur mit Mühe oder überhaupt nicht abzuleiten sind. Ist eine Wortverbindung nicht angeführt, so sollten die einzelnen Bestandteile nachgesehen werden. Auf diese Weise wird sich der Sinn der Zusammensetzung von selbst ergeben.

Grammatik

Wortarten. Sie sind in abgekürzter Form durch Kursivschrift gekennzeichnet (*adj.*, *v.a.* etc.). Eine Erläuterung der Abkürzungen findet sich im Verzeichnis der Abkürzungen. Es wurde nicht für nötig befunden, die Zugehörigkeit von Eigennamen anzuzeigen.

Geschlecht. Im deutsch–englischen Teil sind die Substantive mit ihrem Geschlecht (*m.*, *f.* oder *n.*) gekennzeichnet. Im englisch–deutschen Teil ist das Geschlecht durch den bestimmten Artikel vor dem Substantiv angegeben. In einer Reihe aufeinanderfolgender Definitionen wurde der Artikel dort weggelassen, wo er mit dem vorhergehenden übereinstimmt.

Deklination. Die Endungen des Genitiv Singular und des Nominativ Plural deutscher Substantive sind in Klammern nach der Bezeichnung des Geschlechtes eingefügt. Der

Advice to the User

inseparable verb (*be-*, *ent-*, *zer-* etc.) no such information is given, as it is assumed that the student will be familiar with the function of these prefixes long before he comes to use a dictionary.

Phonetics. Phonetic transcriptions, using the symbols of the International Phonetic Association, are given throughout for all entries in both sections of the dictionary as a help to correct pronunciation. The mark ' precedes the syllable which carries the stress. The glottal stop is not indicated.

Numbers. Only the most common numerals appear in the body of the dictionary. However, fuller coverage is given in the separate Numerical Tables.

Zur Benutzung des Wörterbuches

Plural englischer Substantive wurde nicht berücksichtigt ausser bei einigen stark unregelmässigen Formen. Fälle, die von Präpositionen regiert werden, wurden aufgenommen.

Verben. Im Deutschen wie im Englischen weist die Anmerkung *irr.* den Leser auf die Tabellen unregelmässiger Verben hin. Ist ein zusammengesetztes Verb nicht angeführt, so sind seine Formen mit denen des einfachen Verbs in der Tabelle identisch. "To" vor englischen Infinitivformen wurde durchgehend weggelassen. Deutsche untrennbare Verben werden nur dort als solche gekennzeichnet, wo Zweifel möglich sind, also bei Verben mit präpositionalen Vorsilben. Wo Vorsilben grundsätzlich Teile eines untrennbaren Verbes (*be-*, *ent-*, *zer-* etc.) bilden, ist kein solcher Hinweis angebracht, da angenommen werden darf, dass der Lernende die Funktion dieser Vorsilben kennt, lange bevor er dazu kommt, ein Wörterbuch zu konsultieren.

Phonetik. Jedes einzelne Stichwort ist auch in seiner phonetischen Transkription wiedergegeben. Dabei wurden die phonetischen Symbole der *International Phonetic Association* benutzt. Der Akzent ′ steht jeweils unmittelbar vor der betonten Silbe. Der Knacklaut ist indessen nicht markiert.

Zahlwörter. Nur die gebräuchlichsten Zahlen erscheinen im Hauptteil des Wörterbuches. Eine ausführliche Zusammenstellung findet sich in den besonderen Zahlentabellen.

Key to Pronunciation

Vowels

Phonetic Symbol	German Example	Phonetic Symbol	English Example
a	lassen ['lasən]	i:	seat [si:t]
a:	haben ['ha:bən], Haar [ha:r]	i	finish ['finiʃ], physic ['fizik]
ɛ	häßlich ['hɛslıç], Geld [gɛlt]	e	neck [nek]
ɛ:	Märchen ['mɛ:rçən], Zähne ['tsɛ:nə]	æ	man [mæn], malefactor ['mælifæktə]
e	Medizin [medi'tsi:n]	ɑ:	father ['fɑ:ðə], task [tɑ:sk]
e:	leben ['le:bən], See [ze:], lehnen ['le:nən]	ɔ	block [blɔk], waddle [wɔdl]
ə	rufen ['ru:fən]	ɔ:	shawl [ʃɔ:l], tortoise ['tɔ:təs]
ı	Fisch [fıʃ], Mystik ['mıstık]	o	domain [do'mein]
i	Militär [mili'tɛ:r]	u	good [gud], July [dʒu'lai]
i:	Berlin [bɛr'li:n], Liebe ['li:bə], ihm [i:m]	u:	moon [mu:n], tooth [tu:θ]
ɔ	Kopf [kɔpf]	ʌ	cut [kʌt], somewhere ['sʌmwɛə]
o	mobil [mo'bi:l]	ə:	search [sə:tʃ], surgeon ['sə:dʒən]
o:	Rose ['ro:zə], Boot [bo:t], ohne ['o:nə]	ə	cathedral [kə'θi:drəl], never ['nevə]
œ	Mörder ['mœrdər]		
ø	möblieren [mø'bli:rən]		
ø:	Löwe ['lø:və], Röhre ['rø:rə]		
u	Hund [hunt]		
u:	gut [gu:t], Uhr [u:r]		
y	fünf [fynf], Symbol [zym'bo:l]		
y:	Lübeck ['ly:bɛk], Mühe ['my:ə]		

Diphthongs

Phonetic Symbol	German Example	Phonetic Symbol	English Example
aı	Eis [aıs], Waise ['vaızə]	ei	great [greit]
au	Haus [haus]	ou	show [ʃou]
ɔy	Beute ['bɔytə], Gebäude [gə'bɔydə]	ai	high [hai]
		au	crowd [kraud]
		ɔi	boy [bɔi]
		iə	steer [stiə]
		ɛə	hair [hɛə]
		uə	moor [muə]

Consonants

Phonetic Symbol	German Example	Phonetic Symbol	English Example
ç	Blech [blɛç], ich [ıç]	p	paper ['peipə]
f	Vater ['fa:tər]	b	ball [bɔ:l]
j	ja [ja:]	t	tea [ti:], train [trein]
ŋ	bringen ['brıŋən]	d	deed [di:d]
s	beißen ['baisən], wißen ['visən], los [lo:s]	k	cake [keik], quest [kwest]
ʃ	schon [ʃo:n]	g	game [geim]
ts	Cäcilie [tsɛ'tsi:ljə], Zimmer ['tsimər]	m	mammoth ['mæməθ]
v	weiß [vais]	n	nose [nouz], nanny ['næni]
x	Bach [bax], kochen ['kɔxən], ruchbar ['ru:xba:r]	ŋ	bring [briŋ], finger ['fiŋgə]
z	lesen ['le:zən]	f	fair [fɛə], far [fɑ:]
b	Biene ['bi:nə]	v	vine [vain]
d	Dach [dax]	θ	thin [θin], bath [bɑ:θ]
g	geben ['ge:bən]	ð	thine [ðain], bathe [beið]
h	hier [hi:r]	s	since [sins]
k	Koch [kɔx], quartieren [kwar'ti:rən]	z	busy ['bizi]
l	Lied [li:t]	l	land [lænd], hill [hil]
m	Mirakel [mi'ra:kəl]	ʃ	shield [ʃi:ld], sugar ['ʃugə]
n	Nase ['na:zə]	ʒ	vision ['viʒən]
p	Probe ['pro:bə]	r	rat [ræt], train [trein]
r	rot [ro:t]	h	here [hiə], horse [hɔ:s]
t	Tisch [tiʃ]	x	coronach ['kɔrənæx], loch [lɔx]

Semi-Consonants

j	yellow ['jelou], yes [jes]
w	wall [wɔ:l]

List of Abbreviations

abbr.	abbreviation (of), abbreviated	*m.*	masculine
Acc.	Accusative	*Maths.*	Mathematics
adj.	adjective	*Meas.*	Measurement
adv.	adverb	*Mech.*	Mechanics
Agr.	agriculture	*Med.*	Medicine
Am.	American(ism)	*Met.*	Meteorology
Anat.	Anatomy	*Metall.*	Metallurgy
Archæol.	Archæology	*Mil.*	Military
Archit.	Architecture	*Min.*	Mining
Arith.	Arithmetic	*Motor.*	Motoring
art.	article	*Mount.*	Mountaineering
Astrol.	Astrology	*Mus.*	Music
Astron.	Astronomy	*Myth.*	Mythology
Austr.	Austrian	*n.*	neuter
aux.	auxiliary	*Naut.*	Nautical
Aviat.	Aviation	*Nav.*	Navigation
Bibl.	Biblical	*o.('s)*	one('s)
Bot.	Botany	*o.s.*	oneself
Br.	British	*obs.*	obsolete
Build.	Building	*Orn.*	Ornithology
Carp.	Carpentry	*p.*	person
Chem.	Chemistry	*Parl.*	Parliament
coll.	colloquial	*part.*	particle
collec.	collective	*pej.*	pejorative
Comm.	Commerce	*pers.*	person(al)
comp.	comparative	*Phil.*	Philosophy
conj.	conjunction	*Phonet.*	Phonetics
Cul.	Culinary	*Phot.*	Photography
Dat.	Dative	*Phys.*	Physics
def.	definite	*Physiol.*	Physiology
defect.	defective	*pl.*	plural
dem.	demonstrative	*Poet.*	Poetical
dial.	dialect	*Pol.*	Political
Eccl.	Ecclesiastical	*poss.*	possessive
Econ.	Economics	*p.p.*	past participle
Elec.	Electricity	*prec.*	preceded
emph.	emphatic	*pred.*	predicative
Engin.	Engineering	*prep.*	preposition
Ent.	Entomology	*pron.*	pronoun
excl.	exclamation	*Psych.*	Psychology
f.	feminine	*r.*	reflexive
fig.	figurative	*Rad.*	Radio
Fin.	Finance	*Railw.*	Railways
Footb.	Football	*reg.*	regular
Genit.	Genitive	*Rel.*	Religion
Geog.	Geography	*rel.*	relative
Geol.	Geology	*s.*	substantive
Geom.	Geometry	*Sch.*	School
Gram.	Grammar	*Scot.*	Scottish
Gymn.	Gymnastics	*sing.*	singular
Her.	Heraldry	*sl.*	slang
Hist.	History	*s.th.*	something
Hunt.	Hunting	*Tail.*	Tailoring
imper.	imperative	*Tech.*	Technical
impers.	impersonal	*Teleph.*	Telephone
Ind.	Industry	*temp.*	temporal
indecl.	indeclinable	*Text.*	Textiles
indef.	indefinite	*Theat.*	Theatre
infin.	infinitive	*Theol.*	Theology
insep.	inseparable	*Transp.*	Transport
int.	interjection	*Typ.*	Typography
interr.	interrogative	*Univ.*	University
intim.	intimate	*us.*	usually
iron.	ironical	*v.a.*	active *or* transitive verb
irr.	irregular	*v.n.*	neuter *or* intransitive verb
Ling.	Linguistics	*v.r.*	reflexive verb
Lit.	Literary	*Vet.*	Veterinary Science
Log.	Logic	*vulg.*	vulgar
		Zool.	Zoology

Cassell's German-English Dictionary

A

A, a [a:], *n. das A* (des —s, die —s) the letter A; (*Mus.*) the note A; *A Dur*, A major; *A Moll*, A minor.

Aal [a:l], *m.* (—s, *pl.* —e) eel.

Aas [a:s], *n.* (—es, *pl.* Äser *or* —e) carcass, carrion.

ab [ap], *adv.* off; down; away; (*Theat.*) exit *or* exeunt, — *und zu*, now and again, occasionally; *auf und* —, up and down, to and fro. — *prep.* from; — *Hamburg*, from Hamburg.

abändern ['apɛndərn], *v.a.* alter.

Abart ['apa:rt], *f.* (—, *pl.* —en) variety, species.

Abbau ['apbau], *m.* (—s, *no pl.*) demolition, dismantling; reduction (of staff).

abberufen ['apbəru:fən], *v.a. irr.* recall.

abbestellen ['apbəʃtɛlən], *v.a.* countermand, annul, cancel (an order).

Abbild ['apbɪlt], *n.* (—es, *pl.* —er) copy, image.

Abbildung ['apbɪlduŋ], *f.* (—, *pl.* —en) illustration.

Abbitte ['apbɪtə], *f.* (—, *pl.* —n) apology; — *leisten*, — *tun*, apologise.

abblenden ['apblɛndən], *v.a.* dim (lights).

Abbruch ['apbrux], *m.* (—s, *pl.* ⸚e) breaking off; demolition; *einer Sache* — *tun*, damage s.th.

abdanken ['apdaŋkən], *v.n.* resign, abdicate, retire (from office).

abdecken ['apdɛkən], *v.a.* uncover, unroof; clear (the table).

Abdruck ['apdruk], *m.* (—s, *pl.* —e) impression, copy, reprint, cast.

Abend ['a:bənt], *m.* (—s, *pl.* —e) evening, eve.

Abendbrot ['a:bəntbro:t], *n.* (—s, *no pl.*) evening meal, (*Am.*) supper.

Abendland ['a:bəntlant], *n.* (—es, *no pl.*) occident, west.

Abendmahl ['a:bəntma:l], *n.* (—s, *no pl.*) supper; *das heilige* —, Holy Communion, the Lord's Supper.

abends ['a:bənts], *adv.* in the evening, of an evening.

Abenteuer ['a:bəntɔyər], *n.* (—s, *pl.* —) adventure.

aber ['a:bər], *conj.* but, however; (*emphatic*) — *ja*! yes, indeed! of course! —*prefix.* again, once more.

Aberglaube ['a:bərglaubə], *m.* (—ns, *no pl.*) superstition.

abermals ['a:bərma:ls], *adv.* again, once more.

Abessinien [abɛ'si:njən], *n.* Abyssinia.

abfahren ['apfa:rən], *v.n. irr.* (*aux.* sein) set out, depart, drive off.

Abfall ['apfal], *m.* (—s, *pl.* ⸚e) scrap, remnant; secession; slope; (*pl.*) waste, refuse.

abfallen ['apfalən], *v.n. irr.* (*aux.* sein) fall off; desert; slope.

abfällig ['apfɛlɪç], *adj.* derogatory.

abfangen ['apfaŋən], *v.a. irr.* intercept, catch.

abfärben ['apfɛrbən], *v.n.* (*colours*)run; stain; lose colour.

abfassen ['apfasən], *v.a.* compose, draft.

abfertigen ['apfɛrtɪgən], *v.a.* despatch; deal with, serve (a customer *or* client).

abfeuern ['apfɔyərn], *v.a.* fire (off), launch (rocket, missile).

abfinden ['apfɪndən], *v.a. irr.* indemnify, compound with (o.'s creditors). —*v.r. sich* — *mit*, put up with, come to terms with.

Abflug ['apflu:k], *m.* (—s, *pl.* ⸚e) takeoff, departure (by air).

Abfluß ['apflus], *m.* (—sses, *pl.* ⸚sse) flowing off; drain.

Abfuhr ['apfu:r], *f.* (—, *pl.* —en) removal, collection (of refuse); (*coll.*) rebuff.

abführen ['apfy:rən], *v.a.* arrest, lead away. —*v.n.* (*Med.*) act as a purgative.

Abführmittel ['apfy:rmɪtəl], *n.* (—s, *pl.* —) purgative, laxative.

Abgabe ['apga:bə], *f.* (—, *pl.* —n) delivery, tax, duty, levy.

abgabepflichtig ['apga:bəpflɪçtɪç], *adj.* taxable, subject to duty.

Abgang ['apgaŋ], *m.* (—(e)s, *pl.* ⸚e) wastage, loss; departure; *Schul*—, school-leaving.

abgängig ['apgɛŋɪç], *adj.* lost, missing; (*of goods*) saleable.

abgeben ['apge:bən], *v.a. irr.* deliver, cede; give (an opinion). — *v.r. sich mit etwas*, — concern o.s. with s.th.

abgedroschen ['apgədrɔʃən], *adj.* (*phrases etc.*) trite, hackneyed.

abgefeimt ['apgəfaɪmt], *adj.* cunning, crafty.

abgegriffen ['apgəgrɪfən], *adj.* well thumbed, worn.

abgehen ['apge:ən], *v.n. irr.* (*aux.* sein) leave, retire; branch off; (*Theat.*) make an exit.

abgelebt ['apgəle:pt], *adj.* (*of humans*) decrepit, worn out.

abgelegen ['apgəle:gən], *adj.* remote, distant.

abgemacht ['apgəmaxt], *adj.*, *int.* agreed! done!

abgeneigt ['apgənaɪkt], *adj.* disinclined, averse.

Abgeordnete ['apgəɔrdnətə], *m.*, *f.* (—n, *pl.* —n) political representative, deputy, Member of Parliament.

Abgesandte ['apgəzantə], *m.*, *f.* (—n, *pl.* —n) delegate, ambassador.

abgeschieden [′apgəʃiːdən], *adj.* secluded, remote; deceased.

abgeschmackt [′apgəʃmakt], *adj.* insipid.

abgesehen [′apgəzeːən], *adv.* — *von*, apart from, except for.

abgespannt [′apgəʃpant], *adj.* worn out, run down, exhausted.

abgestorben [′apgəʃtɔrbən], *adj.* dead, numb.

abgetan [′apgətaːn], *adj.* finished, over, done with; *damit ist die Sache* —, that finishes the matter.

abgetragen [′apgətraːgən], *adj.* (*clothes*) shabby, threadbare.

abgewöhnen [′apgəvøːnən], *v.a. einem etwas* —, free (rid) s.o. from (of) a habit, wean from.

abgrasen [′apgraːzən], *v.a.* (*animals*) graze.

Abgrund [′apgrunt], *m.* (—es, *pl.* ⁻e) abyss, precipice.

Abguss [′apgus], *m.* (—es, *pl.* ⁻e) cast, plaster-cast, mould.

abhalten [′aphaltən], *v.a. irr.* restrain, hold back; hold (meeting etc.).

abhandeln [′aphandəln], *v.a. einem etwas* —, bargain for s.th.

abhanden [ap′handən], *adv.* mislaid; — *kommen*, get lost.

Abhandlung [′aphandluŋ], *f.* (—, *pl.* —en) treatise, dissertation; (*pl.*) proceedings.

Abhang [′aphaŋ], *m.* (—es, *pl.* ⁻e) slope; declivity.

abhängen [′aphɛŋən], *v.a. irr.* take off, unhook; *von etwas oder jemandem* —, depend on s.th. or s.o.

abhärten [′aphɛrtən], *v.a.* inure against rigours, toughen.

abheben [′apheːbən], *v.a. irr.* draw (money from bank).

abhold [′aphɔlt], *adj.* averse to (*Dat.*).

abholen [′aphoːlən], *v.a. etwas* —, fetch, collect s.th.; *einen* —, meet s.o. (at the station etc.).

Abitur [abi′tuːr], *n.* (—s, *no pl.*) matriculation examination.

Abiturient [abitu′rjɛnt], *m.* (—en, *pl.* —en) matriculation candidate.

Abkehr [′apkeːr], *f.* (—, *no pl.*) turning away, renunciation.

abklären [′apklɛːrən], *v.a.* (*Chem.*) filter, clear.

Abkommen [′apkɔmən], *n.* (—s, *pl.* —) treaty, agreement, contract.

Abkömmling [′apkœmliŋ], *m.* (—s, *pl.* —e) descendant.

abkühlen [′apkyːlən], *v.a.* cool, chill.

Abkunft [′apkunft], *f.* (—, *no pl.*) descent, origin.

abkürzen [′apkyrtsən], *v.a.* shorten, abridge, curtail.

abladen [′apladən], *v.a. irr.* unload, dump.

Ablaß [′aplas], *m.* (—sses, *pl.* ⁻sse) (*Eccl.*) indulgence.

ablassen [′aplasən], *v.n. irr. von etwas* —, desist from, refrain from s.th.; *v.a. einem etwas billig* —, reduce the price of s.th. for s.o.

Ablauf [′aplauf], *m.* (—es, *no pl.*) (*water*) drainage; (*ticket*) expiration; lapse (of time); (*bill*) maturity.

ablaufen [′aplaufən], *v.n. irr.* (*aux.* sein) (*water*) run off; (*ticket*) expire; *gut* —, turn out well.

Ableben [′apleːbən], *n.* (—s, *no pl.*) decease, death.

ablegen [′apleːgən], *v.a.* (*clothes*) take off; (*documents*) file; *Rechenschaft* —, account for; *eine Prüfung* —, take an examination.

Ableger [′apleːgər], *m.* (—s, *pl.* —) (*Hort.*) cutting.

Ablegung [′apleːguŋ], *f.* (—, *no pl.*) making (of a vow); taking (of an oath).

ablehnen [′apleːnən], *v.a.* refuse, decline.

ableiten [′aplaitən], *v.a.* divert, draw off; (*water*) drain; (*words*) derive from.

ablenken [′aplɛŋkən], *v.a.* (*aux.* haben) *einen von etwas* —, divert s.o.'s attention from s.th., distract.

ablesen [′apleːzən], *v.a. irr.* (*meter*) read off; (*field*) glean.

abliefern [′apliːfərn], *v.a.* deliver.

ablösen [′apløːzən], *v.a. einen* —, take the place of s.o., (*Mil.*) relieve; detach (a stamp from a letter etc.).

abmachen [′apmaxən], *v.a.* undo, detach; settle, arrange.

abmagern [′apmaːgərn], *v.n.* (*aux.* sein) get thinner, waste away.

Abmarsch [′apmarʃ], *m.* (—es, *no pl.*) (*Mil.*) marching off.

abmelden [′apmɛldən], *v.r. sich* —, give notice of departure.

abmessen [′apmɛsən], *v.a. irr.* measure (off), gauge.

abmühen [′apmyːən], *v.r. sich* —, exert o.s., strive.

Abnahme [′apnaːmə], *f.* (—, *pl.* —n) decline, loss of weight; (*moon*) waning; (*goods*) taking delivery.

abnehmen [′apneːmən], *v.n. irr.* lose weight; (*moon*) wane. — *v.a.* (*hat*) take off; *einem etwas* —, relieve s.o. (of trouble *or* work).

Abneigung [′apnaiguŋ], *f.* (—, *pl.* —en) antipathy, dislike.

abnutzen [′apnutsən], *v.a.* wear out by use.

Abonnement [abɔnə′maŋ], *n.* (—s, *pl.* —s) (*newspaper*) subscription; (*railway*) season-ticket.

Abonnent [abɔ′nɛnt], *m.* (—en, *pl.* —en) subscriber.

abonnieren [abɔ′niːrən], *v.a.* subscribe to (a paper).

Abordnung [′apɔrdnuŋ], *f.* (—, *pl.* —en) delegation, deputation.

Abort [a′bɔrt], *m.* (—s, *pl.* —e) lavatory, toilet.

Abortus [a′bɔrtus], *m.* (—us, *no pl.*) (*Med.*) abortion.

abplagen [′applaːgən], *v.r. sich* —, slave, toil.

abprallen [′appralən], *v.n.* (*aux.* sein) *von etwas* —, bounce off, rebound.

abquälen ['apkvɛ:lən], *v.r. sich* —, toil, make o.s. weary (*mit*, with).

abraten ['apra:tən], *v.n. irr. einem von etwas* —, dissuade s.o. from, advise *or* warn s.o. against.

abräumen ['aprɔymən], *v.a.* remove; *den Tisch* —, clear the table.

abrechnen ['aprɛçnən], *v.a.* reckon up. — *v.n. mit einem* —, settle accounts with s.o., (*coll.*) get even with s.o.

Abrede ['apre:də], *f.* (—, *pl.* —**n**) agreement, arrangement; *in* — *stellen*, deny.

abreißen ['apraɪsən], *v.a. irr.* tear off.

abrichten ['aprıçtən], *v.a.* (*dogs*) train, (*horses*) break in.

abriegeln ['apri:gəln], *v.a.* bolt, bar.

Abriß ['aprıs], *m.* (—**sses**, *pl.* —**sse**) sketch; summary, synopsis.

abrollen ['aprɔlən], *v.a.* uncoil. — *v.n.* (*aux. sein*) roll off.

abrücken ['aprʏkən], *v.a.* move away. —*v.n.* (*aux. sein*) (*Mil.*) march off.

Abruf ['apru:f], *m.* (—**es**, *no pl.*) recall (from a post).

abrunden ['aprundən], *v.a.* round off.

abrupfen ['aprupfən], *v.a.* (*feathers*) pluck; (*flowers*) pluck off.

abrüsten ['aprʏstən], *v.n.* disarm.

Abrüstung ['aprʏstuŋ], *f.* (—, *no pl.*) disarmament.

abrutschen ['aprutʃən], *v.n.* (*aux. sein*) slide, slither down.

Absage ['apza:gə], *f.* (—, *pl.* —**n**) cancellation, refusal.

absagen ['apza:gən], *v.n.* refuse, beg to be excused, decline (an invitation).

Absatz ['apzats], *m.* (—**es**, *pl.* ⁝**e**) (*shoe*) heel; (*letter*) paragraph; (*Comm.*) *guter* —, ready sale.

abschaffen ['apʃafən], *v.a.* abolish, do away with.

abschälen ['apʃɛ:lən], *v.a.* peel. — *v.r. sich* —, peel off.

abschätzen ['apʃɛtsən], *v.a.* estimate, appraise; (*taxes*) assess.

Abschaum ['apʃaum], *m.* (—**es**, *no pl.*) scum.

Abscheu ['apʃɔy], *m.* (—**s**, *no pl.*) abhorrence, detestation, loathing.

abscheulich ['apʃɔylıç], *adj.* abominable, repulsive.

abschieben ['apʃi:bən], *v.a. irr.* shove off, push off; *schieb ab!* scram!

Abschied ['apʃi:t], *m.* (—**s**, *pl.* —**e**) leave, departure, farewell; discharge; resignation.

abschießen ['apʃi:sən], *v.a. irr.* shoot off; discharge; (*gun*) fire; *den Vogel* —, win the prize.

abschinden ['apʃındən], *v.r. irr. sich* —, exhaust o.s. with hard work.

abschirren ['apʃırən], *v.a.* unharness.

abschlagen ['apʃla:gən], *v.a. irr.* (*attack*) beat off; (*branches*) lop off; *einem etwas* —, deny s.o. s.th.; *eine Bitte* —, refuse a request.

abschlägig ['apʃlɛgıç], *adj.* negative.

Abschlagszahlung ['apʃlakstsa:luŋ], *f.* (—, *pl.* —**en**) payment by instalments.

abschleifen ['apʃlaɪfən], *v.a. irr.* grind off.

abschleppen ['apʃlɛpən], *v.a.* (*car*) tow (away). — *v.r. sich* —, wear o.s. out by carrying heavy loads.

abschließen ['apʃli:sən], *v.a. irr.* lock up; (*work*) conclude; (*accounts*) balance; *einen Vertrag* —, conclude an agreement.

Abschluß ['apʃlus], *m.* (—**sses**, *pl.* ⁝**sse**) settlement, winding-up.

abschneiden ['apʃnaɪdən], *v.a. irr.* cut off. — *v.n. gut* —, come off well.

Abschnitt ['apʃnıt], *m.* (—**es**, *pl.* —**e**) section; (*book*) paragraph.

abschnüren ['apʃny:rən], *v.a.* lace up, tie up.

abschrecken ['apʃrɛkən], *v.a.* deter, frighten.

abschreiben ['apʃraɪbən], *v.a. irr.* copy, transcribe; crib; *eine Schuld* —, write off a debt.

Abschrift ['apʃrıft], *f.* (—, *pl.* —**en**) copy, transcript, duplicate; *beglaubigte* —, certified copy.

Abschuß ['apʃus], *m.* (—**sses**, *pl.* ⁝**sse**) act of firing (a gun), shooting down (aircraft).

abschüssig ['apʃʏsıç], *adj.* steep.

abschütteln ['apʃʏtəln], *v.a.* shake off, cast off.

abschwächen ['apʃvɛçən], *v.a.* weaken, diminish.

abschweifen ['apʃvaɪfən], *v.n.* (*aux. sein*) digress (from), deviate.

abschwenken ['apʃvɛŋkən], *v.n.* (*aux. sein*) wheel off (*or* aside).

abschwören ['apʃvø:rən], *v.a. irr.* abjure, renounce by oath.

absehbar ['apze:ba:r], *adj.* imaginable, conceivable, foreseeable.

absehen ['apze:ən], *v.a., v.n. irr. einem etwas* —, copy s.th. from s.o.; *auf etwas* —, aim at s.th.; *von etwas* —, waive s.th.; refrain from s.th.

abseits ['apzaɪts], *adv., prep.* (*Genit.*) aside; — *von*, away from.

Absender ['apzɛndər], *m.* (—**s**, *pl.*—) sender; (*Comm.*) consigner.

absetzen ['apzɛtsən], *v.a.* set down; dismiss, deprive of office; depose; (*Comm.*) sell, dispose of.

Absicht ['apzıçt], *f.* (—, *pl.* —**en**) intention, purpose, aim.

absondern ['apzɔndərn], *v.a.* separate, set apart; (*Med.*) secrete. — *v.r. sich* —, seclude o.s. from.

abspannen ['apʃpanən], *v.a.* unharness.

absparen ['apʃpa:rən], *v.n. sich etwas vom Munde* —, stint o.s. for s.th.

abspenstig ['apʃpɛnstıç], *adj.* —*machen*, alienate s.o.'s affections, entice s.o. away; — *werden*, desert.

absperren ['apʃpɛrən], *v.a.* (*door*) lock, shut up; (*street*) close, barricade; (*gas, water*) turn off.

absprechen ['apʃprɛçən], *v.a. irr. einem das Recht* —, deprive s.o. of the right to do s.th.

abspülen [ˈapʃpy:lən], v.a. wash up, rinse.

abstammen [ˈapʃtamən], v.n. (aux. sein) descend from, originate from.

Abstand [ˈapʃtant], m. (—es, pl. ⁓e) distance; von etwas — nehmen, refrain from doing s.th.

abstatten [ˈapʃtatən], v.a. einen Besuch —, pay a visit; einen Bericht —, report on; Dank —, return thanks.

abstechen [ˈapʃtɛçən], v.a. irr. Tiere —, slaughter animals. — v.n. von etwas —, contrast with s.th.

Abstecher [ˈapʃtɛçər], m. (—s, pl. —) short trip, excursion; detour.

abstecken [ˈapʃtɛkən], v.a. mark off, peg out.

absteigen [ˈapʃtaɪgən], v.n. irr. (aux. sein) descend, alight, dismount.

abstellen [ˈapʃtɛlən], v.a. put s.th. down; (gas, water) turn off.

absterben [ˈapʃtɛrbən], v.n. irr. (aux. sein) wither; die.

Abstieg [ˈapʃti:k], m. (—es, no pl.) descent.

Abstimmung [ˈapʃtimuŋ], f. (—, pl. —en) (Parl.) division; referendum, voting.

abstoßen [ˈapʃto:sən], v.a. irr. push off, kick off. —v.n. (Naut.) set sail.

abstoßend [ˈapʃto:sənt], adj. repulsive, repugnant.

abstreifen [ˈapʃtraɪfən], v.a. irr. strip off, pull off; cast, shed.

abstufen [ˈapʃtu:fən], v.a. grade.

abstumpfen [ˈapʃtumpfən], v.a. blunt, dull, take the edge off.

abstürzen [ˈapʃtyrtsən], v.n. (aux. sein) (person) fall; fall down; (Aviat.) crash.

Abt [apt], m. (—es, pl. ⁓e) abbot.

Abtei [ˈaptaɪ], f. (—, pl. —en) abbey.

Abteil [ˈaptaɪl], n. (—s, pl. —e) compartment.

abteilen [ˈaptaɪlən],v.a.divide, partition.

Abteilung [apˈtaɪluŋ], f. (—, pl. —en) section, department.

Äbtissin [ɛpˈtisin], f. (—, pl. —nen) abbess.

abtöten [ˈaptø:tən], v.a. mortify, deaden.

abtragen [ˈaptra:gən], v.a. irr. carry away; (building) demolish; (dress, shoes) wear out; eine Schuld —, pay a debt.

abtreiben [ˈaptraɪbən], v.a. irr. (cattle) drive off; procure an abortion. — v.n. (aux. sein) (ship) drift off.

Abtreibung [ˈaptraɪbuŋ], f. (—, pl. —en) abortion.

abtrennen [ˈaptrɛnən], v.a. (s.th. sewn) unpick; separate.

Abtretung [ˈaptre:tuŋ], f. (—, pl. —en) cession; conveyance.

Abtritt [ˈaptrit], m. (—es, pl. —e) W.C.; (Theat.) exit or exeunt.

abtrocknen [ˈaptrɔknən], v.a. dry.

abtrünnig [ˈaptryniç], adj. disloyal, faithless.

aburteilen [ˈapurtaɪlən], v.a. pass judgment on.

abwägen [ˈapvɛ:gən], v.a. gegeneinander —, weigh against each other.

abwälzen [ˈapvɛltsən], v.a. etwas von sich —, clear o.s. from s.th.

abwandeln [ˈapvandəln], v.a. change; (verbs) conjugate; (nouns) decline.

abwärts [ˈapvɛrts], prep., adv. downward.

abwaschen [ˈapvaʃən], v.a. irr. wash up.

abwechseln [ˈapvɛksəln], v.a. vary, alternate.

Abweg [ˈapve:k], m. (—es, pl. —e) wrong way; auf —e geraten, go astray.

abwehren [ˈapve:rən], v.a. ward off, parry.

abweichen [ˈapvaɪçən], v.n. irr. (aux. sein) — von, deviate from.

abweisen [ˈapvaɪzən], v.a. irr. refuse admittance to, rebuff.

abwenden [ˈapvɛndən], v.a. irr. avert, prevent. — v.r. sich —, turn away from.

abwesend [ˈapve:zənt], adj. absent.

Abwesenheit [ˈapve:zənhaɪt], f. (—, pl. —en) absence.

abwickeln [ˈapvikəln], v.a. uncoil; (business) wind up.

abwischen [ˈapvɪʃən], v.a. wipe clean; sich die Stirn —, mop o.'s brow.

abzahlen [ˈaptsa:lən], v.a. pay off; pay by instalments.

abzehren [ˈaptse:rən], v.n. (aux. sein) waste away.

Abzeichen [ˈaptsaɪçən], n. (—s, pl. —) badge, insignia.

abzeichnen [ˈapsaɪçnən], v.a. sketch, draw from a model. — v.r. sich —, become clear.

abziehen [ˈaptsi:ən], v.a. irr. deduct, subtract; (knife) sharpen; strip (a bed). — v.n. (aux. sein) depart; (Mil.) march off.

Abzug [ˈaptsu:k], m. (—es, pl. ⁓e) retreat, departure; photographic copy; — der Kosten, deduction of charges; (steam, air) outlet.

abzweigen [ˈaptsvaɪgən], v.n. (aux. sein) fork off, branch off.

Achsel [ˈaksəl], f. (—, pl. —n) shoulder; die —n zucken, shrug o.'s shoulders.

Acht [axt], f. (—, no pl.) attention, care, caution, heed; achtgeben, pay attention; sich in — acht nehmen, be careful; ban, excommunication, outlawry; in — und Bann tun, outlaw, proscribe.

acht [axt], num. adj. eight; in — Tagen, in a week; vor — Tagen, a week ago.

achtbar [ˈaxtba:r], adj. respectable.

achten [ˈaxtən], v.a. hold in esteem, value; — auf, pay attention to, keep an eye on.

ächten [ˈɛxtən], v.a. ban, outlaw, proscribe.

achtlos [ˈaxtlo:s], adj. inattentive, negligent.

achtsam [ˈaxtsa:m], adj. attentive, careful.

Achtung [ˈaxtuŋ], f. (—, no pl.) esteem, regard; (Mil.) attention!

Ächtung [ˈɛxtuŋ], f. (—, no pl.) ban, proscription.

achtzehn [ˈaxtse:n], num. adj. eighteen.

achtzig ['axtsɪç], *num. adj.* eighty.

ächzen ['ɛçtsən], *v.n.* groan.

Acker,['akər], *m.* (—s, *pl.* ͏̈) field, arable land; *den — bestellen*, till the soil.

ackern ['akərn], *v.n.* till (the land).

addieren [a'di:rən], *v.a.* add, add up.

Adel ['a:dəl], *m.* (—s, *no pl.*) nobility, aristocracy.

ad(e)lig ['a:dlɪç], *adj.* of noble birth, aristocratic.

Ader ['a:dər], *f.* (—, *pl.* —n) vein; *zu — lassen*, bleed s.o.

Adler ['a:dlər], *m.* (—s, *pl.* —) eagle.

Adresse [a'drɛsə], *f.* (—, *pl.* —n) address.

adrett [a'drɛt], *adj.* neat, adroit, smart.

Affe ['afə], *m.* (—n, *pl.* —n) ape, monkey; (*fig.*) fool.

affektiert [afɛk'ti:rt], *adj.* affected, giving o.s. airs.

äffen ['ɛfən], *v.a.* ape, mimic.

Afghanistan [af'ganistan], *n.* Afghanistan.

Afrika ['a:frika], *n.* Africa.

After ['aftər], *m.* (—s, *pl.* —) anus.

Agentur [agɛn'tu:r], *f.* (—, *pl.* —en) agency.

Agraffe [a'grafə], *f.* (—, *pl.* —n) brooch, clasp.

Agrarier [a'gra:rjər], *m.* (—s, *pl.* —) landed proprietor.

Ägypten [ɛ'gyptən], *n.* Egypt.

Ahle ['a:lə], *f.* (—, *pl.* —n) awl, bodkin.

Ahn [a:n], *m.* (—en, *pl.* —en) ancestor, forefather.

ahnden ['a:ndən], *v.a.* avenge, punish.

Ahne ['a:nə] *see* **Ahn**.

ähneln ['ɛ:nəln], *v.a.* resemble, look like.

ahnen ['a:nən], *v.a., v.n.* have a presentiment, foresee, have a hunch.

ähnlich ['ɛ:nlɪç], *adj.* resembling, like, similar.

Ahnung ['a:nuŋ], *f.* (—, *pl.* —en) foreboding, presentiment, idea, (*Am.*) hunch.

Ahorn ['a:hɔrn], *m.* (—s, *pl.* —e) (*Bot.*) maple.

Ähre ['ɛ:rə], *f.* (—, *pl.* —n) ear of corn.

Akademiker [aka'de:mɪkər], *m.* (—s, *pl.* —) university graduate.

akademisch [aka'de:mɪʃ], *adj.* academic; — *gebildet*, with a university education.

Akazie [a'ka:tsjə], *f.* (—, *pl.* —n) (*Bot.*) acacia.

akklimatisieren [aklimati'zi:rən], *v.r. sich —*, become acclimatised.

Akkord [a'kɔrt], *m.* (—es, *pl.* —e) (*Mus.*) chord; *in — arbeiten*, work on piece-rates.

Akt [akt], *m.* (—es, *pl.* —e) deed, action; (*Theat.*) act; (*Art*) (depiction of) the nude.

Akte ['aktə], *f.* (—, *pl.* —n) document, deed; (*pl.*) records, files; *zu den —n legen*, pigeonhole, shelve.

Aktenstück ['aktənʃtyk], *n.* (—es, *pl.* —e) official document, file.

Aktie ['aktsjə], *f.* (—, *pl.* —n) (*Comm.*) share, (*Am.*) stock.

Aktiengesellschaft ['aktsjəngəzɛlʃaft], *f.* (—, *pl.* —en) joint stock company.

Aktionär [aktsjo'nɛ:r], *m.* (—s, *pl.* —e) shareholder, (*Am.*) stockholder.

Aktiv ['akti:f], *n.* (—s, *pl.* —e) (*Gram.*) active voice.

Aktiva [ak'ti:va], *n. pl.* (*Comm.*) assets.

aktuell [aktu'ɛl], *adj.* topical.

akzentuieren [aktsɛntu'i:rən], *v.a.* accentuate, stress, emphasize.

Albanien [al'ba:njən], *n.* Albania.

albern ['albərn], *adj.* silly, foolish.

Aliment [ali'mɛnt], *n.* (—es, *pl.* —e) (*usually pl.*—e) alimony, maintenance.

Alkali [al'ka:li], *n.* (—s, *pl.* —en) alkali.

Alkohol ['alkoho:l], *m.* (—s, *no pl.*) alcohol.

Alkoholiker [alko'ho:lɪkər], *m.* (—s, *pl.* —) drunkard, alcoholic.

All [al], *n.* (—s, *no pl.*) the universe, (outer) space.

all [al], *adj.* all, entire, whole;ǁ every, each, any.

alle ['alə], *adj.* all, everybody; — *beide*, both of them.

Allee [a'le:], *f.* (—, *pl.* —n) tree-lined walk, avenue.

allein [a'laɪn], *adj.* alone, sole. — *adv.* solely, only, merely. —*conj.* (*obs.*) only, but, however.

alleinig [a'laɪnɪç], *adj.* sole, only, exclusive.

allenfalls [alən'fals], *adv.* possibly, perhaps, if need be.

allenthalben [alənt'halbən], *adv.* everywhere, in all places.

allerdings [alər'dɪŋs], *adv.* of course, indeed, nevertheless.

allerhand [alər'hant], *adj.* of all sorts *or* kinds, various; *das ist ja —! I say!*

Allerheiligen [alər'haɪlɪgən], *pl.* All Saints' Day.

allerlei [alər'laɪ], *adj.* miscellaneous, various.

allerliebst [alər'li:pst], *adj.* (*Am.*) cute; charming.

allerseits ['alərzaɪts], *adv.* generally, on all sides, universally.

alles ['aləs], *adj.* everything, all.

allgemein [algə'maɪn], *adj.* universal, common, general.

alliieren [ali'i:rən], *v.a., v.n.* ally (o.s.).

allmächtig [al'mɛçtɪç], *adj.* omnipotent.

allmählich [al'mɛ:lɪç], *adj.* by degrees, gradual.

allseitig ['alzaɪtɪç], *adj.* universal, (*Am.*) all-round.

Alltag ['alta:k], *m.* (—s,*pl.*—e) working day, week-day.

allwissend [al'vɪsənt], *adj.* omniscient.

allzu ['altzu:], *adv.* too, much too.

Alm [alm], *f.* (—, *pl.* —en) Alpine meadow.

Almosen ['almo:zən], *n.* (—s, *pl.* —) alms, charity.

Alp [alp], *f.*, (—, *pl.* —en) (*mostly pl.*) mountain(s), Alps.

Alpdrücken ['alpdrykən], *n.* (—s, *no pl.*) nightmare.

5

als [als], *conj.* than; *(after comparatives)* than; as, like; but; *er hat nichts — Schulden,* he has nothing but debts; *(temp.)* when, as.

alsbald [als'balt], *adv.* forthwith.

also ['alzo:], *adv.* thus, so, in this manner. — *conj.* consequently, therefore.

Alt [alt], *m.* (—s, *pl.* —e) *(Mus.)* alto.

alt [alt], *adj.* old, ancient; aged; antique.

Altan [al'ta:n], *m.* (—s, *pl.* —e) balcony, gallery.

Altar [al'ta:r], *m.* (—s, *pl.* ¨e) altar.

altbacken ['altbakən], *adj.* stale.

Alter ['altər], *n.* (—s, *no pl.*) age, old age; epoch.

altern ['altərn], *v.n.* *(aux.* sein) grow old.

Altertum ['altərtu:m], *n.* (—s, *pl.* ¨er) antiquity.

Altistin [al'tɪstɪn], *f.* (—, *pl.* —nen) *(Mus.)* contralto.

altklug ['altklu:k], *adj.* precocious.

ältlich ['ɛltlɪç], *adj.* elderly.

Altweibersommer [alt'vaɪbərzɔmər], *m.* (—s, *pl.* —) Indian summer.

Amboß ['ambɔs], *m.* (—sses, *pl.* —sse) anvil.

Ameise ['a:maɪzə], *f.* (—, *pl.* —n) *(Ent.)* ant.

Amerika [a'me:rika], *n.* America.

Amme ['amə], *f.* (—, *pl.* —n) wet nurse.

Ammoniak [amon'jak], *n.* (—s, *no pl.*) ammonia.

Ampel ['ampəl], *f.* (—, *pl.* —n) (hanging) light, lamp, lantern; traffic light.

Ampfer ['ampfər], *m.* (—s, *pl.* —) *(Bot.)* sorrel, dock.

Amsel ['amzəl], *f.* (—, *pl.* —n) *(Orn.)* blackbird.

Amt [amt], *n.* (—es, *pl.* ¨er) office, post, employment; administration, domain, jurisdiction; place of public business.

amtlich ['amtlɪç], *adj.* official.

Amtmann ['amtman], *m.* (—s, *pl.* ¨er) bailiff.

Amtsblatt ['amtsblat], *n.* (—es, *pl.* ¨er) official gazette.

Amtsgericht ['amtsgərɪçt], *n.* (—s, *pl.* —e) county court; *(Am.)* district court.

amüsieren [amy'zi:rən], *v.a.* amuse. — *v.r.* *sich —,* enjoy o.s.

an [an], *prep.* *(Dat. or Acc.),* at, to, on.

analog [ana'lo:k], *adj.* analogous.

Ananas ['ananas], *f.* (—, *pl.* —) pineapple.

Anatom [ana'to:m], *m.* (—en, *pl.* —en) anatomist.

anbahnen ['anba:nən], *v.a.* initiate, open up, pave the way for.

anbändeln ['anbɛndəln], *v.n.* — *mit,* flirt with, make up to.

Anbau ['anbau], *m.* (—s, *pl.* —ten) *(grain)* cultivation; annex(e), wing (of building).

anbauen ['anbauən], *v.a.* cultivate; add to a building.

anbei [an'baɪ], *adv.* enclosed (in letter).

anbeißen ['anbaɪsən], *v.a.* *irr.* bite at,

take a bite of. — *v.n.* *(fish)* bite; *(coll.)* take the bait.

anbelangen ['anbəlaŋən], *v.a.* concern.

anberaumen ['anbəraumən], *v.a.* fix (a date).

anbeten ['anbe:tən], *v.a.* worship, adore, idolise.

anbiedern ['anbi:dərn], *v.r.* *ich mit einem —,* chum up with s.o.

anbieten ['anbi:tən], *v.a.* *irr.* offer.

anbinden ['anbɪndən], *v.a.* *irr.* tie on, bind to; *kurz angebunden sein,* be curt.

Anblick ['anblɪk], *m.* (—s, *no pl.*) view, sight, aspect, spectacle.

anbrechen ['anbreçən], *v.a.* *irr.* begin; break; start on. —*v.n.* dawn.

anbrennen ['anbrɛnən], *v.a.* *irr.* light, set fire to, burn. — *v.n.* *(aux.* sein) catch fire; burn.

anbringen ['anbrɪŋən], *v.a.* *irr.* fit to, place.

Anbruch ['anbrux], *m.* (—s, *no pl.*) beginning; — *der Nacht,* night-fall.

anbrüllen ['anbrylən], *v.a.* roar at.

Andacht ['andaxt], *f.* (—, *pl.* —en) *(Eccl.)* devotion(s).

andächtig ['andɛxtɪç], *adj.* devout.

andauern ['andauərn], *v.n.* last, continue.

Andenken ['andɛŋkən], *n.* (—s, *pl.* —) memory; keepsake; souvenir.

anderer ['andərər], *adj.* other, different; *ein —,* another.

andermal ['andərma:l], *adv.* *ein —,* another time.

ändern ['ɛndərn], *v.a.* alter, change.

andernfalls ['andərnfals], *adv.* otherwise, or else.

anders ['andərs], *adv.* differently, in another manner, otherwise.

anderthalb ['andərthalp], *adj.* one and a half.

anderweitig ['andərvaɪtɪç], *adj.* elsewhere.

andeuten ['andɔytən], *v.a.* hint at, intimate, indicate.

Andrang ['andraŋ], *m.* (—es, *no pl.*) throng, crowd.

aneignen ['anaɪgnən], *v.r.* *sich etwas —,* appropriate s.th.; *(an opinion)* adopt.

anekeln ['ane:kəln], *v.a.* disgust.

Anerbieten ['anɛrbi:tən], *n.* (—s, *pl.* —) offer.

anerkennen ['anɛrkɛnən], *v.a.* *irr.* acknowledge, appreciate, recognize, accept.

anfachen ['anfaxən], *v.a.* kindle (a flame).

Anfahrt ['anfa:rt], *f.* (—, *pl.* —en) drive; *(down a mine)* descent; *(Am.)* drive-way.

Anfall ['anfal], *m.* (—s, *pl.* ¨e) attack, assault; *(Med.)* seizure, fit; *(mood)* fit, burst.

anfallen ['anfalən], *v.a.* *irr.* *einen —,* attack s.o.

Anfang ['anfaŋ], *m.* (—s, *pl.* ¨e) beginning, start, commencement.

anfangen ['anfaŋən], *v.a. irr.* begin, start. — *v.n.* begin, originate.

Anfänger ['anfɛŋər], *m.* (—s, *pl.* —) beginner, novice.

anfänglich ['anfɛŋlɪç], *adv.* in the beginning, at first, initially.

anfassen ['anfasən], *v.a.* take hold of; touch; seize.

anfechtbar ['anfɛçtbaːr], *adj.* disputable, refutable, debatable.

anfechten ['anfɛçtən], *v.a.* (*a will, a verdict*) contest; (*jurors*) challenge.

anfeinden ['anfaɪndən], *v.a.* show enmity to.

anfertigen ['anfɛrtɪgən], *v.a.* make, manufacture, prepare; (*a list*) draw up.

anflehen ['anfleːən], *v.a.* implore, beseech.

Anflug ['anfluːk], *m.* (—s, *pl.* ⁻e) (*Aviat.*) approach; (*beard*) down; touch.

anfordern ['anfɔrdərn], *v.a.* demand, claim.

Anfrage ['anfraːgə], *f.* (—, *pl.* —n) enquiry.

anfügen ['anfyːgən], *v.a.* join to, annex.

anführen ['anfyːrən], *v.a.* lead; adduce, quote (examples), cite; *einen* —, dupe s.o., take s.o. in.

Anführungszeichen ['anfyːruŋtsaɪçən], *n.* (—s, *pl.* —) inverted commas, quotation marks.

anfüllen ['anfʏlən], *v.a. wieder* —, replenish.

Angabe ['angaːbə], *f.* (—, *pl.* —n) declaration, statement; data; instruction; bragging.

angeben ['angeːbən], *v.a. irr.* declare, state; *den Ton* —, lead the fashion; *den Wert* —, declare the value of.— *v.n. groß* —, brag, show off.

Angeber ['angeːbər], *m.* (—s, *pl.* —) informer; braggart.

Angebinde ['angəbɪndə], *n.* (—s, *pl.* —) (*obs.*) present, gift.

angeblich ['angəplɪç], *adj.* ostensible, alleged, so-called.

angeboren ['angəboːrən], *adj.* innate, inborn.

Angebot ['angəboːt], *n.* (—es, *pl.* —e) offer, tender, bid; (*Comm.*) — *und Nachfrage*, supply and demand.

angebracht ['angəbraxt], *adj.* apt, appropriate, opportune.

angedeihen ['angədaɪən], *v.n. einem etwas — lassen*, bestow s.th. on s.o.

angegossen ['angəgɔsən], *adj. das sitzt wie* —, it fits like a glove.

angehen ['angeːən], *v.a. irr. einen um etwas —*, apply to s.o. for s.th.; *das geht Dich nichts an*, that is none of your business.

angehören ['angəhøːrən], *v.n.* belong to.

Angehörige ['angəhøːrɪgə], *m., f.* (—n, *pl.* —n) near relative; next of kin.

Angeklagte ['angəklaːktə], *m., f.* (—n, *pl.* —n) the accused, defendant, prisoner at the bar.

Angel ['aŋəl], *f* (—, *pl.* —n) fishing-rod;

(*door*) hinge, pivot; *zwischen Tür und* —, in passing.

angelegen ['angəleːgən], *adj. sich etwas — sein lassen*, interest o.s. in s.th., concern o.s. in s.th.; *ich werde es mir — sein lassen*, I shall make it my business.

Angelegenheit ['angəleːgənhaɪt], *f.* (—, *pl.* —en) concern, matter, affair.

angeln ['aŋəln], *v.a.* fish, angle.

angemessen ['angəmɛsən], *adj.* proper, suitable, appropriate.

angenehm ['angəneːm], *adj.* acceptable, agreeable, pleasing, pleasant.

angenommen ['angənɔmən], *conj.* — *daß*, given that, supposing that, say.

Anger ['aŋər], *m.* (—s, *pl.* —) grass-plot; green, common.

angesehen ['angəzeːən], *adj.* respected, esteemed, distinguished.

Angesicht ['angəzɪçt] *n.* (—s, *pl.* —er) face, countenance.

angestammt ['angəʃtamt], *adj.* ancestral, hereditary.

Angestellte ['angəʃtɛltə], *m., f.* (—n, *pl.* —n) employee; (*pl.*) staff.

Angler ['aŋlər], *m.* (—s, *pl.* —) angler, fisherman.

angliedern ['angliːdərn], *v.a.* annex, attach.

Anglist [aŋˈglɪst], *m.* (—en, *pl.* —en) (*Univ.*) professor *or* student of English.

angreifen ['angraɪfən], *v.a. irr.* handle, touch; (*capital*) break into; attack, assail; *es greift mich an*, it taxes my strength.

angrenzen ['angrɛntsən], *v.n.* border upon, adjoin.

Angriff ['angrɪf], *m.* (—s, *pl.* —e) offensive, attack, assault.

Angst [aŋst], *f.* (—, *pl.* ⁻e) anxiety; fear; anguish.

ängstigen ['ɛŋstɪgən], *v.a.* alarm, frighten. — *v.r. sich* —, feel uneasy, be afraid.

angucken ['anguːkən], *v.a.* look at.

anhaben ['anhaːbən], *v.a. irr.* have on, be dressed in, wear; *einem etwas* —, hold s.th. against s.o.

anhaften ['anhaftən], *v.n.* stick to, adhere to.

Anhalt ['anhalt], *m.* (—es, *no pl.*) support, basis.

anhalten ['anhaltən], *v.a. irr. einen* —, stop s.o. — *v.n.* stop, pull up, halt; *um ein Mädchen* —, ask for a girl's hand in marriage. — *v.r. sich an etwas halten*, cling to, hang on to s.th.

Anhaltspunkt ['anhaltspuŋkt], *m.* (—es, *pl.* —e) clue, (*Am.*) lead.

Anhang ['anhaŋ], *m.* (—s, *pl.* ⁻e) appendix, supplement.

anhängen ['anhɛŋən], *v.a. irr.* hang on, fasten to, attach.

Anhänger ['anhɛŋər], *m.* (—s, *pl.* —) follower, adherent; (*Footb.*) supporter; pendant (on a necklace); label; (*Transp.*) trailer.

anhänglich ['anhɛŋlɪç], *adj.* attached, affectionate.

Anhängsel ['anhɛŋsəl], *n.* (—s, *pl.* —) appendage.

anhauchen ['anhauxən], *v.a.* breathe upon.

anhäufen ['anhɔyfən], *v.a.* heap up, pile up, amass. —*v.r. sich* —, accumulate.

anheben ['anhe:bən], *v.a. irr.* lift. — *v.n.* (*obs.*) begin.

anheim [an'haim], *adv.* — *stellen,* leave to s.o.'s discretion.

anheimeln ['anhaiməln], *v.a.* remind one of home.

anheischig ['anhaiʃiç], *adj. sich* — *machen,* undertake, pledge o.s.

Anhieb ['anhi:p], *m.* (—s, *pl.* —e) (*fencing*) first stroke; *auf* —, at the first attempt.

Anhöhe ['anhø:ə], *f.* (—, *pl.* —n) hill, rising ground.

anhören ['anhø:rən], *v.a.* listen to; tell by s.o.'s voice *or* accent.

animieren [ani'mi:rən], *v.a.* instigate, egg on.

ankämpfen ['ankɛmpfən], *v.n. gegen etwas* —, struggle against s.th.

ankaufen ['ankaufən], *v.a.* purchase, buy. — *v.r. sich irgendwo* —, buy land somewhere.

Anker ['aŋkər], *m.* (—s, *pl.* —) (*Naut.*) anchor; *den* — *auswerfen,* cast anchor.

ankern ['aŋkərn], *v.a., v.n.* anchor, cast anchor.

Anklage ['ankla:gə], *f.* (—, *pl.* —n) accusation; *gegen einen* — *erheben,* bring a charge against s.o.

Ankläger ['ankle:gər], *m.* (—s, *pl.* —) accuser, prosecutor; plaintiff.

Anklang ['anklaŋ], *m.* (—s, *pl.* ⁻e) reminiscence; — *finden,* please, meet with approval.

ankleben ['ankle:bən], *v.a.* stick to, glue to, paste on.

ankleiden ['anklaidən], *v.a.* dress. — *v.r. sich* —, dress o.s., get dressed.

anklingeln ['ankliŋəln], *v.a.* (*coll.*) *einen* —, ring s.o. up (on the telephone.)

anklopfen ['anklɔpfən], *v.n.* knock.

anknüpfen ['anknypfən], *v.a.* tie; join on to; *ein Gespräch* —, start a conversation; *wieder* —, resume.

ankommen ['ankɔmən], *v.n. irr.* (*aux.* sein) arrive; *es kommt darauf an,* it depends upon.

ankreiden ['ankraidən], *v.a.* chalk up.

ankündigen ['ankyndigən], *v.a.* announce, advertise, give notice of, proclaim.

Ankunft ['ankunft], *f.* (—, *no pl.*) arrival.

ankurbeln ['ankurbəln], *v.a.* (*Motor.*) crank up.

Anlage ['anla:gə], *f.* (—, *pl.* —n) (*capital*) investment; enclosure (*with a letter*); (*industrial*) plant; (*building*) lay-out; *öffentliche* —, pleasure grounds; talent.

anlangen ['anlaŋən], *v.n.* (*aux.* sein) arrive; concern; *was das anlangt,* as far as this is concerned.

Anlaß ['anlas], *m.* (—sses, *pl.* ⁻sse) cause, occasion, motive.

anlassen ['anlasən], *v.a. irr.* keep on; (*Motor.*) start. — *v.r. sich gut* —, promise well.

Anlasser ['anlasər], *m.* (—s, *pl.* —) (*Motor.*) starter.

anläßlich ['anlɛslɪç], *prep.* (*Genit.*) à propos of, on the occasion of.

Anlauf ['anlauf], *m.* (—s, *pl.* ⁻e) start, run, (*Aviat.*) take-off run.

anlaufen ['anlaufən], *v.n. irr.* tarnish; call at (port).

anlegen ['anle:gən], *v.a. Geld* —, invest money; *Kleider* —, don clothes; *einen Garten* —, lay out a garden; *Hand* —, give a helping hand; *auf einen* —, take aim at s.o.; (*Naut.*) land, dock.

Anlegestelle ['anle:gəʃtɛlə], *f.* (—, *pl.* —n) landing place.

anlehnen ['anle:nən], *v.r. sich an etwas* —, lean against s.th.

Anleihe ['anlaiə], *f.* (—, *pl.* —n) loan, *öffentliche* —, government loan; *eine* — *machen,* raise a loan.

anleiten ['anlaitən], *v.a.* train, instruct.

anlernen ['anlɛrnən], *v.a. einen* —, train, apprentice s.o. (in a craft).

Anliegen ['anli:gən], *n.* (—s, *pl.* —) request, petition, concern.

anmachen ['anmaxən], *v.a.* fix, fasten; light (a fire).

anmaßen ['anma:sən], *v.a. sich etwas* —, arrogate s.th.

anmaßend ['anma:sənt], *adj.* arrogant.

anmelden ['anmɛldən], *v.a.* announce, (*claim*) give notice of. — *v.r. sich* —, notify o.'s arrival, make an appointment; *sich* — *lassen,* send in o.'s name.

Anmeldungsformular [an'mɛlduŋsfɔrmula:r], *n.* (—s, *pl.* —e) registration form.

Anmerkung ['anmɛrkuŋ], *f.* (—, *pl.* —en) remark, annotation, footnote.

anmessen ['anmɛsən], *v.a. irr.* measure (s.o. for a garment).

Anmut ['anmu:t], *f.* (—, *no pl.*) grace, charm.

annähen ['annɛ:ən], *v.a.* sew on (to).

annähern ['annɛ:ərn], *v.r. sich* —, approach, draw near; (*Maths.*) approximate.

Annäherung ['annɛ:əruŋ], *f.* (—, *pl.* —en) approach; (*Maths.*) approximation.

Annahme ['anna:mə], *f.* (—, *pl.* —n) acceptance; assumption, hypothesis.

annehmbar ['anne:mba:r], *adj.* acceptable; *ganz* —, passable.

annehmen ['anne:mən], *v.a. irr.* take, accept, take delivery of; suppose, assume, presume; *an Kindes Statt* —, adopt.

Annehmlichkeit ['anne:mlɪçkait], *f.* (—, *pl.* —en) amenity, comfort.

Annonce [an'nɔ̃:sə], *f.* (—, *pl.* —n) (classified) advertisement (in newspaper).

anordnen ['anɔrdnən], *v.a.* arrange, regulate; order, direct.

anorganisch ['anɔrgaːnɪʃ], *adj.* inorganic.

anpacken ['anpakən], *v.a.* get hold of, seize, grasp.

anpassen ['anpasən], *v.a.* fit, suit. — *v.r. sich* —, adapt o.s.

anpflanzen ['anpflantsən], *v.a.* plant, grow.

Anprall ['anpral], *m.* (—s, *no pl.*) impact, bounce, shock.

anpumpen ['anpumpən], *v.a.* (*coll.*) *einen* —, borrow money from s.o.

anrechnen ['anrɛçnən], *v.a. einem etwas* —, charge s.o. with s.th.; *einem etwas hoch* —, think highly of a person for s.th.

Anrecht ['anrɛçt], *n.* (—es, *no pl.*) — *auf*, title to, claim to.

Anrede ['anreːdə], *f.* (—, *pl.* —n) (form of) address, title.

anreden ['anreːdən], *v.a.* address (s.o.).

anregen ['anreːgən], *v.a.* stimulate (s.o.); suggest (s.th.).

Anregung ['anreːguŋ], *f.* (—, *pl.* —en) suggestion, hint.

Anreiz ['anraɪts], *m.* (—es, *no pl.*) incentive; impulse.

Anrichte ['anrɪçtə], *f.* (—, *pl.* —n) dresser, sideboard.

anrichten ['anrɪçtən], *v.a.* (*meal*) prepare, serve (up); *Unheil* —, make mischief.

anrüchig ['anryːçɪç], *adj.* disreputable.

anrücken ['anrykən], *v.a.* bring near to. — *v.n.* (*aux.* sein) approach.

Anruf ['anruːf], *m.* (—s, *pl.* —e) (by *sentry*) challenge; telephone call.

anrufen ['anruːfən], *v.a. irr.* call to, challenge; implore; ring up; *Gott* —, invoke God.

anrühren ['anryːrən], *v.a.* handle, touch; (*Cul.*) mix.

Ansage ['anzaːgə], *f.* (—, *pl.* —n) announcement.

ansagen ['anzaːgən], *v.a.* announce, notify.

Ansager ['anzaːgər], *m.* (—s, *pl.* —) announcer; compere.

ansammeln ['anzaməln], *v.a.* accumulate, gather. — *v.r. sich* —, gather, foregather, congregate, collect.

ansässig ['anzɛsɪç], *adj.* domiciled, resident; *sich* — *machen*, settle.

Ansatz ['anzats], *m.* (—es, *pl.* ⁓e) start; (*Maths.*) construction; disposition (to), tendency (to).

anschaffen ['anʃafən], *v.a.* buy, purchase, get.

anschauen ['anʃauən], *v.a.* look at, view.

anschaulich ['anʃaulɪç], *adj.* clear; *einem etwas* — *machen*, give s.o. a clear idea of s.th.

Anschauung ['anʃauuŋ], *f.* (—, *pl.* —en) view, perception; *nach meiner* —, in my opinion.

Anschein ['anʃaɪn], *m.* (—s, *no pl.*) appearance, semblance.

anscheinend ['anʃaɪnənt], *adj.* apparent, ostensible, seeming.

anschicken ['anʃɪkən], *v.r. sich* — *zu*, prepare for, get ready for.

anschirren ['anʃɪrən], *v.a.* (*horses*) harness.

Anschlag ['anʃlaːk], *m.* (—s, *pl.* ⁓e) poster, placard; — *auf das Leben*, attempt at assassination.

Anschlagbrett ['anʃlaːkbrɛt], *n.* (—es, *pl.* —er) notice-board.

anschlagen ['anʃlaːgən], *v.a. irr.* (*keys of piano or typewriter*) strike, touch; (*knitting*) cast on; *zu hoch* —, overestimate.

anschließen ['anʃliːsən], *v.a. irr.* fasten with a lock. — *v.r. sich* —, join in; (*club*) join.

Anschluß ['anʃlus], *m.* (—sses, *pl.* ⁓sse) (*Railw., telephone*) connection; (*Pol.*) annexation.

Anschlußpunkt ['anʃluspuŋkt], *m.* (—es, *pl.* —e) junction; (*Elec.*) inlet point, power point.

anschmiegen ['anʃmiːgən], *v.r. sich* —, nestle closely to.

anschmieren ['anʃmiːrən], *v.a. einen* —, (*coll.*) deceive, cheat s.o.

anschnallen ['anʃnalən], *v.a.* buckle on.

anschnauzen ['anʃnautsən], *v.a.* snarl at, snap at.

anschneiden ['anʃnaɪdən], *v.a. irr.* cut into; *ein Thema* —, broach a subject.

Anschrift ['anʃrɪft], *f.* (—, *pl.* —en) address.

anschwellen ['anʃvɛlən], *v.n.* (*aux.* sein) swell.

Ansehen ['anzeːən], *n.* (—s, *no pl.*) respect; reputation; authority.

ansehen ['anzeːən], *v.a. irr.* look at *or* upon, consider, regard.

ansehnlich ['anzeːnlɪç], *adj.* considerable, appreciable.

anseilen ['anzaɪlən], *v.a.* (*Mount.*) rope together.

ansetzen ['anzɛtsən], *v.a.* join to; (*Maths.*) start, write out (an equation).

Ansicht ['anzɪçt], *f.* (—, *pl.* —en) opinion; view; (*Comm.*) approval.

ansichtig ['anzɪçtɪç], *adj.* — *werden*, get a glimpse of.

Ansichts(post)karte ['anzɪçts(pɔst)-kartə], *f.* (—, *pl.* —n) picture postcard.

ansiedeln ['anziːdəln], *v.r. sich* —, settle (down), colonize.

Ansinnen ['anzɪnən], *n.* (—s, *pl.* —) demand, suggestion.

anspannen ['anʃpanən], *v.a.* tighten yoke, stretch; harness.

anspielen ['anʃpiːlən], *v.n.* (*Game, Sport*) lead off; *auf etwas* —, allude to s.th.

Ansporn ['anʃpɔrn], *m.* (—s, *no pl.*) spur, incentive.

Ansprache ['anʃpraːxə], *f.* (—, *pl.* —n) address, speech, talk.

ansprechen ['anʃprɛçən], *v.a. irr.* address, accost; please.

anspringen ['anʃprɪŋən], *v.a. irr.* leap at. — *v.n.* (*Motor.*) start.

Anspruch [ˈanʃprux], *m.* (—s, *pl.* ¨e) (*Law*) claim, title.

anspruchsvoll [ˈanʃpruxsfɔl], *adj.* demanding, hard to please.

anstacheln [ˈanʃtaxəln], *v.a.* goad, prod.

Anstalt [ˈanʃtalt], *f.* (—, *pl.* —en) institution, establishment; —*en treffen*, make arrangements (for).

Anstand [ˈanʃtant], *m.* (—es, *no pl.*) propriety; politeness, good manners, good grace; decency; (*Hunt.*) stand, butts.

anständig [ˈanʃtɛndɪç], *adj.* decent, proper, respectable.

Anstandsbesuch [ˈanʃtantsbəzuːx], *m.* (—es, *pl.* —e) formal visit.

anstandshalber [ˈanʃtantshalbər], *adv.* for decency's sake.

anstandslos [ˈanʃtantsloːs], *adv.* unhesitatingly.

anstarren [ˈanʃtarən], *v.a.* stare at.

anstatt [anˈʃtat], *prep.* (*Genit.*), *conj.* instead of, in lieu of, in the place of.

anstecken [ˈanʃtɛkən], *v.a. irr.* pin on; set fire to; infect.

Ansteckung [ˈanʃtɛkuŋ], *f.* (—, *pl.* —en) infection, contagion.

anstehen [ˈanʃteːən], *v.n. irr.* stand in a queue; — *lassen*, put off, delay.

ansteigen [ˈanʃtaɪgən], *v.n. irr.* (*aux.* sein) rise, increase.

anstellen [ˈanʃtɛlən], *v.a. einen* —, appoint s.o. to a post; employ; *Betrachtungen* —, speculate. — *v.r. sich* —, form a queue, line up.

anstellig [ˈanʃtɛlɪç], *adj.* able, skilful, adroit.

Anstellung [ˈanʃtɛluŋ], *f.* (—, *pl.* —en) appointment, employment.

anstiften [ˈanʃtɪftən], *v.a.* instigate.

anstimmen [ˈanʃtɪmən], *v.a.* intone.

Anstoß [ˈanʃtoːs], *m.* (—es, *pl.* ¨e) (*Footb.*) kick-off; — *erregen*, give offence; *den* — *geben zu*, initiate, give an impetus to; *Stein des* —*es*, stumbling block; — *nehmen*, take offence.

anstoßen [ˈanʃtoːsən], *v.a. irr.* knock against, push against; give offence; clink (glasses); border on; *mit der Zunge* —, lisp.

anstößig [ˈanʃtøːsɪç], *adj.* shocking, offensive.

anstreichen [ˈanʃtraɪçən], *v.a. irr.* paint; *Fehler* —, mark wrong.

Anstreicher [ˈanʃtraɪçər], *m.* (—s, *pl.* —) house-painter.

anstrengen [ˈanʃtrɛŋən], *v.a.* strain exert; *eine Klage gegen einen* —, bring an action against s.o. — *v.r. sich* —, exert o.s.

Anstrengung [ˈanʃtrɛŋuŋ], *f.* (—, *pl.* —en) exertion, effort.

Anstrich [ˈanʃtrɪç], *m.* (—s, *pl.* —e) coat of paint.

Ansturm [ˈanʃturm], *m.* (—s, *no pl.*) attack, assault, charge.

Ansuchen [ˈanzuːxən], *n.* (—s, *pl.* —) application, request, petition.

ansuchen [ˈanzuːxən], *v.n. bei einem um etwas* —, apply to s.o. for s.th.

Anteil [ˈantaɪl], *m.* (—s, *pl.* —e) share, portion; sympathy.

Anteilnahme [ˈantaɪlnaːmə], *f.* (—, *no pl.*) sympathy.

Antenne [anˈtɛnə], *f.* (—, *pl.* —n) aerial; antenna.

antik [anˈtiːk], *adj.* antique, ancient, classical.

Antike [anˈtiːkə], *f.* (—, *pl.* —en) (classical) antiquity; ancient work of art (statue etc.).

Antiquar [antiˈkvaːr], *m.* (—s, *pl.* —e) second-hand dealer; antiquary.

Antiquariat [antikvaˈrjaːt], *n.* (—s, *pl.* —e) second-hand bookshop.

antiquarisch [antiˈkvaːrɪʃ], *adj.* antiquarian, second-hand.

Antlitz [ˈantlɪts], *n.* (—es, *pl.* —e) countenance, (*Poet.*) face.

Antrag [ˈantraːk], *m.* (—s, *pl.* ¨e) proposition, proposal, application; *einen* — *stellen*, bring in a motion; make application.

antragen [ˈantraːgən], *v.a. irr.* propose, make a proposal, offer to.

Antragsformular [ˈantraːksfɔrmulaːr], *n.* (—s, *pl.* —e) (*Insurance*) proposal form; application form.

Antragsteller [ˈantraːkʃtɛlər], *m.* (—s, *pl.* —) applicant, mover of a resolution.

antreten [ˈantreːtən], *v.a. irr. ein Amt* —, enter upon an office; *eine Reise* —, set out on a journey. — *v.n.* (*aux.* sein) (*Mil.*) fall in.

Antrieb [ˈantriːp], *m.* (—s, *pl.* —e) impulse, motive; incentive; *aus eigenem* —, voluntarily.

Antritt [ˈantrɪt], *m.* (—s, *no pl.*) start, commencement.

Antrittsvorlesung [ˈantrɪtsfɔrleːzuŋ], *f.* (*Univ.*) inaugural lecture.

antun [ˈantuːn], *v.a. irr. einem etwas* —, do s.th. to s.o.

Antwort [ˈantvɔrt], *f.* (—, *pl.* —en) answer, reply; *abschlägige* —, refusal, rebuff.

antworten [ˈantvɔrtən], *v.a.* answer, reply to.

anvertrauen [ˈanfɛrtrauən], *v.a. einem etwas* —, entrust s.o. with s.th.; confide in s.o.

anverwandt [ˈanfɛrvant] *see* **verwandt**.

Anwalt [ˈanvalt], *m.* (—s, *pl.* ¨e) lawyer, barrister, solicitor, attorney, advocate.

anwandeln [ˈanvandəln], *v.a.* befall.

Anwandlung [ˈanvandluŋ], *f.* (—, *pl.* —en) fit, turn.

Anwartschaft [ˈanvartʃaft], *f.* (—, *pl.* —en) (*Law*) reversion; candidacy.

anweisen [ˈanvaɪzən], *v.a. irr.* instruct, direct; *angewiesen sein auf*, depend upon.

Anweisung [ˈanvaɪzuŋ], *f.* (—, *pl.* —en) instruction, advice, method; (*Comm.*) voucher, credit voucher, cheque.

anwenden [ˈanvɛndən], *v.a. irr.* use, make use of, apply.

anwerben ['anvɛrbən], *v.a.* irr. (*Mil.*) recruit; *sich — lassen*, enlist.

anwesend ['anve:zənt], *adj.* at hand, present.

Anwesenheit ['anve:zənhaɪt], *f.* (—, *no pl.*) presence, attendance.

anwidern ['anvi:dərn], *v.a.* disgust.

Anzahl ['antsa:l], *f.* (—, *no pl.*) number, quantity.

anzahlen ['antsa:lən], *v.a.* pay a deposit.

Anzahlung ['antsa:luŋ], *f.* (—, *pl.* —en) deposit.

Anzeichen ['antsaɪçən], *n.* (—s, *pl.* —) indication, omen.

Anzeige ['antsaɪgə], *f.* (—, *pl.* —n) notice, (classified) advertisement; denunciation; — *erstatten*, to lay information.

anzeigen ['antsaɪgən], *v.a.* point out, indicate; announce; notify; advertise; denounce.

Anzeiger ['antsaɪgər], *m.* (—s, *pl.* —) indicator; (*newspaper*) advertiser.

anzetteln ['antsɛtəln], *v.a.* plot, contrive.

anziehen ['antsi:ən], *v.a.* irr. pull, draw tight, give a tug; attract; stretch; dress; (*screws*) tighten. —, *v.r. sich —*, dress, put on o.'s clothes.

anziehend ['antsi:ənt], *adj.* attractive.

Anziehung ['antsi:uŋ], *f.* (—, *no pl.*) attraction.

Anzug ['antsu:k], *m.* (—s, *pl.* ∵e) (man's) suit; approach.

anzüglich ['antsy:klɪç], *adj.* allusive; suggestive; — *werden*, become offensive.

anzünden ['antsyndən], *v.a.* kindle, ignite.

apart [a'part], *adj.* charming, delightful; (*Am.*) cute.

Apfel ['apfəl], *m.* (—s, *pl.* ∵) apple.

Apfelmost ['apfəlmɔst], *m.* (—s, *no pl.*) cider.

Apfelsine [apfəl'zi:nə], *f.* (—, *pl.* —n) orange.

Apostel [a'pɔstəl], *m.* (—s, *pl.* —) apostle.

Apotheke [apo'te:kə], *f.* (—, *pl.* —n) dispensary, pharmacy, chemist's shop; (*Am.*) drugstore.

Apparat [apa'ra:t], *m.* (—(e)s, *pl.* —e) apparatus; radio *or* television set; telephone.

appellieren [ape'li:rən], *v.n.* — *an*, appeal to.

appetitlich [ape'ti:tlɪç], *adj.* appetising, dainty.

Aprikose [aprɪ'ko:zə], *f.* (—, *pl.* —n) apricot.

Aquarell [akva'rɛl], *n.* (—s, *pl.* —e) water-colour (painting).

Ära ['ɛ:ra], *f.* (—, *no pl.*) era.

Arabien [a'ra:bjən], *n.* Arabia.

Arbeit ['arbaɪt], *f.* (—, *pl.* —en) work, labour; job; employment; workmanship; *an die — gehen*, set to work.

arbeiten ['arbaɪtən], *v.a., v.n.* work, labour, toil.

Arbeiter ['arbaɪtər], *m.* (—s, *pl.* —) worker, workman, labourer, hand.

Arbeiterschaft ['arbaɪtərʃaft], *f.* (—, *no pl.*) working men; workers.

arbeitsam ['arbaɪtza:m], *adj.* industrious, diligent.

Arbeitsamt ['arbaɪtsamt], *n.* (—s, *pl.* ∵er) labour exchange.

arbeitsfähig ['arbaɪtsfɛ:ɪç], *adj.* capable of working, able-bodied.

arbeitslos ['arbaɪtslo:s], *adj.* unemployed, out of work.

Arbeitslosigkeit ['arbaɪtslo:zɪçkaɪt], *f.* (—, *no pl.*) unemployment.

Arbeitsnachweis ['arbaɪtsnaxvaɪs], *m.* (—es, *no pl.*) labour exchange; (*Am.*) labour registry-office.

Arbeitssperre ['arbaɪtsʃperə], *f.* (—, *pl.* —n) (*Ind.*) lock-out.

Archäologe [arçeo'lo:gə], *m.* (—n, *pl.* —n) archaeologist.

Arche ['arçə], *f.* (—, *pl.* —n) ark.

Archipel [arçi'pe:l], *m.* (—s, *pl.* —e) archipelago.

architektonisch [arçɪtɛk'to:nɪʃ], *adj.* architectural.

Archivar [arçi'va:r], *m.* (—s, *pl.* —e) keeper of archives.

arg [ark], *adj.* bad, wicked, mischievous.

Argentinien [argən'ti:njən], *n.* Argentina.

Ärger ['ɛrgər], *m.* (—s, *no pl.*) anger, annoyance.

ärgerlich ['ɛrgərlɪç], *adj.* annoying, aggravating, vexing; angry.

ärgern ['ɛrgərn], *v.a.* annoy, vex, make angry. — *v.r. sich —*, get annoyed.

Ärgernis ['ɛrgərnɪs], *n.* (—ses, *pl.* —se) scandal, nuisance.

arglistig ['arklɪstɪç], *adj.* crafty, sly.

arglos ['arklo:s], *adj.* unsuspecting, guileless, naive.

Argwohn ['arkvo:n], *m.* (—s, *no pl.*) mistrust, suspicion.

argwöhnisch ['arkvø:nɪʃ], *adj.* suspicious, distrustful.

Arie ['a:rjə], *f.* (—, *pl.* —n) (*Mus.*) aria.

Arm [arm], *m.* (—s, *pl.* —e) arm.

arm [arm], *adj.* poor, indigent, needy.

Armaturenbrett [arma'tu:rənbrɛt], *n.* (—s, *no pl.*) dashboard.

Armband ['armbant], *n.* (—s, *pl.* ∵er) bracelet.

Armbanduhr ['armbantu:r], *f.* (—, *pl.* —en) wrist-watch.

Armbrust ['armbrust], *f.* (—, *pl.* —e) cross-bow.

Ärmel ['ɛrməl], *m.* (—s, *pl.* —) sleeve.

Ärmelkanal ['ɛrməlkana:l], *m.* (—s, *no pl.*) English Channel.

Armenien [ar'me:njən], *n.* Armenia.

Armenhaus ['armənhaus], *n.* (—es, *pl.* ∵er) poor-house, almshouse.

Armenpfleger ['armənpfle:gər], *m.* (—s, *pl.* —) almoner.

Armesündermiene [armə'zyndərmi:nə], *f.* (—, *pl.* —n) hangdog look.

ärmlich ['ɛrmlɪç], *adj.* poor, shabby, scanty.

armselig ['armze:lɪç], *adj.* poor, miserable, wretched; paltry.

Armut ['armu:t], *f.* (—, *no pl.*) poverty; *in — geraten*, be reduced to penury.
Arsch [arʃ], *m.* (—es, ¨e) (*vulg.*) arse, backside.
Arsen(ik [ar'ze:n(ɪk)], *n.* (—s, *no pl.*) arsenic.
Art [a:rt], *f.* (—, *pl.* —en) kind, species; race; sort; method, way, manner.
artig ['a:rtɪç], *adj.* well-behaved, polite.
Artigkeit ['a:rtɪçkaɪt], *f.* (—, *pl.* —en) politeness, courtesy.
Artikel [ar'ti:kəl], *m.* (—s, *pl.* —) article; commodity.
Artist [ar'tɪst], *m.* (—en, *pl.* —en) artiste (circus, variety).
Arznei [arts'naɪ], *f.* (—, *pl.* —en) medicine.
Arzneimittel [arts'naɪmɪtəl], *n.* (—s, *pl.*—) medicine, drug.
Arzt [artst], *m.* (—es, *pl.* ¨e) doctor, physician; *praktischer* —, general practitioner.
ärztlich ['ertstlɪç], *adj.* medical.
As (1) [as], *n.* (—, *pl.* —) (*Mus.*) A flat; — *Dur*, A flat major, — *Moll*, A flat minor.
As (2) [as], *n.* (—sses, *pl.* —sse) (*Sport, cards*) ace.
Asbest [as'best], *m.* (—s, *no pl.*) asbestos.
Asche ['aʃə], *f.* (—, *no pl.*) ashes.
Aschenbecher ['aʃənbeçər], *m.* (—s, *pl.* —) ash-tray.
Aschenbrödel ['aʃənbrø:dəl]*or***Aschenputtel** ['aʃənpʊtəl], *n.* Cinderella.
Aschkraut ['aʃkraut], *n.* (—s, *pl.* ¨er) (*Bot.*) cineraria.
Askese [as'ke:zə], *f.* (—, *no pl.*) asceticism.
Asket [as'ke:t], *m.* (—en, *pl.* —en) ascetic.
Assessor [a'sesɔr], *m.* (—s, *pl.* —en) assistant; assistant judge.
Ast [ast], *m.* (—es, *pl.* ¨e) branch, bough.
Astronaut [astro'naut], *m.* (—en, *pl.* —en) astronaut.
Astronom [astro'no:m], *m.* (—en, *pl.* —en) astronomer.
Asyl [a'zy:l], *n.* (—s, *pl.* —e) asylum, sanctuary.
Atem ['a:təm], *m.* (—s, *no pl.*) breath, breathing, respiration.
Atemzug ['a:təmtsu:k], *m.* (—s, *pl.* ¨e) breath.
Äthiopien [ɛti'o:pjən], *n.* Ethiopia.
Atlas (1) ['atlas], *m.* (—sses, *pl.* —sse *and* **Atlanten**) atlas, book of maps.
Atlas (2) ['atlas], *m.* (—sses, *pl.* —asse) satin.
atmen ['a:tmən], *v.n.* breathe.
atomar [ato'ma:r], *adj.* atomic.
Attentat [aten'ta:t], *n.* (—s, *pl.* —e) attempt on s.o.'s life.
Attest [a'test], *n.* (—s, *pl.* —e) (*Med.*) certificate.
ätzen ['etsən], *v.a.* corrode; (*Art*) etch; (*Med.*) cauterise.
auch [aux], *conj., adv.* also, too. likewise, as well.

Au(e) ['au(ə)], *f.* (—, *pl.* —en) green meadow, pasture.
auf [auf], *prep.* on, upon; — *der Straße*, in the road; — *eigene Gefahr*, at your own risk; — *Befehl*, by order; — *einige Tage*, for a few days; — *dem Lande*, in the country; — *keinen Fall*, on no account.
aufatmen ['aufa:tmən], *v.n.* breathe a sigh of relief.
Aufbau ['aufbau], *m.* (—s, *no pl.*) building; (*Lit.*) composition, structure.
aufbauen ['aufbauən], *v.a.* erect, build, construct.
aufbäumen ['aufbɔymən], *v.r. sich* —, (*horses*) rear.
aufbewahren ['aufbəva:rən], *v.a.* keep, store; (*luggage*) take charge of.
Aufbewahrung ['aufbəva:ruŋ], *f.* (—, *pl.* —en) storage, safe keeping.
aufbieten ['aufbi:tən], *v.a. irr.* call up for service; exert (*energies*).
aufbinden ['aufbɪndən], *v.a. irr.* untie; *einem einen Bären* —, to hoax s.o.
aufblähen ['aufblɛ:ən], *v.a.* puff up, swell, inflate.
aufblühen ['aufbly:ən], *v.n.* (*aux. sein*) flourish, unfold.
aufbrausen ['aufbrauzən], *v.n.* (*aux. sein*) fly into a rage.
aufbringen ['aufbrɪŋən], *v.a. irr.* bring up; afford; annoy (s.o.).
Aufbruch ['aufbrux], *m.* (—s, *no pl.*) departure.
aufbürden ['aufbyrdən], *v.a. einem eine Last* —, burden s.o. with a thing.
aufdecken ['aufdɛkən], *v.a.* uncover, unveil.
aufdonnern ['aufdɔnərn], *v.r. sich* — dress up showily.
aufdrängen ['aufdrɛŋən], *v.a. einem etwas* —, press s.th. upon s.o. — *v.r. sich* —, force o.'s company on.
aufdrehen ['aufdre:ən], *v.a.* (*tap*) turn on.
aufdringlich ['aufdrɪŋlɪç], *adj.* importunate, officious, obtrusive.
Aufdruck ['aufdruk], *m.* (—s, *pl.* —e) imprint.
aufdrücken ['aufdrykən], *v.a.* press open; press on s.th.
Aufenthalt ['aufɛnthalt], *m.* (—s, *pl.* —e) stay, sojourn; delay; stop.
auferlegen ['auferle:gən], *v.a.* impose; enjoin.
auferstehen ['auferʃte:ən], *v.n. irr.* (*aux. sein*) (*Rel.*) rise from the dead.
auffahren ['auffa:rən], *v.n. irr.* (*aux. sein*) start (from o.'s sleep); mount; flare up (in anger).
Auffahrt ['auffa:rt], *f.* (—, *pl.* —en) ascent; approach to a house, drive.
auffallen ['auffalən], *v.n. irr.* (*aux. sein*) strike the ground; *einem* —, strike s.o., astonish.
auffangen ['auffaŋən], *v.a. irr.* (*ball*) catch; (*blow*) parry, ward off; (*letter*) intercept.
auffassen ['auffasən], *v.a.* take in, comprehend.

Auffassung ['auffasuŋ], *f.* (—, *pl.* —en) conception, interpretation; view.

aufflackern ['aufflakərn],*v.n.* (*aux.* sein) flare up, flicker.

auffordern ['auffɔrdərn], *v.a.* summon, request, ask, invite.

aufforsten ['auffɔrstən], *v.a.* afforest.

auffressen ['auffresən], *v.a. irr.* devour; (*of animals*) eat up.

auffrischen ['auffrɪʃən], *v.a.* renew, redecorate; (*fig.*) brush up.

aufführen ['auffy:rən], *v.a.* (*Theat.*) perform; *einzeln* —, specify, particularise. — *v.r. sich* —, behave, conduct o.s.

Aufführung ['auffy:ruŋ], *f.* (—, *pl.* —en) (*Theat.*) performance.

Aufgabe ['aufga:bə], *f.* (—, *pl.* —n) giving up, abandonment; (*letters, telegrams*) posting, despatch; (*work*) task; (*Sch.*) exercise; (*Maths.*) problem.

aufgabeln ['aufga:bəln], *v.a.* (*sl.*) pick up.

Aufgang ['aufgaŋ], *m.* (—s, *pl.* ⸚e) ascent, stairs.

aufgeben ['aufge:bən], *v.a. irr.* give up, abandon, relinquish; (*Am.*) quit; (*luggage*) register.

aufgeblasen ['aufgəbla:zən], *adj.* conceited, stuck up.

Aufgebot ['aufgəbo:t], *n.* (—s, *pl.* —e) (*marriage*) banns; (*Mil.*) levy; *mit aller Kräfte*, with the utmost exertion.

aufgebracht ['aufgəbraxt], *adj.* angry, annoyed.

aufgedunsen ['aufgədunzən], *adj.* bloated, sodden.

aufgehen ['aufge:ən], *v.n. irr.* (*aux.* sein) (*knot*) come undone; (*sun*) rise; (*dough*) swell, rise; (*Maths.*) leave no remainder, cancel out.

aufgehoben ['aufgəho:bən], *adj. gut — sein*, be in good hands.

aufgelegt ['aufgəle:kt], *adj.* disposed, inclined.

aufgeräumt ['aufgərɔymt], *adj.* merry, cheerful, in high spirits.

aufgeweckt ['aufgəvɛkt], *adj.* bright, clever, intelligent.

aufgießen ['aufgi:sən], *v.a. irr. Kaffee* —, make coffee.

Aufguß ['aufgus], *m.* (—sses, *pl.* ⸚sse) infusion.

aufhalsen ['aufhalzən], *v.a. einem etwas* —, (*coll.*) saddle s.o. with s.th.

aufhalten ['aufhaltən], *v.a. irr.* (*door*) hold open; *einen* —, delay s.o. — *v.r. sich an einem Ort* —, stay at a place; *sich über etwas* —, find fault with s.th.

aufhängen ['aufhɛŋən], *v.a. irr.* hang (up).

aufhäufen ['aufhɔyfən], *v.a.* pile up. — *v.r. sich* —, accumulate.

Aufheben ['aufhe:bən], *n.* (—s, *no pl.*) lifting up; ado; *viel —s machen*, make a great fuss.

aufheben ['aufhe:bən], *v.a. irr.* lift (up), pick up; keep, preserve; (*laws*) repeal, abolish; (*agreements*) rescind, annul.

Aufhebung ['aufhe:buŋ], *f.* (—, *pl.* —en) abolition, abrogation, annulment, repeal.

aufheitern ['aufhaɪtərn], *v.a.* cheer up; amuse. — *v.r. sich* —, (*weather*) brighten, clear up.

aufhelfen ['aufhɛlfən], *v.n. irr. einem* —, help s.o. up.

aufhellen ['aufhɛlən], *v.r. sich* —, (*weather*) clear up; (*face*) brighten up.

aufhetzen ['aufhɛtsən],*v.a.* rouse (s.o.); *einen — gegen*, incite s.o. against.

aufhorchen ['aufhɔrçən], *v.n.* prick up o.'s ears.

aufhören ['aufhø:rən], *v.n.* cease, stop; (*Am.*) quit; *ohne aufzuhören*, incessantly; *da hört sich doch alles auf!* that is the limit!

aufklären ['aufkle:rən], *v.a.* enlighten; clear up; *einen* —, enlighten s.o. — *v.r. sich* —, (*weather*) brighten.

Aufklärung ['aufkle:ruŋ], *f.* (—, *no pl.*) (age of) Enlightenment.

aufknacken ['aufknakən], *v.a.* crack (open).

aufknöpfen ['aufknœpfən], *v.a.* unbutton; *aufgeknöpft sein*, be in a talkative mood.

aufkommen ['aufkɔmən], *v.n. irr.* (*aux.* sein) come into use, spring up; *für etwas* —, pay for s.th.; *einen nicht — lassen*, give s.o. no chance.

aufkrempeln ['aufkrɛmpəln],*v.a.*(*coll.*) roll up (o.'s sleeves).

aufkündigen ['aufkyndɪgən], *v.a.* (*money*) recall; *einem die Freundschaft* —, break with s.o.

Auflage ['aufla:gə], *f.* (—, *pl.* —n) (*tax*) impost, duty, levy; (*book*) edition, impression; circulation.

auflassen ['auflasən], *v.a. irr.* leave open; (*Law*) cede.

auflauern ['auflauərn], *v.n. einem* —, lie in wait for s.o., waylay s.o.

Auflauf ['auflauf], *m.* (—s, *pl.* ⸚e) tumult, noisy street gathering; soufflé.

auflaufen ['auflaufən], *v.n. irr.* (*aux.* sein) swell, increase; (*ship*) run aground.

aufleben ['aufle:bən], *v.n.* (*aux.* sein) *wieder* —, revive.

auflegen ['aufle:gən], *v.a. irr.* lay upon, put on; (*book*) publish; (*tax, punishment*) impose, inflict.

auflehnen ['aufle:nən], *v.r. sich gegen einen* (or *etwas*) —, rebel against, mutiny, oppose.

auflesen ['aufle:zən], *v.a. irr.* pick up, gather.

aufleuchten ['auflɔyçtən], *v.n.* light up; (*eyes*) shine.

auflockern ['auflɔkərn], *v.a.* loosen.

auflodern ['auflo:dərn], *v.n.* (*aux.* sein) flare up, blaze up.

auflösen

auflösen [′aʊfløːzən], *v.a.* dissolve, loosen; (*puzzle*) solve, guess; (*meeting*) break up; (*business*) wind up; (*partnership*) dissolve; (*army*) disband. — *v.r. sich* —, melt, dissolve, be broken up.

aufmachen [′aʊfmaxən], *v.a.* (*door, packet*) open; (*knot*) undo; *gut* —, pack nicely. — *v.r. sich* —, get going, set out for.

Aufmachung [′aʊfmaxʊŋ], *f.* (—, *pl.* —en) outward appearance, make-up, get-up.

Aufmarsch [′aʊfmarʃ], *m.* (—es, *pl.* ̈e) (*Mil.*) parade.

aufmerksam [′aʊfmɛrkzaːm], *adj.* attentive, observant; civil, kind; *einen* — *machen auf,* draw s.o.'s attention to.

aufmuntern [′aʊfmʊntərn], *v.a.* encourage, cheer up.

Aufnahme [′aʊfnaːmə], *f.* (—, *pl.* —n) reception; (*Phot.*) snap, photograph; (*Geog.*) mapping out, survey; (*Mus.*) recording.

aufnehmen [′aʊfneːmən], *v.a. irr.* take up; receive, give shelter to; (*Phot.*) photograph, film; (*Mus.*) record; (*money*) raise, borrow; (*minutes*) draw up; *den Faden wieder* —, take up the thread; *die Arbeit wieder* —, return to work, resume work; *die Fährte* —, (*Hunt.*) recover the scent; *es mit einem* —, be a match for s.o.; (*Comm.*) *Inventar* —, take stock, draw up an inventory.

aufnötigen [′aʊfnøːtɪgən], *v.a. einem etwas* —, force s.th. upon s.o.

aufpassen [′aʊfpasən], *v.n.* attend to, pay attention to, take notice of, take care of.

aufpeitschen [′aʊfpaɪtʃən], *v.a.* whip up.

aufpflanzen [′aʊfpflantsən], *v.a.* mount, erect. — *v.r. sich vor einem* —, plant o.s. in front of s.o.; *mit aufgepflanztem Bajonett,* with bayonets fixed.

Aufputz [′aʊfpʊts], *m.* (—es, *no pl.*) finery, trimmings.

aufraffen [′aʊfrafən], *v.a.* snatch up, rake up. — *v.r. sich wieder* —, pull o.s. together.

aufräumen [′aʊfrɔʏmən], *v.a.* put in order, clear away; (*room*) tidy up; *mit etwas* —, make a clean sweep of s.th.; *aufgeräumt sein,* be in a jolly mood.

aufrechnen [′aʊfrɛçnən], *v.a.* reckon up; set off against.

aufrecht [′aʊfrɛçt], *adj.* upright, erect; *etwas* — *erhalten,* maintain s.th.; (*opinion*) stick to, adhere to, uphold.

Aufrechterhaltung [′aʊfrɛçtərhaltʊŋ], *f.* (—, *no pl.*) maintenance, preservation.

aufregen [′aʊfreːgən], *v.a.* excite, enrage.

aufreiben [′aʊfraɪbən], *v.a. irr.* rub sore; (*Mil.*) destroy, wipe out. — *v.r. sich* —, exhaust o.s. with worry (*or* work).

aufreizen [′aʊfraɪtsən], *v.a.* incite, provoke.

aufrichten [′aʊfrɪçtən], *v.a.* raise, erect, set upright; (*fig.*) comfort, console. — *v.r. sich* —, rise, sit up.

aufrichtig [′aʊfrɪçtɪç], *adj.* sincere, frank.

aufriegeln [′aʊfriːgəln], *v.a.* unbolt.

Aufriß [′aʊfrɪs], *m.* (—sses, *pl.* —sse) sketch, draft; (*Archit.*) elevation, section.

aufrücken [′aʊfrykən], *v.n.* (*aux.* sein) rise, be promoted (in rank), advance.

Aufruf [′aʊfruːf], *m.* (—s, *pl.* —e) summons, proclamation, appeal; (*Law*) citation.

aufrufen [′aʊfruːfən], *v.a. irr.* summons; (*Sch.*) call upon.

Aufruhr [′aʊfruːr], *m.* (—s, *pl.* —e) uproar, riot, tumult, rebellion, mutiny.

aufrühren [′aʊfryːrən], *v.a.* stir up, agitate, rouse to rebellion.

Aufrüstung [′aʊfrystʊŋ], *f.* (—, *no pl.*) (*Mil.*) (re-)armament.

aufrütteln [′aʊfrytəln], *v.a.* rouse, shake s.o. out of his lethargy.

aufsagen [′aʊfzaːgən], *v.a.* recite.

aufsässig [′aʊfzɛsɪç], *adj.* refractory, rebellious.

Aufsatz [′aʊfzats], *m.* (—es, *pl.* ̈e) top, head-piece, table centre-piece; (*Sch.*) composition, essay; (*newspaper*) article.

aufscheuchen [′aʊfʃɔʏçən], *v.a.* flush (game), startle.

aufschichten [′aʊfʃɪçtən], *v.a.* stack, pile up in layers.

aufschieben [′aʊfʃiːbən], *v.a. irr.* push open; delay, postpone, adjourn; (*Parl.*) prorogue.

Aufschlag [′aʊfʃlaːk], *m.* (—s, *pl.* ̈e) impact, striking; (*sleeve*) cuff; turn-up; (*uniform*) facings; (*Comm.*) increase in price; (*Tennis*) service.

aufschlagen [′aʊfʃlaːgən], *v.n. irr.* (*aux.* sein) hit, strike (open); (*Tennis*) serve. — *v.a. die Augen* —, open o.'s eyes; *ein Lager* —, pitch camp; *ein Buch* —, open a book.

aufschlitzen [′aʊfʃlɪtsən], *v.a.* rip open, slit open.

Aufschluß [′aʊfʃlʊs], *m.* (—sses, *pl.* ̈sse) disclosure, information.

aufschneiden [′aʊfʃnaɪdən], *v.a. irr.* cut open. — *v.n.* brag, boast.

Aufschneider [′aʊfʃnaɪdər], *m.* (-s, *pl.* —) swaggerer, braggart.

Aufschnitt [′aʊfʃnɪt], *m.* (—s, *no pl.*) slice of cold meat *or* sausage.

aufschnüren [′aʊfʃnyːrən], *v.a.* unlace, untie.

Aufschrei [′aʊfʃraɪ], *m.* (—s, *pl.* —e) outcry, screech, scream, shout, shriek.

Aufschrift [′aʊfʃrɪft], *f.* (—, *pl.* —en) inscription, address; heading.

Aufschub [′aʊfʃuːp], *m.* (—s, *pl.* ̈e) delay, adjournment, postponement.

aufschütten [′aʊfʃytən], *v.a.* (*liquid*) pour upon; (*dam*) raise.

aufschwingen [ˈaufʃvɪŋən], *v.r. irr.*
sich —, soar, rise; *ich kann mich dazu
nicht —*, I cannot rise to that.

Aufschwung [ˈaufʃvuŋ], *m.* (—s, *no
pl.*) flight, rising; (*Comm.*) improvement, boom.

Aufsehen [ˈaufzeːən], *n.* (—s, *no pl.*)
sensation, stir.

Aufseher [ˈaufzeːər], *m.* (—s, *pl.* —)
overseer, inspector.

aufsein [ˈaufzaɪn], *v.n. irr.* (*aux.* sein)
be out of bed, be up and about.

aufsetzen [ˈaufzɛtsən], *v.a.* (*hat*) put on;
(*letter, essay*) draft.

Aufsicht [ˈaufzɪçt], *f.* (—, *no pl.*)
inspection, supervision, control.

Aufsichtsrat [ˈaufzɪçtsraːt], *m.* (—s,
pl. ⁓e) (*Comm.*) board of directors.

aufsitzen [ˈaufzɪtsən], *v.n. irr.* sit up,
wait up at night; (*horse*) mount.

aufspannen [ˈaufʃpanən], *v.a.* (*umbrella*)
put up; (*tent*) pitch.

aufspeichern [ˈaufʃpaɪçərn], *v.a.* store
(up), warehouse.

aufsperren [ˈaufʃpɛrən], *v.a.* open
wide, unlock.

aufspielen [ˈaufʃpiːlən], *v.n. zum Tanz
—*, play music for dancing. — *v.r.
sich groß —*, give o.s. airs.

aufspießen [ˈaufʃpiːsən], *v.a.* pierce on
a spit; (*joint*) skewer.

aufspringen [ˈaufʃprɪŋən], *v.n. irr.*
(*aux.* sein) leap up, jump up; (*door*)
fly open; (*hands in winter*) chap.

aufspüren [ˈaufʃpyːrən], *v.a.* track, trace.

aufstacheln [ˈaufʃtaxəln], *v.a.* goad,
incite.

Aufstand [ˈaufʃtant], *m.* (—s, *pl.* ⁓e)
insurrection, revolt, sedition.

aufstapeln [ˈaufʃtaːpəln], *v.a.* pile up,
stack, store.

aufstechen [ˈaufʃtɛçən], *v.a. irr.* (*Med.*)
lance.

aufstehen [ˈaufʃteːən], *v.n. irr.* (*aux.*
sein) (*door*) stand open; stand up; get
up (from bed); rise (from a chair).

aufstellen [ˈaufʃtɛlən], *v.a.* set up,
arrange; erect; (*Pol.*) put forward
(candidate).

Aufstellung [ˈaufʃtɛluŋ], *f.* (—, *pl.*
—en) arrangement; statement; inventory; (*Pol.*) nomination.

aufstemmen [ˈaufʃtɛmən], *v.a.* prise
open.

Aufstieg [ˈaufʃtiːk], *m.* (—s, *pl.* ⁓e)
ascent, rise.

aufstöbern [ˈaufʃtøːbərn], *v.a.* stir (up);
start; (*fig.*) discover, ferret out.

aufstoßen [ˈaufʃtoːsən], *v.a. irr.* push
open; bump against. — *v.n.* belch.

aufstreben [ˈaufʃtreːbən], *v.n.* soar;
(*fig.*) aspire.

aufstreichen [ˈaufʃtraɪçən], *v.a. irr.*
(*paint*) lay on; (*butter*) spread.

aufstülpen [ˈaufʃtylpən], *v.a.* turn up;
(*hat*) clap on o.'s head.

auftakeln [ˈauftaːkəln], *v.a.* (*Naut.*)
rig.

Auftakt [ˈauftakt], *m.* (—s, *pl.* —e)
(*Mus.*) arsis; (*fig.*) opening, prelude.

auftauchen [ˈauftauxən], *v.n.* (*aux.*
sein) appear, emerge, surface.

auftauen [ˈauftauən], *v.n.* (*aux.* sein)
thaw; (*fig.*) lose o.'s reserve.

auftischen [ˈauftɪʃən], *v.a.* dish up.

Auftrag [ˈauftraːk], *m.* (—s, *pl.* ⁓e)
assignment, commission, errand; *im
— von*, on behalf of.

auftragen [ˈauftraːgən], *v.a. irr.* (*food*)
serve up; (*paint*) apply; *einem etwas
—*, charge s.o. with a job; *stark —*,
lay it on thick.

auftreiben [ˈauftraɪbən], *v.a. irr.* raise
(*money*); procure, obtain. — *v.n.*
(*aux.* sein) (*ship*) run aground.

auftrennen [ˈauftrɛnən], *v.a.* unstitch;
(*hem*) unpick.

Auftreten [ˈauftreːtən], *n.* (—s, *no pl.*)
(*Theat.*) appearance; behaviour.

auftreten [ˈauftreːtən], *v.n. irr.* (*aux.*
sein) tread upon, step upon; (*Theat.*)
appear, come on; *energisch —*, take
strong measures, put o.'s foot
down.

Auftritt [ˈauftrɪt], *m.* (—s, *pl.* —e)
(*Theat.*) scene; altercation, row.

auftun [ˈauftuːn], *v.a. irr.* open; *den
Mund —*, speak. — *v.r. sich —*, (*abyss*)
yawn.

auftürmen [ˈauftyrmən], *v.a.* pile up,
heap up. — *v.r. sich —*, tower.

aufwachen [ˈaufvaxən], *v.n.* (*aux.* sein)
awake, wake up.

aufwallen [ˈaufvalən], *v.n.* (*aux.* sein)
boil up, bubble up, rage.

Aufwand [ˈaufvant], *m.* (—s, *no pl.*)
expense, expenditure; sumptuous-
ness.

aufwarten [ˈaufvartən], *v.n.* wait upon,
attend on.

aufwärts [ˈaufvɛrts], *adv.* upward(s),
aloft.

Aufwartung [ˈaufvartuŋ], *f.* (—, *pl.*
—en) attendance; *seine — machen*, pay
a (formal) visit.

aufwaschen [ˈaufvaʃən], *v.a. irr.* wash
the dishes.

aufweisen [ˈaufvaɪzən], *v.a. irr.* show,
produce.

aufwenden [ˈaufvɛndən], *v.a. irr.*
spend upon, expend upon.

aufwickeln [ˈaufvɪkəln], *v.a.* wind up;
unwind.

aufwiegeln [ˈaufviːgəln], *v.a.* stir up,
incite to rebellion.

aufwiegen [ˈaufviːgən], *v.a. irr.* outweigh, counter-balance, make up
for.

aufwischen [ˈaufvɪʃən], *v.a.* wipe away,
mop up.

aufwühlen [ˈaufvyːlən], *v.a.* dig, root
up, (*fig.*) stir.

aufzählen [ˈauftseːlən], *v.a.* count up,
enumerate, list.

aufzäumen [ˈauftsɔymən], *v.a.* bridle
(horses).

aufzehren [ˈauftseːrən], *v.a.* eat up,
consume.

aufzeichnen [ˈauftsaɪçnən], *v.a.* write
down, take a note of, record.

aufziehen ['auftsi:ən], *v.a. irr.* draw up, pull up; pull open;· (*pennant*) hoist; (*clock*) wind up; (*child*) bring up, rear; *einen* —, tease s.o.; *gelindere Saiten* —, be more lenient.

Aufzucht ['auftsuxt], *f.* (—, *no pl.*) breeding, rearing.

Aufzug ['auftsu:k], *m.* (—s, *pl.* ⁼e) lift; (*Am.*) elevator; (*Theat.*) act; dress, array, attire.

aufzwingen ['auftsvɪŋən], *v.a. irr. einem etwas* —, force s.th. on s.o.

Augapfel ['aukapfəl], *m.* (—s, *pl.* ⁼) eye-ball; (*fig.*) apple of o.'s eye.

Auge ['augə], *n.* (—s, *pl.* —n) eye; *aus den* —*n, aus dem Sinn,* out of sight, out of mind; *mit einem blauen* — *davonkommen,* escape by the skin of o.'s teeth, get off cheaply; *es wird mir schwarz vor den* —*n,* I feel faint.

Augenblick ['augənblɪk], *m.* (—s, *pl.* —e) moment, instant; *jeden* —, at any moment.

augenblicklich [augən'blɪklɪç], *adj.* momentary, instantaneous.— *adv.* at present, for the moment, immediately.

Augenbraue ['augənbrauə], *f.* (—, *pl.* —n) eye-brow.

augenfällig ['augənfɛlɪç], *adj.* visible, evident, conspicuous.

Augenglas ['augənglas], *n.* (—es, *pl.* ⁼er) eye-glass.

Augenhöhle ['augənhø:lə], *f.* (—, *pl.* —n) eye-socket.

Augenlicht ['augənlɪçt], *n.* (—s, *no pl.*) eye-sight.

Augenlid ['augənli:t], *n.* (—s, *pl.* —er) eye-lid.

Augenmaß ['augənma:s], *n.* (—es, *no pl.*) *gutes* —, good measuring ability with the eye, a sure eye.

Augenmerk ['augənmɛrk], *n.* (—s, *no pl.*) attention; *sein* — *auf etwas richten,* focus o.'s attention on s.th.

Augenschein ['augənʃain], *m.* (—s, *no pl.*) appearance; *in* — *nehmen,* view.

augenscheinlich ['augənʃainlɪç], *adj.* apparent, evident.

Augenweide ['augənvaidə], *f.* (—, *pl.* —n) delight to the eye, s.th. lovely to look at.

Augenwimper ['augənvɪmpər], *f.* (—, *pl.* —n) eye-lash.

Augenzeuge ['augəntsɔygə], *m.* (—n, *pl.* —n) eye-witness.

August [au'gust], *m.* (—s, *no pl.*) (*month*) August.

Augustiner [augus'ti:nər], *m.* (—s, *pl.* —) (*Eccl.*) Augustinian.

auktionieren [auktsjo'ni:rən], *v.a.* auction(eer), sell by auction.

Aula ['aula], *f.* (—, *pl.* —len) (*Sch., Univ.*) great hall; auditorium maximum.

Aurikel [au'ri:kəl], *f.* (—, *pl.* —n) (*Bot.*) auricula.

aus [aus], *prep.* (*Dat.*) from, out of, of, off. — *adv.* out, over, finished, done with, spent; *es ist alles* —, it is over and done with; *ich weiß weder ein noch* —, I am at my wits' end.

ausarten ['ausartən], *v.n.* (*aux.* sein) degenerate; (*fig.*) deteriorate.

Ausbau ['ausbau], *m.* (—s, *no pl.*) enlargement, extension.

ausbauen ['ausbauən], *v.a.* enlarge (a house); improve on.

ausbedingen ['ausbədɪŋən], *v.a. sich etwas* —, stipulate.

ausbessern ['ausbesərn], *v.a.* (*garment*) mend, repair.

Ausbeute ['ausbɔytə], *f.* (—, *no pl.*) gain, profit, produce.

Ausbeutung ['ausbɔytuŋ], *f.* (—, *no pl.*) exploitation, sweating; (*Min.*) working.

ausbezahlen ['ausbətsa:lən], *v.a.* pay in full.

ausbilden ['ausbɪldən], *v.a.* develop, train; (*Mil.*) drill.

Ausbildung ['ausbɪlduŋ], *f.* (—, *pl.* —en) training, education.

ausbleiben ['ausblaibən], *v.n. irr.* (*aux.* sein) fail to appear, be absent.

Ausblick ['ausblɪk], *m.* (—s, *pl.* —e) view (from window); (*fig.*) prospect, outlook.

ausborgen ['ausbɔrgən], *v.a.* (*sich*) *etwas* —, borrow s.th. from.

ausbreiten ['ausbraitən], *v.a.* spread (things); stretch out (o.'s arms). — *v.r. sich* —, spread, extend.

Ausbreitung ['ausbraituŋ], *f.* (—, *no pl.*) spreading, extension, distribution, expansion.

ausbringen ['ausbrɪŋən], *v.a. irr. einen Toast auf einen* —, drink s.o.'s health.

Ausbruch ['ausbrux], *m.* (—s, *pl.* ⁼e) breaking out, outbreak, eruption, burst (of laughter).

ausbrüten ['ausbry:tən], *v.a.* hatch; (*fig.*) plot.

Ausbund ['ausbunt], *m.* (—s, *pl.* ⁼e) paragon, embodiment.

Ausdauer ['ausdauər], *f.* (—, *no pl.*) perseverance, persistence, stamina.

ausdehnen ['ausde:nən], *v.a.* extend, stretch, distend; (*fig.*) prolong, protract. — *v.r. sich* —, expand, extend, stretch.

Ausdehnung ['ausde:nuŋ], *f.* (—, *pl.* —en) extension, expansion; dilation; (*Phys.*) dimension.

ausdenken ['ausdɛŋkən], *v.a. irr.* think out. — *v.r. sich etwas* —, devise s.th., invent s.th.; *das ist gar nicht auszudenken,* that is unimaginable, inconceivable.

Ausdeutung ['ausdɔytuŋ], *f.* (—, *pl.* —en) interpretation, explanation.

ausdörren ['ausdœrən], *v.a.* parch, dry (up).

ausdrehen ['ausdre:ən], *v.a.* (*gas, light, water*) turn off, switch off.

Ausdruck ['ausdruk], *m.* (—s, *pl.* ⁼e) expression, phrase.

ausdrücken ['ausdrykən], *v.a.* squeeze out, press out; (*fig.*) express.

ausdrücklich ['ausdryklɪç], *adj.* express, explicit.

Ausdrucksweise ['ausdruksvaɪzə], f. (—, pl. —n) enunciation, manner of speech, (mode of) expression, style.

ausdünsten ['ausdynstən], v.a. exhale, perspire.

auseinander [ausaɪn'andər], adv. asunder, apart.

Auseinandersetzung [ausaɪn'andərzetsuŋ], f. (—, pl. —en) altercation; discussion, explanation.

auserkoren ['ausɛrkoːrən], adj. elect, chosen, selected.

auserlesen ['ausɛrleːzən], adj. choice, picked, excellent, first class.

auserwählen ['ausɛrveːlən], v.a. choose, select.

Ausfahrt ['ausfaːrt], f. (—, pl. —en) drive; gateway; exit.

Ausfall ['ausfal], m. (—s, pl. ˙e) falling out; (radioactivity) fall-out; sortie, sally; deficiency, loss, cancellation; result, outcome.

ausfallen ['ausfalən], v.n. irr. (aux. sein) drop out, fall out; be cancelled, be omitted, fail to take place; turn out (well etc.).

ausfallend ['ausfalənt], adj. offensive, abusive.; — werden, become insulting.

ausfertigen ['ausfɛrtɪgən], v.a. despatch, draw up, make out, issue.

ausfindig ['ausfɪndɪç], adj. — machen, find out, locate, discover.

ausflicken ['ausflɪkən], v.a. mend, patch.

Ausflucht ['ausfluxt], f. (—, pl. ˙e) evasion, excuse, subterfuge.

Ausflug ['ausfluːk], m. (—s, pl. ˙e) trip, excursion, outing.

Ausfluß ['ausflus], m. (—sses, pl. ˙sse) (Engin.) outflow, outlet; (Med.) discharge, suppuration.

ausfragen ['ausfraːgən], v.a. einen —, question, quiz s.o.

Ausfuhr ['ausfuːr], f. (—, pl. —en) export.

ausführbar ['ausfyːrbaːr], adj. practicable, feasible; exportable.

ausführen ['ausfyːrən], v.a. take out; lead out; export; carry out, perform, fulfil; point out.

ausführlich [aus'fyːrlɪç], adj. detailed, full.

Ausführung ['ausfyːruŋ], f. (—, pl. —en) execution, carrying out; finish; workmanship.

ausfüllen ['ausfylən], v.a. (forms) fill up, fill in, complete.

ausfüttern ['ausfytərn], v.a. line (a dress).

Ausgabe ['ausgaːbə], f. (—, pl. —en) issue, distribution; (goods) dispatch, issuing counter; delivery; (book) edition; (pl.) expenses, expenditure.

Ausgang ['ausgaŋ], m. (—s, pl. ˙e) going out; exit; result, upshot; end, conclusion; time off (from duty).

Ausgangspunkt ['ausgaŋspuŋkt], m. (—s, pl. —e) starting-point; point of departure.

ausgären ['ausgɛːrən], v.n. irr. (aux. sein) ferment; ausgegoren sein, have fermented.

ausgeben ['ausgeːbən], v.a. irr. (work) give out, distribute; (money) expend, spend; (tickets) issue. —v.r. sich — für, pass o.s. off as.

ausgebreitet ['ausgəbraɪtət], adj. extensive, widespread.

Ausgeburt ['ausgeburt], f. (—, pl. —en) monstrosity; — des Hirns, figment of the imagination.

ausgefahren ['ausgəfaːrən], adj. (street) rutted, well-worn.

ausgehen ['ausgeːən], v.n. irr. (aux. sein) go out; (hair) to fall out; (colour) come off, fade; (breath, patience, money) become exhausted; result, end in.

ausgelassen ['ausgəlasən], adj. boisterous, exuberant, frolicsome, merry, jolly, unbridled.

ausgemacht ['ausgəmaxt], adj. arranged, settled, decided; eine —e Sache, a matter of course, a foregone conclusion; ein —er Schurke, a downright scoundrel.

ausgeschlossen ['ausgəʃlɔsən], p.p. das ist —, that is impossible, out of the question.

ausgewachsen ['ausgəvaksən], adj. full-grown, fully grown.

ausgezeichnet ['ausgətsaɪçnət], adj. excellent, first rate, distinguished.

ausgiebig ['ausgiːbɪç], adj. abundant, plentiful; (soil) fertile, rich.

ausgießen ['ausgiːsən], v.a. irr. pour out.

Ausgleich ['ausglaɪç], m. (—s, no pl.) settlement, compromise, compensation, equalisation.

ausgleichen ['ausglaɪçən], v.a. irr. make even, balance, equalise, compensate; (sport) equalise, draw.

ausgraben ['ausgraːbən], v.a. irr. dig out, dig up, excavate, exhume.

Ausguck ['ausguk], m. (—s, pl. —e) look-out; (Naut.) crow's nest.

Ausguß ['ausgus], m. (—sses, pl. ˙sse) sink, gutter.

aushalten ['aushaltən], v.a. irr. sustain, endure, bear, stand.

aushändigen ['aushɛndɪgən], v.a. deliver up, hand over.

Aushang ['aushaŋ], m. (—s, pl. ˙e) sign, sign-board, placard.

ausharren ['ausharən], v.n. persevere, hold out, wait patiently.

aushecken ['aushɛkən], v.a. hatch (a plot).

aushelfen ['aushɛlfən], v.n. irr. help out.

Aushilfe ['aushɪlfə], f. (—, pl. —n) help, aid, assistance.

aushilfsweise ['aushɪlfsvaɪzə], adv. temporarily, as a stop-gap.

aushöhlen ['aushøːlən], v.a. hollow out, excavate.

ausholen ['aushoːlən], v.a. pump, sound s.o. — v.n. strike out; weit —, go far back (in a narration).

auskehren [ˈauskeːrən], v.a. sweep out.
auskennen [ˈauskɛnən], v.r. irr. sich in etwas —, know all about s.th.
auskleiden [ˈausklaɪdən], v.a. undress.
ausklingen [ˈausklɪŋən], v.n. irr. (aux. sein) (sound) die away.
ausklügeln [ˈausklyːgəln], v.a. puzzle out, contrive.
auskneifen [ˈausknaɪfən], v.n. irr. (aux. sein) (coll.) bolt, run away.
Auskommen [ˈauskɔmən], n. (—s, no pl.) sufficiency, subsistence, livelihood; mit dem ist kein —, there is no getting on with him.
auskommen [ˈauskɔmən], v.n. irr. (aux. sein) mit etwas —, have enough or sufficient of s.th., manage; mit einem gut —, be on good terms with s.o., get on well with s.o.
auskömmlich [ˈauskœmlɪç], adj. sufficient.
auskosten [ˈauskɔstən], v.a. taste or enjoy to the full.
auskramen [ˈauskraːmən], v.a. rummage out; (fig.) reminisce; talk freely.
auskundschaften [ˈauskuntʃaftən], v.a. spy out, reconnoitre, explore.
Auskunft [ˈauskunft], f. (—, pl. ⁝e) information; (Tel.) enquiries; (Mil.) intelligence, enquiry.
auslachen [ˈauslaxən], v.a. laugh at, deride.
ausladen [ˈauslaːdən], v.a. irr. unload, discharge; cancel (invitation).
Auslage [ˈauslaːgə], f. (—, pl. —n) outlay, expenses; advance; shop-window display.
Ausland [ˈauslant], n. (—s, no pl.) foreign country; ins — fahren, go abroad.
Ausländer [ˈauslɛndər], m. (—s, pl. —) foreigner, alien.
auslassen [ˈauslasən], v.a. irr. let off (steam); let out (a dress); melt (butter); leave off, omit. — v.r. sich über etwas —, speak o.'s mind about s.th.
Auslassung [ˈauslasuŋ], f. (—, pl. —en) utterance; omission.
auslaufen [ˈauslaufən], v.n. irr. (aux. sein) run out, leak out; (ship) put to sea; (result) turn out.
Ausläufer [ˈauslɔyfər], m. (—s, pl. —) errand boy; (mountain) spur.
Auslaut [ˈauslaut], m. (—s, pl. —e) (Phonet.) final sound.
auslegen [ˈausleːgən], v.a. lay out, spread out, display; interpret; (money) advance.
ausleihen [ˈauslaɪən], v.a. irr. lend, hire out. — v.r. sich etwas —, borrow s.th.
auslernen [ˈauslɛrnən], v.n. end o.'s apprenticeship.
ausliefern [ˈausliːfərn], v.a. hand over, deliver; surrender, give up, extradite.
auslöschen [ˈauslœʃən], v.a. extinguish, put out (fire).
auslosen [ˈausloːzən], v.a. raffle, draw lots for.

auslösen [ˈausløːzən], v.a. redeem, ransom, recover; (fig.) produce; arouse.
Auslosung [ˈausloːzuŋ], f. (—, pl. —en) raffle, draw.
Auslösung [ˈausløːzuŋ], f. (—, pl. —en) ransom.
auslüften [ˈauslyftən], v.a. air, ventilate.
ausmachen [ˈausmaxən], v.a. decide, settle; amount to; etwas mit einem —, arrange s.th. with s.o.; es macht nichts aus, it does not matter; wieviel macht das aus? how much is this? würde es Ihnen etwas —? would you mind?
Ausmaß [ˈausmaːs], n. (—es, pl. —e) dimension, amount, extent, scale.
ausmeißeln [ˈausmaɪsəln], v.a. chisel out, carve out.
ausmerzen [ˈausmertsən], v.a. expunge, eradicate.
ausmisten [ˈausmɪstən], v.a. clean, clear up (mess).
ausmustern [ˈausmustərn], v.a. eliminate, reject; (Mil.) discharge.
Ausnahme [ˈausnaːmə], f. (—, pl. —n) exception.
ausnehmen [ˈausneːmən], v.a. irr. except, exclude; (poultry) draw; (fish) clean.
ausnutzen [ˈausnutsən], v.a. make the most of s.th.; take advantage of s.th.
ausnützen [ˈausnytsən], v.a. exploit.
auspacken [ˈauspakən], v.a. unpack. — v.n. talk freely; (coll.) open up.
auspfeifen [ˈauspfaɪfən], v.a. irr. (Theat.) hiss at, cat-call.
auspolstern [ˈauspɔlstərn], v.a. stuff.
ausprägen [ˈauspreːgən], v.a. stamp, impress, coin.
ausprobieren [ˈausprobiːrən], v.a. try out.
Auspuff [ˈauspuf], m. (—s, no pl.) (Motor.) exhaust.
auspusten [ˈauspuːstən], v.a. blow out.
ausputzen [ˈausputsən], v.a. clean out; adorn.
ausquartieren [ˈauskvartiːrən], v.a. (Mil.) billet out.
ausquetschen [ˈauskvɛtʃən], v.a. squeeze out.
ausradieren [ˈausradiːrən], v.a. erase.
ausrangieren [ˈausraŋʒiːrən], v.a. cast off, sort out.
ausräuchern [ˈausrɔyçərn], v.a. fumigate.
ausraufen [ˈausraufən], v.a. (obs.) tear or pull out (hair).
ausräumen [ˈausrɔymən], v.a. clear out, clear away.
ausrechnen [ˈausrɛçnən], v.a. reckon, compute, calculate; ausgerechnet du, (emph.) you of all people.
ausrecken [ˈausrɛkən], v.a. sich den Hals —, crane o.'s neck.
Ausrede [ˈausreːdə], f. (—, pl. —n) evasion, excuse, subterfuge.
ausreden [ˈausreːdən], v.a. einem etwas —, dissuade s.o. from s.th. — v.n. finish speaking; einen — lassen, allow s.o. to finish speaking.

ausreichen ['ausraɪçən], v.n. suffice.

ausreißen ['ausraɪsən], v.a. irr. pluck, pull out. — v.n. (aux. sein) run away, bolt.

ausrenken ['ausrɛŋkən], v.a. dislocate, sprain.

ausrichten ['ausrɪçtən], v.a. adjust, make straight; deliver (a message); accomplish; (Mil.) dress.

ausrotten ['ausrɔtən], v.a. root up; exterminate, extirpate.

ausrücken ['ausrykən], v.n. (aux. sein) (Mil.) march out; (coll.) decamp.

Ausruf ['ausru:f], m. (—s, pl. —e) exclamation, interjection, outcry; (public) proclamation.

Ausruf(ungs)zeichen ['ausru:f(uŋs)-tsaɪçən], n. (—s, pl. —) exclamation mark.

ausruhen ['ausru:ən], v.r. sich —, rest, take a rest.

ausrüsten ['ausrystən], v.a. furnish, fit out, equip.

ausrutschen ['ausrutʃən], v.n. (aux. sein) slip.

Aussage ['ausza:gə], f. (—, pl. —n) declaration, statement, evidence; (Law) deposition, affidavit; (Gram.) predicate.

aussagen ['ausza:gən], v.a. say, state, utter, declare; (Law) depose, give evidence.

Aussatz ['auszats], m. (—es, no pl.) leprosy.

Aussätzige ['auszɛtsɪgə], m. (—n, pl. —n) leper.

aussaugen ['auszaugən], v.a. suck dry.

ausschalten ['ausʃaltən], v.a. switch off.

Ausschank ['ausʃank], m. (—s, no pl.) retail (of alcohol); pub, bar.

Ausschau ['ausʃau], f. (—, no pl.) watch; — halten, look out for.

ausscheiden ['ausʃaɪdən], v.a. irr. separate; (Med.) secrete. — v.n. (aux. sein) withdraw from, retire, secede.

Ausscheidung ['ausʃaɪduŋ], f. (—, pl. —en) retirement, withdrawal; (Med.) secretion.

Ausschlag ['ausʃla:k], m. (—s, pl. —e) turn (of the scales); deflection (of the magnetic needle); (Med.) rash, eczema; den — geben, clinch the matter; give the casting vote.

ausschlagen ['ausʃla:gən], v.a. irr. knock out; refuse, decline (an invitation); das schlägt dem Faß den Boden aus, that is the last straw. — v.n. (aux. sein) (Hort.) bud, shoot; gut —, turn out well.

auschlaggebend ['ausʃla:kge:bənt], adj. decisive; (vote) casting.

ausschließen ['ausʃli:sən], v.a. irr. lock out; exclude.

ausschließlich ['ausʃli:slɪç], adj. exclusive, sole.

ausschlüpfen ['ausʃlypfən], v.n. (aux. sein) hatch out.

Ausschluß ['ausʃlus], m. (—sses, pl. ̈sse) exclusion; unter — der Öffentlichkeit, in camera.

ausschmücken ['ausʃmykən], v.a. adorn, decorate, embellish.

Ausschnitt ['ausʃnɪt], m. (—s, pl. —e) cutting out; (newspaper) cutting; (dress) neck (line).

ausschreiben ['ausʃraɪbən], v.a. irr. write down in full; make out a bill; advertise (post) as vacant.

ausschreiten ['ausʃraɪtən], v.n. irr. (aux. sein) step out, stride along.

Ausschreitungen ['ausʃraɪtuŋən], f. pl. rioting; excesses.

Ausschuß ['ausʃus], m. (—sses, pl. ̈sse) dross, refuse, rejects, low quality goods; committee, commission, board.

ausschweifend ['ausʃvaɪfənt], adj. extravagant; licentious, dissolute.

aussehen ['ausze:ən], v.n. irr. look; look like, appear.

außen ['ausən], adv. outside, abroad, outward, without.

Außenhandel ['ausənhandəl], m. (—s, no pl.) export trade.

Außenministerium ['ausənmɪnɪste:r-jum], n. (—s, pl. —terien) Ministry of Foreign Affairs; (U.K.) Foreign Office, (U.S.) State Department.

Außenstände ['ausənʃtɛndə], m. pl. outstanding claims, liabilities.

außer ['ausər], prep. (Dat.) in addition to, besides, apart from; out of, at the outside of, beside, without; — Dienst, retired. — conj. except, save, but.

außerdem ['ausərde:m], adv. besides, moreover, furthermore.

Äußere ['ɔysərə], n. (—n, no pl.) exterior.

außerehelich ['ausəre:əlɪç], adj. illegitimate.

außergewöhnlich ['ausərgəvø:nlɪç], adj. unusual, exceptional.

außerhalb ['ausərhalp], prep. outside.

äußerlich ['ɔysərlɪç], adj. external.

Äußerlichkeit ['ɔysərlɪçkaɪt], f. (—, pl. —en) formality.

äußern ['ɔysərn], v.a. utter, express. — v.r. sich zu etwas —, give o.'s opinion on some question; express o.s. on some subject.

außerordentlich [ausər'ɔrdəntlɪç], adj. extraordinary, unusual; (Univ.) —er Professor, senior lecturer or reader; (Am.) associate professor.

äußerst ['ɔysərst], adj. outermost, most remote; extreme, utmost.

außerstande ['ausərʃtandə], adj. unable.

Äußerung ['ɔysəruŋ], f. (—, pl. —en) utterance, remark, observation.

aussetzen ['auszɛtsən], v.a. set out, put out; offer (a reward); suspend; etwas an einer Sache —, find fault with s.th.; sich einer Gefahr —, expose o.s. to danger, run a risk. — v.n. pause, discontinue; (Motor.) stop, misfire.

Aussicht ['auszɪçt], f. (—, pl. —en) view, panorama; prospect, chance; etwas in — stellen, hold out the prospect of s.th.; in — nehmen, intend.

aussinnen ['auszɪnən],*v. a. irr.* imagine, invent; devise.

aussöhnen ['auszø:nən], *v.r. sich mit einem —,* become reconciled with s.o.

aussondern ['auszɔndərn], *v.a.* single out.

ausspannen ['ausʃpanən], *v.a. (animals)* unharness. — *v.n. (coll.)* relax.

ausspeien ['ausʃpaɪən], *v.a.* spit out, vomit.

aussperren ['ausʃpɛrən], *v.a.* shut out; *(industrial)* lock out.

ausspielen ['ausʃpi:lən], *v.n.* finish playing; *(Sport, Game)* lead (off).

Aussprache ['ausʃpra:xə], *f.* (—, *no pl.*) pronunciation; discussion; confidential talk.

aussprechen ['ausʃprɛçən], *v.a. irr.* have o.'s say; utter; pronounce. — *v.r. sich —,* speak o.'s mind.

Ausspruch ['ausʃprux], *m.* (—s, *pl.* ˙̈e) utterance, dictum.

ausspüren ['ausʃpy:rən], *v.a. (Hunt.)* track down.

ausstaffieren ['ausʃtafi:rən],*v.a.*furnish, equip.

Ausstand ['ausʃtant], *m.* (—s, *pl.* ˙̈e) *(industry)* strike; *(pl.)* outstanding debts, arrears.

ausständig ['ausʃtɛndɪç], *adj.* outstanding; on strike.

ausstatten ['ausʃtatən], *v.a.* endow with, provide with, equip.

Ausstattung ['ausʃtatuŋ], *f.* (—, *pl.* —en) outfit; (bridal) trousseau; *(coll.)* get-up.

ausstechen ['ausʃtɛçən], *v.a. irr.* pierce; *einen —,* (*fig.*) excel s.o.

ausstehen ['ausʃte:ən], *v.n. irr.* stand out; *(money)* be overdue. — *v.a.* endure, suffer, bear, undergo; *ich kann ihn nicht —,* I cannot stand him.

aussteigen ['ausʃtaɪgən], *v.n. irr.* (aux. sein) get out, alight; disembark.

ausstellen ['ausʃtɛlən], *v.a.* exhibit; display; make out (bill etc.).

Aussteller ['ausʃtɛlər], *m.* (—s, *pl.* —) drawer of a cheque); exhibitor.

Ausstellung ['ausʃtɛluŋ], *f.* (—, *pl* —en) exhibition; *(Am.)* exposition.

Aussteuer ['ausʃtɔyər], *f.* (—, *pl.* —n) trousseau.

ausstopfen ['ausʃtɔpfən], *v.a.* stuff.

ausstoßen ['ausʃtosən], *v.a. irr.* push out, expel; utter.

Ausstrahlung ['ausʃtra:luŋ], *f.* (—, *pl.* —en) radiation.

ausstrecken ['ausʃtrɛkən], *v.a.* stretch out, reach out, extend.

ausstreichen ['ausʃtraɪçən], *v.a. irr.* strike out, erase, delete; smoothe.

ausstreuen ['ausʃtrɔyən], *v.a.* scatter, spread, sprinkle; *Gerüchte —,* circulate rumours.

ausstudieren ['ausʃtudi:rən], *v.n.* finish o.'s studies, graduate.

aussuchen ['auszu:xən], *v.a.* select.

Austausch ['austauʃ], *m.* (—es, *pl.* —e) barter, exchange; *(thoughts, letters)* interchange.

austauschen ['austauʃən], *v.a.* barter, exchange; *(thoughts, letters)* interchange.

austeilen ['austaɪlən], *v.a.* distribute, allocate.

Auster ['austər], *f.* (—, *pl.* —n) oyster.

Austerbank ['austərbaŋk], *f.* (—, *pl.* ˙̈e) oyster-bed.

austilgen ['austɪlgən], *v.a.* exterminate, eradicate, extirpate.

Australien [au'stra:ljən], *n.* Australia.

austreiben ['austraɪbən], *v.a. irr.* drive out, expel; exorcise.

austreten ['austre:tən], *v.a. irr.* tread out; stretch (shoes) by walking; *ausgetretene Stufen,* worn steps. — *v.n. (aux.* sein) retire (from business); withdraw (from a club); *(coll.)* go to the lavatory.

Austritt ['austrɪt], *m.* (—s, *pl.* —e) withdrawal, retirement.

ausüben ['ausy:bən], *v.a.* exercise, practise; exert, commit.

Ausverkauf ['ausfɛrkauf], *m.* (—s, *pl.* ˙̈e) selling-off, clearance sale.

Auswahl ['ausva:l], *f.* (—, *pl.* —en) choice, selection.

Auswanderer ['ausvandərər], *m.* (—s, *pl.* —) emigrant.

auswärtig ['ausvɛrtɪç], *adj.* foreign, away.

auswärts ['ausvɛrts], *adv.* outward(s), away from home.

auswechseln ['ausvɛksəln], *v.a.* exchange; fit (spare parts).

Ausweg ['ausve:k], *m.* (—s, *pl.* —e) expedient; way out; *ich weiß keinen —,* I am at my wits' end.

ausweichen ['ausvaɪçən], *v.n. irr. (aux.* sein) give way; evade, parry.

Ausweis ['ausvaɪs], *m.* (—es, *pl.* —e) proof of identity, identity card.

ausweisen ['a ɪsvaɪzən], *v.a. irr.* turn out, banish, exile, deport. — *v.r. (aux.* haben) *sich —,* show proof of o.'s identity.

auswendig ['ausvɛndɪç], *adj.* by heart.

auswirken ['ausvɪrkən], *v.r. sich gut —,* work out well, have a good effect.

Auswuchs ['ausvu:ks], *m.* (—es, *pl.* ˙̈e) sprouting, outgrowth, (*fig.*) excrescence.

Auswurf ['ausvurf], *m.* (—s, *pl.* ˙̈e) excretion; expectoration; — *der Menschheit,* scum of the earth.

auszählen ['austse:lən], *v.n.* count, number. — *v.a.* count out.

Auszahlung ['austsa:luŋ], *f.* (—, *pl.* —en) payment.

auszanken ['austsaŋkən], *v.a.* scold, chide.

auszehren ['austse:rən], *v.n. (aux.* sein) waste away, be consumed.

auszeichnen ['austsaɪçnən], *v.a.* mark out, honour, decorate. — *v.r. sich —,* distinguish o.s.

Auszeichnung ['austsaɪçnuŋ], *f.* (—, *pl.* —en) distinction, medal.

ausziehen ['austsi:ən], *v.a. irr.* undress, take off (clothes); (*Chem.*) extract; stretch. — *v.n.* (*aux.* sein) move out. — *v.r. sich* —, undress.

auszischen ['austsɪʃən], *v.a.* (*Theat.*) hiss, cat-call.

Auszug ['austsu:k], *m.* (—s, *pl.* ̈e) removal (from home); exodus; extract (from a book), abstract (from a deed).

Auto ['auto], *n.* (—s, *pl.* —s) motor-car, (*Am.*) automobile.

Autogramm [auto'gram], *n.* (—s, *pl.* —e) autograph.

Automat [auto'ma:t], *m.* (—en, *pl.* —en) slot machine.

Autor ['autɔr], *m.* (—s, *pl.* —en) author, writer.

Autorität [autori'tɛ:t], *f.* (—, *pl.* —en) authority.

avisieren [avi'zi:rən], *v.a.* notify, advise.

Axt [akst], *f.* (—, *pl.* ̈e) axe.

Azur [a'tsu:r], *m.* (—s, *no pl.*) azure.

B

B [be:], *n.* (—s, *pl.*—s) the letter B; (*Mus.*) B flat; — *Dur*, B flat major; — *Moll*, B flat minor.

Bach [bax], *m.* (—es, *pl.* ̈e) brook, rivulet.

Bachstelze ['baxʃtɛltsə], *f.* (—, *pl.* —n) wagtail.

Backe ['bakə], *f.* (—, *pl.* —n) cheek.

backen ['bakən], *v.a.* bake.

Backenstreich ['bakənʃtraiç], *m.* (—s, *pl.* —e) box on the ear.

Bäcker ['bɛkər], *m.* (—s, *pl.* —) baker.

Backfisch ['bakfiʃ], *m.* (—es, *pl.* —e) (*fig.*) teenage girl.

Backhuhn ['bakhu:n], *n.* (—s, *pl.* ̈er) fried chicken.

Backobst ['bakopst], *n.* (—es, *no pl.*) dried fruit.

Backpfeife ['bakpfaifə], *f.* (—, *pl.* —n) box on the ear.

Backpflaume ['bakpflaumə], *f.* (—, *pl.* —n) prune.

Backstein ['bakʃtain], *m.* (—s, *pl.* —e) brick.

Backwerk ['bakvɛrk], *n.* (—s, *no pl.*) pastry.

Bad [ba:t], *n.* (—es, *pl.* ̈er) bath; spa, watering-place.

Badeanstalt ['ba:dəanʃtalt], *f.* (—, *pl.* —en) public baths.

baden ['ba:dən], *v.n.* bathe, have a bath.

Badewanne ['ba:dəvanə], *f.* (—, *pl.* —n) bath-tub.

Bagage [ba'ga:ʒə], *f.* (—, *no pl.*) luggage; (*Am.*) baggage; (*sl.*) mob, rabble.

Bagger ['bagər], *m.* (—s, *pl.* —) dredger, dredging-machine.

baggern ['bagərn], *v.a.* dredge.

Bahn [ba:n], *f.* (—, *pl.* —en) road, path, course; (*Astr.*) orbit; railway(-line); — *brechen*, open a path.

bahnbrechend ['ba:nbrɛçənt], *adj.* pioneering, epoch-making.

bahnen ['ba:nən], *v.a.* make passable; pave (the way).

Bahngleis ['ba:nglais], *n.* (—es, *pl.* —e) railway-line, railway-track; (*Am.*) railroad-line, railroad-track.

Bahnhof ['ba:nho:f], *m.* (—s, *pl.* ̈e) railway-station, (*Am.*) depot.

Bahnsteig ['ba:nʃtaik], *m.* (—s, *pl.* —e) platform.

Bahnwärter ['ba:nvɛrtər], *m.* (—s, *pl.* —) signal-man.

Bahre ['ba:rə], *f.* (—, *pl.* —n) litter, stretcher; bier.

Bahrtuch ['ba:rtu:x], *n.* (—s, *pl.* ̈er) pall, shroud.

Bai [bai], *f.* (—, *pl.* —en) bay, cove.

Baisse ['bɛsə], *f.* (—, *pl.* —n) (*Comm.*) fall in share prices.

Bakkalaureat [bakalaure'a:t], *n.* (—s, *pl.* —e) bachelor's degree.

Bakterie [bak'te:rjə], *f.* (—, *pl.* —n) bacterium.

bald [balt], *adv.* soon, shortly, directly, presently.

Baldachin ['baldaxin], *m.* (—s, *pl.* —e) canopy.

baldig ['baldiç], *adj.* quick, speedy; *auf —es Wiedersehen*, see you again soon.

Baldrian ['baldria:n], *m.* (—s, *no pl.*) valerian.

Balearen, die [bale'a:rən, di:], *pl.* Balearic Islands.

Balg (1) [balk], *m.* (—s, *pl.* ̈e) skin, slough, husk; bellows (of organ *or* forge).

Balg (2) [balk], *n.* (—s, *pl.* ̈er) brat; naughty child.

balgen ['balgən], *v.r. sich* —, (children) fight, romp.

Balgerei ['balgərai], *f.* (—, *pl.* —en) scuffle, scrimmage.

Balken ['balkən], *m.* (—s, *pl.* —) beam, joist, rafter.

Balkenwerk ['balkənvɛrk], *n.* (—s, *no pl.*) building-frame, timbers, wood-work.

Balkon [bal'kɔ̃], *m.* (—s, *pl.* —s, —e) balcony.

Ball [bal], *m.* (—s, *pl.* ̈e) ball; globe; sphere; dance.

ballen ['balən], *v.a.* form into a ball; clench (o.'s fist).

Ballen ['balən], *m.* (—s, *pl.* —) bale, bundle, package; ball (of the hand *or* foot).

ballförmig ['balfœrmiç], *adj.* spherical.

Ballistik [ba'lɪstɪk], *f.* (—, *no pl.*) ballistics.

Ballon [ba'lɔ̃], *m.* (—s, *pl.* —s, —e) balloon.

Balsam ['balza:m], *m.* (—s, *pl.* —e) balm, balsam.

Baltikum ['baltikum], *n.* (—s, *no pl.*) the Baltic countries.

Bambusrohr ['bambusro:r], *n.* (—s, *pl.* —e) bamboo (cane).

Banane [ba'na:nə], *f.* (—, *pl.* —n) banana.

Banause [ba'nauzə], *m.* (—n, *pl.* —n) narrow-minded person, philistine.

Band (1) [bant], *n.* (—s, *pl.* ⁻er) ribbon, riband, tape; string; (*Bot.*) band; hoop (*for a cask*); (*Anat.*) ligament, tendon.

Band (2) [bant], *n.* (—s, *pl.* —e) (*fig.*) bond, fetter, chain, (*pl.*) bonds, ties (*of friendship*).

Band (3) [bant], *m.* (—es, *pl.* ⁻e) volume.

Bändchen ['bɛntçən], *n.* (—s, *pl.* —) small ribbon, small piece of string; (*book*) small volume.

Bande ['bandə], *f.* (—, *pl.* —n) horde, gang, set.

bändigen ['bɛndɪgən], *v.a.* tame, subdue.

Bandmaß ['bantma:s], *n.* (—es, *pl.* —e) tape-measure.

Bandwurm ['bantvurm], *m.* (—s, *pl.* ⁻er) (*Zool.*) tape-worm.

bange ['baŋə], *adj.* afraid, worried, alarmed.

Bangigkeit ['baŋɪçkaɪt], *f.* (—, *no pl.*) uneasiness, anxiety.

Bank (1) [baŋk], *f.* (—, *pl.* ⁻e) bench, seat (in a park); *auf die lange — schieben,* delay, shelve; *durch die —,* without exception.

Bank (2) [baŋk], *f.* (—, *pl.* —en) bank; *die — sprengen,* break the bank.

Bänkelsänger ['bɛŋkəlzɛŋər], *m.* (—s, *pl.* —) ballad singer.

bank(e)rott [baŋk'rɔt], *adj.* bankrupt.

Bankett [baŋ'kɛt], *n.* (—s, *pl.* —e) banquet.

Bankkonto ['baŋkkɔnto], *n.* (—s, *pl.* —ten) bank-account.

Bann [ban], *m.* (—s, *no pl.*) ban, exile; (*Eccl.*) excommunication; *in den — tun,* outlaw, (*Eccl.*) excommunicate; (*fig.*) charm, spell.

bannen ['banən], *v.a.* banish, exile, cast out.

Banner ['banər], *n.* (—s, *pl.* —) banner, standard.

Bannmeile ['banmaɪlə], *f.* (—, *pl.* —n) boundary.

bar [ba:r], *adv.* in cash, ready money.

Bar [ba:r], *f.* (—, *pl.* —s) bar (for selling drinks etc.).

Bär [bɛ:r], *m.* (—en, *pl.* —en) (*Zool.*) bear; *einem einen — aufbinden,* to lead s.o. up the garden-path.

Barauslagen ['barausla:gən], *f. pl.* cash expenses.

Barbar [bar'ba:r], *m.* (—en, *pl.* —en) barbarian, vandal.

barbarisch [bar'ba:rɪʃ], *adj.* barbarous.

Barbestand ['bar'bəʃtant], *m.* (—s, *pl.* ⁻e) cash reserve, cash balance.

bärbeißig ['bɛːrbaɪsɪç], *adj.* surly, morose.

Barchent ['barçənt], *m.* (—s, *no pl.*) fustian.

Barde ['bardə], *m.* (—n, *pl.* —n) bard, minstrel.

Bärenfell ['bɛːrənfɛl], *n.* (—s, *pl.* —e) bear-skin.

Bärenmütze ['bɛːrənmytsə], *f.* (—, *pl.* —n) (*Mil.*) busby.

Bärenzwinger ['bɛːrəntsvɪŋər], *m.* (—s, *pl.* —) bear-garden.

Barett [ba'rɛt], *n.* (—s, *pl.* —e) cap, beret; (*Eccl.*) biretta.

barfuß ['barfus], *adj.* barefoot(ed).

Bargeld ['bargɛlt], *n.* (—(e)s, *no pl.*) cash.

barhäuptig ['barhɔyptɪç], *adj.* bare-headed.

Barkasse [bar'kasə], *f.* (—, *pl.* —n) launch.

Barke ['barkə], *f.* (—, *pl.* —n) barge, lighter.

barmherzig [barm'hɛrtsɪç], *adj.* merciful, charitable, compassionate.

Barock [ba'rɔk], *n.* (—s, *no pl.*) Baroque.

Baronin [ba'ro:nɪn], *f.* (—, *pl.* —nen) baroness.

Barren ['barən], *m.* (—s, *pl.* —) parallel bars.

Barsch [barʃ], *m.* (—es, *pl.* —e) (*Zool.*) perch.

barsch [barʃ], *adj.* rough, harsh, sharp, abrupt, unfriendly.

Barschaft ['barʃaft], *f.* (—, *pl.* —en) ready money.

Bart [ba:rt], *m.* (—s, *pl.* ⁻e) beard; (*key*) ward.

Bartflechte ['ba:rtflɛçtə], *f.* (—, *pl.* —n) barber's itch.

bärtig ['bɛːrtɪç], *adj.* bearded.

Basalt [ba'zalt], *m.* (—s, *pl.* —e) (*Min.*) basalt.

Base ['ba:zə], *f.* (—, *pl.* —n) female cousin; (*Chem.*) base.

Basis ['ba:zɪs], *f.* (—, *pl.* Basen) base, foundation.

Baskenmütze ['baskənmytsə], *f.* (—, *pl.* —n) tam-o'-shanter, beret.

Baß [bas], *m.* (—sses, *pl.* ⁻sse) (*Mus.*) bass.

Baßschlüssel ['basʃlysəl], *m.* (—s, *pl.* —) (*Mus.*) bass-clef.

Bassin [ba'sɛ̃], *n.* (—s, *pl.* —s) basin, reservoir.

Bast [bast], *m.* (—es, *pl.* —e) inner bark, fibre (*of trees etc.*); bast.

basta ['basta], *int.* and that's that!

Bastei [bas'taɪ], *f.* (—, *pl.* —en) bastion.

basteln ['bastəln], *v.a.* work on a hobby, tinker.

Batist [ba'tɪst], *m.* (—s, *pl.* —e) cambric.

Bau [bau], *m.* (—es, *pl.* —ten) building, structure, edifice; act of building; *im — begriffen,* in course of construction.

Bauart ['bauart], *f.* (—, *pl.* —en) (architectural) style, structure.

Bauch [baux], *m.* (—es, *pl.* ⁻e) belly, stomach.

Bauchfell ['bauxfɛl], *n.* (—s, *pl.* —e) peritoneum.

bauchig ['bauçɪç], *adj.* bulgy.
Bauchredner ['bauxre:dnər], *m.* (—s, *pl.* —) ventriloquist.
bauen ['bauən], *v.a.* build, construct, erect. — *v.n. auf etwas* —, (*fig.*) rely on s.th., count on s.th.
Bauer (1) ['bauər], *m.* (—n, *pl.* —n) farmer, peasant; (*chess*) pawn.
Bauer (2) ['bauər], *n.* (—s, *pl.* —) (*bird*) cage.
Bäuerin ['bɔyərɪn], *f.* (—, *pl.* —nen) farmer's wife.
Bauernfänger ['bauərnfɛŋər], *m.* (—s, *pl.* —) sharper, rook, confidence-trickster.
Bauernstand ['bauərnʃtant], *m.* (—s, *pl.* ⁻e) peasantry.
baufällig ['baufɛlɪç], *adj.* dilapidated, ramshackle.
Baugerüst ['baugəryst], *n.* (—s, *pl.* —e) scaffolding.
Baugewerbe ['baugəvɛrbə], *n.* (—s, *no pl.*) building trade.
Baukunst ['baukunst], *f.* (—, *no pl.*) architecture.
Baum [baum], *m.* (—(e)s, *pl.* ⁻e) tree.
Baumeister ['baumaɪstər], *m.* (—s, *pl.* —) architect, master-builder.
baumeln ['bauməln], *v.n.* dangle.
Baumkuchen ['baumku:xən], *m.* (—s, *pl.* —) pyramid-cake.
Baumschule ['baumʃu:lə], *f.* (—, *pl.* —n) plantation of trees, orchard, tree nursery.
Baumstamm ['baumʃtam], *m.* (—s, *pl.* ⁻e) stem, trunk.
Baumwolle ['baumvɔlə], *f.* (—, *pl.* —n) cotton.
Bauriß ['baurɪs], *m.* (—sses, *pl.* —sse) plan, architect's drawing.
Bausch [bauʃ], *m.* (—es, *pl.* ⁻e) pad, bolster; *in* — *und Bogen*, in the lump; all at once.
bauschig ['bauʃɪç], *adj.* baggy.
Bauwerk ['bauvɛrk] *see* **Gebäude**.
Bayern ['baɪərn], *n.* Bavaria.
Bazar [ba'za:r], *m.* (—s, *pl.* —e) bazaar, fair, emporium.
beabsichtigen [bə'apzɪçtɪgən], *v.a.* aim at, intend, have in view.
beachten [bə'axtən], *v.a.* observe, pay attention to.
Beamte [bə'amtə], *m.* (—n, *pl.* —n) official, officer, civil servant.
Beamtin [bə'amtɪn], *f.* (—, *pl.* —nen) female official, female civil servant.
beängstigen [bə'ɛŋstɪgən], *v.a.* alarm, make afraid.
beanspruchen [bə'anʃpruxən], *v.a.* demand, claim, lay claim to.
beanstanden [bə'anʃtandən], *v.a.* object to, raise objections to, query.
beantragen [bə'antra:gən], *v.a.* move, apply, lodge an application.
beantworten [bə'antvɔrtən], *v.a.* answer, reply to.
bearbeiten [bə'arbaɪtən], *v.a.* work (on); (*book, play*) adapt, arrange, revise; (*Agr.*) cultivate; (*fig.*) *einen* —, try to influence s.o., try to convince s.o.

Bearbeitung [bə'arbaɪtuŋ], *f.* (—, *pl.* —en) working, manipulation, operation; (*Agr.*) culture, cultivation; (*book, play*) adaptation, revision, arrangement.
beargwöhnen [bə'arkvø:nən], *v.a.* suspect, view with suspicion.
beaufsichtigen [bə'aufzɪçtɪgən], *v.a.* control, supervise, superintend.
beauftragen [bə'auftra:gən], *v.a.* commission, charge, authorize.
bebauen [bə'bauən], *v.a.* build upon; (*Agr.*) cultivate.
beben ['be:bən], *v.n.* shake, quake, tremble; *vor Kälte* —, shiver with cold.
Becher ['bɛçər], *m.* (—s, *pl.* —) beaker, cup, goblet, mug; (*dice*) box.
Becken ['bɛkən], *n.* (—s, *pl.* —) basin, bowl; (*Anat.*) pelvis; (*Mus.*) cymbal.
Bedacht [bə'daxt], *m.* (—s, *no pl.*) consideration; *mit* —, deliberately; *ohne* —, thoughtlessly.
bedächtig [bə'dɛçtɪç], *adj.* circumspect, deliberate, cautious, slow.
bedanken [bə'daŋkən], *v.r. sich für etwas* —, thank s.o. for s.th., decline with thanks (*also iron.*).
Bedarf [bə'darf], *m.* (—s, *no pl.*) need, requirement, demand.
bedauerlich [bə'dauərlɪç], *adj.* regrettable, deplorable.
bedauern [bə'dauərn], *v.a.* pity, commiserate, regret; *ich bedaure, daß*, I am sorry that . . .
bedecken [bə'dɛkən], *v.a.* cover (up); *sich mit Ruhm* —, cover o.s. with glory.
bedeckt [bə'dɛkt], *adj.* (*sky*) overcast.
bedenken [bə'dɛŋkən], *v.a. irr.* consider, bear in mind. — *v.r. sich* —, deliberate, hesitate; *sich anders* —, change o.'s mind.
bedenklich [bə'dɛŋklɪç], *adj.* (*persons*) doubtful, dubious; (*things*) risky, delicate, precarious; (*illness*) serious, grave.
Bedenkzeit [bə'dɛŋktsaɪt], *f.* (—, *pl.* —en) time to consider, respite.
bedeuten [bə'dɔytən], *v.a.* signify, mean, imply; direct, order.
bedeutend [bə'dɔytənt], *adj.* important, eminent, considerable, outstanding.
bedeutsam [bə'dɔytza:m], *adj.* significant.
Bedeutung [bə'dɔytuŋ], *f.* (—, *pl.* —en) significance, meaning; consequence, importance; *nichts von* —, nothing to speak of.
bedienen [bə'di:nən], *v.a.* serve, attend to, wait on; (*machine*) operate; (*Cards*) follow suit. — *v.r. sich* —, help o.s., make use of.
Bediente [bə'di:ntə], *m.* (—n, *pl.* —n) servant, attendant, footman, lackey.
Bedienung [bə'di:nuŋ], *f.* (—, *pl.* —en) service, attendance.
bedingen [bə'dɪŋən], *v.a.* stipulate, postulate, condition, cause.

23

bedingt [bə'dɪŋkt], *adj.* conditional.
Bedingung [bə'dɪŋuŋ], *f.* (—, *pl.* —en) stipulation, condition, term; *unter keiner* —, on no account.
bedingungsweise [bə'dɪŋuŋsvaɪzə], *adv.* on condition, conditionally.
bedrängen [bə'drɛŋən], *v.a.* oppress; press hard, afflict.
Bedrängnis [bə'drɛŋnɪs], *f.* (—, *pl.* —se) oppression, distress.
bedrohen [bə'dro:ən], *v.a.* threaten, menace.
bedrohlich [bə'dro:lɪç], *adj.* threatening, menacing, ominous.
bedrücken [bə'drykən], *v.a.* oppress, harass, depress.
Beduine [bedu'i:nə], *m.* (—n, *pl.* —n) Bedouin.
bedünken [bə'dyŋkən], *v.a.* appear, seem; *es bedünkt mich*, methinks.
bedürfen [bə'dyrfən], *v.n. irr.* want, need, be in need of.
Bedürfnis [bə'dyrfnɪs], *n.* (—ses, *pl.* —se) want, need, requirement, necessity; *es ist mir ein* —, I cannot but; *einem dringenden* — *abhelfen*, meet an urgent want *or* need; *ein* — *haben*, (*coll.*) need to relieve o.s.
Bedürfnisanstalt [bə'dyrfnɪsanʃtalt], *f.* (—, *pl.* —en) public lavatory, public convenience.
bedürftig [bə'dyrftɪç], *adj.* needy, indigent, poor.
beeidigen [bə'aɪdɪgən], *v.a.* confirm by oath, swear in.
beeifern [bə'aɪfərn], *v.r. sich* —, exert o.s., strive, be zealous.
beeilen [bə'aɪlən], *v.r. sich* —, hurry, hasten, make haste.
beeindrucken [bə'aɪndrukən], *v.a.* impress.
beeinflussen [bə'aɪnflusən], *v.a.* influence.
beeinträchtigen [bə'aɪntrɛçtigən], *v.a.* injure, lessen, diminish, detract from, curtail.
beenden [bə'ɛndən], *v.a.* end, finish, terminate, conclude.
beendigen [bə'ɛndɪgən], *v.a.* end, finish, terminate, conclude.
beengen [bə'ɛŋən], *v.a.* cramp, narrow.
beerben [bə'ɛrbən], *v.a. einen* —, inherit from s.o.
beerdigen [bə'e:rdɪgən], *v.a.* bury, inter.
Beere ['be:rə], *f.* (—, *pl.* —n) berry.
Beet [be:t], *n.* (—es, *pl.* —e) (flower) bed.
befähigen [bə'fɛ:ɪgən], *v.a.* fit, enable, qualify.
Befähigung [bə'fɛ:ɪguŋ], *f.* (—, *pl.* —en) qualification, capacity, aptitude.
befahren [bə'fa:rən], *v.a. irr.* pass over, travel over, (*Naut.*) navigate.
befallen [bə'falən], *v.a. irr.* befall, fall on; *von Traurigkeit* — *sein*, be overcome by sadness.
befangen [bə'faŋən], *adj.* biased, prejudiced, bashful, embarrassed.

befassen [bə'fasən], *v.a.* touch, handle. — *v.r. sich mit etwas* —, occupy o.s. with s.th.
befehden [bə'fe:dən], *v.a.* make war upon, show enmity towards.
Befehl [bə'fe:l], *m.* (—s, *pl.* —e) order, command; (*Mil.*) *zu* —, very good, sir; (*Mil.*) *den* — *führen über*, command.
befehlen [bə'fe:lən], *v.a. irr.* order, command.
befehligen [bə'fe:lɪgən], *v.a.* (*Mil.*) command, lead.
Befehlshaber [bə'fe:lsha:bər], *m.* (—s, *pl.* —) commander, commanding officer, chief.
befehlswidrig [bə'fe:lsvi:drɪç], *adj.* contrary to orders.
befestigen [bə'fɛstɪgən], *v.a.* fasten, fix, attach, affix; (*Mil.*) fortify; strengthen.
befeuchten [bə'fɔyçtən], *v.a.* wet, moisten, dampen.
Befinden [bə'fɪndən], *n.* (—s, *no pl.*) state of health.
befinden [bə'fɪndən], *v.a. irr.* think, deem, find. — *v.r. sich an einem Ort* —, be in some place; *sich wohl* —, feel well.
befindlich [bə'fɪntlɪç], *adj.* existing; — *sein*, be contained in.
beflecken [bə'flɛkən], *v.a.* stain, spot, blot; defile, pollute.
befleißigen [bə'flaɪsɪgən], *v.r. sich* —, devote o.s. to, take pains to.
beflissen [bə'flɪsən], *adj.* eager to serve, assiduous.
beflügeln [bə'fly:gəln], *v.a.* give wings; (*fig.*) accelerate, animate.
befolgen [bə'fɔlgən], *v.a.* follow, obey; *einen Befehl* —, comply with an order.
befördern [bə'fœrdərn], *v.a.* despatch, forward, send, post, mail, transmit; promote, advance.
Beförderung [bə'fœrdəruŋ], *f.* (—, *pl.* —en) forwarding, transmission; (*office*) promotion, advancement.
Beförderungsmittel [bə'fœrdəruŋsmɪtəl], *n.* (—s, *pl.* —) conveyance, means of transport.
befragen [bə'fra:gən], *v.a.* question, interrogate, examine.
befreien [bə'fraɪən], *v.a.* free, liberate.
befremden [bə'frɛmdən], *v.a.* appear strange, astonish, surprise.
befreunden [bə'frɔyndən], *v.a.* befriend. — *v.r. sich mit einem* —, make friends with s.o.
befriedigen [bə'fri:dɪgən], *v.a.* content, satisfy; appease, calm.
befruchten [bə'fruxtən], *v.a.* fertilise; impregnate.
Befugnis [bə'fu:knɪs], *f.* (—, *pl.* —se) authority, right, warrant.
Befund [bə'funt], *m.* (—s, *pl.* —e) (*Med.*) diagnosis, findings.
befürchten [bə'fyrçtən], *v.a.* fear, be afraid of.
befürworten [bə'fy:rvɔrtən], *v.a.* support, second.

begabt [bə'ga:pt], *adj.* gifted, talented, able.

Begabung [bə'ga:buŋ], *f.* (—, *pl.* —en) ability, talent, gift.

begaffen [bə'gafən], *v.a.* stare at, gape at.

begatten [bə'gatən], *v.r.* sich —, (*Zool.*) copulate.

begeben [bə'ge:bən], *v.r. irr. sich an einen Ort* —, go to a place, betake o.s. to a place; happen, occur.

Begebenheit [bə'ge:bənhaɪt], *f.* (—, *pl.* —en) happening, event, occurrence.

begegnen [bə'ge:gnən], *v.n.* (*aux.* sein) meet, meet with, encounter, befall, happen.

begehen [bə'ge:ən], *v.a. irr.* (*road*) walk along, go over; (*festival*) celebrate; (*crime*) commit, perpetrate.

begehren [bə'ge:rən], *v.a.* desire, wish, covet, want.—*v.n. nach etwas* —, long for s.th.

begehrlich [bə'ge:rlɪç], *adj.* covetous, greedy, desirous.

begeifern [bə'gaɪfərn], *v.a.* spit at; (*fig.*) vilify, besmirch.

begeistern [bə'gaɪstərn], *v.a.* inspire, fill with enthusiasm, enrapture.—*v.r. sich für etwas* —, become enthusiastic about s.th.

Begier(de) [bə'gi:r(də)], *f.* (—, *pl.* —den) desire, lust, appetite.

begierig [bə'gi:rɪç], *adj.* desirous, lustful; anxious; curious (for news).

begießen [bə'gi:sən], *v.a. irr.* (*plants*) water; (*meat etc.*) baste; *etwas festlich* —, celebrate s.th. by drinking; *sich die Nase* —, (*coll.*) get tight.

Beginn [bə'gɪn], *m.* (—s, *no pl.*) beginning, commencement, start.

beginnen [bə'gɪnən], *v.a., v.n. irr.* begin, commence, start.

beglaubigen [bə'glaubɪgən], *v.a.* attest; certify, verify; accredit (an ambassador).

Beglaubigungsschreiben [bə'glaubɪguŋʃraɪbən], *n.* (—s, *pl.* —) credentials.

begleichen [bə'glaɪçən], *v.a. irr.* (*bill*) pay, settle.

begleiten [bə'glaɪtən], *v.a.* accompany, escort, see s.o. off, home etc.

Begleiter [bə'glaɪtər], *m.* (—s, *pl.* —) companion, escort; (*Mus.*) accompanist.

Begleiterscheinung [bə'glaɪtərʃaɪnuŋ], *f.* (—, *pl.* —en) concomitant; (*Med.*) complication, attendant symptom.

Begleitung [bə'glaɪtuŋ], *f.* (—, *pl.* —en) company; (*Mus.*) accompaniment.

beglücken [bə'glykən], *v.a.* make happy.

beglückwünschen [bə'glykvynʃən], *v.a.* congratulate.

begnadet [bə'gna:dət], *adj.* highly talented.

begnadigen [bə'gna:dɪgən], *v.a.* pardon, reprieve.

begnügen [bə'gny:gən], *v.r. sich mit etwas* —, content o.s. with s.th.

Begonie [bə'go:njə], *f.* (—, *pl.* —n) (*Bot.*) begonia.

begraben [bə'gra:bən], *v.a. irr.* bury, inter.

Begräbnis [bə'grɛ:pnɪs], *n.* (—ses, *pl.* —se) burial, funeral, interment.

begreifen [bə'graɪfən], *v.a. irr.* understand, comprehend, conceive.

begreiflich [bə'graɪflɪç], *adj.* comprehensible, conceivable, understandable.

begrenzen [bə'grɛntsən], *v.a.* bound, border, limit.

Begriff [bə'grɪf], *m.* (—s, *pl.* —e) notion, concept, idea, conception; *im* — *sein*, be about to . . . .

begriffen [bə'grɪfən], *adj.* — *sein in*, be engaged in.

begriffsstutzig [bə'grɪfsʃtutsɪç], *adj.* obtuse, dense, slow in the uptake.

begründen [bə'gryndən], *v.a.* base on, justify; found, establish.

begrüßen [bə'gry:sən], *v.a.* greet, salute, welcome.

begünstigen [bə'gynstɪgən], *v.a.* favour, prefer.

Begutachter [bə'gu:taxtər], *m.* (—s, *pl.* —) expert; (*Sch.*) assessor, second examiner.

Begutachtung [bə'gu:taxtuŋ], *f.* (—, *pl.* —en) expert opinion, assessment, report.

begütert [bə'gy:tərt], *adj.* wealthy, rich, well-to-do.

behaart [bə'ha:rt], *adj.* covered with hair, hairy.

behäbig [bə'hɛ:bɪç], *adj.* comfortable; corpulent, portly.

behaften [bə'haftən], *v.a.* charge, burden.

behagen [bə'ha:gən], *v.n.* please, be agreeable; *es behagt mir nicht*, I do not like it.

behaglich [bə'ha:klɪç], *adj.* cosy, comfortable, snug.

behalten [bə'haltən], *v.a. irr.* retain, keep.

Behälter [bə'hɛltər], *m.* (—s, *pl.* —) container; box, bin; (*water*) reservoir; tank.

behandeln [bə'handəln], *v.a.* treat, use; (*Med.*) treat; (*subject*) treat; handle.

Behandlung [bə'handluŋ], *f.* (—, *pl.* —en) treatment, use; (*Med.*) treatment.

Behang [bə'haŋ], *m.* (—es, *pl.* ⁻e) hanging(s); appendage.

behängen [bə'hɛŋən], *v.a. irr.* festoon with, drape.

beharren [bə'harən], *v.n.* persevere; persist, insist.

beharrlich [bə'harlɪç], *adj.* persevering, persistent, constant, firm.

behauen [bə'hauən], *v.a.* (*stones*) hew, cut.

behaupten [bə'hauptən], *v.a.* claim, assert, affirm, maintain.

Behauptung [bə'hauptuŋ], *f.* (—, *pl.* —en.) claim, assertion, affirmation.

Behausung [bə'hauzuŋ], *f.* (—, *pl.* —en.) habitation, housing.

behelfen [bə'hɛlfən], *v.r. irr. sich — mit*, make do with.

behelfsmäßig [bə'hɛlfsmɛːsɪç], *adj.* makeshift, temporary.

behelligen [bə'hɛlɪgən], *v.a.* trouble, molest, disturb.

behend(e) [bə'hɛndə], *adj.* quick, nimble, agile.

beherbergen [bə'hɛrbɛrgən], *v.a.* give shelter to, put up, harbour.

beherrschen [bə'hɛrʃən], *v.a.* rule, govern, dominate; *eine Sache —*, master a subject. — *v.r. sich —*, control o.s.

Beherrschung [bə'hɛrʃuŋ], *f.* (—, *pl.* (*rare*) —en) domination, sway; (*subject*) grasp; (*languages*) command.

beherzigen [bə'hɛrtsɪgən], *v.a.* take to heart, follow, heed.

Beherztheit [bə'hɛrtsthaɪt], *f.* (—, *no pl.*) courage, spirit.

behexen [bə'hɛksən], *v.a.* bewitch.

behilflich [bə'hɪlflɪç], *adj.* helpful, useful.

behindern [bə'hɪndərn], *v.a.* hinder, hamper.

Behörde [bə'hœrdə], *f.* (—, *pl.* —n) the authorities.

behufs [bə'huːfs], *prep.* (*Genit.*) in order to, with a view to.

behüten [bə'hyːtən], *v.a.* guard, protect; *Gott behüte!* Heaven forbid!

behutsam [bə'huːtzaːm], *adj.* careful, cautious.

bei [baɪ], *prep.* (*Dat.*) (*locally*) near by, close by, next to, at.

beibehalten ['baɪbəhaltən], *v.a. irr.* keep, retain.

Beiblatt ['baɪblat], *n.* (—s, *pl.* ¨er) supplement (to a newspaper).

beibringen ['baɪbrɪŋən], *v.a. irr.* adduce (proof); produce (witnesses); (*fig.*) teach; impart to.

Beichte ['baɪçtə], *f.* (—, *pl.* —n) confession.

Beichtstuhl ['baɪçtʃtuːl], *m.* (—s, *pl.* ¨e) confessional.

beide ['baɪdə], *adj.* both, either, the two.

beiderlei ['baɪdərlaɪ], *adj.* of both kinds.

beidrehen ['baɪdreːən], *v.n.* (*Naut.*) heave to.

Beifall ['baɪfal], *m.* (—s, *no pl.*) (*verbal*) approbation; (*shouting*) acclamation, acclaim; (*clapping*) applause.

beifällig ['baɪfɛlɪç], *adj.* favourable, approving, assenting.

beifügen ['baɪfyːgən], *v.a.* enclose, attach.

Beifuß ['baɪfuːs], *m.* (—es, *no pl.*) (*Bot.*) mugwort.

beigeben ['baɪgeːbən], *v.a. irr.* add, join to. — *v.n. klein —*, give in.

Beigeschmack ['baɪgəʃmak], *m.* (—s, *no pl.*) aftertaste, tang.

beigesellen ['baɪgəzɛlən], *v.r. sich —*, associate with.

Beihilfe ['baɪhɪlfə], *f.* (—, *pl.* —n) aid, assistance, subsidy.

beikommen ['baɪkɔmən], *v.n. irr.* (*aux.* sein) *einer Sache —*, to grapple with s.th.; *ich kann ihm nicht —*, I cannot catch him out, get at him.

Beil [baɪl], *n.* (—s, *pl.* —e) hatchet, axe.

Beilage ['baɪlaːgə], *f.* (—, *pl.* —n) enclosure (with a letter); supplement (to a newspaper); *Braten mit —*, joint with vegetables.

beiläufig ['baɪlɔyfɪç], *adv.* by the way, incidentally.

beilegen ['baɪleːgən], *v.a.* add, join; enclose (in letter).

beileibe [baɪ'laɪbə], *int.* — *nicht!* on no account!

Beileid ['baɪlaɪt], *n.* (—s, *no pl.*) condolence, sympathy.

beiliegen ['baɪliːgən], *v.n. irr.* be enclosed with.

beimengen ['baɪmɛŋən], *v.a.* (*Cul.*) mix with, add.

beimessen ['baɪmɛsən], *v.a. irr. einem etwas —*, impute s.th. to s.o.; *einem Glauben —*, credit s.o., give credence to.

Bein [baɪn], *n.* (—s, *pl.* —e) leg; *einem auf die —e helfen*, give a helping hand to s.o.

beinahe [baɪ'naːə], *adv.* almost, nearly.

Beiname ['baɪnaːmə], *m.* (—ns, *pl.* —n) surname; nickname.

Beinbruch ['baɪnbrux], *m.* (—s, *pl.* ¨e) fracture of the leg; (*coll.*) *Hals- und Beinbruch!* good luck!

Beinkleider ['baɪnklaɪdər], *n. pl.* (*obs.*) pants, trousers.

beipflichten ['baɪpflɪçtən], *v.n. einem —*, agree with s.o.

beirren [bə'ɪrən], *v.a. sich nicht — lassen*, not let o.s. be dissuaded *or* put off.

beisammen [baɪ'zamən], *adv.* together.

Beischlaf ['baɪʃlaːf], *m.* (—s, *no pl.*) cohabitation, coition.

Beisein ['baɪzaɪn], *n.* (—s, *no pl.*) *im — von*, in the presence of.

beiseite [baɪ'zaɪtə], *adv.* apart, aside; (*Theat.*) aside.

beisetzen ['baɪzɛtsən], *v.a.* bury, inter, entomb.

Beispiel ['baɪʃpiːl], *n.* (—s, *pl.* —e) example, instance; *zum —* (*abbr.* z.B.), for instance, for example.

beißen ['baɪsən], *v.a. irr.* bite; (*pepper, smoke*) burn, sting.

Beißzange ['baɪstsaŋə], *f.* (—, *pl.* —n) pair of pincers *or* nippers.

Beistand ['baɪʃtant], *m.* (—s, *pl.* ¨e) assistance, help; (*Law*) counsel; — *leisten*, give assistance.

beistehen ['baɪʃteːən], *v.n. irr. einem —*, stand by s.o., help s.o.

beisteuern ['baɪʃtɔyərn], *v.a. zu etwas —*, contribute to s.th.

beistimmen ['baɪʃtɪmən], *v.n.* agree with, assent.

Beistrich ['baɪʃtrɪç], *m.* (—(e)s, *pl.* —e) comma.

beitragen ['baɪtraːgən], *v.a. irr.* contribute; be conducive to.

beitreten ['baɪtreːtən], *v.n. irr.* (*aux.* sein) join (a club); enter into partnership with (a firm).

Beitritt ['baɪtrɪt], *m.* (—s, *no pl.*) accession, joining.

Beiwagen ['baɪvaːgən], *m.* (—s, *pl.* —) trailer, sidecar (on motor cycle).

beiwohnen ['baɪvoːnən], *v.n.* be present at, attend.

Beiwort ['baɪvɔrt], *n.* (—s, *pl.* ꞉er) adjective, epithet.

Beize ['baɪtsə], *f.* (—, *pl.* —n) caustic fluid; (*wood*) stain.

beizeiten [baɪ'tsaɪtən], *adv.* betimes, early, in good time.

beizen ['baɪtsən], *v.a.* cauterise; (*wood*) stain.

bejahen [bə'jaːən], *v.a.* answer in the affirmative.

bejahrt [bə'jaːrt], *adj.* aged, elderly, old.

bejammern [bə'jamərn], *v.a.* bemoan, bewail.

bekannt [bə'kant], *adj.* known, well-known; — *mit*, acquainted with.

Bekannte [bə'kantə], *m.* (—n, *pl.* —n) acquaintance.

bekanntlich [bə'kantlɪç], *adv.* as is well known.

Bekanntmachung [bə'kantmaxuŋ], *f.* (—, *pl.* —en) publication, announcement.

Bekanntschaft [bə'kantʃaft], *f.* (—, *pl.* —en) — *mit einem machen*, strike up an acquaintance with s.o.

bekehren [bə'keːrən], *v.a.* convert. — *v.r. sich* —, be converted *or* become a convert (to); reform.

bekennen [bə'kɛnən], *v.a. irr.* confess, profess; admit, own up to.

Bekenner [bə'kɛnər], *m.* (—s, *pl.* —) Confessor (as title).

Bekenntnis [bə'kɛntnɪs], *n.* (—ses, *pl.* —se) confession (of faith), avowal, creed.

beklagen [bə'klaːgən], *v.a.* lament, bewail, deplore. — *v.r. sich* — *über*, complain of.

Beklagte [bə'klaːktə], *m.* (—n, *pl.* —n) (*Law*) defendant.

bekleiden [bə'klaɪdən], *v.a.* clothe, dress, cover; (*office*) hold.

Bekleidung [bə'klaɪduŋ], *f.* (—, *no pl.*) clothing, clothes; (*office*) administration, holding, exercise.

beklemmen [bə'klɛmən], *v.a. irr.* oppress.

Beklemmung [bə'klɛmuŋ], *f.* (—, *pl.* —en) oppression, anguish.

beklommen [bə'klɔmən], *adj.* anxious, uneasy.

bekommen [bə'kɔmən], *v.a. irr.* obtain, get, receive.

bekömmlich [bə'kœmlɪç], *adj.* beneficial; digestible, wholesome.

beköstigen [bə'kœstɪgən], *v.a.* board; feed.

bekräftigen [bə'krɛftɪgən], *v.a.* aver, corroborate, confirm.

bekränzen [bə'krɛntsən], *v.a.* wreathe, crown (with a garland).

bekreuzigen [bə'krɔytsɪgən], *v.r. sich* —, make the sign of the cross, cross o.s.

bekriegen [bə'kriːgən], *v.a.* make war on.

bekritteln [bə'krɪtəln], *v.a.* criticise, carp at, find fault with.

bekritzeln [bə'krɪtsəln], *v.a.* scrawl on, doodle on.

bekümmern [bə'kymərn], *v.a.* grieve, distress, trouble. — *v.r.* trouble o.s. about, grieve over.

bekunden [bə'kundən], *v.a.* manifest, show; declare.

beladen [bə'laːdən], *v.a. irr.* load.

Belag [bə'laːk], *m.* (—s, *pl.* ꞉e) covering, layer; spread (on sandwiches); fur (on the tongue).

belagern [bə'laːgərn], *v.a.* besiege.

Belang [bə'laŋ], *m.* (—s, *pl.* —e) importance; *von* —, of great moment *or* consequence; (*pl.*) concerns, interests.

belangen [bə'laŋən], *v.a.* (*Law*) sue, prosecute.

belanglos [bə'laŋloːs], *adj.* of small account; irrelevant, unimportant.

belassen [bə'lasən], *v.a. irr. es dabei* —, leave things as they are.

belasten [bə'lastən], *v.a.* load, burden; (*Comm.*) debit, charge; (*Law*) incriminate.

belästigen [bə'lɛstɪgən], *v.a.* bother, pester, molest.

Belastung [bə'lastuŋ], *f.* (—, *pl.* —en) load, burden; (*Comm.*) debiting; (*house*) mortgage; *erbliche* —, hereditary disposition.

Belastungszeuge [bə'lastuŋstsɔygə], *m.* (—n, *pl.* —n) witness for the prosecution.

belaubt [bə'laupt], *adj.* covered with leaves, leafy.

belaufen [bə'laufən], *v.r. irr. sich* — *auf*, amount to, come to.

belauschen [bə'lauʃən], *v.a.* eavesdrop, overhear.

beleben [bə'leːbən], *v.a.* animate, enliven.

Belebtheit [bə'leːpthaɪt], *f.* (—, *no pl.*) animation, liveliness.

Beleg [bə'leːk], *m.* (—s, *pl.* —e) document, proof, receipt, voucher.

belegen [bə'leːgən], *v.a.* cover, overlay; reserve, book (*seat*); support by documents, authenticate, prove.

Belegschaft [bə'leːkʃaft], *f.* (—, *pl.* —en) workers, personnel, staff; (*Min.*) gang, shift.

belegt [bə'leːkt], *adj.* (*tongue*) furred; —*es Brot*, sandwich.

belehnen [bə'leːnən], *v.a.* enfeoff; invest (with a fief).

belehren [bə'leːrən], *v.a.* instruct, advise, inform.

Belehrung [bə'le:ruŋ], *f.* (—, *pl.* —en) information, instruction, advice.

beleibt [bə'laɪpt], *adj.* stout, corpulent, obese.

beleidigen [bə'laɪdɪgən], *v.a.* insult, offend, give offence to.

belesen [bə'le:zən], *adj.* well-read.

beleuchten [bə'lɔʏçtən], *v.a.* illumine, illuminate; (*fig.*) throw light on, elucidate.

Beleuchtungskörper [bə'lɔʏçtuŋskœr-pər], *m.* (—s, *pl.* —) lighting fixture, lamp.

Belgien ['bɛlgjən], *n.* Belgium.

belichten [bə'lɪçtən], *v.a.* (*Phot.*) expose.

belieben [bə'li:bən], *v.a.*, *v.n.* please, like, choose.

beliebig [bə'li:bɪç], *adj.* optional; any, whatever.

beliebt [bə'li:pt], *adj.* popular, well-liked.

Beliebtheit [bə'li:pthaɪt], *f.* (—, *no pl.*) popularity.

bellen ['bɛlən], *v.n.* bark.

beloben [bə'lo:bən], *v.a.* praise, approve.

belohnen [bə'lo:nən], *v.a.* reward, recompense.

belügen [bə'ly:gən], *v.a. irr.* *einen* —, tell lies to s.o., deceive s.o. by lying.

belustigen [bə'lustɪgən], *v.a.* amuse, divert, entertain.

bemächtigen [bə'mɛçtɪgən], *v.r. sich einer Sache* —, take possession of s.th.

bemäkeln [bə'mɛ:kəln], *v.a.* find fault with.

bemalen [bə'ma:lən], *v.a.* paint (over).

bemängeln [bə'mɛŋəln], *v.a.* find fault with.

bemannen [bə'manən], *v.a.* man.

bemänteln [bə'mɛntəln], *v.a.* cloak, hide.

bemeistern [bə'maɪstərn], *v.a.* master.

bemerkbar [bə'mɛrkba:r], *adj.* perceptible, noticeable.

bemerken [bə'mɛrkən], *v.a.* observe, perceive, notice.

Bemerkung [bə'mɛrkuŋ], *f.* (—, *pl.* —en) remark, observation, note.

bemessen [bə'mɛsən], *v.a. irr.* measure; curtail.

bemitleiden [bə'mɪtlaɪdən], *v.a.* pity, be sorry for.

bemittelt [bə'mɪtəlt], *adj.* well-off, well-to-do.

bemoost [bə'mo:st], *adj.* mossy.

bemühen [bə'my:ən], *v.a.* trouble, give trouble (to). — *v.r. sich* —, take pains, strive, endeavour.

bemüht [bə'my:t], *adj.* studious; — *sein*, endeavour, try to.

bemuttern [bə'mutərn], *v.a.* mother.

benachbart [bə'naxba:rt], *adj.* neighbouring, adjacent.

benachrichtigen [bə'naxrɪçtɪgən], *v.a.* inform, give notice of, notify.

benachteiligen [bə'naxtaɪlɪgən], *v.a.* prejudice, discriminate against, handicap.

benagen [bə'na:gən], *v.a.* gnaw at.

benebeln [bə'ne:bəln], *v.a.* befog, cloud; (*fig.*) dim, intoxicate.

benedeien [bene'daɪən], *v.a.* bless, glorify.

Benediktiner [benedɪk'ti:nər], *m.* (—s, *pl.* —) (monk) Benedictine; Benedictine liqueur.

Benefiz [bene'fi:ts], *n.* (—es, *pl.* —e) benefit; benefit performance.

Benehmen [bə'ne:mən], *n.* (—s, *no pl.*) conduct, behaviour.

benehmen [bə'ne:mən], *v.r. irr. sich* —, behave, conduct o.s.

beneiden [bə'naɪdən], *v.a. einen* — *um*, envy s.o. (s.th.).

benennen [bə'nɛnən], *v.a.* name.

benetzen [bə'nɛtsən], *v.a.* moisten.

Bengel ['bɛŋəl], *m.* (—s, *pl.* —) naughty boy, scamp; rascal, lout.

benommen [bə'nɔmən], *adj.* dazed, giddy.

benötigen [bə'nø:tɪgən], *v.a.* be in need of, require.

benutzen [bə'nutsən], *v.a.* make use of, utilise.

Benzin [bɛnt'si:n], *n.* (—s, *no pl.*) benzine; (*Motor.*) petrol; (*Am.*) gas, gasoline.

beobachten [bə'o:baxtən], *v.a.* watch, observe.

bequem [bə'kve:m], *adj.* comfortable, easy; convenient; indolent, lazy.

bequemen [bə'kve:mən], *v.r. sich* —, condescend (to), comply (with).

Bequemlichkeit [bə'kve:mlɪçkaɪt], *f.* (—, *pl.* —en) convenience, ease; indolence.

beraten [bə'ra:tən], *v.a. irr.* advise, assist with advice, counsel. — *v.r. sich* — *mit*, confer with, consult with.

beratschlagen [bə'ra:tʃla:gən], *v.n.* deliberate with.

Beratung [bə'ra:tuŋ], *f.* (—, *pl.* —en) council, deliberation, consultation.

berauben [bə'raubən], *v.a.* rob, deprive (s.o.) of (s.th.).

berauschen [bə'rauʃən], *v.a.* intoxicate.

berechnen [bə'rɛçnən], *v.a.* compute, charge, calculate, estimate.

berechtigen [bə'rɛçtɪgən], *v.a. einen zu etwas* —, entitle s.o. to s.th.; authorise s.o. to have or do s.th.

beredsam [bə're:tza:m], *adj.* eloquent.

beredt [bə're:t], *adj.* eloquent.

Bereich [bə'raɪç], *m. & n.* (—s, *pl.* —e) extent, realm, sphere, scope.

bereichern [bə'raɪçərn], *v.a.* enrich, enlarge.

bereisen [bə'raɪzən], *v.a.* travel over or through, tour (a country).

bereit [bə'raɪt], *adj.* ready, prepared.

bereiten [bə'raɪtən], *v.a.* prepare, get ready.

bereits [bə'raɪts], *adv.* already.

Bereitschaft [bə'raɪtʃaft], *f.* (—, *no pl.*) readiness, preparedness.

bereitwillig [bə'raɪtvɪlɪç], *adj.* willing, ready, obliging.

bereuen [bə'rɔyən], *v.a.* repent, be sorry for, regret.

Berg [bɛrk], *m.* (—es, *pl.* —e) mountain, hill.

bergab [bɛrk'ap], *adj.* downhill.

Bergamt ['bɛrkamt], *n.* (—s, *pl.* ⸚er) mining-office, mine authority.

bergan [bɛrk'an], *adj.* uphill.

Bergarbeiter ['bɛrkarbaItər], *m.* (—s, *pl.* —) miner, collier.

bergauf [bɛrk'auf], *adj.* uphill.

Bergbau ['bɛrkbau], *m.* (—s, *no pl.*) mining, mining industry.

bergen ['bɛrgən], *v.a. irr.* shelter, protect, save; (*flotsam*) save, recover, salvage.

bergig ['bɛrgIç], *adj.* mountainous, hilly.

Bergkristall ['bɛrkkrIstal], *m.* (—s, *pl.* —e) rock-crystal.

Bergleute ['bɛrklɔytə], *pl.* miners, colliers.

Bergmann ['bɛrkman], *m.* (—s, *pl.* Bergleute) miner, collier.

Bergpredigt ['bɛrkpre:dIçt], *f.* (—, *no pl.*) Sermon on the Mount.

Bergschlucht ['bɛrkʃluxt], *f.* (—s, *pl.* —en) ravine, gorge.

Bergsteiger ['bɛrkʃtaIgər], *m.* (—s, *pl.* —) mountaineer.

Bergstock ['bɛrkʃtɔk], *m.* (—s, *pl.* ⸚e) alpenstock.

Bergsturz ['bɛrkʃturts], *m.* (—es, *pl.* ⸚e) landslip, landslide.

Bergung ['bɛrguŋ], *f.* (—, *pl.* —en) sheltering; salvaging; rescue operation.

Bergwerk ['bɛrkvɛrk], *n.* (—s, *pl.* —e) mine, pit.

Bericht [bə'rIçt], *m.* (—s, *pl.* —e) report, account, statement; —*erstatten*, report, give an account of.

Berichterstatter [bə'rIçtɛrʃtatər], *m.* (—s, *pl.* —) reporter.

berichtigen [bə'rIçtIgən], *v.a.* set right, correct, rectify, amend.

berieseln [bə'ri:zəln], *v.a.* irrigate.

beritten [bə'rItən], *adj.* mounted on horseback.

Berlin [bɛr'li:n], *n.* Berlin; —*er Blau*, Prussian blue.

Bern [bɛrn], *n.* Berne.

Bernhardiner [bɛrnhaɾ'di:nər], *m.* (—s, *pl.* —) Cistercian monk; Newfoundland dog, St. Bernard dog.

Bernstein ['bɛrnʃtaIn], *m.* (—s, *no pl.*) amber.

bersten ['bɛrstən], *v.n. irr.* (*aux.* sein) burst.

berüchtigt [bə'ryçtIçt], *adj.* notorious, infamous.

berücken [bə'rykən], *v.a.* enchant, fascinate.

berücksichtigen [bə'rykzIçtIgən], *v.a.* have regard to, take into consideration, allow for.

Beruf [bə'ru:f], *m.* (—s, *pl.* —e) profession, occupation, calling, trade.

berufen [bə'ru:fən], *v.a. irr.* (*meeting*) call, convene; appoint (to an office). — *v.r. sich* — *auf*, appeal to, refer to. — *adj.* competent, qualified.

berufsmäßig [bə'ru:fsmɛ:sIç], *adj.* professional.

Berufung [bə'ru:fuŋ], *f.* (—, *pl.* —en) call, vocation, appointment; (*Law*) appeal.

beruhen [bə'ru:ən], *v.n. auf etwas* —, be based on, be founded on.

beruhigen [bə'ru:Igən], *v.a.* calm, pacify; comfort, console, set at rest.

Beruhigung [bə'ru:Iguŋ], *f.* (—, *pl.* —en) reassurance, quieting, calming.

berühmt [bə'ry:mt], *adj.* famous, celebrated, illustrious, renowned.

berühren [bə'ry:rən], *v.a.* touch, handle; (*subject*) mention, touch upon; *peinlich berührt*, unpleasantly affected.

berußt [bə'ru:st], *adj.* sooty.

Beryll [be'ryl], *m.* (—s, *pl.* —e) beryl.

besagen [bə'za:gən], *v.a.* mean, signify.

besagt [bə'za:kt], *adj.* aforesaid, above-mentioned.

besaiten [bə'zaItən], *v.a.* fit with strings.

Besan [bə'za:n], *m.* (—s, *pl.* —e) (*Naut.*) miz(z)en.

besänftigen [bə'zɛnftIgən], *v.a.* calm, appease, pacify.

Besatz [bə'zats], *m.* (—es, *pl.* ⸚e) trimming, border.

Besatzung [bə'zatsuŋ], *f.* (—, *pl.* —en) crew; (*Mil.*) garrison, occupation.

besaufen [bə'zaufən], *v.r. irr.* (*vulg.*) *sich* —, get drunk.

beschädigen [bə'ʃɛ:dIgən], *v.a.* damage.

beschaffen [bə'ʃafən], *v.a.* procure, get. — *adj.* conditioned, constituted.

Beschaffenheit [bə'ʃafənhaIt], *f.* (—, *no pl.*) nature, kind, quality, condition.

beschäftigen [bə'ʃɛftIgən], *v.a.* occupy, employ.

beschämen [bə'ʃɛ:mən], *v.a.* make ashamed, shame.

beschatten [bə'ʃatən], *v.a.* shade, shadow; follow (s.o.).

Beschau [bə'ʃau], *f.* (—, *no pl.*) examination; inspection.

beschauen [bə'ʃauən], *v.a.* view, look at.

beschaulich [bə'ʃaulIç], *adj.* tranquil, contemplative.

Beschaulichkeit [bə'ʃaulIçkaIt], *f.* (—, *pl.* —en) tranquillity, contemplation.

Bescheid [bə'ʃaIt], *m.* (—s, *pl.* —e) answer, information; (*Law*) decision; — *wissen*, know o.'s way about; know what's what.

bescheiden [bə'ʃaIdən], *v.a. irr.* inform (s.o.); *einen zu sich* —, send for s.o. — *adj.* modest, unassuming.

Bescheidenheit [bə'ʃaIdənhaIt], *f.* (—, *no pl.*) modesty.

bescheinen [bə'ʃaInən], *v.a. irr.* shine upon.

bescheinigen [bə'ʃaInIgən], *v.a. einem etwas* —, attest, certify.

beschenken [bə'ʃɛnkən], *v.a.* give a present to.

bescheren [bə'ʃe:rən], *v.a.* give (a present to), bestow (s.th. on s.o.).

Bescherung [bə'ʃe:ruŋ], *f.* (—, *pl.* —en) giving (of present); *das ist eine schöne —,* (*fig.*) this is a nice mess!

beschicken [bə'ʃɪkən], *v.a. eine Ausstellung —,* contribute to an exhibition.

beschießen [bə'ʃi:sən], *v.a. irr.* shoot at, fire upon, bombard.

beschiffen [bə'ʃɪfən], *v.a.* navigate, sail.

beschimpfen [bə'ʃɪmpfən], *v.a.* insult, abuse, revile.

beschirmen [bə'ʃɪrmən], *v.a.* protect, shelter, defend.

Beschlag [bə'ʃla:k], *m.* (—s, *pl.* ⸚e) mounting; metal fitting; (*on stick*) ferrule; *etwas mit — belegen,* or *in — nehmen,* sequestrate, confiscate, seize.

beschlagen [bə'ʃla:gən], *v.a. irr.* shoe (a horse). — *v.n.* (*window*) mist over.

Beschlagnahme [bə'ʃla:kna:mə], *f.* (—, *pl.* —n) confiscation, seizure.

beschleunigen [bə'ʃlɔynɪgən], *v.a.* hasten, speed up, accelerate.

beschließen [bə'ʃli:sən], *v.a. irr.* shut, lock up; close, conclude, finish; decide, resolve upon.

Beschluß [bə'ʃlus], *m.* (—sses, *pl.* ⸚sse) determination, resolution, decree.

beschmieren [bə'ʃmi:rən], *v.a.* soil, smear.

beschmutzen [bə'ʃmutsən], *v.a.* soil, dirty, foul.

beschneiden [bə'ʃnaɪdən], *v.a. irr.* cut, clip; (*Hort.*) lop, prune; (*animals*) crop; circumcise.

Beschneidung [bə'ʃnaɪduŋ], *f.* (—, *pl.* —en) lopping, pruning; circumcision.

beschönigen [bə'ʃø:nɪgən], *v.a.* palliate, excuse.

beschränken [bə'ʃrɛnkən], *v.a.* limit, restrict.

beschränkt [bə'ʃrɛŋkt], *adj.* limited; *etwas —,* a little stupid; *Gesellschaft mit —er Haftung,* limited (liability) company.

Beschränkung [bə'ʃrɛŋkuŋ], *f.* (—, *pl.* —en) limitation, restriction.

beschreiben [bə'ʃraɪbən], *v.a. irr.* describe; write upon.

beschreiten [bə'ʃraɪtən], *v.a. irr.* tread on.

beschuldigen [bə'ʃuldɪgən], *v.a.* charge (s.o.), accuse.

beschützen [bə'ʃytsən], *v.a.* protect, shelter, guard.

Beschützer [bə'ʃytsər], *m.* (—s, *pl.* —) protector, defender.

Beschwerde [bə'ʃve:rdə], *f.* (—, *pl.* —n) trouble, hardship, difficulty; complaint, grievance.

beschweren [bə'ʃve:rən], *v.a.* make heavier, weight. — *v.r. sich über etwas —,* complain of s.th.

beschwerlich [bə'ʃve:rlɪç], *adj.* burdensome, hard, troublesome.

beschwichtigen [bə'ʃvɪçtɪgən], *v.a.* soothe, appease, still.

beschwindeln [bə'ʃvɪndəln], *v.a.* cheat, swindle (s.o.).

beschwingt [bə'ʃvɪŋkt], *adj.* winged, light-footed.

beschwipst [bə'ʃvɪpst], *adj.* (*coll.*) tipsy.

beschwören [bə'ʃvø:rən], *v.a. irr.* testify on oath; *einen —,* implore s.o.; conjure (up) (ghosts etc.); exorcize.

beseelen [bə'ze:lən], *v.a.* animate.

besehen [bə'ze:ən], *v.a. irr.* look at, inspect.

beseitigen [bə'zaɪtɪgən], *v.a.* remove.

beseligt [bə'ze:lɪçt], *adj.* enraptured, beatified.

Besen ['be:zən], *m.* (—s, *pl.* —) broom, besom.

Besenstiel ['be:zənʃti:l], *m.* (—s, *pl.* —e) broom-stick.

besessen [bə'zesən], *adj.* possessed, obsessed, mad.

besetzen [bə'zetsən], *v.a.* (*dress*) trim, lace; (*Mil.*) occupy, garrison; (*office*) fill; (*Theat.*) cast; (*seat*) occupy, take; *besetzt,* engaged.

Besetzung [bə'zetsuŋ], *f.* (—, *pl.* —en) lacing, trimming; appointment (to post); (*Theat.*) cast.

besichtigen [bə'zɪçtɪgən], *v.a.* view, go over, inspect, examine.

besiedeln [bə'zi:dəln], *v.a.* colonise.

besiegeln [bə'zi:gəln], *v.a.* seal, set o.'s seal to.

besiegen [bə'zi:gən], *v.a.* vanquish, conquer, overcome.

besinnen [bə'zɪnən], *v.r. irr.* reflect; *sich auf etwas —,* recollect, remember, think of.

besinnungslos [bə'zɪnuŋslo:s], *adj.* insensible, unconscious.

Besitz [bə'zɪts], *m.* (—es, *no pl.*) possession, property.

besitzanzeigend [bə'zɪtsantsaɪgənt], *adj.* (*Gram.*) possessive.

besitzen [bə'zɪtsən], *v.a. irr.* possess, own, have.

Besitzergreifung [bə'zɪtsɛrgraɪfuŋ], *f.* (—, *no pl.*) occupation, taking possession (of).

besoffen [bə'zɔfən], *adj.* (*vulg.*) drunk.

besohlen [bə'zo:lən], *v.a.* sole (shoes).

besolden [bə'zɔldən], *v.a.* give a salary to, pay.

besonder [bə'zɔndər], *adj.* special, particular.

Besonderheit [bə'zɔndərhaɪt], *f.* (—, *pl.* —en) particularity, peculiarity, strangeness.

besonders [bə'zɔndərs], *adv.* especially.

besonnen [bə'zɔnən], *adj.* prudent, cautious, collected, circumspect.

besorgen [bə'zɔrgən], *v.a.* take care of, provide, procure.

Besorgnis [bə'zɔrknɪs], *f.* (—, *pl.* —se) care, concern, anxiety, fear.

besorgt [bə'zɔrkt], *adj.* apprehensive, anxious, worried.

Besorgung [bə'zɔrguŋ], *f.* (—, *pl.* —en) care, management; purchase, commission; —*en machen*, go shopping.

bespannen [bə'ʃpanən], *v.a.* string (a musical instrument); put horses (to a carriage).

bespötteln [bə'ʃpœtəln], *v.a.* ridicule.

besprechen [bə'ʃprɛçən], *v.a. irr.* discuss, talk over; (book) review. — *v.r. sich — mit*, confer with.

bespritzen [bə'ʃprɪtsən], *v.a.* sprinkle, splash.

besser ['bɛsər], *adj.* better; *um so —*, so much the better; *je mehr desto —*, the more the better; — *sein als*, be better than, be preferable to; — *werden*, (*weather*) clear up; (*health*) improve.

bessern ['bɛsərn], *v.a.* better, improve. — *v.r. sich —*, reform, improve, mend o.'s ways.

Besserung ['bɛsəruŋ], *f.* (—*pl.* —en) improvement, amendment, reform; (*Med.*) recovery; *gute —*, get well soon.

Besserungsanstalt ['bɛsəruŋsanʃtalt], *f.* (—, *pl.* —en) reformatory.

best ['bɛst], *adj.* best.

bestallen [bə'ʃtalən], *v.a.* appoint.

Bestand [bə'ʃtant], *m.* (—s, *pl.* ¨e) continuance, duration; stock; balance of cash; — *haben*, endure.

Bestandaufnahme [bə'ʃtantaufna:mə], *f.* (—, *pl.* —n) (*Comm.*) stock-taking.

beständig [bə'ʃtɛndɪç], *adj.* continual, perpetual; (*persons*) steady, steadfast, constant.

Bestandteil [bə'ʃtanttail], *m.* (—s, *pl.* —e) constituent part, component, ingredient, essential part.

bestärken [bə'ʃtɛrkən], *v.a.* confirm, strengthen.

bestätigen [bə'ʃtɛ:tɪgən], *v.a.* confirm, ratify, bear out, sanction; *den Empfang eines Briefes —*, acknowledge receipt of a letter.

bestatten [bə'ʃtatən], *v.a.* bury, inter.

bestäuben [bə'ʃtɔybən], *v.a.* cover with dust, spray; (*Bot.*) pollinate.

bestechen [bə'ʃtɛçən], *v.a. irr.* bribe, corrupt; (*fig.*) captivate.

bestechlich [bə'ʃtɛçlɪç], *adj.* corruptible.

Bestechung [bə'ʃtɛçuŋ], *f.* (—, *pl.* —en) corruption, bribery.

Besteck [bə'ʃtɛk], *n.* (—s, *pl.* —e) set of knife, fork and spoon; set *or* case (of instruments).

Bestehen [bə'ʃte:ən], *n.* (—s, *no pl.*) existence.

bestehen [bə'ʃte:ən], *v.a. irr.* undergo, endure, pass (an examination). — *v.n.* exist; *aus etwas —*, consist of s.th.; be composed of s.th.; *auf* (*Dat.*) —, insist upon s.th.

besteigen [bə'ʃtaigən], *v.a. irr.* ascend, mount, climb.

bestellen [bə'ʃtɛlən], *v.a.* order, book; appoint; put in order; (*letter, message*) deliver; (*field*) till.

Bestellung [bə'ʃtɛluŋ], *f.* (—, *pl.* —en) order, commission, delivery (of letter); tilling (of field); appointment; *auf —*, to order.

bestens ['bɛstəns], *adv.* in the best manner.

besteuern [bə'ʃtɔyərn], *v.a.* tax.

bestialisch [bɛstɪ'a:lɪʃ], *adj.* beastly, bestial.

Bestie ['bɛstjə], *f.* (—, *pl.* —n) beast, brute.

bestimmen [bə'ʃtɪmən], *v.a.* fix, settle; decide (s.th.); determine, define.

bestimmt [bə'ʃtɪmt], *adj.* decided, fixed, appointed; *ganz —*, positively, most decidedly.

Bestimmtheit [bə'ʃtɪmthait], *f.* (—, *no pl.*) certainty.

Bestimmung [bə'ʃtɪmuŋ], *f.* (—, *pl.* —en) settlement, decision, determination; provision; destiny.

bestrafen [bə'ʃtra:fən], *v.a.* punish, chastise.

bestrahlen [bə'ʃtra:lən], *v.a.* irradiate; (*Med.*) treat by radiotherapy.

bestreben [bə'ʃtre:bən], *v.r. sich —*, exert o.s., strive (for), endeavour.

Bestrebung [bə'ʃtre:buŋ], *f.* (—, *pl.* —en) effort, endeavour, exertion.

bestreichen [bə'ʃtraiçən], *v.a. irr.* spread.

bestreiten [bə'ʃtraitən], *v.a. irr.* contest, deny, dispute; defray (costs).

bestreuen [bə'ʃtrɔyən], *v.a.* sprinkle, strew, powder.

bestricken [bə'ʃtrɪkən], *v.a.* ensnare, entangle.

bestürmen [bə'ʃtyrmən], *v.a.* storm, assail; (*fig.*) importune.

bestürzen [bə'ʃtyrtsən], *v.a.* dismay, confound, perplex.

Besuch [bə'zu:x], *m.* (—s, *pl.* —e) visit; (*person*) visitor.

besuchen [bə'zu:xən], *v.a.* visit, call on; attend; frequent.

besudeln [bə'zu:dəln], *v.a.* soil, foul.

betagt [bə'ta:kt], *adj.* aged, elderly.

betätigen [bə'tɛ:tɪgən], *v.a.* practise, operate. — *v.r. sich —*, take an active part, work, participate (in).

betäuben [bə'tɔybən], *v.a.* deafen; stun, benumb, anaesthetize.

Betäubung [bə'tɔybuŋ], *f.* (—, *pl.* —en) stupor, stupefaction; *örtliche —*, local anaesthetic.

beteiligen [bə'tailɪgən], *v.a. einen an etwas —*, give s.o. a share of s.th. — *v.r. sich an etwas —*, participate in s.th.; (*Comm.*) have shares in s.th.

Beteiligte [bə'tailɪçtə], *m.* (—n, *pl.* —n) person concerned.

Beteiligung [bə'tailɪguŋ], *f.* (—, *pl.* —en) participation, interest.

beten ['be:tən], *v.n.* pray, say o.'s prayers.

beteuern [bə'tɔyərn], *v.a.* aver, affirm solemnly.

betiteln [bə'ti:təln], *v.a.* entitle, name.

Beton [be'tɔ̃], *m.* (—s, *no pl.*) concrete.

betonen [bə'to:nən], *v.a.* accentuate, stress, emphasise.

Betonung [bə'to:nuŋ], *f.* (—, *pl.* —en) accentuation, emphasis, stress.

betören [bə'tø:rən], *v.a.* delude, infatuate.

Betracht [bə'traxt], *m.* (—s, *no pl.*) consideration, respect, regard.

betrachten [bə'traxtən], *v.a.* consider, look at, view; *etwas aufmerksam —,* contemplate s.th.

beträchtlich [bə'trɛçtlɪç], *adj.* considerable.

Betrachtung [bə'traxtuŋ], *f.* (—, *pl.* —en) contemplation, consideration.

Betrag [bə'tra:k], *m.* (—s, *pl.* ⁓e) amount, sum total.

betragen [bə'tra:gən], *v.a. irr.* amount to, come to. — *v.r. sich —,* behave, conduct o.s.

Betragen [bə'tra:gən], *n.* (—s, *no pl.*) behaviour, conduct, demeanour.

betrauen [bə'trauən], *v.a. einen mit etwas —,* entrust s.o. with s.th.

betrauern [bə'trauərn], *v.a.* mourn for, bemoan.

Betreff [bə'trɛf], *m.* (—s, *no pl.*) reference; *in —,* with regard to.

betreffen [bə'trɛfən], *v.a. irr.* concern, affect, relate to.

Betreiben [bə'traɪbən], *n.* (—s, *no pl.*) *auf — von,* at the instigation of.

betreiben [bə'traɪbən], *v.a. irr.* (*business*) carry on; (*factory*) run; (*trade*) follow, practise.

Betreten [bə'tre:tən], *n.* (—s, *no pl.*) entry, entering.

betreten [bə'tre:tən], *v.a. irr.* step upon, set foot on, enter. — *adj.* disconcerted, embarrassed.

betreuen [bə'trɔyən], *v.a.* care for, attend to.

Betrieb [bə'tri:p], *m.* (—s, *pl.* —e) management, business, factory, plant; *den — einstellen,* close down; *in — sein,* be in operation; *in — setzen,* start working.

betriebsam [bə'tri:pza:m], *adj.* active, busy, industrious, diligent.

Betriebsamkeit [bə'tri:pza:mkaɪt], *f.* (—, *pl.* —en) activity, industry, bustle.

betriebsfertig [bə'tri:psfɛrtɪç], *adj.* ready for service; operational.

Betriebsmaterial [bə'tri:psmaterja:l], *n.* (—s, *pl.* —ien) (*Railw.*) rolling-stock; (*factory*) working-stock.

Betriebspersonal [bə'tri:psperzona:l], *n.* (—s, *no pl.*) workmen, employees, staff.

betrinken [bə'trɪŋkən], *v.r. irr. sich —,* get drunk.

betroffen [bə'trɔfən], *adj.* perplexed, confounded.

betrüben [bə'try:bən], *v.a.* afflict, grieve.

Betrübnis [bə'try:pnɪs], *f.* (—ses, *pl.* —se) affliction, grief, distress, sorrow.

betrübt [bə'try:pt], *adj.* sad, grieved.

Betrug [bə'tru:k], *m.* (—s, *pl.* ⁓ereien) fraud, deceit, deception, imposture; *einen — begehen,* commit a fraud.

betrügen [bə'try:gən], *v.a. irr.* cheat, deceive.

Betrüger [bə'try:gər], *m.* (—s, —) swindler, cheat, deceiver, impostor.

betrunken [bə'truŋkən], *adj.* drunk, drunken, tipsy.

Bett [bɛt], *n.* (—(e)s, *pl.* —en) bed; (*river*) bed, channel.

Bettdecke ['bɛtdɛkə], *f.* (—, *pl.* —n) counterpane; (*Am.*) bedspread; *wollene —,* blanket; *gesteppte —,* quilt.

Bettel ['bɛtəl], *m.* (—s, *no pl.*) trash, trifle.

bettelarm ['bɛtəlarm], *adj.* destitute.

Bettelei [bɛtə'laɪ], *f.* (—, *pl.* —en) begging, beggary, penury.

betteln ['bɛtəln], *v.a.* beg, ask alms.

betten ['bɛtən], *v.a.* bed, lay to rest. — *v.r.* (*fig.*) *sich —,* make o.'s bed.

bettlägerig ['bɛtlɛgərɪç], *adj.* bedridden.

Bettlaken ['bɛtla:kən], *n.* (—s, *pl.* —) sheet.

Bettler ['bɛtlər], *m.* (—s, *pl.* —) beggar.

Bettstelle ['bɛtʃtɛlə], *f.* (—, *pl.* —n) bedstead.

Bettvorleger ['bɛtfo:rle:gər], *m.* (—s, *pl.* —) bedside-carpet *or* rug.

Bettwäsche ['bɛtvɛʃə], *f.* (—, *no pl.*) bed linen, bed clothes.

Bettzeug ['bɛttsɔyk], *n.* (—s, *no pl.*) bedding.

beugen ['bɔygən], *v.a.* bend, bow. — *v.r. sich —,* bend down, stoop.

Beugung ['bɔyguŋ], *f.* (—, *pl.* —en) (*Gram.*) inflection.

Beule ['bɔylə], *f.* (—, *pl.* —n) bruise, bump, swelling, boil.

beunruhigen [bə'unru:ɪgən], *v.a.* alarm, trouble, disquiet.

beurkunden [bə'u:rkundən], *v.a.* authenticate, verify.

beurlauben [bə'u:rlaubən], *v.a.* grant leave of absence. — *v.r. sich —,* take leave.

beurteilen [bə'urtaɪlən], *v.a.* judge, criticise.

Beute ['bɔytə], *f.* (—, *no pl.*) booty, loot; (*animals*) prey; (*Hunt.*) bag.

Beutel ['bɔytəl], *m.* (—s, *pl.* —) bag; (*money*) purse; (*Zool.*) pouch.

Beuteltier ['bɔytəlti:r], *n.* (—s, *pl.* —e) marsupial.

bevölkern [bə'fœlkərn], *v.a.* people, populate.

Bevölkerung [bə'fœlkəruŋ], *f.* (—, *pl.* —en) population.

bevollmächtigen [bə'fɔlmɛçtɪgən], *v.a.* empower, authorise.

bevor [bə'fo:r], *conj.* before, ere, beforehand.

bevormunden [bə'fo:rmundən], *v.a. insep.* act as guardian to; (*fig.*) browbeat.

bevorrechtigt [bə'fo:rrɛçtɪçt], *adj.* privileged.

bevorstehen [bə'fo:rʃte:ən], *v.n. irr.* impend, lie ahead, be imminent; *einem* —, be in store for s.o.

bevorzugen [bə'fo:rtsu:gən], *v.a. insep.* prefer, favour.

bewachen [bə'vaxən], *v.a.* watch over, guard.

bewachsen [bə'vaksən], *adj.* overgrown.

bewaffnen [bə'vafnən], *v.a.* arm, supply with arms.

Bewahranstalt [bə'va:ranʃtalt], *f.* (—, pl. —en) kindergarten, nursery.

bewahren [bə'va:rən], *v.a.* preserve, keep, take care of.

bewähren [bə'vɛ:rən], *v.r. sich* —, prove o.s.

bewahrheiten [bə'va:rhaItən], *v.r. sich* —, come true.

bewährt [bə'vɛ:rt], *adj.* proved.

Bewährung [bə'vɛ:ruŋ], *f.* (—, no pl.) proof, verification.

Bewährungsfrist [bə'vɛ:ruŋsfrIst], *f.* (—, no pl.) probation.

bewaldet [bə'valdət], *adj.* wooded, woody.

bewältigen [bə'vɛltIgən], *v.a.* overcome; manage, master; cope *or* deal with.

bewandert [bə'vandərt], *adj.* versed, skilled, experienced, conversant.

bewandt [bə'vant], *adj.* such; *damit ist es so* —, it is like this.

Bewandtnis [bə'vantnIs], *f.* (—, pl. —se) circumstance, condition, state; *es hat damit folgende* —, the circumstances are as follows.

bewässern [bə'vɛsərn], *v.a.* water, irrigate.

bewegen [bə've:gən], *v.a., v.r.* move, stir; take exercise. — *v.a. irr.* persuade, induce.

Beweggrund [bə've:kgrunt], *m.* (—es, pl. ̈e) motive, reason, motivation.

beweglich [bə've:klIç], *adj.* movable; agile, brisk, sprightly.

Bewegung [bə've:guŋ], *f.* (—, pl. —en) motion, movement; (*mind*) emotion, agitation.

beweinen [bə'vaInən], *v.a.* lament, bemoan, deplore.

Beweis [bə'vaIs], *m.* (—es, pl. —e) proof, evidence; (*Maths.*) demonstration.

beweisen [bə'vaIzən], *v.a. irr.* prove, show, demonstrate.

Beweiskraft [bə'vaIskraft], *f.* (—, no pl.) (*Law*) probative force.

Beweismittel [bə'vaIsmItəl], *n.* (—s, pl. —) evidence, proof.

Bewenden [bə'vɛndən], *n.* (—s, no pl.) *es hat damit sein* —, there the matter rests.

bewenden [bə'vɛndən], *v.n. irr. es dabei* — *lassen*, leave it at that.

bewerben [bə'vɛrbən], *v.r. irr. sich um etwas* —, apply for s.th.

Bewerber [bə'vɛrbər], *m.* (—s, pl. —) applicant, candidate; (*marriage*) suitor.

Bewerbung [bə'vɛrbuŋ], *f.* (—, pl. —en) application, candidature; (*marriage*) courtship.

bewerkstelligen [bə'vɛrkʃtɛlIgən], *v.a.* perform, bring about.

bewerten [bə'vɛrtən], *v.a.* estimate, value.

bewilligen [bə'vIlIgən], *v.a.* grant, allow, permit.

bewillkommnen [bə'vIlkɔmnən], *v.a.* welcome.

bewirken [bə'vIrkən], *v.a.* effect, bring about.

bewirten [bə'vIrtən], *v.a.* entertain, act as host (to).

bewirtschaften [bə'vIrtʃaftən], *v.a.* manage.

bewohnen [bə'vo:nən], *v.a.* inhabit, occupy.

Bewohner [bə'vo:nər], *m.* (—s, pl. —) inhabitant, tenant, resident.

bewölken [bə'vœlkən], *v.r. sich* —, become overcast, become cloudy.

bewundern [bə'vundərn], *v.a.* admire.

bewundernswert [bə'vundərnsvɛrt], *adj.* admirable.

bewußt [bə'vust], *adj.* conscious, aware; *es war mir nicht* —, I was not aware of.

bewußtlos [bə'vustlo:s], *adj.* unconscious; — *werden*, faint, lose consciousness.

Bewußtsein [bə'vustzaIn], *n.* (—s, no pl.) consciousness; *einem etwas zum* — *bringen*, bring s.th. home to s.o.

bezahlbar [bə'tsa:lba:r], *adj.* payable.

bezahlen [bə'tsa:lən], *v.a.* pay; (*bill*) settle.

bezähmen [bə'tsɛ:mən], *v.a.* tame, restrain. — *v.r. sich* —, restrain o.s., control o.s.

bezaubern [bə'tsaubərn], *v.a.* bewitch, enchant, fascinate.

bezeichnen [bə'tsaIçnən], *v.a.* mark, denote, indicate, designate.

bezeichnend [bə'tsaIçnənt], *adj.* indicative, characteristic, significant.

bezeigen [bə'tsaIgən], *v.a.* manifest, show.

bezeugen [bə'tsɔygən], *v.a.* attest, bear witness, testify.

bezichtigen [bə'tsIçtIgən], *v.a.* accuse (s.o.) of (s.th.).

beziehbar [bə'tsi:ba:r], *adj.* (*goods*) obtainable; (*house*) ready for occupation.

beziehen [bə'tsi:ən], *v.a. irr.* cover; (*house etc.*) move into; (*instrument*) string; make up (a bed); *die Wache* —, mount guard. — *v.r. sich* —, (*sky*) cloud over; *sich auf etwas* —, refer to s.th.

Bezieher [bə'tsi:ər], *m.* (—s, pl. —) customer; (*newspaper*) subscriber.

Beziehung [bə'tsi:uŋ], *f.* (—, pl. —en) relation, connection; reference, bearing; *in dieser* —, in this respect; (*Comm.*) *unter* — *auf*, with reference to.

beziehungsweise [bə'tsi:uŋsvaIzə], *adv.* respectively, as the case may be, or.

33

beziffern [bəˈtsɪfərn], v.a. number.
Bezirk [bəˈtsɪrk], m. (—s, pl. —e) district; (Am.) precinct; (Parl.) constituency; (Law) circuit.
Bezirksgericht [bəˈtsɪrksgərɪçt], n. ˙ (—s, pl. —e) county court.
Bezug [bəˈtsuːk], m. (—s, pl. ˙e) (pillow) case, cover; (goods) order, purchase; (fig.) relation; — haben auf, refer to; mit — auf, referring to; (pl.) emoluments, income.
bezüglich [bəˈtsyːklɪç], adj. with regard to, regarding.
Bezugnahme [bəˈtsuːknaːmə], f. (—, pl. —n) reference; unter — auf, with reference to.
Bezugsbedingung [bəˈtsuːksbədɪŋuŋ], f. (—, pl. —en) (usually pl.) (Comm.) conditions or terms of delivery.
Bezugsquelle [bəˈtsuːkskvɛlə], f. (—, pl. —n) source of supply.
bezwecken [bəˈtsvɛkən], v.a. aim at, intend.
bezweifeln [bəˈtsvaɪfəln], v.a. doubt, question.
bezwingen [bəˈtsvɪŋən], v.a. irr. subdue, conquer. — v.r. sich —, restrain o.s.
Bibel [ˈbiːbəl], f. (—, pl. —n) Bible.
Bibelauslegung [ˈbiːbəlauslɛˈguŋ], f. (—, pl. —en) (Biblical) exegesis.
Biber [ˈbiːbər], m. (—s, pl. —) (Zool.) beaver.
Bibliothek [biblioˈteːk], f. (—, pl. —en) library.
Bibliothekar [biblioteˈkaːr], m. (—s, pl. —e) librarian.
biblisch [ˈbiːblɪʃ], adj. biblical, scriptural.
Bickbeere [ˈbɪkbeːrə], f. (—, pl. —n) bilberry.
bieder [ˈbiːdər], adj. upright, honest, decent.
Biederkeit [ˈbiːdərkaɪt], f. (—, no pl.) uprightness, probity.
Biedermann [ˈbiːdərman], m. (—s, pl. ˙er) honourable man; (iron.) Philistine.
biegen [ˈbiːgən], v.a. irr. bend, bow. — v.n. (aux. sein) um die Ecke —, turn the corner. — v.r. sich —, curve; — oder brechen, by hook or by crook.
biegsam [ˈbiːkzaːm], adj. flexible, supple, pliant.
Biegung [ˈbiːguŋ], f. (—, pl. —en) curve, bend; (Gram.) inflexion.
Biene [ˈbiːnə], f. (—, pl. —n) bee.
Bienenhaus [ˈbiːnənhaus], n. (—es, pl. ˙er) apiary.
Bienenkorb [ˈbiːnənkɔrp], m. (—s, pl. ˙e) beehive.
Bienenzüchter [ˈbiːnəntsyçtər], m. (—s, pl. —) apiarist, bee-keeper.
Bier [ˈbiːr], n. (—(e)s, pl. —e) beer.
Bierkanne [ˈbiːrkanə], f. (—, pl. —n) tankard.
Biest [biːst], n. (—es, pl. —er) brute, beast.
bieten [ˈbiːtən], v.a. irr. offer; (auction) bid.

Bieter [ˈbiːtər], m. (—s, pl. —) (auction) bidder.
Bigotterie [bɪgɔtəˈriː], f. (—, no pl.) bigotry.
Bijouterie [bɪʒutəˈriː], f. (—, pl. —n) trinkets, dress-jewellery.
Bilanz [bɪˈlants], f. (—, pl. —en) (Comm.) balance; (financial) statement.
Bild [bɪlt], n. (—es, pl. —er) picture, painting, portrait, image; idea; (coins) effigy; (Cards) court card; (books) illustration; (speech) figure of speech, metaphor.
bilden [ˈbɪldən], v.a. form, shape; (mind) cultivate. — v.r. sich —, improve o.'s mind, educate o.s.
bildend [ˈbɪldənt], adj. instructive, civilising; die —en Künste, the fine arts.
bilderreich [ˈbɪldəraɪç], adj. —e Sprache, flowery language, figurative style.
Bilderschrift [ˈbɪldərʃrɪft], f. (—, pl. —en) hieroglyphics.
Bilderstürmer [ˈbɪldərʃtyrmər], m. (—s, pl. —) iconoclast.
Bildhauer [ˈbɪlthauər], m. (—s, pl. —) sculptor.
bildhübsch [ˈbɪlthypʃ], adj. as pretty as a picture.
bildlich [ˈbɪltlɪç], adj. figurative.
Bildnis [ˈbɪltnɪs], n. (—ses, pl. —se) portrait, figure, image, effigy.
bildsam [ˈbɪltzaːm], adj. plastic, ductile.
bildschön [ˈbɪltʃøːn], adj. very beautiful.
Bildseite [ˈbɪltzaɪtə], f. (—, pl. —n) (coin) face, obverse.
Bildung [ˈbɪlduŋ], f. (—, pl. (rare) —en) formation; (mind) education, culture; knowledge, learning, accomplishments, attainments.
Billard [ˈbɪljart], n. (—s, pl. —s) billiards.
Billett [bɪlˈjɛt], n. (—s, pl. —s) ticket.
billig [ˈbɪlɪç], adj. cheap, inexpensive; equitable, just, fair, reasonable.
billigen [ˈbɪlɪgən], v.a. sanction, approve of, consent to.
Billigkeit [ˈbɪlɪçkaɪt], f. (—, no pl.) cheapness; fairness, equitableness, reasonableness.
Billigung [ˈbɪlɪguŋ], f. (—, no pl.) approbation, approval, sanction.
Bilsenkraut [ˈbɪlzənkraut], n. (—s, pl. ˙er) henbane.
bimmeln [ˈbɪməln], v.n. (coll.) tinkle.
Bimsstein [ˈbɪmsʃtain], m. (—s, pl. —e) pumice stone.
Binde [ˈbɪndə], f. (—, pl. —n) band, bandage; tie; ligature; sanitary towel.
Bindeglied [ˈbɪndəgliːt], n. (—s, pl. —er) connecting link.
Bindehaut [ˈbɪndəhaut], f. (—, pl. ˙e) (Anat.) conjunctiva.
Bindehautentzündung [ˈbɪndəhautɛntsynduŋ], f. (—, pl. —en) conjunctivitis.

binden ['bɪndən], *v.a. irr.* bind, tie, fasten.

Bindestrich ['bɪndəʃtrɪç], *m.* (—(e)s, *pl.* —e) hyphen.

Bindewort ['bɪndəvɔrt], *n.* (—s, *pl.* ⁻er) conjunction.

Bindfaden ['bɪntfa:dən], *m.* (—s, *pl.* ⁻) string, twine.

Bindung ['bɪnduŋ], *f.* (—, *pl.* —en) binding, bond; obligation; (*Mus.*) ligature.

binnen ['bɪnən], *prep.* (*Genit. & Dat.*), *adv.* within.

Binnenhafen ['bɪnənha:fən], *m.* (—s, *pl.* ⁻) inland harbour.

Binnenhandel ['bɪnənhandəl], *m.* (—s, *no pl.*) inland trade.

Binse ['bɪnzə], *f.* (—, *pl.* —n) (*Bot.*) rush, reed.

Biographie [biogra'fi:], *f.* (—, *pl.* —n) biography.

Birke ['bɪrkə], *f.* (—, *pl.* —n) (*Bot.*) birch, birch-tree.

Birma ['bɪrma:], *n.* Burma.

Birnbaum ['bɪrnbaum], *m.* (—s, *pl.* ⁻e) pear-tree.

Birne ['bɪrnə], *f.* (—, *pl.* —n) pear; (*Elec.*) bulb.

birnförmig ['bɪrnfœrmɪç], *adj.* pear-shaped.

bis [bɪs], *prep.* (*time*) till, until; by; (*place*) to, up to; — *auf*, with the exception of. — *conj.* till, until.

Bisam ['bi:zam], *m.* (—s, *pl.* —e) musk.

Bischof ['bɪʃɔf], *m.* (—s, *pl.* ⁻e) bishop.

bischöflich ['bɪʃœflɪç], *adj.* episcopal.

Bischofsstab ['bɪʃɔfsʃta:p], *m.* (—s, *pl.* ⁻e) crosier.

bisher ['bɪshe:r], *adv.* hitherto, till now.

bisherig [bɪs'he:rɪç], *adj.* up to this time, hitherto existing.

Biskayischer Meerbusen [bɪs'ka:ɪʃər 'me:rbu:zən], Bay of Biscay.

Biß [bɪs], *m.* (—sses, *pl.* —sse) bite, sting.

Bißchen ['bɪsçən], *n.* (—s, *pl.* —) morsel; little bit.

Bissen ['bɪsən], *m.* (—s, *pl.* —) bite, morsel.

bissig ['bɪsɪç], *adj.* biting, cutting; sharp, vicious; sarcastic.

Bistum ['bɪstum], *n.* (—s, *pl.* ⁻er) bishopric, diocese; see.

bisweilen [bɪs'vaɪlən], *adv.* sometimes, now and then, occasionally.

Bitte ['bɪtə], *f.* (—, *pl.* —n) request, entreaty.

bitte ['bɪtə], *int.* please.

bitten ['bɪtən], *v.a. irr.* ask; request.

bitter ['bɪtər], *adj.* bitter.

Bitterkeit ['bɪtərkaɪt], *f.* (—, *no pl.*) bitterness.

bitterlich ['bɪtərlɪç], *adv.* (*fig.*) bitterly.

Bittersalz ['bɪtərzalts], *n.* (—es, *no pl.*) Epsom salts.

Bittgang ['bɪtgaŋ], *m.* (—(e)s, *pl.* ⁻e) (*Eccl.*) procession.

Bittsteller ['bɪtʃtɛlər], *m.* (—s, *pl.* —) petitioner, suppli(c)ant.

Biwak ['bi:vak], *m.* (—s, *pl.* —s) bivouac.

blähen ['blɛːən], *v.a.* inflate, puff up, swell.

Blähung ['blɛːuŋ], *f.* (—, *pl.* —en) (*Med.*) flatulence.

blaken ['bla:kən], *v.n.* smoulder; smoke.

Blamage [bla'ma:ʒə], *f.* (—, *pl.* —n) shame, disgrace.

blamieren [bla'mi:rən], *v.a., v.r.* make (o.s.) ridiculous, make a fool of o.s.

blank [blaŋk], *adj.* shining, bright, smooth, polished.

Bläschen ['blɛːsçən], *n.* (—s, *pl.* —) little bubble, blister; (*Med.*) vesicle.

Blase ['bla:zə], *f.* (—, *pl.* —n) (*soap*) bubble; (*skin*) blister; (*Anat.*) bladder.

Blasebalg ['bla:zəbalk], *m.* (—s, *pl.* ⁻e) pair of bellows.

blasen ['bla:zən], *v.a. irr.* blow; (*Mus.*) sound.

Bläser ['blɛːzər], *m.* (—s, *pl.* —) (*glass*) blower; (*Mus.*) wind player.

blasiert [bla'zi:rt], *adj.* blasé, haughty.

Blasrohr ['bla:sro:r], *n.* (—s, *pl.* —e) blow-pipe, pea-shooter.

blaß [blas], *adj.* pale, wan, pallid.

Blässe ['blɛsə], *f.* (—, *no pl.*) paleness, pallor.

Blatt [blat], *n.* (—s, *pl.* ⁻er) leaf; (*paper*) sheet; blade.

Blatter ['blatər], *f.* (—, *pl.* —n) pustule; (*pl.*) smallpox.

blättern ['blɛtərn], *v.a.* turn the leaves (of a book).

Blätterteig ['blɛtərtaɪk], *m.* (—s, *no pl.*) puff pastry.

Blattgold ['blatgɔlt], *n.* (—es, *no pl.*) gold-leaf.

Blattlaus ['blatlaus], *f.* (—, *pl.* ⁻e) (*Ent.*) plant-louse.

Blattpflanze ['blatpflantsə], *f.* (—, *pl.* —n) leaf-plant.

blau [blau], *adj.* blue; —*en Montag machen*, stay away from work; *sein —es Wunder erleben*, be amazed.

blauäugig ['blauɔygɪç], *adj.* blue-eyed.

Blaubeere ['blaubeːrə], *f.* (—, *pl.* —n) bilberry, blueberry.

blaublütig ['blaubly:tɪç], *adj.* aristocratic.

bläuen ['blauən], *v.a.* dye blue, rinse in blue.

bläulich ['blɔylɪç], *adj.* pale blue, bluish.

Blausäure ['blauzɔyrə], *f.* (—, *no pl.*) prussic acid.

Blaustrumpf ['blauʃtrumpf], *m.* (—s, *pl.* ⁻e) blue-stocking.

Blech [blɛç], *n.* (—s, *pl.* —e) tinplate, sheet metal.

blechen ['blɛçən], *v.n.* (*coll.*) fork out money.

blechern ['blɛçərn], *adj.* made of tin, tinny.

Blechinstrument ['blɛçɪnstrumɛnt], *n.* (—s, *pl.* —e) (*Mus.*) brass instrument.

35

Blei [blaɪ], *n.* (—s, *no pl.*) lead.
bleiben ['blaɪbən], *v.n. irr.* (*aux.* sein) remain, stay.
bleich [blaɪç], *adj.* pale, wan, pallid.
Bleiche ['blaɪçə], *f.* (—, *pl.* —n) pallor; (*laundry*) bleaching-place.
bleichen ['blaɪçən], *v.a. irr.* bleach, whiten.
Bleichsucht ['blaɪçzuxt], *f.* (—, *no pl.*) chlorosis, anaemia.
bleiern ['blaɪərn], *adj.* leaden.
Bleiglanz ['blaɪglants], *m.* (—es, *no pl.*) (*Min.*) lead sulphide.
Bleisoldat ['blaɪzɔldaːt], *m.* (—en, *pl.* —en) tin soldier.
Bleistift ['blaɪʃtɪft], *m.* (—s, *pl.* —e) pencil.
Blende ['blɛndə], *f.* (—, *no pl.*) blind; (*Min.*) blende; (*Phot.*) shutter.
blenden ['blɛndən], *v.a.* dazzle, blind.
Blendlaterne ['blɛntlatɛrnə], *f.* (—, *pl.* —n) dark-lantern.
Blendung ['blɛnduŋ], *f.* (—, *pl.* —en) blinding, dazzling.
Blendwerk ['blɛntvɛrk], *n.* (—s, *no pl.*) (optical) illusion, false show.
Blick [blɪk], *m.* (—s, *pl.* —e) glance, look, glimpse.
blicken ['blɪkən], *v.n.* look, glance.
blind [blɪnt], *adj.* blind, sightless; —*er Passagier*, stowaway.
Blinddarm ['blɪntdarm], *m.* (—s, *pl.* ⁓e) appendix.
Blinddarmentzündung ['blɪntdarm-ɛntsynduŋ], *f.* (—, *pl.* —en) appendicitis.
Blindekuh [blɪndəˈkuː], *f.* (—, *no pl.*) blind man's buff.
Blindgänger ['blɪntgɛŋər], *m.* (—s, *pl.* —) misfire, dud, blind.
Blindheit ['blɪnthaɪt], *f.* (—, *no pl.*) blindness.
blindlings ['blɪntlɪŋs], *adv.* blindly; at random.
Blindschleiche ['blɪntʃlaɪçə], *f.* (—, *pl.* —n) (*Zool.*) blind-worm.
blinken ['blɪŋkən], *v.n.* blink, flash, glitter, gleam.
blinzeln ['blɪntsəln], *v.n.* blink.
Blitz [blɪts], *m.* (—es, *pl.* —e) lightning, flash.
Blitzableiter ['blɪtsaplaɪtər], *m.* (—s, *pl.* —) lightning-conductor.
blitzblank ['blɪtsblaŋk], *adj.* as bright as a new pin; shining.
blitzen ['blɪtsən], *v.n.* flash; *es blitzt*, it is lightening; glitter, shine.
Blitzesschnelle ['blɪtsəsʃnɛlə], *f.* (—, *no pl.*) lightning-speed.
Blitzlicht ['blɪtslɪçt], *n.* (—s, *no pl.*) flashlight.
Blitzschlag ['blɪtsʃlaːk], *m.* (—s, *pl.* ⁓e) flash of lightning.
Blitzstrahl ['blɪtsʃtraːl], *m.* (—s, *pl.* —en) flash of lightning.
Block [blɔk], *m.* (—s, *pl.* ⁓e) block, log; pad.
Blockhaus ['blɔkhaus], *n.* (—es, *pl.* ⁓er) log-cabin.

blockieren [blɔˈkiːrən], *v.a.* block (up); (*Mil.*) blockade.
blöde ['bløːdə], *adj.* stupid, dull, thick-headed, dim.
Blödsinn ['bløːtsɪn], *m.* (—s, *no pl.*) nonsense, idiocy.
blöken ['bløːkən], *v.n.* bleat; (*cows*) low.
blond [blɔnt], *adj.* blond, fair, fair-headed.
bloß [bloːs], *adj.* naked, uncovered; bare, mere.
Blöße ['bløːsə], *f.* (—, *pl.* —n) naked-ness, bareness; (*fig.*) weak point.
bloßlegen ['bloːsleːgən], *v.a.* un-cover, lay bare; (*fig.*) reveal, expose.
bloßstellen ['bloːsʃtɛlən], *v.a.* com-promise, show up. — *v.r. sich* —, compromise o.s.
blühen ['blyːən], *v.n.* bloom, blossom, flower, flourish.
Blümchen ['blyːmçən], *n.* (—s, *pl.* —) small flower.
Blume ['bluːmə], *f.* (—, *pl.* —n) flower, bloom; (*wine*) bouquet; (*beer*) froth.
Blumenblatt ['bluːmənblat], *n.* (—s, *pl.* ⁓er) petal.
Blumenerde ['bluːməneːrdə], *f.* (—, *no pl.*) garden mould.
Blumenkelch ['bluːmənkɛlç], *m.* (—es, *pl.* —e) calyx.
Blumenkohl ['bluːmənkoːl], *m.* (—s, *pl.* —e) cauliflower.
Blumenstaub ['bluːmənʃtaup], *m.* (—s, *no pl.*) pollen.
Blumenstrauß ['bluːmənʃtraus], *m.* (—es, *pl.* ⁓e) bunch of flowers, posy, nosegay.
Blumenzucht ['bluːməntsuxt], *f.* (—, *no pl.*) floriculture.
Bluse ['bluːzə], *f.* (—, *pl.* —n) blouse.
Blut [bluːt], *n.* (—es, *no pl.*) blood.
blutarm ['bluːtarm], *adj.* anæmic; (*fig.*) very poor.
Blutbad ['bluːtbaːt], *n.* (—es, *pl.* ⁓er) massacre.
blutdürstig ['bluːtdyrstɪç], *adj.* blood-thirsty.
Blüte ['blyːtə], *f.* (—, *pl.* —n) blossom, flower, bloom.
Blutegel ['bluːteːgəl], *m.* (—s, *pl.* —) leech.
bluten ['bluːtən], *v.n.* bleed.
Bluterguß ['bluːtɛrgus], *m.* (—es, *pl.* ⁓e) effusion of blood.
Blutgefäß ['bluːtgəfɛːs], *n.* (—es, *pl.* —e) blood-vessel.
blutig ['bluːtɪç], *adj.* bloody; cruel.
blutjung ['bluːtjuŋ], *adj.* very young.
Blutkörperchen ['bluːtkœrpərçən], *n.* (—s, *pl.* —) blood-corpuscle.
Blutlassen ['bluːtlasən], *n.* (—s, *no pl.*) (*Med.*) bloodletting.
Blutrache ['bluːtraxə], *f.* (—, *no pl.*) vendetta.
Blutsauger ['bluːtzaugər], *m.* (—s, *pl.* —) vampire.
Blutschande ['bluːtʃandə], *f.* (—, *no pl.*) incest.

blutstillend ['blu:ʃtɪlənt], *adj.* styptic, blood-stanching.

Blutsturz ['blu:tʃturts], *m.* (—es, *no pl.*) haemorrhage; *einen — haben,* burst a blood-vessel.

Blutsverwandte ['blu:tsfɛrvantə], *m. or f.* (—n, *pl.* —n) blood-relation.

Blutvergießen ['blu:tfɛrgi:sən], *n.* (—s, *no pl.*) bloodshed.

Blutvergiftung ['blu:tfɛrgɪftuŋ], *f.* (—, *pl.* —en) blood poisoning.

Blutwurst ['blu:tvurst], *f.* (—, *pl.* ˙e) black-pudding.

Blutzeuge ['blu:ttsɔygə], *m.* (—n, *pl.* —n) martyr.

Bö [bø:], *f.* (—, *pl.* —en) (*Naut.*) squall, gust of wind.

Bock [bɔk], *m.* (—s, *pl.* ˙e) buck; he-goat; (*Gymn.*) horse; (*horse-drawn carriage*) box seat.

bockbeinig ['bɔkbaɪnɪç], *adj.* bow-legged; pigheaded, obstinate.

Bockbier ['bɔkbi:r], *n.* (—s, *no pl.*) bock beer.

bocken ['bɔkən], *v.n.* kick, be refractory; sulk.

Bockfell ['bɔkfɛl], *n.* (—s, *pl.* —e) buckskin.

bockig ['bɔkɪç], *adj.* pigheaded, obstinate.

Bocksbeutel ['bɔksbɔytəl], *m.* (—s, *pl.* —) leather bag; Franconian wine (bottle).

Bockshorn ['bɔkshɔrn], *n.* (—s, *pl.* ˙er) buck horn; *einen ins — jagen,* intimidate s.o.

Boden ['bo:dən], *m.* (—s, *pl.* ˙) ground, bottom, soil, floor; garret, loft.

Bodenfenster ['bo:dənfɛnstər], *n.* (—s, *pl.* —) attic window.

Bodenkammer ['bo:dənkamər], *f.* (—, *pl.* —n) garret, attic.

bodenlos ['bo:dənlo:s], *adj.* bottomless; (*fig.*) unimaginable, enormous.

Bodensatz ['bo:dənzats], *m.* (—es, *pl.* ˙e) sediment, dregs, deposit.

Bodensee ['bo:dənze:], *m.* Lake Constance.

Bogen ['bo:gən], *m.* (—s, *pl.* —, ˙) arch, vault, curve; (*Maths.*) arc; (*violin*) bow; (*paper*) sheet; (*Mus.*) ligature.

bogenförmig ['bo:gənfœrmɪç], *adj.* arch-shaped, arched.

Bogenführung ['bo:gənfy:ruŋ], *f.* (—, *no pl.*) (*Mus.*) bowing (technique).

Bogengang ['bo:gəngaŋ], *m.* (—es, *pl.* ˙e) arcade.

Bogenlampe ['bo:gənlampə], *f.* (—, *pl.* —n) arc-lamp.

Bogenschütze ['bo:gənʃytsə], *m.* (—n, *pl.* —n) archer.

bogig ['bo:gɪç], *adj.* bent, curved, arched.

Bohle ['bo:lə], *f.* (—, *pl.* —n) board, plank.

Böhmen ['bø:mən], *n.* Bohemia.

Bohne ['bo:nə], *f.* (—, *pl.* —n) bean; *grüne —n,* French (*Am.* string) beans; *dicke —n,* broad beans; *blaue —n,* (*fig.*) bullets.

Bohnenstange ['bo:nənʃtaŋə], *f.* (—, *pl.* —n) bean-pole.

Bohnerbürste ['bo:nərbyrstə], *f.* (—, *pl.* —n) polishing-brush.

bohnern ['bo:nərn], *v.a.* polish, wax.

bohren ['bo:rən], *v.a.* bore, pierce, drill.

Bohrer ['bo:rər], *m.* (—s, *pl.* —) gimlet; drill.

Bohrturm ['bo:rturm], *m.* (—s, *pl.* ˙e) derrick.

Boje ['bo:jə], *f.* (—, *pl.* —n) (*Naut.*) buoy.

Bolivien [bo'li:vjən], *n.* Bolivia.

Böller ['bœlər], *m.* (—s, *pl.* —) (*Mil.*) small mortar.

Bollwerk ['bɔlvɛrk], *n.* (—s, *pl.* —e) bulwark.

Bolzen ['bɔltsən], *m.* (—s, *pl.* —) bolt, arrow, pin; (*smoothing iron*) heater.

Bombe ['bɔmbə], *f.* (—, *pl.* —n) bomb, bomb-shell.

Bombenerfolg ['bɔmbənɛrfɔlk], *m.* (—(e)s, *pl.* —e) (*Theat.*) smash hit.

Bonbon [bɔ̃'bɔ̃], *m.* (—s, *pl.* —s) sweet(s), bonbon; (*Am.*) candy.

Bonbonniere [bɔ̃bɔ'nje:rə], *f.* (—, *pl.* —n) box of sweets.

Bonze ['bɔntsə], *m.* (—n, *pl.* —n) (*coll.*) bigwig, (*Am.*) big shot.

Boot [bo:t], *n.* (—es, *pl.* —e) boat.

Bootsanker ['bo:tsaŋkər], *m.* (—s, *pl.* —) grapnel.

Bootsleine ['bo:tslaɪnə], *f.* (—, *pl.* —n) tow-rope.

Bor [bo:r], *n.* (—s, *no pl.*) (*Chem.*) boron.

Bord [bɔrt], *m.* (—s, *pl.* —e) rim; (*Naut.*) board.

Bordell [bɔr'dɛl], *n.* (—s, *pl.* —e) brothel.

borgen ['bɔrgən], *v.a., v.n.* borrow (*von,* from); lend (*Dat.,* to).

Borke ['bɔrkə], *f.* (—, *pl.* —n) bark, rind.

Born [bɔrn], *m.* (—es, *pl.* —e) (*Poet.*) bourn, spring, well, source.

borniert [bɔr'ni:rt], *adj.* narrow-minded.

Borsäure ['bo:rzɔyrə], *f.* (—, *no pl.*) boric acid.

Börse ['bœrzə], *f.* (—, *pl.* —n) purse; (*Comm.*) stock-exchange, bourse.

Börsenbericht ['bœrzənbərɪçt], *m.* (—s, *pl.* —e) stock-market report.

Borste ['bɔrstə], *f.* (—, *pl.* —n) bristle.

borstig ['bɔrstɪç], *adj.* bristly; (*fig.*) irritable.

Borte ['bɔrtə], *f.* (—, *pl.* —n) border, trimming.

bösartig ['bø:sartɪç], *adj.* malevolent, malicious, vicious; (*disease*) malignant.

Böschung ['bøʃuŋ], *f.* (—, *pl.* —en) slope, scarp.

böse ['bø:zə], *adj.* bad, wicked; evil; angry, cross (with, *Dat.*); — *auf* (*Acc.*), angry with s.o., (*Am.*) mad at s.o.

Bösewicht ['bø:zəvɪçt], *m.* (—s, *pl.* —er) villain, ruffian; wretch.

boshaft

boshaft ['bo:ʃaft], *adj.* spiteful, malicious.

Bosheit ['bo:ʃaɪt], *f.* (—, *pl.* —en) malice.

böswillig ['bø:svɪlɪç], *adj.* malevolent.

Botanik [bo'ta:nɪk], *f.* (—, *no pl.*) botany.

Botaniker [bo'ta:nɪkər], *m.* (—s, *pl.* —) botanist.

Botanisiertrommel [botanɪ'zi:rtrɔməl], *f.* (—, *pl.* —n) specimen-box.

Bote ['bo:tə], *m.* (—n, *pl.* —n) messenger.

Botengang ['bo:təŋaŋ], *m.* (—s, *pl.* ⁻e) errand.

botmäßig ['bo:tmɛ:sɪç], *adj.* subject, subordinate.

Botschaft ['bo:tʃaft], *f.* (—, *pl.* —en) message; (*Pol.*) embassy; *gute* —, glad tidings.

Botschafter ['bo:tʃaftər], *m.* (—s, *pl.* —) ambassador.

Böttcher ['bœtçər], *m.* (—s, *pl.* —) cooper.

Bottich ['bɔtɪç], *m.* (—s, *pl.* —e) vat, tub.

Bouillon [bul'jɔ̃], *f.* (—, *no pl.*) broth, meat soup.

Bowle ['bo:lə], *f.* (—, *no pl.*) bowl; spiced wine.

boxen ['bɔksən], *v.n.* box.

brach [bra:x], *adj.* fallow, unploughed, untilled.

Brand [brant], *m.* (—es, *pl.* ⁻e) burning, fire, combustion, conflagration; (*Med.*) gangrene.

Brandblase ['brantbla:zə], *f.* (—, *pl.* —n) blister.

branden ['brandən], *v.n.* surge, break (waves).

brandig ['brandɪç], *adj.* blighted; (*Med.*) gangrenous.

Brandmal ['brantma:l], *n.* (—s, *pl.* —e) burn mark; brand (cattle); (*fig.*) stigma.

brandmarken ['brantmarkən], *v.a.* brand; (*fig.*) stigmatise.

Brandmauer ['brantmauər], *f.* (—, *pl.* —n) fire-proof wall.

brandschatzen ['brantʃatsən], *v.a.* levy contributions (from); pillage, plunder.

Brandsohle ['brantzo:lə], *f.* (—, *pl.* —n) inner sole, welt (of shoe).

Brandstifter ['brantʃtɪftər], *m.* (—s, *pl.* —) incendiary, fire-raiser.

Brandstiftung ['brantʃtɪftuŋ], *f.* (—, *pl.* —en) arson.

Brandung ['branduŋ], *f.* (—, *pl.* —en) breakers, surf, surge (of sea).

Branntwein ['brantvaɪn], *m.* (—s, *pl.* —e) brandy.

Brasilien [bra'zi:ljən], *n.* Brazil.

Braten ['bra:tən], *m.* (—s, *pl.* —) roast (meat), joint.

braten ['bra:tən], *v.a. reg. & irr.* roast, broil, bake, fry, grill. — *v.n.* (*coll.*) bask (in sun), roast.

Brathering ['bra:the:rɪŋ], *m.* (—s, *pl.* —e) grilled herring.

Brathuhn ['bra:thu:n], *n.* (—s, *pl.* ⁻er) roast chicken.

Bratkartoffeln ['bra:tkartɔfəln], *f. pl.* roast *or* fried potatoes.

Bratpfanne ['bra:tpfanə], *f.* (—, *pl.* —n) frying pan.

Bratsche ['bratʃə], *f.* (—, *pl.* —n) (*Mus.*) viola.

Bratspieß ['bra:tʃpi:s], *m.* (—es, *pl.* —e) spit (roasting).

Bratwurst ['bra:tvurst], *f.* (—, *pl.* ⁻e) sausage for frying; fried sausage.

Bräu [brau], **Bräu** [brɔy], *n. & m.* (—s, *no pl.*) brew.

Brauch [braux], *m.* (—es, *pl.* ⁻e) usage, custom, habit.

brauchbar ['brauxba:r], *adj.* useful, serviceable.

brauchen ['brauxən], *v.a.* make use of, employ; need, require, want; (*time*) take.

Braue ['brauə], *f.* (—, *pl.* —n) brow, eye-brow.

brauen ['brauən], *v.a.* brew.

Brauer ['brauər], *m.* (—s, *pl.* —) brewer.

Brauerei ['brauəraɪ], *f.* (—, *pl.* —en) brewery.

Brauhaus ['brauhaus], *n.* (—es, *pl.* ⁻er) brewery.

braun [braun], *adj.* brown.

bräunen ['brɔynən], *v.a.* make brown, tan.

Braunkohl ['braunko:l], *m.* (—s, *no pl.*) (*Bot.*) broccoli.

Braunschweig ['braunʃvaɪk], *n.* Brunswick.

Braus [braus], *m.* (—es, *no pl.*) bustle, tumult; *in Saus und — leben*, lead a riotous life.

Brause ['brauzə], *f.* (—, *pl.* —n) shower (bath); effervescence, (*coll.*) fizzy drink.

Brausekopf ['brauzəkɔpf], *m.* (—es, *pl.* ⁻e) hothead.

Brauselimonade ['brauzəlɪmona:də], *f.* (—, *pl.* —n) effervescent *or* fizzy lemonade.

brausen ['brauzən], *v.n.* roar, bluster, rush; effervesce.

Brausepulver ['brauzəpulvər], *n.* (—s, *pl.* —) effervescent powder.

Braut [braut], *f.* (—, *pl.* ⁻e) bride, betrothed, fiancée.

Brautführer ['brautfy:rər], *m.* (—s, *pl.* —) best man.

Bräutigam ['brɔytɪgam], *m.* (—s, *pl.* —e) bridegroom, betrothed, fiancé.

Brautjungfer ['brautjuŋfər], *f.* (—, *pl.* —n) bridesmaid.

bräutlich ['brɔytlɪç], *adj.* bridal.

Brautpaar ['brautpa:r], *n.* (—es, *pl.* —e) engaged couple.

Brautschau ['brautʃau], *f.* (—, *no pl.*) (*obs.*) search for a wife.

brav [bra:f], *adj.* honest, upright, worthy, honourable; well-behaved, good.

bravo! ['bra:vo], *int.* well done!

Bravourstück [bra'vu:rʃtyk], *n.* (—s, *pl.* —e) feat of valour.

Brechbohnen ['brɛçboːnən], *f. pl.* kidney-beans.

Brecheisen ['brɛçaɪzən], *n.* (—s, *pl.* —) jemmy.

brechen ['brɛçən], *v.a. irr.* break; (*flowers*) pluck, pick; vomit. — *v.n.* (*aux.* sein) break.

Brechmittel ['brɛçmɪtəl], *n.* (—s, *pl.* —) emetic.

Brechruhr ['brɛçruːr], *f.* (—, *no pl.*) cholera.

Brechstange ['brɛçʃtaŋə], *f.* (—, *pl.* —n) crow-bar.

Brechung ['brɛçuŋ], *f.* (—, *pl.* —en) breaking; (*Phys.*) refraction.

Brei [braɪ], *m.* (—s, *pl.* —e) pap, pulp, porridge.

breiartig ['braɪaːrtɪç], *adj.* pulpy.

breiig ['braɪɪç], *adj.* pappy.

breit [braɪt], *adj.* broad, wide.

breitbeinig ['braɪtbaɪnɪç], *adj.* straddle-legged.

Breite ['braɪtə], *f.* (—, *pl.* —n) breadth, width; (*Geog.*) latitude.

Breitengrad ['braɪtəŋɡraːt], *m.* (—es, *pl.* —e) (*Geog.*) degree of latitude.

Breitenkreis ['braɪtənkraɪs], *m.* (—es, *pl.* —e) (*Geog.*) parallel.

breitschultrig ['braɪtʃultrɪç], *adj.* broad-shouldered.

Bremse ['brɛmzə], *f.* (—, *pl.* —n) (*Ent.*) gad-fly; (*Motor.*) brake; (*horse*) barnacle.

bremsen ['brɛmzən], *v.a.* brake, pull up.

brennbar ['brɛnbaːr], *adj.* combustible.

Brenneisen ['brɛnaɪzən], *n.* (—s, *pl.* —) branding iron.

brennen ['brɛnən], *v.a. irr.* burn; (*Med.*) cauterise; (*alcohol*) distil; (*hair*) curl; (*coffee*) roast; (*coal*) char; (*bricks*) bake. — *v.n.* burn; (*fig.*) sting; (*eyes*) smart.

Brenner ['brɛnər], *m.* (—s, *pl.* —) (*person*) distiller; (*Tech.*) burner.

Brennerei [brɛnə'raɪ], *f.* (—, *pl.* —en) distillery.

Brennessel ['brɛnnɛsəl], *f.* (—, *pl.* —n) stinging nettle.

Brennholz ['brɛnhɔlts], *n.* (—es, *no pl.*) firewood.

Brennmaterial ['brɛnmateriaːl], *n.* (—s, *pl.* —ien) fuel.

Brennofen ['brɛnoːfən], *m.* (—s, *pl.* ꞏn) kiln.

Brennpunkt ['brɛnpuŋkt], *m.* (—s, *pl.* —e) focus.

Brennschere ['brɛnʃeːrə], *f.* (—, *pl.* —n) curling-irons.

Brennstoff ['brɛnʃtɔf], *m.* (—(e)s, *pl.* —e) fuel.

brenzlich ['brɛntslɪç], *adj.* smelling (*or* tasting) of burning; (*fig.*) ticklish.

Bresche ['brɛʃə], *f.* (—, *pl.* —n) breach, gap.

Brett [brɛt], *n.* (—s, *pl.* —er) board, plank, shelf.

Brettspiel ['brɛtʃpiːl], *n.* (—s, *pl.* —e) table-game.

Brevier [bre'viːr], *n.* (—s, *pl.* (*rare*) —e) breviary.

Brezel ['breːtsəl], *f.* (—, *pl.* —n) cracknel, pretzel.

Brief [briːf], *m.* (—es, *pl.* —e) letter; epistle.

Briefanschrift ['briːfanʃrɪft], *f.* (—, *pl.* —en) address.

Briefbeschwerer ['briːfbəʃveːrər], *m.* (—s, *pl.* —) letter-weight, paper-weight.

Briefbogen ['briːfboːɡən], *m.* (—s, *pl.* —) sheet of notepaper.

Briefkasten ['briːfkastən], *m.* (—s, *pl.* ꞏꞏ) (*house*) letter-box; (*street*) pillar-box, (*Am.*) post-box.

brieflich ['briːflɪç], *adv.* by letter, in writing.

Briefmarke ['briːfmarkə], *f.* (—, *pl.* —n) postage stamp.

Briefpapier ['briːfpapiːr], *n.* (—s, *no pl.*) notepaper.

Briefporto ['briːfpɔrto], *n.* (—s, *pl.* —ti) postage.

Brieftasche ['briːftaʃə], *f.* (—, *pl.* —n) portfolio, wallet; (*Am.*) pocket-book.

Brieftaube ['briːftaubə], *f.* (—, *pl.* —n) carrier pigeon.

Briefträger ['briːftrɛːɡər], *m.* (—s, *pl.* —) postman.

Briefumschlag ['briːfumʃlaːk], *m.* (—s, *pl.* ꞏe) envelope.

Briefwechsel ['briːfvɛksəl], *m.* (—s, *no pl.*) correspondence.

Brillant [brɪl'jant], *m.* (—en, *pl.* —en) brilliant, diamond. — *adj.* brilliant.

Brille ['brɪlə], *f.* (— *pl.* —n) spectacles, glasses.

Brillenschlange ['brɪlənʃlaŋə], *f.* (—, *pl.* —n) (*Zool.*) hooded cobra.

bringen ['brɪŋən], *v.a. irr.* bring, fetch, carry to, take to, conduct to.

Brise ['briːzə], *f.* (—, *pl.* —n) breeze, light wind.

Britannien [brɪ'tanjən], *n.* Britain.

bröckeln ['brœkəln], *v.a., v.n.* crumble.

Brocken ['brɔkən], *m.* (—s, *pl.* —) bit, piece, fragment, scrap; (*bread*) crumb.

bröcklig ['brœklɪç], *adj.* crumbling.

brodeln ['broːdəln], *v.n.* bubble, simmer.

Brodem ['broːdəm], *m.* (—s, *no pl.*) (*Poet.*) steam, vapour, exhalation.

Brokat [bro'kaːt], *m.* (—s, *pl.* —e) brocade.

Brom [broːm], *n.* (—s, *no pl.*) (*Chem.*) bromine.

Brombeere ['brɔmbeːrə], *f.* (—, *pl.* —n) blackberry, bramble.

Bronze ['brɔ̃ːsə], *f.* (—, *pl.* —n) bronze.

Brosamen ['broːzaːmən], *pl.* crumbs.

Brosche ['brɔʃə], *f.* (—, *pl.* —n) brooch.

Broschüre [brɔ'ʃyːrə], *f.* (—, *pl.* —n) pamphlet, brochure, folder.

Brösel ['brøːzəl], *m.* (—s, *pl.* —) crumb.

Brot [broːt], *n.* (—es, *pl.* —e) bread, loaf; (*fig.*) livelihood.

Brötchen ['brøːtçən], *n.* (—s, *pl.* —) roll, bread-roll.

Broterwerb ['bro:tərvɛrp], *m.* (—s, *no pl.*) livelihood.

Brotgeber ['bro:tge:bər], *m.* (—s, *pl.* —) employer, master.

Brotherr ['bro:thɛr], *m.* (—n, *pl.* —en) employer, master.

Brotkorb ['bro:tkɔrp], *m.* (—s, *pl.* ⁻e) bread-basket.

brotlos ['bro:tlo:s], *adj.* unemployed; (*fig.*) unprofitable.

Brotneid ['bro:tnaIt], *m.* (—s, *no pl.*) professional jealousy.

Bruch [brux], *m.* (—s, *pl.* ⁻e) breakage; rupture; (*Med.*) fracture, rupture, hernia; (*Maths.*) fraction.

Bruchband ['bruxbant], *f.* (—es, *pl.* ⁻er) abdominal belt, truss.

brüchig ['brʏçɪç], *adj.* brittle, full of flaws.

Bruchlandung ['bruxlanduŋ], *f.* (—, —en) (*Aviat.*) crash-landing.

Bruchrechnung ['bruxrɛçnuŋ], *f.* (—, *pl.* —en) (*Arith.*) fractions.

Bruchstück ['bruxʃtyk], *n.* (—s, *pl.* —e) fragment, scrap.

Bruchteil ['bruxtaIl], *m.* (—s, *pl.* —e) fraction.

Brücke ['brykə], *f.* (—, *pl.* —n) bridge.

Brückenpfeiler ['brykənpfaIlər], *m.* (—s, *pl.* —) pier.

Bruder ['bru:dər], *m.* (—s, *pl.* ⁻) brother; (*Eccl.*) friar.

brüderlich ['bry:dərlIç], *adj.* fraternal, brotherly.

Bruderschaft ['bru:dərʃaft], *f.* (—, *pl.* —en) fraternity, brotherhood.

Brügge ['brygə], *n.* Bruges.

Brühe ['bry:ə], *f.* (—, *pl.* —n) broth, meat-soup.

brühen ['bry:ən], *v.a.* scald.

Brühkartoffeln ['bry:kartɔfəln], *f. pl.* potatoes cooked in broth.

brüllen ['brylən], *v.n.* roar howl, yell; (*cows*) low, bellow.

Brummbaß ['brumbas], *m.* (—sses, *pl.* ⁻sse) (*Mus.*) double-bass.

Brummeisen ['brumaIzən], *n.* (—s, *pl.* —) Jew's harp.

brummen ['brumən], *v.n.* growl, grumble, hum.

Brummer ['brumər], *n.* (—s, *pl.* —) (*Ent.*) blue-bottle.

Brunnen ['brunən], *m.* (—s, *pl.* —) well, fountain, spring.

Brunnenkur ['brunənku:r], *f.* (—, *pl.* —en) taking of mineral waters.

Brunst [brunst], *f.* (—, *pl.* ⁻e) (*Zool.*) rut, heat.

Brust [brust], *f.* (—, *pl.* ⁻e) breast; chest; bosom.

Brustbein ['brustbaIn], *n.* (—s, *pl.* —e) breastbone, sternum.

Brustbild ['brustbIlt], *n.* (—s, *pl.* —er) half-length portrait.

brüsten ['brystən], *v.r. sich* —, boast, brag, plume o.s.

Brustfell ['brustfɛl], *n.* (—s, *pl.* —e) pleura.

Brustfellentzündung ['brustfɛlɛntsyn-duŋ], *f.* (—, *no pl.*) pleurisy.

Brusthöhle ['brusthø:lə], *f.* (—, *pl.* —n) thoracic cavity.

Brustkasten ['brustkastən], *m.* (—s, *pl.* ⁻n) chest.

Brusttee ['brustte:], *m.* (—s, *no pl.*) pectoral (herbal) tea.

Brüstung ['brystuŋ], *f.* (—, *pl.* —en) parapet.

Brustwarze ['brustvartsə], *f.* (—, *pl.* —n) nipple.

Brustwehr ['brustve:r], *f.* (—, *pl.* —en) breastwork, parapet.

Brut [bru:t], *f.* (—, *no pl.*) brood; (*fish*) fry.

brutal [bru'ta:l], *adj.* brutal.

brüten ['bry:tən], *v.a.* brood, hatch.

Brutofen ['bru:to:fən], *m.* (—s, *pl.* ⁻) incubator.

brutto ['bruto], *adv.* (*Comm.*) gross.

Bube ['bu:bə], *m.* (—n, *pl.* —n) boy, lad; (*cards*) knave, (*Am.*) jack; rogue, rascal.

Bubenstreich ['bu:bənʃtraIç], *m.* (—s, *pl.* —e) boyish prank; knavish trick.

Bubikopf ['bu:bIkɔpf], *m.* (—(e)s, *pl.* ⁻e) bobbed hair.

Buch [bu:x], *n.* (—s, *pl.* ⁻er) book; quire (of paper).

Buchdruckerei ['bu:xdrukəraI], *f.* (—, —en) printing works, printing office.

Buche ['bu:xə], *f.* (—, *pl.* —n) beech (tree).

buchen ['bu:xən], *v.a.* book, enter, reserve; (*fig.*) score.

Bücherei [by:çə'raI], *f.* (—, *pl.* —en) library.

Buchesche ['bu:xɛʃə], *f.* (—, *pl.* —n) hornbeam.

Buchfink ['bu:xfIŋk], *m.* (—en, *pl.* —en) (*Orn.*) chaffinch.

Buchhalter ['bu:xhaltər], *m.* (—s, *pl.* —) book-keeper.

Buchhändler ['bu:xhɛndlər], *m.* (—s, *pl.* —) bookseller.

Buchmarder ['bu:xmardər], *m.* (—s, *pl.* —) (*Zool.*) pine-marten.

Buchsbaum ['buksbaum], *m.* (—s, *pl.* ⁻e) (*Bot.*) box-tree.

Büchse ['byksə], *f.* (—, *pl.* —n) box, case; tin, can; rifle, gun.

Büchsenfleisch ['byksənflaIʃ], *n.* (—es, *no pl.*) tinned meat.

Büchsenlauf ['byksənlauf], *m.* (—s, *pl.* ⁻e) gun-barrel.

Büchsenöffner ['byksənœfnər], *m.* (—s, *pl.* —) tin-opener.

Buchstabe ['bu:xʃta:bə], *m.* (—n, *pl.* —n) letter, character; *großer* —, capital (letter).

Buchstabenrätsel ['bu:xʃta:bənrɛtsəl], *n.* (—s, *pl.* —) anagram.

buchstabieren [bu:xʃta'bi:rən], *v.a.* spell (out).

buchstäblich ['bu:xʃtɛplIç], *adj.* literal.

Bucht [buxt], *f.* (—, *pl.* —en) inlet, bay, creek, bight.

Buchung ['bu:xuŋ], *f.* (—, *pl.* —en) (*Comm.*) entry (in a book); booking (of tickets).

Buchwissen ['bu:xvɪsən], *n.* (—s, *no pl.*) book-learning.

Buckel ['bukəl], *m.* (—s, *pl.* —) hump, humpback; boss, stud; (*coll.*) back.

bücken ['bykən], *v.r. sich* —, stoop, bow.

bucklig ['buklɪç], *adj.* humpbacked.

Bückling ['byklɪŋ], *m.* (—s, *pl.* —e) smoked herring; kipper.

buddeln ['budəln], *v.n.* (*coll.*) dig.

Bude ['bu:də], *f.* (—, *pl.* —n) booth, stall; (*coll.*) room; (*student's*) digs.

Büfett [by'fɛt], *n.* (—s, *pl.* —s) sideboard; buffet.

Büffel ['byfəl], *m.* (—s, *pl.* —) buffalo.

büffeln ['byfəln], *v.n.* (*coll.*) cram (for an examination), swot.

Bug [bu:k], *m.* (—s, *pl.* ̈e, —e) (*Naut.*) bow, (*Aviat.*) nose.

Buganker ['bu:kaŋkər], *m.* (—s, *pl.* —) bow-anchor.

Bügel ['bygəl], *m.* (—s, *pl.* —) coat-hanger; (*trigger*) guard; (*horse*) stirrup.

bügeln ['bygəln], *v.a.* iron, smoothe, press.

bugsieren [buk'si:rən], *v.a.* tow.

Bugspriet ['bu:kʃpri:t], *n.* (—s, *pl.* —e) bowsprit.

Buhle ['bu:lə], *m.* or *f.* (—n, *pl.* —n) (*Poet.*) paramour, lover.

buhlen ['bu:lən], *v.n.* (*Poet.*) woo, make love (to).

buhlerisch ['bu:lərɪʃ], *adj.* (*Poet.*) amorous, wanton, lewd.

Bühne ['by:nə], *f.* (—, *pl.* —n) (*Theat.*) stage; scaffold, platform.

Bühnenbild ['by:nənbɪlt], *n.* (—es, *pl.* —er) scenery.

Bukett [bu'kɛt], *n.* (—s, *pl.* —s) bunch of flowers, bouquet; bouquet (*wine*).

Bulgarien [bul'ga:rjən], *n.* Bulgaria.

Bulldogge ['buldɔgə], *f.* (—, *pl.* —n) bulldog.

Bulle (1) ['bulə], *m.* (—n, *pl.* —n) bull, bullock.

Bulle (2) ['bulə], *f.* (—, *pl.* —n) (*Eccl.*) (*Papal*) Bull.

bumm [bum], *int.* boom! bang!

Bummel ['buməl], *m.* (—s, *pl.* —) stroll.

Bummelei [bumə'laɪ], *f.* (—, *pl.* —en) idleness, negligence, casualness, carelessness.

bummeln ['buməln], *v.n.* lounge, waste o.'s time, dawdle; stroll.

Bummelzug ['buməltsu:k], *m.* (—s, *pl.* ̈e) slow train.

bums [bums], *int.* bang! crash!

Bund (1) [bunt], *m.* (—es, *pl.* ̈e) bond, tie, league, alliance, federation, confederacy; (*Eccl.*) covenant.

Bund (2) [bunt], *n.* (—es, *pl.* —e) bundle, bunch (of keys).

Bündel ['byndəl], *n.* (—s, *pl.* —) bundle, package.

Bundesgenosse ['bundəsgənɔsə], *m.* (—n, *pl.* —) confederate, ally.

Bundesstaat ['bundəsʃta:t], *m.* (—es, *pl.* —en) federal state; federation.

Bundestag ['bundəsta:k], *m.* (—es, *pl.* —e) federal parliament.

Bundeswehr ['bundəsve:r], *f.* (—, *no pl.*) federal defence; armed forces.

bündig ['byndɪç], *adj.* binding; *kurz und* —, concise, terse, to the point.

Bündnis ['byntnɪs], *n.* (—ses, *pl.* —se) alliance.

Bundschuh ['buntʃu:], *m.* (—s, *pl.* —e) clog, sandal.

bunt [bunt], *adj.* many-coloured, chequered, variegated, motley; *das ist mir zu* —, this is going too far.

buntscheckig ['buntʃɛkɪç], *adj.* dappled, spotted.

Buntspecht ['buntʃpɛçt], *m.* (—s, *pl.* —e) (*Orn.*) (spotted) woodpecker.

Bürde ['byrdə], *f.* (—, *pl.* —n) load, burden.

Bure ['bu:rə], *m.* (—n, *pl.* —n) Boer.

Burg [burk], *f.* (—, *pl.* —en) castle, fortress, citadel, stronghold.

Bürge ['byrgə], *m.* (—n, *pl.* —n) surety, bail, guarantee; *einen* —*n stellen*, offer bail.

bürgen ['byrgən], *v.n.* give security, vouch (for), go bail (for).

Bürger ['byrgər], *m.* (—s, *pl.* —) citizen, townsman, bourgeois, commoner.

bürgerlich ['byrgərlɪç], *adj.* civic; middle-class, bourgeois; —*e Küche*, plain cooking.

Bürgermeister ['byrgərmaɪstər], *m.* (—s, *pl.* —) burgomaster, mayor.

Burggraf ['burkgra:f], *m.* (—en, *pl.* —en) burgrave.

Bürgschaft ['byrkʃaft], *f.* (—, *pl.* —en) bail, surety, guarantee; — *leisten*, provide security.

Burgund [bur'gunt], *n.* Burgundy.

Burgvogt ['burkfo:kt], *m.* (—s, *pl.* —e) (*obs.*) castellan, bailiff.

Burgwarte ['burkvartə], *f.* (—, *pl.* —n) watch-tower.

Büro [by'ro:], *n.* (—s, *pl.* —s) office, bureau, (professional) chambers.

Bursche ['burʃə], *m.* (—n, *pl.* —n) lad, boy, fellow; student; (*Mil.*) batman.

Burschenschaft ['burʃənʃaft], *f.* (—, *pl.* —en) students' association.

Bürste ['byrstə], *f.* (—, *pl.* —n) brush.

Burundi [bu'rundi], *n.* Burundi.

Busch [buʃ], *m.* (—es, *pl.* ̈e) bush, shrub, copse, thicket.

Büschel ['byʃəl], *n.* (—s, *pl.* —) bunch; (*hair*) tuft.

buschig ['buʃɪç], *adj.* bushy, tufted.

Buschklepper ['buʃklɛpər], *m.* (—s, *pl.* —) bushranger.

Busen ['bu:zən], *m.* (—s, *pl.* —) bosom, breast; (*Geog.*) bay, gulf.

Bussard ['busart], *m.* (—s, *pl.* —e) (*Orn.*) buzzard.

Buße ['bu:sə], *f.* (—, *pl.* —n) penance; repentance; penalty.

büßen ['by:sən], *v.a., v.n.* repent, atone, expiate, make amends.

bußfertig ['bu:sfɛrtɪç], *adj.* penitent, repentant.

Büste

Büste ['bystə], f. (—, pl. —n) bust.
Büstenhalter ['bystenhaltər], m. (—s, pl. —) brassière.
Bütte ['bytə], f. (—, pl. —n) tub.
Büttel ['bytəl], m. (—s, pl. —) beadle; bailiff.
Büttenpapier ['bytənpapi:r], n. (—s, no pl.) hand-made paper.
Butter ['butər], f. (—, no pl.) butter.
Butterblume ['butərblu:mə], f. (—, pl. —n) buttercup.
Butterbrot ['butərbro:t], n. (—s, pl. —e) bread and butter.
buttern ['butərn], v.a., v.n. smear with butter; churn.
Butterteig ['butərtaık], m. (—es, pl. —e) puff-pastry.
Butzenscheibe ['butsənʃaıbə], f. (—, pl. —n) bull's-eyed pane.
Byzanz [by'tsants], n. Byzantium, Constantinople.

C

C [tse:], n. (—s, pl. —s) the letter C; (Mus.) C dur, C major; C Moll, C minor; C-Schlüssel, C clef.
Cäsar ['tse:zar], m. Cæsar.
Ceylon ['tseilɔn], n. Ceylon.
Chaiselongue [ʃɛ:zə'lõ:g], f. (—, pl. —s) couch, settee, sofa.
Champagner [ʃam'panjər], m. (—s, pl. —) champagne.
Champignon [ʃampin'jõ], m. (—s, pl. —s) mushroom.
chaotisch [ka'o:tıʃ], adj. chaotic.
Charakter [ka'raktər], m. (—s, pl. —e) character; mental make-up, disposition.
Charakteristik [karaktər'ıstık], f. (—, pl. —en) characterisation.
charakteristisch [karaktər'ıstıʃ], adj. characteristic; typical.
Charge ['ʃarʒə], f. (—, pl. —n) office, appointment; (pl.) (Mil.) non-commissioned officers.
Chaussee [ʃɔ'se:], f. (—, pl. —n) main road, highway.
Chef [ʃɛf], m. (—s, pl. —s) chief, head, employer; (coll.) boss.
Chefredakteur ['ʃefredaktø:r], m. (—s, pl. —e) editor-in-chief.
Chemie [çe'mi:], f. (—, no pl.) chemistry.
Chemikalien [çemi'ka:ljən], f. pl. chemicals.
Chemiker ['çe:mıkər], m. (—s, pl. —) (analytical) chemist.
chemisch ['çe:mıʃ], adj. chemical; — gereinigt, dry-cleaned.
Chiffre ['ʃıfər], f. (—, pl. —n) cipher.
chiffrieren [ʃı'fri:rən], v.a. encipher.
Chile ['tʃi:lə, 'çi:lə], n. Chile.

China ['çi:na], n. China.
Chinarinde [çi:na'rındə], f. (—, no pl.) Peruvian bark.
Chinin [çi'ni:n], n. (—s, no pl.) quinine.
Chirurg [çi'rurk], m. (—en, pl. —en) surgeon.
Chirurgie [çirur'gi:], f. (—, no pl.) surgery.
Chlor [klo:r], n. (—s, no pl.) chlorine.
Chlorkalk ['klo:rkalk], m. (—s, no pl.) chloride of lime.
Chlornatrium [klo:r'na:trjum], n. (—s, no pl.) sodium chloride.
Choleriker [ko'le:rıkər], m. (—s, pl. —) irascible person.
Chor [ko:r], m. (—s, pl. ꞌꞌe) chorus; choir; (Archit.) choir, chancel.
Choral [ko'ra:l], m. (—s, pl. ꞌꞌe) hymn, chorale.
Choramt ['ko:ramt], n. (—s, pl. ꞌꞌer) cathedral service.
Chorgesang ['ko:rgəsaŋ], m. (—s, pl. ꞌꞌe) chorus, choral singing.
Chorhemd ['ko:rhɛmt], n. (—s, pl. —en) surplice.
Chorherr ['ko:rhɛr], m. (—n, pl. —en) canon, prebendary.
Christ [krıst], m. (—en, pl. —en) Christian.
Christbaum ['krıstbaum], m. (—s, pl. ꞌꞌe) Christmas tree.
Christentum ['krıstəntu:m], n. (—s, no pl.) Christendom, Christianity.
Christkind ['krıstkınt], n. (—s, no pl.) Infant Christ, Christ child.
christlich ['krıstlıç], adj. Christian.
Christmette ['krıstmɛtə], f. (—, pl. —n) Christmas matins; midnight mass.
Christus ['krıstus], m. (—i) Christ; vor —, B.C.; nach —, A.D.
Chrom [kro:m], n. (—s, no pl.) chrome.
chromatisch [kro'ma:tıʃ], adj. chromatic.
chromsauer ['kro:mzauər], adj. — chromate of; —es Salz, chromate.
Chronik ['kro:nık], f. (—, pl. —en) chronicle.
chronisch ['kro:nıʃ], adj. chronic.
Chronist [kro'nıst], m. (—en, pl. —en) chronicler.
Chrysantheme [kryzan'te:mə], f. (—, pl. —n) chrysanthemum.
Cis [tsıs], (Mus.) C sharp.
Clique ['klıkə], f. (—, pl. —n) clique, set.
Coeur [kø:r], n. (Cards) hearts.
coulant [ku'lant], adj. polite, friendly; (Comm.) fair, obliging.
Couleur [ku'lø:r], f. (—, pl. —en) colour; students' corporation.
Coupé [ku'pe:], n. (—s, pl. —s) (train) compartment.
Couplet [ku'ple:], n. (—s, pl. —s) comic song.
Coupon [ku'põ], m. (—s, pl. —s) coupon, check, dividend voucher.
Cour [ku:r], f. (—, no pl.) einem Mädchen die — machen, court a girl.

42

Courtage [kur'ta:ʒə], *f.* (—, *pl.* —n) brokerage.
Cousin [ku'zɛ̃], *m.* (—s, *pl.* —s) cousin.
Cousine [ku'zi:nə], *f.* (—, *pl.* —n) (female) cousin.
Cutaway ['katave:], *m.* (—s, *pl.* —s) morning coat.
Czar [tsa:r], *m.* (—en, *pl.* —en) Tsar, Czar.

D

D [de:], *n.* (—s, *pl.* —s) the letter D; (*Mus.*) D *dur*, D major; *D moll*, D minor; *D-Zug*, express train.
da [da:], *adv.* (*local*) there; here; (*temporal*) then, at that moment; (*Mil.*) *wer* —? who goes there? (*Poet. obs.*) where. — *conj.* (*temporal*) when, as; (*causal*) as, because, since.
dabei [da'baɪ], *adv.* nearby; besides, moreover; as well; —*sein*, be present, be about to (*infin.*); — *bleiben*, persist in.
Dach [dax], *n.* (—es, *pl.* ̈er) roof.
Dachboden ['daxbo:dən], *m.* (—s, *pl.* ̈) loft.
Dachdecker ['daxdɛkər], *m.* (—s, *pl.* —) slater, tiler.
Dachgiebel ['daxgi:bəl], *m.* (—s, *pl.* —) gable.
Dachluke ['daxlu:kə], *f.* (—, *pl.* —n) dormer window.
Dachpappe ['daxpapə], *f.* (—, *pl.* —n) roofing felt.
Dachrinne ['daxrɪnə], *f.* (—, *pl.* —n) gutter.
Dachs [daks], *m.* (—es, *pl.* —e) badger.
Dachstube ['daxʃtu:bə], *f.* (—, *pl.* —n) garret, attic (room).
Dachtraufe ['daxtraufə], *f.* (—, *pl.* —n) eaves.
dadurch [da'durç], *adv.* (*local*) through it; in that way; (*causal*) thereby.
dafür [da'fy:r], *adv.* for it; instead of it, in return for it; *ich kann nichts* —, it is not my fault, I can't help it.
Dafürhalten [da'fy:rhaltən], *n.* (—s, *no pl.*) opinion.
dagegen [da'ge:gən], *adv.* against it, compared to it. — *conj.* on the other hand.
daheim [da'haɪm], *adv.* at home.
daher [da'he:r], *adv.* thence, from that. — *conj.* therefore, for that reason.
dahin [da'hɪn], *adv.* thither, to that place; there; this, (*local*) thither; (*temporal*) till then; over, past, lost, gone.
dahinbringen [da'hɪnbrɪŋən], *v.a. irr.* *jemanden* —, induce s.o. to; *es* —, succeed in, manage to.

dahinsiechen [da'hɪnzi:çən], *v.n.* (*aux.* sein) pine away, be failing (in health).
dahinter [da'hɪntər], *adv.* behind that.
Dahlie ['da:ljə], *f.* (—, *pl.* —n) (*Bot.*) dahlia.
Dahome ['daome:], *n.* Dahomey.
damalig ['da:malɪç], *adj.* then; of that time; past.
damals ['da:mals], *adv.* then, at that time.
Damast [da'mast], *m.* (—s, *no pl.*) damask.
Damaszener [damas'tse:nər], *m.* (—s, *pl.* —) Damascene. — *adj.* — *Stahl*, Damascus steel, dagger.
Dame ['da:mə], *f.* (—, *pl.* —n) lady; (*cards, chess*) queen; draughts (*game*).
damit [da'mɪt], *adv.* therewith, with that, with it; *und* — *basta!* and that's all there is to it. — *conj.* in order that, so that; — *nicht*, lest.
dämlich ['dɛ:mlɪç], *adj.* (*coll.*) foolish, silly.
Damm [dam], *m.* (—es, *pl.* ̈e) dam, dyke, mole; (*street*) roadway, causeway; (*rail*) embankment.
dämmen ['dɛmən], *v.a.* dam; (*fig.*) stop, restrain.
dämmerig ['dɛmərɪç], *adj.* dusky.
dämmern ['dɛmərn], *v.n.* grow dusky; dawn.
dämonisch [dɛ'mo:nɪʃ], *adj.* demoniac-(al), demonlike.
Dampf [dampf], *m.* (—es, *pl.* ̈e) vapour, steam, mist, fume; smoke.
dampfen ['dampfən], *v.n.* smoke, fume, steam.
dämpfen ['dɛmpfən], *v.a.* damp, smother, steam; subdue, deaden, muffle, soften down.
Dampfer ['dampfər], *m.* (—s, *pl.* —) steamer.
Dämpfer ['dɛmpfər], *m.* (—s, *pl.* —) damper; (*Mus.*) mute.
Dampfkessel ['dampfkesəl], *m.* (—s, *pl.* —) boiler.
Dämpfung ['dɛmpfuŋ], *f.* (—, *pl.* —en) damping, smothering, suppression; (*Aviat.*) stabilization.
danach [da'na:x], *adv.* after that, thereafter; accordingly, according to that.
daneben [da'ne:bən], *adv.* near it, by it, close by; *es geht* —, it goes amiss. — *conj.* besides.
Dänemark ['dɛ:nəmark], *n.* Denmark.
Dank [daŋk], *m.* (—es, *no pl.*) thanks, gratitude; reward; *Gott sei* —, thank heaven!
dank [daŋk], *prep.* (*Dat.*) owing to, thanks to.
dankbar ['daŋkba:r], *adj.* grateful; thankful.
danken ['daŋkən], *v.n.* (*Dat.*) thank. — *v.a.* owe.
Dankgebet ['daŋkgəbe:t], *n.* (—s, *pl.* —e) (prayer of) thanksgiving.
dann [dan], *adv.* then, at that time, in that case; — *und wann*, now and then, occasionally.
Danzig ['dantsɪç], *n.* Dantzig.

daran

daran, dran [da'ran, dran], *adv.* on it, at it, near that; thereon, thereby; *was liegt —?* what does it matter?

darauf, drauf [da'rauf, drauf], *adv.* (*local*) upon it, on it; (*temporal*) thereupon, thereon, thereafter.

daraufhin [darauf'hın], *adv.* thereupon; on the strength of that.

daraus, draus [da'raus, draus], *adv.* therefrom, hence, from that; *ich mache mir nichts —,* I do not care for it.

darben ['darbən], *v.n.* suffer want, go short; famish.

darbieten ['da:rbi:tən], *v.a. irr.* offer, tender, present.

Darbietung ['da:rbi:tuŋ], *f.* (—, *pl.* —en) offering, presentation, performance.

darbringen ['da:rbrıŋən], *v.a. irr.* bring, present, offer.

darein, drein [da'rın, drın], *adv.* into it, therein.

darin, drin [da'rın, drın], *adv.* therein, in it, within.

darinnen, drinnen [da'rınən, 'drınən], *adv.* inside, in there.

darlegen [da:rle:gən], *v.a.* demonstrate, explain; expound.

Darlehen ['da:rle:ən], *n.* (—s, *pl.* —) loan.

Darm [darm], *m.* (—s, *pl.* ¨e) gut; (*pl.*) intestines, bowels.

Darmsaite ['darmzaıtə], *f.* (—, *pl.* —n) catgut, gut-string.

darob [da'rɔp], *adv.* (*obs.*) on that account, on account of it.

darreichen ['da:raıçən], *v.a.* offer, tender, present; (*Eccl.*) administer (sacraments).

darstellen ['da:rʃtɛlən], *v.a.* represent, delineate; (*Theat.*) perform.

Darstellung ['da:rʃtɛluŋ], *f.* (—, *pl.* —en) representation, exhibition, presentation; (*Theat.*) performance.

dartun ['da:rtu:n], *v.a. irr.* prove, demonstrate.

darüber, drüber [dar'y:bər, 'dry:bər], *adv.* over that, over it; concerning that.

darum, drum [da'rum, drum], *adv.* around it, around that, thereabout; therefore, for that reason.

darunter, drunter [da'runtər, 'druntər], *adv.* under that; thereunder; among; — *und drüber,* topsy-turvy.

das [das], *def. art. n.* the. — *dem. pron., dem. adj.* that, this. — *rel. pron.* which.

Dasein ['da:zaın], *n.* (—s, *no pl.*) presence, being, existence.

daselbst [da:'zɛlpst], *adv.* there, in that very place.

daß [das], *conj.* that; *es sei denn —,* unless; — *nicht,* lest.

dastehen [da:ʃte:ən], *v.n. irr.* stand (there).

datieren [da'ti:rən], *v.a.* date, put a date to.

Dativ ['da:ti:f], *m.* (—s, *pl.* —e) dative.

dato ['da:to], *adv. bis —,* till now, hitherto.

Dattel ['datəl], *f.* (—, *pl.* —n) (*Bot.*) date.

Datum ['da:tum], *n.* (—s, *pl.* **Daten**) date (*calendar*).

Dauer ['dauər], *f.* (—, *no pl.*) duration, length of time; continuance; permanence.

dauerhaft ['dauərhaft], *adj.* durable, lasting; (*colours*) fast.

Dauerkarte ['dauərkartə], *f.* (—, *pl.* —n) season ticket; (*Am.*) commutation ticket.

dauern ['dauərn], *v.n.* continue, last, endure.— *v.a.* move to pity; *er dauert mich,* I am sorry for him.

Dauerpflanze ['dauərpflantsə], *f.* (—, *pl.* —n) perennial plant.

Dauerwelle ['dauərvɛlə], *f.* (—, *pl.* —n) permanent wave, (*coll.*) perm.

Daumen ['daumən], *m.* (—s, *pl.* —) thumb; *einem den — halten,* wish s.o. well, keep o.'s fingers crossed for s.o.

Daune ['daunə], *f.* (—, *pl.* —n) down.

davon [da'fɔn], *adv.* thereof, therefrom, from that; off, away.

davonkommen [da'fɔnkɔmən], *v.n. irr.* (*aux.* sein) get off; *mit einem blauen Auge —,* get off lightly.

davor [da'fo:r], *adv.* before that, before it.

dawider [da'vi:dər], *adv.* against it.

dazu [da'tsu:], *adv.* thereto, to that, to it; in addition to that; for that purpose; *noch —,* besides.

dazumal ['da:tsuma:l], *adv.* then, at that time.

dazwischen [da'tsvıʃən], *adv.* between, among; — *kommen,* intervene, interfere; — *treten,* intervene.

debattieren [deba'ti:rən], *v.a., v.n.* debate.

Debet ['de:bɛt], *n.* (—s, *pl.* —s) debit.

Debüt [de'by:], *n.* (—s, *pl.* —s) first appearance, début.

Dechant [de'çant], *m.* (—en, *pl.* —en) (*Eccl.*) dean.

dechiffrieren [deʃıf'ri:rən], *v.a.* decode, decipher.

Deck [dɛk], *n.* (—s, *pl.* —e) (*Naut.*) deck.

Deckbett ['dɛkbɛt], *n.* (—s, *pl.* —en) coverlet.

Deckblatt ['dɛkblat], *n.* (—s, *pl.* ¨er) (*Bot.*) bractea; (*cigar*) wrapper.

Decke ['dɛkə], *f.* (—, *pl.* —n) cover; blanket, rug; (*bed*) coverlet; (*room*) ceiling.

Deckel ['dɛkəl], *m.* (—s, *pl.* —) lid, top; (*book*) cover; (*coll.*) hat.

decken ['dɛkən], *v.a.* cover; (*Comm.*) secure, reimburse. — *v.r. sich —,* (*Maths.*) coincide; (*fig.*) square, tally.

Deckfarbe ['dɛkfarbə], *f.* (—, *pl.* —n) body colour.

Deckmantel ['dɛkmantəl], *m.* (—s, *pl.* ¨) cloak, disguise.

Deckung ['dɛkuŋ], *f.* (—, *pl.* —en) covering, protection; (*Comm.*) reimbursement; security; (*Mil.*) cover.

dedizieren [dedı'tsi:rən], *v.a.* dedicate.

deduzieren [dedu'tsi:rən], *v.a.* deduce.

defekt [de'fɛkt], *adj.* defective, incomplete, imperfect.

defilieren [defɪ'li:rən], *v.n.* (*Mil.*) pass in review, march past.

definieren [defɪ'ni:rən], *v.a.* define.

Degen ['de:gən], *m.* (—s, *pl.* —) sword; (*fig.*) brave warrior.

degradieren [degra'di:rən], *v.a.* degrade, demote.

dehnbar ['de:nba:r], *adj.* extensible, ductile.

dehnen ['de:nən], *v.a.* extend, expand, stretch. — *v.r. sich* —, stretch o.s.

Deich [daɪç], *m.* (—es, *pl.* —e) dike, dam, embankment.

Deichsel ['daɪksəl], *f.* (—, *pl.* —n) thill, shaft, pole.

deichseln ['daɪksəln], *v.a.* (*fig.*) engineer; (*coll.*) manage; wangle.

dein [daɪn], *poss. adj.* your; (*Poet.*) thy. — *poss. pron.* yours; (*Poet.*) thine.

deinesgleichen [daɪnəs'glaɪçən], *adj.*, *pron.* the like of you, such as you.

deinethalben ['daɪnəthalbən], *adv.* on your account, for your sake, on your behalf.

deinetwegen ['daɪnətve:gən], *adv.* because of you, on your account, for your sake, on your behalf.

deinetwillen ['daɪnətvɪlən], *adv. um* —, on your account, for your sake, on your behalf.

deinige ['daɪnɪgə], *poss. adj.* your; (*Poet.*) thy. — *poss. pron.* yours; (*Poet.*) thine.

Dekan [de'ka:n], *m.* (—s, *pl.* —e) (*Eccl., Univ.*) dean.

Dekanat [deka'na:t], *n.* (—s, *pl.* —e) (*Eccl., Univ.*) deanery, office of dean.

deklamieren [dekla'mi:rən], *v.a., v.n.* recite, declaim.

deklarieren [dekla'ri:rən], *v.a.* declare (for customs duty).

Deklination [deklina'tsjo:n], *f.* (—, *pl.* —en) (*Gram.*) declension; (*Phys.*) declination.

deklinieren [deklɪ'ni:rən], *v.a.* (*Gram.*) decline.

dekolletiert [dekɔle'ti:rt], *adj.* décolleté, low-necked.

Dekret [de'kre:t], *n.* (—s, *pl.* —e) decree, edict, official regulation.

dekretieren [dekre'ti:rən], *v.a.* decree, ordain.

delegieren [dele'gi:rən], *v.a.* delegate.

Delegierte [dele'gi:rtə], *m.* (—n, *pl.* —n) delegate.

delikat [delɪ'ka:t], *adj.* subtle, dainty, tasty; (*coll.*) tricky, difficult.

Delikatesse [delɪka'tesə], *f.* (—, *pl.* —n) delicacy, dainty; (*pl.*) (*Am.*) delicatessen.

Delikt [de'lɪkt], *n.* (—s, *pl.* —e) (*Law*) crime; misdemeanour.

Delle [de'lə], *f.* (—, *pl.* —n) dent.

Delphin [del'fi:n], *m.* (—s, *pl.* —e) dolphin.

deltaförmig ['dɛltafœrmɪç], *adj.* deltoid.

dem [de:m], *def. art. Dat.* to the. — *dem. adj.* to this, to that: — *dem. pron.* to this, to that; *wie* — *auch sei*, however that may be. — *rel. pron.* to whom, to which.

demarkieren [demar'ki:rən], *v.a.* mark, demarcate.

Dementi [de'mɛnti], *n.* (—s, *pl.* —s) (*official*) denial.

dementieren [demɛn'ti:rən], *v.a.* (*Pol.*) deny, contradict.

demgemäß ['de:mgəme:s], *adv.* accordingly.

demnach ['de:mnax], *conj.* therefore, consequently, in accordance with that.

demnächst ['de:mnɛ:çst], *adv.* shortly, soon, in the near future.

demokratisch [demo'kra:tɪʃ], *adj.* democratic.

demolieren [demo'li:rən], *v.a.* demolish.

demonstrieren [demɔn'stri:rən], *v.a., v.n.* demonstrate.

Demut ['de:mu:t], *f.* (—, *no pl.*) humility, meekness.

demütig ['de:mytɪç], *adj.* humble, meek, submissive.

demütigen ['de:mytɪgən], *v.a.* humble, humiliate, subdue.

Denkart ['dɛnka:rt], *f.* (—, *pl.* —en) way of thinking.

denken ['dɛŋkən], *v.a., v.n. irr.* think, reflect (upon); imagine; (*coll.*) guess.

Denker ['dɛŋkər], *m.* (—s, *pl.* —) thinker, philosopher.

Denkmal ['dɛŋkma:l], *n.* (—s, *pl.* ̈er) monument.

Denkmünze ['dɛŋkmyntsə], *f.* (—, *pl.* —n) (commemorative) medal.

Denkschrift ['dɛŋkʃrɪft], *f.* (—, *pl.* —en) memorandum, memoir.

Denkspruch ['dɛŋkʃprux], *m.* (—s, *pl.* ̈e) aphorism, maxim, motto.

Denkungsart ['dɛŋkuŋsart], *f.* (*pl.* —en) *see* **Denkart**.

Denkweise ['dɛŋkvaɪzə], *f.* (—, *pl.* —n) *see* **Denkart**.

denkwürdig ['dɛŋkvyrdɪç], *adj.* memorable.

Denkzettel ['dɛŋktsɛtəl], *m.* (—s, *pl.* —) (*fig.*) reminder, punishment, lesson; *einem einen* — *geben*, give s.o. s.th. to think about *or* a sharp reminder.

denn [dɛn], *conj.* for. — *adv.* then; (*after comparatives*) than; *es sei* — *dass*, unless.

dennoch ['dɛnɔx], *conj.* yet, nevertheless, notwithstanding.

Denunziant [denun'tsjant], *m.* (—en, *pl.* —en) informer.

denunzieren [denun'tsi:rən], *v.a.* inform against, denounce.

Depesche [de'pɛʃə], *f.* (—, *pl.* —n) dispatch; telegram, wire.

deponieren [depo'ni:rən], *v.a.* deposit; (*Law*) depose.

Depositenbank [depo'zi:tənbaŋk], *f.* (—, *pl.* —en) deposit-bank.

deprimieren

deprimieren [deprɪ'mi:rən], *v.a.* depress.

Deputierte [depu'ti:rtə], *m.* (—n, *pl.* —n) deputy.

der [de:r], *def. art. m.* the. — *dem. adj., dem. pron.* this, that. — *rel. pron.* who, which, that.

derart ['de:ra:rt], *adv.* so, in such a manner.

derartig ['de:ra:rtɪç], *adj.* such.

derb [dɛrp], *adj.* firm, solid, coarse, blunt, uncouth; strong, robust.

dereinst [de:r'aɪnst], *adv.* one day (in future).

derenthalben ['de:rənthalbən], *adv.* for her (their) sake, on her (their) account, on whose account.

derentwegen ['de:rəntve:gən], *adv. see* derenthalben.

derentwillen ['de:rəntvɪlən], *adv. see* derenthalben.

dergestalt ['de:rgəʃtalt], *adv.* in such a manner; so.

dergleichen [de:r'glaɪçən], *adv.* such, such as, suchlike.

derjenige ['de:rje:nɪgə], *dem. adj., dem. pron.* that, this; — *welcher*, he who.

derlei ['de:rlaɪ], *adj.* of that sort.

dermaßen ['de:rma:sən], *adv.* to such an extent, to such a degree.

derselbe [de:r'zɛlbə], *pron.* the same.

derweilen [de:r'vaɪlən], *adv.* meanwhile.

Derwisch ['dɛrvɪʃ], *m.* (—(e)s, *pl.* —e) dervish.

derzeit ['de:rtsaɪt], *adv.* at present.

Des [dɛs], *n.* (—, *pl.* —) (*Mus.*) D flat; — *Dur*, D flat major; — *Moll*, D flat minor.

des [dɛs], *def. art. m. & n. Genit. sing.* of the.

desgleichen [dɛs'glaɪçən], *adj.* such, suchlike. — *adv.* likewise, ditto.

deshalb ['dɛshalp], *adv., conj.* therefore.

desinfizieren [dɛsɪnfit'si:rən], *v.a.* disinfect.

dessen ['dɛsən], *dem. pron. m & n. Genit. sing.* of it, of that. — *rel. pron. m. & n. Genit. sing.* whose, of whom, of which, whereof.

dessenungeachtet [dɛsənunge'axtət], *conj.* notwithstanding that, for all that, despite all that.

Destillateur [dɛstɪla'tø:r], *m.* (—s, *pl.* —e) distiller.

destillieren [dɛstɪ'li:rən], *v.a.* distil.

desto ['dɛsto], *adv.* the; — *besser*, so much the better; *je . . . —*, the . . . the.

deswegen ['dɛsve:gən], *adv., conj.* therefore.

Detaillist [deta'jɪst], *m.* (—en, *pl.* —en) retailer.

deucht [dɔyçt] *see* dünken; (*obs.*) *mich deucht*, methinks.

deuten ['dɔytən], *v.a.* point to, show; explain, interpret.

deutlich ['dɔytlɪç], *adj.* clear, distinct; evident, plain.

deutsch [dɔytʃ], *adj.* German.

Deutschland ['dɔytʃlant], *n.* Germany.

Deutschmeister ['dɔytʃmaɪstər], *m.* (—s, *pl.* —) Grand Master of the Teutonic Order.

Deutschtum ['dɔytʃtu:m], *n.* (—s, *no pl.*) German nationality, German customs, German manners.

Deutung ['dɔytuŋ], *f.* (—, *pl.* —en) explanation, interpretation.

Devise [de'vi:zə], *f.* (—, *pl.* —n) device, motto; (*pl.*) foreign currency.

devot [de'vo:t], *adj.* submissive, respectful, humble.

Dezember [de'tsɛmbər], *m.* December.

dezent [de'tsɛnt], *adj.* modest, decent; unobtrusive.

Dezernent [detsɛr'nɛnt], *m.* (—en, *pl.* —en) head of section in ministry or city administration.

dezimieren [detsɪ'mi:rən], *v.a.* decimate, reduce.

Diagramm [dia'gram], *n.* (—s, *pl.* —e) diagram, graph.

Diakon [dia'ko:n], *m.* (—s, *pl.* —e) (*Eccl.*) deacon.

Diakonisse, Diakonissin [diako'nɪsə, diako'nɪsɪn], *f.* (—, *pl.* —nen) deaconess.

Dialektik [dia'lɛktɪk], *f.* (—, *no pl.*) dialectics.

Diamant [dia'mant], *m.* (—en, *pl.* —en) diamond.

diametral [diame'tra:l], *adj.* diametrical.

Diapositiv [diapozi'ti:f], *n.* (—s, *pl.* —e) (*lantern, Phot.*) slide.

Diät [di'ɛ:t], *f.* (—, *pl.* —en) diet; (*pl.*) daily allowance.

dich [dɪç], *pers. pron.* you. — *refl. pron.* yourself.

dicht [dɪçt], *adj.* tight; impervious (to water); dense, compact, solid, firm; — *bei*, hard by, close to.

Dichte ['dɪçtə], *f.* (—, *no pl.*) density.

dichten ['dɪçtən], *v.a., v.n.* write poetry, compose (*verses etc.*); (*Tech.*) tighten; (*Naut.*) caulk.

Dichter ['dɪçtər], *m.* (—s, *pl.* —) poet.

dichterisch ['dɪçtərɪʃ], *adj.* poetic(al).

Dichtigkeit ['dɪçtɪçkaɪt], *f.* (—, *no pl.*) closeness, compactness, thickness, density.

Dichtkunst ['dɪçtkunst], *f.* (—, *no pl.*) (art of) poetry.

Dichtung ['dɪçtuŋ], *f.* (—, *pl.* —en) poetry, poem; fiction; (*Tech.*) caulking; washer, gasket.

dick [dɪk], *adj.* thick; fat; (*books*) bulky; voluminous, stout, obese, corpulent.

Dicke ['dɪkə], *f.* (—, *no pl.*) thickness, stoutness.

dickfellig ['dɪkfɛlɪç], *adj.* thick-skinned.

Dickicht ['dɪkɪçt], *n.* (—s, *pl.* —e) thicket.

die [di:], *def. art. f. & pl.* the. — *dem. adj., dem. pron. f. & pl.* this, these. — *rel. pron. f. & pl.* who, that which.

Dieb [di:p], *m.* (—s, *pl.* —e) thief.

Diebstahl ['di:pʃta:l], *m.* (—s, *pl.* ⸚e) theft.

Diele ['di:lə], *f.* (—, *pl.* —n) floor; (entrance) hall.

dielen ['di:lən], *v.a.* board, floor.

dienen ['di:nən], *v.n. einem —,* serve (s.o.); help (s.o.).

Diener ['di:nər], *m.* (—s, *pl.* —) servant, attendant; (*coll.*) bow.

dienlich ['di:nlɪç], *adj.* serviceable, useful; *für — halten,* think fit.

Dienst [di:nst], *m.* (—es, *pl.* —e) service, employment, duty; *— haben,* be on duty.

Dienstag ['di:nsta:k], *m.* (—s, *pl.* —e) Tuesday.

Dienstalter ['di:nstaltər], *n.* (—s, *pl.* —) seniority.

dienstbar ['di:nstba:r], *adj.* subject, subservient.

Dienstbarkeit ['di:nstba:rkaɪt], *f.* (—, *no pl.*) bondage, servitude.

dienstbeflissen ['di:nstbəflɪsən], *adj.* assiduous.

Dienstbote ['di:nstbo:te], *m.* (—n, *pl.* —n) domestic servant.

dienstfertig ['di:nstfertɪç], *adj.* obliging, ready to serve.

Dienstleistung ['di:nstlaɪstuŋ], *f.* (—, *pl.* —en) service.

dienstlich ['di:nstlɪç], *adj.* official.

Dienstmädchen ['di:nstmɛ:tçən], *n.* (—s, *pl.* —) maidservant.

Dienstmann ['di:nstman], *m.* (—s, *pl.* ̈er) commissionaire, porter.

Dienstpflicht ['di:nstpflɪçt], *f.* (—, *no pl.*) official duty, liability to serve; (*Mil.*) (compulsory) military service.

Dienststunden ['di:nstʃtundən], *f. pl.* office hours.

diensttauglich ['di:nsttaukliç], *adj.* (*Mil.*) fit for service.

Dienstverhältnis ['di:nstferhɛltnɪs], *n.* (—ses, *pl.* —se) (*pl.*) terms of service.

dies [di:s], *abbr.* dieses.

diesbezüglich ['di:sbətsy:klɪç], *adj.* concerning this, relating to this matter.

diese ['di:zə], *dem. adj., dem. pron. f. & pl.* this, these.

dieser ['di:zər], *dem. adj., dem. pron. m.* this.

dieses ['di:zəs], *dem. adj., dem. pron. n.* this.

diesjährig ['di:sjɛ:rɪç], *adj.* of this year, this year's.

diesmal ['di:sma:l], *adv.* this time, for this once.

Dietrich ['di:trɪç], *m.* Derek.

Dietrich (2) ['di:trɪç], *m.* (—s, *pl.* —e) pick lock, master-key, skeleton key.

Differentialrechnung [dɪfərɛnts'ja:l-reçnuŋ], *f.* (—, *pl.* —en) differential calculus.

Differenz [dɪfə'rɛnts], *f.* (—, *pl.* —en) difference; quarrel.

Diktat [dɪk'ta:t], *n.* (—s, *pl.* —e) dictation.

diktatorisch [dɪkta'to:rɪʃ], *adj.* dictatorial.

Diktatur [dɪkta'tu:r], *f.* (—, *pl.* —en) dictatorship.

diktieren [dɪk'ti:rən], *v.a.* dictate.

Ding [dɪŋ], *n.* (—s, *pl.* —e) thing, object, matter.

dingen ['dɪŋən], *v.a.* hire, engage (a manual worker).

dingfest ['dɪŋfest], *adj. — machen,* arrest.

dinglich ['dɪŋlɪç], *adj.* real.

dinieren [di'ni:rən], *v.n.* dine.

Diözese [diø'tse:zə], *f.* (—, *pl.* —n) diocese.

Diphtherie [dɪftə'ri:], *f.* (—, *no pl.*) diphtheria.

Diplom [di'plo:m], *n.* (—s, *pl.* —e) diploma.

Diplomatie [dɪploma'ti:], *f.* (—, *no pl.*) diplomacy.

dir [di:r], *pers. pron. Dat.* to you.

direkt [di'rekt], *adj.* direct; *—er Wagen,* (*railway*) through carriage; *— danach,* immediately afterwards.

Direktion [dɪrekt'sjo:n], *f.* (—, *pl.* —en) direction, management.

Direktor [di'rektɔr], *m.* (—s, *pl.* —en) (managing) director, manager; headmaster, principal.

Direktorium [dɪrek'to:rjum], *n.* (—s, *pl.* —rien) directorate, board of directors.

Direktrice [dɪrek'tri:sə], *f.* (—, *pl.* —n) manageress.

Dirigent [diri'gɛnt], *m.* (—en, *pl.* —en) (*Mus.*) conductor; (*Austr. Admin.*) head of section in Ministry.

dirigieren [diri'gi:rən], *v.a.* direct, manage; (*Mus.*) conduct.

Dirndl ['dɪrndl], *n.* (—s, *pl.* —) (*dial.*) young girl, country wench; (*fig.*) peasant dress, dirndl.

Dirne ['dɪrnə], *f.* (—, *pl.* —n) (*Poet.*) girl; prostitute.

Dis [dɪs], *n.* (—, *no pl.*) (*Mus.*) D sharp.

disharmonisch [dɪshar'mo:nɪʃ], *adj.* discordant.

Diskant [dɪs'kant], *m.* (—s, *pl.* —e) (*Mus.*) treble, soprano.

Diskont [dɪs'kɔnt], *m.* (—(e)s, *pl.* —e) discount, rebate.

diskret [dɪs'kre:t], *adj.* discreet.

Diskurs [dɪs'kurs], *m.* (—es, *pl.* —e) discourse.

diskutieren [dɪsku'ti:rən], *v.a.* discuss, debate.

Dispens [dɪs'pɛns], *m.* (—es, *pl.* —e) dispensation.

dispensieren [dɪspen'zi:rən], *v.a.* dispense (from), exempt (from).

disponieren [dɪspo'ni:rən], *v.n. — über,* dispose of; make plans about.

Dissident [dɪsi'dɛnt], *m.* (—en, *pl.* —en) dissenter, nonconformist.

distanzieren [dɪstan'tsi:rən], *v.r. sich — von,* keep o.'s distance from; dissociate o.s. from.

Distel ['dɪstəl], *f.* (—, *pl.* —n) thistle.

Distelfink ['dɪstəlfɪŋk], *m.* (—s, *pl.* —e) (*Orn.*) gold-finch.

disziplinarisch [dɪstsipli'na:rɪʃ], *adj.* diciplinary.

dito ['di:to], *adv.* ditto.

dividieren

dividieren [dɪvɪ'diːrən], *v.a.* divide.

Diwan ['diːvan], *m.* (—s, *pl.* —e) divan, sofa, couch.

doch [dɔx], *adv., conj.* however, though, although, nevertheless, yet, but; after all, (*emphatic*) yes.

Docht [dɔxt], *m.* (—es, *pl.* —e) wick.

Dock [dɔk], *n.* (—s, *pl.* —s, —e) dock.

Dogge ['dɔgə], *f.* (—, *pl.* —n) bulldog, mastiff; Great Dane.

Dogmatiker [dɔg'maːtɪkər], *m.* (—s, *pl.* —) dogmatist.

dogmatisch [dɔg'maːtɪʃ], *adj.* dogmatic, doctrinal.

Dohle ['doːlə], *f.* (—, *pl.* —n) (*Orn.*) jackdaw.

Doktor ['dɔktɔr], *m.* (—s, *pl.* —en) doctor; physician, surgeon.

Dolch [dɔlç], *m.* (—es, *pl.* —e) dagger, dirk.

Dolde ['dɔldə], *f.* (—, *pl.* —n) (*Bot.*) umbel.

Dolmetscher ['dɔlmɛtʃər], *m.* (—s, *pl.* —) interpreter.

dolmetschen ['dɔlmɛtʃən], *v.a.* interpret.

Dolomiten [doloˈmiːtən], *pl.* Dolomites.

Dom [doːm], *m.* (—s, *pl.* —e) cathedral; dome, cupola.

Domherr ['doːmhɛr], *m.* (—n, *pl.* —en) canon, prebendary.

dominieren [domiˈniːrən], *v.a.* dominate, domineer.

Dominikaner [dominiˈkaːnər], *m.* (—s, *pl.* —) Dominican friar.

dominikanische Republik [dominiˈkaːnɪʃə repuˈbliːk], *f.* Dominican Republic.

Domizil [domiˈtsiːl], *n.* (—s, *pl.* —e) domicile, residence, address.

Domkapitel ['doːmkapiːtəl], *n.* (—s, *pl.* —) dean and chapter.

Dompfaff ['doːmpfaf], *m.* (—s, *pl.* —en) (*Orn.*) bullfinch.

Dompropst ['doːmproːpst], *m.* (—es, *pl.* ⁻e) provost.

Donau ['doːnau], *f.* (—, *no pl.*) Danube.

Donner ['dɔnər], *m.* (—s, *no pl.*) thunder.

donnern ['dɔnərn], *v.n.* thunder; (*fig.*) storm, rage.

Donnerschlag ['dɔnərʃlaːk], *m.* (—s, *pl.* ⁻e) thunderclap.

Donnerstag ['dɔnərstaːk], *m.* (—s, *pl.* —e) Thursday; *Grün —*, Maundy Thursday.

Donnerwetter ['dɔnərvɛtər], *n.* (—s, *pl.* —) thunderstorm; *zum —* (*nochmal*)! hang it all, confound it!

doppeldeutig ['dɔpəldɔytɪç], *adj.* ambiguous.

Doppelgänger ['dɔpəlgɛŋər], *m.* (—s, *pl.* —) double.

Doppellaut ['dɔpəllaut], *m.* (—s, *pl.* —e) diphthong.

doppeln ['dɔpəln] *see* **verdoppeln.**

doppelsinnig ['dɔpəlzɪnɪç] *see* **doppeldeutig.**

doppelt ['dɔpəlt], *adj.* double, twofold.

Doppelzwirn ['dɔpəltsvɪrn], *m.* (—s, *no pl.*) double-thread.

Dorf [dɔrf], *n.* (—es, *pl.* ⁻er) village.

dörflich ['dœrflɪç], *adj.* rural, rustic.

dorisch ['doːrɪʃ], *adj.* Doric.

Dorn [dɔrn], *m.* (—s, *pl.* —en) thorn, prickle; (*Bot.*) spine; (*buckle*) tongue.

dornig ['dɔrnɪç], *adj.* thorny.

Dornröschen ['dɔrnrøːsçən], *n.* (—s, *pl.* —) Sleeping Beauty.

Dorothea [doroˈteːa], *f.* Dorothea, Dorothy.

dorren ['dɔrən] *see* **verdorren.**

dörren ['dœrən], *v.a.* dry, make dry, parch.

Dörrobst ['dœrroːbst], *n.* (—es, *no pl.*) dried fruit.

Dorsch [dɔrʃ], *m.* (—es, *pl.* —e) cod, codfish.

dort [dɔrt], (*Austr.*) **dorten** ['dɔrtən], *adv.* there, yonder; *von — aus*, from that point, from there.

dorther ['dɔrtheːr], *adv.* from there, therefrom, thence.

dorthin ['dɔrthɪn], *adv.* to that place, thereto, thither.

dortig ['dɔrtɪç], *adj.* of that place, local.

Dose ['doːzə], *f.* (—, *pl.* —n) box, tin, can.

dösen ['døːzən], *v.n.* doze, daydream.

Dosis ['doːzɪs], *f.* (—, *pl.* **Dosen**) dose.

Dotter ['dɔtər], *n.* (—s, *pl.* —) yolk (of egg).

Dozent [do'tsɛnt], *m.* (—en, *pl.* —en) university lecturer; (*Am.*) Assistant Professor.

dozieren [do'tsiːrən], *v.n.* lecture.

Drache ['draxə], *m.* (—n, *pl.* —n) dragon; kite; (*fig.*) termagant, shrew.

Dragoner [dra'goːnər], *m.* (—s, *pl.* —) dragoon.

Draht [draːt], *m.* (—es, *pl.* ⁻e) wire.

drahten ['draːtən], *v.a.* (—s, *pl.* —en) wire, telegraph.

Drahtgewebe ['draːtgəveːbə], *n.* (—s, *pl.* —) wire-gauze.

Drahtgitter ['draːtgɪtər], *m.* (—s, *pl.* —) wire grating.

drahtlos ['draːtloːs], *adj.* wireless.

Drahtseilbahn ['draːtzailbaːn], *f.* (—, *pl.* —en) cable (funicular) railway.

Drahtzange ['draːttsaŋə], *f.* (—, *pl.* —n) pliers.

drall [dral], *adj.* buxom, plump.

Drama ['draːma], *n.* (—s, *pl.* —men) drama.

Dramatiker [dra'maːtɪkər], *m.* (—s, *pl.* —) dramatist.

dramatisch [dra'maːtɪʃ], *adj.* dramatic.

dran [dran] *see* **daran.**

Drang [draŋ], *m.* (—s, *no pl.*) urge; rush; throng; pressure; impulse.

drängeln ['drɛŋəln], *v.a.* jostle.

drängen ['drɛŋən], *v.a.* press, urge; *die Zeit drängt*, time presses; *es drängt mich*, I feel called upon.

Drangsal ['draŋzaːl], *f.* or *n.* (—s, *pl.* —e or —en) distress, misery.

drapieren [dra'piːrən], *v.a.* drape.

drastisch ['drastɪʃ], *adj.* drastic.

drauf [drauf] *see* **darauf.**

Draufgänger ['draufgɛŋər], *m.* (—s, *pl.* —) daredevil.

draußen ['drausən], *adv.* outside, without, out of doors.

drechseln ['drɛksəln], *v.a.* turn (on a lathe); *Phrasen* —, turn phrases.

Drechsler ['drɛkslər], *m.* (—s, *pl.* —) turner.

Dreck [drɛk], *m.* (—s, *no pl.*) dirt, mire, dust, filth, dung.

dreckig ['drɛkɪç], *adj.* dirty, filthy, muddy.

drehbar ['dre:ba:r], *adj.* revolving, swivelling.

Drehbuch ['dre:bu:x], *n.* (—s, *pl.* ˙er) (*film*) script.

drehen ['dre:ən], *v.a.* turn; (*film*) shoot. — *v.n.* turn round, veer.

Drehorgel ['dre:ɔrgəl], *f.* (—, *pl.* —n) barrel-organ.

Drehrad ['dre:ra:t], *n.* (—s, *pl.* ˙er) fly-wheel.

Drehung ['dre:uŋ], *f.* (—, *pl.* —en) rotation, turn, revolution.

drei [draɪ], *num. adj.* three.

dreiblätterig ['draɪblɛtərɪç], *adj.* trifoliate.

Dreieck ['draɪɛk], *n.* (—s, *pl.* —e) triangle.

dreieckig ['draɪɛkɪç], *adj.* triangular, three-cornered.

dreieinig [draɪ'aɪnɪç], *adj.* (*Theol.*) triune.

dreifach ['draɪfax], *adj.* threefold, triple.

Dreifaltigkeit [draɪ'faltɪçkaɪt], *f.* (—, *no pl.*) (*Theol.*) Trinity.

Dreifuß ['draɪfu:s], *m.* (—es, *pl.* ˙e) tripod.

dreijährlich ['draɪjɛrlɪç], *adj.* triennial.

Dreikönigsfest [draɪ'kø:nɪksfɛst], *n.* (—es, *no pl.*) Epiphany.

dreimonatlich ['draɪmo:natlɪç], *adj.* quarterly.

Dreirad ['draɪra:t], *n.* (—s, *pl.* ˙er) tricycle.

dreiseitig ['draɪzaɪtɪç], *adj.* trilateral.

dreißig ['draɪsɪç], *num. adj.* thirty.

dreist [draɪst], *adj.* bold, audacious, impudent.

dreistellig ['draɪʃtɛlɪç], *adj.* —*e Zahl*, number of three figures.

dreistimmig ['draɪʃtɪmɪç], *adj.* for three voices.

Dreistufenrakete [draɪ'ʃtu:fənra'ke:tə], *f.* (—, *pl.* —n) three-stage rocket.

dreistündig ['draɪʃtyndɪç], *adj.* lasting three hours.

dreitägig ['draɪtɛ:gɪç], *adj.* lasting three days.

dreiteilig ['draɪtaɪlɪç], *adj.* tripartite, three-piece.

dreizehn ['draɪtse:n], *num. adj.* thirteen.

Drell [drɛl], *m.* (—s, *no pl.*) *see* **Drillich.**

Dresche ['drɛʃə], *f.* (—, *no pl.*) thrashing, beating.

dreschen ['drɛʃən], *v.a. irr.* (*corn*) thresh; (*person*) thrash.

Dreschflegel ['drɛʃfle:gəl], *m.* (—s, *pl.* —) flail.

dressieren [drɛ'si:rən], *v.a.* (*animal*) train; break in.

Dressur [drɛ'su:r], *f.* (—, *pl.* —en) training, breaking-in.

Drillbohrer ['drɪlbo:rər], *m.* (—s, *pl.* —) drill.

drillen ['drɪlən], *v.a.* (*a hole*) bore; (*soldiers*) drill.

Drillich ['drɪlɪç], *m.* (—s, *pl.* —e) drill, canvas.

Drilling ['drɪlɪŋ], *m.* (—s, *pl.* —e) three-barrelled gun; (*pl.*) triplets.

drin [drɪn] *see* **darin.**

dringen ['drɪŋən], *v.n. irr.* penetrate, force o.'s way through; *auf etwas* —, insist on s.th.

dringlich ['drɪŋlɪç], *adj.* urgent, pressing.

drinnen ['drɪnən], *adv.* inside, within.

drittens ['drɪtəns], *adv.* thirdly.

droben ['dro:bən], *adv.* up there, above, aloft, overhead.

Droge ['dro:gə], *f.* (—, *pl.* —n) drug.

Drogerie [dro:gə'ri:], *f.* (—, *pl.* —n) druggist's shop, chemist's; (*Am.*) drugstore.

drohen ['dro:ən], *v.a., v.n.* threaten, menace.

Drohne ['dro:nə], *f.* (—, *pl.* —n) drone.

dröhnen ['drø:nən], *v.n.* boom, roar.

Drohung ['dro:uŋ], *f.* (—, *pl.* —en) threat, menace.

drollig ['drɔlɪç], *adj.* droll, odd, quaint.

Dromedar [drɔmə'da:r], *n.* (—s, *pl.* —e) dromedary.

Droschke ['drɔʃkə], *f.* (—, *pl.* —n) cab, hansom, taxi.

Drossel ['drɔsəl], *f.* (—, *pl.* —n) thrush.

Drosselader ['drɔsəla:dər], *f.* (—, *pl.* —n) jugular vein.

Drosselbein ['drɔsəlbaɪn], *n.* (—s, *pl.* —e) collar-bone.

drosseln ['drɔsəln], *v.a.* throttle. *See also* **erdrosseln.**

drüben ['dry:bən], *adv.* over there, on the other side.

drüber ['dry:bər] *see* **darüber.**

Druck [druk], *m.* (—s, *pl.* ˙e, —e) pressure, squeeze; (*Phys.*) compression; (*Typ.*) impression, print; (*fig.*) hardship.

Druckbogen ['drukbo:gən], *m.* (—s, *pl.* —) proof-sheet, proof.

Druckbuchstabe ['drukbu:xʃta:bə], *m.* (—n, *pl.* —n) letter, type.

Drückeberger ['drykəbergər], *m.* (—s, *pl.* —) slacker, shirker.

drucken ['drukən], *v.a.* print.

drücken ['drykən], *v.a.* press, squeeze; trouble, oppress. — *v.r. sich* —, sneak away, shirk.

Drucker ['drukər], *m.* (—s, *pl.* —) printer.

Drücker ['drykər], *m.* (—s, *pl.* —) (*door*) handle, latch; (*gun*) trigger.

Druckerei ['drukəraɪ], *f.* (—, *pl.* —en) printing shop.

Druckerschwärze

Druckerschwärze ['drukərʃvɛrtsə], f. (—, no pl.) printing-ink.

Druckfehler ['drukfe:lər], m. (—s, pl. —) misprint, printer's error.

druckfertig ['drukfɛrtiç], adj. ready for press.

Drucksache ['drukzaxə], f. (—, pl. —n) (Postal) printed matter.

drum [drum] see darum.

drunten ['druntən], adv. down there, below.

drunter ['druntər] see darunter.

Drüse ['dry:zə], f. (—, pl. —n) gland.

Dschungel ['dʒuŋəl], m. or n. (—s, pl. —) jungle.

du [du:], pers. pron. thou, you.

ducken ['dukən], v.a. bring down, humble. — v.r. sich —, duck, stoop, crouch.

dudeln ['du:dəln], v.n. play the bagpipes; tootle.

Dudelsack ['du:dəlzak], m. (—s, pl. ⁼e) bagpipe(s).

Duft [duft], m. (—s, pl. ⁼e) scent, odour, fragrance, aroma, perfume.

duften ['duftən], v.n. be fragrant.

duftig ['duftiç], adj. fragrant, odoriferous, perfumed.

dulden ['duldən], v.a. suffer, endure, bear, tolerate.

duldsam ['dultza:m], adj. tolerant, indulgent, patient.

dumm [dum], adj. stupid, foolish, dull.

Dummheit ['dumhait], f. (—, pl. —en) stupidity, folly.

dumpf [dumpf], adj. musty; (air) close; (sound) hollow; (fig.) gloomy.

dumpfig ['dumpfiç], adj. damp, musty, stuffy.

Düne ['dy:nə], f. (—, pl. —n) dune, sand-hill.

Düngemittel ['dyŋəmitəl], n. (—s, pl. —) fertilizer.

düngen ['dyŋən], v.a. manure, fertilize.

Dünger ['dyŋər], m. (—s, no pl.) compost, artificial manure.

dunkel ['duŋkəl], adj. dark; (fig.) obscure, mysterious.

Dünkel ['dyŋkəl], m. (—s, no pl.) conceit, arrogance.

dünkelhaft ['dyŋkəlhaft], adj. conceited, arrogant.

Dunkelheit ['duŋkəlhait], f. (—, no pl.) darkness, obscurity.

dunkeln ['duŋkəln], v.n. grow dark.

dünken ['dyŋkən], v.n. (rare) seem, appear. — v.r. sich —, fancy o.s. imagine o.s.

dünn [dyn], adj. thin, slim, weak.

Dunst [dunst], m. (—es, pl. ⁼e) vapour, fume; exhalation; haze; einem blauen — vormachen, humbug a p.

dünsten ['dynstən], v.a. stew.

dunstig ['dunstiç], adj. misty, hazy.

Dunstkreis ['dunstkrais], m. (—es, pl. —e) atmosphere.

Dunstobst ['dunsto:pst], n. (—es, no pl.) stewed fruit.

duodez [duo'de:ts], adj. (Typ.) duodecimo (12mo).

Duodezfürst [duo'de:tsfyrst], m. (—en, pl. —en) petty prince, princeling.

Dur [du:r], n. (Mus.) major; sharp.

durch [durç], prep. (Acc.) (local) through, across; (temporal) during, throughout; (manner) by means of, by. — adv. thoroughly, through.

durchaus [durç'aus], adv. throughout, quite, by all means, absolutely.

Durchblick ['durçblik], m. (—s, pl. —e) vista, view.

durchbohren [durç'bo:rən], v.a. insep. perforate, pierce.

durchbrennen ['durçbrɛnən], v.n. irr. (aux. sein) abscond, bolt.

durchbringen ['durçbriŋən], v.a. irr. bring through, get through; squander (money); pull (a sick person) through. — v.r. sich redlich —, make an honest living.

Durchbruch ['durçbrux], m. (—s, pl. ⁼e) breach, break-through.

durchdrängen ['durçdrɛŋən], v.r. sich —, force o.'s way through.

durchdringen ['durçdriŋən], v.n. irr. sep. (aux. sein) get through. — [durç'driŋən], v.a. irr.insep. penetrate, pierce, permeate, pervade.

durchdrücken ['durçdrykən], v.a. press through; (fig.) carry through.

durcheilen [durç'ailən], v.a. insep. hurry through.

Durcheinander [durçain'andər], n. (—s, no pl.) confusion, muddle.

durcheinander [durçain'andər], adv. in confusion, pell-mell.

Durchfall ['durçfal], m. (—s, no pl.) diarrhoea; (exams etc.) failure.

durchfallen ['durçfalən], v.n. irr. (aux. sein) fall through, come to nought; (exams etc.) fail.

durchflechten [durç'flɛçtən], v.a. irr. interweave, intertwine.

durchfliegen [durç'fli:gən], v.a. irr. fly through; read superficially, skim through.

durchforschen [durç'fɔrʃən], v.a. insep. explore, scrutinise, examine thoroughly.

Durchfuhr ['durçfu:r], f. (—, pl. —en) passage, transit.

durchführbar ['durçfy:rba:r], adj. practicable, feasible.

durchführen ['durçfy:rən], v.a. escort through; (fig.) execute, bring about, carry through.

Durchgang ['durçgaŋ], m. (—s, pl. ⁼e) passage, thoroughfare; (Comm.) transit.

Durchgänger ['durçgɛŋər], m. (—s, pl. —) runaway horse, bolter; (fig.) hothead.

durchgängig ['durçgɛŋiç], adj. general, universal.

durchgehen ['durçge:ən], v.n. irr. (aux. sein) go through; (fig.) abscond; (horse) bolt; (proposal) be carried. — v.a. irr. (aux. sein) peruse, review, go over.

durchgreifen ['durçgraɪfən], *v.n. irr.* act decisively, take strong action.

durchhauen ['durçhauən], *v.a. irr.* cut through; *einen* —, flog s.o.

durchkommen ['durçkɔmən], *v.n. irr.* (*aux.* sein) get through; (*exams etc.*) pass.

durchkreuzen [durç'krɔytsən], *v.a. insep.* cross out; (*fig.*) thwart.

durchlassen ['durçlasən], *v.a. irr.* let pass.

Durchlaucht ['durçlauxt], *f.* (— *pl.* —en) Highness.

durchleuchten [durç'lɔyçtən], *v.a. insep.* (*Med.*) X-ray.

durchlöchern [durç'lœçərn], *v.a. insep.* perforate, riddle.

durchmachen ['durçmaxən], *v.a.* go through, suffer.

Durchmesser ['durçmesər], *m.* (—s, *pl.* —) diameter.

durchnässen [durç'nɛsən], *v.a. insep.* wet to the skin, soak.

durchnehmen ['durçne:mən], *v.a. irr.* go over *or* cover (a subject).

durchpausen ['durçpauzən], *v.a.* trace, copy.

durchqueren [durç'kve:rən], *v.a. insep.* cross, traverse.

Durchsage ['durçza:gə], *f.* (—, *pl.* —n) (radio) announcement.

durchschauen [durç'ʃauən], *v.a. insep.* *einen* —, see through s.o.

durchscheinend ['durçʃaɪnənt], *adj.* transparent, translucent.

Durchschlag ['durçʃla:k], *m.* (—s, *pl.* ˙e) strainer, sieve, colander, filter; carbon copy.

durchschlagen ['durçʃla:gən], *v.a. irr. insep.* strain, filter. — *v.r. irr. sich* —, fight o.'s way through.

durchschlagend ['durçʃla:gənt], *adj.* thorough, complete, effective.

Durchschnitt ['durçʃnɪt], *m.* (—s, *pl.* —e) average; (*Med. etc.*) cross section.

durchschnittlich ['durçʃnɪtlɪç], *adj.* average; ordinary.

durchschossen [durç'ʃɔsən], *adj.* interleaved; interwoven.

durchseihen ['durçzaɪən], *v.a. see* **durchsieben**.

durchsetzen [durç'zɛtsən], *v.a. insep.* intersperse; [durç'zɛtsən], *v.a. sep.* have o.'s way (with s.o.). — *v.r. sep. sich* —, make o.'s way successfully, succeed.

Durchsicht ['durçzɪçt], *f.* (—, *no pl.*) revision, inspection, perusal.

durchsichtig ['durçzɪçtɪç], *adj.* transparent.

durchsickern ['durçzɪkərn], *v.n.* (*aux.* sein) trickle through, ooze through.

durchsieben ['durçzi:bən], *v.a.* strain, filter, sift.

durchsprechen ['durçʃprɛçən], *v.a. irr.* talk over, discuss.

durchstöbern [durç'ʃtø:bərn], *v.a. insep.* rummage through.

durchstreichen ['durçʃtraɪçən], *v.a. irr.* cross out, delete.

durchstreifen [durç'ʃtraɪfən], *v.a. insep.* roam (through).

durchströmen [durç'ʃtrø:mən], *v.a. insep.* flow through, permeate.

durchsuchen [durç'zu:xən], *v.a. insep.* search thoroughly, examine closely.

durchtrieben [durç'tri:bən], *adj.* artful, sly, cunning, crafty.

durchweben [durç've:bən], *v.a.* interweave.

durchweg(s) ['durçvɛk(s)], *adv.* without exception, every time, throughout.

durchwühlen [durç'vy:lən], *v.a. insep.* search; ransack.

durchziehen [durç'tsi:ən], *v.a. irr. insep.* wander through, traverse; ['durçtsi:ən], *v.a. irr. sep.* interlace (with threads); draw through.

durchzucken [durç'tsukən], *v.a. insep.* flash through, convulse.

Durchzug ['durçtsu:k], *m.* (—s, *no pl.*) passage, march through; (*air*) draught.

dürfen ['dyrfən], *v.n. irr.* be permitted; be allowed; dare; be likely.

dürftig ['dyrftɪç], *adj.* paltry, insufficient, poor.

dürr [dyr], *adj.* dry, arid, withered; (*wood*) dead; (*persons*) thin, gaunt.

Dürre ['dyrə], *f.* (—, *pl.* —n) aridity, dryness; drought; (*persons*) thinness.

Durst [durst], *m.* (—es, *no pl.*) thirst.

dürsten ['dyrstən], *v.n.* thirst.

durstig ['durstɪç], *adj.* thirsty.

Dusche ['du:ʃə], *f.* (—, *pl.* —n) shower (bath).

Düse ['dy:zə], *f.* (—, *pl.* —n) jet.

duselig ['du:zəlɪç], *adj.* drowsy; silly.

düster ['dy:stər], *adj.* dark, gloomy; sad, mournful; sombre.

Dutzend ['dutsənt], *n.* (—s, *pl.* —e) dozen.

Duzbruder ['du:tsbru:dər], *m.* (—s, *pl.* ˙) crony, chum; close friend.

duzen ['du:tsen], *v.a.* be on close terms with.

dynamisch [dy'na:mɪʃ], *adj.* dynamic(al).

E

E [e:], *n.* (—s, *pl.* —s) the letter E; (*Mus.*) E *Dur*, E major; E *Moll*, E minor.

Ebbe ['ɛbə], *f.* (—, *pl.* —n) ebb, low tide; — *und Flut*, the tides.

ebben ['ɛbən], *v.n.* ebb.

eben ['e:bən], *adj.* even, level, plane; (*fig.*) plain. — *adv.* precisely, exactly.

Ebenbild ['e:bənbɪlt], *n.* (—es, *pl.* —er) likeness, image.

ebenbürtig ['e:bənbyrtɪç], *adj.* of equal birth *or* rank; equal.

ebenda

ebenda ['e:bəndaː], *adv.* in the same place.

ebendeswegen ['e:bəndɛsveːgən], *adv.* for that very reason.

Ebene ['e:bənə], *f.* (—, *pl.* —n) plain; level ground; (*Maths.*) plane; *schiefe* —, inclined plane.

ebenfalls ['e:bənfals], *adv.* likewise, also, too, as well.

Ebenholz ['e:bənhɔlts], *n.* (—es, *no pl.*) ebony.

Ebenmaß ['e:bənmaːs], *n.* (—es, *pl.* —e) symmetry.

ebenmäßig ['e:bənmɛːsɪç], *adj.* symmetrical.

ebenso ['e:bənzoː], *adv.* in the same way; — *wie*, just as ...

Eber ['e:bər], *m.* (—s, *pl.* —) (*Zool.*) boar.

Eberesche ['e:bərɛʃə], *f.* (—, *pl.* —n) (*Bot.*) mountain ash, rowan.

ebnen ['e:bnən], *v.a.* even out, level; smoothe.

echt [ɛçt], *adj.* genuine, real, true, authentic, pure.

Ecke ['ɛkə], *f.* (—, *pl.* —en) corner, nook.

eckig ['ɛkɪç], *adj.* angular.

Eckzahn ['ɛktsaːn], *m.* (—s, *pl.* —e) eye tooth; canine tooth.

Eckziegel ['ɛktsiːgəl], *m.* (—s, *pl.* —) (*Build.*) header.

edel ['e:dəl], *adj.* noble; well-born, aristocratic; (*metal*) precious.

Edelmann ['e:dəlman], *m.* (—s, *pl.* Edelleute) nobleman, aristocrat.

Edelmut ['e:dəlmuːt], *m.* (—s, *no pl.*) generosity, magnanimity.

Edelstein ['e:dəlʃtain], *m.* (—s, *pl.* —e) precious stone, jewel.

Edeltanne ['e:dəltanə], *f.* (—, *pl.* —n) (*Bot.*) silver fir.

Edelweiß ['e:dəlvais], *n.* (—sses, *no pl.*) (*Bot.*) edelweiss; lion's foot.

Eduard ['e:duart], *m.* Edward.

Efeu ['e:fɔy], *m.* (—s, *no pl.*) (*Bot.*) ivy.

Effekten [ɛ'fɛktən], *m. pl.* goods and chattels; effects; stocks, securities.

Effektenbörse [ɛ'fɛktənbœrzə], *f.* (—, *pl.* —n) Stock Exchange.

Effekthascherei [ɛ'fɛkthaʃərai], *f.* (—, *pl.* —en) sensationalism, clap-trap.

effektuieren [ɛfɛktu'iːrən], *v.a.* (*Comm.*) execute, effectuate.

egal [e'gaːl], *adj.* equal; all the same.

Egge ['ɛgə], *f.* (—, *pl.* —n) harrow.

Egoismus [ego'ɪsmus], *m.* (—, *no pl.*) selfishness, egoism.

egoistisch [ego'ɪstɪʃ], *adj.* selfish, egoistic(al).

Ehe ['e:ə], *f.* (—, *pl.* —n) marriage.

ehe ['e:ə], *conj.* before; *adv.* formerly; *je* —*r*, *desto besser*, the sooner, the better.

Ehebrecher ['e:əbrɛçər], *m.* (—s, *pl.* —) adulterer.

Ehebruch ['e:əbrux], *m.* (—s, *pl.* —e) adultery.

Ehefrau ['e:əfrau], *f.* (—, *pl.* —en) wife, spouse, consort.

Ehegatte ['e:əgatə], *m.* (—n, *pl.* —n) husband, spouse.

ehelich ['e:əlɪç], *adj.* matrimonial; (*children*) legitimate.

Ehelosigkeit ['e:əloːzɪçkait], *f.* (—, *no pl.*) celibacy.

ehemalig ['e:əmaːlɪç], *adj.* former, late.

ehemals ['e:əmaːls], *adv.* formerly, once, of old.

Ehemann ['e:əman], *m.* (—s, *pl.* ̈er) husband.

ehern ['e:ərn], *adj.* brazen; of brass, of bronze.

Ehestand ['e:əʃtant], *m.* (—s, *no pl.*) matrimony.

ehestens ['e:əstəns], *adv.* as soon as possible.

Ehre ['e:rə], *f.* (—, *pl.* —n) honour, reputation, respect, distinction, glory.

ehren ['e:rən], *v.a.* honour, respect, esteem; *sehr geehrter Herr*, dear Sir.

Ehrenbezeigung ['e:rənbətsaigun], *f.* (—, *pl.* —en) mark of respect; (*Mil.*) salute.

Ehrenbürger ['e:rənbyrgər], *m.* (—s, *pl.* —) honorary citizen *or* freeman.

Ehrendame ['e:rəndaːmə], *f.* (—, *pl.* —n) maid of honour.

Ehrenerklärung ['e:rənɛrklɛːrun], *f.* (—, *pl.* —en) reparation, apology.

Ehrengericht ['e:rəngərɪçt], *n.* (—s, *pl.* —e) court of honour.

ehrenhaft ['e:rənhaft], *adj.* honourable, worthy.

Ehrenpreis ['e:rənprais], *m.* (—es, *pl.* —e) prize; (*no pl.*) (*Bot.*) speedwell.

Ehrenrettung ['e:rənrɛtun], *f.* (—, *pl.* —en) vindication.

ehrenrührig ['e:rənryːrɪç], *adj.* defamatory, calumnious.

ehrenvoll ['e:rənfɔl], *adj.* honourable.

ehrenwert ['e:rənvɛrt], *adj.* honourable, respectable.

ehrerbietig ['e:rɛrbiːtɪç], *adj.* reverential, respectful.

Ehrfurcht ['e:rfurçt], *f.* (—, *no pl.*) reverence, awe.

Ehrgefühl ['e:rgəfyːl], *n.* (—s, *no pl.*) sense of honour.

Ehrgeiz ['e:rgaits], *m.* (—es, *no pl.*) ambition.

ehrlich ['e:rlɪç], *adj.* honest; — *währt am längsten*, honesty is the best policy.

ehrlos ['e:rloːs], *adj.* dishonourable, infamous.

ehrsam ['e:rzaːm], *adj.* respectable, honourable.

Ehrwürden ['e:rvyrdən], *m. & f.* (*form of address*) *Euer* —, Reverend Sir, Your Reverence.

ehrwürdig ['e:rvyrdɪç], *adj.* venerable, reverend.

Ei [ai], *n.* (—s, *pl.* —er) egg, ovum.

ei [ai], *int.* ay, indeed.

Eibe ['aibə], *f.* (—, *pl.* —n) (*Bot.*) yew.

Eichamt ['aiçamt], *n.* (—s, *pl.* ̈er) office of weights and measures; (*Am.*) bureau of standards.

Eichapfel ['aɪçapfəl], *m.* (—s, *pl.* ⁀) oak apple.

Eiche ['aɪçə], *f.* (—, *pl.* —n) (*Bot.*) oak.

Eichel ['aɪçəl], *f.* (—, *pl.* —n) acorn; (*Anat.*) glans; (*Cards*) clubs.

eichen (1) ['aɪçən], *v.a.* gauge, calibrate.

eichen (2) ['aɪçən], *adj.* made of oak.

Eichhörnchen ['aɪçhœrnçən] or **Eichkätzchen** ['aɪçkɛtsçən], *n.* (—s, *pl.* —) squirrel.

Eid [aɪt], *m.* (—es, *pl.* —e) oath; *falscher* —, perjury.

Eidam ['aɪdam], *m.* (—s, *pl.* —e) (*obs.*) son-in-law.

eidbrüchig ['aɪtbryçɪç], *adj.* guilty of perjury.

Eidechse ['aɪdɛksə], *f.* (—, *pl.* —n) lizard.

Eidesleistung ['aɪdəslaɪstuŋ], *f.* (—, *pl.* —en) affidavit.

Eidgenosse ['aɪtgənɔsə], *m.* (—n, ⁀*pl.* —n) confederate.

Eidgenossenschaft ['aɪtgənɔsənʃaft], *f.* (—, *pl.* —en) confederacy.

eidlich ['aɪtlɪç], *adj.* by oath, sworn.

Eidotter ['aɪdɔtər], *m. & n.* (—s, *pl.* —) yolk of an egg.

Eierbecher ['aɪərbɛçər], *m.* (—s, *pl.* —) egg cup.

Eierkuchen ['aɪərku:xən], *m.* (—s, *pl.* —) omelet(te), pancake.

Eierschale ['aɪərʃa:lə], *f.* (—, *pl.* —n) egg shell.

Eierspeise ['aɪərʃpaɪzə], *f.* (—, *pl.* —n) dish prepared with eggs.

Eierstock ['aɪərʃtɔk], *m.* (—s, *pl.* ⁀e) ovary.

Eifer ['aɪfər], *m.* (—s, *no pl.*) zeal, eagerness, ardour, haste, passion, vehemence.

Eiferer ['aɪfərər], *m.* (—s, *pl.* —) zealot.

eifern ['aɪfərn], *v.n.* be zealous; *gegen einen* —, inveigh against s.o.

eiförmig ['aɪfœrmɪç], *adj.* oval, egg-shaped.

eifrig ['aɪfrɪç], *adj.* zealous, ardent, eager.

Eigelb ['aɪgɛlp], *n.* (—s, *pl.* —) yolk of (an) egg.

eigen ['aɪgən], *adj.* own; particular, peculiar.

Eigenart ['aɪgəna:rt], *f.* (—, *pl.* —en) peculiarity; idiosyncrasy.

eigenhändig ['aɪgənhɛndɪç], *adj.* with o.'s own hand.

Eigenheit ['aɪgənhaɪt], *f.* (—, *pl.* —en) peculiarity; idiosyncrasy.

eigenmächtig ['aɪgənmɛçtɪç], *adj.* arbitrary, autocratic, high-handed.

Eigenname ['aɪgənna:mə], *m.* (—ns, *pl.* —n) proper name.

Eigennutz ['aɪgənnuts], *m.* (—es, *no pl.*) self-interest, selfishness.

eigennützig ['aɪgənnytsɪç], *adj.* selfish, self-interested, self-seeking.

eigens ['aɪgəns], *adv.* particularly, specially.

Eigenschaft ['aɪgənʃaft], *f.* (—, *pl.* —en) quality, peculiarity; property.

Eigenschaftswort ['aɪgənʃaftsvɔrt], *n.* (—s, *pl.* ⁀er) (*Gram.*) adjective.

Eigensinn ['aɪgənzɪn], *m.* (—s, *no pl.*) obstinacy.

eigentlich ['aɪgəntlɪç], *adj.* true, real; exact, literal.

Eigentum ['aɪgəntu:m], *n.* (—s, *pl.* ⁀er) property, possession, estate.

Eigentümer ['aɪgənty:mər], *m.* (—s, *pl.* —s) owner, proprietor.

eigenwillig ['aɪgənvɪlɪç], *adj.* self-willed.

eignen ['aɪgnən], *v.r. sich — für (zu)*, suit, fit, be suitable *or* fit for (to).

Eilbote ['aɪlbo:tə], *m.* (—n, *pl.* —n) special messenger.

Eile ['aɪlə], *f.* (—, *no pl.*) haste, hurry.

eilen ['aɪlən], *v.n.* (*aux.* sein), *v.r.* (*sich* —), hasten, hurry; be urgent.

eilends ['aɪlənts], *adv.* hastily.

eilfertig ['aɪlfɛrtɪç], *adj.* hasty.

Eilgut ['aɪlgu:t], *n.* (—s, *pl.* ⁀er) express goods.

eilig ['aɪlɪç], *adj.* hasty, speedy; pressing, urgent.

Eilzug ['aɪltsu:k], *m.* (—s, *pl.* ⁀e) fast train.

Eimer ['aɪmər], *m.* (—s, *pl.* —) pail, bucket.

ein(e) ['aɪn(ə)], *indef. art.* a, an; *was für* —; what kind of a(n). — *num. adj.* one; — *jeder*, each one.

einander [aɪn'andər], *adv.* each other, one another.

einarbeiten ['aɪnarbaɪtən], *v.a.* train, familiarize s.o with. —*v.r.* (*aux.* haben) *sich* —, familiarize o.s.

einäschern ['aɪnɛʃərn], *v.a.* reduce to ashes, incinerate; cremate.

einatmen ['aɪna:tmən], *v.a.* breathe in, inhale.

einätzen ['aɪnɛtsən], *v.a.* etch in.

einäugig ['aɪnɔygɪç], *adj.* one-eyed.

Einbahnstraße ['aɪnba:nʃtra:sə], *f.* (—, *pl.* —n) one-way street.

Einband ['aɪnbant], *m.* (—s, *pl.* ⁀e) binding, cover of book.

einbändig ['aɪnbɛndɪç], *adj.* in one volume.

einbauen ['aɪnbauən], *v.a.* build in.

einbegreifen ['aɪnbəgraɪfən], *v.a. irr.* include, comprise.

einberufen ['aɪnbəru:fən], *v.a. irr.* convene, convoke; (*Mil.*) call up.

einbeziehen ['aɪnbətsi:ən], *v.a. irr.* include.

einbiegen ['aɪnbi:gən], *v.n. irr.* turn into (road).

einbilden ['aɪnbɪldən], *v.r. sich* —, imagine, fancy.

Einbildung ['aɪnbɪlduŋ], *f.* (—, *pl.* —en) imagination, fancy, delusion; conceit.

einbinden ['aɪnbɪndən], *v.a. irr.* (*book*) bind.

Einblick ['aɪnblɪk], *m.* (—s, *no pl.*) insight.

Einbrecher ['aɪnbrɛçər], *m.* (—s, *pl.* —) burglar; intruder.

Einbrenne

Einbrenne [ˈaɪnbrɛnə], *f.* (—, *pl.* —n) thickening of soup.

einbringen [ˈaɪnbrɪŋən], *v.a. irr.* bring in, yield, fetch (a price); *wieder* —, retrieve.

einbrocken [ˈaɪnbrɔkən], *v.a.* crumble; *einem etwas* —, (*fig.*) get s.o. into trouble.

Einbruch [ˈaɪnbrux], *m.* (—s, *pl.* ˙e) breaking-in; burglary, house-breaking.

Einbuchtung [ˈaɪnbuxtuŋ], *f.* (—, *pl.* —en) bight, bay.

einbürgern [ˈaɪnbyrgərn], *v.a.* naturalise.

Einbuße [ˈaɪnbuːsə], *f.* (—, *pl.* —n) loss.

einbüßen [ˈaɪnbyːsən], *v.a.* suffer a loss from, lose, forfeit.

eindämmen [ˈaɪndɛmən], *v.a.* dam in (*or* up).

Eindecker [ˈaɪndɛkər], *m.* (—s, *pl.* —) (*Aviat.*) monoplane.

eindeutig [ˈaɪndɔʏtɪç], *adj.* unequivocal, unambiguous.

eindrängen [ˈaɪndrɛŋən], *v.r. sich* —, intrude (into), force o.'s way in (to), interfere.

eindrillen [ˈaɪndrɪlən], *v.a. einem etwas* —, drum s.th. into s.o.

eindringen [ˈaɪndrɪŋən], *v.n. irr.* (*aux.* sein) enter, intrude; invade; penetrate.

eindringlich [ˈaɪndrɪŋlɪç], *adj.* forceful, urgent; impressive.

Eindruck [ˈaɪndruk], *m.* (—s, *pl.* ˙e) impression.

eindrücken [ˈaɪndrykən], *v.a.* press in, squeeze in.

eindrucksfähig [ˈaɪndruksfɛːɪç], *adj.* impressionable.

einengen [ˈaɪnɛŋən], *v.a.* compress, limit, confine, cramp.

Einer [ˈaɪnər], *m.* (—s, *pl.* —) (*Maths.*) digit, unit.

einerlei [ˈaɪnərlaɪ], *adj.* the same, all the same.

einerseits [ˈaɪnərzaɪts], *adv.* on the one hand.

einfach [ˈaɪnfax], *adj.* single; simple, plain, uncomplicated; modest, homely.

einfädeln [ˈaɪnfɛːdəln], *v.a.* thread.

einfahren [ˈaɪnfaːrən], *v.n. irr.* (*aux.* sein) drive in, enter. — *v.a.* run in (new car).

Einfahrt [ˈaɪnfaːrt], *f.* (—, *pl.* —en) entrance, gateway, drive; (*Min.*) descent.

Einfall [ˈaɪnfal], *m.* (—s, *pl.* ˙e) falling-in, downfall, fall; (*Mil.*) invasion; (*fig.*) idea, inspiration.

einfallen [ˈaɪnfalən], *v.n. irr.* (*aux.* sein) fall in, fall into; (*Mil.*) invade; (*fig.*) occur to s.o.

Einfalt [ˈaɪnfalt], *f.* (—, *no pl.*) simplicity; silliness.

Einfaltspinsel [ˈaɪnfaltspɪnzəl], *m.* (—s, *pl.* —) simpleton, dunce.

einfangen [ˈaɪnfaŋən], *v.a. irr.* catch, get hold of.

einfarbig [ˈaɪnfarbɪç], *adj.* of one colour; monochrome.

einfassen [ˈaɪnfasən], *v.a.* border, trim; (*diamonds*) set.

Einfassung [ˈaɪnfasuŋ], *f.* (—, *pl.* —en) bordering, trimming, edging, framing.

einfetten [ˈaɪnfɛtən], *v.a.* grease, lubricate.

einfinden [ˈaɪnfɪndən], *v.r. irr. sich* —, appear, be present.

einflechten [ˈaɪnflɛçtən], *v.a. irr.* plait; (*fig.*) insert.

einfließen [ˈaɪnfliːsən], *v.n. irr.* (*aux.* sein) flow in; — *lassen*, (*fig.*) mention casually, slip in (a word).

einflößen [ˈaɪnfløːsən], *v.a.* infuse; (*fig.*) instil, inspire with.

Einfluß [ˈaɪnflus], *m.* (—sses, *pl.* ˙sse) influx; (*fig.*) influence.

einflußreich [ˈaɪnflusraɪç], *adj.* influential.

einflüstern [ˈaɪnflystərn], *v.n.* suggest, insinuate.

einförmig [ˈaɪnfœrmɪç], *adj.* uniform; monotonous.

einfriedigen [ˈaɪnfriːdɪgən], *v.a.* fence in, enclose.

einfügen [ˈaɪnfyːgən], *v.a.* insert, include, fit in. — *v.r. sich* —, adapt o.s., become a part of.

Einfühlungsvermögen [ˈaɪnfyːluŋsfermøːgən], *n.* (—s, *no pl.*) (*Phil.*) empathy, sympathetic understanding.

Einfuhr [ˈaɪnfuːr], *f.* (—, *pl.* —en) importation, import.

einführen [ˈaɪnfyːrən], *v.a.* introduce; (*goods*) import.

Einführung [ˈaɪnfyːruŋ], *f.* (—, *pl.* —en) introduction; (*goods*) importation.

einfüllen [ˈaɪnfylən], *v.a.* fill in, pour into, bottle.

Eingabe [ˈaɪngaːbə], *f.* (—, *pl.* —n) petitition; application.

Eingang [ˈaɪngaŋ], *m.* (—s, *pl.* ˙e) entry, entrance; arrival.

eingangs [ˈaɪngaŋs], *adv.* in *or* at the beginning.

eingeben [ˈaɪngeːbən], *v.a. irr.* inspire (with); (*petition*) present, deliver; (*claim*) file; (*complaint*) bring; (*medicine*) administer.

eingeboren [ˈaɪngəboːrən], *adj.* native; (*Theol.*) only-begotten.

Eingeborene [ˈaɪngəboːrənə], *m.* (—n, *pl.* —n) native.

Eingebrachte [ˈaɪngəbraxtə], *n.* (—n, *no pl.*) dowry.

Eingebung [ˈaɪngeːbuŋ], *f.* (—, *pl.* —en) inspiration.

eingedenk [ˈaɪngədɛŋk], *prep.* (*Genit.*) mindful of, remembering.

eingefleischt [ˈaɪngəflaɪʃt], *adj.* inveterate, confirmed.

eingehen [ˈaɪngeːən], *v.n. irr.* (*aux.* sein) (*Comm.*) arrive; *auf etwas* —, enter into s.th., agree to s.th.; *auf etwas näher* —, enter into the details of s.th.; (*animals, plants*) die; (*cloth*) shrink.

eingehend [ˈaɪnɡeːənt], *adj.* thorough, exhaustive.

Eingemachte [ˈaɪnɡəmaxtə], *n.* (—n, *no pl.*) preserve.

eingenommen [ˈaɪnɡənɔmən], *adj.* enthusiastic for, infatuated with; — *von sich*, conceited.

Eingeschlossenheit [ˈaɪnɡəʃlɔsənhaɪt], *f.* (—, *no pl.*) isolation, seclusion.

eingeschrieben [ˈaɪnɡəʃriːbən], *adj.* registered (letter).

eingesessen [ˈaɪnɡəzɛsən], *adj.* old-established; resident.

Eingeständnis [ˈaɪnɡəʃtɛntnɪs], *n.* (—ses, *pl.* —se) confession.

eingestehen [ˈaɪnɡəʃteːən], *v.a. irr.* confess to, avow.

Eingeweide [ˈaɪnɡəvaɪdə], *n. pl.* bowels, intestines.

eingewöhnen [ˈaɪnɡəvøːnən], *v.r. sich* —, accustom o.s. to, get used to.

eingießen [ˈaɪnɡiːsən], *v.a. irr.* pour in; pour out.

eingleisig [ˈaɪnɡlaɪzɪç], *adj.* single-track.

eingliedern [ˈaɪnɡliːdərn], *v.r. sich* —, adapt o.s., fit in.

eingreifen [ˈaɪnɡraɪfən], *v.n. irr.* intervene in; interfere with, encroach on.

Eingriff [ˈaɪnɡrɪf], *m.* (—s, *pl.* —e) intervention, encroachment, infringement; (*Med.*) operation.

Einguß [ˈaɪnɡus], *m.* (—sses, *pl.* ⸚sse) infusion; enema.

einhaken [ˈaɪnhaːkən], *v.a.* hook in. — *v.r. sich* —, (*fig.*) take a p.'s arm.

Einhalt [ˈaɪnhalt], *m.* (—s, *no pl.*) stop, check, prohibition, cessation; — *gebieten*, check, suppress.

einhalten [ˈaɪnhaltən], *v.a. irr.* observe, adhere to.

einhändigen [ˈaɪnhɛndɪɡən], *v.a.* hand in, deliver.

einhauen [ˈaɪnhauən], *v.a. irr.* hew in, break open.

Einhebung [ˈaɪnheːbuŋ], *f.* (—, *pl.* —en) (*taxes*) collection.

einheften [ˈaɪnhɛftən], *v.a.* sew in, stitch in; (*papers*) file.

einhegen [ˈaɪnheːɡən], *v.a.* fence in, hedge in.

einheimisch [ˈaɪnhaɪmɪʃ], *adj.* native; (*Bot.*) indigenous.

einheimsen [ˈaɪnhaɪmzən], *v.a.* reap.

Einheit [ˈaɪnhaɪt], *f.* (—, *pl.* —en) unit; unity.

einheitlich [ˈaɪnhaɪtlɪç], *adj.* uniform, consistent.

einheizen [ˈaɪnhaɪtsən], *v.a., v.n.* heat the stove, light the fire.

einhellig [ˈaɪnhɛlɪç], *adj.* unanimous, harmonious.

einher [aɪnˈheːr], *adv.* forth, along, on.

einholen [ˈaɪnhoːlən], *v.a.* obtain; catch up with. — *v.n.* go shopping.

Einhorn [ˈaɪnhɔrn], *n.* (—s, *pl.* ⸚er) unicorn.

einhüllen [ˈaɪnhylən], *v.a.* wrap up, cover, envelop.

einig [ˈaɪnɪç], *adj.* at one. — *adv.* in agreement.

einige [ˈaɪnɪɡə], *adj.* some, several.

einigemal [ˈaɪnɪɡəmaːl], *adv.* several times.

einigen [ˈaɪnɪɡən], *v.a.* unite. — *v.r. sich* — *mit*, come to an agreement with.

einigermaßen [aɪnɪɡərˈmaːsən], *adv.* to a certain extent.

Einigkeit [ˈaɪnɪçkaɪt], *f.* (—, *no pl.*) union, unity, unanimity, harmony.

Einigung [ˈaɪnɪɡuŋ], *f.* (—, *pl.* —en) agreement; union.

einimpfen [ˈaɪnɪmpfən], *v.a.* inoculate, vaccinate.

einjährig [ˈaɪnjeːrɪç], *adj.* one-year-old; annual.

einkassieren [ˈaɪnkasiːrən], *v.a.* cash (*cheque*), collect (*money*).

Einkauf [ˈaɪnkauf], *m.* (—s, *pl.* ⸚e) purchase, buy.

einkaufen [ˈaɪnkaufən], *v.a.* purchase, buy. — *v.n.* go shopping.

Einkäufer [ˈaɪnkɔyfər], *m.* (—s, *pl.* —) (*Comm.*) purchaser, buyer.

Einkehr [ˈaɪnkeːr], *f.* (—, *pl.* —en) stopping (at an inn); (*fig.*) meditation.

einkehren [ˈaɪnkeːrən], *v.n.* (*aux.* sein) stop *or* put up (at an inn).

einkerkern [ˈaɪnkɛrkərn], *v.a.* imprison.

einklagen [ˈaɪnklaːɡən], *v.a.* (*Law*) sue for (money).

einklammern [ˈaɪnklamərn], *v.a.* bracket, enclose in brackets.

Einklang [ˈaɪnklaŋ], *m.* (—s, *no pl.*) accord, unison, harmony.

einkleben [ˈaɪnkleːbən], *v.a.* paste in.

einkleiden [ˈaɪnklaɪdən], *v.a.* clothe; (*fig.*) invest; *sich* — *lassen*, (*Eccl.*) take the veil.

einklemmen [ˈaɪnklemən], *v.a.* squeeze in, jam in.

einkochen [ˈaɪnkɔxən], *v.a.* preserve. — *v.n.* (*aux.* sein) boil down.

Einkommen [ˈaɪnkɔmən], *n.* (—s, *no pl.*) income, revenue.

einkommen [ˈaɪnkɔmən], *v.n. irr.* (*aux.* sein) *bei einem wegen etwas* —, apply to s.o. for s.th.

einkreisen [ˈaɪnkraɪzən], *v.a.* encircle, isolate.

Einkünfte [ˈaɪnkynftə], *f. pl.* income, revenue; emoluments.

einladen [ˈaɪnlaːdən], *v.a. irr.* load in; invite.

Einlage [ˈaɪnlaːɡə], *f.* (—, *pl.* —n) (*letter*) enclosure; (*Theat.*) addition to programme; (*game*) stake; (*Comm.*) investment.

einlagern [ˈaɪnlaːɡərn], *v.a.* (*goods*) store, warehouse; (*Mil.*) billet, quarter.

Einlaß [ˈaɪnlas], *m.* (—sses, *pl.* ⸚sse) admission, admittance; (*water*) inlet.

einlassen [ˈaɪnlasən], *v.a.* admit, allow in; let in. — *v.r. sich auf etwas* —, engage in s.th., enter into s.th.

Einlauf [ˈaɪnlauf], *m.* (—s, *no pl.*) entering; (*Med.*) enema.

55

einlaufen

einlaufen ['aɪnlaufən], *v.n. irr. (aux. sein) (Naut.)* enter harbour, put into port; *(material)* shrink.

einleben ['aɪnle:bən], *v.r. sich —,* grow accustomed to, settle down, acclimatise o.s.

einlegen ['aɪnle:gən], *v.a.* put in, lay in; enclose; *(money)* deposit; *(food)* pickle, preserve; *Fürbitte —,* intercede; *eingelegte Arbeit,* inlaid work.

einleiten ['aɪnlaɪtən], *v.a.* begin, introduce; institute.

Einleitung ['aɪnlaɪtuŋ], *f. (—, pl. —en)* introduction; *(book)* preface; *(Mus.)* prelude; *(Law)* institution.

einlenken ['aɪnleŋkən], *v.n.* turn in; give in, come round.

einleuchten ['aɪnlɔʏçtən], *v.n.* become clear.

einlösen ['aɪnlø:zən], *v.a.* redeem; *(bill)* honour; *(cheque)* cash.

einmachen ['aɪnmaxən], *v.a.* preserve.

einmal ['aɪnma:l], *adv.* once; *es war —,* once upon a time; *auf —,* suddenly; *noch —,* once more; *nicht —,* not even.

Einmaleins ['aɪnma:laɪns], *n. (—es, no pl.)* multiplication table.

einmalig ['aɪnma:lɪç], *adv.* unique, unrepeatable.

Einmaster ['aɪnmastər], *m. (—s, pl. —) (Naut.)* brigantine, cutter.

einmauern ['aɪnmauərn], *v.a.* wall in, immure.

einmengen ['aɪnmeŋən], *v.r. sich —,* meddle with, interfere.

einmieten ['aɪnmi:tən], *v.r. sich —,* take lodgings.

einmischen ['aɪnmɪʃən], *v.r. sich —,* meddle (with), interfere.

einmütig ['aɪnmy:tɪç], *adj.* unanimous, in harmony, united.

Einnahme ['aɪnna:mə], *f. (—, pl. —n)* income, revenue; receipts; *(Mil.)* occupation, capture.

einnehmen ['aɪnne:mən], *v.a. irr.* take in; *(money)* receive; *(medicine)* take; *(taxes)* collect; *(place)* take up, occupy; *(Mil.)* occupy, conquer; *(fig.)* captivate, fascinate.

einnehmend ['aɪnne:mənt], *adj.* fetching, engaging, charming.

einnicken ['aɪnnɪkən], *v.n. (aux. sein)* nod *or* doze off.

einnisten ['aɪnnɪstən], *v.r. sich —,* nestle down; *(fig.)* settle in a place.

Einöde ['aɪnø:də], *f. (—, pl. —n)* desert, solitude.

einordnen ['aɪnɔrdnən], *v.a.* place in order, file, classify.

einpauken ['aɪnpaukən], *v.a.* cram.

einpferchen ['aɪnpferçən], *v.a.* pen in, coop up.

einpökeln ['aɪnpø:kəln], *v.a.* salt, pickle.

einprägen ['aɪnprɛ:gən], *v.a.* imprint, impress.

einquartieren ['aɪnkvarti:rən], *v.a. (Mil.)* quarter, billet.

einrahmen ['aɪnra:mən], *v.a.* frame.

einräumen ['aɪnrɔʏmən], *v.a.* stow (things) away; *einem etwas —,* concede s.th. to s.o.

Einrede ['aɪnre:də], *f. (—, pl. —n)* objection.

einreden ['aɪnre:dən], *v.a. einem etwas —,* persuade s.o. to. *— v.r. sich etwas —,* get s.th. into o.'s head.

einreichen ['aɪnraɪçən], *v.a.* hand in, deliver; tender.

einreihen ['aɪnraɪən], *v.a.* place in line, arrange.

einreihig ['aɪnraɪɪç], *adj.* consisting of a single row; *(Tail.)* single-breasted (suit).

einreißen ['aɪnraɪsən], *v.a. irr.* make a tear in; *(houses)* pull down. *— v.n. (fig.)* gain ground.

einrenken ['aɪnreŋkən], *v.a. (Med.)* set; *(fig.)* settle.

einrichten ['aɪnrɪçtən], *v.a.* put in order, arrange; equip, set up; furnish.

Einrichtung ['aɪnrɪçtuŋ], *f. (—, pl. —en)* arrangement, management; furnishing; *(pl.)* facilities; equipment, amenities.

einrücken ['aɪnrykən], *v.n. (aux. sein)* march in. *— v.a.* insert (in the newspaper).

Eins [aɪns], *f. (—, pl. —en, —er)* one; *(Sch.)* top marks.

eins [aɪns], *num.* one; *es ist mir alles —,* it is all the same to me.

einsalzen ['aɪnzaltsən], *v.a.* salt, pickle, cure.

einsam ['aɪnza:m], *adj.* lonely, solitary, secluded.

Einsamkeit ['aɪnza:mkaɪt], *f. (—, no pl.)* loneliness, solitude, seclusion.

Einsatz ['aɪnzats], *m. (—es, pl. ⁀e)* *(game)* stake, pool; *(dress)* lace inset; *(Mus.)* entry (of a voice), starting intonation; *(Mil.)* sortie, mission.

einsaugen ['aɪnzaugən], *v.a.* suck in; *(fig.)* imbibe.

einsäumen ['aɪnzɔʏmən], *v.a.* hem (in).

einschalten ['aɪnʃaltən], *v.a.* insert, interpolate; switch on; put in gear.

einschärfen ['aɪnʃerfən], *v.a.* impress s.th. on s.o.

einschätzen ['aɪnʃetsən], *v.a.* assess.

einschenken ['aɪnʃeŋkən], *v.a.* pour in *or* out, fill.

einschieben ['aɪnʃi:bən], *v.a.* push in; interpolate, insert.

Einschiebsel ['aɪnʃi:psəl], *n. (—s, pl. —)* interpolation; interpolated part.

einschiffen ['aɪnʃɪfən], *v.a.* embark; *(goods)* ship. *— v.r. sich —,* go aboard, embark.

einschlafen ['aɪnʃla:fən], *v.n. irr. (aux. sein)* fall asleep, go to sleep.

einschläfern ['aɪnʃlɛ:fərn], *v.a.* lull to sleep.

Einschlag ['aɪnʃla:k], *m. (—s, pl. ⁀e)* cover, envelope; *(weaving)* woof, weft; explosion; strike; *(fig.)* streak (of character); touch.

einschlagen ['aɪnʃlaːgən], *v.a. irr.* knock in; (*nail*) drive in; (*parcel*) wrap up; (*road*) take. — *v.n.* (*lightning*) strike; be a success.

einschlägig ['aɪnʃlɛːgɪç], *adj.* bearing on (the subject), pertinent.

einschleppen ['aɪnʃlɛpən], *v.a.* (*disease*) bring in, introduce.

einschließen ['aɪnʃliːsən], *v.a. irr.* lock in *or* up; (*enemy*) surround; (*fig.*) include.

einschlummern ['aɪnʃlumərn], *v.n.* (*aux.* sein) doze off, fall asleep.

Einschluß ['aɪnʃlus], *m.* (—sses, *pl.* ⁝sse) inclusion; *mit — von,* inclusive of.

einschmeicheln ['aɪnʃmaɪçəln], *v.r. sich bei einem —,* ingratiate o.s. with s.o.

einschmelzen ['aɪnʃmɛltsən], *v.a. irr.* melt down.

einschmieren ['aɪnʃmiːrən], *v.a.* smear, grease, oil; (*sore*) put ointment on.

einschneidend ['aɪnʃnaɪdənt], *adj.* important, sweeping, incisive, trenchant.

einschneidig ['aɪnʃnaɪdɪç], *adj.* single-edged.

Einschnitt ['aɪnʃnɪt], *m.* (—s, *pl.* —e) incision, cut, notch; (*verse*) caesura.

einschnüren ['aɪnʃnyːrən], *v.a.* lace up; (*parcel*) tie up.

einschränken ['aɪnʃrɛŋkən], *v.a.* confine, limit, restrict. — *v.r. sich —,* curtail o.'s expenses, economize.

einschrauben ['aɪnʃraʊbən], *v.a.* screw in.

einschreiben ['aɪnʃraɪbən], *v.a. irr.* write in *or* down, inscribe; (*letter*) register. — *v.r. sich —,* enter o.'s name; enrol.

Einschreibesendung ['aɪnʃraɪbəzɛnduŋ], *f.* (—, *pl.* —en) registered letter, registered parcel.

einschreiten ['aɪnʃraɪtən], *v.n. irr.* (*aux.* sein) step in, intervene.

einschrumpfen ['aɪnʃrumpfən], *v.n.* (*aux.* sein) shrink, shrivel.

einschüchtern ['aɪnʃyçtərn], *v.a.* intimidate, overawe.

Einschuß ['aɪnʃus], *m.* (—sses, *pl.* ⁝sse) share, advance of capital; (*weaving*) woof, weft.

einsegnen ['aɪnzeːgnən], *v.a.* consecrate, bless; (*Eccl.*) confirm.

Einsehen ['aɪnzeːən], *n.* (—s, *no pl.*) realisation; *ein — haben,* be reasonable.

einsehen ['aɪnzeːən], *v.a. irr.* look into, glance over; (*fig.*) comprehend, realise.

einseifen ['aɪnzaɪfən], *v.a.* soap, lather; (*fig.*) take s.o. in.

einseitig ['aɪnzaɪtɪç], *adj.* one-sided; (*fig.*) one-track (mind).

Einsenkung ['aɪnzɛŋkuŋ], *f.* (—, *pl.* —en) depression (of the ground).

einsetzen ['aɪnzɛtsən], *v.a.* put in, set in; institute, establish; (*money*) stake; (*Hort.*) plant; (*office*) install s.o. — *v.n.* begin.

Einsetzung ['aɪnzɛtsuŋ], *f.* (—, *pl.* —en) (*office*) investiture, installation; institution.

Einsicht ['aɪnzɪçt], *f.* (—, *no pl.*) inspection, examination; insight, understanding.

einsichtig ['aɪnzɪçtɪç], *adj.* intelligent, sensible, judicious.

Einsichtnahme ['aɪnzɪçtnaːmə], *f. zur —,* (*Comm.*) on approval, for inspection.

Einsiedler ['aɪnziːdlər], *m.* (—s, *pl.* —) hermit, recluse.

einsilbig ['aɪnzɪlbɪç], *adj.* monosyllabic; (*fig.*) taciturn, laconic.

einspannen ['aɪnʃpanən], *v.a.* stretch in a frame; harness; (*coll.*) put to work.

Einspänner ['aɪnʃpɛnər], *m.* (—s, *pl.* —) one-horse vehicle; one-horse cab, fiacre.

einsperren ['aɪnʃpɛrən], *v.a.* lock in, shut up, imprison.

einspinnen ['aɪnʃpɪnən], *v.r. irr. sich —,* spin a cocoon.

einsprengen ['aɪnʃprɛŋən], *v.a.* sprinkle.

einspringen ['aɪnʃprɪŋən], *v.n. irr.* (*aux.* sein) *auf einen —,* leap at; (*lock*) catch, snap; *für einen —,* deputize for s.o.

Einspruch ['aɪnʃprux], *m.* (—s, *pl.* ⁝e) objection, protest; — *erheben,* protest; (*Law*) appeal (against).

einspurig ['aɪnʃpuːrɪç], *adj.* (*Railw.*) single-track line.

einst [aɪnst], *adv.* (*past*) once, once upon a time; (*future*) some day.

Einstand ['aɪnʃtant], *m.* (—s, *no pl.*) (*Tennis*) deuce.

einstecken ['aɪnʃtɛkən], *v.a.* put in; pocket; post (a letter).

einstehen ['aɪnʃteːən], *v.a. irr. zu etwas —,* answer for s.th.; *für einen —,* stand security for s.o.

einsteigen ['aɪnʃtaɪgən], *v.n. irr.* (*aux.* sein) get in, climb on; board.

einstellen ['aɪnʃtɛlən], *v.a.* put in; (*persons*) engage, hire; adjust; (*work*) stop, strike; (*payments*) stop; (*hostilities*) suspend, cease fire. — *v.r. sich —,* turn up, appear.

einstellig ['aɪnʃtɛlɪç], *adj.* (*Maths.*) of one digit.

Einstellung ['aɪnʃtɛluŋ], *f.* (—, *pl.* —en) putting in; (*persons*) engagement, hiring; adjustment; (*work*) stoppage, strike; (*payments*) suspension; (*hostilities*) suspension, cessation; (*fig.*) opinion, attitude.

einstig ['aɪnstɪç], *adj.* (*past*) former, late, erstwhile; (*future*) future, to be, to come.

einstimmen ['aɪnʃtɪmən], *v.n.* join in, chime in.

einstimmig ['aɪnʃtɪmɪç], *adj.* (*Mus.*) (for) one voice, unison; (*fig.*) unanimous.

einstmals ['aɪnstmaːls], *adv.* once, formerly.

57

einstöckig

einstöckig ['aɪnʃtœkɪç], *adj.* one-storied.

einstreichen ['aɪnʃtraɪçən], *v.a. irr.* (*money*) take in, pocket.

einstreuen ['aɪnʃtrɔyən], *v.a.* strew; (*fig.*) intersperse.

einstudieren ['aɪnʃtudi:rən], *v.a.* study; (*Theat., Mus.*) rehearse.

einstürmen ['aɪnʃtyrmən], *v.n.* (*aux.* sein) *auf einen* —, rush at, fall upon.

Einsturz ['aɪnʃturts], *m.* (—es, *pl.* ⸚e) fall, crash; subsidence, collapse.

einstürzen ['aɪnʃtyrtsən], *v.n.* (*aux.* sein) fall in, fall into ruin, fall to pieces, collapse.

einstweilen ['aɪnstvaɪlən], *adv.* in the meantime, meanwhile, for the time being, provisionally.

einstweilig ['aɪnstvaɪlɪç], *adj.* temporary, provisional.

eintägig ['aɪntɛːgɪç], *adj.* one-day, ephemeral.

Eintagsfliege ['aɪntaːksfliːgə], *f.* (—, *pl.* —n) dayfly.

eintauschen ['aɪntauʃən], *v.a.* — *gegen,* exchange for, barter for.

einteilen ['aɪntaɪlən], *v.a.* divide; distribute; classify.

eintönig ['aɪntøːnɪç], *adj.* monotonous.

Eintracht ['aɪntraxt], *f.* (—, *no pl.*) concord, harmony.

einträchtig ['aɪntrɛçtɪç], *adj.* united, harmonious.

Eintrag ['aɪntraːk], *m.* (—s, *pl.* ⸚e) entry (in a book); prejudice, damage, detriment.

eintragen ['aɪntraːgən], *v.a. irr.* enter (in a book), register; bring in, yield.

einträglich ['aɪntrɛklɪç], *adj.* profitable, lucrative.

Eintragung ['aɪntraːguŋ], *f.* (—, *pl.* —en) entry (in a book); enrolment.

einträufeln ['aɪntrɔyfəln], *v.a.* instil.

eintreffen ['aɪntrɛfən], *v.n. irr.* (*aux.* sein) arrive; happen, come true.

eintreiben ['aɪntraɪbən], *v.a. irr.* drive home (*cattle*); collect (debts etc.).

eintreten ['aɪntreːtən], *v.n. irr.* (*aux.* sein) step in, enter; happen, take place; *in einen Verein* —, join a club; *für einen* —, speak up for s.o.

einrichtern ['aɪntrɪçtərn], *v.a. einem etwas* —, cram s.th. into s.o.

Eintritt ['aɪntrɪt], *m.* (—s, *no pl.*) entry, entrance; beginning; *kein* —, no admission.

eintrocknen ['aɪntrɔknən], *v.n.* (*aux.* sein) shrivel, dry up.

einüben ['aɪnyːbən], *v.a.* practise, exercise.

einverleiben ['aɪnfɛrlaɪbən], *v.a.* incorporate in, embody in.

Einvernahme ['aɪnfɛrnaːmə], *f.* (—, *pl.* —n) (*Austr.*) *see* **Vernehmung.**

Einvernehmen ['aɪnfɛrneːmən], *n.* (—s, *no pl.*) understanding; *im besten* —, on the best of terms.

einvernehmen ['aɪnfɛrneːmən], *v.a.* (*aux.* haben) (*Austr.*) *see* **vernehmen.**

einverstanden ['aɪnfɛrʃtandən], (*excl.*) agreed! — *adj.* — *sein,* agree.

Einverständnis ['aɪnfɛrʃtɛntnɪs], *n.* (—ses, *no pl.*) consent, agreement, accord.

Einwand ['aɪnvant], *m.* (—s, *pl.* ⸚e) objection, exception; — *erheben,* raise objections.

einwandern ['aɪnvandərn], *v.n.* (*aux.* sein) immigrate.

einwandfrei ['aɪnvantfraɪ], *adj.* irreproachable, unobjectionable.

einwärts ['aɪnvɛrts], *adv.* inward(s).

einwechseln ['aɪnvɛksəln], *v.a.* change, exchange.

einweichen ['aɪnvaɪçən], *v.a.* steep in water, soak.

einweihen ['aɪnvaɪən], *v.a.* dedicate; (*Eccl.*) consecrate; open (formally), inaugurate; initiate (into).

Einweihung ['aɪnvaɪuŋ], *f.* (—, *pl.* —en) (*Eccl.*) consecration; inauguration, formal opening; initiation.

einwenden ['aɪnvɛndən], *v.a. irr.* object to, raise objections, urge against.

einwerfen ['aɪnvɛrfən], *v.a. irr.* throw in; smash in; interject.

einwickeln ['aɪnvɪkəln], *v.a.* wrap up, envelop.

einwilligen ['aɪnvɪlɪgən], *v.n.* consent, assent, agree, accede.

einwirken ['aɪnvɪrkən], *v.n. auf einen* —, influence s.o.

Einwohner ['aɪnvoːnər], *m.* (—s, *pl.* —) inhabitant.

Einwohnerschaft ['aɪnvoːnərʃaft], *f.* (—, *no pl.*) population, inhabitants.

Einwurf ['aɪnvurf], *m.* (—s, *pl.* ⸚e) (*letter box*) opening, slit; slot; objection.

einwurzeln ['aɪnvurtsəln], *v.r. sich* —, take root; *eingewurzelt,* deep-rooted.

Einzahl ['aɪntsaːl], *f.* (—, *no pl.*) singular.

einzahlen ['aɪntsaːlən], *v.a.* pay in, deposit.

einzäunen ['aɪntsɔynən], *v.a.* fence in.

einzeichnen ['aɪntsaɪçnən], *v.a.* draw in, sketch in. — *v.r. sich* —, enter o.'s name, sign.

Einzelhaft ['aɪntsəlhaft], *f.* (—, *no pl.*) solitary confinement.

Einzelheit ['aɪntsəlhaɪt], *f.* (—, *pl.* —en) detail, particular.

einzeln ['aɪntsəln], *adj.* single; isolated, detached, apart.

einziehen ['aɪntsiːən], *v.a. irr.* draw in, retract; (*Law*) confiscate, impound; (*debts*) collect, call in; (*bill of sight*) discount, cash; (*money*) withdraw (from circulation); (*sails*) furl; (*Mil.*) call up.

einzig ['aɪntsɪç], *adj.* sole; single; unique, only.

Einzug ['aɪntsuːk], *m.* (—s, *pl.* ⸚e) entry, entrance; move (into new house).

einzwängen ['aɪntsvɛŋən], *v.a.* force in, squeeze in.

Eis [aɪs], *n.* (—es, *no pl.*) ice; ice-cream.

E-is ['eːɪs], *n.* (—, *pl.* —) (*Mus.*) E sharp.

Eisbahn ['aɪsbaːn], *f.* (—, *pl.* —en) ice-rink, skating-rink.
Eisbär ['aɪsbɛːr], *m.* (—en, *pl.* —en) polar bear, white bear.
Eisbein ['aɪsbaɪn], *n.* (—s, *pl.* —e) pig's trotters.
Eisberg ['aɪsbɛrk], *m.* (—s, *pl.* —e) iceberg.
Eisblumen ['aɪsbluːmən], *f. pl.* frost patterns (*on glass*).
Eisen ['aɪzən], *n.* (—s, *pl.* —) iron; *altes* —, scrap iron.
Eisenbahn ['aɪzənbaːn], *f.* (—, *pl.* —en) railway.
Eisenfleck ['aɪzənflɛk], *m.* (—s, *pl.* —e) iron mould.
Eisengießerei ['aɪzəngiːsəraɪ], *f.* (—, *pl.* —en) iron foundry, iron forge.
Eisenguß ['aɪzəngus], *m.* (—sses, *pl.* ᵕsse) cast-iron.
Eisenhändler ['aɪzənhɛndlər], *m.* (—s, *pl.* —) ironmonger.
Eisenhütte ['aɪzənhytə], *f.* (—, *pl.* —n) *see* Eisengießerei.
Eisenschlacke ['aɪzənʃlakə], *f.* (—, *no pl.*) iron dross, iron slag.
eisern ['aɪzərn], *adj.* made of iron; (*coll. & fig.*) strong; strict.
Eisgang ['aɪsgaŋ], *m.* (—s, *pl.* ᵕe) drift of ice.
eisgrau ['aɪsgrau], *adj.* hoary.
eiskalt ['aɪskalt], *adj.* icy cold.
Eislauf ['aɪslauf], *m.* (—s, *no pl.*) ice-skating.
Eismeer ['aɪsmeːr], *n.* (—s, *pl.* —e) polar sea; *nördliches* —, Arctic Ocean; *südliches* —, Antarctic Ocean.
Eispickel ['aɪspɪkəl], *m.* (—s, *pl.* —) ice axe.
Eisvogel ['aɪsfoːgəl], *m.* (—s, *pl.* ᵕ) (*Orn.*) kingfisher.
Eiszapfen ['aɪstsapfən], *m.* (—s, *pl.* —) icicle.
eitel ['aɪtəl], *adj.* vain, frivolous, conceited; (*obs.*) pure.
Eiter ['aɪtər], *m.* (—s, *no pl.*) (*Med.*) pus, matter.
Eitergeschwür ['aɪtərgəʃvyːr], *n.* (—s, *pl.* —e) abscess.
eitern ['aɪtərn], *v.n.* suppurate.
Eiterung ['aɪtəruŋ], *f.* (—, *pl.* —en) suppuration.
eitrig ['aɪtrɪç], *adj.* purulent.
Eiweiß ['aɪvaɪs], *n.* (—es, *no pl.*) white of egg; albumen.
Ekel ['eːkəl], *m.* (—s, *no pl.*) nausea, disgust, distaste, aversion.
ekelhaft ['eːkəlhaft], *adj.* loathsome, disgusting, nauseous.
ekeln ['eːkəln], *v.r. sich — vor*, be disgusted (by), feel sick, loathe.
Ekuador [ekua'doːr], *n.* Ecuador.
Elan [e'lã], *m.* (—s, *no pl.*) verve, vigour.
elastisch [e'lastɪʃ], *adj.* elastic, flexible, buoyant.
Elastizität [elastɪtsɪ'tɛːt], *f.* (—, *no pl.*) elasticity; (*mind*) buoyancy.
Elch [ɛlç], *m.* (—s, *pl.* —e) (*Zool.*) elk.
Elegie [ele'giː], *f.* (—, *pl.* —n) elegy.

elektrisieren [elɛktrɪ'ziːrən], *v.a.* electrify.
Elektrizität [elɛktrɪtsɪ'tɛːt], *f.* (—, *no pl.*) electricity.
Elend ['eːlɛnt], *n.* (—s, *no pl.*) misery, distress, wretchedness.
elend ['eːlɛnt], *adj.* miserable, wretched, pitiful; weak; *sich — fühlen*, feel poorly.
elendiglich ['eːlɛndɪklɪç], *adv.* miserably, wretchedly.
Elentier ['eːlɛntiːr], *n.* (—s, *pl.* —e) (*Zool.*) elk.
elf [ɛlf], *num. adj.* eleven.
Elfe ['ɛlfə], *f.* (—, *pl.* —n) fairy.
Elfenbein ['ɛlfənbaɪn], *n.* (—s, *no pl.*) ivory.
Elisabeth [e'liːzabɛt], *f.* Elizabeth.
Ellbogen ['ɛlboːgən], *m.* (—s, *pl.* —) elbow.
Elle ['ɛlə], *f.* (—, *pl.* —n) yard, ell.
Elritze ['ɛlrɪtsə], *f.* (—, *pl.* —n) minnow.
Elsaß ['ɛlzas], *n.* Alsace.
Elster ['ɛlstər], *f.* (—, *pl.* —n) magpie.
Eltern ['ɛltərn], *pl.* parents.
Emaille [e'maːj], *n.* (—s, *no pl.*) enamel.
emailliert [ema(l)'jiːrt], *adj.* covered with vitreous enamel, enamelled.
Empfang [ɛm'pfaŋ], *m.* (—s, *pl.* ᵕe) receipt; reception.
empfangen [ɛm'pfaŋən], *v.a. irr.* receive, accept, take.
Empfänger [ɛm'pfɛŋər], *m.* (—s, *pl.* —) recipient, receiver.
empfänglich [ɛm'pfɛŋlɪç], *adj.* susceptible, impressionable.
Empfängnis [ɛm'pfɛŋnɪs], *f.* (—, *no pl.*) conception.
empfehlen [ɛm'pfeːlən], *v.a. irr.* commend, recommend; give compliments to. — *v.r. sich* —, take leave.
empfinden [ɛm'pfɪndən], *v.a. irr.* feel, perceive.
empfindlich [ɛm'pfɪntlɪç], *adj.* sensitive, susceptible; touchy, thin-skinned.
empfindsam [ɛm'pfɪntsaːm], *adj.* sentimental.
Empfindung [ɛm'pfɪnduŋ], *f.* (—, *pl.* —en) sensation, feeling, sentiment.
empor [ɛm'poːr], *adv.* upward(s), up.
Empore [ɛm'poːrə], *f.* (—, *pl.* —n) gallery (*in church*).
empören [ɛm'pøːrən], *v.a.* excite, enrage, shock. — *v.r. sich* —, revolt, rebel.
Emporkömmling [ɛm'poːrkœmlɪŋ], *m.* (—s, *pl.* —e) upstart.
empört [ɛm'pøːrt], *adj.* furious, shocked, disgusted.
Empörung [ɛm'pøːruŋ], *f.* (—, *pl.* —en) rebellion, revolt, mutiny, insurrection; indignation, disgust.
emsig ['ɛmzɪç], *adj.* assiduous, industrious, busy.
Emsigkeit ['ɛmzɪçkaɪt], *f.* (—, *no pl.*) assiduity, diligence.
Ende ['ɛndə], *n.* (—s, *pl.* —n) end, conclusion.

enden ['ɛndən], v.n. end, finish, conclude. — v.a. terminate, put an end to.

endgültig ['ɛntgʏltɪç], adj. definitive, final.

Endivie [ɛn'diːvjə], f. (—, pl. —n) (Bot.) endive.

endlich ['ɛntlɪç], adj. finite, final, ultimate. — adv. at last, at length, finally.

endlos ['ɛntloːs], adj. endless, never-ending, boundless.

Endung ['ɛnduŋ], f. (—, pl. —en) (Gram.) ending, termination.

Endziel ['ɛntsiːl], n. (—s, pl. —e) final aim.

Energie [ɛnɛr'giː], f. (—, pl. —n) energy.

energisch [e'nɛrgɪʃ], adj. energetic.

eng [ɛŋ], adj. narrow, tight; tight-fitting.

engagieren [āga'ʒiːrən], v.a. engage, hire.

Enge ['ɛŋə], f. (—, pl. —n) narrowness, lack of space; einen in die — treiben drive s.o. into a corner.

Engel ['ɛŋəl], m. (—s, pl. —) angel.

engelhaft ['ɛŋəlhaft], adj. angelic.

Engelschar ['ɛŋəlʃaːr], f. (—, pl. —en) angelic host.

Engelwurzel ['ɛŋəlvurtsəl], f. (—, pl. —n) angelica.

engherzig ['ɛŋhɛrtsɪç], adj. narrow-minded.

England ['ɛŋlant], n. England.

englisch (1) ['ɛŋlɪʃ], adj. (obs.) angelic.

englisch (2) ['ɛŋlɪʃ], adj. English; —e Krankheit, rickets.

Engpaß ['ɛŋpas], m. (—sses, pl. ⁀e) defile, narrow pass; (fig.) bottleneck.

engros [ā'groː], adj. wholesale.

engstirnig ['ɛŋʃtɪrnɪç], adj. narrow-minded.

Enkel ['ɛŋkəl], m. (—s, pl. —) grandchild, grandson.

enorm [e'nɔrm], adj. enormous; (coll.) terrific.

entarten [ɛnt'artən], v.n. (aux. sein) degenerate.

entäußern [ɛnt'ɔysərn], v.r. sich einer Sache —, part with s.th.

entbehren [ɛnt'beːrən], v.a. lack, be in want of; spare.

entbehrlich [ɛnt'beːrlɪç], adj. dispensable, unnecessary, superfluous.

Entbehrung [ɛnt'beːruŋ], f. (—, pl. —en) privation, want.

entbieten [ɛnt'biːtən], v.a. irr. Grüße —, send o.'s respects.

entbinden [ɛnt'bɪndən], v.a. irr. einen von etwas —, release or dispense s.o. from s.th.; (Med.) deliver (a woman of a child).

Entbindung [ɛnt'bɪnduŋ], f. (—, pl. —en) (Med.) delivery, child-birth.

entblättern [ɛnt'blɛtərn], v.a. strip of leaves.

entblößen [ɛnt'bløːsən], v.a., v.r. (sich) —, uncover (o.s.), bare (o.s.).

entdecken [ɛnt'dɛkən], v.a. discover, detect.

Ente ['ɛntə], f. (—, pl. —n) duck; junge —, duckling; (fig.) hoax, fictitious newspaper report.

entehren [ɛnt'eːrən], v.a. dishonour, disgrace; deflower, ravish.

enterben [ɛnt'ɛrbən], v.a. disinherit.

Enterich ['ɛntərɪç], m. (—s, pl. —e) drake.

entfachen [ɛnt'faxən], v.a. set ablaze, kindle.

entfahren [ɛnt'faːrən], v.n. irr. (aux. sein) slip off, escape.

entfallen [ɛnt'falən], v.n. irr. (aux. sein) escape o.'s memory; be left off.

entfalten [ɛnt'faltən], v.a. unfold; display. — v.r. sich —, develop, open up, expand.

entfärben [ɛnt'fɛrbən], v.r. sich —, lose colour, grow pale.

entfernen [ɛnt'fɛrnən], v.a. remove. — v.r. sich —, withdraw.

Entfernung [ɛnt'fɛrnuŋ], f. (—, pl. —en) removal; distance.

entfesseln [ɛnt'fɛsəln], v.a. unfetter; let loose.

Entfettungskur [ɛnt'fɛtuŋskuːr], f. (—, —en) slimming-cure.

entflammen [ɛnt'flamən], v.a. inflame.

entfliegen [ɛnt'fliːgən], v.n. irr. (aux. sein) fly away.

entfliehen [ɛnt'fliːən], v.n. irr. (aux. sein) run away, escape, flee.

entfremden [ɛnt'frɛmdən], v.a. estrange, alienate.

entführen [ɛnt'fyːrən], v.a. abduct, carry off; kidnap; elope with.

entgegen [ɛnt'geːgən], prep. (Dat.), adv. against, contrary to; towards.

Entgegenkommen [ɛnt'geːgənkɔmən], n. (—s, no pl.) obliging behaviour, courtesy.

entgegenkommen [ɛnt'geːgənkɔmən], v.n. irr. (aux. sein) come towards s.o., come to meet s.o.; do a favour, oblige.

entgegennehmen [ɛnt'geːgənneːmən], v.a. irr. receive, accept.

entgegensehen [ɛnt'geːgənzeːən], v.n. irr. await, look forward to.

entgegnen [ɛnt'geːgnən], v.a. reply, retort.

Entgegnung [ɛnt'geːgnuŋ], f. (—, pl. —en) reply, retort, rejoinder.

entgehen [ɛnt'geːən], v.n. irr. (aux. sein) (Dat.) escape; — lassen, let slip.

Entgelt [ɛnt'gɛlt], n. (—s, no pl.) remuneration, recompense.

entgelten [ɛnt'gɛltən], v.a. irr. einen etwas — lassen, make s.o. pay for s.th. or suffer.

entgleisen [ɛnt'glaɪzən], v.n. (aux. sein) run off the rails, be derailed.

enthaaren [ɛnt'haːrən], v.a. depilate.

enthalten [ɛnt'haltən], v.a. irr. hold, contain. — v.r. sich —, abstain from, refrain from.

enthaltsam [ɛnt'haltzaːm], adj. abstinent, abstemious, temperate.

Enthaltung [ɛnt'haltuŋ], f. (—, no pl.) abstention.

enthaupten [ɛnt'hauptən], *v.a.* behead, decapitate.

entheben [ɛnt'he:bən], *v.a. irr. einen einer Sache* —, exempt *or* dispense from, suspend from, relieve of.

entheiligen [ɛnt'haɪlɪgən], *v.a.* profane, desecrate.

enthüllen [ɛnt'hylən], *v.a.* unveil; (*fig.*) reveal.

entkleiden [ɛnt'klaɪdən], *v.a.* unclothe, undress, strip.

entkommen [ɛnt'kɔmən], *v.n. irr.* (*aux.* sein) escape, get off.

entkräften [ɛnt'krɛftən], *v.a.* enfeeble, debilitate, weaken; (*fig.*) refute (an argument).

entladen [ɛnt'la:dən], *v.a. irr.* unload, discharge. — *v.r. sich* —, burst; (*gun*) go off.

Entladung [ɛnt'la:duŋ], *f.* (—, *pl.* —en) unloading, discharge, explosion.

entlang [ɛnt'laŋ], *prep.* along.

entlarven [ɛnt'larfən], *v.a.* unmask; expose.

Entlarvung [ɛnt'larfuŋ], *f.* (—, *pl.* —en) unmasking, exposure.

entlassen [ɛnt'lasən], *v.a. irr.* dismiss; (*Am.*) fire; discharge; pension off.

Entlastung [ɛnt'lastuŋ], *f.* (—, *no pl.*) exoneration; credit (to s.o.'s bank account).

entlaufen [ɛnt'laufən], *v.n. irr.* (*aux.* sein) run away.

entlausen [ɛnt'lauzən], *v.a.* delouse.

entledigen [ɛnt'le:dɪgən], *v.r. sich einer Sache* —, rid o.s. of *or* get rid of a thing; *sich einer Aufgabe* —, perform a task, discharge a commission.

entleeren [ɛnt'le:rən], *v.a.* empty.

entlegen [ɛnt'le:gən], *adj.* remote, distant, far off.

entlehnen [ɛnt'le:nən], *v.a.* borrow from.

entleihen [ɛnt'laɪən], *v.a. irr.* borrow.

entlocken [ɛnt'lɔkən], *v.a.* elicit from.

entmannen [ɛnt'manən], *v.a.* castrate, emasculate.

entmündigen [ɛnt'myndɪgən], *v.a.* place under care of a guardian *or* (*Law*) trustees.

Entmündigung [ɛnt'myndɪguŋ], *f.* (—, *no pl.*) placing under legal control.

entmutigen [ɛnt'mu:tɪgən], *v.a.* discourage, dishearten.

Entnahme [ɛnt'na:mə], *f.* (—, *pl.* —n) (*money*) withdrawal.

entnehmen [ɛnt'ne:mən], *v.a. irr.* (*money*) withdraw; understand, gather *or* infer from.

entnerven [ɛnt'nɛrfən], *v.a.* enervate.

entpuppen [ɛnt'pupən], *v.r. sich* —, burst from the cocoon; (*fig.*) turn out to be.

enträtseln [ɛnt'rɛ:tsəln], *v.a.* decipher, make out.

entreißen [ɛnt'raɪsən], *v.a. irr.* snatch away from; *einer Gefahr* —, save *or* rescue from danger.

entrichten [ɛnt'rɪçtən], *v.a.* pay (off).

entrinnen [ɛnt'rɪnən], *v.n. irr.* (*aux.* sein) escape from.

entrückt [ɛnt rykt], *adj.* enraptured.

entrüsten [ɛnt'rystən], *v.a.* make angry, exasperate. — *v.r. sich* —, become angry, fly into a passion.

entsagen [ɛnt'za:gən], *v.n.* renounce; waive; abdicate.

Entsatz [ɛnt'zats], *m.* (—es, *no pl.*) (*Mil.*) relief.

entschädigen [ɛnt'ʃɛ:dɪgən], *v.a.* indemnify, compensate.

entscheiden [ɛnt'ʃaɪdən], *v.a. irr.* decide. — *v.r. sich* — *für*, come to a decision for, decide in favour of.

Entscheidung [ɛnt'ʃaɪduŋ], *f.* (—, *pl.* —en) decision; verdict.

entschieden [ɛnt'ʃi:dən], *adj.* decided, determined, resolute, peremptory.

Entschiedenheit [ɛnt'ʃi:dənhaɪt], *f.* (—, *no pl.*) resolution, firmness, determination.

entschlafen [ɛnt'ʃla:fən], *v.n. irr.* (*aux.* sein) fall asleep; (*fig.*) die, depart this life.

entschleiern [ɛnt'ʃlaɪərn], *v.a.* unveil.

entschließen [ɛnt'ʃli:sən], *v.r. irr. sich* —, decide (upon), resolve, make up o.'s mind.

Entschlossenheit [ɛnt'ʃlɔsənhaɪt], *f.* (—, *no pl.*) resoluteness, determination.

entschlummern [ɛnt'ʃlumərn], *v.n.* (*aux.* sein) fall asleep.

entschlüpfen [ɛnt'ʃlypfən], *v.n.* (*aux.* sein) slip away; escape.

Entschluß [ɛnt'ʃlus], *m.* (—sses, *pl.* ⁝sse) resolution; *einen* — *fassen*, resolve (to).

entschuldigen [ɛnt'ʃuldɪgən], *v.a.* excuse. — *v.r. sich* —, apologise.

entschwinden [ɛnt'ʃvɪndən], *v.n. irr.* (*aux.* sein) disappear, vanish.

entseelt [ɛnt'ze:lt], *adj.* inanimate, lifeless.

entsenden [ɛnt'zɛndən], *v.a. irr.* send off, despatch.

Entsetzen [ɛnt'zɛtsən], *n.* (—s, *no pl.*) horror, terror.

entsetzen [ɛnt'zɛtsən], *v.a.* (*Mil.*) relieve; frighten, shock, fill with horror. — *v.r. sich* — *über*, be horrified at.

entsetzlich [ɛnt'zɛtslɪç], *adj.* horrible, terrible, dreadful, awful.

entsiegeln [ɛnt'zi:gəln], *v.a.* unseal.

entsinnen [ɛnt'zɪnən], *v.r. sich einer Sache* —, recollect, remember, call s.th. to mind.

entspannen [ɛnt'ʃpanən], *v.a.*, *v.r.* (*sich*) —, relax.

entspinnen [ɛnt'ʃpɪnən], *v.r. irr. sich* —, arise, begin.

entsprechen [ɛnt'ʃprɛçən], *v.n. irr.* respond to, correspond to, meet, suit.

entsprechend [ɛnt'ʃprɛçənt], *adj.* corresponding, suitable.

entsprießen [ɛnt'ʃpri:sən], *v.n. irr.* (*aux.* sein) spring up, sprout.

entspringen [ɛnt'ʃprɪŋən], *v.n. irr.* (*aux.* sein) escape, originate from; (*river*) have its source at, rise.

entstammen [ɛnt'ʃtamən], *v.n.* (*aux.* sein) spring from, originate from.

entstehen [ɛnt'ʃte:ən], *v.n. irr.* (*aux.* sein) arise, originate, begin, result, spring from.

Entstehung [ɛnt'ʃte:uŋ], *f.* (—, *no pl.*) origin, rise.

entstellen [ɛnt'ʃtɛlən], *v.a.* disfigure, deform, distort; (*fig.*) garble.

entsühnen [ɛnt'zy:nən], *v.a.* free from sin, purify, purge.

enttäuschen [ɛnt'tɔyʃən], *v.a.* disappoint.

entthronen [ɛnt'tro:nən], *v.a.* dethrone.

entvölkern [ɛnt'fœlkərn], *v.a.* depopulate.

entwachsen [ɛnt'vaksən], *v.n. irr.* (*aux.* sein) grow out of, outgrow.

entwaffnen [ɛnt'vafnən], *v.a.* disarm.

entwässern [ɛnt'vɛsərn], *v.a.* drain.

entweder [ɛnt've:dər], *conj.* either; — ......*oder*, either ...... or.

entweichen [ɛnt'vaiçən], *v.n. irr.* escape, run away.

entweihen [ɛnt'vaiən], *v.a.* profane, desecrate.

entwenden [ɛnt'vɛndən], *v.a.* take away, steal, embezzle.

entwerfen [ɛnt'vɛrfən], *v.a. irr.* design, sketch, plan, draw up.

entwerten [ɛnt'vɛrtən], *v.a.* reduce in value, depreciate; (*stamps*) cancel.

entwickeln [ɛnt'vɪkəln], *v.a.* unfold, develop; (*ideas*) explain, explicate. — *v.r. sich* —, develop (into), evolve.

Entwicklung [ɛnt'vɪkluŋ], *f.* (—, *pl.* —en) unfolding, development, evolution.

entwinden [ɛnt'vɪndən], *v.a. irr.* wrench from, wrest from.

entwirren [ɛnt'vɪrən], *v.a.* unravel, disentangle.

entwischen [ɛnt'vɪʃən], *v.n.* (*aux.* sein) slip away, escape.

entwöhnen [ɛnt'vø:nən], *v.a.* disaccustom; break off a habit; (*baby*) wean.

entwürdigen [ɛnt'vyrdɪgən], *v.a.* disgrace, degrade.

Entwurf [ɛnt'vurf], *m.* (—s, *pl.* ⁻e) sketch, design, draft, plan, project.

entwurzeln [ɛnt'vurtsəln], *v.a.* uproot.

entziehen [ɛnt'tsi:ən], *v.a. irr.* withdraw, take away, deprive of.

entziffern [ɛnt'tsɪfərn], *v.a.* decipher.

entzücken [ɛnt'tsykən], *v.a.* enchant, delight, charm.

entzündbar [ɛnt'tsyntba:r], *adj.* inflammable.

entzünden [ɛnt'tsyndən], *v.a.* set on fire, light the fire; (*fig.*) inflame. — *v.r. sich* —, catch fire, ignite; (*Med.*) become inflamed.

Entzündung [ɛnt'tsynduŋ], *f.* (—, *pl.* —en) kindling, setting on fire; (*Med.*) inflammation.

entzwei [ɛnt'tsvai], *adv.* in two, broken.

entzweien [ɛnt'tsvaiən], *v.a.* disunite.

Enzian ['ɛntsjan], *m.* (—s, *pl.* —e) (*Bot.*) gentian.

Enzyklopädie [ɛntsyklopɛ'di:], *f.* (—, *pl.* —n) encyclopædia.

Epidemie [epɪde'mi:], *f.* (—, *pl.* —en) epidemic.

epidemisch [epɪ'de:mɪʃ], *adj.* epidemic(al).

Epik ['e:pɪk], *f.* (—, *no pl.*) epic poetry.

episch ['e:pɪʃ], *adj.* epic.

Epos ['e:pɔs], *n.* (—, *pl.* **Epen**) epic poem.

Equipage [ɛkvi'pa:ʒə], *f.* (—, *pl.* —n) carriage.

er [e:r], *pers. pron.* he.

Erachten [ɛr'axtən], *n.* (—s, *no pl.*) opinion, judgment; *meines* —*s*, in my opinion.

erachten [ɛr'axtən], *v.a.* think, consider.

erarbeiten [ɛr'arbaitən], *v.a.* gain *or* achieve by working.

erb ['ɛrb], *adj.* (*in compounds*) hereditary.

erbarmen [ɛr'barmən], *v.r. sich* —, have mercy (on), take pity (on).

erbärmlich [ɛr'bɛrmlɪç], *adj.* miserable, pitiful; contemptible.

erbauen [ɛr'bauən], *v.a.* build, erect; (*fig.*) edify.

erbaulich [ɛr'baulɪç], *adj.* edifying.

Erbauung [ɛr'bauuŋ], *f.* (—, *no pl.*) building, erection; (*fig.*) edification.

Erbbesitz ['ɛrpbəzɪts], *m.* (—es, *pl.* —e) hereditary possession.

Erbe ['ɛrbə], *m.* (—n, *pl.* —n) heir. *n.* (—s, *no pl.*) inheritance; heritage.

erbeben [ɛr'be:bən], *v.n.* (*aux.* sein) shake, tremble, quake.

erbeigen ['ɛrpaigən], *adj.* inherited.

erben ['ɛrbən], *v.a.* inherit.

erbeten [ɛr'be:tən], *v.a. sich etwas* —, ask for s.th. by prayer; request.

erbetteln [ɛr'bɛtəln], *v.a.* obtain by begging.

erbeuten [ɛr'bɔytən], *v.a.* take as booty.

Erbfeind ['ɛrpfaint], *m.* (—s, *pl.* —e) sworn enemy.

Erbfolge ['ɛrpfɔlgə], *f.* (—, *no pl.*) succession.

erbieten [ɛr'bi:tən], *v.r. irr. sich* —, offer to do s.th.; volunteer; *Ehre* —, do homage.

Erbin ['ɛrbɪn], *f.* (—, *pl.* —nen) heiress.

erbitten [ɛr'bɪtən], *v.a. irr.* beg, request, ask for, gain by asking.

erbittern [ɛr'bɪtərn], *v.a.* embitter, anger, exasperate.

erblassen [ɛr'blasən], *v.n.* (*aux.* sein) turn pale.

Erblasser ['ɛrplasər], *m.* (—s, *pl.* —) testator.

erbleichen [ɛr'blaiçən], *v.n. irr.* (*aux.* sein) turn pale, lose colour.

erblich ['ɛrplɪç], *adj.* hereditary, congenital.

erblicken [ɛr'blɪkən], *v.a.* perceive, behold, catch sight of.

erblinden [ɛr'blɪndən], *v.n.* (*aux.* sein) turn blind.

erblos ['ɛrplo:s], *adj.* disinherited; without an heir.

erblühen [ɛr'bly:ən], *v.n. (aux. sein)* blossom (out).

Erbmasse ['ɛrpmasə], *f.* (—, *no pl.*) estate.

erbosen [ɛr'bo:zən], *v.a.* make angry. — *v.r. sich* —, become angry.

erbötig [ɛr'bø:tɪç], *adj.* — *sein,* be willing, be ready.

Erbpacht ['ɛrppaxt], *f.* (—, *pl.* —en) hereditary tenure.

erbrechen [ɛr'brɛçən], *v.a. irr.* break open, open by force. — *v.r. sich* —, vomit.

Erbrecht ['ɛrprɛçt], *n.* (—s, *no pl.*) law (*or* right) of succession.

Erbschaft ['ɛrpʃaft], *f.* (—, *pl.* —en) inheritance, heritage, legacy.

Erbse ['ɛrpsə], *f.* (—, *pl.* —n) pea.

Erbstück ['ɛrpʃtyk], *n.* (—s, *pl.* —e) heirloom.

Erbsünde ['ɛrpzyndə], *f.* (—, *no pl.*) original sin.

Erbteil ['ɛrptail], *n.* (—s, *pl.* —e) portion of inheritance.

Erdapfel ['e:rtapfəl], *m.* (—s, *pl.*) (*Austr.*) potato.

Erdbahn ['e:rtba:n], *f.* (—, *no pl.*) orbit of the earth.

Erdball ['e:rtbal], *m.* (—s, *no pl.*) terrestrial globe.

Erdbeben ['e:rtbe:bən], *n.* (—s, *pl.* —) earthquake.

Erdbeere ['e:rtbe:rə], *f.* (—, *pl.* —n) strawberry.

Erde ['e:rdə], *f.* (—, *pl.* —n) earth, soil ground.

erden ['e:rdən], *v.a.* (*Rad.*) earth.

erdenken [ɛr'dɛŋkən], *v.a.irr.* think out, invent. — *v.r. sich etwas* —, invent s.th., devise s.th.

erdenklich [ɛr'dɛŋklɪç], *adj.* imaginable, conceivable.

Erdenleben ['e:rdənle:bən], *n.* (—s, *no pl.*) life on this earth.

Erdfall ['e:rtfal], *m.* (—s, *pl.* e) landslip.

Erdfläche ['e:rtflɛçə], *f.* (—, *no pl.*) surface of the earth.

Erdgeschoß ['e:rtgəʃɔs], *n.* (—sses, *pl.* —sse) ground floor.

Erdhügel ['e:rthy:gəl], *m.* (—s, *pl.* —) mound of earth.

erdichten ['ɛr'dɪçtən], *v.a.* think out, invent, feign.

Erdkunde ['e:rtkundə], *f.* (—, *no pl.*) geography.

Erdleitung ['e:rtlaituŋ], *f.* (—, *pl.* —en) earth circuit, earth connexion.

Erdmaus ['e:rtmaus], *f.* (—, *pl.* e) field mouse.

Erdmolch ['e:rtmɔlç], *m.* (—s, *pl.* —e) salamander.

Erdnuß ['e:rtnus], *f.* (—, *pl.* sse) groundnut, peanut.

Erdöl ['e:rtø:l], *n.* (—s, *no pl.*) petroleum, mineral oil.

erdolchen [ɛr'dɔlçən], *v.a.* stab (with a dagger).

Erdpech ['e:rtpɛç], *n.* (—s, *no pl.*) bitumen.

erdreisten [ɛr'draɪstən], *v.r. sich* —, dare, have the audacity.

erdrosseln [ɛr'drɔsəln], *v.a.* strangle, throttle.

erdrücken [ɛr'drykən], *v.a.* crush to death.

Erdrutsch ['e:rtrutʃ], *m.* (—es, *no pl.*) landslip, landslide.

Erdschicht ['e:rtʃɪçt], *f.* (—, *pl.* —en) (*Geol.*) layer, stratum.

Erdschnecke ['e:rtʃnɛkə], *f.* (—, *pl.* —n) slug, snail.

Erdscholle ['e:rtʃɔlə], *f.* (—, *pl.* —n) clod (of earth).

Erdsturz ['e:rtʃturts], *m.* (—es, *no pl.*) landslide.

erdulden [ɛr'duldən], *v.a.* suffer, endure.

Erdumseg(e)lung ['e:rtumze:g(ə)luŋ], *f.* (—, *pl.* —en) circumnavigation of the earth.

ereifern [ɛr'aɪfərn], *v.r. sich* —, become heated, get excited.

ereignen [ɛr'aɪgnən], *v.r. sich* —, happen, come to pass.

Ereignis [ɛr'aɪknɪs], *n.* (—ses, *pl.* —se) event, occurrence, happening.

ereilen [ɛr'aɪlən], *v.a.* overtake, befall.

Eremit [ere'mi:t], *m.* (—en, *pl.* —en) hermit, recluse.

erfahren [ɛr'fa:rən], *v.a. irr.* learn, hear; experience. — *adj.* experienced, practised; conversant with, versed in.

Erfahrenheit [ɛr'fa:rənhaɪt], *f.* (—, *no pl.*) experience, skill.

Erfahrung [ɛr'fa:ruŋ], *f.* (—, *pl.* —en) experience, knowledge, expertness, skill; *in* — *bringen,* ascertain, come to know.

erfahrungsgemäß [ɛr'fa:ruŋsgəmɛ:s], *adj.* based on *or* according to experience.

erfahrungsmäßig [ɛr'fa:ruŋsmɛ:sɪç], *adj.* based on experience; empirical.

erfassen [ɛr'fasən], *v.a.* get hold of, seize, comprehend, grasp.

erfinden [ɛr'fɪndən], *v.a. irr.* invent, contrive.

erfinderisch [ɛr'fɪndərɪʃ], *adj.* inventive, ingenious.

Erfindung [ɛr'fɪnduŋ], *f.* (—, *pl.* —en) invention; contrivance.

Erfolg [ɛr'fɔlk], *m.* (—s, *pl.* —e) success; result; effect; — *haben,* succeed, be successful; *keinen* — *haben,* fail.

erfolgen [ɛr'fɔlgən], *v.n.* (*aux.* sein) ensue, follow, result.

erfolgreich [ɛr'fɔlkraɪç], *adj.* successful.

erforderlich [ɛr'fɔrdərlɪç], *adj.* necessary, required.

erfordern [ɛr'fɔrdərn], *v.a.* demand, require.

Erfordernis [ɛr'fɔrdərnɪs], *n.* (—ses, *pl.* —se) necessity, requirement, requisite.

erforschen [ɛr'fɔrʃən], *v.a.* explore, investigate, conduct research into.

erfragen [ɛr'fra:gən], *v.a.* find out by asking, ascertain.

erfreuen [ɛr'frɔyən], *v.a.* gladden, cheer, delight. — *v.r. sich* — *an,* enjoy, take pleasure in.

erfreulich [ɛrˈfrɔylɪç], *adj.* pleasing, gratifying.

erfrieren [ɛrˈfriːrən], *v.n. irr. (aux. sein)* freeze to death, die of exposure; become numb.

erfrischen [ɛrˈfrɪʃən], *v.a.* refresh.

erfüllen [ɛrˈfylən], *v.a.* fulfil, keep (promise); comply with; perform; *seinen Zweck* —, serve its purpose. — *v.r. sich* —, come true, be fulfilled.

Erfüllung [ɛrˈfylʊŋ], *f.* (—, *no pl.*) fulfilment; granting; performance; *in* — *gehen*, come true, be realised.

ergänzen [ɛrˈgɛntsən], *v.a.* complete, complement.

Ergänzung [ɛrˈgɛntsʊŋ], *f.* (—, *pl.* —en) completion; complement, supplement.

ergattern [ɛrˈgatərn], *v.a.* pick up.

ergeben [ɛrˈgeːbən], *v.a. irr.* give, yield, prove, show. — *v.r. sich* —, surrender (to); acquiesce (in); happen, result, follow. — *adj.* devoted, submissive, humble, obedient.

Ergebenheit [ɛrˈgeːbənhaɪt], *f.* (—, *no pl.*) devotion, obedience, humility, fidelity.

ergebenst [ɛrˈgeːbənst], *adj. Ihr —er* (*letter ending*), yours very truly, your obedient servant. — *adv.* respectfully.

Ergebnis [ɛrˈgeːpnɪs], *n.* (—ses, *pl.* —se) outcome, result; (*Agr.*) yield.

Ergebung [ɛrˈgeːbʊŋ], *f.* (—, *no pl.*) submission, resignation; surrender.

Ergehen [ɛrˈgeːən], *n.* (—s, *no pl.*) health, condition, well-being.

ergehen [ɛrˈgeːən], *v.n. irr. (aux. sein)* be promulgated or issued; — *lassen,* issue, publish; *etwas über sich* — *lassen,* submit to or suffer s.th. patiently. — *v.r. sich* —, (*obs.*) take a stroll.

ergiebig [ɛrˈgiːbɪç], *adj.* rich, productive, fertile, profitable.

ergießen [ɛrˈgiːsən], *v.r. irr. sich* —, discharge, flow into.

erglänzen [ɛrˈglɛntsən], *v.n. (aux. sein)* shine forth, sparkle.

erglühen [ɛrˈglyːən], *v.n. (aux. sein)* glow; blush.

ergötzen [ɛrˈgœtsən], *v.a.* (*obs.*) amuse, delight. — *v.r. sich* — *an,* delight in.

ergrauen [ɛrˈgrauən], *v.n. (aux. sein)* become grey; grow old.

ergreifen [ɛrˈgraɪfən], *v.a. irr.* seize, grasp, get hold of; move, touch, affect; *Maßnahmen* —, take measures.

Ergreifung [ɛrˈgraɪfʊŋ], *f.* (—, *no pl.*) seizure; (*measure*) adoption.

ergriffen [ɛrˈgrɪfən], *adj.* moved, touched, impressed.

Ergriffenheit [ɛrˈgrɪfənhaɪt], *f.* (—, *no pl.*) emotion.

ergrimmen [ɛrˈgrɪmən], *v.n. (aux. sein)* grow angry, be enraged.

ergründen [ɛrˈgryndən], *v.a.* get to the bottom of, investigate, fathom.

Erguß [ɛrˈgus], *m.* (—sses, *pl.* ˙sse) outpouring; (*fig.*) effusion.

erhaben [ɛrˈhaːbən], *adj.* sublime, exalted; majestic, elevated.

Erhabenheit [ɛrˈhaːbənhaɪt], *f.* (—, *no pl.*) majesty, sublimity.

erhalten [ɛrˈhaltən], *v.a. irr.* receive, obtain, get, preserve; maintain, keep up. — *v.r. sich* — *von,* subsist on.

erhältlich [ɛrˈhɛltlɪç], *adj.* obtainable.

Erhaltung [ɛrˈhaltʊŋ], *f.* (—, *no pl.*) preservation, conservation; (*family*) maintenance.

erhärten [ɛrˈhɛrtən], *v.a.* make hard; (*fig.*) prove, confirm.

erhaschen [ɛrˈhaʃən], *v.a.* catch, snatch.

erheben [ɛrˈheːbən], *v.a. irr.* lift up, raise; (*fig.*) elevate, exalt; *Klage* —, bring an action; *Geld* —, raise money; *Steuern* —, levy taxes. — *v.r. sich* —, rise, stand up.

erheblich [ɛrˈheːplɪç], *adj.* considerable, weighty, appreciable.

Erhebung [ɛrˈheːbʊŋ], *f.* (—, *pl.* —en) elevation; (*taxes*) levying; revolt, rebellion, rising.

erheischen [ɛrˈhaɪʃən], *v.a.* (*rare*) require, demand.

erheitern [ɛrˈhaɪtərn], *v.a.* cheer, exhilarate.

erhellen [ɛrˈhɛlən], *v.a.* light up, illuminate; (*fig.*) enlighten. — *v.n.* become evident.

erhitzen [ɛrˈhɪtsən], *v.a.* heat; (*fig.*) inflame, excite. — *v.r. sich* —, grow hot; grow angry.

erhöhen [ɛrˈhøːən], *v.a.* heighten, raise, intensify, increase; (*value*) enhance.

erholen [ɛrˈhoːlən], *v.r. sich* —, recover, get better; relax (after work); take a rest.

erholungsbedürftig [ɛrˈhoːlʊŋsbədyrftɪç], *adj.* in need of a rest.

erhören [ɛrˈhøːrən], *v.a.* hear, vouchsafe, grant.

Erich [ˈeːrɪç], *m.* Eric.

erinnerlich [ɛrˈɪnərlɪç], *adj.* remembered; *soweit mir — ist,* as far as I can remember.

erinnern [ɛrˈɪnərn], *v.a.* remind. — *v.r. sich* —, remember, recollect, recall, call to mind.

Erinnerung [ɛrˈɪnərʊŋ], *f.* (—, *pl.* —en) remembrance; recollection; reminiscences.

erjagen [ɛrˈjaːgən], *v.a.* hunt (down), chase.

erkalten [ɛrˈkaltən], *v.n. (aux. sein)* grow cold.

erkälten [ɛrˈkɛltən], *v.r. sich* —, catch cold.

Erkältung [ɛrˈkɛltʊŋ], *f.* (—, *pl.* —en) cold, chill.

erkämpfen [ɛrˈkɛmpfən], *v.a.* obtain by fighting; obtain by great exertion.

erkaufen [ɛrˈkaufən], *v.a.* purchase; bribe, corrupt.

erkennen [ɛrˈkɛnən], *v.a. irr.* recognise, perceive, distinguish, discern; (*Comm.*) credit; *zu — geben,* give to understand; *sich zu — geben,* make o.s. known. — *v.n.* (*Law*) judge; — *auf,* (*Law*) announce verdict, pass sentence.

erkenntlich [ɛr'kɛntlɪç], *adj.* grateful; (*fig.*) *sich — zeigen*, show o.s. grateful.

Erkenntlichkeit [ɛr'kɛntlɪçkaɪt], *f.* (—, *no pl.*) gratitude.

Erkenntnis [ɛr'kɛntnɪs], *f.* (—, *pl.* —se) perception, knowledge, comprehension, understanding; realisation, (*Phil.*) cognition.

Erkennung [ɛr'kɛnuŋ], *f.* (—, *no pl.*) recognition.

Erker ['ɛrkər], *m.* (—s, *pl.* —) alcove bay, turret.

Erkerfenster ['ɛrkərfɛnstər], *n.* (—s, *pl.* —) bay-window.

erklären [ɛr'klɛːrən], *v.a.* explain, expound, account for; make a statement on, declare, state.

erklärlich [ɛr'klɛːrlɪç], *adj.* explicable.

Erklärung [ɛr'klɛːruŋ], *f.* (—, *pl.* —en) explanation; declaration, statement; (*income tax*) return.

erklecklich [ɛr'klɛklɪç],*adj.*considerable.

erklettern [ɛr'klɛtərn], *v.a.* climb.

erklimmen [ɛr'klɪmən], *v.a. irr.* climb.

erklingen [ɛr'klɪŋən], *v.n. irr.* (*aux.* sein) sound, resound.

erkoren [ɛr'koːrən], *adj.* select, chosen.

erkranken [ɛr'kraŋkən], *v.n.* (*aux.* sein) fall ill.

erkühnen [ɛr'kyːnən], *v.r. sich —*, dare, make bold, venture.

erkunden [ɛr'kundən], *v.a.* explore, find out; (*Mil.*) reconnoitre.

erkundigen [ɛr'kundɪgən], *v.r. sich —*, enquire (about), make enquiries.

erlaben [ɛr'laːbən], *v.r. sich —*, (*obs.*) refresh o.s.

erlahmen [ɛr'laːmən],*v.n.* (*aux.*sein)become lame; lose o.'s drive; grow tired.

erlangen [ɛr'laŋən], *v.a.* reach, gain, obtain; acquire; attain.

Erlaß [ɛr'las], *m.* (—sses, *pl.* ⸚sse) remission, exemption, release, dispensation; (*Comm.*) deduction; (*Law, Pol.*) proclamation, edict, decree, writ; (*Eccl.*) indulgence; remission.

erlassen [ɛr'lasən], *v.a. irr.* remit, release, let off; (*Law, Pol.*) enact, promulgate.

erläßlich [ɛr'lɛslɪç], *adj.* remissible, dispensable, venial.

erlauben [ɛr'laubən], *v.a.* permit, allow; *sich etwas —*, take the liberty of, make bold to; have the impertinence to.

Erlaubnis [ɛr'laupnɪs], *f.* (—, *no pl.*) permission, leave, permit; *die — haben*, be permitted; *um — bitten*, beg leave; *mit Ihrer —*, by your leave.

erlaucht [ɛr'lauxt], *adj.* illustrious, noble.

erlauschen [ɛr'lauʃən], *v.a.* overhear.

erläutern [ɛr'lɔytərn], *v.a.* explain, illustrate, elucidate.

Erle ['ɛrlə], *f.* (—, *pl.* —n) (*Bot.*) alder.

erleben [ɛr'leːbən], *v.a.* live to see; go through, experience.

Erlebnis [ɛr'leːpnɪs], *n.* (—ses, *pl.* —se) experience, adventure, occurrence.

erledigen [ɛr'leːdɪgən], *v.a.* settle, finish off, clear up; dispatch; execute (commission etc.).

erledigt [ɛr'leːdɪçt], *adj.* (*coll.*) wornout; exhausted.

erlegen [ɛr'leːgən], *v.a.* slay; pay down.

erleichtern [ɛr'laɪçtərn], *v.a.* lighten, ease, facilitate.

erleiden [ɛr'laɪdən], *v.a. irr.* suffer, endure, bear, undergo.

erlernen [ɛr'lɛrnən], *v.a.* learn, acquire.

erlesen [ɛr'leːzən], *v.a. irr.* select, choose. — *adj.* select, choice.

erleuchten [ɛr'lɔyçtən], *v.a.* illumine, illuminate, floodlight; (*fig.*) enlighten, inspire.

erliegen [ɛr'liːgən], *v.n. irr.* (*aux.* sein) succumb.

Erlkönig ['ɛrlkøːnɪç], *m.* (—s, *pl.* —e) fairy-king, elf-king.

erlogen [ɛr'loːgən], *adj.* false, untrue; trumped-up.

Erlös [ɛr'løːs], *m.* (—es, *no pl.*) proceeds.

erlöschen [ɛr'løːʃən], *v.n. irr.* (*aux.* sein) be extinguished, die out; (*fire*) go out; (*contract*) expire.

erlösen [ɛr'løːzən], *v.a.* redeem; release, save, deliver.

ermächtigen [ɛr'mɛçtɪgən], *v.a.* empower; authorize.

ermahnen [ɛr'maːnən], *v.a.* admonish, exhort, remind.

ermäßigen [ɛr'mɛːsɪgən], *v.a.* reduce.

ermatten [ɛr'matən], *v.a.* weaken, weary, tire. — *v.n.* (*aux.* sein) grow weak, become tired.

Ermessen [ɛr'mɛsən], *n.* (—s, *no pl.*) judgment, opinion.

ermitteln [ɛr'mɪtəln], *v.a.* ascertain, find out.

ermöglichen [ɛr'møːklɪçən], *v.a.* make possible.

ermorden [ɛr'mɔrdən], *v.a.* murder.

ermüden [ɛr'myːdən], *v.a.* tire, fatigue. — *v.n.* (*aux.* sein) get tired, grow weary.

ermuntern [ɛr'muntərn], *v.a.* encourage, cheer up.

ermutigen [ɛr'muːtɪgən],*v.a.*encourage.

ernähren [ɛr'nɛːrən], *v.a.* nourish, feed.

ernennen [ɛr'nɛnən], *v.a. irr.* nominate, appoint.

erneuern [ɛr'nɔyərn], *v.a.* renew repair, renovate.

erniedrigen [ɛr'niːdrɪgən], *v.a.* humble, humiliate, degrade. — *v.r. sich —*, humble o.s., abase o.s.

Ernst (1) [ɛrnst], *m.* Ernest.

Ernst (2) [ɛrnst], *m.* (—es, *no pl.*) earnestness, seriousness.

ernst [ɛrnst], *adj.* earnest, serious.

Ernte ['ɛrntə], *f.* (—, *pl.* —n) harvest crop.

ernüchtern [ɛr'nyçtərn], *v.a.* sober; (*fig.*) disenchant, disillusion.

erobern [ɛr'oːbərn], *v.a.* (*Mil.*) conquer; take, win.

eröffnen [ɛr'œfnən], *v.a.* open, inaugurate; inform, reveal.

erörtern [ɛr'œrtərn], *v.a.* discuss, debate argue.

erpicht [ɛr'pɪçt], *adj.* eager for, bent on.
erpressen [ɛr'prɛsən], *v.a.* extort, blackmail.
erquicken [ɛr'kvɪkən], *v.a.* refresh.
erraten [ɛr'ra:tən], *v.a. irr.* guess.
erregen [ɛr're:gən], *v.a.* cause; stir up, excite, agitate; provoke.
erreichen [ɛr'raɪçən], *v.a.* reach, arrive at; (*fig.*) attain, reach.
erretten [ɛr'rɛtən], *v.a.* save, rescue.
errichten [ɛr'rɪçtən], *v.a.* erect, raise, build.
erringen [ɛr'rɪŋən], *v.a. irr.* obtain (by exertion), achieve.
erröten [ɛr'rø:tən], *v.n.* (*aux.* sein) blush, redden.
Errungenschaft [ɛr'ruŋənʃaft], *f.* (—, *pl.* —en) achievement, acquisition.
Ersatz [ɛr'zats], *m.* (—es, *no pl.*) substitute; compensation, amends; (*Mil. etc.*) replacement.
erschallen [ɛr'ʃalən], *v.n.* (*aux.* sein) resound, sound.
erschaudern [ɛr'ʃaudərn], *v.n.* (*aux.* sein) be seized with horror.
erscheinen [ɛr'ʃaɪnən], *v.n. irr.* (*aux.* sein) appear, make o.'s appearance; seem; be published.
erschießen [ɛr'ʃi:sən], *v.a. irr.* shoot dead.
erschlaffen [ɛr'ʃlafən], *v.n.* (*aux.* sein) flag, slacken.
erschlagen [ɛr'ʃla:gən], *v.a. irr.* slay, kill.
erschließen [ɛr'ʃli:sən], *v.a. irr.* open up.
erschöpfen [ɛr'ʃœpfən], *v.a.* exhaust.
erschrecken [ɛr'ʃrɛkən], *v.a. irr.* startle, shock, terrify. — *v.n.* (*aux.* sein) be startled, be frightened, be terrified.
erschüttern [ɛr'ʃytərn], *v.a.* shake; (*fig.*) move, affect strongly.
erschweren [ɛr'ʃve:rən], *v.a.* (*fig.*) aggravate, make more difficult.
erschwingen [ɛr'ʃvɪŋən], *v.a. irr.* afford, be able to pay.
erschwinglich [ɛr'ʃvɪŋlɪç], *adj.* attainable, within o.'s means.
ersehen [ɛr'ze:ən], *v.a. irr.* — *aus*, gather (from).
ersehnen [ɛr'ze:nən], *v.a.* long for, yearn for.
ersetzen [ɛr'zɛtsən], *v.a.* replace, take the place of; restore, make good; repair; (*money*) refund.
ersichtlich [ɛr'zɪçtlɪç], *adj.* evident.
ersinnen [ɛr'zɪnən], *v.a. irr.* think out, imagine, devise, contrive.
ersparen [ɛr'ʃpa:rən], *v.a.* save.
ersprießlich [ɛr'ʃpri:slɪç], *adj.* useful, profitable, beneficial.
erst [e:rst], *num. adj.* first. — *adv.* first, at first, only, but; — *jetzt*, only now; *nun — recht*, now more than ever.
erstatten [ɛr'ʃtatən], *v.a.* reimburse, compensate, repay; *Bericht* —, report.
Erstattung [ɛr'ʃtatuŋ], *f.* (—, *pl.* —en) reimbursement, restitution.
Erstaufführung ['e:rstauffy:ruŋ], *f.* (—, *pl.* —en) (*Theat.*) first night; première.

Erstaunen [ɛr'ʃtaunən], *n.* (—s, *no pl.*) amazement, astonishment, surprise.
erstechen [ɛr'ʃtɛçən], *v.a. irr.* stab.
erstehen [ɛr'ʃte:ən], *v.n. irr.* (*aux.* sein) rise, arise. — *v.a.* buy, purchase.
ersteigen [ɛr'ʃtaɪgən], *v.a. irr.* climb, mount, ascend.
ersticken [ɛr'ʃtɪkən], *v.a. irr.* choke, stifle, suffocate. — *v.n.* (*aux.* sein) choke, suffocate.
erstmalig ['e:rstma:lɪç], *adj.* first. — *adv.* for the first time.
erstreben [ɛr'ʃtre:bən], *v.a.* strive after.
erstrecken [ɛr'ʃtrɛkən], *v.r. sich* —, extend, reach to.
ersuchen [ɛr'zu:xən], *v.a.* request, ask.
ertappen [ɛr'tapən], *v.a.* catch, detect.
erteilen [ɛr'taɪlən], *v.a.* bestow, impart; *einen Auftrag* —, issue an order; *Unterricht* —, instruct; *die Erlaubnis* —, give permission.
ertönen [ɛr'tø:nən], *v.n.* (*aux.* sein) sound, resound.
Ertrag [ɛr'tra:k], *m.* (—s, *pl.* ⸚e) produce; returns, yield; output; (*sale*) proceeds.
ertragen [ɛr'tra:gən], *v.a. irr.* bear, suffer, endure.
ertränken [ɛr'trɛnkən], *v.a.* drown.
ertrinken [ɛr'trɪŋkən], *v.n. irr.* (*aux.* sein) drown, be drowned.
erübrigen [ɛr'y:brɪgən], *v.a.* save, spare.
erwachen [ɛr'vaxən], *v.n.* (*aux.* sein) awake, wake up.
erwachsen [ɛr'vaksən], *adj.* grown-up, adult. — *v.n. irr.* grow up; ensue, follow, arise.
erwägen [ɛr've:gən], *v.a. irr.* weigh, ponder, consider.
erwähnen [ɛr've:nən], *v.a.* mention.
erwärmen [ɛr'vɛrmən], *v.a.* warm (up), make warm.
erwarten [ɛr'vartən], *v.a.* expect, await.
Erwartung [ɛr'vartuŋ], *f.* (—, *pl.* —en) expectation.
erwecken [ɛr'vɛkən], *v.a.* wake up, awaken, raise; rouse.
erwehren [ɛr've:rən], *v.r. sich* — (*Genit.*), defend o.s.; *ich kann mich des Lachens nicht* —, I cannot help laughing.
erweichen [ɛr'vaɪçən], *v.a.* soften.
erweisen [ɛr'vaɪzən], *v.a. irr.* prove, show; demonstrate.
erweitern [ɛr'vaɪtərn], *v.a.* widen, enlarge, expand.
erwerben [ɛr'vɛrbən], *v.a. irr.* acquire.
erwidern [ɛr'vi:dərn], *v.a.* reply, answer; return.
erwirken [ɛr'vɪrkən], *v.a.* effect, secure.
erwischen [ɛr'vɪʃən], *v.a. see* ertappen.
erwünschen [ɛr'vynʃən], *v.a.* desire, wish for.
erwürgen [ɛr'vyrgən], *v.a.* strangle, throttle.
Erz [ɛrts], (—es, *pl.* —e) ore; brass, bronze.

erzählen [ɛr'tsɛːlən], *v.a.* narrate, relate, tell.

Erzbischof ['ɛrtsbiʃɔf], *m.* (—s, *pl.* ⁓e) archbishop.

erzeugen [ɛr'tsɔygən], *v.a.* engender; beget; produce; (*Elec.*) generate.

Erzherzog ['ɛrtshertsoːk], *m.* (—s, *pl.* ⁓e) archduke.

erziehen [ɛr'tsiːən], *v.a. irr.* educate, train, bring up, rear.

Erziehungsanstalt [ɛr'tsiːuŋsanʃtalt], *f.* (—, *pl.* —en) approved school, reformatory.

erzielen [ɛr'tsiːlən], *v.a.* obtain; fetch, realize (a price); *Gewinn* —, make a profit.

erzittern [ɛr'tsɪtərn], *v.n.* (*aux.* sein) tremble, shake.

Erzofen ['ɛrtsoːfən], *m.* (—s, *pl.* ⁓n) furnace.

erzürnen [ɛr'tsyrnən], *v.a.* make angry. — *v.r. sich* —, grow angry.

Erzvater ['ɛrtsfaːtər], *m.* (—s, *pl.* ⁓) patriarch.

erzwingen [ɛr'tsvɪŋən], *v.a. irr.* enforce, force, compel.

es [ɛs], *pron.* it; — *gibt*, there is; — *sind*, there are; — *lebe*, long live!

Es [ɛs], *n.* (—, *pl.* —) (*Mus.*) E flat.

Esche ['ɛʃə], *f.* (—, *pl.* —n) (*Bot.*) ash, ashtree.

Esel ['eːzəl], *m.* (—s, *pl.* —) ass, donkey.

Eselsohr ['eːzəlsoːr], *n.* (—s, *pl.* —en) (*fig.*) dog's ear.

Eskadron [eska'droːn], *f.* (—, *pl.* —en) squadron.

Espe ['ɛspə], *f.* (—, *pl.* —n) (*Bot.*) asp, aspen.

eßbar ['ɛsbaːr], *adj.* edible.

Esse ['ɛsə], *f.* (—, *pl.* —n) chimney, forge.

Essen ['ɛsən], *n.* (—s, *no pl.*) meal; eating.

essen ['ɛsən], *v.a. irr.* eat, have a meal.

Essenz [ɛ'sɛnts], *f.* (—, *pl.* —en) essence.

Essig ['ɛsɪç], *m.* (—s, *no pl.*) vinegar.

Eßlöffel ['ɛslœfəl], *m.* (—s, *pl.* —) table-spoon.

Estland ['ɛstlant], *n.* Estonia.

Estrade [ɛ'straːdə], *f.* (—, *pl.* —n) platform.

Estrich ['ɛstrɪç], *m.* (—s, *no pl.*) floor, flooring, plaster-floor.

etablieren [eta'bliːrən], *v.a.* establish, set up (business).

Etagenwohnung [e'taːʒənvoːnuŋ], *f.* (—, *pl.* —en) flat; (*Am.*) apartment.

Etappe [e'tapə], *f.* (—, *pl.* —n) stage; (*Mil.*) lines of communication.

Etat [e'taː], *m.* (—s, *pl.* —s) (*Parl.*) estimates, budget; (*Comm.*) statement, balance sheet.

ethisch ['eːtɪʃ], *adj.* ethical.

Etikett [eti'kɛt], *n.* (—s, *pl.* —s) label, ticket, tag.

Etikette [eti'kɛtə], *f.* (—, *no pl.*) etiquette; ceremonial.

etikettieren [etikɛ'tiːrən], *v.a.* label.

etliche ['ɛtlɪçə], *pl. adj. & pron.* some, several, sundry.

Etui [e'tviː], *n.* (—s, *pl.* —s) small case, small box.

etwa ['ɛtva], *adv.* nearly, about; perhaps, perchance, in some way.

etwaig ['ɛtvaɪç], *adj.* possible, any, eventual.

etwas ['ɛtvas], *indef. pron.* some, something. — *adj.* some, any. — *adv.* a little, somewhat.

Etzel ['ɛtsəl], *m.* Attila.

euch [ɔyç], *pers. pron. pl. Dat. & Acc.* you, yourselves.

euer ['ɔyər], *poss. adj.* your. — *poss. pron.* yours.

Eule ['ɔylə], *f.* (—, *pl.* —n) owl.

eurige ['ɔyrɪɡə], *poss. pron.* der, die, das —, yours.

Europa [ɔy'roːpa], *n.* Europe.

Euter ['ɔytər], *n.* (—s, *pl.* —) udder.

evangelisch [evan'ɡeːlɪʃ], *adj.* Evangelical, Protestant.

Evangelium [evan'ɡeːljum], *n.* (—s, *pl.* —lien) gospel.

eventuell [eventu'ɛl], *adj.* possible.

ewig ['eːvɪç], *adj.* eternal; perpetual.

Ewigkeit ['eːvɪçkaɪt], *f.* (—, *pl.* —en) eternity.

explodieren [ɛksplo'diːrən], *v.n.* explode; detonate.

exponieren [ɛkspo'niːrən], *v.a.* set forth, explain at length.

Extemporale [ɛkstɛmpo'raːlə], *n.* (—s, *pl.* —lien) unprepared exercise.

extrahieren [ɛkstra'hiːrən], *v.a.* extract.

Extremitäten [ɛkstremi'tɛːtən], *f. pl.* extremities.

F

F [ɛf], *n.* (—s, *pl.* —s) the letter F; (*Mus.*) *F Dur*, F major; *F Moll*, F minor.

Fabel ['faːbəl], *f.* (—, *pl.* —n) fable; (*fig.*) tale, fiction; (*drama*) plot, story.

fabelhaft ['faːbəlhaft], *adj.* fabulous; phenomenal, gorgeous.

fabeln ['faːbəln], *v.n.* tell fables; talk nonsense.

Fabrik [fa'briːk], *f.* (—, *pl.* —en) factory; plant, works.

Fabrikant [fabri'kant], *m.* (—en, *pl.* —en) manufacturer.

fabrizieren [fabri'tsiːrən], *v.a.* manufacture, make.

fabulieren [fabu'liːrən], *v.n.* tell fables; (*fig.*) tell tall stories.

Fach [fax], *n.* (—s, *pl.* ⁓er) compartment; pigeon-hole, drawer; (*fig.*) subject of study, department, branch.

Fachausdruck ['faxausdruk], *m.* (—s, *pl.* ⁓e) technical term.

Fächer

Fächer ['fɛçər], *m.* (—s, *pl.* —) fan.
Fächertaube ['fɛçərtaubə], *f.* (—, *pl.* —n) fantail.
Fachmann ['faxman], *m.* (—s, *pl.* ⸚er *or* **Fachleute**) expert, specialist.
Fachschule ['faxʃuːlə], *f.* (—, *pl.* —n) technical school.
fachsimpeln ['faxzɪmpəln], *v.n.* talk shop.
Fachwerk ['faxvɛrk], *n.* (—s, *no pl.*) timbered framework.
Fackel ['fakəl], *f.* (—, *pl.* —n) torch.
fade ['faːdə], *adj.* tasteless; boring, insipid.
Faden ['faːdən], *m.* (—s, *pl.* ⸚) thread; (*measure*) fathom.
fadenscheinig ['faːdənʃainɪç], *adj.* threadbare.
Fagott [fa'gɔt], *n.* (—s, *pl.* —e) (*Mus.*) bassoon.
fähig ['fɛːɪç], *adj.* able, capable; talented, gifted, competent.
fahl [faːl], *adj.* pale, sallow.
Fähnchen ['fɛːnçən], *n.* (—s, *pl.* —) small banner; pennon; (*Mil.*) (*obs.*) small troop.
fahnden ['faːndən], *v.a.* search for (officially).
Fahne ['faːnə], *f.* (—, *pl.* —n) flag, banner, standard, colours; (*weather*) vane; (*Typ.*) galley proof.
Fahnenflucht ['faːnənfluxt], *f.* (—, *no pl.*) (*Mil.*) desertion.
Fähnrich ['fɛːnrɪç], *m.* (—s, *pl.* —e) ensign.
Fahrbahn ['faːrbaːn], *f.* (—, *pl.* —en) traffic lane, roadway.
fahrbar ['faːrbaːr], *adj.* passable, navigable, negotiable.
Fähre ['fɛːrə], *f.* (—, *pl.* —n) ferry, ferry-boat.
fahren. ['faːrən], *v.a. irr.* drive. — *v.n.* (*aux.* sein) (*vehicle*) ride (in), be driven; (*vessel*) sail; go, travel.
Fahrer ['faːrər], *m.* (—s, *pl.* —) driver, chauffeur.
Fahrgast ['faːrgast], *m.* (—s, *pl.* ⸚e) passenger.
fahrig ['faːrɪç], *adj.* absent-minded, giddy, thoughtless.
Fahrkarte ['faːrkartə], *f.* (—, *pl.* —n) ticket.
fahrlässig ['faːrlɛsɪç], *adj.* negligent, careless.
Fährmann ['fɛːrman], *m.* (—s, *pl.* ⸚er) ferry-man.
Fahrplan ['faːrplaːn], *m.* (—s, *pl.* ⸚e) timetable, railway-guide.
fahrplanmäßig ['faːrplaːnmɛːsɪç], *adj.* according to the timetable, scheduled.
Fahrpreis ['faːrprais], *m.* (—es, *pl.* —e) cost of ticket, fare.
Fahrrad ['faːrraːt], *n.* (—s, *pl.* ⸚er) cycle, bicycle.
Fahrschein ['faːrʃain], *m.* (—s, *pl.* —e) ticket.
Fahrstraße ['faːrʃtraːsə], *f.* (—, *pl.* —n) roadway.
Fahrstuhl ['faːrʃtuːl], *m.* (—s, *pl.* ⸚e) lift; (*Am.*) elevator.

Fahrt [faːrt], *f.* (—, *pl.* —en) drive, ride, journey; (*sea*) voyage, cruise.
Fährte ['fɛːrtə], *f.* (—, *pl.* —n) track, trace, trail.
Fahrzeug ['faːrtsɔyk], *n.* (—s, *pl.* —e) vehicle, conveyance; vessel, craft.
faktisch ['faktiʃ], *adj.* real, actual.
Faktor ['faktɔr], *m.* (—s, *pl.* —en) foreman, overseer, factor; (*Maths.*) factor, component part.
Faktura [fak'tuːra], *f.* (—, *pl.* —ren) (*Comm.*) invoice.
fakturieren [faktu'riːrən], *v.a.* (*Comm.*) invoice.
Fakultät [fakul'tɛːt], *f.* (—, *pl.* —en) (*Univ.*) faculty.
fakultativ [fakulta'tiːf], *adj.* optional.
Falbel ['falbəl], *f.* (—, *pl.* —n) flounce, furbelow.
Falke ['falkə], *m.* (—n, *pl.* —n) (*Orn.*) falcon, hawk.
Fall [fal], *m.* (—s, *pl.* ⸚e) fall, falling; case; (*Geog.*) decline, incline, gradient; (*fig.*) fall, decline, downfall, failure.
Fallbaum ['falbaum], *m.* (—s, *pl.* ⸚e) tollbar, turnpike.
Fallbeil ['falbail], *n.* (—s, *pl.* —e) guillotine.
Fallbrücke ['falbrykə], *f.* (—, *pl.* —n) draw-bridge.
Falle ['falə], *f.* (—, *pl.* —n) trap, snare.
fallen ['falən], *v.n. irr.* (*aux.* sein) fall, drop; (*Mil.*) be killed.
fällen ['fɛlən], *v.a.* fell, cut down, hew down; *ein Urteil* —, (*Law*) pronounce judgment.
Fallensteller ['falənʃtɛlər], *m.* (—s, *pl.* —) trapper.
fallieren [fa'liːrən], *v.n.* become bankrupt.
fällig ['fɛlɪç], *adj.* due, payable.
Fälligkeit ['fɛlɪçkait], *f.* (—, *pl.* —en) (*Comm.*) maturity.
Fallobst ['falo:pst], *n.* (—es, *no pl.*) windfall (of fruit).
falls [fals], *conj.* in case, if.
Fallschirm ['falʃirm], *m.* (—s, *pl.* —e) parachute.
Fallstrick ['falʃtrik], *m.* (—s, *pl.* —e) snare, trap.
Fallsucht ['falzuxt], *f.* (—, *no pl.*) (*Med.*) epilepsy.
Falltür ['falty:r], *f.* (—, *pl.* —en) trap-door.
Fällung ['fɛluŋ], *f.* (—, *pl.* —en) cutting down.
falsch [falʃ], *adj.* false, incorrect, wrong; disloyal; counterfeit.
fälschen ['fɛlʃən], *v.a.* falsify, forge, tamper with.
Falschheit ['falʃhait], *f.* (—, *pl.* —en) falsehood, deceit, disloyalty.
fälschlich ['fɛlʃlɪç], *adv.* wrongly, falsely.
Fälschung ['fɛlʃuŋ], *f.* (—, *pl.* —en) falsification, forgery.
Falte ['faltə], *f.* (—, *pl.* —n) fold, pleat; (*face*) wrinkle.
falten ['faltən], *v.a.* fold, plait, pleat; wrinkle.

68

Falter ['faltər], *m.* (—s, *pl.* —) (*Ent.*) butterfly.

-fältig [fɛltɪç], *suffix* (*following numbers*). -fold (*e.g.* vierfältig, fourfold).

Falz [falts], *m.* (—es, *pl.* —e) groove, notch; joint.

Falzbein ['faltsbaɪn], *n.* (—s, *pl.* —e) paper-folder, paper-knife.

Falzmaschine ['faltsmaʃiːnə], *f.* (—, *pl.* —n) folding-machine.

familiär [famil'jɛːr], *adj.* familiar, intimate.

Familie [fa'miːljə], *f.* (—, *pl.* —n) family.

famos [fa'moːs], *adj.* (*coll.*) excellent, splendid.

fanatisch [fa'naːtɪʃ], *adj.* fanatic(al), bigoted.

Fanatismus [fana'tɪsmus], *m.* (—, *no pl.*) fanaticism.

Fang [faŋ], *m.* (—es, *pl.* ⁀e) catch, capture; (*bird*) talon, claw.

fangen ['faŋən], *v.a. irr.* catch, seize.

Fangzahn ['faŋtsaːn], *m.* (—s, *pl.* ⁀e) fang, tusk.

Fant [fant], *m.* (—s, *pl.* —e) fop, cockscomb.

Farbe ['farbə], *f.* (—, *pl.* —n) colour, hue, paint, dye.

färben ['fɛrbən], *v.a.* dye, stain.

Farbenbrett ['farbənbrɛt], *n.* (—s, *pl.* —er) palette.

Farb(en)druck ['farpdruk, farbəndruk], *m.* (—s, *pl.* —e) colour-printing.

Farbenspiel ['farbənʃpiːl], *n.* (—s, *no pl.*) iridescence.

Färber ['fɛrbər], *m.* (—s, *pl.* —) dyer.

farbig ['farbɪç], *adj.* coloured.

Farbstift ['farpʃtɪft], *m.* (—s, *pl.* —e) crayon.

Farbstoff ['farpʃtɔf], *m.* (—es, *pl.* —e) dye.

Farbton ['farptoːn], *m.* (—s, *pl.* ⁀e) hue, tone, tinge, shade.

Farn [farn], *m.* (—s, *pl.* —e) (*Bot.*) fern.

Färse ['fɛrzə], *f.* (—, *pl.* —n) (*Zool.*) heifer.

Fasan [fa'zaːn], *m.* (—s, *pl.* —e) (*Orn.*) pheasant.

Fasching ['faʃɪŋ], *m.* (—s, *no pl.*) (*Shrovetide*) carnival.

Faschismus [fa'ʃɪsmus], *m.* (—s, *no pl.*) fascism.

Faselei [fa:zə'laɪ], *f.* (—, *pl.* —en) silly talk, drivel.

faseln ['faːzəln], *v.n.* drivel.

Faser ['faːzər], *f.* (—, *pl.* —n) thread; string; fibre, filament.

fasern ['faːzərn], *v.n.* fray.

Faß [fas], *n.* (—sses, *pl.* ⁀sser) barrel, vat, tun, tub, cask, keg; *Bier vom* —, draught beer; *Wein vom* —, wine from the wood.

Fassade [fa'saːdə], *f.* (—, *pl.* —n) façade.

faßbar ['fasbaːr], *adj.* tangible.

Faßbinder ['fasbɪndər], *m.* (—s, *pl.* —) cooper.

fassen ['fasən], *v.a.* seize, take hold of, grasp; (*jewels*) set; contain, hold. — *v.r.* (*aux.* haben) *sich* —, compose o.s.; *sich kurz* —, be brief.

faßlich ['faslɪç], *adj.* comprehensible, understandable.

Fasson [fa'sõ], *f.* (—, *pl.* —s) fashion; (*fig.*) cut, style.

Fassung ['fasuŋ], *f.* (—, *pl.* —en) (*jewels*) setting; (*speech*) wording, version; (*fig.*) composure.

fassungslos ['fasuŋsloːs], *adj.* bewildered, disconcerted; distraught, speechless.

fast [fast], *adv.* almost, nearly.

fasten ['fastən], *v.n.* fast.

Fastenzeit ['fastəntsaɪt], *f.* (—, *pl.* —en) time of fasting; Lent.

Fastnacht ['fastnaxt], *f.* (—, *no pl.*) Shrove Tuesday; Shrovetide.

fauchen ['fauxən], *v.n.* spit, hiss.

faul [faul], *adj.* (*food*) rotten, putrid, decayed; (*persons*) lazy, idle.

Fäule ['fɔylə], *f.* (—, *no pl.*) rot.

faulen ['faulən], *v.n.* (*aux.* sein) rot.

faulenzen ['faulɛntsən], *v.n.* laze, idle.

Faulenzer ['faulɛntsər], *m.* (—s, *pl.* —) idler, sluggard, lazybones.

Faulenzerei ['faulɛntsəraɪ], *f.* (—, *pl.* —en) idleness, laziness.

Faulheit ['faulhaɪt], *f.* (—, *no pl.*) idleness, laziness, sluggishness.

faulig ['faulɪç], *adj.* putrid, rotten.

Fäulnis ['fɔylnɪs], *f.* (—, *no pl.*) rottenness, putridity.

Faust [faust], *f.* (—, *pl.* ⁀e) fist.

Fäustchen ['fɔystçən], *n.* (—s, *pl.* —) small fist; *sich ins* — *lachen*, laugh in o.'s sleeve.

Faustkampf ['faustkampf], *m.* (—es, *pl.* ⁀e) boxing (match).

Faxen ['faksən], *f. pl.* foolery; — *machen*, play the buffoon.

Fazit ['fatsɪt], *n.* (—s, *no pl.*) sum, amount.

Februar ['feːbruaːr], *m.* (—s, *no pl.*) February.

fechten ['fɛçtən], *v.n. irr.* fight; fence; (*fig.*) beg.

Feder ['feːdər], *f.* (—, *pl.* —n) (*bird*) feather; (*hat*) plume; (*writing*) pen; (*antique*) quill; (*Tech.*) spring.

Federball ['feːdərbal], *m.* (—s, *pl.* ⁀e) shuttle-cock.

federig ['feːdərɪç], *adj.* feathery; (*Tech.*) springy, resilient.

Federlesen(s) ['feːdərleːzən(s)], *n.* (—s, *no pl.*) *nicht viel* — *machen*, make short work of.

Fee [feː], *f.* (—, *pl.* —n) fairy.

feenhaft ['feːənhaft], *adj.* fairy-like, magical.

Fegefeuer ['feːgəfɔyər], *n.* (—s, *no pl.*) purgatory.

fegen ['feːgən], *v.a.* clean, sweep. — *v.n.* (*aux.* sein) tear along.

Fehde ['feːdə], *f.* (—, *pl.* —n) feud, quarrel.

Fehdehandschuh ['feːdəhantʃuː], *m.* (—s, *pl.* —e) gauntlet.

fehlbar ['fe:lba:r], *adj.* fallible.
Fehlbetrag ['fe:lbǝtra:k], *m.* (—s, *pl.* ̈e) deficit.
fehlen ['fe:lǝn], *v.a.* miss. — *v.n.* err, do wrong; be absent; be wanting; *er fehlt mir*, I miss him.
Fehler ['fe:lǝr], *m.* (—s, *pl.* —) fault, defect; mistake, error.
Fehlgeburt ['fe:lgǝburt], *f.* (—, *pl.* —en) miscarriage.
Fehlschlag ['fe:lʃla:k], *m.* (—s, *pl.* ̈e) failure, disappointment.
feien ['faɪǝn], *v.a. einen — gegen*, charm s.o. against; *gefeit*, proof.
Feier ['faɪǝr], *f.* (—, *pl.* —n) celebration, festival, holiday, festive day.
Feierabend ['faɪǝra:bǝnt], *m.* (—s, *pl.* —e) time for leaving off work; — *machen*, knock off (work).
feierlich ['faɪǝrlɪç], *adj.* festive, solemn, stately.
feiern ['faɪǝrn], *v.a.* celebrate; honour, praise. — *v.n.* rest from work.
Feiertag ['faɪǝrta:k], *m.* (—s, *pl.* —e) holiday, festive day.
feig [faɪk], *adj.* cowardly.
Feige ['faɪgǝ], *f.* (—, *pl.* —n) (*Bot.*) fig.
Feigheit ['faɪkhaɪt], *f.* (—, *pl.* —en) cowardice, cowardliness.
Feigling ['faɪklɪŋ], *m.* (—s, *pl.* —e) coward.
Feigwurz ['faɪkvurts], *m.* (—es, *no pl.*) (*Bot.*) fennel.
feil [faɪl], *adj.* (*obs.*) for sale; venal.
feilbieten ['faɪlbi:tǝn], *v.a.* offer for sale.
Feile ['faɪlǝ], *f.* (—, *pl.* —n) file.
feilen ['faɪlǝn], *v.a.* file.
feilhalten ['faɪlhaltǝn], *v.a.* have for sale, be ready to sell.
feilschen ['faɪlʃǝn], *v.n.* bargain, haggle.
Feilspäne ['faɪlʃpɛ:nǝ], *m. pl.* filings.
fein [faɪn], *adj.* fine; neat, pretty, nice; delicate; (*clothes*) elegant; (*behaviour*) refined, polished.
Feinbäckerei ['faɪnbɛkǝraɪ], *f.* (—, *pl.* —en) confectioner's shop.
Feind [faɪnt], *m.* (—es, *pl.* —e) enemy, foe, adversary.
Feindschaft ['faɪntʃaft], *f.* (—, *pl.* —en) enmity, hostility.
feindselig ['faɪntze:lɪç], *adj.* hostile, malignant.
feinfühlend ['faɪnfy:lǝnt], *adj.* delicate, sensitive.
Feinheit ['faɪnhaɪt], *f.* (—, *pl.* —en) fineness, elegance, politeness, delicacy.
Feinschmecker ['faɪnʃmɛkǝr], *m.* (—s, *pl.* —), gourmet.
Feinsliebchen ['faɪns'li:pçǝn], *n.* (—s, *pl.* —) (*Poet. obs.*) sweetheart.
feist [faɪst], *adj.* fat, obese.
Feld [fɛlt], *n.* (—es, *pl.* —er) field, plain; (*chess*) square; (*fig.*) sphere, province.
Feldbett ['fɛltbɛt], *n.* (—s, *pl.* —en) camp-bed.
Feldherr ['fɛlthɛr], *m.* (—n, *pl.* —en) commander, general.

Feldmesser ['fɛltmɛsǝr], *m.* (—s, *pl.* —) land-surveyor.
Feldscher ['fɛltʃe:r], *m.* (—s, *pl.* —e) army-surgeon.
Feldstecher ['fɛltʃtɛçǝr], *m.* (—s, *pl.* —) field-glass(es).
Feldwebel ['fɛltve:bǝl], *m.* (—s, *pl.* —) sergeant-major.
Feldzug ['fɛlttsu:k], *m.* (—es, *pl.* ̈e) campaign, expedition.
Felge ['fɛlgǝ], *f.* (—, *pl.* —n) (*wheel*) felloe, felly, rim.
Fell [fɛl], *n.* (—s, *pl.* —e) hide, skin, pelt.
Felsabhang ['fɛlsaphaŋ], *m.* (—s, *pl.* ̈e) rocky slope.
Felsen ['fɛlzǝn], *m.* (—s, *pl.* —) rock, cliff.
Felsengebirge ['fɛlzǝngǝbɪrgǝ], *n.* Rocky Mountains.
Felsenriff ['fɛlzǝnrɪf], *n.* (—s, *pl.* —e) reef.
felsig ['fɛlzɪç], *adj.* rocky.
Feme ['fe:mǝ], *f.* (—, *pl.* —n) secret tribunal.
Fenchel ['fɛnçǝl], *m.* (—s, *no pl.*) (*Bot.*) fennel.
Fenster ['fɛnstǝr], *n.* (—s, *pl.* —) window.
Fensterbrett ['fɛnstǝrbrɛt], *n.* (—s, *pl.* —er) window-sill.
Fensterflügel ['fɛnstǝrfly:gǝl], *m.* (—s, *pl.* —) (window) casement.
Fensterladen ['fɛnstǝrla:dǝn], *m.* (—s, *pl.* ̈) shutter.
Fensterscheibe ['fɛnstǝrʃaɪbǝ], *f.* (—, *pl.* —n) pane.
Ferien ['fe:rjǝn], *pl.* holidays.
Ferkel ['fɛrkǝl], *n.* (—s, *pl.* —) young pig, piglet.
Fermate [fɛr'ma:tǝ], *f.* (—, *pl.* —n) (*Mus.*) pause, fermata.
fern [fɛrn], *adj.* far, distant, remote.
Fernbleiben ['fɛrnblaɪbǝn], *n.* (—s, *no pl.*) absence.
Ferne ['fɛrnǝ], *f.* (—, *pl.* —n) distance, remoteness.
ferner ['fɛrnǝr], *adv.* further, furthermore, moreover.
fernerhin ['fɛrnǝrhɪn], *adv.* henceforth.
Ferngespräch ['fɛrngǝʃprɛx], *n.* (—s, *pl.* —e) long-distance telephone call, trunk call.
Fernglas ['fɛrngla:s], *n.* (—es, *pl.* ̈er) binoculars.
fernhalten ['fɛrnhaltǝn], *v.a. irr.* keep away.
fernher ['fɛrnhe:r], *adv. von* —, from afar.
fernliegen ['fɛrnli:gǝn], *v.n. irr.* be far from.
Fernrohr ['fɛrnro:r], *n.* (—s, *pl.* —e) telescope.
Fernschreiber ['fɛrnʃraɪbǝr], *m.* (—s, *pl.* —) teleprinter.
Fernsehen ['fɛrnze:ǝn], *n.* (—s, *no pl.*) television.
fernsehen ['fɛrnze:ǝn], *v.n. irr.* watch television.

Fernsehgerät ['fɛrnze:gərɛ:t], *n.* (—s, —e) television set.

Fernsprechamt ['fɛrnʃprɛçamt], *n.* (—s, *pl.* ⁝er) telephone exchange.

Fernsprecher ['fɛrnʃprɛçər], *m.* (—s, *pl.* —) telephone.

Fernstehende ['fɛrnʃte:əndə], *m.* (—n, *pl.* —n) outsider.

Fernverkehr ['fɛrnfɛrke:r], *m.* (—s, *no pl.*) long-distance traffic.

Ferse ['fɛrzə], *f.* (—, *pl.* —n) heel.

Fersengeld ['fɛrzəngɛlt], *n.* (—s, *no pl.*) — *geben*, take to o.'s heels.

fertig ['fɛrtɪç], *adj.* ready, finished; (*coll.*) worn-out, ruined, done for.

Fertigkeit ['fɛrtɪçkaɪt], *f.* (—, *pl.* —en) dexterity, skill.

Fes [fɛs], *n.* (—, *pl.* —) (*Mus.*) F flat.

fesch [fɛʃ], *adj.* smart, stylish; (*dial.*) good-looking.

Fessel ['fɛsəl], *f.* (—, *pl.* —n) fetter, shackle.

Fesselballon ['fɛsəlbaló], *m.* (—s, *pl.* —s) captive balloon.

Fesselbein ['fɛsəlbaɪn], *n.* (—s, *pl.* —e) pastern-joint.

fesseln ['fɛsəln], *v.a.* fetter, shackle, chain; (*fig.*) captivate.

Fest [fɛst], *n.* (—es, *pl.* —e) feast, festival.

fest [fɛst], *adj.* fast, firm; solid, hard; sound; fixed; constant, steadfast.

Feste ['fɛstə], *f.* (—, *pl.* —n) fortress, stronghold.

festigen ['fɛstɪgən], *v.a.* make firm; strengthen.

Festland ['fɛstlant], *n.* (—es, *pl.* ⁝er) continent.

festlich ['fɛstlɪç], *adj.* festive, solemn.

festmachen ['fɛstmaxən], *v.a.* fasten.

Festnahme ['fɛstna:mə], *f.* (—, *no pl.*) apprehension, arrest.

festnehmen ['fɛstne:mən], *v.a. irr.* seize, arrest.

Festrede ['fɛstre:də], *f.* (—, *pl.* —n) formal address.

festschnallen ['fɛstʃnalən], *v.a.* buckle on, fasten.

Festschrift ['fɛstʃrɪft], *f.* (—, *pl.* —en) commemorative volume (in honour of a person or an occasion).

festsetzen ['fɛstzɛtsən], *v.a.* fix, decree.

Festspiel ['fɛstʃpi:l], *n.* (—s, *pl.* —e) festival (play).

feststehen ['fɛstʃte:ən], *v.n. irr.* stand firm; *es steht fest*, it is certain.

feststellen ['fɛstʃtɛlən], *v.a.* ascertain; state; find; determine; diagnose; establish.

Festtag ['fɛstta:k], *m.* (—s, *pl.* —e) feast-day, holiday.

Festung ['fɛstuŋ], *f.* (—, *pl.* —en) fortress, stronghold, citadel.

festziehen ['fɛsttsi:ən], *v.a. irr.* tighten.

Festzug ['fɛsttsu:k], *m.* (—s, *pl.* ⁝e) procession.

Fett [fɛt], *n.* (—s, *pl.* —e) fat, grease, lard.

fett [fɛt], *adj.* fat, greasy.

fettartig ['fɛtartɪç], *adj.* fatty.

fetten ['fɛtən], *v.a.* oil, grease.

Fettfleck ['fɛtflɛk], *m.* (—s, *pl.* —e) spot of grease.

fettgedruckt ['fɛtgədrukt], *adj.* in heavy type.

fetthaltig ['fɛthaltɪç], *adj.* greasy; adipose.

fettig ['fɛtɪç], *adj.* greasy.

fettleibig ['fɛtlaɪbɪç], *adj.* corpulent, obese.

Fetzen ['fɛtsən], *m.* (—s, *pl.* —) piece, rag, tatter, shred.

feucht [fɔyçt], *adj.* moist; (*weather*) muggy, wet; (*room*) damp.

Feuchtigkeit ['fɔyçtɪçkaɪt], *f.* (—, *no pl.*) moisture, humidity, dampness, wetness.

feudal [fɔy'da:l], *adj.* feudal; (*coll.*) distinguished, magnificent.

Feuer ['fɔyər], *n.* (—s, *pl.* —) fire; (*jewels*) brilliancy; (*fig.*) ardour, passion.

feuerbeständig ['fɔyərbəʃtɛndɪç], *adj.* fire-proof.

Feuerbestattung ['fɔyərbəʃtatuŋ], *f.* (—, *pl.* —en) cremation.

Feuereifer ['fɔyəraɪfər], *m.* (—s, *no pl.*) ardour.

feuerfest ['fɔyərfɛst], *adj.* fire-proof, incombustible.

feuergefährlich ['fɔyərgəfɛ:rlɪç], *adj.* inflammable.

Feuerlilie ['fɔyərli:ljə], *f.* (—, *pl.* —n) tiger lily.

Feuermal ['fɔyərma:l], *n.* (—s, *pl.* —e) burn, burn-mark.

Feuermauer ['fɔyərmauər], *f.* (—, *pl.* —n) fire-proof wall, party-wall.

Feuermelder ['fɔyərmɛldər], *m.* (—s, *pl.* —) fire-alarm.

feuern ['fɔyərn], *v.a.* (*Mil.*) fire, discharge; (*coll.*) fire, sack.

Feuerprobe ['fɔyərpro:bə], *f.* (—, *pl.* —n) ordeal by fire.

Feuerrad ['fɔyərra:t], *n.* (—s, *pl.* ⁝er) Catherine wheel.

Feuerrohr ['fɔyərro:r], *n.* (—s, *pl.* —e) gun, matchlock.

Feuersbrunst ['fɔyərsbrunst], *f.* (—, *pl.* ⁝e) (*rare*) fire, conflagration.

Feuerspritze ['fɔyərʃprɪtsə], *f.* (—, *pl.* —n) fire-engine.

Feuerstein ['fɔyərʃtaɪn], *m.* (—s, *no pl.*) flint.

Feuertaufe ['fɔyərtaufə], *f.* (—, *pl.* —n) baptism of fire.

Feuerwarte ['fɔyərvartə], *f.* (—, *pl.* —en) beacon; lighthouse.

Feuerwehr ['fɔyərve:r], *f.* (—, *no pl.*) fire-brigade.

Feuerwerk ['fɔyərvɛrk], *n.* (—, *no pl.*) fireworks.

Feuerwerkskunst ['fɔyərvɛrkskunst], *f.* (—, *no pl.*) pyrotechnics.

Feuerzange ['fɔyərtsaŋə], *f.* (—, *pl.* —n) fire-tongs.

Feuerzeug ['fɔyərtsɔyk], *n.* (—s, *pl.* —e) match-box; cigarette-lighter.

feurig ['fɔyrɪç], *adj.* fiery, burning; (*fig.*) ardent, impassioned, fervent; (*wine*) heady.

Fiaker

Fiaker [fi'akər], *m.* (—s, *pl.* —) (*Austr.*) cab, hansom; (*Am.*) coach.
Fiasko [fi'asko:], *n.* (—s, *pl.* —s) failure.
Fibel ['fi:bəl], *f.* (—, *pl.* —n) primer, spelling-book.
Fiber ['fi:bər], *f.* (—, *pl.* —n) fibre.
Fichte ['fiçtə], *f.* (—, *pl.* —n) (*Bot.*) pine, pine-tree.
fidel [fi'de:l], *adj.* merry, jolly.
Fidibus ['fi:dibus], *m.* (—ses, *pl.* —se) spill, fidibus.
Fidschi ['fɪdʒi:], Fiji.
Fieber ['fi:bər], *n.* (—s, *no pl.*) fever.
fieberhaft ['fi:bərhaft], *adj.* feverish, vehement.
fieberig ['fi:bərɪç], *adj.* feverish, racked by fever.
Fieberkälte ['fi:bərkɛltə], *f.* (—, *no pl.*) chill, shivering (fit).
fiebern ['fi:bərn], *v.n.* have a fever; (*fig.*) rave.
fiebrig ['fi:brɪç], *see* **fieberig**.
Fiedel ['fi:dəl], *f.* (—, *pl.* —n) (*Mus.*) fiddle, violin.
Figur [fi'gu:r], *f.* (—, *pl.* —en) figure, statue, sculpture; chessman.
figürlich [fi'gy:rlɪç], *adj.* figurative.
Filet [fɪ'le:], *n.* (—s, *pl.* —s) netting, net-work; (*meat*) fillet.
Filiale [fɪl'ja:lə], *f.* (—, *pl.* —n) branch, branch-establishment, branch-office.
Filigran [fɪli'gra:n], *n.* (—s, *no pl.*) filigree.
Film [fɪlm], *m.* (—s, *pl.* —e) film; (motion) picture.
Filter ['fɪltər], *m.* (—s, *pl.* —) filter.
filtrieren [fɪl'tri:rən], *v.a.* filter.
Filz [fɪlts], *m.* (—es, *pl.* —e) felt; (*fig.*) niggard, miser, skinflint.
Filzlaus ['fɪltslaus], *f.* (—, *pl.* ⁻e) crab-louse.
Finanzamt [fɪ'nantsamt], *n.* (—s, *pl.* ⁻er) income-tax office; revenue-office.
Finanzen [fɪ'nantsən], *f. pl.* finances, revenue.
Findelkind ['fɪndəlkɪnt], *n.* (—s, *pl.* —er) foundling.
finden ['fɪndən], *v.a. irr.* find. — *v.r. sich* —, *das wird sich* —, we shall see.
Finder ['fɪndər], *m.* (—s, *pl.* —) finder.
findig ['fɪndɪç], *adj.* resourceful, ingenious.
Findling ['fɪntlɪŋ], *m.* (—s, *pl.* —e) foundling.
Finger ['fɪŋər], *m.* (—s, *pl.* —) finger.
Fingerabdruck ['fɪŋərapdruk], *m.* (—s, *pl.* ⁻e) finger-print.
fingerfertig ['fɪŋerfertɪç], *adj.* nimble-fingered.
Fingerhut ['fɪŋərhu:t], *m.* (—s, *pl.* ⁻e) thimble; (*Bot.*) foxglove.
fingern ['fɪŋərn], *v.a.* touch with the fingers, finger.
Fingersatz ['fɪŋərzats], *m.* (—es, *pl.* ⁻e) (*Mus.*) fingering.

Fingerspitze ['fɪŋərʃpɪtsə], *f.* (—, *pl.* —n) finger-tip.
Fingerzeig ['fɪŋərtsaɪk], *m.* (—s, *pl.* —e) hint.
fingieren [fɪŋ'gi:rən], *v.a.* sham.
fingiert [fɪŋ'gi:rt], *adj.* fictitious.
Fink [fɪŋk], *m.* (—en, *pl.* —en) (*Orn.*) finch.
Finne (1) ['fɪnə], *m.* (—n, *pl.* —n) Finn.
Finne (2) ['fɪnə], *f.* (—, *pl.* —n) pimple; (*fish*) fin.
finnig ['fɪnɪç], *adj.* pimpled; (*fish*) finny.
Finnland ['fɪnlant], *n.* Finland.
finster ['fɪnstər], *adj.* dark, obscure; (*fig.*) gloomy, sinister.
Finsternis ['fɪnstərnɪs], *f.* (—, *no pl.*) darkness, gloom.
Finte ['fɪntə], *f.* (—, *pl.* —n) feint; (*fig.*) pretence, trick.
Firlefanz ['fɪrləfants], *m.* (—es, *no pl.*) foolery.
Firma ['fɪrma], *f.* (—, *pl.* —men) (*business*) firm, company.
Firmung ['fɪrmuŋ], *f.* (—, *pl.* —en) (*Eccl.*) confirmation.
Firnis ['fɪrnɪs], *m.* (—ses, *pl.* —se) varnish.
firnissen ['fɪrnɪsən], *v.a.* varnish.
First [fɪrst], *m.* (—es, *pl.* —e) (*house*) roof-ridge; (*mountain*) top.
Fis [fɪs], *n.* (—, *pl.* —) (*Mus.*) F sharp.
Fisch [fɪʃ], *m.* (—es, *pl.* —e) fish.
Fischadler ['fɪʃa:dlər], *m.* (—s, *pl.* —) osprey, sea-eagle.
Fischbein ['fɪʃbaɪn], *n.* (—s, *no pl.*) whalebone.
fischen ['fɪʃən], *v.a., v.n.* fish, angle.
Fischer ['fɪʃər], *m.* (—s, *pl.* —) fisherman, fisher.
Fischerei [fɪʃə'raɪ], *f.* (—, *no pl.*) fishing; fishery.
Fischgerät ['fɪʃərgɛrɛ:t], *n.* (—s, *pl.* —e) fishing-tackle.
Fischgräte ['fɪʃgre:tə], *f.* (—, *pl.* —n) fish-bone.
Fischkelle ['fɪʃkɛlə], *f.* (—, *pl.* —n) fish-slice.
Fischlaich ['fɪʃlaɪç], *m.* (—s, *no pl.*) spawn.
Fischmilch ['fɪʃmɪlç], *f.* (—, *no pl.*) soft roe, milt.
Fischotter ['fɪʃɔtər], *m.* (—s, *pl.* —n) common otter.
Fischreiher ['fɪʃraɪər], *m.* (—s, *pl.* —) (*Orn.*) heron.
Fischreuse ['fɪʃrɔyzə], *f.* (—, *pl.* —n) bow-net; weir.
Fischrogen ['fɪʃro:gən], *m.* (—s, *no pl.*) roe.
Fischschuppe ['fɪʃʃupə], *f.* (—, *pl.* —n) fish-scale.
Fischtran ['fɪʃtra:n], *m.* (—s, *no pl.*) train-oil.
Fischzucht ['fɪʃtsuxt], *f.* (—, *no pl.*) fish-breeding, pisciculture.
Fiskus ['fɪskus], *m.* (—, *pl.* —ken) Treasury, Exchequer.
Fisole [fi'zo:lə], *f.* (—, *pl.* —n) (*Austr.*) French bean.

Fistelstimme ['fɪstəlʃtɪmə], f. (—, no pl.) (Mus.) falsetto.

Fittich ['fɪtɪç], m. (—es, pl. —e) (Poet.) wing, pinion.

fix [fɪks], adj. quick, sharp; — und fertig, quite ready.

Fixum ['fɪksum], n. (—s, pl. —xa) fixed amount; regular salary.

flach [flax], adj. flat, plain, smooth, level; (water) shallow.

Fläche ['flɛçə], f. (—, pl. —n) plain; (Maths.) plane; (crystal) face.

Flächeninhalt ['flɛçənɪnhalt], m. (—s, no pl.) area.

Flächenmaß ['flɛçənma:s], n. (—es, pl. —e) square-measure.

Flächenraum ['flɛçənraum], m. (—es, no pl.) surface area.

Flachheit ['flaxhaɪt], f. (—, no pl.) flatness; (fig.) shallowness.

Flachs [flaks], m. (—es, no pl.) flax.

flackern ['flakərn], v.n. flare, flicker.

Fladen ['fla:dən], m. (—s, pl. —) flat cake; cow-dung.

Flagge ['flagə], f. (—, pl. —n) flag.

Flame ['fla:mə], m. (—n, pl. —n) Fleming.

flämisch ['flɛ:mɪʃ], adj. Flemish.

Flamme ['flamə], f. (—, pl. —n) flame; blaze.

flammen ['flamən], v.n. flame, blaze, sparkle.

Flammeri ['flaməri:], m. (—s, pl. —s) blancmange.

Flandern ['flandərn], n. Flanders.

Flanell [fla'nɛl], m. (—s, pl. —e) flannel.

Flaneur [fla'nø:r], m. (—s, pl. —e) lounger, stroller.

flanieren [fla'ni:rən], v.n. lounge, stroll.

Flanke ['flaŋkə], f. (—, pl. —n) flank; in die — fallen, (Mil.) attack in the flank.

Flasche ['flaʃə], f. (—, pl. —en) bottle, flask.

Flaschenzug ['flaʃəntsu:k], m. (—es, pl. ꞏ̈e) pulley.

flatterhaft ['flatərhaft], adj. fickle, inconstant, flighty.

flattern ['flatərn], v.n. flutter.

flau [flau], adj. insipid, stale; (fig.) dull.

Flaum [flaum], m. (—s, no pl.) down.

Flausch [flauʃ], m. (—es, no pl.) pilot-cloth.

Flaute ['flautə], f. (—, pl. —n) (Nav.) calm; (fig.) (Comm.) depression.

Flechte ['flɛçtə], f. (—, pl. —n) twist, plait, braid; (Med.) eruption, ring-worm; (Bot.) lichen.

flechten ['flɛçtən], v.a. irr. plait; wreathe.

Flechtwerk ['flɛçtvɛrk], n. (—s, no pl.) wicker-work, basketry.

Fleck [flɛk], m. (—s, pl. —e) spot; place, piece (of ground); (fig.) stain, blemish.

Flecken ['flɛkən], m. (—s, pl. —) market town, small town.

fleckenlos ['flɛkənlo:s], adj. spotless.

fleckig ['flɛkɪç], adj. spotted, speckled

Fledermaus ['fle:dərmaus], f. (—, pl. ꞏ̈e) (Zool.) bat.

Flederwisch ['fle:dərvɪʃ], m. (—es, pl. —e) feather-duster.

Flegel ['fle:gəl], m. (—s, pl. —) flail; (fig.) boor.

flegelhaft ['fle:gəlhaft], adj. boorish, churlish, rude.

Flegeljahre ['fle:gəlja:rə], n. pl. years of indiscretion; teens, adolescence.

flehen ['fle:ən], v.a., v.n. implore, supplicate, entreat.

Fleisch [flaɪʃ], n. (—es, no pl.) (raw) flesh; (for cooking) meat; (fruit) pulp.

Fleischbrühe ['flaɪʃbry:ə], f. (—, pl. —n) broth, beef-tea.

Fleischer ['flaɪʃər], m. (—s, pl. —) butcher.

fleischfressend ['flaɪʃfrɛsənt], adj. carnivorous.

Fleischhacker ['flaɪʃhakər], **Fleischhauer** ['flaɪʃhauər], m. (—s, pl. —) butcher.

fleischlich ['flaɪʃlɪç], adj. fleshly, carnal.

fleischlos ['flaɪʃlo:s], adj. vegetarian.

Fleischpastete ['flaɪʃpaste:tə], f. (—, pl. —n) meat-pie.

Fleiß [flaɪs], m. (—es, no pl.) diligence, assiduity, industry.

fleißig ['flaɪsɪç], adj. diligent, assiduous, industrious, hard-working.

fletschen ['flɛtʃən], v.a. die Zähne —, show o.'s teeth.

Flicken ['flɪkən], m. (—s, pl. —) patch.

flicken ['flɪkən], v.a. patch, repair, mend; (shoes) cobble; (stockings) darn.

Flieder ['fli:dər], m. (—s, pl. —) (Bot.) elder, lilac.

Fliege ['fli:gə], f. (—, pl. —n) (Ent.) fly; (beard) imperial.

fliegen ['fli:gən], v.n. irr. (aux. sein) fly; (coll.) get the sack, be fired. — v.a. fly, pilot (an aircraft).

Flieger ['fli:gər], m. (—s, pl. —) airman, aviator; pilot.

fliehen ['fli:ən], v.n. irr. (aux. sein) flee, run away; zu einem —, take refuge with s.o. — v.a. irr. avoid, shun (s.o.).

Fliehkraft ['fli:kraft], f. (—, no pl.) centrifugal force.

Fliese ['fli:zə], f. (—, pl. —n) floor-tile, flagstone.

Fließband ['fli:sbant], n. (—(e)s, pl. ꞏ̈er) (Ind.) assembly line.

fließen ['fli:sən], v.n. irr. (aux. sein) flow.

Fließpapier ['fli:spapi:r], n. (—s, no pl.) blotting-paper.

Flimmer ['flɪmər], m. (—s, no pl.) glittering, sparkling, glimmer.

flimmern ['flɪmərn], v.n. glisten, glitter.

flink [flɪŋk], adj. brisk, agile, quick, sharp, nimble.

Flinte ['flɪntə], *f.* (—, *pl.* —n) gun, musket, rifle.

Flitter ['flɪtər], *m.* (—s, *no pl.*) tinsel, spangle, frippery.

Flitterwochen ['flɪtərvɔxən], *f. pl.* honeymoon.

flitzen ['flɪtsən], *v.n.* (*aux.* sein) *vorbei* —, flit *or* rush past, dash along.

Flocke ['flɔkə], *f.* (—, *pl.* —n) (*snow*) flake; (*wool*) flock.

Floh [flo:], *m.* (—s, *pl.* ⁔e) (*Ent.*) flea.

Flor [flo:r], *m.* (—s, *pl.* —e) bloom; gauze, crape; *in* —, blossoming, blooming.

Florenz [flo'rɛnts], *n.* Florence.

Florett [flo'rɛt], *n.* (—s, *pl.* —e) (*fencing*) foil.

florieren [flo'ri:rən], *v.n.* flourish.

Florstrumpf ['flo:rʃtrumpf], *m.* (—s, *pl.* ⁔e) lisle stocking.

Floskel ['flɔskəl], *f.* (—, *pl.* —n) rhetorical ornament; oratorical flourish; phrase.

Floß [flo:s], *n.* (—es, *pl.* ⁔e) raft.

Flosse ['flɔsə], *f.* (—, *pl.* —n) fin.

flößen ['flø:sən], *v.a.* float.

Flößer ['flø:sər], *m.* (—s, *pl.* —) raftsman.

Flöte ['flø:tə], *f.* (—, *pl.* —n) (*Mus.*) flute.

Flötenzug ['flø:təntsu:k], *m.* (—es, *pl.* ⁔e) (*organ*) flute-stop.

flott [flɔt], *adj.* (*Naut.*) afloat, floating; (*fig.*) gay, jolly, lively, smart; — *leben,* lead a fast life.

Flotte ['flɔtə], *f.* (—, *pl.* —n) fleet, navy.

Flottille [flɔ'tɪljə], *f.* (—, *pl.* —n) flotilla, squadron.

Flöz [flø:ts], *n.* (—es, *pl.* —e) layer, stratum; (*coal*) seam.

Fluch [flu:x], *m.* (—es, *pl.* ⁔e) curse, spell; (*verbal*) curse, oath, swearword.

fluchen ['flu:xən], *v.n.* curse, swear.

Flucht [fluxt], *f.* (—, *pl.* —en) flight, fleeing; suite (of rooms).

flüchten ['flʏçtən], *v.n.* (*aux.* sein), *v.r.* flee, run away, escape.

flüchtig ['flʏçtɪç], *adj.* fugitive; (*Chem.*) volatile; (*fig.*) superficial; evanescent; hasty; slight.

Flüchtling ['flʏçtlɪŋ], *m.* (—s, *pl.* —e) fugitive, refugee.

Flug [flu:k], *m.* (—s, *pl.* ⁔e) (*Aviat.*) flight.

Flugblatt ['flu:kblat], *n.* (—s, *pl.* ⁔er) broadsheet, leaflet.

Flügel ['fly:gəl], *m.* (—s, *pl.* —) wing; (*Mus.*) grand piano; (*door*) leaf.

Flügelschlag ['fly:gəlʃla:k], *m.* (—s, *pl.* ⁔e) wing-stroke.

Flügeltür ['fly:gəlty:r], *f.* (—, *pl.* —en) folding-door.

flügge ['flʏgə], *adj.* fledged.

Flughafen ['flu:kha:fən], *m.* (—s, *pl.* ⁔) airport, aerodrome.

Flugpost ['flu:kpɔst], *f.* (—, *no pl.*) air mail.

flugs [fluks], *adv.* quickly, instantly; (*Lit.*, *obs.*) anon.

Flugsand ['flu:kzant], *m.* (—s, *no pl.*) quicksand, drifting sand.

Flugzeug ['flu:ktsɔyk], *n.* (—s, *pl.* —e) aeroplane; (*Am.*) airplane.

Flugzeugführer ['flu:ktsɔykfy:rər], *m.* (—s, *pl.* —) (*Aviat.*) pilot.

Fluidum ['flu:idum], *n.* (—s, *pl.* —da) fluid; (*fig.*) atmosphere.

Flunder ['flundər], *f.* (—, *pl.* —n) (*fish*) flounder.

Flunkerer ['fluŋkərər], *m.* (—s, *pl.* —) (*coll.*) fibber, story-teller.

Flur (1) [flu:r], *f.* (—, *pl.* —en) field, plain; *auf weiter* —, in the open.

Flur (2) [flu:r], *m.* (—s, *pl.* —e) (*house*) hall, vestibule; corridor.

Flurschaden ['flu:rʃa:dən], *m.* (—s, *pl.* ⁔) damage to crops.

Fluß [flus], *m.* (—sses, *pl.* ⁔sse) river, stream; flow, flowing; flux.

Flußbett ['flusbɛt], *n.* (—s, *pl.* —en) channel, riverbed.

flüssig ['flʏsɪç], *adj.* fluid, liquid; —*e Gelder,* ready cash; liquid assets.

flüstern ['flʏstərn], *v.a.* whisper.

Flut [flu:t], *f.* (—, *pl.* —en) flood; high-tide, high water; torrent; deluge.

fluten ['flu:tən], *v.n.* flow.

Fockmast ['fɔkmast], *m.* (—s, *pl.* —en) foremast.

Focksegel ['fɔkze:gəl], *n.* (—s, *pl.* —) foresail.

Föderalismus [fø:dəra'lɪsmus], *m.* (—, *no pl.*) federalism.

Fohlen ['fo:lən], *n.* (—s, *pl.* —) foal.

fohlen ['fo:lən], *v.n.* foal.

Föhn [fø:n], *m.* (—s, *pl.* —e) (warm) Alpine wind.

Föhre ['fø:rə], *f.* (—, *pl.* —n) (*Bot.*) fir, fir-tree.

Folge ['fɔlgə], *f.* (—, *pl.* —n) succession; series, sequence; continuation; consequence.

folgen ['fɔlgən], *v.n.* (*aux.* sein) follow; succeed; result from, be the consequence of; obey.

folgendermaßen ['fɔlgəndərma:sən], *adv.* as follows.

folgenschwer ['fɔlgənʃve:r], *adj.* momentous, portentous.

folgerichtig ['fɔlgərɪçtɪç], *adj.* consistent, logical.

folgern ['fɔlgərn], *v.a.* draw a conclusion, infer, conclude, deduce.

Folgerung ['fɔlgəruŋ], *f.* (—, *pl.* —en) induction, deduction, inference.

folglich ['fɔlklɪç], *conj.* consequently, therefore.

folgsam ['fɔlkza:m], *adj.* obedient.

Foliant [fo:l'jant], *m.* (—en, *pl.* —en) folio-volume, tome.

Folie ['fo:ljə], *f.* (—, *pl.* —n) foil.

Folter ['fɔltər], *f.* (—, *pl.* —n) rack, torture.

Folterbank ['fɔltərbaŋk], *f.* (—, *pl.* ⁔e) rack.

Fond [fɔ̃:], *m.* (—s, *pl.* —s) back seat.

Fontäne [fɔ'tɛ:nə], *f.* (—, *pl.* —n) fountain.

foppen ['fɔpən], *v.a.* chaff, banter, tease.

Fopperei [fɔpə'raɪ], *f.* (—, *pl.* —en) chaff, banter, teasing.

forcieren [fɔr'si:rən], *v.a.* strain, overdo.

Förderer ['fœrdərər], *m.* (—s, *pl.* —) promoter, backer.

Förderkarren ['fœrdərkarən], *m.* (—s, *pl.* —) (*Min.*) truck, trolley.

förderlich ['fœrdərlɪç], *adj.* useful, conducive (to).

Fördermaschine ['fœrdərmaʃi:nə], *f.* (—, *pl.* —n) winding-machine.

fordern ['fɔrdərn], *v.a.* demand, claim, ask for; (*duel*) challenge.

fördern ['fœrdərn], *v.a.* further, advance, promote, back; hasten; (*Min.*) haul.

Förderschacht ['fœrdərʃaxt], *m.* (—s, *pl.* ⸚e) (*Min.*) winding shaft.

Forderung ['fɔrdəruŋ], *f.* (—, *pl.* —en) demand, claim; (*duel*) challenge.

Förderung ['fœrdəruŋ], *f.* (—, *no pl.*) furtherance, promotion, advancement; (*Min.*) hauling.

Forelle [fo'rɛlə], *f.* (—, *pl.* —n) trout.

Forke ['fɔrkə], *f.* (—, *pl.* —n) pitch-fork, garden-fork.

Form [fɔrm], *f.* (—, *pl.* —en) form, shape, figure; manner; condition; (*casting*) mould; (*grammar*) form, voice.

Formalien [fɔr'ma:ljən], *pl.* formalities.

Formalität [fɔrmalɪ'tɛ:t], *f.* (—, *pl.* —en) formality, form.

Format [fɔr'ma:t], *n.* (—s, *pl.* —e) (*book, paper*) size; format; (*fig.*) stature.

Formel ['fɔrməl], *f.* (—, *pl.* —n) formula.

formell [fɔr'mɛl], *adj.* formal.

Formfehler ['fɔrmfe:lər], *m.* (—s, *pl.* —) faux pas, breach of etiquette.

formieren [fɔr'mi:rən], *v.a.* form. — *v.r. sich* —, fall into line.

förmlich ['fœrmlɪç], *adj.* formal; downright.

formlos ['fɔrmlo:s], *adj.* shapeless; (*fig.*) unconventional, informal, unceremonious.

Formular [fɔrmu'la:r], *n.* (—s, *pl.* —e) (printed) form, schedule.

formulieren [fɔrmu'li:rən], *v.a.* formulate, word.

formvollendet ['fɔrmfɔlɛndət], *adj.* well-rounded, well-finished.

forsch [fɔrʃ], *adj.* dashing.

forschen ['fɔrʃən], *v.n.* search, enquire (after), do research.

Forschung ['fɔrʃuŋ], *f.* (—, *pl.* —en) research, investigation; search, exploration.

Forst [fɔrst], *m.* (—es, *pl.* —e) forest.

Förster ['fœrstər], *m.* (—s, *pl.* —) forester, forest-keeper; (*Am.*) ranger.

Forstfrevel ['fɔrstfre:fəl], *m.* (—s, *no pl.*) infringement of forest-laws.

Forstrevier ['fɔrstrevi:r], *n.* (—s, *pl.* —e) section of forest.

Forstwesen ['fɔrstve:zən], *n.* (—s, *no pl.*) forestry.

Forstwirtschaft ['fɔrstvɪrtʃaft], *f.* (—, *no pl.*) forestry.

fort [fɔrt], *adv.* away; lost, gone, forth, forward.

Fort [fo:rt], *n.* (—s, *pl.* —s) fort.

fortan [fɔrt'an], *adv.* henceforth.

fortbilden ['fɔrtbɪldən], *v.r. sich* —, improve o.s., receive further education.

fortbleiben ['fɔrtblaɪbən], *v.n. irr.* (*aux.* sein) stay away.

Fortdauer ['fɔrtdauər], *f.* (—, *no pl.*) continuance, duration.

fortfahren ['fɔrtfa:rən], *v.n. irr.* (*aux.* sein) drive off; (*Naut.*) set sail; (*fig.*) continue, go on.

Fortgang ['fɔrtgaŋ], *m.* (—s, *no pl.*) going away, departure; (*fig.*) continuation, progress.

Fortkommen ['fɔrtkɔmən], *n.* (—s, *no pl.*) advancement, progress; (*fig.*) livelihood.

fortkommen ['fɔrtkɔmən], *v.n. irr.* (*aux.* sein) *gut* —, prosper, succeed.

fortlassen ['fɔrtlasən], *v.a.* allow to go; leave out, omit; *nicht* —, detain.

fortlaufen ['fɔrtlaufən], *v.n. irr.* (*aux.* sein) run away.

fortpflanzen ['fɔrtpflantsən], *v.r. sich* —, propagate, multiply; (*sickness*) spread.

forträumen ['fɔrtrɔymən], *v.a.* clear away, remove.

fortschaffen ['fɔrtʃafən], *v.a.* carry away, get rid of.

fortscheren ['fɔrtʃe:rən], *v.r. sich* — (*coll.*) beat it, go away.

fortscheuchen ['fɔrtʃɔyçən], *v.a.* scare away.

fortschreiten ['fɔrtʃraɪtən], *v.n. irr.* (*aux.* sein) progress, advance.

Fortschritt ['fɔrtʃrɪt], *m.* (—s, *pl.* —e) progress, advancement, proficiency.

fortsetzen ['fɔrtzɛtsən], *v.a.* continue, carry on.

fortwährend ['fɔrtvɛ:rənt], *adj.* continual, perpetual, unceasing.

Fracht [fraxt], *f.* (—, *pl.* —en) freight, cargo, load.

Frack [frak], *m.* (—s, *pl.* —s, ⸚e) dress-suit, evening dress.

Frage ['fra:gə], *f.* (—, *pl.* —n) question, query.

Fragebogen ['fra:gəbo:gən], *m.* (—s, *pl.* —) questionnaire.

fragen ['fra:gən], *v.a.* ask, enquire, question.

Fragesteller ['fra:gəʃtɛlər], *m.* (—s, *pl.* —) interrogator, questioner.

fraglich ['fra:klɪç], *adj.* questionable, problematic(al).

fragwürdig ['fra:kvyrdɪç], *adj.* doubtful, questionable.

Fraktion [frak'tsjo:n], *f.* (—, *pl.* —en) (*Pol.*) party group.

Frakturschrift

Frakturschrift [frak'tuːrʃrɪft], *f.* (—, *no pl.*) (*lettering*) Gothic type, Old English type, Black Letter type.

Frank [fraŋk], *m.* (—en, *pl.* —en) (*coin*) franc.

Franke ['fraŋkə], *m.* (—n, *pl.* —n) Frank, Franconian.

frankieren [fraŋ'kiːrən], *v.a.* (*post*) prepay, frank.

franko ['fraŋko], *adj.* post-paid; *gratis und* —, gratuitously.

Frankreich ['frankraɪx], *n.* France.

Franse ['franzə], *f.* (—, *pl.* —n) fringe.

Franzose [fran'tsoːzə], *m.* (—n, *pl.* —n) Frenchman.

französisch [fran'tsøːzɪʃ], *adj.* French.

frappant [fra'pant], *adj.* striking.

frappieren [fra'piːrən], *v.a.* strike, astonish.

Fraß [fraːs], *m.* (—es, *no pl.*) (*animals*) feed, fodder; (*sl.*) grub.

Fratz [frats], *m.* (—es, *pl.* —en) brat, little monkey.

Fratze ['fratsə], *f.* (—, *pl.* —en) grimace, caricature.

Frau [frau], *f.* (—, *pl.* —en) woman, wife, lady; (*title*) Mrs.; *gnädige* —, Madam.

Frauenkirche ['frauənkɪrçə], *f.* (—, *no pl.*) Church of Our Lady.

Frauenzimmer ['frauəntsɪmər], *n.* (—s, *pl.* —) (*pej.*) woman, female.

Fräulein ['frɔylaɪn], *n.* (—s, *pl.* —) young lady; (*title*) Miss.

frech [frɛç], *adj.* insolent, impudent, cheeky, pert, saucy.

Frechheit ['frɛçhaɪt], *f.* (—, *pl.* —en) insolence, impudence.

Fregatte [fre'gatə], *f.* (—, *pl.* —n) frigate.

frei [fraɪ], *adj.* free, exempt, unhampered, independent, disengaged; vacant; candid, frank.

Freibeuter ['fraɪbɔytər], *m.* (—s, *pl.* —) freebooter, pirate.

Freibrief ['fraɪbriːf], *m.* (—s, *pl.* —e) patent, licence; permit.

freien ['fraɪən], *v.a.* woo, court.

Freier ['fraɪər], *m.* (—s, *pl.* —) (*obs.*) suitor.

Freigabe ['fraɪgaːbə], *f.* (—, *no pl.*) release.

freigeben ['fraɪgeːbən], *v.a. irr.* release.

freigebig ['fraɪgeːbɪç], *adj.* liberal, generous.

Freigebigkeit ['fraɪgeːbɪçkaɪt], *f.* (—, *no pl.*) liberality, munificence, generosity.

Freigut ['fraɪguːt], *n.* (—s, *pl.* ⁻er) freehold.

Freiheit ['fraɪhaɪt], *f.* (—, *pl.* —en) freedom, liberty, immunity, privilege.

Freiherr ['fraɪhɛr], *m.* (—n, *pl.* —en) baron.

Freikorps ['fraɪkoːr], *n.* (—, *no pl.*) volunteer-corps.

Freilauf ['fraɪlauf], *m.* (—s, *no pl.*) (*bicycle*) free-wheel.

freilich ['fraɪlɪç], *adv.* to be sure, it is true, indeed, of course.

Freilicht- ['fraɪlɪçt], *adj.* (*in compounds*) open-air.

Freimarke ['fraɪmarkə], *f.* (—, *pl.* —n) postage stamp.

freimütig ['fraɪmyːtɪç], *adj.* frank, open, candid.

Freisprechung ['fraɪʃprɛçuŋ], *f.* (—, *no pl.*) acquittal; absolution.

Freistätte ['fraɪʃtɛtə], *f.* (—, *pl.* —n) refuge, asylum.

Freistoß ['fraɪʃtoːs], *m.* (—es, *pl.* ⁻e) (*Footb.*) free kick.

Freitag ['fraɪtaːk], *m.* (—s, *pl.* —e) Friday.

Freitreppe ['fraɪtrɛpə], *f.* (—, *pl.* —n) outside staircase.

Freiübung ['fraɪyːbuŋ], *f.* (—, *pl.* —en) (*mostly pl.*) physical exercises, gymnastics.

freiwillig ['fraɪvɪlɪç], *adj.* voluntary, of o.'s own accord; spontaneous.

Freiwillige ['fraɪvɪlɪgə], *m.* (—n, *pl.* —n) (*Mil.*) volunteer.

fremd [frɛmt], *adj.* strange, foreign, outlandish; odd.

fremdartig ['frɛmtartɪç], *adj.* strange, odd.

Fremde (1) ['frɛmdə], *f.* (—, *no pl.*) foreign country; *in die* — *gehen*, go abroad.

Fremde (2) ['frɛmdə], *m.* (—n, *pl.* —n) stranger, foreigner.

Fremdheit ['frɛmthaɪt], *f.* (—, *no pl.*) strangeness.

Freßbeutel ['frɛsbɔytəl], *m.* (—s, *pl.* —) nose-bag.

Fresse ['frɛsə], *f.* (—, *pl.* —n) (*vulg.*) mouth, snout.

fressen ['frɛsən], *v.a. irr.* (*animals*) eat; (*also fig.*) devour.

Fresserei ['frɛsəraɪ], *f.* (—, *no pl.*) gluttony.

Frettchen ['frɛtçən], *n.* (—s, *pl.* —) (*Zool.*) ferret.

Freude ['frɔydə], *f.* (—, *pl.* —n) joy, joyfulness, gladness, enjoyment, delight, pleasure.

Freudenfest ['frɔydənfest], *n.* (—s, *pl.* —e) feast, jubilee.

Freudenhaus ['frɔydənhaus], *n.* (—es, *pl.* ⁻er) brothel.

Freudenmädchen ['frɔydənmɛːtçən], *n.* (—s, *pl.* —) prostitute.

freudig ['frɔydɪç], *adj.* joyful, cheerful, glad.

freudlos ['frɔytloːs], *adj.* joyless.

freuen ['frɔyən], *v.r. sich* —, rejoice (at), be glad (of); *sich auf etwas* —, look forward to s.th.

Freund [frɔynt], *m.* (—es, *pl.* —e) friend.

freundlich ['frɔyntlɪç], *adj.* friendly, kind, affable, pleasing, cheerful, pleasant, genial.

Freundschaft ['frɔyntʃaft], *f.* (—, *pl.* —en) friendship.

Frevel ['freːfəl], *m.* (—s, *pl.* —) crime, misdeed, offence.

freveln ['fre:fəln], *v.n.* do wrong, trespass, commit an outrage.
Friede(n) ['fri:də(n)], *m.* (—ns, *no pl.*) peace.
friedfertig ['fri:tfertɪç], *adj.* peaceable.
Friedhof ['fri:tho:f], *m.* (—s, *pl.* ˝e) churchyard, cemetery.
friedlich ['fri:tlɪç], *adj.* peaceful.
friedliebend ['fri:tli:bənt], *adj.* peaceable, peace-loving.
Friedrich ['fri:drɪç], *m.* Frederic(k).
friedselig ['fri:tze:lɪç], *adj.* peaceable.
frieren ['fri:rən], *v.n. irr.* feel cold, freeze.
Fries [fri:s], *m.* (—es, *pl.* —e) frieze.
Friese ['fri:zə], *m.* (—n, *pl.* —n) Frisian.
frisch [frɪʃ], *adj.* fresh; new; (*weather*) crisp; (*fig.*) lively, brisk, gay.
Frische ['frɪʃə], *f.* (—, *no pl.*) freshness, liveliness, gaiety.
Friseur ['fri'zø:r], *m.* (—s, *pl.* —e) hairdresser, barber.
Friseuse [fri'zø:zə], *f.* (—, *pl.* —n) female hairdresser.
frisieren [fri'zi:rən], *v.a.* dress (s.o.'s) hair.
Frist [frɪst], *f.* (—, *pl.* —en) time, term, period; (*fixed*) term; delay, respite.
fristen ['frɪstən], *v.a. das Leben* —, gain a bare living.
Frisur [fri'zu:r], *f.* (—, *pl.* —en) coiffure, hair-style.
frivol [fri'vo:l], *adj.* frivolous.
Frivolität [frivo:li'tɛ:t], *f.* (—, *pl.* —en) frivolity.
froh [fro:], *adj.* glad, joyful, joyous.
frohgelaunt ['fro:gəlaunt], *adj.* good-humoured, cheerful.
fröhlich ['frø:lɪç], *adj.* gay, merry.
frohlocken [fro'lɔkən], *v.n.* (*rare*) exult.
Frohsinn ['fro:zɪn], *m.* (—s, *no pl.*) good humour, gaiety.
fromm [frɔm], *adj.* pious, religious, devout.
frommen ['frɔmən], *v.n.* (*obs.*) be of advantage (to s.o.).
Frömmigkeit ['frœmɪçkaɪt], *f.* (—, *no pl.*) piety, devoutness.
Fron [fro:n], *f.* (—, *no pl.*) (feudal) service; statute labour.
frönen ['frø:nən], *v.n.* (*fig.*) be a slave to; indulge in (*Dat.*).
Fronleichnam [fro:n'laɪxna:m], *m.* (*Eccl.*) (feast of) Corpus Christi.
Front [frɔnt], *f.* (—, *pl.* —en) front, forepart; (*building*) elevation; (*Mil.*) front line.
Frosch [frɔʃ], *m.* (—es, *pl.* ˝e) (*Zool.*) frog.
Frost [frɔst], *m.* (—es, *pl.* ˝e) frost; coldness, chill.
Frostbeule ['frɔstbɔylə], *f.* (—, *pl.* —n) chilblain.
frösteln ['frœstəln], *v.n.* feel a chill, shiver.
frostig ['frɔstɪç], *adj.* frosty; cold, chilly.
frottieren [frɔ'ti:rən], *v.a.* rub (down).

Frottiertuch [frɔ'ti:rtu:x], *n.* (—s, *pl.* ˝er) Turkish towel, bath towel.
Frucht [fruxt], *f.* (—, *pl.* ˝e) fruit; (*fig.*) result, effect; (*Med.*) fœtus.
fruchtbar ['fruxtba:r], *adj.* fruitful, productive, fertile.
fruchten ['fruxtən], *v.n.* produce fruit; (*fig.*) be effectual.
Fruchtknoten ['fruxtkno:tən], *m.* (—s, *pl.* —) (*Bot.*) seed-vessel.
früh(e) [fry:(ə)], *adj.* early.
Frühe ['fry:ə], *f.* (—, *no pl.*) early morning, dawn.
früher ['fry:ər], *adv.* earlier (on), formerly.
frühestens ['fry:əstəns], *adv.* at the earliest (possible moment).
Frühjahr ['fry:ja:r], *n.*, **Frühling** ['fry:lɪŋ], *m.* (—s, *pl.* —e) spring.
Frühschoppen ['fry:ʃɔpən], *m.* (—s, *pl.* —) morning pint (beer or wine).
Frühstück ['fry:ʃtyk], *n.* (—s, *pl.* —e) breakfast; *zweites* —, lunch.
Fuchs [fuks], *m.* (—es, *pl.* ˝e) fox; chestnut (horse); (*fig.*) cunning chap; (*student*) freshman.
Fuchsbau ['fuksbau], *m.* (—s, *pl.* —e) fox-hole.
Fuchseisen ['fuksaɪzən], *n.* (—s, *pl.* —) fox-trap.
fuchsen ['fuksən], *v.r. sich* — *über*, be annoyed about.
Fuchsie ['fuksjə], *f.* (—, *pl.* —n) (*Bot.*) fuchsia.
fuchsig ['fuksɪç], *adj.* (*coll.*) very angry.
Füchsin ['fyksɪn], *f.* (—, *pl.* —innen) vixen.
fuchsrot ['fuksro:t], *adj.* fox-coloured, sorrel.
Fuchsschwanz ['fuksʃvants], *m.* (—es, *pl.* ˝e) fox-brush; pad saw.
Fuchtel ['fuxtəl], *f.* (—, *pl.* —n) sword blade; rod, whip.
Fuder ['fu:dər], *n.* (—s, *pl.* —) load, cart-load; wine measure (c. 270 gallons).
Fug ['fu:k], *m.* (—s, *no pl.*) (*rare*) right, justice; *mit* — *und Recht*, with every right.
Fuge (1) ['fu:gə], *f.* (—, *pl.* —n) joint, groove.
Fuge (2) ['fu:gə], *f.* (—, *pl.* —n) (*Mus.*) fugue.
fügen ['fy:gən], *v.a.* fit together, join, dovetail. — *v.r. sich* —, submit (to), accommodate o.s. (to).
fügsam ['fy:kza:m], *adj.* pliant, submissive, yielding.
Fügung ['fy:guŋ], *f.* (—, *pl.* —en) coincidence; dispensation (of Providence); Providence.
fühlbar ['fy:lba:r], *adj.* perceptible; tangible; *sich* — *machen*, make o.s. felt.
fühlen ['fy:lən], *v.a.* feel, touch, sense, be aware of.
Fühler ['fy:lər], *m.* (—s, *pl.* —) tentacle, feeler.

Fühlhorn

Fühlhorn ['fy:lhɔrn], *n.* (—s, *pl.* ̈er) feeler, antenna, tentacle.

Fühlung ['fy:luŋ], *f.* (—, *no pl.*) — *haben mit*, be in touch with.

Fuhre ['fu:rə], *f.* (—, *pl.* —n) conveyance, vehicle, cart-load.

führen ['fy:rən], *v.a.* lead, guide, conduct, command; (*pen*) wield; (*law-suit*) carry on; (*conversation*) have, keep up; (*name*, *title*) bear; (*goods*) stock, deal in; *Krieg* —, wage war; *etwas im Schilde* —, have a plan; *das Wort* —, be spokesman; *einen hinters Licht* —, cheat s.o.

Führer ['fy:rər], *m.* (—s, *pl.* —) leader, guide; head, manager; conductor; driver, pilot.

Führerschaft ['fy:rərʃaft], *f.* (=—, *no pl.*) leadership.

Führerschein ['fy:rərʃain], *m.* (—s, *pl.* —e) driving-licence.

Führersitz ['fy:rərzits], *m.* (—es, *pl.* —e) driver's seat; pilot's cockpit.

Fuhrlohn ['fu:rlo:n], *m.* (—s, *no pl.*) cartage, carriage.

Fuhrmann ['fu:rman], *m.* (—s, *pl.* ̈er) carter, carrier.

Führung ['fy:ruŋ], *f.* (—, *no pl.*) guidance; leadership; conducted tour; management, direction; behaviour, conduct.

Führungszeugnis ['fy:ruŋstsɔyknis], *n.* (—sses, *pl.* —sse) certificate of good conduct.

Fuhrwerk ['fu:rvɛrk], *n.* (—s, *pl.* —e) carriage, vehicle, waggon.

Fuhrwesen ['fu:rve:zən], *n.* (—s, *no pl.*) transport services, transportation.

Fülle ['fylə], *f.* (—, *no pl.*) fullness; abundance, plenty.

Füllen ['fylən], *n.* (—s, *pl.* —) foal.

füllen ['fylən], *v.a.* fill, fill up; stuff.

Füllfederhalter ['fylfe:dərhaltər], *m.* (—s, *pl.* —) fountain-pen.

Füllung ['fyluŋ], *f.* (—, *pl.* —en) filling; stuffing; (*door*) panel.

fummeln ['fuməln], *v.n.* fumble.

Fund [funt], *m.* (—es, *pl.* —e) find; discovery.

Fundbüro ['funtbyro], *n.* (—s, *pl.* —s) lost property office.

Fundgrube ['funtgru:bə], *f.* (—, *pl.* —n) gold-mine, source, treasure-house.

fundieren [fun'di:rən], *v.a.* found; establish.

fünf [fynf], *num. adj.* five.

Fünfeck ['fynfɛk], *n.* (—s, *pl.* —e) pentagon.

Fünffüßler ['fynffy:slər], *m.* (—s, *pl.* —) (*Poet.*) pentameter.

fünfjährig ['fynfjɛ:riç], *num. adj.* five-year-old.

fünfjährlich ['fynfjɛ:rliç], *num. adj.* quinquennial, five-yearly.

fünfzehn ['fynftse:n], *num. adj.* fifteen.

fünfzig ['fynftsiç], *num. adj.* fifty.

fungieren [fuŋ'gi:rən], *v.n.* — *als*, act as, officiate as.

Funk [funk], *m.* (—s, *no pl.*) radio; wireless; telegraphy.

Funke ['funkə], *m.* (—n, *pl.* —n) spark, sparkle.

funkeln ['funkəln], *v.n.* sparkle, glitter; (*stars*) twinkle.

funkelnagelneu ['funkəlna:gəlnɔy], *adj.* (*coll.*) brand-new.

funken ['funkən], *v.a.* flash (*messages*); telegraph, broadcast.

Funker ['funkər], *m.* (—s, *pl.* —) wireless operator.

Funksender ['funkzɛndər], *m.* (—s, *pl.* —) radio-transmitter.

Funkspruch ['funkʃprux], *m.* (—s, *pl.* ̈e) wireless-message.

Funktelegramm ['funktelegram], *n.* (—s, *pl.* —e) radio telegram.

für [fy:r], *prep.* (*Acc.*) for, instead of; *ein — allemal*, once and for all; *an und — sich*, in itself.

Fürbitte ['fy:rbitə], *f.* (—, *pl.* —n) intercession.

Furche ['furçə], *f.* (—, *pl.* —n) furrow; (*face*) wrinkle.

furchen ['furçən], *v.a.* furrow; (*face*) wrinkle.

Furcht [furçt], *f.* (—, *no pl.*) fear, worry, anxiety; dread, fright, terror, apprehension.

furchtbar ['furçtba:r], *adj.* dreadful, terrible, frightful.

fürchten ['fyrçtən], *v.a.* fear, be afraid of. — *v.r. sich — vor*, be afraid of.

fürchterlich ['fyrçtərliç], *adj.* terrible, horrible, awful.

furchtsam ['furçtza:m], *adj.* timid, fearful, apprehensive.

Furie ['fu:riə], *f.* (—, *pl.* —n) fury, virago.

fürlieb [fyr'li:p], *adv. mit etwas — nehmen*, put up with, be content with s.th.

Furnier [fur'ni:r], *n.* (—s, *pl.* —e) veneer, inlay.

Furore [fu'ro:rə], *n.* (—s, *no pl.*) — *machen*, cause a sensation, create an uproar.

Fürsorge ['fy:rzɔrgə], *f.* (—, *no pl.*) solicitude; provision; welfare.

fürsorglich ['fy:rzɔrgliç], *adj.* thoughtful, with loving care.

Fürsprache ['fy:rʃpra:xə], *f.* (—, *no pl.*) advocacy, intercession.

Fürst [fyrst], *m.* (—en, *pl.* —en) prince, sovereign.

Furt [furt], *f.* (—, *pl.* —en) ford.

Furunkel [fu'runkəl], *m.* (—s, *pl.* —) furuncle, boil.

Fürwort ['fy:rvɔrt], *n.* (—s, *pl.* ̈er) pronoun.

Fusel ['fu:zəl], *m.* (—s, *no pl.*) bad liquor, (*Am. sl.*) hooch.

Fuß [fu:s], *m.* (—es, *pl.* ̈e) (*human*) foot; (*object*) base.

Fußangel ['fu:saŋəl], *f.* (—, *pl.* —n) man-trap.

Fußball ['fu:sbal], *m.* (—s, *pl.* ̈e) football.

Fußboden ['fu:sbo:dən], *m.* (—s, *pl.* ː) floor.

fußen ['fu:sən], *v.n.* — *auf*, be based upon.

fußfrei ['fu:sfraɪ], *adj.* ankle-length.

Fußgänger ['fu:sgɛŋər], *m.* (—s, *pl.* —) pedestrian.

Fußgestell ['fu:sgəʃtɛl], *n.* (—s, *pl.* —e) pedestal.

Fußpflege ['fu:spfle:gə], *f.* (—, *no pl.*) chiropody.

Fußpunkt ['fu:spuŋkt], *m.* (—s, *no pl.*) nadir.

Fußtritt ['fu:strɪt], *m.* (—s, *pl.* —e) kick.

futsch [futʃ], *excl.* (*coll.*) gone, lost.

Futter ['futər], *n.* (—s, *no pl.*) (*dress*) lining; (*animals*) fodder, feed.

Futteral [futəˈra:l], *n.* (—s, *pl.* —e) case; sheath.

Futterkräuter ['futərkrɔytər], *n. pl.* herbage.

futtern ['futərn], *v.n.* (*coll.*) feed, stuff o.s.

füttern ['fytərn], *v.a.* feed; (*garment*) line.

G

G [ge:], *n.* (—s, *pl.* —s) the letter G; (*Mus.*) *G Dur,* G major; (*Mus.*) *G Moll,* G minor; (*Mus.*) — *-Saite,* G string.

Gabe ['ga:bə], *f.* (—, *pl.* —n) gift, present; donation; *barmherzige* —, alms; (*fig.*) gift, talent.

Gabel ['ga:bəl], *f.* (—, *pl.* —n) fork; (*deer*) antler; (*cart*) shafts.

gabelig ['ga:bəlɪç], *adj.* forked.

Gabelung ['ga:bəluŋ], *f.* (—, *pl.* —en) bifurcation, branching (of road).

Gabelzinke ['ga:bəltsɪŋkə], *f.* (—, *pl.* —n) prong, tine.

Gabun [ga'bu:n], *n.* Gaboon.

gackern ['gakərn], *v.n.* cackle; (*fig.*) chatter.

gaffen ['gafən], *v.n.* gape (at), stare.

Gage ['ga:ʒə], *f.* (—, *pl.* —n) salary, pay, fee.

gähnen ['gɛ:nən], *v.n.* yawn, gape.

Galan [ga'la:n], *m.* (—s, *pl.* —e) lover, gallant.

galant [ga'lant], *adj.* polite, courteous; —*es Abenteuer,* love affair.

Galanterie [galantə'ri:], *f.* (—, *pl.* —n) courtesy.

Galanteriewaren [galantə'ri:va:rən], *f. pl.* fancy goods.

Galeere [ga'le:rə], *f.* (—, *pl.* —n) galley.

Galerie [galə'ri:], *f.* (—, *pl.* —n) gallery.

Galgen ['galgən], *m.* (—s, *pl.* —) gallows, gibbet; scaffold.

Galgenfrist ['galgənfrɪst], *f.* (—, *no pl.*) short delay, respite.

Galgenhumor ['galgənhumo:r], *m.* (—s, *no pl.*) wry or grim humour.

Galgenvogel ['galgənfo:gəl], *m.* (—s, *pl.* ː) gallows-bird.

Galizien [ga'li:tsjən], *n.* Galicia.

Gallapfel ['galapfəl], *m.* (—s, *pl.* ː) gall-nut.

Galle ['galə], *f.* (—, *pl.* —n) gall, bile.

Gallenblase ['galənbla:zə], *f.* (—, *pl.* —n) gall-bladder.

Gallert ['galərt], *n.* (—s, *no pl.*) jelly.

Gallien ['galjən], *n.* Gaul.

gallig ['galɪç], *adj.* bilious.

galvanisieren [galvanɪ'zi:rən], *v.a.* galvanize.

Gamaschen [ga'maʃən], *f. pl.* spats, gaiters.

Gang [gaŋ], *m.* (—es, *pl.* ːe) walk, gait; (*horse*) pace; (*house*) passage, corridor; (*meal*) course, dish; (*action*) progress, course; (*sport*) round, bout; (*machine*) motion; stroke; (*Motor.*) gear.

gang [gaŋ], *adj.* — *und gäbe,* customary, usual, common.

Gangart ['gaŋa:rt], *f.* (—, *pl.* —en) gait; (*horse*) pace.

gangbar ['gaŋba:r], *adj.* marketable, saleable; (*road*) passable; practicable.

Gans [gans], *f.* (—, *pl.* ːe) (*Orn.*) goose.

Gänseblümchen ['gɛnzəbly:mçən], *n.* (—s, *pl.* —) daisy.

Gänsefüßchen ['gɛnzəfy:sçən], *n. pl.* (*coll.*) inverted commas, quotation marks.

Gänsehaut ['gɛnzəhaut], *f.* (—, *no pl.*) goose-flesh, goose-pimples.

Gänserich ['gɛnzərɪç], *m.* (—s, *pl.* —e) (*Orn.*) gander.

ganz ['gants], *adj.* whole, entire, all; complete, total.

gänzlich ['gɛntslɪç], *adj.* whole, total, entire, full, complete.

gar [ga:r], *adj.* sufficiently cooked, done. — *adv.* very, quite.

garantieren [garan'ti:rən], *v.a.* guarantee, warrant.

Garaus ['ga:raus], *m.* (—, *no pl.*) *einem den — machen,* finish s.o., kill s.o.

Garbe ['garbə], *f.* (—, *pl.* —n) sheaf.

Garde ['gardə], *f.* (—, *pl.* —n) guard, guards.

Garderobe [gardə'ro:bə], *f.* (—, *pl.* —n) wardrobe; cloak-room; (*Theat.*) dressing-room.

Gardine [gar'di:nə], *f.* (—, *pl.* —n) curtain.

Gardist [gar'dɪst], *m.* (—en, *pl.* —en) guardsman.

gären ['gɛ:rən], *v.n.* ferment; effervesce.

Garn [garn], *n.* (—, *pl.* —e) yarn, thread.

Garnele [gar'ne:lə], *f.* (—, *pl.* —n) (*Zool.*) shrimp; *große* —, prawn.

garnieren [gar'ni:rən], *v.a.* trim, garnish.

Garnison [garni'zo:n], *f.* (—, *pl.* —en) garrison.

Garnitur [garni'tu:r], f. (—, pl. —en) trimming; set.

Garnröllchen ['garnrœlçən], n. (—s, pl. —) reel of thread.

garstig ['garstiç], adj. nasty, loathsome, ugly.

Garten ['gartən], m. (—s, pl. ⏝) garden.

Gartenlaube ['gartənlaubə], f. (—, pl. —n) bower, arbour.

Gärtner ['gɛrtnər], m. (—s, pl. —) gardener.

Gärtnerei [gɛrtnə'raɪ], f. (—, pl. —en) horticulture; market-garden; (plant) nursery.

Gärung ['gɛːruŋ], f. (—, pl. —en) fermentation, effervescence.

Gas [gaːs], n. (—es, —e) gas; — geben, (Motor.) accelerate.

gasartig ['ga:sartiç], adj. gaseous.

Gäßchen ['gɛsçən], n. (—s, pl. —) narrow alley; lane.

Gasse ['gasə], f. (—, pl. —n) alleyway, lane; (rare) street.

Gassenbube ['gasənbu:bə] see Gassenjunge.

Gassenhauer ['gasənhauər], m. (—s, pl. —), street-song, vulgar ballad; pop song.

Gassenjunge ['gasənjuŋə], m. (—n, pl. —n) street-urchin.

Gast [gast], m. (—s, pl. ⏝e) guest, visitor.

gastfrei ['gastfraɪ], adj. hospitable.

Gastfreund ['gastfrɔynt], m. (—s, pl. —e) guest; host.

Gastfreundschaft ['gastfrɔyntʃaft], f. (—, no pl.) hospitality.

Gastgeber ['gastge:bər], m. (—s, pl. —) host.

Gasthaus ['gasthaus], n. (—es, pl. ⏝er), Gasthof ['gastho:f], m. (—es, pl. ⏝e) inn, hotel, public house.

gastieren [gas'ti:rən], v.n. (Theat.) appear as a guest artist; star.

gastlich ['gastliç], adj. hospitable.

Gastmahl ['gastma:l], n. (—s, pl. —e) banquet, feast.

Gastrecht ['gastreçt], n. (—s, no pl.) right of hospitality.

Gastspiel ['gastʃpi:l], n. (—s, pl. —e) (Theat.) performance by visiting company.

Gaststätte ['gaststɛtə], f. (—, pl. —n) restaurant.

Gaststube ['gastʃtu:bə], f. (—, pl. —n) hotel lounge; saloon.

Gastwirt ['gastvɪrt], m. (—s, pl. —e) landlord.

Gastwirtin ['gastvɪrtɪn], f. (—, pl. —nen) landlady.

Gastzimmer ['gasttsɪmər], n. (—s, pl. —) see Gaststube; spare bedroom.

Gatte ['gatə], m. (—n, pl. —n) husband, spouse, consort.

Gatter ['gatər], n. (—s, pl. —) grate, lattice, grating.

Gattin ['gatɪn], f. (—, pl. —nen) wife, spouse, consort.

Gattung ['gatuŋ], f. (—, pl. —en) kind, species, sort, class; breed, genus; (Lit.) genre.

Gau [gau], m. (—s, pl. —e) district, province.

gaukeln ['gaukəln], v.n. juggle. — v.a. dazzle.

Gaul [gaul], m. (—s, pl. ⏝e) (old) horse, nag; einem geschenkten — sieht man nicht ins Maul, never look a gift horse in the mouth.

Gaumen ['gaumən], m. (—s, pl. —) palate.

Gauner ['gaunər], m. (—s, pl. —) rogue, sharper, swindler, cheat.

gaunern ['gaunərn], v.n. cheat, trick, swindle.

Gaunersprache ['gaunərʃpra:xə], f. (—, no pl.) thieves' slang.

Gaze ['ga:zə], f. (—, pl. —n) gauze.

Gazelle [ga'tsɛlə], f. (—, pl. —n) (Zool.) gazelle, antelope.

Geächtete [gə'ɛçtətə], m. (—n, pl. —n) outlaw.

Geächze [gə'ɛçtsə], n. (—s, no pl.) moaning, groaning.

Geäder [gə'ɛ:dər], n. (—s, no pl.) veins, arteries; veining.

geädert [gə'ɛ:dərt], adj. veined, streaked; grained.

-geartet [gə'a:rtət], adj. (suffix in compounds) -natured.

Gebäck [gə'bɛk], n. (—s, no pl.) pastry, rolls, cakes.

Gebälk [gə'bɛlk], n. (—s, no pl.) timberwork, timber-frame.

Gebärde [gə'bɛ:rdə], f. (—, pl. —n) gesture.

gebärden [gə'bɛ:rdən], v.r. sich —, behave.

Gebaren [gə'ba:rən], n. (—s, no pl.) demeanour.

gebären [gə'bɛ:rən], v.a. irr. bear, bring forth, give birth to, be delivered of.

Gebärmutter [gə'bɛ:rmutər], f. (—, no pl.) womb, uterus.

Gebäude [gə'bɔydə], n. (—s, pl. —) building, edifice.

Gebein [gə'baɪn], n. (—s, pl. —e) bones, skeleton; (fig.) remains.

Gebell [gə'bɛl], n. (—s, no pl.) barking.

geben ['ge:bən], v.a. irr. give, present; confer, bestow; yield; (cards) deal. — v.r. sich —, show o.s., behave; abate; das gibt sich, that won't last long; es gibt . . ., there is . . .; was gibt's? what's the matter?

Geber ['ge:bər], m. (—s, pl. —) giver, donor.

Gebet [gə'be:t], n. (—s, pl. —e) prayer; sein — verrichten, say o.'s prayers; ins — nehmen, question s.o. thoroughly.

Gebiet [gə'bi:t], n. (—s, pl. —e) district, territory; (Am.) precinct; jurisdiction; (fig.) province, field, sphere, domain.

gebieten [gə'bi:tən], v.a. irr. command, order.

Gebieter [gə'bi:tər], m. (—s, pl. —s) lord, master, ruler.

Gebilde [gə'bɪldə], *n.* (—s, *pl.* —) form, thing; formation, structure; figment.

gebildet [gə'bɪldət], ˙ *adj.* educated, cultured, refined.

Gebirge [gə'bɪrgə], *n.* (—s, *pl.* —) mountains.

Gebirgskamm [gə'bɪrkskam], *m.* (—s, *pl.* ¨e) mountain-ridge.

Gebiß [gə'bɪs], *n.* (—sses, *pl.* —sse) set of (false) teeth, denture; (*horse*) bit.

Gebläse [gə'blɛːzə], *n.* (—s, *pl.* —) bellows; blower.

Gebläsemaschine [gə'blɛːzəmaʃiːnə], *f.* (—, *pl.* —n) blower.

Gebläseofen [gə'blɛːzoːfən], *m.* (—s, *pl.* ¨) blast-furnace.

geblümt [gə'blyːmt], *adj.* flowered.

Geblüt [gə'blyːt], *n.* (—s, *no pl.*) blood; race, line, lineage, stock.

geboren [gə'boːrən], *adj.* born.

geborgen [gə'bɔrgən], *adj.* saved, hidden, sheltered, rescued.

Gebot [gə'boːt], *n.* (—s, *pl.* —e) order, decree, command; (*Bibl.*) Commandment.

geboten [gə'boːtən], *adj.* necessary, advisable.

Gebräu [gə'brɔy], *n.* (—s, *no pl.*) brew, concoction, mixture.

Gebrauch [gə'braux], *m.* (—s, *pl.* ¨e) use; employment; custom, usage, habit, practice; (*rare*) rite.

gebrauchen [gə'brauxən], *v.a.* use, make use of, employ.

gebräuchlich [gə'brɔyçlɪç], *adj.* usual, customary, common.

Gebrauchsanweisung [gə'brauxsanvaɪzuŋ], *f.* (—, *pl.* —en) directions for use.

gebraucht [gə'brauxt], *adj.* used, second-hand.

Gebrechen [gə'brɛçən], *n.* (—s, *pl.* —) infirmity.

gebrechen [gə'brɛçən], *v.n. irr. es gebricht mir an*, I am in want of, I lack.

gebrechlich [gə'brɛçlɪç], *adj.* infirm, frail, weak.

gebrochen [gə'brɔxən], *adj.* broken; —*es Deutsch*, broken German.

Gebrüder [gə'bryːdər], *m. pl.* (*Comm.*) brothers.

Gebrüll [gə'bryl], *n.* (—s, *no pl.*) roaring; (*cows*) lowing.

Gebühr [gə'byːr], *f.* (—, *pl.* —en) charge, due; fee; tax, duty.

gebühren [gə'byːrən], *v.n.* be due to s.o. — *v.r. sich* —, *wie es sich gebührt*, as it ought to be, as is right and proper.

gebunden [gə'bundən], *adj.* (*fig.*) bound, committed; (*Poet.*) metrical.

Geburt [gə'buːrt], *f.* (—, *pl.* —en) birth.

gebürtig [gə'byrtɪç], *adj.* a native of.

Geburtsfehler [gə'buːrtsfeːlər], *m.* (—s, *pl.* —) congenital defect.

Geburtshelfer [gə'buːrtshɛlfər], *m.* (—s, *pl.* —) obstetrician.

Geburtshelferin [gə'buːrtshɛlfərɪn], *f.* (—, *pl.* —nen) midwife.

Geburtsort [gə'buːrtsɔrt], *m.* (—s, *pl.* —e) birthplace.

Geburtsschein [gə'buːrtsʃaɪn], *m.* (—(e)s, *pl.* —e) birth certificate.

Geburtswehen [gə'buːrtsveːən], *f. pl.* birthpangs; labour pains.

Gebüsch [gə'byʃ], *n.* (—es, *no pl.*) bushes, thicket; underwood.

Geck [gɛk], *m.* (—en, *pl.* —en) fop, dandy; (*carnival*) fool.

geckenhaft ['gɛkənhaft], *adj.* foppish, dandyish.

Gedächtnis [gə'dɛçtnɪs], *n.* (—ses, *pl.* —se) memory; remembrance, recollection; *im — behalten*, keep in mind.

Gedanke [gə'daŋkə], *m.* (—ns, *pl.* —n) thought, idea.

Gedankenfolge [gə'daŋkənfɔlgə], *f.* (—, *no pl.*), **Gedankengang** [gə'daŋkəngaŋ], *m.* (—s, *pl.* ¨e) sequence of thought, train of thought.

Gedankenstrich [gə'daŋkənʃtrɪç], *m.* (—s, *pl.* —e) dash; hyphen.

Gedärm [gə'dɛrm], *n.* (—s, *pl.* —e) bowels, intestines, entrails.

Gedeck [gə'dɛk], *n.* (—s, *pl.* —e) cover; menu; place laid at a table.

gedeihen [gə'daɪən], *v.n. irr.* (*aux.* sein) thrive, prosper; progress.

gedeihlich [gə'daɪlɪç], *adj.* thriving, salutary.

gedenken [gə'dɛŋkən], *v.n. irr.* (*Genit.*) think of, remember; — *etwas zu tun*, intend to do s.th.

Gedenken [gə'dɛŋkən], *n.* (—s, *no pl.*) remembrance.

Gedenkfeier [gə'dɛŋkfaɪər], *f.* (—, *pl.* —n) commemoration.

Gedicht [gə'dɪçt], *n.* (—s, *pl.* —e) poem.

gediegen [gə'diːgən], *adj.* solid, sound, genuine, true, honourable, sterling.

Gedränge [gə'drɛŋə], *n.* (—s, *no pl.*) crowd, throng; crush.

Gedrängtheit [gə'drɛnkthaɪt], *f.* (—, *no pl.*) conciseness.

gedrungen [gə'druŋən], *adj.* thick-set, stocky; compact; concise (style).

Geduld [gə'dult], *f.* (—, *no pl.*) patience, forbearance.

gedulden [gə'duldən], *v.r. sich* —, be patient.

geduldig [gə'duldɪç], *adj.* patient, forbearing, indulgent.

Geduld(s)spiel [gə'dult(s)ʃpiːl], *n.* (—s, *pl.* —e) puzzle; (*Cards*) patience.

gedunsen [gə'dunzən], *adj.* bloated.

geeignet [gə'aɪgnət], *adj.* suitable, fit, appropriate, apt.

Gefahr [gə'faːr], *f.* (—, *pl.* —en) danger, peril, hazard, risk; — *laufen*, run the risk.

gefährden [gə'fɛːrdən], *v.a.* endanger, imperil, jeopardize.

gefährlich [gə'fɛːrlɪç], *adj.* dangerous, perilous.

Gefährt [gə'fɛːrt], *n.* (—s, *pl.* —e) (*obs.*) vehicle, conveyance.

Gefährte [gə'fɛːrtə], *m.* (—n, *pl.* —n) comrade, companion, fellow.

Gefälle

Gefälle [gə'fɛlə], n. (—s, pl. —) fall, descent, incline, gradient.

Gefallen [gə'falən], m. (—s, no pl.) pleasure, liking; favour, kindness.

gefallen (1) [gə'falən], v.n. irr. please; es gefällt mir, I like it; wie gefällt Ihnen ...? how do you like ...?

gefallen (2) [gə'falən], adj. (Mil.) fallen, killed in action.

gefällig [gə'fɛlɪç], adj. pleasing, accommodating, obliging, anxious to please; was ist — ? what can I do for you?

Gefälligkeit [gə'fɛlɪçkaɪt], f. (—, pl. —en) courtesy; favour, service, good turn.

gefälligst [gə'fɛlɪçst], adv. if you please.

Gefallsucht [gə'falzuxt], f. (—, no pl.) coquetry.

gefallsüchtig [gə'falzyçtɪç], adj. coquettish.

gefangen [gə'faŋən], adj. in prison, imprisoned, captive.

Gefangene [gə'faŋənə], m., f. (—n, pl. —n) prisoner, captive.

Gefangennahme [gə'faŋənna:mə], f. (—, no pl.) arrest, capture.

Gefangenschaft [gə'faŋənʃaft], f. (—, no pl.) captivity, imprisonment, detention; in — geraten, be taken prisoner.

Gefängnis [gə'fɛŋnɪs], n. (—ses, pl. —se) prison, gaol.

Gefäß [gə'fɛ:s], n. (—es, pl. —e) vessel.

gefaßt [gə'fast], adj. collected, composed, ready; calm; sich auf etwas — machen, prepare o.s. for s.th.

Gefecht [gə'fɛçt], n. (—s, pl. —e) fight, battle, combat; action, engagement.

gefeit [gə'faɪt], adj. proof against.

Gefieder [gə'fi:dər], n. (—s, no pl.) plumage, feathers.

Gefilde [gə'fɪldə], n. (—s, pl. —) (Poet.) fields, plain.

Geflecht [gə'flɛçt], n. (—s, no pl.) wicker-work, texture.

geflissentlich [gə'flɪsəntlɪç], adj. intentional, wilful, with a purpose.

Geflügel [gə'fly:gəl], n. (—s, no pl.) fowls, poultry.

geflügelt [gə'fly:gəlt], adj. winged; —e Worte, household words, familiar quotation.

Geflüster [gə'flystər], n. (—s, no pl.) whispering, whisper.

Gefolge [gə'fɔlgə], n. (—s, no pl.) retinue, following.

gefräßig [gə'frɛ:sɪç], adj. voracious, gluttonous.

Gefreite [gə'fraɪtə], m. (—n, pl. —n) (Mil.) lance-corporal.

gefrieren [gə'fri:rən], v.n. irr. (aux. sein) freeze; congeal.

Gefrierpunkt [gə'fri:rpuŋkt], m. (—s, no pl.) freezing point, zero.

Gefrorene [gə'fro:rənə], n. (—n, no pl.) ice-cream.

Gefüge [gə'fy:gə], n. (—s, no pl.) joints, structure, construction; frame.

gefügig [gə'fy:gɪç], adj. pliant; docile; einen — machen, make s.o. amenable, persuade s.o.

Gefühl [gə'fy:l], n. (—s, pl. —e) feeling, sense, sensation.

gegen ['ge:gən], prep. (Acc.) against; towards; about, near; in comparison with; in the direction of; opposed to; in exchange for; — Quittung, against receipt. — adv., prefix. counter, opposing, contrary.

Gegend ['ge:gənt], f. (—, pl. —en) region, country, part.

Gegengewicht ['ge:gəngəvɪçt], n. (—s, pl. —e) counterweight, counterpoise.

Gegengift ['ge:gəngɪft], n. (—s, pl. —e) antidote.

Gegenleistung ['ge:gənlaɪstuŋ], f. (—, pl. —en) return; service in return; Leistung und —, give and take.

Gegenrede ['ge:gənre:də], f. (—, pl. —n) contradiction; objection.

Gegensatz ['ge:gənzats], m. (—es, pl. ⸚e) contrast, opposition, antithesis.

gegensätzlich ['ge:gənzetslɪç], adj. contrary, adverse.

Gegenseite ['ge:gənzaɪtə], f. (—, pl. —n) opposite side; (coin) reverse.

gegenseitig ['ge:gənzaɪtɪç], adj. reciprocal, mutual.

Gegenstand ['ge:gənʃtant], m. (—s, pl. ⸚e) object; subject, matter.

gegenstandslos [ge:gənʃtantslo:s], adj. superfluous, irrelevant.

Gegenstück ['ge:gənʃtyk], n. (—s, pl. —e) counterpart.

Gegenteil ['ge:gəntaɪl], n. (—s, no pl.) contrary; im —, on the contrary.

gegenüber [ge:gən'y:bər], prep. (Dat.) opposite to, facing. — adv. opposite.

Gegenüberstellung ['ge:gən'y:bərʃteluŋ], f. (—, pl. —en) confrontation.

Gegenwart ['ge:gənvart], f. (—, no pl.) presence; (Gram.) present tense.

Gegenwehr ['ge:gənve:r], f. (—, no pl.) defence, resistance.

Gegenwirkung ['ge:gənvɪrkuŋ], f. (—, pl. —en) reaction, counter-effect.

gegenzeichnen ['ge:gəntsaɪçnən], v.a. countersign.

Gegner ['ge:gnər], m. (—s, pl. —) opponent, adversary, antagonist.

gegnerisch ['ge:gnərɪʃ], adj. adverse, antagonistic.

Gegnerschaft ['ge:gnərʃaft], f. (—, no pl.) antagonism; opposition.

Gehalt (1) [gə'halt], m. (—s, no pl.) contents; (fig.) value, standard.

Gehalt (2) [gə'halt], n. (—s, pl. ⸚er) salary, stipend; pay.

Gehaltszulage [gə'haltstsu:la:gə], f. (—, pl. —n) rise (in salary); increment; (Am.) raise.

gehaltvoll [gə'haltfɔl], adj. substantial.

Gehänge [gə'hɛŋə], n. (—s, pl. —) slope; festoon, garland.

geharnischt [gə'harnɪʃt], adj. armoured, steel-clad; (fig.) severe.

gehässig [gə'hɛsɪç], adj. malicious, spiteful.

Gehäuse [gə'hɔyzə], *n.* (—s, *pl.* —) casing, case; (*snail*) shell.

Gehege [gə'he:gə], *n.* (—s, *pl.* —) enclosure; *einem ins — kommen,* trespass on s.o.'s preserves.

geheim [gə'haɪm], *adj.* secret, clandestine.

Geheimnis [gə'haɪmnɪs], *n.* (—ses, *pl.* —se) secret, mystery.

geheimnisvoll [gə'haɪmnɪsfɔl], *adj.* mysterious.

Geheimrat [gə'haɪmraːt], *m.* (—s, *pl.* ¨e) Privy Councillor.

Geheimschrift [gə'haɪmʃrɪft], *f.* (—, *pl.* —en) cryptography.

Geheimsprache [gə'haɪmʃpraːxə], *f.* (—, *pl.* —en) cipher.

Geheiß [gə'haɪs], *n.* (—es, *no pl.*) command, order, bidding.

gehen [ˈgeːən], *v.n. irr.* (*aux.* sein) go, walk; (*Mach.*) work, function; (*goods*) sell; (*dough*) rise; *er lässt sich —,* he lets himself go; *er lässt es sich gut —,* he enjoys himself; *einem an die Hand —,* lend s.o. a hand, assist s.o.; *in Erfüllung —,* come true; *in sich —,* reflect; *wie geht es dir?* how are you? *es geht mir gut,* I am well.

geheuer [gə'hɔyər], *adj.* (*only in neg.*) *nicht ganz —,* creepy, eerie, uncanny; (*coll.*) fishy.

Gehilfe [gə'hɪlfə], *m.* (—n, *pl.* —n) assistant, helper.

Gehirn [gə'hɪrn], *n.* (—s, *pl.* —e) brain, brains.

Gehirnhautentzündung [gə'hɪrnhautɛntsyndʊŋ], *f.* (—, *pl.* —en) meningitis, cerebral inflammation.

Gehirnschlag [gə'hɪrnʃlaːk], *m.* (—s, *pl.* ¨e) apoplexy.

Gehöft [gə'hœft], *n.* (—es, *pl.* —e) farmstead.

Gehör [gə'høːr], (—s, *no pl.*) hearing; *gutes —,* musical ear.

gehorchen [gə'hɔrçən], *v.n.* obey; *nicht —,* disobey.

gehören [gə'høːrən], *v.n.* belong. — *v.r. sich —,* be the proper thing to do.

gehörig [gə'høːrɪç], *adj. dazu —,* belonging to, referring to; due, fit, proper, thorough; (*fig.*) sound.

Gehörn [gə'hœrn], *n.* (—s, *pl.* —e) horns, antlers.

gehörnt [gə'hœrnt], *adj.* horned; (*fig.*) duped (husband).

Gehorsam [gə'hoːrzaːm], *m.* (—s, *no pl.*) obedience; *— leisten,* show obedience; *den — verweigern,* refuse to obey.

gehorsam [gə'hoːrzaːm], *adj.* obedient, dutiful, submissive.

Gehrock [ˈgeːrɔk], *m.* (—s, *pl.* ¨e) frock-coat.

Geier [ˈgaɪər], *m.* (—s, *pl.* —) (*Orn.*) vulture.

Geifer [ˈgaɪfər], *m.* (—s, *no pl.*) saliva, drivel; (*animals*) foam; (*fig.*) venom, rancour.

geifern [ˈgaɪfərn], *v.n.* slaver, drivel; (*fig.*) foam at the mouth; give vent to o.'s anger.

Geige [ˈgaɪgə], *f.* (—, *pl.* —n) violin, fiddle.

Geigenharz [ˈgaɪgənhaːrts], *n.* (—es, *no pl.*) colophony; rosin.

Geigensteg [ˈgaɪgənʃteːk], *m.* (—s, *pl.* —e) bridge of a violin.

Geiger [ˈgaɪgər], *m.* (—s, *pl.* —) violin-player, violinist.

geil [gaɪl], *adj.* rank; lecherous, lascivious.

Geisel [ˈgaɪzəl], *f.* (—, *pl.* —n) hostage.

Geiß [gaɪs], *f.* (—, *pl.* —en) goat, she-goat.

Geißblatt [ˈgaɪsblat], *n.* (—s, *no pl.*) (*Bot.*) honeysuckle.

Geißbock [ˈgaɪsbɔk], *m.* (—s, *pl.* ¨e) billy-goat.

Geißel [ˈgaɪsəl], *f.* (—, *pl.* —n) scourge.

geißeln [ˈgaɪsəln], *v.a.* scourge, whip, flagellate.

Geist [gaɪst], *m.* (—es, *pl.* —er) spirit, mind; brains, intellect; wit; apparition, ghost.

Geisterbeschwörung [ˈgaɪstərbəʃvøːrʊŋ], *f.* (—, *pl.* —en) evocation (of spirits); necromancy; exorcism.

geisterhaft [ˈgaɪstərhaft], *adj.* ghostly, spectral, weird.

Geisterwelt [ˈgaɪstərvɛlt], *f.* (—, *no pl.*) world of spirits.

geistesabwesend [ˈgaɪstəsapveːzənt], *adj.* absent-minded.

Geistesfreiheit [ˈgaɪstəsfraɪhaɪt], *f.* (—, *no pl.*) freedom of thought.

Geistesgegenwart [ˈgaɪstəsgeːgənvart], *f.* (—, *no pl.*) presence of mind.

Geisteskraft [ˈgaɪstəskraft], *f.* (—, *pl.* ¨e) faculty of the mind.

Geistesstörung [ˈgaɪstəsʃtøːrʊŋ], *f.* (—, *pl.* —en) mental aberration.

Geistesverfassung [ˈgaɪstəsfɛrfasʊŋ], *f.* (—, *no pl.*) state of mind.

geistesverwandt [ˈgaɪstəsfɛrvant], *adj.* congenial.

Geistesverwirrung [ˈgaɪstəsfɛrvɪrʊŋ], *f.* (—, *no pl.*) bewilderment.

Geisteswissenschaften [ˈgaɪstəsvɪsənʃaftən], *f.pl.* (*Univ.*) Arts, Humanities.

Geisteszerrüttung [ˈgaɪstəstsɛrytʊŋ], *f.* (—, *no pl.*) mental derangement, insanity.

geistig [ˈgaɪstɪç], *adj.* intellectual, mental; spiritual; *—e Getränke,* alcoholic liquors.

geistlich [ˈgaɪstlɪç], *adj.* spiritual; religious; ecclesiastical, clerical; *—er Orden,* religious order; *—er Stand,* holy orders, the Clergy.

Geistliche [ˈgaɪstlɪçə], *m.* (—n, *pl.* —n) priest, clergyman, cleric; minister of religion.

Geistlichkeit [ˈgaɪstlɪçkaɪt], *f.* (—, *no pl.*) clergy.

geistlos [ˈgaɪstloːs], *adj.* dull, stupid.

geistreich [ˈgaɪstraɪç], *adj.* clever, witty.

Geiz [gaɪts], *m.* (—es, *no pl.*) avarice, covetousness.

geizen [ˈgaɪtsən], *v.n.* be miserly.

Geizhals

Geizhals ['gaItshals], *m.* (—es, *pl.* ̈-e) miser, niggard.

Geizkragen ['gaItskra:gən], *m.* (—s, *pl.* —) *see* Geizhals.

Gekreisch [gə'kraIʃ], *n.* (—es, *no pl.*) screaming, shrieks.

Gekritzel [gə'krItsəl], *n.* (—s, *no pl.*) scrawling, scribbling.

Gekröse [gə'krø:zə], *n.* (—s, *no pl.*) tripe; (*Anat.*) mesentery.

gekünstelt [gə'kynstəlt], *adj.* artificial, affected.

Gelächter [gə'lɛçtər], *n.* (—s, *no pl.*) laughter.

Gelage [gə'la:gə], *n.* (—s, *pl.* —) (*obs.*) feast, banquet.

Gelände [gə'lɛndə], *n.* (—s, *pl.* —) terrain, region; landscape.

Geländer [gə'lɛndər], *n.* (—s, *pl.* —) railing, balustrade, banister.

gelangen [gə'laŋən], *v.n.* (*aux.* sein) arrive, come (to).

Gelaß [gə'las], *n.* (—sses, *pl.* —sse) (*obs.*) room, chamber.

gelassen [gə'lasən], *adj.* calm, composed, collected.

geläufig [gə'lɔyfIç], *adj.* fluent.

gelaunt [gə'launt], *adj.* disposed.

Geläute [gə'lɔytə], *n.* (—s, *no pl.*) ringing, chiming; bells.

geläutert [gə'lɔytərt], *adj.* purified, cleansed.

gelb [gɛlp], *adj.* yellow, amber.

Gelbschnabel ['gɛlpʃna:bəl], *m.* (—s, *pl.* ̈-) (*Orn.*) fledg(e)ling; greenhorn.

Gelbsucht ['gɛlpzuxt], *f.* (—, *no pl.*) jaundice.

Geld [gɛlt], *n.* (—es, *pl.* —er) money, currency, coin; *bares* —, ready money, hard cash; *kleines* —, small change.

Geldanweisung ['gɛltanvaIzuŋ], *f.* (—, *pl.* —en) money-order.

Geldbuße ['gɛltbu:sə], *f.*(—,*pl.*—n) fine.

Geldkurs ['gɛltkurs], *m.* (—es, *pl.* —e) rate of exchange.

Geldmittel ['gɛltmItəl], *n. pl.* pecuniary resources, financial resources.

Geldschrank ['gɛltʃraŋk], *m.* (—s, *pl.* ̈-e) safe.

Geldstrafe ['gɛltʃtra:fə], *f.* (—, *pl.* —n) fine.

Geldverlegenheit ['gɛltfɛrle:gənhaIt], *f.* (—, *pl.* —en) pecuniary embarrassment, financial difficulty.

Geldwährung ['gɛltvɛ:ruŋ], *f.* (—, *pl.* —en) currency.

Geldwechsel ['gɛltvɛksəl], *m.* (—s, *no pl.*) exchange.

Gelee [ʒə'le:], *n.* (—s, *pl.* —s) jelly.

gelegen [gə'le:gən], *adj.* situated, situate; *das kommt mir gerade* —, that suits me; *mir ist daran* —, *dass*, I am anxious that.

Gelegenheit [gə'le:gənhaIt], *f.* (—, *pl.* —en) occasion, chance, opportunity; facility; *bei* —, one of these days.

Gelegenheitskauf [gə'le:gənhaItskauf], *m.* (—s, *pl.* ̈-e) bargain.

gelegentlich [gə'le:gəntlIç], *adj.* occasional.

gelehrig [gə'le:rIç], *adj.* docile, tractable.

Gelehrsamkeit [gə'le:rza:mkaIt], *f.* (—, *no pl.*) learning, erudition.

gelehrt [gə'le:rt], *adj.* learned, erudite.

Gelehrte [gə'le:rtə], *m.* (—n, *pl.* —n) scholar, man of learning, savant.

Geleise [gə'laIzə], *n.* (—s, *pl.* —) *see* Gleis.

Geleit [gə'laIt], *n.* (—s, *no pl.*) escort, accompaniment; (*Naut.*) convoy; *sicheres* —, safe conduct.

geleiten [gə'laItən], *v.a.* accompany, conduct, escort.

Gelenk [gə'lɛŋk], *n.* (—s, *pl.* —e) (*human*) joint; (*chain*) link.

Gelenkentzündung [gə'lɛŋkɛnttsyn-duŋ], *f.* (—, *pl.* —en) (*Med.*) arthritis.

gelenkig [gə'lɛŋkIç], *adj.* flexible, pliant, nimble, supple.

Gelenkrheumatismus [gə'lɛŋkrɔyma-tIsmUs], *m.* (—, *no pl.*) (*Med.*) rheumatoid arthritis, rheumatic gout.

Gelichter [gə'lIçtər], *n.* (—s, *no pl.*) riff-raff.

Geliebte [gə'li:ptə], *m.* (—n, *pl.* —n) lover, sweetheart, beloved. — *f.* (—n, *pl.* —n) mistress, beloved.

gelinde [gə'lIndə], *adj.* soft, smooth, gentle, mild; — *gesagt*, to say the least.

Gelingen [gə'lIŋən], *n.* (—s, *no pl.*) success.

gelingen [gə'lIŋən], *v.n.* irr. (*aux.* sein) succeed; *es gelingt mir*, I succeed.

gellen ['gɛlən], *v.n.* yell; shrill.

geloben [gə'lo:bən], *v.a.* (*aux.* haben) promise solemnly, vow; *das Gelobte Land*, the Promised Land.

Gelöbnis [gə'lø:pnIs], *n.* (—ses, *pl.* —se) vow, promise.

gelt [gɛlt], *inter.* (*coll.*) isn't it? don't you think so?

gelten ['gɛltən], *v.a. irr.* be worth, cost. — *v.n.* count (as), be valid.

Geltung ['gɛltuŋ], *f.* (—, *no pl.*) value, importance.

Gelübde [gə'lypdə], *n.* (—s, *pl.* —) vow, solemn promise *or* undertaking.

gelungen [gə'luŋən], *adj.* (*coll.*) funny, capital.

Gelüst [gə'lyst], *n.* (—s, *pl.* —e) appetite, desire.

gelüsten [gə'lystən], *v.a.* — *nach*, long for, covet.

Gemach [gə'ma:x], *n.* (—es, *pl.* ̈-er) (*Poet.*) chamber, room; apartment.

gemach [gə'ma:x], *adv.* slowly, softly, by degrees.

gemächlich [gə'mɛçlIç], *adj.* slow, soft, easy, unhurried, leisurely.

Gemahl [gə'ma:l], *m.* (—s, *pl.* —e) spouse, husband, consort.

Gemahlin [gə'ma:lIn], *f.* (—, *pl.* —nen) spouse, wife, consort.

Gemälde [gə'mɛ:ldə], *n.* (—s, *pl.* —) picture, painting, portrait.

gemäß [gə'mɛ:s], *prep.* (*Dat.*) in accordance with, according to.

gemäßigt [gə'mɛ:sɪçt], *adj.* temperate, moderate; —*es Klima*, temperate climate.
Gemäuer [gə'mɔyər], *n.* (—*s, no pl.*) ancient walls, ruins.
gemein [gə'maɪn], *adj.* common, mean, low, vulgar, base.
Gemeinde [gə'maɪndə], *f.* (—, *pl.* —*n*) community, parish, municipality; (*Eccl.*) congregation.
Gemeindevorstand [gə'maɪndefor-ʃtant], *m.* (—*es, no pl.*) town or borough council.
gemeingefährlich [gə'maɪngəfɛ:rlɪç], *adj.* dangerous to the public.
Gemeinheit [gə'maɪnhaɪt], *f.* (—, *pl.* —*en*) meanness; baseness; dirty trick.
gemeinhin [gə'maɪnhɪn], *adv.* commonly.
Gemeinplatz [gə'maɪnplats], *m.* (—*es, pl. ⁓e*) commonplace, truism.
gemeinsam [gə'maɪnza:m], *adj.* common, joint; *der — Markt*, (*Pol.*) Common Market; —*e Sache machen*, make common cause. — *adv.* together.
Gemeinschaft [gə'maɪnʃaft], *f.* (—, *pl.* —*en*) community; association; *in — mit*, jointly; *in — haben*, hold in common.
gemeinschaftlich [gə'maɪnʃaftlɪç], *adj.* common. — *adv.* in common, together.
Gemeinsinn [gə'maɪnzɪn], *m.* (—*s, no pl.*) public spirit.
Gemeinwesen [gə'maɪnve:zən], *n.* (—*s, no pl.*) community.
Gemeinwohl [gə'maɪnvo:l], *n.* (—*s, no pl.*) common weal; common good.
Gemenge [gə'mɛŋə], *n.* (—*s, no pl.*) mixture; (*fig.*) scuffle.
Gemengsel [gə'mɛŋsəl], *n.* (—*s, no pl.*) medley, hotchpotch.
gemessen [gə'mɛsən], *adj.* deliberate.
Gemessenheit [gə'mɛsənhaɪt], *f.* (—, *no pl.*) precision, deliberation.
Gemetzel [gə'mɛtsəl], *n.* (—*s, no pl.*) slaughter, massacre.
Gemisch [gə'mɪʃ], *n.* (—*es, pl.* —*e*) mixture, motley.
Gemme ['gɛmə], *f.* (—, *pl.* —*n*) gem, cameo.
Gemse ['gɛmzə], *f.* (—, *pl.* —*n*) chamois.
Gemüse [gə'my:zə], *n.* (—*s, pl.* —) vegetables, greens.
Gemüsehändler [gə'my:zəhɛndlər], *m.* (—*s, pl.* —) greengrocer.
gemustert [gə'mustərt], *adj.* patterned, figured; (*Comm.*) —*e Sendung*, delivery as per sample.
Gemüt [gə'my:t], *n.* (—*s, pl.* —*er*) mind, soul, heart; disposition, nature, spirit, temper; feeling.
gemütlich [gə'my:tlɪç], *adj.* cosy, snug, comfortable; genial, friendly, pleasant.
Gemütlichkeit [gə'my:tlɪçkaɪt], *f.* (—, *no pl.*) cosiness, snugness; *da hört die — auf*, that is more than I will stand for.

gemütlos [gə'my:tlo:s], *adj.* unfeeling.
Gemütsart [gə'my:tsa:rt], *f.* (—, *no pl.*) disposition; character.
Gemütsbewegung [gə'my:tsbəve:guŋ], *f.* (—, *pl.* —*en*) emotion.
gemütskrank [gə'my:tskraŋk], *adj.* sick in mind; melancholy.
Gemütsleben [gə'my:tsle:bən], *n.* (—*s, no pl.*) emotional life.
Gemütsmensch [gə'my:tsmɛnʃ], *m.* (—*en, pl.* —*en*) man of feeling or sentiment; (*pej.*) sentimentalist.
gemütvoll [gə'my:tfɔl], *adj.* full of feeling, sympathetic.
gen [gɛn], *prep. contraction* of **gegen**, (*Poet.*) towards, to (*Acc.*).
Genannte [gə'nantə], *m.* (—*n, pl.* —*n*) named person, aforesaid.
genäschig [gə'nɛʃɪç], *adj.* fond of sweets, sweet-toothed.
genau [gə'nau], *adj.* precise, exact, accurate; strict, parsimonious.
Genauigkeit [gə'nauɪçkaɪt], *f.* (—, *no pl.*) accuracy, exactitude, precision.
Gendarm [ʒã'darm], *m.* (—*en, pl.* —*en*) policeman, constable.
genehm [gə'ne:m], *adj.* agreeable, acceptable, convenient.
genehmigen [gə'ne:mɪgən], *v.a.* approve of, agree to, permit; (*contract*) ratify.
geneigt [gə'naɪkt], *adj.* inclined (to), disposed (to); prone (to); *einem — sein*, be well disposed towards s.o.; (*Lit.*) *der —e Leser*, gentle reader.
Geneigtheit [gə'naɪkthaɪt], *f.* (—, *no pl.*) inclination, proneness, propensity; favour, kindness.
General [genə'ra:l], *m.* (—*s, pl.* —*e, ⁓e*) general.
Generalfeldmarschall [genə'ra:lfɛlt-marʃal], *m.* (—*s, pl. ⁓e*) field marshal.
Generalkommando [genə'ra:lkɔmando], *n.* (—*s, pl.* —*e*) general's headquarters; (*corps*) headquarters.
Generalkonsul [genə'ra:lkɔnzul], *m.* (—*s, pl.* —*e*) consul-general.
Generalnenner [genə'ra:lnɛnər], *m.* (—*s, pl.* —) (*Maths.*) common denominator.
Generalprobe [genə'ra:lpro:bə], *f.* (—, *pl.* —*n*) dress-rehearsal.
Generalvollmacht [genə'ra:lfɔlmaxt], *f.* (—, *pl.* —*en*) (*Law*) general power of attorney.
generell [genə'rɛl], *adj.* general, common.
generös [genə'rø:s], *adj.* generous, magnanimous.
genesen [gə'ne:zən], *v.n. irr.* (*aux.* sein) recover, be restored to health; convalesce.
Genf [gɛnf], *n.* Geneva.
genial [gen'ja:l], *adj.* ingenious; extremely gifted.
Genick [gə'nɪk], *n.* (—*s, pl.* —*e*) nape, neck.
Genickstarre [gə'nɪkʃtarə], *f.* (—, *no pl.*) (*Med.*) (cerebrospinal) meningitis.
Genie [ʒe'ni:], *n.* (—*s, pl.* —*s*) genius.

genieren [ʒeˈniːrən], *v.a.* trouble, embarrass, disturb. — *v.r. sich* —, feel embarrassed; *sich nicht* —, make o.s. at home.

genießbar [gəˈniːsbaːr], *adj.* eatable, edible, palatable; drinkable; (*fig.*) pleasant, agreeable.

genießen [gəˈniːsən], *v.a. irr.* enjoy; have the use of; (*food*) eat, partake of; *Ansehen* —, enjoy respect.

Geniestreich [ʒeˈniːʃtraɪç], *m.* (—s, *pl.* —e) stroke of genius.

Genitiv [ˈgeːniːtiːf], *m.* (—s, *pl.* —e) (*Gram.*) genitive.

Genosse [gəˈnɔsə], *m.* (—n, *pl.* —n) comrade, mate, colleague; (*crime*) accomplice.

Genossenschaft [gəˈnɔsənʃaft], *f.* (—, *pl.* —en) association, company, confederacy, co-operative, union.

Genre [ʒãr], *n.* (—s, *pl.* —s) genre; style, kind.

Gent [gɛnt], *n.* Ghent.

Genua [ˈgeːnua], *n.* Genoa.

genug [gəˈnuːk], *indecl. adj.* enough, sufficient; —! that will do!

Genüge [gəˈnyːgə], *f.* (—, *no pl.*) *zur* —, sufficiently; *einem* — *leisten*, give satisfaction to s.o.

genügen [gəˈnyːgən], *v.n.* be enough, suffice; *sich etwas* — *lassen*, be content with s.th.

genügsam [gəˈnyːkzaːm], *adj.* easily satisfied; temperate, sober.

Genügsamkeit [gəˈnyːkzaːmkaɪt], *f.* (—, *no pl.*) contentedness, moderation; temperateness, sobriety.

Genugtuung [gəˈnuːktuːuŋ], *f.* (—, *no pl.*) satisfaction; reparation; atonement.

Genuß [gəˈnus], *m.* (—sses, *pl.* ˈsse) enjoyment; use; (*food*) consumption.

Genußmittel [gəˈnusmɪtəl], *n.* (—s, *pl.* —) (*mostly pl.*) luxuries; (*Am.*) delicatessen.

genußreich [gəˈnusraɪç], *adj.* enjoyable, delightful.

Genußsucht [gəˈnussuxt], *f.* (—, *no pl.*) thirst for pleasure.

Geograph [geoˈgraːf], *m.* (—en, *pl.* —en) geographer.

Geographie [geograˈfiː], *f.* (—, *no pl.*) geography.

Geologe [geoˈloːgə], *m.* (—n, *pl.* —n) geologist.

Geologie [geoloˈgiː], *f.* (—, *no pl.*) geology.

Geometer [geoˈmeːtər], *m.* (—s, *pl.* —) geometrician; land-surveyor.

Geometrie [geomeˈtriː], *f.* (—, *no pl.*) geometry.

Georg [geˈɔrk], *m.* George.

Georgine [geɔrˈgiːnə], *f.* (—, *pl.* —n) (*Bot.*) dahlia.

Gepäck [gəˈpɛk], *n.* (—s, *no pl.*) luggage; (*Am.*) baggage.

Gepäckaufbewahrung [gəˈpɛkaufbəvaːruŋ], *f.* (—, *pl.* —en) left luggage office.

Gepäckträger [gəˈpɛktrɛːgər], *m.* (—s, *pl.* —) porter.

Gepflogenheit [gəˈpfloːgənhaɪt], *f.* (—, *pl.* —en) habit, custom, wont.

Geplänkel [gəˈplɛnkəl], *n.* (—s, *pl.* —) (*rare*) skirmish.

Geplärr [gəˈplɛr], *n.* (—s, *no pl.*) bawling.

Geplauder [gəˈplaudər], *n.* (—s, *no pl.*) chatting; small talk.

Gepräge [gəˈprɛːgə], *n.* (—s, *no pl.*) impression, stamp.

Gepränge [gəˈprɛŋə], *n.* (—s, *no pl.*) pomp, ceremony, splendour.

Ger [geːr], *m.* (—s, *pl.* —e) (*rare*) spear, javelin.

Gerade [gəˈraːdə], *f.* (—n, *pl.* —n) (*Maths.*) straight line.

gerade [gəˈraːdə], *adj.* straight, direct, erect, even; (*fig.*) upright, honest. — *adv.* quite, just; *jetzt* —, now more than ever; *fünf* — *sein lassen*, stretch a point; — *heraus*, in plain terms.

geradeaus [gəˈraːdaaus], *adv.* straight on.

gerädert [gəˈrɛːdərt], *adj.* (*fig.*) fatigued, exhausted, worn out.

geradeswegs [gəˈraːdəsveːks], *adv.* straightaway, immediately.

geradezu [gəˈraːdətsuː], *adv.* frankly, downright; *das ist* — *scheußlich*, this is downright nasty.

Geradheit [gəˈraːthaɪt], *f.* (—, *no pl.*) straightness; (*fig.*) straightforwardness.

geradlinig [gəˈraːtliːnɪç], *adj.* rectilinear.

geradsinnig [gəˈraːtzɪnɪç], *adj.* honest, upright.

gerändert [gəˈrɛndərt], *adj.* with a milled edge.

Geranie [gəˈraːnjə], *f.* (—, *pl.* —n) (*Bot.*) geranium.

Gerät [gəˈrɛːt], *n.* (—s, *pl.* —e) tool, implement, device; appliance; (radio, television) set; apparatus.

geraten [gəˈraːtən], *v.n. irr.* (*aux.* sein) turn out; *gut* —, turn out well; — *auf*, come upon.

Geräteturnen [gəˈrɛːtəturnən], *n.* (—s, *no pl.*) gymnastics with apparatus.

Geratewohl [gəˈraːtəvoːl], *n.* (—s, *no pl.*) *aufs* —, at random.

geraum [gəˈraum], *adj.* —e *Zeit*, a long time.

geräumig [gəˈrɔymɪç], *adj.* spacious, large, wide, roomy.

Geräusch [gəˈrɔyʃ], *n.* (—es, *pl.* —e) noise; sound.

gerben [ˈgɛrbən], *v.a.* tan, taw; *einem die Haut* —, give s.o. a hiding.

Gerber [ˈgɛrbər], *m.* (—s, *pl.* —) tanner.

Gerbsäure [ˈgɛrpsɔyrə], *f.* (—, *no pl.*) tannin.

gerecht [gəˈrɛçt], *adj.* just, fair; (*Bibl.*) righteous; *einem* — *werden*, do justice to s.o.

Gerechtigkeit [gəˈrɛçtɪçkaɪt], *f.* (—, *no pl.*) justice, fairness; (*Bibl.*) righteousness.

Gerede [gə're:də], *n.* (—s, *no pl.*) talk, rumour, gossip.

gereichen [gə'raɪçən], *v.n.* turn out to be; *einem zur Ehre —,* redound to s.o.'s honour.

gereizt [gə'raɪtst], *adj.* irritated, annoyed.

gereuen [gə'rɔyən] *see* reuen.

Gerhard ['ge:rhart], *m.* Gerard, Gerald.

Gericht [gə'rɪçt], *n.* (—s, *pl.* —e) court of justice, tribunal; (*food*) course, dish; *das Jüngste —,* Last Judgment.

gerichtlich [gə'rɪçtlɪç], *adj.* judicial, legal; *einen — belangen,* sue s.o.

Gerichtsbarkeit [gə'rɪçtsbarkaɪt], *f.* (—, *no pl.*) jurisdiction.

Gerichtsdiener [gə'rɪçtsdi:nər], *m.* (—s, *pl.* —) (*law court*) usher.

Gerichtshof [gə'rɪçtsho:f], *m.* (—es, *pl.* ˙e) court of justice.

Gerichtskanzlei [gə'rɪçtskantslaɪ], *f.* (—, *pl.* —en) record office.

Gerichtskosten [gə'rɪçtskɔstən], *f. pl.* (*Law*) costs.

Gerichtsordnung [gə'rɪçtsɔrdnuŋ], *f.* (—, *pl* —en) legal procedure.

Gerichtstermin [gə'rɪçtstɛrmi:n], *m.* (—s, *pl.* —e) day fixed for a hearing.

Gerichtsverhandlung [gə'rɪçtsfɛr-handluŋ], *f.* (—, *pl.* —en) hearing; trial.

Gerichtsvollzieher [gə'rɪçtsfɔltsi:ər], *m.* (—s, *pl.* —) bailiff.

gerieben [gə'ri:bən], *adj.* ground; crafty, cunning.

gering [gə'rɪŋ], *adj.* small, little, mean, petty, unimportant, of little value, trifling; low, base.

geringfügig [gə'rɪŋfy:gɪç], *adj.* small, petty, insignificant.

geringschätzig [gə'rɪŋʃɛtsɪç], *adj.* contemptuous, disdainful, supercilious; derogatory.

gerinnen [gə'rɪnən], *v.n. irr.* (*aux.* sein) coagulate, clot; curdle.

Gerinnsel [gə'rɪnzəl], *n.* (—s, *pl.* —) embolism (of the blood); clot.

Gerippe [gə'rɪpə], *n.* (—s, *pl.* —) skeleton; frame; (*Aviat.*) air-frame.

gerippt [gə'rɪpt], *adj.* ribbed, fluted.

gerissen [gə'rɪsən], *adj.* (*coll.*) sharp, cunning.

Germane [gɛr'ma:nə], *m.* (—n, *pl.* —n) Teuton.

Germanist ['gɛrmanɪst], *m.* (—en, *pl.* — en) (*Univ.*) student of *or* expert in German language and/or literature.

gern [gɛrn], *adv.* gladly, willingly, readily, with pleasure; — *haben,* like.

Geröll [gə'rœl], *n.* (—s, *no pl.*) boulders, rubble.

Gerste ['gɛrstə], *f.* (—, *no pl.*) (*Bot.*) barley.

Gerstenschleim ['gɛrstənʃlaɪm], *m.* (—s, *no pl.*) barley water.

Gerte ['gɛrtə], *f.* (—, *pl.* —n) whip, switch, rod.

Geruch [gə'ru:x], *m.* (—s, *pl.* ˙e) smell, odour, scent; *guter —,* fragrance, aroma.

geruchlos [gə'ru:xlo:s], *adj.* scentless, odourless, without smell.

Geruchsinn [gə'ru:xzɪn], *m.* (—es, *no pl.*) sense of smell.

Gerücht [gə'ryçt], *n.* (—s, *pl.* —e) rumour, report.

Gerümpel [gə'rympəl], *n.* (—s, *no pl.*) lumber, trash.

Gerundium [gə'rundjum], *n.* (—s, *pl.* —dien) (*Gram.*) gerund.

Gerüst [gə'ryst], *n.* (—es, *pl.* —e) scaffolding.

Ges [gɛs], *n.* (—, *pl.* —) (*Mus.*) G flat.

gesamt [gə'zamt], *adj.* entire, all, complete.

Gesamtheit [gə'zamthaɪt], *f.* (—, *no pl.*) totality.

Gesandte [gə'zantə], *m.* (—n, *pl.* —n) messenger; ambassador, envoy; *päpstlicher —,* papal nuncio.

Gesandtschaft [gə'zantʃaft], *f.* (—, *pl.* —en) embassy, legation.

Gesang [gə'zaŋ], *m.* (—s, *pl.* ˙e) song, air; hymn; (*Lit.*) canto.

Gesangbuch [gə'zaŋbu:x], *n.* (—s, *pl.* ˙er) hymnal, hymn-book.

Gesäß [gə'zɛ:s], *n.* (—es, *pl.* —e) seat, buttocks.

Geschäft [gə'ʃɛft], *n.* (—s, *pl.* —e) business; trade, commerce; affairs; occupation; shop, (*Am.*) store.

geschäftig [gə'ʃɛftɪç], *adj.* active, bustling, busy.

geschäftlich [gə'ʃɛftlɪç], *adj.* concerning business. — *adv.* on business.

Geschäftsführer [gə'ʃɛftsfy:rər], *m.* (—s, *pl.* —) manager.

Geschäftshaus [gə'ʃɛftshaus], *n.* (—es, *pl.* ˙er) firm; business premises.

geschäftskundig [gə'ʃɛftskundɪç], *adj.* experienced in business.

Geschäftslokal [gə'ʃɛftsloka:l], *n.* (—s, *pl.* —e) business premises, shop.

Geschäftsordnung [gə'ʃɛftsɔrdnuŋ], *f.* (—, *pl.* —en) standing orders; agenda.

Geschäftsträger [gə'ʃɛftstrɛ:gər], *m.* (—s, *pl.* —) (*Comm.*) agent; (*Pol.*) chargé d'affaires.

Geschäftsverkehr [gə'ʃɛftsfərke:r], *m.* (—s, *no pl.*) business dealings.

Geschehen [gə'ʃe:ən], *n.* (—s, *no pl.*) happening.

geschehen [gə'ʃe:ən], *v.n. irr.* (*aux.* sein) happen, occur; take place; be done; *das geschieht dir recht,* it serves you right.

gescheit [gə'ʃaɪt], *adj.* clever, intelligent.

Geschenk [gə'ʃɛŋk], *n.* (—s, *pl.* —e) gift, present, donation.

Geschichte [gə'ʃɪçtə], *f.* (—, *pl.* —n) tale; story; history.

Geschichtenbuch [gə'ʃɪçtənbu:x], *n.* (—es, *pl.* ˙er) story-book.

geschichtlich [gə'ʃɪçtlɪç], *adj.* historical.

Geschichtsschreiber [gə'ʃɪçtsʃraɪbər], *m.* (—s, *pl.* —) historian.

Geschick [gə'ʃɪk], *n.* (—es, *no pl.*) fate, destiny; dexterity, skill, knack, aptitude.

87

Geschicklichkeit [gə'ʃɪklɪçkaɪt], f. (—, pl. —en) dexterity, adroitness, skill.

geschickt [gə'ʃɪkt], adj. skilled, skilful, clever, able.

Geschirr [gə'ʃɪr], n. (—s, no pl.) crockery, plates and dishes; (horses) harness.

Geschlecht [gə'ʃlɛçt], n. (—s, pl. —er) sex; kind, race, species, extraction, family; (Gram.) gender.

geschlechtlich [gə'ʃlɛçtlɪç], adj. sexual; generic.

Geschlechtsart [gə'ʃlɛçtsa:rt], f. (—, pl. —en) generic character.

Geschlechtskrankheit [gə'ʃlɛçtskraŋkhaɪt], f. (—, pl. —en) venereal disease.

Geschlechtskunde [gə'ʃlɛçtskundə], f. (—, no pl.) genealogy.

Geschlechtsreife [gə'ʃlɛçtsraɪfə], f. (—, no pl.) puberty.

Geschlechtsteile [gə'ʃlɛçtstaɪlə], m. pl. genitals.

Geschlechtstrieb [gə'ʃlɛçtstri:p], m. (—s, no pl.) sexual instinct.

Geschlechtswort [gə'ʃlɛçtsvɔrt], n. (—s, pl. ˙er) (Gram.) article.

geschliffen [gə'ʃlɪfən], adj. polished; (glass) cut.

Geschmack [gə'ʃmak], m. (—s, pl. ˙er) taste, flavour.

geschmacklos [gə'ʃmaklo:s], adj. tasteless, insipid; in bad taste.

Geschmacksrichtung [gə'ʃmaksrɪçtuŋ], f. (—, pl. —en) prevailing taste; vogue; tendency.

Geschmeide [gə'ʃmaɪdə], n. (—s, pl. —) jewels, jewellery; trinkets.

geschmeidig [gə'ʃmaɪdɪç], adj. flexible, pliant, supple; (Tech.) malleable.

Geschmeiß [gə'ʃmaɪs], n. (—es, no pl.) dung; vermin; (fig.) rabble.

Geschnatter [gə'ʃnatər], n. (—s, no pl.) cackling.

geschniegelt [gə'ʃni:gəlt], adj. spruce, dressed up.

Geschöpf [gə'ʃœpf], n. (—es, pl. —e) creature.

Geschoß [gə'ʃɔs], n. (—sses, pl. —sse) shot, shell, projectile, missile; (house) storey.

geschraubt [gə'ʃraupt], adj. (style) stilted, affected.

Geschrei [gə'ʃraɪ], n. (—s, no pl.) shrieking, shouting, screaming; (fig.) stir, great noise.

Geschreibsel [gə'ʃraɪpsəl], n. (—s, no pl.) scrawl, scribbling.

Geschütz [gə'ʃyts], n. (—es, pl. —e) artillery, gun; schweres — auffahren, bring o.'s guns into play.

Geschützweite [gə'ʃytsvaɪtə], f. (—, no pl.) calibre.

Geschwader [gə'ʃva:dər], n. (—s, pl.—) squadron.

Geschwätz [gə'ʃvɛts], n. (—es, no pl.) chatter, gossip, prattle, tittle-tattle.

geschweige [gə'ʃvaɪgə], adv. let alone, to say nothing of.

geschwind [gə'ʃvɪnt], adj. quick, nimble, fast, swift, fleet.

Geschwindigkeitsmesser [gə'ʃvɪndɪçkaɪtsmɛsər], m. (—s, pl. —) (Motor.) speedometer.

Geschwister [gə'ʃvɪstər], pl. brothers and sisters.

geschwollen [gə'ʃvɔlən], adj. stilted, turgid, pompous.

Geschworene [gə'ʃvo:rənə], m. (—n, pl. —n), juror, juryman; (pl.) jury.

Geschwulst [gə'ʃvulst], f. (—, pl. ˙e) swelling, tumour.

Geschwür [gə'ʃvy:r], n. (—s, pl. —e) sore, ulcer, abscess.

Geselle [gə'zɛlə], m. (—n, pl. —n) journeyman; companion, comrade, mate.

gesellen [gə'zɛlən], v.a., v.r. join, associate with, keep company with.

gesellig [gə'zɛlɪç], adj. sociable, companionable; gregarious.

Gesellschaft [gə'zɛlʃaft], f. (—, pl. —en) society; community; (formal) party; company, club; geschlossene —, private party; einem — leisten, keep s.o. company; (Comm.) — mit beschränkter Haftung, (abbr.) GmbH, limited company, (abbr.) Ltd.

gesellschaftlich [gə'zɛlʃaftlɪç], adj. social.

Gesellschaftsanzug [gə'zɛlʃaftsantsu:k], m. (—s, pl. ˙e) evening dress.

Gesellschaftsspiel [gə'zɛlʃaftsʃpi:l], n. (—s, pl. —e) round game, party game.

Gesellschaftsvertrag [gə'zɛlʃaftsfɛrtra:k], m. (—es, pl. ˙e) (Law) partnership agreement; deed of partnership.

Gesellschaftszimmer [gə'zɛlʃaftstsɪmər], n. (—s, pl. —) drawing-room, reception room.

Gesetz [gə'zɛts], n. (—es, pl. —e) law, statute, regulation.

Gesetzbuch [gə'zɛtsbu:x], n. (—es, pl. ˙er) code of laws; statute book.

Gesetzentwurf [gə'zɛtsɛntvurf], m. (—es, pl. ˙e) (Parl.) draft bill.

gesetzgebend [gə'zɛtsge:bənt], adj. legislative.

gesetzlich [gə'zɛtslɪç], adj. lawful, legal.

Gesetzlichkeit [gə'zɛtslɪçkaɪt], f. (—, no pl.) lawfulness, legality.

gesetzlos [gə'zɛtslo:s], adj. lawless, anarchical.

gesetzmäßig [gə'zɛtsmɛ:sɪç], adj. conforming to law, lawful, legitimate.

gesetzt [gə'zɛtst], adj. steady, sedate, staid; von —em Alter, of mature age; — daß, supposing that.

Gesetztheit [gə'zɛtsthaɪt], f. (—, no pl.) sedateness, steadiness.

gesetzwidrig [gə'zɛtsvi:drɪç], adj. illegal, unlawful.

Gesicht (1) [gə'zɪçt], n. (—s, pl. —er) face, physiognomy, look.

Gesicht (2) [gə'zɪçt], n. (—s, pl. —e) sight; vision, apparition.

Gesichtsausdruck [gə'zɪçtsausdruk], m. (—s, no pl.) face, mien; expression.

Gesichtsfeld [gə'zıçtsfɛlt], *n.* (—es, *pl.* —er) field of vision.

Gesichtskreis [gə'zıçtskraıs], *m.* (—es, *pl.* —e) horizon.

Gesichtspunkt [gə'zıçtspuŋkt], *m.* (—es, *pl.* —e) point of view.

Gesichtszug [gə'zıçtstsu:k], *m.* (—s, *pl.* ⸚e) feature.

Gesims [gə'zıms], *n.* (—es, *pl.* —e) cornice, moulding, ledge.

Gesinde [gə'zındə], *n.* (—s, *no pl.*) (domestic) servants.

Gesindel [gə'zındəl], *n.* (—s, *no pl.*) mob, rabble.

gesinnt [gə'zınt], *adj.* disposed.

Gesinnung [gə'zınuŋ], *f.* (—, *pl.* —en) disposition, sentiment; conviction.

gesinnungslos [gə'zınuŋslo:s], *adj.* unprincipled.

gesinnungstreu [gə'zınuŋstrɔy], *adj.* loyal, staunch.

Gesinnungswechsel [gə'zınuŋsvɛksəl], *m.* (—s, *no pl.*) change of opinion, volte-face.

gesittet [gə'zıtət], *adj.* civilised, well-mannered.

Gesittung [gə'zıtuŋ], *f.* (—, *no pl.*) (*rare*) civilisation, good manners.

gesonnen [gə'zɔnən] *see* gesinnt.

Gespann [gə'ʃpan], *n.* (—s, *pl.* —e) team, yoke (oxen etc.).

gespannt [gə'ʃpant], *adj.* stretched; intense, thrilled; tense; filled with suspense.

Gespanntheit [gə'ʃpanthaıt], *f.* (—, *no pl.*) tension, strain, suspense.

Gespenst [gə'ʃpɛnst], *n.* (—es, *pl.* —er) ghost, spectre, apparition.

gespenstisch [gə'ʃpɛnstıʃ], *adj.* ghostly, spectral.

Gespiele [gə'ʃpi:lə], *m.* (—n, *pl.* —n) playmate.

Gespielin [gə'ʃpi:lın], *f.* (—, *pl.* —innen) (girl) playmate.

Gespinst [gə'ʃpınst], *n.* (—es, *pl.* —e) web.

Gespött [gə'ʃpœt], *n.* (—s, *no pl.*) mocking, mockery, jeering, derision; (*fig.*) laughing stock.

Gespräch [gə'ʃprɛ:ç], *n.* (—s, *pl.* —e) conversation, discourse, talk; (*phone*) call; *ein — anknüpfen*, start a conversation.

gesprächig [gə'ʃprɛ:çıç], *adj.* talkative, communicative.

gespreizt [gə'ʃpraıtst], *adj.* wide apart; (*fig.*) affected, pompous.

gesprenkelt [gə'ʃprɛŋkəlt], *adj.* speckled.

gesprungen [gə'ʃpruŋən], *adj.* cracked (glass etc.).

Gestade [gə'ʃta:də], *n.* (—s, *pl.* —) shore, coast, bank.

Gestalt [gə'ʃtalt], *f.* (—. *pl.* —en) form, figure, shape; configuration; stature; fashion; manner, way.

gestalten [gə'ʃtaltən], *v.a.* form, shape, fashion, make. — *v.r. sich —*, turn out.

Gestaltung [gə'ʃtaltuŋ], *f.* (—, *pl.* —en) formation; arrangement; planning.

geständig [gə'ʃtɛndıç], *adj.* confessing; — *sein*, confess.

Geständnis [gə'ʃtɛntnıs], *n.* (—ses, *pl.* —se) confession, admission.

Gestank [gə'ʃtaŋk], *m.* (—s, *no pl.*) stink, stench.

gestatten [gə'ʃtatən], *v.a.* permit, allow, grant; *wir — uns*, we beg leave to; — *Sie !* pardon me, excuse me.

Geste ['gɛstə], *f.* (—, *pl.* —n) gesture, gesticulation.

gestehen [gə'ʃte:ən], *v.a. irr.* confess, admit, own; *offen gestanden*, quite frankly.

Gestein [gə'ʃtaın], *n.* (—s, *pl.* —e) (*Poet.*) rock; (*Geol.*) rocks, minerals.

Gestell [gə'ʃtɛl], *n.* (—s, *pl.* —e) rack, frame; (*table*) trestle; (*books*) stand.

Gestellung [gə'ʃtɛluŋ], *f.* (—, *no pl.*) (*Mil.*) reporting for service.

gestern ['gɛstərn], *adv.* yesterday; — *abend*, last night.

gestiefelt [gə'ʃti:fəlt], *adj.* booted; *der —e Kater*, Puss in Boots.

gestielt [gə'ʃti:lt], *adj.* (*axe*) helved; (*Bot.*) stalked, stemmed.

gestikulieren [gɛstiku'li:rən], *v.n.* gesticulate.

Gestirn [gə'ʃtırn], *n.* (—s, *pl.* —e) star, constellation.

gestirnt [gə'ʃtırnt], *adj.* starred, starry.

Gestöber [gə'ʃtø:bər], *n.* (—s, *pl.* —) (*snow, dust*) drift, storm, blizzard.

Gesträuch [gə'ʃtrɔyç], *n.* (—es, *no pl.*) bushes, shrubs; thicket.

gestreift [gə'ʃtraıft], *adj.* striped.

gestreng [gə'ʃtrɛŋ], *adj.* (*obs.*) strict, severe.

gestrig ['gɛstrıç], *adj.* of yesterday.

Gestrüpp [gə'ʃtryp], *n.* (—s, *no pl.*) bushes, underwood, shrubs, shrubbery.

Gestüt [gə'ʃty:t], *n.* (—s, *pl.* —e) stud (-farm).

Gestüthengst [gə'ʃty:thɛŋst], *m.* (—es, *pl.* —e) stallion.

Gesuch [gə'zu:x], *n.* (—s, *pl.* —e) petition, request, application.

gesucht [gə'zu:xt], *adj.* in demand; (*style*) far-fetched; affected; studied.

gesund [gə'zunt], *adj.* healthy, wholesome; *der —e Menschenverstand*, common sense.

Gesundbrunnen [gə'zuntbrunən], *m.* (—s, *pl.* —) mineral waters; spa.

gesunden [gə'zundən], *v.n.* (*aux. sein*) recover o.'s health.

Gesundheit [gə'zunthaıt], *f.* (—, *no pl.*) health.

Gesundheitslehre [gə'zunthaıtsle:rə], *f.* (—, *no pl.*) hygiene.

Getäfel [gə'tɛ:fəl], *n.* (—s, *no pl.*) wainscot, wainscoting, panelling.

Getändel [gə'tɛndəl], *n.* (—s, *no pl.*) (*rare*) flirting, dallying.

Getier [gə'ti:r], *n.* (—s, *no pl.*) (*collective term*) animals.

Getöse [gə'tø:zə], *n.* (—s, *no pl.*) loud noise, din.

89

Getränk [gə'trɛŋk], *n.* (—s, *pl.* —e) drink, beverage.

getrauen [gə'trauən], *v.r. sich* —, dare, venture.

Getreide [gə'traɪdə], *n.* (—s, *pl.* —) corn, grain.

getreu [gə'trɔy], *adj.* faithful, true, loyal.

getreulich [gə'trɔylɪç], *adv.* faithfully, truly, loyally.

Getriebe [gə'tri:bə], *n.* (—s, *pl.* —) machinery; (*Motor.*) gear; drive; *das — der Welt*, the bustle of life.

getrieben [gə'tri:bən], *adj.* (*Tech.*) chased (work.)

Getrödel [gə'trø:dəl], *n.* (—s, *no pl.*) dawdling.

getrost [gə'tro:st], *adj.* confident, cheerful; — *sein*, be of good cheer.

Getto ['gɛto], *n.* (—s, *pl.* —s) ghetto.

Getue [gə'tu:ə], *n.* (—s, *no pl.*) pretence, fuss.

Getümmel [gə'tyməl], *n.* (—s, *no pl.*) bustle, turmoil.

geübt [gə'y:pt], *adj.* skilled, versed.

Geübtheit [gə'y:pthaɪt], *f.* (—, *no pl.*) skill, experience, dexterity.

Gevatter [gə'fatər], *m.* (—s, *pl.* —) (*obs.*) godfather.

gevierteilt [gə'fi:rtaɪlt], *adj.* quartered.

Gewächs [gə'vɛks], *n.* (—es, *pl.* —e) plant, growth; (*Med.*) excrescence.

gewachsen [gə'vaksən], *adj. einem* (*einer Sache*) — *sein*, be equal to s.o. (s.th.).

Gewächshaus [gə'vɛkshaus], *n.* (—es, *pl.* ⁻er) green-house, hot-house, conservatory.

gewagt [gə'va:kt], *adj.* risky, hazardous; daring.

gewählt [gə've:lt], *adj.* choice, select.

gewahr [gə'va:r], *adj. einer Sache — werden*, become aware of s.th., perceive s.th.

Gewähr [gə've:r], *f.* (—, *no pl.*) surety; guarantee; warranty; — *leisten*, guarantee.

gewahren [gə'va:rən], *v.a.* perceive, see, become aware of.

gewähren [gə've:rən], *v.a.* allow, grant; *einen — lassen*, let s.o. do as he pleases, let be.

Gewährleistung [gə've:rlaɪstuŋ], *f.* (—, *pl.* —en) grant of security (*or* bail); guarantee.

Gewahrsam [gə'va:rza:m], *m.* (—s, *no pl.*) safe-keeping, custody.

Gewährsmann [gə've:rsman], *m.* (—es, *pl.* ⁻er) authority; informant.

Gewährung [gə've:ruŋ], *f.* (—, *no pl.*) granting (of request).

Gewalt [gə'valt], *f.* (—, *pl.* —en) power, force, might; authority; violence; *höhere* —, (*Law*) act of God, force majeure; *sich in der — haben*, have control over o.s.

Gewalthaber [gə'valtha:bər], *m.* (—s, *pl.* —) tyrant; despot, autocrat; person in authority.

gewaltig [gə'valtɪç], *adj.* powerful, mighty, enormous, stupendous.

gewaltsam [gə'valtza:m], *adj.* forcible, violent.

Gewaltstreich [gə'valtʃtraɪç], *m.* (—s, *pl.* —e) bold stroke; coup d'état.

Gewalttat [gə'valtta:t], *f.* (—, *pl.* —en) violent action, violence, outrage.

gewalttätig [gə'valtte:tɪç], *adj.* violent, fierce, outrageous.

Gewand [gə'vant], *n.* (—es, *pl.* ⁻er) (*Lit.*) garment, dress; (*Eccl.*) vestment.

gewandt [gə'vant], *adj.* nimble, deft, clever; (*mind*) versatile.

gewärtig [gə'vɛrtɪç], *adj. einer Sache — sein*, expect s.th. to happen.

Gewäsch [gə'vɛʃ], *n.* (—es, *no pl.*) stuff and nonsense; rubbish.

Gewässer [gə'vɛsər], *n.* (—s, *pl.* —) waters.

Gewebe [gə've:bə], *n.* (—s, *pl.* —) (*Physiol.*, *Text.*) tissue; web, weft, texture.

geweckt [gə'vɛkt], *adj.* smart, wideawake.

Gewehr [gə've:r], *n.* (—s, *pl.* —e) gun, fire-arm, rifle.

Gewehrlauf [gə've:rlauf], *m.* (—s, *pl.* ⁻e) barrel.

Geweih [gə'vaɪ], *n.* (—s, *pl.* —e) horns, antlers.

geweiht [gə'vaɪt], *adj.* consecrated; holy.

gewellt [gə'vɛlt], *adj.* corrugated, wavy.

Gewerbe [gə'vɛrbə], *n.* (—s, *pl.* —) trade, profession, business; calling; industry.

Gewerbekunde [gə'vɛrbəkundə], *f.* (—, *no pl.*) technology.

Gewerbeschein [gə'vɛrbəʃaɪn], *m.* (—s, *pl.* —e) trade-licence.

gewerblich [gə'vɛrplɪç], *adj.* industrial.

gewerbsmäßig [gə'vɛrpsme:sɪç], *adj.* professional.

Gewerkschaft [gə'vɛrkʃaft], *f.* (—, *pl.* —en) trade union.

Gewicht [gə'vɪçt], *n.* (—s, *pl.* —e) weight; *schwer ins — fallen*, carry great weight, weigh heavily.

gewichtig [gə'vɪçtɪç], *adj.* weighty, ponderous; (*fig.*) momentous, important, strong.

gewiegt [gə'vi:kt], *adj.* experienced, clever.

gewillt [gə'vɪlt], *adj.* willing.

Gewimmel [gə'vɪməl], *n.* (—s, *no pl.*) milling crowd, swarm, throng.

Gewinde [gə'vɪndə], *n.* (—s, *pl.* —) (*screw*) thread; (*flowers*) garland.

Gewinn [gə'vɪn], *n.* (—s, *pl.* —e) gain, profit; (*lottery*) prize; (*gambling*) winnings.

gewinnen [gə'vɪnən], *v.a. irr.* win, gain, obtain, get, earn.

gewinnend [gə'vɪnənt], *adj.* prepossessing; engaging.

Gewinnung [gə'vɪnuŋ], *f.* (—, *no pl.*) (*Ind.*, *Chem.*) extraction; output, production.

Gewinsel [gə'vɪnzəl], *n.* (—s, *no pl.*) whimpering.

Gewinst [gə'vɪnst], *m.* (—es, *pl.* —e)
(*obs.*) gain, profit.

Gewirr [gə'vɪr], *n.* (—s, *no pl.*) entanglement, confusion.

gewiß [gə'vɪs], *adj.* (*Genit.*) certain,
sure. — *adv.* indeed.

Gewissen [gə'vɪsən], *n.* (—s, *no pl.*)
conscience.

gewissenhaft [gə'vɪsənhaft], *adj.* conscientious, scrupulous.

gewissenlos [gə'vɪsənlo:s], *adj.* unscrupulous.

Gewissensbiß [gə'vɪsənsbɪs],*m.*(—sses,
pl. —sse) (*mostly pl.*) pangs of conscience.

gewissermaßen [gə'vɪsərma:sən], *adv.*
to a certain extent, so to speak.

Gewißheit [gə'vɪshaɪt], *f.* (—, *no pl.*)
certainty.

gewißlich [gə'vɪslɪç], *adv.* surely.

Gewitter [gə'vɪtər], *n.* (—s, *pl.* —)
thunderstorm.

gewittern [gə'vɪtərn], *v.n.* thunder.

gewitzigt, gewitzt [gə'vɪtsɪçt, gə'vɪtst],
adj. knowing, clever; shrewd.

gewogen [gə'vo:gən], *adj.* kindly disposed, favourable; *einem — sein*, be
favourably inclined towards s.o.

Gewogenheit [gə'vo:gənhaɪt], *f.* (—,
no pl.) kindness, favour.

gewöhnen [gə'vø:nən], *v.a.* accustom
to. — *v.r. sich — an*, get used to,
accustom o.s. to.

Gewohnheit [gə'vo:nhaɪt], *f.* (—, *pl.*
—en) (*general*) custom, usage; (*personal*) habit.

gewohnheitsmäßig [gə'vo:nhaɪtsmɛ:-
sɪç], *adj.* habitual. — *adv.* by force of
habit.

Gewohnheitsrecht [gə'vo:nhaɪtsreçt],
n. (—s, *no pl.*) common law.

gewöhnlich [gə'vø:nlɪç], *adj.* customary,
usual; (*fig.*) common, mean, vulgar.

gewohnt [gə'vo:nt], *adj.* accustomed to,
used to.

Gewöhnung [gə'vø:nuŋ], *f.* (—, *no pl.*)
habit, use, habituation.

Gewölbe [gə'vœlbə], *n.* (—s, *pl.* —)
vault, arch.

Gewölk [gə'vœlk], *n.* (—s, *no pl.*)
clouds, cloud formation.

Gewühl [gə'vy:l], *n.* (—s, *no pl.*) crowd,
throng, bustle.

gewunden [gə'vundən], *adj.* tortuous.

Gewürm [gə'vyrm], *n.* (—s, *no pl.*)
reptiles, worms; vermin.

Gewürz [gə'vyrts], *n.* (—es, *pl.* —e)
spice.

Gewürznelke [gə'vyrtsnɛlkə], *f.* (—,
pl. —n) clove.

Gezänk [gə'tsɛŋk], *n.* (—s, *no pl.*)
quarrelling, bickering.

Gezeiten [gə'tsaɪtən], *f. pl.* tides.

Gezeter [gə'tse:tər], *n.* (—s, *no pl.*)
screaming, yelling; (*fig.*) outcry.

geziemen [gə'tsi:mən], *v.r. sich für
einen —*, befit or become s.o.

geziert [gə'tsi:rt], *adj.* affected.

Gezischel [gə'tsɪʃəl], *n.* (—s, *no pl.*)
whispering.

Gezücht [gə'tsyçt], *n.* (—s, *no pl.*)
brood, breed.

Gezweig [gə'tsvaɪk], *n.* (—s, *no pl.*)
branches, boughs.

Gezwitscher [gə'tsvɪtʃər], *n.* (—s, *no
pl.*) chirping.

Gezwungenheit [gə'tsvuŋənhaɪt], *f.*
(—, *no pl.*) constraint.

Gicht [gɪçt], *f.* (—, *no pl.*) (*Med.*) gout.

gichtbrüchig [ˈgɪçtbryçɪç], *adj.* (*obs.*)
paralytic; gouty.

gichtig [ˈgɪçtɪç], *adj.* gouty.

Giebel [ˈgi:bəl], *m.* (—s, *pl.* —) gable.

Giebelfenster [ˈgi:bəlfɛnstər], *n.* (—s,
pl.—) gable-window, dormer-window.

gieb(e)lig [ˈgi:b(ə)lɪç], *adj.* gabled.

Gier [gi:r], *f.* (—, *no pl.*) greediness,
eagerness.

gieren [ˈgi:rən], *v.n.* (*rare*) — *nach*,
thirst for, yearn for.

gierig [ˈgi:rɪç], *adj.* eager, greedy.

Gießbach [ˈgi:sbax], *m.* (—s, *pl.* ˘e)
mountain-torrent.

gießen [ˈgi:sən], *v.a. irr.* (*liquids*) pour,
shed; (*metal*) cast, found.

Gießer [ˈgi:sər], *m.* (—s, *pl.* —) founder.

Gießerei [gi:sə'raɪ], *f.* (—, *pl.* —en)
foundry.

Gießform [ˈgi:sfɔrm], *f.* (—, *pl.* —en)
casting-mould.

Gießkanne [ˈgi:skanə], *f.* (—, *pl.* —n)
watering-can.

Gift [gɪft], *n.* (—es, *pl.* —e) poison,
venom; (*fig.*) virulence; (*coll.*) *darauf
kannst du — nehmen*, you can bet
your life on it.

Giftbaum [ˈgɪftbaum], *m.* (—s, *pl.* ˘e)
upas-tree.

Giftdrüse [ˈgɪftdry:zə], *f.* (—, *pl.* —n)
poison-gland.

giftig [ˈgɪftɪç], *adj.* poisonous; (*fig.*)
venomous; (*Med.*) toxic.

Giftlehre [ˈgɪftle:rə], *f.* (—, *no pl.*)
toxicology.

Giftpilz [ˈgɪftpɪlts], *m.* (—es, *pl.* ˘e)
poisonous toadstool.

Giftschlange [ˈgɪftʃlaŋə], *f.* (—, *pl.*
—n) poisonous snake.

Giftstoff [ˈgɪftʃtɔf], *m.* (—es, *pl.* ˘e)
poison, virus.

Gigant [gɪ'gant], *m.* (—en, *pl.* —en)
giant.

Gigerl [ˈgi:gərl], *m.* (—s, *pl.* —)
(*Austr. dial.*) fop, coxcomb.

Gilde [ˈgɪldə], *f.* (—, *pl.* —n) guild,
corporation.

Gimpel [ˈgɪmpəl], *m.* (—s, *pl.* —)
(*Orn.*) bullfinch, chaffinch; (*fig.*)
simpleton.

Ginster [ˈgɪnstər], *m.* (—s, *no pl.*) (*Bot.*)
gorse, furze, broom.

Gipfel [ˈgɪpfəl], *m.* (—s, *pl.* —) summit, peak; (*fig.*) acme, culmination,
height.

gipfeln [ˈgɪpfəln], *v.n.* culminate.

Gips [gɪps], *m.* (—es, *no pl.*) gypsum,
stucco, plaster of Paris.

Gipsabdruck [ˈgɪpsapdruk], *m.* (—s,
pl. ˘e) plaster-cast.

Gipsbild ['gɪpsbɪlt], *n.* (—s, *pl.* —er) plaster-figure.

Gipsverband ['gɪpsfɐbant], *m.* (—es, *pl.* ·:e) (*Med.*) plaster of Paris dressing.

girieren [ʒiˈriːrən], *v.a.* (*Comm.*) endorse (a bill).

Girlande [gɪrˈlandə], *f.* (—, *pl.* —n) garland.

Girobank ['ʒiːrobaŋk], *f.* (—, *pl.* —en) transfer *or* clearing bank.

Gis [gɪs], *n.* (—, *pl.* —) (*Mus.*) G sharp; — *Moll,* G sharp minor.

gischen ['gɪʃən], *v.n.* foam, froth.

Gischt [gɪʃt], *f.* (—, *pl.* —e) foam, froth; spray.

Gitarre [giˈtarə], *f.* (—, *pl.* —n) guitar.

Gitter ['gɪtər], *n.* (—s, *pl.* —) trellis, grate, fence; railing; lattice; (*colour-printing*) screen.

Gitterwerk ['gɪtərverk], *n.* (—s, *no pl.*) trellis-work.

Glacéhandschuh [glaˈseːhantʃuː], *m.* (—s, *pl.* —e) kid-glove.

Glanz [glants], *m.* (—es, *no pl.*) brightness, lustre, gloss; polish, sheen; (*fig.*) splendour.

glänzen ['glentsən], *v.n.* shine, glitter, glisten; (*fig.*) sparkle.

glänzend ['glentsənt], *adj.* glossy; (*fig.*) splendid, magnificent.

Glanzfirnis ['glantsfɪrnɪs], *m.* (—ses, *pl.* —se) glazing varnish.

Glanzleder ['glantsleːdər], *n.* (—s, *no pl.*) patent leather.

Glanzleinwand ['glantslaɪnvant], *f.* (—, *no pl.*) glazed linen.

glanzlos ['glantsloːs], *adj.* lustreless, dull.

glanzvoll ['glantsfɔl], *adj.* splendid, brilliant.

Glanzzeit ['glantstsaɪt], *f.* (—, *pl.* —en) golden age.

Glas [glaːs], *n.* (—es, *pl.* ·:er) glass, tumbler.

glasartig ['glaːsaːrtɪç], *adj.* vitreous, glassy.

Glaser ['glaːzər], *m.* (—s, *pl.* —) glazier.

Glaserkitt ['glaːzərkɪt], *m.* (—s, *no pl.*) putty.

gläsern ['glɛːzərn], *adj.* vitreous, glassy, made of glass.

Glashütte ['glaːshytə], *f.* (—, *pl.* —n) glass-works.

glasieren [glaˈziːrən], *v.a.* glaze; (*cake etc.*) ice.

glasiert [glaˈziːrt], *adj.* glazed; (*Cul.*) frosted, iced; (*Art.*) varnished.

Glasröhre ['glaːsrøːrə], *f.* (—, *pl.* —n) glass-tube.

Glasscheibe ['glaːsʃaɪbə], *f.* (—, *pl.* —n) glass-pane, sheet of glass.

Glassplitter ['glaːsʃplɪtər], *m.* (—s, *pl.* —) splinter of glass.

Glasur [glaˈzuːr], *f.* (—, *pl.* —en) (*potter's*) glaze, glazing; enamel, varnish; (*cake*) icing.

glatt [glat], *adj.* smooth, sleek; even, plain, glossy; glib; downright. — *adv.* entirely; — *rasiert,* close-shaven.

Glätte ['glɛtə], *f.* (—, *no pl.*) smoothness, evenness, slipperiness; polish.

Glatteis ['glataɪs], *n.* (—es, *no pl.*) slippery ice; sheet ice; (*Am.*) glaze; *einen aufs — führen,* lead s.o. up the garden path.

glätten ['glɛtən], *v.a.* smooth; (*dial.*) iron.

Glatze ['glatsə], *f.* (—, *pl.* —n) bald head.

glatzköpfig ['glatskœpfɪç], *adj.* bald, bald-pated.

Glaube(n) ['glaubə(n)], *m.* (—ns, *no pl.*) faith, belief; creed, religion.

glauben ['glaubən], *v.a.* believe; think, suppose. — *v.n. an etwas* (*Acc.*) —, believe in s.th.

Glaubensbekenntnis ['glaubənsbəkentnɪs], *n.* (—ses, *pl.* —se) confession of faith; creed.

Glaubensgericht ['glaubənsɡərɪçt], *n.* (—es, *no pl.*) inquisition.

Glaubersalz ['glaubərzalts], *n.* (—es, *no pl.*) phosphate of soda, Glauber's salts.

glaubhaft ['glauphaft], *adj.* credible, authentic.

gläubig ['glɔybɪç], *adj.* believing, faithful; (*Eccl.*) *die Gläubigen,* the faithful.

Gläubiger ['glɔybɪgər], *m.* (—s, *pl.* —) creditor.

glaublich ['glauplɪç], *adj.* credible, believable.

glaubwürdig ['glaupvyrdɪç], *adj.* authentic, worthy of belief; plausible.

gleich [glaɪç], *adj.* same, like, equal, even; *auf —e Weise,* likewise; *es ist mir ganz* —, it is all the same to me. — *adv.* alike, at once; almost; just as; *ich komme* —, I shall be there in a moment; — *und* — *gesellt sich gern,* birds of a feather flock together.

gleichaltrig ['glaɪçaltrɪç], *adj.* of the same age.

gleichartig ['glaɪçaːrtɪç], *adj.* of the same kind, homogeneous.

gleichberechtigt ['glaɪçbərɛçtɪçt], *adj.* entitled to equal rights.

Gleiche ['glaɪçə], *n.* (—n, *pl.* —n) the like; the same; *etwas ins* — *bringen,* straighten s.th. out.

gleichen ['glaɪçən], *v.n. irr.* be like, resemble, be equal to.

gleichermaßen ['glaɪçərmaːsən], *adv.* in a like manner, likewise.

gleichfalls ['glaɪçfals], *adv.* likewise, equally, as well; *danke* —, thanks, the same to you.

gleichförmig ['glaɪçfœrmɪç], *adj.* uniform; monotonous.

gleichgesinnt ['glaɪçgəzɪnt], *adj.* congenial, of the same mind.

Gleichgewicht ['glaɪçgəvɪçt], *n.* (—s, *no pl.*) balance, equilibrium.

gleichgültig ['glaɪçgyltɪç], *adj.* indifferent; *es ist mir* —, it's all the same to me.

Gleichheit ['glaɪçhaɪt], *f.* (—, *pl.* —en) equality, likeness.

Gleichklang ['glaɪçklaŋ], m. (—s, pl. ˙ːe) consonance.

gleichmachen ['glaɪçmaxən], v.a. level, equate; *dem Erdboden* —, raze to the ground.

Gleichmaß ['glaɪçmaːs], n. (—es, no pl.) proportion, symmetry.

gleichmäßig ['glaɪçmɛːsɪç], adj. proportionate, symmetrical.

Gleichmut ['glaɪçmuːt], m. (—s, no pl.) equanimity, calm.

gleichmütig ['glaɪçmyːtɪç], adj. even-tempered, calm.

gleichnamig ['glaɪçnaːmɪç], adj. homonymous.

Gleichnis ['glaɪçnɪs], n. (—ses, pl. —se) simile; (Bibl.) parable.

gleichsam ['glaɪçzaːm], adv. as it were, as if.

gleichschenklig ['glaɪçʃɛŋklɪç], adj. (Maths.) isosceles.

gleichseitig ['glaɪçzaɪtɪç], adj. (Maths.) equilateral.

Gleichsetzung ['glaɪçzɛtsuŋ], f. (—, no pl.), **Gleichstellung** ['glaɪçʃtɛluŋ], f. (—, pl. —en) equalisation.

Gleichstrom ['glaɪçʃtroːm], m. (—s, no pl.) (Elec.) direct current.

gleichtun ['glaɪçtuːn], v.a. irr. *es einem —*, emulate s.o.

Gleichung ['glaɪçuŋ], f. (—, pl. —en) (Maths.) equation.

gleichwohl ['glaɪçvoːl], adv., conj. nevertheless, however, yet.

gleichzeitig ['glaɪçtsaɪtɪç], adj. simultaneous, contemporary.

Gleis [glaɪs], n. (—es, pl. —e) (Railw.) track; rails; (Am.) track.

gleiten ['glaɪtən], v.n. irr. (aux. sein) glide, slide, slip.

Gleitflug ['glaɪtfluːk], m. (—es, pl. ˙ːe) (Aviat.) gliding.

Gletscher ['glɛtʃər], m. (—s, pl. —) glacier.

Gletscherspalte ['glɛtʃərʃpaltə], f. (—, pl. —n) crevasse.

Glied [gliːt], n. (—es, pl. —er) limb, joint; member; link; rank, file.

Gliederlähmung ['gliːdərlɛːmuŋ], f. (—, no pl.) paralysis.

gliedern ['gliːdərn], v.a. articulate, arrange, form.

Gliederreißen ['gliːdərraɪsən], n. (—s, no pl.) pain in the limbs, rheumatism, arthritis etc.

Gliederung ['gliːdəruŋ], f. (—, pl. —en) articulation, disposition, structure, arrangement, organisation.

Gliedmaßen ['gliːtmaːsən], f. pl. limbs.

glimmen ['glɪmən], v.n. irr. glimmer, glow, burn faintly; —de Asche, embers.

Glimmer ['glɪmər], m. (—s, no pl.) (Min.) mica.

glimpflich ['glɪmpflɪç], adj. gentle.

glitschen ['glɪtʃən], v.n. (aux. sein) (coll.) slide.

glitschig ['glɪtʃɪç], adj. (coll.) slippery.

glitzern ['glɪtsərn], v.n. glisten, glitter.

Globus ['gloːbus], m. (—ses, pl. —se) globe.

Glöckchen ['glœkçən], n. (—s, pl. —) small bell; hand-bell.

Glocke ['glɔkə], f. (—, pl. —n) bell; *etwas an die große — hängen*, make a great fuss about s.th.

Glockenblume ['glɔkənbluːmə], f. (—, pl. —n) (Bot.) bluebell.

Glockengießer ['glɔkəngiːsər], m. (—s, pl. —) bell-founder.

glockenklar ['glɔkənklaːr], adj. as clear as a bell.

Glockenläuter ['glɔkənlɔʏtər], m. (—s, pl. —) bell-ringer.

Glockenspiel ['glɔkənʃpiːl], n. (—s, pl. —e) chime; (Mus.) glockenspiel, carillon.

Glockenstuhl ['glɔkənʃtuːl], m. (—s, pl. ˙ːe) belfry.

Glockenzug ['glɔkəntsuːk], m. (—s, pl. ˙ːe) bell-rope; (Mus.) bell-stop.

Glöckner ['glœknər], m. (—s, pl. —) bellringer, sexton.

glorreich ['gloːraɪç], adj. glorious.

Glosse ['glɔsə], f. (—, pl. —n) gloss, comment, annotation; —n machen über, comment upon; find fault with; scoff at.

glotzen ['glɔtsən], v.n. stare wide-eyed; gape.

Glück [glyk], n. (—s, no pl.) luck, good luck, fortune, happiness; — haben, be in luck; auf gut —, at random; zum —, fortunately, luckily; viel —, good luck.

Glucke ['glukə], f. (—, pl. —n) (sitting) hen.

glücken ['glykən], v.n. succeed; es ist mir geglückt, I have succeeded in.

glücklich ['glyklɪç], adj. fortunate, lucky, happy.

glückselig [glyk'zeːlɪç], adj. blissful, happy.

glucksen ['gluksən], v.n. gurgle.

Glücksfall ['glyksfal], m. (—es, pl. ˙ːe) lucky chance, windfall, stroke of good fortune.

Glückspilz ['glykspɪlts], m. (—es, pl. —e) (coll.) lucky dog.

glückverheißend ['glykfɛrhaɪsənt], adj. auspicious, propitious.

Glückwunsch ['glykvunʃ], m. (—es, pl. ˙ːe) congratulation; felicitation.

glühen ['glyːən], v.a. make red-hot; (wine) mull. — v.n. glow, be red-hot.

glühend ['glyːənt], adj. glowing, burning; red-hot; (coal) live; (fig.) ardent, fervent.

Glühstrumpf ['glyːʃtrumpf], m. (—es, pl. ˙ːe) incandescent mantle.

Glühwein ['glyːvaɪn], m. (—s, no pl.) mulled wine.

Glut [gluːt], f. (—, no pl.) glowing fire; heat; (fig.) ardour.

glutrot [gluːtroːt], adj. fiery red.

Glyzerin ['glytsəriːn], n. (—s, no pl.) glycerine.

93

Gnade ['gna:də], *f.* (—, *pl.* —n) grace; favour; pardon, clemency, mercy; kindness; *Euer* —n, Your Grace.

Gnadenakt ['gna:dənakt], *m.* (—s, *pl.* —e) act of grace.

Gnadenbrot ['gna:dənbro:t], *n.* (—s, *no pl.*) *das* — *essen*, live on charity.

Gnadenfrist ['gna:dənfrɪst], *f.* (—, *pl.* —en) respite.

Gnadenort ['gna:dənɔrt], *m.* (—(e)s, *pl.* —e) place of pilgrimage.

Gnadenstoß ['gna:dənʃto:s], *m.* (—es, *pl.* ̈e) finishing stroke, coup de grâce, death-blow.

gnadenvoll ['gna:dənfɔl], *adj.* merciful, gracious.

Gnadenweg ['gna:dənve:k], *m.* (—es, *no pl.*) act of grace; *auf dem* —, by reprieve (as an act of grace).

gnädig ['gnɛ:dɪç], *adj.* gracious, merciful, kind; —*e Frau*, Madam; —*er Herr*, Sir.

Gnostiker ['gnɔstɪkər], *m.* (—s, *pl.* —) gnostic.

Gnu [gnu:], *n.* (—s, *pl.* —s) (*Zool.*) gnu.

Gold [gɔlt], *n.* (—(e)s, *no pl.*) gold.

Goldammer ['gɔltamər], *f.* (—, *pl.* —n) (*Orn.*) yellow-hammer.

Goldamsel ['gɔltamzəl], *f.* (—, *pl.* —n) (*Orn.*) yellow-thrush.

Goldarbeiter ['gɔltarbaɪtər], *m.* (—s, *pl.* —) goldsmith.

Goldbarren ['gɔltbarən], *m.* (—s, *pl.* —) ingot of gold.

Goldbergwerk ['gɔltbɛrkvɛrk], *n.* (—s, *pl.* —e) gold-mine.

Goldfisch ['gɔltfɪʃ], *m.* (—es, *pl.* —e) goldfish.

Goldgewicht ['gɔltgəvɪçt], *n.* (—s, *no pl.*) gold-weight, troy-weight.

Goldgrube ['gɔltgru:bə], *f.* (—, *pl.* —n) gold-mine.

goldig ['gɔldɪç], *adj.* golden; (*fig.*) sweet, cute, charming.

Goldklumpen ['gɔltklumpən], *m.* (—s, *pl.* —) nugget (of gold).

Goldlack ['gɔltlak], *m.* (—s, *no pl.*) gold-coloured varnish; (*Bot.*) wall-flower.

Goldmacher ['gɔltmaxər], *m.* (—s, *pl.* —) alchemist.

Goldregen ['gɔltre:gən], *m.* (—s, *pl.* —) (*Bot.*) laburnum.

Goldscheider ['gɔltʃaɪdər], *m.* (—s, *pl.* —) gold-refiner.

Goldschmied ['gɔltʃmi:t], *m.* (—s, *pl.* —e) goldsmith.

Goldschnitt ['gɔltʃnɪt], *m.* (—s, *no pl.*) gilt edge.

Golf (1) [gɔlf], *m.* (—s, *pl.* —e) gulf.

Golf (2) [gɔlf], *n.* (—s, *no pl.*) golf.

Gondel ['gɔndəl], *f.* (—, *pl.* —n) gondola.

gondeln ['gɔndəln], *v.n.* (*aux.* sein) ride in a gondola; (*coll.*) travel, get about.

gönnen ['gœnən], *v.a. einem etwas* —, not grudge s.o. s.th.; *wir* — *es ihm*, we are happy for him.

Gönner ['gœnər], *m.* (—s, *pl.* —) patron, protector.

gönnerhaft ['gœnərhaft], *adj.* patronising.

Gönnerschaft ['gœnərʃaft], *f.* (—, *no pl.*) patronage.

gordisch ['gɔrdɪʃ], *adj.* Gordian; *der* —*e Knoten*, the Gordian knot.

Göre ['gø:rə], *f.* (—, *pl.* —n) (*coll.*) brat; (*Am.*) kid.

Gosse ['gɔsə], *f.* (—, *pl.* —n) gutter.

Gote ['go:tə], *m.* (—n, *pl.* —n) Goth.

Gotik ['go:tɪk], *f.* (—, *no pl.*) Gothic style (architecture etc.).

gotisch ['go:tɪʃ], *adj.* Gothic.

Gott [gɔ:t], *m.* (—es, *pl.* ̈er) God, god; — *befohlen*, goodbye; *grüß* —*!* (*Austr.*) good day; — *sei Dank*, thank God, thank heaven.

gottbegnadet ['gɔtbəgna:dət], *adj.* favoured by God, inspired.

Götterbild ['gœtərbɪlt], *n.* (—es, *pl.* —er) image of a god.

gottergeben ['gɔtɛrge:bən], *adj.* submissive to God's will, devout.

Götterlehre ['gœtərle:rə], *f.* (—, *pl.* —n) mythology.

Götterspeise ['gœtərʃpaɪzə], *f.* (—, *pl.* —n) ambrosia.

Götterspruch ['gœtərʃprux], *m.* (—s, *no pl.*) oracle.

Göttertrank ['gœtərtraŋk], *m.* (—s, *pl.* ̈e) nectar.

Gottesacker ['gɔtəsakər], *m.* (—s, *pl.* —) God's acre, churchyard.

Gottesdienst ['gɔtəsdi:nst], *m.* (—es, *pl.* —e) divine service, public worship.

gottesfürchtig ['gɔtəsfyrçtɪç], *adj.* God-fearing, pious.

Gottesgelehrsamkeit ['gɔtəsgəle:rza:mkaɪt], *f.* (—, *no pl.*) (*rare*) theology, divinity.

Gottesgericht ['gɔtəsgərɪçt], *n.* (—s, *pl.* —e) ordeal.

Gotteshaus ['gɔtəshaus], *n.* (—es, *pl.* ̈er) house of God; (*rare*) church.

Gotteslästerer ['gɔtəslɛstərər], *m.* (—s, *pl.* —) blasphemer.

Gottesleugner ['gɔtəsləygnər], *m.* (—s, *pl.* —) atheist.

Gottfried ['gɔtfri:t], *m.* Godfrey, Geoffrey.

gottgefällig ['gɔtgəfɛlɪç], *adj.* pleasing to God.

Gottheit ['gɔthaɪt], *f.* (—, *pl.* —en) deity, divinity.

Göttin ['gœtɪn], *f.* (—, *pl.* —nen) goddess.

göttlich ['gœtlɪç], *adj.* divine, godlike; (*fig.*) heavenly.

gottlob! [gɔt'lo:p], *excl.* thank God!

gottlos ['gɔtlo:s], *adj.* godless, ungodly, impious; (*fig.*) wicked.

gottvergessen ['gɔtfergɛsən], *adj.* reprobate, impious.

gottverlassen ['gɔtferlasən], *adj.* God-forsaken.

Götze ['gœtsə], *m.* (—n, *pl.* —n) idol, false deity.

Götzenbild ['gœtsənbɪlt], *n.* (—es, *pl.* —er) idol.

Götzendienst ['gœtsəndi:nst], *m.* (—es, *no pl.*) idolatry.

Gouvernante [guvɛr'nantə], *f.* (—, *pl.* —n) governess.

Gouverneur [guvɛr'nø:r], *m.* (—s, *pl.* —e) governor.

Grab [gra:p], *n.* (—s, *pl.* ⁀er) grave, tomb; sepulchre.

Graben ['gra:bən], *m.* (—s, *pl.* ⁀) ditch, trench.

graben ['gra:bən], *v.a. irr.* dig.

Grabgeläute ['gra:pgəlɔytə], *n.* (—s, *no pl.*) death-knell.

Grabhügel ['gra:phy:gəl], *m.* (—s, *pl.* —) tumulus, mound.

Grablegung ['gra:ple:guŋ], *f.* (—, *no pl.*) (*rare*) burial, interment.

Grabmal ['gra:pma:l], *n.* (—s, *pl.* —e, ⁀er) tomb, sepulchre, monument.

Grabschrift ['gra:pʃrɪft], *f.* (—, *pl.* —n) epitaph.

Grabstichel ['gra:pʃtɪçəl], *m.* (—s, *pl.* —) graving-tool.

Grad [gra:t], *m.* (—s, *pl.* —e) degree; rank; grade; extent; point; *in gewissem* —e, to a certain degree; *im höchsten* —e, in the highest degree, extremely.

Gradeinteilung ['gra:taɪntaɪluŋ], *f.* (—, *pl* —en) gradation, graduation.

Gradmesser ['gra:tmɛsər], *m.* (—s, *pl.* —) graduator; (*fig.*) index.

gradweise ['gra:tvaɪzə], *adv.* gradually, by degrees.

Graf [gra:f], *m.* (—en, *pl.* —en) count, earl.

Gräfin ['grɛfɪn], *f.* (—, *pl.* —en) countess.

gräflich ['grɛflɪç], *adj.* belonging to a count *or* earl.

Grafschaft ['gra:fʃaft], *f.* (—, *pl.* —en) county, shire.

Gral [gra:l], *m.* (—s, *no pl.*) Holy Grail.

Gram [gra:m], *m.* (—s, *no pl.*) grief, sorrow.

grämen ['grɛ:mən], *v.a.* grieve. — *v.r. sich* —, grieve, fret, worry.

gramgebeugt ['gra:mgəbɔykt], *adj.* prostrate with grief.

grämlich ['grɛ:mlɪç], *adj.* sullen, morose, ill-humoured.

Gramm [gram], *n.* (—s, *pl.* —e) gramme (15.438 grains); (*Am.*) gram.

Grammatik [gra'matɪk], *f.* (—, *pl.* —en) grammar.

grammatikalisch, grammatisch [gramatɪ'ka:lɪʃ, gra'matɪʃ], *adj.* grammatical.

Gran [gra:n], *n.* (—s, *pl.* —e) (*weight*) grain.

Granat [gra'na:t], *m.* (—s, *pl.* —e) garnet.

Granatapfel [gra'na:tapfəl], *m.* (—s, *pl.* ⁀e) (*Bot.*) pomegranate.

Granate [gra'na:tə], *f.* (—, *pl.* —n) shell, grenade.

Grande ['grandə], *m.* (—n, *pl.* —n) grandee.

Grandezza [gran'dɛtsa], *f.* (—, *no pl.*) grandeur; sententiousness; pomposity.

grandios [grandɪ'o:s], *adj.* grand.

Granit [gra'ni:t], *m.* (—s, *pl.* —e) granite.

Granne ['granə], *f.* (—, *pl.* —n) (*corn*) awn, beard.

graphisch ['gra:fɪʃ], *adj.* graphic.

Graphit [gra'fi:t], *m.* (—s, *no pl.*) blacklead.

Gras [gra:s], *n.* (—es, *pl.* ⁀er) grass; (*coll.*)*ins — beißen*, bite the dust.

grasartig ['gra:sa:rtɪç], *adj.* gramineous.

grasen ['gra:zən], *v.n.* graze.

Grasfleck ['gra:sflɛk], *m.* (—s, *pl.* —e) grass-stain.

Grashalm ['gra:shalm], *m.* (—s, *pl.* —e) grass-blade.

Grashüpfer ['gra:shypfər], *m.* (—s, *pl.* —) (*Ent.*) grass-hopper.

grasig ['gra:zɪç], *adj.* grassy.

Grasmäher ['gra:smɛ:ər], *m.* (—s, *pl.* —) lawn-mower.

Grasmücke ['gra:smykə], *f.* (—, *pl.* —n) (*Orn.*) hedge-sparrow.

grassieren [gra'si:rən], *v.n.* (*epidemics etc.*) spread, rage.

gräßlich ['grɛslɪç], *adj.* hideous, horrible, ghastly.

Grasweide ['gra:svaɪdə], *f.* (—, *pl.* —n) pasture.

Grat [gra:t], *m.* (—s, *pl.* —e) edge, ridge.

Gräte ['grɛ:tə], *f.* (—, *pl.* —n) fish-bone.

Grätenstich ['grɛ:tənʃtɪç], *m.* (—s, *pl.* —e) (*embroidery*) herring-bone stitch.

grätig ['grɛ:tɪç], *adj.* full of fishbones; (*fig.*) grumpy.

gratis ['gra:tɪs], *adj.* gratis; — *und franko*, for nothing.

Gratulation [gratula'tsjo:n], *f.* (—, *pl.* —en) congratulation.

gratulieren [gratu'li:rən], *v.n. einem zu etwas* —, congratulate s.o. on s.th.

grau [grau], *adj.* grey; (*Am.*) gray; *vor —en Zeiten*, in times of yore.

Grauen ['grauən], *n.* (—s, *no pl.*) horror, aversion.

grauen ['grauən], *v.n.* (*morning*) dawn; *es graut mir vor*, I shudder at.

grauenhaft ['grauənhaft], *adj.* horrible, awful, ghastly.

graulen ['graulən], *v.r. sich* —, shudder, be afraid (of ghosts etc.).

graulich ['graulɪç], *adj. mir ist ganz* —, I shudder.

Graupe ['graupə], *f.* (—, *pl.* —n) groats, peeled barley.

graupeln ['graupəln], *v.n. imp.* (*coll.*) drizzle, sleet.

Graus [graus], *m.* (—es, *no pl.*) horror, dread.

grausam ['grauza:m], *adj.* cruel.

Grauschimmel ['grauʃɪməl], *m.* (—s, *pl.* —) grey (horse).

grausen ['grauzən], *v.n. es graust mir vor*, I shudder at.

grausig ['grauzɪç], *adj.* dreadful, gruesome, horrible.

Graveur

Graveur [gra'vø:r], *m.* (—s, *pl.* —e) engraver.

gravieren [gra'vi:rən], *v.a.* engrave.

Gravität [gravi'tɛ:t], *f.* (—, *no pl.*) gravity.

gravitätisch [gravi'tɛ:tiʃ], *adj.* grave, solemn.

Grazie ['gra:tsjə], *f.* (—, *pl.* —n) grace, charm; (*goddess*) Grace.

graziös [gra'tsjø:s], *adj.* graceful.

Greif [graif], *m.* (—(e)s, *pl.* —e) griffin.

greifbar ['graifba:r], *adj.* to hand; (*fig.*) tangible, palpable.

greifen ['graifən], *v.a. irr.* grasp, seize, touch, handle; *etwas aus der Luft —,* invent s.th.; *um sich —,* gain ground.

greinen ['grainən], *v.n.* (*dial. & coll.*) cry, blubber.

Greis [grais], *m.* (—es, *pl.* —e) old man.

greisenhaft ['graizənhaft], *adj.* senile.

grell [grɛl], *adj.* (*colour*) glaring; (*light*) dazzling; (*tone*) shrill, sharp.

Grenadier [grena'di:r], *m.* (—s, *pl.* —e) grenadier.

Grenadiermütze [grena'di:rmytsə], *f.* (—, *pl.* —n) busby, bearskin.

Grenze ['grɛntsə], *f.* (—, *pl.* —n) boundary; frontier; borders; (*fig.*) limit.

grenzen ['grɛntsən], *v.n.* — *an,* border on; (*fig.*) verge on.

Grenzlinie ['grɛntsli:njə], *f.* (—, *pl.* —n) boundary-line, line of demarcation.

Greuel ['grɔyəl], *m.* (—s, *pl.* —) horror, abomination; *das ist mir ein —,* I abominate it.

Greueltat ['grɔyəlta:t], *f.* (—, *pl.* —en) atrocity.

greulich ['grɔyliç], *adj.* horrible, dreadful, shocking, heinous.

Griebe ['gri:bə], *f.* (—, *pl.* —n) (*mostly pl.*) greaves.

Griebs ['gri:ps], *m.* (—es, *pl.* —e) (*dial.*) (*apple*) core.

Grieche ['gri:çə], *m.* (—n, *pl.* —n) Greek.

Griechenland ['gri:çənlant], *n.* Greece.

Griesgram ['gri:sgra:m], *m.* (—s, *pl.* —e) grumbler.

griesgrämig ['gri:sgrɛ:miç], *adj.* morose, grumbling.

Grieß ['gri:s], *m.* (—es, *no pl.*) groats, semolina.

Grießbrei ['gri:sbrai], *m.* (—s, *pl.* —e) gruel.

Griff [grif], *m.* (—s, *pl.* —e) grip, hold, handle.

griffbereit ['grifbərait], *adj.* handy.

Grille ['grilə], *f.* (—, *pl.* —n) (*Ent.*) cricket; (*fig.*) whim; —*n haben,* be capricious; —*n fangen,* be crotchety, be depressed.

grillenhaft ['grilənhaft], *adj.* whimsical; capricious.

Grimasse [gri'masə], *f.* (—, *pl.* —n) grimace.

Grimm [grim], *m.* (—s, *no pl.*) fury, rage, wrath.

Grimmen ['grimən], *n.* (—s, *no pl.*) gripes; (*Med.*) colic.

grimmig ['grimiç], *adj.* fierce, furious; grim.

Grind [grint], *m.* (—s, *pl.* —e) scab, scurf.

grinsen ['grinzən], *v.n.* grin.

Grippe ['gripə], *f.* (—, *pl.* —n) influenza, grippe.

Grips [grips], *m.* (—es, *no pl.*) (*coll.*) sense, brains; *einen beim — nehmen,* take s.o. by the scruff of his neck.

grob [grɔp], *adj.* coarse; rough; gross; rude, crude, uncouth, impolite; (*jewels*) rough, unpolished.

Grobheit ['grɔphait], *f.* (—, *pl.* —en) rudeness; abusive language.

Grobian ['gro:bja:n], *m.* (—s, *pl.* —e) boor, rude fellow.

Grobschmied ['grɔpʃmi:t], *m.* (—s, *pl.* —e) blacksmith.

Grog [grɔk], *m.* (—s, *pl.* —e) grog, toddy.

grölen ['grø:lən], *v.n.* (*coll.*) scream, squall, bawl.

Groll [grɔl], *m.* (—s, *no pl.*) resentment, anger, rancour; *einen — gegen einen haben,* bear s.o. a grudge.

grollen ['grɔlən], *v.n.* (*thunder*) rumble; *einen —,* bear s.o. ill-will; (*Poet.*) be angry (with).

Grönland ['grø:nlant], *n.* Greenland.

Gros (1) [grɔs], *n.* (—ses, *pl.* —se) gross; twelve dozen.

Gros (2) [gro:], *n.* (—s, *no pl.*) bulk, majority; *en —,* wholesale.

Groschen ['grɔʃən], *m.* (—s, *pl.* —) small coin, penny; one 100th of an Austrian shilling; ten-pfennig piece; *einen schönen — verdienen,* make good money.

groß [gro:s], *adj.* great, big, large; tall; vast; eminent, famous; intense; —*e Augen machen,* stare; *Grosser Ozean,* Pacific (Ocean).

großartig ['gro:sa:rtiç], *adj.* grand, sublime, magnificent, splendid.

Großbetrieb ['gro:sbətri:p], *m.* (—s, *pl.* —e) large business; large (industrial) concern.

Großbritannien [gro:sbri'tanjən], *n.* Great Britain.

Größe ['grø:sə], *f.* (—, *pl.* —n) size, largeness, greatness; height; quantity; power; celebrity, star; importance.

Großeltern ['gro:sɛltərn], *pl.* grandparents.

Großenkel ['gro:sɛŋkəl], *m.* (—s, *pl.* —) great-grandson.

Größenverhältnis ['grø:sənferhɛltnis], *n.* (—ses, *pl.* —se) proportion, ratio.

Größenwahn ['grø:sənva:n], *m.* (—s, *no pl.*) megalomania; delusion of grandeur.

Großfürst ['gro:sfyrst], *m.* (—en, *pl.* —en) grand-duke.

Großfürstin ['gro:sfyrstın], *f.* (—, *pl.* —nen) grand-duchess.

Großgrundbesitz ['gro:sgruntbəzıts], *m.* (—es, *pl.* —e) large landed property, estates.

Großhandel ['gro:shandəl], *m.* (—s, *no pl.*) wholesale business.

großherzig ['gro:shertsıç], *adj.* magnanimous.

Grossist [grɔ'sıst], *m.* (—en, *pl.* —en) wholesale merchant.

großjährig ['gro:sjɛ:rıç], *adj.* of age; — *werden*, come of age.

großmächtig ['gro:smɛçtıç], *adj.* (*fig.*) high and mighty.

großmäulig ['gro:smɔylıç], *adj.* bragging, swaggering.

Großmut ['gro:smu:t], *f.* (—, *no pl.*) magnanimity, generosity.

Großmutter ['gro:smutər], *f.* (—, *pl.* ⁏) grandmother.

Großsiegelbewahrer [gro:s'zi:gəlbəva:rər], *m.* (—s, *pl.* —) Lord Chancellor; Keeper of the Great Seal.

Großstadt ['gro:sʃtat], *f.* (—, *pl.* ⁏e) large town, city, metropolis.

Großtat ['gro:sta:t], *f.* (—, *pl.* —en) achievement, exploit, feat.

Großtuer ['gro:stu:ər], *m.* (—s, *pl.* —) boaster, braggart.

großtun ['gro:stu:n], *v.r. irr. sich — mit*, brag of; show off, parade.

Großvater ['gro:sfa:tər], *m.* (—s, *pl.* ⁏) grandfather.

großziehen ['gro:stsi:ən], *v.a. irr.* bring up, rear.

großzügig ['gro:stsy:gıç], *adj.* boldly conceived; grand, generous.

Grotte ['grɔtə], *f.* (—, *pl.* —n) grotto.

Grübchen ['gry:pçən], *n.* (—s, *pl.* —) dimple.

Grube ['gru:bə], *f.* (—, *pl.* —n) hole, pit; (*Min.*) mine; *in die — fahren*, (*Bibl.*) go down to the grave.

Grübelei ['gry:bəlaı], *f.* (—, *pl.* —en) brooding, musing.

grübeln ['gry:bəln], *v.n.* brood (over s.th.)

Grubenarbeiter ['gru:bənarbaıtər], *m.* (—s, *pl.* —) miner.

Grubengas ['gru:bəŋga:s], *n.* (—es, *pl.* —e) fire-damp.

Grubenlampe ['gru:bənlampə], *f.* (—, *pl.* —n) miner's lamp.

Gruft [gruft], *f.* (—, *pl.* ⁏e) tomb, sepulchre; vault, mausoleum.

grün [gry:n], *adj.* green; *grüne Bohnen*, French beans, runner beans; (*fig.*) unripe, immature, inexperienced; *am — en Tisch*, at the conference table; (*fig.*) in theory; *auf einen —en Zweig kommen*, thrive, get on in the world; *einem nicht — sein*, dislike s.o.

Grund [grunt], *m.* (—s, *pl.* ⁏e) ground, soil; earth; land; bottom; foundation, basis; valley; reason, cause, argument; motive.

Grundbedeutung ['gruntbədɔytuŋ], *f.* (—, *pl.* —en) primary meaning, basic meaning.

Grundbesitz ['gruntbəzıts], *m.* (—es, *no pl.*) landed property.

Grundbuch ['gruntbu:x], *n.* (—s, *pl.* ⁏er) land register.

grundehrlich ['grunte:rlıç], *adj.* thoroughly honest.

Grundeigentum ['gruntaıgəntu:m], *n.* (—s, *pl.* ⁏er) landed property.

Grundeis ['gruntaıs], *n.* (—es, *no pl.*) ground-ice.

gründen ['gryndən], *v.a.* found, establish, float (a company); — *v.r. sich — auf*, be based on.

grundfalsch ['gruntfalʃ], *adj.* radically false.

Grundfarbe ['gruntfarbə], *f.* (—, *pl.* —n) primary colour.

Grundfläche ['gruntflɛçə], *f.* (—, *pl.* —n) basis, base.

Grundherr ['grunther], *m.* (—n, *pl.* —en) lord of the manor, freeholder.

grundieren [grun'di:rən], *v.a.* prime, size, paint the undercoat.

Grundkapital ['gruntkapita:l], *n.* (—s, *no pl.*) original stock.

Grundlage ['gruntla:gə], *f.* (—, *pl.* —n) foundation, basis.

Grundlegung ['gruntle:guŋ], *f.* (— *no pl.*) laying the foundation.

gründlich ['gryntlıç], *adj.* thorough, solid.

grundlos ['gruntlo:s], *adj.* bottomless; groundless, unfounded, without foundation.

Grundmauer ['gruntmauər], *f.* (—, *pl.* —n) foundation wall.

Gründonnerstag [gry:n'dɔnərsta:k], *m.* (—s, *pl.* —e) Maundy Thursday.

Grundpfeiler ['gruntpfaılər], *m.* (—s, *pl.* —) (main) pillar.

Grundriß ['gruntrıs], *m.* (—sses, *pl.* —sse) design, groundplan; compendium, elements; blueprint.

Grundsatz ['gruntzats], *m.* (—es, *pl.* ⁏e) principle, maxim; axiom.

grundschlecht ['gruntʃlɛçt], *adj.* thoroughly bad.

Grundschuld ['gruntʃult], *f.* (—, *pl.* —en) mortgage (on land).

Grundstein ['gruntʃtaın], *m.* (—s, *pl.* —e) foundation-stone.

Grundsteuer ['gruntʃtɔyər], *f.* (—, *pl.* —n) land-tax.

Grundstoff ['gruntʃtɔf], *m.* (—es, *pl.* —e) raw material.

Grundstück ['gruntʃtyk], *n.* (—s, *pl.* —e) real estate; plot of land; lot.

Grundtugend ['grunttu:gənt], *f.* (— *pl.* —en) cardinal virtue.

Gründung ['grynduŋ], *f.* (—, *pl.* —en) foundation, establishment.

grundverschieden ['gruntfɛrʃi:dən], *adj.* radically different.

Grundwasser ['gruntvasər], *n.* (—s, *no pl.*) underground water.

Grundzahl ['grunttsa:l], *f.* (—, *pl.* —en) cardinal number.

Grundzug ['grunttsu:k], *m.* (—s, *pl.* ⁏e) characteristic; distinctive feature.

Grüne ['gry:nə], *n.* (—n, *no pl.*) greenness, verdure; *ins — gehen*, take a walk in the open country.

grünen ['gry:nən], *v.n.* become green; (*fig.*) flourish.

Grünfutter ['gry:nfutər], *n.* (—s, *no pl.*) green food.

Grünkohl ['gry:nko:l], *m.* (—s, *no pl.*) green kale.

Grünkramhändler ['gry:nkra:mhɛndlər], *m.* (—s, *pl.* —) greengrocer.

Grünschnabel ['gry:nʃna:bəl], *m.* (—s, *pl.* ⁝) greenhorn.

Grünspan ['gry:nʃpa:n], *m.* (—s, *no pl.*) verdigris.

Grünspecht ['gry:nʃpɛçt], *m.* (—s, *pl.* —e) (*Orn.*) green woodpecker.

grunzen ['gruntsən], *v.n.* grunt.

Grünzeug ['gry:ntsɔyk], *n.* (—s, *no pl.*) greens, herbs.

Gruppe ['grupə], *f.* (—, *pl.* —n) group.

gruppieren [gru'pi:rən], *v.a.* group.

gruselig ['gru:zəlɪç], *adj.* creepy, uncanny.

gruseln ['gru:zəln], *v.a. es gruselt mir* I shudder, it gives me the creeps.

Gruß [gru:s], *m.* (—es, *pl.* ⁝e) salutation, greeting; (*pl.*) regards; *mit herzlichem —*, with kind regards; *einen — ausrichten*, convey s.o.'s regards.

grüßen ['gry:sən], *v.a.* greet; *einen — lassen*, send o.'s regards to s.o.; — *Sie ihn von mir*, remember me to him.

Grütze ['grytsə], *f.* (—, *pl.* —n) peeled grain, groats; (*fig.*) (*coll.*) gumption, brains.

Guatemala [guatə'ma:la], *n.* Guatemala.

gucken ['gukən], *v.n.* look, peep.

Guinea [gɪ'ne:a], *n.* Guinea.

Gulasch ['gulaʃ], *n.* (—s, *no pl.*) goulash.

Gulden ['guldən], *m.* (—s, *pl.* —) florin, guilder.

gülden ['gyldən], *adj.* (*Poet.*) golden.

gültig ['gyltɪç], *adj.* valid; (*money*) current, legal (tender).

Gummi ['gumi:], *m.* (—s, *no pl.*) gum, rubber.

Gummiarabikum [gumia'ra:bɪkum], *n.* gum arabic.

gummiartig ['gumia:rtɪç], *adj.* gummy; like rubber.

Gummiball ['gumibal], *m.* (—s, *pl.* ⁝e) rubber-ball.

Gummiband ['gumibant], *n.* (—s, *pl.* ⁝er) rubber-band, elastic.

Gummielastikum [gumie'lastikum], *n.* indiarubber.

gummieren [gu'mi:rən], *v.a.* gum.

Gummireifen ['gumiraifən], *m.* (—s, *pl.* —) tyre; (*Am.*) tire.

Gummischuhe ['gumiʃu:ə], *m. pl.* galoshes; (*Am.*) rubbers.

Gunst [gunst], *f.* (—, *no pl.*) favour; *zu seinen —en*, in his favour.

Gunstbezeigung ['gunstbətsaɪguŋ], *f.* (—, *pl.* —en) favour, kindness, goodwill.

günstig ['gynstɪç], *adj.* favourable, propitious.

Günstling ['gynstlɪŋ], *m.* (—s, *pl.* —e) favourite.

Gurgel ['gurgəl], *f.* (—, *pl.* —n) gullet, throat.

gurgeln ['gurgəln], *v.n.* gargle; gurgle.

Gurke ['gurkə], *f.* (—, *pl.* —n) (*Bot.*) cucumber; (*pickled*) gherkin.

Gurt [gurt], *m.* (—es, *pl.* —e) belt; strap; harness.

Gürtel ['gyrtəl], *m.* (—s, *pl.* —) girdle, belt; (*Geog.*) zone.

Guß [gus], *m.* (—sses, *pl.* ⁝sse) gush, downpour; founding, cast; (*Cul.*) icing.

Gut [gu:t], *n.* (—(e)s, *pl.* ⁝er) good thing, blessing; property, possession; country seat; estate; (*pl.*) goods.

gut [gu:t], *adj.* good; beneficial; kind; virtuous. — *adv.* well; *es — haben*, be well off; —*er Dinge sein*, be of good cheer; *kurz und —*, in short.

Gutachten ['gu:taxtən], *n.* (—s, *pl.* —) expert opinion, expert evidence.

gutartig ['gu:ta:rtɪç], *adj.* good-natured; benign.

Güte ['gy:tə], *f.* (—, *no pl.*) goodness, kindness, quality.

Güterabfertigung ['gy:tərapfɛrtɪguŋ], *f.* (—, *pl.* —en) (*Railw.*) goods-depot, goods-office.

Güterabtretung ['gy:təraptre:tuŋ], *f.* (—, *pl.* —en) cession of goods; (*Law*) surrender of an estate.

gutgelaunt ['gu:tgəlaunt], *adj.* in good spirits, good-humoured.

gutgemeint ['gu:tgəmaInt], *adj.* well-meant, well-intentioned.

gutgesinnt ['gu:tgəzInt], *adj.* well-intentioned.

Guthaben ['gu:tha:bən], *n.* (—s, *pl.* —) credit-balance, assets.

gutheißen ['gu:thaIsən], *v.a. irr.* approve.

gütig ['gy:tɪç], *adj.* kind, benevolent.

gütlich ['gy:tlɪç], *adj.* amicable, friendly; —*er Vergleich*, amicable settlement; *sich — tun*, indulge o.s.

gutmachen ['gu:tmaxən], *v.a. etwas wieder —*, make amends for s.th., compensate.

gutmütig ['gu:tmy:tɪç], *adj.* good-natured, good-tempered.

Gutsbesitzer ['gu:tsbəzItsər], *m.* (—s, *pl.* —) landowner; proprietor of an estate.

gutschreiben ['gu:tʃraIbən], *v.a. irr. einem etwas —*, enter a sum to s.o.'s credit.

Gutsverwalter ['gu:tsfɛrvaltər], *m.* (—s, *pl.* —) land-steward, agent, bailiff.

gutwillig ['gu:tvIlɪç], *adj.* willing, of o.'s own free will.

Gymnasialbildung [gymnaz'ja:lbIlduŋ], *f.* (—, *no pl.*) classical *or* grammar school education.

Gymnasiast [gymnaz'jast], *m.* (—en, *pl.* —en) grammar-school pupil.

Gymnasium [gym'na:zjum], *n.* (—s, *pl.* —sien) grammar-school.

Gymnastik [gym'nastɪk], *f.* (—, *no pl.*) gymnastics.

gymnastisch [gym'nastɪʃ], *adj.* gymnastic(al); —e Übungen, physical exercises.

H

H [ha:], *n.* (—s, *pl.* —s) the letter H; (*Mus.*) H Dur, B major; H Moll, B minor.

ha! [ha:], *excl.* ha!

Haag, Den [ha:k, de:n], *m.* The Hague.

Haar [ha:r], *n.* (—s, *pl.* —e) hair; wool; nap; aufs —, exactly, to a hair; um ein —, very nearly, within a hair's breadth.

haaren ['ha:rən], *v.r. sich* —, shed o.'s hair.

haargenau ['ha:rgənau], *adj.* (very) exactly; to a nicety.

haarig ['ha:rɪç], *adj.* hairy.

Haarlocke ['ha:rlɔkə], *f.* (—, *pl.* —n) curl, ringlet.

Haarnadel ['ha:rna:dəl], *f.* (—, *pl.* —n) hairpin.

Haaröl ['ha:rø:l], *n.* (—s, *no pl.*) hair-oil.

Haarpinsel ['ha:rpɪnzəl], *m.* (—s, *pl.* —) camel-hair brush.

Haarröhrchen ['ha:rrø:rçən], *n.* (—s, *pl.* —) capillary tube.

Haarschleife ['ha:rʃlaɪfə], *f.* (—, *pl.* —en) bow in the hair.

Haarschnitt ['ha:rʃnɪt], *m.* (—s, *pl.* —e) hair-cut.

Haarschuppen ['ha:rʃupən], *f. pl.* dandruff.

Haarspalterei ['ha:rʃpaltərai], *f.* (—, *pl.* —en) hair-splitting.

haarsträubend ['ha:rʃtrɔybənt], *adj.* hair-raising, monstrous.

Haarwäsche ['ha:rvɛʃə], *f.* (—, *no pl.*) shampooing.

Haarwickel ['ha:rvɪkəl], *m.* (—s, *pl.* —) curler.

Haarzange ['ha:rtsaŋə], *f.* (—, *pl.* —n) tweezers.

Habe ['ha:bə], *f.* (—, *no pl.*) property, belongings, effects; Hab und Gut, all o.'s belongings, goods and chattels.

Haben ['ha:bən], *n.* (—s, *no pl.*) credit; Soll und —, debit and credit.

haben ['ha:bən], *v.a. irr.* have, possess; da hast du's, there you are; es ist nicht zu —, it is not available.

Habenichts ['ha:bənɪçts], *m.* (—es, *no pl.*) have-not.

Habgier ['ha:pgi:r], *f.* (—, *no pl.*) greediness, avarice, covetousness.

habhaft ['ha:phaft], *adj. einer Sache* — werden, get possession of a thing.

Habicht ['ha:bɪçt], *m.* (—s, *pl.* —e) (Orn.) hawk.

Habichtsinseln ['ha:bɪçtsɪnzəln], *f. pl.* the Azores.

Habichtsnase ['ha:bɪçtsna:zə], *f.* (—, *pl.* —n) hooked nose, aquiline nose.

Habilitation [habilita'tsjo:n], *f.* (—, *pl.* —en) admission or inauguration as a university lecturer.

habilitieren [habili'ti:rən], *v.r. sich* —, qualify as a university lecturer.

Habseligkeiten ['ha:pzelɪçkaɪtən], *f. pl.* property, effects, chattels.

Habsucht ['ha:pzuxt], *f.* (—, *no pl.*) avarice, greediness.

Hackbeil ['hakbaɪl], *n.* (—s, *pl.* —e) cleaver, chopping-knife.

Hackbrett ['hakbrɛt], *n.* (—s, *pl.* —er) chopping-board.

Hacke ['hakə], *f.* (—, *pl.* —n) hoe, mattock; heel.

Hacken ['hakən], *m.* (—s, *pl.* —) heel; sich auf die — machen, be off, take to o.'s heels.

hacken ['hakən], *v.a.* hack, chop, hoe; mince; (birds) peck.

Hacker ['hakər], *m.* (—s, *pl.* —) chopper.

Häckerling ['hɛkərlɪŋ], *m.* (—s, *no pl.*) chopped straw.

Hackfleisch ['hakflaɪʃ], *n.* (—es, *no pl.*) mincemeat.

Häcksel ['hɛksəl], *n.* (—s, *no pl.*) chopped straw.

Hader ['ha:dər], *m.* (—s, *no pl.*) quarrel, dispute.

hadern ['ha:dərn], *v.n.* quarrel, have a dispute.

Hafen ['ha:fən], *m.* (—s, *pl.* ˝) harbour, port; refuge, haven.

Hafendamm ['ha:fəndam], *m.* (—s, *pl.* ˝e) jetty, mole, pier.

Hafensperre ['ha:fɛnlpera], *f.* (—, *pl.* —n) embargo, blockade.

Hafenzoll ['ha:fəntsɔl], *m.* (—s, *no pl.*) anchorage, harbour due.

Hafer ['ha:fər], *m.* (—s, *no pl.*) oats; es sticht ihn der —, he is getting cheeky, insolent.

Haferbrei ['ha:fərbraɪ], *m.* (—s, *no pl.*) porridge.

Hafergrütze ['ha:fərgrytsə], *f.* (—, *no pl.*) ground-oats, oatmeal.

Haferschleim ['ha:fərʃlaɪm], *m.* (—s, *no pl.*) oat-gruel, porridge.

Haff [haf], *n.* (—s, *pl.* —e) bay, lagoon.

Haft [haft], *f.* (—, *no pl.*) custody, imprisonment, arrest.

haftbar ['haftba:r], *adj.* answerable; (Law) liable.

Haftbefehl ['haftbəfe:l], *m.* (—s, *pl.* —e) warrant for arrest.

haften ['haftən], *v.n.* stick, cling, adhere; für einen —, go bail for s.o.; für etwas —, answer for, be liable for s.th.

Häftling ['hɛftlɪŋ], *m.* (—s, *pl.* —e) prisoner.

Haftpflicht ['haftpflɪçt], *f.* (—, *no pl.*) liability.

Haftung ['haftuŋ], *f.* (—, *no pl.*) liability, security; (*Comm.*) *Gesellschaft mit beschränkter —,* limited liability company, (*abbr.*) Ltd.

Hag [haːk], *m.* (—es, *pl.* —e) hedge, enclosure.

Hagebuche ['haːgəbuːxə], *f.* (—, *pl.* —n) hornbeam.

Hagebutte ['haːgəbutə], *f.* (—, *pl.* —n) (*Bot.*) hip, haw.

Hagedorn ['haːgədɔrn], *m.* (—s, *no pl.*) (*Bot.*) hawthorn.

Hagel ['haːgəl], *m.* (—s, *no pl.*) hail.

hageln ['haːgəln], *v.n.* hail.

Hagelschauer ['haːgəlʃauər], *m.* (—s, *pl.* —) hailstorm.

hager ['haːgər], *adj.* thin, lean, lank, gaunt.

Häher ['hɛːər], *m.* (—s, *pl.* —) (*Orn.*) jay.

Hahn [haːn], *m.* (—s, *pl.* ¨e) (*Orn.*) cockerel, cock; (*water, gas*) cock, tap, faucet; — *im Korbe sein,* rule the roost; *da kräht kein — danach,* nobody cares two hoots about it.

Hahnenbalken ['haːnənbalkən], *m.* (—s, *pl.* —) cock-loft; hen-roost.

Hahnenfuß ['haːnənfuːs], *m.* (—es, *no pl.*) (*Bot.*) crow-foot.

Hahnensporn ['haːnɛnʃpɔrn], *m.* (—s, *no pl.*) cockspur.

Hahnentritt ['haːnəntrɪt], *m.* (—s, *no pl.*) cock's tread.

Hahnrei ['haːnraɪ], *m.* (—s, *pl.* —e) cuckold; *einen zum — machen,* cuckold s.o.

Hai [haɪ], *m.* (—s, *pl.* —e) (*Zool.*) shark.

Haifisch ['haɪfɪʃ], *m.* (—es, *pl.* —e) (*Zool.*) shark.

Hain [haɪn], *m.* (—s, *pl.* —e) (*Poet.*) grove, thicket.

Haiti [ha'ɪtɪ], *n.* Haiti.

Häkchen ['hɛːkçən], *n.* (—s, *pl.* —) small hook, crotchet; apostrophe.

häkeln ['hɛːkəln], *v.a. v.n.* crochet; (*fig.*) tease; (*Am.*) needle.

Haken ['haːkən], *m.* (—s, *pl.* —) hook, clasp; (*fig.*) hitch, snag.

Hakenkreuz ['haːkənkrɔyts], *n.* (—es, *pl.* —e) swastika.

halb [halp], *adj.* half; *halb neun,* half past eight.

halbieren [hal'biːrən], *v.a.* halve, divide into halves; (*Maths.*) bisect.

Halbinsel ['halpɪnzəl], *f.* (—, *pl.* —n) peninsula.

Halbmesser ['halpmɛsər], *m.* (—s, *pl.* —) radius.

halbpart ['halppart], *adj.* — *mit einem machen,* go halves with s.o.

halbstündig ['halpʃtyndɪç], *adj.* lasting half an hour.

halbstündlich ['halpʃtyntlɪç], *adj.* half-hourly, every half-hour.

halbwegs ['halpveːks], *adv.* (*coll.*) reasonably, tolerably.

Halbwelt ['halpvɛlt], *f.* (—, *no pl.*) demi-monde.

halbwüchsig ['halpvyːksɪç], *adj.* teenage.

Halde ['haldə], *f.* (—, *pl.* —n) declivity, hill; (*Min.*) waste-heap, slag-heap.

Hälfte ['hɛlftə], *f.* (—, *pl.* —n) half; (*obs.*) moiety.

Halfter ['halftər], *f.* (—, *pl.* —n) halter.

Hall [hal], *m.* (—s, *no pl.*) sound, echo.

Halle ['halə], *f.* (—, *pl.* —n) hall, vestibule; portico; porch.

hallen ['halən], *v.n.* sound, resound; clang.

Halm [halm], *m.* (—es, *pl.* —e) stalk; (*grass*) blade.

Hals [hals], *m.* (—es, *pl.* ¨e) neck, throat; — *über Kopf,* head over heels, hastily, hurriedly.

Halsader ['halsaːdər], *f.* (—, *pl.* —n) jugular vein.

Halsbinde ['halsbɪndə], *f.* (—, *pl.* —n) scarf, tie.

Halsentzündung ['halsɛntsynduŋ], *f.* (—, *pl.* —en) inflammation of the throat.

Halskrause ['halskrauzə], *f.* (—, *pl.* —n) frill, ruff.

halsstarrig ['halsʃtarɪç], *adj.* stubborn, obstinate.

Halsweh ['halsveː], *n.* (—s, *no pl.*) sore throat.

Halt [halt], *m.* (—es, *no pl.*) halt; stop; hold; (*also fig.*) support.

haltbar ['haltbaːr], *adj.* durable, strong; tenable, valid.

halten ['haltən], *v.a. irr.* hold; keep; detain; deliver (speech, lecture); observe, celebrate. — *v.n.* stop; stand firm; insist; *halt!* stop! stop it! — *v.r. sich —,* hold out, keep, behave.

haltlos ['haltloːs], *adj.* unprincipled; floundering, unsteady.

Haltung ['haltuŋ], *f.* (—, *pl.* —en) carriage, posture, attitude; (*fig.*) behaviour, demeanour; attitude.

Halunke [ha'luŋkə], *m.* (—n, *pl.* —n) scoundrel, rascal, scamp.

hämisch ['hɛːmɪʃ], *adj.* malicious, spiteful.

Hammel ['haməl], *m.* (—s, *pl.* —) (*meat*) mutton.

Hammelkeule ['haməlkɔylə], *f.* (—, *pl.* —n) leg of mutton.

Hammer ['hamər], *m.* (—s, *pl.* ¨) hammer; *unter den — kommen,* be sold by auction.

Hämorrhoiden [hɛmo'riːdən], *f. pl.* (*Med.*) piles, haemorrhoids.

Hand [hant], *f.* (—, *pl.* ¨e) hand.

Handarbeit ['hantarbaɪt], *f.* (—, *pl.* —en) manual labour; needlework.

Handel ['handəl], *m.* (—s, *no pl.*) trade, commerce; — *treiben,* carry on trade, do business.

Händel ['hɛndəl], *m. pl.* quarrel, difference, dispute.

handeln ['handəln], *v.n.* act; — *in*, deal in; *es handelt sich um . . .* it is a question of . . . ; *es handelt von . . .*, it deals with . . . .

handelseinig ['handəlsaınıç], *adj.* — *werden*, come to terms.

Handelsgenossenschaft ['handəls-gənosənʃaft], *f.* (—, *pl.* —en) trading company.

Handelsgeschäft ['handəlsgəʃeft], *n.* (—es, *pl.* —e) commercial trans-action.

Handelsgesellschaft ['handəlsgəzel-ʃaft], *f.* (—, *pl.* —en) trading com-pany; joint-stock company.

Handelskammer ['handəlskamər], *f.* (—, *pl.* —n) chamber of commerce.

Handelsmarke ['handəlsmarkə], *f.* (—, *pl.* —n) trade-mark.

Handelsreisende ['handəlsraızəndə], *m.* (—n, *pl.* —n) commercial travel-ler.

händelsüchtig ['hendəlzyçtıç], *adj.* quarrelsome; litigious.

Handelsvertrag ['handəlsfertra:k], *m.* (—es, *pl.* —e) commercial treaty; contract.

Handelszweig ['handəlstsvaık], *m.* (—es, *pl.* —e) branch of trade.

Handfeger ['hantfe:gər], *m.* (—s, *pl.* —) hand-broom, handbrush.

Handfertigkeit ['hantfertıçkaıt], *f.* (—, *no pl.*) dexterity, manual skill; handicrafts.

Handfessel ['hantfesəl], *f.* (—, *pl.* —n) handcuff.

handfest ['hantfest], *adj.* robust, strong.

Handgeld ['hantgelt], *n.* (—es, *no pl.*) earnest; (*money*) advance.

Handgelenk ['hantgəleŋk], *n.* (—s, *pl.* —e) wrist.

handgemein ['hantgəmaın], *adj.* — *werden*, come to blows.

Handgemenge ['hantgəmeŋə], *n.* (—s, *no pl.*) fray, scuffle.

handgreiflich ['hantgraıflıç], *adj.* pal-pable; evident, plain.

Handgriff ['hantgrıf], *m.* (—es, *pl.* —e) handle; (*fig.*) knack.

Handhabe ['hantha:bə], *f.* (—, *pl.* —n) (*fig.*) hold, handle.

handhaben ['hantha:bən], *v.a.* handle, manage; operate.

Handlanger ['hantlaŋər], *m.* (—s, *pl.* —) helper, carrier.

Händler ['hendlər], *m.* (—s, *pl.* —). dealer, merchant.

handlich ['hantlıç], *adj.* handy, man-ageable.

Handlung ['handluŋ], *f.* (—, *pl.* —en) shop; (*Am.*) store; commercial house, mercantile business; action, act, deed; (*Lit.*) plot.

Handrücken ['hantrykən], *m.* (—s, *pl.* —) back of the hand.

Handschelle ['hantʃelə], *f.* (—, *pl.* —n) manacle, handcuff.

Handschlag ['hantʃla:k], *m.* (—s, *pl.* —e) handshake.

Handschuh ['hantʃu:], *m.* (—s, *pl.* —e) glove; (*of iron*) gauntlet.

Handstreich ['hantʃtraıç], *m.* (—es, *pl.* —e) (*Mil.*) surprise attack, coup de main.

Handtuch ['hanttu:x], *n.* (—es, *pl.* ̈er) towel.

Handumdrehen ['hantumdre:ən], *n.* (—s, *no pl.*) *im* —, in no time, in a jiffy.

Handwerk ['hantverk], *n.* (—s, *pl.* —e) handicraft, trade, craft.

Handwörterbuch ['hantvœrtərbu:x], *n.* (—es, *pl.* ̈er) compact dictionary.

Handwurzel ['hantvurtsəl], *f.* (—, *pl.* —n) wrist.

Hanf [hanf], *m.* (—es, *no pl.*) hemp.

Hänfling ['henflıŋ], *m.* (—s, *pl.* —e) (*Orn.*) linnet.

Hang [haŋ], *m.* (—es, *pl.* ̈e) slope, declivity; (*fig.*) (*no pl.*) inclination, propensity.

Hängematte ['heŋəmatə], *f.* (—, *pl.* —n) hammock.

hängen ['heŋən], *v.a. irr.* hang, suspend. — *v.r. sich* —, hang o.s. — *v.n.* hang, be suspended; be hanged (*execution*).

Hannover [ha'no:fər], *n.* Hanover.

Hänselei ['henzəlaı], *f.* (—, *pl.* —en) chaffing, leg-pulling, teasing.

hänseln ['henzəln], *v.a.* tease, chaff.

Hantel ['hantəl], *f.* (—, *pl.* —n) dumb-bell.

hantieren [han'ti:rən], *v.n.* busy o.s., work, occupy o.s. (with).

hapern ['ha:pərn], *v.n.* lack, be deficient; *da hapert es*, that's the snag.

Häppchen ['hepçən], *n.* (—s, *pl.* —) morsel.

Happen ['hapən], *m.* (—s, *pl.* —) mouthful.

happig ['hapıç], *adj.* greedy; excessive.

Härchen ['he:rçən], *n.* (—s, *pl.* —) short hair.

Harfe ['harfə], *f.* (—, *pl.* —n) (*Mus.*) harp.

Harke ['harkə], *f.* (—, *pl.* —n) rake.

Harm [harm], *m.* (—es, *no pl.*) grief, sorrow; injury, wrong.

härmen ['hermən], *v.r. sich* — *um*, grieve over.

harmlos ['harmlo:s], *adj.* harmless, innocuous.

Harmonielehre [harmo'ni:le:rə], *f.* (—, *pl.* —n) (*Mus.*) harmonics; harmony.

harmonieren [harmo'ni:rən], *v.n. mit einem* —, be in concord with s.o., agree with s.o.

Harmonika [har'mo:nıka], *f.* (—, *pl.* —ken) (*Mus.*) accordion, concertina; mouth-organ.

Harn [harn], *m.* (—s, *no pl.*) urine.

Harnisch ['harnıʃ], *m.* (—es, *pl.* —e) harness, armour; *in* — *bringen*, enrage.

Harpune [har'pu:nə], *f.* (—, *pl.* —n) harpoon.

harren ['harən], *v.n.* wait for, hope for.

101

harsch [harʃ], *adj.* harsh; rough; unfriendly.

hart [hart], *adj.* hard, severe, cruel, austere.

Härte ['hɛrtə], *f.* (—, *pl.* —n) hardness, severity.

härten ['hɛrtən], *v.a.* harden.

hartleibig ['hartlaɪbɪç], *adj.* constipated.

hartnäckig ['hartnɛkɪç], *adj.* stubborn, obstinate; undaunted.

Harz (1) [harts], *m.* (*Geog.*) (—es, *no pl.*) the Hartz mountains.

Harz (2) [harts], *n.* (—es, *pl.* —e) resin, rosin.

harzig ['hartsɪç], *adj.* resinous.

Hasardspiel [ha'zartʃpiːl], *n.* (—es, *pl.* —e) game of chance, gamble.

Hasche [ha'ʃɛ], *n.* (—s, *pl.* —s) puree, hash, mash.

haschen ['haʃən], *v.a.* catch, snatch, seize. — *v.n.* — *nach*, strain after, snatch at.

Häschen ['hɛ:sçən], *n.* (—s, *pl.* —) (*Zool.*) small hare, leveret.

Häscher ['hɛʃər], *m.* (—s, *pl.* —) bailiff.

Hase ['ha:zə], *m.* (—n, *pl.* —n) (*Zool.*) hare.

Haselrute ['ha:zəlru:tə], *f.* (—, *pl.* —n) hazel-switch.

Hasenfuß ['ha:zənfu:s], *m.* (—es, *no pl.*) coward.

Hasenklein ['ha:zənklaɪn], *n.* (—s, *no pl.*) jugged hare.

Hasenscharte ['ha:zənʃartə], *f.* (—, *pl.* —n) hare-lip.

Haspe ['haspə], *f.* (—, *pl.* —n) hasp, hinge.

Haspel ['haspəl], *f.* (—, *pl.* —n) reel.

haspeln ['haspəln], *v.a.* wind on a reel; (*fig.*) rattle off.

Haß [has], *m.* (—sses, *no pl.*) hatred, hate, detestation.

hassen ['hasən], *v.a.* hate, detest.

haßerfüllt ['hasərfylt], *adj.* full of spite, full of hatred.

häßlich ['hɛslɪç], *adj.* ugly, repulsive; (*fig.*) unpleasant, unkind; unseemly.

Hast [hast], *f.* (—, *no pl.*) haste, hurry, hastiness, rashness.

hastig ['hastɪç], *adj.* hasty, hurried.

hätscheln ['hɛtʃəln], *v.a.* pamper, caress, fondle.

Hatz [hats], *f.* (—, *pl.* —en) baiting; hunt; revelry.

Haube ['haubə], *f.* (—, *pl.* —n) bonnet, cap; (*Motor.*) bonnet, (*Am.*) hood.

Haubenlerche ['haubənlɛrçə], *f.* (—, *pl.* —n) (*Orn.*) crested lark.

Haubitze [hau'bɪtsə], *f.* (—, *pl.* —n) howitzer.

Hauch [haux], *m.* (—es, *no pl.*) breath, whiff; (*fig.*) touch, tinge.

hauchdünn ['haux'dyn], *adj.* extremely thin.

hauchen ['hauxən], *v.n.* breathe.

Hauchlaut ['hauxlaut], *m.* (—es, *pl.* —e) (*Phonet.*) aspirate.

Haudegen ['haude:gən], *m.* (—s, *pl.* —) broad-sword; *ein alter* —, an old bully.

Haue ['hauə], *f.* (—, *no pl.*) (*coll.*) thrashing.

hauen ['hauən], *v.a.* hew; cut; strike; hit; give a hiding to. — *v.n. über die Schnur* —, kick over the traces.

Hauer ['hauər], *m.* (—s, *pl.* —) hewer, cutter; (*animal*) fang, tusk.

Häuer ['hɔyər], *m.* (—s, *pl.* —) miner.

Haufen ['haufən], *m.* (—s, *pl.* —) heap, pile.

häufen ['hɔyfən], *v.a.* heap, pile. — *v.r. sich* —, accumulate, multiply, increase.

häufig ['hɔyfɪç], *adj.* frequent, abundant. — *adv.* frequently, often.

Häufung ['hɔyfuŋ], *f.* (—, *pl.* —en) accumulation.

Haupt [haupt], *n.* (—es, *pl.* ″er) head; leader; chief, principal; (*compounds*) main—; *aufs* — *schlagen*, inflict a total defeat on; *ein bemooste* —, an old student.

Hauptaltar ['hauptalta:r], *m.* (—s, *pl.* —e) (*Eccl.*) high altar.

Hauptbuch ['hauptbu:x], *n.* (—es, *pl.* ″er) ledger.

Häuptling ['hɔyptlɪŋ], *m.* (—s, *pl.* —e) chieftain.

Hauptmann ['hauptman], *m.* (—s, *pl.* ″er, **Hauptleute**) (*Mil.*) captain.

Hauptnenner ['hauptnɛnər], *m.* (—s, *pl.* —) (*Maths.*) common denominator.

Hauptquartier ['hauptkvarti:r], *n.* (—es, *pl.* —e) headquarters.

Hauptsache ['hauptzaxə], *f.* (—, *pl.* —n) main thing, substance, main point; *in der* —, in the main.

hauptsächlich ['hauptzɛçlɪç], *adj.* chief, main, principal, essential.

Hauptsatz ['hauptzats], *m.* (—es, *pl.* ″e) (*Gram.*) principal sentence.

Hauptschriftleiter ['hauptʃrɪftlaɪtər], *m.* (—s, *pl.* —) editor-in-chief.

Hauptschule ['hauptʃu:lə], *f.* (—, *pl.* —n) intermediate school.

Hauptstadt ['hauptʃtat], *f.* (—, *pl.* ″e) capital, metropolis.

Hauptton ['hauptto:n], *m.* (—s, *pl.* ″e) (*Mus.*) key-note; (*Phonet.*) primary accent.

Haupttreffer ['haupttrefər], *m.* (—s, *pl.* —) first prize; jackpot.

Hauptverkehrsstunden ['hauptfer-ke:rsʃtundən], *f. pl.* (*traffic etc.*) rush-hour.

Hauptwache ['hauptvaxə], *f.* (—, *pl.* —n) central guardroom.

Hauptwort ['hauptvort], *n.* (—es, *pl.* ″er) noun, substantive.

Hauptzahl ['haupttsa:l], *f.* (—, *pl.* —en) cardinal number.

Haus [haus], *n.* (—es, *pl.* ″er) house, home; household; firm; *zu* —*e*, at home; *nach* —*e*, home.

Hausarbeit ['hausarbaɪt], *f.* (—, *pl.* —en) housework, domestic work; homework.

Hausarrest ['hausarɛst], *m.* (**—es, *no pl.***) house arrest.

Hausarzt ['hausartst], *m.* (**—es, *pl.* ˙-e**) family doctor.

hausbacken ['hausbakən], *adj.* home-made; homely; humdrum.

Häuschen ['hoysçən], *n.* (**—s, *pl.* —**) small house, cottage; *ganz aus dem — sein,* be beside o.s.

Hausen ['hauzən], *m.* (**—s, *pl.* —**) sturgeon.

hausen ['hauzən], *v.n.* reside, be domiciled; *übel —,* play havoc among.

Hausflur ['hausflu:r], *m.* (**—s, *pl.* —e**) entrance hall (of a house), vestibule.

Hausfrau ['hausfrau], *f.* (**—, *pl.* —en**) housewife, mistress of the house.

Hausfriedensbruch ['hausfri:dənsbrux], *m.* (**—es, *pl.* ˙-e**) (*Law*) intrusion, trespass.

Hausgenosse ['hausgənɔsə], *m.* (**—n, *pl.* —n**) fellow-lodger.

Haushalt ['haushalt], *m.* (**—es, *no pl.***) household.

Haushaltung ['haushaltuŋ], *f.* (**—, *no pl.***) housekeeping.

Hausherr ['hausher], *m.* (**—n, *pl.* —en**) master of the house, householder.

Haushofmeister ['haushofmaɪstər], *m.* (**—s, *pl.* —**) steward; butler.

hausieren [hau'zi:rən], *v.n.* peddle, hawk.

Hauslehrer ['hauslɛ:rər], *m.* (**—s, *pl.* —**) private tutor.

Häusler ['hoyslər], *m.* (**—s, *pl.* —**) cottager.

häuslich ['hoysliç], *adj.* domestic, domesticated.

Hausmädchen ['hausmɛdçən], *n.* (**—s, *pl.* —**) housemaid.

Hausmannskost ['hausmanskɔst], *f.* (**—, *no pl.***) plain fare.

Hausmeister ['hausmaɪstər], *m.* (**—s, *pl.* —**) house-porter, caretaker.

Hausmittel ['hausmɪtəl], *n.* (**—s, *pl.* —**) household remedy.

Hausrat ['hausra:t], *m.* (**—s, *no pl.***) household furnishings, household effects.

Hausschlüssel ['hausʃlysəl], *m.* (**—s, *pl.* —**) latch-key.

Hausschuh ['hausʃu:], *m.* (**—s, *pl.* —e**) slipper.

Hausstand ['hausʃtant], *m.* (**—es, *pl.* ˙-e**) household.

Haustier ['hausti:r], *n.* (**—es, *pl.* —e**) domestic animal.

Hausvater ['hausfa:tər], *m.* (**—s, *pl.* ˙-）** paterfamilias.

Hausverwalter ['hausfɛrvaltər], *m.* (**—s, *pl.* —**) steward, caretaker; (*Am.*) janitor.

Hauswesen ['hausve:zən], *n.* (**—s, *no pl.***) household management *or* affairs.

Hauswirt ['hausvɪrt], *m.* (**—es, *pl.* —e**) landlord.

Hauswirtin ['hausvɪrtɪn], *f.* (**—, *pl.* —nen**) landlady.

Hauswirtschaft ['hausvɪrtʃaft], *f.* (**—, *no pl.***) housekeeping, domestic economy.

Haut [haut], *f.* (**—, *pl.* ˙-e**) (*human*) skin; (*animal*) hide; (*fruit*) peel; (*on liquid*) skin; membrane; film; *aus der — fahren,* flare up.

Hautausschlag ['hautausʃla:k], *m.* (**—s, *pl.* ˙-e**) rash, eczema.

Häutchen ['hoytçən], *n.* (**—s, *pl.* —**) cuticle, pellicle, membrane.

häuten ['hoytən], *v.a.* skin, flay, strip off the skin. — *v.r. sich —,* cast off (skin) *or* slough.

Hebamme ['he:pamə], *f.* (**—, *pl.* —n**) midwife.

Hebel ['he:bəl], *m.* (**—s, *pl.* —**) lever.

heben ['he:bən], *v.a. irr.* raise, lift, hoist, heave; elevate; improve; *aus der Taufe —,* be godfather (godmother) to (s.o.).

Heber ['he:bər], *m.* (**—s, *pl.* —**) siphon.

Hebräer [he'brɛ:ər], *m.* (**—s, *pl.* —**) Hebrew.

Hechel ['hɛçəl], *f.* (**—, *pl.* —n**) hackle, flax-comb.

hecheln ['hɛçəln], *v.a.* dress flax; hackle; (*fig.*) taunt, heckle.

Hecht [hɛçt], *m.* (**—es, *pl.* —e**) (*Zool.*) pike; (*swimming*) dive.

Hechtsprung ['hɛçtʃpruŋ], *m.* header.

Heck [hɛk], *n.* (**—s, *pl.* —e**) (*Naut.*) stern; (*Motor.*) rear; (*Aviat.*) tail.

Heckbord ['hɛkbɔrt], *m.* (**—s, *pl.* —e**) (*Naut.*) taffrail.

Hecke ['hɛkə], *f.* (**—, *pl.* —n**) hedge.

hecken ['hɛkən], *v.n.* breed, bring forth.

Heckpfennig ['hɛkpfɛnɪç], *m.* (**—s, *pl.* —e**) lucky sixpence.

heda! ['he:da:], *excl.* hey, you!

Heer [he:r], *n.* (**—es, *pl.* —e**) army; multitude; *stehendes —,* regular army.

Heeresmacht ['he:rəsmaxt], *f.* (**—, *pl.* ˙-e**) armed forces, troops.

Heerschar ['he:rʃa:r], *f.* (**—, *pl.* —en**) host; corps, legion; (*Bibl.*) *der Herr der —en,* the Lord of Hosts.

Heerschau ['he:rʃau], *f.* (**—, *pl.* —en**) review, muster, parade.

Heerstraße ['he:rʃtra:sə], *f.* (**—, *pl.* —en**) military road; highway; (*Am.*) highroad.

Heerwesen ['he:rve:zən], *n.* (**—s, *no pl.***) military affairs.

Hefe ['he:fə], *f.* (**—, *no pl.***) yeast; dregs, sediment.

Hefeteig ['he:fətaɪk], *m.* (**—s, *pl.* —e**) leavened dough.

Heft [hɛft], *n.* (**—es, *pl.* —e**) exercise-book, copy-book; haft, handle, hilt.

heften ['hɛftən], *v.a.* fasten; baste, stitch, fix, pin.

heftig ['hɛftɪç], *adj.* vehement, violent.

Heftnadel ['hɛftna:dəl], *f.* (**—, *pl.* —n**) stitching-needle.

hegen ['he:gən], *v.a.* enclose, protect, preserve; (*fig.*) cherish; entertain; hold; *— und pflegen,* nurse carefully.

Hehl

Hehl [he:l], *n.* (—es, *no pl.*) concealment, secret.

hehlen ['he:lən], *v.n.* receive stolen goods.

Hehler ['he:lər], *m.* (—s, *pl.* —) receiver of stolen goods, (*sl.*) fence.

hehr [he:r], *adj.* (*Lit.*) exalted, august, sublime.

Heide (1) ['haɪdə], *m.* (—n, *pl.* —n) heathen, pagan.

Heide (2) ['haɪdə], *f.* (—, *pl.* —n) heath.

Heidekraut ['haɪdəkraut], *n.* (—es, *no pl.*) heath, heather.

Heidelbeere ['haɪdəlbe:rə], *f.* (—, *pl.* —n) (*Bot.*) bilberry; (*Am.*) blueberry.

Heidenangst ['haɪdənaŋst], *f.* (—, *no pl.*) (*coll.*) mortal fear.

Heidenlärm ['haɪdənlerm], *m.* (—es, *no pl.*) hullaballoo.

Heidenröschen ['haɪdənrø:sçən], *n.* (—s, *pl.* —) (*Bot.*) sweet-briar.

Heidentum ['haɪdəntu:m], *n.* (—s, *no pl.*) paganism.

heidnisch ['haɪdnɪʃ], *adj.* pagan, heathen.

Heidschnuke ['haɪtʃnu:kə], *f.* (—, *pl.* —n) moorland sheep.

heikel ['haɪkəl], *adj.* delicate, sensitive, critical.

Heil [haɪl], *n.* (—(e)s, *no pl.*) safety, welfare; (*Theol.*) salvation; *sein — versuchen,* have a try, try o.'s luck. *— int.* hail! — *der Königin,* God save the Queen.

heil [haɪl], *adj.* unhurt, intact.

Heiland ['haɪlant], *m.* (—s, *no pl.*) Saviour, Redeemer.

Heilanstalt ['haɪlanʃtalt], *f.* (—, *pl.* —en) sanatorium, convalescent home; (*Am.*) sanitarium.

heilbar ['haɪlba:r], *adj.* curable.

heilbringend ['haɪlbrɪŋənt],*adj.*salutary.

heilen ['haɪlən], *v.a.* cure, heal. — *v.n.* (*aux.* sein) heal.

heilig ['haɪlɪç], *adj.* holy, sacred; *der Heilige Abend,* Christmas Eve; — *sprechen,* canonise; (*before name*) *der, die* —*e,* Saint.

Heiligenschein ['haɪlɪɡənʃaɪn], *m.* (—s, *pl.* —e) halo; (*clouds*) nimbus.

Heiligkeit ['haɪlɪçkaɪt], *f.* (—, *no pl.*) holiness, sanctity, sacredness.

Heiligtum ['haɪlɪçtu:m], *n.* (—s, *pl.* ˮer) sanctuary, shrine; holy relic.

Heiligung ['haɪlɪɡuŋ], *f.* (—, *pl.* —en) sanctification, consecration.

heilkräftig ['haɪlkreftɪç], *adj.* curative, salubrious.

Heilkunde ['haɪlkundə], *f.* (—, *no pl.*) therapeutics.

heillos ['haɪllo:s], *adj.* wicked, mischievous; (*fig.*) awful.

Heilmittel ['haɪlmɪtəl], *n.* (—s, *pl.* —) remedy.

heilsam ['haɪlza:m], *adj.* salubrious, salutary.

Heilsamkeit ['haɪlza:mkaɪt], *f.* (—, *no pl.*) salubrity, salubriousness.

Heilsarmee ['haɪlsarme:], *f.* (—, *no pl.*) Salvation Army.

Heilslehre ['haɪlsle:rə], *f.* (—, *pl.* —n) doctrine of salvation.

Heiltrank ['haɪltraŋk], *m.* (—es, *no pl.*) (medicinal) potion.

Heim [haɪm], *n.* (—es, *pl.* —e) home.

heim [haɪm], *adv. prefix* (*to verbs*) home.

Heimat ['haɪmat], *f.* (—, *no pl.*) native place, home, homeland.

Heimatschein ['haɪmatʃaɪn], *m.* (—es, *pl.* —e) certificate of origin *or* domicile.

Heimchen ['haɪmçən], *n.* (—s, *pl.* —) (*Ent.*) cricket.

heimführen ['haɪmfy:rən], *v.a.* bring home (a bride); (*fig.*) marry.

Heimgang ['haɪmɡaŋ], *m.* (—es, *no pl.*) going home; (*fig.*) decease, death.

heimisch ['haɪmɪʃ], *adj.* native, indigenous; *sich — fühlen,* feel at home.

heimkehren ['haɪmke:rən], *v.n.* return (home).

heimleuchten ['haɪmlɔyçtən], *v.n. einem —,* tell s.o. the plain truth, give s.o. a piece of o.'s mind.

heimlich ['haɪmlɪç], *adj.* secret, clandestine, furtive.

heimsuchen ['haɪmzu:xən], *v.a.* visit; afflict, punish.

Heimtücke ['haɪmtykə], *f.* (—, *no pl.*) malice.

heimwärts ['haɪmverts], *adv.* homeward.

Heimweh ['haɪmve:], *n.* (—s, *no pl.*) homesickness; nostalgia.

heimzahlen ['haɪmtsa:lən], *v.a.* pay back, retaliate.

Hein [haɪn], *m.* (*coll.*) *Freund —,* Death.

Heinzelmännchen ['haɪntsəlmençən], *n.* (—s, *pl.* —) goblin, brownie, imp.

Heirat ['haɪra:t], *f.* (—, *pl.* —en) marriage, wedding.

heiraten ['haɪra:tən], *v.a.* marry, wed.

Heiratsgut ['haɪra:tsɡu:t], *n.* (—es, *pl.* ˮer) dowry.

heischen ['haɪʃən], *v.a.* (*Poet.*) ask, demand.

heiser ['haɪzər], *adj.* hoarse.

heiß [haɪs], *adj.* hot; (*fig.*) ardent; (*climate*) torrid.

heißen ['haɪsən], *v.a. irr.* bid, command. — *v.n.* be called; be said; signify, mean; *es heißt,* it is said; *das heißt (d.h.),* that is to say; *wie — Sie?* what is your name?

heißgeliebt ['haɪsɡəli:pt], *adj.* dearly beloved.

heiter ['haɪtər], *adj.* clear; serene; cheerful.

Heiterkeit ['haɪtərkaɪt], *f.* (—, *no pl.*) serenity; cheerfulness.

heizen ['haɪtsən], *v.a., v.n.* heat.

Heizkissen ['haɪtskɪsən], *n.* (—s, *pl.* —) electric pad *or* blanket.

Heizkörper ['haɪtskœrpər], *m.* (—s, *pl.* —) radiator; heater.

Heizung ['haɪtsuŋ], *f.* (—, *pl.* —en) heating.

hektisch ['hɛktɪʃ], *adj.* hectic.

hektographieren [hɛktogra'fiːrən], *v.a.*
stencil, duplicate.
Hektoliter ['hɛktoliːtər], *m.* (—s, *pl.* —)
hectolitre (22 gallons).
Held [hɛlt], *m.* (—en, *pl.* —en) hero.
Heldengedicht ['hɛldəngədɪçt], *n.*
(—es, *pl.* —e) heroic poem, epic.
heldenhaft ['hɛldənhaft], *adj.* heroic.
— *adv.* heroically.
Heldenmut ['hɛldənmuːt], *m.* (—es,
no pl.) heroism.
helfen ['hɛlfən], *v.n. irr.* (*Dat.*) help,
aid, assist.
Helfershelfer ['hɛlfərshɛlfər], *m.* (—s,
pl. —) accomplice, accessory.
Helgoland ['hɛlgolant], *n.* Heligo-
land.
hell [hɛl], *adj.* clear, bright, light;
(*coll.*) clever, wide awake.
Helldunkel ['hɛlduŋkəl], *n.* (—s, *no pl.*)
twilight; (*Art*) chiaroscuro.
Helle ['hɛlə], *f.* (—, *no pl.*) clearness;
brightness; daylight.
Heller ['hɛlər], *m.* (—s, *pl.* —) small
coin, farthing.
hellhörig ['hɛlhøːrɪç], *adj.* keen of
hearing.
Helligkeit ['hɛlɪçkaɪt], *f.* (—, *no pl.*)
clearness; daylight.
Hellseher ['hɛlzeːər], *m.* (—s, *pl.* —)
clairvoyant.
hellsichtig ['hɛlzɪçtɪç], *adj.* clairvoyant;
clear-sighted.
Helm [hɛlm], *m.* (—es, *pl.* —e)
helmet.
Helmbusch ['hɛlmbuʃ], *m.* (—es, *pl.*
ˁe) crest (of helmet).
Helmgitter ['hɛlmgɪtər], *n.* (—s, *pl.*
—) eye-slit (in helmet).
Helsingfors ['hɛlzɪŋfɔrs], *n.* Helsinki.
Helsingör [hɛlzɪŋ'øːr], *n.* Elsinore.
Hemd [hɛmt], *n.* (—es, *pl.* —en) shirt;
vest.
Hemdenstoff ['hɛmdənʃtɔf], *m.* (—es,
pl. —e) shirting.
hemmen ['hɛmən], *v.a.* stop, hamper,
hinder, restrain; (*fig.*) inhibit.
Hemmschuh ['hɛmʃuː], *m.* (—s, *pl.*
—e) brake; (*fig.*) drag, obstruction.
Hemmung ['hɛmuŋ], *f.* (—, *pl.* —en)
stoppage, hindrance, restraint; (*watch*)
escapement; (*fig.*) inhibition, reluctance.
Hengst [hɛŋkst], *m.* (—es, *pl.* —e)
stallion.
Henkel ['hɛŋkəl], *m.* (—s, *pl.* —)
handle.
henken ['hɛŋkən], *v.a* hang (s.o.).
Henker ['hɛŋkər], *m.* (—s, *pl.* —)
hangman, executioner.
Henne ['hɛnə], *f.* (—, *pl.* —n) (*Zool.*)
hen; *junge* —, pullet.
her [heːr], *adv.* hither, here, to me;
(*temp.*) since, ago; *von alters* —, from
olden times; *von je* —, from time
immemorial; *wo kommst du* —?
where do you come from? *wie lange
ist es* —? how long ago was it?
herab [hɛ'rap], *adv.* downwards, **down**
to; *die Treppe* —, downstairs.

herablassen [hɛ'raplasən], *v.r. irr.
sich — etwas zu tun*, condescend to
do s.th.
herabsehen [hɛ'rapzeːən], *v.n. irr.*
look down; (*fig.*) look down upon s.o.
herabsetzen [hɛ'rapzɛtsən], *v.a.* put
down; degrade; (*value*) depreciate;
(*price*) reduce, lower; (*fig.*) disparage.
herabwürdigen [hɛ'rapvyrdɪgən], *v.a.*
degrade, abase.
herabziehen [hɛ'raptsiːən], *v.a. irr.*
pull down.
Heraldik [hɛ'raldɪk], *f.* (—, *no pl.*)
heraldry.
heran [hɛ'ran], *adv.* up to, on, near.
heranbilden [hɛ'ranbɪldən], *v.a.* train.
— *v.r. sich* —, train, qualify.
herangehen [hɛ'rangeːən], *v.n. irr.*
(*aux.* sein) approach, sidle up (to); *an
etwas* —, set to work on s.th.
heranmachen [hɛ'ranmaxən], *v.r. sich
an etwas* —, set to work on s.th., set
about s.th.
herannahen [hɛ'rannaːən], *v.n.* (*aux.*
sein) approach, draw near.
heranrücken [hɛ'ranrykən], *v.a.* move
near. — *v.n.* (*aux.* sein) advance,
draw near.
heranschleichen [hɛ'ranʃlaɪçən], *v.r.
irr. sich* — *an*, sneak up to.
heranwachsen [hɛ'ranvaksən], *v.n.
irr.* (*aux.* sein) grow up.
heranwagen [hɛ'ranvaːgən], *v.r. sich*
—, venture near.
heranziehen [hɛ'rantsiːən], *v.a. irr.*
draw near; *als Beispiel* —, cite as an
example; (*fig.*) enlist (s.o.'s aid). —
v.n. (*aux.* sein) draw near, approach.
herauf [hɛ'rauf], *adv.* up, upwards.
heraufbeschwören [hɛ'raufbəʃvøːrən],
v.a. conjure up.
heraus [hɛ'raus], *adv.* out, out of.
herausfordern [hɛ'rausfɔrdərn], *v.a.*
challenge.
Herausgabe [hɛ'rausgaːbə], *f.* (—, *pl.*
—n) delivery; (*book*) publication;
editing.
herausgeben [hɛ'rausgeːbən], *v.a. irr.*
give out, deliver; (*money*) give
change; (*book*) publish, edit.
Herausgeber [hɛ'rausgeːbər], *m.* (—s,
pl. —) publisher; editor.
heraushaben [hɛ'raushaːbən], *v.a. irr.
etwas* —, have the knack of s.th.
herausputzen [hɛ'rausputsən], *v.r.
sich* —, dress up.
herausrücken [hɛ'rausrykən], *v.n. mit
Geld* —, fork out money; *mit der
Sprache* —, speak out, come out with.
herausschlagen [hɛ'rausʃlaːgən], *v.a.
irr. die Kosten* —, recover expenses;
viel —, make the most of; profit by.
herausstellen [hɛ'rausʃtɛlən], *v.a.* put
out, expose. — *v.r. sich* — *als*, turn
out to be.
herausstreichen [hɛ'rausʃtraɪçən], *v.a.
irr.* extol, praise.
heraussuchen [hɛ'rausuːxən], *v.a.*
pick out.

herauswollen [hɛ'rausvɔlən], *v.n. nicht mit der Sprache —*, hesitate to speak out.

herb [hɛrp], *adj.* sour, sharp, tart, acrid; (*fig.*) austere, harsh, bitter; (*wine*) dry.

herbei [hɛr'baɪ], *adv.* hither, near.

herbeischaffen [hɛr'baɪʃafən], *v.a.* procure.

herbeiströmen [hɛr'baɪʃtrøːmən], *v.n.* (*aux.* sein) crowd, flock.

Herberge ['hɛrbɛrgə], *f.* (—, *pl.* —n) shelter, lodging, inn.

Herbst [hɛrpst], *m.* (—es, *pl.* —e) autumn; (*Am.*) fall.

Herbstrose ['hɛrpstroːzə], *f.* (—, *pl.* —n) (*Bot.*) hollyhock.

Herbstzeitlose ['hɛrpstsaɪtloːzə], *f.* (—, *pl.* —n) (*Bot.*) meadow-saffron.

Herd [heːrt], *m.* (—es, *pl.* —e) hearth, fireplace; cooking-stove; (*fig.*) focus.

Herde ['heːrdə], *f.* (—, *pl.* —n) flock, herd; (*fig.*) troop.

herein [he'raɪn], *adv.* in, inside. — *int.* —! come in!

hereinbrechen [he'raɪnbrɛçən], *v.n. irr.* (*aux.* sein) *über einen —*, befall s.o., overtake s.o.; (*night*) close in.

hereinfallen [he'raɪnfalən], *v.n. irr.* (*aux.* sein) (*fig.*) be taken in, fall for s.th.

herfallen ['heːrfalən], *v.n. irr.* (*aux.* sein) *über einen —*, go for s.o., set upon s.o.

Hergang ['heːrgaŋ], *m.* (—es, *no pl.*) proceedings, course of events; circumstances; story, plot.

hergeben ['heːrgeːbən], *v.a. irr.* give up, surrender.

hergebracht ['heːrgəbraxt], *adj.* traditional, time-honoured.

hergehen ['heːrgeːən], *v.n. irr.* (*aux.* sein) proceed; *es geht lustig her*, they are having a gay time.

hergelaufen ['heːrgəlaufən], *adj. ein —er Kerl*, an adventurer, an upstart.

herhalten ['heːrhaltən], *v.n. irr.* suffer, serve (as a butt).

Hering ['heːrɪŋ], *m.* (—s, *pl.* —e) (*Zool.*) herring; *geräucherter —*, smoked herring, bloater; *gesalzener —*, pickled herring.

herkommen ['heːrkɔmən], *v.n. irr.* (*aux.* sein) come here; be derived from, descend from.

herkömmlich ['heːrkœmlɪç], *adj.* traditional, customary, usual.

Herkunft ['heːrkunft], *f.* (—, *no pl.*) descent, extraction; origin.

herleiern ['heːrlaɪərn], *v.a.* recite monotonously; reel off.

herleiten ['heːrlaɪtən], *v.a.* derive from.

Hermelin [hɛrmə'liːn], *m.* (—s, *no pl.*) ermine (*fur*).

hermetisch [hɛr'meːtɪʃ], *adj.* hermetical.

hernach [hɛr'naːx], *adv.* after, afterwards; hereafter.

hernehmen ['heːrneːmən], *v.a. irr.* take, get (from); take (s.o.) to task.

hernieder [hɛr'niːdər], *adv.* down.

Herr [hɛr], *m.* (—n, *pl.* —en) master; lord; nobleman; gentleman; (*Theol.*) Lord; principal, governor; *mein —*, Sir; *meine Herren*, gentlemen; *Schmidt*, Mr. Smith; *einer Sache — werden*, master s.th.

Herrenhaus ['hɛrənhaus], *n.* (—es, *pl.* ⸚er) mansion, manor house; (*Parl.*) House of Lords.

Herrenhof ['hɛrənhoːf], *m.* (—es, *pl.* ⸚e) manor, country-seat.

Herrenstand ['hɛrənʃtant], *m.* (—es, *no pl.*) nobility, gentry.

Herrenzimmer ['hɛrəntsɪmər], *n.* (—s, *pl.* —) study.

Herrgott ['hɛrgɔt], the Lord God.

herrichten ['heːrrɪçtən], *v.a.* prepare, fix up.

Herrin ['hɛrɪn], *f.* (—, *pl.* —innen) mistress, lady.

herrisch ['hɛrɪʃ], *adj.* imperious, lordly.

herrlich ['hɛrlɪç], *adj.* magnificent, splendid, glorious, excellent.

Herrnhuter ['hɛrnhuːtər], *m.* (—s, *pl.* —) Moravian; (*pl.*) Moravian brethren.

Herrschaft ['hɛrʃaft], *f.* (—, *pl.* —en) mastery, rule, dominion; master, mistress; *meine —en!* ladies and gentlemen!

herrschaftlich ['hɛrʃaftlɪç], *adj.* belonging to a lord; (*fig.*) elegant, fashionable, distinguished.

herrschen ['hɛrʃən], *v.n.* rule, govern, reign.

Herrscher ['hɛrʃər], *m.* (—s, *pl.* —) ruler.

herrühren ['heːrryːrən], *v.n.* come from, originate in.

hersagen ['heːrzaːgən], *v.a.* recite, reel off.

herschaffen ['heːrʃafən], *v.a.* procure.

herstammen ['heːrʃtamən], *v.n.* come from, stem from, originate from; be derived from.

herstellen ['heːrʃtɛlən], *v.a.* place here; manufacture; *wieder —*, restore; (*sick person*) restore to health.

Herstellung ['heːrʃtɛluŋ], *f.* (—, *no pl.*) manufacture, production.

herstürzen ['heːrʃtyrtsən], *v.n.* (*aux.* sein) *über einen —*, rush at s.o.

herüber [hɛ'ryːbər], *adv.* over, across; *— und hinüber*, there and back.

herum [hɛ'rum], *adv.* round, about; around.

herumbalgen [hɛ'rumbalgən], *v.r. sich —*, scrap; scuffle.

herumbekommen [hɛ'rumbəkɔmən], *v.a. irr.* (*coll.*) talk s.o. over, win s.o. over.

herumbummeln [hɛ'rumbuməln], *v.n.* loaf about.

herumstreichen [hɛ'rumʃtraɪçən], *v.n. irr.* (*aux.* sein) gad about.

herumtreiben [hɛ'rumtraɪbən], *v.r. irr. sich —*, loaf about, gad about.

herumzanken [hɛ'rumtsaŋkən], *v.r. sich —*, squabble, quarrel; live like cat and dog.

Hexenschuß

herumziehen [hɛ'rumtsi:ən], *v.a. irr.* drag about. — *v.n.* (*aux.* sein) wander about, move from place to place.

herunter [hɛ'runtər], *adj.* down, downward; *ich bin ganz* —, I feel poorly.

heruntergekommen [hɛ'runtərgəkɔmən], *adj.* decayed, broken down; in straitened circumstances; depraved.

herunterhandeln [hɛ'runtərhandəln], *v.a. einem etwas* —, beat s.o. down (in price).

herunterwürgen [hɛ'runtərvyrgən], *v.a.* swallow s.th. with dislike.

hervor [hɛr'fo:r], *adv.* forth, forward, out.

hervorheben [hɛr'fo:rhe:bən], *v.a. irr.* emphasize, stress.

hervorragen [hɛr'fo:rra:gən], *v.n.* stand out, project; (*fig.*) be distinguished, excel.

hervorragend [hɛr'fo:rra:gənt], *adj.* prominent; (*fig.*) outstanding, excellent.

hervorrufen [hɛr'fo:rru:fən], *v.a. irr.* call forth; (*fig.*) evoke, bring about, create, cause.

hervorstechen [hɛr'fo:rʃtɛçən], *v.n. irr.* be predominant, stand out.

hervortun [hɛr'fo:rtu:n], *v.r. irr. sich* —, distinguish o.s.

Herz [hɛrts], *n.* (—ens, *pl.* —en) heart; courage; mind; spirit; feeling; core; (*Cards*) hearts; (*coll.*) darling; *einem etwas ans* — *legen*, impress s.th. upon s.o.; *von* —en *gern*, with all my heart; *sich etwas zu* —en *nehmen*, take s.th. to heart.

herzählen [hɛ'rtse:lən], *v.a.* enumerate.

Herzanfall ['hɛrtsanfal], *m.* (—s, *pl.* ⁓e) (*Med.*) heart attack.

Herzbube ['hɛrtsbu:bə], *m.* (—n, *pl.* —n) (*Cards*) knave *or* jack of hearts.

Herzdame ['hɛrtsda:mə], *f.* (—, *pl.* —n) (*Cards*) queen of hearts.

Herzeleid ['hɛrtsəlaɪt], *n.* (—es, *no pl.*) heartbreak, sorrow, anguish, grief.

herzen ['hɛrtsən], *v.a.* hug.

Herzenseinfalt ['hɛrtsənsaɪnfalt], *f.* (—, *no pl.*) simple-mindedness.

Herzensgrund ['hɛrtsənsgrunt], *m.* (—es, *no pl.*) *aus* —, with all my heart.

Herzenslust ['hɛrtsənslust], *f.* (—, *no pl.*) heart's delight; *nach* —, to o.'s heart's content.

Herzfehler ['hɛrtsfe:lər], *m.* (—s, *pl.* —) (*Med.*) cardiac defect; organic heart disease.

Herzfell ['hɛrtsfɛl], *n.* (—s, *pl.* —e) pericardium.

herzförmig ['hɛrtsfœrmɪç], *adj.* heart-shaped.

herzhaft ['hɛrtshaft], *adj.* stout-hearted; courageous, bold; resolute; hearty.

herzig ['hɛrtsɪç], *adj.* lovely, charming, sweet; (*Am.*) cute.

Herzkammer ['hɛrtskamər], *f.* (—, *pl.* —n) ventricle (of the heart).

Herzklappe ['hɛrtsklapə], *f.* (—, *pl.* —n) valve of the heart.

Herzklopfen ['hɛrtsklɔpfən], *n.* (—s, *no pl.*) palpitations.

herzlich ['hɛrtslɪç], *adj.* hearty, cordial, affectionate; —e Grüße, kind regards.

Herzog ['hɛrtso:k], *m.* (—s, *pl.* ⁓e) duke.

Herzogtum ['hɛrtso:ktu:m], *n.* (—s, *pl.* ⁓er) duchy, dukedom.

Herzschlag ['hɛrtsʃla:k], *m.* (—es, *pl.* ⁓e) heartbeat; (*Med.*) heart attack, cardiac failure.

Hetäre [he'tɛ:rə], *f.* (—, *pl.* —n) courtesan.

Hetzblatt ['hɛtsblat], *n.* (—s, *pl.* ⁓er) gutter press.

Hetze ['hɛtsə], *f.* (—, *pl.* —n) chase, hunt, hurry, rush; agitation.

hetzen ['hɛtsən], *v.a.* bait, fluster, chase, hunt, incite. — *v.n. herum* —, rush around.

Hetzer ['hɛtsər], *m.* (—s, *pl.* —) instigator, rabble-rouser.

Heu [hɔy], *n.* (—s, *no pl.*) hay.

Heuboden ['hɔybo:dən], *m.* (—s, *pl.* ⁓) hayloft.

Heuchelei [hɔyçə'laɪ], *f.* (—, *pl.* —en) hypocrisy.

heucheln ['hɔyçəln], *v.n.* play the hypocrite, dissemble. — *v.a.* simulate, affect, feign.

Heuchler ['hɔyçlər], *m.* (—s, *pl.* —) hypocrite.

Heuer ['hɔyər], *f.* (—, *pl.* —n) (*Naut.*) engagement; hire, wages.

heuer ['hɔyər], *adv.* (*dial.*) this year, this season.

heuern ['hɔyərn], *v.a.* (*Naut.*) engage, hire.

Heugabel ['hɔyga:bəl], *f.* (—, *pl.* —n) pitchfork.

heulen ['hɔylən], *v.n.* howl; roar; cry, yell, scream.

Heupferd ['hɔypfɛrt], *n.* (—es, *pl.* —e) (*Ent.*) grasshopper.

heurig ['hɔyrɪç], *adj.* of this year, this year's (*wine etc.*).

Heuschnupfen ['hɔyʃnupfən], *m.* (—s, *no pl.*) hay-fever.

Heuschober ['hɔyʃo:bər], *m.* (—s, *pl.* —) hayrick.

Heuschrecke ['hɔyʃrɛkə], *f.* (—, *pl.* —n) (*Ent.*) locust.

heute ['hɔytə], *adv.* today, this day; — *in acht Tagen*, today week, a week today; — *abend*, tonight.

heutig ['hɔytɪç], *adj.* today's, this day's; modern.

heutzutage ['hɔytsuta:gə], *adv.* nowadays.

Hexe ['hɛksə], *f.* (—, *pl.* —n) witch, sorceress, hag.

hexen ['hɛksən], *v.n.* use witchcraft; practise sorcery.

Hexenschuß ['hɛksənʃus], *m.* (—sses, *no pl.*) (*Med.*) lumbago.

Hexerei

Hexerei ['hɛksə'raɪ], *f.* (—, *pl.* —en) witchcraft, sorcery, juggling.

hie [hi:], *adv.* (*dial.*) here.

Hieb [hi:p], *m.* (—es, *pl.* —e) cut, stroke; hit, blow; (*pl.*) a thrashing.

hienieden [hi:'ni:dən], *adv.* here below, down here.

hier [hi:r], *adv.* here, in this place.

Hiersein ['hi:rzaɪn], *n.* (—s, *no pl.*) presence, attendance.

hiesig ['hi:zɪç], *adj.* of this place, of this country, local.

Hifthorn ['hɪfthɔrn], *n.* (—s, *pl.* ⸚er) hunting-horn.

Hilfe ['hɪlfə], *f.* (—, *pl.* —n) help, aid, assistance, succour, relief.

hilflos ['hɪlflo:s], *adj.* helpless.

hilfreich ['hɪlfraɪç], *adj.* helpful.

Hilfsmittel ['hɪlfsmɪtəl], *n.* (—s, *pl.* —) expedient, remedy.

Hilfsschule ['hɪlfsʃu:lə], *f.* (—, *pl.* —n) school for backward children.

Hilfszeitwort ['hɪlfstsaɪtvɔrt], *n.* (—s, *pl.* ⸚er) (*Gram.*) auxiliary verb.

Himbeere ['hɪmbe:rə], *f.* (—, *pl.* —n) raspberry.

Himmel ['hɪməl], *m.* (—s, *pl.* —) heaven, heavens; sky; firmament.

himmelan [hɪməl'an], *adv.* heavenward.

himmelangst ['hɪmələŋkst], *adv. ihm war* —, he was panic-stricken.

Himmelbett ['hɪməlbɛt], *n.* (—s, *pl.* —en) fourposter.

himmelblau ['hɪməlblau], *adj.* sky-blue.

Himmelfahrt ['hɪməlfaːrt], *f.* (—, *no pl.*) Ascension.

Himmelschlüssel ['hɪməlʃlysəl], *m.* (—s, *pl.* —) (*Bot.*) primrose.

himmelschreiend ['hɪməlʃraɪənt], *adj.* atrocious, revolting.

Himmelsgewölbe ['hɪməlsgəvœlbə], *n.* (—s, *pl.* —) firmament.

Himmelsstrich ['hɪməlsʃtrɪç], *m.* (—s, *pl.* —e) climate, zone.

Himmelszeichen ['hɪməlstsaɪçən], *n.* (—s, *pl.* —) sign of the zodiac.

himmelweit ['hɪməlvaɪt], *adj.* enormous; — *entfernt*, poles apart.

himmlisch ['hɪmlɪʃ], *adj.* celestial, heavenly.

hin [hɪn], *adv.* there, towards that place; finished, gone; ruined; — *und her*, to and fro.

hinab [hɪn'ap], *adv.* down.

hinan [hɪn'an], *adv.* up.

hinarbeiten ['hɪnarbaɪtən], *v.n. auf etwas* —, work towards s.th.

hinauf [hɪn'auf], *adv.* up, up to.

hinaus [hɪn'aus], *adv.* out, out of; *es kommt auf dasselbe* —, it comes to the same thing.

hinauswollen [hɪn'ausvɔlən], *v.n.* wish to go out; (*fig.*) *hoch* —, aim high.

hinausziehen [hɪn'austsi:ən], *v.a. irr.* draw out; drag on; (*fig.*) protract.

Hinblick ['hɪnblɪk], *m.* (—es, *no pl.*) *im* — *auf*, in consideration of, with regard to.

hinbringen ['hɪnbrɪŋən], *v.a. irr.* bring to; escort; *Zeit* —, while away time.

hinderlich ['hɪndərlɪç], *adj.* obstructive, cumbersome.

hindern ['hɪndərn], *v.a.* hinder, obstruct, hamper, impede.

hindeuten ['hɪndɔytən], *v.n. auf etwas* —, point to s.th., hint at s.th.

Hindin ['hɪndɪn], *f.* (—, *pl.* —innen) (*Poet.*) hind.

hindurch [hɪn'durç], *adv.* through; throughout; *die ganze Zeit* —, all the time.

hinein [hɪn'aɪn], *adv.* in, into; *in den Tag* — *leben*, live for the present, lead a life of carefree enjoyment.

hineinfinden [hɪn'aɪnfɪndən], *v.r. irr. sich in etwas* —, reconcile *or* adapt o.s. to s.th.

hinfällig ['hɪnfɛlɪç], *adj.* frail, feeble, weak; shaky, void, invalid.

Hingabe ['hɪnga:bə], *f.* (—, *no pl.*) surrender; (*fig.*) devotion.

hingeben ['hɪnge:bən], *v.a. irr.* give up, surrender. — *v.r. sich einer Sache* —, devote o.s. to a task.

hingegen [hɪn'ge:gən], *adv.* on the other hand.

hinhalten ['hɪnhaltən], *v.a. irr.* (*thing*) hold out; (*person*) keep in suspense, put off.

hinken ['hɪŋkən], *v.n.* limp.

hinlänglich ['hɪnlɛŋlɪç], *adj.* sufficient.

hinlegen ['hɪnle:gən], *v.a.* lay down, put away. — *v.r. sich* —, lie down, go to bed.

hinnehmen ['hɪnne:mən], *v.a. irr.* take, submit to, accept.

hinreichen ['hɪnraɪçən], *v.a.* pass to. — *v.n.* suffice, be sufficient.

Hinreise ['hɪnraɪzə], *f.* (—, *pl.* —n) outward journey.

hinreißen ['hɪnraɪsən], *v.r. irr. sich — lassen*, allow o.s. to be carried away.

hinreißend ['hɪnraɪsənt], *adj.* charming, ravishing, enchanting.

hinrichten ['hɪnrɪçtən], *v.a.* execute, put to death.

hinscheiden ['hɪnʃaɪdən], *v.n. irr.* die, pass away.

hinschlängeln ['hɪnʃlɛŋəln], *v.r. sich* —, meander, wind along.

Hinsicht ['hɪnzɪçt], *f.* (—, *no pl.*) view, consideration, regard.

hinsichtlich ['hɪnzɪçtlɪç], *prep.* (*Genit.*) with regard to.

hinstellen ['hɪnʃtɛlən], *v.a.* put down; make out to be.

hinten ['hɪntən], *adv.* behind; *von* —, from behind.

hinter ['hɪntər], *prep.* (*Dat.*) behind, after.

Hinterachse ['hɪntəraksə], *f.* (—, *pl.*) (*Motor.*) rear-axle.

Hinterbein ['hɪntərbaɪn], *n.* (—s, *pl.* —e) hind-leg; (*fig.*) *sich auf die —e stellen*, get up on o.'s hind-legs.

Hinterbliebene [hɪntər'bli:bənə], *m.*
(**—n**, *pl.* **—n**) survivor; mourner;
(*pl.*) the bereaved.
hinterbringen [hɪntər'brɪŋən], *v.a.*
irr. give information about, (*coll.*)
tell on.
Hinterdeck ['hɪntərdɛk], *n.* (**—s**, *no pl.*)
(*Naut.*) quarter deck.
hinterdrein ['hɪntərdraɪn], *adv.* afterwards, after; behind.
hintereinander [hɪntəraɪn'andər], *adv.*
in succession, one after another.
Hintergedanke ['hɪntərgədaŋkə], *m.*
(**—n**, *pl.* **—n**) mental reservation,
ulterior motive.
hintergehen [hɪntər'ge:ən], *v.a.* *irr.*
deceive, circumvent.
Hintergrund ['hɪntərgrunt], *m.* (**—es**,
pl. ⸚e) background; (*Theat.*) back-
cloth, back-drop.
Hinterhalt ['hɪntərhalt], *m.* (**—s**, *pl.*
—e) ambush; (*fig.*) reserve.
hinterhältig ['hɪntərhɛltɪç], *adj.* furtive, secretive; insidious.
hinterher [hɪntər'he:r], *adv.* behind;
in the rear; afterwards.
Hinterindien ['hɪntərɪndjən], *n.* Indo-
China.
Hinterkopf ['hɪntərkɔpf], *m.* (**—es**, *pl.*
⸚e) occiput, back of the head.
Hinterlader ['hɪntərla:dər], *m.* (**—s**,
pl. **—**) breech-loader.
hinterlassen [hɪntər'lasən], *v.a.* *irr.*
leave (a legacy), bequeath; leave
(word).
Hinterlassenschaft [hɪntər'lasənʃaft],
f. (**—**, *pl.* **—en**) inheritance, bequest.
Hinterlegung [hɪntər'le:guŋ], *f.* (**—**,
pl. **—en**) deposition.
Hinterlist ['hɪntərlɪst], *f.* (**—**, *no pl.*)
fraud, deceit; cunning.
hinterrücks [hɪntər'ryks], *adv.* from
behind; (*fig.*) treacherously, behind
s.o.'s back.
Hintertreffen ['hɪntərtrɛfən], *n.* (**—s**,
no pl.) *ins — geraten*, be left out in the
cold, fall behind.
hintertreiben [hɪntər'traɪbən], *v.a.* *irr.*
prevent, frustrate.
Hintertreppe ['hɪntərtrɛpə], *f.* (**—**, *pl.*
—n) back-stairs.
Hintertreppenroman ['hɪntərtrɛpənro-
roma:n], *m.* (**—s**, *pl.* **—e**) (*Lit.*) cheap
thriller.
hinterziehen ['hɪntərtsi:ən], *v.a.* *irr.*
insep. defraud.
hinträumen ['hɪntrɔymən], *v.n.* *vor
sich —*, daydream.
hinüber [hɪn'y:bər], *adv.* over, across.
hinunter [hɪn'untər], *adv.* down;
den Berg —, downhill.
hinweg [hɪn'vɛk], *adv.* away, off.
hinwegsetzen [hɪn'vɛkzetsən], *v.r. sich
über etwas —*, make light of s.th.
Hinweis ['hɪnvaɪs], *m.* (**—es**, *pl.* **—e**)
hint, indication, reference; *unter —
auf*, with reference to.
hinweisen ['hɪnvaɪzən], *v.a.* *irr. auf
etwas —*, refer to, point to s.th.

hinwerfen ['hɪnvɛrfən], *v.a.* *irr.* throw
down; *hingeworfene Bemerkung*, casual
remark.
hinziehen ['hɪntsi:ən], *v.a.* *irr.* draw
along; attract. — *v.n.* (*aux.* sein)
march along. — *v.r. sich —*, drag on.
hinzielen ['hɪntsi:lən], *v.n. auf etwas —*,
aim at s.th., have s.th. in mind.
hinzu [hɪn'tsu:], *adv.* to, near; besides,
in addition.
hinzufügen [hɪn'tsu:fy:gən], *v.a.* add.
hinzukommen [hɪn'tsu:kɔmən], *v.n.*
irr. (*aux.* sein) be added.
hinzuziehen [hɪn'tsutsi:ən], *v.a.* *irr.*
include, add; call in (expert).
Hiobsbotschaft ['hi:ɔpsbo:tʃaft], *f.* (**—**,
no pl.) bad news.
Hirn [hɪrn], *n.* (**—es**, *pl.* **—e**) brain,
brains. *See also* **Gehirn**.
Hirngespinst ['hɪrngəʃpɪnst], *n.* (**—es**,
pl. **—e**) fancy, chimera, illusion,
figment of the imagination.
hirnverbrannt ['hɪrnfɛrbrant], *adj.*
crazy, insane, mad; (*coll.*) crack-
brained.
Hirsch [hɪrʃ], *m.* (**—es**, *pl.* **—e**) (*Zool.*)
stag, hart.
Hirschbock ['hɪrʃbɔk], *m.* (**—s**, *pl.* ⸚e)
(*Zool.*) stag.
Hirschfänger ['hɪrʃfɛŋər], *m.* (**—s**, *pl.*
—) hunting-knife.
Hirschgeweih ['hɪrʃgəvaɪ], *n.* (**—s**, *pl.*
—e) horns, antlers.
Hirschhorn ['hɪrʃhɔrn], *n.* (**—s**, *no pl.*)
(*Chem.*) hartshorn.
Hirschkäfer ['hɪrʃkɛ:fər], *m.* (**—s**, *pl.*
—) (*Ent.*) stag beetle.
Hirschkeule ['hɪrʃkɔylə], *f.* (**—**, *pl.* **—n**)
haunch of venison.
Hirschkuh ['hɪrʃku:], *f.* (**—**, *pl.* ⸚e)
(*Zool.*) hind, doe.
Hirse ['hɪrzə], *f.* (**—**, *no pl.*) (*Bot.*)
millet.
Hirt [hɪrt], *m.* (**—en**, *pl.* **—en**) shep-
herd, herdsman.
Hirtenbrief ['hɪrtənbri:f], *m.* (**—s**,
pl. **—e**) (*Eccl.*) pastoral letter.
His [hɪs], *n.* (**—**, *pl.* **—**) (*Mus.*) B sharp.
hissen ['hɪsən], *v.a.* hoist (the flag).
Historiker [hɪ'sto:rɪkər], *m.* (**—s**, *pl.*
—) historian.
historisch [hɪ'sto:rɪʃ], *adj.* historical.
Hitzblase ['hɪtsbla:zə], *f.* (**—**, *pl.* **—n**)
blister, heat-rash.
Hitze ['hɪtsə], *f.* (**—**, *no pl.*) heat, hot
weather.
hitzig ['hɪtsɪç], *adj.* hot-headed, hasty,
passionate.
Hitzschlag ['hɪtsʃla:k], *m.* (**—es**, *pl.* ⸚e)
sunstroke, heat-stroke.
Hobel ['ho:bəl], *m.* (**—s**, *pl.* **—**) (*tool*)
plane.
Hoch [ho:x], *n.* (**—s**, *no pl.*) toast
(*drink*); (*Met.*) high.
hoch, hoh [ho:x, ho:], *adj.* high; (*fig.*)
eminent, sublime.
Hochachtung ['ho:xaxtuŋ], *f.* (**—**, *no
pl.*) esteem, regard, respect.
hochachtungsvoll ['ho:xaxtuŋsfɔl],
adj., adv. (*letters*) yours faithfully.

109

Hochamt ['ho:xamt], *n.* (—es, *pl.* ̈er) (*Eccl.*) High Mass.

Hochbau ['ho:xbau], *m.* (—s, *pl.* —ten) superstructure.

hochbetagt ['ho:xbəta:kt], *adj.* advanced in years.

Hochburg ['ho:xburk], *f.* (—, *pl.* —en) (*fig.*) stronghold, citadel.

Hochebene ['ho:xe:bənə], *f.* (—, *pl.* —n) table-land, plateau.

hochfahrend ['ho:xfa:rənt], *adj.* haughty, high-flown; (*coll.*) stuck-up.

Hochgefühl ['ho:xgəfy:l], *n.* (—s, *no pl.*) exaltation.

Hochgenuß ['ho:xgənus], *m.* (—sses, *pl.* ̈sse) exquisite enjoyment; treat.

Hochgericht ['ho:xgərɪçt], *n.* (—s, *pl.* —e) place of execution, scaffold.

hochherzig ['ho:xhɛrtsɪç], *adj.* magnanimous.

Hochmeister ['ho:xmaɪstər], *m.* (—s, *pl.* —) Grand Master.

Hochmut ['ho:xmu:t], *m.* (—s, *no pl.*) haughtiness, pride.

hochnäsig ['ho:xnɛ:zɪç], *adj.* supercilious, stuck-up.

hochnotpeinlich ['ho:xno:tpaɪnlɪç], *adj.* (*obs.*) penal, criminal; —es Verhör, criminal investigation.

Hochofen ['ho:xo:fən], *m.* (—s, *pl.* ̈) blast-furnace.

Hochschule ['ho:xʃu:lə], *f.* (—, *pl.* —n) academy; university.

Hochschüler ['ho:xʃy:lər], *m.* (—s, *pl.* —) student, undergraduate.

höchst [hœ:çst], *adj.* highest, most. — *adv.* most, extremely.

Hochstapler ['ho:xʃta:plər], *m.* (—s, *pl.* —) confidence trickster, swindler.

höchstens ['hœ:çstəns], *adv.* at most, at best.

bochtrabend ['ho:xtra:bənt], *adj.* (*horse*) high-stepping; (*fig.*) high-sounding, bombastic.

hochverdient ['ho:xfɛrdi:nt], *adj.* highly meritorious.

Hochverrat ['ho:xfɛra:t], *m.* (—s, *no pl.*) high treason.

Hochwild ['ho:xvɪlt], *n.* (—es, *no pl.*) deer; big game.

hochwohlgeboren ['ho:xvo:lgəbo:rən], *adj.* (*obs.*) noble; *Euer Hochwohlgeboren*, Right Honourable Sir.

hochwürden ['ho:xvyrdən], *adj. Euer Hochwürden*, Reverend Sir.

Hochzeit ['hɔxtsaɪt], *f.* (—, *pl.* —en) wedding; nuptials.

hochzeitlich ['hɔxtsaɪtlɪç], *adj.* nuptial, bridal.

Hochzeitsreise ['hɔxtsaɪtsraɪzə], *f.* (—, *pl.* —n) honeymoon.

Hocke ['hɔkə], *f.* (—, *pl.* —n) squatting posture; shock, stook.

hocken ['hɔkən], *v.n.* crouch, squat; *zu Hause* —, be a stay-at-home.

Hocker ['hɔkər], *m.* (—s, *pl.* —) stool.

Höcker ['hœkər], *m.* (—s, *pl.* —) hump.

höckerig ['hœkərɪç], *adj.* hump-backed, hunch-backed.

Hode ['ho:də], *f.* (—, *pl.* —n) testicle.

Hof [ho:f], *m.* (—es, *pl.* ̈e) yard, courtyard; farm(stead); (*royal*) court; (*moon*) halo; *einem den* — *machen*, court s.o.

Hofarzt ['ho:fartst], *m.* (—es, *pl.* ̈e) court physician.

hoffähig ['ho:ffɛ:ɪç], *adj.* presentable at court.

Hoffart ['hɔfart], *f.* (—, *no pl.*) pride, arrogance.

hoffärtig ['hɔfɛrtɪç], *adj.* proud, arrogant.

hoffen ['hɔfən], *v.n.* hope; *fest auf etwas* —, trust.

hoffentlich ['hɔfəntlɪç], *adv.* as I hope, I trust that.

Hoffnung ['hɔfnuŋ], *f.* (—, *pl.* —en) hope, expectation, anticipation, expectancy; *guter* — *sein*, be full of hope; be expecting a baby; *sich* — *machen auf*, cherish hopes of.

hoffnungslos ['hɔfnuŋslo:s], *adj.* hopeless, past hope.

hofieren [ho'fi:rən], *v.a.* court.

höfisch ['hø:fɪʃ], *adj.* courtlike, courtly.

höflich ['hø:flɪç], *adj.* courteous, civil, polite.

Hoflieferant ['ho:fli:fərant], *m.* (—en, *pl.* —en) purveyor to His *or* Her Majesty.

Höfling ['hø:flɪŋ], *m.* (—s, *pl.* —e) courtier.

Hofmarschall ['ho:fmarʃal], *m.* (—s, *pl.* —e) Lord Chamberlain.

Hofmeister ['ho:fmaɪstər], *m.* (—s, *pl.* —) (*obs.*) steward; tutor.

Hofnarr ['ho:fnar], *m.* (—en, *pl.* —en) court jester, court fool.

Hofrat ['ho:fra:t], *m.* (—s, *pl.* ̈e) Privy Councillor.

Hofschranze ['ho:fʃrantsə], *m.* (—n, *pl.* —n) courtier; flunkey.

Hofsitte ['ho:fzɪtə], *f.* (—, *pl.* —n) court etiquette.

Höhe ['hø:ə], *f.* (—, *pl.* —n) height, altitude; *bis zur* — *von*, up to the level of; *in die* —, upwards; *in die* — *fahren*, give a start, get excited.

Hoheit ['ho:haɪt], *f.* (—, *pl.* —en) grandeur; sovereignty; (*title*) Highness.

Hohelied [ho:ə'li:t], *n.* (—s, *no pl.*) Song of Solomon.

Höhenmesser ['hø:ənmɛsər], *m.* (—s, *pl.* —) (*Aviat.*) altimeter.

Höhensonne ['hø:ənzɔnə], *f.* (—, *pl.* —n) Alpine sun; (*Med.*) ultra-violet lamp.

Höhenzug ['hø:əntsu:k], *m.* (—s, *pl.* ̈e) mountain range.

Höhepunkt ['hø:əpuŋkt], *m.* (—s, *pl.* —e) climax, culmination, acme; peak.

höher ['hø:ər], *comp. adj.* higher.

hohl [ho:l], *adj.* hollow; (*tooth*) decayed, hollow.

Höhle ['hø:lə], *f.* (—, *pl.* —n) cave, cavern, den.

hohlgeschliffen ['ho:lgəʃlɪfən], *adj.* concave, hollow-ground.

Hohlheit ['ho:lhaɪt], *f.* (—, *no pl.*) hollowness.

Hohlleiste ['ho:llaɪstə], *f.* (—, *pl.* —n) groove, channel.

Hohlmaß ['ho:lma:s], *n.* (—es, *pl.* —e) dry measure.

Hohlmeißel ['ho:lmaɪsəl], *m.* (—s, *pl.* —) gouge.

Hohlsaum ['ho:lzaum], *m.* (—s, *pl.* ̈e) hemstitch.

Hohlspiegel ['ho:lʃpi:gəl], *m.* (—s, *pl.* —) concave mirror.

Höhlung ['hø:luŋ], *f.* (—, *pl.* —en) hollow, cavity.

Hohlziegel ['ho:ltsi:gəl], *m.* (—s, *pl.* —) hollow brick.

Hohn [ho:n], *m.* (—s, *no pl.*) scorn, derision, mockery; sneer.

höhnen ['hø:nən], *v.a.* deride, sneer at; *see* **verhöhnen.**

Höker ['hø:kər], *m.* (—s, *pl.* —) hawker, huckster.

hold [hɔlt], *adj.* kind, friendly; gracious; graceful; sweet.

Holder ['hɔldər] *see* **Holunder.**

holdselig ['hɔltze:lɪç], *adj.* sweet, charming, gracious.

holen ['ho:lən], *v.a.* fetch, collect, get.

Holland ['hɔlant], *n.* Holland.

Hölle ['hœlə], *f.* (—, *no pl.*) hell.

Holm [hɔlm], *m.* (—es, *pl.* —e) islet, holm; (*Gymn.*) bar.

holperig ['hɔlpərɪç], *adj.* rough, bumpy.

holpern ['hɔlpərn], *v.n.* jolt, stumble; (*fig.*) falter.

Holunder [ho'lundər], *m.* (—s, *pl.* —) (*Bot.*) elder; *spanischer* —, lilac.

Holz [hɔlts], *n.* (—es, *pl.* ̈er) wood, timber; (*Am.*) lumber; (*no pl.*) forest; bush.

Holzapfel ['hɔltsapfəl], *m.* (—s, *pl.* ̈) (*Bot.*) crab-apple.

holzartig ['hɔltsartɪç], *adj.* woody, ligneous.

holzen ['hɔltsən], *v.a.* cut *or* gather wood.

hölzern ['hœltsərn], *adj.* wooden; (*fig.*) stiff.

Holzhändler ['hɔltshendlər], *m.* (—s, *pl.* —) timber-merchant; (*Am.*) lumber-merchant.

Holzhauer ['hɔltshauər], *m.* (—s, *pl.* —) wood-cutter.

holzig ['hɔltsɪç], *adj.* woody, wooded; (*asparagus*) woody, hard; (*beans*) stringy.

Holzkohle ['hɔltsko:lə], *f.* (—, *no pl.*) charcoal.

Holzscheit ['hɔltsʃaɪt], *n.* (—s, *pl.* —e) log of wood.

Holzschlag ['hɔltsʃla:k], *m.* (—es, *pl.* ̈e) clearing; felling area.

Holzschnitt ['hɔltsʃnɪt], *m.* (—es, *pl.* —e) wood-cut.

Holzschuh ['hɔltsʃu:], *m.* (—s, *pl.* —e) clog.

Holzweg ['hɔltsve:k], *m.* (—s, *pl.* —e) timbertrack; (*fig.*) *auf dem* — *sein*, be on the wrong tack.

Holzwolle ['hɔltsvɔlə], *f.* (—, *no pl.*) wood shavings.

homogen [homo'ge:n], *adj.* homogeneous.

homolog [homo'lo:g], *adj.* homologous.

honett [ho'nɛt], *adj.* (*obs.*) respectable, genteel.

Honig ['ho:nɪç], *m.* (—s, *no pl.*) honey.

Honigkuchen ['ho:nɪçku:xən], *m.* (—s, *pl.* —) ginger-bread.

Honigwabe ['ho:nɪçva:bə], *f.* (—, *pl.* —n) honeycomb.

Honorar [hono'ra:r], *n.* (—s, *pl.* —e) remuneration; (*professional*) fee; honorarium.

Honoratioren [honora'tsjo:rən], *m. pl.* people of rank; dignitaries.

honorieren [hono'ri:rən], *v.a.* pay a fee to, remunerate.

Hopfen ['hɔpfən], *m.* (—s, *no pl.*) (*Bot.*) hop, hops; *an dem ist* — *und Malz verloren*, he is beyond help.

Hopfenstange ['hɔpfənʃtaŋə], *f.* (—, *pl.* —n) hop-pole; (*fig.*) tall thin person.

hopsen ['hɔpsən], *v.n.* (*aux.* sein) (*coll.*) hop, jump.

hörbar ['hø:rba:r], *adj.* audible.

horchen ['hɔrçən], *v.n.* listen, eavesdrop.

Horde ['hɔrdə], *f.* (—, *pl.* —n) horde.

hören ['hø:rən], *v.a., v.n.* hear.

Hörer ['hø:rər], *m.* (—s, *pl.* —) listener; (*Univ.*) student; (*telephone*) receiver.

Hörerin ['hø:rərɪn], *f.* (—, *pl.* —innen) female listener; (*Univ.*) woman student.

Hörerschaft ['hø:rərʃaft], *f.* (—, *no pl.*) audience.

Hörgerät ['hø:rgere:t], *n.* (—es, *pl.* —e) hearing-aid.

hörig ['hø:rɪç], *adj.* in bondage, a slave to.

Horizont [hori'tsɔnt], *m.* (—es, *pl.* —e) horizon.

Horizontale [horitsɔn'ta:lə], *f.* (—, *pl.* —n) horizontal line.

Horn [hɔrn], *n.* (—s, *pl.* ̈er) horn; (*Mus.*) French horn.

Hörnchen ['hœrnçən], *n.* (—s, *pl.* —) French roll, croissant.

hörnern ['hœrnərn], *adj.* horny, made of horn.

Hornhaut ['hɔrnhaut], *f.* (—, *pl.* ̈te) horny skin; (*eye*) cornea.

Hornhautverpflanzung ['hɔrnhautfərpflantsuŋ], *f.* (—, *no pl.*) corneal graft.

hornig ['hɔrnɪç], *adj.* hard, horny.

Hornisse [hɔr'nɪsə], *f.* (—, *pl.* —n) (*Ent.*) hornet.

horrend [hɔ'rɛnt], *adj.* exorbitant; stupendous.

Hörrohr [hø'rro:r], *n.* (—s, *pl.* —e) ear-trumpet.

Hörsaal ['hø:rza:l], *m.* (—s, *pl.* —säle) auditorium, lecture-room.

Hörspiel ['høːrʃpiːl], *n.* (—s, *pl.* —e) radio play.

Horst [hɔrst], *m.* (—es, *pl.* —e) eyrie.

Hort [hɔrt], *m.* (—es, *pl.* —e) (*Poet.*) treasure; stronghold.

Hortensie [hɔr'tɛnzjə], *f.* (—, *pl.* —n) (*Bot.*) hydrangea.

Hose ['hoːzə], *f.* (—, *pl.* —n) trousers, pants, breeches; (*women*) slacks.

Hosenband ['hoːzənbant], *n.* (—es, *pl.* ⁓er) garter.

Hosenträger ['hoːzəntrɛgər], *m. pl.* braces, (*Am.*) suspenders.

Hospitant [hɔspɪ'tant], *m.* (—en, *pl.* —en) (*Univ.*) temporary student, non-registered student.

hospitieren [hɔspɪ'tiːrən], *v.n.* attend lectures as a visitor.

Hostie ['hɔstjə], *f.* (—, *pl.* —n) (*Eccl.*) the Host.

hüben ['hyːbən], *adv.* on this side; — *und drüben*, on either side.

hübsch [hypʃ], *adj.* pretty, attractive; handsome; good-looking.

Hubschrauber ['huːpʃraubər], *m.* (—s, *pl.* —) (*Aviat.*) helicopter.

huckepack ['hukəpak], *adv.* — *tragen*, carry pick-a-back.

Huf [huːf], *m.* (—es, *pl.* —e) hoof.

Hufe ['huːfə], *f.* (—, *pl.* —n) hide (of land).

Hufeisen ['huːfaizən], *n.* (—s, *pl.* —) horseshoe.

Huflattich ['huːflatɪç], *m.* (—s, *pl.* —e) (*Bot.*) colt's foot.

Hufschlag ['huːfʃlaːk], *m.* (—s, *pl.* ⁓e) (*of a horse*) hoof-beat.

Hüfte ['hyftə], *f.* (—, *pl.* —n) (*Anat.*) hip; (*animals*) haunch.

Hügel ['hyːgəl], *m.* (—s, *pl.* —) hill, hillock.

hügelig ['hyːgəlɪç], *adj.* hilly.

Huhn [huːn], *n.* (—s, *pl.* ⁓er) fowl; hen.

Hühnchen ['hyːnçən], *n.* (—s, *pl.* —) pullet, chicken.

Hühnerauge ['hyːnəraugə], *n.* (—s, *pl.* —n) corn (*on the foot*).

Huld [hult], *f.* (—, *no pl.*) grace, favour.

huldigen ['huldɪgən], *v.n.* pay homage.

huldvoll ['hultfɔl], *adj.* gracious.

Hülle ['hylə], *f.* (—, *pl.* —n) cover, covering; veil; *in — und Fülle*, in abundance, in profusion.

hüllen ['hylən], *v.a.* cover, veil, wrap.

Hülse ['hylzə], *f.* (—, *pl.* —n) hull, husk, shell; cartridge-case.

Hülsenfrucht ['hylzənfruxt], *f.* (—, *pl.* ⁓e) (*Bot.*) leguminous plant.

human [hu'maːn], *adj.* humane.

humanistisch [huma'nɪstɪʃ], *adj.* classical; humanistic.

Hummel ['huməl], *f.* (—, *pl.* —n) (*Ent.*) bumble-bee.

Hummer ['humər], *m.* (—s, *pl.* —) (*Zool.*) lobster.

Humor [hu'moːr], *m.* (—s, *no pl.*) humour.

humoristisch [humo'rɪstɪʃ], *adj.* humorous, witty.

humpeln ['humpəln], *v.n.* hobble, limp.

Humpen ['humpən], *m.* (—s, *pl.* —) deep drinking-cup, bowl, tankard.

Humus ['huːmus], *m.* (—, *no pl.*) garden-mould, humus.

Hund [hunt], *m.* (—es, *pl.* —e) dog; (*hunting*) hound; (*fig.*) rascal, scoundrel.

Hundehaus ['hundəhaus], *n.* (—es, *pl.* ⁓er) dog-kennel.

hundert ['hundərt], *num. adj.* a hundred, one hundred.

Hündin ['hyndɪn], *f.* (—, *pl.* —innen) bitch.

Hundstage ['huntstaːgə], *m. pl.* dog days (July to August).

Hundszahn ['huntstsaːn], *m.* (—es, *pl.* ⁓e) (*Bot.*) dandelion.

Hüne ['hyːnə], *m.* (—n, *pl.* —n) giant, colossus; (*fig.*) tall man.

Hünengrab ['hyːnəngraːp], *n.* (—es, *pl.* ⁓er) tumulus, burial mound, barrow, cairn.

Hunger ['huŋər], *m.* (—s, *no pl.*) hunger; starvation.

hungern ['huŋərn], *v.n.* hunger, be hungry.

Hungertuch ['huŋərtuːx], *n.* (—es, *no pl.*) *am — nagen*, go without food; live in poverty.

hungrig ['huŋrɪç], *adj.* hungry; (*fig.*) desirous of.

Hupe ['huːpə], *f.* (—, *pl.* —n) motorhorn, hooter (of a car).

hüpfen ['hypfən], *v.n.* (*aux.* sein) hop, skip.

Hürde ['hyrdə], *f.* (—, *pl.* —n) hurdle.

Hure ['huːrə], *f.* (—, *pl.* —n) whore, prostitute, harlot; (*coll.*) tart.

hurtig ['hurtɪç], *adj.* nimble, agile; quick, speedy, swift.

Husar [hu'zaːr], *m.* (—en, *pl.* —en) hussar.

husch! [huʃ], *excl.* quick!

huschen ['huʃən], *v.n.* (*aux.* sein) scurry, slip away.

hüsteln ['hyːstəln], *v.n.* cough slightly; clear o.'s throat.

husten ['huːstən], *v.n.* cough.

Hut (1) [huːt], *m.* (—es, *pl.* ⁓e) hat; *steifer —*, bowler.

Hut (2) [huːt], *f.* (—, *no pl.*) guard, keeping, care.

hüten ['hyːtən], *v.a.* guard, tend, care for; *Kinder —*, baby-sit; *das Bett —*, be confined to o.'s bed, be ill in bed. — *v.r. sich — vor*, be on o.'s guard against, beware of.

Hüter ['hyːtər], *m.* (—s, *pl.* —) guardian, keeper; (*cattle*) herdsman.

Hutkrempe ['huːtkrɛmpə], *f.* (—, *pl.* —n) hat-brim.

Hütte ['hytə], *f.* (—, *pl.* —n) hut, cottage; (*Tech.*) furnace, forge, foundry.

Hüttenarbeiter ['hytənarbaitər], *m.* (—s, *pl.* —) smelter, foundry-worker.

Hyäne [hy'ɛːnə], *f.* (—, *pl.* —n) (*Zool.*) hyena.

Hyazinthe [hyat'sɪntə], *f.* (—, *pl.* —n) (*Bot.*) hyacinth.

Hyperbel [hy'pɛrbəl], *f.* (—, *pl.* —n) hyperbola.

hypnotisch [hyp'no:tɪʃ], *adj.* hypnotic.

hypnotisieren [hypnoti'zi:rən], *v.a.* hypnotise.

Hypochonder [hypo'xɔndər], *m.* (—s, *pl.* —) hypochondriac.

Hypothek [hypo'te:k], *f.* (—, *pl.* —en) mortgage.

Hysterie [hyste'ri:], *f.* (—, *no pl.*) hysterics, hysteria.

hysterisch [hys'te:rɪʃ], *adj.* hysterical.

I

I [i:], *n.* (—, *no pl.*) the letter I. — *excl.* *i wo!* (*dial.*) certainly not! of course not!

ich [ɪç], *pers. pron.* I, myself.

ideal [ide'a:l], *adj.* ideal.

idealisieren [ideali'zi:rən], *v.a.* idealise.

Idealismus [idea'lɪsmus], *m.* (—, *no pl.*) idealism.

Idee [i'de:], *f.* (—, *pl.* —n) idea, notion, conception.

identifizieren [idɛntifi'tsi:rən], *v.a.* identify.

identisch [i'dɛntɪʃ], *adj.* identical.

Identität [idɛnti'tɛ:t], *f.* (—, *no pl.*) identity.

idiomatisch [idio'ma:tɪʃ], *adj.* idiomatic.

Idyll [i'dyl], *n.* (—s, *pl.* —e) idyll.

Idylle [i'dylə], *f.* (—, *pl.* —n) idyll.

idyllisch [i'dylɪʃ], *adj.* idyllic.

Igel [i'gəl], *m.* (—s, *pl.* —) (*Zool.*) hedgehog.

ignorieren [ɪgno'ri:rən], *v.a.* ignore, take no notice of.

ihm [i:m], *pers. pron. Dat.* to him, it.

ihn [i:n], *pers. pron. Acc.* him, it.

Ihnen ['i:nən], *pers. pron. Dat.* you, to you.

ihnen ['i:nən], *pers. pron. pl. Dat.* them, to them.

Ihr [i:r], *poss. adj.* your; of your. — *poss. pron.* yours.

ihr [i:r], *pers. pron.* to her; (*pl.*) (*intim.*) you. — *poss. adj.* her, their. — *poss. pron.* hers, theirs.

Ihrer ['i:rər], *pers. pron.* of you. — *poss. adj.* of your.

ihrer ['i:rər], *pers. pron.* of her, of it; (*pl.*) of them. — *poss. adj* of her; to her; (*pl.*) of their.

ihresgleichen ['i:rəsglaɪçən], *adv.* of her, its *or* their kind.

ihrethalben ['i:rəthalbən], *adv.* for her sake, for their sake, on her account, on their account.

ihretwegen ['i:rətve:gən] *see* **ihrethalben**.

ihretwillen ['i:rətvɪlən] *see* **ihrethalben**.

Ihrige [i:rɪgə], *poss. pron.* yours.

ihrige ['i:rɪgə], *poss. pron.* hers, its, theirs.

illegitim [ɪlegi'ti:m], *adj.* illegitimate.

illuminieren [ɪlumi'ni:rən], *v.a.* illuminate, floodlight.

illustrieren [ɪlu'stri:rən], *v.a.* illustrate.

Iltis ['ɪltɪs], *m.* (—ses, *pl.* —se) (*Zool.*) polecat, fitchet.

im [ɪm], *contraction of* **in dem**, in the.

Imbiß ['ɪmbɪs], *m.* (—sses, *pl.* —sse) snack, refreshment, light meal.

Imker ['ɪmkər], *m.* (—s, *pl.* —) bee-keeper.

immatrikulieren [ɪmmatriku'li:rən], *v.a.* (*Univ.*) matriculate, enrol.

Imme ['ɪmə], *f.* (—, *pl.* —n) (*dial.*, *Poet.*) bee.

immer ['ɪmər], *adv.* always, ever; — *mehr*, more and more; — *noch*, still; — *wieder*, time and again; — *größer*, larger and larger; *auf* —, for ever.

immerdar ['ɪmərda:r], *adv.* for ever.

immerhin ['ɪmərhɪn], *adv.* nevertheless, still, after all.

immerzu ['ɪmərtsu:], *adv.* always, constantly.

Immobilien [ɪmo'bi:ljən], *pl.* real estate.

Immortelle [ɪmɔr'tɛlə], *f.* (—, *pl.* —n) (*Bot.*) everlasting flower.

immun [ɪ'mu:n], *adj.* immune.

impfen ['ɪmpfən], *v.a.* vaccinate, inoculate; (*Hort.*) graft.

imponieren [ɪmpo'ni:rən], *v.n.* impress.

Import [ɪm'pɔrt], *m.* (—s, *pl.* —e) import, importation.

imposant [ɪmpo'zant], *adj.* imposing, impressive.

imstande [ɪm'ʃtandə], *adv.* capable, able; — *sein*, be able.

in [ɪn], *prep.* (*Dat.*, *Acc.*) in, into; at; within.

Inangriffnahme [ɪn'angrɪfna:mə], *f.* (—, *no pl.*) start, beginning, inception.

Inbegriff ['ɪnbəgrɪf], *m.* (—es, *no pl.*) essence, epitome.

inbegriffen ['ɪnbəgrɪfən], *adv.* inclusive.

Inbrunst ['ɪnbrunst], *f.* (—, *no pl.*) ardour, fervour.

indem [ɪn'de:m], *adv.* meanwhile. — *conj.* while, whilst; as, because, in that.

indessen [ɪn'dɛsən], *adv.* meanwhile, in the meantime. — *conj.* however, nevertheless, yet.

Indien ['ɪndjən], *n.* India.

Individualität [ɪndividuali'tɛ:t], *f.* (—, *pl.* —en) individuality, personality.

individuell [ɪndividu'ɛl], *adj.* individual.

Individuum [ɪndi'vi:duum], *n.* (—s, *pl.* —duen) individual.

Indizienbeweis [In'di:tsjənbəvaIs], *m.* (—es, *pl.* —e) (*Law*) circumstantial evidence *or* proof.

indossieren [Indɔ'si:rən], *v.a.* endorse.

Industrie [Indus'tri:], *f.* (—, *pl.* —n) industry; manufacture.

industriell [Industri'ɛl], *adj.* industrial.

Industrielle [Industri'ɛlə], *m.* (—n, *pl.* —n) manufacturer, industrialist.

ineinander [Inar'nandər], *adv.* into each other, into one another.

infam [In'fa:m], *adj.* infamous.

Infantin [In'fantIn], *f.* (—, *pl.* —en) Infanta.

infizieren [Infi'tsi:rən], *v.a.* infect.

infolge [In'fɔlgə], *prep.* (*Genit.*) in consequence of, owing to.

informieren [Infor'mi:rən], *v.a.* inform, advise.

Ingenieur [Inʒen'jøːr], *m.* (—s, *pl.* —e) engineer.

Ingrimm ['IngrIm], *m.* (—s, *no pl.*) anger, rage, wrath.

Ingwer ['Iŋvər], *m.* (—s, *no pl.*) ginger.

Inhaber ['Inha:bər], *m.* (—s, *pl.* —) possessor, owner; proprietor; occupant.

inhaftieren [Inhaf'ti:rən], *v.a.* imprison; arrest.

inhalieren [Inha'li:rən], *v.a.* inhale.

Inhalt ['Inhalt], *m.* (—(e)s, *no pl.*) content; contents; tenor.

Inhaltsverzeichnis ['InhaltsfɛrtsaIç-nIs], *n.* (—ses, *pl.* —se) (table of) contents; index.

inhibieren [Inhi'bi:rən], *v.a.* inhibit, prevent.

Inkasso [In'kaso], *n.* (—s, *pl.* —s) encashment.

inklinieren [Inkli'ni:rən], *v.n.* be inclined to.

inklusive [Inklu'zi:və], *adv.* inclusive of, including.

inkonsequent ['Inkɔnzəkvɛnt], *adj.* inconsistent.

Inkrafttreten [In'krafttre:tən], *n.* (—s, *no pl.*) enactment; coming into force.

Inland ['Inlant], *n.* (—s, *no pl.*) inland, interior.

Inländer ['Inlɛndər], *m.* (—s, *pl.* —) native.

Inlett ['Inlɛt], *n.* (—s, *pl.* —e) bed-tick, ticking.

inliegend ['Inli:gənt], *adj.* enclosed.

inmitten [In'mItən], *prep.* (*Genit.*) in the midst of.

innehaben ['Inəha:bən], *v.a. irr.* possess; occupy; hold.

innehalten ['Inəhaltən], *v.a. irr.* (*conditions*) keep to, observe; (*time*) come promptly at. — *v.n.* stop, pause.

innen ['Inən], *adv.* within; *nach* —, inwards; *von* —, from within.

Innenminister ['InənmInIstər], *m.* (—s, *pl.* —) Minister for Internal Affairs; Home Secretary; (*Am.*) Secretary of the Interior.

inner ['Inər], *adj.* inner, interior, internal; intrinsic.

innerhalb ['Inərhalp], *prep.* (*Genit.*) within.

innerlich ['InərlIç], *adj.* internal; inside o.s.; inward.

innerste ['Inərstə], *adj.* inmost, innermost.

innewerden ['Inəve:rdən], *v.a. irr.* (*aux.* sein) perceive, become aware of.

innewohnen ['Inəvo:nən], *v.n.* be inherent in.

innig ['InIç], *adj.* heartfelt, cordial.

Innung ['Inuŋ], *f.* (—, *pl.* —en) guild, corporation.

Insasse ['Inzasə], *m.* (—n, *pl.* —n) inmate; occupant.

insbesondere [Insbə'zɔndərə], *adv.* especially, particularly, in particular.

Inschrift ['InʃrIft], *f.* (—, *pl.* —en) inscription.

Insel ['Inzəl], *f.* (—, *pl.* —n) island.

Inserat [Inzə'ra:t], *n.* (—es, *pl.* —e) classified advertisement; (*coll.*) (small) ad.

inserieren [Inzə'ri:rən], *v.a.* advertise; insert.

insgeheim [Insgə'haIm], *adv.* privately, secretly.

insgesamt [Insgə'zamt], *adv.* altogether, in a body.

insofern [Inzo'fɛrn], *conj.* — *als*, in so far as, inasmuch as, so far as.

inspirieren [Inspi'ri:rən], *v.a.* inspire.

installieren [Insta'li:rən], *v.a.* install, fit.

instandhalten [In'ʃtanthaltən], *v.a. irr.* maintain, preserve, keep in repair.

inständig [In'ʃtɛndIç], *adj.* urgent; fervent.

instandsetzen [In'ʃtantzɛtsən], *v.a.* restore, repair; *einen* — *etwas zu tun,* enable s.o. to do s.th.

Instanz [In'stants], *f.* (—, *pl.* —en) (*Law*) instance; *letzte* —, highest court of appeal, last resort.

Institut [Insti'tu:t], *n.* (—es, *pl.* —e) institute, institution, establishment; (*Univ.*) department.

instruieren [Instru'i:rən], *v.a.* instruct.

Insulaner [Inzu'la:nər], *m* (—s, *pl.* —) islander.

inszenieren [Instse'ni:rən], *v.a.* put on the stage, produce.

Inszenierung [Instse'ni:ruŋ], *f.* (—, *pl.* —en) (*Theat.*) production, staging.

intellektuell [Intelektu'ɛl], *adj.* intellectual.

Intendant [Intɛn'dant], *m.* (—en, *pl.* —en) (*Theat.*) director.

interessant [Intərɛ'sant], *adj.* interesting.

Interesse [Intə'rɛsə], *n.* (—s, *pl.* —n) interest.

Interessent [Intərɛ'sɛnt], *m.* (—en, *pl.* —en) interested party.

interessieren [Intərɛ'si:rən], *v.a.* interest. — *v.r. sich* —, be interested (in).

intern [In'tɛrn], *adj.* internal.

Internat [Intɛr'na:t], *n.* (—es, *pl.* —e) boarding-school.

Interne [ɪn'tɛrnə], *m.* (—n, *pl.* —n) resident (pupil *or* doctor), boarder.
Internist [ɪntɛr'nɪst], *m.* (—en, *pl.* —en) specialist in internal diseases.
interpunktieren [ɪntərpunk'tiːrən], *v.a.* punctuate.
Interpunktion [ɪntərpunkts'joːn], *f.* (—, *pl.* —en) punctuation.
intim [ɪn'tiːm], *adj.* intimate; *mit einem — sein*, be on close terms with s.o.
intonieren [ɪnto'niːrən], *v.n.* intone.
Intrigant [ɪntri'gant], *m.* (—en, *pl.* —en) intriguer, schemer.
intrigieren [ɪntri'giːrən], *v.n.* intrigue, scheme.
Inventar [ɪnvɛn'taːr], *n.* (—s, *pl.* —e) inventory; *ein — aufnehmen*, draw up an inventory.
Inventur [ɪnvɛn'tuːr], *f.* (—, *pl.* —en) stock-taking.
inwärts ['ɪnvɛrts], *adv.* inwards.
inwendig ['ɪnvɛndɪç], *adj.* inward, internal, inner.
inwiefern [ɪnviː'fɛrn], *adv.* to what extent.
inwieweit [ɪnviː'vaɪt], *adv.* how far.
Inzucht ['ɪntsuxt], *f.* (—, *no pl.*) inbreeding.
inzwischen [ɪn'tsvɪʃən], *adv.* meanwhile, in the meantime.
Irak [i'raːk], *m.*, *n.* Iraq.
Iran [i'raːn], *n.* Iran.
irden ['ɪrdən], *adj.* earthen.
irdisch ['ɪrdɪʃ], *adj.* earthly; worldly; terrestrial, temporal.
irgend ['ɪrgənt], *adv.* any, some; *wenn es — geht*, if it can possibly be done.
irgendein [ɪrgənt'aɪn], *pron.* any, some.
Irland ['ɪrlant], *n.* Ireland.
ironisch [i'roːnɪʃ], *adj.* ironic, ironical.
Irre (1) ['ɪrə], *f.* (—, *no pl.*) *in die — gehen*, go astray.
Irre (2) ['ɪrə], *m.* (—n, *pl.* —n) madman, lunatic.
irre ['ɪrə], *adj.* astray; wrong, confused; crazy, demented.
irren ['ɪrən], *v.n.* err, go astray, be wrong. — *v.r. sich —*, be mistaken.
Irrenarzt ['ɪrənartst], *m.* (—es, *pl.* ⸚e) psychiatrist.
Irrenhaus ['ɪrənhaus], *n.* (—es, *pl.* ⸚er) lunatic asylum, mental hospital.
Irrfahrt ['ɪrfaːrt], *f.* (—, *pl.* —en) wandering.
Irrglaube ['ɪrglaubə], *m.* (—ns, *no pl.*) heresy.
irrig ['ɪrɪç], *adj.* erroneous.
irritieren [ɪri'tiːrən], *v.a.* irritate.
Irrlicht ['ɪrlɪçt], *n.* (—s, *pl.* —er) will-o'-the-wisp.
Irrsinn ['ɪrzɪn], *m.* (—s, *no pl.*) madness, insanity, lunacy.
irrsinnig ['ɪrzɪnɪç], *adj.* insane, deranged.
Irrtum ['ɪrtuːm], *m.* (—s, *pl.* ⸚er) error, mistake, fault, oversight.
Irrweg ['ɪrveːk], *m.* (—s, *pl.* —e) wrong track.
Irrwisch ['ɪrvɪʃ], *m.* (—es, *pl.* —e) will-o'-the-wisp.

Ischias ['ɪsçias], *f.*, *m.* (*Med.*) sciatica.
Isegrim ['iːzəgrɪm], *m.* (—s, *pl.* —e) (*fable*) the wolf; a bear (with a sore head) (*also fig.*).
Island ['iːslant], *n.* Iceland.
isolieren [izo'liːrən], *v.a.* (*Electr.*) insulate; (*fig.*) isolate.
Isolierung [izo'liːruŋ], *f.* (—, *pl.* —en) (*Electr.*) insulation; (*fig.*) isolation.
Italien [i'taːljən], *n.* Italy.

J

J [jɔt], *n.* (—, *no pl.*) the letter J.
ja [jaː], *adv.*, *part.* yes; indeed, certainly; even; — *doch*, to be sure; — *freilich*, certainly.
Jacht [jaxt], *f.* (—, *pl.* —en) yacht.
Jacke ['jakə], *f.* (—, *pl.* —n) jacket, tunic.
Jackett [ja'kɛt], *n.* (—s, *pl.* —s) jacket, short coat.
Jagd [jaːkt], *f.* (—, *pl.* —en) hunt, hunting; shooting; chase.
Jagdhund ['jaːkthunt], *m.* (—es, *pl.* —e) retriever, setter; hound.
Jagdrevier ['jaːktreviːr], *n.* (—s, *pl.* —e) hunting-ground.
jagen ['jaːgən], *v.a.* hunt; chase; (*fig.*) tear along.
Jäger ['jɛːgər], *m.* (—s, *pl.* —) hunter, huntsman; game-keeper.
Jägerei [jɛːgə'raɪ], *f.* (—, *no pl.*) huntsmanship.
jäh [jɛː], *adj.* abrupt; steep, precipitous; (*fig.*) hasty, rash, sudden.
jählings ['jɛːlɪŋs], *adv.* abruptly, suddenly, hastily.
Jahr [jaːr], *n.* (—es, *pl.* —e) year.
jähren ['jɛːrən], *v.r. sich —*, (*anniversary*) come round.
Jahresfeier ['jaːrəsfaɪər], *f.* (—, *pl.* —n) anniversary.
Jahresrente ['jaːrəsrɛntə], *f.* (—, *pl.* —n) annuity.
Jahreszeit ['jaːrəstsaɪt], *f.* (—, *pl.* —en) season.
Jahrgang ['jaːrgaŋ], *m.* (—s, *pl.* ⸚e) age group; class; year of publication; vintage.
Jahrhundert [jaːr'hundərt], *n.* (—s, *pl.* —e) century.
jährig ['jɛːrɪç], *adj.* year-old.
jährlich ['jɛːrlɪç], *adj.* yearly, annual. — *adv.* every year.
Jahrmarkt ['jaːrmarkt], *m.* (—s, *pl.* ⸚e) annual fair.
Jahrtausend [jaːr'tauzənt], *n.* (—s, *pl.* —e) millennium.
Jahrzehnt [jaːr'tseːnt], *n.* (—s, *pl.* —e) decade.
Jähzorn ['jɛːtsɔrn], *m.* (—s, *no pl.*) irascibility.

Jalousie [ʒalu'zi:], *f.* (—, *pl.* —n) Venetian blind.

Jamaika [ja'maika], *n.* Jamaica.

Jambus ['jambus], *m.* (—, *pl.* —ben) (*Poet.*) iambic foot.

Jammer ['jamər], *m.* (—s, *no pl.*) lamentation; misery; (*fig.*) pity.

jämmerlich ['jɛmərlɪç], *adj.* lamentable, miserable, wretched, piteous.

jammerschade ['jamərʃa:də], *adv.* a thousand pities.

Jänner ['jɛnər] (*Austr.*) *see* **Januar.**

Januar ['janua:r], *m.* (—s, *pl.* —e) January.

Japan ['ja:pan], *n.* Japan.

Jaspis ['jaspɪs], *m.* (—ses, *pl.* —se) jasper.

jäten ['jɛ:tən], *v.a.* weed.

Jauche ['jauxə], *f.* (—, *pl.* —n) liquid manure.

jauchzen ['jauxtsən], *v.n.* exult, shout with joy.

Jauchzer ['jauxtsər], *m.* (—s, *pl.* —) shout of joy.

jawohl [ja'vo:l], *int.* yes, indeed! certainly, of course.

je [je:], *adv.* ever; at any time; at a time; each; *von — her,* always; — *nachdem,* it depends; — *zwei,* in twos; — *eher — besser,* the sooner the better.

jedenfalls ['je:dənfals], *adv.* at all events, in any case, at any rate, anyway.

jeder, -e, -es ['je:dər], *adj.* every, each; — *beliebige,* any. — *pron.* each, each one; everybody.

jederlei ['je:dərlai], *adj.* of every kind.

jedoch [je'dɔx], *adv.,* however, nevertheless, yet, notwithstanding.

jeglicher, -e, -es ['je:klɪçər], *adj.* every. each. — *pron.* every man, each.

jemals ['je:mals], *adv.* ever, at any time.

jemand ['je:mant], *pron.* somebody, someone; anybody, anyone.

Jemen ['je:mən], *n.* Yemen.

jener, -e, -es ['je:nər], *dem. adj.* that, (*Poet.*) yonder. — *dem. pron.* that one, the former.

Jenseits ['jenzaits], *n.* (—, *no pl.*) the next world, the hereafter, the life to come.

jenseits ['jenzaits], *prep.* (*Genit.*) on the other side, beyond.

jetzig ['jetsɪç], *adj.* present, now existing, current, extant.

jetzt [jetst], *adv.* now, at this time, at present.

jeweilig ['je:vailɪç], *adj.* momentary; actual, for the time being.

Joch [jɔx], *n.* (—es, *pl.* —e) yoke.

Jochbein ['jɔxbain], *n.* (—s, *pl.* —e) cheek-bone.

Jockei ['jɔkai], *m.* (—s, *pl.* —s) jockey.

Jod [jo:t], *n.* (—s, *no pl.*) iodine.

jodeln ['jo:dəln], *v.n.* yodel.

Jodler ['jo:dlər], *m.* (—s, *pl.* —) (*person*) yodeler; (*sound*) yodelling.

Johannisbeere [jo'hanɪsbe:rə], *f.* (—, *pl.* —n) (*Bot.*) red-currant.

Johannisfest [jo'hanɪsfɛst], *n.* (—s, *pl.* —e) Midsummer Day, St. John the Baptist's Day (June 24th).

Johanniskäfer [jo'hanɪskɛːfər], *m.* (—s, *pl.* —) (*Ent.*) glow-worm.

Johannisnacht [jo'hanɪsnaxt], *f.* (—, *pl.* —e) Midsummer Eve.

johlen ['jo:lən], *v.n.* bawl.

Joppe ['jɔpə], *f.* (—, *pl.* —n) shooting-jacket

Jota ['jo:ta], *n.* (—s, *pl.* —s) iota, jot.

Journalismus [ʒurna'lɪsmus], *m.* *see* **Journalistik.**

Journalistik [ʒurna'lɪstɪk], *f.* (—, *no pl.*) journalism.

jubeln ['ju:bəln], *v.n.* rejoice, exult.

Jubilar [ju:bi'la:r], *m.* (—s, *pl.* —e) person celebrating a jubilee.

Jubiläum [ju:bi'lɛ:um], *n.* (—s, *pl.* —läen) jubilee.

jubilieren [ju:bi'li:rən], *v.n.* exult, shout with glee.

juchhe [jux'he:], *excl.* hurrah!

Juchten ['juxtən], *m.* (—, *no pl.*) Russian leather.

jucken ['jukən], *v.a.* scratch. — *v.n.* itch.

Jude ['ju:də], *m.* (—n, *pl.* —n) Jew, Israelite.

Judentum ['ju:dəntu:m], *n.* (—s, *no pl.*) Judaism.

Judenviertel ['ju:dənfi:rtəl], *n.* (—s, *pl.* —) Jewish quarter, ghetto.

Jüdin ['jy:dɪn], *f.* (—, *pl.* —innen) Jewess.

jüdisch ['jy:dɪʃ], *adj.* Jewish.

Jugend ['ju:gənt], *f.* (—, *no pl.*) youth.

jugendlich ['ju:gəntlɪç], *adj.* youthful, juvenile.

Jugoslawien [ju:go'sla:vjən], *n.* Jugoslavia.

Julfest ['ju:lfɛst], *n.* (—es, *pl.* —e) Yule.

Juli ['ju:li], *m.* (—s, *pl.* —s) July.

jung [juŋ], *adj.* young.

Junge (1) ['juŋə], *m.* (—n, *pl.* —n) boy, lad.

Junge (2) ['juŋə], *n.* (—n, *pl.* —n) young animal.

jungenhaft ['juŋənhaft], *adj.* boyish.

Jünger ['jyŋər], *m.* (—s, *pl.* —) disciple, devotee, follower.

Jungfer ['juŋfər], *f.* (—, *pl.* —n) (*obs.*) virgin, maid, maiden; lady's maid.

jüngferlich ['jyŋfərlɪç], *adj.* maidenly, coy, prim.

Jungfrau ['juŋfrau], *f.* (—, *pl.* —en) virgin.

Junggeselle ['juŋgəzɛlə], *m.* (—n, *pl.* —n) bachelor; *eingefleischter —,* confirmed bachelor.

Jüngling ['jyŋlɪŋ], *m.* (—s, *pl.* —e) young man.

jüngst [jyŋst], *adv.* lately, recently.

Juni ['ju:ni], *m.* (—s, *pl.* —s) June.

Junker ['juŋkər], *m.* (—s, *pl.* —) country squire; titled landowner.

Jura ['ju:ra], *n. pl.* jurisprudence, law; (*Univ.*) — *studieren,* read law.

Jurisprudenz [ju:rɪspru'dɛnts], *f.* (—, *no pl.*) jurisprudence.

Jurist [ju:'rɪst], *m.* (—en, *pl.* —en) lawyer, jurist.

juristisch [ju:'rɪstɪʃ], *adj.* juridical; legal.

just [just], *adv.* just now.

Justiz [jus'ti:ts], *f.* (—, *no pl.*) administration of the law *or* of justice.

Justizrat [jus'ti:tsra:t], *m.* (—s, *pl.* ⸚e) (*Law*) Counsellor; King's (Queen's) Counsel.

Jute ['ju:tə], *f.* (—, *no pl.*) jute.

Juwel [ju've:l], *n.* (—s, *pl.* —en) jewel; (*pl.*) jewellery; (*Am.*) jewelry.

Juwelier [juvə'li:r], *m.* (—s, *pl.* —e) jeweller, goldsmith.

K

K [ka:], *n.* (—, *no pl.*) the letter K.

Kabel ['ka:bəl], *n.* (—s, *pl.* —) cable.

Kabeljau [kabəl'jau], *m.* (—s, *pl.* —e) (*Zool.*) cod, codfish.

kabeln [ka'bi:bəln], *v.n.* cable, send a cablegram.

Kabine [ka'bi:nə], *f.* (—, *pl.* —n) cabin, cubicle.

Kabinett [kabi'nɛt], *n.* (—s, *pl.* —e) closet; cabinet.

Kabinettsrat [kabi'nɛtsra:t], *m.* (—s, *pl.* ⸚e) cabinet *or* ministerial committee; political adviser.

Kabüse [ka'by:zə], *f.* (—, *pl.* —n) ship's galley.

Kachel ['kaxəl], *f.* (—, *pl.* —n) glazed tile.

Kadaver [ka'da:vər], *m.* (—s, *pl.* —) carrion, carcass; corpse.

Kadenz [ka'dɛnts], *f.* (—, *pl.* —en) (*Mus.*) cadenza.

Kadett [ka'dɛt], *m.* (—en, *pl.* —en) cadet.

Käfer ['kɛ:fər], *m.* (—s, *pl.* —) (*Ent.*) beetle, (*Am.*) bug.

Kaffee ['kafe], *m.* (—s, *no pl.*) coffee.

Käfig ['kɛ:fɪç], *m.* (—s, *pl.* —e) cage.

kahl [ka:l], *adj.* bald; (*trees*) leafless; (*landscape*) barren; — geschoren, close-cropped.

Kahn ['ka:n], *m.* (—s, *pl.* ⸚e) boat; punt.

Kai [kaɪ], *m.* (—s, *pl.* —s) quay, wharf, landing-place.

Kaimeister ['kaɪmaɪstər], *m.* (—s, *pl.* —) wharfinger.

Kaiser ['kaɪzər], *m.* (—s, *pl.* —) emperor; *um des —s Bart streiten,* quarrel about nothing.

kaiserlich ['kaɪzərlɪç], *adj.* imperial.

Kaiserschnitt ['kaɪzərʃnɪt], *m.* (—es, *pl.* —e) (*Med.*) Caesarean operation.

Kajüte [ka'jy:tə], *f.* (—, *pl.* —n) cabin.

Kakadu ['kakadu:], *m.* (—s, *pl.* —s) (*Orn.*) cockatoo.

Kakao [ka'ka:o], *m.* (—s, *no pl.*) cocoa.

Kalauer ['ka:lauər], *m.* (—s, *no pl.*) pun; stale joke.

Kalb [kalp], *n.* (—es, *pl.* ⸚er) calf; (*roe*) fawn; (*fig.*) colt, calf.

Kalbfleisch ['kalpflaɪʃ], *n.* (—es, *no pl.*) veal.

Kälberei [kɛlbə'raɪ], *f.* (—, *pl.* —en) friskiness.

kälbern ['kɛlbərn], *v.n.* frisk, frolic.

Kalbsbraten ['kalpsbra:tən], *m.* (—s, *pl.* —) roast veal.

Kalbshaxe ['kalpshaksə], *f.* (—, *pl.* —n) knuckle of veal.

Kalbskeule ['kalpskɔylə], *f.* (—, *pl.* —n) leg of veal.

Kalbsmilch ['kalpsmɪlç], *f.* (—, *no pl.*) sweetbread.

Kaldaunen [kal'daunən], *f. pl.* (*dial.*) tripe.

Kalesche [ka'lɛʃə], *f.* (—, *pl.* —n) chaise, light carriage.

Kali ['ka:li], *n.* (—s, *no pl.*) potash.

Kaliber [ka'li:bər], *n.* (—s, *pl.* —) calibre; (*fig.*) sort, quality.

kalibrieren [kali'bri:rən], *v.a.* (*Tech.*) calibrate, graduate, gauge.

Kalifornien [kali'fɔrnjən], *n.* California.

Kalium ['ka:ljum], *n.* (—s, *no pl.*) (*Chem.*) potassium.

Kalk [kalk], *m.* (—s, *pl.* —e) lime; *gebrannter —,* quicklime; *mit — bewerfen,* rough-cast.

kalkartig ['kalka:rtɪç], *adj.* calcareous.

Kalkbewurf ['kalkbəvurf], *m.* (—es, *pl.* ⸚e) coat of plaster.

kalken ['kalkən], *v.a.* whitewash; (*Agr.*) lime.

kalkig ['kalkɪç], *adj.* limy, calcareous.

kalkulieren [kalku'li:rən], *v.n.* calculate, reckon.

kalt [kalt], *adj.* cold, frigid; *mir ist —,* I am cold.

kaltblütig ['kaltbly:tɪç], *adj.* cold-blooded, cool.

Kälte ['kɛltə], *f.* (—, *no pl.*) cold, coldness.

Kaltschale ['kaltʃa:lə], *f.* (—, *pl.* —n) cold beer (*or* wine) soup.

Kambodscha [kam'bɔtʃa], *f.* Cambodia.

Kamee [ka'me:], *f.* (—, *pl.* —n) cameo.

Kamel [ka'me:l], *n.* (—s, *pl.* —e) (*Zool.*) camel.

Kamelziege [ka'me:ltsi:gə], *f.* (—, *pl.* —n) (*Zool.*) Angora-goat, llama.

Kamerad [kamə'ra:t], *m.* (—en, *pl.* —en) comrade, companion, mate.

Kameradschaft [kamə'ra:tʃaft], *f.* (—, *pl.* —en) comradeship, fellowship.

Kamerun [kamə'ru:n], *n.* the Cameroons.

Kamille [ka'mɪlə], *f.* (—, *pl.* —n) camomile.

Kamin [ka'mi:n], *m.* (—s, *pl.* —e) chimney; funnel; fireplace, fireside.

Kaminaufsatz [ka'mi:naufzats], *m.* (—es, *pl.* ⸚e) mantel-piece, over-mantel.

Kaminfeger [ka'mi:nfe:gər], *m.* (—s, *pl.* —) chimney-sweep.

117

Kaminsims [ka'mi:nzIms], *m.* or *n.* (—es, *pl.* —e) mantel-piece.

Kamm [kam], *m.* (—es, *pl.* ⁝e) comb; (*cock*) crest; (*mountains*) ridge.

kämmen ['kɛmən], *v.a.* comb; (*wool*) card.

Kammer ['kamər], *f.* (—, *pl.* —n) chamber, small room; (*Am.*) closet; (*authority*) board; (*Parl. etc.*) chamber.

Kammerdiener ['kamərdi:nər], *m.* (—s, *pl.* —) valet.

Kämmerer ['kɛmərər], *m.* (—s, *pl.* —) Chamberlain, Treasurer.

Kammergericht ['kamərgərɪçt], *n.* (—s, *pl.* —e) Supreme Court of Justice.

Kammergut ['kamərgu:t], *n.* (—s, *pl.* ⁝er) domain, demesne; crown land.

Kammerherr ['kamərhɛr], *m.* (—n, *pl.* —en) chamberlain.

Kammersänger ['kamərzɛŋər], *m.* (—s, *pl.* —) court singer; title given to prominent singers.

Kammgarn ['kamgarn], *n.* (—s, *no pl.*) worsted.

Kammwolle ['kamvɔlə], *f.* (—, *no pl.*) carded wool.

Kampagne [kam'panjə], *f.* (—, *pl.* —n) (*Mil.*) campaign.

Kämpe ['kɛmpə], *m.* (—n, *pl.* —n) (*Poet.*) champion, warrior; *alter* —, old campaigner.

Kampf [kampf], *m.* (—es, *pl.* ⁝e) combat, fight, struggle; (*fig.*) conflict.

kämpfen ['kɛmpfən], *v.n.* fight, combat, struggle.

Kampfer ['kampfər], *m.* (—s, *no pl.*) camphor.

Kämpfer ['kɛmpfər], *m.* (—s, *pl.* —) fighter, combatant.

kampfunfähig ['kampfunfɛ:ɪç], *adj.* (*Mil.*) disabled; — *machen*, disable, put out of action.

kampieren [kam'pi:rən], *v.n.* be encamped, camp.

Kanada ['kanada], *n.* Canada.

Kanal [ka'na:l], *m.* (—s, *pl.* ⁝e) (*natural*) channel; (*artificial*) canal; sewer; *der Ärmelkanal*, the English Channel.

kanalisieren [kanali'zi:rən], *v.a.* canalise; (*streets*) drain by means of sewers.

Kanapee ['kanape:], *n.* (—s, *pl.* —s) sofa, divan.

Kanarienvogel [ka'na:rjənfo:gəl], *m.* (—s, *pl.* ⁝) (*Orn.*) canary.

Kanarische Inseln [ka'na:rɪʃə 'ɪnzəln], *f.pl.* Canary Islands.

Kandare [kan'da:rə], *f.* (—, *pl.* —n) bridle, bit.

Kandelaber [kandə'la:bər], *m.* (—s, *pl.* —) candelabrum, chandelier.

kandidieren [kandi'di:rən], *v.n.* be a candidate (for), apply (for) (*post*); (*Parl.*) stand (for), (*Am.*) run (for election).

kandieren [kan'di:rən], *v.a.* candy.

Kandiszucker ['kandɪstsukər], *m.* (—, *no pl.*) sugar-candy.

Kanevas ['kanəvas], *m.* (—ses, *pl.* —se) canvas.

Känguruh ['kɛŋguru:], *n.* (—s, *pl.* —s) (*Zool.*) kangaroo.

Kaninchen [ka'ni:nçən], *n.* (—s, *pl.* —) (*Zool.*) rabbit.

Kaninchenbau [ka'ni:nçənbau], *m.* (—s, *pl.* —e) rabbit-warren, burrow.

Kanne ['kanə], *f.* (—, *pl.* —n) can, tankard, mug; jug; pot; quart.

Kannegießer ['kanəgi:sər], *m.* (—s, *pl.* —) pot-house politician.

kannelieren [kanə'li:rən], *v.a.* flute, channel.

Kannibale [kani'ba:lə], *m.* (—n, *pl.* —n) cannibal.

Kanoe [ka'nu:], *n. see* Kanu.

Kanone [ka'no:nə], *f.* (—, *pl.* —n) cannon, gun; *unter aller* —, beneath contempt; beneath criticism.

Kanonier [kano'ni:r], *m.* (—s, *pl.* —e) gunner.

Kanonikus [ka'no:nikus], *m.* (—, *pl.* —ker) canon, prebendary.

kanonisieren [kanoni'zi:rən], *v.a.* canonise.

Kante ['kantə], *f.* (—, *pl.* —n) edge, rim, brim, brink, ledge; (*cloth*) list, selvedge.

Kanten ['kantən], *m.* (—s, *pl.* —) (*bread*) crust.

kanten ['kantən], *v.a.* edge, tilt.

Kanthaken ['kantha:kən], *m.* (—s, *pl.* —) cant-hook; grapple; grappling hook.

kantig ['kantɪç], *adj.* angular.

Kantine [kan'ti:nə], *f.* (—, *pl.* —n) canteen, mess.

Kanton [kan'to:n], *m.* (—s, *pl.* —e) (*Swiss*) canton; district, region.

Kantonist [kanto'nɪst], *m.* (—en, *pl.* —en) *unsicherer* —, shifty fellow.

Kantor ['kantɔr], *m.* (—s, *pl.* —en) precentor; organist; cantor.

Kanu [ka'nu:], *n.* (—s, *pl.* —s) canoe.

Kanzel ['kantsəl], *f.* (—, *pl.* —n) pulpit; (*Aviat.*) cockpit.

Kanzlei [kants'lai], *f.* (—, *pl.* —en) office, secretariat; chancellery; chancery-office; lawyer's office.

Kanzleipapier [kants'laipapi:r], *n.* (—s, *no pl.*) foolscap (paper).

Kanzleistil [kants'laiʃti:l], *m.* (—s, *no pl.*) legal jargon.

Kanzler ['kantslər], *m.* (—s, *pl.* —) Chancellor.

Kanzlist [kants'lɪst], *m.* (—en, *pl.* —en) chancery clerk; copying clerk.

Kap [kap], *n.* (—s, *pl.* —s) (*Geog.*) cape, promontory.

Kapaun [ka'paun], *m.* (—s, *pl.* —e) capon.

Kapazität [kapatsi'tɛ:t], *f.* (—, *pl.* —en) capacity; (*fig.*) (*person*) authority.

Kapelle [ka'pɛlə], *f.* (—, *pl.* —n) chapel; (*Mus.*) band.

Kapellmeister [ka'pɛlmaistər], *m.* (—s, *pl.* —) (*Mus.*) band leader, conductor.

Kaper ['ka:pər], *f.* (—, *pl.* —n) (*Bot.*) caper.

kapern ['ka:pərn], *v.a.* capture, catch.
kapieren [ka'pi:rən], *v.a.* (*coll.*) understand, grasp.
Kapital [kapi'ta:l], *n.* (—s, *pl.* —ien) (*money*) capital, stock.
Kapitäl, Kapitell [kapɪ'tɛ:l, kapɪ'tɛl], *n.* (—s, *pl.* —e) (*Archit.*) capital.
Kapitalanlage [kapi'ta:lanla:gə], *f.* (—, *pl.* —n) investment.
kapitalisieren [kapitali'zi:rən], *v.a.* capitalise.
kapitalkräftig [kapi'ta:lkrɛftɪç], *adj.* wealthy, moneyed, affluent; (*business, firm*) sound.
Kapitalverbrechen [kapi'ta:lfɛrbrɛçən], *n.* (—s, *pl.* —) capital offence.
Kapitän [kapi'tɛ:n], *m.* (—s, *pl.* —e) captain (of a ship), master.
Kapitel [ka'pɪtəl], *n.* (—s, *pl.* —) chapter.
Kapitulation [kapitulats'jo:n], *f.* (—, *pl.* —en) surrender.
kapitulieren [kapitu'li:rən], *v.n.* surrender; capitulate.
Kaplan [kap'la:n], *m.* (—s, *pl.* ˙e) chaplain; assistant priest.
Kapotte [ka'pɔtə], *f.* (—, *pl.* —n) hood.
Kappe ['kapə], *f.* (—, *pl.* —n) cap, bonnet; (*shoe*) toe-cap.
Käppi ['kɛpi], *n.* (—s, *pl.* —s) military cap.
Kapriole [kapri'o:lə], *f.* (—, *pl.* —n) caper.
kaprizieren [kapri'tsi:rən], *v.r. sich auf etwas* —, set o.'s heart on s.th., be obstinate about s.th.
kapriziös [kapri'tsjø:s], *adj.* whimsical, capricious.
Kapsel ['kapzəl], *f.* (—, *pl.* —n) capsule.
kaputt [ka'put], *adj.* broken, ruined, done for; — *machen*, break, ruin.
Kapuze [ka'pu:tsə], *f.* (—, *pl.* —n) hood; monk's cowl.
Kapuziner [kapu'tsi:nər], *m.* (—s, *pl.* —) Capuchin (friar); (*coffee*) cappuccino.
Kapuzinerkresse [kapu'tsi:nərkrɛsə], *f.* (—, *no pl.*) (*Bot.*) nasturtium.
Karabiner [kara'bi:nər], *m.* (—s, *pl.* —) (*rifle*) carbine.
Karaffe [ka'rafə], *f.* (—, *pl.* —n) carafe; decanter.
Karambolage [karambo'la:ʒə], *f.* (—, *pl.* —n) collision; (*billiards*) cannon.
Karawane [kara'va:nə], *f.* (—, *pl.* —n) convoy; caravan.
Karbol [kar'bo:l], *n.* (—s, *no pl.*) carbolic acid.
Karbunkel [kar'buŋkəl], *m.* (—s, *pl.* —) (*Med.*) carbuncle.
Karfreitag [kar'fraita:k], *m.* Good Friday.
Karfunkel [kar'fuŋkəl], *m.* (—s, *pl.* —) (*Min.*) carbuncle.
karg [kark], *adj.* scant; meagre; parsimonious.
kargen ['kargən], *v.n.* be stingy, be niggardly.
kärglich ['kɛrklɪç], *adj.* sparing, scanty poor, paltry.

karieren [ka'ri:rən], *v.a.* chequer.
kariert [ka'ri:rt], *adj.* checked, chequered.
Karikatur [karika'tu:r], *f.* (—, *pl.* —en) caricature, cartoon.
karikieren [kari'ki:rən], *v.a.* caricature, distort.
Karl [karl], *m.* Charles; — *der Grosse*, Charlemagne.
Karmeliter [karme'li:tər], *m.* (—s, *pl.* —) Carmelite (friar).
karminrot [kar'mi:nro:t], *adj.* carmine.
karmoisin [karmoa'zi:n], *adj.* crimson.
Karneol [karne'o:l], *m.* (—s, *pl.* —e) (*Min.*) cornelian, carnelian.
Karneval ['karnəval], *m.* (—s, *pl.* —s) carnival; Shrovetide festivities.
Karnickel [kar'nɪkəl], *m.* (—s, *pl.* —) rabbit; *er war das* —, he was the scapegoat.
Kärnten ['kɛrntən], *n.* Carinthia.
Karo ['ka:ro], *n.* (—s, *pl.* —s) check, square; (*cards*) diamonds.
Karosse [ka'rɔsə], *f.* (—, *pl.* —n) statecoach.
Karosserie [karɔsə'ri:], *f.* (—, *pl.* —n) (*Motor.*) body(-work).
Karotte [ka'rɔtə], *f.* (—, *pl.* —n) (*Bot.*) carrot.
Karpfen ['karpfən], *m.* (—s, *pl.* —) (*fish*) carp.
Karre ['karə], *f.* (—, *pl.* —n) cart, wheelbarrow.
Karren ['karən], *m.* (—s, *pl.* —) cart, wheelbarrow, dray.
Karrete [ka're:tə], *f.* (—, *pl.* —n) (*Austr.*) rattletrap, rickety coach.
Karriere [ka'rjɛ:rə], *f.* (—, *pl.* —n) career; — *machen*, get on well.
Kärrner ['kɛrnər], *m.* (—s, *pl.* —) (*obs.*) carter.
Karst [karst], *m.* (—s, *pl.* —e) mattock.
Karthago [kar'ta:go], *n.* Carthage.
Kartätsche [kar'tɛ:tʃə], *f.* (—, *pl.* —n) grape-shot, shrapnel.
Kartäuser [kar'tɔyzər], *m.* (—s, *pl.* —) Carthusian (monk).
Karte ['kartə], *f.* (—, *pl.* —n) card; ticket; map; chart; (*pl.*) pack ((*Am.*) deck) of cards.
Kartei [kar'tai], *f.* (—, *pl.* —en) card index.
Kartell [kar'tɛl], *n.* (—s, *pl.* —e) cartel; ring; syndicate.
Kartoffel [kar'tɔfəl], *f.* (—, *pl.* —n) (*Bot.*) potato.
Kartoffelpuffer [kar'tɔfəlpufər], *m.* (—s, *pl.* —) potato-pancake.
Karton [kar'tɔŋ], *m.* (—s, *pl.* —s) carton, cardboard-box; (*material*) cardboard, paste-board; cartoon.
Kartusche [kar'tuʃə], *f.* (—, *pl.* —n) cartridge.
Karussell [karu'sɛl], *n.* (—s, *pl.* —e) merry-go-round; roundabout.
Karwoche ['ka:rvɔxə], *f.* Holy Week.
Karzer ['kartsər], *m.* (—s, *pl.* —) lock-up, prison.
Kaschmir ['kaʃmi:r], *m.* (—s, *no pl.*) cashmere.

Käse

Käse ['kɛːzə], *m.* (—s, *pl.* —) cheese.

käseartig ['kɛːzəaːrtɪç], *adj.* like cheese; caseous.

Kaserne [ka'zɛrnə], *f.* (—, *pl.* —n) barracks.

kasernieren [kazer'niːrən], *v.a.* put into barracks.

Käsestoff ['kɛːzəʃtɔf], *m.* (—s, *pl.* —e) casein.

käseweiß ['kɛːzəvaɪs], *adj.* deathly pale.

käsig ['kɛːzɪç], *adj.* cheese-like, cheesy, caseous; (*fig.*) sallow.

Kasperle ['kaspɛrlə], *n.* (—s, *pl.* —) Punch.

Kasperl(e)theater ['kaspərl(ə)teaːtər], *n.* (—s, *pl.* —) Punch-and-Judy show.

Kaspisches Meer ['kaspɪʃəsmeːr], *n.* Caspian Sea.

Kasse ['kasə], *f.* (—, *pl.* —n) money-box, till; cash-desk; box-office; **cash,** ready money.

Kassenanweisung ['kasənanvaɪzuŋ], *f.* (—, *pl.* —en) treasury-bill; cash voucher.

Kassenbuch ['kasənbuːx], *n.* (—es, *pl.* ∵er) cash-book.

Kassenschrank ['kasənʃraŋk], *m.* (—s, *pl.* ∵e) strong-box, safe.

Kasserolle [kasə'rɔlə], *f.* (—, *pl.* —n) stew-pot, casserole.

Kassette [ka'sɛtə], *f.* (—, *pl.* —n) deed-box; casket; (*Phot.*) plate-holder.

kassieren [ka'siːrən], *v.a.* cash, collect (money); cashier, annul, discharge.

Kassierer [ka'siːrər], *m.* (—s, *pl.* —) cashier; teller.

Kastagnette [kastan'jɛtə], *f.* (—, *pl.* —n) castanet.

Kastanie [ka'staːnjə], *f.* (—, *pl.* —n) (*Bot.*) chestnut, (*coll.*) conker; chestnut-tree.

Kästchen ['kɛstçən], *n.* (—s, *pl.* —) casket, little box.

Kaste ['kastə], *f.* (—, *pl.* —n) caste.

kasteien [ka'staɪən], *v.r. sich —,* castigate *or* mortify o.s.

Kastell [ka'stɛl], *n.* (—s, *pl.* —e) citadel, small fort; castle.

Kastellan [kastɛ'laːn], *m.* (—s, *pl.* —e) castellan; caretaker.

Kasten ['kastən], *m.* (—s, *pl.* ∵) box, chest, case, crate.

Kastengeist ['kastəngaɪst], *m.* (—es, *no pl.*) exclusiveness; class consciousness.

Kastilien [ka'stiːljən], *n.* Castile.

Kastrat [ka'straːt], *m.* (—en, *pl.* —en) eunuch.

kastrieren [ka'striːrən], *v.a.* castrate.

Katafalk [kata'falk], *m.* (—s, *pl.* —e) catafalque.

katalogisieren [katalogi'ziːrən], *v.a.* catalogue.

Katarakt [kata'rakt], *m.* (—es, *pl.* —e) cataract; waterfall.

Katasteramt [ka'tastəramt], *n.* (—es, *pl.* ∵er) land-registry office.

katechisieren [kateçi'ziːrən], *v.a.* catechise, instruct.

kategorisch [kate'goːrɪʃ], *adj.* categorical, definite.

Kater ['kaːtər], *m.* (—s, *pl.* —) tom-cat; (*fig.*) hangover; *der gestiefelte —,* Puss-in-Boots.

Katheder [ka'teːdər], *n.* (—s, *pl.* —) desk; rostrum; lecturing-desk; (*fig.*) professorial chair.

Kathedrale [kate'draːlə], *f.* (—, *pl.* —n) cathedral.

Katholik [kato'liːk], *m.* (—en, *pl.* —en) (Roman) Catholic.

katholisch [ka'toːlɪʃ], *adj.* (Roman) Catholic.

Kattun [ka'tuːn], *m.* (—s, *pl.* —e) calico, cotton.

Kätzchen ['kɛtsçən], *n.* (—s, *pl.* —) kitten; (*Bot.*) catkin.

Katze ['katsə], *f.* (—, *pl.* —n) cat; *die — im Sack kaufen,* buy a pig in a poke; *für die —,* no good at all, useless.

katzenartig ['katsənaːrtɪç], *adj.* cat-like, feline.

Katzenauge ['katsənaugə], *n.* (—s, *pl.* —n) cat's-eye.

Katzenbuckel ['katsənbukəl], *m.* (—s, *pl.* —) arched back of a cat.

Katzenjammer ['katsənjamər], *m.* (—s, *pl.* —) hangover.

Katzenmusik ['katsənmuziːk], *f.* (—, *no pl.*) caterwauling; cacophony, discordant music.

Katzensprung ['katsənʃpruŋ], *m.* (—es, *no pl.*) (*fig.*) stone's throw.

Kauderwelsch ['kaudərvɛlʃ], *n.* (—es, *no pl.*) gibberish, double-Dutch.

kauen ['kauən], *v.a., v.n.* chew.

kauern ['kauərn], *v.n.* cower, squat, crouch.

Kauf [kauf], *m.* (—es, *pl.* ∵e) purchase, buy; bargain.

Kaufbummel ['kaufbuməl], *m.* (—s, *no pl.*) shopping-spree.

kaufen ['kaufən], *v.a.* (*things*) buy, purchase; (*persons*) bribe.

Käufer ['kɔyfər], *m.* (—s, *pl.* —) buyer, purchaser.

Kaufhaus ['kaufhaus], *n.* (—es, *pl.* ∵er) department-store, emporium.

Kaufladen ['kaufla:dən], *m.* (—s, *pl.* ∵) shop.

käuflich ['kɔyflɪç], *adj.* (*things*) purchasable, marketable; (*persons*) open to bribery, venal.

Kaufmann ['kaufman], *m.* (—s, *pl.* **Kaufleute**) merchant; shopkeeper; (*Am.*) store-keeper.

kaufmännisch ['kaufmɛnɪʃ], *adj.* commercial, mercantile.

Kaugummi ['kaugumi], *m.* (—s, *no pl.*) chewing-gum.

Kaukasus ['kaukazus], *m.* Caucasus (Mountains).

Kaulquappe ['kaulkvapə], *f.* (—, *pl.* —n) (*Zool.*) tadpole.

kaum [kaum], *adv.* scarcely, hardly; no sooner.

Kaurimuschel ['kaurimuʃəl], *f.* (—, *pl.* —n) (*Zool.*) cowrie-shell.

Kautabak ['kautabak], m. (—s, no pl.) chewing-tobacco.

Kaution [kau'tsjo:n], f. (—, pl. —en) security, bail, surety; *eine — stellen*, go, give *or* stand bail.

Kautschuk ['kautʃuk], m. (—s, no pl.) caoutchouc, India-rubber.

Kauz [kauts], m. (—es, pl. ⁏e) (*Orn.*) screech-owl; (*fig.*) *komischer —*, queer customer.

Käuzchen ['kɔytsçən], n. (—s, pl. —) little owl; (*fig.*) imp.

Kavalier [kava'li:r], m. (—s, pl. —e) gentleman; lady's man.

keck [kɛk], adj. bold, daring; pert, saucy.

Kegel ['ke:gəl], m. (—s, pl. —) ninepin, skittle; (*Geom.*) cone; *mit Kind und —*, bag and baggage.

Kegelbahn ['ke:gəlba:n], f. (—, pl. —en) skittle-alley, bowling-alley.

kegelförmig ['ke:gəlfœrmiç], adj. conical.

kegeln ['ke:gəln], v.n. bowl, play at ninepins.

Kehle ['ke:lə], f. (—, pl. —n) throat, windpipe.

Kehlkopf ['ke:lkɔpf], m. (—es, pl. ⁏e) larynx.

Kehllaut ['ke:llaut], m. (—es, pl. —e) (*Phonet.*) guttural sound.

Kehlung ['ke:luŋ], f. (—, pl. —en) channel, flute, groove.

Kehraus ['ke:raus], m. (—, no pl.) last dance; (*fig.*) break-up, end.

kehren ['ke:rən], v.a. sweep; turn; *den Rücken —*, turn o.'s back. — v.r. *sich — an*, pay attention to, regard.

Kehricht ['ke:riçt], m. (—s, no pl.) sweepings; rubbish.

Kehrreim ['ke:rraim], m. (—s, pl. —e) refrain.

Kehrseite ['ke:rzaitə], f. (—, pl. —n) reverse.

kehrtmachen ['ke:rtmaxən], v.n. turn around; (*Mil.*) face about; turn back.

keifen ['kaifən], v.n. scold, nag.

Keil [kail], m. (—s, pl. —e) wedge.

Keile ['kailə], f. (—, no pl.) blows; (*coll.*) hiding; *— kriegen*, get a thrashing.

keilen ['kailən], v.a. wedge; (*coll.*) thrash.

Keilerei [kailə'rai], f. (—, pl. —en) brawl, fight.

keilförmig ['kailfœrmiç], adj. wedge-shaped.

Keilschrift ['kailʃrift], f. (—, pl. —en) cuneiform writing.

Keim [kaim], m. (—es, pl. —e) germ, seed.

keimen ['kaimən], v.n. germinate.

keimfrei ['kaimfrai], adj. sterile, germ-free.

keiner, -e, -es ['kainər], adj. no, not a, not any. — pron. no one, none.

keinerlei ['kainərlai], adj. no, of no sort, no … whatever.

keineswegs ['kainəsve:ks], adv. by no means, on no account.

Keks [ke:ks], m. (—es, pl. —e) biscuit.

Kelch [kɛlç], m. (—es, pl. —e) cup; (*Eccl.*) chalice; (*Bot.*) calyx.

Kelchblatt ['kɛlçblat], n. (—es, pl. ⁏er) sepal.

kelchförmig ['kɛlçfœrmiç], adj. cup-shaped.

Kelle ['kɛlə], f. (—, pl. —n) ladle; (*mason*) trowel.

Keller ['kɛlər], m. (—s, pl. —) cellar, basement.

Kellergewölbe ['kɛlərgəvœlbə], n. (—s, pl. —) vault.

Kellner ['kɛlnər], m. (—s, pl. —) waiter.

keltern ['kɛltərn], v.a. press (*grapes*).

Kenia ['ke:nja], n. Kenya.

kennbar ['kɛnba:r], adj. recognisable, conspicuous.

kennen ['kɛnən], v.a. irr. know, be acquainted with.

Kenner ['kɛnər], m. (—s, pl. —) connoisseur, expert.

Kennkarte ['kɛnkartə], f. (—, pl. —n) identity card.

kenntlich ['kɛntliç], adj. distinguishable.

Kenntnis ['kɛntnis], f. (—, pl. —se) knowledge; (*language*) command.

Kennzeichen ['kɛntsaiçən], n. (—s, pl. —) characteristic, distinguishing mark; sign; symptom; criterion.

Kenterhaken ['kɛntərha:kən], m. (—s, pl. —) grappling-iron.

kentern ['kɛntərn], v.n. (*aux.* sein) capsize.

keramisch [ke'ra:miʃ], adj. ceramic.

Kerbe ['kɛrbə], f. (—, pl. —n) notch, indentation.

kerben ['kɛrbən], v.a. notch.

Kerbholz ['kɛrphɔlts], n. (—es, no pl.) tally; *auf dem —*, on o.'s conscience, charged against o.

Kerbtier ['kɛrpti:r], n. (—es, pl. —e) insect.

Kerker ['kɛrkər], m. (—s, pl. —) prison, jail, gaol; dungeon.

Kerl [kɛrl], m. (—s, pl. —e) fellow, chap; (*Am.*) guy.

Kern [kɛrn], m. (—es, pl. —e) (*nut*) kernel; (*fruit*) stone; (*fig.*) heart, crux; pith; (*Phys.*) nucleus.

kerngesund ['kɛrngəzunt], adj. hale and hearty, fit as a fiddle.

kernig ['kɛrniç], adj. solid, pithy.

Kernphysik ['kɛrnfyzi:k], f. (—, no pl.) nuclear physics.

Kernpunkt ['kɛrnpunkt], m. (—es, pl. —e) gist, essential point.

Kernwaffe ['kɛrnvafə], f. (—, pl. —n) nuclear weapon.

Kerze ['kɛrtsə], f. (—, pl. —n) candle.

Kessel ['kɛsəl], m. (—s, pl. —) kettle, cauldron; (*steam*) boiler.

Kesselschmied ['kɛsəlʃmi:t], m. (—s, pl. —e) boiler-maker.

Kesselstein ['kɛsəlʃtain], m. (—s, no pl.) fur, deposit, scale (on boiler).

Kette ['kɛtə], f. (—, pl. —n) chain.

ketten ['kɛtən], v.a. chain, fetter.

Kettenstich ['kɛtənʃtiç], m. (—es, pl. —e) chain-stitch; (*Naut.*) chain-knot.

Ketzer ['kɛtsər], *m.* (—s, *pl.* —) heretic.
Ketzerei [kɛtsə'raɪ], *f.* (—, *pl.* —en)
heresy.
ketzerisch ['kɛtsərɪʃ], *adj.* heretical.
keuchen ['kɔyçən], *v.n.* pant, puff,
gasp.
Keuchhusten ['kɔyçhu:stən], *m.* (—s,
no pl.) whooping-cough.
Keule ['kɔylə], *f.* (—, *pl.* —n) club;
(*meat*) leg.
keusch [kɔyʃ], *adj.* chaste, pure.
kichern ['kɪçərn], *v.n.* titter, giggle.
Kiebitz ['ki:bɪts], *m.* (—es, *pl.* —e)
(*Orn.*) lapwing, peewit; (*fig.*) onlooker; (*Am.*) rubber-neck (at chess
or cards).
Kiefer (1) ['ki:fər], *m.* (—s, *pl.* —)
jaw, jaw-bone.
Kiefer (2) ['ki:fər], *f.* (—, *pl.* —n)
(*Bot.*) pine.
Kiel [ki:l], *m.* (—es, *pl.* —e) keel; (*pen*)
quill.
Kielwasser ['ki:lvasər], *n.* (—s, *no pl.*)
wake.
Kieme ['ki:mə], *f.* (—, *pl.* —n) (*fish*)
gill.
Kien [ki:n], *m.* (—s, *no pl.*) pine-resin,
resinous pinewood.
Kienspan ['ki:nʃpa:n], *m.* (—s, *pl.* ⸚e)
pine-splinter.
Kiepe ['ki:pə], *f.* (—, *pl.* —n) (*dial.*)
creel, wicker basket.
Kies [ki:s], *m.* (—es, *no pl.*) gravel.
Kiesel ['ki:zəl], *m.* (—s, *pl.* —) pebble;
flint.
Kieselsäure ['ki:zəlzɔyrə], *f.* (—, *no
pl.*) silicic acid.
Kieselstein ['ki:zəlʃtaɪn], *m.* (—s,
pl. —e) pebble.
Kilogramm ['ki:logram], *n.* (—s, *pl.*
—e) kilogramme (1000 grammes).
Kilometer ['ki:lome:tər], *m.* (—s, *pl.*
—) kilometre; (*Am.*) kilometer (1000
metres).
Kimme ['kɪmə], *f.* (—, *pl.* —n) notch.
Kind [kɪnt], *n.* (—es, *pl.* —er) child;
(*law*) infant; — *und Kegel*, bag and
baggage.
Kind(e)l ['kɪnd(ə)l], *n.* (—s, *pl.* —)
(*dial.*) small child, baby; *Münchner* —,
Munich beer.
Kinderei [kɪndə'raɪ], *f.* (—, *pl.* —en)
childishness; childish prank.
Kinderfräulein ['kɪndərfrɔylaɪn], *n.*
(—s, *pl.* —) nurse, (*coll.*) nannie.
Kindergarten ['kɪndərgartən], *m.* (—s,
pl. ⸚) kindergarten, infant-school.
Kinderhort ['kɪndərhɔrt], *m.* (—s,
pl. —e) crèche.
kinderleicht ['kɪndərlaɪçt], *adj.* extremely easy, child's play.
Kindermärchen ['kɪndərmɛːrçən], *n.*
(—s, *pl.* —) fairy-tale.
Kinderstube ['kɪndərʃtu:bə], *f.* (—,
pl. —n) nursery; *eine gute* —, a good
upbringing.
Kinderwagen ['kɪndərva:gən], *m.* (—s,
pl. —) perambulator, pram.
Kindesbeine ['kɪndəsbaɪnə], *n. pl. von
—n an*, from infancy.

Kindeskind ['kɪndəskɪnt], *n.* (—es, *pl.*
—er) (*obs.*) grandchild.
Kindheit ['kɪnthaɪt], *f.* (—, *no pl.*)
childhood, infancy.
kindisch ['kɪndɪʃ], *adj.* childish.
kindlich ['kɪntlɪç], *adj.* childlike;
naive.
Kinn [kɪn], *n.* (—s, *pl.* —e) chin.
Kinnbacken ['kɪnbakən], *m.* (—s,
pl. —) (*Anat.*) jaw-bone.
Kinnbackenkrampf ['kɪnbakən-
krampf], *m.* (—s, *pl.* ⸚e) (*Med.*)
lock-jaw.
Kinnlade ['kɪnla:də], *f.* (—, *pl.* —n)
(*Anat.*) jaw-bone.
Kino ['ki:no], *n.* (—s, *pl.* —s) cinema;
(*coll.*) pictures; (*Am.*) motion picture
theatre; motion pictures, (*coll.*)
movies.
Kipfel ['kɪpfəl], *n.* (—s, *pl.* —) (*dial.*)
roll, croissant.
kippen ['kɪpən], *v.a.* tilt, tip over.
Kirche ['kɪrçə], *f.* (—, *pl.* —n) church.
Kirchenbann ['kɪrçənban], *m.* (—s,
no. pl.) excommunication.
Kirchenbuch ['kɪrçənbu:x], *n.* (—es,
pl. ⸚er) parish-register.
Kirchengut ['kɪrçəngu:t], *n.* (—es,
pl. ⸚er) church-property.
Kirchenlicht ['kɪrçənlɪçt], *n.* (—es,
pl. —er) (*fig.*) shining light, bright
spark.
Kirchenrecht ['kɪrçənrɛçt], *n.* (—es,
no pl.) canon law.
Kirchenschiff ['kɪrçənʃɪf], *n.* (—es,
pl. —e) nave.
Kirchenstuhl ['kɪrçənʃtu:l], *m.* (—es,
pl. ⸚e) pew.
Kirchenversammlung ['kɪrçənfer-
zamluŋ], *f.* (—, *pl.* —en) synod,
convocation.
Kirchenvorsteher ['kɪrçənforʃte:ər], *m.*
(—s, *pl.* —) churchwarden.
kirchlich ['kɪrçlɪç], *adj.* ecclesiastic(al),
religious.
Kirchspiel ['kɪrçʃpi:l], *n.* (—es, *pl.*
—e) parish.
Kirchsprengel ['kɪrçʃprɛŋəl], *m.* (—s,
pl. —) diocese.
Kirchturm ['kɪrçturm], *m.* (—es, *pl.*
⸚e) steeple.
Kirchweih ['kɪrçvaɪ], *f.* (—, *pl.* —en)
(*dial.*) church fair, parish fair.
Kirmes ['kɪrmɛs], *f.* (—, *pl.* —sen) *see*
Kirchweih.
kirre ['kɪrə], *adj.* tame; (*fig.*) amenable.
kirren ['kɪrən], *v.a.* tame, allure. —
v.n. coo.
Kirsch(branntwein) [kɪrʃ(brantvaɪn)],
m. (—s, *no pl.*) cherry-brandy.
Kirsche ['kɪrʃə], *f.* (—, *pl.* —n) (*Bot.*)
cherry; *mit ihr ist nicht gut — n essen*,
she is hard to get on with or not
pleasant to deal with.
Kirschsaft ['kɪrʃzaft], *m.* (—es, *no
pl.*) cherry-juice.
Kirschwasser ['kɪrʃvasər], *n.* (—s, *no
pl.*) cherry-brandy.
Kissen ['kɪsən], *n.* (—s, *pl.* —) cushion,
pillow.

Kiste ['kɪstə], *f.* (—, *pl.* —n) box, case, chest; crate; coffer.

Kitsch [kɪtʃ], *m.* (—es, *no pl.*) trash; rubbish.

Kitt [kɪt], *m.* (—s, *pl.* —e) cement; (*Glazing*) putty.

Kittel ['kɪtəl], *m.* (—s, *pl.* —) smock; overall, tunic; frock.

kitten ['kɪtən], *v.a.* cement, glue.

Kitzchen ['kɪtsçən], *n.* (—s, *pl.* —) kid; fawn; kitten.

Kitzel ['kɪtsəl], *m.* (—s, *no pl.*) tickling, titillation; itch; (*fig.*) desire, appetite.

kitzeln ['kɪtsəln], *v.a.* tickle, titillate.

kitzlich ['kɪtslɪç], *adj.* ticklish; (*fig.*) delicate.

Kladderadatsch ['kladəradatʃ], *m.* (—es, *no pl.*) bang; mess, muddle.

klaffen ['klafən], *v.n.* gape, yawn.

kläffen ['klɛfən], *v.n.* bark, yelp.

Klafter ['klaftər], *f.* (—, *pl.* —n) fathom; (*wood*) cord.

klagbar ['kla:kba:r], *adj.* (*Law*) actionable.

Klage ['kla:gə], *f.* (—, *pl.* —n) complaint; (*Law*) suit, action.

Klagelied ['kla:gəli:t], *n.* (—es, *pl.* —er) dirge, lamentation.

klagen ['kla:gən], *v.n.* complain, lament; (*Law*) sue.

Kläger ['klɛ:gər], *m.* (—s, *pl.* —) complainant; (*Law*) plaintiff.

Klageschrift ['kla:gəʃrɪft], *f.* (—, *pl.* —en) bill of indictment; written complaint.

kläglich ['klɛ:klɪç], *adj.* woeful, pitiful, deplorable.

klaglos ['kla:klo:s], *adj.* uncomplaining.

Klamm [klam], *f.* (—, *pl.* —en) gorge, ravine.

klamm [klam], *adj.* tight, narrow; numb; clammy.

Klammer ['klamər], *f.* (—, *pl.* —n) clamp, clasp, hook; peg; clip; bracket, parenthesis.

klammern ['klamərn], *v.a.* fasten, peg. — *v.r. sich — an*, cling to.

Klang [klaŋ], *m.* (—es, *pl.* —e) sound, tone; *ohne Sang und —*, unheralded and unsung.

klanglos ['klaŋlo:s], *adj.* soundless.

klangnachahmend ['klaŋnaxa:mənt], *adj.* onomatopoeic.

klangvoll ['klaŋfɔl], *adj.* sonorous.

Klappe ['klapə], *f.* (—, *pl.* —en) flap; (*Tech.*) valve; (*vulg.*) *halt die —!* shut up!

klappen ['klapən], *v.n.* flap; (*fig.*) tally, square; *es hat geklappt*, it worked.

Klapper ['klapər], *f.* (—, *pl.* —n) rattle.

klappern ['klapərn], *v.n.* rattle; (*teeth*) chatter.

Klapperschlange ['klapərʃlaŋə], *f.* (—, *pl.* —n) (*Zool.*) rattle-snake.

Klapphut ['klaphu:t], *m.* (—es, *pl.* ˙˙e) opera-hat; chapeau-claque.

Klapps [klaps], *m.* (—es, *pl.* ˙˙e) slap, smack; (*fig.*) touch of madness, kink.

Klappstuhl ['klapʃtu:l], *m.* (—s, *pl.* ˙˙e) camp-stool, folding-chair.

Klapptisch ['klaptɪʃ], *m.* (—es, *pl.* —e) folding-table.

klar [kla:r], *adj.* clear; bright; (*fig.*) evident; plain, distinct.

Kläranlage ['klɛ:ranla:gə], *f.* (—, *pl.* —n) sewage-farm; filter plant.

klären ['klɛ:rən], *v.a.* clear.

Klarheit ['kla:rhaɪt], *f.* (—, *no pl.*) clearness, plainness.

Klarinette [klari'nɛtə], *f.* (—, *pl.* —n) (*Mus.*) clarinet.

Klärmittel ['klɛ:rmɪtəl], *n.* (—s, *pl.* —) clarifier.

Klärung ['klɛ:ruŋ], *f.* (—, *pl.* —en) clarification; (*fig.*) elucidation.

Klasse ['klasə], *f.* (—, *pl.* —n) class, order; (*Sch.*) form.

klassifizieren [klasifi'tsi:rən], *v.a.* classify.

Klassiker ['klasɪkər], *m.* (—s, *pl.* —) classic.

klassisch ['klasɪʃ], *adj.* classic(al), standard.

Klatsch [klatʃ], *m.* (—es, *no pl.*) gossip, scandal.

klatschen ['klatʃən], *v.n.* clap; gossip; (*rain*) patter; *Beifall —*, applaud.

Klatscherei [klatʃə'raɪ], *f.* (—, *pl.* —en) gossip, scandalmongering.

klauben ['klaubən], *v.a.* pick.

Klaue ['klauə], *f.* (—, *pl.* —n) claw, talon; paw.

klauen ['klauən], *v.a.* steal, (*coll.*) pinch.

Klauenseuche ['klauənzɔyçə], *f.* (—, *pl.* —n) *Maul und —*, foot and mouth disease.

Klause ['klauzə], *f.* (—, *pl.* —n) cell, hermitage; (*coll.*) den.

Klausel ['klauzəl], *f.* (—, *pl.* —n) clause, paragraph.

Klausner ['klausnər], *m.* (—s, *pl.* —) hermit, recluse, anchorite.

Klausur [klau'zu:r], *f.* (—, *pl.* —en) seclusion; written examination.

Klaviatur [klavja'tu:r], *f.* (—, *pl.* —en) keyboard.

Klavier [kla'vi:r], *n.* (—s, *pl.* —e) piano, pianoforte.

Klavierstück [kla'vi:rʃtyk], *n.* (—s, *pl.* —e) piece of piano music.

Klebemittel ['kle:bəmɪtəl], *n.* (—s, *pl.* —) adhesive, glue.

kleben ['kle:bən], *v.a.* paste, stick, glue. — *v.n.* stick, adhere.

klebrig ['kle:brɪç], *adj.* sticky; clammy.

Klebstoff ['kle:pʃtɔf], *m.* (—es, *no pl.*) gum; glue.

Klecks [klɛks], *m.* (—es, *pl.* —e) blot; blotch.

Kleckser ['klɛksər], *m.* (—s, *pl.* —) scrawler; (*painter*) dauber.

Klee [kle:], *m.* (—s, *no pl.*) (*Bot.*) clover, trefoil.

Kleid [klaɪt], *n.* (—es, *pl.* —er) frock, garment, dress, gown; (*Poet.*) garb; (*pl.*) clothes; *—er machen Leute*, clothes make the man.

Kleidchen ['klaɪtçən], *n.* (—s, *pl.* —) child's dress.

kleiden ['klaɪdən], *v.a.* dress, clothe.

Kleiderbügel

Kleiderbügel [ˈklaɪdərbyːgəl], *m.* (—s, *pl.* —) coat-hanger.
Kleiderpuppe [ˈklaɪdərpupə], *f.* (—, *pl.* —n) tailor's dummy.
Kleiderschrank [ˈklaɪdərʃraŋk], *m.* (—s, *pl.* Ꞌꞌe) wardrobe.
kleidsam [ˈklaɪtzaːm], *adj.* becoming; well-fitting, a good fit.
Kleidung [ˈklaɪduŋ], *f.* (—, *no pl.*) clothing, clothes, dress.
Kleie [ˈklaɪə], *f.* (—, *no pl.*) bran.
klein [klaɪn], *adj.* little, small; minute; petty; *ein — wenig,* a little bit.
Kleinasien [klaɪnˈaːzjən], *n.* Asia Minor.
Kleinbahn [ˈklaɪnbaːn], *f.* (—, *pl.* —en) narrow-gauge railway.
kleinbürgerlich [ˈklaɪnbyrgərliç], *adj.* (petit) bourgeois.
Kleingeld [ˈklaɪngɛlt], *n.* (—(e)s, *no pl.*) small change.
kleingläubig [ˈklaɪnglɔybɪç], *adj.* faint-hearted.
Kleinhandel [ˈklaɪnhandəl], *m.* (—s, *no pl.*) retail-trade.
Kleinigkeit [ˈklaɪnɪçkaɪt], *f.* (—, *pl.* —en) trifle, small matter.
Kleinkram [ˈklaɪnkraːm], *m.* (—s, *no pl.*) trifles.
kleinlaut [ˈklaɪnlaut], *adj.* subdued, dejected, low-spirited.
kleinlich [ˈklaɪnlɪç], *adj.* petty; mean; narrow-minded; pedantic.
Kleinmut [ˈklaɪnmuːt], *m.* (—es, *no pl.*) faint-heartedness; dejection.
Kleinod [ˈklaɪnoːt], *n.* (—s, *pl.* —ien) jewel; trinket.
Kleinstadt [ˈklaɪnʃtat], *f.* (—, *pl.* Ꞌꞌe) small town.
Kleister [ˈklaɪstər], *m.* (—s, *no pl.*) paste.
Klemme [ˈklɛmə], *f.* (—, *pl.* —n) (*Tech.*) vice; clamp; (*fig.*) difficulty, straits; (*coll.*) fix, jam.
klemmen [ˈklɛmən], *v.a.* pinch, squeeze, jam.
Klemmer [ˈklɛmər], *m.* (—s, *pl.*—) (*eye*) glasses, pince-nez.
Klempner [ˈklɛmpnər], *m.* (—s, *pl.*—) tin-smith; plumber.
Klerus [ˈkleːrus], *m.* (—, *no pl.*) clergy.
Klette [ˈklɛtə], *f.* (—, *pl.* —n) burdock, bur(r); (*fig.*) hanger-on.
klettern [ˈklɛtərn], *v.n.* (*aux.* sein) climb, clamber.
Klima [ˈkliːma], *n.* (—s, *pl.* —s) climate.
Klimaanlage [ˈkliːmaanlaːgə], *f.* (—, *pl.* —n) air conditioning plant.
Klimbim [ˈklɪmˈbɪm], *m.* (—s, *no pl.*) goings-on; festivity; fuss; *der ganze —,* the whole caboodle.
klimpern [ˈklɪmpərn], *v.n.* (*piano*) strum; (*money*) jingle.
Klinge [ˈklɪŋə], *f.* (—, *pl.* —n) blade.
Klingel [ˈklɪŋəl], *f.* (—, *pl.* —n) (*door, telephone*) bell.
Klingelbeutel [ˈklɪŋəlbɔytəl], *m.* (—s, *pl.*—) collecting-bag.
klingeln [ˈklɪŋəln], *v.n.* ring, tinkle.

Klingelzug [ˈklɪŋəltsuːk], *m.* (—es, *pl.* Ꞌꞌe) bell-rope, bell-pull.
klingen [ˈklɪŋən], *v.n. irr.* sound; (*metals*) clang; (*ears*) tingle; *—de Münze,* hard cash, ready money.
Klinke [ˈklɪŋkə], *f.* (—, *pl.* —en) (*door*) handle, latch.
klipp [klɪp], *adv. — und klar,* as clear as daylight.
Klippe [ˈklɪpə], *f.* (—, *pl.* —n) cliff, crag, rock.
klirren [ˈklɪrən], *v.n.* clatter, rattle.
Klischee [kliˈʃeː], *n.* (—s, *pl.* —s) (*Typ.*) plate, printing-block; (*fig.*) cliché, hackneyed expression, tag.
Klistier [klɪˈstiːr], *n.* (—s, *pl.* —e) (*Med.*) enema.
Kloake [kloˈaːkə], *f.* (—, *pl.* —n) sewer, drain.
Kloben [ˈkloːbən], *m.* (—s, *pl.* —) log, block (of wood); pulley.
klopfen [ˈklɔpfən], *v.a., v.n.* knock, beat.
Klöppel [ˈklœpəl], *m.* (—s, *pl.* —) mallet; (*bell*) tongue, clapper; (*drum*) stick; (*lace*) bobbin.
klöppeln [ˈklœpəln], *v.a* make (bone) lace.
Klöppelspitze [ˈklœpəlʃpɪtsə], *f.* (—, *no pl.*) bone-lace.
Klops [klɔps], *m.* (—es, *pl.* —e) meat-dumpling.
Klosett [kloˈzɛt], *n.* (—s, *pl.* —e) lavatory, water-closet, toilet.
Kloß [kloːs], *m.* (—es, *pl.* Ꞌꞌe) dumpling.
Kloster [ˈkloːstər], *n.* (—s, *pl.* Ꞌꞌ) cloister; monastery; convent.
Klostergang [ˈkloːstərgaŋ], *m.* (—es, *pl.* Ꞌꞌe) cloisters.
Klotz [klɔts], *m.* (—es, *pl.* Ꞌꞌe) block, trunk, stump; (*fig.*) *ein grober —,* a great lout.
klotzig [ˈklɔtsɪç], *adj.* cloddy; lumpish; (*sl.*) enormous.
Klub [klup], *m.* (—s, *pl.* —s) club.
Kluft [kluft], *f.* (—, *pl.* Ꞌꞌe) gap; gulf, chasm; (*fig.*) cleavage.
klug [kluːk], *adj.* clever, wise, prudent; judicious, sagacious; *ich kann daraus nicht — werden,* I cannot make head nor tail of it.
klügeln [ˈklyːgəln], *v.n.* ponder; quibble.
Klugheit [ˈkluːkhaɪt], *f.* (—, *no pl.*) cleverness, wisdom, prudence, judiciousness.
Klumpfuß [ˈklumpfuːs], *m.* (—es, *pl.* Ꞌꞌe) club-foot.
Klumpen [ˈklumpən], *m.* (—s, *pl.* —) lump, mass, clod; (*blood*) clot; (*metal*) ingot; (*gold*) nugget.
Klüngel [ˈklyŋəl], *m.* (—s, *pl.* —) clique, set.
knabbern [ˈknabərn], *v.n.* nibble.
Knabe [ˈknaːbə], *m.* (—n, *pl.* —n) boy.
Knäblein [ˈknɛːblaɪn], *n.* (—s, *pl.* —) (*Poet.*) baby boy, small boy.
knack [knak], *int.* crack! snap!
Knäckebrot [ˈknɛkəbroːt], *n.* (—es, *no pl.*) crispbread.
knacken [ˈknakən], *v.a.* crack.

Knackmandel ['knakmandəl], f. (—, pl. —n) shell-almond.

Knackwurst ['knakvurst], f. (—, pl. ‥e) saveloy.

Knacks [knaks], m. (—es, pl. —e) crack.

knacksen ['knaksən], v.n. (coll.) crack.

Knall [knal], m. (—es, pl. —e) report, bang, detonation; — und Fall, quite suddenly, then and there.

Knallbüchse ['knalbyksə], f. (—, pl. —n) pop-gun.

Knalleffekt ['knalɛfɛkt], m. (—s, pl. —e) coup de théâtre; sensation.

knallen ['knalən], v.n. pop, explode, crack.

Knallgas ['knalga:s], n. (—es, no pl.) oxyhydrogen gas.

knallrot ['knalro:t], adj. scarlet; glaring red.

knapp [knap], adj. tight; scarce, insufficient; (style) concise; (majority) narrow, bare.

Knappe ['knapə], m. (—n, pl. —n) esquire, shield-bearer; miner.

Knappheit ['knaphaɪt], f. (—, no pl.) scarcity, shortage.

Knappschaft ['knapʃaft], f. (—, pl. —en) miners' association.

Knarre ['knarə], f. (—, pl. —n) rattle.

knarren ['knarən], v.n. rattle, creak.

Knaster ['knastər], m. (—s, pl. —) tobacco.

knattern ['knatərn], v.n. crackle.

Knäuel ['knɔyəl], m., n. (—s, pl. —) skein, clew, ball.

Knauf [knauf], m. (—es, pl. ‥e) (stick) knob, head; (Archit.) capital.

Knauser ['knauzər], m. (—s, pl. —) niggard, skinflint.

knausern ['knauzərn], v.n. be stingy, scrimp.

Knebel ['kne:bəl], m. (—s, pl. —) cudgel; gag.

knebeln ['kne:bəln], v.a. tie, bind; gag; (fig.) muzzle.

Knecht [knɛçt], m. (—es, pl. —e) servant, farm hand, menial; vassal, slave.

Knechtschaft ['knɛçtʃaft], f. (—, no pl.) servitude, slavery.

kneifen ['knaɪfən], v.a. irr. pinch. — v.n. (fig. coll.) back out (of), shirk.

Kneifer ['knaɪfər], m. (—s, pl. —) pince-nez.

Kneifzange ['knaɪftsaŋə], f. (—, pl. —n) pincers.

Kneipe ['knaɪpə], f. (—, pl. —n) pub; saloon.

kneten ['kne:tən], v.a. knead; massage.

knick(e)beinig ['knɪk(ə)baɪnɪç], adj. knock-kneed.

knicken ['knɪkən], v.a. crack, break.

Knicks [knɪks], m. (—es, pl. —e) curtsy.

knicksen ['knɪksən], v.n. curtsy.

Knie [kni:], n. (—s, pl. —) knee; etwas übers —, brechen, make short work of.

Kniekehle ['kni:ke:lə], f. (—, pl. —n) hollow of the knee.

knien ['kni:ən], v.n. kneel.

Kniescheibe ['kni:ʃaɪbə], f. (—, pl. —n) knee-cap.

Kniff [knɪf], m. (—es, pl. —e) fold; (fig.) trick, knack, dodge.

knipsen ['knɪpsən], v.a. (tickets) clip, punch; (Phot.) take a snap of.

Knirps [knɪrps], m. (—es, pl. —e) pigmy; (fig.) urchin.

knirschen ['knɪrʃən], v.n. crunch, grate, gnash (teeth).

knistern ['knɪstərn], v.n. crackle.

knittern ['knɪtərn], v.a. rumple, wrinkle, crinkle, crease.

Knobel ['kno:bəl], m. pl. dice.

Knoblauch ['kno:blaux], m. (—s, no pl.) (Bot.) garlic.

Knöchel ['knœçəl], m. (—s, pl. —) knuckle, joint; ankle.

Knochen ['knɔxən], m. (—s, pl. —) bone.

Knochengerüst ['knɔxəngərүst], n. (—es, pl. —e) skeleton.

knöchern ['knœçərn], adj. made of bone.

knochig ['knɔxɪç], adj. bony.

Knödel ['knø:dəl], m. (—s, pl. —) dumpling.

Knollen ['knɔlən], m. (—s, pl. —) lump, clod; (Bot.) tuber, bulb.

knollig ['knɔlɪç], adj. knobby, bulbous.

Knopf [knɔpf], m. (—es, pl. ‥e) button; stud; (stick) head, knob.

knöpfen ['knœpfən], v.a. button.

Knorpel ['knɔrpəl], m. (—s, pl. —) gristle, cartilage.

knorplig ['knɔrplɪç], adj. gristly.

knorrig ['knɔrɪç], adj. knotty, gnarled.

Knospe ['knɔspə], f. (—, pl. —n) bud.

Knote ['kno:tə], m. (—n, pl. —n) (fig.) bounder; lout.

Knoten ['kno:tən], m. (—s, pl. —) knot; (fig.) difficulty; (Theat.) plot.

Knotenpunkt ['kno:tənpuŋkt], m. (—es, pl. —e) (Railw.) junction.

Knotenstock ['kno:tənʃtɔk], m. (—es, pl. ‥e) knotty stick.

knotig ['kno:tɪç], adj. knotty, nodular.

knüllen ['knүlən], v.a. crumple.

knüpfen ['knүpfən], v.a. tie; knot; form (a friendship etc.).

Knüppel ['knүpəl], m. (—s, pl. —) cudgel.

knurren ['knurən], v.n. grunt, snarl; (fig.) growl, grumble.

knurrig ['knurɪç], adj. surly, grumpy.

knusprig ['knusprɪç], adj. crisp, crunchy.

Knute ['knu:tə], f. (—, pl. —n) knout.

knutschen ['knu:tʃən], v.r. sich —, (coll.) cuddle; (Am.) neck.

Knüttel [knytəl], m. (—s, pl. —) cudgel, bludgeon.

Knüttelvers ['knytəlfɛrs], m. (—es, pl. —e) doggerel, rhyme.

Kobalt ['ko:balt], m. (—s, no pl.) cobalt.

Kobaltblau ['ko:baltblau], n. (—s, no pl.) smalt.

Koben ['ko:bən], *m.* (—s, *pl.* —) pig-sty.

Kober ['ko:bər], *m.* (—s, *pl.* —) (*dial.*) basket, hamper.

Kobold ['ko:bɔlt], *m.* (—(e)s, *pl.* —e) goblin, hobgoblin.

Koch [kɔx], *m.* (—es, *pl.* ⸚e) cook, chef.

kochen ['kɔxən], *v.a.* cook, boil. — *v.n.* boil; (*fig.*) seethe.

Kocher ['kɔxər], *m.* (—s, *pl.* —) boiler.

Köcher ['kœçər], *m.* (—s, *pl.* —) quiver.

Köchin ['kœçɪn], *f.* (—, *pl.* —nen) (female) cook.

Kochsalz ['kɔxzalts], *n.* (—es, *no pl.*) common salt.

Köder ['kø:dər], *m.* (—s, *pl.* —) bait, lure; (*fig.*) decoy.

ködern ['kø:dərn], *v.a.* bait; (*fig.*) decoy.

Kodex ['ko:dɛks], *m.* (—es, *pl.* —e) codex; old MS.; (*Law*) code.

kodifizieren [ko:difi'tsi:rən], *v.a.* codify.

Koffein [kɔfə:'i:n], *n.* (—s, *no pl.*) caffeine.

Koffer ['kɔfər], *m.* (—s, *pl.* —) box, trunk, suitcase, portmanteau.

Kofferradio ['kɔfərra:djo], *n.* (—s, *pl.* —s) portable radio.

Kofferraum ['kɔfərraum], *m.* (—s, *no pl.*) (*Motor.*) boot, (*Am.*) trunk.

Kohl [ko:l], *m.* (—s, *pl.* —e) (*Bot.*) cabbage; (*no pl.*) (*fig.*) nonsense, rot.

Kohle ['ko:lə], *f.* (—, *pl.* —n) coal.

Kohlenflöz ['ko:lənflø:ts], *n.* (—es, *pl.* —e) coal-seam.

Kohlenoxyd ['ko:lənɔksy:t], *n.* (—s, *no pl.*) carbon monoxide.

Kohlensäure ['ko:lənzɔyrə], *f.* (—, *no pl.*) carbonic acid.

Kohlenstift ['ko:lənʃtɪft], *m.* (—es, *pl.* —e) charcoal-crayon.

Köhler ['kø:lər], *m.* (—s, *pl.* —) charcoal-burner.

Koje ['ko:jə], *f.* (—, *pl.* —n) (*Naut.*) berth, bunk.

Kokarde [Ko'kardə], *f.* (—, *pl.* —n) cockade.

kokett [ko'kɛt], *adj.* coquettish.

Kokette [ko'kɛtə], *f.* (—, *pl.* —n) coquette, flirt.

kokettieren [kokɛ'ti:rən], *v.n.* flirt.

Kokon [ko'kɔ̃], *m.* (—s, *pl.* —s) cocoon.

Kokosnuß [ko'kɔsnus], *f.* (—, *pl.* ⸚sse) (*Bot.*) coconut.

Koks [ko:ks], *m.* (—es, *pl.* —e) coke.

Kolben ['kɔlbən], *m.* (—s, *pl.* —) club: (*rifle*) butt-end; (*engine*) piston; (*Chem.*) retort.

Kolbenstange ['kɔlbənʃtaŋə], *f.* (—, *pl.* —n) piston-rod.

Kolibri ['ko:libri:], *m.* (—s, *pl.* —s) (*Orn.*) humming-bird.

Kolkrabe ['kɔlkra:bə], *m.* (—n, *pl.* —n) (*Orn.*) raven.

Kolleg [ko'le:k], *n.* (—s, *pl.* —ien) course of lectures; lecture.

Kollege [ko'le:gə], *m.* (—n, *pl.* —n) colleague.

Kollekte [kɔ'lɛktə], *f.* (—, *pl.* —n) collection; (*Eccl.*) collect.

Koller ['kɔlər], *m.* (—s, *no pl.*) frenzy, rage.

kollidieren [kɔli'di:rən], *v.n.* collide.

Köln [kœln], *n.* Cologne.

kölnisch ['kœlnɪʃ], *adj.* of Cologne; —*Wasser,* eau de Cologne.

kolonisieren [koloni'zi:rən], *v.a.* colonise.

Kolonnade [kolo'na:də], *f.* (— *pl.* —n) colonnade.

Koloratur [kolora'tu:r], *f.* (—, *pl.* —n) coloratura.

kolorieren [kolo'ri:rən], *v.a.* colour.

Koloß [ko'lɔs], *m.* (—sses, *pl.* —sse) colossus.

Kolportage [kɔlpɔr'ta:ʒə], *f.* (—, *pl.* —n) colportage, door-to-door sale of books; sensationalism.

Kolportageroman [kɔlpɔr'ta:ʒəroma:n], *m.* (—s, *pl.* —e) penny dreadful, shocker.

kolportieren [kɔlpɔr'ti:rən], *v.a.* hawk; spread, disseminate.

Kombinationsgabe [kɔmbina'tsjo:nsga:bə], *f.* (—, *pl.* —n) power of deduction.

kombinieren [kɔmbi'ni:rən], *v.a.* combine; deduce.

Kombüse [kɔm'by:zə], *f.* (— *pl.* —n) galley, caboose.

Komik ['ko:mɪk], *f.* (—, *no pl.*) comicality; humour; funny side.

Komiker ['ko:mɪkər], *m.* (—s, *pl.* —) comedian.

komisch ['ko:mɪʃ], *adj.* comical, funny; peculiar, strange, odd.

Kommandantur [kɔmandan'tu:r], *f.* (—, *pl.* —en) commander's office; garrison headquarters

kommandieren [kɔman'di:rən], *v.a.* command.

Kommanditgesellschaft [kɔman'di:tgəzɛlʃaft], *f.* (—, *pl.* —en) limited partnership.

Kommando [kɔ'mando], *n.* (—s, *pl.* —s) command.

kommen ['kɔmən], *v.n. irr.* (*aux.* sein) come, arrive; come about; *um etwas* —, lose s.th.; *zu etwas* —, come by s.th.; *zu sich* —, come to, regain consciousness.

Kommentar [kɔmen'ta:r], *m.* (—s, *pl.* —e) comment, commentary.

Kommers [kɔ'mɛrs], *m.* (—es, *pl.* —e) students' festivity; drinking party.

Kommersbuch [kɔ'mɛrsbu:x], *n.* (—es, *pl.* ⸚er) students' song-book.

kommerziell [kɔmɛrts'jɛl], *adj.* commercial.

Kommerzienrat [kɔ'mɛrtsjənra:t], *m.* (—s, *pl.* ⸚e) Councillor to the Chamber of Commerce.

Kommilitone [kɔmili'to:nə], *m.* (—n, *pl.* —n) fellow-student.

Kommis [kɔ'mi:], *m.* (—, *pl.* —) clerk.

Kommiß [kɔ'mɪs], *m.* (—sses, *pl.* —) military fatigue-dress; (*fig.*) military service.

Kommissar [kɔmɪ'sa:r], *m.* (—s, *pl.* —e) commissioner.

Kommissariat [kɔmɪsar'ja:t], *n.* (—s, *pl.* —e) commissioner's office.

Kommißbrot [kɔ'mɪsbro:t], *n.* (—es, *no pl.*) (coarse) army bread.

Kommission [kɔmɪs'jo:n], *f.* (—, *pl.* —en) commission, mission, committee.

kommod [kɔ'mo:d], *adj.* (*coll.*) snug, comfortable.

Kommode [kɔ'mo:də], *f.* (—, *pl.* —n) chest of drawers.

Kommune [kɔ'mu:nə], *f.* (—, *pl.* —n) (*coll.*) Communist Party; Reds.

Kommunismus [kɔmu'nɪsmus], *m.* (—, *no pl.*) Communism.

kommunistisch [kɔmu'nɪstɪʃ], *adj.* Communist.

Komödiant [kɔmød'jant], *m.* (—en, *pl.* —en) comedian, player; humbug.

Komödie [kɔ'mø:djə], *f.* (—, *pl.* —n) comedy, play; make-believe; — spielen, (*fig.*) sham, pretend, play-act.

Kompagnon ['kɔmpanjɔ], *m.* (—s, *pl.* —s) partner, associate.

Kompanie [kɔmpa'ni:], *f.* (—, *pl.* —n) (*Mil.*) company; (*Comm.*) partnership, company.

Kompaß ['kɔmpas], *m.* (—sses, *pl.* —sse) compass.

Kompaßrose ['kɔmpasro:zə], *f.* (—, *pl.* —n) compass-card.

kompensieren [kɔmpen'zi:rən], *v.a.* compensate.

komplementär [kɔmplemən'tɛ:r], *adj.* complementary.

komplett [kɔm'plet], *adj.* complete.

komplimentieren [kɔmplimen'ti:rən], *v.a.* compliment, flatter.

Komplize [kɔm'pli:tsə], *m.* (—n, *pl.* —n) accomplice.

kompliziert [kɔmpli'tsi:rt], *adj.* complicated.

Komplott [kɔm'plɔt], *n.* (—s, *pl.* —e) plot, conspiracy.

Komponente [kɔmpo'nentə], *f.* (—, *pl.* —n) component part; constituent.

komponieren [kɔmpo'ni:rən], *v.a.* compose, set to music.

Komponist [kɔmpo'nɪst], *m.* (—en, *pl.* —en) composer.

Kompositum [kɔm'po:zɪtum], *n.* (—s, *pl.* —ta) (*Gram.*) compound word.

Kompott [kɔm'pɔt], *n.* (—s, *pl.* —e) stewed fruit, compote; sweet, dessert.

Kompresse [kɔm'presə], *f.* (—, *pl.* —n) compress.

komprimieren [kɔmpri'mi:rən], *v.a.* compress.

Kompromiß [kɔmpro'mɪs], *m.* (—sses, *pl.* —sse) compromise, settlement.

kompromittieren [kɔmprɔmɪt'ti:rən], *v.a.* compromise. — *v.r.* sich —, compromise o.s.

kondensieren [kɔnden'zi:rən], *v.a.* condense.

Konditor [kɔn'di:tɔr], *m.* (—s, *pl.* —en) confectioner, pastry-cook.

Konditorei [kɔndito'raɪ], *f.* (—, *pl.* —en) confectioner's shop, pastry-shop; café.

kondolieren [kɔndo'li:rən], *v.n.* condole with s.o.

Kondukteur [kɔnduk'tø:r], *m.* (—s, *pl.* —e) (*Swiss & Austr. dial.*) guard (on train), conductor (on tram or bus).

Konfekt [kɔn'fekt], *n.* (—s, *pl.* —e) chocolates; (*Am.*) candy.

Konfektion [kɔnfek'tsjo:n], *f.* (—, *no pl.*) ready-made clothes; outfitting.

Konfektionär [kɔnfektsjo'ne:r], *m.* (—s, *pl.* —e) outfitter.

Konferenz [kɔnfe'rents], *f.* (—, *pl.* —en) conference.

konfessionell [kɔnfesjo'nel], *adj.* denominational, confessional.

Konfirmand [kɔnfɪr'mant], *m.* (—en, *pl.* —en) confirmation candidate.

konfirmieren [kɔnfɪr'mi:rən], *v.a.* (*Eccl.*) confirm.

konfiszieren [kɔnfɪs'tsi:rən], *v.a.* confiscate.

Konfitüren [kɔnfɪ'ty:rən], *f. pl.* confectionery, candied fruit, preserves.

konform [kɔn'fɔrm], *adj.* in conformity (with).

konfus [kɔn'fu:s], *adj.* confused, puzzled, disconcerted.

Kongo ['kɔŋgo], *m.* Congo.

Kongruenz [kɔngru'ents], *f.* (—, *no pl.*) congruity.

König ['kø:nɪç], *m.* (—s, *pl.* —e) king.

Königin ['kø:nɪgɪn], *f.* (—, *pl.* —nen) queen.

königlich ['kø:nɪçlɪç], *adj.* royal, regal, kingly, king-like.

Königreich ['kø:nɪçraɪç], *n.* (—(e)s, *pl.* —e) kingdom.

Königsadler ['kø:nɪçsa:dlər], *m.* (—s, *pl.* —) golden eagle.

Königsschlange ['kø:nɪçʃlaŋə], *f.* (—, *pl.* —n) (*Zool.*) boa constrictor.

Königstiger ['kø:nɪçsti:gər], *m.* (—s, *pl.* —) (*Zool.*) Bengal tiger.

Königtum ['kø:nɪçtu:m], *n.* (—s, *no pl.*) kingship.

Konjunktur [kɔnjuŋk'tu:r], *f.* (—, *pl.* —en) state of the market, (*coll.*) boom.

Konkordat [kɔnkɔr'da:t], *n.* (—s, *pl.* —e) concordat.

konkret [kɔn'kre:t], *adj.* concrete.

Konkurrent [kɔnku'rent], *m.* (—en, *pl.* —en) competitor, (business) rival.

Konkurrenz [kɔnku'rents], *f.* (—, *no pl.*) competition.

konkurrieren [kɔnku'ri:rən], *v.n.* compete.

Konkurs [kɔn'kurs], *m.* (—es, *pl.* —e) bankruptcy.

Konkursmasse [kɔn'kursmasə], *f.* (—, *pl.* —n) bankrupt's estate, bankrupt's stock.

Können ['kœnən], *n.* (—s, *no pl.*) ability; knowledge.

können ['kœnən], *v.a.*, *v.n.* irr. be able to, be capable of; understand; *ich kann*, I can; *er kann Englisch*, he speaks English.

127

konsequent [kɔnzeˈkvɛnt], *adj.* consistent.

Konsequenz [kɔnzeˈkvɛnts], *f.* (—, *pl.* —en) (*characteristic*) consistency; (*result*) consequence.

Konservatorium [kɔnzɛrvaˈtoːrjum], *n.* (—s, *pl.* —rien) (*Mus.*) conservatoire, conservatorium.

Konserve [kɔnˈzɛrvə], *f.* (—, *pl.* —n) preserve; tinned *or* (*Am.*) canned food.

konservieren [kɔnzɛrˈviːrən], *v.a.* preserve.

Konsistorium [kɔnzɪsˈtoːrjum], *n.* (—s, *pl.* —rien) (*Eccl.*) consistory.

Konsole [kɔnˈzoːlə], *f.* (—, *pl.* —n) bracket.

konsolidieren [kɔnzoliˈdiːrən], *v.a.* consolidate.

Konsonant [kɔnzoˈnant], *m.* (—en, *pl.* —en) (*Phonet.*) consonant.

Konsorte [kɔnˈzɔrtə], *m.* (—n, *pl.* —n) associate, accomplice.

Konsortium [kɔnˈzɔrtsjum], *n.* (—s, *pl.* —tien) syndicate.

konstatieren [kɔnstaˈtiːrən], *v.a.* state, note, assert.

konsternieren [kɔnstɛrˈniːrən], *v.a.* dismay, disconcert.

konstituieren [kɔnstituˈiːrən], *v.a.* constitute.

konstitutionell [kɔnstitutsjoˈnɛl], *adj.* constitutional.

konstruieren [kɔnstruˈiːrən], *v.a.* construct; (*Gram.*) construe.

konsularisch [kɔnzuˈlaːrɪʃ], *adj.* consular.

Konsulat [kɔnzuˈlaːt], *n.* (—s, *pl.* —e) consulate.

Konsulent [kɔnzuˈlɛnt], *m.* (—en, *pl.* —en) (*Law*) counsel; consultant.

konsultieren [kɔnzulˈtiːrən], *v.a.* consult.

Konsum [kɔnˈzuːm], *m.* (—s, *no pl.*) (*Econ.*) consumption.

konsumieren [kɔnzuˈmiːrən], *v.a.* consume.

Konsumverein [kɔnˈzuːmfɛraɪn], *m.* (—s, *pl.* —e) cooperative society.

Konterbande [kɔntərˈbandə], *f.* (—, *no pl.*) contraband.

Konterfei [kɔntərˈfaɪ], *n.* (—s, *pl.* —e) (*obs.*) portrait, likeness.

Kontertanz [ˈkɔntərtants], *m.* (—es, *pl.* ⁀e) square dance, quadrille.

kontinuierlich [kɔntinuˈiːrlɪç], *adj.* continuous.

Kontinuität [kɔntinuiˈtɛːt], *f.* (—, *no pl.*) continuity.

Konto [ˈkɔnto], *n.* (—s, *pl.* —ten) (*bank*) account; à —, on account.

Kontokorrent [kɔntokoˈrɛnt], *n.* (—s, *pl.* —e) current account.

Kontor [kɔnˈtoːr], *n.* (—s, *pl.* —e) (*obs.*) office.

Kontorist [kɔntoˈrɪst], *m.* (—en, *pl.* —en) clerk.

Kontrabaß [ˈkɔntrabas], *m.* (—sses, *pl.* ⁀sse) double-bass.

Kontrapunkt [ˈkɔntrapuŋkt], *m.* (—es, *pl.* —e) (*Mus.*) counterpoint.

kontrastieren [kɔntrasˈtiːrən], *v.a., v.n.* contrast.

kontrollieren [kɔntrɔˈliːrən], *v.a.* check, verify.

Kontroverse [kɔntroˈvɛrzə], *f.* (—, *pl.* —n) controversy.

Kontur [kɔnˈtuːr], *f.* (—, *pl.* —en) outline, (*pl.*) contours.

Konvent [kɔnˈvɛnt], *m.* (—s, *pl.* —e) convention, assembly, congress.

konventionell [kɔnvɛntsjoˈnɛl], *adj.* conventional, formal.

Konversationslexikon [kɔnvɛrzaˈtsjoːnslɛksikɔn], *n.* (—s, *pl.* —s) encyclopaedia.

konvertieren [kɔnvɛrˈtiːrən], *v.a., v.n.* convert.

Konvertit [kɔnvɛrˈtɪt], *m.* (—en, *pl.* —en) convert.

Konvolut [kɔnvoˈluːt], *n.* (—s, *pl.* —e) bundle; scroll.

konvulsivisch [kɔnvulˈziːvɪʃ], *adj.* convulsive.

konzentrieren [kɔntsɛnˈtriːrən], *v.a., v.r.* concentrate; *auf etwas* —, centre upon.

konzentrisch [kɔnˈtsɛntrɪʃ], *adj.* concentric.

Konzept [kɔnˈtsɛpt], *n.* (—es, *pl.* —e) rough draft, sketch; *aus dem* — *bringen*, unsettle, disconcert.

Konzeptpapier [kɔnˈtsɛptpapiːr], *n.* (—s, *no pl.*) scribbling paper.

Konzern [kɔnˈtsɛrn], *m.* (—s, *pl.* —e) (*Comm.*) combine.

Konzert [kɔnˈtsɛrt], *n.* (—es, *pl.* —e) concert, (*musical*) recital; concerto.

Konzertflügel [kɔnˈtsɛrtflyːgəl], *m.* (—s, *pl.* —) grand piano.

konzertieren [kɔntsɛrˈtiːrən], *v.n.* give recitals; play in a concert.

Konzertmeister [kɔnˈtsɛrtmaɪstər], *m.* (—s, *pl.* —) leader (*of orchestra*).

Konzession [kɔntsɛˈsjoːn], *f.* (—, *pl.* —en) concession, licence.

konzessionieren [kɔntsɛsjoˈniːrən], *v.a.* license.

Konzil [kɔnˈtsiːl], *n.* (—s, *pl.* —ien) (*Eccl.*) council.

konzipieren [kɔntsiˈpiːrən], *v.a.* draft, plan.

Koordinierung [koːɔrdiˈniːruŋ], *f.* (—, *pl.* —en) co-ordination.

Kopf [kɔpf], *m.* (—es, *pl.* ⁀e) head; top; heading; (*fig.*) mind, brains, judgment; *aus dem* —, by heart.

köpfen [ˈkœpfən], *v.a.* behead, decapitate; (*Bot.*) lop.

Kopfhaut [ˈkɔpfhaut], *f.* (—, *no pl.*) scalp.

Kopfhörer [ˈkɔpfhøːrər], *m.* (—s, *pl.* —) headphone, receiver.

Kopfkissen [ˈkɔpfkɪsən], *n.* (—s, *pl.* —) pillow.

Kopfsalat [ˈkɔpfzalaːt], *m.* (—s, *pl.* —e) (*garden*) lettuce.

kopfscheu [ˈkɔpfʃɔy], *adj.* afraid; alarmed, timid; — *machen*, scare; — *werden*, take fright, jib.

Kopfschmerz ['kɔpfʃmɛrts], *m.* (—es, *pl.* —en) (*mostly pl.*) headache.

Kopfsprung ['kɔpfʃpruŋ], *m.* (—s, *pl.* ⁇e) (*diving*) header.

kopfüber [kɔpf'y:bər], *adv.* head over heels; headlong.

Kopfweh ['kɔpfve:], *n.* (—s, *no pl.*) headache.

Kopfzerbrechen ['kɔpftsɛrbreçən], *n.* (—s, *no pl.*) racking o.'s brains.

Kopie [ko'pi:] *f.* (—, *pl.* —n) copy, duplicate.

kopieren [ko'pi:rən], *v.a.* copy, ape, mimic, take off.

Koppe ['kɔpə], *f. see* **Kuppe**.

Koppel ['kɔpəl], *f.* (—, *pl.* —n) (*dogs*) couple, leash; (*ground*) enclosure, paddock.

koppeln ['kɔpəln], *v.a.* couple, leash.

kopulieren [kopu'li:rən], *v.a.* (*obs.*) marry; pair; (*Hort.*) graft.

Koralle [ko'ralə], *f.* (—, *pl.* —n) coral.

Korallenriff [ko'ralənrif], *n.* (—es, *pl.* —e) coral-reef.

Korb [kɔrp], *m.* (—s, *pl.* ⁇e) basket, hamper; *einen* — *geben,* turn s.o. down, refuse an offer of marriage.

Korbweide ['kɔrpvaidə], *f.* (—, *pl.* —n) (*Bot.*) osier.

Kord [kɔrt], *m.* (—s, *no pl.*) corduroy.

Kordel ['kɔrdəl], *f.* (—, *pl.* —n) cord, twine, thread.

Korea [ko're:a], *n.* Korea.

Korinthe [ko'rintə], *f.* (—, *pl.* —n) (*Bot.*) currant.

Korken ['kɔrkən], *m.* (—s, *pl.* —) cork, stopper.

Korkenzieher ['kɔrkəntsi:ər], *m.* (—s, *pl.* —) cork-screw.

Korn [kɔrn], *n.* (—s, *pl.* —e, ⁇er) (*Bot.*) corn, grain, cereal, rye; (*gun*) sight, *aufs* — *nehmen,* take aim at.

Kornblume ['kɔrnblu:mə], *f.* (—, *pl.* —n) (*Bot.*) corn-flower.

Kornbranntwein ['kɔrnbrantvain], *m.* (—s, *no pl.*) corn-brandy, whisky.

Kornett [kɔr'nɛt], *m.* (—s, *pl.* —e) (*Mil., Mus.*) cornet.

körnig ['kœrniç], *adj.* granular, granulous; grained.

Kornrade ['kɔrnra:də], *f.* (—, *pl.* —n) (*Bot.*) corn-cockle.

Kornspeicher ['kɔrnʃpaiçər], *m.* (—s, *pl.* —) granary, corn-loft.

Körper ['kœrpər], *m.* (—s, *pl.* —) body; (*Phys.*) solid.

Körperbau ['kœrpərbau], *m.* (—s, *no pl.*) build, frame.

Köpergeruch ['kœrpərgəru:x], *m.* (—s, *no pl.*) body odour.

körperlich ['kœrpərliç], *adj.* bodily, physical; —*e Züchtigung,* corporal punishment.

Körpermaß ['kœrpərma:s], *n.* (—es, *pl.* —e) cubic measure.

Körperschaft ['kœrpərʃaft], *f.* (—, *pl.* —en) corporation.

Korps [ko:r], *n.* (—, *pl.* —) (*Mil.*) corps; students' corporation.

Korrektheit [kɔ'rɛkthait], *f.* (—, *no pl.*) correctness.

Korrektionsanstalt [kɔrɛk'tsjo:nsanʃtalt], *f.* (—, *pl.* —en) penitentiary, Borstal institution.

Korrektor [kɔ'rɛktɔr], *m.* (—s, *pl.* —en) proof-reader.

Korrektur [kɔrɛk'tu:r], *f.* (—, *pl.* —en) correction; proof-correction; revision.

Korrekturbogen [kɔrɛk'tu:rbo:gən], *m.* (—s, *pl.* —) (*Typ.*) proof-sheet, galley.

Korrespondenzkarte [kɔrɛspɔn'dɛntskartə], *f.* (—, *pl.* —n) post-card.

korrigieren [kɔri'gi:rən], *v.a.* correct, revise; read (proofs).

Korsett [kɔr'zɛt], *n.* (—s, *pl.* —s) corset, bodice, stays.

Koryphäe [kɔri'fɛ:ə], *m.* (—n, *pl.* —n) celebrity, authority, master mind.

Koseform ['ko:zəfɔrm], *f.* (—, *pl.* —en) term of endearment, pet-name, diminutive.

kosen ['ko:zən], *v.a., v.n.* caress, fondle; make love (to).

Kosinus ['ko:zinus], *m.* (—, *pl.* —) (*Maths.*) cosine.

Kosmetik [kɔs'me:tik], *f.* (—, *no pl.*) cosmetics.

kosmetisch [kɔs'me:tiʃ], *adj.* cosmetic.

kosmisch ['kɔzmiʃ], *adj.* cosmic.

Kosmopolit [kɔsmopo'li:t], *m.* (—en, *pl.* —en) cosmopolitan.

kosmopolitisch [kɔsmopo'li:tiʃ], *adj.* cosmopolitan.

Kost [kɔst], *f.* (—, *no pl.*) food, fare; board.

Kostarika [kɔsta'rika], *n.* Costa Rica.

kostbar ['kɔstba:r], *adj.* valuable, precious, costly.

Kostbarkeit ['kɔstba:rkait], *f.* (—, *pl.* —en) costliness, preciousness; (*pl.*) (*goods*) valuables.

Kosten ['kɔstən], *pl.* cost(s), expenses, charges; (*Law*) costs.

kosten ['kɔstən], *v.a.* taste; (*money*) cost; take, require; *was kostet das?* how much is this?

Kosten(vor)anschlag ['kɔstən(for)anʃla:k], *m.* (—s, *pl.* ⁇e) estimate.

Kostenaufwand ['kɔstənaufvant], *m.* (—s, *pl.* ⁇e) expenditure.

Kostenersatz ['kɔstənɛrzats], *m.* (—es, *no pl.*) refund of expenses, compensation.

kostenfrei ['kɔstənfrai], *adj.* free (of charge), gratis.

kostenlos ['kɔstənlo:s], *see* **kostenfrei**.

Kostgänger ['kɔstgɛŋər], *m.* (—s, *pl.* —) boarder.

Kostgeld ['kɔstgɛlt], *n.* (—es, *no pl.*) maintenance *or* board allowance.

köstlich ['kœstliç], *adj.* excellent, precious; delicious; *ein* —*er Witz,* a capital joke.

kostspielig ['kɔstʃpi:liç], *adj.* expensive, costly.

Kostüm [kɔ'sty:m], *n.* (—s, *pl.* —e) costume; fancy dress.

Kostümfest [kɔ'sty:mfɛst], *n.* (—s, *pl.* —e) fancy-dress ball.

129

kostümieren

kostümieren [kɔsty'miːrən], *v.a.* dress up.

Kot [koːt], *m.* (—es, *no pl.*) mud, dirt; filth, mire; excrement.

Kotelett [kɔt'lɛt], *n.* (—s, *pl.* —s) cutlet.

Köter ['køːtər], *m.* (—s, *pl.* —) cur, mongrel.

Koterie [koːtə'riː], *f.* (—, *pl.* —n) clique, set, coterie.

Kotflügel ['koːtflyːgəl], *m.* (—s, *pl.* —) (*Motor.*) mudguard.

kotig ['koːtɪç], *adj.* dirty, miry.

kotzen ['kɔtsən], *v.n.* (*vulg.*) vomit.

Koweit ['kɔvaɪt], *n.* Kuwait.

Krabbe ['krabə], *f.* (—, *pl.* —n) (*Zool.*) crab; shrimp; (*fig.*) brat, imp.

krabbeln ['krabəln], *v.n.* crawl.

Krach [krax], *m.* (—es, *pl.* —e) crack, crash; din, noise; (*Comm.*) slump; quarrel, row.

krachen ['kraxən], *v.n.* crack, crash.

krächzen ['krɛçtsən], *v.n.* croak.

Kraft [kraft], *f.* (—, *pl.* ⁓e) strength, vigour; force; power, energy; intensity; *in — treten*, come into force.

kraft [kraft], *prep.* (*Genit.*) by virtue of, by authority of, on the strength of.

Kraftausdruck ['kraftausdruk], *m.* (—s, *pl.* ⁓e) forcible expression; expletive.

Kraftbrühe ['kraftbryːə], *f.* (—, *pl.* —n) meat-soup, beef-tea.

Kraftfahrer ['kraftfaːrər], *m.* (—s, *pl.* —) motorist.

kräftig ['krɛftɪç], *adj.* strong, powerful, vigorous, energetic; (*food*) nourishing.

Kraftlehre ['kraftleːrə], *f.* (—, *no pl.*) dynamics.

kraftlos ['kraftloːs], *adj.* weak, feeble.

Kraftwagen ['kraftvaːgən], *m.* (—s, *pl.* —) motor car, automobile, car, lorry, truck.

Kragen ['kraːgən], *m.* (—s, *pl.* —) collar; *es geht mir an den —*, it will cost me dearly.

Krähe ['krɛːə], *f.* (—, *pl.* —n) (*Orn.*) crow.

krähen ['krɛːən], *v.n.* crow.

Krähenfüße ['krɛːənfyːsə], *m. pl.* crow's feet (wrinkles).

Krakau ['kraːkau], *n.* Cracow.

krakeelen [kra'keːlən], *v.n.* (*coll.*) kick up a row.

Kralle ['kralə], *f.* (—, *pl.* —n) claw, talon.

Kram [kraːm], *m.* (—s, *no pl.*) small wares (trade); stuff, rubbish, litter; *es paßt mir nicht in den —*, it does not suit my purpose.

kramen ['kraːmən], *v.n.* rummage.

Krämer ['krɛːmər], *m.* (—s, *pl.* —) retailer, general dealer, shopkeeper.

Kramladen ['kraːmlaːdən], *m.* (—s, *pl.* ⁓) small retail-shop, general shop or store.

Krampe ['krampə], *f.* (—, *pl.* —n) staple.

Krampf [krampf], *m.* (—es, *pl.* ⁓) cramp, spasm, convulsion.

Krampfader ['krampfaːdər], *f.* (—, *pl.* —n) varicose vein.

krampfartig ['krampfaːrtɪç], *adj.* spasmodic.

krampfhaft ['krampfhaft], *adj.* convulsive.

Kran [kraːn], *m.* (—s, *pl.* ⁓e) (*Engin.*) crane.

Kranich ['kraːnɪç], *m.* (—s, *pl.* —e) (*Orn.*) crane.

krank [kraŋk], *adj.* sick, ill.

kränkeln ['krɛŋkəln], *v.n.* be ailing, be in poor health.

kranken ['kraŋkən], *v.n. an etwas —*, suffer from s.th., be afflicted with s.th.

kränken ['krɛŋkən], *v.a.* vex, grieve; offend, insult.

Krankenbahre ['kraŋkənbaːrə], *f.* (—, *pl.* —n) stretcher.

Krankenhaus ['kraŋkənhaus], *n.* (—es, *pl.* ⁓er) hospital.

Krankenkasse ['kraŋkənkasə], *f.* (—, *pl.* —n) sick-fund; health insurance.

Krankenkost ['kraŋkənkɔst], *f.* (—, *no pl.*) invalid diet.

Krankenschwester ['kraŋkənʃvɛstər], *f.* (—, *pl.* —n) nurse.

Krankenstuhl ['kraŋkənʃtuːl], *m.* (—s, *pl.* ⁓e) invalid chair.

Krankenversicherung ['kraŋkənfɛrzɪçəruŋ], *f.* (—, *pl.* —en) health insurance.

Krankenwärter ['kraŋkənvɛrtər], *m.* (—s, *pl.* —) attendant, male nurse.

krankhaft ['kraŋkhaft], *adj.* morbid.

Krankheit ['kraŋkhaɪt], *f.* (—, *pl.* —en) illness, sickness, disease, malady; complaint; *englische —*, rickets.

Krankheitserscheinung ['kraŋkhaɪtsɛrʃaɪnuŋ], *f.* (—, *pl.* —en) symptom.

kränklich ['krɛŋklɪç], *adj.* sickly, infirm, in poor health.

Kränkung ['krɛŋkuŋ], *f.* (—, *pl.* —en) grievance, annoyance; offence, insult.

Kranz [krants], *m.* (—es, *pl.* ⁓e) wreath, garland.

Kränzchen ['krɛntsçən], *n.* (—s, *pl.* —) little garland; (*fig.*) (ladies') weekly tea party; circle, club.

kränzen ['krɛntsən], *v.a.* garland, wreathe.

Krapfen ['krapfən], *m.* (—s, *pl.* —) doughnut.

kraß [kras], *adj.* crass, crude.

Krater ['kraːtər], *m.* (—s, *pl.* —) crater.

Kratzbürste ['kratsbyrstə], *f.* (—, *pl.* —n) scraper; (*fig.*) cross-patch, irritable person.

Krätze ['krɛtsə], *f.* (—, *no pl.*) (*Med.*) scabies, itch, mange.

kratzen ['kratsən], *v.a., v.n.* scratch, scrape, itch.

krauen ['krauən], *v.a.* scratch softly.

kraus [kraus], *adj.* frizzy, curly; crisp, fuzzy; creased; (*fig.*) abstruse; *die Stirn — ziehen*, frown, knit o.'s brow.

Krause ['krauzə], *f.* (—, *pl.* —n) ruff.

kräuseln ['krɔyzəln], *v.a., v.r.* crisp, curl; ripple.

Krauskohl ['krauskoːl], *m.* (—s, *no pl.*) Savoy cabbage.

Kraut [kraut], *n.* (—es, *pl.* ‥er) herb; plant; (*dial.*) cabbage; *wie — und Rüben*, higgledy-piggledy.

krautartig ['krauta:rtɪç], *adj.* herbaceous.

Kräuterkäse ['krɔytərkɛːzə], *m.* (—s, *pl.* —) green cheese.

Kräutertee ['krɔytərte:], *m.* (—s, *no pl.*) herb-tea, infusion of herbs.

Krawall [kra'val], *m.* (—s, *pl.*—e) (*coll.*) row, uproar; shindy.

Krawatte [kra'vatə], *f.* (—, *pl.*—n) cravat, tie.

kraxeln ['kraksəln], *v.n.* (*coll.*) climb, clamber.

Krebs [kre:ps], *m.* (—es, *pl.* —e) (*Zool.*) crayfish, crab; (*Med.*) cancer, carcinoma; (*Geog.*) Tropic of Cancer.

krebsartig ['kre:psa:rtɪç], *adj.* cancerous.

Krebsbutter ['kre:psbutər], *f.* (—, *no pl.*) crab-cheese.

Krebsgang ['kre:psgaŋ], *m.* (—es, *no pl.*) crab's walk, sidling; *den — gehen*, retrograde, decline.

Krebsschaden ['kre:psʃa:dən], *m.* (—s, *pl.* ‥) cancerous sore *or* affection; (*fig.*) canker, inveterate evil.

Kredenz [kre'dɛnts], *f.* (—, *pl.* —en) buffet, serving table, sideboard.

kredenzen [kre'dɛntsən], *v.a.* taste (*wine*); (*obs.*) present, offer.

kreditieren [kredi'ti:rən], *v.a. einem etwas —*, credit s.o. with s.th.

Kreide ['kraɪdə], *f.* (—, *pl.* —n) chalk; (*Art*) crayon.

kreieren [kre'i:rən], *v.a.* create.

Kreis [kraɪs], *m.* (—es, *pl.* —e) circle; (*Astron.*) orbit; district; range; sphere.

Kreisabschnitt ['kraɪsapʃnɪt], *m.* (—s, *pl.* —e) segment.

Kreisausschnitt ['kraɪsausʃnɪt],*m.* (—s, *pl.* —e) sector.

Kreisbogen ['kraɪsbo:gən], *m.* (—s, *pl.* ‥) arc.

kreischen ['kraɪʃən], *v.n.* scream, shriek.

Kreisel ['kraɪzəl], *m.* (—s, *pl.* —) (*toy*) (spinning) top; gyroscope.

kreisen ['kraɪzən], *v.n.* circle, revolve; circulate.

Kreislauf ['kraɪslauf], *m.* (—es, *pl.* ‥e) circular course; (*Astron.*) orbit; (*blood*) circulation.

kreißen ['kraɪsən], *v.n.* (*Med.*) be in labour.

Kreisstadt ['kraɪsʃtat], *f.* (—, *pl.* ‥e) county town.

Kreisumfang ['kraɪsumfaŋ], *m.* (—s, *pl.* ‥e) circumference.

Kreml [kreml], *m.* (—s, *no pl.*) the Kremlin.

Krempe ['krempə], *f.* (—, *pl.* —n) (*hat*) brim.

Krempel ['krempəl], *m.* (—s, *no pl.*) (*coll.*) refuse, rubbish; stuff.

Kren [kre:n], *m.* (—s, *no pl.*) (*Austr.*) horse-radish.

krepieren [kre'pi:rən], *v.n.* (*aux.* sein) (*animals*) die; (*humans*) (*coll.*) perish miserably; explode.

Krepp [krep], *m.* (—s, *no pl.*) crape, crêpe.

Kresse ['kresə], *f.* (—, *pl.* —n) cress.

Kreta ['kre:ta], *n.* Crete.

Kreuz [krɔyts], *n.* (—es, *pl.* —e) cross, crucifix; (*Anat.*) small of the back; (*fig.*) calamity; affliction; *kreuz und quer*, in all directions.

Kreuzband ['krɔytsbant], *n.* (—es, *pl.* ‥er) wrapper (for printed matter).

kreuzbrav ['krɔytsbra:f], *adj.* as good as gold.

kreuzen ['krɔytsən], *v.a.* cross. — *v.r. sich —*, make the sign of the cross.

Kreuzfahrer ['krɔytsfa:rər], *m.* (—s, *pl.* —) crusader.

kreuzfidel ['krɔytsfide:l], *adj.* jolly, merry, as merry as a cricket.

Kreuzgang ['krɔytsgaŋ], *m.* (—es, *pl.* ‥e) cloisters.

kreuzigen ['krɔytsɪgən], *v.a.* crucify.

Kreuzritter ['krɔɪtsrɪtər], *m.* (—s, *pl.* —) Knight of the Cross; crusader.

Kreuzschmerzen ['krɔytsʃmertsən], *m. pl.* lumbago.

Kreuzstich ['krɔytsʃtɪç], *m.* (—es, *no pl.*) (*Embroidery*) cross-stitch.

Kreuzung ['krɔytsuŋ], *f.* (—, *pl.* —en) (*road*) crossing; (*animals*) cross-breeding.

Kreuzverhör ['krɔytsfɛrhø:r], *n.* (—s, *pl.* —e) cross-examination.

Kreuzweg [kredi'tsve:k], *m.* (—s, *pl.* —e) crossroads; (*Eccl.*) Stations of the Cross.

Kreuzworträtsel ['krɔytsvɔrtrɛ:tsəl], *n.* (—s, *pl.* —) crossword-puzzle.

Kreuzzug ['krɔytstsu:k], *m.* (—es, *pl.* ‥e) crusade.

kriechen ['kri:çən], *v.n. irr.* (*aux.* sein) creep, crawl; (*fig.*) cringe, fawn.

kriecherisch ['kri:çərɪʃ], *adj.* fawning, cringing.

Kriechtier ['kri:çti:r], *n.* (—s, *pl.* —e) reptile.

Krieg [kri:k], *m.* (—es, *pl.* —e) war.

kriegen ['kri:gən], *v.a.* get, obtain.

Krieger ['kri:gər], *m.* (—s, *pl.* —) warrior.

kriegerisch ['kri:gərɪʃ], *adj.* warlike, martial.

kriegführend ['kri:kfy:rənt], *adj.* belligerent.

Kriegsfuß ['kri:ksfu:s], *m.* (—es, *no pl.*) *auf —*, at logger-heads.

Kriegsgewinnler ['kri:ksgəvɪnlər], *m.* (—s, *pl.* —) war-profiteer.

Kriegslist ['kri:kslɪst], *f.* (—, *pl.* —en) stratagem.

Kriegsschauplatz ['kri:ksʃauplats], *m.* (—es, *pl.* ‥e) theatre of war.

Kriegsschiff ['kri:ksʃɪf], *n.* (—es, *pl.* —e) man-of-war, warship.

Kriegswesen ['kri:ksve:zən], *n.* (—s, *no pl.*) military affairs.

Kriegszug ['kri:kstsu:k], *m.* (—es, *pl.* ‥e) campaign.

Krim [krɪm], *f.* the Crimea.

Kriminalbeamte [krɪmi'na:lbəamtə], *m.* (—n, *pl.* —n) crime investigator.

Kriminalprozeß [krɪmiˈnaːlprotsɛs], *m.* (—sses, *pl.* —sse) criminal procedure *or* trial.

Krimskrams [ˈkrɪmskrams], *m.* (—, *no pl.*) whatnots, knick-knacks, medley.

Krippe [ˈkrɪpə], *f.* (—, *pl.* —n) crib, manger; crèche.

Krise [ˈkriːzə], *f.* (—, *pl.* —n) crisis.

Kristall [krɪˈstal], *m.* (—s, *pl.* —e) crystal; cut glass.

kristallartig [krɪˈstalaːrtɪç], *adj.* crystalline.

kristallisieren [krɪstaliˈziːrən], *v.a.*, *v.n.* (*aux.* sein), crystallise.

Kristallkunde [krɪˈstalkundə], *f.* (—, *no pl.*) crystallography.

Kriterium [kriˈteːrjum], *n.* (—s, *pl.* —rien) criterion, test.

Kritik [kriˈtiːk], *f.* (—, *pl.* —en) criticism, review; *unter aller* —, extremely bad.

Kritiker [ˈkriːtɪkər], *m.* (—s, *pl.* —) critic.

kritisch [ˈkriːtɪʃ], *adj.* critical; precarious, crucial.

kritisieren [kritiˈziːrən], *v.a.* criticise; review; censure.

kritteln [ˈkrɪtəln], *v.n.* cavil (at), find fault.

Krittler [ˈkrɪtlər], *m.* (—s, *pl.* —) caviller, fault-finder.

Kritzelei [krɪtsəˈlaɪ], *f.* (—, *pl.* —en) scrawling, scribbling.

kritzeln [ˈkrɪtsəln], *v.a.* scrawl, scribble.

Kroatien [kroˈaːtsjən], *n.* Croatia.

Krokodil [krokoˈdiːl], *n.* (—s, *pl.* —e) (*Zool.*) crocodile.

Kronbewerber [ˈkroːnbevɛrbər], *m.* (—s, *pl.* —) aspirant to the crown, pretender.

Krone [ˈkroːnə], *f.* (—, *pl.* —n) crown; (*Papal*) tiara; (*fig.*) head, top, flower.

krönen [ˈkrøːnən], *v.a.* crown.

Kronerbe [ˈkroːnɛrbə], *m.* (—n, *pl.* —n) heir apparent.

Kronleuchter [ˈkroːnlɔyçtər], *m.* (—s, *pl.* —) chandelier.

Kronsbeere [ˈkroːnsbeːrə], *f.* (—, *pl.* —n) (*Bot.*) cranberry.

Krönung [ˈkrøːnuŋ], *f.* (—, *pl.* —en) coronation.

Kropf [krɔpf], *m.* (—es, *pl.* ⸚e) (*human*) goitre, wen; (*birds*) crop, craw.

kropfartig [ˈkrɔpfaːrtɪç], *adj.* goitrous.

kröpfen [ˈkrœpfən], *v.a.* (*birds*) cram.

Kropftaube [ˈkrɔpftaubə], *f.* (—, *pl.* —n) (*Orn.*) pouter-pigeon.

Kröte [ˈkrøːtə], *f.* (—, *pl.* —n) toad.

Krücke [ˈkrykə], *f.* (—, *pl.* —n) crutch; (*fig.*) rake.

Krückstock [ˈkrykʃtɔk], *m.* (—s, *pl.* ⸚e) crutch.

Krug [kruːk], *m.* (—es, *pl.* ⸚e) jug, pitcher, mug; (*fig.*) pub, inn.

Krüger [ˈkryːgər], *m.* (—s, *pl.* —) pub-keeper, tapster.

Krume [ˈkruːmə], *f.* (—, *pl.* —n) crumb.

krüm(e)lig [ˈkryːm(ə)lɪç], *adj.* crumbly, crumby.

krümeln [ˈkryːmeln], *v.n.* crumble.

krumm [krum], *adj.* crooked, curved; *etwas* — *nehmen*, take s.th. amiss.

krummbeinig [ˈkrumbaɪnɪç], *adj.* bandy-legged.

krümmen [ˈkrymən], *v.a.* crook, bend, curve. — *v.r. sich* —, (*fig.*) writhe, cringe.

Krummholz [ˈkrumhɔlts], *n.* (—es, *no pl.*) (*Bot.*) dwarf-pine.

Krummschnabel [ˈkrumʃnaːbəl], *m.* (—s, *pl.* ⸚) (*Orn.*) curlew, crook-bill.

Krümmung [ˈkrymuŋ], *f.* (—, *pl.* —en) curve; turning, winding.

Krüppel [ˈkrypəl], *m.* (—s, *pl.* —) cripple.

krüppelhaft [ˈkrypəlhaft], *adj.* crippled, lame.

krüpp(e)lig [ˈkryp(ə)lɪç], *adj.* crippled, lame.

Kruste [ˈkrustə], *f.* (—, *pl.* —n) crust.

Kübel [ˈkyːbəl], *m.* (—s, *pl.* —) tub, bucket.

Kubikfuß [kuˈbiːkfuːs], *m.* (—es, *pl.* —) cubic foot.

Kubikinhalt [kuˈbiːkɪnhalt], *m.* (—s, *no pl.*) cubic content.

Kubismus [kuˈbɪsmus], *m.* (—, *no pl.*) cubism.

Küche [ˈkyçə], *f.* (—, *pl.* —n) (*room*) kitchen; (*food*) cooking, cookery, cuisine.

Kuchen [ˈkuːxən], *m.* (—s, *pl.* —) cake.

Küchengeschirr [ˈkyçəngəʃɪr], *n.* (—s, *no pl.*) kitchen utensils.

Küchenherd [ˈkyçənheːrt], *m.* (—es, *pl.* —e) kitchen-range.

Küchenlatein [ˈkyçənlatain], *n.* (—s, *no pl.*) dog-Latin.

Küchenmeister [ˈkyçənmaistər], *m.* (—s, *pl.* —) chef, head cook.

Küchenschrank [ˈkyçənʃraŋk], *m.* (—s, *pl.* ⸚e) dresser.

Kuchenteig [ˈkuːxəntaik], *m.* (—s, *pl.* —e) dough (for cake).

Küchenzettel [ˈkyçəntsetəl], *m.* (—s, *pl.* —) bill of fare.

Küchlein [ˈkyːçlain], *n.* (—s, *pl.* —) young chicken, pullet.

Kücken [ˈkykən], *n.* (—s, *pl.* —) young chicken, pullet.

Kuckuck [ˈkukuk], *m.* (—s, *pl.* —e) (*Orn.*) cuckoo; *scher Dich zum* —! go to blazes!

Kufe [ˈkuːfə], *f.* (—, *pl.* —n) tub, vat; (*sleigh*) runner; (*cradle*) rocker.

Küfer [ˈkyːfər], *m.* (—s, *pl.* —) cooper.

Kugel [ˈkuːgəl], *f.* (—, *pl.* —n) ball, bullet, sphere; globe.

kugelfest [ˈkuːgəlfest], *adj.* bullet-proof.

kugelförmig [ˈkuːgəlfœrmɪç], *adj.* spherical, globular.

Kugelgelenk [ˈkuːgəlgəlɛŋk], *n.* (—s, *pl.* —e) ball and socket joint.

Kugellager [ˈkuːgəlaːgər], *n.* (—s, *pl.* —) ball-bearing.

Kugelmaß [ˈkuːgəlmaːs], *n.* (—es, *pl.* —e) ball-calibre.

kugeln [ˈkuːgəln], *v.a.* roll; bowl.

Kugelregen ['ku:gəlre:gən], _m._ (—s, _no pl._) hail of bullets.
kugelrund ['ku:gəlrunt], _adj._ round as a ball, well-fed.
Kugelschreiber ['ku:gəlʃraɪbər], _m._ (—s, _pl._ —) ball-point pen.
Kuh [ku:] _f._ (—, _pl._ ⸚e) cow; _junge_ —, heifer.
Kuhblattern ['ku:blatərn], _f. pl._ cow-pox.
Kuhblume ['ku:blu:mə], _f._ (—, _pl._ —n) (_Bot._) marigold.
Kuhfladen ['ku:fla:dən], _m._ (—s, _pl._ —) cow-dung.
Kuhhaut ['ku:haut], _f._ (—, _pl._ ⸚e) cow-hide; _das geht auf keine_ —, that defies description.
kühl [ky:l], _adj._ cool, fresh; (_behaviour_) reserved.
Kühle ['ky:lə], _f._ (—, _no pl._) coolness, freshness; (_behaviour_) reserve.
kühlen ['ky:lən], _v.a._ cool, freshen.
Kühlraum ['ky:lraum], _m._ (—es, _pl._ ⸚e) refrigerating-chamber.
Kühlschrank ['ky:lʃraŋk], _m._ (—s, _pl._ ⸚e) refrigerator, (_coll._) fridge.
Kühltruhe ['ky:ltru:ə], _f._ (—, _pl._ —n) deep freeze.
Kühlung ['ky:luŋ], _f._ (—, _pl._ —en) refrigeration.
Kuhmist ['ku:mɪst], _m._ (—s, _no pl._) cow-dung.
kühn [ky:n], _adj._ bold, daring, audacious.
Kühnheit ['ky:nhaɪt], _f._ (—, _no pl._) boldness, daring, audacity.
Kujon [ku'jo:n], _m._ (—s, _pl._ —e) bully, scoundrel.
kujonieren [kujo'ni:rən], _v.a._ bully, exploit.
Kukuruz ['kukuruts], _m._ (—es, _no pl._) (_Austr._) maize.
kulant [ku'lant], _adj._ obliging; (_terms_) easy.
Kulanz [ku'lants], _f._ (—, _no pl._) accommodating manner.
Kuli ['ku:li:], _m._ (—s, _pl._ —s) coolie.
kulinarisch [kuli'na:rɪʃ], _adj._ culinary.
Kulisse [ku'lɪsə], _f._ (—, _pl._ —n) (_Theat._) back-drop, side-scene, wings.
Kulissenfieber [ku'lɪsənfi:bər], _n._ (—s, _no pl._) stage-fright.
kulminieren [kulmi'ni:rən], _v.n._ culminate.
kultivieren [kulti'vi:rən], _v.a._ cultivate.
Kultur [kul'tu:r], _f._ (—, _pl._ —en) (_Agr._) cultivation; (_fig._) culture, civilization.
Kultus ['kultus], _m._ (—, _pl._ **Kulte**) cult, worship.
Kultusministerium ['kultusmɪnɪste:rjum], _n._ (—s, _pl._ —**rien**) Ministry of Education.
Kümmel ['kyməl], _m._ (—s, _no pl._) caraway-seed; (_drink_) kümmel.
Kummer ['kumər], _m._ (—s, _no pl._) grief, sorrow, trouble.
kümmerlich ['kymərlɪç], _adj._ miserable, pitiful.
kummerlos ['kumərlo:s], _adj._ untroubled.

kümmern ['kymərn], _v.r. sich_ — _um_, mind, look after, be worried about, care for.
Kümmernis ['kymərnɪs], _f._ (—, _pl._ —**se**) grief, sorrow.
kummervoll ['kumərfɔl], _adj._ sorrowful, painful, grievous.
Kumpan [kum'pa:n], _m._ (—s, _pl._ —e) companion; mate; _lustiger_ —, jolly fellow, good companion.
kund [kunt], _adj._ known, public; _etwas_ — _tun_, make s.th. public; — _und zu wissen sei hiermit_, (_obs._) we hereby give notice.
kundbar ['kuntba:r], _adj._ known; _etwas_ — _machen_, announce s.th., make s.th. known.
kündbar ['kyntba:r], _adj._ (_loan, capital etc._) redeemable; capable of being called in, terminable.
Kunde (1) ['kundə], _m._ (—n, _pl._ —n) customer; _ein schlauer_ —, an artful dodger.
Kunde (2) ['kundə], _f._ (—, _pl._ —n) news; information, notification; (_compounds_) science.
Kundgebung ['kuntge:buŋ], _f._ (—, _pl._ —en) publication; rally; demonstration.
kundig ['kundɪç], _adj._ versed in, conversant with.
Kundige ['kundɪgə], _m._ (—n, _pl._ —n) expert, initiate.
kündigen ['kyndɪgən], _v.n._ give notice (_Dat._).
Kundmachung ['kuntmaxuŋ], _f._ (—, _pl._ —en) publication.
Kundschaft ['kuntʃaft], _f._ (—, _no pl._) clientele, customers; information, reconnaissance.
kundschaften ['kuntʃaftən], _v.n._ reconnoitre, scout.
künftig ['kynftɪç], _adj._ future, prospective, to come.
Kunst [kunst], _f._ (—, _pl._ ⸚e) art; skill.
Kunstbutter ['kunstbutər], _f._ (—, _no pl._) margarine.
Künstelei [kynstə'laɪ], _f._ (—, _pl._ —en) affectation, mannerism.
kunstfertig ['kunstfertɪç], _adj._ skilled, skilful.
Kunstfreund ['kunstfrɔynt], _m._ (—es, _pl._ —e) art-lover.
kunstgerecht ['kunstgəreçt], _adj._ workmanlike.
Kunstgewerbe ['kunstgəverbə], _n._ (—s, _no pl._) arts and crafts.
Kunstgriff ['kunstgrɪf], _m._ (—es, _pl._ —e) trick, dodge, artifice, knack.
Kunsthändler ['kunsthendlər], _m._ (—s, _pl._ —) art-dealer.
Kunstkenner ['kunstkenər], _m._ (—s, _pl._ —) connoisseur.
Künstler ['kynstlər], _m._ (—s, _pl._ —) artist, performer.
künstlerisch ['kynstlərɪʃ], _adj._ artistic, elaborate, ingenious.
künstlich ['kynstlɪç], _adj._ artificial.
kunstlos ['kunstlo:s], _adj._ artless, unaffected.

133

kunstreich ['kunstraɪç], *adj.* ingenious.

Kunstseide ['kunstzaɪdə], *f.* (—, *no pl.*) artificial silk.

Kunststickerei ['kunstʃtɪkəraɪ], *f.* (—, *no pl.*) art needlework.

Kunststoff ['kunstʃtɔf], *m.* (—es, *pl.* —e) plastics.

Kunststopfen ['kunstʃtɔpfən], *n.* (—s, *no pl.*) invisible mending.

Kunststück ['kunstʃtyk], *n.* (—es, *pl.* —e) trick, feat.

Kunstverständige ['kunstferʃtɛndɪgə], *m.* (—n, *pl.* —n) art expert.

Küpe ['ky:pə], *f.* (—, *pl.* —n) large tub; (dyeing) copper.

Kupfer ['kupfər], *n.* (—s, *no pl.*) copper.

Kupferblech ['kupfərblɛç], *n.* (—es, *no pl.*) copper-sheet.

Kupferdraht ['kupfərdra:t], *m.* (—es, *pl.* ⁝e) copper-wire.

kupferhaltig ['kupfərhaltɪç], *adj.* containing copper.

Kupferrost ['kupfərrɔst], *m.* (—es, *no pl.*) verdigris.

Kupferstecher ['kupfərʃteçər], *m.* (—s, *pl.* —) (copperplate) engraver.

kupieren [ku'pi:rən], *v.a.* (*rare*) (*ticket*) punch; (*Austr.*) (*horse*) dock.

Kuppe ['kupə], *f.* (—, *pl.* —n) (*hill*) top, summit.

Kuppel ['kupəl], *f.* (—, *pl.* —n) cupola, dome.

kuppeln ['kupəln], *v.n.* procure, pimp; make a match.

Kuppler ['kuplər], *m.* (—s, *pl.* —) procurer, pimp; matchmaker.

Kupplung ['kupluŋ], *f.* (—, *pl.* —en) (*Railw.*) coupling, joint; (*Motor.*) clutch.

Kur [ku:r], *f.* (—, *pl.* —en) cure; *eine — machen*, undergo medical treatment.

Kuranstalt ['ku:ranʃtalt], *f.* (—, *pl.* —en) sanatorium; (*Am.*) sanitarium.

Küraß ['ky:ras], *m.* (—sses, *pl.* —sse) cuirass.

Kuratel [kura'tɛl], *f.* (—, *pl.* —en) guardianship, trusteeship.

Kuratorium [kura'to:rjum], *n.* (—s, *pl.* —rien) board of guardians or trustees; council, governing body.

Kurbel ['kurbəl], *f.* (—, *pl.* —n) crank, winch.

Kurbelstange ['kurbəlʃtaŋə], *f.* (—, *pl.* —n) connecting rod.

Kurbelwelle ['kurbəlvɛlə], *f.* (—, *pl.* —n) crankshaft.

Kürbis ['kyrbɪs], *m.* (—ses, *pl.* —se) (*Bot.*) pumpkin, gourd.

küren ['ky:rən], *v.a. irr.* (*Poet.*) choose, elect.

Kurfürst ['ku:rfyrst], *m.* (—en, *pl.* —en) Elector (of the Holy Roman Empire).

Kurhaus ['ku:rhaus], *n.* (—es, *pl.* ⁝er) spa; hotel; pump room.

Kurie ['ku:rjə], *f.* (—, *pl.* —n) (*Eccl.*) Curia; Papal Court.

Kurier [ku'ri:r], *m.* (—s, *pl.* —e) courier.

kurieren [ku'ri:rən], *v.a.* cure.

kurios [kur'jo:s], *adj.* curious, queer, strange.

Kuriosität [kurjozi'tɛ:t], *f.* (—, *pl.* —en) curio, curiosity.

Kurort ['ku:rɔrt], *m.* (—es, *pl.* —e) spa, watering-place, health-resort.

Kurrentschrift [ku'rɛntʃrɪft], *f.* (—, *no pl.*) running hand, cursive writing.

Kurs [kurs], *m.* (—es, *pl.* —e) rate of exchange; quotation; circulation; course.

Kursaal ['ku:rza:l], *m.* (—s, *pl.* —säle) hall, (*spa*) pump-room, casino.

Kursbericht ['kursbərɪçt], *m.* (—es, *pl.* —e) market report.

Kursbuch ['kursbu:x], *n.* (—es, *pl.* ⁝er) railway-guide, time-table.

Kürschner ['kyrʃnər], *m.* (—s, *pl.* —) furrier, skinner.

kursieren [kur'zi:rən], *v.n.* be current, circulate.

Kursivschrift [kur'zi:fʃrɪft], *f.* (—, *no pl.*) italics.

Kursstand ['kursʃtant], *m.* (—es, *no pl.*) rate of exchange.

Kursus ['kurzus], *m.* (—, *pl.* **Kurse**) course (of lectures).

Kurszettel ['kursʃtɛtəl], *m.* (—s, *pl.* —) quotation-list.

Kurve ['kurvə], *f.* (—, *pl.* —n) curve.

kurz [kurts], *adj.* short, brief, concise; curt, abrupt.

kurzangebunden [kurts'angəbundən], *adj.* terse, abrupt, curt.

kurzatmig ['kurtsa:tmɪç], *adj.* short-winded, short of breath.

Kürze ['kyrtsə], *f.* (—, *no pl.*) shortness, brevity.

kürzen ['kyrtsən], *v.a.* shorten, abbreviate, condense; (*Maths.*) reduce.

kürzlich ['kyrtslɪç], *adv.* lately, recently, the other day.

Kurzschluß ['kurtsʃlus], *m.* (—sses, *pl.* ⁝sse) short circuit.

Kurzschrift ['kurtsʃrɪft], *f.* (—, *no pl.*) shorthand.

kurzsichtig ['kurtsʃɪçtɪç], *adj.* short-sighted.

kurzum [kurts'um], *adv.* in short.

Kürzung ['kyrtsuŋ], *f.* (—, *pl.* —en) abbreviation, abridgement.

Kurzwaren ['kurtsva:rən], *f. pl.* haberdashery.

kurzweg [kurts've:k], *adv.* simply, offhand, briefly.

Kurzweil ['kurtsvaɪl], *f.* (—, *no pl.*) pastime.

kurzweilig ['kurtsvaɪlɪç], *adj.* amusing, diverting, entertaining.

kusch! [kuʃ], *excl.* (*to dogs*) lie down!

kuschen ['kuʃən], *v.n.*, *v.r.* crouch, lie down.

Kuß [kus], *m.* (—sses, *pl.* ⁝sse) kiss.

küssen ['kysən], *v.a.*, *v.n.*, *v.r.* kiss.

Küste ['kystə], *f.* (—, *pl.* —n) coast, shore.

Küstenstadt ['kystənʃtat], *f.* (—, *pl.* ⁀e) seaside town.
Küster ['kystər], *m.* (—s, *pl.* —) sacristan, sexton, verger.
Kustos ['kustɔs], *m.* (—, *pl.* —oden) custodian; director of museum.
Kutschbock ['kutʃbɔk], *m.* (—s, *pl.* ⁀e) box(-seat).
Kutsche ['kutʃə], *f.* (—, *pl.* —n) coach, carriage.
kutschieren [kut'ʃiːrən], *v.n.* drive a coach.
Kutte ['kutə], *f.* (—, *pl.* —n) cowl.
Kutter ['kutər], *m.* (—s, *pl.* —) (*Naut.*) cutter.
Kuvert [ku'vɛːr], *n.* (—s, *pl.* —s) envelope; (*dinner*) place laid.
kuvertieren [kuvɛr'tiːrən], *v.a.* envelop, wrap.
Kux [kuks], *m.* (—es, *pl.* —e) share in a mining concern.
Kybernetik [kybɛr'neːtɪk], *f.* (—, *no pl.*) cybernetics.

L

L [ɛl], *n.* (—, *pl.* —) the letter L.
Lab [laːp], *n.* (—es, *pl.* —e) rennet.
labbern ['labərn], *v.a.*, *v.n.* dribble, slobber; blab.
Labe ['laːbə], *f.* (—, *no pl.*) (*Poet.*) refreshment; comfort.
laben ['laːbən], *v.a.* refresh, restore, revive.
labil [la'biːl], *adj.* unstable.
Laborant [labo'rant], *m.* (—en, *pl.* —en) laboratory assistant.
Laboratorium [labora'toːrjum], *n.* (—s, *pl.* —rien) laboratory.
laborieren [labo'riːrən], *v.n.* experiment; suffer (from).
Labsal ['laːpzaːl], *n.* (—s, *pl.* —e) restorative, refreshment.
Labung ['laːbuŋ], *f.* (—, *pl.* —en) refreshment, comfort.
Lache ['laxə], *f.* (—, *pl.* —n) pool, puddle.
Lächeln ['lɛçəln], *n.* (—s, *no pl.*) smile; *albernes —*, smirk; *höhnisches —*, sneer.
lächeln ['lɛçəln], *v.n.* smile.
Lachen ['laxən], *n.* (—s, *no pl.*) laugh, laughter.
lachen ['laxən], *v.n.* laugh.
lächerlich ['lɛçərlɪç], *adj.* laughable, ridiculous; preposterous; ludicrous; *sich — machen*, make a fool of o.s.; *etwas — machen*, ridicule s.th.
Lachgas ['laxgaːs], *n.* (—es, *no pl.*) nitrous oxide, laughing-gas.
lachhaft ['laxhaft], *adj.* laughable, ridiculous.

Lachkrampf ['laxkrampf], *m.* (—es, *pl.* ⁀e) hysterical laughter, a fit of laughter.
Lachs [laks], *m.* (—es, *pl.* —e) salmon.
Lachsalve ['laxzalvə], *f.* (—, *pl.* —n) peal of laughter.
Lack [lak], *m.* (—s, *pl.* —e) lac, lacquer, varnish.
lackieren [la'kiːrən], *v.a.* lacquer, varnish.
Lackmus ['lakmus], *n.* (—, *no pl.*) litmus.
Lackschuh ['lakʃuː], *m.* (—s, *pl.* —e) patent-leather shoe.
Lackwaren ['lakvaːrən], *f. pl.* japanned goods.
Lade ['laːdə], *f.* (—, *pl.* —n) box, chest, case, drawer.
Ladebaum ['laːdəbaum], *m.* derrick.
Ladefähigkeit ['laːdəfɛ:ɪçkaɪt], *f.* (—, *pl.* —en), carrying capacity, loading capacity; tonnage.
Ladegeld ['laːdəgɛlt], *n.* (—es, *pl.* —er) loading charges.
Laden ['laːdən], *m.* (—s, *pl.* ⁀) (*window*) shutter; shop, store.
laden ['laːdən], *v.a. irr.* load; (*Elec.*) charge; (*Law*) summon, (*fig.*) incur.
Ladenhüter ['laːdənhyːtər], *m.* (—s, *pl.* —) unsaleable article.
Ladenpreis ['laːdənpraɪs], *m.* (—es, *pl.* —e) retail-price.
Ladentisch ['laːdəntɪʃ], *m.* (—es, *pl.* —e) counter.
Ladeschein ['laːdəʃaɪn], *m.* (—s, *pl.* —e) bill of lading.
Ladestock ['laːdəʃtɔk], *m.* (—es, *pl.* ⁀e) ramrod.
Ladung ['laːduŋ], *f.* (—, *pl.* —en) loading, lading, freight; shipment, cargo; (*gun*) charge; (*Law*) summons.
Laffe ['lafə], *m.* (—n, *pl.* —n) fop.
Lage ['laːgə], *f.* (—, *pl.* —n) site, position, situation; state, condition; stratum, layer.
Lager ['laːgər], *n.* (—s, *pl.* —) couch, bed, divan; (*Geol.*) seam, vein; (*Tech.*) bearing; (*Comm.*) warehouse, store; camp.
Lageraufnahme ['laːgəraufnaːmə], *f.* (—, *pl.* —n) stock-taking, inventory.
Lager(bier) ['laːgər(biːr)], *n.* (—s, *pl.* —e) lager.
Lagergeld ['laːgərgɛlt], *n.* (—es, *pl.* —er) storage charge.
Lagerist [laːgə'rɪst], *m.* (—en, *pl.* —en) warehouse-clerk.
lagern ['laːgərn], *v.a.* store, warehouse.
Lagerstätte ['laːgərʃtɛtə], *f.* (—, *pl.* —n) couch, resting-place; camp site.
Lagerung ['laːgəruŋ], *f.* (—, *pl.* —en) encampment; storage; stratification.
Lagune [la'guːnə], *f.* (—, *pl.* —n) lagoon.
lahm [laːm], *adj.* lame, paralysed, crippled.
lahmen ['laːmən], *v.n.* be lame, limp.
lähmen ['lɛːmən], *v.a.* paralyse.
lahmlegen ['laːmleːgən], *v.a.* paralyse.

Lähmung

Lähmung [ˈlɛ:muŋ], *f.* (—, *pl.* —en) paralysis.

Laib [laɪp], *m.* (—es, *pl.* —e) (*bread*) loaf.

Laich [laɪç], *m.* (—es, *pl.* —e) spawn.

laichen [ˈlaɪçən], *v.n.* spawn.

Laie [ˈlaɪə], *m.* (—n, *pl.* —n) layman, (*pl.*) laity.

Lakai [laˈkaɪ], *m.* (—en, *pl.* —en) lackey, flunkey, footman.

Lake [ˈla:kə], *f.* (—, *pl.* —n) brine, pickle.

Laken [ˈla:kən], *n.* (—s, *pl.* —) (*bed*) sheet.

lakonisch [laˈko:nɪʃ], *adj.* laconic.

Lakritze [laˈkrɪtsə], *f.* (—, *pl.* —n) liquorice.

lallen [ˈlalən], *v.a., v.n.* stammer; babble.

Lama (1) [ˈla:ma:], *n.* (—s, *pl.* —s) (*animal*) llama.

Lama (2) [ˈla:ma:], *m.* (—s, *pl.* —s) (*priest*) lama.

lamentieren [lamɛnˈti:rən], *v.n.* lament, wail.

Lamm [lam], *n.* (—es, *pl.* ⸚er) (*Zool.*) lamb.

Lämmchen [ˈlɛmçən], *n.* (—s, *pl.* —) (*Zool.*) lambkin.

Lämmergeier [ˈlɛmərgaɪər], *m.* (—s, *pl.* —) (*Orn.*) great bearded vulture.

Lampe [ˈlampə], *f.* (—, *pl.* —n) lamp.

Lampenfieber [ˈlampənfi:bər], *n.* (—s, *no pl.*) stage-fright.

Lampenputzer [ˈlampənputsər], *m.* (—s, *pl.* —) lamplighter.

Lampenschirm [ˈlampənʃɪrm], *m.* (—s, *pl.* —e) lampshade.

Lampion [lamˈpjõ], *m. & n.* (—s, *pl.* —s) Chinese lantern.

lancieren [lãˈsi:rən], *v.a.* thrust; launch.

Land [lant], *n.* (—es, *pl.* —e (*Poet.*) and ⸚er) land, country; state; ground, soil; *das Gelobte* —, the Promised Land; *an* — *gehen*, go ashore; *aufs* — *gehen*, go into the country.

Landadel [ˈlanta:dəl], *m.* (—s, *no pl.*) landed gentry.

Landarbeiter [ˈlantarbaɪtər], *m.* (—s, *pl.* —) farm-worker.

Landauer [ˈlandauər], *m.* (—s, *pl.* —) landau.

Landebahn [ˈlandəba:n], *f.* (—, *pl.* —en) (*Aviat.*) runway.

landen [ˈlandən], *v.n.* (*aux. sein*) land, disembark; (*aircraft*) land, touch down.

Landenge [ˈlantəŋə], *f.* (—, *pl.* —n) isthmus.

Ländereien [ˈlɛndəraɪən], *f. pl.* landed property, estate.

Landeserzeugnis [ˈlandəsertsɔyknɪs], *n.* (—sses, *pl.* —sse) home produce.

Landesfürst [ˈlandəsfyrst], *m.* (—en, *pl.* —en) sovereign.

Landesherr [ˈlandəshɛr], *m.* (—n, *pl.* —en) (reigning) prince; sovereign.

Landeshoheit [ˈlandəshohaɪt], *f.* (—, *no pl.*) sovereignty.

Landeskirche [ˈlandəskɪrçə], *f.* (—, *pl.* —n) established church; national church.

Landesschuld [ˈlandəsʃult], *f.* (—, *no pl.*) national debt.

Landessprache [ˈlandəsʃpra:xə], *f.* (—, *pl.* —n) vernacular.

Landestracht [ˈlandəstraxt], *f.* (—, *pl.* —en) national costume.

landesüblich [ˈlandəsy:plɪç], *adj.* conventional, usual, customary.

Landesverweisung [ˈlandəsfɛrvaɪzuŋ], *f.* (—, *pl.* —en) exile, banishment.

landflüchtig [ˈlantflyçtɪç], *adj.* fugitive.

Landfrieden [ˈlantfri:dən], *m.* (—s, *no pl.*) King's (*or* Queen's) peace; (*medieval*) public peace.

Landgericht [ˈlantgərɪçt], *n.* (—es, *pl.* —e) district court; county court.

Landgraf [ˈlantgra:f], *m.* (—en, *pl.* —en) landgrave, count.

Landhaus [ˈlanthaus], *n.* (—es, *pl.* ⸚er) country house.

Landjunker [ˈlantjuŋkər], *m.* (—s, *pl.* —) country squire.

Landkarte [ˈlantkartə], *f.* (—, *pl.* —n) map.

landläufig [ˈlantlɔyfɪç], *adj.* customary, conventional.

ländlich [ˈlɛntlɪç], *adj.* rural, rustic.

Landmann [ˈlantman], *m.* (—es, *pl.* **Landleute**) rustic, peasant.

Landmesser [ˈlantmɛsər], *m.* (—s, *pl.* —) surveyor.

Landpartie [ˈlantparti:], *f.* (—, *pl.* —n) country excursion, picnic.

Landplage [ˈlantpla:gə], *f.* (—, *pl.* —n) scourge, calamity; *eine richtige* —, a public nuisance.

Landrat [ˈlantra:t], *m.* (—s, *pl.* ⸚e) district president *or* magistrate.

Landratte [ˈlantratə], *f.* (—, *pl.* —n) landlubber.

Landrecht [ˈlantrɛçt], *n.* (—es, *no pl.*) common law.

Landregen [ˈlantre:gən], *m.* (—s, *no pl.*) steady downpour; persistent rain.

Landschaft [ˈlantʃaft], *f.* (—, *pl.* —en) landscape.

landschaftlich [ˈlantʃaftlɪç], *adj.* scenic.

Landsknecht [ˈlantsknɛçt], *m.* (—es, *pl.* —e) mercenary; hired soldier.

Landsmann [ˈlantsman], *m.* (—es, *pl.* **Landsleute**) fellow-countryman, compatriot.

Landspitze [ˈlantʃpɪtsə], *f.* (—, *pl.* —n) cape, headland, promontory.

Landstraße [ˈlantʃtra:sə], *f.* (—, *pl.* —n) open road, main road, highway.

Landstreicher [ˈlantʃtraɪçər], *m.* (—s, *pl.* —) vagabond, tramp, (*Am.*) hobo.

Landstrich [ˈlantʃtrɪç], *m.* (—es, *pl.* —e) tract of land.

Landsturm [ˈlantʃturm], *m.* (—s, *no pl.*) (*Milit.*) militia; Home Guard.

Landtag [ˈlantta:k], *m.* (—s, *pl.* —e) (*Parl.*) diet.

Landung [ˈlanduŋ], *f.* (—, *pl.* —en) landing.

Landvermesser *see* **Landmesser**.

Landvogt ['lantfo:kt], *m.* (—es, *pl.* ⁻e) (provincial) governor.

Landweg ['lantve:k], *m.* (—s, *pl.* —e) overland route.

Landwehr ['lantve:r], *f.* (—, *pl.* —en) militia.

Landwirt ['lantvɪrt], *m.* (—s, *pl.* —e) farmer, husbandman.

Landwirtschaft ['lantvɪrtʃaft], *f.* (—, *no pl.*) agriculture.

Landzunge ['lanttsuŋə], *f.* (—, *pl.* —n) spit of land.

lang [laŋ], *adj.* long, tall. — *adv., prep.* (*prec. by Acc.*) for, during, long.

langatmig ['laŋa:tmɪç], *adj.* long-winded.

lange ['laŋə], *adv.* a long time; *wie* —? how long? *so* — *wie*, as long as.

Länge ['lɛŋə], *f.* (—, *pl.* —n) length; (*Geog.*) longitude.

langen ['laŋən], *v.a.* reach, hand, give s.o. s.th. — *v.n.* suffice, be enough.

Längengrad ['lɛŋəngra:t], *m.* (—s, *pl.* —e) degree of longitude.

Längenkreis ['lɛŋənkraɪs], *m.* (—es, *pl.* —e) meridian.

Längenmaß ['lɛŋənma:s], *n.* (—es, *pl.* —e) linear measure.

Langeweile ['laŋəvaɪlə], *f.* (—, *no pl.*) boredom, ennui.

Langfinger ['laŋfɪŋər], *m.* (—s, *pl.* —) pickpocket.

langjährig ['laŋjɛ:rɪç], *adj.* of long standing.

Langlebigkeit ['laŋle:bɪçkaɪt], *f.* (—, *no pl.*) longevity.

länglich ['lɛŋlɪç], *adj.* oblong.

Langmut ['laŋmu:t], *f.* (—, *no pl.*) forbearance, patience.

längs [lɛŋs], *prep.* (*Genit., Dat.*) along.

langsam ['laŋza:m], *adj.* slow; deliberate.

längst [lɛŋst], *adv.* long ago, long since.

längstens ['lɛŋstəns], *adv.* at the longest; at the latest.

Languste [laŋ'gustə], *f.* (—, *pl.* —n) (*Zool.*) spiny lobster.

langweilen ['laŋvaɪlən], *v.a.* (*insep.*) bore, tire. — *v.r. sich* —, feel bored, be bored.

langwierig ['laŋvi:rɪç], *adj.* lengthy, protracted, wearisome.

Lanze ['lantsə], *f.* (—, *pl.* —n) lance, spear; *eine* — *brechen*, take up the cudgels, stand up for (s.th. *or* s.o.).

Lanzenstechen ['lantsənʃteçən], *n.* (—s, *no pl.*) tournament.

Lanzette [lan'tsetə], *f.* (—, *pl.* —n) lancet.

Lanzknecht ['lantsknɛçt], *m.* (—es, *pl.* —e) *see* **Landsknecht**.

Laos ['la:ɔs], *n.* Laos.

Lappalie [la'pa:ljə], *f.* (—, *pl.* —n) trifle.

Lappen ['lapən], *m.* (—s, *pl.* —) rag, duster, patch; (*ear*) lobe.

Läpperschulden ['lɛpərʃuldən], *f. pl.* petty debts.

läppisch ['lɛpɪʃ], *adj.* silly, foolish, trifling.

Lappland ['lapland], *n.* Lapland.

Lärche ['lɛrçə], *f.* (—, *pl.* —n) (*Bot.*) larch.

Lärm [lɛrm], *m.* (—s, *no pl.*) noise, din.

lärmen ['lɛrmən], *v.n.* make a noise, brawl.

Larve ['larfə], *f.* (—, *pl.* —n) mask; (*Ent.*) grub, larva.

lasch [laʃ], *adj.* limp; insipid.

Lasche ['laʃə], *f.* (—, *pl.* —n) flap; (*shoe*) gusset, strip.

lassen ['lasən], *v.a., v.n. irr.* let, allow, suffer, permit; leave; make, cause; order, command; desist.

läßlich ['lɛslɪç], *adj.* (*Eccl.*) venial (*sin*).

lässig ['lɛsɪç], *adj.* indolent, sluggish, inactive.

Lässigkeit ['lɛsɪçkaɪt], *f.* (—, *no pl.*) lassitude, inaction, indolence; negligence.

Last [last], *f.* (—, *pl.* —en) load, burden, weight, charge.

lasten ['lastən], *v.n.* be heavy; weigh (on).

lastenfrei ['lastənfraɪ], *adj.* unencumbered.

Laster ['lastər], *n.* (—s, *pl.* —) vice.

Lästerer ['lɛstərər], *m.* (—s, *pl.* —) slanderer, calumniator; blasphemer.

lasterhaft ['lastərhaft], *adj.* vicious, wicked; corrupt.

Lasterhöhle ['lastərhø:lə], *f.* (—, *pl.* —n) den of vice.

lästerlich ['lɛstərlɪç], *adj.* blasphemous.

lästern ['lɛstərn], *v.a.* slander, defame; blaspheme.

lästig ['lɛstɪç], *adj.* tiresome, troublesome.

Lasttier ['lastti:r], *n.* (—es, *pl.* —e) beast of burden.

Lastwagen ['lastva:gən], *m.* (—s, *pl.* —) lorry, (*Am.*) truck.

Lasur [la'zu:r], *m.* (—s, *pl.* —e) lapis-lazuli; ultramarine.

Latein [la'taɪn], *n.* (—s, *no pl.*) Latin.

lateinisch [la'taɪnɪʃ], *adj.* Latin.

Laterne [la'tɛrnə], *f.* (—, *pl.* —n) lantern; (*street*) lamp.

latschen ['la:tʃən], *v.n.* shuffle along.

Latte ['latə], *f.* (—, *pl.* —n) lath, batten; *eine lange* —, lanky person.

Lattich ['latɪç], *m.* (—s, *pl.* —e) lettuce.

Latz [lats], *m.* (—es, *pl.* ⁻e) flap, bib; pinafore.

lau [lau], *adj.* tepid, lukewarm, insipid; (*fig.*) half-hearted.

Laub [laup], *n.* (—es, *no pl.*) foliage, leaves.

Laube ['laubə], *f.* (—, *pl.* —n) arbour, summer-house.

Laubengang ['laubəngaŋ], *m.* (—es, *pl.* ⁻e) arcade, covered walk.

Laubfrosch ['laupfrɔʃ], *m.* (—es, *pl.* ⁻e) (*Zool.*) tree-frog.

Laubsäge ['laupzɛ:gə], *f.* (—, *pl.* —n) fret-saw.

Lauch [laux], *m.* (—es, *no pl.*) (*Bot.*) leek.

Lauer ['lauər], *f.* (—, *no pl.*) ambush, hiding-place; *auf der* — *sein*, lie in wait.

lauern ['lauərn], *v.n.* lurk, lie in wait (for), watch (for).

Lauf [lauf], *m.* (—es, *pl.* ⁝e) course, run; running; operation; (*river*) current; (*gun*) barrel; (*fig.*) rein.

Laufbahn ['laufbaːn], *f.* (—, *pl.* —en) career, *die medizinische — einschlagen*, enter upon a medical career.

Laufband ['laufbant], *n.* (—s, *pl.* ⁝er) (*baby*) rein, leading-string; (*Tech.*) conveyor-belt.

Laufbrücke ['laufbrykə], *f.* (—, *pl.* —n) gangway.

Laufbursche ['laufburʃə], *m.* (—n, *pl.* —n) errand-boy.

laufen ['laufən], *v.n.* irr. (*aux.* sein) run; walk; (*wheel*) turn; flow, trickle down.

laufend ['laufənt], *adj.* current.

Läufer ['lɔyfər], *m.* (—s, *pl.* —) runner; (*carpet*) rug; (*Chess*) bishop; (*Footb.*) half-back.

Lauffeuer ['lauffɔyər], *n.* (—s, *no pl.*) wildfire.

Laufgraben ['laufgraːbən], *m.* (—s, *pl.* ⁝) trench.

läufig ['lɔyfiç], *adj.* (*animals*) ruttish.

Laufpaß ['laufpas], *m.* (—sses, *no pl.*) *den — geben*, give (s.o.) the sack.

Laufschritt ['laufʃrit], *m.* (—es, *pl.* —e) march; *im —*, at the double.

Laufzeit ['laufsait], *f.* (—, *pl.* —en) running-time; currency; (*animals*) rutting time.

Lauge ['laugə], *f.* (—, *pl.* —en) (*Chem.*) lye, alkali.

Lauheit ['lauhait], *f.* (—, *no pl.*) tepidity, lukewarmness; (*fig.*) half-heartedness.

Laune ['launə], *f.* (—, *pl.* —n) humour, temper, mood, whim.

launenhaft ['launənhaft], *adj.* moody.

launig ['launiç], *adj.* humorous.

launisch ['launiʃ], *adj.* moody, fitful, bad-tempered.

Laus [laus], *f.* (—, *pl.* ⁝e) (*Zool.*) louse.

Lausbub ['lausbuːp], *m.* (—en, *pl.* —en) young scamp, rascal.

lauschen ['lauʃən], *v.n.* listen, eavesdrop.

Lausejunge ['lauzəjuŋə], *m.* (—n, *pl.* —n) rascal, lout.

lausig ['lauziç], *adj.* (*vulg.*) sordid, lousy.

laut [laut], *adj.* loud, noisy, audible, clamorous. — *prep.* (*Genit.*) as per, according to, in virtue of.

Laut [laut], *m.* (—es, *pl.* —e) sound.

lautbar ['lautbaːr], *adj.* — *machen*, make known.

Laute ['lautə], *f.* (—, *pl.* —n) (*Mus.*) lute.

lauten ['lautən], *v.n.* purport, run, read.

läuten ['lɔytən], *v.a.*, *v.n.* ring; toll; *es läutet*, the bell is ringing.

lauter ['lautər], *adj.* clear, pure; (*fig.*) single-minded; genuine; nothing but. — *adv.* merely.

Lauterkeit ['lautərkait], *f.* (—, *no pl.*) clearness, purity; (*fig.*) single-mindedness, integrity.

läutern ['lɔytərn], *v.a.* clear, purify; refine.

Läuterung ['lɔytəruŋ], *f.* (—, *pl.* —en) clearing, purification; refinement.

lautieren [lau'tiːrən], *v.a.* read phonetically.

Lautlehre ['lautleːrə], *f.* (—, *no pl.*) phonetics.

lautlich ['lautliç], *adj.* phonetic.

lautlos ['lautloːs], *adj.* mute, silent; noiseless.

Lautmalerei ['lautmaːlərai], *f.* (—, *no pl.*) onomatopoeia.

Lautsprecher ['lautʃprɛçər], *m.* (—s, *pl.* —) loudspeaker.

Lautverschiebung ['lautfɛrʃiːbuŋ], *f.* (—, *pl.* —en) sound shift.

lauwarm ['lauvarm], *adj.* lukewarm, tepid; (*fig.*) half-hearted.

Lava ['laːva], *f.* (—, *no pl.*) lava.

Lavendel [la'vɛndəl], *m.* (—s, *no pl.*) (*Bot.*) lavender.

lavieren [la'viːrən], *v.n.* tack; (*fig.*) wangle.

Lawine [la'viːnə], *f.* (—, *pl.* —n) avalanche.

lax [laks], *adj.* lax, loose.

Laxheit ['lakshait], *f.* (—, *pl.* —en) laxity.

Laxiermittel [lak'siːrmitəl], *n.* (—s, *pl.* —) laxative, aperient.

Lazarett [latsa'rɛt], *n.* (—s, *pl.* —e) infirmary, military hospital.

Lebemann ['leːbəman], *m.* (—es, *pl.* ⁝er) man about town.

Leben ['leːbən], *n.* (—s, *pl.* —) life; (*fig.*) existence; activity; animation, bustle, stir.

leben ['leːbən], *v.n.* live, be alive.

lebend ['leːbənt], *adj.* alive, living; (*language*) modern.

lebendig [le'bɛndiç], *adj.* living, alive, quick.

Lebensanschauung ['leːbənsanʃauuŋ], *f.* (—, *pl.* —en) conception of life, philosophy of life.

Lebensart ['leːbənsaːrt], *f.* (—, *no pl.*) way of living; (*fig.*) behaviour; *gute* —, good manners.

lebensfähig ['leːbənsfɛːiç], *adj.* capable of living, viable.

lebensgefährlich ['leːbənsgəfɛːrliç], *adj.* perilous, extremely dangerous.

Lebensgeister ['leːbənsgaistər], *m. pl.* spirits.

lebensgroß ['leːbənsgroːs], *adj.* life-size.

lebenslänglich ['leːbənslɛŋliç], *adj.* lifelong, for life; —*e Rente*, life annuity.

Lebenslauf ['leːbənslauf], *m.* (—es, *pl.* ⁝e) curriculum vitae.

Lebensmittel ['leːbənsmitəl], *n. pl.* food, provisions, victuals.

lebensmüde ['leːbənsmyːdə], *adj.* weary of life.

Lebensunterhalt ['leːbənsuntərhalt], *m.* (—s, *no pl.*) livelihood.

Lebenswandel ['leːbənsvandəl], *m.* (—s, *no pl.*) conduct, mode of life.

Lebensweise ['le:bǝnsvaɪzǝ], f. (—, no pl.) habits, way of life.

Leber ['le:bǝr], f. (—, pl. —n) liver; frisch von der — weg, frankly, without mincing matters.

Leberblümchen ['le:bǝrbly:mçǝn], n. (—s, pl. —) (Bot.) liverwort.

Leberfleck ['le:bǝrflɛk], m. (—s, pl. —e) mole.

Lebertran ['le:bǝrtra:n], m. (—s, no pl.) cod-liver oil.

Leberwurst ['le:bǝrvurst], f. (—, pl. ⁻e) liver sausage.

Lebewesen ['le:bǝve:zǝn], n. (—s, pl. —) living creature.

Lebewohl ['le:bǝvo:l], n., excl. farewell, good-bye; — sagen, bid farewell.

lebhaft ['le:phaft], adj. lively, vivacious, brisk, animated.

Lebkuchen ['le:pku:xǝn], m. (—s, pl. —) gingerbread.

Lebzeiten ['le:ptsaɪtǝn], f. pl. zu — von (Genit.), in the lifetime of.

lechzen ['lɛçtsǝn], v.n. be parched with thirst; nach etwas —, (fig.) long for s.th., pine for s.th.

Leck [lɛk], n. (—s, pl. —e) leak; ein — bekommen, spring a leak.

leck [lɛk], adj. leaky.

lecken ['lɛkǝn], v.a. lick, lap.

lecker ['lɛkǝr], adj. delicate, delicious, dainty.

Leckerbissen ['lɛkǝrbisǝn], m. (—s, pl. —) delicacy; dainty, tit-bit.

Leckerei [lɛkǝ'raɪ], f. (—, pl. —en) delicacy.

Leder ['le:dǝr], n. (—s, no pl.) leather.

ledern ['le:dǝrn], adj. (of) leather, leathery; (fig.) dull, boring.

ledig ['le:dɪç], adj. unmarried, single; (fig.) rid of, free from.

lediglich ['le:dɪklɪç], adv. merely, only, solely.

leer [le:r], adj. empty, void; blank; (fig.) hollow, futile, empty, vain, inane.

Leere ['le:rǝ], f. (—, no pl.) emptiness, void, vacuum.

leeren ['le:rǝn], v.a. empty, evacuate.

Leerlauf ['le:rlauf], m. (—s, no pl.) (Motor.) idling; (gear) neutral.

legalisieren [legali'zi:rǝn], v.a. legalise, authenticate.

Legat (1) [le'ga:t], m. (—en, pl. —en) legate.

Legat (2) [le'ga:t], n. (—s, pl. —e) legacy, bequest.

Legationsrat [lega'tsjo:nsra:t], m. (—s, pl. ⁻e) counsellor in a legation.

legen ['le:gǝn], v.a. lay, put, place. — v.r. sich —, lie down; cease, subside.

Legende [le'gɛndǝ], f. (—, pl. —n) legend.

Legierung [lǝ'gi:ruŋ], f. (—, pl. —en) alloy.

Legion [le'gjo:n], f. (—, pl. —en) legion.

Legionär [le:gjo'nɛ:r], m. (—s, pl. —e) legionary.

legitim [legi'ti:m], adj. legitimate.

Legitimation [legitima'tsjo:n], f. (—, pl. —en) proof of identity.

legitimieren [legiti'mi:rǝn], v.a. legitimise. — v.r. sich —, prove o.'s identity.

Lehen ['le:ǝn], n. (—s, pl. —) fief; zu — geben, invest with, enfeoff; zu — tragen, hold in fee.

Lehensdienst see **Lehnsdienst**.

Lehenseid see **Lehnseid**.

Lehensmann see **Lehnsmann**.

Lehm [le:m], m. (—s, no pl.) loam, clay, mud.

lehmig ['le:mɪç], adj. clayey, loamy.

Lehne ['le:nǝ], f. (—, pl. —n) support, prop; (chair) back, arm-rest.

lehnen ['le:nǝn], v.a., v.n. lean. — v.r. sich — an, lean against.

Lehnsdienst ['le:nsdi:nst], m. (—es, pl. —e) feudal service.

Lehnseid ['le:nsaɪt], m. (—es, pl. —e) oath of allegiance.

Lehnsmann ['le:nsman], m. (—es, pl. ⁻er) feudal tenant, vassal.

Lehnstuhl ['le:nʃtu:l], m. (—s, pl. ⁻e) armchair, easy chair.

Lehramt ['le:ramt], n. (—es, pl. ⁻er) professorship; teaching post or profession.

Lehrbrief ['le:rbri:f], m. (—es, pl. —e) apprentice's indentures; certificate of apprenticeship.

Lehrbuch ['le:rbu:x], n. (—es, pl. ⁻er) textbook, manual.

Lehre ['le:rǝ], f. (—, pl. —n) teaching, advice, rule, doctrine, dogma, moral; (craft) apprenticeship.

lehren ['le:rǝn], v.a. teach, inform, instruct; profess.

Lehrer ['le:rǝr], m. (—s, pl. —) teacher, instructor, schoolmaster.

Lehrgang ['le:rgaŋ], m. (—es, pl. ⁻e) course (of instruction).

Lehrgegenstand ['le:rge:gǝnʃtant], m. (—es, pl. ⁻e) subject of instruction; branch of study.

Lehrgeld ['le:rgɛlt], n. (—es, pl. —er) premium for apprenticeship; — zahlen, (fig.) pay for o.'s experience.

Lehrkörper ['le:rkœrpǝr], m. (—s, no pl.) teaching staff; (Univ.) faculty.

Lehrling ['le:rlɪŋ], m. (—s, pl. —e) apprentice.

Lehrmädchen ['le:rmɛ:tçǝn], n. (—s, pl. —) girl apprentice.

Lehrmeister ['le:rmaɪstǝr], m. (—s, pl. —) teacher, instructor, master.

Lehrmittel ['le:rmɪtǝl], n. (—s, pl. —) teaching appliance or aid.

lehrreich ['le:rraɪç], adj. instructive.

Lehrsatz ['le:rzats], m. (—es, pl. ⁻e) tenet, dogma, rule; (Maths.) theorem.

Lehrstuhl ['le:rʃtu:l], m. (—s, pl. ⁻e) (Univ.) chair; professorship.

Lehrzeit ['le:rtsaɪt], f. (—, pl. —en) apprenticeship.

Leib [laɪp], m. (—es, pl. ⁻er) body; abdomen; womb.

Leibarzt ['laɪpa:rtst], m. (—es, pl. ⁻e) court surgeon.

Leibbinde

Leibbinde [ˈlaɪpbɪndə], *f.* (—, *pl.* —n) abdominal belt.

Leibchen [ˈlaɪpçən], *n.* (—s, *pl.* —) bodice, corset; vest.

leibeigen [laɪpˈaɪgən], *adj.* in bondage, in thraldom, in serfdom.

Leibeserbe [ˈlaɪbəsˌɛrbə], *m.* (—n, *pl.* —n) heir, descendant, offspring; (*pl.*) issue.

Leibesfrucht [ˈlaɪbəsfruxt], *f.* (—, *pl.* ˀe) embryo, foetus.

Leibeskraft [ˈlaɪbəskraft], *f.* (—, *pl.* ˀe) bodily strength; *aus —en*, with might and main.

Leibesübung [ˈlaɪbəsyːbuŋ], *f.* (—, *pl.* —en) physical exercise; (*pl.*) gymnastic exercises.

Leibgericht [ˈlaɪpgəriçt], *n.* (—s, *pl.* —e) favourite dish.

leibhaftig [laɪpˈhaftɪç], *adj.* real, incarnate, in person.

leiblich [ˈlaɪplɪç], *adj.* bodily, corporeal.

Leibrente [ˈlaɪprɛntə], *f.* (—, *pl.* —n) life-annuity.

Leibschmerzen [ˈlaɪpʃmɛrtsən], *m. pl.* stomach-ache.

Leibspeise [ˈlaɪpʃpaɪzə], *f.* (—, *pl.* —n) favourite dish.

Leibwache [ˈlaɪpvaxə], *f.* (—, *no pl.*) body-guard.

Leibwäsche [ˈlaɪpvɛʃə], *f.* (—, *no pl.*) underwear.

Leiche [ˈlaɪçə], *f.* (—, *pl.* —n) (dead) body, corpse; (*dial.*) funeral.

Leichenbegängnis [ˈlaɪçənbəgɛŋnɪs], *n.* (—ses, *pl.* —se) funeral, burial, interment.

Leichenbeschauer [ˈlaɪçənbəʃauər], *m.* (—s, *pl.* —) coroner.

Leichenbestatter [ˈlaɪçənbəʃtater], *m.* (—s, *pl.* —) undertaker; (*Am.*) mortician.

leichenhaft [ˈlaɪçənhaft], *adj.* corpse-like, cadaverous.

Leichenschau [ˈlaɪçənʃau], *f.* (—, *no pl.*) post mortem (examination), (coroner's) inquest.

Leichentuch [ˈlaɪçəntuːx], *n.* (—es, *pl.* ˀer) shroud, pall.

Leichenverbrennung [ˈlaɪçənfɛrbrenuŋ], *f.* (—, *pl.* —en) cremation.

Leichenwagen [ˈlaɪçənvaːgən], *m.* (—s, *pl.* —) hearse.

Leichenzug [ˈlaɪçəntsuːk], *m.* (—es, *pl.* ˀe) funeral procession.

Leichnam [ˈlaɪçnaːm], *m.* (—s, *pl.* —e) (dead) body, corpse.

leicht [laɪçt], *adj.* light; slight; weak; easy.

leichtfertig [ˈlaɪçtfɛrtɪç], *adj.* frivolous, irresponsible.

leichtgläubig [ˈlaɪçtglɔybɪç], *adj.* credulous, gullible.

leichthin [ˈlaɪçthɪn], *adv.* lightly.

Leichtigkeit [ˈlaɪçtɪçkaɪt], *f.* (—, *no pl.*) ease, facility.

Leichtsinn [ˈlaɪçtzɪn], *m.* (—s, *no pl.*) thoughtlessness, carelessness; frivolity.

Leid [laɪt], *n.* (—es, *no pl.*) sorrow, grief; harm, hurt; *einem etwas zu —e tun*, harm s.o.

leid [laɪt], *adj. es tut mir —*, I am sorry; *du tust mir —*, I am sorry for you.

Leiden [ˈlaɪdən], *n.* (—s, *pl.* —) suffering, misfortune; (*illness*) affliction, complaint; *das — Christi*, the Passion.

leiden [ˈlaɪdən], *v.a., v.n. irr.* suffer, bear, endure, undergo.

Leidenschaft [ˈlaɪdənʃaft], *f.* (—, *pl.* —en) passion.

leider [ˈlaɪdər], *adv.* unfortunately.

leidig [ˈlaɪdɪç], *adj.* tiresome, unpleasant.

leidlich [ˈlaɪtlɪç], *adj.* tolerable, moderate.

leidtragend [ˈlaɪttraːgənt], *adj.* in mourning.

Leidtragende [ˈlaɪttraːgəndə], *m.* or *f.* (—n, *pl.* —n) mourner.

Leidwesen [ˈlaɪtveːzən], *n.* (—s, *no pl.*) *zu meinem —*, to my regret.

Leier [ˈlaɪər], *f.* (—, *pl.* —n) lyre.

Leierkasten [ˈlaɪərkastən], *m.* (—s, *pl.* ˀ) barrel organ.

leiern [ˈlaɪərn], *v.n.* drone, drawl on.

leihen [ˈlaɪən], *v.a. irr. einem etwas —*, lend s.o. s.th.; *von einem etwas —*, borrow s.th. from s.o.

Leim [laɪm], *m.* (—s, *no pl.*) glue; *einem auf den — gehen*, be taken in by s.o., fall for s.th.

Leimfarbe [ˈlaɪmfarbə], *f.* (—, *pl.* —en) water-colour, distemper.

Lein [laɪn], *m.* (—s, *pl.* —e) linseed, flax.

Leine [ˈlaɪnə], *f.* (—, *pl.* —n) line, cord.

Leinen [ˈlaɪnən], *n.* (—s, *no pl.*) linen.

Leinöl [ˈlaɪnøːl], *n.* (—s, *no pl.*) linseed oil.

Leintuch [ˈlaɪntuːx], *n.* (—es, *pl.* ˀer) linen sheet, sheeting.

Leinwand [ˈlaɪnvant], *f.* (—, *no pl.*) linen, sheeting; (*Art*) canvas; (*film*) screen.

leise [ˈlaɪzə], *adj.* low, soft, gentle, faint, slight; delicate.

Leiste [ˈlaɪstə], *f.* (—, *pl.* —n) ledge, border; groin.

Leisten [ˈlaɪstən], *m.* (—s, *pl.* —) (*shoe*) last, form.

leisten [ˈlaɪstən], *v.a.* do, perform; accomplish; *ich kann es mir nicht —*, I cannot afford it.

Leistenbruch [ˈlaɪstənbrux], *m.* (—es, *pl.* ˀe) hernia, rupture.

Leistung [ˈlaɪstuŋ], *f.* (—, *pl.* —en) performance, accomplishment, achievement.

leistungsfähig [ˈlaɪstuŋsfɛːɪç], *adj.* efficient.

leiten [ˈlaɪtən], *v.a.* lead, guide, manage; preside over.

Leiter (1) [ˈlaɪtər], *m.* (—s, *pl.* —) leader, manager; conductor; head.

Leiter (2) [ˈlaɪtər], *f.* (—, *pl.* —n) ladder.

Leiterwagen [ˈlaɪtərvaːgən], *m.* (—s, *pl.* —) rack-wagon; (*Austr.*) small hand-cart.

Leitfaden ['laɪtfaːdən], *m.* (—s, *pl.* ⸚) (*book*) manual, textbook, guide.

Leitstern ['laɪtʃtɛrn], *m.* (—s, *pl.* —e) pole-star; (*fig.*) lodestar, guiding star.

Leitung ['laɪtuŋ], *f.* (—, *pl.* —en) management, direction; (*Elec.*) lead, connection; line; (water- *or* gas-) main(s); pipeline; *eine lange — haben*, be slow in the uptake.

Leitungsvermögen ['laɪtuŋsfɛrmøː-gən], *n.* (—s, *no pl.*) conductivity.

Leitwerk ['laɪtvɛrk], *n.* (—s, *no pl.*) (*Aviat.*) tail unit.

Lektion [lɛkts'joːn], *f.* (—, *pl.* —en) lesson; *einem eine — geben*, lecture s.o.

Lektor ['lɛktɔr], *m.* (—s, *pl.* —en) publisher's reader; teacher, lector.

Lektüre [lɛk'tyːrə], *f.* (—, *pl.* —n) reading matter, books.

Lende ['lɛndə], *f.* (—, *pl.* —n) (*Anat.*) loin.

lendenlahm ['lɛndənlaːm], *adj.* weak-kneed, lame.

lenkbar ['lɛŋkbaːr], *adj.* dirigible, manageable, tractable, governable.

lenken ['lɛŋkən], *v.a.* drive, steer; (*fig.*) direct, rule, manage.

Lenkstange ['lɛŋkʃtaŋə], *f.* (—, *pl.* —n) connecting-rod; (*bicycle*) handle-bar.

Lenz [lɛnts], *m.* (—es, *pl.* —e) (*Poet.*) spring.

Lepra ['leːpra], *f.* (—, *no pl.*) leprosy.

Lerche ['lɛrçə], *f.* (—, *pl.* —n) (*Orn.*) lark, skylark.

lernbegierig ['lɛrnbəgiːrɪç], *adj.* studious, eager to learn.

lernen ['lɛrnən], *v.a.* learn; study; *einen kennen —*, make s.o.'s acquaintance; *auswendig —*, learn by heart.

Lesart ['leːsaːrt], *f.* (—, *pl.* —en) reading, version.

lesbar ['leːsbaːr], *adj.* legible; readable.

Lese ['leːzə], *f.* (—, *pl.* —n) gathering (of fruit); vintage.

lesen ['leːzən], *v.a. irr.* gather; glean; read; *die Messe —*, celebrate *or* say mass; *über etwas —*, (*Univ.*) lecture on s.th.

lesenswert ['leːzənsvɛrt], *adj.* worth reading.

Leser ['leːzər], *m.* (—s, *pl.* —) gatherer, gleaner; reader.

leserlich ['leːzərlɪç], *adj.* legible.

Lettland ['lɛtlant], *n.* Latvia.

letzen ['lɛtsən], *v.a.* (*Poet.*) comfort, cheer, refresh.

letzt [lɛtst], *adj.* last, extreme, ultimate, final.

letztens ['lɛtstəns], *adv.* lastly, in the end.

letztere ['lɛtstərə], *adj.* latter.

letzthin ['lɛtsthɪn], *adv.* (*rare*) lately, the other day, recently.

Leu [lɔy], *m.* (—en, *pl.* —en) (*Poet.*) lion.

Leuchte ['lɔyçtə], *f.* (—, *pl.* —n) light, lamp, lantern; (*fig.*) luminary, star.

leuchten ['lɔyçtən], *v.n.* light, shine.

leuchtend ['lɔyçtənt], *adj.* shining, bright; luminous.

Leuchter ['lɔyçtər], *m.* (—s, *pl.* —) candlestick, candelabrum.

Leuchtrakete ['lɔyçtrakeːtə], *f.* (—, *pl.* —n) Roman candle; flare.

Leuchtturm ['lɔyçtturm], *m.* (—s, *pl.* ⸚e) lighthouse.

leugnen ['lɔygnən], *v.a.* deny, disclaim; *nicht zu —*, undeniable.

Leumund ['lɔymunt], *m.* (—es, *no pl.*) renown, reputation.

Leute ['lɔytə], *pl.* persons, people, men; servants, domestic staff.

Leutnant ['lɔytnant], *m.* (—s, *pl.* —s) lieutenant.

leutselig ['lɔytzeːlɪç], *adj.* affable, friendly; condescending.

Levkoje [lɛf'koːjə], *f.* (—, *pl.* —n) (*Bot.*) stock.

Lexikon ['lɛksɪkɔn], *n.* (—s, *pl.* —s, —ka) dictionary, lexicon, encyclopaedia.

Libanon ['liːbanɔn], *m.* Lebanon.

Libelle [li'bɛlə], *f.* (—, *pl.* —n) (*Ent.*) dragonfly.

Liberia [li'beːrja], *n.* Liberia.

Libyen ['liːbɪən], *n.* Libya.

Licht [lɪçt], *n.* (—es, *pl.* —er) light, candle; luminary.

licht [lɪçt], *adj.* light, clear, open.

Lichtbild ['lɪçtbɪlt], *n.* (—es, *pl.* —er) photograph.

Lichtbrechung ['lɪçtbrɛçuŋ], *f.* (—, *pl.* —en) refraction of light.

lichten ['lɪçtən], *v.a.* clear, thin; *den Anker —*, weigh anchor.

lichterloh ['lɪçtərloː], *adj.* blazing, ablaze.

Lichthof ['lɪçthoːf], *m.* (—s, *pl.* ⸚e) well of a court, quadrangle.

Lichtmeß ['lɪçtmɛs], *f.* (—, *no pl.*) (*Eccl.*) Candlemas.

Lichtschirm ['lɪçtʃɪrm], *m.* (—s, *pl.* —e) screen, lamp-shade.

Lichtspieltheater ['lɪçtʃpiːlteaːtər], *n.* (—s, *pl.* —) cinema.

Lichtung ['lɪçtuŋ], *f.* (—, *pl.* —en) glade, clearing.

Lid [liːt], *n.* (—s, *pl.* —er) eye-lid.

lieb [liːp], *adj.* dear; beloved; good; *das ist mir —*, I am glad of it; *der —e Gott*, God; *unsere —e Frau*, Our Lady; *bei einem — Kind sein*, be a favourite with s.o., curry favour with s.o.

liebäugeln ['liːpɔygəln], *v.n. insep.* ogle.

Liebchen ['liːpçən], *n.* (—s, *pl.* —) sweetheart, love, darling.

Liebe ['liːbə], *f.* (—, *no pl.*) love.

Liebelei [liːbə'laɪ], *f.* (—, *pl.* —en) flirtation.

lieben ['liːbən], *v.a.* love, like, be fond of.

liebenswürdig ['liːbənsvyrdɪç], *adj.* amiable, kind, charming.

lieber ['liːbər], *adv.* rather, better, sooner; *etwas — tun*, prefer to do s.th.

Liebhaber ['liːphaːbər], *m.* (—s, *pl.* —) lover; (*fig.*) amateur, dilettante; (*Theat.*) leading man.

Liebhaberin ['liːphaːbərɪn], *f.* leading lady.

liebkosen ['li:pko:zən], _v.a. insep._ fondle, caress.

lieblich ['li:pliç], _adj._ lovely, charming, sweet.

Liebling ['li:pliŋ], _m._ (—s, _pl._ —e) darling, favourite.

lieblos ['li:plo:s], _adj._ hard-hearted; unkind.

Liebreiz ['li:praits], _m._ (—es, _no pl._) charm, attractiveness.

liebreizend ['li:praitsənt], _adj._ charming.

Liebschaft ['li:pʃaft], _f._ (—, _pl._ —en) love affair.

Lied [li:t], _n._ (—es, _pl._ —er) song, air, tune; _geistliches_ —, hymn.

liederlich ['li:dərliç], _adj._ careless, slovenly; dissolute, debauched; —es _Leben_, profligacy.

Lieferant [li:fə'rant], _m._ (—en, _pl._ —en) supplier, purveyor, contractor; _Eingang für_ —en, tradesmen's entrance.

liefern ['li:fərn], _v.a._ deliver, furnish, supply.

Lieferschein ['li:fərʃain], _m._ (—s, _pl._ —e) delivery note.

liegen ['li:gən], _v.n. irr._ lie; be situated; _es liegt mir daran_, it is of importance to me, I have it at heart; _es liegt mir nichts daran_, it is of no consequence to me.

Liegenschaft ['li:gənʃaft], _f._ (—, _pl._ —en) landed property, real estate.

Liga ['li:ga:], _f._ (—, _pl._ —gen) league.

Liguster [li'gustər], _m._ (—s, _no pl._) privet.

liieren [li'i:rən], _v.r._ (_aux._ haben) _sich_ — _mit_, unite with, combine with.

Likör [li'kø:r], _m._ (—s, _pl._ —e) liqueur.

lila ['li:la:] _adj._ (_colour_) lilac.

Lilie ['li:ljə], _f._ (—, _pl._ —n) (_Bot._) lily.

Limonade [limo'na:də], _f._ (—, _pl._ —n) lemonade.

lind [lint], _adj._ soft, gentle, mild.

Linde ['lində], _f._ (—, _pl._ —n) (_Bot._) lime-tree, linden.

lindern ['lindərn], _v.a._ soften, assuage, mitigate, soothe, allay.

Lindwurm ['lintvurm], _m._ (—s, _pl._ —er) (_Poet._) dragon.

Lineal [line'a:l], _n._ (—s, _pl._ —e) ruler, rule.

Linie ['li:njə], _f._ (—, _pl._ —n) line; lineage, descent; _in erster_ —, in the first place.

Linienschiff ['li:njənʃif], _n._ (—es, _pl._ —e) (_Naut._) liner.

lin(i)ieren [lin'(j)i:rən], _v.a._ rule.

linkisch ['liŋkiʃ], _adj._ awkward, clumsy.

links [liŋks], _adv._ to the left, on the left-hand side; —_um_! left about turn!

Linnen ['linən], _n._ (—s, _no pl._) (_Poet._) linen.

Linse ['linzə], _f._ (—, _pl._ —n) (_vegetable_) lentil; (_optical_) lens.

linsenförmig ['linzənfœrmiç], _adj._ lens-shaped.

Linsengericht ['linzəngəriçt], _n._ (—s, _pl._ —e) (_Bibl._) mess of pottage.

Lippe ['lipə], _f._ (—, _pl._ —n) lip; (_coll._) _eine_ — _riskieren_, be cheeky.

Lippenlaut ['lipənlaut], _m._ (—s, _pl._ —e) (_Phonet._) labial.

Lippenstift ['lipənʃtift], _m._ (—s, _pl._ —e) lipstick.

liquidieren [likvi'di:rən], _v.a._ liquidate, wind up, settle; charge.

lispeln ['lispəln], _v.n._ lisp.

Lissabon ['lisa'bɔn], _n._ Lisbon.

List [list], _f._ (—, _pl._ —en) cunning, craft; trick, stratagem, ruse.

Liste ['listə], _f._ (—, _pl._ —n) list, roll, catalogue.

listig ['listiç], _adj._ cunning, crafty, sly.

Listigkeit ['listiçkait], _f._ (—, _no pl._) slyness, craftiness.

Litanei [lita'nai], _f._ (—, _pl._ —en) litany.

Litauen ['litauən], _n._ Lithuania.

Liter ['li:tər], _m. & n._ (—s, _pl._ —) litre.

literarisch [litə'ra:riʃ], _adj._ literary.

Literatur [litəra'tu:r], _f._ (—, _pl._ —en) literature, letters.

Litfaßsäule ['litfaszɔylə], _f._ (—, _pl._ —n) advertisement pillar.

Liturgie [litur'gi:], _f._ (—, _pl._ —n) liturgy.

Litze ['litsə], _f._ (—, _pl._ —n) lace, braid, cord; (_Elec._) flex.

Livland ['li:flant], _n._ Livonia.

Livree [li'vre:], _f._ (—, _pl._ —n) livery.

Lizenz [li'tsents], _f._ (—, _pl._ —en) licence.

Lob [lo:p], _n._ (—es, _no pl._) praise, commendation.

loben ['lo:bən], _v.a._ praise, commend.

lobesam ['lo:bəza:m], _adj._ (_Poet._) worthy, honourable.

Lobgesang ['lo:pgəzaŋ], _m._ (—s, _pl._ ⁓e) hymn of praise.

Lobhudelei [lo:phu:də'lai], _f._ (—, _pl._ —en) adulation, flattery, toadying.

löblich ['lø:pliç], _adj._ laudable, commendable, meritorious.

lobpreisen ['lo:ppraizən], _v.a. insep._ eulogise, extol.

Lobrede ['lo:pre:də], _f._ (—, _pl._ —n) panegyric, eulogy.

Loch [lɔx], _n._ (—es, _pl._ ⁓er) hole.

Lochbohrer ['lɔxbo:rər], _m._ (—s, _pl._ —) auger.

lochen ['lɔxən], _v.a._ perforate, punch.

Locher ['lɔxər], _m._ (—s, _pl._ —) perforator, punch.

löcherig ['lœçəriç], _adj._ full of holes.

Lochmeißel ['lɔxmaisəl], _m._ (—s, _pl._ —) mortice-chisel.

Locke ['lɔkə], _f._ (—, _pl._ —n) curl, lock, ringlet, tress.

locken ['lɔkən], _v.a._ allure, decoy, entice.

locker ['lɔkər], _adj._ loose; slack; spongy; dissolute; _nicht_ — _lassen_, stick to o.'s guns.

lockern ['lɔkərn], _v.a._ loosen.

lockig ['lɔkiç], _adj._ curled, curly.

Lockmittel ['lɔkmitəl], _n._ (—s, _pl._ —) inducement, lure, bait.

Lockspeise ['lɔkʃpaizə], _f._ (—, _pl._ —n) lure, bait.

Lockung ['lɔkuŋ], *f.* (—, *pl.* —en) allurement, enticement.

Lockvogel ['lɔkfoːgəl], *m.* (—s, *pl.* ∵) decoy-bird.

Loden ['loːdən], *m.* (—s, *pl.* —) coarse cloth, frieze.

lodern ['loːdərn], *v.n.* blaze, flame.

Löffel ['lœfəl], *m.* (—s, *pl.* —) spoon; (*animal*) ear; *einen über den — barbieren*, take s.o. in.

Logarithmus [loga'rɪtmus], *m.* (—, *pl.* —men) logarithm.

Logbuch ['lɔkbuːx], *n.* (—es, *pl.* ∵er) logbook.

Loge ['loːʒə], *f.* (—, *pl.* —n) (*Theat.*) box; (*Freemasonry*) lodge.

Logenschließer ['loʒənʃliːsər], *m.* (—s, *pl.* —) (*Theat.*) attendant.

logieren [lo'ʒiːrən], *v.n.* board (with).

Logis [lo'ʒiː], *n.* (—, *pl.* —) lodgings.

logisch ['loːgɪʃ], *adj.* logical.

Lohe ['loːhə], *f.* (—, *pl.* —n) tanning bark; flame.

Lohgerber ['loːgɛrbər], *m.* (—s, *pl.* —) tanner.

Lohn [loːn], *m.* (—s, *pl.* ∵e) wages, pay; reward; recompense.

lohnen ['loːnən], *v.a.* reward, recompense, remunerate; pay wages to; *es lohnt sich nicht,* it is not worth while.

Lohnstopp ['loːnʃtɔp], *m.* (—s, *pl.* —s) pay pause, wage freeze.

Löhnung ['løːnuŋ], *f.* (—, *pl.* —en) pay, payment.

Lokal [loˈkaːl], *n.* (—s, *pl* —e) locality, premises; inn, pub, café.

lokalisieren [lokaliˈziːrən], *v.a.* localise.

Lokalität [lokaliˈtɛːt], *f.* (—, *pl.* —en) *see* Lokal.

Lokomotive [lokomoˈtiːvə], *f.* (—, *pl.* —n) (*Railw.*) locomotive, engine.

Lokomotivführer [lokomoˈtiːffyːrər], *m.* (—s, *pl.* —) (*Railw.*) engine-driver.

Lombard [lɔmˈbart], *m.* (—s, *pl.* —e) deposit-bank, loan bank.

Lombardei [lɔmbarˈdai], *f.* Lombardy.

Lorbeer ['lɔrbeːr], *m.* (—s, *pl.* —en) laurel.

Lorbeerbaum ['lɔrbeːrbaum], *m.* (—s, *pl.* ∵e) laurel-tree, bay-tree.

Lorbeerspiritus ['lɔrbeːrʃpiːritus], *m.* (—, *no pl.*) bay rum.

Lorgnon [lɔrnˈjõ], *n.* (—s, *pl.* —s) monocle, eye-glass.

Los [loːs], *n.* (—es, *pl.* —e) share, ticket; lot, fate; *das große —,* first prize.

los [loːs], *adj.* loose, untied; free from; released from, rid of; (*Am.*) quit of; *was ist los?* what is going on? what's the matter? *etwas — werden,* get rid of s.th.; *schieß los!* fire away!

lösbar ['løːsbaːr], *adj.* (*question, riddle*) soluble.

losbinden ['loːsbɪndən], *v.a. irr.* untie, unbind, loosen.

losbrechen ['loːsbrɛçən], *v.a. irr.* break off. — *v.n.* (*aux.* sein) break loose.

Löschblatt ['lœʃblat], *n.* (—es, *pl.* ∵er) blotting-paper.

Löscheimer ['lœʃaimər], *m.* (—s, *pl.* —) fire-bucket.

löschen ['lœʃən], *v.a.* put out; extinguish; (*debt*) cancel; (*writing*) efface, blot; (*freight*) (*Naut.*) unload; (*thirst*) quench.

Löschpapier ['lœʃpapiːr], *n.* (—s, *no pl.*) blotting-paper.

Löschung ['lœʃuŋ], *f.* (—, *pl.* —en) (*freight*) (*Naut.*) discharging, landing, unloading.

losdrücken ['loːsdrykən], *v.n.* discharge, fire.

lose ['loːzə], *adj.* loose, slack; (*fig.*) dissolute; —*s Maul,* malicious tongue.

Lösegeld ['løːzəgɛlt], *n.* (—es, *pl.* —er) ransom.

losen ['loːzən], *v.n.* draw lots.

lösen ['løːzən], *v.a.* loosen, untie; absolve, free, deliver; dissolve; solve; (*relations*) break off; (*tickets*) take, buy.

losgehen ['loːsgeːən], *v.n. irr.* (*aux.* sein) begin; (*gun*) go off; *auf einen —,* go for s.o.; *jetzt kann's —,* now for it.

loskaufen ['loːskaufən], *v.a.* redeem, ransom.

loskommen ['loːskɔmən], *v.n. irr.* (*aux.* sein) come loose; *von etwas —,* get rid of s.th.

löslich ['løːslɪç], *adj.* (*Chem.*) soluble.

loslösen ['loːsløːzən], *v.a.* detach.

losmachen ['loːsmaxən], *v.a.* free from. — *v.r. sich — von,* disengage o.s. from.

losreißen ['loːsraisən], *v.a. irr.* pull away, separate. — *v.n.* (*aux.* sein), break loose. — *v.r. sich — von,* tear o.s. away from.

lossagen ['loːszaːgən], *v.r. sich — von,* renounce s.th., dissociate o.s. from s.th.

losschlagen ['loːsʃlaːgən], *v.a.* knock loose; let fly; (*fig.*) sell, dispose of.

lossprechen ['loːsʃprɛçən], *v.a. irr.* (*Eccl.*) absolve; (*Law*) acquit.

lossteuern ['loːsʃtɔyərn], *v.n. — auf,* make for.

Losung ['loːzuŋ], *f.* (—, *pl.* —en) watchword, motto, password, slogan.

Lösung ['løːzuŋ], *f.* (—, *pl.* —en) loosening; solution.

losziehen ['loːstsiːən], *v.n. irr.* (*Mil.*) set out; *gegen einen —,* inveigh against s.o.; (*fig., coll.*) run s.o. down.

Lot [loːt], *n.* (—es, *pl.* —e) lead, plummet; (*weight*) half an ounce; (*Maths.*) perpendicular (line).

Löteisen ['løːtaizən], *n.* (—s, *pl.* —) soldering iron.

loten [loːtən], *v.a., v.n.* (*Naut.*) take soundings, plumb.

löten ['løːtən], *v.a.* solder.

Lothringen ['loːtrɪŋən], *n.* Lorraine.

Lötkolben ['løːtkɔlbən], *m.* (—s, *pl.* —) soldering iron.

Lotleine ['loːtlainə], *f.* (—, *pl.* —n) sounding-line.

Lotrechtstarter ['loːtrɛçtʃtartər], *m.* (—s, *pl.* —) (*Aviat.*) vertical take-off plane (V.T.O.L.).

143

Lötrohr ['løːtroːr], n. (—s, pl. —e) soldering-pipe.

Lotse ['loːtsə], m. (—n, pl. —n) (Naut.) pilot.

Lotterbett ['lɔtərbɛt], n. (—es, pl. —en) bed of idleness; (obs.) couch.

Lotterie [lɔtə'riː], f. (—, pl. —n) lottery, sweep-stake.

Lotterleben ['lɔtərleːbən], n. (—s, no pl.) dissolute life.

Löwe ['løːvə], m. (—n, pl. —n) (Zool.) lion.

Löwenbändiger ['løːvənbɛndɪgər], m. (—s, pl. —) lion tamer.

Löwengrube ['løːvəngruːbə], f. (—, pl. —n) lion's den.

Löwenmaul ['løːvənmaul], n. (—s, no pl.) (Bot.) snapdragon.

Löwenzahn ['løːvəntsaːn], m. (—s, no pl.) (Bot.) dandelion.

Löwin ['løːvɪn], f. (—, pl. —nen) (Zool.) lioness.

Luchs [luks], m. (—es, pl. —e) lynx.

Lücke ['lykə], f. (—, pl. —n) gap, breach; (fig.) omission, defect, blank.

Lückenbüßer ['lykənbyːsər], m. (—s, pl. —) stop-gap, stand-in.

lückenhaft ['lykənhaft], adj. fragmentary, incomplete, imperfect.

Luder ['luːdər], n. (—s, pl. —) (rare) carrion; (vulg.) beast, trollop; dummes —, silly ass, fathead.

Luderleben ['luːdərleːbən], n. (—s, no pl.) dissolute life.

ludern ['luːdərn], v.n. lead a dissolute life.

Luft [luft], f. (—, pl. "e) air.

Luftbrücke ['luftbrykə], f. (—, no pl.) air-lift.

Lüftchen ['lyftçən], n. (—s, pl. —) gentle breeze.

luftdicht ['luftdɪçt], adj. airtight.

Luftdruck ['luftdruk], m. (—s, no pl.) air pressure, atmospheric pressure; blast.

Luftdruckmesser ['luftdrukmɛsər], m. (—s, pl. —) barometer, pressure-gauge.

lüften ['lyftən], v.a. air, ventilate.

luftförmig ['luftfœrmɪç], adj. gaseous.

luftig ['luftɪç], adj. airy, windy.

Luftklappe ['luftklapə], f. (—, pl. —n) air-valve.

Luftkurort ['luftkuːrɔrt], m. (—s, pl. —e) health resort.

Luftlinie ['luftliːnjə], f. (—, pl. —n) bee-line; in der —, as the crow flies; (Aviat.) airline.

Luftloch ['luftlɔx], m. (—s, pl. "er) air-pocket.

Luftraum ['luftraum], m. (—s, no pl.) atmosphere; air space.

Luftröhre ['luftrøːrə], f. (—, pl. —n) windpipe.

Luftschiff ['luftʃɪf], n. (—es, pl. —e) air-ship.

Luftschiffahrt ['luftʃifaːrt], f. (—, no pl.) aeronautics.

Luftspiegelung ['luftʃpiːgəluŋ], f. (—, pl. —en) mirage.

Luftsprung ['luftʃpruŋ], m. (—s, pl. "e) caper, gambol; "e machen, caper, gambol.

Lüftung ['lyftuŋ], f. (—, no pl.) airing, ventilation.

Lug [luːk], m. (—s, no pl.) (obs.) lie; — und Trug, a pack of lies.

Lüge ['lyːgə], f. (—, pl. —n) lie, false-hood, fib; einen — strafen, give s.o. the lie.

lügen ['lyːgən], v.n. irr. lie, tell a lie.

lügenhaft ['lyːgənhaft], adj. lying, false, untrue.

Lügner ['lyːgnər], m. (—s, pl. —) liar.

Luke ['luːkə], f. (—, pl. —n) dormer-window; (ship) hatch.

Lümmel ['lyməl], m. (—s, pl. —) lout; hooligan.

Lump ['lump], m. (—s, —en, pl. —e, —en) scoundrel, blackguard.

Lumpen ['lumpən], m. (—s, pl. —) rag, tatter.

Lumpengesindel ['lumpəngəzɪndəl], n. (—s, no pl.) rabble, riffraff.

Lumpenpack ['lumpənpak], n. (—s, no pl.) rabble, riffraff.

Lumpensammler ['lumpənzamlər], m. (—s, pl. —) rag-and-bone-man.

Lumperei [lumpə'raɪ], f. (—, pl. —en) shabby trick; meanness; trifle.

lumpig ['lumpɪç], adj. ragged; (fig.) shabby, mean.

Lunge ['luŋə], f. (—, pl. —n) (human) lung; (animals) lights.

Lungenentzündung ['luŋənɛntsynduŋ], f. (—, pl. —en) pneumonia.

Lungenkrankheit ['luŋənkraŋkhaɪt], f. (—, pl. —en) pulmonary disease.

Lungenkraut ['luŋənkraut], n. (—s, pl. "er) lungwort.

Lungenschwindsucht ['luŋənʃvɪntzuxt], f. (—, no pl.) pulmonary consumption, tuberculosis.

lungern ['luŋərn], v.n. idle, loiter.

Lunte ['luntə], f. (—, pl. —n) fuse, slow-match; — riechen, smell a rat.

Lupe ['luːpə], f. (—, pl. —n) magnifying glass, lens; etwas durch die — besehen, examine s.th. closely, scrutinise s.th.; unter die — nehmen, examine closely.

lüpfen ['lypfən], v.a. lift.

Lupine [lu'piːnə], f. (—, pl. —n) (Bot.) lupin.

Lust [lust], f. (—, pl. "e) enjoyment, pleasure, delight; desire, wish, inclination, liking; — bekommen zu, feel inclined to; — haben auf, have a mind to, feel like; nicht übel — haben, have half a mind to.

Lustbarkeit ['lustbaːrkaɪt], f. (—, pl. —en) amusement, diversion, entertainment, pleasure.

Lustdirne ['lustdɪrnə], f. (—, pl. —n) prostitute.

lüstern ['lystərn], adj. lustful, lascivious.

lustig ['lustɪç], adj. gay, merry, cheerful, amusing, funny; — sein, make merry; sich über einen — machen, poke fun at s.o.

Lüstling ['lystlɪŋ], *m.* (—s, *pl.* —e) libertine, lecher.

Lustmord ['lustmɔrt], *m.* (—es, *pl.* —e) sex murder.

Lustreise ['lustraɪzə], *f.* (—, *pl.* —n) pleasure trip.

Lustschloß ['lustʃlɔs], *n.* (—sses, *pl.* ⸚sser) country house, country seat.

Lustspiel ['lustʃpi:l], *n.* (—s, *pl.* —e) comedy.

lustwandeln ['lustvandəln], *v.n. insep.* (*aux.* sein) stroll, promenade.

Lutherisch ['lutərɪʃ], *adj.* Lutheran.

lutschen ['lutʃən], *v.a.* suck.

Lüttich ['lytɪç], *n.* Liège.

Luxus ['luksus], *m.* (—, *no pl.*) luxury.

Luzern [lu'tsɛrn], *n.* Lucerne.

Luzerne [lut'sɛrnə], *f.* (—, *pl.* —n) (*Bot.*) lucerne.

Lymphe ['lymfə], *f.* (—, *pl.* —n) lymph.

lynchen ['lynçən], *v.a.* lynch.

Lyrik ['ly:rɪk], *f.* (—, *no pl.*) lyric poetry.

lyrisch ['ly:rɪʃ], *adj.* lyric(al).

Lyzeum [ly'tse:um], *n.* (—s, *pl.* Lyzeen) lyceum, grammar school *or* high school for girls.

M

M [ɛm], *n.* (—s, *pl.* —s) the letter M.

Maas [ma:s], *f.* River Meuse.

Maat [ma:t], *m.* (—s, *pl.* —s, —en) (*Naut.*) mate.

Mache ['maxə], *f.* (—, *no pl.*) put-up job, humbug, sham, eyewash.

machen ['maxən], *v.a.* make, do, produce, manufacture; cause; amount to; *mach schon*, be quick; *das macht nichts*, it does not matter; *mach's kurz*, cut it short; *etwas — lassen*, have s.th. made; *sich auf den Weg —*, set off; *sich viel (wenig) aus etwas —*, care much (little) for s.th.; *mach, daß du fortkommst*, get out, scram.

Macherlohn ['maxərlo:n], *m.* (—es, *pl.* ⸚e) charge for making s.th.

Macht [maxt], *f.* (—, *pl.* ⸚e) might, power; force, strength; authority; *mit aller —*, with might and main.

Machtbefugnis ['maxtbəfu:knɪs], *f.* (—, *pl.* —se) competence.

Machtgebot ['maxtgəbo:t], *n.* (—s, *pl.* —e) authoritative order.

Machthaber ['maxtha:bər], *m.* (—s, *pl.* —) potentate, ruler.

mächtig ['mɛçtɪç], *adj.* mighty, powerful; *einer Sache — sein*, to have mastered s.th.

machtlos ['maxtlo:s], *adj.* powerless.

Machtspruch ['maxtʃprux], *m.* (—s, *pl.* ⸚e) authoritative dictum; command; decree.

Machtvollkommenheit ['maxtfɔlkɔmənhaɪt], *f.* (—, *pl.* —en) absolute power; sovereignty; *aus eigner —*, of o.'s own authority.

Machtwort ['maxtvɔrt], *n.* (—es, *pl.* ⸚e) word of command; fiat; *ein — sprechen*, bring o.'s authority to bear, speak with authority.

Machwerk ['maxvɛrk], *n.* (—s, *pl.* —e) shoddy product; bad job; concoction; (*story*) pot-boiler.

Madagaskar [mada'gaskar], *n.* Madagascar.

Mädchen ['mɛːtçən], *n.* (—s, *pl.* —) girl; (*servant*) maid; — *für alles*, maid-of-all-work.

mädchenhaft ['mɛːtçənhaft], *adj.* girlish, maidenly.

Mädchenhandel ['mɛːtçənhandəl], *m.* (—s, *no pl.*) white slave trade.

Made ['ma:də], *f.* (—, *pl.* —n) maggot, mite.

Mädel ['mɛːdəl], *n.* (—s, *pl.* —) (*coll.*) see **Mädchen**.

madig ['ma:dɪç], *adj.* maggoty.

Magazin [maga'tsi:n], *n.* (—s, *pl.* —e) warehouse, storehouse; journal.

Magd [ma:kt], *f.* (—, *pl.* ⸚e) maid, maidservant; (*Poet.*) maiden.

Magen ['ma:gən], *m.* (—s, *pl.* —) (*human*) stomach; (*animals*) maw.

Magengrube ['ma:gəngru:bə], *f.* (—, *pl.* —n) pit of the stomach.

Magensaft ['ma:gənzaft], *m.* (—es, *pl.* ⸚e) gastric juice.

mager ['ma:gər], *adj.* lean, thin, slender, slim; (*fig.*) meagre.

Magerkeit ['ma:gərkaɪt], *f.* (—, *no pl.*) leanness, thinness, slenderness.

Magie [ma'gi:], *f.* (—, *no pl.*) magic.

Magier ['ma:gjər], *m.* (—s, *pl.* —) magician.

Magister [ma'gɪstər], *m.* (—s, *pl.* —) schoolmaster; (*Univ.*) Master; — *der freien Künste*, Master of Arts.

Magistrat [magɪs'tra:t], *m.* (—s, *pl.* —e) municipal board, local authority.

magnetisch [mag'ne:tɪʃ], *adj.* magnetic.

magnetisieren [magneti'zi:rən], *v.a.* magnetise.

Magnetismus [magne'tɪsmus], *m.* (—, *pl.* —men) magnetism; (*person*) mesmerism; *Lehre vom —*, magnetics.

Magnifizenz [magnifi'tsɛnts], *f.* (—, *pl.* —en) magnificence; *seine —*, (*Univ.*) title of Vice-Chancellor.

Mahagoni [maha'go:ni], *n.* (—s, *no pl.*) mahogany.

Mahd [ma:t], *f.* (—, *pl.* —en) mowing.

mähen ['mɛːən], *v.a.* mow.

Mäher ['mɛːər], *m.* (—s, *pl.* —) mower.

Mahl [ma:l], *n.* (—s, *pl.* —e, ⸚er) meal, repast.

mahlen ['ma:lən], *v.a.* grind.

Mahlstrom ['ma:lʃtro:m], *m.* (—s, *no pl.*) maelstrom, whirlpool, eddy.

Mahlzahn ['ma:ltsa:n], *m.* (—s, *pl.* ⸚e) molar, grinder.

Mahlzeit ['ma:ltsaɪt], *f.* (—, *pl.* —en) meal, repast.

Mähmaschine ['mɛ:maʃi:nə], *f.* (—, *pl.* —n) reaping-machine; lawn-mower.

Mähne ['mɛ:nə], *f.* (—, *pl.* —n) mane.

mahnen ['ma:nən], *v.a.* remind, admonish, warn; (*debtor*) demand payment, dun.

Mähre ['mɛ:rə], *f.* (—, *pl.* —n) mare.

Mähren ['mɛ:rən], *n.* Moravia.

Mai [maɪ], *m.* (—s, *pl.* —e) May.

Maid [maɪt], *f.* (—, *no pl.*) (*Poet.*) maiden.

Maiglöckchen ['maɪɡlœkçən], *n.* (—s, *pl.* —) (*Bot.*) lily of the valley.

Maikäfer ['maɪkɛ:fər], *m.* (—s, *pl.* —) (*Ent.*) cockchafer.

Mailand ['maɪlant], *n.* Milan.

Mais [maɪs], *m.* (—es, *no pl.*) (*Bot.*) maize, Indian corn.

Majestät [majɛs'tɛ:t], *f.* (—, *pl.* —en) majesty.

majestätisch [majɛs'tɛ:tiʃ], *adj.* majestic.

Major [ma'jo:r], *m.* (—s, *pl.* —e) (*Mil.*) major.

Majoran [majo'ra:n], *m.* (—s, *no pl.*) (*Bot.*) marjoram.

Majorat [majo'ra:t], *n.* (—s, *pl.* —e) primogeniture; entail.

majorenn [majo'rɛn], *adj.* (*obs.*) of age, over twenty-one.

Majorität [majori'tɛ:t], *f.* (—, *pl.* —en) majority.

Makel ['ma:kəl], *m.* (—s, *pl.* —) spot, blot; (*fig.*) blemish, flaw, defect.

Mäkelei [mɛ:kə'laɪ], *f.* (—, *pl.* —en) fault-finding, carping; fastidiousness.

makellos ['ma:kəllo:s], *adj.* spotless, immaculate.

mäkeln ['mɛ:kəln], *v.n.* find fault (with), cavil (at).

Makkabäer [maka'bɛ:ər], *m.* Maccabee.

Makler ['ma:klər], *m.* (—s, *pl.* —) broker.

Mäkler ['mɛ:klər], *m.* (—s, *pl.* —) fault-finder, caviller.

Maklergebühr ['ma:klərɡəby:r], *f.* (—, *pl.* —en) brokerage.

Makrele [ma'kre:lə], *f.* (—, *pl.* —n) (*Zool.*) mackerel.

Makrone [ma'kro:nə], *f.* (—, *pl.* —n) macaroon.

Makulatur [makula'tu:r], *f.* (—, *no pl.*) waste paper.

Mal [ma:l], *n.* (—s, *pl.* —e) mark, sign, token; monument; mole, birth-mark; stain; time; *dieses* —, this time, this once; *manches* —, sometimes; *mehrere* —*e*, several times; *mit einem* —, all of a sudden.

mal [ma:l], *adv. & part.* once; *noch*—, once more; (*coll.*) *hör* —, I say.

Malaya [ma'laɪa], *n.* Malaya.

malen ['ma:lən], *v.a.* paint.

Maler ['ma:lər], *m.* (—s, *pl.* —) painter.

Malerei [ma:lə'raɪ], *f.* (—, *pl.* —en) painting; picture.

malerisch ['ma:lərɪʃ], *adj.* picturesque.

Malerleinwand ['ma:lərlaɪnvant], *f.* (—, *no pl.*) canvas.

Malheur [ma'lø:r], *n.* (—s, *pl.* —e) misfortune, mishap.

Mali [ma:li] *n.* Mali.

maliziös [mali'tsjø:s], *adj.* malicious.

Malkasten ['ma:lkastən], *m.* (—s, *pl.* ⸚) paint-box.

Malstein ['ma:lʃtaɪn], *m.* (—s, *pl.* —e) monument; boundary stone.

Malstock ['ma:lʃtɔk], *m.* (—s, *pl.* ⸚e) maulstick, mahlstick.

Malteserorden [mal'te:zərɔrdən], *m.* (—s, *no pl.*) Order of the Knights of Malta.

malträtieren [maltrɛ'ti:rən], *v.a.* ill-treat.

Malve ['malvə], *f.* (—, *pl.* —n) (*Bot.*) mallow.

Malz [malts], *n.* (—es, *no pl.*) malt; *an ihm ist Hopfen und — verloren,* he is hopeless.

Malzbonbon ['maltsbɔbɔ], *m.* (—s, *pl.* —s) cough-lozenge, malt drop.

Mälzer ['mɛltsər], *m.* (—s, *pl.* —) maltster.

Mama [ma'ma:], *f.* (—, *pl.* —s) (*fam.*) mummy, mum, (*Am.*) mammy.

Mammon ['mamɔn], *m.* (—s, *no pl.*) mammon; *schnöder* —, filthy lucre.

Mammut ['mamut], *n.* (—s, *pl.* —e) mammoth.

Mamsell [mam'zɛl], *f.* (—, *pl.* —en) housekeeper.

man [man], *indef. pron.* one, they, people, men; — *sagt,* they say.

manch [manç], *pron.* (—er, —e, —es) many a, some, several.

mancherlei [mançər'laɪ], *adj.* several; of several kinds.

Manchester [man'çɛstər], *m.* (—s, *no pl.*) corduroy.

manchmal ['mançma:l], *adv.* sometimes.

Mandant [man'dant], *m.* (—en, *pl.* —en) client.

Mandantin [man'dantin], *f.* (—, *pl.* —innen) female client.

Mandarine [manda'ri:nə], *f.* (—, *pl.* —n) mandarin (orange), tangerine.

Mandat [man'da:t], *n.* (—s, *pl.* —e) mandate.

Mandel ['mandəl], *f.* (—, *pl.* —n) almond; (*Anat.*) tonsil; (*quantity*) fifteen; *eine* — *Eier,* fifteen eggs.

Mandoline [mando'li:nə], *f.* (—, *pl.* —n) mandolin.

Mangan [maŋ'ga:n], *n.* (—s, *no pl.*) (*Chem.*) manganese.

Mangel (1) ['maŋəl], *f.* (—, *pl.* —n) mangle, wringer.

Mangel (2) ['maŋəl], *m.* (—s, *pl.* ⸚) deficiency, defect; blemish; lack, shortage, want; *aus* — *an,* for want of; — *haben an,* be short of, lack (s.th.).

mangelhaft ['maŋəlhaft], *adj.* defective, imperfect.

mangeln (1) ['maŋəln], *v.a.* (*laundry*) mangle.

mangeln (2) ['maŋəln], *v.n.* be in want of, be short of; *es mangelt uns an ...*, we lack ....

mangels ['maŋəls], *prep.* (*Genit.*) for lack of, for want of.

Mangold ['maŋgɔlt], *m.* (—s, *no pl.*) (*Bot.*) beet, mangel-wurzel.

Manie [ma'ni:], *f.* (—, *pl.* —n) mania, craze.

Manier [ma'ni:r], *f.* (—, *pl.* —en) manner, habit; *gute —en haben*, have good manners.

maniriert [mani'ri:rt], *adj.* affected; (*Art*) mannered.

manierlich [ma'ni:rlɪç], *adj.* well behaved, civil, polite.

manipulieren [manipu'li:rən], *v.a.* manipulate.

Manko ['maŋko:], *n.* (—s, *pl.* —s) deficit, deficiency.

Mann [man], *m.* (—(e)s, *pl.* ̈er, (*Poet.*) —en) man; husband; *etwas an den — bringen*, get s.th. off o.'s hands, dispose of s.th.; *seinen — stehen*, hold o.'s own; *bis auf den letzten —*, to a man.

Mannbarkeit ['manba:rkait], *f.* (—, *no pl.*) puberty; marriageable age.

Männchen ['mɛnçən], *n.* (—s, *pl.* —) little man, manikin; (*Zool.*) male; *mein —*, (*coll.*) my hubby; *— machen*, (*dogs*) sit on the hindlegs, beg.

mannhaft ['manhaft], *adj.* manly, stout, valiant.

mannigfaltig ['manɪçfaltɪç], *adj.* manifold, multifarious.

männlich ['mɛnlɪç], *adj.* male; (*fig.*) manly; (*Gram.*) masculine.

Mannsbild ['mansbɪlt], *n.* (—es, *pl.* —er) (*coll.*) man, male person.

Mannschaft ['manʃaft], *f.* (—, *pl.* —en) men; crew, team.

mannstoll ['manstɔl], *adj.* man-mad.

Mannszucht ['manstsuxt], *f.* (—, *no pl.*) discipline.

Manöver [ma'nøːvər], *n.* (—s, *pl.* —) manoeuvre.

manövrieren [manø'vri:rən], *v.a.* manoeuvre.

Mansarde [man'zardə], *f.* (—, *pl.* —n) garret, attic.

manschen ['manʃən], *v.a., v.n.* dabble; splash (about).

Manschette [man'ʃetə], *f.* (—, *pl.* —n) cuff.

Mantel ['mantəl], *m.* (—s, *pl.* ̈) cloak, overcoat, coat, mantle, wrap; *den — nach dem Winde hängen*, be a time-server.

Manufaktur [manufak'tu:r], *f.* (—, *pl.* —en) manufacture.

Mappe ['mapə], *f.* (—, *pl.* —n) portfolio, case, file.

Mär [mɛ:r], *f.* (—, *pl.* —en) (*Poet.*) tale, tidings, legend.

Märchen ['mɛ:rçən], *n.* (—s, *pl.* —) fairy-tale, fable; fib.

märchenhaft ['mɛ:rçənhaft], *adj.* fabulous, legendary; (*coll.*) marvellous.

Marder ['mardər], *m.* (—s, *pl.* —) (*Zool.*) marten.

Maria [ma'ri:a], *f.* Mary; *die Jungfrau —*, the Virgin Mary.

Marienbild [ma'ri:ənbɪlt], *n.* (—es, *pl.* —er) image of the Virgin Mary.

Marienblume [ma'ri:ənblu:mə], *f.* (—, *pl.* —n) (*Bot.*) daisy.

Marienglas [ma'ri:ənglas], *n.* (—es, *no pl.*) mica.

Marienkäfer [ma'ri:ənkɛ:fər], *m.* (—s, *pl.* —) (*Ent.*) lady-bird.

Marine [ma'ri:nə], *f.* (—, *pl.* —n) navy.

marinieren [mari'ni:rən], *v.a.* pickle.

Marionette [mario'netə], *f.* (—, *pl.* —n) puppet, marionette.

Mark (1) [mark], *n.* (—s, *no pl.*) (*bone*) marrow; (*fruit*) pith, pulp.

Mark (2) [mark], *f.* (—, *pl.* —en) boundary, frontier province.

Mark (3) [mark], *f.* (—, *pl.* —) (*coin*) mark.

markant [mar'kant], *adj.* striking, prominent; (*remark*) pithy.

Marke ['markə], *f.* (—, *pl.* —n) (*trade*) mark, brand; (*postage*) stamp; (*game*) counter.

markieren [mar'ki:rən], *v.a.* mark.

markig ['markɪç], *adj.* marrowlike; (*fig.*) pithy, strong.

Markise [mar'ki:zə], *f.* (—, *pl.* —n) (sun)blind, awning.

Markt [markt], *m.* (—es, *pl.* ̈e) market, market-square, fair.

Marktflecken ['marktflekən], *m.* (—s, *pl.* —) borough; (small) market town.

Marktschreier ['marktʃraiər], *m.* (—s, *pl.* —) cheap-jack, quack, charlatan.

Markus ['markus], *m.* Mark.

Marmel ['marməl], *f.* (—, *pl.* —n) (*obs.*) marble.

Marmelade [marmə'la:də], *f.* (—, *pl.* —n) marmalade, jam.

Marmor ['marmɔr], *m.* (—s, *no pl.*) marble.

Marokko [ma'rɔko], *n.* Morocco.

Marone [ma'ro:nə], *f.* (—, *pl.* —n) sweet chestnut.

Maroquin [maro'kɛ̃], *n.* (—s, *no pl.*) Morocco leather.

Marotte [ma'rɔtə], *f.* (—, *pl.* —n) whim; fad.

Marquise [mar'ki:zə], *f.* (—, *pl.* —n) marchioness.

Marsch (1) [marʃ], *m.* (—es, *pl.* ̈e) march; *sich in — setzen*, set out; march off.

Marsch (2) [marʃ], *f.* (—, *pl.* —en) fen, marsh.

marsch! [marʃ], *int.* march! be off! get out!

Marschboden ['marʃbo:dən], *m.* (—s, *no pl.*) marshy soil, marshland.

marschieren [mar'ʃi:rən], *v.n.* (*aux.* sein) march.

Marstall ['marʃtal], *m.* (—s, *pl.* ̈e) royal stud.

Marter ['martər], *f.* —, *pl.* —n) torture, torment.

martern

martern ['martərn], *v.a.* torture, torment.

Märtyrer ['mɛrtyrər], *m.* (—s, *pl.* —) martyr.

Martyrium [mar'ty:rjum], *n.* (—s, *pl.* —rien) martyrdom.

März [mɛrts], *m.* (—es, *pl.* —e) (*month*) March.

Masche ['maʃə], *f.* (—, *pl.* —n) mesh; (*knitting*) stitch; (*dial.*) bow tie; (*coll.*) racket.

Maschine [ma'ʃi:nə], *f.* (—, *pl.* —n) machine; engine; *mit der — geschrieben,* typewritten.

Maschinengarn [ma'ʃi:nəngarn], *n.* (—s, *no pl.*) twist.

Maschinerie [maʃinə'ri:], *f.* (—, *pl.* —en) machinery.

Maser ['ma:zər], *f.* (—, *pl.* —n) (*wood*) vein, streak.

Masern ['ma:zərn], *f. pl.* measles.

Maske ['maskə], *f.* (—, *pl.* —n) mask, visor.

Maskerade [maskə'ra:də], *f.* (—, *pl.* —n) masquerade.

maskieren [mas'ki:rən], *v.a.* mask. — *v.r. sich* —, put on a mask.

Maß (1) [ma:s], *n.* (—es, *pl.* —e) measure, size; moderation, propriety; degree, extent; proportion; — *halten,* be moderate; *einem — nehmen,* measure s.o. (for); *in starkem —,* to a high degree; *mit —,* in moderation; *nach —,* to measure; *ohne — und Ziel,* immoderately, with no holds barred; *über alle —en,* exceedingly.

Maß (2) [ma:s], *m. & f.* (—, *pl.* —e) (*drink*) quart.

massakrieren [masa'kri:rən], *v.a.* massacre, slaughter.

Maßarbeit ['ma:sarbaɪt], *f.* (—, *pl.* —en) (*work*) made to measure; bespoke tailoring.

Masse ['masə], *f.* (—, *pl.* —n) mass, bulk; multitude; *eine —,* a lot.

Maßeinheit ['ma:saɪnhaɪt], *f.* (—, *pl.* —n) measuring-unit.

massenhaft ['masənhaft], *adj.* abundant.

Maßgabe ['ma:sga:bə], *f.* (—, *pl.* —n) *nach —,* according to, in proportion to.

maßgebend ['ma:sge:bənt], *adj.* standard; (*fig.*) authoritative.

massieren [ma'si:rən], *v.a.* massage.

mäßig ['mɛ:sɪç], *adj.* moderate, temperate, frugal.

Mäßigkeit ['mɛ:sɪçkaɪt], *f.* (—, *no pl.*) moderation, temperance, frugality.

Mäßigung ['mɛ:sɪguŋ], *f.* (—, *no pl.*) moderation.

Massiv [ma'si:f], *n.* (—s, *pl.* —e) (*mountains*) massif, range.

Maßliebchen ['ma:sli:pçən], *n.* (—s, *pl.* —) (*Bot.*) daisy.

maßlos ['ma:slo:s], *adj.* immoderate; (*fig.*) extravagant.

Maßnahme ['ma:sna:mə], *f.* (—, *pl.* —n) measure; —*n ergreifen,* take steps.

Maßregel ['ma:sre:gəl], *f.* (—, *pl.* —n) measure.

maßregeln ['ma:sre:gəln], *v.a.* reprove, reprimand.

Maßstab ['ma:sʃta:p], *m.* (—es, *pl.* ⸚e) standard; (*maps*) scale; *in kleinem (großem) —,* on a small (large) scale.

maßvoll ['ma:sfɔl], *adj.* moderate.

Mast (1) [mast], *m.* (—es, *pl.* —e) mast; pylon.

Mast (2) [mast], *f.* (—, *no pl.*) fattening.

Mastbaum ['mastbaum], *m.* (—s, *pl.* ⸚e) mast.

Mastdarm ['mastdarm], *m.* (—s, *pl.* ⸚e) rectum.

mästen ['mɛstən], *v.a.* feed, fatten.

Mastkorb ['mastkɔrp], *m.* (—s, *pl.* ⸚e) masthead.

Mästung ['mɛstuŋ], *f.* (—, *no pl.*) fattening, cramming.

Materialwaren [mate'rjalva:rən], *f. pl.* groceries; household goods.

materiell [mate'rjɛl], *adj.* material, real; materialistic.

Mathematik [matema'ti:k], *f.* (—, *no pl.*) mathematics.

mathematisch [mate'ma:tɪʃ], *adj.* mathematical.

Matratze [ma'tratsə], *f.* (—, *pl.* —n) mattress.

Matrikel [ma'tri:kəl], *f.* (—, *pl.* —n) register, roll.

Matrize [ma'tri:tsə], *f.* (—, *pl.* —n) matrix, die, stencil.

Matrose [ma'tro:zə], *m.* (—n, *pl.* —n) sailor, seaman.

Matsch [matʃ], *m.* (—es, *no pl.*) slush; mud.

matt [mat], *adj.* tired, exhausted, spent; languid; weak, feeble; (*light*) dim; (*gold*) dull; (*silver*) tarnished; (*Chess*) (check-)mate; — *setzen,* (*Chess*) to (check-)mate.

Matte ['matə], *f.* (—, *pl.* —n) mat, matting.

Matthäus [ma'tɛ:us], *m.* Matthew.

Mattheit ['mathaɪt], *f.* (—, *no pl.*) tiredness, exhaustion, languor, feebleness; (*light*) dimness; (*gold*) dullness.

mattherzig ['mathɛrtsɪç], *adj.* poorspirited, faint-hearted.

Matura [ma'tu:ra], *f.* (—, *pl.* —en) (*Austr.*) school-leaving *or* matriculation examination.

Mätzchen ['mɛtsçən], *n.* (—s, *pl.* —) nonsense; trick; *mach keine —,* don't be silly.

Mauer ['mauər], *f.* (—, *pl.* —n) wall.

Mauerkelle ['mauərkelə], *f.* (—, *pl.* —n) trowel.

mauern ['mauərn], *v.a.* build. — *v.n.* lay bricks, construct a wall.

Mauerwerk ['mauərverk], *n.* (—s, *no pl.*) brick-work.

Maul [maul], *n.* (—es, *pl.* ⸚er) (*animals*) mouth, muzzle; (*vulg.*) mouth; *das — halten,* shut up, hold o.'s tongue; *ein loses — haben,* have a loose tongue; *nicht aufs — gefallen sein,* have a quick tongue; (*vulg.*) *halt's —,* shut up.

Maulaffe ['maulafə], *m.* (—n, *pl.* —n) booby; —n feilhalten, stand gaping.

Maulbeere ['maulbe:rə], *f.* (—, *pl.* —n) (*Bot.*) mulberry.

maulen ['maulən], *v.n.* pout, sulk.

Maulesel ['maule:zəl], *m.* (—s, *pl.* —) (*Zool.*) mule.

maulfaul ['maulfaul], *adj.* tongue-tied; taciturn.

Maulheld ['maulhɛlt], *m.* (—en *pl.* —en) braggart.

Maulkorb ['maulkɔrp], *m.* (—s, *pl.* ·e) muzzle.

Maulschelle ['maulʃɛlə], *f.* (—, *pl.* —n) box on the ear.

Maultier ['maulti:r], *n.* (—s, *pl.* —e) (*Zool.*) mule.

Maulwerk ['maulvɛrk], *n.* (—s, *no pl.*) ein großes — haben, (*coll.*) have the gift of the gab.

Maulwurf ['maulvurf], *m.* (—s, *pl.* ·e) (*Zool.*) mole.

Maurer ['maurər], *m.* (—s, *pl.* —) mason, bricklayer.

Maus [maus], *f.* (—, *pl.* ·e) mouse.

Mausefalle ['mauzəfalə], *f.* (—, *pl.* —n) mouse-trap.

mausen ['mauzən], *v.n.* catch mice. — *v.a.* (*fig.*) pilfer, pinch.

Mauser ['mauzər], *f.* (—, *no pl.*) moulting.

mausern ['mauzərn], *v.r. sich* —, moult.

mausetot ['mauzəto:t], *adj.* dead as a door-nail.

mausig ['mauzɪç], *adj. sich* — *machen*, put on airs.

Maxime [mak'si:mə], *f.* (—, *pl.* —n) maxim, motto, device.

Mazedonien [matsə'do:njən], *n.* Macedonia.

Mäzen [mɛ:'tse:n], *m.* (—s, *pl.* —e) patron of the arts, Maecenas.

Mechanik [me'ça:nɪk], *f.* (—, *no pl.*) mechanics.

Mechaniker [me'ça:nɪkər], *m.* (—s, *pl.* —) mechanic.

mechanisch [me'ça:nɪʃ], *adj.* mechanical.

meckern ['mɛkərn], *v.n.* bleat; (*fig.*) grumble, complain.

Medaille [me'daljə], *f.* (—, *pl.* —n) medal.

Medaillon [medal'jõ], *n.* (—s, *pl.* —s) locket.

meditieren [medi'ti:rən], *v.n.* meditate.

Medizin [medi'tsi:n], *f.* (—, *pl.* —en) medicine, physic.

Mediziner [medi'tsi:nər], *m.* (—s, *pl.* —) physician, medical practitioner, student of medicine.

medizinisch [medi'tsi:nɪʃ], *adj.* medical, medicinal.

Meer [me:r], *n.* (—es, *pl.* —e) sea, ocean; offnes —, high seas; am —, at the seaside; auf dem —, at sea; übers —, overseas.

Meerbusen ['me:rbu:zən], *m.* (—s, *pl.* —) bay, gulf, bight.

Meerenge ['me:rɛŋə], *f.* (—, *pl.* —n) straits.

Meeresspiegel ['me:rəsʃpi:gəl], *m.* (—s, *no pl.*) sea-level.

Meerkatze ['me:rkatsə], *f.* (—, *pl.* —n) long-tailed monkey.

Meerrettich ['me:rrɛtɪç], *m.* (—s, *pl.* —e) (*Bot.*) horse-radish.

Meerschaum ['me:rʃaum], *m.* (—s, *no pl.*) sea-foam; (*pipe*) meerschaum.

Meerschwein ['me:rʃvain], *n.* (—s, *pl.* —e) (*Zool.*) porpoise.

Meerschweinchen ['me:rʃvainçən], *n.* (—s, *pl.* —) (*Zool.*) guinea-pig.

Mehl [me:l], *n.* (—es, *no pl.*) flour; meal; dust, powder.

Mehlkleister ['me:lklaistər], *m.* (—s, *no pl.*) flour paste.

Mehlspeise ['me:lʃpaizə], *f.* (—, *pl.* —n) (*dial.*) pudding, sweet.

mehr [me:r], *indecl. adj., adv.* more; umso —, all the more; immer —, more and more; — als genug, enough and to spare.

Mehrbetrag ['me:rbətra:k], *m.* (—s, *pl.* ·e) surplus.

mehrdeutig ['me:rdɔytɪç], *adj.* ambiguous.

mehren ['me:rən], *v.r. sich* —, multiply, increase in numbers.

mehrere ['me:rərə], *pl. adj.* several.

mehrfach ['me:rfax], *adj.* repeated.

Mehrheit ['me:rhait], *f.* (—, *pl.* —en) majority.

mehrmals ['me:rma:ls], *adv.* several times.

Mehrzahl ['me:rtsa:l], *f.* (—, *no pl.*) (*Gram.*) plural; majority, bulk.

meiden ['maidən], *v.a. irr.* shun, avoid.

Meierei [maiə'rai], *f.* (—, *pl.* —en) (*dairy*) farm.

Meile ['mailə], *f.* (—, *pl.* —n) mile; league.

Meiler ['mailər], *m.* (—s, *pl.* —) charcoal-kiln, charcoal-pile.

mein(e) ['main(ə)], *poss. adj.* my. —*poss. pron.* mine.

Meineid ['mainait], *m.* (—s, *pl.* —e) perjury; einen — schwören, perjure o.s.

meineidig ['mainaidɪç], *adj.* perjured, forsworn.

meinen ['mainən], *v.a.* mean, intend, think.

meinerseits ['mainərzaits], *adv.* I, for my part.

meinethalben ['mainəthalbən], *adv.* on my account, speaking for myself, for my sake; I don't care, I don't mind.

meinetwegen ['mainətve:gən], *adv.* see **meinethalben**.

meinetwillen ['mainətvilən], *adv.* um —, for my sake, on my behalf.

meinige ['mainigə], *poss. pron.* mine.

Meinung ['mainuŋ], *f.* (—, *pl.* —en) opinion; meaning; notion; öffentliche —, public opinion; der — sein, be of the opinion, hold the opinion; einem die — sagen, give s.o. a piece of o.'s mind; meiner — nach, in my opinion.

Meinungsverschiedenheit

Meinungsverschiedenheit ['maɪnuŋs-fɛrʃiːdənhaɪt], *f.* (—, *pl.* —en) difference of opinion, disagreement.

Meise ['maɪzə], *f.* (—, *pl.* —n) (*Orn.*) titmouse.

Meißel ['maɪsəl], *m.* (—s, *pl.* —) chisel.

meißeln ['maɪsəln], *v.a.* chisel, sculpt.

meist [maɪst], *adj.* most. — *adv.* usually, generally.

meistens ['maɪstəns], *adv.* mostly.

Meister ['maɪstər], *m.* (—s, *pl.* —) (*craft*) master; (*sport*) champion; *seinen* — *finden*, meet o.'s match.

meisterhaft ['maɪstərhaft], *adj.* masterly.

meisterlich ['maɪstərlɪç], *adj.* masterly.

meistern ['maɪstərn], *v.a.* master.

Meisterschaft ['maɪstərʃaft], *f.* (—, *pl.* —en) mastery; (*sport*) championship.

Mekka ['mɛka], *n.* Mecca.

Meldeamt ['mɛldəamt], *n.* (—s, *pl.* ⁻er) registration office.

melden ['mɛldən], *v.a.* announce, inform, notify; (*Mil.*) report. — *v.r.* *sich* —, answer the phone; *sich* — *lassen*, send in o.'s name, have o.s. announced; *sich zu etwas* —, apply for s.th.

Meldezettel ['mɛldətsetəl], *m.* (—s, *pl.* —) registration form.

meliert [me'liːrt], *adj.* mixed; (*hair*) iron grey, streaked with grey.

melken ['mɛlkən], *v.a. irr.* milk.

Melodie [melo'diː], *f.* (—, *pl.* —n) melody, tune.

Melone [me'loːnə], *f.* (—, *pl.* —n) (*Bot.*) melon; (*coll.*) bowler hat.

Meltau ['meːltau], *m.* (—s, *no pl.*) mildew.

Membrane [mɛm'braːnə], *f.* (—, *pl.* —n) membrane, diaphragm.

Memme ['mɛmə], *f.* (—, *pl.* —n) coward, poltroon.

memorieren [memo'riːrən], *v.a.* memorise, learn by heart.

Menage [me'naːʒə], *f.* (—, *pl.* —n) household.

Menge ['mɛŋə], *f.* (—, *pl.* —n) quantity, amount; multitude, crowd; *eine* —, a lot.

mengen ['mɛŋən], *v.a.* mix. — *v.r.* *sich* — *in*, interfere in.

Mensch (1) [mɛnʃ], *m.* (—en, *pl.* —en) human being; man; person; *kein* —, nobody.

Mensch (2) [mɛnʃ], *n.* (—es, *pl.* —er) (*vulg.*) wench.

Menschenfeind ['mɛnʃənfaɪnt], *m.* (—es, *pl.* —e) misanthropist.

Menschenfreund ['mɛnʃənfrɔynt], *m.* (—es, *pl.* —e) philanthropist.

Menschengedenken ['mɛnʃəngədɛŋkən], *n.* (—s, *no pl.*) *seit* —, from time immemorial.

Menschenhandel ['mɛnʃənhandəl], *m.* (—s, *no pl.*) slave-trade.

Menschenkenner ['mɛnʃənkɛnər], *m.* (—s, *pl.* —) judge of character.

Menschenmenge ['mɛnʃənmɛŋə], *f.* (—, *no pl.*) crowd.

Menschenraub ['mɛnʃənraup], *m.* (—s, *no pl.*) kidnapping.

Menschenverstand ['mɛnʃənfɛrʃtant], *m.* (—es, *no pl.*) human understanding; *gesunder* —, commonsense.

Menschheit ['mɛnʃhaɪt], *f.* (—, *no pl.*) mankind, human race.

menschlich ['mɛnʃlɪç], *adj.* human.

Menschwerdung ['mɛnʃverduŋ], *f.* (—, *no pl.*) incarnation.

Mensur [mɛn'zuːr], *f.* (—, *pl.* —en) students' duel.

Mergel ['mɛrgəl], *m.* (—s, *no pl.*) marl.

merkbar ['mɛrkbaːr], *adj.* perceptible, noticeable.

merken ['mɛrkən], *v.a.* note, perceive, observe, notice; *sich etwas* —, bear in mind; *sich nichts* — *lassen*, show no sign.

merklich ['mɛrklɪç], *adj.* perceptible, appreciable.

Merkmal ['mɛrkmaːl], *n.* (—s, *pl.* —e) mark, characteristic, feature.

merkwürdig ['mɛrkvyrdɪç], *adj.* remarkable, curious, strange.

Merle ['mɛrlə], *f.* (—, *pl.* —n) (*dial.*) blackbird.

Mesner ['mɛsnər], *m.* (—s, *pl.* —) sexton, sacristan.

meßbar ['mɛsbaːr], *adj.* measurable.

Meßbuch ['mɛsbuːx], *n.* (—es, *pl.* ⁻er) missal.

Messe ['mɛsə], *f.* (—, *pl.* —n) (*Eccl.*) Mass; *stille* —, Low Mass; (*Comm.*) fair; (*Mil.*) mess.

messen ['mɛsən], *v.a. irr.* measure, gauge. — *v.r.* *sich mit einem* —, pit oneself against s.o.

Messer (1) ['mɛsər], *m.* (—s, *pl.* —) gauge, meter.

Messer (2) ['mɛsər], *n.* (—s, *pl.* —) knife.

Messerheld ['mɛsərhɛlt], *m.* (—en, *pl.* —en) cut-throat, hooligan, rowdy.

Messias [mɛ'siːas], *m.* Messiah.

Meßgewand ['mɛsgəvant], *n.* (—es, *pl.* ⁻er) chasuble, vestment.

Meßkunst ['mɛskunst], *f.* (—, *no pl.*) surveying.

Messing ['mɛsɪŋ], *n.* (—s, *no pl.*) brass; *aus* —, brazen.

Metall [me'tal], *n.* (—s, *pl.* —e) metal; *unedle* —*e*, base metals.

Metallkunde [me'talkundə], *f.* (—, *no pl.*) metallurgy.

meteorologisch [meteoro'loːgɪʃ], *adj.* meteorological.

Meter ['meːtər], *n. & m.* (—s, *pl.* —) (*linear measure*) metre; (*Am.*) meter; (*Poet.*) metre.

methodisch [me'toːdɪʃ], *adj.* methodical.

Metrik ['meːtrɪk], *f.* (—, *no pl.*) prosody, versification.

Mette ['mɛtə], *f.* (—, *pl.* —n) (*Eccl.*) matins.

Metze ['mɛtsə], *f.* (—, *pl.* —n) (*obs.*) prostitute.

Metzelei [mɛtsə'laɪ], *f.* (—, *pl.* —en) slaughter, massacre.

metzeln ['mɛtsəln], *v.a.* massacre, butcher.

Metzger ['mɛtsgər], *m.* (—s, *pl.* —) butcher.

Meuchelmörder ['mɔyçəlmœrdər], *m.* (—s, *pl.* —) assassin.

meucheln ['mɔyçəln], *v.a.* assassinate.

meuchlings ['mɔyçlɪŋs], *adv.* treacherously, insidiously.

Meute ['mɔytə], *f.* (—, *pl.* —n) pack of hounds; (*fig.*) gang.

Meuterei [mɔytə'raɪ], *f.* (—, *pl.* —en) mutiny, sedition.

meutern ['mɔytərn], *v.n.* mutiny.

Mezzanin ['mɛtsanɪn], *n.* (—s, *pl.* —e) half-storey, mezzanine.

miauen [mi'auən], *v.n.* mew.

mich [mɪç], *pers. pron.* me, myself.

Michaeli(s) [mɪça'e:li(s)], *n.* Michaelmas.

Michel ['mɪçəl], *m.* Michael; *deutscher* —, plain honest German.

Mieder ['mi:dər], *n.* (—s, *pl.* —) bodice.

Miene ['mi:nə], *f.* (—, *pl.* —n) mien, air; (*facial*) expression.

Miete ['mi:tə], *f.* (—, *pl.* —n) rent; hire; (*corn*) rick, stack.

mieten ['mi:tən], *v.a.* rent, hire.

Mieter ['mi:tər], *m.* (—s, *pl.* —) tenant, lodger.

Mietskaserne ['mi:tskazernə], *f.* (—, *pl.* —en) tenement house.

Mietszins ['mi:tstsɪns], *m.* (—es, *pl.* —e) rent.

Milbe ['mɪlbə], *f.* (—, *pl.* —n) mite.

Milch [mɪlç], *f.* (—, *no pl.*) milk; (*fish*) soft roe; *abgerahmte* —, skim(med) milk; *geronnene* —, curdled milk.

Milchbart ['mɪlçba:rt], *m.* (—s, *pl.* ⁰e) milksop.

Milchbruder ['mɪlçbru:dər], *m.* (—s, *pl.* ⁰) foster-brother.

milchen ['mɪlçən], *v.n.* yield milk.

Milcher ['mɪlçer], *m.* (—s, *pl.* —) (*fish*) milter.

Milchgesicht ['mɪlçgəzɪçt], *n.* (—s, *pl.* —er) baby face; smooth complexion.

Milchglas ['mɪlçglas], *n.* (—es, *no pl.*) opalescent glass, frosted glass.

Milchstraße ['mɪlçʃtra:sə], *f.* (—, *no pl.*) Milky Way.

Milde ['mɪldə], *f.* (—, *no pl.*) mildness, softness; (*fig.*) gentleness, (*rare*) charity, generosity.

mildern ['mɪldərn], *v.a.* soften, alleviate, mitigate, soothe, allay; *—de Umstände*, extenuating circumstances.

Milderung ['mɪldəruŋ], *f.* (—, *pl.* —en) mitigation, moderation; soothing.

mildtätig ['mɪltte:tɪç], *adj.* charitable, benevolent, munificent.

Militär [mili'te:r], *n.* (—s, *no pl.*) military, army; *beim — sein*, serve in the army.

Miliz [mi'li:ts], *f.* (—, *no pl.*) militia.

Milliarde [mɪl'jardə], *f.* (—, *pl.* —n) a thousand millions; (*Am.*) billion.

Million [mɪl'jo:n], *f.* (—, *pl.* —en) million.

Millionär [mɪljo'nɛ:r], *m.* (—s, *pl.* —e) millionaire.

Milz [mɪlts], *f.* (—, *pl.* —en) spleen.

Mime ['mi:mə], *m.* (—n, *pl.* —n) mime, actor.

Mimik ['mi:mɪk], *f.* (—, *no pl.*) mime, miming.

Mimiker ['mi:mɪkər], *m.* (—s, *pl.* —) mimic.

Mimose [mi'mo:zə], *f.* (—, *pl.* —n) (*Bot.*) mimosa.

minder ['mɪndər], *adj.* lesser, smaller, minor, inferior.

Minderheit ['mɪndərhaɪt], *f.* (—, *pl.* —en) minority.

minderjährig ['mɪndərje:rɪç], *adj.* (*Law*) under age.

mindern ['mɪndərn], *v.a.* diminish, lessen.

minderwertig ['mɪndərvertɪç], *adj.* inferior, of poor quality.

Minderwertigkeitskomplex ['mɪndərvertɪçkaɪtskɔmpleks], *m.* (—es, *pl.* —e) inferiority complex.

mindest ['mɪndəst], *adj.* least, smallest, minimum, lowest; *nicht im —en*, not in the least, not at all.

mindestens ['mɪndəstəns], *adv.* at least.

Mine ['mi:nə], *f.* (—, *pl.* —n) mine; (*ball point pen*) refill; (*pencil*) lead.

minimal [mini'ma:l], *adj.* infinitesimal, minimum.

Ministerialrat [minister'ja:lra:t], *m.* (—s, *pl.* ⁰e) senior civil servant.

ministeriell [minister'jɛl], *adj.* ministerial.

Ministerium [mini'ste:rjum], *n.* (—s, *pl.* —rien) ministry.

Ministerpräsident [mi'nɪstərpre:zidɛnt], *m.* (—en, *pl.* —en) prime minister; premier.

Ministerrat [mi'nɪstərra:t], *m.* (—s, *pl.* ⁰e) cabinet, council of ministers.

Ministrant [mini'strant], *m.* (—en, *pl.* —en) acolyte; sacristan.

Minne ['mɪnə], *f.* (—, *no pl.*) (*obs.*, *Poet.*) love.

Minnesänger [mɪnə'zɛŋər], *m.* (—s, *pl.* —) minnesinger; troubadour, minstrel.

Minus ['mi:nus], *n.* (—, *no pl.*) deficit.

Minze ['mɪntsə], *f.* (—, *pl.* —n) (*Bot.*) mint.

mir [mi:r], *pers. pron.* to me.

Mirakel [mi'ra:kəl], *n.* (—s, *pl.* —) miracle, marvel, wonder.

mischen ['mɪʃən], *v.a.* mix; (*Cards*) shuffle; (*coffee, tea*) blend.

Mischling ['mɪʃlɪŋ], *m.* (—s, *pl.* —e) mongrel, hybrid.

Mischrasse

Mischrasse ['mɪʃrasə], *f.* (—, *pl.* —n) cross-breed.

Mischung ['mɪʃuŋ], *f.* (—, *pl.* —en) mixture, blend.

Misere [mi'ze:rə], *f.* (—, *no pl.*) unhappiness, misery.

Mispel ['mɪspəl], *f.* (—, *pl.* —n) (*Bot.*) medlar (tree).

mißachten [mɪs'axtən], *v.a.* disregard, despise.

mißarten [mɪs'a:rtən], *v.n.* (*aux.* sein) degenerate.

Mißbehagen ['mɪsbəha:gən], *n.* (—s, *no pl.*) displeasure, uneasiness.

mißbilligen [mɪs'bɪlɪgən], *v.a.* object (to), disapprove (of).

Mißbrauch ['mɪsbraux], *m.* (—s, *pl.* ⁓e) abuse, misuse.

missen ['mɪsən], *v.a.* lack, be without, feel the lack of.

Missetat ['mɪsəta:t], *f.* (—, *pl.* —en) misdeed, felony.

mißfallen [mɪs'falən], *v.n. irr.* displease.

mißförmig ['mɪsfœrmɪç], *adj.* deformed, misshapen.

Mißgeburt ['mɪsgəburt], *f.* (—, *pl.* —en) abortion; monster.

mißgelaunt ['mɪsgəlaunt], *adj.* ill-humoured.

Mißgeschick ['mɪsgəʃɪk], *n.* (—s, *no pl.*) mishap, misfortune.

mißgestimmt ['mɪsgəʃtɪmt], *adj.* grumpy, out of sorts.

mißglücken [mɪs'glykən], *v.n.* (*aux.* sein) fail, be unsuccessful.

Mißgriff ['mɪsgrɪf], *m.* (—s, *pl.* —e) blunder, mistake.

Mißgunst ['mɪsgunst], *f.* (—, *no pl.*) jealousy, envy.

mißhandeln [mɪs'handəln], *v.a.* ill-treat.

Missionar [mɪsjo'na:r], *m.* (—s, *pl.* —e) missionary.

mißlich ['mɪslɪç], *adj.* awkward; difficult, unpleasant.

mißliebig ['mɪsli:bɪç], *adj.* unpopular, odious.

mißlingen [mɪs'lɪŋən], *v.n. irr.* (*aux.* sein) miscarry, go wrong, misfire, prove a failure, turn out badly.

mißraten [mɪs'ra:tən], *v.n. irr.* (*aux.* sein) miscarry, turn out badly.

Mißstand ['mɪsʃtant], *m.* (—es, *pl.* ⁓e) grievance, abuse.

Mißton ['mɪsto:n], *m.* (—s, *pl.* ⁓e) dissonance.

mißtrauen [mɪs'trauən], *v.n.* distrust, mistrust.

Mißverhältnis ['mɪsferhɛltnɪs], *n.* (—ses, *no pl.*) disproportion.

Mißverständnis ['mɪsferʃtɛntnɪs], *n.* (—ses, *pl.* ⁓se) misunderstanding.

Mist [mɪst], *m.* (—es, *no pl.*) dung, manure, muck; (*fig.*) rubbish.

Mistel ['mɪstəl], *f.* (—, *pl.* —n) (*Bot.*) mistletoe.

Mistfink ['mɪstfɪŋk], *m.* (—s, *pl.* —e) (*fig.*) dirty child; mudlark.

mit [mɪt], *prep.* (*Dat.*) with. — *adv.* also, along with,

mitarbeiten ['mɪtarbaɪtən], *v.n.* collaborate, cooperate; (*lit. work*) contribute.

mitbringen ['mɪtbrɪŋən], *v.a. irr.* bring along.

Mitbürger ['mɪtbyrgər], *m.* (—s, *pl.* —) fellow-citizen.

mitempfinden ['mɪtempfɪndən], *v.a. irr.* sympathise with.

Mitesser ['mɪtesər], *m.* (—s, *pl.* —) (*Med.*) blackhead.

mitfahren ['mɪtfa:rən], *v.n. irr.* (*aux.* sein) ride with s.o.; *einen — lassen*, give s.o. a lift.

mitfühlen ['mɪtfy:lən], *v.n.* sympathise.

mitgehen ['mɪtge:ən], *v.n. irr.* (*aux.* sein) go along (with), accompany (s.o.); *etwas — heißen* or *lassen*, pilfer, pocket, pinch.

Mitgift ['mɪtgɪft], *f.* (—, *no pl.*) dowry.

Mitglied ['mɪtgli:t], *n.* (—s, *pl.* —er) member, fellow, associate.

mithin [mɪt'hɪn], *adv.*, *conj.* consequently, therefore.

Mitläufer ['mɪtlɔyfər], *m.* (—s, *pl.* —) (*Polit.*) fellow-traveller.

Mitlaut ['mɪtlaut], *m.* (—s, *pl.* —e) (*Phonet.*) consonant.

Mitleid ['mɪtlaɪt], *n.* (—s, *no pl.*) compassion, sympathy, pity; *mit einem — haben*, take pity on s.o.

Mitleidenschaft ['mɪtlaɪdənʃaft], *f.* (—, *no pl.*) *einen in — ziehen*, involve s.o., implicate s.o.

mitmachen ['mɪtmaxən], *v.a.*, *v.n.* join in, participate (in), do as others do; go through, suffer.

Mitmensch ['mɪtmenʃ], *m.* (—en, *pl.* —en) fellow-man; fellow-creature.

mitnehmen ['mɪtne:mən], *v.a. irr.* take along, take with o.; strain, take it out of o., weaken.

mitnichten [mɪt'nɪçtən], *adv.* by no means.

mitreden ['mɪtre:dən], *v.n.* join in a conversation; contribute.

mitsamt [mɪt'zamt], *prep.* (*Dat.*) together with.

Mitschuld ['mɪtʃult], *f.* (—, *no pl.*) complicity.

Mitschüler ['mɪtʃy:lər], *m.* (—s, *pl.* —) schoolfellow, fellow-pupil, fellow-student, classmate.

Mittag ['mɪta:k], *m.* (—s, *pl.* —e) midday, noon, noontide; *zu — essen*, have dinner *or* lunch.

Mittagessen ['mɪta:kesən], *n.* (—s, *pl.* —) lunch, luncheon.

Mittagsseite ['mɪta:kszaɪtə], *f.* (—, *no pl.*) south side.

Mittäter ['mɪtte:tər], *m.* (—s, *pl.* —) accomplice.

Mitte ['mɪtə], *f.* (—, *no pl.*) middle, midst.

mitteilen ['mɪttaɪlən], *v.a.* (*Dat.*) communicate, inform, impart.

mitteilsam ['mɪttaɪlza:m], *adj.* communicative.

Mitteilung ['mɪttaɪluŋ], *f.* (—, *pl.* —en) communication.

Mittel ['mɪtəl], *n.* (—s, *pl.*) means, expedient, way, resource; remedy; (*pl.*) money, funds; *als — zum Zweck*, as a means to an end; *sich ins — legen*, mediate, intercede.

Mittelalter ['mɪtəlaltər], *n.* (—s, *no pl.*) Middle Ages.

mittelbar ['mɪtəlba:r], *adj.* indirect.

Mittelding ['mɪtəldɪŋ], *n.* (—s, *pl.* —e) medium; something in between.

Mittelgebirge ['mɪtəlgəbɪrgə], *n.* (—s, *pl.* —) hills; (subalpine) mountains.

mittelländisch ['mɪtəllɛndɪʃ], *adj.* Mediterranean.

mittellos ['mɪtəllo:s], *adj.* penniless, impecunious.

Mittelmaß ['mɪtəlma:s], *n.* (—es, *pl.* —e) average.

mittelmäßig ['mɪtəlmɛːsɪç], *adj.* mediocre.

Mittelmeer ['mɪtəlme:r], *n.* (—s, *no pl.*) Mediterranean.

Mittelpunkt ['mɪtəlpuŋkt], *m.* (—s, *pl.* —e) centre; focus.

mittels ['mɪtəls], *prep.* (*Genit.*) by means of.

Mittelschule ['mɪtəlʃu:lə], *f.* (—, *pl.* —n) secondary (intermediate) school; (*Austr.*) grammar school; (*Am.*) high school.

Mittelstand ['mɪtəlʃtant], *m.* (—es, *no pl.*) middle class.

mittelste ['mɪtəlstə], *adj.* middlemost, central.

Mittelstürmer ['mɪtəlʃtyrmər], *m.* (—s, *pl.* —) (*Footb.*) centre-forward.

Mittelwort ['mɪtəlvɔrt], *n.* (—es, *pl.* ⁓er) (*Gram.*) participle.

mitten ['mɪtən], *adv.* in the midst; *— am Tage*, in broad daylight.

Mitternacht ['mɪtərnaxt], *f.* (—, *no pl.*) midnight.

Mittler ['mɪtlər], *m.* (—s, *pl.* —) mediator.

mittlere ['mɪtlərə], *adj.* middle; average; mean.

Mittwoch ['mɪtvɔx], *m.* (—s, *pl.* —e) Wednesday.

mitunter [mɪt'untər], *adv.* now and then, occasionally, sometimes.

mitunterzeichnen ['mɪtuntərtsaɪçnən], *v.a., v.n.* countersign; add o.'s signature (to).

Miturheber ['mɪtu:rhe:bər], *m.* (—s, *pl.* —) co-author.

Mitwelt ['mɪtvɛlt], *f.* (—, *no pl.*) the present generation, contemporaries, our own times; the world outside.

mitwirken ['mɪtvɪrkən], *v.n.* cooperate.

Mnemotechnik [mne:mo'tɛçnɪk], *f.* (—, *no pl.*) mnemonics.

Möbel ['møːbəl], *n.* (—s, *pl.* —) piece of furniture; (*pl.*) furniture.

mobil [mo'bi:l], *adj.* mobile, active, quick; *— machen*, mobilise, put in motion.

Mobiliar [mobil'ja:r], *n.* (—s, *pl.* Mobilien) furniture, movables.

mobilisieren [mobili'zi:rən], *v.a.* mobilise.

möblieren [mø'bli:rən], *v.a.* furnish; *neu —*, refurnish.

Mode ['mo:də], *f.* (—, *pl.* —n) mode, fashion; custom, use; *in der —*, in fashion, in vogue.

Modell [mo'dɛl], *n.* (—s, *pl.* —e) model; *— stehen*, model; (*fig.*) be the prototype.

modellieren [modɛ'li:rən], *v.a.* (*dresses*) model; (*Art*) mould.

Moder ['mo:dər], *m.* (—s, *no pl.*) mould.

moderig ['mo:drɪç] *see* **modrig**.

modern(1) ['mo:dərn], *v.n.* moulder, rot.

modern(2) [mo'dɛrn], *adj.* modern, fashionable, up-to-date.

modernisieren [moderni'zi:rən], *v.a.* modernise.

modifizieren [modifi'tsi:rən], *v.a.* modify.

modisch ['mo:dɪʃ], *adj.* stylish, fashionable.

Modistin [mo'dɪstɪn], *f.* (—, *pl.* —nen) milliner.

modrig ['mo:drɪç], *adj.* mouldy.

modulieren [modu'li:rən], *v.a.* modulate.

Modus ['mo:dus], *m.* (—, *pl.* Modi) (*Gram.*) mood; mode, manner.

mogeln ['mo:gəln], *v.n.* cheat.

mögen ['mø:gən], *v.n. irr.* like, desire, want, be allowed, have a mind to; (*modal auxiliary*) may, might; *ich möchte gern*, I should like to.

möglich ['mø:klɪç], *adj.* possible, practicable; feasible; *sein —stes tun*, do o.'s utmost; *nicht —!* you don't say (so)!

Möglichkeit ['mø:klɪçkaɪt], *f.* (—, *pl.* —en) possibility, feasibility, practicability; (*pl.*) potentialities; contingencies, prospects (of career).

Mohn [mo:n], *m.* (—es, *no pl.*) poppy-(seed).

Mohr [mo:r], *m.* (—en, *pl.* —en) Moor; negro.

Möhre ['mø:rə], *f.* (—, *pl.* —n) carrot.

Mohrenkopf ['mo:rənkopf], *m.* (—es, *pl.* ⁓e) chocolate éclair.

Mohrrübe ['mo:rry:bə], *f.* (—, *pl.* —n) carrot.

mokieren [mɔ'ki:rən], *v.r. sich — über*, sneer at, mock at, be amused by.

Mokka ['mɔka], *m.* (—s, *no pl.*) Mocha coffee.

Molch [mɔlç], *m.* (—es, *pl.* —e) (*Zool.*) salamander.

Moldau ['mɔldau], *f.* Moldavia.

Mole ['mo:lə], *f.* (—, *pl.* —n) breakwater, jetty, pier.

Molekül [mole'ky:l], *n.* (—s, *pl.* —e) molecule.

Molke ['mɔlkə], *f.* (—, *pl.* —n) whey.

Molkerei [mɔlke'raɪ], *f.* (—, *pl.* —en dairy.

moll [mɔl], *adj.* (*Mus.*) minor.

Molluske

Molluske [mɔ'luskə], *f.* (—, *pl.* —n) (*Zool.*) mollusc.

Moment (1) [mo'mɛnt], *m.* (—s, *pl.* —e) moment, instant.

Moment (2) [mo'mɛnt], *n.* motive, factor; (*Phys.*) momentum.

Momentaufnahme [mo'mɛntaufna:-mə], *f.* (—, *pl.* —n) snapshot.

momentan [momɛn'ta:n], *adv.* at the moment, for the present, just now.

Monarch [mo'narç], *m.* (—en, *pl.* —en) monarch.

Monarchie [monar'çi:], *f.* (—, *pl.* —n) monarchy.

Monat ['mo:nat], *m.* (—s, *pl.* —e) month.

monatlich ['mo:natlıç], *adj.* monthly.

Monatsfluß ['mo:natsflus], *m.* (—sses, *pl.* ∵sse) menses.

Monatsschrift ['mo:natsʃrıft], *f.* (—, *pl.* —en) monthly (*journal*).

Mönch [mœnç], *m.* (—es, *pl.* —e) monk, friar.

Mönchskappe ['mœnçskapə], *f.* (—, *pl.* —n) cowl, monk's hood.

Mönchskutte ['mœnçskutə], *f.* (—, *pl.* —n) cowl.

Mond [mo:nt], *m.* (—es, *pl.* —e) moon; *zunehmender* —, waxing moon; *abnehmender* —, waning moon.

Mondfinsternis ['mo:ntfɪnstərnıs], *f.* (—, *pl.* —se) eclipse of the moon.

mondsüchtig ['mo:ntzyçtıç], *adj.* given to sleep-walking; (*fig.*) moonstruck.

Mondwandlung ['mo:ntvandluŋ], *f.* (—, *pl.* —en) phase of the moon.

Moneten [mo'ne:tən], *pl.* (*sl.*) money, cash, funds.

Mongolei [mɔŋgo'laɪ], *f.* Mongolia.

monieren [mo'ni:rən], *v.a.* remind (a debtor); censure.

monogam [mono'ga:m], *adj.* monogamous.

Monopol [mono'po:l], *n.* (—s, *pl.* —e) monopoly.

monoton [mono'to:n], *adj.* monotonous.

Monstrum ['mɔnstrum], *n.* (—s, *pl.* Monstra) monster, monstrosity.

Monsun [mɔn'zu:n], *m.* (—s, *pl.* —e) monsoon.

Montag ['mo:nta:k], *m.* (—s, *pl.* —e) Monday; *blauer* —, Bank Holiday Monday.

Montage [mɔn'ta:ʒə], *f.* (—, *pl.* —n) fitting (up), setting up, installation, assembling.

Montanindustrie [mɔn'ta:nɪndustri:], *f.* (—, *no pl.*) mining industry.

Montanunion [mɔn'ta:nunjo:n], *f.* (—, *no pl.*) (*Pol.*) European Coal and Steel Community.

Monteur [mɔn'tø:r], *m.* (—s, *pl.* —e) fitter.

montieren [mɔn'ti:rən], *v.a.* fit (up), set up, mount, install.

Montur [mɔn'tu:r], *f.* (—, *pl.* —en) uniform, livery.

Moor [mo:r], *n.* (—es, *pl.* —e) swamp, fen, bog.

Moos [mo:s], *n.* (—es, *pl.* —e) moss; (*sl.*) cash.

Moped ['mo:pɛt], *n.* (—s, *pl.* —s) moped, motorised pedal cycle.

Mops [mɔps], *m.* (—es, *pl.* ∵e) pug (dog).

mopsen ['mɔpsən], *v.r. sich* —, feel bored.

Moral [mo'ra:l], *f.* (—, *no pl.*) moral, morals.

moralisch [mo'ra:lıʃ], *adj.* moral.

Morast [mo'rast], *m.* (—es, *pl.* ∵e) morass, bog, fen, mire.

Moratorium [mora'to:rjum], *n.* (—s, *pl.* —rien) (*payments etc.*) respite.

Morchel ['mɔrçəl], *f.* (—, *pl.* —n) (*Bot.*) morel (edible fungus).

Mord [mɔrt], *m.* (—es, *pl.* —e) murder.

morden ['mɔrdən], *v.a., v.n.* murder.

Mörder ['mœrdər], *m.* (—s, *pl.* —) murderer.

Mordsgeschichte ['mɔrtsgəʃıçtə], *f.* (—, *pl.* —n) (*coll.*) cock-and-bull story.

Mordskerl ['mɔrtskerl], *m.* (—s, *pl.* —e) devil of a fellow; (*Am.*) great guy.

Mordtat ['mɔrtta:t], *f.* (—, *pl.* —en) murder.

Morelle [mo'rɛlə], *f.* (—, *pl.* —n) (*Bot.*) morello cherry.

Morgen ['mɔrgən], *m.* (—s, *pl.* —) morning, daybreak; (*Poet.*) east; measure of land; *eines* —s, one morning.

morgen ['mɔrgən], *adv.* tomorrow; — *früh*, tomorrow morning; *heute* —, this morning.

Morgenblatt ['mɔrgənblat], *n.* (—s, *pl.* ∵er) morning paper.

morgendlich ['mɔrgəntlıç], *adj.* of *or* in the morning; matutinal.

Morgenland ['mɔrgənlant], *n.* (—es, *pl.* —) orient, east.

Morgenrot ['mɔrgənro:t], *n.* (—s, *no pl.*) dawn, sunrise.

morgens ['mɔrgəns], *adv.* in the morning.

morgig ['mɔrgıç], *adj.* tomorrow's.

Morphium ['mɔrfjum], *n.* (—s, *no pl.*) morphia, morphine.

morsch [mɔrʃ], *adj.* brittle, rotten, decayed.

Mörser ['mœrzər], *m.* (—s, *pl.* —) mortar.

Mörserkeule ['mœrzərkɔylə], *f.* (—, *pl.* —n) pestle.

Mörtel ['mœrtəl], *m.* (—s, *no pl.*) mortar, plaster.

Mörtelkelle ['mœrtəlkɛlə], *f.* (—, *pl.* —n) trowel.

Mosaik [moza'i:k], *n.* (—s, *pl.* —e) mosaic (work); inlaid work.

mosaisch [mo'za:ıʃ], *adj.* Mosaic.

Moschee [mo'ʃe:], *f.* (—, *pl.* —n) mosque.

Moschus ['mɔʃus], *m.* (—, *no pl.*) musk.

Mosel ['mo:zəl], *f.* Moselle.

Moskau ['mɔskau], *n.* Moscow.

Moskito [mɔs'ki:to], *m.* (**—s**, *pl.* **—s**) (*Ent.*) mosquito.

Most [mɔst], *m.* (**—es**, *no pl.*) new wine, cider.

Mostrich ['mɔstrɪç], *m.* (**—s**, *no pl.*) mustard.

Motiv [mo'ti:f], *n.* (**—es**, *pl.* **—e**) motive; (*Mus.*, *Lit.*) motif, theme.

motivieren [moti'vi:rən], *v.a.* motivate.

Motorrad ['mo:tɔrra:t], *n.* (**—es**, *pl.* ⁚er) motor-cycle.

Motte ['mɔtə], *f.* (**—**, *pl.* **—n**) (*Ent.*) moth.

moussieren [mu'si:rən], *v.n.* effervesce, sparkle.

Möwe ['mø:və], *f.* (**—**, *pl.* **—n**) (*Orn.*) seagull.

Mucke ['mukə], *f.* (**—**, *pl.* **—n**) whim, caprice; obstinacy.

Mücke ['mykə], *f.* (**—**, *pl.* **—n**) (*Ent.*) gnat, fly, mosquito.

Muckerei [mukə'raɪ], *f.* (**—**, *pl.* **—en**) cant.

mucksen ['muksən], *v.n.* stir, move, budge.

müde ['my:də], *adj.* tired, weary; **— machen**, tire.

Muff [muf], *m.* (**—es**, *pl.* **—e**) muff.

muffig ['mufɪç], *adj.* musty, fusty, stuffy.

Mühe ['my:ə], *f.* (**—**, *pl.* **—n**) trouble, pains; effort, labour, toil; *sich —* **geben**, take pains.

mühelos ['my:əlo:s], *adj.* effortless, easy.

mühen ['my:ən], *v.r. sich —*, exert o.s., take pains.

Mühewaltung ['my:əvaltuŋ], *f.* (**—**, *pl.* **—en**) exertion, effort.

Mühle ['my:lə], *f.* (**—**, *pl.* **—n**) (*flour*) mill; (*coffee*) grinder; game.

Muhme ['mu:mə], *f.* (**—**, *pl.* **—n**) (*obs.*) aunt.

Mühsal ['my:za:l], *f.* (**—**, *pl.* **—e**) hardship, misery, toil.

mühsam ['my:za:m], *adj.* troublesome, laborious.

mühselig ['my:ze:lɪç], *adj.* painful, laborious; miserable.

Mulatte [mu'latə], *m.* (**—n**, *pl.* **—n**) mulatto.

Mulde ['muldə], *f.* (**—**, *pl.* **—n**) trough.

muldenförmig ['muldənfœrmɪç], *adj.* trough-shaped.

Mull [mul], *m.* (**—s**, *no pl.*) Indian muslin.

Müll [myl], *m.* (**—s**, *no pl.*) dust, rubbish; (*Am.*) garbage.

Müller ['mylər], *m.* (**—s**, *pl.* **—**) miller.

mulmig ['mulmɪç], *adj.* dusty, mouldy, decayed.

multiplizieren [multipli'tsi:rən], *v.a.* multiply.

Mumie ['mu:mjə], *f.* (**—**, *pl.* **—n**) (*Archæol.*) mummy.

Mummenschanz ['mumənʃants], *m.* (**—es**, *no pl.*) mummery, masquerade.

München ['mynçən], *n.* Munich.

Mund [munt], *m.* (**—es**, *pl.* **—e**, ⁚er) mouth; *den — halten*, keep quiet; *einen großen — haben*, talk big; *sich den — verbrennen*, put o.'s foot in it.

Mundart ['munda:rt], *f.* (**—**, *pl.* **—en**) (local) dialect.

Mündel ['myndəl], *m.*, *f. & n.* (**—s**, *pl.* **—**) ward, minor, child under guardianship.

mündelsicher ['myndəlzɪçər], *adj.* gilt-edged.

munden ['mundən], *v.n. es mundet mir*, I like the taste, I relish it.

münden ['myndən], *v.n.* discharge (into), flow (into).

mundfaul ['muntfaul], *adj.* tongue-tied; taciturn.

mundgerecht ['muntgəreçt], *adj.* palatable; (*fig.*) suitable.

Mundharmonika ['muntharmo:nika], *f.* (**—**, *pl.* **—kas**, **—ken**) mouth organ.

mündig ['myndɪç], *adj.* of age; **— werden**, come of age.

mündlich ['myntlɪç], *adj.* verbal, oral, by word of mouth; (*examination*) viva voce.

Mundschenk ['muntʃɛŋk], *m.* (**—s**, *pl.* **—e**) cupbearer.

mundtot ['muntto:t], *adj.* **— machen**, silence, gag.

Mündung ['mynduŋ], *f.* (**—**, *pl.* **—en**) (*river*) estuary, mouth; (*gun*) muzzle.

Mundvorrat ['muntforra:t], *m.* (**—s**, *pl.* ⁚e) provisions, victuals.

Mundwerk ['muntvɛrk], *n.* (**—s**, *no pl.*) mouth; (*fig.*) gift of the gab.

Munition [muni'tsjo:n], *f.* (**—**, *no pl.*) ammunition.

munkeln ['muŋkəln], *v.n.* whisper; *man munkelt*, it is rumoured.

Münster ['mynstər], *n.* (**—s**, *pl.* **—**) minster, cathedral.

munter ['muntər], *adj.* awake; lively, active, sprightly, vivacious, cheerful, gay.

Münze ['myntsə], *f.* (**—**, *pl.* **—n**) coin.

Münzeinheit ['myntsaɪnhaɪt], *f.* (**—**, *no pl.*) monetary unit.

Münzfälscher ['myntsfɛlʃər], *m.* (**—s**, *pl.* **—**) (counterfeit) coiner.

Münzkunde ['myntskundə], *f.* (**—**, *no pl.*) numismatics.

Münzprobe ['myntspro:bə], *f.* (**—**, *pl.* **—n**) assay of a coin.

mürbe ['myrbə], *adj.* mellow; (*meat*) tender; (*cake*) crisp; brittle; *einen — machen*, soften s.o. up, force s.o. to yield.

Murmel ['murməl], *f.* (**—**, *pl.* **—n**) (*toy*) marble.

murmeln ['murməln], *v.n.* murmur, mutter.

Murmeltier ['murməlti:r], *n.* (**—s**, *pl.* **—e**) (*Zool.*) marmot; *wie ein — schlafen*, sleep like a log.

murren ['murən], *v.n.* grumble, growl.

mürrisch ['myrɪʃ], *adj.* morose, surly, sulky, peevish, sullen.

Mus [muːs], *n.* (—es, *no pl.*) purée, (apple) sauce; pulp.

Muschel ['muʃəl], *f.* (—, *pl.* —n) mussel, shell; (*telephone*) ear-piece.

Muse ['muːzə], *f.* (—, *pl.* —n) muse.

Muselman ['muːzəlman], *m.* (—en, *pl.* —en) Muslim, Moslem.

Musik [muˈziːk], *f.* (—, *no pl.*) music.

musikalisch [muziˈkaːlɪʃ], *adj.* musical.

Musikant [muziˈkant], *m.* (—en, *pl.* —en) musician; performer.

Musiker ['muːzɪkər], *m.* (—s, *pl.* —) musician.

musizieren [muziˈtsiːrən], *v.n.* play music.

Muskateller [muskaˈtɛlər], *m.* (—s, *no pl.*) muscatel (wine).

Muskatnuß [musˈkaːtnus], *f.* (—, *pl.* ⸚sse) nutmeg.

Muskel ['muskəl], *m.* (—s, *pl.* —n) muscle.

muskelig ['muskliç] *see* **musklig**.

Muskete [musˈkeːtə], *f.* (—, *pl.* —n) musket.

Musketier [muskeˈtiːr], *m.* (—s, *pl.* —e) musketeer.

musklig ['muskliç], *adj.* muscular.

muskulös [muskuˈløːs], *adj.* muscular.

Muße ['muːsə], *f.* (—, *no pl.*) leisure; *mit* —, leisurely, at leisure.

Musselin [musəˈliːn], *m.* (—s, *pl.* —e) muslin.

müssen ['mysən], *v.n. irr.* have to, be forced, be compelled, be obliged; *ich muß*, I must, I have to.

müßig ['myːsɪç], *adj.* idle, lazy, unemployed.

Müßiggang ['myːsɪçgaŋ], *m.* (—s, *no pl.*) idleness, laziness, sloth.

Muster ['mustər], *n.* (—s, *pl.* —) sample; pattern; (proto-)type; (*fig.*) example.

Musterbild ['mustərbɪlt], *n.* (—s, *pl.* —er) paragon.

mustergültig ['mustərgyltɪç], *adj.* exemplary; standard; excellent.

musterhaft ['mustərhaft], *adj.* exemplary.

mustern ['mustərn], *v.a.* examine, muster, scan; (*troops*) review, inspect.

Musterung ['mustəruŋ], *f.* (—, *pl.* —en) review; examination, inspection.

Mut ['muːt], *m.* (—es, *no pl.*) courage, spirit; — *fassen*, take heart, muster up courage.

Mutation [mutaˈtsjoːn], *f.* (—, *pl.* —en) change.

mutieren [muˈtiːrən], *v.n.* change; (*voice*) break.

mutig ['muːtɪç], *adj.* courageous, brave.

mutlos ['muːtloːs], *adj.* discouraged, dejected, despondent.

mutmaßen ['muːtmaːsən], *v.a. insep.* surmise, suppose, conjecture.

Mutter ['mutər], *f.* (—, *pl.* ⸚) mother; (*screw*) nut.

Mutterkorn ['mutərkɔrn], *n.* (—s, *no pl.*) ergot.

Mutterkuchen ['mutərkuːxən], *m.* (—s, *pl.* —) placenta, after-birth.

Mutterleib ['mutərlaɪp], *m.* (—s, *no pl.*) womb, uterus.

Muttermal ['mutərmaːl], *n.* (—s, *pl.* —e) birth-mark.

Mutterschaft ['mutərʃaft], *f.* (—, *no pl.*) motherhood, maternity.

mutterseelenallein ['mutərzeːlənalaɪn], *adj.* quite alone; (*coll.*) all on o.'s own.

Muttersöhnchen ['mutərzøːnçən], *n.* (—s, *pl.* —) mother's darling, spoilt child.

Mutterwitz ['mutərvɪts], *m.* (—es, *no pl.*) mother-wit, native wit, common sense.

Mutwille ['muːtvɪlə], *m.* (—ns, *no pl.*) mischievousness, wantonness.

Mütze ['mytsə], *f.* (—, *pl.* —n) cap; bonnet; beret.

Myrrhe ['mɪrə], *f.* (—, *pl.* —n) myrrh.

Myrte ['mɪrtə], *f.* (—, *pl.* —n) (*Bot.*) myrtle.

Mysterium [mɪsˈteːrjum], *n.* (—s, *pl.* —rien) mystery.

Mystik ['mɪstɪk], *f.* (—, *no pl.*) mysticism.

Mythologie [mytoloˈgiː], *f.* (—, *pl.* —n) mythology.

Mythus ['mytus], *m.* (—, *pl.* **Mythen**) myth.

N

N [ɛn], *n.* (—s, *pl.* —s) the letter N.

na [na], *int.* well, now; —*mu!* well, I never! — *und?* so what?

Nabe ['naːbə], *f.* (—, *pl.* —n) hub.

Nabel ['naːbəl], *m.* (—s, *pl.* —) navel.

Nabelschnur ['naːbəlʃnuːr], *f.* (—, *pl.* ⸚e) umbilical cord.

nach [naːx], *prep.* (*Dat.*) after, behind, following; to, towards; according to, in conformity *or* accordance with; in imitation of. — *adv.*, *prefix*. after, behind; afterwards, later; — *und* —, little by little, by degrees, gradually.

nachäffen ['naːxɛfən], *v.a.* ape, mimic, imitate; (*coll.*) take off.

nachahmen ['naːxaːmən], *v.a.* imitate, copy; counterfeit.

nacharbeiten ['naːxarbaɪtən], *v.n.* work after hours *or* overtime. — *v.a.* copy (*Dat.*).

nacharten ['naːxaːrtən], *v.n.* (*aux.* sein) resemble, (*coll.*) take after.

Nachbar ['naːxbaːr], *m.* (—s, —n, *pl.* —n) neighbour.

Nachbarschaft ['naːxbaːrʃaft], *f.* (—, *no pl.*) neighbourhood, vicinity; (*people*) neighbours.

nachbestellen ['naːxbəʃtɛlən], *v.a.* order more, re-order.

nachbilden ['na:xbɪldən], *v.a.* copy, reproduce.

nachdem [na:x'de:m], *adv.* afterwards, after that. — *conj.* after, when; *je —*, according to circumstances, that depends.

nachdenken ['na:xdɛŋkən], *v.n. irr.* think (over), meditate, muse, ponder.

nachdenklich ['na:xdɛŋklɪç], *adj.* reflective, pensive, wistful; — *stimmen*, set thinking.

Nachdruck ['na:xdruk], *m.* (—s, *pl.* —e) reprint; stress, emphasis.

nachdrucken ['na:xdrukən], *v.a.* reprint.

nachdrücklich ['na:xdryklɪç], *adj.* emphatic; — *betonen*, emphasise.

nacheifern ['na:xaɪfərn], *v.n. einem —*, emulate s.o.

nacheinander ['na:xaɪnandər], *adv.* one after another.

nachempfinden ['na:xɛmpfɪndən], *v.a. irr.* sympathize with, feel for.

Nachen ['naxən], *m.* (—s, *pl.* —) (*Poet.*) boat, skiff.

Nachfolge ['na:xfɔlgə], *f.* (—, *pl.* —n) succession.

nachfolgend ['na:xfɔlgənt], *adj.* following, subsequent.

Nachfolger ['na:xfɔlgər], *m.* (—s, *pl.* —) successor.

nachforschen ['na:xfɔrʃən], *v.a.* search after; enquire into, investigate.

Nachfrage ['na:xfra:gə], *f.* (—, *no pl.*) enquiry; (*Comm.*) demand; *Angebot und —*, supply and demand.

nachfühlen ['na:xfy:lən], *v.a. einem etwas —*, enter into s.o.'s feelings, sympathize with s.o.

nachfüllen ['na:xfylən], *v.a.* replenish, fill up.

nachgeben ['na:xge:bən], *v.n. irr.* relax, slacken, yield; give in, relent, give way.

nachgehen ['na:xge:ən], *v.n. irr.* (*aux.* sein) *einem —*, follow s.o., go after s.o.; (*clock*) be slow; follow up, investigate.

nachgerade ['na:xgəra:də], *adv.* by this time, by now; gradually.

nachgiebig ['na:xgi:bɪç], *adj.* yielding, compliant.

nachgrübeln ['na:xgry:bəln], *v.n.* speculate.

Nachhall ['na:xhal], *m.* (—s, *no pl.*) echo, resonance.

nachhaltig ['na:xhaltɪç], *adj.* lasting, enduring.

nachhängen ['na:xhɛŋən], *v.n. irr. seinen Gedanken —*, muse.

nachher ['na:xhe:r], *adv.* afterwards, later on.

nachherig ['na:xhe:rɪç], *adj.* subsequent, later.

Nachhilfestunde ['na:xhɪlfəʃtundə], *f.* (—, *pl.* —n) private coaching.

nachholen ['na:xho:lən], *v.a.* make good; make up for.

Nachhut ['na:xhu:t], *f.* (—, *no pl.*) (*Mil.*) rearguard.

nachjagen ['na:xja:gən], *v.n.* (*aux* sein) pursue.

Nachklang ['na:xklaŋ], *m.* (—s, *pl.* ⁓e) echo; (*fig.*) after-effect, reminiscence.

Nachkomme ['na:xkɔmə], *m.* (—n, *pl.* —n) descendant, offspring.

nachkommen ['na:xkɔmən], *v.n. irr.* (*aux.* sein) come after, follow; *seiner Pflicht —*, do o.'s duty; comply with; *einem Versprechen —*, keep a promise; *seinen Verpflichtungen nicht — können*, be unable to meet o.'s commitments.

Nachkommenschaft ['na:xkɔmənʃaft], *f.* (—, *no pl.*) descendants, offspring, issue, progeny.

Nachlaß ['na:xlas], *m.* (—sses, *pl.* ⁓sse) inheritance, estate, bequest; remission, discount, allowance.

nachlassen ['na:xlasən], *v.a. irr.* leave behind, bequeath; (*trade*) give a discount of. — *v.n.* abate, subside, slacken.

nachlässig ['na:xlɛsɪç], *adj.* negligent, remiss, careless.

nachlaufen ['na:xlaufən], *v.n. irr.* (*aux.* sein) *einem —*, run after s.o.

Nachlese ['na:xle:zə], *f.* (—, *pl.* —n) gleaning.

nachliefern ['na:xli:fərn], *v.a.* supply subsequently, complete delivery of.

nachmachen ['na:xmaxən], *v.a.* copy, imitate; counterfeit, forge.

nachmals ['na:xma:ls], *adv.* afterwards, subsequently.

Nachmittag ['na:xmɪta:k], *m.* (—s, *pl.* —e) afternoon.

Nachnahme ['na:xna:mə], *f.* (—, *no pl.*) *per —*, cash *or* (*Am.*) collect (payment) on delivery (*abbr.* C.O.D.).

nachplappern ['na:xplapərn], *v.a.* repeat mechanically.

Nachrede ['na:xre:də], *f.* (—, *pl.* —n) epilogue; *üble —*, slander.

Nachricht ['na:xrɪçt], *f.* (—, *pl.* —en) news, information; (*Mil.*) intelligence; — *geben*, send word.

nachrücken ['na:xrykən], *v.n.* (*aux.* sein) move up.

Nachruf ['na:xru:f], *m.* (—s, *pl.* —e) obituary.

nachrühmen ['na:xry:mən], *v.a. einem etwas —*, speak well of s.o.

Nachsatz ['na:xzats], *m.* (—es, *pl.* ⁓e) concluding clause; postscript.

nachschauen ['na:xʃauən], *v.n. jemandem —*, gaze after s.o.

nachschlagen ['na:xʃla:gən], *v.a. irr.* look up, consult (a book).

Nachschlagewerk ['na:xʃla:gəverk], *n.* (—s, *pl.* —e) work of reference, reference book.

Nachschlüssel ['na:xʃlysəl], *m.* (—s, *pl.* —) master-key, skeleton-key.

Nachschrift ['na:xʃrɪft], *f.* (—, *pl.* —en) postscript, (*abbr.* P.S.).

Nachschub ['na:xʃu:p], *m.* (—s, *pl.* ⁓e) (fresh) supply; (*Mil.*) reinforcements.

Nachsehen ['na:xze:ən], *n.* (—s, *no pl.*) *das — haben*, be left out in the cold.

nachsehen ['na:xze:ən], *v.a.*, *v.n. irr.*
look for, look s.th. up, refer to s.th.;
einem etwas —, be indulgent with s.o.

Nachsicht ['na:xzɪçt], *f.* (—, *no pl.*)
forbearance, indulgence.

Nachsilbe ['na:xzɪlbə], *f.* (—, *pl. —n*)
suffix.

nachsinnen ['na:xzɪnən], *v.n.* muse,
reflect.

nachsitzen ['na:xzɪtsən], *v.n.* be kept
in after school.

Nachsommer ['na:xzɔmər], *m.* (—s,
pl. —) Indian summer.

Nachspeise ['na:xʃpaɪzə], *f.* (—, *pl. —n*)
dessert.

nachspüren ['na:xʃpy:rən], *v.n. einem
—*, trace, track.

nächst [nɛ:çst], *prep.* (*Dat.*) next to,
nearest to. — *adj.* next.

Nächste ['nɛ:çstə], *m.* (—n, *pl. —n*)
fellow-man, neighbour.

nachstehen ['na:xʃte:ən], *v.n. irr.
einem —*, be inferior to s.o.; *keinem
—*, be second to none.

nachstehend ['na:xʃte:ənt], *adv.* below,
hereinafter. — *adj.* following.

nachstellen ['na:xʃtelən], *v.n. einem —*,
lie in wait for s.o.

Nachstellung ['na:xʃtelʊŋ], *f.* (—, *pl.
—en*) persecution, ambush; (*Gram.*)
postposition.

nächstens ['nɛ:çstəns], *adv.* soon,
shortly.

nachstöbern ['na:xʃtø:bərn], *v.n.* rummage.

nachströmen ['na:xʃtrø:mən], *v.n.*
(*aux. sein*) crowd after.

Nacht [naxt], *f.* (—, *pl. ˨e*) night;
die ganze — hindurch, all night;
bei —, at night; *gute — wünschen*,
bid goodnight; *über —*, overnight;
in der —, during the night; *bei — und
Nebel*, in the dead of night.

Nachteil ['na:xtaɪl], *m.* (—s, *pl. —e*)
disadvantage, damage.

Nachtessen ['naxtesən], *n.* (—s, *pl. —*)
supper; evening meal.

Nachtfalter ['naxtfaltər], *m.* (—s, *pl. —*)
(*Ent.*) moth.

Nachtgeschirr ['naxtgəʃɪr], *n.* (—s,
pl. —e) chamber-pot.

Nachtgleiche ['naxtglaɪçə], *f.* (—, *pl.
—n*) equinox.

Nachthemd ['naxtɛmt], *n.* (—es, *pl.
—en*) night-dress, night-gown.

Nachtigall ['naxtɪgal], *f.* (—, *pl. —en*)
(*Orn.*) nightingale.

nächtigen ['nɛçtɪgən], *v.n.* spend the
night.

Nachtisch ['naxtɪʃ], *m.* (—es, *pl. —e*)
dessert.

Nachtlager ['naxtla:gər], *n.* (—s, *pl.
—*) lodgings for the night; (*Mil.*)
bivouac.

Nachtmahl ['naxtma:l], *n.* (—s, *pl.
—e*) (*Austr.*) supper.

nachtönen ['na:xtø:nən], *v.n.* resound.

Nachtrag ['na:xtra:k], *m.* (—s, *pl. ˨e*)
supplement, postscript, addition; (*pl.*)
addenda.

nachtragen ['na:xtra:gən], *v.a. irr.*
carry after; add; (*fig.*) *einem etwas —*,
bear s.o. a grudge.

nachträglich ['na:xtre:klɪç], *adj.* subsequent; supplementary; additional;
further; later.

Nachtrupp ['na:xtrup], *m.* (—s, *no pl.*)
rearguard.

Nachtschwärmer ['naxtʃvɛrmər], *m.*
(—s, *pl. —*) night-reveller.

Nachttisch ['naxtɪʃ], *m.* (—es, *pl. —e*)
bedside-table.

nachtun ['na:xtu:n], *v.a. irr. einem
etwas —*, imitate s.o., emulate s.o.

Nachtwächter ['naxtvɛçtər], *m.* (—s,
pl. —) night-watchman.

Nachtwandler ['naxtvandlər], *m.* (—s,
pl. —) sleep-walker, somnambulist.

Nachwahl ['na:xva:l], *f.* (—, *pl. —en*)
by(e)-election.

Nachwehen ['na:xve:ən], *f. pl.* after-
math; unpleasant consequences.

Nachweis ['na:xvaɪs], *m.* (—es, *pl.
—e*) proof; (*Lit.*) reference; agency.

nachweisen ['na:xvaɪzən], *v.a. irr.*
prove, establish; (*Lit.*) refer.

Nachwelt ['na:xvɛlt], *f.* (—, *no pl.*)
posterity.

Nachwort ['na:xvɔrt], *n.* (—es, *pl. —e*)
epilogue.

Nachwuchs ['na:xvu:ks], *m.* (—es, *no
pl.*) coming generation; recruits.

Nachzahlung ['na:xtsa:lʊŋ], *f.* (—, *pl.
—en*) additional payment, supplementary payment.

Nachzählung ['na:xtse:lʊŋ], *f.* (—, *pl.
—en*) recount.

nachziehen ['na:xtsi:ən], *v.a. irr.*
drag, tow; tighten; trace, pencil. —
v.n. follow.

Nachzügler ['na:xtsy:glər], *m.* (—s, *pl.
—*) straggler.

Nacken ['nakən], *m.* (—s, *pl. —*) nape,
scruff of the neck.

nackend ['nakənt], *adj.* naked.

nackt [nakt], *adj.* nude, naked; (*bird*)
callow; (*fig.*) bare; *sich — ausziehen*,
strip.

Nadel ['na:dəl], *f.* (—, *pl. —n*) needle,
pin; *wie auf —n sitzen*, be on tenterhooks.

Nadelöhr ['na:dələø:r], *n.* (—s, *pl. —e*)
eye of a needle.

Nagel ['na:gəl], *m.* (—s, *pl. ˨*) nail;
(*wooden*) peg; (*ornament*) stud; *etwas
an den — hängen*, lay s.th. aside, give
s.th. up.

nagelneu ['na:gəlnɔy], *adj.* brand new.

nagen ['na:gən], *v.a., v.n.* gnaw; (*fig.*)
rankle.

Näharbeit ['nɛ:arbaɪt], *f.* (—, *pl. —en*)
sewing, needlework.

nahe ['na:ə], *adj., adv.* near, close, nigh;
— bei, close to; *— daran sein*, be on
the point of; *es geht mir —*, it grieves
me, it touches me; *einem zu —
treten*, hurt s.o.'s feelings; *es liegt —*,
it is obvious, it suggests itself.

Nähe ['nɛ:ə], *f.* (—, *no pl.*) nearness,
proximity; *in der —*, at hand, close by.

nahen ['na:ən], *v.n.* (*aux.* sein) draw near, approach.

nähen ['nɛ:ən], *v.a.* sew, stitch.

Nähere ['nɛ:ərə], *n.* (—n, *no pl.*) details, particulars.

Näherin ['nɛ:ərɪn], *f.* (—, *pl.* — innen) seamstress, needlewoman.

nähern ['nɛ:ərn], *v.r. sich* —, draw near, approach.

nahestehen ['na:əʃte:ən], *v.n.* be closely connected *or* friendly (with s.o.).

Nährboden ['nɛ:rbo:dən], *m.* (—s, *pl.* ⸚) rich soil; (*Med., Biol.*) culture-medium.

nähren ['nɛ:rən], *v.a.* nourish, feed. — *v.r. sich — von*, feed on; (*fig.*) gain a livelihood.

nahrhaft ['na:rhaft], *adj.* nourishing, nutritive, nutritious.

Nährstand ['nɛ:rʃtant], *m.* (—es, *no pl.*) peasants, producers.

Nahrung ['na:ruŋ], *f.* (—, *no pl.*) nourishment.

Nahrungsmittel ['na:ruŋsmɪtəl], *n.* (—s, *pl.* —) food, provisions, victuals.

Naht [na:t], *f.* (—, *pl.* ⸚e) seam.

Nähzeug ['nɛ:tsɔyk], *n.* (—s, *no pl.*) sewing kit, work box.

naiv [na'i:f], *adj.* naïve, artless, guileless.

Naivität [naivi'tɛ:t], *f.* (—, *no pl.*) artlessness, guilelessness, naïveté.

Name ['na:mə], *m.* (—ns, *pl.* —n) name; *guter* —, good name, renown, reputation; *dem —n nach*, by name; *etwas beim rechten —n nennen*, call a spade a spade.

namens ['na:məns], *adv.* called; by the name of.

Namensvetter ['na:mənsfɛtər], *m.* (—s, *pl.* —n) namesake.

namentlich ['na:məntlɪç], *adj.* by name; particularly.

Namenverzeichnis ['na:mənfɛrtsaɪçnɪs], *n.* (—ses, *pl.* —se) list of names; (*scientific*) nomenclature.

namhaft ['na:mhaft], *adj.* distinguished, renowned; considerable; *— machen*, name.

nämlich ['nɛ:mlɪç], *adv.* namely, to wit.

Napf [napf], *m.* (—es, *pl.* ⸚e) bowl, basin.

Napfkuchen ['napfku:xən], *m.* (—s, *pl.* —) pound-cake, large cake.

Narbe ['narbə], *f.* (—, *pl.* —n) scar; (*leather*) grain.

Narkose [nar'ko:zə], *f.* (—, *pl.* —n) anaesthesia; narcosis.

Narr [nar], *m.* (—en, *pl.* —en) fool; jester, buffoon; *einen zum —en haben*, make a fool of s.o.; *an einem einen —en gefressen haben*, dote on, be infatuated with s.o.

Narrheit ['narhaɪt], *f.* (—, *pl.* —en) foolishness, folly.

närrisch ['nɛrɪʃ], *adj.* foolish, comical; odd; merry; eccentric, mad; *— werden*, go mad.

Narzisse [nar'tsɪsə], *f.* (—, *pl.* —n) (*Bot.*) narcissus; *gelbe —*, daffodil.

naschen ['naʃən], *v.a., v.n.* pilfer titbits; nibble at, eat sweets.

Näscherei [nɛʃər'aɪ], *f.* (—, *pl.* —en) sweets, dainties, sweetmeats.

naschhaft ['naʃhaft], *adj.* sweet-toothed.

Naschkatze ['naʃkatsə], *f.* (—, *pl.* —n) sweet tooth.

Nase ['na:zə], *f.* (—, *pl.* —n) nose; (*animal*) snout; scent; *stumpfe —*, snub nose; *gebogene —*, Roman nose; *immer der — nach*, follow your nose; *die — hoch tragen*, be stuck-up; *eine feine (gute) — haben*, be good at; *nicht miss much*; *die — rümpfen*, turn up o.'s nose; *seine — in alles stecken*, poke o.'s nose into everything; *einem etwas unter die — reiben*, bring s.th. home to s.o.

näseln ['nɛ:zəln], *v.n.* speak with a twang.

Nasenbein ['na:zənbaɪn], *n.* (—s, *pl.* —e) nasal bone.

Nasenbluten ['na:zənblu:tən], *n.* (—s, *no pl.*) nose-bleed.

Nasenflügel ['na:zənfly:gəl], *m.* (—s, *pl.* —) side of the nose; nostril.

naseweis ['na:zəvaɪs], *adj.* pert, saucy.

Nashorn ['na:shɔrn], *n.* (—s, *pl.* ⸚er) (*Zool.*) rhinoceros.

Naß [nas], *n.* (—sses, *no pl.*) (*Poet.*) fluid.

naß [nas], *adj.* wet, moist, damp.

Nässe ['nɛsə], *f.* (—, *no pl.*) wetness, dampness, moisture, humidity.

nationalisieren [natsjonali'zi:rən], *v.a.* nationalise.

Nationalität [natsjonali'tɛ:t], *f.* (—, *pl.* —en) nationality.

Natrium ['na:trjum], *n.* (—s, *no pl.*) sodium.

Natron ['natrɔn], *n.* (—s, *no pl.*) sodium carbonate; *doppelkohlensaures —*, sodium bicarbonate; bicarbonate of soda.

Natter ['natər], *f.* (—, *pl.* —n) (*Zool.*) adder, viper.

Natur [na'tu:r], *f.* (—, *pl.* —en) nature; (*body*) constitution; (*mind*) disposition; *von —*, by nature, constitutionally; *nach der — zeichnen*, draw from nature.

naturalisieren [naturali'zi:rən], *v.a.* naturalise.

Naturalleistung [natu'ra:llaɪstuŋ], *f.* (—, *pl.* —en) payment in kind.

Naturell [natu'rɛl], *n.* (—s, *pl.* —e) natural disposition, temper.

Naturforscher [na'tu:rfɔrʃər], *m.* (—s, *pl.* —) naturalist.

naturgemäß [na'tu:rgəmɛ:s], *adj.* natural.

Naturgeschichte [na'tu:rgəʃɪçtə], *f.* (—, *no pl.*) natural history.

naturgetreu [na'tu:rgətrɔy], *adj.* true to nature, lifelike.

Naturkunde [na'tu:rkundə], *f.* (—, *no pl.*) natural history.

Naturlehre [na'tu:rle:rə], *f.* (—, *no pl.*) natural philosophy; physics.

natürlich

natürlich [na'ty:rlıç], *adj.* natural; innate, inherent; unaffected, artless. — *adv.* of course, naturally.

Naturspiel [na'tu:rʃpi:l], *n.* (—s, *pl.* —e) freak of nature.

Naturtrieb [na'tu:rtri:p], *m.* (—s, *no pl.*) natural impulse, instinct.

naturwidrig [na'tu:rvi:drıç], *adj.* contrary to nature, unnatural.

Naturwissenschaft [na'tu:rvɪsənʃaft], *f.* (—, *pl.* —en) (natural) science.

naturwüchsig [na'tu:rvy:ksıç], *adj.* original; unsophisticated.

Nautik ['nautık], *f.* (—, *no pl.*) nautical science.

nautisch ['nautıʃ], *adj.* nautical.

Nazi ['na:tsi], *abbr.* National Socialist.

Neapel [ne'a:pəl], *n.* Naples.

Nebel ['ne:bəl], *m.* (—s, *pl.* —) fog; *leichter* —, haze, mist; *dichter* —, (*London*) pea-souper; (*with soot*) smog.

Nebelschicht ['ne:bəlʃıçt], *f.* (—, *pl.* —n) fog-bank.

neben ['ne:bən], *prep.* (*Dat.*, *Acc.*) near, by, beside, besides, close to, next to; (*in compounds*) secondary, subsidiary, side-. — *adv.* beside, besides.

nebenan [ne:bən'an], *adv.* next door, nearby.

nebenbei [ne:bən'baɪ], *adv.* besides, by the way, incidentally.

Nebenbuhler ['ne:bənbu:lər], *m.* (—s, *pl.* —) rival.

nebeneinander [ne:bənaɪn'andər], *adv.* side by side, abreast.

Nebenfluß ['ne:bənflus], *m.* (—sses, *pl.* ˙˙sse) tributary, affluent.

nebenher [ne:bən'he:r], *adv.* by the side of, along with.

Nebenmensch ['ne:bənmɛnʃ], *m.* (—en, *pl.* —en) fellow creature.

Nebensatz ['ne:bənzats], *m.* (—es, *pl.* ˙˙e) (*Gram.*) subordinate clause.

Nebenzimmer ['ne:bəntsɪmər], *n.* (—s, *pl.* —) adjoining room.

neblig ['ne:blıç], *adj.* foggy, misty, hazy.

nebst [ne:pst], *prep.* (*Dat.*) together with, including.

necken ['nɛkən], *v.a.* tease, chaff, banter.

neckisch ['nɛkıʃ], *adj.*, droll, playful, arch.

Neffe ['nɛfə], *m.* (—n, *pl.* —n) nephew.

Neger ['ne:gər], *m.* (—s, *pl.* —) Negro.

negerartig ['ne:gəra:rtıç], *adj.* Negroid.

negieren [ne'gi:rən], *v.a.* deny, negate, negative.

nehmen ['ne:mən], *v.a. irr.* take, seize; receive, accept; *einem etwas* —, take s.th. from s.o.; *das lasse ich mir nicht* —, I insist on that, I am not to be done out of that; *ein Ende* —, come to an end; *etwas in die Hand* —, take s.th. in hand; *Schaden* —, suffer damage; *einen beim Wort* —, take s.o. at his word; *sich in acht* —, take care.

Nehrung ['ne:run], *f.* (—, *pl.* —en) narrow tongue of land, spit.

Neid [naɪt], *m.* (—es, *no pl.*) envy, grudge.

Neidhammel ['naɪthaməl], *m.* (—s, *pl.* —) dog in the manger.

neidisch ['naɪdıʃ], *adj.* envious, grudging, jealous.

Neige ['naɪgə], *f.* (—, *pl.* —n) remnant, sediment; *zur* — *gehen*, be on the decline, run short, dwindle.

neigen ['naɪgən], *v.a.*, *v.n.* incline, bow, bend; *zu etwas* —, be inclined to, be prone to. — *v.r. sich* —, bow.

Neigung ['naɪgun], *f.* (—, *pl.* —en) inclination, proneness; affection; (*ground*) dip, slope, gradient; (*ship*) list.

Neigungsfläche ['naɪgunsflɛçə], *f.* (—, *pl.* —n) inclined plane.

nein [naɪn], *adv.* no.

Nekrolog [nekro'lo:k], *m.* (—(e)s, *pl.* —e) obituary.

Nelke ['nɛlkə], *f.* (—, *pl.* —n) (*Bot.*) pink, carnation; (*condiment*) clove.

nennen ['nɛnən], *v.a. irr.* name, call by name, term, style.

Nenner ['nɛnər], *m.* (—s, *pl.* —) denominator.

Nennung ['nɛnuŋ], *f.* (—, *pl.* —en) naming, mentioning.

Nennwert ['nɛnve:rt], *m.* (—s, *pl.* —e) nominal value.

Nepal ['ne:pal], *n.* Nepal.

Nerv [nɛrf], *m.* (—s, *pl.* —en) nerve, sinew; *einem auf die* —*en gehen*, get on s.o.'s nerves.

Nervenlehre ['nɛrfənle:rə], *f.* (—, *no pl.*) neurology.

nervig ['nɛrvıç], *adj.* strong; (*fig.*) pithy.

nervös [nɛr'vø:s], *adj.* nervous, irritable, fidgety.

Nerz [nɛrts], *m.* (—es, *pl.* —e) mink.

Nessel ['nɛsəl], *f.* (—, *pl.* —n) nettle.

Nesseltuch ['nɛsəltu:x], *n.* (—es, *no pl.*) muslin.

Nest [nɛst], *n.* (—es, *pl.* —er) nest; (*eagle*) eyrie; *kleines* —, small town.

Nesthäkchen ['nɛsthɛ:kçən], *n.* (—s, *pl.* —) youngest child.

nett [nɛt], *adj.* nice, kind, friendly; neat, trim.

netto ['nɛto], *adv.* (*Comm.*) net, clear.

Netz [nɛts], *n.* (—es, *pl.* —e) net; (*Electr.*) grid; *Eisenbahn* —, railway network *or* system.

netzen ['nɛtsən], *v.a.* (*obs.*, *Poet.*) wet, moisten.

Netzhaut ['nɛtshaut], *f.* (—, *pl.* ˙˙e) retina.

neu [nɔy], *adj.* new, fresh; modern; recent; *aufs* —*e*, *von* —*em*, anew, afresh; —*e*, —*ere Sprachen*, modern languages.

Neuenburg ['nɔyənburk], *n.* Neuchâtel.

neuerdings ['nɔyərdıns], *adv.* newly, lately.

Neuerer ['nɔyərər], *m.* (—s, *pl.* —) innovator.

neuerlich ['nɔyərliç], *adj.* late, repeated.

Neufundland [nɔy'funtlant], *n.* Newfoundland.

Neugier(de) ['nɔygi:r(də)], *f.* (—, *no pl.*) inquisitiveness, curiosity.

neugierig ['nɔygi:riç], *adj.* curious, inquisitive.

Neuheit ['nɔyhaɪt], *f.* (—, *pl.* —en) novelty.

Neuigkeit ['nɔyɪçkaɪt], *f.* (—, *pl.* —en) piece of news.

neulich ['nɔyliç], *adv.* lately, recently.

Neuling ['nɔylɪŋ], *m.* (—s, *pl.* —e) novice, beginner, tyro, newcomer; (*Am.*) greenhorn.

neumodisch ['nɔymo:dɪʃ], *adj.* newfangled, in vogue.

Neumond ['nɔymo:nt], *m.* (—s, *pl.* —e) new moon.

neun [nɔyn], *num. adj.* nine.

Neunauge ['nɔynaugə], *n.* (—s, *pl.* —n) river lamprey.

neunzehn ['nɔyntse:n], *num. adj.* nineteen.

neunzig ['nɔyntsɪç], *num. adj.* ninety.

Neuregelung ['nɔyre:gəluŋ], *f.* (—, *pl.* —en) rearrangement.

Neuseeland [nɔy'ze:lant], *n.* New Zealand.

neutralisieren [nɔytrali'zi:rən], *v.a.* neutralise.

Neutralität [nɔytrali'tɛ:t], *f.* (—, *no pl.*) neutrality.

Neutrum ['nɔytrum], *n.* (—s, *pl.* —ren) (*Gram.*) neuter.

Neuzeit ['nɔytsaɪt], *f.* (—, *no pl.*) modern times.

nicht [nɪçt], *adv.* not; *auch* —, nor; — *doch*, don't; — *einmal*, not even; *durchaus* —, not at all, by no means; — *mehr*, no more, no longer; not any more; *noch* —, not yet; — *wahr?* isn't it? aren't you? (*in compounds*) non–, dis–, a– (*negativing*).

Nichte ['nɪçtə], *f.* (—, *pl.* —n) niece.

nichten ['nɪçtən], *adv.* (*obs.*) *mit*—, by no means, not at all.

nichtig ['nɪçtɪç], *adj.* null, void, invalid.

Nichtigkeit ['nɪçtɪçkaɪt], *f.* (—, *no pl.*) invalidity, nullity.

nichts [nɪçts], *pron.* nothing, nought; — *als*, nothing but.

nichtsdestoweniger [nɪçtsdésto've:nɪgər], *adv.* nevertheless.

Nichtsnutz ['nɪçtsnuts], *m.* (—es, *pl.* —e) good for nothing.

Nickel ['nɪkəl], *n.* (—s, *no pl.*) (*metal*) nickel.

nicken ['nɪkən], *v.n.* nod.

nie [ni:], *adv.* never, at no time.

nieder ['ni:dər], *adj.* low, lower, nether; mean, inferior. — *adv.* down.

niedergeschlagen ['ni:dərgəʃla:gən], *adj.* dejected, low-spirited, depressed.

niederkommen ['ni:dərkɔmən], *v.n. irr.* (*aux.* sein) (*rare*) be confined.

Niederkunft ['ni:dərkunft], *f.* (—, *no pl.*) confinement, childbirth.

Niederlage ['ni:dərla:gə], *f.* (—, *pl.* —n) (*enemy*) defeat, overthrow; (*goods*) depot, warehouse; (*Am.*) agency.

Niederlande ['ni:dərlandə], *n. pl.* the Netherlands.

niederlassen ['ni:dərlasən], *v.a. irr.* let down. — *v.r. sich* —, sit down, take a seat; settle; establish o.s. in business.

Niederlassung ['ni:dərlasuŋ], *f.* (—, *pl.* —en) establishment; settlement, colony; branch, branch establishment.

niederlegen ['ni:dərle:gən], *v.a.* lay down, put down; (*office*) resign, abdicate. — *v.r. sich* —, lie down.

Niederschlag ['ni:dərʃla:k], *m.* (—s, *pl.* ⸚e) precipitation, sediment, deposit; rain.

niederschlagen ['ni:dərʃla:gən], *v.a. irr.* strike down; (*fig.*) depress, discourage; (*Law*) quash, cancel; (*eyes*) cast down; (*Chem.*) precipitate; (*Boxing*) knock out.

Niedertracht ['ni:dərtraxt], *f.* (—, *no pl.*) baseness, meanness, villainy, beastliness.

Niederung ['ni:dəruŋ], *f.* (—, *pl.* —en) low ground, marsh.

niedlich ['ni:tlɪç], *adj.* pretty, dainty; (*Am.*) cute.

niedrig ['ni:drɪç], *adj.* low; (*fig.*) base, vile.

niemals ['ni:ma:ls], *adv.* never, at no time.

niemand ['ni:mant], *pron.* nobody, no one.

Niere ['ni:rə], *f.* (—, *pl.* —n) kidney.

Nierenbraten ['ni:rənbra:tən], *m.* (—s, *no pl.*) roast loin.

Nierenfett ['ni:rənfet], *n.* (—s, *no pl.*) suet.

nieseln ['ni:zəln], *v.n. imp.* drizzle.

niesen ['ni:zən], *v.n.* sneeze.

Nießbrauch ['ni:sbraux], *m.* (—s, *no pl.*) usufruct, benefit.

Niete ['ni:tə], *f.* (—, *pl.* —n) blank; (*Engin.*) rivet; failure.

Niger ['ni:gər], *n.* Niger.

Nigeria [ni'ge:rja], *n.* Nigeria.

Nikaragua [nika'ra:gua], *n.* Nicaragua.

Nikolaus ['nikolaus], *m.* Nicholas; *Sankt* —, Santa Claus.

Nil [ni:l], *m.* (—s, *no pl.*) Nile.

Nilpferd ['ni:lpfe:rt], *n.* (—s, *pl.* —e) (*Zool.*) hippopotamus.

nimmer (mehr) ['nɪmər (me:r)], *adv.* never, never again.

nippen ['nɪpən], *v.a., v.n.* sip, (take a) nip (of).

Nippsachen ['nɪpzaxən], *f. pl.* knick-knacks.

nirgends ['nɪrgənts], *adv.* nowhere.

Nische ['ni:ʃə], *f.* (—, *pl.* —n) niche.

Nisse ['nɪsə], *f.* (—, *pl.* —n) nit.

nisten ['nɪstən], *v.n.* nest.

Niveau [ni'vo:], *n.* (—s, *pl.* —s) level, standard.

nivellieren [nive'li:rən], *v.a.* level.

Nixe ['nɪksə], *f.* (—, *pl.* —n) water-nymph, mermaid, water-sprite.

Nizza ['nɪtsa], *n.* Nice.

nobel ['no:bəl], *adj.* noble, smart; (*Am.*) swell; munificent, open-handed, magnanimous.

noch [nɔx], *adv.* still, yet; — *einmal,* — *mals,* once more; *weder* ... — ..., neither ... nor ...; — *nicht,* not yet; — *nie,* never yet, never before.

nochmalig ['nɔxma:lɪç], *adj.* repeated.

Nomade [no'ma:də], *m.* (—n, *pl.* —n) nomad.

nominell [nomi'nɛl], *adj.* nominal.

nominieren [nomi'ni:rən], *v.a.* nominate.

Nonne ['nɔnə], *f.* (—, *pl.* —n) nun.

Noppe ['nɔpə], *f.* (—, *pl.* —n) nap.

Norden ['nɔrdən], *m.* (—s, *no pl.*) north.

nördlich ['nœrtlɪç], *adj.* northern, northerly.

Nordsee ['nɔrtze:], *f.* North Sea.

nörgeln ['nœrgəln], *v.n.* find fault, cavil, carp, nag.

Norm ['nɔrm], *f.* (—, *pl.* —en) standard, rule, norm.

normal [nɔr'ma:l], *adj.* normal, standard.

Norwegen ['nɔrve:gən], *n.* Norway.

Not [no:t], *f.* (—, *pl.* —e) need, necessity; misery, want, trouble, distress; (*in compounds*) emergency.

not [no:t], *pred. adj.* — *tun,* be necessary.

Nota ['no:ta], *f.* (—, *pl.* —s) bill, statement.

Notar [no'ta:r], *m.* (—s, *pl.* —e) notary.

Notdurft ['notdurft], *f.* (—, *pl.* —e) want, necessaries, necessity; *seine* — *verrichten,* ease o.s.

notdürftig ['no:tdyrftɪç], *adj.* scanty, makeshift.

Note ['no:tə], *f.* (—, *pl.* —n) note; (*Mus.*) note; (*School*) mark(s); *nach* —*n,* (*fig.*) with a vengeance.

Notenbank ['no:tənbaŋk], *f.* (—, *pl.* —en) bank of issue.

Notenblatt ['no:tənblat], *n.* (—s, *pl.* —er) sheet of music.

notgedrungen ['no:tgədruŋən], *adj.* compulsory, forced; perforce.

Nothelfer ['no:thelfər], *m.* (—s, *pl.* —) helper in time of need.

notieren [no'ti:rən], *v.a.* note, book; (*Comm.*) quote.

notifizieren [notifi'tsi:rən], *v.a.* notify.

nötig ['nø:tɪç], *adj.* necessary; — *haben,* want, need.

nötigen ['nø:tɪgən], *v.a.* compel, press, force, urge; necessitate; *sich* — *lassen,* stand upon ceremony.

Notiz [no'ti:ts], *f.* (—, *pl.* —en) note, notice; — *nehmen von,* take notice of; (*pl.*) notes, jottings.

notleidend ['no:tlaɪdənt], *adj.* financially distressed, indigent, needy.

notorisch [no'to:rɪʃ], *adj.* notorious.

Notstand ['no:tʃtant], *m.* (—s, *no pl.*) state of distress; emergency.

Notverband ['no:tfɛrband], *m.* (—es, *pl.* —e) first-aid dressing.

Notwehr ['no:tve:r], *f.* (—, *no pl.*) self-defence.

notwendig ['no:tvɛndɪç], *adj.* necessary, essential, needful.

Notzucht ['no:ttsuxt], *f.* (—, *no pl.*) rape, violation.

Novelle [no'vɛlə], *f.* (—, *pl.* —n) (*Lit.*) novella, short story, short novel.

Novize [no'vi:tsə], *m.* (—n, *pl.* —n) or *f.* (—, *pl.* —n) novice.

Nu [nu:], *m. & n.* (—s, *no pl.*) moment; *im* —, in no time, in an instant.

Nubien ['nu:bjən], *n.* Nubia.

nüchtern ['nyçtərn], *adj.* fasting; sober; jejune; (*fig.*) dry, matter-of-fact, realistic.

Nüchternheit ['nyçtərnhaɪt], *f.* (—, *no pl.*) sobriety; (*fig.*) dryness.

Nudel ['nu:dəl], *f.* (—, *pl.* —n) noodles, macaroni, vermicelli; *eine komische* —, a funny person.

Null [nul], *f.* (—, *pl.* —en) nought, zero; (*fig.*) nonentity.

null [nul], *adj.* null; nil; — *und nichtig,* null and void; *etwas für* — *und nichtig erklären,* annul.

numerieren [nume'ri:rən], *v.a.* number.

Nummer ['numər], *f.* (—, *pl.* —n) number, size, issue.

nun [nu:n], *adv., conj.* now, at present; since; —*!* now! well! *von* — *an,* henceforth; — *und nimmermehr,* nevermore; *was* —*?* what next?

nunmehr ['nu:nme:r], *adv.* now, by this time.

Nunzius ['nuntsjus], *m.* (—, *pl.* —zien) (Papal) nuncio.

nur [nu:r], *adv.* only, solely, merely, but; *wenn* —, if only, provided that; — *das nicht,* anything but that; — *zu,* go to it!

Nürnberg ['nyrnberk], *n.* Nuremberg.

Nuß [nus], *f.* (—, *pl.* —sse) nut.

Nußhäher ['nushe:ər], *m.* (—s, *pl.* —) (*Orn.*) jay.

Nüster ['nystər], *f.* (—, *pl.* —n) (*horse*) nostril.

Nutzanwendung ['nutsanvenduŋ], *f.* (—, *pl.* —en) practical application.

nutzbar ['nutsba:r], *adj.* useful, usable, productive.

nütze ['nytsə], *adj.* useful, of use.

Nutzen ['nutsən], *m.* (—s, *pl.* —) use, utility; profit, gain, advantage, benefit; — *bringen,* yield profit; — *ziehen aus,* derive profit from.

nützen ['nytsən], *v.a.* make use of, use. — *v.n.* be of use, serve, be effective, work.

nützlich ['nytslɪç], *adj.* useful.

nutzlos ['nutslo:s], *adj.* useless.

Nutznießer ['nutsni:sər], *m.* (—s, *pl.* —) beneficiary, usufructuary.

Nymphe ['nymfə], *f.* (—, *pl.* —en) nymph.

O

O [o:], n. (—s, pl. —s) the letter O.
ol [o:], excl. oh!
Oase [o'a:zə], f. (—, pl. —n) oasis.
ob [ɔp], conj. whether; if; als —, as if; und —! rather! yes, indeed! — prep. (Genit., Dat.) on account of; upon, on.
Obacht ['o:baxt], f. (—, no pl.) heed, care; — geben, pay attention, look out.
Obdach ['ɔpdax], n. (—es, no pl.) shelter, lodging.
Obduktion [ɔpduk'tsjo:n], f. (—, pl. —en) post-mortem examination.
oben [o:bən], adv. above, aloft, on top; (house) upstairs; (water) on the surface; von — bis unten, from top to bottom; von — herab, from above; (fig.) haughtily, superciliously.
obendrein [o:bən'draɪn], adv. besides, into the bargain.
obengenannt ['o:bəngənant], adj. above-mentioned.
Ober ['o:bər], m. (—s, pl. —) head waiter; Herr —!, waiter!; (in compounds) upper, chief.
ober ['o:bər], adj. upper, higher; chief; superior.
Oberfläche ['o:bərfleçə], f. (—, pl. —n) surface.
oberflächlich ['o:bərfleçlɪç], adj. superficial, casual.
oberhalb ['o:bərhalp], adv., prep. (Genit.) above.
Oberin ['o:bərɪn], f. (—, pl. —innen) (Eccl.) Mother Superior; hospital matron.
Oberschule ['o:bərʃu:lə], f. (—, pl. —n) high school, secondary school.
Oberst ['o:bərst], m. (—en, pl. —en) colonel.
Oberstaatsanwalt ['o:bərʃta:tsanvalt], m. (—s, pl. ⸚e) Attorney-General.
oberste ['o:bərstə], adj. uppermost, highest, supreme.
Oberstimme ['o:bərʃtɪmə], f. (—, pl. —n) (Mus.) treble, soprano.
Oberstübchen ['o:bərʃty:pçən], n. (—s, pl. —) (fig.) nicht richtig im — sein, have bats in the belfry.
Obervolta ['o:bərvolta], n. Upper Volta.
obgleich [ɔp'glaɪç], conj. though, although.
Obhut ['ɔphu:t], f. (—, no pl.) keeping, care, protection.
obig ['o:bɪç], adj. foregoing, above-mentioned, aforementioned, aforesaid.
objektiv [ɔpjɛk'ti:f], adj. objective, impartial, unprejudiced.
Oblate [o'bla:tə], f. (—, pl. —n) wafer; (Eccl.) Host.

obliegen ['ɔpli:gən], v.n. irr. be incumbent upon s.o.; be o.'s duty; apply o.s. to.
Obmann ['ɔpman], m. (—es, pl. ⸚er) chairman; (jury) foreman.
Obrigkeit ['o:brɪçkaɪt], f. (—, pl. —en) authorities.
obschon [ɔp'ʃo:n] see under obwohl.
Observatorium [ɔpzɛrva'to:rjum], n. (—s, pl. —rien) observatory.
obsiegen ['ɔpzi:gən], v.n. (rare) be victorious.
Obst [o:pst], n. (—es, no pl.) fruit.
obszön [ɔps'tsø:n], adj. obscene.
obwalten ['ɔpvaltən], v.n. (rare) exist, prevail, obtain; unter den —den Umständen, in the circumstances, as matters stand.
obwohl [ɔp'vo:l] (also **obschon** [ɔp'ʃo:n], **obzwar** [ɔp'tsva:r]), conj. though, although.
Ochse ['ɔksə], m. (—n, pl. —n) (Zool.) ox; bullock; (fig.) blockhead.
ochsen ['ɔksən], v.n. (sl.) swot, cram.
Ochsenauge ['ɔksənaugə], n. (—s, pl. —n) ox-eye, bull's eye; (Archit.) oval dormer window; porthole light.
Ochsenziemer ['ɔksəntsi:mər], m. (—s, pl. —) (obs.) horse-whip.
Ocker ['ɔkər], m. (—s, no pl.) ochre.
Öde ['ø:də], f. (—, pl. —n) wilderness.
öde ['ø:də], adj. desolate, bleak, dreary.
Odem ['o:dəm], m. (—s, no pl.) (Poet.) breath.
oder ['o:dər], conj. or; — aber, or else; — auch, or rather.
Ofen ['o:fən], m. (—s, pl. ⸚) stove; oven, furnace.
Ofenpest [o:fən'pɛst], n. Budapest.
offen ['ɔfən], adj. open; (fig.) candid, sincere, frank; — gestanden, frankly speaking.
offenbar [ɔfən'ba:r], adj. obvious, manifest, evident.
offenbaren [ɔfən'ba:rən], v.a. insep. make known, reveal, disclose. — v.r. sich einem —, open o.'s heart to s.o.; unbosom o.s.
Offenheit ['ɔfənhaɪt], f. (—, no pl.) frankness, candour.
offenkundig ['ɔfənkundɪç], adj. obvious, manifest.
offensichtlich ['ɔfənzɪçtlɪç], adj. obvious; apparent.
öffentlich ['œfəntlɪç], adj. public.
offerieren [ɔfə'ri:rən], v.a. offer.
Offerte [ɔ'fɛrtə], f. (—, pl. —n) offer, tender.
offiziell [ɔfi'tsjɛl], adj. official.
Offizier [ɔfi'tsi:r], m. (—s, pl. —e) officer, lieutenant.
Offizierspatent [ɔfi'tsi:rspatɛnt], n. (—s, pl. —e) (Mil.) commission.
offiziös [ɔfi'tsjø:s], adj. semi-official.
öffnen ['œfnən], v.a. open.
oft [ɔft], **oftmals** ['ɔftma:ls], adv. often, frequently.
öfters ['œftərs], adv. often, frequently.

163

Oheim ['o:haɪm], *m.* (—s, *pl* —e) (*Poet.*) uncle.

ohne ['o:nə], *prep.* (*Acc.*) without, but for, except.

ohnehin ['o:nəhɪn], *adv.* as it is.

Ohnmacht ['o:nmaxt], *f.* (—, *pl.* —en) fainting-fit, swoon; impotence; *in — fallen*, faint.

Ohr [o:r], *n.* (—es, *pl.* —en) ear; *bis über beide —en*, head over heels; *die —en spitzen*, prick up o.'s ears.

Ohrenbläser ['o:rənblɛ:zər], *m.* (—s, *pl.* —) tale-bearer.

Ohrensausen ['o:rənzauzən], *n.* (—s, *no pl.*) humming in the ears.

Ohrenschmaus ['o:rənʃmaus], *m.* (—es, *no pl.*) musical treat.

Ohrfeige ['o:rfaɪgə], *f.* (—, *pl.* —n) box on the ear.

Ohrläppchen ['o:rlɛpçən], *n.* (—s, *pl.* —) lobe of the ear.

Ohrmuschel ['o:rmuʃəl], *f.* (—, *pl.* —n) auricle.

oktav [ɔk'ta:f], *adj.* octavo.

Oktober [ɔk'to:bər], *m.* (—s, *pl.* —) October.

oktroyieren [ɔktroa'ji:rən], *v.a.* dictate, force s.th. upon s.o.

okulieren [oku'li:rən], *v.a.* (*trees*) graft.

Öl [ø:l], *n.* (—s, *pl.* —e) oil; (*rare*) olive-oil.

Ölanstrich ['ø:lanʃtrɪç], *m.* (—s, *pl.* —e) coat of oil-paint.

ölen ['ø:lən], *v.a.* oil, lubricate; (*rare*) anoint.

Ölgemälde ['ø:lgəmɛ:ldə], *n.* (—s, *pl.* —) oil painting.

Ölung ['ø:luŋ], *f.* (—, *pl.* —en) oiling; anointing; (*Eccl.*) *die letzte —*, Extreme Unction.

Olymp [o'lymp], *m.* Mount Olympus.

olympisch [o'lympɪʃ], *adj.* Olympian.

Omelett [omə'lɛt], *n.* (—s, *pl.* —s) omelette.

Onkel ['ɔŋkəl], *m.* (—s, *pl.* —) uncle.

Oper ['o:pər], *f.* (—, *pl.* —n) opera.

operieren [opə'ri:rən], *v.a.*, *v.n.* operate (on); *sich — lassen*, be operated on; undergo an operation.

Opfer ['ɔpfər], *n.* (—s, *pl.* —) sacrifice; victim.

opfern ['ɔpfərn], *v.a.*, *v.n.* offer (up), sacrifice, immolate.

opponieren [ɔpo'ni:rən], *v.n.* oppose.

Optiker ['ɔptɪkər], *m.* (—s, *pl.* —) optician.

oratorisch [ora'to:rɪʃ], *adj.* oratorical.

Orchester [ɔr'kɛstər], *n.* (—s, *pl.* —) orchestra, band.

orchestrieren [ɔrkɛs'tri:rən], *v.a.* orchestrate, score for orchestra.

Orchidee [ɔrçi'de:], *f.* (—, *pl.* —n) (*Bot.*) orchid.

Orden ['ɔrdən], *m.* (—s, *pl.* —) medal; (*Eccl.*) (religious) order.

ordentlich ['ɔrdəntlɪç], *adj.* orderly, tidy, methodical, neat; regular; respectable, steady; sound; *—er Professor*, (full) professor.

Order ['ɔrdər], *f.* (—, *pl.* —s) (*Comm.*) order.

ordinär [ɔrdi'nɛ:r], *adj.* common, vulgar.

Ordinarius [ɔrdi'na:rjus], *m.* (—, *pl.* —ien) (*Univ.*) professor; (*Eccl.*) ordinary.

ordnen ['ɔrdnən], *v.a.* put in order, tidy, arrange, dispose.

Ordnung ['ɔrdnuŋ], *f.* (—, *pl.* —en) order, arrangement, disposition, routine; tidiness; class, rank; *in —*, all right, in good trim; *nicht in —*, out of order, wrong.

ordnungsgemäß ['ɔrdnuŋsgəmɛ:s], *adv.* duly.

ordnungsmäßig ['ɔrdnuŋsmɛsɪç], *adj.* regular.

ordnungswidrig ['ɔrdnuŋsvi:drɪç], *adj.* irregular.

Ordnungszahl ['ɔrdnuŋstsa:l], *f.* (—, *pl.* —en) ordinal number.

Ordonnanz [ɔrdɔ'nants], *f.* (—, *pl.* —en) ordinance; (*Mil.*) orderly.

Organ [ɔr'ga:n], *n.* (—s, *pl.* —e) organ.

organisieren [ɔrgani'zi:rən], *v.a.* organise.

Orgel ['ɔrgəl], *f.* (—, *pl.* —n) (*Mus.*) organ.

Orgelzug ['ɔ:rgəltsu:k], *m.* (—s, *pl.* -e) organ-stop.

Orgie ['ɔrgjə], *f.* (—, *pl.* —n) orgy.

orientalisch [orjɛn'ta:lɪʃ], *adj.* oriental, eastern.

orientieren [orjɛn'ti:rən], *v.a.* inform, orientate; set s.o. right. — *v.r. sich — über*, orientate o.s., find out about; get o.'s bearings.

Orkan [ɔr'ka:n], *m.* (—s, *pl.* —e) hurricane, gale, typhoon.

Ornat [ɔr'na:t], *m.* (—es, *pl.* —e) official robes; vestments.

Ort [ɔrt], *m.* (—es, *pl.* —e, -er) place, spot; region; (*in compounds*) local.

örtlich ['œrtlɪç], *adj.* local.

Ortschaft ['ɔrtʃaft], *f.* (—, *pl.* —en) place, township, village.

Öse ['ø:zə], *f.* (—, *pl.* —n) loop; *Haken und —*, hooks and eyes.

Ostasien ['ɔsta:zjən], *n.* Eastern Asia, the Far East.

Ost(en) ['ɔst(ən)], *m.* (—s, *no pl.*) east.

ostentativ [ɔstɛnta'ti:f], *adj.* ostentatious.

Osterei ['o:stəraɪ], *n.* (—s, *pl.* —er) Easter egg.

Ostern ['o:stərn], *f. pl.* (*used as n. sing.*) Easter.

Österreich ['ø:stərraɪç], *n.* Austria.

Ostindien ['ɔstɪndjən], *n.* the East Indies.

östlich ['œstlɪç], *adj.* eastern, easterly.

Oxyd [ɔk'sy:t], *n.* (—es, *pl.* —e) oxide.

oxydieren [ɔksy'di:rən], *v.a.*, *v.n.* oxidise.

Ozean ['o:tsea:n], *m.* (—s, *pl.* —e) ocean, sea; *Grosser —*, Pacific (Ocean).

Ozon [o'tso:n], *n.* (—s, *no pl.*) ozone.

P

P [pe:], *n.* (—s, *pl.* —s) the letter P.
Paar [pa:r], *n.* (—es, *pl.* —e) pair, couple.
paar [pa:r], *adj.* ein —, a few, some.
Pacht [paxt], *f.* (—, *pl.* —en) lease; *in — nehmen*, take on lease.
Pachthof ['paxtho:f], *m.* (—s, *pl.* ¨e) leasehold estate, farm.
Pack (1) [pak], *m.* (—s, *pl.* ¨e) pack, bale, packet; *mit Sack und —*, (with) bag and baggage.
Pack (2) [pak], *n.* (—s, *no pl.*) rabble, mob.
Päckchen ['pɛkçən], *n.* (—s, *pl.* —) pack, packet; (small) parcel.
packen ['pakən], *v.a.* pack; seize; (*fig.*) —d, thrilling; *pack dich!* be off! scram!
pädagogisch [pɛ:da'go:gɪʃ], *adj.* educational, pedagogic(al).
paddeln ['padəln], *v.n.* paddle.
paff [paf], *excl.* bang! *ich bin ganz —*, I am astounded.
paffen ['pafən], *v.n.* puff; draw (at a pipe).
Page ['pa:ʒə], *m.* (—n, *pl.* —n) page-boy.
Paket [pa'ke:t], *n.* (—s, *pl.* —e) packet, package, parcel.
paktieren [pak'ti:rən], *v.n.* come to terms.
Palast [pa'last], *m.* (—es, *pl.* ¨e) palace.
Palästina [palɛ'sti:na], *n.* Palestine.
Paletot ['paləto:], *m.* (—s, *pl.* —s) overcoat.
Palisanderholz [pali'zandərhɔlts], *n.* (—es, *no pl.*) rosewood.
Palme ['palmə], *f.* (—, *pl.* —n) (*Bot.*) palm-tree.
Palmkätzchen ['palmkɛtsçən], *n.* (—s, *pl.* —) (*Bot.*) catkin.
Palmwoche ['palmvɔxə], *f.* Holy Week.
Pampelmuse ['pampəlmu:zə], *f.* (—, *pl.* —n) (*Bot.*) grapefruit.
Panama ['pa:nama], *n.* Panama.
Panier [pa'ni:r], *n.* (—s, *pl.* —e) standard, banner.
panieren [pa'ni:rən], *v.a.* dress (*meat etc.*), roll in bread-crumbs.
Panne ['panə], *f.* (—, *pl.* —n) puncture; (*Motor.*) break-down; mishap.
panschen ['panʃən], *v.n.* splash about in water. — *v.a.* adulterate.
Pantoffel [pan'tɔfəl], *m.* (—s, *pl.* —n) slipper; *unter dem — stehen*, be henpecked.
Pantoffelheld [pan'tɔfəlhɛlt], *m.* (—en, *pl.* —en) henpecked husband.

Panzer ['pantsər], *m.* (—s, *pl.* —) armour, breast-plate, coat of mail; (*Mil.*) tank.
Papagei [papa'gaɪ], *m.* (—s, *pl.* —en) (*Orn.*) parrot.
Papier [pa'pi:r], *n.* (—s, *pl.* —e) paper; (*Comm.*) stocks; (*pl.*) papers, documents; *ein Bogen —*, a sheet of paper.
Papierkrieg [pa'pi:rkri:k], *m.* (—s, *no pl.*) (*coll.*) red tape.
Papierwaren [pa'pi:rva:rən], *f. pl.* stationery.
Pappdeckel ['papdɛkəl], *m.* (—s, *pl.* —) pasteboard.
Pappe ['papə], *f.* (—, *no pl.*) paste, cardboard, pasteboard.
Pappel ['papəl], *f.* (—, *pl.* —n) poplar.
pappen ['papən], *v.a.* stick; glue, paste.
Pappenstiel ['papənʃti:l], *m.* (—s, *pl.* —e) trifle.
papperlapapp ['papərlapap], *excl.* fiddlesticks! nonsense!
Papst [pa:pst], *m.* (—es, *pl.* ¨e) Pope.
päpstlich ['pɛ:pstlɪç], *adj.* papal; *—er als der Papst*, fanatically loyal, outheroding Herod; over-zealous.
Parabel [pa'ra:bəl], *f.* (—, *pl.* —n) parable; (*Maths.*) parabola.
paradieren [para'di:rən], *v.n.* parade, make a show.
Paradies [para'di:s], *n.* (—es, *pl.* —e) paradise.
paradox [para'dɔks], *adj.* paradoxical.
Paragraph [para'gra:f], *m.* (—en, *pl.* —en) paragraph, article, clause, section.
Paraguay ['paragvaɪ, para'gua:ɪ], *n.* Paraguay.
Paralyse [para'ly:zə], *f.* (—, *pl.* —n) paralysis.
parat [pa'ra:t], *adj.* prepared, ready.
Pardon [par'dɔ̃], *m.* (—s, *no pl.*) pardon, forgiveness.
Parfüm [par'fy:m], *n.* (—s, *pl.* —e) perfume, scent.
pari ['pa:ri], *adv.* at par.
parieren [pa'ri:rən], *v.a.* parry, keep off. — *v.n.* obey; *aufs Wort —*, obey implicitly *or* to the letter.
Parität [pari'tɛ:t], *f.* (—, *no pl.*) parity; (religious) equality.
Parkanlagen [park'anla:gən], *f. pl.* parks; public gardens.
parken ['parkən], *v.a.* park.
Parkett [par'kɛt], *n.* (—s, *pl.* —e) parquet flooring; (*Theat.*) stalls.
Parkuhr [park'u:r], *f.* (—, *pl.* —en) parking-meter.
Parlament [parla'mɛnt], *n.* (—s, *pl.* —e) parliament.
Parlamentär [parlamɛn'tɛ:r], *m.* (—s, *pl.* —e) officer negotiating a truce.
Parlamentarier [parlamɛn'ta:rjər], *m.* (—s, *pl.* —) parliamentarian, member of a parliament.
Parole [pa'ro:lə], *f.* (—, *pl.* —n) watchword, cue, motto, slogan, password.

Partei

Partei [par'taɪ], *f.* (—, *pl.* —en) party, faction; — *nehmen für*, side with.

Parteigänger [par'taɪgɛŋər], *m.* (—s, *pl.* —) partisan.

Parteigenosse [par'taɪgənɔsə], *m.* (—n, *pl.* —n) party member (especially National Socialist); comrade.

parteiisch [par'taɪɪʃ], *adj.* partial, biased, prejudiced.

Parteinahme [par'taɪnaːmə], *f.* (—, *no pl.*) partisanship.

Parteitag [par'taɪtaːk], *m.* (—s, *pl.* —e) party conference; congress.

Parterre [par'tɛrə], *n.* (—s, *pl.* —s) ground floor; (*Theat.*) pit; stalls.

Partie [par'tiː], *f.* (—, *pl.* —n) (*Comm.*) parcel; (*marriage*) match; (*chess etc.*) game; (*bridge*) rubber; outing, excursion, trip.

Partitur [parti'tuːr], *f.* (—, *pl.* —en) (*Mus.*) score.

Partizip [parti'tsiːp], *n.* (—s, *pl.* —e, —ien) (*Gram.*) participle.

Parzelle [par'tsɛlə], *f.* (—, *pl.* —n) allotment, lot, parcel.

paschen ['paʃən], *v.a.* smuggle.

Paß [pas], *m.* (—sses, *pl.* ̈sse) (*mountain*) pass; (*travelling*) passport; (*horse*) amble.

Passagier [pasa'ʒiːr], *m.* (—s, *pl.* —e) passenger; *blinder* —, stowaway.

Passant [pa'sant], *m.* (—en, *pl.* —en) passer-by.

Passatwind [pa'saːtvɪnt], *m.* (—s, *pl.* —e) trade-wind.

passen ['pasən], *v.n.* fit, suit, be suitable, be convenient; (*Cards*) pass.

passieren [pa'siːrən], *v.a.* sieve; (*road*) pass, cross, negotiate. — *v.n.* (*aux. sein*) pass; happen, take place, come about.

Passif, Passivum [pa'siːf *or* 'pasiːf, pa'siːvum], *n.* (—s, *pl.* —e; —, *pl.* —va) (*Gram.*) passive voice; (*Comm.*) (*pl.*) debts, liabilities.

Passus ['pasus], *m.* (—, *pl.* —) passage (in book).

Pasta, Paste ['pasta, 'pastə], *f.* (—, *pl.* —ten) paste.

Pastell [pa'stɛl], *m.* (—s, *pl.* —e) pastel, crayon; — *malen*, draw in pastel.

Pastete [pa'steːtə], *f.* (—, *pl.* —n) pie, pastry.

Pastille [pa'stɪlə], *f.* (—, *pl.* —n) lozenge, pastille.

Pastor ['pastɔr], *m.* (—s, *pl.* —en) minister, pastor; parson; vicar, rector.

Pate ['paːtə], *m.* (—n, *pl.* —n) godparent; — *stehen*, be godfather to.

patent [pa'tɛnt], *adj.* fine, grand, (*sl.*) smashing.

Patent [pa'tɛnt], *n.* (—(e)s, *pl.* —e) patent; charter, licence.

patentieren [paten'tiːrən], *v.a.* patent, license.

pathetisch [pa'teːtɪʃ], *adj.* elevated, solemn, moving.

Patin ['paːtɪn], *f.* (—, *pl.* —innen) godmother.

patriotisch [patri'oːtɪʃ], *adj.* patriotic.

Patrone [pa'troːnə], *f.* (—, *pl.* —n) cartridge; stencil, pattern.

Patrouille [pa'truljə], *f.* (—, *pl.* —n) (*Mil.*) patrol.

Patsche ['patʃə], *f.* (—, *pl.* —n) (*dial.*) hand; (*fig.*) mess, pickle; *in eine* — *geraten*, get into a jam.

patschen ['patʃən], *v.n.* (*aux. sein*) splash.

Patt [pat], *n.* (—s, *pl.* —s) (*Chess*) stalemate.

patzig ['patsɪç], *adj.* rude; cheeky, saucy.

Pauke ['paukə], *f.* (—, *pl.* —n) kettledrum; *mit* —n *und Trompeten*, with drums beating and colours flying.

pauken ['paukən], *v.n.* beat the kettledrum; (*coll.*) swot, plod, grind; fight a duel.

pausbackig ['pausbakɪç], *adj.* chubby-faced, bonny.

Pauschale [pau'ʃaːlə], *f.* (—, *pl.* —n) lump sum.

Pause ['pauzə], *f.* (—, *pl.* —n) pause, stop; (*Theat.*) interval; (*Sch.*) playtime, break; (*Tech.*) tracing.

pausen ['pauzən], *v.a.* trace.

pausieren [pau'ziːrən], *v.n.* pause.

Pavian ['paːvjaːn], *m.* (—s, *pl.* —e) (*Zool.*) baboon.

Pech [pɛç], *n.* (—es, *no pl.*) pitch; (*shoemaker's*) wax; (*fig.*) bad luck, rotten luck.

pechschwarz ['pɛçʃvarts], *adj.* black as pitch.

Pechvogel ['pɛçfoːgəl], *m.* (—s, *pl.* ̈) unlucky fellow.

Pedell [pe'dɛl], *m.* (—s, *pl.* —e) beadle; porter, caretaker; (*Univ. sl.*) bulldog.

Pegel ['peːgəl], *m.* (—s, *pl.* —) water-gauge.

peilen ['paɪlən], *v.a.*, *v.n.* sound, measure, take bearings (of).

Pein [paɪn], *f.* (—, *no pl.*) pain, torment.

peinigen ['paɪnɪgən], *v.a.* torment; harass, distress.

peinlich ['paɪnlɪç], *adj.* painful, disagreeable; embarrassing; delicate; strict, punctilious; (*Law*) capital, penal.

Peitsche ['paɪtʃə], *f.* (—, *pl.* —n) whip.

pekuniär [pekun'jɛːr], *adj.* financial.

Pelerine [peləˈriːnə], *f.* (—, *pl.* —n) cape.

Pelle ['pɛlə], *f.* (—, *pl.* —n) peel, husk.

Pellkartoffeln ['pɛlkartɔfəln], *f. pl.* potatoes in their jackets.

Pelz [pɛlts], *m.* (—es, *pl.* —e) pelt, fur; fur coat.

pelzig ['pɛltsɪç], *adj.* furry.

Pendel ['pɛndəl], *n.* (—s, *pl.* —) pendulum.

pendeln ['pɛndəln], *v.n.* swing, oscillate.

pennen ['pɛnən], *v.n.* (*sl.*) sleep.

166

Pfiffikus

Pension [pãˈsjoːn], *f.* (—, *pl.* —en) pension; boarding-house; board and lodging.

Pensionat [pãsjoˈnaːt], *n.* (—s, *pl.* —e) boarding-school.

pensionieren [pãsjoˈniːrən], *v.a.* pension off; *sich — lassen*, retire.

Pensum [ˈpɛnzum], *n.* (—s, *pl.* —sen) task; curriculum, syllabus.

per [pɛr], *prep.* — *Adresse*, care of.

Perfekt [perˈfɛkt], *n.* (—s, *pl.* —e) (*Gram.*) perfect (tense).

perforieren [perfoˈriːrən], *v.a.* perforate, punch.

Pergament [pɛrgaˈmɛnt], *n.* (—s, *pl.* —e) parchment, vellum.

Perle [ˈpɛrlə], *f.* (—, *pl.* —n) pearl; (*glass*) bead; (*fig.*) gem, treasure.

perlen [ˈpɛrlən], *v.n.* sparkle.

Perlgraupe [ˈpɛrlgraupə], *f.* (—, *no pl.*) (*Bot.*) pearl-barley.

Perlhuhn [ˈpɛrlhuːn], *n.* (—s, *pl.* ˝er) (*Zool.*) guinea-fowl.

Perlmutter [ˈpɛrlmutər], *f.* (—, *no pl.*) mother-of-pearl.

Perpendikel [perpɛnˈdiːkəl], *m. & n.* (—s, *pl.* —) pendulum.

Perser [ˈpɛrzər], *m.* (—s, *pl.* —) Persian; *echter —*, genuine Persian carpet.

Persien [ˈpɛrzjən], *n.* Persia.

Personal [perzoˈnaːl], *n.* (—s, *no pl.*) personnel, staff.

Personalien [perzoˈnaːljən], *n. pl.* particulars (of a person).

Personenverkehr [perˈzoːnənferkeːr], *m.* (—s, *no pl.*) passenger-traffic.

Personenzug [perˈzoːnəntsuːk], *m.* (—s, *pl.* ˝e) (slow) passenger train.

personifizieren [perzonifiˈtsiːrən], *v.a.* personify, embody, impersonate.

Persönlichkeit [perˈzøːnlɪçkaɪt], *f.* (—, *pl.* —en) personality, person.

perspektivisch [perspɛkˈtiːvɪʃ], *adj.* perspective.

Peru [peˈruː], *n.* Peru.

Perücke [peˈrykə], *f.* (—, *pl.* —n) wig.

Pest [pɛst], *f.* (—, *no pl.*) plague, pestilence.

pestartig [ˈpɛsta:rtɪç], *adj.* pestilential.

Petersilie [peːtərˈziːljə], *f.* (—, *no pl.*) (*Bot.*) parsley.

petitionieren [petitsjoˈniːrən], *v.a.* petition.

Petschaft [ˈpɛtʃaft], *n.* (—s, *pl.* —e) seal, signet.

Petz [pɛts], *m.* (—es, *pl.* —e) *Meister —*, Bruin (the bear).

petzen [ˈpɛtsən], *v.n.* tell tales (about), sneak.

Pfad [pfaːt], *m.* (—s, *pl.* —e) path.

Pfadfinder [ˈpfaːtfɪndər], *m.* (—s, *pl.* —) Boy Scout.

Pfaffe [ˈpfafə], *m.* (—n, *pl.* —n) (*pej.*) cleric, priest.

Pfahl [pfaːl], *m.* (—s, *pl.* ˝e) post, stake.

Pfahlbauten [ˈpfaːlbautən], *m. pl.* lake dwellings.

pfählen [ˈpfɛːlən], *v.a.* fasten with stakes; impale.

Pfand [pfant], *n.* (—s, *pl.* ˝er) pawn, pledge; security; (*game*) forfeit; *ein — einlösen*, redeem a pledge.

pfänden [ˈpfɛndən], *v.a.* take in pledge; seize.

Pfänderspiel [ˈpfɛndərʃpiːl], *n.* (—s, *pl.* —e) game of forfeits.

Pfandgeber [ˈpfantgeːbər], *m.* (—s, *pl.* —) pawner.

Pfandleiher [ˈpfantlaɪər], *m.* (—s, *pl.* —) pawnbroker.

Pfandrecht [ˈpfantrɛçt], *n.* (—s, *no pl.*) lien.

Pfändung [ˈpfɛnduŋ], *f.* (—, *pl.* —en) seizure, attachment, distraint.

Pfanne [ˈpfanə], *f.* (—, *pl.* —n) pan, frying-pan.

Pfannkuchen [ˈpfankuːxən], *m.* (—s, *pl.* —) pancake; *Berliner —*, doughnut.

Pfarre [ˈpfarə], *f.* (—, *pl.* —n) living, parish; (*house*) vicarage, parsonage, manse.

Pfarrer [ˈpfarər], *m.* (—s, *pl.* —) parson; vicar, (parish) priest.

Pfau [pfau], *m.* (—en, *pl.* —en) (*Orn.*) peacock.

Pfauenauge [ˈpfauənaugə], *n.* (—s, *pl.* —n) (*Ent.*) peacock butterfly.

Pfeffer [ˈpfɛfər], *m.* (—s, *no pl.*) pepper; *spanischer —*, red pepper, cayenne.

Pfefferkuchen [ˈpfɛfərkuːxən], *m.* (—s, *pl.* —) gingerbread, spiced cake.

Pfefferminz [ˈpfɛfərmɪnts], *n.* (—, *no pl.*) peppermint.

Pfeife [ˈpfaɪfə], *f.* (—, *pl.* —n) whistle, fife; pipe.

pfeifen [ˈpfaɪfən], *v.a., v.n. irr.* whistle, play the fife; (*Theat.*) boo, hiss; (*bullets*) whiz(z).

Pfeifenrohr [ˈpfaɪfənroːr], *n.* (—s, *pl.* —e) pipe-stem.

Pfeil [pfaɪl], *m.* (—es, *pl.* —e) arrow, dart, bolt.

Pfeiler [ˈpfaɪlər], *m.* (—s, *pl.* —) pillar.

Pfeilwurz [ˈpfaɪlvurts], *f.* (—, *no pl.*) (*Bot.*) arrow root.

Pfennig [ˈpfɛnɪç], *m.* (—s, *pl.* —e) one hundredth of a mark; (*loosely*) penny.

Pferch [pfɛrç], *m.* (—es, *pl.* —e) fold, pen.

Pferd [pfeːrt], *n.* (—es, *pl.* —e) horse; *zu —*, on horseback; *vom — steigen*, dismount.

Pferdeknecht [ˈpfeːrdəknɛçt], *m.* (—es, *pl.* —e) groom.

Pferdestärke [ˈpfeːrdəʃtɛrkə], *f.* (—, *no pl.*) horse-power (*abbr.* PS).

Pfiff [pfɪf], *m.* (—es, *pl.* —e) whistle.

Pfifferling [ˈpfɪfərlɪŋ], *m.* (—s, *pl.* —e) (*Bot.*) mushroom; chanterelle; *einen — wert*, worthless.

pfiffig [ˈpfɪfɪç], *adj.* cunning, sly, crafty.

Pfiffikus [ˈpfɪfikus], *m.* (—, *pl.* —se) (*coll.*) sly dog.

Pfingsten

Pfingsten ['pfɪŋkstən], *n.* Whitsun (-tide), Pentecost.

Pfingstrose ['pfɪŋkstroːzə], *f.* (—, *pl.* (*Bot.*) peony.

Pfirsich ['pfɪrzɪç], *m.* (—s, *pl.* —e) (*Bot.*) peach.

Pflanze ['pflantsə], *f.* (—, *pl.* —n) plant.

pflanzen ['pflantsən], *v.a.* plant.

Pflanzer ['pflantsər], *m.* (—s, *pl.* —) planter.

pflanzlich ['pflantslɪç], *adj.* vegetable, botanical.

Pflänzling ['pflɛntslɪŋ], *m.* (—s, *pl.* —e) seedling, young plant.

Pflanzung ['pflantsuŋ], *f.* (—, *pl.* —en) plantation.

Pflaster ['pflastər], *n.* (—s, *pl.* —) (*Med.*) plaster; (*street*) pavement; *ein teures* —, an expensive place to live in.

Pflaume ['pflaumə], *f.* (—, *pl.* —n) plum; *getrocknete* —, prune.

Pflege ['pfleːgə], *f.* (—, *no pl.*) care, attention, nursing, fostering.

Pflegeeltern ['pfleːgəɛltərn], *pl.* foster-parents.

pflegen ['pfleːgən], *v.a.* nurse, look after, take care of; *Umgang* — *mit*, associate with. — *v.n.* be used to, be in the habit of.

Pflegling ['pfleːklɪŋ], *m.* (—s, *pl.* —e) foster-child, ward.

Pflicht [pflɪçt], *f.* (—, *pl.* —en) duty, obligation.

Pflichtgefühl ['pflɪçtgəfyːl], *n.* (—s, *no pl.*) sense of duty.

pflichtgemäß ['pflɪçtgəmɛːs], *adj.* dutiful.

pflichtschuldig ['pflɪçtʃuldɪç], *adj.* in duty bound.

Pflock [pflɔk], *m.* (—s, *pl.* ⁔e) plug, peg.

pflücken ['pflykən], *v.a.* pluck, pick, gather.

Pflug [pfluːk], *m.* (—es, *pl.* ⁔e) plough.

Pflugschar ['pfluːkʃaːr], *f.* (—, *pl.* —en) ploughshare.

Pforte ['pfɔrtə], *f.* (—, *pl.* —n) gate, door, porch.

Pförtner ['pfœrtnər], *m.* (—s, *pl.* —) door-keeper, porter.

Pfosten ['pfɔstən], *m.* (—s, *pl.* —) post, stake; (*door*) jamb.

Pfote ['pfoːtə], *f.* (—, *pl.* —n) paw.

Pfriem [pfriːm], *m.* (—es, *pl.* —e) awl.

Pfropf [pfrɔpf], ['pfrɔpf(ən)], *m.* (—s, *pl.* —en) cork, stopper; (*gun*) wad.

pfropfen ['pfrɔpfən], *v.a.* graft; cork.

Pfründe ['pfryndə], *f.* (—, *pl.* —n) living, benefice.

Pfuhl [pfuːl], *m.* (—es, *pl.* —e) pool, puddle.

Pfühl [pfyːl], *m.* (—es, *pl.* —e) (*Poet.*) bolster, pillow, cushion.

pfui! [pfui], *excl.* shame! ugh! — *Teufel!* shame! a damned shame!

Pfund [pfunt], *n.* (—es, *pl.* —e) pound.

pfuschen ['pfuʃən], *v.n.* botch; *einem ins Handwerk* —, poach on s.o. else's preserve.

Pfütze ['pfytsə], *f.* (—, *pl.* —n) puddle.

Phänomen [fɛːnoˈmeːn], *n.* (—s, *pl.* —e) phenomenon.

Phantasie [fantaˈziː], *f.* (—, *pl.* —n) fancy, imagination; (*Mus.*) fantasia.

phantasieren [fantaˈziːrən], *v.n.* indulge in fancies; (*sick person*) rave, wander, be delirious; (*Mus.*) improvise.

Phantast [fanˈtast], *m.* (—en, *pl.* —en) dreamer, visionary.

Pharisäer [fariˈzɛːər], *m.* (—s, *pl.* —) Pharisee.

Phase ['faːzə], *f.* (—, *pl.* —n) phase, stage (of process *or* development).

Philippinen [filiˈpiːnən], *f. pl.* Philippines.

Philister [fiˈlɪstər], *m.* (—s, *pl.* —) Philistine.

philisterhaft [fiˈlɪstərhaft], *adj.* philistine, narrow-minded, conventional.

Philologie [filoloˈgiː], *f.* (—, *no pl.*) philology; study of languages.

Philosoph [filoˈzoːf], *m.* (—en, *pl.* —en) philosopher.

Philosophie [filozoˈfiː], *f.* (—, *pl.* —n) philosophy.

Phiole [fiˈoːlə], *f.* (—, *pl.* —n) phial, vial.

Phlegma ['flɛgma], *n.* (—s, *no pl.*) phlegm.

Phonetik [foˈneːtɪk], *f.* (—, *no pl.*) phonetics.

photogen [fotoˈgeːn], *adj.* photogenic.

Photograph [fotoˈgraːf], *m.* (—en, *pl.* —en) photographer.

Photographie [fotograˈfiː], *f.* (—, *pl.* —n) photograph, photo; (*Art*) photography.

photographieren [fotograˈfiːrən], *v.a.* photograph.

Physik [fyˈziːk], *f.* (—, *no pl.*) physics.

physikalisch [fyziˈkaːlɪʃ], *adj.* physical (of physics).

Physiker ['fyˈzɪkər], *m.* (—s, *pl.* —) physicist.

Physiologe [fyˈzjoˈloːgə], *m.* (—en, *pl.* —en) physiologist.

physiologisch [fyˈzjoˈloːgɪʃ], *adj.* physiological.

physisch ['fyˈzɪʃ], *adj.* physical.

Picke ['pɪkə], *f.* (—, *pl.* —n) pickaxe, axe.

Pickel ['pɪkəl], *m.* (—s, *pl.* —) pimple.

Piedestal ['pjeˈdɛstaːl], *n.* (—s, *pl.* —e) pedestal.

piepen ['piːpən], *v.n.* squeak, chirp.

piepsen ['piːpsən], *v.n.* squeak, chirp.

Pietät [pieˈtɛːt], *f.* (—, *no pl.*) piety, reverence.

Pik [piːk], *n.* (—s, *pl.* —s) (*cards*) spades.

pikant [piˈkant], *adj.* piquant, spicy; (*fig.*) risqué.

Pikee [piˈkeː], *m.* (—s, *pl.* —s) piqué.

pikiert [piˈkiːrt], *adj.* irritated, annoyed, piqued.

Pikkolo ['pɪkolo], *m.* (—s, *pl.* —s) apprentice waiter, boy (waiter); (*Mus.*) piccolo, flute.

Pilger ['pɪlgər], *m.* (—s, *pl.* —) pilgrim.
Pille ['pɪlə], *f.* (—, *pl.* —n) pill.
Pilz [pɪlts], *m.* (—es, *pl.* —e) fungus, mushroom.
Piment [pi'mɛnt], *n.* (—s, *pl.* —e) pimento, Jamaican pepper, all-spice.
pimplig ['pɪmplɪç], *adj.* effeminate.
Pinguin ['pɪŋgu'i:n], *m.* (—s, *pl.* —e) (*Orn.*) penguin.
Pinie ['pi:njə], *f.* (—, *pl.* —n) (*Bot.*) stone-pine.
Pinne ['pɪnə], *f.* (—, *pl.* —n) drawing-pin; peg.
Pinscher ['pɪnʃər], *m.* (—s, *pl.* —) terrier.
Pinsel ['pɪnzəl], *m.* (—s, *pl.* —) (*Painting*) brush, pencil; (*fig.*) simpleton.
Pinzette [pɪn'tsɛtə], *f.* (—, *pl.* —n) pincers, tweezers.
Pirsch [pɪrʃ], *f.* (—, *no pl.*) (deer-) stalking.
Piste ['pɪstə], *f.* (—, *pl.* —n) track; (*Aviat.*) runway.
pittoresk [pɪto'rɛsk], *adj.* picturesque.
placken ['plakən], *v.r. sich* —, toil, drudge.
plädieren [plɛ'di:rən], *v.n.* plead.
Plädoyer [plɛ:doa'je:], *n.* (—s, *pl.* —s) speech for the prosecution *or* the defence (in a court of law), plea, pleading.
Plage ['pla:gə], *f.* (—, *pl.* —n) torment, trouble; calamity; plague.
plagen ['pla:gən], *v.a.* plague, trouble, torment, vex. — *v.r. sich* —, toil.
Plagiat [plag'ja:t], *n.* (—es, *pl.* —e) plagiarism.
Plaid [plɛ:t], *n.* (—s, *pl.* —s) travelling-rug.
Plakat [pla'ka:t], *n.* (—(e)s, *pl.* —e) poster, placard, bill.
Plan [pla:n], *n.* (—es, *pl.* ⸚e) plan, scheme, plot; map, ground-plan.
Plane ['pla:nə], *f.* (—, *pl.* —n) awning, cover.
planieren [pla'ni:rən], *v.a.* level, plane down; bulldoze, flatten.
Planke ['plaŋkə], *f.* (—, *pl.* —n) plank, board.
Plänkelei [plɛnkə'laɪ], *f.* (—, *pl.* —en) skirmish.
planmäßig ['pla:nmɛ:sɪç], *adj.* according to plan.
planschen ['planʃən], *v.n.* splash; paddle.
Plantage [plan'ta:ʒə], *f.* (—, *pl.* —n) plantation.
planvoll ['pla:nfɔl], *adj.* systematic, well-planned.
Planwagen ['pla:nva:gən], *m.* (—s, *pl.* ⸚) tilt-cart.
plappern ['plapərn], *v.n.* prattle, chatter.
plärren ['plɛrən], *v.n.* blubber, bawl.
Plastik ['plastɪk], *f.* (—, *pl.* —en) plastic art; plastic (material).
Platane [pla'ta:nə], *f.* (—, *pl.* —n) plane-tree.

Platin ['pla:ti:n], *n.* (—s, *no pl.*) platinum.
platonisch [pla'to:nɪʃ], *adj.* platonic.
plätschern ['plɛtʃərn], *v.n.* splash about.
platt [plat], *adj.* flat, level, even; insipid; downright; —*e Redensart*, commonplace, platitude; (*coll.*) *ich bin ganz* —, I am astonished *or* dumbfounded.
Plättbrett ['plɛtbrɛt], *n.* (—es, *pl.* —er) ironing board.
plattdeutsch ['platdɔytʃ], *adj.* Low German.
Platte ['platə], *f.* (—, *pl.* —n) plate; dish; board; slab; sheet; ledge; (*fig.*) bald head; (*Mus.*) (gramophone) record.
plätten ['plɛtən], *v.a.* iron (clothes).
Plattfisch ['platfɪʃ], *n.* (—es, *pl.* —e) (*Zool.*) plaice.
Plattfuß ['platfu:s], *n.* (—es, *pl.* ⸚e) flat foot.
Plattheit ['plathaɪt], *f.* (—, *pl.* —en) flatness; (*fig.*) platitude.
Platz [plats], *m.* (—es, *pl.* ⸚e) place, town, spot, site; space, room; (*town*) square; seat; — *nehmen*, take a seat, be seated.
Platzanweiserin ['platsanvaɪzərɪn], *f.* (—, *pl.* —nen) usherette.
Plätzchen ['plɛtsçən], *n.* (—s, *pl.* —) small place; drop; biscuit.
platzen ['platsən], *v.n.* (*aux.* sein) burst, explode.
Platzregen ['platsre:gən], *m.* (—s, *no pl.*) downpour, heavy shower.
Plauderei [plaudə'raɪ], *f.* (—, *pl.* —en) chat.
Plaudertasche ['plaudərtaʃə], *f.* (—, *pl.* —n) chatterbox.
Pleite ['plaɪtə], *f.* (—, *pl.* —n) (*coll.*) bankruptcy; — *machen*, go bankrupt.
Plenum ['ple:num], *n.* (—s, *no pl.*) plenary session.
Pleuelstange ['plɔyəlʃtaŋə], *f.* (—, *pl.* —n) connecting-rod.
Plinsen ['plɪnzən], *f. pl.* (*Austr.*) fritters.
Plissee [plɪ'se:], *n.* (—s, *pl.* —s) pleating.
Plombe ['plɔmbə], *f.* (—, *pl.* —n) lead, seal; (*teeth*) filling.
plombieren [plɔm'bi:rən], *v.a.* seal with lead; (*teeth*) fill.
plötzlich ['plœtslɪç], *adj.* sudden.
plump [plump], *adj.* clumsy, ungainly, awkward; crude, coarse.
plumps [plumps], *excl.* bump! oops!
Plunder ['plundər], *m.* (—s, *no pl.*) lumber, trash.
plündern ['plyndərn], *v.a.* plunder, pillage.
Plüsch [ply:ʃ], *m.* (—es, *no pl.*) plush.
pneumatisch [pnɔy'ma:tɪʃ], *adj.* pneumatic.
Pöbel ['pø:bəl], *m.* (—s, *no pl.*) mob, rabble.
pochen ['pɔxən], *v.a., v.n.* knock, beat, throb.

Pocke

Pocke ['pɔkə], *f.* (—, *pl.* —n) pockmark; (*pl.*) smallpox.

pockennarbig ['pɔkənnarbɪç], *adj.* pockmarked.

Podagra ['po:dagra:], *n.* (—s, *no pl.*) (*Med.*) gout.

Pointe [po'ɛ̃tə], *f.* (—, *pl.* —n) (*of a story*) point.

Pokal [po'ka:l], *m.* (—s, *pl.* —e) goblet, cup; trophy.

Pökelfleisch ['pø:kəlflaɪʃ], *n.* (—es, *no pl.*) salted meat.

Pol [po:l], *m.* (—s, *pl.* —e) pole.

polemisch [po'le:mɪʃ], *adj.* polemic(al), controversial.

Polen ['po:lən], *n.* Poland.

Police [po'li:sə], *f.* (—, *pl.* —n) insurance policy.

polieren [po'li:rən], *v.a.* polish, furbish, burnish.

Poliklinik ['po:likli:nɪk], *f.* (—, *pl.* —en) (*Med.*) out-patients' department.

Politik [poli'ti:k], *f.* (—, *no pl.*) politics; policy.

politisieren [politi'zi:rən], *v.n.* talk politics.

Politur [poli'tu:r], *f.* (—, *no pl.*) polish, gloss.

Polizei [poli'tsaɪ], *f.* (—, *no pl.*) police.

polizeilich [poli'tsaɪlɪç], *adj.* of the police.

Polizeistunde [poli'tsaɪʃtundə], *f.* (—, *no pl.*) closing time.

Polizeiwache [poli'tsaɪvaxə], *f.* (—, *pl.* —n) police station.

Polizist [poli'tsɪst], *m.* (—en, *pl.* —en) policeman, constable.

Polizze [po'lɪtsə], *f.* (—, *pl.* —n) (*Austr. dial.*) insurance policy.

polnisch ['pɔlnɪʃ], *adj.* Polish.

Polster ['pɔlstər], *n.* (—s, *pl.* —) cushion, bolster.

Polterabend ['pɔltəra:bənt], *m.* (—s, *pl.* —e) wedding-eve party.

Poltergeist ['pɔltərgaɪst], *m.* (—es, *pl.* —er) poltergeist, hobgoblin.

poltern ['pɔltərn], *v.n.* rumble; make a noise; bluster.

Polyp [po'ly:p], *m.* (—en, *pl.* —en) (*Zool.*) polyp; (*Med.*) polypus.

Pomeranze [pomə'rantsə], *f.* (—, *pl.* —n) (*Bot.*) orange.

Pommern ['pɔmərn], *n.* Pomerania.

Pope ['po:pə], *m.* (—n, *pl.* —n) Greek Orthodox priest.

Popo [po'po:], *m.* (—s, *pl.* —s) (*coll.*) backside, bottom.

populär [popu'lɛ:r], *adj.* popular.

porös [po'rø:s], *adj.* porous.

Porree ['pɔre:], *m.* (—s, *no pl.*) leek.

Portefeuille [pɔrt'fœj], *n.* (—s, *pl.* —s) portfolio.

Portier [pɔr'tje:], *m.* (—s, *pl.* —s) doorkeeper, caretaker; porter.

Porto ['pɔrto:], *n.* (—s, *pl.* Porti) postage.

Porzellan [pɔrtsə'la:n], *n.* (—s, *pl.* —e) china, porcelain; *Meißner* —, Dresden china.

Posamenten [poza'mɛntən], *n. pl.* trimmings.

Posaune [po'zaunə], *f.* (—, *pl.* —n) (*Mus.*) trombone.

Positur [pozi'tu:r], *f.* (—, *pl.* —en) posture; *sich in — setzen*, strike an attitude.

Posse ['pɔsə], *f.* (—, *pl.* —n) (*Theat.*) farce, skit.

Possen ['pɔsən], *m.* (—s, *pl.* —) trick; *einem einen — spielen*, play a trick on s.o.

possierlich [pɔ'si:rlɪç], *adj.* droll, funny, comic(al).

Post [pɔst], *f.* (—, *pl.* —en) post, mail; (*building*) post-office.

Postament [pɔsta'mɛnt], *n.* (—s, *pl.* —e) plinth, pedestal.

Postanweisung ['pɔstanvaɪzuŋ], *f.* (—, *pl.* —en) postal order, money order.

Posten ['pɔstən], *m.* (—s, *pl.* —) post, station; place; (*goods*) parcel, lot, job lot; (*Comm.*) item; (*Mil.*) outpost; *— stehen*, stand sentry; *nicht auf dem — sein*, be unwell.

Postfach ['pɔstfax], *n.* (—es, *pl.* ̈er) post-office box.

postieren [pɔs'ti:rən], *v.a.* post, place, station.

postlagernd ['pɔstla:gərnt], *adj.* poste restante, to be called for.

Postschalter ['pɔstʃaltər], *m.* (—s, *pl.* —) post-office counter.

postulieren [pɔstu'li:rən], *v.a.* postulate.

postwendend ['pɔstvɛndənt], *adj.* by return of post.

Postwertzeichen ['pɔstve:rttsaɪçən], *n.* (—s, *pl.* —) stamp.

Potenz [po'tɛnts], *f.* (—, *pl.* —en) (*Maths.*) power; *zur dritten —*, cubed, to the power of three.

potenzieren [potɛn'tsi:rən], *v.a.* (*Math.*) raise; intensify.

Pottasche ['pɔtaʃə], *f.* (—, *no pl.*) potash.

potzblitz ['pɔtsblɪts], *excl.* good Heavens! good gracious!

potztausend ['pɔtstauzənt], *excl.* great Scott! good Heavens!

Pracht [praxt], *f.* (—, *no pl.*) splendour, magnificence; (*in compounds*) de luxe.

prächtig ['prɛçtɪç], *adj.* splendid, magnificent, sumptuous.

prachtvoll ['praxtfɔl], *adj.* gorgeous, magnificent.

Prädikat [prɛ:di'ka:t], *n.* (—s, *pl.* —e) mark; (*Gram.*) predicate.

Prag [pra:k], *n.* Prague.

prägen ['prɛ:gən], *v.a.* coin, mint, stamp.

prägnant [prɛg'nant], *adj.* meaningful, precise.

prahlen ['pra:lən], *v.n.* boast, brag, talk big, show off.

Praktikant [praktɪ'kant], *m.* (—en, *pl.* —en) probationer; apprentice.

Praktiken ['praktɪkən], *f. pl.* machinations.

praktisch ['praktɪʃ], *adj.* practical; —*er Arzt*, general practitioner.

praktizieren [prakti'tsi:rən], *v.a.* practise.

Prall [pral], *m.* (—es, *pl.* —e) impact.

prall [pral], *adj.* tense, tight; (*cheeks*) chubby.

prallen ['pralən], *v.n.* (*aux.* sein) *auf etwas* —, bounce against s.th.

Prämie ['prɛ:mjə], *f.* (—, *pl.* —n) prize; (*insurance*) premium; (*dividend*) bonus.

prangen ['praŋən], *v.n.* shine, glitter, make a show.

Pranger ['praŋər], *m.* (—s, *pl.* —) pillory; *etwas an den* — *stellen*, expose s.th., pillory.

präparieren [prɛpa'ri:rən], *v.a.*, *v.r.* prepare.

Präsens ['prɛ:zɛns], *n.* (—, *pl.* —ntia) (*Gram.*) present tense.

präsentieren [prɛzɛn'ti:rən], *v.a.* present; *präsentiert das Gewehr!* present arms!

prasseln ['prasəln], *v.n.* (*fire*) crackle; rattle.

prassen ['prasən], *v.n.* revel, gorge (*o.s.*), guzzle, feast.

Prätendent [prɛtɛn'dɛnt], *m.* (—en, *pl.* —en) pretender, claimant.

Präteritum [prɛ'te:ritum], *n.* (—s, *pl.* —ta) (*Gram.*) preterite, past tense.

Praxis ['praksɪs], *f.* (—, *no pl.*) practice.

präzis [prɛ'tsi:s], *adj.* precise, exact.

präzisieren [prɛtsi'zi:rən], *v.a.* define exactly.

predigen ['pre:dɪgən], *v.a.*, *v.n.* preach.

Predigt ['pre:dɪçt], *f.* (—, *pl.* —en) sermon; (*fig.*) homily, lecture.

Preis [praɪs], *m.* (—es, *pl.* —e) price, rate, value; (*reward*) prize; praise; *um jeden* —, at any price, at all costs; *um keinen* —, not for all the world; *feste* —*e*, fixed prices; no rebate, no discount.

Preisausschreiben ['praɪsausʃraɪbən], *n.* (—s, *pl.* —) prize competition.

Preiselbeere ['praɪzəlbe:rə], *f.* (—, *pl.* —n) (*Bot.*) bilberry, cranberry.

preisen ['praɪzən], *v.a. irr.* praise, laud; glorify.

preisgeben ['praɪsge:bən], *v.a. irr.* give up, abandon, part with; *dem Spott preisgegeben sein*, become a laughing-stock.

Preisunterbietung ['praɪsuntərbi:tuŋ], *f.* (—, *pl.* —en) under-cutting.

Prellbock ['prɛlbɔk], *m.* (—s, *pl.* ⁀e) buffer (-block).

prellen ['prɛlən], *v.a.* cheat, defraud.

Prellstein ['prɛlʃtaɪn], *m.* (—s, *pl.* —e) kerbstone.

pressant [prɛ'sant], *adj.* (*Austr*) urgent.

Presse ['prɛsə], *f.* (—, *pl.* —n) press; newspapers; (*coll.*) coaching establishment, crammer.

pressieren [prɛ'si:rən], *v.n.* be urgent.

Preßkohle ['prɛsko:lə], *f.* (—, *no pl.*) briquette(s).

Preßkolben ['prɛskɔlbən], *m.* (—s, *pl.* —) piston.

Preßluft ['prɛsluft], *f.* (—, *no pl.*) compressed air.

Preußen ['prɔysən], *n.* Prussia.

prickeln ['prɪkəln], *v.n.* prick, prickle, sting, tickle.

Prieme ['pri:mə], *f.* (—, *pl.* —n) chew, quid.

Priester ['pri:stər], *m.* (—s, *pl.* —) priest; *zum* — *weihen*, ordain to the priesthood.

Prima ['pri:ma:], *f.* (—, *pl.* **Primen**) highest form at a grammar school (sixth form).

prima ['pri:ma:], *adj.* excellent, splendid, first-rate.

Primaner [pri'ma:nər], *m.* (—s, *pl.* —) pupil in the highest form at a grammar school, sixth form boy.

Primel ['pri:məl], *f.* (—, *pl.* —n) (*Bot.*) primrose, primula.

Primus ['pri:mus], *m.* (—, *no pl.*) (*School*) head boy, captain of the school.

Prinzip [prɪnt'si:p], *n.* (—s, *pl.* —ien) principle.

Priorität [priori'tɛ:t], *f.* (—, *no pl.*) priority, precedence.

Prise ['pri:zə], *f.* (—, *pl.* —n) pinch of snuff.

Prisma ['prɪsma:], *n.* (—s, *pl.* —men) prism.

Pritsche ['prɪtʃə], *f.* (—, *pl.* —n) plank-bed.

Privatdozent [pri'va:tdotsɛnt], *m.* (—en, *pl.* —en) (*Univ.*) (unsalaried) lecturer.

privatisieren [privati'zi:rən], *v.n.* have private means.

Probe ['pro:bə], *f.* (—, *pl.* —n) experiment, trial, probation, test; (*Theat.*, *Mus.*) rehearsal; sample, pattern; *auf* —, on trial; *auf die* — *stellen*, put to the test *or* on probation.

Probeabzug ['pro:bəaptsu:k], *m.* (—s, *pl.* ⁀e) (*Printing*) proof.

proben ['pro:bən], *v.a.* rehearse.

probieren [pro'bi:rən], *v.a.* try, attempt; taste.

Probst [pro:pst], *m.* (—es, *pl.* ⁀e) provost.

Produzent [produ'tsɛnt], *m.* (—en, *pl.* —en) producer (of goods), manufacturer.

produzieren [produ'tsi:rən], *v.a.* produce (goods). — *v.r. sich* —, perform, show off.

profanieren [profa'ni:rən], *v.a.* desecrate, profane.

Professur [profɛ'su:r], *f.* (—, *pl.* —en) (*Univ.*) professorship, Chair.

profitieren [profi'ti:rən], *v.a.*, *v.n.* profit (by), take advantage (of).

projizieren [proji'tsi:rən], *v.a.* project.

Prokura [pro'ku:ra:], *f.* (—, *no pl.*) (*Law*) power of attorney.

Prokurist [proku'rɪst], *m.* (—en, *pl.* —en) confidential clerk; company secretary.

prolongieren

prolongieren [proloŋ'gi:rən], *v.a.* prolong, extend.

promenieren [promə'ni:rən], *v.n.* take a stroll.

Promotion [promo'tsjo:n], *f.* (—, *pl.* —en) graduation, degree ceremony.

promovieren [promo'vi:rən], *v.n.* graduate, take a degree.

promulgieren [promul'gi:rən], *v.a.* promulgate.

Pronomen [pro'no:mən], *n.* (—s, *pl.* —mina) (*Gram.*) pronoun.

prophezeien [profe'tsaɪən], *v.a.* prophesy, predict, forecast.

prophylaktisch [profy'laktɪʃ], *adj.* preventive, prophylactic.

Propst [pro:pst], *m.* (—es, *pl.* ⸚e) provost.

Prosa ['pro:za:], *f.* (—, *no pl.*) prose.

prosit ['pro:zɪt], *excl.* cheers! here's to you! your health!

Prospekt [pro'spɛkt], *m.* (—es, *pl.* —e) prospect; (*booklet*) prospectus.

Prostituierte [prostitu'i:rtə], *f.* (—n, *pl.* —n) prostitute; (*coll.*) tart.

protegieren [prote'ʒi:rən], *v.a.* favour, patronize.

Protektion [protek'tsjo:n], *f.* (—, *no pl.*) patronage, favouritism.

protestieren [protes'ti:rən], *v.n.* make a protest, protest (against s.th.).

Protokoll [proto'kɔl], *n.* (—s, *pl.* —e) minutes, record; protocol; regulations.

Protokollführer [proto'kɔlfy:rər], *m.* (—s, *pl.* —) recorder, clerk of the minutes.

Protz [prɔts], *m.* (—en, *pl.* —en) snob, upstart; show-off.

Proviant [pro'vjant], *m.* (—s, *no pl.*) provisions, stores.

provinziell [provɪn'tsjɛl], *adj.* provincial.

Provinzler [pro'vɪntslər], *m.* (—s, *pl.* —) provincial.

Provision [provi'zjo:n], *f.* (—, *pl.* —en) (*Comm.*) commission, brokerage.

Provisor [pro'vi:zɔr], *m.* (—s, *pl.* —en) dispenser.

provisorisch [provi'zo:rɪʃ], *adj.* provisional, temporary.

provozieren [provo'tsi:rən], *v.a.* provoke.

Prozedur [protse'du:r], *f.* (—, *pl.* —en) proceedings, procedure.

Prozent [pro'tsɛnt], *m. & n.* (—s, *pl.* —e) per cent.

Prozentsatz [pro'tsɛntzats], *m.* (—es, *pl.* ⸚e) percentage, rate of interest.

Prozeß [pro'tsɛs], *m.* (—es, *pl.* —e) process; lawsuit, litigation; trial; *mit etwas kurzen — machen*, deal summarily with.

Prozeßwesen [pro'tsɛsve:zən], *n.* (—s, *no pl.*) legal procedure.

prüde ['pry:də], *adj.* prudish, prim.

prüfen ['pry:fən], *v.a.* test, examine.

Prüfung ['pry:fuŋ], *f.* (—, *pl.* —en) trial, test; examination; (*fig.*) temptation, affliction.

172

Prügel ['pry:gəl], *m.* (—s, *pl.* —) cudgel; (*pl.*) thrashing; *eine Tracht —*, a good hiding.

prügeln ['pry:gəln], *v.a.* beat, give a hiding to.

Prunk [pruŋk], *m.* (—(e)s, *no pl.*) splendour, ostentation, pomp.

prusten ['pru:stən], *v.n.* snort.

Psalm [psalm], *m.* (—es, *pl.* —e) psalm.

Psalter ['psaltər], *m.* (—s, *pl.* —) (*book*) psalter; (*instrument*) psaltery.

Psychiater [psyçi'a:tər], *m.* (—s, *pl.* —) psychiatrist.

Psychologe [psyço'lo:gə], *m.* (—n, *pl.* —n) psychologist.

Pubertät [puber'tɛ:t], *f.* (—, *no pl.*) puberty.

Publikum ['pu:blikum], *n.* (—s, *no pl.*) public; (*Theat.*) audience.

publizieren [publi'tsi:rən], *v.a.* publish; promulgate.

Pudel ['pu:dəl], *m.* (—s, *pl.* —) poodle; *des —s Kern*, the gist of the matter.

Puder ['pu:dər], *m.* (—s, *no pl.*) powder, face-powder.

pudern ['pu:dərn], *v.a.* powder.

Puff [puf], *m.* (—es, *pl.* ⸚e) cuff, thump.

puffen ['pufən], *v.a.* cuff, thump.

Puffer ['pufər], *m.* (—s, *pl.* —) buffer.

Puffspiel ['pufʃpi:l], *n.* (—s, *pl.* —e) backgammon.

pullen ['pulən], *v.n.* rein in (a horse); (*coll.*) piddle.

Pulsader ['pulsa:dər], *f.* (—, *pl.* —n) artery; aorta.

pulsieren [pul'zi:rən], *v.n.* pulsate; pulse, throb.

Pulsschlag ['pulsʃla:k], *m.* (—s, *pl.* ⸚e) pulse-beat; pulsation.

Pult [pult], *n.* (—es, *pl.* —e) desk, writing-table; lectern.

Pulver ['pulvər], *n.* (—s, *pl.* —) powder.

Pump [pump], *m.* (—s, *no pl.*) (*sl.*) credit; *auf —*, on tick.

pumpen ['pumpən], *v.a., v.n.* pump; (*fig.*) (*sl.*) *sich etwas —*, borrow s.th., touch s.o. for s.th.; lend.

Pumpenschwengel ['pumpənʃveŋəl], *m.* (—s, *pl.* —) pump-handle.

Pumpernickel ['pumpərnikəl], *m.* (—s, *pl.* —) black bread, Westphalian rye-bread.

Pumphosen ['pumpho:zən], *f. pl.* plus-fours.

Punkt [puŋkt], *m.* (—es, *pl.* —e) point, dot, spot; (*Gram.*) full stop.

punktieren [puŋk'ti:rən], *v.a.* dot; punctuate.

pünktlich ['pyŋktlɪç], *adj.* punctual.

punktum ['puŋktum], *excl. und damit —*, that's the end of it; that's it.

Puppe ['pupə], *f.* (—, *pl.* —n) doll; (*Ent.*) pupa, chrysalis.

pur [pu:r], *adj.* pure, sheer; (*drink*) neat.

Puritaner [puri'taːnər], *m.* (—s, *pl.* —) puritan.

Purpur ['purpur], *m.* (—s, *no pl.*) purple.

Purzelbaum ['purtsəlbaum], *m.* (—s, *pl.* ⁓e) somersault.

purzeln ['purtsəln], *v.n.* tumble.

Pustel ['pustəl], *f.* (—, *pl.* —n) pustule.

pusten ['puːstən], *v.n.* puff, blow.

Pute ['puːtə], *f.* (—, *pl.* —n) (*Orn.*) turkey-hen; *dumme* —, silly goose.

Puter ['puːtər], *m.* (—s, *pl.* —) turkey-cock.

puterrot ['puːtərroːt], *adj.* as red as a turkey-cock.

Putsch [putʃ], *m.* (—es, *pl.* —e) coup de main, insurrection, riot.

Putz [puts], *m.* (—es, *no pl.*) finery; cleaning; rough-cast.

putzen ['putsən], *v.a.* polish, shine; clean. — *v.r. sich* —, dress up.

Putzfrau ['putsfrau], *f.* (—, *pl.* —en) charwoman.

Putzmacherin ['putsmaxərɪn], *f.* (—, *pl.* —nen) milliner.

Pyramide [pyra'miːdə], *f.* (—, *pl.* —n) pyramid.

Pyrenäen [pyra'nɛːən], *pl.* Pyrenees; —*halbinsel*, Iberian Peninsula.

Q

Q [kuː], *n.* (—s, *pl.* —s) the letter Q.

quabbeln ['kvabəln], *v.n.* shake, wobble.

Quacksalber ['kvakzalbər], *m.* (—s, *pl.* —) quack, mountebank.

Quacksalberei [kvakzalbə'rai], *f.* (—, *pl.* —en) quackery.

Quaderstein ['kvaːdərʃtain], *m.* (—s, *pl.* —e) ashlar, hewn stone.

Quadrat [kva'draːt], *n.* (—es, *pl.* —e) square; *zum* (or *ins*) — *erheben*, square (a number).

Quadratur [kvadra'tuːr], *f.* (—, *pl.* —en) quadrature; *die* — *des Kreises finden*, square the circle.

quadrieren [kva'driːrən], *v.a.* square.

quaken ['kvaːkən], *v.n.* (*frog*) croak; (*duck*) quack.

quäken ['kvɛːkən], *v.n.* squeak.

Quäker ['kvɛːkər], *m.* (—s, *pl.* —) Quaker.

Qual [kvaːl], *f.* (—, *pl.* —en) anguish, agony, torment.

quälen ['kvɛːlən], *v.a.* torment, torture, vex. — *v.r. sich* —, toil.

qualifizieren [kvalifi'tsiːrən], *v.a.* qualify.

Qualität [kvali'tɛːt], *f.* (—, *pl.* —en) quality.

Qualle ['kvalə], *f.* (—, *pl.* —n) (*Zool.*) jelly-fish.

Qualm [kvalm], *m.* (—es, *no pl.*) dense smoke.

Quantität [kvanti'tɛːt], *f.* (—, *pl.* —en) quantity.

Quantum ['kvantum], *n.* (—s, *pl.* —ten) portion, quantity.

Quappe ['kvapə], *f.* (—, *pl.* —n) (*Zool.*) tadpole.

Quarantäne [kvaran'tɛːnə], *f.* (—, *no pl.*) quarantine.

Quark [kvark], *m.* (—s, *no pl.*) curds; cream-cheese; (*fig.*) trash, rubbish, nonsense, bilge.

Quarta ['kvarta], *f.* (—, *no pl.*) fourth form.

Quartal [kvar'taːl], *n.* (—s, *pl.* —e) quarter of a year; term.

Quartier [kvar'tiːr], *m.* (—s, *pl.* —e) quarters, lodging; (*Mil.*) billet.

Quarz [kvarts], *m.* (—es, *no pl.*) quartz.

Quaste ['kvastə], *f.* (—, *pl.* —n) tassel.

Quatember [kva'tembər], *m.* (—s, *pl.* —) quarter day; (*Eccl.*) Ember Day.

Quatsch [kvatʃ], *m.* (—es, *no pl.*) nonsense, drivel.

Quecke ['kvɛkə], *f.* (—, *pl.* —n) couch-grass, quick-grass.

Quecksilber ['kvɛkzɪlbər], *n.* (—s, *no pl.*) quicksilver, mercury.

Quelle ['kvɛlə], *f.* (—, *pl.* —n) well, spring, fountain; (*fig.*) source; *aus sicherer* —, on good authority.

Quentchen ['kvɛntçən], *n.* (—s, *pl.* —) small amount, dram.

quer [kveːr], *adj.* cross, transverse, oblique, diagonal. — *adv.* across; *kreuz und* —, in all directions.

Querbalken ['kveːrbalkən], *m.* (—s, *pl.* —) cross-beam.

querdurch ['kveːrdurç], *adv.* across.

querfeldein ['kveːrfɛltain], *adv.* cross-country.

Querkopf ['kveːrkɔpf], *m.* (—es, *pl.* ⁓e) crank.

Quersattel ['kveːrzatəl], *m.* (—s, *pl.* ⁓) side-saddle.

Querschiff ['kveːrʃif], *n.* (—es, *pl.* —e) (*church*) transept.

Querschnitt ['kveːrʃnit], *m.* (—s, *pl.* —e) cross-section; (*fig.*) average.

Querulant [kveru'lant], *m.* (—en, *pl.* —en) grumbler.

quetschen ['kvetʃən], *v.a.* squeeze, crush, mash; bruise.

Queue [køː], *m.* (—s, *pl.* —s) (*Billiards*) cue.

quieken ['kviːkən], *v.n.* squeak.

Quinta ['kvinta], *f.* (—, *no pl.*) fifth form.

Quinte ['kvintə], *f.* (—, *pl.* —n) (*Mus.*) fifth.

Quirl [kvɪrl], *m.* (—s, *pl.* —e) whisk; (*Bot.*) whorl.

quitt [kvɪt], *adj.* — *sein*, be quits.

Quitte ['kvɪtə], *f.* (—, *pl.* —n) (*Bot.*) quince.

quittegelb [ˈkvɪtəgɛlp], *adj.* bright yellow.
quittieren [kvɪˈtiːrən], *v.a.* receipt; give a receipt; *den Dienst* —, leave the service.
Quittung [ˈkvɪtuŋ], *f.* (—, *pl.* —en) receipt.
Quodlibet [ˈkvɔdlɪbɛt], *n.* (—s, *pl.* —s) medley.
Quote [ˈkvoːtə], *f.* (—, *pl.* —n) quota, share.
quotieren [kvoˈtiːrən], *v.a.* (*stock exchange*) quote (prices).

R

R [ɛr], *n.* (—s, *pl.* —s) the letter R.
Rabatt [raˈbat], *m.* (—s, *pl.* —e) rebate, discount.
Rabatte [raˈbatə], *f.* (—, *pl.* —n) flower-border.
Rabbiner [raˈbiːnər], *m.* (—s, *pl.* —) rabbi.
Rabe [ˈraːbə], *m.* (—n, *pl.* —n) (*Orn.*) raven; *ein weißer* —, a rare bird.
Rabenaas [ˈraːbənaːs], *n.* (—es, *pl.* —e) carrion.
rabiat [raˈbjaːt], *adj.* furious, rabid.
Rache [ˈraxə], *f.* (—, *no pl.*) revenge, vengeance.
Rachen [ˈraxən], *m.* (—s, *pl.* —) jaws, throat.
rächen [ˈrɛːçən], *v.a.* avenge. — *v.r. sich* —, avenge o.s., take vengeance.
Rachenbräune [ˈraxənbrɔynə], *f.* (—, *no pl.*) croup, quinsy.
Rachitis [raˈxiːtɪs], *f.* (—, *no pl.*) (*Med.*) rickets.
rachsüchtig [ˈraxzyçtɪç], *adj.* vindictive, vengeful.
rackern [ˈrakərn], *v.r. sich* —, (*coll.*) toil, work hard.
Rad [raːt], *n.* (—es, *pl.* ̈er) wheel; bicycle; *ein* — *schlagen*, turn a cart-wheel; (*peacock*) spread the tail.
Radau [raˈdau], *m.* (—s, *no pl.*) noise, din, shindy.
Rade [ˈraːdə], *f.* (—, *pl.* —n) corn-cockle.
radebrechen [ˈraːdəbrɛçən], *v.a. insep.* murder a language.
radeln [ˈraːdəln], *v.n.* (*aux.* sein) (*coll.*) cycle.
Rädelsführer [ˈrɛːdəlsfyːrər], *m.* (—s, *pl.* —) ringleader.
rädern [ˈrɛːdərn], *v.a.* break on the wheel; *gerädert sein*, (*fig.*) ache in all o.'s bones, be exhausted.
Radfahrer [ˈraːtfaːrər], *m.* (—s, *pl.* —) cyclist.
radieren [raˈdiːrən], *v.n.* erase; etch.
Radierung [raˈdiːruŋ], *f.* (—, *pl.* —en) etching.

Radieschen [raˈdiːsçən], *n.* (—s, *pl.* —) (*Bot.*) radish.
Radio [ˈraːdjo], *n.* (—s, *pl.* —s) wireless, radio.
raffen [ˈrafən], *v.a.* snatch up, gather up.
Raffinade [rafiˈnaːdə], *f.* (—, *no pl.*) refined sugar.
Raffinement [rafinəˈmã], *n.* (—s, *no pl.*) elaborateness.
raffinieren [rafiˈniːrən], *v.a.* refine.
raffiniert [rafiˈniːrt], *adj.* refined; elaborate, crafty, wily, cunning.
ragen [ˈraːgən], *v.n.* tower, soar.
Rahm [raːm], *m.* (—es, *no pl.*) cream; *den* — *abschöpfen*, skim; (*fig.*) skim the cream off.
Rahmen [ˈraːmən], *m.* (—s, *pl.* —) frame; milieu, limit, scope, compass; *im* — *von*, within the framework of.
rahmig [ˈraːmɪç], *adj.* creamy.
raisonnieren [rɛzɔˈniːrən], *v.n.* reason, argue; (*fig.*) grumble, answer back.
Rakete [raˈkeːtə], *f.* (—, *pl.* —n) rocket, sky-rocket.
Rakett [raˈkɛt], *n.* (—s, *pl.* —s) (*tennis*) racket.
rammen [ˈramən], *v.a.* ram.
Rampe [ˈrampə], *f.* (—, *pl.* —n) ramp, slope; platform; (*Theat.*) apron.
ramponiert [rampoˈniːrt], *adj.* battered, damaged.
Ramsch [ramʃ], *m.* (—es, *pl.* ̈e) odds and ends; (*Comm.*) job lot.
Rand [rant], *m.* (—es, *pl.* ̈er) edge, border, verge, rim; (*book*) margin; (*hat*) brim; *am* — *des Grabes*, with one foot in the grave; *außer* — *und Band geraten*, get completely out of hand.
randalieren [randaˈliːrən], *v.n.* kick up a row.
Randbemerkung [ˈrantbəmɛrkuŋ], *f.* (—, *pl.* —en) marginal note, gloss.
rändern [ˈrɛndərn], *v.a.* border, edge, mill.
Ränftchen [ˈrɛnftçən], *n.* (—s, *pl.* —) crust (of bread).
Rang [raŋ], *m.* (—es, *pl.* ̈e) rank, grade, rate; order, class; standing (in society); (*Theat.*) circle, tier, gallery.
Range [ˈraŋə], *m.* (—s, *pl.* —n) scamp, rascal. — *f.* (—, *pl.* —n) tomboy, hoyden.
rangieren [rãˈʒiːrən], *v.a.* (*Railw.*) shunt. — *v.n.* rank.
Ranke [ˈraŋkə], *f.* (—, *pl.* —n) tendril, shoot.
Ränke [ˈrɛŋkə], *m. pl.* intrigues, tricks.
ranken [ˈraŋkən], *v.r.* (*aux.* haben) *sich* —, (*plant*) climb (with tendrils).
Ränkeschmied [ˈrɛŋkəʃmiːt], *m.* (—es, *pl.* —e) plotter, intriguer.
Ranzen [ˈrantsən], *m.* (—s, *pl.* —) satchel, knapsack, rucksack.
ranzig [ˈrantsɪç], *adj.* rancid, rank.
Rappe [ˈrapə], *m.* (—n, *pl.* —n) black horse.

Rappel ['rapəl], *m.* (—s, *no pl.*) (*coll.*) slight madness; rage, fit.

Rappen ['rapən], *m.* (—s, *pl.* —) small Swiss coin; centime.

rapportieren [rapɔr'tiːrən], *v.a.* report.

Raps [raps], *m.* (—es, *no pl.*) rapeseed.

rar [raːr], *adj.* rare, scarce; exquisite.

rasch [raʃ], *adj.* quick, swift.

rascheln ['raʃəln], *v.n.* rustle.

Rasen ['raːzən], *m.* (—s, *pl.* —) lawn, turf, sod.

rasen ['raːzən], *v.n.* rave, rage, be delirious; rush, speed; *in —der Eile*, in a tearing hurry.

Raserei [raːzə'raɪ], *f.* (—, *pl.* —en) madness; fury.

Rasierapparat [ra'ziːrapaːt], *m.* (—s, *pl.* —e) (safety-)razor; shaver.

rasieren [ra'ziːrən], *v.a.* shave; *sich — lassen*, be shaved, get a shave.

Rasierzeug [ra'ziːrtsɔyk], *n.* (—s, *no pl.*) shaving-tackle.

Raspel ['raspəl], *f.* (—, *pl.* —n) rasp.

Rasse ['rasə], *f.* (—, *pl.* —n) race; breed; *reine —*, thoroughbred; *gekreuzte —*, cross-breed.

Rassel ['rasəl], *f.* (—, *pl.* —n) rattle.

rasseln ['rasəln], *v.n.* rattle, clank.

Rassendiskriminierung ['rasəndɪskrimiːniːruŋ], *f.* (—, *no pl.*) racial discrimination.

Rast [rast], *f.* (—, *no pl.*) rest, repose.

rasten ['rastən], *v.n.* rest, take a rest; halt.

Raster ['rastər], *m.* (—s, *pl.* —) (*Phot.*) screen.

rastlos ['rastloːs], *adj.* restless.

Rat (1) [raːt], *m.* (—es, *pl.* —schläge) advice, counsel; deliberation; *mit — und Tat*, with advice and assistance; *einem einen — geben*, give s.o. advice, counsel s.o.; *einen um — fragen*, consult s.o.; *— schaffen*, find ways and means.

Rat (2) [raːt], *m.* (—es, *pl.* —e) council, councillor.

Rate ['raːtə], *f.* (—, *pl.* —n) instalment, rate.

raten ['raːtən], *v.a., v.n., irr.* advise; guess, conjecture.

Ratgeber ['raːtgeːbər], *m.* (—s, *pl.* —) adviser, counsellor.

Rathaus ['raːthaus], *n.* (—es, *pl.* —er) town-hall.

Ratifizierung [ratifi'tsiːruŋ], *f.* (—, *pl.* —en) ratification.

Ration [ra'tsjoːn], *f.* (—, *pl.* —en) ration, share, portion.

rationell [ratsjo'nɛl], *adj.* rational.

ratlos ['raːtloːs], *adj.* helpless, perplexed.

ratsam ['raːtzaːm], *adj.* advisable.

Ratschlag ['raːtʃlaːk], *m.* (—s, *pl.* —e) advice, counsel.

Ratschluß ['raːtʃlus], *m.* (—sses, *pl.* —sse) decision, decree.

Ratsdiener ['raːtsdiːnər], *m.* (—s, *pl.* —) beadle, tipstaff, summoner.

Rätsel ['rɛːtsəl], *n.* (—s, *pl.* —) riddle, puzzle, mystery, enigma, conundrum.

Ratsherr ['raːtshɛr], *m.* (—n, *pl.* —en) alderman, (town-)councillor, senator.

Ratte ['ratə], *f.* (—, *pl.* —n) (*Zool.*) rat.

Raub [raup], *m.* (—es, *no pl.*) robbery; booty, prey.

rauben ['raubən], *v.a.* rob, plunder; *es raubt mir den Atem*, it takes my breath away.

Räuber ['rɔybər], *m.* (—s, *pl.* —) robber, thief; highwayman; *— und Gendarm*, cops and robbers.

Raubgier ['raupgiːr], *f.* (—, *no pl.*) rapacity.

Rauch [raux], *m.* (—s, *no pl.*) smoke, vapour.

Rauchen ['rauxən], *n.* (—s, *no pl.*) smoking; *— verboten*, no smoking.

rauchen ['rauxən], *v.a., v.n.* smoke.

räuchern ['rɔyçərn], *v.a.* (*meat, fish*) smoke-dry, cure; (*disinfect*) fumigate. *— v.n.* (*Eccl.*) burn incense.

Rauchfang ['rauxfaŋ], *m.* (—s, *pl.* —e) chimney-flue.

Räude ['rɔydə], *f.* (—, *no pl.*) mange.

Raufbold ['raufbɔlt], *m.* (—s, *pl.* —e) brawler, bully.

raufen ['raufən], *v.a.* (*hair*) tear out, pluck. *— v.n.* fight, brawl. *— v.r. sich — mit*, scuffle with, fight, have a scrap with.

rauh [rau], *adj.* rough; (*fig.*) harsh, rude; hoarse; (*weather*) raw, inclement.

Rauheit ['rauhaɪt], *f.* (—, *no pl.*) roughness; hoarseness; (*fig.*) harshness, rudeness; (*weather*) inclemency; (*landscape*) ruggedness.

rauhen ['rauən], *v.a.* (*cloth*) nap.

Raum [raum], *m.* (—es, *pl.* —e) space, room; outer space; (*fig.*) scope; *dem Gedanken — geben*, entertain an idea.

räumen ['rɔymən], *v.a.* clear, empty; quit, leave; *das Feld —*, abandon the field, clear out.

Rauminhalt ['raumɪnhalt], *m.* (—s, *no pl.*) volume.

räumlich ['rɔymlɪç], *adj.* spatial; (*in compounds*) space-.

Räumlichkeiten ['rɔymlɪçkaɪtən], *f. pl.* premises.

Raumschiff ['raumʃɪf], *n.* (—es, *pl.* —e) spaceship, spacecraft.

Räumung ['rɔymuŋ], *f.* (—, *pl.* —en) evacuation.

raunen ['raunən], *v.a., v.n.* whisper.

Raupe ['raupə], *f.* (—, *pl.* —n) (*Ent.*) caterpillar.

Rausch [rauʃ], *m.* (—es, *pl.* —e) intoxication; delirium, frenzy; *einen — haben*, be drunk, intoxicated; *seinen — ausschlafen*, sleep it off.

rauschen ['rauʃən], *v.n.* rustle, rush, roar.

Rauschgift ['rauʃgɪft], *n.* (—s, *pl.* —e) drug; narcotic.

Rauschgold ['rauʃgɔlt], *n.* (—es, *no pl.*) tinsel.

räuspern ['rɔyspərn], *v.r. sich —*, clear o.'s throat.

Raute ['rautə], *f.* (—, *pl.* —n) (*Maths.*) rhombus; lozenge; (*Bot.*) rue.

Razzia ['ratsja], *f.* (—, *pl.* —zzien) (police-)raid, swoop.

reagieren [rea'gi:rən], *v.n.* react (on).

realisieren [reali'zi:rən], *v.a.* convert into money, realise.

Realschule [re'a:lʃu:lə], *f.* (—, *pl.* —n) technical grammar school; secondary modern school.

Rebe ['re:bə], *f.* (—, *pl.* —n) vine.

Rebell [re'bel], *m.* (—en, *pl.* —en) rebel, mutineer, insurgent.

Rebensaft ['re:bənzaft], *m.* (—s, *pl.* ⁓e) grape-juice, wine.

Rebhuhn ['re:phu:n], *n.* (—s, *pl.* ⁓er) (*Orn.*) partridge.

Reblaus ['re:plaus], *f.* (—, *pl.* ⁓e) (*Ent.*) phylloxera.

Rechen ['reçən], *m.* (—s, *pl.* —) (*garden*) rake; (*clothes*) rack.

Rechenaufgabe ['reçənaufga:bə], *f.* (—, *pl.* —n) sum; mathematical *or* arithmetical problem.

Rechenmaschine ['reçənmaʃi:nə], *f.* (—, *pl.* —n) calculating machine, adding-machine.

Rechenschaft ['reçənʃaft], *f.* (—, *no pl.*) account; — *ablegen,* account for; *zur* — *ziehen,* call to account.

Rechenschieber ['reçənʃi:bər], *m.* (—s, *pl.* —) slide-rule.

Rechentabelle ['reçəntabelə], *f.* (—, *pl.* —n) ready reckoner.

rechnen ['reçnən], *v.a., v.n.* reckon, calculate, do sums, compute; *auf etwas* —, count on s.th.; *auf einen* —, rely on s.o.

Rechnung ['reçnuŋ], *f.* (—, *pl.* —en) reckoning, account, computation; (*document*) invoice, bill, statement, account; *einer Sache* — *tragen,* make allowances for s.th.; take s.th. into account; *einem einen Strich durch die* — *machen,* put a spoke in s.o.'s wheel; *eine* — *begleichen,* settle an account.

Rechnungsabschluß ['reçnuŋsapʃlus], *m.* (—sses, *pl.* ⁓sse) balancing of accounts, balance-sheet.

Rechnungsprüfer ['reçnuŋspry:fər], *m.* (—s, *pl.* —) auditor.

Rechnungsrat ['reçnuŋsra:t], *m.* (—s, *pl.* ⁓e) member of the board of accountants, (senior government) auditor.

Recht [reçt], *n.* (—es, *pl.* —e) right, justice; claim on, title to; law, jurisprudence; *von* —*s wegen,* by right; — *sprechen,* administer justice; *die* —*e studieren,* study law.

recht [reçt], *adj.* right; just; real, true; suitable; proper; *zur* —*en Zeit,* in time; *es geht nicht mit* —*en Dingen zu,* there is s.th. queer about it; *was dem einen* —, *ist dem andern billig,* what is sauce for the goose is sauce for the gander; *einem* — *geben,* agree with s.o.; — *haben,* be (in the) right.

Rechteck ['reçtek], *n.* (—s, *pl.* —e) rectangle.

rechten ['reçtən], *v.n. mit einem* —, dispute, remonstrate with s.o.

rechtfertigen ['reçtfertigən], *v.a. insep.* justify. — *v.r. sich* —, exculpate o.s.

rechtgläubig ['reçtgləybiç], *adj.* orthodox.

rechthaberisch ['reçtha-bəriʃ], *adj.* stubborn, obstinate.

rechtlich ['reçtliç], *adj.* legal, lawful, legitimate; (*Law*) judicial, juridical.

rechtmäßig ['reçtmɛ:siç], *adj.* lawful, legitimate, legal.

rechts [reçts], *adv.* to the right, on the right.

Rechtsabtretung ['reçtsaptre:tuŋ], *f.* (—, *pl.* —en) cession, assignment.

Rechtsanwalt ['reçtsanvalt], *m.* (—s, *pl.* ⁓e) lawyer, solicitor, attorney.

Rechtsbeistand ['reçtsbaiʃtant], *m.* (—s, *pl.* ⁓e) (legal) counsel.

rechtschaffen ['reçtʃafən], *adj.* upright, honest, righteous.

Rechtschreibung ['reçtʃraibuŋ], *f.* (—, *no pl.*) orthography, spelling.

Rechtshandel ['reçtshandəl], *m.* (—s, *pl.* ⁓) action, case, lawsuit.

rechtskräftig ['reçtskreftiç], *adj.* legal, valid.

Rechtslehre ['reçtsle:rə], *f.* (—, *pl.* —n) jurisprudence.

Rechtsspruch ['reçtsʃprux], *m.* (—(e)s, *pl.* ⁓e) verdict.

Rechtsverhandlung ['reçtsferhandluŋ], *f.* (—, *pl.* —en) legal proceedings.

Rechtsweg ['reçtsve:k], *m.* (—(e)s, *pl.* —e) course of law.

rechtswidrig ['reçtsvi:driç], *adj.* against the law, illegal.

Rechtszuständigkeit ['reçtstsu:ʃtendiçkait], *f.* (—, *pl.* —en) (legal) competence.

rechtwinklig ['reçtviŋkliç], *adj.* rectangular.

rechtzeitig ['reçttsaitiç], *adj.* opportune. — *adv.* in time, at the right time.

Reck [rek], *n.* (—s, *pl.* —e) horizontal bar.

Recke ['rekə], *m.* (—n, *pl.* —n) (*Poet.*) hero.

recken ['rekən], *v.a.* stretch, extend.

Redakteur [redak'tø:r], *m.* (—s, *pl.* —e) editor (newspaper, magazine).

Redaktion [redak'tsjo:n], *f.* (—, *pl.* —en) editorship, editorial staff; (*room*) editorial office.

Rede ['re:də], *f.* (—, *pl.* —n) speech, oration; address; *es geht die* —, people say; *es ist nicht der* — *wert,* it is not worth mentioning; *eine* — *halten,* deliver a speech; *zur* — *stellen,* call to account.

reden ['re:dən], *v.a.* speak, talk, discourse; *einem nach dem Munde* —, humour s.o.; *in den Wind* —, speak in vain, preach to the winds; *mit sich* — *lassen,* be amenable to reason.

Redensart ['re:dɔnsaːrt], *f.* (—, *pl.*
—en) phrase, idiom; cliché; *einen mit
leeren —en abspeisen*, put s.o. off with
fine words.
Redewendung ['re:dɔvɛnduŋ], *f.* (—,
pl. —en) turn of phrase.
redigieren [redi'giːrən], *v.a.* edit.
redlich ['re:tlɪç], *adj.* honest, upright.
Redner ['re:dnɔr], *m.* (—s, *pl.* —)
speaker, orator.
Reede ['re:dɔ], *f.* (—, *pl.* —n) (*Naut.*)
roadstead.
Reederei [re:dɔ'raɪ], *f.* (—, *pl.* —en)
shipping-business.
reell [re'ɛl], *adj.* honest, fair, sound,
bona fide.
Reep [re:p], *n.* (—s, *pl.* —e) (*Naut.*)
rope.
Referat [refe'raːt], *n.* (—s, *pl.* —e)
report; paper (to a learned society),
lecture.
Referendar [referɛn'daːr], *m.* (—s, *pl.*
—e) junior barrister *or* teacher.
Referent [refe'rɛnt], *m.* (—en, *pl.*
—en) reporter, reviewer; lecturer;
expert (adviser).
Referenz [refe'rɛnts], *f.* (—, *pl.* —en)
reference (to s.o. *or* s.th.).
referieren [refe'riːrən], *v.a., v.n.* report
(on), give a paper (on).
reflektieren [reflɛk'tiːrən], *v.a.* reflect.
— *v.n. auf etwas* —, be a prospective
buyer of s.th., have o.'s eye on s.th.
Reformator [refor'maːtɔr], *m.* (—s,
pl. —en) reformer.
reformieren [refor'miːrən], *v.a.* reform.
Regal [re'gaːl], *n.* (—s, *pl.* —e) shelf.
rege ['re:gɔ], *adj.* brisk, lively, animated.
Regel ['re:gɔl], *f.* (—, *pl.* —n) rule
precept, principle; *in der* —, as a
rule, generally.
regelmäßig ['re:gɔlmɛːsɪç], *adj.* regular.
regeln ['re:gɔln], *v.a.* regulate, arrange,
order.
Regelung ['re:gɔluŋ], *f.* (—, *pl.* —en)
regulation.
regelwidrig ['re:gɔlviːdrɪç], *adj.* contrary to rule, irregular, foul.
Regen ['re:gɔn], *m.* (—s, *no pl.*) rain.
regen ['re:gɔn], *v.r. sich* —, move,
stir.
Regenbogen ['re:gɔnboːgɔn], *m.* (—s,
pl. —) rainbow.
Regenbogenhaut ['re:gɔnboːgɔnhaut],
f. (—, *pl.* ˙e) (*eye*) iris.
Regenguß ['re:gɔngus], *m.* (—sses,
pl. ˙sse) downpour, violent shower.
Regenmantel ['re:gɔnmantɔl], *m.* (—s,
pl. ˙) waterproof, raincoat, mac.
Regenpfeifer ['re:gɔnpfaifɔr], *m.* (—s,
pl. —) (*Orn.*) plover.
Regenrinne ['re:gɔnrinɔ], *f.* (—, *pl.*
—n) eaves.
Regenschirm ['re:gɔnʃirm], *m.* (—s,
pl. —e) umbrella.
Regentschaft [re'gɛntʃaft], *f.* (—, *pl.*
—en) regency.

Regie [re'ʒiː], *f.* (—, *pl.* —n) stage
management, production, direction.
regieren [re'giːrən], *v.a.* rule, reign
over, govern. — *v.n.* reign; (*fig.*)
prevail, predominate.
Regierung [re'giːruŋ], *f.* (—, *pl.* —en)
government; reign.
Regierungsrat [re'giːruŋsraːt], *m.* (—s,
pl. ˙e) government adviser.
Regiment (1) [regi'mɛnt], *n.* (—s, *pl.*
—e) rule, government.
Regiment (2) [regi'mɛnt], *n.* (—s, *pl.*
—er) (*Mil.*) regiment.
Regisseur [reʒi'søːr], *m.* (—s, *pl.* —e)
stage-manager, producer, director.
Registrator [regɪs'traːtɔr], *m.* (—s, *pl.*
—en) registrar, recorder; registering
machine.
Registratur [regɪstra'tuːr], *f.* (—, *pl.*
—en) record office, registry; filing-
cabinet.
registrieren [regɪs'triːrən], *v.a.* register, record, file.
reglos ['re:kloːs], *adj.* motionless.
regnen ['re:gnɔn], *v.n.* rain; *es regnet
in Strömen*, it is raining cats and
dogs.
Regreß [re'grɛs], *m.* (—sses, *pl.*
—sse) recourse, remedy.
regsam ['re:kzaːm], *adj.* quick, alert,
lively.
regulieren [regu'liːrən], *v.a.* regulate.
Regung ['re:guŋ], *f.* (—, *pl.* —en)
movement; impulse.
Reh [re:], *n.* (—(e)s, *pl.* —e) doe, roe.
rehabilitieren [rehabili'tiːrən], *v.a.*
rehabilitate.
Rehbock ['re:bɔk], *m.* (—s, *pl.* ˙e)
(*Zool.*) roe-buck.
Rehkeule ['re:kɔylɔ], *f.* (—, *pl.* —n)
haunch of venison.
reiben ['raibɔn], *v.a. irr.* rub, grate,
grind; *einem etwas unter die Nase* —,
throw s.th. in s.o.'s teeth, bring s.th.
home to s.o.
Reibung ['raibuŋ], *f.* (—, *pl.* —en)
friction.
Reich [raɪç], *n.* (—(e)s, *pl.* —e) kingdom, realm, empire, state.
reich [raɪç], *adj.* rich, wealthy, opulent.
reichen ['raɪçɔn], *v.a.* reach, pass,
hand; *einem die Hand* —, shake hands
with s.o. — *v.n.* reach, extend; be
sufficient.
reichhaltig ['raɪçhaltɪç], *adj.* abundant, copious.
reichlich ['raɪçlɪç], *adj.* ample, plentiful.
Reichskammergericht [raɪçs'kamɔr-
gɔrɪçt], *n.* (—s, *no pl.*) Imperial
High Court of Justice (*Holy Roman
Empire*).
Reichskanzlei ['raɪçskantslai], *f.* (—,
pl. —en) (Imperial) Chancery.
Reichskanzler ['raɪçskantslɔr], *m.* (—s,
pl. —) (Imperial) Chancellor.
Reichsstände ['raɪçsʃtɛndɔ], *m. pl.*
Estates (of the Holy Roman Empire).
Reichstag ['raɪçstaːk], *m.* (—s, *pl.*
—e) Imperial Parliament, Reichstag,
Diet.

Reichtum ['raɪçtuːm], *m.* (—s, *pl.* ˙-er) riches, wealth, opulence.

Reif (1) [raɪf], *m.* (—s, *no pl.*) hoar-frost.

Reif (2) [raɪf], *m.* (—s, *pl.* —e) ring.

reif [raɪf], *adj.* ripe, mature.

Reifen ['raɪfən], *m.* (—s, *pl.* —) hoop; tyre; — *schlagen*, trundle a hoop.

reifen ['raɪfən], *v.n.* (*aux.* sein) ripen, mature, grow ripe.

Reifeprüfung ['raɪfəpryːfuŋ], *f.* (—, *pl.* —en) matriculation examination.

reiflich ['raɪflɪç], *adj. sich etwas — überlegen*, give careful consideration to s.th.

Reigen ['raɪgən], *m.* (—s, *pl.* —) round-dance, roundelay.

Reihe ['raɪə], *f.* (—, *pl.* —n) series; file; row; progression, sequence; (*Theat.*) tier; *in — und Glied*, in closed ranks; *nach der —*, in turns; *ich bin an der —*, it is my turn.

Reihenfolge ['raɪənfɔlgə], *f.* (—, *no pl.*) succession.

Reiher ['raɪər], *m.* (—s, *pl.* —) (*Orn.*) heron.

Reim [raɪm], *m.* (—(e)s, *pl.* —e) rhyme.

rein [raɪn], *adj.* clean, pure, clear, neat; *—e Wahrheit*, plain truth; *ins —e bringen*, settle, clear up; *ins —e schreiben*, make a fair copy of; *einem —en Wein einschenken*, have a straight talk with s.o.

Reineke ['raɪnəkə], *m.* (—, *no pl.*) — *Fuchs*, Reynard the Fox.

Reinertrag ['raɪnɛrtraːk], *m.* (—(e)s, *pl.* ˙-e) net proceeds.

Reinfall ['raɪnfal], *m.* (—s, *pl.* ˙-e) sell, wild-goose chase; disappointment.

reinfallen ['raɪnfalən], *v.n. irr.* (*aux.* sein) be unsuccessful.

Reingewinn ['raɪngəvɪn], *m.* (—s, *pl.* —e) net proceeds.

Reinheit ['raɪnhaɪt], *f.* (—, *no pl.*) purity.

reinigen ['raɪnɪgən], *v.a.* clean, cleanse; dry-clean; purge.

Reinigung ['raɪnɪguŋ], *f.* (—, *pl.* —en) cleaning; (*fig.*) purification, cleansing; *chemische —*, dry-cleaning.

reinlich ['raɪnlɪç], *adj.* clean, neat.

Reis (1) [raɪs], *m.* (—es, *no pl.*) rice.

Reis (2) [raɪs], *n.* (—es, *pl.* —er) twig, sprig; scion; cutting.

Reisbesen ['raɪsbeːzən], *m.* (—s, *pl.* —) birch-broom, besom.

Reise ['raɪzə], *f.* (—, *pl.* —n) tour, trip, journey, travels; voyage; *gute —!* bon voyage!

reisefertig ['raɪzəfɛrtɪç], *adj.* ready to start.

Reisegeld ['raɪzəgɛlt], *n.* (—es, *pl.* —er) travel allowance.

reisen ['raɪzən], *v.n.* (*aux.* sein) travel, tour, journey, take a trip.

Reisende ['raɪzəndə], *m.* (—n, *pl.* —n) traveller; commercial traveller.

Reisig ['raɪzɪç], *n.* (—s, *no pl.*) brush-wood.

Reisige ['raɪzɪgə], *m.* (—n, *pl.* —n) (*obs.*) trooper, horseman.

Reißaus [raɪsʼaus], *n.* (—, *no pl.*) — *nehmen*, take to o.'s heels.

Reißbrett ['raɪsbrɛt], *n.* (—es, *pl.* —er) drawing-board.

reißen ['raɪsən], *v.a. irr.* tear; rend; pull; snatch; *etwas an sich —*, seize s.th., usurp.

reißend ['raɪsənt], *adj.* rapid; ravening; carnivorous; (*Comm.*) brisk, rapid (sales).

Reißnagel ['raɪsnaːgəl], *m. see* **Reißzwecke**.

Reißschiene ['raɪsʃiːnə], *f.* (—, *pl.* —n) T-square.

Reißverschluß ['raɪsfɛrʃlus], *m.* (—sses, *pl.* ˙-sse) zip-fastener.

Reißzwecke ['raɪstsvɛkə], *f.* (—, *pl.* —n) drawing-pin.

reiten ['raɪtən], *v.a. irr.* ride (a horse). — *v.n.* (*aux.* sein) ride, go on horseback.

Reiterei [raɪtəʼraɪ], *f.* (—, *pl.* —en) cavalry.

Reitknecht ['raɪtknɛçt], *m.* (—es, *pl.* —e) groom.

Reiz [raɪts], *m.* (—es, *pl.* —e) charm, attraction, fascination, allure; stimulus; irritation; (*Phys.*) impulse.

reizbar ['raɪtsbaːr], *adj.* susceptible, irritable.

reizen ['raɪtsən], *v.a.* irritate; stimulate, charm, entice.

reizend ['raɪtsənt], *adj.* charming.

Reizmittel ['raɪtsmɪtəl], *n.* (—s, *pl.* —) stimulant; irritant.

rekeln ['reːkəln], *v.r.* (*dial.*) *sich —*, loll about.

Reklame [reˈklaːmə], *f.* (—, *pl.* —n) propaganda, advertisement, advertising, publicity.

reklamieren [reklaˈmiːrən], *v.a.* claim, reclaim. — *v.a.* complain.

rekognoszieren [rekɔgnɔsˈtsiːrən], *v.a.* reconnoitre.

rekommandieren [rekɔmanˈdiːrən], *v.a.* (*Austr.*) register (a letter).

Rekonvaleszent [rekɔnvalɛsˈtsɛnt], *m.* (—en, *pl.* —en) convalescent.

Rekrut [reˈkruːt], *m.* (—en, *pl.* —en) recruit.

rekrutieren [rekruˈtiːrən], *v.a.* recruit. — *v.r. sich — aus*, be recruited from.

rektifizieren [rɛktifiˈtsiːrən], *v.a.* rectify.

Rektor ['rɛktɔr], *m.* (—s, *pl.* —en) (school) headmaster; (*Univ.*) chancellor.

Rektorat [rɛktoˈraːt], *n.* (—es, *pl.* —e) rectorship, chancellorship.

relativ [relaˈtiːf], *adj.* relative, comparative.

relegieren [releˈgiːrən], *v.a.* expel; (*Univ.*) send down, rusticate.

Relief [rɛlˈjef], *n.* (—s, *pl.* —s) (*Art*) relief.

religiös [reliˈgjøːs], *adj.* religious.

Reliquie [reˈliːkvjə], *f.* (—, *pl.* —n) (*Rel.*) relic.

Remise [re'mi:zə], _f._ (—, _pl._ —n) coach-house.

Remittent [remɪ'tɛnt], _m._ (—en, _pl._ —en) remitter.

Renegat [rene'ga:t], _m._ (—en, _pl._ —en) renegade.

Renette [rɛ'netə], _f._ (—, _pl._ —n) rennet(-apple).

renken ['rɛŋkən], _v.a._ wrench, bend, twist.

Rennbahn ['rɛnba:n], _f._ (—, _pl._ —en) race-course; (cinder-)track; (_Motor._) racing-circuit.

rennen ['rɛnən], _v.n. irr._ (_aux._ sein) run, race, rush.

Renommé [rɛnɔ'me:], _n._ (—s, _no pl._) renown, repute, reputation.

renommieren [rɛnɔ'mi:rən], _v.n._ brag, boast.

renovieren [reno'vi:rən], _v.a._ renovate, restore, redecorate, renew.

rentabel [rɛn'ta:bəl], _adj._ profitable, lucrative.

Rente ['rɛntə], _f._ (—, _pl._ —n) pension, annuity.

Rentier [rɛn'tje:], _m._ (—s, _pl._ —s) rentier, person of independent means.

rentieren [rɛn'ti:rən], _v.r. sich —_, be profitable, be worthwhile, pay.

Rentner ['rɛntnər], _m._ (—s, _pl._ —) pensioner.

Reparatur [rapara'tu:r], _f._ (—, _pl._ —en) repair.

reparieren [repa'ri:rən], _v.a._ repair.

Repräsentant [reprɛzen'tant], _m._ (—en, _pl._ —en) representative.

Repräsentantenkammer [reprɛzen'tantənkamər], _f._ (—, _pl._ —n) (_Am._) House of Representatives.

Repressalien [reprɛ'sa:ljən], _f. pl._ reprisals, retaliation.

reproduzieren [reprodu'tsi:rən], _v.a._ reproduce.

Republikaner [republi'ka:nər], _m._ (—s, _pl._ —) republican.

requirieren [rekvi'ri:rən], _v.a._ requisition.

Reseda [re'ze:da], _f._ (—, _pl._ —s) (_Bot._) mignonette.

Reservat [rezer'va:t], _n._ (—es, _pl._ —e) reservation, reserve.

Residenz [rezi'dɛnts], _f._ (—, _pl._ —en) residence, seat of the Court.

residieren [rezi'di:rən], _v.n._ reside.

Residuum [re'zi:duum], _n._ (—s, _pl._ —duen) residue, dregs.

resignieren [rezig'ni:rən], _v.n., v.r._ resign; be resigned (to s.th.); give up.

Respekt [re'spɛkt], _m._ (—es, _no pl._) respect, regard; _mit — zu sagen_, with all due respect.

respektieren [respɛk'ti:rən], _v.a._ respect, honour.

Ressort [re'so:r], _n._ (—s, _pl._ —s) department, domain.

Rest [rɛst], _m._ (—es, _pl._ —e) rest, residue, remainder; remnant; (_money_) balance.

restaurieren [rɛsto'ri:rən], _v.a._ restore, renovate.

Resultat [rezul'ta:t], _n._ (—es, _pl._ —e) result, outcome.

Resümee [rezy'me:], _n._ (—s, _pl._ —s) résumé, précis, digest, summary, synopsis, abstract.

retten ['rɛtən], _v.a._ save, preserve; rescue, deliver; _die Ehre —_, vindicate o.'s honour.

Rettich ['rɛtɪç], _m._ (—s, _pl._ —e) radish.

Rettung ['rɛtuŋ], _f._ (—, _pl._ —en) saving, rescue, deliverance.

retuschieren [retu'ʃi:rən], _v.a._ retouch.

Reue ['rɔyə], _f._ (—, _no pl._) repentance, remorse, contrition.

reuen ['rɔyən], _v.a., v.n._ repent, regret; _es reut mich_, I am sorry.

Reugeld ['rɔygɛlt], _n._ (—es, _pl._ —er) forfeit-money, penalty.

reüssieren [rey'si:rən], _v.n._ succeed.

Revanche [re'vã:ʃə], _f._ (—, _pl._ —n) revenge; (_fig._) return.

revanchieren [revã'ʃi:rən], _v.r. sich —_, repay a service, have or take o.'s revenge.

Reverenz [reve'rɛnts], _f._ (—, _pl._ —en) bow, curtsy.

revidieren [revi'di:rən], _v.a._ revise, check.

Revier [re'vi:r], _n._ (—s, _pl._ —e) district, precinct, quarter; preserve.

Revisor [re'vi:zɔr], _m._ (—s, _pl._ —en) accountant, auditor.

revoltieren [revɔl'ti:rən], _v.n._ rise, revolt.

revolutionieren [revolutsjo'ni:rən], _v.a._ revolutionise.

Revolverblatt [re'vɔlvərblat], _n._ (—s, _pl._ ̈er) gutter press.

Revue [re'vy:], _f._ (—, _pl._ —n) revue; review; _— passieren lassen_, pass in review.

Rezensent [retsen'zɛnt], _m._ (—en, _pl._ —en) reviewer, critic.

rezensieren [retsɛn'zi:rən], _v.a._ review.

Rezept [re'tsɛpt], _n._ (—es, _pl._ —e) (_Med._) prescription; (_Cul._) recipe.

rezitieren [retsi'ti:rən], _v.a._ recite.

Rhabarber [ra'barbər], _m._ (—s, _no pl._) (_Bot._) rhubarb.

Rhein [raɪn], _m._ (—s, _no pl._) (River) Rhine.

Rhodesien [ro'de:zjən], _n._ Rhodesia.

Rhodus ['ro:dus], _n._ Rhodes.

Rhythmus ['rytmus], _m._ (—, _pl._ —men) rhythm.

Richtbeil ['rɪçtbaɪl], _n._ (—s, _pl._ —e) executioner's axe.

richten ['rɪçtən] _v.a., v.n._ direct, point at; prepare; _die Augen — auf_, fix o.'s eyes upon; _einen zugrunde —_, ruin s.o.; judge, try, pass sentence on, condemn. _—v.r. sich nach_ (_Dat._) _—_, be guided by.

Richter ['rɪçtər], _m._ (—s, _pl._ —) judge; justice.

richtig ['rɪçtɪç], _adj._ right, correct, exact, true; _nicht ganz — sein_, be not quite right in the head.

Richtlot ['rɪçtlo:t], *n.* (—s, *pl.* —e) plumb-line.

Richtschnur ['rɪçtʃnu:r], *f.* (—, *pl.* —en) plumb-line; (*fig.*) rule, precept.

Richtung ['rɪçtuŋ], *f.* (—, *pl.* —en) direction.

riechen ['ri:çən], *v.a., v.n. irr.* smell, scent, reek; *Lunte* —, smell a rat.

Riege ['ri:gə], *f.* (—, *pl.* —n) row, section.

Riegel ['ri:gəl], *m.* (—s, *pl.* —) bar, bolt; *ein* — *Schokolade*, a bar of chocolate.

Riemen ['ri:mən], *m.* (—s, *pl.* —) strap, thong; oar.

Ries [ri:s], *n.* (—es, *pl.* —e) (*paper*) ream.

Riese ['ri:zə], *m.* (—n, *pl.* —n) giant.

rieseln ['ri:zəln], *v.n.* murmur, babble, ripple, trickle; drizzle.

Riesenschlange ['ri:zənʃlaŋə], *f.* (—, *pl.* —n) anaconda.

Riff [rɪf], *n.* (—es, *pl.* —e) reef.

rigoros [rigo'ro:s], *adj.* strict, rigorous.

Rille ['rɪlə], *f.* (—, *pl.* —n) groove, small furrow; (*Archit.*) flute, chamfer.

Rind [rɪnt], *n.* (—es, *pl.* —er) ox, cow; (*pl.*) cattle, horned cattle, head of cattle.

Rinde ['rɪndə], *f.* (—, *pl.* —n) rind, bark, peel; (*bread*) crust.

Rinderbraten ['rɪndərbra:tən], *m.* (—s, *pl.* —) roast beef.

Rindfleisch ['rɪntflaɪʃ], *n.* (—es, *no pl.*) beef.

Rindvieh ['rɪntfi:], *n.* (—s, *no pl.*) cattle; (*fig.*) blockhead, ass.

Ring [rɪŋ], *m.* (—(e)s, *pl.* —e) ring; (*chain*) link; (*under the eye*) dark circle; (*Comm.*) syndicate, trust.

Ringelblume ['rɪŋəlblu:mə], *f.* (—, *pl.* —n) (*Bot.*) marigold.

ringeln ['rɪŋəln], *v.r. sich* —, curl.

ringen ['rɪŋən], *v.a. irr.* wring. — *v.n.* wrestle.

Ringer ['rɪŋər], *m.* (—s, *pl.* —) wrestler.

Ringmauer ['rɪŋmauər], *f.* (—, *pl.* —n) city *or* town wall.

rings [rɪŋs], *adv.* around.

ringsum(her) [rɪŋ'sum(he:r)], *adv.* round about.

Rinne ['rɪnə], *f.* (—, *pl.* —n) furrow, gutter; groove.

rinnen ['rɪnən], *v.n. irr.* (*aux,* sein) run, leak, drip.

Rinnsal ['rɪnza:l], *n.* (—s, *pl.* —e) channel, water-course.

Rinnstein ['rɪnʃtaɪn], *m.* (—s, *pl.* —e) gutter.

Rippe ['rɪpə], *f.* (—, *pl.* —n) rib.

Rippenfellentzündung ['rɪpənfɛlɛnttsynduŋ], *f.* (—, *pl.* —en) pleurisy.

Rippenspeer ['rɪpənʃpe:r], *m.* (—s, *pl.* —e) (*Casseler*) —, spare-rib, ribs of pork.

Rippenstoß ['rɪpənʃto:s], *m.* (—es, *pl.* —e) dig in the ribs, nudge.

Rips [rɪps], *m.* (—es, *no pl.*) rep.

Risiko ['ri:ziko], *n.* (—s, *pl.* —ken) risk.

riskant [rɪs'kant], *adj.* risky.

riskieren [rɪs'ki:rən], *v.a.* risk.

Riß [rɪs], *m.* (—sses, *pl.* —sse) rent, tear; sketch, design, plan.

rissig ['rɪsɪç], *adj.* cracked, torn.

Ritt [rɪt], *m.* (—(e)s, *pl.* —e) ride.

Ritter ['rɪtər], *m.* (—s, *pl.* —) knight; *einen zum* — *schlagen*, dub s.o. a knight.

ritterlich ['rɪtərlɪç], *adj.* knightly; (*fig.*) chivalrous, valiant, gallant.

Ritterschlag ['rɪtərʃla:k], *m.* (—(e)s, *pl.* —e) accolade.

Rittersporn ['rɪtərʃpɔrn], *m.* (—s, *pl.* —e) (*Bot.*) larkspur.

rittlings ['rɪtlɪŋs], *adv.* astride.

Rittmeister ['rɪtmaɪstər], *m.* (—s, *pl.* —) captain (of cavalry).

Ritus ['ri:tus], *m.* (—, *pl.* **Riten**) rite.

Ritz [rɪts], *m.* (—es, *pl.* —e) chink, fissure, cleft, crevice; (*glacier*) crevasse.

ritzen ['rɪtsən], *v.a.* scratch.

Rivale [ri'va:lə], *m.* (—n, *pl.* —n) rival.

Rivalität [rivali'tɛ:t], *f.* (—, *pl.* —en) rivalry.

Rizinusöl ['ri:tsinusø:l], *n.* (—s, *no pl.*) castor oil.

Robbe ['rɔbə], *f.* (—, *pl.* —n) (*Zool.*) seal.

Robe ['ro:bə], *f.* (—, *pl.* —n) dress, robe; gown.

röcheln ['ræçəln], *v.n.* rattle in o.'s throat.

rochieren [rɔ'xi:rən], *v.n.* (*Chess*) castle.

Rock [rɔk], *m.* (—(e)s, *pl.* —e) (*woman*) skirt; (*man*) coat.

rodeln ['ro:dəln], *v.n.* (*aux.* haben & sein) toboggan.

roden ['ro:dən], *v.a.* clear, weed, thin out (plants).

Rogen ['ro:gən], *m.* (—s, *no pl.*) (*fish*) roe, spawn.

Roggen ['rɔgən], *m.* (—s, *no pl.*) rye.

roh [ro:], *adj.* raw; rough, rude, coarse, crude; *ein* —*er Mensch*, a brute; (*in compounds*) rough-; preliminary, unrefined.

Rohbilanz ['ro:bilants], *f.* (—, *pl.* —en) trial balance.

Roheisen ['ro:aɪzən], *n.* (—s, *no pl.*) pig-iron.

Roheit ['ro:haɪt], *f.* (—, *pl.* —en) coarseness, rudeness, crudity.

Rohr [ro:r], *n.* (—es, *pl.* —e, —en) tube, pipe; reed, cane; (*gun*) barrel.

Rohrdommel ['ro:rdɔmǝl], *f.* (—, *pl.* —n) (*Orn.*) bittern.

Röhre ['rø:rə], *f.* (—, *pl.* —n) tube, pipe; (*Radio*) valve.

Röhricht ['rø:rɪçt], *n.* (—s, *pl.* —e) reeds.

Rohrpfeife ['ro:rpfaɪfə], *f.* (—, *pl.* —n) reed-pipe.

Rohrpost ['ro:rpɔst], *f.* (—, *no pl.*) pneumatic post.

Rohrzucker ['ro:rtsukər], *m.* (—s, *no pl.*) cane-sugar.

Rolladen [ˈrɔladən], *m.* (—s, *pl.* ⸚) sliding shutter, roller blind.

Rollbahn [ˈrɔlbaːn], *f.* (—, *pl.* —en) (*Aviat.*) runway, tarmac.

Rolle [ˈrɔlə], *f.* (—, *pl.* —n) reel, roll; pulley; (*Theat.*) part; rôle; (*laundry*) mangle.

rollen [ˈrɔlən], *v.a.* roll, reel; (*laundry*) mangle. — *v.n.* (*aux.* sein) roll (along); (*thunder*) roar, roll.

Roller [ˈrɔlər], *m.* (—s, *pl.* —) scooter.

Rollmops [ˈrɔlmɔps], *m.* (—es, *pl.* ⸚e) soused herring.

Rollschuh [ˈrɔlʃuː], *m.* (—s, *pl.* —e) roller-skate.

Rollstuhl [ˈrɔlʃtuːl], *m.* (—s, *pl.* ⸚e) wheel-chair, bath-chair.

Rolltreppe [ˈrɔltrɛpə], *f.* (—, *pl.* —n) escalator, moving staircase.

Rom [roːm], *n.* Rome.

Roman [roˈmaːn], *m.* (—s, *pl.* —e) novel.

romanisch [roˈmaːnɪʃ], *adj.* Romanesque.

Romanliteratur [roˈmaːnlitəratuːr], *f.* (—, *no pl.*) fiction.

Romanschriftsteller [roˈmaːnʃrɪftʃtelər], *m.* (—s, *pl.* —) novelist.

Römer [ˈrøːmər], *m.* (—s, *pl.* —) Roman; (*glass*) rummer.

Rondell [rɔnˈdɛl], *n.* (—s, *pl.* —e) circular flower-bed.

Röntgenstrahlen [ˈrœntgənʃtraːlən], *m. pl.* X-rays.

rosa [ˈroːzaː], *adj.* pink, rose-coloured.

Rose [ˈroːzə], *f.* (—, *pl.* —n) rose.

Rosenkranz [ˈroːzənkrants], *m.* (—es, *pl.* ⸚e) garland of roses; (*Eccl.*) rosary.

Rosenkreuzer [ˈroːzənkrɔytsər], *m.* (—s, *pl.* —) Rosicrucian.

Rosine [roˈziːnə], *f.* (—, *pl.* —n) sultana, raisin.

Rosmarin [ˈrɔsmariːn], *m.* (—s, *no pl.*) (*Bot.*) rosemary.

Roß [rɔs], *n.* (—sses, *pl.* —sse) horse, steed.

Roßbremse [ˈrɔsbrɛmzə], *f.* (—, *pl.* —n) (*Ent.*) horsefly, gadfly.

Rössel [ˈrøsəl], *n.* (—s, *pl.* —) (*Chess*) knight.

Roßhaarmatratze [ˈrɔshaːrmatrats], *f.* (—, *pl.* —n) hair-mattress.

Roßkastanie [ˈrɔskastaːnjə], *f.* (—, *pl.* —n) (*Bot.*) horse-chestnut.

Rost (1) [rɔst], *m.* (—es, *no pl.*) rust.

Rost (2) [rɔst], *m.* (—s, *pl.* —e) grate; gridiron.

Rostbraten [ˈrɔstbraːtən], *m.* (—s, *pl.* —) roast meat.

rosten [ˈrɔstən], *v.n.* go rusty; rust; *alte Liebe rostet nicht*, love that's old rusts not away.

rösten [ˈrøːstən], *v.a.* toast, roast, grill.

rot [roːt], *adj.* red; — *werden*, redden, blush.

Rotauge [ˈroːtaugə], *n.* (—s, *pl.* —n) (*Zool.*) roach.

Röte [ˈrøːtə], *f.* (—, *no pl.*) redness, red colour.

Röteln [ˈrøːtəln], *m. pl.* (*Med.*) German measles, rubella.

Rotfink [ˈroːtfɪŋk], *m.* (—en, *pl.* —en) (*Orn.*) bullfinch.

Rotfuchs [ˈroːtfuks], *m.* (—es, *pl.* ⸚e) (*Zool.*) sorrel horse.

rotieren [roˈtiːrən], *v.n.* rotate.

Rotkäppchen [ˈroːtkɛpçən], *n.* Little Red Riding Hood.

Rotkehlchen [ˈroːtkeːlçən], *n.* (—s, *pl.* —) robin.

Rotlauf [ˈroːtlauf], *m.* (—s, *no pl.*) (*Med.*) erysipelas.

Rotschimmel [ˈroːtʃɪməl], *m.* (—s, *pl.* —) roan-horse.

Rotspon [ˈroːtʃpoːn], *m.* (—s, *no pl.*) (*dial.*) claret.

Rotte [ˈrɔtə], *f.* (—, *pl.* —n) band, gang, rabble; (*Mil.*) file, squad.

Rotwild [ˈroːtvɪlt], *n.* (—s, *no pl.*) red deer.

Rotz [rɔts], *m.* (—es, *no pl.*) (*vulg.*) mucus; snot.

Rouleau [ruˈloː], *n.* (—s, *pl.* —s) sun-blind, roller-blind.

routiniert [rutiˈniːrt], *adj.* smart; experienced.

Rübe [ˈryːbə], *f.* (—, *pl.* —n) (*Bot.*) turnip; *rote* —, beetroot; *gelbe* —, carrot.

Rubel [ˈruːbəl], *m.* (—s, *pl.* —) rouble.

Rübenzucker [ˈryːbəntsukər], *m.* (—s, *no pl.*) beet-sugar.

Rubin [ruˈbiːn], *m.* (—s, *pl.* —e) ruby.

Rubrik [ruˈbriːk], *f.* (—, *pl.* —en) rubric; title, heading, category, column.

Rübsamen [ˈryːpzaːmən], *m.* (—s, *no pl.*) rape-seed.

ruchbar [ˈruːxbaːr], *adj.* manifest, known, notorious.

ruchlos [ˈruːxloːs], *adj.* wicked, profligate, vicious.

Ruck [ruk], *m.* (—(e)s, *pl.* —e) pull, jolt, jerk.

Rückblick [ˈrykblɪk], *m.* (—s, *pl.* —e) retrospect, retrospective view.

Rücken [ˈrykən], *m.* (—s, *pl.* —) back; (*mountains*) ridge; *einem den kehren*, turn o.'s back upon s.o.

rücken [ˈrykən], *v.a.* move, push. — *v.n.* move along.

Rückenmark [ˈrykənmark], *n.* (—s, *no pl.*) spinal marrow.

Rückenwirbel [ˈrykənvɪrbəl], *m.* (—s, *pl.* —) dorsal vertebra.

rückerstatten [ˈrykərʃtatən], *v.a.* refund.

Rückfahrkarte [ˈrykfaːrkartə], *f.* (—, *pl.* —n) return ticket.

Rückfall [ˈrykfal], *m.* (—s, *pl.* ⸚e) relapse.

rückgängig [ˈrykgɛŋɪç], *adj.* — *machen*, cancel, annul, reverse (a decision).

Rückgrat [ˈrykgraːt], *n.* (—s, *pl.* —e) backbone, spine.

Rückhalt [ˈrykhalt], *m.* (—s, *no pl.*) reserve; support, backing.

Rückkehr

Rückkehr ['rykke:r], *f.* (—, *no pl.*) return.

Rücklicht ['ryklıçt], *n.* (—s, *pl.* —er) (*Motor. etc.*) tail-light.

rücklings ['ryklıŋks], *adv.* from behind.

Rucksack ['rukzak], *m.* (—s, *pl.* ⁓e) rucksack; knapsack.

Rückschritt ['rykʃrıt], *m.* (—es, *pl.* —e) step backward, retrograde step, regression.

Rücksicht ['rykzıçt], *f.* (—, *pl.* —en) consideration, regard.

Rücksprache ['rykʃpra:xə], *f.* (—, *pl.* —n) conference, consultation; — *nehmen mit*, consult, confer with.

rückständig ['rykʃtɛndıç], *adj.* outstanding; old-fashioned; backward.

Rücktritt ['ryktrıt], *m.* (—s, *no pl.*) resignation.

ruckweise ['rukvaızə], *adv.* by fits and starts; jerkily.

Rückwirkung ['rykvırkuŋ], *f.* (—, *pl.* —en) reaction, retroaction.

Rüde ['ry:də], *m.* (—n, *pl.* —n) male (dog, fox etc.).

Rudel ['ru:dəl], *n.* (—s, *pl.* —) flock, herd, pack.

Ruder ['ru:dər], *n.* (—s, *pl.* —) oar, rudder, paddle; *am* — *sein*, be at the helm; (*Pol.*) be in power.

rudern ['ru:dərn], *v.a., v.n.* row.

Ruf [ru:f], *m.* (—(e)s, *pl.* —e) call; shout; reputation, renown; *einen guten* (*schlechten*) — *haben*, have a good (bad) reputation, be well (ill) spoken of.

rufen ['ru:fən], *v.a., v.n. irr.* call, shout; *einen* — *lassen*, send for s.o.

Rüffel ['ryfəl], *m.* (—s, *pl.* —) (*coll.*) reprimand; (*sl.*) rocket.

Rüge ['ry:gə], *f.* (—, *pl.* —n) censure, blame, reprimand.

Ruhe ['ru:ə], *f.* (—, *no pl.*) rest, repose; quiet, tranquillity; *sich zur* — *setzen*, retire (from business etc.).

Ruhegehalt ['ru:əgəhalt], *n.* (—es, *pl.* ⁓er) retirement pension, superannuation.

ruhen ['ru:ən], *v.n.* rest, repose, take a rest.

Ruhestand ['ru:əʃtant], *m.* (—es, *no pl.*) retirement.

ruhig ['ru:ıç], *adj.* quiet, tranquil, peaceful, calm; *sich* — *verhalten*, keep quiet.

Ruhm [ru:m], *m.* (—(e)s, *no pl.*) glory, fame, renown; *einem zum* — *gereichen*, be *or* redound to s.o.'s credit.

rühmen ['ry:mən], *v.a.* praise, extol, glorify. — *v.r. sich* —, boast.

Ruhr (1) [ru:r], *f.* (River) Ruhr.

Ruhr (2) [ru:r], *f.* (—, *no pl.*) dysentery.

Rührei ['ry:raı], *n.* (—s, *pl.* —er) scrambled egg.

rühren ['ry:rən], *v.a.* stir, move, touch. — *v.r. sich* —, move, stir; get a move on.

rührig ['ry:rıç], *adj.* active, alert.

rührselig ['ry:rze:lıç], *adj.* oversentimental; lachrymose.

Rührung ['ry:ruŋ], *f.* (—, *no pl.*) emotion.

Ruin [ru'i:n], *m.* (—s, *no pl.*) (*fig.*) ruin; decay; bankruptcy.

Ruine [ru'i:nə], *f.* (—, *pl.* —n) ruin(s).

rülpsen ['rylpsən], *v.n.* belch.

Rum [rum], *m.* (—s, *no pl.*) rum.

Rumänien [ru'mɛ:njən], *n.* Rumania.

Rummel ['ruməl], *m.* (—s, *no pl.*) tumult, row, hubbub.

Rumor [ru'mo:r], *m.* (—s, *no pl.*) noise; rumour.

rumoren [ru'mo:rən], *v.n.* make a noise.

Rumpelkammer ['rumpəlkamər], *f.* (—, *pl.* —n) lumber-room, junkroom.

rumpeln ['rumpəln], *v.n.* rumble.

Rumpf [rumpf], *m.* (—(e)s, *pl.* ⁓e) (*Anat.*) trunk; (*ship*) hull; (*Aviat.*) fuselage.

rümpfen ['rympfən], *v.a. die Nase* —, turn up o.'s nose.

rund [runt], *adj.* round, rotund; — *heraus*, flatly; *etwas* — *abschlagen*, refuse s.th. flatly; — *herum*, round about.

Runde ['rundə], *f.* (—, *pl.* —n) round; (*Sport*) round, bout; *die* — *machen*, (*watchman*) patrol.

Rundfunk ['runtfuŋk], *m.* (—s, *no pl.*) broadcasting, wireless; radio.

Rundgang ['runtgaŋ], *m.* (—s, *pl.* ⁓e) round, tour (of inspection).

rundlich ['runtlıç], *adj.* plump.

Rundschau ['runtʃau], *f.* (—, *no pl.*) panorama; review, survey.

Rundschreiben ['runtʃraıbən], *n.* (—s, *pl.* —) circular letter.

rundweg ['runtve:k], *adv.* flatly, plainly.

Rune ['ru:nə], *f.* (—, *pl.* —n) rune; runic writing.

Runkelrübe ['ruŋkəlry:bə], *f.* (—, *pl.* —n) beetroot.

Runzel ['runtsəl], *f.* (—, *pl.* —n) wrinkle, pucker.

Rüpel ['ry:pəl], *m.* (—s, *pl.* —) bounder, lout.

rupfen ['rupfən], *v.a.* pluck; *einen* —, (*fig.*) fleece s.o.

Rupie ['ru:pjə], *f.* (—, *pl.* —n) rupee.

ruppig ['rupıç], *adj.* unfriendly, rude; scruffy.

Ruprecht ['ru:prɛçt], *m. Knecht* —, Santa Claus.

Rüsche ['ry:ʃə], *f.* (—, *pl.* —n) ruche.

Ruß [ru:s], *m.* (—es, *no pl.*) soot.

Rüssel ['rysəl], *m.* (—s, *pl.* —) snout; (*elephant*) trunk.

Rußland ['ruslant], *n.* Russia.

rüsten ['rystən], *v.a.* prepare, fit (out); equip; (*Mil.*) arm, mobilise.

Rüster ['rystər], *f.* (—, *pl.* —n) elm.

rüstig ['rystıç], *adj.* vigorous, robust.

Rüstung ['rystuŋ], *f.* (—, *pl.* —en) armour; preparation; (*Mil.*) armament.

Rüstzeug ['rysttsɔyk], *n.* (—s, *no pl.*) equipment.
Rute ['ru:tə], *f.* (—, *pl.* —n) rod, twig; (*fox*) brush.
Rutengänger ['ru:təngeŋər], *m.* (—s, *pl.* —) water-diviner.
rutschen ['rutʃən], *v.n.* (*aux.* sein) slip, slide, skid, slither.
rütteln ['rytəln], *v.a.*, *v.n.* shake, jolt.

S

S [ɛs], *n.* (—s, *pl.* —s) the letter S.
Saal [za:l], *m.* (—(e)s, *pl.* **Säle**) hall, large room.
Saat [za:t], *f.* (—, *pl.* —en) seed; sowing; standing corn.
Sabbat ['zabat], *m.* (—s, *pl.* —e) sabbath.
sabbern ['zabərn], *v.n.* (*sl.*) slaver, drivel.
Säbel ['zɛ:bəl], *m.* (—s, *pl.* —) sabre; *krummer* —, falchion, scimitar.
säbeln ['zɛ:bəln], *v.a.* sabre, hack at.
sachdienlich ['zaxdi:nlɪç], *adj.* relevant, pertinent.
Sache ['zaxə], *f.* (—, *pl.* —n) thing, matter, affair; (*Law*) action, case; *die* — *ist* (*die*) *daß*, the fact is that; *das gehört nicht zur* —, that is beside the point; *bei der* — *sein*, pay attention to the matter in hand; *das ist meine* —, that is my business; *die* — *der Unterdrückten verteidigen*, take up the cause of the oppressed.
Sachlage ['zaxla:gə], *f.* (—, *no pl.*) state of affairs.
sachlich ['zaxlɪç], *adj.* pertinent; objective.
sächlich ['zɛçlɪç], *adj.* (*Gram.*) neuter.
Sachse ['zaksə], *m.* (—n, *pl.* —n) Saxon.
Sachsen ['zaksən], *n.* Saxony.
sachte ['zaxtə], *adj.* soft, slow, quiet, careful, gentle.
Sachverhalt ['zaxfɛrhalt], *m.* (—s, *no pl.*) facts (of a case), state of things, circumstances.
sachverständig ['zaxfɛrʃtɛndɪç], *adj.* expert, competent, experienced.
Sachwalter ['zaxvaltər], *m.* (—s, *pl.* —) manager, counsel, attorney.
Sack [zak], *m.* (—(e)s, *pl.* ⁀e) sack, bag; *mit* — *und Pack*, (with) bag and baggage.
Säckel ['zɛkəl], *m.* (—s, *pl.* —) purse.
Sackgasse ['zakgasə], *f.* (—, *pl.* —n) cul-de-sac, blind alley; *einen in eine* — *treiben*, corner s.o.
Sackpfeife ['zakpfaɪfə], *f.* (—, *pl.* —n) bagpipe.
Sacktuch ['zaktu:x], *n.* (—es, *pl.* ⁀er) sacking; (*dial.*) pocket-handkerchief.

säen ['zɛ:ən], *v.a.* sow.
Saffian ['zafja:n], *m.* (—s, *no pl.*) morocco-leather.
Saft [zaft], *m.* (—(e)s, *pl.* ⁀e) juice; (*tree*) sap; (*meat*) gravy; *ohne* — *und Kraft*, insipid; *im eigenen* — *schmoren*, stew in o.'s own juice.
Sage ['za:gə], *f.* (—, *pl.* —n) legend, fable, myth; *es geht die* —, it is rumoured.
Säge ['zɛ:gə], *f.* (—, *pl.* —n) saw.
sagen ['za:gən], *v.a.* say, tell; *einem etwas* — *lassen*, send word to s.o.; *es hat nichts zu* —, it does not matter; *was Du nicht sagst!* you don't say (so)!
sägen ['zɛ:gən], *v.a.*, *v.n.* saw; (*fig.*) snore.
sagenhaft ['za:gənhaft], *adj.* legendary, mythical; (*fig.*) fabulous.
Sahne ['za:nə], *f.* (—, *no pl.*) cream.
Saite ['zaɪtə], *f.* (—, *pl.* —n) string; *strengere* —*n aufziehen*, (*fig.*) take a stricter line.
Sakko ['zako], *m.* (—s, *pl.* —s) lounge jacket.
Sakristei [zakrɪ'staɪ], *f.* (—, *pl.* —en) vestry.
Salat [za'la:t], *m.* (—(e)s, *pl.* —e) salad; (*plant*) lettuce; (*sl.*) mess.
salbadern ['zalba:dərn], *v.n.* prate, talk nonsense.
Salbe ['zalbə], *f.* (—, *pl.* —n) ointment, salve.
Salbei ['zalbaɪ], *m.* (—s, *no pl.*) (*Bot.*) sage.
salben ['zalbən], *v.a.* anoint.
salbungsvoll ['zalbuŋsfɔl], *adj.* unctuous.
Saldo ['zaldo], *m.* (—s, *pl.* —s) balance.
Saline [za'li:nə], *f.* (—, *pl.* —n) salt-mine, salt-works.
Salkante ['za:lkantə], *f.* (—, *pl.* —n) selvedge, border.
Salm [zalm], *m.* (—s, *pl.* —e) (*Zool.*) salmon.
Salmiakgeist ['zalmjakgaɪst], *m.* (—s, *no pl.*) ammonia.
Salon [za'lɔ̃], *m.* (—s, *pl.* —s) salon; saloon; drawing-room.
salonfähig [za'lɔ̃fɛ:ɪç], *adj.* presentable, socially acceptable.
salopp [za'lɔp], *adj.* careless, slovenly, shabby, sloppy.
Salpeter [zal'pe:tər], *m.* (—s, *no pl.*) nitre, saltpetre.
salutieren [zalu'ti:rən], *v.a.*, *v.n.*, salute.
Salve ['zalvə], *f.* (—, *pl.* —n) volley, discharge, salute.
Salz [zalts], *n.* (—es, *pl.* —e) salt.
Salzfaß ['zaltsfas], *n.* (—sses, *pl.* ⁀sser) salt-cellar.
Salzlake ['zaltsla:kə], *f.* (—, *pl.* —n) brine.
Salzsäure ['zaltszɔyrə], *f.* (—, *no pl.*) hydrochloric acid.
Sämann ['zɛ:man], *m.* (—s, *pl.* ⁀ner) sower.
Sambia ['zambia], *n.* Zambia.

Same(n)

Same(n) ['za:mə(n)], *m.* (**—ns**, *pl.* **—n**) seed; sperm; spawn.

Samenstaub ['za:mənʃtaup], *m.* (**—s**, *no pl.*) pollen.

Sämereien [zɛ:mə'raɪən], *f. pl.* seeds, grain.

sämisch ['zɛ:mɪʃ], *adj.* chamois.

Sammelband ['zaməlbant], *m.* (**—es**, *pl.* ⁈e) miscellany, anthology.

sammeln ['zaməln], *v.a.* collect, gather. — *v.r.* **sich** —, meet; collect o.'s thoughts, compose o.s.

Sammler ['zamlər], *m.* (**—s**, *pl.* **—**) collector; accumulator.

Samstag ['zamsta:k], *m.* (**—s**, *pl.* **—e**) Saturday.

Samt [zamt], *m.* (**—(e)s**, *pl.* **—e**) velvet.

samt [zamt], *adv.* together, all together; — *und sonders*, jointly and severally.— *prep.* (*Dat.*) together with.

sämtlich ['zɛmtlɪç], *adj.* each and every.

Sand [zant], *m.* (**—es**, *no pl.*) sand; *feiner* —, grit; *grober* —, gravel.

Sandtorte ['zanttɔrtə], *f.* (**—**, *pl.* **—n**) sponge-cake, madeira-cake.

Sanduhr ['zantu:r], *f.* (**—**, *pl.* **—en**) hourglass.

sanft [zanft], *adj.* soft, gentle.

Sänfte ['zɛnftə], *f.* (**—**, *pl.* **—n**) sedanchair.

Sang [zaŋ], *m.* (**—es**, *pl.* **Gesänge**) song; *ohne* — *und Klang*, (*fig.*) unostentatiously, without fuss, without ceremony.

sanieren [za'ni:rən], *v.a.* cure; (*company*) reconstruct, put on a sound financial basis.

sanitär [zani'tɛ:r], *adj.* sanitary.

Sanitäter [zani'tɛ:tər], *m.* (**—s**, *pl.*—) medical orderly; ambulance man.

Sankt [zaŋkt], *indecl. adj.* Saint; (*abbr.*) St.

sanktionieren [zaŋktsjo'ni:rən], *v.a.* sanction.

Sansibar ['zanziba:r], *n.* Zanzibar.

Sardelle [zar'dɛlə], *f.* (**—**, *pl.* **—n**) (*Zool.*) anchovy.

Sardinien [zar'di:njən], *n.* Sardinia.

Sarg [zark], *m.* (**—es**, *pl.* ⁈e) coffin.

sarkastisch [zar'kastɪʃ], *adj.* sarcastic.

Satellit [zatə'li:t], *m.* (**—en**, *pl.* **—en**) satellite.

Satiriker [za'ti:rɪkər], *m.* (**—s**, *pl.* **—**) satirist.

satt [zat], *adj.* sated, satiated, satisfied; (*colours*) deep, rich; *sich* — *essen*, eat o.'s fill; *einer Sache* — *sein*, be sick of s.th., have had enough of s.th.

Sattel ['zatəl], *m.* (**—s**, *pl.* ⁈) saddle; *einen aus dem* — *heben*, (*fig.*) oust s.o.; *fest im* — *sitzen*, (*fig.*) be master of a situation; *in allen ⁈n gerecht*, versatile.

satteln ['zatəln], *v.a.* saddle.

Sattheit ['zathaɪt], *f.* (**—**, *no pl.*) satiety.

sättigen ['zɛtɪgən], *v.a.* satisfy, sate, satiate; (*Chem.*) saturate.

sattsam ['zatza:m], *adv.* enough, sufficiently.

saturieren [zatu'ri:rən], *v.a.* (*Chem.*) saturate.

Satz [zats], *m.* (**—es**, *pl.* ⁈e) sentence; proposition; thesis; (*Mus.*) movement; (*Typ.*) composition; (*dregs*) sediment; (*gambling*) stake; *mit einem* —, with one leap (*or* jump *or* bound).

Satzbildung ['zatsbɪlduŋ], *f.* (**—**, *pl.* **—en**) (*Gram.*) construction; (*Chem.*) sedimentation.

Satzlehre ['zatsle:rə], *f.* (**—**, *no pl.*) syntax.

Satzung ['zatsuŋ], *f.* (**—**, *pl.* **—en**) statute.

Satzzeichen ['zatstsaɪçən], *n.* (**—s**, *pl.* **—**) punctuation-mark.

Sau [zau], *f.* (**—**, *pl.* ⁈e) sow; (*vulg.*) dirty person, slut.

sauber ['zaubər], *adj.* clean, neat, tidy.

säubern ['zɔybərn], *v.a.* clean, cleanse; (*fig.*) purge.

Saubohne ['zaubo:nə], *f.* (**—**, *pl.* **—n**) broad bean.

Saudiarabien ['zaudiara:bjən], *n.* Saudi Arabia.

sauer ['zauər], *adj.* sour, acid; (*fig.*) troublesome; morose.

Sauerbrunnen ['zauərbrunən], *m.* (**—s**, *pl.* **—**) mineral water.

Sauerei [zauə'raɪ], *f.* (**—**, *pl.* **—en**) (*sl.*) filthiness; mess.

Sauerkraut ['zauərkraut], *n.* (**—s**, *no pl.*) pickled cabbage.

säuerlich ['zɔyərlɪç], *adj.* acidulous.

Sauerstoff ['zauərʃtɔf], *m.* (**—(e)s**, *no pl.*) oxygen.

Sauerteig ['zauərtaɪk], *m.* (**—(e)s**, *pl.* **—e**) leaven.

sauertöpfisch ['zauərtœpfɪʃ], *adj.* morose, peevish.

saufen ['zaufən], *v.a.*, *v.n. irr.* (*animals*) drink; (*humans*) drink to excess.

Säufer ['zɔyfər], *m.* (**—s**, *pl.* **—**) drunkard, drinker, alcoholic.

saugen ['zaugən], *v.a.*, *v.n.* suck.

säugen ['zɔygən], *v.a.* suckle.

Säugetier ['zɔygəti:r], *n.* (**—s**, *pl.* **—e**) mammal.

Saugheber ['zaukhe:bər], *m.* (**—s**, *pl.* **—**) suction-pump; siphon.

Säugling ['zɔyklɪŋ], *m.* (**—s**, *pl.* **—e**) suckling, baby.

Saugwarze ['zaukvartsə], *f.* (**—**, *pl.* **—n**) nipple.

Säule ['zɔylə], *f.* (**—**, *pl.* **—n**) pillar, column.

Säulenbündel ['zɔylənbyndəl], *n.* (**—s**, *pl.* **—**) (*Archit.*) clustered column.

Säulenfuß ['zɔylənfu:s], *m.* (**—es**, *pl.* ⁈e) (*Archit.*) base, plinth.

Säulengang ['zɔyləngaŋ], *m.* (**—s**, *pl.* ⁈e) colonnade.

Saum [zaum], *m.* (**—(e)s**, *pl.* ⁈e) seam, hem, border, edge; selvedge.

saumäßig ['zaumɛ:sɪç], *adj.* (*sl.*) beastly, filthy, piggish; enormous.

säumen (1) ['zɔymən], *v.a.* hem.

säumen (2) ['zɔymən], *v.n.* delay, tarry.

säumig ['zɔymɪç], *adj.* tardy, slow, dilatory.

Saumpferd [ˈzaumpfeːrt], *n.* (—s, *pl.* —e) pack-horse.

saumselig [ˈzaumzeːlɪç], *adj.* tardy, dilatory.

Säure [ˈzɔyrə], *f.* (—, *pl.* —n) acid; (*Med.*) acidity.

Saurier [ˈzaurjər], *m.* (—s, *pl.* —) saurian.

Saus [zaus], *m.* (—es, *no pl.*) rush; revel, riot; *in — und Braus leben,* live a wild life, live riotously.

säuseln [ˈzɔyzəln], *v.n.* rustle, murmur.

sausen [ˈzauzən], *v.n.* bluster, blow, howl, whistle; (*coll.*) rush, dash.

Saustall [ˈzauʃtal], *m.* (—s, *pl.* ˙e) pigsty.

Schabe [ˈʃaːbə], *f.* (—, *pl.* —n) (*Ent.*) cockroach.

schaben [ˈʃaːbən], *v.a.* scrape, shave, rub.

Schabernack [ˈʃaːbərnak], *m.* (—s, *pl.* —e) practical joke, trick.

schäbig [ˈʃeːbɪç], *adj.* shabby.

Schablone [ʃaˈbloːnə], *f.* (—, *pl.* —n) model, mould, pattern, stencil; (*fig.*) routine.

Schach [ʃax], *n.* (—(e)s, *no pl.*) chess; — *bieten,* check; — *spielen,* play chess; *in — halten,* keep in check.

Schacher [ˈʃaxər], *m.* (—s, *no pl.*) haggling, bargaining, barter.

Schächer [ˈʃeçər], *m.* (—s, *pl.* —) wretch, felon, robber.

Schacht [ʃaxt], *m.* (—(e)s, *pl.* ˙e) shaft.

Schachtel [ˈʃaxtəl], *f.* (—, *pl.* —n) box, (cardboard) box, (small) case.

Schachtelhalm [ˈʃaxtəlhalm], *m.* (—s, *pl.* —e) (*grass*) horse-tail.

Schächter [ˈʃeçtər], *m.* (—s, *pl.* —) (kosher) butcher.

schade [ˈʃaːdə], *int.* a pity, a shame, unfortunate; *wie* —, what a pity; *sehr* —, a great pity.

Schädel [ˈʃeːdəl], *m.* (—s, *pl.* —) skull.

Schaden [ˈʃaːdən], *m.* (—s, *pl.* ˙) damage, injury, detriment; *zu — kommen,* come to grief.

schaden [ˈʃaːdən], *v.n.* do harm, do damage, do injury; *es schadet nichts,* it does not matter.

Schadenersatz [ˈʃaːdənerzats], *m.* (—es, *no pl.*) indemnity, compensation, indemnification; (*money*) damages.

Schadenfreude [ˈʃaːdənfrɔydə], *f.* (—, *no pl.*) malicious pleasure.

Schadensforderung [ˈʃaːdənsfordəruŋ], *f.* (—, *pl.* —en) claim (for damages).

schadhaft [ˈʃaːthaft], *adj.* defective, faulty.

schädlich [ˈʃeːtlɪç], *adj.* injurious, noxious, pernicious, noisome.

schadlos [ˈʃaːtloːs], *adj.* indemnified; *einen — halten,* indemnify s.o., compensate s.o.; *sich an einem — halten,* recoup o.s. from s.o.

Schadlosigkeit [ˈʃaːtloːzɪçkaɪt], *f.* (—, *no pl.*) harmlessness.

Schaf [ʃaːf], *n.* (—(e)s, *pl.* —e) sheep.

Schafblattern [ˈʃaːfblatərn], *f. pl.* (*Med.*) chicken-pox.

Schafdarm [ˈʃaːfdarm], *m.* (—s, *pl.* ˙e) sheep-gut.

Schäfer [ˈʃeːfər], *m.* (—s, *pl.* —) shepherd.

Schäferstündchen [ˈʃeːfərʃtyntçən], *n.* (—s, *pl.* —) tryst; rendezvous.

schaffen [ˈʃafən], *v.a.,* *v.n. irr.* make, produce, create. — *v.a. reg.* provide; manage; *aus dem Wege* —, remove. — *v.n. reg.* work; *einem zu — machen,* give s.o. trouble.

Schaffner [ˈʃafnər], *m.* (—s, *pl.* —) (*Railw. etc.*) guard, conductor.

Schafgarbe [ˈʃaːfgarbə], *f.* (—, *pl.* —n) (*Bot.*) common yarrow.

Schafhürde [ˈʃaːfhyrdə], *f.* (—, *pl.* —n) sheep-fold.

Schafott [ʃaˈfɔt], *n.* (—(e)s, *pl.* —e) scaffold.

Schafschur [ˈʃaːfʃuːr], *f.* (—, *pl.* —en) sheep-shearing.

Schaft [ʃaft], *m.* (—(e)s, *pl.* ˙e) shaft; (*gun*) stock.

Schafwolle [ˈʃaːfvɔlə], *f.* (—, *no pl.*) sheep's wool, fleece.

Schakal [ʃaˈkaːl], *m.* (—s, *pl.* —e) (*Zool.*) jackal.

Schäkerei [ʃeːkəˈraɪ], *f.* (—, *pl.* —en) playfulness, teasing, dalliance, flirtation.

Schal [ʃaːl], *m.* (—s, *pl.* —e) scarf, shawl.

schal [ʃaːl], *adj.* stale, flat, insipid.

Schale [ˈʃaːlə], *f.* (—, *pl.* —n) (*nut, egg*) shell; (*fruit*) peel, rind; dish, bowl; (*Austr.*) cup; (*fig.*) outside.

schälen [ˈʃeːlən], *v.a.* shell; peel.

Schalk [ʃalk], *m.* (—(e)s, *pl.* —e) knave, rogue; wag, joker.

Schall [ʃal], *m.* (—(e)s, *no pl.*) sound.

Schallbecken [ˈʃalbekən], *n.* (—s, *pl.* —) cymbal.

Schallehre [ˈʃaleːrə], *f.* (—, *no pl.*) acoustics.

schallen [ˈʃalən], *v.n.* sound, reverberate.

Schalmei [ʃalˈmaɪ], *f.* (—, *pl.* —en) (*Poet., Mus.*) shawm.

Schallplatte [ˈʃalplatə], *f.* (—, *pl.* —n) (gramophone) record.

schalten [ˈʃaltən], *v.n.* rule; switch; (*Motor.*) change gear; — *und walten,* manage.

Schalter [ˈʃaltər], *m.* (—s, *pl.* —) (*Elec.*) switch; booking-office; counter.

Schalthebel [ˈʃalthebəl], *m.* (—s, *pl.* —). (*Motor.*) gear lever.

Schaltier [ˈʃaltiːr], *n.* (—s, *pl.* —e) (*Zool.*) crustacean.

Schaltjahr [ˈʃaltjaːr], *n.* (—s, *pl.* —e) leap year.

Schalttafel [ˈʃalttafəl], *f.* (—, *pl.* —n) switch-board.

Scham [ʃaːm], *f.* (—, *no pl.*) shame, modesty; private parts.

schämen [ˈʃeːmən], *v.r. sich* —, be ashamed (of).

schamlos [ˈʃaːmloːs], *adj.* shameless.

schamrot [ˈʃaːmroːt], *adj.* blushing; — *werden,* blush.

schandbar [ˈʃantbaːr], *adj.* ignominious, infamous.

Schande [ˈʃandə], *f.* (—, *no pl.*) shame, disgrace; dishonour, ignominy.

schänden [ˈʃɛndən], *v.a.* dishonour, disgrace; violate, ravish.

Schandfleck [ˈʃantflɛk], *m.* (—s, *pl.* —e) stain, blemish.

schändlich [ˈʃɛntliç], *adj.* shameful, disgraceful, infamous.

Schändung [ˈʃɛnduŋ], *f.* (—, *pl.* —en) violation.

Schank [ʃaŋk], *m.* (—s, *no pl.*) sale of liquor.

Schanzarbeiter [ˈʃantsarbaɪtər], *m.* (—s, *pl.* —) sapper.

Schanze [ˈʃantsə], *f.* (—, *pl.* —n) redoubt, bulwark; *in die — schlagen*, risk, venture.

Schar [ʃaːr], *f.* (—, *pl.* —en) troop, band; host.

Scharade [ʃaˈraːdə], *f.* (—, *pl.* —n) charade.

scharen [ˈʃaːrən], *v.r. sich — um*, assemble, congregate, gather round.

Schären [ˈʃɛːrən], *f. pl.* reefs, skerries.

scharf [ʃarf], *adj.* sharp, keen, acute, acrid, pungent; piercing; (*fig.*) severe, rigorous.

Schärfe [ˈʃɛrfə], *f.* (—, *no pl.*) sharpness, keenness, acuteness; pungency, acridness; severity, rigour.

schärfen [ˈʃɛrfən], *v.a.* sharpen, whet; (*fig.*) strengthen, intensify.

Scharfrichter [ˈʃarfriçtər], *m.* (—s, *pl.* —) executioner.

scharfsichtig [ˈʃarfziçtiç], *adj.* sharp-eyed, (*fig.*) penetrating, astute.

scharfsinnig [ˈʃarfzɪniç], *adj.* clear-sighted, sagacious, ingenious.

Scharlach [ˈʃarlax], *m.* (—s, *no pl.*) scarlet; (*Med.*) scarlet-fever.

Scharlatan [ˈʃarlataːn], *m.* (—s, *pl.* —e) charlatan, humbug.

scharmant [ʃarˈmant], *adj.* charming.

Scharmützel [ʃarˈmytsəl], *n.* (—s, *pl.* —) skirmish.

Scharnier [ʃarˈniːr], *n.* (—s, *pl.* —e) hinge, joint.

Schärpe [ˈʃɛrpə], *f.* (—, *pl.* —n) sash.

Scharpie [ʃarˈpiː], *f.* (—, *no pl.*) lint.

scharren [ˈʃarən], *v.a.*, *v.n.* scrape, rake.

Scharte [ˈʃartə], *f.* (—, *pl.* —n) notch, crack; *eine — auswetzen*, repair a mistake, make up for s.th.

Scharteke [ʃarˈteːkə], *f.* (—, *pl.* —n) worthless book, trash; *eine alte —*, an old fuddy-duddy, frump.

scharwenzeln [ʃarˈvɛntsəln], *v.n.* dance attendance, be obsequious.

Schatten [ˈʃatən], *m.* (—s, *pl.* —) shade, shadow.

Schattenbild [ˈʃatənbɪlt], *n.* (—s, *pl.* —er) silhouette.

Schattenriß [ˈʃatənrɪs], *m.* (—sses, *pl.* —sse) silhouette.

schattieren [ʃaˈtiːrən], *v.a.* shade (drawing).

schattig [ˈʃatiç], *adj.* shady.

Schatulle [ʃaˈtulə], *f.* (—, *pl.* —n) cash-box; privy purse.

Schatz [ʃats], *m.* (—es, *pl* ¨e)¹ treasure; (*fig.*) sweetheart, darling.

Schatzamt [ˈʃatsamt], *n.* (—s, *pl.* ¨er) Treasury, Exchequer.

schätzbar [ˈʃɛtsbaːr], *adj.* estimable.

Schätzchen [ˈʃɛtsçən], *n.* (—s, *pl.* —) (*coll.*) sweetheart.

schätzen [ˈʃɛtsən], *v.a.* value, estimate; esteem; reckon at.

Schatzkammer [ˈʃatskamər], *f.* (—, *pl.* —n) treasury.

Schatzmeister [ˈʃatsmaɪstər], *m.* (—s, *pl.* —) treasurer.

Schätzung [ˈʃɛtsuŋ], *f.* (—, *pl.* —en) valuation, estimate; (*fig.*) esteem.

Schau [ʃau], *f.* (—, *pl.* —en) show, view, spectacle; *zur — stellen*, display; parade.

Schauder [ˈʃaudər], *m.* (—s, *pl.* —) shudder, shiver; horror.

schaudern [ˈʃaudərn], *v.n.* shudder, shiver.

schauen [ˈʃauən], *v.a.* see, view. — *v.n.* look, gaze (*auf*, at), *schau mal*, look here.

Schauer [ˈʃauər], *m.* (—s, *pl.* —) shiver, paroxysm; (*fig.*) thrill, awe; (*rain*) shower.

schauern [ˈʃauərn], *v.n.* shudder, shiver; (*rain*) shower.

Schauerroman [ˈʃauərromaːn], *m.* (—s, *pl.* —e) (*novel*) penny dreadful, thriller.

Schaufel [ˈʃaufəl], *f.* (—, *pl.* —n) shovel.

Schaufenster [ˈʃaufɛnstər], *n.* (—s, *pl.* —) shop-window.

Schaukel [ˈʃaukəl], *f.* (—, *pl.* —n) swing.

schaulustig [ˈʃaulustiç], *adj.* curious.

Schaum [ʃaum], *m.* (—es, *pl.* ¨e) foam, froth; bubbles; scum; *— schlagen*, whip cream.

schäumen [ˈʃɔymən], *v.n.* foam, froth, sparkle.

Schauplatz [ˈʃauplats], *m.* (—es, *pl.* ¨e) scene, stage.

schaurig [ˈʃauriç], *adj.* grisly, horrid, horrible.

Schauspiel [ˈʃauʃpiːl], *n.* (—s, *pl.* —e) spectacle; drama, play.

Schauspieler [ˈʃauʃpiːlər], *m.* (—s, *pl.* —) actor, player.

Schaustellung [ˈʃauʃtɛluŋ], *f.* (—, *pl.* —en) exhibition.

Scheck [ʃɛk], *m.* (—s, *pl.* —s) cheque.

scheckig [ˈʃɛkiç], *adj.* piebald, spotted, dappled.

scheel [ʃeːl], *adj.* squint-eyed; envious; *einen — ansehen*, look askance at s.o.

Scheffel [ˈʃɛfəl], *m.* (—s, *pl.* —) bushel.

scheffeln [ˈʃɛfəln], *v.a.* rake in; accumulate.

Scheibe [ˈʃaɪbə], *f.* (—, *pl.* —n) disc; (*window*) pane; (*shooting*) target; (*bread*) slice.

Scheibenhonig [ˈʃaɪbənhoːniç], *m.* (—s, *no pl.*) honey in the comb.

Scheibenschießen [ˈʃaɪbənʃiːsən], *n.* (—s, *no pl.*) target-practice.

Scheich [ʃaɪç], *m.* (—s, *pl.* —e) sheikh.

Scheide [ˈʃaɪdə], *f.* (—, *pl.* —n) sheath, scabbard; (*Anat.*) vagina.

Scheidemünze [ˈʃaɪdəmyntsə], *f.* (—, *pl.* —n) small coin, change.

scheiden [ˈʃaɪdən], *v.a. irr.* divide; separate, divorce; *sich — lassen*, obtain a divorce. — *v.n.* (*aux.* sein) part, depart; *aus dem Amte —*, resign office.

Scheidewand [ˈʃaɪdəvant], *f.* (—, *pl.* ⸚e) partition-wall.

Scheideweg [ˈʃaɪdəveːk], *m.* (—s, *pl.* —e) cross-roads; *am — stehen*, be at the parting of the ways.

Scheidung [ˈʃaɪduŋ], *f.* (—, *pl.* —en) divorce.

Schein [ʃaɪn], *m.* (—(e)s, *no pl.*) shine, sheen, lustre, splendour; semblance, pretence; *den — wahren*, keep up appearances; *der — trügt*, appearances are deceptive; (*in compounds*) mock, would-be, apparent; (*pl.* —e) (piece of) paper, chit, note; (*fig.*) attestation, certificate.

scheinbar [ˈʃaɪnbaːr], *adj.* apparent; ostensible, seeming. — *adv.* seemingly.

scheinen [ˈʃaɪnən], *v.n. irr.* shine, sparkle; seem, appear.

scheinheilig [ˈʃaɪnhaɪlɪç], *adj.* hypocritical.

Scheinheiligkeit [ˈʃaɪnhaɪlɪçkaɪt], *f.* (—, *no pl.*) hypocrisy.

scheintot [ˈʃaɪntoːt], *adj.* in a cataleptic trance; seemingly dead.

Scheinwerfer [ˈʃaɪnverfər], *m.* (—s, *pl.* —) headlight; searchlight; floodlight.

Scheit [ʃaɪt], *n.* (—(e)s, *pl.* —e) piece of wood, billet.

Scheitel [ˈʃaɪtəl], *m.* (—s, *pl.* —) (*hair*) parting; top, vertex.

Scheiterhaufen [ˈʃaɪtərhaufən], *m.* (—s, *pl.* —) stake; funeral pyre.

scheitern [ˈʃaɪtərn], *v.n.* (*aux.* sein) (*ship*) founder, be wrecked; (*fig.*) miscarry, fail.

Schelle [ˈʃɛlə], *f.* (—, *pl.* —n) bell.

Schellen [ˈʃɛlən], *f. pl.* (*Cards*) diamonds.

schellen [ˈʃɛlən], *v.n.* ring the bell.

Schellfisch [ˈʃɛlfɪʃ], *m.* (—es, *pl.* —e) (*Zool.*) haddock.

Schelm [ʃɛlm], *m.* (—(e)s, *pl.* —e) rogue, knave, villain.

schelten [ˈʃɛltən], *v.a. irr.* scold, chide, rebuke, reprimand.

Schema [ˈʃeːma], *n.* (—s, *pl.* —s) schedule, model, plan, scheme.

Schemel [ˈʃeːməl], *m.* (—s, *pl.* —) foot-stool.

Schenk [ʃɛŋk], *m.* (—en, *pl.* —en) cupbearer; publican.

Schenke [ˈʃɛŋkə], *f.* (—, *pl.* —n) ale-house, tavern, pub.

Schenkel [ˈʃɛŋkəl], *m.* (—s, *pl.* —) thigh; (*Geom.*) side of triangle.

schenken [ˈʃɛŋkən], *v.a.* present s.o. with, donate, give.

Schenkstube [ˈʃɛŋkʃtuːbə], *f.* (—, *pl.* —n) tap-room.

Scherbe [ˈʃɛrbə], *f.* (—, *pl.* —n) potsherd; fragment of glass etc.

Schere [ˈʃeːrə], *f.* (—, *pl.* —n) scissors; (*garden*) shears; (*crab*) claw.

scheren [ˈʃeːrən], *v.a.* shave; clip, shear; bother, concern. — *v.r. sich —*, clear off; *scher dich zum Teufel!* go to blazes!

Scherereien [ʃeːrəˈraɪən], *f. pl.* vexation, bother, trouble.

Scherflein [ˈʃɛrflaɪn], *n.* (—s, *pl.* —) mite; *sein — beitragen*, contribute o.'s share.

Scherge [ˈʃɛrɡə], *m.* (—n, *pl.* —n) (*obs.*) beadle.

Scherz [ʃɛrts], *m.* (—es, *pl.* —e) jest, joke; *— beiseite*, joking apart.

scheu [ʃɔy], *adj.* shy, bashful, timid; skittish.

scheuchen [ˈʃɔyçən], *v.a.* scare away.

scheuen [ˈʃɔyən], *v.a.* shun, avoid, fight shy of, fear. — *v.n.* take fright.

Scheuer [ˈʃɔyər], *f.* (—, *pl.* —n) barn.

scheuern [ˈʃɔyərn], *v.a.* scour, scrub.

Scheuklappe [ˈʃɔyklapə], *f.* (—, *pl.* —n) blinker.

Scheune [ˈʃɔynə], *f.* (—, *pl.* —n) barn.

Scheusal [ˈʃɔyzaːl], *n.* (—s, *pl.* —e) monster.

scheußlich [ˈʃɔyslɪç], *adj.* frightful, dreadful, abominable, hideous.

Schicht [ʃɪçt], *f.* (—, *pl.* —en) layer, stratum, seam; (*society*) class; (*work*) shift.

schick [ʃɪk], *adj.* stylish, chic.

schicken [ˈʃɪkən], *v.a.* send, despatch, convey. — *v.r. sich —*, be proper; *sich in etwas —*, put up with s.th., resign o.s. to s.th.

schicklich [ˈʃɪklɪç], *adj.* proper, becoming, suitable, seemly.

Schicksal [ˈʃɪkzaːl], *n.* (—s, *pl.* —e) fate, destiny, lot.

Schickung [ˈʃɪkuŋ], *f.* (—, *pl.* —en) Divine Will, Providence.

schieben [ˈʃiːbən], *v.a. irr.* shove, push; *die Schuld auf einen —*, put the blame on s.o.

Schieber [ˈʃiːbər], *m.* (—s, *pl.* —) bolt, slide; (*fig.*) profiteer, spiv.

Schiedsgericht [ˈʃiːtsɡərɪçt], *n.* (—es, *pl.* —e) arbitration tribunal.

Schiedsrichter [ˈʃiːtsrɪçtər], *m.* (—s, *pl.* —) referee, umpire, arbiter.

schief [ʃiːf], *adj.* slanting, oblique, bent, crooked; wry; *—e Ebene*, inclined plane; *— gehen*, go wrong.

Schiefe [ˈʃiːfə], *f.* (—, *no pl.*) obliquity.

Schiefer [ˈʃiːfər], *m.* (—s, *no pl.*) slate.

schiefrig [ˈʃiːfrɪç], *adj.* slaty.

schielen [ˈʃiːlən], *v.n.* squint, be cross-eyed.

Schienbein [ˈʃiːnbaɪn], *n.* (—s, *pl.* —e) shin-bone, shin.

Schiene

Schiene ['ʃiːnə], *f.* (—, *pl.* —n) rail; (*Med.*) splint.

schier [ʃiːr], *adj.* (*rare*) sheer, pure. — *adv.* almost, very nearly.

Schierling ['ʃiːrlɪŋ], *m.* (—s, *pl.* —e) (*Bot.*) hemlock.

schießen ['ʃiːsən], *v.a., v.n. irr.* shoot, fire, discharge; (*fig.*) rush; *etwas — lassen,* let go of s.th.; *die Zügel — lassen,* loosen o.'s hold on the reins; *ein Kabel — lassen,* pay out a cable; *das ist zum —,* that's very funny.

Schiff [ʃɪf], *n.* (—(e)s, *pl.* —e) ship, vessel, boat; (*church*) nave.

schiffbar ['ʃɪfbaːr], *adj.* navigable.

Schiffbruch ['ʃɪfbrux], *m.* (—s, *pl* —e) shipwreck.

Schiffbrücke ['ʃɪfbrykə], *f.* (—, *pl.* —n) pontoon-bridge.

schiffen ['ʃɪfən], *v.n.* sail; navigate.

Schiffsboden ['ʃɪfsboːdən], *m.* (—s, *pl.* ⸚) (ship's) hold.

Schiffsmaat ['ʃɪfsmaːt], *m.* (—s, *pl.* —e) shipmate.

Schiffsrumpf ['ʃɪfsrumpf], *m.* (—es, *pl.* ⸚e) hull.

Schiffsschnabel ['ʃɪfsʃnaːbəl], *m.* (—s, *pl.* ⸚) prow, bows.

Schiffsvorderteil ['ʃɪfsfɔrdərtaɪl], *n.* (—s, *pl.* —e) forecastle, prow.

Schiffszwieback ['ʃɪfstsviːbak], *m.* (—s, *no pl.*) ship's biscuit.

Schikane [ʃiˈkaːnə], *f.* (—, *pl.* —n) chicanery.

Schild (1) [ʃɪlt], *m.* (—(e)s, *pl.* —e) shield, buckler, escutcheon; *etwas im — führen,* have designs on s.th., plan s.th.

Schild (2) [ʃɪlt], *n.* (—s, *pl.* —er) signboard, plate.

Schilderhaus ['ʃɪldərhaus], *n.* (—es, *pl.* ⸚er) sentry-box.

Schildermaler ['ʃɪldərmaːlər], *m.* (—s, *pl.* —) sign-painter.

schildern ['ʃɪldərn], *v.a.* describe, depict.

Schildknappe ['ʃɪltknapə], *m.* (—n, *pl.* —n) shield-bearer, squire.

Schildkrot ['ʃɪltkroːt], *n.* (—s, *no pl.*) tortoise-shell.

Schildkröte ['ʃɪltkrøːtə], *f.* (—, *pl.* —n) (*Zool.*) turtle, tortoise.

Schildpatt ['ʃɪltpat], *n.* (—s, *no pl.*) tortoise-shell.

Schildwache ['ʃɪltvaxə], *f.* (—, *pl.* —n) sentinel, sentry; — *stehen,* be on sentry duty, stand guard.

Schilf(rohr) ['ʃɪlf(roːr)], *n.* (—(e)s, *no pl.*) (*Bot.*) reed, rush, sedge.

schillern ['ʃɪlərn], *v.n.* opalesce, glitter, change colour, be iridescent.

Schilling ['ʃɪlɪŋ], *m.* (—s, *pl.* —e) Austrian coin; shilling.

Schimmel (1) ['ʃɪməl], *m.* (—s, *pl.* —) white horse.

Schimmel (2) ['ʃɪməl], *m.* (—s, *no pl.*) mould, mustiness.

schimmeln ['ʃɪməln], *v.n.* (*aux.* sein) go mouldy, moulder.

Schimmer ['ʃɪmər], *m.* (—s, *pl.* —) glitter, gleam; *ich habe keinen —,* I haven't a clue.

schimmlig ['ʃɪmlɪç], *adj.* mouldy, musty, mildewed.

Schimpanse [ʃɪmˈpanzə], *m.* (—n, *pl.* —n) (*Zool.*) chimpanzee.

Schimpf [ʃɪmpf], *m.* (—es, *no pl.*) abuse, affront, insult; *mit — und Schande,* in disgrace.

schimpfen ['ʃɪmpfən], *v.n.* curse, swear; — *auf,* (*fig.*) run (s.o.) down. — *v.a.* insult (s.o.), call (s.o.) names; scold.

Schindel ['ʃɪndəl], *f.* (—, *pl.* —n) shingle.

schinden ['ʃɪndən], *v.a. irr.* flay; (*fig.*) grind, oppress, sweat. — *v.r. sich —,* slave, drudge.

Schindluder ['ʃɪntluːdər], *n.* (—s, *pl.* —) worn-out animal; *mit einem — treiben,* exploit s.o.

Schinken ['ʃɪŋkən], *m.* (—s, *pl.* —) ham.

Schinkenspeck ['ʃɪŋkənʃpɛk], *m.* (—s, *no pl.*) bacon.

Schippe ['ʃɪpə], *f.* (—, *pl.* —n) shovel, spade.

Schirm [ʃɪrm], *m.* (—(e)s, *pl.* —e) screen; umbrella; parasol, sunshade; lampshade; (*fig.*) shield, shelter, cover.

schirmen ['ʃɪrmən], *v.a.* protect (from), shelter.

Schirmherr ['ʃɪrmhɛr], *m.* (—s, *pl.* —en) protector, patron.

Schlacht [ʃlaxt], *f.* (—, *pl.* —en) battle; fight; *eine — liefern,* give battle; *die — gewinnen,* carry the day, win the battle.

Schlachtbank ['ʃlaxtbaŋk], *f.* (—, *pl.* ⸚e) shambles; *zur — führen,* lead to the slaughter.

schlachten ['ʃlaxtən], *v.a.* kill, butcher, slaughter.

Schlachtenbummler ['ʃlaxtənbumlər], *m.* (—s, *pl.* —) camp follower.

Schlachtfeld ['ʃlaxtfelt], *n.* (—s, *pl.* —er) battlefield.

Schlachtruf ['ʃlaxtruːf], *m.* (—s, *pl.* —e) battle-cry.

Schlacke ['ʃlakə], *f.* (—, *pl.* —n) slag, clinker, dross.

Schlackwurst ['ʃlakvurst], *f.* (—, *pl.* ⸚e) (*North German*) sausage.

Schlaf [ʃlaːf], *m.* (—(e)s, *no pl.*) sleep; slumber, rest; *in tiefem —,* fast asleep; *in den — wiegen,* rock to sleep.

Schläfchen ['ʃleːfçən], *n.* (—s, *pl.* —) nap; *ein — machen,* have forty winks.

Schläfe ['ʃleːfə], *f.* (—, *pl.* —n) temple.

schlafen ['ʃlaːfən], *v.n. irr.* sleep; *schlaf wohl,* sleep well; — *gehen,* go to bed.

schlaff [ʃlaf], *adj.* slack, loose, lax, flabby; weak; remiss.

schlaflos ['ʃlaːfloːs], *adj.* sleepless.

Schlafmittel ['ʃlaːfmɪtəl], *n.* (—s, *pl.* —) soporific, sleeping tablet, sleeping draught.

schläfrig ['ʃleːfrɪç], *adj.* drowsy, sleepy.

Schlafrock [ˈʃlaːfrɔk], *m.* (—s, *pl.* ⏜e) dressing-gown; *Äpfel im —*, apple fritters.

schlafwandeln [ˈʃlaːfvandəln], *v.n.* (*aux.* sein) walk in o.'s sleep, sleepwalk.

Schlag [ʃlaːk], *m.* (—(e)s, *pl.* ⏜e) blow, stroke; beat; (*Elec.*) shock; *ein Mann von gutem —*, a good type of man; *vom — gerührt*, struck by apoplexy; *— fünf*, at five o'clock sharp.

Schlagader [ˈʃlaːkaːdər], *f.* (—, *pl.* —n) artery.

Schlaganfall [ˈʃlaːkanfal], *m.* (—s, *pl.* ⏜e) stroke, apoplexy.

Schlagballspiel [ˈʃlaːkbalʃpiːl], *n.* (—s, *pl.* —e) rounders.

Schlagbaum [ˈʃlaːkbaum], *m.* (—s, *pl.* ⏜e) turnpike.

schlagen [ˈʃlaːgən], *v.a.* *irr.* beat, strike, hit; (*tree*) fell; (*money*) coin; *Alarm —*, sound the alarm; *ans Kreuz —*, crucify; *ein Kreuz —*, make the sign of the cross. — *v.n.* (*clock*) strike; (*heart*) beat; (*birds*) warble; *aus der Art —*, degenerate. — *v.r. sich —*, fight; *sich auf Säbel —*, fight with sabres; *sich an die Brust —*, beat o.'s breast.

Schlager [ˈʃlaːgər], *m.* (—s, *pl.* —) hit, pop song; (*fig.*) success.

Schläger [ˈʃlɛːgər], *m.* (—s, *pl.* —) rapier; bat; (tennis-)racket; (golf-)club.

Schlägerei [ʃlɛːgəˈraɪ], *f.* (—, *pl.* —en) fray, scuffle.

schlagfertig [ˈʃlaːkfɛrtɪç], *adj.* quick-witted.

Schlagkraft [ˈʃlaːkkraft], *f.* (—, *no pl.*) striking power.

Schlaglicht [ˈʃlaːklɪçt], *n.* (—s, *pl.* —er) strong direct light.

Schlagsahne [ˈʃlaːkzaːnə], *f.* (—, *no pl.*) double cream, raw cream; whipped cream.

Schlagschatten [ˈʃlaːkʃatən], *m.* (—s, *pl.* —) deep shadow.

Schlagseite [ˈʃlaːkzaɪtə], *f.* (—, *no pl.*) — *bekommen*, (*Naut.*) list.

Schlagwort [ˈʃlaːkvɔrt], *n.* (—s, *pl.* ⏜er) catchword, slogan; trite saying.

Schlagzeile [ˈʃlaːktsaɪlə], *f.* (—, *pl.* —n) headline.

Schlamm [ʃlam], *m.* (—(e)s, *no pl.*) mud, mire.

Schlampe [ˈʃlampə], *f.* (—, *pl.* —n) slut.

Schlange [ˈʃlaŋə], *f.* (—, *pl.* —n) snake, serpent; (*fig.*) queue.

schlängeln [ˈʃlɛŋəln], *v.r. sich —*, wind, meander.

schlangenartig [ˈʃlaŋənaːrtɪç], *adj.* snaky, serpentine.

schlank [ʃlaŋk], *adj.* slim, slender.

schlapp [ʃlap], *adj.* limp, tired, weak, slack; *— machen*, break down, collapse.

Schlappe [ˈʃlapə], *f.* (—, *pl.* —n) reverse, defeat; *eine — erleiden*, suffer a set-back.

Schlappschwanz [ˈʃlapʃvants], *m.* (—es, *pl.* ⏜e) weakling; milksop.

Schlaraffenland [ʃlaˈrafənlant], *n.* (—(e)s, *pl.* ⏜er) land of milk and honey.

schlau [ʃlau], *adj.* cunning, crafty, sly, shrewd.

Schlauch [ʃlaux], *m.* (—(e)s, *pl.* ⏜e) hose; tube.

Schlaukopf [ˈʃlaukɔpf], *m.* (—(e)s, *pl.* ⏜e) slyboots; (*Am.*) wiseacre.

schlecht [ʃlɛçt], *adj.* bad, evil, wicked; poor; *mir ist —*, I feel ill; *—e Zeiten*, hard times; *—es Geld*, base money.

schlechterdings [ˈʃlɛçtərdɪŋs], *adv.* simply, positively, absolutely.

schlechthin [ˈʃlɛçthɪn], *adv.* simply, plainly.

Schlechtigkeit [ˈʃlɛçtɪçkaɪt], *f.* (—, *pl.* —en) wickedness, baseness.

Schlegel [ˈʃleːgəl], *m.* (—s, *pl.* —) mallet; drumstick; (*bell*) clapper.

Schlehdorn [ˈʃleːdɔrn], *m.* (—s, *pl.* —e) blackthorn, sloe-tree.

schleichen [ˈʃlaɪçən], *v.n.* *irr.* (*aux.* sein) sneak, prowl, slink; *—de Krankheit*, lingering illness.

Schleichhandel [ˈʃlaɪçhandəl], *m.* (—s, *no pl.*) smuggling, black marketeering.

Schleie [ˈʃlaɪə], *f.* (—, *pl.* —n) tench.

Schleier [ˈʃlaɪər], *m.* (—s, *pl.* —) veil.

Schleife [ˈʃlaɪfə], *f.* (—, *pl.* —n) bow, loop, noose.

schleifen [ˈʃlaɪfən], *v.a.* *irr.* drag along, trail; grind, polish, sharpen, whet, hone; cut.

Schleim [ʃlaɪm], *m.* (—(e)s, *no pl.*) slime, mucus, phlegm.

Schleimhaut [ˈʃlaɪmhaut], *f.* (—, *pl.* ⏜e) mucous membrane.

Schleimsuppe [ˈʃlaɪmzupə], *f.* (—, *pl.* —n) gruel.

schleißen [ˈʃlaɪsən], *v.a.* *irr.* split, slit; (*feathers*) strip.

schlemmen [ˈʃlɛmən], *v.n.* carouse, gormandise.

schlendern [ˈʃlɛndərn], *v.n.* (*aux.* sein) saunter along, stroll.

Schlendrian [ˈʃlɛndriaːn], *m.* (—s, *no pl.*) old jog-trot, routine.

schlenkern [ˈʃlɛŋkərn], *v.a.* dangle, swing.

Schleppdampfer [ˈʃlɛpdampfər], *m.* (—s, *pl.* —) steam-tug, tug-boat, tow-boat.

Schleppe [ˈʃlɛpə], *f.* (—, *pl.* —n) train (of a dress).

schleppen [ˈʃlɛpən], *v.a.* carry (s.th. heavy), drag, tow.

Schleppenträger [ˈʃlɛpəntrɛːgər], *m.* (—s, *pl.* —) train-bearer.

Schleppnetz [ˈʃlɛpnɛts], *n.* (—es, *pl.* —e) dragnet.

Schlesien [ˈʃleːzjən], *n.* Silesia.

Schleuder [ˈʃlɔydər], *f.* (—, *pl.* —n) sling; catapult.

schleudern [ˈʃlɔydərn], *v.a.* sling, throw, fling away. — *v.n.* (*Motor.*) skid; (*Comm.*) sell cheaply, under-sell.

schleunigst ['ʃlɔynɪçst], *adv.* very quickly, with the utmost expedition, promptly.

Schleuse ['ʃlɔyzə], *f.* (—, *pl.* —n) sluice, flood-gate, lock.

Schlich [ʃlɪç], *m.* (—es, *pl.* —e) trick, dodge; *einem hinter seine —e kommen*, be up to s.o.'s tricks.

schlicht [ʃlɪçt], *adj.* plain, simple, homely; *—er Abschied*, curt dismissal.

schlichten ['ʃlɪçtən], *v.a.* level; (*argument*) settle; adjust, compose.

Schlichtheit ['ʃlɪçthaɪt], *f.* (—, *no pl.*) plainness, simplicity, homeliness.

schließen ['ʃliːsən], *v.a. irr.* shut, close; contract; *etwas — aus*, conclude s.th. from; (*meeting*) close; *Frieden —*, make peace; *einen in die Arme —*, embrace s.o.; *etwas in sich —*, imply, entail.

Schließer ['ʃliːsər], *m.* (—s, *pl.* —) doorkeeper; (*prison*) jailer, turnkey.

schließlich ['ʃliːslɪç], *adv.* lastly, finally, in conclusion.

Schliff [ʃlɪf], *m.* (—(e)s, *no pl.*) polish, refinement.

schlimm [ʃlɪm], *adj.* bad, evil, ill; sad; serious, sore; disagreeable; naughty; *um so —er*, so much the worse, worse luck.

Schlinge ['ʃlɪŋə], *f.* (—, *pl.* —n) loop, knot; noose, snare.

Schlingel ['ʃlɪŋəl], *m.* (—s, *pl.* —) little rascal.

schlingen ['ʃlɪŋən], *v.a. irr.* sling, wind; swallow, devour.

Schlips [ʃlɪps], *m.* (—es, *pl.* —e) (neck-)tie, cravat.

Schlitten ['ʃlɪtən], *m.* (—s, *pl.* —) sledge, sled, sleigh.

Schlittschuh ['ʃlɪtʃuː], *m.* (—s, *pl.* —e) skate; *— laufen*, skate.

Schlitz [ʃlɪts], *m.* (—es, *pl.* —e) slit.

schlohweiß ['ʃloːvaɪs], *adj.* white as sloe-blossom, snow-white.

Schloß [ʃlɔs], *n.* (—sses, *pl.* ¨sser) (*door*) lock, padlock; (*gun*) lock; palace, castle; *unter — und Riegel*, under lock and key.

Schloße ['ʃloːsə], *f.* (—, *pl.* —n) hailstone.

Schlosser ['ʃlɔsər], *m.* (—s, *pl.* —) locksmith.

Schlot [ʃloːt], *m.* (—(e)s, *pl.* —e) chimney, funnel.

schlottern ['ʃlɔtərn], *v.n.* wobble, dodder; tremble.

Schlucht [ʃluxt], *f.* (—, *pl.* —en) deep valley, defile, cleft, glen, ravine, gorge.

schluchzen ['ʃluxtsən], *v.n.* sob.

schlucken ['ʃlukən], *v.a.* gulp down, swallow. — *v.n.* hiccup.

Schlucker ['ʃlukər], *m.* (—s, *pl.* —) *armer —*, poor wretch.

Schlummer ['ʃlumər], *m.* (—s, *no pl.*) slumber.

Schlumpe ['ʃlumpə], *f.* (—, *pl.* —n) slut, slattern.

Schlund [ʃlunt], *m.* (—(e)s, *pl.* ¨e) throat, gorge, gullet; gulf, abyss.

schlüpfen ['ʃlypfən], *v.n.* (*aux.* sein) slip, slide, glide.

Schlüpfer ['ʃlypfər], *m. pl.* knickers.

schlüpfrig ['ʃlypfrɪç], *adj.* slippery; (*fig.*) obscene, indecent.

schlürfen ['ʃlyrfən], *v.a.* drink noisily, lap up. — *v.n.* (*aux.* sein) (*dial.*) shuffle along.

Schluß [ʃlus], *m.* (—sses, *pl.* ¨sse) end, termination; conclusion.

Schlüssel ['ʃlysəl], *m.* (—s, *pl.* —) key; (*Mus.*) clef.

Schlüsselbein ['ʃlysəlbaɪn], *n.* (—s, *pl.* —e) collar-bone.

Schlüsselblume ['ʃlysəlbluːmə], *f.* (—, *pl.* —n) (*Bot.*) cowslip, primrose.

Schlußfolgerung ['ʃlusfɔlgərʊŋ], *f.* (—, *pl.* —en) conclusion, inference, deduction.

schlüssig ['ʃlysɪç], *adj.* resolved, determined; sure; (*Law*) well-grounded; *sich — werden über*, resolve on.

Schmach [ʃmaːx], *f.* (—, *no pl.*) disgrace, ignominy.

schmachten ['ʃmaxtən], *v.n.* languish, pine.

schmächtig ['ʃmɛçtɪç], *adj.* slender, slim, spare.

schmackhaft ['ʃmakhaft], *adj.* tasty, savoury.

schmähen ['ʃmɛːən], *v.a.* revile, abuse, calumniate.

Schmähschrift ['ʃmɛːʃrɪft], *f.* (—, *pl.* —en) lampoon.

schmal [ʃmaːl], *adj.* narrow.

schmälen ['ʃmɛːlən], *v.a.* chide, scold.

schmälern ['ʃmɛːlərn], *v.a.* lessen, diminish, curtail; detract from, belittle.

Schmalz [ʃmalts], *n.* (—es, *no pl.*) grease, lard, fat.

schmarotzen [ʃmaˈrɔtsən], *v.n.* sponge on others.

Schmarren [ˈʃmarən], *m.* (—s, *pl.* —) trash; (*dial.*) omelette.

Schmatz [ʃmats], *m.* (—es, *pl.* ¨e) (*dial.*) smacking kiss.

schmauchen [ˈʃmauxən], *v.a., v.n.* smoke.

Schmaus [ʃmaus], *m.* (—es, *pl.* —e) feast, banquet.

schmecken [ˈʃmɛkən], *v.a.* taste. — *v.n.* taste; *es schmeckt mir*, I like it.

Schmeichelei [ʃmaɪçəˈlaɪ], *f.* (—, *pl.* —en) flattery, adulation.

schmeicheln [ˈʃmaɪçəln], *v.n.* flatter; fondle, pet.

schmeißen [ˈʃmaɪsən], *v.a. irr.* throw, hurl, fling; (*sl.*) *ich werde die Sache schon —*, I shall pull it off.

Schmeißfliege [ˈʃmaɪsfliːgə], *f.* (—, *pl.* —n) (*Ent.*) bluebottle.

Schmelz [ʃmɛlts], *m.* (—es, *no pl.*) enamel; melting; (*voice*) mellowness.

schmelzbar [ˈʃmɛltsbaːr], *adj.* fusible.

schmelzen [ˈʃmɛltsən], *v.a. irr.* smelt, melt. — *v.n.* (*aux.* sein) (*ice*) melt; (*fig.*) decrease, diminish.

Schmelztiegel [ˈʃmɛltstiːgəl], *m.* (—s, *pl.* —) crucible; melting pot.

Schmelztopf [ˈʃmɛltstɔpf], *m. see* **Schmelztiegel.**

Schmerbauch [ˈʃmeːrbaux], *m.* (—(e)s, *pl.* ⁝e) (*coll.*) paunch, belly.

Schmerz [ʃmɛrts], *m.* (—es, *pl.* —en) ache, pain; grief, sorrow; *einem —en verursachen,* give *or* cause s.o. pain.

schmerzlich [ˈʃmɛrtsliç], *adj.* painful, distressing.

Schmetterling [ˈʃmɛtərlɪŋ], *m.* (—s, *pl.* —e) (*Ent.*) butterfly, moth.

schmettern [ˈʃmɛtərn], *v.n.* resound; (*trumpets*) blare; (*bird*) warble.

Schmied [ʃmiːt], *m.* (—s, *pl.* —e) (black)smith.

Schmiede [ˈʃmiːdə], *f.* (—, *pl.* —n) forge, smithy.

schmiegen [ˈʃmiːgən], *v.r. sich —,* bend, yield; *sich an einen —,* cling to s.o., nestle against s.o.

Schmiere [ˈʃmiːrə], *f.* (—, *pl.* —n) grease, salve; (*Theat.*) troop of strolling players.

schmieren [ˈʃmiːrən], *v.a.* smear, grease, spread; (*fig.*) bribe; (*bread*) butter. — *v.n.* scrawl, scribble.

Schmierfink [ˈʃmiːrfɪŋk], *m.* (—en, *pl.* —en) dirty person; muckraker.

Schmiermittel [ˈʃmiːrmɪtəl], *n.* (—s, *pl.* —) lubricant.

Schmierseife [ˈʃmiːrzaɪfə], *f.* (—, *no pl.*) soft soap.

Schminke [ˈʃmɪŋkə], *f.* (—, *pl.* —n) greasepaint; rouge; make-up, cosmetics.

Schmirgel [ˈʃmɪrgəl], *m.* (—s, *no pl.*) emery.

Schmiß [ʃmɪs], *m.* (—sses, *pl.* —sse) cut in the face, (duelling) scar; (*fig.*) smartness, verve.

Schmöker [ˈʃmøːkər], *m.* (—s, *pl.* —) trashy book.

schmollen [ˈʃmɔlən], *v.n.* sulk, pout.

Schmorbraten [ˈʃmoːrbraːtən], *m.* (—s, *pl.* —) stewed meat.

Schmuck [ʃmuk], *m.* (—(e)s, *pl.* —stücke) ornament, jewels, jewellery; (*Am.*) jewelry.

schmuck [ʃmuk], *adj.* neat, spruce, dapper, smart.

schmücken [ˈʃmʏkən], *v.a.* adorn, embellish.

Schmucksachen [ˈʃmukzaxən], *f. pl.* jewels, finery, jewellery, articles of adornment; (*Am.*) jewelry.

schmuggeln [ˈʃmugəln], *v.a.* smuggle.

schmunzeln [ˈʃmuntsəln], *v.n.* smirk, grin.

Schmutz [ʃmuts], *m.* (—es, *no pl.*) dirt, filth.

schmutzen [ˈʃmutsən], *v.n.* get soiled, get dirty.

Schmutzkonkurrenz [ˈʃmutskɔnkurɛnts], *f.* (—, *no pl.*) unfair competition.

Schnabel [ˈʃnaːbəl], *m.* (—s, *pl.* ⁝) bill, beak; (*ship*) prow; *halt den —, wie ihm*

der — gewachsen ist, he calls a spade a spade.

Schnabeltier [ˈʃnaːbəltiːr], *n.* (—s, *pl.* —e) duck-bill, duck-billed platypus.

Schnaderhüpfel [ˈʃnaːdərhypfəl], *n.* (—s, *pl.* —) (*dial.*) Alpine folk-song.

Schnalle [ˈʃnalə], *f.* (—, *pl.* —n) buckle.

schnalzen [ˈʃnaltsən], *v.n.* click; snap.

schnappen [ˈʃnapən], *v.n.* snap; snatch at s.th.; *nach Luft —,* gasp for breath.

Schnaps [ʃnaps], *m.* (—es, *pl.* ⁝e) spirits, brandy, gin.

schnarchen [ˈʃnarçən], *v.n.* snore.

Schnarre [ˈʃnarə], *f.* (—, *pl.* —n) rattle.

schnattern [ˈʃnatərn], *v.n.* cackle; gabble; chatter.

schnauben [ˈʃnaubən], *v.n.* puff and blow; snort; *vor Zorn —,* fret and fume.

schnaufen [ˈʃnaufən], *v.n.* breathe heavily, pant.

Schnauze [ˈʃnautsə], *f.* (—, *pl.* —n) (*animals*) snout; (*vulg.*) mouth, trap; nozzle.

schnauzen [ˈʃnautsən], *v.n.* snarl, shout (at).

Schnecke [ˈʃnɛkə], *f.* (—, *pl.* —n), (*Zool.*) snail, slug.

Schnee [ʃneː], *m.* (—s, *no pl.*) snow.

Schneegestöber [ˈʃneːgəʃtøːbər], *n.* (—s, *pl.* —) snow-storm.

Schneeglöckchen [ˈʃneːglœkçən], *n.* (—s, *pl.* —) (*Bot.*) snowdrop.

Schneeschläger [ˈʃneːʃlɛːgər], *m.* (—s, *pl.* —) whisk.

Schneetreiben [ˈʃneːtraɪbən], *n.* (—s, *no pl.*) snow-storm, blizzard.

Schneewittchen [ʃneːˈvɪtçən], *n.* (—s, *no pl.*) Snow White.

Schneid [ʃnaɪt], *m.* (—s, *no pl.*) go, push, dash, courage.

Schneide [ˈʃnaɪdə], *f.* (—, *pl.* —n) edge.

Schneidebohne [ˈʃnaɪdəboːnə], *f.* (—, *pl.* —n) French bean, string-bean.

Schneidemühle [ˈʃnaɪdəmyːlə], *f.* (—, *pl.* —n) saw mill.

schneiden [ˈʃnaɪdən], *v.a. irr.* cut, trim, carve; (*fig.*) ignore, cut; *Gesichter —,* make faces. — *v.r. sich —,* cut o.s.; (*Maths.*) intersect; *sich die Haare — lassen,* have o.'s hair cut.

Schneider [ˈʃnaɪdər], *m.* (—s, *pl.* —) tailor.

Schneiderei [ʃnaɪdəˈraɪ], *f.* (—, *no pl.*) tailoring; dressmaking.

Schneidezahn [ˈʃnaɪdətsaːn], *m.* (—s, *pl.* ⁝e) incisor.

schneidig [ˈʃnaɪdɪç], *adj.* dashing.

schneien [ˈʃnaɪən], *v.n.* snow.

Schneise [ˈʃnaɪzə], *f.* (—, *pl.* —n) (*forest*) glade, cutting.

schnell [ʃnɛl], *adj.* quick, swift, speedy, fast, rapid; *mach —,* hurry up.

Schnelle [ˈʃnɛlə], *f.* (—, *pl.* —n) (*river*) rapids.

schnellen [ˈʃnɛlən], *v.n.* spring, jump.

Schnelligkeit [ˈʃnɛlɪçkaɪt], *f.* (—, *no pl.*) quickness, speed, swiftness, rapidity; (*Tech.*) velocity.

Schnepfe [ˈʃnɛpfə], *f.* (—, *pl.* —n) (*Orn.*) snipe, woodcock.

schneuzen [ˈʃnɔytsən], *v.r.* *sich* (*die Nase*) —, blow o.'s nose.

schniegeln [ˈʃniːgəln], *v.r.* *sich* —, (*coll.*) dress up, deck out; *geschniegelt und gebügelt*, spick and span.

Schnippchen [ˈʃnɪpçən], *n.* (—s, *pl.* —) *einem ein* — *schlagen*, play a trick on s.o.

schnippisch [ˈʃnɪpɪʃ], *adj.* pert, perky.

Schnitt [ʃnɪt], *m.* (—(e)s, *pl.* —e) cut, incision; section; (*beer*) small glass; (*dress*) cut-out pattern; (*book*) edge.

Schnittbohne [ˈʃnɪtboːnə], *f.* (—, *pl.* —n) (*Bot.*) French bean.

Schnitte [ˈʃnɪtə], *f.* (—, *pl.* —n) slice (of bread).

Schnitter [ˈʃnɪtər], *m.* (—s, *pl.* —) reaper.

Schnittlauch [ˈʃnɪtlaux], *m.* (—s, *no pl.*) (*Bot.*) chives.

Schnittmuster [ˈʃnɪtmʊstər], *n.* (—s, *pl.* —) cut-out pattern.

Schnittwaren [ˈʃnɪtvaːrən], *f. pl.* dry goods, drapery.

Schnitzel [ˈʃnɪtsəl], *n.* (—s, *pl.* —) (*Cul.*) cutlet; *Wiener* —, veal cutlet; snip; (*pl.*) shavings.

schnitzen [ˈʃnɪtsən], *v.a.* carve (in wood).

schnodd(e)rig [ˈʃnɔd(ə)rɪç], *adj.* (*coll.*) cheeky, insolent.

schnöde [ˈʃnøːdə], *adj.* base, heinous, mean, vile; —*r Mammon*, filthy lucre; —*r Undank*, rank ingratitude.

Schnörkel [ˈʃnœrkəl], *m.* (—s, *pl.* —) (*writing*) flourish.

schnorren [ˈʃnɔrən], *v.n.* (*rare*) cadge, beg.

schnüffeln [ˈʃnyfəln], *v.n.* sniff; (*fig.*) pry, snoop.

Schnuller [ˈʃnʊlər], *m.* (—s, *pl.* —) baby's dummy; (*Am.*) comforter.

Schnupfen [ˈʃnʊpfən], *m.* (—s, *pl.* —) cold (in the head); *den* — *haben*, have a (running) cold; *den* — *bekommen*, catch cold.

schnupfen [ˈʃnʊpfən], *v.a.*, *v.n.* take snuff.

Schnupftuch [ˈʃnʊpftuːx], *n.* (—(e)s, *pl.* ˙er) (*dial.*) (pocket-) handkerchief.

schnuppe [ˈʃnʊpə], *adj.* (*sl.*) *mir ist alles* —, it is all the same to me, I don't care.

schnuppern [ˈʃnʊpərn], *v.n.* smell, snuffle.

Schnur [ʃnuːr], *f.* (—, *pl.* —en, ˙e) twine, cord, string; (*Elec.*) lead, flex.

Schnürchen [ˈʃnyːrçən], *n.* (—s, *pl.* —) *wie am* —, like clockwork.

schnüren [ˈʃnyːrən], *v.a.* lace, tie up; *sein Ränzel* —, pack o.'s bag.

Schnurrbart [ˈʃnʊrbaːrt], *m.* (—s,

pl. ˙e) moustache; *sich einen* — *wachsen lassen*, grow a moustache.

Schnurre [ˈʃnʊrə], *f.* (—, *pl.* —n) funny story, yarn.

schnurren [ˈʃnʊrən], *v.n.* purr.

Schnürsenkel [ˈʃnyːrzɛŋkəl], *m.* (—s, *pl.* —) (*shoe*) lace.

schnurstracks [ˈʃnuːrʃtraks], *adv.* directly, immediately, on the spot.

Schober [ˈʃoːbər], *m.* (—s, *pl.* —) stack, rick.

Schock (1) [ʃɔk], *n.* (—(e)s, *pl.* —e) sixty, three score.

Schock (2) [ʃɔk], *m.* (—(e)s, *pl.* —s) shock; blow; stroke.

Schöffe [ˈʃœfə], *m.* (—n, *pl.* —n) (*Law*) juror; member of jury.

Schokolade [ʃokoˈlaːdə], *f.* (—, *pl.* —n) chocolate; *eine Tafel* —, a bar of chocolate.

Scholle [ˈʃɔlə], *f.* (—, *pl.* —n) plaice; (*ice*) floe; clod; soil.

schon [ʃoːn], *adv.* already; indeed; yet; *na wenn* —, so what; — *gut*, that'll do; — *gestern*, as early as yesterday.

schön [ʃøːn], *adj.* beautiful, fair, handsome, lovely; —*e Literatur*, belleslettres, good books.

schonen [ˈʃoːnən], *v.a.* spare, save; treat considerately.

Schoner [ˈʃoːnər], *m.* (—s, *pl.* —) antimacassar; (*Naut.*) schooner.

Schönheit [ˈʃøːnhaɪt], *f.* (—, *no pl.*) beauty.

Schonung [ˈʃoːnuŋ], *f.* (—, *pl.* —en) forbearance, considerate treatment; (*forest*) plantation of young trees.

Schonzeit [ˈʃoːntsaɪt], *f.* (—, *pl.* —en) close season.

Schopf [ʃɔpf], *m.* (—es, *pl.* ˙e) tuft, head of hair; (*bird*) crest; *das Glück beim* —*e fassen*, take time by the forelock, make hay while the sun shines.

Schöpfbrunnen [ˈʃœpfbrunən], *m.* (—s, *pl.* —) (draw-)well.

schöpfen [ˈʃœpfən], *v.a.* (*water*) draw; derive; *Verdacht* —, become suspicious; *frische Luft* —, get a breath of fresh air; *Mut* —, take heart.

Schöpfer [ˈʃœpfər], *m.* (—s, *pl.* —) creator.

Schöpfkelle [ˈʃœpfkɛlə], *f.* (—, *pl.* —n) scoop.

Schopflerche [ˈʃɔpflɛrçə], *f.* (—, *pl.* —n) (*Orn.*) crested lark.

Schöpfung [ˈʃœpfuŋ], *f.* (—, *pl.* —en) creation.

Schoppen [ˈʃɔpən], *m.* (—s, *pl.* —) (*approx.*) half a pint.

Schöps [ʃœps], *m.* (—es, *pl.* —e) (*Zool.*) wether; (*fig.*) simpleton.

Schorf [ʃɔrf], *m.* (—(e)s, *pl.* —e) scab, scurf.

Schornstein [ˈʃɔrnʃtaɪn], *m.* (—s, *pl.* —e) chimney; (*ship*) funnel.

Schoß [ʃoːs], *m.* (—es, *pl.* ˙e) lap; (*Poet.*) womb; skirt; tail; *die Hände in den* — *legen*, be idle, fold o.'s arms, twiddle o.'s thumbs.

Schößling [ˈʃœsliŋ], m. (—s, pl. —e) shoot, sprig.

Schote [ˈʃoːtə], f. (—, pl. —n) pod, husk, shell; (pl.) green peas.

Schotter [ˈʃɔtər], m. (—s, no pl.) road-metal, broken stones, gravel.

Schottland [ˈʃɔtlant], n. Scotland.

schraffieren [ʃraˈfiːrən], v.a. (Art) hatch.

schräg [ʃrɛːk], adj. oblique, sloping, slanting, diagonal.

Schramme [ˈʃramə], f. (—, pl. —n) scratch, scar.

Schrank [ʃraŋk], m. (—(e)s, pl. ˙˙e) cupboard, wardrobe.

Schranken [ˈʃraŋkən], f. pl. barriers, (level crossing) gates, limits, bounds; *in — halten*, limit, keep within bounds.

schränken [ˈʃrɛŋkən], v.a. cross; fold.

Schranze [ˈʃrantsə], m. (—n, pl. —n) sycophant, toady.

Schraube [ˈʃraubə], f. (—, pl. —n) screw; bolt; propeller.

Schraubengewinde [ˈʃraubəngəvində], n. (—s, pl. —) thread of a screw.

Schraubenmutter [ˈʃraubənmutər], f. (—, pl. —n) female screw, nut.

Schraubenzieher [ˈʃraubəntsiːər], m. (—s, pl. —) screw-driver.

Schraubstock [ˈʃraupʃtɔk], m. (—s, pl. ˙˙e) (tool) vice.

Schreck(en) [ˈʃrek(ən)], m. (—s, pl. —) fright, terror, alarm, horror; shock.

Schrecknis [ˈʃreknis], n. (—ses, pl. —se) terror, horror.

Schrei [ʃrai], m. (—s, pl. —e) cry; scream.

Schreiben [ˈʃraibən], n. (—s, pl. —) letter, missive.

schreiben [ˈʃraibən], v.a. irr. write; *ins Reine —*, make a fair copy.

Schreibfehler [ˈʃraipfeːlər], m. (—s, pl. —) slip of the pen.

Schreibkrampf [ˈʃraipkrampf], m. (—(e)s, pl. ˙˙e) writer's cramp.

Schreibmaschine [ˈʃraipmaʃiːnə], f. (—, pl. —n) typewriter.

Schreibwaren [ˈʃraipvaːrən], f. pl. stationery.

Schreibweise [ˈʃraipvaizə], f. (—, pl. —n) style; spelling.

schreien [ˈʃraiən], v.a., v.n. irr. cry, shout, scream, yell.

Schreihals [ˈʃraihals], m. (—es, pl. ˙˙e) cry-baby, noisy child.

Schrein [ʃrain], m. (—(e)s, pl. —e) box, chest; shrine.

schreiten [ˈʃraitən], v.n. irr. (aux. sein) stride, step, pace.

Schrift [ʃrift], f. (—, pl. —en) writing; handwriting, calligraphy; publication; type; *Heilige —*, Holy Writ, Holy Scripture.

Schriftführer [ˈʃriftfyːrər], m. (—s, pl. —) secretary.

Schriftgießerei [ˈʃriftgiːsərai], f. (—, pl. —en) type-foundry.

Schriftleiter [ˈʃriftlaitər], m. (—s, pl. —) editor.

schriftlich [ˈʃriftliç], adj. written. — adv. in writing, by letter.

Schriftsetzer [ˈʃriftzetsər], m. (—s, pl. —) compositor.

Schriftsteller [ˈʃriftʃtelər], m. (—s, pl. —) writer, author.

Schriftstück [ˈʃriftʃtyk], n. (—s, pl. —e) document, deed.

Schriftwechsel [ˈʃriftvɛksəl], m. (—s, no pl.) exchange of notes, correspondence.

Schriftzeichen [ˈʃriftsaiçən], n. (—s, pl. —) character, letter (of alphabet).

schrill [ʃril], adj. shrill.

Schritt [ʃrit], m. (—(e)s, pl. —e) step, pace, move; *lange —e machen*, stride; *— halten*, keep pace; *— fahren*, drive slowly, drive at walking pace; *aus dem —*, out of step; *in einer Sache —e tun*, make a move or take steps about s.th.

schrittweise [ˈʃritvaizə], adv. step by step, gradually.

schroff [ʃrɔf], adj. steep, precipitous; (fig.) gruff, blunt, rough, harsh.

schröpfen [ˈʃrœpfən], v.a. (Med.) cup; (fig.) fleece.

Schrot [ʃroːt], m. & n. (—(e)s, pl. —e) grape-shot, small shot; *ein Mann vom alten —*, a man of the utmost probity.

Schrotbrot [ˈʃroːtbroːt], n. (—es, no pl.) wholemeal bread.

Schrott [ʃrɔt], m. (—(e)s, pl. —e), old iron, scrap metal.

Schrulle [ˈʃrulə], f. (—, pl. —n) fad, whim.

schrumpfen [ˈʃrumpfən], v.n. (aux. sein) shrink, shrivel.

Schub [ʃup], m. (—s, pl. ˙˙e) shove, push; batch.

Schubkarren [ˈʃupkarən], m. (—s, pl. —) wheelbarrow.

Schublade [ˈʃuplaːdə], f. (—, pl. —n) drawer.

schüchtern [ˈʃyçtərn], adj. shy, bashful, timid.

Schuft [ʃuft], m. (—(e)s, pl. —e) blackguard, scoundrel.

schuften [ˈʃuftən], v.n. work hard, toil.

Schufterei [ʃuftəˈrai], f. (—, no pl.) drudgery.

schuftig [ˈʃuftiç], adj. rascally, mean.

Schuh [ʃuː], m. (—s, pl. —e) shoe; *einem etwas in die — schieben*, lay the blame at s.o.'s door.

Schuhwerk [ˈʃuːverk], n. (—s, no pl.) footwear.

Schuhwichse [ˈʃuːviksə], f. (—, no pl.) shoe-polish.

Schuld [ʃult], f. (—, pl. —en) guilt, offence, sin; fault; blame; cause; (money) debt; *in —en geraten*, run into debt.

schuld [ʃult], adj. *ich bin —*, it is my fault, I am to blame.

schulden [ˈʃuldən], v.a. owe, be indebted to.

schuldig [ˈʃuldiç], adj. guilty, culpable; *sich — bekennen*, plead guilty; *einen — sprechen*, pronounce s.o. guilty;

ihm ist Anerkennung —, appreciation is due to him.
Schuldigkeit [ˈʃuldɪçkaɪt], *f.* (—, *no pl.*) obligation, duty.
schuldlos [ˈʃultlo:s], *adj.* innocent, guiltless.
Schuldner [ˈʃuldnər], *m.* (—s, *pl.* —) debtor.
Schule [ˈʃu:lə], *f.* (—, *pl.* —n) school; *in die — gehen,* go to school, attend school; *die — schwänzen,* play truant; *hohe —, (Riding)* advanced horsemanship.
schulen [ˈʃu:lən], *v.a.* train, instruct.
Schüler [ˈʃy:lər], *m.* (—s, *pl.* —) schoolboy, pupil, student, scholar.
Schulklasse [ˈʃu:lklasə], *f.* (—, *pl.* —n) class, form.
Schulleiter [ˈʃu:llaɪtər], *m.* (—s, *pl.* —) headmaster.
Schulrat [ˈʃu:lra:t], *m.* (—s, *pl.* ⁻e) school-inspector.
Schulter [ˈʃultər], *f.* (—, *pl.* —n) shoulder.
Schulterblatt [ˈʃultərblat], *n.* (—s, *pl.* ⁻er) shoulder-blade.
Schultheiß [ˈʃulthaɪs], *m.* (—en, *pl.* —en) village magistrate, mayor.
Schulunterricht [ˈʃu:luntərrɪçt], *m.* (—s, *no pl.*) school teaching, lessons.
schummeln [ˈʃuməln], *v.n. (coll.)* cheat.
Schund [ʃunt], *m.* (—(e)s, *no pl.*) trash.
Schuppe [ˈʃupə], *f.* (—, *pl.* —n) scale; *(pl.)* dandruff.
Schuppen [ˈʃupən], *m.* (—s, *pl.* —) shed.
Schuppentier [ˈʃupənti:r], *n.* (—s, *pl.* —e) *(Zool.)* armadillo.
Schur [ʃu:r], *f.* (—, *pl.* —en) shearing.
schüren [ˈʃy:rən], *v.a. (fire)* poke, rake; *(fig.)* stir up, fan, incite.
schürfen [ˈʃyrfən], *v.a.* scratch. — *v.n. (Min.)* prospect.
schurigeln [ˈʃu:rɪgəln], *v.a.* bully, pester.
Schurke [ˈʃurkə], *m.* (—n, *pl.* —n) scoundrel, villain, blackguard.
Schurz [ʃurts], *m.* (—es, *pl.* —e) apron, overall.
Schürze [ˈʃyrtsə], *f.* (—, *pl.* —n) apron, pinafore.
schürzen [ˈʃyrtsən], *v.a.* tuck up, pin up.
Schürzenjäger [ˈʃyrtsənjɛ:gər], *m.* (—s, *pl.* —) ladies' man.
Schurzfell [ˈʃurtsfɛl], *n.* (—s, *pl.* —e) leather apron.
Schuß [ʃus], *m.* (—sses, *pl.* ⁻sse) shot, report; dash; *weit vom —,* out of harm's way; wide of the mark.
Schüssel [ˈʃysəl], *f.* (—, *pl.* —n) dish.
Schußwaffe [ˈʃusvafə], *f.* (—, *pl.* —n) fire-arm.
Schuster [ˈʃu:stər], *m.* (—s, *pl.* —) shoemaker, cobbler; *auf —s Rappen,* on Shanks's pony.
schustern [ˈʃu:stərn], *v.n.* cobble, make *or* mend shoes.
Schutt [ʃut], *m.* (—(e)s, *no pl.*) rubbish, refuse; rubble; *— abladen,*

dump refuse.
Schütte [ˈʃytə], *f.* (—, *pl.* —n) *(dial.* bundle, truss.
schütteln [ˈʃytəln], *v.a.* shake, jolt.
schütten [ˈʃytən], *v.a.* shoot, pour; pour out.
schütter [ˈʃytər], *adj. (dial.) (hair)* thin; scarce.
Schutz [ʃuts], *m.* (—es, *no pl.*) protection, shelter, cover; *einen in — nehmen gegen,* defend s.o. against.
Schutzbefohlene [ˈʃutsbəfo:lənə], *m.* (—n, *pl.* —n) charge, person in o.'s care, ward.
Schutzbündnis [ˈʃutsbyntnɪs], *n.* (—ses, *pl.* —se) defensive alliance.
Schütze [ˈʃytsə], *m.* (—n, *pl.* —n) rifleman, sharpshooter, marksman; *(Astrol.)* Sagittarius.
schützen [ˈʃytsən], *v.a.* protect, shelter, defend. — *v.r. sich — vor,* guard o.s. against.
Schützengraben [ˈʃytsəngra:bən], *m.* (—s, *pl.* ⁻) trench.
Schutzgebiet [ˈʃutsgəbi:t], *n.* (—s, *pl.* —e) protectorate.
Schutzgitter [ˈʃutsgɪtər], *n.* (—s, *pl.* —) grid, guard.
Schutzheilige [ˈʃutshaɪlɪgə], *m.* (—n, *pl.* —n) patron saint.
Schützling [ˈʃytslɪŋ], *m.* (—s, *pl.* —e) protégé, charge.
Schutzmann [ˈʃutsman], *m.* (—s, *pl.* ⁻er, **Schutzleute**) policeman, constable.
Schutzmarke [ˈʃutsmarkə], *f.* (—, *pl.* —n) trade-mark.
Schutzzoll [ˈʃutstsol], *m.* (—s, *pl.* ⁻e) protective duty, tariff.
Schwaben [ˈʃva:bən], *n.* Swabia.
Schwabenstreich [ˈʃva:bənʃtraɪç], *m.* (—s, *pl.* —e) tomfoolery.
schwach [ʃvax], *adj.* weak, frail, feeble; *(noise)* faint; *(pulse)* low; *—e Seite,* foible; *—e Stunde,* unguarded moment.
Schwäche [ˈʃvɛçə], *f.* (—, *pl.* —n) weakness, faintness; infirmity.
schwächen [ˈʃvɛçən], *v.a.* weaken, debilitate.
Schwächling [ˈʃvɛçlɪŋ], *m.* (—s, *pl.* —e) weakling.
Schwachsinn [ˈʃvaxzɪn], *m.* (—s, *no pl.*) feeble-mindedness.
Schwächung [ˈʃvɛçuŋ], *f.* (—, *pl.* —en) weakening, lessening.
Schwadron [ʃva'dro:n], *f.* (—, *pl.* —en) squadron.
Schwadroneur [ʃvadro'nø:r], *m.* (—s, *pl.* —e) swaggerer.
schwadronieren [ʃvadro'ni:rən], *v.n.* talk big, swagger.
schwafeln [ˈʃva:fəln], *v.n. (sl.)* talk nonsense, waffle.
Schwager [ˈʃva:gər], *m.* (—s, *pl.* ⁻) brother-in-law.
Schwägerin [ˈʃvɛ:gərɪn], *f.* (—, *pl.* —nen) sister-in-law.
Schwalbe [ˈʃvalbə], *f.* (—, *pl.* —n) *(Orn.)* swallow.

Schwalbenschwanz ['ʃvalbənʃvants], *m.* (—es, *pl.* ⸚e) (*butterfly*) swallow's tail; (*joinery*) dovetail.

Schwall [ʃval], *m.* (—(e)s, *no pl.*) flood; (*fig.*) deluge, torrent.

Schwamm [ʃvam], *m.* (—(e)s, *pl.* ⸚e) sponge; fungus, mushroom; dry rot.

schwammig ['ʃvamɪç], *adj.* spongy, fungous.

Schwan [ʃva:n], *m.* (—(e)s, *pl.* ⸚e) swan; *junger —*, cygnet.

schwanen ['ʃva:nən], *v.n. imp. es schwant mir*, I have a foreboding.

Schwang [ʃvaŋ], *m. in —e sein*, be in fashion, be the rage.

schwanger ['ʃvaŋər], *adj.* pregnant.

schwängern ['ʃvɛŋərn], *v.a.* make pregnant, get with child; (*fig.*) impregnate.

Schwangerschaft ['ʃvaŋərʃaft], *f.* (—, *pl.* —en) pregnancy.

Schwank [ʃvaŋk], *m.* (—(e)s, *pl.* ⸚e) funny story, joke; (*Theat.*) farce.

schwank [ʃvaŋk], *adj.* flexible, supple; *ein —es Rohr*, a reed shaken by the wind.

schwanken ['ʃvaŋkən], *v.n.* totter, stagger; (*fig.*) waver, vacillate; (*prices*) fluctuate.

Schwanz [ʃvants], *m.* (—es, *pl.* ⸚e) tail.

schwänzeln ['ʃvɛntsəln], *v.n.* (*animal*) wag the tail; (*fig.*) fawn, cringe.

schwänzen ['ʃvɛntsən], *v.a. die Schule —*, play truant.

Schwären ['ʃvɛːrən], *m.* (—s, *pl.* —) ulcer, abscess.

schwären ['ʃvɛːrən], *v.n.* fester, suppurate.

Schwarm [ʃvarm], *m.* (—(e)s, *pl.* ⸚e) (*insects*) swarm; (*humans*) crowd; (*birds*) flight.

Schwärmerei [ʃvɛrmə'raɪ], *f.* (—, *pl.* —en) enthusiasm, passion, craze.

Schwarte ['ʃvartə], *f.* (—, *pl.* —n) rind; crust; *alte —*, (*fig.*) old volume; tome.

schwarz [ʃvarts], *adj.* black.

Schwarzamsel ['ʃvartsamzəl], *f.* (—, *pl.* —n) (*Orn.*) blackbird.

Schwarzdorn ['ʃvartsdɔrn], *m.* (—s, *no pl.*) (*Bot.*) blackthorn, sloe.

Schwärze ['ʃvɛrtsə], *f.* (—, *no pl.*) blackness; printer's ink.

schwärzen ['ʃvɛrtsən], *v.a.* blacken.

Schwarzkünstler ['ʃvartskynstlər], *m.* (—s, *pl.* —) magician, necromancer.

Schwarzwald ['ʃvartsvalt], *m.* Black Forest.

Schwarzwild ['ʃvartsvɪlt], *n.* (—(e)s, *no pl.*) wild boar.

schwatzen ['ʃvatsən], *v.n.* chat, chatter, prattle.

Schwätzer ['ʃvɛtsər], *m.* (—s, *pl.* —) chatterbox.

Schwatzhaftigkeit ['ʃvatshaftɪçkaɪt], *f.* (—, *no pl.*) loquacity, talkativeness.

Schwebe ['ʃveːbə], *f.* (—, *pl.* —n) suspense; suspension.

Schwebebaum ['ʃveːbəbaum], *m.* (—s, *pl.* ⸚e) horizontal bar.

schweben ['ʃveːbən], *v.n.* be suspended, hover; (*fig.*) be pending; *in Gefahr —*, be in danger; *es schwebt mir auf der Zunge*, it is on the tip of my tongue.

Schwede ['ʃveːdə], *m.* (—n, *pl.* —n) Swede; *alter —*, (*fig.*) old boy.

Schweden ['ʃveːdən], *n.* Sweden.

Schwedenhölzer ['ʃveːdənhœltsər], *n. pl.* (*rare*) matches.

Schwefel ['ʃveːfəl], *m.* (—s, *no pl.*) sulphur, brimstone.

Schwefelhölzchen ['ʃveːfəlhœltsçən], *n.* (—s, *pl.* —) (*obs.*) match.

schwefeln ['ʃveːfəln], *v.a.* impregnate with sulphur, fumigate.

Schwefelsäure ['ʃveːfəlzɔyrə], *f.* (—, *no pl.*) sulphuric acid.

Schweif [ʃvaɪf], *m.* (—(e)s, *pl.* —e) tail.

schweifen ['ʃvaɪfən], *v.n.* (*aux.* sein) ramble, stray, wander.

schweifwedeln ['ʃvaɪfveːdəln], *v.n.* fawn.

Schweigegeld ['ʃvaɪɡəɡelt], *n.* (—(e)s, *pl.* —er) (*coll.*) hush-money.

Schweigen ['ʃvaɪɡən], *n.* (—s, *no pl.*) silence.

schweigen ['ʃvaɪɡən], *v.n. irr.* be silent; be quiet; *ganz zu — von*, to say nothing of.

schweigsam ['ʃvaɪkza:m], *adj.* taciturn.

Schwein [ʃvaɪn], *n.* (—(e)s, *pl.* —e) pig, hog; swine; *wildes —*, boar; (*fig.*) luck, fluke; *— haben*, be lucky.

Schweinekoben ['ʃvaɪnəko:bən], *m.* (—s, *pl.* —) pigsty.

Schweinerei [ʃvaɪnə'raɪ], *f.* (—, *pl.* —en) filth; (*fig.*) smut, filthiness, obscenity; mess.

Schweineschmalz ['ʃvaɪnəʃmalts], *n.* (—es, *no pl.*) lard.

Schweinigel ['ʃvaɪnɪɡəl], *m.* (—s, *pl.* —) (*Zool.*) hedgehog, porcupine; (*fig.*) dirty pig, filthy wretch.

Schweinskeule ['ʃvaɪnskɔylə], *f.* (—, *pl.* —n) leg of pork.

Schweiß [ʃvaɪs], *m.* (—es, *no pl.*) sweat, perspiration.

schweißen ['ʃvaɪsən], *v.a.* weld, solder.

Schweiz [ʃvaɪts], *f.* Switzerland.

Schweizer ['ʃvaɪtsər], *m.* (—s, *pl.* —) Swiss; (*fig.*) dairyman.

Schweizerei [ʃvaɪtsə'raɪ], *f.* (—, *pl.* —en) dairy.

schwelen ['ʃveːlən], *v.n.* burn slowly, smoulder.

schwelgen ['ʃvɛlɡən], *v.n.* carouse, revel.

Schwelgerei [ʃvɛlɡə'raɪ], *f.* (—, *pl.* —en) revelry.

schwelgerisch ['ʃvɛlɡərɪʃ], *adj.* luxurious, voluptuous.

Schwelle ['ʃvɛlə], *f.* (—, *pl.* —n) threshold; (*Railw.*) sleeper.

schwellen ['ʃvɛlən], *v.n. irr.* (*aux.* sein) swell; (*water*) rise.

Schwellung ['ʃvɛluŋ], *f.* (—, *pl.* —en) swelling.

schwemmen

schwemmen [ˈʃvɛmən], *v.a.* wash, soak, carry off.

Schwengel [ˈʃvɛŋəl], *m.* (—s, *pl.* —) (*bell*) clapper; (*pump*) handle.

schwenken [ˈʃvɛŋkən], *v.a.* swing; shake, brandish; (*glasses*) rinse.

Schwenkung [ˈʃvɛŋkuŋ], *f.* (—, *pl.* —en) change; (*Mil.*) wheeling.

schwer [ʃve:r], *adj.* heavy; difficult, hard; ponderous; severe; — *von Begriff*, obtuse, slow in the uptake; —*e Speise*, indigestible food; *einem das Herz* — *machen*, grieve s.o.

schwerblütig [ˈʃve:rbly:tɪç], *adj.* phlegmatic.

Schwere [ˈʃve:rə], *f.* (—, *no pl.*) weight, heaviness; gravity.

Schwerenöter [ˈʃve:rənøːtər], *m.* (—s, *pl.* —) gay dog, ladies' man.

schwerfällig [ˈʃve:rfɛlɪç], *adj.* ungainly, cumbrous, unwieldy; (*fig.*) thickheaded, dense.

Schwergewicht [ˈʃve:rgəvɪçt], *n.* (—s, *no pl.*) (*Sport*) heavyweight; (*fig.*) emphasis.

schwerhörig [ˈʃve:rhøːrɪç], *adj.* hard of hearing, deaf.

Schwerkraft [ˈʃve:rkraft], *f.* (—, *no pl.*) gravity.

schwerlich [ˈʃve:rlɪç], *adv.* hardly, scarcely.

schwermütig [ˈʃve:rmy:tɪç], *adj.* melancholy.

Schwerpunkt [ˈʃve:rpuŋkt], *m.* (—s, *pl.* —e) centre of gravity.

Schwert [ʃve:rt], *n.* (—(e)s, *pl.* —er) sword.

Schwertgriff [ˈʃve:rtɡrɪf], *m.* (—s, *pl.* —e) hilt.

Schwertlilie [ˈʃve:rtli:ljə], *f.* (—, *pl.* —n) (*Bot.*) iris; fleur-de-lys.

Schwertstreich [ˈʃve:rtʃtraɪç], *m.* (—(e)s, *pl.* —e) sword-blow, swordstroke.

schwerwiegend [ˈʃve:rvi:ɡənt], *adj.* weighty.

Schwester [ˈʃvɛstər], *f.* (—, *pl.* —n) sister; *barmherzige* —, sister of mercy.

Schwesternschaft [ˈʃvɛstərnʃaft], *f.* (—, *pl.* —en) sisterhood; (*Am.*) sorority.

Schwibbogen [ˈʃvɪpbo:ɡən], *m.* (—s, *pl.* —) (*Archit.*) flying buttress.

Schwiegersohn [ˈʃvi:ɡərzo:n], *m.* (—s, *pl.* —̈e) son-in-law.

Schwiegertochter [ˈʃvi:ɡərtɔxtər], *f.* (—, *pl.* —̈) daughter-in-law.

Schwiele [ˈʃvi:lə], *f.* (—, *pl.* —n) hard skin, callus, weal.

schwielig [ˈʃvi:lɪç], *adj.* callous, horny.

schwierig [ˈʃvi:rɪç], *adj.* difficult, hard.

Schwierigkeit [ˈʃvi:rɪçkaɪt], *f.* (—, *pl.* —en) difficulty; *auf* —*en stoßen*, meet with difficulties.

schwimmen [ˈʃvɪmən], *v.n. irr.* (*aux.* sein) swim, float.

Schwimmer [ˈʃvɪmər], *m.* (—s, *pl.* —) swimmer.

Schwimmgürtel [ˈʃvɪmɡyrtəl], *m.* (—s, *pl.* —) life-belt.

Schwindel [ˈʃvɪndəl], *m.* (—s, *pl.* —) giddiness, dizziness, vertigo; swindle, fraud.

Schwindelanfall [ˈʃvɪndəlanfal], *m.* (—s, *pl.* —̈e) attack of giddiness, vertigo.

Schwindelei [ʃvɪndəˈlaɪ], *f.* (—, *pl.* —en) swindle, fraud, deceit.

schwindelhaft [ˈʃvɪndəlhaft], *adj.* fraudulent.

schwinden [ˈʃvɪndən], *v.n. irr.* (*aux.* sein) dwindle; disappear, vanish.

Schwindler [ˈʃvɪndlər], *m.* (—s, *pl.* —) swindler, humbug; cheat.

schwindlig [ˈʃvɪndlɪç], *adj.* dizzy, giddy.

Schwindsucht [ˈʃvɪntzuxt], *f.* (—, *no pl.*) (*Med.*) tuberculosis, consumption.

schwindsüchtig [ˈʃvɪntzyçtɪç], *adj.* (*Med.*) tubercular.

Schwinge [ˈʃvɪŋə], *f.* (—, *pl.* —n) wing.

schwingen [ˈʃvɪŋən], *v.a. irr.* brandish. — *v.n.* swing, vibrate. — *v.r. sich* —, vault; *sich auf den Thron* —, usurp *or* take possession of the throne.

Schwingung [ˈʃvɪŋuŋ], *f.* (—, *pl.* —en) vibration, oscillation.

Schwips [ʃvɪps], *m.* (—es, *pl.* —e) (*coll.*) tipsiness; *einen* — *haben*, be tipsy.

schwirren [ˈʃvɪrən], *v.n.* whir, buzz.

Schwitzbad [ˈʃvɪtsba:t], *n.* (—es, *pl.* —̈er) Turkish bath, steam-bath.

schwitzen [ˈʃvɪtsən], *v.n.* sweat, perspire.

schwören [ˈʃvøːrən], *v.a., v.n. irr.* swear, take an oath; *darauf kannst du* —, you can be quite sure of that, you bet; *falsch* —, forswear o.s., perjure o.s.

schwül [ʃvy:l], *adj.* sultry, close.

Schwüle [ˈʃvy:lə], *f.* (—, *no pl.*) sultriness.

Schwulst [ʃvulst], *m.* (—es, *no pl.*) bombast.

schwülstig [ˈʃvylstɪç], *adj.* bombastic, turgid.

Schwülstigkeit [ˈʃvylstɪçkaɪt], *f.* (—, *pl.* —en) bombastic style, turgidity.

Schwund [ʃvunt], *m.* (—(e)s, *no pl.*) dwindling, decline; shrinkage.

Schwung [ʃvuŋ], *m.* (—(e)s, *pl.* —̈e) swing, leap, bound; (*fig.*) verve, élan; (*Poet.*) flight, soaring.

schwunghaft [ˈʃvuŋhaft], *adj.* flourishing, soaring.

Schwungkraft [ˈʃvuŋkraft], *f.* (—, *no pl.*) centrifugal force; (*mental*) resilience.

Schwungrad [ˈʃvuŋra:t], *n.* (—s, *pl.* —̈er) fly-wheel.

schwungvoll [ˈʃvuŋfɔl], *adj.* spirited.

Schwur [ʃvu:r], *m.* (—(e)s, *pl.* —̈e) oath.

Schwurgericht [ˈʃvu:rɡərɪçt], *n.* (—s, *pl.* —e) (*Law*) assizes.

sechs [zɛks], *num. adj.* six.

Sechseck [ˈzɛksɛk], *n.* (—s, *pl.* —e) hexagon.

sechseckig [ˈzɛksɛkɪç], *adj.* hexagonal.

Sechser ['zɛksər], m. (—s, pl. —) coin of small value.

sechsspännig ['zɛksʃpɛnɪç], adj. drawn by six horses.

sechzehn ['zɛçtseːn], num. adj. sixteen.

sechzig ['zɛçtsɪç], num. adj. sixty.

Sediment [zediˈmɛnt], n. (—s, pl. —e) sediment.

See (1) [zeː], m. (—s, pl. —n) lake, pool.

See (2) [zeː], f. (—, no pl.) sea, ocean; hohe —, high seas; zur — gehen, go to sea, become a sailor.

Seeadler ['zeːadlər], m. (—s, pl. —) (Orn.) osprey.

Seebad ['zeːbaːt], n. (—s, pl. ˵er) seaside resort; bathe in the sea.

Seebär ['zeːbɛːr], m. (—en, pl. —en) (fig.) old salt.

Seefahrer ['zeːfaːrər], m. (—s, pl. —) mariner, navigator.

Seefahrt ['zeːfaːrt], f. (—, pl. —en) seafaring; voyage, cruise.

seefest ['zeːfɛst], adj. (ship) seaworthy; (person) a good sailor.

Seefischerei ['zeːfɪʃəraɪ], f. (—, no pl.) deep-sea fishing.

Seeflotte ['zeːflɔtə], f. (—, pl. —n) navy, fleet.

Seegang ['zeːgaŋ], m. (—s, no pl.) swell.

Seegras ['zeːgraːs], n. (—es, no pl.) seaweed.

Seehandel ['zeːhandəl], m. (—s, no pl.) maritime trade.

Seehund ['zeːhunt], m. (—s, pl. —e) (Zool.) seal.

Seeigel ['zeːiːgəl], m. (—s, pl. —) (Zool.) sea-urchin.

Seejungfrau ['zeːjuŋfrau], f. (—, pl. —en) mermaid.

Seekadett ['zeːkadɛt], m. (—en, pl. —en) midshipman; (naval) cadet.

Seekarte ['zeːkartə], f. (—, pl. —n) chart.

seekrank ['zeːkraŋk], adj. seasick.

Seekrieg ['zeːkriːk], m. (—s, pl. —e) naval war.

Seeküste ['zeːkystə], f. (—, pl. —n) sea-coast, shore, beach.

Seele ['zeːlə], f. (—, pl. —n) soul; mit ganzer —, with all my heart.

Seelenamt ['zeːlənamt], n. (—s, pl. ˵er) (Eccl.) office for the dead, requiem.

Seelenangst ['zeːlənaŋkst], f. (—, pl. ˵e) anguish, agony.

Seelenheil ['zeːlənhaɪl], n. (—s, no pl.) (Theol.) salvation.

Seelenhirt ['zeːlənhɪrt], m. (—en, pl. —en) pastor.

seelenlos ['zeːlənloːs], adj. inanimate.

Seelenmesse ['zeːlənmɛsə], f. (—, pl. —n) requiem; Mass for the dead.

Seelenruhe ['zeːlənruːə], f. (—, no pl.) tranquillity of mind.

seelenruhig ['zeːlənruːɪç], adj. cool, calm, collected, unperturbed.

Seelenstärke ['zeːlənʃtɛrkə], f. (—, no pl.) fortitude; composure.

seelenvergnügt ['zeːlənfɛrgnyːkt], adj. blissfully happy.

Seelenverwandtschaft ['zeːlənfɛrvant-ʃaft], f. (—, pl. —en) mental affinity, (mutual) understanding.

seelenvoll ['zeːlənfɔl], adj. wistful, soulful.

Seelenwanderung ['zeːlənvandəruŋ], f. (—, no pl.) transmigration of souls, metempsychosis.

Seeleute ['zeːlɔytə] see under **Seemann.**

seelisch ['zeːlɪʃ], adj. mental, psychological, psychic(al).

Seelsorge ['zeːlsɔrgə], f. (—, no pl.) (Eccl.) cure of souls; pastoral duties or work.

Seemann ['zeːman], m. (—s, pl. ˵er. Seeleute) seaman, sailor, mariner.

Seemeile ['zeːmaɪlə], f. (—, pl. —n) knot, nautical mile.

Seemöwe ['zeːmøːvə], f. (—, pl. —n) (Orn.) seagull.

Seemuschel ['zeːmuʃəl], f. (—, pl. —n) sea-shell.

Seepflanze ['zeːpflantsə], f. (—, pl. —n) marine plant.

Seerabe ['zeːraːbə], m. (—n, pl. —n) (Orn.) cormorant.

Seeräuber ['zeːrɔybər], m. (—s, pl. —) pirate.

Seerose ['zeːroːzə], f. (—, pl. —n) (Bot.) water-lily.

Seesalz ['zeːzalts], n. (—es, no pl.) bay salt, sea salt.

Seeschlacht ['zeːʃlaxt], f. (—, pl. —en) naval engagement, naval battle.

Seestern ['zeːʃtɛrn], m. (—s, pl. —e) (Zool.) starfish.

Seestille ['zeːʃtɪlə], f. (—, no pl.) calm (at sea).

Seetang ['zeːtaŋ], m. (—s, no pl.) (Bot.) seaweed.

seetüchtig ['zeːtyçtɪç], adj. seaworthy.

Seeuhr ['zeːuːr], f. (—, pl. —en) marine chronometer.

Seeuntüchtigkeit ['zeːuntyçtɪçkaɪt], f. (—, no pl.) unseaworthiness.

Seewasser ['zeːvasər], n. (—s, no pl.) sea-water, brine.

Seewesen ['zeːvezən], n. (—s, no pl.) naval affairs.

Seezunge ['zeːtsuŋə], f. (—, pl. —n) sole (fish).

Segel ['zeːgəl], n. (—s, pl. —) sail; großes —, mainsail; unter — gehen, set sail, put to sea; die — streichen, strike sail.

segelfertig ['zeːgəlfɛrtɪç], adj. ready to sail; sich — machen, get under sail.

Segelflugzeug ['zeːgəlfluːktsɔyk], n. (—s, pl. —e) glider(-plane).

Segelschiff ['zeːgəlʃɪf], n. (—s, pl. —e) sailing-vessel.

Segelstange ['zeːgəlʃtaŋə], f. (—, pl. —n) sail-yard.

Segen ['zeːgən], m. (—s, no pl.) blessing, benediction; (fig.) abundance; — sprechen, give the blessing, say grace.

segensreich ['ze:gǝnsraiç], *adj.* blessed, full of blessings; prosperous.

Segenswunsch ['ze:gǝnsvunʃ], *m.* (—es, *pl.* ˙˙e) good wish.

segnen ['ze:gnǝn], *v.a.* bless.

sehen ['ze:ǝn], *v.a. irr.* see, behold, perceive; *etwas gern* —, like s.th., approve of s.th. — *v.n.* look, see; *sich — lassen*, parade, show o.s., *wir werden —*, that remains to be seen, we shall see.

sehenswert ['ze:ǝnsve:rt], *adj.* worth seeing.

Sehenswürdigkeit ['ze:ǝnsvyrdiçkait], *f.* (—, *pl.* —en) curiosity, object of interest, tourist attraction; *(pl.)* sights.

Seher ['ze:ǝr], *m.* (—s, *pl.* —) seer, prophet.

Sehne ['ze:nǝ], *f.* (—, *pl.* —n) sinew, tendon; string.

sehnig ['ze:niç], *adj.* sinewy, muscular; *(meat)* tough.

sehnlich ['ze:nliç], *adj.* earnest, passionate, eager.

Sehnsucht ['ze:nzuxt], *f.* (—, *no pl.*) longing, yearning, desire.

sehr [ze:r], *adv.* very, much, greatly, very much; *zu* —, too much; — *gut*, very good; — *wohl*, very well.

Sehweite ['ze:vaitǝ], *f.* (—, *no pl.*) range of vision.

seicht [zaiçt], *adj.* shallow, superficial.

Seide ['zaidǝ], *f.* (—, *pl.* —n) silk.

Seidel ['zaidǝl], *n.* (—s, *pl.* —) *(dial.)* mug, tankard; pint.

seiden ['zaidǝn], *adj.* silk, silken, silky.

Seidenpapier ['zaidǝnpapi:r], *n.* (—s, *no pl.*) tissue-paper.

Seidenraupe ['zaidǝnraupǝ], *f.* (—, *pl.* —n) *(Ent.)* silkworm.

Seidenstoff ['zaidǝnʃtɔf], *m.* (—es, *pl.* —e) spun silk.

Seife ['zaifǝ], *f.* (—, *pl.* —n) soap; *ein Stück* —, a cake of soap.

seifen ['zaifǝn], *v.a.* soap.

Seifenschaum ['zaifǝnʃaum], *m.* (—s, *no pl.*) lather.

Seifenwasser ['zaifǝnvasǝr], *n.* (—s, *no pl.*) soap-suds.

seifig ['zaifiç], *adj.* soapy, saponaceous.

seihen ['zaiǝn], *v.a.* strain, filter.

Seil [zail], *n.* (—(e)s, *pl.* —e) rope; *straffes* —, taut rope, tight rope; *schlaffes* —, slack rope.

Seilbahn ['zailba:n], *f.* (—, *pl.* —en) funicular railway; cable car.

Seilbrücke ['zailbrykǝ], *f.* (—, *pl.* —n) rope bridge.

Seiltänzer ['zailtɛntsǝr], *m.* (—s, *pl.* —) tight-rope walker.

Seilziehen ['zailtsi:ǝn], *n.* (—s, *no pl.*) tug of war.

Seim [zaim], *m.* (—(e)s, *pl.* —e) strained honey.

Sein [zain], *n.* (—s, *no pl.*) being, existence.

sein (1) [zain], *v.n. irr.* *(aux.* sein) be, exist.

sein (2) [zain], *poss. adj.* his, her, its; one's. — *pers. pron.* his.

seinerseits ['zainǝrzaits], *adv.* for his part.

seinerzeit ['zainǝrtsait], *adv.* at that time, at the time, formerly.

seinesgleichen ['zainǝsglaiçǝn], *indecl. adj. & pron.* of his sort, such as he.

seinethalben ['zainǝthalbǝn], *adv.* on his account, for his sake, on his behalf.

seinetwegen ['zainǝtve:gǝn], *adv.* on his account, for his sake, on his behalf.

Seinige ['zainigǝ], *n.* (—n, *pl.* —n) his, his property; *(pl.)* his family, his people; *das* — *tun*, do o.'s share.

seit [zait], *prep. (Dat.)* since, for; — *gestern*, since yesterday, from yesterday onwards; — *einiger Zeit*, for some time past. — *conj.* see **seitdem**.

seitdem [zait'de:m], *adv.* since then, since that time. — *conj.* since.

Seite ['zaitǝ], *f.* (—, *pl.* —n) side, flank; *(book)* page; *etwas auf die* — *bringen*, put s.th. aside; *ich bin auf seiner* —, I side with him, I am on his side; *er hat seine guten* —*n*, he has his good points.

Seitenansicht ['zaitǝnanziçt], *f.* (—, *pl.* —en) profile.

Seitengleis ['zaitǝnglais], *n.* (—es, *pl.* —e) (railway) siding.

Seitenhieb ['zaitǝnhi:p], *m.* (—s, *pl.* —e) innuendo, sly hit, dig.

seitens ['zaitǝns], *prep. (Genit.)* on the part of.

Seitensprung ['zaitǝnʃpruŋ], *m.* (—s, *pl.* ˙˙e) side-leap, caper; *(fig.)* (amorous) escapade.

Seitenstraße ['zaitǝnʃtra:sǝ], *f.* (—, *pl.* —n) side-street.

Seitenstück ['zaitǝnʃtyk], *n.* (—s, *pl.* —e) companion-piece.

Seitenzahl ['zaitǝntsa:l], *f.* (—, *pl.* —en) page-number; number of pages.

seither [zait'he:r], *adv.* since that time, since then.

seitlich ['zaitliç], *adj.* lateral.

Sekretär [zekre'tɛ:r], *m.* (—s, *pl.* —e) secretary.

Sekretariat [zekreta'rja:t], *n.* (—s, *pl.* —e) secretariat, secretary's office.

Sekt [zɛkt], *m.* (—s, *pl.* —e) champagne.

Sekte ['zɛktǝ], *f.* (—, *pl.* —n) sect.

Sektierer [zɛk'ti:rǝr], *m.* (—s, *pl.* —) sectarian.

Sektion [zɛk'tsjo:n] *f.* (—, *pl.* —en) section; *(Med.)* dissection.

Sekundaner [zekun'da:nǝr], *m.* (—s, *pl.* —) pupil in the second (highest) form.

Sekundant [zekun'dant], *m.* (—en, *pl.* —en) *(Duelling)* second.

sekundär [zekun'dɛ:r], *adj.* secondary.

Sekunde [ze'kundǝ], *f.* (—, *pl.* —n) *(time)* second.

Sekundenzeiger [ze'kundǝntsaigǝr], *m.* (—s, *pl.* —) *(clock)* second-hand.

sekundieren [zekun'di:rǝn], *v.n. einem* —, second s.o.

selber ['zɛlbǝr], *indecl. adj. & pron.* self.

selb(ig) ['zɛlb(ig)], *adj.* the same.

selbst [zɛlpst], *indecl. adj. & pron.* self; — *ist der Mann*, depend on yourself; *von* —, of its own accord, spontaneously. — *adv.* even; — *wenn*, even if, even though; — *dann nicht*, not even then.

selbständig ['zɛlpʃtɛndɪç], *adj.* independent.

Selbstbestimmung ['zɛlpstbəʃtɪmuŋ], *f.* (—, *no pl.*) self-determination, autonomy.

selbstbewußt ['zɛlpstbəvust], *adj.* self-assertive, self-confident, conceited.

selbstherrlich ['zɛlpstherlɪç], *adj.* autocratic, tyrannical.

Selbstlaut ['zɛlpstlaut], *m.* (—s, *pl.* —e) vowel.

selbstlos ['zɛlpstlo:s], *adj.* unselfish, selfless, altruistic.

Selbstlosigkeit [zɛlpst'lo:zɪçkaɪt], *f.* (—, *no pl.*) unselfishness, altruism.

Selbstmord ['zɛlpstmɔrt], *m.* (—s, *pl.* —e) suicide.

selbstredend ['zɛlpstre:dənt], *adj.* self-evident, obvious.

Selbstsucht ['zɛlpstzuxt], *f.* (—, *no pl.*) selfishness, ego(t)ism.

selbstsüchtig ['zɛlpstzyçtɪç], *adj.* selfish, ego(t)istic(al).

selbstverständlich ['zɛlpstferʃtɛntlɪç], *adj.* self-evident. — *adv.* of course, obviously.

Selbstzweck ['zɛlpstsvek], *m.* (—s, *no pl.*) end in itself.

selig ['ze:lɪç], *adj.* blessed, blissful; (*fig.*) delighted; deceased, late; — *sprechen*, beatify.

Seligkeit ['ze:lɪçkaɪt], *f.* (—, *pl.* —en) bliss, blissfulness; (*Eccl.*) salvation, beatitude.

Seligsprechung ['ze:lɪçʃprɛçuŋ], *f.* (—, *pl.* —en) beatification.

Sellerie ['zɛləri:], *m.* (—s, *pl.* —s) (*Bot.*) celery.

selten ['zɛltən], *adj.* rare, scarce; (*fig.*) remarkable. — *adv.* seldom, rarely, infrequently.

Seltenheit ['zɛltənhaɪt], *f.* (—, *pl.* —en) rarity, curiosity, scarcity; (*fig.*) remarkableness.

Selterwasser ['zɛltərvasər], *n.* (—s, *no pl.*) soda-water.

seltsam ['zɛltza:m], *adj.* strange, unusual, odd, curious.

Semester [ze'mɛstər], *n.* (—s, *pl.* —) university term, semester.

Semit [ze'mi:t], *m.* (—en, *pl.* —en) Semite, Jew.

semmelblond ['zɛməlblɔnt], *adj.* flaxen-haired.

Semmelkloß ['zɛməlklo:s], *m.* (—es, *pl.* ⸚e) bread dumpling.

Senator [ze'na:tɔr], *m.* (—s, *pl.* —en) senator.

senden ['zɛndən], *v.a. irr.* send, despatch; (*money*) remit. — *v.a. reg.* (*Rad.*) broadcast.

Sender ['zɛndər], *m.* (—s, *pl.* —) sender; (*Rad.*) (broadcasting) station, transmitter.

Sendling ['zɛntlɪŋ], *m.* (—s, *pl.* —e) (*Poet.*) emissary.

Sendschreiben ['zɛntʃraɪbən], *n.* (—s, *pl.* —) epistle, missive.

Sendung ['zɛnduŋ], *f.* (—, *pl.* —en) (*Comm.*) shipment, consignment; (*fig.*) mission; (*Rad.*) broadcast, transmission.

Senegal ['ze:nəgal], *n.* Senegal.

Senf [zɛnf], *m.* (—s, *no pl.*) mustard.

sengen ['zɛŋən], *v.a.* singe, scorch; — *und brennen*, lay waste.

Senkblei ['zɛŋkblaɪ], *n.* (—s, *pl.* —e) plummet.

Senkel ['zɛŋkəl], *m.* (—s, *pl.* —) shoe-lace.

senken ['zɛŋkən], *v.a.* lower, sink. — *v.r. sich* —, sink, go down; dip, slope, subside.

senkrecht ['zɛŋkrɛçt], *adj.* perpendicular.

Senkung ['zɛŋkuŋ], *f.* (—, *pl.* —en) depression, dip, subsidence.

Senn(e) ['zɛn(ə)], *m.* (—n, *pl.* —(e)n) Alpine herdsman.

Sennerin ['zɛnərɪn], *f.* (—, *pl.* —nen) Alpine dairy-woman.

Senneschoten ['zɛnəʃo:tən], *f. pl.* senna pods.

Sennhütte ['zɛnhytə], *f.* (—, *pl.* —n) Alpine dairy; chalet.

sensationell [zɛnzatsjo'nɛl], *adj.* sensational.

Sense ['zɛnzə], *f.* (—, *pl.* —n) scythe.

sensibel [zɛn'zi:bəl], *adj.* sensitive.

Sentenz [zɛn'tɛnts], *f.* (—, *pl.* —en) aphorism.

sentimental [zɛntimɛn'ta:l], *adj.* sentimental.

separat [zepa'ra:t], *adj.* separate, special.

September [zɛp'tɛmbər], *m.* (—s, *pl.* —) September.

Serbien ['zɛrbjən], *n.* Serbia.

Serie ['ze:rjə], *f.* (—, *pl.* —n) series.

Service [zɛr'vi:s], *n.* (—s, *pl.* —) dinner-set, dinner-service.

servieren [zɛr'vi:rən], *v.a., v.n.* serve, wait at table.

Serviertisch [zɛr'vi:rtɪʃ], *m.* (—es, *pl.* —e) sideboard.

Sessel ['zɛsəl], *m.* (—s, *pl.* —) armchair, easy-chair; (*Austr. dial.*) chair.

seßhaft ['zɛshaft], *adj.* settled, domiciled.

setzen ['zɛtsən], *v.a.* set, put, place; (*monument*) erect; (*bet*) stake; (*Typ.*) compose. — *v.r. sich* —, sit down; (*coffee*) settle; *sich bei einem in Gunst* —, ingratiate o.s. with s.o.

Setzer ['zɛtsər], *m.* (—s, *pl.* —) compositor.

Setzling ['zɛtslɪŋ], *m.* (—s, *pl.* —e) young tree, young plant.

Seuche ['zɔyçə], *f.* (—, *pl.* —n) pestilence; epidemic.

seufzen ['zɔyftsən], *v.n.* sigh.

Seufzer ['zɔyftsər], *m.* (—s, *pl.* —) sigh.

Sexta ['zɛksta:], *f.* (—, *pl.* —s) (*Sch.*) sixth form, lowest form.

Sextant

Sextant [zɛks'tant], *m.* (—en, *pl.* —en) sextant.

sexuell [zɛksu'ɛl], *adj.* sexual.

sezieren [ze'tsi:rən], *v.a.* dissect.

Seziersaal [ze'tsi:rza:l], *m.* (—s, *pl.* —säle) dissecting-room.

Sibirien [zi'bi:rjən], *n.* Siberia.

sich [zɪç], *pron.* oneself, himself, herself, itself, themselves; each other.

Sichel ['zɪçəl], *f.* (—, *pl.* —n) sickle.

sicher ['zɪçər], *adj.* certain, sure, secure, safe; confident, positive; *seiner Sache — sein*, be sure of o.'s ground; — *stellen*, secure.

Sicherheit ['zɪçərhaɪt], *f.* (—, *pl.* —en) certainty; security, safety; confidence, positiveness; *in — bringen*, secure.

sichern ['zɪçərn], *v.a.* secure, make secure; assure, ensure.

Sicherung ['zɪçəruŋ], *f.* (—, *pl.* —en) securing; (*Elec.*) fuse; (*gun*) safety-catch.

Sicht [zɪçt], *f.* (—, *no pl.*) sight.

sichtbar ['zɪçtba:r], *adj.* visible; conspicuous.

sichten ['zɪçtən], *v.a.* sift, sort out; sight.

sichtlich ['zɪçtlɪç], *adv.* visibly.

Sichtwechsel ['zɪçtvɛksəl], *m.* (—s, *pl.* —) (*Banking*) sight-bill, bill payable on sight.

Sichtweite ['zɪçtvaɪtə], *f.* (—, *no pl.*) range of vision.

sickern ['zɪkərn], *v.n.* (*aux.* sein) leak, ooze, seep.

Sie [zi:], *pron.* (*formal*) you.

sie [zi:], *pers. pron.* she, her; they, them.

Sieb [zi:p], *n.* (—(e)s, *pl.* —e) sieve; riddle; colander.

sieben (1) ['zi:bən], *v.a.* (*Cul.*) sift, strain.

sieben (2) ['zi:bən], *num. adj.* seven; *meine — Sachen*, my belongings.

Siebeneck ['zi:bənɛk], *n.* (—s, *pl.* —e) heptagon.

Siebengestirn ['zi:bəngəʃtɪrn], *n.* (—s, *no pl.*) Pleiades.

siebenmal ['zi:bənma:l], *adv.* seven times.

Siebenmeilenstiefel [zi:bən'maɪlənʃti:fəl], *m. pl.* seven-league boots.

Siebenschläfer ['zi:bənʃlɛ:fər], *m.* (—s, *pl.* —) lazy-bones.

siebzehn ['zi:ptse:n], *num. adj.* seventeen.

siebzig ['zi:ptsɪç], *num. adj.* seventy.

siech [zi:ç], *adj.* (*rare*) sick, infirm.

siechen ['zi:çən], *v.n.* be in bad health.

sieden ['zi:dən], *v.a., v.n.* boil, seethe.

siedeln ['zi:dəln], *v.n.* settle.

Siedlung ['zi:dluŋ], *f.* (—, *pl.* —en) settlement; housing estate.

Sieg [zi:k], *m.* (—(e)s, *pl.* —e) victory; *den — davontragen*, win the day.

Siegel ['zi:gəl], *n.* (—s, *pl.* —) seal; *Brief und —*, sign and seal.

Siegelbewahrer ['zi:gəlbəva:rər], *m.* (—s, *pl.* —) Lord Privy Seal; keeper of the seal.

Siegellack ['zi:gəllak], *n.* (—s, *no pl.*) sealing wax.

siegeln ['zi:gəln], *v.a.* seal.

siegen ['zi:gən], *v.n.* conquer, win, be victorious, triumph (over).

Sieger ['zi:gər], *m.* (—s, *pl.* —) victor, conqueror.

Siegesbogen ['zi:gəsbo:gən], *m.* (—s, *pl.* ·:) triumphal arch.

Siegeszeichen ['zi:gəstsaɪçən], *n.* (—s, *pl.* —) sign of victory, trophy.

sieghaft ['zi:khaft], *adj.* victorious, triumphant.

siegreich ['zi:kraɪç], *adj.* victorious, triumphant.

siehe! ['zi:ə], *excl.* see! look! lo and behold!

Sierra Leone ['siɛra le'o:nə], *f.* Sierra Leone.

Signal [zɪg'na:l], *n.* (—s, *pl.* —e) signal.

Signalement [zɪgnalə'mã], *n.* (—s, *pl.* —s) personal description.

Signalglocke [zɪg'na:lglɔkə], *f.* (—, *pl.* —n) warning-bell.

signalisieren [zɪgnali'zi:rən], *v.a.* signal.

Signatarmacht [zɪgna'ta:rmaxt], *f.* (—, *pl.* ·:e) signatory power.

signieren [zɪg'ni:rən], *v.a.* sign.

Silbe ['zɪlbə], *f.* (—, *pl.* —n) syllable.

Silbenmaß ['zɪlbənma:s], *n.* (—es, *pl.* —e) (*Poet.*) metre.

Silbenrätsel ['zɪlbənrɛ:tsəl], *n.* (—s, *pl.* —) charade.

Silber ['zɪlbər], *n.* (—s, *no pl.*) silver; plate.

Silberbuche ['zɪlbərbu:xə], *f.* (—, *pl.* —n) white beech(-tree).

Silberfuchs ['zɪlbərfuks], *m.* (—es, *pl.* ·:e) (*Zool.*) silver fox.

silbern ['zɪlbərn], *adj.* made of silver, silvery.

Silberpappel ['zɪlbərpapəl], *f.* (—, *pl.* —n) (*Bot.*) white poplar(-tree).

Silberschimmel ['zɪlbərʃɪməl],'*m.* (—s, *pl.* —) grey-white horse.

Silberzeug ['zɪlbərtsɔyk], *n.* (—s, *no pl.*) (silver) plate.

Silvester [zɪl'vɛstər], *m.* (—s, *pl.* —) New Year's Eve.

Similistein ['zi:miliʃtaɪn], *m.* (—s, *pl.* —e) imitation or paste jewellery.

Sims [zɪms], *m.* (—es, *pl.* —e) cornice, moulding, shelf, ledge.

Simulant [zimu'lant], *m.* (—en, *pl.* —en) malingerer.

simulieren [zimu'li:rən], *v.a.* simulate.

simultan [zimul'ta:n], *adj.* simultaneous.

Singapur [zɪŋga'pu:r], *n.* Singapore.

Singdrossel ['zɪŋdrɔsəl], *f.* (—, *pl.* —n) (*Orn.*) common thrush.

singen ['zɪŋən], *v.a., v.n. irr.* sing.

Singspiel ['zɪŋʃpi:l], *n.* (—s, *pl.* —e) musical comedy, light opera, opera buffa.

Singular ['zɪŋgula:r], *m.* (—s, *pl.* —e) singular.

sinken ['zɪŋkən], *v.n. irr. (aux. sein)*
sink; *(price)* decline, drop, fall; *den
Mut* — *lassen*, lose heart.

Sinn [zɪn], *m.* (—(e)s, *pl.* —e) sense;
intellect, mind; consciousness, memory; taste, meaning, purport; wish;
etwas im — *haben*, have s.th. in mind,
intend s.th.; *leichter* —, lightheartedness; *andern* —*es werden*, change o's
mind; *das hat keinen* —, there is no
sense in that; *von* —*en sein*, be out of
o.'s senses; *seine fünf* —*e beisammen
haben*, be in o.'s right mind; *sich etwas
aus dem* — *schlagen*, dismiss s.th.
from o.'s mind; *es kommt mir in den*
—, it occurs to me.

Sinnbild ['zɪnbɪlt], *n.* (—s, *pl.* —er)
symbol, emblem.

sinnen ['zɪnən], *v.n. irr.* meditate,
reflect.

Sinnesänderung ['zɪnəsɛndəruŋ], *f.*
(—, *pl.* —en) change of mind.

Sinnesart ['zɪnəsaːrt], *f.* (—, *no pl.*)
disposition, character.

Sinnesorgan ['zɪnəsɔrgaːn], *n.* (—s,
pl. —e) sense-organ.

Sinnestäuschung ['zɪnəstɔyʃuŋ], *f.* (—,
pl. —en) illusion, hallucination.

sinnfällig ['zɪnfɛlɪç], *adj.* obvious,
striking.

Sinngedicht ['zɪngədɪçt], *n.* (—es,
pl. —e) epigram.

sinnig ['zɪnɪç], *adj.* thoughtful, meaningful; judicious, fitting.

sinnlich ['zɪnlɪç], *adj.* sensual, sensuous.

Sinnlichkeit ['zɪnlɪçkaɪt], *f.* (—, *no
pl.*) sensuality, sensuousness.

sinnlos ['zɪnloːs], *adj.* senseless, meaningless, pointless.

sinnreich ['zɪnraɪç], *adj.* ingenious.

Sinnspruch ['zɪnʃprux], *m.* (—es,
pl. —e) sentence, maxim, device,
motto.

sinnverwandt ['zɪnfɛrvant], *adj.* synonymous.

sinnvoll ['zɪnfɔl], *adj.* meaningful,
significant.

sinnwidrig ['zɪnviːdrɪç], *adj.* nonsensical, absurd.

Sintflut ['zɪntfluːt], *f.* (—, *no pl.*)
(Bibl.) the Flood.

Sinus ['ziːnus], *m.* (—, *pl.* —se) *(Maths.)*
sine.

Sippe ['zɪpə], *f.* (—, *pl.* —n) kin, tribe,
family, clan.

Sippschaft ['zɪpʃaft], *f.* (—, *pl.* —en)
kindred; *die ganze* —, the whole
caboodle.

Sirene [ziˈreːnə], *f.* (—, *pl.* —n) siren.

Sirup ['ziːrup], *m.* (—s, *no pl.*) syrup,
treacle.

Sitte ['zɪtə], *f.* (—, *pl.* —n) custom,
mode, fashion; *(pl.)* manners, morals;
—*n und Gebräuche*, manners and
customs.

Sittengesetz ['zɪtəngəzɛts], *n.* (—es,
pl. —e) moral law.

Sittenlehre ['zɪtənleːrə], *f.* (—, *no pl.*)
moral philosophy, ethics.

sittenlos ['zɪtənloːs], *adj.* immoral,
profligate, licentious.

Sittenprediger ['zɪtənpreːdɪgər], *m.*
(—s, *pl.* —) moraliser.

Sittich ['zɪtɪç], *m.* (—s, *pl.* —e)
(Orn.) budgerigar; parakeet.

sittig ['zɪtɪç], *adj.* well-behaved.

sittlich ['zɪtlɪç], *adj.* moral.

Sittlichkeit ['zɪtlɪçkaɪt], *f.* (—, *no pl.*)
morality, morals.

sittsam ['zɪtzaːm], *adj.* modest, demure.

situiert [zɪtuˈiːrt], *adj. gut (schlecht)* —,
well (badly) off.

Sitz [zɪts], *m.* (—es, *pl.* —e) seat,
chair; residence, location, place;
(Eccl.) see.

Sitzarbeit ['zɪtsarbaɪt], *f.* (—, *pl.* —en)
sedentary work.

Sitzbad ['zɪtsbaːt], *n.* (—(e)s, *pl.* —er)
hip bath.

sitzen ['zɪtsən], *v.n. irr.* sit, be seated;
(fig.) be in prison; *(dress)* fit; —
lassen, throw over, jilt; — *bleiben*,
remain seated; *(school)* stay in the same
class, not be moved up; be a wallflower; remain unmarried.

Sitzfleisch ['zɪtsflaɪʃ], *n.* (—es, *no pl.*)
(coll.) kein — *haben*, be restless,
lack application.

Sitzplatz ['zɪtsplats], *m.* (—es, *pl.* —e)
seat.

Sitzung ['zɪtsuŋ], *f.* (—, *pl.* —en)
meeting, sitting, session.

Sitzungsprotokoll ['zɪtsuŋsprotokɔl],
n. (—s, *pl.* —e) minutes (of a meeting).

Sitzungssaal ['zɪtsuŋszaːl], *m.* (—s,
pl. —säle) board-room, conference
room.

Sizilien [ziˈtsiːljən], *n.* Sicily.

Skala ['skaːla], *f.* (—, *pl.* —len) scale;
(Mus.) gamut.

Skandal [skanˈdaːl], *m.* (—s, *pl.* —e)
scandal; row, riot; — *machen*, kick
up a row.

skandalös [skandaˈløːs], *adj.* scandalous.

skandieren [skanˈdiːrən], *v.a. (Poet.)*
scan.

Skandinavien [skandɪˈnaːvjən], *n.* Scandinavia.

Skelett [skeˈlɛt], *n.* (—s, *pl.* —e)
skeleton.

Skepsis ['skɛpsɪs], *f.* (—, *no pl.*) scepticism, doubt.

skeptisch ['skɛptɪʃ], *adj.* sceptical,
doubtful.

Skizze ['skɪtsə], *f.* (—, *pl.* —n) sketch.

skizzieren [skɪˈtsiːrən], *v.a.* sketch.

Sklave ['sklaːvə], *m.* (—n, *pl.* —n) slave;
zum —*n machen*, enslave.

Sklavendienst ['sklaːvəndiːnst], *m.*
(—es, *no pl.*) slavery.

Sklaverei [sklaːvəˈraɪ], *f.* (—, *no pl.*)
slavery, thraldom.

Skonto ['skɔnto], *m. & n.* (—s, *pl.* —s)
discount.

Skrupel ['skruːpəl], *m.* (—s, *pl.* —)
scruple; *sich* — *machen*, have scruples.

skrupulös [skrupuˈløːs], *adj.* scrupulous, meticulous.

Skulptur [skulp'tuːr], *f.* (—, *pl.* —en) sculpture.

skurril [sku'riːl], *adj.* ludicrous.

Slawe ['slaːvə], *m.* (—n, *pl.* —n) Slav.

slawisch ['slaːvɪʃ], *adj.* Slav, Slavonic.

Slowake [slo'vaːkə], *m.* (—n, *pl.* —n) Slovakian.

Slowene [slo've:nə], *m.* (—n, *pl.* —n) Slovenian.

Smaragd [sma'rakt], *m.* (—(e)s, *pl.* —e) emerald.

smaragden [sma'raktən], *adj.* emerald.

Smoking ['smo:kɪŋ], *m.* (—s, *pl.* —s) dinner-jacket.

so [zo:], *adv.* so, thus, in this way, like this; —? really? —*ist es*, that is how it is; —*daß*, so that; — . . . *wie*, as . . . as; *na — was!* well, I never! — *conj.* then, therefore.

sobald [zo'balt], *conj.* as soon as, directly.

Socke ['zɔkə], *f.* (—, *pl.* —n) sock.

Sockel ['zɔkəl], *m.* (—s, *pl.* —) pedestal, plinth, stand, base.

Soda ['zo:da], *n.* (—s, *no pl.*) (carbonate of) soda.

sodann [zo'dan], *adv. conj.* then.

Sodbrennen ['zo:tbrɛnən], *n.* (—s, *no pl.*) heartburn.

soeben [zo'e:bən], *adv.* just now.

sofern [zo'fɛrn], *conj.* if, in case, so far as.

sofort [zo'fɔrt], *adv.* at once, immediately.

Sog [zo:k], *m.* (—(e)s, *pl.* —e) undertow, suction.

sogar [zo'ga:r], *adv.* even.

sogenannt [zogə'nant], *adj.* so-called, would-be.

sogleich [zo'glaiç], *adv.* at once, immediately.

Sohle ['zo:lə], *f.* (—, *pl.* —n) sole; (*mine*) floor.

Sohn [zo:n], *m.* (—(e)s, *pl.* —e) son; *der verlorene* —, the prodigal son.

solange [zo'laŋə], *conj.* as long as.

Solbad ['zo:lba:t], *n.* (—s, *pl.* —er) saline bath.

solch [zɔlç], *adj., dem. pron.* such.

solcherlei ['zɔlçərlai], *adj.* of such a kind, suchlike.

Sold [zɔlt], *m.* (—(e)s, *no pl.*) army pay.

Soldat [zɔl'da:t], *m.* (—en, *pl.* —en) soldier.

Soldateska [zɔlda'tɛska], *f.* (—, *pl.* —s) soldiery.

Söldner ['zœldnər], *m.* (—s, *pl.* —) mercenary, hireling.

Sole ['zo:lə], *f.* (—, *pl.* —n) salt-water, brine.

Solei ['zo:lai], *n.* (—s, *pl.* —er) pickled egg.

solidarisch [zoli'da:rɪʃ], *adj.* joint, jointly responsible; unanimous.

Solidarität [zolidari'tɛ:t], *f.* (—, *no pl.*) solidarity.

Solist [zo'lɪst], *m.* (—en, *pl.* —en) soloist.

Soll [zɔl], *n.* (—s, *no pl.*) debit; — *und Haben*, debit and credit.

sollen ['zɔlən], *v.n. irr.* be obliged, be compelled; have to; be supposed to; (*aux.*) shall, should etc.; *ich soll*, I must, I am to; *er soll krank sein*, he is said to be ill; *ich sollte eigentlich*, I really ought to.

Söller ['zœlər], *m.* (—s, *pl.* —) loft, garret, balcony.

Somali [zo'ma:li], *n.* Somalia.

somit [zo'mɪt], *adv.* consequently, therefore, accordingly.

Sommer ['zɔmər], *m.* (—s, *pl.* —) summer.

Sommerfäden ['zɔmərfɛ:dən], *m. pl.* gossamer.

Sommerfrische ['zɔmərfrɪʃə], *f.* (—, *pl.* —n) holiday resort.

Sommergetreide ['zɔmərgətraidə], *n.* (—s, *no pl.*) spring corn.

Sommersonnenwende ['zɔmərzɔnənvendə], *f.* (—, *pl.* —n) summer solstice.

Sommersprosse ['zɔmərʃprɔsə], *f.* (—, *pl.* —n) freckle.

sonach [zo'na:x], *adv.* therefore, consequently.

Sonate [zo'na:tə], *f.* (—, *pl.* —n) sonata.

Sonde ['zɔndə], *f.* (—, *pl.* —n) sounding-lead, plummet; probe.

sonder ['zɔndər], (*obs.*) *prep.* (*Acc.*) without.

Sonderausgabe ['zɔndərausga:bə], *f.* (—, *pl.* —n) separate edition; special edition.

Sonderausschuß ['zɔndərausʃus], *m.* (—sses, *pl.* ⁻sse) select committee.

sonderbar ['zɔndərba:r], *adj.* strange, odd, queer, singular, peculiar.

sonderlich ['zɔndərlɪç], *adj.* special, especial, particular. — *adv. nicht* —, not much.

Sonderling ['zɔndərlɪŋ], *m.* (—s, *pl.* —e) freak, odd character, crank.

sondern ['zɔndərn], *v.a.* separate, distinguish, differentiate. — *conj.* but; *nicht nur*, . . . — *auch*, not only . . . but also.

Sonderrecht ['zɔndərrɛçt], *n.* (—s, *pl.* —e) special privilege.

sonders ['zɔndərs], *adv. samt und* —, all and each, all and sundry.

Sonderstellung ['zɔndərʃteluŋ], *f.* (—, *no pl.*) exceptional position.

Sonderung ['zɔndəruŋ], *f.* (—, *pl.* —en) separation.

Sonderzug ['zɔndərtsu:k], *m.* (—s, *pl.* ⁻e) special train.

sondieren [zɔn'di:rən], *v.a.* (*wound*) probe; (*ocean*) plumb; (*fig.*) sound.

Sonett [zo'nɛt], *n.* (—(e)s, *pl.* —e) sonnet.

Sonnabend ['zɔna:bənt], *m.* (—s, *pl.* —e) Saturday.

Sonne ['zɔnə], *f.* (—, *pl.* —n) sun.

sonnen ['zɔnən], *v.r. sich* —, sun o.s., bask in the sun, sunbathe.

Sonnenaufgang ['zɔnənaufgaŋ], *m.* (—s, *pl.* ⁻e) sunrise.

Sonnenbrand ['zɔnənbrant], *m.* (—s, *pl.* ⁻e) sunburn.

Sonnendeck ['zɔnəndɛk], *n.* (—s, *pl.* —e) awning.

Sonnenfinsternis ['zɔnənfɪnstərnɪs], *f.* (—, *pl.* —se) eclipse of the sun.

sonnenklar ['zɔnənkla:r], *adj.* very clear, as clear as daylight.

Sonnenschirm ['zɔnənʃɪrm], *m.* (—s, *pl.* —e) parasol, sunshade.

Sonnenstich ['zɔnənʃtɪç], *n.* (—(e)s, *no pl.*) sunstroke.

Sonnenuhr ['zɔnənu:r], *f.* (—, *pl.* —en) sundial.

Sonnenuntergang ['zɔnənuntərgaŋ], *m.* (—s, *pl.* ꞏe) sunset.

Sonnenwende ['zɔnənvɛndə], *f.* (—, *no pl.*) solstice.

Sonntag ['zɔnta:k], *m.* (—s, *pl.* —e) Sunday.

sonntags ['zɔnta:ks], *adv.* on Sundays, of a Sunday.

Sonntagsjäger ['zɔnta:ksjɛ:gər], *m.* (—s, *pl.* —) amateur sportsman.

sonor [zo'no:r], *adj.* sonorous.

sonst [zɔnst], *adv.* else, otherwise, besides, at other times; — *noch etwas?* anything else?

sonstig ['zɔnstɪç], *adj.* other, existing besides.

sonstwo ['zɔnstvo], *adv.* elsewhere, somewhere else.

Sopran [zo'pra:n], *m.* (—s, *pl.* —e) soprano.

Sorbett ['zɔrbɛt], *n.* (—s, *pl.* —s) sherbet.

Sorge ['zɔrgə], *f.* (—, *pl.* —n) care; grief, worry; sorrow; anxiety; concern; (*pl.*) troubles, worries; — *tragen dass* . . . , see to it that . . . ; — *tragen zu,* take care of; — *um,* concern for.

sorgen ['zɔrgən], *v.n.* — *für,* care for, provide for, look after. — *v.r. sich* — *um,* worry about.

sorgenvoll ['zɔrgənfɔl], *adj.* uneasy, troubled, anxious.

Sorgfalt ['zɔrkfalt], *f.* (—, *no pl.*) care, attention.

sorgfältig ['zɔrkfɛltɪç], *adj.* careful, painstaking; elaborate.

sorglos ['zɔrklo:s], *adj.* careless, irresponsible, unconcerned, indifferent; carefree.

sorgsam ['zɔrkza:m], *adj.* careful, heedful.

Sorte ['zɔrtə], *f.* (—, *pl.* —n) sort, kind, species, brand.

sortieren [zɔr'ti:rən], *v.a.* sort (out).

Sortiment [zɔrti'mɛnt], *n.* (—s, *pl.* —e) assortment; bookshop.

Sortimentsbuchhändler [zɔrti'mɛntsbu:xhɛndlər], *m.* (—s, *pl.* —) retail bookseller.

Soße ['zo:sə], *f.* (—, *pl.* —n) sauce, gravy.

Souffleur [suf'lø:r], *m.* (—s, *pl.* —e) prompter.

Soutane [su'ta:nə], *f.* (—, *pl.* —n) cassock, soutane.

Souterrain [sutɛ'rɛ̃], *n.* (—s, *pl.* —s) basement.

souverän [su:və'rɛ:n], *adj.* sovereign; (*fig.*) supremely good.

Souveränität [su:vərɛ:ni'tɛ:t], *f.* (—, *no pl.*) sovereignty.

soviel [zo'fi:l], *adv.* so much; — *wie,* as much as. — *conj.* so far as; — *ich weiß,* as far as I know.

sowie [zo'vi:], *conj.* as, as well as, as soon as.

Sowjet [sɔv'jet], *m.* (—s, *pl.* —s) Soviet.

sowohl [zo'vo:l], *conj.* — *wie,* as well as.

sozial [zo'tsja:l], *adj.* social.

sozialisieren [zotsjali'zi:rən], *v.a.* nationalise.

Sozialwissenschaft [zo'tsja:lvɪsənʃaft], *f.* (—, *pl.* —en) sociology; social science.

Sozietät [zotsje'tɛ:t], *f.* (—, *pl.* —en) partnership.

Sozius ['zotsjus], *m.* (—, *pl.* —se, **Socii**) partner; pillion-rider; —*sitz,* (*motor cycle*) pillion (seat).

sozusagen ['zo:tsuza:gən], *adv.* as it were, so to speak.

Spagat [ʃpa'ga:t], *m.* (—(e)s, *no pl.*) (*dial.*) string, twine; (*Dancing*) the splits.

spähen ['ʃpɛ:ən], *v.n.* look out, watch; (*Mil.*) scout; spy.

Späher ['ʃpɛ:ər], *m.* (—s, *pl.* —) scout; spy.

Spalier [ʃpa'li:r], *n.* (—s, *pl.* —e) trellis; — *bilden,* form a lane (*of people*).

Spalierobst [ʃpa'li:ro:pst], *n.* (—(e)s, *no pl.*) wall-fruit.

Spalt [ʃpalt], *m.* (—(e)s, *pl.* —e) crack, rift, cleft, rent; (*glacier*) crevasse.

Spalte ['ʃpaltə], *f.* (—, *pl.* —n) (*newspaper*) column.

spalten ['ʃpaltən], *v.a.* split, cleave, slit. — *v.r. sich* —, divide, break up, split up; (*in two*) bifurcate.

Spaltholz ['ʃpalthɔlts], *n.* (—es, *no pl.*) fire-wood.

Spaltpilz ['ʃpaltpɪlts], *m.* (—es, *pl.* —e) fission-fungus.

Spaltung ['ʃpaltuŋ], *f.* (—, *pl.* —en) cleavage; (*atomic*) fission; (*fig.*) dissension, rupture; (*Eccl.*) schism.

Span [ʃpa:n], *m.* (—(e)s, *pl.* ꞏe) chip, chippings, shavings.

Spange ['ʃpaŋə], *f.* (—, *pl.* —n) clasp, buckle.

Spanien ['ʃpa:njən], *n.* Spain.

spanisch ['ʃpa:nɪʃ], *adj.* Spanish; —*e Wand,* folding screen; *es kommt mir* — *vor,* it is Greek to me.

Spann [ʃpan], *m.* (—(e)s, *pl.* ꞏe) instep.

Spanne ['ʃpanə], *f.* (—, *pl.* —n) span; *eine* — *Zeit,* a short space of time.

spannen ['ʃpanən], *v.a.* stretch, strain, span.

spannend ['ʃpanənt], *adj.* thrilling, tense.

Spannkraft ['ʃpankraft], *f.* (—, *no pl.*) elasticity.

Spannung ['ʃpanuŋ], *f.* (—, *pl.* —en) tension, suspense, strain; (*fig.*) eager expectation, curiosity, suspense, close attention; (*Elec.*) voltage.

Sparbüchse

Sparbüchse ['ʃpaːrbyksə], *f.* (—, *pl.* —n) money-box.

sparen ['ʃpaːrən], *v.a.*, *v.n.* save, economise, put by, lay by.

Spargel ['ʃpargəl], *m.* (—s, *pl.* —) asparagus.

Spargelder ['ʃpaːrgɛldər], *n. pl.* savings.

Sparkasse ['ʃpaːrkasə], *f.* (—, *pl.* —n) savings bank.

spärlich ['ʃpɛːrlɪç], *adj.* scant, scanty, sparse.

Sparpfennig ['ʃpaːrpfɛnɪç], *m.* (—s, *pl.* —e) nest-egg.

Sparren ['ʃparən], *m.* (—s, *pl.* —) spar, rafter; *er hat einen —*, he has a screw loose.

sparsam ['ʃpaːrzaːm], *adj.* economical, thrifty, frugal.

Spaß [ʃpaːs], *m.* (—es, *pl.* ¨e) jest, fun, joke; *aus —, im —, zum —*, in fun; *— verstehen*, take a joke; *es macht mir —*, it amuses me, it is fun for me.

spaßen ['ʃpaːsən], *v.n.* jest, joke.

spaßhaft ['ʃpaːshaft], *adj.* funny, facetious, jocular.

Spaßverderber ['ʃpaːsfɛrdɛrbər], *m.* (—s, *pl.* —) spoil-sport.

Spaßvogel ['ʃpaːsfoːgəl], *m.* (—s, *pl.* ¨) wag.

Spat [ʃpaːt], *m.* (—(e)s, *pl.* —e) (*Min.*) spar.

spät [ʃpɛːt], *adj.* late; *wie — ist es?* what is the time? *zu — kommen*, be late.

Spätabend ['ʃpɛːtaːbənt], *m.* (—s, *pl.* —e) latter part of the evening, late evening.

Spatel ['ʃpaːtəl], *m.* (—s, *pl.* —) spatula.

Spaten ['ʃpaːtən], *m.* (—s, *pl.* —) spade.

Spatenstich ['ʃpaːtənʃtɪç], *m.* (—(e)s, *pl.* —e) *den ersten — tun*, turn the first sod.

später ['ʃpɛːtər], *adv.* later (on), afterwards.

spätestens ['ʃpɛːtəstəns], *adv.* at the latest.

Spätling ['ʃpɛːtlɪŋ], *m.* (—s, *pl.* —e) late arrival; late fruit.

Spätsommer ['ʃpɛːtzɔmər], *m.* (—s, *pl.* —) Indian summer.

Spatz [ʃpats], *m.* (—en *pl.* —en) (*Orn.*) sparrow.

spazieren [ʃpaˈtsiːrən], *v.n.* (*aux.* sein) walk leisurely, stroll; *— gehen*, go for a walk, take a stroll; *— führen*, take for a walk.

Spazierfahrt [ʃpaˈtsiːrfaːrt], *f.* (—, *pl.* —en) (pleasure-)drive.

Spazierstock [ʃpaˈtsiːrʃtɔk], *m.* (—s, *pl.* ¨e) walking-stick.

Spazierweg [ʃpaˈtsiːrveːk], *m.* (—s, *pl.* —e) walk, promenade.

Specht [ʃpɛçt], *m.* (—(e)s, *pl.* —e) (*Orn.*) woodpecker.

Speck [ʃpɛk], *m.* (—(e)s, *no pl.*) bacon; *eine Scheibe —*, a rasher of bacon.

speckig ['ʃpɛkɪç], *adj.* fat.

Speckschwarte ['ʃpɛkʃvarte], *f.* (—, *pl.* —n) bacon-rind.

Speckseite ['ʃpɛkzaɪtə], *f.* (—, *pl.* —n) flitch of bacon.

spedieren [ʃpeˈdiːrən], *v.a.* forward; despatch.

Spediteur [ʃpediˈtøːr], *m.* (—s, *pl.* —e) forwarding agent, furniture-remover, carrier.

Spedition [ʃpediˈtsjoːn], *f.* (—, *pl.* —en) conveyance; forwarding agency.

Speer [ʃpeːr], *m.* (—(e)s, *pl.* —e) spear, lance.

Speiche ['ʃpaɪçə], *f.* (—, *pl.* —n) spoke.

Speichel ['ʃpaɪçəl], *m.* (—s, *no pl.*) spittle, saliva.

Speicher ['ʃpaɪçər], *m.* (—s, *pl.* —) granary, warehouse, storehouse; loft.

speien ['ʃpaɪən], *v.a.*, *v.n. irr.* spit; vomit, be sick.

Speise ['ʃpaɪzə], *f.* (—, *pl.* —n) food, nourishment, dish.

Speisekammer ['ʃpaɪzəkamər], *f.* (—, *pl.* —n) larder, pantry.

Speisekarte ['ʃpaɪzəkartə], *f.* (—, *pl.* —n) bill of fare, menu.

speisen ['ʃpaɪzən], *v.a.* feed, give to eat. — *v.n.* eat, dine, sup, lunch.

Speiseröhre ['ʃpaɪzərøːrə], *f.* (—, *pl.* —n) gullet.

Speisewagen ['ʃpaɪzəvaːgən], *m.* (—s, *pl.* —) (*Railw.*) dining-car.

Spektakel [ʃpɛkˈtaːkəl], *m.* (—s, *no pl.*) uproar, hubbub; shindy, rumpus; noise, row.

Spektrum ['ʃpɛktrum], *n.* (—s, *pl.* Spektren) spectrum.

Spekulant [ʃpekuˈlant], *m.* (—en, *pl.* —en) speculator.

spekulieren [ʃpekuˈliːrən], *v.n.* speculate; theorise.

Spende ['ʃpɛndə], *f.* (—, *pl.* —n) gift, donation; bounty.

spenden ['ʃpɛndən], *v.a.* bestow, donate, contribute.

Spender ['ʃpɛndər], *m.* (—s, *pl.* —) donor, giver, benefactor.

spendieren [ʃpɛnˈdiːrən], *v.a.* (give a) treat, pay for, stand.

Sperber ['ʃpɛrbər], *m.* (—s, *pl.* —) (*Orn.*) sparrow-hawk.

Sperling ['ʃpɛrlɪŋ], *m.* (—s, *pl.* —e) (*Orn.*) sparrow.

sperrangelweit ['ʃpɛraŋəlvaɪt], *adv.* wide open.

Sperre ['ʃpɛrə], *f.* (—, *pl.* —n) shutting, closing, blockade, blocking; closure; ban; (*Railw.*) barrier.

sperren ['ʃpɛrən], *v.a.* spread out; (*Typ.*) space; shut, close, block; cut off; *ins Gefängnis —*, put in prison. — *v.r. sich — gegen*, offer resistance to.

Sperrhaken ['ʃpɛrhaːkən], *m.* (—s, *pl.* —) catch, ratchet.

Sperrsitz ['ʃpɛrzɪts], *m.* (—es, *pl.* —e) (*Theat.*) stall.

Sperrung ['ʃpɛruŋ], *f.* (—, *pl.* —en) barring, obstruction, block, blockade; (*Comm.*) embargo.

Sperrzeit ['ʃpɛrtsaɪt], *f.* (—, *pl.* —en) closing-time.

Spesen ['ʃpeːzən], *f. pl.* charges, expenses.

spesenfrei ['ʃpeːzənfraɪ], *adj.* free of charge; expenses paid.

Spezereien [ʃpeːtsəˈraɪən], *f. pl.* spices.

spezialisieren [ʃpetsjaliˈziːrən], *v.a.* specify. — *v.r. sich* —, specialise.

Spezialist [ʃpetsjaˈlɪst], *m.* (—en, *pl.* —en) specialist, expert.

Spezialität [ʃpetsjaliˈtɛːt], *f.* (—, *pl.* —en) speciality, (*Am.*) specialty.

speziell [ʃpeˈtsjɛl], *adj.* special, particular.

Spezies ['ʃpeːtsjɛs], *f.* (—, *pl.* —) species; (*Maths.*) rule.

Spezifikation [ʃpetsifikaˈtsjoːn], *f.* (—, *pl.* —en) specification.

spezifisch [ʃpeˈtsiːfɪʃ], *adj.* specific.

spezifizieren [ʃpetsifiˈtsiːrən], *v.a.* specify.

Spezifizierung [ʃpetsifiˈtsiːruŋ], *f.* (—, *pl.* —en) specification.

Spezimen ['ʃpeːtsimən], *n.* (—s, *pl.* —mina) specimen.

Sphäre ['sfɛːrə], *f.* (—, *pl.* —n) sphere.

sphärisch ['sfɛːrɪʃ], *adj.* spherical.

Spickaal ['ʃpɪkaːl], *m.* (—s, *pl.* —e) smoked eel.

spicken ['ʃpɪkən], *v.a.* lard; *den Beutel* —, fill o.'s purse.

Spiegel ['ʃpiːgəl], *m.* (—s, *pl.* —) mirror, looking-glass.

spiegelblank ['ʃpiːgəlblaŋk], *adj.* sparkling, shiny, polished.

Spiegelei ['ʃpiːgəlaɪ], *n.* (—s, *pl.* —er) fried egg.

Spiegelfechterei ['ʃpiːgəlfɛçtəraɪ], *f.* (—, *pl.* —en) shadow-boxing, make-believe.

Spiegelfenster ['ʃpiːgəlfɛnstər], *n.* (—s, *pl.* —) plate-glass window.

spiegeln ['ʃpiːgəln], *v.n.* glitter, shine. — *v.a.* reflect. — *v.r. sich* —, be reflected.

Spiegelscheibe ['ʃpiːgəlʃaɪbə], *f.* (—, *pl.* —n) plate-glass pane.

Spiegelung ['ʃpiːgəluŋ], *f.* (—, *pl.* —en) reflection; mirage.

Spiel [ʃpiːl], *n.* (—(e)s, *pl.* —e) play; game; sport; (*Theat.*) acting, performance; (*Mus.*) playing; *ehrliches* (*unehrliches*) —, fair (foul) play; *leichtes* —, walk-over; *auf dem stehen*, be at stake; *aufs — setzen*, stake, risk; *die Hand im — haben*, have a finger in the pie; *gewonnenes — haben*, gain o.'s point; *ein gewagtes — treiben*, play a bold game; *sein — mit einem treiben*, trifle with s.o.

Spielart ['ʃpiːlaːrt], *f.* (—, *pl.* —en) manner of playing; variety.

Spielbank ['ʃpiːlbaŋk], *f.* (—, *pl.* —en) casino; gambling-table.

Spieldose ['ʃpiːldoːzə], *f.* (—, *pl.* —n) musical box.

spielen ['ʃpiːlən], *v.a., v.n.* play; gamble; (*Mus.*) play; (*Theat.*) act; *eine Rolle* —, play a part; *mit dem Gedanken* —, toy with the idea.

spielend ['ʃpiːlənt], *adv.* easily.

Spieler ['ʃpiːlər], *m.* (—s, *pl.* —) player; gambler; gamester.

Spielerei [ʃpiːləˈraɪ], *f.* (—, *pl.* —en) child's play; trivialities.

Spielhölle ['ʃpiːlhœlə], *f.* (—, *pl.* —n) gambling-den.

Spielmann ['ʃpiːlman], *m.* (—s, *pl.* **Spielleute**) musician, fiddler; (*Middle Ages*) minstrel.

Spielmarke ['ʃpiːlmarkə], *f.* (—, *pl.* —n) counter, chip.

Spielplan ['ʃpiːlplaːn], *m.* (—s, *pl.* ∵e) (*Theat.*) repertory.

Spielplatz ['ʃpiːlplats], *m.* (—es, *pl.* ∵e) playground.

Spielraum ['ʃpiːlraum], *m.* (—s, *no pl.*) elbow-room; (*fig.*) scope; margin; clearance.

Spielsache ['ʃpiːlzaxə], *f.* (—, *pl.* —n) toy, plaything.

Spielschule ['ʃpiːlʃuːlə], *f.* (—, *pl.* —n) infant-school, kindergarten.

Spieltisch ['ʃpiːltɪʃ], *m.* (—es, *pl.* —e) card-table.

Spieluhr ['ʃpiːluːr], *f.* (—, *pl.* —en) musical clock.

Spielverderber ['ʃpiːlfɛrdɛrbər], *m.* (—s, *pl.* —) spoilsport.

Spielwaren ['ʃpiːlvaːrən], *f. pl.* toys.

Spielzeit ['ʃpiːltsaɪt], *f.* (—, *pl.* —en) playtime; (*Theat.*) season.

Spielzeug ['ʃpiːltsɔyk], *n.* (—s, *pl.* —e) plaything, toy.

Spieß [ʃpiːs], *m.* (—es, *pl.* —e) spear, pike; (*Cul.*) spit.

Spießbürger ['ʃpiːsbyrgər], *m.* (—s, *pl.* —) Philistine.

spießen ['ʃpiːsən], *v.a.* spear, pierce.

Spießer ['ʃpiːsər], *m.* (—s, *pl.* —) Philistine.

Spießgeselle ['ʃpiːsgəzɛlə], *m.* (—n, *pl.* —n) accomplice, companion *or* partner in crime.

spießig ['ʃpiːsɪç], *adj.* (*coll.*) Philistine, uncultured, narrow-minded.

Spießruten ['ʃpiːsruːtən], *f. pl.* — *laufen*, run the gauntlet.

Spinat [ʃpiˈnaːt], *m.* (—s, *no pl.*) spinach.

Spind [ʃpɪnt], *n.* (—(e)s, *pl.* —e) cupboard.

Spindel ['ʃpɪndəl], *f.* (—, *pl.* —n) spindle; distaff; (*staircase*) newel.

spindeldürr ['ʃpɪndəldyr], *adj.* as thin as a lath.

Spindelholz ['ʃpɪndəlhɔlts], *n.* (—es, *no pl.*) spindle-tree wood.

Spinett [ʃpiˈnɛt], *n.* (—s, *pl.* —e) spinet.

Spinne ['ʃpɪnə], *f.* (—, *pl.* —n) spider.

spinnefeind ['ʃpɪnəfaɪnt], *adj. einander* — *sein*, hate each other like poison.

spinnen ['ʃpɪnən], *v.a. irr.* spin. — *v.n.* (*coll.*) be off o.'s head, be crazy.

Spinnerei [ʃpɪnəˈraɪ], *f.* (—, *pl.* —en) spinning-mill.

Spinngewebe ['ʃpɪŋgəveːbə], *n.* (—s, *pl.* —) cobweb.

Spinnrocken ['ʃpɪnrɔkən], *m.* (—s, *pl.* —) distaff.

spintisieren [ʃpɪntiˈziːrən], *v.n.* muse, meditate.

Spion [ʃpi'o:n], *m.* (—s, *pl.* —e) spy.

spionieren [ʃpio'ni:rən], *v.n.* spy, pry.

Spirale [ʃpi'ra:lə], *f.* (—, *pl.* —n) spiral.

Spirituosen [ʃpiritu'o:zən], *pl.* spirits, liquors.

Spiritus [ʃpi'ritus], *m.* (—, *pl.* —se) alcohol, spirits of wine; *denaturierter* —, methylated spirits.

Spiritusbrennerei [ʃpi:ritusbrenəraɪ], *f.* (—, *pl.* —en) distillery.

Spiritusgehalt [ʃpi:ritusgəhalt], *m.* (—s, *pl.* —e) (*alcoholic*) strength, proof.

Spital [ʃpi'ta:l], *n.* (—s, *pl.* ˙ˑer) infirmary; hospital.

Spitz [ʃpits], *m.* (—es, *pl.* —e) Pomeranian dog; *einen — haben,* (*coll.*) be slightly tipsy.

spitz [ʃpits], *adj.* pointed; (*fig.*) snappy, biting.

Spitzbart [ʃpitsba:rt], *m.* (—s, *pl.* ˙ˑe) imperial (beard), pointed beard.

Spitzbogen [ʃpitsbo:gən], *m.* (—s, *pl.* —) pointed arch, Gothic arch.

Spitzbogenfenster [ʃpitsbo:gənfenstər], *n.* (—s, *pl.* —) lancet window.

Spitzbube [ʃpitsbu:bə], *m.* (—n, *pl.* —n) rogue; rascal; scamp.

Spitzbubenstreich [ʃpitsbu:bən-ʃtraɪç], *m.* (—(e)s, *pl.* —e) act of roguery, knavery.

spitzbübisch [ʃpitsby:biʃ], *adj.* roguish.

Spitze [ʃpitsə], *f.* (—, *pl.* —n) point; tip; top, peak; extremity; (*pipe*) mouthpiece; (*cigarette*) holder; (*pen*) nib; lace; *etwas auf die — treiben,* carry s.th. to extremes; *an der — stehen,* be at the head of.

Spitzel [ʃpitsəl], *m.* (—s, *pl.* —) police-agent; informer.

spitzen [ʃpitsən], *v.a.* sharpen; *die Ohren —,* prick up o.'s ears; *sich auf etwas —,* await s.th. eagerly, be all agog for s.th.

Spitzenbelastung [ʃpitsənbəlastuŋ], *f.* (—, *pl.* —en) peak load.

Spitzenleistung [ʃpitsənlaɪstuŋ], *f.* (—, *pl.* —en) maximum output; peak performance.

Spitzentuch [ʃpitsəntu:x], *n.* (—(e)s, *pl.* ˙ˑer) lace scarf.

spitzfindig [ʃpitsfindiç], *adj.* subtle, crafty; hair-splitting.

Spitzhacke [ʃpitshakə], *f.* (—, *pl.* —n) pickaxe.

spitzig [ʃpitsiç], *adj.* pointed, sharp; (*fig.*) biting, poignant.

Spitzmaus [ʃpitsmaus], *f.* (—, *pl.* ˙ˑe) (*Zool.*) shrew.

Spitzname [ʃpitsna:mə], *m.* (—ns, *pl.* —n) nickname.

spitzwinklig [ʃpitsviŋkliç], *adj.* acute-angled.

spleißen [ʃplaɪsən], *v.a. irr.* split, cleave.

Splitter [ʃplitər], *m.* (—s, *pl.* —) splinter, chip.

splittern [ʃplitərn], *v.n.* (*aux.* sein) splinter.

splitternackt [ʃplitərnakt], *adj.* stark naked.

spontan [ʃpɔn'ta:n], *adj.* spontaneous.

sporadisch [ʃpo'ra:diʃ], *adj.* sporadic.

Spore [ʃpo:rə], *f.* (—, *pl.* —n) spore.

Sporn [ʃpɔrn], *m.* (—s, *pl.* **Sporen**) spur.

spornstreichs [ʃpɔrnʃtraɪçs], *adv.* post-haste, at once.

Sportler [ʃpɔrtlər], *m.* (—s, *pl.* —) athlete, sportsman.

sportlich [ʃpɔrtliç], *adj.* athletic; sporting.

sportsmäßig [ʃpɔrtsme:siç], *adj.* sportsmanlike.

Spott [ʃpɔt], *m.* (—(e)s, *no pl.*) mockery; scorn; *Gegenstand des —s,* laughing-stock; *— treiben mit,* mock, deride; *zum Schaden den — hinzufügen,* add insult to injury.

spottbillig [ʃpɔtbiliç], *adj.* ridiculously cheap, dirt-cheap.

Spöttelei [ʃpœtə'laɪ], *f.* (—, *pl.* —en) sarcasm.

spötteln [ʃpœtəln], *v.n.* mock, jeer.

spotten [ʃpɔtən], *v.a., v.n.* deride, scoff (at); *es spottet jeder Beschreibung,* it defies description.

Spötter [ʃpœtər], *m.* (—s, *pl.* —) mocker, scoffer.

Spötterei [ʃpœtə'raɪ], *f.* (—, *pl.* —en) mockery, derision.

Spottgedicht [ʃpɔtgədiçt], *n.* (—(e)s, *pl.* —e) satirical poem.

spöttisch [ʃpœtiʃ], *adj.* mocking, satirical, ironical, scoffing.

spottlustig [ʃpɔtlustiç], *adj.* flippant, satirical.

Spottschrift [ʃpɔtʃrift], *f.* (—, *pl.* —en) satire, lampoon.

Sprache [ʃpra:xə], *f.* (—, *pl.* —n) speech, language, tongue; expression; diction; discussion; *etwas zur — bringen,* bring a subject up; *zur — kommen,* come up for discussion; *heraus mit der —!* speak out!

Sprachfehler [ʃpra:xfe:lər], *m.* (—s, *pl.* —) impediment in o.'s speech.

sprachfertig [ʃpra:xfertiç], *adj.* having a ready tongue; a good linguist, fluent.

Sprachgebrauch [ʃpra:xgəbraux], *m.* (—(e)s, *pl.* ˙ˑe) (linguistic) usage.

Sprachkenner [ʃpra:xkenər], *m.* (—s, *pl.* —) linguist.

sprachkundig [ʃpra:xkundiç], *adj.* proficient in languages.

Sprachlehre [ʃpra:xle:rə], *f.* (—, *no pl.*) grammar.

sprachlich [ʃpra:xliç], *adj.* linguistic.

sprachlos [ʃpra:xlo:s], *adj.* speechless, tongue-tied; — *dastehen,* be dumb-founded.

Sprachrohr [ʃpra:xro:r], *n.* (—s, *pl.* —e) megaphone, speaking-tube; (*fig.*) mouthpiece.

Sprachschatz [ʃpra:xʃats], *m.* (—es, *no pl.*) vocabulary.

Sprachvergleichung [ʃpra:xferglaɪçuŋ], *f.* (—, *no pl.*) comparative philology.

Sprachwerkzeug ['ʃpraːxvərktsɔyk], *n.* (—s, *pl.* —e) organ of speech.

Sprachwissenschaft ['ʃpraːxvisənʃaft], *f.* (—, *pl.* —en) linguistics, philology.

sprechen ['ʃprɛçən], *v.a.,v.n. irr.* speak, declare, say; talk; *für einen* —, put in a good word for s.o., speak up for s.o.; *er ist nicht zu* —, he is not available; *auf einen gut zu* — *sein,* feel well disposed towards s.o.; *schuldig* —, pronounce guilty; *das Urteil* —, pass sentence.

sprechend ['ʃprɛçənt], *adj.* expressive; — *ähnlich,* strikingly alike.

Sprecher ['ʃprɛçər], *m.* (—s, *pl.* —) speaker, orator, spokesman; (*Rad.*) announcer.

Sprechstunde ['ʃprɛçʃtundə], *f.* (—, *pl.* —n) consulting hours, surgery hours; office hours.

Sprechzimmer ['ʃprɛçtsimər], *n.* (—s, *pl.*—) consulting-room.

spreizen ['ʃpraitsən], *v.a.* spread open; *die Beine* —, plant o.'s legs wide apart, straddle. — *v.r. sich* —, give o.s. airs.

Sprengbombe ['ʃprɛŋbɔmbə], *f.* (—, *pl.* —n) (high explosive) bomb.

Sprengel ['ʃprɛŋəl], *m.* (—s, *pl.* —) diocese.

sprengen ['ʃprɛŋən], *v.a.* sprinkle; water; burst, explode; burst open, blow up; *eine Versammlung* —, break up a meeting. — *v.n.* (*aux.* sein) ride at full speed, gallop.

Sprengpulver ['ʃprɛŋpulvər], *n.* (—s, *no pl.*) blasting-powder.

Sprengstoff ['ʃprɛŋʃtɔf], *m.* (—es, *pl.* —e) explosive.

Sprengwagen ['ʃprɛŋvaːgən], *m.* (—s, *pl.* —) sprinkler; water-cart.

sprenkeln ['ʃprɛŋkəln], *v.a.* speckle.

Spreu ['ʃprɔy], *f.* (—, *no pl.*) chaff.

Sprichwort ['ʃpriçvɔrt], *n.* (—s, *pl.* ˸er) proverb, adage, saying.

sprießen ['ʃpriːsən], *v.n. irr.* sprout, shoot, germinate.

Springbrunnen ['ʃpriŋbrunən], *m.* (—s, *pl.* —) fountain.

springen ['ʃpriŋən], *v.n. irr.* (*aux.* sein) spring, leap, jump; (*glass*) burst; *etwas* — *lassen,* (*coll.*) treat s.o. to s.th.

Springer ['ʃpriŋər], *m.* (—s, *pl.* —) jumper, acrobat; (*Chess*) knight.

Springflut ['ʃpriŋfluːt], *f.* (—, *pl.* —en) spring-tide.

Springtau ['ʃpriŋtau], *n.* (—s, *pl.* —e) skipping-rope; (*Naut.*) slip-rope.

Sprit [ʃprit], *m.* (—s, *pl.* —e) spirit alcohol; (*sl.*) fuel, petrol.

Spritze ['ʃpritsə], *f.* (—, *pl.* —n) squirt, syringe; fire-engine; (*coll.*) injection.

spritzen ['ʃpritsən], *v.a.* squirt, spout, spray, sprinkle; (*coll.*) inject. — *v.n.* gush forth.

Spritzkuchen ['ʃpritskuːxən], *m.* (—s, *pl.* —) fritter.

Spritztour ['ʃpritstuːr], *f.* (—, *pl.* —en) (*coll.*) pleasure trip, outing; (*coll.*) spin.

spröde ['ʃprøːdə], *adj.* (*material*) brittle; (*person*) stubborn; coy, prim, prudish.

Sprödigkeit ['ʃprøːdiçkait], *f.* (—, *no pl.*) (*material*) brittleness; (*person*) stubbornness; coyness, primness, prudery.

Sproß [ʃprɔs], *m.* (—sses, *pl.* —sse) sprout, shoot, germ; (*fig.*) scion, offspring.

Sprosse ['ʃprɔsə], *f.* (—, *pl.* —n) (*ladder*) step, rung.

Sprößling ['ʃprøːsliŋ], *m.* (—s, *pl.* —e) scion, offspring.

Sprotte ['ʃprɔtə], *f.* (—, *pl.* —n) sprat.

Spruch [ʃprux], *m.* (—(e)s, *pl.* ˸e) saying, aphorism; proverb; (*obs.*) saw; (*judge*) sentence, verdict.

spruchreif ['ʃpruxraif], *adj.* ripe for judgment; ready for a decision.

Sprudel ['ʃpruːdəl], *m.* (—s, *pl.* —) bubbling spring; (*coll.*) soda water.

sprudeln ['ʃpruːdəln], *v.n.* bubble, gush.

sprühen ['ʃpryːən], *v.a.* sprinkle, scatter, spray. — *v.n.* sparkle, emit sparks; (*rain*) drizzle.

sprühend ['ʃpryːənt], *adj.* (*fig.*) sparkling, scintilating, brilliant.

Sprühregen ['ʃpryːreːgən], *m.* (—s, *no pl.*) drizzling rain, drizzle.

Sprung [ʃpruŋ], *m.* (—(e)s, *pl.* ˸e) leap, bound, jump; chink, crack; *nur auf einen* — *zu Besuch kommen,* pay a flying visit; *auf dem* — *sein zu,* be on the point of; *sich auf den* — *machen,* cut and run, (*coll.*) fly; *große ˸e machen,* (*coll.*) live it up, cut a dash.

Sprungfeder ['ʃpruŋfeːdər], *f.* (—, *pl.* —n) spring.

Sprungkraft ['ʃpruŋkraft], *f.* (—, *no pl.*) springiness, elasticity, buoyancy.

Spucke ['ʃpukə], *f.* (—, *no pl.*) spittle, saliva.

spucken ['ʃpukən], *v.a., v.n.* spit.

Spuk [ʃpuːk], *m.* (—s, *pl.* —e) haunting; ghost, spectre, apparition; (*coll.*) spook.

spuken ['ʃpuːkən], *v.n.* haunt; be haunted.

spukhaft ['ʃpuːkhaft], *adj.* uncanny, phantom-like, ghost-like, spooky.

Spule ['ʃpuːlə], *f.* (—, *pl.* —n) spool; (*Elec.*) coil.

Spüleimer ['ʃpyːlaimər], *m.* (—s, *pl.* —e) slop-pail.

spülen ['ʃpyːlən], *v.a.* rinse, wash.

Spülicht ['ʃpyːliçt], *n.* (—s, *no pl.*) dish-water.

Spund [ʃpunt], *m.* (—(e)s, *pl.* ˸e) bung.

Spundloch ['ʃpuntlɔx], *n.* (—s, *pl.* ˸er) bung-hole.

Spur [ʃpuːr], *f.* (—, *pl.* —en) footprint, track, trail; spoor; (*fig.*) trace, vestige; *frische* —, hot scent; *einer Sache auf die* — *kommen,* be on the track of s.th.; *keine* — *von,* not a trace of, not an inkling of.

spüren ['ʃpyːrən], *v.a.* trace, track (down); feel, sense; notice.

Spürhund ['ʃpyːrhunt], *m.* (—s, *pl.* —e) tracker dog, setter, beagle; (*fig.*) spy, sleuth.

spurlos ['ʃpuːrloːs], *adj.* trackless, without a trace; *es ging — an ihm vorüber*, it left no mark on him; *— verschwinden*, vanish into thin air.

Spürsinn ['ʃpyːrzɪn], *m.* (—s, *no pl.*) scent; flair; sagacity, shrewdness.

Spurweite ['ʃpuːrvaɪtə], *f.* (—, *pl.* —n) gauge, width of track.

sputen ['ʃpuːtən], *v.r. sich —*, make haste, hurry.

Staat [ʃtaːt], *m.* (—(e)s, *pl.* —en) state; government; pomp, show, parade; *— machen*, make a show of.

Staatenbund ['ʃtaːtənbunt], *m.* (—(e)s, *pl.* ⁀e) confederacy, federation.

staatlich ['ʃtaːtlɪç], *adj.* belonging to the state, public, national.

Staatsangehörige ['ʃtaːtsangəhøːrɪgə], *m.* (—n, *pl.* —n) citizen (of a country), subject, national.

Staatsangehörigkeit ['ʃtaːtsangəhøːrɪçkaɪt], *f.* (—, *pl.* —en) nationality.

Staatsanwalt ['ʃtaːtsanvalt], *m.* (—s, *pl.* ⁀e) public prosecutor, Attorney-General.

Staatsbeamte ['ʃtaːtsbəamtə], *m.* (—n, *pl.* —n) civil servant, employee of the state.

Staatsbürger ['ʃtaːtsbyrgər], *m.* (—s, *pl.* —) citizen, national.

Staatsdienst ['ʃtaːtsdiːnst], *m.* (—(e)s, *pl.* ⁀e) civil service, government service.

Staatseinkünfte ['ʃtaːtsaɪnkynftə], *f. pl.* public revenue.

Staatsgesetz ['ʃtaːtsgəzɛts], *n.* (—es, *pl.* ⁀e) statute law.

Staatsgewalt ['ʃtaːtsgəvalt], *f.* (—, *no pl.*) executive power.

Staatshaushalt ['ʃtaːtshaushalt], *m.* (—s, *no pl.*) state finances, budget.

Staatshaushaltsanschlag ['ʃtaːtshaushaltsanʃlaːk], *m.* (—s, *pl.* ⁀e) budget estimates.

Staatskanzler ['ʃtaːtskantslər], *m.* (—s, *pl.* —) Chancellor.

Staatskasse ['ʃtaːtskasə], *f.* (—, *no pl.*) public exchequer, treasury.

Staatskörper ['ʃtaːtskœrpər], *m.* (—s, *pl.* —) body politic.

Staatskosten ['ʃtaːtskɔstən], *f. pl. auf —*, at (the) public expense.

Staatskunst ['ʃtaːtskunst], *f.* (—, *no pl.*) statesmanship; statecraft.

Staatsminister ['ʃtaːtsminɪstər], *m.* (—s, *pl.* —) cabinet minister; minister of state.

Staatsrat ['ʃtaːtsraːt], *m.* (—s, *no pl.*) council of state; (*pl.* ⁀e) councillor of state.

Staatsrecht ['ʃtaːtsrɛçt], *n.* (—(e)s, *no pl.*) constitutional law.

Staatssiegel ['ʃtaːtsziːgəl], *n.* (—s, *pl.* —) Great Seal, official seal.

Staatsstreich ['ʃtaːtsʃtraɪç], *m.* (—(e)s, *pl.* ⁀e) coup d'état.

Staatswirtschaft ['ʃtaːtsvɪrtʃaft], *f.* (—, *no pl.*) political economy.

Staatszimmer ['ʃtaːtstsɪmər], *n.* (—s, *pl.* —) state apartment.

Stab [ʃtaːp], *m.* (—(e)s, *pl.* ⁀e) staff; stick, rod, pole; crosier; mace; (*Mil.*) field-officers, staff; *den — über einen brechen*, condemn s.o. (to death).

stabil [ʃtaˈbiːl], *adj.* steady, stable, firm.

stabilisieren [ʃtabiliˈziːrən], *v.a.* stabilise.

Stabreim ['ʃtaːpraɪm], *m.* (—s, *no pl.*) alliteration.

Stabsarzt ['ʃtaːpsartst], *m.* (—es, *pl.* ⁀e) (*Mil.*) medical officer.

Stabsquartier ['ʃtaːpskvartiːr], *n.* (—s, *pl.* ⁀e) (*Mil.*) headquarters.

Stachel ['ʃtaxəl], *m.* (—s, *pl.* —n) (*animal*) sting; (*plant*) prickle, thorn; (*fig.*) keen edge, sting; stimulus; *wider den — löcken*, kick against the pricks.

Stachelbeere ['ʃtaxəlbeːrə], *f.* (—, *pl.* —n) (*Bot.*) gooseberry.

Stachelschwein ['ʃtaxəlʃvaɪn], *n.* (—s, *pl.* ⁀e) (*Zool.*) hedgehog, porcupine.

stachlig ['ʃtaxlɪç], *adj.* prickly, thorny; (*fig.*) disagreeable.

Stadion ['ʃtaːdjon], *n.* (—s, *pl.* —dien) sports-arena, stadium.

Stadium ['ʃtaːdjum], *n.* (—s, *pl.* —dien) stage (of development), phase.

Stadt [ʃtat], *f.* (—, *pl.* ⁀e) town; city.

Stadtbahn ['ʃtatbaːn], *f.* (—, *pl.* —en) metropolitan railway.

Städtchen ['ʃtɛtçən], *n.* (—s, *pl.* —) small town, township.

Städter ['ʃtɛtər], *m.* (—s, *pl.* —) townsman.

Stadtgemeinde ['ʃtatgəmaɪndə], *f.* (—, *pl.* —n) municipality.

städtisch ['ʃtɛtɪʃ], *adj.* municipal.

Stadtmauer ['ʃtatmauər], *f.* (—, *pl.* —n) town wall, city wall.

Stadtrat ['ʃtatraːt], *m.* (—s, *no pl.*) town council; (*pl.* ⁀e) town councillor; alderman.

Stadtteil ['ʃtattaɪl], *m.* (—s, *pl.* —e) ward, district, part of a town.

Stadttor ['ʃtattoːr], *n.* (—s, *pl.* —e) city-gate.

Stadtverordnete ['ʃtatfɛrɔrdnətə], *m.* (—n, *pl.* —n) town councillor.

Stafette [ʃtaˈfeːtə], *f.* (—, *pl.* —n) courier; relay.

Staffel ['ʃtafəl], *f.* (—, *pl.* —n) step, rundle, rung, round; relay; (*fig.*) degree; (*Aviat.*) squadron.

Staffelei [ʃtafəˈlaɪ], *f.* (—, *pl.* —en) easel.

staffeln ['ʃtafəln], *v.a.* grade; differentiate; stagger.

Staffelung ['ʃtafəluŋ], *f.* (—, *pl.* —en) gradation.

stagnieren [ʃtagˈniːrən], *v.n.* stagnate.

Stahl [ʃtaːl], *m.* (—(e)s, *pl.* ⁀e) steel.

stählen ['ʃtɛːlən], *v.a.* steel, harden, temper; brace.

stählern ['ʃtɛːlərn], *adj.* made of steel, steely.

Stahlquelle ['ʃtaːlkvɛlə], *f.* (—, *pl.* —n) chalybeate spring; mineral spring.

Stahlstich ['ʃtaːlʃtɪç], *m.* (—(e)s, *pl.* —e) steel-engraving.

Stählung ['ʃtɛ:luŋ], *f.* (—, *no pl.*) steeling; (*fig.*) bracing.
Stahlwaren ['ʃta:lva:rən], *f. pl.* hardware, cutlery.
Stall [ʃtal], *m.* (—(e)s, *pl.* ⁻e) stable; (*pig*) sty; (*dog*) kennel.
Stallbursche ['ʃtalburʃə], *m.* (—n, *pl.* —n) stable-boy, groom.
Stallungen ['ʃtaluŋən], *f. pl.* stabling, stables.
Stambul ['stambul], *n.* Istanbul.
Stamm [ʃtam], *m.* (—(e)s, *pl.* ⁻e) (*tree*) trunk; (*people*) tribe, family, race; (*words*) stem; root.
Stammaktie ['ʃtamaktsjə], *f.* (—, *pl.* —n) (*Comm.*) original share.
Stammbaum ['ʃtambaum], *m.* (—s, *pl.* ⁻e) pedigree; family tree.
Stammbuch ['ʃtambu:x], *n.* (—(e)s, *pl.* ⁻er) album.
stammeln ['ʃtaməln], *v.a., v.n.* stammer, stutter; falter.
stammen ['ʃtamən], *v.n.* (*aux.* sein) be descended from, spring from, originate from, stem from; be derived from.
Stammesgenosse ['ʃtaməsgənɔsə], *m.* (—n, *pl.* —n) kinsman, clansman.
Stammgast ['ʃtamgast], *m.* (—es, *pl.* ⁻e) regular customer.
Stammgut ['ʃtamgu:t], *n.* (—s, *pl.* ⁻er) family estate.
Stammhalter ['ʃtamhaltər], *m.* (—s, *pl.* —) son and heir; eldest son.
Stammhaus ['ʃtamhaus], *n.* (—es, *pl.* ⁻er) ancestral mansion; (*royalty*) dynasty; (*Comm.*) business headquarters, head office.
stämmig ['ʃtɛmɪç], *adj.* sturdy, strong.
Stammler ['ʃtamlər], *m.* (—s, *pl.* —) stammerer, stutterer.
Stammsilbe ['ʃtamzilbə], *f.* (—, *pl.* —n) (*Ling.*) radical syllable.
Stammtafel ['ʃtamta:fəl], *f.* (—, *pl.* —n) genealogical table.
Stammvater ['ʃtamfa:tər], *m.* (—s, *pl.* ⁻) ancestor, progenitor.
stammverwandt ['ʃtamfɛrvant], *adj.* cognate, kindred.
stampfen ['ʃtampfən], *v.a.* stamp, pound, ram down. — *v.n.* stamp, trample.
Stand [ʃtant], *m.* (—(e)s, *pl.* ⁻e) stand; (*market*) stall; situation, state (of affairs), condition; reading, position; rank, station (in life); (*pl.*) the classes, the estates.
Standarte [ʃtan'dartə], *f.* (—, *pl.* —n) standard, banner.
Standbild ['ʃtantbɪlt], *n.* (—(e)s, *pl.* ⁻er) statue.
Ständchen ['ʃtɛntçən], *n.* (—s, *pl.* —) serenade; *einem ein — bringen*, serenade s.o.
Ständehaus ['ʃtɛndəhaus], *n.* (—es, *pl.* ⁻er) state assembly-hall.
Ständer ['ʃtɛndər], *m.* (—s, *pl.* —) stand, pedestal; post; (upright) desk.
Standesamt ['ʃtandəsamt], *n.* (—s, *pl.* ⁻er) registry office.

Standesbeamte ['ʃtandəsbəamtə], *m.* (—n, *pl.* —n) registrar (of births, marriages and deaths).
Standesbewußtsein ['ʃtandəsbəvustzain], *n.* (—s, *no pl.*) class-feeling, class-consciousness.
Standesperson ['ʃtandəsperzo:n], *f.* (—, *pl.* —en) person of rank.
Standgericht ['ʃtantgərɪçt], *n.* (—es, *pl.* —e) court-martial; summary court of justice.
standhaft ['ʃtanthaft], *adj.* constant, firm, steadfast.
standhalten ['ʃtanthaltən], *v.n. irr.* bear up, stand o.'s ground, withstand, resist.
ständig ['ʃtɛndɪç], *adj.* permanent.
ständisch ['ʃtɛndɪʃ], *adj.* relating to the estates (of the realm).
Standort ['ʃtantɔrt], *m.* (—s, *pl.* —e) location; station.
Standpauke ['ʃtantpaukə], *f.* (—, *pl.* —n) (*coll.*) harangue; severe reprimand.
Standpunkt ['ʃtantpuŋkt], *m.* (—(e)s, *pl.* —e) standpoint; point of view; *den — vertreten*, take the line; *einem den — klar machen*, give s.o. a piece of o.'s mind.
Standrecht ['ʃtantreçt], *n.* (—(e)s, *no pl.*) martial law.
Standuhr ['ʃtantu:r], *f.* (—, *pl.* —en) grandfather-clock.
Stange ['ʃtaŋə], *f.* (—, *pl.* —n) stick, pole; *bei der — bleiben*, stick to the point, persevere.
Stank [ʃtaŋk], *m.* (—s, *no pl.*) (*dial.*) stench; discord, trouble.
Stänker ['ʃtɛŋkər], *m.* (—s, *pl.* —) (*coll.*) mischief-maker, quarrelsome person.
stänkern ['ʃtɛŋkərn], *v.n.* pick quarrels; ferret about, make trouble.
Stanniol [ʃta'njo:l], *n.* (—s, *no pl.*) tinfoil.
stanzen ['ʃtantsən], *v.a.* punch, stamp.
Stapel ['ʃta:pəl], *m.* (—s, *pl.* —) pile, heap; (*Naut.*) slipway; *ein Schiff vom — lassen*, launch a ship.
Stapellauf ['ʃta:pəllauf], *m.* (—s, *pl.* ⁻e) (*Naut.*) launch, launching.
stapeln ['ʃta:pəln], *v.a.* pile up.
Stapelnahrung ['ʃta:pəlna:ruŋ], *f.* (—, *no pl.*) staple diet.
Stapelplatz ['ʃta:pəlplats], *m.* (—es, *pl.* ⁻e) mart, emporium.
Stapelware ['ʃta:pəlva:rə], *f.* (—, *pl.* —n) staple goods.
Stapfen ['ʃtapfən], *m.* or *f. pl.* footsteps.
Star (1) [ʃta:r], *m.* (—(e)s, *pl.* —e) (*Med.*) cataract; *einen den — stechen*, operate for cataract; (*fig.*) open s.o.'s eyes.
Star (2) [ʃta:r], *m.* (—(e)s, *pl.* —en) (*Orn.*) starling.
stark [ʃtark], *adj.* strong, stout; robust; vigorous; heavy; considerable; *—er Esser*, hearty eater. — *adv.* very much.

Stärke ['ʃtɛrkə], f. (—, no pl.) strength, vigour, robustness; strong point; starch.

Stärkekleister ['ʃtɛrkəklaɪstər], m. (—s, no pl.) starch-paste.

Stärkemehl ['ʃtɛrkəme:l], n. (—s, no pl.) starch-flour.

stärken ['ʃtɛrkən], v.a. strengthen; corroborate; starch. — v.r. sich —, take some refreshment.

stärkend ['ʃtɛrkənt], adj. strengthening, restorative; —es Mittel, tonic.

starkleibig ['ʃtarklaɪbɪç], adj. corpulent, stout, obese.

Stärkung ['ʃtɛrkuŋ], f. (—, pl. —en) strengthening, invigoration; refreshment.

starr [ʃtar], adj. stiff, rigid; fixed; inflexible; stubborn; einen — ansehen, stare at s.o.

starren ['ʃtarən], v.n. stare.

Starrheit ['ʃtarhaɪt], f. (—, no pl.) stiffness, rigidity; fixedness; inflexibility; stubbornness.

starrköpfig ['ʃtarkœpfɪç], adj. headstrong, stubborn, obstinate, pigheaded.

Starrkrampf ['ʃtarkrampf], m. (—(e)s, no pl.) (Med.) tetanus.

Starrsinn ['ʃtarzɪn], m. (—s, no pl.) stubbornness, obstinacy.

Station [ʃta'tsjo:n], f. (—, pl. —en) (Railw.) station; (main) terminus; stop, stopping-place; (hospital) ward; freie —, board and lodging found.

stationär [ʃtatsjo'nɛ:r], adj. stationary.

stationieren [ʃtatsjo'ni:rən], v.a. station.

Stationsvorsteher [ʃtat'sjo:nsfɔrʃte:ər], m. (—s, pl. —) station-master.

statisch ['ʃta:tɪʃ], adj. static.

Statist [ʃta'tɪst], m. (—en, pl. —en) (Theat.) extra, walking-on part; (pl.) supers.

Statistik [ʃta'tɪstɪk], f. (—, pl. —en) statistics.

Statistiker [ʃta'tɪstɪkər], m. (—s, pl. —) statistician.

Stativ [ʃta'ti:f], n. (—s, pl. —e) stand, tripod.

Statt [ʃtat], f. (—, no pl.) place, stead; an seiner —, in his place.

statt [ʃtat], prep. (Genit.) instead of, in lieu of.

Stätte ['ʃtɛtə], f. (—, pl. —n) place, abode.

stattfinden ['ʃtatfɪndən], v.n. irr. take place.

stattgeben ['ʃtatge:bən], v.n. irr. einer Bitte —, grant a request.

statthaft ['ʃtathaft], adj. admissible, allowable, lawful.

Statthalter ['ʃtathaltər], m. (—s, pl. —) governor.

stattlich ['ʃtatlɪç], adj. stately, handsome, distinguished, comely; portly; considerable; eine —e Summe, a tidy sum.

statuieren [ʃtatu'i:rən], v.a. decree; ein Exempel —, make an example of.

Statut [ʃta'tu:t], n. (—s, pl. —en) statute, regulation.

Staub [ʃtaup], m. (—(e)s, no pl.) dust, powder; sich aus dem — machen, take French leave; abscond.

Stäubchen ['ʃtɔypçən], n. (—s, pl. —) mote, particle of dust.

stauben ['ʃtaubən], v.n. es staubt, it is dusty.

Staubgefäß ['ʃtaupɡəfɛ:s], n. (—es, pl. —e) stamen.

staubig ['ʃtaubɪç], adj. dusty.

Staubkamm ['ʃtaupkam], m. (—s, pl. ̈e) fine-tooth comb.

Staublappen ['ʃtauplapən], m. (—s, pl. —) duster.

Staubmantel ['ʃtaupmantəl], m. (—s, pl. ̈) overall, smock; dust(er)coat, (Am.) duster.

Staubsauger ['ʃtaupzauɡər], m. (—s, pl. —) vacuum cleaner.

Staubtuch ['ʃtauptu:x], n. (—es, pl. ̈er) duster.

Staubwedel ['ʃtaupve:dəl], m. (—s, pl. —) feather duster.

Staubwolke ['ʃtaupvɔlkə], f. (—, pl. —n) cloud of dust.

Staubzucker ['ʃtauptsukər], m. (—s, no pl.) castor-sugar, icing-sugar.

Staudamm ['ʃtaudam], m. (—s, pl. ̈e) dam, dyke.

Staude ['ʃtaudə], f. (—, pl. —n) shrub, bush.

stauen ['ʃtauən], v.a. stow; (water) dam. — v.r. sich —, be congested.

staunen ['ʃtaunən], v.n. be astonished, be surprised, wonder (at).

Staupe ['ʃtaupə], f. (—, pl. —n) (animals) distemper.

stäupen ['ʃtɔypən], v.a. (obs.) scourge, flog.

Stauung ['ʃtauuŋ], f. (—, pl. —en) stowage; (water) damming-up, swell, rising; (blood) congestion; (traffic) jam, build-up.

stechen ['ʃtɛçən], v.a. irr. prick, sting; stab; (cards) trump.

stechend ['ʃtɛçənt], adj. pungent, biting.

Stechmücke ['ʃtɛçmykə], f. (—, pl. —n) (Ent.) gnat, mosquito.

Stechpalme ['ʃtɛçpalmə], f. (—, pl. —n) (Bot.) holly.

Steckbrief ['ʃtɛkbri:f], m. (—s, pl. —e) warrant (for arrest).

stecken ['ʃtɛkən], v.a. stick into, put, place, fix; (plants) set, plant; in Brand —, set on fire, set fire to. — v.n. irgendwo —, be about somewhere; — bleiben, get stuck, break down; — er steckt dahinter, he is at the bottom of it. — v.r. sich hinter einen —, shelter behind s.o.

Stecken ['ʃtɛkən], m. (—s, pl. —) stick, staff.

Stecker ['ʃtɛkər], m. (—s, pl. —) (Elec.) plug.

Steckkontakt ['ʃtɛkkɔntakt], m. (—(e)s, pl. —e) (Elec.) plug, point.

Stecknadel ['ʃtɛkna:dəl], f. (—, pl. —n) pin.

Steg [ʃte:k], m. (—(e)s, pl. —e) plank, foot-bridge; jetty; (violin) bridge.

Stegreif ['ʃte:kraɪf], *m.* (—s, *pl.* —e) (*obs.*) stirrup; *aus dem — sprechen,* extemporise, improvise.

stehen ['ʃte:ən], *v.n. irr.* stand; be; stand still; *einem gut —,* fit *or* suit s.o. well; *mit einem gut —,* be on good terms with s.o.; *gut —,* be in a fair way, look promising; *was steht zu Diensten?* what can I do for you? *— bleiben,* stand still, stop, pull up.

stehlen ['ʃte:lən], *v.a. irr.* steal.

Steiermark ['ʃtaɪərmark], *f.* Styria.

steif [ʃtaɪf], *adj.* stiff; (*grog*) strong; awkward; ceremonious, punctilious, formal. — *adv. etwas — und fest behaupten,* swear by all that's holy.

steifen ['ʃtaɪfən], *v.a.* stiffen, starch.

Steifheit ['ʃtaɪfhaɪt], *f.* (—, *no pl.*) stiffness; (*fig.*) formality.

Steifleinen ['ʃtaɪflaɪnən], *n.* (—s, *no pl.*) buckram.

Steig [ʃtaɪk], *m.* (—(e)s, *pl.* —e) path, (mountain) track.

Steigbügel ['ʃtaɪkby:gəl], *m.* (—s, *pl.* —) stirrup.

Steigen ['ʃtaɪgən], *n.* (—s, *no pl.*) rising, increase; (*price*) advance, rise; *im —,* on the increase.

steigen ['ʃtaɪgən], *v.n. irr.* (*aux.* sein) climb, mount, ascend; (*barometer*) rise; (*population*) increase; (*horse*) rear; (*price*) advance, rise.

Steiger ['ʃtaɪgər], *m.* (—s, *pl.* —) climber, mountaineer; mining-surveyor, overseer.

steigern ['ʃtaɪgərn], *v.a.* (*price*) raise; (*fig.*) enhance, increase. — *v.r. sich —,* increase.

Steigerung ['ʃtaɪgəruŋ], *f.* (—, *pl.* —en) raising; (*fig.*) enhancement; increase; (*Gram.*) comparison.

Steigung ['ʃtaɪguŋ], *f.* (—, *pl.* —en) gradient.

steil [ʃtaɪl], *adj.* steep.

Stein [ʃtaɪn], *m.* (—(e)s, *pl.* —e) stone, rock; flint; jewel, gem; monument; (*Chess*) piece, chessman; (*Draughts*) man; (*fruit*) stone, kernel; — *des Anstoßes,* stumbling block; *mir fällt ein — vom Herzen,* it is a load off my mind; *bei einem einen — im Brett haben,* be in s.o.'s good books; *einem —e in den Weg legen,* put obstacles in s.o.'s way; *der — des Weisen,* the philosopher's stone.

Steinadler ['ʃtaɪna:dlər], *m.* (—s, *pl.* —) (*Orn.*) golden eagle.

steinalt ['ʃtaɪnalt], *adj.* very old.

Steinbock ['ʃtaɪnbɔk], *m.* (—s, *pl.* ⸚e) ibex; (*Astrol.*) Capricorn.

Steinbruch ['ʃtaɪnbrux], *m.* (—s, *pl.* ⸚e) stone-pit, quarry.

Steinbutt ['ʃtaɪnbut], *m.* (—s, *pl.* —e) (*Zool.*) turbot.

Steindruck ['ʃtaɪndruk], *m.* (—s, *no pl.*) lithography.

steinern ['ʃtaɪnərn], *adj.* stony; built of stone.

Steingut ['ʃtaɪngu:t], *n.* (—s, *no pl.*) earthenware, stoneware, pottery.

Steinhagel ['ʃtaɪnha:gəl], *m.* (—s, *no pl.*) shower of stones.

Steinhaue ['ʃtaɪnhauə], *f.* (—, *pl.* —n) pickaxe.

Steinhügel ['ʃtaɪnhy:gəl], *m.* (—s, *pl.* —) cairn.

steinig ['ʃtaɪnɪç], *adj.* stony, rocky.

steinigen ['ʃtaɪnɪgən], *v.a.* stone.

Steinkalk ['ʃtaɪnkalk], *m.* (—s, *no pl.*) quicklime.

Steinkohle ['ʃtaɪnko:lə], *f.* (—, *no pl.*) pit-coal.

Steinkrug ['ʃtaɪnkru:k], *m.* (—s, *pl.* ⸚e) stone jar.

Steinmarder ['ʃtaɪnmardər], *m.* (—s, *pl.* —) (*Zool.*) stone-marten.

Steinmetz ['ʃtaɪnmets], *m.* (—es, *pl.* —e) stone-cutter, stone-mason.

Steinobst ['ʃtaɪno:pst], *n.* (—es, *no pl.*) stone-fruit.

Steinplatte ['ʃtaɪnplatə], *f.* (—, *pl.* —n) slab, flagstone.

steinreich ['ʃtaɪnraɪç], *adj.* as rich as Croesus.

Steinsalz ['ʃtaɪnzalts], *n.* (—es, *no pl.*) rock-salt, mineral-salt.

Steinwurf ['ʃtaɪnvurf], *m.* (—s, *pl.* ⸚e) *einen — entfernt,* within a stone's throw.

Steiß [ʃtaɪs], *m.* (—es, *pl.* —e) rump; (*coll.*) buttocks, posterior.

Stellage [ʃte'la:ʒə], *f.* (—, *pl.* —n) stand, frame.

Stelldichein ['ʃteldɪçaɪn], *n.* (—s, *no pl.*) assignation, rendezvous, tryst; (*coll.*) date.

Stelle ['ʃtelə], *f.* (—, *pl.* —n) place, spot; job, position; situation; (*book*) passage; figure, digit; department; *offene —,* vacancy; *auf der —,* at once, immediately; *an deiner —,* if I were you; *nicht von der — kommen,* remain stationary; *zur — sein,* be at hand.

stellen ['ʃtelən], *v.a.* put, place, set; *richtig —,* regulate, correct, amend; (*clock*) set right; *seinen Mann —,* play o.'s part, pull o.'s weight. — *v.r. sich —,* come forward; pretend; *sich krank —,* feign illness, malinger, pretend to be ill.

Stellenbewerber ['ʃtelənbəverbər], *m.* (—s, *pl.* —) applicant (for a job).

Stellengesuch ['ʃteləngəzu:x], *n.* (—s, *pl.* —e) application (for a job).

Stellenvermittlung ['ʃtelənfermɪtluŋ], *f.* (—, *pl.* —en) employment office, employment exchange.

stellenweise ['ʃtelənvaɪzə], *adv.* in parts, here and there.

Stellmacher ['ʃtelmaxər], *m.* (—s, *pl.* —) wheelwright.

Stellung ['ʃteluŋ], *f.* (—, *pl.* —en) position, posture; attitude; situation; job; (*Mil.*) trenches; — *nehmen zu,* express o.'s views on.

Stellvertreter ['ʃtelfertre:tər], *m.* (—s, *pl.* —) representative, deputy; substitute, supply, proxy, relief; (*doctor*) locum.

Stelzbein ['ʃteltsbaɪn], *n.* (—s, *pl.* —e) wooden leg.

Stemmeisen

Stemmeisen [ˈʃtɛmaɪzən], *n.* (—s, *pl.* —) crowbar.

stemmen [ˈʃtɛmən], *v.a.* (*water*) stem, dam; (*weight*) lift. — *v.r. sich* — *gegen*, resist fiercely.

Stempel [ˈʃtɛmpəl], *m.* (—s, *pl.* —) stamp, rubber-stamp, die; pounder; (*Bot.*) pistil.

Stempelgebühr [ˈʃtɛmpəlgəbyːr], *f.* (—, *pl.* —en) stamp-duty.

stempeln [ˈʃtɛmpəln], *v.a.* stamp, hallmark; brand; cancel (*postage stamp*). — *v.n.* (*coll.*) — *gehen*, be on the dole.

Stengel [ˈʃtɛŋəl], *m.* (—s, *pl.* —) stalk.

Stenografie [ʃtenograˈfiː], *f.* (—, *no pl.*) stenography, shorthand.

stenografisch [ʃtenoˈgraːfiʃ], *adj.* in shorthand.

Stenogramm [ʃtenoˈgram], *n.* (—s, *pl.* —e) shorthand-note.

Stenotypistin [ʃtenotyˈpɪstɪn], *f.* (—, *pl.* —nen) shorthand-typist.

Stephan [ˈʃtefan], *m.* Stephen.

Steppdecke [ˈʃtɛpdɛkə], *f.* (—, *pl.* —n) quilt.

Steppe [ˈʃtɛpə], *f.* (—, *pl.* —n) steppe.

steppen [ˈʃtɛpən], *v.a.* stitch, quilt.

Sterbeglocke [ˈʃtɛrbəglɔkə], *f.* (—, *pl.* —n) passing bell, death bell.

Sterbehemd [ˈʃtɛrbəhɛmt], *n.* (—(e)s, *pl.* —en) shroud, winding-sheet.

sterben [ˈʃtɛrbən], *v.n. irr.* (*aux. sein*) die.

Sterbenswörtchen [ˈʃtɛrbənsvœrtçən], *n.* (—s, *pl.* —) *nicht ein* —, not a syllable.

Sterbesakramente [ˈʃtɛrbəzakramɛntə], *n. pl.* (*Eccl.*) last sacraments, last rites.

sterblich [ˈʃtɛrplɪç], *adj.* mortal; — *verliebt*, desperately in love.

Sterblichkeit [ˈʃtɛrplɪçkaɪt], *f.* (—, *no pl.*) mortality.

stereotyp [stereoˈtyːp], *adj.* stereotyped.

sterilisieren [steriliˈziːrən], *v.a.* sterilise.

Sterilität [steriliˈtɛːt], *f.* (—, *no pl.*) sterility.

Stern [ʃtɛrn], *m.* (—(e)s, *pl.* —e) star; (*Typ.*) asterisk.

Sternbild [ˈʃtɛrnbɪlt], *n.* (—s, *pl.* —er) constellation.

Sterndeuter [ˈʃtɛrndɔytər], *m.* (—s, *pl.* —) astrologer.

Sterndeutung [ˈʃtɛrndɔytuŋ], *f.* (—, *no pl.*) astrology.

Sternenschimmer [ˈʃtɛrnənʃɪmər], *m.* (—s, *no pl.*) starlight.

sternförmig [ˈʃtɛrnfœrmɪç], *adj.* starlike, star-shaped.

Sterngucker [ˈʃtɛrnɡukər], *m.* (—s, *pl.* —) stargazer.

sternhagelvoll [ˈʃtɛrnhaːɡəlfɔl], *adj.* (*coll.*) as drunk as a lord.

Sternkunde [ˈʃtɛrnkundə], *f.* (—, *no pl.*) astronomy.

Sternkundige [ˈʃtɛrnkundɪɡə], *m.* (—n, *pl.* —n) astronomer.

Sternschnuppe [ˈʃtɛrnʃnupə], *f.* (—, *pl.* —n) falling star, shooting star, meteorite.

Sternwarte [ˈʃtɛrnvartə], *f.* (—, *pl.* —n) observatory.

stetig [ˈʃteːtɪç], *adj.* continual, continuous, constant.

stets [ʃteːts], *adv.* always, ever, continually.

Steuer (1) [ˈʃtɔyər], *n.* (—s, *pl.* —) rudder, helm, steering wheel.

Steuer (2) [ˈʃtɔyər], *f.* (—, *pl.* —n) tax; (*local*) rate; (*import*) customs duty.

Steueramt [ˈʃtɔyəramt], *n.* (—s, *pl.* ⸚er) inland revenue office, tax office.

Steuerbeamte [ˈʃtɔyərbəamtə], *m.* (—n, *pl.* —n) revenue officer, tax collector.

Steuerbord [ˈʃtɔyərbort], *n.* (—s, *no pl.*) starboard.

Steuereinnehmer [ˈʃtɔyəraɪnneːmər], *m.* (—s, *pl.* —) tax collector.

steuerfrei [ˈʃtɔyərfraɪ], *adj.* duty-free, exempt from taxes.

Steuerhinterziehung [ˈʃtɔyərhɪntərtsiːuŋ], *f.* (—, *pl.* —en) tax evasion.

steuerlos [ˈʃtɔyərloːs], *adj.* rudderless, adrift.

Steuermann [ˈʃtɔyərman], *m.* (—s, *pl.* ⸚er) mate; helmsman.

steuern [ˈʃtɔyərn], *v.a.* steer; *einem Unheil* —, avoid *or* steer clear of an evil.

steuerpflichtig [ˈʃtɔyərpflɪçtɪç], *adj.* taxable, liable to tax, dutiable.

Steuerrad [ˈʃtɔyərraːt], *n.* (—s, *pl.* ⸚er) steering-wheel.

Steuerung [ˈʃtɔyəruŋ], *f.* (—, *no pl.*) steering, controls.

Steuerveranlagung [ˈʃtɔyərfɛranlaːguŋ], *f.* (—, *pl.* —en) tax-assessment.

stibitzen [ʃtiˈbɪtsən], *v.a.* (*coll.*) pilfer, filch.

Stich [ʃtɪç], *m.* (—(e)s, *pl.* —e) sting; prick; stitch; stab; (*Cards*) trick; (*Art*) engraving; *einen im* — *lassen*, leave s.o. in the lurch.

Stichel [ˈʃtɪçəl], *m.* (—s, *pl.* —) (*Art*) graver.

Stichelei [ʃtɪçəˈlaɪ], *f.* (—, *pl.* —en) taunt, sneer, gibe.

sticheln [ˈʃtɪçəln], *v.a.* taunt, nag.

stichhaltig [ˈʃtɪçhaltɪç], *adj.* valid, sound.

Stichhaltigkeit [ˈʃtɪçhaltɪçkaɪt], *f.* (—, *no pl.*) validity, cogency.

Stichprobe [ˈʃtɪçproːbə], *f.* (—, *pl.* —n) sample taken at random, sampling.

Stichwahl [ˈʃtɪçvaːl], *f.* (—, *pl.* —en) second ballot.

Stichwort [ˈʃtɪçvort], *n.* (—s, *pl.* —e) key-word; (*Theat.*) cue.

sticken [ˈʃtɪkən], *v.a., v.n.* embroider.

Stickerei [ʃtɪkəˈraɪ], *f.* (—, *pl.* —en) embroidery.

Stickgarn [ˈʃtɪkɡarn], *n.* (—s, *pl.* —e) embroidery cotton *or* silk.

Stickhusten [ˈʃtɪkhuːstən], *m.* (—s, *no pl.*) choking cough.

stickig [ˈʃtɪkɪç], *adj.* stuffy.

Stickmuster [ˈʃtɪkmustər], *n.* (—s, *pl.* —) embroidery-pattern.

Stickstoff [ˈʃtɪkʃtɔf], *m.* (—(e)s, *no pl.*) nitrogen.

stieben [ˈʃtiːbən], *v.n.* (*aux.* sein) scatter, spray; *auseinander* —, disperse.

Stiefbruder [ˈʃtiːfbruːdər], *m.* (—s, *pl.* ˙) step-brother.

Stiefel [ˈʃtiːfəl], *m.* (—s, *pl.* —) boot.

Stiefelknecht [ˈʃtiːfəlknɛçt], *m.* (—(e)s, *pl.* —e) boot-jack.

Stiefelputzer [ˈʃtiːfəlputsər], *m.* (—s, *pl.* —) shoe-black; (*Am.*) shoe-shine; (*hotel*) boots.

Stiefeltern [ˈʃtiːfɛltern], *pl.* step-parents.

Stiefmütterchen [ˈʃtiːfmytərçən], *n.* (—s, *pl.* —) (*Bot.*) pansy.

stiefmütterlich [ˈʃtiːfmytərlɪç], *adj.* like a stepmother; niggardly.

Stiefsohn [ˈʃtiːfzoːn], *m.* (—s, *pl.* ˙e) stepson.

Stiege [ˈʃtiːgə], *f.* (—, *pl.* —n) staircase.

Stieglitz [ˈʃtiːglɪts], *m.* (—es, *pl.* —e) goldfinch.

Stiel [ʃtiːl], *m.* (—(e)s, *pl.* —e) handle; (*plant*) stalk.

Stier [ʃtiːr], *m.* (—(e)s, *pl.* —e) bull; *junger* —, bullock; (*Astrol.*) Taurus.

stieren [ˈʃtiːrən], *v.n.* stare (at), goggle.

Stift (1) [ʃtɪft], *m.* (—(e)s, *pl.* —e) tack, pin, peg; pencil; (*coll.*) apprentice; young chap.

Stift (2) [ʃtɪft], *n.* (—(e)s, *pl.* —e) charitable *or* religious foundation.

stiften [ˈʃtɪftən], *v.a.* establish, give, donate; found, set on foot, originate; *Frieden* —, bring about peace.

Stifter [ˈʃtɪftər], *m.* (—s, *pl.* —) founder, originator, donor.

Stiftung [ˈʃtɪftuŋ], *f.* (—, *pl.* —en) establishment, foundation; institution; charitable foundation; endowment, donation.

Stil [ʃtiːl], *m.* (—(e)s, *pl.* —e) style; (*fig.*) manner.

stilisieren [ʃtili:ˈziːrən], *v.a.* word, draft.

Stilistik [ʃtiːˈlɪstɪk], *f.* (—, *no pl.*) art of composition.

stilistisch [ʃtiːˈlɪstɪʃ], *adj.* stylistic.

still [ʃtɪl], *adj.* quiet, still, silent; calm; —*er Teilhaber*, sleeping partner; *im* —*en*, secretly, on the sly.

Stille [ˈʃtɪlə], *f.* (—, *no pl.*) silence, quietness, tranquillity; calm, calmness; *in der* —, silently; *in der* — *der Nacht*, at dead of night.

stillen [ˈʃtɪlən], *v.a.* allay; (*blood*) staunch; (*baby*) suckle, feed, nurse; (*thirst*) quench; (*hunger*) appease.

stillos [ˈʃtiːloːs], *adj.* incongruous; in bad taste.

Stillung [ˈʃtɪluŋ], *f.* (—, *no pl.*) allaying; (*blood*) staunching; (*baby*) suckling, feeding, nursing; (*thirst*) quenching; (*hunger*) appeasing.

stilvoll [ˈʃtiːlfɔl], *adj.* harmonious; stylish; in good taste.

Stimmband [ˈʃtɪmbant], *n.* (—s, *pl.* ˙er) vocal chord.

stimmberechtigt [ˈʃtɪmbərɛçtɪçt], *adj.* entitled to vote, enfranchised.

Stimmbruch [ˈʃtɪmbrux], *m.* (—s, *no pl.*) breaking of the voice.

Stimme [ˈʃtɪmə], *f.* (—, *pl.* —n) voice; (*election*) vote, suffrage; *die* — *abgeben*, vote.

stimmen [ˈʃtɪmən], *v.a.* (*piano*) tune; *einen günstig* —, dispose s.o. favourably towards s.th. — *v.n.* agree, tally (with), square (with), accord (with); vote.

Stimmeneinheit [ˈʃtɪmənaɪnhaɪt], *f.* (—, *no pl.*) unanimity.

Stimmengleichheit [ˈʃtɪmənglaɪçhaɪt], *f.* (—, *no pl.*) equality of votes, tie.

Stimmer [ˈʃtɪmər], *m.* (—s, *pl.* —) (*piano*) tuner.

Stimmführer [ˈʃtɪmfyːrər], *m.* (—s, *pl.* —) leader, spokesman.

Stimmgabel [ˈʃtɪmgaːbəl], *f.* (—, *pl.* —n) tuning fork.

stimmhaft [ˈʃtɪmhaft], *adj.* (*Phonet.*) voiced.

Stimmlage [ˈʃtɪmlaːgə], *f.* (—, *pl.* —n) (*Mus.*) register.

stimmlos [ˈʃtɪmloːs], *adj.* voiceless; (*Phonet.*) unvoiced.

Stimmrecht [ˈʃtɪmrɛçt], *n.* (—s, *no pl.*) suffrage, right to vote; *allgemeines* —, universal suffrage.

Stimmung [ˈʃtɪmuŋ], *f.* (—, *no pl.*) tuning; (*fig.*) disposition, humour, mood; atmosphere; *in guter* —, in high spirits, *in gedrückter* —, in low spirits.

stimmungsvoll [ˈʃtɪmuŋsfɔl], *adj.* impressive, full of atmosphere.

Stimmwechsel [ˈʃtɪmvɛksəl], *m.* (—s, *no pl.*) breaking of the voice.

Stimmzettel [ˈʃtɪmtsetəl], *m.* (—s, *pl.* —) ballot-paper.

stinken [ˈʃtɪŋkən], *v.n. irr.* stink, reek, smell.

Stinktier [ˈʃtɪŋktiːr], *n.* (—s, *pl.* —e) (*Zool.*) skunk.

Stipendium [ʃtiˈpɛndjum], *n.* (—s, *pl.* —dien) scholarship.

Stirn [ʃtɪrn], *f.* (—, *pl.* —en) forehead, brow; *die* — *runzeln*, frown, knit o.'s brow; *die* — *haben zu*, have the cheek to; *einem die* — *bieten*, face s.o., defy s.o.

Stirnhöhle [ˈʃtɪrnhøːlə], *f.* (—, *pl.* —en) frontal cavity.

Stirnseite [ˈʃtɪrnzaɪtə], *f.* (—, *pl.* —n) front.

stöbern [ˈʃtøːbərn], *v.n.* rummage about; (*snow*) drift.

stochern [ˈʃtɔxərn], *v.a.*, *v.n.* (*food*) pick (at); (*teeth*) pick.

Stock (1) [ʃtɔk], *m.* (—(e)s, *pl.* ˙e) stick, cane, walking-stick; *über* — *und Stein*, over hedges and ditches.

Stock (2) [ʃtɔk], *m.* (—es, *pl.* —werke) storey, floor.

stocken

stocken ['ʃtɔkən], v.n. stop; (*blood*) run cold; (*linen*) go mildewed; hesitate, falter; (*conversation*) flag.

stockfinster ['ʃtɔkfɪnstər], adj. pitch dark.

Stockfisch ['ʃtɔkfɪʃ], m. (—es, pl. —e) dried cod; dried fish.

stöckisch ['ʃtœkɪʃ], adj. obstinate, stubborn.

Stockrose ['ʃtɔkro:zə], f. (—, pl. —n) (*Bot.*) hollyhock.

Stockschnupfen ['ʃtɔkʃnupfən], m. (—s, no pl.) heavy or chronic cold.

stocksteif ['ʃtɔkʃtaɪf], adj. stiff as a poker.

stockstill ['ʃtɔkʃtɪl], adj. quite still, stock-still.

stocktaub ['ʃtɔktaup], adj. deaf as a post.

Stockung ['ʃtɔkuŋ], f. (—, pl. —en) stagnation; hesitation; block, blockage; stopping, standstill.

Stockwerk ['ʃtɔkvɛrk], n. (—s, pl. —e) storey, floor.

Stoff [ʃtɔf], m. (—(e)s, pl. —e) fabric, material; substance; subject matter.

Stoffwechsel ['ʃtɔfvɛksəl], m. (—s, no pl.) metabolism.

stöhnen ['ʃtø:nən], v.n. groan, moan.

Stoiker ['sto:ɪkər], m. (—s, pl. —) stoic.

Stola ['sto:la:], f. (—, pl. —ien) (*Eccl.*) stole.

Stollen ['ʃtɔlən], m. (—s, pl. —) fruitcake; (*Min.*) gallery, adit.

stolpern ['ʃtɔlpərn], v.n. (*aux.* sein) stumble, trip.

Stolz [ʃtɔlts], m. (—es, no pl.) haughtiness, pride.

stolz [ʃtɔlts], adj. haughty, proud; stuck-up, conceited; (*fig.*) majestic.

stolzieren [ʃtɔl'tsi:rən], v.n. (*aux.* sein) strut; prance.

stopfen ['ʃtɔpfən], v.a. stuff; fill; darn, mend; *einem den Mund* —, cut s.o. short.

Stopfgarn ['ʃtɔpfgarn], n. (—s, pl. —e) darning-thread.

Stoppel ['ʃtɔpəl], f. (—, pl. —n) stubble.

stoppeln ['ʃtɔpəln], v.a. glean; *etwas zusammen* —, compile s.th. badly.

Stöpsel ['ʃtœpsəl], m. (—s, pl. —) stopper, cork; *kleiner* —, little mite.

stöpseln ['ʃtœpsəln], v.a. cork.

Stör [ʃtø:r], m. (—(e)s, pl. —e) (*Zool.*) sturgeon.

Storch [ʃtɔrç], m. (—(e)s, pl. ⁀e) (*Orn.*) stork.

Storchschnabel ['ʃtɔrçʃna:bəl], m. (—s, pl. ⁀) stork's bill; (*Tech.*) pantograph.

stören ['ʃtø:rən], v.a. disturb, trouble; (*Rad.*) jam. — v.n. intrude, be in the way.

Störenfried ['ʃtø:rənfri:d], m. (—s, pl. —e) intruder, mischief-maker, nuisance.

Störer ['ʃtø:rər], m. (—s, pl. —) disturber.

stornieren [stɔr'ni:rən], v.a. cancel, annul.

störrisch ['ʃtœrɪʃ], adj. stubborn, obstinate.

Störung ['ʃtø:ruŋ], f. (—, pl. —en) disturbance, intrusion; (*Rad.*) jamming.

Stoß [ʃto:s], m. (—es, pl. ⁀e) push, thrust; impact; blow, stroke, jolt; (*papers*) heap, pile; (*documents*) bundle.

Stoßdegen ['ʃto:sde:gən], m. (—s, pl. —) rapier.

Stößel ['ʃtø:səl], m. (—s, pl. —) pestle; (*Motor.*) tappet.

stoßen ['ʃto:sən], v.a. irr. thrust, push; pound; *vor den Kopf* —, offend. — v.n. bump, jolt; — *an*, border upon; *auf etwas* —, come across s.th., stumble on s.th.; *ins Horn* —, blow a horn. — v.r. *sich* —, hurt o.s.; *sich an etwas* —, take offence at s.th., take exception to s.th.

Stoßseufzer ['ʃto:szɔyftsər], m. (—s, pl. —) deep sigh.

Stoßwaffe ['ʃto:svafə], f. (—, pl. —n) thrusting or stabbing weapon.

stoßweise ['ʃto:svaɪzə], adv. by fits and starts.

Stotterer ['ʃtɔtərər], m. (—s, pl. —) stutterer, stammerer.

stottern ['ʃtɔtərn], v.n. stutter, stammer.

stracks [ʃtraks], adv. straight away, directly.

Strafanstalt ['ʃtra:fanʃtalt], f. (—, pl. —en) penitentiary, prison.

Strafarbeit ['ʃtra:farbaɪt], f. (—, pl. —en) (*Sch.*) imposition.

strafbar ['ʃtra:fba:r], adj. punishable, criminal, culpable.

Strafbarkeit ['ʃtra:fba:rkaɪt], f. (—, no pl.) culpability.

Strafe ['ʃtra:fə], f. (—, pl. —n) punishment; (*money*) fine, penalty; *bei* — *von*, on pain of.

strafen ['ʃtra:fən], v.a. punish, rebuke; (*money*) fine.

Straferlaß ['ʃtra:fərlas], m. (—sses, pl. —sse) remission of penalty, amnesty.

straff [ʃtraf], adj. tight, tense, taut.

Strafgericht ['ʃtra:fgərɪçt], n. (—es, no pl.) punishment; judgment; (*Law*) Criminal Court.

Strafgesetzbuch ['ʃtra:fgəzɛtsbu:x], n. (—(e)s, pl. ⁀er) penal code.

sträflich ['ʃtrɛ:flɪç], adj. punishable; culpable; reprehensible, blameworthy.

Sträfling ['ʃtrɛ:flɪŋ], m. (—s, pl. —e) convict.

Strafporto ['ʃtra:fpɔrto], n. (—s, pl. —ti) excess postage.

Strafpredigt ['ʃtra:fpre:dɪçt], f. (—, pl. —en) severe admonition, stern reprimand.

Strafprozess ['ʃtra:fprotsɛs], m. (—es, pl. —e) criminal proceedings.

Strafrecht ['ʃtra:frɛçt], n. (—(e)s, no pl.) criminal law.

Strafverfahren ['ʃtra:ffɛrfa:rən], n. (—s, pl. —) criminal procedure.

214

Strahl [ʃtraːl], *m.* (—(e)s, *pl.* —en) beam, ray; (*water etc.*) jet, spout; (*lightning*) flash; —en werfen, emit rays.

Strahlantrieb [ʃtraːlantriːp], *m.* (—s, *no pl.*) (*Aviat.*) jet propulsion.

strahlen [ʃtraːlən], *v.n.* radiate, shine, beam, emit rays; (*fig.*) beam (with joy).

strählen [ʃtreːlən], *v.a.* (*rare*) comb.

Strahlenbrechung [ʃtraːlənbrɛçuŋ], *f.* (—, *pl.* —en) refraction.

strahlenförmig [ʃtraːlənfœrmɪç], *adj.* radiate.

Strahlenkrone [ʃtraːlənkroːnə], *f.* (—, *pl.* —n) aureole, halo.

Strahlung [ʃtraːluŋ], *f.* (—, *pl.* —en) radiation; (*fig.*) radiance.

Strähne [ʃtreːnə], *f.* (—, *pl.* —n) skein, hank; eine — Pech, a spell of bad luck.

Stramin [ʃtraˈmiːn], *m.* (—s, *pl.* —e) embroidery canvas.

stramm [ʃtram], *adj.* tight; rigid; sturdy, strapping.

strampeln [ʃtrampəln], *v.n.* struggle; (*baby*) kick.

Strand [ʃtrant], *m.* (—(e)s, *pl.* —e) shore, beach, strand.

stranden [ʃtrandən], *v.n.* be stranded, founder.

Strandkorb [ʃtrantkɔrp], *m.* (—s, *pl.* ⁀e) beach-chair.

Strandwache [ʃtrantvaxə], *f.* (—, *no pl.*) coast-guard.

Strang [ʃtraŋ], *m.* (—(e)s, *pl.* ⁀e) rope, cord; über die ⁀e schlagen, kick over the traces; zum — verurteilen, condemn to be hanged.

strangulieren [ʃtranɡuˈliːrən], *v.a.* strangle.

Strapaze [ʃtraˈpatsə], *f.* (—, *pl.* —n) over-exertion, fatigue, hardship.

strapazieren [ʃtrapaˈtsiːrən], *v.a.* over-exert, fatigue.

strapaziös [ʃtrapaˈtsjøːs], *adj.* fatiguing, exacting.

Straße [ʃtraːsə], *f.* (—, *pl.* —n) (*city*) street; (*country*) road, highway; (*sea*) strait; auf der —, in the street; über die — gehen, cross the street.

Straßenbahn [ʃtraːsənbaːn], *f.* (—, *pl.* —en) tram; tramcar, (*Am.*) streetcar.

Straßendamm [ʃtraːsəndam], *m.* (—s, *pl.* ⁀e) roadway.

Straßendirne [ʃtraːsəndɪrnə], *f.* (—, *pl.* —n) prostitute, street-walker.

Straßenfeger [ʃtraːsənfeːɡər], *m.* (—s, *pl.* —) roadman, road-sweeper, scavenger, crossing-sweeper.

Straßenpflaster [ʃtraːsənpflastər], *n.* (—s, *no pl.*) pavement.

Straßenraub [ʃtraːsənraup], *m.* (—s, *no pl.*) highway-robbery.

Stratege [ʃtraˈteːɡə], *m.* (—n, *pl.* —n) strategist.

sträuben [ʃtrɔybən], *v.r. sich —*, bristle; (*fig.*) struggle (against), oppose.

Strauch [ʃtraux], *m.* (—(e)s, *pl.* ⁀er) bush, shrub.

straucheln [ʃtrauxəln], *v.n.* (*aux.* sein) stumble.

Strauchritter [ʃtrauxrɪtər], *m.* (—s, *pl.* —) footpad, vagabond, highwayman.

Strauß (1) [ʃtraus], *m.* (—es, *pl.* ⁀e) (*Poet.*) fight, tussle; (*flowers*) bunch, bouquet, nosegay.

Strauß (2) [ʃtraus], *m.* (—es, *pl.* —e) (*Orn.*) ostrich.

Sträußchen [ʃtrɔysçən], *n.* (—s, *pl.* —) small bunch of flowers, nosegay.

Straußfeder [ʃtrausfeːdər], *f.* (—, *pl.* —n) ostrich-feather.

Strazze [ʃtratsə], *f.* (—, *pl.* —n) scrapbook.

Strebe [ʃtreːbə], *f.* (—, *pl.* —n) buttress, prop, stay.

Strebebogen [ʃtreːbəboːɡən], *m.* (—s, *pl.* —) (*Archit.*) arch, buttress; flying buttress.

Streben [ʃtreːbən], *n.* (—s, *no pl.*) ambition, aspiration; effort, endeavour, striving.

streben [ʃtreːbən], *v.n.* strive, aspire, endeavour.

Streber [ʃtreːbər], *m.* (—s, *pl.* —) pushing person, (social) climber. (*Am. coll.*) go-getter.

strebsam [ʃtreːpzaːm], *adj.* ambitious, assiduous, industrious.

streckbar [ʃtrɛkbaːr], *adj.* ductile, extensible.

Streckbett [ʃtrɛkbɛt], *n.* (—s, *pl.* —en) orthopaedic bed.

Strecke [ʃtrɛkə], *f.* (—, *pl.* —n) stretch, reach, extent; distance; tract; line; zur — bringen, (*Hunt.*) bag, run to earth.

strecken [ʃtrɛkən], *v.a.* stretch, extend; (*metal*) lengthen out; make (s.th.) last; die Waffen —, lay down arms.

Streich [ʃtraɪç], *m.* (—(e)s, *pl.* —e) stroke, blow; (*fig.*) prank; trick; dummer —, piece of folly, lark.

streicheln [ʃtraɪçəln], *v.a.* stroke, caress.

streichen [ʃtraɪçən], *v.a. irr.* stroke, touch; paint, spread; cancel; strike; (*sail*) lower. — *v.n.* move past, fly past; wander.

Streichholz [ʃtraɪçhɔlts], *n.* (—es, *pl.* ⁀er) match.

Streichinstrument [ʃtraɪçɪnstruˈmɛnt], *n.* (—s, *pl.* —e) stringed instrument.

Streif [ʃtraɪf], *m.* (—(e)s, *pl.* —e) stripe, strip, streak.

Streifband [ʃtraɪfbant], *n.* (—s, *pl.* ⁀er) wrapper.

Streifblick [ʃtraɪfblɪk], *m.* (—s, *pl.* —e) glance.

Streife [ʃtraɪfə], *f.* (—, *pl.* —n) raid; patrol (*police etc.*).

Streifen [ʃtraɪfən], *m.* (—s, *pl.* —) stripe, streak; (*Mil.*) bar.

streifen ['ʃtraɪfən], v.a. graze, touch in passing; take off (remove). — v.n. (aux. sein) ramble, roam, rove.

streifig ['ʃtraɪfɪç], adj. striped, streaky.

Streik [ʃtraɪk], m. (—(e)s, pl. —s) strike; in den — treten, go on strike.

Streikbrecher ['ʃtraɪkbrɛçər], m. (—s, pl. —) blackleg.

streiken ['ʃtraɪkən], v.n. (workers) strike, be on strike.

Streit [ʃtraɪt], m. (—(e)s, pl. —e) dispute, quarrel, conflict; (words) argument; einen — anfangen, pick a quarrel.

Streitaxt ['ʃtraɪtakst], f. (—, pl. ˙˙e) battle-axe.

streitbar ['ʃtraɪtba:r], adj. warlike, martial.

streiten ['ʃtraɪtən], v.n. irr. quarrel, fight; —de Kirche, Church Militant.

Streitfrage ['ʃtraɪtfra:gə], f. (—, pl. —n) moot point, point at issue; controversy.

Streithammel ['ʃtraɪthaməl], m. (—s, pl. —) squabbler.

Streithandel ['ʃtraɪthandəl], m. (—s, pl. ˙˙) law-suit.

streitig ['ʃtraɪtɪç], adj. disputable, doubtful, at issue; einem etwas — machen, contest s.o.'s right to s.th.

Streitkräfte ['ʃtraɪtkrɛftə], f. pl. (Mil.) forces.

streitlustig ['ʃtraɪtlustɪç], adj. argumentative.

Streitschrift ['ʃtraɪtʃrɪft], f. (—, pl. —en) pamphlet, polemical treatise.

Streitsucht ['ʃtraɪtzuxt], f. (—, no pl.) quarrelsomeness; (Law) litigiousness.

streitsüchtig ['ʃtraɪtzyçtɪç], adj. quarrelsome, litigious.

streng [ʃtrɛŋ], adj. severe, strict, rigorous; —e Kälte, biting cold; im —sten Winter, in the depth of winter. — adv. —genommen, strictly speaking.

Strenge ['ʃtrɛŋə], f. (—, no pl.) severity, rigour.

strenggläubig ['ʃtrɛŋglɔybɪç], adj. strictly orthodox.

Streu [ʃtrɔy], f. (—, pl. —en) litter, bed of straw.

Streubüchse ['ʃtrɔybyksə], f. (—, pl. —n) castor.

streuen ['ʃtrɔyən], v.a. strew, scatter, sprinkle.

streunen ['ʃtrɔynən], v.n. roam (about).

Streuung ['ʃtrɔyuŋ], f. (—, pl. —en) strewing; (shot) dispersion.

Streuzucker ['ʃtrɔytsukər], m. (—s, no pl.) castor-sugar.

Strich [ʃtrɪç], m. (—(e)s, pl. —e) stroke, line, dash; (land) tract; (Art) touch; region; gegen den —, against the grain; einen einen — durch die Rechnung machen, put a spoke in s.o.'s wheel, frustrate s.o.

Strichpunkt ['ʃtrɪçpuŋkt], m. (—s, pl. —e) semicolon.

Strichregen ['ʃtrɪçre:gən], f. (—s, pl. —) passing shower.

Strick [ʃtrɪk], m. (—(e)s, pl. —e) cord, line, rope; du —, (fig.) you scamp! einem einen — drehen, give s.o. enough rope to hang himself, lay a trap for s.o.

stricken ['ʃtrɪkən], v.a., v.n. knit.

Strickerei [ʃtrɪkə'raɪ], f. (—, pl. —en) knitting; knitting business, workshop.

Strickleiter ['ʃtrɪklaɪtər], f. (—, pl. —n) rope-ladder.

Strickzeug ['ʃtrɪktsɔyk], n. (—s, pl. —e) knitting.

Striegel ['ʃtri:gəl], m. (—s, pl. —) curry-comb.

striegeln ['ʃtri:gəln], v.a. curry.

Strieme ['ʃtri:mə], f. (—, pl. —n) weal, stripe.

Strippe ['ʃtrɪpə], f. (—, pl. —n) strap, band, string; cord.

strittig ['ʃtrɪtɪç], adj. contentious, debatable.

Stroh [ʃtro:], n. (—s, no pl.) straw; (roof) thatch; mit — decken, thatch; leeres — dreschen, beat the air.

Strohfeuer ['ʃtro:fɔyər], n. (—s, no pl.) (fig.) flash in the pan; short-lived enthusiasm.

Strohhalm ['ʃtro:halm], m. (—s, pl. —e) straw.

Strohhut ['ʃtro:hu:t], m. (—s, pl. ˙˙e) straw-hat.

Strohkopf ['ʃtro:kɔpf], m. (—(e)s, pl. ˙˙e) (coll.) stupid person.

Strohmann ['ʃtro:man], m. (—s, pl. ˙˙er) (coll.) man of straw; (Cards) dummy.

Strohmatte ['ʃtro:matə], f. (—, pl. —n) straw-mat.

Strohwitwe ['ʃtro:vɪtvə], f. (—, pl. —n) grass-widow.

Strolch [ʃtrɔlç], m. (—(e)s, pl. —e) vagabond; (fig.) scamp.

Strom [ʃtro:m], m. (—(e)s, pl. ˙˙e) river, torrent; (also fig.) flood; stream; (also Elec.) current; (coll.) electricity; gegen den — schwimmen, swim against the current, be an individualist.

stromab ['ʃtro:map], adv. downstream.

stromauf ['ʃtro:mauf], adv. upstream.

strömen ['ʃtrø:mən], v.n. (aux. sein) flow, stream; (rain) pour; (people) flock.

Stromer ['ʃtro:mər], m. (—s, pl. —) vagabond, tramp, vagrant.

Stromkreis ['ʃtro:mkraɪs], m. (—es, pl. —e) (Elec.) circuit.

Stromschnelle ['ʃtro:mʃnɛlə], f. (—, pl. —n) rapids.

Strömung ['ʃtrø:muŋ], f. (—, pl. —en) current; (fig.) tendency.

Strophe ['ʃtro:fə], f. (—, pl. —n) verse, stanza.

strotzen ['ʃtrɔtsən], v.n. be puffed up; overflow, burst, teem.

strotzend ['ʃtrɔtsənt], adj. vor Gesundheit —, bursting with health.

Strudel ['ʃtru:dəl], m. (—s, pl. —) whirl, whirlpool, vortex, eddy; pastry.

Struktur [ʃtruk'tu:r], f. (—, pl. —en) structure.

Strumpf [ʃtrumpf], *m.* (—(e)s, *pl.* ⁻e) stocking; (*short*) sock.

Strumpfband [ˈʃtrumpfbant], *n.* (—(e)s, *pl.* ⁻er) garter.

Strumpfwaren [ˈʃtrumpfvaːrən], *f. pl.* hosiery.

Strumpfwirker [ˈʃtrumpfvɪrkər], *m.* (—s, *pl.* —) stocking-weaver.

Strunk [ʃtruŋk], *m.* (—(e)s, *pl.* ⁻e) (*tree*) stump, trunk; (*plant*) stalk.

struppig [ˈʃtrupɪç], *adj.* rough, unkempt, frowsy.

Stube [ˈʃtuːbə], *f.* (—, *pl.* —n) room, chamber; *gute —*, sitting-room.

Stubenarrest [ˈʃtuːbənarɛst], *m.* (—s, *pl.* —e) confinement to quarters.

Stubenhocker [ˈʃtuːbənhɔkər], *m.* (—s, *pl.* —) stay-at-home.

Stubenmädchen [ˈʃtuːbənmɛːtçən], *n.* (—s, *pl.* —) housemaid.

Stuck [ʃtuk], *m.* (—(e)s, *no pl.*) stucco, plaster.

Stück [ʃtyk], *n.* (—(e)s, *pl.* —e) piece; part; lump; (*Theat.*) play; *aus freien —en*, of o.'s own accord; *große —e auf einen halten*, think highly of s.o.

Stückarbeit [ˈʃtykarbaɪt], *f.* (—, *pl.* —en) piece-work.

Stückchen [ˈʃtykçən], *n.* (—s, *pl.* —) small piece, morsel, bit.

stückeln [ˈʃtykəln], *v.a.* cut in(to) pieces; patch, mend.

stückweise [ˈʃtykvaɪzə], *adv.* piecemeal.

Stückwerk [ˈʃtykvɛrk], *n.* (—s, *no pl.*) (*fig.*) patchy *or* imperfect work, a bungled job.

Stückzucker [ˈʃtyktsukər], *m.* (—s, *no pl.*) lump sugar.

Student [ʃtuˈdɛnt], *m.* (—en, *pl.* —en) (*Univ.*) student, undergraduate.

studentenhaft [ʃtuˈdɛntənhaft], *adj.* student-like.

Studentenverbindung [ʃtuˈdɛntənfɛrbɪnduŋ], *f.* (—, *pl.* —en) students' association *or* union.

Studie [ˈʃtuːdjə], *f.* (—, *pl.* —n) study, (*Art*) sketch; (*Lit.*) essay; (*pl.*) studies.

Studienplan [ˈʃtuːdjənplaːn], *m.* (—s, *pl.* ⁻e) curriculum.

Studienrat [ˈʃtuːdjənraːt], *m.* (—s, *pl.* ⁻e) grammar school teacher, assistant master.

studieren [ʃtuˈdiːrən], *v.a.*, *v.n.* study, read (a subject); be at (the) university.

studiert [ʃtuˈdiːrt], *adj.* educated; (*fig.*) affected, deliberate, studied.

Studierte [ʃtuˈdiːrtə], *m.* (*coll.*) egghead.

Studium [ˈʃtuːdjum], *n.* (—s, *pl.* —dien) study, pursuit; university education.

Stufe [ˈʃtuːfə], *f.* (—, *pl.* —n) step; (*fig.*) degree; *auf gleicher — mit*, on a level with.

stufenweise [ˈʃtuːfənvaɪzə], *adv.* gradually, by degrees.

Stuhl [ʃtuːl], *m.* (—s, *pl.* ⁻e) chair, seat; *der Heilige —*, the Holy See.

Stuhlgang [ˈʃtuːlgaŋ], *m.* (—s, *no pl.*) (*Med.*) stool, evacuation (of the bowels), movement, motion.

Stukkatur [ʃtukaˈtuːr], *f.* (—, *no pl.*) stucco-work.

Stulle [ˈʃtulə], *f.* (—, *pl.* —n) (*dial.*) slice of bread and butter.

Stulpe [ˈʃtulpə], *f.* (—, *pl.* —n) cuff.

stülpen [ˈʃtylpən], *v.a.* turn up, invert.

Stulpnase [ˈʃtulpnaːzə], *f.* (—, *pl.* —n) turned-up nose, pug-nose.

Stulpstiefel [ˈʃtulpʃtiːfəl], *m.* (—s, *pl.* —) top-boot.

stumm [ʃtum], *adj.* mute, dumb, silent.

Stumme [ˈʃtumə], *m.* & *f.* (—n, *pl.* —n) dumb person, mute.

Stummel [ˈʃtuməl], *m.* (—s, *pl.* —) stump; (*cigarette*) end, butt.

Stummheit [ˈʃtumhaɪt], *f.* (—, *no pl.*) dumbness.

Stümper [ˈʃtympər], *m.* (—s, *pl.* —) bungler, botcher.

stümperhaft [ˈʃtympərhaft], *adj.* bungling, botchy.

stümpern [ˈʃtympərn], *v.a.*, *v.n.* bungle, botch.

Stumpf [ʃtumpf], *m.* (—(e)s, *pl.* ⁻e) stump, trunk; *mit — und Stiel ausrotten*, destroy root and branch.

stumpf [ʃtumpf], *adj.* blunt; (*angle*) obtuse; (*fig.*) dull; *— machen*, blunt, dull.

Stumpfsinn [ˈʃtumpfzɪn], *m.* (—s, *no pl.*) stupidity, dullness.

stumpfwinklig [ˈʃtumpfvɪŋkliç], *adj.* obtuse-angled.

Stunde [ˈʃtundə], *f.* (—, *pl.* —n) hour; lesson.

stunden [ˈʃtundən], *v.a.* give a respite, allow time (to pay up).

Stundenglas [ˈʃtundənglaːs], *n.* (—es, *pl.* ⁻er) hour-glass.

Stundenplan [ˈʃtundənplaːn], *m.* (—s, *pl.* ⁻e) (*Sch.*) time-table.

Stundenzeiger [ˈʃtundəntsaɪgər], *m.* (—s, *pl.* —) hour-hand.

Stündlein [ˈʃtyntlaɪn], *n.* (—s, *pl.* —) *sein — hat geschlagen*, his last hour has come.

Stundung [ˈʃtunduŋ], *f.* (—, *pl.* —en) respite, grace.

stupend [ʃtuˈpɛnt], *adj.* stupendous.

stur [ʃtuːr], *adj.* obdurate, unwavering, stolid, dour, stubborn.

Sturm [ʃturm], *m.* (—(e)s, *pl.* ⁻e) storm, gale, tempest, hurricane; (*Mil.*) attack, assault; *— und Drang*, (*Lit.*) Storm and Stress; *— im Wasserglas*, storm in a teacup; *— laufen gegen*, storm against.

Sturmband [ˈʃturmbant], *n.* (—s, *pl.* ⁻er) chinstrap.

Sturmbock [ˈʃturmbɔk], *m.* (—s, *pl.* ⁻e) battering-ram.

stürmen [ˈʃtyrmən], *v.a.* storm, take by assault. *— v.n.* be violent, be stormy; (*Mil.*) advance.

Stürmer [ˈʃtyrmər], *m.* (—s, *pl.* —) assailant; (*football*) centre-forward.

Sturmglocke [ˈʃturmglɔkə], *f.* (—, *pl.* —n) tocsin, alarm-bell.

Sturmhaube [ˈʃturmhaubə], *f.* (—, *pl.* —en) (*Mil.*) morion, helmet.

stürmisch [ˈʃtyrmɪʃ], *adj.* stormy, tempestuous; (*fig.*) boisterous, turbulent, tumultuous, impetuous; —*er Beifall*, frantic applause; —*e Überfahrt*, rough crossing.

Sturmschritt [ˈʃturmʃrɪt], *m.* (—s, *no pl.*) double march.

Sturmvogel [ˈʃturmfoːɡəl], *m.* (—s, *pl.* ⁀) (*Orn.*) stormy petrel.

Sturz [ʃturts], *m.* (—es, *pl.* ⁀e) fall, tumble; crash; collapse; (*Comm.*) failure, smash; (*government*) overthrow.

Sturzacker [ˈʃturtsakər], *m.* (—s, *pl.* ⁀) freshly ploughed field.

Sturzbach [ˈʃturtsbax], *m.* (—(e)s, *pl.* ⁀e) torrent.

Stürze [ˈʃtyrtsə], *f.* (—, *pl.* —n) pot-lid, cover.

stürzen [ˈʃtyrtsən], *v.a.* hurl, overthrow; ruin. — *v.n.* (*aux.* sein) (*person*) have a fall; (*object*) tumble down; (*business*) fail; crash; plunge; (*water*) rush. — *v.r.* throw oneself; *sich — auf*, rush at, plunge into.

Sturzhelm [ˈʃturtshɛlm], *m.* (—s, *pl.* —e) crash-helmet.

Sturzsee [ˈʃturtszeː], *f.* (—, *no pl.*) heavy sea.

Sturzwelle [ˈʃturtsvɛlə], *f.* (—, *pl.* —n) breaker, roller.

Stute [ˈʃtuːtə], *f.* (—, *pl.* —n) mare.

Stutzbart [ˈʃtutsbaːrt], *m.* (—s, *pl.* ⁀e) short beard.

Stütze [ˈʃtytsə], *f.* (—, *pl.* —n) prop, support, stay.

Stutzen [ˈʃtutsən], *m.* (—s, *pl.* —) short rifle, carbine.

stutzen [ˈʃtutsən], *v.a.* (*hair*) clip, trim; (*horse*) dock, crop; (*tree*) prune, lop. — *v.n.* be taken aback, hesitate.

stützen [ˈʃtytsən], *v.a.* prop, support; base *or* found (on). — *v.r.* *sich — auf*, lean upon; (*fig.*) rely upon.

Stutzer [ˈʃtutsər], *m.* (—s, *pl.* —) dandy, fop, beau.

stutzerhaft [ˈʃtutsərhaft], *adj.* dandified.

stutzig [ˈʃtutsɪç], *adj.* startled, puzzled; — *werden*, be nonplussed, be taken aback *or* puzzled.

Stützmauer [ˈʃtytsmauər], *f.* (—, *pl.* —n) buttress, retaining wall.

Stützpunkt [ˈʃtytspuŋkt], *m.* (—s, *pl.* —e) point of support; foothold; (*Mil.*) base; (*Tech.*) fulcrum.

Subjekt [zupˈjɛkt], *n.* (—s, *pl.* —e) subject; (*fig.*) creature.

subjektiv [zupjɛkˈtiːf], *adj.* subjective, personal, prejudiced.

sublimieren [zubliˈmiːrən], *v.a.* sublimate.

Substantiv [zupstanˈtiːf], *n.*ˑ (—(e)s, *pl.* —e) (*Gram.*) substantive, noun.

subtil [zupˈtiːl], *adj.* subtle.

subtrahieren [zuptraˈhiːrən], *v.a.* subtract.

Subvention [zupvɛnˈtsjoːn], *f.* (—, *pl.* —en) subsidy, grant-in-aid.

Suche [ˈzuːxə], *f.* (—, *no pl.*) search, quest; *auf der — nach*, in quest of.

suchen [ˈzuːxən], *v.a.*, *v.n.* seek, look for; attempt, endeavour.

Sucht [zuxt], *f.* (—, *pl.* ⁀e) mania, addiction, passion.

süchtig [ˈzyçtɪç], *adj.* addicted (to).

Sud [zuːd], *m.* (—(e)s, *pl.* —e) boiling, brewing; suds.

Sudan [ˈzuːdan], *m.* the Sudan.

sudeln [ˈzuːdəln], *v.a.*, *v.n.* smear, daub, make a mess (of).

Süden [ˈzyːdən], *m.* (—s, *no pl.*) south.

Südfrüchte [ˈzyːtfryçtə], *f. pl.* Mediterranean *or* tropical fruit.

südlich [ˈzyːtlɪç], *adj.* southern, southerly; *in —er Richtung*, southward.

Südosten [zyːtˈʔostən], *m.* (—s, *no pl.*) south-east.

Suff [zuf], *m.* (—(e)s, *no pl.*) (*sl.*) boozing, tippling.

suggerieren [zugeˈriːrən], *v.a.* suggest.

Sühne [ˈzyːnə], *f.* (—, *no pl.*) expiation, atonement.

sühnen [ˈzyːnən], *v.a.* expiate, atone for.

Sühneopfer [ˈzyːnəʔopfər], *n.* (—s, *pl.* —) expiatory sacrifice; atonement.

Suite [ˈsviːtə], *f.* (—, *pl.* —n) retinue, train.

sukzessiv [zuktsɛˈsiːf], *adj.* gradual, successive.

Sülze [ˈzyltsə], *f.* (—, *pl.* —n) brawn, aspic, jelly.

Summa [zuˈmaː], *f.* (—, *pl.* **Summen**) — *summarum*, sum total.

summarisch [zuˈmaːrɪʃ], *adj.* summary.

Summe [ˈzumə], *f.* (—, *pl.* —n) sum, amount.

summen [ˈzumən], *v.a.*, *v.n.* hum. — *v.n.* buzz, hum.

summieren [zuˈmiːrən], *v.a.* sum up, add up. — *v.r. sich —*, mount up.

Sumpf [zumpf], *m.* (—(e)s, *pl.* ⁀e) bog, morass, marsh, moor, swamp.

sumpfig [ˈzumpfɪç], *adj.* boggy, marshy.

Sund [zunt], *m.* (—(e)s, *pl.* —e) straits, sound.

Sünde [ˈzyndə], *f.* (—, *pl.* —n) sin.

Sündenbock [ˈzyndənbɔk], *m.* (—s, *pl.* ⁀e) scapegoat.

Sündenfall [ˈzyndənfal], *m.* (—s, *no pl.*) (*Theol.*) fall of man.

Sündengeld [ˈzyndənɡɛlt], *n.* (—(e)s, *no pl.*) ill-gotten gains; (*coll.*) vast sum of money.

sündenlos [ˈzyndənloːs], *adj.* sinless, impeccable.

Sündenpfuhl [ˈzyndənpfuːl], *m.* (—s, *pl.* —e) sink of iniquity.

Sünder [ˈzyndər], *m.* (—s, *pl.* —) sinner; *armer —*, poor devil; *du alter —*, you old scoundrel.

sündhaft [ˈzynthaft], *adj.* sinful, iniquitous.

sündig [ˈzyndɪç], *adj.* sinful.

sündigen [ˈzyndɪɡən], *v.n.* sin, err.

Sündigkeit [ˈzyndɪçkait], *f.* (—, *no pl.*) sinfulness.

Superlativ [ˈzuːpərlatiːf], *m.* (—s, *pl.* —e) superlative (degree).

Suppe ['zupə], *f.* (—, *pl.* —n) soup;
eingebrannte —, thick soup; *einem
die* — *versalzen*, spoil s.o.'s little game.
Suppenfleisch ['zupənflaɪʃ], *n.* (—es,
no pl.) stock-meat.
Suppenkelle ['zupənkɛlə], *f.* (—,
pl. —n) soup ladle.
Suppenterrine ['zupəntɛriːnə], *f.* (—,
pl. —n) tureen.
Surrogat [zuro'gaːt], *n.* (—s, *pl.* —e)
substitute.
süß [zyːs], *adj.* sweet.
Süße ['zyːsə], *f.* (—, *no pl.*) sweetness.
süßen ['zyːsən], *v.a.* sweeten.
Süßholz ['zyːshɔlts], *n.* (—es, *no pl.*)
liquorice; — *raspeln*, talk sweet
nothings, pay compliments.
Süßigkeit ['zyːsɪçkaɪt], *f.* (—, *pl.* —en)
sweetness; (*pl.*) sweets.
süßlich ['zyːslɪç], *adj.* sweetish; (*fig.*)
fulsome, mawkish, cloying.
Süßspeise ['zyːsʃpaɪzə], *f.* (—, *pl.* —n)
dessert.
Süßwasser ['zyːsvasər], *n.* (—s, *no pl.*)
fresh water.
Symbolik [zym'boːlɪk], *f.* (—, *no pl.*)
symbolism.
symbolisch [zym'boːlɪʃ], *adj.* sym-
bolic(al).
symbolisieren [zymbɔlɪ'ziːrən], *v.a.*
symbolize.
symmetrisch [zy'meːtrɪʃ], *adj.* symmetrical.
Sympathie [zympa'tiː], *f.* (—, *pl.* —n)
fondness, congeniality, sympathy.
sympathisch [zym'paːtɪʃ], *adj.* congenial, likeable.
Synagoge [zyna'goːgə], *f.* (—, *pl.* —n)
synagogue.
synchronisieren [zynkroni'ziːrən], *v.a.*
synchronise.
Syndikus ['zyndikus], *m.* (—, *pl.*
Syndizi) syndic.
Synode [zy'noːdə], *f.* (—, *pl.* —n) synod.
synthetisch [zyn'teːtɪʃ], *adj.* synthetic.
Syrien [zyːrjən], *n.* Syria.
systematisch [zyste'maːtɪʃ], *adj.* sys-
tematic(al).
Szenarium [stse'naːrjum], *n.* (—s,
pl. —rien) scenario, stage, scene.
Szene ['stseːnə], *f.* (—, *pl.* —n) scene;
in — *setzen*, stage, produce; (*coll.*)
get up; *sich in* — *setzen*, show off.
Szenerie [stsenə'riː], *f.* (—, *pl.* —n)
scenery.
szenisch ['stseːnɪʃ], *adj.* scenic.
Szepter ['stsɛptər], *n.* (—s, *pl.* —)
sceptre, mace.

T

T [teː], *n.* (—, *pl.* —) the letter T.
Tabak ['tabak], *m.* (—s, *pl.* —e)
tobacco.

Tabaksbeutel ['tabaksbɔytəl], *m.* (—s,
pl. —) tobacco-pouch.
Tabatiere [taba'tjeːrə], *f.* (—, *pl.* —n)
snuff-box.
tabellarisch [tabɛ'laːrɪʃ], *adj.* in tables,
tabular.
Tabelle [ta'bɛlə], *f.* (—, *pl.* —n)
table, index, schedule.
Tablett [ta'blɛt], *n.* (—s, *pl.* —s)
tray.
Tablette [ta'blɛtə], *f.* (—, *pl.* —n)
tablet, pill.
Tabulatur [tabula'tuːr], *f.* (—, *pl.* —en)
tablature, tabling, index.
Tadel ['taːdəl], *m.* (—s, *pl.* —) blame,
censure, reproach; (*Sch.*) bad mark;
ohne —, blameless.
tadellos ['taːdəlloːs], *adj.* blameless,
faultless, impeccable.
tadeln ['taːdəln], *v.a.* blame, censure,
find fault with; reprimand.
tadelnswert ['taːdəlnsveːrt], *adj.* blameworthy, culpable.
Tafel ['taːfəl], *f.* (—, *pl.* —n) board;
(*Sch.*) blackboard; slate; (*fig.*) (*obs.*)
dinner, banquet; festive fare; (*chocolate*) slab, bar.
Täfelchen ['tɛːfəlçən], *n.* (—s, *pl.* —)
tablet.
tafelförmig ['taːfəlfœrmɪç], *adj.* tabular.
tafeln ['taːfəln], *v.n.* dine, feast.
täfeln ['tɛːfəln], *v.a.* wainscot, panel.
Täfelung ['tɛːfəluŋ], *f.* (—, *pl.* —en)
wainscoting, panelling.
Taft, Taffet [taft, 'tafət], *m.* (—(e)s,
pl. —e) taffeta.
Tag [taːk], *m.* (—(e)s, *pl.* —e) day;
(*fig.*) light; *der jüngste* —, Doomsday;
bei —*e*, in the daytime, by daylight;
sich etwas bei —*e besehen*, examine
s.th. in the light of day; — *für* —,
day by day; *von* — *zu* —, from day
to day; *dieser* —*e*, one of these days,
shortly; *etwas an den* — *bringen*,
bring s.th. to light; *in den* — *hinein
leben*, live improvidently; — *und
Nachtgleiche*, equinox.
Tagbau ['taːkbau], *m.* (—s, *no pl.*)
opencast mining.
Tageblatt ['taːgəblat], *n.* (—s, *pl.* ⸚er)
daily paper.
Tagebuch ['taːgəbuːx], *n.* (—(e)s, *pl.*
⸚er) diary, journal.
Tagedieb ['taːgədiːp], *m.* (—(e)s, *pl.*
—e) idler, wastrel.
Tagelöhner ['taːgəløːnər], *m.* (—s, *pl.*
—) day-labourer.
tagen ['taːgən], *v.n.* dawn; (*gathering*)
meet; (*Law*) sit.
Tagesanbruch ['taːgəsanbrux], *m.* (—s,
pl. ⸚e) daybreak, dawn.
Tagesbericht ['taːgəsbərɪçt], *m.*
(—(e)s, *pl.* —e) daily report.
Tagesgespräch ['taːgəsgəʃprɛːç], *n.*
(—(e)s, *pl.* —e) topic of the day.
Tagesordnung ['taːgəsɔrdnuŋ], *f.* (—,
pl. —en) agenda.
Tagewerk ['taːgəverk], *n.* (—s, *no pl.*)
day's work, daily round.
täglich ['tɛːklɪç], *adj.* daily.

tagsüber ['ta:ksy:bər], *adv.* in the daytime, during the day.

Taille ['taljə], *f.* (—, *pl.* —n) waist.

takeln ['ta:kəln], *v.a.* tackle, rig.

Takelwerk ['ta:kəlverk], *n.* (—s, *no pl.*) rigging.

Takt (1) [takt], *m.* (—es, *pl.* —e) (*Mus.*) time, measure, bar; — *schlagen*, beat time.

Takt (2) [takt], *m.* (—es, *no pl.*) tact, discretion.

taktfest ['taktfest], *adj.* (*Mus.*) good at keeping time; (*fig.*) firm.

taktieren [tak'ti:rən], *v.n.* (*Mus.*) beat time.

Taktik ['taktik], *f.* (—, *pl.* —en) tactics.

Taktiker ['taktikər], *m.* (—s, *pl.* —) tactician.

taktisch ['taktiʃ], *adj.* tactical.

taktlos ['taktlo:s], *adj.* tactless.

Taktmesser ['taktmesər], *m.* (—s, *pl.* —) metronome.

Taktstock ['taktʃtɔk], *m.* (—s, *pl.* ˑe) baton.

Tal [ta:l], *n.* (—(e)s, *pl.* ˑer) valley, dale, glen.

talab [ta:l'ap], *adv.* downhill.

Talar [ta'la:r], *m.* (—s, *pl.* —e) gown.

Talent [ta'lent], *n.* (—(e)s, *pl.* —e) talent, accomplishment, gift.

talentiert [talən'ti:rt], *adj.* talented, gifted, accomplished.

talentvoll [ta'lentfɔl], *adj.* talented, gifted, accomplished.

Taler ['ta:lər], *m.* (—s, *pl.* —) old German coin; thaler.

Talfahrt ['ta:lfa:rt], *f.* (—, *pl.* —en) descent.

Talg [talk], *m.* (—(e)s, *no pl.*) tallow.

Talk [talk], *m.* (—(e)s, *no pl.*) talc.

Talkerde ['talke:rdə], *f.* (—, *no pl.*) (*Geog.*) hollow, narrow valley.

Talmulde ['ta:lmuldə], *f.* (—, *pl.* —n) narrow valley, trough.

Talsohle ['ta:lzo:lə], *f.* (—, *pl.* —n) floor of a valley.

Talsperre ['ta:lʃperə], *f.* (—, *pl.* —n) dam (across valley); barrage.

Tambour ['tambu:r], *m.* (—s, *pl.* —e) drummer.

Tamtam ['tamtam], *n.* (—s, *no pl.*) tom-tom; (*fig.*) palaver.

Tand [tant], *m.* (—(e)s, *no pl.*) knick-knack, trifle; rubbish.

Tändelei [tendə'laɪ], *f.* (—, *pl.* —en) trifling, toying; (*fig.*) flirting.

Tändelmarkt ['tendəlmarkt], *m.* (—s, *pl.* ˑe) rag-fair.

tändeln ['tendəln], *v.n.* trifle, dally, toy; (*fig.*) flirt.

Tang [taŋ], *m.* (—s, *pl.* —e) (*Bot.*) seaweed.

Tanganjika [taŋga'nji:ka], *n.* Tanganyika.

Tangente [taŋ'gentə], *f.* (—, *pl.* —n) tangent.

Tanger ['taŋər], *n.* Tangier.

Tank [taŋk], *m.* (—(e)s, *pl.* —e) tank.

tanken ['taŋkən], *v.n.* refuel; fill up (with petrol).

Tankstelle ['taŋkʃtelə], *f.* (—, *pl.* —n) filling-station.

Tanne ['tanə], *f.* (—, *pl.* —n) (*Bot.*) fir.

Tannenbaum ['tanənbaum], *m.* (—s, *pl.* ˑe) (*Bot.*) fir-tree.

Tannenholz ['tanənhɔlts], *n.* (—es, *no pl.*) (*timber*) deal.

Tannenzapfen ['tanəntsapfən], *m.* (—s, *pl.* —) (*Bot.*) fir-cone.

Tansania [tanza'ni:a], *n.* Tanzania.

Tante ['tantə], *f.* (—, *pl.* —n) aunt.

Tantieme [tã'tje:mə], *f.* (—, *pl.* —n) royalty, share (in profits), percentage.

Tanz [tants], *m.* (—es, *pl.* ˑe) dance.

Tanzboden ['tantsbo:dən], *m.* (—s, *pl.* ˑ) ballroom, dance-hall.

tänzeln ['tentsəln], *v.n.* skip about, frisk; (*horses*) amble.

tanzen ['tantsən], *v.a., v.n.* dance.

tanzlustig ['tantslustiç], *adj.* fond of dancing.

Tapet [ta'pe:t], *n.* (—s, *no pl.*) *aufs* — *bringen*, broach, bring up for discussion.

Tapete [ta'pe:tə], *f.* (—, *pl.* —n) wall-paper.

tapezieren [tapə'tsi:rən], *v.a.* paper.

Tapezierer [tapə'tsi:rər], *m.* (—s, *pl.* —) paperhanger; upholsterer.

tapfer ['tapfər], *adj.* brave, valiant, gallant, courageous.

Tapferkeit ['tapfərkaɪt], *f.* (—, *no pl.*) valour, bravery, gallantry.

Tapisserie [tapisə'ri:], *f.* (—, *no pl.*) needlework; tapestry.

tappen ['tapən], *v.n.* grope about.

täppisch ['tepiʃ], *adj.* clumsy, awkward, unwieldy.

tarnen ['tarnən], *v.a.* camouflage.

Tasche ['taʃə], *f.* (—, *pl.* —n) pocket; bag, pouch; *in die* — *stecken*, pocket; *in die* — *greifen*, pay, fork out, put o.'s hand in o.'s pocket.

Taschendieb ['taʃendi:p], *m.* (—(e)s, *pl.* —e) pickpocket; *vor* —*en wird gewarnt*, beware of pickpockets.

Taschenformat ['taʃənfɔrma:t], *n.* (—s, *no pl.*) pocket-size.

Taschenspieler ['taʃənʃpi:lər], *m.* (—s, *pl.* —) juggler, conjurer.

Taschentuch ['taʃəntu:x], *n.* (—s, *pl.* ˑer) (pocket-)handkerchief.

Taschenuhr ['taʃənu:r], *f.* (—, *pl.* —en) pocket-watch.

Tasse ['tasə], *f.* (—, *pl.* —n) cup.

Tastatur [tasta'tu:r], *f.* (—, *pl.* —en) keyboard.

Taste ['tastə], *f.* (—, *pl.* —n) (*Mus.*) key.

tasten ['tastən], *v.n.* grope about, feel o.'s way.

Tastsinn ['tastzɪn], *m.* (—s, *no pl.*) sense of touch.

Tat [ta:t], *f.* (—, *pl.* —en) deed, act, action; feat, exploit; *in der* —, in fact, indeed; *auf frischer* —, in the very act; *einem mit Rat und* — *beistehen*, give s.o. advice and guidance, help by word and deed.

Tatbestand ['ta:tbəʃtant], *m.* (—es, *pl.* e) (*Law*) facts of the case.

Tatendrang ['ta:təndraŋ], *m.* (—(e)s, *no pl.*) urge for action; impetuosity.

tatenlos ['ta:tənlo:s], *adj.* inactive.

Täter ['tɛ:tər], *m.* (—s, *pl.* —) perpetrator, doer; culprit.

tätig ['tɛ:tɪç], *adj.* active, busy.

Tätigkeit ['tɛ:tɪçkaɪt], *f.* (—, *pl.* —en) activity.

Tätigkeitswort ['tɛ:tɪçkaɪtsvɔrt], *n.* (—(e)s, *pl.* er) (*Gram.*) verb.

Tatkraft ['ta:tkraft], *f.* (—, *no pl.*) energy.

tätlich ['tɛ:tlɪç], *adj.* — *werden*, become violent.

tätowieren [tɛ:to'vi:rən], *v.a.* tattoo.

Tatsache ['ta:tzaxə], *f.* (—, *pl.* —en) fact, matter of fact.

tatsächlich ['ta:tzɛçlɪç], *adj.* actual. — *excl.* really!

tätscheln ['tɛ:tʃəln], *v.a.* fondle.

Tatterich ['tatərɪç], *m.* (—s, *no pl.*) (*coll.*) trembling, shakiness.

Tatze ['tatsə], *f.* (—, *pl.* —n) paw.

Tau (1) [tau], *m.* (—s, *no pl.*) thaw; dew.

Tau (2) [tau], *n.* (—s, *pl.* —e) rope, cable.

taub [taup], *adj.* deaf; (*nut*) hollow, empty; — *machen*, deafen; — *sein gegen*, turn a deaf ear to.

Täubchen ['tɔypçən], *n.* (—s, *pl.* —) little dove; (*fig.*) sweetheart.

Taube ['taubə], *f.* (—, *pl.* —n) (*Orn.*) pigeon, dove.

Taubenschlag ['taubənʃla:k], *m.* (—s, *pl.* e) dovecote.

Taubenschwanz ['taubənʃvants], *m.* (—es, *pl.* e) (*Ent.*) hawkmoth.

Tauber ['taubər], *m.* (—s, *pl.* —) (*Orn.*) cock-pigeon.

Taubheit ['tauphaɪt], *f.* (—, *no pl.*) deafness.

Taubnessel ['taupnɛsəl], *f.* (—, *pl.* —n) (*Bot.*) deadnettle.

taubstumm ['taupʃtum], *adj.* deaf and dumb, deaf-mute.

tauchen ['tauçən], *v.n.* (*aux.* haben & sein) dive, plunge. — *v.a.* immerse, dip.

Tauchsieder ['tauçzi:dər], *m.* (—s, *pl.* —) (*Elec.*) immersion heater.

tauen ['tauən], *v.a.*, *v.n.* thaw, melt.

Taufbecken ['taufbɛkən], *n.* (—s, *pl.* —) (baptismal) font.

Taufe ['taufə], *f.* (—, *pl.* —n) baptism, christening; *aus der* — *heben*, stand godparent.

taufen ['taufən], *v.a.* baptise, christen.

Taufkleid ['taufklaɪt], *n.* (—s, *pl.* er) christening robe.

Täufling ['tɔyflɪŋ], *m.* (—s, *pl.* e) infant presented for baptism; neophyte.

Taufname ['taufna:mə], *n.* (—ns, *pl.* —n) Christian name.

Taufpate ['taufpa:tə], *m.* (—n, *pl.* —n) godfather, godmother.

Taufstein ['taufʃtaɪn], *n.* (—s, *pl.* —e) (baptismal) font.

taugen ['taugən], *v.n.* be good for, be fit for; *nichts* —, be good for nothing.

Taugenichts ['taugənɪçts], *m.* (—, *pl.* —e) ne'er-do-well, scapegrace, good-for-nothing.

tauglich ['tauklɪç], *adj.* able; useful, fit, suitable.

Taumel ['tauməl], *m.* (—s, *no pl.*) giddiness, dizziness, staggering; (*fig.*) whirl; ecstasy, frenzy, delirium, intoxication.

taumeln ['tauməln], *v.n.* (*aux.* sein) reel, stagger.

Tausch [tauʃ], *m.* (—es, *no pl.*) exchange, barter.

tauschen ['tauʃən], *v.a.* exchange for, barter against, swop; *die Rollen* —, change places.

täuschen ['tɔyʃən], *v.a.* deceive, delude. — *v.r. sich* —, be mistaken.

Tauschhandel ['tauʃhandəl], *m.* (—s, *no pl.*) barter.

Tauschmittel ['tauʃmɪtəl], *n.* (—s, *pl.* —) medium of exchange.

Täuschung ['tɔyʃuŋ], *f.* (—, *pl.* —en) deceit, deception; illusion.

Täuschungsversuch ['tɔyʃuŋsfɛrzu:ç], *m.* (—es, *pl.* —e) attempt at deception; (*Mil.*) diversion.

tausend ['tauzənt], *num. adj.* a thousand.

tausendjährig ['tauzəntjɛ:rɪç], *adj.* millennial, of a thousand years; *das* —*e Reich*, the millennium.

Tausendsasa ['tauzəntzasa], *m.* (—s, *pl.* —) devil of a fellow.

Tautropfen ['tautrɔpfən], *m.* (—s, *pl.* —) dew-drop.

Tauwetter ['tauvɛtər], *n.* (—s, *no pl.*) thaw.

Taxameter [taksa'me:tər], *m.* (—s, *pl.* —) taximeter.

Taxe ['taksə], *f.* (—, *pl.* —n) set rate, tariff; (taxi)cab; *nach der* — *verkauft werden*, be sold *ad valorem*.

taxieren [tak'si:rən], *v.a.* appraise, value.

Taxus ['taksus,] *m.* (—, *pl.* —) (*Bot.*) yew(-tree).

Technik ['tɛçnɪk], *f.* (—, *pl.* —en) technology, engineering; technique; skill, execution.

Techniker ['tɛçnɪkər], *m.* (—s, *pl.* —) technician, technical engineer.

Technikum ['tɛçnɪkum], *n.* (—s, *pl.* —s) technical school, college.

technisch ['tɛçnɪʃ], *adj.* technical; —*er Ausdruck*, technical term; —*e Störung*, technical hitch *or* breakdown.

technologisch [tɛçno'lo:gɪʃ], *adj.* technological.

Techtelmechtel

Techtelmechtel ['tɛçtəlmɛçtəl], *n.* (—s, *pl.* —) (*coll.*) love affair, flirtation.

Tee [te:], *m.* (—s, *no pl.*) tea.

Teedose ['te:do:zə], *f.* (—, *pl.* —n) tea-caddy.

Teekanne ['te:kanə], *f.* (—, *pl.* —n) tea-pot.

Teelöffel ['te:lœfəl], *m.* (—s, *pl.* —) tea-spoon.

Teemaschine ['te:maʃi:nə], *f.* (—, *pl.* —n) tea-urn.

Teer [te:r], *m.* (—(e)s, *no pl.*) tar.

Teerleinwand ['te:rlaɪnvant], *f.* (—, *no pl.*) tarpaulin.

Teerose ['te:ro:zə], *f.* (—, *pl.* —n) (*Bot.*) tea rose.

Teerpappe ['te:rpapə], *f.* (—, *no pl.*) roofing-felt.

teeren ['te:rən], *v.a.* tar.

Teesieb ['te:zi:p], *n.* (—(e)s, *pl.* —e) tea-strainer.

Teich [taɪç], *m.* (—es, *pl.* —e) pond.

Teig [taɪk], *m.* (—(e)s, *pl.* —e) dough, paste.

teigig ['taɪgɪç], *adj.* doughy.

Teigrolle ['taɪkrɔlə], *f.* (—, *pl.* —n) rolling-pin.

Teil [taɪl], *m. & n.* (—(e)s, *pl.* —e) part; portion; piece, component; share; *edler* —, vital part; *zum* —, partly; *zu gleichen* —*en*, share and share alike.

teilbar ['taɪlba:r], *adj.* divisible.

Teilchen ['taɪlçən], *n.* (—s, *pl.* —) particle.

teilen ['taɪlən], *v.a.* divide; share; partition off. — *v.r. sich* —, share in; (*road*) fork.

Teiler ['taɪlər], *m.* (—s, *pl.* —) divider; (*Maths.*) divisor.

teilhaben ['taɪlha:bən], *v.n. irr.* (have a) share in, participate in.

Teilhaber ['taɪlha:bər], *m.* (—s, *pl.* —) partner.

teilhaftig ['taɪlhaftɪç], *adj.* sharing, participating; *einer Sache* — *werden*, partake of s.th., come in for s.th.

Teilnahme ['taɪlna:mə], *f.* (—, *no pl.*) participation; (*fig.*) sympathy, interest.

teilnahmslos ['taɪlna:mslo:s], *adj.* unconcerned, indifferent.

Teilnahmslosigkeit ['taɪlna:mslo:zɪçkaɪt], *f.* (—, *no pl.*) unconcern; listlessness, indifference.

teilnahmsvoll ['taɪlna:msfɔl], *adj.* solicitous.

teilnehmen ['taɪlne:mən], *v.n. irr.* take part (in), participate, partake; (*fig.*) sympathise.

Teilnehmer ['taɪlne:mər], *m.* (—s, *pl.* —) member, participant; (*telephone*) subscriber.

teils [taɪls], *adv.* partly.

Teilstrecke ['taɪlʃtrɛkə], *f.* (—, *pl.* —n) section (of a railway).

Teilung ['taɪluŋ], *f.* (—, *pl.* —en) division, partition; distribution.

Teilungszahl ['taɪluŋtsa:l], *f.* (—, *pl.* —en) (*Maths.*) dividend; quotient.

teilweise ['taɪlvaɪzə], *adv.* partly, in part.

Teilzahlung ['taɪltsa:luŋ], *f.* (—, *pl.* —en) part-payment, instalment.

Teint [tɛ̃], *m.* (—s, *no pl.*) complexion.

telephonieren [telefo'ni:rən], *v.a., v.n.* telephone.

Telegraphie [telegra'fi:], *f.* (—, *no pl.*) telegraphy.

telegraphisch [tele'gra:fiʃ], *adj.* telegraphic, by telegram.

Telegramm [tele'gram], *n.* (—s, *pl.* —e) telegram, wire, cable.

Telegrammadresse [tele'gramadrɛsə], *f.* (—, *pl.* —n) telegraphic address.

Telegrammformular [tele'gramformula:r], *n.* (—s, *pl.* —e) telegram-form.

Teleskop [telɛs'ko:p], *n.* (—s, *pl.* —e) telescope.

Teller ['tɛlər], *m.* (—s, *pl.* —) plate.

Tempel ['tɛmpəl], *m.* (—s, *pl.* —) temple.

Temperament [tɛmpəra'mɛnt], *n.* (—s, *pl.* —e) temperament, disposition; (*fig.*) spirits.

temperamentvoll [tɛmpəra'mɛntfɔl], *adj.* full of spirits, vivacious; lively.

Temperatur [tɛmpəra'tu:r], *f.* (—, *pl.* —en) temperature.

Temperenzler [tɛmpə'rɛntslər], *m.* (—s, *pl.* —) total abstainer, tee-totaller.

temperieren [tɛmpə'ri:rən], *v.a.* temper.

Tempo ['tɛmpo:], *n.* (—s, *pl.* —s, Tempi) time, measure, speed.

temporisieren [tɛmpori'zi:rən], *v.n.* temporise.

Tendenz [tɛn'dɛnts], *f.* (—, *pl.* —en) tendency.

tendenziös [tɛndɛn'tsjø:s], *adj.* biased, coloured, tendentious.

Tender ['tɛndər], *m.* (—s, *pl.* —) (*Railw.*) tender.

Tenne ['tɛnə], *f.* (—, *pl.* —n) threshing floor.

Tenor [te'no:r], *m.* (—s, *pl.* ⸚e) (*Mus.*) tenor.

Teppich ['tɛpɪç], *m.* (—s, *pl.* —e) carpet.

Termin [tɛr'mi:n], *m.* (—s, *pl.* —e) time, date, appointed day; *einen* —*ansetzen*, fix a day (for a hearing, examination etc.).

Termingeschäft [tɛr'mi:ngəʃɛft], *n.* (—s, *pl.* —e) (business in) futures.

Terminologie [tɛrminolo'gi:], *f.* (—, *pl.* —n) terminology.

Terpentin [tɛrpɛn'ti:n], *n.* (—s, *no pl.*) turpentine.

Terrain [tɛ'rɛ̃], *n.* (—s, *pl.* —s) ground, terrain.

Terrasse [tɛ'rasə], *f.* (—, *pl.* —n) terrace.

Terrine [tɛ'ri:nə], *f.* (—, *pl.* —n) tureen.

territorial [tɛrɪto'rja:l], *adj.* territorial.

Territorium [tɛrɪ'to:rjum], *n.* (—s, *pl.* —torien) territory.

tertiär [tɛr'tsjɛːr], *adj.* tertiary.

Terzett [tɛr'tsɛt], *n.* (—s, *pl.* —e) trio.

Testament [testa'mɛnt], *n.* (—s, *pl.* —e) testament, will; (*Bibl.*) Testament; *ohne* —, intestate.

testamentarisch [testamen'taːrɪʃ], *adj.* testamentary.

Testamentseröffnung [testa'mentsɛrœfnuŋ], *f.* (—, *pl.* —en) reading of the will.

Testamentsvollstrecker [testa'mentsfɔlʃtrɛkər], *m.* (—s, *pl.* —) executor.

teuer ['tɔyər], *adj.* dear; costly, expensive; *einem* — *zu stehen kommen*, cost s.o. dear.

Teuerung ['tɔyəruŋ], *f.* (—, *pl.* —en) scarcity, dearth.

Teufel ['tɔyfəl], *m.* (—s, *pl.* —) devil, fiend; *armer* —, poor devil; *scher dich zum* —, go to blazes; *den* — *an die Wand malen*, talk of the devil.

Teufelei [tɔyfə'laɪ], *f.* (—, *pl.* —en) devilry, devilish trick.

teuflisch ['tɔyflɪʃ], *adj.* devilish, diabolical.

Thailand ['taɪlant], *n.* Thailand.

Theater [te'aːtər], *n.* (—s, *pl.* —) theatre, stage.

Theaterkarte [te'aːtərkartə], *f.* (—, *pl.* —n) theatre-ticket.

Theaterkasse [te'aːtərkasə], *f.* (—, *pl.* —n) box-office.

Theaterstück [te'aːtərʃtyk], *n.* (—(e)s, *pl.* —e) play, drama.

Theatervorstellung [te'aːtərfoːrʃtɛluŋ], *f.* (—, *pl.* —en) theatre performance.

Theaterzettel [te'aːtərtsetəl], *m.* (—s, *pl.* —) play-bill.

theatralisch [tea'traːlɪʃ], *adj.* theatrical; dramatic; histrionic.

Thema ['teːmaː], *n.* (—s, *pl.* —men, **Themata**) theme, subject, topic.

Themse ['tɛmzə], *f.* Thames.

Theologe [teo'loːgə], *m.* (—n, *pl.* —n) theologian.

Theologie [teolo'giː], *f.* (—, *no pl.*) theology, divinity.

theoretisch [teo're:tɪʃ], *adj.* theoretical.

theoretisieren [teoreti'ziːrən], *v.n.* theorise.

Theorie [teo'riː], *f.* (—, *pl.* —n) theory.

Therapie [tera'piː], *f.* (—, *no pl.*) therapy.

Therme ['tɛrmə], *f.* (—, *pl.* —n) hot spring.

Thermometer [tɛrmo'meːtər], *n.* (—s, *pl.* —) thermometer.

Thermosflasche ['tɛrmɔsflaʃə], *f.* (—, *pl.* —n) thermos-flask.

These ['teːzə], *f.* (—, *pl.* —n) thesis.

Thron [troːn], *m.* (—(e)s, *pl.* —e) throne; *auf den* — *setzen*, place on the throne, enthrone; *vom* — *stoßen*, dethrone, depose.

Thronbesteigung ['troːnbəʃtaɪguŋ], *f.* (—, *pl.* —en) accession (to the throne).

Thronbewerber ['troːnbəvɛrbər], *m.* (—s, *pl.* —) claimant to the throne, pretender.

thronen ['troːnən], *v.n.* sit enthroned.

Thronerbe ['troːnɛrbə], *m.* (—n, *pl.* —n) heir apparent, crown prince.

Thronfolge ['troːnfɔlgə], *f.* (—, *no pl.*) line *or* order of succession.

Thronfolger ['troːnfɔlgər], *m.* (—s, *pl.* —) heir to the throne, heir apparent.

Thronhimmel ['troːnhɪməl], *m.* (—s, *pl.* —) canopy.

Thronrede ['troːnreːdə], *f.* (—, *pl.* —n) speech from the throne.

Thunfisch ['tuːnfɪʃ], *m.* (—es, *pl.* —e) (*Zool.*) tunny, (*Am.*) tuna.

Thüringen ['tyːrɪŋən], *n.* Thuringia.

Thymian ['tyːmjaːn], *m.* (—s, *no pl.*) (*Bot.*) thyme.

ticken ['tɪkən], *v.n.* tick.

tief [tiːf], *adj.* deep, profound, low; far; extreme; (*voice*) bass; (*fig.*) profound; *in —ster Nacht*, in the dead of night; *aus —stem Herzen*, from the bottom of o.'s heart. — *adv.* — *atmen*, take a deep breath; — *in Schulden*, head over ears in debt; — *verletzt*, cut to the quick.

Tiefbau ['tiːfbau], *m.* (—s, *no pl.*) underground workings.

tiefbedrückt ['tiːfbədrykt], *adj.* deeply distressed; very depressed.

tiefbewegt ['tiːfbəveːkt], *adj.* deeply moved.

Tiefe ['tiːfə], *f.* (—, *pl.* —en) depth; (*fig.*) profundity.

tiefgebeugt ['tiːfgəbɔykt], *adj.* bowed down.

tiefgreifend ['tiːfgraɪfənt], *adj.* radical, sweeping.

tiefschürfend ['tiːfʃyrfənt], *adj.* profound; thoroughgoing.

Tiefsee ['tiːfzeː], *f.* (—, *no pl.*) deep sea.

Tiefsinn ['tiːfzɪn], *m.* (—s, *no pl.*) pensiveness, melancholy.

tiefsinnig ['tiːfzɪnɪç], *adj.* pensive, melancholy, melancholic(al).

Tiegel ['tiːgəl], *m.* (—s, *pl.* —) crucible; saucepan.

Tier [tiːr], *n.* (—(e)s, *pl.* —e) animal, beast; *ein großes* —, (*coll.*) a V.I.P., a bigwig; (*Am.*) a swell, a big shot.

Tierart ['tiːraːrt], *f.* (—, *pl.* —en) (*Zool.*) species.

Tierarzt ['tiːraːrtst], *m.* (—es, *pl.* ⁖e) veterinary surgeon.

Tierbändiger ['tiːrbɛndɪgər], *m.* (—s, *pl.* —) animal-tamer.

Tiergarten ['tiːrgartən], *m.* (—s, *pl.* ⁖) zoological gardens, zoo.

tierisch ['tiːrɪʃ], *adj.* animal, brute, brutal, bestial.

Tierkreis ['tiːrkraɪs], *m.* (—es, *no pl.*) zodiac.

Tierkunde ['tiːrkundə], *f.* (—, *no pl.*) zoology.

Tierquälerei ['tiːrkvɛːləraɪ], *f.* (—, *pl.* —en) cruelty to animals.

Tierreich ['tiːrraɪç], *n.* (—(e)s, *no pl.*) animal kingdom.

Tierschutzverein ['tiːrʃutsfəraɪn], *m.* (—s, *pl.* —e) society for the prevention of cruelty to animals.

Tierwärter

Tierwärter ['ti:rvɛrtər], m. (—s, pl. —) keeper (at a zoo).

Tiger ['ti:gər], m. (—s, pl. —) (Zool.) tiger.

Tigerin ['ti:gərɪn], f. (—, pl. —nen) (Zool.) tigress.

tilgbar ['tɪlkba:r], adj. extinguishable; (debt) redeemable.

tilgen ['tɪlgən], v.a. strike out, efface, annul; (debt) discharge; (sin) expiate, atone for.

Tilgung ['tɪlguŋ], f. (—, pl. —en) striking out, obliteration; annulment, payment; redemption.

Tilgungsfonds ['tɪlguŋsfɔ̃], m. (—, pl. —) sinking fund.

Tingeltangel ['tɪŋəltaŋəl], m. & n. (—s, pl. —) (coll.) music-hall.

Tinktur [tɪŋk'tu:r], f. (—, pl. —en) tincture.

Tinte ['tɪntə], f. (—, pl. —n) ink; in der — sein, be in a jam, be in the soup.

Tintenfaß ['tɪntənfas], n. (—sses, pl. —sser) ink-pot, ink-stand.

Tintenfisch ['tɪntənfɪʃ], m. (—es, pl. —e) (Zool.) cuttle-fish.

Tintenfleck ['tɪntənflɛk], m. (—s, pl. —e) blot, ink-spot.

Tintenklecks ['tɪntənklɛks], m. (—es, pl. —e) blot.

Tintenstift ['tɪntənʃtɪft], m. (—s, pl. —e) indelible pencil.

Tintenwischer ['tɪntənvɪʃər], m. (—s, pl. —) pen-wiper.

tippen ['tɪpən], v.a. tap; (coll.) type.

Tirol [ti'ro:l], n. Tyrol.

Tisch [tɪʃ], m. (—es, pl. —e) table, board; den — decken, lay the table; zu — gehen, sit down to dinner.

Tischdecke ['tɪʃdɛkə], f. (—, pl. —n) tablecloth.

Tischgebet ['tɪʃgəbe:t], n. (—s, pl. —e) grace.

Tischler ['tɪʃlər], m. (—s, pl. —) joiner, cabinet-maker, carpenter.

Tischlerei [tɪʃlə'raɪ], f. (—, no pl.) joinery, cabinet-making, carpentry.

Tischrede ['tɪʃre:də], f. (—, pl. —n) after-dinner speech.

Tischrücken ['tɪʃrykən], n. (—s, no pl.) table-turning.

Tischtennis ['tɪʃtɛnɪs], n. (—, no pl.) table-tennis, ping-pong.

Tischtuch ['tɪʃtu:x], n. (—(e)s, pl. —er) tablecloth.

Tischzeit ['tɪʃtsaɪt], f. (—, pl. —en) mealtime.

Titane [ti'ta:nə], m. (—n, pl. —n) Titan.

titanenhaft [ti'ta:nənhaft], adj. titanic.

Titel ['ti:təl], m. (—s, pl. —) title; claim; heading, headline.

Titelbild ['ti:təlbɪlt], n. (—(e)s, pl. —er) frontispiece.

Titelblatt ['ti:təlblat], n. (—(e)s, pl. —er) title page.

Titelrolle ['ti:təlrɔlə], f. (—, pl. —n) title role.

titulieren [titu'li:rən], v.a. style, address.

---

toben ['to:bən], v.n. rave; rage, roar; be furious; be wild.

tobsüchtig ['to:pzyçtɪç], adj. raving, mad.

Tochter ['tɔxtər], f. (—, pl. ⁼) daughter.

töchterlich ['tœçtərlɪç], adj. filial, daughterly.

Tod [to:t], m. (—es, pl. —esfälle or (rare) —e) death, decease, demise; dem — geweiht, doomed; Kampf auf — und Leben, fight to the death; zum — verurteilen, condemn to death.

Todesangst ['to:dəsaŋst], f. (—, pl. ⁼e) agony, mortal terror.

Todesanzeige ['to:dəsantsaɪgə], f. (—, pl. —n) announcement of death; obituary notice.

Todesfall ['to:dəsfal], m. (—(e)s, pl. ⁼e) death, decease; fatality.

Todesgefahr ['to:dəsgəfa:r], f. (—, pl. —en) mortal danger.

Todeskampf ['to:dəskampf], m. (—(e)s, pl. ⁼e) death agony.

todesmutig ['to:dəsmu:tɪç], adj. death-defying.

Todesstoß ['to:dəsʃto:s], m. (—es, pl. ⁼e) death-blow.

Todesstrafe ['to:dəsʃtra:fə], f. (—, no pl.) capital punishment.

Todfeind ['to:tfaɪnt], m. (—es, pl. —e) mortal enemy.

todkrank ['to:tkraŋk], adj. sick unto death, dangerously or mortally ill.

tödlich ['tœ:tlɪç], adj. mortal, deadly, fatal.

todmüde ['to:tmy:də], adj. tired to death.

Todsünde ['to:tzyndə], f. (—, pl. —n) mortal sin.

Togo ['to:go], n. Togo.

Toilette [toa'lɛtə], f. (—, pl. —n) lavatory, toilet; (fig.) dress.

tolerant [tole'rant], adj. tolerant.

Toleranz [tole'rants], f. (—, no pl.) toleration; tolerance.

tolerieren [tole'ri:rən], v.a. tolerate.

toll [tɔl], adj. mad, frantic; wild; —er Streich, mad prank; zum — werden, enough to drive o. mad.

Tolle ['tɔlə], f. (—, pl. —n) (dial.) forelock, tuft of hair, top-knot.

Tollhaus ['tɔlhaus], n. (—es, pl. ⁼er) madhouse, lunatic asylum.

Tollheit ['tɔlhaɪt], f. (—, pl. —en) foolhardiness, mad prank.

Tollkirsche ['tɔlkɪrʃə], f. (—, pl. —n) belladonna, deadly nightshade.

Tollwut ['tɔlvu:t], f. (—, no pl.) frenzy; rabies.

Tolpatsch ['tɔlpatʃ], m. (—es, pl. —e) clumsy person.

Tölpel ['tœlpəl], m. (—s, pl. —) blockhead, lout, hobbledehoy.

Tölpelei [tœlpə'laɪ], f. (—, pl. —en) clumsiness, awkwardness.

tölpelhaft ['tœlpəlhaft], adj. clumsy, doltish, loutish.

Tomate [to'ma:tə], f. (—, pl. —n) tomato.

Ton (1) [to:n], *m.* (—(e)s, *pl.* ˙·e) sound, tone, accent, note; shade; manners; *guter (schlechter)* —, good (bad) form, etiquette; *den* — *angeben*, set the fashion.

Ton (2) [to:n], *m.* (—s, *no pl.*) clay, potter's earth.

Tonabnehmer ['to:napne:mər], *m.* (—s, *pl.* —) *(gramophone)* pick-up.

tonangebend ['to:nange:bənt], *adj.* leading in fashion, setting the pace; leading, fashionable.

Tonart ['to:na:rt], *f.* (—, *pl.* —en) *(Mus.)* key.

Tonbandgerät ['to:nbantgɛrɛ:t], *n.* (—s, *pl.* —e) tape-recorder.

tönen ['tø:nən], *v.n.* sound.

Tonerde ['to:ne:rdə], *f.* (—, *no pl.*) clay.

tönern ['tø:nərn], *adj.* earthen.

Tonfall ['to:nfal], *m.* (—s, *no pl.*) cadence, intonation (of voice).

Tonfolge ['to:nfɔlgə], *f.* (—, *pl.* —n) *(Mus.)* succession of notes.

Tonführung ['to:nfy:ruŋ], *f.* (—, *no pl.*) modulation.

Tonkunst ['to:nkunst], *f.* (—, *no pl.*) music.

Tonkünstler ['to:nkynstlər], *m.* (—s, *pl.* —) musician.

Tonleiter ['to:nlaItər], *f.* (—, *pl.* —n) scale, gamut.

Tonne ['tɔnə], *f.* (—, *pl.* —n) tun, cask, barrel; ton.

Tonnengewölbe ['tɔnəngəvœlbə], *n.* (—s, *pl.* —) cylindrical vault.

Tonpfeife ['to:npfaIfə], *f.* (—, *pl.* —n) clay-pipe.

Tonsatz ['to:nzats], *m.* (—es, *pl.* ˙·e) *(Mus.)* composition.

Tonsur [tɔn'zu:r], *f.* (—, *pl.* —en) tonsure.

Tonwelle ['to:nvɛlə], *f.* (—, *pl.* —n) sound-wave.

Topas [to'pa:s], *m.* (—es, *pl.* —e) topaz.

Topf [tɔpf], *m.* (—(e)s, *pl.* ˙·e) pot; *alles in einen* — *werfen*, lump everything together.

Topfblume ['tɔpfblu:mə], *f.* (—, *pl.* —n) pot-plant.

Topfdeckel ['tɔpfdɛkəl], *m.* (—s, *pl.* —) lid of a pot.

Töpfer ['tœpfər], *m.* (—s, *pl.* —) potter.

Töpferarbeit ['tœpfərarbaIt], *f.* (—, *pl.* —en) pottery.

Töpferscheibe ['tœpfərʃaIbə], *f.* (—, *pl.* —n) potter's wheel.

Töpferware ['tœpfərva:rə], *f.* (—, *pl.* —n) pottery, earthenware.

Topfgucker ['tɔpfgukər], *m.* (—s, *pl.* —) busybody; inquisitive person.

Topographie [topogra'fi:], *f.* (—, *no pl.*) topography.

Tor (1) [to:r], *m.* (—en, *pl.* —en) *(obs.)* fool, simpleton.

Tor (2) [to:r], *n.* (—(e)s, *pl.* —e) gate; *(Footb.)* goal.

Torangel ['to:raŋəl], *f.* (—, *pl.* —n) hinge.

Tor(es)schluß ['to:r(əs)ʃlus], *m.* (—es, *no pl.*) shutting of the gate; *noch gerade vor* —, at the eleventh hour.

Torf [tɔrf], *m.* (—(e)s, *no pl.*) peat, turf.

Torfgrube ['tɔrfgru:bə], *f.* (—, *pl.* —n) turf-pit.

Torfmoor ['tɔrfmo:r], *n.* (—s, *pl.* —e) peat-bog.

Torfstecher ['tɔrfʃtɛçər], *m.* (—s, *pl.* —) peat-cutter.

Torheit ['to:rhaIt], *f.* (—, *pl.* —en) foolishness, folly.

Torhüter ['to:rhy:tər], *m.* (—s, *pl.* —) gate-keeper.

töricht ['tø:rIçt], *adj.* foolish, silly.

Törin ['tø:rIn], *f.* (—, *pl.* —nen) *(rare)* foolish woman.

torkeln ['tɔrkəln], *v.n.* *(aux. sein)* *(coll.)* stagger, reel.

Tornister [tɔr'nIstər], *m.* (—s, *pl.* —) knapsack, satchel.

Torpedo [tɔr'pe:do], *m.* (—s, *pl.* —s) torpedo.

Torso ['tɔrzo], *m.* (—s, *pl.* —s) trunk, torso.

Tort [tɔrt], *m.* (—s, *no pl.*) injury, wrong; *einem einen* — *antun*, wrong s.o., play a trick on s.o.

Torte ['tɔrtə], *f.* (—, *pl.* —n) cake, pastry, tart.

Tortur [tɔr'tu:r], *f.* (—, *pl.* —en) torture.

Torwächter ['to:rvɛçtər], *m.* (—s, *pl.* —) gate-keeper; porter.

tosen ['to:zən], *v.n.* roar.

tot [to:t], *adj.* dead, deceased.

total [to'ta:l], *adj.* total, complete.

Totalisator [totali'za:tɔr], *m.* (—s, *pl.* —en) totalisator; *(coll.)* tote.

Totalleistung [to'ta:llaIstuŋ], *f.* (—, *pl.* —en) full effect; total output.

Tote ['to:tə], *m., f.* (—n, *pl.* —n) dead person, the deceased.

töten ['tø:tən], *v.a.* kill, put to death.

Totenacker ['to:tənakər], *m.* (—s, *pl.* ˙·) churchyard, cemetery.

Totenamt ['to:tənamt], *n.* (—s, *no pl.*) office for the dead, requiem, Mass for the dead.

Totenbahre ['to:tənba:rə], *f.* (—, *pl.* —n) bier.

Totengräber ['to:təngrɛ:bər], *m.* (—s, *pl.* —) grave-digger.

Totenhemd ['to:tənhɛmt], *n.* (—(e)s, *pl.* —en) shroud, winding-sheet.

Totenklage ['to:tənkla:gə], *f.* (—, *no pl.*) lament.

Totenschein ['to:tənʃaIn], *m.* (—(e)s, *pl.* —e) death-certificate.

Totenstille ['to:tənʃtIlə], *f.* (—, *no pl.*) dead calm.

Totenwache ['to:tənvaxə], *f.* (—, *no pl.*) wake.

totgeboren ['to:tgəbo:rən], *adj.* stillborn, born dead.

Totschlag ['to:tʃla:k], *m.* (—s, *no pl.*) manslaughter.

totschlagen ['to:tʃla:gən], *v.a.* *irr.* kill, strike dead.

Totschläger

Totschläger ['to:tʃlɛ:gər], *m.* (—s, *pl.* —) loaded cane, life-preserver.

totschweigen ['to:tʃvaɪgən], *v.a. irr.* hush up.

Tötung ['tø:tuŋ], *f.* (—, *pl.* —en) killing.

Tour [tu:r], *f.* (—, *pl.* —en) tour, excursion; *in einer* —, ceaselessly; *auf —en bringen,* (*coll.*) (*Motor.*) rev up.

Tournee [tur'ne:], *f.* (—, *pl.* —n) (*Theat.*) tour.

Trab [tra:p], *m.* (—(e)s, *no pl.*) trot.

Trabant [tra'bant], *m.* (—en, *pl.* —en) satellite.

traben [tra:bən], *v.n.* (*aux.* sein) trot.

Trabrennen ['tra:prɛnən], *n.* (—s, *pl.* —) trotting-race.

Tracht [traxt], *f.*\(—, *pl.* —en) dress, costume; national costume; native dress; *eine — Prügel,* a good hiding.

trachten ['traxtən], *v.n.* strive, aspire, endeavour; *einem nach dem Leben —,* seek to kill s.o.

trächtig ['trɛçtɪç], *adj.* (*animal*) pregnant, with young.

Trafik [tra'fik¹], *m.* (—s, *pl.* —s) (*Austr.*) tobacco-kiosk.

Tragbahre ['tra:kba:rə], *f.* (—, *pl.* —n) stretcher.

Tragbalken ['tra:kbalkən], *m.* (—s *pl.,* —) girder.

tragbar ['tra:kba:r], *adj.* portable; tolerable.

träge ['trɛ:gə], *adj.* lazy, indolent, inert, sluggish.

tragen ['tra:gən], *v.a. irr.* bear, carry; (*dress*) wear; (*fig.*) bear, endure; *Bedenken —,* hesitate, have doubts; *Zinsen —,* yield interest; *einen auf Händen —,* care lovingly for s.o.

Träger ['trɛ:gər], *m.* (—s, *pl.* —) porter, carrier; girder.

Trägheit ['trɛ:khaɪt], *f.* (—, *no pl.*) indolence, laziness, inertia.

tragisch ['tra:gɪʃ], *adj.* tragic(al).

Tragkraft ['tra:kkraft], *f.* (—, *no pl.*) carrying *or* load capacity; lifting power.

Tragödie [tra'gø:djə], *f.* (—, *pl.* —n) tragedy.

Tragsessel ['tra:kzɛsəl], *m.* (—s, *pl.* —) sedan-chair.

Tragweite ['tra:kvaɪtə], *f.* (—, *no pl.*) significance, importance, range.

trainieren [trɛ'ni:rən], *v.a.* train.

Traktat [trak'ta:t], *n.* (—s, *pl.* —e) treatise, tract.

Traktätchen [trak'tɛ:tçən], *n.* (—s, *pl.* —) (short) tract.

traktieren [trak'ti:rən], *v.a.* treat; treat badly.

trällern ['trɛlərn], *v.n.* trill, hum.

Trambahn ['tramba:n], *f.* (—, *pl.* —en) tram; (*Am.*) streetcar.

Trampel ['trampəl], *n.* (—s, *pl.* —) clumsy person, bumpkin; (*Am.*) hick.

trampeln ['trampəln], *v.n.* trample.

Trampeltier ['trampəlti:r], *n.* (—s, *pl.* —e) camel; (*fig.*) clumsy person.

Tran [tra:n], *m.* (—(e)s, *no pl.*) whale-oil.

tranchieren [trã'ʃi:rən], *v.a.* carve.

Tranchiermesser [trã'ʃi:rmɛsər], *n.* (—s, *pl.* —) carving-knife.

Träne ['trɛ:nə], *f.* (—, *pl.* —n) tear, teardrop; *zu —n gerührt,* moved to tears.

tränen ['trɛ:nən], *v.n.* (*eyes*) water.

Tränendrüse ['trɛ:nəndry:zə], *f.* (—, *pl.* —n) lachrymal gland.

tränenleer ['trɛ:nənle:r], *adj.* tearless.

Tränenstrom ['trɛ:nənʃtro:m], *m.* (—s, *pl.* ⁻e) flood of tears.

tränenvoll ['trɛ:nənfɔl], *adj.* tearful.

tranig ['tra:nɪç], *adj.* dull, slow.

Trank [traŋk], *m.* (—(e)s, *pl.* ⁻e) drink, beverage, potion.

Tränke ['trɛŋkə], *f.* (—, *pl.* ⁻n) (*horse*) watering-place.

tränken ['trɛŋkən], *v.a.* give to drink, water; impregnate, saturate.

transitiv ['tranziti:f], *adj.* transitive.

Transitlager ['tranzɪtla:gər], *n.* (—s, *pl.* —) bonded warehouse; transit camp.

transitorisch [tranzi'to:rɪʃ], *adj.* transitory.

transpirieren [transpi'ri:rən], *v.n.* perspire.

transponieren [transpo'ni:rən], *v.a.* transpose.

Transportkosten [trans'pɔrtkɔstən]¹, *f. pl.* shipping charges.

Transportmittel [trans'pɔrtmɪtəl], *n.* (—s, *pl.* —) means of carriage, conveyance, transport.

Trapez [tra'pe:ts], *n.* (—es, *pl.* —e) trapeze; (*Maths.*) trapezoid.

Tratsch [tra:tʃ], *m.* (—es, *no pl.*) (*coll.*) gossip, tittle-tattle.

tratschen ['tra:tʃən], *v.n.* (*coll.*) gossip.

Tratte ['tratə], *f.* (—, *pl.* —n) (*Comm.*) draft, bill of exchange.

Traube ['traubə], *f.* (—, *pl.* —n) (*Bot.*) grape, bunch of grapes.

Traubensaft ['traubənzaft], *m.* (—s, *pl.* ⁻e) grape-juice; (*Poet.*) wine.

traubig ['traubɪç], *adj.* clustered, grape-like.

trauen ['trauən], *v.a.* marry; join in marriage; *sich — lassen,* get married. — *v.n. einem —,* trust s.o., confide in s.o. — *v.r. sich —,* dare, venture.

Trauer ['trauər], *f.* (—, *no pl.*) mourning; sorrow, grief.

Trauermarsch ['trauərmarʃ], *m.* (—es, *pl.* ⁻e) funeral march.

trauern ['trauərn], *v.n.* mourn, be in mourning.

Trauerspiel ['trauərʃpi:l], *n.* (—s, *pl.* —e) tragedy.

Trauerweide ['trauərvaɪdə], *f.* (—, *pl.* —n) (*Bot.*) weeping willow.

Traufe ['traufə], *f.* (—, *pl.* —n) eaves; *vom Regen in die —,* out of the frying pan into the fire.

träufeln ['trɔyfəln], *v.a.* drip, drop.

Traufröhre ['traufrø:rə], *f.* (—, *pl.* —n) gutter-pipe.

traulich ['traulɪç], *adj.* familiar, homely, cosy.

Traum [traum], *m.* (—(e)s, *pl.* ˙e) dream; *das fällt mir nicht im —e ein*, I should not dream of it.

Traumbild ['traumbɪlt], *n.* (—s, *pl.* —er) vision.

Traumdeutung ['traumdɔytuŋ], *f.* (—, *no pl.*) interpretation of dreams.

träumen ['trɔymən], *v.n.* dream; *sich etwas nicht — lassen*, have no inkling of, not dream of s.th.; not believe s.th.

Träumer ['trɔymər], *m.* (—s, *pl.* —) dreamer; (*fig.*) visionary.

Träumerei [trɔymə'raɪ], *f.* (—, *pl.* —en) dreaming, reverie.

traumhaft ['traumhaft], *adj.* dream-like.

traurig ['traurɪç], *adj.* sad, mournful, sorrowful.

Traurigkeit ['traurɪçkaɪt], *f.* (—, *no pl.*) sadness, melancholy.

Trauring ['traurɪŋ], *m.* (—s, *pl.* —e) wedding-ring.

Trauschein ['trauʃaɪn], *m.* (—s, *pl.* —e) marriage certificate.

traut [traut], *adj.* dear, beloved; cosy; *—es Heim Glück allein*, east, west, home's best; there's no place like home.

Trauung ['trauuŋ], *f.* (—, *pl.* —en) marriage ceremony.

Trauzeuge ['trautsɔygə], *m.* (—n, *pl.* —n) witness to a marriage.

trecken ['trɛkən], *v.a.* (*dial.*) draw, drag, tug.

Trecker ['trɛkər], *m.* (—s, *pl.* —) tractor.

Treff [trɛf], *n.* (—s, *no pl.*) (*Cards*) clubs.

Treffen ['trɛfən], *n.* (—s, *pl.* —) action, battle, fight; meeting, gathering; *etwas ins — führen*, put s.th. forward, urge s.th.

treffen ['trɛfən], *v.a. irr.* hit, meet; *nicht —*, miss; *wie vom Donner getroffen*, thunderstruck; *ins Schwarze —*, hit the mark, score a bull's eye. — *v.r. sich —*, happen.

treffend ['trɛfənt], *adj.* appropriate, pertinent.

Treffer ['trɛfər], *m.* (—s, *pl.* —) (*lottery*) win, prize; (*Mil.*) hit.

trefflich ['trɛflɪç], *adj.* excellent.

Treffpunkt ['trɛfpuŋkt], *m.* (—s, *pl.* —e) meeting-place.

Treffsicherheit ['trɛfzɪçərhaɪt], *f.* (—, *no pl.*) accurate aim.

Treibeis ['traɪpaɪs], *n.* (—es, *no pl.*) floating-ice, ice floe.

treiben ['traɪbən], *v.a. irr.* drive, urge; incite; (*trade*) carry on, ply; *Studien —*, study; *was treibst du?* what are you doing? *etwas zu weit —*, carry s.th. too far; *einen in die Enge —*, drive s.o. into a corner. — *v.n.* be adrift, drift.

Treiben ['traɪbən], *n.* (—s, *no pl.*) driving; doings; bustle.

Treiber ['traɪbər], *m.* (—s, *pl.* —) (*Hunt.*) driver; beater.

Treibhaus ['traɪphaus], *n.* (—es, *pl.* ˙er) hothouse, greenhouse.

Treibkraft ['traɪpkraft], *f.* (—, *no pl.*) impulse, driving power.

Treibriemen ['traɪpri:mən], *m.* (—s, *pl.* —) driving-belt.

Treibsand ['traɪpzant], *m.* (—s, *no pl.*) quicksand, shifting sand.

Treibstange ['traɪpʃtaŋə], *f.* (—, *pl.* —en) main rod, connecting-rod.

Treibstoff ['traɪpʃtɔf], *m.* (—(e)s, *pl.* —e) fuel.

treideln ['traɪdəln], *v.a.* (*Naut.*) tow.

Treidelsteig ['traɪdəlʃtaɪk], *m.* (—s, *pl.* —e) towpath.

trennbar ['trɛnba:r], *adj.* separable.

trennen ['trɛnən], *v.a.* separate, sever. — *v.r. sich —*, part.

Trennung ['trɛnuŋ], *f.* (—, *pl.* —en) separation, segregation; parting; division.

Trennungsstrich ['trɛnuŋsʃtrɪç], *m.* (—es, *pl.* —e) hyphen, dash.

treppab [trɛp'ap], *adv.* downstairs.

treppauf [trɛp'auf], *adv.* upstairs.

Treppe ['trɛpə], *f.* (—, *pl.* —n) stairs, staircase, flight of stairs.

Treppenabsatz ['trɛpənapzats], *m.* (—es, *pl.* ˙e) (*staircase*) landing.

Treppengeländer ['trɛpəngəlɛndər], *n.* (—s, *pl.* —) balustrade, banisters.

Treppenhaus ['trɛpənhaus], *n.* (—es, *pl.* ˙er) stair-well, staircase.

Treppenläufer ['trɛpənlɔyfər], *m.* (—s, *pl.* —) stair-carpet.

Treppenstufe ['trɛpənʃtu:fə], *f.* (—, *pl.* —n) step, stair.

Treppenwitz ['trɛpənvɪts], *m.* (—es, *no pl.*) afterthought, esprit de l'escalier.

Tresor [tre'zo:r], *m.* (—s, *pl.* —e) safe, strongroom.

Tresse ['trɛsə], *f.* (—, *pl.* —n) braid, lace, galloon.

treten ['tre:tən], *v.a., v.n. irr.* tread, step, trample upon; go; — *Sie näher*, step this way; *in Verbindung — mit*, make contact with; *in den Ehestand —*, get married; *einem zu nahe —*, offend s.o., tread on s.o.'s toes.

treu [trɔy], *adj.* faithful, loyal, true; conscientious.

Treubruch ['trɔybrux], *m.* (—(e)s, *pl.* ˙e) breach of faith, disloyalty.

Treue ['trɔyə], *f.* (—, *no pl.*) faithfulness, loyalty, fidelity; *meiner Treu!* upon my soul! *auf Treu und Glauben*, on trust.

Treueid ['trɔyaɪt], *m.* (—s, *pl.* —e) oath of allegiance.

Treuhänder ['trɔyhɛndər], *m.* (—s, *pl.* —) trustee.

treuherzig ['trɔyhɛrtsɪç], *adj.* guileless, trusting.

treulich ['trɔylɪç], *adv.* faithfully.

treulos ['trɔylo:s], *adj.* faithless, perfidious; unfaithful.

Treulosigkeit

Treulosigkeit [ˈtrɔylo:zɪçkaɪt], *f.* (—, *no pl.*) faithlessness, perfidy, disloyalty.

Tribüne [triˈbyːnə], *f.* (—, *pl.* —n) tribune, platform; (*racing*) grandstand.

Tribut [triˈbuːt], *m.* (—s, *pl.* —e) tribute.

tributpflichtig [triˈbuːtpflɪçtɪç], *adj.* tributary.

Trichter [ˈtrɪçtər], *m.* (—s, *pl.* —) funnel.

trichterförmig [ˈtrɪçtərfœrmɪç], *adj.* funnel-shaped.

Trieb [triːp], *m.* (—(e)s, *pl.* —e) (*plant*) shoot, growth; instinct, bent, propensity, inclination; (*Psych.*) drive.

Triebfeder [ˈtriːpfeːdər], *f.* (—, *pl.* —n) mainspring; (*fig.*) motive, guiding principle.

Triebkraft [ˈtriːpkraft], *f.* (—, *pl.* ⁻e) motive power.

Triebwagen [ˈtriːpvaːgən], *m.* (—s, *pl.* —) rail-car.

Triebwerk [ˈtriːpvɛrk], *n.* (—s, *pl.* —e) power unit, drive.

triefen [ˈtriːfən], *v.n. irr. & reg.* trickle, drip; be wet through, be soaking wet.

Trient [triˈɛnt], *n.* Trent.

Trier [triːr], *n.* Trèves.

Triest [triˈɛst], *n.* Trieste.

Trift [trɪft], *f.* (—, *pl.* —en) pasture, pasturage, common, meadow.

triftig [ˈtrɪftɪç], *adj.* weighty, valid, conclusive, cogent.

Trikot [triˈkoː], *m. & n.* (—s, *pl.* —s) stockinet; (*circus, ballet*) tights.

Triller [ˈtrɪlər], *m.* (—s, *pl.* —) (*Mus.*) trill, shake.

trillern [ˈtrɪlərn], *v.n.* trill, quaver, shake; warble.

Trinität [triniˈtɛːt], *f.* (—, *no pl.*) Trinity.

trinkbar [ˈtrɪŋkbaːr], *adj.* drinkable.

Trinkbecher [ˈtrɪŋkbeçər], *m.* (—s, *pl.* —) drinking-cup.

trinken [ˈtrɪŋkən], *v.a., v.n. irr.* drink.

Trinker [ˈtrɪŋkər], *m.* (—s, *pl.* —) drinker, drunkard.

Trinkgelage [ˈtrɪŋkgəlaːgə], *n.* (—s, *pl.* —) drinking-bout.

Trinkgeld [ˈtrɪŋkgɛlt], *n.* (—s, *pl.* —er) tip, gratuity.

Trinkhalle [ˈtrɪŋkhalə], *f.* (—, *pl.* —n) (*spa*) pump-room.

Trinkspruch [ˈtrɪŋkʃprux], *m.* (—(e)s, *pl.* ⁻e) toast.

Trinkstube [ˈtrɪŋkʃtuːbə], *f.* (—, *pl.* —n) tap-room.

Tripolis [ˈtriːpolɪs], *n.* Tripoli.

trippeln [ˈtrɪpəln], *v.n.* trip (daintily), patter.

Tripper [ˈtrɪpər], *m.* (—s, *no pl.*) (*Med.*) gonorrhoea.

Tritt [trɪt], *m.* (—(e)s, *pl.* —e) step, pace; kick.

Trittbrett [ˈtrɪtbrɛt], *n.* (—s, *pl.* —er) foot-board; carriage-step; (*organ*) pedal.

Triumph [triˈumf], *m.* (—(e)s, *pl.* —e) triumph.

Triumphzug [triˈumftsuːk], *m.* (—(e)s, *pl.* ⁻e) triumphal procession.

Trivialität [trivjaliˈtɛːt], *f.* (—, *pl.* —en) triviality, platitude.

trocken [ˈtrɔkən], *adj.* dry, arid; (*fig.*) dull, dry as dust; (*wine*) dry.

Trockenboden [ˈtrɔkənboːdən], *m.* (—s, *pl.* ⁻) loft.

Trockenfäule [ˈtrɔkənfɔylə], *f.*, **Trockenfäulnis** [ˈtrɔkənfɔylnɪs], *f.* (—, *no pl.*) dry rot.

Trockenfutter [ˈtrɔkənfutər], *n.* (—s, *no pl.*) fodder.

Trockenfütterung [ˈtrɔkənfytəruŋ], *f.* (—, *pl.* —en) dry feeding.

Trockenhaube [ˈtrɔkənhaubə], *f.* (—, *pl.* —n) hair drier.

Trockenheit [ˈtrɔkənhaɪt], *f.* (—, *no pl.*) dryness; drought.

Trockenschleuder [ˈtrɔkənʃlɔydər], *f.* (—, *pl.* —n) spin-drier.

trocknen [ˈtrɔknən], *v.a., v.n.* dry, air.

Troddel [ˈtrɔdəl], *f.* (—, *pl.* —n) tassel.

Trödel [ˈtrøːdəl], *m.* (—s, *no pl.*) junk, lumber, rubbish.

Trödelladen [ˈtrøːdəlaːdən], *m.* (—s, *pl.* ⁻) junk-shop.

Trödelmarkt [ˈtrøːdəlmarkt], *m.* (—s, *no pl.*) kettle market, jumble sale.

trödeln [ˈtrøːdəln], *v.n.* dawdle, loiter.

Trödler [ˈtrøːdlər], *m.* (—s, *pl.* —) second-hand dealer; (*coll.*) dawdler, loiterer.

Trog [troːk], *m.* (—(e)s, *pl.* ⁻e) trough.

Troja [ˈtroːja], *n.* Troy.

trollen [ˈtrɔlən], *v.r. sich* —, decamp, toddle off, make o.s. scarce.

Trommel [ˈtrɔməl], *f.* (—, *pl.* —n) drum; cylinder, barrel; tin box; *die* — *rühren*, beat the big drum.

Trommelfell [ˈtrɔməlfɛl], *n.* (—s, *pl.* —e) drum-skin; ear-drum.

trommeln [ˈtrɔməln], *v.n.* drum, beat the drum.

Trommelschlegel [ˈtrɔməlʃleːgəl], *m.* (—s, *pl.* —) drumstick.

Trommelwirbel [ˈtrɔməlvɪrbəl], *m.* (—s, *pl.* —) roll of drums.

Trommler [ˈtrɔmlər], *m.* (—s, *pl.* —) drummer.

Trompete [trɔmˈpeːtə], *f.* (—, *pl.* —n) trumpet; *die* — *blasen*, blow the trumpet.

trompeten [trɔmˈpeːtən], *v.n.* trumpet, sound the trumpet.

Trompetengeschmetter [trɔmˈpeːtəngəʃmɛtər], *n.* (—s, *no pl.*) flourish of trumpets.

Tropen [ˈtroːpən], *f. pl.* the tropics.

Tropenfieber [ˈtroːpənfiːbər], *n.* (—s, *no pl.*) tropical fever.

tröpfeln [ˈtrœpfəln], *v.a., v.n.* trickle, sprinkle.

Tropfen [ˈtrɔpfən], *m.* (—s, *pl.* —) drop; *steter* — *höhlt den Stein*, constant dripping wears away a stone.

tropfen [ˈtrɔpfən], *v.n.* drop, drip.

Trophäe [tro'fɛə], *f.* (—, *pl.* —n) trophy.

tropisch ['tro:pɪʃ], *adj.* tropical, tropic.

Troß [trɔs], *m.* (—sses, *pl.* -sse) (*Mil.*) baggage-train; (*fig.*) hangers-on, camp-followers.

Troßpferd ['trɔspfeːrt], *n.* (—s, *pl.* —e) pack-horse.

Trost [tro:st], *m.* (—es, *no pl.*) consolation, comfort; *geringer* —, cold comfort; *du bist wohl nicht bei* —? have you taken leave of your senses?

trösten ['trø:stən], *v.a.* comfort, console; *tröste dich,* cheer up.

Tröster ['trø:stər], *m.* (—s, *pl.* —) comforter, consoler; (*Theol.*) Holy Ghost, Comforter.

tröstlich ['trø:stlɪç], *adj.* consoling, comforting.

trostlos ['tro:stlo:s], *adj.* disconsolate, inconsolable; desolate, bleak.

Trostlosigkeit ['tro:stlo:zɪçkaɪt], *f.* (—, *no pl.*) disconsolateness; (*fig.*) wretchedness; dreariness.

Trott [trɔt], *m.* (—s, *no pl.*) trot.

Trottel ['trɔtəl], *m.* (—s, *pl.* —) (*coll.*) idiot.

Trottoir [trɔto'aːr], *n.* (—s, *pl.* —e) pavement, footpath; (*Am.*) sidewalk.

trotz [trɔts], *prep.* (*Genit., Dat.*) in spite of, despite; — *alledem,* all the same.

Trotz [trɔts], *m.* (—es, *no pl.*) defiance, obstinacy, refractoriness; *einem* — *bieten,* defy s.o.; *einem etwas zum* — *machen,* do s.th. in defiance of s.o.

trotzdem [trɔts'deːm], *conj.* notwithstanding that, albeit, although. — *adv.* nevertheless.

trotzen ['trɔtsən], *v.n.* defy; sulk, be obstinate; *Gefahren* —, brave dangers.

trotzig ['trɔtsɪç], *adj.* defiant; sulky, refractory; headstrong, stubborn, obstinate.

Trotzkopf ['trɔtskɔpf], *m.* (—(e)s, *pl.* —e) obstinate child; pig-headed person.

trübe ['try:bə], *adj.* dim, gloomy; (*weather*) dull, cloudy, overcast; (*water*) troubled; (*glass*) misted; —*s Lächeln,* wan smile.

Trubel ['tru:bəl], *m.* (—s, *no pl.*) tumult, turmoil, disturbance.

trüben ['try:bən], *v.a.* darken, sadden, trouble; (*glass*) mist; (*metal*) tarnish; (*fig.*) obscure.

Trübsal ['try:pza:l], *f.* (—, *pl.* —e), *n.* (—s, *pl.* —e) misery, trouble, distress; — *blasen,* mope.

trübselig ['try:pze:lɪç], *adj.* woeful, lamentable; woebegone, forlorn.

Trübsinn ['try:pzɪn], *m.* (—s, *no pl.*) sadness, dejection.

trübsinnig ['try:pzɪnɪç], *adj.* sad, dejected.

Trüffel ['tryfəl], *f.* (—, *pl.* —n) truffle.

Trug [tru:k], *m.* (—(e)s, *no pl.*) deceit, fraud; *Lug und* —, a pack of lies.

Trugbild ['tru:kbɪlt], *n.* (—es, *pl.* —er) phantom.

trügen ['try:gən], *v.a. irr.* deceive.

trügerisch ['try:gərɪs], *adj.* deceptive, illusory, fallacious.

Truggewebe ['tru:kgəve:bə], *n.* (—s, *pl.* —) tissue of lies.

Trugschluß ['tru:kʃlus], *m.* (—sses, *pl.* -sse) fallacy, false deduction.

Truhe ['tru:ə], *f.* (—, *pl.* —n) chest, trunk, coffer.

Trumm [trum], *m.* (—s, *pl.* —er) lump, broken piece.

Trümmer ['trymər], *m. pl.* fragments, debris, ruins; *in* — *gehen,* go to wrack and ruin; *in* — *schlagen,* wreck.

Trümmerhaufen ['trymərhaufən], *m.* (—s, *pl.* —) heap of ruins, heap of rubble.

Trumpf [trumpf], *m.* (—(e)s, *pl.* —e) trump, trump-card.

trumpfen ['trumpfən], *v.a.* trump.

Trumpffarbe ['trumpffarbə], *f.* (—, *pl.* —n) trump-suit.

Trunk [truŋk], *m.* (—(e)s, *pl.* —e) draught, potion, drinking; *sich dem* — *ergeben,* take to drink.

trunken ['truŋkən], *adj.* drunk, intoxicated; (*fig.*) elated.

Trunkenbold ['truŋkənbɔlt], *m.* (—s, *pl.* —e) drunkard.

Trunkenheit ['truŋkənhaɪt], *f.* (—, *no pl.*) drunkenness, intoxication.

Trunksucht ['truŋkzuxt], *f.* (—, *no pl.*) dipsomania, alcoholism.

trunksüchtig ['truŋkzyçtɪç], *adj.* dipsomaniac, addicted to drinking.

Trupp [trup], *m.* (—s, *pl.* —s) troop, band.

Truppe ['trupə], *f.* (—, *pl.* —n) (*Mil.*) company, troops, forces; (*actors*) troupe.

Truppengattung ['trupəngatuŋ], *f.* (—, *pl.* —en) branch of the armed forces.

Truthahn ['tru:tha:n], *m.* (—s, *pl.* —e) (*Orn.*) turkey cock.

Truthenne ['tru:thənə], *f.* (—, *pl.* —n) (*Orn.*) turkey hen.

Truthühner ['tru:thy:nər], *n. pl.* (*Orn.*) turkey-fowl.

Trutz [truts], *m.* (—es, *no pl.*) (*Poet.*) defiance; *zum Schutz und* —, offensively and defensively.

Tschad [tʃat], *n.* Chad.

Tschechoslowakei [tʃeçoslova'kaɪ], *f.* Czechoslovakia.

Tuch (1) [tu:x], *n.* (—(e)s, *pl.* —er) shawl, wrap.

Tuch (2) [tu:x], *n.* (—s, *pl.* —e) cloth, fabric.

Tuchhändler ['tu:xhɛndlər], *m.* (—s, *pl.* —) draper, clothier.

tüchtig ['tyçtɪç], *adj.* able, competent, efficient. — *adv.* largely, much, heartily.

Tüchtigkeit ['tyçtɪçkaɪt], *f.* (—, *no pl.*) ability, competence, efficiency.

Tücke ['tykə], *f.* (—, *pl.* —n) malice, spite.

tückisch ['tykɪʃ], *adj.* malicious, insidious.

Tugend ['tu:gənt], *f.* (—, *pl.* —en) virtue.

Tugendbold ['tu:gəntbɔlt], *m.* (—s, *pl.* —e) paragon.

tugendhaft ['tu:gənthaft], *adj.* virtuous.

Tugendlehre ['tu:gəntle:rə], *f.* (—, *no pl.*) ethics, morals.

Tüll [tyl], *m.* (—s, *pl.* —e) tulle.

Tulpe ['tulpə], *f.* (—, *pl.* —n) (*Bot.*) tulip.

Tulpenzwiebel ['tulpəntsvi:bəl], *f.* (—, *pl.* —n) tulip-bulb.

tummeln ['tuməln], *v.r. sich* —, romp about; make haste.

Tummelplatz ['tuməlplats], *m.* (—es, *pl.* ¨e) playground, fairground.

Tümpel ['tympəl], *m.* (—s, *pl.* —) pond, pool, puddle.

Tun [tu:n], *n.* (—s, *no pl.*) doing; *sein — und Lassen*, his conduct.

tun [tu:n], *v.a. irr.* do, make; put; *tut nichts*, it does not matter; *viel zu — haben*, have a lot to do, be busy; *not —*, be necessary; *Buße —*, repent.

Tünche ['tynçə], *f.* (—, *pl.* —n) whitewash.

tünchen ['tynçən], *v.a.* whitewash.

Tunichtgut ['tu:nɪçtgu:t], *m.* (—s, *no pl.*) ne'er-do-well, scamp.

Tunke ['tuŋkə], *f.* (—, *pl.* —n) sauce, gravy.

tunken ['tuŋkən], *v.a.* dip, steep; (*Am.*) dunk.

tunlich ['tu:nlɪç], *adj.* feasible, practicable, expedient.

tunlichst ['tu:nlɪçst], *adv.* if possible, possibly.

Tunnel ['tunəl], *m.* (—s, *pl.* —) tunnel.

Tunnelbau ['tunəlbau], *m.* (—s, *no pl.*) tunnelling.

tüpfeln ['typfəln], *v.a.* dot, spot.

Tupfen ['tupfən], *m.* (—s, *pl.* —) dot, polka-dot.

Tür [ty:r], *f.* (—, *pl.* —en) door; *einem die — weisen*, show s.o. the door; *vor der — stehen*, be imminent; *kehr vor deiner eigenen —*, mind your own business; put your own house in order; *offene —en einrennen*, flog a willing horse; *zwischen — und Angel stecken*, be undecided.

Türangel ['ty:raŋəl], *f.* (—, *pl.* —n) door-hinge.

Türhüter ['ty:rhy:tər], *m.* (—s, *pl.* —) doorkeeper.

Türkei [tyr'kai], *f.* Turkey.

Türkensäbel ['tyrkənze:bəl], *m.* (—s, *pl.* —) scimitar.

Türkis [tyr'ki:s], *m.* (—es, *pl.* —e) turquoise.

Türklinke ['ty:rklɪŋkə], *f.* (—, *pl.* —n) door-handle.

Turm [turm], *m.* (—(e)s, *pl.* ¨e) tower; spire, steeple; belfry; (*Chess*) castle.

Turmalin [turma'li:n], *m.* (—s, *pl.* —e) tourmaline.

Türmchen ['tyrmçən], *n.* (—s, *pl.* —) turret.

türmen ['tyrmən], *v.a.* pile up. — *v.n.* (*coll.*) bolt, run away. — *v.r. sich* —, rise high, be piled high.

Turmspitze ['turmʃpɪtsə], *f.* (—, *pl.* —n) spire.

turnen ['turnən], *v.n.* do exercises *or* gymnastics.

Turnen ['turnən], *n.* (—s, *no pl.*) gymnastics, physical training.

Turner ['turnər], *m.* (—s, *pl.* —) gymnast.

Turngerät ['turngərɛ:t], *n.* (—es, *pl.* —e) gymnastic apparatus.

Turnhalle ['turnhalə], *f.* (—, *pl.* —n) gymnasium.

Turnier [tur'ni:r], *n.* (—s, *pl.* —e) tournament.

Turnübung ['turny:buŋ], *f.* (—, *pl.* —en) gymnastic exercise.

Turnverein ['turnfərain], *m.* (—s, *pl.* —e) athletics club, gymnastics club.

Türpfosten ['ty:rpfɔstən], *m.* (—s, *pl.* —) door-post.

Türriegel ['ty:rri:gəl], *m.* (—s, *pl.* —) bolt.

Türschild ['ty:rʃɪlt], *n.* (—(e)s, *pl.* —e) (door)plate.

Türschloß ['ty:rʃlɔs], *n.* (—sses, *pl.* ¨sser) lock.

Türschlüssel ['ty:rʃlysəl], *m.* (—s, *pl.* —) door-key, latch-key.

Türschwelle ['ty:rʃvɛlə], *f.* (—, *pl.* —n) threshold.

Tusch [tuʃ], *m.* (—es, *pl.* —e) (*Mus.*) flourish.

Tusche ['tuʃə], *f.* (—, *pl.* —n) watercolour; Indian ink.

tuscheln ['tuʃəln], *v.n.* whisper.

tuschen ['tuʃən], *v.a.* draw in Indian ink.

Tuschkasten ['tuʃkastən], *m.* (—s, *pl.* ¨) paint-box.

Tüte ['ty:tə], *f.* (—, *pl.* —n) paper bag.

Tutel [tu'te:l], *f.* (—, *no pl.*) guardianship.

tuten ['tu:tən], *v.n.* hoot, honk, blow a horn.

Tütendreher ['ty:təndre:ər], *m.* (—s, *pl.* —) (*sl.*) small shopkeeper.

Typ [ty:p], *m.* (—s, *pl.* —en) type.

Type ['ty:pə], *f.* (—, *pl.* —n) (*Typ.*) type; (*fig.*) queer fish.

Typhus ['ty:fus], *m.* (—, *no pl.*) (*Med.*) typhoid (fever).

typisch ['ty:pɪʃ], *adj.* typical.

Typus ['ty:pus], *m.* (—, *pl.* **Typen**) type.

Tyrann [ty'ran], *m.* (—en, *pl.* —en) tyrant.

Tyrannei [tyra'nai], *f.* (—, *pl.* —en) tyranny, despotism.

tyrannisch [ty'ranɪʃ], *adj.* tyrannical, despotic.

tyrannisieren [tyrani'zi:rən], *v.a.* tyrannise over, oppress, bully.

U

U [u:], *n.* (—s, *pl.* —s) the letter U.

U-Bahn ['u:ba:n], *f.* (—, *no pl.*) underground (railway); tube, (*Am.*) subway.

Übel ['y:bəl], *n.* (—s, *pl.* —) evil, trouble; misfortune; disease.

übel ['y:bəl], *adj.* evil, ill, bad; *mir ist —,* I feel sick; *nicht —,* not too bad; *— daran sein,* be in a bad way, be in a mess.

übelgesinnt ['y:bəlgəzɪnt], *adj.* evil-minded; ill-disposed; *einem — sein,* bear s.o. a grudge.

Übelkeit ['y:bəlkaɪt], *f.* (—, *pl.* —en) nausea, sickness.

übellaunig ['y:bəllaunɪç], *adj.* ill-humoured, bad-tempered.

übelnehmen ['y:bəlne:mən], *v.a. irr.* take amiss, resent, be offended at.

übelnehmerisch ['y:bəlne:mərɪʃ], *adj.* touchy, easily offended.

Übelstand ['y:bəlʃtant], *m.* (—(e)s, *pl.* ⸚e) inconvenience, drawback; (*pl.*) abuses.

Übeltat ['y:bəlta:t], *f.* (—, *pl.* —en) misdeed.

Übeltäter ['y:bəltɛ:tər], *m.* (—s, *pl.* —) evildoer, malefactor.

übelwollend ['y:bəlvɔlənt], *adj.* malevolent.

üben ['y:bən], *v.a.* practise, exercise; *Rache —,* wreak vengeance.

über ['y:bər], *prep.* (*Dat., Acc.*) over, above; across; about; more than, exceeding; via, by way of; concerning, on. — *adv.* over, above; *— und —,* all over; *— kurz oder lang,* sooner or later; *heute —s Jahr,* a year from today.

überall ['y:bəral], *adv.* everywhere, anywhere.

überanstrengen [y:bər'anʃtrɛŋən], *v.a. insep.* overtax s.o.'s strength, strain. — *v.r. sich —,* overtax o.'s strength, overexert o.s.

Überanstrengung [y:bər'anʃtrɛŋuŋ], *f.* (—, *pl.* —en) over-exertion, strain.

überantworten [y:bər'antvɔrtən], *v.a. insep.* deliver up, surrender.

überarbeiten [y:bər'arbaɪtən], *v.a. insep.* revise, do again. — *v.r. sich —,* overwork o.s.

überarbeitet [y:bər'arbaɪtət], *adj.* overwrought, overworked.

überaus ['y:bəraus], *adv.* exceedingly, extremely.

überbauen [y:bər'bauən], *v.a. insep.* build over.

überbieten [y:bər'bi:tən], *v.a. irr. insep.* outbid (s.o.); (*fig.*) surpass.

Überbleibsel ['y:bərblaɪpsəl], *n.* (—s, *pl.* —) remainder, remnant, residue, rest.

Überblick ['y:bərblɪk], *m.* (—(e)s, *pl.* —e) survey, general view.

überblicken [y:bər'blɪkən], *v.a. insep.* survey, look over.

überbringen [y:bər'brɪŋən], *v.a. irr. insep.* bear, deliver, hand in.

Überbringung [y:bər'brɪŋuŋ], *f.* (—, *no pl.*) delivery.

überbrücken [y:bər'brykən], *v.a. insep.* bridge, span.

überdachen [y:bər'daxən], *v.a. insep.* roof (over).

überdauern [y:bər'dauərn], *v.a. insep.* outlast; tide over.

überdenken [y:bər'dɛŋkən], *v.a. irr. insep.* think over, consider.

überdies [y:bər'di:s], *adv.* besides, moreover.

überdrucken [y:bər'drukən], *v.a. insep.* overprint.

Überdruß ['y:bərdrus], *m.* (—sses, *no pl.*) weariness; disgust; *zum —,* ad nauseam.

überdrüssig ['y:bərdrysɪç], *adj.* weary of.

Übereifer ['y:bəraɪfər], *m.* (—s, *no pl.*) excessive zeal.

übereifrig ['y:bəraɪfrɪç], *adj.* excessively zealous, officious.

übereilen [y:bər'aɪlən], *v.r. insep. sich —,* hurry too much, overshoot the mark.

übereilt [y:bər'aɪlt], *adj.* overhasty, rash.

übereinkommen [y:bər'aɪnkɔmən], *v.n. irr.* (*aux.* sein) agree.

Übereinkunft [y:bər'aɪnkunft], *f.* (—, *pl.* ⸚e) agreement, convention.

übereinstimmen [y:bər'aɪnʃtɪmən], *v.n.* agree, concur, harmonize, be of one mind, be of the same opinion; (*things*) tally, square.

Übereinstimmung [y:bər'aɪnʃtɪmuŋ], *f.* (—, *no pl.*) accord, agreement, conformity, harmony.

überfahren (1) [y:bər'fa:rən], *v.a. irr. insep.* traverse, pass over; run over (s.o.).

überfahren (2) ['y:bərfa:rən], *v.a. irr. insep.* ferry across. — *v.n.* (*aux.* sein) cross.

Überfahrt ['y:bərfa:rt], *f.* (—, *pl.* —en) passage, crossing.

Überfall ['y:bərfal], *m.* (—s, *pl.* ⸚e) sudden attack, raid.

überfallen (1) ['y:bərfalən], *v.n. irr.* (*aux.* sein) (*p.p.* übergefallen) fall over.

überfallen (2) [y:bər'falən], *v.a. irr. insep.* (*p.p.* überfallen) attack suddenly, raid.

überfällig ['y:bərfɛlɪç], *adj.* overdue.

überfliegen [y:bər'fli:gən], *v.a. irr. insep.* fly over; (*fig.*) glance over, skim.

überfließen ['y:bərfli:sən], *v.n. irr.* (*aux.* sein) overflow.

überflügeln

überflügeln [y:bər'fly:gəln], *v.a. insep.* surpass, outstrip.

Überfluß ['y:bərflus], *m.* (—sses, *no pl.*) abundance, plenty, profusion; surplus; — *haben an*, abound in, have too much of.

überflüssig ['y:bərflysıç], *adj.* superfluous, unnecessary.

überfluten [y:bər'flu:tən], *v.a. insep.* overflow, flood.

überführen (1) ['y:bərfy:rən], *v.a.* convey, conduct (across).

überführen (2) [y:bər'fy:rən], *v.a. insep.* convict; transport a coffin.

Überführung [y:bər'fy:ruŋ], *f.* (—, *pl.* —en) conviction (for a crime); transport (of a coffin).

Überfüllung [y:bər'fyluŋ], *f.* (—, *no pl.*) overcrowding.

Übergabe ['y:bərga:bə], *f.* (—, *no pl.*) surrender, yielding up; delivery, handing over.

Übergang ['y:bərgaŋ], *m.* (—s, *pl.* -̈e) passage; (*Railw.*) crossing; (*fig.*) change-over, transition.

übergeben [y:bər'ge:bən], *v.a. irr. insep.* deliver up, hand over. — *v.r. sich* —, vomit.

übergehen (1) ['y:bərge:ən], *v.n. irr.* (*aux.* sein) (*p.p.* übergegangen) go over, change over, turn (into); *zum Feinde* —, go over to the enemy; *in andre Hände* —, change hands.

übergehen (2) [y:bər'ge:ən], *v.a. irr. insep.* (*p.p.* übergangen) pass over, pass by.

Übergehung [y:bər'ge:uŋ], *f.* (—, *no pl.*) omission; passing over.

übergeordnet ['y:bərgəordnət], *adj.* superior.

Übergewicht ['y:bərgəvıçt], *n.* (—(e)s, *no pl.*) overweight; (*fig.*) preponderance, superiority.

übergießen [y:bər'gi:sən], *v.a. irr. insep.* pour over, douse with.

überglücklich ['y:bərglyklıç], *adj.* overjoyed.

übergreifen ['y:bərgraıfən], *v.n. irr.* overlap; encroach (upon); spread.

Übergriff ['y:bərgrıf], *m.* (—(e)s, *pl.* -e) encroachment.

übergroß ['y:bərgro:s], *adj.* excessively large, overlarge.

überhaben ['y:bərha:bən], *v.a. irr.* have enough of, be sick of.

überhandnehmen [y:bər'hantne:mən], *v.n. irr.* gain the upper hand; run riot.

überhangen ['y:bərhaŋən], *v.n. irr.* hang over.

überhängen ['y:bərheŋən], *v.a. irr.* cover, hang upon.

überhäufen [y:bər'hɔyfən], *v.a. insep.* overwhelm.

überhaupt [y:bər'haupt], *adv.* in general, altogether, at all; after all.

überheben [y:bər'he:bən], *v.r. irr. insep. sich* —, strain o.s. by lifting; (*fig.*) be overbearing.

überheblich [y:bər'he:plıç], *adj.* overbearing, arrogant.

überheizen [y:bər'haıtsən], *v.a. insep.* overheat.

überhitzt [y:bər'hıtst], *adj.* overheated; impassioned.

überholen [y:bər'ho:lən], *v.a. insep.* overtake, out-distance; (*fig.*) overhaul.

überhören [y:bər'hø:rən], *v.a. insep.* hear s.o.'s lessons; ignore; miss (s.th.).

überirdisch ['y:bərırdıʃ], *adj.* celestial, superterrestrial.

Überkleid ['y:bərklaıt], *n.* (—(e)s, *pl.* -̈er) outer garment; overall.

überklug ['y:bərklu:k], *adj.* too clever by half, conceited.

überkochen [y:bər'kɔxən], *v.n.* (*aux.* sein) boil over.

überkommen [y:bər'kɔmən], *adj.* — *sein von*, be seized with.

überladen [y:bər'la:dən], *v.a. irr. insep.* overload. — *adj.* overdone, too elaborate; bombastic.

überlassen [y:bər'lasən], *v.a irr. insep.* leave, relinquish, give up, yield.

überlasten [y:bər'lastən], *v.a. insep.* overburden.

überlaufen (1) ['y:bərlaufən], *v.a. irr.* run over; (*to the enemy*) desert.

überlaufen (2) [y:bər'laufən], *v.a. insep.* (*p.p.* überlaufen) overrun.

Überläufer ['y:bərlɔyfər], *m.* (—s, *pl.* —) deserter, runaway.

überleben [y:bər'le:bən], *v.a. insep.* survive, outlive; (*fig.*) live (s.th.) down; *sich überlebt haben*, be out of date, be dated.

Überlebende [y:bər'le:bəndə], *m.* (—n, *pl.* —n) survivor.

überlegen (1) ['y:bərle:gən], *v.a.* lay over, cover.

überlegen (2) [y:bər'le:gən], *v.a. insep.* (*p.p.* überlegt) think over, consider, turn over in o.'s mind. — *adj.* superior; — *sein*, outdo, be superior to.

Überlegenheit [y:bər'le:gənhaıt], *f.* (—, *no pl.*) superiority.

Überlegung [y:bər'le:guŋ], *f.* (—, *pl.* —en) consideration, deliberation; *bei näherer* —, on second thoughts, on thinking it over.

überliefern [y:bər'li:fərn], *v.a. insep.* hand down (to posterity), hand on, pass on.

Überlieferung [y:bər'li:fəruŋ], *f.* (—, *pl.* —en) tradition.

überlisten [y:bər'lıstən], *v.a. insep.* outwit.

Übermacht ['y:bərmaxt], *f.* (—, *no pl.*) superiority, superior force.

übermalen [y:bər'ma:lən], *v.a. insep.* paint over.

übermangansauer [y:bərmaŋ'ga:nzauər], *adj.* permanganate of; —*es Kali*, permanganate of potash.

übermannen [y:bər'manən], *v.a. insep.* overpower.

Übermaß ['y:bərma:s], *n.* (—es, *no pl.*) excess; *im* —, to excess.

übermäßig [´y:bərmɛːsɪç], *adj.* excessive, immoderate.

Übermensch [´y:bərmɛnʃ], *m.* (—en, *pl.* —en) superman.

übermenschlich [´y:bərmɛnʃlɪç], *adj.* superhuman.

übermitteln [y:bər´mɪtəln], *v.a. insep.* convey.

übermorgen [´y:bərmɔrgən], *adv.* the day after tomorrow.

Übermut [´y:bərmuːt], *m.* (—s, *no pl.*) wantonness; high spirits.

übermütig [´y:bərmyːtɪç], *adj.* wanton; full of high spirits.

übernachten [y:bər´naxtən], *v.n. insep.* pass *or* spend the night.

übernächtig [´y:bərnɛçtɪç], *adj.* haggard, tired by a sleepless night.

Übernahme [´y:bərnaːmə], *f.* (—, *no pl.*) taking possession, taking charge.

übernatürlich [´y:bərnaty:rlɪç], *adj.* supernatural.

übernehmen [y:bər´neːmən], *v.a. irr. insep.* take possession of, take upon o.s., take over. — *v.r. sich* —, overtax o.'s strength.

überordnen [´y:bərɔrdnən], *v.a.* place above.

überprüfen [y:bər´pryːfən], *v.a. insep.* examine, overhaul.

überquellen [´y:bərkvɛlən], *v.n. irr. insep.* (*aux.* sein) bubble over.

überqueren [y:bər´kveːrən], *v.a. insep.* cross.

überragen [y:bər´raːgən], *v.a. insep.* tower above, overtop; (*fig.*) surpass, outstrip.

überraschen [y:bər´raʃən], *v.a. insep.* surprise, take by surprise.

Überraschung [y:bər´raʃuŋ], *f.* (—, *pl.* —en) surprise.

überreden [y:bər´reːdən], *v.a. insep.* persuade, talk (s.o.) into (s.th.).

Überredung [y:bər´reːduŋ], *f.* (—, *no pl.*) persuasion.

überreichen [y:bər´raɪçən], *v.a. insep.* hand over, present formally.

überreichlich [´y:bərraɪçlɪç], *adj.* superabundant.

Überreichung [y:bər´raɪçuŋ], *f.* (—, *no pl.*) formal presentation.

überreizen [y:bər´raɪtsən], *v.a. insep.* over-excite, over-stimulate.

überrennen [y:bər´rɛnən], *v.a. irr. insep.* take by storm, overrun.

Überrest [´y:bərrɛst], *m.* (—es, *pl.* —e) remainder, remnant, residue.

überrumpeln [y:bər´rumpəln], *v.a. insep.* catch unawares, surprise.

übersättigen [y:bər´zɛtɪgən], *v.a. insep.* saturate; surfeit, cloy.

Übersättigung [y:bər´zɛtɪguŋ], *f.* (—, *no pl.*) saturation; surfeit.

Überschallgeschwindigkeit [´y:bərʃalgəʃvɪndɪçkaɪt], *f.* (—, *no pl.*) supersonic speed.

überschatten [y:bər´ʃatən], *v.a. insep.* overshadow.

überschätzen [y:bər´ʃɛtsən], *v.a. insep.* overrate, over-estimate.

überschauen [y:bər´ʃauən], *v.a. insep.* survey.

überschäumen [´y:bərʃɔymən], *v.n.* (*aux.* sein) bubble over.

überschäumend [´y:bərʃɔymənt], *adj.* ebullient, exuberant.

Überschlag [´y:bərʃlaːk], *m.* (—s, *pl.* ˵e) somersault; estimate.

überschlagen [y:bər´ʃlaːgən], *v.a. irr. insep.* (*pages*) miss, skip; estimate, compute. — *v.r. sich* —, turn a somersault, overturn. — *adj.* tepid, lukewarm.

überschnappen [´y:bərʃnapən], *v.n.* (*aux.* sein) snap; (*fig.*, *coll.*) go out of o.'s mind.

überschreiben [y:bər´ʃraɪbən], *v.a. irr. insep.* superscribe, entitle.

überschreiten [y:bər´ʃraɪtən], *v.a. irr. insep.* cross; go beyond, exceed.

Überschrift [´y:bərʃrɪft], *f.* (—, *pl.* —en) heading, headline.

Überschuß [´y:bərʃus], *m.* (—sses, *pl.* ˵sse) surplus.

überschüssig [´y:bərʃysɪç], *adj.* surplus, remaining.

überschütten [y:bər´ʃytən], *v.a. insep.* shower with, overwhelm with.

Überschwang [´y:bərʃvaŋ], *m.* (—s, *no pl.*) exaltation, rapture.

überschwemmen [y:bər´ʃvɛmən], *v.a. insep.* flood, inundate.

Überschwemmung [y:bər´ʃvɛmuŋ], *f.* (—, *pl.* —en) inundation, flood, deluge.

überschwenglich [y:bər´ʃvɛŋlɪç], *adj.* exuberant, exalted.

Übersee [´y:bərzeː], *f.* (—, *no pl.*) overseas.

übersehen [y:bər´zeːən], *v.a. irr. insep.* survey, look over; overlook, disregard.

übersenden [y:bər´zɛndən], *v.a. irr. insep.* send, forward, transmit; (*money*) remit.

Übersendung [y:bər´zɛnduŋ], *f.* (—, *pl.* —en) sending, forwarding, transmission; remittance.

übersetzen (1) [´y:bərzɛtsən], *v.a.* (*p.p.* übergesetzt) ferry across, cross (a river).

übersetzen (2) [y:bər´zɛtsən], *v.a. insep.* (*p.p.* übersetzt) translate.

Übersetzer [y:bər´zɛtsər], *m.* (—s, *pl.* —) translator.

Übersetzung [y:bər´zɛtsuŋ], *f.* (—, *pl.* —en) translation.

Übersicht [´y:bərzɪçt], *f.* (—, *pl.* —en) survey, summary; epitome.

übersichtlich [´y:bərzɪçtlɪç], *adj.* clearly arranged, readable at a glance, lucid.

übersiedeln [y:bər´ziːdəln], *v.n.* (*aux.* sein) remove, move, settle in a different place.

Übersiedlung [y:bər´ziːdluŋ], *f.* (—, *pl.* —en) removal.

überspannen [y:bər´ʃpanən], *v.a. insep.* overstretch.

überspannt [y:bər´ʃpant], *adj.* eccentric, extravagant.

Überspanntheit [yːbərˈʃpanthaɪt], *f.*
(—, *pl.* —en) eccentricity.

überspringen [yːbərˈʃprɪŋən], *v.a. irr.*
insep. jump over; (*fig.*) skip.

übersprudeln [ˈyːbərʃpruːdəln], *v.n.*
(*aux.* sein) bubble over.

überstechen [yːbərˈʃteçən], *v.a. irr.*
(*cards*) trump higher.

überstehen [yːbərˈʃteːən], *v.a. irr.*
insep. overcome, endure, get over,
weather.

übersteigen [yːbərˈʃtaɪgən], *v.a. irr.*
insep. exceed, surpass.

überstrahlen [yːbərˈʃtraːlən], *v.a. insep.*
outshine, surpass in splendour.

überstreichen [yːbərˈʃtraɪçən], *v.a. irr.*
insep. paint over.

überströmen [yːbərˈʃtrøːmən], *v.a.*
insep. flood, overflow.

Überstunde [ˈyːbərʃtundə], *f.* (—, *pl.*
—n) extra working time, overtime.

überstürzen [yːbərˈʃtyrtsən], *v.r. insep.*
sich —, act in haste.

übertäuben [yːbərˈtɔybən], *v.a. insep.*
deafen.

überteuern [yːbərˈtɔyərn], *v.a. insep.*
overcharge.

übertölpeln [yːbərˈtœlpəln], *v.a. insep.*
cheat.

übertönen [yːbərˈtøːnən], *v.a. insep.*
(*sound*) drown.

übertragen [yːbərˈtraːgən], *v.a. irr.*
insep. transfer, hand over; convey;
broadcast; translate; (*Comm.*) carry
over; *einem ein Amt* —, confer an
office on s.o.

Übertragung [yːbərˈtraːguŋ], *f.* (—, *pl.*
—en) cession; transference; handing
over; (*Comm.*) carrying over; (*Rad.*)
transmission; (*Med.*) transfusion.

übertreffen [yːbərˈtrefən], *v.a. irr.*
insep. surpass, excel, outdo.

übertreiben [yːbərˈtraɪbən], *v.a. irr.*
insep. exaggerate.

Übertreibung [yːbərˈtraɪbuŋ], *f.* (—,
pl. —en) exaggeration.

übertreten (1) [ˈyːbərtreːtən], *v.n. irr.*
(*aux.* sein) go over to; (*river*) overflow; (*religion*) change to, join (*church,
party*).

übertreten (2) [yːbərˈtreːtən], *v.a. irr.*
insep. transgress, trespass against,
infringe, violate.

Übertretung [yːbərˈtreːtuŋ], *f.* (—, *pl.*
—en) transgression, trespass, violation, infringement.

übertrieben [yːbərˈtriːbən], *adj.* excessive, immoderate, exaggerated.

Übertritt [ˈyːbərtrɪt], *m.* (—s, *no pl.*)
defection, going over; (*Rel.*) change,
conversion.

übertünchen [yːbərˈtynçən], *v.a. insep.*
whitewash, rough-cast; (*fig.*) gloss
over.

Übervölkerung [yːbərˈfœlkəruŋ], *f.*
(—, *no pl.*) overpopulation.

übervoll [ˈyːbərfɔl], *adj.* overful, brimful, chock-full.

übervorteilen [yːbərˈfoːrtaɪlən], *v.a.*
insep. cheat, defraud.

überwachen [yːbərˈvaxən], *v.a. insep.*
watch over, superintend, supervise.

Überwachung [yːbərˈvaxuŋ], *f.* (—,
no pl.) superintendence, supervision.

überwachsen [yːbərˈvaksən], *v.a. irr.*
insep. overgrow.

überwältigen [yːbərˈvɛltɪgən], *v.a.*
insep. overcome, overpower, subdue.

überwältigend [yːbərˈvɛltɪgənt], *adj.*
overwhelming.

Überwältigung [yːbərˈvɛltɪguŋ], *f.*
(—, *no pl.*) overpowering.

überweisen [yːbərˈvaɪzən], *v.a. irr.*
insep. assign; (*money*) remit.

Überweisung [yːbərˈvaɪzuŋ], *f.* (—, *pl.*
—en) assignment; (*money*) remittance.

überwerfen (1) [ˈyːbərvɛrfən], *v.a. irr.*
throw over; (*clothes*) slip on.

überwerfen (2) [yːbərˈvɛrfən], *v.r. irr.*
insep. sich — *mit*, fall out with s.o.

überwiegen [yːbərˈviːgən], *v.n. irr.*
insep. prevail.

überwiegend [yːbərˈviːgənt], *adj.* paramount, overwhelming, predominant.

überwinden [yːbərˈvɪndən], *v.a. irr.*
insep. overcome, conquer. — *v.r.*
sich —, prevail upon o.s., bring o.s.
(to).

Überwindung [yːbərˈvɪnduŋ], *f.* (—,
no pl.) conquest; reluctance.

überwintern [yːbərˈvɪntərn], *v.n. insep.*
winter, hibernate.

Überwinterung [yːbərˈvɪntəruŋ], *f.*
(—, *no pl.*) hibernation.

überwölkt [yːbərˈvœlkt], *adj.* overcast.

Überwurf [ˈyːbərvurf], *m.* (—s, *pl.* ⁻e)
wrap, shawl, cloak.

Überzahl [ˈyːbərtsaːl], *f.* (—, *no pl.*) *in
der* —, in the majority.

überzählig [ˈyːbərtsɛːlɪç], *adj.* super-
numerary, surplus.

überzeichnen [yːbərˈtsaɪçnən], *v.a.*
insep. (*Comm.*) over-subscribe.

überzeugen [yːbərˈtsɔygən], *v.a. insep.*
convince. — *v.r. sich* —, satisfy o.s.

Überzeugung [yːbərˈtsɔyguŋ], *f.* (—,
no pl.) conviction, certainty.

überziehen (1) [ˈyːbərtsiːən], *v.a. irr.*
put on (a garment).

überziehen (2) [yːbərˈtsiːən], *v.a. irr.*
insep. cover; (*bed*) put fresh linen on;
(*Bank*) overdraw.

Überzieher [ˈyːbərtsiːər], *m.* (—s, *pl.*
—) overcoat.

Überzug [ˈyːbərtsuːk], *m.* (—s, *pl.* ⁻e)
case, cover; bed-tick; coating.

üblich [ˈyːplɪç], *adj.* usual, customary;
nicht mehr —, out of use, obsolete.

übrig [ˈyːbrɪç], *adj.* remaining, left
over; *die —en*, the others; — *bleiben*,
be left, remain; — *haben*, have left;
— *sein*, be left; *im —en*, for the rest;
ein —es tun, stretch a point; *für
einen etwas* —, *haben*, like s.o.

übrigens [ˈyːbrɪgəns], *adv.* besides,
moreover; by the way.

Übung [ˈyːbuŋ], *f.* (—, *pl.* —en)
exercise, practice.

Ufer ['u:fər], *n.* (—s, *pl.* —) (*river*) bank; (*sea*) shore, beach.

Uganda [u'ganda], *n.* Uganda.

Uhr [u:r], *f.* (—, *pl.* —en) clock; watch; *elf* —, eleven o'clock; *wieviel* — *ist es?* what is the time?

Uhrmacher ['u:rmaxər], *m.* (—s, *pl.* —) watchmaker, clockmaker.

Uhrwerk ['u:rvɛrk], *n.* (—s, *pl.* —e) clockwork.

Uhrzeiger ['u:rtsaɪɡər], *m.* (—s, *pl.* —) hand (of clock *or* watch).

Uhu ['u:hu:], *m.* (—s, *pl.* —s) (*Orn.*) eagle-owl.

ulkig ['ulkɪç], *adj.* funny.

Ulme ['ulmə], *f.* (—, *pl.* —en) (*Bot.*) elm, elm-tree.

Ultrakurzwelle ['ultrakurtsvɛlə], *f.* (—, *pl.* —n) ultra-short wave.

ultrarot ['ultraro:t], *adj.* infra-red.

Ultrastrahlung ['ultraʃtra:luŋ], *f.* (—, *pl.* —en) cosmic radiation.

ultraviolett ['ultraviolet], *adj.* ultra-violet.

um [um], *prep.* (*Acc.*) about, around; approximately, near; for, because of; by; — *Geld bitten*, ask for money; — *5 Uhr*, at five o'clock. — *conj.* to, in order to. — *adv.* up, past, upside down; round about; around.

umarbeiten ['umarbaɪtən], *v.a.* do again, remodel, revise; recast.

umarmen [um'armən], *v.a.* insep. embrace.

Umarmung [um'armuŋ], *f.* (—, *pl.* —en) embrace.

umbauen (1) ['umbauən], *v.a.* rebuild.

umbauen (2) [um'bauən], *v.a.* insep. surround with buildings.

umbiegen ['umbi:ɡən], *v.a.* irr. bend.

umbilden ['umbɪldən], *v.a.* transform, reform, recast, remould.

umbinden ['umbɪndən], *v.a. irr. sich etwas* —, tie s.th. around o.s.

umblicken ['umblɪkən], *v.r. sich* —, look round.

umbringen ['umbrɪŋən], *v.a.* irr. kill, slay, murder.

umdrehen ['umdre:ən], *v.a.* turn over, turn round, revolve. — *v.r. sich* —, turn round.

Umdrehung [um'dre:uŋ], *f.* (—, *pl.* —en) revolution, rotation.

umfahren (1) [um'fa:rən], *v.a.* irr. insep. drive round, circumnavigate.

umfahren (2) ['umfa:ren], *v.a.* irr. run down.

umfallen ['umfalən], *v.n.* irr. (*aux.* sein) fall down, fall over.

Umfang ['umfaŋ], *m.* (—s, *pl.* ⏜e) circumference; (*fig.*) extent.

umfangen [um'faŋən], *v.a. irr. insep.* encircle, embrace.

umfangreich [um'faŋraɪç], *adj.* extensive, voluminous.

umfassen [um'fasən], *v.a. insep.* comprise, contain.

umfassend [um'fasənt], *adj.* comprehensive.

umfließen [um'fli:sən], *v.a. irr. insep.* surround by water.

umformen ['umfɔrmən], *v.a.* transform, remodel.

Umformung ['umfɔrmuŋ], *f.* (—, *pl.* —en) transformation, remodelling.

Umfrage ['umfra:ɡə], *f.* (—, *pl.* —n) enquiry, poll, quiz.

Umfriedung [um'fri:duŋ], *f.* (—, *pl.* —en) enclosure.

Umgang ['umɡaŋ], *m.* (—s, *pl.* ⏜e) circuit, procession; (*fig.*) acquaintance, association; relations, connection; — *haben mit*, associate with.

umgänglich ['umɡɛŋlɪç], *adj.* sociable, companionable.

Umgangsformen ['umɡaŋsfɔrmən], *f. pl.* manners.

Umgangssprache ['umɡaŋsʃpra:xə], *f.* (— *pl.* —en) colloquial speech.

umgeben [um'ge:bən], *v.a. irr. insep.* surround.

Umgebung [um'ge:buŋ], *f.* (—, *pl.* —en) environment, surroundings.

umgehen (1) ['umge:ən], *v.n. irr.* (*aux.* sein) associate with s.o.; handle s.th.; — *in*, haunt.

umgehen (2) [um'ge:ən], *v.a. irr. insep.* go round; (*flank*) turn; (*fig.*) evade, shirk.

umgehend ['umge:ənt], *adv.* immediately; (*letter*) by return of post.

Umgehung [um'ge:uŋ], *f.* (—, *pl.* —en) shirking, evasion; detour; (*Mil.*) flank movement, turning.

umgekehrt ['umgəke:rt], *adj.* reverse. — *adv.* conversely.

umgestalten ['umgəʃtaltən], *v.a.* transform, recast.

Umgestaltung ['umgəʃtaltuŋ], *f.* (—, *pl.* —en) transformation; recasting.

umgraben ['umgra:bən], *v.a. irr.* dig up.

umgrenzen [um'grɛntsən], *v.a. insep.* limit, set bounds to.

Umgrenzung [um'grɛntsuŋ], *f.* (—, *pl.* —en) boundary; limitation.

umgucken ['umgukən], *v.r. sich* —, look about o.

umhalsen [um'halzən], *v.a. insep.* hug, embrace.

Umhang ['umhaŋ], *m.* (—s, *pl.* ⏜e) shawl, cloak.

umher [um'he:r], *adv.* around, round, about.

umherblicken [um'he:rblɪkən], *v.n.* look round.

umherflattern [um'he:rflatərn], *v.n.* (*aux.* sein) flutter about.

umherlaufen [um'he:rlaufən], *v.n. irr.* (*aux.* sein) run about; roam about, ramble, wander.

umherziehend [um'he:rtsi:ənt], *adj.* itinerant.

umhüllen [um'hylən], *v.a. insep.* envelop, wrap up.

Umkehr ['umke:r], *f.* (—, *no pl.*) return; change; (*fig.*) conversion.

umkehren

umkehren [ˈumkeːrən], *v.a.* turn (back), upset, overturn. — *v.n.* (*aux.* sein) turn back, return.

Umkehrung [ˈumkeːruŋ], *f.* (—, *pl.* —en) inversion.

umkippen [ˈumkɪpən], *v.a.* upset, overturn. — *v.n.* (*aux.* sein) capsize, tilt over.

umklammern [umˈklamərn], *v.a. insep.* clasp; clutch; (*fig.*) cling to.

umkleiden (1) [ˈumklaɪdən], *v.r. sich* —, change o.'s clothes.

umkleiden (2) [umˈklaɪdən], *v.a. insep.* cover.

umkommen [ˈumkəmən], *v.n. irr.* (*aux.* sein) perish, die.

Umkreis [ˈumkraɪs], *m.* (—es, *pl.* —e) circumference, compass.

Umlauf [ˈumlauf], *m.* (—s, *no pl.*) circulation; *in — bringen*, put into circulation.

Umlaut [ˈumlaut], *m.* (—s, *pl.* —e) (*Phonet.*) modification of vowels.

umlegen [ˈumleːgən], *v.a.* lay down, move, shift, put about; (*sl.*) kill.

umleiten [ˈumlaɪtən], *v.a.* (*traffic*) divert.

umlernen [ˈumlɛrnən], *v.a., v.n.* relearn; retrain (for new job).

umliegend [ˈumliːgənt], *adj.* surrounding.

ummodeln [ˈumoːdəln], *v.a.* remodel, recast, change, fashion differently.

Umnachtung [umˈnaxtuŋ], *f.* (—, *no pl.*) mental derangement.

umpacken [ˈumpakən], *v.a.* repack.

umpflanzen [ˈumpflantsən], *v.a.* transplant.

Umpflanzung [ˈumpflantsuŋ], *f.* (—, *pl.* —en) transplantation.

umrahmen [umˈraːmən], *v.a. insep.* frame, surround.

umrändern [umˈrɛndərn], *v.a. insep.* border, edge.

umrechnen [ˈumrɛçnən], *v.a.* (*figures*) reduce, convert.

umreißen (1) [ˈumraɪsən], *v.a. irr.* pull down, break up.

umreißen (2) [umˈraɪsən], *v.a. irr. insep.* sketch, outline.

umrennen [ˈumrɛnən], *v.a. irr.* run down, knock over.

umringen [umˈrɪŋən], *v.a. insep.* encircle, surround.

Umriß [ˈumrɪs], *m.* (—sses, *pl.* —sse) outline, contour.

umrühren [ˈumryːrən], *v.a.* (*Cul.*) stir.

umsatteln [ˈumzatəln], *v.n.* (*fig.*) change o.'s profession.

Umsatz [ˈumzats], *m.* (—es, *pl.* ¨e) turnover.

umschalten [ˈumʃaltən], *v.a.* (*Elec.*) switch (over); reverse (current).

Umschau [ˈumʃau], *f.* (—, *no pl.*) review, survey; *— halten*, look round, muster, review.

umschauen [ˈumʃauən], *v.r. sich* —, look round.

umschichtig [ˈumʃɪçtɪç], *adv.* turn and turn about, in turns.

umschiffen (1) [ˈumʃɪfən], *v.a.* transship, transfer (cargo, passengers).

umschiffen (2) [umˈʃɪfən], *v.a. insep.* sail round, circumnavigate.

Umschlag [ˈumʃlaːk], *m.* (—(e)s, *pl.* ¨e) (*weather*) break, sudden change; (*letter*) envelope; (*Med.*) poultice, compress.

umschlagen [ˈumʃlaːgən], *v.n. irr.* (*aux.* sein) (*weather*) change suddenly; capsize; turn sour.

umschließen [umˈʃliːsən], *v.a. irr. insep.* enclose, surround; comprise.

umschlingen [umˈʃlɪŋən], *v.a. irr. insep.* embrace.

umschnallen [ˈumʃnalən], *v.a.* buckle on.

umschreiben (1) [ˈumʃraɪbən], *v.a. irr.* rewrite, write differently.

umschreiben (2) [umˈʃraɪbən], *v.a. irr. insep.* circumscribe, paraphrase.

Umschreibung [umˈʃraɪbuŋ], *f.* (—, *pl.* —en) paraphrase.

Umschweife [ˈumʃvaɪfə], *m.pl.* fuss, talk; circumlocution; *ohne —*, point-blank.

Umschwung [ˈumʃvuŋ], *m.* (—s, *no pl.*) sudden change, revolution.

umsegeln [umˈzeːgəln], *v.a. insep.* sail round.

umsehen [ˈumzeːən], *v.r. irr. sich* —, look round; look out (for), cast about (for).

Umsicht [ˈumzɪçt], *f.* (—, *no pl.*) circumspection.

umsichtig [ˈumzɪçtɪç], *adj.* cautious, circumspect.

umsinken [ˈumzɪŋkən], *v.n. irr.* (*aux.* sein) sink down.

umsonst [umˈzɔnst], *adv.* without payment, gratis, for nothing; in vain, vainly, to no purpose.

umspannen (1) [ˈumʃpanən], *v.a.* change horses.

umspannen (2) [umˈʃpanən], *v.a. insep.* encompass, span.

umspringen [ˈumʃprɪŋən], *v.n. irr.* (*aux.* sein) (*wind*) change suddenly; *mit einem —*, (*fig.*) deal with s.o.

Umstand [ˈumʃtant], *m.* (—s, *pl.* ¨e) circumstance; fact; factor; (*pl.*) fuss; *in anderen ¨en sein*, be expecting a baby; *unter keinen ¨en*, on no account.

umständlich [ˈumʃtɛntlɪç], *adj.* circumstantial; ceremonious; complicated, fussy.

Umstandswort [ˈumʃtantsvɔrt], *n.* (—es, *pl.* ¨er) (*Gram.*) adverb.

umstehend [ˈumʃteːənt], *adv.* on the next page.

Umstehenden [ˈumʃteːəndən], *pl.* bystanders.

umsteigen [ˈumʃtaɪgən], *v.n. irr.* (*aux.* sein) change (trains etc.).

umstellen (1) [ˈumʃtɛlən], *v.a.* place differently, transpose, change over.

umstellen (2) [umˈʃtɛlən], *v.a. insep.* surround, beset.

Umstellung [ˈumʃtɛluŋ], *f.* (—, *pl.* —en) transposition; (*Gram.*) inversion; change of position in team.

umstimmen [ˈumʃtɪmən], *v.a.* turn s.o. from his opinion, bring s.o. round to (s.th.).

umstoßen [ˈumʃtoːsən], *v.a. irr.* knock down, upset, overthrow; (*judgment*) reverse.

umstricken [umˈʃtrɪkən], *v.a. insep.* ensnare.

umstritten [umˈʃtrɪtən], *adj.* controversial, disputed.

umstülpen [ˈumʃtylpən], *v.a.* turn up, turn upside down.

Umsturz [ˈumʃturts], *m.* (—es, *no pl.*) downfall; subversion; revolution.

umstürzen [ˈumʃtyrtsən], *v.a.* upset, overturn; overthrow.

umtaufen [ˈumtaufən], *v.a.* rename, rechristen.

Umtausch [ˈumtauʃ], *m.* (—s, *no pl.*) exchange.

umtauschen [ˈumtauʃən], *v.a.* exchange, change.

Umtriebe [ˈumtriːbə], *m. pl.* plots, goings-on, intrigues.

umtun [ˈumtuːn], *v.r. irr. sich — nach,* look for, cast about for.

Umwälzung [ˈumvɛltsuŋ], *f.* (—, *pl.* —en) turning-about; (*fig.*) revolution.

umwandeln [ˈumvandəln], *v.a.* change, transform; (*Gram.*) inflect.

umwechseln [ˈumvɛksəln], *v.a.* exchange.

Umweg [ˈumveːk], *m.* (—s, *pl.* —e) roundabout way, detour.

Umwelt [ˈumvɛlt], *f.* (—, *no pl.*) environment, milieu.

umwenden [ˈumvɛndən], *v.a. irr.* turn round; turn over. — *v.r. sich —,* turn round.

umwerben [umˈvɛrbən], *v.a. irr. insep.* court.

umwerfen [ˈumvɛrfən], *v.a. irr.* overturn, knock over, upset.

umwickeln [umˈvɪkəln], *v.a. insep.* wrap round, wind round.

umwölken [umˈvœlkən], *v.r. insep. sich —,* (*sky*) darken, become overcast.

umzäunen [umˈtsɔynən], *v.a. insep.* hedge in, fence in, enclose.

umziehen (1) [ˈumtsiːən], *v.a. irr.* change (clothes). — *v.n.* (*aux.* sein) move house. — *v.r. sich —,* change o.'s clothes.

umziehen (2) [umˈtsiːən], *v.r. irr. insep. sich —,* get overcast, cloud over.

umzingeln [umˈtsɪŋəln], *v.a. insep.* surround.

Umzug [ˈumtsuːk], *m.* (—s, *pl.* —e) procession; removal; move.

unabänderlich [unapˈɛndərlɪç], *adj.* unalterable, irrevocable.

Unabänderlichkeit [ˈunapɛndərlɪçkait], *f.* (—, *no pl.*) unchangeableness, irrevocability.

unabhängig [ˈunaphɛŋɪç], *adj.* independent, autonomous; unrelated.

Unabhängigkeit [ˈunaphɛŋɪçkait], *f.* (—, *no pl.*) independence, self-sufficiency.

unabkömmlich [ˈunapkœmlɪç], *adj.* indispensable.

unablässig [ˈunaplɛsɪç], *adj.* unceasing, continual, unremitting.

unabsehbar [ˈunapzeːbaːr], *adj.* immeasurable, immense; unfathomable.

unabsichtlich [ˈunapzɪçtlɪç], *adj.* unintentional, accidental.

unabwendbar [unapˈvɛntbaːr], *adj.* irremediable; unavoidable.

unachtsam [ˈunaxtzaːm], *adj.* inattentive, inadvertent, negligent, careless.

Unachtsamkeit [ˈunaxtzaːmkait], *f.* (—, *pl.* —en) inadvertence, inattention, negligence, carelessness.

unähnlich [ˈunɛːnlɪç], *adj.* unlike, dissimilar.

unanfechtbar [ˈunanfɛçtbaːr], *adj.* indisputable, incontestable.

unangebracht [ˈunangəbraxt], *adj.* out of place, inapposite.

unangefochten [ˈunangəfɔxtən], *adj.* undisputed, uncontested.

unangemeldet [ˈunangəmɛldət], *adj.* unannounced, unheralded.

unangemessen [ˈunangəmɛsən], *adj.* unsuitable, inappropriate, inadequate.

unangenehm [ˈunangəneːm], *adj.* disagreeable, unpleasant; *einen — berühren,* jar, grate on s.o.

unangetastet [ˈunangətastət], *adj.* untouched.

unangreifbar [ˈunangraifbaːr], *adj.* unassailable, secure.

unannehmbar [ˈunanne-mbaːr], *adj.* unacceptable.

Unannehmlichkeit [ˈunanne-mlɪçkait], *f.* (—, *pl.* —en) unpleasantness, annoyance.

unansehnlich [ˈunanze-nlɪç], *adj.* insignificant; unattractive.

unanständig [ˈunanʃtɛndɪç], *adj.* improper, indecent.

Unanständigkeit [ˈunanʃtɛndɪçkait], *f.* (—, *pl.* —en) indecency, immodesty, impropriety.

unantastbar [ˈunantastbaːr], *adj.* unimpeachable.

unappetitlich [ˈunapetiːtlɪç], *adj.* distasteful, unsavoury, unappetising.

Unart [ˈunaːrt], *f.* (—, *pl.* —en) bad habit, naughtiness.

unartig [ˈunaːrtɪç], *adj.* ill-behaved, naughty.

unästhetisch [ˈunɛste-tɪʃ], *adj.* offensive, coarse; inartistic.

unauffällig [ˈunauffɛlɪç], *adj.* unobtrusive.

unaufgefordert [ˈunaufgəfɔrdərt], *adj.* unbidden.

unaufgeklärt [ˈunaufgəkle-rt], *adj.* unexplained, unsolved.

unaufgeschnitten [ˈunaufgəʃnɪtən], *adj.* uncut.

unaufhaltsam [ˈunaufhaltzaːm], *adj.* incessant, irresistible.

unaufhörlich ['unaufhøːrlɪç], *adj.* incessant, continual.

unauflöslich ['unaufløːslɪç], *adj.* indissoluble.

unaufmerksam ['unaufmɛrkzaːm], *adj.* inattentive.

unaufrichtig ['unaufrɪçtɪç], *adj.* insincere.

unaufschiebbar ['unaufʃiːpbaːr], *adj.* urgent, pressing, brooking no delay.

unausbleiblich ['unausblaɪplɪç], *adj.* inevitable, unfailing.

unausführbar ['unausfyːrbaːr], *adj.* impracticable.

unausgebildet ['unausgəbɪldət], *adj.* untrained, unskilled.

unausgefüllt ['unausgəfylt], *adj.* not filled up; (*form*) blank.

unausgegoren ['unausgəgoːrən], *adj.* crude; (*wine*) unfermented.

unausgesetzt ['unausgəzɛtst], *adj.* continual, continuous.

unausgesprochen ['unausgəʃprɔxən], *adj.* unsaid; (*fig.*) implied.

unauslöschlich ['unausløʃlɪç], *adj.* indelible, inextinguishable.

unaussprechlich ['unausʃprɛçlɪç], *adj.* inexpressible, unspeakable.

unausstehlich ['unausʃteːlɪç], *adj.* insufferable.

unausweichlich ['unausvaɪçlɪç], *adj.* inevitable.

unbändig ['unbɛndɪç], *adj.* intractable, unmanageable; (*fig.*) extreme.

unbarmherzig ['unbarmhɛrtsɪç], *adj.* merciless.

unbeabsichtigt ['unbəapzɪçtɪçt], *adj.* unintentional.

unbeanstandet ['unbəanʃtandət], *adj.* unexceptionable; unopposed; with impunity.

unbeantwortbar ['unbəantvɔrtbaːr], *adj.* unanswerable.

unbeaufsichtigt ['unbəaufzɪçtɪçt], *adj.* unattended to, not looked after; without supervision.

unbebaut ['unbəbaut], *adj.* (*Agr.*) uncultivated; undeveloped (by building).

unbedacht ['unbədaxt], *adj.* thoughtless.

unbedenklich ['unbədɛŋklɪç], *adj.* harmless, innocuous. — *adv.* without hesitation.

unbedeutend ['unbədɔytənt], *adj.* insignificant.

unbedingt ['unbədɪŋkt], *adj.* unconditional, unlimited, absolute. — *adv.* quite definitely; without fail.

unbeeinflußt ['unbəaɪnflust], *adj.* uninfluenced.

unbefahrbar ['unbəfaːrbaːr], *adj.* impassable, impracticable.

unbefangen ['unbəfaŋən], *adj.* unbiased, unprejudiced; easy, unselfconscious, unembarrassed, uninhibited; natural.

Unbefangenheit ['unbəfaŋənhaɪt], *f.*

(—, *no pl.*) impartiality; ease of manner, unselfconsciousness, openness, naturalness.

unbefestigt ['unbəfɛstɪçt], *adj.* unfortified.

unbefleckt ['unbəflɛkt], *adj.* immaculate; —*e Empfängnis*, Immaculate Conception.

unbefriedigend ['unbəfriːdɪgənt], *adj.* unsatisfactory.

unbefriedigt ['unbəfriːdɪçt], *adj.* not satisfied, unsatisfied.

unbefugt ['unbəfuːkt], *adj.* unauthorised.

unbegreiflich ['unbəgraɪflɪç], *adj.* incomprehensible, inconceivable.

unbegrenzt ['unbəgrɛntst], *adj.* unlimited, unbounded.

unbegründet ['unbəgryndət], *adj.* unfounded, groundless.

Unbehagen ['unbəhaːgən], *n.* (—s, *no pl.*) uneasiness, discomfort.

unbehaglich ['unbəhaːklɪç], *adj.* uncomfortable; *sich — fühlen*, feel ill at ease.

unbehelligt ['unbəhɛlɪçt], *adj.* unmolested.

unbeholfen ['unbəhɔlfən], *adj.* awkward, clumsy.

unbeirrt ['unbaɪrt], *adj.* unswerving, uninfluenced, unperturbed.

unbekannt ['unbəkant], *adj.* unknown, unacquainted; *ich bin hier* —, I am a stranger here.

unbekümmert ['unbəkymərt], *adj.* unconcerned, careless, indifferent.

unbelehrt ['unbəleːrt], *adj.* uninstructed.

unbeliebt ['unbəliːpt], *adj.* unpopular.

unbemannt ['unbəmant], *adj.* without crew, unmanned.

unbemerkbar ['unbəmɛrkbaːr], *adj.* unnoticeable, imperceptible.

unbemerkt ['unbəmɛrkt], *adj.* unnoticed.

unbemittelt ['unbəmɪtəlt], *adj.* impecunious, poor.

unbenommen ['unbənɔmən], *adj.* *es bleibt dir* —, you are free to.

unbenutzt ['unbənutst], *adj.* unused.

unbequem ['unbəkveːm], *adj.* uncomfortable, inconvenient, troublesome.

Unbequemlichkeit ['unbəkveːmlɪçkaɪt], *f.* (—, *pl.* —en) inconvenience.

unberechenbar ['unbərɛçənbaːr], *adj.* incalculable; (*fig.*) erratic.

unberechtigt ['unbərɛçtɪçt], *adj.* unwarranted, unjustified.

unberücksichtigt ['unbərykzɪçtɪçt], *adj.* disregarded; — *lassen*, ignore.

unberufen ['unbəruːfən], *adj.* unauthorized. — *excl.* touch wood!

unbeschadet ['unbəʃaːdət], *prep.* (*Genit.*) without prejudice to.

unbeschädigt ['unbəʃɛːdɪçt], *adj.* undamaged.

unbeschäftigt ['unbəʃɛftɪçt], *adj.* unemployed, disengaged.

unbescheiden ['unbəʃaɪdən], *adj.* presumptuous, greedy, immodest; unblushing; exorbitant; arrogant.

Unbescheidenheit ['unbəʃaɪdənhaɪt], *f.* (—, *no pl.*) presumptuousness, greed.

unbescholten ['unbəʃɔltən], *adj.* irreproachable, of unblemished character.

Unbescholtenheit ['unbəʃɔltənhaɪt], *f.* (—, *no pl.*) blamelessness, good character, unsullied reputation.

unbeschränkt ['unbəʃrɛŋkt], *adj.* unlimited, unbounded; —*e Monarchie*, absolute monarchy.

unbeschreiblich ['unbəʃraɪplɪç], *adj.* indescribable.

unbeschrieben ['unbəʃriːbən], *adj.* unwritten; *ein* —*es Papier*, a blank sheet of paper.

unbeschwert ['unbəʃveːrt], *adj.* unburdened; easy.

unbeseelt ['unbəzeːlt], *adj.* inanimate.

unbesiegbar [unbəˈziːkbaːr], *adj.* invincible.

unbesoldet ['unbəzɔldət], *adj.* unpaid, unsalaried.

unbesonnen ['unbəzɔnən], *adj.* thoughtless, rash.

Unbesonnenheit ['unbəzɔnənhaɪt], *f.* (—, *pl.* —en) thoughtlessness.

unbesorgt ['unbəzɔrkt], *adj.* unconcerned; *sei* —, never fear.

unbeständig ['unbəʃtɛndɪç], *adj.* fickle, inconstant; (*weather*) unsettled.

unbestechlich ['unbəʃtɛçlɪç], *adj.* incorruptible.

unbestellbar ['unbəʃtɛlbaːr], *adj.* not deliverable; (*letters etc.*) address(ee) unknown.

unbestellt ['unbəʃtɛlt], *adj.* not ordered; (*Agr.*) uncultivated, untilled.

unbestimmt ['unbəʃtɪmt], *adj.* uncertain, not settled; indefinite; irresolute; vague.

unbestraft ['unbəʃtraːft], *adj.* unpunished; without previous conviction.

unbestreitbar ['unbəʃtraɪtbaːr], *adj.* indisputable, incontestable.

unbestritten ['unbəʃtrɪtən], *adj.* uncontested, undoubted, undisputed.

unbeteiligt ['unbətaɪlɪçt], *adj.* unconcerned, indifferent.

unbeträchtlich ['unbətrɛçtlɪç], *adj.* inconsiderable, trivial.

unbetreten ['unbətreːtən], *adj.* untrodden, untouched.

unbeugsam ['unbɔʏkzaːm], *adj.* inflexible, unyielding.

unbewacht ['unbəvaxt], *adj.* unguarded.

unbewaffnet ['unbəvafnət], *adj.* unarmed; *mit* —*em Auge*, with the naked eye.

unbewandert ['unbəvandərt], *adj.* unversed in, unfamiliar with.

unbezahlt ['unbətsaːlt], *adj.* unpaid.

unbezähmbar ['unbətseːmbaːr], *adj.* uncontrollable, indomitable.

unbezwinglich ['unbətsvɪŋlɪç], *adj.* invincible, unconquerable.

Unbildung ['unbɪlduŋ], *f.* (—, *no pl.*) lack of education *or* knowledge *or* culture.

Unbill ['unbɪl], *f.* (—, *pl.* **Unbilden**) injustice, wrong, injury; (*weather*) inclemency.

unbillig ['unbɪlɪç], *adj.* unreasonable, unfair.

Unbilligkeit ['unbɪlɪçkaɪt], *f.* (—, *no pl.*) unreasonableness, injustice, unfairness.

unbotmäßig ['unboːtmɛːsɪç], *adj.* unruly, insubordinate.

unbußfertig ['unbuːsfertɪç], *adj.* impenitent, unrepentant.

und [unt], *conj.* and; — *nicht*, nor; — *so weiter* (abbr. *usw.*), etc., and so on, and so forth; — *wenn*, even if.

Undank ['undaŋk], *m.* (—s, *no pl.*) ingratitude.

undankbar ['undaŋkbaːr], *adj.* ungrateful; *eine* —*e Aufgabe*, a thankless task.

Undankbarkeit ['undaŋkbaːrkaɪt], *f.* (—, *no pl.*) ingratitude.

undenkbar ['undɛŋkbaːr], *adj.* unthinkable, unimaginable, inconceivable.

undenklich ['undɛŋklɪç], *adj. seit* —*en Zeiten*, from time immemorial.

undeutlich ['undɔʏtlɪç], *adj.* indistinct; inarticulate; (*fig.*) unintelligible.

Unding ['undɪŋ], *n.* (—s, *no pl.*) absurdity.

unduldsam ['undultzaːm], *adj.* intolerant.

undurchdringlich ['undurçdrɪŋlɪç], *adj.* impenetrable.

undurchführbar ['undurçfyːrbaːr], *adj.* impracticable, unworkable.

undurchsichtig ['undurçzɪçtɪç], *adj.* opaque, not transparent.

uneben ['uneːbən], *adj.* uneven, rugged; (*coll.*) *nicht* —, not bad.

unecht ['unɛçt], *adj.* false, not genuine, spurious, counterfeit.

unedel ['uneːdəl], *adj.* (*metal*) base.

unehelich ['uneːəlɪç], *adj.* illegitimate.

Unehre ['uneːrə], *f.* (—, *no pl.*) dishonour, disgrace, discredit.

unehrlich ['uneːrlɪç], *adj.* dishonest.

Unehrlichkeit ['uneːrlɪçkaɪt], *f.* (—, *pl.* —en) dishonesty.

uneigennützig ['unaɪɡənnytsɪç], *adj.* unselfish, disinterested, public-spirited.

uneingedenk ['unaɪŋɡədɛŋk], *adj.* (*Genit.*) unmindful, forgetful.

uneingeschränkt ['unaɪŋɡəʃrɛŋkt], *adj.* unrestrained, unlimited.

uneinig ['unaɪnɪç], **uneins** ['unaɪns], *adj.* disunited, divided; — *werden*, fall out; — *sein*, disagree.

Uneinigkeit ['unaɪnɪçkaɪt], *f.* (—, *pl.* —en) disharmony, discord.

uneinnehmbar ['unaɪnneːmbaːr], *adj.* unconquerable, impregnable.

239

uneins *see under* **uneinig.**

unempfänglich ['unɛmpfɛŋlɪç], *adj.* insusceptible; unreceptive.

unempfindlich ['unɛmpfɪntlɪç], *adj.* insensitive, indifferent; unfeeling.

unendlich [un'ɛntlɪç], *adj.* endless, infinite.

unentbehrlich ['unɛntbe:rlɪç], *adj.* indispensable, (absolutely) essential.

unentgeltlich [unɛnt'gɛltlɪç], *adj.* free (of charge).

unentschieden ['unɛntʃi:dən], *adj.* undecided, undetermined; irresolute; (*game*) drawn, tied.

unentschlossen ['unɛntʃlɔsən], *adj.* irresolute.

Unentschlossenheit ['unɛntʃlɔsənhaɪt], *f.* (—, *no pl.*) irresolution, indecision.

unentschuldbar ['unɛntʃultba:r], *adj.* inexcusable.

unentstellt ['unɛntʃtɛlt], *adj.* undistorted.

unentwegt ['unɛntve:kt], *adj.* steadfast, unflinching, unswerving.

unentwickelt ['unɛntvɪkəlt], *adj.* undeveloped; —*e Länder,* underdeveloped countries.

unentwirrbar ['unɛntvɪrba:r], *adj.* inextricable.

unentzifferbar ['unɛntʦɪfərba:r], *adj.* indecipherable.

unentzündbar ['unɛnttsyntba:r], *adj.* non-inflammable.

unerachtet ['unɛraxtət], *prep.* (*Genit.*) (*obs.*) notwithstanding.

unerbeten ['unɛrbe:tən], *adj.* unsolicited.

unerbittlich ['unɛrbɪtlɪç], *adj.* inexorable.

unerfahren ['unɛrfa:rən], *adj.* inexperienced.

unerforschlich ['unɛrfɔrʃlɪç], *adj.* inscrutable.

unerfreulich ['unɛrfrɔylɪç], *adj.* unpleasant, displeasing, disagreeable.

unerfüllbar ['unɛrfylba:r], *adj.* unrealisable.

unerfüllt ['unɛrfylt], *adj.* unfulfilled.

unergründlich ['unɛrgryntlɪç], *adj.* unfathomable, impenetrable.

unerheblich ['unɛrhe:plɪç], *adj.* trifling, unimportant.

unerhört ['unɛrhø:rt], *adj.* unprecedented, unheard of, shocking, outrageous; not granted; turned down.

unerkannt ['unɛrkant], *adj.* unrecognised.

unerkennbar ['unɛrkɛnba:r], *adj.* unrecognisable.

unerklärlich ['unɛrklɛ:rlɪç], *adj.* inexplicable.

unerläßlich ['unɛrlɛslɪç], *adj.* indispensable.

unerlaubt ['unɛrlaupt], *adj.* unlawful, illicit.

unermeßlich ['unɛrmɛslɪç], *adj.* immense, vast.

unermüdlich ['unɛrmy:tlɪç], *adj.* untiring, indefatigable.

unerquicklich ['unɛrkvɪklɪç], *adj.* unedifying, disagreeable.

unerreichbar ['unɛrraɪçba:r], *adj.* unattainable, inaccessible.

unerreicht ['unɛrraɪçt], *adj.* unequalled.

unersättlich ['unɛrzɛtlɪç], *adj.* insatiable, greedy.

unerschöpflich ['unɛrʃœpflɪç], *adj.* inexhaustible.

unerschöpft ['unɛrʃœpft], *adj.* unexhausted.

unerschrocken ['unɛrʃrɔkən], *adj.* intrepid, undaunted.

unerschütterlich ['unɛrʃytərlɪç], *adj.* imperturbable.

unerschüttert ['unɛrʃytərt], *adj.* unshaken, unperturbed.

unerschwinglich ['unɛrʃvɪŋlɪç], *adj.* prohibitive, exorbitant, unattainable.

unersetzlich ['unɛrzɛtslɪç], *adj.* irreplaceable.

unersprießlich ['unɛrʃpri:slɪç], *adj.* unprofitable.

unerträglich ['unɛrtrɛ:klɪç], *adj.* intolerable, insufferable.

unerwartet ['unɛrvartət], *adj.* unexpected.

unerwidert ['unɛrvi:dərt], *adj.* (*love*) unrequited; (*letter*) unanswered.

unerwünscht ['unɛrvynʃt], *adj.* undesirable, unwelcome.

unerzogen ['unɛrtso:gən], *adj.* uneducated; ill-bred, unmannerly.

unfähig ['unfɛ:ɪç], *adj.* incapable, unable, unfit.

Unfähigkeit ['unfɛ:ɪçkaɪt], *f.* (—, *no pl.*) incapability, inability, unfitness.

Unfall ['unfal], *m.* (—s, *pl.* —e) accident.

unfaßbar ['unfasba:r], *adj.* incomprehensible, inconceivable.

unfehlbar ['unfe:lba:r], *adj.* inevitable; infallible.

Unfehlbarkeit ['unfe:lba:rkaɪt], *f.* (—, *no pl.*) infallibility.

unfein ['unfaɪn], *adj.* indelicate, coarse, impolite.

unfern ['unfɛrn], *prep.* (*Genit., Dat.*) not far from.

unfertig ['unfɛrtɪç], *adj.* unfinished, unready.

unflätig ['unflɛ:tɪç], *adj.* obscene, nasty, filthy.

unfolgsam ['unfɔlkza:m], *adj.* disobedient, recalcitrant.

unförmig ['unfœrmɪç], *adj.* deformed, ill-shaped, misshapen.

unförmlich ['unfœrmlɪç], *adj.* shapeless; free and easy, unceremonious.

unfrankiert ['unfraŋki:rt], *adj.* (*letter*) not prepaid, unstamped, unfranked.

unfrei ['unfraɪ], *adj.* not free; subjugated; constrained.

unfreiwillig ['unfraɪvɪlɪç], *adj.* involuntary.

unfreundlich ['unfrɔyntlɪç], *adj.* unfriendly, unkind; (*weather*) inclement.

Unfreundlichkeit ['unfrɔyntlɪçkaɪt], *f.* (—, *pl.* —en) unfriendliness, unkindness; (*weather*) inclemency.

Unfrieden ['unfri:dən], *m.* (—s, *no pl.*) discord, dissension.

unfruchtbar ['unfruxtba:r], *adj.* barren, sterile; (*fig.*) fruitless.

Unfug ['unfu:k], *m.* (—s, *no pl.*) disturbance, misconduct; mischief; *grober* —, public nuisance.

unfühlbar ['unfy:lba:r], *adj.* imperceptible.

ungangbar ['unganba:r], *adj.* impassable.

Ungarn ['ungarn], *n.* Hungary.

ungastlich ['ungastlɪç], *adj.* inhospitable.

ungeachtet ['ungəaxtət], *prep.* (*Genit.*) notwithstanding.

ungeahndet ['ungəa:ndət], *adj.* unpunished, with impunity.

ungeahnt ['ungəa:nt], *adj.* unexpected, unsuspected, undreamt of.

ungebändigt ['ungəbɛndɪçt], *adj.* untamed.

ungebärdig ['ungəbɛ:rdɪç], *adj.* unmannerly, refractory.

ungebeten ['ungəbe:tən], *adj.* uninvited, unbidden.

ungebleicht ['ungəblaɪçt], *adj.* unbleached.

ungebraucht ['ungəbrauxt], *adj.* unused.

Ungebühr ['ungəby:r], *f.* (—, *no pl.*) unseemliness, impropriety, excess.

ungebührlich ['ungəby:rlɪç], *adj.* unseemly.

ungebunden ['ungəbundən], *adj.* unbound, in sheets; unrestrained, loose; unlinked; —*e Rede*, prose.

Ungeduld ['ungədult], *f.* (—, *no pl.*) impatience.

ungeduldig ['ungəduldɪç], *adj.* impatient.

ungeeignet ['ungəaɪgnət], *adj.* unfit, unsuitable.

ungefähr ['ungəfɛ:r], *adj.* approximate, rough. — *adv.* approximately, roughly, about, round.

ungefährlich ['ungəfɛ:rlɪç], *adj.* not dangerous, harmless, safe.

ungefällig ['ungəfɛlɪç], *adj.* ungracious, disobliging.

ungefärbt ['ungəfɛrpt], *adj.* uncoloured; (*fig.*) unvarnished.

ungefüge ['ungəfy:gə], *adj.* clumsy.

ungehalten ['ungəhaltən], *adj.* indignant, angry.

ungeheißen ['ungəhaɪsən], *adj.* unbidden. — *adv.* of o.'s own accord.

ungehemmt ['ungəhɛmt], *adj.* unchecked, uninhibited.

ungeheuchelt ['ungəhɔyçəlt], *adj.* unfeigned.

Ungeheuer ['ungəhɔyər], *n.* (—s, *pl.* —) monster, monstrosity.

ungeheuer ['ungəhɔyər], *adj.* huge, immense; atrocious, frightful.

ungehobelt ['ungəhobəlt], *adj.* unplaned; (*fig.*) boorish, uncultured, unpolished.

ungehörig ['ungəhø:rɪç], *adj.* unseemly, improper.

Ungehorsam ['ungəho:rza:m], *m.* (—s, *no pl.*) disobedience.

ungehorsam ['ungəho:rza:m], *adj.* disobedient; — *sein*, disobey.

Ungehorsamkeit ['ungəho:rza:mkaɪt], *f.* (—, *pl.* —en) disobedience, insubordination.

ungekämmt ['ungəkɛmt], *adj.* unkempt.

ungekünstelt ['ungəkynstəlt], *adj.* artless, unstudied.

ungeladen ['ungəla:dən], *adj.* (*gun*) unloaded, not charged; uninvited.

ungeläutert ['ungəlɔytərt], *adj.* unrefined; unpurified.

ungelegen ['ungəle:gən], *adj.* inconvenient, inopportune.

Ungelegenheit ['ungəle:gənhaɪt], *f.* (—, *pl.* —en) inconvenience, trouble.

ungelehrig ['ungəle:rɪç], *adj.* intractable, unintelligent.

ungelenk ['ungəlɛnk], *adj.* clumsy, awkward; ungainly.

ungelöscht ['ungəlœʃt], *adj.* unquenched; (*lime*) unslaked; (*mortgage*) unredeemed.

Ungemach ['ungəma:x], *n.* (—(e)s, *no pl.*) adversity, toil, privation.

ungemein ['ungəmaɪn], *adj.* uncommon, extraordinary. — *adv.* very much, exceedingly.

ungemütlich ['ungəmy:tlɪç], *adj.* uncomfortable, cheerless, unpleasant.

ungeniert ['unʒeni:rt], *adj.* free and easy, unceremonious, unabashed.

ungenießbar ['ungəni:sba:r], *adj.* unpalatable, uneatable, inedible.

ungenügend ['ungənygənt], *adj.* insufficient, unsatisfactory.

ungenügsam ['ungəny:kza:m], *adj.* insatiable, greedy.

ungeordnet ['ungəɔrdnət], *adj.* illassorted, confused.

ungepflegt ['ungəpfle:kt], *adj.* uncared for, neglected.

ungerade ['ungəra:də], *adj.* uneven; — *Zahl*, odd number.

ungeraten ['ungəra:tən], *adj.* abortive, unsuccessful, spoiled; undutiful; illbred.

ungerecht ['ungərɛçt], *adj.* unjust, unfair.

ungerechtfertigt ['ungərɛçtfertɪçt], *adj.* unwarranted, unjustified.

Ungerechtigkeit ['ungərɛçtɪçkaɪt], *f.* (—, *pl.* —en) injustice.

ungeregelt ['ungəre:gəlt], *adj.* not regulated, irregular.

ungereimt ['ungəraɪmt], *adj.* rhymeless; —*es Zeug*, nonsense, absurdity.

ungern ['ungɛrn], *adv.* unwillingly, reluctantly.

ungerufen

ungerufen ['ʊngəruːfən], *adj.* un-bidden.

ungerührt ['ʊngəryːrt], *adj.* unmoved.

ungesäumt ['ʊngezɔymt], *adj.* un-seamed, unhemmed; (*fig.*) im-mediate. — *adv.* immediately, without delay.

ungeschehen ['ʊngəʃeːən], *adj.* un-done; — *machen*, undo.

Ungeschick ['ʊngəʃɪk], *n.* (—s, *no pl.*) awkwardness, clumsiness.

Ungeschicklichkeit ['ʊngəʃɪklɪçkaɪt], *f.* (—, *pl.* —en) awkwardness, clumsi-ness.

ungeschickt ['ʊngəʃɪkt], *adj.* awkward, clumsy, unskilful.

ungeschlacht ['ʊngəʃlaxt], *adj.* un-couth, unwieldy; coarse, rude.

ungeschliffen ['ʊngəʃlɪfən], *aaj.* un-polished; (*fig.*) coarse.

Ungeschliffenheit ['ʊngəʃlɪfənhaɪt], *f.* (—, *no pl.*) coarseness, uncouthness.

ungeschmälert ['ʊngəʃmɛːlərt], *adj.* undiminished, unimpaired.

ungeschminkt ['ʊngəʃmɪŋkt], *adj.* without cosmetics *or* make-up, not made up; (*truth*) plain, unvarnished.

ungeschoren ['ʊngəʃoːrən], *adj.* un-shorn; *laß mich* —, leave me alone.

ungeschult ['ʊngəʃuːlt], *adj.* un-trained.

ungeschwächt ['ʊngəʃvɛçt], *adj.* un-impaired.

ungesellig ['ʊngəzelɪç], *adj.* unsociable.

ungesetzlich ['ʊngəzetslɪç], *adj.* illegal, unlawful, illicit.

ungesetzmäßig ['ʊngəzetsmɛːsɪç], *adj.* illegitimate, lawless; exceptional; not regular.

ungesiegelt ['ʊngəziːgəlt], *adj.* un-sealed.

Ungestalt ['ʊngəʃtalt], *f.* (—, *no pl.*) deformity.

ungestalt ['ʊngəʃtalt], *adj.* misshapen, deformed.

ungestempelt ['ʊngəʃtempəlt], *adj.* unstamped, uncancelled, not post-marked.

ungestillt ['ʊngəʃtɪlt], *adj.* unquenched, unslaked; not fed, unsatisfied.

ungestört ['ʊngəʃtøːrt], *adj.* undis-turbed.

ungestraft ['ʊngəʃtraːft], *ʾadj.* un-punished. — *adv.* with impunity.

ungestüm ['ʊngəʃtyːm], *adj.* im-petuous.

Ungestüm ['ʊngəʃtyːm], *m. & n.* (—s, *no pl.*) impetuosity.

ungesund ['ʊngəzunt], *adj.* unwhole-some, unhealthy, sickly; (*fig.*) un-natural, morbid.

ungetan ['ʊngətaːn], *adj.* not done, left undone.

ungetreu ['ʊngətrɔy], *adj.* disloyal, faithless.

ungetrübt ['ʊngətryːpt], *adj.* un-troubled.

ungewandt ['ʊngəvant], *adj.* unskilful.

ungewaschen ['ʊngəvaʃən], *adj.* un-washed; (*sl.*) —*es Mundwerk*, mal-icious tongue.

ungeweiht ['ʊngəvaɪt], *adj.* uncon-secrated.

ungewiß ['ʊngəvɪs], *adj.* uncertain, doubtful.

Ungewißheit ['ʊngəvɪshaɪt], *f.* (—, *no pl.*) uncertainty, suspense.

Ungewitter ['ʊngəvɪtər], *n.* (—s, *pl.* —) storm, thunderstorm.

ungewöhnlich ['ʊngəvøːnlɪç], *adj.* un-usual, uncommon.

Ungewohntheit ['ʊngəvoːnthaɪt], *f.* (—, *no pl.*) strangeness; want of practice.

ungezähmt ['ʊngətsɛːmt], *adj.* un-tamed; (*fig.*) uncurbed.

Ungeziefer ['ʊngətsiːfər], *n.* (—s, *pl.* —) vermin.

ungeziert ['ʊngətsiːrt], *adj.* unaffected, natural.

ungezogen ['ʊngətsoːgən], *adj.* ill-mannered, naughty.

ungezügelt ['ʊngətsyːgəlt], *adj.* un-bridled; (*fig.*) unruly.

ungezwungen ['ʊngətsvuŋən], *adj.* unforced; (*fig.*) unaffected.

Ungezwungenheit ['ʊngətsvuŋənhaɪt], *f.* (—, *no pl.*) naturalness, ease.

Unglaube ['ʊnglaubə], *m.* (—ns, *no pl.*) disbelief.

unglaubhaft ['ʊnglauphaft], *adj.* un-authenticated, incredible.

ungläubig ['ʊnglɔybɪç], *adj.* incredu-lous, disbelieving.

Ungläubige ['ʊnglɔybɪgə], *m.* (—n, *pl.* —n) unbeliever.

unglaublich ['ʊnglauplɪç], *adj.* in-credible, unbelievable.

unglaubwürdig ['ʊnglaupvyrdɪç], *adj.* unauthenticated, incredible.

ungleichartig ['ʊnglaɪçaːrtɪç], *adj.* dissimilar, heterogeneous.

ungleichförmig ['ʊnglaɪçfœrmɪç], *adj.* not uniform; dissimilar.

Ungleichheit ['ʊnglaɪçhaɪt], *f.* (—, *pl.* —en) inequality; unlikeness, dis-similarity; unevenness.

ungleichmäßig ['ʊnglaɪçmɛːsɪç], *adj.* unequal, irregular; changeable, fitful.

Unglimpf ['ʊnglɪmpf], *m.* (—(e)s, *no pl.*) harshness; insult.

Unglück ['ʊnglyk], *n.* (—s, *pl.* —fälle) misfortune, adversity, ill-luck; acci-dent, disaster; distress, sorrow, affliction.

unglückbringend ['ʊnglykbrɪŋənt], *adj.* disastrous, unpropitious.

unglücklich ['ʊnglyklɪç], *adj.* un-fortunate, unhappy, unlucky; —*e Liebe*, unrequited love.

unglücklicherweise ['ʊnglyklɪçər-vaɪzə], *adv.* unfortunately, unluckily.

Unglücksbotschaft ['ʊnglyksboːtʃaft], *f.* (—, *pl.* —en) bad news.

unglückselig ['ʊnglykzeːlɪç], *adj.* luck-less, wretched, unfortunate, calamitous.

Unglücksfall ['ʊnglyksfal], *m.* (—(e)s, *pl.* ⁻e) accident.

Unglücksgefährte [ˈunglyksgəfɛːrtə], *m.* (—n, *pl.* —n) companion in misfortune.

Ungnade [ˈungnaːdə], *f.* (—, *no pl.*) disgrace.

ungültig [ˈungyltɪç], *adj.* invalid, void; — *machen*, invalidate, annul.

Ungunst [ˈungunst], *f.* (—, *no pl.*) disfavour; unpropitiousness; (*weather*) inclemency.

ungünstig [ˈungynstɪç], *adj.* unfavourable, adverse.

ungut [ˈunguːt], *adv. etwas für — nehmen*, take s.th. amiss.

unhaltbar [ˈunhaltbaːr], *adj.* untenable.

Unheil [ˈunhaɪl], *n.* (—s, *no pl.*) mischief, harm; disaster.

unheilbar [ˈunhaɪlbaːr], *adj.* incurable.

unheilbringend [ˈunhaɪlbrɪŋənt], *adj.* ominous, unlucky; disastrous.

Unheilstifter [ˈunhaɪlʃtɪftər], *m.* (—s, *pl.* —) mischief-maker.

unheilvoll [ˈunhaɪlfɔl], *adj.* calamitous, disastrous.

unheimlich [ˈunhaɪmlɪç], *adj.* weird, eerie, uncanny.

unhöflich [ˈunhøːflɪç], *adj.* impolite, uncivil, discourteous.

Unhold [ˈunhɔlt], *m.* (—s, *pl.* —e) fiend, monster.

Unhörbarkeit [ˈunhøːrbaːrkaɪt], *f.* (—, *no pl.*) inaudibility.

Uniformität [uniformiˈtɛːt], *f.* (—, *no pl.*) uniformity.

Unikum [ˈuːnikum], *n.* (—s, *pl.* —s) unique thing *or* person; eccentric.

Universalmittel [univerˈzaːlmɪtəl], *n.* (—s, *pl.* —) panacea, universal remedy.

Universität [univerziˈtɛːt], *f.* (—, *pl.* —en) university.

Universitätsdozent [univerziˈtɛːtsdotsɛnt], *m.* (—en, *pl.* —en) university lecturer.

Universum [uniˈverzum], *n.* (—s, *no pl.*) universe.

unkaufmännisch [ˈunkaufmɛnɪʃ], *adj.* unbusinesslike.

Unke [ˈuŋkə], *f.* (—, *pl.* —n) (*Zool.*) toad; (*fig.*) grumbler, pessimist.

unken [ˈuŋkən], *v.n.* grumble, grouse.

unkenntlich [ˈunkɛntlɪç], *adj.* indiscernible, unrecognisable.

Unkenntlichkeit [ˈunkɛntlɪçkaɪt], *f.* (—, *no pl.*) *bis zur* —, past recognition.

Unkenntnis [ˈunkɛntnɪs], *f.* (—, *no pl.*) ignorance.

unklug [ˈunkluːk], *adj.* imprudent.

Unkosten [ˈunkɔstən], *f. pl.* expenses, costs, charges; overheads.

Unkraut [ˈunkraut], *n.* (—s, *no pl.*) weed(s).

unkündbar [ˈunkyntbaːr], *adj.* irredeemable; irrevocable, permanent.

unkundig [ˈunkundɪç], *adj.* ignorant (of), unacquainted (with).

unlängst [ˈunlɛŋst], *adv.* recently, lately, not long ago.

unlauter [ˈunlautər], *adj.* sordid, squalid; unfair.

unleidlich [ˈunlaɪtlɪç], *adj.* intolerable.

unleserlich [ˈunleːzərlɪç], *adj.* illegible.

unleugbar [ˈunlɔykbaːr], *adj.* undeniable, indisputable.

unlieb [ˈunliːp], *adj.* disagreeable.

unliebenswürdig [ˈunliːbənsvyrdɪç], *adj.* sullen, surly.

unlösbar [ˈunløːsbaːr], *adj.* insoluble.

unlöslich [ˈunløːslɪç], *adj.* (*substance*) indissoluble, insoluble.

Unlust [ˈunlust], *f.* (—, *no pl.*) aversion, disinclination; slackness.

unlustig [ˈunlustɪç], *adj.* averse, disinclined.

unmanierlich [ˈunmaniːrlɪç], *adj.* ill-mannered.

unmännlich [ˈunmɛnlɪç], *adj.* unmanly, effeminate.

Unmaß [ˈunmaːs], *n.* (—es, *no pl.*) excess.

Unmasse [ˈunmasə], *f.* (—, *pl.* —n) vast quantity.

unmaßgeblich [ˈunmaːsgeːplɪç], *adj.* unauthoritative, open to correction; (*fig.*) humble.

unmäßig [ˈunmɛːsɪç], *adj.* intemperate, excessive.

Unmenge [ˈunmeŋə], *f.* (—, *pl.* —n) vast quantity.

Unmensch [ˈunmɛnʃ], *m.* (—en, *pl.* —en) brute.

unmenschlich [ˈunmɛnʃlɪç], *adj.* inhuman, brutal; (*coll.*) vast.

unmerklich [ˈunmerklɪç], *adj.* imperceptible.

unmeßbar [ˈunmɛsbaːr], *adj.* immeasurable.

unmittelbar [ˈunmɪtəlbaːr], *adj.* immediate, direct.

unmöglich [ˈunmøːklɪç], *adj.* impossible.

unmündig [ˈunmyndɪç], *adj.* under age, minor.

Unmündige [ˈunmyndɪgə], *m.* (—n, *pl.* —n) (*Law*) minor.

Unmündigkeit [ˈunmyndɪçkaɪt], *f.* (—, *no pl.*) minority.

Unmut [ˈunmuːt], *m.* (—s, *no pl.*) ill-humour; displeasure, indignation, petulance.

unmutig [ˈunmuːtɪç], *adj.* ill-humoured, petulant, indignant.

unnachahmlich [ˈunnaxaːmlɪç], *adj.* inimitable.

unnachgiebig [ˈunnaxgiːbɪç], *adj.* relentless, unyielding.

unnachsichtig [ˈunnaxzɪçtɪç], *adj.* unrelenting, relentless.

unnahbar [ˈunnaːbaːr], *adj.* unapproachable, stand-offish.

unnennbar [ˈunnɛnbaːr], *adj.* unutterable.

unnütz [ˈunnyts], *adj.* useless.

unordentlich [ˈunɔrdəntlɪç], *adj.* untidy, slovenly.

Unordnung [ˈunɔrdnuŋ], *f.* (—, *no pl.*) disorder, untidiness, muddle, confusion.

unparteiisch ['unpartaɪʃ], *adj.* impartial, unbiased, objective.

unpassend ['unpasənt], *adj.* unsuitable, inappropriate; improper.

unpassierbar ['unpasiːrbaːr], *adj.* impassable.

unpäßlich ['unpɛslɪç], *adj.* indisposed, unwell, out of sorts.

Unpäßlichkeit ['unpɛslɪçkaɪt], *f.* (—, *pl.* —en) indisposition.

unproportioniert ['unprɔpɔrtsjoniːrt], *adj.* disproportionate; unshapely.

unqualifizierbar ['unkvalifitsiːrbaːr], *adj.* unspeakable, nameless.

Unrat ['unraːt], *m.* (—(e)s, *no pl.*) dirt, rubbish.

unratsam ['unraːtzaːm], *adj.* inadvisable.

Unrecht ['unrɛçt], *n.* (—(e)s, *no pl.*) wrong, injustice; — *haben*, be in the wrong.

unrecht ['unrɛçt], *adj.* wrong, unjust.

unrechtmäßig ['unrɛçtmɛːsɪç], *adj.* unlawful, illegal.

unredlich ['unreːtlɪç], *adj.* dishonest.

unregelmäßig ['unreːgəlmɛːsɪç], *adj.* irregular.

unreif ['unraɪf], *adj.* unripe, immature; (*fig.*) crude, raw.

Unreife ['unraɪfə], *f.* (—, *no pl.*) immaturity.

unrein ['unraɪn], *adj.* unclean; (*fig.*) impure.

Unreinheit ['unraɪnhaɪt], *f.* (—, *pl.* —en) impurity.

Unreinlichkeit ['unraɪnlɪçkaɪt], *f.* (—, *no pl.*) uncleanliness.

unrentabel ['unrɛntaːbəl], *adj.* unprofitable.

unrettbar ['unrɛtbaːr], *adj.* irretrievable, hopelessly lost.

unrichtig ['unrɪçtɪç], *adj.* incorrect, erroneous, wrong.

Unrichtigkeit ['unrɪçtɪçkaɪt], *f.* (—, *no pl.*) error, falsity, incorrectness.

Unruhe ['unruːə], *f.* (—, *pl.* —en) unrest, restlessness; disquiet, uneasiness; riot, disturbance; (*clock*) balance.

Unruhestifter ['unruːəʃtɪftər], *m.* (—s, *pl.* —) disturber (of the peace); troublemaker.

unruhig ['unruːɪç], *adj.* restless; troublesome, turbulent, uneasy (about), fidgety.

unrühmlich ['unryːmlɪç], *adj.* inglorious.

uns [uns], *pers. pron.* us, ourselves; to us.

unsachlich ['unzaxlɪç], *adj.* subjective; irrelevant.

unsagbar ['unzaːkbaːr], *adj.* unutterable, unspeakable.

unsanft ['unzanft], *adj.* harsh, violent.

unsauber ['unzaubər], *adj.* unclean, dirty; (*fig.*) squalid.

unschädlich ['unʃɛːtlɪç], *adj.* harmless, innocuous.

unschätzbar ['unʃɛtsbaːr], *adj.* invaluable.

unscheinbar ['unʃaɪnbaːr], *adj.* plain, homely, insignificant.

unschicklich ['unʃɪklɪç], *adj.* unbecoming, indecent, improper, unseemly.

unschlüssig ['unʃlysɪç], *adj.* irresolute, undecided.

Unschuld ['unʃult], *f.* (—, *no pl.*) innocence; *verfolgte* —, injured innocence.

unschuldig ['unʃuldɪç], *adj.* innocent, guiltless; chaste; —*es Vergnügen*, harmless pleasure.

unschwer ['unʃveːr], *adv.* easily.

Unsegen ['unzeːgən], *m.* (—s, *no pl.*) misfortune; curse.

unselbständig ['unzɛlpʃtɛndɪç], *adj.* dependent.

unselig ['unzeːlɪç], *adj.* unfortunate, luckless, fatal.

unser ['unzər], *poss. adj.* our. — *pers. pron.* of us.

unsereiner ['unzəraɪnər], *pron.* s.o. in our position; one of us, people in our position.

unserthalben, unsertwegen ['unzərthalbən, unzərtveːgən], *adv.* for our sake, on our account.

unsertwillen ['unzərtvɪlən], *adv. um* —, for our sake, on our account.

unsicher ['unzɪçər], *adj.* unsafe; uncertain, doubtful; (*route*) precarious; (*hand*) unsteady; (*legs*) shaky.

unsichtbar ['unzɪçtbaːr], *adj.* invisible.

Unsinn ['unzɪn], *m.* (—s, *no pl.*) nonsense.

unsinnig ['unzɪnɪç], *adj.* nonsensical; mad, insane.

Unsitte ['unzɪtə], *f.* (—, *pl.* —n) abuse, nuisance; bad habit.

unsittlich ['unzɪtlɪç], *adj.* immoral.

unstät, unstet ['unʃtɛːt, 'unʃteːt], *adj.* unsteady, inconstant; restless.

unstatthaft ['unʃtathaft], *adj.* illicit.

unsterblich ['unʃtɛrplɪç], *adj.* immortal.

Unsterblichkeit ['unʃtɛrplɪçkaɪt], *f.* (—, *no pl.*) immortality.

unstillbar ['unʃtɪlbaːr], *adj.* unappeasable, unquenchable.

unstreitig ['unʃtraɪtɪç], *adj.* indisputable, unquestionable.

Unsumme ['unzumə], *f.* (—, *pl.* —n) vast amount (of money).

unsympathisch ['unzympaːtɪʃ], *adj.* uncongenial, disagreeable; *er ist mir* —, I dislike him.

untadelhaft, untadelig ['unta:dəlhaft, 'unta:dəlɪç], *adj.* blameless, irreproachable, unimpeachable.

Untat ['untaːt], *f.* (—, *pl.* —en) misdeed, crime.

untätig ['untɛːtɪç], *adj.* inactive, idle, supine.

untauglich ['untauklɪç], *adj.* unfit, useless; incompetent; (*Mil.*) disabled.

unteilbar ['unˈtaɪlbaːr], *adj.* indivisible.

unten [ˈʊntən], *adv.* below, beneath; (*house*) downstairs.

unter [ˈʊntər], *prep.* (*Dat., Acc.*) under, beneath, below, among, between.

Unterbau [ˈʊntərbau], *m.* (—s, *pl.* —ten) substructure, foundation.

Unterbewußtsein [ˈʊntərbəvustzaɪn], *n.* (—s, *no pl.*) subconscious mind, subconsciousness.

unterbieten [untərˈbiːtən], *v.a. irr. insep.* underbid, undersell.

Unterbilanz [ˈʊntərbilants], *f.* (—, *pl.* —en) deficit.

unterbinden [untərˈbɪndən], *v.a. irr. insep.* tie up, bind up; (*fig.*) prevent, check.

unterbleiben [untərˈblaɪbən], *v.n. irr. insep.* (*aux.* sein) remain undone, be left undone, cease.

unterbrechen [untərˈbrɛçən], *v.a. irr. insep.* interrupt; (*journey*) break; (*speech*) cut short.

Unterbrechung [untərˈbrɛçuŋ], *f.* (—, *pl.* —en) interruption.

unterbreiten (1) [ˈʊntərbraɪtən], *v.a.* spread under.

unterbreiten (2) [untərˈbraɪtən], *v.a. insep.* submit, lay before.

unterbringen [ˈʊntərbrɪŋən], *v.a. irr.* provide (*a place*) for; (*goods*) dispose of; (*money*) invest; (*people*) accommodate, put up.

Unterbringung [ˈʊntərbrɪŋuŋ], *f.* (—, *no pl.*) provision for; (*goods*) disposal of; (*money*) investment; (*people*) accommodation.

unterdessen [untərˈdɛsən], *adv., conj.* in the meantime, meanwhile.

unterdrücken [untərˈdrykən], *v.a. insep.* suppress, curb, check; oppress.

Unterdrückung [untərˈdrykuŋ], *f.* (—, *no pl.*) oppression, suppression.

untereinander [untəraɪnˈandər], *adv.* with each other, mutually, among themselves.

unterfangen [untərˈfaŋən], *v.r. irr. insep. sich* —, dare, venture, presume.

Untergang [ˈʊntərgaŋ], *m.* (—s, *pl.* ̈e) (*sun*) setting; (*ship*) sinking; (*fig.*) decline.

untergeben [untərˈgeːbən], *adj.* subject, subordinate.

Untergebene [untərˈgeːbənə], *m.* (—n, *pl.* —n) subordinate.

untergehen [ˈʊntərgeːən], *v.n. irr.* (*aux.* sein) (*sun*) go down, set; (*ship*) sink; (*fig.*) perish; decline.

Untergeschoß [ˈʊntərgəʃɔs], *n.* (—sses, *pl.* —sse) ground floor.

Untergestell [ˈʊntərgəʃtɛl], *n.* (—s, *pl.* —e) undercarriage, chassis.

untergraben [untərˈgraːbən], *v.a. irr. insep.* undermine.

unterhalb [ˈʊntərhalp], *prep.* (*Genit.*) below, under.

Unterhalt [ˈʊntərhalt], *m.* (—s, *no pl.*) maintenance, support, livelihood.

unterhalten (1) [ˈʊntərhaltən], *v.a. irr.* hold under.

unterhalten (2) [untərˈhaltən], *v.a. irr. insep.* maintain, keep, support; entertain. — *v.r. sich* —, converse, make conversation; *sich gut* —, enjoy o.s.

unterhaltend [untərˈhaltənt], *adj.* entertaining, amusing, lively.

Unterhaltskosten [ˈʊntərhaltskɔstən], *f. pl.* maintenance; (*house*) cost of repairs.

Unterhaltung [untərˈhaltuŋ], *f.* (—, *pl.* —en) maintenance; conversation; amusement, entertainment.

Unterhaltungslektüre [untərˈhaltuŋslɛktyːrə], *f.* (—, *no pl.*) light reading, fiction.

unterhandeln [untərˈhandəln], *v.n. insep.* negotiate.

Unterhändler [ˈʊntərhɛndlər], *m.* (—s, *pl.* —) negotiator, mediator.

Unterhandlung [untərˈhandluŋ], *f.* (—, *pl.* —en) negotiation.

Unterhaus [ˈʊntərhaus], *n.* (—es, *pl.* ̈er) ground floor; (*Parl.*) lower house; House of Commons.

Unterhemd [ˈʊntərhɛmt], *n.* (—(e)s, *pl.* —en) vest.

unterhöhlen [untərˈhøːlən], *v.a. insep.* undermine.

Unterholz [ˈʊntərhɔlts], *n.* (—es, *no pl.*) undergrowth, underwood.

Unterhosen [ˈʊntərhoːzən], *f. pl.* (*women*) briefs; (*men*) underpants.

unterirdisch [ˈʊntərɪrdɪʃ], *adj.* subterranean, underground.

unterjochen [untərˈjɔxən], *v.a. insep.* subjugate, subdue.

Unterkiefer [ˈʊntərkiːfər], *m.* (—s, *pl.* —) lower jaw.

Unterkleid [ˈʊntərklaɪt], *n.* (—s, *pl.* —er) under-garment.

unterkommen [ˈʊntərkɔmən], *v.n. irr.* (*aux.* sein) find accommodation *or* shelter; (*fig.*) find employment.

Unterkommen [ˈʊntərkɔmən], *n.* (—s, *no pl.*) shelter, accommodation; (*fig.*) employment, place.

Unterkörper [ˈʊntərkœrpər], *m.* (—s, *pl.* —s) lower part of the body.

unterkriegen [ˈʊntərkriːgən], *v.a.* get the better of; *lass dich nicht* —, stand firm.

Unterkunft [ˈʊntərkunft], *f.* (—, *pl.* ̈e) shelter, accommodation; employment.

Unterlage [ˈʊntərlaːgə], *f.* (—, *pl.* —n) foundation, base; blotting pad; (*pl.*) documents, files.

unterlassen [untərˈlasən], *v.a. irr. insep.* omit (to do), fail (to do), neglect; forbear.

Unterlassung [untərˈlasuŋ], *f.* (—, *pl.* —en) omission, neglect.

Unterlassungssünde [untərˈlasuŋszyndə], *f.* (—, *pl.* —n) sin of omission.

Unterlauf [ˈʊntərlauf], *m.* (—(e)s, *pl.* ̈e) (*river*) lower course.

unterlaufen [untər'laufən], *v.n. irr. insep. (aux.* sein) run under; *(mistake)* creep in. — *adj.* suffused, blood-shot.

unterlegen (1) ['untərle:gən], *v.a.* lay under; *einen anderen Sinn* —, put a different construction upon.

unterlegen (2) [untər'le:gən], *adj.* inferior.

Unterleib ['untərlaip], *m.* (—s, *no pl.*) abdomen.

unterliegen [untər'li:gən], *v.n. irr. insep. (aux.* sein) succumb, be overcome; be subject (to).

Untermieter ['untərmi:tər], *m.* (—s, *pl.* —) subtenant.

unterminieren [untərmi'ni:rən], *v.a. insep.* undermine.

unternehmen [untər'ne:mən], *v.a. irr. insep.* undertake, take upon o.s., attempt.

Unternehmen [untər'ne:mən], *n.* (—s, *pl.* —) enterprise, undertaking.

unternehmend [untər'ne:mənt], *adj.* bold, enterprising.

Unternehmer [untər'ne:mər], *m.* (—s, *pl.* —) contractor, entrepreneur.

Unteroffizier ['untərofitsi:r], *m.* (—s, *pl.* —e) *(army)* non-commissioned officer; *(navy)* petty officer.

unterordnen ['untərordnən], *v.a.* subordinate. — *v.r. sich* —, submit (to).

Unterordnung ['untərordnuŋ], *f.* (—, *no pl.*) subordination, submission; *(Biol.)* sub-order.

Unterpacht ['untərpaxt], *f.* (—, *no pl.*) sublease.

Unterpfand ['untərpfant], *n.* (—(e)s, *no pl.*) *(obs.)* pawn, pledge.

Unterredung [untər're:duŋ], *f.* (—, *pl.* —en) conference, interview, talk.

Unterricht ['untərrIçt], *m.* (—(e)s, *no pl.*) instruction, tuition, teaching.

unterrichten [untər'rIçtən], *v.a. insep.* instruct, teach.

Unterrichtsanstalt ['untərrIçtsanʃtalt], *f.* (—, *pl.* —en) educational establishment *or* institution.

Unterrichtsgegenstand ['untərrIçtsge:gənʃtant], *m.* (—s, *pl.* ⁀e) subject of instruction.

Unterrock ['untərrɔk], *m.* (—s, *pl.* ⁀e) petticoat, slip; underskirt.

untersagen [untər'za:gən], *v.a. insep.* forbid; *Rauchen untersagt,* smoking prohibited.

Untersatz ['untərzats], *m.* (—es, *pl.* ⁀e) basis, holder, stand, trestle; saucer.

unterschätzen [untər'ʃetsən], *v.a. insep.* underrate, underestimate.

unterscheiden [untər'ʃaidən], *v.a. irr. insep.* distinguish, discriminate, discern, differentiate. — *v.r. sich* —, differ; *ich kann sie nicht* —, I cannot tell them apart.

Unterscheidung [untər'ʃaiduŋ], *f.* (—, *pl.* —en) distinction, differentiation.

Unterscheidungsmerkmal [untər-'ʃaiduŋsmerkma:l], *n.* (—s, *pl.* —e) distinctive mark, characteristic.

Unterscheidungsvermögen [untər-'ʃaiduŋsfermø:gən], *n.* (—s, *no pl.*) power of discrimination.

Unterscheidungszeichen [untər'ʃaiduŋstsaIçən], *n.* (—s, *pl.* —) criterion.

Unterschenkel ['untərʃeŋkəl], *m.* (—s, *pl.* —) shank, lower part of the thigh.

Unterschicht ['untərʃIçt], *f.* (—, *pl.* —en) substratum, subsoil.

unterschieben (1) ['untərʃi:bən], *v.a. irr.* substitute; interpolate; forge; foist upon.

unterschieben (2) [untər'ʃi:bən], *v.a. irr. insep.* (*fig.*) attribute falsely, pass s.o. off as.

Unterschiebung [untər'ʃi:buŋ], *f.* (—, *pl.* —en) substitution; forgery.

Unterschied ['untərʃi:t], *m.* (—(e)s, *pl.* —e) difference.

unterschiedlich ['untərʃi:tlIç], *adj.* different, diverse.

unterschiedslos ['untərʃi:tslo:s], *adv.* indiscriminately.

unterschlagen [untər'ʃla:gən], *v.a. irr. insep.* embezzle, intercept.

Unterschlagung [untər'ʃla:guŋ], *f.* (—, *pl.* —en) embezzlement.

Unterschlupf ['untərʃlupf], *m.* (—es, *pl.* ⁀e) shelter, refuge.

unterschlüpfen ['untərʃlypfən], *v.n. (aux.* sein) find shelter, slip away; (*fig.*) hide.

unterschreiben [untər'ʃraibən], *v.a. irr. insep.* sign, subscribe to.

Unterschrift ['untərʃrIft], *f.* (—, *pl.* —en) signature.

Unterseeboot ['untərze:bo:t], *n.* (—s, *pl.* —e) submarine.

untersetzt [untər'zetst], *adj.* thickset, dumpy.

untersinken ['untərzIŋkən], *v.n. irr. (aux.* sein) go down.

unterst ['untərst], *adj.* lowest, undermost, bottom.

Unterstaatssekretär [untər'ʃta:tszekrete:r], *m.* (—s, *pl.* —e) undersecretary of state.

unterstehen (1) ['untərʃte:ən], *v.n. irr. (aux.* sein) find shelter (under).

unterstehen (2) [untər'ʃte:ən], *v.n. irr. insep.* be subordinate. — *v.r. sich* —, dare, venture.

unterstellen (1) ['untərʃtelən], *v.a.* place under. — *v.r. sich* —, take shelter (under).

unterstellen (2) [untər'ʃtelən], *v.a. insep.* put under the authority of; impute (s.th. to s.o.).

Unterstellung [untər'ʃteluŋ], *f.* (—, *pl.* —en) imputation, insinuation.

unterstreichen [untər'ʃtraIçən], *v.a. irr. insep.* underline.

Unterstreichung [untər'ʃtraIçuŋ], *f.* (—, *pl.* —en) underlining.

Unterströmung ['untərʃtrø:muŋ], *f.* (—, *pl.* —en) undercurrent.

unterstützen [untər'ʃtytsən], *v.a. insep.* support, assist, aid; (*fig.*) countenance.

Unterstützung [untər'ʃtytsuŋ], *f.* (—, *pl.* —en) support, aid, assistance, relief.

Unterstützungsanstalt [untər'ʃtytsuŋsanʃtalt], *f.* (—, *pl.* —en) charitable institution.

unterstützungsbedürftig [untər'ʃtytsuŋsbədyrftiç], *adj.* indigent.

untersuchen [untər'zu:xən], *v.a. insep.* investigate, examine, look over.

Untersuchung [untər'zu:xuŋ], *f.* (—, *pl.* —en) investigation, inquiry; *(medical)* examination.

Untersuchungshaft [untər'zu:xuŋshaft], *f.* (—, *no pl.*) imprisonment pending investigation.

Untersuchungsrichter [untər'zu:xuŋsriçtər], *m.* (—s, *pl.* —) examining magistrate.

Untertan ['untərta:n], *m.* (—s, *pl.* —en) subject.

untertan ['untərta:n], *adj.* subject.

untertänig ['untərte:niç], *adj.* humble, obsequious, submissive, servile.

Untertasse ['untərtasə], *f.* (—, *pl.* —n) saucer.

untertauchen ['untərtauxən], *v.a.* dip, duck, submerge. — *v.n. (aux.* sein) dive.

unterwegs [untər've:ks], *adv.* on the way.

unterweisen [untər'vaizən], *v.a. irr. insep.* teach, instruct.

Unterweisung [untər'vaizuŋ], *f.* (—, *pl.* —en) instruction, teaching.

Unterwelt ['untərvelt], *f.* (—, *no pl.*) Hades, the underworld.

unterwerfen [untər'verfən], *v.a. irr. insep.* subject, subdue. — *v.r. sich* —, submit (to), resign o.s. (to).

Unterwerfung [untər'verfuŋ], *f.* (—, *no pl.*) subjection, submission.

unterwühlen [untər'vy:lən], *v.a. insep.* root up; (*fig.*) undermine.

unterwürfig [untər'vyrfiç], *adj.* submissive, subject; obsequious.

Unterwürfigkeit [untər'vyrfiçkait], *f.* (—, *no pl.*) submissiveness; obsequiousness.

unterzeichnen [untər'tsaiçnən], *v.a. insep.* sign.

Unterzeichner [untər'tsaiçnər], *m.* (—s, *pl.* —) signatory; *(insurance)* underwriter.

Unterzeichnete [untər'tsaiçnətə], *m.* (—n, *pl.* —n) undersigned.

Unterzeichnung [untər'tsaiçnuŋ], *f.* (—, *pl.* —en) signature.

unterziehen [untər'tsi:ən], *v.r. irr. insep. sich* —, submit to, undertake; *(operation)* undergo.

Untiefe ['unti:fə], *f.* (—, *pl.* —n) shallow water, flat, shoal, sands.

Untier ['unti:r], *n.* (—s, *pl.* —e) monster.

untilgbar ['untilkba:r], *adj.* indelible; *(debt)* irredeemable.

untrennbar ['untrɛnba:r], *adj.* inseparable.

untreu ['untrɔy], *adj.* faithless, unfaithful, disloyal, perfidious.

Untreue ['untrɔyə], *f.* (—, *no pl.*) faithlessness, unfaithfulness, disloyalty, perfidy.

untröstlich ['untrø:stliç], *adj.* inconsolable, disconsolate.

untrüglich ['untry:kliç], *adj.* unmistakable, infallible.

untüchtig ['untyçtiç], *adj.* inefficient; incompetent.

unüberlegt ['uny:bərle:kt], *adj.* inconsiderate, thoughtless; rash.

unübersehbar ['uny:bərze:ba:r], *adj.* immense, vast.

unübersteiglich ['uny:bərʃtaikliç], *adj.* insurmountable.

unübertrefflich ['uny:bərtrefliç], *adj.* unsurpassable, unequalled, unrivalled.

unübertroffen ['uny:bərtrofən], *adj.* unsurpassed.

unüberwindlich ['uny:bərvintliç], *adj.* invincible, unconquerable.

unumgänglich ['unumgɛŋliç], *adj.* indispensable, unavoidable, inevitable.

unumschränkt ['unumʃrɛŋkt], *adj.* unlimited, absolute.

unumstößlich ['unumʃtø:sliç], *adj.* irrefutable.

unumwunden ['unumvundən], *adj.* frank, plain.

ununterbrochen ['ununtərbrɔxən], *adj.* uninterrupted, unremitting.

unveränderlich ['unfɛrɛndərliç], *adj.* unchangeable, unalterable.

unverändert ['unfɛrɛndərt], *adj.* unchanged, unaltered.

unverantwortlich ['unfɛrantvortliç], *adj.* irresponsible, inexcusable, unjustifiable.

unveräußerlich ['unfɛrɔysərliç], *adj.* not for sale; inalienable.

unverbesserlich ['unfɛrbesərliç], *adj.* incorrigible.

unverbindlich ['unfɛrbintliç], *adj.* not binding, without prejudice, without obligation.

unverblümt ['unfɛrbly:mt], *adj.* blunt, point-blank.

unverbrennlich ['unfɛrbrɛnliç], *adj.* incombustible.

unverbrüchlich ['unfɛrbryçliç], *adj.* inviolable.

unverbürgt ['unfɛrbyrkt], *adj.* unwarranted, unofficial; unconfirmed.

unverdaulich ['unfɛrdauliç], *adj.* indigestible.

unverdaut ['unfɛrdaut], *adj.* undigested.

unverdient ['unfɛrdi:nt], *adj.* unmerited, undeserved.

unverdientermaßen ['unfɛrdi:ntərma:sən], *adv.* undeservedly.

unverdorben ['unfɛrdɔrbən], *adj.* unspoiled, uncorrupted, innocent.

unverdrossen ['unfɛrdrɔsən], *adj.* indefatigable.

unvereidigt ['unfɛraidiçt], *adj.* unsworn.

unvereinbar ['unfɛrainba:r], *adj.* incompatible, inconsistent.

Unvereinbarkeit

Unvereinbarkeit ['unfɛraɪnba:rkaɪt], *f.* (—, *no pl.*) incompatibility, inconsistency.

unverfälscht ['unfɛrfɛlʃt], *adj.* unadulterated, genuine, pure.

unverfänglich ['unfɛrfɛŋlɪç], *adj.* harmless.

unverfroren ['unfɛrfro:rən], *adj.* cheeky, impudent.

unvergeßlich ['unfɛrgɛslɪç], *adj.* memorable, not to be forgotten, unforgettable.

unvergleichlich ['unfɛrglaɪçlɪç], *adj.* incomparable.

unverhältnismäßig ['unfɛrhɛltnɪsmɛ:sɪç], *adj.* disproportionate.

unverheiratet ['unfɛrhaɪra:tət], *adj.* unmarried.

unverhofft ['unfɛrhɔft], *adj.* unexpected.

unverhohlen ['unfɛrho:lən], *adj.* unconcealed, undisguised, candid.

unverkennbar ['unfɛrkɛnba:r], *adj.* unmistakable.

unverlangt ['unfɛrlaŋkt], *adj.* unsolicited, not ordered.

unverletzlich ['unfɛrlɛtslɪç], *adj.* invulnerable; (*fig.*) inviolable.

unverletzt ['unfɛrlɛtst], *adj.* (*persons*) unhurt; (*things*) undamaged, intact.

unvermeidlich ['unfɛrmaɪtlɪç], *adj.* inevitable, unavoidable.

unvermindert ['unfɛrmɪndərt], *adj.* undiminished.

unvermittelt ['unfɛrmɪtəlt], *adj.* sudden, abrupt.

Unvermögen ['unfɛrmø:gən], *n.* (—s, *no pl.*) inability, incapacity.

unvermögend ['unfɛrmø:gənt], *adj.* incapable; impecunious.

unvermutet ['unfɛrmu:tət], *adj.* unexpected, unforeseen.

unverrichtet ['unfɛrrɪçtət], *adj.* —*er Sache,* empty-handed; unsuccessfully.

unverschämt ['unfɛrʃɛ:mt], *adj.* impudent, brazen.

unverschuldet ['unfɛrʃuldət], *adj.* not in debt, unencumbered; (*fig.*) undeserved.

unversehens ['unfɛrze:əns], *adv.* unexpectedly, unawares.

unversehrt ['unfɛrze:rt], *adv.* (*persons*) unhurt, safe; (*things*) undamaged.

unversiegbar ['unfɛrzi:kba:r], *adj.* inexhaustible.

unversiegt ['unfɛrzi:kt], *adj.* unexhausted.

unversöhnlich ['unfɛrzø:nlɪç], *adj.* implacable, irreconcilable.

unversöhnt ['unfɛrzø:nt], *adj.* unreconciled.

unversorgt ['unfɛrzɔrkt], *adj.* unprovided for.

Unverstand ['unfɛrʃtant], *m.* (—(e)s, *no pl.*) want of judgment, indiscretion.

unverständig ['unfɛrʃtɛndɪç], *adj.* foolish, unwise, imprudent.

unverständlich ['unfɛrʃtɛntlɪç], *adj.* unintelligible, incomprehensible.

unversteuert ['unfɛrʃtɔyərt], *adj.* with duty *or* tax unpaid.

unversucht ['unfɛrzu:xt], *adj.* untried; *nichts — lassen,* leave no stone unturned.

unverträglich ['unfɛrtrɛ:klɪç], *adj.* quarrelsome.

unverwandt ['unfɛrvant], *adj.* unrelated; fixed, constant; immovable.

unverwundbar ['unfɛrvuntba:r], *adj.* invulnerable.

unverwüstlich ['unfɛrvy:stlɪç], *adj.* indestructible.

unverzagt ['unfɛrtsa:kt], *adj.* undaunted, intrepid.

unverzeihlich ['unfɛrtsaɪlɪç], *adj.* unpardonable.

unverzinslich ['unfɛrtsɪnslɪç], *adj.* (*money*) gaining no interest.

unverzollt ['unfɛrtsɔlt], *adj.* duty unpaid.

unverzüglich ['unfɛrtsy:klɪç], *adj.* immediate.

unvollendet ['unfɔlɛndət], *adj.* unfinished.

unvollständig ['unfɔlʃtɛndɪç], *adj.* incomplete.

unvorbereitet ['unfo:rbəraɪtət], *adj.* unprepared.

unvordenklich ['unfo:rdɛŋklɪç], *adj.* *seit —en Zeiten,* from time immemorial.

unvorhergesehen ['unfo:rhe:rgəze:ən], *adj.* unforeseen, unlooked for.

unvorsichtig ['unfo:rzɪçtɪç], *adj.* imprudent, incautious, careless.

unvorteilhaft ['unfo:rtaɪlhaft], *adj.* unprofitable, disadvantageous; — *aussehen,* not look o.'s best.

unwägbar ['unvɛ:kba:r], *adj.* imponderable.

unwahr ['unva:r], *adj.* untrue, false.

Unwahrhaftigkeit ['unva:rhaftɪçkaɪt], *f.* (—, *no pl.*) want of truthfulness, unreliability, dishonesty.

Unwahrheit ['unva:rhaɪt], *f.* (—, *pl.* —en) lie, untruth, falsehood.

unwegsam ['unve:kza:m], *adj.* impassable, impracticable.

unweigerlich ['unvaɪgərlɪç], *adj.* unhesitating, unquestioning. — *adv.* without fail.

unweit ['unvaɪt], *prep.* (*Genit.*) not far from, near.

Unwesen ['unve:zən], *n.* (—s, *no pl.*) nuisance; *sein — treiben,* be up to o.'s tricks.

Unwetter ['unvɛtər], *n.* (—s, *pl.* —) bad weather, thunderstorm.

unwichtig ['unvɪçtɪç], *adj.* unimportant; insignificant, of no consequence.

unwiderleglich ['unvi:dərle:klɪç], *adj.* irrefutable.

unwiderruflich ['unvi:dərru:flɪç], *adj.* irrevocable.

unwidersprechlich ['unvi:dərʃprɛçlɪç], *adj.* incontestable.

unwidersprochen ['unvi:dərʃprɔxən], *adj.* uncontradicted.

unwiderstehlich ['unvi:dərʃte:lıç], *adj.* irresistible.

unwiederbringlich ['unvi:dərbrıŋlıç], *adj.* irrecoverable, irretrievable.

Unwille ['unvılə], *m.* (**—ns**, *no pl.*) displeasure, indignation.

unwillkürlich ['unvılky:rlıç], *adj.* involuntary; instinctive.

unwirsch ['unvırʃ], *adj.* petulant, testy; curt, uncivil.

unwirtlich ['unvırtlıç], *adj.* inhospitable.

unwirtschaftlich ['unvırtʃaftlıç], *adj.* not economic, uneconomic.

unwissend ['unvısənt], *adj.* illiterate, ignorant.

Unwissenheit ['unvısənhaıt], *f.* (—, *no pl.*) ignorance.

unwissenschaftlich ['unvısənʃaftlıç], *adj.* unscholarly; unscientific.

unwissentlich ['unvısəntlıç], *adv.* unknowingly, unconsciously.

unwohl ['unvo:l], *adj.* unwell, indisposed.

Unwohlsein ['unvo:lzaın], *n.* (**—s**, *no pl.*) indisposition.

unwürdig ['unvyrdıç], *adj.* unworthy, undeserving.

Unzahl ['untsa:l], *f.* (—, *no pl.*) vast number.

unzählbar [un'tsɛ:lba:r], *adj.* innumerable, numberless.

unzählig [un'tsɛ:lıç], *adj.* innumerable; —*e Male*, over and over again.

unzart ['untsa:rt], *adj.* indelicate, rude, rough; unceremonious.

Unzeit ['untsaıt], *f.* (—, *no pl.*) *zur* —, out of season, inopportunely.

unzeitgemäß ['untsaıtgəmɛ:s], *adj.* out of date, behind the times; unfashionable.

unzeitig ['untsaıtıç], *adj.* unseasonable; untimely, inopportune.

unziemlich ['untsi:mlıç], *adj.* unseemly, unbecoming.

Unzier ['untsi:r], *f.* (—, *no pl.*) disfigurement; flaw.

Unzucht ['untsuxt], *f.* (—, *no pl.*) unchastity; lewdness; fornication.

unzüchtig ['untsyçtıç], *adj.* unchaste, lascivious, lewd.

unzufrieden ['untsufri:dən], *adj.* discontented, dissatisfied.

unzugänglich ['untsugeŋlıç], *adj.* inaccessible.

unzulänglich ['untsuleŋlıç], *adj.* inadequate, insufficient.

Unzulänglichkeit ['untsuleŋlıçkaıt], *f.* (—, *no pl.*) inadequacy.

unzulässig ['untsulesıç], *adj.* inadmissible.

unzurechnungsfähig ['untsurɛçnuŋsfɛ:ıç], *adj.* not accountable (for o.'s actions), non compos mentis, insane.

Unzurechnungsfähigkeit ['untsurɛçnuŋsfɛ:ıçkaıt], *f.* (—, *no pl.*) irresponsibility; feeblemindedness.

unzusammenhängend ['untsuzamənhɛŋənt], *adj.* incoherent.

unzuständig ['untsuʃtendıç], *adj.* incompetent, not competent (*Law etc.*).

unzuträglich ['untsutre:klıç], *adj.* unwholesome.

unzutreffend ['untsutrefənt], *adj.* inapposite; unfounded; inapplicable.

unzuverlässig ['untsuferlesıç], *adj.* unreliable.

unzweckmäßig ['untsvɛkmɛ:sıç], *adj.* inexpedient.

unzweideutig ['untsvaıdɔytıç], *adj.* unequivocal, explicit, unambiguous.

üppig ['ypıç], *adj.* abundant; opulent, luxurious, luxuriant, voluptuous.

uralt ['u:ralt], *adj.* very old, old as the hills; ancient.

uranfänglich ['u:ranfɛŋlıç], *adj.* primordial, primeval.

Uraufführung ['u:rauffy:ruŋ], *f.* (—, *pl.* —en) (*Theat.*) first night, première.

urbar ['u:rba:r], *adj.* arable, under cultivation; — *machen*, cultivate.

Urbarmachung ['u:rba:rmaxuŋ], *f.* (—, *no pl.*) cultivation.

Urbild ['u:rbılt], *n.* (**—(e)s**, *pl.* **—er**) prototype; (*fig.*) ideal.

ureigen ['u:raıgən], *adj.* quite original; idiosyncratic.

Ureltern ['u:rɛltərn], *pl.* ancestors.

Urenkel ['u:rɛŋkəl], *m.* (**—s**, *pl.* —) great-grandson, great-grandchild.

Urenkelin ['u:rɛŋkəlın], *f.* (—, *pl.* **—nen**) great-granddaughter.

Urfehde ['u:rfe:də], *f.* (—, *no pl.*) oath to keep the peace.

Urform ['u:rfɔrm], *f.* (—, *pl.* **—en**) primitive form; original form; archetype.

Urgroßmutter ['u:rgro:smutər], *f.* (—, *pl.* ⁀) great-grandmother.

Urgroßvater ['u:rgro:sfa:tər], *m.* (**—s**, *pl.* ⁀) great-grandfather.

Urheber ['u:rhe:bər], *m.* (**—s**, *pl.* —) author, originator.

Urheberrecht ['u:rhe:bərrɛçt], *n.* (**—s**, *pl.* **—e**) copyright.

Urheberschaft ['u:rhe:bərʃaft], *f.* (—, *no pl.*) authorship.

Urin [u'ri:n], *m.* (**—s**, *no pl.*) urine.

Urkunde ['u:rkundə], *f.* (—, *pl.* **—n**) document, deed, charter; *zur* — *dessen*, (*obs.*) in witness whereof.

Urkundenbeweis ['u:rkundənbəvaıs], *m.* (**—es**, *pl.* **—e**) documentary evidence.

urkundlich ['u:rkuntlıç], *adj.* documentary.

Urlaub ['u:rlaup], *m.* (**—s**, *pl.* **—e**) leave of absence; vacation; (*Mil.*) furlough.

urplötzlich ['u:rplœtslıç], *adj.* sudden. — *adv.* all at once, suddenly.

Urquell ['u:rkvɛl], *m.* (**—s**, *pl.* **—en**) fountain-head, original source.

Ursache ['u:rzaxa], *f.* (—, *pl.* **—n**) cause; *keine* —, don't mention it.

Urschrift ['u:rʃrıft], *f.* (—, *pl.* **—en**) original text.

Ursprache ['u:rʃpra:xə], *f.* (—, *pl.* **—n**) original language.

Ursprung ['u:rʃpruŋ], *m.* (**—s**, *pl.* ⁀e) origin; extraction.

249

ursprünglich [ˈuːrʃpryŋlɪç], *adj.* original.

Urteil [ˈurtaɪl], *n.* (—s, *pl.* —e) opinion; (*Law*) judgment, verdict, sentence; *ein — fällen*, pass judgment on; *nach meinem —*, in my opinion.

urteilen [ˈurtaɪlən], *v.n.* judge.

Urteilsspruch [ˈurtaɪlsʃprux], *m.* (—s, *pl.* ⁓e) judgment, sentence.

Uruguay [uruˈgwaːɪ], *n.* Uruguay.

Urureltern [ˈuːruːrɛltərn], *pl.* ancestors.

Urvater [ˈuːrfaːtər], *m.* (—s, *pl.* ⁓) forefather.

Urvolk [ˈuːrfɔlk], *n.* (—(e)s, *pl.* ⁓er) primitive people, aborigines.

Urwald [ˈuːrvalt], *m.* (—(e)s, *pl.* ⁓er) primæval forest, virgin forest.

Urwelt [ˈuːrvɛlt], *f.* (—, *no pl.*) primæval world.

Urzeit [ˈuːrtsaɪt], *f.* (—, *pl.* —en) prehistoric times.

V

V [fau], *n.* (—s, *pl.* —s) the letter V.

vag [vaːk], *adj.* vague.

Vagabund [vagaˈbunt], *m.* (—en, *pl.* —en) vagabond, tramp; (*Am.*) hobo.

Vakuumbremse [ˈvaːkuumbrɛmzə], *f.* (—, *pl.* —n) air-brake, vacuum-brake.

Vase [ˈvaːzə], *f.* (—, *pl.* —n) vase.

Vater [ˈfaːtər], *m.* (—s, *pl.* ⁓) father.

Vaterland [ˈfaːtərlant], *n.* (—(e)s, *pl.* ⁓er) mother-country, native country; *—sliebe*, patriotism.

vaterländisch [ˈfaːtərlendɪʃ], *adj.* patriotic.

vaterlandslos [ˈfaːtərlantsloːs], *adj.* having no mother country; unpatriotic.

väterlich [ˈfɛːtərlɪç], *adj.* fatherly, paternal. — *adv.* like a father.

vaterlos [ˈfaːtərloːs], *adj.* fatherless.

Vatermord [ˈfaːtərmɔrt], *m.* (—(e)s, *pl.* —e) parricide; patricide.

Vatermörder [ˈfaːtərmœrdər], *m.* (—s, *pl.* —) parricide; (*fig.*) high *or* stand-up collar.

Vaterschaft [ˈfaːtərʃaft], *f.* (—, *no pl.*) paternity.

Vatersname [ˈfaːtərsnaːmə], *m.* (—ns, *pl.* —n) surname, family name.

Vaterstadt [ˈfaːtərʃtat], *f.* (—, *pl.* ⁓e) native town.

Vaterstelle [ˈfaːtərʃtelə], *f.* (—, *pl.* —n) — *vertreten*, act as a father, be a father (to).

Vaterunser [faːtərˈunzər], *n.* (—s, *pl.* —) Lord's Prayer.

Vatikan [vatiˈkaːn], *m.* (—s, *no pl.*) Vatican.

vegetieren [vegeˈtiːrən], *v.n.* vegetate.

Veilchen [ˈfaɪlçən], *n.* (—s, *pl.* —) (*Bot.*) violet.

Vene [ˈveːnə], *f.* (—, *pl.* —n) vein.

Venezuela [vɛnɛtsuˈeːla], *n.* Venezuela.

Ventil [vɛnˈtiːl], *n.* (—s, *pl.* —e) valve.

ventilieren [vɛntiˈliːrən], *v.a.* ventilate, air; (*fig.*) discuss, ventilate.

verabfolgen [fɛrˈapfɔlgən], *v.a.* deliver, hand over, remit; serve.

Verabfolgung [fɛrˈapfɔlguŋ], *f.* (—, *no pl.*) delivery.

verabreden [fɛrˈapreːdən], *v.a.* agree (upon); stipulate; *etwas mit einem —*, agree on s.th. with s.o. — *v.r. sich mit einem —*, make an appointment with s.o.; (*coll.*) have a date.

Verabredung [fɛrˈapreːduŋ], *f.* (—, *pl.* —en) agreement, arrangement, appointment; (*coll.*) date.

verabreichen [fɛrˈapraɪçən], *v.a.* deliver, dispense.

verabsäumen [fɛrˈapzɔymən], *v.a.* neglect, omit.

verabscheuen [fɛrˈapʃɔyən], *v.a.* detest, loathe, abhor.

Verabscheuung [fɛrˈapʃɔyuŋ], *f.* (—, *no pl.*) abhorrence, detestation, loathing.

verabscheuungswürdig [fɛrˈapʃɔyuŋsvyrdɪç], *adj.* abominable, detestable.

verabschieden [fɛrˈapʃiːdən], *v.a.* dismiss, discharge. — *v.r. sich —*, take leave, say good-bye; (*Pol.*) pass (of an Act).

Verabschiedung [fɛrˈapʃiːduŋ], *f.* (—, *no pl.*) dismissal; discharge; (*Pol.*) passing (of an Act).

verachten [fɛrˈaxtən], *v.a.* despise, scorn.

verächtlich [fɛrˈɛçtlɪç], *adj.* despicable, contemptible; contemptuous, scornful.

Verachtung [fɛrˈaxtuŋ], *f.* (—, *no pl.*) contempt, disdain, scorn.

verallgemeinern [fɛralgəˈmaɪnərn], *v.a., v.n.* generalise.

veralten [fɛrˈaltən], *v.n.* (*aux.* sein) become obsolete, date.

veraltet [fɛrˈaltət], *adj.* obsolete.

Veranda [veˈranda], *f.* (—, *pl.* —den) verandah, porch.

veränderlich [fɛrˈɛndərlɪç], *adj.* changeable, variable; (*fig.*) inconstant, fickle.

verändern [fɛrˈɛndərn], *v.a.* change, alter. — *v.r. sich —*, change, vary; change o.'s job.

verankern [fɛrˈaŋkərn], *v.a.* anchor.

veranlagt [fɛrˈanlaːkt], *adj.* inclined; gifted; having a propensity (to); *gut —*, talented; (*tax*) assessed.

Veranlagung [fɛrˈanlaːguŋ], *f.* (—, *pl.* —en) bent; talent; predisposition; (*tax*) assessment.

veranlassen [fɛrˈanlasən], *v.a.* bring about, cause, motivate; *einen —*, induce s.o., cause s.o.; *etwas —*, bring s.th. about, cause s.th.

Veranlassung [fɛr'anlasuŋ], *f.* (—, *no pl.*) cause, motive; occasion; inducement; *auf seine* —, at his suggestion; *ohne irgend eine* —, without the slightest provocation.

veranschaulichen [fɛr'anʃaulɪçən], *v.a.* illustrate, make clear.

veranschlagen [fɛr'anʃla:gən], *v.a.* estimate, assess.

Veranschlagung [fɛr'anʃla:guŋ], *f.* (—, *pl.* —en) estimate.

veranstalten [fɛr'anʃtaltən], *v.a.* organise, arrange.

Veranstalter [fɛr'anʃtaltər], *m.* (—s, *pl.* —) organiser.

Veranstaltung [fɛr'anʃtaltuŋ], *f.* (—, *pl.* —en) arrangement; entertainment; show; event; (sporting) fixture.

verantworten [fɛr'antvɔrtən], *v.a.* account for. — *v.r. sich* —, answer (for), justify o.s.

verantwortlich [fɛr'antvɔrtlɪç], *adj.* responsible, answerable, accountable.

Verantwortlichkeit [fɛr'antvɔrtlɪçkait], *f.* (—, *no pl.*) responeibility.

Verantwortung [fɛr'antvɔrtuŋ], *f.* (—, *no pl.*) responsibility, justification, excuse; defence; *auf deine* —, at your own risk; *einen zur* — *ziehen,* call s.o. to account.

verantwortungsvoll [fɛr'antvɔrtuŋs-fɔl], *adj.* responsible.

verarbeiten [fɛr'arbaitən], *v.a.* manufacture, process; (*fig.*) digest.

Verarbeitung [fɛr'arbaituŋ], *f.* (—, *no pl.*) manufacture; process; finish; (*fig.*) digestion.

verargen [fɛr'argən], *v.a. einem etwas* —, blame or reproach s.o. for s.th.

verärgern [fɛr'ɛrgərn], *v.a.* annoy, make angry.

Verarmung [fɛr'armuŋ], *f.* (—, *no pl.*) impoverishment.

verausgaben [fɛr'ausga:bən], *v.r. sich* —, overspend, run short of money; spend o.s., wear o.s. out.

veräußern [fɛːˈɔysərn], *v.a.* dispose of, sell.

Veräußerung [fɛːˈɔysəruŋ], *f.* (—, *no pl.*) sale; alienation.

Verband [fɛr'bant], *m.* (—s, *pl.* ̈e) bandage, dressing; association, union; unit.

verbannen [fɛr'banən], *v.a.* banish, exile, outlaw.

Verbannte [fɛr'bantə], *m.* (—n, *pl.* —n) exile, outlaw.

Verbannung [fɛr'banuŋ], *f.* (—, *pl.* —en) banishment, exile.

verbauen [fɛr'bauən], *v.n.* obstruct; build up; use up or spend in building.

verbeißen [fɛr'baisən], *v.a. irr. sich etwas* —, suppress s.th.; *sich das Lachen* —, stifle a laugh. — *v.r. sich in etwas* —, stick doggedly to s.th.

verbergen [fɛr'bɛrgən], *v.a. irr.* conceal, hide.

verbessern [fɛr'bɛsərn], *v.a.* improve, correct, mend.

Verbesserung [fɛr'bɛsəruŋ], *f.* (—, *pl.* —en) improvement; correction.

verbeugen [fɛr'bɔygən], *v.r. sich* —, bow.

Verbeugung [fɛr'bɔyguŋ], *f.* (—, *pl.* —en) bow, obeisance.

verbiegen [fɛr'bi:gən], *v.a. irr.* twist, distort, bend the wrong way.

verbieten [fɛr'bi:tən], *v.a. irr.* forbid, prohibit.

verbilligen [fɛr'bɪlɪgən], *v.a.* cheapen, reduce the price of.

verbinden [fɛr'bɪndən], *v.a. irr.* tie up, bind up, connect; (*Med.*) dress, bandage; unite, join; *die Augen* —, blindfold. — *v.r. sich* —, unite, join; (*Chem.*) combine.

verbindlich [fɛr'bɪntlɪç], *adj.* binding; obligatory; obliging; —*en Dank,* my best thanks.

Verbindlichkeit [fɛr'bɪntlɪçkait], *f.* (—, *pl.* —en) liability, obligation; compliment.

Verbindung [fɛr'bɪnduŋ], *f.* (—, *pl.* —en) connexion, connection, junction; association; alliance; (*Railw.*) connection; (*Chem.*) compound.

Verbindungsglied [fɛr'bɪnduŋsgli:t], *n.* (—(e)s, *pl.* —er) connecting link.

Verbindungslinie [fɛr'bɪnduŋsli:njə], *f.* (—, *pl.* —n) line of communication.

verbissen [fɛr'bɪsən], *adj.* obstinate, grim; soured. — *adv.* doggedly.

verbitten [fɛr'bɪtən], *v.a. irr. sich etwas* —, forbid s.th. determinedly; insist on s.th. not being done, object to.

verbittern [fɛr'bɪtərn], *v.a.* embitter.

Verbitterung [fɛr'bɪtəruŋ], *f.* (—, *no pl.*) exasperation.

verblassen [fɛr'blasən], *v.n.* (*aux. sein*) turn pale.

Verbleib [fɛr'blaip], *m.* (—(e)s, *no pl.*) whereabouts.

verbleiben [fɛr'blaibən], *v.n. irr.* (*aux. sein*) remain.

verblenden [fɛr'blɛndən], *v.a.* dazzle, delude, blind.

Verblendung [fɛr'blɛnduŋ], *f.* (—, *no pl.*) infatuation; delusion.

verblüffen [fɛr'blyfən], *v.n.* amaze, stagger, dumbfound.

Verblüffung [fɛr'blyfuŋ], *f.* (—, *no pl.*) bewilderment.

verblühen [fɛr'bly:ən], *v.n.* (*aux. sein*) wither, fade.

verblümt [fɛr'bly:mt], *adj.* veiled.

verbluten [fɛr'blu:tən], *v.n.* (*aux. sein*) bleed to death.

verborgen (1) [fɛr'bɔrgən], *v.a.* lend out.

verborgen (2) [fɛr'bɔrgən], *adj.* concealed, hidden; *im* —*en,* secretly.

Verborgenheit [fɛr'bɔrgənhait], *f.* (—, *no pl.*) concealment, seclusion.

Verbot [fɛr'bo:t], *n.* (—(e)s, *pl.* —e) prohibition.

verboten [fɛr'bo:tən], *adj.* forbidden, prohibited.

verbrämen [fɛr'brɛ:mən], *v.a.* (*garment*) edge, border.

verbrauchen

verbrauchen [fɛr'brauxən], *v.a.* consume, use up; spend.
Verbraucher [fɛr'brauxər], *m.* (—s, *pl.* —) consumer.
Verbrechen [fɛr'brɛçən], *n.* (—s, *pl.* —) crime.
verbrechen [fɛr'brɛçən], *v.a. irr.* commit, perpetrate.
Verbrecher [fɛr'brɛçər], *m.* (—s, *pl.* —) criminal.
Verbrecheralbum [fɛr'brɛçəralbum], *n.* (—s, *no pl.*) rogues' gallery.
verbreiten [fɛr'braItən], *v.a.* spread, diffuse.
verbreitern [fɛr'braItərn], *v.a.* widen.
Verbreitung [fɛr'braItuŋ], *f.* (—, *no pl.*) spread(ing), propaganda, extension.
verbrennbar [fɛr'brɛnba:r], *adj.* combustible.
verbrennen [fɛr'brɛnən], *v.a. irr.* burn; cremate; *von der Sonne verbrannt,* sunburnt. — *v.n.* (*aux.* sein) get burnt. — *v.r. sich* —, scald o.s., burn o.s.
Verbrennung [fɛr'brɛnuŋ], *f.* (—, *pl.* —en) burning, combustion; cremation.
verbrieft [fɛr'bri:ft], *adj.* vested; documented.
verbringen [fɛr'brIŋən], *v.a. irr.* (*time*) spend, pass.
verbrüdern [fɛr'bry:dərn], *v.r. sich* —, fraternise.
verbrühen [fɛr'bry:ən], *v.a.* scald.
verbummeln [fɛr'buməln], *v.a. die Zeit* —, fritter the time away.
verbunden [fɛr'bundən], *adj. einem* — *sein,* be obliged to s.o.
verbünden [fɛr'byndən], *v.r. sich* — *mit,* ally o.s. with.
Verbündete [fɛr'byndətə], *m.* (—n, *pl.* —n) ally, confederate.
verbürgen [fɛr'byrgən], *v.a.* warrant, guarantee. — *v.r. sich für etwas* —, vouch for s.th.; guarantee s.th.
Verdacht [fɛr'daxt], *m.* (—(e)s, *no pl.*) suspicion.
verdächtig [fɛr'dɛçtIç], *adj.* suspicious, doubtful, questionable.
verdächtigen [fɛr'dɛçtIgən], *v.a.* throw suspicion on, suspect.
verdammen [fɛr'damən], *v.a.* condemn, damn.
verdammenswert [fɛr'damənsve:rt], *adj.* damnable.
Verdammung [fɛr'damuŋ], *f.* (—, *no pl.*) condemnation.
verdampfen [fɛr'dampfən], *v.n.* (*aux.* sein) evaporate.
verdanken [fɛr'daŋkən], *v.a. einem etwas* —, be indebted to s.o. for s.th.; owe s.th. to s.o.
verdauen [fɛr'dauən], *v.a.* digest.
verdaulich [fɛr'daulIç], *adj.* digestible.
Verdauung [fɛr'dauuŋ], *f.* (—, *no pl.*) digestion.
Verdauungsstörung [fɛr'dauuŋʃtø:-ruŋ], *f.* (—, *pl.* —en) indigestion.
Verdeck [fɛr'dɛk], *n.* (—s, *pl.* —e) awning; (*Naut.*) deck.

verdecken [fɛr'dɛkən], *v.a.* cover, hide.
verdenken [fɛr'dɛŋkən], *v.a. irr. einem etwas* —, blame s.o. for s.th.
Verderb [fɛr'dɛrp], *m.* (—s, *no pl.*) ruin, decay.
verderben [fɛr'dɛrbən], *v.a. irr.* spoil, corrupt, pervert. — *v.n.* (*aux.* sein) decay, go bad.
Verderben [fɛr'dɛrbən], *n.* (—s, *no pl.*) corruption, ruin.
Verderber [fɛr'dɛrbər], *m.* (—s, *pl.*—) corrupter, perverter.
verderblich [fɛr'dɛrplIç], *adj.* ruinous, pernicious, destructive; (*goods*) perishable.
Verderbnis [fɛr'dɛrpnIs], *f.* (—, *no pl.*) corruption, depravity; perversion; perdition.
Verderbtheit [fɛr'dɛrpthaIt], *f.* (—, *no pl.*) corruption, perversion, depravity.
verdeutlichen [fɛr'dɔytlIçən], *v.a.* illustrate, clarify.
verdichten [fɛr'dIçtən], *v.a., v.r.* thicken, condense, liquefy.
Verdichtung [fɛr'dIçtuŋ], *f.* (—, *no pl.*) condensation; solidification.
verdicken [fɛr'dIkən], *v.a.* thicken; solidify.
verdienen [fɛr'di:nən], *v.a.* earn; deserve.
Verdienst (1) [fɛr'di:nst], *m.* (—es, *pl.* —e) profit, gain, earnings.
Verdienst (2) [fɛr'di:nst], *n.* (—es, *pl.* —e) merit, deserts.
verdienstvoll [fɛr'di:nstfɔl], *adj.* meritorious, deserving; distinguished.
verdient [fɛr'di:nt], *adj. sich* — *machen um,* deserve well of, serve well (a cause etc.).
verdientermaßen [fɛr'di:ntərmasən], *adv.* deservedly.
verdingen [fɛr'dIŋən], *v.r. irr. sich* —, enter service (with), take a situation (with).
verdolmetschen [fɛr'dɔlmɛtʃən], *v.a.* interpret, translate.
verdoppeln [fɛr'dɔpəln], *v.a.* double.
verdorben [fɛr'dɔrbən], *adj.* spoilt; corrupted, depraved, debauched.
verdrängen [fɛr'drɛŋən], *v.a.* crowd out; (*Phys.*) displace; (*fig.*) supplant, supersede; (*Psych.*) inhibit, repress.
Verdrängung [fɛr'drɛŋuŋ], *f.* (—, *no pl.*) supplanting; (*Phys.*) displacement; (*Psych.*) inhibition, repression.
verdrehen [fɛr'dre:ən], *v.a.* twist (the wrong way); (*fig.*) misrepresent, distort.
verdreht [fɛr'dre:t], *adj.* cracked, cranky, crazy, queer.
Verdrehtheit [fɛr'dre:thaIt], *f.* (—, *no pl.*) crankiness.
Verdrehung [fɛr'dre:uŋ], *f.* (—, *pl.* —en) distortion; (*fig.*) misrepresentation.
verdrießen [fɛr'dri:sən], *v.a. irr.* vex, annoy.
verdrießlich [fɛr'dri:slIç], *adj.* (*thing*) vexatious, tiresome; (*person*) morose, peevish.

verdrossen [fɛr'drɔsən], *adj.* annoyed; fretful, sulky.

Verdrossenheit [fɛr'drɔsənhaɪt], *f.* (—, *no pl.*) annoyance; fretfulness, sulkiness.

verdrücken [fɛr'drykən], *v.a.* (*sl.*) eat o.'s fill of. — *v.r.* (*coll.*) sich —, slink away; sneak away.

Verdruß [fɛr'drus], *m.* (—sses, *no pl.*) vexation, annoyance; — *bereiten*, give trouble, cause annoyance.

verduften [fɛr'duftən], *v.n.* (*aux.* sein) evaporate; (*fig.*) (*coll.*) take French leave, clear out.

verdummen [fɛr'dumən], *v.n.* (*aux.* sein) become stupid.

verdunkeln [fɛr'duŋkəln], *v.a.* black-out, obscure; (*fig.*) eclipse.

Verdunk(e)lung [fɛr'duŋk(ə)luŋ], *f.* (—, *no pl.*) darkening, eclipse; black-out.

Verdunk(e)lungsgefahr [vɛr'duŋk(ə)-luŋsɡəfaːr], *f.* (—, *no pl.*) (*Law*) danger of prejudicing the course *or* administration of justice.

verdünnen [fɛr'dynən], *v.a.* thin out, dilute.

Verdünnung [fɛr'dynuŋ], *f.* (—, *no pl.*) attenuation; dilution.

verdunsten [fɛr'dunstən], *v.n.* (*aux.* sein) evaporate.

verdursten [fɛr'durstən], *v.n.* (*aux.* sein) die of thirst, perish with thirst.

verdüstern [fɛr'dyːstərn], *v.a.* darken, make gloomy.

verdutzen [fɛr'dutsən], *v.a.* disconcert, bewilder, nonplus.

Veredlung [fɛr'eːdluŋ], *f.* (—, *no pl.*) improvement, refinement.

verehelichen [fɛr'eːəlɪçən], *v.r.* (*obs.*) sich —, get married.

verehren [fɛr'eːrən], *v.a.* respect, revere, esteem; worship, adore.

Verehrer [fɛr'eːrər], *m.* (—s, *pl.* —) admirer; lover.

verehrlich [fɛr'eːrlɪç], *adj.* venerable.

verehrt [fɛr'eːrt], *adj.* honoured; *sehr —er Herr*, dear Sir.

Verehrung [fɛr'eːruŋ], *f.* (—, *no pl.*) reverence, veneration; worship, adoration.

verehrungswürdig [fɛr'eːruŋsvyrdɪç], *adj.* venerable.

vereidigt [fɛr'aɪdɪçt], *adj.* sworn in, bound by oath, under oath; *—er Bücherrevisor*, chartered accountant.

Vereidigung [fɛr'aɪdɪguŋ], *f.* (—, *no pl.*) swearing in; oathtaking.

Verein [fɛr'aɪn], *m.* (—s, *pl.* —e) union, association, society; club.

vereinbar [fɛr'aɪnbaːr], *adj.* compatible.

vereinbaren [fɛr'aɪnbaːrən], *v.a.* agree upon, arrange.

Vereinbarung [fɛr'aɪnbaːruŋ], *f.* (—, *pl.* —en) arrangement, agreement.

vereinen [fɛr'aɪnən], *v.a.* unite.

vereinfachen [fɛr'aɪnfaxən], *v.a.* simplify.

vereinigen [fɛr'aɪnɪgən], *v.a.* unite. — *v.r.* sich — *mit*, associate o.s. with, join with.

Vereinigung [fɛr'aɪnɪguŋ], *f.* (—, *pl.* —en) union; association.

vereinnahmen [fɛr'aɪnnaːmən], *v.a.* receive, take (*money*).

vereinsamen [fɛr'aɪnzaːmən], *v.n.* (*aux.* sein) become isolated, become lonely.

vereint [fɛr'aɪnt], *adj.* united, joined. — *adv.* in concert, (all) together.

vereinzelt [fɛr'aɪntsəlt], *adj.* sporadic, isolated. — *adv.* here and there, now and then.

Vereinzelung [fɛr'aɪntsəluŋ], *f.* (—, *pl.* —en) isolation; individualization.

vereisen [fɛr'aɪzən], *v.n.* become frozen, freeze; congeal.

Vereisung [fɛr'aɪzuŋ], *f.* (—, *pl.* —en) freezing, icing (up).

vereiteln [fɛr'aɪtəln], *v.a.* frustrate, thwart.

Vereitelung [fɛr'aɪtəluŋ], *f.* (—, *pl.* —en) frustration, thwarting.

vereitern [fɛr'aɪtərn], *v.n.* suppurate.

Vereiterung [fɛr'aɪtəruŋ], *f.* (—, *pl.* —en) suppuration.

verenden [fɛr'ɛndən], *v.n.* (*aux.* sein) (*animal*) die.

verengen [fɛr'ɛŋən], *v.a.* narrow, straighten, constrict.

Verengung [fɛr'ɛŋuŋ], *f.* (—, *pl.* —en) narrowing, straightening, contraction.

vererben [fɛr'ɛrbən], *v.a.* leave (by will), bequeath. — *v.r.* sich — *auf*, devolve upon, be hereditary.

vererblich [fɛr'ɛrplɪç], *adj.* (in)heritable, hereditary.

Vererbung [fɛr'ɛrbuŋ], *f.* (—, *no pl.*) heredity.

verewigen [fɛr'eːvɪgən], *v.a.* immortalise.

Verewigte [fɛr'eːvɪçtə], *m.* (—n, *pl.* —n) (*Poet.*) deceased.

Verfahren [fɛr'faːrən], *n.* (—s, *pl.* —) process; (*Law*) procedure; proceedings; *das — einstellen*, quash proceedings.

verfahren [fɛr'faːrən], *v.n. irr.* (*aux.* sein) proceed, act, operate. — *v.a.* spend (*money etc.*) on travelling. — *v.r.* sich —, (*Motor.*) lose o.'s way.

Verfall [fɛr'fal], *m.* (—s, *no pl.*) decay, decline; downfall, ruin; (*Comm.*) expiration, maturity; *in — geraten*, fall into ruin, decay.

verfallen [fɛr'falən], *v.n. irr.* (*aux.* sein) decay; go to ruin; lapse; (*Comm.*) fall due, expire; (*pledge*) become forfeit; *einem —*, become the property of, accrue to, devolve upon s.o.; (*fig.*) become the slave of s.o.; (*health*) decline, fail; *auf etwas —*, hit upon an idea. — *adj.* decayed, ruined.

Verfalltag [fɛr'faltaːk], *m.* (—s, *pl.* —e) day of payment; maturity.

verfälschen [fɛr'fɛlʃən], *v.a.* falsify; adulterate.

Verfälschung [fɛr'fɛlʃuŋ], *f.* (—, *pl.* —en) falsification; adulteration.

verfangen [fɛrˈfaŋən], *v.r. irr. sich* —, get entangled; *sich in ein Lügennetz* —, entangle o.s. in a tissue of lies.

verfänglich [fɛrˈfɛŋlɪç], *adj.* risky; insidious.

verfärben [fɛrˈfɛrbən], *v.r. sich* —, change colour.

verfassen [fɛrˈfasən], *v.a.* compose, write, be the author of.

Verfasser [fɛrˈfasər], *m.* (—s, *pl.* —) author, writer.

Verfassung [fɛrˈfasuŋ], *f.* (—, *pl.* —en) composition; (*state*) constitution; state, condition, disposition.

verfassungsgemäß [fɛrˈfasuŋsɡəmɛːs], *adj.* constitutional.

verfassungswidrig [fɛrˈfasuŋsviːdrɪç], *adj.* unconstitutional.

verfaulen [fɛrˈfaulən], *v.n.* (*aux.* sein) rot, putrefy.

verfechten [fɛrˈfɛçtən], *v.a. irr.* defend, advocate; maintain.

verfehlen [fɛrˈfeːlən], *v.a.* fail, miss; fail to meet; fail to do; *den Weg* —, lose o.'s way.

verfehlt [fɛrˈfeːlt], *adj.* unsuccessful, false, abortive; *eine* —*e Sache*, a failure.

Verfehlung [fɛrˈfeːluŋ], *f.* (—, *pl.* —en) lapse.

verfeinern [fɛrˈfainərn], *v.a.* refine, improve.

Verfeinerung [fɛrˈfainəruŋ], *f.* (—, *pl.* —en) refinement, polish.

verfertigen [fɛrˈfɛrtɪɡən], *v.a.* make, manufacture.

verfilmen [fɛrˈfɪlmən], *v.a.* make a film of, film.

verfinstern [fɛrˈfɪnstərn], *v.r. sich* —, get dark; be eclipsed.

verflechten [fɛrˈflɛçtən], *v.a. irr.* interweave, interlace. — *v.r. sich* —, (*fig.*) become entangled, become involved.

verfließen [fɛrˈfliːsən], *v.n. irr.* (*aux.* sein) flow away; (*time*) elapse, pass.

verflossen [fɛrˈflɔsən], *adj.* past, bygone.

verfluchen [fɛrˈfluːxən], *v.a.* curse, execrate.

verflucht [fɛrˈfluːxt], *excl.* damn!

verflüchtigen [fɛrˈflʏçtɪɡən], *v.r. sich* —, become volatile; evaporate; (*coll.*) make off, make o.s. scarce.

Verfluchung [fɛrˈfluːxuŋ], *f.* (—, *pl.* —en) malediction, curse.

Verfolg [fɛrˈfɔlk], *m.* (—(e)s, *no pl.*) progress, course.

verfolgen [fɛrˈfɔlɡən], *v.a.* pursue; persecute; prosecute.

Verfolger [fɛrˈfɔlɡər], *m.* (—s, *pl.* —) pursuer; persecutor.

Verfolgung [fɛrˈfɔlɡuŋ], *f.* (—, *pl.* —en) pursuit; persecution; prosecution.

Verfolgungswahn [fɛrˈfɔlɡuŋsvaːn], *m.* (—s, *no pl.*) persecution mania.

verfrüht [fɛrˈfryːt], *adj.* premature.

verfügbar [fɛrˈfyːkbaːr], *adj.* available.

verfügen [fɛrˈfyːɡən], *v.a.* decree, order. — *v.n.* — *über etwas*, have control of s.th, have s.th. at o.'s disposal.

Verfügung [fɛrˈfyːɡuŋ], *f.* (—, *pl.* —en) decree, ordinance; disposition, disposal; *einem zur* — *stehen*, be at s.o.'s service *or* disposal.

verführen [fɛrˈfyːrən], *v.a.* seduce.

verführerisch [fɛrˈfyːrərɪʃ], *adj.* seductive, alluring; (*coll.*) fetching.

Verführung [fɛrˈfyːruŋ], *f.* (—, *no pl.*) seduction.

vergällen [fɛrˈɡɛlən], *v.a.* spoil, mar.

vergallopieren [fɛrɡaloˈpiːrən], *v.r.* (*coll.*) *sich* —, blunder, overshoot the mark.

vergangen [fɛrˈɡaŋən], *adj.* past, gone, last.

Vergangenheit [fɛrˈɡaŋənhait], *f.* (—, *no pl.*) past, time past; (*Gram.*) past tense.

vergänglich [fɛrˈɡɛŋlɪç], *adj.* transient, transitory.

Vergaser [fɛrˈɡaːzər], *m.* (—s, *pl.* —) (*Motor.*) carburettor.

vergeben [fɛrˈɡeːbən], *v.a. irr.* give away; forgive, pardon; confer, bestow.

vergebens [fɛrˈɡeːbəns], *adv.* in vain, vainly.

vergeblich [fɛrˈɡeːplɪç], *adj.* vain, futile, fruitless. — *adv.* in vain.

Vergebung [fɛrˈɡeːbuŋ], *f.* (—, *no pl.*) forgiveness, pardon; (*office*) bestowal.

vergegenwärtigen [fɛrɡeːɡənˈvɛrtɪɡən], *v.a.* bring to mind, imagine.

Vergehen [fɛrˈɡeːən], *n.* (—s, *pl.* —) offence lapse.

vergehen [fɛrˈɡeːən], *v.n. irr.* (*aux.* sein) go away, pass (away); elapse; perish; (*time*) pass. — *v.r. sich* —, go wrong; offend; violate (*Law, person*).

vergelten [fɛrˈɡɛltən], *v.a. irr.* repay, reward, recompense.

Vergeltung [fɛrˈɡɛltuŋ], *f.* (—, *no pl.*) requital, retribution; reward, recompense.

vergessen [fɛrˈɡɛsən], *v.a. irr.* forget; *bei einem* —, leave behind.

Vergessenheit [fɛrˈɡɛsənhait], *f.* (— *no pl.*) oblivion.

vergeßlich [fɛrˈɡɛslɪç], *adj.* forgetful.

vergeuden [fɛrˈɡɔydən], *v.a.* waste, squander.

vergewaltigen [fɛrɡəˈvaltɪɡən], *v.a.* assault criminally, rape, violate; (*fig.*) coerce, force.

Vergewaltigung [fɛrɡəˈvaltɪɡuŋ], *f.* (—, *no pl.*) criminal assault, rape; (*fig.*) coercion.

vergewissern [fɛrɡəˈvɪsərn], *v.r. sich* —, ascertain, make sure.

vergießen [fɛrˈɡiːsən], *v.a. irr.* spill; shed.

vergiften [fɛrˈɡɪftən], *v.a.* poison.

Vergiftung [fɛrˈɡɪftuŋ], *f.* (—, *pl.* —en) poisoning.

vergilbt [fɛrˈɡɪlpt], *adj.* yellow with age.

Vergißmeinnicht [fɛrˈɡɪsmainnɪçt], *n.* (—s, *pl.* —e) (*Bot.*) forget-me-not.

Vergleich [fɛr'glaɪç], *m.* (—(e)s, *pl.* —e) comparison; agreement; (*Law*) compromise.

vergleichbar [fɛr'glaɪçbaːr], *adj.* comparable.

vergleichen [fɛr'glaɪçən], *v.a. irr.* compare.

vergleichsweise [fɛr'glaɪçsvaɪzə], *adv.* by way of comparison; comparatively; (*Law*) by way of agreement.

Vergnügen [fɛr'gnyːgən], *n.* (—s, *no pl.*) pleasure, enjoyment, fun.

vergnügen [fɛr'gnyːgən], *v.a.* amuse, delight.

Vergnügung [fɛr'gnyːguŋ], *f.* (—, *pl.* —en) entertainment, amusement.

vergönnen [fɛr'gœnən], *v.a.* grant, allow; not (be)grudge.

vergöttern [fɛr'gœtərn], *v.a.* idolise, worship.

vergraben [fɛr'graːbən], *v.a. irr.* hide in the ground, bury.

vergrämt [fɛr'grɛːmt], *adj.* careworn.

vergreifen [fɛr'graɪfən], *v.r. irr. sich — an,* lay violent hands on, violate.

vergriffen [fɛr'grɪfən], *adj.* out of stock, out of print.

vergrößern [fɛr'grøːsərn], *v.a.* enlarge, expand; increase; magnify; (*fig.*) exaggerate.

Vergrößerung [fɛr'grøːsəruŋ], *f.* (—, *pl.* —en) magnification, enlargement, increase.

Vergrößerungsglas [fɛr'grøːsəruŋs-glas], *n.* (—es, *pl.* ⸚er) magnifying glass.

Vergünstigung [fɛr'gynstɪguŋ], *f.* (—, *pl.* —en) privilege, favour, special facility, concession.

vergüten [fɛr'gyːtən], *v.a. einem etwas —,* compensate s.o. for s.th.; reimburse s.o. for s.th.

Vergütung [fɛr'gyːtuŋ], *f.* (—, *pl.* —en) indemnification, compensation, reimbursement.

verhaften [fɛr'haftən], *v.a.* arrest.

Verhaftung [fɛr'haftuŋ], *f.* (—, *pl.* —en) arrest.

verhallen [fɛr'halən], *v.n.* (*aux.* sein) (*sound*) fade, die away.

verhalten [fɛr'haltən], *v.r. irr. sich —,* act, behave.

Verhalten [fɛr'haltən], *n.* (—s, *no pl.*) behaviour, conduct, demeanour.

Verhältnis [fɛr'hɛltnɪs], *n.* (—ses, *pl.* —se) (*Maths.*) proportion, ratio; relation; footing; love-affair, liaison; (*coll.*) mistress.

verhältnismäßig [fɛr'hɛltnɪsmɛːsɪç], *adj.* proportionate, comparative.

Verhältniswort [fɛr'hɛltnɪsvɔrt], *n.* (—es, *pl.* ⸚er) preposition.

Verhältniszahl [fɛr'hɛltnɪstsaːl], *f.* (—, *pl.* —en) proportional number.

Verhaltungsmaßregel [fɛr'haltuŋs-maːsreːgəl], *f.* (—, *pl.* —n) rule of conduct; instruction.

verhandeln [fɛr'handəln], *v.a.* discuss, transact. — *v.n.* negotiate.

Verhandlung [fɛr'handluŋ], *f.* (—, *pl.* —en) discussion, negotiation, transaction; (*Law*) proceedings.

verhängen [fɛr'hɛŋən], *v.a.* cover with; decree; inflict (a penalty) on s.o.

Verhängnis [fɛr'hɛŋnɪs], *n.* (—ses, *pl.* —se) fate, destiny; misfortune.

Verhängnisglaube [fɛr'hɛŋnɪsglaubə], *m.* (—ns, *no pl.*) fatalism.

verhängnisvoll [fɛr'hɛŋnɪsfɔl], *adj.* fateful, portentous; fatal.

verhärmt [fɛr'hɛrmt], *adj.* careworn.

verharren [fɛr'harən], *v.n.* remain; persist.

Verhärtung [fɛr'hɛrtuŋ], *f.* (—, *pl.* —en) hardening, hardened state; (*skin*) callosity; (*fig.*) obduracy.

verhaßt [fɛr'hast], *adj.* hated, odious.

verhätscheln [fɛr'hɛtʃəln], *v.a.* pamper, coddle.

verhauen [fɛr'hauən], *v.a.* beat, thrash.

Verheerung [fɛr'heːruŋ], *f.* (—, *pl.* —en) devastation.

verhehlen [fɛr'heːlən], *v.a.* conceal, hide.

verheilen [fɛr'haɪlən], *v.n.* (*aux.* sein) heal.

verheimlichen [fɛr'haɪmlɪçən], *v.a.* keep secret, hush up.

verheiraten [fɛr'haɪraːtən], *v.a.* give in marriage, marry off. — *v.r. sich —,* marry, get married.

verheißen [fɛr'haɪsən], *v.a. irr.* promise.

Verheißung [fɛr'haɪsuŋ], *f.* (—, *pl.* —en) promise.

verhelfen [fɛr'hɛlfən], *v.n. irr. einem zu etwas —,* help s.o. to s.th.

Verherrlichung [fɛr'hɛrlɪçuŋ], *f.* (—, *no pl.*) glorification.

Verhetzung [fɛr'hɛtsuŋ], *f.* (—, *pl.* —en) incitement, instigation.

verhexen [fɛr'hɛksən], *v.a.* bewitch.

verhindern [fɛr'hɪndərn], *v.a.* hinder, prevent.

Verhinderung [fɛr'hɪndəruŋ], *f.* (—, *pl.* —en) prevention, obstacle.

verhöhnen [fɛr'høːnən], *v.a.* deride, scoff at, jeer at.

Verhöhnung [fɛr'høːnuŋ], *f.* (—, *pl.* —en) derision.

Verhör [fɛr'høːr], *n.* (—s, *pl.* —e) hearing; (judicial) examination; *ins — nehmen,* question, interrogate, cross-examine.

verhören [fɛr'høːrən], *v.a.* examine judicially, interrogate. — *v.r. sich —,* misunderstand.

verhüllen [fɛr'hylən], *v.a.* cover, wrap up, veil.

verhungern [fɛr'huŋərn], *v.n.* (*aux.* sein) starve.

verhungert [fɛr'huŋərt], *adj.* famished.

verhunzen [fɛr'huntsən], *v.a.* spoil, bungle.

verhüten [fɛr'hyːtən], *v.a.* prevent, avert.

Verhütung [fɛr'hyːtuŋ], *f.* (—, *no pl.*) prevention, warding off.

verirren [fɛr'ɪrən], *v.r. sich —,* go astray, lose o.'s way.

verirrt

verirrt [fɛrˈɪrt], *adj.* stray, straying, lost.
verjagen [fɛrˈjaːgən], *v.a.* drive away, chase away.
verjährt [fɛrˈjɛːrt], *adj.* statute-barred; prescriptive; obsolete; old.
verjubeln [fɛrˈjuːbəln], *v.a.* play ducks and drakes with; squander.
verjüngen [fɛrˈjyŋən], *v.a.* make younger; (*Archit.*) taper. — *v.r. sich* —, grow younger.
Verjüngung [fɛrˈjyŋuŋ], *f.* (—, *pl.* —en) rejuvenation.
verkannt [fɛrˈkant], *adj.* misunderstood.
verkappt [fɛrˈkapt], *adj.* disguised, secret, in disguise.
Verkauf [fɛrˈkauf], *m.* (—(e)s, *pl.* ⁓e) sale.
verkaufen [fɛrˈkaufən], *v.a.* sell.
Verkäufer [fɛrˈkɔyfər], *m.* (—s, *pl.* —) seller; shop assistant, salesman.
verkäuflich [fɛrˈkɔyflɪç], *adj.* for sale, saleable; mercenary.
Verkaufspreis [fɛrˈkaufspraɪs], *m.* (—es, *pl.* —e) selling-price.
Verkehr [fɛrˈkeːr], *m.* (—s, *no pl.*) traffic; commerce; intercourse; communication; — *mit*, association with; service (*trains, buses etc.*), transport.
verkehren [fɛrˈkeːrən], *v.a.* turn upside down; transform; pervert. — *v.n.* frequent (a place), visit, associate (with); run, operate.
Verkehrsstockung [fɛrˈkeːrsʃtɔkuŋ], *f.* (—, *pl.* —en) traffic jam.
Verkehrsstraße [fɛrˈkeːrsʃtraːsə], *f.* (—, *pl.* —n) thoroughfare.
verkehrt [fɛrˈkeːrt], *adj.* upside down; (*fig.*) wrong.
Verkehrtheit [fɛrˈkeːrthaɪt], *f.* (—, *pl.* —en) absurdity, piece of folly.
Verkehrung [fɛrˈkeːruŋ], *f.* (—, *pl.* —en) turning; inversion; perversion; misrepresentation; (*Gram.*) inversion.
verkennen [fɛrˈkɛnən], *v.a. irr.* mistake, fail to recognize; misjudge (s.o.'s intentions).
verklagen [fɛrˈklaːgən], *v.a.* sue; accuse.
verklären [fɛrˈklɛːrən], *v.a.* transfigure, illumine.
verklärt [fɛrˈklɛːrt], *adj.* transfigured; radiant.
verkleben [fɛrˈkleːbən], *v.a.* paste over.
verkleiden [fɛrˈklaɪdən], *v.a., v.r.* disguise (o.s.).
Verkleidung [fɛrˈklaɪduŋ], *f.* (— *pl.* —en) disguise.
verkleinern [fɛrˈklaɪnərn], *v.a.* make smaller, diminish, reduce; belittle, disparage.
Verkleinerung [fɛrˈklaɪnəruŋ], *f.* (—, *pl.* —en) diminution, reduction; belittling, detraction.
Verkleinerungswort [fɛrˈklaɪnəruŋsvɔrt], *n.* (—s, *pl.* ⁓er) (*Gram.*) diminutive.
verkneifen [fɛrˈknaɪfən], *v.r. irr.* (*coll.*) *sich etwas* —, deny o.s. s.th.

verkniffen [fɛrˈknɪfən], *adj.* pinched; shrewd; hard-bitten.
verknöchern [fɛrˈknœçərn], *v.n.* (*aux.* sein) ossify; (*fig.*) become fossilised *or* inflexible.
Verknöcherung [fɛrˈknœçəruŋ], *f.* (—, *pl.* —en) ossification; (*fig.*) fossilisation.
verknüpfen [fɛrˈknypfən], *v.a.* tie, connect, link.
verkochen [fɛrˈkɔxən], *v.n.* (*aux.* sein) boil away.
verkommen [fɛrˈkɔmən], *v.n. irr.* (*aux.* sein) go from bad to worse, go to seed, decay, become depraved. — *adj.* demoralised, down and out, depraved.
Verkommenheit [fɛrˈkɔmənhaɪt], *f.* (—, *no pl.*) demoralisation; depravity.
verkörpern [fɛrˈkœrpərn], *v.a.* embody.
verkrachen [fɛrˈkraxən], *v.r. sich* —, quarrel, (*coll.*) have a row.
verkriechen [fɛrˈkriːçən], *v.r. irr. sich* —, creep *or* crawl away; slink away, lie low.
verkümmern [fɛrˈkymərn], *v.n.* (*aux.* sein) wear away, waste away; pine away.
verkünden [fɛrˈkyndən], *v.a.* proclaim, announce, publish, prophesy.
Verkündigung [fɛrˈkyndɪguŋ], *f.* (—, *pl.* —en) announcement, proclamation; prediction.
Verkündung [fɛrˈkynduŋ], *f.* (—, *pl.* —en) publication, proclamation.
Verkürzung [fɛrˈkyrtsuŋ], *f.* (—, *pl.* —en) shortening, curtailment.
verlachen [fɛrˈlaxən], *v.a.* laugh at, deride.
verladen [fɛrˈlaːdən], *v.a. irr.* load, ship, freight.
Verladung [fɛrˈlaːduŋ], *f.* (—, *pl.* —en) loading, shipping.
Verlag [fɛrˈlaːk], *m.* (—(e)s, *pl.* —e) publication; publishing house, (firm of) publishers.
Verlagsrecht [fɛrˈlaːksrɛçt], *n.* (—s, *pl.* —e) copyright.
Verlangen [fɛrˈlaŋən], *n.* (—s, *no pl.*) demand, request; longing, desire.
verlangen [fɛrˈlaŋən], *v.a.* ask, demand, request.
verlängern [fɛrˈlɛŋərn], *v.a.* lengthen, prolong, extend.
Verlängerung [fɛrˈlɛŋəruŋ], *f.* (—, *pl.* —en) lengthening; (*period*) prolongation, extension.
verlangsamen [fɛrˈlaŋzaːmən], *v.a.* slow down, slacken, decelerate.
Verlaß [fɛrˈlas], *m.* (—sses, *no pl.*) *es ist kein* — *auf dich*, you cannot be relied on.
verlassen [fɛrˈlasən], *v.a. irr.* leave, abandon. — *v.r. sich* — *auf*, rely on, depend upon. — *adj.* forlorn, forsaken, deserted, desolate, lonely.
Verlassenheit [fɛrˈlasənhaɪt], *f.* (—, *no pl.*) desolation, loneliness, solitude.
verläßlich [fɛrˈlɛslɪç], *adj.* reliable, trustworthy.

256

Verlauf [fɛr'lauf], *m.* (—(e)s, *no pl.*) lapse, expiration; course.

verlaufen [fɛr'laufən], *v.n. irr. (aux. sein) (time)* pass; *(period)* expire, elapse; develop(e), turn out. — *v.r. sich —,* lose o.'s way; *(colour)* run.

verlauten [fɛr'lautən], *v.n.* transpire.

verleben [fɛr'le:bən], *v.a.* pass, spend.

verlebt [fɛr'le:pt], *adj.* worn out; spent; *(Am.)* played out.

verlegen [fɛr'le:gən], *v.a. (domicile)* move, remove; *(things)* mislay; *(books)* publish; obstruct; adjourn; change to another date *or* place. — *v.r. sich auf etwas —,* devote o.s. to s.th. — *adj.* embarrassed, ill at ease.

Verlegenheit [fɛr'le:gənhaɪt], *f.* (—, *pl.* —en) embarrassment, perplexity; predicament, embarrassment.

Verleger [fɛr'le:gər], *m.* (—s, *pl.* —) publisher.

verleiden [fɛr'laɪdən], *v.a. einem etwas* —, spoil s.th. for s.o.

verleihen [fɛr'laɪən], *v.a. irr.* lend; *(honour, title)* confer, bestow, award.

Verleiher [fɛr'laɪər], *m.* (—s, *pl.* —) lender.

Verleihung [fɛr'laɪuŋ], *f.* (—, *pl.* —en) lending, loan; *(medal, prize)* investiture; grant, conferring.

verleiten [fɛr'laɪtən], *v.a.* mislead, entice, induce; seduce.

Verleitung [fɛr'laɪtuŋ], *f.* (—, *no pl.*) misleading, enticement, inducement; seduction.

verlernen [fɛr'lɛrnən], *v.a.* unlearn; forget.

verlesen [fɛr'le:zən], *v.a. irr.* read aloud, read out, recite. — *v.r. sich —,* misread.

verletzen [fɛr'lɛtsən], *v.a.* injure, hurt, wound, violate.

verletzend [fɛr'lɛtsənt], *adj.* offensive, insulting; cutting.

verletzlich [fɛr'lɛtslɪç], *adj.* vulnerable.

Verletzlichkeit [fɛr'lɛtslɪçkaɪt], *f.* (—, *no pl.*) vulnerability.

Verletzung [fɛr'lɛtsuŋ], *f.* (—, *pl.* —en) hurt, wound; *(Law)* violation.

verleugnen [fɛr'lɔygnən], *v.a.* deny, renounce, disown.

Verleugnung [fɛr'lɔygnuŋ], *f.* (—, *pl.* —en) denial, abnegation.

verleumden [fɛr'lɔymdən], *v.a.* slander, calumniate, traduce.

Verleumdung [fɛr'lɔymduŋ], *f.* (—, *pl.* —en) slander, libel, calumny.

verlieben [fɛr'li:bən], *v.r. sich — in,* fall in love with.

Verliebte [fɛr'li:ptə], *m. or f.* (—n, *pl.* —n) person in love, lover.

Verliebtheit [fɛr'li:pthaɪt], *f.* (—, *no pl.*) infatuation, amorousness.

verlieren [fɛr'li:rən], *v.a. irr.* lose.

Verlierer [fɛr'li:rər], *m.* (—s, *pl.* —) loser.

Verlies [fɛr'li:s], *n.* (—(s)es, *pl.* —(s)e) dungeon.

verloben [fɛr'lo:bən], *v.r. sich — mit,* become engaged to.

Verlöbnis [fɛr'lø:pnɪs], *n.* (—ses, *pl.* —se) *(rare)* engagement.

Verlobte [fɛr'lo:ptə], *m.* (—n, *pl.* —n) and *f.* (—n, *pl.* —n) fiancé(e), betrothed.

Verlobung [fɛr'lo:buŋ], *f.* (—, *pl.* —en) engagement, betrothal.

verlocken [fɛr'lɔkən], *v.a.* tempt, entice.

verlogen [fɛr'lo:gən], *adj.* lying, mendacious.

Verlogenheit [fɛr'lo:gənhaɪt], *f.* (—, *no pl.*) mendacity.

verlohnen [fɛr'lo:nən], *v. impers.* be worth while.

verlöschen [fɛr'lœʃən], *v.a.* extinguish.

verlosen [fɛr'lo:zən], *v.a.* raffle; draw *or* cast lots for.

Verlosung [fɛr'lo:zuŋ], *f.* (—, *pl.* —en) raffle, lottery.

verlöten [fɛr'lø:tən], *v.a.* solder.

verlottern [fɛr'lɔtərn], *v.n. (aux. sein)* go to the dogs.

Verlust [fɛr'lust], *m.* (—es, *pl.* —e) loss; *(death)* bereavement; *(Mil.)* casualty.

verlustig [fɛr'lustɪç], *adj.* — *gehen,* lose s.th., forfeit s.th.

vermachen [fɛr'maxən], *v.a. einem etwas* —, bequeath s.th. to s.o.

Vermächtnis [fɛr'mɛçtnɪs], *n.* (—ses, *pl.* —sse) will; legacy, bequest; *(fig.) heiliges —,* sacred trust.

vermahlen [fɛr'ma:lən], *v.a.* grind (down).

Vermählung [fɛr'mɛ:luŋ], *f.* (—, *pl.* —en) marriage, wedding.

Vermahnung [fɛr'ma:nuŋ], *f.* (—, *pl.* —en) admonition, exhortation.

vermauern [fɛr'mauərn], *v.a.* wall up.

vermehren [fɛr'me:rən], *v.a.* augment, multiply, increase. — *v.r. sich —,* multiply.

Vermehrung [fɛr'me:ruŋ], *f.* (—, *pl.* —en) increase, multiplication.

vermeiden [fɛr'maɪdən], *v.a. irr.* avoid, shun, shirk.

vermeidlich [fɛr'maɪtlɪç], *adj.* avoidable.

Vermeidung [fɛr'maɪduŋ], *f.* (—, *no pl.*) avoidance.

vermeintlich [fɛr'maɪntlɪç], *adj.* supposed, alleged, pretended; *(heir)* presumptive.

vermelden [fɛr'mɛldən], *v.a.* announce, notify.

vermengen [fɛr'mɛŋən], *v.a.* mingle, mix.

Vermerk [fɛr'mɛrk], *m.* (—s, *pl.* —e) entry, notice, note.

vermerken [fɛr'mɛrkən], *v.a.* observe, jot down.

vermessen [fɛr'mɛsən], *v.a. irr.* measure; *(land)* survey. — *adj.* bold, daring, audacious; arrogant.

Vermessenheit [fɛr'mɛsənhaɪt], *f.* (—, *no pl.*) boldness, audacity; arrogance.

Vermesser [fɛr'mɛsər], *m.* (—s, *pl.*—) *(land)* surveyor.

T K   257

Vermessung

Vermessung [fɛr'mɛsuŋ], *f.* (—, *pl.* —en) (*land*) survey; measuring.

vermieten [fɛr'mi:tən], *v.a.* let, lease, hire out.

Vermieter [fɛr'mi:tər], *m.* (—s, *pl.* —) landlord; hirer.

vermindern [fɛr'mɪndərn], *v.a.* diminish, lessen.

Verminderung [fɛr'mɪndəruŋ], *f.* (—, *pl.* —en) diminution, reduction, decrease, lessening.

vermischen [fɛr'mɪʃən], *v.a.* mix, mingle, blend.

vermissen [fɛr'mɪsən], *v.a.* miss; *vermißt sein*, be missing; *vermißt werden*, be missed.

vermitteln [fɛr'mɪtəln], *v.n.* mediate. — *v.a.* adjust; negotiate, secure.

Vermittler [fɛr'mɪtlər], *m.* (—s, *pl.* —) mediator; agent, middleman.

Vermittlung [fɛr'mɪtluŋ], *f.* (—, *pl.* —en) mediation, intervention.

vermöbeln [fɛr'mø:bəln], *v.a.* (*sl.*) *einen* —, thrash s.o.

vermodern [fɛr'mo:dərn], *v.n.* (*aux.* sein) moulder, rot.

vermöge [fɛr'mø:gə], *prep.* (*Genit.*) by virtue of, by dint of, on the strength of.

Vermögen [fɛr'mø:gən], *n.* (—s, *pl.* —) faculty, power; means, assets; fortune, wealth, riches; *er hat* —, he is a man of property; *nach bestem* —, to the best of o.'s ability.

vermögen [fɛr'mø:gən], *v.a. irr.* be able to, have the power to, be capable of.

vermögend [fɛr'mø:gənt], *adj.* wealthy.

Vermögensbestand [fɛr'mø:gənsbə-ʃtant], *m.* (—s, *pl.* ̈-e) assets.

Vermögenssteuer [fɛr'mø:gənsʃtɔyər], *f.* (—, *pl.* —n) property tax.

vermorscht [fɛr'mɔrʃt], *adj.* mouldering, rotten.

vermuten [fɛr'mu:tən], *v.a.* suppose, conjecture, surmise, presume; guess.

vermutlich [fɛr'mu:tlɪç], *adj.* likely, probable.

Vermutung [fɛr'mu:tuŋ], *f.* (—, *pl.* —en) guess, supposition, conjecture.

vernachlässigen [fɛr'naxlɛsɪgən], *v.a.* neglect.

Vernachlässigung [fɛr'naxlɛsɪguŋ], *f.* (—, *pl.* —en) neglect, negligence.

vernarren [fɛr'narən], *v.r. sich* — (*in, Acc.*), become infatuated (with).

vernarrt [fɛr'nart], *adj.* madly in love.

vernaschen [fɛr'naʃən], *v.a.* squander (money) on sweets.

vernehmbar [fɛr'ne:mba:r], *adj.* audible; *sich* — *machen*, make o.s. heard.

Vernehmen [fɛr'ne:mən], *n.* (—s, no *pl.*) *dem* — *nach*, from what o. hears.

vernehmen [fɛr'ne:mən], *v.a. irr.* hear, learn; (*Law*) examine, interrogate.

vernehmlich [fɛr'ne:mlɪç], *adj.* audible, distinct, clear.

Vernehmlichkeit [fɛr'ne:mlɪçkaɪt], *f.* (—, no *pl.*) audibility.

Vernehmung [fɛr'ne:muŋ], *f.* (—, *pl.* —en) (*Law*) interrogation, examination.

verneigen [fɛr'naɪgən], *v.r. sich* —, curts(e)y, bow.

Verneigung [fɛr'naɪguŋ], *f.* (—, *pl.* —en) curts(e)y, bow.

verneinen [fɛr'naɪnən], *v.a.* deny, answer in the negative.

Verneinung [fɛr'naɪnuŋ], *f.* (—, *pl.* —en) negation, denial; (*Gram.*) negation, negative.

vernichten [fɛr'nɪçtən], *v.a.* annihilate, destroy utterly, exterminate.

Vernichtung [fɛr'nɪçtuŋ], *f.* (—, *no pl.*) annihilation, extinction, destruction.

vernieten [fɛr'ni:tən], *v.a.* rivet.

Vernunft [fɛr'nunft], *f.* (—, *no pl.*) reason, sense, intelligence, judgment; *gesunde* —, common sense; — *annehmen*, listen to reason; *einen zur* — *bringen*, bring s.o. to his senses.

vernünftig [fɛr'nynftɪç], *adj.* sensible, reasonable, rational.

veröden [fɛr'ø:dən], *v.n.* (*aux.* sein) become desolate, become devastated.

Verödung [fɛr'ø:duŋ], *f.* (—, *no pl.*) devastation, desolation.

veröffentlichen [fɛr'œfəntlɪçən], *v.a.* publish.

Veröffentlichung [fɛr'œfəntlɪçuŋ], *f.* (—, *pl.* —en) publication.

verordnen [fɛr'ɔrdnən], *v.a.* order, command, ordain; (*Med.*) prescribe.

Verordnung [fɛr'ɔrdnuŋ], *f.* (—, *pl.* —en) order; (*Law*) decree, edict, statute; (*Med.*) prescription.

verpassen [fɛr'pasən], *v.a.* lose by delay, let slip; (*train etc.*) miss.

verpfänden [fɛr'pfɛndən], *v.a.* pawn, pledge.

Verpfänder [fɛr'pfɛndər], *m.* (—s, *pl.* —) mortgager.

Verpfändung [fɛr'pfɛnduŋ], *f.* (—, *pl.* —en) pawning, pledging.

verpflanzen [fɛr'pflantsən], *v.a.* transplant.

Verpflanzung [fɛr'pflantsuŋ], *f.* (—, *pl.* —en) transplantation.

verpflegen [fɛr'pfle:gən], *v.a.* board, provide food for, feed; nurse.

Verpflegung [fɛr'pfle:guŋ], *f.* (—, *no pl.*) board, catering; food.

Verpflegungskosten [fɛr'pfle:guŋskɔstən], *f. pl.* (cost of) board and lodging.

verpflichten [fɛr'pflɪçtən], *v.a.* bind, oblige, engage.

verpflichtend [fɛr'pflɪçtənt], *adj.* obligatory.

Verpflichtung [fɛr'pflɪçtuŋ], *f.* (—, *pl.* —en) obligation, duty; liability, engagement.

verplaudern [fɛr'plaudərn], *v.a.* spend (time) chatting.

verplempern [fɛr'plɛmpərn], *v.a.* (*coll.*) spend foolishly, fritter away.

verpönt [fɛr'pø:nt], *adj.* frowned upon; taboo.

verprassen [fɛr'prasən], *v.a.* squander (money) in riotous living.

verpuffen [fɛrˈpufən], v.n. (aux. sein) (coll.) fizzle out.

verpulvern [fɛrˈpulvərn], v.a. fritter away.

Verputz [fɛrˈputs], m. (—es, no pl.) plaster.

verquicken [fɛrˈkvikən], v.a. amalgamate; mix up.

Verrat [fɛrˈraːt], m. (—(e)s, no pl.) treachery, treason.

verraten [fɛrˈraːtən], v.a. irr. betray; disclose; das verrät die Hand des Künstlers, this proclaims the hand of the artist.

Verräter [fɛrˈrɛːtər], m. (—s, pl. —) traitor.

verräterisch [fɛrˈrɛːtərɪʃ], adj. treacherous, treasonable, perfidious; (fig.) tell-tale.

verrauchen [fɛrˈrauxən], v.n. (aux. sein) evaporate; (fig.) blow over; cool down.

verräuchern [fɛrˈrɔyçərn], v.a. smoke, fill with smoke.

verräumen [fɛrˈrɔymən], v.a. misplace, mislay.

verrauschen [fɛrˈrauʃən], v.n. (aux. sein) (sound) die away; pass away.

verrechnen [fɛrˈrɛçnən], v.a. reckon up. — v.r. sich —, miscalculate.

Verrechnung [fɛrˈrɛçnuŋ], f. (—, pl. —en) reckoning-up.

Verrechnungsscheck [fɛrˈrɛçnuŋsʃɛk], m. (—s, pl. —e, —s) crossed cheque.

verregnen [fɛrˈreːgnən], v.a. spoil by rain.

verreiben [fɛrˈraibən], v.a. irr. rub away; rub hard.

verreisen [fɛrˈraizən], v.n. (aux. sein) go on a journey.

verrenken [fɛrˈrɛŋkən], v.a. sprain, dislocate.

Verrenkung [fɛrˈrɛŋkuŋ], f. (—, pl. —en) sprain, dislocation.

verrichten [fɛrˈrɪçtən], v.a. do, perform, acquit o.s. of; execute; (prayer) say.

verriegeln [fɛrˈriːgəln], v.a. bolt.

verringern [fɛrˈrɪŋərn], v.a. reduce, diminish.

Verringerung [fɛrˈrɪŋəruŋ], f. (—, no pl.) diminution, reduction.

verrinnen [fɛrˈrɪnən], v.n. irr. (aux. sein) run off; (fig.) pass, elapse.

verrosten [fɛrˈrɔstən], v.n. (aux. sein) rust.

verrottet [fɛrˈrɔtət], adj. rotten.

verrucht [fɛrˈruːxt], adj. villainous, atrocious, heinous, infamous.

Verruchtheit [fɛrˈruːxthait], f. (—, no pl.) villainy.

verrücken [fɛrˈrykən], v.a. shift, displace.

verrückt [fɛrˈrykt], adj. crazy, mad.

Verrückte [fɛrˈryktə], m. (—n, pl. —n) madman. — f. (—n, pl. —n) madwoman.

Verrücktheit [fɛrˈrykthait], f. (—, pl. —en) craziness; mad act.

Verruf [fɛrˈruːf], m. (—s, no pl.) discredit, ill repute.

verrufen [fɛrˈruːfən], adj. notorious, of ill repute.

Vers [fɛrs], m. (—es, pl. —e) verse.

versagen [fɛrˈzaːgən], v.a. einem etwas —, deny s.o. s.th., refuse s.o. s.th. — v.n. fail, break down; (voice) falter; sich etwas —, abstain from s.th., deny o.s. s.th.

Versager [fɛrˈzaːgər], m. (—s, pl. —) misfire; failure, unsuccessful person, flop.

versammeln [fɛrˈzaməln], v.a. gather around, convene. — v.r. sich —, assemble, meet.

Versammlung [fɛrˈzamluŋ], f. (—, pl. —en) assembly, meeting, gathering, convention.

Versand [fɛrˈzant], m. (—s, no pl.) dispatch, forwarding, shipping, shipment.

versanden [fɛrˈzandən], v.n. (aux. sein) silt up.

Versandgeschäft [fɛrˈzantgəʃɛft], n. (—s, pl. —e) export business; mail order business.

Versatzamt [fɛrˈzatsamt], n. (—s, pl. ⸚er) pawn-shop.

versauen [fɛrˈzauən], v.a. (sl.) make a mess of.

versauern [fɛrˈzauərn], v.n. (aux. sein) turn sour; (fig.) become morose.

versaufen [fɛrˈzaufən], v.a. irr. (sl.) squander (money) on drink, drink away.

versäumen [fɛrˈzɔymən], v.a. miss, omit, lose by delay; leave undone; neglect.

Versäumnis [fɛrˈzɔymnis], n. (—ses, pl. —se) neglect, omission; (time) loss.

Versbau [ˈfɛrsbau], m. (—s, no pl.) versification; verse structure.

verschachern [fɛrˈʃaxərn], v.a. barter away.

verschaffen [fɛrˈʃafən], v.a. provide, procure, obtain, get.

verschämt [fɛrˈʃɛːmt], adj. shamefaced, bashful.

verschanzen [fɛrˈʃantsən], v.a. fortify.

Verschanzung [fɛrˈʃantsuŋ], f. (—, pl. —en) fortification, entrenchment.

verschärfen [fɛrˈʃɛrfən], v.a. heighten, intensify, sharpen.

verscharren [fɛrˈʃarən], v.a. cover with earth; bury hurriedly.

verscheiden [fɛrˈʃaidən], v.n. irr. (aux. sein) die, pass away.

verschenken [fɛrˈʃɛŋkən], v.a. make a present of, give away.

verscherzen [fɛrˈʃɛrtsən], v.a. sich etwas —, forfeit s.th.

verscheuchen [fɛrˈʃɔyçən], v.a. scare away, frighten away; Sorgen —, banish care.

verschicken [fɛrˈʃikən], v.a. send on, send out, forward, transmit; evacuate.

Verschickung [fɛrˈʃikuŋ], f. (—, no pl.) forwarding, transmission; evacuation; banishment, exile.

verschieben

verschieben [fɛrˈʃiːbən], v.a. irr. shift, move; delay, put off, defer, postpone.
Verschiebung [fɛrˈʃiːbuŋ], f. (—, pl. —en) removal; postponement; (fig.) black marketeering.
verschieden [fɛrˈʃiːdən], adj. different, diverse; deceased, departed; (pl.) some, several, sundry.
verschiedenartig [fɛrˈʃiːdənˌrtɪç], adj. varied, various, heterogeneous.
verschiedenerlei [fɛrˈʃiːdənərlaɪ], indecl. adj. diverse, of various kinds.
Verschiedenheit [fɛrˈʃiːdənhaɪt], f. (—, pl. —en) difference; diversity, variety.
verschiedentlich [fɛrˈʃiːdəntlɪç], adv. variously, severally; repeatedly.
verschiffen [fɛrˈʃɪfən], v.a. export, ship.
verschimmeln [fɛrˈʃɪməln], v.n. (aux. sein) go mouldy.
verschlafen [fɛrˈʃlaːfən], v.a. irr. sleep through, sleep away. — v.r. sich —, oversleep. — adj. sleepy, drowsy.
Verschlag [fɛrˈʃlaːk], m. (—s, pl. ⸚e) partition, box, cubicle.
verschlagen [fɛrˈʃlaːgən], v.a. irr. es verschlägt mir den Atem, it takes my breath away. — adj. cunning, crafty, sly.
verschlechtern [fɛrˈʃlɛçtərn], v.a. worsen, make worse. — v.r. sich —, deteriorate.
Verschlechterung [fɛrˈʃlɛçtəruŋ], f. (—, no pl.) deterioration.
verschleiern [fɛrˈʃlaɪərn], v.a. veil.
Verschleierung [fɛrˈʃlaɪəruŋ], f. (—, pl. —en) veiling, concealment; camouflage.
verschleißen [fɛrˈʃlaɪsən], v.a. irr. wear out, waste.
verschlemmen [fɛrˈʃlɛmən], v.a. squander on eating and drinking.
verschleppen [fɛrˈʃlɛpən], v.a. carry off, deport; kidnap; protract, spread; put off, procrastinate.
verschleudern [fɛrˈʃlɔydərn], v.a. waste; sell at cut prices.
verschließen [fɛrˈʃliːsən], v.a. irr. lock, lock up.
verschlimmern [fɛrˈʃlɪmərn], v.a. make worse. — v.r. sich —, get worse, worsen, deteriorate.
Verschlimmerung [fɛrˈʃlɪmeruŋ], f. (—, no pl.) worsening, deterioration.
verschlingen [fɛrˈʃlɪŋən], v.a. irr. swallow up, devour.
verschlossen [fɛrˈʃlɔsən], adj. reserved, uncommunicative, withdrawn.
Verschlossenheit [fɛrˈʃlɔsənhaɪt], f. (—, no pl.) reserve.
verschlucken [fɛrˈʃlukən], v.a. swallow, gulp down; (fig.) suppress. — v.r. sich —, swallow the wrong way.
verschlungen [fɛrˈʃluŋən], adj. intricate, complicated.
Verschluß [fɛrˈʃlus], m. (—sses. pl. ⸚sse) lock; clasp; fastening; unter haben, keep under lock and key.
Verschlußlaut [fɛrˈʃluslaut], m. (—s, pl.—e) (Phon.) explosive, plosive, stop.

verschmachten [fɛrˈʃmaxtən], v.n. (aux. sein) languish, pine; be parched.
Verschmähung [fɛrˈʃmɛːuŋ], f. (—, no pl.) disdain, scorn, rejection.
Verschmelzung [fɛrˈʃmɛltsuŋ], f. (—, no pl.) coalescence, fusion, blending.
verschmerzen [fɛrˈʃmɛrtsən], v.a. get over; bear stoically, make the best of.
verschmitzt [fɛrˈʃmɪtst], adj. cunning, crafty, mischievous.
verschmutzen [fɛrˈʃmutsən], v.n. (aux. sein) get dirty.
verschnappen [fɛrˈʃnapən], v.r. sich —, blurt out a secret, give o.s. away, let the cat out of the bag.
verschneiden [fɛrˈʃnaɪdən], v.a. irr. (wings) clip; (trees) prune; (animals) castrate; (wine) blend.
verschneien [fɛrˈʃnaɪən], v.n. (aux. sein) be snowed up, be covered with snow, be snowbound.
Verschnitt [fɛrˈʃnɪt], m. (—s, no pl.) blended wine, blend.
Verschnittene [fɛrˈʃnɪtənə], m. (—n, pl. —n) eunuch.
verschnörkelt [fɛrˈʃnœrkəlt], adj. adorned with flourishes.
verschnupft [fɛrˈʃnupft], adj. — sein, have a cold in the head; (fig.) be vexed.
verschnüren [fɛrˈʃnyːrən], v.a. (shoes) lace up; (parcel) tie up.
verschonen [fɛrˈʃoːnər], v.a. spare, exempt from.
verschönern [fɛrˈʃøːnərn], v.a. embellish, beautify.
Verschönerung [fɛrˈʃøːnəruŋ], f. (—, pl. —en) embellishment, adornment.
Verschonung [fɛrˈʃoːnuŋ], f. (—, no pl.) exemption; forbearance.
verschossen [fɛrˈʃɔsən], adj. faded, discoloured; (fig.) madly in love.
verschreiben [fɛrˈʃraɪbən], v.a. irr. prescribe. — v.r. sich —, make a mistake in writing.
verschrien [fɛrˈʃriːən], adj. notorious.
verschroben [fɛrˈʃroːbən], adj. cranky, eccentric.
Verschrobenheit [fɛrˈʃroːbənhaɪt], f. (—, pl. —en) crankiness, eccentricity.
verschrumpfen [fɛrˈʃrumpfən], v.n. (aux. sein) shrivel up.
verschüchtern [fɛrˈʃyçtərn], v.a. intimidate.
verschulden [fɛrˈʃuldən], v.a. bring on, be the cause of; be guilty of.
verschuldet [fɛrˈʃuldət], adj. in debt.
Verschuldung [fɛrˈʃulduŋ], f. (—, no pl.) indebtedness.
verschütten [fɛrˈʃytən], v.a. spill; bury alive.
verschwägern [fɛrˈʃvɛːgərn], v.r. sich —, become related by marriage.
Verschwägerung [fɛrˈʃvɛːgəruŋ], f. (—, no pl.) relationship by marriage.
verschwatzen [fɛrˈʃvatsən], v.a. gossip (the time) away, spend o.'s time gossiping.
verschweigen [fɛrˈʃvaɪgən], v.a. irr. keep secret, keep (news) from, hush up.

verschwenden [fɛrˈʃvɛndən], *v.a.* squander, waste.

verschwenderisch [fɛrˈʃvɛndərɪʃ], *adj.* prodigal, profuse, lavish; wasteful.

Verschwendung [fɛrˈʃvɛnduŋ], *f.* (—, *no pl.*) waste; extravagance.

Verschwendungssucht [fɛrˈʃvɛnduŋs-zuxt], *f.* (—, *no pl.*) prodigality; extravagance.

verschwiegen [fɛrˈʃviːgən], *adj.* discreet, close, secretive.

Verschwiegenheit [fɛrˈʃviːgənhaɪt], *f.* (—, *no pl.*) discretion, secrecy.

verschwimmen [fɛrˈʃvɪmən], *v.n. irr.* (*aux.* sein) become blurred.

verschwinden [fɛrˈʃvɪndən], *v.n. irr.* (*aux.* sein) disappear, vanish.

verschwommen [fɛrˈʃvɔmən], *adj.* vague, blurred.

verschwören [fɛrˈʃvøːrən], *v.r. irr. sich* —, plot, conspire.

Verschwörer [fɛrˈʃvøːrer], *m.* (—s, *pl.* —) conspirator.

Verschwörung [fɛrˈʃvøːruŋ], *f.* (—, *pl.* —en) conspiracy.

Versehen [fɛrˈzeːən], *n.* (—s, *pl.* —) error, mistake, oversight.

versehen [fɛrˈzeːən], *v.a. irr.* provide; perform; fill (an office); *einen* — *mit*, furnish s.o. with. — *v.r. sich* —, make a mistake.

versehren [fɛrˈzeːrən], *v.a.* wound; disable.

versenden [fɛrˈzɛndən], *v.a. irr.* forward, consign, send off.

Versender [fɛrˈzɛndər], *m.* (—s, *pl.*—) consigner, exporter.

Versendung [fɛrˈzɛnduŋ], *f.* (—, *no pl.*) transmission, shipping.

Versendungskosten [fɛrˈzɛnduŋskɔs-tən], *f. pl.* forwarding charges.

versengen [fɛrˈzɛŋən], *v.a.* singe, scorch.

versenken [fɛrˈzɛŋkən], *v.a.* sink; (*ship*) scuttle.

Versenkung [fɛrˈzɛŋkuŋ], *f.* (—, *no pl.*) sinking; hollow; (*ship*) scuttling; (*Theat.*) trap-door.

versessen [fɛrˈzɛsən], *adj.* — *sein auf,* be bent upon, be mad on.

versetzen [fɛrˈzɛtsən], *v.a.* transplant, remove; give; pawn, pledge; transfer; (*pupil*) promote to a higher form. — *v.r. sich in die Lage eines anderen* —, put o.s. in s.o. else's position.

versichern [fɛrˈzɪçərn], *v.a.* assert, declare, aver, assure (s.o. of s.th) insure (s.th.).

Versicherung [fɛrˈzɪçəruŋ], *f.* (—, *pl.* —en) assurance, assertion; insurance.

Versicherungsgesellschaft [fɛrˈzɪçə-ruŋsgəzɛlʃaft], *f.* (—, *pl.* —en) insurance company.

Versicherungsprämie [fɛrˈzɪçəruŋs-prɛːmjə], *f.* (—, *pl.* —n) insurance premium.

versiegbar [fɛrˈziːkbaːr], *adj.* exhaustible.

versiegeln [fɛrˈziːgəln], *v.a.* seal (up).

versiegen [fɛrˈziːgən], *v.n.* (*aux.* sein) dry up, be exhausted.

versilbern [fɛrˈzɪlbərn], *v.a.* plate with silver; (*fig.*) convert into money.

versinken [fɛrˈzɪŋkən], *v.n. irr.* sink; (*ship*) founder; sink; *versunken sein,* be absorbed (in s.th.).

Versmaß [ˈfɛrsmaːs], *n.* (—es, *pl.* —e) metre.

versoffen [fɛrˈzɔfən], *adj.* (*vulg.*) drunken.

versohlen [fɛrˈzoːlən], *v.a.* (*coll.*) thrash (s.o.).

versöhnen [fɛrˈzøːnən], *v.r. sich mit einem* —, become reconciled with s.o.

versöhnlich [fɛrˈzøːnlɪç], *adj.* propitiatory, conciliatory.

Versöhnung [fɛrˈzøːnuŋ], *f.* (—, *no pl.*) reconciliation.

versorgen [fɛrˈzɔrgən], *v.a.* provide with; take care of; support, maintain.

Versorger [fɛrˈzɔrgər], *m.* (—s, *pl.* —) provider.

Versorgung [fɛrˈzɔrguŋ], *f.* (—, *no pl.*) provision, maintenance.

verspäten [fɛrˈʃpɛːtən], *v.r. sich* —, be late, be behind time; (*train*) be overdue.

Verspätung [fɛrˈʃpɛːtuŋ], *f.* (—, *no pl.*) delay; lateness.

verspeisen [fɛrˈʃpaɪzən], *v.a.* eat up.

versperren [fɛrˈʃpɛrən], *v.a.* block up, barricade, close.

verspielen [fɛrˈʃpiːlən], *v.a.* lose (at play); gamble away. — *v.r. sich* —, play wrong.

verspielt [fɛrˈʃpiːlt], *adj.* playful.

verspotten [fɛrˈʃpɔtən], *v.a.* deride, scoff at.

versprechen [fɛrˈʃprɛçən], *v.a. irr.* promise. — *v.r. sich* —, make a slip of the tongue.

Versprechen [fɛrˈʃprɛçən], *n.* (—s, *pl.* —) promise.

versprengen [fɛrˈʃprɛŋən], *v.a.* disperse.

verspüren [fɛrˈʃpyːrən], *v.a.* feel, perceive.

verstaatlichen [fɛrˈʃtaːtlɪçən], *v.a.* nationalise.

Verstand [fɛrˈʃtant], *m.* (—(e)s, *no pl.*) intellect, intelligence, sense; understanding, reason, mind.

verstandesmäßig [fɛrˈʃtandəsmɛːsɪç], *adj.* rational, reasonable.

Verstandesschärfe [fɛrˈʃtandəsʃɛrfə], *f.* (—, *no pl.*) penetration, acumen.

verständig [fɛrˈʃtɛndɪç], *adj.* judicious, sensible, reasonable.

verständigen [fɛrˈʃtɛndɪgən], *v.a.* inform, notify. — *v.r. sich mit einem* —, come to an agreement with s.o.

Verständigung [fɛrˈʃtɛndɪguŋ], *f.* (—, *pl.* —en) understanding, agreement; information; arrangement.

verständlich [fɛrˈʃtɛntlɪç], *adj.* intelligible, clear, understandable.

Verständnis [fɛrˈʃtɛntnɪs], (—ses, *no pl.*) comprehension, understanding, perception, insight.

verständnisinnig

verständnisinnig [fɛrˈʃtɛntnɪsɪnɪç], *adj.* sympathetic; having profound insight.

verstärken [fɛrˈʃtɛrkən], *v.a.* strengthen, reinforce, intensify.

Verstärker [fɛrˈʃtɛrkər], *m.* (—s, *pl.* —) amplifier; magnifier.

Verstärkung [fɛrˈʃtɛrkuŋ], *f.* (—, *pl.* —en) strengthening, intensification, amplification; (*Mil.*) reinforcements.

verstauben [fɛrˈʃtaubən], *v.n.* (*aux.* sein) get dusty.

verstauchen [fɛrˈʃtauxən], *v.a.* wrench, sprain, dislocate.

verstauen [fɛrˈʃtauən], *v.a.* stow away.

Versteck [fɛrˈʃtɛk], *n.* (—s, *pl.* —e) hiding-place; place of concealment; —(en) spielen, play hide-and-seek.

verstecken [fɛrˈʃtɛkən], *v.a.* hide, conceal.

versteckt [fɛrˈʃtɛkt], *adj.* indirect, veiled.

verstehen [fɛrˈʃteːən], *v.a. irr.* understand, comprehend.

versteigen [fɛrˈʃtaɪgən], *v.r. irr. sich* —, climb too high; (*fig.*) go too far.

versteigern [fɛrˈʃtaɪgərn], *v.a.* sell by auction.

Versteigerung [fɛrˈʃtaɪgəruŋ], *f.* (—, *pl.* —en) auction, public sale.

versteinern [fɛrˈʃtaɪnərn], *v.n.* (*aux.* sein) turn into stone, petrify.

verstellbar [fɛrˈʃtɛlbaːr], *adj.* adjustable.

verstellen [fɛrˈʃtɛlən], *v.a.* adjust; (*voice*) disguise. — *v.r. sich* —, sham, pretend.

versterben [fɛrˈʃtɛrbən], *v.n. irr.* (*aux.* sein) (*Poet.*) die.

versteuern [fɛrˈʃtɔyərn], *v.a.* pay tax on.

verstiegen [fɛrˈʃtiːgən], *adj.* eccentric, extravagant.

verstimmen [fɛrˈʃtɪmən], *v.a.* (*Mus.*) put out of tune; (*fig.*) put out of humour, annoy.

Verstimmtheit [fɛrˈʃtɪmthaɪt], *f.* (—, *no pl.*) ill-humour, ill-temper, pique.

Verstimmung [fɛrˈʃtɪmuŋ], *f.* (—, *pl.* —en) bad temper, ill-feeling.

verstockt [fɛrˈʃtɔkt], *adj.* stubborn, obdurate.

Verstocktheit [fɛrˈʃtɔkthaɪt], *f.* (—, *no pl.*) stubbornness, obduracy.

verstohlen [fɛrˈʃtoːlən], *adj.* surreptitious, clandestine, furtive.

verstopfen [fɛrˈʃtɔpfən], *v.a.* stop up; block (up); *verstopft sein*, be constipated.

Verstopfung [fɛrˈʃtɔpfuŋ], *f.* (—, *pl.* —en) obstruction; constipation.

verstorben [fɛrˈʃtɔrbən], *adj.* deceased, late.

verstört [fɛrˈʃtøːrt], *adj.* troubled, worried; distracted.

Verstörtheit [fɛrˈʃtøːrthaɪt], *f.* (—, *no pl.*) consternation, agitation; distraction; haggardness.

Verstoß [fɛrˈʃtoːs], *m.* (—es, *pl.* ⁀e) blunder, mistake; offence.

verstoßen [fɛrˈʃtoːsən], *v.a. irr.* cast off, disown, repudiate. — *v.n.*

gegen, offend against, act in a manner contrary to.

verstreichen [fɛrˈʃtraɪçən], *v.n. irr.* (*aux.* sein) (*time*) elapse, pass away.

verstricken [fɛrˈʃtrɪkən], *v.a.* entangle, ensnare.

Verstrickung [fɛrˈʃtrɪkuŋ], *f.* (—, *pl.* —en) entanglement.

verstümmeln [fɛrˈʃtyməln], *v.a.* mutilate, mangle.

verstummen [fɛrˈʃtumən], *v.n.* (*aux.* sein) grow silent; become speechless.

Verstümmlung [fɛrˈʃtymluŋ], *f.* (—, *pl.* —en) mutilation.

Versuch [fɛrˈzuːx], *m.* (—s, *pl.* —e) attempt, trial, endeavour; (*science*) experiment; (*Lit.*) essay.

versuchen [fɛrˈzuːxən], *v.a.* try, attempt, endeavour; (*food*) taste; *einen* —, tempt s.o.

Versucher [fɛrˈzuːxər], *m.* (—s, *pl.* —) tempter.

Versuchskaninchen [fɛrˈzuːxskaniːnçən], *n.* (—s, *pl.* —) (*fig.*) guinea-pig.

Versuchung [fɛrˈzuːxuŋ], *f.* (—, *pl.* —en) temptation.

versündigen [fɛrˈzyndɪgən], *v.r. sich* —, sin (against).

Versunkenheit [fɛrˈzuŋkənhaɪt], *f.* (—, *no pl.*) absorption, preoccupation.

vertagen [fɛrˈtaːgən], *v.a.* adjourn, prorogue.

Vertagung [fɛrˈtaːguŋ], *f.* (—, *pl.* —en) adjournment, prorogation.

vertauschen [fɛrˈtauʃən], *v.a.* exchange, barter, mistake, confuse.

verteidigen [fɛrˈtaɪdɪgən], *v.a.* defend, uphold, vindicate; (*fig.*) maintain.

Verteidiger [fɛrˈtaɪdɪgər], *m.* (—s, *pl.* —) defender; (*Law*) counsel for the defence.

Verteidigung [fɛrˈtaɪdɪguŋ], *f.* (—, *no pl.*) defence; justification.

Verteidigungskrieg [fɛrˈtaɪdɪguŋskriːk], *m.* (—(e)s, *pl.* —e) defensive war.

verteilen [fɛrˈtaɪlən], *v.a.* distribute, allot, allocate.

Verteilung [fɛrˈtaɪluŋ], *f.* (—, *pl.* —en) distribution, apportionment.

verteuern [fɛrˈtɔyərn], *v.a.* make dearer, raise the price of.

verteufelt [fɛrˈtɔyfəlt], *adj.* devilish. — *adv.* (*coll.*) awfully, infernally.

vertiefen [fɛrˈtiːfən], *v.a.* deepen.

vertieft [fɛrˈtiːft], *adj.* absorbed, deep in thought.

Vertiefung [fɛrˈtiːfuŋ], *f.* (—, *pl.* —en) cavity, recess, hollow; (*knowledge*) deepening; (*fig.*) absorption.

vertilgen [fɛrˈtɪlgən], *v.a.* wipe out, exterminate; (*food*) (*coll.*) polish off.

Vertilgung [fɛrˈtɪlguŋ], *f.* (—, *no pl.*) extermination, extirpation.

Vertrag [fɛrˈtraːk], *m.* (—(e)s, *pl.* ⁀e) contract, agreement; (*Pol.*) treaty, pact, convention.

vertragen [fɛrˈtraːgən], *v.a. irr.* suffer, endure; (*food*) digest. — *v.r. sich mit*, get on well with.

vertraglich [fɛr'traːklɪç], *adj.* as per contract, according to agreement.

verträglich [fɛr'trɛːklɪç], *adj.* accommodating, peaceable.

vertragsmäßig [fɛr'traːksmɛːsɪç], *adj.* according to contract.

vertragswidrig [fɛr'traːksviːdrɪç], *adj.* contrary to contract.

vertrauen [fɛr'trauən], *v.n.* rely (upon), trust (in).

Vertrauen [fɛr'trauən], *n.* (—s, *no pl.*) confidence, trust, reliance.

vertrauenerweckend [fɛr'trauənɛrvɛkənt], *adj.* inspiring confidence.

Vertrauensbruch [fɛr'trauənsbrux], *m.* (—es, *pl.* ⸚e) breach of faith.

Vertrauensmann [fɛr'trauənsman], *m.* (—s, *pl.* ⸚er) confidant; delegate; person entrusted with s.th.; (*Ind.*) shop steward.

vertrauensselig [fɛr'trauənszeːlɪç], *adj.* confiding, trusting.

Vertrauensvotum [fɛr'trauənsvoːtum], *n.* (—s, *pl.* —ten) vote of confidence.

vertrauenswürdig [fɛr'trauənsvyrdɪç], *adj.* trustworthy.

vertraulich [fɛr'traulɪç], *adj.* confidential; familiar.

Vertraulichkeit [fɛr'traulɪçkaɪt], *f.* (—, *pl.* —en) familiarity.

verträumt [fɛr'trɔymt], *adj.* dreamy.

vertraut [fɛr'traut], *adj.* intimate, familiar; conversant.

Vertraute [fɛr'trautə], *m.* (—n, *pl.* —n) close friend, confidant.

Vertrautheit [fɛr'trauthaɪt], *f.* (—, *no pl.*) familiarity.

vertreiben [fɛr'traɪbən], *v.a. irr.* drive away, expel; eject; (*person*) banish; (*time*) pass, kill; (*goods*) sell.

Vertreibung [fɛr'traɪbuŋ], *f.* (—, *no pl.*) expulsion; banishment.

vertreten [fɛr'treːtən], *v.a. irr.* represent (s.o.), deputise for (s.o.).

Vertreter [fɛr'treːtər], *m.* (—s, *pl.* —) representative, deputy; (*Comm.*) agent.

Vertretung [fɛr'treːtuŋ], *f.* (—, *pl.* —en) representation, agency.

Vertrieb [fɛr'triːp], *m.* (—s, *pl.* —e) sale; distribution.

vertrinken [fɛr'trɪŋkən], *v.a. irr.* spend *or* waste money on drink.

vertrocknen [fɛr'trɔknən], *v.n.* (*aux.* sein) dry up, wither.

vertrödeln [fɛr'trøːdəln], *v.a.* fritter (o.'s time) away.

vertrösten [fɛr'trøːstən], *v.a.* console; put off; put (s.o.) off with fine words; fob (s.o.) off with vain hopes.

Vertröstung [fɛr'trøːstuŋ], *f.* (—, *pl.* —en) comfort; empty promises.

vertun [fɛr'tuːn], *v.a. irr.* squander, waste.

vertuschen [fɛr'tuʃən], *v.a.* hush up.

verübeln [fɛr'yːbəln], *v.a.* take amiss.

verüben [fɛr'yːbən], *v.a.* commit, perpetrate.

verunehren [fɛr'uneːrən], *v.a.* dishonour, disgrace.

verunglimpfen [fɛr'unglɪmpfən], *v.a.* bring into disrepute; defame, calumniate.

Verunglimpfung [fɛr'unglɪmpfuŋ], *f.* (—, *pl.* —en) defamation, detraction, calumny.

verunglücken [fɛr'unglykən], *v.n.* (*aux.* sein) (*person*) meet with an accident; be killed; (*thing*) misfire, fail.

verunreinigen [fɛr'unraɪnɪgən], *v.a.* contaminate.

Verunreinigung [fɛr'unraɪnɪguŋ], *f.* (—, *pl.* —en) contamination.

verunstalten [fɛr'unʃtaltən], *v.a.* disfigure, deface.

Verunstaltung [fɛr'unʃtaltuŋ], *f.* (—, *pl.* —en) disfigurement.

Veruntreuung [fɛr'untrɔyuŋ], *f.* (—, *pl.* —en) embezzlement, misappropriation.

verunzieren [fɛr'untsiːrən], *v.a.* disfigure, spoil.

verursachen [fɛr'uːrzaxən], *v.a.* cause, occasion.

verurteilen [fɛr'urtaɪlən], *v.a.* condemn; (*Law*) sentence.

Verurteilung [fɛr'urtaɪluŋ], *f.* (—, *no pl.*) condemnation; (*Law*) sentence.

vervielfältigen [fɛr'fiːlfɛltɪgən], *v.a.* multiply; duplicate, make copies of.

Vervielfältigung [fɛr'fiːlfɛltɪguŋ], *f.* (—, *pl.* —en) multiplication; duplication, copying.

vervollkommnen [fɛr'fɔlkɔmnən], *v.a.* improve, perfect.

Vervollkommnung [fɛr'fɔlkɔmnuŋ], *f.* (—, *no pl.*) improvement, perfection.

vervollständigen [fɛr'fɔlʃtɛndɪgən], *v.a.* complete.

Vervollständigung [fɛr'fɔlʃtɛndɪguŋ], *f.* (—, *no pl.*) completion.

verwachsen [fɛr'vaksən], *v.n. irr.* (*aux.* sein) grow together; be overgrown. — *adj.* deformed.

verwahren [fɛr'vaːrən], *v.a.* take care of, preserve, secure. — *v.r. sich gegen*, protest against.

verwahrlosen [fɛr'vaːrloːzən], *v.a.* neglect. — *v.n.* (*aux.* sein) be in need of care and protection, be neglected.

Verwahrlosung [fɛr'vaːrloːzuŋ], *f.* (—, *no pl.*) neglect.

Verwahrung [fɛr'vaːruŋ], *f.* (—, *no pl.*) keeping; charge; *in — geben*, deposit, give into s.o.'s charge; *— einlegen gegen*, enter a protest against.

verwalten [fɛr'valtən], *v.a.* manage, administer.

Verwalter [fɛr'valtər], *m.* (—s, *pl.* —) administrator, manager; steward, bailiff.

Verwaltung [fɛr'valtuŋ], *f.* (—, *pl.* —en) administration, management; Civil Service.

Verwaltungsbezirk [fɛr'valtuŋsbətsɪrk], *m.* (—s, *pl.* —e) administrative district.

Verwandlung [fɛr'vandluŋ], *f.* (—, *pl.* —en) alteration, transformation.

Verwandlungskünstler

Verwandlungskünstler [fɛr'vandluŋs-kynstlər], *m.* (—s, *pl.* —) quick-change artist.

verwandt [fɛr'vant], *adj.* related; cognate; congenial.

Verwandte [fɛr'vantə], *m.* (—n, *pl.* —n) relative, relation; kinsman; *der nächste* —, next of kin.

Verwandtschaft [fɛr'vantʃaft], *f.* (—, *pl.* —en) relationship; relations, family; congeniality, sympathy.

verwarnen [fɛr'varnən], *v.a.* admonish, forewarn.

Verwarnung [fɛr'varnuŋ], *f.* (—, *pl.* —en) admonition.

Verwässerung [fɛr'vɛsəruŋ], *f.* (—, *pl.* —en) dilution.

verwechseln [fɛr'vɛksəln], *v.a.* confuse; mistake for.

Verwechslung [fɛr'vɛksluŋ], *f.* (—, *pl.* —en) confusion, mistake.

verwegen [fɛr've:gən], *adj.* bold, audacious.

Verwegenheit [fɛr've:gənhaɪt], *f.* (—, *pl.* —en) boldness, audacity.

verweichlichen [fɛr'vaɪçlɪçən], *v.a.* coddle. — *v.n.* (*aux.* sein) become effeminate.

verweigern [fɛr'vaɪgərn], *v.a.* refuse, deny; reject.

Verweigerung [fɛr'vaɪgəruŋ], *f.* (—, *pl.* —en) refusal, denial; rejection.

verweilen [fɛr'vaɪlən], *v.n.* remain; tarry; stay (with), dwell (on).

verweint [fɛr'vaɪnt], *adj.* (*eyes*) red with weeping.

Verweis [fɛr'vaɪs], *m.* (—es, *pl.* —e) reproof, reprimand, rebuke.

verweisen [fɛr'vaɪzən], *v.a. irr.* reprimand; banish, exile; — *auf etwas*, refer to s.th., hint at s.th.

Verweisung [fɛr'vaɪzuŋ], *f.* (—, *pl.* —en) banishment, exile; reference.

verweltlichen [fɛr'vɛltlɪçən], *v.a.* secularise, profane.

verwenden [fɛr'vɛndən], *v.a.* use, make use of; apply to, employ in, utilize.

Verwendung [fɛr'vɛnduŋ], *f.* (—, *pl.* —en) application, use, expenditure, employment.

verwerfen [fɛr'vɛrfən], *v.a. irr.* reject, disapprove of.

verwerflich [fɛr'vɛrflɪç], *adj.* objectionable.

Verwertung [fɛr've:rtuŋ], *f.* (—, *no pl.*) utilisation.

verwesen [fɛr've:zən], *v.a.* administer. — *v.n.* (*aux.* sein) rot, decompose, putrefy.

Verweser [fɛr've:zər], *m.* (—s, *pl.* —) administrator.

Verwesung [fɛr've:zuŋ], *f.* (—, *no pl.*) (*office*) administration; putrefaction, rotting.

verwickeln [fɛr'vɪkəln], *v.a.* entangle, involve.

verwickelt [fɛr'vɪkəlt], *adj.* intricate, complicated, involved.

Verwicklung [fɛr'vɪkluŋ], *f.* (—, *pl.* —en) entanglement, involvement, complication.

verwildern [fɛr'vɪldərn], *v.n.* (*aux.* sein) run wild.

verwildert [fɛr'vɪldərt], *adj.* wild, uncultivated, overgrown; (*fig.*) intractable.

Verwilderung [fɛr'vɪldəruŋ], *f.* (—, *no pl.*) running wild, growing wild.

verwirken [fɛr'vɪrkən], *v.a.* forfeit.

verwirklichen [fɛr'vɪrklɪçən], *v.a.* realise. — *v.r. sich* —, materialise, come true.

Verwirklichung [fɛr'vɪrklɪçuŋ], *f.* (—, *no pl.*) realisation, materialisation.

Verwirkung [fɛr'vɪrkuŋ], *f.* (—, *no pl.*) forfeiture.

verwirren [fɛr'vɪrən], *v.a.* disarrange, throw into disorder, entangle; puzzle, bewilder, confuse, disconcert.

Verwirrung [fɛr'vɪruŋ], *f.* (—, *pl.* —en) bewilderment, confusion.

verwischen [fɛr'vɪʃən], *v.a.* blot out, smudge, obliterate.

verwittern [fɛr'vɪtərn], *v.n.* (*aux.* sein) be weather-beaten.

verwöhnen [fɛr'vø:nən], *v.a.* spoil, pamper, coddle.

verworfen [fɛr'vɔrfən], *adj.* profligate; rejected, reprobate.

verworren [fɛr'vɔrən], *adj.* confused, perplexed; intricate; (*speech*) rambling.

verwundbar [fɛr'vuntba:r], *adj.* vulnerable.

verwunden [fɛr'vundən], *v.a.* wound, hurt, injure.

verwundern [fɛr'vundərn], *v.r. sich* —, be surprised, wonder, be amazed.

Verwunderung [fɛr'vundəruŋ], *f.* (—, *no pl.*) surprise, astonishment, amazement.

Verwundung [fɛr'vunduŋ], *f.* (—, *pl.* —en) wounding, wound, injury.

verwunschen [fɛr'vunʃən], *adj.* enchanted, spellbound, bewitched.

verwünschen [fɛr'vynʃən], *v.a.* curse; cast a spell on, bewitch.

verwünscht [fɛr'vynʃt], *excl.* confound it!

Verwünschung [fɛr'vynʃuŋ], *f.* (—, *pl.* —en) curse, malediction.

verwüsten [fɛr'vy:stən], *v.a.* devastate, ravage, lay waste.

Verwüstung [fɛr'vy:stuŋ], *f.* (—, *pl.* —en) devastation.

verzagen [fɛr'tsa:gən], *v.n.* (*aux.* sein) lose heart, lose courage.

verzagt [fɛr'tsa:kt], *adj.* fainthearted, discouraged.

Verzagtheit [fɛr'tsa:kthaɪt], *f.* (—, *no pl.*) faintheartedness.

verzählen [fɛr'tsɛ:lən], *v.r. sich* —, miscount.

verzapfen [fɛr'tsapfən], *v.a.* sell (liquor) on draught; (*fig.*) tell (a story), talk (nonsense).

verzärteln [fɛr'tsɛ:rtəln], *v.a.* pamper, coddle; spoil.

verzaubern [fɛr'tsaubərn], *v.a.* bewitch, charm, put a spell on.

verzehren [fɛr'tseːrən], *v.a.* consume, eat. — *v.r. sich* — *in*, pine away with, be consumed with.

Verzehrung [fɛr'tseːruŋ], *f.* (—, *no pl.*) (*obs.*) consumption, tuberculosis.

verzeichnen [fɛr'tsaɪçnən], *v.a.* draw badly; note down, register, record.

Verzeichnis [fɛr'tsaɪçnɪs], *n.* (—**ses,** *pl.* —**se**) catalogue, list, register.

verzeihen [fɛr'tsaɪən], *v.a. irr.* forgive, pardon.

verzeihlich [fɛr'tsaɪlɪç], *adj.* pardonable, forgivable, excusable, venial.

Verzeihung [fɛr'tsaɪuŋ], *f.* (—, *no pl.*) pardon, forgiveness; *ich bitte um —,* I beg your pardon.

verzerren [fɛr'tsɛrən], *v.a.* distort.

Verzerrung [fɛr'tsɛruŋ], *f.* (—, *pl.* —en) distortion; (*face*) grimace.

verzetteln [fɛr'tsɛtəln], *v.a.* disperse, scatter.

Verzicht [fɛr'tsɪçt], *m.* (—(e)s, *no pl.*) renunciation, resignation.

verzichten [fɛr'tsɪçtən], *v.n.* forgo, renounce.

verziehen [fɛr'tsiːən], *v.a. irr.* distort; spoil (*child*). — *v.n.* (*aux.* sein) go away, move away.

Verzierung [fɛr'tsiːruŋ], *f.* (—, *pl.* —en) decoration, ornament.

verzögern [fɛr'tsøːgərn], *v.a.* delay, defer, retard, protract, procrastinate. — *v.r. sich* —, be delayed.

Verzögerung [fɛr'tsøːgəruŋ], *f.* (—, *pl.* —en) delay, retardation, procrastination; time-lag.

verzollen [fɛr'tsɔlən], *v.a.* pay duty on.

Verzückheit [fɛr'tsykhaɪt], *f.* (—, *no pl.*) ecstasy, rapture.

Verzug [fɛr'tsuːk], *m.* (—s, *no pl.*) delay.

verzweifeln [fɛr'tsvaɪfəln], *v.n.* despair, be desperate.

Verzweiflung [fɛr'tsvaɪfluŋ], *f.* (—, *no pl.*) despair.

verzwickt [fɛr'tsvɪkt], *adj.* complicated, intricate, tricky.

Vesuv [veˈzuːf], *m.* Mount Vesuvius.

Vetter ['vɛtər], *m.* (—s, *pl.* —n) cousin.

Vetternwirtschaft ['vɛtərnvɪrtʃaft], *f.* (—, *no pl.*) nepotism.

Vexierbild [vɛ'ksiːrbɪlt], *n.* (—s, *pl.* —er) picture-puzzle.

Vexierspiegel [vɛ'ksiːrʃpiːgəl], *m.* (—s, *pl.*—) distorting mirror.

vibrieren [viˈbriːrən], *v.n.* vibrate.

Vieh [fiː], *n.* (—s, *no pl.*) cattle, livestock.

Viehfutter ['fiːfutər], *n.* (—s, *no pl.*) forage, fodder, feeding-stuff.

viehisch ['fiːɪʃ], *adj.* beastly, brutal.

Viehwagen ['fiːvaːgən], *m.* (—s, *pl.* —) cattle-truck.

Viehweide ['fiːvaɪdə], *f.* (—, *pl.* —n) pasture, pasturage.

Viehzüchter ['fiːtsyçtər], *m.* (—s, *pl.* —) cattle-breeder.

viel [fiːl], *adj.* much, a great deal, a lot; (*pl.*) many.

vielartig ['fiːlartɪç], *adj.* multifarious.

vieldeutig ['fiːldɔytɪç], *adj.* ambiguous, equivocal.

Vieleck ['fiːlɛk], *n.* (—s, *pl.* —e) polygon.

vielerlei ['fiːlərlaɪ], *adj.* of many kinds, various.

vielfältig ['fiːlfɛltɪç], *adj.* manifold.

vielfarbig ['fiːlfarbɪç], *adj.* multi-coloured, variegated.

Vielfraß ['fiːlfraːs], *m.* (—es, *pl.* —e) glutton.

vielgeliebt ['fiːlgəliːpt], *adj.* much loved, well-beloved, dearly loved.

vielgereist ['fiːlgəraɪst], *adj.* much travelled.

vielleicht [fi'laɪçt], *adv.* perhaps, maybe.

vielmals ['fiːlmaːls], *adv.* many times, frequently, much.

Vielmännerei [fiːlmɛnəˈraɪ], *f.* (—, *no pl.*) polyandry.

vielmehr [fiːlˈmeːr], *adv.* rather, much more. — *conj.* rather, on the other hand.

vielsagend ['fiːlzaːgənt], *adj.* expressive, full of meaning.

vielseitig [fiːlˈzaɪtɪç], *adj.* multilateral; (*fig.*) versatile.

Vielseitigkeit ['fiːlzaɪtɪçkaɪt], *f.* (—, *no pl.*) versatility.

vielverheißend ['fiːlfɛrhaɪsənt], *adj.* promising, auspicious.

Vielweiberei [fiːlvaɪbəˈraɪ], *f.* (—, *no pl.*) polygamy.

vier [fiːr], *num. adj.* four.

Viereck ['fiːrɛk], *n.* (—s, *pl.* —e) square, quadrangle.

viereckig ['fiːrɛkɪç], *adj.* square.

vierfüßig ['fiːrfyːsɪç], *adj.* four-footed.

vierhändig ['fiːrhɛndɪç], *adj.* four-handed; — *spielen*, (*piano*) play duets.

vierschrötig ['fiːrʃrøːtɪç], *adj.* robust, thick-set, stocky.

vierseitig ['fiːrzaɪtɪç], *adj.* quadrilateral.

vierstimmig ['fiːrʃtɪmɪç], *adj.* (*Mus.*) four-part; for four voices.

vierteilen [fiːrˈtaɪlən], *v.a.* quarter, divide into four parts.

Viertel ['fɪrtəl], *n.* (—s, *pl.* —) quarter, fourth part.

Viertelstunde [fɪrtəlˈʃtundə], *f.* (—, *pl.* —n) quarter of an hour.

viertens ['fiːrtəns], *num. adv.* fourthly, in the fourth place.

Vierwaldstättersee [fiːrˈvaltʃtɛtərzeː], *m.* Lake Lucerne.

vierzehn ['fɪrtseːn], *num. adj.* fourteen; — *Tage,* a fortnight.

vierzig ['fɪrtsɪç], *num. adj.* forty.

Vietnam [viɛtˈnaːm], *n.* Vietnam.

Violinschlüssel [violiːnˈʃlysəl], *m.* (—s, *pl.* —) (*Mus.*) treble clef.

Virtuosität [vɪrtuoziˈtɛːt], *f.* (—, *no pl.*) mastery, virtuosity.

Visage [viˈzaːʒə], *f.* (—, *pl.* —n) (*coll.*) face.

Visier [viˈziːr], *n.* (—, *pl.* —e) visor; (*gun*) sight.

Vision [viˈzjoːn], *f.* (—, *pl.* —en) vision.

Visionär

Visionär [vizjo'nɛːr], *m.* (—s, *pl.* —e) visionary.

Visitenkarte [vi'ziːtənkartə], *f.* (—, *pl.* —n) card, visiting card.

Visum ['viːzum], *n.* (—s, *pl.* Visa) visa.

Vizekönig ['viːtsəkøːnɪç], *m.* (—s, *pl.* —e) viceroy.

Vlies [fliːs], *n.* (—es, *pl.* —e) fleece.

Vogel ['foːgəl], *m.* (—s, *pl.* ⁻) bird; (*coll.*) fellow; *einen* — *haben,* be off o.'s head.

Vogelbauer ['foːgəlbauər], *n.* (—s, *pl.* —) bird-cage.

Vogelfänger ['foːgəlfɛŋər], *m.* (—s, *pl.* —) fowler, bird-catcher.

vogelfrei ['foːgəlfrai], *adj.* outlawed, proscribed.

Vogelfutter ['foːgəlfutər], *n.* (—s, *no pl.*) bird-seed.

Vogelhändler ['foːgəlhɛndlər], *m.* (—s, *pl.* —) bird-dealer.

Vogelhaus ['foːgəlhaus], *n.* (—es, *pl.* ⁻er) aviary.

Vogelkenner ['foːgəlkɛnər], *m.* (—s, *pl.* —) ornithologist.

Vogelkunde ['foːgəlkundə], *f.* (—, *no pl.*) ornithology.

Vogelperspektive ['foːgəlpɛrspɛktiːvə], *f.* (—, *no pl.*) bird's-eye view.

Vogelschau ['foːgəlʃau], *f.* (—, *no pl.*) bird's-eye view.

Vogelsteller ['foːgəlʃtɛlər], *m.* (—s, *pl.* —) fowler, bird-catcher.

Vogesen [vo'geːzən], *pl.* Vosges Mountains.

Vogler ['foːglər], *m.* (—s, *pl.* —) fowler.

Vogt [foːkt], *m.* (—(e)s, *pl.* ⁻e) prefect, bailiff, steward, provost.

Vogtei [foːk'tai], *f.* (—, *pl.* —en) prefecture, bailiwick.

Vokabel [vo'kaːbəl], *f.* (—, *pl.* —n) word, vocable.

Vokabelbuch [vo'kaːbəlbuːx], *n.* (—(e)s, *pl.* ⁻er) vocabulary (book).

Vokal [vo'kaːl], *m.* (—s, *pl.* —e) vowel.

Vokativ [voka'tiːf], *m.* (—s, *pl.* —e) (*Gram.*) vocative.

Volk [fɔlk], *n.* (—(e)s, *pl.* ⁻er) people, nation; *das gemeine* —, mob, the common people.

Völkerkunde ['fœlkərkundə], *f.* (—, *no pl.*) ethnology.

Völkerrecht ['fœlkərrɛçt], *n.* (—s, *no pl.*) international law.

Völkerschaft ['fœlkərʃaft], *f.* (—, *pl.* —en) tribe, people.

Völkerwanderung ['fœlkərvandəruŋ], *f.* (—, *pl.* —en) mass migration.

Volksabstimmung ['fɔlksapʃtɪmuŋ], *f.* (—, *pl.* —en) referendum.

Volksausgabe ['fɔlksausgaːbə], *f.* (—, *pl.* —n) popular edition.

Volksbeschluß ['fɔlksbəʃlus], *m.* (—sses, *pl.* ⁻sse) plebiscite.

Volksbibliothek ['fɔlksbiblioteːk], *f.* (—, *pl.* —en) public library.

Volkscharakter ['fɔlkskaraktər], *m.* (—s, *no pl.*) national character.

Volksentscheid ['fɔlksɛntʃait], *m.* (—s, *pl.* —e) plebiscite.

Volksführer ['fɔlksfyːrər], *m.* (—s, *pl.* —) demagogue.

Volksheer ['fɔlksheːr], *n.* (—s, *pl.* —e) national army.

Volksherrschaft ['fɔlkshɛrʃaft], *f.* (—, *no pl.*) democracy.

Volkshochschule ['fɔlkshoxʃuːlə], *f.* (—, *no pl.*) adult education (classes).

Volksjustiz ['fɔlksjustiːts], *f.* (—, *no pl.*) lynch-law.

Volkskunde ['fɔlkskundə], *f.* (—, *no pl.*) folklore.

Volkslied ['fɔlksliːt], *n.* (—s, *pl.* —er) folk-song.

Volksschicht ['fɔlksʃɪçt], *f.* (—, *pl.* —en) class.

Volksschule ['fɔlksʃuːlə], *f.* (—, *pl.* —n) primary school; elementary school.

Volkssitte ['fɔlkszɪtə], *f.* (—, *pl.* —n) national custom.

Volkssprache ['fɔlksʃpraːxə], *f.* (—, *pl.* —n) vernacular.

Volksstamm ['fɔlksʃtam], *m.* (—s, *pl.* ⁻e) tribe.

Volkstracht ['fɔlkstraxt], *f.* (—, *pl.* —en) national costume.

volkstümlich ['fɔlkstyːmlɪç], *adj.* national, popular.

Volksvertretung ['fɔlksfɛrtreːtuŋ], *f.* (—, *no pl.*) representation of the people, parliamentary representation.

Volkswirt ['fɔlksvɪrt], *m.* (—s, *pl.* —e) political economist.

Volkswirtschaft ['fɔlksvɪrtʃaft], *f.* (—, *no pl.*) political economy.

Volkszählung ['fɔlkstsɛːluŋ], *f.* (—, *pl.* —en) census.

voll [fɔl], *adj.* full, filled; whole, complete, entire.

vollauf ['fɔlauf], *adv.* abundantly.

Vollbart ['fɔlbaːrt], *m.* (—s, *pl.* ⁻e) beard.

vollberechtigt ['fɔlbərɛçtɪçt], *adj.* fully entitled.

Vollbild ['fɔlbɪlt], *n.* (—s, *pl.* —er) full-length portrait, full-page illustration.

Vollblut ['fɔlbluːt], *n.* (—s, *pl.* ⁻er) thoroughbred.

vollblütig ['fɔlblyːtɪç], *adj.* full-blooded, thoroughbred.

vollbringen [fɔl'brɪŋən], *v.a. irr.* accomplish, achieve, complete.

Vollbringung [fɔl'brɪŋuŋ], *f.* (—, *no pl.*) achievement.

Volldampf ['fɔldampf], *m.* (—es, *no pl.*) full steam.

vollenden [fɔl'ɛndən], *v.a.* finish, complete.

vollendet [fɔl'ɛndət], *adj.* finished; accomplished.

vollends ['fɔlɛnts], *adv.* quite, altogether, wholly, entirely, moreover.

Vollendung [fɔl'ɛnduŋ], *f.* (—, *no pl.*) completion; perfection.

Völlerei [fœlə'rai], *f.* (—, *pl.* —en) gluttony.

vollführen [fɔl'fy:rən], *v.a.* execute, carry out.

Vollgefühl ['fɔlgəfy:l], *n.* (—s, *no pl.*) consciousness, full awareness.

Vollgenuß ['fɔlgənus], *m.* (—sses, *no pl.*) full enjoyment.

vollgültig ['fɔlgyltɪç], *adj.* fully valid; unexceptionable.

Vollheit ['fɔlhaɪt], *f.* (—, *no pl.*) fullness, plenitude.

völlig ['fœlɪç], *adj.* entire, whole, complete.

vollinhaltlich ['fɔlɪnhaltlɪç], *adv.* to its full extent.

volljährig ['fɔljɛ:rɪç], *adj.* of age.

Volljährigkeit ['fɔljɛ:rɪçkaɪt], *f.* (—, *no pl.*) adult years, majority.

vollkommen ['fɔlkɔmən], *adj.* perfect. — *adv.* entirely.

Vollkommenheit [fɔl'kɔmənhaɪt], *f.* (—, *no pl.*) perfection.

Vollmacht ['fɔlmaxt], *f.* (—, *pl.* —en) authority; fullness of power; power of attorney.

vollsaftig ['fɔlzaftɪç], *adj.* juicy, succulent.

vollständig ['fɔlʃtɛndɪç], *adj.* complete, full. — *adv.* entirely.

vollstrecken [fɔl'ʃtrɛkən], *v.a.* execute, carry out.

Vollstrecker [fɔl'ʃtrɛkər], *m.* (—s, *pl.* —) executor.

volltönig ['fɔltø:nɪç], *adj.* sonorous.

vollwertig ['fɔlvɛrtɪç], *adj.* standard, sterling.

vollzählig ['fɔltsɛ:lɪç], *adj.* complete.

vollziehen [fɔl'tsi:ən], *v.a. irr.* execute, carry out, ratify.

vollziehend [fɔl'tsi:ənt], *adj.* executive.

Vollziehungsgewalt [fɔl'tsi:uŋsgəvalt], *f.* (—, *no pl.*) executive power.

Vollzug [fɔl'tsu:k], *m.* (—s, *no pl.*) execution; fulfilment.

Volontär [vɔlɔ'tɛ:r], *m.* (—s, *pl.* —e) volunteer.

von [fɔn] (*von dem* becomes **vom**), *prep.* (*Dat.*) by, from; of; on; concerning, about; — *Shakespeare*, by Shakespeare; — *Beruf*, by profession; *er kommt* — *London*, he comes from London; — *fern*, from afar; — *jetzt an*, from now on; — *einem versprechen*, speak of s.o.; *dein Breif vom 15.*, your letter of the 15th.

vonnöten [fɔn'nø:tən], *adv.* — *sein*, be necessary.

vonstatten [fɔn'ʃtatən], *adv.* — *gehen*, progress; go off.

vor [fo:r], *prep.* (*Dat., Acc.*) (*place*) before, ahead of, in front of; (*time*) before, prior to, earlier than; from; of; with; above; in presence of, because of; more than; — *dem Hause*, in front of the house; — *Sonnenaufgang*, before sunrise; —*zwei Tagen*, two days ago; *sich verstecken*, hide from s.o.; *sich hüten* —, beware of; — *starr* — *Kälte*, stiff with cold; — *allem*, above all. — *adv.* before; *nach wie* —, now as before.

Vorabend ['fo:ra:bənt], *m.* (—s, *pl.* —e) eve.

Vorahnung ['fo:ra:nuŋ], *f.* (—, *pl.* —en) presentiment, foreboding.

voran [fo'ran], *adv.* before, in front, forward, on.

vorangehen [fo'range:ən], *v.n. irr.* (*aux.* sein) take the lead, go ahead.

Voranzeige ['fo:rantsaɪgə], *f.* (—, *pl.* —n) advance notice; (*film*) trailer.

Vorarbeiter ['fo:rarbaɪtər], *m.* (—s, *pl.* —) foreman.

voraus [fo'raus], *adv.* before, in front, foremost; in advance; *im* or *zum* —, beforehand; (*thanks*) in anticipation.

vorauseilen [fo'rausaɪlən], *v.n.* (*aux.* sein) run ahead.

vorausgehen [fo'rausge:ən], *v.n. irr.* (*aux.* sein) walk ahead; *einem* —, go before; precede s.o.

voraushaben [fo'rausha:bən], *v.n. irr.* *etwas vor einem* —, have the advantage over s.o.

Voraussage [fo'rausza:gə], *f.* (—, *pl.* —n) prediction, prophecy; (*weather*) forecast.

voraussagen [fo'rausza:gən], *v.a.* predict, foretell; (*weather*) forecast.

voraussehen [fo'rausze:ən], *v.a. irr.* foresee.

voraussetzen [fo'rauszɛtsən], *v.a.* presuppose, take for granted.

Voraussetzung [fo'rauszɛtsuŋ], *f.* (—, *pl.* —en) supposition, presupposition; *unter der* —, on the understanding.

Voraussicht [fo'rauszɪçt], *f.* (—, *no pl.*) foresight, forethought; *aller* — *nach*, in all probability.

voraussichtlich [fo'rauszɪçtlɪç], *adj.* prospective, presumptive, probable, expected. — *adv.* probably, presumably.

Vorbau ['fo:rbau], *m.* (—s, *pl.* —ten) frontage.

Vorbedacht ['fo:rbədaxt], *m.* (—s, *no pl.*) premeditation; *mit* —, on purpose, deliberately.

vorbedacht ['fo:rbədaxt], *adj.* premeditated.

Vorbedeutung ['fo:rbədɔytuŋ], *f.* (—, *pl.* —en) omen.

Vorbehalt ['fo:rbəhalt], *m.* (—s, *pl.* —e) reservation, proviso.

vorbehalten ['fo:rbəhaltən], *v.a. irr.* reserve; make reservation that.

vorbehaltlich ['fo:rbəhaltlɪç], *prep.* (*Genit.*) with the proviso that.

vorbei [fo:r'baɪ], *adv.* by; along; past, over, finished, gone.

vorbeigehen [fo:r'baɪge:ən], *v.n. irr.* (*aux.* sein) pass by; go past; march past.

vorbeilassen [fo:r'baɪlasən], *v.a. irr.* let pass.

Vorbemerkung ['fo:rbəmɛrkuŋ], *f.* (—, *pl.* —en) preface, prefatory note.

vorbereiten ['fo:rbəraɪtən], *v.a.* prepare.

Vorbereitung ['fo:rbəraɪtuŋ], *f.* (—, *pl.* —en) preparation.

Vorbesitzer

Vorbesitzer [ˈfoːrbəzɪtsər], *m.* (**—s**, *pl.* **—**) previous owner.

Vorbesprechung [ˈfoːrbəʃprɛçuŋ], *f.* (**—**, *pl.* **—en**) preliminary discussion.

vorbestimmen [ˈfoːrbəʃtɪmən], *v.a.* predestine, predetermine.

Vorbestimmung [ˈfoːrbəʃtɪmuŋ], *f.* (**—**, *no pl.*) predestination.

vorbestraft [ˈfoːrbəʃtraːft], *adj.* previously convicted.

vorbeten [ˈfoːrbeːtən], *v.n.* lead in prayer.

vorbeugen [ˈfoːrbɔygən], *v.n.* prevent, preclude, obviate. — *v.r.* **sich —**, bend forward.

Vorbeugung [ˈfoːrbɔyguŋ], *f.* (**—**, *no pl.*) prevention; prophylaxis.

Vorbeugungsmaßnahme [ˈfoːrbɔyguŋsmaːsnaːmə], *f.* (**—**, *pl.* **—n**) preventive measure.

Vorbild [ˈfoːrbɪlt], *n.* (**—s**, *pl.* **—er**) model, example, pattern, ideal.

vorbildlich [ˈfoːrbɪltlɪç], *adj.* exemplary; typical; — **sein**, be a model.

Vorbildung [ˈfoːrbɪlduŋ], *f.* (**—**, *no pl.*) preparatory training.

Vorbote [ˈfoːrboːtə], *m.* (**—n**, *pl.* **—n**) herald, precursor, forerunner.

vorbringen [ˈfoːrbrɪŋən], *v.a. irr.* produce, proffer; advance, utter, allege, assert, claim.

vordatieren [ˈfoːrdatiːrən], *v.a.* antedate.

vordem [forˈdeːm], *adv.* (*obs.*) formerly, once.

Vorderachse [ˈfordəraksə], *f.* (**—**, *pl.* **—n**) front axle.

Vorderansicht [ˈfordəranzɪçt], *f.* (**—**, *pl.* **—en**) front view.

Vorderarm [ˈfordərarm], *m.* (**—s**, *pl.* **—e**) forearm.

Vordergrund [ˈfordərgrunt], *m.* (**—s**, *pl.* **—e**) foreground

vorderhand [ˈfordərhant], *adv.* for the present.

Vorderseite [ˈfordərzaɪtə], *f.* (**—**, *pl.* **—n**) front.

vorderst [ˈfordərst], *adj.* foremost, first.

Vordertür [ˈfordərtyːr], *f.* (**—**, *pl.* **—en**) front door.

Vordertreffen [ˈfordərtrɛfən], *n.* (**—s**, *no pl.*) **ins — kommen**, be in the vanguard, come to the fore.

vordrängen [ˈfoːrdrɛŋən], *v.r.* **sich —**, press forward, jump the queue.

vordringen [ˈfoːrdrɪŋən], *v.n. irr.* (*aux.* sein) advance, push forward.

vordringlich [ˈfoːrdrɪŋlɪç], *adj.* urgent; forward, importunate.

Vordruck [ˈfoːrdrúk], *m.* (**—s**, *pl.* **—e**) (*printed*) form.

voreilen [ˈfoːraɪlən], *v.n.* (*aux.* sein) rush forward.

voreilig [ˈfoːraɪlɪç], *adj.* over-hasty, rash.

Voreiligkeit [ˈfoːraɪlɪçkaɪt], *f.* (**—**, *no pl.*) hastiness, rashness.

voreingenommen [ˈfoːraɪŋənɔmən], *adj.* biased, prejudiced.

Voreingenommenheit [ˈfoːraɪŋənɔmənhaɪt], *f.* (**—**, *no pl.*) bias, prejudice.

Voreltern [ˈfoːrɛltərn], *pl.* forefathers, ancestors.

vorenthalten [ˈfoːrɛnthaltən], *v.a. irr. sep. & insep.* withhold.

Vorentscheidung [ˈfoːrɛntʃaɪduŋ], *f.* (**—**, *pl.* **—en**) preliminary decision.

vorerst [foːrˈeːrst], *adv.* first of all, firstly; for the time being.

vorerwähnt [ˈfoːrɛrvɛːnt], *adj.* aforementioned.

Vorfahr [ˈfoːrfaːr], *m.* (**—en**, *pl.* **—en**) ancestor.

vorfahren [ˈfoːrfaːrən], *v.n. irr.* (*aux.* sein) drive up (to a house *etc.*).

Vorfall [ˈfoːrfal], *m.* (**—s**, *pl.* **—e**) occurrence, incident.

vorfinden [ˈfoːrfɪndən], *v.a. irr.* find, find present, meet with.

Vorfrage [ˈfoːrfraːgə], *f.* (**—**, *pl.* **—n**) preliminary question.

vorführen [ˈfoːrfyːrən], *v.a.* bring forward, produce.

Vorführung [ˈfoːrfyːruŋ], *f.* (**—**, *pl.* **—en**) production, presentation; performance.

Vorgang [ˈfoːrgaŋ], *m.* (**—s**, *pl.* **—e**) occurrence, event, happening; proceeding, precedent; procedure.

Vorgänger [ˈfoːrgɛŋər], *m.* (**—s**, *pl.* **—**) predecessor.

Vorgarten [ˈfoːrgartən], *m.* (**—s**, *pl.* **—**) front garden.

vorgeben [ˈfoːrgeːbən], *v.a. irr.* pretend; allow (in advance).

Vorgebirge [ˈfoːrgəbɪrgə], *n.* (**—s**, *no pl.*) cape, promontory.

vorgeblich [ˈfoːrgeːplɪç], *adj.* pretended; ostensible.

vorgefaßt [ˈfoːrgəfast], *adj.* preconceived.

Vorgefühl [ˈfoːrgəfyːl], *n.* (**—s**, *pl.* **—e**) presentiment.

vorgehen [ˈfoːrgeːən], *v.n. irr.* (*aux.* sein) advance, walk ahead; proceed; (*clock*) be fast, gain; (*fig.*) take precedence; occur, happen; *was geht hier vor?* what's going on here?

Vorgehen [ˈfoːrgeːən], *n.* (**—s**, *no pl.*) (course of) action, (manner of) procedure.

vorgenannt [ˈfoːrgənant], *adj.* aforenamed.

Vorgericht [ˈfoːrgərɪçt], *n.* (**—s**, *pl.* **—e**) hors d'œuvre, entrée.

Vorgeschichte [ˈfoːrgəʃɪçtə], *f.* (**—**, *no pl.*) prehistory; early history; antecedents.

vorgeschichtlich [ˈfoːrgəʃɪçtlɪç], *adj.* prehistoric.

Vorgeschmack [ˈfoːrgəʃmak], *m.* (**—s**, *no pl.*) foretaste.

Vorgesetzte [ˈfoːrgəzɛtstə], *m.* (**—n**, *pl.* **—n**) superior, senior; boss.

vorgestern [ˈfoːrgɛstərn], *adv.* the day before yesterday.

vorgreifen [ˈfoːrgraɪfən], *v.n. irr.* anticipate, forestall.

Vorhaben ['fo:rha:bən], *m.* (—s, *no pl.*) intention, purpose, design.

vorhaben ['fo:rha:bən], *v.a. irr.* intend; be busy with; *etwas mit einem* —, have designs on s.o.; have plans for s.o.

Vorhalle ['fo:rhalə], *f.* (—, *pl.* —n) vestibule, hall, porch.

vorhalten ['fo:rhaltən], *v.a. irr.* hold s.th. before s.o.; (*fig.*) remonstrate (with s.o. about s.th.); reproach. — *v.n.* last.

Vorhaltungen ['fo:rhaltuŋən], *f. pl.* remonstrances, expostulations.

vorhanden [for'handən], *adj.* at hand, present, in stock, on hand.

Vorhandensein [for'handənzaɪn], *n.* (—s, *no pl.*) existence; availability.

Vorhang ['fo:rhaŋ], *m.* (—s, *pl.* ⁓e) curtain.

Vorhängeschloß ['fo:rhɛŋəʃlɔs], *n.* (—sses, *pl.* ⁓sser) padlock.

vorher ['fo:rhe:r], *adv.* before, beforehand, in advance.

vorhergehen [fo:r'he:rge:ən], *v.n. irr.* (*aux.* sein) go before, precede.

vorhergehend [fo:r'he:rge:ənt], *adj.* foregoing, aforesaid, preceding.

vorherig [fo:r'he:rɪç], *adj.* preceding, previous, former.

vorherrschen ['fo:rhɛrʃən], *v.n.* prevail, predominate.

vorhersagen [fo:r'he:rza:gən], *v.a.* predict, foretell.

vorhersehen [fo:r'he:rze:ən], *v.a. irr.* foresee.

vorheucheln ['fo:rhɔyçəln], *v.a. einem etwas* —, pretend s.th. to s.o.

vorhin [fo:r'hɪn], *adv.* just before, a short while ago.

Vorhof ['fo:rho:f], *m.* (—s, *pl.* ⁓e) forecourt.

Vorhölle ['fo:rhœlə], *f.* (—, *no pl.*) limbo.

Vorhut ['fo:rhu:t], *f.* (—, *no pl.*) vanguard.

vorig ['fo:rɪç], *adj.* former, preceding.

Vorjahr ['fo:rja:r], *n.* (—s, *pl.* —e) preceding year.

vorjammern ['fo:rjamərn], *v.n. einem etwas* —, moan to s.o. about s.th.

Vorkämpfer ['fo:rkɛmpfər], *m.* (—s, *pl.* —) champion; pioneer.

vorkauen ['fo:rkauən], *v.a.* (*fig.*) predigest; spoon-feed.

Vorkaufsrecht ['fo:rkaufsrɛçt], *n.* (—s, *no pl.*) right of first refusal, right of pre-emption.

Vorkehrung ['fo:rke:ruŋ], *f.* (—, *pl.* —en) preparation; precaution; (*pl.*) arrangements.

Vorkenntnisse ['fo:rkɛntnɪsə], *f. pl.* rudiments, elements, grounding; previous knowledge.

vorkommen ['fo:rkɔmən], *v.n. irr.* (*aux.* sein) occur, happen; be found.

Vorkommnis ['fo:rkɔmnɪs], *n.* (—ses, *pl.* —se) occurrence, event, happening.

Vorkriegs- ['fo:rkri:ks], *prefix.* pre-war.

Vorladung ['fo:rla:duŋ], *f.* (—, *pl.* —en) summons, writ, subpœna.

Vorlage ['fo:rla:gə], *f.* (—, *pl.* —n) pattern, master-copy.

vorlagern ['fo:rla:gərn], *v.n.* (*aux.* sein) extend (in front of).

Vorland ['fo:rlant], *n.* (—s, *pl.* ⁓er) cape, foreland, foreshore.

vorlassen ['fo:rlasən], *v.a. irr.* give precedence to; admit, show in.

Vorläufer ['fo:rlɔyfər], *m.* (—s, *pl.* —) forerunner, precursor.

vorläufig ['fo:rlɔyfɪç], *adj.* provisional, preliminary, temporary. — *adv.* for the time being.

vorlaut ['fo:rlaut], *adj.* pert, forward.

Vorleben ['fo:rle:bən], *n.* (—s, *no pl.*) antecedents, past life.

vorlegen ['fo:rle:gən], *v.a.* put before s.o.; submit, propose; (*food*) serve.

Vorleger ['fo:rle:gər], *m.* (—s, *pl.* —) rug, mat.

Vorlegeschloß ['fo:rle:gəʃlɔs], *n.* (—sses, *pl.* ⁓sser) padlock.

vorlesen ['fo:rle:zən], *v.a. irr.* read aloud, read out.

Vorlesung ['fo:rle:zuŋ], *f.* (—, *pl.* —en) lecture.

vorletzte ['fo:rlɛtstə], *adj.* last but one, penultimate.

Vorliebe ['fo:rli:bə], *f.* (—, *no pl.*) predilection, partiality.

vorliebnehmen [fo:r'li:pne:mən], *v.n.* — *mit etwas*, be content with s.th., take pot luck.

vorliegen ['fo:rli:gən], *v.n. irr.* (*aux.* sein) be under consideration.

vorlügen ['fo:rly:gən], *v.a. irr. einem etwas* —, tell lies to s.o.

vormachen ['fo:rmaxən], *v.a. einem etwas* —, show s.o. how a thing is done; (*fig.*) play tricks on s.o., deceive s.o.

vormalig ['fo:rma:lɪç], *adj.* former, erstwhile, late.

vormals ['fo:rma:ls], *adv.* formerly.

Vormarsch ['fo:rmarʃ], *m.* (—es, *pl.* ⁓e) (*Mil.*) advance.

vormerken ['fo:rmɛrkən], *v.a.* make a note of, take down; book.

Vormittag ['fo:rmɪta:k], *m.* (—s, *pl.* —e) morning, forenoon.

vormittags ['fo:rmɪta:ks], *adv.* in the morning; before noon.

Vormund ['fo:rmunt], *m.* (—s, *pl.* ⁓er) guardian.

Vormundschaft ['fo:rmuntʃaft], *f.* (—, *pl.* —en) guardianship.

Vormundschaftsgericht ['fo:rmuntʃaftsgərɪçt], *n.* (—s, *pl.* —e) Court of Chancery.

vorn [fɔrn], *adv.* before, in front of; in front; (*Naut.*) fore.

Vorname ['fo:rna:mə], *m.* (—ns, *pl.*—n) first name, Christian name.

vornehm ['fo:rne:m], *adj.* of noble birth, refined; distinguished, elegant.

vornehmen ['fo:rne:mən], *v.a. irr.* take in hand; *sich etwas* —, undertake s.th.; plan *or* intend to do s.th.

Vornehmheit ['fo:rne:mhaɪt], *f.* (—, *no pl.*) refinement, distinction.

vornehmlich ['fo:rne:mlɪç], *adv.* chiefly, principally, especially.

vornherein ['fɔrnhɛraɪn], *adv. von* —, from the first; from the beginning.

Vorort ['fo:rɔrt], *m.* (—s, *pl.* —e) suburb.

Vorortsbahn ['fo:rɔrtsba:n], *f.* (—, *pl.* —en) suburban (railway) line.

Vorplatz ['fo:rplats], *m.* (—es, *pl.* ⁻e) forecourt.

Vorposten ['fo:rpɔstən], *m.* (—s, *pl.* —) (*Mil.*) outpost, pickets.

Vorpostengefecht ['fo:rpɔstəngəfɛçt], *n.* (—s, *pl.* —e) outpost skirmish.

Vorprüfung ['fo:rpry:fuŋ], *f.* (—, *pl.* —en) preliminary examination.

Vorrang ['fo:rraŋ], *m.* (—s, *no pl.*) precedence, first place, priority.

Vorrat ['fo:rra:t], *m.* (—s, *pl.* ⁻e) store, stock, provision.

Vorratskammer ['fo:rra:tskamər], *f.* (—, *pl.* —n) store-room; larder.

Vorrecht ['fo:rrɛçt], *n.* (—s, *pl.* —e) privilege, prerogative.

Vorrede ['fo:rre:də], *f.* (—, *pl.* —n) preface; introduction.

Vorredner ['fo:rre:dnər], *m.* (—s, *pl.* —) previous speaker.

vorrichten ['fo:rrɪçtən], *v.a.* prepare, fix up, get ready.

Vorrichtung ['fo:rrɪçtuŋ], *f.* (—, *pl.* —en) appliance, device, contrivance.

vorrücken ['fo:rrykən], *v.a.* move forward, advance; (*clock*) put on. — *v.n.* (*aux.* sein) (*Mil.*) advance.

Vorsaal ['fo:rza:l], *m.* (—s, *pl.* —säle) hall, entrance hall.

Vorsatz ['fo:rzats], *m.* (—es, *pl.* ⁻e) purpose, design, intention.

vorsätzlich ['fo:rzɛtslɪç], *adj.* intentional, deliberate.

Vorschein ['fo:rʃaɪn], *m.* *zum* — *kommen*, turn up; appear.

vorschießen ['fo:rʃi:sən], *v.a. irr.* (*money*) advance, lend.

Vorschlag ['fo:rʃla:k], *m.* (—s, *pl.* ⁻e) proposal, offer, proposition.

vorschlagen ['fo:rʃla:gən], *v.a. irr.* put forward, propose, suggest; recommend.

vorschnell ['fo:rʃnel], *adj.* hasty, rash, precipitate.

vorschreiben ['fo:rʃraɪbən], *v.a. irr.* write out (for s.o.); (*fig.*) prescribe, order.

Vorschrift ['fo:rʃrɪft], *f.* (—, *pl.* —en) prescription, direction, order, command, regulation.

vorschriftsmäßig ['fo:rʃrɪftsmɛ:sɪç], *adj.* according to regulations.

vorschriftswidrig ['fo:rʃrɪftsvi:drɪç], *adj.* contrary to regulations.

Vorschub ['fo:rʃup], *m.* (—s, *no pl.*) aid, assistance; — *leisten*, countenance, encourage, abet.

Vorschule ['fo:rʃu:lə], *f.* (—, *pl.* —n) preparatory school.

Vorschuß ['fo:rʃus], *m.* (—sses, *pl.* ⁻sse) advance (of cash).

vorschützen ['fo:rʃytsən], *v.a.* use as a pretext, pretend, plead.

vorschweben ['fo:rʃve:bən], *v.n.* be present in o.'s mind.

vorsehen ['fo:rze:ən], *v.r. irr. sich* —, take heed; be careful, look out, beware.

Vorsehung ['fo:rze:uŋ], *f.* (—, *no pl.*) Providence.

vorsetzen ['fo:rzɛtsən], *v.a.* set before; serve; (*word*) prefix.

Vorsicht ['fo:rzɪçt], *f.* (—, *no pl.*) care, precaution, caution, circumspection.

vorsichtig ['fo:rzɪçtɪç], *adj.* cautious, careful, circumspect.

vorsichtshalber ['fo:rzɪçtshalbər], *adv.* as a precautionary measure.

Vorsichtsmaßnahme ['fo:rzɪçtsma:s-na:mə], *f.* (—, *pl.* —n) precautionary measure, precaution.

Vorsilbe ['fo:rzɪlbə], *f.* (—, *pl.* —n) prefix.

vorsintflutlich ['fo:rzɪntflu:tlɪç], *adj.* antediluvian; (*fig.*) out-of-date.

Vorsitzende ['fo:rzɪtsəndə], *m.* (—n, *pl.* —n) chairman, president.

Vorsorge ['fo:rzɔrgə], *f.* (—, *no pl.*) care, precaution.

vorsorglich ['fo:rzɔrklɪç], *adj.* provident, careful.

vorspiegeln ['fo:rʃpi:gəln], *v.a. einem etwas* —, deceive s.o.; pretend.

Vorspiegelung ['fo:rʃpi:gəluŋ], *f.* (—, *pl.* —en) pretence; — *falscher Tatsachen*, false pretences.

Vorspiel ['fo:rʃpi:l], *n.* (—s, *pl.* —e) prelude; overture.

vorsprechen ['fo:rʃprɛçən], *v.n. irr. bei einem* —, call on s.o. — *v.a. einem etwas* —, say s.th. for s.o.; repeat.

vorspringen ['fo:rʃprɪŋən], *v.n. irr.* (*aux.* sein) leap forward; jut out, project.

Vorsprung ['fo:rʃpruŋ], *m.* (—s, *pl.* ⁻e) projection, prominence; (*fig.*) advantage (over), start, lead.

Vorstadt ['fo:rʃtat], *f.* (—, *pl.* ⁻e) suburb.

vorstädtisch ['fo:rʃtɛtɪʃ], *adj.* suburban.

Vorstand ['fo:rʃtant], *m.* (—s, *pl.* ⁻e) board of directors; director, principal.

Vorstandssitzung ['fo:rʃtantszɪtsuŋ], *f.* (—, *pl.* —en) board meeting.

vorstehen ['fo:rʃte:ən], *v.n. irr.* project, protrude; (*office*) administer, govern, direct, manage.

vorstehend ['fo:rʃte:ənt], *adj.* projecting, protruding; above-mentioned, foregoing.

Vorsteher ['fo:rʃte:ər], *m.* (—s, *pl.* —) director, manager; supervisor.

Vorsteherdrüse ['fo:rʃte:ərdry:zə], *f.* (—, *pl.* —n) prostate gland.

vorstellbar ['fo:rʃtelba:r], *adj.* imaginable.

vorstellen ['fo:rʃtelən], *v.a.* (*thing*) put forward; (*person*) present, introduce; (*Theat.*) impersonate; represent; (*clock*) put on; *sich etwas* —, visualise s.th., imagine s.th.

vorstellig ['foːrʃtɛlɪç], *adj.* — *werden*, petition; lodge a complaint.

Vorstellung ['foːrʃtɛluŋ], *f.* (—, *pl.* —en) (*person*) presentation, introduction; (*Theat.*) performance; idea, notion, image; representation.

Vorstellungsvermögen ['foːrʃtɛluŋsfɛr'møːgən], *n.* (—s, *no pl.*) imagination, imaginative faculty.

Vorstoß ['foːrʃtoːs], *m.* (—es, *pl.* ⁀e) (*Mil.*) sudden advance, thrust.

vorstoßen ['foːrʃtoːsən], *v.a. irr.* push forward. — *v.n.* (*aux.* sein) (*Mil.*) advance suddenly.

Vorstrafe ['foːrʃtraːfə], *f.* (—, *pl.* —n) previous conviction.

vorstrecken ['foːrʃtrɛkən], *v.a.* stretch forward, protrude; (*money*) advance.

Vorstufe ['foːrʃtuːfə], *f.* (—, *pl.* —n) first step.

Vortänzerin ['foːrtɛntsərɪn], *f.* (—, *pl.* —nen) prima ballerina.

Vorteil ['fortaɪl], *m.* (—s, *pl.* —e) advantage, profit.

vorteilhaft ['fortaɪlhaft], *adj.* advantageous, profitable, lucrative.

Vortrag ['foːrtraːk], *m.* (—s, *pl.* ⁀e) recitation, delivery, rendering; statement, report; talk, speech, lecture.

vortragen ['foːrtraːgən], *v.a. irr.* make a report; (*poem*) recite, declaim; make a request; (*Comm.*) carry forward; lecture on.

Vortragskunst ['foːrtraːkskunst], *f.* (—, *no pl.*) elocution; (art of) public speaking.

vortrefflich ['foːrtrɛflɪç], *adj.* excellent, splendid.

Vortrefflichkeit [for'trɛflɪçkaɪt], *f.* (—, *no pl.*) excellence.

vortreten ['foːrtreːtən], *v.n. irr.* (*aux.* sein) step forward.

Vortritt ['foːrtrɪt], *m.* (—s, *no pl.*) precedence.

vorüber [for'yːbər], *adv.* past, gone, over, finished, done with.

vorübergehen [for'yːbərgeːən], *v.n. irr.* (*aux.* sein) pass by, pass, go past.

vorübergehend [for'yːbərgeːənt], *adj.* passing, temporary, transitory.

Vorübung ['foːryːbuŋ], *f.* (—, *pl.* —en) preliminary exercise.

Voruntersuchung ['foːruntɐrzuːxuŋ], *f.* (—, *pl.* —en) preliminary inquiry; trial in magistrate's court.

Vorurteil ['foːrurtaɪl], *n.* (—s, *pl.* —e) bias, prejudice.

vorurteilslos ['foːrurtaɪlsloːs], *adj.* impartial, unprejudiced, unbiased.

Vorvater ['foːrfaːtər], *m.* (—s, *pl.* ⁀) progenitor, ancestor.

Vorverkauf ['foːrfɛrkauf], *m.* (—s, *pl.* ⁀e) booking in advance, advance booking.

vorwagen ['foːrvaːgən], *v.r. sich* —, dare to go (or come) forward.

vorwaltend ['foːrvaltənt], *adj.* prevailing, predominating.

Vorwand ['foːrvant], *m.* (—s, *pl.* ⁀e) pretence, pretext; *unter dem* —, under pretence of.

vorwärts ['foːrvɛrts], *adv.* forward.

vorwärtskommen ['foːrvɛrtskɔmən], *v.n. irr.* (*aux.* sein) make headway, get on.

vorweg [for'vɛk], *adv.* before.

vorwegnehmen [for'vɛkneːmən], *v.a. irr.* anticipate.

vorweisen ['foːrvaɪzən], *v.a. irr.* show, produce, exhibit.

Vorwelt ['foːrvɛlt], *f.* (—, *no pl.*) primitive world; former ages.

vorweltlich ['foːrvɛltlɪç], *adj.* primæval, prehistoric.

vorwerfen ['foːrvɛrfən], *v.a. irr. einem etwas* —, blame s.o. for s.th.; charge s.o. with s.th., tax s.o. with s.th.

vorwiegen ['foːrviːgən], *v.n. irr.* prevail.

vorwiegend ['foːrviːgənt], *adv.* mostly, for the most part.

Vorwissen ['foːrvɪsən], *n.* (—s, *no pl.*) foreknowledge, prescience.

Vorwitz ['foːrvɪts], *m.* (—es, *no pl.*) pertness.

vorwitzig ['foːrvɪtsɪç], *adj.* forward, pert, meddlesome.

Vorwort (1) ['foːrvɔrt], *n.* (—s, *pl.* —e) preface.

Vorwort (2) ['foːrvɔrt], *n.* (—s, *pl.* ⁀er) (*Gram.*) preposition.

Vorwurf ['foːrvurf], *m.* (—s, *pl.* ⁀e) reproach; theme, subject.

vorwurfsfrei ['foːrvurfsfraɪ], *adj.* free from blame, irreproachable.

vorwurfsvoll ['foːrvurfsfɔl], *adj.* reproachful.

Vorzeichen ['foːrtsaɪxən], *n.* (—s, *pl.* —) omen, token; (*Maths.*) sign.

vorzeigen ['foːrtsaɪgən], *v.a.* show, produce, exhibit, display.

Vorzeit ['foːrtsaɪt], *f.* (—, *no pl.*) antiquity, olden times.

vorzeiten [for'tsaɪtən], *adv.* (*Poet.*) in olden times, formerly.

vorzeitig ['foːrtsaɪtɪç], *adj.* premature.

vorziehen ['foːrtsiːən], *v.a. irr.* prefer.

Vorzimmer ['foːrtsɪmər], *n.* (—s, *pl.* —) anteroom, antechamber.

Vorzug ['foːrtsuːk], *m.* (—s, *pl.* ⁀e) preference, advantage; excellence, superiority.

vorzüglich [for'tsyːklɪç], *adj.* superior, excellent, exquisite.

Vorzüglichkeit [for'tsyːklɪçkaɪt], *f.* (—, *no pl.*) excellence, superiority.

Vorzugsaktie ['foːrtsuːksaktsjə], *f.* (—, *pl.* —n) preference share.

vorzugsweise ['foːrtsuːksvaɪzə], *adv.* for choice, preferably.

vulgär [vul'gɛːr], *adj.* vulgar.

Vulkan [vul'kaːn], *m.* (—s, *pl.* —e) volcano.

vulkanisch [vul'kaːnɪʃ], *adj.* volcanic.

W

W

W [ve:] *n.* (—s, *pl.* —s) the letter W.
Waage ['va:gə], *f.* (—, *pl.* —n) balance, pair of scales.
waag(e)recht ['va:g(ə)rɛçt], *adj.* horizontal.
Waagschale ['va:kʃa:lə], *f.* (—, *pl.* —n) pan of a balance.
Wabe ['va:bə], *f.* (—, *pl.* —n) honeycomb.
Waberlohe ['va:bərlo:ə], *f.* (—, *no pl.*) (*Poet.*) flickering flames, magic fire.
wach [vax], *adj.* awake; alert; *völlig* —, wide awake.
Wachdienst ['vaxdi:nst], *m.* (—es, *no pl.*) guard, sentry duty.
Wache ['vaxə], *f.* (—, *pl.* —n) guard, watch; (*person*) sentry, sentinel.
wachen ['vaxən], *v.n.* be awake; guard; — *über*, watch, keep an eye on.
Wacholder [va'xɔldər], *m.* (—s, *pl.* —) (*Bot.*) juniper.
wachrufen [vax'ru:fən], *v.a. irr.* (*fig.*) call to mind.
Wachs [vaks], *n.* (—es, *no pl.*) wax.
wachsam ['vaxza:m], *adj.* watchful, vigilant.
Wachsamkeit ['vaxza:mkaɪt], *f.* (—, *no pl.*) watchfulness, vigilance.
Wachsbild ['vaksbɪlt], *n.* (—s, *pl.* —er) waxen image.
wachsen ['vaksən], *v.n. irr.* (*aux.* sein) grow, increase.
wächsern ['vɛksərn], *adj.* waxen, made of wax.
Wachsfigur ['vaksfigu:r], *f.* (—, *pl.* —en) wax figure.
Wachsfigurenkabinett ['vaksfigu:rənkabinet], *n.* (—s, *pl.* —e) waxworks.
Wachsleinwand ['vakslaɪnvant], *f.* (—, *no pl.*) oil-cloth.
Wachstuch ['vakstu:x], *n.* (—(e)s, *no pl.*) oil-cloth; American cloth.
Wachstum ['vakstu:m], *n.* (—s, *no pl.*) growth, increase.
Wacht [vaxt], *f.* (—, *pl.* —en) watch, guard.
Wachtdienst ['vaxtdi:nst], *see* **Wachtdienst.**
Wachtel ['vaxtəl], *f.* (—, *pl.* —n) (*Orn.*) quail.
Wachtelhund ['vaxtəlhunt], *m.* (—(e)s, *pl.* —e) (*Zool.*) spaniel.
Wächter ['vɛçtər], *m.* (—s, *pl.* —) watchman, warder, guard.
wachthabend ['vaxtha:bənt], *adj.* on duty.
Wachtmeister ['vaxtmaɪstər], *m.* (—s, *pl.* —) sergeant.

Wachtparade [vaxtpara:də], *f.* (—, *pl.* —n) mounting of the guard.
Wachtposten ['vaxtpɔstən], *m.* (—s, *pl.* —) guard, picket.
Wachtraum ['vaxtraum], *m.* (—s, *pl.* ⁻e) day-dream, waking dream.
Wachtturm ['vaxtturm], *m.* (—s, *pl.* ⁻e) watch-tower.
wackeln ['vakəln], *v.n.* totter, shake, wobble.
wacker ['vakər], *adj.* gallant, brave, valiant; upright.
wacklig ['vaklɪç], *adj.* tottering, shaky; (*furniture*) rickety; (*tooth*) loose.
Wade ['va:də], *f.* (—, *pl.* —n) calf (of the leg).
Wadenbein ['va:dənbaɪn], *n.* (—s, *pl.* —e) shin-bone.
Waffe ['vafə], *f.* (—, *pl.* —n) weapon, arm; *die* —*n strecken*, surrender.
Waffel ['vafəl], *f.* (—, *pl.* —n) wafer; waffle.
Waffeleisen ['vafəlaɪzən], *n.* (—s, *pl.* —) waffle-iron.
Waffenbruder ['vafənbru:dər], *m.* (—s, *pl.* ⁻) brother-in-arms, comrade.
waffenfähig ['vafənfe:ɪç], *adj.* able to bear arms.
Waffengewalt ['vafəngəvalt], *f.* (—, *no pl.*) *mit* —, by force of arms.
Waffenglück ['vafənglyk], *n.* (—s, *no pl.*) fortunes of war.
Waffenrock ['vafənrɔk], *m.* (—s, *pl.* ⁻e) tunic.
Waffenruf ['vafənru:f], *m.* (—s, *no pl.*) call to arms.
Waffenschmied [vafənʃmi:t], *m.* (—s, *pl.* —e) armourer.
Waffenstillstand ['vafənʃtɪlʃtant], *m.* (—s, *no pl.*) armistice, truce.
waffnen ['vafnən], *v.a.* arm.
Wage *see* **Waage.**
Wagebalken ['va:gəbalkən], *m.* (—s, *pl.* —) scale-beam.
Wagen ['va:gən], *m.* (—s, *pl.* —) vehicle, conveyance, carriage, coach, car, cab, wagon, cart, truck, van, dray.
wagen ['va:gən], *v.a., v.n.* dare, venture, risk.
wägen ['ve:gən], *v.a., irr.* weigh, balance; (*words*) consider.
Wagenverkehr ['va:gənferke:r], *m.* (—s, *no pl.*) vehicular traffic.
wagerecht *see* **waagerecht.**
Waggon [va'gɔ̃], *m.* (—s, *pl.* —s) railway carriage; goods van.
waghalsig ['va:khalzɪç], *adj.* foolhardy, rash, daring.
Wagnis ['va:knɪs], *n.* (—ses, *pl.* —se) venture, risky undertaking; risk.
Wagschale *see* **Waagschale.**
Wahl [va:l], *f.* (—, *pl.* —en) choice; election; selection; alternative.
Wahlakt ['va:lakt], *m.* (—s, *pl.* —e) poll, election.
Wahlaufruf ['va:laufru:f], *m.* (—s, *pl.* —e) manifesto, election address.
wählbar ['ve:lba:r], *adj.* eligible.
Wählbarkeit ['ve:lba:rkaɪt], *f.* (—, *no pl.*) eligibility.

wahlberechtigt ['va:lbərɛçtɪçt], *adj.* entitled to vote.

wählen ['vɛːlən], *v.a.* choose; (*Parl.*) elect; (*Telephone*) dial.

Wähler ['vɛːlər], *m.* (—s, *pl.* —) elector; constituent.

wählerisch ['vɛːlərɪʃ], *adj.* fastidious, particular.

Wählerschaft ['vɛːlərʃaft], *f.* (—, *pl.* —en) constituency.

wahlfähig ['va:lfɛːɪç], *adj.* eligible.

Wahlliste ['va:llɪstə], *f.* (—, *pl.* —n) electoral list, register (of electors).

wahllos ['va:llo:s], *adj.* indiscriminate.

Wahlrecht ['va:lrɛçt], *n.* (—s, *no pl.*) franchise.

Wahlspruch ['va:lʃprux], *m.* (—s, *pl.* ̈e) device, motto.

wahlunfähig ['va:lunfɛːɪç], *adj.* ineligible.

Wahlurne ['va:lurnə], *f.* (—, *pl.* —n) ballot-box.

Wahlverwandtschaft ['va:lfɛrvantʃaft], *f.* (—, *no pl.*) elective affinity, congeniality.

Wahlzettel ['va:ltsɛtəl], *m.* (—s, *pl.* —) ballot-paper.

Wahn [va:n], *m.* (—(e)s, *no pl.*) delusion.

Wahnbild ['va:nbɪlt], *n.* (—s, *pl.* —er) hallucination, delusion; phantasm.

wähnen ['vɛːnən], *v.a.* fancy, believe.

Wahnsinn ['va:nzɪn], *m.* (—s, *no pl.*) madness, lunacy.

wahnsinnig ['va:nzɪnɪç], *adj.* insane, mad, lunatic; (*coll.*) terrific.

Wahnsinnige ['va:nzɪnɪgə], *m.* (—n, *pl.* —n) madman, lunatic.

Wahnwitz ['va:nvɪts], *m.* (—es, *no pl.*) madness.

wahnwitzig ['va:nvɪtsɪç], *adj.* mad.

wahr [va:r], *adj.* true, real, genuine.

wahren ['va:rən], *v.a.* guard, watch over.

währen ['vɛːrən], *v.n.* last.

während ['vɛːrənt], *prep.* (*Genit.*) during. — *conj.* while, whilst; whereas.

wahrhaft ['va:rhaft], *adj.* truthful, veracious.

wahrhaftig [va:r'haftɪç], *adv.* truly, really, in truth.

Wahrhaftigkeit [va:r'haftɪçkaɪt], *f.* (—, *no pl.*) truthfulness, veracity.

Wahrheit ['va:rhaɪt], *f.* (—, *pl.* —en) truth; reality; *die — sagen*, tell the truth.

Wahrheitsliebe ['va:rhaɪtsli:bə], *f.* (—, *no pl.*) love of truth, truthfulness.

wahrlich [va:rlɪç], *adv.* truly, in truth.

wahrnehmbar ['va:rne:mba:r], *adj.* perceptible.

wahrnehmen ['va:rne:mən], *v.a. irr.* perceive, observe.

Wahrnehmung ['va:rne:muŋ], *f.* (—, *pl.* —en) perception, observation.

wahrsagen ['va:rza:gən], *v.n.* prophesy; tell fortunes.

Wahrsager ['va:rza:gər], *m.* (—s, *pl.* —) fortune-teller, soothsayer.

wahrscheinlich [va:r'ʃaɪnlɪç], *adj.* likely, probable; *es wird — regnen*, it will probably rain.

Wahrscheinlichkeit [va:r'ʃaɪnlɪçkaɪt], *f.* (—, *pl.* —en) likelihood, probability.

Wahrung ['va:ruŋ], *f.* (—, *no pl.*) protection, preservation, maintenance.

Währung ['vɛːruŋ], *f.* (—, *pl.* —en) currency, standard.

Wahrzeichen ['va:rtsaɪçən], *n.* (—s, *pl.* —) landmark; (*fig.*) sign, token.

Waibling(er) ['vaɪblɪŋ(ər)], *m.* Ghibelline.

Waidmann ['vaɪtman], *m.* (—s, *pl.* ̈er) huntsman, hunter.

waidmännisch ['vaɪtmɛnɪʃ], *adj.* sportsmanlike.

Waise ['vaɪzə], *f.* (—, *pl.* —n) orphan.

Waisenhaus ['vaɪzənhaus], *n.* (—es, *pl.* ̈er) orphanage.

Waisenmutter ['vaɪzənmutər], *f.* (—, *pl.* ̈) foster-mother.

Waisenvater ['vaɪzənfa:tər], *m.* (—s, *pl.* ̈) foster-father.

Wald [valt], *m.* (—es, *pl.* ̈er) wood, forest; woodland.

Waldbrand ['valtbrant], *m.* (—s, *pl.* ̈e) forest-fire.

Waldlichtung ['valtlɪçtuŋ], *f.* (—, *pl.* —en) forest glade, clearing.

Waldmeister ['valtmaɪstər], *m.* (—s, *no pl.*) (*Bot.*) woodruff.

Waldung ['valduŋ], *f.* (—, *pl.* —en) woods, woodland.

Waldwiese ['valtvi:zə], *f.* (—, *pl.* —en) forest-glade.

Walfisch ['va:lfɪʃ], *m.* (—es, *pl.* —e) whale.

Walfischfang ['va:lfɪʃfaŋ], *m.* (—s, *no pl.*) whaling.

Walfischfänger ['va:lfɪʃfɛŋər], *m.* (—s, *pl.* —) whaler, whale fisher.

Walfischtran ['va:lfɪʃtra:n], *m.* (—s, *no pl.*) train-oil.

Walküre [val'ky:rə], *f.* (—, *pl.* —n) Valkyrie.

Wall [val], *m.* (—(e)s, *pl.* ̈e) rampart, dam, vallum; mound.

Wallach ['valax], *m.* (—s, *pl.* —e) castrated horse, gelding.

wallen ['valən], *v.n.* bubble, boil up; wave, undulate.

Wallfahrer ['valfa:rər], *m.* (—s, *pl.* —) pilgrim.

Wallfahrt ['valfa:rt], *f.* (—, *pl.* —en) pilgrimage.

wallfahrten ['valfa:rtən], *v.n.* (*aux.* sein) go on a pilgrimage.

Walnuß ['valnus], *f.* (—, *pl.* ̈sse) (*Bot.*) walnut.

Walpurgisnacht [val'purgɪsnaxt], *f.* witches' sabbath.

Walroß ['valrɔs], *n.* (—sses, *pl.* —sse) sea-horse, walrus.

Walstatt ['valʃtat], *f.* (—, *pl.* ̈en) (*Poet.*) battlefield.

walten ['valtən], *v.n.* rule; *seines Amtes —*, do o.'s duty, carry out o.'s duties.

Walze ['valtsə], *f.* (—, *pl.* —n) roller, cylinder.

walzen ['valtsən], *v.a.* roll. — *v.n.* waltz.

wälzen ['vɛltsən], *v.a.* roll, turn about.

walzenförmig ['valtsənfœrmɪç], *adj.* cylindrical.

Walzer ['valtsər], *m.* (—s, *pl.* —) waltz.

Wälzer ['vɛltsər], *m.* (—s, *pl.* —) tome; thick volume.

Walzwerk ['valtsvɛrk], *n.* (—s, *pl.* —e) rolling-mill.

Wams [vams], *n.* (—es, *pl.* ꞉e) (*obs.*) doublet, jerkin.

Wand [vant], *f.* (—, *pl.* ꞉e) wall; side.

Wandbekleidung ['vantbəklaɪduŋ], *f.* (—, *pl.* —en) wainscot, panelling.

Wandel ['vandəl], *m.* (—s, *no pl.*) mutation, change; behaviour, conduct; *Handel und* —, trade and traffic.

wandelbar ['vandəlba:r], *adj.* changeable, inconstant.

Wandelgang ['vandəlgaŋ], *m.* (—s, *pl.* ꞉e) lobby; lounge, foyer; (*in the open*) covered way, covered walk.

wandeln ['vandəln], *v.a.* (*aux.* haben) change. — *v.n.* (*aux.* sein) walk, wander. — *v.r. sich* —, change.

Wanderbursche ['vandərburʃə], *m.* (—n, *pl.* —n) travelling journeyman.

Wanderer ['vandərər], *m.* (—s, *pl.* —) wanderer, traveller; hiker.

Wanderleben ['vandərle:bən], *n.* (—s, *no pl.*) nomadic life.

Wanderlehrer ['vandərle:rər], *m.* (—s, *pl.* —) itinerant teacher.

Wanderlust ['vandərlust], *f.* (—, *no pl.*) urge to travel; call of the open.

wandern ['vandərn], *v.n.* (*aux.* sein) wander, travel; migrate.

Wanderschaft ['vandərʃaft], *f.* (—, *no pl.*) wanderings.

Wandersmann ['vandərsman], *m.* (—s, *pl.* ꞉er) wayfarer.

Wandertruppe ['vandərtrupə], *f.* (—, *pl.* —n) (*Theat.*) strolling players.

Wanderung ['vandəruŋ], *f.* (—, *pl.* —en) walking tour; hike.

Wandervolk ['vandərfɔlk], *n.* (— (e)s, *pl.* ꞉er) nomadic tribe.

Wandgemälde ['vantgəmɛ:ldə], *n.* (—s, *pl.* —) mural painting, mural.

Wandlung ['vandluŋ], *f.* (—, *pl.* —en) transformation; (*Theol.*) transubstantiation.

Wandspiegel ['vantʃpi:gəl], *m.* (—s, *pl.* —) pier-glass.

Wandtafel ['vantta:fəl], *f.* (—, *pl.* —n) blackboard.

Wange ['vaŋə], *f.* (—, *pl.* —n) cheek.

Wankelmut ['vaŋkəlmu:t], *m.* (—s, *no pl.*) fickleness, inconstancy.

wankelmütig ['vaŋkəlmy:tɪç], *adj.* inconstant, fickle.

wanken ['vaŋkən], *v.n.* totter, stagger; (*fig.*) waver, be irresolute.

wann [van], *adv.* when; *dann und* —, now and then, sometimes.

Wanne ['vanə], *f.* (—, *pl.* —n) tub, bath.

wannen ['vanən], *adv.* (*obs.*) von —, whence.

Wannenbad ['vanənba:t], *n.* (—s, *pl.* ꞉er) bath.

Wanst [vanst], *m.* (—es, *pl.* ꞉e) belly, paunch.

Wanze ['vantsə], *f.* (—, *pl.* —n) (*Ent.*) bug.

Wappen ['vapən], *n.* (—s, *pl.* —) crest, coat-of-arms.

Wappenbild ['vapənbɪlt], *n.* (—s, *pl.* —er) heraldic figure.

Wappenkunde ['vapənkundə], *f.* (—, *no pl.*) heraldry.

Wappenschild ['vapənʃɪlt], *m.* (—s, *pl.* —e) escutcheon.

Wappenspruch ['vapənʃprux], *m.* (—(e)s, *pl.* ꞉e) motto, device.

wappnen ['vapnən], *v.a.* arm.

Ware ['va:rə], *f.* (—, *pl.* —n) article, commodity; (*pl.*) merchandise, goods, wares.

Warenausfuhr ['va:rənausfu:r], *f.* (—, *no pl.*) exportation, export.

Warenbörse ['va:rənbœrzə], *f.* (—, *pl.* —n) commodity exchange.

Wareneinfuhr ['va:rənaɪnfu:r], *f.* (—, *no pl.*) importation, import.

Warenhaus ['va:rənhaus], *n.* (—es, *pl.* ꞉er) department store, emporium; (*Am.*) store.

Warenlager ['va:rənla:gər], *n.* (—s, *pl.* —) magazine; stock; warehouse.

Warensendung ['va:rənzɛnduŋ], *f.* (—, *pl.* —en) consignment of goods.

Warentausch ['va:rəntauʃ], *m.* (—es, *no pl.*) barter.

warm [varm], *adj.* warm, hot.

warmblütig ['varmbly:tɪç], *adj.* warm-blooded.

Wärme ['vɛrmə], *f.* (—, *no pl.*) warmth; heat.

Wärmeeinheit ['vɛrməaɪnhaɪt], *f.* (—, *pl.* —en) thermal unit; calorie.

Wärmegrad ['vɛrməgra:t], *m.* (—s, *pl.* —e) degree of heat; temperature.

Wärmeleiter ['vɛrməlaɪtər], *m.* (—s, *pl.* —) conductor of heat.

Wärmemesser ['vɛrməmɛsər], *m.* (—s, *pl.* —) thermometer.

wärmen ['vɛrmən], *v.a.* warm, heat.

Wärmflasche ['vɛrmflaʃə], *f.* (—, *pl.* —n) hot-water bottle.

warnen ['varnən], *v.a.* warn; caution.

Warnung ['varnuŋ], *f.* (—, *pl.* —en) warning, caution, admonition; notice.

Warschau ['varʃau], *n.* Warsaw.

Warte ['vartə], *f.* (—, *pl.* —n) watch-tower, belfry, look-out.

Wartegeld ['vartəgɛlt], *n.* (—s, *pl.* —er) half pay; (*ship*) demurrage charges.

warten ['vartən], *v.n.* wait; — *auf* (*Acc.*), wait for, await. — *v.a.* tend, nurse.

Wärter ['vɛrtər], *m.* (—s, *pl.* —) keeper, attendant; warder; male nurse.

Wartesaal ['vartəza:l], *m.* (—s, *pl.* —säle) (*Railw.*) waiting-room.

Wartung ['vartuŋ], *f.* (—, *no pl.*) nursing, attendance; servicing; maintenance.

Weberei

warum [va'rum], *adv., conj.* why, for what reason.

Warze ['vartsə], *f.* (—, *pl.* —n) wart.

was [vas], *interr. pron.* what? — *rel. pron.* what, that which.

Waschanstalt ['vaʃanʃtalt], *f.* (—, *pl.* —en) laundry.

waschbar ['vaʃbaːr], *adj.* washable.

Waschbär ['vaʃbɛːr], *m.* (—en, *pl.* —en) (*Zool.*) raccoon.

Waschbecken ['vaʃbɛkən], *n.* (—s, *pl.* —) wash-basin.

Wäsche ['vɛʃə], *f.* (—, *no pl.*) washing, wash, laundry; linen.

waschecht ['vaʃɛçt], *adj.* washable; (*fig.*) genuine.

waschen ['vaʃən], *v.a. irr.* wash.

Wäscherin ['vɛʃərin], *f.* (—, *pl.* —nen) washerwoman, laundress.

Waschhaus ['vaʃhaus], *n.* (—es, *pl.* ˗er) wash-house, laundry; (*reg. trade name*) launderette.

Waschkorb ['vaʃkɔrp], *m.* (—s, *pl.* ˗e) clothes-basket.

Waschküche ['vaʃkyçə], *f.* (—, *pl.* —en) wash-house.

Waschlappen ['vaʃlapən], *m.* (—s, *pl.* —) face-flannel, face-cloth, face-washer; (*fig.*) milksop.

Waschleder ['vaʃleːdər], *n.* (—s, *no pl.*) chamois leather, wash-leather.

Waschmaschine ['vaʃmaʃiːnə], *f.* (—, *pl.* —n) washing-machine.

Waschtisch ['vaʃtiʃ], *m.* (—es, *pl.* —e) wash-stand.

Waschwanne ['vaʃvanə], *f.* (—, *pl.* —n) wash-tub.

Wasser ['vasər], *n.* (—s, *pl.* —) water; *stille — sind tief,* still waters run deep.

wasserarm ['vasərarm], *adj.* waterless, dry, arid.

Wasserbehälter ['vasərbəhɛltər], *m.* (—s, *pl.* —) reservoir, cistern, tank.

Wasserblase ['vasərblaːzə], *f.* (—, *pl.* —en) bubble.

Wässerchen ['vɛsərçən], *n.* (—s, *pl.* —) brook, streamlet; *er sieht aus, als ob er kein — trüben könnte,* he looks as if butter would not melt in his mouth.

Wasserdampf ['vasərdampf], *m.* (—(e)s, *no pl.*) steam.

wasserdicht ['vasərdiçt], *adj.* water-proof.

Wasserdruck ['vasərdruk], *m.* (—s, *no pl.*) hydrostatic pressure, hydraulic pressure.

Wassereimer ['vasəraimər], *m.* (—s, *pl.* —) pail, water-bucket.

Wasserfall ['vasərfal], *m.* (—s, *pl.* ˗e) waterfall, cataract, cascade.

Wasserfarbe ['vasərfarbə], *f.* (—, *pl.* —n) water-colour.

Wasserheilanstalt ['vasərhailanʃtalt], *f.* (—, *pl.* —en) spa.

wässerig ['vɛsəriç], *adj.* watery; (*fig.*) insipid, flat, diluted.

Wasserkanne ['vasərkanə], *f.* (—, *pl.* —n) pitcher, ewer.

Wasserkessel ['vasərkɛsəl], *m.* (—s, *pl.* —) boiler; kettle.

Wasserkopf ['vasərkɔpf], *m.* (—(e)s, *pl.* ˗e) (*Med.*) hydrocephalus.

Wasserkur ['vasərkuːr], *f.* (—, *pl.* —en) hydropathic treatment.

Wasserleitung ['vasərlaituŋ], *f.* (—, *pl.* —en) aqueduct; water main.

Wasserlinsen ['vasərlinzən], *f. pl.* (*Bot.*) duck-weed.

Wassermann ['vasərman], *m.* (—s, *no pl.*) (*Astrol.*) Aquarius.

wässern ['vɛsərn], *v.a.* water, irrigate, soak.

Wassernixe ['vasərniksə], *f.* (—, *pl.* —n) water nymph.

Wassernot ['vasərnoːt], *f.* (—, *no pl.*) drought, scarcity of water.

Wasserrabe ['vasərraːbə], *m.* (—n, *pl.* —n) (*Orn.*) cormorant.

Wasserrinne ['vasərrinə], *f.* (—, *pl.* —n) gutter.

Wasserröhre ['vasərrøːrə], *f.* (—, *pl.* —n) water-pipe.

Wasserscheide ['vasərʃaidə], *f.* (—, *pl.* —n) watershed.

Wasserscheu ['vasərʃɔy], *f.* (—, *no pl.*) hydrophobia.

Wasserspiegel ['vasərʃpiːgəl], *m.* (—s, *pl.* —) water-level.

Wasserspritze ['vasərʃpritsə], *f.* (—, *pl.* —n) squirt; sprinkler.

Wasserstand ['vasərʃtant], *m.* (—s, *no pl.*) water-level.

Wasserstiefel ['vasərʃtiːfəl], *m.* (—s, *pl.* —) wader, gumboot.

Wasserstoff ['vasərʃtɔf], *m.* (—(e)s, *no pl.*) hydrogen.

Wassersucht ['vasərzuxt], *f.* (—, *no pl.*) dropsy.

Wassersuppe ['vasərzupə], *f.* (—, *pl.* —n) water-gruel.

Wässerung ['vɛsəruŋ], *f.* (—, *pl.* —en) watering, irrigation.

Wasserverdrängung ['vasərfɛrdrɛŋuŋ], *f.* (—, *no pl.*) displacement (of water).

Wasserwaage ['vasərvaːgə], *f.* (—, *pl.* —n) water-balance, water-level; hydrometer.

Wasserweg ['vasərveːk], *m.* (—s, *pl.* —e) waterway; *auf dem —,* by water, by sea.

Wasserzeichen ['vasərtsaiçən], *n.* (—s, *pl.* —) watermark.

waten ['vaːtən], *v.n.* (*aux.* sein) wade.

watscheln ['vaːtʃəln], *v.n.* (*aux.* sein) waddle.

Watt (1) [vat], *n.* (—s, *pl.* —e) sandbank; (*pl.*) shallows.

Watt (2) [vat], *n.* (—s, *pl.* —) (*Elec.*) watt.

Watte ['vatə], *f.* (—, *no pl.*) wadding, cotton-wool.

wattieren [va'tiːrən], *v.a.* pad.

Webe ['veːbə], *f.* (—, *pl.* —n) web, weft.

weben ['veːbən], *v.a.* weave.

Weber ['veːbər], *m.* (—s, *pl.* —) weaver.

Weberei [veːbə'rai], *f.* (—, *pl.* —en) weaving-mill.

Weberschiffchen

Weberschiffchen ['ve:bərʃɪfçən], *n.* (—s, *pl.* —) shuttle.

Wechsel ['vɛksəl], *m.* (—s, *pl.* —) change; turn, variation; vicissitude; (*Comm.*) bill of exchange.

Wechselbalg ['vɛksəlbalk], *m.* (—s, *pl.* ˙e) changeling.

Wechselbank ['vɛksəlbaŋk], *f.* (—, *pl.* ˙e) discount-bank.

Wechselbeziehung ['vɛksəlbətsi:uŋ], *f.* (—, *pl.* —en) reciprocal relation, correlation.

Wechselfälle ['vɛksəlfɛlə], *m. pl.* vicissitudes.

Wechselfieber ['vɛksəlfi:bər], *n.* (—s, *pl.* —) intermittent fever.

Wechselfolge ['vɛksəlfɔlgə], *f.* (—, *no pl.*) rotation, alternation.

Wechselgeld ['vɛksəlgɛlt], *n.* (—(e)s, *no pl.*) change.

wechseln ['vɛksəln], *v.a.* change, exchange. — *v.n.* change, alternate, change places.

wechselseitig ['vɛksəlzaɪtɪç], *adj.* reciprocal, mutual.

Wechselstrom ['vɛksəlʃtro:m], *m.* (—s, *no pl.*) alternating current.

Wechselstube ['vɛksəlʃtu:bə], *f.* (—, *pl.* —n) exchange office.

wechselvoll ['vɛksəlfɔl], *adj.* eventful, chequered; changeable.

wechselweise ['vɛksəlvaɪzə], *adv.* reciprocally, mutually; by turns, alternately.

Wechselwinkel ['vɛksəlvɪŋkəl], *m.* (—s, *pl.* —) alternate angle.

Wechselwirkung ['vɛksəlvɪrkuŋ], *f.* (—, *pl.* —en) reciprocal effect.

Wechselwirtschaft ['vɛksəlvɪrtʃaft], *f.* (—, *no pl.*) rotation of crops.

Wecken ['vɛkən], *m.* (—s, *pl.* —) (*dial.*) bread-roll.

wecken ['vɛkən], *v.a.* wake, rouse, awaken.

Wecker ['vɛkər], *m.* (—s, *pl.* —) alarm-clock.

Weckuhr ['vɛku:r], *f.* (—, *pl.* —en) alarm-clock.

Wedel ['ve:dəl], *m.* (—s, *pl.* —) feather-duster, fan; tail.

wedeln ['ve:dəln], *v.n. mit dem Schwanze* —, wag its tail.

weder ['ve:dər], *conj.* neither; — ... *noch*, neither . . . nor.

Weg [ve:k], *m.* (—(e)s, *pl.* —e) way, path, route, road; walk, errand; *am* —, by the wayside.

weg [vɛk], *adv.* away, gone, off, lost.

weggeben ['vɛkbge:bən], *v.r. irr. sich* —, go away, leave.

wegbekommen ['vɛkbəkɔmən], *v.a. irr. etwas* —, get the hang of s.th.; *get s.th. off or away.*

Wegbereiter ['ve:kbəraɪtər], *m.* (—s, *pl.* —) forerunner, pathfinder, pioneer.

wegblasen ['vɛkbla:zən], *v.a. irr.* blow away; *wie weggeblasen,* without leaving a trace.

wegbleiben ['vɛkblaɪbən], *v.n. irr.* (*aux.* sein) stay away.

wegblicken ['vɛkblɪkən], *v.n.* look the other way.

wegbringen ['vɛkbrɪŋən], *v.a. irr. einen* —, get s.o. away.

wegdrängen ['vɛkdrɛŋən], *v.a.* push away.

Wegebau ['ve:gəbau], *m.* (—s, *no pl.*) road-making.

wegeilen ['vɛkaɪlən], *v.n.* (*aux.* sein) hasten away, hurry off.

wegelagern ['vɛkgəla:gərn], *v.a.* way-lay.

wegen ['ve:gən], *prep.* (*Genit., Dat.*) because of, on account of, owing to, by reason of.

Wegfall ['vɛkfal], *m.* (—s, *no pl.*) omission.

wegfallen ['vɛkfalən], *v.n. irr.* (*aux.* sein) fall off; be omitted; cease.

Weggang ['vɛkgaŋ], *m.* (—s, *no pl.*) departure, going away.

weggießen ['vɛkgi:sən], *v.a. irr.* pour away.

weghaben ['vɛkha:bən], *v.a. irr. etwas* —, understand how to do s.th, have the knack of doing s.th.

wegkommen ['vɛkkɔmən], *v.n. irr.* (*aux.* sein) get away; be lost.

wegkönnen ['vɛkkœnən], *v.n. irr. nicht* —, not be able to get away.

Weglassung ['vɛklasuŋ], *f.* (—, *pl.* —en) omission.

wegmachen ['vɛkmaxən], *v.r. sich* —, decamp, make off.

wegmüssen ['vɛkmysən], *v.n. irr.* be obliged to go; have to go.

Wegnahme ['vɛkna:mə], *f.* (—, *no pl.*) taking, seizure, capture.

Wegreise ['vɛkraɪzə], *f.* (—, *no pl.*) departure.

Wegscheide ['ve:kʃaɪdə], *f.* (—, *pl.* —n) crossroads, crossways.

wegscheren ['vɛkʃe:rən], *v.a.* clip; shave off. — *v.r. sich* —, be off.

wegschnappen ['vɛkʃnapən], *v.a.* snatch away.

wegsehnen ['vɛkze:nən], *v.r. sich* —, wish o.s. far away; long to get away.

wegsein ['vɛkzaɪn], *v.n. irr.* (*aux.* sein) (*person*) be gone, be away; have gone off; (*things*) be lost; *ganz* —, (*coll.*) be beside o.s. *or* amazed.

wegsetzen ['vɛkzɛtsən], *v.a.* put away.

wegspülen ['vɛkʃpy:lən], *v.a.* wash away.

Wegstunde ['ve:kʃtundə], *f.* (—, *pl.* —n) an hour's walk.

Wegweiser ['ve:kvaɪzər], *m.* (—s, *pl.* —) signpost, road-sign.

wegwenden ['vɛkvɛndən], *v.r. irr. sich* —, turn away.

wegwerfen ['vɛkvɛrfən], *v.a. irr.* throw away.

wegwerfend ['vɛkvɛrfənt], *adj.* disparaging, disdainful.

Wegzehrung ['ve:ktse:ruŋ], *f.* (—, *no pl.*) food for the journey; (*Eccl.*) viaticum.

wegziehen ['vɛktsiːən], *v.a. irr.* draw away, pull away. — *v.n. (aux.* sein) march away; (*fig.*) move, remove.

Wegzug ['vɛktsuːk], *m.* (—s, *no pl.*) removal; moving away.

Weh [veː], *n.* (—s, *no pl.*) pain; grief, pang; misfortune.

weh [veː], *adj.* painful, sore; *mir ist — ums Herz,* I am sick at heart; my heart aches. — *adv.* — *tun,* ache; pain, hurt, offend, distress, grieve. — *int.* — *mir!* woe is me!

Wehen ['veːən], *n. pl.* birth-pangs, labour-pains.

wehen ['veːən], *v.n. (wind)* blow.

Wehgeschrei ['veːgəʃraɪ], *n.* (—s, *no pl.*) wailings.

Wehklage ['veːklaːgə], *f.* (—, *pl.* —n) lamentation.

wehklagen ['veːklaːgən], *v.n. insep.* lament, wail.

wehleidig ['veːlaɪdɪç], *adj.* tearful; easily hurt; self-pitying.

wehmütig ['veːmyːtɪç], *adj.* sad, melancholy, wistful.

Wehr (1) [veːr], *n.* (—s, *pl.* —e) weir.

Wehr (2) [veːr], *f.* (—, *pl.* —en) defence, bulwark.

wehren ['veːrən], *v.r. sich* —, defend o.s., offer resistance.

wehrhaft ['veːrhaft], *adj.* capable of bearing arms, able-bodied.

wehrlos ['veːrloːs], *adj.* defenceless, unarmed; (*fig.*) weak, unprotected.

Wehrpflicht ['veːrpflɪçt], *f.* (—, *no pl.*) compulsory military service, conscription.

Wehrstand ['veːrʃtant], *m.* (—s, *no pl.*) the military.

Weib [vaɪp], *n.* (—(e)s, *pl.* —er) woman; (*Poet.*) wife.

Weibchen ['vaɪpçən], *n.* (—s, *pl.* —) (*animal*) female.

Weiberfeind ['vaɪbərfaɪnt], *m.* (—s, *pl.* —e) woman-hater, misogynist.

Weiberherrschaft ['vaɪbərhɛrʃaft], *f.* (—, *no pl.*) petticoat rule.

weibisch ['vaɪbɪʃ], *adj.* womanish, effeminate.

weiblich ['vaɪplɪç], *adj.* female, feminine; womanly.

Weiblichkeit ['vaɪplɪçkaɪt], *f.* (—, *no pl.*) womanliness, femininity.

Weibsbild ['vaɪpsbɪlt], *n.* (—s, *pl.* —er) (*sl.*) female; wench.

weich [vaɪç], *adj.* weak; soft; tender, gentle; effeminate; sensitive; — *machen,* soften; — *werden,* relent.

Weichbild ['vaɪçbɪlt], *n.* (—s, *no pl.*) precincts; city boundaries.

Weiche ['vaɪçə], *f.* (—, *pl.* —n) (*Railw.*) switch, points.

weichen (1) ['vaɪçən], *v.a.* steep, soak, soften.

weichen (2) ['vaɪçən], *v.n. irr. (aux.* sein) yield, make way, give ground.

Weichensteller ['vaɪçənʃtɛlər], *m.* (—s, *pl.* —) (*Railw.*) pointsman, signalman.

Weichheit ['vaɪçhaɪt], *f.* (—, *no pl.*) softness; (*fig.*) weakness, tenderness.

weichherzig ['vaɪçhɛrtsɪç], *adj.* soft-hearted, tender-hearted.

weichlich ['vaɪçlɪç], *adj.* soft; (*fig.*) weak, effeminate.

Weichling ['vaɪçlɪŋ], *m.* (—s, *pl.* —e) weakling.

Weichsel ['vaɪksəl], *f.* Vistula.

Weichselkirsche ['vaɪksəlkɪrʃə], *f.* (—, *pl.* —n) sour cherry; morello.

Weide ['vaɪdə], *f.* (—, *pl.* —n) pasture, pasturage; (*Bot.*) willow.

Weideland ['vaɪdəlant], *n.* (—s, *pl.* ˟er) pasture-ground.

weiden ['vaɪdən], *v.a., v.n.* pasture, feed.

Weidenbaum ['vaɪdənbaum], *m.* (—s, *pl.* ˟e) willow-tree.

Weiderich ['vaɪdərɪç], *m.* (—s, *pl.* —e) willow-herb, loose-strife, rose bay.

Weidgenosse ['vaɪtgənɔsə], *m.* (—en, *pl.* —en) fellow huntsman.

weidlich ['vaɪtlɪç], *adv. (rare)* greatly, thoroughly.

Weidmann ['vaɪtman], *m.* (—s, *pl.* ˟er) sportsman, huntsman.

Weidmannsheil! ['vaɪtmanshaɪl], *excl.* tally-ho!

weigern ['vaɪgərn], *v.r. sich* —, refuse, decline.

Weigerung ['vaɪgəruŋ], *f.* (—, *pl.* —en) refusal, denial.

Weih [vaɪ], *m.* (—en, *pl.* —en) (*Orn.*) kite.

Weihbischof ['vaɪbɪʃɔf], *m.* (—s, *pl.* ˟e) suffragan bishop.

Weihe ['vaɪə], *f.* (—, *pl.* —en) consecration; (*priest*) ordination; initiation; (*fig.*) solemnity.

weihen ['vaɪən], *v.a.* bless, consecrate; ordain. — *v.r. sich* —, devote o.s. (to).

Weiher ['vaɪər], *m.* (—s, *pl.* —) pond, fishpond.

weihevoll ['vaɪəfɔl], *adj.* solemn.

Weihnachten ['vaɪnaxtən], *n. or f.* Christmas.

Weihnachtsabend ['vaɪnaxtsaːbənt], *m.* (—s, *pl.* —e) Christmas Eve.

Weihnachtsfeiertag ['vaɪnaxtsfaɪərtaːk], *m.* (—s, *pl.* —e) Christmas Day; *zweiter* —, Boxing Day.

Weihnachtsgeschenk ['vaɪnaxtsgəʃɛŋk], *n.* (—s, *pl.* —e) Christmas box, Christmas present.

Weihnachtslied ['vaɪnaxtsliːt], *n.* (—(e)s, *pl.* —er) Christmas carol.

Weihnachtsmann ['vaɪnaxtsman], *m.* (—(e)s, *pl.* ˟er) Santa Claus, Father Christmas.

Weihrauch ['vaɪraux], *m.* (—s, *no pl.*) incense.

Weihwasser ['vaɪvasər], *n.* (—s, *no pl.*) holy water.

weil [vaɪl], *conj.* because, as, since.

weiland ['vaɪlant], *adv. (obs.)* formerly, once.

Weile ['vaɪlə], *f.* (—, *no pl.*) while, short time; leisure.

weilen ['vaɪlən], *v.n.* tarry, stay, abide.

Wein [vaɪn], *m.* (—(e)s, *pl.* —e) wine; (*plant*) vine; *einem reinen — einschenken,* tell s.o. the truth.

Weinbau

Weinbau ['vaɪnbau], *m.* (—s, *no pl.*) vine growing, viticulture.

Weinbeere ['vaɪnbeːrə], *f.* (—, *pl.* —n) grape.

Weinberg ['vaɪnbɛrk], *m.* (—s, *pl.* —e) vineyard.

Weinbrand ['vaɪnbrant], *m.* (—s, *no pl.*) brandy.

weinen ['vaɪnən], *v.n.* weep, cry.

Weinernte ['vaɪnɛrntə], *f.* (—, *pl.* —n) vintage.

Weinessig ['vaɪnɛsɪç], *m.* (—s, *no pl.*) (wine) vinegar.

Weinfaß ['vaɪnfas], *n.* (—sses, *pl.* ˙sser) wine-cask.

Weingeist ['vaɪngaɪst], *m.* (—es, *no pl.*) spirits of wine, alcohol.

Weinhändler ['vaɪnhɛndlər], *m.* (—s, *pl.* —) wine merchant.

Weinkarte ['vaɪnkartə], *f.* (—, *pl.* —n) wine-list.

Weinkeller ['vaɪnkɛlər], *m.* (—s, *pl.* —) wine-cellar; wine-tavern.

Weinkellerei ['vaɪnkɛləraɪ], *f.* (—, *pl.* —en) wine-store.

Weinkelter ['vaɪnkɛltər], *f.* (—, *pl.* —n) wine-press.

Weinkneipe ['vaɪnknaɪpə], *f.* (—, *pl.* —n) wine-tavern.

Weinkoster ['vaɪnkɔstər], *m.* (—s, *pl.* —) wine-taster.

Weinlaub ['vaɪnlaup], *n.* (—s, *no pl.*) vine-leaves.

Weinlese ['vaɪnleːzə], *f.* (—, *pl.* —n) vintage, grape harvest.

Weinranke ['vaɪnraŋkə], *f.* (—, *pl.* —n) vine-branch, tendril.

Weinschenke ['vaɪnʃɛŋkə], *f.* (—, *pl.* —n) wine-house, tavern.

weinselig ['vaɪnzeːlɪç], *adj.* tipsy.

Weinstein ['vaɪnʃtaɪn], *m.* (—s, *no pl.*) tartar.

Weinsteinsäure ['vaɪnʃtaɪnzɔyrə], *f.* (—, *no pl.*) tartaric acid.

Weinstock ['vaɪnʃtɔk], *m.* (—s, *pl.* ˙e) vine.

Weintraube ['vaɪntraubə], *f.* (—, *pl.* —n) grape, bunch of grapes.

weinumrankt ['vaɪnumraŋkt], *adj.* vine-clad.

weise ['vaɪzə], *adj.* wise, prudent.

Weise (1) ['vaɪzə], *m.* (—n, *pl.* —n) wise man, sage.

Weise (2) ['vaɪzə], *f.* (—, *pl.* —n) manner, fashion; method, way; tune, melody.

weisen ['vaɪzən], *v.a. irr.* point to, point out, show.

Weiser ['vaɪzər], *m.* (—s, *pl.* —) signpost; indicator; (*clock*) hand.

Weisheit ['vaɪshaɪt], *f.* (—, *pl.* —en) wisdom, prudence.

Weisheitszahn ['vaɪshaɪtstsaːn], *m.* (—s, *pl.* ˙e) wisdom tooth.

weislich ['vaɪslɪç], *adv.* wisely, prudently, advisedly.

weismachen ['vaɪsmaxən], *v.a. einem etwas* —, (*coll.*) spin a yarn to s.o.; *laß dir nichts* —, don't be taken in.

weiß [vaɪs], *adj.* white, clean, blank.

weissagen ['vaɪsza:gən], *v.a. insep.* prophesy, foretell.

Weissager ['vaɪsza:gər], *m.* (—s, *pl.* —) prophet, soothsayer.

Weissagung ['vaɪsza:guŋ], *f.* (—, *pl.* —en) prophecy.

Weißbuche ['vaɪsbuːxə], *f.* (—, *pl.* —n) (*Bot.*) hornbeam.

Weiße ['vaɪsə], *f.* (—, *no pl.*) whiteness; (*fig.*) (*dial.*) pale ale.

weißglühend ['vaɪsgly:ɔnt], *adj.* at white heat, incandescent, white hot.

Weißnäherin ['vaɪsnɛːərɪn], *f.* (—, *pl.* —nen) seamstress.

Weißwaren ['vaɪsvaːrən], *f. pl.* linen.

Weisung ['vaɪzuŋ], *f.* (—, *pl.* —en) order, direction, instruction; directive.

weit [vaɪt], *adj.* distant, far, far off; wide, broad, vast, extensive; (*clothing*) loose, too big.

weitab [vaɪt'ap], *adv.* far away.

weitaus [vaɪt'aus], *adv.* by far.

weitblickend ['vaɪtblɪkənt], *adj.* far-sighted.

Weite ['vaɪtə], *f.* (—, *pl.* —n) width, breadth; distance.

weiten ['vaɪtən], *v.a.* widen, expand.

weiter ['vaɪtər], *adj.* further, farther, wider.

weiterbefördern ['vaɪtərbəfœrdərn], *v.a.* send on, forward, send on.

weiterbilden ['vaɪtərbɪldən], *v.a.* improve, develop(e), extend.

Weitere ['vaɪtərə], *n.* (—n, *no pl.*) rest, remainder.

weiterführen ['vaɪtərfy:rən], *v.a.* continue, carry on.

weitergeben ['vaɪtərge:bən], *v.a. irr.* pass on.

weitergehen ['vaɪtərge:ən], *v.n. irr.* (*aux.* sein) walk on.

weiterhin ['vaɪtərhɪn], *adv.* furthermore; in time to come; in future.

weiterkommen ['vaɪtərkɔmən], *v.n. irr.* (*aux.* sein) get on.

Weiterung ['vaɪtəruŋ], *f.* (—, *pl.* —en) widening, enlargement.

weitgehend ['vaɪtge:ənt], *adj.* far-reaching, sweeping.

weitläufig ['vaɪtlɔyfɪç], *adj.* ample, large; detailed, elaborate; distant, widespread; diffuse, long-winded.

weitschweifig ['vaɪtʃvaɪfɪç], *adj.* prolix, diffuse, rambling.

weitsichtig ['vaɪtzɪçtɪç], *adj.* long-sighted.

weittragend ['vaɪttra:gənt], *adj.* portentous, far-reaching.

weitverbreitet ['vaɪtfɛrbraɪtət], *adj.* widespread.

Weizen ['vaɪtsən], *m.* (—s, *no pl.*) wheat.

Weizengrieß ['vaɪtsəngri:s], *m.* (—es, *no pl.*) semolina; grits.

welch [vɛlç], *pron.* what (a).

welcher, -e, -es ['vɛlçər], *interr. pron.* which? what? — *rel. pron.* who, which, that; (*indef.*) (*coll.*) some.

278

welcherlei ['vɛlçərlaı], *indecl. adj.* of what kind.

Welfe ['vɛlfə], *m.* (**—n**, *pl.* **—n**) Guelph.

welk [vɛlk], *adj.* faded, withered; — *werden*, fade, wither.

welken ['vɛlkən], *v.n.* (*aux.* sein) wither, fade, decay.

Wellblech ['vɛlblɛç], *n.* (**—s**, *no pl.*) corrugated iron.

Welle ['vɛlə], *f.* (**—**, *pl.* **—n**) wave, billow.

wellen ['vɛlən], *v.a.* wave.

Wellenbewegung ['vɛlənbəveːɡuŋ], *f.* (**—**, *pl.* **—en**) undulation.

Wellenlinie ['vɛlənliːnjə], *f.* (**—**, *pl.* **—n**) wavy line.

wellig ['vɛlıç], *adj.* wavy, undulating.

welsch [vɛlʃ], *adj.* foreign; Italian; French.

Welschkohl ['vɛlʃkoːl], *m.* (**—s**, *no pl.*) (*Bot.*) savoy cabbage.

Welschkorn ['vɛlʃkɔrn], *n.* (**—s**, *no pl.*) (*Bot.*) Indian corn.

Welt [vɛlt], *f.* (**—**, *pl.* **—en**) world, earth; universe; society.

Weltall ['vɛltal], *n.* (**—s**, *no pl.*) universe, cosmos; (outer) space.

Weltanschauung ['vɛltanʃauuŋ], *f.* (**—**, *pl.* **—en**) view of life, philosophy of life, ideology.

Weltbeschreibung ['vɛltbəʃraıbuŋ], *f.* (**—**, *no pl.*) cosmography.

Weltbürger ['vɛltbyrɡər], *m.* (**—s**, *pl.* **—**) cosmopolitan.

welterschütternd ['vɛltərʃytərnt], *adj.* world-shaking.

weltfremd ['vɛltfrɛmt], *adj.* unworldy, unsophisticated.

Weltgeschichte ['vɛltɡəʃıçtə], *f.* (**—**, *no pl.*) world history.

Weltherrschaft ['vɛlthɛrʃaft], *f.* (**—**, *no pl.*) world dominion.

Weltkenntnis ['vɛltkɛntnıs], *f.* (**—**, *no pl.*) worldly wisdom.

weltklug ['vɛltkluːk], *adj.* astute, worldly-wise.

Weltkrieg ['vɛltkriːk], *m.* (**—es**, *pl.* **—e**) world war.

weltlich ['vɛltlıç], *adj.* worldly; (*Eccl.*) temporal, secular.

Weltmacht ['vɛltmaxt], *f.* (**—**, *pl.* **—e**) world power, great power.

Weltmeer ['vɛltmeːr], *n.* (**—s**, *pl.* **—e**) ocean.

Weltmeisterschaft ['vɛltmaıstərʃaft], *f.* (**—**, *pl.* **—en**) world championship.

Weltordnung ['vɛltɔrdnuŋ], *f.* (**—** *pl.* **—en**) cosmic order.

Weltraum ['vɛltraum], *m.* (**—s**, *no pl.*) space.

Weltraumflug ['vɛltraumfluːk], *m.* (**—(e)s**, *pl.* **—e**) space flight.

Weltraumforschung ['vɛltraumfɔr-ʃuŋ], *f.* (**—**, *no pl.*) space exploration.

Weltraumgeschoß ['vɛltraumɡəʃoːs], *n.* (**—sses**, *pl.* **—sse**) space rocket.

Weltruf ['vɛltruːf], *m.* (**—s**, *no pl.*) world-wide renown.

Weltschmerz ['vɛltʃmɛrts], *m.* (**—es**, *no pl.*) world-weariness, Wertherism; melancholy.

Weltsprache ['vɛltʃpraːxə], *f.* (**—**, *pl.* **—en**) universal language; world language.

Weltstadt ['vɛltʃtat], *f.* (**—**, *pl.* **—e**) metropolis.

Weltumseglung ['vɛltumzeːɡluŋ], *f.* (**—**, *pl.* **—en**) circumnavigation (of the globe).

Weltuntergang ['vɛltuntərɡaŋ], *m.* (**—s**, *no pl.*) end of the world.

Weltwirtschaft ['vɛltvırtʃaft], *f.* (**—**, *no pl.*) world trade.

wem [veːm], *pers. pron.* (*Dat. of* **wer**) to whom. — *interr. pron.* to whom?

wen [veːn], *pers. pron.* (*Acc. of* **wer**) whom. — *interr. pron.* whom?

Wende ['vɛndə], *f.* (**—**, *pl.* **—n**) turn, turning(-point).

Wendekreis ['vɛndəkraıs], *m.* (**—es**, *pl.* **—e**) tropic.

Wendeltreppe ['vɛndəltrɛpə], *f.* (**—**, *pl.* **—n**) spiral staircase.

wenden ['vɛndən], *v.a.* reg. & irr. turn.

Wendepunkt ['vɛndəpuŋkt], *m.* (**—es**, *pl.* **—e**) turning point; crisis.

Wendung ['vɛnduŋ], *f.* (**—**, *pl.* **—en**) turn, turning; crisis; (*speech*) phrase.

wenig ['veːnıç], *adj.* little, few; *ein* **—**, a little.

weniger ['veːnıɡər], *adj.* less, fewer.

wenigstens ['veːnıçstəns], *adv.* at least.

wenn [vɛn], *conj.* if; when; whenever; in case; — *nicht*, unless.

wenngleich [vɛnˈɡlaıç], *conj.* though, although.

wer [veːr], *rel. pron.* who, he who; — *auch*, whoever. — *interr. pron.* who? which? — *da?* who goes there?

Werbekraft ['vɛrbəkraft], *f.* (**—**, *no pl.*) (*Advertising*) attraction; appeal; publicity value.

werben ['vɛrbən], *v.n. irr.* advertise, canvass; court, woo. — *v.a.* (*soldiers*) recruit.

Werbung ['vɛrbuŋ], *f.* (**—**, *pl.* **—en**) advertising, publicity, propaganda; recruiting; courtship.

Werdegang ['veːrdəɡaŋ], *m.* (**—s**, *no pl.*) evolution, development.

werden ['veːrdən], *v.n. irr.* (*aux.* sein) become, get; grow; turn; *Arzt* **—**, become a doctor; *alt* **—**, grow old; *bleich* — turn pale.

werdend ['veːrdənt], *adj.* becoming; nascent, incipient, budding.

werfen ['vɛrfən], *v.a. irr.* throw, cast.

Werft (1) [vɛrft], *m.* (**—(e)s**, *pl.* **—e**) warp.

Werft (2) [vɛrft], *f.* (**—**, *pl.* **—en**) dockyard, shipyard, wharf.

Werk [vɛrk], *n.* (**—(e)s**, *pl.* **—e**) work, action, deed; undertaking; (*Ind.*) works, plant, mill, factory.

Werkführer ['vɛrkfyːrər], *m.* (**—s**, *pl.* **—**) foreman.

Werkleute ['vɛrklɔytə], *pl.* workmen.

Werkmeister ['vɛrkmaıstər], *m.* (**—s**, *pl.* **—**) overseer, foreman.

werktätig ['vɛrkteːtıç], *adj.* active, practical; hard-working.

Werkzeug ['vɛrktsɔyk], *n.* (—s, *pl.* —e) implement, tool, jig, instrument.

Wermut ['vɛːrmuːt], *m.* (—s, *no pl.*) absinthe, vermouth.

Wert [veːrt], *m.* (—(e)s, *pl.* —e) value, worth, price; use; merit; importance.

wert [veːrt], *adj.* valuable; worth; dear, esteemed.

Wertangabe ['veːrtaŋaːbə], *f.* (—, *pl.* —n) valuation; declared value.

Wertbestimmung ['veːrtbəʃtɪmuŋ], *f.* (—, *no pl.*) appraisal, assessment, valuation.

Wertbrief ['veːrtbriːf], *m.* (—s, *pl.* —e) registered letter.

werten ['veːrtən], *v.a.* value.

Wertgegenstand ['veːrtgeːgənʃtant], *m.* (—s, *pl.* ̈e) article of value.

Wertmesser ['veːrtmɛsər], *m.* (—s, *pl.* —) standard.

Wertpapiere ['veːrtpapiːrə], *n. pl.* securities.

Wertsachen ['veːrtzaxən], *f. pl.* valuables.

wertschätzen ['veːrtʃɛtsən], *v.a.* esteem (highly).

wertvoll ['veːrtfɔl], *adj.* of great value, valuable.

Wertzeichen ['veːrttsaɪçən], *n.* (—s, *pl.* —) stamp; coupon.

wes [vɛs], *pers. pron.* (*obs.*) whose.

Wesen ['veːzən], *n.* (—s, *pl.* —) being, creature; reality; essence, nature, substance; character, demeanour; (*in compounds*) organisation; affairs.

wesenlos ['veːzənloːs], *adj.* disembodied, unsubstantial, shadowy; trivial.

wesensgleich ['veːzənsglaɪç], *adj.* identical, substantially the same.

wesentlich ['veːzəntlɪç], *adj.* essential, material.

weshalb [vɛs'halp], *conj., adv.* wherefore, why; therefore.

Wespe ['vɛspə], *f.* (—, *pl.* —n) (*Ent.*) wasp.

Wespennest ['vɛspənnɛst], *n.* (—s, *pl.* —er) wasps' nest; *in ein — stechen*, stir up a hornets' nest.

wessen ['vɛsən], *pers. pron.* (*Genit. of* wer) whose. — *interr. pron.* whose?

Weste ['vɛstə], *f.* (—, *pl.* —n) waistcoat.

Westen ['vɛstən], *m.* (—s, *no pl.*) west; *nach* —, westward.

Westfalen [vɛst'faːlən], *n.* Westphalia.

Westindien [vɛst'ɪndjən], *n.* the West Indies.

weswegen [vɛs'veːgən] *see* **weshalb**.

Wettbewerb ['vɛtbəvɛrp], *m.* (—s, *pl.* —e) competition, rivalry; *unlauterer* —, unfair competition.

Wettbewerber ['vɛtbəvɛrbər], *m.* (—s, *pl.* —) rival, competitor.

Wette ['vɛtə], *f.* (—, *pl.* —n) bet, wager; *um die* — *laufen*, race one another.

Wetteifer ['vɛtaɪfər], *m.* (—s, *no pl.*) rivalry.

wetteifern ['vɛtaɪfərn], *v.n. insep.* vie (with), compete.

wetten ['vɛtən], *v.a., v.n.* bet, lay a wager, wager.

Wetter ['vɛtər], *n.* (—s, *pl.* —) weather; bad weather, storm; *schlagende* —, (*Min.*) fire-damp.

Wetterbeobachtung ['vɛtərbəobaxtuŋ], *f.* (—, *pl.* —en) meteorological observation.

Wetterbericht ['vɛtərbərɪçt], *m.* (—s, *pl.* —e) weather report *or* forecast.

Wetterfahne ['vɛtərfaːnə], *f.* (—, *pl.* —en) weather-cock, vane; (*fig.*) turncoat.

wetterfest ['vɛtərfɛst], *adj.* weather-proof.

Wetterglas ['vɛtərglaːs], *n.* (—es, *pl.* ̈er) barometer.

Wetterhahn ['vɛtərhaːn], *m.* (—s, *pl.* ̈e) weather-cock.

Wetterkunde ['vɛtərkundə], *f.* (—, *no pl.*) meteorology.

Wetterleuchten ['vɛtərlɔyçtən], *n.* (—s, *no pl.*) summer lightning; sheet lightning.

wettern ['vɛtərn], *v.n.* be stormy; (*fig.*) curse, swear, thunder (against), storm.

Wettervorhersage ['vɛtərfoːrheːrzaːgə], *f.* (—, *pl.* —n) weather forecast.

wetterwendisch ['vɛtərvɛndɪʃ], *adj.* changeable; irritable, peevish.

Wettkampf ['vɛtkampf], *m.* (—(e)s, *pl.* ̈e) contest, tournament.

Wettlauf ['vɛtlauf], *m.* (—s, *pl.* ̈e) race.

wettmachen ['vɛtmaxən], *v.a.* make up for.

Wettrennen ['vɛtrɛnən], *n.* (—s, *pl.* —) race.

Wettstreit ['vɛtʃtraɪt], *m.* (—s, *pl.* —e) contest, contention.

wetzen ['vɛtsən], *v.a.* whet, hone, sharpen.

Wichse ['vɪksə], *f.* (—, *pl.* —n) blacking, shoe-polish; (*fig.*) thrashing.

wichsen ['vɪksən], *v.a.* black, shine; (*fig.*) thrash.

Wicht [vɪçt], *m.* (—(e)s, *pl.* —e) creature; (*coll.*) chap.

Wichtelmännchen ['vɪçtəlmɛnçən], *n.* (—s, *pl.* —) pixie, goblin.

wichtig ['vɪçtɪç], *adj.* important; weighty; significant; *sich* — *machen*, put on airs.

Wichtigkeit ['vɪçtɪçkaɪt], *f.* (—, *no pl.*) importance; significance.

Wicke ['vɪkə], *f.* (—, *pl.* —n) (*Bot.*) vetch.

Wickel ['vɪkəl], *m.* (—s, *pl.* —) roller; (*hair*) curler; (*Med.*) compress.

Wickelkind ['vɪkəlkɪnt], *n.* (—s, *pl.* —er) babe in arms.

wickeln ['vɪkəln], *v.a.* roll, coil; wind; wrap (up); (*babies*) swaddle; (*hair*) curl.

Widder ['vɪdər], *m.* (—s, *pl.* —) ram; (*Astrol.*) Aries.

wider ['viːdər], *prep.* (*Acc.*) against, in opposition to, contrary to.

widerfahren [vi:dər'fa:rən], *v.n.* *irr.* *insep.* (*aux.* sein) happen to s.o., befall s.o.; *einem Gerechtigkeit — lassen*, give s.o. his due.

Widerhaken ['vi:dərha:kən], *m.* (**—s**, *pl.* **—**) barb.

Widerhall ['vi:dərhal], *m.* (**—s**, *pl.* **—e**) echo, resonance; (*fig.*) response.

widerlegen [vi:dər'le:gən], *v.a. insep.* refute, disprove, prove (s.o.) wrong.

Widerlegung [vi:dər'le:guŋ], *f.* (**—**, *pl.* **—en**) refutation, rebuttal.

widerlich ['vi:dərlɪç], *adj.* disgusting, nauseating, repulsive.

widernatürlich ['vi:dərnaty:rlɪç], *adj.* unnatural; perverse.

widerraten [vi:dər'ra:tən], *v.a. irr. insep.* advise against; dissuade from.

widerrechtlich ['vi:dərrɛçtlɪç], *adj.* illegal, unlawful.

Widerrede ['vi:dərre:də], *f.* (**—**, *pl.* **—n**) contradiction.

Widerruf ['vi:dərru:f], *m.* (**—s**, *pl.* **—e**) revocation, recantation.

widerrufen [vi:dər'ru:fən], *v.a. irr. insep.* recant, retract, revoke.

Widersacher ['vi:dərzaxər], *m.* (**—s**, *pl.* **—**) adversary, antagonist.

Widerschein ['vi:dərʃaɪn], *m.* (**—s**, *no pl.*) reflection.

widersetzen [vi:dər'zɛtsən], *v.r. insep.* *sich —*, resist, (*Dat.*) oppose.

widersetzlich [vi:dər'zɛtslɪç], *adj.* refractory, insubordinate.

Widersinn ['vi:dərzɪn], *m.* (**—s**, *no pl.*) nonsense, absurdity; paradox.

widersinnig ['vi:dərzɪnɪç], *adj.* nonsensical, absurd; paradoxical.

widerspenstig ['vi:dərʃpɛnstɪç], *adj.* refractory, rebellious, obstinate, stubborn.

widerspiegeln [vi:dər'ʃpi:gəln], *v.a.* reflect, mirror.

widersprechen [vi:dər'ʃprɛçən], *v.n. irr. insep.* (*Dat.*) contradict, gainsay.

Widerspruch ['vi:dərʃprux], *m.* (**—es**), *pl.* ⸚e) contradiction.

widerspruchsvoll ['vi:dərʃpruxsfɔl], *adj.* contradictory.

Widerstand ['vi:dərʃtant], *m.* (**—s**, *pl.* ⸚e) resistance, opposition.

widerstandsfähig ['vi:dərʃtantsfɛ:ɪç], *adj.* resistant, hardy.

widerstehen [vi:dər'ʃte:ən], *v.n. irr. insep.* (*Dat.*) resist, withstand; be distasteful (to).

Widerstreben [vi:dər'ʃtre:bən], *n.* (**—s**, *no pl.*) reluctance.

widerstreben [vi:dər'ʃtre:bən], *v.n. insep.* (*Dat.*) strive against, oppose; be distasteful to a p.

Widerstreit ['vi:dərʃtraɪt], *m.* (**—s**, *no pl.*) contradiction, opposition; conflict.

widerwärtig ['vi:dərvɛrtɪç], *adj.* unpleasant, disagreeable, repugnant, repulsive; hateful, odious.

Widerwille ['vi:dərvɪlə], *m.* (**—ns**, *no pl.*) aversion (to).

widmen ['vɪdmən], *v.a.* dedicate.

Widmung ['vɪdmuŋ], *f.* (**—**, *pl.* **—en**) dedication.

widrig ['vi:drɪç], *adj.* contrary, adverse, inimical, unfavourable.

widrigenfalls ['vi:drɪgənfals], *adv.* failing this, otherwise, else.

wie [vi:], *adv.* how. — *conj.* as, just as, like; — *geht's?* how are you?

wieder ['vi:dər], *adv.* again, anew, afresh; back, in return.

Wiederabdruck ['vi:dərapdruk], *m.* (**—s**, *pl.* **—e**) reprint.

Wiederaufbau [vi:dər'aufbau], *m.* (**—s**, *no pl.*) rebuilding.

Wiederaufnahme [vi:dər'aufna:mə], *f.* (**—**, *no pl.*) resumption.

Wiederbelebungsversuch ['vi:dərbə-le:buŋsfɛrzu:x], *m.* (**—es**, *pl.* **—e**) attempt at resuscitation.

Wiederbezahlung ['vi:dərbətsa:luŋ], *f.* (**—**, *pl.* **—en**) reimbursement.

wiederbringen ['vi:dərbrɪŋən], *v.a. irr.* bring back, restore.

Wiedereinrichtung ['vi:dəraɪnrɪçtuŋ], *f.* (**—**, *no pl.*) reorganisation, re-establishment.

Wiedereinsetzung ['vi:dəraɪnzɛtsuŋ], *f.* (**—**, *pl.* **—en**) restoration, reinstatement, rehabilitation.

wiedererkennen ['vi:dərɛrkɛnən], *v.a. irr.* recognise.

Wiedererstattung ['vi:dərɛrʃtatuŋ], *f.* (**—**, *no pl.*) restitution.

Wiedergabe ['vi:dərga:bə], *f.* (**—**, *no pl.*) restitution, return; (*fig.*) rendering, reproduction.

wiedergeben ['vi:dərge:bən], *v.a. irr.* return, give back; (*fig.*) render.

Wiedergeburt ['vi:dərgəbu:rt], *f.* (**—**, *no pl.*) rebirth, regeneration, renascence.

Wiedergutmachung [vi:dər'gu:t-maxuŋ], *f.* (**—**, *no pl.*) reparation.

Wiederherstellung [vi:dər'he:rʃteluŋ], *f.* (**—**, *no pl.*) restoration; recovery.

Wiederherstellungsmittel [vi:dər-'he:rʃteluŋsmɪtəl], *n.* (**—s**, *pl.* **—**) restorative, tonic.

wiederholen [vi:dər'ho:lən], *v.a. insep.* repeat, reiterate.

Wiederholung [vi:dər'ho:luŋ], *f.* (**—**, *pl.* **—en**) repetition.

Wiederkäuer ['vi:dərkɔyər], *m.* (**—s**, *pl.* **—**) ruminant.

Wiederkehr ['vi:dərke:r], *f.* (**—**, *no pl.*) return; recurrence.

wiederkehren ['vi:dərke:rən], *v.n.* (*aux.* sein) return.

wiederklingen ['vi:dərklɪŋən], *v.n. irr.* reverberate.

wiederkommen ['vi:dərkɔmən], *v.n. irr.* (*aux.* sein) return, come back.

Wiedersehen ['vi:dərze:ən], *n.* (**—s**, *no pl.*) reunion, meeting after separation; *auf —*, good-bye; so long! see you again!

wiedersehen ['vi:dərze:ən], *v.a. irr.* see again, meet again.

wiederum ['viːdərum], *adv.* again, anew, afresh.

Wiedervereinigung ['viːdərfɛraɪnɪguŋ], *f.* (—, *pl.* —en) reunion, reunification.

Wiedervergeltung ['viːdərfɛrgɛltuŋ], *f.* (—, *no pl.*) requital, retaliation, reprisal.

Wiederverkauf ['viːdərfɛrkauf], *m.* (—s, *no pl.*) resale.

Wiederverkäufer ['viːdərfɛrkɔyfər], *m.* (—s, *pl.* —) retailer.

Wiederversöhnung ['viːdərfɛrzøːnuŋ], *f.* (—, *no pl.*) reconciliation.

Wiederwahl ['viːdərvaːl], *f.* (—, *no pl.*) re-election.

Wiege ['viːgə], *f.* (—, *pl.* —n) cradle.

wiegen ['viːgən], *v.a.* rock (the cradle). — *v.r. sich — in*, delude o.s. with. — *v.a., v.n. irr.* weigh.

Wiegenfest ['viːgənfɛst], *n.* (—es, *pl.* —e) (*Poet., Lit.*) birthday.

Wiegenlied ['viːgənliːt], *n.* (—s, *pl.* —er) cradle-song, lullaby.

wiehern ['viːərn], *v.n.* neigh.

Wien [viːn], *n.* Vienna.

Wiese ['viːzə], *f.* (—, *pl.* —n) meadow.

Wiesel ['viːzəl], *n.* (—s, *pl.* —) (*Zool.*) weasel.

wieso [vi'zoː] *adv.* why? how do you mean? in what way?

wieviel [vi'fiːl], *adv.* how much, how many; *den —ten haben wir heute?* what is the date today?

wiewohl [vi'voːl], *conj.* although, though.

Wild [vɪlt], *n.* (—(e)s, *no pl.*) game; venison.

wild [vɪlt], *adj.* wild, savage, fierce; furious.

Wildbach ['vɪltbax], *m.* (—s, *pl.* ⸚e) (mountain) torrent.

Wilddieb ['vɪltdiːp], *m.* (—(e)s, *pl.* —e) poacher.

Wilde ['vɪldə], *m.* (—n, *pl.* —n) savage.

wildern ['vɪldərn], *v.n.* poach.

Wildfang ['vɪltfaŋ], *m.* (—s, *pl.* ⸚e) scamp, tomboy.

wildfremd ['vɪltfrɛmt], *adj.* completely strange.

Wildhüter ['vɪlthyːtər], *m.* (—s, *pl.* —) gamekeeper.

Wildleder ['vɪltleːdər], *n.* (—s, *no pl.*) suède, doeskin, buckskin.

Wildnis ['vɪltnɪs], *f.* (—, *pl.* —se) wilderness, desert.

Wildpark ['vɪltpark], *m.* (—s, *pl.* —s) game-reserve.

Wildpret ['vɪltprɛt], *n.* (—s, *no pl.*) game; venison.

Wildschwein ['vɪltʃvaɪn], *n.* (—s, *pl.* —e) wild boar.

Wille ['vɪlə], *m.* (—ns, *no pl.*) will, wish, design, purpose.

willenlos ['vɪlənloːs], *adj.* weak-minded.

willens ['vɪləns], *adv.* — *sein*, be willing, have a mind to.

Willenserklärung ['vɪlənsɛrklɛːruŋ], *f.* (—, *pl.* —en) (*Law*) declaratory act.

Willensfreiheit ['vɪlənsfraɪhaɪt], *f.* (—, *no pl.*) free will.

Willenskraft ['vɪlənskraft], *f.* (—, *no pl.*) strength of will, will-power.

willentlich ['vɪləntlɪç], *adv.* purposely, on purpose, intentionally, wilfully.

willfahren [vɪl'faːrən], *v.n. insep.* (*Dat.*) comply with, gratify.

willfährig ['vɪlfɛːrɪç], *adj.* compliant, complaisant.

willig ['vɪlɪç], *adj.* willing, ready, docile.

willkommen [vɪl'kɔmən], *adj.* welcome; — *heißen*, welcome.

Willkür ['vɪlkyːr], *f.* (—, *no pl.*) free will; discretion; caprice, arbitrariness.

willkürlich ['vɪlkyːrlɪç], *adj.* arbitrary.

wimmeln ['vɪməln], *v.n.* swarm, teem (with).

wimmern ['vɪmərn], *v.n.* whimper.

Wimpel ['vɪmpəl], *m.* (—s, *pl.* —) pennon, pennant, streamer.

Wimper ['vɪmpər], *f.* (—, *pl.* —n) eyelash; *ohne mit der — zu zucken*, without turning a hair, without batting an eyelid.

Wind [vɪnt], *m.* (—(e)s, *pl.* —e) wind, breeze; *von etwas — bekommen*, get wind of.

Windbeutel ['vɪntbɔytəl], *m.* (—s, *pl.* —) cream puff; (*fig.*) windbag.

Windbüchse ['vɪntbyksə], *f.* (—, *pl.* —n) air-gun.

Winde ['vɪndə], *f.* (—, *pl.* —n) (*Tech.*) windlass; (*Bot.*) bindweed.

Windel ['vɪndəl], *f.* (—, *pl.* —n) (baby's) napkin; (*Am.*) diaper.

windelweich ['vɪndəlvaɪç], *adj.* very soft, limp; *einen — schlagen*, beat s.o. to a jelly.

winden ['vɪndən], *v.a. irr.* wind, reel; wring; (*flowers*) make a wreath of. — *v.r. sich —*, writhe.

Windeseile ['vɪndəsaɪlə], *f.* (—, *no pl.*) lightning speed.

Windfahne ['vɪntfaːnə], *f.* (—, *pl.* —n) weather-cock, vane.

windfrei ['vɪntfraɪ], *adj.* sheltered.

Windhund ['vɪnthunt], *m.* (—s, *pl.* —e) greyhound; (*fig.*) windbag.

windig ['vɪndɪç], *adj.* windy.

Windklappe ['vɪntklapə], *f.* (—, *pl.* —n) air-valve.

Windlicht ['vɪntlɪçt], *n.* (—s, *pl.* —er) torch; storm lantern.

Windmühle ['vɪntmyːlə], *f.* (—, *pl.* —n) windmill.

Windpocken ['vɪntpɔkən], *f. pl.* (*Med.*) chicken-pox.

Windrichtung ['vɪntrɪçtuŋ], *f.* (—, *pl.* —en) direction of the wind.

Windrose ['vɪntroːzə], *f.* (—, *pl.* —n) compass card; windrose.

Windsbraut ['vɪntsbraut], *f.* (—, *no pl.*) gust of wind, squall; gale.

windschief ['vɪntʃiːf], *adj.* warped, bent.

Windschutzscheibe ['vɪntʃutsʃaɪbə], *f.* (—, *pl.* —n) (*Motor.*) windscreen.

Windseite ['vɪntzaɪtə], *f.* (—, *pl.* —n) windward side.

Windspiel ['vɪntʃpiːl], *n.* (—s, *pl.* —e) greyhound.

windstill ['vɪntʃtɪl], *adj.* calm.

Windung ['vɪnduŋ], *f.* (—, *pl.* —en) winding; convolution; twist, loop; coil; meandering.

Wink [vɪŋk], *m.* (—(e)s, *pl.* —e) sign, nod; (*fig.*) hint, suggestion.

Winkel ['vɪŋkəl], *m.* (—s, *pl.* —) corner; (*Maths.*) angle.

Winkeladvokat ['vɪŋkəlatvoːkaːt], *m.* (—en, *pl.* —en) quack lawyer.

Winkelmaß ['vɪŋkəlmaːs], *n.* (—es, *pl.* —e) set-square.

Winkelmesser ['vɪŋkəlmɛsər], *m.* (—s, *pl.* —) protractor.

Winkelzug ['vɪŋkəltsuːk], *m.* (—s, *pl.* —e) evasion, trick, shift.

winken ['vɪŋkən], *v.n.* signal, nod, beckon, wave.

winklig ['vɪŋklɪç], *adj.* angular.

winseln ['vɪnzəln], *v.n.* whimper, whine, wail.

Winter ['vɪntər], *m.* (—s, *pl.* —) winter.

Wintergarten ['vɪntərgartən], *m.* (—s, *pl.* -̈) conservatory.

Wintergewächs ['vɪntərgəvɛks], *n.* (—es, *pl.* —e) perennial plant.

Wintergrün ['vɪntərgryːn], *n.* (—s, *no pl.*) evergreen; wintergreen.

wintern ['vɪntərn], *v.n.* become wintry.

Winterschlaf ['vɪntərʃlaːf], *m.* (—s, *no pl.*) hibernation; *den* — *halten,* hibernate.

Winzer ['vɪntsər], *m.* (—s, *pl.* —) vine-grower.

winzig ['vɪntsɪç], *adj.* tiny, diminutive.

Wipfel ['vɪpfəl], *m.* (—s, *pl.* —) top (of a tree), tree-top.

Wippe ['vɪpə], *f.* (—, *pl.* —n) seesaw.

wippen ['vɪpən], *v.n.* balance, see-saw.

wir [viːr], *pers. pron.* we.

Wirbel ['vɪrbəl], *m.* (—s, *pl.* —) (*water*) whirlpool, eddy; whirlwind; (*drum*) roll; (*head*) crown; (*back*) vertebra.

wirbeln ['vɪrbəln], *v.a., v.n.* whirl.

Wirbelsäule ['vɪrbəlzɔylə], *f.* (—, *pl.* —n) spine, vertebral column.

Wirbelwind ['vɪrbəlvɪnt], *m.* (—s, *pl.* —e) whirlwind.

Wirken ['vɪrkən], *n.* (—s, *no pl.*) activity.

wirken ['vɪrkən], *v.a.* effect, work; bring to pass; (*materials*) weave; (*dough*) knead. — *v.n.* work.

Wirker ['vɪrkər], *m.* (—s, *pl.* —) weaver.

wirklich ['vɪrklɪç], *adj.* real, actual; true, genuine.

Wirklichkeit ['vɪrklɪçkaɪt], *f.* (—, *no pl.*) reality.

wirksam ['vɪrkzaːm], *adj.* effective, efficacious.

Wirksamkeit ['vɪrkzaːmkaɪt], *f.* (—, *no pl.*) efficacy, efficiency.

Wirkung ['vɪrkuŋ], *f.* (—, *pl.* —en) working, operation; reaction; efficacy; effect, result, consequence; force, in-

fluence; *eine* — *ausüben auf,* have an effect on; influence s.o. *or* s.th.

Wirkungskreis ['vɪrkuŋskraɪs], *m.* (—es, *pl.* —e) sphere of activity.

wirkungslos ['vɪrkuŋsloːs], *adj.* ineffectual.

wirkungsvoll ['vɪrkuŋsfɔl], *adj.* effective, efficacious; (*fig.*) impressive.

wirr [vɪr], *adj.* tangled, confused; — *durcheinander,* higgledy-piggledy; *mir ist ganz* — *im Kopf,* my head is going round.

Wirren ['vɪrən], *f. pl.* troubles, disorders, disturbances.

wirrköpfig ['vɪrkœpfɪç], *adj.* muddle-headed.

Wirrsal ['vɪrzaːl], *n.* (—s, *pl.* —e) confusion, disorder.

Wirrwarr ['vɪrvar], *m.* (—s, *no pl.*) jumble, hurly-burly, hubbub.

Wirt [vɪrt], *m.* (—(e)s, *pl.* —e) host; innkeeper; landlord.

Wirtin ['vɪrtɪn], *f.* (—, *pl.* —innen) hostess, landlady, innkeeper's wife.

wirtlich ['vɪrtlɪç], *adj.* hospitable.

Wirtschaft ['vɪrtʃaft], *f.* (—, *pl.* —en) housekeeping; administration; economy; household; housekeeping; inn, ale-house; (*coll.*) mess.

wirtschaften ['vɪrtʃaftən], *v.n.* keep house, housekeep; administer, run; (*coll.*) rummage.

Wirtschafterin ['vɪrtʃaftərɪn], *f.* (—, *pl.* —innen) housekeeper.

wirtschaftlich ['vɪrtʃaftlɪç], *adj.* economical, thrifty.

Wirtschaftlichkeit ['vɪrtʃaftlɪçkaɪt], *f.* (—, *no pl.*) economy; profitability.

Wirtschaftsgeld ['vɪrtʃaftsgɛlt], *n.* (—s, *pl.* —er) housekeeping-money.

Wirtshaus ['vɪrtshaus], *n.* (—es, *pl.* -̈er) inn.

Wisch [vɪʃ], *m.* (—es, *pl.* —e) scrap of paper, rag.

wischen ['vɪʃən], *v.a.* wipe.

wispern ['vɪspərn], *v.a., v.n.* whisper.

Wißbegier(de) ['vɪsbəgiːr(də)], *f.* (—, *no pl.*) craving for knowledge; curiosity.

Wissen ['vɪsən], *n.* (—s, *no pl.*) knowledge, learning, erudition.

wissen ['vɪsən], *v.a. irr.* know, be aware of (a fact); be able to.

Wissenschaft ['vɪsənʃaft], *f.* (—, *pl.* —en) learning, scholarship; science.

wissenschaftlich ['vɪsənʃaftlɪç], *adj.* learned, scholarly; scientific.

wissenswert ['vɪsənsveːrt], *adj.* worth knowing.

Wissenszweig ['vɪsənstsvaɪk], *m.* (—s, *pl.* —e) branch of knowledge.

wissentlich ['vɪsəntlɪç], *adj.* deliberate, wilful. — *adv.* knowingly.

wittern ['vɪtərn], *v.a.* scent, smell; (*fig.*) suspect.

Witterung ['vɪtəruŋ], *f.* (—, *no pl.*) weather; trail; scent.

Witterungsverhältnisse ['vɪtəruŋsfɛr-hɛltnɪsə], *n. pl.* atmospheric conditions.

Witterüngswechsel ['vɪtərunsveksəl], *m.* (—s, *no pl.*) change in the weather.

Witwe ['vɪtvə], *f.* (—, *pl.* —n) widow.

Witwer ['vɪtvər], *m.* (—s, *pl.* —) widower.

Witz [vɪts], *m.* (—es, *pl.* —e) wit, brains; joke, jest, witticism; funny story.

Witzblatt ['vɪtsblat], *n.* (—s, *pl.* ∵er) satirical *or* humorous journal.

Witzbold ['vɪtsbɔlt], *m.* (—es, *pl.* —e) wag; wit.

witzeln ['vɪtsəln], *v.n.* poke fun (at).

witzig ['vɪtsɪç], *adj.* witty; funny, comical; bright.

wo [vo:], *interr. adv.* where? — *conj.* when.

wobei [vo:'baɪ], *adv.* by which, at which, in connection with which; whereby; in doing so.

Woche ['vɔxə], *f.* (—, *pl.* —n) week.

Wochenbericht ['vɔxənbərɪçt], *m.* (—s, *pl.* —e) weekly report.

Wochenbett ['vɔxənbɛt], *n.* (—s, *no pl.*) confinement.

Wochenblatt ['vɔxənblat], *n.* (—s, *pl.* ∵er) weekly (paper).

Wochenlohn ['vɔxənlo:n], *m.* (—s, *pl.* ∵e) weekly wage(s).

Wochenschau ['vɔxənʃau], *f.* (—, *no pl.*) newsreel.

Wochentag ['vɔxənta:k], *m.* (—s, *pl.* —e) week-day.

wöchentlich ['vœçəntlɪç], *adj.* weekly, every week.

wodurch [vo:'durç], *adv.* whereby, by which, through which; (*interr.*) by what?

wofern [vo:'fɛrn], *conj.* if, provided that.

wofür [vo:'fy:r], *adv.* for what, for which, wherefore.

Woge ['vo:gə], *f.* (—, *pl.* —n) wave, billow.

wogegen [vo:'ge:gən], *adv.* against what, against which, in return for which.

wogen ['vo:gən], *v.n.* heave, sway; (*fig.*) fluctuate.

woher [vo:'he:r], *adv.* whence, from what place, how.

wohin [vo:'hɪn], *adv.* whither, where.

wohingegen [vo:hɪn'ge:gən], *conj.* (*obs.*) whereas.

Wohl [vo:l], *n.* (—(e)s, *no pl.*) welfare, health; *auf dein* —, your health! cheers!

wohl [vo:l], *adv.* well, fit; indeed, doubtless, certainly; *ja* —, to be sure.

wohlan! [vo:'lan], *excl.* well! now then!

wohlauf! [vo:'lauf], *excl.* cheer up! — *sein*, be in good health.

wohlbedacht ['vo:bədaxt], *adj.* well considered.

Wohlbefinden ['vo:bəfɪndən], *n.* (—s, *no pl.*) good health.

Wohlbehagen ['vo:bəha:gən], *n.* (—s, *no pl.*) comfort, ease, wellbeing.

wohlbehalten ['vo:bəhaltən], *adj.* safe.

wohlbekannt ['vo:bəkant], *adj.* well known.

wohlbeleibt ['vo:bəlaɪpt], *adj.* corpulent, stout.

wohlbestallt ['vo:bəʃtalt], *adj.* duly installed.

Wohlergehen ['vo:lɛrge:ən], *n.* (—s, *no pl.*) welfare, wellbeing.

wohlerhalten ['vo:lɛrhaltən], *adj.* well preserved.

wohlerzogen ['vo:lɛrtso:gən], *adj.* well bred, well brought up.

Wohlfahrt ['vo:lfa:rt], *f.* (—, *no pl.*) welfare, prosperity.

wohlfeil ['vo:lfaɪl], *adj.* cheap, inexpensive.

Wohlgefallen ['vo:lgəfalən], *n.* (—s, *no pl.*) pleasure, delight, approval.

wohlgefällig ['vo:lgəfɛlɪç], *adj.* pleasant, agreeable.

Wohlgefühl ['vo:lgəfy:l], *n.* (—s, *no pl.*) comfort, ease.

wohlgelitten ['vo:lgəlɪtən], *adj.* popular.

wohlgemeint ['vo:lgəmaɪnt], *adj.* well meant.

wohlgemerkt ['vo:lgəmɛrkt], *adv.* mind you! mark my words!

wohlgemut ['vo:lgəmu:t], *adj.* cheerful, merry.

wohlgeneigt ['vo:lgənaɪkt], *adj.* well disposed (towards).

wohlgepflegt ['vo:lgəpfle:kt], *adj.* well kept.

wohlgeraten ['vo:lgəra:tən], *adj.* successful; well turned out; good, well behaved.

Wohlgeruch ['vo:lgəru:x], *m.* (—es, *pl.* ∵e) sweet scent, perfume, fragrance.

Wohlgeschmack ['vo:lgəʃmak], *m.* (—s, *no pl.*) pleasant flavour, agreeable taste.

wohlgesinnt ['vo:lgəzɪnt], *adj.* well disposed.

wohlgestaltet ['vo:lgəʃtaltət], *adj.* well shaped.

wohlgezielt ['vo:lgətsi:lt], *adj.* well aimed.

wohlhabend ['vo:lha:bənt], *adj.* well-to-do, wealthy, well off.

wohlig ['vo:lɪç], *adj.* comfortable, cosy.

Wohlklang ['vo:lklaŋ], *m.* (—s, *pl.* ∵e) harmony, euphony.

wohlklingend ['vo:lklɪŋənt], *adj.* harmonious, euphonious, sweet-sounding.

Wohlleben ['vo:lle:bən], *n.* (—s, *no pl.*) luxurious living.

wohllöblich ['vo:llø:plɪç], *adj.* worshipful.

wohlmeinend ['vo:lmaɪnənt], *adj.* well-meaning.

wohlschmeckend ['vo:lʃmɛkənt], *adj.* savoury, tasty, delicious.

Wohlsein ['vo:lzaɪn], *n.* (—s, *no pl.*) good health, wellbeing.

Wohlstand ['vo:lʃtant], *m.* (—s, *no pl.*) prosperity.

Wohltat ['vo:lta:t], *f.* (—, *pl.* —en) benefit; kindness; (*pl.*) benefaction, charity; (*fig.*) treat.

Wohltäter ['vo:ltɛ:tər], *m.* (—s, *pl.* —) benefactor.

Wohltätigkeit ['vo:ltɛ:tɪçkaɪt], *f.* (—, *no pl.*) charity.

wohltuend ['vo:ltu:ənt], *adj.* soothing.

wohltun ['vo:ltu:n], *v.n. irr.* do good; be comforting.

wohlweislich ['vo:lvaɪslɪç], *adj.* wisely.

Wohlwollen ['vo:lvɔlən], *n.* (—s, *no pl.*) benevolence; favour, patronage.

wohnen ['vo:nən], *v.n.* reside, dwell, live.

wohnhaft ['vo:nhaft], *adj.* domiciled, resident; — *sein*, reside, be domiciled.

Wohnhaus ['vo:nhaus], *n.* (—es, *pl.* ̈er) dwelling-house.

wohnlich ['vo:nlɪç], *adj.* comfortable; cosy.

Wohnort ['vo:nɔrt], *m.* (—s, *pl.* —e) place of residence.

Wohnsitz ['vo:nzɪts], *m.* (—es, *pl.* —e) domicile, abode, residence.

Wohnstätte ['vo:nʃtɛtə], *f.* (—, *pl.* —n) abode, home.

Wohnung ['vo:nuŋ], *f.* (—, *pl.* —en) residence, dwelling; house, flat, lodging; apartment.

Wohnungsmangel ['vo:nuŋsmaŋəl], *m.* (—s, *no pl.*) housing shortage.

Wohnwagen ['vo:nva:gən], *m.* (—s, *pl.* —) caravan.

Wohnzimmer ['vo:ntsɪmər], *n.* (—s, *pl.* —) sitting-room, living-room.

wölben ['vœlbən], *v.r. sich —*, vault, arch.

Wölbung ['vœlbuŋ], *f.* (—, *pl.* —en) vault, vaulting.

Wolf [vɔlf], *m.* (—(e)s, *pl.* ̈e) wolf.

Wolke ['vɔlkə], *f.* (—, *pl.* —n) cloud.

Wolkenbruch ['vɔlkənbrux], *m.* (—s, *pl.* ̈e) cloudburst, violent downpour.

Wolkenkratzer ['vɔlkənkratsər], *m.* (—s, *pl.* —) sky-scraper.

Wolkenkuckucksheim [vɔlkən'kukukshaɪm], *n.* (—s, *no pl.*) Utopia, cloud cuckoo land.

Wolldecke ['vɔldɛkə], *f.* (—, *pl.* —n) blanket.

Wolle ['vɔlə], *f.* (—, *pl.* —n) wool.

wollen (1) ['vɔlən], *v.a., v.n. irr.* wish, want to, be willing, intend; *was — Sie*, what do you want?

wollen (2) ['vɔlən], *adj.* woollen, made of wool.

Wollgarn ['vɔlgarn], *n.* (—s, *pl.* —e) woollen yarn.

Wollhandel ['vɔlhandəl], *m.* (—s, *no pl.*) wool-trade.

wollig ['vɔlɪç], *adj.* woolly.

Wollsamt ['vɔlzamt], *m.* (—s, *no pl.*) plush, velveteen.

Wollust ['vɔlust], *f.* (—, *pl.* ̈e) voluptuousness; lust.

wollüstig ['vɔlystɪç], *adj.* voluptuous.

Wollwaren ['vɔlva:rən], *f. pl.* woollen goods.

Wollzupfen ['vɔltsupfən], *n.* (—s, *no pl.*) wool-picking.

womit [vo:'mɪt], *adv.* wherewith, with which; (*interr.*) with what?

womöglich [vo:'mø:klɪç], *adv.* if possible, perhaps.

wonach [vo:'na:x], *adv.* whereafter, after which; according to which.

Wonne ['vɔnə], *f.* (—, *pl.* —n) delight, bliss, rapture.

wonnetrunken ['vɔnətruŋkən], *adj.* enraptured.

wonnig ['vɔnɪç], *adj.* delightful.

woran [vo:'ran], *adv.* whereat, whereby; (*interr.*) by what? at what?

worauf [vo:'rauf], *adv.* upon which, at which; whereupon; (*interr.*) on what?

woraufhin [vo:rauf'hɪn], *conj.* whereupon.

woraus [vo:'raus], *adv.* (*rel. & interr.*) whence, from which; by *or* out of which.

worein [vo:'raɪn], *adv.* (*rel. & interr.*) into which; into what.

worin [vo:'rɪn], *adv.* (*rel.*) wherein; (*interr.*) in what?

Wort [vɔrt], *n.* (—(e)s, *pl.* ̈er, —e) word, term; expression, saying.

wortarm ['vɔrtarm], *adj.* poor in words, deficient in vocabulary.

Wortarmut ['vɔrtarmu:t], *f.* (—, *no pl.*) paucity of words, poverty of language.

Wortbildung ['vɔrtbɪlduŋ], *f.* (—, *pl.* —en) word-formation.

wortbrüchig ['vɔrtbryçɪç], *adj.* faithless, disloyal.

Wörterbuch ['vœrtərbu:x], *n.* (—(e)s, *pl.* ̈er) dictionary.

Worterklärung ['vɔrtɛrkle:ruŋ], *f.* (—, *pl.* —en) definition.

Wortforschung ['vɔrtfɔrʃuŋ], *f.* (—, *no pl.*) etymology.

Wortfügung ['vɔrtfy:guŋ], *f.* (—, *no pl.*) syntax.

Wortführer ['vɔrtfy:rər], *m.* (—s, *pl.* —) spokesman.

Wortgefecht ['vɔrtgəfɛçt], *n.* (—es, *pl.* —e) verbal battle.

wortgetreu ['vɔrtgətrɔy], *adj.* literal, verbatim.

wortkarg ['vɔrtkark], *adj.* laconic, sparing of words, taciturn.

Wortlaut ['vɔrtlaut], *m.* (—s, *pl.* —e) wording, text.

wörtlich ['vœrtlɪç], *adj.* verbal; literal; word for word.

wortlos ['vɔrtlo:s], *adj.* speechless. — *adv.* without uttering a word.

wortreich ['vɔrtraɪç], *adj.* (*language*) rich in words; (*fig.*) verbose, wordy.

Wortreichtum ['vɔrtraɪçtum], *m.* (—s, *no pl.*) (*language*) wealth of words; (*fig.*) verbosity, wordiness.

Wortschwall ['vɔrtʃval], *m.* (—s, *no pl.*) bombast; torrent of words.

Wortspiel ['vɔrtʃpi:l], *n.* (—s, *pl.* —e) pun.

Wortversetzung ['vɔrtfɛrzɛtsuŋ], *f.* (—, *pl.* —en) inversion (of words).

Wortwechsel ['vɔrtvɛksəl], *m.* (—s, *pl.* —) dispute, altercation.

worüber [vo:'ry:bər], *adv.* (*rel.*) about which, whereof; (*interr.*) about what?

worunter [vo'runtər], *adv.* (*rel.*) whereunder; (*interr.*) under what?

woselbst [vo:'zɛlpst], *adv.* where.

wovon [vo:'fɔn], *adv.* (*rel.*) whereof; (*interr.*) of what?

wovor [vo:'fo:r], *adv.* (*rel.*) before which; (*interr.*) before what?

wozu [vo:'tsu:], *adv.* (*rel.*) whereto; (*interr.*) why? for what purpose? to what end?

Wrack [vrak], *n.* (—s, *pl.* —s) wreck.

wringen ['vrɪŋən], *v.a.* wring.

Wringmaschine ['vrɪŋmaʃi:nə], *f.* (—, *pl.* —n) wringer, mangle.

Wucher ['vu:xər], *m.* (—s, *no pl.*) usury.

wucherisch ['vu:xərɪʃ], *adj.* usurious, extortionate.

wuchern ['vu:xərn], *v.n.* practise usury; (*plants*) luxuriate, grow profusely.

Wucherungen ['vu:xəruŋən], *f. pl.* (*Med.*) excrescence, growth.

Wuchs [vu:ks], *m.* (—es, *no pl.*) growth; shape, build.

Wucht [vuxt], *f.* (—, *no pl.*) power, force; weight; impetus.

wuchten ['vuxtən], *v.n.* (*Poet.*) press heavily. — *v.a.* prise up.

wuchtig ['vuxtɪç], *adj.* weighty, forceful.

Wühlarbeit ['vy:larbaɪt], *f.* (—, *pl.* —en) subversive activity.

wühlen ['vy:lən], *v.a., v.n.* dig, burrow; (*fig.*) agitate.

Wühler ['vy:lər], *m.* (—s, *pl.* —) agitator, demagogue.

Wühlmaus ['vy:lmaus], *f.* (—, *pl.* ̈e) (*Zool.*) vole.

Wulst [vulst], *m.* (—es, *pl.* ̈e) roll, pad; swelling.

wülstig ['vylstɪç], *adj.* padded, stuffed; swollen.

wund [vunt], *adj.* sore, wounded.

Wundarzt ['vuntartst], *m.* (—es, *pl.* ̈e) (*obs.*) surgeon.

Wundbalsam ['vuntbalzam], *m.* (—s, *pl.* —e) balm.

Wunde ['vundə], *f.* (—, *pl.* —n) wound, hurt.

Wunder ['vundər], *n.* (—s, *pl.* —) marvel, wonder, miracle.

wunderbar ['vundərba:r], *adj.* wonderful, marvellous.

Wunderding ['vundərdɪŋ], *n.* (—s, *pl.* —e) marvel.

Wunderdoktor ['vundərdɔktor], *m.* (—s, *pl.* —en) quack doctor.

Wunderglaube ['vundərglaubə], *m.* (—ns, *no pl.*) belief in miracles.

wunderhübsch [vundər'hypʃ], *adj.* exceedingly pretty.

Wunderkind ['vundərkɪnt], *n.* (—s, *pl.* —er) infant prodigy.

Wunderlampe ['vundərlampə], *f.* (—, *pl.* —n) magic lantern.

wunderlich ['vundərlɪç], *adj.* strange, odd, queer.

wundern ['vundərn], *v.r. sich — über*, be surprised at, be astonished at.

wundersam ['vundərza:m], *adj.* wonderful, strange.

wunderschön ['vundərʃø:n], *adj.* lovely, gorgeous; exquisite.

Wundertat ['vundərta:t], *f.* (—, *pl.* —en) miraculous deed.

wundertätig ['vundərtɛ:tɪç], *adj.* miraculous.

Wundertier ['vundərti:r], *n.* (—s, *pl.* —e) monster; (*fig.*) prodigy.

Wunderwerk ['vundərvɛrk], *n.* (—s, *pl.* —e) miracle.

Wundmal ['vuntma:l], *n.* (—s, *pl.* —e) scar.

Wunsch [vunʃ], *m.* (—es, *pl.* ̈e) wish, desire, aspiration.

Wünschelrute ['vynʃəlru:tə], *f.* (—, *pl.* —n) divining-rod.

wünschen ['vynʃən], *v.a.* wish, desire, long for.

wünschenswert ['vynʃənsve:rt], *adj.* desirable.

Wunschform ['vunʃfɔrm], *f.* (—, *no pl.*) (*Gram.*) optative form.

wuppdich! ['vupdɪç], *excl.* here goes!

Würde ['vyrdə], *f.* (—, *pl.* —n) dignity, honour.

Würdenträger ['vyrdəntrɛ:gər], *m.* (—s, *pl.* —) dignitary.

würdevoll ['vyrdəfɔl], *adj.* dignified.

würdig ['vyrdɪç], *adj.* worthy (of), deserving, meritorious.

würdigen ['vyrdɪgən], *v.a.* honour; *ich weiss es zu —*, I appreciate it.

Würdigung ['vyrdɪguŋ], *f.* (—, *pl.* —en) appreciation.

Wurf [vurf], *m.* (—(e)s, *pl.* ̈e) cast, throw.

Würfel ['vyrfəl], *m.* (—s, *pl.* —) die; (*Geom.*) cube; — *spielen*, play at dice.

würfelförmig ['vyrfəlfœrmɪç], *adj.* cubic, cubiform.

würfeln ['vyrfəln], *v.n.* play at dice.

Wurfgeschoß ['vurfgəʃo:s], *n.* (—sses, *pl.* —sse) missile, projectile.

Wurfmaschine ['vurfmaʃi:nə], *f.* (—, *pl.* —n) catapult.

Wurfscheibe ['vurfʃaɪbə], *f.* (—, *pl.* —n) discus, quoit.

Wurfspieß ['vurfʃpi:s], *m.* (—es, *pl.* —e) javelin.

würgen ['vyrgən], *v.a.* strangle, throttle. — *v.n.* choke.

Würgengel ['vyrgeŋəl], *m.* (—s, *no pl.*) avenging angel.

Würger ['vyrgər], *m.* (—s, *pl.* —) strangler, murderer; (*Poet.*) slayer; (*Orn.*) shrike, butcher-bird.

Wurm [vurm], *m.* (—(e)s, *pl.* ̈er) worm; (*apple*) maggot.

wurmen ['vurmən], *v.a.* vex.

wurmstichig ['vurmʃtɪçɪç], *adj.* worm-eaten.

Wurst [vurst], *f.* (—, *pl.* ̈e) sausage.

wurstig ['vurstɪç], *adj.* (*sl.*) quite indifferent.

Wurstigkeit ['vurstɪçkaɪt], *f.* (—, *no pl.*) callousness, indifference.

Würze ['vyrtsə], *f.* (—, *pl.* —n) seasoning, spice, condiment.

Wurzel ['vurtsəl], *f.* (—, *pl.* —n) root.

wurzeln ['vurtsəln], *v.n.* be rooted.

würzen ['vyrtsən], *v.a.* season, spice.

würzig ['vyrtsɪç], *adj.* spicy, fragrant.

Zahn

Wust [vust], *m.* (—es, *no pl.*) chaos, trash.
wüst [vy:st], *adj.* waste, desert; desolate; dissolute.
Wüste ['vy:stə], *f.* (—, *pl.* —n) desert, wilderness.
Wüstling ['vy:stlɪŋ], *m.* (—s, *pl.* —e) profligate, libertine.
Wut [vu:t], *f.* (—, *no pl.*) rage, fury, passion.
wüten ['vy:tən], *v.n.* rage, storm, fume.
wutentbrannt ['vu:təntbrant], *adj.* enraged, infuriated.
Wüterich ['vy:tərɪç], *m.* (—s, *pl.* —e) tyrant; ruthless fellow.
Wutgeschrei ['vu:tgəʃraɪ], *n.* (—s, *no pl.*) yell of rage.
wutschnaubend ['vu:tʃnaubənt], *adj.* foaming with rage.

X

X [ɪks], *n.* (—s, *pl.* —s) the letter X.
X-Beine ['ɪksbaɪnə], *n. pl.* knock-knees.
x-beliebig ['ɪksbəli:bɪç], *adj.* any, whatever (one likes).
Xenie ['kse:njə], *f.* (—, *pl.* —n) epigram.
Xereswein ['kse:rəsvaɪn], *m.* (—s, *pl.* —e) sherry.
x-mal ['ɪksma:l], *adv.* (*coll.*) so many times, umpteen times.
X-Strahlen ['ɪksʃtra:lən], *m. pl.* X-rays.
Xylographie [ksylogra'fi:], *f.* (—, *no pl.*) wood-engraving.
Xylophon [ksylo'fo:n], *n.* (—s, *pl.* —e) (*Mus.*) xylophone.

Y

Y ['ypsilɔn], *n.* (—s, *pl.* —s) the letter Y
Yak [jak], *m.* (—s, *pl.* —s) (*Zool.*) yak.
Yamswurzel ['jamsvurtsəl], *f.* (—, *pl.* —n) yam.
Ysop [y'zo:p], *m.* (—s, *no pl.*) hyssop.

Z

Z [tsɛt], *n.* (—s, *pl.* —s) the letter Z.
Zabel ['tsa:bəl], *m.* (—s, *pl.* —) (*obs.*) chess-board.

Zacke ['tsakə], *f.* (—, *pl.* —n) tooth, spike; (*fork*) prong.
zackig ['tsakɪç], *adj.* pronged, toothed, indented; (*rock*) jagged; (*sl.*) smart.
zagen ['tsa:gən], *v.n.* quail, blench, be disheartened, be fainthearted.
zaghaft ['tsa:khaft], *adj.* faint-hearted.
Zaghaftigkeit ['tsa:khaftɪçkaɪt], *f.* (—, *no pl.*) faintheartedness, timidity.
zäh [tsɛ:], *adj.* tough.
Zähigkeit ['tsɛ:ɪçkaɪt], *f.* (—, *no pl.*) toughness.
Zahl [tsa:l], *f.* (—, *pl.* —en) number, figure.
zahlbar ['tsa:lba:r], *adj.* payable, due.
zählbar ['tsɛ:lba:r], *adj.* calculable.
zahlen ['tsa:lən], *v.a.* pay; *Ober!* —, waiter! the bill, please.
zählen ['tsɛ:lən], *v.a.*, *v.n.* count, number.
Zahlenfolge ['tsa:lənfɔlgə], *f.* (—, *no pl.*) numerical order.
Zahlenlehre ['tsa:lənle:rə], *f.* (—, *no pl.*) arithmetic.
Zahlenreihe ['tsa:lənraɪə], *f.* (—, *pl.* —n) numerical progression.
Zahlensinn ['tsa:lənzɪn], *m.* (—s, *no pl.*) head for figures.
Zahler ['tsa:lər], *m.* (—s, *pl.* —) payer.
Zähler ['tsɛ:lər], *m.* (—s, *pl.* —) counter, teller; meter; (*Maths.*) numerator.
Zahlkellner ['tsa:lkɛlnər], *m.* (—s, *pl.* —) head waiter.
Zahlmeister ['tsa:lmaɪstər], *m.* (—s, *pl.* —) paymaster, treasurer, bursar.
zahlreich ['tsa:lraɪç], *adj.* numerous.
Zahltag ['tsa:lta:k], *m.* (—s, *pl.* —e) pay-day.
Zahlung ['tsa:luŋ], *f.* (—, *pl.* —en) payment; — *leisten*, make payment; *die —en einstellen*, stop payment.
Zählung ['tsɛ:luŋ], *f.* (—, *pl.* —en) counting, computation; census.
Zahlungseinstellung ['tsa:luŋsaɪnʃtɛluŋ], *f.* (—, *pl.* —en) suspension of payment.
zahlungsfähig ['tsa:luŋsfɛ:ɪç], *adj.* solvent.
Zahlungsmittel ['tsa:luŋsmɪtəl], *n.* (—s, *pl.* —) means of payment; *gesetzliches* —, legal tender.
Zahlungstermin ['tsa:luŋstermi:n], *m.* (—s, *pl.* —e) time of payment.
zahlungsunfähig ['tsa:luŋsunfe:ɪç], *adj.* insolvent.
Zahlwort ['tsa:lvɔrt], *n.* (—s, *pl.* ⸚er) (*Gram.*) numeral.
zahm [tsa:m], *adj.* tame; domestic(ated); — *machen*, tame.
zähmen ['tsɛ:mən], *v.a.* tame, domesticate.
Zähmer ['tsɛ:mər], *m.* (—s, *pl.* —) tamer.
Zahmheit ['tsa:mhaɪt], *f.* (—, *no pl.*) tameness.
Zähmung ['tsɛ:muŋ], *f.* (—, *no pl.*) taming, domestication.
Zahn [tsa:n], *m.* (—(e)s, *pl.* ⸚e) tooth; (*wheel*) cog.

Zahnarzt ['tsa:nartst], *m.* (—es, *pl.* ¨e) dentist, dental surgeon.

Zahnbürste ['tsa:nbyrstə], *f.* (—, *pl.* —n) tooth-brush.

Zähneklappern ['tsɛ:nəklapərn], *n.* (—s, *no pl.*) chattering of teeth.

Zähneknirschen ['tsɛ:nəknirʃən], *n.* (—s, *no pl.*) gnashing of teeth.

zahnen ['tsa:nən], *v.n.* teethe, cut o.'s teeth.

zähnen ['tsɛ:nən], *v.a.* indent, notch.

Zahnfleisch ['tsa:nflaiʃ], *n.* (—es, *no pl.*) gums.

Zahnfüllung ['tsa:nfyluŋ], *f.* (—, *pl.* —en) filling, stopping (of tooth).

Zahnheilkunde ['tsa:nhailkundə], *f.* (—, *no pl.*) dentistry, dental surgery.

Zahnlücke ['tsa:nlykə], *f.* (—, *pl.* —n) gap in the teeth.

Zahnpaste ['tsa:npastə], *f.* (—, *no pl.*) tooth-paste.

Zahnpulver ['tsa:npulvər], *n.* (—s, *no pl.*) tooth-powder.

Zahnrad ['tsa:nra:t], *n.* (—s, *pl.* ¨er) cog-wheel.

Zahnradbahn ['tsa:nra:tba:n], *f.* (—, *pl.* —en) rack-railway.

Zahnschmerzen ['tsa:nʃmɛrtsən], *m. pl.* toothache.

Zahnstocher ['tsa:nʃtɔxər], *m.* (—s, *pl.* —) tooth-pick.

Zähre ['tsɛ:rə], *f.* (—, *pl.* —n) (*Poet.*) tear.

Zander ['tsandər], *m.* (—s, *pl.* —) (*fish*) pike.

Zange ['tsaŋə], *f.* (—, *pl.* —n) tongs; pincers; tweezers; nippers; (*Med.*) forceps.

Zank [tsaŋk], *m.* (—es, *pl.* ¨ereien) quarrel, altercation, tiff.

Zankapfel ['tsaŋkapfəl], *m.* (—s, *pl.* ¨) bone of contention.

zanken ['tsaŋkən], *v.r. sich* —, quarrel, dispute.

zänkisch ['tsɛnkiʃ], *adj.* quarrelsome.

Zanksucht ['tsaŋkzuxt], *f.* (—, *no pl.*) quarrelsomeness.

zanksüchtig ['tsaŋkzyçtiç], *adj.* quarrelsome, cantankerous.

Zapfen ['tsapfən], *m.* (—s, *pl.* —) pin, peg; (*cask*) bung, spigot; (*fir*) cone.

zapfen ['tsapfən], *v.a.* tap, draw.

Zapfenstreich ['tsapfənʃtraiç], *m.* (—s, *no pl.*) (*Mil.*) tattoo, retreat.

zapp(e)lig ['tsap(ə)liç], *adj.* fidgety.

zappeln ['tsapəln], *v.n.* kick, struggle, wriggle.

Zar [tsa:r], *m.* (—en, *pl.* —en) Czar, Tsar.

zart [tsart], *adj.* tender, sensitive, delicate, gentle; — *besaitet*, (*iron.*) sensitive, highly strung.

Zartgefühl ['tsartgəfy:l], *n.* (—s, *no pl.*) delicacy, sensitivity.

Zartheit ['tsarthait], *f.* (—, *no pl.*) tenderness, gentleness.

zärtlich ['tsɛ:rtliç], *adj.* loving, amorous, tender.

Zärtlichkeit ['tsɛ:rtliçkait], *f.* (—, *pl.* —en) tenderness; caresses.

Zartsinn ['tsartzin], *m.* (—s, *no pl.*) delicacy.

Zauber ['tsaubər], *m.* (—s, *no pl.*) charm, spell, enchantment; magic; fascination.

Zauberei [tsaubə'rai], *f.* (—, *pl.* —en) magic, witchcraft, sorcery.

Zauberer ['tsaubərər], *m.* (—s, *pl.* —) magician, sorcerer, wizard.

zauberisch ['tsaubəriʃ], *adj.* magical; (*fig.*) enchanting.

Zauberkraft ['tsaubərkraft], *f.* (—, *no pl.*) magic power, witchcraft.

Zaubermittel ['tsaubərmitəl], *n.* (—s, *pl.* —) charm.

zaubern ['tsaubərn], *v.n.* practise magic; conjure.

Zauberspruch ['tsaubərʃprux], *m.* (—s, *pl.* ¨e) spell, charm.

Zauberstab ['tsaubərʃta:p], *m.* (—s, *pl.* ¨e) magic wand.

Zauderer ['tsaudərər], *m.* (—s, *pl.* —) loiterer, temporizer, procrastinator.

zaudern ['tsaudərn], *v.n.* delay; hesitate, procrastinate.

Zaum [tsaum], *m.* (—(e)s, *pl.* ¨e) bridle; *im* — *halten*, check, restrain.

zäumen ['tsɔymən], *v.a.* bridle.

Zaun [tsaun], *m.* (—(e)s, *pl.* ¨e) hedge, fence; *einen Streit vom* — *brechen*, pick a quarrel.

Zaungast ['tsaungast], *m.* (—s, *pl.* ¨e) onlooker, outsider; intruder.

Zaunkönig ['tsaunkø:niç], *m.* (—s, *pl.* —e) (*Orn.*) wren.

Zaunpfahl ['tsaunpfa:l], *m.* (—s, *pl.* ¨e) pale, hedge-pole; *mit dem* — *winken*, give s.o. a broad hint.

Zaunrebe ['tsaunre:bə], *f.* (—, *pl.* —n) (*Bot.*) Virginia creeper.

zausen ['tsauzən], *v.a.* tousle; (*hair*) disarrange, ruffle.

Zechbruder ['tsɛçbru:dər], *m.* (—s, *pl.* ¨) tippler, toper.

Zeche ['tsɛçə], *f.* (—, *pl.* —n) bill (in a restaurant); mine; *die* — *bezahlen*, foot the bill, pay the piper.

Zeder ['tse:dər], *f.* (—, *pl.* —n) (*Bot.*) cedar.

zedieren [tsɛ'di:rən], *v.a.* cede.

Zehe ['tse:ə], *f.* (—, *pl.* —n) toe.

Zehenspitze ['tse:ənʃpitsə], *f.* (—, *pl.* —n) tip of the toe, tiptoe.

zehn [tse:n], *num. adj.* ten.

Zehneck ['tse:nɛk], *n.* (—s, *pl.* —e) decagon.

Zehnte ['tse:ntə], *m.* (—n, *pl.* —n) tithe.

zehren ['tse:rən], *v.n. von etwas* —, live on s.th., prey upon s.th.

Zehrfieber ['tse:rfi:bər], *n.* (—s, *no pl.*) hectic fever.

Zehrgeld ['tse:rgɛlt], *n.* (—s, *pl.* —er) subsistence, allowance.

Zehrvorrat ['tse:rfo:rra:t], *m.* (—s, *pl.* ¨e) provisions.

Zehrung ['tse:ruŋ], *f.* (—, *pl.* —en) consumption; victuals; (*Eccl.*) *letzte* —, viaticum.

Zeichen ['tsaiçən], *n.* (—s, *pl.* —) sign, token, symptom, omen; indication; badge; signal.

Zeichenbrett ['tsaɪçənbret], *n.* (—s, *pl.* —er) drawing-board.

Zeichendeuter ['tsaɪçəndɔytər], *m.* (—s, *pl.* —) astrologer.

Zeichendeuterei [tsaɪçəndɔytə'raɪ], *f.* (—, *no pl.*) astrology.

Zeichenerklärung ['tsaɪçənerklɛːruŋ], *f.* (— *pl.* —en) legend, key.

Zeichensprache ['tsaɪçənʃpraːxə], *f.* (—, *no pl.*) sign-language.

Zeichentinte ['tsaɪçəntɪntə], *f.* (—, *no pl.*) marking ink.

zeichnen ['tsaɪçnən], *v.a.* draw; mark; (*money*) subscribe; (*letter*) sign.

Zeichner ['tsaɪçnər], *m.* (—s, *pl.* —) draughtsman, designer.

Zeichnung ['tsaɪçnuŋ], *f.* (—, *pl.* —en) drawing.

Zeigefinger ['tsaɪgəfɪŋər], *m.* (—s, *pl.* —) forefinger, index finger.

zeigen ['tsaɪgən], *v.a.* show, point to, prove.

Zeiger ['tsaɪgər], *m.* (—s, *pl.* —) indicator; hand (of watch, clock).

zeihen ['tsaɪən], *v.a. irr. einen einer Sache* —, tax s.o. with s.th.

Zeile ['tsaɪlə], *f.* (—, *pl.* —n) line; furrow; (*pl.*) letter.

Zeisig ['tsaɪzɪç], *m.* (—s, *pl.* —e) (*Orn.*) siskin.

Zeit [tsaɪt], *f.* (—, *pl.* —en) time; *zur* —, at present; *auf* —, on credit.

Zeitabschnitt ['tsaɪtapʃnɪt], *m.* (—s, *pl.* —e) period; epoch.

Zeitalter ['tsaɪtaltər], *n.* (—s, *pl.* —) age, era.

Zeitdauer ['tsaɪtdauər], *f.* (—, *no pl.*) space of time.

Zeitfrage ['tsaɪtfraːgə], *f.* (—, *pl.* —n) topical question; question of time.

Zeitgeist ['tsaɪtgaɪst], *m.* (—s, *no pl.*) spirit of the age.

zeitgemäß ['tsaɪtgəmɛːs], *adj.* timely, seasonable, opportune, modern.

Zeitgenosse ['tsaɪtgənɔsə], *m.* (—n, *pl.* —n) contemporary.

zeitig ['tsaɪtɪç], *adj.* early, timely.

zeitigen ['tsaɪtɪgən], *v.a.* engender, generate. — *v.n.* mature, ripen.

Zeitkarte ['tsaɪtkartə], *f.* (—, *pl.* —n) season ticket.

Zeitlauf ['tsaɪtlauf], *m.* (—s, *pl.* ᵞe) course of time, conjuncture.

zeitlebens ['tsaɪtleːbəns], *adv.* for life, (for) all his (*or* her) life.

zeitlich ['tsaɪtlɪç], *adj.* temporal, earthly; secular; temporary, transient.

zeitlos ['tsaɪtloːs], *adj.* lasting, permanent.

Zeitmangel ['tsaɪtmaŋəl], *m.* (—s, *no pl.*) lack of time.

Zeitmesser ['tsaɪtmesər], *m.* (—s, *pl.* —) chronometer, timepiece; metronome.

Zeitpunkt ['tsaɪtpuŋkt], *m.* (—s, *pl.* —e) moment, date; point of time.

zeitraubend ['tsaɪtraubənt], *adj.* time-consuming.

Zeitraum ['tsaɪtraum], *m.* (—s, *pl.* ᵞe) space of time, period.

Zeitschrift ['tsaɪtʃrɪft], *f.* (—, *pl.* —en) periodical, journal, magazine.

Zeitung ['tsaɪtuŋ], *f.* (—, *pl.* —en) newspaper.

Zeitungsente ['tsaɪtuŋsentə], *f.* (—, *pl.* —n) canard, newspaper hoax.

Zeitungskiosk ['tsaɪtuŋskiosk], *m.* (—s, *pl.* —e) newspaper-stall.

Zeitungsnachricht ['tsaɪtuŋsnaːxrɪçt], *f.* (—, *pl.* —en) newspaper report.

Zeitungswesen ['tsaɪtuŋsveːzən], *n.* (—s, *no pl.*) journalism.

Zeitverlust ['tsaɪtferlust], *m.* (—s, *no pl.*) loss of time; *ohne* —, without delay.

Zeitvertreib ['tsaɪtfertraɪp], *m.* (—s, *no pl.*) pastime, amusement; *zum* —, to pass the time.

zeitweilig ['tsaɪtvaɪlɪç], *adj.* temporary.

zeitweise ['tsaɪtvaɪzə], *adv.* from time to time.

Zeitwort ['tsaɪtvɔrt], *n.* (—s, *pl.* ᵞer) (*Gram.*) verb.

Zelle ['tsɛlə], *f.* (—, *pl.* —n) cell.

Zelt [tsɛlt], *n.* (—(e)s, *pl.* —e) tent.

Zeltdecke ['tsɛltdekə], *f.* (—, *pl.* —n) awning, marquee.

Zement [tse'mɛnt], *m.* (—s, *no pl.*) cement.

Zenit [tse'niːt], *m.* (—s, *no pl.*) zenith.

zensieren [tsɛn'ziːrən], *v.a.* review, censure; (*Sch.*) mark.

Zensor ['tsɛnzɔr], *m.* (—s, *pl.* —en) censor.

Zensur [tsɛn'zuːr], *f.* (—, *pl.* —en) censure; (*Sch.*) report, mark; censorship.

Zentimeter ['tsɛntimeːtər], *m.* (—s, *pl.* —) centimetre.

Zentner ['tsɛntnər], *m.* (—s, *pl.* —) hundredweight.

zentral [tsɛn'traːl], *adj.* central.

Zentrale [tsɛn'traːlə], *f.* (—, *pl.* —n) control room; head office.

zentralisieren [tsɛntrali'ziːrən], *v.a.* centralise.

Zentrum ['tsɛntrum], *n.* (—s, *pl.* —tren) centre; (*Am.*) center.

Zephir ['tsefiːr], *m.* (—s, *pl.* —e) zephyr.

Zepter ['tsɛptər], *m. & n.* (—s, *pl.* —e) sceptre, mace.

zerbrechen [tsɛr'breçən], *v.a.*, *v.n. irr.* (*aux.* sein) break to pieces; shatter; *sich den Kopf* —, rack o.'s brains.

zerbrechlich [tsɛr'breçlɪç], *adj.* brittle, fragile.

zerbröckeln [tsɛr'brœkəln], *v.a.*, *v.n.* (*aux.* sein) crumble.

zerdrücken [tsɛr'drykən], *v.a.* crush, bruise.

Zeremonie [tseremo'niː], *f.* (—, *pl.* —n) ceremony.

zeremoniell [tseremo'njɛl], *adj.* ceremonial, formal.

Zerfahrenheit [tsɛr'faːrənhaɪt], *f.* (—, *no pl.*) absent-mindedness.

Zerfall [tsɛr'fal], *m.* (—s, *no pl.*) disintegration; decay.

zerfallen [tsɛr'falən], *v.n. irr.* (*aux.* sein) fall to pieces. — *adj.* in ruins.

zerfleischen [tsɛr'flaɪʃən], *v.a.* lacerate, tear to pieces.

zerfließen [tsɛr'fliːsən], *v.n. irr.* (*aux.* sein) dissolve, melt.

zerfressen [tsɛr'frɛsən], *v.a. irr.* gnaw, corrode.

zergehen [tsɛr'geːən], *v.n. irr.* (*aux.* sein) dissolve, melt.

zergliedern [tsɛr'gliːdərn], *v.a.* dissect; (*fig.*) analyse.

zerhauen [tsɛr'hauən], *v.a.* hew in pieces, chop up.

zerkauen [tsɛr'kauən], *v.a.* chew.

zerkleinern [tsɛr'klaɪnərn], *v.a.* cut into small pieces; (*firewood*) chop.

zerklüftet [tsɛr'klyftət], *adj.* rugged.

zerknirscht [tsɛr'knɪrʃt], *adj.* contrite.

Zerknirschung [tsɛr'knɪrʃuŋ], *f.* (—, *no pl.*) contrition.

zerknittern [tsɛr'knɪtərn], *v.a.* crumple.

zerknüllen [tsɛr'knylən], *v.a.* rumple.

zerlassen [tsɛr'lasən], *v.a. irr.* melt, liquefy.

zerlegen [tsɛr'leːgən], *v.a.* resolve; take to pieces; cut up, carve; (*fig.*) analyse.

zerlumpt [tsɛr'lumpt], *adj.* ragged, tattered.

zermahlen [tsɛr'maːlən], *v.a.* grind to powder.

zermalmen [tsɛr'malmən], *v.a.* crush.

zermartern [tsɛr'martərn], *v.a.* torment; *sich das Hirn —*, rack o.'s brains.

zernagen [tsɛr'naːgən], *v.a.* gnaw (away).

zerquetschen [tsɛr'kvɛtʃən], *v.a.* squash, crush.

zerraufen [tsɛr'raufən], *v.a.* dishevel.

Zerrbild ['tsɛrbɪlt], *n.* (—s, *pl.* —er) caricature.

zerreiben [tsɛr'raɪbən], *v.a. irr.* grind to powder, pulverise.

zerreißen [tsɛr'raɪsən], *v.a. irr.* tear, rend, tear up; break; rupture. — *v.n.* (*aux.* sein) be torn; (*clothes*) wear out.

zerren ['tsɛrən], *v.a.* pull, tug, drag; strain.

zerrinnen [tsɛr'rɪnən], *v.n. irr.* (*aux.* sein) dissolve, melt; (*fig.*) vanish.

zerrütten [tsɛr'rytən], *v.a.* unsettle, disorder, unhinge; ruin, destroy.

zerschellen [tsɛr'ʃɛlən], *v.n.* (*aux.* sein) be dashed to pieces, be wrecked.

zerschlagen [tsɛr'ʃlaːgən], *v.a. irr.* break, smash to pieces, batter.

zerschmettern [tsɛr'ʃmɛtərn], *v.a.* dash to pieces, break, crush; shatter, overwhelm.

zersetzen [tsɛr'zɛtsən], *v.a., v.r.* break up; disintegrate.

zerspalten [tsɛr'ʃpaltən], *v.a.* cleave, split, slit.

zersprengen [tsɛr'ʃprɛŋən], *v.a.* explode, burst; (*crowd*) disperse; (*Mil.*) rout.

zerspringen [tsɛr'ʃprɪŋən], *v.n. irr.* (*aux.* sein) crack; fly to pieces, split.

zerstampfen [tsɛr'ʃtampfən], *v.a.* crush, pound.

zerstäuben [tsɛr'ʃtɔybən], *v.a.* spray, atomize.

zerstörbar [tsɛr'ʃtøːrbaːr], *adj.* destructible.

zerstören [tsɛr'ʃtøːrən], *v.a.* destroy, devastate.

Zerstörer [tsɛr'ʃtøːrər], *m.* (—s, *pl.* —) destroyer.

Zerstörung [tsɛr'ʃtøːruŋ], *f.* (—, *pl.* —en) destruction.

Zerstörungswut [tsɛr'ʃtøːruŋsvuːt], *f.* (—, *no pl.*) vandalism.

zerstoßen [tsɛr'ʃtoːsən], *v.a. irr.* bruise, pound.

zerstreuen [tsɛr'ʃtrɔyən], *v.a.* scatter, disperse; divert.

zerstreut [tsɛr'ʃtrɔyt], *adj.* absent-minded.

Zerstreuung [tsɛr'ʃtrɔyuŋ], *f.* (—, *pl.* —en) dispersion; amusement, diversion, distraction.

zerstückeln [tsɛr'ʃtykəln], *v.a.* dismember.

Zerstückelung [tsɛr'ʃtykəluŋ], *f.* (—, *no pl.*) dismemberment.

zerteilen [tsɛr'taɪlən], *v.a.* divide, separate; disperse, dissipate. — *v.r. sich —*, dissolve.

Zertifikat [tsɛrtifi'kaːt], *n.* (—s, *pl.* —e) certificate, attestation.

zertrennen [tsɛr'trɛnən], *v.a.* rip up, unstitch.

zertrümmern [tsɛr'trymərn], *v.a.* destroy, break up, demolish.

Zerwürfnis [tsɛr'vyrfnɪs], *n.* (—ses, *pl.* —se) discord, dissension.

zerzausen [tsɛr'tsauzən], *v.a.* dishevel, tousle.

zerzupfen [tsɛr'tsupfən], *v.a.* pick to pieces, pluck.

Zession [tsɛs'joːn], *f.* (—, *pl.* —en) cession, assignment, transfer.

Zetergeschrei ['tseːtərgəʃraɪ], *n.* (—s, *no pl.*) outcry, hullabaloo.

zetern ['tseːtərn], *v.n.* yell; (*coll.*) kick up a row.

Zettel ['tsɛtəl], *m.* (—s, *pl.* —) slip of paper; label, chit.

Zettelkasten ['tsɛtəlkastən], *m.* (—s, *pl.* ⁓) card-index, filing cabinet.

Zeug [tsɔyk], *n.* (—(e)s, *no pl.*) stuff, material; implements, kit, utensils; (*coll.*) things.

Zeuge ['tsɔygə], *m.* (—n, *pl.* —n) witness; *zum —n aufrufen*, call to witness.

zeugen ['tsɔygən], *v.a.* beget, generate, engender. — *v.n.* give evidence.

Zeugenaussage ['tsɔygənauszaːgə], *f.* (—, *pl.* —n) evidence, deposition.

Zeugenbeweis ['tsɔygənbəvaɪs], *m.* (—es, *pl.* —e) evidence, proof.

Zeugeneid ['tsɔygənaɪt], *m.* (—s, *pl.* —e) oath of a witness.

Zeughaus ['tsɔykhaus], *n.* (—es, *pl.* ⁓er) (*obs.*) arsenal.

Zeugin ['tsɔygɪn], *f.* (—, *pl.* —**innen**) female witness.

Zinne

Zeugnis ['tsɔyknɪs], n. (—ses, pl. —se)
(Law.) deposition; testimonial, cer-
tificate, reference; character; school
report; — ablegen, give evidence,
bear witness; einem ein gutes —
ausstellen, give s.o. a good reference.
Zeugung ['tsɔyguŋ], f. (—, pl. —en)
procreation, generation.
Zeugungskraft ['tsɔyguŋskraft], f. (—,
no pl.) generative power.
Zeugungstrieb ['tsɔyguŋstri:p], m.
(—s, no pl.) procreative instinct.
Zichorie [tsɪ'çoːrjə], f. (—, pl. —n)
chicory.
Zicke ['tsɪkə], f. (—, pl. —n) dial. for
Ziege.
Ziege ['tsiːgə], f. (—, pl. —n) goat.
Ziegel ['tsiːgəl], m. (—s, pl. —) (roof)
tile; (wall) brick.
Ziegelbrenner ['tsiːgəlbrɛnər], m. (—s,
pl. —) tile-maker, tiler; brickmaker.
Ziegelbrennerei [tsiːgəlbrɛnə'raɪ], f.
(—, pl. —en) tile-kiln; brickyard.
Ziegeldach ['tsiːgəldax], n. (—s, pl.
-̈er) tiled roof.
Ziegeldecker ['tsiːgəldɛkər], m. (—s,
pl. —) tiler.
Ziegelei [tsiːgə'laɪ], f. (—, pl. —en)
brickyard, brickworks.
Ziegelerde ['tsiːgələ:rdə], f. (—, no
pl.) brick-clay.
Ziegenbart ['tsiːgənbaːrt], m. (—s, pl.
-̈e) goat's beard; (human) goatee.
Ziegenleder ['tsiːgənleːdər], n. (—s,
no pl.) kid (leather).
Ziegenpeter ['tsiːgənpeːtər], m. (—s,
no pl.) (Med.) mumps.
ziehen ['tsiːən], v.a. irr. draw, pull,
drag; pull out; cultivate; breed;
(game) move. — v.n. draw, be an
attraction; (aux. sein) go, move. —
v.r. sich —, extend.
Ziehkind ['tsiːkɪnt], n. (—s, pl. —er)
foster-child.
Ziehmutter ['tsiːmutər], f. (—, pl. -̈)
foster-mother.
Ziehung ['tsiːuŋ], f. (—, pl. —en)
draw (in a lottery).
Ziehvater ['tsiːfaːtər], m. (—s, pl. -̈)
foster-father.
Ziel [tsiːl], n. (—s, pl. —e) goal, aim,
purpose, intention, end; butt, target;
(Mil.) objective; (sports) winning-
post.
zielbewußt ['tsiːlbəvust], adj. purposeful; systematic.
zielen ['tsiːlən], v.n. aim (at), take
aim (at).
Ziellosigkeit ['tsiːlloːzɪçkaɪt], f. (—,
no pl.) aimlessness.
Zielscheibe ['tsiːlʃaɪbə], f. (—, pl.
—en) target, butt.
ziemen ['tsiːmən], v.r. sich —, become
s.o., behove s.o., be proper for,
befit.
Ziemer ['tsiːmər], n. & m. (—s, pl. —)
whip.
ziemlich ['tsiːmlɪç], adj. moderate,
tolerable, middling, fairly considerable, fair. — adv. rather, fairly.

Zier [tsiːr], f. (—, pl. —den) ornament.
Zieraffe ['tsiːrafə], m. (—n, pl. —n)
fop, affected person.
Zierat ['tsiːraːt], m. (—s, no pl.)
ornament, finery.
Zierde ['tsiːrdə], f. (—, pl. —n)
decoration, embellishment; (fig.)
credit, pride.
Ziererei [tsiːrə'raɪ], f. (—, pl. —en)
affectation.
Ziergarten ['tsiːrgårtən], m. (—s, pl.
-̈) flower-garden, ornamental garden.
zierlich ['tsiːrlɪç], adj. dainty, graceful,
pretty.
Zierpflanze ['tsiːrpflantsə], f. (—, pl.
—n) ornamental plant.
Zierpuppe ['tsiːrpupə], f. (—, pl.
—n) overdressed woman.
Ziffer ['tsɪfər], f. (—, pl. —n) figure,
numeral.
Zifferblatt ['tsɪfərblat], n. (—s, pl.
-̈er) dial, face.
ziffernmäßig ['tsɪfərnmɛːsɪç], adj.
statistical.
Ziffernschrift ['tsɪfərnʃrɪft], f. (—, pl.
—en) code.
Zigarette [tsiga'rɛtə], f. (—, pl. —n)
cigarette.
Zigarettenetui [tsiga'rɛtənetvi:], n.
(—s, pl. —s) cigarette-case.
Zigarettenspitze [tsiga'rɛtənʃpɪtsə], f.
(—, pl. —n) cigarette-holder.
Zigarettenstummel [tsiga'rɛtənʃtu-
məl], m. (—s, pl. —) cigarette-end.
Zigarre [tsi'garə], f. (—, pl. —n) cigar.
Zigarrenkiste [tsi'garənkɪstə], f. (—,
pl. —n) cigar-box.
Zigarrenstummel [tsi'garənʃtuməl],
m. (—s, pl. —) cigar-end.
Zigeuner [tsi'gɔynər], m. (—s, pl. —)
gipsy.
Zikade [tsi'kaːdə], f. (—, pl. —n)
(Ent.) grasshopper.
Zimmer ['tsɪmər], n. (—s, pl. —)
room.
Zimmermädchen ['tsɪmɛrmɛːtçən], n.
(—s, pl. —) chambermaid.
Zimmermann ['tsɪmərman], m. (—s,
pl. Zimmerleute) carpenter, joiner.
zimmern ['tsɪmərn], v.a. carpenter,
construct, build.
Zimmernachweis ['tsɪmərnaːxvaɪs], m.
(—es, pl. —e) accommodation
bureau.
Zimmerreihe ['tsɪmərraɪə], f. (—, pl.
—n) suite of rooms.
Zimmervermieter ['tsɪmərfɛrmiːtər],
m. (—s, pl. —) landlord.
zimperlich ['tsɪmpərlɪç], adj. sim-
pering; prim; finicky, hypersensitive.
Zimt [tsɪmt], m. (—(e)s, no pl.) cinnamon.
Zink [tsɪŋk], n. (—s, no pl.) zinc.
Zinke ['tsɪŋkə], f. (—, pl. —n) prong,
tine.
Zinn [tsɪn], n. (—s, no pl.) tin; pewter.
Zinnblech ['tsɪnblɛç], n. (—s, no pl.)
tin-plate.
Zinne ['tsɪnə], f. (—, pl.—n) battlement,
pinnacle.

291

zinnern ['tsɪnern], *adj.* made of pewter, of tin.

Zinnober [tsɪn'o:bər], *m.* (—s, *no pl.*) cinnabar; (*coll.*) fuss.

Zinnsäure ['tsɪnzɔyrə], *f.* (—, *no pl.*) stannic acid.

Zins [tsɪns], *m.* (—es, *pl.* —en) duty, tax; rent; (*pl.*) interest.

zinsbar ['tsɪnsba:r], *adj.* tributary; — *anlegen*, invest at interest; — *machen*, force to pay a tribute.

Zinsen ['tsɪnzən], *m. pl.* interest.

zinsentragend ['tsɪnzəntra:gənt], *adj.* interest-bearing.

Zinseszins ['tsɪnzəstsɪns], *m.* (—, *no pl.*) compound interest.

Zinsfuß ['tsɪnsfu:s], *m.* (—es, *pl.* ⁻e) rate of interest.

zinspflichtig ['tsɪnspflɪçtɪç], *adj.* subject to tax.

Zinsrechnung ['tsɪnsrɛçnuŋ], *f.* (—, *pl.* —en) interest account, calculation of interest.

Zinsschein ['tsɪnsʃaɪn], *m.* (—s, *pl.* —e) coupon, dividend warrant.

Zipfel ['tsɪpfəl], *m.* (—s, *pl.* —) tassel, edge, point, tip.

Zipperlein ['tsɪpərlaɪn], *n.* (—s, *no pl.*) (*coll.*) gout.

zirka ['tsɪrka], *adv.* circa, about, approximately.

Zirkel ['tsɪrkəl], *m.* (—s, *pl.* —) circle; (*Maths.*) pair of compasses; gathering.

zirkulieren [tsɪrku'li:rən], *v.n.* circulate; — *lassen*, put in circulation.

Zirkus ['tsɪrkus], *m.* (—, *pl.* —se) circus.

zirpen ['tsɪrpən], *v.n.* chirp.

zischeln ['tsɪʃəln], *v.n.* whisper.

zischen ['tsɪʃən], *v.n.* hiss; sizzle.

Zischlaut ['tsɪʃlaut], *m.* (—s, *pl.* —e) (*Phon.*) sibilant.

Zisterne [tsɪs'tɛrnə], *f.* (—, *pl.* —n) cistern.

Zisterzienser [tsɪstɛr'tsjɛnzər], *m.* (—s, *pl.* —) Cistercian (monk).

Zitadelle [tsɪta'dɛlə], *f.* (—, *pl.* —n) citadel.

Zitat [tsi'ta:t], *n.* (—(e)s, *pl.* —e) quotation, reference; *falsches* —, misquotation.

Zither ['tsɪtər], *f.* (—, *pl.* —n) zither.

zitieren [tsi'ti:rən], *v.a.* cite, quote; *falsch* —, misquote.

Zitronat [tsitro'na:t], *n.* (—s, *no pl.*) candied lemon peel.

Zitrone [tsi'tro:nə], *f.* (—, *pl.* —n) lemon.

Zitronenlimonade [tsi'tro:nənlimona:də], *f.* (—, *pl.* —n) lemonade, lemon drink.

Zitronensaft [tsi'tro:nənzaft], *m.* (—s, *pl.* ⁻e) lemon-juice.

Zitronensäure [tsi'tro:nənzɔyrə], *f.* (—, *no pl.*) citric acid.

Zitronenschale [tsi'tro:nənʃa:lə], *f.* (—, *pl.* —n) lemon-peel.

zitterig ['tsɪtərɪç], *adj.* shaky, shivery.

zittern ['tsɪtərn], *v.n.* tremble, shiver, quake.

Zitterpappel ['tsɪtərpapəl], *f.* (—, *pl.* —n) (*Bot.*) aspen-tree.

Zivil [tsi'vi:l], *n.* (—s, *no pl.*) civilians, *in* —, in plain clothes; (*coll.*) in civvies *or* mufti.

Zivilbeamte [tsi'vi:lbəamtə], *m.* (—n, *pl.* —n) civil servant.

Zivildienst [tsi'vi:ldi:nst], *m.* (—es, *no pl.*) civil service.

Zivilehe [tsi'vi:le:ə], *f.* (—, *pl.* —n) civil marriage.

Zivilgesetzbuch [tsi'vi:lgəzɛtsbu:x], *n.* (—s, *pl.* ⁻er) code of civil law.

Zivilingenieur [tsi'vi:lɪnʒɛnjø:r], *m.* (—s, *pl.* —e) civil engineer.

Zivilisation [tsiviliza'tsjo:n], *f.* (—, *pl.* —en) civilisation.

zivilisatorisch [tsiviliza'to:rɪʃ], *adj.* civilising.

zivilisieren [tsivili'zi:rən], *v.a.* civilise.

Zivilist [tsivi'lɪst], *m.* (—en, *pl.* —en) civilian.

Zivilkleidung [tsi'vi:lklaɪduŋ], *f.* (—, *no pl.*) civilian dress, plain clothes.

Zobel ['tso:bəl], *m.* (—s, *pl.* —) sable.

Zobelpelz ['tso:bəlpɛlts], *m.* (—es, *pl.* —e) sable fur; sable-coat.

Zofe ['tso:fə], *f.* (—, *pl.* —n) lady's maid.

zögern ['tsø:gərn], *v.n.* hesitate, tarry, delay.

Zögerung ['tsø:gəruŋ], *f.* (—, *pl.* —en) hesitation, delay.

Zögling ['tsø:klɪŋ], *m.* (—s, *pl.* —e) (*obs.*) pupil; charge, ward.

Zölibat [tsø:li'ba:t], *m. & n.* (—s, *no pl.*) celibacy.

Zoll (1) [tsɔl], *m.* (—s, *no pl.*) inch.

Zoll (2) [tsɔl], *m.* (—s, *pl.* ⁻e) customs duty; (*bridge*) toll.

Zollabfertigung ['tsɔlapfɛrtɪguŋ], *f.* (—, *no pl.*) customs clearance.

Zollamt ['tsɔlamt], *n.* (—s, *pl.* ⁻er) custom house.

Zollaufschlag ['tsɔlaufʃla:k], *m.* (—s, *pl.* ⁻e) additional duty.

Zollbeamte ['tsɔlbəamtə], *m.* (—n, *pl.* —n) customs officer.

zollbreit ['tsɔlbraɪt], *adj.* one inch wide.

zollen ['tsɔlən], *v.a. Ehrfurcht* —, pay o.'s respects; *Beifall* —, applaud; *Dank* —, show gratitude.

zollfrei ['tsɔlfraɪ], *adj.* duty-free, exempt from duty.

Zöllner ['tsœlnər], *m.* (—s, *pl.* —) tax-gatherer.

zollpflichtig ['tsɔlpflɪçtɪç], *adj.* liable to duty, dutiable.

Zollsatz ['tsɔlzats], *m.* (—es, *pl.* ⁻e) customs tariff.

Zollverein ['tsɔlfəraɪn], *m.* (—s, *no pl.*) customs union.

Zollverschluß ['tsɔlfɛrʃlus], *m.* (—sses, *pl.* ⁻sse) bond.

Zone ['tso:nə], *f.* (—, *pl.* —n) zone.

Zoologe [tso:o'lo:gə], *m.* (—n, *pl.* —n) zoologist.

Zoologie [tso:olo'gi:], *f.* (—, *no pl.*) zoology.

zoologisch [tso:o'lo:gɪʃ], *adj.* zoo-logical; *—er Garten*, zoological gar-dens, zoo.

Zopf [tsɔpf], *m.* (—(e)s, *pl.* ¨e) plait, pigtail; (*coll.*) (old-fashioned) pe-dantry.

Zorn [tsɔrn], *m.* (—(e)s, *no pl.*) wrath, anger, indignation; *seinen — auslassen*, vent o.'s anger; *in — geraten*, get angry.

zornglühend ['tsɔrngly:ənt], *adj.* boil-ing with rage.

zornig ['tsɔrnɪç], *adj.* angry, wrathful, irate; *— werden*, get angry.

Zote ['tso:tə], *f.* (—, *pl.* —n) smutty story, ribaldry, bawdiness.

zotig ['tso:tɪç], *adj.* loose, ribald, smutty.

zottig ['tsɔtɪç], *adj.* shaggy.

zu [tsu:], *prep.* (*Dat.*) to, towards; in addition to; at, in, on; for; *— Anfang*, in the beginning; *— Fuß*, on foot; *— Hause*, at home; *— Wasser*, at sea, by sea; *— deinem Nutzen*, for your benefit. *— adv. & prefix*, to, towards; closed; too; *— sehr*, too; *— viel*, too much.

Zubehör ['tsu:bəhø:r], *n.* (—s, *no pl.*) accessory, appurtenance.

zubekommen ['tsu:bəkɔmən], *v.a. irr.* get in addition.

Zuber ['tsu:bər], *m.* (—s, *pl.* —) tub.

zubereiten ['tsu:bəraɪtən], *v.a.* prepare.

Zubereitung ['tsu:bəraɪtuŋ], *f.* (—, *no pl.*) preparation.

zubilligen ['tsu:bɪlɪgən], *v.a.* allow, grant.

zubleiben ['tsu:blaɪbən], *v.n. irr.* (*aux.* sein) remain shut.

zubringen ['tsu:brɪŋən], *v.a. irr. die Zeit —*, spend the time.

Zubringerdienst ['tsu:brɪŋərdi:nst], *m.* (—es, *pl.* —) shuttle-service, tender-service.

Zubuße ['tsu:bu:sə], *f.* (—, *pl.* —n) (additional) contribution.

Zucht [tsuxt], *f.* (—, *no pl.*) race, breed; discipline; breeding, rearing; edu-cation, discipline; (good) manners; *in — halten*, keep in hand.

züchten ['tsyçtən], *v.a.* cultivate; rear, breed; grow.

Züchter ['tsyçtər], *m.* (—s, *pl.* —) (*plants*) nurseryman; (*animals*) breeder.

Zuchthaus ['tsuxthaus], *n.* (—es, *pl.* ¨er) penitentiary, convict prison.

Zuchthäusler ['tsuxthɔyslər], *m.* (—s, *pl.* —) convict.

Zuchthengst ['tsuxthɛŋst], *m.* (—es, *pl.* —e) stallion.

züchtig ['tsyçtɪç], *adj.* modest, chaste.

züchtigen ['tsyçtɪgən], *v.a.* chastise, lash.

Züchtigkeit ['tsyçtɪçkaɪt], *f.* (—, *no pl.*) modesty, chastity.

Züchtigung ['tsyçtɪguŋ], *f.* (—, *pl.* —en) chastisement; *körperliche —*, corporal punishment.

Zuchtlosigkeit ['tsuxtlo:zɪçkaɪt], *f.* (—, *no pl.*) want of discipline.

Zuchtmeister ['tsuxtmaɪstər], *m.* (—s, *pl.* —) disciplinarian, taskmaster.

Zuchtochse ['tsuxtɔksə], *m.* (—n, *pl.* —n) bull.

Zuchtstute ['tsuxtʃtu:tə], *f.* (—, *pl.* —n) brood-mare.

Züchtung ['tsyçtuŋ], *f.* (—, *pl.* —en) (*plants*) cultivation; (*animals*) rearing, breeding.

Zuchtvieh ['tsuxtfi:], *n.* (—s, *no pl.*) breeding stock.

Zuchtwahl ['tsuxtva:l], *f.* (—, *no pl.*) (*breeding*) selection.

zucken ['tsukən], *v.n.* quiver, twitch; wince; start, jerk.

Zucken ['tsukən], *n.* (—s, *no pl.*) palpitation, convulsion, twitch, tic.

Zucker ['tsukər], *m.* (—s, *no pl.*) sugar.

Zuckerbäcker ['tsukərbɛkər], *m.* (—s, *pl.* —) confectioner.

Zuckerguß ['tsukərgus], *m.* (—es, *no pl.*) (sugar-)icing.

Zuckerkandis ['tsukərkandɪs], *m.* (—, *no pl.*) sugar-candy.

zuckerkrank ['tsukərkraŋk], *adj.* (*Med.*) diabetic.

Zuckerkrankheit ['tsukərkraŋkhaɪt], *f.* (—, *no pl.*) (*Med.*) diabetes.

zuckern ['tsukərn], *v.a.* sugar.

Zuckerpflanzung ['tsukərpflantsuŋ], *f.* (—, *pl.* —en) sugar-plantation.

Zuckerraffinerie ['tsukərrafinəri:], *f.* (—, *pl.* —n) sugar-refinery.

Zuckerrohr ['tsukərro:r], *n.* (—s, *no pl.*) sugar-cane.

Zuckerrübe ['tsukərry:bə], *f.* (—, *pl.* —n) sugar-beet.

Zuckerwerk ['tsukərvɛrk], *n.* (—s, *no pl.*) confectionery.

Zuckerzange ['tsukərtsaŋə], *f.* (—, *pl.* —n) sugar-tongs.

Zuckung ['tsukuŋ], *f.* (—, *pl.* —en) convulsion, spasm.

zudecken ['tsu:dɛkən], *v.a.* cover up.

zudem [tsu'de:m], *adv.* besides, more-over.

Zudrang ['tsu:draŋ], *m.* (—s, *no pl.*) crowd(ing); rush (on), run (on).

zudrehen ['tsu:dre:ən], *v.a.* turn off.

zudringlich ['tsu:drɪŋlɪç], *adj.* im-portunate; intruding.

zudrücken ['tsu:drykən], *v.a.* close (by pressing), shut.

zueignen ['tsu:aɪgnən], *v.a.* dedicate.

zuerkennen ['tsu:ɛrkɛnən], *v.a. irr.* award, adjudicate.

zuerst [tsu'e:rst], *adv.* at first, first, in the first instance.

Zufahrt ['tsu:fa:rt], *f.* (—, *no pl.*) approach, drive.

Zufall ['tsu:fal], *m.* (—s, *pl.* ¨e) chance, coincidence; *durch —*, by chance.

zufallen ['tsu:falən], *v.n. irr.* (*aux.* sein) close, fall shut; *einem —*, devolve upon s.o., fall to s.o.'s lot.

zufällig ['tsu:fɛlɪç], *adj.* accidental, casual, fortuitous. *— adv.* by chance.

Zuflucht ['tsu:fluxt], *f.* (—, *no pl.*) refuge, shelter, haven, recourse.

Zufluchtsort ['tsu:fluxtsɔrt], *m.* (—(e)s, *pl.* —e) asylum, shelter, place of refuge.

Zufluß ['tsu:flus], *m.* (—sses, *pl.* ⁻sse) supply; influx.

zuflüstern ['tsu:flystərn], *v.a.* einem etwas —, whisper s.th. to s.o.

zufolge [tsu'fɔlgə], *prep.* (*Genit.*, *Dat.*) in consequence of, owing to, due to, on account of.

zufrieden [tsu'fri:dən], *adj.* content, contented, satisfied; — lassen, leave alone.

zufriedenstellen [tsu'fri:dənʃtɛlən], *v.a.* satisfy.

zufügen ['tsu:fy:gən], *v.a.* add (to); inflict.

Zufuhr ['tsu:fu:r], *f.* (—, *pl.* —en) (*goods*) supplies.

Zug [tsu:k], *m.* (—(e)s, *pl.* ⁻e) drawing, pull, tug; draught; march, procession; (*Railw.*) train; (*face*) feature; (*chess*) move; (*character*) trait; (*pen*) stroke; (*birds*) flight; migration; (*mountains*) range.

Zugabe ['tsu:ga:bə], *f.* (—, *pl.* —n) addition, make-weight, extra; (*concert*) encore; als —, into the bargain.

Zugang ['tsu:gaŋ], *m.* (—s, *pl.* ⁻e) approach, entry, entrance, admittance, access.

zugänglich ['tsu:gɛŋlɪç], *adj.* accessible, available; (*person*) affable.

Zugbrücke ['tsu:kbrykə], *f.* (—, *pl.* —n) drawbridge.

zugeben ['tsu:ge:bən], *v.a. irr.* give in addition; concede, admit.

zugegen [tsu'ge:gən], *adv.* present.

zugehen ['tsu:ge:ən], *v.n. irr.* (*aux.* sein) (*door*) shut (of itself), close; happen; auf einen —, walk towards s.o.; so geht es im Leben zu, such is life; das geht nicht mit rechten Dingen zu, there is something uncanny about it.

zugehörig ['tsu:gəhø:rɪç], *adj.* belonging, appertaining.

zugeknöpft ['tsu:gəknœpft], *adj.* reserved, taciturn.

Zügel ['tsy:gəl], *m.* (—s, *pl.* —) rein, bridle.

zügeln ['tsy:gəln], *v.a.* bridle, curb, check.

zugesellen ['tsu:gəzɛlən], *v.r.* sich —, associate with, join.

Zugeständnis ['tsu:gəʃtɛntnɪs], *n.* (—sses, *pl.* —sse) admission; concession.

zugestehen ['tsu:gəʃte:ən], *v.a. irr.* admit; concede; einem etwas —, allow s.o. s.th.

zugetan ['tsu:gəta:n], *adj.* attached, devoted.

Zugführer ['tsu:kfy:rər], *m.* (—s, *pl.* —) (*Railw.*) guard; (*Mil.*) platoon commander.

zugießen ['tsu:gi:sən], *v.a. irr.* fill up, pour on.

zugig ['tsu:gɪç], *adj.* windy, draughty.

Zugkraft ['tsu:kkraft], *f.* (—, *no pl.*) tractive power, magnetic attraction;

(*fig.*) pull, attraction; publicity value.

zugleich [tsu'glaɪç], *adv.* at the same time; — mit, together with.

Zugluft ['tsu:kluft], *f.* (—, *no pl.*) draught (of air).

zugreifen ['tsu:graɪfən], *v.n. irr.* grab; lend a hand; (*at table*) help o.s.

Zugrolle ['tsu:krɔlə], *f.* (—, *pl.* —n) pulley.

zugrunde [tsu'grundə], *adv.* — gehen, perish, go to ruin, go to the dogs; — legen, base upon.

Zugstück ['tsu:kʃtyk], *n.* (—s, *pl.* —e) (*Theat.*) popular show; (*coll.*) success, hit.

zugucken ['tsu:gukən], *v.n.* look on, watch.

zugunsten [tsu'gunstən], *prep.* (*Genit.*) for the benefit of.

zugute [tsu'gu:tə], *adv.* — halten, make allowances.

Zugvogel ['tsu:kfo:gəl], *m.* (—s, *pl.* ⁻) bird of passage.

zuhalten ['tsu:haltən], *v.a. irr.* keep closed.

Zuhälter ['tsu:hɛltər], *m.* (—s, *pl.* —) souteneur; pimp.

Zuhilfenahme [tsu'hɪlfəna:mə], *f.* (—, *no pl.*) unter —, with the help of, by means of.

zuhören ['tsu:hø:rən], *v.n.* listen to, attend to.

Zuhörerschaft ['tsu:hø:rərʃaft], *f.* (—, *pl.* —en) audience.

zujubeln ['tsu:ju:bəln], *v.n.* einem —, acclaim s.o., cheer s.o.

zukehren ['tsu:ke:rən], *v.a.* einem den Rücken —, turn o.'s back on s.o.

zuknöpfen ['tsu:knœpfən], *v.a.* button (up).

zukommen ['tsu:kɔmən], *v.n. irr.* (*aux.* sein) auf einen —, advance towards s.o.; einem —, be due to s.o.; become s.o.; reach s.o.

Zukost ['tsu:kɔst], *f.* (—, *no pl.*) (*food*) trimmings, extras.

Zukunft ['tsu:kunft], *f.* (—, *no pl.*) future; prospects.

zukünftig ['tsu:kynftɪç], *adj.* future, prospective.

Zukunftsmusik ['tsu:kunftsmuzi:k], *f.* (—, *no pl.*) daydreams, pipe-dreams.

zulächeln ['tsu:lɛçəln], *v.a.* einem —, smile at s.o.

Zulage ['tsu:la:gə], *f.* (—, *pl.* —n) addition; increase of salary, rise; (*Am.*) raise.

zulangen ['tsu:laŋən], *v.n.* be sufficient; (*at table*) help o.s.

zulänglich ['tsu:lɛŋlɪç], *adj.* sufficient, adequate.

zulassen ['tsu:lasən], *v.a. irr.* leave unopened; allow; admit; permit.

zulässig ['tsu:lɛsɪç], *adj.* admissible; das ist nicht —, that is not allowed.

Zulassung ['tsu:lasuŋ], *f.* (—, *pl.* —en) admission.

Zulauf ['tsu:lauf], *m.* (—s, *no pl.*) run (of customers); crowd, throng.

294

zulaufen [ˈtsuːlaufən], *v.n. irr. (aux.* sein) *auf einen* —, run towards s.o.; *spitz* —, taper, come to a point.

zulegen [ˈtsuːleːgən], *v.a.* add; increase; *sich etwas* —, make o.s. a present of s.th.; get s.th.

zuletzt [tsuˈlɛtst], *adv.* last, at last, lastly, finally, eventually, in the end.

zuliebe [tsuˈliːbə], *adv. einem etwas* — *tun,* oblige s.o.; do s.th. for s.o.'s sake.

zum = **zu dem.**

zumachen [ˈtsuːmaxən], *v.a.* shut, close.

zumal [tsuˈmaːl], *adv.* especially, particularly. — *conj.* especially since.

zumeist [tsuˈmaɪst], *adv.* mostly, for the most part.

zumute [tsuˈmuːtə], *adv. mir ist nicht gut* —, I don't feel well.

zumuten [ˈtsuːmuːtən], *v.a. einem etwas* —, expect *or* demand s.th. of s.o.

Zumutung [ˈtsuːmuːtuŋ], *f.* (—, *pl.* —en) unreasonable demand.

zunächst [tsuˈnɛːçst], *adv.* first, above all.

Zunahme [ˈtsuːnaːmə], *f.* (—, *pl.* —n) increase.

Zuname [ˈtsuːnaːmə], *m.* (—ns, *pl.* —n) surname, family name.

zünden [ˈtsyndən], *v.n.* catch fire, ignite.

Zunder [ˈtsundər], *m.* (—s, *no pl.*) tinder.

Zünder [ˈtsyndər], *m.* (—s, *pl.* —) lighter, detonator, fuse.

Zündholz [ˈtsyntholts], *n.* (—es, *pl.* ˙er) match.

Zündkerze [ˈtsyntkɛrtsə], *f.* (—, *pl.* —n) (*Motor.*) sparking-plug.

Zündstoff [ˈtsyntʃtɔf], *m.* (—s, *pl.* —e) fuel.

Zündung [ˈtsynduŋ], *f.* (—, *pl.* —en) ignition; detonation.

zunehmen [ˈtsuːneːmən], *v.n. irr.* increase, put on weight; (*moon*) wax.

zuneigen [ˈtsuːnaɪgən], *v.r. sich* —, incline towards.

Zuneigung [ˈtsuːnaɪguŋ], *f.* (—, *pl.* —en) affection, inclination.

Zunft [tsunft], *f.* (—, *pl.* ˙e) company, guild, corporation; (*fig.*) brotherhood.

Zunftgenosse [ˈtsunftgənɔsə], *m.* (—n, *pl.* —n) member of a guild.

zünftig [ˈtsynftɪç], *adj.* professional; proper.

zunftmäßig [ˈtsunftmɛːsɪç], *adj.* professional; competent.

Zunge [ˈtsuŋə], *f.* (—, *pl.* —n) tongue; (*buckle*) catch; (*fig.*) language; (*fish*) sole.

züngeln [ˈtsyŋəln], *v.n.* (*flame*) shoot out, lick.

Zungenband [ˈtsuŋənbant], *n.* (—s, *pl.* ˙er) ligament of the tongue.

zungenfertig [ˈtsuŋənfɛrtɪç], *adj.* voluble, glib.

Zungenlaut [ˈtsuŋənlaut], *m.* (—s, *pl.* —e) (*Phon.*) lingual sound.

Zungenspitze [ˈtsuŋənʃpɪtsə], *f.* (—, *pl.* —n) tip of the tongue.

zunichte [tsuˈnɪçtə], *adv.* — *machen,* ruin, undo, destroy; — *werden,* come to nothing.

zupfen [ˈtsupfən], *v.a.* pick, pluck.

zurechnungsfähig [ˈtsuːrɛçnuŋsfɛːɪç], *adj.* accountable, of sane mind, compos mentis.

zurecht [tsuˈrɛçt], *adv.* aright, right(ly), in order.

zurechtfinden [tsuˈrɛçtfɪndən], *v.r. irr. sich* —, find o.'s way about.

zurechtkommen [tsuˈrɛçtkɔmən], *v.n. irr. (aux.* sein) arrive in (good) time; *mit einem gut* —, get on well with s.o.

zurechtlegen [tsuˈrɛçtleːgən], *v.a.* put in order, get ready.

zurechtmachen [tsuˈrɛçtmaxən], *v.a.* get s.th. ready, prepare s.th. — *v.r. sich* —, prepare o.s.; (*women*) make up; (*coll.*) put on o.'s face.

zurechtweisen [tsuˈrɛçtvaɪzən], *v.a. irr.* reprove (s.o.), set (s.o.) right; direct.

Zurechtweisung [tsuˈrɛçtvaɪzuŋ], *f.* (—, *pl.* —en) reprimand.

Zureden [ˈtsuːreːdən], *n.* (—s, *no pl.*) encouragement; entreaties.

zureden [ˈtsuːreːdən], *v.n.* encourage (s.o.), persuade (s.o.)

zureichen [ˈtsuːraɪçən], *v.a.* reach, hand. — *v.n.* be sufficient, be enough, suffice.

zurichten [ˈtsuːrɪçtən], *v.a. etwas* (*einen*) *übel* —, maltreat s.th. (s.o.).

zürnen [ˈtsyrnən], *v.n.* be angry (with).

zurück [tsuˈryk], *adv.* back; behind; backwards; — *excl.* stand back!

zurückbegeben [tsuˈrykbəgeːbən], *v.r. irr. sich* —, go back, return.

zurückbehalten [tsuˈrykbəhaltən], *v.a. irr.* retain, keep back.

zurückbekommen [tsuˈrykbəkɔmən], *v.a. irr.* get back, recover (s.th.).

zurückberufen [tsuˈrykbəruːfən], *v.a. irr.* recall.

zurückfordern [tsuˈrykfɔrdərn], *v.a.* demand back, demand the return of.

zurückführen [tsuˈrykfyːrən], *v.a.* lead back; *auf etwas* —, attribute to; trace back to.

zurückgeblieben [tsuˈrykgəbliːbən], *adj.* retarded, mentally deficient, backward.

zurückgezogen [tsuˈrykgətsoːgən], *adj.* secluded, retired.

zurückhalten [tsuˈrykhaltən], *v.a. irr.* keep back, retain.

zurückhaltend [tsuˈrykhaltənt], *adj.* reserved.

zurückkehren [tsuˈrykkeːrən], *v.n. (aux.* sein) return.

zurückkommen [tsuˈrykkɔmən], *v.n. irr. (aux.* sein) come back.

zurücklassen [tsuˈryklasən], *v.a. irr.* leave behind, abandon.

zurücklegen [tsu'rykle:gən], *v.a.* lay aside, put by; *eine Strecke* —, cover a distance. — *v.r. sich* —, lean back; *zurückgelegter Gewinn*, undistributed profits.

zurückmüssen [tsu'rykmysən], *v.n. irr.* be obliged to return.

zurücknehmen [tsu'rykne:mən], *v.a. irr.* take back.

zurückschrecken [tsu'rykʃrekən], *v.a.* frighten away. — *v.n. irr. (aux.* sein) recoil (from).

zurücksehnen [tsu'rykze:nən], *v.r. sich* —, long to return, wish o.s. back.

zurücksetzen [tsu'rykzɛtsən], *v.a.* put back; slight; discriminate against; neglect.

Zurücksetzung [tsu'rykzɛtsuŋ], *f.* (—, *pl.* —en) slight, rebuff.

zurückstrahlen [tsu'rykʃtra:lən], *v.a.* reflect.

zurücktreten [tsu'ryktre:tən], *v.n. irr. (aux.* sein) stand back, withdraw; resign.

zurückverlangen [tsu'rykfɛrlaŋən], *v.a.* demand back, request the return of.

zurückversetzen [tsu'rykfɛrzɛtsən], *v.a. (Sch.)* put in a lower form. — *v.r. sich* —, turn o.'s thoughts back (to), hark back.

zurückweichen [tsu'rykvaɪçən], *v.n. irr. (aux.* sein) withdraw, retreat.

zurückweisen [tsu'rykvaɪzən], *v.a. irr.* refuse, reject, repulse.

zurückwollen [tsu'rykvɔlən], *v.n.* wish to return.

zurückziehen [tsu'ryktsi:ən], *v.a. irr.* draw back; *(fig.)* withdraw, retract, countermand. — *v.r. sich* —, retire, withdraw.

Zuruf ['tsu:ru:f], *m.* (—s, *pl.* —e) call, acclaim, acclamation.

Zusage ['tsu:za:gə], *f.* (—, *pl.* —n) promise; acceptance.

zusagen ['tsu:za:gən], *v.a.* promise; *es sagt mir zu*, I like it. — *v.n.* accept.

zusagend ['tsu:za:gənt], *adj.* affirmative; agreeable.

zusammen [tsu'zamən], *adv.* together, jointly.

zusammenbeißen [tsu'zamənbaɪsən], *v.a. irr. die Zähne* —, set o.'s teeth.

zusammenbetteln [tsu'zamənbɛtəln], *v.a. sich etwas* —, collect (by begging).

zusammenbrechen [tsu'zamənbre-çən], *v.n. irr. (aux.* sein) break down, collapse.

Zusammenbruch [tsu'zamənbrux], *m.* (—s, *pl.* ̈e) breakdown, collapse, débâcle.

zusammendrängen [tsu'zaməndreŋ-ən], *v.a.* press together; *(fig.)* abridge, condense.

zusammendrücken [tsu'zaməndry-kən], *v.a.* compress.

zusammenfahren [tsu'zamənfa:rən], *v.n. irr. (aux.* sein) collide; give a start.

zusammenfallen [tsu'zamənfalən], *v.n. irr. (aux.* sein) collapse.

zusammenfassen [tsu'zamənfasən], *v.a.* sum up, summarize.

Zusammenfassung [tsu'zamənfasuŋ], *f.* (—, *no pl.*) summing-up, summary.

zusammenfinden [tsu'zamənfɪndən], *v.r. irr. sich* —, discover a mutual affinity, come together.

Zusammenfluß [tsu'zamənflus], *m.* (—sses, *pl.* ̈sse) confluence.

zusammengeben [tsu'zamənge:bən], *v.a. irr.* join in marriage.

Zusammengehörigkeit [tsu'zaməngə-hø:rɪçkaɪt], *f.* (—, *no pl.*) solidarity; *(Am.)* togetherness.

zusammengesetzt [tsu'zaməngəzɛtst], *adj.* composed (of), consisting (of); complicated; *(Maths.)* composite.

zusammengewürfelt [tsu'zaməngə-vyrfəlt], *adj.* motley, mixed.

Zusammenhalt [tsu'zamənhalt], *m.* (—s, *no pl.*) holding together; unity.

Zusammenhang [tsu'zamənhaŋ], *m.* (—s, *pl.* ̈e) coherence; connection, context.

zusammenhängen [tsu'zamənheŋən], *v.n. irr.* hang together, cohere; *(fig.)* be connected (with).

Zusammenklang [tsu'zamənklaŋ], *m.* (—s, *pl.* ̈e) unison, harmony.

Zusammenkunft [tsu'zamənkunft], *f.* (—, *pl.* ̈e) meeting, convention, conference; reunion.

zusammenlaufen [tsu'zamənlaufən], *v.n. irr. (aux.* sein) crowd together, converge; flock together; *(milk)* curdle; *(material)* shrink.

zusammenlegen [tsu'zamənle:gən], *v.a.* put together; *(money)* collect; *(letter)* fold up.

zusammennehmen [tsu'zamənne:-mən], *v.a. irr.* gather up. — *v.r. sich* —, get a firm grip on o.s., pull o.s. together.

zusammenpassen [tsu'zamənpasən], *v.n.* fit together, match; agree; be compatible.

zusammenpferchen [tsu'zamənpfer-çən], *v.a.* pen up, crowd together in a small space.

zusammenpressen [tsu'zamənpresən], *v.a.* squeeze together.

zusammenraffen [tsu'zamənrafən], *v.a.* gather up hurriedly, collect. — *v.r. sich* —, pluck up courage; pull o.s. together.

zusammenrechnen [tsu'zamənreç-nən], *v.a.* add up.

zusammenreimen [tsu'zamənraɪmən], *v.a. sich etwas* —, figure s.th. out.

zusammenrücken [tsu'zamənrykən], *v.a.* move together, draw closer. — *v.n.* move closer together, move up.

zusammenschießen [tsu'zamənʃi:sən], *v.a. irr.* shoot to pieces, shoot down; *Geld* —, club together, raise a subscription.

zusammenschlagen [tsu'zamənʃla:-gən], *v.a. irr.* beat up; strike together; clap, fold.

zusammenschließen [tsu'zamənʃli:-sən], *v.r. irr. sich* —, join, unite, ally o.s. (with).

zusammenschweißen [tsu'zamənʃvai-sən], *v.a.* weld together.

Zusammensein [tsu'zamənzain], *n.* (—s, *no pl.*) meeting, social gathering.

Zusammensetzung [tsu'zamənzɛtsuŋ], *f.* (—, *pl.* —en) construction; composition.

Zusammenspiel [tsu'zamənʃpi:l], *n.* (—s, *no pl.*) (*Theat., Mus.*) ensemble.

zusammenstellen [tsu'zamənʃtɛlən], *v.a.* compose, concoct; put together, compile.

Zusammenstellung [tsu'zamənʃtɛluŋ], *f.* (—, *pl.* —en) combination, compilation; juxtaposition.

zusammenstoppeln [tsu'zamənʃtɔp-əln], *v.a.* string together, patch up.

Zusammenstoß [tsu'zamənʃto:s], *m.* (—es, *pl.* ⁝e) clash, conflict; collision.

zusammenstoßen [tsu'zamənʃto:sən], *v.n. irr.* (*aux.* sein) clash; crash, come into collision, collide.

zusammentragen [tsu'zaməntra:gən], *v.a. irr.* collect, compile.

zusammentreffen [tsu'zaməntrɛfən], *v.n. irr.* meet; coincide.

zusammentreten [tsu'zaməntre:tən], *v.n. irr.* (*aux.* sein) meet.

zusammentun [tsu'zaməntu:n], *v.r. irr. sich* — *mit*, associate with, join.

zusammenwirken [tsu'zamənvɪrkən], *v.n.* cooperate, collaborate.

zusammenwürfeln [tsu'zamənvyr-fəln], *v.a.* jumble up.

zusammenzählen [tsu'zaməntsɛ:lən], *v.a.* add up.

zusammenziehen [tsu'zaməntsi:ən], *v.n. irr.* (*aux.* sein) move in together. — *v.a.* draw together, contract. — *v.r. sich* —, shrink; (*storm*) gather; *Zahlen* —, add up.

Zusammenziehung [tsu'zaməntsi:uŋ], *f.* (—, *no pl.*) contraction.

Zusatz [tsu:zats], *m.* (—es, *pl.* ⁝e) addition, supplement, admixture; (*will*) codicil.

zuschanzen ['tsu:ʃantsən], *v.a. einem etwas* —, obtain s.th. for s.o.

zuschauen ['tsu:ʃauən], *v.n.* look on, watch.

Zuschauer ['tsu:ʃauər], *m.* (—s, *pl.* —) onlooker, spectator.

Zuschauerraum ['tsu:ʃauərraum], *m.* (—s, *pl.* ⁝e) (*Theat.*) auditorium.

zuschaufeln ['tsu:ʃaufəln], *v.a.* shovel in, fill up.

zuschieben ['tsu:ʃi:bən], *v.a. irr.* push towards; shut; *einem etwas* —, shove (blame) on to s.o.

zuschießen ['tsu:ʃi:sən], *v.a. irr. Geld* —, put money into (an undertaking).

Zuschlag ['tsu:ʃla:k], *m.* (—s, *pl.* ⁝e) addition; (*Railw.*) excess fare.

zuschlagen ['tsu:ʃla:gən], *v.a. irr.* add; (*door*) bang; (*auction*) knock down to (s.o.). — *v.n.* strike hard.

zuschlag(s)pflichtig ['tsu:ʃla:k(s)pflɪç-tɪç], *adj.* liable to a supplementary charge.

zuschmeißen ['tsu:ʃmaisən], *v.a. irr.* (*door*) slam to, bang.

zuschneiden ['tsu:ʃnaidən], *v.a. irr.* (*pattern*) cut out; cut up.

Zuschneider ['tsu:ʃnaidər], *m.* (—s, *pl.*—) (*Tail.*) cutter.

Zuschnitt ['tsu:ʃnɪt], *m.* (—s, *no pl.*) (*clothing*) cut.

zuschreiben ['tsu:ʃraibən], *v.a. irr. einem etwas* —, impute s.th. to s.o.; attribute *or* ascribe s.th. to s.o.

Zuschrift ['tsu:ʃrɪft], *f.* (—, *pl.* —en) communication, letter.

Zuschuß ['tsu:ʃus], *m.* (—sses, *pl.* ⁝sse) additional money, supplementary allowance, subsidy.

zuschütten ['tsu:ʃytən], *v.a.* fill up.

Zusehen ['tsu:ze:ən], *n.* (—s, *no pl.*) *das* — *haben*, be left out in the cold.

zusehen ['tsu:ze:ən], *v.n. irr.* look on, watch; be a spectator; see to it.

zusehends ['tsu:ze:ənts], *adv.* visibly.

zusetzen ['tsu:zɛtsən], *v.a.* add to, admix; lose. — *v.n. einem* —, pester s.o.; attack s.o.

zusichern ['tsu:zɪçərn], *v.a.* promise, assure.

Zusicherung ['tsu:zɪçəruŋ], *f.* (—, *pl.* —en) promise, assurance.

Zuspeise ['tsu:ʃpaizə], *f.* (—, *no pl.*) (*dial.*) (*food*) trimmings; vegetables.

zusperren ['tsu:ʃpɛrən], *v.a.* shut, close, lock up.

zuspitzen ['tsu:ʃpɪtsən], *v.a.* sharpen to a point. — *v.r. sich* —, come to a climax.

zusprechen ['tsu:ʃprɛçən], *v.n. irr. dem Wein* —, drink heavily. — *v.a. Mut* —, comfort.

Zuspruch ['tsu:ʃprux], *m.* (—s, *pl.* ⁝e) exhortation; consolation.

Zustand ['tsu:ʃtant], *m.* (—s, *pl.* ⁝e) condition, state of affairs, situation.

zustande [tsu:'ʃtandə], *adv.* — *kommen*, come off, be accomplished; — *bringen*, accomplish.

zuständig ['tsu:ʃtɛndɪç], *adj.* competent; appropriate.

Zuständigkeit ['tsu:ʃtɛndɪçkait], *f.* (—, *no pl.*) competence.

zustecken ['tsu:ʃtɛkən], *v.a.* pin up; *einem etwas* —, slip s.th. into s.o.'s hand.

zustehen ['tsu:ʃte:ən], *v.n. irr.* be due to, belong to; be s.o.'s business to.

zustellen ['tsu:ʃtɛlən], *v.a.* deliver, hand over; (*Law*) serve (a writ).

Zustellung ['tsu:ʃtɛluŋ], *f.* (—, *pl.* —en) delivery; (*Law*) service.

zusteuern ['tsu:ʃtɔyərn], *v.a.* contribute. — *v.n.* (*aux.* sein) steer for; (*fig.*) aim at.

zustimmen ['tsu:ʃtɪmən], *v.n.* agree to.

Zustimmung ['tsu:ʃtɪmuŋ], *f.* (—, *pl.* —en) assent, consent, agreement.

zustopfen ['tsu:ʃtɔpfən], *v.a.* fill up, stop up, plug; darn, mend.

zustoßen ['tsu:ʃto:sən], *v.a. irr.* push to, shut.

zustürzen ['tsu:ʃtyrtsən], *v.n.* (*aux.* sein) *auf einen —,* rush at or towards s.o.

Zutaten ['tsu:ta:tən], *f. pl.* ingredients, garnishings.

zuteil [tsu'taɪl], *adv. — werden,* fall to s.o.'s share.

zutragen ['tsu:tra:gən], *v.a. irr.* report, tell. *— v.r. sich —,* happen.

Zuträger ['tsu:trɛ:gər], *m.* (—s, *pl.* —) informer, tale-bearer.

zuträglich ['tsu:trɛ:klɪç], *adj.* advantageous, wholesome.

Zutrauen ['tsu:trauən], *n.* (—s, *no pl.*) confidence.

zutrauen ['tsu:trauən], *v.a. einem etwas —,* credit s.o. with s.th.

zutraulich ['tsu:traulɪç], *adj.* trusting; familiar, intimate; tame.

zutreffen ['tsu:trɛfən], *v.n. irr.* prove correct, take place.

zutreffend ['tsu:trɛfənt], *adj.* apposite, pertinent.

Zutritt ['tsu:trɪt], *m.* (—s, *no pl.*) entry; access, admittance; *— verboten,* no admittance.

zutunlich ['tsu:tu:nlɪç], *adj.* confiding, obliging.

zuverlässig ['tsu:fɛrlɛsɪç], *adj.* reliable; authentic.

Zuversicht ['tsu:fɛrzɪçt], *f.* (—, *no pl.*) trust, confidence.

zuversichtlich ['tsu:fɛrzɪçtlɪç], *adj.* confident.

zuvor [tsu'fo:r], *adv.* before, first, formerly.

zuvorkommend [tsu'fo:rkɔmənt], *adj.* obliging, polite.

Zuwachs ['tsu:vaks], *m.* (—es, *no pl.*) increase, accretion, growth.

zuwachsen ['tsu:vaksən], *v.n. irr.* (*aux.* sein) become overgrown.

zuwandern ['tsu:vandərn], *v.n.* (*aux.* sein) immigrate.

zuwegebringen [tsu've:gəbrɪŋən], *v.a. irr.* bring about, effect.

zuweilen [tsu'vaɪlən], *adv.* sometimes, at times.

zuweisen ['tsu:vaɪzən], *v.a. irr.* assign, apportion.

zuwenden ['tsu:vɛndən], *v.a.* turn towards; give.

zuwerfen ['tsu:vɛrfən], *v.a. irr.* throw towards, cast; (*door*) slam.

zuwider ['tsu:vi:dər], *prep.* (*Dat.*) against, contrary to. — *adv.* repugnant.

Zuwiderhandlung [tsu'vi:dərhandluŋ], *f.* (—, *pl.* —en) contravention.

zuwiderlaufen [tsu'vi:dərlaufən], *v.n. irr.* (*aux.* sein) be contrary to, fly in the face of.

zuzählen ['tsu:tsɛ:lən], *v.a.* add to.

zuziehen ['tsu:tsi:ən], *v.a. irr.* draw together; tighten; consult; (*curtain*) draw. *— v.r. sich eine Krankheit —,* catch a disease.

Zuzug ['tsu:tsu:k], *m.* (—s, *no pl.*) immigration; population increase.

zuzüglich ['tsu:tsy:klɪç], *prep.* (*Genit.*) in addition to, including, plus.

Zwang [tsvaŋ], *m.* (—s, *no pl.*) coercion, force; compulsion; (*fig.*) constraint; *sich — auferlegen,* restrain o.s.; *u deinen Gefühlen keinen — an,* let yourself go.

zwanglos ['tsvaŋlo:s], *adj.* informal, free and easy.

Zwangsarbeit ['tsvaŋsarbaɪt], *f.* (—, *pl.* —en) forced labour.

Zwangsjacke ['tsvaŋsjakə], *f.* (—, *pl.* —en) strait-jacket.

Zwangsmaßnahme ['tsvaŋsma:sna:-mə], *f.* (—, *pl.* —en) compulsory measure, compulsion.

Zwangsversteigerung ['tsvaŋsfɛrʃtaɪgəruŋ], *f.* (—, *pl.* —en) enforced sale.

Zwangsvollstreckung ['tsvaŋsfɔlʃtrekuŋ], *f.* (—, *pl.* —en) distraint.

zwangsweise ['tsvaŋsvaɪzə], *adv.* by force, compulsorily.

Zwangswirtschaft ['tsvaŋsvɪrtʃaft], *f.* (—, *no pl.*) price control, controlled economy.

zwanzig ['tsvantsɪç], *num. adj.* twenty.

zwar [tsva:r], *adv.* to be sure, indeed, it is true, true; (*Am.*) sure.

Zweck [tsvɛk], *m.* (—(e)s, *pl.* —e) end, object, purpose.

zweckdienlich ['tsvɛkdi:nlɪç], *adj.* useful, expedient.

Zwecke ['tsvɛkə], *f.* (—, *pl.* —n) tack, drawing-pin.

zweckentsprechend ['tsvɛkɛntʃpreçənt], *adj.* suitable, appropriate.

zweckmäßig ['tsvɛkmɛ:sɪç], *adj.* expedient, suitable, proper.

zwecks [tsvɛks], *prep.* (*Genit.*) for the purpose of.

zwei [tsvaɪ], *num. adj.* two.

zweibändig ['tsvaɪbɛndɪç], *adj.* in two volumes.

zweideutig ['tsvaɪdɔytɪç], *adj.* ambiguous, equivocal; (*fig.*) suggestive.

Zweideutigkeit ['tsvaɪdɔytɪçkaɪt], *f.* (—, *pl.* —en) ambiguity.

Zweifel ['tsvaɪfəl], *m.* (—s, *pl.* —) doubt, scruple; *ohne —,* no doubt.

zweifelhaft ['tsvaɪfəlhaft], *adj.* doubtful, dubious.

zweifellos ['tsvaɪfəllo:s], *adv.* doubtless.

zweifeln ['tsvaɪfəln], *v.n.* doubt, question; *ich zweifle nicht daran,* I have no doubt about it.

Zweifelsfall ['tsvaɪfəlsfal], *m.* (—s, *pl.* ⁀e) doubtful matter; *im —,* in case of doubt.

Zweifler ['tsvaɪflər], *m.* (—s, *pl.* —) doubter, sceptic.

Zweig [tsvaɪk], *m.* (—(e)s, *pl.* —e) twig, bough, branch.

zweigen ['tsvaɪgən], *v.r. sich —,* bifurcate, fork, branch.

Zweigniederlassung ['tsvaɪkni:dərlasuŋ], *f.* (—, *pl.* —en) branch establishment.

zweihändig ['tsvaɪhɛndɪç], *adj.* two-handed; (*keyboard music*) solo.

Zweihufer ['tsvaɪhuːfər], *m.* (**—s**, *pl.* **—**) cloven-footed animal.

zweijährig ['tsvaɪjɛːrɪç], *adj.* two-year-old; of two years' duration.

zweijährlich ['tsvaɪjɛːrlɪç], *adj.* biennial. — *adv.* every two years.

Zweikampf ['tsvaɪkampf], *m.* (**— (e)s**, *pl.* ⸚e) duel.

zweimal ['tsvaɪmal], *adv.* twice; — *soviel*, twice as much.

zweimotorig ['tsvaɪmotoːrɪç], *adj.* twin-(or two-) engined.

Zweirad ['tsvaɪraːt], *n.* (**—s**, *pl.* ⸚er) bicycle.

zweireihig ['tsvaɪraɪɪç], *adj.* (*suit*) double-breasted.

zweischneidig ['tsvaɪʃnaɪdɪç], *adj.* two-edged.

zweiseitig ['tsvaɪzaɪtɪç], *adj.* two-sided, bilateral.

zweisprachig ['tsvaɪʃpraːxɪç], *adj.* bilingual, in two languages.

zweitälteste ['tsvaɪtɛltəstə], *adj.* second (eldest).

zweitbeste ['tsvaɪtbɛstə], *adj.* second best.

zweite ['tsvaɪtə], *num. adj.* second; *aus —r Hand*, secondhand; *zu zweit*, in twos, two of (us, them).

Zweiteilung ['tsvaɪtaɪluŋ], *f.* (**—**, *pl.* **—en**) bisection.

zweitens ['tsvaɪtəns], *adv.* secondly, in the second place.

zweitletzte ['tsvaɪtletstə], *adj.* last but one, penultimate.

zweitnächste ['tsvaɪtnɛçstə], *adj.* next but one.

Zwerchfell ['tsvɛrçfel], *n.* (**—s**, *pl.* **—e**) diaphragm, midriff.

zwerchfellerschütternd ['tsvɛrçfelerʃytərnt], *adj.* side-splitting.

Zwerg [tsvɛrk], *m.* (**—s**, *pl.* **—e**) dwarf, pigmy.

zwerghaft ['tsvɛrkhaft], *adj.* dwarfish.

Zwetsche ['tsvɛtʃə], *f.* (**—**, *pl.* **—n**) (*Bot.*) damson.

Zwickel ['tsvɪkəl], *m.* (**—s**, *pl.* **—**) gusset; *komischer* —, (*coll.*) queer fish.

zwicken ['tsvɪkən], *v.a.* pinch, nip.

Zwicker ['tsvɪkər], *m.* (**—s**, *pl.* **—**) pince-nez.

Zwickmühle ['tsvɪkmyːlə], *f.* (**—**, *pl.* **—n**) *in der — sein*, be on the horns of a dilemma, be in a jam.

Zwickzange ['tsvɪktsaŋə], *f.* (**—**, *pl.* **—n**) pincers.

Zwieback ['tsviːbak], *m.* (**—s**, *pl.* **—e**) rusk.

Zwiebel ['tsviːbəl], *f.* (**—**, *pl.* **—n**) onion; bulb.

zwiebelartig ['tsviːbəlaːrtɪç], *adj.* bulbous.

zwiebeln ['tsviːbəln], *v.a. einen* —, bully, torment s.o.

Zwielicht ['tsviːlɪçt], *n.* (**—s**, *no pl.*) twilight.

Zwiespalt ['tsviːʃpalt], *m.* (**—s**, *pl.* **—e**) difference, dissension; schism.

Zwiesprache ['tsviːʃpraːxə], *f.* (**—**, *pl.* **—n**) dialogue; discussion.

Zwietracht ['tsviːtraxt], *f.* (**—**, *no pl.*) discord, disharmony.

zwieträchtig ['tsviːtrɛçtɪç], *adj.* discordant, at variance.

Zwillich ['tsvɪlɪç], *m.* (**—s**, *pl.* **—e**) ticking.

Zwilling ['tsvɪlɪŋ], *m.* (**—s**, *pl.* **—e**) twin; (*pl.*) (*Astrol.*) Gemini.

Zwingburg ['tsvɪŋburk], *f.* (**—**, *pl.* **—en**) stronghold.

Zwinge ['tsvɪŋə], *f.* (**—**, *pl.* **—n**) ferrule.

zwingen ['tsvɪŋən], *v.a. irr.* force, compel; master, overcome, get the better of. — *v.r. sich* —, force o.s. (to), make a great effort (to).

zwingend ['tsvɪŋənt], *adj.* cogent, imperative, convincing.

Zwinger ['tsvɪŋər], *m.* (**—s**, *pl.* **—**) keep, donjon, fort; bear-pit.

Zwingherrschaft ['tsvɪŋherʃaft], *f.* (**—**, *pl.* **—en**) despotism, tyranny.

zwinkern ['tsvɪŋkərn], *v.n.* wink; (*stars*) twinkle.

Zwirn [tsvɪrn], *m.* (**—(e)s**, *pl.* **—e**) thread, sewing cotton.

Zwirnrolle ['tsvɪrnrɔlə], *f.* (**—**, *pl.* **—n**) ball of thread, reel of cotton.

zwischen ['tsvɪʃən], *prep.* (*Dat., Acc.*) between; among, amongst.

Zwischenakt ['tsvɪʃənakt], *m.* (**—s**, *pl.* **—e**) (*Theat.*) interval.

Zwischenbemerkung ['tsvɪʃənbəmerkuŋ], *f.* (**—**, *pl.* **—en**) interruption, digression.

Zwischendeck ['tsvɪʃəndɛk], *n.* (**—s**, *pl.* **—e**) (*ship*) steerage, between decks.

zwischendurch ['tsvɪʃəndurç], *adv.* in between, at intervals.

Zwischenfall ['tsvɪʃənfal], *m.* (**—s**, *pl.* ⸚e) incident; episode.

Zwischengericht ['tsvɪʃəngərɪçt], *n.* (**—s**, *pl.* **—e**) (*food*) entrée, entremets.

Zwischenglied ['tsvɪʃəngliːt], *n.* (**—s**, *pl.* **—er**) link.

Zwischenhändler ['tsvɪʃənhendlər], *m.* (**—s**, *pl.* **—**) middleman.

Zwischenpause ['tsvɪʃənpauzə], *f.* (**—**, *pl.* **—n**) interval; pause.

Zwischenraum ['tsvɪʃənraum], *m.* (**—s**, *pl.* ⸚e) intermediate space, gap.

Zwischenrede ['tsvɪʃənreːdə], *f.* (**—**, *pl.* **—n**) interruption.

Zwischenruf ['tsvɪʃənruːf], *m.* (**—s**, *pl.* **—e**) interruption, interjection.

Zwischensatz ['tsvɪʃənzats], *m.* (**—es**, *pl.* ⸚e) parenthesis; interpolation.

Zwischenspiel ['tsvɪʃənʃpiːl], *n.* (**—s**, *pl.* **—e**) interlude, intermezzo.

Zwischenzeit ['tsvɪʃəntsaɪt], *f.* (**—**, *no pl.*) interval, interim, meantime; *in der* —, meanwhile.

Zwist [tsvɪst], *m.* (**—es**, *pl.* **—e**) discord, quarrel, dispute.

Zwistigkeiten ['tsvɪstɪçkaɪtən], *f. pl.* hostilities.

zwitschern ['tsvɪtʃərn], *v.n.* chirp, twitter.

Zwitter

Zwitter ['tsvɪtər], *m.* (—s, *pl.* —)
hybrid, cross-breed, mongrel; hermaphrodite.
zwitterhaft ['tsvɪtərhaft], *adj.* hybrid;
bisexual.
zwölf [tsvœlf], *num. adj.* twelve.
Zwölffingerdarm ['tsvœlffɪŋərdarm],
m. (—s, *pl.* ⁻e) duodenum.
Zyankali [tsy:an'ka:li], *n.* (—s, *no pl.*)
potassium cyanide.
Zyklon [tsy'klo:n], *m.* (—s, *pl.* —e)
cyclone.
Zyklus ['tsyklus], *m.* (—, *pl.* **Zyklen**)
cycle; course, series.

zylinderförmig [tsy'lɪndərfœrmɪç], *adj.*
cylindric(al).
Zylinderhut [tsy'lɪndərhu:t], *m.* (—s,
pl. ⁻e) top-hat, silk-hat.
zylindrisch [tsy'lɪndrɪʃ], *adj.* cylindric(al).
Zyniker ['tsy:nɪkər], *m.* (—s, *pl.* —)
cynic.
zynisch ['tsy:nɪʃ], *adj.* cynical.
Zynismus [tsy'nɪsmus], *m.* (—, *no pl.*)
cynicism.
Zypern ['tsy:pərn], *n.* Cyprus.
Zypresse [tsy'presə], *f.* (—, *pl.* —n)
(*Bot.*) cypress.

A

A [ei]. das A (*also Mus.*).

a [ə, ei] (**an** [ən, æn] *before vowel or silent* h), *indef. art.* ein, eine, ein; *two at a time*, zwei auf einmal; *many a*, mancher; *two shillings a pound*, zwei Schilling das Pfund.

abacus ['æbəkəs], *s.* das Rechenbrett.

abandon [ə'bændən], *v.a.* (*give up*) aufgeben; (*forsake*) verlassen; (*surrender*) preisgeben.

abandonment [ə'bændənmənt], *s.* das Verlassen (*active*); das Verlassensein (*passive*); die Wildheit, das Sichgehenlassen.

abasement [ə'beismənt], *s.* die Demütigung, Erniedrigung.

abash [ə'bæʃ], *v.a.* beschämen.

abate [ə'beit], *v.n.* nachlassen.

abbess ['æbes], *s.* die Äbtissin.

abbey ['æbi], *s.* die Abtei.

abbot ['æbət], *s.* der Abt.

abbreviate [ə'bri:vieit], *v.a.* abkürzen.

abbreviation [əbri:vi'eiʃən], *s.* die Abkürzung.

abdicate ['æbdikeit], *v.a., v.n.* entsagen (*Dat.*), abdanken.

abdomen [æb'doumən, 'æbdəmən], *s.* (*Anat.*) der Unterleib, Bauch.

abdominal [æb'dɔminəl], *adj.* (*Anat.*) Bauch-, Unterleibs-.

abduct [æb'dʌkt], *v.a.* entführen.

abed [ə'bed], *adv.* zu Bett, im Bett.

aberration [æbə'reiʃən], *s.* die Abirrung; die Verirrung; (*Phys.*) die Strahlenbrechung.

abet [ə'bet], *v.a.* helfen (*Dat.*), unterstützen.

abeyance [ə'beiəns], *s.* die Unentschiedenheit, (der Zustand der) Ungewißheit; *in —*, unentschieden.

abhor [əb'hɔ:], *v.a.* verabscheuen.

abhorrence [əb'hɔrəns], *s.* die Abscheu (*of*, vor, *Dat.*).

abhorrent [əb'hɔrənt], *adj.* widerlich, ekelhaft.

abide [ə'baid], *v.n. irr.* bleiben, verweilen; (*last*) dauern. — *v.a.* aushalten.

ability [ə'biliti], *s.* die Fähigkeit, Tüchtigkeit; (*pl.*) die Geisteskräfte, *f. pl.*

abject ['æbdʒekt], *adj.* elend; (*submissive*) unterwürfig, verächtlich.

ablaze [ə'bleiz], *adj., adv.* in Flammen.

able [eibl], *adj.* fähig; (*clever*) geschickt; (*efficient*) tüchtig.

ablution [ə'blu:ʃən], *s.* die Abwaschung, Waschung.

abnormal [æb'nɔ:məl], *adj.* abnorm, ungewöhnlich.

abnormality [æbnɔ:'mæliti], *s.* die Ungewöhnlichkeit.

aboard [ə'bɔ:d], *adv.* an Bord.

abode [ə'boud], *s.* der Wohnsitz, Wohnort.

abolish [ə'bɔliʃ], *v.a.* aufheben, abschaffen.

abolition [æbo'liʃən], *s.* die Abschaffung, Aufhebung.

abominable [ə'bɔminəbl], *adj.* abscheulich, scheußlich.

abominate [ə'bɔmineit], *v.a.* verabscheuen.

abomination [əbɔmi'neiʃən], *s.* der Abscheu, Greuel.

aboriginal [æbə'ridʒinəl], *adj.* eingeboren, einheimisch. — *s.* der Eingeborene.

aborigines [æbə'ridʒini:z], *s. pl.* die Eingeborenen, Ureinwohner.

abortion [ə'bɔ:ʃən], *s.* die Fehlgeburt; die Abtreibung.

abortive [ə'bɔ:tiv], *adj.* mißlungen.

abound [ə'baund], *v.n.* wimmeln von (*Dat.*).

about [ə'baut], *prep.* um; (*toward*) gegen; *about 3 o'clock*, gegen drei; (*concerning*) über, betreffend. — *adv.* umher, herum; (*round*) rund herum; (*nearly*) etwa, ungefähr; (*everywhere*) überall; *to be — to*, im Begriffe sein *or* stehen zu . . .

above [ə'bʌv], *prep.* über; — *all things*, vor allen Dingen; *this is — me*, das ist mir zu hoch; — *board*, offen, ehrlich. — *adv.* oben, darüber, *over and —*, obendrein; —*mentioned*, obenerwähnt.

abrade [ə'breid], *v.a.* abschaben, abschürfen.

abrasion [ə'breiʒən], *s.* die Abschürfung; Abnutzung.

abreast [ə'brest], *adj., adv.* nebeneinander, Seite an Seite; *keep —*, (sich) auf dem Laufenden halten; *Schritt halten* (mit).

abridge [ə'bridʒ], *v.a.* (ab)kürzen.

abridgement [ə'bridʒmənt], *s.* die (Ab)kürzung; (*book etc.*) der Auszug.

abroad [ə'brɔ:d], *adv.* im Ausland, auswärts; *to go —*, ins Ausland reisen.

abrogate ['æbrogeit], *v.a.* abschaffen.

abrogation [æbro'geiʃən], *s.* (*Pol.*) die Abschaffung.

abrupt [ə'brʌpt], *adj.* plötzlich; (*curt*) schroff; kurz; jäh.

abruptness [ə'brʌptnis], *s.* (*speech*) die Schroffheit; (*suddenness*) die Plötzlichkeit; (*drop*) die Steilheit.

abscess ['æbses], *s.* das Geschwür, die Schwellung, der Abszeß.

abscond

abscond [əb'skɔnd], *v.n.* sich davon-machen.

absence ['æbsəns], *s.* die Abwesenheit; *leave of* —, der Urlaub.

absent (1) ['æbsənt], *adj.* abwesend; — *minded*, zerstreut.

absent (2) [æb'sent], *v.r.* — *oneself*, fehlen, fernbleiben; (*go away*) sich ent-fernen.

absentee [æbsən'ti:], *s.* der Abwesende.

absolute ['æbsəlu:t], *adj.* absolut, un-umschränkt.

absolve [əb'zɔlv], *v.a.* freisprechen (*from*, von), lossprechen, entbinden.

absorb [əb'sɔ:b], *v.a.* absorbieren, aufsaugen; (*attention*) in Anspruch nehmen.

absorbed [əb'sɔ:bd], *adj.* versunken.

absorbent [əb'sɔ:bənt], *adj.* absorbie-rend.

absorption [əb'sɔ:pʃən], *s.* (*Chem.*) die Absorption; (*attention*) das Versun-kensein.

abstain [əb'stein], *v.n.* sich enthalten; — *from voting*, sich der Stimme enthalten.

abstainer [əb'steinə], *s.* der Abstinenz-ler, Antialkoholiker.

abstemious [əb'sti:miəs], *adj.* enthalt-sam.

abstention [əb'stenʃən], *s.* die Enthaltung.

abstinence ['æbstinəns], *s.* die Ent-haltsamkeit, das Fasten (*food*).

abstract [æb'strækt], *v.a.* abstrahieren, abziehen; (*summarize*) kürzen, aus-ziehen. —['æbstrækt], *adj.* abstrakt; (*Maths.*) rein. — *s.* der Auszug, Abriß (*of article, book, etc.*).

abstracted [æb'stræktid], *adj.* zerstreut, geistesabwesend.

abstraction [æb'strækʃən], *s.* die Ab-straktion; der abstrakte Begriff.

abstruse [æb'stru:s], *adj.* schwerver-ständlich, tiefsinnig.

absurd [əb'sə:d], *adj.* absurd, töricht; (*unreasonable*) unvernünftig, gegen alle Vernunft; (*laughable*) lächerlich.

absurdity [əb'sə:diti], *s.* die Torheit, Unvernünftigkeit.

abundance [ə'bʌndəns], *s.* die Fülle, der Überfluß.

abundant [ə'bʌndənt], *adj.* reichlich.

abuse [ə'bju:z], *v.a.* mißbrauchen; (*insult*) beschimpfen; (*violate*) schän-den. —[ə'bju:s], *s.* der Mißbrauch; (*language*) die Beschimpfung; (*vio-lation*) die Schändung.

abusive [ə'bju:siv], *adj.* (*language*) grob; schimpfend, schmähend.

abut [ə'bʌt], *v.n.* anstoßen, angrenzen.

abysmal [ə'bizməl], *adj.* bodenlos.

abyss [ə'bis], *s.* der Abgrund, Schlund.

Abyssinian [æbi'sinjən], *adj.* abes-sinisch. — *s.* der Abessinier.

acacia [ə'keiʃə], *s.* (*Bot.*) die Akazie.

academic [ækə'demik], *adj.* akademisch. — *s.* der Akademiker.

academy [ə'kædəmi], *s.* die Akademie.

acajon ['ækəʒu:], *s.* (*Bot.*) der Nieren-baum.

accede [æk'si:d], *v.n.* beistimmen; ein-willigen; — *to the throne*, den Thron besteigen.

accelerate [æk'seləreit], *v.a.* beschleu-nigen. — *v.n.* schneller fahren.

acceleration [ækselə'reiʃən], *s.* die Beschleunigung.

accelerator [æk'seləreitə], *s.* (*Motor.*) der Gashebel, das Gaspedal.

accent (1), **accentuate** [æk'sent, æk-'sentjueit], *v.a.* akzentuieren, betonen.

accent (2) ['æksənt], *s.* (*Phon.*) der Ton, Wortton, die Betonung; der Akzent (*dialect*), die Aussprache.

accentuation [æksentju'eiʃən], *s.* die Aussprache, Akzentuierung, Beto-nung.

accept [æk'sept], *v.a.* annehmen.

acceptable [æk'septəbl], *adj.* angenehm, annehmbar, annehmlich.

acceptance [æk'septəns], *s.* die An-nahme; (*Comm.*) das Akzept.

access ['ækses], *s.* der Zugang, Zutritt.

accessible [æk'sesibl], *adj.* erreichbar, zugänglich.

accession [æk'seʃən], *s.* der Zuwachs; — *to the throne*, die Thronbesteigung.

accessory [æk'sesəri], *adj.* zugehörig; hinzukommend; (*Law*) mitschuldig; (*subsidiary*) nebensächlich. — *s.* (*Law*) der Mitschuldige; (*pl.*) das Zubehör.

accidence ['æksidəns], *s.* (*Gram.*) die Flexionslehre.

accident ['æksidənt], *s.* (*chance*) der Zufall; (*mishap*) der Unfall, Unglücks-fall.

accidental [æksi'dentəl], *adj.* zufällig; (*inessential*) unwesentlich; durch Un-fall.

acclaim [ə'kleim], *v.a.* akklamieren, mit Beifall aufnehmen. — *v.n.* zujubeln. — *s.* der Beifall.

acclamation [æklə'meiʃən], *s.* der Beifall, Zuruf.

acclimatize [ə'klaimətaiz], *v.a., v.r.* akklimatisieren; sich anpassen, einge-wöhnen.

accommodate [ə'kɔmədeit], *v.a.* (*adapt*) anpassen; (*lodge*) unter-bringen, beherbergen, aufnehmen; einem aushelfen (*with money*) jeman-dem Geld leihen. — *v.r.* — *oneself to*, sich an etwas anpassen, sich in etwas fügen.

accommodating [ə'kɔmədeitiŋ], *adj.* gefällig, entgegenkommend.

accommodation [əkɔmə'deiʃən], *s.* (*adaptation*) die Anpassung; (*dispute*) die Beilegung; (*room*) die Unterkunft.

accompaniment [ə'kʌmpənimənt], *s.* die Begleitung.

accompany [ə'kʌmpəni], *v.a.* begleiten.

accomplice [ə'kʌmplis *or* ə'kɔmplis], *s.* der Komplize, Mitschuldige, Mit-täter.

accomplish [ə'kʌmpliʃ *or* ə'kɔmpliʃ], *v.a.* vollenden, zustandebringen, voll-bringen; (*objective*) erreichen.

accomplished [ə'kʌmpliʃd *or* ə'kɔm-pliʃd], *adj.* vollendet.

accomplishment [ə'kʌmpliʃmənt *or* ə'kɔmpliʃmənt], *s.* (*of project*) die Ausführung; (*of task*) die Vollendung; (*of prophecy*) die Erfüllung; (*pl.*) die Talente, *n. pl.*, Gaben, Kenntnisse, *f. pl.*

accord '[ə'kɔ:d], *s.* (*agreement*) die Übereinstimmung; (*unison*) die Eintracht. — *v.n.* übereinstimmen (*with*, mit). — *v.a.* bewilligen.

accordance [ə'kɔ:dəns], *s.* die Übereinstimmung.

according [ə'kɔ:diŋ], *prep.* — *to*, gemäß, nach, laut.

accordingly [ə'kɔ:diŋli], *adv.* demgemäß, demnach, folglich.

accordion [ə'kɔ:diən], *s.* (*Mus.*) die Ziehharmonika, das Akkordeon.

accost [ə'kɔst], *v.a.* ansprechen, anreden.

account [ə'kaunt], *s.* die Rechnung; (*report*) der Bericht; (*narrative*) die Erzählung; (*importance*) die Bedeutung; (*Fin.*) das Konto, Guthaben; *cash* —, die Kassenrechnung; *on no* —, auf keinen Fall; *on his* —, seinetwegen, um seinetwillen; *on* — *of*, wegen (*Genit.*); *on that* —, darum; *of no* —, unbedeutend. — *v.n.* — *for*, Rechenschaft ablegen über (*Acc.*); (*explain*) erklären.

accountable [ə'kauntəbl], *adj.* verrechenbar (*item*); verantwortlich (*person*).

accountant [ə'kauntənt], *s.* der Bücherrevisor, Rechnungsführer; *junior* —, der Buchhalter.

accredit [ə'kredit], *v.a.* akkreditieren, beglaubigen, (*authorize*) ermächtigen, bevollmächtigen.

accretion [ə'kri:ʃən], *s.* der Zuwachs.

accrue [ə'kru:], *v.n.* (*Comm.*) zuwachsen, erwachsen, zufallen.

accumulate [ə'kju:mjuleit], *v.a.*, *v.n.* anhäufen; sich anhäufen, zunehmen, sich ansammeln.

accumulation [əkju:mju'leiʃən], *s.* die Ansammlung, Anhäufung.

accuracy ['ækjurəsi], *s.* die Genauigkeit.

accurate ['ækjurit], *adj.* genau, richtig.

accursed [ə'kə:sid], *adj.* verflucht, verwünscht.

accusation [ækju'zeiʃən], *s.* die Anklage.

accusative [ə'kju:zətiv], *s.* (*Gram.*) der Akkusativ.

accuse [ə'kju:z], *v.a.* anklagen, beschuldigen (*of*, *Genit.*).

accustom [ə'kʌstəm], *v.a.* gewöhnen (*to*, an, *Acc.*).

ace [eis], *s.* (*Cards*) das As, die Eins.

acerbity [ə'sə:biti], *s.* die Rauheit, Herbheit; (*manner*) die Grobheit.

acetate ['æsiteit], *s.* das Azetat; essigsaures Salz.

acetic [ə'si:tik, ə'setik], *adj.* essigsauer.

acetylene [ə'setili:n], *s.* das Azetylen.

ache [eik], *s.* der Schmerz. — *v.n.* schmerzen, weh(e)tun.

achieve [ə'tʃi:v], *v.a.* erreichen, erlangen; (*accomplish*) vollenden; (*perform*) ausführen; (*gain*) erlangen, erwerben.

achievement [ə'tʃi:vmənt], *s.* (*accomplishment*) die Leistung, der Erfolg; die Errungenschaft; (*gain*) die Erwerbung.

achromatic [ækro'mætik], *adj.* achromatisch, farblos.

acid ['æsid], *adj.* sauer, scharf. — *s.* (*Chem.*) die Säure.

acidulated [ə'sidjuleitid], *adj.* (*Chem.*) angesäuert.

acknowledge [æk'nɔlidʒ], *v.a.* anerkennen; (*admit*) zugeben; (*confess*) bekennen; (*letter*) den Empfang bestätigen.

acknowledgement [æk'nɔlidʒmənt], *s.* die Anerkennung, (*receipt*) Bestätigung, Quittung; (*pl.*) die Dankesbezeigung; die Erkenntlichkeit.

acme ['ækmi], *s.* der Gipfel, Höhepunkt.

acorn ['eikɔ:n], *s.* (*Bot.*) die Eichel.

acoustics [ə'ku:stiks], *s. pl.* die Akustik; (*subject*, *study*) die Schallehre.

acquaint [ə'kweint], *v.a.* bekanntmachen; (*inform*) mitteilen (*Dat.*), informieren; unterrichten.

acquaintance [ə'kweintəns], *s.* die Bekanntschaft; der Bekannte, die Bekannte (*person*); die Kenntnis (*with*, von).

acquiesce [ækwi'es], *v.n.* einwilligen, sich fügen.

acquiescence [ækwi'esəns], *s.* die Einwilligung (*in*, in, *Acc.*), Zustimmung (*in*, zu, *Dat.*)

acquiescent [ækwi'esənt], *adj.* fügsam.

acquire [ə'kwaiə], *v.a.* erlangen, erwerben; (*language*) erlernen.

acquisition [ækwi'ziʃən], *s.* die Erlangung, Erwerbung.

acquit [ə'kwit], *v.a.* freisprechen.

acre ['eikə], *s.* der Acker (*appr.* 0.4 *Hektar*).

acrid ['ækrid], *adj.* scharf, beißend.

acrimonious [ækri'mouniəs], *adj.* scharf, bitter.

across [ə'krɔs, ə'krɔ:s], *adv.* kreuzweise, (quer) hinüber. — *prep.* quer durch, über; *come* —, (zufällig) treffen; *come* — *a problem*, auf ein Problem stoßen.

act [ækt], *s.* (*deed*) die Tat; (*Theat.*) der Akt; (*Parl. etc.*) die Akte. — *v.a.* (*Theat.*) spielen. — *v.n.* handeln (*do something*); sich benehmen *or* tun, als ob (*act as if*, *pretend*); (*Theat.*) spielen; (*Chem.*) wirken (*react*).

action ['ækʃən], *s.* die Handlung (*play*, *deed*); Wirkung (*effect*); (*Law*) der Prozeß; der Gang.

active ['æktiv], *adj.* (*person*, *Gram.*) aktiv; tätig; rührig (*industrious*); wirksam (*effective*).

activity [æk'tiviti], *s.* die Tätigkeit; (*Chem.*) Wirksamkeit.

actor ['æktə], *s.* der Schauspieler.

actress ['æktrəs], die Schauspielerin.

actual ['æktjuəl], *adj.* tatsächlich, wirklich.

actuality [æktju'æliti], *s.* die Wirklichkeit.

actuary ['æktjuəri], *s.* der Aktuar, Versicherungsbeamte.

actuate ['æktjueit], *v.a.* betreiben, in Bewegung setzen.

acuity [ə'kju:iti], *s.* der Scharfsinn (*mind*), die Schärfe (*vision etc.*).

acute [ə'kju:t], *adj.* scharf, scharfsinnig (*mind*); spitz (*angle*); fein (*sense*); — *accent*, der Akut.

adage ['ædidʒ], *s.* das Sprichwort.

adamant ['ædəmənt], *adj.* sehr hart, unerbittlich (*inexorable*).

adapt [ə'dæpt], *v.a.* anpassen, angleichen; bearbeiten.

adaptable [ə'dæptəbl], *adj.* anpassungsfähig.

adaptation [ædæp'teiʃən], *s.* die Anpassung, die Bearbeitung (*of book*).

adaptive [ə'dæptiv], *adj.* anpassungsfähig.

add [æd], *v.a.* hinzufügen, (*Maths.*) addieren.

adder ['ædə], *s.* (*Zool.*) die Natter.

addict ['ædikt], *s.* der Süchtige.

addiction [ə'dikʃən], *s.* die Sucht.

addicted [ə'diktid], *adj.* verfallen.

addition [ə'diʃən], *s.* die Hinzufügung, Zugabe, (*Maths.*) Addition.

additional [ə'diʃənəl], *adj.* zusätzlich, nachträglich.

address [ə'dres], *s.* die Anschrift, Adresse (*letter*); die Ansprache (*speech*). — *v.a.* (*letter*) adressieren, richten an (*Acc.*).

addressee [ædre'si:], *s.* der Adressat, der Empfänger.

adduce [ə'dju:s], *v.a.* anführen (*proof*, Beweis).

adenoid ['ædinɔid], *s.* (*usually pl.*) (*Med.*) die Wucherung.

adept ['ædept], *adj.* geschickt, erfahren.

adequacy ['ædikwəsi], *s.* die Angemessenheit, das Gewachsensein, die Zulänglichkeit.

adequate ['ædikwət], *adj.* gewachsen (*Dat.*); angemessen, hinreichend (*sufficient*).

adhere [əd'hiə], *v.n.* haften, anhängen; — *to one's opinion*, bei seiner Meinung bleiben.

adherence [əd'hiərəns], *s.* das Festhalten (an, *Dat.*).

adhesion [əd'hi:ʒən], *s.* (*Phys.*) die Adhäsion; das Anhaften.

adhesive [əd'hi:ziv], *adj.* haftend, klebrig; — *plaster*, das Heftpflaster.

adipose ['ædipous], *adj.* fett, feist.

adjacent [ə'dʒeisənt], *adj.* naheliegend, benachbart, angrenzend.

adjective ['ædʒəktiv], *s.* (*Gram.*) das Adjektiv; Eigenschaftswort.

adjoin [ə'dʒɔin], *v.a.* anstoßen, angrenzen.

adjourn [ə'dʒə:n], *v.a.* vertagen, aufschieben.

adjudicate [ə'dʒu:dikeit], *v.a.* beurteilen, richten.

adjunct ['ædʒʌŋkt], *s.* der Zusatz.

adjust [ə'dʒʌst], *v.a.* ordnen; (*adapt*) anpassen; regulieren, einstellen.

adjustable [ə'dʒʌstəbl], *adj.* verstellbar, einstellbar.

adjustment [ə'dʒʌstmənt], *s.* die Einstellung, Anpassung; (*Law*) Schlichtung; Berichtigung.

administer [əd'ministə], *v.a.* verwalten (*an enterprise*); verabreichen (*medicine*); abnehmen (*an oath*, einen Eid).

administration [ədminis'treiʃən], *s.* die Verwaltung, Regierung; die Darreichung (*sacraments*).

administrative [əd'ministrətiv], *adj.* Verwaltungs-; verwaltend.

admirable ['ædmirəbl], *adj.* bewundernswert.

admiral ['ædmirəl], *s.* der Admiral.

Admiralty ['ædmirəlti], *s.* die Admiralität.

admiration [ædmi'reiʃən], *s.* die Bewunderung.

admire [əd'maiə], *v.a.* bewundern, verehren.

admirer [əd'maiərə], *s.* der Bewunderer, Verehrer.

admissible [əd'misibl], *adj.* zulässig.

admission [əd'miʃən], *s.* die Zulassung, (*entry*) der Eintritt; Zutritt; (*confession*) das Eingeständnis, Zugeständnis.

admit [əd'mit], *v.a.* zulassen; aufnehmen; zugeben (*deed*); gelten lassen (*argument*).

admittance [əd'mitəns], *s.* der Zugang, Eintritt, Zutritt.

admixture [əd'mikstʃə], *s.* die Beimischung, Beigabe.

admonish [əd'mɔniʃ], *v.a.* ermahnen, mahnen, warnen.

admonition [ædmə'niʃən], *s.* die Ermahnung, Warnung.

ado [ə'du:], *s.* der Lärm, das Tun, das Treiben; *without further* —, ohne weiteres.

adolescence [ædo'lesəns], *s.* die Adoleszenz, Jugend, Jugendzeit.

adolescent [ædo'lesənt], *s.* der Jugendliche. — *adj.* jugendlich.

adopt [ə'dɔpt], *v.a.* (*Law*) annehmen, adoptieren.

adoption [ə'dɔpʃən], *s.* (*Law*) die Annahme, Adoption.

adoptive [ə'dɔptiv], *adj.* Adoptiv-, angenommen.

adorable [ə'dɔ:rəbl], *adj.* anbetungswürdig, (*coll.*) wunderbar, schön.

adoration [ædo'reiʃən], *s.* die Anbetung.

adore [ə'dɔ:], *v.a.* anbeten; verehren.

adorn [ə'dɔ:n], *v.a.* (aus)schmücken, zieren.

Adriatic (Sea) [eidri:'ætik (si:)], *das* adriatische Meer.

adrift [ə'drift], *adv.* treibend; *cut o.s.* —, sich absondern.

adroit [ə'drɔit], *adj.* gewandt, geschickt.

adroitness [ə'drɔitnis], *s.* die Gewandtheit, die Geschicklichkeit.

adulation [ædju'leiʃən], s. die Schmeichelei.

adulator ['ædjuleitə], s. der Schmeichler.

adulatory ['ædjuleitəri], adj. schmeichlerisch.

adult [ə'dʌlt or 'ædʌlt], adj. erwachsen. — s. der Erwachsene.

adulterate [ə'dʌltəreit], v.a. verfälschen; verwässern.

adulterer [ə'dʌltərə], s. der Ehebrecher.

adultery [ə'dʌltəri], s. der Ehebruch.

adumbrate [ə'dʌmbreit or 'æd-], v.a. skizzieren, entwerfen, andeuten.

advance [əd'va:ns], v.a. fördern (a cause); vorschießen (money); geltend machen (claim). — v.n. vorrücken, vorstoßen; (make progress, gain promotion) aufsteigen. — s. der Fortschritt (progress); der Vorschuß (money); in —, im voraus.

advancement [əd'va:nsmənt], s. der Fortschritt (progress), der Aufstieg, die Beförderung (promotion); die Förderung (of a cause).

advantage [əd'va:ntidʒ], s. der Vorteil, Nutzen; (superiority) die Überlegenheit.

Advent ['ædvent]. (Eccl.) der Advent.

advent ['ædvənt], s. die Ankunft.

adventitious [ædven'tiʃəs], adj. zufällig.

adventure [əd'ventʃə], s. das Abenteuer. — v.n. auf Abenteuer ausgehen, wagen.

adventurer [əd'ventʃərə], s. der Abenteurer.

adventurous [əd'ventʃərəs], adj. abenteuerlich, unternehmungslustig.

adverb ['ædvə:b], s. (Gram.) das Adverb(ium), Umstandswort.

adverbial [əd'və:biəl], adj. adverbial.

adversary ['ædvəsəri], s. der Gegner, Widersacher.

adverse ['ædvə:s], adj. widrig, feindlich, ungünstig.

adversity [əd'və:siti], s. das Unglück, Mißgeschick; in —, im Unglück.

advert [əd'və:t], v.n. hinweisen.

advertise ['ædvətaiz], v.a. anzeigen; annoncieren (in press), Reklame machen.

advertisement [əd'və:tizmənt], s. die Anzeige, Annonce; Reklame.

advertiser ['ædvətaizə], s. der Anzeiger.

advice [əd'vais], s. der Rat, Ratschlag; die Nachricht (information).

advise [əd'vaiz], v.a. raten (Dat.), beraten; benachrichtigen (inform); verständigen.

advisable [əd'vaizəbl], adj. ratsam.

advisedly [əd'vaizidli], adv. absichtlich, mit Bedacht.

adviser [əd'vaizə], s. der Berater.

advisory [əd'vaizəri], adj. beratend, ratgebend, Rats-.

advocacy ['ædvəkəsi], s. (Law) die Verteidigung; die Fürsprache (championing of, für, Acc.); die Vertretung (of view).

Aegean (Sea) [i:'dʒi:ən (si:)]. das ägäische Meer.

aerated ['eəreitid], adj. kohlensauer.

aerial ['eəriəl], s. (Rad.) die Antenne. — adj. luftig, Luft-.

aerie ['eəri, 'iəri], s. see **eyrie**.

aerodrome ['eərodroum], s. der Flugplatz, Flughafen.

aeronautical [eəro'nɔ:tikəl], adj. aeronautisch.

aeronautics [eəro'nɔ:tiks], s. pl. die Aeronautik, Luftfahrt.

aeroplane, (Am.) **airplane** ['eəroplein, 'eərplein], s. das Flugzeug.

aesthetic(al) [i:s'θetik(əl)], adj. ästhetisch.

aesthetics [i:s'θetiks], s. die Ästhetik.

afar [ə'fa:], adv. fern, weit entfernt; from —, von weitem, (von) weit her.

affability [æfə'biliti], s. die Leutseligkeit, Freundlichkeit.

affable ['æfəbl], adj. freundlich, leutselig.

affair [ə'feə], s. die Affäre; die Angelegenheit (matter); das Anliegen (concern).

affect [ə'fekt], v.a. beeinflußen; rühren; wirken auf; vortäuschen (pretend); zur Schau tragen (exhibit).

affectation [æfek'teiʃən], s. die Ziererei, das Affektieren, die Affektiertheit.

affected [ə'fektid], adj. affektiert, gekünstelt, geziert; befallen, angegriffen (illness).

affection [ə'fekʃən], s. die Zuneigung, Zärtlichkeit.

affectionate [ə'fekʃənit], adj. zärtlich, liebevoll; (in letters) yours —ly, herzlichst.

affinity [ə'finiti], s. (Chem.) die Affinität; die Verwandtschaft (relationship).

affirm [ə'fə:m], v.a. behaupten, bestätigen, versichern; bekräftigen (confirm).

affirmation [æfə'meiʃən], s. die Behauptung, Bekräftigung.

affirmative [ə'fə:mətiv], adj. bejahend, positiv; in the —, bejahend.

affix [ə'fiks], v.a. anheften, aufkleben (stick); anbringen (join to, an, Acc.).

afflict [ə'flikt], v.a. quälen, plagen.

affliction [ə'flikʃən], s. die Plage, Qual; das Mißgeschick; die Not; das Leiden.

affluence ['æfluəns], s. der Überfluß (abundance); der Reichtum.

affluent ['æfluənt], adj. reich, wohlhabend. — s. der Nebenfluß (tributary).

afford [ə'fɔ:d], v.a. geben, bieten; (sich) leisten (have money for); gewähren (give); hervorbringen (yield).

afforest [ə'fɔrist], v.a. aufforsten.

affray [ə'frei], s. die Schlägerei.

African ['æfrikən], adj. afrikanisch. — s. der Afrikaner.

affront [ə'frʌnt], s. die Beleidigung. — v.a. beleidigen.

Afghan ['æfgæn], adj. afghanisch. — s. der Afghane.

afield [ə'fi:ld], adj., adv. im Felde; weit umher; weit weg.

afire [ə'faiə], adv., adv. in Flammen.

aflame [əˈfleim], *adj., adv.* in Flammen.
afloat [əˈflout], *adj., adv.* schwimmend, dahintreibend.
afoot [əˈfut], *adj., adv.* im Gange.
afore [əˈfɔː], *adv.* vorher.
aforesaid [əˈfɔːsed], *adj. the* —, das Obengesagte, der Vorhergenannte.
afraid [əˈfreid], *adj.* ängstlich, furchtsam; *be* —, fürchten (*of s.th.*, etwas, *Acc.*); sich fürchten.
afresh [əˈfreʃ], *adv.* von neuem.
aft [ɑːft], *adv.* (*Naut.*) achtern.
after [ˈɑːftə], *prep.* nach (*time*); nach, hinter (*place*); *the day* — *tomorrow*, übermorgen. — *adj.* hinter, später. — *adv.* hinterher, nachher (*time*); darauf, dahinter (*place*). — *conj.* nachdem.
afternoon [ɑːftəˈnuːn], *s.* der Nachmittag.
afterwards [ˈɑːftəwədz], *adv.* nachher, daraufhin, später.
again [əˈgein], *adv.* wieder, abermals, noch einmal; zurück (*back*); dagegen (*however*); *as much* —, noch einmal soviel; — *immer* wieder.
against [əˈgeinst], *prep.* gegen, wider; nahe bei (*near, Dat.*); bis an (*up to, Acc.*); — *the grain*, wider *or* gegen den Strich.
agate [ˈægeit], *s.* der Achat.
agave [əˈgeivi], *s.* (*Bot.*) die Agave.
age [eidʒ], *s.* das Alter (*person*); das Zeitalter (*period*); die Reife; *come of* —, volljährig werden; mündig werden; *old* —, das Greisenalter; *for* —*s*, seit einer Ewigkeit. — *v.n.* altern, alt werden.
aged [ˈeidʒid], *adj.* bejahrt.
agency [ˈeidʒənsi], *s.* die Agentur (*firm*); die Mitwirkung (*participation*); die Hilfe (*assistance*); die Vermittlung (*mediation*).
agenda [əˈdʒendə], *s.* das Sitzungsprogramm; die Tagesordnung.
agent [ˈeidʒənt], *s.* der Agent, Vertreter.
agglomerate [əˈgloməreit], *v.a.* zusammenhäufen. — *v.n.* sich zusammenhäufen, sich ballen.
aggrandisement [əˈgrændizmənt], *s.* die Überhebung, Übertreibung, Erweiterung.
aggravate [ˈægrəveit], *v.a.* verschlimmern; ärgern.
aggravation [ægrəˈveiʃən], *s.* die Verschlimmerung (*of condition*); der Ärger (*annoyance*).
aggregate [ˈægrigit], *adj.* gesamt, vereinigt, vereint. — *s.* das Aggregat.
aggregation [ægriˈgeiʃən], *s.* (*Geol., Chem.*) die Vereinigung, Anhäufung, Ansammlung.
aggression [əˈgreʃən], *s.* der Angriff, Überfall.
aggressive [əˈgresiv], *adj.* aggressiv, angreifend.
aggressor [əˈgresə], *s.* der Angreifer.
aggrieve [əˈgriːv], *v.a.* kränken.

aghast [əˈgɑːst], *adj.* bestürzt; sprachlos; entsetzt.
agile [ˈædʒail], *adj.* behend, flink, beweglich.
agitate [ˈædʒiteit], *v.a.* bewegen; beunruhigen; aufrühren; stören.
agitation [ædʒiˈteiʃən], *s.* (*Pol.*) die Agitation; die Unruhe (*unrest*); der Aufruhr (*revolt*).
agitator [ˈædʒiteitə], *s.* (*Pol.*) der Agitator; der Aufwiegler (*inciter*).
aglow [əˈglou], *adv.* glühend.
agnostic [ægˈnɔstik], *s.* der Agnostiker.
ago [əˈgou], *adv.* vor; *long* —, vor langer Zeit; *not long* —, kürzlich; *a month* —, vor einem Monat.
agog [əˈgɔg], *adv.* erregt, gespannt, neugierig (*for, auf, Acc.*).
agonize [ˈægənaiz], *v.a.* quälen, martern. — *v.n.* Qual erleiden; mit dem Tode ringen *or* kämpfen.
agonising [ˈægənaiziŋ], *adj.* schmerzhaft, qualvoll.
agony [ˈægəni], *s.* die Pein, Qual; der Todeskampf; — *column*, die Seufzerspalte.
agrarian [əˈgreəriən], *adj.* landwirtschaftlich; — *party*, die Bauernpartei.
agree [əˈgriː], *v.n.* übereinstimmen (*be in agreement*); übereinkommen (*come to an agreement*), sich einigen.
agreeable [əˈgriːəbl], *adj.* angenehm, gefällig.
agreement [əˈgriːmənt], *s.* die Übereinstimmung, das Übereinkommen; der Vertrag, die Verständigung (*understanding*).
agricultural [ægriˈkʌltʃərəl], *adj.* landwirtschaftlich.
agriculture [ˈægrikʌltʃə], *s.* die Landwirtschaft.
aground [əˈgraund], *adj., adv.* (*Naut.*) gestrandet; *to run* —, stranden.
ague [ˈeigjuː], *s.* (*Med.*) der Schüttelfrost.
ah! [ɑː], *interj.* ach!; aha! (*surprise*).
aha! [ɑˈhɑː], *interj.* ach so!
ahead [əˈhed], *adv.* vorwärts, voran (*movement*), voraus (*position*), *go* — (*carry on*), fortfahren; *go* — (*make progress*), vorwärtskommen.
ahoy! [əˈhɔi], *interj.* (*Naut.*) ahoi!
aid [eid], *v.a.* helfen (*Dat.*), unterstützen (*Acc.*), beistehen (*Dat.*). — *s.* die Hilfe, der Beistand.
aide-de-camp [ˈeiddəˈkɑ̃], *s.* der Adjutant (*eines Generals*).
ail [eil], *v.n.* schmerzen; krank sein.
ailing [ˈeiliŋ], *adj.* kränklich, leidend.
ailment [ˈeilmənt], *s.* das Leiden.
aim [eim], *v.a.* (*weapon, blow etc.*) richten (*at, auf*). — *v.n.* zielen (*auf, Acc.*); trachten (*nach, strive for*). — *s*, das Ziel, der Zweck (*purpose*); die Absicht (*intention*).
aimless [ˈeimlis], *adj.* ziellos, zwecklos.

air [ɛə], s. die Luft; die Melodie (*tune*);
die Miene (*mien*); *air force*, die Luft-
waffe; *air pocket*, das Luftloch; *air
raid*, der Luftangriff; *in the open* —,
im Freien; *on the* —, im Rundfunk; *to
give oneself* —*s*, vornehm tun. — *v.a.*
lüften (*room*); trocknen (*washing*);
aussprechen (*views*).

airbase [ˈɛəbeis], s. der Fliegerstütz-
punkt.

airconditioning [ˈɛəkəndiʃəniŋ], s. die
Klimaanlage.

aircraft [ˈɛəkrɑ:ft], s. das Luftfahrzeug,
Flugzeug.

airgun [ˈɛəgʌn], s. die Windbüchse,
das Luftgewehr.

airiness [ˈɛərinis], s. die Luftigkeit,
Leichtigkeit.

airletter [ˈɛəletə], s. der Luftpostbrief.

airliner [ˈɛəlainə], s. das Verkehrs-
flugzeug.

airmail [ˈɛəmeil], s. die Luftpost.

airman [ˈɛəmən], s. der Flieger.

airplane *see* **aeroplane.**

airport [ˈɛəpɔ:t], s. der Flughafen.

airtight [ˈɛətait], adj. luftdicht.

airy [ˈɛəri], adj. luftig.

aisle [ail], s. das Seitenschiff (*church*);
der Gang.

Aix-la-Chapelle [ˈeikslaʃæˈpel].Aachen,
n.

ajar [əˈdʒɑ:], adv. angelehnt, halb
offen.

akimbo [əˈkimbou], adv. Hände an den
Hüften, Arme in die Seiten gestemmt.

akin [əˈkin], adj. verwandt (*to*, mit,
Dat.).

alack [əˈlæk], interj. ach! oh, weh! *alas
and* —, ach und wehe!

alacrity [əˈlækriti], s. die Bereitwilligkeit; Munterkeit.

alarm [əˈlɑ:m], s. der Alarm; Lärm
(*noise*); die Warnung; Angst, Bestürzung; — *clock*, der Wecker. — *v.a.*
erschrecken.

alas! [əˈlæs], interj. ach, wehe!

Albanian [ælˈbeiniən], adj. albanisch.
— s. der Albanier.

album [ˈælbəm], s. das Album.

albumen [ælˈbju:mən], s. das Eiweiß,
(*Chem.*) der Eiweißstoff.

albuminous [ælˈbju:minəs], adj. eiweiß-
haltig, Eiweiß-.

alchemist [ˈælkimist], s. der Alchimist.

alchemy [ˈælkimi], s. die Alchimie.

alcohol [ˈælkəhɔl], s. der Alkohol.

alcoholic [ælkəˈhɔlik], adj. alkoholisch.
— s. der Trinker, Alkoholiker.

alcove [ˈælkouv], s. der Alkoven.

alder [ˈɔ:ldə], s. (*Bot.*) die Erle.

alderman [ˈɔ:ldəmən], s. der Ratsherr,
der Stadtrat.

ale [eil], s. englisches Bier.

alert [əˈlə:t], adj. wachsam, aufmerksam; *on the* —, auf der Hut.

algebra [ˈældʒibrə], s. die Algebra.

Algerian [ælˈdʒiəriən], adj. algerisch.
— s. der Algerier.

Algiers [ælˈdʒiəz]. Algier, *n.*

alias [ˈeiliəs], adv. sonst genannt.

alien [ˈeiliən], adj. fremd, ausländisch.
— s. der Fremde, Ausländer.

alienate [ˈeiliəneit], v.a. entfremden.

alienation [eiliəˈneiʃən], s. die Entfremdung; — *of mind*, die Geisteser-
krankung, Geistesgestörtheit.

alienist [ˈeiliənist], s. der Irrenarzt.

alight (1) [əˈlait], v.n. absteigen (*from
horse*); aussteigen (*from carriage etc.*).

alight (2) [əˈlait], adj. brennend, in
Flammen.

alike [əˈlaik], adj. gleich, ähnlich. —
adv. *great and small* —, sowohl große
wie kleine.

alimentary [æliˈmentəri], adj. Nah-
rungs-, Verdauungs-; — *canal*, (*Anat.*)
der Darmkanal.

alimentation [ælimenˈteiʃən], s. die
Beköstigung; (*Law*) der Unterhalt.

alimony [ˈælimoni], s. der Unterhalts-
beitrag; (*pl.*) Alimente. , *n.pl.*

alive [əˈlaiv], adj. lebendig; — *and
kicking*, wohlauf, munter; — *to*,
empfänglich für.

alkali [ˈælkəlai], s. (*Chem.*) das Laugen-
salz, Alkali.

alkaline [ˈælkəlain], adj. (*Chem.*) alka-
lisch, laugensalzig.

all [ɔ:l], adj., pron. all, ganz (*whole*);
sämtliche, alle; *above* —, vor allem;
once and for —, ein für allemal; *not
at* —, keineswegs; *All Saints*, Allerheiligen; *All Souls*, Allerseelen. —
adv. ganz, gänzlich, völlig; — *the
same*, trotzdem; — *the better*, umso
besser.

allay [əˈlei], v.a. lindern, beruhigen,
unterdrücken.

allegation [æliˈgeiʃən], s. die Behauptung.

allege [əˈledʒ], v.a. behaupten, aussagen.

allegiance [əˈli:dʒəns], s. die Treue,
Ergebenheit; Untertanenpflicht.

allegorical [æliˈgɔrikəl], adj. allego-
risch, sinnbildlich.

alleviate [əˈli:vieit], v.a. erleichtern,
mildern.

alleviation [əli:viˈeiʃən], s. die Erleichterung, Milderung.

alley [ˈæli], s. die Gasse; Seitenstraße;
bowling —, die Kegelbahn.

alliance [əˈlaiəns], s. (*Pol.*) die Allianz,
das Bündnis (*treaty*); der Bund
(*league*).

allied [əˈlaid, ˈælaid], adj. verbündet,
vereinigt; alliiert; verwandt.

alliteration [əlitəˈreiʃən], s. die Alliteration, der Stabreim.

allocate [ˈælokeit], v.a. zuweisen,
zuteilen.

allot [əˈlɔt], v.a. zuteilen (*assign*);
verteilen (*distribute*).

allotment [əˈlɔtmənt], s. der Anteil;
die Zuteilung; die Landparzelle; die
Laubenkolonie, der Schrebergarten
(*garden*).

allow [əˈlau], v.a. gewähren (*grant*);
erlauben (*permit*); zulassen (*admit*). —
v.n. — *for*, Rücksicht nehmen auf
(*Acc.*); in Betracht ziehen.

allowance

allowance [ə'lauəns], *s.* die Rente; das Taschengeld (*money*); die Erlaubnis (*permission*); die Genehmigung (*approval*); die Nachsicht (*indulgence*).

alloy [ə'lɔi, 'ælɔi], *s.* die Legierung. — *v.a.* (Metall.) legieren.

allude [ə'lu:d], *v.a.* anspielen (*to*, auf).

allure [ə'ljuə], *v.a.* locken, anlocken.

allurement [ə'ljuəmənt], *s.* der Reiz, die Lockung.

allusion [ə'lu:ʒən], *s.* die Anspielung.

alluvial [ə'lu:viəl], *adj.* angeschwemmt.

alluvium [ə'lu:viəm], *s.* das Schwemmgebiet, Schwemmland.

ally ['ælai], *s.* der Verbündete, Bundesgenosse, Alliierte. — [ə'lai], *v.a., v.r.* (sich) vereinigen, (sich) verbünden.

almanac ['ɔ:lmənæk], *s.* der Almanach.

almighty [ɔ:l'maiti], *adj.* allmächtig; *God Almighty!* allmächtiger Gott!

almond ['a:mənd], *s.* (Bot.) die Mandel.

almoner ['ælmənə], *s.* der Wohlfahrtsbeamte, die Fürsorgerin.

almost ['ɔ:lmoust], *adv.* fast, beinahe.

alms [a:mz], *s.* das Almosen.

aloe ['ælou], *s.* (Bot.) die Aloe.

aloft [ə'lɔft], *adv.* droben, (hoch) oben; empor.

alone [ə'loun], *adj., adv.* allein; *all —*, ganz allein; *leave —*, in Ruhe lassen; *let —*, geschweige (denn).

along [ə'lɔŋ], *adv.* längs, der Länge nach; entlang, weiter; *come —!* komm mit!; *get — (with)*, auskommen. — *prep.* längs; entlang.

alongside [əlɔŋ'said], *adv.* nebenan. — [ə'lɔŋsaid], *prep.* neben.

aloof [ə'lu:f], *adj., adv.* fern, weitab; *keep —*, sich fernhalten.

aloofness [ə'lu:fnis], *s.* das Sichfernhalten; das Vornehmtun.

aloud [ə'laud], *adj., adv.* laut; hörbar.

alphabet ['ælfəbet], *s.* das Alphabet, Abc.

Alpine ['ælpain], *adj.* alpinisch, Alpen-.

Alps, The [ælps, ði], die Alpen, *pl.*

already [ɔ:l'redi], *adv.* schon, bereits.

Alsatian [æl'seiʃən], *adj.* elsässisch. — *s.* der Elsässer; (*dog*) der Wolfshund, deutscher Schäferhund.

also [ɔ:lsou], *adv.* (*likewise*) auch, ebenfalls; (*moreover*) ferner.

altar ['ɔ:ltə], *s.* der Altar.

alter ['ɔ:ltə], *v.a.* ändern, verändern. — *v.n.* sich (ver)ändern.

alterable ['ɔ:ltərəbl], *adj.* veränderlich.

alteration [ɔ:ltə'reiʃən], *s.* die Änderung, Veränderung.

altercation [ɔ:ltə'keiʃən], *s.* der Zank, Streit; Wortwechsel.

alternate ['ɔ:ltəneit], *v.a., v.n.* abwechseln lassen, abwechseln.

alternative [ɔ:l'tə:nativ], *adj.* abwechselnd, alternativ, zur Wahl gestellt. — *s.* die Alternative, die Wahl.

although [ɔ:l'ðou], *conj.* obgleich, obwohl, obschon.

altimeter ['æltimi:tə], *s.* der Höhenmesser.

altitude ['æltitju:d], *s.* die Höhe.

alto ['æltou], *s.* (Mus.) die Altstimme, der Alt.

altogether [ɔ:ltu'geðə], *adv.* zusammen, zusammengenommen, allesamt; (*wholly*) ganz und gar, durchaus.

alum ['æləm], *s.* (Chem.) der Alaun.

aluminium [ælju'minjəm], (*Am.*) **aluminum** [ə'lu:minəm], *s.* das Aluminium.

always ['ɔ:lweiz], *adv.* immer, stets.

am [æm] *see* **be**.

amalgamate [ə'mælgəmeit], *v.a.* amalgamieren. — *v.n.* sich vereinigen, vermischen.

amalgamation [əmælgə'meiʃən], *s.* die Verbindung, Vereinigung.

amass [ə'mæs], *v.a.* anhäufen, zusammentragen.

amateur [æmə'tə: or 'æmətjuə], *s.* der Amateur, Liebhaber.

amatory ['æmətəri], *adj.* Liebes-, verliebt, sinnlich.

amaze [ə'meiz], *v.a.* erstaunen, in Erstaunen versetzen; verblüffen (*baffle*).

amazement [ə'meizmənt], *s.* das Erstaunen, Staunen, die Verwunderung.

amazing [ə'meiziŋ], *adj.* erstaunlich, wunderbar.

Amazon (1) ['æməzən], *s.* (Myth.) die Amazone.

Amazon (2) ['æməzən], *s.* (*river*) der Amazonas.

ambassador [æm'bæsədə], *s.* der Botschafter.

ambassadorial [æmbæsə'dɔ:riəl], *adj.* Botschafts-.

amber ['æmbə], *s.* der Bernstein.

ambidextrous [æmbi'dekstrəs], *adj.* (mit beiden Händen gleich) geschickt.

ambiguity [æmbi'gju:iti], *s.* die Zweideutigkeit, der Doppelsinn.

ambiguous [æm'bigjuəs], *adj.* zweideutig; dunkel (*sense*).

ambit ['æmbit], *s.* der Umkreis, die Umgebung.

ambition [æm'biʃən], *s.* die Ambition, der Ehrgeiz.

ambitious [æm'biʃəs], *adj.* ehrgeizig.

amble [æmbl], *v.n.* schlendern, (gemächlich) spazieren.

ambulance ['æmbjuləns], *s.* der Krankenwagen.

ambush ['æmbuʃ], *v.a.* überfallen (*Acc.*), auflauern (*Dat.*). — *s.* die Falle, der Hinterhalt.

ameliorate [ə'mi:liəreit], *v.a.* verbessern.

amenable [ə'mi:nəbl], *adj.* zugänglich; unterworfen.

amend [ə'mend], *v.a.* verbessern, berichtigen; ändern.

amendment [ə'mendmənt], *s.* die Verbesserung; der Zusatz, die zusätzliche Änderung (*proposal*).

amends [ə'mendz], *s. pl.* der Schadenersatz; *make —*, Schadenersatz leisten; wiedergutmachen.

amenity [ə'mi:niti *or* ə'meniti], *s.* die Behaglichkeit, Annehmlichkeit; (*pl.*) die Vorzüge, *m pl.*; die Einrichtungen, *f. pl.*

American [ə'merikən], *adj.* amerikanisch; — *cloth*, das Wachstuch. — *s.* der Amerikaner.

amiability [eimjə'biliti], *s.* die Liebenswürdigkeit.

amiable ['eimjəbl], *adj.* liebenswürdig.

amicable ['æmikəbl], *adj.* freundschaftlich.

amidst [ə'midst], *prep.* mitten in, mitten unter (*Dat.*), inmitten (*Gen.*).

amiss [ə'mis], *adj.*, *adv.* übel; verkehrt; *take* —, übelnehmen.

amity ['æmiti], *s.* die Freundschaft.

ammonia [ə'mouniə], *s.* das Ammoniak; *liquid* —, der Salmiakgeist.

ammunition [æmju'niʃən], *s.* die Munition.

amnesty ['æmnisti], *s.* die Amnestie, Begnadigung.

among(st) [ə'mʌŋ(st)], *prep.* (mitten) unter, zwischen, bei.

amorous ['æmərəs], *adj.* verliebt.

amorphous [ə'mɔ:fəs], *adj.* amorph, gestaltlos, formlos.

amortization [əmɔ:ti'zeiʃən], *s.* die Amortisierung (*debt*); (*Comm.*) Tilgung, Abtragung.

amount [ə'maunt], *s.* der Betrag (*sum of money*); die Menge (*quantity*). — *v.n.* betragen; — *to*, sich belaufen auf (*Acc.*).

amphibian [æm'fibiən], *adj.* amphibisch. — *s.* (*Zool.*) die Amphibie.

amphibious [æm'fibiəs], *adj.* amphibienhaft.

ample [æmpl], *adj.* weit, breit (*scope*); voll, reichlich; ausgebreitet; genügend.

amplification [æmplifi'keiʃən], *s.* die Ausbreitung; Verbreiterung, Erklärung, Erweiterung; (*Elec.*) die Verstärkung (*sound*).

amplifier ['æmplifaiə], *s.* der Verstärker; der Lautsprecher.

amplify ['æmplifai], *v.a.* erweitern, ausführen, vergrößern; verstärken (*sound*).

amputate ['æmpjuteit], *v.a.* amputieren.

amputation [æmpju'teiʃən], *s.* die Amputation.

amuck [ə'mʌk], *adv.* amok.

amulet ['æmjulit], *s.* das Amulett.

amuse [ə'mju:z], *v.a.* unterhalten, amüsieren.

amusement [ə'mju:zmənt], *s.* die Unterhaltung, das Vergnügen.

an *see under* **a**.

Anabaptist [ænə'bæptist], *s.* der Wiedertäufer.

anachronism [ə'nækrənizm], *s.* der Anachronismus.

anaemia [ə'ni:miə], *s.* (*Med.*) die Blutarmut.

anaemic [ə'ni:mik], *adj.* (*Med.*) blutarm.

anaesthetic [ænəs'θetik], *adj.* schmerzbetäubend. — *s.* die Narkose.

analogous [ə'næləgəs], *adj.* analog.

analogy [ə'nælədʒi], *s.* die Analogie.

analyse ['ænəlaiz], *v.a.* analysieren.

analysis [ə'nælisis], *s.* die Analyse.

anarchic(al) [ə'na:kik(əl)], *adj.* anarchisch.

anarchy ['ænəki], *s.* die Anarchie.

anathema [ə'næθimə], *s.* (*Eccl.*) der Kirchenbann.

anatomical [ænə'tɔmikəl], *adj.* anatomisch.

anatomist [ə'nætəmist], *s.* der Anatom.

anatomize [ə'nætəmaiz], *v.a.* zergliedern, zerlegen.

anatomy [ə'nætəmi], *s.* die Anatomie.

ancestor ['ænsəstə], *s.* der Vorfahre, Ahnherr.

ancestry ['ænsəstri], *s.* die Ahnenreihe, Herkunft, der Stammbaum (*family tree*).

anchor ['æŋkə], *s.* der Anker. — *v.a.* verankern. — *v.n.* ankern.

anchorage ['æŋkəridʒ], *s.* die Verankerung; der Ankerplatz.

anchovy [æn'tʃouvi *or* 'æntʃəvi], *s.* (*Zool.*) die Sardelle.

ancient ['einʃənt], *adj.* alt, uralt, antik; althergebracht (*traditional*). — ' *s.* (*pl.*) die Alten (Griechen und Römer).

and [ænd], *conj.* und.

Andes, the ['ændi:z, ði]. die Anden, *pl.*

anecdote ['ænekdout], *s.* die Anekdote.

anemone [ə'neməni], *s.* (*Bot.*) die Anemone, das Windröschen; (*Zool.*) *sea* —, die Seeanemone.

anew [ə'nju:], *adv.* von neuem.

angel ['eindʒəl], *s.* der Engel.

angelic [æn'dʒelik], *adj.* engelhaft, engelgleich.

anger ['æŋgə], *s.* der Zorn, Unwille, Ärger. — *v.a.* erzürnen, verärgern, ärgerlich machen.

angle [æŋgl], *s.* (*Geom.*) der Winkel; die Angel (*fishing*). — *v.n.* angeln (*for*, nach).

Angles [æŋglz], *s. pl.* die Angeln, *m. pl.*

Anglo-Saxon [æŋglou'sæksən], *adj.* angelsächsisch. — *s.* der Angelsachse.

anglicism ['æŋglisizm], *s.* der Anglizismus (*style*).

anguish ['æŋgwiʃ], *s.* die Qual, Pein.

angular ['æŋgjulə], *adj.* winklig, eckig.

anhydrous [æn'haidrəs], *adj.* wasserfrei, (*Chem.*) wasserlos.

aniline ['ænilain], *s.* das Anilin. — *adj.* — *dye*, die Anilinfarbe.

animal ['æniməl], *s.* das Tier, Lebewesen.

animate ['ænimeit], *v.a.* beleben, beseelen; (*fig.*) anregen.

animated ['ænimeitid], *adj.* belebt; munter.

animation [æni'meiʃən], *s.* die Belebung.

animosity [æni'mɔsiti], *s.* die Feindseligkeit, Abneigung, Erbitterung.

anise ['ænis], *s.* (*Bot.*) der Anis.

ankle

ankle [ˈæŋkl], *s.* (*Anat.*) der Fußknöchel; — *socks*, kurze Socken.

anklet [ˈæŋklit], *s.* der Fußring.

annalist [ˈænəlist], *s.* der Chronist, Geschichtsschreiber.

annals [ˈænəlz], *s. pl.* die Annalen (*f. pl.*); die Chronik (*sing.*).

anneal [əˈniːl], *v.a.* ausglühen.

annex [əˈneks], *v.a.* annektieren, angliedern, sich aneignen.

annex(e) [ˈæneks], *s.* der Anhang, der Anbau.

annexation [ænekˈseiʃən], *s.* die Angliederung, Aneignung.

annihilate [əˈnaiileit], *v.a.* vernichten, zerstören.

annihilation [ənaiiˈleiʃən], *s.* die Vernichtung, Zerstörung.

anniversary [æniˈvəːsəri], *s.* der Jahrestag, die Jahresfeier.

annotate [ˈænoteit], *v.a.* anmerken, mit Anmerkungen versehen.

annotation [ænoˈteiʃən], *s.* die Anmerkung, Notiz.

announce [əˈnauns], *v.a.* melden, ankündigen; anzeigen; (*Rad.*) ansagen.

announcement [əˈnaunsmənt], *s.* die Ankündigung, Bekanntmachung; (*Rad.*) die Ansage.

announcer [əˈnaunsə], *s.* (*Rad.*) der Ansager.

annoy [əˈnɔi], *v.a.* ärgern; belästigen.

annoyance [əˈnɔiəns], *s.* das Ärgernis; die Belästigung.

annual [ˈænjuəl], *adj.* jährlich, Jahres-. — *s.* der Jahresband (*serial publication*); das Jahrbuch; (*Bot.*) die einjährige Pflanze.

annuity [əˈnjuːiti], *s.* die Jahresrente, Lebensrente.

annul [əˈnʌl], *v.a.* annullieren, ungültig machen, für ungültig erklären.

annulment [əˈnʌlmənt], *s.* die Annullierung, Ungültigkeitserklärung.

Annunciation [ənʌnsiˈeiʃən], *s.* (*Eccl.*) die Verkündigung.

anode [ˈænoud], *s.* die Anode.

anodyne [ˈænodain], *adj.* schmerzstillend.

anoint [əˈnɔint], *v.a.* salben.

anomalous [əˈnɔmələs], *adj.* abweichend, unregelmäßig, anomal.

anomaly [əˈnɔməli], *s.* die Anomalie, Abweichung, Unregelmäßigkeit.

anon [əˈnɔn], *adv.* sogleich, sofort.

anonymous [əˈnɔniməs], *adj.* (*abbr.* **anon.**) anonym; namenlos; unbekannt.

anonymity [ænoˈnimiti], *s.* die Anonymität.

another [əˈnʌðə], *adj. & pron.* ein anderer; ein zweiter; noch einer; *one* —, einander.

answer [ˈɑːnsə], *v.a.* beantworten. — *v.n.* antworten. — *s.* die Antwort, Erwiderung.

answerable [ˈɑːnsərəbl], *adj.* verantwortlich (*responsible*); beantwortbar (*capable of being answered*).

ant [ænt], *s.* (*Ent.*) die Ameise.

antagonise [ænˈtægənaiz], *v.a.* sich (*Dat.*) jemanden zum Gegner machen.

antagonism [ænˈtægənizm], *s.* der Widerstreit, Konflikt; der Antagonismus.

Antarctic [æntˈɑːktik], *adj.* Südpol-, antarktisch. — *s.* der südliche Polarkreis.

antecedence [æntiˈsiːdəns], *s.* der Vortritt (*rank*).

antecedent [æntiˈsiːdənt], *s.* (*pl.*) das Vorhergehende, die Vorgeschichte.

antedate [ˈæntideit], *v.a.* vordatieren.

antediluvian [æntidiˈluːviən], *adj.* vorsintflutlich;(*fig.*) überholt; altmodisch.

antelope [ˈæntiloup], *s.* (*Zool.*) die Antilope.

antenna [ænˈtenə], *s.* (*Ent.*) der Fühler; (*Rad.*) die Antenne.

anterior [ænˈtiəriə], *adj.* vorder (*in space*), älter, vorherig, vorhergehend, (*in time*).

anteroom [ˈæntiruːm], *s.* das Vorzimmer.

anthem [ˈænθəm], *s.* die Hymne, der Hymnus.

anther [ˈænθə], *s.* (*Bot.*) der Staubbeutel.

antic [ˈæntik], *s.* die Posse; (*pl.*) komisches Benehmen.

anticipate [ænˈtisipeit], *v.a.* vorwegnehmen; zuvorkommen; ahnen (*guess*); erwarten (*await*); vorgreifen.

anticipation [æntisiˈpeiʃən], *s.* die Vorwegnahme; die Erwartung.

antidote [ˈæntidout], *s.* das Gegengift.

antipathy [ænˈtipəθi], *s.* die Antipathie, der Widerwille.

antipodal [ænˈtipədəl], *adj.* antipodisch; entgegengesetzt.

antiquarian [æntiˈkwɛəriən], *adj.* altertümlich; antiquarisch.

antiquary [ˈæntikwəri], *s.* der Altertumsforscher, Antiquar.

antiquated [ˈæntikweitid], *adj.* überholt, unmodern, veraltet.

antique [ænˈtiːk], *s.* die Antike; das alte Kunstwerk. — *adj.* alt, antik; altmodisch.

antiquity [ænˈtikwiti], *s.* die Antike, das Altertum; die Vorzeit (*period of history*).

antiseptic [æntiˈseptik], *adj.* antiseptisch — *s.* das antiseptische Mittel.

antler [ˈæntlə], *s.* die Geweihsprosse; (*pl.*) das Geweih.

anvil [ˈænvil], *s.* der Amboß.

anxiety [æŋˈzaiəti], *s.* die Angst (*fear*); Besorgnis (*uneasiness*); Unruhe.

anxious [ˈæŋkʃəs], *adj.* ängstlich (*afraid*); besorgt (*worried*); eifrig bemüht (*keen*, um, *on*, *Acc.*).

any [ˈeni], *adj. & pron.* jeder; irgendein; etwas; (*pl.*) einige; (*neg.*) *not* —, kein.

anybody, anyone [ˈenibɔdi, ˈeniwʌn], *pron.* irgendwer; jemand; jeder.

anyhow, anyway [ˈenihau, ˈeniwei], *adv.* irgendwie, auf irgendeine Weise; auf alle Fälle.

anyone *see under* **anybody.**

apprentice

anything ['eniθiŋ], s. irgend etwas; alles.
anyway see under anyhow.
anywhere ['enihweə], adv. irgendwo; überall; not —, nirgends.
apace [ə'peis], adv. geschwind, hurtig, flink.
apart [ə'pɑ:t], adv. für sich, abgesondert; einzeln; poles —, weit entfernt; take —, zerlegen; — from, abgesehen von.
apartment [ə'pɑ:tmənt], s. das Zimmer; (Am.) die Wohnung (flat).
apathy ['æpəθi], s. die Apathie, Interesselosigkeit, Gleichgültigkeit.
apathetic [æpə'θetik], adj. apathisch, uninteressiert; teilnahmslos.
ape [eip], s. (Zool.) der Affe. — v.a. nachäffen, nachahmen.
aperient [ə'piəriənt], adj. (Med.) abführend. — s. (Med.) das Abführmittel.
aperture ['æpətʃə], s. die Öffnung.
apex ['eipeks], s. die Spitze, der Gipfel.
aphorism ['æfərizm], s. der Aphorismus.
apiary ['eipiəri], s. das Bienenhaus.
apiece [ə'pi:s], adv. pro Stück, pro Person.
apologetic [əpɔlə'dʒetik], adj. entschuldigend, reumütig; verteidigend.
apologize [ə'pɔlədʒaiz], v.n. sich entschuldigen (for, wegen; to, bei).
apology [ə'pɔlədʒi], s. die Entschuldigung; Abbitte; Rechtfertigung.
apoplectic [æpə'plektik], adj. (Med.) apoplektisch.
apoplexy [æpəpleksi], s. (Med.) der Schlagfluß, Schlaganfall (fit).
apostle [ə'pɔsl], s. der Apostel.
apostolic [æpəs'tɔlik], adj. apostolisch.
apostrophe [ə'pɔstrəfi], s. der Apostroph (punctuation); die Anrede (speech).
apostrophize [ə'pɔstrəfaiz], v.a. apostrophieren; anreden (speak to).
apotheosis [əpɔθi'ousis], s. die Apotheose.
appal [ə'pɔ:l], v.a. erschrecken.
appalling [ə'pɔ:liŋ], adj. schrecklich.
apparatus [æpə'reitəs], s. das Gerät, die Apparatur; (coll.) der Apparat.
apparel [ə'pærəl], s. die Kleidung.
apparent [ə'pærənt], adj. scheinbar; offensichtlich; augenscheinlich; heir —, der rechtmäßige Erbe.
apparition [æpə'riʃən], s. die Erscheinung; der Geist, das Gespenst (ghost).
appeal [ə'pi:l], v.n. appellieren (make an appeal); (Law) Berufung einlegen; gefallen (please). — s. (public, Mil.) der Appell; die Bitte (request).
appear [ə'piə], v.n. erscheinen; scheinen; auftreten.
appearance [ə'piərəns], s. die Erscheinung; das Auftreten (stage, etc.); der Schein (semblance); keep up —s, den Schein wahren; to all —s, allem Anschein nach.

appease [ə'pi:z], v.a. besänftigen.
appeasement [ə'pi:zmənt], s. die Besänftigung, (Pol.) die Befriedung.
appellation [æpe'leiʃən], s. die Benennung.
append [ə'pend], v.a. anhängen, beifügen.
appendicitis [əpendi'saitis], s. (Med.) die Blinddarmentzündung.
appendix [ə'pendiks], s. der Anhang; (Med.) der Blinddarm.
appertain [æpə'tein], v.n. gehören (to, zu).
appetite ['æpitait], s. der Appetit.
appetizing ['æpitaiziŋ], adj. appetitlich, appetitanregend.
applaud [ə'plɔ:d], v.a., v.n. applaudieren, Beifall klatschen (Dat.).
applause [ə'plɔ:z], s. der Applaus, Beifall.
apple [æpl], s. der Apfel.
appliance [ə'plaiəns], s. das Gerät, die Vorrichtung.
applicable ['æplikəbl], adj. anwendbar, passend (to, auf).
applicant ['æplikənt], s. der Bewerber (for, um).
application [æpli'keiʃən], s. die Bewerbung (for, um); das Gesuch; die Anwendung (to, auf); letter of —, der Bewerbungsbrief; — form, das Bewerbungsformular.
apply [ə'plai], v.a. anwenden (auf, to, Acc.); gebrauchen. — v.n. sich bewerben (um, for, Acc.); (Dat.) this does not —, das trifft nicht zu; — within, drinnen nachfragen.
appoint [ə'pɔint], v.a. bestimmen; ernennen; ausrüsten.
appointment [ə'pɔintmənt], s. die Festsetzung; die Ernennung; die Bestellung, die Stellung (position); make an —, jemanden ernennen (fill a post), sich verabreden (arrange to meet); by —, Hoflieferant (to, Genit.).
apportion [ə'pɔ:ʃən], v.a. zuteilen, zuweisen, zumessen.
apposite ['æpəzit], adj. passend, angemessen.
appositeness ['æpəzitnis], s. die Angemessenheit.
appraise [ə'preiz], v.a. beurteilen.
appraisal [ə'preizəl], s. die Beurteilung, Abschätzung.
appreciable [ə'pri:ʃəbl], adj. merklich; nennenswert.
appreciate [ə'pri:ʃieit], v.a. würdigen, schätzen.
appreciation [əpri:ʃi'eiʃən], s. die Schätzung, Würdigung.
apprehend [æpri'hend], v.a. verhaften, ergreifen (arrest); befürchten (fear).
apprehension [æpri'henʃən], s. die Verhaftung (arrest); die Befürchtung (fear).
apprehensive [æpri'hensiv], adj. besorgt, in Furcht (for, um), furchtsam.
apprentice [ə'prentis], s. der Lehrling; Praktikant. — v.a. in die Lehre geben (with, bei, Dat.).

apprenticeship

apprenticeship [ə'prentiʃip], *s.* die Lehre, Lehrzeit, Praktikantenzeit; *student* —, die Studentenpraxis.

apprise [ə'praiz], *v.a.* benachrichtigen, informieren.

approach [ə'proutʃ], *v.a., v.n.* sich nähern (*Dat.*). — *s.* die Annäherung, das Herankommen, Näherrücken.

approachable [ə'proutʃəbl], *adj.* zugänglich, freundlich.

approbation [æpro'beiʃən], *s.* die (offizielle) Billigung, Zustimmung.

appropriate [ə'proupriit], *adj.* angemessen, gebührend, geeignet (*suitable*). — [ə'prouprieit], *v.a.* requirieren, sich aneignen.

appropriation [əproupri'eiʃən], *s.* die Requisition, Aneignung, Übernahme, Besitznahme.

approval [ə'pru:vəl], *s.* die Billigung, der Beifall, die Zustimmung.

approve [ə'pru:v], *v.a.* loben, billigen; genehmigen; annehmen (*work*).

approved [ə'pru:vd], *adj.* anerkannt.

approximate [ə'prɔksimit], *adj.* ungefähr, annähernd. — [ə'prɔksimeit], *v.a., v.n.* sich nähern.

approximation [əprɔksi'meiʃən], *s.* die Annäherung.

approximative [ə'prɔksimətiv], *adj.* annähernd.

appurtenance [ə'pə:tənəns], *s.* das (*or* der) Zubehör.

appurtenant [ə'pə:tənənt], *adj.* zugehörig.

apricot ['eiprikɔt], *s.* (*Bot.*) die Aprikose.

April ['eipril]. der April.

apron ['eiprən], *s.* die Schürze; der Schurz; — *stage*, die Vorbühne, das Proszenium.

apropos [apro'pou], *adv.* beiläufig; mit Bezug auf, diesbezüglich.

apse [æps], *s.* (*Archit.*) die Apsis.

apt [æpt], *adj.* geeignet, passend; fähig.

aptitude ['æptitju:d], *s.* die Eignung, Fähigkeit.

aptness ['æptnis], *s.* die Angemessenheit, Eignung.

aquatic [ə'kwɔtik *or* ə'kwætik], *adj.* Wasser-, wasser-; — *display*, Wasserkünste. — *s.* (*pl.*) der Wassersport.

aqueduct ['ækwidʌkt], *s.* die Wasserleitung; der Aquädukt.

aqueous ['eikwiəs], *adj.* (*Chem.*) wässerig.

aquiline ['ækwilain], *adj.* adlerartig, Adler-.

Arab ['ærəb], *s.* der Araber.

Arabian [ə'reibiən], *adj.* arabisch; — *Nights*, Tausend-und-eine-Nacht.

Arabic ['ærəbik], *adj.* arabisch (*language, literature*).

arable ['ærəbl], *adj.* pflügbar, bestellbar.

arbiter ['a:bitə], *s.* der Schiedsrichter.

arbitrary ['a:bitrəri], *adj.* willkürlich.

arbitrate ['a:bitreit], *v.n.* vermitteln.

arbitration [a:bi'treiʃən], *s.* die Vermittlung; Entscheidung; (*Comm.*) Arbitrage.

arboriculture ['a:bɔrikʌltʃə], *s.* die Baumzucht.

arbour ['a:bə], *s.* die Laube, Gartenlaube.

arc [a:k], *s.* (*Geom.*) der Bogen; — *lamp*, die Bogenlampe; — *welding*, das Lichtschweißen.

arcade [a:'keid], *s.* die Arkade.

Arcadian [a:'keidiən], *adj.* arkadisch. — *s.* der Arkadier.

arch [a:tʃ], *s.* der Bogen, die Wölbung; —*way*, der Bogengang. — *v.a., v.n.* wölben, sich wölben. — *adj.* schelmisch, listig. — *prefix.* oberst; erst, Haupt-; — *-enemy*, der Erzfeind.

archaeological [a:kiə'lɔdʒikəl], *adj.* archäologisch.

archaeologist [a:ki'ɔlədʒist], *s.* der Archäologe.

archaeology [a:ki'ɔlədʒi], *s.* die Archäologie.

archaic [a:'keiik], *adj.* altertümlich.

archaism ['a:keiizm], *s.* der Archaismus (*style*).

archbishop [a:tʃ'biʃəp], *s.* der Erzbischof.

archduke [a:tʃ'dju:k], *s.* der Erzherzog.

archer ['a:tʃə], *s.* der Bogenschütze.

archery ['a:tʃəri], *s.* das Bogenschießen.

architect ['a:kitekt], *s.* der Architekt, Baumeister.

architecture ['a:kitektʃə], *s.* die Architektur, Baukunst.

archives ['a:kaivz], *s. pl.* das Archiv.

Arctic ['a:ktik], *adj.* arktisch. — *s.* die Nordpolarländer, *n. pl.*

ardent ['a:dənt], *adj.* heiß, glühend, brennend.

ardour ['a:də], *s.* die Hitze, die Inbrunst, der Eifer.

arduous ['a:djuəs], *adj.* schwierig; mühsam.

area ['ɛəriə], *s.* das Areal (*measurement*); das Gebiet, die Zone; die Fläche (*region*).

arena [ə'ri:nə], *s.* die Arena, der Kampfplatz.

Argentine ['a:dʒəntain], *adj.* argentinisch. — (*Republic*), Argentinien, *n.*

Argentinian [a:dʒən'tiniən], *adj.* argentinisch. — *s.* der Argentin(i)er.

argue ['a:gju:], *v.n.* disputieren, streiten; folgern, schließen.

argument ['a:gjumənt], *s.* das Argument; (*Log.*) der Beweis; der Streit (*dispute*).

argumentative [a:gju'mentətiv], *adj.* streitsüchtig.

arid ['ærid], *adj.* trocken, dürr.

aright [ə'rait], *adv.* richtig, zurecht.

arise [ə'raiz], *v.n. irr.* aufstehen; sich erheben; entstehen (*originate*); *arising from the minutes*, es ergibt sich aus dem Protokoll.

aristocracy [æris'tɔkrəsi], *s.* die Aristokratie, der Adel.

aristocratic [æristo'krætik], *adj.* aristokratisch, adlig.

arithmetic [ə'riθmətik], *s.* die Arithmetik.

arithmetical [æriθ'metikəl], *adj.* arithmetisch.

ark [ɑːk], *s.* die Arche; — *of the Covenant*, die Bundeslade.

arm (1) [ɑːm], *s.* (*Anat.*) der Arm.

arm (2) [ɑːm], *s.* die Waffe; *up in —s*, in Aufruhr. — *v.a., v.n.* bewaffnen, sich bewaffnen, rüsten, sich rüsten.

armament ['ɑːməmənt], *s.* die Rüstung, Bewaffnung.

armature ['ɑːmətiuə], *s.* die Armatur.

armchair ['ɑːmtʃɛə], *s.* der Lehnstuhl; der Sessel.

Armenian [ɑːˈmiːniən], *adj.* armenisch. — *s.* der Armenier.

armistice ['ɑːmistis], *s.* der Waffenstillstand.

armour ['ɑːmə], *s.* die Rüstung, der Harnisch; —*plated*, gepanzert; —*ed car*, der Panzerwagen.

armourer ['ɑːmərə], *s.* der Waffenschmied.

armoury ['ɑːməri], *s.* die Rüstkammer, Waffenschmiede.

army ['ɑːmi], *s.* die Armee, das Heer.

aroma [əˈroumə], *s.* das Aroma, die Duft.

aromatic [ærəˈmætik], *adj.* aromatisch. —*s.* (*Chem.*) das Aromat.

around [ə'raund], *adv.* herum, rundringsherum, umher, im Kreise; *stand —*, herumstehen; *be —*, sich in der Nähe halten. — *prep.* um; bei, um ... herum.

arouse [ə'rauz], *v.a.* aufwecken, aufrütteln.

arraignment [ə'reinmənt], *s.* die Anklage.

arrange [ə'reindʒ], *v.a.* anordnen, arrangieren, einrichten, vereinbaren.

arrangement [ə'reindʒmənt], *s.* die Anordnung; die Einrichtung; die Vereinbarung (*agreement*); (*Law*) die Vergleichung, der Vergleich.

arrant ['ærənt], *adj.* durchtrieben.

array [ə'rei], *v.a.* schmücken, aufstellen. — *s.* die Ordnung; Aufstellung.

arrears [ə'riəz], *s. pl.* der Rückstand, die Schulden.

arrest [ə'rest], *v.a.* (*Law*) festnehmen, verhaften; festhalten; aufhalten (*hinder*). — *s.* die Festnahme; die Festhaltung.

arrival [ə'raivəl], *s.* die Ankunft.

arrive [ə'raiv], *v.n.* ankommen.

arrogance ['ærəgəns], *s.* die Anmaßung, Überheblichkeit.

arrogant ['ærəgənt], *adj.* anmaßend, hochfahrend, überheblich.

arrow ['ærou], *s.* der Pfeil.

arrowroot ['ærouruːt], *s.* (*Bot.*) die Pfeilwurz.

arsenal ['ɑːsinəl], *s.* das Arsenal, Zeughaus.

arsenic ['ɑːsənik], *s.* das Arsen.

arson [ɑːsn], *s.* die Brandstiftung.

art [ɑːt], *s.* die Kunst; *fine —*, schöne Kunst; (*Univ.*) —*s faculty*, die philosophische Fakultät; —*s* (*subject*), das humanistische Fach, die Geisteswissenschaften.

arterial [ɑːˈtiəriəl], *adj.* Pulsader-, Schlagader-; — *road*, die Hauptverkehrsader, die Hauptstraße.

artery ['ɑːtəri], *s.* die Pulsader, Schlagader; der Hauptverkehrsweg.

artesian [ɑːˈtiːʒən], *adj.* artesisch.

artful ['ɑːtful], *adj.* listig, schlau.

article ['ɑːtikl], *s.* (*Gram., Law, Press*) der Artikel; der Posten (*item in list*). — *v.a. be* —*d to a solicitor*, bei einem Advokaten assistieren.

articulate [ɑːˈtikjuleit], *v.a.* artikulieren (*pronounce clearly*); — [—lit], *adj.* deutlich (*speech*).

articulation [ɑːtikjuˈleiʃən], *s.* die Artikulation, deutliche Aussprache.

artifice ['ɑːtifis], *s.* der Kunstgriff, die List.

artificer [ɑːˈtifisə], *s.* der Handwerker.

artificial [ɑːtiˈfiʃəl], *adj.* künstlich, Kunst-; — *silk*, die Kunstseide.

artillery [ɑːˈtiləri], *s.* die Artillerie.

artisan [ɑːtiˈzæn], *s.* der Handwerker.

artist ['ɑːtist], *s.* der Künstler, die Künstlerin.

artistic [ɑːˈtistik], *adj.* künstlerisch.

artless ['ɑːtlis], *adj.* arglos, natürlich, naiv.

Aryan ['ɛəriən], *adj.* arisch. — *s.* der Arier.

as [æz], *adv., conj.* so, als, wie, ebenso; als, während, weil; — *big* —, so groß wie; — *well* —, sowohl als auch; *such* —, wie; — *it were*, gleichsam.

asbestos [æz'bestəs], *s.* der Asbest.

ascend [ə'send], *v.a., v.n.* ersteigen, besteigen; emporsteigen.

ascendancy, -ency [ə'sendənsi], *s.* der Aufstieg; der Einfluß; das Übergewicht.

ascendant, -ent [ə'sendənt], *s. in the —*, aufsteigend.

ascent [ə'sent], *s.* der Aufstieg, die Besteigung.

ascension [ə'senʃən], *s.* (*Astron.*) das Aufsteigen; *Ascension Day*, Himmelfahrt(stag).

ascertain [æsə'tein], *v.a.* in Erfahrung bringen, erkunden, feststellen.

ascertainable [æsə'teinəbl], *adj.* erkundbar, feststellbar.

ascetic [ə'setik], *adj.* asketisch.

asceticism [ə'setisizm], *s.* die Askese.

ascribe [ə'skraib], *v.a.* zuschreiben.

ascribable [ə'skraibəbl], *adj.* zuzuschreiben, zuschreibbar.

ash (1) [æʃ], *s.* (*Bot.*) die Esche.

ash (2) [æʃ], *s.* die Asche.

ashamed [ə'ʃeimd], *adj.* beschämt; *be —*, sich schämen.

ashcan ['æʃkæn] (*Am.*) *see* dustbin.

ashen ['æʃən], *adj.* aschgrau, aschfarben.

ashore [ə'ʃɔː], *adv.* am Land; am Ufer, ans Ufer *or* Land.

ashtray ['æʃtrei], *s.* der Aschenbecher.

Ash Wednesday [æʃ'wenzdei], *s.* der Aschermittwoch.

Asiatic [eiʃi'ætik], *adj.* asiatisch. — *s.* der Asiat.

aside [ə′said], *adv.* seitwärts, zur Seite; abseits.

ask [ɑ:sk], *v.a., v.n.* fragen (*question*); bitten (*request*); fordern (*demand*); einladen (*invite*).

asleep [ə′sli:p], *pred. adj., adv.* schlafend, im Schlaf; eingeschlafen.

asp [æsp], *s.* (*Zool.*) die Natter.

asparagus [æs′pærəgəs], *s.* (*Bot.*) der Spargel.

aspect [′æspekt], *s.* der Anblick, die Ansicht (*view, angle*); der Gesichtspunkt.

aspen [′æspən], *s.* (*Bot.*) die Espe.

asperity [æs′periti], *s.* die Härte; die Rauheit.

aspersion [æs′pə:ʃən], *s.* die Verleumdung; Schmähung.

asphalt [′æsfælt], *s.* der Asphalt.

asphyxia [æs′fiksjə], *s.* (*Med.*) die Erstickung.

aspirant [ə′spaiərənt, ′æsp-], *s.* der Bewerber, Anwärter.

aspirate [′æspireit], *v.a.* (*Phon.*) aspirieren. — [—rit] *adj.* aspiriert. — *s.* der Hauchlaut.

aspiration [æspi′reiʃən], *s.* der Atemzug; das Streben (*striving*) ; (*Phon.*) die Aspiration.

aspire [ə′spaiə], *v.n.* streben, verlangen.

ass [æs], *s.* der Esel.

assail [ə′seil], *v.a.* angreifen, anfallen.

assailable [ə′seiləbl], *adj.* angreifbar.

assassin [ə′sæsin], *s.* der Meuchelmörder.

assassinate [ə′sæsineit], *v.a.* meuchlings ermorden.

assassination [əsæsi′neiʃən], *s.* der Meuchelmord, die Ermordung.

assault [ə′sɔ:lt], *v.a.* angreifen, überfallen. — *s.* der Überfall, Angriff.

assay [ə′sei], *s.* die Metallprobe. — *v.a.* (auf Edelmetall hin) prüfen.

assemble [ə′sembl], *v.a., v.n.* versammeln, sich versammeln.

assembly [ə′sembli], *s.* die Versammlung (*assemblage*); — line, das laufende Band, das Fließband.

assent [ə′sent], *v.n.* beistimmen (*Dat.*), billigen (*Acc.*). — *s.* die Zustimmung (zu, *Dat.*), Billigung (*Genit.*).

assert [ə′sə:t], *v.a.* behaupten.

assertion [ə′sə:ʃən], *s.* die Behauptung.

assess [ə′ses], *v.a.* schätzen, beurteilen.

assessment [ə′sesmənt], *s.* die Beurteilung, Schätzung, Wertung.

assessor [ə′sesə], *s.* der Beurteiler, Einschätzer, Bewerter, Assessor; der Beisitzer (*second examiner*).

assets [′æsets], *s. pl.* (*Comm.*) die Aktiva; Vorzüge (*personal*).

assiduity [æsi′dju:iti], *s.* der Fleiß, die Emsigkeit.

assiduous [ə′sidjuəs], *adj.* fleißig, unablässig, emsig.

assign [ə′sain], *v.a.* zuteilen, anweisen, zuweisen (*apportion*), festsetzen (*fix*).

assignable [ə′sainəbl], *adj.* zuteilbar; bestimmbar.

assignation [æsig′neiʃən], *s.* die Zuweisung; (*Law*) die Übertragung; die Verabredung.

assignment [ə′sainmənt], *s.* die Zuweisung, Übertragung; die Aufgabe.

assimilate [ə′simileit], *v.a., v.n.* assimilieren, angleichen; sich assimilieren, sich angleichen, ähnlich werden.

assist [ə′sist], *v.a., v.n.* beistehen (*Dat.*), helfen (*Dat.*), unterstützen (*Acc.*).

assistance [ə′sistəns], *s.* der Beistand, die Hilfe; die Aushilfe; (*financial*) der Zuschuß.

assistant [ə′sistənt], *s.* der Assistent, Helfer.

assize [ə′saiz], *s.* die Gerichtssitzung; (*pl.*) das Schwurgericht.

associate [ə′souʃieit], *v.a.* verbinden (*link*). — *v.n.* verkehren (*company*); sich verbinden (*Comm.*) sich vereinigen. — [—iit], *s.* (*Comm.*) der Partner.

association [əsousi′eiʃən], *s.* die Vereinigung, der Bund, Verein; die Gesellschaft; der Verkehr.

assonance [′æsənəns], *s.* (*Phon.*) die Assonanz, der Gleichlaut.

assort [ə′sɔ:t], *v.a.* ordnen, aussuchen, sortieren; —ed sweets, gemischte Bonbons.

assortment [ə′sɔ:tmənt], *s.* die Sammlung, Mischung, Auswahl.

assuage [ə′sweidʒ], *v.a.* mildern, besänftigen, stillen.

assume [ə′sju:m], *v.a.* annehmen; übernehmen, ergreifen.

assuming [ə′sju:miŋ], *adj.* anmaßend; — that, angenommen daß . . ., gesetzt den Fall.

assumption [ə′sʌmpʃən], *s.* die Annahme (*opinion*); Übernahme (*taking up*); Aneignung (*appropriation*); *Assumption of the Blessed Virgin*, Mariä Himmelfahrt.

assurance [ə′ʃuərəns], *s.* die Versicherung; Sicherheit (*manner*).

assure [ə′ʃuə], *v.a.* versichern, sicher stellen, ermutigen.

assuredly [ə′ʃuəridli], *adv.* sicherlich, gewiß.

aster [′æstə], *s.* (*Bot.*) die Aster.

asterisk [′æstərisk], *s.* (*Typ.*) das Sternchen.

astern [ə′stə:n], *adv.* (*Naut.*) achteraus.

asthma [′æsθmə], *s.* das Asthma.

asthmatic [æsθ′mætik], *adj.* asthmatisch.

astir [ə′stə:], *adv.* wach, in Bewegung.

astonish [ə′stɔniʃ], *v.a.* in Erstaunen versetzen, verblüffen.

astonishment [ə′stɔniʃmənt], *s.* das Erstaunen, die Verwunderung; die Bestürzung.

astound [ə′staund], *v.a.* in Erstaunen versetzen, bestürzen.

astounding [ə′staundiŋ], *adj.* erstaunlich, verblüffend.

astral [′æstrəl], *adj.* Stern(en)-, gestirnt.

astray [ə'strei], *pred. adj.*, *adv.* irre; *go* —, sich verirren; (*fig.*) abschweifen.
astride [ə'straid], *pred.adj.,adv.* rittlings.
astringent [ə'strindʒənt], *adj.* zusammenziehend.
astrologer [ə'strɔlədʒə], *s.* der Sterndeuter, Astrolog(e).
astrological [æstrə'lɔdʒikəl], *adj.* astrologisch.
astrology [æ'strɔlədʒi], *s.* die Astrologie, Sterndeuterei.
astronaut [ˈæstrɔnɔːt], *s.* der Astronaut.
astronomer [ə'strɔnəmə], *s.* der Astronom.
astronomical [æstrə'nɔmikəl], *adj.* astronomisch.
astronomy [ə'strɔnəmi], *s.* die Astronomie, Sternkunde.
astute [ə'stjuːt], *adj.* listig, schlau.
astuteness [ə'stjuːtnis], *s.* die Schlauheit, Listigkeit, der Scharfsinn.
asunder [ə'sʌndə], *adv.* auseinander, entzwei.
asylum [ə'sailəm], *s.* das Asyl, der Zufluchtsort (*refuge*); *lunatic* —, das Irrenhaus.
at [æt], *prep.* an; auf; bei, für; in, nach; mit, gegen; um, über; von, aus, zu; — *my expense*, auf meine Kosten; — *all*, überhaupt; — *first*, zuerst; — *last*, zuletzt, endlich; — *peace*, in Frieden; *what are you driving* —? worauf wollen sie hinaus?
atheism [ˈeiθiizm], *s.* der Atheismus.
atheist [ˈeiθiist], *s.* der Atheist.
atheistic [eiθiˈistik], *adj.* atheistisch, gottlos.
Athenian [ə'θiːnjən], *s.* der Athener. — *adj.* athenisch.
Athens [ˈæθɔnz]. Athen, *n.*
athlete [ˈæθliːt], *s.* der Athlet.
athletic [æθ'letik], *adj.* athletisch.
athletics [æθ'letiks], *s. pl.* die Leichtathletik, Athletik.
Atlantic (Ocean) [ət'læntik ('ouʃən)]. der Atlantik.
atlas [ˈætləs], *s.* der Atlas.
atmosphere [ˈætməsfiə], *s.* die Atmosphäre.
atmospheric(al) [ætməs'ferik(əl)], *adj.* atmosphärisch. — *s.* (*pl.*) atmosphärische Störungen, *f. pl.*
atoll [ə'tɔl], *s.* die Koralleninsel, das Atoll.
atom [ˈætəm], *s.* das Atom.
atomic [ə'tɔmik], *adj.* (*Phys.*) Atom-, atomisch, atomar; (*theory*) atomistisch; — *bomb*, die Atombombe; — *pile*, der Atomreaktor; — *armament*, die atomare Aufrüstung.
atone [ə'toun], *v.n.* sühnen, büßen.
atonement [ə'tounmənt], *s.* die Buße, Sühne, Versöhnung.
atonic [ei'tɔnik], *adj.* tonlos, unbetont.
atrocious [ə'trouʃəs], *adj.* gräßlich, schrecklich, entsetzlich.
atrocity [ə'trɔsiti], *s.* die Gräßlichkeit, Grausamkeit, Greueltat.
atrophy [ˈætrəfi], *s.* (*Med.*) die Abmagerung, Atrophie. — [ˈætrəfai], *v.n.* absterben, auszehren.

attach [ə'tætʃ], *v.a.* anheften, beilegen, anhängen; (*fig.*) beimessen (*attribute*).
attachment [ə'tætʃmənt], *s.* das Anhaften (*sticking to*, an, *Acc.*); das Anhängsel (*appendage*); die Freundschaft (*to*, für, *Acc.*); die Anhänglichkeit (*loyalty*, an, *Acc.*).
attack [ə'tæk], *v.a.* angreifen. — *s.* die Attacke, der Angriff; (*Med.*) der Anfall.
attain [ə'tein], *v.a.* erreichen, erlangen.
attainable [ə'teinəbl], *adj.* erreichbar.
attainment [ə'teinmənt], *s.* die Erlangung, Erreichung; Errungenschaft; (*pl.*) Kenntnisse, *f. pl.*
attempt [ə'tempt], *s.* der Versuch. — *v.a.* versuchen.
attend [ə'tend], *v.a.*, *v.n.* begleiten, anwesend sein (*be present*, *at*, bei, *Dat.*); beiwohnen (*be present as guest*); zuhören (*listen to*); bedienen (*customer*); behandeln (*patient*).
attendance [ə'tendəns], *s.* die Begleitung (*accompaniment*); die Anwesenheit (*presence*); die Zuhörerschaft (*audience*); — *to be in* —, Dienst tun (*at*, bei); anwesend sein (*be present*).
attendant [ə'tendənt], *s.* der Diener, Wärter.
attention [ə'tenʃən], *s.* die Aufmerksamkeit, Achtung.
attentive [ə'tentiv], *adj.* aufmerksam.
attenuate [ə'tenjueit], *v.a.* verdünnen (*dilute*). — *v.n.* abmagern.
attest [ə'test], *v.a.* attestieren, bezeugen, bescheinigen.
attestation [ætes'teiʃən], *s.* die Bescheinigung; das Zeugnis.
Attic [ˈætik], *adj.* attisch, klassisch.
attic [ˈætik], *s.* die Dachkammer, die Dachstube.
attire [ə'taiə], *v.a.* ankleiden, kleiden. — *s.* die Kleidung.
attitude [ˈætitjuːd], *s.* die Haltung, Stellung (*toward*, zu), Einstellung.
attorney [ə'təːni], *s.* der Anwalt; *Attorney-General*, der Kronanwalt, (*Am.*) der Staatsanwalt; — *at law*, Rechtsanwalt.
attract [ə'trækt], *v.a.* anziehen.
attraction [ə'trækʃən], *s.* die Anziehung; der Reiz (*appeal*); die Anziehungskraft.
attractive [ə'træktiv], *adj.* anziehend, reizvoll.
attribute [ə'tribjuːt], *v.a.* zuschreiben, beimessen. — *s.* [ˈætribjuːt], (*Gram.*) das Attribut, die Eigenschaft.
attributive [ə'tribjutiv], *adj.* (*Gram.*) attributiv; beilegend.
attrition [ə'triʃən], *s.* die Zermürbung, Aufreibung, Reue.
attune [ə'tjuːn], *v.a.* (*Mus.*) stimmen, anpassen (*adapt to*, an, *Acc.*).
auburn [ˈɔːbəːn], *adj.* rotbraun.
auction [ˈɔːkʃən], *s.* die Auktion, die Versteigerung.
auctioneer [ɔːkʃə'niə], *s.* der Auktionator, Versteigerer.

audacious [ɔ:'deiʃəs], *adj.* waghalsig, kühn, dreist.

audacity [ɔ:'dæsiti], *s.* die Kühnheit (*valour*); Frechheit (*impudence*).

audible ['ɔ:dibl], *adj.* hörbar.

audibility [ɔ:di'biliti], *s.* die Hörbarkeit, Vernehmbarkeit.

audience [ɔ:'djəns], *s.* die Audienz (*of the Pope*, beim Papst); (*Theat.*) das Publikum; (*listeners*) die Zuhörer.

audit ['ɔ:dit], *s.* die Rechnungsprüfung, Revision. — *v.a.* revidieren, prüfen.

auditor ['ɔ:ditə], *s.* der Rechnungsrevisor, Buchprüfer.

auditory ['ɔ:ditəri], *adj.* Gehör-, Hör-.

auditorium [ɔ:di'tɔ:riəm], *s.* der Hörsaal, Vortragssaal.

auger ['ɔ:gə], *s.* der (große) Bohrer.

aught [ɔ:t], *pron.* (*obs.*) irgend etwas (*opp. to naught*).

augment [ɔ:g'ment], *v.a., v.n.* vermehren, vergrößern; zunehmen.

augmentation [ɔ:gmen'teiʃən], *s.* die Vergrößerung, Erhöhung, Zunahme.

augur ['ɔ:gə], *v.a.* weissagen, prophezeien.

August ['ɔ:gəst]. der August.

august [ɔ:'gʌst], *adj.* erhaben.

aunt [ɑ:nt], *s.* die Tante.

aurora [ɔ:'rɔ:rə], *s.* die Morgenröte.

auscultation [ɔ:skəl'teiʃən], *s.*(*Med.*) die Auskultation, Untersuchung.

auspices ['ɔ:spisiz], *s.* die Auspizien.

auspicious [ɔ:'spiʃəs], *adj.* unter glücklichem Vorzeichen, verheißungsvoll, günstig.

austere [ɔ:s'tiə], *adj.* streng, ernst, schmucklos.

austerity [ɔ:s'teriti], *s.* die Strenge.

Australian [ɔ'streiljən], *adj.* australisch. — *s.* der Australier.

Austrian ['ɔ:striən], *adj.* österreichisch. — *s.* der Österreicher.

authentic [ɔ:'θentik], *adj.* authentisch, echt.

authenticity [ɔ:θen'tisiti], *s.* die Authentizität, Echtheit.

author, authoress ['ɔ:θə, ɔ:θər'es], *s.* der Autor, die Autorin; der Verfasser, die Verfasserin.

authoritative [ɔ:'θɔritətiv], *adj.* autoritativ, maßgebend.

authority [ɔ:'θɔriti], *s.* die Autorität, Vollmacht (*power of attorney*); das Ansehen; *the authorities*, die Behörden.

authorization [ɔ:θɔrai'zeiʃən], *s.* die Bevollmächtigung, Befugnis.

authorize ['ɔ:θəraiz], *v.a.* autorisieren, bevollmächtigen, berechtigen.

authorship ['ɔ:θəʃip], *s.* die Autorschaft.

autobiographical [ɔ:tobaiə'græfikl], *adj.* autobiographisch.

autobiography [ɔ:tobai'ɔgrəfi], *s.* die Autobiographie.

autocracy [ɔ:'tɔkrəsi], *s.* die Selbstherrschaft.

autocrat ['ɔ:tokræt], *s.* der Autokrat, Selbstherrscher.

autograph ['ɔ:togræf, -grɑ:f], *s.* die eigene Handschrift, Unterschrift; das Autogramm.

automatic [ɔ:to'mætik], *adj.* automatisch.

automatize [ɔ:'tɔmətaiz], *v.a.* automatisieren, auf Automation umstellen.

automation [ɔ:to'meiʃən], *s.* (*Engin.*) die Automation; Automatisierung.

automaton [ɔ:'tɔmətən], *s.* der Automat.

automobile ['ɔ:tomobi:l], *s.* der Kraftwagen, das Auto.

autonomous [ɔ:'tɔnəməs], *adj.* autonom, unabhängig.

autonomy [ɔ:'tɔnəmi], *s.* die Autonomie, Unabhängigkeit.

autopsy ['ɔ:tɔpsi], *s.* die Autopsie; Obduktion, Leichenschau.

autumn ['ɔ:təm], *s.* der Herbst.

autumnal [ɔ:'tʌmnəl], *adj.* herbstlich.

auxiliary [ɔ:g'ziljəri], *adj.* Hilfs-.

avail [ə'veil], *v.n.* nützen, helfen, von Vorteil sein. — *v.r.* — *o.s of a th.*, sich einer Sache bedienen. — *s.* der Nutzen; *of no* —, nutzlos.

available [ə'veiləbl], *adj.* vorrätig, verfügbar, zur Verfügung (stehend).

avalanche ['ævəlɑ:nʃ], *s.* die Lawine.

avarice ['ævəris], *s.* der Geiz, die Habsucht, Gier.

avaricious [ævə'riʃəs], *adj.* geizig, habsüchtig, habgierig.

avenge [ə'vendʒ], *v.a.* rächen.

avenue ['ævənju:], *s.* die Allee; der Zugang.

average ['ævəridʒ], *adj.* durchschnittlich; *not more than* —, mäßig. — *s.* der Durchschnitt; *on an* —, durchschnittlich, im Durchschnitt. — *v.a.* den Durchschnitt nehmen.

averse [ə'və:s], *adj.* abgeneigt (*to, Dat.*).

aversion [ə'və:ʃən], *s.* die Abneigung, der Widerwille.

avert [ə'və:t], *v.a.* abwenden.

aviary ['eiviəri], *s.* das Vogelhaus.

aviation [əivi'eiʃən], *s.* das Flugwesen.

aviator ['eivieitə], *s.* der Flieger.

avid ['ævid], *adj.* begierig (*of* or *for*, nach).

avidity [æ'viditi], *s.* die Begierde, Gier (*for*, nach).

avoid [ə'vɔid], *v.a.* vermeiden.

avoidable [ə'vɔidəbl], *adj.* vermeidlich, vermeidbar.

avoidance [ə'vɔidəns], *s.* die Vermeidung, das Meiden.

avow [ə'vau], *v.a.* eingestehen, anerkennen (*acknowledge*).

avowal [ə'vauəl], *s.* das Geständnis; die Erklärung.

await [ə'weit], *v.a.* erwarten, warten auf (*Acc.*).

awake(n) [ə'weik(ən)], *v.a., v.n. irr.* aufwecken, wecken; aufwachen (*wake up*). — *adj. wide awake*, schlau, auf der Hut.

award [ə'wɔ:d], *s.* die Zuerkennung, Auszeichnung; Belohnung (*money*); (*Law*) das Urteil. — *v.a.* zuerkennen; — *damages*, Schadenersatz zusprechen; verleihen (*grant*).

aware [ə'wɛə], *adj.* gewahr, bewußt (*Genit.*).

away [ə'wei], *adv.* weg; hinweg, fort.

awe [ɔ:], *s.* die Ehrfurcht; Furcht.

awful ['ɔ:ful], *adj.* furchtbar, schrecklich.

awhile [ə'wail], *adv.* eine Weile, eine kurze Zeit.

awkward ['ɔ:kwəd], *adv.* ungeschickt, unbeholfen, ungelenk; unangenehm (*difficult*); — *situation*, peinliche Situation, Lage.

awkwardness ['ɔkwədnis], *s.* die Ungeschicklichkeit, Unbeholfenheit.

awl [ɔ:l], *s.* die Ahle, der Pfriem.

awning ['ɔ:niŋ], *s.* die Plane; das Sonnendach.

awry [ə'rai], *adj.* schief, verkehrt.

axe [æks], *s.* die Axt, das Beil.

axiom ['æksiəm], *s.* das Axiom, **der** Satz, Lehrsatz, Grundsatz.

axiomatic [æksiə'mætik], *adj.* axiomatisch, grundsätzlich; gewiß.

axis ['æksis], *s.* die Achse.

axle [æksl], *s.* die Achse.

ay(e) (1) [ai], *adv.* ja, gewiß.

ay(e) (2) [ei], *adv.* ständig, ewig.

azalea [ə'zeiliə], *s.* (*Bot.*) die Azalie.

azure ['æʒə, 'eiʒə], *adj.* himmelblau, azurblau.

B

B [bi:]. das B; (*Mus.*) das **H**.

baa [ba:], *v.n.* blöken.

babble [bæbl], *v.n.* schwatzen, schwätzen. — *s.* das Geschwätz; das Murmeln (*water*).

babe, baby [beib, 'beibi], *s.* der Säugling, das Baby, das kleine Kind, das Kindlein.

baboon [bə'bu:n], *s.* (*Zool.*) der Pavian.

bachelor ['bætʃələ], *s.* der Junggeselle; (*Univ.*) Bakkalaureus.

back [bæk], *s.* der Rücken, die Rückseite. — *adj.* Hinter-, Rück-; — *door*, die Hintertür; — *stairs*, die Hintertreppe. — *adv.* rückwärts, zurück. — *v.a.* unterstützen; (*Comm.*) indossieren; gegenzeichnen; wetten auf (*Acc.*) (*bet on*).

backbone ['bækboun], *s.* (*Anat.*) das Rückgrat.

backfire ['bækfaiə], *s.* (*Motor.*) die Frühzündung; (*gun*) die Fehlzündung. — [bæk'faiə], *v.n.* (*Motor.*) frühzünden; (*gun*) fehlzünden.

backgammon [bæk'gæmən], *s.* das Bordspiel, das Puffspiel.

background ['bækgraund], *s.* der Hintergrund.

backhand ['bækhænd], *s.* (*Sport*) die Rückhand; *a — ed compliment*, eine verblümte Grobheit.

backside [bæk'said], *s.* (*vulg.*) der Hintere.

backslide [bæk'slaid], *v.n.* abfallen, abtrünnig werden.

backward ['bækwəd], *adj.* zurückgeblieben. **backward(s)** *adv.* rückwärts, zurück.

backwater ['bækwɔ:tə], *s.* das Stauwasser.

backwoods ['bækwudz], *s. pl.* der Hinterwald.

bacon ['beikən], *s.* der Speck.

bad [bæd], *adj.* schlecht, schlimm; böse (*immoral*); (*coll.*) unwohl (*unwell*); *not too —*, ganz gut; *from — to worse*, immer schlimmer; — *language*, unanständige Worte, das Fluchen; — *luck*, Unglück, Pech; *want —ly*, nötig brauchen.

badge [bædʒ], *s.* das Abzeichen; Kennzeichen (*mark*).

badger (1) ['bædʒə], *s.* (*Zool.*) der Dachs.

badger (2) ['bædʒə], *v.a.* ärgern, stören, belästigen.

badness ['bædnis], *s.* die Schlechtigkeit, Bosheit, das schlechte Wesen, die Bösartigkeit.

baffle [bæfl], *v.a.* täuschen, verblüffen. — *s.* (*obs.*) die Täuschung; (*Build.*) Verkleidung; (*Elec.*) Verteilerplatte.

bag [bæg], *s.* der Sack, Beutel; die Tasche; *shopping —*, Einkaufstasche; *travelling —*, Reisehandtasche. — *v.a.* einstecken, als Beute behalten (*hunt*).

bagatelle [bægə'tel], *s.* die Bagatelle, Lappalie, Kleinigkeit; das Kugelspiel (*pin-table ball-game*).

baggage ['bægidʒ], *s.* das Gepäck.

bagging ['bægiŋ], *s.* die Sackleinwand.

baggy ['bægi], *adj.* ungebügelt; bauschig.

bagpipe ['bægpaip], *s.* der Dudelsack.

bagpiper ['bægpaipə], *s.* der Dudelsackpfeifer.

bail [beil], *s.* der Bürge; die Bürgschaft; *stand —*, für einen bürgen; *allow —*, Bürgschaft zulassen. — *v.a.* Bürgschaft leisten; — *out*, (durch Kaution) in Freiheit setzen.

bailiff ['beilif], *s.* der Amtmann; Gerichtsvollzieher.

bait [beit], *s.* der Köder. — *v.a.* ködern, locken (*attract*).

baiter ['beitə], *s.* der Hetzer, Verfolger.

baiting ['beitiŋ], *s.* die Hetze.

bake [beik], *v.a., v.n.* backen.

baker ['beikə], *s.* der Bäcker; *—'s dozen*, 13 Stück.

bakery ['beikəri], *s.* die Bäckerei.

baking ['beikiŋ], *s.* das Backen.

balance

balance ['bæləns], s. die Waage (scales); die Bilanz (audit); das Gleichgewicht (equilibrium); (Comm.) der Saldo, der Überschuß (profit); die Unruhe (watch). — v.a., v.n. wägen, abwägen (scales); ausgleichen (— up); einen Saldo ziehen (— an account); ins Gleichgewicht bringen (bring into equilibrium).

balcony ['bælkəni], s. der Balkon, der Söller (castle); Altan (villa).

bald [bɔːld], adj. kahl, haarlos; (fig.) armselig, schmucklos.

baldness ['bɔːldnis], s. die Kahlheit (hairlessness); Nacktheit (bareness).

bale (1) [beil], s. der Ballen.

bale (2) [beil], v.n. — out, abspringen; aussteigen.

Balearic Islands [bæli'ærik ailəndz], s. pl. die Balearen, Balearischen Inseln. — adj. balearisch.

baleful ['beilful], adj. unheilvoll.

balk [bɔːk], v.a. aufhalten, hemmen. — v.n. scheuen, zurückscheuen (at, vor).

ball (1) [bɔːl], s. der Ball; die Kugel; — cock, der Absperrhahn; —point pen, der Kugelschreiber.

ball (2) [bɔːl], s. der Ball (dance).

ballad ['bæləd], s. die Ballade.

ballast ['bæləst], s. der Ballast.

ballet ['bælei], s. das Ballett.

balloon [bə'luːn], s. der Ballon.

ballot ['bælət], s. die geheime Wahl, Abstimmung; —box, die Wahlurne; —-paper, der Stimmzettel. —v. n. wählen, abstimmen.

balm [baːm], s. der Balsam.

balsam ['bɔlsəm], s. der Balsam.

Baltic ['bɔːltik], adj. baltisch. — (Sea), die Ostsee; — Provinces, das Baltikum, die Ostseeprovinzen.

balustrade ['bæləstreid], s. die Balustrade, das Geländer.

bamboo [bæm'buː], s. (Bot.) der Bambus.

bamboozle [bæm'buːzl], v.a. verblüffen; beschwindeln (cheat).

ban [bæn], v.a. bannen, verbannen; verbieten. — s. der Bann, das Verbot.

banal [bæ'næl, 'beinəl], adj. banal.

banality [bə'næliti], s. die Banalität, Trivialität.

banana [bə'nɑːnə], s. die Banane.

band [bænd], s. das Band (ribbon etc.); (Mus.) die Kapelle; die Bande (robbers). — v.n. — together, sich verbinden; sich zusammentun.

bandage ['bændidʒ], s. der Verband, die Bandage.

bandit ['bændit], s. der Bandit.

bandmaster ['bændmɑːstə], s. der Kapellmeister.

bandstand ['bændstænd], s. der Musikpavillon.

bandy ['bændi], adj. —-legged, krummbeinig. — v.a. — words, Worte wechseln; streiten.

bane [bein], s. das Gift; (fig.) Verderben.

baneful ['beinful], adj. verderblich.

bang [bæŋ], s. der Knall (explosion), das Krachen (clap). — v.n. knallen, krachen lassen. — v.a. — a door, eine Türe zuwerfen.

banish ['bæniʃ], v.a. verbannen, bannen.

banisters ['bænistəz], s. pl. das Treppengeländer.

bank [bæŋk], s. (Fin.) die Bank; das Ufer (river); der Damm (dam). — v.a. einlegen, einzahlen, auf die Bank bringen (sum of money); eindämmen (dam up). — v.n. ein Konto haben (have an account, with, bei).

banker ['bæŋkə], s. der Bankier.

bankrupt ['bæŋkrʌpt], adj. bankrott; zahlungsunfähig; (coll.) pleite.

bankruptcy ['bæŋkrʌptsi], s. der Bankrott.

banns [bænz], s. pl. das Heiratsaufgebot.

banquet ['bæŋkwit], s. das Banquet, Festessen.

bantam ['bæntəm], s. das Bantamhuhn, Zwerghuhn; (Boxing) — -weight, das Bantamgewicht.

banter ['bæntə], v.n. scherzen, necken. — s. das Scherzen, der Scherz.

baptism ['bæptizm], s. die Taufe.

Baptist ['bæptist], s. der Täufer, Baptist.

baptize [bæp'taiz], v.a. taufen.

bar [baː], s. die Barre, Stange (pole); der Riegel; Balken; Schlagbaum (barrier); (fig.) das Hindernis; der Schenktisch, die Bar (in public house); prisoner at the —, Gefangener vor (dem) Gericht; call to the —, zur Gerichtsadvokatur (or als Anwalt) zulassen; (Mus.) der Takt. — v.a. verriegeln (door); (fig.) hindern (from action); verbieten (prohibit); ausschließen (exclude).

barb [baːb], s. die Spitze (of wire); der Widerhaken (hook).

barbed [baːbd], adj. spitzig; — remark, die spitze Bemerkung; — wire, der Stacheldraht.

barbarian [baː'beəriən], s. der Barbar. — adj. barbarisch.

barbarism ['baːbərizm], s. die Roheit; der Barbarismus.

barber ['baːbə], s. der Barbier, Friseur.

barberry ['baːbəri], s. (Bot.) die Berberitze.

bard [baːd], s. der Barde, Sänger.

bare [beə], adj. nackt, bloß; — -headed, barhäuptig. — v.a. entblößen.

barefaced ['beəfeist], adj. schamlos.

barely ['beəli], adv. kaum.

bargain ['baːgin], s. der Kauf, Gelegenheitskauf; der Handel (trading); das Geschäft; into the —, noch dazu, obendrein. — v.n. feilschen, handeln (haggle) (for, um).

barge [baːdʒ], s. der Lastkahn, die Barke. — v.n. (coll.) — in, stören.

bargee [baː'dʒiː], s. der Flußschiffer, Bootsmann.

baritone ['bæritoun], s. (Mus.) der Bariton.

bark (1) [baːk], *s.* die Rinde (*of tree*).
bark (2) [baːk], *v.n.* bellen (*dog*); — *up the wrong tree*, auf falscher Fährte sein. — *s.* das Gebell (*dog*).
barley ['baːli], *s.* (*Bot.*) die Gerste.
barmaid ['baːmeid], *s.* die Kellnerin.
barman ['baːmən], *s.* der Kellner.
barn [baːn], *s.* die Scheune; — *owl*, die Schleiereule.
barnacle ['baːnəkl], *s.* die Entenmuschel; die Klette.
barnstormer ['baːnstɔːmə], *s.* der Schmierenkomödiant.
barometer [bə'rɔmitə], *s.* das Barometer.
baron ['bærən], *s.* der Baron, Freiherr.
barony ['bærəni], *s.* die Baronswürde.
baroque [bə'rɔk], *adj.* barock. — *s.* das Barock.
barque [baːk], *s.* die Bark.
barracks ['bærəks], *s. pl.* die Kaserne.
barrage ['bæraːʒ, 'bæridʒ], *s.* das Sperrfeuer (*firing*); das Wehr, der Damm.
barrel ['bærəl], *s.* das Faß (*vat*), die Tonne (*tun*); der Gewehrlauf (*rifle*); die Trommel (*cylinder*); — *organ*, die Drehorgel.
barren ['bærən], *adj.* unfruchtbar, dürr.
barrenness ['bærənnis], *s.* die Unfruchtbarkeit.
barricade [bæri'keid], *s.* die Barrikade. — *v.a.* verrammeln, verschanzen.
barrier ['bæriə], *s.* die Barriere, der Schlagbaum; das Hindernis; (*Railw.*) die Schranke.
barrister ['bæristə], *s.* der Rechtsanwalt, Advokat.
barrow (1) ['bærou], *s.* der Schubkarren, Handkarren; — *-boy*, der Höker, Schnellverkäufer.
barrow (2) ['bærou], *s.* (*Archaeol.*) das Hünengrab, Heldengrab.
barter ['baːtə], *v.a.* tauschen, austauschen. — *s.* der Tauschhandel.
Bartholomew [baː'θɔləmjuː]. Bartholomäus, *m.*; *Massacre of St. Bartholomew's Eve*, Bartholomäusnacht, Pariser Bluthochzeit.
basalt ['bæsɔːlt, bæ'sɔːlt], *s.* der Basalt.
base [beis], *s.* die Basis, Grundlage; der Sockel; (*Chem.*) die Base. — *adj.* niedrig, gemein; (*Metall.*) unedel. — *v.a.* basieren, beruhen, fundieren (*upon*, auf).
baseless ['beislis], *adj.* grundlos.
basement ['beismənt], *s.* das Kellergeschoß.
baseness ['beisnis], *s.* die Gemeinheit, Niedrigkeit.
bashful ['bæʃful], *adj.* verschämt, schamhaft, schüchtern.
basic ['beisik], *adj.* grundlegend.
basin ['beisən], *s.* das Becken.
basis ['beisis], *s.* die Basis, Grundlage.
bask [baːsk], *v.n.* sich sonnen.
basket ['baːskit], *s.* der Korb.
bass (1) [beis], *s.* (*Mus.*) der Baß, die Baßstimme.

bass (2) [bæs], *s.* (*Zool.*) der Barsch.
bassoon [bə'suːn], *s.* (*Mus.*) das Fagott.
bastard ['bæstəd], *s.* der Bastard.
baste [beist], *v.a.* mit Fett begießen (*roast meat*); (*coll.*) prügeln.
bastion ['bæstiən], *s.* die Bastion, Festung, das Bollwerk.
bat (1) [bæt], *s.* die Fledermaus.
bat (2) [bæt], *s.* der Schläger. — *v.n.* (den Ball) schlagen; (*cricket*) am Schlagen sein (*be batting*).
batch [bætʃ], *s.* der Stoß (*pile*); die Menge (*people*); (*Mil.*) der Trupp.
bath [baːθ], *s.* das Bad; (*Am.*) —*robe*, der Schlafrock, Bademantel; — *tub*, die Badewanne.
bathe [beið], *v.n.* baden; *bathing pool*, das Schwimmbad; *bathing suit*, der Badeanzug.
batman ['bætmən], *s.* der Offiziersbursche.
baton ['bætən], *s.* der Stab.
batsman ['bætsmən], *s.* der Schläger (*cricket*).
batten [bætn], *s.* die Holzlatte. — *v.a.* mästen, füttern. — *v.n.* fett werden.
batter ['bætə], *s.* der Schlagteig. — *v.a.* schlagen, zertrümmern; —*ing ram*, (*Mil.*) der Sturmbock.
battery ['bætəri], *s.* die Batterie.
battle [bætl], *s.* die Schlacht; — *cruiser*, der Schlachtkreuzer; —*ship*, das Schlachtschiff. — *v.n.* kämpfen (*for*, um).
Bavarian [bə'vɛəriən], *adj.* bayrisch. — *s.* der Bayer.
bawl [bɔːl], *v.n.* plärren, schreien.
bay (1) [bei], *adj.* rötlich braun.
bay (2) [bei], *s.* die Bucht, Bai; — *window*, das Erkerfenster.
bay (3) [bei], *s.* *keep at* —, in Schach halten, *stand at* —, sich zur Wehr setzen.
bay (4) [bei], *s.* (*Bot.*) der Lorbeer.
bay (5) [bei], *v.n.* bellen, heulen; — *for the moon*, das Unmögliche wollen.
bayonet ['beiənet], *s.* das Bajonett.
bazaar [bə'zaː], *s.* der Basar.
be [biː], *v.n. irr.* sein, existieren; sich befinden; vorhanden sein; — *off*, sich fortmachen (*move*); ungenießbar sein (*meat, food*); nicht mehr da sein (— *off the menu*).
beach [biːtʃ], *s.* der Strand, das Gestade.
beacon ['biːkən], *s.* das Leuchtfeuer; der Leuchtturm; das Lichtsignal.
bead [biːd], *s.* das Tröpfchen (*drop*); die Perle (*pearl*); (*pl.*) die Perlschnur; der Rosenkranz.
beadle [biːdl], *s.* (*Univ.*) der Pedell; (*Eccl.*) Kirchendiener.
beagle [biːgl], *s.* der Jagdhund, Spürhund.
beak [biːk], *s.* der Schnabel.
beaker ['biːkə], *s.* der Becher.
beam [biːm], *s.* der Balken (*wood*); der Strahl (*ray*), Glanz. — *v.n.* strahlen.

bean

bean [bi:n], s. (*Bot.*) die Bohne; *not a* —, keinen Heller *or* Pfennig.

bear (1) [bɛə], s. (*Zool.*) der Bär.

bear (2) [bɛə], *v.a. irr.* tragen, ertragen; gebären (*a child*); hegen (*sorrow etc.*). — *v.n.* — *upon*, drücken auf (*pressure*), Einfluß haben (*effect*); — *up*, geduldig sein.

bearable ['bɛərəbl], *adj.* tragbar, erträglich.

beard [biəd], s. der Bart. — *v.a.* trotzen (*Dat.*).

bearded ['biədid], *adj.* bärtig.

bearer ['bɛərə], s. der Träger, Überbringer.

bearing ['bɛəriŋ], s. das Benehmen, die Haltung (*manner*); (*pl.*) (*Geog.*) die Richtung; *lose o.'s* —*s*, sich verlaufen; *ball* —*s*, (*Engin.*) das Kugellager.

bearpit ['bɛəpit], s. der Bärenzwinger.

beast [bi:st], s. das Tier; die Bestie.

beastliness ['bi:stlinis], s. das tierische Benehmen; die Grausamkeit (*cruelty*); die Gemeinheit.

beastly ['bi:stli], *adj.* grausam, (*coll.*) schrecklich.

beat [bi:t], s. der Schlag, das Schlagen; (*Mus.*) der Takt; die Runde, das Revier (*patrol district*). — *v.a. irr.* schlagen; — *time*, den Takt schlagen; — *carpets*, Teppich klopfen. — *v.n.* — *it*, sich davonmachen.

beater ['bi:tə], s. (*Hunt.*) der Treiber.

beatify [bi:'ætifai], *v.a.* seligsprechen.

beau [bou], s. der Stutzer, Geck.

beautiful ['bju:tiful], *adj.* schön.

beautify ['bju:tifai], *v.a.* schön machen, verschönern.

beauty ['bju:ti], s. die Schönheit; — *salon*, der Schönheitssalon; *Sleeping Beauty*, das Dornröschen.

beaver ['bi:və], s. (*Zool.*) der Biber.

becalm [bi'ka:m], *v.a.* besänftigen.

because [bi'kɔz], *conj.* weil, da; — *of*, wegen, um ... willen.

beck [bek], s. der Wink; *be at s.o.'s* — *and call*, jemandem zu Gebote stehen.

beckon ['bekən], *v.a., v.n.* winken, heranwinken, zuwinken (*Dat.*).

become [bi'kʌm], *v.n. irr.* werden. — *v.a.* anstehen, sich schicken, passen (*Dat.*).

becoming [bi'kʌmiŋ], *adj.* passend, kleidsam.

bed [bed], s. das Bett; Beet (*flowers*); (*Geol.*) das Lager, die Schicht. — *v.a.* betten, einbetten.

bedaub [bi'dɔ:b], *v.a.* beflecken, beschmieren.

bedding ['bediŋ], s. das Bettzeug.

bedevil [bi'devəl], *v.a.* behexen, verhexen.

bedew [bi'dju:], *v.a.* betauen.

bedlam ['bedləm], s. (*coll.*) das Irrenhaus; *this is* —, die Hölle ist los.

Bedouin [bi'du:in], s. der Beduine.

bedpost ['bedpoust], s. der Bettpfosten.

bedraggle [bi'drægl], *v.a.* beschmutzen.

bedridden ['bedridn], *adj.* bettlägerig, ans Bett gefesselt.

bedroom ['bedru:m], s. das Schlafzimmer.

bedtime ['bedtaim], s. die Schlafenszeit.

bee [bi:], s. (*Ent.*) die Biene; *have a* — *in o.'s bonnet*, einen Vogel haben.

beech [bi:tʃ], s. (*Bot.*) die Buche.

beef [bi:f], s. das Rindfleisch; — *tea*, die Fleischbrühe.

beehive ['bi:haiv], s. der Bienenkorb.

beeline ['bi:lain], s. die Luftlinie, gerade Linie; *make a* — *for s.th.*, schnurstracks auf etwas losgehen.

beer [biə], s. das Bier; *small* —, Dünnbier, (*fig.*) unbedeutend.

beet [bi:t], s. (*Bot.*) die Runkelrübe; *sugar* —, die Zuckerrübe.

beetle [bi:tl], s. (*Ent.*) der Käfer; — *brows*, buschige Augenbrauen.

beetroot ['bi:tru:t], s. (*Bot.*) die rote Rübe.

befall [bi'fɔ:l], *v.a. irr.* widerfahren (*Dat.*). — *v.n.* zustoßen (*happen, Dat.*).

befit [bi'fit], *v.a.* sich geziemen, sich gebühren.

befog [bi'fɔg], *v.a.* in Nebel hüllen; umnebeln.

before [bi'fɔ:], *adv.* vorn; voraus, voran; (*previously*) vorher, früher; (*already*) bereits, schon. — *prep.* vor. — *conj.* bevor, ehe.

beforehand [bi'fɔ:hænd], *adv.* im voraus, vorher.

befoul [bi'faul], *v.a.* beschmutzen.

befriend [bi'frend], *v.a.* befreunden, unterstützen (*support*).

beg [beg], *v.a., v.n.* betteln (um, *for*); ersuchen, bitten (*request*).

beget [bi'get], *v.a. irr.* zeugen.

beggar ['begə], s. der Bettler.

begin [bi'gin], *v.a., v.n. irr.* beginnen, anfangen.

beginner [bi'ginə], s. der Anfänger.

beginning [bi'giniŋ], s. der Anfang.

begone ! [bi'gɔn], *interj.* hinweg! fort! mach dich fort!

begrudge [bi'grʌdʒ], *v.a.* nicht gönnen, mißgönnen.

beguile [bi'gail], *v.a.* bestricken, betrügen; — *the time*, die Zeit vertreiben.

behalf [bi'ha:f], s. *on* — *of*, um ... (*Genit.*) willen; im Interesse von, im Namen von.

behave [bi'heiv], *v.n.* sich benehmen, sich betragen.

behaviour [bi'heivjə], s. das Benehmen, Gebaren.

behead [bi'hed], *v.a.* enthaupten.

behind [bi'haind], *adv.* hinten, zurück, hinterher. — *prep.* hinter.

behindhand [bi'haindhænd], *adj., adv.* im Rückstand (*in arrears*); zurück (*backward*).

behold [bi'hould], *v.a. irr.* ansehen; er blicken; *lo and* — *!* siehe da!

beholden [bi'houldən], *adj.* verpflichtet (*to, Dat.*).

beholder [bi'houldə], s. der Zuschauer.

behove [bi'houv], *v.a.* sich geziemen, ziemen, gebühren.

being ['bi:iŋ], *pres. part for the time* —, vorläufig, für jetzt. — *s.* das Sein, die Existenz; das Wesen (*creature*).

belated [bi'leitid], *adj.* verspätet.

belch [beltʃ], *v.n.* rülpsen, aufstoßen.

belfry ['belfri], *s.* der Glockenturm.

Belgian ['beldʒən], *adj.* belgisch. — *s.* der Belgier.

belie [bi'lai], *v.a.* täuschen, Lügen strafen.

belief [bi'li:f], *s.* der Glaube, die Meinung.

believable [bi'li:vəbl], *adj.* glaubhaft, glaublich.

believe [bi'li:v], *v.a., v.n.* glauben (*an, Acc.*), vertrauen (*Dat.*).

believer [bi'li:və], *s.* der Gläubige.

belittle [bi'litl], *v.a.* schmälern, verkleinern, verächtlich machen.

bell [bel], *s.* die Glocke; Schelle, Klingel; — *founder,* der Glockengießer; — *-boy, (Am.)* — *-hop,* der Hotelpage.

belligerent [bi'lidʒərənt], *adj.* kriegführend. — *s.* der Kriegführende.

bellow ['belou], *v.n.* brüllen. — *s.* das Gebrüll.

bellows ['belouz], *s.* der Blasebalg.

belly ['beli], *s.* der Bauch.

belong [bi'lɔŋ], *v.n.* gehören (*Dat.*), angehören (*Dat.*).

belongings [bi'lɔŋiŋz], *s. pl.* die Habe, das Hab und Gut, der Besitz.

beloved [bi'lʌvd, -vid], *adj.* geliebt, lieb.

below [bi'lou], *adv.* unten. — *prep.* unterhalb (*Genit.*), unter (*Dat.*).

Belshazzar [bel'ʃæzə]. Belsazar, *m.*

belt [belt], *s.* der Gürtel, Gurt; der Riemen; (*Tech.*) Treibriemen; *below the* —, unfair. — *v.a.* umgürten; (*coll.*) prügeln.

bemoan [bi'moun], *v.a.* beklagen.

bench [bentʃ], *s.* die Bank; der Gerichtshof (*court of law*); *Queen's Bench,* der oberste Gerichtshof.

bend [bend], *v.a., v.n. irr.* biegen; beugen; sich krümmen. — *s.* die Biegung, Krümmung, Kurve.

bendable ['bendəbl], *adj.* biegsam.

beneath [bi'ni:θ] *see below.*

Benedictine [beni'dikti:n], *s.* der Benediktiner.

benediction [beni'dikʃən], *s.* der Segensspruch, der Segen; die Segnung.

benefaction [beni'fækʃən], *s.* die Wohltat.

benefactor ['benifæktə], *s.* der Wohltäter.

benefactress ['benifæktris], *s.* die Wohltäterin.

beneficent [be'nefisənt], *adj.* wohltätig.

beneficial [beni'fiʃəl], *adj.* vorteilhaft, gut (*for,* für), wohltuend.

benefit ['benifit], *s.* der Vorteil, Nutzen. — *v.n.* Nutzen ziehen. — *v.a.* nützen.

benevolence [be'nevələns], *s.* das Wohlwollen.

benevolent [be'nevələnt], *adj.* wohlwollend; — *society,* der Unterstützungsverein, — *fund,* der Unterstützungsfond.

Bengali [ben'gɔ:li], *adj.* bengalisch. — *s.* der Bengale.

benign [bi'nain], *adj.* gütig, mild.

bent [bent], *adj.* gebogen, krumm; — *on something,* versessen auf etwas. — *s.* die Neigung, der Hang; — *for,* Vorliebe für.

benzene ['benzi:n], *s.* das Benzol, Kohlenbenzin.

benzine ['benzi:n], *s.* das Benzin.

bequeath [bi'kwi:θ], *v.a.* vermachen, hinterlassen.

bequest [bi'kwest], *s.* das Vermächtnis.

bereave [bi'ri:v], *v.a. irr.* berauben (durch Tod).

bereavement [bi'ri:vmənt], *s.* der Verlust (durch Tod).

beret ['berei], *s.* die Baskenmütze.

Bernard ['bə:nəd]. Bernhard, *m.; St.* — *dog,* der Bernhardiner.

berry ['beri], *s.* die Beere.

berth [bə:θ], *s.* (*Naut.*) der Ankerplatz; die Koje. — *v.a., v.n.* anlegen; *vor Anker gehen* (*boat*).

beseech [bi'si:tʃ], *v.a. irr.* bitten, anflehen.

beset [bi'set], *v.a. irr.* bedrängen, bedrücken, umringen.

beside [bi'said], *prep.* außer, neben, nahe bei; — *the point,* unwesentlich; *quite* — *the mark,* weit vom Schuß.

besides [bi'saidz], *adv.* überdies, außerdem.

besiege [bi'si:dʒ], *v.a.* belagern.

besmirch [bi'smə:tʃ], *v.a.* besudeln.

besom ['bi:zəm], *s.* der Besen.

bespatter [bi'spætə], *v.a.* bespritzen.

bespeak [bi'spi:k], *v.a. irr.* bestellen; (*Tail.*) *bespoke,* nach Maß gemacht *or* gearbeitet.

best [best], *adj.* (*superl. of* **good**) best; — *adv.* am besten. — *s. want the* — *of both worlds,* alles haben wollen; *to the* — *of my ability,* nach besten Kräften; *to the* — *of my knowledge,* soviel ich weiß.

bestial ['bestjəl], *adj.* bestialisch, tierisch.

bestow [bi'stou], *v.a.* verleihen, erteilen.

bet [bet], *s.* die Wette. — *v.a., v.n. irr.* wetten.

betray [bi'trei], *v.a.* verraten.

betrayal [bi'treiəl], *s.* der Verrat.

betrayer [bi'treiə], *s.* der Verräter.

betroth [bi'trouð], *v.a.* verloben.

betrothal [bi'trouðəl], *s.* die Verlobung.

better ['betə], *adj.* (*comp. of* **good**) besser. — *adv. you had* — *go,* es wäre besser, Sie gingen; *think* — *of it,* sich eines Besseren besinnen, sich's überlegen. — *s. get the* — *of,* überwinden; *so much the* —, desto *or* umso besser. — *v.a.* verbessern; — *oneself,* seine Lage verbessern.

betterment ['betəmənt], s. die Verbesserung.

between [bi'twi:n], adv. dazwischen. — prep. zwischen; unter (among).

bevel ['bevəl], s. der Winkelpasser; die Schräge. — v.a. abkanten.

beverage ['bevəridʒ], s. das Getränk.

bevy ['bevi], s. die Schar (of beauties, von Schönen).

bewail [bi'weil], v.a., v.n. betrauern, beweinen; trauern um.

beware [bi'wɛə], v.n. sich hüten (of, vor).

bewilder [bi'wildə], v.a. verwirren.

bewitch [bi'witʃ], v.a. bezaubern.

beyond [bi'jɔnd], adv. jenseits, drüben. — prep. über ... hinaus; jenseits; außer.

biannual [bai'ænjuəl], adj. halbjährlich.

bias ['baiəs], s. die Neigung; das Vorurteil (prejudice). — v.a. beeinflussen.

bias(s)ed ['baiəsd], adj. voreingenommen.

bib [bib], s. der Schürzenlatz; das Lätzchen.

Bible [baibl], s. die Bibel.

Biblical ['biblikəl], adj. biblisch.

bibliography [bibli'ɔgrəfi], s. die Bibliographie.

bibliophile ['bibliəfail], s. der Bücherfreund.

biceps ['baiseps], s. der Bizeps, Armmuskel.

bicker ['bikə], v.n. zanken, hadern.

bickering ['bikəriŋ], s. das Gezänk, Hadern, der Hader.

bicycle ['baisikl], (coll.) **bike** [baik], s. das Fahrrad.

bicyclist ['baisiklist], s. der Radfahrer.

bid [bid], v.a., v.n. irr. gebieten, befehlen (Dat.) (order); bieten (at auction); — farewell, Lebewohl sagen. — s. das Gebot, Angebot (at auction).

bidding ['bidiŋ], s. der Befehl (order); das Bieten (at auction); die Einladung (invitation).

bide [baid], v.n. irr. verbleiben, verharren (in, by, bei).

biennial [bai'eniəl], adj. zweijährig, alle zwei Jahre.

bier [biə], s. die Bahre, Totenbahre.

big [big], adj. groß, dick (fat); talking —, großsprecherisch; talk —, prahlen.

bigamy ['bigəmi], s. die Bigamie, die Doppelehe.

bigness ['bignis], s. die Größe, Dicke.

bigoted ['bigətid], adj. bigott, fanatisch.

bigotry ['bigətri], s. die Bigotterie.

bigwig ['bigwig], s. (coll.) die vornehme Person, der Würdenträger.

bike see **bicycle**.

bilberry ['bilbəri], s. (Bot.) die Heidelbeere.

bile [bail], s. die Galle.

bilge [bildʒ], s. die Bilge, der Schiffsboden; (coll.) Unsinn (nonsense).

bilious ['biljəs], adj. gallig.

bill (1) [bil], s. der Schnabel (bird).

bill (2) [bil], die Rechnung (account); — of exchange, der Wechsel; — of entry, die Zolldeklaration; — of fare, die Speisekarte; (Parl.) der Gesetzentwurf; das Plakat (poster). — v.a. anzeigen.

billboard ['bilbɔ:d], s. (Am.) das Anschlagbrett.

billet ['bilit], s. das Billett (card); das Quartier, die Unterkunft (army).

billfold ['bilfould], s. (Am.) die Brieftasche.

billhook ['bilhuk], s. die Hippe.

billiards ['biljədz], s. das Billardspiel.

billow ['bilou], s. die Woge. — v.n. wogen.

bin [bin], s. der Behälter.

bind [baind], v.a. irr. binden, verpflichten; (Law) — over, zu gutem Benehmen verpflichten.

binder ['baində], s. der Binder, Buchbinder.

bindery ['baindəri], s. die Buchbinderei, Binderwerkstatt.

binding ['baindiŋ], s. der Einband.

binnacle ['binəkl], s. das Kompaßhäuschen.

binocular [bi'nɔkjulə], adj. für beide Augen. — s. (pl.) das Fernglas, der Feldstecher.

binomial [bai'noumiəl], adj. binomisch. — s. (pl.) (Maths.) das Binom, der zweigliedrige Ausdruck.

biochemical [baio'kemikəl], adj. biochemisch.

biochemistry [baio'kemistri], s. die Biochemie.

biographer [bai'ɔgrəfə], s. der Biograph.

biographical [baio'græfikəl], adj. biographisch.

biography [bai'ɔgrəfi], s. die Biographie, die Lebensbeschreibung.

biological [baio'lɔdʒikəl], adj. biologisch.

biology [bai'ɔlədʒi], s. die Biologie.

biometric(al) [baio'metrik(əl)], adj. biometrisch.

biometry [bai'ɔmitri], s. die Biometrie.

biophysical [baio'fizikəl], adj. biophysisch.

biophysics [baio'fiziks], s. die Biophysik.

biped ['baiped], s. der Zweifüßler.

biplane ['baiplein], s. (Aviat.) der Doppeldecker.

birch [bə:tʃ], s. (Bot.) die Birke; die Birkenrute, Rute (cane). — v.a. (mit der Rute) züchtigen.

bird [bə:d], s. der Vogel; — of passage, der Wandervogel, Zugvogel; —cage, der Vogelkäfig, das Vogelbauer; — fancier, der Vogelzüchter; —'s-eye view, die Vogelperspektive.

birth [bə:θ], s. die Geburt; — certificate, der Geburtsschein.

birthday ['bə:θdei], s, der Geburtstag.

biscuit ['biskit], s. der or das Keks; der Zwieback.

bisect [bai'sekt], *v.a.* entzweischneiden, halbieren.

bisection [bai'sekʃən], *s.* die Zweiteilung, Halbierung.

bishop ['biʃəp], *s.* der Bischof; (*Chess*) der Läufer.

bishopric ['biʃəprik], *s.* das Bistum.

bismuth ['bizməθ], *s.* der *or* das Wismut.

bison ['baisən], *s.* (*Zool.*) der Bison.

bit [bit], *s.* der Bissen (*bite*), das Bißchen (*little* —); das Gebiß (*bridle*); der Bart (*of key*).

bitch [bitʃ], *s.* die Hündin.

bite [bait], *v.a. irr.* beißen. — *s.* das Beißen (*mastication*); der Biß (*morsel*).

biting ['baitiŋ], *adj.* (*also fig.*) beißend, scharf. — *adv.* — *cold*, bitterkalt.

bitter ['bitə], *adj.* bitter.

bittern ['bitə:n], *s.* (*Orn.*) die Rohrdommel.

bitterness ['bitənis], *s.* die Bitterkeit.

bitumen [bi'tju:mən], *s.* der Bergteer, Asphalt.

bivouac ['bivuæk], *s.* (*Mil.*) das Biwak, Lager.

bizarre [bi'za:], *adj.* bizarr, wunderlich.

blab [blæb], *v.a., v.n.* schwatzen, ausplaudern (*give away*).

blabber ['blæbə], *s.* (*coll.*) der Schwätzer.

black [blæk], *adj.* schwarz; — *sheep*, der Taugenichts; — *pudding*, die Blutwurst; *Black Forest*, der Schwarzwald; *Black Maria*, der Polizeiwagen; (*coll.*) die grüne Minna; *Black Sea*, das schwarze Meer.

blackberry ['blækbəri], *s.* (*Bot.*) die Brombeere.

blackbird ['blækbə:d], *s.* (*Orn.*) die Amsel.

blackguard ['blæga:d], *s.* der Spitzbube, Schurke.

blackmail ['blækmeil], *v.a.* erpressen. — *s.* die Erpressung.

blacksmith ['blæksmiθ], *s.* der Grobschmied.

bladder ['blædə], *s.* (*Anat.*) die Blase.

blade [bleid], *s.* die Klinge (*razor*); der Halm (*grass*); *shoulder* —, das Schulterblatt.

blamable ['bleiməbl], *adj.* tadelnswert, tadelhaft.

blame [bleim], *s.* der Tadel, die Schuld. — *v.a.* tadeln, beschuldigen, die Schuld zuschreiben (*Dat.*).

blameless ['bleimlis], *adj.* tadellos, schuldlos.

blanch [bla:ntʃ], *v.n.* erbleichen, weiß werden. — *v.a.* weiß machen.

bland [blænd], *adj.* mild, sanft.

blandish ['blændiʃ], *v.a.* schmeicheln (*Dat.*).

blandishment ['blændiʃmənt], *s.* (*mostly in pl.*) die Schmeichelei.

blandness ['blændnis], *s.* die Milde, Sanftheit.

blank [blæŋk], *adj.* blank, leer; reimlos (*verse*); *leave a* —, einen Raum freilassen; — *cartridge*, die Platzpatrone.

blanket ['blæŋkit], *s.* die Decke; (*coll.*) *a wet* —, ein langweiliger Kerl, der Spielverderber.

blare [blɛə], *v.n.* schmettern.

blaspheme [blæs'fi:m], *v.a., v.n.* lästern, fluchen.

blasphemous ['blæsfiməs], *adj.* lästerlich.

blasphemy ['blæsfəmi], *s.* die Gotteslästerung.

blast [bla:st], *v.a.* sprengen, zerstören. — *s.* der Windstoß (*gust*); der Stoß (*trumpets*); die Explosion (*bomb*); — *furnace*, der Hochofen. — *excl.* (*sl.*) — *!* zum Teufel!

blasting ['bla:stiŋ], *s.* das Sprengen.

blatant ['bleitənt], *adj.* laut, lärmend; dreist.

blaze [bleiz], *s.* die Flamme (*flame*); das Feuer; der Glanz (*colour etc.*). — *v.n.* flammen; leuchten (*shine*). — *v.a.* ausposaunen, bekannt machen (*make known*).

blazer ['bleizə], *s.* die Sportjacke, Klubjacke.

blazon ['bleizən], *v.a.* verkünden.

bleach [bli:tʃ], *v.a.* bleichen. — *s.* das Bleichmittel.

bleak [bli:k], *adj.* öde, rauh; trübe, freudlos.

bleakness ['bli:knis], *s.* die Öde (*scenery*); Traurigkeit, Trübheit.

bleary ['bliəri], *adj.* trübe; — *eyed*, triefäugig.

bleat [bli:t], *v.n.* blöken.

bleed [bli:d], *v.n. irr.* bluten. — *v.a.* bluten lassen; erpressen (*blackmail*).

blemish ['blemiʃ], *s.* der Makel, der Fehler. — *v.a.* schänden, entstellen.

blench [blentʃ], *v.n.* zurückweichen, stutzen.

blend [blend], *v.a., v.n.* mischen, vermengen; sich mischen. — *s.* die Mischung, Vermischung.

bless [bles], *v.a.* segnen; beglücken; loben.

blessed [blest, 'blesid], *adj.* gesegnet, selig.

blessing ['blesiŋ], *s.* der Segen.

blight [blait], *s.* der Meltau. — *v.a.* verderben.

blind [blaind], *adj.* blind; — *man's buff*, Blinde Kuh; — *spot*, der schwache Punkt. — *s.* die Blende, das Rouleau; *Venetian* —, die Jalousie. — *v.a.* blind machen, täuschen.

blindfold ['blaindfould], *adj.* mit verbundenen Augen.

blindness ['blaindnis], *s.* die Blindheit.

blindworm ['blaindwə:m], *s.* (*Zool.*) die Blindschleiche.

blink [bliŋk], *s.* das Blinzeln. — *v.n.* blinzeln, blinken. — *v.a.* nicht sehen wollen.

blinkers ['bliŋkəz], *s. pl.* die Scheuklappen.

bliss [blis], *s.* die Wonne, Seligkeit.

blissful ['blisful], *adj.* wonnig, selig.

blister ['blistə], *s.* die Blase. — *v.n.* Blasen ziehen, Blasen bekommen.

blithe

blithe [blaið], *adj.* munter, lustig, fröhlich.

blitheness ['blaiðnis], *s.* die Munterkeit, Fröhlichkeit.

blizzard ['blizəd], *s.* der Schneesturm.

bloated ['bloutid], *adj.* aufgeblasen, aufgedunsen.

bloater ['bloutə], *s.* (*Zool.*) der Bückling.

blob [blɔb], *s.* der Kleks.

block [blɔk], *s.* der Block, Klotz (*wood*); Häuserblock (*houses*); — *letters,* große Druckschrift. — *v.a.* blockieren, hemmen (*hinder*); sperren (*road*).

blockade [blɔ'keid], *s.* die Blockade.

blockhead ['blɔkhed], *s.* der Dummkopf.

blonde [blɔnd], *adj.* blond. — *s.* die Blondine.

blood [blʌd], *s.* das Blut; — *vessel,* das Blutgefäß.

bloodcurdling ['blʌdkə:dliŋ], *adj.* haarsträubend.

bloodless ['blʌdlis], *adj.* blutlos, unblutig.

bloodthirsty ['blʌdθə:sti], *adj.* blutdürstig.

bloody ['blʌdi], *adj.* blutig; (*vulg.*) verflucht.

bloom [blu:m], *s.* die Blüte; die Blume. — *v.n.* blühen.

bloomers ['blu:məz], *s. pl.* altmodische Unterhosen für Damen.

blooming ['blu:miŋ], *adj.* blühend.

blossom ['blɔsəm], *s.* die Blüte. — *v.n.* blühen, Blüten treiben.

blot [blɔt], *s.* der Kleks; Fleck; (*fig.*) der Schandfleck. — *v.a.* beflecken; löschen (*ink*); — *out,* ausmerzen, austilgen; *blotting paper,* das Löschpapier.

blotch [blɔtʃ], *s.* der Hautfleck; die Pustel; der Kleks (*blot*).

blotter ['blɔtə], *s.* der Löscher.

blouse [blauz], *s.* die Bluse.

blow (1) [blou], *s.* der Schlag.

blow (2) [blou], *v.a. irr.* blasen; wehen; — *o.'s own trumpet,* prahlen; anfachen (*fire*) — *o.'s nose,* sich schneuzen; — *v.n.* schnaufen, keuchen; — *up,* in die Luft sprengen.

blower ['blouə], *s.* das Gebläse; der Bläser.

blowpipe ['bloupaip], *s.* das Lötrohr.

blubber ['blʌbə], *s.* der Walfischspeck, der Tran. — *v.n.* schluchzen, heulen, flennen.

bludgeon ['blʌdʒən], *s.* der Knüppel; die Keule (*club*). — *v.a.* niederschlagen.

blue [blu:], *adj.* blau; schwermütig (*sad*); — *blooded,* aus edlem Geblüte.

bluebell ['blu:bel], *s.* (*Bot.*) die Glockenblume.

bluebottle ['blu:bɔtl], *s.* (*Ent.*) die Schmeißfliege.

bluestocking ['blu:stɔkiŋ], *s.* der Blaustrumpf.

bluff [blʌf], *adj.* grob, schroff. — *s.* der Bluff, die Täuschung, der Trick. — *v.a., v.n.* vortäuschen (*pretend*), bluffen; verblüffen (*deceive*).

blunder ['blʌndə], *s.* der Fehler, Schnitzer. — *v.n.* einen Fehler machen.

blunderer ['blʌndərə], *s.* der Tölpel.

blunderbuss ['blʌndəbʌs], *s.* die Donnerbüchse.

blunt [blʌnt], *adj.* stumpf (*edge*); derb, offen (*speech*). — *v.a.* abstumpfen; verderben (*appetite*).

bluntness ['blʌntnis], *s.* die Stumpfheit (*edge*); die Derbheit (*speech*).

blur [blə:], *s.* der Fleck. — *v.a.* verwischen.

blurt [blə:t], *v.a.* — *out,* herausplatzen.

blush [blʌʃ], *v.n.* erröten. — *s.* die Schamröte, das Erröten.

bluster ['blʌstə], *s.* das Toben, Brausen. — *v.n.* toben, brausen.

blustering ['blʌstəriŋ], *adj.* lärmend, tobend.

boa ['bouə], *s.* (*Zool.*) die Boa.

boar [bɔ:], *s.* (*Zool.*) der Eber.

board [bɔ:d], *s.* das Brett (*wood*); die Tafel (*notice* —); die Verpflegung (*food*); — *and lodging,* die Vollpension; die Behörde, der Ausschuß (*officials*). — *v.a.* — *up,* vernageln, zumachen; — *someone,* verpflegen; — *a steamer,* an Bord gehen; — *ing school,* das Internat, das Pensionat.

boarder ['bɔ:də], *s.* der Internatsschüler; der Pensionär.

boast [boust], *v.n.* prahlen, sich rühmen. — *s.* der Stolz (*pride*).

boastful ['boustful], *adj.* prahlerisch.

boat [bout], *s.* das Boot; *rowing* —, das Ruderboot; der Kahn.

bob [bɔb], *s.* der Knicks; (*coll.*) der Schilling. — *v.n.* baumeln; springen; *bobbed hair,* der Bubikopf.

bobbin ['bɔbin], *s.* die Spule, der Klöppel.

bobsleigh ['bɔbslei], *s.* der Bob(sleigh), Rennschlitten.

bodice ['bɔdis], *s.* das Mieder, Leibchen.

bodied ['bɔdid], *adj. suffix; able-* —, gesund, stark.

body ['bɔdi], *s.* der Körper; die Körperschaft (*organisation*).

bodyguard ['bɔdigɑ:d], *s.* die Leibwache.

Boer ['bouə], *s.* der Bure.

bog [bɔg], *s.* der Sumpf. — *v.a.* (*coll.*) — *down,* versinken.

Bohemian [bo'hi:mjən], *s.* der Böhme. — *adj.* böhmisch; künstlerhaft.

boil (1) [bɔil], *v.a., v.n.* kochen, sieden. — *s.* das Kochen; —*ing point,* der Siedepunkt.

boil (2) [bɔil], *s.* (*Med.*) die Beule, der Furunkel.

boisterous ['bɔistərəs], *adj.* ungestüm; laut (*noisy*).

boisterousness ['bɔistərəsnis], *s.* die Heftigkeit, Lautheit.

bold [bould], *adj.* kühn, dreist; *make* —, sich erkühnen.

boldness ['bouldnis], *s.* die Kühnheit, Dreistigkeit.

Bolivian [bə'livjən], *adj.* bolivianisch. —*s.* der Bolivianer.

bolster ['boulstə], *s.* das Polster, Kissen.

bolt [boult], *s.* der Bolzen, Riegel (*on door*); der Pfeil (*arrow*). — *v.a.* verriegeln (*bar*); verschlingen (*devour*). — *v.n.* davonlaufen (*run away*), durchgehen (*abscond*).

bomb [bom], *s.* die Bombe. — *v.a.* bombardieren.

bombard [bom'ba:d], *v.a.* bombardieren.

bombardment [bom'ba:dmənt], *s.* die Beschießung.

bombastic [bom'bæstik], *adj.* schwülstig, bombastisch (*style*).

bombproof ['bompru:f], *adj.* bombensicher.

bond [bond], *s.* das Band (*link*); die Schuldverschreibung (*debt*); *in* —, unter Zollverschluß; (*pl.*) die Fesseln (*fetters*). — *v.a.* (*Chem.*) binden; (*Comm.*) zollpflichtig erklären (*declare dutiable*).

bondage ['bondidʒ], *s.* die Knechtschaft.

bone [boun], *s.* der Knochen; die Gräte (*fish*); — *china*, feines Geschirr, das Porzellan; — *of contention*, der Zankapfel; — *dry*, staubtrocken; — *idle*, stinkfaul; — *lace*, die Klöppelspitze. — *v.a.* Knochen oder Gräten entfernen.

bonfire ['bonfaiə], *s.* das Freudenfeuer.

bonnet ['bonit], *s.* die Haube, das Häubchen.

bonny ['boni], *adj.* hübsch, nett.

bony ['bouni], *adj.* beinern, knöchern.

book [buk], *s.* das Buch. — *v.a.* belegen (*seat*); eine Karte lösen (*ticket*); engagieren (*engage*).

bookbinder ['bukbaində], *s.* der Buchbinder.

bookcase ['bukkeis], *s.* der Bücherschrank.

bookie *see* bookmaker.

booking-office ['bukiŋofis], *s.* der Fahrkartenschalter; die Kasse (*Theat. etc.*)

book-keeper ['bukki:pə], *s.* der Buchhalter.

book-keeping ['bukki:piŋ], *s.* die Buchhaltung; *double entry* —, doppelte Buchführung, *single entry* —, einfache Buchführung.

bookmaker ['bukmeikə], *s.* (*abbr.* **bookie** ['buki]), *s.* (*Racing*) der Buchmacher.

bookmark(er) ['bukma:k(ə)], *s.* das Lesezeichen.

bookseller ['bukselə], *s.* der Buchhändler.

bookshop ['bukʃop], *s.* die Buchhandlung.

bookstall ['buksto:l], *s.* der Bücherstand.

bookworm ['bukwə:m], *s.* der Bücherwurm.

boom (1) [bu:m], *s.* der Aufschwung; Boom; (*Comm.*) die Konjunktur; Hausse.

boom (2) [bu:m], *v.n.* dröhnen, (dumpf) schallen.

boon [bu:n], *s.* die Wohltat.

boor [buə], *s.* der Lümmel.

boorish ['buəriʃ], *adj.* lümmelhaft.

boot [bu:t], *s.* der Stiefel, hohe Schuh. — *v.a.* mit dem Stiefel stoßen, kicken.

booth [bu:ð], *s.* die (Markt) Bude; Kabine, Zelle.

bootlace ['bu:tleis], *s.* der Schnürsenkel, der Schnürriemen.

booty ['bu:ti], *s.* die Beute.

booze [bu:z], *v.n.* (*coll.*) saufen.

boozy ['bu:zi], *adj.* (*coll.*) angeheitert, leicht betrunken.

border ['bo:də], *s.* der Rand; die Grenze. — *v.a., v.n.* angrenzen (*on*); einsäumen (*surround*).

borderer ['bo:dərə], *s.* der Grenzbewohner.

bore [bo:], *v.a.* bohren; langweilen (*be boring*). — *s.* das Bohrloch (*drill-hole*), die Bohrung (*drilling*); der langweilige Kerl (*person*).

boredom ['bo:dəm], *s.* die Langeweile.

borer ['bo:rə], *s.* der Bohrer (*drill*).

born [bo:n], *adj.* geboren.

borrow ['borou], *v.a.* borgen, entlehnen.

borrowing ['borouiŋ], *s.* das Borgen, Entlehnen.

bosom ['buzəm], *s.* der Busen.

boss [bos], *s.* der Beschlag, der Buckel; (*coll.*) der Chef.

botanical [bo'tænikəl], *adj.* botanisch.

botanist ['botənist], *s.* der Botaniker.

botany ['botəni], *s.* die Botanik.

botch [botʃ], *s.* das Flickwerk. — *v.a.* verderben, verhunzen.

both [bouθ], *adj., pron.* beide, beides; — *of them*, beide. — *conj.* — ... *and*, sowohl ... als auch.

bother ['boðə], *v.a.* plagen, stören, belästigen; — *it!* zum Henker damit! — *v.n.* sich bemühen. — *s.* die Belästigung, das Ärgernis.

bottle ['botl], *s.* die Flasche. — *v.a.* in Flaschen abfüllen.

bottom ['botəm], *s.* der Boden, Grund (*ground*); die Ursache (*cause*); (*Naut.*) der Schiffsboden.

bottomless ['botəmlis], *adj.* grundlos, bodenlos.

bough [bau], *s.* der Zweig, Ast.

boulder ['bouldə], *s.* der Felsblock.

bounce [bauns], *v.a.* aufprallen lassen (*ball*). — *v.n.* aufprallen. — *s.* der Rückprall, Aufprall.

bound (1) [baund], *s.* der Sprung; *by leaps and* —*s*, sehr schnell, sprunghaft. — *v.n.* springen, prallen.

bound (2) [baund], *v.a.* begrenzen, einschränken. — *adj.* verpflichtet; *he is* — *to* (*inf.*), er wird sicherlich ...

bound (3) [baund], *adj.* — *for*, auf dem Wege nach.

boundary ['baundəri], *s.* die Grenzlinie, Grenze.

bounder ['baundə], *s.* der ungezogene Bursche.

boundless ['baundlis], *adj.* grenzenlos, unbegrenzt.

bounteous ['bauntiəs], *adj.* freigebig; reichlich (*plenty*).

bounty ['baunti], *s.* die Freigebigkeit (*generosity*); (*Comm.*) Prämie.

bouquet [bu'kei], *s.* das Bukett, der Blumenstrauß; die Blume (*wine*).

bourgeois ['buəʒwa:], *s.* der Bürger; Philister. — *adj.* kleinbürgerlich, philisterhaft.

bow (1) [bau], *s.* (*Naut.*) der Bug; —*sprit*, das Bugspriet.

bow (2) [bau], *s.* die Verbeugung, Verneigung. — *v.n.* sich verneigen, sich verbeugen. — *v.a.* neigen.

bow (3) [bou], *s.* (*Mus.*) der Bogen; die Schleife (*ribbon*). — *v.a.* streichen (*violin*).

bowel ['bauəl], *s.* der Darm; (*pl.*) die Eingeweide.

bowl (1) [boul], *s.* die Schale, der Napf, die Schüssel.

bowl (2) [boul], *s.* die Holzkugel; (*pl.*) das Rasenkugelspiel, Bowlingspiel. — *v.n.* (*Cricket*) den Ball werfen.

bowler (1) ['boulə], *s.* (*hat*) der steife Hut, die Melone.

bowler (2) ['boulə], *s.* (*Sport*) der Ballmann.

box (1) [bɔks], *s.* (*Bot.*) der Buchsbaum.

box (2) [bɔks], *s.* die Büchse, Dose, Schachtel, der Kasten; (*Theat.*) die Loge; — *office*, die Theaterkasse.

box (3) [bɔks], *s.* der Schlag; — *on the ear*, die Ohrfeige. — *v.n.* boxen.

boxer ['bɔksə], *s.* der Boxer; Boxkämpfer.

Boxing Day ['bɔksiŋ'dei], der zweite Weihnachtstag.

boy [bɔi], *s.* der Junge, Knabe; Diener (*servant*).

boyish ['bɔiiʃ], *adj.* knabenhaft.

boyhood ['bɔihud], *s.* das Knabenalter.

brace [breis], *s.* das Band; die Klammer (*clamp*); — *of partridges*, das Paar Rebhühner; die Spange (*denture*). — *v.a.* spannen, straffen. — *v.r.* — *yourself!* stähle dich!

bracelet ['breislit], *s.* das Armband.

braces ['breisiz], *s. pl.* die Hosenträger.

bracken ['brækən], *s.* (*Bot.*) das Farnkraut.

bracket ['brækit], *s.* die Klammer; *income* —, die Einkommensgruppe. — *v.a.* (ein-)klammern; (*Maths.*) in Klammern setzen.

brackish ['brækiʃ], *adj.* salzig.

brad [bræd], *s.* der kopflose Nagel; — *awl*, der Vorstechbohrer.

brag [bræg], *v.n.* prahlen.

braggart ['brægət], *s.* der Prahlhans.

Brahmin ['bra:min], *s.* der Brahmane.

braid [breid], *s.* die Borte; der Saumbesatz. — *v.a.* (mit Borten) besetzen.

Braille [breil], *s.* die Blindenschrift.

brain [brein], *s.* das Gehirn, Hirn; *scatter-* —*ed*, zerstreut.

brainwave ['breinweiv], *s.* der Geistesblitz.

brake [breik], *s.* die Bremse. — *v.a.* bremsen.

bramble [bræmbl], *s.* der (*Bot.*) Brombeerstrauch.

bran [bræn], *s.* die Kleie.

branch [bra:ntʃ], *s.* der Ast, Zweig; (*Comm.*) die Zweigstelle, Filiale. — *v.n.* — *out*, sich verzweigen; — *out into*, sich ausbreiten, etwas Neues anfangen; — *off*, abzweigen.

brand [brænd], *s.* der (Feuer) Brand; das Brandmal (*on skin*); die Sorte, Marke (*make*); — *new*, funkelnagelneu. — *v.a.* brandmarken, kennzeichnen.

brandish ['brændiʃ], *v.a.* schwingen, herumschwenken.

brandy ['brændi], *s.* der Branntwein, Kognac, Weinbrand.

brass [bra:s], *s.* das Messing; — *band*, die Blechmusik, Militärmusikkapelle; — *founder*, Erzgießer, Gelbgießer; (*sl.*) die Frechheit (*impudence*).

brassiere ['bræsiɛə], *s.* der Büstenhalter.

brat [bræt], *s.* (*coll.*) das Kind, der Balg.

brave [breiv], *adj.* tapfer, kühn. — *v.a.* trotzen, standhalten (*Dat.*). — *s.* der Held, Krieger; der Indianer (*redskin*).

bravery ['breivəri], *s.* die Tapferkeit.

brawl [brɔ:l], *s.* der Krawall, die Rauferei. — *v.n.* zanken, lärmen.

brawn [brɔ:n], *s.* die Sülze; (*fig.*) die Körperkraft, Stärke.

brawny ['brɔ:ni], *adj.* stark, sehnig.

bray [brei], *v.n.* iah sagen, Eselslaute von sich geben (*donkey*). — *s.* das Iah des Esels, das Eselsgeschrei.

brazen [breizn], *adj.* (*Metall.*) aus Erz; unverschämt (*shameless*).

brazenfaced ['breiznfeisd], *adj.* unverschämt.

brazier ['breiziə], *s.* der Kupferschmied; die Kohlenpfanne.

Brazil [brə'zil]. Brasilien, *n.*; — *nut*, die Paranuß.

Brazilian [brə'ziliən], *adj.* brasilianisch. — *s.* der Brasilianer.

breach [bri:tʃ], *s.* die Bresche; der Bruch (*break*); die Verletzung; der Vertragsbruch (*of contract*); der Verstoß (*of*, gegen, *etiquette etc.*).

bread [bred], *s.* das Brot; *brown* —, das Schwarzbrot; — *and butter*, das Butterbrot.

breadth [bretθ], *s.* die Breite, Weite.

break [breik], *s.* der Bruch (*breach*); die Lücke (*gap*); die Chance (*chance*); *a lucky* —, ein glücklicher Zufall, ein Glücksfall; die Pause (*from work*). — *v.a., v.n. irr.* brechen; — *off*, Pause machen; — *in*, unterbrechen (*interrupt*); — *in*, (*horse*) einschulen, zureiten; — *up*, abbrechen (*school, work*); — *away*, sich trennen, absondern; — *down*, zusammenbrechen (*health*); (*Am.*) analysieren; auflösen.

breakage ['breikidʒ], *s.* der Bruch, der Schaden (*damage*).

breakdown ['breikdoun], *s.* der Zusammenbruch (*health*); die Panne (*car*); (*Am.*) die Analyse (*analysis*).

breaker ['breikə], *s.* die Brandungswelle, Brandung.

breakfast ['brekfəst], *s.* das Frühstück. — *v.n.* frühstücken.

breast [brest], *s.* die Brust.

breath [breθ], *s.* der Atem; der Hauch (*exhalation*); *with bated* —, mit verhaltenem Atem.

breathe [bri:ð], *v.a., v.n.* atmen.

breathing ['bri:ðiŋ], *s.* die Atmung.

breathless ['breθlis], *adj.* atemlos.

breech [bri:tʃ], *s.* der Boden.

breeches ['britʃiz], *s.pl.* Reithosen, *f. pl.*

breed [bri:d], *v.a. irr.* zeugen, züchten (*cattle, etc.*). — *v.n.* sich vermehren. — *s.* die Zucht, die Art (*type*); die Rasse (*race*).

breeder ['bri:də], *s.* der Züchter.

breeding ['bri:diŋ], *s.* die gute Kinderstube (*manners*); die Erziehung; das Züchten (*of plants, cattle etc.*).

breeze [bri:z], *s.* die Briese.

breezy ['bri:zi], *adj.* windig; lebhaft (*manner*), beschwingt (*tone*).

brethren ['breðrən], *s. pl.* (*obs.*) die Brüder.

Breton [bretn], *adj.* bretonisch. — *s.* der Bretagner, Bretone.

brevet ['brevit], *s.* das Patent.

breviary ['bri:viəri], *s.* das Brevier.

brevity ['breviti], *s.* die Kürze.

brew [bru:], *v.a.* brauen. — *s.* das Gebräu, Bräu (*beer*).

brewer ['bru:ə], *s.* der Brauer, Bierbrauer.

brewery ['bru:əri], *s.* die Brauerei, das Brauhaus.

briar, brier ['braiə], *s.* (*Bot.*) der Dornstrauch, die wilde Rose.

bribe [braib], *v.a.* bestechen. — *s.* das Bestechungsgeld.

bribery ['braibəri], *s.* die Bestechung.

brick [brik], *s.* der Ziegel, Backstein; *drop a* —, eine Taktlosigkeit begehen, einen Schnitzer machen.

bricklayer ['brikleiə], *s.* der Maurer.

bridal [braidl], *adj.* bräutlich.

bride [braid], *s.* die Braut.

bridegroom ['braidgru:m], *s.* der Bräutigam.

bridesmaid ['braidzmeid], *s.* die Brautjungfer.

bridge [bridʒ], *s.* die Brücke. — *v.a.* überbrücken; — *the gap*, die Lücke füllen.

bridle [braidl], *s.* der Zaum, Zügel. — *v.a.* aufzäumen. — *v.n.* sich brüsten.

brief [bri:f], *adj.* kurz, bündig, knapp. — *s.* der Schriftsatz, der Rechtsauftrag, die Instruktionen, *f. pl.* (*instructions*). — *v.a.* instruieren, beauftragen; informieren (*inform*).

brigade [bri'geid], *s.* die Brigade.

brigand ['brigənd], *s.* der Brigant, Straßenräuber.

bright [brait], *adj.* hell, glänzend (*shiny*); klug, intelligent (*clever*).

brighten [braitn], *v.a.* glänzend machen (*polish etc.*); erhellen, aufheitern(*cheer*).

brightness ['braitnis], *s.* der Glanz; die Helligkeit; die Klugheit (*cleverness*).

brill [bril], *s.* (*Zool.*) der Glattbutt.

brilliance, brilliancy ['briljəns, -jənsi], *s.* der Glanz, die Pracht.

brim [brim], *s.* der Rand (*glass*); die Krempe (*hat*). — *v.n.* — (*over*) *with*, überfließen von.

brimful ['brimful], *adj.* übervoll.

brimstone ['brimstoun], *s.* der Schwefel; — *butterfly*, der Zitronenfalter.

brindled [brindld], *adj.* scheckig, gefleckt.

brine [brain], *s.* die Salzsole, das Salzwasser.

bring [briŋ], *v.a. irr.* bringen; — *about*, zustande bringen; — *forth*, hervorbringen; gebären; — *forward*, fördern; anführen; — *on*, herbeiführen; — *up*, erziehen, aufziehen.

brink [briŋk], *s.* (*fig.*) der Rand; — *of a precipice*, Rand eines Abgrundes.

briny ['braini], *adj.* salzig.

brisk [brisk], *adj.* frisch, munter, feurig (*horse*).

brisket ['briskit], *s.* die Brust (eines Tieres).

briskness ['brisknis], *s.* die Lebhaftigkeit.

bristle [brisl], *s.* die Borste. — *v.n.* sich sträuben.

British ['britiʃ], *adj.* britisch.

Britisher, Briton ['britiʃə, 'britən], *s.* der Brite.

brittle [britl], *adj.* zerbrechlich, spröde.

brittleness ['britlnis], *s.* die Sprödigkeit, Zerbrechlichkeit.

broach [broutʃ], *v.a.* anzapfen, anschneiden; — *a subject*, ein Thema berühren.

broad [brɔ:d], *adj.* breit, weit; ordinär, derb (*joke*); — *minded*, duldsam, weitherzig.

broadcast ['brɔ:dka:st], *v.a.* senden, übertragen (*radio*). — *s.* die Sendung, das Programm.

broadcaster ['brɔ:dka:stə], *s.* der im Radio Vortragende *or* Künstler (*artist*); Ansager.

broadcasting ['brɔ:dka:stiŋ], *s.* das Senden, der Rundfunk; — *station*, der Sender, die Rundfunkstation.

broadcloth ['brɔ:dklɔθ], *s.* das feine Tuch.

broaden [brɔ:dn], *v.a.* erweitern, verbreitern.

brocade [bro'keid], *s.* der Brokat.

brogue [broug], *s.* der grobe Schuh; der irische Akzent.

broil [brɔil], *v.a.* braten, rösten.

broke [brouk], *adj.* (*coll.*) pleite.

broken ['broukən], *adj.* gebrochen; zerbrochen; unterbrochen (*interrupted*).

broker ['broukə], *s.* der Makler.

bronchial ['brɔŋkjəl], *adj.* (*Anat.*) bronchial, in or von der Luftröhre, Luftröhren-.

bronchitis [brɔŋ'kaitis], *s.* (*Med.*) die Luftröhrenentzündung, Bronchitis.

bronze [brɔnz], *s.* (*Metall.*) die Bronze, Bronzefarbe.

brooch [broutʃ], *s.* die Brosche.

brood [bru:d], *s.* die Brut. — *v.n.* brüten; grübeln (*meditate*).

brook (1) [bruk], *s.* der Bach.

brook (2) [bruk], *v.a.* ertragen, leiden.

brooklet ['bruklit], *s.* das Bächlein.

broom [bru:m], *s.* der Besen; (*Bot.*) der Ginster.

broth [brɔθ], *s.* die Brühe; *meat —*, Fleischbrühe.

brothel ['brɔθəl], *s.* das Bordell.

brother ['brʌðə], *s.* der Bruder; *— -in-law*, der Schwager.

brotherhood ['brʌðəhud], *s.* die Bruderschaft.

brotherly ['brʌðəli], *adj.* brüderlich.

brow [brau], *s.* die Braue, Augenbraue; der Kamm (*hill*); die Stirn(e) (*forehead*).

browbeat ['braubi:t], *v.a.* einschüchtern.

brown [braun], *adj.* braun; *in a — study*, in tiefem Nachsinnen.

browse [brauz], *v.n.* weiden (*cattle*); stöbern, (durch-)blättern (*in books etc.*).

Bruin ['bru:in]. Braun, Meister Petz, der Bär.

bruise [bru:z], *v.a.* quetschen, stoßen; (wund) schlagen. — *s.* die Quetschung.

Brunswick ['brʌnzwik]. Braunschweig, *n.*

brunt [brʌnt], *s.* der Anprall; *bear the —*, der Wucht ausgesetzt sein, den Stoß auffangen.

brush [brʌʃ], *s.* die Bürste (*clothes*); der Pinsel (*paint, painting*); *— stroke*, der Pinselstrich. — *v.a., v.n.* bürsten, abbürsten; *— against s.o.*, mit jemandem zusammenstoßen, streifen (*an, Acc.*); *— up one's English*, das Englisch auffrischen; *— off*, abschütteln.

brushwood ['brʌʃwud], *s.* das Gestrüpp.

brusque [brusk], *adj.* brüsk, barsch.

Brussels ['brʌsəlz]. Brüssel, *n.*; *— sprouts*, (*Bot.*) der Rosenkohl.

brutal [bru:tl], *adj.* brutal, grausam.

brutality [bru:'tæliti], *s.* die Brutalität.

brute [bru:t], *s.* der Unmensch.

bubble [bʌbl], *s.* die Blase; (*fig.*) der Schwindel (*swindle*). — *v.n.* sprudeln, wallen, schäumen.

buccaneer [bʌkə'niə], *s.* der Seeräuber.

buck [bʌk], *s.* (*Zool.*) der Bock; (*Am. sl.*) der Dollar. — *v.a. — up*, aufmuntern. — *v.n. — up*, sich zusammenraffen.

bucket ['bʌkit], *s.* der Eimer, Kübel.

buckle [bʌkl], *s.* die Schnalle. — *v.a.* zuschnallen; biegen. — *v.n.* sich krümmen.

buckler ['bʌklə], *s.* der Schild.

buckram ['bʌkrəm], *s.* die Steifleinwand.

buckskin ['bʌkskin], *s.* das Wildleder.

buckwheat ['bʌkwi:t], *s.* (*Bot.*) der Buchweizen.

bucolic [bju:'kɔlik], *adj.* bukolisch, ländlich, Schäfer-.

bud [bʌd], *s.* (*Bot.*) die Knospe. — *v.n.* knospen.

buddy ['bʌdi], *s.* (*Am.*) der Freund, Kamerad.

budge [bʌdʒ], *v.n.* sich rühren, sich regen.

budget ['bʌdʒit], *s.* das Budget; der Haushaltsplan; der Etat; *present the —*, den Staatsetat vorlegen. — *v.n.* voranschlagen (*for*), planen.

buff [bʌf], *adj.* ledergelb.

buffalo ['bʌfəlou], *s.* (*Zool.*) der Büffel.

buffer ['bʌfə], *s.* der Puffer.

buffet (1) ['bʌfit], *s.* der Puff, Faustschlag (*blow*). — *v.a.* schlagen, stoßen.

buffet (2) ['bufei], *s.* das Buffet, der Anrichtetisch.

buffoon [bʌ'fu:n], *s.* der Possenreißer.

buffoonery [bʌ'fu:nəri], *s.* die Possen, *f. pl.*; das Possenreißen.

bug [bʌg], *s.* (*Ent.*) die Wanze; (*Am.*) der Käfer; (*coll.*) das Insekt.

buggy ['bʌgi], *s.* der Einspänner.

bugle [bju:gl], *s.* (*Mus.*) das Signalhorn, die Signaltrompete.

bugler ['bju:glə], *s.* (*Mus.*) der Trompeter.

build [bild], *v.a., v.n. irr.* bauen; errichten; *— on*, sich verlassen auf (*rely on*). — *s.* die Statur, Figur (*figure*).

builder ['bildə], *s.* der Bauherr, Baumeister (*employer*); Bauarbeiter (*worker*).

building ['bildiŋ], *s.* das Gebäude, der Bau; *— site*, der Bauplatz.

bulb [bʌlb], *s.* (*Bot.*) der Knollen, die Zwiebel; *Dutch —*, die Tulpe; (*Elec.*) die Birne.

bulbous ['bʌlbəs], *adj.* zwiebelartig; dickbäuchig.

Bulgarian [bʌl'gɛəriən], *adj.* bulgarisch. — *s.* der Bulgare.

bulge [bʌldʒ], *s.* die Ausbauchung; die Ausbuchtung (*in fighting line*). — *v.n.* herausragen, anschwellen.

bulk [bʌlk], *s.* die Masse, Menge; *buy in —*, im Großen einkaufen.

bulky [ˈbʌlki], *adj.* schwer (*heavy*); massig (*stodgy*); unhandlich.
bull (1) [bul], *s.* (*Zool.*) der Bulle, Stier; —'s *eye,* das Schwarze (*target*).
bull (2) [bul], *s.* (*Papal*) die Bulle, der Erlass.
bulldog [ˈbuldɔg], *s.* der Bullenbeißer.
bullet [ˈbulit], *s.* die Kugel, das Geschoß.
bulletin [ˈbulitin], *s.* das Bulletin, der Tagesbericht.
bullfight [ˈbulfait], *s.* der Stierkampf.
bullfinch [ˈbulfintʃ], *s.* (*Orn.*) der Dompfaff.
bullfrog [ˈbulfrɔg], *s.* (*Zool.*) der Ochsenfrosch.
bullion [ˈbuljən], *s.* der Goldbarren, Silberbarren.
bullock [ˈbulək], *s.* (*Zool.*) der Ochse.
bully [ˈbuli], *s.* der Raufbold, Angeber, Großtuer (*braggart*); der Tyrann. — *v.a.* tyrannisieren, einschüchtern.
bulrush [ˈbulrʌʃ], *s.* (*Bot.*) die Binse.
bulwark [ˈbulwək], *s.* das Bollwerk, die Verteidigung.
bump [bʌmp], *s.* der Schlag, der Stoß. — *v.a.* stoßen.
bun [bʌn], *s.* das Rosinenbrötchen; das süße Brötchen; (*hair*) der Knoten.
bunch [bʌntʃ], *s.* der Bund (*keys*); der Strauß (*flowers*); die Traube (*grapes*). — *v.a.* zusammenfassen, zusammenbinden, zusammenraffen.
bundle [bʌndl], *s.* das Bündel.
bung [bʌŋ], *s.* der Spund (*in barrel*).
bungle [bʌŋgl], *v.a.* verpfuschen, verderben.
bungler [ˈbʌŋglə], *s.* der Stümper.
bunion [ˈbʌnjən], *s.* die Fußschwiele.
bunk (1) [bʌŋk], *s.* die (Schlaf-)Koje.
bunk (2) [bʌŋk], *s.* (*coll.*) der Unsinn.
bunker [ˈbʌŋkə], *s.* der Kohlenraum, Bunker.
bunting [ˈbʌntiŋ], *s.* das Flaggentuch.
buoy [bɔi], *s.* die Boje.
buoyant [ˈbɔiənt], *adj.* schwimmend; lebhaft, heiter.
buoyancy [ˈbɔiənsi], *s.* die Schwimmkraft; die Schwungkraft.
burden (1) [bəːdn], *s.* die Bürde, Last. — *v.a.* belasten, beladen.
burden (2) [bəːdn], *s.* der Refrain; der Hauptinhalt.
burdensome [ˈbəːdnsəm], *adj.* beschwerlich.
bureau [bjuəˈrou], *s.* der Schreibtisch; das Büro.
bureaucracy [bjuəˈrɔkrəsi], *s.* die Bürokratie.
burgess [ˈbəːdʒis], *s.* der Bürger.
burglar [ˈbəːglə], *s.* der Einbrecher.
burglary [ˈbəːgləri], *s.* der Einbruch, der Diebstahl.
burgomaster [ˈbəːgɔmaːstə], *s.* der Bürgermeister.
Burgundian [bəːˈgʌndiən], *adj.* burgundisch. —*s.* der Burgunder.
Burgundy (1) [ˈbəːgəndi], das Burgund.
Burgundy (2) [ˈbəːgəndi], *s.* der Burgunder(-wein).

burial [ˈberiəl], das Begräbnis; — *ground,* der Kirchhof, Friedhof; — *service,* die Totenfeier, Trauerfeier.
burlesque [bəːˈlesk], *s.* die Burleske, Posse.
burly [ˈbəːli], *adj.* dick, stark.
Burmese [bəːˈmiːz], *adj.* birmesisch. — *s.* der Birmese.
burn [bəːn], *v.a., v.n. irr.* brennen, verbrennen. — *s.* das Brandmal.
burner [ˈbəːnə], *s.* der Brenner.
burnish [ˈbəːniʃ], *v.a.* polieren.
burred [bəːd], *adj.* überliegend; (*Metall.*) ausgehämmert; — *over,* (*Metall.*) breitgeschmiedet.
burrow [ˈbʌrou], *s.* der Bau, (*rabbits etc.*). — *v.n.* sich eingraben; wühlen.
burst [bəːst], *v.a., v.n. irr.* bersten, platzen, explodieren (*explode*); — *out laughing,* laut auflachen; — *into tears,* in Tränen ausbrechen; — *into flames,* aufflammen; sprengen (*blow up*). — *s.* der Ausbruch; die Explosion.
bury [ˈberi], *v.a.* begraben; beerdigen.
bus [bʌs], *s.* der Autobus, Omnibus.
busby [ˈbʌzbi], *s.* (*Mil.*) die Bärenmütze.
bush [buʃ], *s.* der Busch.
bushel [ˈbuʃl], *s.* der Scheffel.
bushy [ˈbuʃi], *adj.* buschig.
business [ˈbiznis], *s.* das Geschäft; die Beschäftigung, die Tätigkeit (*activity*); Aufgabe, Obliegenheit; der Handel (*trade*); *on* —, geschäftlich.
businesslike [ˈbiznislaik], *adj.* geschäftsmäßig, nüchtern, praktisch.
businessman [ˈbiznismæn], *s.* der Geschäftsmann.
bust (1) [bʌst], *s.* die Büste.
bust (2) [bʌst], *v.a., v.n.* (*coll.*) sprengen; *go* —, bankrott machen.
bustard [ˈbʌstəd], *s.* (*Orn.*) die Trappe.
bustle [bʌsl], *s.* der Lärm, die Aufregung. — *v.n.* aufgeregt umherlaufen; rührig sein (*be active*).
busy [ˈbizi], *adj.* geschäftig (*active*); beschäftigt (*engaged,* mit, *in*); *be* —, zu tun haben.
but [bʌt], *conj.* aber, jedoch; sondern. — *adv.* nur, bloß; — *yesterday,* erst gestern. — *prep.* außer; *all* — *two,* alle außer zwei.
butcher [ˈbutʃə], *s.* der Metzger, Fleischer; —'s *knife,* das Fleischmesser.
butchery [ˈbutʃəri], *s.* die Schlächterei; das Blutbad, das Gemetzel.
butler [ˈbʌtlə], *s.* der oberste Diener; Kellermeister.
butt [bʌt], *s.* das dicke Ende; der Kolben (*rifle*); der Stoß (*blow*); die Zielscheibe (*target*). — *v.a.* stoßen, spießen.
butter [ˈbʌtə], *s.* die Butter. — *v.a.* mit Butter bestreichen; — *up,* schmeicheln (*Dat.*).
butterfly [ˈbʌtəflai], *s.* (*Ent.*) der Schmetterling.
buttery [ˈbʌtəri], *s.* die Speisekammer.

buttock(s) ['bʌtək(s)], s. der Hintere, das Gesäß.

button [bʌtn], s. der Knopf. — v.a. — up, knöpfen, zumachen.

buttress ['bʌtris], s. der Strebepfeiler.

buxom ['bʌksəm], adj. drall, gesund.

buy [bai], v.a. irr. kaufen.

buzz [bʌz], s. das Summen. — v.n. summen.

buzzard ['bʌzəd], s. (Orn.) der Bussard.

by [bai], prep. (beside) neben, an; (near) nahe; (before) gegen, um, bei; (about) bei; (from, with) durch, von, mit; — the way, nebenbei bemerkt; — way of, mittels. — adv. (nearby) nahe; nebenan.

by-election ['baiilekʃən], s. die Nachwahl; Ersatzwahl.

bygone ['baigɔn], adj. vergangen.

bylaw, byelaw ['bailɔ:], s. die Bestimmung.

Byzantine [bai'zæntain], adj. byzantinisch.

C

C [si:]. das C (also Mus.).

cab [kæb], s. (horse-drawn) die Droschke, der Wagen; das Taxi; —stand, der Droschkenhalteplatz; (Motor.) der Taxiplatz, Taxistand.

cabaret ['kæbərei], s. das Kabarett, die Kleinbühne.

cabbage ['kæbidʒ], s. (Bot.) der Kohl.

cabin ['kæbin], s. die Kabine (boat); die Hütte (hut); — -boy, der Schiffsjunge.

cabinet ['kæbinet], s. das Kabinett (government); der Schrank (cupboard); das kleine Zimmer or Nebenzimmer (mainly Austr.); (Rad.) das Gehäuse; — maker, der Kunsttischler.

cable [keibl], s. das Kabel (of metal), das Seil (metal or rope); das Telegramm. — v.a. kabeln, telegraphieren.

cablegram ['keiblgræm], s. die (Kabel-) Depesche.

cabman ['kæbmən], s. der Taxichauffeur.

caboose [kə'bu:s], s. die Schiffsküche.

cabriolet [kæbrio'lei], s. das Kabriolett.

cackle [kækl], v.n. gackern (hens); schnattern (geese); (fig.) schwatzen.

cacophony [kə'kɔfəni], s. der Mißklang.

cad [kæd], s. der gemeine Kerl, Schuft.

cadaverous [kə'dævərəs], adj. leichenhaft.

caddie ['kædi], s. der Golfjunge.

caddy ['kædi], s. tea —, die Teebüchse, Teedose.

cadence ['keidəns], s. (Phonet.) der Tonfall; (Mus.) die Kadenz.

cadet [kə'det], s. (Mil.) der Kadett.

cadge [kædʒ], v.a. erbetteln.

Caesar ['si:zə]. Cäsar, m.

Caesarean [si'zɛəriən], adj. cäsarisch; — operation or section, (Med.) der Kaiserschnitt.

cafeteria [kæfə'tiəriə], s. das Selbstbedienungsrestaurant.

cage [keidʒ], s. (Zool.) der Käfig; (Orn.) das Vogelbauer. — v.a. einfangen, einsperren.

cagey ['keidʒi], adj. (coll.) argwöhnisch, zurückhaltend; schlau.

cairn [kɛən], s. (Archaeol.) der Steinhaufen, der Grabhügel.

caitiff ['keitif], adj. niederträchtig. — s. der Schuft.

cajole [kə'dʒoul], v.a. schmeicheln (Dat.).

cake [keik], s. der Kuchen; — of soap, das Stück Seife; have o.'s — and eat it, alles haben. — v.a., v.n. zusammenbacken; —d with dirt, mit Schmutz beschmiert.

calamity [kə'læmiti], s. das Unheil, Unglück; Elend.

calcareous [kæl'kɛəriəs], adj. (Geol.) kalkartig.

calculate ['kælkjuleit], v.a. berechnen.

calculation [kælkju'leiʃən], s. die Berechnung.

calendar ['kæləndə], s. der Kalender.

calf [kɑ:f], s. (Zool.) das Kalb; (Anat.) die Wade; — love, die Jugendliebe.

calibre ['kælibə], s. das Kaliber.

calico ['kælikou], s. der Kaliko, Kattun.

Caliph ['keilif], s. der Kalif.

calk (1) [kɔ:k], v.a. beschlagen (horse).

calk (2), **caulk** [kɔ:k], v.a. (Naut.) abdichten.

call [kɔ:l], v.a., v.n. rufen, herbeirufen; (Am.) antelefonieren, anrufen (ring up); (name) nennen; — to account, zur Rechenschaft ziehen; (summon) kommen lassen; — for, abholen; this —s for, das berechtigt zu. — s. der Ruf, Anruf; die (innere) Berufung, der Beruf.

callbox ['kɔ:lbɔks] see phone box.

calling ['kɔ:liŋ], s. der Beruf, das Gewerbe (occupation).

callous ['kæləs], adj. schwielig (hands); (fig.) unempfindlich, hart, gemein.

callow ['kælou], adj. ungefiedert (bird); (fig.) unerfahren.

calm [kɑ:m], adj. ruhig, still; gelassen. — s. die Ruhe; (Naut.) Windstille. — v.a. beruhigen. — v.n. — down, sich beruhigen, sich legen (storm etc.).

caloric [kæ'lɔrik], adj. Wärme-, warm; (Chem.) kalorisch.

calorie, calory ['kæləri], s. die Kalorie.

calumny ['kæləmni], s. die Verleumdung.

calve [kɑ:v], v.n. kalben, Kälber kriegen.

cambric ['kæmbrik], s. der Batist (textile).

camel ['kæməl], s. (Zool.) das Kamel.

cameo ['kæmiou], s. die Kamee.

camera ['kæmərə], s. (Phot.) die Kamera.

camomile ['kæməmail], s. (Bot.) die Kamille.

camp [kæmp], s. das Lager; Zeltlager.
— v.n. sich lagern, ein Lager aufschlagen, zelten.

campaign [kæm'pein], s. der Feldzug.
— v.n. einen Feldzug mitmachen;
(fig.) Propaganda machen.

camphor ['kæmfə], s. der Kampfer.

camping ['kæmpiŋ], s. die Lagerausrüstung (equipment); das Lagern (activity), das Zelten.

can (1) [kæn], s. die Kanne; die Büchse; watering —, die Gießkanne. — v.a. (Am.) einmachen, einkochen (fruit).

can (2) [kæn], v. aux. irr. können, imstande sein, vermögen.

Canadian [kə'neidiən], adj. kanadisch.
— s. der Kanadier.

canal [kə'næl], s. der Kanal; — lock, die Kanalschleuse.

canalize ['kænəlaiz], v.a. kanalisieren, leiten.

cancel ['kænsəl], v.a. widerrufen, absagen (show); aufheben, ungültig machen.

cancellation [kænsə'leiʃən], s. die Aufhebung, Absage, Widerrufung.

cancer ['kænsə], s. (Med., Astrol.) der Krebs.

cancerous ['kænsərəs], adj. (Med.) krebsartig.

candelabra [kændi'lɑ:brə], s. der Kandelaber, Leuchter.

candid ['kændid], adj. offen, aufrichtig.

candidate ['kændideit], s. der Kandidat, Bewerber.

candidature ['kændiditʃə], s. die Kandidatur, die Bewerbung.

candied ['kændid], adj. gezuckert, kandiert (fruit).

candle [kændl], s. die Kerze, das Licht.

Candlemas ['kændlməs]. (Eccl.) Lichtmeß.

candlestick ['kændlstik], s. der Kerzenleuchter.

candlewick ['kændlwik], s. der Kerzendocht (textile).

candour ['kændə], s. die Offenheit, Aufrichtigkeit.

candy ['kændi], s. (Am.) das Zuckerwerk, (pl.) Süßigkeiten. — v.a. verzuckern.

cane [kein], s. (Bot.) das Rohr, der Rohrstock; Spazierstock. — v.a. (mit dem Stock) schlagen.

canine ['kænain], adj. Hunde-, hündisch; — tooth, der Eckzahn.

canister ['kænistə], s. die Blechbüchse, der Kanister.

canker ['kæŋkə], s. (Bot.) der Brand; (Bot.) der Pflanzenrost; (fig.) eine zerfressende Krankheit.

cannibal ['kænibəl], s. der Kannibale, Menschenfresser.

cannon ['kænən], s. die Kanone, das Geschütz.

canoe [kə'nu:], s. das Kanu.

canon ['kænən], s. (Mus., Eccl.) der Kanon; die Regel; (Eccl.) der Domherr; — law, das kanonische Recht.

canonize ['kænənaiz], v.a. (Eccl.) kanonisieren, heiligsprechen.

canopy ['kænəpi], s. der Baldachin.

cant [kænt], s. die Heuchelei.

can't, cannot [kɑ:nt,'kænɔt] see can (2).

cantankerous [kæn'tæŋkərəs], adj. zänkisch, mürrisch.

cantata [kæn'tɑ:tə], s. (Mus.) die Kantate.

canteen [kæn'ti:n], s. die Kantine (restaurant); die Besteckgarnitur (set of cutlery).

canter ['kæntə], s. der Galopp, der Kurzgalopp.

canticle ['kæntikl], s. (Eccl.) der Lobgesang, das Loblied.

canto ['kæntou], s. (Lit.) der Gesang.

canton ['kæntən], s. (Pol.) der Kanton, der Bezirk.

canvas ['kænvəs], s. das Segeltuch; (Art) die Malerleinwand; die Zeltplane (tent).

canvass ['kænvəs], v.a., v.n. (Pol.) um Stimmen werben.

canvasser ['kænvəsə], s. (Pol.) der Werber, Stimmensammler.

cap [kæp], s. die Kappe, Mütze; die Haube; der Deckel. — v.a. übertreffen.

capability [keipə'biliti], s. die Fähigkeit.

capable ['keipəbl], adj. fähig (Genit.), imstande (of, zu); tüchtig.

capacious [kə'peiʃəs], adj. geräumig.

capacity [kə'pæsiti], s. der Inhalt, die Geräumigkeit; die Fassungskraft (intellect); die Leistungsfähigkeit (ability); der Fassungsraum (space).

cape (1) [keip], s. (Tail.) der Kragenmantel.

cape (2) [keip], s. (Geog.) das Kap, das Vorgebirge.

caper ['keipə], s. der Sprung, Luftsprung. — v.n. in die Luft springen.

capillary [kə'piləri], adj. haarfein; — tubing, die Haarröhre, die Kapillarröhre.

capital ['kæpitl], s. (Comm.) das Kapital; die Hauptstadt (capital city); — punishment, die Todesstrafe; — letter, der Großbuchstabe. — adj. (coll.) ausgezeichnet, vorzüglich.

capitalize ['kæpitəlaiz], v.a. (Comm.) kapitalisieren; ausnutzen.

capitation [kæpi'teiʃən], s. die Kopfsteuer.

capitulate [kə'pitjuleit], v.n. kapitulieren.

capon ['keipən], s. (Zool.) der Kapaun.

caprice [kə'pri:s], s. die Kaprize, Laune.

capricious [kə'priʃəs], adj. launenhaft, eigensinnig.

Capricorn ['kæprikɔ:n]. (Astrol.) der Steinbock; tropic of —, der Wendekreis des Steinbocks.

capriole ['kæprioul], s. der Luftsprung.

capsize [kæp'saiz], v.n. umkippen, kentern (boat).

capstan ['kæpstən], s. (Engin.) die Ankerwinde; (Mech.) die Erdwinde; (Naut.) das Gangspill.

capsular ['kæpsjulə], adj. kapselförmig.

capsule ['kæpsju:l], s. die Kapsel.

captain ['kæptin], s. (Naut.) der Kapitän; (Mil.) der Hauptmann.

captious

captious ['kæpʃəs], *adj.* zänkisch, streitsüchtig; verfänglich.

captivate ['kæptiveit], *v.a.* einnehmen, gewinnen.

captive ['kæptiv], *s.* der Gefangene. — *adj.* gefangen.

capture ['kæptʃə], *s.* die Gefangennahme (*men*); Erbeutung (*booty*).

Capuchin ['kæputʃin], *s.* (*Eccl.*) der Kapuziner.

car [ka:], *s.* (*Motor.*) der Wagen; das Auto; (*Am.*) der Eisenbahnwagen.

carafe [kə'ræf], *s.* die Karaffe, Wasserflasche.

caravan ['kærəvæn], *s.* die Karawane; der Wohnwagen.

caraway ['kærəwei],*s.*(*Bot.*)derKümmel.

carbine ['ka:bain], *s.* der Karabiner.

carbolic [ka:'bolik], *adj.* — *acid*, (*Chem.*) die Karbolsäure.

carbon ['ka:bən], *s.* (*Chem.*) der Kohlenstoff.

carbonate ['ka:bəneit], *s.* (*Chem.*) das kohlensaure Salz, Karbonat.

carbonize ['ka:bənaiz], *v.a.* verkohlen. — *v.n.* (*Chem., Geol.*) zu Kohle werden.

carbuncle ['ka:bʌnkl], *s.* (*Min.*) der Karfunkel; (*Med.*) der Karbunkel.

carburettor [ka:bju'retə], *s.* (*Motor.*) der Vergaser.

carcase, carcass ['ka:kəs], *s.* der Kadaver.

card (1) [ka:d], *s.* die Karte, Postkarte; *playing* —, die Spielkarte; *put your* —*s on the table*, rück mit der Wahrheit heraus!

card (2) [ka:d], *v.a.* krempeln (*wool*); kardätschen (*cotton*).

cardboard ['ka:dbo:d], *s.* die Pappe, der Pappendeckel.

cardiac ['ka:diæk], *adj.* (*Med.*) Herz-.

cardinal ['ka:dinl], *s.* (*Eccl.*) der Kardinal. — *adj.* Kardinal-, grundlegend.

cardiogram ['ka:diogræm], *s.* (*Med.*) das Kardiogramm.

cardsharper ['ka:dʃa:pə], *s.* der Falschspieler.

care [kɛə], *s.* die Sorge (*anxiety*, um, *for*); *with* —, mit Sorgfalt, genau; *care of* (*abbr. c/o on letters*), bei; *take* —, sich in acht nehmen. — *v.n.* — *for*, sich interessieren, gern haben.

careen [kə'ri:n], *v.a.* (*Naut.*) kielholen, umlegen.

career [kə'riə], *s.* die Karriere, Laufbahn.

careful ['kɛəful], *adj.* sorgfältig, vorsichtig, umsichtig.

carefulness ['kɛəfulnis], *s.* die Vorsicht, Sorgfalt, Umsicht.

careless ['kɛəlis], *adj.* unachtsam, nachlässig.

carelessness ['kɛəlisnis], *s.* die Nachlässigkeit, Unachtsamkeit.

caress [kə'res], *v.a.* liebkosen, herzen. — *s.* die Liebkosung, die Zärtlichkeit.

caretaker ['kɛəteikə], *s.* der Hausmeister.

careworn ['kɛəwɔ:n], *adj.* abgehärmt, von Sorgen gebeugt.

cargo ['ka:gou], *s.* die Fracht, die Ladung.

caricature [kærikə'tjuə *or* 'kærikətʃə], *s.* die Karikatur. — *v.a.* karikieren, verzerren.

Carinthian [kə'rinθjən], *adj.* kärntnerisch.

carmine ['ka:main], *s.* der Karmin.

carnage ['ka:nidʒ], *s.* das Blutbad.

carnal [ka:nl], *adj.* fleischlich, sinnlich.

carnation [ka:'neiʃən], *s.* (*Bot.*) die Nelke.

carnival ['ka:nivl], *s.* der Karneval.

carnivorous [ka:'nivərəs], *adj.* fleischfressend.

carol ['kærəl], *s. Christmas* —, das Weihnachtslied.

carotid [kə'rɔtid], *s.* (*Anat.*) die Halspulsader.

carousal [kə'rauzəl], *s.* das Gelage, das Gezeche.

carouse [kə'rauz], *v.n.* zechen, schmausen.

carp (1) [ka:p], *s.* (*Zool.*) der Karpfen.

carp (2) [ka:p], *v.n.* bekritteln, tadeln.

Carpathian Mountains [ka:'peiθjən 'mauntinz]. die Karpathen, *f. pl.*

carpenter ['ka:pəntə], *s.* der Zimmermann; Tischler.

carpentry ['ka:pəntri], *s.* die Tischlerei, das Zimmerhandwerk.

carpet ['ka:pit], *s.* der Teppich; — *bag*, die Reisetasche.

carriage ['kæridʒ], *s.* der Wagen, Waggon; das Verhalten, die Haltung (*bearing*); (*Comm.*) — *paid*, einschließlich Zustellung; — *way*, der Straßendamm.

carrier ['kæriə], *s.* der Fuhrmann, Fuhrunternehmer.

carrion ['kæriən], *s.* das Aas.

carrot ['kærət], *s.* (*Bot.*) die Mohrrübe; die Karotte.

carry ['kæri], *v.a.* tragen; bringen; führen (*on vehicle*), fahren (*convey*); — *interest*, Zinsen tragen; (*Comm.*) — *forward*, übertragen; — *two* (*in adding up*), zwei weiter; — *on*, weitermachen, fortfahren; — *through*, durchführen, durchhalten. — *v.n.* vernehmbar sein (*of sound*); — *on*, weiterarbeiten, weiterexistieren.

cart [ka:t], *s.* der Karren, Frachtwagen.

cartel [ka:'tel], *s.* (*Comm.*) das Kartell.

Carthage ['ka:θidʒ]. Karthago, *n.*

carthorse ['ka:thɔ:s], *s.* das Zugpferd.

cartilage ['ka:tilidʒ], *s.* der Knorpel.

carton ['ka:tən], *s.* (*cardboard box*) der Karton, die Schachtel.

cartoon [ka:'tu:n], *s.* die Karikatur; — *film*, der Trickfilm.

cartridge ['ka:tridʒ], *s.* die Patrone.

cartwright ['ka:trait], *s.* der Stellmacher, Wagenbauer.

carve [ka:v], *v.a.* schneiden (*cut*); schnitzen (*wood*), meißeln (*stone*), tranchieren (*meat*).

carver ['kɑːvə], s. der Schnitzer (*wood*); das Tranchiermesser (*carving knife*).

cascade [kæs'keid], s. der Wasserfall.

case (1) [keis], s. der Kasten, Behälter; das Futteral, Etui (*spectacles*); das Gehäuse (*watch*); die Kiste (*wooden box*); (*Typ.*) der Schriftkasten.

case (2) [keis], s. der Fall (*event*); (*Law*) der Rechtsfall, der Umstand (*circumstance*); in —, falls.

casement ['keismənt], s. der Fensterflügel, das Fenster (*frame*).

caseous ['keisjəs], adj. käsig.

cash [kæʃ], s. bares Geld; die Barzahlung; — *box*, die Kasse. — v.a. einlösen (*cheque*).

cashier [kæ'ʃiə], s. der Kassierer. — v.a. (*Mil.*) entlassen.

cashmere ['kæʃiə], s. die Kaschmirwolle (*wool*).

casing ['keisiŋ], s. die Hülle; das Gehäuse (*case*); die Haut (*sausage skin*).

cask ['kɑːsk], s. das Faß.

casket ['kɑːskit], s. das Kästchen; (*Am.*) der Sarg.

Caspian (Sea) ['kæspiən (siː)]. das kaspische Meer.

cassock ['kæsək], s. die Soutane.

cast [kɑːst], v.a. irr. werfen (*throw*); (*Metall.*) gießen (*Theat.*) besetzen; (*plaster*) formen; — *off*, abwerfen; — *anchor*, ankern; — *o.'s skin*, sich häuten; — *down*, niederschlagen; — *a vote*, die Stimme abgeben. — s. der Wurf; (*Metall.*) der Guß; (*Theat.*) die Besetzung; der Abguß (plaster). — adj. — *iron*, das Gußeisen; — *steel*, der Gußstahl.

castanets [kæstə'nets], s. pl. (*Mus.*) die Kastagnetten, f. pl.

castaway ['kɑːstəwei], adj. weggeworfen; (*Naut.*) schiffbrüchig.

caste [kɑːst], s. die Kaste.

caster ['kɑːstə], s. der Streuer, die Streubüchse; — *sugar*, Streuzucker.

casting ['kɑːstiŋ], s. (*Metall.*) das Gießen, der Guß.

castle [kɑːsl], s. die Burg, das Schloß; (*Chess*) der Turm.

castor (1) ['kɑːstə], s. (*Zool.*) der Biber.

castor (2) ['kɑːstə] see **caster.**

castor (3) **oil** ['kɑːstər 'ɔil], s. das Rizinusöl.

castrate [kæs'treit], v.a. kastrieren.

castration [kæs'treiʃən], s. die Kastration.

casual ['kæʒjuəl], adj. zufällig, gelassen (*manner*); gelegentlich; flüchtig.

casualty ['kæʒjuəlti], s. der Unglücksfall; — *ward*, die Unfallstation; (*pl.*) die Verluste, m. pl.

cat [kæt], s. die Katze; *tom* —, der Kater; — *burglar*, der Fassadenkletterer; —'*s eye*, das Katzenauge, der Rückstrahler; der Reflektor.

cataclysm ['kætəklizm], s. die Sintflut, die Überschwemmung.

catacomb ['kætəkuːm], s. die Katakombe.

catalogue ['kætələɡ], s. der Katalog,

das Verzeichnis. — v.a. im Katalog verzeichnen, katalogisieren.

catapult ['kætəpult], s. die Schleuder (*hand*); (*Mil.*) die Wurfmaschine. — v.a. schleudern.

cataract ['kætərækt], s. der Wasserfall (*water*); (*Med.*) der Star.

catarrh [kə'tɑː], s. (*Med.*) der Katarrh.

catastrophe [kə'tæstrəfi], s. die Katastrophe, das Unglück.

catastrophic [kætəs'trɔfik], adj. katastrophal, unheilvoll.

catch [kætʃ], v.a. irr. fangen, auffangen, fassen; überfallen (— *unawares, ambush*); — *a cold*, sich einen Schnupfen zuziehen, sich erkälten; erreichen (*train, etc.*); — *redhanded*, bei frischer Tat ertappen. — s. der Fang (*fish*); die Beute (*prey, booty*); der Haken (*hook, also fig.*).

catchpenny ['kætʃpeni], s. der Flitterkram, Lockartikel. — adj. marktschreierisch.

catchphrase, catchword ['kætʃfreiz, 'kætʃwɔːd], s. das (billige) Schlagwort.

catechism ['kætikizm], s. der Katechismus.

categorical [kæti'ɡɔrikəl], adj. kategorisch, entschieden.

category ['kætiɡəri], s. die Kategorie, Klasse, Gruppe, Gattung.

cater ['keitə], v.n. Lebensmittel einkaufen; verpflegen; (*fig.*) sorgen (*for, für*).

caterer ['keitərə], s. der Lebensmittellieferant.

catering ['keitəriŋ], s. die Verpflegung.

caterpillar ['kætəpilə], s. (*Ent.*) die Raupe; —*tractor*, der Raupenschlepper.

caterwaul ['kætəwɔːl], v.n. miauen.

cathedral [kə'θiːdrəl], s. der Dom, die Kathedrale.

Catholic ['kæθəlik], adj. katholisch. — s. der Katholik.

catholic ['kæθəlik], adj. allumfassend.

Catholicism [kə'θɔlisizm], s. der Katholizismus.

catkin ['kætkin], s. (*Bot.*) das Kätzchen; *pussy-willow* —, das Palmkätzchen.

cattle [kætl], s. pl. das Vieh; — *plague*, die Rinderpest; — *show*, die Viehausstellung.

caucus ['kɔːkəs], s. die Wahlversammlung; der Wahlausschuß.

caul [kɔːl], s. das Haarnetz; (*Anat.*) die Eihaut.

cauldron ['kɔːldrən], s. der Kessel.

cauliflower ['kɔliflauə], s. (*Bot.*) der Blumenkohl.

caulk [kɔːk], v.a. kalfatern (*see under* calk (2)).

causal ['kɔːzəl], adj. ursächlich.

causality [kɔː'zæliti], s. der ursächliche Zusammenhang; (*Log.*) die Kausalität.

cause [kɔːz], s. die Ursache. — v.a. verursachen.

causeway ['kɔːzwei], s. der Damm.

caustic ['kɔːstik], adj. ätzend; beißend.

cauterize

cauterize ['kɔ:təraiz], v.a. (Med.) ätzen, ausbrennen.
caution ['kɔ:ʃən], s. die Vorsicht (care); die Warnung (warning). — v.a. (Law) ermahnen; warnen.
cautionary ['kɔ:ʃənəri], adj. warnend.
cautious ['kɔ:ʃəs], adj. vorsichtig, behutsam.
cautiousness ['kɔ:ʃəsnis], s. die Vorsicht, Behutsamkeit.
cavalcade [kævəl'keid], s. die Kavalkade; (Mil.) der Reiterzug.
cavalry ['kævəlri], s. die Kavallerie, die Reiterei.
cave [keiv], s. die Höhle. — v.a. aushöhlen. — v.n. — in, einstürzen, einfallen.
caveat ['keiviæt], s. (Law) die Warnung; der Vorbehalt.
cavern ['kævən], s. die Höhle.
cavernous ['kævənəs], adj. (Geog., Geol.) voll Höhlen.
caviare [kævi'a:], s. der Kaviar.
cavil ['kævil], v.n. nörgeln (at, über), tadeln (Acc.).
cavity ['kæviti], s. die Höhlung.
caw [kɔ:], v.n. (Orn.) krächzen.
cease [si:s], v.a. einstellen. — v.n. aufhören.
ceaseless ['si:slis], adj. unaufhörlich.
cedar ['si:də], s. (Bot.) die Zeder.
cede [si:d], v.a. überlassen. — v.n. nachgeben.
ceiling ['si:liŋ], s. die Decke (room); (Comm.) die Preisgrenze.
celebrate ['selibreit], v.a. feiern; zelebrieren.
celebrated ['selibreitid], adj. berühmt.
celebration [seli'breiʃən], s. die Feier.
celebrity [si'lebriti], s. die Berühmtheit; der „Star“.
celerity [si'leriti], s. die Behendigkeit, Schnelligkeit.
celery ['seləri], s. (Bot.) der Sellerie.
celestial [si'lestjəl], adj. himmlisch.
celibacy ['selibəsi], s. die Ehelosigkeit; (Eccl.) das Zölibat.
celibate ['selibit], adj. unverheiratet.
cell [sel], s. die Zelle.
cellar ['selə], s. der Keller; salt —, das Salzfaß.
cellarage ['seləridʒ], s. die Kellerei; die Einkellerung (storage).
cellarer ['selərə], s. der Kellermeister.
cellular ['seljulə], adj. zellartig, Zell-.
Celt [kelt, selt], s. der Kelte.
Celtic ['keltik, 'seltik], adj. keltisch.
cement [si'ment], s. der Zement, Mörtel. — v.a. auszementieren, verkitten.
cemetery ['semətri], s. der Kirchhof, der Friedhof.
cenotaph ['senotæf or -ta:f], s. das Ehrengrabmal, Ehrendenkmal.
censer ['sensə], s. (Eccl.) das Weihrauchfaß.
censor ['sensə], s. der Zensor.
censorious [sen'sɔ:riəs], adj. kritisch, tadelsüchtig.
censure ['senʃə], s. der Tadel, Verweis. — v.a. tadeln.

census ['sensəs], s. die Volkszählung.
cent [sent], s. (Am.) der Cent (coin); (Comm.) per —, das Prozent.
centenarian [senti'nɛəriən], adj. hundertjährig. — s. der Hundertjährige.
centenary [sen'ti:nəri], s. die Hundertjahrfeier.
centennial [sen'tenjəl], adj. alle hundert Jahre, hundertjährig.
centipede ['sentipi:d], s. (Zool.) der Tausendfüßler.
central ['sentrəl], adj. zentral.
centralize ['sentrəlaiz], v.a. zentralisieren.
centre ['sentə], s. das Zentrum, der Mittelpunkt; die Mitte.
centric(al) ['sentrik(əl)], adj. (Engin., Maths.) zentral.
centrifugal [sen'trifjugəl], adj. zentrifugal.
centrifuge ['sen'trifju:dʒ], s. die Zentrifuge.
centripetal [sen'tripitl], adj. zentripetal, zum Mittelpunkt hinstrebend.
century ['sentʃuri], s. das Jahrhundert.
cereal ['siəriəl], adj. vom Getreide, Getreide—. — s. die Kornmehlspeise.
cerebral ['seribrəl], adj. Gehirn-.
ceremonial [seri'mounjəl], adj. feierlich, förmlich (formal). — s. das Zeremoniell.
ceremonious [seri'mounjəs], adj. feierlich, zeremoniell.
ceremony ['seriməni], s. die Zeremonie, die Feier.
certain ['sə:tin], adj. sicher, gewiß.
certainty ['sə:tinti], s. die Gewißheit.
certificate [sə:'tifikit], s. das Zeugnis, die Bescheinigung.
certification [sə:tifi'keiʃən], s. die Bescheinigung, Bezeugung.
certify ['sə:tifai], v.a. bescheinigen, bezeugen, beglaubigen.
certitude ['sə:titju:d], s. die Gewißheit.
cerulean [si'ru:ljən], adj. himmelblau.
cesspool ['sespu:l], s. die Senkgrube.
cessation [se'seiʃən], s. das Aufhören; (of hostilities) der Waffenstillstand.
cession ['seʃən], s. die Abtretung, der Verzicht (of, auf).
chafe [tʃeif], v.a. wärmen, warmreiben; erzürnen (annoy); wundreiben (skin). — v.n. toben, wüten.
chafer ['tʃeifə], s. (Ent.) der Käfer.
chaff [tʃa:f], s. die Spreu; die Neckerei (teasing). — v.a. necken.
chaffer ['tʃæfə], v.n. handeln, schachern (haggle).
chaffinch ['tʃæfintʃ], s. (Orn.) der Buchfink.
chagrin [ʃæ'gri:n], s. der Verdruß, der Ärger.
chain [tʃein], s. die Kette. — v.a. anketten.
chair [tʃɛə], s. der Stuhl; (Univ.) Lehrstuhl. — v.a. vorsitzen (Dat.).
chairman ['tʃɛəmən], s. der Vorsitzende.
chalice ['tʃælis], s. (Eccl.) der Kelch.

chalk [tʃɔ:k], *s.* die Kreide. — *v.a.* —
up, ankreiden, anschreiben.

chalky [ˈtʃɔ:ki], *adj.* (*Geol.*) kreidig,
kreideartig.

challenge [ˈtʃælindʒ], *v.a.* herausfordern; in Frage stellen (*question*);
anhalten (*of a sentry*). — *s.* die Herausforderung; das Anhalten (*by a
sentry*); die Einwendung.

chalybeate [kəˈlibiət], *adj.* (*Med.*)
eisenhaltig.

chamber [ˈtʃeimbə], *s.* das Zimmer, die
Kammer.

chamberlain [ˈtʃeimbəlin], *s.* der
Kammerherr.

chambermaid [ˈtʃeimbəmeid], *s.* das
Zimmermädchen, Kammermädchen.

chameleon [kəˈmi:ljən], *s.* (*Zool.*) das
Chamäleon.

chamois [ˈʃæmwɑ:], *s.* (*Zool.*) die Gemse.

champagne [ʃæmˈpein], *s.* der Champagner, der Sekt.

champion [ˈtʃæmpjən], *s.* der Meister,
Verteidiger. — *v.a.* vertreten (*cause*);
beschützen (*person*).

chance [tʃɑ:ns], *s.* der Zufall; die
Gelegenheit (*opportunity*); die
Möglichkeit (*possibility*); *take a* —,
es darauf ankommen lassen; *by* —,
zufällig. — *v.a.* zufällig tun, geraten;
riskieren (*risk*).

chancel [ˈtʃɑ:nsəl], *s.* (*Eccl.*) der Chor,
der Altarplatz.

chancellor [ˈtʃɑ:nsələ], *s.* der Kanzler.

chancery [ˈtʃɑ:nsəri], *s.* das Kanz-
leigericht.

chandelier [ʃændəˈliə], *s.* der Arm-
leuchter, Kronleuchter.

chandler [ˈtʃɑ:ndlə], *s.* der Lichtzieher;
Krämer; (*corn merchant*) der Korn-
händler.

change [tʃeindʒ], *s.* die Änderung; das
Umsteigen (*trains*); *small* —, das
Kleingeld; die Veränderung; Abwechs-
lung. — *v.a.* ändern (*alter*); wechseln
(*money*); umsteigen (*trains*); eintauschen, umtauschen (*exchange*); sich
umziehen (*clothes*). — *v.n.* sich (ver)-
ändern, anders werden, umschlagen;
(*Railw.*) — *for*, umsteigen nach.

changeable [ˈtʃeindʒəbl], *adj.* veränderlich.

changeling [ˈtʃeindʒliŋ], *s.* der Wechselbalg.

changeover [ˈtʃeindʒouvə], *s.* der
Wechsel; der Umschalter; die Umstellung.

channel [ˈtʃænəl], *s.* der Kanal. — *v.a.*
leiten, kanalisieren.

chant [tʃɑ:nt], *v.a., v.n.* (*Eccl.*) singen.
— *s.* (*Mus.*) der Kantus, der litur-
gische Gesang.

chaos [ˈkeiɔs], *s.* das Chaos.

chaotic [keiˈɔtik], *adj.* chaotisch.

chap (1) [tʃæp], *s.* der Riss (*skin etc.*).
— *v.n.* Risse bekommen.

chap (2) [tʃæp], *s.* (*usually in pl.*) der
Kinnbacken.

chap (3) [tʃæp], *s.* (*coll.*) der Kerl, der
Bursche.

chapel [ˈtʃæpəl], *s.* (*Eccl.*) die Kapelle.

chaperon [ˈʃæpəroun], *s.* die Anstands-
dame. — *v.a.* begleiten, bemuttern.

chaplain [ˈtʃæplin], *s.* der Kaplan.

chapter [ˈtʃæptə], *s.* das Kapitel.

char [tʃɑ:], *v.a.* verkohlen. — *v.n.*
(*coll.*) putzen, Hausarbeit verrichten
(*do housework*). — *s.* (*coll.*) die Haus-
hilfe, die Hausgehilfin, Putzfrau.

character [ˈkærəktə], *s.* der Charakter
(*personality*); das Zeichen (*sign, symbol*); (*Maths.*) die Ziffer; das Zeugnis
(*testimonial*).

characteristic [kærəktəˈristik], *adj.*
charakteristisch, typisch.

characterize [ˈkærəktəraiz], *v.a.* charakterisieren, kennzeichnen.

charade [ʃəˈrɑ:d], *s.* die Scharade, das
Silbenrätsel.

charcoal [ˈtʃɑ:koul], *s.* die Holzkohle;
— *burner*, der Köhler.

charge [tʃɑ:dʒ], *v.a.* laden, aufladen;
(*Law*) beschuldigen; (*Mil.*) angreifen;
belasten (*with a bill*); — *up to s.o.*,
jemandem etwas anrechnen; verlangen
(*price*). — *s.* die Ladung, der Auftrag
(*order*); die Aufsicht; *to be in* —, die
Aufsicht haben; (*Law*) die Beschuldi-
gung, Anklage; das Mündel (*of a
guardian*); (*pl.*) die Kosten, Spesen.

chargeable [ˈtʃɑ:dʒəbl], *adj.* anzurech-
nend; steuerbar (*of objects*).

charger [ˈtʃɑ:dʒə], *s.* das Schlachtroß.

chariness [ˈtʃɛərinis], *s.* die Behutsamkeit.

chariot [ˈtʃæriət], *s.* der Kriegswagen.

charioteer [tʃæriəˈtiə], *s.* der Wagen-
lenker.

charitable [ˈtʃæritəbl], *adj.* wohltätig,
mild, mildtätig.

charitableness [ˈtʃæritəblnis], *s.* die
Wohltätigkeit, Milde.

charity [ˈtʃæriti], *s.* die Güte; Näch-
stenliebe; Mildtätigkeit (*alms*); die
Barmherzigkeit (*charitableness*); der
wohltätige Zweck (*cause*); *sister of* —,
barmherzige Schwester.

charlatan [ˈʃɑ:lətən], *s.* der Scharlatan,
Pfuscher.

charm [tʃɑ:m], *s.* der Zauber (*magic*);
der Reiz. — *v.a.* bezaubern.

chart [tʃɑ:t], *s.* (*Geog.*) die Karte. — *v.a.*
auf der Karte einzeichnen.

charter [ˈtʃɑ:tə], *s.* die Urkunde. — *v.a.*
(*Naut.*) die Schiffsmiete. — *v.a.*
mieten, chartern, heuern (*ship, plane*);
ein Privileg geben, bevorrechtigen.

charwoman [ˈtʃɑ:wumən], *s.* die
Putzfrau, Reinemacherin.

chary [ˈtʃɛəri], *adj.* behutsam; vorsichtig (*cautious*); sparsam (*thrifty*).

chase [tʃeis], *v.a.* jagen, verfolgen. — *s.*
die Jagd (*hunt*); das Gehege (*game
preserve*).

chaser [ˈtʃeisə], *s.* der Verfolger (*pursuer*); die Schiffskanone (*gun*).

chasm [kæzm], *s.* die Kluft; der
Abgrund.

chassis [ˈʃæsi], *s.* (*Motor.*) das Fahr-
gestell.

chaste [tʃeist], *adj.* keusch, züchtig.
chasten [tʃeisn], *v.a.* züchtigen; reinigen.
chastize [tʃæs'taiz], *v.a.* züchtigen.
chastity [ˈtʃæstiti], *s.* die Keuschheit, Züchtigkeit.
chasuble [ˈtʃæzjubl], *s.* (*Eccl.*) das Meßgewand.
chat [tʃæt], *v.n.* plaudern. — *s.* das Geplauder.
chattel [tʃætl], *s.* (*usually in pl.*) die Habe; *goods and* —s, Hab und Gut.
chatter [ˈtʃætə], *v.n.* schwätzen; schnattern. — *s.* das Geschwätz (*talk*).
chatterbox [ˈtʃætəbɔks], *s.* die Plaudertasche.
chatty [ˈtʃæti], *adj.* geschwätzig.
chauffeur [ˈʃoufə, ʃouˈfɔː], *s.* (*Motor.*) der Fahrer.
chauffeuse [ʃouˈfɔːz], *s.* die Fahrerin.
chauvinism [ˈʃouvinizm], *s.* der Chauvinismus.
cheap [tʃiːp], *adj.* billig.
cheapen [ˈtʃiːpən], *v.a.* herabsetzen, erniedrigen (*value*).
cheapness [ˈtʃiːpnis], *s.* die Billigkeit (*price*).
cheat [tʃiːt], *v.a.*, *v.n.* betrügen. — *s.* der Betrüger.
cheating [ˈtʃiːtiŋ], *s.* das Betrügen; der Betrug.
check [tʃek], *s.* der Einhalt, der Halt; die Kontrolle; das Hindernis (*obstacle*); (*Chess*) Schach; (*Am.*) *see* **cheque.** — *v.a.* zurückhalten, aufhalten (*stop*); überprüfen. — *v.n.* Schach bieten (*Dat.*).
checker *see under* **chequer.**
checkmate [ˈtʃekmeit], *s.* das Schachmatt.
cheek [tʃiːk], *s.* die Wange, die Backe; die Unverschämtheit (*impertinence*). — *v.a.* unverschämt sein *or* handeln (*s.o.*, an jemandem).
cheeky [ˈtʃiːki], *adj.* frech, unverschämt.
cheer [tʃiə], *v.a.* anfeuern, anspornen; zujubeln; — *up*, aufmuntern. — *v.n.* — *up*, Mut fassen. — *s.* der Zuruf; der Beifallsruf (*acclaim*); *three* —s, ein dreifaches Hoch (*for*, auf).
cheerful [ˈtʃiəful], *adj.* fröhlich, froh.
cheerless [ˈtʃiəlis], *adj.* unfreundlich, freudlos.
cheese [tʃiːz], *s.* der Käse; — *straw,* die Käsestange.
cheesecloth [ˈtʃiːzklɔθ], *s.* (*Am.*) das Nesseltuch.
cheeseparing [ˈtʃiːzpɛəriŋ], *adj.* knauserig.
cheesy [ˈtʃiːzi], *adj.* käsig; schlecht aussehend.
cheetah [ˈtʃiːitə], *s.* (*Zool.*) der Jagdleopard.
chemical [ˈkemikəl], *adj.* chemisch. — *s.* die Chemikalie, das chemische Element; das chemische Produkt.
chemise [ʃiˈmiːz], *s.* das Frauenhemd.
chemist [ˈkemist], *s.* der Chemiker; Drogist; Apotheker (*dispenser*).

chemistry [ˈkemistri], *s.* die Chemie.
cheque, (*Am.*) **check** [tʃek], *s.* (*Fin.*) der Scheck.
chequer, checker [ˈtʃekə], *s.* das scheckige Muster, Würfelmuster. — *v.a.* würfelig machen, bunt machen.
cherish [ˈtʃeriʃ], *v.a.* hegen, wertschätzen, lieben.
cherry [ˈtʃeri], *s.* (*Bot.*) die Kirsche; — *brandy,* das Kirschwasser.
chess [tʃes], *s.* das Schachspiel; —*man,* die Schachfigur; —*board,* das Schachbrett.
chest [tʃest], *s.* die Truhe (*box*); die Kiste; (*Anat.*) Brust; — *of drawers,* die Kommode.
chestnut [ˈtʃestnʌt], *s.* (*Bot.*) die Kastanie; (*horse*) der Braune. — *adj.* kastanienbraun.
chew [tʃuː], *v.a.* kauen; —*ing gum,* der Kaugummi.
chic [ʃiːk], *adj.* elegant, schick.
chicanery [ʃiˈkeinəri], *s.* die Schikane, Haarspalterei, Kleinlichkeit.
chicken [ˈtʃikin], *s.* das Huhn, Kücken; — *soup,* die Hühnersuppe.
chickenpox [ˈtʃikinpɔks], *s.* (*Med.*) die Windpocken.
chicory [ˈtʃikəri], *s.* (*Bot.*) die Zichorie.
chide [tʃaid], *v.a. irr.* schelten.
chief [tʃiːf], *s.* der Häuptling (*of tribe*); (*Am. coll.*) der Chef (*boss*). — *adj.* hauptsächlich, Haupt-, oberst.
chieftain [ˈtʃiːftin], *s.* der Häuptling (*of tribe*); Anführer (*leader*).
chilblain [ˈtʃilblein], *s.* die Frostbeule.
child [tʃaild], *s.* das Kind.
childbirth [ˈtʃaildbəːθ], *s.* die Niederkunft.
childhood [ˈtʃaildhud], *s.* die Kindheit.
childish [ˈtʃaildiʃ], *adj.* kindisch.
childlike [ˈtʃaildlaik], *adj.* kindlich, wie ein Kind.
Chilean [ˈtʃiliən], *adj.* chilenisch. — *s.* der Chilene.
chill [tʃil], *s.* die Kälte, der Frost; die Erkältung. — *v.a.* kalt machen (*freeze*); erstarren lassen (*make rigid*); entmutigen (*discourage*).
chilly [ˈtʃili], *adj.* frostig, eisig, eiskalt.
chime [tʃaim], *s.* das Glockengeläute. — *v.n.* klingen, läuten.
chimera [kiˈmiərə], *s.* das Hirngespinst, das Trugbild.
chimney [ˈtʃimni], *s.* der Kamin, der Schornstein; —*pot,* —*stack,* der Schornstein; —*sweep,* der Kaminfeger, Schornsteinfeger.
chimpanzee [tʃimpænˈziː], *s.* (*Zool.*) der Schimpanse.
chin [tʃin], *s.* (*Anat.*) das Kinn.
china [ˈtʃainə], *s.* das Porzellan; — *ware,* das Küchengeschirr.
chine (1) [tʃain], *s.* das Rückgrat.
chine (2) [tʃain], *s.* (*Geog.*) der Kamm.
Chinaman [ˈtʃainəmən], *s.* (*obs.*) der Chinese.
Chinese [tʃaiˈniːz], *adj.* chinesisch. — *s.* der Chinese.
chink [tʃiŋk], *s.* die Ritze, der Spalt.

chip [tʃip], *v.a.* schnitzeln (*wood*); ausbrechen (*stone*); in kleine Stücke schneiden. — *v.n.* — *off*, abbröckeln; — *in₂* (*coll.*) sich hineinmischen. —*s.* der Span (*wood*); der Splitter (*glass, stone*); (*pl.*) Pommes frites (*pl.*) (*potatoes*).

chiromancy [ˈkaiərɔmænsi], *s.* das Handlesen.

chiropodist [kiˈrɔpədist], *s.* der Fußpfleger.

chirp [tʃəːp], *v.n.* zwitschern (*birds*), zirpen (*crickets*).

chirping [ˈtʃəːpiŋ], *s.* das Gezwitscher (*birds*), das Gezirpe (*crickets*).

chisel [ˈtʃizl], *s.* der Meißel. — *v.a.* meißeln.

chit [tʃit], *s.* das Stück Papier; (*coll.*) junges Ding; —*chat*, das Geplauder.

chivalrous [ˈʃivəlrəs], *adj.* ritterlich; tapfer (*brave*).

chivalry [ˈʃivəlri], *s.* die Ritterlichkeit (*courtesy*); Tapferkeit (*bravery*).

chive [tʃaiv], *s.* (*Bot.*) der Schnittlauch.

chlorate [ˈklɔːreit], *s.* (*Chem.*) das Chlorsalz.

chlorine [ˈklɔːriːn], *s.* (*Chem.*) das Chlor, Chlorgas.

chloroform [ˈklɔrəfɔːm], *s.* das Chloroform. — *v.a.* chloroformieren.

chocolate [ˈtʃɔkəlit], *s.* die Schokolade. — *adj.* schokoladefarben.

choice [tʃɔis], *s.* die Wahl; Auswahl (*selection*). — *adj.* auserlesen.

choir [ˈkwaiə], *s.* der Chor.

choke [tʃouk], *v.a.*, *v.n.* ersticken; verstopfen (*block*). — *s.* (*Elec.*) die Drosselspule; (*Motor.*) die Starterklappe.

choler [ˈkɔlə], *s.* die Galle; (*fig.*) der Zorn (*anger*).

cholera [ˈkɔlərə], *s.* (*Med.*) die Cholera.

choleric [ˈkɔlərik], *adj.* jähzornig, cholerisch.

choose [tʃuːz], *v.a. irr.* wählen, auswählen (*select*).

choosy [ˈtʃuːzi], *adj.* wählerisch.

chop [tʃɔp], *v.a.* abhacken (*cut off*), hacken (*meat*). — *s.* das Kotelett (*meat*).

chopper [ˈtʃɔpə], *s.* das Hackbeil (*axe*); das Hackmesser (*knife*).

choppy [ˈtʃɔpi], *adj.* bewegt (*sea*), stürmisch.

chopstick [ˈtʃɔpstik], *s.* das Eßstäbchen.

choral [ˈkɔːrəl], *adj.* Chor-; — *society*, der Gesangverein.

chorale [kɔˈrɑːl], *s.* (*Eccl.*, *Mus.*) der Choral.

chord [kɔːd], *s.* die Saite; (*Geom.*) die Sehne; (*Mus.*) der Akkord.

chorister [ˈkɔristə], *s.* der Chorknabe (*boy*), Chorsänger.

chorus [ˈkɔːrəs], *s.* der Chor (*opera*); der Refrain (*song*).

Christ [kraist], Christus, *m.*

christen [krisn], *v.a.* taufen (*baptize*); nennen (*name*).

Christendom [ˈkrisndəm], *s.* die Christenheit.

christening [ˈkrisniŋ], *s.* die Taufe.

Christian [ˈkristjən], *s.* der Christ (*believer in Christ*). — *adj.* christlich; — *name*, der Vorname.

Christianity [kristiˈæniti], *s.* die christliche Religion, das Christentum.

Christmas [ˈkrisməs], *s.* (die) Weihnachten; das Weihnachtsfest; — *Eve*, der heilige Abend.

chromatic [kroˈmætik], *adj.* (*Mus.*) chromatisch.

chrome [kroum], *s.* das Chrom.

chronic [ˈkrɔnik], *adj.* chronisch.

chronicle [ˈkrɔnikl], *s.* die Chronik. — *v.a.* (in einer Chronik) verzeichnen.

chronological [krɔnəˈlɔdʒikəl], *adj.* chronologisch.

chronology [krəˈnɔlədʒi], *s.* die Chronologie.

chronometer [krəˈnɔmitə], *s.* das Chronometer.

chrysalis [ˈkrisəlis], *s.* (*Ent.*) die Puppe.

chrysanthemum [kriˈzænθəməm], *s.* (*Bot.*) die Chrysantheme.

chub [tʃʌb], *s.* (*Zool.*) der Döbel.

chubby [ˈtʃʌbi], *adj.* pausbäckig, plump.

chuck [tʃʌk], *v.a.* (*coll.*) — *out*, hinauswerfen. — *v.n.* glucken (*chicken*).

chuckle [tʃʌkl], *v.n.* kichern. — *s.* das Kichern.

chum [tʃʌm], *s.* (*coll.*) der Freund, Kamerad. — *v.n.* (*coll.*) — *up*, sich befreunden (*with*, mit).

chump [tʃʌmp], *s.* der Klotz (*wood*).

chunk [tʃʌŋk], *s.* das große Stück (*meat etc.*).

church [tʃəːtʃ], *s.* die Kirche.

churchwarden [tʃəːtʃˈwɔːdn], *s.* der Kirchenvorsteher.

churchyard [ˈtʃəːtʃjaːd], *s.* der Friedhof.

churl [tʃəːl], *s.* der Grobian, der grobe Kerl.

churlish [ˈtʃəːliʃ], *adj.* grob, unfein.

churn [tʃəːn], *s.* das Butterfaß. — *v.a.* mischen, schütteln (*butter etc.*); *up*, aufwühlen (*stir up*).

chute [ʃuːt], *s.* die Gleitbahn.

cider [ˈsaidə], *s.* der Apfelmost.

cigar [siˈgɑː], *s.* die Zigarre; — *case*, das Zigarrenetui.

cigarette [sigəˈret], *s.* die Zigarette; — *holder*, die Zigarettenspitze; — *lighter*, das Feuerzeug.

cinder [ˈsində], *s.* (*usually in pl.*) die Asche (*fire*); die Schlacke (*furnace*).

Cinderella [sindəˈrelə], das Aschenbrödel, Aschenputtel.

cinema [ˈsinimə], *s.* das Kino.

cinematography [siniməˈtɔgrəfi], *s.* die Filmkunst.

Cingalese *see* Singhalese.

cinnamon [ˈsinəmən], *s.* der Zimt.

cipher [ˈsaifə], *s.* die Ziffer; die Geheimschrift (*code*). — *v.n.* rechnen. — *v.a.* chiffrieren (*code*).

Circassian [səːˈkæsiən], *adj.* tscherkessisch. — *s.* der Tscherkesse.

circle [ˈsəːkl], *s.* der Zirkel, Kreis; (*social*) Gesellschaftskreis; (*Theat.*) der Rang. — *v.a.* umringen. — *v.n.* umkreisen; sich drehen (*revolve*).

circuit [ˈsəːkit], *s.* der Kreislauf; (*Elec.*) der Stromkreis.

circuitous [səːˈkjuːitəs], *adj.* weitschweifig, weitläufig.

circular [ˈsəːkjulə], *adj.* rund, kreisförmig, Rund-; — *tour*, die Rundreise. — *s.* das Rundschreiben (*letter*); der Werbebrief (*advertising*).

circulate [ˈsəːkjuleit], *v.a.* in Umlauf setzen. — *v.n.* umlaufen, kreisen, zirkulieren.

circulation [səːkjuˈleiʃən], *s.* die Zirkulation, der Kreislauf (*blood*); die Verbreitung, Auflage (*newspaper*); der Umlauf (*banknotes*).

circumcise [ˈsəːkəmsaiz], *v.a.* beschneiden.

circumference [səːˈkʌmfərəns], *s.* der Umfang.

circumscribe [ˈsəːkəmskraib], *v.a.* beschränken, einengen (*narrow down*); umschreiben (*paraphrase*).

circumspect [ˈsəːkəmspekt], *adj.* umsichtig, vorsorglich.

circumspection [səːkəmˈspekʃən], *s.* die Umsicht, Vorsicht.

circumstance [ˈsəːkəmstæns, -stɑːns], *s.* der Umstand; *pomp and* —, großer Aufmarsch.

circumstantial [səːkəmˈstænʃəl], *adj.* umständlich; zu einem Umstand gehörig; eingehend; — *evidence*, der Indizienbeweis.

circumvent [səːkəmˈvent], *v.a.* überlisten, hintergehen.

circus [ˈsəːkəs], *s.* der Zirkus; der Platz.

cirrhus [ˈsirəs], *s.* die Federwolke.

Cistercian [sisˈtəːʃən], *s.* der Zisterzienser (*monk*).

cistern [ˈsistən], *s.* die Zisterne, der Wasserbehälter.

citadel [ˈsitədəl], *s.* die Zitadelle, die Burg.

citation [saiˈteiʃən], *s.* das Zitat; (*Law*) die Zitierung, Vorladung; (*Mil.*) die rühmliche Erwähnung.

cite [sait], *v.a.* zitieren (*quote*); (*Law*) vorladen.

citizen [ˈsitizən], *s.* der Bürger, Staatsbürger (*national*); *fellow* —, der Mitbürger.

citizenship [ˈsitizənʃip], *s.* das Bürgerrecht, die Staatsangehörigkeit.

citrate [ˈsitreit], *s.* (*Chem.*) das Zitrat.

citric [ˈsitrik], *adj.* (*Chem.*) Zitronen-.

citron [ˈsitrən], *s.* die Zitrone. — *adj.* zitronenfarben.

city [ˈsiti], *s.* die Stadt; die Großstadt; die City. — *adj.* städtisch.

civic [ˈsivik], *adj.* Stadt-, städtisch (*ceremonial*); bürgerlich.

civil [ˈsivil], *adj.* zivil; höflich (*polite*); — *engineer*, der Zivilingenieur; — *service*, der Beamtendienst, die Beamtenlaufbahn, der Staatsdienst; — *war*, der Bürgerkrieg.

civilian [siˈviljən], *s.* der Zivilist.

civility [siˈviliti], *s.* die Höflichkeit.

civilization [sivilaiˈzeiʃən], *s.* die Zivilisation.

civilize [ˈsivilaiz], *v.a.* zivilisieren, verfeinern (*refine*).

clack [klæk], *v.n.* klappern (*wood etc.*); plaudern, plappern.

clad [klæd], *adj.* gekleidet.

claim [kleim], *v.a.* Anspruch erheben (*to*, auf); fordern (*demand*); behaupten (*assert*). — *s.* der Anspruch; die Forderung (*demand*); das Recht.

claimant [ˈkleimənt], *s.* der Beanspruchende, Ansprucherheber.

clairvoyance [kleəˈvɔiəns], *s.* das Hellsehen.

clairvoyant [kleəˈvɔiənt], *s.* der Hellseher.

clam [klæm], *s.* (*Zool.*) die Venusmuschel; *shut up like a* —, verschwiegen sein.

clamber [ˈklæmbə], *v.n.* klettern.

clamminess [ˈklæminis], *s.* die Feuchtigkeit, Klebrigkeit.

clammy [ˈklæmi], *adj.* feucht, klebrig.

clamorous [ˈklæmərəs], *adj.* lärmend, laut, ungestüm.

clamour [ˈklæmə], *s.* das Geschrei, der Lärm. — *v.n.* laut schreien (*for*, nach, *Dat.*).

clamp [klæmp], *s.* die Klammer, die Klampe. — *v.a.* festklammern.

clan [klæn], *s.* die Sippe, die Familie.

clandestine [klænˈdestin], *adj.* heimlich, verstohlen.

clang [klæŋ], *s.* der Schall, das Geklirr. — *v.n.* erschallen. — *v.a.* erschallen lassen.

clangour [ˈklæŋə], *s.* das Getöse, der Lärm.

clank [klæŋk], *s.* das Geklirre, das Gerassel (*metal*).

clannish [ˈklæniʃ], *adj.* stammesbewußt; engherzig (*narrow*).

clap [klæp], *v.a.* schlagen, zusammenschlagen (*hands*). — *v.n.* Beifall klatschen (*Dat.*).

clapperboard [ˈklæpəbɔːd], *s.* (*Film*) das Klappbrett, die Klapptafel; der Klöppel (*beater*, in *lacemaking*).

claptrap [ˈklæptræp], *s.* der billige Effekt, das eitle Geschwätz (*gossip*).

claret [ˈklærit], *s.* der Rotwein.

clarification [klærifiˈkeiʃən], *s.* die Klarstellung, Aufklärung.

clarify [ˈklærifai], *v.a.* klarstellen.

clari(o)net [klæri(ə)ˈnet], *s.* (*Mus.*) die Klarinette.

clarion [ˈklæriən], *s.* (*Mus.*) die Zinke, Trompete; — *call*, der laute Ruf.

clash [klæʃ], *v.a.* zusammenschlagen. — *v.n.* aufeinanderprallen, zusammenfallen (*dates*); widerstreiten (*views*). — *s.* (*fig.*) der Zusammenstoß, der Widerstreit.

clasp [klɑːsp], *v.a.* ergreifen, festhalten. — *s.* der Haken (*hook*); die Schnalle, die Spange (*buckle*, *brooch*); — *knife*, das Taschenmesser.

class [klɑːs], *s.* die Klasse.
classic(al) [ˈklæsik(əl)], *adj.* klassisch.
classics [ˈklæsiks], *s. pl.* die Klassiker, *m. pl.*; die klassische Philologie (*subject of study*).
classification [klæsifiˈkeiʃən], *s.* die Klassifizierung.
classify [ˈklæsifai], *v.a.* klassifizieren.
clatter [ˈklætə], *s.* das Getöse, Geklirr. — *v.a., v.n.* klappern, klirren.
Claus [klɔːz]. Claus, Nicholas, *m.*; Santa —, der heilige Nikolaus, Knecht Ruprecht, Weihnachtsmann.
clause [klɔːz], *s.* (*Gram.*) der Nebensatz; die Klausel (*contract*); (*Law*) der Vertragspunkt.
claw [klɔː], *s.* die Klaue, die Kralle. — *v.a.* kratzen.
clay [klei], *s.* der Ton, Lehm.
clayey [kleii], *adj.* lehmig, tonig.
clean [kliːn], *adj.* rein, reinlich (*habits*); sauber; — *shaven,* glattrasiert. — *v.a.* reinigen, putzen.
cleaner [ˈkliːnə], *s.* die Reinemacherin, die Putzfrau.
cleanliness [ˈklenlinis], *s.* die Reinlichkeit, Sauberkeit.
cleanse [klenz], *v.a.* reinigen.
clear [kliə], *adj.* klar, hell; deutlich (*meaning*); schuldlos (*not guilty*). — *s. in the* —, nicht betroffen, schuldlos. — *v.a.* (*Chem.*) klären; (*Law*) für unschuldig erklären; verzollen (*pass through customs*); springen (über, *Acc.*). — *v.n.* (— *up*), sich aufklären, aufhellen (*weather*).
clearance [ˈkliərəns], *s.* die Räumung; — *sale,* der Ausverkauf; die Verzollung (*customs*).
clearing [ˈkliəriŋ], *s.* die Lichtung (*in wood*); (*Comm.*) die Verrechnung.
clearness [ˈkliənis], *s.* die Deutlichkeit, die Klarheit, Helle.
cleave [kliːv], *v.a., v.n. irr.* spalten (*wood*). — *v.n.* sich spalten.
cleaver [ˈkliːvə], *s.* das Hackmesser.
cleek [kliːk], *s.* der Golfschläger.
clef [klef], *s.* (*Mus.*) der Schlüssel.
cleft [kleft], *s.* der Spalt. — *adj.* — *palate,* die Gaumenspalte.
clemency [ˈklemənsi], *s.* die Milde, Gnade (*mercy*).
clement [ˈklemənt], *adj.* mild (*climate*); gnädig (*merciful*).
clench [klentʃ], *v.a.* zusammenpressen; ballen (*fist*).
clergy [ˈkləːdʒi], *s.* (*Eccl.*) die Geistlichkeit.
clergyman [ˈkləːdʒimən], *s.* (*Eccl.*) der Geistliche.
clerical [ˈklerikl], *adj.* (*Eccl.*) geistlich; beamtlich, Beamten-, Büro- (*office*); — *work,* die Büroarbeit.
clerk [klɑːk], *s.* der Schreiber, der Bürogehilfe (*junior*), der Bürobeamte, Büroangestellte (*senior*); bank —, der Bankbeamte.
clever [ˈklevə], *adj.* klug; intelligent; geschickt (*deft*); gewandt, listig (*cunning*).

cleverness [ˈklevənis], *s.* die Klugheit (*intelligence*); die Schlauheit (*cunning*); die Begabung (*talent*); die Geschicklichkeit (*skill*).
clew [kluː] *see* **clue.**
click [klik], *v.a., v.n.* einschnappen (*lock*); zusammenschlagen (*o.'s heels,* die Hacken); schnalzen (*o.'s tongue*); (*sl.*) zusammenpassen (*of two people*). — *s.* das Einschnappen (*lock*); das Zusammenschlagen (*heels*); das Schnalzen (*tongue*).
client [ˈklaiənt], *s.* (*Law*) der Klient; (*Comm.*) der Kunde.
clientele [kliːənˈtel], *s.* die Klientel, die Kundschaft.
cliff [klif], *s.* die Klippe.
climate [ˈklaimit], *s.* das Klima.
climatic [klaiˈmætik], *adj.* klimatisch.
climax [ˈklaimæks], *s.* der Höhepunkt.
climb [klaim], *v.a.* erklettern, erklimmen. — *v.n.* klettern, bergsteigen; (*Aviat.*) steigen. — *s.* der Aufstieg, die Ersteigung.
climber [ˈklaimə], *s.* der Bergsteiger (*mountaineer*); (*Bot.*) die Schlingpflanze.
clinch [klintʃ], *v.a.* vernieten, befestigen; — *a deal,* einen Handel abschließen. — *s.* der feste Griff; die Umklammerung (*boxing*).
cling [kliŋ], *v.n. irr.* sich anklammern, festhalten (*to,* an).
clinic [ˈklinik], *s.* die Klinik.
clinical [ˈklinikl], *adj.* klinisch.
clink [kliŋk], *s.* das Geklirre; (*coll.*) das Gefängnis. — *v.a.* — *glasses,* mit den Gläsern anstoßen.
clinker [ˈkliŋkə], *s.* der Backstein; die Schlacke.
clip (1) [klip], *v.a.* stutzen, beschneiden; lochen (*ticket*).
clip (2) [klip], *v.a.* befestigen. — *s. paper* —, die Büroklammer.
clippings [ˈklipiŋz], *s. pl.* die Abschnitte; die Schnitzel (*waste*); Zeitungsausschnitte, *m. pl.*
cloak [klouk], *s.* der Mantel, der Deckmantel (*cover*). — *v.a.* verbergen.
cloakroom [ˈkloukruːm], *s.* die Garderobe; — *free,* keine Garderobegebühr; (*Railw.*) die Gepäckaufbewahrung.
clock [klɔk], *s.* die (große) Uhr, Wanduhr; — *face,* das Zifferblatt. — *v.n.* — *in,* die Zeitkarte (Kontrollkarte) stempeln lassen, eintreffen (*arrive*).
clockwise [ˈklɔkwaiz], *adv.* im Uhrzeigersinne.
clod [klɔd], *s.* die Erdscholle, der Erdklumpen; (*sl.*) der Lümmel (*lout*).
clog [klɔg], *v.a.* belasten, hemmen, verstopfen. — *v.n.* sich verstopfen. — *s.* der Holzschuh.
cloisters [ˈklɔistəz], *s. pl.* (*Eccl., Archit.*) der Kreuzgang.

close

close [klouz], *v.a.* schließen, verschließen; beenden (*meeting etc.*). — *v.n.* — *in on*, über einen hereinbrechen, umzingeln. — *s.* das Ende, der Schluß; [klous] der Domplatz. — [klous], *adj.* nahe (*near*); knapp (*narrow*); nahestehend, vertraut (*friend*); schwül (*weather*); geizig (*miserly*).

closeness [ˈklousnis], *s.* die Nähe (*nearness*); die Schwüle (*weather*); die Vertrautheit (*familiarity*).

closet [ˈklozit], *s.* der Wandschrank (*cupboard*); das kleine Zimmer; das Klosett (*W.C.*). — *v.r.* — *o.s. with*, sich mit jemandem zurückziehen, sich vertraulich beraten.

closure [ˈklouʒə], *s.* der Schluß; der Abschluß (einer Debatte).

clot [klɔt], *s.* das Klümpchen. — *v.n.* sich verdicken, gerinnen; —*ted cream*, dicke Sahne.

cloth [klɔθ], *s.* das Tuch; der Stoff; die Leinwand (*bookbinding*); American —, das Wachstuch; — *printing*, der Zeugdruck.

clothe [klouð], *v.a.* kleiden. — *v.r.* sich kleiden.

clothes [klouðz], *s. pl.* die Kleider, *n. pl.*; die Kleidung; die Wäsche (*washing*); — *basket*, der Wäschekorb; — *press*, der Kleiderschrank.

clothier [ˈklouðiə], *s.* der Tuchmacher (*manufacturer*); der Tuchhändler (*dealer*).

clothing [ˈklouðiŋ], *s.* die Kleidung.

cloud [klaud], *s.* die Wolke; under a —, in Ungnade; —*burst*, der Wolkenbruch. — *v.a.* bewölken, verdunkeln. — *v.n.* — *over*, sich umwölken.

cloudiness [ˈklaudinis], *s.* die Umwölkung, der Wolkenhimmel.

cloudy [ˈklaudi], *adj.* wolkig, bewölkt, umwölkt.

clout [klaut], *s.* (*obs.*) der Lappen (*rag*); (*coll.*) der Schlag (*hit*). — *v.a.* schlagen (*hit*).

clove [klouv], *s.* die Gewürznelke (*spice*).

clove(n) [klouv(n)], *adj.* gespalten.

clover [ˈklouvə], *s.* (*Bot.*) der Klee; *to be in* —, Glück haben, es gut haben.

clown [klaun], *s.* der Hanswurst. — *v.n.* den Hanswurst spielen.

clownish [ˈklauniʃ], *adj.* tölpelhaft.

clownishness [ˈklauniʃnis], *s.* die Derbheit, Tölpelhaftigkeit.

cloy [klɔi], *v.n.* übersättigen, anwidern, anekeln.

club (1) [klʌb], *s.* die Keule (*stick*). — *v.a.* (einen) mit einer Keule schlagen.

club (2) [klʌb], *s.* der Klub, der Verein. — *v.n.* — *together*, zusammen beitragen, zusammensteuern (*contribute jointly*).

club (3) [klʌb], *s.* (*cards*) das Treff, die Eichel (*German cards*).

clubfoot [ˈklʌbfut], *s.* der Klumpfuß.

cluck [klʌk], *v.n.* glucken (*hen*).

clue [klu:], *s.* der Anhaltspunkt, Leitfaden, die Richtlinie, die Angabe (*crossword*); *no* —, keine blasse Ahnung.

clump [klʌmp], *s.* der Klumpen; **die Gruppe.**

clumsiness [ˈklʌmzinis], *s.* die Unbeholfenheit, Ungeschicklichkeit.

clumsy [ˈklʌmzi], *adj.* unbeholfen, schwerfällig, ungeschickt.

Cluniac [ˈkluːnjæk]. (*Eccl.*) der Kluniazenser.

cluster [ˈklʌstə], *s.* die Traube (*grapes*), der Büschel. — *v.n.* in Büscheln wachsen *or* stehen, dicht gruppiert sein.

clutch [klʌtʃ], *v.a.* ergreifen, packen (*grip*). — *s.* der Griff; (*Motor.*) die Kupplung.

coach [koutʃ], *s.* die Kutsche; der Wagen, der Autobus; der Privatlehrer (*teacher*). — *v.a.* unterrichten, vorbereiten (*for examinations etc.*).

coachman [ˈkoutʃmən], *s.* der Kutscher.

coagulate [kouˈægjuleit], *v.a.* gerinnen lassen. — *v.n.* gerinnen.

coagulation [kouægjuˈleiʃən], *s.* das Gerinnen.

coal [koul], *s.* die Kohle; — *mine*, das Kohlenbergwerk; die Kohlengrube; — *miner*, der Bergmann.

coalesce [kouəˈles], *v.n.* zusammenwachsen, sich vereinigen.

coalescence [kouəˈlesəns], *s.* die Verschmelzung.

coalition [kouəˈliʃən], *s.* (*Pol.*) die Koalition, das Bündnis.

coarse [kɔːs], *adj.* grob; gemein (*manner*).

coarseness [ˈkɔːsnis], *s.* die Grobheit, Unfeinheit.

coast [koust], *s.* die Küste. — *v.n.* (an der Küste) entlangfahren; gleiten, rodeln.

coat [kout], *s.* der Mantel, Rock; die Jacke (*jacket*); das Fell (*animal*); — *of arms*, das Wappenschild; — *of mail*, das Panzerhemd; — *of paint*, der Anstrich. — *v.a.* überziehen, bemalen (*paint*).

coathanger [ˈkouthæŋə], *s.* der Kleiderbügel.

coating [ˈkoutiŋ], *s.* der Überzug.

coax [kouks], *v.a.* beschwatzen; überreden (*persuade*).

cob (1) [kɔb], *s.* der Gaul.

cob (2) [kɔb], *s.* (*Orn.*) der Schwan.

cob (3) [kɔb], *s.* der (Mais)Kolben (*corn on the* —).

cobble [kɔbl], *v.a.* flicken (*shoes*).

cobbled [ˈkɔbld], *adj.* mit Kopfsteinen gepflastert.

cobbler [ˈkɔblə], *s.* der Schuhflicker.

cobble(stone) [ˈkɔbl(stoun)], *s.* das Kopfsteinpflaster.

cobweb [ˈkɔbweb], *s.* das Spinngewebe.

cock [kɔk], *s.* (*Orn.*) der Hahn; (*Engin.*) der Sperrhahn, Hahn; — *sparrow*, das Sperlingsmännchen; —*-a-doodle-doo!* kikeriki!

cockade [kɔˈkeid], *s.* die Kokarde.

cockatoo [kɔkəˈtuː], *s.* (*Orn.*) der Kakadu.

collier

cockchafer ['kɔktʃeifə], *s.* (*Ent.*) der Maikäfer.

cockerel ['kɔkərəl], *s.* (*Orn.*) der junge Hahn.

cockle [kɔkl], *s.* (*Zool.*) die Herzmuschel.

cockney ['kɔkni], *s.* der geborene Londoner.

cockpit ['kɔkpit], *s.* (*Aviat.*) der Pilotensitz, die Kanzel, der Führerraum.

cockroach ['kɔkroutʃ], *s.* (*Ent.*) die Schabe.

cocksure ['kɔkʃuə], *adj.* zuversichtlich, allzu sicher.

cockswain [kɔksn] *see* **coxswain.**

cocoa ['koukou], *s.* der Kakao.

coconut ['koukonʌt], *s.* die Kokosnuß.

cocoon [kə'ku:n], *s.* der Kokon, die Puppe (*of silkworm*).

cod [kɔd], *s.* der Kabeljau, Dorsch; — *liver oil*, der Lebertran; *dried* —, der Stockfisch.

coddle [kɔdl], *v.a.* verhätscheln, verweichlichen.

code [koud], *s.* das Gesetzbuch, der Kodex; die Chiffre (*cipher*). — *v.a.* chiffrieren, schlüsseln.

codify ['koudifai], *v.a.* kodifizieren.

coerce [kou'ə:s], *v.a.* zwingen.

coercion [kou'ə:ʃən], *s.* der Zwang.

coercive [kou'ə:siv], *adj.* zwingend.

coeval [kou'i:vəl], *adj.* gleichaltrig, gleichzeitig.

coexist [kouig'zist], *v.n.* zugleich existieren, nebeneinander leben.

coffee ['kɔfi], *s.* der Kaffee; — *grinder*, die Kaffeemühle; — *grounds*, der Kaffeesatz; — *pot*, die Kaffeekanne; — *set*, das Kaffeeservice.

coffer ['kɔfə], *s.* der Kasten, die Truhe.

coffin ['kɔfin], *s.* der Sarg.

cog [kɔg], *s.* der Zahn (*on wheel*); — *wheel*, das Zahnrad.

cogency ['koudʒənsi], *s.* die zwingende Kraft, Triftigkeit.

cogent ['koudʒənt], *adj.* zwingend, triftig.

cogitate ['kɔdʒiteit], *v.n.* nachdenken.

cogitation [kɔdʒi'teiʃən], *s.* die Überlegung, das Nachdenken.

cognate ['kɔgneit], *adj.* verwandt.

cognition [kɔg'niʃən], *s.* die Kenntnis, das Erkennen.

cognizance ['kɔgnizəns], *s.* die Erkenntnis; die Kenntnisnahme; (*Law*) die gerichtliche Kenntnisnahme.

cognizant ['kɔgnizənt], *adj.* wissend, in vollem Wissen (*of, Genit.*).

cohabit [kou'hæbit], *v.n.* zusammenleben.

cohabitation [kouhæbi'teiʃən], *s.* das Zusammenleben.

coheir [kou'ɛə], *s.* der Miterbe.

cohere [kou'hiə], *v.n.* zusammenhängen.

coherence [kou'hiərəns], *s.* der Zusammenhang.

coherent [kou'hiərənt], *adj.* zusammenhängend.

cohesion [kou'hi:ʒən], *s.* (*Phys.*) die Kohäsion.

coiffure [kwæ'fjuə], *s.* die Frisur, die Haartracht.

coil [kɔil], *s.* (*Elec.*) die Spule; die Windung. — *v.a.* aufwickeln; umwickeln, (auf)spulen. — *v.n.* sich winden.

coin [kɔin], *s.* die Münze, das Geldstück. — *v.a.* münzen, prägen; — *a phrase*, eine Redewendung prägen.

coinage ['kɔinidʒ], *s.* die Prägung.

coincide [kouin'said], *v.n.* zusammenfallen, zusammentreffen.

coincidence [kou'insidəns], *s.* das Zusammenfallen, Zusammentreffen; der Zufall (*chance*).

coincident [kou'insidənt], *adj.* zusammentreffend.

coke [kouk], *s.* der Koks.—*v.a.* (*Chem., Engin.*) verkoken.

cold [kould], *adj.* kalt; gefühllos, kühl. — *s.* die Kälte (*temperature*); die Erkältung (*indisposition*).

coldish ['kouldiʃ], *adj.* kühl.

coldness ['kouldnis], *s.* die Kälte (*temperature*); die Kaltherzigkeit (*heartlessness*).

colic ['kɔlik], *s.* die Kolik.

collaborate [kə'læbəreit], *v.n.* zusammenarbeiten.

collaboration [kəlæbə'reiʃən], *s.* die Zusammenarbeit; die Mitwirkung, Mitarbeit (*assistance*).

collaborator [kə'læbəreitə], *s.* der Mitarbeiter.

collapse [kə'læps], *s.* der Zusammenbruch. — *v.n.* zusammenbrechen (*disintegrate*); zerfallen, einstürzen.

collapsible [kə'læpsibl], *adj.* zerlegbar, zusammenlegbar, zusammenklappbar.

collar ['kɔlə], *s.* der Kragen; — *bone*, das Schlüsselbein (*Anat.*); *dog* —, das Halsband; (*coll.*) der Priesterkragen; —*stud*, der Kragenknopf. — *v.a.* beim Kragen fassen, ergreifen.

collate [kɔ'leit], *v.a.* vergleichen (*texts etc.*).

collateral [kɔ'lætərəl], *adj.* Seiten-, von beiden Seiten. — *s.* (*Am.*) die Garantie, Bürgschaft.

collation [kɔ'leiʃən], *s.* die Vergleichung, der Vergleich (*texts etc.*); der Imbiß.

colleague ['kɔli:g], *s.* der Kollege, die Kollegin.

collect [kə'lekt], *v.a.* sammeln, zusammenbringen. — *v.n.* sich versammeln. — ['kɔlikt], *s.* (*Eccl.*) die Kollekte.

collection [kə'lekʃən], *s.* die Sammlung.

collective [kə'lektiv], *adj.* kollektiv, gemeinsam. — *s.* (*Pol.*) das Kollektiv.

collector [kə'lektə], *s.* der Sammler.

college ['kɔlidʒ], *s.* das Kollegium; das College; die Hochschule, Universität.

collide [kə'laid], *v.n.* zusammenstoßen.

collie ['kɔli], *s.* der Schäferhund.

collier ['kɔliə], *s.* der Kohlenarbeiter; das Kohlenfrachtschiff (*boat*).

341

collision [kə'liʒən], *s.* der Zusammen-stoß, Zusammenprall.

collocate ['kɔləkeit], *v.a.* ordnen.

collodion [kə'loudjən], *s.* (*Chem.*) das Kollodium.

colloquial [kə'loukwiəl], *adj.* umgangs-sprachlich, Umgangs-.

colloquy ['kɔləkwi], *s.* die Unterredung, das Gespräch (*formal*).

collusion [kə'lu:ʒən], *s.* das heimliche Einverständnis, die unstatthafte Part-nerschaft; die Verdunkelung.

collusive [kə'lu:ziv], *adj.* abgekartet.

Cologne [kə'loun]. Köln, *n.*; *eau de* —, Kölnisch Wasser.

Colombian [kɔ'lɔmbjən], *adj.* kolum-bisch. — *s.* der Kolumbier.

colon (1) ['koulən], *s.* das Kolon, der Doppelpunkt.

colon (2) ['koulɔn], *s.* (*Med.*) der Dickdarm.

colonel [kə:nl], *s.* (*Mil.*) der Oberst; — -*in-chief*, der Generaloberst, der ober-ste Befehlshaber; *lieutenant-* —, der Oberstleutnant.

colonial [kə'lounjəl], *adj.* kolonial, aus den Kolonien.

colonist ['kɔlənist], *s.* der Siedler; Ansiedler.

colonization [kɔlənai'zeiʃən], *s.* die Kolonisierung, Besiedelung.

colonize ['kɔlənaiz], *v.a.* besiedeln, kolonisieren.

colonnade [kɔlə'neid], *s.* die Kolonnade, der Säulengang.

colony ['kɔləni], *s.* die Kolonie.

colophony [kɔ'lɔfəni], *s.* das Kolo-phonium (*resin*).

coloration [kʌlə'reiʃən], *s.* die Färbung, Tönung.

colossal [kə'lɔsəl], *adj.* kolossal, riesig, riesenhaft.

colour ['kʌlə], *s.* die Farbe; (*com-plexion*) die Gesichtsfarbe; (*paint*) die Farbe, der Anstrich; (*dye*) die Färbung. — *v.a.* färben; anstreichen (*paint house etc.*).

colt [koult], *s.* das Füllen.

columbine ['kɔləmbain], *s.* (*Bot.*) die Akelei.

column ['kɔləm], *s.* die Säule; die Spalte (*press*); (*also Mil.*) die Kolonne.

colza ['kɔlzə], *s.* (*Bot.*) der Raps.

coma ['koumə], *s.* (*Med.*) das Koma, die Schlafsucht.

comb [koum], *s.* der Kamm. — *v.a.* kämmen; (*fig.*) genau untersuchen.

combat ['kʌmbət, 'kɔmbət], *s.* der Kampf, das Gefecht; *in single* —, im Duell, Zweikampf. — *v.a.* kämpfen, bekämpfen.

combatant ['kʌmbətənt, 'kɔmb-], *s.* der Kämpfer.

comber ['koumə], *s.* der Wollkämmer.

combination [kɔmbi'neiʃən], *s.* die Kombination, die Verbindung.

combine [kəm'bain], *v.a.* kombinieren, verbinden. — *v.n.* sich verbinden. — ['kɔmbain], *s.* (*Comm.*) der Trust, Ring.

combustible [kəm'bʌstibl], *adj.* ver-brennbar; feuergefährlich.

combustion [kəm'bʌstʃən], *s.* die Verbrennung.

come [kʌm], *v.n. irr.* kommen; — *about*, sich ereignen (*event*); — *across*, stoßen auf (*Acc.*); — *by* (*s.th.*), ergattern, erwerben; — *for*, abholen; — *forth, forward*, hervorkommen, hervortreten; — *from*, herkommen von, — *in*, hereinkommen; — *off*, (*of object*) loskommen, (*succeed*) glücken; — *out* (*appear*), herauskommen; — *to o.'s*, zu sich kommen; — *of age*, mündig werden; — *to o.'s senses*, zur Besinnung *or* Vernunft kommen; *that is still to* —, das steht uns noch bevor.

comedian [kə'mi:djən], *s.* der Komö-diant, Komiker (*stage*).

comedy ['kɔmədi], *s.* die Komödie, das Lustspiel.

comeliness ['kʌmlinis], *s.* die Anmut, Schönheit.

comely ['kʌmli], *adj.* anmutig, schön.

comestible [kə'mestibl], *s.* (*usually pl.*) die Eßwaren, *f. pl.*

comet ['kɔmit], *s.* der Komet.

comfit ['kʌmfit], *s.* das Konfekt, die Bonbons.

comfort ['kʌmfət], *s.* der Trost (*solace*); der Komfort, die Bequemlichkeit. — *v.a.* trösten.

comforter ['kʌmfətə], *s.* der Tröster; (*Am.*) die Steppdecke.

comfortless ['kʌmfətlis], *adj.* trostlos, unbehaglich.

comic ['kɔmik], *adj.* komisch; — *writer*, humoristischer Schriftsteller. — *s.* die Bilderzeitung (*children's paper*).

comical ['kɔmikl], *adj.* lächerlich, zum Lachen, komisch.

comma ['kɔmə], *s.* das Komma, der Beistrich; *inverted* —s, die Anfüh-rungszeichen.

command [kə'mɑ:nd], *v.a., v.n.* (*Mil.*) kommandieren; über jemanden ver-fügen (*have s.o. at o.'s disposal*). — *s.* der Befehl.

commandant [kɔmən'dænt], *s.* der Kommandant, Befehlshaber.

commander [kə'mɑ:ndə], *s.* der Be-fehlshaber.

commandment [kə'mɑ:ndmənt], *s.* (*Rel.*) das Gebot.

commemorate [kə'meməreit], *v.a.* feiern, gedenken (*Genit.*).

commemoration [kəmemə'reiʃən], *s.* die Feier, die Gedächtnisfeier.

commemorative [kə'memərətiv], *adj.* Gedächtnis-.

commence [kə'mens], *v.a., v.n.* be-ginnen, anfangen.

commencement [kə'mensmənt], *s.* der Anfang, der Beginn.

commend [kə'mend], *v.a.* empfehlen, loben (*praise*).

commendable [kə'mendəbl], *adj.* emp-fehlenswert.

commendation [komen'deiʃən], *s.* die Empfehlung.

commensurable, commensurate [kə'menʃərəbl, kə'menʃərit], *adj.* kommensurabel, entsprechend; angemessen.

comment ['koment], *v.n.* kommentieren (*on*, zu, *Dat.*). — *s.* der Kommentar; die Bemerkung (*remark*).

commentary ['koməntəri], *s.* der Kommentar.

commentator ['komənteitə], *s.* der Kommentator, Berichterstatter.

commerce ['komə:s], *s.* der Handel; *college of* —, die Handelsschule.

commercial [kə'mə:ʃəl], *adj.* kommerziell, kaufmännisch, Handels-; — *traveller*, der Handelsreisende, Vertreter; — *manager*, der geschäftliche Leiter.

commingle [kə'miŋgl], *v.a.* vermischen|gefühl.

commiserate [kə'mizəreit], *v.n.* bemitleiden; — *with s.o.*, mit einem Mitgefühl haben.

commissariat [komi'sɛəriət], *s.* (*Pol.*) das Kommissariat.

commissary ['komisəri], *s.* der Kommissar. — *adj.* kommissarisch.

commission [kə'miʃən], *s.* die Kommission; (*Mil.*) der Offiziersrang; die Begehung (*of crime*); (*Law*) die (offizielle) Kommission; der Auftrag, die Bestellung (*order*).

commissionaire [kəmiʃən'ɛə], *s.* der Portier.

commissioned [kə'miʃənd], *adj.* bevollmächtigt.

commissioner [kə'miʃənə], *s.* (*Pol.*) der Kommissar, der Bevollmächtigte.

commit [kə'mit], *v.a.* begehen (*do*); übergeben (*consign*); anvertrauen (*entrust*). — *v.r.* sich verpflichten.

committal [kə'mitl], *s.* das Übergeben; die Überantwortung.

committee [kə'miti], *s.* das Kommitee, der Ausschuß.

commodious [kə'moudiəs], *adj.* bequem, geräumig.

commodity [kə'moditi], *s.* (*Comm.*) die Ware, der Artikel.

commodore ['komədo:], *s.* (*Naut.*) der Kommodore, der Kommandant eines Geschwaders.

common ['komən], *adj.* gewöhnlich (*usual*); gemein (*vulgar*); allgemein (*general*); *in* —, gemeinschaftlich; — *sense*, der gesunde Menschenverstand; *the* — *man*, der kleine Mann. — *n. pl. House of Commons*, das Unterhaus.

commoner ['komənə], *s.* der Bürger; (*Parl.*) Mitglied des Unterhauses.

commonness ['komənnis], *s.* die Gemeinheit (*vulgarity*); das häufige Vorkommen (*frequency*).

commonplace ['komənpleis], *adj.* alltäglich. — *s.* der Gemeinplatz.

commonwealth ['komənwelθ], *s.* die Staatengemeinschaft, der Staatenbund; das Commonwealth.

commotion [kə'mouʃən], *s.* die Erschütterung; der Aufruhr; der Lärm.

communal ['komjunəl], *adj.* gemeinschaftlich, allgemein; (*Pol.*) Kommunal-.

commune ['komju:n], *s.* (*Pol.*) die Kommune. — [kə'mju:n], *v.n.* sich unterhalten.

communicable [kə'mju:nikəbl], *adj.* mitteilbar; übertragbar.

communicate [kə'mju:nikeit], *v.a.* mitteilen; verkünden (*proclaim*); benachrichtigen. — *v.n.* in Verbindung stehen.

communication [kəmju:ni'keiʃən], *s.* die Mitteilung; Verlautbarung; die Verkündigung (*proclamation*); die Information; (*Elec.*) die Verbindung; (*pl.*), die Verbindungslinie; —*s engineering*, Fernmeldetechnik.

communion [kə'mju:njən], *s.* (*Eccl.*) die Kommunion; das heilige Abendmahl; die Gemeinschaft (*fellowship*).

Communism ['komjunizm], *s.* (*Pol.*) der Kommunismus.

Communist ['komjunist], *s.* der Kommunist. — *adj.* kommunistisch.

community [kə'mju:niti], *s.* die Gemeinschaft.

commutable [kə'mju:təbl], *adj.* umtauschbar, auswechselbar.

commutation [komju'teiʃən], *s.* der Austausch; (*Law*) die Herabsetzung (*of sentence*).

commutator ['komjuteitə], *s.* (*Elec.*) der Umschalter.

commute [kə'mju:t], *v.n.* hin und her fahren, pendeln, mit Zeitkarte fahren (*travel*). — *v.a.* herabsetzen (*sentence*).

compact ['kompækt], *adj.* kompakt, fest; gedrängt (*succinct*); kurz, bündig (*short*).

companion [kəm'pænjən], *s.* der Gefährte, die Gefährtin.

companionable [kəm'pænjənəbl], *adj.* gesellig, freundlich.

companionship [kəm'pænjənʃip], *s.* die Geselligkeit; die Gesellschaft.

company ['kampəni], *s.* die Gesellschaft; (*Mil.*) die Kompanie; der Freundeskreis (*circle of friends*); (*Comm.*) die Handelsgesellschaft; *limited* (*liability*) —, Gesellschaft mit beschränkter Haftung; *public* (*private*) —, Gesellschaft des öffentlichen (privaten) Rechtes.

comparative [kəm'pærətiv], *adj.* vergleichend, relativ. — *s.* (*Gram.*) der Komparativ.

compare [kəm'pɛə], *v.a.* vergleichen. — *v.n.* sich vergleichen lassen.

comparison [kəm'pærisən], *s.* der Vergleich; das Gleichnis (*simile*).

compartment [kəm'pɑ:tmənt], *s.* (*Railw.*) das Abteil; die Abteilung.

compass ['kampəs], *s.* der Umkreis, Umfang (*scope*); (*Naut.*) der Kompaß; *point of the* —, der Kompaßstrich; (*Engin.*) der Zirkel.

compassion [kəm'pæʃən], s. die Barmherzigkeit, das Mitleid, das Erbarmen.
compassionate [kəm'pæʃənit], adj.
mitleidig; (Mil.) — leave, der Son-
derurlaub.
compatibility [kəmpæti'biliti], s. die
Verträglichkeit, Vereinbarkeit.
compatible [kəm'pætibl], adj. verträglich, vereinbar.
compatriot [kəm'peitriət], s. der
Landsmann.
compel [kəm'pel], v.a. zwingen, nötigen.
compendium [kəm'pendjəm], s. das
Kompendium, die kurze Schrift, die
kurze Darstellung.
compensate ['kɔmpənseit], v.a. kompensieren, einem Ersatz leisten.
compensation [kɔmpən'seiʃən], s. der
Ersatz, die Wiedergutmachung.
compensatory [kɔmpən'seitəri], adj.
ausgleichend, Ersatz-.
compete [kəm'piːt], v.n. wetteifern,
konkurrieren.
competence, competency ['kɔmpitəns,
-nsi], s. die Kompetenz; Zuständigkeit; Befähigung (capability); Tüchtigkeit (ability).
competent ['kɔmpitənt], adj. kom-
petent; zuständig; fähig (capable);
tüchtig (able).
competition [kɔmpi'tiʃən], s. die Konkurrenz; die Mitbewerbung (for job).
competitive [kəm'petitiv], adj. Kon-
kurrenz-, konkurrierend.
competitor [kəm'petitə], s. (Comm.)
der Konkurrent; der Mitbewerber
(fellow applicant), Teilnehmer (sport).
complacent [kəm'pleisənt], adj. selbst-
zufrieden, selbstgefällig.
complain [kəm'plein], v.n. sich beklagen (of, über, Acc.).
complaint [kəm'pleint], s. die Klage;
Beschwerde (grievance); das Leiden
(illness).
complement ['kɔmplimənt], s. die
Ergänzung, Gesamtzahl. — [-'ment],
v.a. ergänzen.
complementary [kɔmpli'mentəri], adj.
Ergänzungs-, ergänzend.
complete [kəm'pliːt], adj. komplett;
voll (full up); vollkommen (perfect).
— v.a. vollenden (end); ergänzen
(make whole).
completeness [kəm'pliːtnis], s. die
Vollendung (condition); Ganzheit
(wholeness).
completion [kəm'pliːʃən], s. die Vollendung (fulfilment); die Beendigung
(ending); der Abschluß.
complex ['kɔmpleks], adj. (Maths.)
komplex; kompliziert (complicated).
— s. der Komplex (Archit., Psych.).
complexion [kəm'plekʃən], s. die
Gesichtsfarbe; (fig.) das Aussehen.
complexity [kəm'pleksiti], s. die
Kompliziertheit; die Schwierigkeit.
compliance [kəm'plaiəns], s. die
Willfährigkeit, Einwilligung.
compliant [kəm'plaiənt], adj. willig,
willfährig.

complicate ['kɔmplikeit], v.a. kom-
plizieren, erschweren.
complication [kɔmpli'keiʃən], s. die
Komplikation, die Erschwerung.
complicity [kəm'plisiti], s. (Law) die
Mitschuld.
compliment ['kɔmplimənt], s. das
Kompliment. — [-'ment], v.n. Kom-
plimente machen.
complimentary [kɔmpli'mentəri], adj.
lobend; — ticket, die Freikarte.
comply [kəm'plai], v.n. einwilligen
(with, in, Acc.); sich halten (an, Acc.).
compose [kəm'pouz], v.a., v.n. (Mus.)
komponieren; beruhigen (the mind);
(Lit.) verfassen; (Typ.) setzen.
composed [kəm'pouzd], adj. ruhig,
gefaßt.
composer [kəm'pouzə], s. (Mus.) der
Komponist.
composite ['kɔmpəzit], adj. zusammengesetzt.
composition [kɔmpə'ziʃən], s. (Mus.
etc.) die Komposition; Beschaffenheit
Zusammensetzung.
compositor [kəm'pɔzitə], s. (Typ.) der
Schriftsetzer.
compost ['kɔmpɔst], s. (Agr.) der
Dünger, Kompost.
composure [kəm'pouʒə], s. die Gelassenheit, die Gemütsruhe, die Fassung.
compound ['kɔmpaund], s. (Chem.)
die Verbindung; die Zusammensetzung. — adj. zusammengesetzt;
kompliziert; (Comm.) — interest, die
Zinseszinsen. — [kəm'paund], v.a.
(Chem.) mischen, zusammensetzen.
comprehend [kɔmpri'hend], v.a. verstehen (understand); einschließen (include).
comprehensible [kɔmpri'hensibl], adj.
verständlich, begreiflich.
comprehension [kɔmpri'henʃən], s.
das Verstehen, das Erfassen; (Psych.)
— tests, die Verständnisprüfung.
comprehensive [kɔmpri'hensiv], adj.
umfassend.
compress [kəm'pres], v.a. komprimieren; zusammendrücken (press together). — ['kɔmpres], s. (Med.) die
Kompresse, der Umschlag (poultice).
compression [kəm'preʃən], s. der
Druck; das Zusammendrücken (pressing together); die Kürzung (abridg-
ment).
comprise [kəm'praiz], v.a. umfassen,
einschließen.
compromise ['kɔmprəmaiz], v.a. kompromittieren. — v.n. einen Kompromiß schließen. — s. der or das Kompromiß.
compulsion [kəm'pʌlʃən], s. der
Zwang.
compulsory [kəm'pʌlsəri], adj. zwingend; Zwangs-; — subject, das
obligatorische Fach.
compunction [kəm'pʌnkʃən], s. die
Gewissensbisse, m. pl.
computation [kɔmpju'teiʃən], s. die
Berechnung.

compute [kəm'pju:t], *v.a.*, *v.n.* berechnen.

computer [kəm'pju:tə], *s.* die automatische Rechenmaschine.

comrade ['kɔmrid], *s.* der Kamerad.

comradeship ['kɔmridʃip], *s.* die Kameradschaft.

con [kɔn], *v.a.* genau betrachten, studieren; (*ship*) steuern.

concave ['kɔnkeiv], *adj.* (*Phys.*) konkav.

conceal [kən'si:l], *v.a.* verbergen, verstecken.

concealment [kən'si:lmənt], *s.* die Verhehlung, die Verheimlichung (*act of concealing*); *place of —*, das Versteck.

concede [kən'si:d], *v.a.* zugestehen, einräumen.

conceit [kən'si:t], *s.* die Einbildung, der Eigendünkel (*presumption*); (*obs.*) die Idee; (*Lit.*) die (gedankliche) Spielerei.

conceited [kən'si:tid], *adj.* eingebildet, eitel.

conceivable [kən'si:vəbl], *adj.* denkbar; begreiflich (*understandable*).

conceive [kən'si:v], *v.a.*, *v.n.* empfangen (*become pregnant*); begreifen (*understand*).

concentrate ['kɔnsəntreit], *v.a.* konzentrieren. — *v.n.* sich konzentrieren (*on*, auf, *Acc.*). — *s.* (*Chem.*) das Konzentrat.

concentrated ['kɔnsəntreitid], *adj.* konzentriert.

concentration [kɔnsən'treiʃən], *s.* die Konzentration.

concentric [kən'sentrik], *adj.* (*Geom.*) konzentrisch.

conception [kən'sepʃən], *s.* die Vorstellung, der Begriff (*idea*); die Empfängnis (*of a child*).

concern [kən'sə:n], *v.a.* (*affect*) betreffen, angehen; *be concerned with*, zu tun haben (mit, *Dat.*). — *s.* die Angelegenheit (*affair*); die Sorge (*care, business*); das Geschäft, das Unternehmen; *cause grave —*, tiefe Besorgnis erregen.

concerned [kən'sə:nd], *adj.* (*worried*) besorgt; (*involved*) interessiert (*in*, an, *Dat.*).

concerning [kən'sə:niŋ], *prep.* betreffend (*Acc.*), hinsichtlich (*Genit.*).

concert ['kɔnsət], *s.* (*Mus.*) das Konzert; Einverständnis.

concerted [kən'sə:tid], *adj.* gemeinsam, gemeinschaftlich.

concertina [kɔnsə'ti:nə], *s.* (*Mus.*) die Ziehharmonika.

concerto [kən'tʃə:tou], *s.* (*Mus.*) das Konzert.

concession [kən'seʃən], *s.* die Konzession (*licence*); das Zugeständnis.

conch [kɔŋk], *s.* die (große) Muschel.

conciliate [kən'silieit], *v.a.* versöhnen.

conciliation [kənsili'eiʃən], *s.* die Versöhnung.

conciliatory [kən'siliətəri], *adj.* versöhnlich.

concise [kən'sais], *adj.* kurz, knapp.

conciseness [kən'saisnis], *s.* die Kürze, Knappheit.

conclave ['kɔnkleiv], *s.* (*Eccl.*) das Konklave.

conclude [kən'klu:d], *v.a.*, *v.n.* schließen, beenden (*speech etc.*); (*infer*) folgern (*from*, aus, *Dat.*); abschließen (*treaty*).

conclusion [kən'klu:ʒən], *s.* der Abschluß (*treaty*); die Folgerung (*inference*); der Beschluß (*decision*).

conclusive [kən'klu:siv], *adj.* entscheidend, überzeugend.

concoct [kən'kɔkt], *v.a.* zusammenbrauen, aushecken.

concoction [kən'kɔkʃən], *s.* das Gebräu, die Mischung.

concomitant [kən'kɔmitənt], *adj.* begleitend; Begleit-, Neben-. — *s.* der Begleitumstand.

concord ['kɔnkɔ:d], *s.* die Eintracht, die Harmonie.

concordance [kən'kɔ:dəns], *s.* die Übereinstimmung; die Konkordanz (*of Bible etc.*).

concordant [kən'kɔ:dənt], *adj.* in Eintracht (mit), übereinstimmend (mit) (*Dat.*).

concordat [kən'kɔ:dæt], *s.* (*Eccl.*, *Pol.*) das Konkordat.

concourse ['kɔnkɔ:s], *s.* das Gedränge (*crowd*).

concrete ['kɔnkri:t], *s.* (*Build.*) der Beton; (*Log.*) das Konkrete. — *adj.* konkret, wirklich.

concur [kən'kə:], *v.n.* übereinstimmen (*with*, mit, *Dat.*).

concurrence [kən'kʌrəns], *s.* die Übereinstimmung.

concurrent [kən'kʌrənt], *adj.* gleichzeitig (*simultaneous*); mitwirkend (*accompanying*).

concussion [kən'kʌʃən], *s.* (*Med.*) die (Gehirn)Erschütterung.

condemn [kən'dem], *v.a.* verurteilen, verdammen.

condemnable [kən'demnəbl], *adj.* verwerflich, verdammenswert.

condemnation [kɔndem'neiʃən], *s.* die Verurteilung, die Verdammung.

condensate ['kɔndenseit], *s.* (*Chem.*) das Kondensat, das Ergebnis der Kondensation.

condensation [kɔnden'seiʃən], *s.* die Kondensation; Verdichtung.

condensed [kən'densd], *adj.* (*Chem.*) kondensiert; (*Chem.*, *Engin.*) verdichtet; gekürzt (*abridged*).

condenser [kən'densə], *s.* (*Chem.*, *Engin.*) der Kondensator; (*Elec.*) der Verstärker.

condescend [kɔndi'send], *v.n.* sich herablassen.

condescending [kɔndi'sendiŋ], *adj.* herablassend.

condescension [kɔndi'senʃən], *s.* die Herablassung.

condiment [kɔndimənt], *s.* die Würze.

condition [kən'diʃən], *s.* der Zustand; Umstand; die Bedingung (*proviso*); der Gesundheitszustand (*physical state*).

345

conditional

conditional [kən'diʃənəl], *adj.* bedingt; unter der Bedingung; konditionell.
conditioned [kən'diʃənd], *adj.* vorbereitet (*for action*); geartet.
condole [kən'doul], *v.n.* Beileid ausdrücken (*with, Dat.*), kondolieren (*with, Dat.*).
condolence [kən'douləns], *s.* das Beileid.
condone [kən'doun], *v.a.* verzeihen.
conducive [kən'dju:siv], *adj.* förderlich, dienlich, nützlich (*to, Dat.*).
conduct [kən'dʌkt], *v.a.* leiten, führen; (*Phys.*) ein Leiter sein; (*Mus.*) dirigieren. — *v.r.* sich aufführen, sich benehmen. — ['kəndʌkt], *s.* das Benehmen (*behaviour*); — *of a war*, die Kriegsführung.
conductive [kən'dʌktiv], *adj.* (*Elec.*) leitend.
conductor [kən'dʌktə], *s.* der Leiter, Führer (*leader*); (*Phys., Elec.*) der Leiter; (*Am.*) der Schaffner (*train*); (*Mus.*) der Dirigent.
conduit ['kʌn-, 'kəndit], *s.* die Leitung, die Röhre.
cone [koun], *s.* (*Geom.*) der Kegel; (*Bot.*) der Zapfen.
coney ['kouni], *s.* (*Zool.*) das Kaninchen.
confection [kən'fekʃən], *s.* das Konfekt.
confectioner [kən'fekʃənə], *s.* der Zuckerbäcker, Konditor.
confectionery [kən'fekʃənəri], *s.* die Zuckerwaren, *f.pl.* (*sweets*); Konditoreiwaren, *f.pl.* (*cakes*); die Zuckerbäckerei (*sweet shop*); die Konditorei.
confederacy [kən'fedərəsi], *s.* der Bund (*of states*); das Bündnis (*treaty*).
confederate [kən'fedərit], *s.* der Bundesgenosse, der Verbündete. — *adj.* verbündet; — *state*, der Bundesstaat. — [-reit], *v.n.* sich verbünden (*with*, mit, *Dat.*).
confederation [kənfedə'reiʃən], *s.* das Bündnis (*treaty*); der Bund (*state*).
confer [kən'fə:], *v.a.* verleihen (*degree, title*). — *v.n.* beraten (*with*, mit, *Dat.*), unterhandeln (*negotiate*).
conference ['kənfərəns], *s.* die Konferenz, die Besprechung, die Beratung, Tagung.
confess [kən'fes], *v.a.* bekennen; beichten (*sin*); zugestehen (*acknowledge*).
confession [kən'feʃən], *s.* das Bekenntnis; die Beichte (*sin*); das Glaubensbekenntnis (*creed*).
confessor [kən'fesə], *s.* der Bekenner; *father* —, der Beichtvater.
confidant [kənfi'dænt], *s.* der Vertraute.
confide [kən'faid], *v.a.* anvertrauen. — *v.n.* vertrauen (*Dat.*).
confidence ['kənfidəns], *s.* das Vertrauen; die Zuversicht; — *trick*, die Bauernfängerei, der Schwindel.
confident ['kənfidənt], *adj.* zuversichtlich; dreist (*bold*).
confidential [kənfi'denʃəl], *adj.* vertraulich, privat.

confine [kən'fain], *v.a.* einschränken (*hem in*); einsperren; *be* —*d to bed*, bettlägerig sein.
confinement [kən'fainmənt], *s.* die Einschränkung (*limitation*); das Wochenbett, die Niederkunft (*childbirth*).
confines ['kənfainz], *s. pl.* die Grenzen, *f. pl.* (*physical*); die Einschränkungen, *f. pl.* (*limitations*).
confirm [kən'fə:m], *v.a.* bestätigen, bekräftigen (*corroborate*); (*Eccl.*) firmen, konfirmieren.
confirmation [kənfə'meiʃən], *s.* die Bestätigung (*corroboration*); (*Eccl.*) die Firmung, Konfirmation.
confirmed [kən'fə:md], *adj.* eingefleischt; unverbesserlich.
confiscate ['kənfiskeit], *v.a.* konfiszieren, einziehen, beschlagnahmen.
confiscation [kənfis'keiʃən], *s.* die Konfiszierung, die Einziehung, die Beschlagnahme (*customs etc.*).
conflagration [kənflə'greiʃən], *s.* der (große) Brand.
conflict ['kənflikt], *s.* der Konflikt, der Zusammenstoß. — [kən'flikt], *v.n.* in Konflikt geraten; in Widerspruch stehen.
confluence ['kənfluəns], *s.* (*Geog.*) der Zusammenfluß.
confluent ['kənfluənt], *adj.* zusammenfließend. — *s.* der Nebenfluß (*tributary*).
conform [kən'fə:m], *v.n.* sich anpassen.
conformation [kənfə:'meiʃən], *s.* die Anpassung.
conformist [kən'fə:mist], *adj.* fügsam. — *s.* das Mitglied der Staatskirche.
conformity [kən'fə:miti], *s.* die Gleichförmigkeit; *in* — *with*, gerade so; gemäß (*Dat.*); die Gleichheit (*equality*).
confound [kən'faund], *v.a.* verwirren (*confuse*); vernichten (*overthrow*).
confounded [kən'faundid], *adj.* verdammt, verwünscht.
confront [kən'frʌnt], *v.a.* (*Law*) — *s.o. with*, gegenüberstellen (*put in front of*); gegenüberstehen (*stand in front of*).
confrontation [kənfrʌn'teiʃən], *s.* die Gegenüberstellung.
confuse [kən'fju:z], *v.a.* verwirren (*muddle*); bestürzen (*perplex*); verwechseln (*mix up*).
confusion [kən'fju:ʒən], *s.* die Verwirrung, das Durcheinander (*muddle*); die Bestürzung (*astonishment*); die Verlegenheit (*dilemma*).
confutation [kənfju:'teiʃən], *s.* die Widerlegung.
confute [kən'fju:t], *v.a.* widerlegen.
congeal [kən'dʒi:l], *v.n.* gefrieren (*freeze*); gerinnen.
congenial [kən'dʒi:niəl], *adj.* geistesverwandt, geistig ebenbürtig, sympathisch.
congeniality [kəndʒi:ni'æliti], *s.* die Geistesverwandtschaft.
conger ['kəŋgə], *s.* (*Zool.*) der Meeraal.

congest [kən'dʒest], *v.a.* anhäufen, überfüllen.

congestion [kən'dʒestʃən], *s.* die Überfüllung; Stauung; die Übervölkerung (*overpopulation*); (*Med.*) der Blutandrang.

conglomerate [kən'glɔməreit], *v.n.* sich zusammenballen. — [-rit], *s.* das Konglomerat, die Ballung.

conglomeration [kənglɔmə'reiʃən], *s.* die Zusammenhäufung, Zusammenballung.

Congolese [kɔŋgo'li:z], *adj.* kongolesisch. — *s.* der Kongolese.

congratulate [kən'grætjuleit], *v.n.* gratulieren (*on*, zu, *Dat.*).

congratulation [kəngrætju'leiʃən], *s.* (*usually pl.*) die Glückwünsche, *m. pl.*

congratulatory [kən'grætjuleitəri], *adj.* Glückwunsch-.

congregate [ˈkɔŋgrigeit], *v.a.* sammeln. — *v.n.* sich versammeln, sich scharen (*round*, um, *Acc.*).

congregation [kɔŋgri'geiʃən], *s.* die Versammlung, die Schar; (*Eccl.*) die Gemeinde.

congregational [kɔŋgri'geiʃənəl], *adj.* (*Eccl.*) Gemeinde-; *Congregational Church*, unabhängige Gemeindekirche.

congress [ˈkɔŋgres], *s.* der Kongreß.

congruence [ˈkɔŋgruəns], *s.* (*Geom.*) die Kongruenz.

congruent [ˈkɔŋgruənt], *adj.* (*Geom.*) kongruent.

congruity [kɔŋ'gru:iti], *s.* (*Geom.*) die Übereinstimmung; die Kongruenz.

congruous [ˈkɔŋgruəs], *adj.* übereinstimmend, angemessen.

conic(al) [ˈkɔnik(əl)], *adj.* konisch, kegelförmig; (*Geom.*) – *section*, der Kegelschnitt.

conifer [ˈkɔnifə], *s.* (*Bot.*) der Nadelbaum.

conjecture [kən'dʒəktʃə], *s.* die Mutmaßung, die Annahme. — *v.a.* mutmaßen, annehmen.

conjoin [kɔn'dʒɔin], *v.a.* (*Law*) verbinden.

conjugal [ˈkɔndʒugəl], *adj.* ehelich.

conjugate [ˈkɔndʒugeit], *v.a.* (*Gram.*) konjugieren.

conjugation [kɔndʒu'geiʃən], *s.* (*Gram.*) die Konjugation.

conjunction [kən'dʒʌŋkʃən], *s.* (*Gram.*) das Bindewort.

conjunctive [kən'dʒʌŋktiv], *adj.* verbindend; (*Gram.*) — *mood*, der Konjunktiv.

conjunctivitis [kəndʒʌŋkti'vaitis], *s.* (*Med.*) die Bindehautentzündung.

conjuncture [kən'dʒʌŋktʃə], *s.* der Wendepunkt; die Krise (*of events*).

conjure [ˈkʌndʒə], *v.a.* beschwören; — *up*, heraufbeschwören. — *v.n.* zaubern.

conjurer [ˈkʌndʒərə], *s.* der Zauberer.

connect [kə'nekt], *v.a.* verbinden, in Zusammenhang bringen.

connection, connexion [kə'nekʃən],*s* die Verbindung, der Zusammenhang.

connivance [kə'naivəns], *s.* die Nachsicht, das Gewährenlassen.

connive [kə'naiv], *v.n.* nachsichtig sein (*at*, bei, *Dat.*); gewähren lassen.

connoisseur [kɔnə'sə:], *s.* der Kenner.

connubial [kə'nju:biəl], *adj.* ehelich.

conquer [ˈkɔŋkə], *v.a.* besiegen (*foe*); erobern (*place*).

conqueror [ˈkɔŋkərə], *s.* der Eroberer, der Sieger.

conquest [ˈkɔŋkwest], *s.* der Sieg, die Eroberung.

consanguinity [kɔnsæŋ'gwiniti], *s.* die Blutsverwandtschaft.

conscience [ˈkɔnʃəns], *s.* das Gewissen; *in all* — wahrhaftig.

conscientious [kɔnʃi'enʃəs], *adj.* gewissenhaft.

conscientiousness [kɔnʃi'enʃəsnis], *s.* die Gewissenhaftigkeit.

conscious [ˈkɔnʃəs], *adj.* bewußt (*Genit.*).

consciousness [ˈkɔnʃəsnis], *s.* das Bewußtsein.

conscript [kən'skript], *v.a.* (*Mil.*) einziehen, einberufen. — [ˈkɔnskript], *s.* (*Mil.*) der Rekrut, der Dienstpflichtige.

conscription [kən'skripʃən], *s.* die allgemeine Wehrpflicht.

consecrate [ˈkɔnsikreit], *v.a.* weihen, widmen.

consecrated [ˈkɔnsikreitid], *adj.* geweiht (*Dat.*).

consecration [kɔnsi'kreiʃən], *s.* die Weihe, Einweihung (*of church*); die Weihung.

consecutive [kən'sekjutiv], *adj.* aufeinanderfolgend, fortlaufend.

consecutiveness [kən'sekjutivnis], *s.* die Aufeinanderfolge.

consent [kən'sent], *v.n.* zustimmen, beistimmen (*to*, *Dat.*). — *s.* die Zustimmung, die Einwilligung.

consequence [ˈkɔnsikwəns], *s.* die Konsequenz; (*Log.*) Folgerung; die Folge; die Wichtigkeit (*importance*).

consequent [ˈkɔnsikwənt], *adj.* folgend, nachfolgend.

consequential [kɔnsi'kwenʃəl], *adj.* wichtigtuend, anmaßend; (*Log.*) folgerichtig.

consequently [ˈkɔnsikwəntli], *adv.* folglich, infolgedessen.

conservatism [kən'sə:vətizm], *s.* (*Pol.*) der Konservatismus; die konservative Denkweise.

conservative [kən'sə:vətiv], *adj.* (*Pol.*) konservativ.

conservatoire [kən'sə:vətwa:], *s.* (*Mus.*) das Konservatorium, die Musikhochschule.

conservatory [kən'sə:vətəri], *s.* (*Bot.*) das Gewächshaus.

conserve [kən'sə:v], *v.a.* konservieren, erhalten, einmachen. — *s.* (*fruit*) das Eingemachte.

consider [kən'sidə], *v.a.* betrachten, in Betracht ziehen (*think over*, *look at*); berücksichtigen (*have regard to*); nachdenken über (*Acc.*) (*ponder*).

considerable

considerable [kən'sidərəbl], *adj.* beträchtlich, ansehnlich.

considerate [kən'sidərit], *adj.* rücksichtsvoll (*thoughtful*).

consideration [kənsidə'reiʃən], *s.* die Betrachtung (*contemplation*); die Rücksicht (*regard*) (*for*, auf, *Acc.*); die Entschädigung (*compensation*); die Belohnung (*reward*).

considering [kən'sidəriŋ], *prep.* in Anbetracht (*Genit.*).

consign [kən'sain], *v.a.* überliefern (*hand over*); übersenden (*remit*).

consignee [kɔnsai'niː], *s.* (*Comm.*) der Empfänger, der Adressat (*recipient*).

consigner [kən'sainə], *s.* der Absender (*of goods*).

consignment [kən'sainmənt], *s.* die Sendung (*of goods*).

consist [kən'sist], *v.n.* bestehen (*of*, aus, *Dat.*).

consistency [kən'sistənsi], *s.* die Festigkeit, Dichtigkeit; (*Chem.*) die Konsistenz.

consistent [kən'sistənt], *adj.* konsequent; — *with*, übereinstimmend, gemäß (*Dat.*); (*Chem.*) dicht, fest.

consistory [kən'sistəri], *s.* (*Eccl.*) das Konsistorium.

consolable [kən'souləbl], *adj.* tröstlich, zu trösten.

consolation [kɔnso'leiʃən], *s.* der Trost; draw —, Trost schöpfen.

console (1) [kən'soul], *v.a.* trösten.

console (2) ['kɔnsoul], *s.* (*Archit.*) die Konsole.

consolidate [kən'sɔlideit], *v.a.* befestigen, konsolidieren. — *v.n.* fest werden.

consolidation [kənsɔli'deiʃən], *s.* die Befestigung; Festigung, Bestärkung (*confirmation*).

consonance ['kɔnsənəns], *s.* (*Phonet.*) die Konsonanz; der Einklang, die Harmonie.

consonant ['kɔnsənənt], *adj.* in Einklang (*with*, mit, *Dat.*). — *s.* der Konsonant.

consort ['kɔnsɔːt], *s.* der Gemahl, Gatte; die Gemahlin, die Gattin. — [kən'sɔːt], *v.n.* verkehren (*with*, mit, *Dat.*).

conspicuous [kən'spikjuəs], *adj.* auffallend, deutlich sichtbar, hervorragend.

conspiracy [kən'spirəsi], *s.* die Verschwörung.

conspirator [kən'spirətə], *s.* der Verschwörer.

conspire [kən'spaiə], *v.n.* sich verschwören.

constable ['kʌnstəbl], *s.* der Polizist, der Schutzmann.

Constance ['kɔnstəns], Konstanze, *f.* (*name*); Konstanz, *n.* (*town*); Lake —, der Bodensee.

constancy ['kɔnstənsi], *s.* die Beständigkeit, Treue.

constant ['kɔnstənt], *adj.* (*Chem.*) konstant; treu, beständig.

constellation [kɔnstə'leiʃən], *s.* die Konstellation; das Sternbild.

consternation [kɔnstə'neiʃən], *s.* die Bestürzung.

constipation [kɔnsti'peiʃən], *s.* die Verstopfung.

constituency [kən'stitjuənsi], *s.* der Wahlkreis (*electoral district*); die Wählerschaft (*voters*).

constituent [kən'stitjuənt], *adj.* wesentlich. — *s.* der Bestandteil (*component*); (*Pol.*) der Wähler.

constitute ['kɔnstitjuːt], *v.a.* ausmachen (*make up*); bilden (*form*); festsetzen (*establish*); (*Pol.*) errichten (*set up*).

constitution [kɔnsti'tjuːʃən], *s.* die Konstitution (*physique*); die Errichtung (*establishment*); die Beschaffenheit, Natur (*nature*); (*Pol.*) die Verfassung.

constitutional [kɔnsti'tjuːʃənəl], *adj.* körperlich bedingt; (*Pol.*) verfassungsmäßig.

constrain [kən'strein], *v.a.* nötigen, zwingen.

constraint [kən'streint], *s.* der Zwang.

constrict [kən'strikt], *v.a.* zusammenziehen.

constriction [kən'strikʃən], *s.* die Zusammenziehung, Beengtheit.

construct [kən'strʌkt], *v.a.* errichten, bauen, konstruieren.

construction [kən'strʌkʃən], *s.* die Errichtung, der Bau, die Konstruktion.

constructive [kən'strʌktiv], *adj.* (*Engin.*) konstruktiv; behilflich (*positive*).

constructor [kən'strʌktə], *s.* der Konstrukteur, der Erbauer (*builder*).

construe [kən'struː], *v.a.* konstruieren, deuten (*interpret*).

consul ['kɔnsəl], *s.* der Konsul; — *general*, der Generalkonsul.

consular ['kɔnsjulə], *adj.* konsularisch.

consulate ['kɔnsjulit], *s.* das Konsulat; — *general*, das Generalkonsulat.

consult [kən'sʌlt], *v.a.* konsultieren, zu Rate ziehen; nachschlagen (*a book*). — *v.n.* sich beraten (*with*, mit, *Dat.*); (*Comm.*) als Berater hinzuziehen.

consultant [kən'sʌltənt], *s.* (*Med.*) der Facharzt; der Berater.

consultation [kɔnsəl'teiʃən], *s.* die Beratung (*advice*); die Besprechung (*discussion*); (*Med.*, *Engin.*) die Konsultation.

consume [kən'sjuːm], *v.a.* verzehren (*eat up*); verbrauchen (*use up*).

consumer [kən'sjuːmə], *s.* der Verbraucher; (*Comm.*) der Konsument.

consummate [kən'sʌmit], *adj.* vollendet. — ['kɔnsəmeit], *v.a.* vollenden, vollziehen.

consummation [kɔnsə'meiʃən], *s.* die Vollziehung, Vollendung.

consumption [kən'sʌmpʃən], *s.* (*Comm.*) der Verbrauch; (*Med.*) die Schwindsucht.

consumptive [kən'sʌmptiv], *adj.* (*Med.*) schwindsüchtig.

contact ['kɔntækt], *v.a.* berühren (*touch*); in Verbindung treten (mit) (*get into touch (with)*). — *s.* (*Elec.*) der Kontakt; die Berührung (*touch*); die Verbindung (*connexion*).

contagion [kən'teidʒən], *s.* (*Med.*) die Ansteckung.

contagious[kən'teidʒəs],*adj.*ansteckend.

contain [kən'tein], *v.a.* enthalten (*hold*); zurückhalten (*restrain*).

container [kən'teinə], *s.* der Behälter.

contaminate [kən'tæmineit], *v.a.* verunreinigen; vergiften.

contemplate ['kɔntəmpleit], *v.a.* betrachten (*consider*). — *v.n.* nachdenken (*ponder*).

contemplation [kɔntəm'pleiʃən], *s.* die Betrachtung (*consideration*); das Sinnen (*pondering*).

contemplative [kən'templətiv], *adj.* nachdenklich, kontemplativ.

contemporaneous [kɔntempə'reiniəs], *adj.* gleichzeitig.

contemporary [kən'tempərəri], *adj.* zeitgenössisch. — *s.* der Zeitgenosse.

contempt [kən'tempt], *s.* die Verachtung, — *of court*, die Gerichtsbeleidigung.

contemptible [kən'temptibl], *adj.* verächtlich, verachtungswert.

contemptibleness [kən'temptiblnis], *s.* die Verächtlichkeit.

contemptuous [kən'temptjuəs], *adj.* höhnisch, verachtungsvoll.

contemptuousness [kən'temptjuəsnis], *s.* der Hohn, der verachtungsvolle Ton, der Hochmut.

contend [kən'tend], *v.n.* streiten; bestreiten, behaupten.

content [kən'tent], *adj.* zufrieden. — *v.a.* zufriedenstellen. — ['kɔntent], *s.* (*often pl.*) der Inhalt.

contented [kən'tentid], *adj.* zufrieden.

contentedness, contentment [kən-'tentidnis, kən'tentmənt], *s.* die Zufriedenheit.

contention [kən'tenʃən], *s.* der Streit, die Behauptung.

contentious [kən'tenʃəs], *adj.* streitsüchtig (*person*); strittig (*question*).

contest ['kɔntest], *s.* der Streit, Wettstreit, Wettkampf. — [kən'test], *v.a.* um etwas streiten, bestreiten.

context ['kɔntekst], *s.* der Zusammenhang.

contexture [kən'tekstʃə], *s.* (*Engin.*) der Bau, die Zusammensetzung; das Gewebe (*textile*).

contiguity [kɔnti'gju:iti], *s.* die Berührung; die Nachbarschaft.

contiguous [kən'tigjuəs], *adj.* anstossend, anliegend.

continence ['kɔntinəns], *s.* die Mäßigung (*moderation*); die Enthaltsamkeit (*abstemiousness*).

continent (1) ['kɔntinənt], *adj.* enthaltsam, mässig.

continent (2) ['kɔntinənt], *s.* das Festland, der Kontinent.

contingency [kən'tindʒənsi], *s.* der Zufall; die Möglichkeit (*possibility*).

contingent [kən'tindʒənt], *s.* der Beitrag, das Kontingent (*share*). — *adj.* möglich.

continual [kən'tinjuəl], *adj.* fortwährend, beständig.

continuance [kən'tinjuəns], *s.* die Fortdauer.

continuation [kəntinju'eiʃən], *s.* die Fortsetzung.

continue [kən'tinju:], *v.a.* fortsetzen (*go on with*); verlängern (*prolong*). — *v.n.* weitergehen, weiterführen (*of story*).

continuity [kɔnti'nju:iti], *s.* der Zusammenhang, die ununterbrochene Folge, Kontinuität (*Film*); — *girl*, die Drehbuchsekretärin.

continuous [kən'tinjuəs], *adj.* zusammenhängend, ununterbrochen, andauernd.

contort [kən'tɔ:t], *v.a.* verdrehen.

contortion [kən'tɔ:ʃən], *s.* die Verdrehung, Verkrümmung, Verzerrung.

contortionist [kən'tɔ:ʃənist], *s.* der Schlangenmensch.

contour ['kɔntuə], *s.* die Kontur, der Umriß.

contraband ['kɔntrəbænd], *adj.* Schmuggel-, geschmuggelt. — *s.* die Bannware, Schmuggelware.

contract [kən'trækt], *v.a.* zusammenziehen (*pull together*); verengen (*narrow down*); verkürzen (*shorten*); sich eine Krankheit zuziehen (— *a disease*); Schulden machen (— *debts*). — *v.n.* sich zusammenziehen, kürzer werden; einen Kontrakt abschließen (*come to terms*). — ['kɔntrækt], *s.* der Vertrag (*pact*); (*Comm.*) der Kontrakt.

contraction [kən'trækʃən], *s.* die Zusammenziehung; (*Phonet.*) die Kürzung.

contractor [kən'træktə], *s.* (*Comm.*) der Kontrahent; der Lieferant (*supplier*); *building* —, der Bauunternehmer.

contradict [kɔntrə'dikt], *v.n.* widersprechen (*Dat.*).

contradiction [kɔntrə'dikʃən], *s.* der Widerspruch.

contradictory [kɔntrə'diktəri], *adj.* in Widerspruch stehend, widersprechend.

contrarily ['kɔntrərili], *adv.* im Gegensatz dazu, hingegen, dagegen.

contrary ['kɔntrəri], *adj.* entgegengesetzt, *on the* —, im Gegenteil; [kən'trɛəri], widersprechend.

contrast [kən'trɑ:st], *v.a.* einander entgegenstellen, gegenüberstellen. — *v.n.* einen Gegensatz darstellen *or* bilden. — ['kɔntrɑ:st], *s.* der Kontrast (*colours*); der Gegensatz.

contravene [kɔntrə'vi:n], *v.a.* übertreten, zuwiderhandeln (*Dat.*).

contribute [kən'tribju:t], *v.a.* beitragen; beisteuern (*money, energy*).

contribution [kɔntri'bju:ʃən], *s.* der Beitrag.

contributive, contributory [kən'tri-bjutiv, kən'tribjutəri], *adj.* beitragend, Beitrags-.

contributor [kən'tribjutə], *s.* der Beitragende, der Spender (*of money*); der Mitarbeiter (*journalist etc.*).

contrite ['kɔntrait], *adj.* zerknirscht, reuevoll.

contrition [kən'triʃən], *s.* die Zerknirschung, die Reue.

contrivance [kən'traivəns], *s.* die Vorrichtung, die Erfindung.

contrive [kən'traiv], *v.a.* ausdenken, erfinden; fertigbringen (*accomplish*).

control [kən'troul], *v.a.* kontrollieren (*check*); die Leitung haben (*have command of*); die Aufsicht führen (*supervise*). — *s.* die Kontrolle; die Aufsicht; die Leitung; (*pl.*) (*Motor.*) die Steuerung; (*Aviat.*) das Leitwerk.

controller [kən'troulə], *s.* der Aufseher (*supervisor*); der Direktor (*of corporation*); der Revisor (*examiner, auditor*).

controversial [kɔntro'və:ʃəl], *adj.* umstritten, strittig.

controversy ['kɔntrovə:si], *s.* die Kontroverse, die Streitfrage.

controvert ['kɔntrovə:t], *v.a.* bestreiten, widersprechen (*Dat.*).

contumacious [kɔntju'meiʃəs], *adj.* widerspenstig, halsstarrig.

contumacy ['kɔntjuməsi], *s.* die Widerspenstigkeit (*obstreperousness*); der Ungehorsam (*disobedience*).

contumelious [kɔntju'mi:liəs], *adj.* frech, unverschämt (*insolent*).

contuse [kən'tju:z], *v.a.* quetschen.

conundrum [kə'nʌndrəm], *s.* das Scherzrätsel.

convalescence [kɔnvə'lesəns], *s.* die Gesundung, die Genesung.

convalescent [kɔnvə'lesənt], *adj.* genesend. — *s.* der Genesende, der Rekonvaleszent.

convene [kən'vi:n], *v.a.* zusammenrufen, versammeln. — *v.n.* zusammentreten, sich versammeln.

convenience [kən'vi:niəns], *s.* die Bequemlichkeit; *at your early* —, umgehend; *public* —, öffentliche Bedürfnisanstalt.

convenient [kən'vi:niənt], *adj.* bequem, gelegen; passend (*time*).

convent ['kɔnvənt], *s.* das (Nonnen)-Kloster.

convention [kən'venʃən], *s.* die Konvention, der Kongress (*meeting*); der Vertrag (*treaty*); die Sitte (*tradition, custom*).

conventional [kən'venʃənəl], *adj.* herkömmlich, traditionell.

conventual [kən'ventjuəl], *adj.* klösterlich.

conversation [kɔnvə'seiʃən], *s.* die Konversation, Unterhaltung; das Gespräch.

conversational [kɔnvə'seiʃənəl], *adj.* gesprächig, umgangssprachlich.

converse (1) [kən'və:s], *v.n.* sich unterhalten (*with*, mit, *Dat.*).

converse (2) ['kɔnvə:s], *adj.* umgekehrt.

conversely ['kɔnvə:sli], *adv.* hingegen, dagegen.

conversion [kən'və:ʃən], *s.* die Umkehrung (*reversal*); (*Rel.*) die Bekehrung; (*Comm.*) die Umwechslung.

convert ['kɔnvə:t], *s.* (*Rel.*) der Bekehrte, die Bekehrte; der Konvertit. — [kən'və:t], *v.a.* (*Rel.*) bekehren; (*Comm.*) umwechseln.

converter [kən'və:tə], *s.* (*Rel.*) der Bekehrer; (*Metall., Elec.*) der Umformer.

convertible [kən'və:tibl], *adj.* umwandelbar. — *s.* (*Motor.*) der *or* das Konvertible.

convex ['kɔnveks], *adj.* (*Phys.*) konvex.

convey [kən'vei], *v.a.* transportieren; führen (*bear, carry*); mitteilen (*impart*).

conveyance [kən'veiəns], *s.* die Beförderung (*transport*); das Fuhrwerk (*vehicle*); die Übertragung; (*Law*) das Übertragungsdokument.

conveyancing [kən'veiənsin], *s.* (*Law*) die legale *or* rechtliche Übertragung.

convict ['kɔnvikt], *s.* der Sträfling. — [kən'vikt], *v.a.* für schuldig erklären.

conviction [kən'vikʃən], *s.* die Überzeugung; (*Law*) die Überführung, die Schuldigsprechung.

convince [kən'vins], *v.a.* überzeugen.

convivial [kən'viviəl], *adj.* gesellig (*sociable*).

conviviality [kənvivi'æliti], *s.* die Geselligkeit.

convocation [kɔnvə'keiʃən], *s.* die Zusammenberufung, Festversammlung; (*Eccl.*) die Synode.

convoke [kən'vouk], *v.a.* zusammenberufen.

convolvulus [kən'vɔlvjuləs], *s.* (*Bot.*) die Winde.

convoy ['kɔnvɔi], *s.* das Geleit, die Bedeckung; (*Mil.*) der Begleitzug. — [kən'vɔi], *v.a.* geleiten; (*Mil.*) im Geleitzug mitführen.

convulse [kən'vʌls], *v.a.* erschüttern.

convulsion [kən'vʌlʃən], *s.* der Krampf, die Zuckung.

convulsive [kən'vʌlsiv], *adj.* krampfhaft, zuckend.

coo [ku:], *v.n.* girren (*of birds*); *bill and* —, schnäbeln.

cook [kuk], *v.a., v.n.* kochen; (*coll.*) — *the books*, die Bücher(Bilanz)fälschen *or* frisieren. — *s.* der Koch, die Köchin; *too many cooks* (*spoil the broth*), zu viele Köche (verderben den Brei).

cookery ['kukəri], *s.* die Kochkunst; — *school*, die Kochschule.

cool [ku:l], *adj.* kühl (*climate*); kaltblütig (*coldblooded*); unverschämt (*brazen*). — *s.* die Kühle. — *v.a.* abkühlen; (*fig.*) besänftigen. — *v.n.* sich abkühlen.

cooler ['ku:lə], *s.* (*Chem.*) das Kühlfaß; (*coll.*) das Gefängnis; (*sl.*) das Kittchen.

coop [ku:p], *s.* die Kufe; das Faß; *hen* —, der Hühnerkorb. — *v.a.* — *up*, einsperren.

cooper [ˈku:pə], *s.* der Böttcher, der Faßbinder.

cooperate [kouˈɔpəreit], *v.n.* zusammenarbeiten; mitarbeiten, mitwirken.

cooperation [kouɔpəˈreiʃən], *s.* die Zusammenarbeit, die Mitarbeit.

cooperative [kouˈɔpərətiv], *adj.* willig; mitwirkend. — *s.* die Konsumgenossenschaft, der Konsum.

coordinate [kouˈɔ:dineit], *v.a.* koordinieren, beiordnen. — [-nit], *adj.* (*Gram.*) koordiniert.

coordination [kouɔ:diˈneiʃən], *s.* die Koordinierung.

coot [ku:t], *s.* (*Orn.*) das Wasserhuhn.

copartnership [kouˈpɑ:tnəʃip], *s.* die Teilhaberschaft; die Partnerschaft in der Industrie.

cope (1) [koup], *s.* (*Eccl.*) das Pluviale, der Priesterrock; (*Build.*) die Decke.

cope (2) [koup], *v.n.* — *with s.th.*, mit etwas fertig werden, — es schaffen.

coping [ˈkoupiŋ], *s.* (*Build.*) die Kappe; — *-stone* or *copestone*, der Firststein, Schlußstein, Kappstein.

copious [ˈkoupiəs], *adj.* reichlich; wortreich (*style*).

copiousness [ˈkoupiəsnis], *s.* die Reichhaltigkeit, Fülle.

copper [ˈkɔpə], *s.* (*Metall.*) das Kupfer; (*sl.*) der Polizist; (*coll.*) der Penny, das Pennystück. — *adj.* kupfern.

copperplate [ˈkɔpəpleit], *s.* der Kupferstich (*etching*); (*Typ.*) die Kupferplatte.

coppery [ˈkɔpəri], *adj.* Kupfer-, kupfern, kupferfarben (*colour*).

coppice, copse [ˈkɔpis, kɔps], *s.* das Unterholz, das Dickicht.

copulate [ˈkɔpjuleit], *v.n.* sich paaren, begatten.

copulation [kɔpjuˈleiʃən], *s.* die Paarung; der Beischlaf (*human*).

copy [ˈkɔpi], *v.a.* kopieren, abschreiben (*write*); imitieren, nachahmen (*imitate*). — *s.* die Kopie; *carbon* —, die Durchschrift; Abschrift; die Nachahmung (*imitation*); die Fälschung (*forgery*).

copybook [ˈkɔpibuk], *s.* das Heft.

copyist [ˈkɔpiist], *s.* der Kopist.

coquet, coquette (1) [kɔˈket], *v.n.* kokettieren.

coquette (2) [kɔˈket], *s.* die Kokette.

coquettish [kɔˈketiʃ], *adj.* kokett.

coral [ˈkɔrəl], *s.* die Koralle. — *adj.* Korallen-.

cord [kɔ:d], *s.* die Schnur, der Strick (*rope*); (*Am.*) der Bindfaden (*string*); die Klafter (*wood measure*); der Kordstoff (*textile*); *vocal* —, das Stimmband.

cordage [ˈkɔ:didʒ], *s.* (*Naut.*) das Tauwerk.

cordial (1) [ˈkɔ:diəl], *adj.* herzlich.

cordial (2) [ˈkɔ:diəl], *s.* der Fruchtsaft (konzentriert), Magenlikör.

cordiality [kɔ:diˈæliti], *s.* die Herzlichkeit.

corduroy [ˈkɔ:djurɔi], *s.* der Kordsamt.

core [kɔ:], *s.* der Kern; das Innere (*innermost part*).

cork [kɔ:k], *s.* der Kork, der Korken. — *v.a.* verkorken.

corkscrew [ˈkɔ:kskru:], *s.* der Korkzieher.

cormorant [ˈkɔ:mərənt], *s.* (*Orn.*) der Kormoran, die Scharbe.

corn (1) [kɔ:n], *s.* das Korn, das Getreide (*wheat etc.*); (*Am.*) *sweet* —, der Mais.

corn (2) [kɔ:n], *s.* das Hühnerauge (*on foot*).

corned [kɔ:nd], *adj.* eingesalzt; — *beef*, das Pökelrindfleisch.

cornea [ˈkɔ:niə], *s.* (*Anat.*) die Hornhaut.

cornel-tree [ˈkɔ:nəltri:], *s.* (*Bot.*) der Kornelkirschbaum.

cornelian [kɔ:ˈni:liən], *s.* (*Geol.*) der Karneol.

corner [ˈkɔ:nə], *s.* die Ecke; (*Footb.*) der Eckstoß. — *v.a.* in eine Ecke treiben; in die Enge treiben (*force*).

cornered [ˈkɔ:nəd], *adj.* eckig (*angular*); in die Enge getrieben, gefangen (*caught*).

cornet [ˈkɔ:nit], *s.* (*Mus.*) die Zinke, das Flügelhorn; (*Mil.*) der Kornett, der Fähnrich.

cornflower [ˈkɔ:nflauə], *s.* (*Bot.*) die Kornblume.

cornice [ˈkɔ:nis], *s.* (*Archit.*) das Gesims.

cornucopia [kɔ:njuˈkoupjə], *s.* das Füllhorn.

corollary [kəˈrɔləri], *s.* (*Log.*) der Folgesatz; die Folgeerscheinung (*consequence*).

corona [kəˈrounə], *s.* (*Astron.*) der Hof, Lichtkranz.

coronation [kɔrəˈneiʃən], *s.* die Krönung.

coroner [ˈkɔrənə], *s.* der Leichenbeschauer.

coronet [ˈkɔrənet], *s.* die Adelskrone.

corporal (1) [ˈkɔ:pərəl], *s.* (*Mil.*) der Korporal, der Unteroffizier, Obergefreite.

corporal (2) [ˈkɔ:pərəl], *adj.* körperlich; — *punishment*, die Züchtigung.

corporate [ˈkɔ:pərit], *adj.* (*Law, Comm.*) als Körperschaft; gemeinschaftlich, einheitlich (*as a group or unit*).

corporation [kɔ:pəˈreiʃən], *s.* (*Law, Comm.*) die Körperschaft; die Korporation; die Gemeinde (*municipal*); (*sl.*) der Schmerbauch (*stoutness*).

corps [kɔ:], *s.* das Korps.

corpse [kɔ:ps], *s.* der Leichnam.

corpulence [ˈkɔ:pjuləns], *s.* die Korpulenz, die Beleibtheit.

corpulent [ˈkɔ:pjulənt], *adj.* korpulent, dick.

Corpus Christi [ˈkɔ:pəs ˈkristi]. (der) Fronleichnam, das Fronleichnamsfest.

corpuscle [ˈkɔ:pʌsl], *s.* (*Anat.*) das Körperchen.

correct [kə'rekt], *v.a.* korrigieren (*remove mistakes*); verbessern; tadeln (*reprove*); berichtigen (*rectify*). — *adj.* korrekt, tadellos, richtig.

correction [kə'rekʃən], *s.* die Korrektur (*of mistakes*); die Verbesserung (*improvement*); die Richtigstellung (*restoration*); der Verweis (*censure*).

corrective [kə'rektiv], *adj.* zur Besserung. — *s.* das Korrektiv.

correctness [kə'rektnis], *s.* die Korrektheit (*of manner, action etc.*).

corrector [kə'rektə], *s.* der Korrektor (*proof reader etc.*).

correlate ['kɔrileit], *v.a.* in Beziehung setzen, aufeinander beziehen. — [-lit], *s.* (*Log.*) das Korrelat.

correlative [kɔ'relətiv], *adj.* in Wechselbeziehung stehend.

correspond [kɔris'pɔnd], *v.n.* korrespondieren (*exchange letters*); entsprechen (*to, Dat.*).

correspondence [kɔris'pɔndəns], *s.* die Korrespondenz; der Briefwechsel (*letters*); die Übereinstimmung (*harmony*).

correspondent [kɔris'pɔndənt], *s.* der Korrespondent (*letter-writer*); der Journalist, Berichterstatter (*newspaper*).

corridor ['kɔridɔː], *s.* der Korridor; der Gang.

corrigible ['kɔridʒibl], *adj.* verbesserlich.

corroborate [kə'rɔbəreit], *v.a.* bestätigen (*confirm*); bestärken (*strengthen*).

corroboration [kərɔbə'reiʃən], *s.* die Bestätigung, die Bekräftigung.

corroborative [kə'rɔbərətiv], *adj.* bekräftigend.

corrode [kə'roud], *v.a.* zerfressen, zersetzen, ätzen (*acid*).

corrosion [kə'rouʒən], *s.* die Anfressung, Ätzung.

corrosive [kə'rouziv], *adj.* ätzend.

corrugated ['kɔrugeitid], *adj.* gewellt, Well-; — *iron,* das Wellblech; — *paper,* die Wellpappe.

corrupt [kə'rʌpt], *v.a.* verderben (*spoil*); bestechen (*bribe*). — *adj.* korrupt (*morals*); verdorben (*spoilt*).

corruptible [kə'rʌptibl], *adj.* verderblich; bestechlich.

corruption [kə'rʌpʃən], *s.* die Korruption; die Bestechung (*bribery*).

corruptness [kə'rʌptnis], *s.* die Verdorbenheit, der Verfall.

corsair ['kɔːsɛə], *s.* der Korsar, der Seeräuber.

corset ['kɔːsit], *s.* das Korsett.

coruscate ['kɔrəskeit], *v.n.* schimmern, leuchten.

corvette [kɔː'vet], *s.* (*Naut.*) die Korvette.

cosine ['kousain], *s.* (*Maths.*) der Kosinus.

cosiness ['kouzinis], *s.* die Bequemlichkeit, die Behaglichkeit (*comfort*).

cosmetic [kɔz'metik], *adj.* kosmetisch. — *s.* (*pl.*) das *or* die (*pl.*) Schönheitsmittel.

cosmic ['kɔzmik], *adj.* kosmisch.

cosmopolitan [kɔzmo'pɔlitən], *adj.* kosmopolitisch, weltbürgerlich. — *s.* der Kosmopolit, der Weltbürger.

Cossack ['kɔsæk], *s.* der Kosak.

cost [kɔst], *v.a. irr.* kosten. — *v.n. irr.* zu stehen kommen. — *s.* die Kosten, *f. pl.* (*expenses*); *at all* —*s,* um jeden Preis.

costermonger ['kɔstəmʌŋgə], *s.* der Straßenhändler.

costly ['kɔstli], *adj.* kostspielig.

costume ['kɔstjuːm], *s.* das Kostüm; — *play,* das Zeitstück.

cosy ['kouzi], *adj.* behaglich, bequem.

cot (1) [kɔt], *s.* das Bettchen, Kinderbett.

cot (2) [kɔt], *s.* (*obs.*) die Hütte (*hut*).

cottage ['kɔtidʒ], *s.* die Hütte, das Häuschen.

cottager ['kɔtidʒə], *s.* der Kleinhäusler.

cotton [kɔtn], *s.* die Baumwolle. — *v.n.* — *on to,* (*coll.*) sich anhängen, sich anschließen (*Dat.*); — *on,* folgen können (*understand*).

couch [kautʃ], *s.* die Chaiselongue, der Diwan. — *v.a.* (*express*) in Worte fassen.

cough [kɔf], *v.n.* husten. — *s.* der Husten; *whooping* —, der Keuchhusten.

council ['kaunsil], *s.* der Rat (*body*); die Ratsversammlung.

councillor ['kaunsilə], *s.* der Rat, das Ratsmitglied; der Stadtrat.

counsel ['kaunsəl], *s.* der Rat (*advice*); der Berater (*adviser*); der Anwalt (*lawyer*). — *v.a.* einen Rat geben, beraten (*Acc.*).

counsellor ['kaunsələ], *s.* der Ratgeber; der Ratsherr; (*Am.*) der Anwalt (*lawyer*).

count (1) [kaunt], *v.a., v.n.* zählen; — *on s.o.,* sich auf jemanden verlassen. — *s.* die Zählung.

count (2) [kaunt], *s.* der Graf.

countenance ['kauntənəns], *s.* das Gesicht, die Miene. — *v.a.* begünstigen, unterstützen, zulassen.

counter (1) ['kauntə], *s.* der Rechner, der Zähler (*chip*); die Spielmarke; der Zahltisch (*desk*); Ladentisch (*in shop*); Schalter (*in office*).

counter (2) ['kauntə], *adv.* entgegen.

counteract [kauntə'rækt], *v.a.* entgegenwirken (*Dat.*).

counteraction [kauntə'rækʃən], *s.* die Gegenwirkung; der Widerstand (*resistance*).

counterbalance ['kauntəbæləns], *s.* das Gegengewicht. — [-'bæləns], *v.a.* ausbalancieren, ausgleichen.

countercharge ['kauntətʃɑːdʒ], *s.* die Gegenklage.

counterfeit ['kauntəfiːt, -fit], *s.* die Fälschung (*forgery*); die Nachahmung (*imitation*). — *adj.* gefälscht, falsch.

counterfoil ['kauntəfɔil], *s.* das Kontrollblatt; der Kupon.

counter–intelligence ['kauntərintelidʒəns], *s.* die Spionageabwehr.

countermand [kauntə'mɑ:nd], *v.a.* widerrufen.

counterpane ['kauntəpein], *s.* die Steppdecke.

counterpart ['kauntəpɑ:t], *s.* das Gegenbild, das Gegenstück.

counterplot ['kauntəplɔt], *s.* der Gegenplan. — *v.n.* einen Gegenplan machen.

counterpoint ['kauntəpɔint], *s.* (*Mus.*) der Kontrapunkt.

counterpoise ['kauntəpɔiz], *s.* das Gegengewicht. — *v.a.* das Gleichgewicht halten.

countersign ['kauntəsain], *v.a.* gegenzeichnen, mitunterschreiben. — *s.* das Gegenzeichen.

countess ['kauntes], *s.* die Gräfin.

counting-house ['kauntiŋhaus], *s.* das Kontor.

countless ['kauntlis], *adj.* zahllos.

country ['kʌntri], *s.* das Land. — *adj.* Land-, ländlich, Bauern-.

county ['kaunti], *s.* die Grafschaft (*British*); der Landbezirk (*U.S.A.*).

couple [kʌpl], *s.* das Paar. — *v.a.* paaren, verbinden. — *v.n.* sich paaren (*pair*); sich verbinden.

couplet ['kʌplit], *s.* das Verspaar.

coupling ['kʌpliŋ], *s.* (*Mech.*) die Kupplung.

courage ['kʌridʒ], *s.* der Mut.

courageous [kə'reidʒəs], *adj.* mutig, tapfer.

courier ['kuriə], *s.* der Eilbote (*messenger*); der Reisebegleiter (*tour leader*).

course [kɔ:s], *s.* der Kurs; der Lauf (*time*); der Ablauf (*lapse of a period etc.*); die Bahn (*racing track*); *in due* —, zu gegebener Zeit; *of* —, natürlich.

courser ['kɔ:sə], *s.* das schnelle Pferd.

court [kɔ:t], *s.* der Hof (*royal etc.*); (*Law*) der Gerichtshof. — *v.a.* (*a lady*) den Hof machen (*Dat.*); — *disaster*, das Unglück herausfordern.

courteous ['kə:tiəs], *adj.* höflich.

courtesan ['kɔ:tizən *or* kɔ:ti'zæn], *s.* die Kurtisane, die Buhlerin.

courtesy ['kə:təsi], *s.* die Höflichkeit; *by* — *of*, mit freundlicher Erlaubnis von.

courtier ['kɔ:tiə], *s.* der Höfling.

courtly ['kɔ:tli], *adj.* höfisch, Hof-.

court-martial [kɔ:t'mɑ:ʃəl], *s.* das Kriegsgericht.

courtship ['kɔ:tʃip], *s.* das Werben, die Werbung, das Freien.

courtyard ['kɔ:tjɑ:d], *s.* der Hof, der Hofraum.

cousin [kʌzn], *s.* der Vetter (*male*); die Kusine (*female*).

cove [kouv], *s.* die (kleine) Bucht.

covenant ['kʌvənənt], *s.* (*Bibl.*) der Bund; (*Comm.*) der Vertrag.

cover ['kʌvə], *v.a.* decken, bedecken (*table etc.*); schützen (*protect*); — *up*, bemänteln. — *s.* die Decke (*blanket*); der Deckel (*lid*); der Einband (*book*); das Gedeck (*table*); (*Comm.*) die Deckung; — *point*, (*Cricket*) die Deckstellung; *under* —, (*Mil.*) verdeckt, unter Deckung; — *girl*, das Mädchen auf dem Titelblatt (einer Illustrierten.)

covering ['kʌvəriŋ], *s.* die Bedeckung, die Bekleidung (*clothing*).

coverlet, coverlid ['kʌvəlit, 'kʌvəlid], *s.* die Bettdecke.

covert ['kʌvə:t], *s.* der Schlupfwinkel (*hideout*); das Dickicht (*thicket*). — *adj.* verborgen, bedeckt (*covered*); heimlich (*secret*).

covet ['kʌvit], *v.a.*, *v.n.* begehren (*Acc.*), gelüsten (nach (*Dat.*)).

covetous ['kʌvitəs], *adj.* begierig, habsüchtig.

covetousness ['kʌvitəsnis], *s.* die Begierde, die Habsucht.

covey ['kʌvi], *s.* der Flug *or* die Kette (Rebhühner, *partridges*).

cow (1) [kau], *s.* die Kuh; — — *shed*, der Kuhstall.

cow (2) [kau], *v.a.* einschüchtern.

coward ['kauəd], *s.* der Feigling.

cowardice ['kauədis], *s.* die Feigheit.

cower ['kauə], *v.n.* sich kauern.

cowherd ['kauhə:d], *s.* der Kuhhirt.

cowl [kaul], *s.* die Kappe (*of monk*), die Kapuze (*hood*).

cowslip ['kauslip], *s.* (*Bot.*) die Primel, die Schlüsselblume.

coxswain ['kɔksn], *s.* (*Naut.*) der Steuermann.

coy [kɔi], *adj.* scheu, spröde, zurückhaltend.

coyness ['kɔinis], *s.* die Sprödigkeit.

crab [kræb], *s.* (*Zool.*) die Krabbe; — *apple*, (*Bot.*) der Holzapfel.

crabbed ['kræbd], *adj.* mürrisch (*temper*); unleserlich (*handwriting*).

crack [kræk], *s.* der Riß (*fissure*); der Krach, Schlag; der Sprung; die komische Bemerkung (*remark*). — *adj.* (*coll.*) erstklassig; — *shot*, der Meisterschütze. — *v.a.* aufbrechen; aufknacken (*nut, safe*); — *a joke*, eine witzige Bemerkung machen. — *v.n.* — *under strain*, unter einer Anstrengung zusammenbrechen; bersten (*break*).

cracked, crackers [krækd, 'krækəz], *adj.* (*coll.*) verrückt.

cracker ['krækə], *s.* der Keks; der Frosch (*firework*).

crackle [krækl], *v.n.* knistern, prasseln (*fire*); knallen, platzen (*rocket*).

cracknel ['kræknəl], *s.* die Brezel.

crackpot ['krækpɔt], *s.* (*coll.*) der verrückte Kerl.

cradle [kreidl], *s.* die Wiege. — *v.a.* einwiegen.

craft [krɑ:ft], *s.* die Fertigkeit (*skill*); das Handwerk (*trade*); die List (*cunning*); *arts and* —*s*, die Handwerkskünste.

craftsman ['krɑːftsmən], *s.* der (ge-
lernte) Handwerker.
crafty ['krɑːfti], *adj.* listig, schlau.
crag [kræg], *s.* die Klippe.
cragged, craggy [krægd, 'krægi],
adj. felsig, schroff.
cram [kræm], *v.a.* vollstopfen (*stuff
full*); (*coll.*) pauken (*coach*). — *v.n.*
büffeln.
crammer ['kræmə], *s.* (*coll.*) der
Einpauker, Privatlehrer (*tutor*).
cramp [kræmp], *s.* (*Med.*) der Krampf;
die Klammer (*tool*). — *v.a.* einengen
(*narrow*); verkrampfen.
cramped [kræmpd], *adj.* krampfhaft;
eingeengt, beengt (*enclosed*).
cranberry ['krænbəri], *s.* (*Bot.*) die
Preiselbeere.
crane [krein], *s.* (*Orn.*) der Kranich;
(*Engin.*) der Kran. — *v.a.* — *o.'s neck,*
den Hals ausrecken.
crank (1) [kræŋk], *s.* (*Motor.*) die
Kurbel; —*handle,* die Andrehwelle;
(*Motor., Engin.*) —*shaft,* die Kurbelwelle, die Kurbel.
crank (2) [kræŋk], *s.* der Sonderling,
der sonderbare Kauz (*eccentric*).
cranky ['kræŋki], *adj.* sonderbar.
cranny ['kræni], *s.* der Spalt, der Riß;
nook and —, Eck und Spalt.
crape [kreip], *s.* der Krepp, Flor.
crash [kræʃ], *s.* der Krach; (*Motor.*)
Zusammenstoß; (*Aviat.*) Absturz. —
v.n. krachen (*noise*); stürzen, abstürzen (*fall*).
crass [kræs], *adj.* derb, grob, kraß.
crate [kreit], *s.* der Packkorb (*basket*);
die Kiste (*wood*).
crater ['kreitə], *s.* (*Geol.*) der Krater.
cravat [krə'væt], *s.* die breite Halsbinde,
das Halstuch (*scarf*); die Krawatte.
crave [kreiv], *v.a.* (dringend) verlangen
(*for,* nach, *Dat.*)
craven ['kreivn], *adj.* feig, mutlos. — *s.*
der Feigling.
craving ['kreiviŋ], *s.* das starke Verlangen.
craw [krɔː], *s.* (*Zool.*) der Vogelkropf.
crawl [krɔːl], *v.n.* kriechen; kraulen
(*swim*).
crawling ['krɔːliŋ], *s.* das Kriechen; das
Kraulschwimmen.
crayon ['kreiən], *s.* der Farbstift, der
Pastellstift.
craze [kreiz], *s.* die Manie; die verrückte
Mode (*fashion*).
craziness ['kreizinis], *s.* die Verrücktheit.
crazy ['kreizi], *adj.* verrückt.
creak [kriːk], *v.n.* knarren.
cream [kriːm], *s.* der Rahm, die Sahne;
whipped —, die Schlagsahne, (*Austr.*)
der Schlagobers. — *v.a.* — *off,* (die
Sahne) abschöpfen; (*fig.*) das Beste
abziehen.
creamery ['kriːməri], *s.* die Molkerei.
creamy ['kriːmi], *adj.* sahnig.
crease [kriːs], *s.* die Falte (*trousers etc.*);
— *resistant,* knitterfrei.— *v.a.* falten
(*fold*). — *v.n.* knittern.

create [kri'eit], *v.a.* erschaffen, schaffen.
creation [kri'eiʃən], *s.* die Schöpfung.
creative [kri'eitiv], *adj.* schöpferisch.
creator [kri'eitə], *s.* der Schöpfer.
creature ['kriːtʃə], *s.* das Geschöpf.
credence ['kriːdəns], *s.* der Glaube.
credentials [kri'denʃəlz], *s. pl.* das
Zeugnis, das Beglaubigungsschreiben;
die Legitimation (*proof of identity*).
credibility [kredi'biliti], *s.* die Glaubwürdigkeit.
credible ['kredibl], *adj.* glaubwürdig,
glaublich.
credit ['kredit], *s.* (*Comm.*) der Kredit;
der gute Ruf (*reputation*); das Guthaben (*assets*). — *v.a.* — *s.o. with s.th.,*
jemandem etwas gutschreiben; glau-
ben (*believe*).
creditable ['kreditəbl], *adj.* ehrenwert,
lobenswert.
creditor ['kreditə], *s.* (*Comm.*) der
Gläubiger.
credulity [kre'djuːliti], *s.* die Leicht-
gläubigkeit.
credulous ['kredjuləs], *adj.* leichtgläubig.
creed [kriːd], *s.* das Glaubensbekenntnis.
creek [kriːk], *s.* die kleine Bucht; das
Flüßchen (*small river*).
creel [kriːl], *s.* der Fischkorb.
creep [kriːp], *s.* (*Geol.*) der Rutsch;
(*pl., coll.*) the —s, die Gänsehaut, das
Gruseln. — *v.a.* — *s.o.* with *s.th.,*
sich einschleichen.
creeper ['kriːpə], *s.* die Schlingpflanze,
das Rankengewächs; (*Sch.*) der
Kriecher; *Virginia —,* der wilde Wein.
creepy ['kriːpi], *adj.* kriechend; gruselig
(*frightening*).
cremate [kri'meit], *v.a.* einäschern.
cremation [kri'meiʃən], *s.* die Verbrennung, Einäscherung.
crematorium, (*Am.*) **crematory** [kre-
mə'tɔːriəm, 'kremətəri], *s.* das Krema-
torium.
Creole ['kriːoul], *s.* der Kreole.
crepuscular [kri'pʌskjulə], *adj.* dämmerig.
crescent ['kresənt], *adj.* wachsend,
zunehmend. — *s.* der (zunehmende)
Mond, die Mondsichel; das Hörnchen.
cress [kres], *s.* (*Bot.*) die Kresse; *mustard
and —,* die Gartenkresse.
crest [krest], *s.* der Kamm (*cock*); der
Gipfel (*hill*); der Kamm (*wave*); der
Busch (*helmet*); das Wappenschild
(*Heraldry*).
crestfallen ['krestfɔːlən], *adj.* ent-
mutigt, mutlos, niedergeschlagen.
Cretan ['kriːtən], *adj.* kretisch. — *s.* der
Kreter, die Kreterin.
cretonne ['kretən], *s.* die Kretonne.
crevasse [krə'væs], *s.* die Gletscherspalte.
crevice ['krevis], *s.* der Riß.
crew (1) [kruː], *s.* (*Naut., Aviat.*) die
Besatzung; (*Naut.*) die Schiffsmann-
schaft; die Mannschaft (*team*); (*Am.*)
— *cut,* die Bürstenfrisur.

cruet

crew (2) [kru:] see crow.
crib [krib], s. die Krippe (Christmas);
die Wiege (cradle); (Sch.) die Esels-
brücke. — v.a. (Sch.) abschreiben
(copy).
crick [krik], s. (in neck) der steife Hals.
cricket ['krikit], s. (Ent.) das Heimchen,
die Grille; (Sport) das Cricket(spiel).
crime [kraim], s. das Verbrechen; —
fiction, die Detektivromane, m. pl.
criminal ['kriminəl], s. der Verbrecher.
— adj. — case, der Kriminalfall;
verbrecherisch (act); — investigation, die Fahndung.
crimp [krimp], v.a. kräuseln (hair).
crimson ['krimzən], adj. karmesinrot.
cringe [krindʒ], v.n. kriechen.
crinkle [kriŋkl], v.a., v.n. kräuseln.—s.
die Falte.
crinoline ['krinəlin], s. der Reifrock.
cripple [kripl], s. der Krüppel. — v.a.
verkrüppeln; lahmlegen (immobilize).
crisis ['kraisis], s. die Krise, der
Wendepunkt; die Notlage.
crisp [krisp], adj. kraus (hair); knusperig (bread); frisch.
criss-cross ['kriskrəs], adv. kreuz und
quer.
criterion [krai'tiəriən], s. das Kennzeichen, das Kriterium.
critic ['kritik], s. der Kritiker; Rezensent (reviewer).
critical ['kritikəl], adj. kritisch.
criticism ['kritisizm], s. die Kritik (of,
an, Dat.); Rezension, Besprechung
(review).
criticize ['kritisaiz], v.a. kritisieren.
croak [krouk], v.n. krächzen (raven);
quaken (frog).
croaking ['kroukiŋ], s. das Krächzen,
das Gekrächze (raven); das Quaken
(frog).
Croat ['krouæt], s. der Kroate.
Croatian [krou'eiʃən], adj. kroatisch.
crochet ['krouʃei], s. die Häkelei; —
hook, die Häkelnadel. — v.a., v.n.
häkeln.
crock [krɔk], s. der Topf, der irdene
Krug; der alte Topf; (coll.) old —, der
Invalide, Krüppel.
crockery ['krɔkəri], s. (Comm.) die
Töpferware; das Geschirr (household).
crocodile ['krɔkədail], s. das Krokodil.
crocus ['kroukəs], s. (Bot.) der Krokus,
die Safranblume.
croft [krɔft], s. das Kleinbauerngut.
crofter ['krɔftə], s. der Kleinbauer.
crone [kroun], s. das alte Weib; die
Hexe (witch).
crony ['krouni], s. (coll.) old —, der alte
Freund.
crook [kruk], s. der Krummstab (staff);
der Schwindler (cheat). — v.a.
krümmen, biegen.
crooked ['krukid], adj. krumm; (fig.)
schwindlerisch, verbrecherisch.
crookedness ['krukidnis], s. die Krumm-
heit; die Durchtriebenheit (slyness).
croon [kru:n], v.n. leise singen; (Am.)
im modernen Stil singen.

crooner ['kru:nə], s. der Jazzsänger.
crop [krɔp], s. der Kropf (bird); die
Ernte (harvest); der (kurze) Haarschnitt; riding —, die Reitpeitsche.
— v.a. stutzen (cut short). — v.n.
— up, auftauchen.
crosier ['krouziə], s. (Eccl.) der Bischofsstab.
cross [krɔs], s. das Kreuz. — v.a. (Zool.,
Bot.) kreuzen; überqueren (road,
on foot); — s.o.'s path, einem in die
Quere kommen. — v.n. überfahren
(übers Wasser); hinübergehen; —
over, übersetzen (on boat or ferry).
— v.r. sich bekreuzigen. — adj.
mürrisch (grumpy), verstimmt; at —
purposes, ohne einander zu verstehen;
make —, verstimmen. — adv. kreuz-
- weise; —-eyed, schielend; —-grained,
wider den Strich, schlecht aufgelegt.
crossbow ['krɔsbou], s. die Armbrust.
crossbreed ['krɔsbri:d], s. die Mischrasse, der Mischling.
cross-examine [krɔsig'zæmin], v.a.,
v.n. (Law) ins (Kreuz-)Verhör
nehmen.
crossing ['krɔsiŋ], s. die Straßen-
kreuzung; (Naut.) die Überfahrt; der
Straßenübergang; Kreuzweg.
crossroads ['krɔsroudz], s. der Kreuzweg, die Kreuzung.
crossword ['krɔswə:d], s. das Kreuzworträtsel.
crotch [krɔtʃ], s. der Haken.
crotchet ['krɔtʃit], s. (Mus.) die
Viertelnote; die Grille (mood).
crotchety ['krɔtʃiti], adj. grillenhaft,
verschroben.
crouch [krautʃ], v.n. sich ducken
(squat); sich demütigen (cringe).
croup (1) [kru:p], s. (Med.) der Krupp.
croup (2) [kru:p], s. die Kruppe.
crow [krou], s. (Orn.) die Krähe; das
Krähen (of cock). — v.n. irr. krähen
(cock).
crowbar ['kroubɑ:], s. das Brecheisen.
crowd [kraud], s. die Menge (multitude);
das Gedränge (throng). — v.n.
— in, sich hineindrängen, dazu-
drängen; — around, sich herum-
scharen um (Acc.).
crown [kraun], s. die Krone (diadem
or coin); der Gipfel (mountain);
(Anat.) der Scheitel; — lands,
Krongüter (n. pl.), Landeigentum der
Krone, n.; — prince, der Kronprinz;
of thorns, die Dornenkrone. — v.a.
krönen.
crucial ['kru:ʃəl], adj. entscheidend,
kritisch.
crucifix ['kru:sifiks], s. das Kruzifix.
crucify ['kru:sifai], v.a. kreuzigen.
crude [kru:d], adj. roh, ungekocht,
unreif; grob (manners); ungeschliffen.
crudity ['kru:diti], s. die Rohheit;
Grobheit (manners).
cruel ['kru:əl], adj. grausam.
cruelty ['kru:əlti], s. die Grausamkeit.
cruet ['kru:it], s. das Salz- oder Pfeffer-
fäßchen; das Fläschchen.

355

cruise [kru:z], *v.n.* (*Naut.*) kreuzen. — *s.* die Seefahrt, die Seereise; *pleasure* —, die Vergnügungsreise (zu Wasser).

cruiser ['kru:zə], *s.* (*Naut.*) der Kreuzer; *battle* —, der Panzerkreuzer.

crumb [krʌm], *s.* die Krume. — *v.a.* zerbröckeln, zerkrümeln.

crumble [krʌmbl], *v.n.* zerfallen, zerbröckeln.

crumpet ['krʌmpit], *s.* das Teebrötchen, das Teeküchlein.

crumple [krʌmpl], *v.a.* zerknittern (*material*). — *v.n.* — *up*, zusammenbrechen.

crunch [krʌntʃ], *v.a.* zerstoßen, zermalmen. — *v.n.* knirschen.

crusade [kru:'seid], *s.* der Kreuzzug.

crusader [kru:'seidə], *s.* der Kreuzfahrer.

crush [krʌʃ], *v.a.* zerdrücken; zerstoßen (*pulverize*); drängen (*crowd*); zertreten (*tread down*); (*fig.*) vernichten. — *s.* das Gedränge (*throng*); (*coll.*) *have a — on*, verknallt sein, in einen verliebt sein.

crust [krʌst], *s.* die Kruste, die Rinde (*bread*). — *v.a.* mit einer Kruste bedecken. — *v.n.* verkrusten.

crustaceous [krʌs'teiʃəs], *adj.* (*Zool.*) krustenartig, Krustentier-.

crusty ['krʌsti], *adj.* krustig, knusperig (*pastry, bread*); mürrisch (*grumpy*).

crutch [krʌtʃ], *s.* die Krücke.

crux [krʌks], *s.* der entscheidende Punkt, der springende Punkt, die Schwierigkeit.

cry [krai], *v.n.* schreien, rufen; weinen (*weep*). — *v.a.* — *down*, niederschreien. — *s.* der Schrei; der Zuruf (*call*).

crypt [kript], *s.* (*Eccl.*) die Krypta, die Gruft.

crystal ['kristəl], *s.* der Kristall.

crystallize ['kristəlaiz], *v.n.* sich kristallisieren, Kristalle bilden.

cub [kʌb], *s.* (*Zool.*) das Junge. — *v.n.* Junge haben, Junge werfen.

Cuban ['kju:bən], *adj.* kubanisch. — *s.* der Kubaner.

cube [kju:b], *s.* der Würfel; (*Maths.*) — *root*, die Kubikwurzel. — *v.a.* zur Dritten (Potenz) erheben; kubieren.

cubic(al) ['kju:bik(əl)], *adj.* kubisch, zur dritten Potenz.

cubit ['kju:bit], *s.* die Elle.

cuckoo ['kuku:], *s.* (*Orn.*) der Kuckuck.

cucumber ['kju:kʌmbə], *s.* (*Bot.*) die Gurke; *cool as a* —, ruhig und gelassen.

cud [kʌd], *s.* das wiedergekäute Futter; *chew the* —, wiederkauen (*also fig.*).

cuddle [kʌdl], *v.a.* liebkosen, an sich drücken. — *v.n.* sich anschmiegen.

cudgel ['kʌdʒəl], *s.* der Knüttel; *take up the* —*s for*, sich für etwas einsetzen.

cue (1) [kju:], *s.* (*Theat.*) das Stichwort. — *v.a.* einem (*Theat.*) das Stichwort *or* (*Mus.*) den Einsatz geben.

cue (2) [kju:], *s.* der Billardstock. — *v.a.* (*Billiards*) abschießen.

cuff (1) [kʌf], *s.* die Manschette, der Aufschlag (*shirt*); —*links*, die Manschettenknöpfe, *m.pl.*

cuff (2) [kʌf], *s.* der Schlag. — *v.a.* schlagen, puffen.

culinary ['kju:linəri], *adj.* kulinarisch; Küchen-, Eß-, Speisen-.

cull [kʌl], *v.a.* auswählen, auslesen (*from books*).

culminate ['kʌlmineit], *v.n.* kulminieren, den Höhepunkt erreichen.

culpable ['kʌlpəbl], *adj.* schuldig; strafbar.

culprit ['kʌlprit], *s.* der Schuldige, Verbrecher.

cult [kʌlt], *s.* der Kult, die Verehrung; der Kultus.

cultivate ['kʌltiveit], *v.a.* kultivieren; (*Agr.*) anbauen; pflegen (*acquaintance*); bilden (*mind*).

cultivation [kʌlti'veiʃən], *s.* (*Agr.*) der Anbau; die Bildung (*mind*).

culture ['kʌltʃə], *s.* die Kultur, die Bildung.

cumbersome ['kʌmbəsəm], *adj.* beschwerlich, lästig.

cunning ['kʌniŋ], *s.* die List, die Schlauheit. — *adj.* listig, schlau.

cup [kʌp], *s.* die Tasse (*tea*—); der Becher (*handleless*); (*Eccl.*) der Kelch; der Pokal (*sports*); — *final*, das Endspiel. — *v.a.* (*Med.*) schröpfen.

cupboard ['kʌbəd], *s.* der Schrank.

cupola ['kju:pələ], *s.* (*Archit.*, *Metall.*) die Kuppel.

cur [kə:], *s.* der Köter; (*fig*). der Schurke.

curable ['kjuərəbl], *adj.* heilbar.

curate ['kjuərit], *s.* der Hilfsgeistliche.

curative ['kjuərətiv], *adj.* heilsam, heilend.

curator [kjuə'reitə], *s.* der Kurator, Verwalter, Direktor.

curb [kə:b], *v.a.* zügeln, bändigen. — *s.* der Zaum (*bridle*).

curd [kə:d], *s.* der Rahmkäse, der Milchkäse; (*pl.*) der Quark.

curdle [kə:dl], *v.a.* gerinnen lassen. — *v.n.* gerinnen; erstarren.

cure [kjuə], *s.* die Kur, die Heilung. — *v.a.* kurieren, wieder gesundmachen; einpökeln (*foodstuffs*).

curfew ['kə:fju:], *s.* die Abendglocke (*bells*); das Ausgehverbot, die Polizeistunde (*police*).

curio ['kjuəriou], *s.* die Kuriosität, das Sammlerstück; die Rarität.

curiosity [kjuəri'ɔsiti], *s.* die Neugier; Merkwürdigkeit.

curious ['kjuəriəs], *adj.* neugierig (*inquisitive*); seltsam, sonderbar (*strange*).

curl [kə:l], *v.a.* kräuseln, (in Locken) wickeln. — *v.n.* sich kräuseln. — *s.* die Haarlocke.

curler ['kə:lə], *s.* der Lockenwickler.

curlew ['kə:lju:], *s.*(*Orn.*)der Brachvogel.

curly ['kə:li], *adj.* lockig.

currant ['kʌrənt], *s.* (*Bot.*) die Korinthe, die Johannisbeere.

currency ['kʌrənsi], *s.* die Währung (*money*); der Umlauf (*circulation*).

current ['kʌrənt], *adj.* im Umlauf; allgemein gültig, eben gültig; jetzig (*modern*). — *s.* (*Elect.*) der Strom; die Strömung (*river*); der Zug (*air*).

curry (1) ['kʌri], *v.a.* gerben (*tan*); — *comb,* der Pferdestriegel; — *favour,* sich einschmeicheln.

curry (2) ['kʌri], *s.* das indische Ragout. — *v.a.* würzen.

curse [kəːs], *v.a., v.n.* verfluchen; verwünschen. — *s.* der Fluch; die Verwünschung.

cursive ['kəːsiv], *adj.* kursiv, Kursiv-.

cursory ['kəːsəri], *adj.* kursorisch, oberflächlich.

curt [kəːt], *adj.* kurz angebunden (*speech, manner*).

curtail [kəːˈteil], *v.a.* stutzen, beschränken (*scope*); verkürzen (*time*).

curtain ['kəːtin], *s.* die Gardine; der Vorhang; (*Mil.*) — *fire,* das Sperrfeuer; — *lecture,* die Gardinenpredigt; — *speech,* die Ansprache vor dem Vorhang. — *v.a.* verhüllen (*hide*); mit Vorhängen versehen (*hang curtains*).

curtness ['kəːtnis], *s.* die Kürze; die Barschheit.

curts(e)y ['kəːtsi], *s.* der Knicks. — *v.n.* knicksen, einen Knicks machen.

curve [kəːv], *s.* die Krümmung; (*Geom.*) die Kurve. — *v.a.* krümmen, biegen. — *v.n.* sich biegen.

curved [kəːvd], *adj.* krumm, gebogen.

cushion ['kuʃən], *s.* das Kissen. — *v.a.* polstern.

custody ['kʌstədi], *s.* die Obhut; Bewachung, Haft.

custom ['kʌstəm], *s.* die Sitte, die Tradition; der Gebrauch, Brauch (*usage*); die Kundschaft (*trade*); (*pl.*) der Zoll (*duty*).

customary ['kʌstəməri], *adj.* gewohnt, althergebracht, gebräuchlich.

customer ['kʌstəmə], *s.* der Kunde, die Kundin.

cut [kʌt], *v.a. irr.* schneiden; — (*s.o.*) ignorieren; — *o.'s teeth,* zahnen; *this won't — any ice,* das wird nicht viel nützen; — *both ways,* das ist ein zweischneidiges Schwert; — *a lecture,* eine Vorlesung schwänzen; — *short,* unterbrechen. — *adj.* — *out for,* wie gerufen zu *or* für; — *to the quick,* aufs tiefste verletzt; — *glass,* das geschliffene Glas; — *price,* verbilligt. — *s.* der Schnitt (*section*); der Hieb (*gash*); (*Art*) der Stich; — *in salary,* eine Gehaltskürzung; die Abkürzung, die Kürzung (*abridgement*).

cute [kjuːt], *adj.* klug, aufgeweckt; (*Am.*) süß, niedlich.

cutler ['kʌtlə], *s.* der Messerschmied.

cutlery ['kʌtləri], *s.* das Besteck (*tableware*); (*Comm.*) die Messerschmiedwaren, *f. pl.*

cutlet ['kʌtlit], *s.* das Kotelett, das Rippchen.

cut-throat ['kʌtθrout], *s.* der Halsabschneider; — *competition,* Konkurrenz auf Leben und Tod.

cuttle [kʌtl], *s.* (*Zool.*) der Tintenfisch.

cyanide ['saiənaid], *s.* (*Chem.*) zyanidsaures Salz; das Zyanid, die Blausäure.

cyclamen ['sikləmən], *s.* (*Bot.*) das Alpenveilchen.

cycle [saikl], *s.* (*Geom.*) der Kreis; (*Mus., Zool.*) der Zyklus; (*coll.*) das Fahrrad. — *v.n.* (*coll.*) radfahren; zirkulieren (*round,* um, *Acc.*).

cyclone ['saikloun], *s.* der Wirbelwind, der Wirbelsturm.

cyclopaedia [saiklo'piːdjə] *see* **encyclopædia.**

cylinder ['silində], *s.* der Zylinder; die Walze.

cymbal ['simbəl], *s.* (*Mus.*) die Zimbel, das Becken.

cynic ['sinik], *s.* der Zyniker.

cynical ['sinikəl], *adj.* zynisch.

cypress ['saiprəs], *s.* (*Bot.*) die Zypresse.

Cypriot ['sipriət], *adj.* zyprisch. — *s.* der Zypriote.

czar [zɑː], *s.* der Zar.

Czech, Czechoslovak(ian) [tʃek, tʃeko'slovæk, tʃekoslo'vækjən], *adj.* tschechisch. —*s.* der Tscheche.

D

D [diː]. das D (*also Mus.*).

dab [dæb], *v.a.* leicht berühren. — *s.* der leichte Schlag (*blow*).

dabble [dæbl], *v.n.* sich in etwas versuchen, pfuschen (*in,* in, *Dat.*).

dabbler ['dæblə], *s.* der Pfuscher, Stümper.

dace [deis], *s.* (*Zool.*) der Weißfisch.

dad, daddy [dæd, 'dædi], *s.* der Papa; Vati; *daddy longlegs,* die Bachmücke, die langbeinige Mücke.

dado ['deidou], *s.* die Täfelung.

daffodil ['dæfədil], *s.* (*Bot.*) die Narzisse.

dagger ['dægə], *s.* der Dolch; *at —s drawn,* spinnefeind; *look —s,* mit Blicken durchbohren.

dahlia ['deiljə], *s.* (*Bot.*) die Dahlie, die Georgine.

daily ['deili], *adj.* täglich; Tages-. — *s.* (*newspaper*) die Tageszeitung; (*woman*) die Putzfrau.

dainties ['deintiz], *s. pl.* das Backwerk, das kleine Gebäck, das Teegebäck.

daintiness ['deintinis], *s.* die Feinheit; die Kleinheit; die Leckerhaftigkeit.

dainty ['deinti], *adj.* fein, klein, zierlich; lecker (*food*).

dairy ['dɛəri],*s.* die Molkerei, die Meierei.

dairyman ['dɛərimən], *s.* der Milchmann; der Senne (*in Alps*).

dais [deis, 'deiis], *s.* das Podium.

daisy

daisy ['deizi], *s.* (*Bot.*) das Gänseblümchen, das Marienblümchen.
dale [deil], *s.* das Tal.
dalliance ['dæliəns], *s.* die Tändelei, Liebelei; Verzögerung.
dally ['dæli], *v.n.* die Zeit vertrödeln.
dam (1) [dæm], *s.* der Damm. — *v.a.* eindämmen, abdämmen.
dam (2) [dæm], *s.* (*Zool.*) die Tiermutter.
damage ['dæmidʒ], *s.* der Schaden; der Verlust (*loss*); (*pl.*) (*Law*) der Schadenersatz. — *v.a.* beschädigen.
damageable ['dæmidʒəbl], *adj.* leicht zu beschädigen.
damask ['dæməsk], *s.* der Damast (*textile*). — *adj.* damasten, aus Damast.
dame [deim], *s.* die Dame (*title*); (*Am.*) (*coll.*) die junge Dame, das Fräulein.
damn [dæm], *v.a.* verdammen.
damnable ['dæmnəbl], *adj.* verdammenswert, verdammt.
damnation [dæm'neiʃən], *s.* die Verdammung, Verdammnis.
damn(ed) [dæm(d)], *adj. & adv.* verwünscht, verdammt.
damp [dæmp], *adj.* feucht, dumpfig. — *s.* die Feuchtigkeit; (*Build.*) — *course*, die Schutzschicht. — *v.a.* dämpfen, befeuchten; — *the spirits*, die gute Laune verderben.
damsel ['dæmzəl], *s.* die Jungfer; das Mädchen.
damson ['dæmzən], *s.* (*Bot.*) die Damaszenerpflaume.
dance [dɑ:ns], *v.a., v.n.* tanzen. — *s.* der Tanz; *lead s.o. a* —, einem viel Mühe machen.
dandelion ['dændilaiən], *s.* (*Bot.*) der Löwenzahn.
dandle [dændl], *v.a.* hätscheln; schaukeln.
dandy ['dændi], *s.* der Geck, der Stutzer.
Dane [dein], *s.* der Däne.
dane [dein], *s.* *great* —, die Dogge.
Danish ['deiniʃ], *adj.* dänisch.
danger ['deindʒə], *s.* die Gefahr.
dangerous ['deindʒərəs], *adj.* gefährlich.
dangle [dæŋgl], *v.a.* baumeln lassen. — *v.n.* baumeln, hängen.
dank [dæŋk], *adj.* feucht, naßkalt.
Danube ['dænju:b], die Donau.
dapper ['dæpə], *adj.* schmuck; niedlich; elegant.
dappled ['dæpld], *adj.* scheckig, bunt.
Dardanelles, The [dɑ:dəˈnelz], die Dardanellen, *pl.*
dare [dɛə], *v.n. irr.* wagen; *I* — *say*, das meine ich wohl, ich gebe zu.
daredevil ['dɛədevl], *s.* der Wagehals, der Draufgänger.
daring ['dɛəriŋ], *s.* die Kühnheit.
dark [dɑ:k], *adj.* dunkel, finster. — *s.* die Dunkelheit; *shot in the* —, ein Schuß aufs Geratewohl, ins Blaue.
darken ['dɑ:kən], *v.a.* verdunkeln, verfinstern. — *v.n.* dunkel werden.

darkish ['dɑ:kiʃ], *adj.* nahezu dunkel.
darkness ['dɑ:knis], *s.* die Dunkelheit, Finsternis.
darkroom ['dɑ:kru:m], *s.* die Dunkelkammer.
darling ['dɑ:liŋ], *s.* der Liebling. — *adj.* lieb, teuer.
darn (1) [dɑ:n], *v.a.* stopfen.
darn (2) [dɑ:n], *v.a.* verdammen.
darn(ed) [dɑ:n(d)], (*excl.*) verdammt.
darning ['dɑ:niŋ], *s.* das Stopfen; — *needle*, die Stopfnadel.
dart [dɑ:t], *s.* der Pfeil; der Spieß (*spear*); (*pl.*) das Pfeilwurfspiel. — *v.n.* losstürmen, sich stürzen.
dash [dæʃ], *v.a.* zerschmettern, zerstören (*hopes*). — *v.n.* stürzen. — *s.* der Schlag (*blow*); die Eleganz; (*Typ.*) der Gedankenstrich; (*Motor.*)— *board*, das Schaltbrett, Armaturenbrett.
dashing ['dæʃiŋ], *adj.* schneidig.
dastard ['dæstəd], *s.* der Feigling, die Memme.
dastardly ['dæstədli], *adj., adv.* feige.
data ['deitə], *s. pl.* (*Science*) die Angaben, die Daten.
date (1) [deit], *s.* das Datum; (*Am.*) die Verabredung; *out of* —, vertetal (*antiquated*), altmodisch (*out of fashion*). — *v.a.* datieren; (*Am.*) ausführen. — *v.n.* das Datum tragen.
date (2) [deit], *s.* (*Bot.*) die Dattel.
dative ['deitiv], *s.* (*Gram.*) der Dativ.
daub [dɔ:b], *v.a.* bekleksen; (*coll.*) bemalen. — *s.* die Kleckserei; (*coll.*) die Malerei.
daughter ['dɔ:tə], *s.* die Tochter;— -*inlaw*, die Schwiegertochter.
daunt [dɔ:nt], *v.a.* einschüchtern.
dauphin ['dɔ:fin], *s.* der Dauphin.
daw [dɔ:], *s.* (*Orn.*) die Dohle.
dawdle [dɔ:dl], *v.n.* trödeln, die Zeit vertrödeln.
dawdler ['dɔ:dlə], *s.* der Trödler, Tagedieb, die Schlafmütze.
dawn [dɔ:n], *s.* das Morgengrauen, die Morgendämmerung. — *v.n.* dämmern, tagen.
day [dei], *s.* der Tag; *the other* —, neulich; *every* —, täglich; *one* —, eines Tages; *by* —, bei or am Tage.
daybreak ['deibreik], *s.* der Tagesanbruch.
daytime ['deitaim], *s. in the* —, bei Tage.
daze [deiz], *v.a.* blenden (*dazzle*); betäuben (*stupefy*).
dazzle [dæzl], *v.a.* blenden.
deacon ['di:kən], *s.* (*Eccl.*) der Diakon.
deaconess ['di:kənes], *s.* (*Eccl.*) die Diakonisse.
dead [ded], *adj.* tot; *stop* —, plötzlich anhalten; *as* — *as mutton*, mausetot; — *from the neck up*, (*coll.*) dumm wie die Nacht. — *adv.* — *beat*, erschöpft; (*Am.*)—*sure*, ganz sicher. — *s. in the* — *of night*, in tiefster Nacht; (*pl.*) die Toten.

decompose

deaden [dedn], *v.a.* abschwächen (*weaken*); abtöten (*anæsthetise*).
deadly ['dedli], *adj.* tödlich.
deadness ['dednis], *s.* die Leblosigkeit; Mattheit (*tiredness*).
deaf [def], *adj.* taub; — *and dumb*, taubstumm.
deafen [defn], *v.a.* betäuben.
deafmute ['defmju:t], *s.* der Taubstumme.
deal (1) [di:l], *s.* das Geschäft; die Anzahl; *a fair or square* —, eine anständige Behandlung; *a good* —, beträchtlich; *a great* — *of*, sehr viel; *make a* —, ein Geschäft abschliessen; *it's a* — *!* abgemacht! — *v.a. irr.* austeilen; Karten geben (*cards*); — *a blow*, einen Schlag erteilen. — *v.n. irr.* — *with s.th.*, etwas behandeln.
deal (2) [di:l], *s.* (*Bot.*) das Kiefernholz, die Kiefer; — *board*, das Kiefernholzbrett.
dealer ['di:lə], *s.* der Händler.
dean [di:n], *s.* der Dekan.
dear [diə], *adj.* teuer, lieb (*beloved*); teuer, kostspielig (*expensive*); — *me!* ach, Du lieber Himmel! —, —! du liebe Zeit! — *John!* Lieber Hans!
dearness ['diənis], *s.* die Teuerung, das Teuersein.
dearth [də:θ], *s.* der Mangel (*of*, an, *Dat.*).
death [deθ], *s.* der Tod; der Todesfall; — *penalty*, die Todesstrafe; — *warrant*, das Todesurteil.
deathbed ['deθbed], *s.* das Totenbett, Sterbebett.
deathblow ['deθblou], *s.* der Todesstoß.
deathless ['deθlis], *adj.* unsterblich.
debar [di'ba:], *v.a.* ausschließen (*from*, von, *Dat.*).
debase [di'beis], *v.a.* erniedrigen, verschlechtern.
debatable [di'beitəbl], *adj.* strittig.
debate [di'beit], *s.* die Debatte. — *v.a., v.n.* debattieren.
debauch [di'bɔ:tʃ], *v.a., v.n.* verführen; verderben.
debauchee [di'bɔ:tʃi:], *s.* der Schwelger, der Wüstling.
debenture [di'bentʃə], *s.* der Schuldschein.
debilitate [di'biliteit], *v.a.* schwächen.
debit ['debit], *s.* die Schuldseite, das Soll (*in account*). — *v.a.* belasten.
debt [det], *s.* die Schuld; *run into* — *or incur* —*s*, Schulden machen.
debtor ['detə], *s.* der Schuldner.
decade ['dekəd, 'dekeid], *s.* das Jahrzehnt; die Dekade.
decadence ['dekədəns], *s.* die Dekadenz, der Verfall.
decalogue ['dekəlɔg], *s.* (*Bibl.*) die zehn Gebote.
decamp [di'kæmp], *v.n.* aufbrechen, ausreißen.
decant [di'kænt], *v.a.* abfüllen, abgießen.
decanter [di'kæntə], *s.* die Karaffe.

decapitate [di'kæpiteit], *v.a.* enthaupten köpfen.
decapitation [di:kæpi'teiʃən], *s.* die Enthauptung.
decay [di'kei], *v.n.* in Verfall geraten. — *s.* der Verfall, die Verwesung.
decease [di'si:s], *s.* das Hinscheiden, der Tod. — *v.n.* sterben, dahinscheiden, verscheiden.
deceit [di'si:t], *s.* der Betrug; die List (*cunning*).
deceive [di'si:v], *v.a.* betrügen.
deceiver [di'si:və], *s.* der Betrüger.
December [di'sembə], *s.* der Dezember.
decency ['di:sənsi], *s.* der Anstand; die Anständigkeit, Ehrlichkeit; die Schicklichkeit.
decent ['di:sənt], *adj.* anständig.
decentralize [di:'sentrəlaiz], *v.a.* dezentralisieren.
deception [di'sepʃən], *s.* der Betrug.
deceptive [di'septiv], *adj.* trügerisch.
decide [di'said], *v.a., v.n.* entscheiden; bestimmen (*determine*).
decimal ['desiməl], *adj.* dezimal.
decimate ['desimeit], *v.a.* dezimieren, herabsetzen (*reduce*).
decipher [di'saifə], *v.a.* entziffern (*read*); dechiffrieren (*decode*).
decision [di'siʒən], *s.* die Entscheidung, der Beschluß (*resolution*); die Entschlossenheit (*decisiveness*).
decisive [di'saisiv], *adj.* entscheidend.
decisiveness [di'saisivnis], *s.* die Entschiedenheit.
deck [dek], *s.* (*Naut.*) das Deck; — *chair*, der Liegestuhl. — *v.a.* — (*out*), ausschmücken.
declaim [di'kleim], *v.a.* deklamieren.
declamation [deklə'meiʃən], *s.* die Deklamation.
declamatory [di'klæmətəri], *adj.* Deklamations-, deklamatorisch, Vortrags-.
declaration [deklə'reiʃən], *s.* die Erklärung; die Deklaration.
declare [di'kleə], *v.a.* erklären. — *v.n.* sich erklären.
declared [di'kleəd], *adj.* erklärt, offen.
declension [di'klenʃən], *s.* (*Gram.*) die Deklination, die Abwandlung.
declinable [di'klainəbl], *adj.* (*Gram.*) deklinierbar.
declination [dekli'neiʃən], *s.* (*Phys.*) die Abweichung, Deklination.
decline [di'klain], *v.n.* abweichen (*deflect*); abnehmen (*decrease*); sich weigern (*refuse*); fallen (*price*). — *v.a.* (*Gram.*) deklinieren; ablehnen (*turn down*). — *s.* die Abnahme (*decrease*); der Verfall (*decadence*); der Abhang (*slope*).
declivity [di'kliviti], *s.* der Abhang.
decode [di'koud], *v.a.* entziffern, dechiffrieren.
decompose [di:kəm'pouz], *v.n.* verwesen; zerfallen, sich zersetzen. — *v.a.* auflösen.

359

decorate ['dekəreit], *v.a.* dekorieren (*honour*); ausschmücken (*beautify*); ausmalen (*paint*).

decoration [dekə'reiʃən], *s.* die Dekoration, der Orden (*medal*); die Ausschmückung (*ornamentation*); die Ausmalung (*décor*).

decorator ['dekəreitə], *s.* der Zimmermaler.

decorous ['dekərəs *or* di'kɔːrəs], *adj.* anständig, sittsam.

decorum [di'kɔːrəm], *s.* das Dekorum, das anständige Benehmen.

decoy [di'kɔi], *s.* der Köder (*bait*). — *v.a.* locken, verlocken.

decrease [di'kriːs], *v.a.* vermindern, verringern. — *v.n.* abnehmen. — ['diːkriːs], *s.* die Abnahme, die Verringerung.

decree [di'kriː], *s.* der Beschluß (*resolution*); (*Law*) das Urteil; — *nisi*, das provisorische Scheidungsurteil. — *v.a.*, eine Verordnung erlassen; beschließen (*decide*).

decrepit [di'krepit], *adj.* abgelebt; gebrechlich (*frail*).

decry [di'krai], *v.a.* verrufen; in Verruf bringen.

dedicate ['dedikeit], *v.a.* widmen, weihen, zueignen (*to, Dat.*).

dedication [dedi'keiʃən], *s.* die Widmung, Weihung; die Zueignung.

dedicatory ['dedikeitəri], *adj.* zueignend.

deduce [di'djuːs], *v.a.* schließen (*conclude*); ableiten (*derive*).

deduct [di'dʌkt], *v.a.* abziehen (*subtract*); abrechnen (*take off*).

deduction [di'dʌkʃən], *s.* der Abzug (*subtraction*); die Folgerung (*inference*); der Rabatt (*in price*).

deductive [di'dʌktiv], *adj.* (*Log.*) deduktiv.

deed [diːd], *s.* die Tat, die Handlung (*action*); (*Law*) die Urkunde, das Dokument.

deem [diːm], *v.a.* erachten, halten für.

deep [diːp], *adj.* tief; — *freeze*, die Tiefkühlung; (*fig.*) dunkel. — *s.* die Tiefe (*des Meeres*).

deepen [diːpn], *v.a.* vertiefen. — *v.n.* tiefer werden; sich vertiefen.

deer [diə], *s.* (*Zool.*) das Rotwild, der Hirsch; — *stalking*, die Pirsch.

deface [di'feis], *v.a.* entstellen, verunstalten.

defalcate [di'fælkeit], *v.n.* Gelder unterschlagen.

defamation [defə'meiʃən], *s.* die Verleumdung.

defamatory [di'fæmətəri], *adj.* verleumderisch.

defame [di'feim], *v.a.* verleumden.

default [di'fɔːlt], *v.n.* (vor Gericht) ausbleiben. — *s.* der Fehler (*error*); die Unterlassung (*omission*).

defaulter [di'fɔːltə], *s.* der Pflichtvergessene; (*Law*) der Schuldige.

defeat [di'fiːt], *v.a.* schlagen, besiegen. — *s.* die Niederlage.

defect [di'fekt], *s.* der Fehler, Makel. — *v.n.* abfallen (*desert, from*, von, *Dat.*).

defection [di'fekʃən], *s.* der Abfall.

defective [di'fektiv], *adj.* fehlerhaft, mangelhaft.

defectiveness [di'fektivnis], *s.* die Mangelhaftigkeit, die Fehlerhaftigkeit.

defence [di'fens], *s.* die Verteidigung.

defenceless [di'fenslis], *adj.* wehrlos.

defencelessness [di'fenslisnis], *s.* die Wehrlosigkeit.

defend [di'fend], *v.a.* verteidigen.

defendant [di'fendənt], *s.* (*Law*) der Angeklagte.

defensive [di'fensiv], *adj.* verteidigend. — *s.* die Defensive; *be on the* —, sich verteidigen.

defer [di'fəː], *v.a.* aufschieben (*postpone*). — *v.n.* sich unterordnen, sich fügen (*to, Dat.*).

deference ['defərəns], *s.* der Respekt, die Achtung (*to, vor, Dat.*).

deferential [defə'renʃəl], *adj.* ehrerbietig, respektvoll.

defiance [di'faiəns], *s.* der Trotz, die Herausforderung.

defiant [di'faiənt], *adj.* trotzig, herausfordernd.

deficiency [di'fiʃənsi], *s.* die Unzulänglichkeit, der Mangel (*quantity*); die Fehlerhaftigkeit (*quality*).

deficient [di'fiʃənt], *adj.* unzulänglich (*quantity*); fehlerhaft (*quality*).

deficit ['defisit], *s.* das Defizit, der Fehlbetrag.

defile (1) [di'fail], *v.a.* schänden, beflecken.

defile (2) ['diːfail], *v.n.* vorbeimarschieren (*march past*) (an, *Dat.*). — *s.* der Engpaß.

defilement [di'failmənt], *s.* die Schändung.

define [di'fain], *v.a.* definieren, begrenzen; bestimmen (*determine*).

definite ['definit], *adj.* bestimmt (*certain*); klar, deutlich (*clear*); endgültig (*final*).

definition [defi'niʃən], *s.* die Definition, die Klarheit; (*Maths.*) die Bestimmung.

definitive [di'finitiv], *adj.* definitiv, endgültig (*final*); bestimmt (*certain*).

deflect [di'flekt], *v.a.* ablenken (*divert*). — *v.n.* abweichen (von, *Dat.*).

defoliation [diːfouli'eiʃən], *s.* der Blätterfall.

deform [di'fɔːm], *v.a.* verunstalten, entstellen. — *v.n.* (*Metall.*) sich verformen.

deformity [di'fɔːmiti], *s.* die Entstellung; die Häßlichkeit (*ugliness*).

defraud [di'frɔːd], *v.a.* betrügen.

defray [di'frei], *v.a.* bestreiten, bezahlen (*costs*).

deft [deft], *adj.* geschickt, gewandt.

deftness ['deftnis], *s.* die Gewandtheit, die Geschicktheit.

defunct [di'fʌŋkt], *adj.* verstorben. — *s.* der Verstorbene.

defy [di'fai], *v.a.* trotzen (*Dat.*).

degenerate [di'dʒenəreit], *v.n.* entarten; herabsinken (*sink low*). —[-rit], *adj.* degeneriert, entartet.

degradation [degri'deiʃən], *s.* die Absetzung, Entsetzung, Degradierung.

degrade [di'greid], *v.a.* (*Mil.*) degradieren; entwürdigen; vermindern.

degraded [di'greidid], *adj.* heruntergekommen.

degrading [di'greidiŋ], *adj.* entehrend.

degree [di'gri:], *s.* (*Meas., Univ.*) der Grad; (*Univ.*) die akademische Würde; die Stufe (*step, stage*); die Ordnung, die Klasse (*order, class*); *by* —*s,* nach und nach, allmählich.

deify ['di:ifai], *v.a.* vergöttern.

deign [dein], *v.n.* geruhen, belieben.

deity ['di:iti], *s.* die Gottheit.

dejected [di'dʒektid], *adj.* niedergeschlagen.

dejection [di'dʒekʃən], *s.* die Niedergeschlagenheit.

delay [di'lei], *v.a., v.n.* aufschieben (*put off*); verzögern (*retard*). — *s.* der Aufschub; die Verzögerung.

delectable [di'lektəbl], *adj.* erfreulich, köstlich.

delectation [delek'teiʃən], *s.* die Freude, das Ergötzen (*in, an, Dat.*).

delegate ['deligit], *s.* der Delegierte, Abgeordnete; der Vertreter. — ['deligeit], *v.a.* delegieren, entsenden.

delegation [deli'geiʃən], *s.* die Delegation, die Abordnung.

delete [di'li:t], *v.a.* tilgen, (aus)streichen, auslöschen (*writing*).

deleterious [deli'tiəriəs], *adj.* schädlich.

deletion [di'li:ʃən], *s.* die Tilgung, die Auslöschung.

delf [delf], *s.* das Delfter Porzellan.

deliberate [di'libərit], *adj.* absichtlich (*intentional*); vorsichtig (*careful*); bedächtig (*thoughtful*). — [-reit], *v.n.* beratschlagen, Rat halten. — *v.a.* überlegen, bedenken.

deliberateness [di'libəritnis], *s.* die Bedächtigkeit (*thoughtfulness*); die Absichtlichkeit (*intention*).

deliberation [dilibə'reiʃən], *s.* die Überlegung, die Beratung.

delicacy ['delikəsi], *s.* die Feinheit, Zartheit (*manner*); der Leckerbissen (*luxury food*); die Schwächlichkeit (*health*).

delicate ['delikit], *adj.* fein (*manner*); schwächlich (*sickly*); kitzlig, heikel (*difficult*).

delicious [di'liʃəs], *adj.* köstlich (*food*).

deliciousness [di'liʃəsnis], *s.* die Köstlichkeit.

delight [di'lait], *s.* das Entzücken, das Vergnügen; *Turkish* —, türkisches Konfekt; *take* — *in,* an etwas Gefallen finden, sich freuen (*an, über*). — *v.a., v.n.* entzücken, erfreuen (*in, an, Dat.*).

delightful [di'laitful], *adj.* entzückend, bezaubernd.

delimit [di:'limit], *v.a.* abgrenzen, begrenzen.

delimitation [di:limi'teiʃən], *s.* die Begrenzung, Abgrenzung.

delineate [di'linieit], *v.a.* umreißen, entwerfen, skizzieren (*draft, sketch*); schildern, beschreiben (*describe*).

delineation [dilini'eiʃən], *s.* die Skizze, der Entwurf (*sketch, draft*); die Schilderung (*description*).

delinquency [di'liŋkwənsi], *s.* das Verbrechen.

delinquent [di'liŋkwənt], *adj.* verbrecherisch. — *s.* der Verbrecher, Missetäter (*criminal*).

deliquesce [deli'kwes], *v.n.* (*Chem.*) zergehen, zerschmelzen.

deliquescence [deli'kwesəns], *s.* das Zerschmelzen, die Schmelzbarkeit.

deliquescent [deli'kwesənt], *adj.* leicht schmelzbar (*melting*); leicht zerfliessend (*butter etc.*).

delirious [di'liriəs], *adj.* (*Med.*) phantasierend, wahnsinnig.

delirium [di'liriəm], *s.* (*Med.*) das Delirium; der Wahnsinn (*madness*); das Phantasieren (*raving*); — *tremens,* der Säuferwahnsinn.

deliver [di'livə], *v.a.* abliefern, überreichen (*hand over*); liefern (*goods*); befreien (*free*); erlösen (*redeem*); zustellen (*letters etc.*); entbinden (*woman of child*).

deliverance [di'livərəns], *s.* die Erlösung (*redemption*); die Befreiung (*liberation*); die Übergabe.

delivery [di'livəri], *s.* die Befreiung (*liberation*); (*Med.*) die Niederkunft, Entbindung; der Vortrag (*speech*); die Lieferung, die Zustellung (*goods*); — *man,* der Zustellbote; — *van,* der Lieferwagen.

dell [del], *s.* das enge Tal.

delude [di'lu:d], *v.a.* betrügen, täuschen.

deluge ['delju:dʒ], *s.* die Überschwemmung. — *v.a.* überschwemmen.

delusion [di'lu:ʒən], *s.* die Täuschung, das Blendwerk.

delusive, delusory [di'lu:ziv, di'lu:zəri], *adj.* täuschend, trügerisch.

delve [delv], *v.n.* graben.

demagogic(al) [demə'gɔdʒik(əl)], *adj.* demagogisch.

demagogue ['deməgɔg], *s.* der Demagoge, der Aufrührer.

demand [di'mɑ:nd], *v.a.* verlangen, fordern. — *s.* die Forderung, das Begehren (*desire*); *on* —, auf Verlangen; *in great* —, viel gefragt; *supply and* —, Angebot und Nachfrage.

demarcate ['di:mɑ:keit], *v.a.* abgrenzen; abstecken (*field*).

demarcation [di:mɑ:'keiʃən], *s.* die Abgrenzung; — *line,* die Grenzlinie.

demeanour [di'mi:nə], *s.* das Benehmen.

demented [di'mentid], *adj.* wahnsinnig, von Sinnen, toll.

demerit [di:'merit], *s.* der Fehler.

demesne [di'mi:n *or* -'mein], *s.* das Erbgut; die Domäne.

demi- ['demi], *prefix.* halb-.

demigod ['demigɔd], *s.* der Halbgott.

demijohn ['demidʒɔn], *s.* der Glasballon.

demise [di'maiz], *s.* der Tod, das Hinscheiden. — *v.a.* (*Law*) vermachen.

demisemiquaver ['demisemikweivə], *s.* (*Mus.*) die Zweiunddreißigstelnote.

demobilize [di:'moubilaiz], *v.a.* demobilisieren.

democracy [di'mɔkrəsi], *s.* die Demokratie.

democratic [demo'krætik], *adj.* demokratisch.

demolish [di'mɔliʃ], *v.a.* demolieren, zerstören, niederreißen.

demon ['di:mən], *s.* der Dämon, der Teufel; *a — for work,* ein unersättlicher Arbeiter.

demoniac [di'mouniæk], **demoniacal** [di:mə'naiəkl], *adj.* besessen, teuflisch.

demonstrable [di'mɔnstrəbl], *adj.* beweisbar, nachweislich (*verifiable*).

demonstrate ['demənstreit], *v.a., v.n.* beweisen (*prove*); demonstrieren.

demonstration [demən'streiʃən], *s.* der Beweis (*theoretical*); die Demonstration (*practical*); (*Pol.*) Kundgebung.

demonstrative [di'mɔnstrətiv], *adj.* (*Gram.*) demonstrativ; überschwenglich (*emotional*).

demoralize [di:'mɔrəlaiz], *v.a.* demoralisieren.

demote [di:'mout], *v.a.* (*Mil., official*) degradieren.

demotion [di:'mouʃən], *s.* (*Mil., official*) die Degradierung.

demur [di'mə:], *v.n.* Anstand nehmen; Einwendungen machen (*raise objections*); zögern, zaudern (*hesitate*). — *s.* der Zweifel, der Skrupel.

demure [di'mjuə], *adj.* sittsam, zimperlich; spröde (*prim*).

demureness [di'mjuənis], *s.* die Sittsamkeit; die Sprödigkeit (*primness*).

den [den], *s.* die Höhle, Grube; *lion's —,* die Löwengrube.

denial [di'naiəl], *s.* die Verneinung, das Dementi (*negation*); das Ableugnen (*disclaimer*); die Absage (*refusal*).

denizen ['denizən], *s.* der Bürger, der Alteingesessene.

denominate [di'nɔmineit], *v.a.* nennen, benennen (*name*).

denomination [dinɔmi'neiʃən], *s.* die Bezeichnung; der Nennwert (*currency*); (*Rel.*) das Bekenntnis.

denominational [dinɔmi'neiʃənəl], *adj.* konfessionell.

denominator [di'nɔmineitə], *s.* (*Maths.*) der Nenner.

denote [di'nout], *v.a.* bezeichnen, kennzeichnen.

dénouement [dei'nu:mā:], *s.* die Entwicklung, die Darlegung, die Lösung.

denounce [di'nauns], *v.a.* denunzieren, angeben; (*Law*) anzeigen.

dense [dens], *adj.* dicht; (*coll.*) beschränkt (*stupid*).

density ['densiti], *s.* die Dichte; — *of population,* die Bevölkerungsdichte.

dent (1) [dent], *s.* die Beule.

dent (2) [dent], *s.* die Kerbe (*in wood*); der Einschnitt (*cut*).

dental [dentl], *adj.* Zahn-; — *studies,* zahnärztliche Studien; — *treatment,* die Zahnbehandlung. — *s.* (*Phonet.*) der Zahnlaut.

dentist ['dentist], *s.* der Zahnarzt.

dentistry ['dentistri], *s.* die Zahnheilkunde.

denude [di'nju:d], *v.a.* entblößen; berauben (*of, Genit.*).

denunciation [dinʌnsi'eiʃən], *s.* die Denunzierung, die Anzeige.

deny [di'nai], *v.a.* verneinen (*negate*); abschlagen (*refuse*); verleugnen (*refuse to admit*).

deodorant, deodorizer [di:'oudərənt, di:'oudəraizə], *s.* der Geruchsentzieher (*apparatus*); der Deodorant.

deodorize [di:'oudəraiz], *v.a.* geruchlos machen.

depart [di'pa:t], *v.n.* abreisen, abfahren (*for, nach, Dat.*); scheiden.

department [di'pa:tmənt], *s.* die Abteilung; — *store,* das Kaufhaus.

departmental [di:pa:t'mentl], *adj.* Abteilungs-.

departure [di'pa:tʃə], *s.* die Abreise, die Abfahrt.

depend [di'pend], *v.n.* abhängen, abhängig sein (*upon,* von, *Dat.*); sich verlassen (*upon,* auf, *Acc.*); *that —s,* das kommt darauf an.

dependable [di'pendəbl], *adj.* verläßlich, zuverlässig.

dependant [di'pendənt], *s.* das abhängige Familienmitglied (*member of family*); der Angehörige, Abhängige.

dependence [di'pendəns], *s.* die Abhängigkeit (*need*); das Vertrauen, der Verlaß (*reliance*).

dependency [di'pendənsi], *s.* (*Pol.*) die abhängige Kolonie.

dependent [di'pendənt], *adj.* abhängig (*upon,* von, *Dat.*).

depict [di'pikt], *v.a.* schildern, beschreiben.

deplete [di'pli:t], *v.a.* entleeren (*make empty*); erschöpfen (*exhaust*).

depletion [di'pli:ʃən], *s.* die Entleerung.

deplorable [di'plɔ:rəbl], *adj.* bedauernswert, bedauerlich.

deplore [di'plɔ:], *v.a.* beklagen.

deploy [di'plɔi], *v.a.* entfalten. — *v.n.* sich entfalten; (*Mil.*) aufmarschieren.

deployment [di'plɔimənt], *s.* (*Mil.*) das Deployieren, die Entfaltung.

deponent [di'pounənt], *s.* (*Law*) der vereidigte Zeuge. — *adj.* (*Gram.*) (*verb*) das Deponens.

depopulate [di:'pɔpjuleit], *v.a.* entvölkern.

deport [di'pɔ:t], *v.a.* deportieren.

deportation [di:pɔ:'teiʃən], *s.* die Deportation.

deportment [di'pɔ:tmənt], — s. die körperliche Haltung (*physical*); das Benehmen (*social*).

depose [di'pouz], *v.a.* absetzen (*remove from office*); (*Law*) zu Papier bringen (*write down*); schriftlich erklären (*declare in writing*).

deposit [di'pɔzit], *s.* (*Comm.*) die Anzahlung; (*Geol., Chem.*) der Niederschlag; (*Geol.*) die Ablagerung; (*Comm.*) — *account*, das Depositenkonto. — *v.a.* (*Geol., Chem.*) absetzen; (*Comm.*) anzahlen, einzahlen.

deposition [di:pə'ziʃən], *s.* die Niederschrift, die schriftliche Erklärung; die Absetzung (*removal from office*).

depositor [di'pɔzitə], *s.* (*Comm.*) der Einzahler.

depository [di'pɔzitəri], *s.* das Lagerhaus.

depot ['depou], *s.* das Depot, das Lagerhaus (*store*); (*Am.*) der Bahnhof.

deprave [di'preiv], *v.a.* verderben.

depraved [di'preivd], *adj.* (moralisch) verdorben.

depravity [di'præviti], *s.* die Verdorbenheit, die Verworfenheit.

deprecate ['deprikeit], *v.a.* mißbilligen (*disapprove of*; *Acc.*); sich verbitten.

deprecation [depri'keiʃən], *s.* die Abbitte; die Mißbilligung (*disapproval*).

depreciate [di'pri:ʃieit], *v.a.* abwerten, herabwürdigen. — *v.n.* an Wert verlieren, im Wert sinken.

depreciation [dipri:ʃi'eiʃən], *s.* die Abwertung; der Verlust (*loss*); (*Pol., Comm.*) die Entwertung.

depredation [depri'deiʃən], *s.* das Plündern, der Raub.

depress [di'pres], *v.a.* niederdrücken (*press down*); deprimieren (*morale*).

depressed [di'prest], *adj.* niedergeschlagen.

depression [di'preʃən], *s.* das Niederdrücken (*action*); (*Pol.*) die Depression; die Niedergeschlagenheit (*despondency*); das Tief (*weather*).

deprivation [depri'veiʃən], *s.* der Verlust (*lack*); die Beraubung (*robbery*).

deprive [di'praiv], *v.a.* berauben (*of, Genit.*); wegnehmen (*of, Acc.*).

depth [depθ], *s.* die Tiefe; — *charge,* die Unterwasserbombe; *in the —s of night,* in tiefster Nacht; (*Phys.*) — *of focus,* die Tiefenschärfe; *be out of o.'s* —, den Grund unter seinen Füßen verloren haben, ratlos sein (*be helpless*); — *sounder,* das Echolot.

deputation [depju'teiʃən], *s.* die Deputation, die Abordnung.

depute [di'pju:t], *v.a.* abordnen, entsenden.

deputize ['depjutaiz], *v.n.* vertreten (*for, Acc.*).

deputy ['depjuti], *s.* der Abgeordnete, der Deputierte (*delegate*); der Vertreter (*replacement*).

derail [di:'reil], *v.a.* zum Entgleisen bringen. — *v.n.* entgleisen.

derailment [di:'reilmənt], *s.* die Entgleisung.

derange [di'reindʒ], *v.a.* verwirren, stören.

derangement [di'reindʒmənt], *s.* die Verwirrung; die Geistesstörung (*madness*).

derelict ['derilikt], *adj.* verlassen.

dereliction [deri'likʃən], *s.* das Verlassen; — *of duty,* die Pflichtvergessenheit.

deride [di'raid], *v.a.* verlachen, verhöhnen.

derision [di'riʒən], *s.* die Verhöhnung.

derisive [di'raisiv], *adj.* höhnisch, spöttisch.

derivable [di'raivəbl], *adj.* ableitbar.

derivation [deri'veiʃən], *s.* die Ableitung.

derivative [di'rivətiv], *adj.* abgeleitet. — *s.* das abgeleitete Wort.

derive [di'raiv], *v.a., v.n.* ableiten, herleiten.

derogation [dero'geiʃən], *s.* die Herabsetzung.

derrick ['derik], *s.* der Ladebaum.

dervish ['də:viʃ], *s.* der Derwisch.

descant ['deskænt], *s.* (*Mus.*) der Diskant *or* der Sopran. — [dis'kænt], *v.n.* sich verbreiten (*on,* über, *Acc.*).

descend [di'send], *v.n.* hinab- *or* herabsteigen (*go down*); abstammen (*stem from*).

descendant [di'sendənt], *s.* der Nachkomme.

descent [di'sent], *s.* der Abstieg (*going down*); der Fall (*decline*); die Abstammung (*forebears*); der Abhang (*slope*); (*Aviat.*) die Landung.

describable [dis'kraibəbl], *adj.* zu beschreiben, beschreibbar.

describe [dis'kraib], *v.a.* beschreiben, schildern.

description [dis'kripʃən], *s.* die Beschreibung; *of any* —, jeder Art.

descriptive [dis'kriptiv], *adj.* schildernd, beschreibend.

desecrate ['desikreit], *v.a.* entweihen, entheiligen.

desecration [desi'kreiʃən], *s.* die Entweihung, die Schändung.

desert (1) ['dezət], *s.* die Wüste.

desert (2) [di'zə:t], *v.a.* verlassen, im Stiche lassen. — *v.n.* desertieren.

desert (3) [di'zə:t], *s.* (*usually pl.*) das Verdienst.

desertion [di'zə:ʃən], *s.* (*Mil.*) die Fahnenflucht.

deserve [di'zə:v], *v.a.* verdienen.

deserving [di'zə:viŋ], *adj.* verdienstvoll.

design [di'zain], *v.a.* entwerfen (*plan*); vorhaben (*intend*); bestimmen (*determine*). — *s.* der Entwurf (*sketch*); der Plan (*draft*); die Absicht, das Vorhaben (*intention*); das Muster (*pattern*).

designate

designate ['dezigneit], *v.a.* bezeichnen (*mark*); ernennen (*appoint*). — [–nit], *adj.* ernannt; *chairman* —, der künftige Vorsitzende.

designation [dezig'neiʃən], *s.* die Bestimmung, Ernennung (*appointment*); die Bezeichnung (*mark*).

designer [di'zainə], *s.* der Zeichner, der Graphiker (*artist*); der Ränkeschmied (*schemer*).

designing [di'zainiŋ], *adj.* hinterlistig, schlau.

desirable [di'zaiərəbl], *adj.* erwünscht, wünschenswert.

desire [di'zaiə], *s.* der Wunsch, die Begierde; das Verlangen, die Sehnsucht (*longing*). — *v.a.* verlangen, begehren.

desirous [di'zaiərəs], *adj.* begierig (*of, inf.*).

desist [di'zist], *v.n.* ablassen, aufhören.

desk [desk], *s.* der Schreibtisch; das Pult; — *lamp*, die Tischlampe *or* Bürolampe.

desolate ['desəlit], *adj.* verlassen, öde; trostlos (*sad*). — [–leit], *v.a.* verwüsten (*lay waste*).

desolation [desə'leiʃən], *s.* die Verwüstung (*of land*); die Trostlosigkeit (*sadness*).

despair [dis'pɛə], *v.n.* verzweifeln (*of, an, Dat.*). — *s.* die Verzweiflung.

despatch, dispatch [dis'pætʃ], *v.a.* absenden, befördern (*post*); abfertigen (*send*); erledigen (*deal with*); töten (*kill*). — *s.* die Abfertigung (*clearance*); die Eile (*speed*); die Depesche (*message*).

desperado [despə'reidou, -'ra:dou], *s.* der Wagehals, der Draufgänger.

desperate ['despərit], *adj.* verzweifelt.

desperation [despə'reiʃən], *s.* die Verzweiflung.

despicable ['despikəbl], *adj.* verächtlich.

despise [dis'paiz], *v.a.* verachten.

despite [dis'pait], *prep.* trotz (*Genit., Dat.*).

despoil [dis'pɔil], *v.a.* plündern, ausrauben.

despondency [dis'pɔndənsi], *s.* die Verzweiflung, Verzagtheit.

despondent [dis'pɔndənt], *adj.* verzagend, verzweifelnd, mutlos.

despot ['despɔt], *s.* der Despot, der Tyrann.

despotic [des'pɔtik], *adj.* despotisch.

despotism ['despətizm], *s.* (*Pol.*) der Despotismus.

dessert [di'zə:t], *s.* das Dessert, der Nachtisch.

destination [desti'neiʃən], *s.* die Bestimmung, das Ziel; der Bestimmungsort (*address*); das Reiseziel (*journey*).

destine ['destin], *v.a.* bestimmen.

destiny ['destini], *s.* das Geschick; das Schicksal, das Verhängnis (*fate*).

destitute ['destitju:t], *adj.* verlassen (*deserted*); hilflos, mittellos (*poor*); in bitterer Not (*in great distress*).

destitution [desti'tju:ʃən], *s.* die Notlage, die bittere Not.

destroy [dis'trɔi], *v.a.* zerstören (*buildings*); verwüsten; vernichten (*lives*).

destroyer [dis'trɔiə], *s.* der Zerstörer.

destructible [dis'trʌktibl], *adj.* zerstörbar.

destruction [dis'trʌkʃən], *s.* die Zerstörung (*of buildings*), die Verwüstung; die Vernichtung.

destructive [dis'trʌktiv], *adj.* zerstörend, verderblich.

destructiveness [dis'trʌktivnis], *s.* die Zerstörungswut, der Zerstörungssinn.

desultory ['dezəltəri], *adj.* unmethodisch, sprunghaft; oberflächlich (*superficial*).

detach [di'tætʃ], *v.a.* absondern, trennen.

detachment [di'tætʃmənt], *s.* die Absonderung (*separation*); (*Mil.*) das Kommando.

detail [di'teil], *v.a.* im einzelnen beschreiben (*describe minutely*); (*Mil.*) abkommandieren. — ['di:teil], *s.* die Einzelheit.

detailed [di'teild], *adj.* ausführlich, detailliert, ins Einzelne gehend (*report etc.*); [di'teild], (*Mil.*) abkommandiert.

detain [di'tein], *v.a.* aufhalten, zurückhalten; festhalten (*in prison*).

detect [di'tekt], *v.a.* entdecken, aufdecken.

detection [di'tekʃən], *s.* die Entdeckung, die Aufdeckung.

detective [di'tektiv], *s.* der Detektiv.

detention [di'tenʃən], *s.* (*Law*) die Haft; die Vorenthaltung (*of articles*).

deter [di'tə:], *v.a.* abschrecken.

detergent [di'tə:dʒənt], *s.* das Reinigungsmittel.

deteriorate [di'tiəriəreit], *v.n.* sich verschlimmern, verschlechtern.

deterioration [ditiəriə'reiʃən], *s.* die Verschlimmerung.

determinable [di'tə:minəbl], *adj.* bestimmbar.

determinate [ditə'minit], *adj.* festgesetzt, bestimmt.

determination [di'tə:mi'neiʃən], *s.* die Entschlossenheit (*resoluteness*); die Bestimmung (*identification*); der Entschluß (*resolve*).

determine [di'tə:min], *v.a.* bestimmen (*ascertain*); beschließen (*resolve*).

deterrent [di'terənt], *s.* das Abschreckungsmittel.

detest [di'test], *v.a.* verabscheuen.

detestable [di'testəbl], *adj.* abscheulich.

detestation [detes'teiʃən], *s.* der Abscheu (*of, vor, Dat.*).

dethrone [di:'θroun], *v.a.* entthronen, vom Thron verdrängen.

detonate ['di:- *or* 'detoneit], *v.n.* detonieren, explodieren. — *v.a.* explodieren, detonieren lassen, zum Detonieren bringen.

dice

detonation [deto'neiʃən], s. die Detonation, die Explosion.

detonator ['detoneitə], s. der Zünder, die Zündpatrone; (Railw.) die Knallpatrone.

detour ['deituə or di'tuə], s. der Umweg; (Civil Engin.) die Umleitung. — v.n. (Am.) einen Umweg machen. — v.a. (Am.) umleiten (re-route).

detract [di'trækt], v.a., v.n. abziehen; schmälern.

detraction [di'trækʃən], s. die Schmälerung, die Verleumdung (slander).

detractive [di'træktiv], adj. verleumderisch.

detractor [di'træktə], s. der Verleumder.

detriment ['detrimənt], s. der Nachteil, der Schaden.

detrimental [detri'mentl], adj. nachteilig; abträglich; schädlich (harmful).

deuce (1) [dju:s], s. die Zwei (game); (Tennis) der Einstand.

deuce (2) [dju:s], s. (coll.) der Teufel.

devastate ['devəsteit], v.a. verwüsten, verheeren.

devastating ['devəsteitiŋ], adj. schrecklich, verheerend.

devastation [devəs'teiʃən], s. die Verheerung, die Verwüstung.

develop [di'veləp], v.a. entwickeln. — v.n. sich entwickeln; sich entfalten (prove, turn out).

developer [di'veləpə], s. (Phot.) das Entwicklungsmittel.

development [di'veləpmənt], s. die Entwicklung.

developmental [diveləp'mentl], adj. Entwicklungs-.

deviate ['di:vieit], v.n. abweichen.

deviation [di:vi'eiʃən], s. die Abweichung.

device [di'vais], s. die Vorrichtung (equipment); der Kunstgriff (trick).

devil [devl], s. der Teufel; der Lehrling, Laufbursche (printer's, lawyer's); the — take the hindmost! der Teufel hol was dann kommt! — v.n. in der Lehre sein (for, bei, Dat.).

devilish ['devəliʃ], adj. teuflisch.

devilment, devilry ['devəlmənt, 'devəlri], s. die Teufelei, die Teufelslaune.

devious ['di:viəs], adj. abweichend; abgelegen; abwegig.

deviousness ['di:viəsnis], s. die Abschweifung, Verirrung.

devise [di'vaiz], v.a. erfinden (invent); ersinnen (think out).

deviser, devisor [di'vaizə], s. der Erfinder (inventor); der Erblasser (testator).

devoid [di'vɔid], adj. frei (of, von, Dat.); ohne (Acc.).

devolve [di'vɔlv], v.a. übertragen (transfer); abwälzen (pass on burden) (to, auf, Acc.). — v.n. zufallen (Dat.).

devote [di'vout], v.a. widmen; aufopfern (sacrifice).

devoted [di'voutid], adj. ergeben (affectionate); geweiht (consecrated).

devotee [devo'ti:], s. der Anhänger; der Verehrer (fan).

devotion [di'vouʃən], s. die Hingabe; die Aufopferung (sacrifice); die Andacht (prayer).

devotional [di'vouʃənəl], adj. Andachts-.

devour [di'vauə], v.a. verschlingen.

devout [di'vaut], adj. andächtig, fromm.

devoutness [di'vautnis], s. die Frömmigkeit.

dew [dju:], s. der Tau.

dewy [dju:i], adj. betaut, taufeucht.

dexterity [deks'teriti], s. die Gewandtheit, die Fertigkeit.

dexterous ['dekstərəs], adj. gewandt, geschickt.

diabetes [daiə'bi:ti:z], s. (Med.) die Zuckerkrankheit.

diabetic [daiə'betik], s. (Med.) der Zuckerkranke. — adj. zuckerkrank.

diabolic(al) [daiə'bɔlik(əl)], adj. teuflisch.

diadem ['daiədem], s. das Diadem, das Stirnband.

diæresis [dai'iərəsis], s. die Diärese.

diagnose [daiəg'nouz], v.a. diagnostizieren, als Diagnose finden, befinden.

diagnosis [daiəg'nousis], s. die Diagnose, der Befund.

diagonal [dai'ægənəl], adj. diagonal, schräg. — s. (Geom.) die Diagonale.

diagram ['daiəgræm], s. das Diagramm.

dial ['daiəl], s. das Zifferblatt; (Teleph.) die Wählerscheibe. — v.a., v.n. (Teleph.) wählen.

dialect ['daiəlekt], s. der Dialekt, die Mundart.

dialectic [daiə'lektik], s. (Phil.) die Dialektik.

dialektical [daiə'lektikəl], adj. dialektisch, logisch.

dialogue ['daiəlɔg], s. der Dialog, das Zwiegespräch.

diameter [dai'æmitə], s. der Durchmesser.

diametrical [daiə'metrikəl], adj. diametral; gerade entgegengesetzt.

diamond ['daiəmənd], s. der Diamant; (Cards) das Karo.

diaper ['daiəpə], s. (Am.) die Windel.

diaphragm ['daiəfræm], s. (Anat.) das Zwerchfell; (Phys.) die Membran.

diarrhœa [daiə'riə], s. (Med.) der Durchfall.

diary ['daiəri], s. das Tagebuch, der Kalender.

diatribe ['daiətraib], s. der Tadel, der Angriff (verbal), die Schmähschrift (written).

dibble [dibl], s. der Pflanzstock. — v.n. Pflanzen stecken, anpflanzen.

dice [dais], s. pl. die Würfel (sing. die). — v.a. würfeln, werfen.

dicker

dicker [′dikə], *v.n.* (*Am.*) feilschen, handeln.

dicky [′diki], *s.* das Vorhemd.

dictate [dik′teit], *v.a., v.n.* diktieren, vorschreiben.

dictation [dik′teiʃən], *s.* (*Sch.*) das Diktat.

dictator [dik′teitə], *s.* der Diktator.

dictatorship [dik′teitəʃip], *s.* die Diktatur.

diction [′dikʃən], *s.* die Ausdrucksweise (*speech*).

dictionary [′dikʃənri], *s.* das Wörterbuch.

didactic [di′dæktik], *adj.* lehrhaft, Lehr-.

die (1) [dai], *v.n.* sterben (*of*, an, *Dat.*); — *away,* verebben.

die (2) [dai], *s.* der Würfel (*cube*); die Gießform (*mould*); der Stempel (*punch*); (*Metall.*) das Gesenk (*swage*); — *casting,* der Spritzguß; — *castings,* die Spritzgußteile, Gußteile; — *forging,* das Gesenkschmiedestück.

die (3) [dai] *see under* dice.

dielectric [daii′lektrik], *adj.* dielektrisch.

diet (1) [′daiət], *s.* (*Pol.*) der Landtag, Reichstag.

diet (2) [′daiət], *s.* (*Med.*) die Diät. — *v.n.* (*Med.*) eine Diät halten. — *v.a.* (*Med.*) eine Diät vorschreiben.

dietary, dietetic [′daiətəri, daiə′tetik], *adj.* diätetisch.

differ [′difə], *v.n.* sich unterscheiden (*be different from,* von, *Dat.*); anderer Meinung sein (*be of different opinion*).

difference [′difərəns], *s.* (*Maths.*) die Differenz; der Unterschied (*discrepancy*); die Meinungsverschiedenheit (*divergence of opinion*).

different [′difərənt], *adj.* verschieden, verschiedenartig.

differentiate [difə′renʃieit], *v.n.* (*Maths.*) differenzieren; einen Unterschied machen (*between,* zwischen, *Dat.*).

difficult [′difikəlt], *adj.* schwierig, schwer.

difficulty [′difikəlti], *s.* die Schwierigkeit.

diffidence [′difidəns], *s.* die Schüchternheit.

diffident [′difidənt], *adj.* schüchtern.

diffraction [di′frækʃən], *s.* die Ablenkung, (*Phys., Optics*) die Brechung.

diffuse [di′fju:z], *v.a.* ausgießen (*pour*); verbreiten (*spread*). — [di′fju:s], *adj.* verbreitet, weitschweifig (*style*); zerstreut.

diffuseness [di′fju:snis], *s.* die Weitläufigkeit (*style*).

diffusion [di′fju:ʒən], *s.* (*Phys.*) die Diffusion, die Zerstreuung, die Verbreitung.

dig (1) [dig], *v.a. irr.* graben; — *in the ribs,* in die Rippen stoßen. — *v.n.* (*coll.*) wohnen (*live in lodgings*).

dig (2) [dig], *v.a.* (*coll.*) verstehen.

digest [di′dʒest], *v.a.* (*Anat.*) verdauen. — [′daidʒest], *s.* (*Am.*) die Sammlung von Auszügen; (*pl.*) Pandekten.

digestibility [didʒesti′biliti], *s.* die Verdaulichkeit.

digestible [di′dʒestibl], *adj.* verdaulich.

digestion [di′dʒestʃən], *s.* die Verdauung.

digestive [di′dʒestiv], *adj.* Verdauungs-; — *biscuit,* das Kornmehlkeks; — *organs,* die Verdauungsorgane.

digger [′digə], *s.* der Gräber; (*coll.*) der Australier.

digit [′didʒit], *s.* (*Maths.*) die (einstellige) Zahl; der Zahlenwert.

digitalis [didʒi′teilis], *s.* (*Bot.*) der Fingerhut.

dignified [′dignifaid], *adj.* würdig, würdevoll.

dignify [′dignifai], *v.a.* ehren (*honour*); zieren (*decorate*).

dignitary [′dignitəri], *s.* der Würdenträger.

dignity [′digniti], *s.* die Würde.

digress [dai′gres], *v.n.* abweichen, abschweifen.

digression [dai′greʃən], *s.* die Abweichung, die Abschweifung.

digressive [dai′gresiv], *adj.* abschweifend (*style*).

digs [digz], *s. pl.* (*coll.*) das (möblierte) Zimmer, die Wohnung.

dike [daik], *s.* der Graben, der Deich. — *v.a.* eindeichen, eindämmen.

dilapidated [di′læpideitid], *adj.* baufällig.

dilapidation [dilæpi′deiʃən], *s.* die Baufälligkeit, der Verfall.

dilate [d(a)i′leit], *v.a.* erweitern, ausdehnen. — *v.n.* sich ausdehnen; sich auslassen (*speak*) (*on,* über, *Acc.*).

dilation [d(a)i′leiʃən], *s.* die Erweiterung (*expansion*); die Auslassung (*speaking*).

dilatoriness [′dilətərinis], *s.* die Saumseligkeit.

dilatory [′dilətəri], *adj.* zögernd, aufschiebend, saumselig.

dilemma [d(a)i′lemə], *s.* das Dilemma, die Klemme.

diligence [′dilidʒəns], *s.* der Fleiß, die Emsigkeit.

diligent [′dilidʒənt], *adj.* fleißig, arbeitsam.

dilly-dally [′dili′dæli], *v.n.* tändeln, zaudern, Zeit vertrödeln.

dilute [d(a)i′lju:t], *v.a.* (*Chem.*) verdünnen; schwächen (*weaken*).

dilution [d(a)i′lju:ʃən], *s.* die Verdünnung.

diluvial, diluvian [d(a)i′lju:viəl, -iən], *adj.* Diluvial-, des Diluviums; sintflutlich.

dim [dim], *adj.* trübe, unklar; (*Phys.*) abgeblendet. — *v.a.* abdunkeln, abblenden.

dimension [d(a)i′menʃən], *s.* die Dimension, das Maß.

dimensional [d(a)i′menʃənəl], *adj.* dimensional.

diminish [di'miniʃ], *v.a.* vermindern. — *v.n.* sich vermindern.

diminution [dimi'nju:ʃən], *s.* die Verringerung, die Verminderung.

diminutive [di'minjutiv], *adj.* verkleinernd, klein. — *s.* (*Gram.*) das Verkleinerungswort.

dimness ['dimnis], *s.* die Trübheit; die Düsterkeit (*dark*).

dimple [dimpl], *s.* das Grübchen.

dimpled [dimpld], *adj.* mit einem Grübchen.

din [din], *s.* das Getöse, der Lärm.

dine [dain], *v.n.* speisen, essen.

dinginess ['dindʒinis], *s.* die Dunkelheit, die Schäbigkeit.

dingy ['dindʒi], *adj.* dunkel, schäbig.

dinner ['dinə], *s.* das Essen; das Festessen (*formal*); — *jacket*, der Smoking.

dint [dint], *s.* der Nachdruck, der Schlag; *by — of*, mittels (*Genit.*).

diocesan [dai'ɔsisən], *adj.* (*Eccl.*) einer Diözese angehörig, Diözesan-.

diocese ['daiəsis], *s.* (*Eccl.*) die Diözese.

dip [dip], *v.a.* eintauchen, eintunken; abblenden (*lights*). — *v.n.* (unter)tauchen; sinken; sich flüchtig einlassen (*into*, in). — *s.* die Senke; der Abhang (*slope*).

diphtheria [dif'θiəriə], *s.* (*Med.*) die Diphtherie.

diphthong ['difθɔŋ], *s.* (*Phonet.*) der Diphthong.

diploma [di'ploumə], *s.* das Diplom; *teaching —*, das Lehrerdiplom.

diplomacy [di'plouməsi], *s.* die Diplomatie.

diplomatic [diplo'mætik], *adj.* diplomatisch, taktvoll; urkundlich (*documents*). — *s.* (*pl.*) das Studium der Urkunden.

diplomat(ist) ['diplomæt, di'ploumətist], *s.* (*Pol.*) der Diplomat.

dipper ['dipə], *s.* der Taucher.

dire [daiə] *adj.* fürchterlich, schrecklich; — *necessity*, bittere Not.

direct [d(a)i'rekt], *adj.* direkt, unmittelbar. — *v.a.* leiten (*be in charge of*); hinweisen, hinlenken; den Weg zeigen (*tell the way to*); anordnen (*arrange for*).

direction [d(a)i'rekʃen], *s.* die Leitung (*management*); (*Geogr.*) die Richtung, Himmelsrichtung; die Anordnung (*arrangement, order*); —*s for use*, die Gebrauchsanweisung.

director [d(a)i'rektə], *s.* der Direktor; der Leiter.

directory [d(a)i'rektəri], *s.* das Adreßbuch; das Telephonbuch.

dirge [də:dʒ], *s.* der Trauergesang.

dirigible ['diridʒibl], *adj.* lenkbar, leitbar.

dirt [də:t], *s.* der Schmutz, der Kot, Dreck. — *adj.* — *cheap*, spottbillig.

dirty ['də:ti], *adj.* schmutzig; gemein (*joke*).

disability [disə'biliti], *s.* die Unfähigkeit, das Unvermögen (*inability*); die Schädigung (*impairment of health*).

disable [dis'eibl], *v.a.* unfähig *or* untauglich machen.

disablement [dis'eiblmənt], *s.* die Versehrung, die Verkrüppelung.

disabuse [disə'bju:z], *v.a.* aufklären, eines Besseren belehren.

disaccustom [disə'kʌstəm], *v.a.* entwöhnen, abgewöhnen.

disadvantage [disəd'va:ntidʒ], *s.* der Nachteil.

disaffection [disə'fekʃən], *s.* die Abneigung; der Widerwille.

disagree [disə'gri:], *v.n.* nicht übereinstimmen, nicht einer Meinung sein.

disagreeable [disə'griəbl], *adj.* unangenehm, verdrießlich; unfreundlich.

disagreement [disə'gri:ment], *s.* die Uneinigkeit (*disunity*); die Meinungsverschiedenheit (*difference of opinion*).

disallow [disə'lau], *v.a.* nicht gestatten; in Abrede stellen.

disappear [disə'piə], *v.n.* verschwinden.

disappearance [disə'piərəns], *s.* das Verschwinden.

disappoint [disə'point], *v.a.* enttäuschen.

disappointment [disə'pointmənt], *s.* die Enttäuschung.

disapprobation [disæpro'beiʃan], *s.* die Mißbilligung.

disapproval [disə'pru:vəl], *s.* die Mißbilligung.

disapprove [disə'pru:v], *v.a.* mißbilligen (*of*, *Acc.*).

disarm [dis'a:m], *v.a.* entwaffnen. —*v.n.* abrüsten.

disarmament [dis'a:məmənt], *s.* die Abrüstung.

disarray [disə'rei], *v.a.* in Unordnung bringen. — *s.* die Unordnung (*disorder*); die Verwirrung (*confusion*).

disaster [di'za:stə], *s.* das Unglück; das Unheil, die Katastrophe.

disastrous [di'za:strəs], *adj.* unheilvoll, schrecklich.

disavow [disə'vau], *v.a.* ableugnen.

disavowal [disə'vauəl], *s.* das Ableugnen.

disband [dis'bænd], *v.a.* entlassen (*dismiss*); auflösen (*dissolve*).

disbar [dis'ba:], *v.a.* (*Law*) von der Rechtspraxis ausschließen.

disbelief [disbi'li:f], *s.* der Unglaube (*incredulity*); der Zweifel (*doubt*).

disbelieve [disbi'li:v], *v.a.* nicht glauben; bezweifeln.

disburse [dis'bə:s], *v.a.* auszahlen, ausgeben.

disbursement [dis'bə:smənt], *s.* die Auszahlung, die Ausgabe.

disc [disk], *s.* (*also Med.*) die Scheibe; die Platte (*record*).

discard [dis'ka:d], *v.a.* ablegen, beiseite legen, aufgeben.

discern [di'zə:n *or* di'sə:n], *v.a.* unterscheiden; wahrnehmen, bemerken.

discernment [di'sə:nmənt], *s.* die Urteilskraft (*powers of judgment*); die Einsicht.

discharge

discharge [dis'tʃɑːdʒ], *v.a.* entlassen (*dismiss*); abfeuern (*pistol*); abladen, ausladen (*cargo*); bezahlen (*debt*); tun, erfüllen (*duty*). — *s.* die Entladung (*gun*); die Entlassung (*dismissal*); die Bezahlung (*debt*); die Erfüllung (*duty*).

disciple [di'saipl], *s.* (*Bibl.*) der Jünger; der Schüler.

disciplinarian [disipli'nɛəriən], *s.* der Zuchtmeister.

disciplinary ['disiplinəri], *adj.* disziplinarisch.

discipline ['disiplin], *s.* die Disziplin, die Zucht. — *v.a.* disziplinieren, züchtigen.

disclaim [dis'kleim], *v.a.* verleugnen (*deny*); nicht anerkennen (*refuse to acknowledge*); verzichten (*renounce*).

disclaimer [dis'kleimə], *s.* der Widerruf.

disclose [dis'klouz], *v.a.* eröffnen, enthüllen.

disclosure [dis'klouʒə], *s.* die Eröffnung, die Enthüllung.

discoloration [diskʌlə'reiʃən], *s.* die Entfärbung, Verfärbung.

discomfiture [dis'kʌmfitʃə], *s.* die Verwirrung.

discomfort [dis'kʌmfət], *s.* das Unbehagen; die Beschwerde.

disconcert [diskən'səːt], *v.a.* außer Fassung bringen (*upset*); vereiteln (*frustrate*).

disconnect [diskə'nekt], *v.a.* trennen (*separate*); abstellen.

disconsolate [dis'kɔnsəlit], *adj.* trostlos, untröstlich.

discontent [diskən'tent], *s.* die Unzufriedenheit, das Mißvergnügen. — *v.a.* mißvergnügt stimmen.

discontinuance [diskən'tinjuəns], *s.* die Beendigung (*finish*); das Aufhören (*suspension*); die Unterbrechung (*interruption*).

discontinue [diskən'tinjuː], *v.a.* nicht fortsetzen; unterbrechen (*interrupt*); einstellen.

discord ['diskɔːd], *s.* die Zwietracht (*disagreement*); (*Mus.*) der Mißklang.

discordance [dis'kɔːdəns], *s.* die Uneinigkeit.

discordant [dis'kɔːdənt], *adj.* uneinig, widersprechend.

discount ['diskaunt], *s.* (*Comm.*) der Abzug, der Rabatt; *allow a* —, einen Rabatt gewähren; *be at a* —, unbeliebt sein, nicht geschätzt sein; *sell at a* —, unter dem Preis verkaufen. — [dis'kaunt], *v.a.* (*Comm.*) diskontieren, einen Rabatt gewähren; nur mit Vorsicht aufnehmen (*accept with doubt*).

discountable [dis'kauntəbl], *adj.* diskontierbar, in Abzug zu bringen.

discountenance [dis'kauntinəns], *v.a.* mißbilligen.

discourage [dis'kʌridʒ], *v.a.* entmutigen; abraten (*from*, von, *Dat.*).

discouragement [dis'kʌridʒmənt], *s.* die Entmutigung.

discourse [dis'kɔːs], *v.n.* einen Vortrag halten (*on*, über, *Acc.*); sprechen. — ['diskɔːs], *s.* der Vortrag; das Gespräch, die Rede.

discourteous [dis'kəːtiəs], *adj.* unhöflich.

discourtesy [dis'kəːtəsi], *s.* die Unhöflichkeit.

discover [dis'kʌvə], *v.a.* entdecken.

discovery [dis'kʌvəri], *s.* die Entdeckung.

discredit [dis'kredit], *s.* der üble Ruf; die Schande. — *v.a.* in schlechten Ruf bringen; diskreditieren.

discreditable [dis'kreditəbl], *adj.* schimpflich.

discreet [dis'kriːt], *adj.* diskret, verschwiegen; vorsichtig (*cautious*).

discrepancy [dis'krepənsi], *s.* die Diskrepanz, der Widerspruch; der Unterschied (*difference*).

discretion [dis'kreʃən], *s.* die Diskretion; die Klugheit; der Takt (*tact*); die Verschwiegenheit (*silence*); *at your* —, nach Ihrem Belieben; *use your* —, handle nach deinem Ermessen; handeln Sie nach Ihrem Ermessen.

discretionary [dis'kreʃənəri], *adj.* willkürlich, uneingeschränkt.

discriminate [dis'krimineit], *v.a., v.n.* unterscheiden (*distinguish*); absondern (*separate*).

discriminating [dis'krimineitiŋ], *adj.* scharfsinnig; einsichtig.

discriminatory [dis'krimineitəri], *adj.* einen Unterschied machend; — *legislation*, das Ausnahmegesetz.

discursive [dis'kəːsiv], *adj.* diskursiv, ohne Zusammenhang.

discuss [dis'kʌs], *v.a.* besprechen, erörtern.

discussion [dis'kʌʃən], *s.* die Diskussion, das Gespräch.

disdain [dis'dein], *s.* die Verachtung. — *v.a.* verachten, verschmähen; herabsetzen (*belittle*).

disdainful [dis'deinful], *adj.* geringschätzig, verächtlich.

disease [di'ziːz], *s.* die Krankheit.

diseased [di'ziːzd], *adj.* krank.

disembark [disim'bɑːk], *v.n.* aussteigen, landen. — *v.a.* aussteigen lassen, ausschiffen.

disembarkation [disembɑː'keiʃən], *s.* die Ausschiffung; die Landung.

disenchant [disin'tʃɑːnt], *v.a.* ernüchtern.

disenchantment [disin'tʃɑːntmənt], *s.* die Ernüchterung.

disengage [disin'geidʒ], *v.a.* losmachen, befreien (*release*); freigeben. — *v.n.* (*Mil.*) sich absetzen.

disengaged [disin'geidʒd], *adj.* frei (*unoccupied*).

disentangle [disin'tæŋgl], *v.a.* entwirren; befreien (*free*).

disentanglement [disin'tæŋglmənt], *s.* die Entwirrung, die Befreiung.

disfavour [dis'feivə], *s.* die Ungunst, die Ungnade.

disfigure [dis'figə], *v.a.* entstellen, verunstalten.

disfiguration [disfigjuə'reiʃən], *s.* die Entstellung, die Verunstaltung.

disfranchise [dis'fræntʃaiz], *v.a.* das Wahlrecht entziehen (*Dat.*).

disgorge [dis'gɔ:dʒ], *v.a.* ausspeien.

disgrace [dis'greis], *v.a.* entehren, Schande bringen. — *s.* die Ungnade, Schande (*shame*); die Entehrung (*putting to shame*).

disgraceful [dis'greisful], *adj.* schändlich, entehrend.

disgruntled [dis'grʌntld], *adj.* verstimmt, unzufrieden.

disguise [dis'gaiz], *v.a.* verkleiden (*dress*); (*fig.*) verstellen. — *s.* die Verkleidung; die Verstellung.

disgust [dis'gʌst], *s.* der Ekel, der Widerwille. — *v.a.* anekeln; *be —ed*, sehr ärgerlich sein; *be —ed with s. th.*, etwas verabscheuen.

dish [diʃ], *s.* die Schüssel (*bowl*); das Gericht (*food*). — *v.a.* (*coll.*) abtun (*frustrate*); — *up*, auftragen (*food*).

dishcloth [ˈdiʃklɔθ], *s.* das Wischtuch; der Abwaschlappen.

dishearten [dis'hɑ:tn], *v.a.* entmutigen, verzagt machen.

dishevelled [di'ʃevəld], *adj.* aufgelöst (*hair*); zerzaust (*hair, clothes*).

dishonest [dis'ɔnist], *adj.* unehrlich.

dishonesty [dis'ɔnisti], *s.* die Unehrlichkeit.

dishonour [dis'ɔnə], *s.* die Schande. — *v.a.* schänden, Schande bringen (über, *Acc.*).

dishonourable [dis'ɔnərəbl], *adj.* ehrlos, schimpflich.

dishwater [ˈdiʃwɔ:tə], *s.* das Spülwasser.

disillusion [disi'lu:ʒən], *s.* die Enttäuschung, die Ernüchterung. — *v.a.* enttäuschen, ernüchtern.

disinclination [disinkli'neiʃən], *s.* die Abneigung.

disincline [disin'klain], *v.a.* abgeneigt machen (*Dat.*).

disinfect [disin'fekt], *v.a.* desinfizieren.

disinfectant [disin'fektənt], *s.* das Desinfektionsmittel.

disinfection [disin'fekʃən], *s.* die Desinfektion.

disingenuous [disin'dʒenjuəs], *adj.* unaufrichtig, unredlich.

disinherit [disin'herit], *v.a.* enterben.

disinter [disin'tə:], *v.a.* exhumieren, ausgraben.

disinterested [dis'intrəstid], *adj.* uneigennützig.

disinterestedness [dis'intrəstidnis], *s.* die Selbstlosigkeit, die Uneigennützigkeit.

disjoin [dis'dʒɔin], *v.a.* trennen.

disjoint [dis'dʒɔint], *v.a.* zerlegen, zerstücken.

disjointedness [dis'dʒɔintidnis], *s.* die Zerstücktheit, die Zusammenhangslosigkeit (*style of writing etc.*).

disjunction [dis'dʒʌŋkʃən], *s.* die Trennung, die Abtrennung.

disjunctive [dis'dʒʌŋktiv], *adj.* (*Gram.*) trennend, disjunktiv.

disk [disk] *see* disc.

dislike [dis'laik], *v.a.* nicht leiden mögen, nicht gerne haben. — *s.* die Abneigung (*of*, gegen, *Acc.*).

dislocate [ˈdislokeit], *v.a.* verrenken (*bone*); (*fig.*) in Unordnung bringen.

dislocation [dislo'keiʃən], *s.* (*Med.*) die Verrenkung; die Verwirrung (*traffic etc.*).

dislodge [dis'lɔdʒ], *v.a.* vertreiben (*drive out*); entfernen (*remove*).

disloyal [dis'lɔiəl], *adj.* ungetreu; verräterisch.

disloyalty [dis'lɔiəlti], *s.* die Untreue (*sentiment*); der Verrat (*act*).

dismal [ˈdizməl], *adj.* trostlos, traurig (*mood*); düster, trüb (*weather*).

dismantle [dis'mæntl], *v.a.* niederreißen, zerlegen; abbauen.

dismay [dis'mei], *v.a.* erschrecken, entmutigen. — *s.* die Furcht, der Schrecken, die Bangigkeit.

dismember [dis'membə], *v.a.* zerstückeln.

dismemberment [dis'membəmənt], *s.* die Zerstückelung, die Aufteilung.

dismiss [dis'mis], *v.a.* entlassen (*person*); aufgeben (*idea*).

dismissal [dis'misəl], *s.* die Entlassung; (*Law*) die Abweisung.

dismount [dis'maunt], *v.n.* vom Pferd absteigen. — *v.a.* (*die Truppen*) absteigen lassen.

disobedience [disə'bi:djəns], *s.* der Ungehorsam.

disobedient [disə'bi:djənt], *adj.* ungehorsam.

disobey [disə'bei], *v.a.*, *v.n.* nicht gehorchen.

disoblige [disə'blaidʒ], *v.a.* verletzen, unhöflich behandeln.

disorder [dis'ɔ:də], *s.* die Unordnung; der Aufruhr (*riot*). — *v.a.* verwirren, in Unordnung bringen.

disorderliness [dis'ɔ:dəlinis], *s.* die Unordentlichkeit.

disorderly [dis'ɔ:dəli], *adj.* unordentlich (*unsystematic*); aufrührerisch, liederlich.

disorganization [disɔ:gəni'zeiʃən *or* -nai'zeiʃən], *s.* die Zerrüttung, die Auflösung (*dissolution*).

disorganize [dis'ɔ:gənaiz], *v.a.* auflösen.

disown [dis'oun], *v.a.* verleugnen.

disparage [dis'pæridʒ], *v.a.* verunglimpfen (*slight*); herabsetzen (*minimize*).

disparagement [dis'pæridʒmənt], *s.* die Herabsetzung.

disparity [dis'pæriti], *s.* die Ungleichheit.

dispatch [dis'pætʃ] *see* despatch.

dispel [dis'pel], *v.a.* vertreiben, verscheuchen.

dispensable

dispensable [dis'pensəbl], *adj.* erläßlich, entbehrlich.

dispensary [dis'pensəri], *s.* die Apotheke.

dispensation [dispen'seiʃən], *s.* die Austeilung; (*Eccl.*) die Dispensation.

dispense [dis'pens], *v.a.* ausgeben, austeilen (*distribute*); — *with*, entbehren können, verzichten (auf, *Acc.*).

dispenser [dis'pensə], *s.* der Apotheker, der Pharmazeut.

dispersal [dis'pə:səl], *s.* das Zerstreuen, die Verteilung.

disperse [dis'pə:s], *v.a.* zerstreuen. — *v.n.* sich zerstreuen, sich verteilen.

dispirit [dis'pirit], *v.a.* mutlos machen, entmutigen.

displace [dis'pleis], *v.a.* verlegen, versetzen; (*Phys.*) verdrängen; *—d person,* der Heimatlose, der Verschleppte, der Flüchtling.

displacement [dis'pleismənt], *s.* die Versetzung (*from one place to another*); die Entwurzelung (*uprooting*); (*Phys.*) die Verdrängung; (*Naut.*) das Deplacement.

display [dis'plei], *v.a.* entfalten, ausstellen, zur Schau stellen (*show*). — *s.* die Entfaltung (*showing*), die Schaustellung, Ausstellung (*exhibition*).

displease [dis'pli:z], *v.a.* mißfallen (*Dat.*).

displeased [dis'pli:zd], *adj.* ungehalten (*at*, über, *Acc.*).

displeasure [dis'pleʒə], *s.* das Mißvergnügen, das Mißfallen (— *at*, an, *Dat.*).

disposable [dis'pouzəbl], *adj.* (*Comm.*) disponibel; zur Verfügung stehend.

disposal [dis'pouzl], *s.* die Verfügung (*ordering*); die Übergabe (*handing over*); *at o.'s —,* zur Verfügung; *bomb —,* die Unschädlichmachung der Bomben.

dispose [dis'pouz], *v.a.* einrichten (*thing*); geneigt machen (*person*); — *of,* etwas loswerden (*Acc.*). — *v.n.* anordnen (*ordain*).

disposed [dis'pouzd], *adj.* geneigt; *be well — towards s.o.,* jemandem zugeneigt sein *or* wohlwollend gegenüberstehen; *well —,* (in) guter Laune.

disposition [dispə'ziʃən], *s.* (*Psych.*) die Anlage; die Gemütsart (*temperament*); die Anordnung (*sequence*); der Plan, die Anlage (*of book etc.*); die Verfügung (*arrangement*).

dispossess [dispə'zes], *v.a.* enteignen, (des Besitzes) berauben (*Genit.*).

disproof [dis'pru:f], *s.* die Widerlegung.

disproportion [disprə'pɔ:ʃən], *s.* das Mißverhältnis.

disproportionate [disprə'pɔ:ʃnit], *adj.* unverhältnismäßig.

disprove [dis'pru:v], *v.a.* widerlegen.

disputable [dis'pju:təbl], *adj.* bestreitbar.

disputant ['dispjutənt], *s.* der Opponent, der Disputant.

disputation [dispju'teiʃən], *s.* der gelehrte Streit, die Disputation.

dispute [dis'pju:t], *s.* der Disput, die Meinungsverschiedenheit. — *v.a.,* *v.n.* streiten, verschiedener Ansicht sein; disputieren (*debate*); mit Worten streiten (*argue*).

disqualification [diskwɔlifi'keiʃən], *s.* die Disqualifizierung.

disqualify [dis'kwɔlifai], *v.a.* disqualifizieren, ausschließen.

disquiet [dis'kwaiət], *v.a.* beunruhigen, stören. — *s.* die Unruhe, die Störung.

disquisition [diskwi'ziʃən], *s.* die (lange) Abhandlung *or* Rede.

disregard [disri'gɑ:d], *v.a.* mißachten, nicht beachten. — *s.* die Außerachtlassung, die Mißachtung.

disreputable [dis'repjutəbl], *adj.* verrufen, in üblem Rufe stehend.

disrepute [disri'pju:t], *s.* der schlechte Name, der üble Ruf.

disrespect [disris'pekt], *s.* die Geringschätzung, der Mangel an Respekt. — *v.a.* (*obs.*) mißachten, geringschätzen, respektlos behandeln.

disrespectful [disris'pektful], *adj.* respektlos, unhöflich.

disrobe [dis'roub], *v.a.* entkleiden. — *v.n.* sich entkleiden.

disrupt [dis'rʌpt], *v.a.* abreißen, unterbrechen, stören (*disturb*).

disruption [dis'rʌpʃən], *s.* die Störung, die Unterbrechung (*interruption*); der Bruch.

dissatisfaction [dissætis'fækʃən], *s.* die Unzufriedenheit.

dissatisfied [dis'sætisfaid], *adj.* unzufrieden, unbefriedigt.

dissatisfy [dis'sætisfai], *v.a.* unzufrieden lassen.

dissect [di'sekt], *v.a.* zergliedern, zerlegen; (*Anat.*) sezieren.

dissection [di'sekʃən], *s.* die Zergliederung; (*Anat.*) die Sektion.

dissemble [di'sembl], *v.a.,* *v.n.* heucheln; sich verstellen.

disseminate [di'semineit], *v.a.* verbreiten.

dissemination [disemi'neiʃən], *s.* die Verbreitung.

dissension [di'senʃən], *s.* die Uneinigkeit, der Zwist (*conflict*).

dissent [di'sent], *v.n.* anderer Meinung sein; abweichen (*from*, von, *Dat.*). — *s.* die Abweichung, die abweichende Meinung.

dissenter [di'sentə], *s.* der Dissenter, das Mitglied der Freikirche.

dissertation [disə'teiʃən], *s.* die Dissertation, die Abhandlung.

dissever [di'sevə], *v.a.* trennen (*separate*); zerteilen (*divide*).

dissidence ['disidəns], *s.* die Uneinigkeit.

dissident ['disidənt], *adj.* uneinig, anders denkend.

dissimilar [di'similə], *adj.* unähnlich, ungleichartig.

dissimilarity [disimi'læriti], *s.* die Unähnlichkeit, die Ungleichartigkeit.

dissimulate [di'simjuleit], *v.a.* verhehlen (*conceal*). — *v.n.* sich verstellen, heucheln.

dissimulation [disimju'leiʃən], *s.* die Verstellung, Heuchelei, das Vorgeben (*pretence*).

dissipate ['disipeit], *v.a.* zerstreuen (*spread*); verschwenden (*waste*).

dissipation [disi'peiʃən], *s.* die Zerstreuung, die Verschwendung; die Ausschweifung.

dissociate [di'souʃieit], *v.a.* trennen, lösen. — *v.r.* abrücken (von).

dissociation [disouʃi'eiʃən], *s.* die Trennung; die Dissoziation.

dissolubility [disɔlju'biliti], *s.* die Auflösbarkeit.

dissoluble [di'sɔljubl], *adj.* auflösbar.

dissolute ['disɔlju:t], *adj.* ausschweifend, lose, liederlich.

dissolution [disə'lju:ʃən], *s.* die Auflösung; der Tod (*death*).

dissolvable [di'zɔlvəbl], *adj.* auflösbar, löslich.

dissolve [di'zɔlv], *v.a.* auflösen; lösen. — *v.n.* sich auflösen, zergehen (*melt*).

dissonance ['disənəns], *s.* die Dissonanz, der Mißklang.

dissonant ['disənənt], *adj.* (*Mus.*) dissonant; mißhellig (*discordant*).

dissuade [di'sweid], *v.a.* abraten (*from*, von, *Dat.*).

dissuasion [di'sweiʒən], *s.* das Abraten.

dissuasive [di'sweisiv], *adj.* abratend.

distaff ['dista:f], *s.* der Spinnrocken (*spinning*); *on the* — *side*, auf der weiblichen Linie.

distance ['distəns], *s.* die Entfernung; die Ferne (*remoteness*). — *v.a.* hinter sich lassen, sich distanzieren (von, *Dat.*).

distant ['distənt], *adj.* entfernt, fern (*space*); kühl (*manner*).

distaste [dis'teist], *s.* die Abneigung (vor, *Dat.*); der Widerwille (gegen, *Acc.*).

distasteful [dis'teistful], *adj.* widerwärtig, zuwider.

distastefulness [dis'teistfulnis], *s.* die Widerwärtigkeit.

distemper (1) [dis'tempə], *s.* die Krankheit; die Staupe (*dogs*).

distemper (2) [dis'tempə], *s.* die Wasserfarbe (*paint*). — *v.a.* mit Wasserfarbe streichen.

distend [dis'tend], *v.a.* (*Med.*) ausdehnen, strecken. — *v.n.* sich ausdehnen.

distension, distention [dis'tenʃən], *s.* das Dehnen; (*Med.*) die Ausdehnung, die Streckung.

distich ['distik], *s.* (*Poet.*) das Distichon.

distil [dis'til], *v.a.* destillieren. — *v.n.* (*Chem.*) destillieren, herauströpfeln.

distillation [disti'leiʃən], *s.* die Destillierung, (*Chem.*) der Destilliervorgang.

distiller [dis'tilə], *s.* der Branntweinbrenner.

distillery [dis'tiləri], *s.* die (Branntwein)brennerei.

distinct [dis'tiŋkt], *adj.* deutlich, klar; — *from*, verschieden von (*Dat.*).

distinction [dis'tiŋkʃən], *s.* der Unterschied, die Unterscheidung (*differentiation*); die Auszeichnung (*eminence*).

distinctive [dis'tiŋktiv], *adj.* unterscheidend (*differentiating*); deutlich (*clear*); leicht zu unterscheiden (*easy to distinguish*).

distinctiveness [dis'tiŋktivnis], *s.* die Deutlichkeit (*of voice etc.*); die Eigenart, Eigentümlichkeit (*peculiarity*).

distinguish [dis'tiŋgwiʃ], *v.a.* unterscheiden. — *v.r.* — *o.s.*, sich auszeichnen.

distinguishable [dis'tiŋgwiʃəbl], *adj.* unterscheidbar.

distinguished [dis'tiŋgwiʃd], *adj.* berühmt, vornehm.

distort [dis'tɔ:t], *v.a.* verdrehen; verzerren, verrenken.

distortion [dis'tɔ:ʃən], *s.* die Verdrehung, Verzerrung; (*fig.*) die Entstellung (*of truth etc.*).

distract [dis'trækt], *v.a.* abziehen, ablenken (*divert*); stören (*disturb*).

distracted [dis'træktid], *adj.* zerstreut; verrückt (*mentally deranged*).

distraction [dis'trækʃən], *s.* die Ablenkung; die Störung (*disturbance*); *to* —, bis zur Raserei.

distrain [dis'trein], *v.a.* beschlagnahmen, in Beschlag nehmen.

distraint [dis'treint], *s.* die Beschlagnahme.

distress [dis'tres], *s.* die Not, die Trübsal. — *v.a.* betrüben (*sadden*); quälen (*torture*).

distribute [dis'tribju:t], *v.a.* verteilen, austeilen (*among*, unter, *Acc.*).

distribution [distri'bju:ʃən], *s.* die Verteilung; die Austeilung (*giving out*); (*Comm.*) der Vertrieb.

distributive [dis'tribjutiv], *adj.* (*Gram.*) distributiv; — *trades*, die Vertriebsgewerbe.

district ['distrikt], *s.* (*Geog.*, *Pol.*) der Bezirk; die Gegend (*region*); der Kreis (*administrative*); — *commissioner*, der Kreisbeamte, Kreisvorsteher.

distrust [dis'trʌst], *v.a.* mißtrauen (*Dat.*). — *s.* das Mißtrauen (*of*, gegen, *Acc.*).

distrustful [dis'trʌstful], *adj.* mißtrauisch (*of*, gegen, *Acc.*).

disturb [dis'tə:b], *v.a.* stören (*trouble*); in Unordnung bringen (*disorder*).

disturbance [dis'tə:bəns], *s.* die Störung (*interruption etc.*); der Aufruhr (*riot*).

disunion [dis'ju:njən], *s.* die Entzweiung, die Zwietracht.

disunite [disju'nait], *v.a.* entzweien, Zwietracht säen zwischen. — *v.n.* sich trennen.

disuse [dis'ju:z], *v.a.* außer Gebrauch setzen. — [-'ju:s], *s.* der Nichtgebrauch (*abeyance*); die Entwöhnung (*cessation of practice*).

ditch [ditʃ], *s.* der Graben; *dull as —water*, uninteressant, langweilig. — *v.a.* mit einem Graben umgeben (*dig around*); graben.

ditto ['ditou], *adv.* desgleichen, dito.

ditty ['diti], *s.* das Liedchen.

diurnal [dai'ə:nəl], *adj.* täglich.

divan [di'væn], *s.* der Diwan.

dive [daiv], *v.n.* tauchen, springen (ins Wasser); (*Aviat.*) sturzfliegen, einen Sturzflug machen. — *s.* der Hechtsprung (ins Wasser); der Wassersprung; der Kopfsprung; (*Aviat.*) der Sturzflug.

diver ['daivə], *s.* (*Sport, Orn.*) der Taucher.

diverge [dai'və:dʒ], *v.n.* abweichen, auseinandergehen.

divergence [dai'və:dʒəns], *s.* die Abweichung, die Divergenz, Meinungsverschiedenheit.

divergent [dai'və:dʒənt], *adj.* auseinandergehend, abweichend.

divers ['daivəz], *adj. pl.* etliche, verschiedene.

diverse [dai'və:s], *adj.* verschieden, mannigfaltig.

diversify [dai'və:sifai], *v.a.* verschieden machen.

diversion [dai'və:ʃən], *s.* die Zerstreuung; (*Traffic*) die Umleitung.

diversity [dai'və:siti], *s.* die Verschiedenheit; die Ungleichheit (*disparity*).

divert [dai'və:t], *v.a.* ablenken, zerstreuen.

divest [di'vest *or* dai'-], *v.a.* entkleiden, berauben (*of office*, eines Amtes). — *v.r.* — *o.s. of*, auf etwas verzichten (*give up*).

divide [di'vaid], *v.a.* (*Maths.*) dividieren; teilen (*share*); aufteilen (*proportion*); sondern, trennen (*separate*). — *v.n.* sich teilen; (*Maths.*) sich dividieren lassen.

dividend ['dividənd], *s.* (*Comm.*) die Dividende; (*Maths.*) der Dividend.

dividers [di'vaidəz], *s.pl.* der Stechzirkel.

divination [divi'neiʃən], *s.* die Wahrsagung (*prophecy*); die Ahnung.

divine [di'vain], *v.a.* weissagen (*prophesy*); erraten (*guess*). — *adj.* göttlich; (*coll.*) herrlich. —*s.* (*obs.*) der Geistliche (*clergyman*).

divinity [di'viniti], *s.* die Göttlichkeit; die Gottheit (*deity*); die Theologie.

divisibility [divizi'biliti], *s.* (*Maths.*) die Teilbarkeit.

divisible [di'vizibl], *adj.* teilbar.

division [di'viʒən], *s.* (*Maths., Mil.*) die Division; die Teilung (*partition*); die Abteilung (*department*); (*Parl.*) die Abstimmung.

divisor [di'vaizə], *s.* (*Maths.*) der Divisor; der Teiler.

divorce [di'vɔ:s], *s.* (*Law*) die Scheidung; die Trennung (*separation*). — *v.a.* sich von einem scheiden lassen.

divulge [dai'vʌldʒ], *v.a.* ausplaudern; verraten (*betray*); verbreiten (*spread*).

dizziness ['dizinis], *s.* der Schwindel.

dizzy ['dizi], *adj.* schwindlig.

do [du:], *v.a. irr.* tun, machen; — *o.'s duty*, seine Pflicht erfüllen; — *o.'s bit*, das Seinige leisten; — *o.'s homework*, seine Aufgaben machen; — *a favour*, einen Gefallen erweisen; vollbringen (*accomplish*); — *away with*, abschaffen (*Acc.*); einpacken. — *v.n. this will* —, das genügt; *this won't* —, so geht's nicht; — *without*, ohne etwas auskommen; *how* — *you* — ? sehr angenehm (*on introduction to people*).

docile ['dousail], *adj.* gelehrig, lenksam, fügsam.

docility [do'siliti], *s.* die Gelehrigkeit, die Fügsamkeit.

dock (1) [dɔk], *s.* (*Bot.*) das Ampferkraut; — *leaf*, das Ampferblatt.

dock (2) [dɔk], *s.* (*Naut.*) die Dock; —*yard*, die Schiffswerft; (*Law*) die Anklagebank. — *v.a.* (*Naut.*) ein Schiff ins Dock bringen.

dock (3) [dɔk], *v.a.* stutzen (*clip*); kürzen (*wages*).

docket ['dɔkit], *s.* der Zettel (*chit*); der Lieferschein.

doctor ['dɔktə], *s.* (*Med.*) der Arzt, der Doktor. — *v.a.* operieren, kastrieren (*a cat etc.*).

doctorate ['dɔktərit], *s.* das Doktorat, die Doktorwürde.

doctrinaire [dɔktri'neə], *s.* der Doktrinär. — *adj.* doktrinär.

doctrinal [dɔk'trainəl], *adj.* Lehr-.

doctrine ['dɔktrin], *s.* die Lehre, die Doktrin.

document ['dɔkjumənt], *s.* das Dokument, die Urkunde.

documentary [dɔkju'mentəri], *adj.* Dokumentar- (*film*); dokumentarisch (*evidence*).

documentation [dɔkjumen'teiʃən], *s.* die Dokumentation, Heranziehung von Dokumenten.

dodge [dɔdʒ], *v.a.* ausweichen (*Dat.*). — *s.* der Kniff.

dodger ['dɔdʒə], *s.* der Schwindler.

doe [dou], *s.* (*Zool.*) das Reh.

doeskin ['douskin], *s.* das Rehleder.

doff [dɔf], *v.a.* abnehmen, ablegen (*clothes*).

dog [dɔg], *s.* der Hund; —*'s ear*, das Eselsohr (*in book*). — *v.a.* verfolgen, auf Schritt und Tritt folgen (*Dat.*) (*follow closely*).

dogfish ['dɔgfiʃ], *s.* (*Zool.*) der Dornhai.

dogged ['dɔgid], *adj.* unverdrossen, zäh.

doggedness ['dɔgidnis], *s.* die Zähigkeit.

doggerel ['dɔgərəl], *s.* der Knüttelvers.

dogma ['dɔgmə], *s.* das Dogma, der Glaubenssatz.

dower

dogmatic [dɔg'mætik], *adj.* dogmatisch.

dogmatism ['dɔgmətizm], *s.* der Dogmatismus.

dogmatize ['dɔgmətaiz], *v.n.* dogmatisieren.

doldrums ['douldrəmz], *s. pl.* die Schwermut, die Depression; (*Naut.*) die Windstillen, *f.pl.*

dole [doul], *s.* das Almosen; die Arbeitslosenunterstützung (*unemployment benefit*); *be on the —*, stempeln gehen, Arbeitslosenunterstützung beziehen. — *v.a. — out*, austeilen, verteilen.

doleful ['doulful], *adj.* traurig, bekümmert.

doll [dɔl], *s.* die Puppe.

dollar ['dɔlə], *s.* der Dollar.

dolman ['dɔlmən], *s.* der Dolman.

dolorous ['dɔlərəs], *adj.* (*Lit.*) schmerzlich, schmerzhaft.

dolphin ['dɔlfin], *s.* (*Zool.*) der Delphin.

dolt [doult], *s.* der Tölpel.

doltish ['doultiʃ], *adj.* tölpelhaft.

doltishness ['doultiʃnis], *s.* die Tölpelhaftigkeit.

domain [do'mein], *s.* das Gebiet, der Bereich.

dome [doum], *s.* (*Archit.*) die Kuppel, die Wölbung; der Dom.

domed [doumd], *adj.* gewölbt.

domestic [do'mestik], *adj.* Haus-, häuslich; — *animal*, das Haustier.

domesticate [do'mestikeit], *v.a.* zähmen (*tame*), zivilisieren.

domesticity [dɔmes'tisiti], *s.* die Häuslichkeit.

domicile ['dɔmisail], *s.* das Domizil; der Wohnort.

domiciled ['dɔmisaild], *adj.* wohnhaft (*at*, in, *Dat.*).

dominant ['dɔminənt], *adj.* vorherrschend. — *s.* (*Mus.*) die Dominante.

dominate ['dɔmineit], *v.a.* beherrschen. — *v.n.* herrschen.

domination [dɔmi'neiʃən], *s.* die Herrschaft.

domineer [dɔmi'niə], *v.n.* tyrannisieren.

domineering [dɔmi'niəriŋ], *adj.* überheblich, gebieterisch.

Dominican [do'minikən], *s.* der Dominikaner (*friar*).

dominion [do'minjən], *s.* die Herrschaft (*rule*); das Dominion (*Br. Commonwealth*).

domino ['dɔminou], *s.* (*pl. —noes*) der Domino (*mask*); (*pl.*) das Domino (*game*).

don (1) [dɔn], *s.* der Universitätsgelehrte, Universitätsdozent (*scholar*); Don (*Spanish nobleman*).

don (2) [dɔn], *v.a.* anziehen.

donate [do'neit], *v.a.* schenken, stiften.

donation [do'neiʃən], *s.* die Schenkung, die Stiftung; die Gabe (*gift*).

donkey ['dɔŋki], *s.* (*Zool.*) der Esel; — *engine*, die Hilfsmaschine.

donor ['dounə], *s.* der Spender, der Stifter; *blood —*, der Blutspender.

doom [du:m], *s.* die Verurteilung (*judgment*); der Untergang; das jüngste Gericht.

doomed [du:md], *adj.* verurteilt, verdammt (*to*, zu, *Dat.*).

Doomsday ['du:msdei]. der jüngste Tag, der Tag des jüngsten Gerichtes.

door [dɔ:], *s.* die Tür(e); *next —*, nebenan; *out of —s*, draußen, im Freien; *—bell*, die Türklingel; *—latch*, die Klinke.

doorman ['dɔ:mæn], *s.* der Türsteher, der Pförtner.

dormant ['dɔ:mənt], *adj.* schlafend; unbenutzt.

dormer window ['dɔ:mə 'windou], *s.* das Dachfenster.

dormitory ['dɔ:mitri], *s.* der Schlafsaal.

dormouse ['dɔ:maus], *s.* (*Zool.*) die Haselmaus.

dose [dous], *s.* (*Med.*) die Dosis. — *v.a.* dosieren.

dot [dɔt], *s.* der Punkt, das Tüpfel. — *v.a.* punktieren; *sign on the —ted line*, unterschreiben; *— the i's and cross the t's*, äußerst genau sein.

dotage ['doutidʒ], *s.* die Altersschwäche, das Greisenalter.

dotard ['doutəd], *s.* der alte Dummkopf.

dote [dout], *v.n.* vernarrt sein (*on*, in, *Acc.*).

double [dʌbl], *adj.* (*Maths.*) doppelt; zweideutig (*meaning*); falsch (*false*); *— entry book-keeping*, doppelte Buchführung. — *s.* der Doppelgänger, die Doppelgängerin; *at the —*, im Sturmschritt. — *v.a.* (*Maths.*) verdoppeln; zusammenlegen (*fold in two*). — *v.n. — up with pain*, sich vor Schmerzen winden *or* krümmen.

doublet ['dʌblit], *s.* der Wams; *— and hose*, Wams und Hosen; der Pasch (*dice*); (*Ling.*) die Dublette, Doppelform.

doubt [daut], *s.* der Zweifel. — *v.a.* zweifeln (an, *Dat.*); bezweifeln.

doubtful ['dautful], *adj.* zweifelhaft, fraglich (*uncertain*).

doubtless ['dautlis], *adj.* zweifellos, ohne Zweifel.

douche [du:ʃ], *s.* die Dusche.

dough [dou], *s.* der Teig.

doughnut ['dounʌt], *s.* der Krapfen, Pfannkuchen.

doughy ['doui], *adj.* weich, teigig.

douse [daus], *v.a.* begießen, mit Wasser beschütten.

dove [dʌv], *s.* (*Orn.*) die Taube.

dovecote ['dʌvkout], *s.* der Taubenschlag.

dovetail ['dʌvteil], *v.a., v.n.* einpassen; fügen; *—ing*, die Einpassung, die Verzinkung.

dowager ['dauədʒə], *s.* die Witwe (*of noble family*, von Stande).

dowdy ['daudi], *adj.* schlampig, unordentlich, unelegant.

dower ['dauə], *s.* die Mitgift, die Ausstattung.

down

down (1) [daun], *s.* der Flaum, die Daune.

down (2) [daun], *s.* das Hügelland.

down (3) [daun], *adv.* hinunter, herunter; nieder; unter; hinab. — *prep.* herab; hinunter. — *adj.* the — *train*, der Zug aus London. — *v.a.* niederzwingen, hinunterstürzen.

downcast ['daunkɑ:st], *adj.* niedergeschlagen.

downfall ['daunfɔ:l], *s.* der Sturz.

downhill [daun'hil], *adv.* bergab. — ['daunhil], *adj.* abschüssig.

downpour ['daunpɔ:], *s.* der Platzregen.

downright ['daunrait], *adj.* völlig. — *adv.* geradezu.

downward ['daunwəd], *adj.* abschüssig. — *adv.* (*also* **downwards**) *see* **down**.

dowry ['dauri] *see* **dower**.

doze [douz], *v.n.* dösen, schlummern.

dozen [dʌzn], *s.* das Dutzend.

drab [dræb], *adj.* eintönig; langweilig (*boring*).

draft [drɑ:ft], *s.* (*Comm.*) die Tratte; der Entwurf (*sketch*); (*Mil.*) das Detachement. — *v.a.* entwerfen (*sketch*); (*Mil.*) abordnen; (*Am.*) einziehen.

drag [dræg], *v.a.* schleppen. — *s.* (*Engin.*) die Schleppbremse, der Dregghaken; der Hemmschuh (*wedge*); —*net*, das Schleppnetz; —*wheel*, das Schlepprad.

dragoman ['drægomən], *s.* der Dolmetscher.

dragon ['drægən], *s.* der Drache.

dragonfly ['drægənflai], *s.* (*Ent.*) die Libelle.

dragoon [drə'gu:n], *v.a.* unterdrücken. — *s.* (*Mil.*) der Dragoner.

drain [drein], *v.a.* entwässern, austrocknen; trockenlegen. — *v.n.* ablaufen, abfließen, auslaufen. — *s.* der Abguß, Abzug, die Gosse (*in street*); (*Engin.*) die Dränage; —*ing board*, das Ablauf- *or* Abwaschbrett; (*Phot.*) —*ing rack*, der Trockenständer; *a* — *on o.'s income*, eine Belastung des Einkommens.

drainage ['dreinidʒ], *s.* die Trockenlegung, die Kanalisierung.

drainpipe ['dreinpaip], *s.* das Abflußrohr; — *trousers*, die Röhrenhosen, *f. pl.*

drake [dreik], *s.* (*Orn.*) der Enterich.

dram [dræm], *s.* der Trunk; Schluck (*spirits*).

drama ['drɑ:mə], *s.* das Drama, das Schauspiel.

dramatic [drə'mætik], *adj.* dramatisch.

dramatist ['drɑ:m-*or*'dræmətist], *s.* der Dramatiker.

dramatize ['dræmətaiz], *v.a.* dramatisieren.

drape [dreip], *v.a.* drapieren, bedecken; einhüllen (*wrap*). — *s.* (*Am.*) der Vorhang.

draper ['dreipə], *s.* der Stoffhändler, der Tuchhändler.

drapery ['dreipəri], *s.* — *department*, die Stoff- *or* Tuchabteilung; die Tuchhandlung (*shop*).

drastic ['drɑ:stik *or* 'dræstik], *adj.* drastisch, radikal.

draught [drɑ:ft], *s.* der Zug (*air*); der Tiefgang (— *of ship*); der Schluck (*drink*); der Schlaftrunk (*sleeping* —); — *horse*, das Zugpferd; — *beer*, das Faßbier; —*board*, das Damespielbrett; (*pl.*) das Damespiel.

draw [drɔ:], *v.a.* *irr.* ziehen (*pull*); zeichnen (*sketch*); anlocken (*attract*); ausschreiben (*cheque*); —*well*, der Ziehbrunnen; — *s.* das Los, die Verlosung (*lottery*); (*Sport*) das Unentschieden.

drawback ['drɔ:bæk], *s.* der Nachteil, die Schattenseite.

drawbridge ['drɔ:bridʒ], *s.* die Zugbrücke.

drawer ['drɔ:ə], *s.* die Schublade; *chest of* —*s*, die Kommode; (*pl.*) die Unterhosen, *f. pl.*

drawing ['drɔ:iŋ], *s.* (*Art*) die Zeichnung; — *board*, das Reißbrett; — *office*, das Zeichenbüro, der Zeichensaal.

drawing room ['drɔ:iŋ rum], *s.* das Wohnzimmer, der Salon.

drawl [drɔ:l], *v.n.* gedehnt sprechen. — *s.* die gedehnte Sprechweise.

drawn [drɔ:n], *adj.* (*Sport*) unentschieden.

dray [drei], *s.* der Rollwagen, der Karren; —*man*, der Kutscher, der Fuhrmann.

dread [dred], *s.* der Schrecken. — *adj.* schrecklich. — *v.a.* fürchten. — *v.n.* sich fürchten (vor, *Dat.*).

dreadful ['dredful], *adj.* schrecklich, furchtbar.

dreadnought ['drednɔ:t], *s.* (*Naut.*) das große Schlachtschiff.

dream [dri:m], *s.* der Traum. — *v.n. irr.* träumen; *I would not* — *of it*, es würde mir nicht im Traum einfallen, ich denke nicht daran.

dreamt [dremt] *see* **dream**.

dreamy ['dri:mi], *adj.* verträumt, träumerisch.

dreariness ['driərinis], *s.* die Öde.

dreary ['driəri], *adj.* traurig, öde.

dredge [dredʒ], *s.* das Schleppnetz. — *v.a.* (*Engin.*) ausbaggern; (*Naut.*) dreggen.

dredger ['dredʒə], *s.* der Bagger, das Baggerschiff; (*Cul.*) die Streubüchse.

dregs [dregz], *s. pl.* der Bodensatz (*in cup etc.*); die Hefe (*yeast*).

drench [drentʃ], *v.a.* durchnässen, tränken.

Dresden ['drezdən]. (*china*) das Meißner Porzellan.

dress [dres], *s.* das Kleid; die Kleidung; *evening* —, die Abendkleidung; *full* —, die Gala(kleidung); — *circle*, erster Rang; —*maker*, die Schneiderin; — *rehearsal*, die Generalprobe; — *shirt*, das Frackhemd; — *suit*, der Frackanzug. — *v.a.*, *v.n.* (sich) anziehen.

dresser ['dresə], *s.* der Ankleider (*valet*);
der Anrichtetisch (*table*).

dressing ['dresiŋ], *s.* (*Build.*) die Verkleidung; der Verband (*bandage*); der
Verputz (*interior decoration*); — *gown*,
der Schlafrock, Bademantel; (*Theat.*)
— *room*, das Künstlerzimmer; An-
kleidezimmer; — *table*, der Toilet-
tentisch.

dressy ['dresi], *adj.* elegant; mode-
süchtig.

dribble ['dribl], *v.n.* tröpfeln (*trickle*);
geifern (*slaver*); (*Footb.*) dribbeln.

driblet ['driblit], *s.* die Kleinigkeit, die
Lappalie.

drift [drift], *s.* die Richtung (*direction*);
die Strömung (*stream*); das Treiben;
Gestöber (*snow*). — *v.a.* treiben.
— *v.n.* dahintreiben.

drill (1) [dril], *v.a.* drillen, bohren
(*bore*); (*Mil.*) exerzieren; (*Agr.*) eine
Furche ziehen; einstudieren (*coach*).
— *s.* (*Mil.*) das Exerzieren; (*Agr.*) die
Furche; der Bohrer (*tool*); — *hall*,
die Übungs- or Exerzierhalle.

drill (2) [dril], *s.* der Drillich (*textile*).

drily ['draili], *adv.* trocken.

drink [driŋk], *v.a., v.n. irr.* trinken. —
s. das Getränk, der Trank (*potion*);
etwas zum Trinken (*a —*); *come, have
a —*, trinken wir ein Glas (zusammen); *strong —*, geistiges Getränk.

drinkable ['driŋkəbl], *adj.* trinkbar;
zum Trinken.

drinker ['driŋkə], *s.* der Trinker, Säufer;
der Zecher; der Trunkenbold (*drunk-
ard*).

drip [drip], *v.n.* tröpfeln. — *s.* das
Tröpfeln.

dripping ['dripiŋ], *s.* (*Cul.*) das Braten-
fett, das Schmalz.

drive [draiv], *v.a. irr.* treiben (*sheep
etc.*); fahren (*a car*). — *v.n.* fahren;
dahinfahren (— *along*). — *s.* die
Ausfahrt, Fahrt (*trip*); die Einfahrt
(*approach to house*).

driving ['draiviŋ], *s.* das Fahren; —
licence, der Führerschein; — *school*,
die Fahrschule; — *test*, die Fahr-
prüfung.

drivel ['drivl], *s.* der Geifer; der
Unsinn (*nonsense*). — *v.n.* Unsinn
reden.

driver ['draivə], *s.* der Fahrer, der
Chauffeur; (*Railw.*) Führer; (*Hunt.*)
der Treiber.

drizzle [drizl], *v.n.* rieseln; leicht
regnen. — *s.* das Rieseln, der feine
Regen, der Sprühregen.

droll [droul], *adj.* drollig, possierlich.

drollery ['drouləri], *s.* die Possierlich-
keit; die Schnurre.

dromedary ['drʌmədəri or 'drɔm-], *s.*
(*Zool.*) das Dromedar.

drone (1) [droun], *s.* das Gedröhn, das
Gesumme (*noise*). — *v.n.* dröhnen,
summen (*hum loudly*).

drone (2) [droun], *s.* (*Ent.*) die Drohne;
der Faulpelz (*lazybones*).

droop [dru:p], *v.a.* hängen lassen. —
v.n. herabhängen; verwelken (*flowers*);
ermatten (*tire*).

drop [drɔp], *s.* der Tropfen (*liquid*);
das Fallen (*fall*). — *v.a.* fallen
lassen; — *a brick*, eine taktlose Bemerkung machen; — *a hint*, andeuten,
auf etwas hindeuten. — *v.n.* fallen.

droppings ['drɔpiŋz], *s. pl.* der Mist,
Dünger (*of animals*).

dropsical ['drɔpsikəl], *adj.* (*Med.*)
wassersüchtig.

dropsy ['drɔpsi], *s.* (*Med.*) die Wassersucht.

dross [drɔs], *s.* (*Metall.*) die Schlacke;
der Unrat, das wertlose Zeug.

drought [draut], *s.* die Dürre, die
Trockenheit.

drove [drouv], *s.* die Herde, die Trift
(*cattle*).

drover ['drouvə], *s.* der Viehtreiber.

drown [draun], *v.a.* ertränken; überschwemmen (*flood*); übertönen
(*noise*). — *v.n.* ertrinken.

drowse [drauz], *v.n.* schlummern,
schläfrig sein.

drowsy ['drauzi], *adj.* schläfrig.

drub [drʌb], *v.a.* prügeln.

drudge [drʌdʒ], *s.* das Packtier; der
Sklave, der Knecht.

drudgery ['drʌdʒəri], *s.* die Plackerei,
die Plagerei (*hard toil*).

drug [drʌg], *s.* die Droge; die Medizin;
das Rauschgift. — *v.a.* betäuben.

drugget ['drʌgit], *s.* der (grobe)
Wollstoff.

drum [drʌm], *s.* die Trommel. —
v.n. trommeln, austrommeln.

drunk [drʌŋk], *adj.* betrunken.

drunkard ['drʌŋkəd], *s.* der Trunkenbold.

drunkenness ['drʌŋkənnis], *s.* die
Trunkenheit.

dry [drai], *adj.* trocken, dürr; aus-
getrocknet, durstig (*thirsty*). — *v.a.*
austrocknen, trocken machen, dörren.
— *v.n.* trocken werden, trocknen.

dryad ['draiæd], *s.* (*Myth.*) die Baumnymphe
Dryade.

dryness ['drainis], *s.* die Trockenheit,
die Dürre.

dual ['dju:əl], *adj.* doppelt; Zwei-.

dub (1) [dʌb], *v.a.* zum Ritter schlagen;
nennen (*name*).

dub (2) [dʌb], *v.a.* (*Films*) synchronisieren.

dubious ['dju:bjəs], *adj.* zweifelhaft.

ducal ['dju:kəl], *adj.* herzoglich.

duchess ['dʌtʃis], *s.* die Herzogin.

duchy ['dʌtʃi], *s.* das Herzogtum.

duck (1) [dʌk], *s.* (*Orn.*) die Ente.

duck (2) [dʌk], *v.n.* sich ducken, sich
bücken; untertauchen (*in water*).—
v.a. untertauchen, ins Wasser tauchen.

duckling ['dʌkliŋ], *s.* (*Orn.*) das Ent-
chen.

duct [dʌkt], *s.* (*Anat.*) der Kanal; die
Röhre.

ductile ['dʌktail], *adj.* dehnbar; fügsam.

dud [dʌd], *s.* (*Mil.*) der Blindgänger; der Fehlschlag.

dude [dju:d], *s.* (*Am.*) der Geck.

dudgeon [ˈdʌdʒən], *s.* der Groll, der Unwille; *in high* —, sehr aufgebracht.

due [dju:], *adj.* gebührend, fällig, schuldig (*to, Dat.*); angemessen, recht; *this is* — *to carelessness,* das ist auf Nachlässigkeit zurückzuführen. — *adv.* direkt, gerade. — *s.* (*pl.*) die Gebühren.

duel [ˈdju:əl], *s.* das Duell. — *v.n.* sich duellieren (mit, *Dat.*).

duet [dju:ˈet], *s.* (*Mus.*) das Duett.

duffer [ˈdʌfə], *s.* der Tölpel; (*obs.*) der Hausierer.

duffle, duffel [dʌfl], *s.* der Düffel, das Düffeltuch.

dug [dʌg], *s.* die Zitze.

dug-out [ˈdʌg-aut], *s.* der Unterstand, der Bunker.

duke [dju:k], *s.* der Herzog; *Grand Duke,* der Großherzog.

dukedom [ˈdju:kdəm], *s.* das Herzogtum.

dull [dʌl], *adj.* fade, langweilig (*boring*); träge, schwerfällig (*slow to grasp*); stumpfsinnig (*obtuse*); schal, abgeschmackt (*tasteless*); schwach (*perception*); dumpf (*thud, noise*); matt (*colour*); trüb, überwölkt (*weather*); flau (*trade*). — *v.a.* abstumpfen (*senses*).

dullness [ˈdʌlnis], *s.* die Stumpfheit (*senses*); die Langweile (*boredom*); die Schwerfälligkeit (*stolidity*); die Schwäche (*vision etc.*); die Stumpfsinnigkeit (*stupidity*).

dumb [dʌm], *adj.* stumm; (*sl.*) dumm; —*founded,* verblüfft; — *show,* die Pantomime; —*bell,* (*Gymn.*) die Hantel.

dumbness [ˈdʌmnis], *s.* die Stummheit.

dummy [ˈdʌmi], *s.* der Strohmann (*cards*); die Kleiderpuppe (*wax figure*); der Blindgänger (*dud shell*); der Schnuller (*baby's*).

dump [dʌmp], *v.a.* kippen, abladen; —*ing ground,* der Abladeplatz. — *s.* (*Am. coll.*) das Bumslokal.

dumpling [ˈdʌmpliŋ], *s.* der Kloß, (*Austr.*) der Knödel.

dumps [dʌmps], *s. pl.* der Unmut, der Mißmut, die Depression.

dumpy [ˈdʌmpi], *adj.* untersetzt, kurz und dick.

dun (1) [dʌn], *adj.* schwarzbraun.

dun (2) [dʌn], *s.* der Gläubiger. — *v.a.* energisch mahnen.

dunce [dʌns], *s.* der Dummkopf.

dune [dju:n], *s.* die Düne.

dung [dʌŋ], *s.* der Dünger. — *v.a.* düngen.

dungeon [ˈdʌndʒən], *s.* der Kerker.

dupe [dju:p], *s.* der Betrogene. — *v.a.* betrügen.

duplicate [ˈdju:plikeit], *v.a.* verdoppeln; doppelt schreiben *or* ausfüllen (*write twice*); vervielfältigen (*stencil*). — [-kit], *s.* das Duplikat.

duplicity [dju:ˈplisiti], *s.* die Falschheit, die Doppelzüngigkeit.

durability [djuərəˈbiliti], *s.* die Dauerhaftigkeit.

durable [ˈdjuərəbl], *adj.* dauerhaft.

duration [djuəˈreiʃən], *s.* die Dauer, die Länge (*time*).

duress [djuəˈres], *s.* der Zwang; *under* —, zwangsweise.

during [ˈdjuəriŋ], *prep.* während.

dusk [dʌsk], *s.* die Dämmerung.

dusky [ˈdʌski], *adj.* dunkel, trüb; düster.

dust [dʌst], *s.* der Staub. — *v.a.* abstauben (*clean*); bestäuben (*pollinate*); bestreuen.

dustbin [ˈdʌstbin], *s.* der Mülleimer.

dusty [ˈdʌsti], *adj.* staubig; *not so* —, (*coll.*) nicht so übel.

Dutch [dʌtʃ], *adj.* holländisch; niederländisch; — *treat,* auf getrennte Kosten; *double* —, Kauderwelsch, Unsinn.

Dutchman [ˈdʌtʃmən], *s.* der Holländer, der Niederländer.

dutiful [ˈdju:tiful], *adj.* gehorsam, pflichttreu, pflichtbewußt.

duty [ˈdju:ti], *s.* die Pflicht; die Abgabe (*tax*); *customs* —, der Zoll; *be on* —, Dienst haben; (*being*) *on* —, diensthabend; *off* —, dienstfrei; — *free,* zollfrei; *in* — *bound,* von Rechts wegen, pflichtgemäß.

dwarf [dwɔ:f], *s.* der Zwerg. — *v.a.* am Wachstum hindern (*stunt*); klein erscheinen lassen (*overshadow*).

dwell [dwel], *v.n. irr.* wohnen (*be domiciled*); verweilen (*remain*).

dwelling [ˈdweliŋ], *s.* die Wohnung; — *place,* der Wohnort.

dwindle [dwindl], *v.n.* abnehmen, kleiner werden.

dye [dai], *v.a.* färben. — *s.* die Farbe; (*Chem.*) der Farbstoff.

dyeing [ˈdaiiŋ], *s.* das Färben; Färbereigewerbe.

dyer [ˈdaiə], *s.* der Färber.

dying [ˈdaiiŋ], *s.* das Sterben; *the* —, (*pl.*) die Sterbenden, *pl.* — *adj.* sterbend.

dynamic [daiˈnæmik], *adj.* dynamisch.

dynamics [daiˈnæmiks], *s. pl.* die Dynamik.

dynamite [ˈdainəmait], *s.* das Dynamit.

dynamo [ˈdainəmou], *s.* der Dynamo, die Dynamomaschine.

dynasty [ˈdinəsti], *s.* die Dynastie.

dysentery [ˈdisəntri], *s.* (*Med.*) die Ruhr.

dyspepsia [disˈpepsiə], *s.* (*Med.*) die Magenverstimmung.

dyspeptic [disˈpeptik], *adj.* mit verstimmten Magen; schlecht aufgelegt (*grumpy*).

E

E [i:]. das E (*also Mus.*); *E flat,* Es; *E sharp,* Eis; *E minor,* E-moll.

each [i:tʃ], *adj., pron.* jeder, jede, jedes; — *other*, einander; — *one*, jeder einzelne.

eager ['i:gə], *adj.* eifrig, begierig.

eagerness ['i:gənis], *s.* der Eifer, die Begierde.

eagle [i:gl], *s.* (*Orn.*) der Adler; (*Am.*) das Zehndollarstück.

ear [iə], *s.* das Ohr; —*lap*, das Ohrläppchen; —*phones*, die Kopfhörer; — *piece*, die Hörmuschel; —*drum*, das Trommelfell; — *of corn*, die Ähre.

earl [ə:l], *s.* der Graf.

earldom ['ə:ldəm], *s.* die (englische) Grafschaft.

early ['ə:li], *adj.* früh, frühzeitig.

earmark ['iəmɑ:k], *v.a.* kennzeichnen, bezeichnen.

earn [ə:n], *v.a.* verdienen; erwerben.

earnest ['ə:nist], *s.* der Ernst; der ernste Beweis, das Handgeld; (*Comm.*) die Anzahlung; (*fig.*) der Vorgeschmack. — *adj.* ernst, ernsthaft.

earnings ['ə:niŋz], *s.* das Einkommen.

earshot ['iəʃɔt], *s.* die Hörweite.

earth [ə:θ], *s.* die Erde; der Erdboden (*soil*); der Fuchsbau (*of fox*); *down to* —, praktisch denkend; *move heaven and* —, alles daransetzen; *where on* —, wo in aller Welt.

earthen ['ə:θən], *adj.* irden, aus Erde; —*ware*, das Steingut.

earthquake ['ə:θkweik], *s.* das Erdbeben.

earthly ['ə:θli], *adj.* irdisch.

earthworm ['ə:θwə:m], *s.* (*Zool.*) der Regenwurm.

earthy ['ə:θi], *adj.* erdig; irdisch.

earwig ['iəwig], *s.* (*Ent.*) der Ohrwurm.

ease [i:z], *s.* die Leichtigkeit (*facility*); die Bequemlichkeit (*comfort*); *feel at* —, sich wie zu Hause fühlen; (*Mil.*) *stand at* —! rührt euch! *ill at* —, unbehaglich. — *v.a.* erleichtern, leichter machen; lindern (*pain*). — *v.n.* — *off*, (*Mil.*) sich auflockern.

easel [i:zl], *s.* das Gestell; die Staffelei.

easiness ['i:zinis], *s.* die Leichtigkeit, die Ungezwungenheit.

east [i:st], *adj., adv.* Ost-, ostwärts (*direction*). — *s.* der Osten, der Orient.

Easter ['i:stə]. das *or* (*n.* or *f. pl.*) die Ostern.

eastern ['i:stən], *adj.* östlich; morgenländisch, orientalisch (*oriental*).

easy ['i:zi], *adj.* leicht, frei; — *chair*, der Lehnstuhl, Sessel; *stand* —! rührt Euch! *take it* —, nimm's nicht so ernst; es sich (*Dat.*) bequem machen (*make o.s. comfortable*); (*Comm.*) — *terms*, Zahlungserleichterungen; — *-going*, gemütlich.

eat [i:t], *v.a., v.n. irr.* essen, speisen (*dine*); fressen (*of animals*); — *humble pie*, sich demütigen; — *o.'s hat*, einen Besen fressen; — *o.'s words* seine Worte bereuen.

eatable ['i:təbl], *adj.* genießbar, eßbar.

eaves [i:vz], *s. pl.* die Dachrinne, die Traufe.

eavesdrop ['i:vzdrɔp], *v.n.* belauschen (*on s.o.*, *Acc.*).

eavesdropper ['i:vzdrɔpə], *s.* der Lauscher.

ebb [eb], *s.* die Ebbe. — *v.n.* nachlassen, abebben, abfließen.

ebonize ['ebənaiz], *v.a.* wie Ebenholz *or* schwarz beizen.

ebony ['ebəni], *s.* das Ebenholz.

ebullient [i'bʌljənt], *adj.* aufwallend.

eccentric [ik'sentrik], *adj.* exzentrisch, überspannt, wunderlich.

eccentricity [eksen'trisiti], *s.* die Exzentrizität, die Überspanntheit.

ecclesiastic [ikli:zi'æstik], *s.* der Geistliche. — *adj.* (*also* -ical) geistlich, kirchlich.

echo ['ekou], *s.* das Echo, der Widerhall. — *v.a., v.n.* widerhallen (*resound*); wiederholen (*repeat*).

eclectic [i'klektik], *adj.* eklektisch. — *s.* der Eklektiker.

eclecticism [i'klektisizm], *s.* (*Phil.*) der Eklektizismus.

eclipse [i'klips], *s.* die Verfinsterung, Finsternis (*darkness*); die Verdunklung (*darkening*). — *v.a.* verdunkeln.

ecliptic [i'kliptik], *s.* die Ekliptik, die Sonnenbahn.

economic [i:kə'nɔmik], *adj.* ökonomisch, wirtschaftlich.

economical [i:kə'nɔmikl], *adj.* (*frugal*) sparsam, wirtschaftlich.

economics [i:kə'nɔmiks], *s.* (*pl.*) die Wirtschaftslehre, die Ökonomie.

economist [i'kɔnəmist], *s.* der Ökonom der Wirtschaftsfachmann.

economize [i'kɔnəmaiz], *v.n.* sparen (*on*, mit, *Dat.*); sparsam sein mit (*Dat.*).

economy [i'kɔnəmi], *s.* die Wirtschaft; *political* —, die Nationalökonomie, Staatswirtschaftslehre.

ecstasy ['ekstəsi], *s.* die Ekstase, die Entzückung, die Verzückung.

ecstatic [iks'tætik], *adj.* ekstatisch, verzückt; entzückt (*delighted*).

Ecuadorean [ekwə'dɔ:riən], *adj.* ekuadorianisch. — *n.* der Ekuadorianer.

ecumenical [i:kju'menikəl], *adj.* ökumenisch.

eddy ['edi], *s.* der Wirbel, Strudel. — *v.n.* wirbeln.

edge [edʒ], *s.* die Schärfe, die Schneide (*blade*); die Kante (*ledge*); der Rand (*brink*); der Saum (*border*); die Ecke (*corner*); der Schnitt (*book*); die Schärfe (*wit, keenness*); *put an* — *on*, schärfen; *be on* —, nervös sein. — *v.a.* besetzen (*decorate*); umgeben; *double—d*, zweischneidig; *two—d*, zweischneidig, zweikantig; *—d with lace*, mit Spitze eingefaßt. — *v.n.* sich bewegen; — *forward*, langsam vorrücken; — *off*, sich abseits halten, sich drücken; — *away from*, abrücken.

edgy ['edʒi], *adj.* kantig, eckig; (*fig.*) nervös, reizbar.

edible ['edibl], *adj.* eßbar.

edict ['i:dikt], *s.* die Verordnung.
edification [edifi'keiʃən], *s.* die Erbauung.
edifice ['edifis], *s.* der Bau, das Gebäude.
edify ['edifai], *v.a.* erbauen.
edit ['edit], *v.a.* herausgeben (*book etc.*).
edition [i'diʃən], *s.* die Ausgabe.
editor ['editə], *s.* der Herausgeber, der Schriftleiter; (*newspaper*) der Redakteur.
editorial [edi'tɔ:riəl], *adj.* Redaktions-. — *s.* der Leitartikel.
editorship ['editəʃip], *s.* die Redaktion; die Schriftleitung.
educate ['edjukeit], *v.a.* erziehen, (heran)bilden.
education [edju'keiʃən], *s.* die Erziehung (*upbringing*); die Bildung (*general culture*); das Bildungwesen, das Schulwesen (*educational system*); *primary* —, die Grundschulung, das Volksschulwesen; *secondary* —, das Mittelschulwesen, das höhere Schulwesen; *university* —, das Hochschulwesen (*system*), die Universitätsbildung (*of individual*); *local* — *authority*, das Schulamt, die Schulbehörde; *Professor of Education*, Professor der Pädagogik; *further* —, *adult* —, weitere Ausbildung, Erwachsenenbildung.
educational [edju'keiʃənəl], *adj.* erzieherisch (*educative*); Bildungs-, Unterrichts- (*for education*); — *attainment*, der Bildungsgrad, die Schulstufe (*grade*); — *facilities*, die Lehrmittel, Bildungs- *or* Schulungsmöglichkeiten, *f. pl.*
education(al)ist [edju'keiʃən(əl)ist], *s.* der Erzieher, der Pädagoge; der Erziehungsfachmann (*theorist*).
eel [i:l], *s.* (*Zool.*) der Aal.
eerie ['iəri], *adj.* gespenstisch, unheimlich.
efface [i'feis], *v.a.* auslöschen, austilgen.
effacement [i'feismənt], *s.* die Austilgung; *self-* —, die Selbstaufopferung.
effect [i'fekt], *s.* die Wirkung; die Folge, das Ergebnis (*consequence*); der Eindruck (*impression*); *of no* —, ohne jede Wirkung; *carry into* —, ausführen; *take* — *from*, vom . . . in Kraft treten. — *v.a.* bewirken (*bring about*).
effective [i'fektiv], *adj.* wirksam (*having an effect*); gültig (*in force*); dienstfähig (*usable*); wirklich (*actual*).
effectual [i'fektjuəl], *adj.* wirksam (*effective*); kräftig, energisch (*strong*).
effectuate [i'fektjueit], *v.a.* bewerkstelligen (*get done*); bewirken (*bring about*).
effeminacy [i'feminəsi], *s.* die Verweichlichung.
effeminate [i'feminit], *adj.* weichlich, verweichlicht.
effervescence [efə'vesəns], *s.* das Aufbrausen, Schäumen.
effervescent [efə'vesənt], *adj.* aufbrausend, aufschäumend.

effete [i'fi:t], *adj.* abgenutzt, erschöpft.
efficacious [efi'keiʃəs], *adj.* wirksam. energisch.
efficacy ['efikəsi], *s.* die Wirksamkeit, die Energie.
efficiency [i'fiʃənsi], *s.* die Tüchtigkeit (*of person*); die Wirksamkeit; die Leistung.
efficient [i'fiʃənt], *adj.* tüchtig; leistungsfähig; wirksam (*drug etc.*).
effigy ['efidʒi], *s.* das Bild, das Abbild.
efflorescent [eflɔ:'resənt], *adj.* aufblühend.
effluent ['efluənt], *adj.* ausfließend.
effluvium [i'flu:viəm], *s.* die Ausdünstung.
effort ['efət], *s.* die Anstrengung, die Bemühung; *make an* —, sich bemühen, sich anstrengen; *make every* —, alle Kräfte anspannen.
effrontery [i'frʌntəri], *s.* die Frechheit (*cheek*); die Unverschämtheit (*impertinence*).
effortless ['efətlis], *adj.* mühelos.
effulgence [i'fʌldʒəns], *s.* der Glanz, das Strahlen.
effulgent [i'fʌldʒənt], *adj.* schimmernd, strahlend.
effusion [i'fju:ʒən], *s.* die Ausgießung; der Erguß (*verse etc.*); der Überschwang.
effusive [i'fju:ziv], *adj.* überschwenglich.
egg [eg], *s.* das Ei; *fried* —, das Spiegelei; *scrambled* —, das Rührei; — *flip*, der Eierpunsch; —*shell*, die Eierschale. — *v.a.* — *on*, anspornen, anreizen.
eglantine ['eglәntain], *s.* (*Bot.*) die wilde Rose.
egoism ['egouizm], *s.* der Egoismus.
ego(t)ist ['ego(t)ist], *s.* der Egoist.
egregious [i'gri:dʒəs], *adj.* ungeheuer-(lich).
egress ['i:gres], *s.* der Ausgang, der Ausfluß (*water etc.*).
Egyptian [i'dʒipʃən], *adj.* ägyptisch. — *s.* der Ägypter.
eiderdown ['aidədaun], *s.* die Daunendecke, Steppdecke.
eiderduck ['aidədʌck], *s.* (*Orn.*) die Eidergans.
eight [eit], *num. adj.* acht.
eighteen [ei'ti:n], *num. adj.* achtzehn.
eighty ['eiti], *num. adj.* achtzig.
either ['aiðə], *adj.*, *pron.* einer von beiden. — *conj.* entweder (*or*, oder).
ejaculate [i'dʒækjuleit], *v.a.*, *v.n.* ausstoßen.
eject [i'dʒekt], *v.a.* hinauswerfen; ausstoßen.
ejection [i'dʒekʃən], *s.* die Ausstoßung.
eke [i:k], *v.a.* — *out*, verlängern, ergänzen; — *out an existence*, ein spärliches Auskommen finden.
elaborate [i'læbəreit], *v.a.* ausarbeiten, im einzelnen ausarbeiten. — [-rit], *adj.* detailliert, ausgearbeitet; kunstvoll (*intricate*); umständlich (*involved*).

elaboration [ilæbə'reiʃən], *s.* die Ausar-
beitung (im einzelnen); die Detailar-
beit.

elapse [i'læps], *v.n.* verstreichen, verfließen (*time*).

elastic [i'læstik], *adj.* elastisch. — *s.*
das Gummiband.

elasticity [elæs'tisiti], *s.* (*Phys.*) die
Elastizität.

elate [i'leit], *v.a.* stolz machen; ermutigen.

elated [i'leitid], *adj.* in gehobener
Stimmung.

elation [i'leiʃən], *s.* der Stolz; die
Begeisterung.

elbow [ˈelbou], *s.* (*Anat.*) der Ellen-
bogen; *at o.'s* —, bei der Hand; —
room, der Spielraum. — *v.a.* — *o.'s
way through*, sich durchdrängen.

elder (1) [ˈeldə], *comp. adj.* älter. — *s.*
der Alte, der Älteste; Kirchenälteste.

elder (2) [ˈeldə], *s.* (*Bot.*) der Holunder.

elderly [ˈeldəli], *adj.* älter; alt; ältlich.

elect [i'lekt], *v.a.* erwählen (*to*, zu,
Dat.); auswählen (*choose*). — *adj.*
erwählt, auserwählt; *chairman* —, der
gewählte Vorsitzende.

election [i'lekʃən], *s.* die Auswahl
(*selection*); (*Pol.*) die Wahlen, *f. pl.*; die
Wahl (*choice*); *by(e)* - —, die Bezirks-
wahl, die Neuwahl; — —*broadcast*, eine
Radiowahlrede.

electioneering [ilekʃən'iəriŋ], *s.* das
Wahlmanöver, die Wahlpropaganda,
der Wahlkampf.

elective [i'lektiv], *adj.* durch Wahl
bestimmt; Wahl-.

elector [i'lektə], *s.* (*Pol.*) der Wähler;
das Mitglied eines Wahlausschusses
(*academic etc.*); der Kurfürst (*prince*).

electorate [i'lektərit], *s.* die Wählerschaft.

electress [i'lektrəs], *s.* die Kurfürstin
(*princess*).

electric(al) [i'lektrik(əl)], *adj.* elektrisch;
electrical engineer, der Elektrotechni-
ker; der Student der Elektrotechnik
(*trainee*); *electric switch*, der elek-
trische Schalter; — *razor*, der elek-
trische Rasierapparat.

electrician [elek'triʃən], *s.* der Elek-
triker.

electricity [ilek- *or* elek'trisiti], *s.* die
Elektrizität.

electrocution [ilektro'kju:ʃən], *s.* die
Hinrichtung *or* der Unfall (*accidental*)
durch Elektrizität.

electron [i'lektron], *s.* das Elektron.

electroplate [i'lektropleit], *v.a.* galvanisch versilbern.

electrotype [i'lektrotaip], *s.* der galva-
nische Abdruck, die Galvanographie.

elegance [ˈeligəns], *s.* die Eleganz.

elegant [ˈeligənt], *adj.* elegant, fein.

elegy [ˈelidʒi], *s.* (*Lit.*) die Elegie.

element [ˈelimənt], *s.* das Element; der
Bestandteil (*component*).

elemental [eli'mentl], *adj.* elementar.

elementary [eli'mentri], *adj.* einfach
(*simple*); elementar (*for beginners*).

elephant [ˈelifənt], *s.* (*Zool.*) der
Elefant.

elevate [ˈeliveit], *v.a.* erheben, erhöhen.

elevation [eli'veiʃən], *s.* die Erhebung
(*lifting*); (*Geom.*) die Elevation; die
Erhöhung (*rise*); der Aufriß (*Engin.
drawing*).

elevator [ˈeliveitə], *s.* (*Am.*) der Lift,
der Aufzug, der Fahrstuhl; (*Agr.*) der
Getreideheber.

eleven [i'levn], *num. adj.* elf.

elf [elf], *s.* der Elf, der Kobold.

elfin [ˈelfin], *adj.* Elfen-, elfenhaft.

elicit [i'lisit], *v.a.* herauslocken, entlocken.

eligibility [elidʒi'biliti], *s.* die Wählbarkeit.

eligible [ˈelidʒibl], *adj.* wählbar, passend.

eliminate [i'limineit], *v.a.* ausschalten,
ausscheiden, eliminieren.

elimination [ilimi'neiʃən], *s.* die Aus-
schaltung, die Ausscheidung.

elision [i'liʒən], *s.* (*Phonet.*) die Auslassung, die Weglassung.

elixir [i'liksə], *s.* das Elixier.

elk [elk], *s.* (*Zool.*) der Elch.

ell [el], *s.* die Elle.

ellipse [i'lips], *s.* (*Geom.*) die Ellipse.

ellipsis [i'lipsis], *s.* (*Gram.*) die
Ellipse.

elliptic(al) [i'liptik(əl)], *adj.* (*Gram.,
Geom.*) elliptisch.

elm [elm], *s.* (*Bot.*) die Ulme.

elocution [elə'kju:ʃən], *s.* der Vortrag
(*delivery*); die Vortragskunst.

elocutionist [elə'kju:ʃənist], *s.* der
Vortragskünstler.

elongate [ˈi:lɔŋgeit], *v.a.* verlängern.

elongation [i:lɔŋ'geiʃən], *s.* die Verlängerung.

elope [i'loup], *v.n.* entlaufen, von
zu Hause fliehen.

elopement [i'loupmənt], *s.* das Entlaufen, die Flucht von zu Hause.

eloquence [ˈeləkwəns], *s.* die Bered-
samkeit.

eloquent [ˈeləkwənt], *adj.* beredt,
redegewandt.

else [els], *adv.* sonst, außerdem, anders;
or —, sonst . . .; *how* — ? wie denn
sonst? *nobody* —, sonst niemand;
anyone — ? sonst noch jemand? — *conj.*
sonst.

elsewhere [els'wɛə], *adv.* anderswo;
anderswohin.

Elsinore [ˈelsinɔː]. Helsingör, *n.*

elucidate [i'lju:sideit], *v.a.* erläutern,
erklären (*to s.o., Dat.*).

elucidation [ilju:si'deiʃən], *s.* die
Erläuterung, die Erklärung.

elude [i'lju:d], *v.a.* ausweichen, entgehen (*Dat.*).

elusive [i'lju:siv], *adj.* schwer faßbar,
täuschend.

Elysian [i'liziən], *adj.* elysisch.

emaciate [i'meiʃieit], *v.a.* abmagern,
dünn werden.

emaciation [imeiʃi'eiʃən], *s.* die Abmagerung.

379

emanate ['emǝneit], v.n. ausgehen, herrühren (derive); ausstrahlen (radiate).

emancipate [i'mænsipeit], v.a. befreien, emanzipieren.

emancipation [imænsi'peiʃǝn], s. die Emanzipation.

embalm [im'ba:m], v.a. einbalsamieren.

embankment [im'bæŋkmǝnt], s. der Flußdamm, der Eisenbahndamm; die Eindämmung.

embarcation see **embarkation**.

embargo [im'ba:gou], s. die Handelssperre.

embark [im'ba:k], v.a. einschiffen. — v.n. sich einschiffen; — upon s.th., an etwas herangehen, unternehmen.

embarkation [emba:'keiʃǝn], s. die Einschiffung.

embarrass [im'bærǝs], v.a. verlegen machen, in Verlegenheit bringen.

embarrassment [im'bærǝsmǝnt], s. die Verlegenheit.

embassy ['embǝsi], s. (Pol.) die Botschaft, die Gesandtschaft.

embed [im'bed], v.a. einbetten.

embellish [im'beliʃ], v.a. verschönern, ausschmücken; ausmalen (story).

embers ['embǝz], s. pl. die glühende Asche; die Kohlen, f. pl.; Ember Days, (Eccl.) die Quatembertage, m. pl.

embezzle [im'bezl], v.a. veruntreuen, unterschlagen.

embitter [im'bitǝ], v.a. verbittern.

emblazon [im'bleizn], v.a. ausmalen, auf ein Schild setzen.

emblem ['emblǝm], s. das Emblem, das Abzeichen.

emblematic(al) [emblǝ'mætik(ǝl)], adj. sinnbildlich, symbolisch.

embodiment [im'bɔdimǝnt], s. die Verkörperung.

embody [im'bɔdi], v.a. verkörpern.

embolden [im'bouldn], v.a. erkühnen, anfeuern, anspornen; be emboldened, sich erkühnen.

emboss [im'bɔs], v.a. in getriebener Arbeit verfertigen, prägen.

embossed [im'bɔst], adj. getrieben, in erhabener Arbeit; gestanzt.

embrace [im'breis], v.a. (fig.) umarmen, umfassen. — s. die Umarmung.

embrasure [im'breiʒǝ], s. die Schießscharte.

embrocation [embro'keiʃǝn], s. die Einreibung (act); (Pharm.) die Einreibsalbe.

embroider [im'brɔidǝ], v.a. sticken; verzieren, ausschmücken (adorn).

embroidery [im'brɔidǝri], s. die Stickerei; die Verzierung, Ausschmückung (of story etc.).

embroil [im'brɔil], v.a. verwickeln.

embryo ['embriou], s. der Keim; Embryo.

embryonic [embri'ɔnik], adj. im Embryostadium, im Werden.

emend [i'mend], v.a. verbessern (text), berichtigen.

emendation [i:men'deiʃǝn], s. die Textverbesserung.

emendator ['i:mendeitǝ], s. der Berichtiger.

emerald ['emǝrǝld], s. der Smaragd.

emerge [i'mǝ:dʒ], v.n. auftauchen, hervortreten, an den Tag kommen.

emergence [i'mǝ:dʒǝns], s. das Auftauchen, das Hervortreten.

emergency [i'mǝ:dʒǝnsi], s. der Notfall; die kritische Lage; in case of —, im Notfalle; — exit, der Notausgang; — landing, die Notlandung; — measures, Notmaßnahmen; — brake, die Notbremse.

emery ['emǝri], s. — paper, das Schmirgelpapier.

emetic [i'metik], s. das Brechmittel.

emigrant ['emigrǝnt], s. der Auswanderer.

emigrate ['emigreit], v.n. auswandern.

emigration [emi'greiʃǝn], s. die Auswanderung.

eminence ['eminǝns], s. die Anhöhe; die Eminenz, der hohe Ruf (fame); die eminente Stellung, die Autorität (authority); Your Eminence, Eure Eminenz.

eminent ['eminǝnt], adj. eminent, hervorragend.

emissary [i'emisǝri], s. der Abgesandte, der Sendbote.

emission [i'miʃǝn], s. die Aussendung (sending out); die Ausstrahlung (radiation).

emit [i'mit], v.a. aussenden; ausstrahlen; ausströmen.

emolument [i'mɔljumǝnt], s. das (Neben)einkommen, das Zusatzgehalt, das Honorar (fee).

emotion [i'mouʃǝn], s. die Rührung, die Bewegung, das Gefühl, die Gemütsbewegung.

emotional [i'mouʃǝnǝl], adj. gefühlvoll.

emperor ['empǝrǝ], s. der Kaiser.

emphasis ['emfǝsis], s. der Nachdruck.

emphasize ['emfǝsaiz], v.a. betonen.

empire ['empaiǝ], s. das Reich, das Kaiserreich.

empiric(al) [emp'irik(ǝl)], adj. (Phil.) empirisch.

empiricism [em'pirisizm], s. (Phil.) der Empirizismus.

employ [im'plɔi], v.a. benutzen (thing); beschäftigen, anstellen (person).

employee [im'plɔii:], s. der Angestellte.

employer [im'plɔiǝ], s. der Arbeitgeber.

employment [im'plɔimǝnt], s. die Beschäftigung, die Arbeit.

emporium [em'pɔ:riǝm], s. der Handelsplatz; (Naut.) der Stapelplatz; das Warenhaus (stores).

empower [em'pauǝ], v.a. bevollmächtigen.

empress ['empres], s. die Kaiserin.

emptiness ['emptinis], s. die Leere, die Öde.

empty ['empti], adj. leer; — -headed, geistlos.

emulate ['emjuleit], *v.a.* nacheifern (*Dat.*).

emulation [emju'leiʃən], *s.* der Wetteifer, das Nacheifern.

emulous ['emjuləs], *adj.* nacheifernd, wetteifernd; eifersüchtig (*jealous*).

emulsion [i'mʌlʃən], *s.* (*Pharm.*) die Emulsion.

enable [i'neibl], *v.a.* befähigen; ermächtigen (*empower*).

enact [i'nækt], *v.a.* (*Pol.*) verordnen; verfügen (*order*); darstellen, aufführen (*on stage*).

enactment [i'næktmənt], *s.* die Verordnung.

enamel [i'næml], *v.a.* emaillieren. — *s.* die Emaille; (*Med.*) der Schmelz.

enamour [i'næmə], *v.a.* verliebt machen.

encamp [in'kæmp], *v.n.* (sich) lagern, das Lager aufschlagen.

encampment [in'kæmpmənt], *s.* das Lager.

encase [in'keis], *v.a.* einschließen, in ein Gehäuse schließen.

encashment [in'kæʃmənt], *s.* (*Comm.*) das Inkasso, die Einkassierung.

enchain [in'tʃein], *v.a.* in Ketten legen, anketten.

enchant [in'tʃɑ:nt], *v.a.* bezaubern.

enchantment [in'tʃɑ:ntmənt], *s.* die Bezauberung; der Zauber (*spell*).

encircle [in'sə:kl], *v.a.* umringen, umkreisen; (*Mil.*) einkreisen.

encirclement [in'sə:klmənt], *s.* die Einkreisung.

enclose [in'klouz], *v.a.* einschließen; einlegen (*in letter*).

enclosure [in'klouʒə], *s.* die Einfriedigung; die Beilage, Einlage (*in letter*).

encompass [in'kʌmpəs], *v.a.* umfassen, umspannen (*comprise*).

encore ['ɔnkɔ:, ɔn'kɔ:], *int.* noch einmal! —*s.* die Wiederholung, Zugabe.

encounter [in'kauntə], *v.a.* treffen; begegnen (*Dat.*). — *s.* das Zusammentreffen.

encourage [in'kʌridʒ], *v.a.* ermutigen; anspornen.

encouragement [in'kʌridʒmənt], *s.* die Ermutigung; die Förderung (*promotion*).

encroach [in'kroutʃ], *v.n.* eingreifen (*interfere*); übergreifen.

encroachment [in'kroutʃmənt], *s.* der Eingriff, der Übergriff.

encrust [in'krʌst], *v.a.* inkrustieren; verkrusten.

encumber [in'kʌmbə], *v.a.* belasten.

encumbrance [in'kʌmbrəns], *s.* die Belastung, das Hindernis.

encyclical [en'siklikl], *s.* das (päpstliche) Rundschreiben, die Enzyklika.

encyclopaedia [insaiklo'pi:djə], *s.* das Lexikon, die Enzyklopädie.

encyclopaedic [insaiklo'pi:dik], *adj.* enzyklopädisch.

end [end], *s.* das Ende; der Schluß; das Ziel (*aim*); die Absicht (*intention*); *in the* —, am Ende, letzten Endes; *to*

that —, zu dem Zweck; *put an* — *to*, einer Sache ein Ende machen; *make* —*s meet*, sein Auskommen finden; *burn the candle at both* —*s*, seine Kräfte verschwenden. — *v.a.* beenden. — *v.n.* enden, Schluß machen.

ending ['endiŋ], *s.* das Ende (*of play etc.*); (*Gram.*) die Endung.

endanger [in'deindʒə], *v.a.* gefährden, in Gefahr bringen.

endear [in'diə], *v.a.* beliebt machen. — *v.r.* — *o.s. to*, sich lieb Kind machen bei.

endearment [in'diəmənt], *s. term of* —, ein Kosewort.

endeavour [in'devə], *v.n.* sich bemühen, sich bestreben. — *s.* das Streben, die Bestrebung, die Bemühung.

endemic(al) [en'demik(əl)], *adj.* einheimisch; endemisch.

endive ['endiv], *s.* (*Bot.*) die Endivie.

endless ['endlis], *adj.* unendlich, endlos.

endorse [in'dɔ:s], *v.a.* bestätigen (*confirm*); beipflichten; (*Fin.*) indossieren (*cheque*).

endorsement [in'dɔ:smənt], *s.* die Bestätigung (*confirmation*); (*Fin.*) das Indossament (*cheque*).

endow [en'dau], *v.a.* begaben (*talents*); ausstatten (*equip*); stiften.

endowment [en'daumənt], *s.* die Begabung (*talents*); die Stiftung; — *policy*, die abgekürzte Lebensversicherung.

endurable [in'djuərəbl], *adj.* erträglich.

endurance [in'djuərəns], *s.* die Ausdauer (*toughness*); die Dauer, Fortdauer (*time*); das Ertragen (*suffering*); — *test*, die Dauerprüfung; (*fig.*) die Geduldsprobe (*patience*).

endure [in'djuə], *v.a.* aushalten, ertragen; leiden (*suffer*).

endways, endwise ['endweiz, -waiz], *adv.* mit dem Ende nach vorne; aufrecht (*vertical*).

enemy ['enəmi], *s.* der Feind, der Gegner.

energetic [enə'dʒetik], *adj.* energisch, tatkräftig.

energy ['enədʒi], *s.* die Energie, die Tatkraft; der Nachdruck (*vehemence*).

enervate ['enə:veit], *v.a.* entkräften, schwächen.

enervation [enə:'veiʃən], *s.* die Entkräftigung, die Schwächung.

enfeeble [in'fi:bl], *v.a.* entkräften, schwächen.

enfold [in'fould], *v.a.* umschließen, umfassen; einhüllen (*veil*).

enforce [in'fɔ:s], *v.a.* erzwingen, durchsetzen.

enforcement [in'fɔ:smənt], *s.* die Erzwingung, die Durchsetzung.

enfranchise [in'fræntʃaiz], *v.a.* freilassen, befreien (*emancipate*); (*Pol.*) das Stimmrecht geben.

enfranchisement [in'fræntʃizmənt], *s.* die Befreiung, die Gewährung des Stimmrechts.

engage [in'geidʒ], *v.a.* verpflichten, engagieren (*pledge, bind*); anstellen (*employ*); verwickeln (*in conversation*); become —*d*, sich verloben. — *v.n.* — *in*, sich einlassen in (*Acc.*), sich befassen mit (*Dat.*).

engagement [in'geidʒmənt], *s.* die Verpflichtung (*pledge*); die Verlobung (*betrothal*); die Verabredung (*appointment*); das Gefecht (*with enemy*).

engaging [in'geidʒiŋ], *adj.* freundlich, verbindlich (*smile etc.*); einnehmend.

engender [in'dʒendə], *v.a.* erzeugen, hervorrufen (*cause*).

engine ['endʒin], *s.* die Maschine; der Motor; (*Railw.*) die Lokomotive; fire —, die Feuerspritze; — driver, (*Railw.*) der Lokomotivführer.

engineer [endʒi'niə], *s.* der Ingenieur (*professional*); der Techniker (*technician*); (*Am.*) der Lokomotivführer (*engine driver*).

engineering [endʒi'niəriŋ], *s.* das Ingenieurwesen; der Maschinenbau; chemical —, die chemische Technik or Technologie; civil —, das Zivilingenieurwesen; electrical —, die Elektrotechnik or die Elektrotechnologie; mechanical —, der Maschinenbau, die Strukturtechnik; — laboratory, das technische Labor; — workshop, die technische Werkstatt.

English ['iŋgliʃ], *adj.* englisch; britisch. — *s.* die englische Sprache, das Englisch; (*pl.*) the —, die Engländer, *m.pl.*

Englishman ['iŋgliʃmən], *s.* der Engländer.

Englishwoman ['iŋgliʃwumən], *s.* die Engländerin.

engrain [in'grein], *v.a.* tief einprägen.

engrave [in'greiv], *v.a.* gravieren, eingravieren (*art*); einprägen (*impress*).

engraver [in'greivə], *s.* der Graveur, der Kupferstecher.

engraving [in'greiviŋ], *s.* der Kupferstich.

engross [in'grous], *v.a.* ganz in Anspruch nehmen, gefangen halten (*mind*).

engulf [in'gʌlf], *v.a.* verschlingen.

enhance [in'hɑːns], *v.a.* erhöhen (*raise*); steigern (*increase*).

enhancement [in'hɑːnsmənt], *s.* die Erhöhung (*pleasure*); die Steigerung (*growth*).

enigma [i'nigmə], *s.* das Rätsel.

enigmatic(al) [enig'mætik(ə)l], *adj.* rätselhaft (*puzzling*); dunkel (*obscure*).

enjoin [in'dʒɔin], *v.a.* (an)befehlen (*s.o., Dat.*), einschärfen (*s.o., Dat.*).

enjoy [in'dʒɔi], *v.a.* genießen (*Acc.*); sich freuen (über, *Acc.*). — *v.r.* — *o.s.*, sich amüsieren.

enjoyable [in'dʒɔiəbl], *adj.* erfreulich, angenehm, genießbar.

enjoyment [in'dʒɔimənt], *s.* der Genuß, die Freude (*of*, an, *Dat.*).

enlarge [in'lɑːdʒ], *v.a.* vergrößern (*premises etc.*); erweitern (*expand*). —

v.n. sich verbreiten (*on* or *upon*, über, *Acc.*).

enlargement [in'lɑːdʒmənt], *s.* die Vergrößerung (*also Phot.*).

enlighten [in'laitn], *v.a.* erleuchten, aufklären (*explain to*).

enlightenment [in'laitnmənt], *s.* (*Eccl.*) die Erleuchtung;(*Phil.*)die Aufklärung.

enlist [in'list], *v.a.* anwerben (*Mil.*); gewinnen (*cooperation*). — *v.n.* (*Mil.*) sich anwerben lassen.

enliven [in'laivn], *v.a.* beleben, aufmuntern.

enmity ['enmiti], *s.* die Feindschaft.

ennoble [i'noubl], *v.a.* adeln; veredeln.

enormity [i'nɔːmiti], *s.* die Ungeheuerlichkeit.

enormous [i'nɔːməs], *adj.* ungeheuer; ungeheuerlich.

enough [i'nʌf], *adj., adv.* genug; ausreichend; sure —, gewiß!; well —, ziemlich gut.

enquire *see under* **inquire**.

enquiry *see under* **inquiry**.

enrage [in'reidʒ], *v.a.* wütend machen.

enraged [in'reidʒd], *adj.* wütend, entrüstet.

enrapture [in'ræptʃə], *v.a.* in Entzückung versetzen, entzücken (*delight*).

enrich [in'ritʃ], *v.a.* bereichern; (*Chem.*) verbessern.

enrol [in'roul], *v.a.* einschreiben (*inscribe*); (*Mil.*) anwerben. — *v.n.* sich einschreiben; beitreten (*Dat.*).

enrolment [in'roulmənt], *s.* die Einschreibung; — form, das Einschreibeformular.

ensconce [in'skɔns], *v.r.* — *o.s.*, sich niederlassen.

enshrine [in'ʃrain], *v.a.* umhüllen, einschließen; in einem Schrein aufbewahren.

enshroud [in'ʃraud], *v.a.* einhüllen.

ensign ['ensin or 'enzən, 'ensain], *s.* (*Naut.*) die Fahne, die Flagge; (*Mil. rank*) der Fähnrich.

enslave [in'sleiv], *v.a.* unterjochen, versklaven.

ensnare [in'snɛə], *v.a.* umgarnen, verführen (*seduce*).

ensue [in'sjuː], *v.n.* folgen.

ensure [in'ʃuə], *v.a.* versichern (*assure*); sicherstellen (*make sure*).

entail [in'teil], *v.a.* zur Folge haben, mit sich bringen.

entangle [in'tæŋgl], *v.a.* verwickeln, verwirren (*confuse*).

entanglement [in'tæŋglmənt], *s.* die Verwicklung; die Verwirrung (*confusion*).

enter ['entə], *v.a.* betreten; eintreten; — *o.'s name*, seinen Namen einschreiben. — *v.n.* eintreten (*in*, in, *Acc.*); — into agreement, einen Vertrag eingehen; — on, sich einlassen in (*Acc.*); — upon a career, eine Laufbahn antreten.

enterprise ['entəpraiz], *s.* das Unternehmen; das Wagnis (*daring*); private —, das Privatunternehmen; (*Econ.*)

die freie Wirtschaft; *public* —, **das** staatliche *or* Staatsunternehmen.

enterprising ['entəpraiziŋ], *adj.* unternehmungslustig.

entertain [entə'tein], *v.a.* unterhalten (*amuse*); zu Tisch haben (*person*); hegen (*opinion*).

entertaining [entə'teiniŋ], *adj.* amüsant, unterhaltend.

entertainment [entə'teinmənt], *s.* die Unterhaltung, Vergnügung.

enthral [in'θrɔːl], *v.a.* fesseln, bannen.

enthrone [in'θroun], *v.a.* auf den Thron bringen *or* setzen.

enthusiasm [in'θjuːziæzm], *s.* die Begeisterung; die Schwärmerei.

enthusiast [in'θjuːziæst], *s.* der Enthusiast, der Schwärmer.

enthusiastic [inθjuːzi'æstik], *adj.* enthusiastisch, begeistert, schwärmerisch.

entice [in'tais], *v.a.* locken, anlocken, verlocken (*lure*).

enticement [in'taismənt], *s.* die Lockung.

entire [in'taiə], *adj.* gesamt, ganz; völlig; vollständig (*complete*).

entirety [in'taiəriti], *s.* die Gesamtheit (*totality*); das Ganze (*total*).

entitle [in'taitl], *v.a.* berechtigen; betiteln (*title*).

entitlement [in'taitlmənt], *s.* die Berechtigung.

entity ['entiti], *s.* das Wesen.

entomb [in'tuːm], *v.a.* begraben.

entomologist [entə'mɔlədʒist], *s.* der Entomologe.

entomology [entə'mɔlədʒi], *s.* die Entomologie.

entrails ['entreilz], *s. pl.* die Eingeweide, *n.pl.*

entrain [in'trein], *v.a.* (*Railw.*, *Mil.*) einsteigen lassen. — *v.n.* (*Railw.*) (in den Zug) einsteigen.

entrance (1) [in'trɑːns], *s.* der Eingang (*door*); — *fee*, der Eintritt; — *hall*, der Hausflur, die Vorhalle; *university* —, Zulassung zur Universität.

entrance (2) [in'trɑːns], *v.a.* entzücken, hinreißen.

entrant ['entrənt], *s.* (*to school, university etc.*) der (neu) Zugelassene; Teilnehmer.

entrap [in'træp], *v.a.* fangen, verstricken.

entreat [in'triːt], *v.a.* anflehen, ersuchen.

entreaty [in'triːti], *s.* die flehentliche *or* dringende Bitte, (*obs.*) das Ansuchen.

entrench [in'trentʃ], *v.a.* verschanzen, festsetzen.

entrenchment [in'trentʃmənt], *s.* (*Mil.*) die Verschanzung.

entrust [in'trʌst], *v.a.* anvertrauen (*s. th.*); betreuen (*s.o. with*, mit, *Dat.*).

entry ['entri], *s.* das Eintreten, der Eintritt; der Eingang (*house*); (*Comm.*) die Eintragung (*book-keeping*); *double* —, doppelte Buchführung; die Einfuhr (*import*); — *permit*, **die**

Einreisebewilligung; *no* —, Eintritt verboten!

entwine [in'twain], *v.a.* verflechten, herumwickeln.

enumerate [i'njuːməreit], *v.a.* aufzählen.

enumeration [injuːmə'reiʃən], *s.* die Aufzählung.

enunciate [i'nʌnsieit], *v.a.* aussprechen.

enunciation [inʌnsi'eiʃən], *s.* (*Phonet.*) die Aussprache; die Kundgebung (*declaration*).

envelop [in'veləp], *v.a.* einhüllen, umhüllen.

envelope ['enviloup, 'ɔnvəloup], *s.* die Hülle; der Umschlag, Briefumschlag (*letter*).

enviable ['enviəbl], *adj.* beneidenswert.

envious ['enviəs], *adj.* neidisch (*of s.o.*, auf, *Acc.*).

environment [in'vaiərənmənt], *s.* die Umgebung; (*Geog.*, *Zool.*) die Umwelt.

environs [in'vaiərənz], *s. pl.* die Umgebung, die Umgegend.

envisage [in'vizidʒ], *v.a.* sich vorstellen.

envoy ['envɔi], *s.* (*Pol.*) der Gesandte, der Bote.

envy ['envi], *s.* der Neid. — *v.a.* beneiden.

epaulette [epə'let], *s.* (*Mil.*) das Achselstück, die Epaulette.

ephemeral [i'femərəl], *adj.* Eintags-, Tages-; eintägig, vergänglich (*transient*).

epic ['epik], *adj.* episch. — *s.* das Epos.

epicure ['epikjuə], *s.* der Epikureer, der Feinschmecker, der Genießer.

epidemic [epi'demik], *s.* die Epidemie.

epigram ['epigræm], *s.* das Epigramm.

epigrammatic [epigrə'mætik], *adj.* epigrammatisch, kurz; treffend (*apt*).

epilepsy ['epilepsi], *s.* (*Med.*) die Epilepsie, die Fallsucht.

epileptic [epi'leptik], *s.* (*Med.*) der Epileptiker.

epilogue ['epilɔg], *s.* der Epilog.

Epiphany [i'pifəni]. (*Eccl.*) das Fest der heiligen drei Könige, Epiphanias.

episcopal [i'piskəpəl], *adj.* bischöflich.

episcopate [i'piskəpit], *s.* die Bischofswürde, das Episkopat (*collective*).

episode ['episoud], *s.* die Episode.

epistle [i'pisl], *s.* die Epistel, das Sendschreiben.

epistolary [i'pistələri], *adj.* brieflich, Brief-.

epitaph ['epitaːf], *s.* die Grabschrift.

epithet ['epiθet], *s.* das Beiwort, die Benennung.

epitome [i'pitəmi], *s.* die Epitome, der Auszug; der Abriß (*summary*).

epitomize [i'pitəmaiz], *v.a.* kürzen; einen Auszug machen von (*Dat.*).

epoch ['iːpɔk], *s.* die Epoche; — - *making*, bahnbrechend.

equable ['ekwəbl], *adj.* gleich, gleichmäßig; gleichmütig (*tranquil*).

equal ['iːkwəl], *adj.* gleich, ebenbürtig (*to, Dat.*).

equality [i'kwɔliti], *s.* die Gleichheit, Ebenbürtigkeit.

equalization [i:kwəlai'zeiʃən], *s.* der Ausgleich; — *of burdens,* der Lastenausgleich.

equalize ['i:kwəlaiz], *v.a.* gleichmachen. — *v.n.* (*Footb.*) ausgleichen.

equanimity [i:kwə'nimiti], *s.* der Gleichmut.

equate [i'kweit], *v.a.* (*Maths.*) gleichsetzen.

equation [i'kweiʃən], *s.* die Gleichung.

equator[i'kweitə], *s.* (*Geog.*)der Äquator.

equatorial [ekwə'tɔ:riəl], *adj.* (*Geog.*) äquatorial.

equerry ['ekwəri], *s.* der Stallmeister; diensttuender Kammerherr (*of King*).

equestrian [i'kwestriən], *adj.* beritten; Reit-; — *art,* die Reitkunst.

equidistant [i:kwi'distənt], *adj.* gleich weit entfernt.

equilateral [i:kwi'lætərəl], *adj.* gleichseitig.

equilibrium [i:kwi'libriəm], *s.* das Gleichgewicht.

equine ['i:kwain], *adj.* Pferd-, pferdeartig.

equinoctial [i:kwi'nɔkʃəl], *adj.* äquinoktial.

equinox ['i:kwinɔks], *s.* die Tag- und Nachtgleiche.

equip [i'kwip], *v.a.* (*Mil.*) ausrüsten; ausstatten (*furnish*).

equipment [i'kwipmənt], *s.* die Ausrüstung, die Ausstattung; das Zeug.

equitable ['ekwitəbl], *adj.* unparteiisch, gerecht, billig.

equity ['ekwiti], *s.* die Billigkeit, die Unparteilichkeit.

equivalence [i'kwivələns], *s.* die Gleichwertigkeit, die Gleichheit.

equivalent [i'kwivələnt], *adj.* gleichwertig. — *s.* das Äquivalent, der gleiche Wert, der Gegenwert.

equivocal [i'kwivəkəl], *adj.* zweideutig, doppelsinnig, zweifelhaft.

era ['iərə], *s.* die Ära, die Zeitrechnung.

eradicate [i'rædikeit], *v.a.* ausrotten, austilgen, vertilgen.

eradication [irædi'keiʃən], *s.* die Ausrottung, die Vertilgung.

erase [i'reiz], *v.a.* ausradieren.

eraser [i'reizə], *s.* der Radiergummi (*India rubber*).

erasure [i'reiʒə], *s.* die Ausradierung; die Auskratzung (*scratching*).

ere [εə], *prep.* (*obs.*) vor. — *conj.* (*obs.*) ehe, bevor.

erect [i'rekt], *adj.* aufrecht, gerade. — *v.a.* aufrichten; errichten (*build*).

erection [i'rekʃən], *s.* die Errichtung (*structure*); die Aufrichtung (*putting up*).

ermine ['ə:min], *s.* der *or* das Hermelin.

erode [i'roud], *v.a.* (*Geog., Geol.*) ausfressen.

erosion [i'rouʒən], *s.* die Erosion.

erotic [i'rɔtik], *adj.* erotisch.

err [ə:], *v.n.* irren.

errand ['erənd], *s.* der Auftrag, Gang; der Botengang; — *boy,* der Laufbursche.

errant ['erənt], *adj.* herumstreifend; *knight* —, fahrender Ritter.

errata *see under* **erratum**.

erratic [i'rætik], *adj.* regellos, unberechenbar, ohne Verlaß.

erratum [e'reitəm, e'ra:təm], *s.* (*pl.* **errata** [e'reitə, e'ra:tə]) der Druckfehler.

erroneous [i'rouniəs], *adj.* irrig, irrtümlich.

error ['erə], *s.* der Irrtum, der Fehler.

erudite ['erudait], *adj.* gelehrt.

erudition [eru'diʃən], *s.* die Gelehrsamkeit.

erupt [i'rʌpt], *v.n.* ausbrechen.

eruption [i'rʌpʃən], *s.* der Ausbruch.

eruptive [i'rʌptiv], *adj.* Ausbruchs-, ausbrechend.

escalator ['eskəleitə], *s.* die Rolltreppe.

escapade [eskə'peid], *s.* der Streich (*prank*).

escape [is'keip], *v.a., v.n.* entkommen, entgehen, entfliehen.

escapism [is'keipizm], *s.* die Philosophie der Weltflucht.

escapist [is'keipist], *s.* der Weltflüchtling.

escarpment [is'ka:pmənt], *s.* die Böschung.

eschew [is'tʃu:], *v.a.* vermeiden.

escort [is'kɔ:t], *v.a.* geleiten; decken (*cover*). — ['eskɔ:t], *s.* (*Mil.*) die Garde, die Deckung; Begleitung (*persons*); (*Mil.*) das Geleit (*conduct*).

escutcheon [is'kʌtʃən], *s.* das Wappenschild.

esoteric [eso'terik], *adj.* (*Phil.*) esoterisch, geheim, dunkel.

espalier [es'pæljə], *s.* (*Mil.*) das Spalier.

especial [is'peʃəl], *adj.* besonder, außergewöhnlich.

espionage ['espiənɑːʒ *or* -nidʒ], *s.* die Spionage, das Spionieren.

espouse [is'pauz], *v.a.* (ver)-heiraten; (*fig.*) eintreten (für, *Acc.*).

espy [is'pai], *v.a.* ausspähen, erspähen.

essay [e'sei], *v.a.* versuchen, probieren. — ['esei], *s.* der Versuch; der Aufsatz, Essay (*composition*).

essayist ['esiist], *s.* der Essayist.

essence ['esəns], *s.* (*Phil., Chem.*) die Essenz.

essential [i'senʃəl], *adj.* wesentlich, wichtig (*important*).

establish [is'tæbliʃ], *v.a.* feststellen, (*ascertain*); gründen (*found*); —*ed Church,* die englische Staatskirche.

establishment [is'tæbliʃmənt], *s.* die Feststellung (*ascertainment*); die Gründung (*foundation*); die Unternehmung, das Geschäft (*business*); (*Mil.*) die Aufstellung, der Bestand; (*Eccl.*) die Staatskirche.

estate [is'teit], *s.* (*Pol.*) der Stand; das Vermögen; das Gut; (*property*) — *duty,* die Vermögensteuer; — *manager,* der Gutsverwalter; — *agent,* der

Grundstückmakler; *real* —, der Grundbesitz; (*pl.*) Immobilien, *pl.*

esteem [is'tiːm], *v.a.* schätzen (*value*); achten (*respect*). — *s.* die Wertschätzung, die Achtung.

estimable ['estiməbl], *adj.* schätzenswert.

estimate ['estimeit], *v.a.* schätzen (*evaluate*); berechnen (*calculate*). — ['estimit], *s.* die Schätzung, der Voranschlag.

estimation [esti'meiʃən], *s.* die Wertschätzung; die Achtung (*respect*).

Estonian [es'touniən], *adj.* estnisch, estländisch. — *s.* der Este, Estländer.

estrange [is'treindʒ], *v.a.* entfremden.

estrangement [is'treindʒmənt], *s.* die Entfremdung.

estuary ['estjuəri], *s.* die Mündung (*river*); der Meeresarm (*bay*).

etch [etʃ], *v.a.* (*Metall.*) ätzen; (*Art*) radieren.

etching ['etʃiŋ], *s.* (*Art*) die Radierung.

eternal [i'təːnl], *adj.* ewig; immerwährend.

eternity [i'təːniti], *s.* die Ewigkeit.

ether ['iːθə], *s.* der Äther.

ethereal [i'θiəriəl], *adj.* ätherisch, luftig

ethical ['eθikl], *adj.* ethisch, sittlich.

ethics ['eθiks], *s. pl.* die Ethik, die Sittenlehre; *professional* —, das Berufsethos.

Ethiopian [iːθi'oupiən], *adj.* äthiopisch. — *s.* der Äthiopier.

ethnography [eθ'nɔgrəfi], *s.* die Ethnographie, die Völkerkunde.

etymology [eti'mɔlədʒi], *s.* die Etymologie, die Wortableitung.

eucharist ['juːkərist], *s.* (*Eccl.*) die Eucharistie; das heilige Abendmahl.

eulogize ['juːlədʒaiz], *v.a.* loben, preisen.

euphonium [juˈfouniəm], *s.* (*Mus.*) das Bombardon, Baritonhorn.

euphony ['juːfəni], *s.* der Wohlklang.

European [juərə'piən], *adj.* europäisch. — *s.* der Europäer.

euphemism ['juːfimizm], *s.* der Euphemismus.

euphuism ['juːfjuizm], *s.* (*Lit.*) die gezierte Stilart.

evacuate [i'vækjueit], *v.a.* evakuieren, räumen.

evacuation [ivækju'eiʃən], *s.* die Evakuierung, die Räumung.

evade [i'veid], *v.a.* ausweichen (*Dat.*); entgehen (*escape, Dat.*).

evanescent [evə'nesənt], *adj.* verschwindend.

evangelical [iːvæn'dʒelikəl], *adj.* evangelisch.

evangelist [i'vændʒəlist], *s.* der Evangelist.

evangelize [i'vændʒəlaiz], *v.a.*, *v.n.* das Evangelium lehren *or* predigen.

evaporate [i'væpəreit], *v.a.* verdunsten lassen, verdampfen lassen. — *v.n.* (*Chem.*) verdunsten.

evaporation [ivæpə'reiʃən], *s.* die Verdampfung, die Verdunstung.

evasion [i'veiʒən], *s.* die Flucht (*escape*) (*from*, von, *Dat.*); die Ausflucht, das Ausweichen.

evasive [i'veiziv], *adj.* ausweichend.

eve, even (1) [iːv,iːvn], *s.* (*Poet.*) der Vorabend; Abend.

even (2) [iːvn], *adj.* eben, glatt (*smooth*); gerade (*number*); quitt (*quits*); gelassen (*temper*); gleich (*equal*). — *v.a.* — *out*, gleichmachen, ebnen.

even (3) [iːvn], *adv.* gerade, selbst, sogar (*emphatic*); *not* —, nicht einmal; — *though*, obwohl.

evening ['iːvniŋ], *s.* der Abend; — *gown*, das Abendkleid; — *dress*, der Abendanzug; der Smoking (*dinner jacket*); der Frack (*tails*).

evenness ['iːvənnis], *s.* die Ebenheit (*of surface*); die Gelassenheit (*of temper*).

event [i'vent], *s.* die Begebenheit, der Vorfall (*happening*); das (große) Ereignis (*state occasion*); *at all* —*s*, auf alle Fälle; *in the* —, im Falle, daß.

eventful [i'ventful], *adj.* ereignisreich.

eventual [i'ventjuəl], *adj.* schließlich, endlich.

ever ['evə], *adv.* je; immer, stets; nur, überhaupt; *for* —, für immer; — *so*, so sehr, sehr; — *since*, seitdem.

evergreen ['evəgriːn], *adj.* immergrün. — *s.* (*Bot.*) das Immergrün.

everlasting [evə'lɑːstiŋ], *adj.*ewig; dauernd; fortwährend (*continual*).

every ['evri], *adj.* jeder, jeder einzelne (*pl.* alle); — *one*, jeder einzelne; — *now and then*, dann und wann; — *other day*, jeden zweiten Tag; — *day*, alle Tage.

everybody, everyone ['evribɔdi, 'evriwʌn], *s.* jedermann, ein jeder.

everyday ['evridei], *adj.* alltäglich.

everyone *see under* **everybody**.

everything ['evriθiŋ], *s.* alles.

everywhere ['evrihweə], *adv.* überall.

evict [i'vikt], *v.a.* vertreiben (*eject*); (*Law*) (gerichtlich) kündigen (*Dat.*).

eviction [i'vikʃən], *s.* die Kündigung, die Vertreibung.

evidence ['evidəns], *s.* der Beweis (*proof*); (*Law*) das Zeugnis; *documentary* —, (*Law*) das Beweisstück; (*Law*) *give* —, eine Zeugenaussage machen.

evident ['evidənt], *adj.* klar, deutlich (*obvious*); augenscheinlich (*visible*); *self-* —, selbstverständlich.

evil [i'vil], *s.* das Übel, das Böse. — *adj.* übel, böse; — *speaking*, die üble Nachrede.

evildoer ['iːvilduːə], *s.* der Übeltäter.

evince [i'vins], *v.a.* zeigen, dartun, an den Tag legen.

evocation [iːvo'keiʃən], *s.* die Beschwörung (*magic*); das Hervorrufen.

evocative [i'vɔkətiv], *adj.* hervorrufend, voll Erinnerungen (*of, Genit.*).

evoke [i'vouk], *v.a.* hervorrufen (*call forth*); beschwören (*conjure up*).

evolution [iːvo'ljuːʃən, ev-], *s.* die Entwicklung, Evolution.

evolutionary [i:və'lju:ʃənri], *adj.* Evolutions-, Entwicklungs-.

evolve [i'vɔlv], *v.a.* entwickeln. — *v.n.* sich entwickeln.

ewe [ju:], *s.* (*Zool.*) das Mutterschaf.

ewer ['jua], *s.* die Wasserkanne.

exact [ig'zækt], *adj.* genau, gewissenhaft, exakt. — *v.a.* fordern; erpressen; eintreiben (*dept.*).

exacting [ig'zæktiŋ], *adj.* genau, anspruchsvoll.

exactitude [ig'zæktitju:d], *s.* die Genauigkeit.

exactly [ig'zæktli], *adv.* (*coll.*) ganz richtig!

exactness [ig'zæktnis], *s.* die Genauigkeit.

exaggerate [ig'zædʒəreit], *v.a.* übertreiben.

exaggeration [igzædʒə'reiʃən], *s.* die Übertreibung.

exalt [ig'zɔ:lt], *v.a.* erhöhen, erheben.

exaltation [egzɔ:l'teiʃən], *s.* die Erhöhung, die Erhebung.

exalted [ig'zɔ:ltid], *adj.* erhaben, hoch.

examination [igzæmi'neiʃən], *s.* die Prüfung; (*Med.*) die Untersuchung; (*Law*) das Verhör, das Untersuchungsverhör; die Ausfragung (*scrutiny*); — *board*, die Prüfungskommission.

examine [ig'zæmin], *v.a.* prüfen; (*Med.*) untersuchen; (*Law*) verhören; ausfragen.

examiner [ig'zæminə], *s.* der Examinator.

example [ig'zɑ:mpl], *s.* das Beispiel; *for* —, zum Beispiel; *set an* —, ein Beispiel geben.

exasperate [ig'zæspəreit], *v.a.* aufreizen; ärgern, aufbringen.

exasperation [igzæspə'reiʃən], *s.* die Entrüstung, die Erbitterung.

excavate ['ekskəveit], *v.a.* ausgraben.

excavation [ekskə'veiʃən], *s.* die Ausgrabung.

exceed [ik'si:d], *v.a.* überschreiten (*go beyond*); übertreffen (*surpass*). — *v.n.* zu weit gehen.

exceeding [ik'si:diŋ], *adj.* (*obs.*) übermäßig, übertrieben.

exceedingly [ik'si:diŋli], *adv.* außerordentlich; äußerst.

excel [ik'sel], *v.a.* übertreffen. — *v.n.* sich auszeichnen (*in*, in, *Dat.*).

excellence ['eksələns], *s.* die Vortrefflichkeit.

excellent ['eksələnt], *adj.* ausgezeichnet, hervorragend.

except [ik'sept], *v.a.* ausnehmen, ausschließen. — *conj.* außer (es sei denn) daß. — *prep.* ausgenommen, mit Ausnahme von (*Dat.*).

exception [ik'sepʃən], *s.* die Ausnahme (*exemption*); der Einwand, Einwurf (*objection*).

exceptionable [ik'sepʃənəbl], *adj.* anfechtbar (*disputable*); anstößig.

exceptional [ik'sepʃənəl], *adj.* außergewöhnlich.

exceptionally [ik'sepʃənəli], *adv.* ausnahmsweise.

excerpt [ik'sə:pt], *v.a.* ausziehen, exzerpieren. — ['eksə:pt], *s.* der Auszug, das Exzerpt.

excess [ik'ses], *s.* das Übermaß; *carry to* —, übertreiben; — *fare*, der Zuschlag; — *luggage*, das Übergewicht.

excessive [ik'sesiv], *adj.* übermäßig, allzuviel.

exchange [iks'tʃeindʒ], *s.* der Austausch; *stock* —, die Börse; *rate of* —, der Kurs; *bill of* —, der Wechsel; der Tausch (*barter*). — *v.a.* wechseln; tauschen (*barter*) (*against*, für, *Acc.*); austauschen (*messages etc.*).

exchangeable [iks'tʃeindʒəbl], *adj.* (*Comm.*) austauschbar.

exchequer [iks'tʃekə], *s.* die Staatskasse; das Finanzamt (*office*); *Chancellor of the Exchequer*, der Schatzkanzler.

excise (1) ['eksaiz], *s.* die Akzise; *customs and* —, das Zollamt, der Zoll; — *officer*, der Zollbeamte, Steuerbeamte.

excise (2) [ek'saiz], *v.a.* (her)ausschneiden.

excision [ek'siʒən], *s.* das Ausschneiden, die Entfernung.

excitable [ik'saitəbl], *adj.* erregbar, reizbar.

excitation [eksi'teiʃən], *s.* (*Phys.*, *Chem.*) die Erregung.

excitement [ik'saitmənt], *s.* die Erregung, Aufregung (*mood*).

exciting [ik'saitiŋ], *adj.* erregend, aufregend, packend (*thrilling*).

exclaim [iks'kleim], *v.a.* ausrufen.

exclamation [eksklə'meiʃən], *s.* der Ausruf (*interjection*); das Geschrei (*shouting*).

exclude [iks'klu:d], *v.a.* ausschließen.

exclusion [iks'klu:ʒən], *s.* der Ausschluß.

exclusive [iks'klu:siv], *adj.* ausschließlich (*sole*); exklusiv (*select*).

exclusiveness [iks'klu:sivnis], *s.* der exklusive Charakter, die Exklusivität.

excommunicate [ekskə'mju:nikeit], *v.a.* (*Eccl.*) von der Kirchengemeinde ausschließen, bannen, exkommunizieren.

excommunication [ekskəmju:ni'keiʃən], *s.* (*Eccl.*) die Exkommunikation, der Bann.

excoriate [eks'kɔ:rieit], *v.a.* häuten; abschälen (*peel*).

excrement ['ekskrimənt], *s.* das Exkrement, der Kot.

excrescence [iks'kresəns], *s.* der Auswuchs.

excretion [eks'kri:ʃən], *s.* die Ausscheidung, der Auswurf.

excruciate [iks'kru:ʃieit], *v.a.* martern, peinigen; *excruciatingly funny*, furchtbar komisch.

exculpate ['ekskʌlpeit], *v.a.* rechtfertigen, entschuldigen.

exculpation [ekskʌl'peiʃən], *s.* die Entschuldigung, die Rechtfertigung.

excursion [iks'kə:ʃən], *s.* der Ausflug, die Exkursion (*outing*); die Digression (*irrelevance*); der Abstecher (*deviation*).

excusable [iks'kju:zəbl], *adj.* entschuldbar, verzeihlich.

excuse [iks-'kju:s], *s.* die Entschuldigung. — [-'kju:z], *v.a.* entschuldigen (*Acc.*), verzeihen (*Dat.*).

execrable ['eksikrəbl], *adj.* abscheulich.

execrate ['eksikreit], *v.a.* verfluchen, verwünschen.

execute ['eksikju:t], *v.a.* ausführen (*carry out*); (*Law*) hinrichten (*kill*).

execution [eksi'kju:ʃən], *s.* die Ausführung (*of an order*); (*Law*) die Hinrichtung; die Pfändung (*official forfeit*).

executioner [eksi'kju:ʃənə], *s.* der Henker, der Scharfrichter.

executive [ik'sekjutiv], *adj.* ausübend, vollziehend (*of power etc.*). — *s.* (*Pol.*) die Exekutive; (*Comm.*) das Direktionsmitglied.

executor [ik'sekjutə], *s.* der Testamentsvollstrecker (*of a will*).

exemplar [ig'zemplə], *s.* das Muster, das Beispiel.

exemplary [ig'zempləri], *adj.* musterhaft, vorbildlich.

exemplify [ig'zemplifai], *v.a.* durch Beispiel(e) erläutern.

exempt [ig'zempt], *v.a.* ausnehmen, befreien, verschonen (*spare*).

exemption [ig'zempʃən], *s.* die Ausnahme.

exequies ['eksikwiz], *s. pl.* das Leichenbegängnis, die Totenfeier.

exercise ['eksəsaiz], *s.* die Übung (*practice*); die körperliche Betätigung (*exertion*). — *v.a.* üben; — *o.'s rights*, von seinen Rechten Gebrauch machen; — *discretion*, Diskretion walten lassen; (*Mil.*) — *troops*, exerzieren.

exert [ig'zə:t], *v.a.* ausüben; — *pressure*, Druck ausüben (*upon*, auf, *Acc.*). — *v.r.* — *o.s.*, sich anstrengen.

exertion [ig'zə:ʃən], *s.* die Anstrengung, die Bemühung.

exhalation [ekshə'leiʃən], *s.* die Ausatmung, die Ausdünstung.

exhale [eks'heil], *v.a.* ausatmen; aushauchen; ausdünsten.

exhaust [ig'zə:st], *v.a.* erschöpfen. — *s.* (*Motor.*) der Auspuff.

exhaustible [ig'zə:stibl], *adj.* erschöpflich.

exhaustion [ig'zə:stʃən], *s.* die Erschöpfung.

exhibit [ig'zibit], *v.a.* ausstellen (*display*); zeigen (*demonstrate*). — ['eksibit], *s.* das Ausstellungsobjekt; (*Law*) das Beweisstück.

exhibition [eksi'biʃən], *s.* die Ausstellung (*display*); (*Films*) die Vorführrung (*showing*); das Stipendium (*scholarship*).

exhibitioner [eksi'biʃənə], *s.* der Stipendiat.

exhilarate [ig'ziləreit], *v.a.* aufheitern.

exhilaration [igzilə'reiʃən], *s.* die Aufheiterung.

exhort [ig'zə:t], *v.a.* ermahnen.

exhortation [egzə:'teiʃən], *s.* die Ermahnung.

exigence, exigency ['eksidʒəns, -si], *s.* das Bedürfnis, Erfordernis (*necessity*); der dringende Notfall (*emergency*).

exigent ['eksidʒənt], *adj.* dringend.

exile ['eksail], *s.* der Verbannte (*person*); das Exil, die Verbannung (*state*). — *v.a.* verbannen; des Landes verweisen.

exist [ig'zist], *v.n.* existieren.

existence [ig'zistəns], *s.* das Dasein, die Existenz.

existent [ig'zistənt], *adj.* seiend, wirklich, existierend.

existentialism [egzis'tenʃəlizm], *s.* der Existentialismus.

exit ['eksit], *s.* der Ausgang; (*Theat.*) der Abgang.

exonerate [ig'zonəreit], *v.a.* entlasten.

exorbitant [ig'zə:bitənt], *adj.* übertrieben, übermäßig.

exorcise ['eksə:saiz], *v.a.* bannen, beschwören.

exorcism ['eksə:sizm], *s.* die Geisterbeschwörung.

exotic [ig'zətik], *adj.* exotisch.

expand [iks'pænd], *v.a.* erweitern, ausbreiten, ausdehnen. — *v.n.* sich erweitern (*broaden*); sich ausdehnen (*stretch*).

expansion [iks'pænʃən], *s.* die Ausdehnung, die Ausbreitung.

expansive [iks'pænsiv], *adj.* ausgedehnt; Ausdehnungs- (*forces*); (*fig.*) mitteilsam.

expatiate [iks'peiʃieit], *v.n.* sich verbreiten (*on*, über, *Acc.*).

expatriate [eks'peitrieit], *v.a.* verbannen.

expect [iks'pekt], *v.a.* erwarten (*wait for*); glauben (*believe*); hoffen (*hope for*); — *a baby*, ein Kind erwarten.

expectant [iks'pektənt], *adj.* schwanger (*with child*); voll Erwartung.

expectation [ekspek'teiʃən], *s.* die Erwartung, die Hoffnung.

expedience, expediency [iks'pi:diəns, -si], *s.* die Zweckmäßigkeit, die Schicklichkeit.

expedient [iks'pi:diənt], *adj.* zweckmäßig, schicklich, ratsam. — *s.* das Mittel; der Ausweg.

expedite ['ekspidait], *v.a.* beschleunigen.

expedition [ekspi'diʃən], *s.* (*Mil. etc.*) die Expedition; die schnelle Abfertigung.

expeditious [ekspi'diʃəs], *adj.* schleunig, schnell.

expel [iks'pel], *v.a.* vertreiben, austreiben; (*Sch.*) verweisen (*from*, von, aus).

expend [iks'pend], *v.a.* ausgeben.

expenditure [iks'penditʃə], *s.* (*Comm.*) die Ausgabe; der Aufwand (*of energy*).

expense

expense [iks'pens], *s.* die Ausgabe; (*pl.*) die Kosten, Auslagen, Spesen, *f. pl.*

expensive [iks'pensiv], *adj.* teuer, kostspielig.

experience [iks'piəriəns], *s.* die Erfahrung, das Erlebnis. — *v.a.* erfahren.

experienced [iks'piəriənsd], *adj.* erfahren.

experiment [iks'perimənt], *s.* das Experiment, der Versuch. — *v.n.* experimentieren, Versuche machen.

experimental [iksperi'mentl], *adj.* Probe-, probeweise, experimentell.

expert ['ekspə:t], *s.* der Fachmann; der Sachverständige.

expertise [ekspə'ti:z], *s.* die Expertise, die Fachkenntnis.

expertness [iks'pə:tnis], *s.* die Gewandtheit.

expiable ['ekspiəbl], *adj.* sühnbar.

expiation [ekspi'eiʃən], *s.* die Sühnung, die Sühne.

expiration [ekspi'reiʃən], *s.* das Ausatmen; (*fig.*) der Tod; der Ablauf (*time*); die Verfallszeit (*lapse of validity*).

expire [iks'paiə], *v.n.* aushauchen (*breathe*); ablaufen (*run out*); sterben (*die*).

expiry [iks'pairi], *s.* die Ablaufsfrist (*of papers*).

explain [iks'plein], *v.a.* erklären, erläutern.

explanation [eksplə'neiʃən], *s.* die Erklärung, Erläuterung.

expletive [iks'pli:tiv], *s.* das Fluchwort, der Kraftausdruck.

explicable ['eksplikəbl], *adj.* erklärlich, erklärbar.

explication [ekspli'keiʃən], *s.* die Erklärung.

explicit [iks'plisit], *adj.* ausdrücklich, deutlich.

explicitness [iks'plisitnis], *s.* die Deutlichkeit, die Bestimmtheit.

explode [iks'ploud], *v.n.* explodieren; (*Mil.*) platzen (*of a shell*). — *v.a.* explodieren lassen.

exploit [iks'ploit], *v.a.* ausbeuten; ausnützen (*utilize*). — ['eksploit], *s.* die Heldentat, die Großtat.

exploitation [eksploi'teiʃən], *s.* die Ausbeutung, die Ausnützung.

exploration [eksplɔ:'reiʃən], *s.* die Erforschung.

explore [iks'plɔ:], *v.a.* erforschen, untersuchen (*investigate*).

explosion [iks'plouʒən], *s.* die Explosion.

explosive [iks'plousiv], *adj.* explosiv. — *s.* der Sprengstoff.

exponent [iks'pounənt], *s.* (*Maths.*) der Exponent; der Vertreter (*of a theory*).

export [eks'pɔ:t], *v.a.* ausführen, exportieren. — ['ekspɔ:t], *s.* der Export, die Ausfuhr.

exporter [eks'pɔ:tə], *s.* der Exporteur, der Ausfuhrhändler, der Exportkaufmann.

expose [iks'pouz], *v.a.* entblößen; aussetzen (*to cold etc.*); bloßstellen (*display*); (*Phot.*) belichten; darlegen (*set forth*); ausstellen (*exhibit*).

exposition [ekspo'ziʃən], *s.* die Aussetzung; die Auslegung (*interpretation*); die Darlegung (*deposition, declaration*); die Ausstellung (*exhibition*).

exposure [iks'pouʒə], *s.* die Aussetzung (*to cold etc.*); die Bloßstellung; (*Phot.*) die Belichtung.

expostulate [iks'pɔstjuleit], *v.n.* zur Rede stellen.

expound [iks'paund], *v.a.* auslegen, darlegen.

express [iks'pres], *v.a.* ausdrücken; zum Ausdruck bringen. — *adj.* ausdrücklich, eilig, Eil-; besonder; — *letter*, der Eilbrief; — *train*, der Schnellzug. — *s.* der Eilzug.

expression [iks'preʃən], *s.* der Ausdruck.

expressive [iks'presiv], *adj.* ausdrucksvoll.

expressly [iks'presli], *adv.* ausdrücklich, besonders.

expropriate [eks'prouprieit], *v.a.* enteignen.

expropriation [eksproupri'eiʃən], *s.* die Enteignung.

expulsion [iks'pʌlʃən], *s.* die Ausstoßung; der Ausschluß; die Vertreibung (*of a large number*).

expunge [iks'pʌndʒ], *v.a.* austilgen, auslöschen.

expurgate ['ekspə:geit], *v.a.* reinigen.

exquisite ['ekskwizit], *adj.* auserlesen, vortrefflich.

extant ['ekstənt, ek'stænt], *adj.* noch vorhanden, existierend.

extempore [eks'tempəri], *adv.* aus dem Stegreif, extemporiert.

extemporize [eks'tempəraiz], *v.a.* extemporieren, improvisieren.

extend [iks'tend], *v.a.* ausdehnen (*boundaries etc.*); ausstrecken (*a helping hand*); verlängern (*time*); bieten (*a welcome*); erweitern (*enlarge*). — *v.n.* sich erstrecken, sich ausdehnen; dauern (*time*).

extensible [iks'tensibl], *adj.* ausdehnbar.

extension [iks'tenʃən], *s.* die Ausdehnung; die Verlängerung (*time*); *university — classes*, Abendkurse, *m. pl.* (der Erwachsenenbildung); (*Telephone*) der Apparat.

extensive [iks'tensiv], *adj.* ausgedehnt, umfassend.

extent [iks'tent], *s.* die Ausdehnung, die Weite; die Größe (*size*); *to a certain —*, bis zu einem gewissen Grade; *to the — of £x*, bis zu einem Betrage von x Pfund.

extenuate [iks'tenjueit], *v.a.* beschönigen; mildern; *extenuating circumstances*, (*Law*) mildernde Umstände, *m. pl.*

extenuation [ikstenju'eiʃən], *s.* die Beschönigung, die Abschwächung.

exterior [eks'tiəriə], *adj.* äußerlich. — *s.* das Äußere.

exterminate [iks'tə:mineit], *v.a.* ausrotten, vertilgen.

extermination [ikstə:mi'neiʃən], *s.* die Ausrottung, die Vertilgung.

external [eks'tə:nl], *adj.* äußerlich; auswärtig.

extinct [iks'tiŋkt], *adj.* ausgestorben.

extinction [iks'tiŋkʃən], *s.* das Erlöschen (*dying*); die Vernichtung (*annihilation*); das Aussterben.

extinguish [iks'tiŋgwiʃ], *v.a.* auslöschen; vernichten (*annihilate*). — *v.n.* auslöschen, ausgehen (*of fire or life*).

extirpate ['ekstə:peit], *v.a.* ausrotten.

extol [iks'toul], *v.a.* preisen, erheben.

extort [iks'tə:t], *v.a.* erpressen.

extortion [iks'tə:ʃən], *s.* die Erpressung.

extortionate [iks'tə:ʃənit], *adj.* erpresserisch.

extra ['ekstrə], *adj.* zusätzlich. — *s.* (*pl.*) die Nebenausgaben, *f. pl.*

extract [iks'trækt], *v.a.* (aus)ziehen (*pull out*). — ['ekstrækt], *s.* (*Chem.*) der Extrakt; der Auszug (*book*).

extraction [iks'trækʃən], *s.* das Ausziehen (*pulling out*); das Zahnziehen (*tooth*); das Verfertigen eines Auszuges (*book*); die Herkunft (*origin*).

extradite ['ekstrədait], *v.a.* (*Pol.*) ausliefern.

extradition [ekstrə'diʃən], *s.* (*Pol.*) die Auslieferung.

extraneous [eks'treiniəs], *adj.* nicht zur Sache gehörig, unwesentlich.

extraordinary [iks'trɔ:dnəri], *adj.* außerordentlich.

extravagance [iks'trævəgəns], *s.* die Extravaganz; die Verschwendung (*waste*).

extravagant [iks'trævəgənt], *adj.* extravagant; verschwenderisch.

extravaganza [ikstrævə'gænzə], *s.* fantastisches Werk, die Burleske, Posse.

extreme [iks'tri:m], *adj.* äußerst (*uttermost*); höchst (*highest*); extrem (*stringent*); letzt (*last*); — *unction*, (*Eccl.*) die Letzte Ölung; *in the* —, äußerst.

extremity [iks'tremiti], *s.* die äußerste Grenze (*limit*); die Notlage (*straits*, *emergency*); (*pl.*) die Extremitäten, *f. pl.*

extricate ['ekstrikeit], *v.a.* herauswinden, herauswickeln (*disentangle*), befreien.

extrude [eks'tru:d], *v.a.* ausstoßen (*Metall.*) ausziehen.

extrusion [eks'tru:ʒən], *s.* die Ausstoßung; die Ausziehung (*of steel etc.*).

exuberant [ig'zju:bərənt], *adj.* überschwenglich, überschäumend.

exude [ik'sju:d], *v.a.* ausschwitzen; von sich geben (*give out*).

exult [ig'zʌlt], *v.n.* frohlocken.

exultant [ig'zʌltənt], *adj.* triumphierend.

exultation [egzʌl'teiʃən], *s.* das Frohlocken, der Jubel.

eye [ai], *v.a.* ansehen, betrachten. — *s.* das Auge; — *of a needle*, das Nadelöhr; *an* — *for an* —, Aug' um Auge; — *witness*, der Augenzeuge.

eyeball ['aibɔ:l], *s.* der Augapfel.

eyebrow ['aibrau], *s.* die Augenbraue.

eyeglass ['aiglɑ:s], *s.* der Zwicker, Klemmer.

eyelash ['ailæʃ], *s.* die Augenwimper.

eyelid ['ailid], *s.* das Augenlid.

eyesight ['aisait], *s.* die Sehkraft, das Augenlicht.

eyrie ['ɛəri, 'iəri], *s.* der Adlerhorst.

F

F [ef]. das F (*also Mus.*).

fable [feibl], *s.* die Fabel; das Märchen.

fabric ['fæbrik], *s.* das Gewebe, der Stoff.

fabricate ['fæbrikeit], *v.a.* herstellen; (*fig.*) fabrizieren; erfinden.

fabrication [fæbri'keiʃən], *s.* (*fig.*) die Erdichtung, die Erfindung.

fabulous ['fæbjuləs], *adj.* fabelhaft; wunderbar.

façade [fə'sɑ:d], *s.* die Fassade.

face [feis], *v.a.* jemandem ins Gesicht sehen (*s.o.*); gegenüberstehen, gegenüberliegen (*lie opposite*, *Dat.*); — *west*, nach Westen gehen (*of house*, *window*). — *v.n.* — *about*, sich umdrehen. — *s.* das Gesicht, (*Poet.*) das Angesicht; — *to* — *with*, gegenüber (*Dat.*); *on the* — *of it*, auf den ersten Blick; *lose* —, sich blamieren; *have the* — *to*, die Frechheit haben etwas zu tun.

facet ['fæsit], *s.* die Facette; der Zug (*feature*).

facetious [fə'si:ʃəs], *adj.* scherzhaft.

facetiousness [fə'si:ʃəsnis], *s.* die Scherzhaftigkeit, die Witzigkeit.

facile ['fæsail], *adj.* leicht.

facilitate [fə'siliteit], *v.a.* erleichtern, leicht machen.

facility [fə'siliti], *s.* die Leichtigkeit (*ease*); die Gewandtheit (*deftness*); die Möglichkeit (*possibility*); (*pl.*) die Einrichtungen, die Möglichkeiten, *f. pl.* (*amenities*).

facing ['feisiŋ], *s.* (*Tail.*) der Besatz, der Aufschlag; (*Build.*) die Verkleidung; (*Mil.*) die Schwenkung, die Wendung.

facsimile [fæk'simili], *s.* das Faksimile.

fact [fækt], *s.* die Tatsache; *as a matter of* —, tatsächlich, in Wirklichkeit; —*s and figures*, der Bericht mit Tatsachen und Zahlen; *in* —, tatsächlich; *in point of* —, in der Tat, in Wirklichkeit.

faction ['fækʃən], *s.* (*Pol.*) die Partei, die Faktion.

factitious [fæk'tiʃəs], *adj.* nachgemacht, künstlich.

factor ['fæktə], *s.* der Faktor; (*Comm.*) der Agent; der Umstand (*fact*).

factory

factory ['fæktəri], *s.* die Fabrik; — *hand*, der Fabrikarbeiter.
factual ['fæktjuel], *adj.* Tatsachen-, tatsächlich.
faculty ['fækəlti], *s.* (*Univ.*) die Fakultät; die Fähigkeit (*sense*); (*pl.*) die Talente, *n. pl.*, die Begabung; Kräfte, *f. pl.*
fad [fæd], *s.* die Grille, die Laune; die Marotte.
faddy ['fædi], *adj.* schrullig.
fade [feid], *v.n.* verschießen (*colour*); verwelken (*flower*); vergehen.
fag [fæg], *v.a.* ermüden. — *v.n.* (*Sch.*) Dienste tun, Diener sein (*for*, für). — *s.* die Plackerei; (*coll.*) die Zigarette; (*Sch.*) der Fuchs, der neue Schüler; — *end*, der Zigarettenstummel; (*Naut.*) das offene Tauende; der letzte Rest (*remnant*).
faggot ['fægət], *s.* das Reisigbündel.
fail [feil], *v.a.* im Stiche lassen (*let down*); (*Sch.*) durchfallen (*an examination*, in einer Prüfung). — *v.n.* — *to do*, etwas nicht tun, fehlgehen, scheitern; versagen.
failing ['feiliŋ], *adj.* schwach, versagend. — *s.* der Mangel, Fehler.
failure ['feiljə], *s.* der Fehlschlag; das Versagen (*weakness*); das Nichteinhalten (*non-compliance*); das Durchfallen (*in examinations*); der Versager (*person*).
fain [fein], *adv.* (*obs.*) gern, gerne.
faint [feint], *v.n.* in Ohnmacht fallen, ohnmächtig werden. — *adj.* leise, schwach (*noise etc.*); — *hearted*, kleinmütig.
fair (1) [fɛə], *adj.* hübsch, schön (*beautiful*); unparteiisch, fair (*impartial*); anständig, angemessen (*equitable*); blond.
fair (2) [fɛə], *s.* der Jahrmarkt (*market*); (*Comm.*) die Messe, die Handelsmesse.
fairness ['fɛənis], *s.* die Schönheit (*beauty*); die Unparteilichkeit, Fairneß (*objectivity*); die Sportlichkeit (*sportsmanship*); die Anständigkeit (*equity*).
fairy ['fɛəri], *s.* die Fee.
faith [feiθ], *s.* der Glaube; die Treue (*loyalty*); das Vertrauen (*trust*).
faithful ['feiθful], *adj.* (*Rel.*) gläubig; treu (*loyal*); ergeben (*devoted*).
faithless ['feiθlis], *adj.* (*Rel.*) ungläubig; treulos, untreu (*disloyal*).
fake [feik], *s.* der Schwindel.
falcon ['fɔ:(l)kən], *s.* (*Orn.*) der Falke.
falconer ['fɔ:(l)knə], *s.* der Falkner.
falconry ['fɔ:(l)kənri], *s.* die Falknerei.
fall [fɔ:l], *v.n. irr.* fallen, abfallen (*leaves*); einbrechen (*night*); sich legen (*wind*); heruntergehen, sinken (*price*); geboren werden (*pigs, lambs*); — *through*, mißlingen, zunichte werden. — *s.* der Fall; (*Am.*) der Herbst (*autumn*); der Abhang (*precipice*); der Verfall (*decay*); der Untergang (*decline*).
fallacious [fə'leifəs], *adj.* trügerisch, trüglich, falsch (*assumption etc.*).

fallacy ['fæləsi], *s.* die Täuschung, der Irrtum, Trugschluß.
fallible ['fælibl], *adj.* fehlbar.
falling ['fɔ:liŋ], *s.* das Fallen; — *sickness*, die Fallsucht; — *off*, das Abnehmen (*decrease*); — *out*, der Zwist, der Streit (*disunity*). — *adj.* — *star*, die Sternschnuppe.
fallow (1) ['fælou], *adj.* brach.
fallow (2) ['fælou], *adj.* fahl.
false [fɔ:ls], *adj.* falsch, unrichtig (*untrue*); — *alarm*, der blinde Alarm; — *bottom*, der Doppelboden; — *start*, der Fehlstart; — *step*, der Fehltritt; — *verdict*, das Fehlurteil; — *pretences*, die Vorspiegelung falscher Tatsachen.
falsehood ['fɔ:lshud], *s.* die Lüge, die Unwahrheit.
falseness ['fɔ:lsnis], *s.* die Falschheit; die Unaufrichtigkeit (*insincerity*).
falsify ['fɔl:sifai], *v.a.* (ver-)fälschen.
falsity ['fɔ:lsiti] *see* falseness.
falter ['fɔ:ltə], *v.n.* straucheln (*stumble*); stammeln (*stammer*).
fame [feim], *s.* der Ruhm; der Ruf; *ill* —, der üble Ruf.
familiar [fə'miljə], *adj.* vertraut, wohlbekannt, intim; gewohnt (*habitual*); *be on* — *terms*, auf vertrautem Fuß stehen.
familiarity [fəmili'æriti], *s.* die Vertrautheit, die Vertraulichkeit (*intimacy*).
familiarize [fə'miljəraiz], *v.a.* vertraut machen, bekannt machen.
family ['fæmili], *s.* die Familie; — *doctor*, der Hausarzt; (*Chem.*) die Gruppe; *be in the* — *way*, in anderen Umständen sein, guter Hoffnung sein, schwanger sein; — *tree*, der Stammbaum.
famine ['fæmin], *s.* die Hungersnot; — *relief*, Hilfe für die Hungernden.
famish ['fæmiʃ], *v.n.* verhungern, hungern; verschmachten.
famous ['feiməs], *adj.* berühmt, wohlbekannt (*for*, wegen).
fan [fæn], *s.* der Fächer (*lady's*); der Ventilator; (*sl.*) der leidenschaftliche Anhänger, der Fan; (*coll.*) Fanatiker (*admirer*). — *v.a.* fächeln; anfachen (*flames*); entfachen (*hatred*). — *v.n.* (*Mil.*) — *out*, sich ausbreiten, ausschwärmen.
fanatic [fə'nætik], *s.* der Fanatiker.
fanatical [fə'nætikəl], *adj.* fanatisch.
fanaticism [fə'nætisizm], *s.* der Fanatismus, die Schwärmerei.
fancier ['fænsiə] *s.* *pigeon* —, der Taubenzüchter; *bird* —, der Vogelzüchter.
fanciful ['fænsiful], *adj.* schwärmerisch, wunderlich.
fancy ['fænsi], *s.* die Vorliebe (*preference*); die Phantasie; die Laune (*whim*); *take a* — *to*, leibgewinnen. — *adj.* — *dress*, der Maskenanzug, das Kostüm; — *goods*, Galanteriewaren; — *cakes*, Torten, *f.pl.*; das Feingebäck. — *v.a.* denken, gern haben; (*coll.*) — *oneself*, sich einbilden, man sei; *just*—! denk doch mal! denk mal an!

fanfare ['fænfɛə], s. (Mus.) die Fanfare, der Tusch.

fang [fæŋ], s. (Zool.) der Hauzahn, der Giftzahn (of snake); (Engin.) der Zapfen. — v.a. (Engin.) vollpumpen, aufpumpen und in Tätigkeit setzen.

fanlight ['fænlait], s. die Lünette, das Lichtfenster.

fantastic(al) [fæn'tæstik(əl)], adj. fantastisch.

fantasy ['fæntəsi], s. (Poet., Mus.) die Phantasie; das Hirngespinst (chimæra).

far [fɑː], adj. weit; fern, entfernt (distant). — adv. — and wide, weit und breit; by —, bei weitem; go too —, zu weit gehen; he will go —, er wird seinen Weg machen; — sighted, weitsichtig.

farce [fɑːs], s. die Farce, die Posse.

fare [fɛə], s. das Fahrgeld; der Fahrpreis (of taxi etc.); der Fahrgast (one travelling in taxi); — stage, die Fahr or Teilstrecke; das Essen, die Kost (food); bill of —, die Speisekarte. — v.n. ergehen (Dat.), daran sein.

farewell [fɛə'wel], interj. lebewohl! — dinner, das Abschiedsessen; — party, die Abschiedsgesellschaft.

farinaceous [færi'neiʃəs], adj. mehlig, aus Mehl.

farm [fɑːm], s. der Pachthof, der Bauernhof; die Farm; — hand, der Landarbeiter, der Farmarbeiter; — bailiff, der Gutsverwalter. — v.a. bebauen; — out, verpachten. — v.n. Landwirt sein.

farmer ['fɑːmə], s. der Bauer, Landwirt; der Pächter (tenant).

farmland ['fɑːmlænd], s. das Ackerland.

farmyard ['fɑːmjɑːd], s. der Bauernhof, Gutshof.

farrier ['færiə], s. der Hufschmid.

farrow ['færou], s. der Wurf (pigs). — v.n. ferkeln, Junge haben.

farther ['fɑːðə], comp. adj., adv. ferner, weiter.

farthest ['fɑːðist], superl. adj., adv. fernst, weitest.

farthing ['fɑːðiŋ], s. der Farthing, der Heller.

fascinate ['fæsineit], v.a. bezaubern, faszinieren.

fascination [fæsi'neiʃən], s. die Bezauberung; der Reiz, der Zauberbann (spell).

fascism ['fæʃizm], s. (Pol.) der Faschismus.

fashion ['fæʃən], s. die Mode; out of —, außer Mode; die Art und Weise (manner). — v.a. gestalten, bilden (shape); fully —ed, vollgeformt or geformt, angepaßt.

fashionable ['fæʃnəbl], adj. modisch, modern; elegant.

fast (1) [fɑːst], adj. schnell (runner); fest (firm); my watch is —, meine Uhr geht vor; a — woman, eine leichtlebige Frau; — train, der Schnellzug; — and furious, schnell wie der Wind. — adv. fest.

fast (2) [fɑːst], v.n. (Rel.) fasten; (Rel.) — day, der Fasttag.

fasten [fɑːsn], v.a. festbinden, festmachen (fix). — v.n. sich festhalten (on to, an, Dat.).

fastidious [fəs'tidiəs], adj. wählerisch, anspruchsvoll.

fastidiousness [fəs'tidiəsnis], s. die anspruchsvolle Art.

fat [fæt], adj. fett; dick (person). — s. das Fett; (Cul.) das Speisefett.

fatal ['feitəl], adj. tödlich (lethal); verhängnisvoll.

fatalism ['feitəlizm], s. der Fatalismus.

fatality [fə'tæliti], s. das Verhängnis; der Todesfall; der tödliche Unfall.

fate [feit], s. das Schicksal, Geschick; das Verhängnis (doom, destiny).

fated ['feitid], adj. dem Verderben (Untergang) geweiht.

fateful ['feitful], adj. verhängnisvoll, unselig.

father ['fɑːðə], s. der Vater; (Eccl.) Pater; — -in-law, der Schwiegervater. — v.a. Vater sein or werden von (Dat.); zeugen (procreate).

fatherland ['fɑːðəlænd], s. das Vaterland.

fatherly ['fɑːðəli], adj. väterlich; wie ein Vater.

fathom ['fæðəm], s. die Klafter. — v.a. ergründen, erforschen.

fatigue [fə'tiːg], s. die Ermüdung, die Erschöpfung; (Mil.) der Arbeitsdienst. — v.a. ermüden, erschöpfen.

fatling ['fætliŋ], s. (Agr.) das Mastvieh.

fatness ['fætnis], s. die Beleibtheit (person); die Fettheit (animals).

fatten [fætn], v.a. — up, mästen (animals); fett werden lassen. — v.n. fett werden, sich mästen (an, Dat.).

fatty ['fæti], adj. (Chem.) fett, fettig. — s. (coll.) der Dickwanst.

fatuity [fə'tjuːiti], s. die Albernheit, die Dummheit.

fatuous ['fætjuəs], adj. albern, dumm, nichtssagend.

faucet ['fɔːsit], s. der Zapfen, der Hahn.

fault [fɔːlt], s. der Fehler; die Schuld; find — with, etwas kritisieren; tadeln; it is my —, es ist meine Schuld; at —, im Irrtum.

faultless ['fɔːltlis], adj. fehlerlos, fehlerfrei.

faultlessness ['fɔːltlisnis], s. die Fehlerlosigkeit, die fehlerlose Ausführung.

faulty ['fɔːlti], adj. fehlerhaft, mangelhaft.

faun [fɔːn], s. (Myth.) der Faun.

fauna ['fɔːnə], s. die Fauna, die Tierwelt.

favour ['feivə], s. die Gunst, das Wohlwollen; (Comm.) in — of, zugunsten; do a —, einen Gefallen tun or erweisen; be in —, sehr begehrt sein, in hoher Gunst stehen. — v.a. bevorzugen, begünstigen, wohlwollend gegenüberstehen (Dat.).

favourable ['feivərəbl], adj. günstig, vorteilhaft.

favourite

favourite ['feivərit], s. der Favorit, der Liebling; der Günstling (of kings). — adj. Lieblings-, bevorzugt.

fawn (1) [fɔ:n], s. (Zool.) das junge Reh, das Rehkalb; — coloured, rehfarben. — adj. rehfarben, hellbraun.

fawn (2) [fɔ:n], v.n. schmeicheln, kriecherisch sein ((up)on, Dat.).

fawning ['fɔ:niŋ], adj. kriecherisch, kriechend.

fear [fiə], s. die Furcht, die Angst; stand in — of s.o., sich vor jemandem fürchten; for — of, aus Angst vor (Dat.). — v.a. fürchten, befürchten.

fearful ['fiəful], adj. furchtsam (full of fear); furchtbar (causing fear).

fearless ['fiəlis], adj. furchtlos (of, vor, Dat.).

fearlessness ['fiəlisnis], s. die Furchtlosigkeit.

feasibility [fi:zi'biliti], s. die Tunlichkeit, die Möglichkeit.

feasible ['fi:zibl], adj. tunlich, möglich.

feast [fi:st], s. das Fest, der Festtag; der Schmaus (good meal). — v.n. schmausen (upon, von, Dat.). — v.a. festlich bewirten.

feat [fi:t], s. die Tat, die Heldentat; das Kunststück.

feather ['feðə], s. die Feder; show the white —, Feigheit an den Tag legen; — bed, das Federbett. — v.a. federn; — o.'s nest, sein Schäfchen ins Trockene bringen.

feature ['fi:tʃə], s. der Zug (characteristic); der Gesichtszug (facial). — v.a. charakterisieren; (Film) in der Hauptrolle zeigen.

February ['februəri], der Februar.

feckless ['feklis], adj. hilflos, unfähig.

feculence ['fekjuləns], s. (Chem.) der Bodensatz, der Hefesatz.

fecund ['fekənd], adj. fruchtbar.

fecundate ['fekəndeit], v.a. fruchtbar machen, befruchten.

fecundity [fi'kʌnditi], s. die Fruchtbarkeit.

federacy ['fedərəsi], s. der Bund, die Föderation.

federal ['fedərəl], adj. Bundes-, föderativ.

federalism ['fedərəlizm], s. der Föderalismus.

federalize ['fedərəlaiz], v.a. verbünden.

federation [fedə'reiʃən], s. die Föderation, die Verbündung; (Pol.) der Bund.

fee [fi:], s. die Gebühr (official dues); das Honorar (of doctor etc.); (pl.) (Sch.) das Schulgeld.

feeble [fi:bl], adj. schwach, matt; — minded, schwachsinnig.

feed [fi:d], v.a. irr. füttern; verkösten (humans); unterhalten (maintain); zuführen (into machine, Dat.); be fed up with, etwas satt haben; — pipe, die Speiseröhre. — v.n. sich nähren (on, von, Dat.); weiden (graze).

feeder ['fi:də], s. der Kinderlatz (bib); (Tech.) der Zubringer.

feel [fi:l], v.n. irr. sich fühlen (sense); meinen (think). — v.a. berühren, betasten (touch); empfinden (be aware of).

feeler ['fi:lə], s. der Fühler; put out a —, einen Fühler ausstrecken.

feeling ['fi:liŋ], s. das Gefühl; with —, bewegt, gerührt (moved); grimmig (in anger).

feign [fein], v.a. vortäuschen, heucheln.

feint [feint], s. die Verstellung (disguise); die Finte (fencing).

felicitate [fi'lisiteit], v.a. Glück wünschen (upon, zu, Dat.), beglückwünschen (Acc.).

felicitation [filisi'teiʃən], s. die Beglückwünschung, der Glückwunsch.

felicitous [fi'lisitəs], adj. glücklich ausgedrückt, gut gesagt (in speaking).

felicity [fi'lisiti], s. die Glückseligkeit; die glückliche Ausdruckweise (style).

feline ['fi:lain], adj. Katzen-, katzenartig.

fell (1) [fel], adj. grausam; at one — swoop, mit einem wilden Schwung.

fell (2) [fel], v.a. fällen (timber); töten (kill).

fell (3) [fel], s. das Gebirge, das Felsengelände.

fell (4) [fel], s. das Fell, die Haut (skin).

fellow ['felou], s. der Gefährte, Genosse (companion); das Mitglied eines College or einer Universität; (coll.) der Kerl; queer —, seltsamer Kauz; — feeling, das Mitgefühl; — traveller, der Weggenosse; (Pol.) der Mitläufer.

fellowship ['felouʃip], s. die Mitgliedschaft (einer Hochschule etc.) (membership); die Freundschaft (friendship); good —, die Geselligkeit.

felly, felloe ['feli, 'felou], s. die Radfelge.

felon ['felən], s. der Verbrecher.

felonious [fi'louniəs], adj. verbrecherisch.

felt [felt], s. der Filz.

female ['fi:meil], adj. weiblich. — s. (Zool.) das Weibchen.

feminine ['feminin], adj. weiblich. — s. (Gram.) das weibliche Geschlecht; das Weibliche.

fen [fen], s. das Moor, das Marschland.

fence [fens], s. der Zaun, das Staket. — v.a. umzäunen, einzäunen (enclose). — v.n. fechten (fight with rapiers).

fencing ['fensiŋ], s. die Einzäunung (fence); das Fechten (with rapiers); — master, der Fechtmeister.

fend [fend], v.a. — off, abwehren, parieren. — v.n. — for oneself, sich allein behelfen.

fennel [fenl], s. (Bot.) der Fenchel.

ferment [fə:'ment], v.a. zur Gärung bringen. — v.n. gären, fermentieren. — ['fə:ment], s. das Gärmittel (also fig.); (Chem.) das Gärungsprodukt.

fermentation [fə:men'teiʃən], s. die Gärung.

fern [fə:n], s. (Bot.) das Farnkraut.

ferocious [fə'rouʃəs], adj. wild, grimmig.

ferocity [fə'rɔsiti], s. die Wildheit.
ferret ['ferit], s. (Zool.) das Frett, das Frettchen. — v.a. — out, ausspüren.
ferry ['feri], s. die Fähre. — v.a. — across, hinüberrudern, hinüberfahren, übersetzen.
fertile ['fə:tail], adj. fruchtbar.
fertility [fə'tiliti], s. die Fruchtbarkeit.
fertilize ['fə:tilaiz], v.a. befruchten.
fertilizer ['fə:tilaizə], s. das Düngemittel, der Dünger.
fervent ['fə:vənt], adj. inbrünstig (prayer); heiß (wish).
fervid ['fə:vid], adj. glühend, heiß (with zeal).
fervour ['fə:və], s. die Inbrunst (prayer); die Sehnsucht (wish).
fester ['festə], v.n. schwären, eitern.
festival ['festivəl], s. das Fest, die Festspiele, n. pl.
festive ['festiv], adj. festlich, Fest-.
festivity [fes'tiviti], s. die Festlichkeit.
festoon [fes'tu:n], s. die Girlande. — v.a. behängen, mit Girlanden verzieren, schmücken.
fetch [fetʃ], v.a. holen, bringen.
fetching ['fetʃiŋ], adj. einnehmend.
fetter ['fetə], v.a. fesseln, binden. — s. (pl.) die Fesseln, f. pl.
feud [fju:d], s. die Fehde.
feudal ['fju:dl], adj. feudal, Lehns-.
fever ['fi:və], s. das Fieber.
few [fju:], adj. einige; wenige; a — , ein paar.
fiancé [fi'ɔ:nsei], s. der Verlobte, Bräutigam.
fiancée [fi'ɔ:nsei], s. die Verlobte, Braut.
fib [fib], s. (coll.) die Lüge. — v.n. (coll.) lügen.
fibre ['faibə], s. die Fiber, Faser.
fibrous ['faibrəs], adj. faserartig.
fickle [fikl], adj. unbeständig, wankelmütig.
fiction ['fikʃən], s. die Erdichtung (figment); (Lit.) die Romanliteratur.
fictitious [fik'tiʃəs], adj. erdichtet, in der Phantasie.
fiddle [fidl], s. (coll.) die Geige, Fiedel, Violine. — v.n. (coll., Mus.) geigen; schwindeln (cheat).
fiddlesticks! [fidlstiks], int. Unsinn!
fidelity [fi'deliti], s. die Treue (loyalty); Genauigkeit; (Engin.) high — , Präzision, High Fidelity.
fidget ['fidʒit], v.n. unruhig sein.
fidgety ['fidʒiti], adj. nervös.
fie! [fai], int. pfui!
field [fi:ld], s. das Feld; (fig.) das Gebiet; — glass, der Feldstecher; (Hunt.) — sports, die Feldübungen, der Jagdsport. — v.a., v.n. abfangen, abpassen (cricket).
fiend [fi:nd], s. der Unhold, böse Geist; fresh air — , ein Freund der frischen Luft.
fiendish ['fi:ndiʃ], adj. teuflisch, boshaft.
fierce [fiəs], adj. wild, wütend (beast); — weather, — cold, die grimmige Kälte, der grimmige Winter.

fiery ['faiəri], adj. feurig; hitzig.
fife [faif], s. (Mus.) die Querpfeife.
fifteen [fif'ti:n], num. adj. fünfzehn.
fifth [fifθ], num. adj. der fünfte.
fifty ['fifti], num. adj. fünfzig.
fig [fig], s. (Bot.) die Feige.
fight [fait], v.a., v.n. irr. kämpfen, bekämpfen (in battle); raufen (of boys). — s. der Kampf; die Rauferei.
figment ['figmənt], s. die Erdichtung.
figurative ['figjuərətiv], adj. bildlich (style).
figure ['figə], s. die Figur (body); die Gestalt, Form (shape); (Maths.) die Zahl, die Ziffer; cut a — , einen Eindruck machen; a fine — of a man! ein fabelhafter Kerl! — v.a. — out, ausdenken, ausrechnen. — v.n. eine Rolle spielen, rangieren.
figured ['figəd], adj. figuriert.
figurehead ['figəhed], s. der scheinbare Leiter, die Representationsfigur.
filament ['filəmənt], s. der Faden, der Glühfaden (bulb).
filbert ['filbə:t], s. (Bot.) die Haselnuß.
filch [filtʃ], v.a. stehlen, klauen.
file [fail], s. (Engin.) die Feile; (Mil.) die Reihe; (Comm.) der Aktenstoß, das Aktenbündel, der Ordner; (pl.) die Akten, f. pl.; single — , im Gänsemarsch; rank and — , die große Masse; on the — , in den Akten. — v.a. feilen (metal); zu den Akten legen (papers); einreichen (petition).
filial ['filiəl], adj. kindlich.
filibuster ['filibastə], s. der Freibeuter; (Am.) (Pol.) die Obstruktion.
filigree ['filigri:], s. die Filigranarbeit.
filing ['failiŋ], s. (pl.) die Feilspäne; das Einheften (of papers); — cabinet, die Kartei.
fill [fil], v.a. füllen; ausfüllen (place, job); plombieren (tooth); — up, tanken (with petrol). — s. das volle Maß; eat o.'s — , sich satt essen.
fillet ['filit], s. das Filet (meat); das Band, die Binde (band).
filling ['filiŋ], s. die Plombe (in tooth); — station, die Tankstelle.
filly ['fili], s. das Füllen.
film [film], s. der Film (cinema, Phot.); die Haut, das Häutchen (skin); der Belag (coating). — v.a. aufnehmen, verfilmen, filmen (photograph).
filter ['filtə], v.a. filtrieren, filtern. — v.n. durchfiltern. — s. das Filter.
filth [filθ], s. der Schmutz.
filthy ['filθi], adj. schmutzig.
filtration [fil'treiʃən], s. das Filtrieren, das Durchsickern.
fin [fin], s. (Zool.) die Finne, die Flosse.
final [fainl], adj. letzt, endlich; endgültig. — s. (Sport) die Endrunde, das Endspiel.
finale [fi'nɑ:li], s. (Mus.) das Finale.
finality [fai'næliti], s. die Endgültigkeit.
finance [fi'næns or 'fai-], s. die Finanz, das Finanzwesen. — v.a. finanzieren.

financial [fi'nænʃəl], *adj.* finanziell, Geld-, Finanz-.

finch [fintʃ], *s.* (*Orn.*) der Fink.

find [faind], *v.a. irr.* finden; — *fault with*, jemanden kritisieren; *all found*, volle Verpflegung (inbegriffen). — *s.* der Fund.

finding ['faindiŋ], *s.* das Finden, der Befund; (*Law*) der Wahrspruch.

fine (1) [fain], *adj.* fein (*delicate*); dünn (*thin*); schön (*beautiful*); scharf (*distinct*); großartig(*splendid*).

fine (2) [fain], *v.a.* zu einer Geldstrafe verurteilen. — *s.* die Geldstrafe.

finery ['fainəri], *s.* der Putz; (*Engin.*) der Frischofen.

finger ['fiŋgə], *s.* der Finger; *have a — in the pie*, die Hand im Spiel haben. — *v.a.* berühren, antasten.

finish ['finiʃ], *v.a.* beenden, fertig machen, vollenden; —*ing touch*, die lezte Hand. — *v.n.* aufhören, enden. — *s.* das Ende (*end*); der letzte Schliff; die Appretur, die Fertigung.

finite ['fainait], *adj.* endlich.

Finn [fin], *s.* der Finne.

Finnish ['finiʃ], *adj.* finnisch.

fir [fə:], *s.* (*Bot.*) die Föhre, die Tanne; — *cone*, der Tannenzapfen.

fire [faiə], *s.* das Feuer; — *brigade*, die Feuerwehr; — *damp*, (*Min.*) schlagende Wetter, *n.pl.*; — *engine*, die Feuerspritze; — *extinguisher*, der Löschapparat, Feuerlöscher; — *escape*, die Rettungsleiter. — *v.a.* brennen (*clay*); anzünden, in Gang setzen (*furnace*); anspornen (*enthuse*); (*coll.*) entlassen (*dismiss*). — *v.n.* feuern (*at*, auf, *Acc.*).

firebrand ['faiəbrænd], *s.* der Aufwiegler.

fireman ['faiəmən], *s.* der Heizer.

fireplace ['faiəpleis], *s.* der Kamin.

fireproof ['faiəpru:f], *adj.* feuerfest.

fireside ['faiəsaid], *s.* der (häusliche) Herd, der Kamin.

firewood ['faiəwud], *s.* das Brennholz.

firework ['faiəwə:k], *s.* (*usually pl.*) das Feuerwerk.

firm [fə:m], *adj.* fest, hart (*solid*); entschlossen (*decided*). — *s.* die Firma.

firmament ['fə:məmənt], *s.* das Firmament, Himmelsgewölbe; der Sternenhimmel.

firmness ['fə:mnis], *s.* die Festigkeit, Entschlossenheit.

first [fə:st], *num. adj., adv.* erst; zuerst; — *of all*, zuallererst; — *born*, erstgeboren; — *rate*, erstklassig. — *s. from the* —, von Anfang an.

fiscal ['fiskəl], *adj.* fiskalisch, von der Staatskasse, Finanz-.

fish [fiʃ], *s.* der Fisch; *like a — out of water*, nicht in seinem Element; *a queer* —, ein seltsamer Kauz; — *bone*, die Gräte. — *v.n.* fischen; — *for compliments*, nach Lob haschen, nach Komplimenten fischen.

fisherman ['fiʃəmən], *s.* der Fischer.

fishery ['fiʃəri], *s.* der Fischfang.

fishing ['fiʃiŋ], *s.* das Fischen, der Fischfang; — *fly*, die Angelfliege; — *line*, die Angelschnur; — *rod*, die Angelrute; — *tackle*, das Angelgerät.

fishy ['fiʃi], *adj.* (*coll.*) anrüchig, verdächtig.

fissile ['fisail], *adj.* (*Phys.*) spaltbar.

fission ['fiʃ(ə)n], *s.* (*Phys.*) die Spaltung.

fist [fist], *s.* die Faust; *hand over* —, im Überfluß; *tight* —*ed*, geizig.

fisticuffs ['fistikʌfs], *s.* die Schlägerei, das Raufen.

fistula ['fistjulə], *s.* (*Anat.*) die Fistel.

fit (1) [fit], *v.a.* passen, anpassen (*Dat.*); einfügen (— *into s.th.*); — *in*, hineinpassen; — *on a suit*, einen Anzug anprobieren (*Dat.*); — *for a career*, zu einer Laufbahn vorbereiten; — *out*, ausrüsten. — *v.n.* passen, sich fügen (— *into*); — *in*, passen (*in*, zu, *Dat.*). — *adj.* geeignet, fähig (*suitable*); — *to drop*, todmüde; gesund, stark (*healthy*); schicklich (*proper*); (*Sport*) in guter Form.

fit (2) [fit], *s.* der Anfall; *by* —*s and starts*, ruckweise.

fitful ['fitful], *adj.* launenhaft; unbeständig.

fitness ['fitnis], *s.* die Tauglichkeit (*health*); die Schicklichkeit (*propriety*); die Fähigkeit (*ability*) (*Sport*) die gute Form.

fitter ['fitə], *s.* der Monteur.

fitting, fitment ['fitiŋ, 'fitmənt], *s.* die Armatur; die Montage. — *adj.* passend (*suitable*); geeignet (*appropriate*).

five [faiv], *num. adj.* fünf.

fiver ['faivə], *s.* (*coll.*) die Fünfpfundnote.

fix [fiks], *v.a.* festmachen, befestigen (*make firm*); festsetzen (*a time*); (*Am.*) herrichten, anrichten (*a meal*); — *with a glare* or *stare*, mit den Augen fixieren, scharf ansehen; — *up* (*coll.*), etwas erledigen (*something*); bedienen (*serve s.o.*). — *s.* (*coll.*) die Klemme, die Schwierigkeit, das Dilemma.

fixture ['fikstʃə], *s.* (*Sport*) die Veranstaltung; das Inventarstück (*furniture*).

fizz [fiz], *v.n.* brausen (*drink*).

fizzle ['fizl], *v.n.* zischen (*flame*); — *out*, verebben, ausgehen, zunichte werden; (*Am.*, *coll.*) durchfallen (*fail in school*).

fizzy ['fizi], *adj.* mit Kohlensäure, sprudelnd.

flabbergast ['flæbəga:st], *v.a.* (*coll.*) verblüffen.

flabby ['flæbi], *adj.* schlaff.

flaccid ['flæksid], *adj.* schlapp, schlaff.

flag (1) [flæg], *s.* (*Mil.*) die Flagge; die Fahne; — *officer*, der Flaggoffizier; —*staff*, die Fahnenstange.

flag (2) [flæg], *v.n.* ermatten, erschlaffen.

flag (3) [flæg], *s.* (—*stone*) der Fliessstein, die Fliese. — *v.a.* mit Fliesen auslegen, mit Fliessteinen pflastern.

flagon ['flægən], *s.* die Doppelflasche.
flagrant ['fleigrənt], *adj.* entsetzlich (*shocking*); schamlos (*impudent*).
flail [fleil], *s.* der Dreschflegel.
flair [flɛə], *s.* der Instinkt; (*coll.*) die Nase (*for*, für, *Acc.*).
flake [fleik], *s.* die Flocke. — *v.n.* — *off*, abblättern.
flame [fleim], *s.* die Flamme; (*coll.*) *old* —, die (alte) Liebe, Geliebte(r), die Flamme. — *v.n.* flammen, lodern.
flamingo [flə'mingou], *s.* (*Orn.*) der Flamingo.
flange [flændʒ], *s.* (*Engin.*) der Flan(t)sch.
flank [flæŋk], *s.* die Flanke, die Seite; die Weiche (*of animal*). — *v.a.* flankieren.
flannel [flænl], *s.* der Flanell.
flap [flæp], *s.* die Klappe; das Ohrläppchen (*earlobe*); der Flügelschlag (— *of wings*).
flare [flɛə], *v.n.* flammen, flackern; — *up*, aufbrausen (*in temper*). — *s.* das Aufflammen, das Aufflackern; die Leuchtkugel.
flash [flæʃ], *s.* der Blitz (*of lightning*); das Afflammen; (*phot.*) —*light*, das Blitzlicht. — *v.a.* aufflammen lassen, aufblitzen lassen. — *v.n.* aufflammen, aufblitzen.
flashy ['flæʃi], *adj.* großtuend, angeberisch (*bragging*); buntfarbig (*gaudy*).
flask [flɑːsk], *s.* die kleine Flasche, das Fläschchen.
flat [flæt], *adj.* flach, eben; abgestanden, schal (*drink*); (*Mus.*) zu tief, vermindert; platt, albern (*conversation*); — *footed*, plattfüßig; — *tyre*, die Panne. — *adv.* — *out*, ausgepumpt, erschöpft. — *s.* die Mietwohnung, Wohnung (*lodgings*); (*Mus.*) das B; (*pl.*) das Flachland; (*Theat.*) (*pl.*) die Bühnenbilder, *n. pl.*
flatness ['flætnis], *s.* die Flachheit, die Plattheit (*of conversation etc.*).
flatten [flætn], *v.a.* flach machen; glätten (*smooth*).
flatter ['flætə], *v.a.* schmeicheln (*Dat.*).
flattery ['flætəri], *s.* die Schmeichelei.
flaunt [flɔːnt], *v.a.* prahlen, prunken (*s.th.*, mit, *Dat.*).
flavour ['fleivə], *s.* der Geschmack, die Würze; das Aroma; die Blume (*bouquet of wine*). — *v.a.* würzen.
flaw [flɔː], *s.* der Riß (*chink*); der Fehler (*fault*).
flawless ['flɔːlis], *adj.* fehlerlos.
flax [flæks], *s.* (*Bot.*) der Flachs.
flay [flei], *v.a.* schinden, die Haut abziehen (*Dat.*).
flea [fliː], *s.* (*Ent.*) der Floh.
fleck [flek], *v.a.* sprenkeln.
fledge [fledʒ], *v.a.* befiedern; *fully* —*d*, flügge; selbständig.
fledgling ['fledʒliŋ], *s.* der Grünschnabel, der Novize.
flee [fliː], *v.a., v.n.* irr. fliehen, entfliehen (*from*, von, *Dat.*); flüchten (vor, *Dat.*).

fleece [fliːs], *s.* das Vlies. — *v.a.* scheren (*sheep*); ausnützen (*exploit*); berauben.
fleet [fliːt], *s.* die Flotte. — *adj.* (*Poet.*) schnellfüßig.
Fleming ['flemiŋ], *s.* der Flame.
Flemish ['flemiʃ], *adj.* flämisch.
flesh [fleʃ], *s.* das (lebende) Fleisch; die Frucht (*of fruit*).
flex [fleks], *s.* (*Elec.*) die Kontaktschnur.
flexible ['fleksibl], *adj.* biegsam; (*fig.*) anpassungsfähig.
flexion ['flekʃən], *s.* (*Gram.*) die Flexion, die Biegung.
flick [flik], *s.* der leichte Schlag. — *v.a.* leicht schlagen, berühren.
flicker ['flikə], *s.* das Flackern, das Flimmern. — *v.n.* flackern, flimmern.
flight [flait], *s.* (*Aviat.*) der Flug; die Flucht (*escape*); — *of stairs*, die Treppe, Treppenflucht.
flimsy ['flimzi], *adj.* hauchdünn (*material*); schwach (*argument*).
flinch [flintʃ], *v.n.* zurückweichen, zurückzucken (*from*, vor, *Dat.*).
fling [fliŋ], *v.a. irr.* schleudern, werfen, — *s.* der Wurf; *highland* —, schottischer Tanz; *have a last* —, sich zum letzten Mal austoben.
flint [flint], *s.* der Feuerstein.
flippancy ['flipənsi], *s.* die Leichtfertigkeit.
flippant ['flipənt], *adj.* leichtfertig, leichtsinnig, schnippisch.
flirt [fləːt], *v.n.* flirten, liebeln, (*with*, mit, *Dat.*).
flirtation [flə'teiʃən], *s.* die Liebelei.
flit [flit], *v.n.* hin und her flitzen; huschen.
flitch [flitʃ], *s.* die Speckseite.
flitter ['flitə], *v.n.* flattern.
float [flout], *v.n.* obenauf schwimmen, dahingleiten; —*ing ice*, das Treibeis. — *v.a.* schwimmen lassen; (*Naut.*) flott machen; (*Comm.*) gründen (*a company*); ausgeben (*a loan*). — *s.* das Floß (*raft*); der ausgeschmückte Wagen (*decorated vehicle*).
flock [flok], *s.* die Herde (*sheep*). — *v.n.* zusammenlaufen, sich scharen.
floe [flou], *s.* die Eisscholle.
flog [flog], *v.a.* peitschen (*whip*); antreiben; (*coll.*) verkaufen; — *a dead horse*, sich umsonst bemühen.
flood [flʌd], *s.* die Flut; das Hochwasser, die Überschwemmung (*flooding*); (*fig.*) die Fülle; — *gate*, die Schleuse. — *v.a.* überfluten, überschütten (*with requests*). — *v.n.* überschwemmen (*of river*).
floodlight ['flʌdlait], *s.* das Flutlicht, Scheinwerferlicht.
floor [flɔː], *s.* der Boden, der Fußboden; das Stockwerk, der Stock (*storey*); *from the* —, aus dem Plenum; — *walker*, die Aufsicht (*in stores*). — *v.a.* zu Boden strecken, überrumpeln (*surprise*).
flop [flop], *v.n.* (*coll.*) hinsinken, hinplumpsen; versagen (*fail*). — *s.* der Versager, Mißerfolg (*play*, *film etc.*).

Florentine

Florentine ['flɔrəntain], *adj.* florentinisch. — *s.* der Florentiner.

florid ['flɔrid], *adj.* blühend; überladen.

florin ['flɔrin], *s.* das Zweischillingstück.

florist ['flɔrist], *s.* der Blumenhändler.

flotsam ['flɔtsəm], *s.* das Strandgut, Wrackgut.

flounce (1) [flauns], *v.n.* hastig bewegen.

flounce (2) [flauns], *v.a.* mit Falbeln besetzen (*dress*). — *s.* die Falbel (*on dress*).

flounder (1) ['flaundə], *v.n.* umhertappen, unsicher sein.

flounder (2) ['flaundə], *s.* (*Zool.*) die Flunder.

flour ['flauə], *s.* das Mehl.

flourish ['flʌriʃ], *v.n.* blühen; wirken; gedeihen (*thrive*); schnörkeln, verzieren (*in writing*); Fanfaren blasen, schmettern (*trumpets*). — *s.* der Schnörkel; der Trompetenstoß, Tusch (*of trumpets*).

flout [flaut], *v.a.* verhöhnen, verspotten. — *s.* der Hohn, der Spott.

flow [flou], *v.n. irr.* fließen; strömen. — *s.* der Fluß (*of water, goods etc.*); — *of words*, der Redeschwall.

flower ['flauə], *s.* die Blume; die Blüte (*blossom*). — *v.n.* blühen, in Blüte stehen.

flowery ['flauəri], *adj.* gewählt, umständlich, geziert (*style*).

fluctuate ['flʌktjueit], *v.n.* schwanken.

fluctuation [flʌktju'eiʃen], *s.* das Schwanken.

flue [flu:], *s.* der Rauchfang (*of chimney*).

fluency ['flu:ənsi], *s.* das fließende Sprechen, die Geläufigkeit.

fluent ['flu:ənt], *adj.* geläufig, fließend.

fluid ['flu:id], *adj.* fließend, flüssig (*liquid*). — *s.* die Flüssigkeit.

fluke [flu:k], *s.* der glückliche Zufall (*chance*).

flunkey ['flʌŋki], *s.* der Diener, der Bediente.

flurry ['flʌri], *s.* die Unruhe; die Aufregung (*excitement*).

flush (1) [flʌʃ], *s.* das Erröten (*blushing*); die Aufwallung (*of anger*). — *v.a.* nachspülen (*basin*); erröten machen (*make blush*). — *v.n.* erröten.

flush (2) [flʌʃ], *adj.* in gleicher Ebene, eben.

flush (3) [flʌʃ], *v.a.* (*Hunt.*) aufscheuchen.

fluster ['flʌstə], *v.a.* verwirren (*muddle*); aufregen (*excite*).

flute [flu:t], *s.* (*Mus.*) die Flöte; (*Carp.*) die Hohlkehle. — *v.a.* (*Carp., Archit.*) aushöhlen. — *v.n.* (*Mus.*) flöten, Flöte spielen.

flutter ['flʌtə], *v.n.* flattern, unruhig sein. — *s.* die Unruhe.

flux [flʌks], *s.* das Fließen; *be in* —, in der Schwebe sein.

fly [flai], *v.a. irr.* wehen lassen, hissen (*flag*). — *v.n. irr.* (*Aviat.*) fliegen;

fliehen (*escape*); eilen (*hurry*). — *s.* (*Ent.*) die Fliege.

flyleaf ['flaili:f], *s.* das Vorsatzblatt.

flying ['flaiiŋ], *adj.* fliegend, Flug-; — *squad*, das Überfallkommando.

flyover ['flaiouvə], *s.* die Brückenkreuzung, Überführung.

flywheel ['flaiwi:l], *s.* das Schwungrad.

foal [foul], *s.* (*Zool.*) das Füllen. — *v.n.* fohlen.

foam [foum], *s.* der Schaum; — *rubber*, der Schaumgummi. — *v.n.* schäumen.

fob [fɔb], *v.a.* — *off*, abfertigen, abspeisen.

focus ['foukəs], *s.* der Brennpunkt; der Mittelpunkt (*of interest*). — *v.a.* (*Phot.*) einstellen. — *v.n.* — *upon*, sich konzentrieren auf (*Acc.*).

fodder ['fɔdə], *s.* das Futter.

foe [fou], *s.* der Feind.

fog [fɔg], *s.* der Nebel.

fogey ['fougi], *s.* der Kerl, Kauz.

foible [fɔibl], *s.* die Schwäche, die schwache Seite.

foil (1) [fɔil], *v.a.* vereiteln.

foil (2) [fɔil], *s.* die Folie; der Hintergrund (*background*).

foil (3) [fɔil], *s.* das Florett (*fencing*).

foist [fɔist], *v.a.* aufschwatzen (*upon, Dat.*).

fold (1) [fould], *v.a.* falten (*clothes etc.*); umarmen (*in o.'s arms*). — *v.n.* schließen, sich falten. — *s.* die Falte; (*Geol.*) die Vertiefung.

fold (2) [fould], *s.* die Herde (*sheep*); *return to the* —, zu den Seinen zurückkehren.

folder ['fouldə], *s.* die Mappe (*papers*); das Falzbein.

folding ['fouldiŋ], *adj.* Klapp-; — *chair*, der Klappstuhl; — *door*, die Flügeltür.

foliage ['fouljidʒ], *s.* (*Bot.*) das Laub.

folio ['fouliou], *s.* das Folio, der Foliant.

folk [fouk], *s.* (*also pl.*) die Leute; (*pl.*) (*Am.*) Freunde (*mode of address*).

folklore ['fouklɔ:] *s.* die Volkskunde.

folksong ['fouksɔŋ], *s.* das Volkslied.

follow ['fɔlou], *v.a., v.n.* folgen (*Dat.*); — *suit*, dasselbe tun, Farbe bekennen.

follower ['fɔlouə], *s.* der Anhänger (*supporter*); der Nachfolger (*successor*); *camp* —, der Mitläufer.

folly ['fɔli], *s.* die Narrheit; die törichte Handlung (*action*).

foment [fo'ment], *v.a.* anregen (*stimulate*); pflegen (*cultivate*); warm baden.

fond [fɔnd], *adj.* zärtlich, lieb; *be* — *of*, gern haben.

fondle [fɔndl], *v.a.* liebkosen.

fondness ['fɔndnis], *s.* die Zärtlichkeit, die (Vor-)liebe.

font [fɔnt], *s.* der Taufstein (*baptismal*).

food [fu:d], *s.* die Nahrung, Speise (*nourishment*); Lebensmittel (*n.pl.*); das Futter (*for animals*); *some* —, etwas zum Essen; — *store*, das Lebensmittelgeschäft.

fool [fu:l], *s.* der Narr, Tor. — *v.a.* zum Narren halten, übertölpeln.

foolish ['fuːliʃ], *adj.* töricht, albern, närrisch (*person*); unsinnig (*act*).

foolscap ['fuːlskæp], *s.* das Kanzlei-papier.

foot [fut], *s.* der Fuß; *on* —, zu Fuß; — *board*, das Trittbrett; *put o.'s* — *in it*, eine taktlose Bemer-kung fallen lassen, ins Fettnäpfchen treten. — *v.a.* — *the bill*, bezahlen.

footage ['futidʒ], *s.* die Länge in Fuß.

football ['futbɔːl], *s.* der Fußball.

footbridge ['futbridʒ], *s.* der Steg.

footing ['futiŋ], *s.* die Grundlage, Basis.

footlight ['futlait], *s.* (*usually pl.*) die Rampenlichter, *n. pl.*

footman ['futmən], *s.* der Bediente.

footprint ['futprint], *s.* die Fußstapfe.

footstool ['futstuːl], *s.* der Schemel.

fop [fɔp], *s.* der Geck.

for [fɔː], *prep.* für (*Acc.*); anstatt (*Genit.*) (*instead of*); *in exchange* —, für, um; — *example*, zum Beispiel; *heaven's sake*, um Himmels willen; — *two days*, zwei Tage lang; auf zwei Tage; seit zwei Tagen; *now you are* — *it!* jetzt hast du's! *as* — *me*, meinet-wegen, was mich anbelangt; — *all that*, trotz alledem. — *conj.* denn, weil.

forage ['fɔridʒ], *s.* das Futter. — *v.n.* furagieren.

forasmuch [fɔrəz'mʌtʃ], *conj.* (*obs.*) — *as*, insofern als.

foray ['fɔrei], *s.* der Raubzug.

forbear [fɔː'bɛə], *v.a. irr.* vermeiden, unterlassen (*avoid*); sich enthalten (*abstain*). — *v.n.* (geduldig) hinneh-men, ertragen.

forbid [fə'bid], *v.a. irr.* verbieten; *God* —*!* Gott behüte!

forbidding [fə'bidiŋ], *adj.* ab-schreckend.

force [fɔːs], *s.* (*Phys.*) die Kraft; die Macht (*might*); die Gewalt (*brute* —); (*pl.*) die Streitkräfte, *f. pl.*; (*Phys.*) die Kräfte. — *v.a.* zwingen, nötigen.

forceful ['fɔːsful], *adj.* kräftig, ener-gisch, kraftvoll.

forceps ['fɔːseps], *s.* (*Med.*) die Zange; die Pinzette.

forcible ['fɔːsibl], *adj.* heftig, stark (*strong*); gewaltsam (*violent*).

ford [fɔːd], *s.* die Furt.

fore- [fɔː], *pref.* Vorder-, vorder.

forebear ['fɔːbɛə], *s.* der Vorfahre.

forebode [fɔː'boud], *v.a.* voraussagen, vorbedeuten.

forecast [fɔː'kaːst], *v.a.* vorhersagen, voraussagen. — ['fɔːkaːst], *s.* die Vor-hersage.

foreclose [fɔː'klouz], *v.a.* ausschließen.

forefather ['fɔːfaːðə], *s.* der Ahne, der Vorvater.

forefinger ['fɔːfiŋgə], *s.* (*Anat.*) der Zeigefinger.

forego [fɔː'gou], *v.a. irr.* vorhergehen.

foreground ['fɔːgraund], *s.* der Vorder-grund.

forehead ['fɔrid], *s.* die Stirne.

foreign ['fɔrin], *adj.* fremd; auslän-disch.

foreigner ['fɔrinə], *s.* der Fremde, der Ausländer.

foreland ['fɔːlənd], *s.* das Vorgebirge.

foreman ['fɔːmən], *s.* der Werkführer, Vorarbeiter.

foremast ['fɔːmaːst], *s.* (*Naut.*) der Fockmast.

foremost ['fɔːmoust], *adj.* vorderst, vornehmlichst, führend. — *adv.* zuerst; *first and* —, zuallererst.

forenoon ['fɔːnuːn], *s.* der Vormittag.

forensic [fɔ'rensik], *adj.* forensisch, gerichtsmedizinisch.

forerunner ['fɔːrʌnə], *s.* der Vorläufer.

foresail ['fɔːseil, 'fɔːsəl], *s.* (*Naut.*) das Focksegel.

foresee [fɔː'siː], *v.a. irr.* vorhersehen.

foreshadow [fɔː'ʃædou], *v.a.* vorher andeuten.

foreshorten [fɔː'ʃɔːtn], *v.a.* verkürzen.

foresight ['fɔːsait], *s.* die Vorsorge, der Vorbedacht.

forest ['fɔrist], *s.* der Wald; der Urwald (*jungle*).

forestall [fɔː'stɔːl], *v.a.* vorwegnehmen, zuvorkommen (*Dat.*).

forester ['fɔristə], *s.* der Förster.

forestry ['fɔristri], *s.* die Forstwissen-schaft (*science*); das Forstwesen (*management*).

foretaste ['fɔːteist], *s.* der Vorge-schmack.

foretell [fɔː'tel], *v.a. irr.* voraussagen.

forethought ['fɔːθɔːt], *s.* der Vorbe-dacht.

forewarn [fɔː'wɔːn], *v.a.* warnen.

forfeit ['fɔːfit], *s.* das Pfand (*pledge*); die Einbuße (*fine*); (*pl.*) das Pfänder-spiel. — *v.a.* verlieren, verwirken.

forfeiture ['fɔːfitʃə], *s.* die Verwirkung, die Einbuße, der Verlust.

forge [fɔːdʒ], *s.* die schmieden (*iron*); fälschen (*falsify*). — *v.n.* — *ahead*, sich vorwärtsarbeiten. — *s.* die Schmiede (*iron*); der Eisenhammer (*hammer*).

forget [fə'get], *v.a., v.n. irr.* vergessen; —*me-not*, das Vergißmeinnicht.

forgetful [fə'getful], *adj.* vergeßlich.

forgive [fə'giv], *v.a., v.n. irr.* vergeben, verzeihen.

forgo [fɔː'gou], *v.a. irr.* verzichten; aufgeben.

fork [fɔːk], *s.* die Gabel; die Abzwei-gung (*road*). — *v.n.* sich gabeln, sich spalten.

forlorn [fɔː'lɔːn], *adj.* verlassen, ver-loren, elend.

form [fɔːm], *s.* die Form, die Gestalt (*shape*); die Formalität (*formality*); das Formular (*document*); *in good* —, (*Sport*) in guter Form; *bad* —, gegen den guten Ton; *a matter of* —, eine Formsache. — *v.a.* formen, gestalten (*shape*); bilden (*an association etc. of*, über, *Acc.*).

formal ['fɔːməl], *adj.* formal, äußer-lich; formell.

formality [fɔː'mæliti], *s.* die For-malität.

formation [fɔːˈmeiʃən], s. (Mil.) die Formation; (Geol.) die Bildung; die Formung; die Aufstellung (sports team).

former [ˈfɔːmə], adj. früher, vorig.

formidable [ˈfɔːmidəbl], adj. schrecklich, furchtbar.

formula [ˈfɔːmjulə], s. die Formel.

formulate [ˈfɔːmjuleit], v.a. formulieren.

forsake [fɔːˈseik], v.a. irr. verlassen, im Stich lassen.

forsooth [fɔːˈsuːθ], adv. (Poet.) wahrlich, wirklich!

forswear [fɔːˈswɛə], v.a. irr. abschwören; — oneself, einen Meineid schwören.

fort [fɔːt], s. das Fort, die Festung.

forth [fɔːθ], adv. vorwärts; weiter (further); and so —, und so weiter (u.s.w.); fort (away).

forthcoming [fɔːθˈkʌmiŋ], adj. bevorstehend.

forthwith [fɔːθˈwiθ], adv. sogleich.

fortieth [ˈfɔːtiəθ], num. adj. vierzigst. — s. der Vierzigste.

fortification [fɔːtifiˈkeiʃən], s. die Befestigung.

fortify [ˈfɔːtifai], v.a. befestigen; bestärken.

fortitude [ˈfɔːtitjuːd], s. die Tapferkeit.

fortnight [ˈfɔːtnait], s. vierzehn Tage, m. pl.

fortress [ˈfɔːtris] see fort.

fortuitous [fɔːˈtjuːitəs], adj. zufällig.

fortunate [ˈfɔːtʃənit], adj. glücklich, günstig.

fortune [ˈfɔːtjuːn], s. das Glück, das Schicksal; das Vermögen (wealth); — teller, die Wahrsagerin.

forty [ˈfɔːti], num. adj. vierzig.

forward [ˈfɔːwəd], adj. vorder (in front); voreilig, vorlaut (rash); früh (early). — adv. vorne; — march! vorwärts! carry —, (Comm.) übertragen. — s. (Footb.) der Stürmer; — line, der Angriff. — v.a. weiterleiten, expedieren; (letter) please—, bitte nachsenden.

forwardness [ˈfɔːwədnis], s. die Frühreife; die Voreiligkeit, Dreistigkeit.

fossil [ˈfɔsil], s. das Fossil.

foster [ˈfɔstə], v.a. nähren (feed); aufziehen (bring up); — a thought, einen Gedanken hegen; — mother, die Pflegemutter; — brother, der Pflegebruder.

foul [faul], adj. schmutzig; faul (rotten). — v.a. beschmutzen. — v.n. (Footb.) einen Verstoß begehen. — s. (Footb.) der Verstoß.

found (1) [faund], v.a. gründen, begründen.

found (2) [faund], v.a. (Metall.) gießen (cast).

foundation [faunˈdeiʃən], s. das Fundament; die Unterlage; die Begründung, die Gründung (initiation); die Stiftung (establishment); — stone, der Grundstein.

founder (1) [ˈfaundə], s. der Gründer, Stifter.

founder (2) [ˈfaundə], v.n. scheitern, Schiffbruch erleiden (on, an, Dat.).

foundling [ˈfaundliŋ], s. das Findelkind, der Findling.

foundry [ˈfaundri], s. (Metall.) die Gießerei.

fount (1) [faunt], s. (Typ.) der Schriftguss.

fount (2) [faunt] (Poet.) see fountain.

fountain [ˈfauntin], s. die Quelle, der Brunnen; der Springbrunnen; — pen, die Füllfeder; — head, der Urquell.

four [fɔː], num. adj. vier; — -in-hand, das Viergespann.

fowl [faul], s. (Orn.) das Huhn, das Geflügel.

fowler [ˈfaulə], s. der Vogelsteller, Vogelfänger.

fox [fɔks], s. (Zool.) der Fuchs; (fig.) der listige Kauz, Schlauberger (cunning fellow). — v.a. (coll.) überlisten, täuschen.

fraction [ˈfrækʃən], s. (Maths.) der Bruch; (Mech.) der Bruchteil.

fractional [ˈfrækʃənəl], adj. (Maths.) Bruch-, gebrochen.

fractionate [ˈfrækʃəneit], v.a. (Chem.) fraktionieren (oil).

fractious [ˈfrækʃəs], adj. zänkisch, streitsüchtig.

fracture [ˈfræktʃə], s. (Med.) der Bruch. — v.a. brechen; — o.'s leg, sich das Bein brechen.

fragile [ˈfrædʒail], adj. zerbrechlich; gebrechlich (feeble).

fragment [ˈfrægmənt], s. das Bruchstück, das Fragment.

fragrance [ˈfreigrəns], s. der Wohlgeruch, Duft.

fragrant [ˈfreigrənt], adj. wohlriechend, duftend.

frail [freil], adj. gebrechlich, schwach (feeble).

frailty [ˈfreilti], s. die Schwäche.

frame [freim], s. der Rahmen (of picture); das Gerüst (scaffold); die Form (shape). — v.a. einrahmen (a picture); (Am.) in die Enge treiben, reinlegen (get s.o. wrongly blamed); (Comm.) entwerfen (a letter).

framework [ˈfreimwəːk], s. der Rahmen (outline); das Fachwerk (construction).

franchise [ˈfræntʃaiz], s. das Wahlrecht.

Franciscan [frænˈsiskən], s. der Franziskaner (friar).

frank [fræŋk], adj. offen, aufrichtig. — v.a. frankieren (letter). — s. der Frankovermerk.

frankincense [ˈfræŋkinsens], s. der Weihrauch.

frantic [ˈfræntik], adj. wahnsinnig, außer sich.

fraternal [frəˈtəːnəl], adj. brüderlich.

fraternity [frəˈtəːniti], s. die Bruderschaft; (Am.) der Studentenbund, -klub.

fraternize ['frætənaiz], *v.n.* sich verbrüdern, fraternisieren.

fraud [frɔːd], *s.* der Betrug.

fraudulent ['frɔːdjulənt], *adj.* be-
trügerisch.

fraught [frɔːt], *adj.* voll (*with*, von,
Dat.).

fray (1) [frei], *v.a.* abnutzen; —
the nerves, auf die Nerven gehen
(*Dat.*).

fray (2) [frei], *s.* der Kampf, die
Schlägerei.

freak [friːk], *s.* das Monstrum, die
Mißgeburt.

freakish ['friːkiʃ], *adj.* seltsam; gro-
tesk.

freckle [frekl], *s.* die Sommersprosse.

freckled [frekld], *adj.* sommersprossig.

free [friː], *adj.* frei; offen (*frank*); —
trade area, die Freihandelszone; *of
my own — will*, aus freien Stücken.
— *v.a.* befreien.

freebooter ['friːbuːtə], *s.* der Freibeuter.

freedom ['friːdəm], *s.* die Freiheit; —
of a city, das Ehrenbürgerrecht.

freehold ['friːhould], *s.* der freie
Grundbesitz, der Freigrundbesitz.

freeholder ['friːhouldə], *s.* der (freie)
Grundbesitzer.

freeman ['friːmən], *s.* der Freibürger,
Ehrenbürger.

freemason ['friːmeisn], *s.* der Frei-
maurer.

freewheel ['friːˈwiːl], *s.* der Freilauf,
das Freilaufrad. — *v.n.* mit Freilauf
fahren.

freeze [friːz], *v.a.* *irr.* gefrieren lassen.
— *v.n.* frieren, gefrieren; — *up*,
zufrieren.

freight [freit], *s.* die Fracht. — *v.a.*
verfrachten.

freighter ['freitə], *s.* (*Naut.*) der
Frachtdampfer.

French [frentʃ], *adj.* französisch; —
bean, die Schnittbohne; — *horn*, (*Mus.*)
das Horn.

Frenchman ['frentʃmən], *s.* der Franzose.

Frenchwoman ['frentʃwumən], *s.* die
Französin.

frenzied ['frenzid], *adj.* wahnsinnig,
außer sich.

frequency ['friːkwənsi], *s.* (*Phys.*) die
Frequenz; die Häufigkeit (*of occurrence*).

frequent ['friːkwənt], *adj.* häufig. —
[friˈkwent], *v.a.* (häufig) besuchen.

fresh [freʃ], *adj.* frisch, neu; ungesalzen
(*water*); (*sl.*) frech; — *water*, das
Süßwasser.

fresher, freshman ['freʃə, 'freʃmən], *s.*
der Neuankömmling; (*Univ.*) der
Fuchs, Anfänger.

fret (1) [fret], *s.* (*Carp.*) das Gitterwerk, Laubsägewerk. — *v.a.* (*Carp.*)
durchbrochen verzieren.

fret (2) [fret], *s.* der Verdruß, Ärger.
— *v.n.* sich Sorgen machen.

fretful ['fretful], *adj.* verdrießlich,
ärgerlich, mißmutig.

fretsaw ['fretsɔː], *s.* (*Carp.*) die Laubsäge.

friar ['fraiə], *s.* (*Eccl.*) der Mönch,
Bettelmönch.

friction ['frikʃən], *s.* die Reibung; (*fig.*)
die Unstimmigkeit.

Friday ['fraid(e)i]. der Freitag; *Good
—*, der Karfreitag.

friend [frend], *s.* der (die) Freund(in).

friendly ['frendli], *adj.* freundlich.

friendship ['frendʃip], *s.* die Freundschaft.

frigate ['frigit], *s.* (*Naut.*) die Fregatte.

fright [frait], *s.* die Furcht, der Schreck,
das Entsetzen.

frighten [fraitn], *v.a.* erschrecken (*s.o.*).

frightful ['fraitful], *adj.* schrecklich.

frigid ['fridʒid], *adj.* kalt, frostig;
kühl.

frill [fril], *s.* die Krause; die Ausschmückung (*style*).

frilly ['frili], *adj.* gekräuselt, geziert.

fringe [frindʒ], *s.* die Franse (*fringed
edge*); der Rand (*edge, brink*). — *v.a.*
mit Fransen besetzen, einsäumen.
— *v.n.* — *on*, grenzen an (*Acc.*).

Frisian ['friːʒən], *adj.* friesisch.

frisk [frisk], *v.a.* (*sl.*) durchsuchen
(*search*). — *v.n.* hüpfen (*of animals*).
— *s.* der Sprung (*of animals*).

frisky ['friski], *adj.* lebhaft, munter.

fritter ['fritə], *s.* der Pfannkuchen;
apple —, Äpfel im Schlafrock. —
v.a. zerstückeln (*cut up*); vertrödeln
(*waste*), vergeuden.

frivolity [friˈvɔliti], *s.* der Leichtsinn,
die Leichtfertigkeit.

frivolous ['frivələs], *adj.* leichtsinnig,
leichtfertig.

fro [frou], *adv.* *to and —*, auf und ab,
hin und her.

frock [frɔk], *s.* der Kittel, das Kleid;
(*Eccl.*) die Soutane, Kutte.

frog [frɔg], *s.* (*Zool.*) der Frosch.

frogman ['frɔgmən], *s.* der Tauch-
schwimmer, Froschmann.

frolic ['frɔlik], *s.* der Scherz; der
Spaß. — *v.n.* scherzen, ausgelassen
sein.

from [frɔm], *prep.* von; von ... her
(*hence*); aus ... heraus (*out of*); von
... an (*starting —*); vor (*in the face of*).

front [frʌnt], *s.* die Stirn; die Vorderseite; (*Mil.*) die Front; *in — of*,
vor (*Dat.*); — *door*, die Haustür.

frontage ['frʌntidʒ], *s.* die Front,
Vorderfront (*of building*).

frontal ['frʌntl], *adj.* Stirn-, Vorder-;
(*Mil.*) — *attack*, der Frontalangriff.
— *s.* (*Eccl.*) die Altardecke.

frontier ['frʌntjə], *s.* die Grenze; —
police, die Grenzpolizei.

frontispiece ['frʌntispiːs], *s.* das Titelbild.

frost [frɔst], *s.* der Frost, der Reif.

frostbite ['frɔstbait], *s.* die Frostbeule.

frosted ['frɔstid], *adj.* bereift.

froth [frɔθ], *s.* der Schaum. — *v.n.*
schäumen.

frown [fraun], *v.n.* die Stirn runzeln, finster dreinschauen. — *s.* das Stirnrunzeln.

frugal ['fru:gǝl], *adj.* frugal, sparsam, einfach.

fruit [fru:t], *s.* die Frucht (*singular*); das Obst (*plural or collective*). — *v.n.* (*Bot.*) Früchte tragen.

frustrate [frʌs'treit], *v.a.* verhindern; vereiteln (*bring to nought*).

fry (1) [frai], *v.a.* braten; *fried potatoes*, Bratkartoffeln, *f. pl.*

fry (2) [frai], *s.* der Rogen (*of fish*); (*fig.*) die Brut, Menge. — (*Mus.*) die Fuge.

frying pan ['fraiiŋpæn], *s.* die Bratpfanne; *out of the — into the fire*, vom Regen in die Traufe.

fuchsia ['fju:ʃǝ], *s.* (*Bot.*) die Fuchsie.

fudge [fʌdʒ], *s.* weiches Zuckerwerk; (*coll.*) Unsinn!

fuel ['fjuǝl], *s.* der Brennstoff, Treibstoff; das Heizmaterial. — *v.a.*, *v.n.* tanken.

fugitive ['fju:dʒitiv], *adj.* flüchtig, auf der Flucht. — *s.* der Flüchtling.

fugue [fju:g], *s.* (*Mus.*) die Fuge.

fulcrum ['fʌlkrǝm], *s.* der Stützpunkt, Hebelpunkt.

fulfil [ful'fil], *v.a.* erfüllen; — *a requirement*, einem Gesetz genüge tun.

full [ful], *adj.* voll; vollständig (*complete*); —*time*, hauptberuflich.

fuller ['fulǝ], *s.* der Walker.

fullness ['fulnis], *s.* die Fülle.

fulsome ['fulsǝm], *adj.* widerlich, ekelhaft; übermäßig.

fumble [fʌmbl], *v.n.* tappen (*for*, nach, *Dat.*).

fume [fju:m], *s.* der Rauch, Dunst; der Zorn (*anger*). — *v.n.* zornig sein, wüten (*be angered*).

fun [fʌn], *s.* der Spaß, Scherz; *have —*, sich gut unterhalten, sich amüsieren; *make — of*, zum besten haben.

function ['fʌŋkʃǝn], *s.* (*also Maths.*) die Funktion; das Amt (*office*); die Feier(lichkeit) (*formal occasion*). — *v.n.* funktionieren (*be in working order*); fungieren (*officiate*).

fund [fʌnd], *s.* der Fonds (*financial*); (*fig.*) die Fülle (*of*, an); *public —s*, die Staatsgelder.

fundamental [fʌndǝ'mentl], *adj.* grundsätzlich, wesentlich. — *s.* (*pl.*) die Grundlagen, *f.pl.*

funeral ['fju:nǝrǝl], *s.* die Bestattung, Beerdigung.

funereal [fju:'niǝriǝl], *adj.* wie bei einem Begräbnis, betrübt, traurig.

fungus ['fʌŋgǝs], *s.* (*Bot.*) der Pilz; der Schwamm (*mushroom*).

funk [fʌŋk], *s.* (*sl.*) die Angst, Panik. — *v.a.* fürchten.

funnel [fʌnl], *s.* der Trichter.

funny ['fʌni], *adj.* spaßhaft, komisch.

fur [fǝ:], *s.* der Pelz, das Fell (*coat of animal*); (*Med.*) der Belag (*on tongue*).

furbelow ['fǝ:bilou], *s.* die Falbel.

furbish ['fǝ:biʃ], *v.a.* aufputzen.

furious ['fjuǝriǝs], *adj.* wild, rasend, wütend.

furl [fǝ:l], *v.a.* (zusammen-)rollen; (*Naut.*) aufrollen.

furlong ['fǝ:lɔŋ], *s.* ein Achtel einer englischen Meile.

furlough ['fǝ:lou], *s.* der Urlaub.

furnace ['fǝ:nis], *s.* der Ofen, Hochofen (*steel*); (*Metall.*) der Schmelzofen.

furnish ['fǝ:niʃ], *v.a.* ausstatten, versehen (*equip*); möblieren (*a room* etc.).

furnisher ['fǝ:niʃǝ], *s.* der Möbelhändler; der Lieferant.

furniture ['fǝ:nitʃǝ], *s.* die Möbel, *n. pl.*; die Einrichtung.

furrier ['fʌriǝ], *s.* der Kürschner.

furrow ['fʌrou], *s.* die Furche (*field*); die Runzel (*brow*). — *v.a.* runzeln (*brow*); Furchen ziehen (*plough up*).

further ['fǝ:ðǝ], *comp. adj.*, *adv. see* **farther**. — *v.a.* fördern (*advance*).

furtherance ['fǝ:ðǝrǝns], *s.* die Förderung (*advancement*).

furthermore ['fǝ:ðǝmɔ:], *adv.* ferner.

furthest ['fǝ:ðist], *superl. adj.*, *adv. see* **farthest**.

furtive ['fǝ:tiv], *adj.* verstohlen, heimlich.

fury ['fjuǝri], *s.* die Wut; (*Myth.*) die Furie.

furze [fǝ:z], *s.* (*Bot.*) der Stechginster.

fuse [fju:z], *v.a.*, *v.n.* schmelzen (*melt*); vereinigen (*unite*). — *s.* (*Elec.*) die Sicherung; *blow a —*, eine Sicherung durchbrennen; — *box*, der Sicherungskasten; — *wire*, der Schmelzdraht.

fuselage ['fju:zilɑ:ʒ *or* -lidʒ], *s.* (*Aviat.*) der (Flugzeug-)rumpf.

fusible ['fju:zibl], *adj.* schmelzbar.

fusilier [fju:zi'liǝ], *s.* (*Mil.*) der Füsilier.

fusion ['fju:ʒǝn], *s.* die Verschmelzung; die Vereinigung.

fuss [fʌs], *s.* das Getue, die Umständlichkeit; *make a — about*, viel Aufhebens machen.

fussy ['fʌsi], *adj.* übertrieben genau; umständlich; geschäftig (*busy*); — *about*, genau in (*Dat.*).

fusty ['fʌsti], *adj.* moderig, muffig.

futile ['fju:tail], *adj.* nutzlos, vergeblich.

futility [fju:'tiliti], *s.* die Nutzlosigkeit.

future ['fju:tʃǝ], *s.* die Zukunft. — *adj.* (zu-)künftig.

fuzzy ['fʌzi], *adj.* kraus.

G

G [dʒi:], das G (*also Mus.*); — *sharp*, das Gis; — *flat*, das Ges; *key of —*, der G Schlüssel, Violinschlüssel.

gab [gæb], s. das Geschwätz; *the gift of the* —, ein gutes Mundwerk.

gabble [gæbl], *v.n.* schwatzen.

gable [geibl], s. der Giebel.

gad [gæd], *v.n.* — *about*, umherstreifen.

gadfly ['gædflai], s. (*Ent.*) die Bremse.

gag [gæg], s. der Knebel; (*sl.*) der Witz. — *v.a.* knebeln.

gaiety ['geiəti], s. die Fröhlichkeit.

gain [gein], *v.a.* gewinnen, erwerben (*earn*); — *possession*, Besitz ergreifen. — s. der Gewinn, Vorteil.

gainful ['geinful], *adj.* — *employment*, die einträgliche Beschäftigung.

gainsay ['geinsei *or* gein'sei], *v.a.* widersprechen (*pers.*, *Dat.*).

gait [geit], s. das Schreiten, der Schritt, Gang.

gaiter ['geitə], s. die Gamasche.

galaxy ['gæləksi], s. (*Astron.*) die Milchstraße; (*fig.*) die glänzende Versammlung.

gale [geil], s. der Sturm.

gall [gɔːl], s. die Galle. — *v.a.* verbittern, ärgern.

gallant ['gælənt], *adj.* tapfer (*of soldier*); gallant, höflich (*polite*).

gallantry ['gæləntri], s. die Tapferkeit; die Höflichkeit, Galanterie.

gallery ['gæləri], s. die Gallerie.

galley ['gæli], s. (*Naut.*) die Galeere; (*Typ.*) — *proof*, der Fahnenabzug.

gallon ['gælən], s. die Gallone.

gallop ['gæləp], *v.n.* galoppieren. — s. der Galopp.

gallows ['gælouz], s. der Galgen.

galosh [gə'lɔʃ], s. die Galosche.

galvanic [gæl'vænik], *adj.* galvanisch.

galvanize ['gælvənaiz], *v.a.* galvanisieren.

gamble [gæmbl], *v.n.* um Geld spielen; — *away*, verspielen. — s. das Risiko.

gambol [gæmbl], *v.n.* herumspringen.

game [geim], s. das Spiel (*play*); das Wild, Wildbret (*pheasants etc.*); *fair* —, Freiwild, *n.*, offene Beute, *f.*

gamecock ['geimkɔk], s. (*Orn.*) der Kampfhahn.

gamekeeper ['geimkiːpə], s. der Wildhüter.

gammon ['gæmən], s. der (geräucherte) Schinken (*bacon*).

gamut ['gæmət], s. die Tonleiter.

gander ['gændə], s. (*Orn.*) der Gänserich.

gang [gæŋ], s. die Bande; die Mannschaft (*workmen*). — *v.n.* — *up*, eine Bande bilden; — *up on s.o.*, sich gegen jemanden verbünden.

gangrene ['gæŋgriːn], s. (*Med.*) der Brand; die Fäulnis.

gangway ['gæŋwei], s. die Planke, der Laufgang (*on boat*); der Durchgang.

gaol, jail [dʒeil], s. das Gefängnis. — *v.a.* einsperren.

gaoler, jailer ['dʒeilə], s. der Kerkermeister.

gap [gæp], s. die Lücke; die Bresche (*breach*).

gape [geip], *v.n.* gähnen, (*fig.*) klaffen.

garage ['gærɑːʒ *or* 'gæridʒ], s. die Garage, die Tankstelle.

garb [gɑːb], s. die Tracht, Kleidung.

garbage ['gɑːbidʒ], s. der Abfall; (*Am.*) — *can*, der Mülleimer.

garble [gɑːbl], *v.a.* verstümmeln.

garden [gɑːdn], s. der Garten. — *v.n.* im Garten arbeiten.

gardener ['gɑːdnə], s. der Gärtner.

gargle [gɑːgl], *v.n.* gurgeln, spülen.

gargoyle ['gɑːgɔil], s. (*Archit.*) der Wasserspeier.

garish ['gæriʃ], *adj.* grell, auffallend.

garland ['gɑːlənd], s. der Blumenkranz, die Girlande.

garlic ['gɑːlik], s. (*Bot.*) der Knoblauch.

garment ['gɑːmənt], s. das Gewand.

garner ['gɑːnə], *v.a.* aufspeichern (*store*).

garnet ['gɑːnit], s. der Granat.

garnish ['gɑːniʃ], *v.a.* ausschmücken, verzieren.

garret ['gærət], s. die Dachkammer.

garrison ['gærisən], s. (*Mil.*) die Garnison. — *v.a.* stationieren.

garrulity [gæ'ruːliti], s. die Schwatzhaftigkeit.

garter ['gɑːtə], s. das Strumpfband, das Hosenband; *Order of the Garter*, der Hosenbandorden.

gas [gæs], s. das Gas; (*Am.*) *see* **gasoline**.

Gascon ['gæskən], s. der Gaskogner.

gaseous ['geisiəs], *adj.* gasförmig, gasartig.

gash [gæʃ], s. die Schnittwunde.

gasoline ['gæsoliːn], s. (*Am.*) das Benzin.

gasp [gɑːsp], *v.n.* keuchen; nach Luft schnappen. — s. das Keuchen, das Luftschnappen.

gastric ['gæstrik], *adj.* (*Anat.*) gastrisch; — *ulcer*, das Magengeschwür.

gate [geit], s. das Tor, der Eingang. — *v.a.* einsperren, Hausarrest geben (*Dat.*).

gateway ['geitwei], s. die Einfahrt.

gather ['gæðə], *v.a.* sammeln, einsammeln (*collect*); versammeln (*assemble*). — *v.n.* entnehmen, schließen (*infer*); sich versammeln (*come together*); aufziehen (*storm*).

gathering ['gæðəriŋ], s. die Versammlung (*meeting*).

gauche [gouʃ], *adj.* linkisch, ungeschickt.

gaudy ['gɔːdi], *adj.* übertrieben, grell, prunkhaft.

gauge [geidʒ], *v.a.* (*Engin.*) ausmessen, kalibrieren; eichen (*officially*). — s. der Maßstab (*scale*); (*Railw.*) die Spurweite.

gauger ['geidʒə], s. der Eichmeister.

Gaul [gɔːl], s. der Gallier.

gaunt [gɔːnt], *adj.* mager; hager.

gauntlet ['gɔːntlit], s. der (Panzer)handschuh.

gauze [gɔːz], s. die Gaze.

gavotte [gə'vɔt], s. (*Mus.*) die Gavotte.

gay [gei], *adj.* fröhlich, heiter; bunt (*colour*).

gaze [geiz], *v.n.* starren.

gazelle [gə'zel], *s.* (*Zool.*) die Gazelle.

gazette [gə'zet], *s.* die (amtliche) Zeitung; das Amtsblatt.

gear [giə], *s.* das Gerät; (*Mech.*) das Triebwerk; (*Naut.*) das Geschirr; *switch*—, das Schaltgerät; (*Motor.*) der Gang; — *ratio*, die Übersetzung; *differential* —, der Achsenantrieb; *steering* —, die Lenkung (*of car*); — *box*, das Schaltgetriebe, die Gangschaltung; *out of* —, in Unordnung; *in top* —, mit Höchstgeschwindigkeit; *change to bottom* —, auf erste Geschwindigkeit (*or*, auf langsam) einschalten. — *v.a.* — *down*, herabsetzen; (*Engin.*) — *up*, übersetzen; — *to*, anpassen.

gelatine ['dʒeləti:n], *s.* die Gallerte, die Geleemasse.

gem [dʒem], *s.* die Gemme, der Edelstein.

gender ['dʒendə], *s.* (*Gram.*) das Geschlecht.

gene [dʒi:n], *s.* (*Biol.*) das Gen.

geneaology [dʒi:ni'ælədʒi], *s.* die Genealogie; der Stammbaum (*family tree*).

general ['dʒenərəl], *s.* (*Mil.*) der General; *lieutenant*- —, der Generalleutnant. — *adj.* allgemein, General-; — -*purpose*, für alle Zwecke; Allzweck-.

generalization [dʒenərəlai'zeiʃən], *s.* die Verallgemeinerung.

generalize ['dʒenərəlaiz], *v.a.* verallgemeinern.

generate ['dʒenəreit], *v.a.* erzeugen; (*Elec.*) Strom erzeugen.

generation [dʒenə'reiʃən], *s.* die Generation (*contemporaries*); das Zeugen (*production*); (*Elec.*) die Stromerzeugung.

generosity [dʒenə'rɔsiti], *s.* die Großmut (*magnanimity*); die Freigebigkeit (*liberality*).

generous ['dʒenərəs], *adj.* großmütig; freigebig (*with gifts*).

Genevan [dʒi'ni:vən], *adj.* genferisch. — *s.* der Genfer.

genial ['dʒi:niəl], *adj.* freundlich, mild.

geniality [dʒi:ni'æliti], *s.* die Freundlichkeit, Leutseligkeit.

genital ['dʒenitəl], *adj.* Zeugungs-. — *s.* (*pl.*) die Geschlechtsteile, Genitalien, *pl.*

genitive ['dʒenitiv], *s.* (*Gram.*) der Wesfall, Genitiv.

genius ['dʒi:niəs], *s.* das Genie; der Genius.

Genoese [dʒenou'i:z], *adj.* genuesisch. — *s.* der Genuese.

Gentile ['dʒentail], *s.* heidnisch; nicht jüdisch.

gentility [dʒen'tiliti], *s.* die Herkunft aus vornehmem Haus, Vornehmheit.

gentle [dʒentl], *adj.* sanft, mild; gelind (*breeze*).

gentlefolk ['dʒentlfouk], *s.* bessere *or* vornehme Leute, *pl.*

gentleman ['dʒentlmən], *s.* der Gentleman, Herr; feiner Herr.

gentleness ['dʒentlnis], *s.* die Milde, Sanftheit.

gentry ['dʒentri], *s.* der niedere Adel.

genuine ['dʒenjuin], *adj.* echt.

genus ['dʒi:nəs], *s.* (*Biol.*) die Gattung.

geographer [dʒi'ɔgrəfə], *s.* der Geograph.

geographical [dʒi:o'græfikəl], *adj.* geographisch.

geography [dʒi'ɔgrəfi], *s.* die Geographie, Erdkunde.

geological [dʒi:o'lɔdʒikəl], *adj.* geologisch.

geologist [dʒi'ɔlədʒist], *s.* der Geologe.

geology [dʒi'ɔlədʒi], *s.* die Geologie.

geometric(al) [dʒi:o'metrik(əl)], *adj.* geometrisch.

geometrist [dʒi'ɔmətrist], *s.* der Geometer.

geometry [dʒi'ɔmətri], *s.* die Geometrie.

geranium [dʒə'reiniəm], *s.* (*Bot.*) die Geranie, das Geranium.

germ [dʒə:m], *s.* der Keim; (*pl.*) die Bakterien, *f. pl.*

German ['dʒə:mən], *adj.* deutsch. — *s.* der, die Deutsche.

germane [dʒə:'mein], *adj.* zur Sache gehörig, zugehörig.

Germanic [dʒə:'mænik], *adj.* germanisch.

germinate ['dʒə:mineit], *v.n.* keimen.

gerund ['dʒerənd], *s.* (*Gram.*) das Gerundium.

gerundive [dʒe'rʌndiv], *s.* (*Gram.*) das Gerundiv(um).

gesticulate [dʒes'tikjuleit], *v.n.* Gebärden machen, gestikulieren.

gesture ['dʒestʃə], *s.* die Geste; der Gebärde.

get [get], *v.a. irr.* bekommen, (*coll.*) kriegen; erhalten (*receive*); erwischen (*catch up with*); einholen (*fetch*); — *over or across*, klar machen. — *v.n.* gelangen (*arrive*); werden (*become*); — *along*, weiterkommen; — *on or* (*Am.*) *along with s.o.*, mit jemandem auskommen; — *on in the world*, Karriere machen; — *away*, entkommen; — *down to it*, zur Sache kommen; — *in*, hineinkommen; — *off*, aussteigen; *show s.o. where he — s off*, jemandem seine Meinung sagen; (*Sch.*) — *through*, durchkommen (*in examination*); — *up*, aufstehen.

get-up ['getʌp], *s.* das Kostüm; die Ausstattung (*attire*).

Ghanaian [gɑ:'neiən], *adj.* ghanaisch. — *s.* der Ghanaer.

ghastly ['gɑ:stli], *adj.* furchtbar, schrecklich.

gherkin ['gə:kin], *s.* (*Bot.*) die Essiggurke.

ghost [goust], *s.* der Geist, das Gespenst.

giant ['dʒaiənt], *s.* der Riese.

gibberish ['dʒibəriʃ], *s.* das Kauderwelsch.

gibbet ['dʒibit], *s.* der Galgen.

gibe [dʒaib], *v.n.* spotten, höhnen (*at, über, Acc.*). — *s.* der Spott, Hohn; die spöttische Bemerkung (*remark*).

giblets ['dʒiblits], *s. pl.* das Gänseklein.

giddiness ['gidinis], *s.* das Schwindelgefühl.

giddy ['gidi], *adj.* schwindelig.

gift [gift], *s.* die Gabe, das Geschenk.

gifted ['giftid], *adj.* begabt.

gig [gig], *s.* der leichte Wagen; (*Naut.*) der Nachen, das Gig.

gigantic [dʒai'gæntik], *adj.* riesig, riesengroß.

giggle [gigl], *v.n.* kichern. — *s.* das Kichern, Gekicher.

gild [gild], *v.a.* vergolden; verschönern; —*ing the pill*, etwas Unangenehmes (die Pille) versüßen.

gill (1) [gil], *s.* (*Biol.*) die Kieme.

gill (2) [dʒil], *s.* das Viertel einer Pinte (0.14 *l.*).

gilt [gilt], *s.* die Vergoldung; — *edged*, mit Goldschnitt; (*Comm.*) hochwertige *or* mündelsichere Staatspapiere.

gimlet ['gimlit], *s.* (*Carp.*) der Handbohrer.

gin [dʒin], *s.* der Gin, der Wachholderbranntwein; — *and tonic*, Gin und Tonic.

ginger ['dʒindʒə], *s.* der Ingwer; — *haired*, rothaarig; — *nut*, das Ingweror Pfeffernüßchen, Ingwerkeks; — *beer*, Ingwerbier. — *v.a.* — *up*, aufstacheln, anreizen.

gingerbread ['dʒindʒəbred], *s.* der Lebkuchen, Pfefferkuchen.

gipsy ['dʒipsi], *s.* der Zigeuner.

giraffe [dʒi'rɑːf], *s.* (*Zool.*) die Giraffe.

gird [gəːd], *v.a.* reg. & irr. (*Poet.*) gürten.

girder ['gəːdə], *s.* der Balken, Träger.

girdle [gəːdl], *v.a.* gürten, umgürten; — *the earth*, die Erde umkreisen.

girl [gəːl], *s.* das Mädchen.

girlhood ['gəːlhud], *s.* die Mädchenzeit, die Mädchenjahre, *n. pl.*

girlish ['gəːliʃ], *adj.* mädchenhaft, wie ein Mädchen.

gist [dʒist], *s.* das Wesentliche.

give [giv], *v.a. irr.* geben; — *out*, bekanntgeben, bekanntmachen; — *up*, aufgeben; — *way to*, Platz machen. — *v.n.* sich dehnen, sich strecken (*of wood, metal etc.*); — *in*, nachgeben (*to, Dat.*).

glacial ['gleisjəl], *adj.* eisig, Gletscher-.

glacier ['glæsiə], *s.* der Gletscher.

glad [glæd], *adj.* froh, erfreut (*at, über, Acc.*).

gladden [glædn], *v.a.* erheitern, erfreuen.

glade [gleid], *s.* die Lichtung.

glamorous ['glæmərəs], *adj.* bezaubernd, blendend glanzvoll.

glamour ['glæmə], *s.* der Zauber; — der Glanz.

glance [glɑːns], *s.* der Blick; *at a* —, auf den ersten Blick. — *v.n.* flüchtig blicken.

gland [glænd], *s.* (*Anat.*) die Drüse.

glandular ['glændjulə], *adj.* Drüsen-, drüsig.

glare [glɛə], *s.* der blendende Glanz, das Schimmern; der (scharf) durchbohrende Blick (*stare*).

glaring ['glɛəriŋ], *adj.* schreiend (*of colour*); auffallend (*obvious*).

glass [glɑːs], *s.* das Glas; der Spiegel (*mirror*); das Wetterglas (*barometer*); (*pl.*) die Brille (*spectacles*).

glassblower ['glɑːsblouə], *s.* der Glasbläser.

glassworks ['glɑːswəːks], *s.* die Glashütte.

glassy ['glɑːsi], *adj.* gläsern.

glaze [gleiz], *s.* die Glasur. — *v.a.* glasieren; verglasen.

glazier ['gleiziə], *s.* der Glaser.

gleam [gliːm], *v.n.* strahlen, glänzen (*with*, vor, *Dat.*). — *s.* der Glanz, das Strahlen.

glean [gliːn], *v.a.* auflesen; erfahren (*learn*).

glebe [gliːb], *s.* das Pfarrgut.

glee (1) [gliː], *s.* die Freude, Heiterkeit.

glee (2) [gliː], *s.* (*Mus.*) der Rundgesang; — *club*, die Liedertafel.

glen [glen], *s.* das enge Tal.

glib [glib], *adj.* glatt, geläufig, zungenfertig.

glide [glaid], *v.n.* gleiten. — *s.* das Gleiten.

glider ['glaidə], *s.* (*Aviat.*) das Segelflugzeug.

glimmer ['glimə], *s.* der Schimmer, Glimmer. — *v.n.* schimmern, glimmen.

glimpse [glimps], *s.* der (flüchtige) Blick; *catch a* —, einen Blick erhaschen. — *v.a.* flüchtig blicken (*auf, Acc.*).

glisten ['glisn], *v.n.* glitzern, glänzen.

glitter ['glitə], *v.n.* glänzen, schimmern.

gloaming ['gloumiŋ], *s.* die Dämmerung.

globe [gloub], *s.* der Globus, der Erdball; die Kugel.

globular ['glɔbjulə], *adj.* kugelförmig.

gloom [gluːm], *s.* das Dunkel; der Trübsinn, die Traurigkeit.

gloomy ['gluːmi], *adj.* deprimiert, trübsinnig, düster.

glorify ['glɔːrifai], *v.a.* verherrlichen.

glorious ['glɔːriəs], *adj.* herrlich; (*Mil.*) glorreich.

glory ['glɔːri], *s.* die Herrlichkeit, der Ruhm. — *v.n.* frohlocken (*in*, über, *Acc.*).

gloss [glɔs], *s.* der Glanz; (*Lit.*) die Glosse, Anmerkung. — *v.a.* — *over*, beschönigen; (*Lit.*) glossieren, mit Anmerkungen versehen.

glossary ['glɔsəri], *s.* das Glossar, die Spezialwörterliste; das Wörterbuch.

glossy ['glɔsi], *adj.* glänzend.

glove [glʌv], *s.* der Handschuh.

glow [glou], *v.n.* glühen. — *s.* die Glut, das Glühen; Wohlbehagen.

glower ['glauə], *v.n.* — *at*, feindselig ansehen, anstarren.

glue [glu:], *s.* der Leim. — *v.a.* leimen, zusammenleimen.

glum [glʌm], *adj.* mürrisch, finster.

glut [glʌt], *s.* die Überfülle. — *v.a.* überladen, überfüllen.

glutinous [ˈgluːtinəs], *adj.* zähe, klebrig.

glutton [glʌtn], *s.* der Vielfraß.

gluttony [ˈglʌtəni], *s.* die Schwelgerei, Gefräßigkeit.

glycerine [ˈglisəriːn], *s.* das Glyzerin.

gnarled [nɑːld], *adj.* knorrig.

gnash [næʃ], *v.a.* knirschen (*teeth*).

gnat [næt], *s.* (*Ent.*) die Mücke.

gnaw [nɔː], *v.a.*, *v.n.* nagen (an, *Dat.*), zernagen, zerfressen (at, *Acc.*).

gnome [noum], *s.* der Erdgeist, der Zwerg, Gnom.

go [gou], *v.n. irr.* gehen, fahren, laufen; arbeiten (*engine*); verlaufen (*event*); sich erstrecken (*distance*); — *down in the general esteem*, in der Achtung sinken; — *on*, fortfahren; — *mad*, verrückt werden; — *bald*, die Haare verlieren; — *without*, leer ausgehen, entbehren; *let* —, loslassen; — *for*, auf jemanden losgehen; — *in for*, sich interessieren für (*Acc.*); — *all out for*, energisch unternehmen; *a* —*ing concern*, ein gutgehendes Unternehmen; —*ing on for 20*, fast 20 Jahre. — *s.* der Versuch; (*coll.*) *plenty of* —, recht lebhaft, voller Schwung.

goad [goud], *v.a.* anstacheln.

goal [goul], *s.* das Ziel; (*Footb.*) das Tor.

goalkeeper [ˈgoulkiːpə], *s.* der Torwart.

goalpost [ˈgoulpoust], *s.* der Torpfosten.

goat [gout], *s.* (*Zool.*) die Geiß, Ziege; *billy* —, der Ziegenbock; *nanny* —, die Geiß.

gobble [gɔbl], *v.a.* verschlingen, gierig essen.

goblet [ˈgɔblit], *s.* der Becher.

goblin [ˈgɔblin], *s.* der Kobold, der Gnom; der Schelm.

go-cart [ˈgoukɑːt], *s.* der Kinderwagen, Gängelwagen.

God [gɔd], Gott.

god [gɔd], *s.* der Gott.

godchild [ˈgɔdtʃaild], *s.* das Patenkind.

goddess [ˈgɔdes], *s.* die Göttin.

godfather [ˈgɔdfɑːðə], *s.* der Pate.

godhead [ˈgɔdhed], *s.* die Gottheit.

godless [ˈgɔdlis], *adj.* gottlos, ungläubig.

godmother [ˈgɔdmʌðə], *s.* die Patin.

goggle [gɔgl], *v.n.* glotzen, starren (*stare*). — *s.* (*pl.*) die Schutzbrille.

going [ˈgouin], *s.* das Gehen, das Funktionieren (*of machinery*); *while the* — *is good*, zur rechten Zeit.

gold [gould], *s.* das Gold; (*Fin.*) — *standard*, die Goldwährung.

goldfinch [ˈgouldfintʃ], *s.* (*Orn.*) der Stieglitz.

goldsmith [ˈgouldsmiθ], *s.* der Goldschmied.

gondola [ˈgɔndələ], *s.* die Gondel.

good [gud], *adj.* gut; artig, brav; *for* —, auf immer; *in* — *time*, rechtzeitig; — *and proper*, (*coll.*) wie es sich gehört, anständig; *as* — *as*, so gut wie; — *looking*, hübsch; — *natured*, gutmütig. — *s. for your own* —, in Ihrem eigenen Interesse; *that's no* —, das taugt nichts; (*pl.*) die Güter, *n.pl.*, Waren, *f.pl.*; *goods station*, der Frachbahnhof; *goods train*, der Güterzug; *goods yard*, der Güterstapelplatz.

goodbye [gudˈbai], *interj.*, *s.*—*!* leb wohl! auf Wiedersehen!

goodness [ˈgudnis], *s.* die Güte.

goodwill [gudˈwil], *s.* das Wohlwollen; (*Comm.*) die Kundschaft.

goose [guːs], *s.* (*Orn.*) die Gans.

gooseberry [ˈguzbəri], *s.* (*Bot.*) die Stachelbeere.

gore [gɔː], *s.* das geronnene Blut. — *v.a.* durchbohren (*pierce, stab*).

gorge [gɔːdʒ], *s.* die Felsenschlucht (*ravine*); (*Anat.*) die Kehle. — *v.a.* gierig verschlingen.

gorgeous [ˈgɔːdʒəs], *adj.* prachtvoll, prächtig.

gorse [gɔːs], *s.* (*Bot.*) der Stechginster.

gory [ˈgɔːri], *adj.* blutig.

goshawk [ˈgɔshɔːk], *s.* (*Orn.*) der Hühnerhabicht.

gosling [ˈgɔzlin], *s.* (*Orn.*) das Gänschen.

gospel [ˈgɔspəl], *s.* das Evangelium; *the* — *according to*, das ... Evangelium, das Evangelium des ...

gossamer [ˈgɔsəmə], *s.* das feine Gewebe; die Sommerfäden.

gossip [ˈgɔsip], *v.n.* klatschen; schwatzen, plaudern. — *s.* der Klatsch; der Schwätzer; die Klatschbase.

Gothic [ˈgɔθik], *adj.* gotisch.

gouge [gaudʒ], *s.* der Hohlmeißel. — *v.a.* aushöhlen, ausstechen.

gourd [ˈguəd], *s.* der Kürbis.

gout [gaut], *s.* (*Med.*) die Gicht.

govern [ˈgʌvən], *v.a.*, *v.n.* (*Pol.*) regieren; beherrschen; (*fig.*) leiten, herrschen.

governable [ˈgʌvənəbl], *adj.* lenkbar, lenksam.

governess [ˈgʌvənis], *s.* die Erzieherin, die Gouvernante.

government [ˈgʌvənmənt], *s.* die Regierung; (*Pol.*) — *benches*, die Regierungssitze; — *loan*, die Staatsanleihe.

governor [ˈgʌvənə], *s.* der Gouverneur, Statthalter.

gown [gaun], *s.* das Kleid (*lady's*); (*Univ.*) der Talar; (*official robe*) die Amtstracht.

grab [græb], *v.a.* packen, ergreifen. — *s.* der Zugriff.

grace [greis], *s.* die Gnade; Gunst (*favour*); die Anmut (*gracefulness*); *Your Grace*, Euer Gnaden; das Tischgebet (*prayer at table*); (*Mus.*) — *note*, die Fermate; *ten minutes'* —, zehn Minuten Aufschub. — *v.a.* schmücken, zieren, ehren.

graceful [ˈgreisful], *adj.* anmutig, reizend; graziös (*movement*).

graceless ['greislis], *adj.* ungraziös.
gracious ['greiʃəs], *adj.* gnädig, huldreich.
gradation [grə'deiʃən], *s.* die Abstufung, die Stufenleiter.
grade [greid], *s.* der Grad, Rang (*rank*); (*Am.*) (*Sch.*) die Klasse. — *v.a.* sortieren, ordnen.
gradient ['greidiənt], *s.* (*Geog.*) die Steigung; der Steigungswinkel (*angle*).
gradual ['grædjuəl], *adj.* allmählich.
graduate ['grædjueit], *v.n.* promovieren (*receive degree*); — *as a doctor*, als Doktor promovieren, den Doktor machen.—[-djuit], *s.* der Akademiker, Graduierte.
graft (1) [grɑ:ft], *s.* (*Hort., Med.*) die (Haut)übertragung. — *v.a.* (*Hort., Med.*) übertragen, anheften (*on to*, auf, *Acc.*).
graft (2) [grɑ:ft], *s.* (*Am.*) der unerlaubte Gewinn; das Schmiergeld; der Betrug (*swindle*).
grain [grein], *s.* das Korn, Samenkorn; das Getreide; das Gran (=0·065 *gramme*); die Maserung (*in wood*); *against the* —, gegen den Strich.
grammar ['græmə], *s.* die Grammatik; — *school*, das Gymnasium.
grammatical [grə'mætikəl], *adj.* grammatisch.
gramme [græm], *s.* das Gramm.
gramophone ['græməfoun], *s.* das Grammophon.
granary ['grænəri], *s.* der (Korn)speicher, die Kornkammer.
grand [grænd], *adj.* groß, großartig; wunderbar; *Grand Duke*, der Großherzog. — *s.* (*Am.*) (*sl.*) 1000 Dollar; (*piano*) der Flügel; *baby* —, der Stutzflügel.
grandchild ['grændtʃaild], *s.* der Enkel, die Enkelin.
grandee [græn'di:], *s.* der spanische Grande.
grandeur ['grændjə], *s.* die Größe, Pracht.
grandfather ['grændfɑ:ðə], *s.* der Großvater.
grandiloquent [græn'dilokwənt], *adj.* großsprecherisch.
grandmother ['grændmʌðə], *s.* die Großmutter.
grange [greindʒ], *s.* der Meierhof, das Landhaus.
granite ['grænit], *s.* der Granit.
grannie, granny ['græni], *s.* (*coll.*) die Oma.
grant [grɑ:nt], *s.* die Gewährung (*of permission etc.*); die Zuwendung (*subsidy*); (*Sch.*) das Stipendium. — *v.a.* geben, gewähren; *take for* —*ed*, als selbstverständlich hinnehmen.
granular ['grænjulə], *adj.* körnig.
granulated ['grænjuleitid], *adj.* feinkörnig, Kristall- (*sugar*).
grape [greip], *s.* (*Bot.*) die Weinbeere, die Traube; — *sugar*, der Traubenzucker; *bunch of* —*s*, Weintrauben, *f. pl.*
grapefruit ['greipfru:t], *s.* die Pampelmuse.

graphic ['græfik], *adj.* (*Art*) graphisch; deutlich, bildhaft, anschaulich.
grapnel ['græpnəl], *s.* (*Naut.*) der Dregganker.
grapple [græpl], *v.n.* — *with*, raufen, (miteinander) ringen.
grasp [grɑ:sp], *v.a.* (mit der Hand) ergreifen, erfassen. — *s.* das Fassungsvermögen, die Auffassung; der Griff (*hand*).
grasping ['grɑ:spiŋ], *adj.* habgierig, gewinnsüchtig.
grass [grɑ:s], *s.* (*Bot.*) das Gras; der Rasen (*lawn*); — *widow*, die Strohwitwe.
grasshopper ['grɑ:shɔpə], *s.* (*Ent.*) die Heuschrecke.
grate (1) [greit], *s.* der Feuerrost, der Kamin.
grate (2) [greit], *v.a.* reiben (*cheese*); schaben, kratzen. — *v.n.* knirschen; auf die Nerven gehen.
grateful ['greitful], *adj.* dankbar.
grater ['greitə], *s.* das Reibeisen; die Reibe (*electrical*).
gratification [grætifi'keiʃən], *s.* die Genugtuung, Befriedigung.
gratify ['grætifai], *v.a.* befriedigen, erfreuen.
grating ['greitiŋ], *s.* das Gitter.
gratis ['greitis], *adv.* gratis, umsonst, frei, unentgeltlich.
gratitude ['grætitju:d], *s.* die Dankbarkeit.
gratuitous [grə'tju:itəs], *adj.* frei, freiwillig (*voluntary*); unentgeltlich (*free of charge*); grundlos (*baseless*).
gratuity [grə'tju:iti], *s.* das Trinkgeld (*tip*); die Gratifikation.
grave (1) [greiv], *adj.* schwer, ernst (*serious*); feierlich (*solemn*). —*s.* (*Mus.*) das Grave.
grave (2) [greiv], *s.* das Grab (*tomb*).
gravel [grævl], *s.* der Kies.
graveyard ['greivjɑ:d], *s.* der Friedhof.
gravitate ['græviteit], *v.n.* gravitieren, hinstreben.
gravitation [grævi'teiʃən], *s.* die Schwerkraft.
gravitational [grævi'teiʃənəl], *adj.* (*Phys.*) Schwerkrafts-.
gravity ['græviti], *s.* der Ernst (*seriousness*); (*Phys.*) die Schwere, Schwerkraft.
gravy ['greivi], *s.* die Sauce, Soße; der Saft des Fleisches, des Bratens; — *boat*, die Sauciere.
gray, grey [grei], *adj.* grau.
graze (1) [greiz], *v.n.* weiden.
graze (2) [greiz], *v.a.* streifen (*pass closely*), abschürfen.
grazier ['greiziə], *s.* der Viehzüchter.
grease [gri:s], *s.* das Fett; das Schmieröl (*machine*). — *v.a.* einfetten (*pans*); schmieren, einschmieren (*machinery*).
greasy ['gri:si], *adj.* fett, schmierig, ölig.
great [greit], *adj.* groß, bedeutend, wichtig; (*Am.*) wundervoll, wunderbar.

greatcoat ['greitcout], *s.* der Winter-
mantel.
great-grandfather [greit'grændfɑ:ðə],
s. der Urgroßvater.
greatly ['greitli], *adv.* stark, sehr.
greatness ['greitnis], *s.* die Größe,
Bedeutung.
greedy ['gri:di], *adj.* gierig; gefräßig
(*eater*).
Greek [gri:k], *adj.* griechisch. — *s.* der
Grieche.
green [gri:n], *adj.* grün; neu (*new*),
frisch (*fresh*).
greengage ['gri:ngeidʒ], *s.* (*Bot.*) die
Reineclaude.
greengrocer ['gri:ngrousə], *s.* der
Grünwarenhändler, Gemüsehändler.
greenhorn ['gri:nhɔ:n], *s.* der Grünschnabel.
greenhouse ['gri:nhaus], *s.* das Gewächshaus, Treibhaus.
Greenlander ['gri:nləndə], *s.* der Grön-
länder.
greet [gri:t], *v.a.* grüßen, begrüßen.
greeting ['gri:tiŋ], *s.* die Begrüßung;
(*pl.*) Grüße, *m. pl.*
gregarious [gri'gɛəriəs], *adj.* gesellig.
grenade [grɪ'neid], *s.* die Granate.
grey *see under* **gray**.
greyhound ['greihaund], *s.* (*Zool.*) das
Windspiel, der Windhund.
grid [grid], *s.* (*Elec.*) das Stromnetz;
(*Phys.*) das Gitter.
gridiron ['gridaiən], *s.* der Bratrost, das
Bratrostgitter.
grief [gri:f], *s.* der Kummer, die Trauer.
grievance ['gri:vəns], *s.* die Klage,
Beschwerde.
grieve [gri:v], *v.a.* kränken. — *v.n.*
sich grämen, sich kränken (*over*, über,
Acc., wegen, *Genit.*).
grievous ['gri:vəs], *adj.* schmerzlich.
grill [gril], *s.* der Rostbraten, Bratrost.
— *v.a.* grillieren, rösten (*meat*);
verhören (*question closely*).
grilling ['griliŋ], *s.* das Verhör.
grim [grim], *adj.* grimmig, finster.
grimace [gri'meis], *s.* die Grimasse, die
Fratze.
grime [graim], *s.* der Schmutz, der Ruß.
grimy ['graimi], *adj.* schmutzig, rußig.
grin [grin], *v.n.* grinsen; (*coll.*) —
and bear it, mach gute Miene zum
bösen Spiel. — *s.* das Grinsen.
grind [graind], *v.a. irr.* zerreiben (*rub*);
schleifen (*sharpen*); mahlen (*pulverize*); — *o.'s teeth*, mit den Zähnen
knirschen. — *s.* (*coll.*) die ungeheuere
Anstrengung, die Plackerei.
grinder ['graində], *s. coffee* —, die
Kaffeemühle; *knife* —, der Schleifer,
Wetzer; der Backzahn (*molar*).
grindstone ['graindstoun], *s.* der Schleif-
stein; *keep o.'s nose to the* —, fest bei
der Arbeit bleiben.
grip [grip], *s.* der Griff; *lose o.'s* —,
nicht mehr bewältigen können (wie
bisher); (*Tech.*) der Handgriff (*handle*).
— *v.a.* ergreifen, festhalten.
gripe [graip], *v.n.* (*sl.*) meckern.

gripes [graips], *s. pl.* (*Med.*) das Bauch-
grimmen, die Kolik.
gripping ['gripiŋ], *adj.* fesselnd (*story*).
grisly ['grizli], *adj.* scheußlich, gräßlich.
grist [grist], *s.* das Mahlgut, Gemah-
lene; — *to o.'s mill*, Wasser auf seine
Mühle.
gristle [grisl], *s.* der Knorpel.
grit [grit], *s.* das Schrot, der Kies; der
Mut (*courage*).
gritty ['griti], *adj.* körnig, kiesig,
sandig.
grizzled [grizld], *adj.* grau, grau-
meliert.
groan [groun], *v.n.* stöhnen.
groats [grouts], *s. pl.* die Hafergrütze.
grocer ['grousə], *s.* der Kolonialwaren-
händler, Feinkosthändler.
groin [grɔin], *s.* (*Anat.*) die Leiste;
(*Archit.*) die Gewölbekante, Rippe.
groom [gru:m], *s.* der Stallknecht
(*stables*); (*obs.*) der Junge (*inn*). — *v.a.*
schniegeln, bürsten; schön machen.
groove [gru:v], *s.* die Rinne; die Rille
(*of gramophone record*). — *v.a.* rillen;
furchen (*dig a furrow*).
grope [group], *v.n.* tappen, tasten
(*around*, umher).
gross [grous], *adj.* dick (*fat*); plump
(*heavy-handed*); grob (*ill-mannered*);
— *weight*, das Bruttogewicht; ungeheuer (*error*).
grotto ['grɔtou], *s.* die Grotte.
ground [graund], *s.* der Grund, Boden
(*also pl.*); die Ursache (*cause*); —
floor, das Erdgeschoß. — *v.n.* stranden
(*of ship*).
groundwork ['graundwə:k], *s.* die
Grundlagen, *f. pl.*
group [gru:p], *s.* die Gruppe. — *v.a.*
gruppieren, anordnen.
grouse (1) [graus], *v.n.* (*coll.*) meckern,
sich beklagen. — *s.* der Grund zur
Klage, die Beschwerde.
grouse (2) [graus], *s.* (*Orn.*) das Birk-
huhn, Moorhuhn.
grove [grouv], *s.* der Hain, das Wäld-
chen.
grovel [grɔvl], *v.n.* kriechen, schöntun
(*Dat.*).
grow [grou], *v.n. irr.* wachsen, sich
mehren (*increase*); werden (*become*).
— *v.a.* anbauen, anpflanzen.
growl [graul], *v.n.* brummen, knurren.
— *s.* das Gebrumme, Geknurre.
grown-up [groun'ʌp], *s.* der Erwachsene. — *adj.* erwachsen.
growth [grouθ], *s.* das Anwachsen
(*increase*); das Wachstum (*growing*).
grub [grʌb], *s.* (*Zool.*) die Larve; (*coll.*)
das Essen. — *v.n.* — *about*, wühlen.
grudge [grʌdʒ], *s.* der Groll; Neid
(*jealousy*). — *v.a.* mißgönnen (*envy*).
— *v.n.* — *doing s.th.*, etwas ungerne
tun.
gruel ['gru:əl], *s.* der Haferschleim.
gruesome ['gru:səm], *adj.* schauerlich,
schrecklich.
gruff [grʌf], *adj.* mürrisch.
grumble [grʌmbl], *v.n.* murren, klagen.

grumbler ['grʌmblə], s. der Unzu-friedene, Nörgler.

grunt [grʌnt], v.n. grunzen. — s. das Grunzen.

guarantee [gærən'tiː], v.a. bürgen, garantieren. — s. die Bürgschaft; (Comm.) die Garantie.

guarantor [gærən'tɔː], s. der Bürge; (Comm.) der Garant.

guard [gaːd], s. die Wache (watch or watchman); (Railw.) der Schaffner; die Schutzvorrichtung (protective device); (fire) —, das Kamingitter; (for sword) das Stichblatt. — v.a. be-wachen; behüten (protect). — v.n. auf der Hut sein; — against, sich hüten (vor, Dat.); vorbeugen.

guarded ['gaːdid], adj. behutsam, vorsichtig.

guardian ['gaːdjən], s. der Vormund (of child); der Wächter.

guardianship ['gaːdjənʃip], s. (Law) die Vormundschaft.

Guatemalan [gwæti'maːlən], adj. guatemaltekisch. — s. der Guatemal-teke.

Guelph [gwelf], s. der Welfe.

guess [ges], v.a. raten (a riddle). — v.n. (Am.) glauben, meinen. — s. die Vermutung; have a —, rate mal!

guest [gest], s. der Gast; paying —, der Pensionär.

guffaw [gʌ'fɔː], s. das (laute) Gelächter.

guidance ['gaidəns], s. die Führung, Anleitung.

guide [gaid], s. der Führer, Wegweiser, Reiseführer; (Phot.) die Führung. — v.a. führen, anleiten.

guided ['gaidid], adj. gelenkt; — missile, das Ferngeschoß, die Rakete.

guild [gild], s. die Gilde, Zunft, In-nung.

guildhall ['gildhɔːl], s. das Rathaus.

guile [gail], s. der Betrug, die Arglist.

guileless ['gaillis], adj. arglos.

guilt [gilt], s. die Schuld.

guilty ['gilti], adj. schuldig.

guinea ['gini], s. die Guinee (21 shil-lings); — fowl, das Perlhuhn; — pig, das Meerschweinchen.

guise [gaiz], s. die Verkleidung (cos-tume); die Erscheinung (appearance).

guitar [gi'taː], s. (Mus.) die Gitarre.

gulf [gʌlf], s. der Meerbusen, Golf; der Abgrund (abyss).

gull [gʌl], s. (Orn.) die Möwe.

gullet ['gʌlit], s. (Anat.) der Schlund, die Gurgel.

gullible ['gʌlibl], adj. leichtgläubig.

gully ['gʌli], s. die Schlucht (abyss).

gulp [gʌlp], v.a. schlucken. — s. der Schluck, Zug.

gum (1) [gʌm], s. (Bot.) der Gummi. — v.a. gummieren; (coll.) — up, verderben (spoil).

gum (2) [gʌm], s. (Anat.) das Zahn-fleisch.

gun [gʌn], s. das Gewehr (rifle); die Kanone (cannon); — carriage, die Lafette.

gunpowder ['gʌnpaudə], s. das Schieß-pulver.

gunsmith ['gʌnsmiθ], s. der Büchsen-macher.

gurgle [gə:gl], v.n. glucksen.

gush [gʌʃ], v.n. sich ergießen; schwär-men.

gusset ['gʌsit], s. (Tail.) der Zwickel.

gust [gʌst], s. der Windstoß.

gut [gʌt], s. (Anat.) der Darm; (pl.) die Eingeweide, n. pl.;(pl.) (coll.) der Mut. — v.a. ausnehmen; ausleeren.

gutter ['gʌtə], s. die Rinne, Gosse.

guttersnipe ['gʌtəsnaip], s. der Lausbube.

guttural ['gʌtərəl], adj. Kehl-. — s. (Phon.) der Kehllaut.

guy [gai], s. die Vogelscheuche, die verkleidete Puppe; (Am.) der Kerl.

guzzle [gʌzl], v.n. schlemmen.

gymnasium [dʒim'neiziəm], s. die Turnhalle.

gymnastics [dʒim'næstiks], s. pl. das Turnen; die Gymnastik.

gypsum ['dʒipsəm], s. der Gips; der schwefelsaure Kalk.

gyrate [dʒaiə'reit], v.n. sich im Kreise bewegen, sich drehen, kreisen.

H

H [eitʃ], das H.

haberdasher ['hæbədæʃə], s. der Kurz-warenhändler.

haberdashery ['hæbədæʃəri], s. die Kurzwarenhandlung.

habit ['hæbit], s. die Gewohnheit (custom); force of —, aus Gewohnheit, die Macht der Gewohnheit; die Kleidung (costume); riding —, das Reitkostüm.

habitable ['hæbitəbl], adj. bewohnbar.

habitation [hæbi'teiʃən], s. die Woh-nung.

habitual [hə'bitjuəl], adj. gewohn-heitsmäßig.

habituate [hə'bitjueit], v.a. gewöhnen.

hack (1) [hæk], v.a. hacken (wood); treten.

hack (2) [hæk], s. der Lohnschreiber; der (alte) Gaul, das Mietpferd (horse).

hackle [hækl], v.a. hecheln.

hackney ['hækni], s. — carriage, die Mietskutsche; das Taxi.

haddock ['hædək], s. (Zool.) der Schell-fisch.

haemorrhage ['hemərid3], s. (Med.) die Blutung, der Blutsturz.

haemorrhoids ['hemərɔidz], s.pl.(Med.) die Hämorrhoiden, f. pl.

hag [hæg], s. das alte Weib; die Hexe (witch).

haggard

haggard ['hægəd], *adj.* hager (*lean*); häßlich, abgehärmt.

haggle [hægl], *v.n.* feilschen.

haggler ['hæglə], *s.* der Feilscher.

hail (1) [heil], *s.* der Hagel. — *v.n.* hageln.

hail (2) [heil], *v.a.* (mit einem Ruf) begrüßen; rufen. — *interj.* Heil, willkommen! — *s.* der Zuruf, Gruß.

hair [hɛə], *s.* das Haar; *split* —s, Haarspalterei treiben.

haircut ['hɛəkʌt], *s.* der Haarschnitt.

hairdresser ['hɛədrɛsə], *s.* der Friseur.

hale [heil], *adj.* — *and hearty*, frisch und gesund, rüstig.

half [hɑːf], *adj.* halb. — *adv.* — *baked*, unreif; unterentwickelt (*stupid*); (*coll.*) *not* —, und wie! sehr gern. — *s.* die Hälfte; *too clever by* —, allzu gescheit.

halfcaste ['hɑːfkɑːst], *s.* der Mischling.

halfpenny ['heipni], *s.* der halbe Penny.

halfwit ['hɑːfwit], *s.* der Dummkopf.

halibut ['hælibət], *s.* (*Zool.*) der Heilbutt.

hall [hɔːl], *s.* der Saal; die Halle; der Hausflur (*entrance* —); (*Univ.*) — (*of residence*), das Studentenheim; — *porter*, der Portier.

hallmark ['hɔːlmɑːk], *s.* das Kennzeichen.

hallow ['hæləu], *v.a.* weihen, heiligen.

Halloween [hæləu'iːn]. der Allerheiligenabend.

hallucination [həluːsi'neiʃən], *s.* die Halluzination.

halo ['heiləu], *s.* der Heiligenschein (*of saint*); der Hof (*round the moon*).

halt [hɔːlt], *v.n.* halten, haltmachen; zögern (*tarry*). — *! Halt! —ing speech*, die Sprechhemmung. — *v.a.* anhalten, zum Halten bringen. — *s.* (*Railw.*) die (kleine) Haltestelle.

halve [hɑːv], *v.a.* halbieren.

ham [hæm], *s.* (*Cul.*) der Schinken; (*Anat.*) der Schenkel; — *acting*, das Schmierentheater.

hammer ['hæmə], *s.* der Hammer. — *v.a., v.n.* hämmern; — *away at*, an etwas emsig arbeiten; — *out a problem*, ein Problem zur Lösung bringen.

hammock ['hæmək], *s.* die Hängematte.

hamper (1) ['hæmpə], *s.* der Packkorb.

hamper (2) ['hæmpə], *v.a.* behindern.

hand [hænd], *s.* die Hand; *a fair* —, eine gute Handschrift; der Uhrzeiger (*on watch, clock*); die Seite (*right, left* —); die Karten, *f. pl.* (*card game*); *play a strong* —, starke Karten halten *or* spielen; *on* —, vorrätig, auf Lager; *get out of* —, unkontrollierbar werden. — *v.a.* — *in*, einhändigen, einreichen; — *out*, austeilen; — *over*, übergeben, einhändigen.

handbag ['hændbæg], *s.* die Handtasche.

handbill ['hændbil], *s.* der Zettel, Reklamezettel (*advertising*).

handful ['hændful], *s.* die Handvoll; *to be quite a* —, genug zu schaffen geben; das Sorgenkind.

handicap ['hændikæp], *s.* das Hindernis. — *v.a.* hindern, behindern.

handicraft ['hændikrɑːft], *s.* das Handwerk; Kunsthandwerk.

handkerchief ['hæŋkətʃif], *s.* das Taschentuch.

handle [hændl], *s.* der Griff; der Henkel (*pot, vase*). — *v.a.* handhaben (*machine*); behandeln (*person*); anpacken (*problem*).

handlebar ['hændlbɑː], *s.* die Lenkstange (*bicycle*).

handmaid(en) ['hændmeid(n)], *s.* (*obs.*) die Magd.

handrail ['hændreil], *s.* das Geländer.

handshake ['hændʃeik], *s.* der Händedruck.

handsome ['hænsəm], *adj.* hübsch, schön, stattlich.

handy ['hændi], *adj.* geschickt; — *man*, der Gelegenheitsarbeiter, Mann für alles.

hang [hæŋ], *v.a. reg. & irr.* hängen; aufhängen (*suspend*); — *it!* zum Henker; — *paper*, ein Zimmer austapezieren; — *dog expression*, den Kopf hängen lassen, die betrübte Miene. — *v.n.* hängen; (*coll.*) — *on!* warte einen Moment! — *about*, herumstehen; herumlungern (*loiter*).

hanger-on [hæŋər'ɔn], *s.* der Anhänger, Mitläufer.

hangman ['hæŋmən], *s.* der Henker.

hanker ['hæŋkə], *v.n.* sich sehnen.

Hanoverian [hæno'viəriən], *adj.* hannöversch. — *s.* der Hannoveraner.

hansom ['hænsəm], *s.* die zweirädrige Droschke.

haphazard [hæp'hæzəd], *s.* der Zufall, das Geratewohl.

hapless ['hæplis], *adj.* unglücklich.

happen [hæpn], *v.n.* sich ereignen, passieren; — *to . . .*, zufällig . . .

happiness ['hæpinis], *s.* das Glück; die Glückseligkeit.

happy ['hæpi], *adj.* glücklich, glückselig.

harangue [hə'ræŋ], *s.* die Ansprache. — *v.a.* einsprechen (auf, *Acc.*); anreden.

harass ['hærəs], *v.a.* plagen, quälen.

harbinger ['hɑːbindʒə], *s.* der Vorbote, Bote.

harbour ['hɑːbə], *s.* der Hafen. — *v.a.* beherbergen (*shelter*); hegen (*cherish*).

hard [hɑːd], *adj.* schwer (*difficult*); hart (*tough*); hartherzig (*miserly*); — *up*, in Not, in Geldverlegenheit; — *of hearing*, schwerhörig.

harden ['hɑːdn], *v.a.* härten. — *v.n.* hart werden.

hardiness ['hɑːdinis], *s.* die Kraft, Stärke; die Rüstigkeit.

hardly ['hɑːdli], *adv.* kaum.

hardship ['hɑːdʃip], *s.* die Not, Bedrängnis (*need*); die Beschwerde (*complaint*).

hardware ['hɑːdwɛə], *s.* die Eisen-ware(n).

hardy ['hɑːdi], *adj.* abgehärtet, stark; (*Bot.*) — *annual*, ein widerstands-fähiges Jahresgewächs.

hare [hɛə], *s.* (*Zool.*) der Hase; — *brained*, unbedacht, gedankenlos; — *lip*, die Hasenscharte.

harebell ['hɛəbel], *s.* (*Bot.*) die Glocken-blume.

haricot ['hærikou], *s.* (*Bot.*) — *bean*, die welsche Bohne.

hark [hɑːk], *v.n.* horchen.

harlequin ['hɑːlikwin], *s.* der Harlekin.

harlot ['hɑːlət], *s.* die Hure.

harm [hɑːm], *s.* das Leid, Unrecht; *do* — *to*, Schaden zufügen (*Dat.*). — *v.a.* verletzen (*hurt*); schaden (*dam-age, Dat.*).

harmful ['hɑːmful], *adj.* schädlich.

harmless ['hɑːmlis], *adj.* harmlos.

harmonious [hɑːˈmouniəs], *adj.* har-monisch; einmütig (*of one mind*).

harmonize ['hɑːmənaiz], *v.a.* in Ein-klang bringen. — *v.n.* harmonieren, in Einklang stehen.

harmony ['hɑːməni], *s.* (*Mus.*) die Harmonie; (*fig.*) der Einklang, die Einmütigkeit.

harness ['hɑːnis], *s.* der Harnisch. — *v.a.* anschirren, anspannen (*horse*); (*fig.*) nutzbar machen.

harp [hɑːp], *s.* (*Mus.*) die Harfe. — *v.n.* (*coll.*) — *upon*, herumreiten auf (*Dat.*).

harpoon [hɑːˈpuːn], *s.* die Harpune. — *v.a.* harpunieren.

harrow ['hærou], *s.* die Egge, Harke. — *v.a.* harken, eggen; quälen.

harry ['hæri], *v.a.* verheeren, quälen.

harsh [hɑːʃ], *adj.* herb, rauh (*rough*); streng (*severe*).

hart [hɑːt], *s.* (*Zool.*) der Hirsch.

harvest ['hɑːvist], *s.* die Ernte; — *home*, das Erntefest.

hash [hæʃ], *v.a.* zerhacken; vermischen (*mix up*). — *s.* das Hackfleisch; *make a — of things*, verpfuschen, alles verderben.

hasp [hæsp *or* hɑːsp], *s.* der Haken, die Spange.

haste [heist], *s.* die Hast, Eile (*hurry*); die Voreiligkeit (*rashness*).

hasten [heisn], *v.n.* eilen, sich beeilen.

hasty ['heisti], *adj.* voreilig.

hat [hæt], *s.* der Hut; (*coll.*) *talk through o.'s* —, Unsinn reden.

hatch (1) [hætʃ], *s.* die Brut (*chickens*). — *v.a., v.n.* (aus-)brüten; aushecken (*cunning*).

hatch (2) [hætʃ], *s.* das Servierfenster (*for serving food*); (*Naut.*) die Luke.

hatch (3) [hætʃ], *v.a.* (*Art*) schraffieren.

hatchet ['hætʃit], *s.* das Beil, die Axt; *bury the* —, das Kriegsbeil begraben.

hate [heit], *v.a., v.n.* hassen; — *to . . .*, nicht . . . wollen. — *s.* der Haß, Widerwille, die Abneigung.

hateful ['heitful], *adj.* verhaßt (*hated*); gehässig (*hating*).

hatred ['heitrid], *s.* der Haß.

hatter ['hætə], *s.* der Hutmacher.

haughty ['hɔːti], *adj.* übermütig (*super-cilious*); hochmütig, stolz (*proud*); hochnäsig (*giving o.s. airs*).

haul [hɔːl], *v.a.* schleppen, ziehen. — *s.* das Schleppen; (*coll.*) die Beute.

haulage ['hɔːlidʒ], *s.* der Schleppdienst, die Spedition.

haunch [hɔːntʃ], *s.* (*Anat.*) die Hüfte; der Schenkel (*horse*); die Keule (*venison*).

haunt [hɔːnt], *v.a.* heimsuchen, spuken (*in, Dat.*); *it is* —*ed*, hier spukt es.

have [hæv], *v.a. irr.* haben, besitzen (*possess*); erhalten; lassen; — *to*, müs-sen; — *s.th. made, done*, etwas machen lassen.

haven [heivn], *s.* der Zufluchtsort.

haversack ['hævəsæk], *s.* der Brot-beutel.

havoc ['hævək], *s.* die Verwüstung, Verheerung.

hawk (1) [hɔːk], *s.* (*Orn.*) der Habicht; der Falke (*falcon*).

hawk (2) [hɔːk], *v.a.* hausieren.

hawker ['hɔːkə], *s.* der Hausierer.

hawthorn ['hɔːθɔːn], *s.* (*Bot.*) der Hagedorn.

hay [hei], *s.* das Heu; — *fever*, der Heuschnupfen; — *loft*, der Heuboden; — *rick*, der Heuschober.

hazard ['hæzəd], *s.* der Zufall (*chance*); die Gefahr (*danger*); das Risiko (*risk*). — *v.a.* aufs Spiel setzen, riskieren.

hazardous ['hæzədəs], *adj.* gefährlich, gewagt.

haze [heiz], *s.* der Dunst, Nebeldunst.

hazel [heizl], *s.* (*Bot.*) die Haselstaude; — *nut*, die Haselnuß.

hazy ['heizi], *adj.* dunstig, nebelig.

he [hiː], *pers. pron.* er; — *who*, der-jenige, welcher, wer.

head [hed], *s.* der Kopf; die Spitze (*of arrow*); der Leiter (*of firm*); (*Sch.*) der Direktor; die Überschrift (*heading*); die Krisis (*climax*); (*Pol.*) der Führer, das (Staats-)Oberhaupt. — *v.a.* anführen, führen; (*Mil.*) befehligen; — *v.n.* (*Naut.*) — *for*, Kurs nehmen auf (*Acc.*).

headache ['hedeik], *s.* (*Med.*) die Kopfschmerzen, *m. pl.*

headlamp ['hedlæmp], *s.* der Schein-werfer.

headphone ['hedfoun], *s.* (*usually pl.*) der Kopfhörer.

headstrong ['hedstrɔŋ], *adj.* halsstar-rig.

heady ['hedi], *adj.* hastig, ungestüm; be-rauschend (*liquor*).

heal [hiːl], *v.a.* heilen. — *v.n.* (zu)heilen, verheilen.

health [helθ], *s.* die Gesundheit; — *resort*, der Kurort; *your (good)* —*!* Gesundheit! auf Ihr Wohl! Prosit! (*drinking toast*).

healthy ['helθi], *adj.* gesund.

heap [hiːp], *s.* der Haufen, die Menge. — *v.a.* häufen, aufhäufen.

hear [hiə], *v.a., v.n. irr.* hören; erfahren (*learn*); (*Law*) verhören (*evidence*).

hearing ['hiəriŋ], *s.* das Gehör (*auditory perception*); *within* —, in Hörweite; (*Law*) das Verhör.

hearsay ['hiəsei], *s.* das Hörensagen.

hearse [həːs], *s.* der Leichenwagen.

heart [haːt], *s.* das Herz; der Mut (*courage*); das Innerste (*core*); *by* —, auswendig; *take to* —, beherzigen; *take* — *from*, Mut fassen (aus, *Dat.*).

heartburn ['haːtbəːn], *s.* (*Med.*) das Sodbrennen.

heartfelt ['haːtfelt], *adj.* herzlich.

hearth [haːθ], *s.* der Herd.

hearty ['haːti], *adj.* herzlich; aufrichtig (*sincere*); herzhaft.

heat [hiːt], *s.* die Hitze, Wärme; die Brunst (*animals*). — *v.a.* heizen (*fuel*); erhitzen (*make hot*).

heath [hiːθ], *s.* die Heide.

heathen [hiːðən], *s.* der Heide, Ungläubige.

heather ['heðə], *s.* (*Bot.*) das Heidekraut.

heating ['hiːtiŋ], *s.* die Heizung.

heave [hiːv], *v.a. reg. & irr.* heben, hieben. — *v.n.* sich heben und senken.

heaven [hevn], *s.* der Himmel; *good* —*s!* ach, du lieber Himmel!

heaviness ['hevinis], *s.* die Schwere.

heavy ['hevi], *adj.* schwer; schwerwiegend (*grave*).

Hebrew ['hiːbruː], *adj.* hebräisch. — *s.* der Hebräer, der Jude.

hectic ['hektik], *adj.* hektisch, aufgeregt.

hector ['hektə], *v.a.* tyrannisieren (*bully*). — *v.n.* renommieren, prahlen.

hedge [hedʒ], *s.* die Hecke. — *v.a.* einhegen, einzäunen.

hedgehog ['hedʒhɔg], *s.* (*Zool.*) der Igel.

hedgerow ['hedʒrou], *s.* die Baumhecke.

heed [hiːd], *s.* die Hut, Aufmerksamkeit. — *v.a.* beachten.

heedless ['hiːdlis], *adj.* unachtsam.

heel [hiːl], *s.* die Ferse (*foot*); der Absatz (*shoe*); *take to o.'s* —*s*, die Flucht ergreifen; (*Am. sl.*) der Lump.

heifer ['hefə], *s.* (*Zool.*) die junge Kuh.

height [hait], *s.* die Höhe, Anhöhe; die Größe (*tallness*); der Hügel (*hill*).

heighten [haitn], *v.a.* erhöhen.

heir [ɛə], *s.* der Erbe (*to, Genit.*).

heiress ['ɛəres], *s.* die Erbin.

heirloom ['ɛəluːm], *s.* das Erbstück.

helicopter ['helikɔptə], *s.* (*Aviat.*) der Hubschrauber.

hell [hel], *s.* die Hölle. — *interj.* zum Teufel!

hellish ['heliʃ], *adj.* höllisch.

helm [helm], *s.* das Steuer, Steuerruder.

helmet ['helmit], *s.* der Helm.

helmsman ['helmzmən], *s.* (*Naut.*) der Steuermann.

help [help], *v.a., v.n.* helfen (*Dat.*); *I cannot* — *laughing*, ich muß lachen; *I cannot* — *it*, ich kann nichts dafür. — *v.r.* — *o.s.*, sich bedienen. — *s.* die Hilfe, Unterstützung.

helpful ['helpful], *adj.* behilflich, hilfreich.

helping ['helpiŋ], *s.* die Portion.

helpless ['helplis], *adj.* hilflos.

helpmate, helpmeet ['helpmeit, -miːt], *s.* der Gehilfe, die Gehilfin.

helter-skelter ['heltə'skeltə], *adv.* Hals über Kopf.

hem [hem], *s.* der Saum. — *v.a.* (*Tail.*) einsäumen, säumen.

hemisphere ['hemisfiə], *s.* die Halbkugel, Hemisphäre.

hemlock ['hemlɔk], *s.* der Schierling.

hemp [hemp], *s.* der Hanf.

hemstitch ['hemstitʃ], *s.* der Hohlsaum.

hen [hen], *s.* die Henne (*poultry*); das Weibchen (*other birds*).

hence [hens], *adv.* von hier; von jetzt an.

henceforth ['hens'fɔːθ], *adv.* fortan, von nun an.

henpecked ['henpekd], *adj.* unter dem Pantoffel stehend.

her [həː], *pers. pron.* sie (*Acc.*), ihr (*Dat.*). — *poss. adj.* ihr.

herald ['herəld], *s.* der Herold. — *v.a.* ankündigen.

heraldry ['herəldri], *s.* die Wappenkunde.

herb [həːb], *s.* (*Bot.*) das Kraut.

herbaceous [həːˈbeiʃəs], *adj.* krautartig.

herbage ['həːbidʒ], *s.* das Gras; (*Law*) das Weiderecht.

herbal ['həːbəl], *adj.* krautartig, Kräuter-, Kraut-.

herd [həːd], *s.* die Herde. — *v.n.* sich zusammenfinden.

here [hiə], *adv.* hier.

hereafter [hiərˈɑːftə], *adv.* hernach, künftig. — *s.* die Zukunft; das Jenseits.

hereby [hiəˈbai], *adv.* hiermit.

hereditary [hiˈreditəri], *adj.* erblich.

heredity [hiˈrediti], *s.* (*Biol.*) die Erblichkeit, Vererbung.

heresy ['herisi], *s.* die Ketzerei.

heretic ['heritik], *s.* der Ketzer.

heretofore ['hiətuˈfɔː], *adv.* zuvor, vormals.

heritage ['heritidʒ], *s.* die Erbschaft.

hermetic [həːˈmetik], *adj.* luftdicht.

hermit ['həːmit], *s.* der Eremit, Einsiedler.

hero ['hiərou], *s.* der Held.

heroic [hiˈrouik], *adj.* heldenhaft, heldenmütig.

heroine ['heroin], *s.* die Heldin.

heroism ['heroizm], *s.* der Heldenmut.

heron ['herən], *s.* (*Orn.*) der Reiher.

herring ['heriŋ], *s.* (*Zool.*) der Hering; *red* —, die Ablenkungsfinte, das Ablenkungsmanöver; — *bone*, die Gräte; *pickled* —, der eingemachte Hering.

hers [həːz], *poss. pron.* ihr, der ihre, der ihrige.

herself [həːˈself], *pers. pron.* sich; sie selbst.

hesitate ['heziteit], *v.n.* zögern, zaudern; unschlüssig sein (*be undecided*).

hesitation [hezi'teiʃən], s. das Zögern, Zaudern; das Bedenken (deliberation).

Hessian ['heʃən], adj. hessisch. — s. der Hesse.

hessian ['hesiən], s. die Sackleinwand (textile).

heterodox ['hetərədɔks], adj. irrgläubig.

heterogeneous [hetəro'dʒi:niəs], adj. heterogen, ungleichartig.

hew [hju:], v.a. irr. hauen.

hexagonal [hek'sægənəl], adj. sechseckig.

hiatus [hai'eitəs], s. die Lücke.

hibernate ['haibəneit], v.n. überwintern.

hibernation [haibə'neiʃən], s. der Winterschlaf.

hiccup ['hikʌp], s. (usually pl.) (Med.) der Schlucken, Schluckauf.

hickory ['hikəri], s. (Bot.) das Hickoryholz.

hide (1) [haid], v.a. irr. verstecken, verbergen. — v.n. irr. sich verbergen; — and seek, das Versteckspiel.

hide (2) [haid], s. die Haut (of animal), das Fell, (tanned) das Leder.

hideous ['hidiəs], adj. häßlich, scheußlich, furchtbar.

hiding (1) ['haidiŋ], s. das Versteck.

hiding (2) ['haidiŋ], s. die Tracht Prügel.

hierarchy ['haiərɑːki], s. die Hierarchie.

higgle [higl] see haggle.

higgledy-piggledy ['higldi'pigldi], adv. wüst durcheinander.

high [hai], adj. hoch; erhaben, vornehm; angegangen (meat); — school, die höhere Schule; — time, höchste Zeit; (Am.) vergnügliche Zeit; High Church, die Hochkirche. — s. (Meteor.) das Hoch.

Highness ['hainis], s. die Hoheit (title).

highroad, highway ['hairoud, 'haiwei], s. die Haupt- or Landstraße.

highwayman ['haiweimən], s. der Straßenräuber.

hike [haik], v.n. wandern, einen Ausflug machen. — s. die Wanderung, der Ausflug.

hilarious [hi'lɛəriəs], adj. fröhlich, lustig, ausgelassen.

hill [hil], s. der Hügel, Berg.

hilt [hilt], s. der Griff.

him [him], pers. pron. ihn, ihm.

himself [him'self], pers. pron. sich; er selbst.

hind [haind], s. (Zool.) die Hirschkuh, Hindin.

hinder ['hində], v.a. hindern.

hindmost ['haindmoust], adj. hinterst; the devil take the —, den letzten hol der Teufel! nach mir die Sintflut!

hindrance ['hindrəns], s. das Hindernis; (Law) without let or —, ohne Hinderung.

Hindu [hin'du:], s. der Hindu.

hinge [hindʒ], s. die Angel, der Angelpunkt. — v.n. sich um etwas drehen; von etwas abhängen (on, Dat.).

hint [hint], v.n. zu verstehen geben, auf etwas hindeuten (at, auf, Acc.), andeuten. — s. die Andeutung, der Fingerzeig.

hip (1) [hip], s. (Anat.) die Hüfte.

hip (2) [hip], s. (Bot.) die Hagebutte.

hire ['haiə], v.a. (ver-)mieten (car etc.); anstellen (man etc.). — s. die Miete; der Lohn (wage); — purchase, der Abzahlungskauf, die Ratenzahlung.

hireling ['haiəliŋ], s. der Mietling.

hirsute ['hə:sju:t], adj. behaart, haarig.

his [hiz], poss. adj. sein, seine. — poss. pron. sein, der seinige, der seine.

hiss [his], v.n. zischen (at, auf, Acc.). — s. das Zischen.

historian [his'tɔ:riən], s. der Historiker, der Geschichtsschreiber.

historical [his'tɔrikəl], adj. historisch, geschichtlich.

history ['histəri], s. die Geschichte, die Geschichtswissenschaft.

histrionic [histri'ɔnik], adj. schauspielerisch.

hit [hit], v.a. irr. schlagen, stoßen. — s. der Schlag, der Treffer (on the target); (Am.) der Schlager, Erfolg (success); — parade, die Schlagerparade.

hitch [hitʃ], v.a. anhaken (hook); anhängen; — a lift, — hike, per Anhalter fahren. — s. der Nachteil, der Haken.

hither ['hiðə], adv. hierher.

hitherto [hiðə'tu:], adv. bisher.

hive [haiv], s. der Bienenkorb; Bienenstock; — of bees, der Schwarm.

hoar [hɔ:], adj. eisgrau, weißlich; — frost, der Reif.

hoard [hɔ:d], v.a. hamstern. — s. der Vorrat, Schatz.

hoarding ['hɔ:diŋ], s. die Umzäunung, die Bretterwand; die Reklamewand.

hoarse [hɔ:s], adj. heiser.

hoarseness ['hɔ:snis], s. die Heiserkeit.

hoax [houks], s. der Betrug, die Irreführung; der Schabernack (in fun). — v.a. betrügen; foppen (in fun).

hobble [hɔbl], v.n. humpeln. — v.a. an den Füßen fesseln.

hobby ['hɔbi], s. das Steckenpferd, Hobby, die Liebhaberei.

hobgoblin [hɔb'gɔblin], s. der Kobold.

hobnail ['hɔbneil], s. der Hufnagel.

hobnailed ['hɔbneild], adj. — boots, genagelte Stiefel, m. pl.

hobnob ['hɔbnɔb], v.n. (coll.) vertraulich sein.

hock (1) [hɔk], s. (Anat.) das Sprunggelenk.

hock (2) [hɔk], s. (wine) der Rheinwein.

hod [hɔd], s. (Build.) der Trog; der Eimer (coal).

hodge-podge see under hotchpotch.

hoe [hou], s. die Hacke, Harke. — v.a., v.n. hacken, harken.

hog [hɔg], s. das Schwein. — v.a. verschlingen (food); an sich reißen (grasp).

hogshead ['hɔgzhed], s. das Oxhoft.

hoist [hɔist], v.a. hissen.

hold [hould], *v.a.*, *v.n.* *irr.* halten (*keep*); enthalten (*contain*); behaupten (*assert*); meinen (*think*); gelten (*be valid*); — *forth*, deklamieren; — *good*, sich bewähren; — *out*, hinhalten (*hope*); (*endure*) aushalten;—*up*, aufhalten. — *s.* (*Naut.*) der Schiffsraum; der Macht (*power*).

holder ['houldə], *s.* der Inhaber, Besitzer.

holding ['houldiŋ], *s.* das Pachtgut (*farm*); der Besitz (*property*); (*Comm.*) der Trust.

hole [houl], *s.* das Loch; die Höhle (*cavity*). — *v.a.* aushöhlen; (*Golf*) ins Loch spielen.

holiday ['hɔlidei], *s.* der Feiertag; der Urlaub (*vacation*); (*pl.*) die Ferien, *pl.*

holiness ['houlinis], *s.* die Heiligkeit.

hollow ['hɔlou], *adj.* hohl. — *s.* die Höhlung; die Höhle.

holly ['hɔli], *s.* (*Bot.*) die Stechpalme.

hollyhock ['hɔlihɔk], *s.* (*Bot.*) die Stockrose.

holocaust ['hɔlokɔːst], *s.* das Brandopfer; die Katastrophe.

holster ['houlstə], *s.* die Pistolentasche, die Halfter.

holy ['houli], *adj.* heilig; *Holy Week*, die Karwoche.

homage ['hɔmidʒ], *s.* die Huldigung; *pay* —, huldigen (*Dat.*).

home [houm], *s.* das Heim, die Wohnung; die Heimat; *at* —, zu Hause; *Home Office*, das Innenministerium; — *Rule*, (*Pol.*) die Selbstverwaltung.

homer ['houmə] (*Am.*) *see* **homing pigeon**.

homesick ['houmsik], *adj.* an Heimweh leidend.

homestead ['houmsted], *s.* der Bauernhof.

homicide ['hɔmisaid], *s.* der Mord (*crime*); der Mörder (*killer*).

homily ['hɔmili], *s.* die Predigt; Moralpredigt.

homing pigeon ['houmiŋ'pidʒən], *s.* die Brieftaube.

homogeneous [hɔmə'dʒiːniəs], *adj.* homogen; gleichartig.

hone [houn], *s.* der Wetzstein. — *v.a.* (*blade, knife*) abziehen.

honest ['ɔnist], *adj.* ehrlich, aufrichtig.

honesty ['ɔnisti], *s.* die Ehrlichkeit.

honey ['hʌni], *s.* der Honig; (*Am.,* *coll.*) Liebling!

honeycomb ['hʌnikoum], *s.* die Honigwabe.

honeymoon ['hʌnimuːn], *s.* die Flitterwochen.

honorarium [ɔnə'reəriəm], *s.* das Honorar.

honorary ['ɔnərəri], *adj.* Ehren-, ehrenamtlich.

honour ['ɔnə], *s.* die Ehre; *your* —, Euer Ehrwürden; Euer Gnaden (*title*). — *v.a.* ehren, auszeichnen.

honourable ['ɔnərəbl], *adj.* ehrenwert, ehrenvoll; Hochwohlgeboren (*title*).

hood [hud], *s.* die Kapuze; das akademische Gradabzeichen über dem Talar; (*Hunt.*) die Haube; —*ed* *falcon*, der Jagdfalke (mit Haube).

hoodwink ['hudwiŋk], *v.a.* täuschen.

hoof [huːf *or* huf], *s.* der Huf (*horse*); die Klaue.

hook [huk], *s.* der Haken; *by* — *or by crook*, mit allen Mitteln. — *v.a.* angeln, fangen.

hooked [hukd], *adj.* gekrümmt, hakenförmig.

hooligan ['huːligən], *s.* der Rowdy.

hoop [huːp], *s.* der Reifen. — *v.a.* (ein Faß) binden.

hooper ['huːpə], *s.* der Böttcher.

hoopoe ['huːpou], *s.* (*Orn.*) der Wiedehopf.

hoot [huːt], *v.n.* schreien (*owl*); ertönen (*siren*); hupen (*car*).

hooter ['huːtə], *s.* die Sirene (*siren*); die Hupe (*car*).

hop (1) [hɔp], *v.n.* hüpfen, tanzen; —*ping mad*, ganz verrückt.

hop (2) [hɔp], *s.* (*Bot.*) der Hopfen. — *v.a.* (*beer*) hopfen, Hopfen zusetzen (*Dat.*). — *v.n.* Hopfen ernten.

hope [houp], *s.* die Hoffnung. — *v.n.* hoffen (*for*, auf, *Acc.*).

hopeless ['houplis], *adj.* hoffnungslos.

horizon [hə'raizən], *s.* der Horizont.

horizontal [hɔri'zɔntl], *adj.* horizontal, waagrecht.

horn [hɔːn], *s.* das Horn; (*Mus.*) *French* —, das Waldhorn, Horn; (*Motor.*) die Hupe.

hornet ['hɔːnit], *s.* (*Ent.*) die Hornisse.

hornpipe ['hɔːnpaip], *s.* (*Mus.*) der Matrosentanz; die Hornpfeife.

horrible ['hɔribl], *adj.* schrecklich.

horrid ['hɔrid], *adj.* abscheulich.

horrific [hɔ'rifik], *adj.* schrecklich, schreckenerregend.

horror ['hɔrə], *s.* der Schrecken, das Entsetzen; (*fig.*) der Greuel.

horse [hɔːs], *s.* das Pferd, Roß; *on* —*back*, zu Pferd.

horseman ['hɔːsmən], *s.* der Reiter.

horsepower ['hɔːspauə], *s.* die Pferdestärke.

horseradish ['hɔːsrædiʃ], *s.* der Meerrettich.

horseshoe ['hɔːsʃuː], *s.* das Hufeisen.

horticulture ['hɔːtikʌltʃə], *s.* der Gartenbau.

hose [houz], *s.* die Strümpfe, *m. pl.* (*stockings*); der Schlauch (*water pipe*).

hosiery ['houʒəri], *s.* die Strumpfwarenindustrie; die Strumpfwaren.

hospitable [hɔs'pitəbl], *adj.* gastlich, gastfreundlich.

hospital ['hɔspitl], *s.* das Krankenhaus.

hospitality [hɔspi'tæliti], *s.* die Gastlichkeit, Gastfreundschaft.

host (1) [houst], *s.* der Gastwirt (*landlord*); der Gastgeber.

host (2) [houst], *s.* (*Rel.*) *angelic* —, die Engelschar; (*Mil.*) das Heer, die Heerschar.

host (3) [houst], *s.* (*Eccl.*) die Hostie.

hostage ['hɔstidʒ], *s.* die Geisel.

hostess ['houstis *or* –tes], *s.* die Gastgeberin; der —, die Stewardeß.

hostile ['hɔstail], *adj.* feindlich; feindselig (*inimical*).

hot [hɔt], *adj.* heiß; hitzig (*temperament*); scharf, gewürzt (*of spices*); (*fig.*) heftig, erbittert.

hotchpotch, hodge-podge ['hɔtʃpɔtʃ, 'hɔdʒpodʒ], *s.* das Mischmasch.

hotel [(h)ou'tel], *s.* das Hotel, der Gasthof.

hothouse ['hɔthaus], *s.* das Treibhaus.

hound [haund], *s.* (*Zool.*) der Jagdhund. — *v.a.* hetzen.

hour ['auə], *s.* die Stunde; — *hand*, der Stundenzeiger; *for* —*s*, stundenlang; *keep early* (*late*) —*s*, früh (spät) zu Bett gehen.

hourglass ['auəgla:s], *s.* die Sanduhr.

hourly ['auəli], *adj., adv.* stündlich.

house [haus], *s.* das Haus; (*Comm.*) die Firma. — [hauz], *v.a.* beherbergen, unterbringen.

houseboat ['hausbout], *s.* das Wohnboot.

housebreaking ['hausbreikiŋ], *s.* der Einbruch.

household ['haushould], *s.* der Haushalt.

housekeeper ['hauski:pə], *s.* die Haushälterin.

housewife ['hauswaif], *s.* die Hausfrau.

housing ['hauziŋ], *s.* die Unterbringung; — *department*, das Wohnungsamt.

hovel ['hɔvl *or* hʌvl], *s.* die Hütte.

hover ['hɔvə *or* 'hʌvə], *v.n.* schweben, schwanken.

how [hau], *adv.* wie; — *do you do?* (*in introduction*) sehr angenehm; — *are you?* wie geht es Ihnen *or* Dir?

however [hau'evə], *adv.* wie immer, wie auch immer, wie sehr auch. — *conj.* doch, jedoch, dennoch.

howl [haul], *v.n.* heulen. — *s.* das Geheul.

hoyden ['hɔidn], *s.* das wilde Mädchen.

hub [hʌb], *s.* die Nabe (am Rad); — *of the universe*, die Mitte der Welt.

hubbub ['hʌbʌb], *s.* der Tumult, Lärm.

huckaback ['hʌkəbæk], *s.* der Zwillich (*textile*).

huckle [hʌkl], *s.* die Hüfte.

huddle [hʌdl], *v.n.* sich drängen, sich zusammendrücken. — *s.* das Gedränge.

hue [hju:], *s.* der Farbton, die Tönung.

huff [hʌf], *s.* die schlechte Laune, die Mißstimmung.

huffy ['hʌfi], *adj.* mißmutig, übel gelaunt.

hug [hʌg], *v.a.* umarmen. — *s.* die Umarmung.

huge [hju:dʒ], *adj.* riesig, groß, ungeheuer.

Huguenot ['hju:gənou *or* –nɔt], *s.* der Hugenotte. — *adj.* hugenottisch, Hugenotten-.

hulk [hʌlk], *s.* (*Naut.*) das Schiffsinnere, der Schiffsrumpf; der schwerfällige Mensch.

hull [hʌl], *s.* die Hülse, Schale; (*Naut., Aviat.*) der Rumpf. — *v.a.* (*Engin.*) hülsen.

hullo! [hə'lou], *interj.* hallo!

hum [hʌm], *v.n.* summen, brummen. — *s.* das Summen, Brummen, Gemurmel (*murmuring*).

human ['hju:mən], *adj.* menschlich. — *s.* der Mensch.

humane [hju:'mein], *adj.* menschenfreundlich.

humanity [hju:'mæniti], *s.* die Menschheit (*mankind*); die Menschlichkeit (*compassion*); (*pl.*) die klassischen Fächer, *n. pl.*, die humanistischen Wissenschaften, *f. pl.*

humanize ['hju:mənaiz], *v.a.* menschlich oder gesittet machen.

humble [hʌmbl], *adj.* demütig; bescheiden (*modest*); unterwürfig (*servile*). — *v.a.* erniedrigen (*humiliate*).

humbug ['hʌmbʌg], *s.* die Schwindelei (*swindle*); der Schwindler (*crook*); der Unsinn (*nonsense*).

humdrum ['hʌmdrʌm], *adj.* langweilig, eintönig.

humid ['hju:mid], *adj.* feucht.

humidity [hju:'miditi], *s.* die Feuchtigkeit.

humiliate [hju:'milieit], *v.a.* erniedrigen.

humility [hju:'militi], *s.* die Demut.

humming-bird ['hʌmiŋbə:d], *s.* (*Orn.*) der Kolibri.

humming-top ['hʌmiŋtɔp], *s.* der Brummkreisel.

humorous ['hju:mərəs], *adj.* humoristisch, spaßhaft, komisch.

humour ['hju:mə], *s.* der Humor, die (gute) Laune. — *v.a.* in guter Laune erhalten, gut stimmen; willfahren (*Dat.*).

hump [hʌmp], *s.* der Buckel, der Höcker.

hunch [hʌntʃ], *s.* der Buckel; *have a* —, das Gefühl haben.

hunchback ['hʌntʃbæk], *s.* der Bucklige.

hundred ['hʌndrəd], *num. adj.* a —, hundert.

hundredweight ['hʌndrədweit], *s.* der (englische) Zentner.

Hungarian [hʌŋ'gɛəriən], *adj.* ungarisch. — *s.* der Ungar.

hunger ['hʌŋgə], *s.* der Hunger.

hungry ['hʌŋgri], *adj.* hungrig.

hunt [hʌnt], *s.* die Jagd. — *v.a., v.n.* jagen.

hunter ['hʌntə], *s.* der Jäger.

hurdle [hə:dl], *s.* die Hürde.

hurdy-gurdy ['hə:digə:di], *s.* der Leierkasten.

hurl [hə:l], *v.a.* schleudern, werfen.

hurly-burly ['hə:libə:li], *s.* der Wirrwarr.

hurricane ['hʌrikin], *s.* der Orkan; — *lamp*, die Sturmlaterne.

hurried ['hʌrid], *adj.* eilig, hastig.

hurry ['hʌri], v.n. eilen, sich beeilen; — to do, eiligst tun. — v.a. beschleunigen. — s. die Eile, Hast, Beschleunigung.

hurt [həːt], v.a. irr. verletzen; wehetun (Dat.); (verbally) kränken. — s. die Verletzung, Kränkung.

hurtful ['həːtful], adj. schädlich, kränkend.

husband ['hʌzbənd], s. der Mann, Ehemann, Gemahl. — v.a. verwalten, sparsam verfahren mit (Dat.).

husbandman ['hʌzbəndmən], s. der Landwirt.

husbandry ['hʌzbəndri], s. die Landwirtschaft.

hush [hʌʃ], v.a. zum Schweigen bringen. — s. die Stille; — money, das Schweigegeld.

husky (1) ['hʌski], adj. heiser (voice).

husky (2) ['hʌski], s. (Zool.) der Eskimohund.

hussy ['hʌzi], s. (coll.) das Frauenzimmer.

hustings ['hʌstiŋz], s. die Wahltribüne.

hustle [hʌsl], v.a. drängen, stoßen. — s. das Gedränge.

hut [hʌt], s. die Hütte, Baracke.

hutch [hʌtʃ], s. der Trog, Kasten (chest).

hybrid ['haibrid], adj. Bastard-. — s. der Bastard.

hydraulic [hai'drɔːlik], adj. hydraulisch.

hydroelectric [haidroui'lektrik], adj. hydroelektrisch.

hydrogen ['haidrədʒən], s. der Wasserstoff.

hyena [hai'iːnə], s. (Zool.) die Hyäne.

hygiene ['haidʒiːn], s. die Hygiene, Gesundheitslehre.

hymn [him], s. die Hymne, das Kirchenlied.

hymnal ['himnəl], s. das Gesangbuch.

hyper- ['haipə], prefix. über-.

hyperbole [hai'pəːbəli], s. die Übertreibung.

hyphen ['haifən], s. der Bindestrich.

hypnosis [hip'nousis], s. die Hypnose.

hypochondriac [haipo'kɔndriæk], adj. hypochondrisch. — s. der Hypochonder.

hypocrisy [hi'pɔkrisi], s. die Heuchelei.

hypocrite ['hipəkrit], s. der Heuchler.

hypothesis [hai'pɔθisis], s. die Hypothese.

hypothetical [haipə'θetikəl], adj. hypothetisch, angenommen.

hysteria [his'tiəriə], s. die Hysterie.

I

I [ai]. das I.
I [ai], pers. pron. ich.

ice [ais], s. das Eis; — bound, eingefroren; (Naut.) — breaker, der Eisbrecher; (Am.) —box, der Kühlschrank; — cream, das Eis; das Gefrorene. — v.a. (confectionery) verzuckern; (cake) glasieren.

Icelander ['aislændə], s. der Isländer.

Icelandic [ais'lændik], adj. isländisch.

icicle ['aisikl], s. der Eiszapfen.

icy ['aisi], adj. eisig.

idea [ai'diə], s. die Idee.

ideal [ai'diəl], adj. ideal. — s. das Ideal.

idealize [ai'diəlaiz], v.a. idealisieren.

identical [ai'dentikəl], adj. identisch, gleich.

identification [aidentifi'keiʃən], s. die Gleichsetzung, Identifizierung.

identify [ai'dentifai], v.a. identifizieren, gleichsetzen.

identity [ai'dentiti], s. die Identität, Gleichheit.

idiocy ['idiəsi], s. der Blödsinn.

idiom ['idiəm], s. das Idiom, die sprachliche Eigentümlichkeit.

idiomatic [idio'mætik], adj. idiomatisch.

idiosyncrasy [idio'siŋkrəsi], s. die Empfindlichkeit, die Abneigung (gegen, Acc.); die Idiosynkrasie.

idiot ['idiət], s. der Idiot.

idle [aidl], adj. unnütz (useless); müßig, faul (lazy). — v.n. träge sein.

idleness ['aidlnis], s. der Müßiggang, die Faulheit.

idol [aidl], s. das Götzenbild; das Idol.

idolatry [ai'dɔlətri], s. die Götzenverehrung.

idolize ['aidolaiz], v.a. vergöttern, abgöttisch lieben.

idyll ['aidil or 'idil], s. die Idylle, das Idyll.

idyllic [ai'dilik or i'dilik], adj. idyllisch.

if [if], conj. wenn, falls (in case); ob (whether).

igneous ['igniəs], adj. feurig.

ignite [ig'nait], v.a. entzünden. — v.n. zur Entzündung kommen, sich entzünden.

ignition [ig'niʃən], s. die Zündung.

ignoble [ig'noubl], adj. unedel, gemein.

ignominious [igno'miniəs], adj. schimpflich, schmählich.

ignominy ['ignomini], s. die Schande, Schmach.

ignoramus [ignə'reiməs], s. der Unwissende.

ignorance ['ignərəns], s. die Unwissenheit, Unkenntnis.

ignorant ['ignərənt], adj. unwissend.

ignore [ig'nɔː], v.a. ignorieren, nicht beachten.

ill [il], adj. böse, schlimm (bad); krank (sick); — feeling, die Verstimmung. — adv. — at ease, unbequem, verlegen can — afford, kann sich kaum leisten …; —timed, zu unrechter Zeit.

illbred [il'bred], adj. ungezogen.

illegal [i'liːgəl], adj. illegal, ungesetzlich.

illegibility [iledʒi'biliti], s. die Unleserlichkeit.

illegible [i'ledʒibl], *adj.* unleserlich.
illegitimacy [ili'dʒitiməsi], *s.* die Unehelichkeit, Illegitimität.
illegitimate [ili'dʒitimit], *adj.* illegitim, unehelich.
illicit [[i'lisit], *adj.* unerlaubt.
illiteracy [i'litərəsi], *s.* die Unkenntnis des Schreibens und Lesens, das Analphabetentum.
illiterate [i'litərit], *s.* der Analphabet.
illness ['ilnis], *s.* die Krankheit.
illogical [i'lɔdʒikəl], *adj.* unlogisch.
illuminate [i'lju:mineit], *v.a.* erleuchten; (*fig.*) aufklären.
illuminating [i'lju:mineitiŋ], *adj.* aufschlußreich.
illumination [ilju:mi'neiʃən], *s.* die Erleuchtung; die Erklärung (*explanation*).
illusion [i'lju:ʒən], *s.* die Illusion, Täuschung.
illusive, illusory [i'lju:ziv, i'lju:zəri], *adj.* trügerisch, täuschend.
illustrate ['iləstreit], *v.a.* erläutern; illustrieren (*with pictures*).
illustration [iləs'treiʃən], *s.* die Illustration (*pictorial*); Erläuterung, Erklärung; das Beispiel (*instance*).
illustrious [i'lʌstriəs], *adj.* glänzend, berühmt.
image ['imidʒ], *s.* das Bild; das Ebenbild; die Erscheinung (*appearance*).
imagery ['imidʒəri], *s.* der Gebrauch von Stilbildern (*style*), die Bildersprache.
imaginable [i'mædʒinəbl], *adj.* denkbar.
imaginary [i'mædʒinəri], *adj.* eingebildet, nicht wirklich, vermeintlich.
imagination [imædʒi'neiʃən], *s.* die Einbildung; die Vorstellung; die Phantasie.
imaginative [i'mædʒinətiv], *adj.* erfinderisch, voll Phantasie.
imagine [i'mædʒin], *v.a.* sich vorstellen, sich denken.
imbecile ['imbisail *or* 'imbisi:l], *adj.* schwachsinnig. — *s.* der Idiot.
imbecility [imbi'siliti], *s.* der Schwachsinn.
imbibe [im'baib], *v.a.* trinken; (*fig.*) in sich aufnehmen.
imbroglio [im'brouliou], *s.* die Verwicklung.
imbue [im'bju:], *v.a.* erfüllen, sättigen (*fig.*).
imitate ['imiteit], *v.a.* nachahmen, imitieren.
imitation [imi'teiʃən], *s.* die Nachahmung, Imitation; — *leather*, das Kunstleder.
immaculate [i'mækjulit], *adj.* unbefleckt, makellos.
immaterial [imə'tiəriəl], *adj.* unwesentlich, unwichtig.
immature [imə'tjuə], *adj.* unreif.
immeasurable [i'meʒərəbl], *adj.* unermeßlich, unmeßbar.
immediate [i'mi:djit], *adj.* unmittelbar, direkt, sofortig.

immediately [i'mi:djətli], *adv.* sofort.
immemorial [imi'mɔ:riəl], *adj.* undenklich, ewig.
immense [i'mens], *adj.* unermeßlich, ungeheuer.
immerse [i'mə:s], *v.a.* eintauchen.
immersion [i'mə:ʃən], *s.* das Eintauchen, die Versenkung; — *heater*, der Tauchsieder.
immigrant ['imigrənt], *s.* der Einwanderer.
imminent ['iminənt], *adj.* bevorstehend.
immobile [i'moubail], *adj.* unbeweglich.
immoderate [i'mɔdərit], *adj.* unmäßig.
immodest [i'mɔdist], *adj.* unbescheiden; unsittlich, unanständig (*immoral*).
immodesty [i'mɔdisti], *s.* die Unanständigkeit (*indecency*); Unbescheidenheit (*presumption*).
immolate ['iməleit], *v.a.* opfern.
immoral [i'mɔrəl], *adj.* unsittlich, unmoralisch.
immortal [i'mɔ:tl], *adj.* unsterblich.
immortalize [i'mɔ:təlaiz], *v.a.* verewigen, unsterblich machen.
immovable [i'mu:vəbl], *adj.* unbeweglich (*fig.*).
immunity [i'mju:niti], *s.* die Freiheit, Straffreiheit; Immunität.
immutable [im'ju:təbl], *adj.* unabänderlich; unveränderlich.
imp [imp], *s.* der Knirps, Kobold, kleine Schelm.
impair [im'pɛə], *v.a.* beeinträchtigen; vermindern (*reduce*).
impale [im'peil], *v.a.* aufspießen; durchbohren.
impalpable [im'pælpəbl], *adj.* unfühlbar, unmerklich.
impart [im'pa:t], *v.a.* erteilen; verleihen (*confer*); mitteilen (*inform*).
impartial [im'pa:ʃəl], *adj.* unparteiisch.
impartiality [impa:ʃi'æliti], *s.* die Unparteilichkeit, Objektivität.
impassable [im'pa:səbl], *adj.* unwegsam, unpassierbar.
impasse [im'pæs], *s.* der völlige Stillstand.
impassioned [im'pæʃənd], *adj.* leidenschaftlich.
impassive [im'pæsiv], *adj.* unempfindlich.
impatience [im'peiʃəns], *s.* die Ungeduld.
impatient [im'peiʃənt], *adj.* ungeduldig.
impeach [im'pi:tʃ], *v.a.* anklagen.
impeachment [im'pi:tʃmənt], *s.* die Anklage.
impecunious [impi'kju:niəs], *adj.* unbemittelt, mittellos.
impede [im'pi:d], *v.a.* behindern, verhindern.
impediment [im'pedimənt], *s.* das Hindernis.
impel [im'pel], *v.a.* antreiben; zwingen (*force*).

impending

impending [im'pendiŋ], *adj.* bevorstehend, drohend.

impenetrable [im'penitrəbl], *adj.* undurchdringlich, unerforschlich.

impenitent [im'penitənt], *adj.* reuelos, unbußfertig.

imperative [im'perətiv], *adj.* zwingend (*cogent*); dringend notwendig. — *s.* (*Gram.*) der Imperativ, die Befehlsform.

imperceptible [impə'septibl], *adj.* unmerklich.

imperfect [im'pə:fikt], *adj.* unvollständig, unvollkommen; fehlerhaft (*goods etc.*). — *s.* (*Gram.*) das Imperfekt.

imperial [im'piəriəl], *adj.* kaiserlich, Kaiser-, Reichs-.

imperil [im'peril], *v.a.* gefährden; in Gefahr bringen, einer Gefahr aussetzen.

imperious [im'piəriəs], *adj.* gebieterisch.

imperishable [im'periʃəbl], *adj.* unverwüstlich, unvergänglich.

impermeable [im'pə:miəbl], *adj.* undurchdringlich.

impersonal [im'pə:sənəl], *adj.* unpersönlich.

impersonate [im'pə:səneit], *v.a.* verkörpern, darstellen; sich ausgeben als.

impertinence [im'pə:tinəns], *s.* die Anmaßung, Frechheit, Unverschämtheit.

impertinent [im'pə:tinənt], *adj.* anmaßend, frech, unverschämt.

imperturbable [impə'tə:bəbl], *adj.* unerschütterlich, ruhig, gelassen.

impervious [im'pə:viəs], *adj.* unwegsam, undurchdringlich.

impetuous [im'petjuəs], *adj.* ungestüm, heftig.

impetus ['impitəs], *s.* die Triebkraft, der Antrieb.

impinge [im'pindʒ], *v.n.* verstoßen (*on, gegen*); übergreifen (*on, in*).

implacable [im'plækəbl], *adj.* unversöhnlich.

implement ['implimənt], *s.* das Gerät. — [impli'ment], *v.a.* (*Law*) erfüllen, in Wirkung setzen, in Kraft treten lassen.

implementation [implimen'teiʃən], *s.* das Inkrafttreten, die Erfüllung, Ausführung.

implicate ['implikeit], *v.a.* verwickeln.

implicit [im'plisit], *adj.* unbedingt; einbegriffen.

implore [im'plɔ:], *v.a.* anflehen.

imply [im'plai], *v.a.* besagen, meinen; andeuten.

impolite [impə'lait], *adj.* unhöflich, grob.

impolitic [im'pɔlitik], *adj.* unklug, unpolitisch, undiplomatisch.

imponderable [im'pɔndərəbl], *adj.* unwägbar. — *s. pl.* unwägbare, unvorhersehbare Umstände, *m.pl.*

import [im'pɔ:t], *v.a.* einführen, importieren; bedeuten, besagen. —

['impɔ:t], *s.* (*Comm.*) die Einfuhr, der Import; die Bedeutung (*importance, meaning*), Wichtigkeit (*significance*); (*Comm.*) — *licence*, die Einfuhrgenehmigung.

importance [im'pɔ:təns], *s.* die Bedeutung, Wichtigkeit.

important [im'pɔ:tənt], *adj.* bedeutend, wichtig.

importation [impɔ:'teiʃən], *s.* die Einfuhr.

importune [impɔ:'tju:n], *v.a.* belästigen, angehen, dringend bitten.

impose [im'pouz], *v.a.* aufbürden, auferlegen. — *v.n.* — *upon s.o.*, einen belästigen.

imposition [impə'ziʃən], *s.* die Belästigung; (*Sch.*) die Strafarbeit.

impossible [im'pɔsibl], *adj.* unmöglich.

impostor [im'pɔstə], *s.* der Schwindler, Betrüger.

impotent ['impətənt], *adj.* schwach, machtlos; impotent (*sexually*).

impound [im'paund], *v.a.* beschlagnahmen, in Beschlag nehmen.

impoverish [im'pɔvəriʃ], *v.a.* arm machen.

impoverished [im'pɔvəriʃd], *adj.* verarmt, armselig.

impracticability [impræktikə'biliti], *s.* die Unmöglichkeit, Unausführbarkeit.

impracticable [im'præktikəbl], *adj.* unausführbar.

imprecate ['imprikeit], *v.a.* verwünschen.

impregnable [im'pregnəbl], *adj.* uneinnehmbar, unbezwinglich.

impregnate [im'pregneit], *v.a.* impregnieren; (*Chem.*) sättigen.

impress [im'pres], *v.a.* beeindrucken, imponieren (*fig.*); einprägen, einpressen (*print*). — ['impres], *s.* der Eindruck, (*Typ.*) Abdruck.

impression [im'preʃən], *s.* (*fig.*) der Eindruck; die Auflage (*books*).

impressionable [im'preʃənəbl], *adj.* eindrucksfähig, empfänglich.

impressive [im'presiv], *adj.* ergreifend, eindrucksvoll.

imprint ['imprint], *s.* der Name des Verlags oder Druckers. — [im'print], *v.a.* drucken.

imprison [im'prizn], *v.a.* gefangensetzen, in Haft nehmen.

imprisonment [im'priznmənt], *s.* die Haft; (*Law*) der Arrest.

improbability [imprɔbə'biliti], *s.* die Unwahrscheinlichkeit.

improbable [im'prɔbəbl], *adj.* unwahrscheinlich.

improbity [im'prɔubiti], *s.* die Unredlichkeit.

impromptu [im'prɔmptju:], *adj., adv.* aus dem Stegreif, unvorbereitet.

improper [im'prɔpə], *adj.* unpassend; unanständig (*indecent*).

impropriety [impro'praiiti], *s.* die Unanständigkeit (*indecency*); die Ungehörigkeit.

improve [im'pru:v], *v.a.* verbessern; (*Hort.*) veredeln. — *v.n.* besser werden, sich bessern; (*Med.*) sich erholen.

improvement [im'pru:vmənt], *s.* die Verbesserung; (*Med.*) die Besserung, der Fortschritt.

improvident [im'prɔvidənt], *adj.* unvorsichtig, nicht auf die Zukunft bedacht.

improvise ['imprəvaiz], *v.a.* improvisieren.

imprudent [im'pru:dənt], *adj.* unklug, unvorsichtig.

impudent ['impjudənt], *adj.* unverschämt.

impugn [im'pju:n], *v.a.* anfechten, angreifen.

impulse ['impʌls], *s.* der Impuls; der Anstoß.

impulsive [im'pʌlsiv], *adj.* impulsiv.

impunity [im'pju:niti], *s.* die Straffreiheit.

impure [im'pjuə], *adj.* (*also Metall.*, *Chem.*) unrein, unedel; unsauber.

impute [im'pju:t], *v.a.* beimessen; zurechnen, die Schuld geben für.

in [in], *prep.* in; an; zu, auf; bei; nach, unter; über; von; mit; — *the morning*, vormittags; — *case*, falls; — *any case*, auf jeden Fall; — *German*, auf deutsch; — *my opinion*, meiner Meinung nach; — *the street*, auf der Straße; — *time*, rechtzeitig. — *adv.* drinnen, innen; herein, hinein; zu Hause.

inability [inə'biliti], *s.* die Unfähigkeit.

inaccessible [inæk'sesibl], *adj.* unzugänglich.

inaccurate [i'nækjurit], *adj.* ungenau.

inaction [i'nækʃən], *s.* die Untätigkeit.

inactive [i'næktiv], *adj.* untätig.

inadequate [i'nædikwit], *adj.* unzulänglich.

inadmissible [inəd'misibl], *adj.* unzulässig.

inadvertent [inəd'və:tənt], *adj.* unbeabsichtigt; unachtsam.

inadvertently [inəd'və:təntli], *adv.* unversehens; versehentlich.

inalienable [in'eiliənəbl], *adj.* unveräußerlich.

inane [i'nein], *adj.* hohl, leer, sinnlos.

inanimate [i'nænimit], *adj.* unbeseelt, leblos.

inanity [i'næniti], *s.* die Leere, Nichtigkeit.

inapplicable [i'næplikəbl], *adj.* unanwendbar; unzutreffend.

inappropriate [inə'proupriit], *adj.* unpassend.

inarticulate [ina:'tikjulit], *adj.* unartikuliert.

inasmuch [inəz'mʌtʃ], *adv.* insofern (als).

inattentive [inə'tentiv], *adj.* unaufmerksam.

inaudible [i'nɔ:dibl], *adj.* unhörbar.

inaugural [i'nɔ:gjurəl], *adj.* Inaugural-, Eröffnungs-, Antritts-.

inaugurate [i'nɔ:gjureit], *v.a.* einweihen, eröffnen.

inauspicious [inɔ:'spiʃəs], *adj.* ungünstig.

inborn ['inbɔ:n], *adj.* angeboren.

inbred ['inbred], *adj.* in Inzucht geboren; angeboren, ererbt.

inbreeding ['inbri:diŋ], *s.* die Inzucht.

incalculable [in'kælkjuləbl], *adj.* unberechenbar.

incandescence [inkæn'desəns], *s.* die Weißglut.

incandescent [inkæn'desənt], *adj.* weißglühend.

incantation [inkæn'teiʃən], *s.* die Beschwörung.

incapable [in'keipəbl], *adj.* unfähig (*of doing s.th.*, etwas zu tun).

incapacitate [inkə'pæsiteit], *v.a.* unfähig machen.

incapacity [inkə'pæsiti], *s.* die Unfähigkeit.

incarcerate [in'ka:səreit], *v.a.* einkerkern, einsperren.

incarnate [in'ka:nit], *adj.* eingefleischt; (*Theol.*) verkörpert.

incarnation [inka:'neiʃən], *s.* die Verkörperung; (*Theol.*) Menschwerdung.

incautious [in'kɔ:ʃəs], *adj.* unvorsichtig.

incendiary [in'sendjəri], *adj.* Brand-, brennend. — *s.* der Brandstifter.

incense [in'sens], *v.a.* aufregen, erzürnen (*make angry*); (*Eccl.*) beweihräuchern. — ['insens], *s.* (*Eccl.*) der Weihrauch.

incentive [in'sentiv], *adj.* Ansporn-, Anreiz-. — *s.* der Ansporn, Anreiz; (*Comm.*) — *scheme*, das Inzentivsystem, Akkordsystem.

incessant [in'sesənt], *adj.* unaufhörlich, ununterbrochen.

incest ['insest], *s.* die Blutschande.

incestuous [in'sestjuəs], *adj.* blutschänderisch.

inch [intʃ], *s.* der Zoll. — *v.n.* — *away*, abrücken.

incident ['insidənt], *s.* der Vorfall, Zwischenfall; das Ereignis.

incidental [insi'dentl], *adj.* zufällig. — *s.* (*pl.*) zufällige Ausgaben, *f. pl.*; das Zusätzliche, Nebenausgaben, *f. pl.*

incipient [in'sipiənt], *adj.* beginnend, anfangend.

incise [in'saiz], *v.a.* einschneiden, (*Med.*) einen Einschnitt machen.

incision [in'siʒən], *s.* der Einschnitt.

incisive [in'saisiv], *adj.* einschneidend; energisch (*person*).

incite [in'sait], *v.a.* aufreizen, anspornen.

incivility [insi'viliti], *s.* die Unhöflichkeit.

inclement [in'klemənt], *adj.* unfreundlich (*weather, climate*).

inclination [inkli'neiʃən], *s.* die Neigung (*also fig.*).

incline [in'klain], *v.n.* neigen, sich neigen. — ['inklain], *s.* der Neigungswinkel; der Abhang.

include [in'klu:d], *v.a.* einschließen (*contain*); umfassen (*enclose*).

including

including [in'klu:diŋ], *prep.* einschließlich.
inclusive [in'klu:siv], *adj.* einschließlich, mitgerechnet.
incoherent [inko'hiərənt], *adj.* unzusammenhängend.
incombustible [inkəm'bʌstibl], *adj.*
unverbrennbar.
income ['inkʌm], *s.* das Einkommen.
**incommensurable, incommensu-
rate** [inkə'menʃərəbl, inkə'menʃərit],
adj. unvereinbar, unmeßbar.
incomparable [in'kɔmpərəbl], *adj.* unvergleichlich.
incompatible [inkəm'pætibl], *adj.* unvereinbar.
incompetence, incompetency [in-
'kɔmpitəns, -tənsi], *s.* die Inkompe-
tenz; Unzulänglichkeit.
incompetent [in'kɔmpitənt], *adj.* unzuständig, inkompetent; unzulänglich.
incomplete [inkəm'pli:t], *adj.* unvollständig.
incomprehensible [inkɔmpri'hensibl],
adj. unverständlich.
inconceivable [inkən'si:vəbl], *adj.* unbegreiflich.
inconclusive [inkən'klu:siv], *adj.* unvollständig (*incomplete*); unüberzeu-
gend; ergebnislos.
incongruity [inkɔn'gru:iti], *s.* (*Maths.*)
die Inkongruenz; (*fig.*) die Unan-
gemessenheit.
incongruous [in'kɔŋgruəs], *adj.* in-
kongruent; unangemessen.
inconsequent [in'kɔnsikwənt], *adj.* fol-
gewidrig.
inconsequential [inkɔnsi'kwenʃəl], *adj.*
inkonsequent (*inconsistent*); unzusammenhängend.
inconsiderate [inkən'sidərit], *adj.* rücksichtslos, unbedachtsam.
inconsistent [inkən'sistənt], *adj.* inkonsequent.
inconsolable [inkən'souləbl], *adj.* untröstlich.
inconstancy [in'kɔnstənsi], *s.* die Unbeständigkeit; Untreue (*fickleness*).
incontestable [inkən'testəbl], *adj.* unanfechtbar, unbestreitbar.
incontinent [in'kɔntinənt], *adj.* unent-
haltsam.
incontrovertible [inkɔntro'və:tibl], *adj.*
unstreitig, unanfechtbar.
inconvenience [inkən'vi:niəns], *s.* die
Unbequemlichkeit, Unannehmlich-
keit.
inconvenient [inkən'vi:niənt], *adj.* unangenehm, unpassend.
inconvertible [inkən'və:tibl], *adj.* unveränderlich; (*Comm.*) unumsetzbar.
incorporate [in'kɔ:pəreit], *v.a.* einverleiben (*Dat.*), eingliedern (*Acc.*).
incorporated [in'kɔ:pəreitid], *adj.*
(*Am.*) eingetragene Körperschaft,
eingetragener Verein.
incorrect [inkə'rekt], *adj.* unrichtig,
fehlerhaft; unschicklich, unpassend.
incorrigible [in'kɔridʒibl], *adj.* unverbesserlich.

incorruptible [inkə'rʌptibl], *adj.* unbestechlich.
increase [in'kri:s], *v.a.* vermehren,
vergrößern (*size, volume*); steigern
(*heat, intensity*); erhöhen (*price*). —
v.n. sich vermehren, sich erhöhen;
wachsen (*grow*). — ['inkri:s], *s.* die
Zunahme; der Zuwachs (*family*); die
Erhöhung.
incredible [in'kredibl], *adj.* unglaublich.
incredulity [inkre'dju:liti], *s.* die
Ungläubigkeit, der Unglaube.
incredulous [in'kredjuləs], *adj.* ungläubig, schwer zu überzeugen.
increment ['inkrimənt], *s.* (*Comm.*) die
Zulage, Gehaltserhöhung.
incriminate [in'krimineit], *v.a.* beschuldigen, inkriminieren.
incubate ['inkjubeit], *v.a.* brüten, ausbrüten. — *v.n.* brüten.
incubator ['inkjubeitə], *s.* der Brutap-
parat.
inculcate ['inkʌlkeit], *v.a.* einprägen.
inculpate ['inkʌlpeit], *v.a.* beschuldigen.
incumbent [in'kʌmbənt], *adj.* (*upon,
Dat.*) obliegend, nötig. — *s.* der
Pfründner, Amtsinhaber.
incur [in'kə:], *v.a.* auf sich laden, sich
zuziehen.
incurable [in'kjuərəbl], *adj.* unheilbar.
incursion [in'kə:ʃən], *s.* der Einfall,
Streifzug.
indebted [in'detid], *adj.* verpflichtet,
dankbar (*grateful*); verschuldet (*in
debt*).
indecent [in'di:sənt], *adj.* unschicklich,
unanständig.
indecision [indi'siʒən], *s.* die Unentschlossenheit.
indecisive [indi'saisiv], *adj.* unentschlossen.
indeclinable [indi'klainəbl], *adj.*
(*Gram.*) undeklinierbar.
indecorous [indi'kɔ:rəs *or* in'dekərəs],
adj. unrühmlich, unanständig.
indeed [in'di:d], *adv.* in der Tat,
tatsächlich.
indefatigable [indi'fætigəbl], *adj.* unermüdlich.
indefensible [indi'fensibl], *adj.* unhaltbar; unverzeihlich (*unforgivable*).
indefinable [indi'fainəbl], *adj.* unbestimmbar, undefinierbar.
indefinite [in'definit], *adj.* unbestimmt.
indelible [in'delibl], *adj.* unauslöschlich.
indelicate [in'delikit], *adj.* unfein.
indemnify [in'demnifai], *v.a.* entschädigen.
indemnity [in'demniti], die Entschädigung.
indent [in'dent], *v.a.* auszacken, einschneiden.
indenture [in'dentʃə], *s.* der Lehrbrief
(*apprentice*); Vertrag.
independence [indi'pendəns], *s.* die
Unabhängigkeit, Freiheit.
independent [indi'pendənt], *adj.* unabhängig, frei.

indescribable [indi'skraibəbl], *adj.* unbeschreiblich.

indestructible [indi'strʌktibl], *adj.* unverwüstlich; unzerstörbar.

indeterminable [indi'tə:minəbl], *adj.* unbestimmbar.

indeterminate [indi'tə:minit], *adj.* unbestimmt.

index ['indeks], *s.* (*pl.* **indexes**) das Inhaltsverzeichnis; (*pl.* **indices**) (*Maths.*) der Exponent; — *finger*, der Zeigefinger; (*pl.*) die Finger, Zeiger, *m. pl.* (*pointers*).

India ['indjə], das Indien; — *paper*, das Dünnpapier.

Indian ['indjən], *adj.* indisch; — *ink*, die Tusche. — *s.* der Ind(i)er.

indiarubber ['indjə'rʌbə], *s.* der Radiergummi.

indicate ['indikeit], *v.a.* anzeigen, angeben.

indication [indi'keiʃən], *s.* das Anzeichen, Merkmal, der Hinweis.

indicative [in'dikətiv], *adj.* bezeichnend (für, *Acc.*). — *s.* (*Gram.*) der Indikativ.

indict [in'dait], *v.a.* anklagen.

indictment [in'daitmənt], *s.* die Anklage.

indifference [in'difrəns], *s.* die Gleichgültigkeit.

indifferent [in'difrənt], *adj.* gleichgültig.

indigence ['indidʒəns], *s.* die Armut.

indigenous [in'didʒinəs], *adj.* eingeboren, einheimisch.

indigent ['indidʒənt], *adj.* arm, dürftig.

indigestible [indi'dʒestibl], *adj.* unverdaulich.

indigestion [indi'dʒestʃən], *s.* die Magenbeschwerden, *f. pl.*; die Magenverstimmung.

indignant [in'dignənt], *adj.* empört, unwillig, entrüstet.

indignation [indig'neiʃən], *s.* die Entrüstung, der Unwille.

indignity [in'digniti], *s.* die Schmach, der Schimpf.

indirect [indi'rekt], *adj.* indirekt, mittelbar.

indiscreet [indis'kri:t], *adj.* indiskret, unvorsichtig; unbescheiden (*immodest*); taktlos.

indiscretion [indis'kreʃən], *s.* die Indiskretion, Taktlosigkeit.

indiscriminate [indis'kriminit], *adj.* ohne Unterschied, wahllos, kritiklos.

indispensable [indis'pensəbl], *adj.* unerläßlich, unentbehrlich.

indisposed [indis'pouzd], *adj.* unwohl (*health*); unwillig (*unwilling*).

indisposition [indispə'ziʃən], *s.* das Unwohlsein (*health*); das Abgeneigtsein (*disinclination*).

indisputable [indis'pju:təbl], *adj.* unbestreitbar.

indissoluble [indi'sɔljubl], *adj.* unauflöslich.

indistinct [indis'tiŋkt], *adj.* undeutlich.

indistinguishable [indis'tiŋgwiʃəbl], *adj.* nicht zu unterscheiden, ununterscheidbar.

individual [indi'vidjuəl], *adj.* individuell, persönlich; einzeln (*single*). — *s.* das Individuum, Einzelwesen.

individuality [individju'æliti], *s.* die Individualität.

indivisible [indi'vizibl], *adj.* unteilbar.

Indo-Chinese [indotʃai'ni:z], *adj.* hinterindisch. — *s.* der Hinterind(i)er.

indolent ['indələnt], *adj.* indolent, träge.

Indonesian [indo'ni:ʒən], *adj.* indonesisch. — *s.* der Indonesier.

indoor ['indɔ:], *adj.* im Haus; drinnen (*inside*).

indoors [in'dɔ:z], *adv.* im Hause, zu Hause.

indubitable [in'dju:bitəbl], *adj.* zweifellos, unzweifelhaft.

induce [in'dju:s], *v.a.* veranlassen, bewegen, verleiten (*incite*).

inducement [in'dju:smənt], *s.* der Beweggrund (*cause*); der Anlaß (*reason*); die Verleitung (*incitement*).

induction [in'dʌkʃən], *s.* die Einführung; (*Elec.*) die Induktion.

inductive [in'dʌktiv], *adj.* (*Log.*, *Elec.*) induktiv.

indulge [in'dʌldʒ], *v.a.* nachgeben (*Dat.*); verwöhnen. — *v.n.* — *in*, frönen (*Dat.*).

indulgence [in'dʌldʒəns], *s.* die Nachsicht; das Wohlleben; (*Eccl.*) der Ablaß.

industrial [in'dʌstriəl], *adj.* industriell, Industrie-.

industrious [in'dʌstriəs], *adj.* fleißig, arbeitsam.

industry ['indəstri], *s.* die Industrie (*production*); der Fleiß (*industriousness*).

inebriate [i'ni:brieit], *v.a.* berauschen. — [-iit], *adj.* berauscht.

ineffable [i'nefəbl], *adj.* unaussprechlich.

ineffective, ineffectual [ini'fektiv, ini'fektjuəl], *adj.* unwirksam, wirkungslos; unfähig.

inefficiency [ini'fiʃənsi], *s.* die Erfolglosigkeit, Untauglichkeit.

inefficient [ini'fiʃənt], *adj.* untauglich, untüchtig.

ineligible [in'elidʒibl], *adj.* nicht wählbar.

inept [i'nept], *adj.* untüchtig, albern, dumm.

ineptitude [i'neptitju:d], *s.* die Unfähigkeit; die Dummheit (*stupidity*).

inequality [ini'kwɔliti], *s.* die Ungleichheit.

inert [i'nə:t], *adj.* träg.

inestimable [in'estiməbl], *adj.* unschätzbar.

inevitable [in'evitəbl], *adj.* unumgänglich, unvermeidlich.

inexcusable [iniks'kju:zəbl], *adj.* unverzeihlich, unentschuldbar.

inexhaustible [inig'zɔ:stibl], *adj.* unerschöpflich.

inexpedient

inexpedient [iniks'pi:djənt], *adj.* un-zweckmäßig, unpraktisch, unpassend.

inexpensive [iniks'pensiv], *adj.* billig, nicht kostspielig.

inexperience [iniks'piəriəns], *s.* die Unerfahrenheit, Naivität.

inexpert [iniks'pə:t], *adj.* ungeübt, unerfahren.

inexpiable [i'nekspiəbl], *adj.* unsühn-bar, nicht wieder gut zu machen.

inexplicable [i'neksplikəbl], *adj.* un-erklärlich.

inexpressible [iniks'presibl], *adj.* un-aussprechlich.

inexpressive [iniks'presiv], *adj.* aus-druckslos.

inextinguishable [iniks'tiŋgwiʃəbl], *adj.* unauslöschlich.

inextricable [i'nekstrikəbl], *adj.* un-entwirrbar.

infallible [in'fælibl], *adj.* unfehlbar.

infamous ['infəməs], *adj.* verrufen, abscheulich, berüchtigt.

infamy ['infəmi], *s.* die Schande; Ehrlosigkeit (*dishonour*).

infancy ['infənsi], *s.* die Kindheit, Un-mündigkeit; (*fig.*) der Anfang.

infant ['infənt], *s.* das Kind; (*Law*) der Unmündige, das Mündel.

infantry ['infəntri], *s.* die Infanterie.

infatuate [in'fætjueit], *v.a.* betören.

infect [in'fekt], *v.a.* anstecken, infizie-ren.

infection [in'fekʃən], *s.* (*Med.*) die Ansteckung, Infektion.

infectious [in'fekʃəs], *adj.* (*Med.*) an-steckend.

infer [in'fə:], *v.a.* schließen, herleiten, folgern.

inference ['infərəns], *s.* die Folge-rung.

inferior [in'fiəriə], *comp. adj.* geringer; untergeordnet (*subordinate*); schlech-ter (*worse*).

inferiority [infiəri'ɔriti], *s.* die In-feriorität, Minderwertigkeit.

infernal [in'fə:nəl], *adj.* höllisch.

infest [in'fest], *v.a.* heimsuchen, plagen.

infidel ['infidəl], *adj.* ungläubig. — *s.* der Heide, Ungläubige.

infiltrate ['infiltreit], *v.n.* durchsickern, durchdringen, infiltrieren.

infinite ['infinit], *adj.* unendlich.

infinitive [in'finitiv], *s.* (*Gram.*) der Infinitiv, die Nennform.

infirm [in'fə:m], *adj.* gebrechlich, schwach; siech (*sick*).

infirmary [in'fə:məri], *s.* das Kranken-haus.

infirmity [in'fə:miti], *s.* die Schwäche, Gebrechlichkeit.

inflame [in'fleim], *v.a.* entzünden.

inflammation [inflə'meiʃən], *s.* die Entzündung.

inflate [in'fleit], *v.a.* aufblasen, auf-blähen; (*Comm.*) künstlich erhöhen (*values*).

inflation [in'fleiʃən], *s.* die Aufblähung; (*Comm.*) die Inflation.

inflect [in'flekt], *v.a.* (*Gram.*) biegen, flektieren, deklinieren, konjugieren.

inflection [in'flekʃən], *s.* (*Gram.*) die Biegung; (*Phonet.*) der Tonfall.

inflexible [in'fleksibl], *adj.* unbiegsam.

inflexion *see* **inflection**.

inflict [in'flikt], *v.a.* auferlegen (*im-pose*); beibringen (*administer*).

infliction [in'flikʃən], *s.* die Ver-hängung, das Beibringen.

influence ['influəns], *v.a.* beeinflussen. — *s.* der Einfluß.

influential [influ'enʃəl], *adj.* einfluß-reich.

influenza [influ'enzə], *s.* (*Med.*) die Grippe.

inform [in'fɔ:m], *v.a., v.n.* informieren, benachrichtigen; — *against*, jemanden denunzieren.

informal [in'fɔ:məl], *adj.* nicht formell; ungezwungen, zwanglos.

informant [in'fɔ:mənt], *s.* der Angeber.

information [infə'meiʃən], *s.* die In-formation, Nachricht, Auskunft.

infrequent [in'fri:kwənt], *adj.* selten.

infringe [in'frindʒ], *v.r.* übertreten.

infuriate [in'fjuərieit], *v.a.* wütend machen.

infuse [in'fju:z], *v.a.* einflößen, auf-gießen, begießen.

infusion [in'fju:ʒən], *s.* die Eingießung; der Aufguß (*tea*); (*Chem.*) die In-fusion.

ingenious [in'dʒi:niəs], *adj.* geistreich, genial.

ingenuity [indʒi'nju:iti], *s.* der Scharf-sinn.

ingenuous [in'dʒenjuəs], *adj.* offen, unbefangen, arglos.

ingot ['iŋgət], *s.* der Barren.

ingrained [in'greind], *adj.* eingefleischt.

ingratiate [in'greiʃieit], *v.r. — o.s.*, sich beliebt machen, sich einschmeicheln (*with*, bei).

ingratitude [in'grætitju:d], *s.* die Un-dankbarkeit.

ingredient [in'gri:diənt], *s.* der Be-standteil; die Zutat.

inhabit [in'hæbit], *v.a.* bewohnen.

inhabitant [in'hæbitənt], *s.* der Bewoh-ner; Einwohner.

inhale [in'heil], *v.a.* einatmen.

inherent [in'hiərənt], *adj.* eigen, an-geboren (*innate*); in der Sache selbst (*intrinsic*).

inherit [in'herit], *v.a.* erben.

inheritance [in'heritəns], *s.* die Erb-schaft, das Erbgut (*patrimony*); (*fig.*) das Erbe.

inhibit [in'hibit], *v.a.* hindern; —*ing factor*, der Hemmfaktor.

inhibition [ini'biʃən], *s.* (*Psych.*) die Hemmung.

inhospitable [inhɔs'pitəbl], *adj.* un-gastlich, ungastfreundlich.

inhuman [in'hju:mən], *adj.* unmensch-lich.

inhume [in'hju:m], *v.a.* beerdigen.

inimical [i'nimikəl], *adj.* feindlich (gesinnt), feindselig.

inimitable [i'nimitəbl], *adj.* unnachahmlich.

iniquitous [i'nikwitəs], *adj.* ungerecht, schlecht, boshaft.

iniquity [i'nikwiti], *s.* die Ungerechtigkeit (*injustice*); die Schändlichkeit (*shame*).

initial [i'niʃəl], *adj.* anfänglich. — *s.* (*Typ.*) der Anfangsbuchstabe.

initiate [i'niʃieit], *v.a.* einweihen, anfangen.

initiative [i'niʃiətiv], *s.* die Initiative; der erste Anstoß (*impulse*).

injection [in'dʒekʃən], *s.* (*Med.*) die Einspritzung, Injektion.

injudicious [indʒu'diʃəs], *adj.* unbedacht, unbesonnen; übereilt (*rash*).

injunction [in'dʒʌŋkʃən], *s.* die Vorschrift, (*Law*) die gerichtliche Verfügung.

injure ['indʒə], *v.a.* verletzen.

injurious [in'dʒuəriəs], *adj.* verletzend; schädlich (*harmful*).

injury ['indʒəri], *s.* die Verletzung, Verwundung; der Schaden (*damage*).

injustice [in'dʒʌstis], *s.* die Ungerechtigkeit.

ink [iŋk], *s.* die Tinte.

inkling ['iŋkliŋ], *s.* die Ahnung.

inkstand ['iŋkstænd], *s.* das Schreibzeug.

inlaid [in'leid], *adj.* eingelegt.

inland [in'lənd], *adj.* inländisch, Binnen-; — *revenue office*, das Steueramt, Finanzamt.

inlet ['inlit], *s.* (*Geog.*) die kleine Bucht.

inmate ['inmeit], *s.* der Insasse, Bewohner.

inmost ['inmoust], *adj.* innerst.

inn [in], *s.* der Gasthof, das Wirtshaus; *Inns of Court*, die Londoner Rechtskammern, *pl. pl.*

innate [i'neit], *adj.* angeboren.

inner ['inə], *adj.* inner; geheim (*secret*).

innings ['iniŋz], *s.* das Daransein (*in Cricket*); die Reihe.

innocence ['inəsəns], *s.* die Unschuld.

innocuous [i'nɔkjuəs], *adj.* unschädlich.

innovate ['inoveit], *v.a., v.n.* als Neuerung einführen, Neuerungen machen.

innovation [ino'veiʃən], *s.* die Neuerung.

innuendo [inju'endou], *s.* das Innuendo, die Anspielung.

innumerable [i'nju:mərəbl], *adj.* unzählig, unzählbar.

inoculate [i'nɔkjuleit], *v.a.* impfen.

inoffensive [ino'fensiv], *adj.* harmlos, unschädlich.

inopportune [in'ɔpətju:n], *adj.* ungelegen.

inordinate [i'nɔ:dinit], *adj.* unmäßig.

inorganic [inɔ:'gænik], *adj.* anorganisch.

inquest [in'kwest], *s.* die gerichtliche Untersuchung (*Law*); *coroner's* —, die Leichenschau.

inquire, enquire [in'kwaiə], *v.n.* sich erkundigen (*after*, nach, *Dat.*), nachfragen.

inquiry, enquiry [in'kwaiəri], *s.* die Nachfrage; — *office*, die Auskunftsstelle.

inquisition [inkwi'ziʃən], *s.* (*Eccl.*) die Inquisition; die gerichtliche Untersuchung.

inquisitive [in'kwizitiv], *adj.* neugierig.

inquisitiveness [in'kwizitivnis], *s.* die Neugier(de).

inroad ['inroud], *s.* der Eingriff, Überfall.

insane [in'sein], *adj.* wahnsinnig.

insanity [in'sæniti], *s.* der Wahnsinn.

insatiable [in'seiʃəbl], *adj.* unersättlich.

inscribe [in'skraib], *v.a.* einschreiben (*enrol*); widmen (*book*).

inscription [in'skripʃən], *s.* die Inschrift.

inscrutable [in'skru:təbl], *adj.* unergründlich, unerforschlich.

insect ['insekt], *s.* das Insekt, Kerbtier.

insecure [insi'kjuə], *adj.* unsicher.

insensate [in'sensit], *adj.* unsinnig (*senseless*); gefühllos..

insensible [in'sensibl], *adj.* unempfindlich; gefühllos.

insensitive [in'sensitiv], *adj.* ohne feineres Gefühl, unempfindlich.

inseparable [in'sepərəbl], *adj.* unzertrennlich, untrennbar.

insert [in'sə:t], *v.a.* einsetzen, einschalten (*add*); inserieren (*in newspaper*).

insertion [in'sə:ʃən], *s.* die Einschaltung (*addition*); die Annonce, das Inserat (*press*).

inside [in'said], *adj.* inner. — *adv.* im Innern. — *prep.* innerhalb. — *s.* das Innere.

insidious [in'sidiəs], *adj.* heimtückisch.

insight ['insait], *s.* der Einblick.

insignia [in'signiə], *s. pl.* die Insignien.

insignificance [insig'nifikəns], *s.* die Geringfügigkeit, Bedeutungslosigkeit.

insignificant [insig'nifikənt], *adj.* unbedeutend, geringfügig.

insincere [insin'siə], *adj.* unaufrichtig.

insincerity [insin'seriti], *s.* die Unaufrichtigkeit.

insinuate [in'sinjueit], *v.a.* zu verstehen geben, andeuten, anspielen auf (*Acc.*).

insinuation [insinju'eiʃən], *s.* der Wink, die Andeutung, Anspielung.

insipid [in'sipid], *adj.* schal, geschmacklos.

insist [in'sist], *v.n.* bestehen (*upon*, auf, *Dat.*).

insistence [in'sistəns], *s.* das Bestehen, Beharren.

insolence ['insələns], *s.* die Frechheit.

insolent ['insələnt], *adj.* frech, unverschämt.

insoluble [in'sɔljubl], *adj.* unlösbar; (*Chem.*) unlöslich.

insolvent [in'sɔlvənt], *adj.* insolvent, zahlungsunfähig, bankrott.

inspect [in'spekt], *v.a.* inspizieren; besichtigen.

inspection [in'spekʃən], *s.* die Inspektion; Besichtigung.

inspiration [inspi'reiʃən], *s.* die Inspiration, Erleuchtung, Begeisterung.

inspire [in'spaiə], *v.a.* inspirieren, begeistern.

instability [instə'biliti], *s.* die Unbeständigkeit, Labilität.

install [in'stɔːl], *v.a.* einsetzen (*in office*); einbauen.

installation [instə'leiʃən], *s.* die Einsetzung (*inauguration*); die Installation.

instalment [in'stɔːlmənt], *s.* die Rate; *by* —*s*, auf Abzahlung; die Fortsetzung (*serial*).

instance ['instəns], *s.* das Beispiel (*example*); (*Law*) die Instanz; *at my* —, auf meine dringende Bitte; *for* —, zum Beispiel. — *v.a.* als Beispiel anführen.

instant ['instənt], *s.* der Augenblick. — *adj.* gegenwärtig; sofortig; laufend (*current month*).

instantaneous [instən'teiniəs], *adj.* augenblicklich, sofortig.

instead [in'sted], *adv.* dafür, stattdessen; — *of*, (an)statt (*Genit.*).

instep ['instep], *s.* (*Anat.*) der Rist.

instigate ['instigeit], *v.a.* aufhetzen, anreizen, anstiften.

instil [in'stil], *v.a.* einflößen.

instinct ['instiŋkt], *s.* der Instinkt, Naturtrieb.

institute ['institjuːt], *s.* das Institut. — *v.a.* einrichten (*install*); stiften (*found*).

institution [insti'tjuːʃən], *s.* die Stiftung (*foundation*); die Anstalt (*establishment*).

instruct [in'strʌkt], *v.a.* unterrichten, unterweisen.

instruction [in'strʌkʃən], *s.* der Unterricht (*in schools etc.*); (*pl.*) die Instruktionen, *f. pl.*; die Direktive.

instructive [in'strʌktiv], *adj.* instruktiv, lehrreich.

instrument ['instrumənt], *s.* das Instrument; Werkzeug (*tool*).

insubordination [insəbɔːdi'neiʃən], *s.* der Ungehorsam.

insufferable [in'sʌfərəbl], *adj.* unerträglich.

insufficient [insə'fiʃənt], *adj.* ungenügend, unzulänglich.

insular ['insjulə], *adj.* Insel-; insular (*narrow-minded*).

insulate ['insjuleit], *v.a.* absondern (*separate*); (*Elec.*) isolieren; *insulating tape*, das Isolierband.

insult [in'sʌlt], *v.a.* beleidigen.

insuperable [in'sjuːpərəbl], *adj.* unüberwindlich.

insupportable [insə'pɔːtəbl], *adj.* unhaltbar (*argument*); unerträglich (*insufferable*).

insurance [in'ʃuərəns], *s.* die Versicherung; — *policy*, die Police; — *premium*, die Prämie; — *broker*, der Versicherungsmakler.

insure [in'ʃuə], *v.a.* versichern.

insurgent [in'səːdʒənt], *s.* der Aufständische, Aufrührer.

insurmountable [insə'mauntəbl], *adj.* unüberwindlich.

insurrection [insə'rekʃən], *s.* der Aufstand, Aufruhr; die Empörung.

intact [in'tækt], *adj.* unversehrt, intakt.

intangible [in'tændʒibl], *adj.* unberührbar (*untouchable*); (*Log.*) abstrakt. — *s. pl.* (*Log.*) die Intangibilien, *pl.*

integer ['intidʒə], *s.* (*Maths.*) das Ganze, die ganze Zahl.

integral ['intigrəl], *adj.* wesentlich; vollständig. — *s.* (*Maths.*) das Integral.

integrate ['intigreit], *v.a.* (*Maths.*) integrieren.

integration [inti'greiʃən], *s.* (*Maths.*) die Integrierung; (*fig.*) die Integration, das völlige Aufgehen.

integrity [in'tegriti], *s.* die Rechtschaffenheit, Redlichkeit (*probity*).

intellect ['intilekt], *s.* der Geist, Intellekt, Verstand.

intellectual [inti'lektjuəl], *adj.* intellektuell. — *s.* der Intellektuelle.

intelligence [in'telidʒəns], *s.* die Intelligenz; die Nachricht (*news*).

intelligent [in'telidʒənt], *adj.* intelligent.

intelligible [in'telidʒibl], *adj.* verständlich.

intemperance [in'tempərəns], *s.* die Unmäßigkeit.

intemperate [in'tempərit], *adj.* unmäßig.

intend [in'tend], *v.a.* beabsichtigen, vorhaben.

intendant [in'tendənt], *s.* der Intendant, Verwalter.

intense [in'tens], *adj.* intensiv, heftig.

intent [in'tent], *adj.* gespannt, begierig, bedacht (*on*, auf, *Acc.*). — *s.* die Absicht.

intention [in'tenʃən], *s.* die Absicht.

intentioned [in'tenʃənd], *adj. well-* —, wohlgesinnt.

inter [in'təː], *v.a.* beerdigen.

intercede [intə'siːd], *v.n.* vermitteln (*between*); sich verwenden (*on behalf of*, für, *Acc.*).

intercept [intə'sept], *v.a.* abfangen, auffangen, hemmen.

intercession [intə'seʃən], *s.* die Vermittlung, Fürsprache, Fürbitte.

interchange [intə'tʃeindʒ], *s.* der Austausch. — [-'tʃeindʒ], *v.a.* austauschen.

intercourse ['intəkɔːs], *s.* der Verkehr, Umgang.

interdict [intə'dikt], *v.a.* untersagen, verbieten.

interest ['intrəst], *s.* das Interesse; die Beteiligung; (*Comm.*) die Zinsen, *m. pl.*; *compound* —, die Zinseszinsen, *m. pl.* — *v.a.* interessieren.

interested ['intrəstid], *adj.* (*in*, an, *Dat.*) interessiert; *be* — *in*, sich interessieren für.

interesting ['intrəstiŋ], *adj.* interessant.
interfere [intə'fiə], *v.n.* sich einmischen, eingreifen (*in*, in, *Acc.*)
interference [intə'fiərəns], *s.* die Einmischung; (*Rad.*) die Störung.
interim ['intərim], *adj.* vorläufig, Zwischen-.
interior [in'tiəriə], *adj.* innerlich. — *s.* das Innere; das Binnenland; — *decorator*, der Innenraumgestalter, der Innenarchitekt; *Ministry of the Interior*, das Innenministerium.
interjection [intə'dʒekʃən], *s.* die Interjektion; der Ausruf.
interlace [intə'leis], *v.a.* einflechten.
interleave [intə'li:v], *v.a.* durchschießen (*a book*).
interlinear [intə'liniə], *adj.* zwischenzeilig.
interlocutor [intə'lɔkjutə], *s.* der Gesprächspartner.
interloper ['intəloupə], *s.* der Eindringling.
interlude ['intəlju:d], *s.* das Zwischenspiel.
intermarry [intə'mæri], *v.n.* untereinander heiraten.
intermediate [intə'mi:diit], *adj.* Mittel-; (*Sch.*) — *certificate*, das Mittelstufenzeugnis.
interment [in'tə:mənt], *s.* die Beerdigung.
interminable [in'tə:minəbl], *adj.* endlos, langwierig.
intermingle [intə'miŋgl], *v.n.* sich vermischen.
intermission [intə'miʃən], *s.* die Pause, Unterbrechung.
intermit [intə'mit], *v.a.* unterbrechen.
intermittent [intə'mitənt], *adj.* Wechsel-, aussetzend.
internal [in'tə:nl], *adj.* intern, innerlich.
international [intə'næʃənəl], *adj.* international; — *law*, das Völkerrecht.
interpolate [in'tə:poleit], *v.a.* interpolieren, einschalten.
interpose [intə'pouz], *v.a.* dazwischenstellen. — *v.n.* vermitteln (*mediate*).
interpret [in'tə:prit], *v.a.* verdolmetschen; erklären (*explain*); auslegen, interpretieren.
interpretation [intə:pri'teiʃən], *s.* die Auslegung, Interpretation.
interpreter [in'tə:pritə], *s.* der Dolmetscher.
interrogate [in'terogeit], *v.a.* ausfragen, befragen, vernehmen.
interrogation [intero'geiʃən], *s.* die Befragung; (*Law*) das Verhör, die Vernehmung.
interrogative [intə'rɔgətiv], *adj.* (*Gram.*) Frage-, Interrogativ-.
interrupt [intə'rʌpt], *v.a.* unterbrechen; stören (*disturb*).
interruption [intə'rʌpʃən], *s.* die Unterbrechung; Störung (*disturbance*).
intersect [intə'sekt], *v.a.* durchschneiden.

intersperse [intə'spə:s], *v.a.* untermengen, vermischen, einstreuen.
intertwine [intə'twain], *v.a.*, *v.n.* (sich) durchflechten.
interval ['intəvəl], *s.* der Zwischenraum; die Pause; (*Mus.*) das Interval.
intervene [intə'vi:n], *v.n.* eingreifen; als Vermittler dienen (*act as mediator*).
intervention [intə'venʃən], *s.* die Vermittlung, Intervention.
interview ['intəvju:], *v.a.* zur Vorsprache einladen (*a candidate*); interviewen. — *s.* die Vorsprache, das Interview.
intestate [in'testit], *adj.* ohne Testament.
intestines [in'testinz], *s. pl.* (*Anat.*) die Eingeweide, *n. pl.*
intimacy ['intiməsi], *s.* die Vertraulichkeit, Intimität.
intimate ['intimit], *adj.* intim, vertraut, vertraulich. — [-meit], *v.a.* andeuten, zu verstehen geben.
intimation [inti'meiʃən], *s.* der Wink, die Andeutung.
intimidate [in'timideit], *v.a.* einschüchtern.
into ['intu], *prep.* (*Acc.*) in, in ... hinein (*towards*).
intolerable [in'tɔlərəbl], *adj.* unerträglich.
intolerance [in'tɔlərəns], *s.* die Unduldsamkeit, Intoleranz.
intonation [into'neiʃən], *s.* (*Phonet.*) die Intonation; (*Mus.*) das Anstimmen, der Tonansatz (*of instruments*).
intoxicate [in'tɔksikeit], *v.a.* berauschen.
intractable [in'træktəbl], *adj.* unbändig, unlenksam.
intransitive [in'trænsitiv *or* in'trɑ:ns-], *adj.* (*Gram.*) intransitiv.
intrepid [in'trepid], *adj.* unerschrocken, furchtlos.
intricacy ['intrikəsi], *s.* die Verwicklung (*tangle*), Schwierigkeit (*difficulty*).
intricate ['intrikit], *adj.* verwickelt, schwierig.
intrigue [in'tri:g], *s.* die Intrige. — *v.n.* intrigieren.
intrinsic [in'trinsik], *adj.* wesentlich; innerlich (*inner*).
introduce [intrə'dju:s], *v.a.* einführen, einleiten (*book etc.*); vorstellen (*person*).
introduction [intrə'dʌkʃən], *s.* die Einführung, das Bekanntmachen; die Einleitung (*preface*); die Vorstellung (*presentation to s.o.*, *Dat.*).
introductory [intrə'dʌktəri], *adj.* einführend.
introspection [intrə'spekʃən], *s.* die Selbstbetrachtung, Introspektion.
introspective [intrə'spektiv], *adj.* nachdenklich, beschaulich.
intrude [in'tru:d], *v.n.* eindringen, sich eindrängen; stören (*be in the way*).
intrusion [in'tru:ʒən], *s.* das Eindringen.

intuition [intju'iʃən], *s.* die Intuition, Eingebung.
intuitive [in'tju:itiv], *adj.* intuitiv, gefühlsmäßig.
inundate ['inʌndeit], *v.a.* überschwemmen.
inure [i'njuə], *v.a.* gewöhnen; abhärten (*harden*).
invade [in'veid], *v.a.* angreifen, einfallen (in, *Dat.*).
invalid [in'vælid], *adj.* ungültig (*void*); ['invəlid] krank (*sick*). — *s.* der Kranke, Invalide.
invalidate [in'vælideit], *v.a.* ungültig machen, für ungültig erklären.
invalidity [invə'liditi], *s.* die Ungültigkeit.
invaluable [in'væljuəbl], *adj.* von hohem Wert, wertvoll, unschätzbar.
invariable [in'vɛəriəbl], *adj.* unveränderlich. — *s.* (*Maths.*) die unveränderliche Größe, die Konstante, Unveränderliche.
invasion [in'veiʒən], *s.* die Invasion, der Einfall; Angriff (*of*, auf, *Acc.*).
invective [in'vektiv], *adj.* schmähend. — *s.* die Schmähung.
inveigh [in'vei], *v.n.* schmähen, losziehen (gegen); schimpfen (auf, *Acc.*).
inveigle [in'veigl], *v.a.* verleiten, verführen.
invent [in'vent], *v.a.* erfinden.
invention [in'venʃən], *s.* die Erfindung.
inventor [in'ventə], *s.* der Erfinder.
inventory ['invəntri], *s.* der Bestand, das Inventar; die Liste (*list*).
inverse [in'və:s, 'invə:s], *adj.* umgekehrt.
inversion [in'və:ʃən], *s.* die Umkehrung; (*Gram., Maths.*) die Inversion.
invert [in'və:t], *v.a.* umstellen, umkehren. — ['invə:t], *s.* (*Chem.*) — *sugar*, der Invertzucker.
invest [in'vest], *v.a.* bekleiden; bedecken; (*Comm.*) investieren, anlegen.
investigate [in'vestigeit], *v.a.* untersuchen, erforschen.
investiture [in'vestitʃə], *s.* die Investitur; die Belehnung.
investment [in'vestmənt], *s.* die Investierung, Kapitalanlage.
inveterate [in'vetərit], *adj.* eingewurzelt, eingefleischt.
invidious [in'vidiəs], *adj.* neiderregend, verhaßt.
invigorate [in'vigəreit], *v.a.* stärken, beleben.
invincible [in'vinsibl], *adj.* unbesiegbar, unüberwindlich.
inviolable [in'vaiələbl], *adj.* unverletzlich.
invisible [in'vizibl], *adj.* unsichtbar.
invitation [invi'teiʃən], *s.* die Einladung.
invite [in'vait], *v.a.* einladen.
invocation [invo'keiʃən], *s.* die Anrufung.
invoice ['invɔis], *s.* die Rechnung, Faktura. — *v.a.* fakturieren.
invoke [in'vouk], *v.a.* anrufen.
involuntary [in'vɔləntri], *adj.* unfreiwillig (*unwilling*); unwillkürlich (*reflex*).

involve [in'vɔlv], *v.a.* verwickeln.
involved [in'vɔlvd], *adj.* schwierig, verwickelt, kompliziert.
invulnerable [in'vʌlnərəbl], *adj.* unverwundbar, unverletzlich.
inward ['inwəd], *adj.* inner(lich). — *adv.* (*also* **inwards**) einwärts, nach innen, ins Innere.
iodine ['aiədain *or* 'aiədi:n], *s.* (*Chem.*) das Jod.
Iraki, Iraqi [i'rɑ:ki], *adj.* irakisch. — *s.* der Iraker.
Iranian [i'reinjən], *adj.* iranisch. — *s.* der Iranier.
irascible [i'ræsibl], *adj.* jähzornig, aufbrausend.
irate [ai'reit], *adj.* erzürnt, zornig.
ire [aiə], *s.* (*Poet.*) der Zorn.
iridescent [iri'desənt], *adj.* irisierend, schillernd.
iris ['aiəris], *s.* (*Anat.*) die Regenbogenhaut; (*Bot.*) die Schwertlilie.
Irish ['airiʃ], *adj.* irisch, ersisch. — *s.* (*pl.*) the —, die Irländer, Iren, *pl.*
Irishman ['airiʃmən], *s.* der Irländer, Ire.
irk [ə:k], *v.a.* verdrießen, verärgern.
irksome ['ə:ksəm], *adj.* lästig, ärgerlich.
iron ['aiən], *s.* (*Metall.*) das Eisen; (*pl.*) die eisernen Fesseln. — *adj.* eisern, Eisen-. — *v.a.* bügeln, plätten; — *out*, schlichten, beilegen.
ironical [ai'rɔnikəl], *adj.* ironisch.
ironmonger ['aiənmʌŋgə], *s.* der Eisenhändler.
ironmould ['aiənmould], *s.* der Rostfleck.
irony ['aiərəni], *s.* die Ironie.
irradiate [i'reidieit], *v.a.* bestrahlen.
irrational [i'ræʃənəl], *adj.* (*Log.,Maths.*) irrational; unvernünftig (*without reason*).
irreconcilable [irekən'sailəbl], *adj.* unversöhnlich; unvereinbar (*incompatible*).
irregular [i'regjulə], *adj.* unregelmäßig, gegen die Regel.
irrelevant [i'reləvənt], *adj.* belanglos.
irremediable [iri'mi:diəbl], *adj.* unheilbar; nicht wieder gut zu machen.
irreparable [i'repərəbl], *adj.* unersetzlich.
irrepressible [iri'presibl], *adj.* nicht zu unterdrücken, unbezähmbar.
irreproachable [iri'proutʃəbl], *adj.* untadelhaft, tadellos.
irresistible [iri'zistibl], *adj.* unwiderstehlich.
irresolute [i'rezolju:t], *adj.* unschlüssig, unentschlossen.
irrespective [iris'pektiv], *adj.* ohne Rücksicht (*of*, auf, *Acc.*).
irresponsible [iris'pɔnsibl], *adj.* unverantwortlich.
irretrievable [iri'tri:vəbl], *adj.* unersetzlich, unwiederbringlich.
irreverent [i'revərənt], *adj.* unehrerbietig.
irrevocable [i'revəkəbl], *adj.* unwiderruflich.

irrigate ['irigeit], *v.a.* bewässern.
irritable ['iritəbl], *adj.* reizbar.
irritant ['iritənt], *s.* das Reizmittel.
irritate ['iriteit], *v.a.* reizen (*also Med.*), ärgern.
irritation [iri'teiʃən], *s.* die Reizung, das Reizen; die Erzürnung.
irruption [i'rʌpʃən], *s.* der Einbruch.
island ['ailənd], *s.* die Insel.
isle [ail], *s.* (*Poet.*) die Insel.
isolate ['aisəleit], *v.a.* (*Med.*) isolieren; absondern; (*Chem.*) darstellen.
isolation [aisə'leiʃən], *s.* die Absonderung, Isolierung.
Israeli [iz'reili], *adj.* den Staat Israel betreffend. — *s.* der Israeli.
Israelite ['izreiəlait], *adj.* israelitisch. — *s.* der Israelit.
issue ['isju: *or* 'iʃu:], *s.* der Ausgang, Erfolg (*result*); *main* —, der Hauptpunkt; die Nachkommenschaft (*children*); die Ausgabe (*edition*); Herausgabe (*publication*). — *v.a.* herausgeben; erlassen (*proclaim*); veröffentlichen (*publish*). — *v.n.* herrühren, stammen (*from*).
isthmus ['isθməs], *s.* die Landenge.
it [it], *pron.* es; *with* —, damit.
Italian [i'tæljən], *adj.* italienisch. — *s.* der Italiener.
italics [i'tæliks], *s. pl.* (*Typ.*) der Kursivdruck, die Kursivschrift.
itch [itʃ], *s.* die Krätze. — *v.n.* jucken; — *to do s.th.*, (*coll.*) darauf brennen, etwas zu tun.
item ['aitəm], *s.* der Posten (*in bill*); der Programmpunkt (*agenda*); die Einzelheit.
itemize ['aitəmaiz], *v.a.* (*Comm.*) aufführen; verzeichnen.
iterate ['itəreit], *v.a.* wiederholen.
itinerant [i'tinərənt], *adj.* wandernd.
its [its], *poss. adj.* sein, ihr; dessen, deren.
itself [it'self], *pron.* selber, sich; *of* —, von selbst.
ivory ['aivəri], *s.* das Elfenbein. — *adj.* aus Elfenbein, elfenbeinern.
ivy ['aivi], *s.* (*Bot.*) der Efeu.

J

J [dʒei]. das J.
jabber ['dʒæbə], *v.n.* schnattern.
Jack [dʒæk]. Hans; *Union* —, die britische Flagge; (*Cards*) der Bube.
jack [dʒæk], *s.* (*Motor.*) der Wagenheber. — *v.a.* — *up*, (*Motor.*) hochwinden.
jackal ['dʒækɔːl], *s.* (*Zool.*) der Schakal.
jackass ['dʒækæs], *s.* (*Zool.*) der Esel.
jackdaw ['dʒækdɔː], *s.* die Dohle.
jacket ['dʒækit], *s.* das Jackett, die Jacke; *dinner* —, der Smoking;

potatoes in their —*s*, Kartoffeln in der Schale, *f. pl.*
jade [dʒeid], *s.* der Nierenstein.
jaded ['dʒeidid], *adj.* abgeplagt, abgehärmt, ermüdet.
jag [dʒæg], *s.* die Kerbe. — *v.a.* kerben, zacken.
jagged ['dʒægid], *adj.* zackig.
jail *see under* gaol.
jailer *see under* gaoler.
jam (1) [dʒæm], *s.* die Marmelade, Konfitüre.
jam (2) [dʒæm], *s. traffic* —, die Verkehrsstauung; (*coll.*) *in a* —, in der Klemme. — *v.a.* zusammenpressen (*press together*); (*Rad.*) stören.
Jamaican [dʒə'meikən], *adj.* jamaikanisch. — *s.* der Jamaikaner.
jamb [dʒæm], *s.* der Türpfosten.
jangle ['dʒæŋgl], *v.n.* klirren, rasseln. — *s.* das Geklirr, Gerassel.
janitor ['dʒænitə], *s.* der Portier.
January ['dʒænjuəri]. der Januar.
Japan [dʒə'pæn], *s.* lakierte Arbeit. — *v.a.* lackieren.
Japanese [dʒæpə'niːz], *adj.* japanisch. — *s.* der Japaner.
jar (1) [dʒɑː], *s.* der Topf, das Glas (*preserves*).
jar (2) [dʒɑː], *v.n.* offenstehen (*door*); mißtönen, knarren.
jargon ['dʒɑːgən], *s.* der Jargon.
jasmine ['dʒæzmin], *s.* (*Bot.*) der Jasmin.
jasper ['dʒæspə], *s.* der Jaspis.
jaundice ['dʒɔːndis], *s.* (*Med.*) die Gelbsucht; (*fig.*) der Neid (*envy*); —*d outlook*, die Verbitterung, Mißstimmung.
jaunt [dʒɔːnt], *s.* der Ausflug, Spaziergang. — *v.n.* herumstreifen, spazieren.
jaunty ['dʒɔːnti], *adj.* leicht, munter, lebhaft.
jaw [dʒɔː], *s.* (*Anat.*) der Kinnbacken; der Rachen (*animals*).
jay [dʒei], *s.* (*Orn.*) der Häher.
jazz [dʒæz], *s.* die Jazzmusik.
jealous ['dʒeləs], *adj.* eifersüchtig.
jealousy ['dʒeləsi], *s.* die Eifersucht.
jeer ['dʒiə], *v.a.*, *v.n.* spotten, verhöhnen.
jejune [dʒi'dʒuːn], *adj.* nüchtern, trocken.
jelly ['dʒeli], *s.* das Gelee.
jellyfish ['dʒelifiʃ], *s.* (*Zool.*) die Qualle.
jeopardize ['dʒepədaiz], *v.a.* gefährden.
jeopardy ['dʒepədi], *s.* die Gefahr.
jerk [dʒəːk], *v.a.* rucken, stoßen (*push*); plötzlich bewegen (*move suddenly*). — *v.n.* zusammenzucken. — *s.* (*Am. coll.*) der Kerl; der Ruck, Stoß.
jersey ['dʒəːzi], *s.* die Wolljacke.
jessamine ['dʒesəmin], *s.* (*Bot.*) der Jasmin.
jest [dʒest], *s.* der Spaß, Scherz. — *v.n.* scherzen.
jester ['dʒestə], *s.* der Spaßmacher, Hofnarr.

jet

jet (1) [dʒet], s. der Strahl, Wasserstrahl; (*Aviat.*) die Düse; — *engine*, der Düsenmotor; — *plane*, das Düsenflugzeug. — *v.n.* hervorspringen.

jet (2) [dʒet], s. der Gagat; — *black*, pechschwarz.

jetsam ['dʒetsəm], s. das Strandgut.

jetty ['dʒeti], s. der Hafendamm, die Landungsbrücke (*landing stage*).

Jew [dʒu:], s. der Jude.

jewel ['dʒuəl], s. das Juwel, der Edelstein.

jewel(le)ry ['dʒuəlri], s. der Schmuck; die Juwelen, n. pl.

Jewish ['dʒu:iʃ], adj. jüdisch.

Jewry ['dʒuəri], s. die Judenschaft, das Judentum.

jiffy ['dʒifi], s. (*coll.*) der Augenblick.

jig (1) [dʒig], s. die Gigue (*dance*).

jig (2) [dʒig], s. das Werkzeug (*tool*); —*saw*, die Säge; —*saw puzzle*, das Zusammenlegspiel, -setzspiel.

jilt [dʒilt], v.a. sitzen lassen.

jingle ['dʒiŋgl], v.a. klimpern, klimpern lassen (*coins etc.*). — s. das Geklimper.

job [dʒɔb], s. die Arbeit, Anstellung; die Stellung; das Geschäft; — *in hand*, die Beschäftigung.

jobber ['dʒɔbə], s. der Makler, Spekulant (*stock exchange*).

jockey ['dʒɔki], s. der Jockei, Reiter.

jocular ['dʒɔkjulə], adj. scherzhaft, lustig.

jocund ['dʒɔkənd], adj. munter, heiter.

jog [dʒɔg], v.a. stoßen, antreiben. — v.n. gemächlich traben, trotten. — s. der Trott.

join [dʒɔin], v.a. verbinden, zusammenfügen; (*club etc.*) beitreten (*Dat.*). — v.n. (*rivers*) zusammenfließen (mit, *Dat.*); (*Comm.*) sich vereinigen (mit, *Dat.*).

joiner ['dʒɔinə], s. der Tischler, Schreiner.

joint [dʒɔint], s. (*Anat.*) das Gelenk; das Stück Fleisch, der Braten (*meat*); (*sl.*) das Lokal, die Spelunke. — adj. vereint, gemeinsam; (*Comm.*) — *stock company*, die Aktiengesellschaft; — *heir*, der Miterbe.

joist [dʒɔist], s. (*Carp.*) der Querbalken.

joke [dʒouk], s. der Scherz, Witz.

jollity ['dʒɔliti], s. die Heiterkeit.

jolly ['dʒɔli], adj. fröhlich, heiter, lustig.

jolt [dʒoult], v.a. schütteln, erschüttern (*shake up*). — s. der Stoß.

jostle [dʒɔsl], v.a. stoßen, drängen. — v.n. drängeln.

jot [dʒɔt], s. der Punkt, das Iota. — v.a. — (*down*), notieren, niederschreiben.

journal ['dʒə:nəl], s. die Zeitschrift (*periodical*).

journalism ['dʒə:nəlizm], s. das Zeitungswesen, der Journalistenberuf.

journalist ['dʒə:nəlist], s. der Journalist.

journey ['dʒə:ni], s. die Reise.

joust [dʒu:st], s. das Turnier.

jovial ['dʒouviəl], adj. jovial, freundlich; lustig (*gay*).

joy [dʒɔi], s. die Freude.

jubilant ['dʒu:bilənt], adj. frohlockend.

jubilation [dʒu:bi'leiʃən], s. der Jubel.

jubilee ['dʒu:bili:], s. das Jubiläum.

Judaism [dʒu'deiizm], s. das Judentum.

judge [dʒʌdʒ], s. der Richter. — v.a. richten, beurteilen, entscheiden.

judgment ['dʒʌdʒmənt], s. das Urteil; das Urteilsvermögen (*discretion*), die Urteilskraft.

judicial [dʒu:'diʃəl], adj. richterlich, gerichtlich.

judicious [dʒu:'diʃəs], adj. klug, scharfsinnig.

jug [dʒʌg], s. der Krug.

juggle [dʒʌgl], v.n. jonglieren, gaukeln.

juggler ['dʒʌglə], s. der Jongleur.

Jugoslav see **Yugoslav.**

jugular ['dʒu:g- or 'dʒʌgjulə], adj. Kehl-, Hals-, Gurgel-. — s. (*vein*) die Halsader.

juice [dʒu:s], s. der Saft.

July [dʒu'lai], s. der Juli.

jumble ['dʒʌmbl], v.a. zusammenmischen, vermischen. — s. das gemischte Zeug; — *sale*, der Verkauf, Ausverkauf gebrauchter Dinge, Ramschverkauf.

jump [dʒʌmp], v.n. springen. — s. der Sprung.

junction ['dʒʌŋkʃən], s. (*Railw.*) der Knotenpunkt; die Kreuzung.

juncture ['dʒʌŋktʃə], s. der (kritische) Zeitpunkt.

June [dʒu:n], s. der Juni.

jungle [dʒʌŋgl], s. der Dschungel.

junior ['dʒu:njə], adj. jünger; Unter-.

juniper ['dʒu:nipə], s. (*Bot.*) der Wacholder.

junk [dʒʌŋk], s. (*coll.*) das alte Zeug, alte Möbelstücke, n. pl.

junket ['dʒʌŋkit], s. der Schmaus, das Fest; (*Cul.*) dicke Milch mit Sahne. — v.n. schmausen, feiern (*celebrate*).

juridical [dʒuə'ridikəl], adj. rechtlich; gerichtlich (*in Court*).

jurisdiction [dʒuəriz'dikʃən], s. die Gerichtsbarkeit.

juror ['dʒuərə], s. der, die Geschworene.

jury ['dʒuəri], s. die Jury, das Geschworenengericht.

just [dʒʌst], adj. gerecht; rechtschaffen (*decent*); gehörig (*proper*). — adv. soeben, eben; — *as*, eben als, gerade wie.

justice ['dʒʌstis], s. die Gerechtigkeit; der Richter (*judge*).

justifiable ['dʒʌstifaiəbl], adj. zu rechtfertigen, berechtigt.

justify ['dʒʌstifai], v.a. rechtfertigen.

jut [dʒʌt], v.n. — (*out*), hervorragen. — s. der Vorsprung.

jute [dʒu:t], s. die Jute.

juvenile ['dʒu:vənail], adj. jugendlich, unreif.

juxtaposition [dʒʌkstəpə'ziʃən], s. die Nebeneinanderstellung, Gegenüberstellung.

K

K [kei]. das K.
kale [keil], *s.* (*Bot.*) der Krauskohl.
kaleidoscope [kə'laidəskoup], *s.* das Kaleidoskop.
kangaroo [kæŋgə'ru:], *s.* (*Zool.*) das Känguruh.
keel [ki:l], *s.* der Kiel; *on an even —*, bei ruhiger See; (*also fig.*) ruhig. — *v.n. — over*, umkippen.
keen [ki:n], *adj.* eifrig (*intent*); scharfsinnig (*perspicacious*); scharf (*blade*).
keenness [ki:nnis], *s.* der Eifer; Scharfsinn; die Schärfe (*blade*).
keep [ki:p], *v.a. irr.* halten (*hold*); behalten (*retain*); führen (*a shop*); hüten (*gate, dog etc.*). — *v.n. — doing*, in etwas fortfahren, — *going*, weitergehen; — *away*, sich fernhalten; — *in*, indoors, zu Hause bleiben; — *off*, abhalten; sich fernhalten; — *out*, draußen bleiben; — *up*, aufrechterhalten. — *s.* das Burgverlies; der Unterhalt.
keeper [ki:pə], *s.* der Hüter, Wärter; Museumsbeamte.
keeping [ki:piŋ], *s.* die Verwahrung; *in safe —*, in guten Händen, in guter Obhut.
keepsake [ki:pseik], *s.* das Andenken.
keg [keg], *s.* das Fäßchen.
ken [ken], *s.* die Kenntnis; *in my —*, meines Wissens. — *v.a.* (*Scottish*) kennen.
kennel [kenl], *s.* die Hundehütte.
kerb(stone) [kə:b(stoun)], *s.* der Prellstein.
kerchief [kə:tʃif], *s.* das Kopftuch, Halstuch.
kernel [kə:nl], *s.* der Kern.
kettle [ketl], *s.* der Kessel; — *drum*, die Kesselpauke.
key [ki:], *s.* der Schlüssel; (*Mus.*) die Tonart; die Taste (*on piano etc.*); — *man*, eine wichtige Person, Person in einer Schlüsselstellung. — *v.a. — (in)*, einfügen, befestigen.
keyboard [ki:bɔ:d], *s.* die Klaviatur; Tastatur (*typewriter*); — *instrument*, das Tasteninstrument.
keyhole [ki:houl], *s.* das Schlüsselloch.
keystone [ki:stoun], *s.* der Schlußstein.
kick [kik], *v.a., v.n.* mit dem Fuße stoßen *or* treten; — *against s.th.*, sich wehren. — *s.* der Fußstoß, Tritt; (*Footb.*) — *off*, der Anstoß; *free —*, der Freistoß; *penalty —*, der Strafstoß, der Elfmeterstoß.
kid (1) [kid], *s.* (*Zool.*) das Geißlein, Zicklein; *with — gloves*, mit Glacéhandschuhen; (*coll.*) das Kind.
kid (2) [kid], *v.a.* (*Am. coll.*) zum Narren haben, aufziehen (*tease*).

kidnap [kidnæp], *v.a.* entführen.
kidney [kidni], *s.* (*Anat.*) die Niere; — *bean*, die französische Bohne.
kill [kil], *v.a.* töten; schlachten (*animal*).
kiln [kiln], *s.* der Darrofen; der Ziegelofen (*tiles, bricks*).
kilt [kilt], *s.* der Schottenrock.
kin [kin], *s.* die Verwandtschaft; *kith and —*, die Verwandten, *m. pl.*
kind [kaind], *s.* die Art, Gattung, Art und Weise. — *adj.* freundlich, gütig, liebenswürdig.
kindle [kindl], *v.a.* anzünden, anfachen.
kindliness, kindness [kaindlinis, kaindnis], *s.* die Güte, Freundlichkeit.
kindred [kindrid], *adj.* verwandt.
king [kiŋ], *s.* der König.
kingdom [kiŋdəm], *s.* das Königreich.
kink [kiŋk], *s.* der Knoten; (*coll.*) der Vogel, die Grille (*obsession etc.*).
kinship [kinʃip], *s.* die Sippe, Verwandtschaft.
kipper [kipə], *s.* der geräucherte Hering.
kiss [kis], *v.a.* küssen. — *s.* der Kuß.
kit [kit], *s.* (*Mil.*) die Ausrüstung.
kitbag [kitbæg], *s.* der Tornister.
kitchen [kitʃən], *s.* die Küche; — *garden*, der Gemüsegarten.
kite [kait], *s.* der Drache, Papierdrache; *fly a —*, einen Drachen steigen lassen; (*Orn.*) der Gabelweih, der (rote) Milan; (*sl.*) der Schwindler.
kith [kiθ], *s.* now only in — *and kin*, die Verwandten, *m. pl.*
kitten [kitn], *s.* das Kätzchen.
knack [næk], *s.* der Kniff, Kunstgriff.
knacker [nækə], *s.* der Abdecker (*horse*).
knapsack [næpsæk], *s.* der Rucksack, Tornister.
knave [neiv], *s.* der Kerl, Schurke; Bube (*cards*).
knead [ni:d], *v.a.* kneten.
knee [ni:], *s.* (*Anat.*) das Knie.
kneel [ni:l], *v.n. irr.* knieen, niederknieen.
knell [nel], *s.* die Totenglocke.
knick-knack [niknæk], *s.* die Nippsache.
knife [naif], *s.* das Messer. — *v.a.* erstechen.
knight [nait], *s.* der Ritter; der Springer (*chess*).
knit [nit], *v.a., v.n. reg. & irr.* stricken; *knitting needle*, die Stricknadel.
knob [nɔb], *s.* der (Tür)knopf, die Türklinke; der Knorren (*wood*).
knock [nɔk], *v.n.* klopfen, schlagen. — *s.* der Schlag, Stoß.
knoll [noul], *s.* der kleine Hügel.
knot [nɔt], *s.* der Knoten; die Schwierigkeit (*difficulty*).
know [nou], *v.a. irr.* kennen (*be acquainted with*); wissen (*possess knowledge (of)*).
knowing [nouiŋ], *adj.* wissend.
knowledge [nɔlidʒ], *s.* die Kenntnis (*acquaintance with*); das Wissen (*by*

knuckle

study, information etc.); die Kenntnisse (of language etc.).
knuckle [nakl], s. (Anat.) der Knöchel.
— v.n. — under, sich fügen.
Kremlin ['kremlin], s. der Kreml.
kudos ['kju:dɔs], s. der Ruhm, das
Ansehen.

L

L [el]. das L.
label [leibl], s. die Etikette, das Schildchen.
labial ['leibiəl], adj. (Phonet.) labial,
Lippen-. — s. (Phonet.) der Lippenlaut.
laboratory [lə'bɔrətəri, (Am.) 'læbərə-
təri], s. das Laboratorium, (coll.) das
Labor.
laborious [lə'bɔːriəs], adj. mühsam.
labour ['leibə], s. die Arbeit, Mühe;
Labour Party, die Arbeiterpartei;
(Med.) die Geburtswehen, f. pl. —
v.n. sich abmühen, leiden; sich
anstrengen.
labourer ['leibərə], s. der Arbeiter,
Taglöhner.
lace [leis], s. die Spitze, Tresse. — v.a.
verbrämen (trim with lace); zu-
schnüren (shoe); stärken (coffee with
rum etc.).
lacerate ['læsəreit], v.a. zerreißen.
lack [læk], v.a. ermangeln (Genit.). —
v.n. fehlen (an, Dat.). — s. der Mangel,
das Fehlen.
lackadaisical [lækə'deizikəl], adj.
schlaff, (coll.) schlapp, unbekümmert.
lackey ['læki], s. der Lakai, Diener,
Bediente.
laconic [lə'kɔnik], adj. lakonisch.
lacquer ['lækə], s. der Lack. — v.a.
lackieren.
lad [læd], s. der Bursche, Junge.
ladder ['lædə], s. die Leiter.
lading ['leidiŋ], s. (Comm.) das Laden;
die Fracht; bill of —, der Frachtbrief.
ladle [leidl], s. der Schöpflöffel, Sup-
penlöffel; die Kelle. — v.a. ausschöpfen, austeilen.
lady ['leidi], s. die Dame; —in-waiting,
die Hofdame.
ladybird ['leidibə:d], s. (Ent.) der
Marienkäfer.
ladyship ['leidiʃip], s. (Title) gnädige
Frau.
lag [læg], v.n. zurückbleiben. — v.a.
verkleiden, isolieren (tank).
laggard ['lægəd], s. der Zauderer. —
adj. zögernd, zaudernd.
lagoon [lə'gu:n], s. die Lagune.
lair [lɛə], s. das Lager (of animal).
laird [lɛəd], s. der schottische Guts-
herr.

laity ['leiiti], s. die Laien, m. pl.
lake [leik], s. der See.
lamb [læm], s. (Zool.) das Lamm. —
v.n. lammen.
lambent ['læmbənt], adj. brennend,
lodernd, strahlend.
lame [leim], adj. lahm. — v.a. lähmen.
lament [lə'ment], v.a., v.n. betrauern,
beweinen. — s. das Klagelied, die
Wehklage.
lamp [læmp], s. die Lampe; —post,
der Laternenpfahl.
lampoon [læm'pu:n], v.a. schmähen,
lächerlich machen. — s. die Schmähschrift.
lamprey ['læmpri], s. (Zool.) das
Neunauge.
lance [lɑːns], s. (Mil.) die Lanze. —
v.a. durchbohren; (Med.) lancieren.
lancer ['lɑːnsə], s. (Mil.) der Ulan.
lancet ['lɑːnsit], s. (Med.) die Lanzette.
land [lænd], s. das Land; das Grundstück (plot); — tax, die Grundsteuer.
— v.a. ans Land bringen, fangen
(fish). — v.n. landen.
landlord ['lændlɔːd], s. der Eigentümer,
der Hausherr; Wirt (pub).
landmark ['lændmɑːk], s. der Grenz-
stein, das Wahrzeichen.
landscape ['lændskeip], s. die Landschaft.
landslide, landslip ['lændslaid, 'lænd-
slip], s. der Erdrutsch.
lane [lein], s. der Heckenweg, Pfad; die
Gasse; (Motor.) die Fahrbahn.
language ['læŋgwidʒ], s. die Sprache.
languid ['læŋgwid], adj. flau, matt.
languor ['læŋgə], s. die Mattigkeit,
Flauheit.
lank [læŋk], adj. mager, schlank.
lantern ['læntən], s. die Laterne.
Laotian ['lauʃən], adj. laotisch. — s. der
Laote.
lap (1) [læp], s. der Schoß.
lap (2) [læp], s. das Plätschern (of
waves). — v.a. auflecken (lick up). —
v.n. plätschern.
lapel [lə'pel], s. der Aufschlag (of
jacket).
lapidary ['læpidəri], adj. lapidarisch;
wuchtig.
lapse [læps], v.n. gleiten, fallen; verlaufen (time). — s. der Verlauf (time);
der Fehler (mistake); das Verfallen
(into laziness etc.).
lapwing ['læpwiŋ], s. (Orn.) der Kiebitz.
larceny ['lɑːsəni], s. der Diebstahl.
larch [lɑːtʃ], s. (Bot.) die Lärche.
lard [lɑːd], s. das Schweinefett, Schweineschmalz.
larder ['lɑːdə], s. die Speisekammer.
large [lɑːdʒ], adj. groß; weit; dick, stark.
largesse ['lɑːdʒes], s. die Freigebigkeit
(generosity); die Schenkung (donation).
lark (1) [lɑːk], s. (Orn.) die Lerche.
lark (2) [lɑːk], s. (coll.) der Scherz. —
v.n. scherzen.
larkspur ['lɑːkspə:], s. (Bot.) der
Rittersporn.
larva ['lɑːvə], s. (Zool.) die Larve.

larynx ['læriŋks], *s.* (*Anat.*) der Kehlkopf.
lascivious [lə'siviəs], *adj.* wollüstig.
lash [læʃ], *s.* die Wimper (*eye*); die Peitschenschnur (*whip*); der Peitschenhieb (*stroke of whip*). — *v.a.* peitschen.
lass [læs], *s.* (*coll.*) das Mädchen.
lassitude ['læsitjuːd], *s.* die Mattigkeit.
lasso [lə'suː *or* 'læsou], *s.* das Lasso. — *v.a.* mit einem Lasso fangen.
last (1) [lɑːst], *adj.* letzt, vorig, äußerst; *at long* —, endlich.
last (2) [lɑːst], *s.* der Leisten (*shoemaking*).
last (3) [lɑːst], *v.n.* dauern, anhalten; hinreichen (*be sufficient*).
lastly ['lɑːstli], *adv.* zuletzt.
latch [lætʃ], *v.a.* verschließen.
latchkey ['lætʃkiː], *s.* der Hausschlüssel.
late [leit], *adj.* spät; verspätet; verstorben, selig (*deceased*); neulich (*recent*); *the train is* —, der Zug hat Verspätung; *of late*, jüngst.
latent ['leitənt], *adj.* (*Med.*) latent; verborgen.
lateral ['lætərəl], *adj.* seitlich, Seiten-.
lath [lɑːθ], *s.* die Latte.
lathe [leið], *s.* die Drehbank.
lather ['læðə], *s.* der Seifenschaum. — *v.n., v.a.* (sich) einseifen.
Latin ['lætin], *adj.* lateinisch. — *s.* das Latein, die lateinische Sprache.
latitude ['lætitjuːd], *s.* die geographische Breite; die Weite (*width*); (*fig.*) der Spielraum (*scope*).
latter ['lætə], *adj.* letzter; später (*later*). — *s.* der Letzte.
latterly ['lætəli], *adv.* neulich, neuerdings.
lattice ['lætis], *s.* das Gitter. — *v.a.* vergittern.
Latvian ['lætviən], *adj.* lettisch. — *s.* der Lette.
laud [lɔːd], *v.a.* loben, preisen.
laudable ['lɔːdəbl], *adj.* lobenswert.
laudatory ['lɔːdətəri], *adj.* belobend.
laugh [lɑːf], *v.n.* lachen; —*ing stock*, der Gegenstand des Gelächters.
laughter ['lɑːftə], *s.* das Lachen, Gelächter.
launch [lɔːntʃ], *s.* die Barkasse. — *v.a.* vom Stapel lassen.
launching ['lɔːntʃiŋ], *s.* der Stapellauf.
laundress ['lɔːndris], *s.* die Wäscherin.
laundry ['lɔːndri], *s.* die Wäsche (*clothes*); Wäscherei (*place*).
laureate ['lɔːriit], *s.* der Hofdichter.
laurel ['lɔrəl], *s.* (*Bot.*) der Lorbeer.
lavatory ['lævətri], *s.* das W.C., der Abort, Waschraum; die Toilette; *public* —, die Bedürfnisanstalt.
lavender ['lævəndə], *s.* (*Bot.*) der Lavend l.
lavish ['læviʃ], *adj.* freigebig, verschwenderisch. — *v.a.* vergeuden.
lavishness ['læviʃnis], *s.* die Freigebigkeit, Verschwendung.
law [lɔː], *s.* das Gesetz (*statute*); das Recht (*justice*); die Jura, Jurispru-

denz (*subject of study*).
lawful ['lɔːful], *adj.* gesetzlich, gesetzmäßig.
lawless ['lɔːlis], *adj.* gesetzlos; unrechtmäßig (*illegal*).
lawn (1) [lɔːn], *s.* der Rasen.
lawn (2) [lɔːn], *s.* der Batist.
lawsuit ['lɔːsuːt], *s.* der Prozeß.
lawyer ['lɔːjə], *s.* der Advokat, Rechtsanwalt, Jurist.
lax [læks], *adj.* locker, lax.
laxative ['læksətiv], *s.* das Abführmittel.
laxity ['læksiti], *s.* die Schlaffheit, Lockerheit (*of rope etc.*).
lay (1) [lei], *v.a. irr.* legen; setzen (*put*); stellen (*place*); bannen (*ghost*); — *up*, sammeln. — *v.n.* legen (*eggs*); wetten (*wager*); — *about one*, um sich schlagen.
lay (2) [lei], *s.* (*Poet.*) das Lied.
lay (3) [lei], *adj.* Laien-.
layer ['leiə], *s.* die Schicht; — *cake*, die Cremetorte.
layman ['leimən], *s.* der Laie.
laziness ['leizinis], *s.* die Faulheit.
lazy ['leizi], *adj.* faul, träge.
lea [liː], *s.* (*Poet.*) die Aue.
lead (1) [liːd], *v.a., v.n. irr.* führen, leiten; ausspielen (*cards*). — *s.* die Führung; (*Elec.*) Leitung.
lead (2) [led], *s.* das Blei; Bleilot (*plumb-line*).
leader ['liːdə], *s.* der Führer; (*Mus.*) der Konzertmeister; der Leitartikel (*leading article*).
leaf [liːf], *s.* (*Bot.*) das Blatt; (*Build.*) der Türflügel. — *v.a.* (*coll.*) — *through*, durchblättern.
leafy ['liːfi], *adj.* belaubt.
league (1) [liːg], *s.* drei englische Meilen, *f.pl.*
league (2) [liːg], *s.* das Bündnis (*pact*); *be in* —, verbündet sein; *League of Nations*, der Völkerbund.
leak [liːk], *v.n.* lecken, ein Loch haben. — *s.* das Loch; (*Naut.*) das Leck.
leaky ['liːki], *adj.* leck.
lean (1) [liːn], *v.n. irr.* (sich) lehnen (an, *Acc.*), stützen (auf, *Acc.*).
lean (2) [liːn], *adj.* mager, hager.
leap [liːp], *v.n. irr.* springen. — *s.* der Sprung; — *year*, das Schaltjahr.
learn [ləːn], *v.a. irr.* lernen, erfahren.
learned ['ləːnid], *adj.* gelehrt.
learning ['ləːniŋ], *s.* die Gelehrsamkeit.
lease [liːs], *s.* die Pacht, der Mietvertrag (*of house*). — *v.a.* (ver)pachten.
leasehold ['liːshould], *s.* die Pachtung.
leash [liːʃ], *v.a.* koppeln, anbinden. — *s.* die Koppel.
least [liːst], *adj.* wenigst, geringst, mindest, kleinst. — *s. at* (*the*) —, wenigstens, mindestens.
leather ['leðə], *s.* das Leder. — *adj.* Leder-, ledern.
leave [liːv], *v.a. irr.* verlassen (*quit*); lassen (*let*); hinterlassen (*bequeath*). — *v.n.* Abschied nehmen, abreisen. — *s.* der Urlaub; der Abschied (*farewell*); die Erlaubnis (*permission*).

leaven

leaven [levn], *s.* der Sauerteig. — *v.a.* säuern.

Lebanese [lebə'ni:z], *adj.* libanesisch. — *s.* der Libanese.

lecture ['lektʃə], *s.* die Vorlesung; der Vortrag.

lecturer ['lektʃərə], *s.* (*Univ.*) der Dozent; der Vortragende (*speaker*).

ledge [ledʒ], *s.* der Sims (*window*).

ledger ['ledʒə], *s.* (*Comm.*) das Hauptbuch.

lee [li:], *s.* die Leeseite (*shelter*).

leech [li:tʃ], *s.* (*Zool.*) der Blutegel.

leek [li:k], *s.* (*Bot.*) der Lauch.

leer ['liə], *s.* das Starren; der Seitenblick. — *v.n.* schielen (*at*, auf, nach); starren.

lees [li:z], *s. pl.* der Bodensatz, die Hefe.

left [left], *adj.* link. — *adv.* inks. — *s.* die linke Seite.

leg [leg], *s.* (*Anat.*) das Bein; der Schaft.

legacy ['legəsi], *s.* das Vermächtnis, das Erbe, Erbgut.

legal ['li:gəl], *adj.* gesetzlich.

legality [li'gæliti], *s.* die Gesetzlichkeit.

legatee [legə'ti:], *s.* (*Law*) der Erbe, die Erbin.

legation [li'geiʃən], *s.* die Gesandtschaft.

legend ['ledʒənd], *s.* die Legende, Sage; die Inschrift (*inscription*).

legendary ['ledʒəndəri], *adj.* legendär, sagenhaft.

leggings ['leginz], *s. pl.* die Gamaschen.

legible ['ledʒibl], *adj.* leserlich.

legislation [ledʒis'leiʃən], *s.* die Gesetzgebung.

legislative ['ledʒislətiv], *adj.* gesetzgebend.

legislator ['ledʒisleitə], *s.* der Gesetzgeber.

legitimacy [li'dʒitiməsi], *s.* die Gesetzmäßigkeit; (*Law*) die eheliche Geburt (*of birth*).

legitimate [li'dʒitimit], *adj.* gesetzmäßig; (*Law*) ehelich (*child*). — [-meit], *v.a.* für gesetzlich erklären.

legitimize [li'dʒitimaiz], *v.a.* legitimieren.

leguminous [li'gju:minəs], *adj.* Hülsen—; hülsentragend.

leisure ['leʒə], *s.* die Freizeit, Muße.

leisurely ['leʒəli], *adj.*, *adv.* gelassen, gemächlich.

lemon ['lemən], *s.* (*Bot.*) die Zitrone.

lemonade [lemən'eid], *s.* die Limonade.

lend [lend], *v.a. irr.* leihen; —*ing library*, die Leihbibliothek.

length [leŋθ], *s.* die Länge (*extent*); die Dauer (*duration*); *at* —, ausführlich.

lengthen ['leŋθən], *v.a.*, *v.n.* (sich) verlängern.

lengthy ['leŋθi], *adj.* langwierig, lang.

lenient ['li:niənt], *adj.* nachsichtig, milde.

lens [lenz], *s.* die Linse (*optics*); das Objektiv.

Lent [lent]. die Fastenzeit.

lentil ['lentil], *s.* (*Bot.*) die Linse.

leprosy ['leprəsi], *s.* der Aussatz, die Leprakrankheit.

leprous ['leprəs], *adj.* aussätzig.

lesion ['li:ʒən], *s.* die Verletzung.

less [les], *comp. adj.*, *adv.* weniger, kleiner.

lessee [le'si:], *s.* der Pächter, Mieter.

lessen [lesn], *v.a.*, *v.n.* (sich) verringern, vermindern.

lesser ['lesə], *comp. adj.* geringer; kleiner.

lesson [lesn], *s.* die Lehrstunde, Lektion; (*pl.*) der Unterricht; (*Rel.*) der Bibeltext.

lessor ['lesə], *s.* der Eigentümer, Vermieter.

lest [lest], *conj.* damit nicht; aus Furcht, daß.

let [let], *v.a. irr.* lassen; zulassen; vermieten; (*room*); — *down*, blamieren, enttäuschen; *off*, abschießen. — *s. without* — *or hindrance*, ohne Hinderung.

lethal ['li:θəl], *adj.* tödlich.

letter ['letə], *s.* der Brief; der Buchstabe (*character*); — *box*, der Briefkasten; (*pl.*) die Literatur.

letterpress ['letəpres], *s.* die Kopierpresse.

lettuce ['letis], *s.* (*Bot.*) der Salat.

level [levl], *adj.* eben, gleich. — *s.* die Ebene; das Niveau. — *v.a.* ebnen, ausgleichen; (*Build.*) planieren.

lever ['li:və], *s.* der Hebel.

levity ['leviti], *s.* der Leichtsinn.

levy ['levi], *v.a.* erheben (*tax*); auferlegen (*penalty*). — *s.* die Steuer.

lewd [lju:d *or* lu:d], *adj.* liederlich, gemein, unzüchtig.

liability [laiə'biliti], *s.* die Verantwortlichkeit; *limited* —, beschränkte Haftung; die Steuerpflichtigkeit (*to tax*), Zollpflichtigkeit (*to duty*).

liable ['laiəbl], *adj.* haftbar, zahlungspflichtig.

liar ['laiə], *s.* der Lügner.

libel ['laibəl], *s.* die Verleumdung. — *v.a.* verleumden, schmähen.

libellous ['laibələs], *adj.* verleumderisch.

liberal ['libərəl], *adj.* (*Pol.*) liberal; freigebig (*generous*); — *arts*, Geisteswissenschaften, *f. pl.*

liberate ['libəreit], *v.a.* befreien, freisetzen; (*Law*) in Freiheit setzen.

Liberian [lai'bi:riən], *adj.* liberisch. — *s.* der Liberier.

libertine ['libati:n], *s.* der Wüstling.

liberty ['libəti], *s.* die Freiheit; die Erlaubnis (*permit*).

librarian [lai'brɛəriən], *s.* der Bibliothekar, die Bibliothekarin.

library ['laibrəri], *s.* die Bibliothek.

Libyan ['libjən], *adj.* libysch. — *s.* der Libyer.

licence ['laisəns], *s.* die Genehmigung, Erlaubnis (*permit*); *driving* —, der Führerschein; die Zügellosigkeit (*licentiousness*).

license ['laisəns], *v.a.* genehmigen, bewilligen; *licensing laws*, Ausschanksgesetze, *n. pl.* (*for alcohol*).

licentiate [lai'senʃiit], *s.* der Lizenziat (*degree*).

licentious [lai'senʃəs], *adj.* ausschweifend, liederlich, locker (*in morals*).

lichen ['laikən, 'litʃən], *s.* (*Bot.*) die Flechte.

lichgate ['litʃgeit], *s.* das Friedhofstor.

lick [lik], *v.a.* lecken; (*Am.*) prügeln, verhauen.

lid [lid], *s.* das Augenlid; der Deckel.

lie [lai], (1) *v.n.* lügen. — *s.* die Lüge (*untruth*).

lie [lai], (2) *v.n. irr.* liegen; — *down*, sich legen, hinlegen; sich fügen (*fig.*).

lieu [lju:], *s. in* —, an Stelle, anstatt (*Genit.*).

lieutenant [lef'tenənt], *s.* der Leutnant.

life [laif], *s.* das Leben.

lifebelt ['laifbelt], *s.* der Rettungsgürtel.

lifeboat ['laifbout], *s.* das Rettungsboot.

lifetime ['laiftaim], *s.* die Lebenszeit, Zeit seines Lebens.

lift [lift], *s.* der Aufzug, Fahrstuhl; (*coll.*) *give a — to*, mitnehmen (*im* Auto). — *v.a.* heben; aufheben (*abolish*); (*coll.*) klauen, stehlen.

ligament ['ligəmənt], *s.* das Band; (*Anat.*) die Flechse, die Sehne.

ligature ['ligətʃə], *s.* (*Typ.*) die Ligatur; die Verbindung.

light [lait], *adj.* hell, licht; blond (*hair*); leicht (*weight*). — *s.* das Licht; *give a —*, ein Streichholz geben, Feuer geben. — *v.a. irr.* beleuchten (*room*); anzünden (*fire*). — *v.n. irr.* — (*up*), hell werden, leuchten; (*fig.*) aufleuchten.

lighten [laitn], *v.a.* erhellen (*brighten*); erleichtern (*ease*).

lighter ['laitə], *s.* das Feuerzeug (*smoker's*); (*Naut.*) das Lichterschiff.

lighthouse ['laithaus], *s.* der Leuchtturm.

lightning ['laitniŋ], *s.* der Blitz; — *conductor*, der Blitzableiter; — *speed*, die Blitzesschnelle.

ligneous ['liɡniəs], *adj.* holzig.

lignite ['liɡnait], *s.* die Braunkohle.

like (1) [laik], *v.a.* gern haben; *I — to sing*, ich singe gern. — *v.n.* belieben, wollen; *as you —*, wie Sie wollen. — *s. his —s and dislikes*, seine Wünsche und Abneigungen.

like (2) [laik], *adj.* gleich, ähnlich. — *s. his —*, seinesgleichen. — *prep.* gleich, wie; *just — him!* das sieht ihm ähnlich! *feel —*, möchte gern; *what is it —?* wie sieht es aus?

likelihood ['laiklihud], *s.* die Möglichkeit; Wahrscheinlichkeit (*probability*).

likely ['laikli], *adj.* möglich; wahrscheinlich (*probable*).

liken ['laikən], *v.a.* vergleichen.

likeness ['laiknis], *s.* die Ähnlichkeit.

likewise ['laikwaiz], *adv.* ebenso, gleichfalls, auch.

liking ['laikiŋ], *s.* die Vorliebe (*for*, für, *Acc.*); Neigung (*for*, zu, *Dat.*); *to my*

—, nach meinem Geschmack *or* Wunsch.

lilac ['lailək], *s.* (*Bot.*) der Flieder.

lilt [lilt], *v.a.*, *v.n.* trällern, summen. — *s.* die Melodie, Weise.

lily ['lili], (*Bot.*) *s.* die Lilie; — *of the valley*, das Maiglöckchen.

limb [lim], *s.* das Glied.

limber ['limbə], *adj.* geschmeidig.

lime (1) [laim], *s.* der Leim, Kalk (*chalk*).

lime (2) [laim], *s.* (*Bot.*) die Linde (*tree*); die Limone (*fruit*); — *juice*, der Limonensaft.

limestone ['laimstoun], *s.* der Kalkstein.

limit ['limit], *s.* die Grenze, das Ende. — *v.a.* begrenzen, beschränken.

limitation [limi'teiʃən], *s.* die Begrenzung.

limn [lim], *v.a.* (*Art.*) zeichnen, malen.

limp [limp], *v.n.* hinken. — *adj.* müde, schlaff.

limpid ['limpid], *adj.* klar, durchsichtig.

linden ['lindən], *s.* (*Bot.*) die Linde.

line (1) [lain], *s.* die Linie, Eisenbahnlinie (*Railw.*); die Zeile; der Strich; (*Mil.*) die Reihe; — *of business*, die Geschäftsbranche; (*Genealogy*) die Abstammung; *take a strong —*, entschlossen auftreten.

line (2) [lain], *v.a.* füttern (*a garment*).

lineage ['liniidʒ], *s.* die Abstammung.

lineament ['liniəmənt], *s.* der Gesichtszug.

linear ['liniə], *adj.* linear, geradlinig.

linen ['linin], *s.* die Leinwand; *bed —*, die Laken, Bettwäsche. — *adj.* leinen.

liner ['lainə], *s.* (*Naut.*) das Passagierschiff.

linger ['liŋgə], *v.n.* zögern; verweilen.

lingerie ['lɛ̃ʒəri:], *s.* die Damenunterwäsche.

linguist ['liŋgwist], *s.* der Sprachkundige, Philologe, Linguist.

liniment ['linimənt], *s.* (*Med.*) die Salbe.

lining ['lainiŋ], *s.* das Futter (*of garment*).

link [liŋk], *s.* das Glied (*in chain*); die Verbindung (*connexion*). — *v.a.* verbinden, verknüpfen.

linnet ['linit], *s.* (*Orn.*) der Hänfling.

linseed ['linsi:d], *s.* der Leinsamen; — *oil*, das Leinöl.

lint [lint], *s.* die Scharpie, das Verbandzeug.

lion ['laiən], *s.* (*Zool.*) der Löwe.

lioness ['laiənes], *s.* (*Zool.*) die Löwin.

lip [lip], *s.* (*Anat.*, *Bot.*) die Lippe (*mouth*); der Rand (*of jug*).

lipstick ['lipstik], *s.* der Lippenstift.

liquefy ['likwifai], *v.a.*, *v.n.* flüssig machen *or* werden.

liqueur [li'kjuə], *s.* der Likör.

liquid ['likwid], *adj.* flüssig. — *s.* die Flüssigkeit.

liquidate ['likwideit], *v.a.* liquidieren; (*Comm.*) flüssig machen (*assets*); bezahlen (*pay off*).

431

liquor ['likə], *s.* der Alkohol.
liquorice ['likəris], *s.* die Lakritze.
lisp [lisp], *v.n.* lispeln. — *s.* der Sprachfehler, das Anstoßen, Lispeln.
list [list], *s.* die Liste, das Verzeichnis; (*Naut.*) die Schlagseite.
listen [lisn], *v.n.* horchen, zuhören.
listless ['listlis], *adj.* teilnahmslos.
litany ['litəni], *s.* (*Eccl.*) die Litanei.
literal ['litərəl], *adj.* buchstäblich.
literary ['litərəri], *adj.* literarisch, Literatur-.
literature ['litrətʃə], *s.* die Literatur.
lithe [laið], *adj.* geschmeidig.
Lithuanian [liθju'einiən], *adj.* litauisch. — *s.* der Litauer.
litigate ['litigeit], *v.n.* einen Prozeß anstrengen, litigieren, prozessieren.
litigation [liti'geiʃən], *s.* die Litigation, der Prozeß.
litter ['litə], *s.* (*Zool.*) die Jungen, *n. pl.*; die Brut; die Sänfte (*carriage*); der Abfall, die Abfälle (*waste paper etc.*). — *v.n.* (*Zool.*) Junge haben, werfen. — *v.a.* Abfälle wegwerfen, unsauber machen.
little [litl], *adj.* klein (*size, value*); gering (*value*); — *by* —, nach und nach.
liturgy ['litədʒi], *s.* (*Eccl.*) die Liturgie.
live [liv], *v.n.* leben; wohnen (*dwell*).
livelihood ['laivlihud], *s.* der Lebensunterhalt.
liveliness ['laivlinis], *s.* die Lebhaftigkeit.
lively ['laivli], *adj.* lebhaft.
liven [laivn], *v.a.* — *up*, beleben.
liver ['livə], *s.* (*Anat.*) die Leber.
livery ['livəri], *s.* die Livree (*uniform*); — *company*, die Zunftgenossenschaft.
livid ['livid], *adj.* bleich, blaß.
living ['liviŋ], *s.* das Auskommen, der Unterhalt; die Lebensweise; (*Eccl.*) die Pfründe, Pfarrstelle.
lizard ['lizəd], *s.* (*Zool.*) die Eidechse.
lo! [lou], *excl.* (*obs.*) sieh, da! siehe!
load [loud], *s.* die Last, Belastung. — *v.a.* beladen, belasten. — *v.n.* laden, aufladen.
loadstone *see* **lodestone.**
loaf [louf], *s.* der Laib (*bread*); *sugar* —, der Zuckerhut. — *v.n.* herumlungern, nichts tun.
loafer ['loufə], *s.* der Faulenzer, Drückeberger.
loam [loum], *s.* der Lehm.
loan [loun], *s.* die Anleihe. — *v.a.* leihen.
loath [louθ], *adj.* unwillig, abgeneigt.
loathe [louð], *v.a.* verabscheuen, hassen.
loathing ['louðiŋ], *s.* der Abscheu, Ekel.
loathsome ['louθsəm], *adj.* abscheulich, ekelhaft.
lobby ['lɔbi], *s.* die Vorhalle. — *v.a.* (*Pol.*) einen beeinflußen.
lobe [loub], *s.* das Läppchen.
lobster ['lɔbstə], *s.* (*Zool.*) der Hummer.
local ['loukəl], *adj.* lokal, örtlich. — *s.* (*coll.*) das Stammgasthaus (*pub*).

locality [lo'kæliti], *s.* die Lokalität, die Örtlichkeit, der Ort.
localize ['loukəlaiz], *v.a.* lokalisieren, auf einen Ort beschränken.
locate [lo'keit], *v.a.* finden (*find*); ausfindig machen.
location [lo'keiʃən], *s.* die Plazierung (*position*); die Lage; der Standort; *on* —, auf dem Gelände, auf Außenaufnahme (*film*).
loch [lɔx], *s.* (*Scot.*) der See.
lock [lɔk], *s.* das Schloß (*on door*); die Schleuse (*on waterway*); die Locke (*hair*). — *v.a.* schließen, abschließen (*door*); hemmen (*wheel*). — *v.n.* sich schließen; — *in*, ineinandergreifen (*cogs*).
locker ['lɔkə], *s.* der Schließschrank, das Schließfach.
locket ['lɔkit], *s.* das Medaillon.
locksmith ['lɔksmiθ], *s.* der Schlosser.
lock-up ['lɔkʌp], *s.* der Arrest, die Haftzelle; (*coll.*) die Garage.
locust ['loukəst], *s.* (*Ent.*) die Heuschrecke.
lodestone ['loudstoun], *s.* der Magnetstein, Magnet.
lodge [lɔdʒ], *v.n.* wohnen; logieren (*temporary*). — *v.a.* beherbergen (*accommodate*); einbringen (*a complaint, protest*). — *s.* das Haus, das Häuschen; die Loge (*Freemasons*).
lodger ['lɔdʒə], *s.* der (Unter)mieter.
lodgings ['lɔdʒiŋz], *s. pl.* das möblierte Zimmer, die Wohnung.
loft [lɔft], *s.* der Boden, Dachboden.
lofty ['lɔfti], *adj.* hoch; erhaben; stolz (*proud*).
log [lɔg], *s.* der Holzklotz, das Scheit; —*cabin*, —*house*, das Blockhaus; (*Naut.*) das Log, das Schiffstagebuch. — *v.a.* (*Naut.*) eintragen.
loggerheads ['lɔgəhedz], *s. pl. at* —, in Widerspruch, Widerstreit, im Konflikt.
logic ['lɔdʒik], *s.* die Logik.
logical ['lɔdʒikəl], *adj.* logisch.
loin [lɔin], *s.* (*Anat.*) die Lende.
loincloth ['lɔinklɔθ], *s.* der Lendenschurz.
loiter ['lɔitə], *v.n.* herumlungern; bummeln.
loiterer ['lɔitərə], *s.* der Lungerer, Faulenzer.
loitering ['lɔitəriŋ], *s.* das Herumlungern, Herumstehen, Faulenzen.
loll [lɔl], *v.n.* herumlungern.
lollipop ['lɔlipɔp], *s.* das Zuckerwerk, die Süßigkeit; (*fig.*) der Leckerbissen.
loneliness ['lounlinis], *s.* die Einsamkeit.
lonely (*Am.*) **lonesome** ['lounli, 'lounsəm], *adj.* einsam.
long [lɔŋ], *adj.* lang. — *adv.* — *ago*, vor langer Zeit; *before* —, in kurzer Zeit. — *v.n.* sich sehnen (*for*, nach, *Dat.*).
longitude ['lɔndʒitjuːd], *s.* die Länge; (*Geog.*) der Längengrad.

longitudinal [lɔndʒi'tjuːdinəl], adj. in der geographischen Länge, Längen-.

look [luk], v.n. blicken, sehen, schauen (at, auf, Acc.); — to it, dafür sorgen; — out for, Ausschau halten nach (Dat.); — out! paß auf! — after s.o., sich um jemanden kümmern; — into, prüfen, untersuchen; — forward to, sich freuen (auf, Acc.); — over, durchsehen. — s. der Blick (glance); das Aussehen (appearance).

looking-glass ['lukiŋglɑːs], s. der Spiegel.

look-out ['lukaut], s. der Ausblick; die Ausschau.

loom [luːm], s. der Webstuhl. — v.n. in der Ferne auftauchen (emerge).

loon [luːn], s. (Orn.) der Eisvogel, Eistaucher; (coll.) der Narr.

loony ['luːni], adj. (coll.) wahnsinnig, närrisch.

loop [luːp], s. die Schlinge, das Schlingband; (Railw.) — line, die Schleife.

loophole ['luːphoul], s. der Ausweg, die Hintertür.

loose [luːs], adj. locker, lose; liederlich (morals). — v.a. lösen.

loosen [luːsn], v.a. auflockern, locker machen.

lop [lɔp], v.a. stutzen (trees).

lopsided [lɔp'saidid], adj. einseitig.

loquacious [lo'kweiʃəs], adj. geschwätzig.

loquacity [lo'kwæsiti], s. die Schwatzhaftigkeit.

Lord [lɔːd], s. (Rel.) the —, Gott der Herr; der Lord (nobleman's title); — Mayor, der Oberbürgermeister.

lord [lɔːd], s. der Herr.

lordly ['lɔːdli], adj. vornehm, stolz.

lore [lɔː], s. die Kunde.

lose [luːz], v.a., v.n. irr. verlieren; nachgehen (of timepiece).

loser ['luːzə], s. der Verlierende.

loss [lɔs], s. der Verlust.

lot [lɔt], s. das Los (der Anteil (share); die Menge (quantity); die Partie (auction); (Am.) das Stück Land.

loth see loath.

lotion ['louʃən], s. das Waschmittel, das Wasser.

loud [laud], adj. laut; grell (colour).

lounge [laundʒ], s. der Gesellschaftsraum; (Obs.) die Chaiselongue; — suit, der Straßenanzug. — v.n. nichts tun, herumlungern, herumsitzen.

louse [laus], s. (Zool.) die Laus.

lout [laut], s. der Tölpel.

lovable ['lʌvəbl], adj. liebenswürdig, liebenswert.

love [lʌv], s. die Liebe; for the — of God, um Gottes Willen; for —, um nichts; not for — nor money, weder für Geld noch gute Worte, auf keinen Fall. — v.a., v.n. lieben; — to, gern tun.

lover ['lʌvə], s. der Liebhaber, der or die Geliebte.

low [lou], adj. niedrig; nieder, tief; leise; (Mus.) tief; (spirits) niedergeschlagen. — v.n. muhen (of cattle).

lowlands ['loulǝndz], s. pl. die Niederungen, f.pl.; die Ebene; das Unterland.

lowliness ['loulinis], s. die Demut, Bescheidenheit.

lowness ['lounis], s. die Niedrigkeit; Tiefe.

loyal ['lɔiǝl], adj. treu, ergeben, loyal.

loyalty ['lɔiǝlti], s. die Treue, Ergebenheit, Loyalität.

lozenge ['lɔzindʒ], s. die Pastille; (Geom.) die Raute.

lubricant ['luːbrikǝnt], s. das Schmiermittel, Schmieröl.

lubricate ['luːbrikeit], v.a. ölen, schmieren.

lucid ['luːsid], adj. klar, deutlich.

lucidity [luː'siditi], s. die Klarheit.

luck [lʌk], s. das Glück, der Glücksfall.

luckily ['lʌkili], adv. glücklicherweise.

lucky ['lʌki], adj. mit Glück gesegnet, glücklich.

lucrative ['luːkrǝtiv], adj. einträglich.

lucre ['luːkǝ], s. der Gewinn.

ludicrous ['luːdikrǝs], adj. lächerlich, komisch.

lug [lʌg], v.a. schleifen, zerren; (burden) schleppen.

luggage ['lʌgidʒ], s. das Gepäck.

lugger ['lʌgǝ], s. (Naut.) der Logger, Lugger.

lugubrious [luː'gjuːbriǝs], adj. traurig.

lukewarm ['luːkwɔːm], adj. lauwarm.

lull [lʌl], s. die (Wind)stille. — v.a. einlullen, beschwichtigen.

lullaby ['lʌlǝbai], s. das Wiegenlied.

lumbago [lʌm'beigou], s. (Med.) der Hexenschuß.

lumbar ['lʌmbǝ], adj. (Anat.) zu den Lenden gehörig, Lenden-.

lumber ['lʌmbǝ], s. der Kram, das alte Zeug; (timber) das Bauholz; — room, die Rumpelkammer.

luminous ['luːminǝs], adj. leuchtend, Leucht-.

lump [lʌmp], s. der Klumpen, Haufen; — sugar, der Würfelzucker; — sum, die Pauschalsumme. — v.a. — (together), zusammenwerfen.

lumpy ['lʌmpi], adj. klumpig.

lunacy ['luːnǝsi], s. der Wahnsinn.

lunatic ['luːnǝtik], adj. wahnsinnig. — s. der Wahnsinnige; — asylum, das Irrenhaus, die Irrenanstalt.

lunch [lʌntʃ], v.n. zu Mittag essen. — s. (also luncheon ['lʌntʃǝn]) das Mittagessen.

lung [lʌŋ], s. (Anat.) die Lunge.

lunge [lʌndʒ], v.n. stoßen, stürzen. — s. der Stoß.

lurch [lǝːtʃ], s. leave in the —, im Stiche lassen. — v.n. taumeln.

lure [luǝ], v.a. locken, ködern (bait). — s. der Köder (bait), die Lockung.

lurid ['ljuǝrid], adj. unheimlich, grell.

lurk [lǝːk], v.n. lauern.

luscious ['lʌʃǝs], adj. saftig, süß.

lush [lʌʃ], adj. üppig (vegetation); übermäßig.

lust [lʌst], s. die Wollust, Sucht. — v.n. gelüsten (for, nach, Dat.).
lustre ['lʌstə], s. der Glanz.
lusty ['lʌsti], adj. kräftig, laut.
lute [luːt], s. (Mus.) die Laute.
lutanist ['luːtənist], s. (Mus.) der Lautenspieler.
Lutheran ['luːθərən], adj. lutherisch. — s. der Lutheraner.
luxuriate [lʌg'zjuərieit, lʌk'sjuə-], v.n. schwelgen; (Bot.) üppig wachsen.
luxurious [lʌg'zjuəriəs, lʌk'sjuə-], adj. üppig; (rich) reich ausgeschmückt, prächtig, luxuriös.
luxury ['lʌkʃəri], s. der Luxus, Aufwand.
lymph [limf], s. die Lymphe.
lynx [links], s. (Zool.) der Luchs.
lyric ['lirik], s. die Lyrik.
lyrical ['lirikəl], adj. lyrisch.

M

M [em]. das M.
macaroon [mækə'ruːn], s. die Makrone.
mace [meis], s. das Zepter.
macerate ['mæsəreit], v.a. abzehren.
machination [mæki'neiʃən], s. die Machenschaft, Ränke, m.pl.
machine [mə'ʃiːn], s. die Maschine.
mackerel ['mækərəl], s. (Zool.) die Makrele.
mackintosh ['mækintɔʃ], s. der Regenmantel.
mad [mæd], adj. verrückt, wahnsinnig.
madam ['mædəm], s. (addr.) gnädige Frau.
madden [mædn], v.a. verrückt machen.
madman ['mædmən], s. der Wahnsinnige.
madness ['mædnis], s. der Wahnsinn.
magazine [mægə'ziːn], s. die (illustrierte) Zeitschrift; (gun) der Ladestock; der Lagerraum (storeroom).
maggot ['mægət], s. (Ent.) die Made.
magic ['mædʒik], adj. zauberhaft; — lantern, die Laterna Magica. — s. der Zauber; die Magie, Zauberei.
magician [mə'dʒiʃən], s. der Zauberer.
magistracy ['mædʒistrəsi], s. die Obrigkeit (authority).
magistrate ['mædʒistr(e)it], s. der Richter.
magnanimity [mægnə'nimiti], s. der Großmut.
magnanimous [mæg'næniməs], adj. großmütig.
magnate ['mægneit], s. der Magnat, Großunternehmer.
magnet ['mægnit], s. der Magnet.
magnetic [mæg'netik], adj. magnetisch.
magnetize ['mægnitaiz], v.a. magnetisieren.

magnificence [mæg'nifisəns], s. die Herrlichkeit.
magnificent [mæg'nifisənt], adj. herrlich, großartig.
magnify ['mægnifai], v.a. vergrößern (make larger); (Rel.) verherrlichen.
magnitude ['mægnitjuːd], s. die Größe; order of —, die Größenordnung.
magpie ['mægpai], s. (Orn.) die Elster.
Magyar ['mægjaː], adj. madjarisch. — s. der Magyar, Madjar.
mahogany [mə'hɔgəni], s. das Mahagoni(holz).
maid [meid], s. (Poet.) das Mädchen; das Stubenmädchen (servant).
maiden [meidn], s. (Poet.) die Jungfrau, das Mädchen; — aunt, die unverheiratete Tante.
mail (1) [meil], s. die Post. — v.a. aufgeben, mit der Post senden.
mail (2) [meil], s. (Mil.) der Panzer.
maim [meim], v.a. verstümmeln, lähmen.
main (1) [mein], adj. hauptsächlich, Haupt-; (Railw.) — line, die Hauptstrecke. — s. der Hauptteil; in the —, hauptsächlich; (Poet.) das Weltmeer; (pl.) das Hauptrohr, die Hauptleitung.
main (2) [mein], s. with might and —, mit allen Kräften.
mainstay ['meinstei], s. die Hauptgrundlage, Hauptstütze.
maintain [mein'tein], v.a. erhalten, unterhalten (keep); behaupten (assert).
maintenance ['meintənəns], s. der Unterhalt, die Unterhaltskosten, pl. die Erhaltung.
maize [meiz], s. (Bot.) der Mais.
majestic [mə'dʒestik], adj. majestätisch, prunkvoll.
majesty ['mædʒəsti], s. die Majestät.
major ['meidʒə], adj. größer, älter (elder brother); wichtig (more important). — s. (Mil.) der Major; (Law) der Mündige. — v.n. (Am.) sich spezialisieren.
majority [mə'dʒɔriti], s. die Mehrheit (in numbers); (Law) die Mündigkeit; (Mil.) der Majorsrang.
make [meik], v.a. irr. machen, schaffen, herstellen (produce); (coll.) verdienen (money); he has made it! (coll.) er hat's geschafft!; — out, ausfüllen (cheque etc.); entziffern (decipher); — up, erfinden (invent); schminken (o.'s face). — v.n. what do you — of him? was halten Sie von ihm? — s. die Marke.
make-believe ['meikbəliːv], s. der Vorwand. — adj. vorgetäuscht.
maladjustment [mælə'dʒʌstmənt], s. die Unfähigkeit sich anzupassen; die falsche Einstellung; das Missverhältnis.
maladroit [mælə'drɔit], adj. ungeschickt, ungewandt.
malady ['mælədi], s. das Leiden, die Krankheit.

Malagasy [mælə'gæsi], *adj.* madagassich. — *s.* der Madagasse.
Malaysian [mə'leiziən], *adj.* malaysisch. — *s.* der Malaysier.
malcontent ['mælkəntent], *adj.* mißvergnügt.
male [meil], *adj.* männlich; — *screw,* die Schraubenspindel. — *s.* der Mann; (*Zool.*) das Männchen.
malefactor ['mælifæktə], *s.* der Übeltäter.
malice ['mælis], *s.* die Bosheit.
malicious [mə'liʃəs], *adj.* boshaft, böswillig.
malign [mə'lain], *v.a.* lästern, verleumden.
malignant [mə'lignənt], *adj.* bösartig.
malignity [mə'ligniti], *s.* die Bösartigkeit.
malinger [mə'liŋgə], *v.n.* sich krank stellen.
malleable ['mæliəbl], *adj.* (*Metall.*) leicht zu hämmern; (*fig.*) geschmeidig.
mallet ['mælit], *s.* der Schlegel, Holzhammer.
mallow ['mælou], *s.* (*Bot.*) die Malve.
malpractice [mæl'præktis], *s.* das gesetzwidrige Handeln, der Mißbrauch; die Amtsvergehung.
malt [mɔ:lt], *s.* das Malz.
Maltese [mɔ:l'ti:z], *adj.* maltesisch. — *s.* der Malteser.
maltreat [mæl'tri:t], *v.a.* mißhandeln.
mammal ['mæməl], *s.* (*Zool.*) das Säugetier.
man [mæn], *s.* der Mann (*adult male*); der Mensch (*human being*); — *of war,* das Kriegschiff. — *v.a.* bemannen.
manacle ['mænəkl], *s.* die Handschelle. — *v.a.* fesseln.
manage ['mænidʒ], *v.a.* leiten, handhaben, verwalten; *how did you* — *it?* wie haben Sie's fertiggebracht?
management ['mænidʒmənt], *s.* die Leitung, Führung.
manager ['mænədʒə], *s.* der Leiter, Geschäftsführer, Manager.
mandatary *see* mandatory.
mandate ['mændeit], *s.* das Mandat.
mandatory ['mændətəri], *adj.* befehlend, bevollmächtigt, beauftragt. — *s.* der Bevollmächtigte, Beauftragte.
mandrake ['mændreik], *s.* der Alraun.
mane [mein], *s.* die Mähne.
manganese ['mæŋgəni:z], *s.* (*Chem.*) das Mangan.
mange [meindʒ], *s.* die Räude.
manger ['meindʒə], *s.* die Krippe.
mangle (1) [mæŋgl], *s.* die Mangel. — *v.a.* rollen; mangeln (*laundry*).
mangle (2) [mæŋgl], *v.a.* verstümmeln (*disfigure*).
mango ['mæŋgou], *s.* (*Bot.*) die Mangofrucht.
manhood ['mænhud], *s.* die Mannbarkeit, das Mannesalter.
mania ['meiniə], *s.* der Wahnsinn, die Manie.
maniac ['meiniæk], *s.* der Wahnsinnige. — *adj.* wahnsinnig.

manifest ['mænifest], *adj.* deutlich, klar, offenbar.
manifestation [mænifes'teiʃən], *s.* die Offenbarung.
manifesto [mæni'festou], *s.* das Manifest.
manifold ['mænifould], *adj.* mannigfach.
manipulate [mə'nipjuleit], *v.a.* manipulieren, handhaben.
mankind [mæn'kaind], *s.* die Menschheit.
manly ['mænli], *adj.* mannhaft, männlich.
manner ['mænə], *s.* die Art, Sitte (*custom*); die Manier (*bearing*); das Benehmen (*behaviour*); (*pl.*) gute Sitten.
mannered ['mænəd], *adj.* gesittet, geartet; manieriert, gekünstelt (*artificial*).
manor ['mænə], *s.* — *house,* das Herrenhaus, Schloß.
manorial [mə'nɔ:riəl], *adj.* des Herrenhauses, herrschaftlich.
manservant ['mænsə:vənt], *s.* der Bediente, Diener.
mansion ['mænʃən], *s.* das (herrschaftliche) Wohnhaus, Herrenhaus.
manslaughter ['mænslɔ:tə], *s.* der Totschlag.
mantelpiece ['mæntlpi:s], *s.* der Kaminsims.
mantle [mæntl], *s.* (*gas*) der Glühstrumpf; (*Tail.*) der Mantel. — *v.a.* verhüllen (*cloak*).
manual ['mænjuəl], *s.* das Handbuch; (*Mus.*) das Handregister. — *adj.* Hand-.
manufacture [mænju'fæktʃə], *s.* die Herstellung, Erzeugung (*production*); (*Comm.*) das Fabrikat (*product*).
manufacturer [mænju'fæktʃərə], *s.* der Fabrikant, Erzeuger.
manure [mə'njuə], *s.* der Dünger; der Mist. — *v.a.* düngen.
manuscript ['mænjuskript], *s.* die Handschrift, das Manuskript.
many ['meni], *adj.* viele; *as* — *as,* ganze ... (*emphatically*); — *a,* mancher.
map [mæp], *s.* die Landkarte. — *v.a.* —(*out*), nach der Karte planen.
maple [meipl], *s.* (*Bot.*) der Ahorn.
mar [ma:], *v.a.* verderben.
marauder [mə'rɔ:də], *s.* der Plünderer.
marble [ma:bl], *s.* der Marmor (*rock*); (*pl.*) die Murmel (*game*). — *adj.* marmorn.
March [ma:tʃ]. der März.
march [ma:tʃ], *s.* der Marsch. — *v.n.* marschieren; *steal a* — *on s.o.,* jemandem zuvorkommen.
marchioness [ma:ʃə'nes], *s.* die Marquise.
mare [mɛə], *s.* (*Zool.*) die Stute.
margin ['ma:dʒin], *s.* der Rand.
marginal [ma:dʒinəl], *adj.* Rand-, am Rande gelegen.
marigold ['mærigould], *s.* (*Bot.*) die Dotterblume.

marine

marine [mə'ri:n], *adj.* Marine-, See-.
— *s.* (*Mil.*) der Seesoldat; *tell that to
the Marines!* erzähle das der Großmutter!

mariner ['mærinə], *s.* der Seemann.

marital ['mæritəl], *adj.* ehelich.

maritime ['mæritaim], *adj.* Meeres-,
See-.

mark [ma:k], *s.* das Zeichen (*sign*);
(*Sch.*) die Zensur, Note; (*Comm.*) die
Marke; *wide of the* —, auf dem
Holzwege. — *v.a.* markieren (*make
sign on*); — *my words,* merk dir das!
paß auf! (*Comm.*) — *down,* den Preis
heruntersetzen; ins Auge fassen
(*observe closely*); *a* —*ed man,* ein
Gezeichneter.

market ['ma:kit], *s.* der Markt. — *v.a.*
auf den Markt bringen.

marksman ['ma:ksmən], *s.* der Schütze.

marl [ma:l], *s.* der Mergel.

marmalade ['ma:məleid], *s.* die Oran-
genmarmelade.

marmot ['ma:mət], *s.* (*Zool.*) das
Murmeltier.

maroon (1) [mə'ru:n], *adj.* kastanienbraun, rotbraun.

maroon (2) [mə'ru:n], *v.a.* aussetzen.

marquee [ma:'ki:], *s.* das große Zelt.

marquess, marquis ['ma:kwis], *s.* der
Marquis.

marriage ['mæridʒ], *s.* die Ehe, Heirat;
die Hochzeit (*wedding*).

marriageable ['mæridʒəbl], *adj.*
heiratsfähig.

married ['mærid], *adj.* verheiratet.

marrow ['mærou], *s.* (*Anat.*) das
Mark; (*Bot.*) der Kürbis.

marry ['mæri], *v.a.* heiraten; trauen
(*perform marriage ceremony*); — *off,*
verheiraten (*o.'s daughter*). — *v.n.*
sich verheiraten.

marsh [ma:ʃ], *s.* der Morast, Sumpf.

marshal ['ma:ʃəl], *s.* der Marschall.

marshy ['ma:ʃi], *adj.* morastig, sumpfig.

marten ['ma:tin], *s.* (*Zool.*) der Marder.

martial ['ma:ʃəl], *adj.* Kriegs-, kriegerisch.

martin ['ma:tin], *s.* (*Orn.*) die Mauer-
schwalbe.

martyr ['ma:tə], *s.* der Märtyrer.

martyrdom ['ma:tədəm], *s.* das
Märtyrertum, der Märtyrertod.

marvel [ma:vl], *v.n.* staunen (*at,* über,
Acc.).

marvellous ['ma:v(ə)ləs], *adj.* wunderbar, erstaunlich.

masculine ['mæskjulin], *adj.* männlich.
— *s.* (*Gram.*) das Maskulinum, das
männliche Geschlecht.

mash [mæʃ], *v.a.* zerquetschen, zerdrücken. — *s.* der Brei.

mask [ma:sk], *v.a., v.n.* maskieren, sich
vermummen. — *s.* die Maske.

mason ['meisən], *s.* der Maurer.

masonic [mə'sɔnik], *adj.* freimaurerisch.

masquerade [mæskə'reid], *s.* der
Mummenschanz, die Maskerade.

Mass [mæs, ma:s], *s.* (*Eccl.*) die Messe;
Low Mass, die stille Messe; *High*
Mass, das Hochamt; *Requiem Mass,*
die Seelenmesse.

mass [mæs], *s.* die Masse; die
Menge. — *v.a., v.n.* (sich) massen,
ansammeln.

massacre ['mæsəkə], *s.* das Blutbad.

massive ['mæsiv], *adj.* massiv, schwer.

mast [ma:st], *s.* der Mast. — *v.a.*
(*Naut.*) bemasten.

Master ['ma:stə], *s.* (*Univ.*) der Magister;
der junge Herr (*before boy's name.*)

master ['ma:stə], *s.* der Meister (*of a
craft*); der Herr, Arbeitgeber (*employer*); — *key,* der Hauptschlüssel.
— *v.a.* meistern, beherrschen.

masticate ['mæstikeit], *v.a.* kauen.

mastiff ['mæstif], *s.* (*Zool.*) der Ketten-
hund, Mastiff.

mat [mæt], *s.* die Matte.

match (1) [mætʃ], *s.* das Streichholz,
Zündholz.

match (2) [mætʃ], *s.* der ebenbürtige
Partner (*suitable partner*); *find o.'s* —,
seinesgleichen finden; (*Sport*) das
Wettspiel, der Wettkampf; Fußball-
kampf; (*Cricket*) das Cricketspiel. —
v.a., v.n. passen zu, anpassen; ebenbürtig sein (*be equal*).

matchless ['mætʃlis], *adj.* unvergleichlich, ohnegleichen.

mate (1) [meit], *s.* der Gefährte,
Genosse; (*Naut.*) der Maat, Steuermann; (*coll.*) Freund. — *v.n.* sich
paaren, sich verheiraten.

mate (2) [meit], *v.a.* (*Chess*) matt setzen.

material [mə'tiəriəl], *s.* das Material,
der Stoff. — *adj.* wesentlich (*essential*); materiell (*tangible*).

materialism [mə'tiəriəlizm], *s.* der
Materialismus.

maternal [mə'tə:nəl], *adj.* mütterlich.

maternity [mə'tə:niti], *s.* die Mutterschaft; — *ward,* die Geburtsklinik.

mathematical [mæθə'mætikəl], *adj.*
mathematisch.

mathematics [mæθə'mætiks], *s.* die
Mathematik.

matins ['mætinz], *s.* (*Eccl.*) die Früh-
mette.

matriculate [mə'trikjuleit], *v.n.* sich
immatrikulieren (lassen).

matrimonial [mætri'mouniəl], *adj.*
Ehe-, ehelich.

matrimony ['mætriməni], *s.* die Ehe.

matron ['meitrən], *s.* die Oberschwester,
Oberin (*in hospital etc.*); die Matrone
(*older woman*).

matter ['mætə], *s.* der Stoff (*substance*);
die Sache, der Gegenstand (*subject*);
die Angelegenheit (*case*); *printed* —,
Drucksache; *what is the* —? was ist
los?; *the heart of the* —, des Pudels
Kern; *as a* — *of fact,* tatsächlich,
ernst gesprochen. — *v.n.* bedeutsam
sein, wichtig sein.

mattock ['mætək], *s.* die Haue.

mattress ['mætrəs], *s.* die Matratze.

mature [mə'tjuə], *adj.* reif; (*fig.*)
gereift. — *v.a., v.n.* reifen, zur Reife
bringen; (*Comm.*) fällig werden.

matured [mə'tjuəd], *adj.* abgelagert.

maturity [mə'tjuəriti], *s.* die Reife; (*Comm.*) die Fälligkeit.

maudlin ['mɔ:dlin], *adj.* rührselig, sentimental.

maul [mɔ:l], *v.a.* mißhandeln.

Maundy Thursday ['mɔ:ndi'θə:zd(e)i]. der Gründonnerstag.

mauve [mouv], *adj.* malvenfarbig; violett.

maw [mɔ:], *s.* (*Zool.*) der Magen.

mawkish ['mɔ:kiʃ], *adj.* abgeschmackt, sentimental, rührselig.

maxim ['mæksim], *s.* der Grundsatz.

May [mei]. der Mai.

may (1) [mei], *v.n. aux. irr.* mögen, können; (*permissive*) dürfen.

may (2) [mei], *s.* (*Bot.*) der Weißdorn.

mayor [mɛə], *s.* der Bürgermeister.

maypole ['meipoul], *s.* der Maibaum.

maze [meiz], *s.* das Labyrinth.

me [mi:], *pers. pron.* (*Acc.*) mich; (*Dat.*) mir.

mead [mi:d], *s.* der Met.

meadow ['medou], *s.* die Wiese.

meagre ['mi:gə], *adj.* mager, karg (*lean, poor*); dürftig.

meal (1) [mi:l], *s.* das Mahl, Essen, die Mahlzeit.

meal (2) [mi:l], *s.* das Mehl (*flour*).

mealy ['mi:li], *adj.* mehlig; —*mouthed*, frömmelnd; kleinlaut (*shy*).

mean (1) [mi:n], *v.a. irr.* bedeuten (*signify*); meinen (*wish to express*); vorhaben (*intend*).

mean (2) [mi:n], *adj.* mittelmäßig, Mittel- (*average*). — *s.* die Mitte.

mean (3) [mi:n], *adj.* gemein, niedrig (*despicable*); geizig.

meander [mi'ændə], *s.* die Windung, das Wellenmuster. — *v.n.* sich winden, sich schlängeln.

meaning ['mi:niŋ], *s.* die Bedeutung (*significance, connotation*); der Sinn.

meaningless ['mi:niŋlis], *adj.* bedeutungslos.

means [mi:nz], *s.* das Mittel; *by all* —, auf jeden Fall, unbedingt; *by no* —, keinesfalls; *by—of*, mittels (*Genit.*).

meantime, meanwhile ['mi:ntaim, 'mi:nwail], *s.* die Zwischenzeit.—*adv.* in der Zwischenzeit, indessen.

measles [mi:zlz], *s.* (*Med.*) die Masern, *f. pl.*; *German* —, die Röteln, *m. pl.*

measurable ['meʒərəbl], *adj.* meßbar.

measure ['meʒə], *s.* das Maß; der Maßstab (*scale*); (*Mus.*) der Takt; das Zeitmaß.—*v.a.* messen, abmessen.

meat [mi:t], *s.* das Fleisch.

mechanic [mi'kænik], *s.* der Mechaniker.

mechanical [mi'kænikəl], *adj.* mechanisch, automatisch; — *engineering*, der Maschinenbau.

mechanics [mi'kæniks], *s.* die Mechanik.

medal [medl], *s.* die Medaille, der Orden.

meddle [medl], *v.n.* sich einmischen (in, *in, Acc.*).

mediæval, medieval [medi'i:vəl], *adj.* mittelalterlich.

mediate ['mi:dieit], *v.n.* vermitteln, intervenieren. — *adj.* mittelbar.

mediator ['mi:dieitə], *s.* der Vermittler.

medical ['medikəl], *adj.* medizinisch, ärztlich; — *orderly*, der Krankenwärter.

medicate ['medikeit], *v.a.* medizinisch behandeln.

medicine ['medsən], *s.* die Medizin, Arznei.

medieval *see* mediæval.

mediocre ['mi:dioukə], *adj.* mittelmäßig.

mediocrity [mi:di'ɔkriti], *s.* die Mittelmäßigkeit.

meditate ['mediteit], *v.n.* nachdenken, sinnen.

meditation [medi'teiʃən], *s.* das Sinnen, Nachdenken.

Mediterranean [meditə'reiniən], *adj.* mittelländisch. — *s.* das Mittelmeer, mittelländische Meer.

medium ['mi:djəm], *s.* das Medium; das Mittel (*means*), *adj.* mittelgroß.

medlar ['medlə], *s.* (*Bot.*) die Mispel.

medley ['medli], *s.* (*Mus.*) das Potpourri; das Gemisch (*mixture*).

meek [mi:k], *adj.* sanft, mild.

meet [mi:t], *v.a., v.n. irr.* treffen (*Acc.*), sich treffen (mit, *Dat.*), begegnen (*Dat.*). — *s.* (*Hunt.*) das Jagen.

meeting ['mi:tiŋ], *s.* das Zusammentreffen; die Tagung, Sitzung (*conference*).

melancholy ['melənkɔli], *adj.* melancholisch, schwermütig. — *s.* die Melancholie, die Schwermut.

mellifluous [me'lifluəs], *adj.* lieblich, süß (*of sounds*).

mellow ['melou], *adj.* mild, weich, mürbe (*fruit etc.*); freundlich (*mood*). — *v.a.* mürbe machen, reifen lassen. — *v.n.* weich werden.

melodious [mə'loudiəs], *adj.* klangvoll, wohlklingend, melodisch.

melodrama ['melədrɑ:mə], *s.* das Melodrama.

melody ['melədi], *s.* die Melodie.

melon ['melən], *s.* (*Bot.*) die Melone.

melt [melt], *v.a., v.n. reg. & irr.* schmelzen.

member ['membə], *s.* das Mitglied (*of club*); (*Parl.*) der Abgeordnete, das Glied.

membrane ['membrein], *s.* die Membran; (*Anat.*) das Häutchen.

memento [mi'mentou], *s.* das Andenken.

memoir ['memwɑ:], *s.* die Denkschrift; (*pl.*) die Memoiren, *n. pl.*

memorable ['memərəbl], *adj.* denkwürdig.

memorandum [memə'rændəm], *s.* das Memorandum, die Denkschrift.

memorial [mi'mɔ:riəl], *s.* das Denkmal (*monument*). — *adj.* Gedenk-, zum Gedenken, Gedächtnis-.

memory ['meməri], *s.* die Erinnerung; das Gedächtnis (*faculty*); das Andenken (*remembrance*).

menace ['menis], *s.* die Drohung. — *v.a.* bedrohen.

mend [mend], *v.a.* reparieren; verbessern, ausbessern. — *v.n.* sich bessern.

mendacious [men'deiʃəs], *adj.* lügnerisch, verlogen (*lying*).

mendacity [men'dæsiti], *s.* die Lügenhaftigkeit, Verlogenheit.

mendicant ['mendikənt], *adj.* bettlerisch. — *s.* der Bettler.

mendicity [men'disiti], *s.* die Bettelei.

menial ['mi:niəl], *adj.* gemein, grob (*job*).

mental [mentl], *adj.* geistig; (*coll.*) geisteskrank.

mention ['menʃən], *v.a.* erwähnen; *don't — it*, gern geschehen! — *s.* die Erwähnung.

mentor ['mentə], *s.* der Ratgeber.

menu ['menju:], *s.* die Speisekarte.

mercantile ['mə:kəntail], *adj.* Handels-, kaufmännisch.

mercenary ['mə:sənəri], *adj.* für Geld zu haben, käuflich, feil; materiell eingestellt. — *s.* der Söldner.

mercer ['mə:sə], *s.* der Seidenhändler.

mercerised ['mə:səraizd], *adj.* (*Textile*) merzerišiert.

merchandise ['mə:tʃəndaiz], *s.* die Ware.

merchant ['mə:tʃənt], *s.* der Kaufmann.

merchantman ['mə:tʃəntmən], *s.* (*Naut.*) das Handelsschiff, Frachtschiff.

merciful ['mə:siful], *adj.* barmherzig, gnädig.

Mercury ['mə:kjuəri]. (*Myth.*) Merkur, *m.*

mercury ['mə:kjuəri], *s.* (*Chem.*) das Quecksilber.

mercy ['mə:si], *s.* die Barmherzigkeit, Gnade.

mere (1) [miə], *adj.* bloß, allein.

mere (2) [miə], *s.* der Teich.

meretricious [meri'triʃəs], *adj.* falsch, täuschend.

merge [mə:dʒ], *v.n.* aufgehen lassen, verschmelzen (*combine*).

merger ['mə:dʒə], *s.* (*Comm.*) die Fusion, Vereinigung, Zusammenlegung.

meridian [mə'ridiən], *s.* der Meridian; (*fig.*) der Gipfel.

merit ['merit], *s.* das Verdienst, der Wert. — *v.a.* verdienen.

meritorious [meri'tɔ:riəs], *adj.* verdienstlich.

mermaid ['mə:meid], *s.* die Wasserjungfer, Nixe.

merriment ['merimənt], *s.* die Belustigung, das Fröhlichsein, die Fröhlichkeit.

merry ['meri], *adj.* froh, fröhlich; — *go-round*, das Karussell.

mesh [meʃ], *s.* das Netz; die Masche (*knitting*). — *v.a.* einfangen.

mess (1) [mes], *s.* (*Mil.*) die Offiziersmesse.

mess (2) [mes], *s.* die Unordnung (*disorder*).

message ['mesidʒ], *s.* die Nachricht, Mitteilung, Botschaft.

messenger ['mesindʒə], *s.* der Bote.

Messiah [mi'saiə], *s.* der Messias.

metal [metl], *s.* das Metall.

metallurgy ['metələ:dʒi], *s.* die Metallurgie, Hüttenkunde.

metaphor ['metəfɔ:], *s.* die Metapher.

metaphorical [metə'fɔrikəl], *adj.* bildlich.

meter ['mi:tə], *s.* der Messer, Zähler (*gauge*); (*Am.*) *see* **metre** (1).

methinks [mi'θiŋks], *v. impers.* (*obs.*) mich dünkt, ich meine, mir scheint.

method ['meθəd], *s.* die Methode.

methodical [mi'θɔdikəl], *adj.* methodisch, systematisch.

methylate ['meθileit], *v.a.* (*Chem.*) denaturieren.

metre (1) ['mi:tə], *s.* der *or* das Meter (*unit of measurement*).

metre (2) ['mi:tə], *s.* (*Poet.*) das Versmaß.

metric ['metrik], *adj.* metrisch (*system of measurement*).

metrical ['metrikəl], *adj.* (*Poet.*) im Metrum, metrisch, Vers–.

metropolis [mi'trɔpəlis], *s.* die Metropole.

metropolitan [metrə'pɔlitən], *adj.* hauptstädtisch. — *s.* (*Eccl.*) der Erzbischof.

mettle [metl], *s.* der Mut (*courage*); *put s.o. on his —*, einen anspornen.

mew [mju:], *s.* das Miauen (*of cat*). — *v.n.* miauen.

mews [mju:z], *s. pl.* die Stallung.

Mexican ['meksikən], *adj.* mexikanisch. — *s.* der Mexikaner.

microphone ['maikrəfoun], *s.* das Mikrophon.

mid- [mid], *prefix.* mittel, Mittel-, mittler.

midday [mid'dei], *s.* der Mittag.

middle [midl], *s.* die Mitte, das Zentrum.

middling ['midliŋ], *adj.* (*coll.*) mittelmäßig.

midget ['midʒit], *s.* der Zwerg (*dwarf*).

midnight ['midnait], *s.* die Mitternacht.

midriff ['midrif], *s.* das Zwerchfell.

midshipman ['midʃipmən], *s.* (*Naut.*) der Seekadett.

midwife ['midwaif], *s.* die Hebamme.

mien [mi:n], *s.* die Miene.

might [mait], *s.* die Macht, Gewalt.

mighty ['maiti], *adj.* mächtig, stark.

mignonette [minjə'net], *s.* (*Bot.*) die Reseda.

migrate [mai'greit], *v.n.* wandern, migrieren; (*birds*) ziehen.

migratory ['maigrətəri], *adj.* Zug-, Wander-.

Milanese [milə'n:iz], *adj.* mailändisch. — *s.* der Mailänder.

mild [maild], *adj.* mild, sanft.

mildew ['mildju:], *s.* der Meltau.

mile [mail], *s.* die (englische) Meile.

mileage ['mailidʒ], *s.* die Meilenzahl.

milfoil ['milfɔil], *s.* (*Bot.*) die Schafgarbe (*yarrow*).

military ['militəri], *adj.* militärisch. — *s.* das Militär.

militia [mi'liʃə], *s.* die Miliz.

milk [milk], *v.a.* melken. — *s.* die Milch.

milksop ['milksɔp], *s.* die Memme.

milky ['milki], *adj.* milchig; *Milky Way*, die Milchstraße.

mill [mil], *s.* die Mühle; die Spinnerei (*textile*); *rolling* —, das Walzwerk; *run of the* —, gewöhnlich; *through the* —, wohl erfahren, lebenserfahren. — *v.a.* mahlen (*flour*); rollen, walzen (*steel*); rändern (*coins*); —*ed edge*, die Rändelkante. —*v.n.* — (*around*), sich drängen.

miller ['milə], *s.* der Müller.

millet ['milit], *s.* die Hirse.

milliner ['milinə], *s.* die Modistin, Putzmacherin.

millinery ['milinəri], *s.* die Putzwaren, Modewaren, *f. pl.*

million ['miljən], *s.* die Million.

milt [milt], *s.* die Fischmilch; (*Anat.*) die Milz.

mimic ['mimik], *s.* der Mimiker. — *v.a.* nachahmen.

mimicry ['mimikri], *s.* die Nachahmung; (*Zool.*) die Anpassung (*in colour*).

mince [mins], *v.a.* kleinhacken (*meat*); — *o.'s words*, affektiert sprechen; *not* — *o.'s words*, kein Blatt vor den Mund nehmen. — *s.* gehacktes Fleisch; — *pie*, die Dörrobstpastete.

mincemeat ['minsmi:t], *s.* die (gehackte) Dörrobstmischung.

mincing ['minsiŋ], *adj.* affektiert; — *steps*, trippelnde Schritte.

mind [maind], *s.* der Geist, das Gemüt; die Meinung; der Sinn; der Verstand; *what is on your* —? was bedrückt Sie?; *bear in* —, daran denken; *have a* —, Lust haben; *make up o.'s* —, sich entschließen; *with an open* —, unparteiisch. — *v.a.* beachten, achten (auf, *Acc.*). — *v.n. do you* —? macht es Ihnen etwas aus? *never* —, macht nichts; *I don't* —, mir ist's recht, meinetwegen.

minded ['maindid], *adj.* gesinnt, eingestellt.

mine (1) [main], *poss. pron.* mein, meinig.

mine (2) [main], *s.* das Bergwerk (*general*), die Grube (*coal*). — *v.a.* abbauen, graben (*Acc.*, nach, *Dat.*).

miner ['mainə], *s.* der Bergmann, Bergarbeiter; (*coll.*) der Kumpel.

mineral ['minərəl], *s.* das Mineral; (*pl.*) Mineralwasser.

mingle [miŋgl], *v.a., v.n.* (sich) mischen.

minimize ['minimaiz], *v.a.* (möglichst) klein machen.

mining ['mainiŋ], *s.* die Hüttenkunde (*theory*); der Bergbau.

minion ['minjən], *s.* der Liebling.

minister ['ministə], *s.* (*Pol.*) der Minister; *Prime Minister*, der Ministerpräsident; (*Eccl.*) der Geistliche, Pfarrer. — *v.n.* einen Gottesdienst abhalten; dienen (*to, Dat.*).

ministration [minis'treiʃən], *s.* der Dienst, die Dienstleistung.

ministry ['ministri], *s.* das Ministerium (*department of state*); (*Eccl.*) der Beruf *or* das Amt des Geistlichen.

minnow ['minou], *s.* (*Zool.*) die Elritze.

minor ['mainə], *adj.* kleiner, geringer; (*Sch.*) jünger (*after boy's name*). — *s.* (*Law*) der Minderjährige, Unmündige.

minority [mai'nɔriti], *s.* die Minorität (*in numbers*); (*Law*) die Unmündigkeit.

minster ['minstə], *s.* (*Eccl.*) das Münster.

minstrel ['minstrəl], *s.* der Spielmann.

mint (1) [mint], *s.* (*Bot.*) die Minze.

mint (2) [mint], *s.* die Münzstätte. — *v.a.* münzen.

minuet [minju'et], *s.* (*Mus.*) das Menuett.

minute (1) ['minit], *s.* die Minute (*time*); (*pl.*) das Protokoll (*of meeting*). — *v.a.* zu Protokoll nehmen, protokollieren.

minute (2) [mai'nju:t], *adj.* winzig, klein.

minutiae [mi'nju:ʃii], *s.pl.* die Details, *n. pl.*, die Einzelheiten, *f. pl.*

miracle ['mirəkl], *s.* das Wunder.

miraculous [mi'rækjuləs], *adj.* wunderbar; wundertätig.

mirage [mi'rɑ:ʒ], *s.* die Luftspiegelung, die Fata Morgana.

mire [maiə], *s.* der Schlamm, Kot.

mirror ['mirə], *s.* der Spiegel. — *v.a.* reflektieren, spiegeln.

mirth [mə:θ], *s.* der Frohsinn.

misadventure [misəd'ventʃə], *s.* das Mißgeschick.

misalliance [misə'laiəns], *s.* die Mißheirat, Mesalliance.

misapply [misə'plai], *v.a.* falsch anwenden.

misapprehend [misæpri'hend], *v.a.* mißverstehen.

misapprehension [misæpri'henʃən], *s.* das Mißverständnis.

misappropriate [misə'prouprieit], *v.a.* unrechtmäßig erwerben, unterschlagen.

misbehave [misbi'heiv], *v.n.* sich schlecht benehmen.

miscalculate [mis'kælkjuleit], *v.a., v.n.* sich verrechnen.

miscarriage [mis'kæridʒ], *s.* das Mißlingen; (*Med.*) die Fehlgeburt.

miscarry [mis'kæri], *v.n.* mißlingen; (*Med.*) fehlgebären.

miscellaneous [misə'leiniəs], *adj.* vermischt.

miscellany [mi'seləni], *s.* der Sammelband (*of writers*); die Mischung, das Gemisch.

mischief ['mistʃif], *s.* der Unfug; *out to make —*, darauf aus, Unfug zu stiften; *— maker*, der Unheilstifter.

mischievous ['mistʃivəs], *adj.* boshaft.

misconceive [miskən'si:v], *v.a.* mißverstehen.

misconception [miskən'sepʃən], *s.* das Mißverständnis.

misconduct [mis'kɔndʌkt], *s.* das unkorrekte Verhalten; der Fehltritt.

misconstruction [miskən'strʌkʃən], *s.* die Mißdeutung.

misconstrue [miskən'stru:], *v.a.* mißdeuten.

misdeed [mis'di:d], *s.* die Missetat.

misdemeanour [misdi'mi:nə], *s.* (*Law.*) das Vergehen; die Missetat.

miser ['maizə], *s.* der Geizhals.

miserable ['mizərəbl], *adj.* elend, kläglich (*wretched*); nichtswürdig (*base*).

miserly ['maizəli], *adj.* geizig.

misery ['mizəri], *s.* das Elend, die Not.

misfortune [mis'fɔ:tʃən], *s.* das Unglück.

misgiving [mis'givin], *s.* die Befürchtung, der Zweifel (*doubt*).

misguide [mis'gaid], *v.a.* irreführen, verleiten.

mishap [mis'hæp], *s.* der Unfall.

misinform [misin'fɔ:m], *v.a.* falsch informieren, falsch unterrichten.

misinterpret [misin'tə:prit], *v.a.* mißdeuten.

misjudge [mis'dʒʌdʒ], *v.a.* falsch beurteilen.

mislay [mis'lei], *v.a. irr.* verlegen.

mislead [mis'li:d], *v.a. irr.* verführen, irreführen.

misnomer [mis'noumə], *s.* der falsche Name.

misogynist [mi'sɔdʒinist], *s.* der Weiberfeind.

misplace [mis'pleis], *v.a.* übel anbringen (*remark*); verlegen (*thing*).

misprint [mis'print], *v.a.* verdrucken, falsch drucken. — ['misprint], *s.* der Druckfehler.

misquote [mis'kwout], *v.a.* falsch zitieren.

misrepresent [misrepri'zent], *v.a.* falsch darstellen.

misrule [mis'ru:l], *s.* die schlechte Regierung; die Unordnung (*disorder*).

miss (1) [mis], *s.* das Fräulein.

miss (2) [mis], *v.a.* vermissen (*yearn for*); versäumen (*a train, lesson etc.*); verfehlen (*target*); *— the boat*, den Anschluß verpassen; *be missing*, fehlen.

missal [misl], *s.* (*Eccl.*) das Meßbuch.

misshapen [mis'ʃeipən], *adj.* mißgestaltet.

missile ['misail], *s.* das Geschoß; *ballistic —*, das Raketengeschoß; *guided —*, ferngesteuertes Raketengeschoss.

mission ['miʃən], *s.* die Mission; Sendung; der Auftrag (*task*).

missionary ['miʃənəri], *adj.* Missions-. *— s.* der Missionar.

missive ['misiv], *s.* das Sendschreiben.

misspell [mis'spel], *v.a.* falsch buchstabieren, falsch schreiben.

mist [mist], *s.* der Dunst; Nebel (*fog*).

mistake [mis'teik], *s.* der Fehler. *— v.a. irr.* verkennen.

mistaken [mis'teikn], *adj.* im Unrecht; irrig; *be —*, sich irren.

mistimed [mis'taimd], *adj.* zur Unzeit, unzeitig.

mistletoe ['misltou], *s.* (*Bot.*) die Mistel, der Mistelzweig.

mistress ['mistrəs], *s.* die Herrin; Hausfrau; Geliebte (*paramour*); Lehrerin (*Sch.*).

mistrust [mis'trʌst], *v.a.* mißtrauen.

misunderstand [misʌndə'stænd], *v.a. irr.* mißverstehen.

misuse [mis'ju:z], *v.a.* mißbrauchen.

mite (1) [mait], *s.* (*Zool.*) die Milbe.

mite (2) [mait], *s.* das Scherflein (*coin*); (*coll.*) das Kindchen, das Kerlchen.

mitigate ['mitigeit], *v.a.* mildern.

mitre ['maitə], *s.* die Bischofsmütze, Mitra.

mitten [mitn], *s.* der Fäustling, Fausthandschuh.

mix [miks], *v.a.* mischen, vermischen. *— v.n.* verkehren.

mixed [miksd], *adj. a — blessing*, eine fragliche Wohltat.

mizzle [mizl], *v.n.* sprühen, rieseln.

mnemonics [ni'mɔniks], *s.* die Gedächtniskunst.

moan [moun], *v.n.* stöhnen (*wail*); klagen (*complain*). *— s.* (*coll.*) die Klage.

moat [mout], *s.* der Burggraben, Wassergraben.

mob [mɔb], *s.* der Pöbel.

mobility [mo'biliti], *s.* die Beweglichkeit.

mobilize ['moubilaiz], *v.a.* mobilisieren.

mock [mɔk], *v.a.* verspotten (*tease*); täuschen (*mislead*). *— v.n.* spotten. *— s.* der Spott, die Täuschung. *— adj.* Schein-; *— heroic*, komischheroisch.

modal [moudl], *adj.* (*Gram.*) modal, der Aussageweise nach; (*Mus.*) dem Modus nach.

mode [moud], *s.* (*Mus.*) der Modus, die Art; die Mode (*fashion*).

model [mɔdl], *s.* das Modell; das Muster (*pattern*). *— v.a., v.n.* modellieren.

moderate ['mɔdərit], *adj.* mäßig; (*climate*) gemäßigt. *— [-reit], v.a.* mäßigen; abändern.

modern ['mɔdən], *adj.* modern.

modernize ['mɔdənaiz], *v.a.* modernisieren.

modest ['mɔdist], *adj.* bescheiden.

modesty ['mɔdisti], *s.* die Bescheidenheit.

modify ['mɔdifai], *v.a.* abändern, modifizieren.

modish ['moudiʃ], *adj.* nach der neuesten Mode, modisch.

modulate ['mɔdjuleit], *v.a.* modulieren.

moil [mɔil], *v.n.* sich plagen.

moist [mɔist], *adj.* feucht.

moisten [mɔisn], *v.a.* befeuchten.

moisture ['mɔistʃə], *s.* die Feuchtigkeit.

molasses [mo'læsiz], *s.* die Melasse.

mole (2) [moul], *s.* (*Zool.*) der Maulwurf.

mole (3) [moul], *s.* das Muttermal (*skin mark*).

mole (3) [moul], *s.* der Seedamm, Hafendamm.

molecular [mo'lekjulə], *adj.* molekular.

molecule ['mɔl-, 'moulikju:l], *s.* das Molekül.

molest [mo'lest], *v.a.* belästigen.

mollify ['mɔlifai], *v.a.* besänftigen.

mollusc ['mɔləsk], *s.* (*Zool.*) die Molluske.

molt *see under* **moult**.

molten ['moultən], *adj.* geschmolzen.

moment ['moumənt], *s.* der Augenblick, Moment (*instant*); die Wichtigkeit (*importance*).

momentary ['mouməntəri], *adj.* momentan, einen Augenblick lang.

momentum [mo'mentəm], *s.* das Moment, die Triebkraft.

monarch ['mɔnək], *s.* der Monarch.

monarchy ['mɔnəki], *s.* die Monarchie.

monastery ['mɔnəstri], *s.* das (Mönchs-)kloster.

monastic [mə'næstik], *adj.* klösterlich.

Monday ['mʌndi], der Montag.

money ['mʌni], *s.* das Geld; *ready* —, bares Geld; *make* —, Geld verdienen; — *order*, die Postanweisung.

Mongolian [mɔŋ'gouliən], *adj.* mongolisch. — *s.* der Mongole.

mongrel ['mʌŋgrəl], *s.* (*Zool.*) der Mischling.

monitor ['mɔnitə], *s.* der Ermahner; (*Rad.*) der Abhörer.

monitoring ['mɔnitəriŋ], *adj.* — *service*, der Abhördienst.

monk [mʌŋk], *s.* (*Eccl.*) der Mönch.

monkey ['mʌŋki], *s.* (*Zool.*) der Affe.

monomania [mɔno'meiniə], *s.* die Monomanie, fixe Idee.

monopolize [mə'nɔpəlaiz], *v.a.* monopolisieren.

monopoly [mə'nɔpəli], *s.* das Monopol.

monosyllabic [mɔnəsi'læbik], *adj.* einsilbig.

monotonous [mə'nɔtənəs], *adj.* monoton, eintönig.

monsoon [mɔn'su:n], *s.* der Monsun.

monster ['mɔnstə], *s.* das Ungeheuer.

monstrance ['mɔnstrəns], *s.* (*Eccl.*) die Monstranz.

monstrosity [mɔns'trɔsiti], *s.* die Ungeheuerlichkeit.

monstrous ['mɔnstrəs], *adj.* ungeheuerlich.

month [mʌnθ], *s.* der Monat.

monthly ['mʌnθli], *adj.* monatlich, Monats-.

mood [mu:d], *s.* die Stimmung, Laune; (*Gram., Mus.*) der Modus.

moodiness ['mu:dinis], *s.* die Launenhaftigkeit.

moody ['mu:di], *adj.* launenhaft.

moon [mu:n], *s.* der Mond.

moonlight ['mu:nlait], *s.* das Mondlicht, der Mondschein.

moonshine ['mu:nʃain], *s.* der Mondschein; (*fig.*) Unsinn.

moonstruck ['mu:nstrʌk], *adj.* mondsüchtig; verliebt.

Moor [muə], *s.* der Mohr, Neger.

moor [muə], *s.* das Moor, Heideland.

moorage ['muəridʒ], *s.* der Ankerplatz.

moorhen ['mɔ:hen], *s.* (*Orn.*) das Moorhuhn, Wildhuhn.

moorish ['muəriʃ], *adj.* maurisch.

moot [mu:t], *v.a.* erörtern, besprechen. — *adj. a* — *point*, ein strittiger Punkt.

mop [mɔp], *s.* der Wischlappen, Mop. — *v.a.* aufwischen (*floor*), wischen (*brow*).

mope [moup], *v.n.* traurig sein.

moral ['mɔrəl], *adj.* moralisch (*high principled*); sittlich (*decent*). — *s.* die Moral (*precept*); (*pl.*) die Sitten, *f. pl.*; die Sittlichkeit.

moralize ['mɔrəlaiz], *v.n.* moralisieren, Moral predigen (*Dat.*).

morass [mo'ræs], *s.* der Morast.

morbid ['mɔ:bid], *adj.* krankhaft.

more [mɔ:], *comp. adj.*, *adv.* mehr; *once* —, noch einmal; *all the* —, umso mehr; *the* — *the better*, je mehr desto besser.

moreover [mɔ:'rouvə], *adv.* zudem, überdies, weiterhin.

morning ['mɔ:niŋ], *s.* der Morgen, Vormittag; — *coat*, der Cutaway, Frack.

Moroccan [mə'rɔkən], *adj.* marokkanisch. — *s.* der Marokkaner.

Morocco [mə'rɔkou], Marokko, *n.*

morocco [mə'rɔkou], *s.* der Saffian, das Maroquinleder.

moron ['mɔ:rɔn], *s.* der Schwachsinnige.

morose [mə'rous], *adj.* mürrisch.

morrow ['mɔrou], *s.* (*Poet.*) der Morgen.

morsel [mɔ:sl], *s.* der Bissen, das Stück.

mortal [mɔ:tl], *adj.* sterblich, tödlich; — *sin*, die Todsünde. — *s.* der Sterbliche, der Mensch.

mortality [mɔ:'tæliti], *s.* die Sterblichkeit.

mortar ['mɔ:tə], *s.* (*Build.*) der Mörtel; (*Mil.*) der Mörser.

mortgage ['mɔ:gidʒ], *s.* die Hypothek. — *v.a.* verpfänden; eine Hypothek aufnehmen (auf, *Acc.*).

mortgagee [mɔ:gi'dʒi:], *s.* der Hypothekengläubiger.

mortician [mɔ:'tiʃən], *s.* (*Am.*) *see* **undertaker**.

mortify ['mɔ:tifai], *v.a.* kasteien (*chasten*); kränken (*humiliate*).

mortise ['mɔ:tis], *s.* (*Build.*) das Zapfenloch.

mortuary ['mɔːtjuəri], *s.* die Leichen-halle.

mosque [mɔsk], *s.* (*Rel.*) die Moschee.

mosquito [mɔs'kiːtou], *s.* (*Ent.*) der Moskito.

moss [mɔs], *s.* (*Bot.*) das Moos.

most [moust], *superl. adj.* meist; (*pl.*) die meisten. — *adv.* meist, meistens; höchst (*before adjectives*).

mostly ['moustli], *adv.* meistenteils.

mote [mout], *s.* das Stäubchen.

moth [mɔθ], *s.* (*Ent.*) die Motte.

mother ['mʌðə], *s.* die Mutter; — *-in-law,* die Schwiegermutter; —*of-pearl,* die Perlmutter.

motherly ['mʌðəli], *adj.* mütterlich.

motion ['mouʃən], *s.* die Bewegung, der Gang; (*Parl., Rhet.*) der Antrag. — *v.a.* bewegen. — *v.n.* zuwinken (*Dat.*).

motive ['moutiv], *s.* das Motiv, der Beweggrund.

motley ['mɔtli], *adj.* scheckig, bunt.

motor ['moutə], *s.* der Motor.

motoring ['moutəriŋ], *s.* das Autofahren, der Autosport.

mottled [mɔtld], *adj.* gescheckt, gesprenkelt.

metto ['mɔtou], *s.* das Motto, der Wahlspruch.

mould (1) [mould], *s.* die Form; Guß-form (*casting*); die Schablone. — *v.a.* formen; (*Metall.*) gießen, formen.

mould (2) [mould], *s.* der Schimmel (*fungus*); (*Hort.*) die Gartenerde. — *v.n.* schimmeln.

moulder (1) ['mouldə], *s.* der Bildner; (*Metall.*) der Gießer.

moulder (2) ['mouldə], *v.n.* vermodern.

mouldy ['mouldi] *adj.* moderig, schimmelig.

moult (*Am.*) **molt** [moult], *v.n.* (*Zool.*) sich mausern.

mound [maund], *s.* der Erdhügel.

mount [maunt], *v.a.* besteigen (*horse, hill*); montieren, anbringen (*apparatus*). — *v.n.* sich belaufen (*bill*), betragen. — *s.* (*Poet.*) der Berg.

mountain ['mauntin], *s.* der Berg.

mountaineer [maunti'niə], *s.* der Berg-steiger.

mountainous ['mauntinəs], *adj.* gebirgig.

mourn [mɔːn], *v.a., v.n.* (be)trauern.

mourner ['mɔːnə], *s.* der Leidtragende.

mournful ['mɔːnful], *adj.* traurig.

mourning ['mɔːniŋ], *s.* die Trauer.

mouse [maus], *s.* (*Zool.*) die Maus.

moustache [mə'staːʃ], *s.* der Schnurrbart.

mouth [mauθ], *s.* (*Anat.*) der Mund; (*Geog.*) die Mündung.

movable ['muːvəbl], *adj.* beweglich, verschiebbar.

move [muːv], *v.a.* bewegen; (*emotionally*) rühren; den Antrag stellen (*a motion*). — *v.n.* umziehen; übersiedeln (*change residence*).

movement ['muːvmənt], *s.* die Bewegung (*motion*); (*Mus.*) der Satz; das Gehwerk (*mechanism*).

movies ['muːviz], *s. pl.* (*coll.*) das Kino, der Film.

mow [mou], *v.a. irr.* mähen.

much [mʌtʃ], *adj.* viel. — *adv.* sehr, bei weitem; *as — as,* ganze . . .; *as — again,* noch einmal so viel.

mud [mʌd], *s.* der Schmutz, Schlamm.

muddle [mʌdl], *v.a.* verwirren. — *s.* die Verwirrung.

muff (1) [mʌf], *s.* der Muff.

muff (2) [mʌf], *v.a.* verderben (*mar*).

muffin ['mʌfin], *s.* der dünne Kuchen, der Butterkuchen.

muffle [mʌfl], *v.a.* umwickeln; dämpfen (*a sound*).

muffler ['mʌflə], *s.* das Halstuch; (*Motor.*) der Schalldämpfer.

mug [mʌg], *s.* der Krug; (*coll.*) der Tölpel.

muggy ['mʌgi], *adj.* schwül; feucht (*humid*).

mulatto [mju'lætou], *s.* der Mulatte.

mulberry ['mʌlbəri], *s.* (*Bot.*) die Maulbeere.

mule [mjuːl], *s.* (*Zool.*) das Maultier, der Maulesel.

muleteer [mjuːli'tiə], *s.* der Maulesel-treiber.

mulish ['mjuːliʃ], *adj.* störrisch.

mull (1) [mʌl], *v.a.* würzen (*add spices to*); *mulled wine,* der Glühwein.

mull (2) [mʌl], *v.a., v.n. — over,* überlegen, überdenken.

multifarious [mʌlti'feəriəs], *adj.* mannigfaltig.

multiple ['mʌltipl], *s.* das Vielfache. — *adj.* vielfach.

multiply ['mʌltiplai], *v.a., v.n.* multiplizieren, (sich) vervielfachen.

multitude ['mʌltitjuːd], *s.* die Menge.

multitudinous [mʌlti'tjuːdinəs], *adj.* zahlreich, massenhaft.

mumble [mʌmbl], *v.a., v.n.* murmeln.

mummery ['mʌməri], *s.* der Mummen-schanz.

mummy (1) ['mʌmi], *s.* die Mumie.

mummy (2) ['mʌmi], *s.* (*coll.*) die Mutti.

mumps [mʌmps], *s.* (*Med.*) der Ziegen-peter.

munch [mʌntʃ], *v.a., v.n.* kauen.

mundane ['mʌndein], *adj.* weltlich.

municipal [mju'nisipəl], *adj.* städtisch.

municipality [mjunisi'pæliti], *s.* die Stadtgemeinde.

munificence [mju'nifisəns], *s.* die Freigebigkeit.

munificent [mju'nifisənt], *adj.* freigebig.

mural ['mjuərəl], *s.* die Wandmalerei; das Wandgemälde. — *adj.* Wand-.

murder ['məːdə], *s.* der Mord. — *v.a.* ermorden, morden.

murderer ['məːdərə], *s.* der Mörder.

murderous ['məːdərəs], *adj.* mörderisch.

murky ['məːki], *adj.* trübe, unklar.

murmur ['məːmə], *s.* das Gemurmel.

muscle [mʌsl], *s.* (*Anat.*) der Muskel.

muscular ['mʌskjulə], *adj.* (*Anat.*) muskulös, Muskel-.

muse (1) [mju:z], *v.n.* nachdenken, sinnen.

muse (2) [mju:z], *s.* (*Myth.*) die Muse.

museum [mju:'ziəm], *s.* das Museum.

mushroom ['mʌʃrum], *s.* (*Bot.*) der (eßbare) Pilz.

music ['mju:zik], *s.* die Musik; — stand, das Notenpult.

musician [mju:'ziʃən], *s.* der Musiker.

musk [mʌsk], *s.* der Moschus, Bisam.

musket ['mʌskit], *s.* die Muskete, Flinte.

muslin ['mʌzlin], *s.* der Musselin.

mussel [mʌsl], *s.* (*Zool.*) die Muschel.

must [mʌst], *v. aux. irr.* müssen; (*with neg.*) dürfen.

mustard ['mʌstəd], *s.* der Senf.

muster ['mʌstə], *v.a.* mustern. — *v.n.* sich sammeln. — *s.* die Musterung; pass —, die Prüfung bestehen.

musty ['mʌsti], *adj.* dumpf, dumpfig, muffig.

mutable ['mju:təbl], *adj.* veränderlich.

mutation [mju'teiʃən], *s.* die Veränderung; (*Maths.*, *Genetics*) die Mutation.

mute [mju:t], *adj.* stumm. — *v.a.* (*Mus.*) dämpfen. — *s.* (*Mus.*) der Dämpfer.

mutilate ['mju:tileit], *v.a.* verstümmeln.

mutinous ['mju:tinəs], *adj.* aufrührerisch.

mutiny ['mju:tini], *s.* die Meuterei.

mutter ['mʌtə], *v.a.*, *v.n.* murmeln.

mutton [mʌtn], *s.* das Hammelfleisch; — chop, das Hammelkotelett.

mutual ['mju:tjuəl], *adj.* gegenseitig.

muzzle [mʌzl], *s.* der Maulkorb (*of dog*); die Mündung (*of rifle*).

my [mai], *poss. adj.* mein.

myrrh [mə:], *s.* die Myrrhe.

myrtle ['mə:tl], *s.* (*Bot.*) die Myrte.

myself [mai'self], *pron.* ich selbst; (*refl.*) mir, mich.

mysterious [mis'tiəriəs], *adj.* geheimnisvoll.

mystery ['mistəri], *s.* das Geheimnis.

mystic ['mistik], *s.* der Mystiker.

mystic(al) ['mistik(əl)], *adj.* mystisch, geheimnisvoll, dunkel.

mystification [mistifi'keiʃən], *s.* die Täuschung, Irreführung.

mystify ['mistifai], *v.a.* täuschen, verblüffen.

myth [miθ], *s.* der Mythos, die Mythe, Sage.

N

N [en]. das N.

nag (1) [næg], *v.a.* nörgeln.

nag (2) [næg], *s.* der Gaul.

nail [neil], *s.* der Nagel. — *v.a.* annageln.

naïve ['naii:v], *adj.* naiv.

naïveté, naïvety [nai'i:vti], *s.* die Naivität, Einfalt.

naked ['neikid], *adj.* nackt.

name [neim], *s.* der Name. — *v.a.* nennen, heißen.

nameless ['neimlis], *adj.* namenlos.

namely ['neimli], *adv.* nämlich.

namesake ['neimseik], *s.* der Namensvetter.

nap [næp], *s.* das Schläfchen. — *v.n.* schlummern, einnicken.

nape [neip], *s.* (*Anat.*) das Genick.

napkin ['næpkin], *s.* die Serviette; Windel (*baby's*).

narrate [nə'reit], *v.a.* erzählen.

narrative ['nærətiv], *s.* die Erzählung, Geschichte.

narrator [nə'reitə], *s.* der Erzähler; (*Rad.*) der Sprecher.

narrow ['nærou], *adj.* eng, schmal; — gauge, die Schmalspur; — minded, engstirnig.

nasty ['nɑ:sti], *adj.* widerlich, unangenehm.

natal [neitl], *adj.* Geburts-.

nation ['neiʃən], *s.* die Nation, das Volk.

nationality [næʃə'næliti], *s.* die Staatsangehörigkeit, Nationalität.

native ['neitiv], *adj.* einheimisch, eingeboren. — *s.* der Eingeborene.

natural ['nætʃərəl], *adj.* natürlich.

naturalist ['nætʃərəlist], *s.* der Naturforscher.

naturalization [nætʃərəlai'zeiʃən], *s.* die Naturalisierung, Einbürgerung.

naturalize ['nætʃərəlaiz], *v.a.*, *v.n.* naturalisieren, einbürgern.

nature ['neitʃə], *s.* die Natur, das Wesen.

naught [nɔ:t], *s.* die Null.

naughty ['nɔ:ti], *adj.* unartig.

nausea ['nɔ:siə], *s.* (*Med.*) der Brechreiz, das Erbrechen.

nautical ['nɔ:tikəl], *adj.* nautisch, Schiffs-.

naval ['neivəl], *adj.* Marine-.

nave [neiv], *s.* (*Archit.*) das Schiff.

navigable ['nævigəbl], *adj.* schiffbar.

navigate ['nævigeit], *v.a.*, *v.n.* steuern.

navigation [nævi'geiʃən], *s.* die Schiffahrt (*shipping*); das Steuern, die Navigation.

navy ['neivi], *s.* die Flotte, Marine.

Neopolitan [niə'politən], *adj.* neapolitanisch. — *s.* der Neapolitaner.

near [niə], *adj.*, *adv.* nahe, in der Nähe. — *prep.* nahe (an *or* bei).

nearly ['niəli], *adv.* beinahe, fast.

nearness ['niənis], *s.* die Nähe.

neat [ni:t], *adj.* nett, sauber (*tidy*); rein, unvermischt, pur (*unmixed*).

neatness ['ni:tnis], *s.* die Sauberkeit.

necessary ['nesəsəri], *adj.* notwendig.

necessity [ni'sesiti], *s.* die Not, Notwendigkeit; (*pl.*) das zum Leben Nötige.

neck [nek], *s.* (*Anat.*) der Hals; stick o.'s — out, es riskieren. — *v.n.* (*Am. sl.*) knutschen.

necklace ['neklis], *s.* das Halsband, die Halskette.

necktie ['nektai], *s.* der Schlips, die Krawatte.

need [ni:d], *s.* die Not, der Bedarf. — *v.a.* brauchen, nötig haben.

needful ['ni:dful], *adj.* notwendig.

needle [ni:dl], *s.* die Nadel. — *v.a.* (*coll.*) sticheln, ärgern (*annoy*).

needy ['ni:di], *adj.* in Not befindlich, arm, bedürftig.

nefarious [ni'fɛəriəs], *adj.* nichtswürdig, schändlich.

negative ['negətiv], *adj.* negativ, verneinend. — *s.* (*Phot.*) das Negativ; die Verneinung (*denial*); *in the —*, verneinend.

neglect [ni'glekt], *v.a.* vernachlässigen, außer acht lassen. — *s.* die Vernachlässigung.

neglectful [ni'glektful], *adj.* nachlässig.

negligence ['neglidʒəns], *s.* die Nachlässigkeit.

negotiate [ni'gouʃieit], *v.a., v.n.* verhandeln, unterhandeln.

negotiation [nigouʃi'eiʃən], *s.* die Unterhandlung.

Negro ['ni:grou], *s.* der Neger.

neigh [nei], *v.n.* wiehern.

neighbour ['neibə], *s.* der Nachbar.

neighbourhood ['neibəhud], *s.* die Nachbarschaft, Umgebung.

neighbouring ['neibəriŋ], *adj.* Nachbar-, benachbart.

neighbourliness ['neibəlinis], *s.* das gute nachbarliche Verhältnis, die Geselligkeit.

neither ['naiðə *or* 'ni:ðə], *adj., pron.* keiner (von beiden). — *conj.* auch nicht; — . . . *nor*, weder . . . noch.

Nepalese [nepə'li:z], *adj.* nepalesisch. — *s.* der Nepalese.

nephew ['nefju *or* 'nevju], *s.* der Neffe.

nerve [nə:v], *s.* der Nerv; der Mut (*courage*); die Frechheit (*impudence*); (*pl.*) die Angst, Nervosität.

nervous ['nə:vəs], *adj.* nervös; — *of*, furchtsam vor (*Dat.*), ängstlich wegen (*Genit.*).

nest [nest], *s.* das Nest; (*fig.*) — *egg*, die Ersparnisse, *f.pl.* — *v.n.* nisten.

nestle [nesl], *v.n.* sich anschmiegen.

net (1) [net], *s.* das Netz. — *v.a.* (Fische) fangen, ins Netz bekommen.

net (2) [net], *adj.* netto; ohne Verpackung; — *weight*, das Nettogewicht.

nettle [netl], *s.* (*Bot.*) die Nessel. — *v.a.* sticheln, ärgern.

neurosis [njuə'rousis], *s.* (*Med.*) die Neurose.

neutrality [nju:'træliti], *s.* die Neutralität.

never ['nevə], *adv.* nie, niemals; — *mind*, mach Dir (machen Sie sich) nichts draus!

nevertheless [nevəðə'les], *conj.* trotzdem, nichtsdestoweniger.

new [nju:], *adj.* neu; *New Year's Day*, der Neujahrstag; *New Zealander*, der

Neuseeländer. — *s.* (*pl.*) die Nachrichten, *f. pl.*

newspaper ['nju:speipə], *s.* die Zeitung.

next [nekst], *adj.* nächst. — *adv.* danach.

nib [nib], *s.* die Spitze (*of pen*).

nibble [nibl], *v.a., v.n.* knabbern, nagen (*at, an, Dat.*).

nice [nais], *adj.* fein (*scrupulous*); nett, angenehm (*pleasant*).

nicety ['naisəti], *s.* die Feinheit (*of distinction etc.*).

nickel [nikl], *s.* das Nickel; (*Am.*) das Fünfcentstück.

nickname ['nikneim], *s.* der Spitzname.

niece [ni:s], *s.* die Nichte.

Nigerian [nai'dʒiəriən], *adj.* nigerisch. — *s.* der Nigerier.

niggardly ['nigədli], *adj.* geizig.

nigh [nai], *adj., adv.* (*Poet.*) nahe.

night [nait], *s.* die Nacht; *last —*, gestern abend; *the — before last*, vorgestern abend; *at —*, nachts.

nightingale ['naitiŋgeil], *s.* (*Orn.*) die Nachtigall.

nightmare ['naitmɛə], *s.* der Alpdruck.

nimble [nimbl], *adj.* flink; geschickt (*deft*).

nine [nain], *num. adj.* neun.

nineteen [nain'ti:n], *num. adj.* neunzehn.

ninety ['nainti], *num. adj.* neunzig.

ninth [nainθ], *num. adj.* neunte.

nip [nip], *v.a.* zwicken.

nipple [nipl], *s.* (*Anat.*) die Brustwarze.

nitrogen ['naitrədʒən], *s.* (*Chem.*) der Stickstoff.

no [nou], *part.* nein. — *adj.* kein. — *adv.* nicht; — *one*, niemand.

nobility [no'biliti], *s.* der Adel.

noble [noubl], *adj.* edel; großmütig (*magnanimous*); adlig (*well born*).

nobody ['noubədi], *pron.* niemand.

nod [nɔd], *v.n.* nicken.

noise [nɔiz], *s.* der Lärm, das Geräusch.

noiseless ['nɔizlis], *adj.* geräuschlos.

noisy ['nɔizi], *adj.* laut, lärmend.

nominal ['nɔminəl], *adj.* nominell.

nominate ['nɔmineit], *v.a.* nennen (*name*); ernennen (*appoint*).

nomination [nɔmi'neiʃən], *s.* die Nennung, Ernennung.

none [nʌn], *pron.* keiner, niemand.

nonsense ['nɔnsəns], *s.* der Unsinn.

nook [nuk], *s.* die Ecke, der Winkel.

noon [nu:n], *s.* der Mittag.

noose [nu:s], *s.* die Schlinge.

nor [nɔ:], *conj.* auch nicht; *neither . . . —*, weder . . . noch.

normal [nɔ:məl], *adj.* normal.

normalize ['nɔ:məlaiz], *v.a.* normalisieren.

Norman ['nɔ:mən], *adj.* normannisch. — *s.* der Normanne.

north [nɔ:θ], *s.* der Norden. — *adj.* nördlich.

northerly, northern ['nɔ:ðəli, 'nɔ:ðən], *adj.* nördlich, von Norden.

Norwegian [nɔ:'wi:dʒən], *adj.* norwegisch. — *s.* der Norweger.

nose [nouz], *s.* (*Anat.*) die Nase; — *dive*, der Sturzflug.

nosey ['nouzi], *adj.* (*coll.*) neugierig.

nostalgia [nɔs'tældʒə], *s.* das Heimweh, die Sehnsucht.

nostril ['nɔstril], *s.* (*Anat.*) das Nasenloch.

not [nɔt], *adv.* nicht; — *at all*, keineswegs.

notable ['noutəbl], *adj.* berühmt, wohlbekannt; bemerkenswert.

notary ['noutəri], *s.* der Notar.

notch [nɔtʃ], *s.* die Kerbe. — *v.a.* kerben, einkerben.

note [nout], *s.* die Notiz, der Zettel; (*Mus.*) die Note; die Bedeutung; *take* —*s*, Notizen machen; *take — of*, zur Kenntnis nehmen. — *v.a.* notieren, aufzeichnen.

notepaper ['noutpeipə], *s.* das Briefpapier.

noteworthy ['noutwə:ði], *adj.* beachtenswert.

nothing ['nʌθiŋ], *pron. s.* nichts; *for* —, umsonst; *good for* —, der Taugenichts.

notice ['noutis], *s.* die Kenntnis (*attention*); die Anzeige (*in press etc.*); Notiz; Bekanntmachung; *give* —, kündigen. — *v.a.* bemerken.

noticeable ['noutisəbl], *adj.* bemerkbar.

notification [noutifi'keiʃən], *s.* die Benachrichtigung, Bekanntmachung.

notify ['noutifai], *v.a.* benachrichtigen, informieren.

notion ['nouʃən], *s.* der Begriff (*concept*); die Idee (*idea*); die Meinung (*opinion*).

notoriety [noutə'raiiti], *s.* der üble Ruf.

notorious [no'tɔ:riəs], *adj.* berüchtigt.

notwithstanding [nɔtwið'stændiŋ], *prep.* ungeachtet (*Genit.*). — *adv.* trotzdem, dennoch. — *conj.* — *that*, obgleich.

nought [nɔ:t], *s.* die Null (*figure 0*); nichts (*nothing*).

noun [naun], *s.* (*Gram.*) das Hauptwort, Substantiv.

nourish ['nʌriʃ], *v.a.* nähren; ernähren.

nourishment ['nʌriʃmənt], *s.* die Nahrung.

Nova Scotian ['nouvə'skouʃən], *adj.* neuschottisch.

novel [nɔvl], *s.* (*Lit.*) der Roman. — *adj.* neu; neuartig (*modern*).

novelty ['nɔvlti], *s.* die Neuheit.

November [no'vembə]. der November.

novice ['nɔvis], *s.* der Neuling (*greenhorn*); (*Eccl.*) der, die Novize.

novitiate [no'viʃiit], *s.* die Lehrzeit; (*Eccl.*) das Noviziat.

now [nau], *adv.* nun, jetzt; — *and then*, dann und wann, hin und wieder. — *conj.* — (*that*), da nun.

nowadays ['nauədeiz], *adv.* heutzutage.

nowhere ['nouhwɛə], *adv.* nirgends.

noxious ['nɔkʃəs], *adj.* (*Med., Bot.*) schädlich.

nozzle [nɔzl], *s.* die Düse; (*sl.*) die Schnauze.

nuclear ['nju:kliə], *adj.* (*Phys.*) nuklear, Kern-.

nucleus ['nju:kliəs], *s.* der Kern.

nude [nju:d], *adj.* nackt, bloß.

nudge [nʌdʒ], *v.a.* leicht anstoßen.

nudity ['nju:diti], *s.* die Nacktheit.

nugget ['nʌgit], *s.* der Klumpen.

nuisance ['nju:səns], *s.* die Plage, Lästigkeit; das Ärgernis (*annoyance*).

null [nʌl], *adj.* null und nichtig; ungültig.

nullify ['nʌlifai], *v.a.* annullieren, ungültig machen.

nullity ['nʌliti], *s.* die Ungültigkeit.

numb [nʌm], *adj.* erstarrt, gefühllos. — *v.a.* erstarren lassen.

number ['nʌmbə], *s.* die Zahl, Nummer (*telephone etc.*); die Anzahl (*quantity*); *cardinal* —, die Grundzahl; *ordinal* —, die Ordnungszahl. — *v.a.* nummerieren; zählen (*count*).

numbness ['nʌmnis], *s.* die Erstarrung.

numeral ['nju:mərəl], *s.* (*Gram.*) das Zahlwort.

numerical [nju:'merikəl], *adj.* (*Maths.*) Zahlen-, numerisch.

numerous ['nju:mərəs], *adj.* zahlreich.

numismatics [nju:miz'mætiks], *s.* die Münzkunde.

numskull ['nʌmskʌl], *s.* der Dummkopf.

nun [nʌn], *s.* (*Eccl.*) die Nonne.

nunnery ['nʌnəri], *s.* (*Eccl.*) das Nonnenkloster.

nuptials ['nʌpʃəlz], *s. pl.* (*Lit., Poet.*) die Hochzeit, das Hochzeitsfest.

nurse [nə:s], *s.* die Krankenschwester, Pflegerin; die Amme (*wet nurse*). — *v.a.* pflegen.

nursery ['nə:səri], *s.* das Kinderzimmer; (*Bot.*) die Pflanzschule, Baumschule (*for trees*); — *school*, der Kindergarten.

nurture ['nə:tʃə], *v.a.* nähren, aufziehen.

nut [nat], *s.* (*Bot.*) die Nuß; (*Tech.*) die Schraubenmutter; (*Am. coll.*) *nuts*, verrückt.

nutcracker ['nʌtkrækə], *s.* (*usually pl.*) der Nußknacker.

nutmeg ['nʌtmeg], *s.* (*Cul.*) die Muskatnuß.

nutriment ['nju:trimənt], *s.* die Nahrung; (*animals*) das Futter.

nutrition [nju'triʃən], *s.* die Ernährung.

nutritious [nju'triʃəs], *adj.* nahrhaft.

nutshell ['nʌtʃel], *s.* die Nußschale; (*fig.*) *put in a* —, kurz ausdrücken.

nymph [nimf], *s.* (*Myth.*) die Nymphe.

O

O [ou]. das O. — *int.* oh!

oaf [ouf], *s.* der Tölpel.

oak [ouk], *s.* (*Bot.*) die Eiche.

oaken ['oukən], *adj.* eichen, aus Eichenholz.

oar [ɔ:], *s.* das Ruder; *put o.'s — in,* sich einmengen.

oasis [ou'eisis], *s.* die Oase.

oath [ouθ]; *s.* der Eid; der Fluch (*curse*); *commissioner for —s,* der öffentliche Notar; *take an —,* einen Eid schwören *or* leisten.

oats [outs], *s. pl.* (*Bot.*) der Hafer; *sow o.'s wild —s,* sich austoben, sich die Hörner ablaufen.

obdurate ['ɔbdjurit], *adj.* halsstarrig.

obedience [o'bi:djəns], *s.* der Gehorsam.

obedient [o'bi:djənt], *adj.* gehorsam.

obeisance [o'beisəns], *s.* die Verbeugung, Ehrfurchtsbezeigung.

obese [o'bi:s], *adj.* fettleibig, beleibt.

obey [o'bei], *v.a., v.n.* gehorchen (*Dat.*).

obituary [o'bitjuəri], *s.* der Nachruf, der Nekrolog.

object ['ɔbdʒikt], *s.* der Gegenstand (*thing*); (*Gram.*) das Objekt; der Zweck (*objective, purpose*). — [əb'dʒekt], *v.n.* — *to,* einwenden (*gainsay*); vorhalten (*remonstrate*).

objection [əb'dʒekʃən], *s.* der Einwand.

objectionable [əb'dʒekʃənəbl], *adj.* anstößig.

objective [əb'dʒektiv], *adj.* objektiv, unparteiisch. — *s.* das Ziel (*aim*).

obligation [ɔbli'geiʃən], *s.* die Verpflichtung.

obligatory [o'bligətəri, 'ɔblig-], *adj.* verbindlich, obligatorisch.

oblige [o'blaidʒ], *v.a.* verpflichten; *much obliged,* vielen Dank; *can you — me?* können Sie mir aushelfen?

obliging [o'blaidʒiŋ], *adj.* gefällig, zuvorkommend.

oblique [o'bli:k], *adj.* schräg, schief; (*fig.*) indirekt.

obliterate [o'blitəreit], *v.a.* auslöschen (*extinguish*); vertilgen (*destroy*).

oblivion [o'bliviən], *s.* die Vergessenheit.

oblivious [o'bliviəs], *adj.* vergeßlich.

oblong ['ɔblɔŋ], *adj.* länglich. — *s.* das Rechteck.

obloquy ['ɔbləkwi], *s.* die Schmähung, Schande.

obnoxious [ɔb'nɔkʃəs], *adj.* verhaßt, scheußlich.

obscene [ɔb'si:n], *adj.* anstößig, obszön.

obscenity [ɔb'sen-, ɔb'si:niti], *s.* die Obszönität.

obscure [əb'skjuə], *adj.* dunkel (*dark*); unbekannt (*unknown*).

obscurity [əb'skjuəriti], *s.* die Dunkelheit (*darkness*); die Unbekanntheit.

obsequies ['ɔbsikwiz], *s. pl.* das Leichenbegängnis.

obsequious [əb'si:kwiəs], *adj.* unterwürfig.

observance [əb'zə:vəns], *s.* die Befolgung, Beobachtung, das Einhalten (*Law etc.*).

observant [əb'zə:vənt], *adj.* aufmerksam; achtsam.

observation [ɔbzə'veiʃən], *s.* die Beobachtung (*watching*); die Bemerkung (*remark*).

observatory [əb'zə:vətri], *s.* die Sternwarte.

observe [əb'zə:v], *v.a.* beobachten (*watch*); bemerken (*notice, remark on*).

obsession [əb'seʃən], *s.* die Besessenheit, fixe Idee.

obsolete ['ɔbsəli:t], *adj.* veraltet.

obstacle ['ɔbstəkl], *s.* das Hindernis.

obstinacy ['ɔbstinəsi], *s.* die Hartnäckigkeit.

obstinate ['ɔbstinit], *adj.* hartnäckig.

obstruct [əb'strʌkt], *v.a.* hemmen, hindern.

obstruction [əb'strʌkʃən], *s.* das Hindernis, die Hemmung, Verstopfung.

obtain [əb'tein], *v.a.* erhalten, erlangen; bekommen (*get*).

obtrude [ɔb'tru:d], *v.n.* sich aufdrängen. — *v.a.* aufdrängen.

obtrusive [əb'tru:siv], *adj.* aufdringlich.

obtuse [ɔb'tju:s], *adj.* stumpf; dumm (*stupid*).

obviate ['ɔbvieit], *v.a.* vorbeugen (*Dat.*).

obvious ['ɔbviəs], *adj.* klar, offenbar, selbstverständlich.

occasion [o'keiʒən], *s.* die Gelegenheit (*chance*); der Anlaß; die Veranlassung (*cause*). — *v.a.* veranlassen; verursachen (*cause*).

occasional [o'keiʒənəl], *adj.* gelegentlich.

occident ['ɔksidənt], *s.* das Abendland, der Westen.

occult [ɔ'kʌlt], *adj.* geheim, Okkult-.

occupancy ['ɔkjupənsi], *s.* der Besitz, das Innehaben (*holding*).

occupant ['ɔkjupənt], *s.* der Inhaber; der Bewohner (*of house*), Insasse.

occupation [ɔkju'peiʃən], *s.* die Besetzung; (*Mil.*) *army of —,* die Besatzung; der Beruf, die Beschäftigung (*job*); — *with,* das Befassen mit (*Dat.*).

occupy ['ɔkjupai], *v.a.* (*Mil.*) besetzen, in Besitz nehmen; beschäftigen (*engage*); bekleiden (*office*).

occur [ə'kə:], *v.n.* geschehen, sich ereignen; — *to s.o.,* jemandem einfallen.

occurrence [ə'kʌrəns], *s.* das Geschehen, Ereignis, der Vorfall.

ocean ['ouʃən], *s.* der Ozean, die See, das Meer. — *adj.* Meeres-.

octagon ['ɔktəgən], *s.* das Achteck.

octagonal [ɔk'tægənəl], *adj.* achteckig.

October [ɔk'toubə] der Oktober.

octogenarian [ɔktodʒi'nɛəriən], *s.* der Achtzigjährige.

ocular ['ɔkjulə], *adj.* Augen-.

oculist ['ɔkjulist],*s.*(*Med.*)derAugenarzt.

odd [ɔd], *adj.* ungerade; seltsam (*queer*); einzeln (*solitary*). — *s.* (*pl.*) die Wahrscheinlichkeit.

oddity ['ɔditi], *s.* die Seltenheit, Sonderbarkeit.

oddment ['ɔdmənt], *s.* (*pl.*) die Reste, *m. pl.*

ode [oud], *s.* (*Poet.*) die Ode.

odious ['oudiəs], *adj.* verhaßt, widerwärtig.

odium ['oudiəm], *s.* der Haß.
odorous ['oudərəs], *adj.* duftend, duftig.
odour ['oudə], *s.* der Geruch, Duft.
of [ɔv], *prep.* von (*Dat.*); aus (*out of*) (*Dat.*); — *course,* natürlich.
off [ɔf, ɔ:f], *adv.* fort, weg; entfernt; *make* —, sich davonmachen; *far* —, weit weg; — *and on,* ab und zu; *well* —, wohlhabend. — *prep.* von (*from*); fort von; entfernt von (*distant from*).
offal [ɔfl], *s.* der Abfall.
offence [o'fens], *s.* (*Law*) das Vergehen; die Beleidigung (*insult*).
offend [o'fend], *v.a.* beleidigen (*insult*). — *v.n.* (*Law*) sich vergehen (gegen, *Acc.*).
offensive [o'fensiv], *adj.* beleidigend (*insulting*); anstößig (*indecent*). — *s.* die Offensive, der Angriff (*against,* auf, *Acc.*).
offer ['ɔfə], *v.a.* bieten (*auction*); anbieten (*hold out*). — *s.*das Anerbieten; (*Comm.*) das Angebot, der Antrag.
offering ['ɔfəriŋ], *s.* das Opfer.
office ['ɔfis], *s.* das Amt; die Stellung (*position*); die Funktion (*duties*); das Büro; (*Eccl.*) der Gottesdienst; *high* —, das hohe Amt; — *bearer,* der Amtswalter.
officer ['ɔfisə], *s.* (*Mil.*) der Offizier; der Beamte (*functionary*); *honorary* —, der ehrenamtliche Beamte, der Beamte im Ehrenamt.
official [o'fiʃəl], *adj.* offiziell, amtlich. — *s.* der Beamte.
officiate [o'fiʃieit], *v.n.* amtieren; fungieren.
officious [o'fiʃəs], *adj.* zudringlich, (übertrieben) dienstfertig.
offing ['ɔfiŋ], *s.* (*Naut.*) die hohe See; *in the* —, bevorstehend.
offset [ɔf'set], *v.a.* (*Comm.*) ausgleichen; (*Typ.*) offset drucken, im Offset drucken; (*fig.*) unschädlich machen, wettmachen. — ['ɔfset], *s.* (*Comm.*) die Gegenrechnung, der Ausgleich; (*Typ.*) der Offsetdruck.
offshoot ['ɔfʃu:t], *s.* der Sprößling.
offspring ['ɔfspriŋ], *s.* die Nachkommenschaft.
often, (*Poet.*) **oft** [ɔfn,ɔft], *adv.*oft, häufig.
ogle [ougl], *v.a., v.n.* äugeln, beäugeln, glotzen, anglotzen.
ogre ['ougə], *s.* der Menschenfresser.
oil [ɔil], *s.* das Öl. — *v.a.* einölen, einschmieren.
oilcloth ['ɔilklɔθ], *s.* das Wachstuch.
ointment ['ɔintmənt], *s.* die Salbe.
old [ould], *adj.* alt; —*fashioned,* altmodisch.
olive ['ɔliv], *s.* (*Bot.*) die Olive; *the Mount of Olives,* der Ölberg.
Olympic [o'limpik], *adj.* olympisch; *the — Games,* die Olympischen Spiele.
omelette ['ɔmǝlit], *s.* (*Cul.*) das Omelett, der Eierkuchen.
omen ['oumən], *s.* das (böse) Vorzeichen, das Omen.

ominous ['ɔminəs], *adj.* von schlimmer Vorbedeutung, ominös.
omission [o'miʃən], *s.* die Unterlassung; (*Typ.*) die Auslassung.
omit [o'mit], *v.a.* unterlassen (*leave undone*); auslassen (*leave out*).
omnibus ['ɔmnibəs], *s.* der Omnibus, der Autobus.
omnipotent [ɔm'nipətənt], *adj.* allmächtig.
omniscient [ɔm'nisiənt], *adj.* allwissend.
on [ɔn], *prep.* an; auf; über; vor; bei; zu; nach; um; *call* — (*s.o.*), vorsprechen (bei, *Dat.*); — *fire,* in Flammen; — *condition,* unter der Bedingung (*Comm.*); — *account,* a Konto; — *high,* hoch oben; — *my honour,* auf mein Ehrenwort; — *purpose,* absichtlich; — *sale,* zum Verkauf. — *adv.* weiter, fort (*forward*); gültig, zutreffend (*correct, valid*); *get* —, vorwärtskommen; *get* — *with s.th.,* weitermachen; *get* — *with s.o.,* auskommen (mit, *Dat.*).
once [wʌns], *adv.* einmal; einst (*long ago*); — *more,* nochmals, noch einmal; — *and for all,* ein für alle Mal; *at* —, sogleich; — *in a while,* ab und zu. — *conj.* sobald.
one [wʌn], *num. adj.* ein, eine, ein; — *way street,* die Einbahnstraße. — *pron.* man (*impersonal*). — *s. little* —, der Kleine; — *by* —, eins nach dem anderen, einzeln.
onerous ['ɔnərəs], *adj.* beschwerlich.
onion ['ʌnjən], *s.* (*Bot.*) die Zwiebel.
onlooker ['ɔnlukə], *s.* der Zuschauer.
only ['ounli], *adj.* einzig, allein. — *adv.* nur, bloß. — *conj.* jedoch.
onset ['ɔnset], *s.* der Angriff (*attack*); der Anfang (*beginning*).
onslaught ['ɔnslɔ:t], *s.* der Angriff, Überfall.
onward ['ɔnwəd], *adj.* fortschreitend. — *adv.* (*also onwards*) vorwärts.
ooze [u:z], *s.* der Schlamm. — *v.n.* träufeln, sickern.
opacity [o'pæsiti], *s.* (*Phys.*) die Dunkelheit, Undurchsichtigkeit.
opal [oupl], *s.* der Opal.
opaque [o'peik], *adj.* (*Phys.*) dunkel, undurchsichtig.
open [oupn], *adj.* offen; offenherzig (*frank*); — *to suggestions,* einem Vorschlag zugänglich. — *v.a.* öffnen; eröffnen (*start*); — *an account,* ein Konto eröffnen. — *v.n.* sich öffnen, sich auftun.
opening ['oupniŋ], *s.* das Öffnen; die freie Stelle; die Gelegenheit (*opportunity*). — *adj.* einleitend; — *gambit,* (*Chess*) der Eröffnungszug.
openness ['oupənnis], *s.* die Offenheit, Ehrlichkeit (*frankness*).
opera ['ɔpərə], *s.* (*Mus.*) die Oper; *comic* —, die komische Oper; — *hat,* der Zylinderhut, Klapphut.
operatic [ɔpə'rætik], *adj.* (*Mus.*) Opern-.

operate

operate ['ɔpəreit], *v.a., v.n. (Engin.)* bedienen; *(Med.)* operieren *(on, Acc.)*.

operation [ɔpə'reiʃən], *s. (Med., Mil.)* die Operation; die Bedienung *(of engine etc.)*.

operative ['ɔpərətiv], *adj.* wirksam *(effective). — s.* der Arbeiter.

opiate ['oupiit], *s.* das Schlafmittel. — *adj.* einschläfernd.

opine [o'pain], *v.n.* meinen.

opinion [o'pinjən], *s.* die Meinung; *in my* —, meiner Meinung nach.

opinionated [o'pinjəneitid], *adj.* von sich eingenommen, selbstgefällig.

opium ['oupjəm], *s.* das Opium.

opponent [ə'pounənt], *s.* der Gegner.

opportune ['ɔpətjuːn], *adj.* gelegen, günstig.

opportunity [ɔpə'tjuːniti], *s.* die Gelegenheit, Chance; die Möglichkeit.

oppose [ə'pouz], *v.a.* bekämpfen; widerstehen, entgegentreten *(Dat.)*.

opposite ['ɔpəzit], *adj.* entgegengesetzt; gegenüberliegend; gegensätzlich *(contrary). — prep.* gegenüber *(Dat.)*. — *s.* das Gegenteil.

opposition [ɔpə'ziʃən], *s. (Parl.)* die Opposition; der Widerstand.

oppress [ə'pres], *v.a.* unterdrücken.

oppression [ə'preʃən], *s.* die Unterdrückung.

oppressive [ə'presiv], *adj.* drückend, tyrannisch.

opprobrious [ə'proubriəs], *adj.* schändlich, schimpflich.

opprobrium [ə'proubriəm], *s.* die Schande.

optician [ɔp'tiʃən], *s.* der Optiker.

optics ['ɔptiks], *s.* die Optik.

optimism ['ɔptimizm], *s.* der Optimismus.

option ['ɔpʃən], *s.* die Wahl.

optional ['ɔpʃənəl], *adj.* Wahl-, frei, beliebig.

opulence ['ɔpjuləns], *s.* der Reichtum *(an, Dat.)*, die Üppigkeit.

opulent ['ɔpjulənt], *adj.* reich, üppig.

or [ɔː], *conj.* oder; noch *(after neg.)*; *either . . . —*, entweder . . . oder.

oracle ['ɔrəkl], *s.* das Orakel.

oral ['ɔːrəl], *adj.* mündlich. — *s.* die mündliche Prüfung.

orange ['ɔrindʒ,], *s. (Bot.)* die Orange, Apfelsine.

oration [o'reiʃən], *s.* die feierliche Rede, Ansprache.

orator ['ɔrətə], *s.* der Redner.

oratorio [ɔrə'tɔːriou], *s. (Mus.)* das Oratorium.

oratory ['ɔrətəri], *s. (Eccl.)* die Kapelle; *(Rhet.)* die Redekunst.

orb [ɔːb], *s.* die Kugel; der Reichsapfel; *(Poet.)* der Himmelskörper.

orbit ['ɔːbit], *s. (Astron.)* die Bahn (der Gestirne), Planetenbahn.

orchard ['ɔːtʃəd], *s.* der Obstgarten.

orchestra ['ɔːkistrə], *s. (Mus.)* das Orchester.

ordain [ɔː'dein], *v.a.* ordinieren, anordnen; *(Eccl.)* zum Priester weihen.

ordeal ['ɔːdiəl], *s.* die Feuerprobe; Heimsuchung.

order ['ɔːdə], *s.* die Ordnung *(system)*; die Verordnung *(command etc.)*; *(Mil.)* der Befehl; *(Comm.)* die Bestellung; *(Biol.)* die Ordnung; der Orden *(Eccl.; also decoration)*; *take (holy)* —*s*, ordiniert werden, Priester werden; *in — to*, um zu; *in — that*, so daß; *by —*, auf (den) Befehl. — *v.a.* befehlen, verordnen, anordnen; *(Comm.)* bestellen.

orderly ['ɔːdəli], *adj.* ordentlich, ruhig. —*s. (Mil.)* die Ordonanz; *(Med.)* der Gehilfe, Krankenwärter.

ordinal ['ɔːdinl], *adj., s. (number)* die Ordnungszahl.

ordinance ['ɔːdinəns], *s.* die Verordnung.

ordinary ['ɔːdinəri], *adj.* gewöhnlich.

ordnance ['ɔːdnəns], *s.* das schwere Geschütz; *(Mil., Geog.) — survey*, die Landesvermessung.

ore [ɔː], *s.* das Erz, Metall.

organ ['ɔːgən], *s.* das Organ; *(Mus.)* die Orgel; *— grinder*, der Leierkastenmann.

organic [ɔː'gænik], *adj.* organisch. edi

organisation [ɔːgənai'zeiʃən], *s.* Organisation.

organise ['ɔːgənaiz], *v.a.* organisieren.

organism ['ɔːgənizm], *s. (Biol.)* der Organismus.

organist ['ɔːgənist], *s. (Mus.)* der Organist.

orgy ['ɔːdʒi], *s.* die Orgie.

oriel ['ɔːriəl], *s.* der Erker; *— window*, das Erkerfenster.

orient ['ɔːriənt], *s.* der Orient, Osten.

oriental [ɔːri'entl], *adj.* östlich.

orifice ['ɔrifis], *s.* die Öffnung, Mündung.

origin ['ɔridʒin], *s.* der Ursprung, die Herkunft.

original [ə'ridʒinl], *adj.* Ursprungs-, ursprünglich; originell *(creative)*. — *s.* das Original.

originality [əridʒi'næliti], *s.* die Originalität.

originate [ə'ridʒineit], *v.n.* entstehen, entspringen. — *v.a.* hervorbringen, entstehen lassen.

ornament ['ɔːnəmənt], *s.* das Ornament; die Verzierung *(decoration)*.

ornate [ɔː'neit], *adj.* geziert, geschmückt.

orphan ['ɔːfən], *s.* der, die Waise.

orphanage ['ɔːfənidʒ], *s.* das Waisenhaus.

orthodoxy ['ɔːθədɔksi], *s.* die Orthodoxie, die Rechtgläubigkeit.

orthography [ɔː'θɔgrəfi], *s.* die Rechtschreibung.

orthopaedic [ɔːθə'piːdik], *adj.* orthopädisch.

oscillate ['ɔsileit], *v.n.* oszillieren, schwingen.

oscillatory ['ɔsileitəri], *adj.* schwingend, oszillierend.

osier ['ouʒjə], *s. (Bot.)* die Korbweide.

osprey ['ɔsprei], *s. (Orn.)* der Seeadler.

overhead

ossify ['ɔsifai], v.a. verknöchern lassen; versteinern lassen (stone). — v.n. verknöchern; versteinern (stone).

ostensible [ɔs'tensibl], adj. scheinbar, anscheinend, vorgeblich.

ostentation [ɔsten'teiʃən], s. die Großtuerei, der Prunk.

ostentatious [ɔsten'teiʃəs], adj. großtuerisch, prahlerisch, protzig.

ostler ['ɔslə], s. (obs.) der Stallknecht.

ostracize ['ɔstrəsaiz], v.a. verbannen, ausschließen.

ostrich ['ɔstritʃ], s. (Orn.) der Strauß.

other ['ʌðə], adj. ander. — pron., s. the —, der, die, das andere.

otherwise ['ʌðəwaiz], conj. sonst. — adv. andernfalls.

otter ['ɔtə], s. (Zool.) die Otter.

ought [ɔ:t], v. aux. defect. sollte, müßte.

ounce [auns], s. die Unze.

our ['auə], poss. adj. unser, uns(e)re, unser.

ours ['auəz], poss. pron. unsrig, unser, uns(e)re, unser.

ourselves [auə'selvz], pers. pron. wir, wir selbst, uns selbst; (refl.) uns.

ousel [u:zl], s. (Orn.) die Amsel.

out [aut], adv. aus; draußen (outside); außerhalb (outside, externally); heraus; hinaus (outward, away from the speaker). — prep. — of, aus, von (Dat.).

outer ['autə], adj. äußer.

outfit ['autfit], s. die Ausrüstung.

outing ['autiŋ], s. der Ausflug.

outhouse ['authaus], s. das Nebengebäude, der Anbau.

outlaw ['autlɔ:], s. der Verbannte, der Vogelfreie.

outlay ['autlei], s. (Comm.) die Auslagen, die Spesen, f. pl.

outlet ['autlit], s. der Ausfluß, Abfluß; (fig.) das Ventil.

outline ['autlain], s. der Umriß, Entwurf. — [aut'lain], v.a. skizzieren, umreißen, kurz beschreiben.

outlive [aut'liv], v.a. überleben.

outlook ['autluk], s. die Aussicht, der Ausblick; die Weltanschauung (philosophy).

outlying ['autlaiiŋ], adj. außenliegend, außerhalb liegend, entlegen.

outnumber [aut'nʌmbə], v.a. an Zahl übertreffen.

outpatient ['autpeiʃənt], s. der ambulante Patient.

outrage ['autreidʒ], s. die Beleidigung (insult); die Gewalttat. — [aut'reidʒ], v.a. verletzen, beleidigen, schänden.

outrageous [aut'reidʒəs], adj. schändlich, schimpflich, unerhört; übertrieben (exaggerated).

outright ['autrait], adj. völlig. — [aut'rait], adv. gerade heraus, gänzlich.

outrun [aut'rʌn], v.a. irr. überholen, einholen.

outset ['autset], s. der Anfang.

outshine [aut'ʃain], v.a. irr. übertreffen.

outside [aut'said], adv. außen, draußen. — ['autsaid], prep. außerhalb (Genit.).

— adj. äußere, außenstehend. — s. das Äußere, die Außenseite.

outskirts ['autskə:ts], s. pl. die Umgebung, Vorstadt.

outstanding [aut'stændiŋ], adj. hervorragend (excellent); noch unbeglichen (unpaid); unerledigt (undone).

outstay [aut'stei], v.a. länger bleiben, zu lange bleiben.

outvote [aut'vout], v.a. überstimmen.

outward ['autwəd], adj. äußere, äußerlich, außerhalb befindlich. — adv. (also outwards) auswärts, nach außen.

outweigh [aut'wei], v.a. schwerer wiegen als, überwiegen.

outwit [aut'wit], v.a. überlisten.

oval [ouvl], adj. oval. — s. das Oval.

ovary ['ouvəri], s. (Anat.) der Eierstock.

ovation [o'veiʃən], s. die Huldigung, Ovation.

oven [ʌvn], s. der Backofen; (kleine) Schmelzofen.

over ['ouvə], prep. über; oberhalb. — adv. über; herüber; drüben; — there, drüben; hinüber (across); vorüber (past).

overact [ouvər'ækt], v.n. übertreiben.

overawe [ouvər'ɔ:], v.a. einschüchtern.

overbalance [ouvə'bæləns], v.a. überwiegen. — v.n. überkippen.

overbear [ouvə'bɛə], v.a. irr. überwältigen.

overbearing [ouvə'bɛəriŋ], adj. anmaßend.

overboard ['ouvəbɔ:d], adv. über Bord.

overburden [ouvə'bə:dn], v.a. überlasten.

overcast [ouvə'kɑ:st], adj. bewölkt.

overcharge [ouvə'tʃɑ:dʒ], v.a. zu viel berechnen (pers., Dat.), übervorteien; überladen (overload). — s. die Übervorteilung; (Tech.) der Überdruck.

overcoat ['ouvəkout], s. der Mantel; light —, der Überzieher.

overcome [ouvə'kʌm], v.a., v.n. irr. überwinden.

overdo [ouvə'du:], v.a. irr. übertreiben.

overdone [ouvə'dʌn], adj. übergar, zu lange gekocht.

overdrive [ouvə'draiv], v.a. irr. abhetzen, zu weit treiben. — ['ouvədraiv] s. (Motor.) der Schnellgang.

overdue [ouvə'dju:], adj. überfällig, verfallen.

overflow [ouvə'flou], v.a., v.n. überfließen; überfluten (banks). — ['ouvəflou], s. der Überfluß (flood); die Überschwemmung.

overgrow [ouvə'grou], v.a. irr. überwachsen, überwuchern. — v.n. zu groß werden.

overhang [ouvə'hæŋ], v.a. irr. überhängen.

overhaul [ouvə'hɔ:l], v.a. überholen. — ['ouvəhɔ:l], s. die Überholung.

overhead [ouvə'hed], adv. droben; oben (above). — ['ouvəhed], s. (pl.) (Comm.) laufende Unkosten, pl.

overhear [ouvə'hiə], v.a. irr. zufällig hören.
overjoyed [ouvə'dʒɔid], adj. entzückt.
overlap [ouvə'læp], v.n. überschneiden, zusammenfallen (dates etc.).—['ouvə-læp], s. die Überschneidung, das Zusammenfallen.
overload [ouvə'loud], v.a. überlasten; (Elec.) überladen.
overlook [ouvə'luk], v.a. übersehen; verzeihen (disregard).
overmuch [ouvə'mʌtʃ], adv. allzusehr.
overpay (ouvə'pei], v.a., v.n. zu viel bezahlen.
overpopulated [ouvə'pɔpjuleitid], adj. übervölkert.
overpower [ouvə'pauə], v.a. überwältigen.
overrate [ouvə'reit], v.a. überschätzen.
overreach [ouvə'ri:tʃ], v.a. übervorteilen.
override [ouvə'raid], v.a. irr. überreiten; unterdrücken (suppress).
overrule [ouvə'ru:l], v.a. nicht gelten lassen, verwerfen.
overseer ['ouvəsiə], s. der Aufseher.
oversleep [ouvə'sli:p], v.n. irr. sich verschlafen.
overstep [ouvə'step], v.a. überschreiten.
overstrain [ouvə'strein], v.a., v.n. (sich) zu sehr anstrengen, überanstrengen.
overt [ou'və:t], adj. offenkundig; öffentlich (public).
overtake [ouvə'teik], v.a. irr. einholen; (Mot.) überholen.
overtax [ouvə'tæks], v.a. zu hoch besteuern; (fig.) überanstrengen (strain).
overthrow [ouvə'θrou], v.a. irr. umstürzen; (Pol.) stürzen. — ['ouvəθrou], s. der Sturz.
overtime ['ouvətaim], s. Überstunden, f. pl.
overture ['ouvətjuə], s. die Ouvertüre.
overturn [ouvə'tə:n], v.a. umstürzen. — v.n. überschlagen.
overweening [ouvə'wi:niŋ], adj. eingebildet.
overweight ['ouvəweit], s. das Übergewicht.
overwhelm [ouvə'welm], v.a. überwältigen.
overwork [ouvə'wə:k], v.n. sich überarbeiten.
overwrought [ouvə'rɔ:t], adj. übermäßig erregt, aufgeregt, überreizt.
owe [ou], v.a. schulden. — v.n. verdanken (be in debt).
owing ['ouiŋ], pred. adj. — to, dank (Dat.), zufolge (Dat.).
owl [aul], s. (Orn.) die Eule.
own (1) [oun], v.a. besitzen (possess). — adj. eigen.
own (2) [oun], v.a. anerkennen (acknowledge).
owner ['ounə], s. der Besitzer, Eigentümer.
ox [ɔks], s. (Zool.) der Ochse.
oxidate ['ɔksideit] see oxidise.

oxide ['ɔksaid], s. (Chem.) das Oxyd.
oxidise ['ɔksidaiz], v.a., v.n. (Chem.) oxydieren.
oxtail ['ɔksteil], s. der Ochsenschwanz.
oxygen ['ɔksidʒən], s. (Chem.) der Sauerstoff.
oyster ['ɔistə], s. (Zool.) die Auster.
ozone [ou'zoun], s. (Chem.) das Ozon.

P

P [pi:]. das P.
pa [pɑ:], s. (coll.) Papa, der Vater.
pace [peis], s. der Gang, Schritt (step); das Tempo (rate). — v.n. — up and down, auf- und abschreiten. — v.a. einschulen (horse).
Pacific, The [pə'sifik, ðə]. der Stille Ozean.
pacific [pə'sifik], adj. friedlich, still.
pacify ['pæsifai], v.a. Frieden stiften, beruhigen.
pack [pæk], s. das or der Pack; der Ballen (bale); das Rudel (wolves); das Spiel (cards); das Paket, die Packung. — v.a. packen (a case); parteiisch zusammensetzen; die Karten schlecht mischen (cheat at cards); packed like sardines, dichtgedrängt, eingepfercht. — v.n. packen; seine Sachen einpacken.
package ['pækidʒ], s. der Ballen (bale); das Gepäckstück, Paket.
packet ['pækit] s. das Paket; (Naut.) — boat, das Paketboot, Postschiff.
pact [pækt], s. der Pakt, Vertrag.
pad [pæd], s. das Polster, Kissen; der Notizblock (writing block). — v.a. auspolstern; padded cell, die Gummizelle.
padding ['pædiŋ], s. (Tail.) das Futter; (fig.) die (nichtssagende) Ausfüllung, das leere Geschwätz.
paddle ['pædl], v.a., v.n. rudern, paddeln. — s. das Paddel, (Doppel) ruder, das Schaufelruder; — steamer, der Raddampfer.
paddock ['pædək], s. der Sattelplatz; das Gehege.
padlock ['pædlɔk], s. das Vorhängeschloß, Vorlegeschloß.
pagan ['peigən], adj. heidnisch. — s. der Heide.
paganism ['peigənizm], s. das Heidentum.
page (1) [peidʒ], s. der Page (court attendant); Hoteljunge (hotel boy). — v.a. durch Pagen suchen lassen.
page (2) [peidʒ], s. die Seite (of book). — v.a. paginieren (book).
pageant ['pædʒənt], s. der Aufzug, der Prunkzug; das Schaustück (dramatic).
pail [peil], s. der Eimer.

pain [pein], *s.* der Schmerz, die Pein; (*pl.*) die Mühe; *go to a lot of* —*s*, sich große Mühe geben. — *v.a.* schmerzen; bekümmern (*mentally*).

paint [peint], *s.* die Farbe (*dye*); die Schminke (*make-up*). — *v.a.* anstreichen, malen.

painter ['peintə], *s.* der Maler.

painting ['peintiŋ], *s.* das Gemälde.

pair [pɛə], *s.* das Paar; *two* —*s of shoes*, zwei Paar Schuhe; *a* — *of spectacles*, die Brille; *a* — *of scissors*, die Schere. — *v.a.* paaren. — *v.n.* sich paaren.

pajamas [pə'dʒɑːməz] *see under* **pyjamas**.

Pakistani [pɑːki'stɑːni], *adj.* pakistanisch. — *s.* der Pakistaner.

palace ['pæləs], *s.* der Palast.

palatable ['pælətəbl], *adj.* schmackhaft.

palatal ['pælətl], *adj.* (*Phonet.*) palatal, Gaumen-, Vordergaumen-. — *s.* (*Phonet.*) der Gaumenlaut.

palate ['pælit], *s.* der Gaumen.

Palatinate, The [pə'lætinit, ðə]. die Pfalz, Pfalzgrafschaft.

palaver [pə'lɑːvə], *s.* die Unterredung; das Palaver.

pale (1) [peil], *adj.* blaß, bleich.

pale (2) [peil], *s.* der Pfahl; *beyond the* —, unkultiviert.

Palestinian [pælis'tiniən], *adj.* palästinisch. — *s.* der Palästiner.

palette ['pælit], *s.* die Palette (*see also* **pallet** (1)).

paling ['peiliŋ], *s.* der Lattenzaun; (*pl.*) der Pfahlbau.

pall (1) [pɔːl], *s.* das Leichentuch.

pall (2) [pɔːl], *v.n.* schal werden (*become stale*).

pallet (1) ['pælit], *s.* die Palette (*painter's*); — *knife*, das Streichmesser (*potter's* etc.).

pallet (2) ['pælit], *s.* der Strohsack.

palliative ['pæliətiv], *s.* linderndes Mittel; (*fig.*) die Beschönigung.

pallid ['pælid], *adj.* blaß, bleich.

pallor ['pælə], *s.* die Blässe.

palm (1) [pɑːm], *s.* die Handfläche. — *v.a.* — (*off*) *on to s.o.*, an jemanden loswerden, jemandem etwas andrehen.

palm (2) [pɑːm], *s.* (*Bot.*) die Palme; *Palm Sunday*, Palmsonntag.

palmer ['pɑːmə], *s.* (*obs.*) der Pilger (*pilgrim*).

palmist ['pɑːmist], *s.* der Handleser, Wahrsager.

palmistry ['pɑːmistri], *s.* die Handwahrsagerei.

palmy ['pɑːmi], *adj.* glorreich.

palpable ['pælpəbl], *adj.* handgreiflich, greifbar, klar.

palpitate ['pælpiteit], *v.n.* klopfen (*of heart*).

palsied ['pɔːlzid], *adj.* (*Med.*) gelähmt.

palsy ['pɔːlzi], *s.* (*Med.*) die Lähmung.

paltry ['pɔːltri], *adj.* erbärmlich, armselig.

pamper ['pæmpə], *v.a.* verwöhnen.

pan (1) [pæn], *s.* die Pfanne. — *v.n.* —

out, sich ausbreiten, sich weiten.

pan (2) [pæn], *v.a.* (*Phot.*) kreisen, im Bogen führen.

panacea [pænə'siə], *s.* das Universalmittel.

pancake ['pænkeik], *s.* der Pfannkuchen.

pander ['pændə], *v.n.* fröhnen (*Dat.*), nachgeben.

pane [pein], *s.* die Glasscheibe.

panel [pænl], *s.* die Holzfüllung, Täfelung (*in room*); die Liste; die Kommission (*of experts* etc.).

pang [pæŋ], *s.* die Angst, Pein; der Schmerz, Stich (*stab of pain*).

panic ['pænik], *s.* die Panik, der Schrecken.

panoply ['pænəpli], *s.* (*Poet.*) die Rüstung.

pansy ['pænzi], *s.* (*Bot.*) das Stiefmütterchen; (*sl.*) der Weichling, Feigling.

pant [pænt], *v.n.* keuchen, schwer atmen.

pantaloons [pæntə'luːnz] (*usually abbr.* **pants** [pænts]), *s. pl.* die Unterhosen, Hosen, *f. pl.*

panther ['pænθə], *s.* (*Zool.*) der Panther.

pantomime ['pæntəmaim], *s.* die Pantomime, das Weihnachtsstück.

pantry ['pæntri], *s.* die Speisekammer.

pap [pæp], *s.* der Kinderbrei.

papacy ['peipəsi], *s.* das Papsttum.

papal ['peipəl], *adj.* päpstlich.

paper ['peipə], *s.* das Papier (*material*); die Zeitung (*daily* —); die Abhandlung (*essay*); — *knife*, der Brieföffner. — *v.a.* tapezieren (*a room*).

paperhanger ['peipəhæŋə], *s.* der Tapezierer.

paperweight ['peipəweit], *s.* der Briefbeschwerer.

par [pɑː], *s.* die Gleichheit, das Pari.

parable ['pærəbl], *s.* die Parabel, das Gleichnis.

parabola [pə'ræbələ], *s.* (*Geom.*) die Parabel.

parabolic [pærə'bɔlik], *adj.* parabolisch, gleichnishaft.

parachute ['pærəʃuːt], *s.* (*Aviat.*) der Fallschirm.

parade [pə'reid], *s.* die Parade, der Aufmarsch. — *v.a.* herausstellen; zur Schau tragen (*show off*). — *v.n.* (*Mil.*) vorbeimarschieren.

paradise ['pærədais], *s.* das Paradies.

paraffin ['pærəfin], *s.* das Paraffin.

paragon ['pærəgən], *s.* das Musterkind, Musterbeispiel, Vorbild.

paragraph ['pærəgrɑːf], *s.* der Abschnitt, Absatz, Paragraph.

Paraguayan [pærə'gwaiən], *adj.* paraguayisch. — *s.* der Paraguayer.

parallel ['pærəlel], *adj.* parallel. — *s.* die Parallele.

paralyse ['pærəlaiz], *v.a.* lähmen.

paralysis [pə'rælisis], *s.* die Lähmung.

paramount ['pærəmaunt], *adj.* oberst.

paramour ['pærəmuə], *s.* der *or* die Geliebte.

parapet

parapet [ˈpærəpit], *s.* das Geländer, die Brüstung.

paraphrase [ˈpærəfreiz], *s.* die Umschreibung. — *v.a.* umschreiben.

parasite [ˈpærəsait], *s.* der Schmarotzer, Parasit.

parasol [ˈpærəsɔl], *s.* der Sonnenschirm.

parboil [ˈpɑːbɔil], *v.a.* aufkochen lassen.

parcel [pɑːsl], *s.* das Paket; Bündel (*bundle*). — *v.a.* — *up*, einpacken.

parch [pɑːtʃ], *v.a.* austrocknen.

parchment [ˈpɑːtʃmənt], *s.* das Pergament.

pardon [pɑːdn], *v.a.* vergeben, verzeihen (*Dat.*); begnadigen (*Acc.*) (*give amnesty*). — *s.* der Pardon, die Verzeihung; — *!, I beg your* — *!* bitte um Entschuldigung; *I beg your* —? wie bitte?

pare [pɛə], *v.a.* beschneiden (*nails*); schälen (*fruit*).

parent [ˈpɛərənt], *s.* der Vater, die Mutter, (*pl.*) die Eltern, *pl.*

parentage [ˈpɛərəntidʒ], *s.* die Abkunft, Herkunft.

parenthesis [pəˈrenθisis], *s.* die Parenthese, die Klammer.

parish [ˈpæriʃ], *s.* das Kirchspiel, die Gemeinde, die Pfarre.

parishioner [pəˈriʃənə], *s.* das Gemeindemitglied.

Parisian [pəˈriziən], *adj.* parisisch. — *s.* der Pariser.

park [pɑːk], *s.* der Park; (*Motor.*) der Wagenpark, Parkplatz. — *v.a., v.n.* parken.

parking [ˈpɑːkiŋ], *s.* (*Motor.*) das Parken; — *meter*, die Parkuhr, der Parkometer.

parley [ˈpɑːli], *s.* die Unterredung, Verhandlung. — *v.n.* verhandeln.

parliament [ˈpɑːləmənt], *s.* das Parlament.

parlour [ˈpɑːlə], *s.* das Wohnzimmer, die gute Stube; —*maid*, das Dienstmädchen; — *trick*, das Kunststück.

parochial [pəˈroukiəl], *adj.* Pfarr-, Gemeinde-; (*fig.*) engstirnig.

parody [ˈpærədi], *s.* die Parodie. — *v.a.* parodieren.

parole [pəˈroul], *s.* das Ehrenwort; (*Mil.*) das Losungswort.

paroxysm [ˈpærəksizm], *s.* der heftige Anfall.

parquet [ˈpɑːki], *s.* das Parkett; — *floor*, der Parkettfußboden.

parrot [ˈpærət], *s.* (*Orn.*) der Papagei.

parry [ˈpæri], *v.a.* parieren, abwehren.

parse [pɑːs, pɑːz], *v.a.* (*Gram.*) analysieren.

parsimony [ˈpɑːsiməni], *s.* die Sparsamkeit.

parsley [ˈpɑːsli], *s.* (*Bot.*) die Petersilie.

parson [pɑːsn], *s.* der Pastor, Pfarrer.

parsonage [ˈpɑːsənidʒ], *s.* das Pfarrhaus.

part [pɑːt], *s.* der Teil; Anteil (*share*); (*Theat.*) die Rolle; (*Mus.*) die Stimme;

(*Geog.*) die Gegend; *for his* —, seinerseits. — *v.n.* — (*with*), sich trennen (von, *Dat.*); — *company*, auseinandergehen.

partake [pɑːˈteik], *v.n.* teilnehmen, teilhaben (*in*, an, *Dat.*).

partial [pɑːʃl], *adj.* Teil-; parteiisch (*subjective*); — *to*, eingenommen für.

participate [pɑːˈtisipeit], *v.n.* teilnehmen (*in*, an, *Dat.*).

participation [pɑːtisiˈpeiʃən], *s.* die Teilnahme.

participle [ˈpɑːtisipl], *s.* (*Gram.*) das Mittelwort, Partizip(ium).

particle [ˈpɑːtikl], *s.* die Partikel, das Teilchen.

particular [pəˈtikjulə], *adj.* besonder (*special*); einzel (*individual*); sonderbar (*queer*); ungewöhnlich; genau. — *s.* (*pl.*) die Details, *n. pl.*, Einzelheiten, *f. pl.*

parting [ˈpɑːtiŋ], *s.* der Abschied (*taking leave*); der Scheitel (*hair*).

partisan [pɑːtiˈzæn], *s.* der Partisane, Parteigänger.

partition [pɑːˈtiʃən], *s.* die Teilung (*division*); die Scheidewand (*dividing wall*). — *v.a.* teilen; aufteilen (*divide up*).

partly [ˈpɑːtli], *adv.* zum Teil, teils.

partner [ˈpɑːtnə], *s.* der Partner; Teilhaber (*in business etc.*).

partnership [ˈpɑːtnəʃip], *s.* die Partnerschaft.

partridge [ˈpɑːtridʒ], *s.* (*Orn.*) das Rebhuhn.

party [ˈpɑːti], *s.* (*Pol.*) die Partei; (*Law*) die Partei, Seite; die Gesellschaft, die Party (*social gathering*); *throw* or *give a* —, einen Gesellschaftsabend (*or* eine Party) geben; *guilty* —, der schuldige Teil (*Build.*) — *wall*, die Brandmauer.

Paschal [ˈpɑːskəl], *adj.* Oster-.

pass [pɑːs], *v.a.* passieren; vorbeigehen (an, *Dat.*); durchlassen (*let through*); (*Law*) — *sentence*, das Urteil fällen. — *v.n.* fortgehen, vergehen, geschehen (*happen*); vorübergehen (*of time*); — *for*, gelten; (*Sch.*) durchkommen (*exam*); *come to* —, sich ereignen. — *s.* der Paß; (*Theat.*) die Freikarte.

passable [ˈpɑːsəbl], *adj.* gangbar; (*fig.*) leidlich, erträglich.

passage [ˈpæsidʒ], *s.* der Durchgang (*thoroughfare*); das Vergehen (*of time*); die Seereise; die Stelle (*book*).

passenger [ˈpæsindʒə], *s.* der Reisende, Passagier; — *train*, der Personenzug.

passer-by [ˈpɑːsəbai], *s.* der Passant, Vorübergehende.

passing [ˈpɑːsiŋ], *s.* das Vorbeigehen, das Vorübergehen; (*Parl.*) das Durchgehen; das Hinscheiden (*death*). — *adj.* vorübergehend, zeitweilig.

Passion [ˈpæʃən], *s.* (*Eccl.*) das Leiden; (*Mus.*) die Passion; — *Week*, die Karwoche; — *flower*, die Passionsblume.

passion [ˈpæʃən], *s.* die Leidenschaft;

fly into a —, aufbrausen.

passive ['pæsiv], *adj.* passiv. — *s.* (*Gram.*) das Passiv(um).

Passover ['pɑ:souvə], *s.* (*Rel.*) das Passahfest.

passport ['pɑ:spɔ:t], *s.* der Reisepaß.

past [pɑ:st], *adj.* vergangen. — *adv.* vorbei. — *prep.* nach (*time*). — *s.* die Vergangenheit; (*Gram.*) das Imperfekt, Präteritum.

paste [peist], *s.* die Paste, der Brei; der Kleister (*glue*). — *v.a.* kleben, kleistern.

pasteboard ['peistbɔ:d], *s.* die Pappe.

pastime ['pɑ:staim], *s.* der Zeitvertreib.

pastor ['pɑ:stə], *s.* (*Rel.*) der Seelsorger, Pfarrer.

pastoral ['pɑ:stərəl], *adj.* Hirten-, pastoral. — *s.* (*Poet*). das Hirtengedicht.

pastry ['peistri], *s.* (*Cul.*) die Pastete; das Gebäck; — *cook*, der Konditor, Zuckerbäcker.

pasture ['pɑ:stʃə], *s.* die Weide, das Grasland. — *v.n.* weiden, grasen.

pasty ['pɑ:sti, 'pæsti], *s.* (*Cul.*) die Pastete. — ['peisti], *adj.* teigig.

pat [pæt], *s.* der Klaps; der Schlag (*slap*). — *v.a.* leicht schlagen, streicheln (*gently*).

patch [pætʃ], *v.a.* flicken, ausbessern. — *s.* der Fleck (*mending material*); der Flecken (*land*); (*coll.*) *no — on him*, kein Vergleich mit ihm; *nicht zu vergleichen mit ihm.*

patent ['peitənt *or* 'pætənt], *adj.* offen, klar, patent; — *leather*, das Glanzleder. — *s.* das Patent.

patentee [peitən'ti:], *s.* der Patentinhaber.

paternal [pə'tə:nəl], *adj.* väterlich.

path [pɑ:θ], *s.* der Pfad, Weg, Fußsteig.

pathetic [pə'θetik], *adj.* pathetisch, rührend; armselig.

pathology [pə'θɔlədʒi], *s.* (*Med.*) die Pathologie.

pathway ['pɑ:θwei], *s.* der Fußweg, Fußsteig.

patience ['peiʃəns], *s.* die Geduld; die Patience (*card game*).

patient ['peiʃənt], *adj.* geduldig. — *s.* (*Med.*) der Patient.

patrician [pə'triʃən], *adj.* patrizisch. — *s.* der Patrizier.

patrimony ['pætriməni], *s.* das (väterliche) Erbgut.

patriot ['peitriət, 'pætriət], *s.* der Patriot.

patriotism ['peitriətizm, 'pæt-], *s.* die Vaterlandsliebe, der Patriotismus.

patrol [pə'troul], *s.* die Patrouille, Streife. — *v.n.* auf Patrouille gehen.

patron ['peitrən], *s.* der Schutzherr, der Gönner; (*Comm.*) der Kunde; — *saint*, der Schutzheilige.

patronage ['pætrənidʒ], *s.* die Gönnerschaft, Huld.

patronize ['pætrənaiz], *v.a.* besuchen (*frequent*); begünstigen (*favour*).

patronizing ['pætrənaiziŋ], *adj.* herablassend.

patten [pætn], *s.* (*Archit.*) der Sockel; der Holzschuh (*clog*).

patter (1) ['pætə], *s.* das Geplätscher (*rain etc.*). — *v.n.* plätschern.

patter (2) ['pætə], *s.* das Geplauder (*chatter*). — *v.n.* schwätzen.

pattern ['pætən], *s.* das Muster; die Schablone (*in material*).

paucity ['pɔ:siti], *s.* die geringe Anzahl, der Mangel.

paunch [pɔ:ntʃ], *s.* der Wanst.

pauper ['pɔ:pə], *s.* der Arme.

pauperize ['pɔ:pəraiz], *v.a.* arm machen, verarmen lassen.

pause [pɔ:z], *s.* die Pause. — *v.n.* innehalten.

pave [peiv], *v.a.* pflastern.

pavement ['peivmənt], *s.* das Pflaster; der Bürgersteig, Gehsteig.

pavilion [pə'viljən], *s.* das Gartenhaus; der Pavillon.

paw [pɔ:], *s.* die Pfote; die Tatze. — *v.a.* streicheln, betasten.

pawn (1) [pɔ:n], *s.* das Pfand. — *v.a.* verpfänden.

pawn (2) [pɔ:n], *s.* (*Chess*) der Bauer.

pawnbroker ['pɔ:nbroukə], *s.* der Pfandleiher.

pay [pei], *v.a. irr.* zahlen; bezahlen, begleichen (*bill*); — *attention*, aufpassen, Aufmerksamkeit schenken; — *o.'s respects*, Respekt zollen. — *v.n. irr.* sich bezahlt machen, sich lohnen (*it — s to . . .*). — *s.* (*Mil.*) der Sold; (*Comm.*) der Lohn (*wage*), die Bezahlung (*payment*).

payable ['peiəbl], *adj.* zahlbar, zu bezahlen.

payee [pei'i:], *s.* der Empfänger, Präsentant.

payer ['peiə], *s.* der Zahler; (*Comm.*) der Trassat.

payment ['peimənt], *s.* die Bezahlung, Begleichung (*of sum*).

pea [pi:], *s.* (*Bot.*) die Erbse (*see also* **peas(e)**).

peace [pi:s], *s.* der Friede(n); die Ruhe (*restfulness*).

peaceable ['pi:səbl], *adj.* friedlich; friedliebend.

peaceful ['pi:sful], *adj.* friedlich, ruhig (*restful*).

peach [pi:tʃ], *s.* (*Bot.*) der *or* (*Austr.*) die Pfirsich.

peacock ['pi:kɔk], *s.* (*Orn.*) der Pfau.

peahen ['pi:hen], *s.* (*Orn.*) die Pfauhenne.

peak [pi:k], *s.* der Gipfel, die Spitze; der Schirm (*of cap*); — *hour*, die Stunde des Hochbetriebs, Hauptverkehrsstunde.

peal [pi:l], *v.a.* läuten. — *v.n.* erschallen. — *s.* das Läuten, Geläute.

peanut ['pi:nat], *s.* (*Bot.*) die Erdnuß.

pear [pɛə], *s.* (*Bot.*) die Birne.

pearl [pə:l], *s.* die Perle; — *barley*, die Perlgraupen, *f. pl.*; *mother of* —, die Perlmutter.

peasant ['pezənt], s. der Bauer.
peasantry ['pezəntri], s. das Bauern-volk, die Bauernschaft.
peas(e) [pi:z], s. pl. *pease pudding*, der Erbsenbrei, das Erbsenpüree.
peat [pi:t], s. der Torf.
pebble [pebl], s. der Kiesel(stein).
peck (1) [pek], s. der Viertelscheffel (=9 litres.)
peck (2) [pek], s. das Picken (*of hen*); (*coll.*) der Kuß. — v.a. hacken, hauen.
pecker ['pekə], s. die Picke, Haue; *keep your — up!* Mut bewahren!
peckish ['pekiʃ], adj. hungrig.
pectoral ['pektərəl], adj. Brust-. — s. das Brustmittel.
peculiar [pi'kju:liə], adj. eigenartig, eigentümlich (*strange*); — *to*, eigen (*Dat.*); besonder (*special*).
peculiarity [pikju:li'æriti], s. die Eigen-tümlichkeit, Eigenartigkeit.
pecuniary [pi'kju:niəri], adj. Geld-, geldlich, finanziell, pekuniär.
pedagogue ['pedəgɔg], s. der Päda-gog(e), Erzieher.
pedal [pedl] s. das Pedal; (*Motor.*) der Fußhebel. — v.n. radfahren; (*coll.*) radeln.
pedant ['pedənt], s. der Pedant.
pedantic [pi'dæntik], adj. pedantisch.
pedantry ['pedəntri], s. die Pedanterie.
peddle [pedl], v.a. hausieren.
peddling ['pedliŋ], adj. kleinlich, un-bedeutend.
pedestal ['pedistl], s. der Sockel.
pedestrian [pi'destriən], s. der Fuß-gänger. — adj. Fuß-, Fußgänger-.
pedigree ['pedigri:], s. der Stamm-baum.
pediment ['pedimənt], s. (*Archit.*) der Ziergiebel.
pedlar ['pedlə], s. der Hausierer.
peel [pi:l], s. die Schale (*of fruit*). — v.a. schälen. — v.n. sich schälen.
peep [pi:p], v.n. gucken. — s. der (schnelle) Blick, das Gucken; — *show*, der Guckkasten.
peer (1) [piə], s. (*Parl.*) der Pair, Lord; der Ebenbürtige (*equal*).
peer (2) [piə], v.n. gucken, blicken, schauen.
peerage ['piəridʒ], s. der (Reichs)adel.
peeress ['piəres], s. die Gattin eines Pairs.
peerless ['piəlis], adj. unvergleichlich.
peevish ['pi:viʃ], adj. n ürrisch.
pe(e)wit ['pi:wit], s. (*Orn.*) der Kiebitz.
peg ['peg], s. der Pflock (*stake*); der Holzstift (*in wall*); *clothes —*, die Wäscheklammer. — v.a. anpflocken (*to ground*).
pelican ['pelikən], s. (*Orn.*) der Pelikan.
pellet ['pelit], s. das Kügelchen.
pell-mell ['pel'mel], adv. durchein-ander.
pelt (1) [pelt], v.a. — *with*, bewerfen mit, — *a person with*, werfen nach einem (*Acc.*). — v.n. strömen (*rain etc.*); rennen (*hasten*).
pelt (2) [pelt], s. der Pelz (*of animal*).

pen (1) [pen], s. *quill —*, die Feder; *fountain —*, die Füllfeder; *ballpoint —*, der Kugelschreiber. — v.a. schrei-ben; verfassen (*compose*).
pen (2) [pen], s. das Gehege. — v.a. einschliessen (*sheep*).
penal ['pi:nəl], adj. Straf-; — *servitude*, die Zuchthausstrafe.
penalize ['pi:nəlaiz], v.a. bestrafen.
penalty ['penəlti], s. die Strafe.
penance ['penəns], s. die Buße.
pence [pens] *see under* penny.
pencil ['pensl], s. der Bleistift; der Stift; (*Geom.*) der Strahl. — v.a. niederschreiben, notieren.
pendant ['pendənt], s. das Ohrgehänge; (*fig.*) das Gegenstück.
pendent ['pendənt], adj. hängend, schwebend.
pending ['pendiŋ], adj. in der Schwebe; unentschieden (*undecided*). — prep. während (*during*); bis (zu) (*until*).
pendulum ['pendjuləm], s. das Pendel.
penetrate ['penitreit], v.a. durch-dringen.
peninsula [pi'ninsjulə], s. die Halb-insel.
penitent ['penitənt], s. der Büßer. — adj. bußfertig.
penitentiary [peni'tenʃəri], s. (*Am.*) das Zuchthaus (*prison*).
penknife ['pennaif], s. das Taschen-messer.
pennant ['penənt], s. der Wimpel, das Fähnchen.
penniless ['penilis], adj. mittellos, ohne einen Heller Geld, arm.
pennon ['penən] *see* pennant.
penny ['peni], s. (*pl.* **pence** [pens], **pennies** [peniz]) der Penny; (*Am.*) das Centstück; — *farthing*, das Hoch-rad; — *whistle*, die Blechpfeife; *a pretty —*, hübsches Geld.
pension ['penʃən], s. die Pension; das Ruhegehalt. — v.a. (*off*) pensionieren, in den Ruhestand versetzen.
pensive ['pensiv], adj. nachdenklich.
Pentecost ['pentikɔst]. das *or* (*pl.*) die Pfingsten.
penthouse ['penthaus], s. das Wetter-dach.
penurious [pi'njuəriəs], adj. unbe-mittelt, arm (*poor*); dürftig, karg (*meagre*).
penury ['penjuəri], s. die Not, Armut.
peony ['piəni], s. (*Bot.*) die Päonie, Pfingstrose.
people [pi:pl], s. *pl.* das Volk (*nation*); die Leute, Menschen (*pl.*). — v.a. bevölkern.
pepper ['pepə], s. der Pfeffer. — v.a. pfeffern.
per [pə:], prep. pro; per; durch; *as — account*, laut Rechnung.
peradventure [pə:rəd'ventʃə], adv. (*obs.*) von ungefähr; vielleicht (*per-haps*).
perambulator [pə'ræmbjuleitə] (*abbr. coll.*) **pram** [præm]), s. der Kinder-wagen.

perceive [pə'si:v], *v.a.* wahrnehmen, merken.

percentage [pə'sentidʒ], *s.* der Prozentsatz (*of interest*); Prozente, *n. pl.*

perceptible [pə'septibl], *adj.* wahrnehmbar, merklich.

perception [pə'sepʃən], *s.* die Wahrnehmung, Empfindung.

perch (1) [pə:tʃ], *v.n.* aufsitzen; sitzen (*of birds*). — *s.* die Stange.

perch (2) [pə:tʃ], *s.* (*Zool.*) der Barsch.

perchance [pə'tʃɑ:ns], *adv.* vielleicht.

percolate ['pə:kəleit], *v.n.* durchsickern, durchtröpfeln.

percolator ['pə:kəleitə], *s.* die Kaffeemaschine.

percussion [pə'kʌʃən], *s.* (*Mus.*) das Schlagzeug.

peremptory ['perəmptəri, pə'remptəri], *adj.* entschieden, bestimmt (*decided*); absprechend.

perennial [pə'reniəl], *adj.* (*Bot.*) perennierend; Dauer-.

perfect ['pə:fikt], *adj.* vollkommen, vollendet, perfekt. — *s.* (*tense*) (*Gram.*) das Perfekt(um). — [pə'fekt], *v.a.* vollenden.

perfection [pə'fekʃən], *s.* die Vollendung, Vollkommenheit; *to* —, vollkommen.

perfidious [pə'fidiəs], *adj.* treulos, untreu; tückisch.

perfidy ['pə:fidi], *s.* die Treulosigkeit.

perforate ['pə:fəreit], *v.a.* durchlöchern, perforieren (*paper*); durchbohren (*pierce*).

perforce [pə'fɔ:s], *adv.* mit Gewalt, notgedrungen.

perform [pə'fɔ:m], *v.a.* ausführen (*carry out*); (*Theat.*) aufführen. — *v.n.* spielen, auftreten (*of actor*).

performance [pə'fɔ:məns], *s.* die Ausführung; Verrichtung (*execution of duty etc.*); (*Theat.*) die Aufführung.

perfume ['pə:fju:m], *s.* das Parfüm; der Duft (*scent*). — *v.a.* parfümieren.

perfunctory [pə'fʌŋktəri], *adj.* nachlässig, oberflächlich, flüchtig.

perhaps [pə'hæps], *adv.* vielleicht.

peril ['peril], *s.* die Gefahr.

period ['piəriəd], *s.* die Periode (*time*); der Zeitraum (*span*); (*Am.*) der Punkt (*full stop*).

periodical [piəri'ɔdikəl], *adj.* periodisch. — *s.* die Zeitschrift.

perish ['periʃ], *v.n.* zugrunde gehen, umkommen.

perishable ['periʃəbl], *adj.* vergänglich; (leicht) verderblich (*of food*).

periwig ['periwig], *s.* die Perücke.

periwinkle (1) ['periwiŋkl], *s.* (*Zool.*) die Uferschnecke.

periwinkle (2) ['periwiŋkl], (*Bot.*) das Immergrün.

perjure ['pə:dʒə], *v.r.* meineidig werden.

perjurer ['pə:dʒərə], *s.* der Meineidige.

perjury ['pə:dʒəri], *s.* der Meineid.

permanence, permanency ['pə:mə-nəns, 'pə:mənənsi], *s.* die Dauer, Beständigkeit.

permanent ['pə:mənənt], *adj.* Dauer-, dauerhaft, beständig; — *wave*, die Dauerwelle.

permeability [pə:miə'biliti], *s.* die Durchdringbarkeit, Durchlässigkeit.

permeable ['pə:miəbl], *adj.* durchdringlich.

permeate ['pə:mieit], *v.a.* durchdringen.

permissible [pə'misibl], *adj.* zulässig, statthaft.

permission [pə'miʃən], *s.* die Erlaubnis.

permit [pə'mit], *v.a.* zulassen, erlauben. — ['pə:mit], *s.* die Erlaubnis; (*official*) die Genehmigung.

permutation [pə:mju'teiʃən], *s.* (*Maths.*) die Permutation.

pernicious [pə'niʃəs], *adj.* verderblich, schädlich, bösartig.

perorate ['perəreit], *v.n.* eine (lange) Rede beschließen.

perpendicular [pə:pən'dikjulə], *adj.* senkrecht. — *s.* die Senkrechte.

perpetrate ['pə:pitreit], *v.a.* begehen (*commit*).

perpetration [pə:pi'treiʃən], *s.* die Verübung, Begehung.

perpetrator ['pə:pitreitə], *s.* der Begeher, Täter.

perpetual [pə'petjuəl], *adj.* (an-)dauernd; ewig.

perpetuate [pə'petjueit], *v.a.* verewigen.

perpetuity [pə:pi'tju:iti], *s.* die Ewigkeit.

perplex [pə'pleks], *v.a.* bestürzen, verblüffen.

perplexity [pə'pleksiti], *s.* die Bestürzung, Verwirrung.

persecute ['pə:sikju:t], *v.a.* verfolgen.

persecution [pə:si'kju:ʃən], *s.* die Verfolgung.

perseverance [pə:si'viərəns], *s.* die Ausdauer, Beharrlichkeit.

persevere [pə:si'viə], *v.n.* beharren (*in*, bei, *Dat.*).

Persian ['pə:ʃən], *adj.* persisch. — *s.* der Perser.

persist [pə'sist], *v.n.* beharren (*in*, auf, *Dat.*).

persistence [pə'sistəns], *s.* die Beharrlichkeit.

person ['pə:sən], *s.* die Person; *in* —, persönlich.

personal ['pə:sənəl], *adj.* persönlich.

personality [pə:sə'næliti], *s.* die Persönlichkeit.

personify [pə'sɔnifai], *v.a.* verkörpern.

personnel [pə:sə'nel], *s.* das Personal; (*Comm.*) — *manager*, der Personalchef.

perspective [pə'spektiv], *s.* die Perspektive. — *adj.* perspektivisch.

perspicacious [pə:spi'keiʃəs], *adj.* scharfsichtig, scharfsinnig.

perspicacity [pə:spi'kæsiti], *s.* der Scharfblick, Scharfsinn.

perspicuity [pə:spi'kju:iti], *s.* die Durchsichtigkeit, Klarheit.

perspicuous [pə'spikjuəs], *adj.* deutlich, klar.

perspiration [pə:spi'reiʃən], *s.* der Schweiß.

perspire [pə'spaiə], *v.n.* schwitzen.

persuade [pə'sweid], *v.a.* überreden.

persuasion [pə'sweiʒən], *s.* die Überredung.

persuasive [pə'sweiziv], *adj.* überzeugend, überredend.

pert [pə:t], *adj.* naseweis, keck.

pertain [pə'tein], *v.n.* (an)gehören (*to* Dat.).

pertinacious [pə:ti'neiʃəs], *adj.* beharrlich, halsstarrig.

pertinacity [pə:ti'næsiti], *s.* die Beharrlichkeit, Halsstarrigkeit.

pertinence, pertinency ['pə:tinəns, 'pə:tinənsi], *s.* die Angemessenheit.

pertinent ['pə:tinənt], *adj.* angemessen, passend.

pertness ['pə:tnis], *s.* die Keckheit, der Vorwitz.

perturb [pə'tə:b], *v.a.* verwirren, stören, beunruhigen.

perturbation [pə:tə'beiʃən], *s.* die Verwirrung, Störung, Beunruhigung.

peruke [pə'ru:k], *s.* die Perücke.

peruse [pə'ru:z], *v.a.* durchlesen.

Peruvian [pə'ru:viən], *adj.* peruanisch. — *s.* der Peruaner.

pervade [pə'veid], *v.a.* durchdringen.

perverse [pə'və:s], *adj.* verkehrt.

perversion [pə'və:ʃən], *s.* die Perversion.

perversity [pə'və:siti], *s.* die Verdorbenheit, Widernatürlichkeit.

pervert [pə'və:t], *v.a.* verkehren, verderben. — ['pə:və:t], *s.* der Verdorbene, der perverse Mensch.

perverted [pə'və:tid], *adj.* pervers (*sexually*).

pervious ['pə:viəs], *adj.* zugänglich, passierbar; durchlässig.

pessimist ['pesimist], *s.* der Pessimist.

pest [pest], *s.* (*Med.*) die Pest; (*fig.*) die Plage.

pester ['pestə], *v.a.* quälen, auf die Nerven gehen (*Dat.*).

pestiferous [pes'tifərəs], *adj.* verpestend.

pestilence ['pestiləns], *s.* (*Med.*) die Pest, Seuche.

pestle [pesl], *s.* die Mörserkeule.

pet [pet], *s.* das Haustier; der Liebling; — *name*, der Kosename. — *v.a.* liebkosen, streicheln.

petition [pi'tiʃən], *s.* die Bittschrift. — *v.n.* mit einer Bittschrift herantreten an (*Acc.*).

petrel ['petrəl], *s.* (*Orn.*) der Sturmvogel.

petrification [petrifi'keiʃən], *s.* die Versteinerung.

petrify ['petrifai], *v.a.* versteinern; (*fig.*) starr machen, bestürzen; *petrified with fright*, starr vor Entsetzen. — *v.n.* zu Stein werden.

petrol ['petrəl], *s.* das Benzin; (*crude oil*) das Petroleum; — *station*, die Tankstelle.

petticoat ['petikout], *s.* der Unterrock.

pettifogging ['petifɔgin], *adj.* Winkel-, kleinlich, schikanös (*petty*).

pettiness ['petinis], *s.* die Kleinlichkeit.

pettish ['petiʃ], *adj.* verdrießlich.

petty ['peti], *adj.* klein, gering, kleinlich.

petulance ['petjuləns], *s.* die Launenhaftigkeit, Gereiztheit.

petulant ['petjulənt], *adj.* launenhaft.

pew [pju:], *s.* (*Eccl.*) der Kirchensitz; (*coll.*) der Sitz, Stuhl.

pewit ['pi:wit] *see* **pe(e)wit**.

pewter ['pju:tə], *s.* das Zinn; die Zinnwaren, *f. pl.* (*wares*).

pewterer ['pju:tərə], *s.* der Zinngießer.

phantom ['fæntəm], *s.* das Phantom, Trugbild; das Gespenst (*ghost*).

Pharisee ['færisi:], *s.* der Pharisäer.

pharmaceutical [fɑ:mə'sju:tikəl], *adj.* pharmazeutisch.

pharmacy ['fɑ:məsi], *s.* die Apothekerkunst (*dispensing*); die Apotheke (*dispensary*); die Pharmazeutik (*discipline*).

phase [feiz], *s.* die Phase.

pheasant ['fezənt], *s.* (*Orn.*) der Fasan.

phenomenal [fi'nɔminəl], *adj.* außerordentlich, phänomenal.

phenomenon [fi'nɔminən], *s.* das Phänomen.

phial ['faiəl], *s.* die Phiole, das Fläschchen.

philanthropist [fi'lænθrəpist], *s.* der Philanthrop.

philanthropy [fi'lænθrəpi], *s.* die Philanthropie.

philatelist [fi'lætəlist], *s.* der Philatelist, Markensammler.

philately [fi'lætəli], *s.* das Markensammeln, die Philatelie, Briefmarkenkunde.

Philippine ['filipi:n], *adj.* philippinisch.

Philistine ['filistain], *s.* der Philister; (*fig.*) der Spießbürger.

philologist [fi'lɔlədʒist], *s.* der Philologe.

philology [fi'lɔlədʒi], *s.* die Philologie.

philosopher [fi'lɔsəfə], *s.* der Philosoph.

philosophize [fi'lɔsəfaiz], *v.n.* philosophieren.

philosophy [fi'lɔsəfi], *s.* die Philosophie.

phlegm [flem], *s.* das Phlegma (*mood*); (*Med.*) der Schleim.

phlegmatic [fleg'mætik], *adj.* phlegmatisch, gelassen.

phone [foun] *see under* **telephone**.

phonetics [fə'netiks], *s.* die Phonetik.

phosphorescent [fɔsfə'resənt], *adj.* phosphoreszierend, leuchtend.

phosphorus ['fɔsfərəs], *s.* (*Chem.*) der Phosphor.

photograph ['foutəgræf *or* -grɑ:f], *s.* die Photographie, das Lichtbild (*picture*). — *v.a.* photographieren, aufnehmen, (*coll.*) knipsen.

photographer [fə'tɔgrəfə], *s.* der Photograph.

photography [fə'tɔgrəfi], s. die Photographie.

phrase [freiz], s. die Phrase. — v.a. phrasieren, fassen, ausdrücken.

phrenology [fre'nɔlədʒi], s. die Phrenologie, Schädellehre.

phthisis ['θaisis], s. (Med.) die Schwindsucht.

physic ['fizik], s. (obs.) die Medizin, Arznei.

physical ['fizikəl], adj. körperlich (bodily); physikalisch (of physics).

physician [fi'ziʃən], s. der Arzt.

physics ['fiziks], s. die Physik.

physiognomy [fizi'ɔnəmi or -'ɔgnəmi], s. die Physiognomie, die Gesichtsbildung.

physiologist [fizi'ɔlədʒist], s. der Physiolog.

physiology [fizi'ɔlədʒi], s. die Physiologie.

piano(forte) ['pjænou('fɔ:ti)], s. das Klavier.

pick [pik], v.a. pflücken (flowers); hacken (hack); — up, auflesen; auswählen (select); gewaltsam öffnen (a lock); anfangen (a quarrel). — v.n. why — on me? warum gerade mich auswählen? — s. die Picke, Spitzhacke (axe); die Auswahl; — of the bunch, (coll.) das Beste von allen.

picket ['pikit], s. die Wache; der Streikposten (of strikers); der Pflock (wood). — v.a. bewachen. — v.n. Wache stehen.

pickle [pikl], s. (Cul.) der Pökel, das Gepökelte; (coll.) die unangenehme Lage (calamity). — v.a. einpökeln.

pickpocket ['pikpɔkit], s. der Taschendieb.

picnic ['piknik], s. das Picknick. — v.n. picknicken.

pictorial [pik'tɔ:riəl], adj. illustriert.

picture ['piktʃə], s. das Bild; — book, das Bilderbuch; — postcard, die Ansichtskarte; pretty as a —, bildhübsch; der Film; (pl.) das Kino. — v.a. sich vorstellen.

picturesque [piktʃə'resk], adj. pittoresk, malerisch.

pie [pai], s. (Cul.) die Pastete (savoury); das Törtchen (sweet).

piebald ['paibɔ:ld], adj. scheckig. — s. der Schecke (horse).

piece [pi:s], s. das Stück. — v.a. — together, zusammenflicken (mend), zusammensetzen (compose).

piecemeal ['pi:smi:l], adv. stückweise.

pied [paid] see piebald.

pier [piə], s. der Hafendamm; der Pfeiler (column).

pierce [piəs], v.a. durchstechen, durchbohren.

pierglass ['piəglɑ:s], s. der Pfeilerspiegel.

piety ['paiəti], s. die Pietät, Frömmigkeit.

pig [pig], s. (Zool.) das Schwein.

pigeon ['pidʒən], s. (Orn.) die Taube.

pigeonhole ['pidʒənhoul], s. das Fach.

pigheaded [pig'hedid], adj. starrköpfig, dickköpfig.

piglet ['piglit], s. (Zool.) das Ferkel.

pigment ['pigmənt], s. das Pigment, der (natürliche) Farbstoff.

pigtail ['pigteil], s. der Haarzopf.

pike [paik], s. (Zool.) der Hecht; die Pike (weapon).

pile (1) [pail], s. der Haufen, Stoß (paper). — v.a. aufhäufen.

pile (2) [pail], s. (Archit.) der Pfahl; Pfeiler (stone).

pile (3) [pail], s. (Text.) der Teppichflausch (carpet), die Noppe (cloth).

piles [pailz], s. pl. (Med. coll.) die Haemorrhoiden, pl.

pilfer ['pilfə], v.a. stehlen, mausen.

pilferer ['pilfərə], s. der Dieb.

pilgrim ['pilgrim], s. der Pilger.

pill [pil], s. (Med.) die Pille.

pillage ['pilidʒ], s. die Plünderung. — v.a. ausplündern.

pillar ['pilə], s. der Pfeiler, die Säule; — box, der Briefkasten.

pillion ['piljən], s. der zweite Sitz, Sozius (motorcycle).

pillory ['piləri], s. der Pranger. — v.a. anprangern.

pillow ['pilou], s. das Kopfkissen.

pilot ['pailət], s. der Pilot; (Naut.) der Lotse. — v.a. (Aviat.) steuern, (Naut.) lotsen.

pimento [pi'mentou], s. (Bot.) der Jamaikapfeffer.

pimp [pimp], s. der Kuppler.

pimple [pimpl], s. der Pickel; (pl.) der Ausschlag.

pin [pin], s. die Stecknadel; (Engin.) der Bolzen, Stift; (skittles) der Kegel. — v.a. — down, festlegen.

pinafore ['pinəfɔ:], s. die Schürze, Kinderschürze.

pincers ['pinsəz], s. pl. die Kneifzange, Zange.

pinch [pintʃ], v.a. kneifen, zwicken; (coll.) klauen, stehlen. — v.n. sparen, darben. — s. die Prise (tobacco); at a —, wenn es sein muß.

pine (1) [pain], s. (Bot.) die Kiefer, Föhre.

pine (2) [pain], v.n. — for, schmachten (nach, Dat.), sich sehnen.

pineapple ['painæpl], s. (Bot.) die Ananas.

pinion ['pinjən], s. der Flügel (wing); (Poet.) die Schwinge; (Mech.) das Zahnrad; — shaft, die Ritzelwelle; — spindle, die Zahnradwelle. — v.a. binden, fesseln.

pink [piŋk], adj. rosa. — s. (Bot.) die (rosa) Nelke; (Hunt.) der (rote) Jagdrock; in the — (of condition), in bester Gesundheit, in bester Form.

pinnacle ['pinəkl], s. die Zinne, Spitze; (fig.) der Gipfel.

pint [paint], s. die Pinte (0.57 litre); (beer) der Schoppen.

pioneer [paiə'niə], s. der Pionier. — v.a. bahnbrechend sein, bahnen.

pious ['paiəs], adj. fromm.

pip [pip], *s.* der Obstkern; (*Mil. coll.*) der Leutnantsstern.

pipe [paip], *s.* die Pfeife; (*Engin.*) das Rohr; die Röhre; (*Mus.*) die Pfeife. — *v.a.* pfeifen; durch Rohre leiten.

piping ['paipiŋ], *adj.* — *hot*, kochend heiß.

pipkin ['pipkin], *s.* das Töpfchen.

piquant ['pi:kənt], *adj.* pikant; scharf (*taste*).

pique [pi:k], *s.* der Groll. — *v.a.* reizen.

piracy ['pairəsi], *s.* die Seeräuberei.

pirate ['pairit], *s.* der Pirat, Seeräuber. — [pai'reit], *v.a.* (*fig.*) plagiieren, ohne Erlaubnis drucken (*books*).

pistil ['pistil], *s.* (*Bot.*) der Stempel.

pistol ['pistəl], *s.* die Pistole.

piston ['pistən], *s.* (*Mech.*) der Kolben.

pit [pit], *s.* die Grube; (*Min.*) der Schacht, das Bergwerk; (*Theat.*, *Mus.*) der Orchesterraum; (*Theat.*) das Parterre.

pitch (1) [pitʃ], *s.* der Grad, Gipfel (*height*); (*Mus.*) der Ton, die Tonhöhe (*level*); (*Sport*) das Spielfeld. — *v.a.* werfen; feststecken; (*Mus.*) stimmen; befestigen; (*tent*) (ein Zelt) aufschlagen; — *in*, sich ins Zeug legen.

pitch (2) [pitʃ], *s.* das Pech (*tar*); — *dark*, pechschwarz.

pitchblende ['pitʃblend], *s.* die Pechblende.

pitcher ['pitʃə], *s.* der Krug.

pitchfork ['pitʃfɔ:k], *s.* die Heugabel.

piteous ['pitiəs], *adj.* erbärmlich.

pitfall ['pitfɔ:l], *s.* die Falle.

pith [piθ], *s.* das Mark; (*fig.*) der Kern, das Wesentliche; die Kraft (*strength*).

pithy ['piθi], *adj.* markig, kräftig; prägnant.

pitiable ['pitiəbl], *adj.* erbärmlich.

pitiful ['pitiful], *adj.* erbärmlich (*pitiable*); mitleidig (*sympathetic*).

pitiless ['pitilis], *adj.* erbarmungslos, grausam.

pittance ['pitəns], *s.* der Hungerlohn, das Bißchen, die Kleinigkeit.

pity ['piti], *s.* das Mitleid. — *v.a.* bemitleiden, bedauern.

pivot ['pivət], *s.* (*Mech.*) der Drehpunkt, Zapfen; (*fig.*) der Mittelpunkt, Angelpunkt. — *v.n.* zum Mittelpunkt haben, sich drehen (um).

placard ['plæka:d], *s.* das Plakat.

placate [plə'keit], *v.a.* versöhnen.

place [pleis], *s.* der Platz, Ort, die Stelle; — *name*, der Ortsname; (*rank*) der Rang, die Rangstufe. — *v.a.* plazieren (*in a job*); legen, setzen, stellen; — *an order*, einen Auftrag geben.

placid ['plæsid], *adj.* gelassen, sanft, gutmütig.

plagiarism ['pleidʒiərizm], *s.* das Plagiat, das Plagiieren.

plague [pleig], *s.* (*Med.*) die Pest, Seuche; (*fig.*) die Plage. — *v.a.* belästigen, plagen.

plaice [pleis], *s.* (*Zool.*) die Scholle.

plain [plein], *s.* die Ebene, Fläche. — *adj.* eben, flach (*even*); schlicht,

einfach, klar; — *dealing*, ehrliche Handlungsweise; — *speaking*, offenes Sprechen, aufrichtiges Reden; (*Mus.*) — *song*, der einstimmige Chorgesang, die gregorianische Kirchenmusik.

plaintiff ['pleintif], *s.* (*Law*) der Kläger.

plaintive ['pleintiv], *adj.* klagend.

plait [plæt], *s.* der Zopf, die Flechte. — *v.a.* flechten (*hair*); falten.

plan [plæn], *s.* der Plan, Grundriß. — *v.a.* planen, entwerfen.

plane (1) [plein], *v.a.* hobeln (*wood*). — *s.* die Fläche (*surface*); die Stufe (*level*); (*coll.*) das Flugzeug (*aeroplane*).

plane (2) see **plane-tree**.

planet ['plænit], *s.* (*Astron.*) der Planet.

plane-tree ['pleintri:], *s.* (*Bot.*) die Platane.

planish ['plæniʃ], *v.a.* (*woodwork*) polieren, glätten.

plank [plæŋk], *s.* die Planke; (*Pol.*) der Programmpunkt.

plant [pla:nt], *s.* (*Bot.*) die Pflanze; (*Ind.*) die Anlage, der Betrieb. — *v.a.* anpflanzen, anlegen; — *suspicion*, Verdacht einflößen (*of*, *against*, gegen, *Acc.*).

plantain ['plæntein], *s.* (*Bot.*) der Wegerich; (*fruit*) der Pisang.

plantation [plæn'teiʃən], *s.* die Pflanzung, Plantage.

plaster ['pla:stə], *s.* das Pflaster (*adhesive*); (*Build.*) der Mörtel, der Mauerbewurf; — *cast*, der Gipsabdruck; — *of Paris*, der Stuck, der feine Gipsmörtel. — *v.a.* bepflastern, verputzen; (*fig.*) dick auftragen.

plastic ['plæstik], *adj.* plastisch; (*malleable*) formbar; — *surgery*, plastische Chirurgie. — *s.* der Kunststoff.

Plate, River [pleit, 'rivə]. der La Plata Strom.

plate [pleit], *s.* der Teller (*dish*), die Platte, Scheibe; (*coll.*) — *glass*, das Spiegelglas; das Geschirr (*service of crockery*); *gold* —, das Goldgeschirr. — *v.a.* überziehen, versilbern, verchromen.

platform ['plætfɔ:m], *s.* (*Railw.*) der Bahnsteig; die Bühne, das Podium.

platinum ['plætinəm], *s.* das Platin.

platitude ['plætitju:d], *s.* die Plattheit, der Gemeinplatz.

platitudinous [plæti'tju:dinəs], *adj.* nichtssagend.

platoon [plə'tu:n], *s.* (*Mil.*) der Zug.

plaudit ['plɔ:dit], *s.* der Beifall.

plausible ['plɔ:zibl], *adj.* wahrscheinlich, glaubwürdig, einleuchtend.

play [plei], *s.* das Spiel (*game*); (*Theat.*) das Stück. — *v.a.*, *v.n.* spielen.

player ['pleiə], *s.* der Spieler; (*Theat.*) der Schauspieler.

playful ['pleiful], *adj.* spielerisch, spielend.

playground ['pleigraund], *s.* der Spielplatz.

playhouse ['pleihaus], *s.* das Schauspielhaus.

playmate ['pleimeit], *s.* der Spiel-
gefährte.

playwright ['pleirait], *s.* der Dramatiker, Schauspieldichter.

plea [pli:], *s.* die Bitte; das Gesuch; der
Vorwand.

plead [pli:d], *v.a.*, *v.n.* plädieren, sich
berufen auf; vorschützen (*claim*).

pleasant ['plezənt], *adj.* angenehm,
freundlich.

pleasantry ['plezəntri], *s.* das freund-
liche Wort, der Scherz (*joke*).

please [pli:z], *v.a.*, *v.n.* gefallen; einen
Gefallen tun (*do a favour*); — *!* bitte,
haben Sie die Güte!; *if you* —, wenn
Sie nichts dagegen haben.

pleasing ['pli:ziŋ], *adj.* einnehmend,
angenehm.

pleasure ['pleʒə], *s.* das Vergnügen; *at
your* —, nach Belieben; *take* — *in*,
Vergnügen finden an (*Dat.*).

pleat [pli:t], *v.a.* plissieren. — *s.* die
Falte, das Plissee.

pledge [pledʒ], *s.* das Pfand, die Bürgschaft (*guarantee*); das Versprechen
(*promise*). — *v.a.* sich verbürgen,
versprechen (*promise*); zutrinken (*drink to*).

plenary ['pli:nəri], *adj.* Plenar-, vollständig.

plenipotentiary [plenipo'tenʃəri], *s.*
der Bevollmächtigte.

plenitude ['plenitju:d], *s.* die Fülle.

plenteous, plentiful ['plentiəs, 'plenti-
ful], *adj.* reichlich, in Fülle.

plenty ['plenti], *s.* die Fülle.

pleurisy ['pluərəsi], *s.* (*Med.*) die
Brustfellentzündung.

pliable, pliant ['plaiəbl, 'plaiənt], *adj.*
geschmeidig, biegsam.

pliers ['plaiəz], *s.* *pl.* die Drahtzange.

plight (1) [plait], *s.* die Notlage.

plight (2) [plait], *v.a.* feierlich versprechen.

plod [plɔd], *v.n.* schwerfällig gehen
(*walk*); sich plagen (*work hard*).

plot (1) [plɔt], *s.* das Stück Land, der
Bauplatz.

plot (2) [plɔt], *s.* das Komplott, die
Verschwörung; die Handlung (*book,
play etc.*). — *v.a.* aushecken (*ambush
etc.*), planen.

plough, plow [plau], *s.* der Pflug. —
v.a. pflügen; (*coll.*) *be* —*ed*, durchfallen (*in,* in, *Dat.*).

ploughshare ['plauʃeə], *s.* die Pflugschar.

plover ['plʌvə], *s.* (*Orn.*) der Kiebitz,
Regenpfeifer.

plow *see under* **plough**.

pluck (1) [plʌk], *v.a.* pflücken (*flowers*);
rupfen (*feathers*); — *up courage*, Mut
fassen.

pluck (2) [plʌk], *s.* (*coll.*) der Mut.

plucky ['plʌki], *adj.* mutig.

plug [plʌg], *s.* (*Elec.*) der Stecker; der
Stöpsel (*stopper*); *sparking* —, (*Motor.*)
die Zündkerze. — *v.a.* stöpseln,
zustopfen (*block*); (*fig.*) betonen,
herausstellen (*repeat for advertisement*).

plum [plʌm], *s.* (*Bot.*) die Pflaume;
(*coll.*) das Beste.

plumage ['plu:midʒ], *s.* (*Orn.*) das
Gefieder.

plumb [plʌm], *s.* das Senkblei, Lot;
— *-rule*, die Senkwaage. — *adv.*
senkrecht, gerade, lotrecht.

plume [plu:m], *s.* die (Schmuck)
feder.

plump [plʌmp], *adj.* dick, drall.

plunder ['plʌndə], *v.a.*, *v.n.* plündern.
— *s.* die Beute, der Raub.

plunge [plʌndʒ], *v.a.*, *v.n.* untertauchen, stoßen, hinabstürzen.

plunger ['plʌndʒə], *s.* der Taucher;
(*Engin.*) der Tauchkolben.

pluperfect [plu:'pə:fikt], *s.* (*Gram.*) das
Plusquamperfektum.

plural ['pluərəl], *s.* (*Gram.*) der Plural,
die Mehrzahl.

plurality [pluə'ræliti], *s.* die Mehrzahl,
der Plural.

plus [plʌs], *prep.* plus, zuzüglich.

plush [plʌʃ], *s.* (*Text.*) der Plüsch.

ply [plai], *s.* die Falte (*fold*), Lage
(*layer*). — *v.a.* ausüben (*trade*).

plywood ['plaiwud], *s.* das Sperrholz,
die Sperrholzplatte.

pneumonia [nju'mouniə], *s.* (*Med.*) die
Lungenentzündung.

poach (1) [poutʃ], *v.n.* wildern; — *on*,
übergreifen auf.

poach (2) [poutʃ], *v.a.* ohne Schale
kochen; *poached eggs*, verlorene Eier,
n. pl.

poacher ['poutʃə], *s.* der Wilderer,
Wilddieb.

pocket ['pɔkit], *s.* die Tasche; — *book*,
die Brieftasche; das Taschenbuch;
— *money*, das Taschengeld.

pod [pɔd], *s.* (*Bot.*) die Schote.

poem ['pouim], *s.* das Gedicht.

poet ['pouit], *s.* der Dichter.

poetic(al) [pou'etik(l)], *adj.* dichterisch.

poignancy ['pɔinjənsi], *s.* die Schärfe.

poignant ['pɔinjənt], *adj.* scharf, beißend, schmerzlich.

point [pɔint], *s.* der Punkt (*of remark,
sentence*); die Sache; der Zweck; die
Spitze (*of pencil etc.*); *make a* —, es
sich zur Aufgabe machen; *in* — *of
fact*, tatsächlich; *come to the* —, zur
Sache kommen. — *v.a.*, *v.n.* spitzen,
zuspitzen (*pencil*); — *out*, zeigen,
(hin)deuten; — *to*, hinweisen auf; —
the moral, die Moral erklären.

pointblank ['pɔint'blæŋk], *adj.*, *adv.*
schnurgerade, direkt.

pointed ['pɔintid], *adj.* scharf, spitzig,
deutlich (*remark*).

pointer ['pɔintə], *s.* der Zeiger; (*fig.*)
der Fingerzeig (*hint*).

poise [pɔiz], *s.* das Gleichgewicht; (*fig.*)
angemessenes Benehmen, die Grazie.
— *v.a.* abwägen; im Gleichgewicht
halten. — *v.n.* schweben; —*d for
action*, tatbereit.

poison [pɔizn], *s.* das Gift. — *v.a.*
vergiften.

poke

poke (1) [pouk], *v.a.* schüren (*fire*); stoßen; — *fun at*, sich lustig machen über. — *s.* der Stoß; — *in the ribs*, ein Rippenstoß.

poke (2) [pouk], *s.* der Sack; *a pig in a* —, die Katze im Sack.

poker (1) ['poukə], *s.* der Schürhaken, das Schüreisen.

poker (2) ['poukə], *s.* (*Cards*) das Pokerspiel.

polar ['poulə], *adj.* (*Geog.*) Polar-; (*Phys.*) polar.

polarity [po'læriti], *s.* die Polarität.

Pole [poul], *s.* der Pole.

pole (1) [poul], *s.* (*Geog.*) der Pol.

pole (2) [poul], *s.* die Stange (*rod*); der Pfahl (*upright*).

poleaxe ['poulæks], *s.* die Streitaxt.

polecat ['poulkæt], *s.* (*Zool.*) der Iltis.

polemic [pə'lemik], *s.* die Polemik, der Streit.

police [pə'li:s], *s.* die Polizei. — *v.a.* polizeilich beaufsichtigen.

policeman [pə'li:smən], *s.* der Polizist.

policy (1) ['polisi], *s.* die Politik.

policy (2) ['polisi], *s.* (*Insurance*) die Police.

Polish ['pouliʃ], *adj.* polnisch.

polish ['poliʃ], *v.a.* polieren. — *s.* die Politur, der Glanz.

polished ['poliʃd], *adj.* glatt (*smooth*); (*fig.*) wohlerzogen, fein (*manners*).

polite [pə'lait], *adj.* höflich.

politeness [pə'laitnis], *s.* die Höflichkeit.

politic ['politik], *adj.* politisch; schlau (*cunning*).

political [pə'litikəl], *adj.* politisch; staatskundig.

politician [poli'tiʃən], *s.* der Politiker, Staatsmann.

politics ['politiks], *s.* (*sometimes pl.*) die Politik, politische Gesinnung.

poll [poul], *s.* die Wahl (*election*). — *v.n.* abstimmen, wählen, seine Stimme abgeben.

pollard ['poləd], *s.* (*Bot.*) der gekappte Baum; (*Zool.*) das hornlose Tier.

pollen ['polən], *s.* (*Bot.*) der Blütenstaub.

pollinate ['polineit], *v.a.* (*Bot.*) bestäuben.

polling ['pouliŋ], *s.* die Wahl, der Wahlgang (*election*); — *station*, das Wahllokal.

pollute [pə'lju:t], *v.a.* verunreinigen.

pollution [pə'lju:ʃən], *s.* die Verunreinigung.

poltroon [pol'tru:n], *s.* die Memme.

poly- ['poli], *pref.* viel-.

Polynesian [poli'ni:ziən], *adj.* polynesisch. — *s.* der Polynesier.

polytechnic [poli'teknik], *s.* das Technikum; polytechnische Fachschule.

pomegranate ['pom-, 'pʌmgrænit], *s.* (*Bot.*) der Granatapfel.

Pomeranian [pomə'reiniən], *adj.* pommerisch. — *s.* der Pommer; der Spitz (*dog*).

pommel [pʌml], *s.* der Sattelknopf; der Knauf (*sword*). — *v.a.* schlagen.

pomp [pomp], *s.* der Pomp, das Gepränge.

pompous ['pompəs], *adj.* hochtrabend, prahlerisch; (*manner*) schwerfällig, wichtigtuerisch.

pond [pond], *s.* der Teich.

ponder ['pondə], *v.a., v.n.* bedenken, überlegen.

ponderous ['pondərəs], *adj.* schwer, schwerfällig.

pontiff ['pontif], *s.* der Hohepriester; der Papst.

pontifical [pon'tifikəl], *adj.* bischöflich, päpstlich. — *s. pl.* die bischöfliche Amtstracht.

pontificate [pon'tifikit], *s.* das (*or* der) Pontifikat. — [-keit], *v.n.* (*coll.*) predigen.

pontoon (1) [pon'tu:n], *s.* die Schiffsbrücke, der Brückenkahn.

pontoon (2) [pon'tu:n], *s.* (*cards*) das Einundzwanzig, Vingt-et-un.

pony ['pouni], *s.* (*Zool.*) der *or* das Pony.

poodle [pu:dl], *s.* (*Zool.*) der Pudel.

pooh-pooh [pu:'pu:], *v.a.* verspotten.

pool (1) [pu:l], *s.* die Lache, der Pfuhl.

pool (2) [pu:l], *s.* (*fig.*) der gemeinsame Einsatz (*money, forces etc.*). — *v.a.* zusammenschließen.

poop [pu:p], *s.* (*Naut.*) das Heck, Hinterteil.

poor [puə], *adj.* arm, dürftig; *in* — *health*, bei schwacher Gesundheit; (*fig.*) armselig, schlecht.

pop [pop], *v.n.* knallen, explodieren. — *v.a.* (*coll.*) schnell versetzen, verpfänden.

Pope [poup], *s.* (*Eccl.*) der Papst.

poplar ['poplə], *s.* (*Bot.*) die Pappel.

poppy ['popi], *s.* (*Bot.*) der Mohn.

populace ['popjulis], *s.* der Pöbel.

popular ['popjulə], *adj.* volkstümlich, beliebt.

popularity [popju'læriti], *s.* die Beliebtheit.

populate ['popjuleit], *v.a.* bevölkern.

population [popju'leiʃən], *s.* die Bevölkerung.

populous ['popjuləs], *adj.* dicht bevölkert.

porcelain ['po:slin], *s.* das Porzellan, das Geschirr.

porch [po:tʃ], *s.* die Eingangshalle, Vorhalle.

porcupine ['po:kjupain], *s.* (*Zool.*) das Stachelschwein.

pore (1) [po:], *s.* die Pore.

pore (2) [po:], *v.n.* sich vertiefen (*over, in*), brüten (*über*).

pork [po:k], *s.* das Schweinefleisch.

porosity [po:'rositi], *s.* die Porosität.

porous ['po:rəs], *adj.* porös.

porpoise ['po:pəs], *s.* (*Zool.*) der Tümmler, das Meerschwein.

porridge ['poridʒ], *s.* (*Cul.*) der Haferbrei.

porringer ['porindʒə], *s.* (*Cul.*) der Napf.

port (1) [po:t], *s.* der Hafen.

port (2) [po:t], *s.* der Portwein (*wine*).

practise

portable ['pɔ:təbl], *adj.* tragbar; Koffer- (*radio etc.*).

portcullis [pɔ:t'kʌlis], *s.* das Fallgatter.

portend [pɔ:'tend], *v.a.* vorbedeuten, ahnen lassen.

portent ['pɔ:tent], *s.* die Vorbedeutung.

porter ['pɔ:tə], *s.* (*Railw.*) der Gepäckträger; der Pförtner, Portier (*caretaker, janitor*); das Porterbier (*beer*).

porterage ['pɔ:təridʒ], *s.* der Trägerlohn, die Zustellkosten, *f.pl.*

portfolio [pɔ:t'fouliou], *s.* die Mappe; (*Pol.*) das Ressort; das Portefeuille.

portico ['pɔ:tikou], *s.* (*Archit.*) die Säulenhalle.

portion ['pɔ:ʃən], *s.* die Portion, der Anteil. — *v.a.* aufteilen, austeilen (*share out*).

portliness ['pɔ:tlinis], *s.* die Stattlichkeit (*dignity*); Behäbigkeit (*corpulence*).

portly ['pɔ:tli], *adj.* stattlich (*dignified*); behäbig (*corpulent*).

portmanteau [pɔ:t'mæntou], *s.* der Handkoffer.

portrait ['pɔ:trit], *s.* (*Art*) das Bildnis, Porträt.

portray [pɔ:'trei], *v.a.* im Bilde darstellen, porträtieren; (*fig.*) schildern, darstellen (*describe*).

Portuguese [pɔ:tju'gi:z], *adj.* portugiesisch. — *s.* der Portugiese.

pose [pouz], *s.* die Haltung, Stellung (*of model etc.*). — *v.a.* in Pose stellen; aufwerfen (*question*). — *v.n.* (*as model*) stehen, sitzen; *as*, posieren, sich ausgeben als (*pretend to be*).

poser ['pouzə], *s.* die schwierige Frage.

position [pə'ziʃən], *s.* die Lage (*situation*); die Stellung (*job*); der Stand, Rang (*rank*); (*Astron., Mil.*) die Position.

positive ['pɔzitiv], *adj.* positiv; (*fig.*) ausdrücklich, sicher (*sure*).

possess [pə'zes], *v.a.* besitzen.

possession [pə'zeʃən], *s.* der Besitz, Besitztum.

possessive [pə'zesiv], *adj.* (*Gram.*) besitzanzeigend, possessiv; (*fig.*) besitzgierig.

possibility [pɔsi'biliti], *s.* die Möglichkeit.

possible ['pɔsibl], *adj.* möglich.

post (1) [poust], *s.* der Pfosten (*pillar*).

post (2) [poust], *s.* die Post (*mail*); der Posten (*job*). — *v.a.* zur Post geben; (*coll.*) einstecken (*letter*).

postage ['poustidʒ], *s.* das Porto; *stamp,* die Briefmarke.

postal [poustl], *adj.* Post-.

poster ['poustə], *s.* das Plakat.

posterity [pɔs'teriti], *s.* die Nachwelt.

posthumous ['pɔstjuməs], *adj.* hinterlassen, nach dem Tode, postum.

postman ['poustmən], *s.* der Briefträger.

postmark ['poustmɑ:k], *s.* der Poststempel.

post-mortem [poust'mɔ:təm], *s.* — — —

(*examination*), die Obduktion, Leichenschau.

post-office ['poustɔfis], *s.* das Postamt.

postpone [poust'poun], *v.a.* verschieben, aufschieben.

postscript ['poustskript], *s.* die Nachschrift.

postulate ['pɔstjuleit], *v.a.* postulieren, voraussetzen.

posture ['pɔstʃə], *s.* die Positur, Haltung (*of body*).

pot [pɔt], *s.* der Topf; die Kanne (*beer*); (*coll.*) *go to* —, zugrunde gehen. — *v.a.* einkochen, einmachen; (*fig.*) kürzen.

potash ['pɔtæʃ], *s.* (*Chem.*) die Pottasche.

potassium [pə'tæsiəm], *s.* (*Chem.*) das Kalium.

potato [pə'teitou], *s.* (*Bot.*) die Kartoffel.

potent ['poutənt], *adj.* kräftig, stark, wirksam.

potential [pə'tenʃəl], *s.* das Potential. — *adj.* möglich, potentiell (*possible*).

potter ['pɔtə], *s.* der Töpfer.

pottery ['pɔtəri], *s.* die Töpferei; die Töpferwaren, Tonwaren, *f. pl.* (*goods*).

pouch [pautʃ], *s.* der Beutel.

poulterer ['poultərə], *s.* der Geflügelhändler.

poultice ['poultis], *s.* der Umschlag.

poultry ['poultri], *s.* das Geflügel.

pounce (1) [pauns], *s.*(*obs.*) die Klaue. — *v.n.* — *upon,* herfallen (über, *Acc.*).

pounce (2) [pauns], *s.* das Bimssteinpulver. — *v.a.* (mit Bimsstein) abreiben.

pound (1) [paund], *s.* das Pfund; das Pfund Sterling.

pound (2) [paund], *v.a.* zerstoßen.

poundage ['paundidʒ], *s.* das Pfundgeld, die Gebühr pro Pfund.

pour [pɔ:], *v.a.* gießen, schütten, einschenken. — *v.n.* strömen.

pout [paut], *v.n.* schmollen.

poverty ['pɔvəti], *s.* die Armut.

powder ['paudə], *s.* (*Mil.*) das Pulver; der Puder (*face etc.*). — *v.a.* zu Pulver machen, stoßen; (*face*) pudern.

power [pauə], *s.* die Macht; Gewalt; Kraft; Fähigkeit; — *of attorney,* die Vollmacht; (*Maths.*) die Potenz; (*Elec.*) der Strom; — *house,* — *station,* das Elektrizitätswerk; — *cut,* die Stromstörung.

powerful ['pauəful], *adj.* kräftig, mächtig, einflußreich.

powerless ['pauəlis], *adj.* kraftlos, machtlos.

pox [pɔks], *s.* (*Med.*) die Pocken, *f. pl.*; die Syphilis.

practicable ['præktikəbl], *adj.* ausführbar, tunlich.

practical ['præktikəl], *adj.* praktisch.

practice ['præktis], *s.* die Ausübung (*doing, carrying out*); die Praxis.

practise ['præktis], *v.a.* ausführen, ausüben (*a profession etc.*); üben (*rehearse*). — *v.n.* sich üben.

461

practised

practised ['præktisd], *adj.* geübt, geschult (in).

practitioner [præk'tiʃənə], *s.* (*Med.*) praktischer Arzt; (*Law*) Advokat.

pragmatic [præg'mætik], *adj.* pragmatisch.

prairie ['prɛəri], *s.* die Prärie.

praise [preiz], *v.a.* preisen, loben. — *s.* das Lob.

pram *see under* **perambulator.**

prance [prɑːns], *v.n.* sich bäumen; (*fig.*) sich brüsten (*brag*).

prank [præŋk], *s.* der Streich.

prate [preit], *v.n.* plappern, schwatzen.

prattle [prætl], *v.n.* plaudern, schwatzen. — *s.* das Geschwätz.

prawn [prɔːn], *s.* (*Zool.*) die Steingarnele.

pray [prei], *v.n.* beten. — *v.a.* bitten, ersuchen (*beseech*).

prayer [prɛə], *s.* das Gebet.

preach [priːtʃ], *v.a.*, *v.n.* predigen.

preacher ['priːtʃə], *s.* der Prediger.

preamble [priː'æmbl], *s.* die Vorrede, der Einleitungsparagraph.

precarious [pri'kɛəriəs], *adj.* unsicher, prekär.

precaution [pri'kɔːʃən], *s.* die Vorsichtsmaßregel.

precede [pri'siːd], *v.a.*, *v.n.* vorausgehen, den Vortritt haben.

precedence ['presidəns *or* pri'siːdəns], *s.* der Vortritt, Vorrang.

precedent ['presidənt], *s.* der Präzedenzfall.

precept ['priːsept], *s.* die Vorschrift, Regel.

preceptor [pri'septə], *s.* der Lehrer, Lehrmeister.

precinct ['priːsiŋkt], *s.* das Gebiet, der Bezirk; (*pl.*) die Grenzen, *f. pl.*

precious ['preʃəs], *adj.* wertvoll, kostbar; — *metal*, das Edelmetall.

precipice ['presipis], *s.* der Abgrund.

precipitous [pri'sipitəs], *adj.* jäh, abschüssig.

precise [pri'sais], *adj.* genau, bestimmt.

precision [pri'siʒən], *s.* die Präzision, Genauigkeit; (*Engin.*) — *tool*, das Präzisionswerkzeug.

preclude [pri'kluːd], *v.a.* ausschließen.

precocious [pri'kouʃəs], *adj.* frühreif.

preconceive [priːkən'siːv], *v.a.* vorher denken.

preconceived [priːkən'siːvd], *adj.* vorgefaßt.

preconception [priːkən'sepʃən], *s.* das Vorurteil.

precursor [pri'kəːsə], *s.* der Vorläufer.

predatory ['predətəri], *adj.* räuberisch, Raub-.

predecessor ['priːdisesə], *s.* der Vorgänger.

predestin(at)e [priː'destin(eit)], *v.a.* vorher bestimmen; (*Theol.*) prädestinieren.

predicament [pri'dikəmənt], *s.* die Verlegenheit.

predicate ['predikit], *s.* (*Gram.*) das Prädikat. — [-keit], *v.a.* behaupten.

predict [pri'dikt], *v.a.* voraussagen, vorhersagen.

prediction [pri'dikʃən], *s.* die Vorhersage (*weather etc.*); die Weissagung (*prophecy*).

predilection [priːdi'lekʃən], *s.* die Vorliebe.

predispose [priːdis'pouz], *v.a.* vorbereiten; empfänglich machen.

predominant [pri'dɔminənt], *adj.* vorherrschend.

predominate [pri'dɔmineit], *v.n.* vorherrschen.

pre-eminence [priː'eminəns], *s.* der Vorrang.

prefabricate [priː'fæbrikeit], *v.a.* vorfabrizieren, als Fertigteil herstellen, in der Fabrik herstellen.

prefabrication [priːfæbri'keiʃən], *s.* die Vorfabrizierung.

preface ['prefis], *s.* das Vorwort.

prefatory ['prefətəri], *adj.* einleitend.

prefect ['priːfekt], *s.* der Präfekt.

prefer [pri'fəː], *v.a.* vorziehen.

preference ['prefərəns], *s.* der Vorzug; (*Comm.*) — *share*, die Vorzugsaktie.

preferment [pri'fəːmənt], *s.* die Beförderung.

prefix ['priːfiks], *s.* die Vorsilbe. — [priː'fiks], *v.a.* vorsetzen.

pregnancy ['pregnənsi], *s.* die Schwangerschaft.

pregnant ['pregnənt], *adj.* schwanger.

prejudge [priː'dʒʌdʒ], *v.a.* vorher urteilen, voreilig urteilen.

prejudice ['predʒudis], *s.* das Vorurteil. — *v.a.* beeinträchtigen.

prejudicial [predʒu'diʃəl], *adj.* schädlich.

prelate ['prelit], *s.* (*Eccl.*) der Prälat.

preliminary [pri'liminəri], *adj.* vorläufig, Präliminar-. — *s.* (*pl.*) die Vorbereitungen, *f. pl.*

prelude ['prelju:d], *s.* das Vorspiel.

premature ['premətʃə], *adj.* vorschnell, übereilt, vorzeitig.

premeditate [pri'mediteit], *v.a.* (*Law*) vorher überlegen.

Premier ['premiə], *s.* der Premierminister.

premise (1) ['premis], *s.* (*Log.*) die Prämisse; (*pl.*) das Haus, Grundstück; die Stätte, der Ort; das Lokal (*inn etc.*).

premise (2) [pri'maiz], *v.a.* vorausschicken.

premium ['priːmiəm], *s.* die Prämie.

premonition [priːmə'niʃən], *s.* die Vorahnung.

preoccupation [priːɔkju'peiʃən], *s.* die Zerstreutheit.

preoccupied [priː'ɔkjupaid], *adj.* besorgt; zerstreut (*absent-minded*).

preparation [prepə'reiʃən], *s.* die Vorbereitung; Zubereitung (*of meals*).

preparatory [pri'pærətri], *adj.* vorbereitend; — *school*, die Vorschule.

prepare [pri'pɛə], *v.a.*, *v.n.* vorbereiten (*for*, auf); zubereiten (*meals*).

prepay [priː'pei], *v.a. irr.* vorausbezahlen; (*post*) frankieren.

preponderant [pri'pɔndərənt], *adj.* überwiegend.

preponderate [pri'pɔndəreit], *v.a.,* *v.n.* überwiegen.

preposition [prepə'ziʃən], *s.* (*Gram.*) die Präposition.

prepossess [pri:pə'zes], *v.a.* einnehmen, beeindrucken.

preposterous [pri'pɔstərəs], *adj.* töricht, lächerlich, unerhört.

prerogative [pri'rɔgətiv], *s.* das Vorrecht.

presage [pri'seidʒ], *v.a.* prophezeien. — ['presidʒ], *s.* die Prophezeiung.

prescient ['presiənt, 'pri:–], *adj.* vorahnend, vorherwissend.

prescribe [pri'skraib], *v.a., v.n.* vorschreiben; (*Med.*) verschreiben, verordnen.

prescription [pri'skripʃən], *s.* die Vorschrift(*precept*); (*Med.*) das Rezept.

presence ['prezəns], *s.* die Gegenwart, Anwesenheit (*attendance*); das Äußere (*appearance*); — *of mind,* die Geistesgegenwart.

present (1) ['prezənt], *adj.* anwesend, gegenwärtig; jetzig. — *s.* (*Gram.*) das Präsens, die Gegenwart; (*time*) die Gegenwart, heutige Zeit.

present (2) [pri'zent], *v.a.* darstellen (*on stage*); vorstellen (*introduce*); präsentieren (*arms*); schenken, geben (*gifts*). — ['prezənt], *s.* das Geschenk (*gift*).

presentation [prezən'teiʃən], *s.* die Darstellung (*stage, art*); die Vorstellung (*introduction*); die Überreichung (*of gift*).

presentiment [pri'zentimənt], *s.* das Vorgefühl, die Vorahnung.

presently ['prezəntli], *adv.* bald, sogleich.

preservation [prezə'veiʃən], *s.* die Erhaltung, Bewahrung.

preservative [pri'zə:vətiv], *s.* das Konservierungsmittel.

preserve [pri'zə:v], *v.a.* bewahren, erhalten; (*fruit*) einmachen. — *s.* (*Hunt.*) das Jagdgehege, Jagdrevier, (*pl.*) die Konserven, *f. pl.*

preside [pri'zaid], *v.n.* (*over*) den Vorsitz führen.

president ['prezidənt], *s.* der Präsident.

press [pres], *v.a., v.n.* drücken (*push*); bügeln, plätten (*iron*); nötigen (*force*); dringend bitten (*entreat*). — *s.* die Presse (*newspapers, printing*); der Schrank (*cupboard*); das Gedränge (*crowd*).

pressing ['presiŋ], *adj.* dringend.

pressure ['preʃə], *s.* der Druck.

prestige [pres'ti:ʒ], *s.* das Prestige, Ansehen.

presumable [pri'zju:məbl], *adj.* mutmaßlich, vermutlich.

presume [pri'zju:m], *v.a., v.n.* vermuten; — *on,* sich anmaßen.

presumption [pri'zʌmpʃən], *s.* die Annahme; die Anmaßung (*arrogance*).

presumptive [pri'zʌmptiv], *adj.* mutmaßlich.

presumptuous [pri'zʌmptjuəs], *adj.* anmaßend, dreist, vermessen.

presuppose [pri:sə'pouz], *v.a.* voraussetzen.

pretence [pri'tens], *s.* der Vorwand.

pretend [pri'tend], *v.a., v.n.* vortäuschen, vorgeben.

pretension [pri'tenʃən], *s.* die Anmaßung, der Anspruch (*to,* auf).

pretentious [pri'tenʃəs], *adj.* anspruchsvoll.

preterite ['pretərit], *s.* (*Gram.*) das Präteritum.

pretext ['pri:tekst], *s.* der Vorwand.

pretty ['priti], *adj.* hübsch, nett. — *adv.* (*coll.*) ziemlich.

prevail [pri'veil], *v.n.* vorherrschen, die Oberhand gewinnen.

prevalence ['prevələns], *s.* das Vorherrschen.

prevaricate [pri'værikeit], *v.n.* Ausflüchte machen.

prevent [pri'vent], *v.a.* verhindern.

prevention [pri'venʃən], *s.* die Verhinderung.

preventive [pri'ventiv], *adj.* vorbeugend.

previous ['pri:viəs], *adj.* vorhergehend.

prey [prei], *s.* die Beute, der Raub. — *v.n.* rauben, nachstellen.

price [prais], *s.* der Preis, Wert.

priceless ['praislis], *adj.* unschätzbar, unbezahlbar.

prick [prik], *s.* der Stachel, Stich (*stab*). — *v.a.* stechen (*stab*); punktieren (*puncture*).

prickle [prikl], *s.* (*Bot.*) der Stachel.

pride [praid], *s.* der Stolz. — *v.r.* — *o.s.,* sich brüsten, stolz sein (*on,* auf, *Acc.*).

priest [pri:st], *s.* (*Eccl.*) der Priester.

prig [prig], *s.* der eingebildete Tropf; Tugendheld.

priggish ['prigiʃ], *adj.* dünkelhaft, selbstgefällig.

prim [prim], *adj.* steif, spröde.

primacy ['praiməsi], *s.* der, das Primat.

primæval [prai'mi:vəl], *adj.* Ur-, anfänglich, ursprünglich.

primary ['praiməri], *adj.* erst, ursprünglich; Haupt– (*main*). — *s.* (*pl.*) (*Am.*) die Vorwahlen, *f. pl.* (*Presidential elections*).

prime [praim], *adj.* erst, wichtigst. — *s.* die Blüte, Vollendung, Vollkraft.

primer ['praimə], *s.* das Elementarbuch, die Fibel.

primitive ['primitiv], *adj.* primitiv; ursprünglich (*original*).

primness ['primnis], *s.* die Geziertheit, Steifheit.

primrose ['primrouz], *s.* (*Bot.*) die Primel.

prince [prins], *s.* der Prinz; Fürst (*rank*).

princess [prin'ses], *s.* die Prinzessin.

principal ['prinsipl], *s.* der Direktor (*business*); Rektor (*school etc.*); (*Comm.*) das Kapital; (*Mus.*) der erste Spieler. — *adj.* erst, Haupt–.

principality [prinsi'pæliti], *s.* das Fürstentum.

principle

principle ['prinsipl], *s.* das Prinzip, der Grundsatz.

print [print], *v.a.* drucken, abdrucken. — *s.* (*Typ., Art*) der Druck; *out of* —, vergriffen.

printer ['printə], *s.* der Buchdrucker.

prior [praiə], *adj.* früher, eher; — *to*, vor (*Dat.*). — *s.* (*Eccl.*) der Prior.

priority [prai'ɔriti], *s.* die Priorität, der Vorrang.

prise [praiz], *v.a.* — *open*, gewaltsam öffnen, aufbrechen.

prism [prizm], *s.* das Prisma.

prison [prizn], *s.* das Gefängnis.

prisoner ['prizənə], *s.* der Gefangene, Sträfling.

pristine ['pristain] *adj.* ehemalig, vormalig, ursprünglich.

privacy ['praivəsi *or* 'privəsi], *s.* die Zurückgezogenheit, Stille.

private ['praivit], *adj.* privat, persönlich, vertraulich (*confidential*). — *s.* (*Mil.*) der Gemeine, Landser.

privation [prai'veiʃən], *s.* der Mangel, die Entbehrung (*lack*); die Beraubung (*deprivation*).

privilege ['privilidʒ], *s.* das Privileg, Vorrecht. — *v.a.* ausnehmen, privilegieren.

privy ['privi], *s.* der Abtritt, Abort. — *adj.* — *to*, mitwissend; *Privy Council*, der Staatsrat.

prize [praiz], *s.* der Preis, die Belohnung; — *v.a.* hochschätzen.

prizewinner ['praizwinə], *s.* der Preisträger; *Nobel* —, der Nobelpreisträger.

probability [prɔbə'biliti], *s.* die Wahrscheinlichkeit.

probable ['prɔbəbl], *adj.* wahrscheinlich.

probate ['proubeit], *s.* (*Law*) die Testamentsbestätigung.

probation [pro'beiʃən], *s.* die Bewährung, Bewährungsfrist (*period*).

probationary [pro'beiʃənəri], *adj.* Bewährungs-.

probe [proub], *v.a.* sondieren, untersuchen. — *s.* die Sonde; Prüfung.

probity ['proubiti], *s.* die Redlichkeit, Anständigkeit.

problem ['prɔbləm], *s.* das Problem.

problematic [prɔblə'mætik], *adj.* zweifelhaft, problematisch.

proboscis [prə'bɔsis], *s.* (*Ent.*) der Rüssel.

procedure [prə'siːdʒə], *s.* der Vorgang, das Verfahren.

proceed [prə'siːd], *v.n.* vorgehen, verfahren.

proceeds ['prousiːdz], *s. pl.* der Ertrag.

process (1) ['prouses], *s.* der Vorgang, Prozeß. — *v.a.* verarbeiten, fertigen.

process (2) [pro'ses], *v.n.* in einem Zuge gehen.

procession [prə'seʃən], *s.* der (feierliche) Umzug, die Prozession.

proclaim [prə'kleim], *v.a.* (*Pol.*) proklamieren, ausrufen.

proclamation [prɔklə'meiʃən], *s.* (*Pol.*) die Ausrufung, Proklamation.

proclivity [prə'kliviti], *s.* der Hang, die Neigung (*tendency*).

procrastinate [prə'kræstineit], *v.a.* aufschieben. — *v.n.* zögern, zaudern.

procreate ['proukrieit], *v.a.* zeugen, hervorbringen.

procurable [prə'kjuərəbl], *adj.* zu verschaffen, erhältlich.

procure [prə'kjuə], *v.a.* verschaffen, besorgen.

prod [prɔd], *v.a.* stoßen.

prodigal ['prɔdigəl], *adj.* verschwenderisch, vergeudend; — *son*, der verlorene Sohn.

prodigious [prə'didʒəs], *adj.* erstaunlich, ungeheuer.

prodigy ['prɔdidʒi], *s.* das Wunderkind.

produce [prə'djuːs], *v.a.* erzeugen, produzieren. — ['prɔdjuːs], *s.* das Produkt, Erzeugnis.

producer [prə'djuːsə], *s.* der Erzeuger; (*Theat., Cinema*) der Regisseur.

product ['prɔdʌkt], *s.* das Produkt, Erzeugnis.

production [prə'dʌkʃən], *s.* die Produktion; die Erzeugung (*industrial*); das Zeigen, Vorweisen (*of documents*); (*Theat.*) die Regie.

productive [prə'dʌktiv], *adj.* produktiv, schöpferisch (*mind*); fruchtbar (*soil*).

profane [prə'fein], *adj.* profan; ruchlos.

profanity [prə'fæniti], *s.* die Profanierung; das Lästern.

profess [prə'fes], *v.a., v.n.* bekennen, erklären, sich bekennen zu.

profession [prə'feʃən], *s.* der (höhere) Beruf; (*Eccl.*) das Bekenntnis; die Beteuerung (*protestation*).

professional [prə'feʃənəl], *adj.* beruflich, berufsmäßig.

professor [prə'fesə], *s.* der (Universitäts) Professor.

professorship [prə'fesəʃip], *s.* die Professur.

proffer ['prɔfə], *v.a.* anbieten (*offer*).

proficiency [prə'fiʃənsi], *s.* die Tüchtigkeit; (*skill*) die Beherrschung.

proficient [prə'fiʃənt], *adj.* bewandert, tüchtig; (*in language*) fließend.

profile ['proufail], *s.* das Profil.

profit ['prɔfit], *s.* der Profit, Gewinn, Nutzen. — *v.n.* Nutzen ziehen. — *v.a.* von Nutzen sein (*Dat.*).

profound [prə'faund], *adj.* tief; gründlich (*thorough*).

profuse [prə'fjuːs], *adj.* reichlich, verschwenderisch.

profusion [prə'fjuːʒən], *s.* der Überfluß.

progeny ['prɔdʒəni], *s.* der Nachkomme; die Nachkommenschaft.

prognosticate [prɔg'nɔstikeit], *v.a.* vorhersagen.

prognostication [prɔgnɔsti'keiʃən], *s.* die Voraussage.

programme, (*Am.*) **program** ['prougræm], *s.* das Programm.

progress ['prougres], *s.* der Fortschritt. — [pro'gres], *v.n.* fortschreiten, Fortschritte machen.

progression [pro'greʃən], *s.* (*Maths.*) die Reihe, Progression.

progressive [pro'gresiv], *adj.* fortschrittlich (*modern*); fortschreitend (*continuous*); progressiv.

prohibit [prou'hibit], *v.a.* verbieten.

prohibition [proui'biʃən], *s.* das Verbot.

project [prə'dʒekt], *v.a.* projizieren; entwerfen. — ['prɔdʒekt], *s.* das Projekt, der Plan.

projectile [prə'dʒektail], *s.* das Geschoß.

projection [prə'dʒekʃən], *s.* die Projektion (*film*); der Entwurf (*plan*); der Vorsprung (*jutting out*).

proletarian [prouli'tɛəriən], *adj.* proletarisch. — *s.* der Prolet(arier).

prolific [prə'lifik], *adj.* fruchtbar.

prolix ['prouliks], *adj.* weitschweifig.

prologue ['proulɔg], *s.* der Prolog.

prolong [prə'lɔŋ], *v.a.* verlängern, prolongieren.

prominent ['prɔminənt], *adj.* prominent, hervorragend.

promiscuous [prə'miskjuəs], *adj.* unterschiedslos (*indiscriminate*); vermischt (*mixed*).

promise ['prɔmis], *v.a.* versprechen. — *v.n.* Erwartungen erwecken. — *s.* das Versprechen.

promissory ['prɔmisəri], *adj.* versprechend; (*Comm.*) — *note*, der Schuldschein.

promontory ['prɔməntəri], *s.* das Vorgebirge.

promote [prə'mout], *v.a.* befördern; fördern (*foster*).

promotion [prə'mouʃən], *s.* die Beförderung (*advancement*); Förderung (*fostering*); (*Am.*) die Reklame (*publicity*).

prompt [prɔmpt], *adj.* prompt, pünktlich. — *v.a.* (*Theat.*) soufflieren; treiben (*inspire*).

prompter ['prɔmptə], *s.* (*Theat.*) der Souffleur.

promptitude ['prɔmptitju:d], *s.* die Promptheit, Pünktlichkeit.

promulgate ['prɔmʌlgeit], *v.a.* bekanntmachen, verbreiten.

prone [proun], *adj.* geneigt, neigend.

prong [prɔŋ], *s.* die Zinke, Gabel.

pronominal [pro'nɔminəl], *adj.* (*Gram.*) pronominal.

pronoun ['prounaun], *s.* das Fürwort, Pronomen.

pronounce [prə'nauns], *v.a.*, *v.n.* aussprechen (*words*); feierlich erklären (*proclaim*).

pronunciation [prənʌnsi'eiʃən], *s.* die Aussprache.

proof [pru:f], *s.* der Beweis, die Probe; (*Typ.*) der Korrekturbogen. — *v.a.* (*Engin.*, *Chem.*) impregnieren.

prop [prɔp], *s.* die Stütze, der Stützpfahl. — *v.a.* stützen.

propaganda [prɔpə'gændə], *s.* die Propaganda, Reklame.

propagate ['prɔpəgeit], *v.a.* propagieren; (*Bot.*) fortpflanzen.

propel [prə'pel], *v.a.* forttreiben, vorwärtstreiben.

propeller [prə'pelə], *s.* der Propeller, die Schraube.

propensity [prə'pensiti], *s.* die Neigung, der Hang.

proper ['prɔpə], *adj.* schicklich (*manners*); eigentümlich, eigen (*peculiar*).

property ['prɔpəti], *s.* das Eigentum (*possession*); die Eigenschaft (*quality*).

prophecy ['prɔfisi], *s.* die Prophezeiung, Weissagung.

prophesy ['prɔfisai], *v.a.* prophezeien.

propitiate [prə'piʃieit], *v.a.* versöhnen.

propitiation [prəpiʃi'eiʃən], *s.* die Versöhnung.

propitious [prə'piʃəs], *adj.* gnädig, günstig, geneigt.

proportion [prə'pɔ:ʃən], *s.* das Verhältnis; die Proportion; der Anteil (*portion*); das Ebenmaß (*in art*).

proportionate [prə'pɔ:ʃənit], *adj.* im Verhältnis, verhältnismäßig, proportioniert.

proposal [prə'pouzəl], *s.* der Vorschlag, Antrag.

propose [prə'pouz], *v.a.* antragen, beantragen, vorschlagen. — *v.n.* — *to a lady*, einen Heiratsantrag machen.

proposition [prɔpə'ziʃən], *s.* der Vorschlag, Antrag; die Idee.

propound [prə'paund], *v.a.* vorlegen, vorbringen (*a theory etc.*).

proprietor [prə'praiətə], *s.* der Eigentümer.

propriety [prə'praiəti], *s.* die Schicklichkeit.

propulsion [prə'pʌlʃən], *s.* der Antrieb.

prorogue [prə'roug], *v.a.* vertagen.

prosaic [prə'zeiik], *adj.* prosaisch, nüchtern.

proscribe [pro'skraib], *v.a.* verbieten, ächten.

proscription [pro'skripʃən], *s.* die Verbannung, das Verbot.

prose [prouz], *s.* die Prosa.

prosecute ['prɔsikju:t], *v.a.* verfolgen; (*Law*) gerichtlich verfolgen, anklagen.

prosecutor ['prɔsikju:tə], *s.* (*public*) der Staatsanwalt; der Kläger.

proselyte ['prɔsəlait], *s.* der Neubekehrte, Proselyt.

prospect ['prɔspekt], *s.* die Aussicht; (*pl.*) die Aussichten, Chancen, *f.pl.* — [prɔs'pekt], *v.n.* suchen (*for*, nach, *Dat.*).

prospectus [prə'spektəs], *s.* der Prospekt.

prosper ['prɔspə], *v.n.* gedeihen, blühen. — *v.a.* segnen.

prosperity [prɔs'periti], *s.* der Wohlstand; der Reichtum; das Gedeihen (*thriving*).

prosperous ['prɔspərəs], *adj.* glücklich, wohlhabend.

prostitute ['prɔstitju:t], *s.* die Prostituierte, Dirne. — *v.a.* erniedrigen.

prostrate ['prɔstreit], *adj.* hingestreckt, niedergeworfen, fußfällig. — [prɔs'treit], *v.a.* niederwerfen.

prosy

prosy ['prouzi], *adj.* prosaisch, weitschweifig, langweilig.

protect [prə'tekt], *v.a.* beschützen.

protection [prə'tekʃən], *s.* der Schutz; die Protektion (*favour*).

protective [prə'tektiv], *adj.* Schutz-, schützend.

protector [prə'tektə], *s.* der Beschützer; (*Engin.*) der Schutz.

protest [prə'test], *v.a., v.n.* protestieren, einwenden. — ['proutest], *s.* der Protest, Einspruch.

Protestant ['prɔtistənt], *adj.* protestantisch. — *s.* der Protestant.

protestation [prɔtes'teiʃən], *s.* die Beteuerung, Verwahrung.

protocol ['proutəkɔl], *s.* das Protokoll.

prototype ['proutotaip], *s.* das Urbild, Modell, der Prototyp.

protract [prə'trækt], *v.a.* in die Länge ziehen; hinausziehen.

protractor [prə'træktə], *s.* der Winkelmesser, Transporteur, die Schmiege.

protrude [prə'tru:d], *v.n.* herausragen, hervorstehen, vordringen.

protuberance [prə'tju:bərəns], *s.* der Höcker, der Auswuchs, die Protuberanz.

proud [praud], *adj.* stolz (*of*, auf, *Acc.*).

prove [pru:v], *v.a.* beweisen. — *v.n.* sich erweisen (*turn out*).

provender ['prɔvində], *s.* das Viehfutter.

proverb ['prɔvə:b], *s.* das Sprichwort.

proverbial [prə'və:biəl], *adj.* sprichwörtlich.

provide [prə'vaid], *v.a., v.n.* vorsehen, versorgen, verschaffen.

provided [prə'vaidid], *conj.* vorausgesetzt.

providence ['prɔvidəns], *s.* die Vorsehung.

provident ['prɔvidənt], *adj.* vorsorglich.

providential [prɔvi'denʃəl], *adj.* von der Vorsehung bestimmt.

province ['prɔvins], *s.* die Provinz, das Gebiet (*also fig.*).

provincial [prə'vinʃəl], *adj.* ländlich, Provinz-; provinziell.

provision [prə'viʒən], *s.* die Versorgung (*supply*); der Vorrat (*stock*); (*pl.*) die Lebensmittel (*victuals*).

provisional [prə'viʒənəl], *adj.* vorläufig.

proviso [prə'vaizou], *s.* der Vorbehalt.

provocation [prɔvə'keiʃən], *s.* die Herausforderung.

provoke [prə'vouk], *v.a.* herausfordern, provozieren.

prow [prau], *s.* (*Naut.*) der Bug.

prowess ['praues], *s.* die Stärke (*physical*); die körperliche Tüchtigkeit; Tapferkeit.

prowl [praul], *v.n.* herumstreichen.

proximity [prɔk'simiti], *s.* die Nähe.

proxy ['prɔksi], *s.* der Stellvertreter.

prudence ['pru:dəns], *s.* die Klugheit, Vorsicht.

prudent ['pru:dənt], *adj.* klug, vorsichtig.

prudery ['pru:dəri], *s.* die Sprödigkeit.

prudish ['pru:diʃ], *adj.* prüde, spröde, zimperlich.

prune (1) [pru:n], *s.* (*Cul.*) die Backpflaume.

prune (2) [pru:n], *v.a.* beschneiden, stutzen.

Prussian ['prʌʃən], *adj.* preußisch; — *blue*, das Berlinerblau. — *s.* der Preuße.

prussic ['prʌsik], *adj.* blausauer; — *acid*, die Blausäure.

pry [prai], *v.n.* spähen, ausforschen.

psalm [sɑ:m], *s.* der Psalm.

psychology [sai'kɔlədʒi], *s.* die Psychologie.

pub [pʌb], *s.* das Wirtshaus, die Kneipe.

puberty ['pju:bəti], *s.* die Pubertät, Mannbarkeit.

public ['pʌblik], *adj.* öffentlich. — *s.* das Publikum; die Öffentlichkeit.

publican ['pʌblikən], *s.* der Gastwirt.

publication [pʌbli'keiʃən], *s.* die Veröffentlichung, Herausgabe.

publicity [pʌb'lisiti], *s.* die Werbung, die Reklame; — *manager*, der Reklamechef, Werbeleiter.

publicize ['pʌblisaiz], *v.a.* weithin bekannt machen, publizieren.

publish ['pʌbliʃ], *v.a.* veröffentlichen; verlegen (*books*); — *ing house*, der Verlag.

publisher ['pʌbliʃə], *s.* der Verleger.

pucker ['pʌkə], *v.a.* falten; runzeln (*wrinkle*). — *s.* die Falte.

pudding ['pudiŋ], *s.* der Pudding.

puddle [pʌdl], *s.* die Pfütze. — *v.a.* puddeln (*iron*).

puerile ['pjuərail], *adj.* kindisch, knabenhaft.

puff [pʌf], *v.a., v.n.* puffen, paffen, blasen; —*ed-up*, aufgebläht, stolz. — *s.* der Windstoß; — *pastry*, der Blätterteig.

pug [pʌg], *s.* (*Zool.*) der Mops.

pugnacious [pʌg'neiʃəs], *adj.* kampfsüchtig, kampflustig.

puisne ['pju:ni], *adj.* (*Law*) jünger, Unter-.

puissant ['pwi:sənt], *adj.* mächtig, stark.

puke [pju:k], *v.n.* sich erbrechen.

pull [pul], *v.a., v.n.* ziehen, reißen; zerren. — *s.* der Zug, Ruck.

pullet ['pulit], *s.* (*Orn.*) das Hühnchen.

pulley ['puli], *s.* der Flaschenzug.

pulmonary, pulmonic ['pʌlmənəri, pʌl'mɔnik], *adj.* Lungen-.

pulp [pʌlp], *s.* der Brei; das Fleisch (*of fruit*); das Mark (*marrow*); die Pulpa (*tooth*). — *v.a.* zerstampfen, zu Brei stampfen.

pulpit ['pulpit], *s.* (*Eccl.*) die Kanzel.

pulsate [pʌl'seit]. *v.n.* pulsieren, schlagen.

pulse (1) [pʌls], *s.* der Puls.

pulse (2) [pʌls], *s.* (*Bot.*) die Hülsenfrüchte, *f. pl.*

pulverize ['pʌlvəraiz], *v.a.* zu Pulver stoßen, zerstoßen.

pumice ['pʌmis], *s.* der Bimsstein.
pump (1) [pʌmp], *s.* die Pumpe. — *v.a.*, *v.n.* pumpen; ausfragen (*question*).
pump (2) [pʌmp], *s.* der Tanzschuh (*dancing shoe*).
pumpkin ['pʌmpkin], *s.* (*Bot.*) der Kürbis.
pun [pʌn], *s.* das Wortspiel. — *v.n.* Wortspiele machen.
Punch [pʌntʃ]. das Kasperle; — *and Judy*, Hanswurst und seine Frau.
punch (1) [pʌntʃ], *v.a.* schlagen, boxen (*box*). — *s.* der Schlag (*hit*); der Faustschlag (*boxing*).
punch (2) [pʌntʃ], *v.a.* lochen (*card*). — *s.* der Pfriem (*tool*).
punch (3) [pʌntʃ], *s.* der Punsch (*drink*).
punchy ['pʌntʃi], *adj.* kurz, dick, untersetzt.
punctilious [pʌŋk'tiliəs], *adj.* sorgfältig, spitzfindig.
punctual ['pʌŋktjuəl], *adj.* pünktlich.
punctuate ['pʌŋktjueit], *v.a.* (*Gram.*) interpunktieren; (*fig.*) betonen.
punctuation [pʌŋktju'eiʃən], *s.* (*Gram.*) die Interpunktion.
puncture ['pʌŋktʃə], *s.* (*Motor.*) der Reifendefekt, die Panne; (*Med.*) der Punktur, der Einstich. — *v.a.* (*Med.*) punktieren.
pungent ['pʌndʒənt], *adj.* scharf, stechend.
punish ['pʌniʃ], *v.a.* bestrafen (*s.o.*); strafen.
punishable ['pʌniʃəbl], *adj.* strafbar.
punishment ['pʌniʃmənt], *s.* die Strafe, Bestrafung.
punt [pʌnt], *s.* das kleine Boot, Flachboot.
puny ['pju:ni], *adj.* schwach, winzig.
pup [pʌp], *s.* der junge Hund; *be sold a —*, einen schlechten Kauf machen. — *v.n.* Junge werfen.
pupil (1) ['pju:pil], *s.* der Schüler.
pupil (2) ['pju:pil], *s.* die Pupille (*eye*).
pupil(l)age ['pju:pilidʒ], *s.* die Minderjährigkeit (*of minor*).
puppet ['pʌpit], *s.* die Puppe, Marionette; der Strohmann (*human tool*).
puppy ['pʌpi] *see* pup.
purblind ['pə:blaind], *adj.* halbblind.
purchase ['pə:tʃis], *s.* der Kauf, Einkauf. — *v.a.* kaufen.
pure ['pjuə], *adj.* pur, rein.
purge [pə:dʒ], *v.a.* reinigen. — *s.* die Reinigung; (*Pol.*) die Säuberung.
purify ['pjuərifai], *v.a.* läutern, reinigen.
purl (1) [pə:l], *s.* die Borte; (*knitting*) die Häkelkante.
purl (2) [pə:l], *v.n.* sich drehen, wirbeln; (*sl.*) umkippen.
purl (3) [pə:l], *s.* das Murmeln, Rieseln (*of brook*). — *v.n.* murmeln, rieseln.
purloin [pə:'lɔin], *v.a.* stehlen.
purple [pə:pl], *adj.* purpurn; — *patch*, die Glanzstelle. — *s.* der Purpur.
purport [pə:'pɔ:t], *v.a.* bedeuten, Sinn haben. — ['pə:pət], *s.* der Sinn, die Bedeutung.
purpose ['pə:pəs], *s.* die Absicht, der Zweck.

purposeful ['pə:pəsful], *adj.* zweckbewußt, energisch, zielbewußt.
purr [pə:], *v.n.* schnurren (*of cat*).
purse [pə:s], *s.* die Börse, Geldtasche; das Portemonnaie.
pursuance [pə'sju:əns], *s.* (*Law*) die Verfolgung, Ausführung.
pursuant [pə'sju:ənt], *adj.* (*Law*) zufolge, gemäß (*to, Dat.*).
pursue [pə'sju:], *v.a.* verfolgen.
pursuit [pə'sju:t], *s.* die Verfolgung; (*pl.*) die Geschäfte, *n. pl.*; Beschäftigung.
purvey [pə'vei], *v.a.* versorgen, liefern.
purview ['pə:vju:], *s.* der Spielraum; das Blickfeld.
push [puʃ], *v.a.* stoßen, drücken, schieben, drängen; *be —ed for*, in der Klemme sein. — *s.* der Stoß, Schub, das Drängen; *at a —*, wenn absolut nötig.
pusillanimous [pju:si'lænimǝs], *adj.* kleinmütig.
puss, pussy [pus, 'pusi], *s.* (*coll.*) die Katze, das Kätzchen, Miezchen.
put [put], *v.a. & irr.* setzen (*set*), legen (*lay*), stellen (*stand*); — *off*, aufschieben, aus der Fassung bringen (*disconcert*); — *on*, anziehen, auflegen; — *it on thickly*, es dick auftragen. — *v.n.* (*Naut.*) — *in*, anlegen.
putrefy ['pju:trifai], *v.a., v.n.* faul werden (*rot*), verwesen.
putrid ['pju:trid], *adj.* faul (*rotten*).
puttee ['pʌti:], *s.* (*Mil.*) die Wickelgamasche.
putty ['pʌti], *s.* der Kitt.
puzzle [pʌzl], *s.* das Rätsel. — *v.a.* zu denken geben (*Dat.*).
pygmy ['pigmi], *s.* der Pygmäe.
pyjamas, (*Am.*) **pajamas** [pi'dʒɑ:məz, pǝ-], *s. pl.* der Schlafanzug.
pyramid ['pirəmid], *s.* die Pyramide.
pyre [paiə], *s.* der Scheiterhaufen.
pyrotechnics [paiǝro'tekniks], *s. pl.* das Feuerwerk, die Feuerwerkskunst.
python ['paiθən], *s.* (*Zool.*) die Riesenschlange.

Q

Q [kju:]. das Q.
qua [kwei], *conj.* als.
quack [kwæk], *v.n.* quaken; (*coll.*) quacksalbern. — *s.* der Quacksalber.
quadrangle ['kwɔdræŋgl], *s.* (*abbr.* **quad** [kwɔd]), das Viereck; der Hof (*in college etc*).
quadrant ['kwɔdrənt], *s.* der Quadrant, Viertelkreis; (*Engin.*) der Winkelmesser.
quadrille [kwɔ'dril], *s.* die Quadrille, der Kontertanz.

quadruped

quadruped ['kwɔdruped], *s.* (*Zool.*) das vierfüßige Tier.

quadruple ['kwɔdrupl], *adj.* vierfach.

quaff [kwæf], *v.a.* schlucken. — *v.n.* zechen (*drink heavily*).

quagmire ['kwægmaiə], *s.* der Sumpf.

quail (1) [kweil], *s.* (*Orn.*) die Wachtel.

quail (2) [kweil], *v.n.* verzagen.

quaint [kweint], *adj.* seltsam, wunderlich, eigenartig.

quake [kweik], *v.n.* erzittern, beben.

Quaker ['kweikə], *s.* der Quäker.

qualification [kwɔlifi'keiʃən], *s.* die Befähigung. Qualifikation (*ability*); die Einschränkung (*proviso*).

qualify ['kwɔlifai], *v.a.* befähigen (*make able*); beschränken, mäßigen, qualifizieren (*modify*). — *v.n.* sich qualifizieren, das Studium abschließen.

qualitative ['kwɔlitətiv], *adj.* qualitätsmäßig, Wert-, qualitativ.

quality ['kwɔliti], *s.* die Qualität (*high class*); der Wert (*standard*).

qualm [kwɑːm], *s.* der Skrupel.

quantitative ['kwɔntitətiv], *adj.* quantitativ.

quantity ['kwɔntiti], *s.* die Quantität, Menge.

quantum ['kwɔntəm], *s.* die Menge; das Quantum; — *theory*, die Quantentheorie.

quarantine ['kwɔrəntiːn], *s.* die Quarantäne.

quarrel ['kwɔrəl], *s.* der Streit, Zwist. — *v.n.* streiten, zanken.

quarry (1) ['kwɔri], *s.* der Steinbruch.

quarry (2) ['kwɔri], *s.* die Beute (*prey*).

quart [kwɔːt], *s.* das Viertelmaß (*1.15 litre*).

quarter ['kwɔːtə] *s.* das Viertel(jahr); (*Arith.*) das Viertel (*also of town*); (*pl.*) das Quartier.

quartermaster ['kwɔːtəmɑːstə], *s.* (*Mil.*) der Feldzeugmeister.

quartet(te) [kwɔː'tet], *s.* das Quartett.

quarto ['kwɔːtou], *s.* das Quartoformat.

quartz [kwɔːts], *s.* der Quartz.

quash [kwɔʃ], *v.a.* unterdrücken (*suppress*); (*Law*) annullieren.

quaver ['kweivə], *s.* (*Mus.*) die Achtelnote; der Triller (*trill*). — *v.n.* tremolieren, trillern.

quay [kiː], *s.* der Kai, Hafendamm.

queen [kwiːn], *s.* die Königin.

queer [kwiə], *adj.* seltsam, sonderlich.

quell [kwel], *v.a.* unterdrücken.

quench [kwentʃ], *v.a.* löschen; stillen (*thirst*).

querulous ['kweruləs], *adj.* mürrisch, jämmerlich; zänkisch.

query ['kwiəri], *s.* die Frage. — *v.a.* in Frage stellen.

quest [kwest], *s.* das Suchen, Streben; die Suche.

question ['kwestʃən], *s.* die Frage; — *mark*, das Fragezeichen. — *v.a.* fragen, in Frage stellen; ausfragen (*s.o.*).

questionable ['kwestʃənəbl], *adj.* zweifelhaft, fraglich, bedenklich.

queue [kjuː], *s.* die Schlange, das Anstellen. — *v.n.* Schlange stehen.

quibble [kwibl], *s.* das Wortspiel, die Ausflucht. — *v.n.* um Worte streiten.

quick [kwik], *adj.* schnell (*fast*); lebendig (*live*).

quicken ['kwikən], *v.a.* beleben, anfeuern.

quicklime ['kwiklaim], *s.* der ungelöschte Kalk.

quicksand ['kwiksænd], *s.* der Flugsand.

quicksilver ['kwiksilvə], *s.* (*Chem.*) das Quecksilber.

quid (1) [kwid], *s.* (*sl.*) das Pfund Sterling.

quid (2) [kwid], *s.* (*Lat.*) etwas; — *pro quo*, Gleiches mit Gleichem.

quiescence [kwi'esəns], *s.* die Ruhe.

quiet ['kwaiət], *adj.* ruhig.

quietism ['kwaiətizm], *s.* der Quietismus.

quietness ['kwaiətnis], *s.* die Ruhe, Stille.

quill [kwil], *s.* der Federkiel, die Feder. — *v.a.* falten, fälteln.

quilt [kwilt], *s.* die Steppdecke.

quince [kwins], *s.* (*Bot.*) die Quitte.

quinine [kwi'niːn], *s.* (*Med.*) das Chinin.

quinquennial [kwin'kweniəl], *adj.* fünfjährig, fünfjährlich, alle fünf Jahre.

quinsy ['kwinzi], *s.* (*Med.*) die Bräune.

quint [kwint], *s.* (*Mus.*) die Quinte.

quintessence [kwin'tesəns], *s.* die Quintessenz, der Kern, der Inbegriff.

quintuple ['kwintjupl], *adj.* fünffach.

quip [kwip], *s.* die Stichelei; die witzige Bemerkung.

quire [kwaiə], *s.* das Buch Papier.

quirk [kwəːk], *s.* die (unerwartete) Wendung; Spitzfindigkeit.

quit [kwit], *v.a.,* *v.n.* verlassen; weggehen; (*Am.*) aufhören. — *adj.* (*pl.*) (**quits**) quitt, bezahlt.

quite [kwait], *adv.* ganz, völlig.

quiver (1) ['kwivə], *s.* der Köcher.

quiver (2) ['kwivə], *v.n.* erzittern, schauern.

quiz [kwiz], *s.* das Fragespiel, Quizprogramm (*Radio etc.*).

quoit [kɔit], *s.* die Wurfscheibe.

quorum ['kwɔːrəm], *s.* die beschlußfähige Anzahl.

quota ['kwoutə], *s.* die Quote.

quotation [kwo'teiʃən], *s.* das Zitat; (*Comm.*) der Kostenanschlag, die Notierung.

quote [kwout], *v.a.* zitieren; (*Comm.*) einen Preis zitieren, notieren.

R

R [ɑː(r)]. das R.

rabbet ['ræbit], *s.* die Fuge, Nute. — *v.a.* einfugen.

rabbi ['ræbai], s. (Rel.) der Rabbiner.
rabbit ['ræbit], s. (Zool.) das Kaninchen.
rabble [ræbl], s. der Pöbel.
rabid ['ræbid], adj. wütend, rasend.
race (1) [reis], s. die Rasse; das Geschlecht (stock).
race (2) [reis], s. das Rennen (horses etc.); der Wettlauf (run); — course, die Rennbahn. — v.a., v.n. um die Wette laufen.
racial ['reiʃəl], adj. rassisch.
raciness ['reisinis], s. das Rassige, die Urwüchsigkeit.
rack [ræk], s. die Folterbank; das Reck (gymnasium); (Railw.) das Gepäcknetz. — v.a. recken, strecken; — o.'s brains, sich den Kopf zerbrechen.
racket (1), **racquet** ['rækit], s. der Tennisschläger.
racket (2) ['rækit], s. der Lärm (noise, din).
racket (3) ['rækit], s. (coll.) der Schwindel.
racketeer [ræki'tiə], s. der Schwindler.
racy ['reisi], adj. stark; pikant.
radar ['reidɑː], s. das Radar.
radiance ['reidiəns], s. der Glanz, das Strahlen.
radiant ['reidiənt], adj. strahlend.
radiate ['reidieit], v.a., v.n. strahlen, ausstrahlen.
radiator ['reidieitə], s. der Heizapparat, Heizkörper; (Motor.) der Kühler.
radical ['rædikəl], adj. (Pol.) radikal; gründlich (thorough). — s. (Pol.) der Radikale; (Phonet.) der Grundlaut, Wurzellaut.
radio ['reidiou], s. das Radio, der Rundfunk.
radioactive [reidiou'æktiv], adj. radioaktiv.
radish ['rædiʃ], s. (Bot.) der Rettich.
radius ['reidiəs], s. der Radius, Halbmesser; (Phys., Maths.) der Strahl (line).
raffle [ræfl], s. die Auslosung. — v.a. auslosen, ausspielen.
raft [rɑːft], s. das Floß.
rafter ['rɑːftə], s. der Dachsparren.
rag (1) [ræg], s. der Lumpen.
rag (2) [ræg], v.a. necken, zum Besten haben (tease).
ragamuffin ['rægəmʌfin], s. der Lumpenkerl.
rage [reidʒ], s. die Wut, Raserei; die Manie, Mode (fashion). — v.n. wüten, rasen.
ragged ['rægid], adj. zerlumpt; zackig, rauh (rough).
ragout [ra'guː], s. (Cul.) das Ragout.
raid [reid], s. der Streifzug, die Razzia; der Angriff. — v.a. überfallen.
rail (1) [reil], s. (Railw.) die Schiene; by —, mit der Eisenbahn.
rail (2) [reil], v.n. schmähen; spotten (Genit.).
railing ['reiliŋ], s. das Geländer, Gitter.
raillery ['reiləri], s. die Spöttelei, das Schmähen.

railway, (Am.) **railroad** ['reilwei, 'reilroud], s. die Eisenbahn.
raiment ['reimənt], s. (Poet.) die Kleidung.
rain [rein], s. der Regen. — v.n. regnen.
rainbow ['reinbou], s. der Regenbogen.
raincoat ['reinkout], s. der Regenmantel.
raise [reiz], v.a. heben (lift); steigern (prices); aufbringen (army, money); züchten (breed); aufziehen (children). — s. (Am.) die Steigerung, Erhöhung (salary).
raisin ['reizin], s. (Bot.) die Rosine.
rake (1) [reik], s. der Rechen (tool). — v.a. zusammenrechen, harken; bestreichen (fire at).
rake (2) [reik], s. der Schlemmer (roué).
rakish ['reikiʃ], adj. liederlich.
rally ['ræli], v.a. sammeln, versammeln; v.n. sich versammeln, sich scharen. — s. die Massenversammlung, Kundgebung; das Treffen.
ram [ræm], s. der Widder; (Mil.) die Ramme. — v.a. rammen.
ramble [ræmbl], v.n. (im Grünen) wandern; herumschweifen; einen Ausflug machen. — s. der Ausflug.
rambler ['ræmblə], s. der Wanderer (hiker); (Bot.) die Heckenrose.
ramification [ræmifi'keiʃən], s. die Verzweigung, Verästelung (also fig.); (pl.) Zweige, m. pl. (also fig.).
ramp [ræmp], v.n. sich ranken (of plants). — s. die Rampe.
rampant ['ræmpənt], adj. zügellos, grassierend (wild); (Her.) sich bäumend.
rampart ['ræmpɑːt], s. der Wall.
ramshackle ['ræmʃækl], adj. wackelig, baufällig.
rancid ['rænsid], adj. ranzig.
rancour ['ræŋkə], s. der Groll, die Erbitterung.
random ['rændəm], s. at —, aufs Geratewohl. — adj. zufällig, Zufalls-.
range [reindʒ], s. die Reihe (row, series); (Geog.) die Bergkette; der Küchenherd (stove); (Mil.) die Schießstätte (shooting ground); die Schußweite, Reichweite (distance). — v.n. sich reihen; sich erstrecken (stretch). — v.a. rangieren, anordnen, durchstreifen.
rangefinder ['reindʒfaində], s. (Phot.) der Entfernungsmesser.
ranger ['reindʒə], s. der Förster, Forstgehilfe; (Mil.) der leichte Reiter.
rank (1) [ræŋk], s. die Klasse; der Rang (order); — and file, die Mannschaft (of members); die Mitgliedschaft, Masse. — v.n. sich reihen; gelten.
rank (2) [ræŋk], adj. übermäßig, üppig, allzu stark; ranzig (of fat etc.).
rankle [ræŋkl], v.n. nagen.
ransack ['rænsæk], v.a. plündern.
ransom ['rænsəm], s. das Lösegeld; hold to —, (gegen Lösegeld) gefangen halten. — v.a. loskaufen.

rant [rænt], *v.n.* wüten; großtun; groß-
sprechen.
rap [ræp], *v.a., v.n.* schlagen, klopfen.
rapacious [rə'peiʃəs], *adj.* raubgierig.
rape (1) [reip], *v.a.* vergewaltigen. — *s.*
die Vergewaltigung.
rape (2) [reip], *s.* (*Bot.*) der Raps.
rapid ['ræpid], *adj.* rasch, schnell,
reißend (*river*). — *s.* (*pl.*) die Stromschnelle.
rapier ['reipiə], *s.* der Degen; (*fencing*)
das Rapier.
rapine ['ræpain], *s.* (*Poet.*) der Raub.
rapt [ræpt], *adj.* entzückt; versunken.
rapture ['ræptʃə], *s.* das Entzücken.
rare (1) [rɛə], *adj.* selten.
rare (2) [rɛə], *adj.* (*meat*) rar.
rarity ['rɛəriti], *s.* die Seltenheit.
rascal ['rɑ:skəl], *s.* der Schurke.
rash (1) [ræʃ], *adj.* unbesonnen.
rash (2) [ræʃ], *s.* der Ausschlag (*skin*).
rasher ['ræʃə], *s.* die Speckschnitte.
rasp [rɑ:sp], *s.* die Raspel, Feile. —
v.a., v.n. raspeln; heiser sein (*speech*).
raspberry ['rɑ:zbəri], *s.* (*Bot.*) die
Himbeere.
rat [ræt], *s.* (*Zool.*) die Ratte; (*fig.*) der
Verräter.
ratable ['reitəbl], *adj.* steuerpflichtig.
rate (1) [reit], *s.* die Mass; der Tarif;
die Geschwindigkeit (*speed*); Gemein-
deabgabe (*tax*); das Verhältnis (*proportion*). — *v.a.* schätzen (*estimate*);
(*Am.*) einschätzen, halten für.
rate (2) [reit], *v.a.* schelten (*berate*).
rather ['rɑ:ðə], *adv.* vielmehr, eher,
lieber (*in comparisons*); — *good*, ziemlich gut.
ratification [rætifi'keiʃən], *s.* die Bestätigung; (*Pol.*) die Ratifizierung.
ratify ['rætifai], *v.a.* bestätigen; (*Pol.*)
ratifizieren.
ratio ['reiʃiou], *s.* das Verhältnis.
ration ['ræʃən], *s.* die Ration.
rational ['ræʃənəl], *adj.* Vernunfts-,
rationell, vernunftgemäß.
rattle [rætl], *s.* das Geklapper (*noise*);
die Klapper (*toy etc.*); *death* —, das
Todesröcheln. — *v.a.* klappern,
Lärm machen; (*fig.*) aus der Fassung
bringen; — *off*, herunterleiern. —
v.n. rasseln, klappern.
raucous ['rɔ:kəs], *adj.* heiser, rauh.
ravage ['rævidʒ], *v.a.* verheeren. — *s.*
(*pl.*) die Verheerung, Verwüstung.
rave [reiv], *v.n.* vernarrt sein (*about*, in);
schwärmen (*für*).
raven [reivn], *s.* (*Orn.*) der Rabe.
ravenous ['rævənəs], *adj.* gefräßig,
gierig.
ravine [rə'vi:n], *s.* die Schlucht.
ravish ['ræviʃ], *v.a.* schänden, entehren; (*delight*) entzücken.
raw [rɔ:], *adj.* rauh (*rough*); roh (*meat*);
jung, grün (*novice*); *a* — *deal*, die
unfaire Behandlung.
ray (1) [rei], *s.* (*Phys.*) der Strahl. —
v.n. strahlen.
ray (2) [rei], *s.* (*Zool.*) der Rochen.
raze [reiz], *v.a.* radieren (*erase*); zer-

stören (*destroy*).
razor ['reizə], *s.* der Rasierapparat;
— *strop*, der Streichriemen.
re* [ri:], *pref.* wieder —, noch einmal,
zurück-.

* In the following pages, only those
compounds are listed in which the
meaning is different from the root
word or where no simple stem exists.

reach [ri:tʃ], *v.a.* reichen, erlangen
(*attain*); reichen (*hand*); erreichen.
— *s.* der Bereich, (*fig.*) die Weite.
react [ri'ækt], *v.n.* reagieren (*to*, auf,
Acc.).
read (1) [ri:d], *v.a., v.n.* irr. lesen; anzeigen (*meter etc.*); — *for a degree*,
studieren.
read (2) [red], *adj. well—*, belesen.
readable ['ri:dəbl], *adj.* gut zu lesen,
lesenswert; leserlich (*legible*).
reader ['ri:də], *s.* der Leser; (*Univ.*)
der außerordentliche Professor; (*fig.*)
das Lesebuch.
readiness ['redinis], *s.* die Bereitschaft,
Bereitwilligkeit.
ready ['redi], *adj.* bereit, fertig; prompt;
— *money*, das Bargeld.
real [riəl], *adj.* wirklich, wahr, tatsächlich; echt; — *estate*, der Grundbesitz.
realistic [riə'listik], *adj.* realistisch.
reality [ri'æliti], *s.* die Wirklichkeit.
realize ['riəlaiz], *v.a.* (*understand*) begreifen; (*sell*) veräußern; verwirklichen.
realm [relm], *s.* das Reich.
reap [ri:p], *v.a.* ernten.
rear (1) [riə], *adj.* hinter, nach-. — *s.*
der Hintergrund; (*Mil.*) die Nachhut.
rear (2) [riə], *v.a.* aufziehen, erziehen
(*bring up*). — *v.n.* sich bäumen.
reason ['ri:zən], *s.* die Ursache, der
Grund (*cause*); die Vernunft (*reasonableness*). — *v.n.* argumentieren,
debattieren.
reasonable ['ri:zənəbl], *adj.* vernünftig;
verständig.
reasonably ['ri:zənəbli], *adv.* ziemlich,
verhältnismäßig.
rebate ['ri:beit], *s.* der Rabatt.
rebel [rebl], *s.* der Rebell. — [ri'bel],
v.n. sich empören.
rebound [ri'baund], *v.n.* zurückprallen.
—['ri:baund], *s.* der Rückprall.
rebuff [ri'bʌf], *s.* die Abweisung. —
v.a. abweisen, zurückweisen.
rebuke [ri'bju:k], *v.a.* zurechtweisen,
tadeln. — *s.* der Tadel, die Kritik (an).
rebut [ri'bʌt], *v.a.* zurückweisen.
rebuttal [ri'bʌtl], *s.* die Widerlegung.
recalcitrant [ri'kælsitrənt], *adj.* widerspenstig, störrisch.
recall [ri'kɔ:l], *v.a.* zurückrufen; (*remember*) sich erinnern.
recant [ri'kænt], *v.a., v.n.* widerrufen.
recapitulate [ri:kə'pitjuleit], *v.a.* re-
kapitulieren, wiederholen.
recast [ri:'kɑ:st], *v.a.* neu fassen, umarbeiten.
recede [ri'si:d], *v.n.* zurückgehen;
heruntergehen (*prices etc.*).

receipt [ri'si:t], *s.* die Empfangsbestätigung, Quittung. — *v.a.* quittieren.
receive [ri'si:v], *v.a.* erhalten, empfangen; (*Law*) Diebesgut annehmen.
receiver [ri'si:və], *s.* der Empfänger; (*Law*) der Hehler; (*Telephone*) der Hörer; (*Rad.*) der Apparat.
recent ['ri:sənt], *adj.* jüngst, neuest.
recently ['ri:səntli], *adv.* vor kurzem.
reception [ri'sepʃən], *s.* der Empfang.
receptive [ri'septiv], *adj.* empfänglich.
recess [ri'ses], *s.* (*Parl.*) die Ferien, *pl.*; die Pause; die Nische (*nook*).
recession [ri'seʃən], *s.* (*Econ.*) die Rezession, die Baisse.
recipe ['resipi], *s.* (*Cul.*) das Rezept.
recipient [ri'sipiənt], *s.* der Empfänger (*of donation etc.*).
reciprocal [ri'siprəkəl], *adj.* gegenseitig, wechselseitig.
reciprocate [ri'siprəkeit], *v.a.*, *v.n.* erwidern, vergelten.
recital [ri'saitl], *s.* der Vortrag; (*Mus.*) das Solokonzert, Kammerkonzert.
recite [ri'sait], *v.a.* vortragen; (*story*) erzählen, aufsagen.
reckless ['reklis], *adj.* leichtsinnig.
reckon ['rekən], *v.n.* rechnen (*on*, mit, *Dat.*); dafür halten, denken (*think*).
reclamation [reklə'meiʃən], *s.* (*Agr.*) die Urbarmachung; (*fig.*) die Beschwerde, Reklamation.
recline [ri'klain], *v.n.* sich zurücklehnen.
recluse [ri'klu:s], *s.* der Einsiedler.
recognition [rekəg'niʃən], *s.* die Anerkennung.
recognize ['rekəgnaiz], *v.a.* anerkennen (als) (*acknowledge*); erkennen (*know again*).
recoil [ri'kɔil], *v.n.* zurückprallen, zurückfahren.
recollect [rekə'lekt], *v.a.* sich erinnern (an, *Acc.*).
recollection [rekə'lekʃən], *s.* die Erinnerung, das Gedächtnis.
recommend [rekə'mend], *v.a.* empfehlen.
recompense ['rekəmpens], *v.a.* vergelten, entschädigen, belohnen.
reconcile ['rekənsail], *v.a.* versöhnen.
reconciliation [rekənsili'eiʃən], *s.* die Versöhnung.
recondite ['rekəndait], *adj.* dunkel, verborgen, wenig bekannt.
reconnoitre [rekə'nɔitə], *v.a.* auskundschaften.
record [ri'kɔ:d], *v.a.* notieren, eintragen (*enter*), festhalten; aufnehmen (*tape etc.*). — ['rekɔ:d], *s.* die Aufzeichnung (*in writing*); die Schallplatte (*gramophone*); (*Sports*) der Rekord.
recorder [ri'kɔ:də], *s.* der Protokollführer; (*Law*) der Richter; Syndikus, Registrator; (*Mus.*) die Blockflöte.
recount [ri'kaunt], *v.a.* erzählen.
recourse [ri'kɔ:s], *s.* die Zuflucht.
recover [ri'kʌvə], *v.a.* wiedererlangen. — *v.n.* sich erholen.

recovery [ri'kʌvəri], *s.* die Wiedererlangung (*regaining*); (*Med.*) die Genesung, Erholung.
recreation [rekri'eiʃən], *s.* die Erholung.
recrimination [rekrimi'neiʃən], *s.* die Gegenklage.
recruit [ri'kru:t], *v.a.* rekrutieren, anwerben. — *s.* der Rekrut.
rectangle ['rektæŋgl], *s.* das Rechteck.
rectify ['rektifai], *v.a.* richtigstellen; (*Elec.*) gleichrichten, umformen.
rectilinear [rekti'liniə], *adj.* geradlinig.
rectitude ['rektitju:d], *s.* die Aufrichtigkeit.
rector ['rektə], *s.* (*Eccl.*) der Pfarrer; der Rektor, Vorstand (*institution*).
recuperate [ri'kju:pəreit], *v.n.* sich erholen.
recur [ri'kə:], *v.n.* sich wieder ereignen, sich wiederholen.
recurrence [ri'kʌrəns], *s.* die Wiederholung.
red [red], *adj.* rot; — *hot*, glühend heiß.
redbreast ['redbrest], *s.* (*Orn.*) das Rotkehlchen.
redeem [ri'di:m], *v.a.* erlösen.
redemption [ri'dempʃən], *s.* die Erlösung.
redolent ['redolənt], *adj.* duftend.
redound [ri'daund], *v.n.* gereichen, sich erweisen.
redress [ri'dres], *v.a.* abhelfen (*Dat.*); wieder herstellen. — *s.* die Abhilfe.
reduce [ri'dju:s], *v.a.* vermindern, herabsetzen; (*fig.*) degradieren. — *v.n.* (*weight*) abnehmen.
reduction [ri'dʌkʃən], *s.* die Herabsetzung (*price etc.*); die Verminderung (*decrease*); (*Chem.*) die Reduktion.
redundant [ri'dʌndənt], *adj.* überflüssig.
reduplicate [ri:'dju:plikeit], *v.a.* verdoppeln.
reed [ri:d], *s.* (*Bot.*) das Schilfrohr; (*Mus.*) die Rohrpfeife.
reef [ri:f], *s.* das Riff, Felsenriff; (*Naut.*) das Reff.
reek [ri:k], *v.n.* rauchen, dampfen, riechen. — *s.* der Rauch, Dampf, der Gestank.
reel [ri:l], *s.* die Spule, Rolle, Haspel. — *v.a.* — *off*, abrollen; (*fig.*) mechanisch hersagen. — *v.n.* taumeln.
refectory [ri'fektəri], *s.* der Speisesaal; das Refektorium (*in monastery etc.*).
refer [ri'fə:], *v.n.* — *to s.th.*, weiterleiten; überweisen; — *to*, sich beziehen (auf, *Acc.*).
referee [refə'ri:], *s.* der Referent; (*Sport*) der Schiedsrichter.
reference ['refərəns], *s. with — to,* in or mit Bezug auf; die Referenz, Empfehlung; Verweisung (*to*, auf); — *library*, die Nachschlagebibliothek; — *index*, das (Nachschlags)verzeichnis.
refine [ri'fain], *v.a.* (*Chem.*) raffinieren; (*manners*) verfeinern; (*products*) läutern, veredeln.

reflect

reflect [ri'flɛkt], *v.a.* widerspiegeln (*mirror*); ein Licht werfen (auf, *Acc.*). — *v.n.* — *on*, überlegen (*think over*).

reflection, reflexion [ri'flɛkʃən], *s.* die Überlegung, das Nachdenken; die Spiegelung, Reflexion.

reform [ri:'fɔːm], *s.* die Reform, Verbesserung. — *v.a.* reformieren; ['ri:'fɔːm] (sich) neu bilden. — *v.n.* sich bessern.

refractory [ri'fræktəri], *adj.* widerspenstig.

refrain (1) [ri'frein], *v.n.* — *from*, sich enthalten (*Genit.*); absehen von (*Dat.*).

refrain (2) [ri'frein], *s.* (*Mus., Poet.*) der Kehrreim.

refresh [ri'freʃ], *v.a.* erfrischen.

refrigerator [ri'fridʒəreitə], *s.* der Kühlschrank.

refuge ['refjuːdʒ], *s.* die Zuflucht.

refugee [refjuːdʒiː], *s.* der Flüchtling. — *adj.* Flüchtlings-.

refund [ri:'fʌnd], *v.a.* ersetzen, zurückzahlen. — ['ri:fʌnd], *s.* die Rückvergütung.

refusal [ri'fjuːzəl], *s.* die Verweigerung.

refuse [ri'fjuːz], *v.a.* verweigern, abschlagen. — *v.n.* — *to*, sich weigern. — ['refjuːs], *s.* der Müll.

refute [ri'fjuːt], *v.a.* widerlegen.

regal ['riːgəl], *adj.* königlich.

regale [ri'geil], *v.a.* bewirten.

regalia [ri'geiliə], *s. pl.* die Kronjuwelen, *n. pl.*; (*fig.*) die Amtstracht, der Amtsschmuck.

regard [ri'gɑːd], *v.a.* ansehen (*as*, als); beachten (*heed*); *as* —*s*, was ... betrifft. — *s.* die Hochachtung, Achtung (*esteem*);(*pl.*)die Grüsse,*m.pl.*

regarding [ri'gɑːdiŋ], *prep.* bezüglich, mit Bezug auf.

regardless [ri'gɑːdlis], *adj.* rücksichtslos, ohne Rücksicht auf.

regency ['riːdʒənsi], *s.* die Regentschaft.

regent ['riːdʒənt], *s.* der Regent.

regiment ['redʒimənt], *s.* (*Mil.*) das Regiment. — [-ment], *v.a.* (*fig.*) regimentieren.

region ['riːdʒən], *s.* die Gegend.

regional ['riːdʒənəl], *adj.* örtlich, lokal, Bezirks-.

register ['redʒistə], *s.* das Register, die Liste. — *v.n.* sich eintragen.

registrar ['redʒistrɑː], *s.* der Registrator; der Standesbeamte (*births etc.*); der Kanzleidirektor (*institution*).

registry ['redʒistri], *s.* die Registratur.

regret [ri'gret], *v.a.* bereuen, bedauern. — *s.* die Reue; das Bedauern (*in formal apology*); *with* —, mit Bedauern.

regular ['regjulə], *adj.* regelmäßig; (*Am.*) anständig. — *s.* (*Mil.*) der Berufssoldat.

regulate ['regjuleit], *v.a.* regulieren, regeln.

regulation [regju'leiʃən], *s.* die Regelung; die Anordung (*order*).

rehabilitate [ri:hə'biliteit], *v.a.* rehabilitieren.

rehearsal [ri'həːsl], *s.* (*Theat., Mus.*) die Probe.

rehearse [ri'həːs], *v.a.* proben, wiederholen.

reign [rein], *v.n.* herrschen, regieren. — *s.* die Herrschaft, Regierung.

rein [rein], *s.* der Zügel, der Zaum.

reindeer ['reindiə], *s.* (*Zool.*) das Ren, Rentier.

reinforce [ri:in'fɔːs], *v.a.* betonen, verstärken.

reinforced [ri:in'fɔːsd], *adj.* verstärkt; — *concrete*, der Eisenbeton.

reject [ri'dʒekt], *v.a.* ausschlagen, verwerfen.

rejection [ri'dʒekʃən], *s.* die Ablehnung, Verwerfung.

rejoice [ri'dʒɔis], *v.n.* sich freuen.

rejoin [ri:'dʒɔin],*v.a.* wiedervereinigen. — [ri'dʒɔin], *v.n.* erwidern.

rejoinder [ri'dʒɔində], *s.* die Erwiderung.

relapse [ri'læps], *s.* der Rückfall. — *v.n.* fallen, zurückfallen.

relation [ri'leiʃən], *s.* die Beziehung (*connexion*); der, die Verwandte (*relative*); (*pl.*) die Verwandtschaft (*family*).

relative ['relətiv], *adj.* relativ; verhältnismäßig (*in proportion*). — *s.* der, die Verwandte.

relax [ri'læks], *v.n.* sich ausruhen; nachlassen. — *v.a.* entspannen.

relay [ri'lei], *v.a.* (*Rad.*) übertragen. — ['riːlei], *s.* — *race*, der Staffellauf.

release [ri'liːs], *v.a.* freilassen, freisetzen (*prisoner*); freigeben (*news*). — *s.* die Freigabe (*news etc.*); die Freisetzung (*liberation*).

relegate ['religeit], *v.a.* verweisen, zurückweisen.

relent [ri'lent], *v.n.* nachgeben.

relentless [ri'lentlis], *adj.* unerbittlich, unnachgiebig.

relevance ['reləvəns], *s.* die Wichtigkeit.

relevant ['reləvənt], *adj.* wichtig, sachdienlich.

reliable [ri'laiəbl], *adj.* verläßlich, zuverlässig.

reliance [ri'laiəns], *s.* das Vertrauen.

relic ['relik], *s.* das Überbleibsel; das Andenken; (*Eccl.*) die Reliquie.

relief (1) [ri'liːf], *s.* die Erleichterung, Linderung, (*easement*); die Ablösung (*guard etc.*); die Aushilfe (*extra staff etc.*).

relief (2) [ri'liːf], *s.* (*Art*) das Relief.

relieve [ri'liːv], *v.a.* erleichtern; lindern (*pain*); ablösen (*from duty*).

religion [ri'lidʒən], *s.* die Religion.

religious [ri'lidʒəs], *adj.* religiös, gläubig, fromm.

relinquish [ri'liŋkwiʃ], *v.a.* verlassen, aufgeben.

relish [′reliʃ], *v.a.* Geschmack finden an. — *v.n.* schmecken. — *s.* der Geschmack, die Würze.

reluctance [ri′lʌktəns], *s.* der Widerwille, das Zögern.

reluctant [ri′lʌktənt], *adj.* widerwillig, widerstrebend. — *v.a.* abhelfen (*Dat.*).

rely [ri′lai], *v.n.* sich verlassen (*on, auf*); vertrauen (*auf*).

remain [ri′mein], *v.n.* bleiben, zurückbleiben, übrigbleiben.

remainder [ri′meində], *s.* der Rest.

remand [ri′mɑ:nd], *v.a.* — *in custody,* in die Untersuchungshaft zurückschicken. — *s.* — *home,* die Besserungsanstalt.

remark [ri′mɑ:k], *s.* die Bemerkung. — *v.a.* bemerken.

remarkable [ri′mɑ:kəbl], *adj.* bemerkenswert, außerordentlich.

remedial [rə′mi:diəl], *adj.* Heil-, abhelfend.

remedy [′remədi], *s.* das Heilmittel, Hilfsmittel. — *v.a.* abhelfen (*Dat.*).

remember [ri′membə], *v.a.* sich erinnern an; — *s.o. to s.o. else,* jemanden von jemandem grüßen lassen.

remembrance [ri′membrəns], *s.* die Erinnerung.

remind [ri′maind], *v.a.* erinnern (*of, an*), mahnen.

reminiscence [remi′nisəns], *s.* die Erinnerung.

remiss [ri′mis], *adj.* nachlässig.

remission [ri′miʃən], *s.* der Nachlaß; (*Rel.*) die Vergebung (*of sins*).

remit [ri′mit], *v.a.* (*Comm.*) überweisen, einsenden; erlassen (*forgive*).

remittance [ri′mitəns], *s.* (*Comm.*) die Rimesse, die Überweisung.

remnant [′remnənt], *s.* der Überrest.

remonstrate [′remənstreit], *v.n.* Vorstellungen machen.

remorse [ri′mɔ:s], *s.* die Reue.

remote [ri′mout], *adj.* fern, entlegen.

removal [ri′mu:vəl], *s.* das Wegschaffen (*taking away*); die Übersiedlung, der Umzug.

remove [ri′mu:v], *v.a.* entfernen. — *v.n.* umziehen. — *s.* (*Sch.*) die Versetzungsklasse; der Verwandtschaftsgrad (*relationship*).

removed [ri′mu:vd], *adj.* entfernt; *cousin once* —, der Vetter ersten Grades.

remuneration [rimju:nə′reiʃən], *s.* die Besoldung, Entlöhnung.

rend [rend], *v.a.* reißen, zerreißen.

render [′rendə], *v.a.* leisten (*service*); übersetzen (*translate*); wiedergeben; (*Comm.*) — *account,* Rechnung vorlegen.

rendering [′rendəriŋ], *s.* die Wiedergabe, der Vortrag (*of song etc.*); (*Comm.*) die Vorlage; die Übersetzung (*translation*).

renegade [′renigeid], *s.* der Abtrünnige.

renewal [ri′nju:əl], *s.* die Erneuerung; die Verlängerung (*extension*).

rennet [′renit], *s.* das Lab.

renounce [ri′nauns], *v.a.* entsagen (*Dat.*), verzichten auf (*Acc.*).

renown [ri′naun], *s.* der Ruhm.

rent (1) [rent], *v.a.* mieten, pachten. — *s.* die Miete, Pacht (*of land, farm*).

rent (2) [rent], *s.* der Riß (*tear*).

rental [rentl], *s.* die Miete.

renunciation [rinʌnsi′eiʃən], *s.* die Entsagung, der Verzicht.

repair [ri′pɛə], *v.a.* ausbessern, reparieren. — *s.* die Reparatur; *beyond* —, nicht reparierbar.

reparations [repə′reiʃənz], *s. pl.* (*Pol.*) die Reparationen, Wiedergutmachungskosten, *f. pl.*

repartee [repɑː′tiː], *s.* die treffende Antwort.

repast [ri′pɑːst], *s.* die Mahlzeit.

repeal [ri′piːl], *v.a.* (*Parl.*) aufheben, widerrufen. — *s.* die Aufhebung.

repeat [ri′piːt], *v.a.* wiederholen.

repent [ri′pent], *v.a.* bereuen.

repercussion [ri:pə′kʌʃən], *s.* der Rückstoß, die Rückwirkung.

repertory [′repətəri], *s.* (*Theat. etc.*) das Repertoire, der Spielplan.

repetition [repi′tiʃən], *s.* die Wiederholung.

replace [ri:′pleis], *v.a.* ersetzen.

replete [ri′pliːt], *adj.* voll, angefüllt.

reply [ri′plai], *v.n.* antworten, erwidern. — *s.* die Antwort.

report [ri′pɔːt], *v.a., v.n.* berichten. — *s.* der Bericht; (*Sch.*) das Zeugnis; der Knall (*of explosion*).

repose [ri′pouz], *v.n.* ruhen. — *v.a.* setzen (*in, auf*). — *s.* die Ruhe, der Friede.

repository [ri′pɔzitəri], *s.* die Niederlage, Aufbewahrungsstätte, Fundstätte.

reprehensible [repri′hensibl], *adj.* tadelnswert.

represent [repri′zent], *v.a.* repräsentieren, vertreten.

representative [repri′zentətiv], *adj.* repräsentativ, typisch. — *s.* der Stellvertreter; (*Pol.*) der Repräsentant.

repress [ri′pres], *v.a.* unterdrücken.

reprieve [ri′priːv], *v.a.* begnadigen. — *s.* die Gnadenfrist.

reprimand [repri′mɑːnd], *v.a.* verweisen, tadeln. — *s.* der Tadel.

reprint [ri:′print], *v.a.* neu drucken. — [′ri:print], *s.* der Neudruck.

reprisal [ri′praizəl], *s.* die Vergeltungsmaßregel; (*pl.*) die Repressalien, *f. pl.*

reproach [ri′proutʃ], *v.a.* vorwerfen (*Dat.*), tadeln. — *s.* der Vorwurf, Tadel.

reprobate [′reprəbeit], *adj.* ruchlos, verworfen.

reproduce [ri:prə′djuːs], *v.a.* reproduzieren, erzeugen.

reproof [ri′pruːf], *s.* der Vorwurf, Tadel.

reprove [ri′pruːv], *v.a.* tadeln, rügen (*a person*), mißbilligen (*a practice*).

republic

republic [ri'pʌblik], *s.* die Republik.

repudiate [ri'pju:dieit], *v.a.* zurückweisen, verwerfen.

repugnant [ri'pʌgnənt], *adj.* widerwärtig, ekelhaft.

repulse [ri'pʌls], *v.a.* (*Mil.*) zurückschlagen; abweisen (*s.o.*). — *s.* (*Mil.*) das Zurückschlagen; (*fig.*) die Zurückweisung.

repulsive [ri'pʌlsiv], *adj.* widerwärtig.

reputation [repju'teiʃən], *s.* der (gute) Ruf.

request [ri'kwest], *v.a.* ersuchen. — *s.* das Ersuchen, Ansuchen, die Bitte.

requiem ['rekwiəm], *s.* (*Eccl.*) das Requiem, die Totenmesse.

require [ri'kwaiə], *v.a.* fordern, verlangen, brauchen.

requirement [ri'kwaiəmənt], *s.* die Anforderung, das Erfordernis.

requisite ['rekwizit], *adj.* erforderlich.

requisition [rekwi'ziʃən], *s.* (*Mil.*) die Requisition; die Forderung.

requite [ri'kwait], *v.a.* vergelten.

rescind [ri'sind], *v.a.* für ungültig erklären, aufheben.

rescue ['reskju:], *v.a.* retten. — *s.* die Rettung.

research [ri'sə:tʃ], *v.n.* forschen, Forschung treiben. — *s.* die Forschung.

resemble [ri'zembl], *v.a.* ähnlich sein (*Dat.*), gleichen (*Dat.*).

resent [ri'zent], *v.a.* übelnehmen.

resentful [ri'zentful], *adj.* nachträgerisch; empfindlich (*over-sensitive*).

resentment [ri'zentmənt], *s.* die Empfindlichkeit; der Groll (*spite*).

reservation [rezə'veiʃən], *s.* die Reservierung (*of seat*); der Vorbehalt (*doubt*).

reserve [ri'zə:v], *v.a.* reservieren, belegen (*seat*); (*fig.*) vorbehalten (*o.'s position*). — *s.* die Reserve, die Verschlossenheit (*shyness*); die Einschränkung (*limitation*); die Reserven, *f. pl.* (*money*).

reside [ri'zaid], *v.n.* wohnen.

resident ['rezidənt], *adj.* wohnhaft. — *s.* der Ansässige.

residual [ri'zidjuəl], *adj.* übrig bleibend.

residue ['rezidju:], *s.* der Rückstand, Rest.

resign [ri'zain], *v.a.* abtreten, aufgeben; (ein Amt) niederlegen. — *v.n.* abdanken. — *v.r.* — *o.s.* *to,* sich in etwas fügen, zurücktreten.

resignation [rezig'neiʃən], *s.* die Resignation, der Rücktritt (*from office*); die Fügung, Resignation (*attitude*).

resin ['rezin], *s.* das Harz.

resist [ri'zist], *v.a., v.n.* widerstehen, Widerstand leisten (*Dat.*).

resistance [ri'zistəns], *s.* der Widerstand.

resolute ['rezəlju:t], *adj.* entschlossen.

resolution [rezə'lju:ʃən], *s.* die Entschlossenheit (*determination*); die Entscheidung (*decision*); der Vorsatz, Entschluß (*vow*).

resolve [ri'zɔlv], *v.a.* auflösen (*solve*); beschließen (*conclude*). — *v.n.* entscheiden (*decide*). — *s.* der Beschluß, die Entscheidung.

resonance ['rezənəns], *s.* die Resonanz.

resort [ri'zɔ:t], *v.n.* — *to,* seine Zuflucht nehmen (zu). — *s. seaside* —, das Seebad, *health* —, der Kurort (*spa*).

resound [ri'zaund], *v.n.* widerhallen.

resource [ri'zɔ:s], *s.* das Hilfsmittel; (*pl.*) die Mittel, *n. pl.*

respect [ri'spekt], *v.a.* respektieren, achten; berücksichtigen (*have regard to*). — *s.* der Respekt, die Achtung; *with* — *to,* mit Bezug auf; *in* — *of,* bezüglich (*Genit.*).

respectability [rispektə'biliti], *s.* die Anständigkeit; Achtbarkeit.

respective [ris'pektiv], *adj.* respektiv.

respectively [ris'pektivli], *adv.* beziehungsweise.

respiration [respi'reiʃən], *s.* die Atmung.

respiratory [ris'paiərətri *or* 'respireitəri], *adj.* Atmungs-.

respire [ris'paiə], *v.n.* atmen.

respite ['respit], *s.* die Frist, der Aufschub.

resplendent [ri'splendənt], *adj.* glänzend.

respond [ri'spɔnd], *v.n.* antworten, eingehen (*to, auf*).

respondent [ri'spɔndənt], *s.* (*Law*) der Beklagte.

response [ri'spɔns], *s.* die Antwort, Aufnahme, Reaktion; (*fig.*) der Widerhall.

responsibility [rispɔnsi'biliti], *s.* die Verantwortung, Verantwortlichkeit.

responsible [ri'spɔnsibl], *adj.* verantwortlich.

responsive [ri'spɔnsiv], *adj.* empfänglich, zugänglich.

rest (1) [rest], *v.n.* ruhen, rasten. — *s.* die Ruhe, Rast; (*Mus.*) die Pause.

rest (2) [rest], *v.n.* bleiben (*stay*); — *assured,* sei (seien Sie) versichert. — *s.* der Rest; die übrigen, *pl.*

restaurant ['restərɑ̃], *s.* das Restaurant.

restful ['restful], *adj.* ruhig.

restitution [resti'tju:ʃən], *s.* die Wiedergutmachung.

restive ['restiv], *adj.* unruhig, ruhelos.

restless ['restlis], *adj.* rastlos, unruhig.

restoration [restɔ:'reiʃən], *s.* die Wiederherstellung; (*Hist.*) die Restauration.

restore [ri'stɔ:], *v.a.* wiederherstellen.

restrain [ri'strein], *v.a.* zurückhalten, einschränken.

restraint [ri'streint], *s.* die Zurückhaltung.

restrict [ri'strikt], *v.a.* beschränken.

restriction [ri'strikʃən], *s.* die Einschränkung.

restrictive [ri'striktiv], *adj.* einschränkend.

result [ri'zʌlt], *v.n.* folgen, sich ergeben; (*come about*) erfolgen. — *s.* das Ergebnis, Resultat; (*consequence*) die Folge.

resume [ri'zju:m], *v.a.* wiederaufnehmen; (*narrative*) fortsetzen. — *v.n.* fortfahren.

résumé ['rezjumei], *s.* das Resümee, die Zusammenfassung.

resumption [ri'zʌmpʃən], *s.* die Wiederaufnahme.

resurrection [rezə'rekʃən], *s.* (*Rel.*) die Auferstehung.

resuscitate [ri'sʌsiteit], *v.a.* wiederbeleben.

retail ['ri:teil], *s.* der Kleinhandel, Einzelhandel. — [ri'teil], *v.a.* im Detail handeln, verkaufen.

retain [ri'tein], *v.a.* behalten.

retainer [ri'teinə], *s.* der Diener; Gefolgsmann; der Vorschuß (*fee*).

retake [ri:'teik], *v.a. irr.* (*Mil.*) wieder erobern; (*Phot., Film*) noch einmal aufnehmen. — *s.* (*Am.*) die Neuaufnahme (*Phot., Film*).

retaliate [ri'tælieit], *v.n.* sich rächen, vergelten.

retard [ri'ta:d], *v.a.* verzögern, verlangsamen.

retch [retʃ], *v.n.* sich erbrechen.

retentive [ri'tentiv], *adj.* behaltend, gut (*memory*).

reticent ['retisənt], *adj.* schweigsam, einsilbig.

retina ['retinə], *s.* (*Anat.*) die Netzhaut.

retinue ['retinju:], *s.* das Gefolge.

retire [ri'taiə], *v.n.* sich zurückziehen (*withdraw*); in den Ruhestand treten (*from work*). — *v.a.* pensionieren.

retirement [ri'taiəmənt], *s.* die Pension, der Ruhestand; die Zurückgezogenheit (*seclusion*).

retort [ri'tɔ:t], *s.* (*Chem.*) die Retorte; die scharfe Antwort (*debate*). — *v.n.* scharf erwidern.

retouch [ri:'tʌtʃ], *v.a.* (*Phot.*) retouchieren.

retrace [ri:'treis], *v.a.* zurückverfolgen.

retreat [ri'tri:t], *v.n.* sich zurückziehen. — *s.* der Rückzug (*Mil.*); Zufluchtsort.

retrench [ri'trentʃ], *v.a.* einschränken (*restrict*); verkürzen (*shorten*). — *v.n.* sich einschränken.

retribution [retri'bju:ʃən], *s.* die Vergeltung.

retrieve [ri'tri:v], *v.a.* wieder bekommen, wieder gewinnen.

retriever [ri'tri:və], *s.* (*Zool.*) der Apportierhund, Stöberhund.

retrograde ['retrəgreid], *adj.* rückgängig, rückwärts.

retrospect ['retrospekt], *s.* der Rückblick.

retrospective [retro'spektiv], *adj.* rückblickend.

return [ri'tə:n], *v.a.* zurückgeben; erwidern (*reciprocate*); abordnen, entsenden (*to Parl.*); (*figures*) einsenden. — *v.n.* zurückkehren, zurückkommen.

— *s.* die Rückkehr; (*Fin.*) der Gewinn; (*Parl.*) die Entsendung, Mandatierung; (*pl.*) (*figures*) die Einsendung; *by* — *of post*, umgehend, postwendend; — *ticket*, die Rückfahrkarte.

reunion [ri:'ju:niən], *s.* die Wiedervereinigung.

reveal [ri'vi:l], *v.a.* enthüllen, offenbaren (*show*); verraten (*betray*).

reveille [ri'væli], *s.* (*Mil.*) das Wecken Wecksignal.

revel [revl], *v.n.* schwelgen.

revelation [revə'leiʃən], *s.* die Offenbarung.

revelry ['revəlri], *s.* die Schwelgerei.

revenge [ri'vendʒ], *s.* die Rache, Revanche. — *v.r.* (also *be revenged*) sich rächen (*on, an, Dat.*).

revenue ['revənju:], *s.* das Einkommen; *Inland* —, die Steuereinnahmen.

reverberate [ri'və:bəreit], *v.n.* widerhallen.

revere [ri'viə], *v.a.* verehren.

reverence ['revərəns], *s.* die Ehrerbietung der Respekt; *show* —, Ehrerbietung zollen.

Reverend ['revərənd]. (*abbr.* Rev.) (*Eccl.*) *The* —, Seine Ehrwürden; *The Very* —, Seine Hochwürden.

reverent, reverential ['revərənt, revə-'renʃəl], *adj.* ehrerbietig.

reverie ['revəri], *s.* die Träumerei.

reversal [ri'və:səl], *s.* die Umkehrung, Umstoßung.

reverse [ri'və:s], *v.a., v.n.* umkehren, umdrehen. — *s.* das Gegenteil (*contrary*); die Kehrseite (*of coin*).

revert [ri'və:t], *v.a., v.n.* umkehren, zurückkehren.

review [ri'vju:], *v.a.* durchsehen, prüfen (*examine*); rezensieren (*book etc.*). — *s.* die Revision; (*Mil.*) die Parade, Truppenmusterung; die Rezension, Besprechung (*book etc.*).

revile [ri'vail], *v.a., v.n.* schmähen.

revise [ri'vaiz], *v.a.* korrigieren (*correct*); wiederholen (*recapitulate*); umarbeiten (*modify*).

revision [ri'viʒən], *s.* die Revision; Korrektur; Umarbeitung; Wiederholung (*recapitulation*).

revolt [ri'voult], *v.n.* sich empören, revoltieren. — *v.a.* empören. — *s.* die Empörung.

revolting [ri'voultiŋ], *adj.* ekelhaft, empörend.

revolution [revə'lju:ʃən], *s.* (*Pol.*) die Revolution; (*Motor.*) die Umdrehung.

revolve [ri'vɔlv], *v.n.* rotieren, sich drehen.

revolver [ri'vɔlvə], *s.* der Revolver.

revue [ri'vju:], *s.* (*Theat.*) die Revue.

revulsion [ri'vʌlʃən], *s.* der Ekel; der Umschwung.

reward [ri'wɔ:d], *v.a.* belohnen (*person*); vergelten (*deed*). — *s.* die Belohnung.

rhetoric ['retərik], *s.* die Redekunst.

rheumatic [ru:'mætik], *adj.* (*Med.*)

rheumatism

rheumatisch.

rheumatism ['ru:mətizm], s. (Med.) der Rheumatismus.

Rhodesian [ro'di:ʃən, -'di:ʒən], adj. rhodesisch. — s. der Rhodesier.

rhododendron [roudo'dendrən], s. (Bot.) die Alpenrose.

rhubarb ['ru:ba:b], s. (Bot.) der Rhabarber.

rhyme [raim], s. der Reim; no — nor reason, sinnlos.

rhythm [riðm], s. der Rhythmus.

rib [rib], s. (Anat.) die Rippe.

ribald ['ribəld], adj. liederlich; (joke) unanständig.

ribbon ['ribən], s. das Band.

rice [rais], s. der Reis.

rich [ritʃ], adj. reich; fruchtbar (fertile).

rick [rik], s. der Schober.

rickets ['rikits], s. (Med.) die englische Krankheit, die Rachitis.

rickety ['rikiti], adj. gebrechlich, wacke-lig, baufällig.

rid [rid], v.a. irr. befreien, freimachen (of, von); — o.s., sich entledigen (of, Genit.); get — of, loswerden (Acc.); be — of, los sein (Acc.).

riddance ['ridəns], s. die Befreiung, das Loswerden.

riddle (1) [ridl], s. das Rätsel (puzzle).

riddle (2) [ridl], s. das grobe Sieb (sieve). — v.a. sieben (sieve); durch-löchern.

ride [raid], v.a., v.n. irr. reiten (on horse), fahren (on bicycle etc.); — at anchor, vor Anker liegen. — s. der Ritt (on horse), die Fahrt (in vehicle).

rider ['raidə], s. der Reiter (horseman); der Fahrer (cyclist etc.); der Zusatz (addition).

ridge [ridʒ], s. der Rücken (edge); die Bergkette; die Furche (furrow). — v.a. furchen.

ridicule ['ridikju:l], s. der Spott. — v.a. lächerlich machen.

ridiculous [ri'dikjuləs], adj. lächerlich.

rife [raif], adj. häufig, weitverbreitet.

rifle (1) [raifl], s. die Büchse, das Gewehr.

rifle (2) [raifl], v.a. ausplündern.

rift [rift], s. der Riß, Spalt, die Spalte. — v.a. spalten.

rig [rig], s. (Naut.) die Takelung; (fig.) — out, die Ausstattung. — v.a. (Naut.) (auf)takeln; (Am.) fälschen (fake); — out, ausstatten.

right [rait], adj. recht; richtig; wahr; gesund; korrekt; — hand, rechtsseitig; you are —, Sie haben recht; that's —, das stimmt. — s. das Recht; by right(s), rechtmäßig; drive on the —, rechts fahren.

righteous ['raitʃəs], adj. rechtschaffen, aufrecht.

rightful ['raitful], adj. rechtmäßig.

rigid ['ridʒid], adj. steif; unbeugsam; streng (severe).

rigidity [ri'dʒiditi], s. die Steifheit, Unnachgiebigkeit; die Strenge.

rigmarole ['rigməroul], s. die Salba-derei, das Gewäsch.

rigorous ['rigərəs], adj. streng; genau.

rigour ['rigə], s. die Strenge; die Härte.

rill [ril], s. (Poet.) das Bächlein.

rim [rim], s. der Rand, die Felge.

rime [raim], s. (Poet.) der Reif.

rind [raind], s. die Rinde.

ring (1) [riŋ], s. der Ring.

ring (2) [riŋ], s. der Schall, das Läuten (bell); der Anruf (telephone); das Geläute (bells). — v.a. irr. läuten, klingeln (bell). — v.n. läuten; ertönen, tönen (call, voice).

ringleader ['riŋli:də], s. der Rädels-führer.

rink [riŋk], s. die Eisbahn; Rollschuh-bahn.

rinse [rins], v.a. spülen, waschen. — s. das Abspülen.

riot ['raiət], s. der Aufruhr. — v.n. Aufruhr stiften; meutern.

rip [rip], v.a. reißen, aufreißen. — s. der Riß.

ripe [raip], adj. reif.

ripen ['raipən], v.n. reifen. — v.a. reifen lassen.

ripple [ripl], s. die Welle, Kräuselwelle (water). — v.n. kräuseln (water); (Bot.) riffeln.

rise [raiz], v.n. irr. aufstehen (get up); auf-steigen (ascend); anschwellen (swell); steigen (price). — s. die Erhöhung; (Comm.) der Anstieg; die Steigerung; Erhöhung (salary); der Ursprung (origin).

rising ['raiziŋ], s. der Aufstand (rebel-lion).

risk [risk], s. das Risiko. — v.a. wagen, riskieren.

rite [rait], s. der Ritus.

ritual ['ritjuəl], s. das Ritual.

rival [raivl], s. der Rivale, Nebenbuhler. — adj. nebenbuhlerisch, konkurrie-rend. — v.a. konkurrieren, wetteifern.

river ['rivə], s. der Fluß.

rivet ['rivit], s. die Niete. — v.a. nieten.

roach [routʃ], s. (Zool.) die Plötze.

road [roud], s. die Straße; der Weg.

roam [roum], v.n. herumstreichen.

roan [roun], s. der Rotschimmel (horse).

roar [rɔ:], v.n. brüllen (animals); brausen (storm). — s. das Gebrüll (animal); das Getöse, Brausen, Rauschen.

roast [roust], v.a., v.n. braten, rösten. — s. der Braten.

rob [rɔb], v.a. berauben.

robbery ['rɔbəri], s. der Raub, die Räuberei.

robe [roub], s. die Robe.

robin ['rɔbin], s. (Orn.) das Rotkehl-chen.

rock [rɔk], s. der Felsen, die Klippe. — v.a. schaukeln, wiegen. — v.n. wackeln, taumeln.

rocket ['rɔkit], s. die Rakete; (sl.) die Rüge. — v.n. hochfliegen; hochgehen (prices).

rocky ['rɔki], adj. felsig.

rod [rɔd], s. die Rute; (*fishing*) die Angelrute; die Stange (*pole*).

rodent ['roudənt], s. (*Zool.*) das Nagetier.

roe (1) [rou], s. der Fischrogen.

roe (2) [rou], s. (*Zool.*) das Reh, die Hirschkuh.

rogation [ro'geiʃən], s. das Gebet, die Litanei; *Rogation Sunday*, der Sonntag Rogate.

rogue [roug], s. der Schelm.

role [roul], s. (*Theat.*, *fig.*) die Rolle.

roll [roul], s. die Liste; — *call*, der Aufruf, die Parade; die Rolle; die Semmel, das Brötchen (*bread*). — *v.a.* rollen; wälzen. — *v.n.* rollen; sich wälzen; sich drehen; schlingen (*ship*); schlenkern (*person*).

roller ['roulə], s. die Rolle; — *bandage*, das Wickelband; — *skates*, die Rollschuhe.

rollick ['rɔlik], *v.n.* herumtollen, lustig sein.

rolling stock ['rouliŋ stɔk], s. (*Railw.*) der Wagenbestand.

romance [rou'mæns], s. die Romanze.

romantic [rou'mæntik], *adj.* romantisch.

romp [rɔmp], s. der Wildfang, das Tollen. — *v.n.* toben.

roof [ru:f], s. das Dach. — *v.a.* decken.

rook (1) [ruk], s. (*Orn.*) die Saatkrähe.

rook (2) [ruk], s. (*Chess*) der Turm.

room [ru:m, rum], s. der Raum, das Zimmer. — *v.n.* (*Am.*) ein Zimmer teilen (*with*, mit).

roomy ['ru:mi], *adj.* geräumig.

roost [ru:st], s. der Hühnerstall. — *v.n.* aufsitzen, schlafen.

root [ru:t], s. die Wurzel. — *v.n.* wurzeln.

rooted ['ru:tid], *adj.* eingewurzelt.

rope [roup], s. das Seil. — *v.a.* anseilen (*in climbing*); (*coll.*) — *in*, verwickeln, hereinziehen.

rosary ['rouzəri], s. (*Rel.*) der Rosenkranz.

rose [rouz], s. (*Bot.*) die Rose.

Rosemary ['rouzməri]. Rosemarie.

rosemary ['rouzməri], s. (*Bot.*) der Rosmarin.

rosin ['rɔzin] see resin.

rosy ['rouzi], *adj.* rosig.

rot [rɔt], *v.n.* faulen, modern. — s. die Fäulnis, Verwesung; (*coll.*) der Unsinn.

rotate [ro'teit], *v.a.*, *v.n.* (sich) drehen, rotieren.

rote [rout], s. *by* —, mechanisch, auswendig.

rotten [rɔtn], *adj.* faul, verdorben, schlecht.

rotund [ro'tʌnd], *adj.* rundlich, rund.

rough [rʌf], *adj.* rauh, grob; flüchtig, ungefähr (*approximate*); ungehobelt (*ill-mannered*).

roughshod ['rʌfʃɔd], *adj.* rücksichtslos.

round [raund], *adj.* rund. — s. die Runde. — *prep.* (rund) um; um ... herum. — *adv.* (rings)herum; (*around*) ungefähr; etwa (*approximately*).

roundabout ['raundəbaut], s. das Karussel. — *adj.* umständlich.

Roundhead ['raundhed], s. (*Eng. Hist.*) der Puritaner.

rouse [rauz], *v.a.* erwecken.

rout [raut], s. (*Mil.*) die wilde Flucht. — *v.a.* in die Flucht jagen.

route [ru:t], s. der Weg; die Route.

rover ['rouvə], s. der Wanderer, älterer Pfadfinder (*scout*); der Seeräuber (*pirate*).

row (1) [rou], s. die Reihe.

row (2) [rau], s. der Lärm, Streit. — *v.n.* (*coll.*) lärmend streiten, zanken.

row (3) [rou], *v.n.* rudern.

rowdy ['raudi], s. der Raufbold. — *adj.* laut, lärmend.

royal ['rɔiəl], *adj.* königlich.

royalty ['rɔiəlti], s. das Mitglied des Königshauses, die königliche Hoheit; (*pl.*) (*Law*) die Tantieme.

rub [rʌb], *v.a.*, *v.n.* (sich) reiben. — s. die Reibung; die heikle Stelle, das Problem.

rubber (1) ['rʌbə], s. der Gummi; Radiergummi.

rubber (2) ['rʌbə], s. (*Whist*) der Robber.

rubbish ['rʌbiʃ], s. der Abfall, Mist; (*fig.*) der Schund (*book*), der Unsinn (*nonsense*).

ruby ['ru:bi], s. der Rubin.

rudder ['rʌdə], s. das Steuerruder.

ruddy ['rʌdi], *adj.* rötlich.

rude [ru:d], *adj.* roh; grob; ungebildet; unhöflich.

rudiment ['ru:dimənt], s. die Anfangsgründe, die Grundlage.

rue (1) [ru:], s. (*Bot.*) die Raute.

rue (2) [ru:], *v.a.* beklagen, bereuen.

ruff [rʌf], s. die Halskrause.

ruffian ['rʌfiən], s. der Raufbold.

ruffle [rʌfl], *v.a.* zerzausen (*hair*); verwirren (*muddle*). — s. die Krause (*on dress*); die Aufregung.

rug [rʌg], s. die Wolldecke, der Vorleger.

rugged ['rʌgid], *adj.* rauh; uneben.

ruin ['ru:in], s. die Ruine; (*fig.*) der Zusammenbruch. — *v.a.* ruinieren.

rule [ru:l], s. die Regel, Vorschrift; die Herrschaft; *slide* —, der Rechenschieber. — *v.a.* beherrschen; regeln; lin(i)ieren (*draw lines on*). — *v.n.* herrschen (*reign*; *be valid*); lin(i)ieren (*draw lines*); entscheiden (*decide*).

ruling ['ru:liŋ], s. die Regelung, Entscheidung.

rum (1) [rʌm], s. der Rum.

rum (2) [rʌm], *adj.* (*sl.*) seltsam.

Rumanian [ru:'meiniən], *adj.* rumänisch. — s. der Rumäne.

rumble [rʌmbl], *v.n.* poltern, rasseln, rumpeln; (*stomach*) knurren.

ruminate ['ru:mineit], *v.n.* wiederkäuen; nachsinnen.

rummage ['rʌmidʒ], *v.a.*, *v.n.* durchstöbern.

rumour ['ru:mə], s. das Gerücht.

rump [rʌmp], s. der Rumpf, Steiß; — *steak*, das Rumpsteak.

run [rʌn], *v.n. irr.* laufen, rennen; eilen; verkehren (*bus*); fließen (*flow*); (*Theat.*) gegeben werden; lauten (*text*). — *s.* der Lauf, das Rennen; (*Theat.*) die Spieldauer; *in the long* —, am Ende, auf die Dauer.

runaway ['rʌnəwei], *adj.* entlaufen. — *s.* der Ausreißer.

rung [rʌŋ], *s.* die Sprosse.

runway ['rʌnwei], *s.* (*Aviat.*) die Rollbahn, Startbahn, Landebahn.

rupture ['rʌptʃə], *s.* (*Med.*) der Leistenbruch.

rural ['ruərəl], *adj.* ländlich.

rush (1) [rʌʃ], *s.* (*Bot.*) die Binse.

rush (2) [rʌʃ], *s.* der Ansturm, Andrang; die Hetze; der Hochbetrieb. — *v.n.* stürzen, in Eile sein.

Russian ['rʌʃən], *adj.* russisch. — *s.* der Russe.

rust [rʌst], *s.* der Rost. — *v.n.* verrosten.

rustic ['rʌstik], *adj.* ländlich.

rut (1) [rʌt], *s.* die Spur; das Geleise.

rut (2) [rʌt], *s.* (*animals*) die Brunst.

ruthless ['ru:θlis], *adj.* grausam, rücksichtslos.

rye [rai], *s.* (*Bot.*) der Roggen.

S

S [es]. das S.

sable [seibl], *s.* der Zobel. — *adj.* schwarz.

sabotage ['sæbotɑ:ʒ], *s.* die Sabotage. — *v.a.* sabotieren.

sabre ['seibə], *s.* der Säbel.

sack (1) [sæk], *s.* der Sack; (*coll.*) die Entlassung (*get the* —). — *v.a.* (*coll.*) entlassen.

sack (2) [sæk], *v.a.* plündern (*pillage*).

sack (3) [sæk], *s.* (*obs.*) der Weißwein.

sacrament ['sækrəmənt], *s.* das Sakrament.

sacred ['seikrid], *adj.* heilig.

sacrifice ['sækrifais], *s.* das Opfer. — *v.a.* opfern.

sacrilege ['sækrilidʒ], *s.* das Sakrileg, der Frevel.

sad [sæd], *adj.* traurig.

sadden [sædn], *v.a.* betrüben.

saddle [sædl], *s.* der Sattel. — *v.a.* satteln; (*coll.*) — *s.o. with s.th.*, einem etwas aufhalsen.

safe [seif], *adj.* sicher (*secure*); wohlbehalten (*arrival etc.*). — *s.* der Geldschrank, das Safe.

safeguard ['seifgɑ:d], *v.a.* beschützen, garantieren. — *s.* der Schutz, die Sicherheit.

safety ['seifti], *s.* die Sicherheit.

saffron ['sæfrən], *s.* der Safran. — *adj.* safrangelb.

sagacious [sə'geiʃəs], *adj.* scharfsinnig.

sagacity [sə'gæsiti], *s.* der Scharfsinn.

sage (1) [seidʒ], *s.* (*Bot.*) der, die Salbei.

sage (2) [seidʒ], *s.* der Weise. — *adj.* weise, klug.

sail [seil], *s.* das Segel. — *v.n.* segeln, (*Naut.*) fahren.

sailor ['seilə], *s.* der Matrose, Seemann.

Saint [seint, sənt]. (*abbr.* **S.** *or* **St.**) Sankt (*before name*).

saint [seint], *s.* der *or* die Heilige.

sake [seik], *s.* *for my son's* —, um meines Sohnes willen; *for the* — *of peace*, um des Friedens willen.

salacious [sə'leiʃəs], *adj.* geil; zotig (*joke*).

salad ['sæləd], *s.* der Salat.

salary ['sæləri], *s.* das Gehalt.

sale [seil], *s.* der Verkauf; *annual* —, (*Comm.*) der Ausverkauf.

salesman ['seilzmən], *s.* der Verkäufer.

salient ['seiliənt], *adj.* hervorspringend, wichtig, Haupt-.

saline ['seilain], *s.* die Salzquelle. — *adj.* salzhaltig.

saliva [sə'laivə], *s.* der Speichel.

sallow ['sælou], *adj.* blaß, bleich.

sally ['sæli], *s.* der Ausfall, (*fig.*) der komische Einfall. — *v.n.* ausfallen; — *forth*, losgehen.

salmon ['sæmən], *s.* (*Zool.*) der Lachs.

saloon [sə'lu:n], *s.* der Salon; (*Am.*) das Wirtshaus, die Kneipe.

salt [sɔ:lt], *s.* das Salz; — *cellar*, das Salzfäßchen; (*coll.*) *old* —, der alte Matrose. — *v.a.* salzen.

saltpetre [sɔ:lt'pi:tə], *s.* der Salpeter.

salubrious [sə'lju:briəs], *adj.* gesund (*climate, neighbourhood*).

salutary ['sæljutəri], *adj.* heilsam (*lesson, experience*).

salute [sə'lju:t], *v.a.* grüßen. — *s.* der Gruß, (*Mil.*) Salut.

salvage ['sælvidʒ], *s.* die Bergung, Rettung; das Bergegut. — *v.a.* retten, bergen.

salvation [sæl'veiʃən], *s.* die Rettung; (*Rel.*) die Erlösung, das Heil.

salve [sælv, sɑ:v], *v.a.* einsalben; heilen. — *s.* die Salbe.

salver ['sælvə], *s.* der Präsentierteller.

salvo ['sælvou], *s.* (*Mil.*) die Salve.

Samaritan [sə'mæritən], *s.* der Samariter; (*fig.*) der Wohltäter.

same [seim], *adj.* der-, die-, dasselbe.

sample [sɑ:mpl], *s.* die Probe, das Muster (*test, pack etc.*). — *v.a.* probieren; kosten (*food*).

sampler ['sɑ:mplə], *s.* das Stickmuster.

sanctify ['sæŋktifai], *v.a.* heiligen.

sanctimonious [sæŋkti'mouniəs], *adj.* scheinheilig.

sanction ['sæŋkʃən], *s.* (*Pol.*) die Sanktion; (*fig.*) Genehmigung. — *v.a.* genehmigen, sanktionieren.

sanctuary ['sæŋktjuəri], *s.* das Heiligtum.

sand [sænd], *s.* der Sand. — *v.a.* sanden, bestreuen; (*floors*) abreiben.

sandal [sændl], *s.* die Sandale.

sandwich ['sænwitʃ], s. das belegte (Butter)brot.

sane [sein], adj. gesund (mind); vernünftig.

sanguine ['sæŋgwin], adj. optimistisch.

sanitary ['sænitəri], adj. Gesundheits-, Sanitäts-; —towel, die (Damen)binde.

sanity ['sæniti], s. die Vernunft, der gesunde Menschenverstand; (Law) die Zurechnungsfähigkeit.

Santa Claus [sæntə'klɔːz]. der heilige Nikolaus, Knecht Ruprecht.

sap (1) [sæp], s. der Saft; (fig.) der Lebenskraft.

sap (2) [sæp], v.a. untergraben, schwächen.

sapling ['sæpliŋ], s. (Bot.) das Bäumchen, der junge Baum.

sapper ['sæpə], s. (Mil.) der Sappeur; der Schanzgräber, Pionier.

sapphire ['sæfaiə], s. der Saphir.

sarcasm ['saːkæzm], s. der Sarkasmus.

sarcastic [saː'kæstik], adj. sarkastisch.

sash (1) [sæʃ], s. die Schärpe.

sash (2) [sæʃ], s. — window, das Schiebefenster; — cord, die Fensterschnur.

Satan ['seitən]. der Satan.

satchel ['sætʃəl], s. die Leder(schul)-tasche.

sate [seit], v.a. sättigen.

satellite ['sætəlait], s. der Satellit, Trabant.

satin ['sætin], s. (Text.) der Atlas.

satire ['sætaiə], s. die Satire.

satisfaction [sætis'fækʃən], s. die Befriedigung, Zufriedenheit.

satisfactory [sætis'fæktri], adj. befriedigend, genügend; zufriedenstellend.

satisfy ['sætisfai], v.a. befriedigen, sättigen; (fig.) zufriedenstellen.

saturate ['sætʃureit], v.a. (Chem.) saturieren, sättigen.

Saturday ['sætədei]. der Samstag, Sonnabend.

sauce [sɔːs], s. (Cul.) die Sauce, Tunke; (coll.) die Unverschämtheit.

saucepan ['sɔːspæn], s. (Cul.) der Kochtopf.

saucer ['sɔːsə], s. die Untertasse.

saucy ['sɔːsi], adj. (coll.) unverschämt, frech.

saunter ['sɔːntə], v.n. schlendern, spazieren.

sausage ['sɔsidʒ], s. die Wurst.

savage ['sævidʒ], adj. wild. — s. der Wilde.

save [seiv], v.a. retten (life); (Theol.) erlösen (money); sich ersparen (trouble, labour); aufheben (keep). — v.n. sparen, sparsam sein. —prep., conj. außer, außer daß, ausgenommen.

saving ['seiviŋ], s. das Ersparnis; savings bank, die Sparkasse.

saviour ['seivjə], s. der Retter; (Rel.) der Heiland.

savour ['seivə], s. der Geschmack; die Würze. — v.n. schmecken (of, nach, Dat.).

savoury ['seivəri], adj. schmackhaft. — s. pikantes Vor- or Nachgericht.

saw (1) [sɔː], v.a. sägen. — s. die Säge.

saw (2) [sɔː], s. (obs.) das Sprichwort.

sawyer ['sɔːjə], s. der Sägearbeiter, Säger.

Saxon ['sæksən], adj. sächsisch. — s. der Sachse.

say [sei], v.a. irr. sagen; (lines, prayer) hersagen. — v.n. (Am. coll.) —! sagen Sie mal! — s. das entscheidende Wort.

saying ['seiiŋ], s. das Sprichwort, der Spruch.

scab [skæb], s. der Schorf, die Krätze.

scabbard ['skæbəd], s. die Degenscheide.

scaffold ['skæfəld], s. (Build.) das Gerüst; das Schafott (place of execution).

scald [skɔːld], v.a. verbrühen; —ing hot, brühheiß.

scale (1) [skeil], s. die Waagschale (balance).

scale (2) [skeil], s. (Mus.) die Skala, Tonleiter.

scale (3) [skeil], s. (Geog. etc.) die Skala, das Ausmaß, der Maßstab; on a large —, im großen (Maßstabe). — v.a. erklettern (climb); — down, im Maßstab verringern.

scale (4) [skeil], s. (fish etc.) die Schuppe. — v.a. schuppen, abschälen (remove —s).

scallop ['skɔləp], s. (Zool.) die Kammuschel.

scalp [skælp], s. (Anat.) die Kopfhaut. — v.a. skalpieren, die Kopfhaut abziehen.

scamp [skæmp], s. (coll.) der Taugenichts.

scan [skæn], v.a. (Poet.) skandieren; (Rad.) absuchen.

scandalize ['skændəlaiz], v.a. empören, verärgern.

scant [skænt], adj. selten; knapp, sparsam.

Scandinavian [skændi'neivjən], adj. skandinavisch. — s. der Skandinavier.

scanty ['skænti], adj. spärlich, knapp.

scapegoat ['skeipgout], s. der Sündenbock.

scar [skaː], s. die Narbe.

scarce [skɛəs], adj. selten, spärlich.

scarcely ['skɛəsli], adv. kaum.

scarcity ['skɛəsiti], s. die Seltenheit, Knappheit.

scare [skɛə], v.a. erschrecken, ängstigen. — s. der Schreck.

scarecrow ['skɛəkrou], s. die Vogelscheuche.

scarf [skaːf], s. der Schal, das Halstuch.

scarlet ['skaːlit], adj. scharlachrot. — s. der Scharlach.

scarp [skaːp], s. die Böschung.

scatter ['skætə], v.a., v.n. (sich) zerstreuen, (sich) verbreiten; streuen.

scavenge ['skævindʒ], v.a. ausreinigen, auswaschen; säubern.

scavenger ['skævindʒə], s. der Straßenkehrer; Aasgeier.

scene

scene [si:n], *s.* die Szene, der Schauplatz; *behind the* —*s,* hinter den Kulissen; — *shifter,* der Kulissenschieber.

scenery ['si:nəri], *s.* die Landschaft (*nature*); (*Theat.*) das Bühnenbild, die Kulissen, *f. pl.*

scent [sent], *s.* der Geruch, Duft, das Parfüm (*perfume*); die Witterung, Fährte (*trail of hunted animal*).

sceptic ['skeptik], *s.* der Skeptiker.

sceptre ['septə], *s.* das Zepter.

schedule ['ʃedju:l, (*Am.*) 'ske-], *s.* der Plan; die Liste; der (Fahr-, Stunden-) plan; (*Law*) der Zusatz (*in documents*). — *v.a.* (*Am.*) einteilen, zuteilen (*apportion*); aufzeichnen.

scheme [ski:m], *s.* das Schema; der Plan; — *of things,* die Gesamtplanung. — *v.n.* aushecken; Ränke schmieden.

scholar ['skɔlə], *s.* der Gelehrte, der Wissenschaftler; der Schuljunge, Schüler; (*Univ.*) der Stipendiat.

scholarly ['skɔləli], *adj.* gelehrt.

scholarship ['skɔləʃip], *s.* die Gelehrsamkeit (*learning*); das Stipendium (*award*).

scholastic [skɔ'læstik], *adj.* scholastisch. — *s.* der Scholastiker.

school [sku:l], *s.* die Schule. — *v.a.* abrichten; schulen; erziehen.

schoolboy ['sku:lbɔi], *s.* der Schüler.

schoolgirl ['sku:lgə:l], *s.* die Schülerin.

schoolmaster ['sku:lma:stə], *s.* der Lehrer.

schoolmistress ['sku:lmistrəs], *s.* die Lehrerin.

schooner ['sku:nə], *s.* (*Naut.*) der Schoner.

science ['saiəns], *s.* die Wissenschaft, Naturwissenschaft (*natural* —*s*).

scientific [saiən'tifik], *adj.* wissenschaftlich, naturwissenschaftlich.

scientist ['saiəntist], *s.* der Gelehrte; Naturwissenschaftler, Naturforscher.

scintillate ['sintileit], *v.n.* funkeln, glänzen.

scion ['saiən], *s.* der Sprößling.

scissors ['sizəz], *s. pl.* die Schere.

scoff [skɔf], *v.a.* verspotten, verhöhnen. — *v.n.* spotten. —*s.* der Spott, Hohn.

scold [skould], *v.a.* schelten. — *v.n.* zanken.

scoop [sku:p], *v.a.* aushöhlen (*hollow out*); ausschöpfen (*ladle out*). — *s.* die Schippe, Schöpfkelle; (*fig.*) die Sensation, Erstmeldung.

scooter ['sku:tə], *s.* der (Motor)roller.

scope [skoup], *s.* der Wirkungskreis, Spielraum.

scorch [skɔ:tʃ], *v.a.* versengen, verbrennen. — *v.n.* versengt werden; (*coll.*) dahinrasen (*speed*).

score [skɔ:], *s.* die Zwanzig; die Rechnung; (*Mus.*) die Partitur; das Spielergebnis (*in game*).

scorn [skɔ:n], *v.a.* verachten. — *s.* der Spott (*scoffing*); die Geringschätzung, Verachtung.

Scot, Scotsman [skɔt, 'skɔtsmən], *s.* der Schotte.

Scotch [skɔtʃ], *s.* der Whisky.

scotch [skɔtʃ], *v.a.* ritzen; (*fig.*) vernichten.

Scotswoman ['skɔtswumən], *s.* die Schottin.

Scottish ['skɔtiʃ], *adj.* schottisch.

scoundrel ['skaundrəl], *s.* der Schurke.

scour ['skauə], *v.a.* scheuern, reinigen.

scourge [skə:dʒ], *s.* die Geißel. — *v.a.* geißeln.

scout [skaut], *s.* der Kundschafter; (*Boy Scout*) der Pfadfinder.

scowl [skaul], *v.n.* finster dreinsehen. — *s.* das finstere Gesicht.

scraggy ['skrægi], *adj.* hager, dürr.

scramble ['skræmbl], *v.n.* klettern. — *v.a.* verrühren; *scrambled eggs,* das Rührei.

scrap [skræp], *s.* das Stückchen, der Brocken, Fetzen; — *merchant,* der Altwarenhändler. — *v.a.* zum alten Eisen werfen, verschrotten.

scrapbook ['skræpbuk], *s.* das Sammelbuch, Bilderbuch.

scrape [skreip], *v.a.,v.n.* (sich) schaben, kratzen; (*coll.*) — *up,* auflesen. — *s.* (*coll.*) die Klemme (*difficulty*).

scraper ['skreipə], *s.* der Fußabstreifer.

scratch [skrætʃ], *v.a.,v.n.* kratzen; sich kratzen; (*Sport*) zurückziehen. — *s.* der Kratzer; *come up to* —, seinen Mann stellen.

scrawl [skrɔ:l], *v.a., v.n.* kritzeln (*scribble*); (*coll.*) unleserlich schreiben. — *s.* das Gekritzel.

scream [skri:m], *v.n.* schreien; kreischen. — *s.* der Schrei; (*coll.*) zum Schreien, zum Lachen.

screech [skri:tʃ], *v.n.* schreien, kreischen (*hoarsely*). — *s.* das Gekreisch.

screen [skri:n], *s.* der Schirm (*protection*); (*Cinema*) die Leinwand. — *v.a.* abschirmen (*shade*); (*Film*) durchspielen, vorführen; (*question*) untersuchen; ausfragen.

screening ['skri:niŋ], *s.* (*Cinema*) die Vorführung; (*Pol.*) die Befragung, Untersuchung.

screw [skru:], *v.a.* schrauben. — *s.* die Schraube.

screwdriver ['skru:draivə], *s.* der Schraubenzieher.

scribble ['skribl], *v.a., v.n.* kritzeln, (unleserlich) schreiben. — *s.* das Gekritzel.

scribe [skraib], *s.* der Schreiber.

script [skript], *s.* das Manuskript; (*Film*) das Drehbuch.

scripture ['skriptʃə], *s.* die Heilige Schrift.

scroll [skroul], *s.* die Schriftrolle; (*Typ.*) der Schnörkel; die Urkunde (*document etc.*).

scrub [skrʌb], *v.a.* schrubben, reiben, scheuern.

scruff [skrʌf], *s.* (*of the neck*) das Genick.

scruple [skru:pl], *s.* der Skrupel.

scrupulous ['skru:pjuləs], *adj.* genau, gewissenhaft; allzu bedenklich.

scrutinize ['skru:tinaiz], *v.a.* genau prüfen, untersuchen.

scrutiny ['skru:tini], *s.* die genaue Prüfung; die Untersuchung.

scuffle [skʌfl], *v.n.* sich raufen. — *s.* die Balgerei, Rauferei.

scull [skʌl], *s.* das kurze Ruder.

scullery ['skʌləri], *s.* die Abwaschküche.

scullion ['skʌliən], *s.* (*obs.*) der Küchenjunge.

sculptor ['skʌlptə], *s.* der Bildhauer.

sculpture ['skʌlptʃə], *s.* die Bildhauerei (*activity*); die Skulptur (*piece*).

scum [skʌm], *s.* der Abschaum.

surf [skə:f], *s.* der Schorf, Grind.

scurrilous ['skʌriləs], *adj.* gemein.

scurvy ['skə:vi], *s.* (*Med.*) der Skorbut. — *adj.* niederträchtig.

scutcheon ['skʌtʃən] *see* escutcheon.

scuttle (1) [skʌtl], *s.* (*Naut.*) die Springluke. — *v.a.* (*Naut.*) ein Schiff zum Sinken bringen, versenken.

scuttle (2) [skʌtl], *s.* der Kohleneimer.

scuttle (3) [skʌtl], *v.n.* eilen (*hurry*).

scythe [saið], *s.* die Sense.

sea [si:], *s.* die See, das Meer.

seal (1) [si:l], *s.* das Siegel, Petschaft. — *v.a.* (be)siegeln.

seal (2) [si:l], *s.* (*Zool.*) der Seehund, die Robbe.

seam [si:m], *s.* der Saum; die Naht; (*Min.*) der Ader, das Flöz; (*Metall.*) die Naht. — *v.a.* einsäumen.

seamstress ['si:mstrəs], *s.* die Näherin.

sear [siə], *v.a.* sengen (*burn*); trocknen; verdorren. — *adj. see* sere.

search [sə:tʃ], *v.n.* suchen (*for*, nach, *Dat.*); forschen (*for*, nach, *Dat.*). — *v.a.* untersuchen, durchsuchen (*house*, *case etc.*). — *s.* die Suche (*for person*); die Untersuchung (*of house etc.*).

searchlight ['sə:tʃlait], *s.* der Scheinwerfer.

seasick ['si:sik], *adj.* seekrank.

seaside ['si:said], *s.* die Küste, der Strand.

season [si:zn], *s.* die Jahreszeit, Saison; — *ticket*, die Dauerkarte. — *v.a.* würzen (*spice*). — *v.n.* reifen (*mature*).

seasoning ['si:zniŋ], *s.* die Würze.

seat [si:t], *s.* der Sitz, Sitzplatz, Stuhl. — *v.a.* setzen; fassen (*of room capacity*); *be —ed*, Platz nehmen.

seaweed ['si:wi:d], *s.* (*Bot.*) der Seetang.

secession [si'seʃən], *s.* die Loslösung, Trennung, Spaltung.

seclude [si'klu:d], *v.a.* abschließen, absondern.

seclusion [si'klu:ʒən], *s.* die Abgeschlossenheit.

second ['sekənd], *num. adj.* zweit; (*repeat*) noch ein. — *s.* die Sekunde (*time*); (*Sport*) der Sekundant; — *v.a.* sekundieren (*Dat.*), beipflichten; [si'kɔnd] abkommandieren (zu).

secondary ['sekəndri], *adj.* zweitrangig, sekundär.

secondhand ['sekəndhænd], *adj.* antiquarisch, gebraucht.

secrecy ['si:krəsi], *s.* die Heimlichkeit; *pledge to —*, die Verschwiegenheit.

secret ['si:krit], *s.* das Geheimnis. — *adj.* geheim.

secretary ['sekrətəri], *s.* der Sekretär, die Sekretärin.

secrete [si'kri:t], *v.a.* ausscheiden, absondern.

secretion [si'kri:ʃən], *s.* die Ausscheidung; (*Med.*) das Sekret.

sect [sekt], *s.* die Sekte.

section ['sekʃən], *s.* die Sektion, Abteilung (*department*); der Teil (*part*); Abschnitt (*in book etc.*).

secular ['sekjulə], *adj.* weltlich, säkulär.

secure [sə'kjuə], *adj.* sicher, gesichert. — *v.a.* sichern (*make safe*); besorgen (*obtain*).

security [sə'kjuəriti], *s.* die Sicherheit; (*Comm.*) die Garantie, Bürgschaft; (*pl.*) die Staatspapiere, Wertpapiere, *n. pl.*, Aktien, *f. pl.*

sedate [si'deit], *adj.* gesetzt, ruhig (*placid*).

sedative ['sedətiv], *adj.* beruhigend. — *s.* das Beruhigungsmittel.

sedentary ['sedəntri], *adj.* sitzend, Sitz-.

sediment ['sedimənt], *s.* der Bodensatz; (*Geol.*) das Sediment.

sedition [si'diʃən], *s.* der Aufstand.

seditious [si'diʃəs], *adj.* aufrührerisch.

seduce [si'dju:s], *v.a.* verführen.

sedulous ['sedjuləs], *adj.* emsig, fleißig.

see (1) [si:], *s.* (*Eccl.*) das (Erz)bistum; *Holy See*, der Heilige Stuhl.

see (2) [si:], *v.a.*, *v.n. irr.* sehen; einsehen, verstehen (*understand*).

seed [si:d], *s.* die Saat; der Same (*grain*). — *v.a.* (*Sport*) aussetzen, setzen.

seediness ['si:dinis], *s.* die Schäbigkeit; Armseligkeit, das Elend.

seedy ['si:di], *adj.* elend; schäbig.

seeing ['si:iŋ], *conj.* — *that*, da doch.

seek [si:k], *v.a. irr.* suchen (*object*). — *v.n.* trachten (*to*, *infin.*).

seem [si:m], *v.n.* scheinen, erscheinen.

seemly ['si:mli], *adj.* schicklich, anständig.

seer [siə], *s.* der Prophet.

seesaw ['si:sɔ:], *s.* die Schaukel.

seethe [si:ð], *v.n.* kochen, (*fig.*) sieden.

segment ['segmənt], *s.* (*Geom.*) der Abschnitt.

segregate ['segrigeit], *v.a.* absondern.

segregation [segri'geiʃən], *s. racial —*, die Rassentrennung.

seize [si:z], *v.a.* ergreifen, packen (*arrest*, *grasp*); beschlagnahmen (*impound*).

seizure ['si:ʒə], *s.* die Beschlagnahme (*of goods*); (*Med.*) der Anfall.

seldom ['seldəm], *adv.* selten.

select [si'lekt], *v.a.* auswählen; auslesen. — *adj.* auserlesen.

selection [si'lekʃən], *s.* die Wahl, Auswahl.

self [self], *s.* das Selbst; — *— consciousness*, die Befangenheit; — *— denial*, die Selbstverleugnung, Selbstaufopferung.

selfish

selfish ['selfiʃ], *adj.* egoistisch, selbst-süchtig.

sell [sel], *v.a. irr.* verkaufen; *(sl.)* — *(s.o.) out,* jemanden verraten.

semblance ['sembləns], *s.* der Anschein, die Ähnlichkeit.

semi- ['semi], *pref.* halb.

semibreve ['semibri:v], *s. (Mus.)* die ganze Note.

semicircle ['semisə:kl], *s.* der Halb-kreis.

semicolon ['semikoulən], *s.* der Strich-punkt.

semiquaver ['semikweivə], *s. (Mus.)* die Sechzehntelnote.

senate ['senit], *s.* der Senat.

send [send], *v.a. irr.* senden, schicken; — *for,* holen lassen; — *-off,* die Abschiedsfeier.

Senegalese [seniɡə'li:z], *adj.* senegal-. — *s.* der Senegalese.

senile ['si:nail], *adj.* altersschwach.

senior ['si:njə], *adj.* älter; dienstälter *(in position).*

seniority [si:ni'ɔriti], *s.* der Rangvor-tritt, das Dienstalter.

sensation [sen'seiʃən], *s.* die Empfin-dung; Sensation.

sensational [sen'seiʃənəl], *adj.* sen-sationell.

sense [sens], *v.a.* fühlen, empfinden. — *s.* der Sinn; das Empfinden, Gefühl; *common* —, gesunder Men-schenverstand.

senseless ['senslis], *adj.* sinnlos.

sensibility [sensi'biliti], *s.* die Empfind-lichkeit.

sensible ['sensibl], *adj.* vernünftig.

sensitive ['sensitiv], *adj.* feinfühlend, empfindlich.

sensitize ['sensitaiz], *v.a. (Phot. etc.)* empfindlich machen.

sensual ['sensjuəl], *adj.* sinnlich, wol-lüstig.

sensuous ['sensjuəs], *adj.* sinnlich.

sentence ['sentəns], *s. (Gram.)* der Satz; *(Law)* das Urteil. — *v.a.* verur-teilen.

sententious [sen'tenʃəs], *adj.* spruch-reich; affektiert.

sentiment ['sentimənt], *s.* die Emp-findung, das Gefühl; die Meinung *(opinion).*

sentimental [senti'mentl], *adj.* senti-mental, gefühlvoll; empfindsam.

sentinel ['sentinəl], *s. (Mil.)* die Schild-wache, Wache.

separable ['sepərəbl], *adj.* trennbar.

separate ['sepəreit], *v.a.* trennen. — [-rit], *adj.* getrennt.

separation [sepə'reiʃən], *s.* die Tren-nung.

September [sep'tembə]. der Septem-ber.

sequel ['si:kwəl], *s.* die Folge, Fortset-zung *(serial).*

sequence ['si:kwəns], *s.* die Ordnung, Reihenfolge, Aufeinanderfolge.

sequester [si'kwestə], *v.a.* absondern, entfernen.

sere [siə], *adj.* trocken, dürr.

serene [si'ri:n], *adj.* heiter; gelassen, ruhig *(quiet).*

serf [sə:f], *s.* der Leibeigene.

sergeant ['sɑ:dʒənt], *s. (Mil.)* der Feldwebel.

series ['siəri:z *or* 'siərii:z], *s.* die Reihe.

serious ['siəriəs], *adj.* ernst, seriös.

sermon ['sə:mən], *s.* die Predigt.

serpent ['sə:pənt], *s. (Zool.)* die Schlange.

serpentine ['sə:pəntain], *adj.* schlangen-artig, sich schlängelnd.

serrated [se'reitid], *adj. (Bot., Engin.)* zackig, gezackt.

serried ['serid], *adj.* dichtgedrängt.

servant ['sə:vənt], *s.* der Bediente, Diener; die Magd, das Mädchen, Dienstmädchen.

serve [sə:v], *v.a., v.n.* dienen *(Dat.)*; *(Law)* abbüßen, absitzen *(sentence)*; servieren *(food)*; *(Tennis)* angeben.

service ['sə:vis], *s.* der Dienst, die Bedienung; *(Mil.)* der Militärdienst; das Service, Geschirr, Porzellan *(china).*

serviceable ['sə:visəbl], *adj.* brauch-bar, dienlich, benutzbar.

servile ['sə:vail], *adj.* knechtisch.

servility [sə:'viliti], *s.* die Kriecherei.

servitude ['sə:vitju:d], *s.* die Knecht-schaft.

session ['seʃən], *s.* die Sitzung; das Studienjahr, Hochschuljahr.

set [set], *v.a. irr.* setzen; stellen *(stand)*; legen *(lay)*; ordnen (— *out*); — *a saw,* eine Säge schärfen, wetzen; fassen *(stone)*; — *fire to,* in Brand setzen; — *aside,* beiseitelegen; — *to music,* vertonen; — *about,* anfangen, sich anschicken; herfallen über *(s.o.)*; — *up,* einrichten. — *v.n.* — *forth, forward,* aufbrechen; — *out to,* stre-ben, trachten; *(sun)* untergehen; fest werden *(solidify).* — *s.* der Satz *(com-plete collection)*; die Garnitur *(gar-ments)*; der Kreis, die Clique *(circle of people)*; *(Theat.)* das Bühnenbild.

settee [se'ti:], *s.* das Sofa.

setter ['setə], *s. (Zool.)* der Vorsteh-hund; *red* —, der Hühnerhund.

setting ['setiŋ], *s.* das Setzen; die Szene *(of play etc.)*; die Sonnenunter-gang *(of the sun)*; *(Typ.)* — *up,* die Auslegung, Aufstellung.

settle (1) [setl], *v.a.* ordnen, schlichten; *(Comm.)* begleichen, bezahlen. — *v.n.* sich niederlassen, siedeln; *(wea-ther)* sich aufklären.

settle (2) [setl], *s.* der Ruhesitz.

settlement ['setlmənt], *s. (Comm.)* die Begleichung; die Siedlung *(habita-tion).*

seven [sevn], *num. adj.* sieben.

seventeen ['sevnti:n], *num. adj.* siebzehn.

seventh [sevnθ], *num. adj.* siebente.

seventy ['sevnti], *num. adj.* siebzig.

sever ['sevə], *v.a.* trennen.

several ['sevərəl], *adj. pl.* verschiedene, mehrere.

severance ['sevərəns], s. die Trennung.
severe [si'viə], adj. streng.
severity [si'veriti], s. die Strenge.
sew [sou], v.a., v.n. nähen.
sewage ['sju:idʒ], s. das Abfuhrwasser, Kloakenwasser, Kanalwasser.
sewer (1) ['sju:ə], s. die Kanalanlage, der Abzugskanal.
sewer (2) ['souə], s. der Näher, die Näherin.
sewing ['souiŋ], s. das Nähen; — machine, die Nähmaschine.
sex [seks], s. das Geschlecht.
sexagenarian [seksədʒə'neəriən], s. der Sechzigjährige.
sextant ['sekstənt], s. der Sextant.
sexton ['sekstən], s. (Eccl.) der Küster, Totengräber.
sexual ['seksjuəl], adj. geschlechtlich, sexuell.
shabby ['ʃæbi], adj. schäbig; (fig.) erbärmlich.
shackle [ʃækl], v.a. fesseln. — s. (usually pl.) die Fesseln, f. pl.
shade [ʃeid], s. der Schatten; (pl.) (Am.) die Jalousien, f. pl. (blinds). — v.a. beschatten; (Art) schattieren, verdunkeln.
shadow ['ʃædou], s. der Schatten. — v.a. verfolgen.
shady ['ʃeidi], adj. schattig; (fig.) verdächtig.
shaft [ʃɑːft], s. der Schaft (handle); (Min.) der Schacht; die Deichsel (cart); der Pfeil (arrow).
shag [ʃæg], s. der Tabak.
shaggy ['ʃægi], adj. zottig.
shake [ʃeik], v.a. irr. schütteln; rütteln; (fig.) erschüttern. — v.n. zittern (tremble); wanken (waver). — s. das Zittern, Beben; (Mus.) der Triller.
shaky ['ʃeiki], adj. zitternd, wankend; rissig, wackelig (wobbly); (fig.) unsicher (insecure).
shall [ʃæl], v. aux. sollen (be supposed to); werden (future).
shallow ['ʃælou], adj. flach, seicht. — s. die Untiefe (sea).
sham [ʃæm], adj. falsch, unecht. — v.a. vortäuschen.
shambles [ʃæmblz], s. die Unordnung; (fig.) das Schlachtfeld.
shame [ʃeim], s. die Scham (remorse); die Schande (dishonour); what a —! wie schade! — v.a. beschämen.
shamefaced ['ʃeimfeisd], adj. verschämt.
shameful ['ʃeimful], adj. schändlich (despicable).
shampoo [ʃæm'puː], s. das Haarwaschmittel. — v.a. das Haar waschen.
shamrock ['ʃæmrɔk], s. (Bot.) der irische Klee.
shank [ʃæŋk], s. der Unterschenkel; (coll.) on Shanks's pony, zu Fuß.
shanty (1) ['ʃænti], s. die Hütte.
shanty (2) ['ʃænti], s. sea —, das Matrosenlied.
shape [ʃeip], s. die Gestalt, Figur, Form. — v.a. gestalten, formen. — v.n. Gestalt annehmen.

shapely ['ʃeipli], adj. wohlgestaltet, schön gestaltet.
share [ʃeə], v.a., v.n. (sich) teilen. — s. der Teil, Anteil; (Comm.) die Aktie (in company).
shareholder ['ʃeəhouldə], s. der Aktionär.
shark [ʃɑːk], s. (Zool.) der Haifisch, Hai; (fig.) der Wucherer (profiteer) Hochstapler.
sharp [ʃɑːp], adj. scharf; (fig.) intelligent. — s. (Mus.) das Kreuz.
sharpen [ʃɑːpn], v.a. schärfen; spitzen (pencil).
sharpener ['ʃɑːpnə], s. pencil —, der Bleistiftspitzer.
shatter ['ʃætə], v.a. zerschmettern. — v.n. zerbrechen.
shave [ʃeiv], v.a., v.n. (sich) rasieren; abschaben (pare). — s. die Rasur, das Rasieren.
shavings ['ʃeiviŋz], s. pl. die Hobelspäne, m. pl.
shawl [ʃɔːl], s. der Schal, das Umschlagetuch.
she [ʃiː], pers. pron. sie.
sheaf [ʃiːf], s. die Garbe.
shear [ʃiə], v.a. irr. scheren (sheep etc.).
shears [ʃiəz], s. pl. die Schere.
sheath [ʃiːθ], s. die Scheide.
sheathe [ʃiːð], v.a. in die Scheide stecken.
shed (1) [ʃed], s. der Schuppen.
shed (2) [ʃed], v.a. irr. vergießen (blood, tears); ausschütten.
sheen [ʃiːn], s. der Glanz.
sheep [ʃiːp], s. (Zool.) das Schaf.
sheer (1) [ʃiə], adj. rein, lauter; senkrecht.
sheer (2) [ʃiə], v.n. (Naut.) gieren, abgieren.
sheet [ʃiːt], s. das Bettuch; das Blatt, der Bogen (paper); die Platte (metal); — metal, — iron, das Eisenblech; — lightning, das Wetterleuchten.
shelf [ʃelf], s. das Brett, Regal; der Sims (mantel); (Geog.) die Sandbank; (coll.) on the —, sitzengeblieben.
shell [ʃel], s. die Schale (case); die Muschel (mussel); (Mil.) die Bombe, Granate. — v.a. schälen (peas); bombardieren, beschiessen (town).
shelter ['ʃeltə], s. das Obdach (lodging); der Unterstand, Schuppen; der Schutz (protection). — v.a. Obdach gewähren (Dat.); beschützen (protect). — v.n. sich schützen, unterstellen.
shelve [ʃelv], v.a. auf ein Brett legen; (fig.) aufschieben (postpone).
shelving ['ʃelviŋ], s. das Regal.
shepherd ['ʃepəd], s. der Schäfer, Hirt.
sheriff ['ʃerif], s. der Sheriff.
shew [ʃou] see show.
shield [ʃiːld], s. der Schild. — v.a. schützen.
shift [ʃift], v.a. verschieben. — v.n. die Lage ändern. — s. die Veränderung, der Wechsel; (Industry) die Schicht.
shifty ['ʃifti], adj. unstet; durchtrieben.

shin [ʃin], *s.* (*Anat.*) das Schienbein.
shindy [ʃindi], *s.* der Lärm.
shine [ʃain], *v.n. irr.* scheinen (*sun*); glänzen. — *s.* der Glanz.
shingle (1) [ʃiŋgl], *s.* (*Build.*) die Schindel; (*Hair*) der Herrenschnitt.
shingle (2) [ʃiŋgl], *s.* (*Geol.*) der Kiesel.
shingles [ʃiŋglz], *s. pl.* (*Med.*) die Gürtelrose.
ship [ʃip], *s.* das Schiff. — *v.a.* verschiffen, (*Comm.*) versenden.
shipping [ʃipiŋ], *s.* die Schiffahrt; (*Comm.*) der Versand, die Verfrachtung, Verschiffung.
shire [ʃaiə], *s.* die Grafschaft.
shirk [ʃə:k], *v.a.* vermeiden, sich drücken (vor, *Dat.*).
shirt [ʃə:t], *s.* das Hemd.
shirting [ʃə:tiŋ], *s.* der Hemdenstoff.
shiver [ʃivə], *v.n.* zittern, beben. — *s.* der Schauer, Schauder.
shoal [ʃoul], *s.* der Schwarm; (*Naut.*) die Untiefe.
shock (1) [ʃɔk], *v.a.* entsetzen; erschrecken; schockieren. — *s.* der Schock, das Entsetzen.
shock (2) [ʃɔk], *s.* — *of hair*, zottiges Haar.
shoddy [ʃɔdi], *adj.* schlecht, wertlos.
shoe [ʃu:], *s.* der Schuh. — *v.a.* beschuhen; (*horse*) beschlagen.
shoelace, **shoestring** [ʃu:leis, ʃu:striŋ], *s.* der Schuhsenkel, (*Austr.*) das Schuhschnürl; *on a shoestring*, fast ohne Geld.
shoeshine [ʃu:ʃain], *s.* (*Am.*) der Schuhputzer.
shoestring *see under* **shoelace**.
shoot [ʃu:t], *v.a. irr.* schießen. — *v.n.* sprossen, hervorschießen; (*film*) aufnehmen. — *s.* (*Bot.*) der Sproß.
shooting [ʃu:tiŋ], *s.* das Schießen; — *range*, der Schießstand. — *adj.* — *star*, die Sternschnuppe.
shop [ʃɔp], *s.* der Laden, das Geschäft; (*work*) die Werkstatt; *talk* — , fachsimpeln; — *window*, das Schaufenster. — *v.n.* einkaufen.
shopkeeper [ʃɔpki:pə], *s.* der Kaufmann, Krämer.
shoplifter [ʃɔpliftə], *s.* der Ladendieb.
shore [ʃɔ:], *s.* das Gestade, die Küste; die Stütze. — *v.a.* — *up*, stützen.
short [ʃɔ:t], *adj.* kurz, klein, knapp; (*curt*) kurz angebunden; — *of money*, in Geldnot; *run* — , knapp werden; — *sighted*, kurzsichtig; *be on* — *time working*, kurz arbeiten. — *s.* (*Elect.*) (*coll.*) der Kurzschluß (*short circuit*); (*pl.*) die Kniehose, kurze Hose.
shortcoming [ʃɔ:tkʌmiŋ], *s.* der Fehler, Mangel.
shorten [ʃɔ:tn], *v.a.* verkürzen, abkürzen. — *v.n.* kürzer werden.
shorthand [ʃɔ:thænd], *s.* die Stenographie; — *typist*, die Stenotypistin.
shot [ʃɔt], *s.* der Schuß; (*man*) der Schütze.

shoulder [ʃouldə], *s.* (*Anat.*) die Schulter. — *v.a.* schultern, auf sich nehmen, auf die Achsel nehmen.
shout [ʃaut], *v.n.* schreien, rufen. — *s.* der Schrei, Ruf.
shove [ʃʌv], *v.a.* schieben, stoßen. — *s.* der Schub, Stoß.
shovel [ʃʌvl], *s.* die Schaufel. — *v.a.* schaufeln.
show [ʃou], *v.a. irr.* zeigen; (*fig.*) dartun. — *v.n.* sich zeigen, zu sehen sein; — *off*, prahlen, protzen. — *v.r.* — *o.s. to be*, sich erweisen als. — *s.* (*Theat.*) die Schau, Aufführung.
shower [ʃauə], *s.* der Schauer (*rain*); (*fig.*) die Fülle, der Überfluß; — (*bath*), die Dusche; *take a* — (*bath*), brausen. — *v.a., v.n.* herabregnen; überschütten.
showing [ʃouiŋ], *s.* die Vorführung, der Beweis.
showy [ʃoui], *adj.* protzig, angeberisch.
shred [ʃred], *s.* der Fetzen; (*fig.*) die Spur (*of evidence*). — *v.a.* zerreißen, zerfetzen.
shrew [ʃru:], *s.* die Spitzmaus; (*fig.*) das zänkische Weib.
shrewd [ʃru:d], *adj.* schlau, verschlagen, listig.
shriek [ʃri:k], *v.n.* kreischen. — *s.* der Schrei, das Gekreisch.
shrift [ʃrift], *s. give s.o. short* — , mit einem kurzen Prozeß machen.
shrill [ʃril], *adj.* schrill, gellend, durchdringend.
shrimp [ʃrimp], *s.* (*Zool.*) die Garnele.
shrine [ʃrain], *s.* der (Reliquien)schrein; der Altar.
shrink [ʃriŋk], *v.n. irr.* eingehen, einschrumpfen. — *v.a.* eingehen lassen.
shrinkage [ʃriŋkidʒ], *s.* das Eingehen (*fabric*); (*Geol.*) die Schrumpfung.
shrivel [ʃrivl], *v.n.* einschrumpfen, sich runzeln.
shroud [ʃraud], *s.* das Leichentuch. — *v.a.* einhüllen.
Shrove [ʃrouv] **Tuesday**, die Fastnacht.
shrub [ʃrʌb], *s.* (*Bot.*) der Strauch, die Staude.
shrug [ʃrʌg], *v.a.* (*shoulders*) die Achseln zucken. — *s.* das Achselzucken.
shudder [ʃʌdə], *s.* der Schauder. — *v.n.* schaudern.
shuffle [ʃʌfl], *v.a.* (*cards*) mischen. — *v.n.* schlürfen, schleppend gehen.
shun [ʃʌn], *v.a.* meiden.
shunt [ʃʌnt], *v.a., v.n.* rangieren.
shut [ʃʌt], *v.a. irr.* schließen. — *v.n.* sich schließen, zugehen; (*coll.*) — *up!* halt's Maul!
shutter [ʃʌtə], *s.* der Fensterladen.
shuttle [ʃʌtl], *s.* (*Mech.*) das Weberschiff.
shuttlecock [ʃʌtlkɔk], *s.* der Federball.
shy (1) [ʃai], *adj.* scheu, schüchtern. — *v.n.* scheuen (*of horses*).
shy (2) [ʃai], *s.* der Wurf.
sick [sik], *adj.* krank; unwohl, übel; leidend (*suffering*); (*fig.*) — *of*, überdrüssig (*Genit.*).

sicken [sikn], *v.n.* krank werden *or* sein; sich ekeln (*be nauseated*). — *v.a.* anekeln.

sickle [sikl], *s.* die Sichel.

sickness ['siknis], *s.* die Krankheit.

side [said], *s.* die Seite. — *v.n.* — *with*, Partei ergreifen für.

sideboard ['saidbɔːd], *s.* das Büffet, die Anrichte.

sidereal [sai'diəriəl], *adj.* (*Maths.*, *Phys.*) Sternen-, Stern-.

sidewalk ['saidwɔːk] (*Am.*) *see* **pavement**.

siding ['saidiŋ],*s.*(*Railw.*)das Nebengleis.

sidle [saidl], *v.n.* — *up to*, sich heranmachen.

siege [siːdʒ], *s.* die Belagerung.

sieve [siv], *s.* das Sieb. — *v.a.* sieben.

sift [sift], *v.a.* sieben; (*fig.*) prüfen.

sigh [sai], *v.n.* seufzen. — *s.* der Seufzer.

sight [sait], *s.* die Sicht (*view*); die Sehkraft (*sense of*); der Anblick; *at* —, auf den ersten Blick; *out of* —, *out of mind*, aus den Augen, aus dem Sinn; (*pl.*) die Sehenswürdigkeiten, *f. pl.*; —*seeing*, die Besichtigung (der Sehenswürdigkeiten). — *v.a.* sichten.

sign [sain], *s.* das Zeichen; der Wink (*hint*); das Aushängeschild (*of pub, shop etc.*). — *v.a.* unterschreiben, unterzeichnen. — *v.n.* winken.

signal ['signəl], *s.* das Signal.

signboard ['sainbɔːd], *s.* das Aushängeschild.

signet ['signit], *s.* das Siegel; — *ring*, der Siegelring.

significance [sig'nifikəns], *s.* die Bedeutung, der Sinn.

significant [sig'nifikənt], *adj.* bedeutend, wichtig.

signify ['signifai], *v.a.* bedeuten (*mean*); anzeigen (*denote*).

silence ['sailəns], *s.* das Schweigen, die Ruhe.

silent ['sailənt], *adj.* still; schweigsam (*taciturn*).

Silesian [sai'liːʃən], *adj.* schlesisch. — *s.* der Schlesier.

silk [silk], *s.* (*Text.*) die Seide.

silkworm ['silkwəːm], *s.* (*Ent.*) die Seidenraupe.

sill [sil], *s.* die Schwelle; *window* —, das Fensterbrett.

silly ['sili], *adj.* albern, dumm.

silver ['silvə], *s.* das Silber. — *v.a.* versilbern. — *adj.* silbern.

similar ['similə], *adj.* ähnlich.

simile ['simili], *s.* (*Lit.*) das Gleichnis.

simmer ['simə], *v.n.*, *v.a.* langsam kochen.

simper ['simpə], *v.n.* lächeln, grinsen.

simple [simpl], *adj.* einfach; (*fig.*) einfältig.

simpleton ['simpltən], *s.* der Einfaltspinsel, Tor.

simplicity [sim'plisiti], *s.* die Einfachheit; (*fig.*) die Einfalt.

simplify ['simplifai], *v.a.* vereinfachen.

simulate ['simjuleit], *v.a.* nachahmen, heucheln, vortäuschen.

simultaneous [siməl'teinjəs], *adj.* gleichzeitig.

sin [sin], *s.* die Sünde. — *v.n.* sündigen.

since [sins], *prep.* seit (*Dat.*). — *conj.* seit (*time*); weil, da (*cause*). — *adv.* seither, seitdem.

sincere [sin'siə], *adj.* aufrichtig.

sincerely [sin'siəli], *adv.* yours —, Ihr ergebener (*letters*).

sincerity [sin'seriti], *s.* die Aufrichtigkeit.

sine [sain], *s.* (*Maths.*) der Sinus, die Sinuskurve.

sinecure ['sainikjuə], *s.* der Ruheposten, die Sinekure.

sinew ['sinjuː], *s.* (*Anat.*) die Sehne, der Nerv.

sinful ['sinful], *adj.* sündig, sündhaft.

sing [siŋ], *v.a.*, *v.n. irr.* singen; — *of*, besingen.

singe [sindʒ], *v.a.* sengen.

Singhalese [siŋgə'liːz], *adj.* singhalesisch. — *s.* der Singhalese, die Singhalesin.

single [siŋgl], *adj.* einzeln; ledig (*unmarried*; *single-handed*, allein. — *v.a.* — *out*, auswählen.

singlet ['siŋglit], *s.* die Unterjacke.

singly ['siŋgli], *adv.* einzeln (*one by one*).

singular ['siŋgjulə], *adj.* einzigartig, einzig. — *s.* (*Gram.*) die Einzahl.

sinister ['sinistə], *adj.* böse, unheimlich, finster.

sink [siŋk], *v.a. irr.* versenken; (*fig.*) (*differences etc.*) begraben. — *v.n.* versinken; (*Naut.*) sinken, versinken. — *s.* das Abwaschbecken, Ausgußbecken.

sinker ['siŋkə], *s.* der Schachtarbeiter (*man*); (*Naut.*) das Senkblei.

sinuous ['sinjuəs], *adj.* gewunden.

sinus ['sainəs], *s.* (*Anat.*) die Knochenhöhle; die Bucht.

sip [sip], *v.a.* schlürfen, nippen. — *s.* das Schlückchen.

siphon ['saifən], *s.* (*Phys.*) der Heber; die Siphonflasche. — *v.a.* auspumpen.

Sir (1) [səː] (*title preceding Christian name*) Herr von ... (*baronet or knight*).

sir (2) [səː], *s.* Herr (*respectful form of address*); *dear* —, sehr geehrter Herr (*in letters*).

sire [saiə], *s.* der Ahnherr, Vater. — *v.a.* zeugen (*horses etc.*).

siren ['saiərən], *s.* die Sirene.

sirloin ['səːlɔin], *s.* das Lendenstück.

siskin ['siskin], *s.* (*Orn.*) der Zeisig.

sister ['sistə], *s.* die Schwester; (*Eccl.*) Nonne; —*in-law*, die Schwägerin.

sit [sit], *v.n. irr.* sitzen. — *v.a.* — *an examination*, eine Prüfung machen.

site [sait], *s.* die Lage, der Platz.

sitting ['sitiŋ], *s.* die Sitzung; — *room*, das Wohnzimmer.

situated ['sitjueitid], *adj.* gelegen.

situation [sitju'eiʃən], *s.* die Lage, Situation; der Posten, die Stellung (*post*).

six [siks], *num. adj.* sechs; *be at —es and sevens*, durcheinander, uneinig sein.
sixteen [siks'ti:n], *num. adj.* sechzehn.
sixth [siksθ], *num. adj.* sechste.
sixty ['siksti], *num. adj.* sechzig.
size [saiz], *s.* die Größe, das Maß; (*fig.*) der Umfang.
skate (1) [skeit], *s.* der Schlittschuh. — *v.n.* Schlittschuh laufen.
skate (2) [skeit], *s.* (*Zool.*) der Glattrochen.
skeleton ['skelitǝn], *s.* das Skelett, Knochengerüst; — *key*, der Dietrich.
sketch [sketʃ], *s.* die Skizze, der Entwurf. — *v.a.* skizzieren, entwerfen. — *v.n.* Skizzen entwerfen.
sketchy ['sketʃi], *adj.* flüchtig.
skew [skju:], *adj.* schief, schräg.
skewer [skju:ǝ], *s.* der Fleischspieß.
ski [ski:], *s.* der Schi.
skid [skid], *v.n.* gleiten, schleudern, rutschen. — *v.a.* hemmen, bremsen (*wheel*). — *s.* der Hemmschuh, die Bremse (*of wheel*).
skiff [skif], *s.* (*Naut.*) der Nachen, Kahn.
skilful ['skilful], *adj.* geschickt, gewandt; (*fig.*) erfahren.
skill [skil], *s.* die Geschicklichkeit, Gewandtheit; (*fig.*) die Erfahrung.
skim [skim], *v.a.* abschöpfen, abschäumen.
skimp [skimp], *v.a.* knausern, sparsam sein (mit, *Dat.*).
skimpy ['skimpi], *adj.* knapp.
skin [skin], *s.* die Haut; die Schale (*fruit*); — *deep*, oberflächlich. — *v.a.* häuten, schinden.
skinflint ['skinflint], *s.* der Geizhals.
skinner ['skinǝ], *s.* der Kürschner.
skip [skip], *v.n.* springen, hüpfen. — *v.a.* (*coll.*) auslassen, überspringen. — *s.* der Sprung.
skipper ['skipǝ], *s.* (*Naut.*) der Kapitän; (*coll.*) der Chef.
skipping rope ['skipiŋ roup], *s.* das Springseil.
skirmish ['skǝ:miʃ], *s.* das Scharmützel. — *v.n.* scharmützeln.
skirt [skǝ:t], *s.* der Rock, Rockschoß (*woman's garment*); der Saum (*edge*). — *v.a.* einsäumen (*seam, edge*); grenzen, am Rande entlang gehen.
skirting (board) ['skǝ:tiŋ (bɔ:d)], *s.* die Fußleiste.
skit [skit], *s.* die Stichelei, die Parodie, Satire.
skittish ['skitiʃ], *adj.* leichtfertig.
skulk [skʌlk], *v.n.* lauern, herumlungern.
skull [skʌl], *s.* der Schädel; — *and crossbones*, der Totenkopf.
skunk [skʌŋk], *s.* (*Zool.*) das Stinktier; (*coll.*) der Schuft.
sky [skai], *s.* der (sichtbare) Himmel.
skylark ['skailɑ:k], *s.* (*Orn.*) die Feldlerche.
skylarking ['skailɑ:kiŋ], *s.* das Possenreißen, die Streiche.
skyline ['skailain], *s.* der Horizont.
skyscraper ['skaiskreipǝ], *s.* der Wolkenkratzer.

slab [slæb], *s.* die Platte (*stone*); die Tafel, das Stück.
slack [slæk], *adj.* schlaff (*feeble*); locker (*loose*). — *s.* der Kohlengrus. — *v.n.* nachlassen, locker werden, faulenzen.
slacken [slækn], *v.a., v.n.* locker werden, nachlassen.
slackness ['slæknis], *s.* die Schlaffheit, Faulheit.
slag [slæg], *s.* die Schlacke.
slake [sleik], *v.a.* dämpfen, löschen, stillen.
slam (1) [slæm], *v.a.* zuwerfen, zuschlagen (*door*). — *s.* der Schlag.
slam (2) [slæm], *v.a.* (*Cards*) Schlemm ansagen, Schlemm machen. — *s.* (*Cards*) der Stich.
slander ['slɑ:ndǝ], *v.a.* verleumden. — *s.* die Verleumdung.
slanderer ['slɑ:ndǝrǝ], *s.* der Verleumder.
slang [slæŋ], *s.* der Slang.
slant [slɑ:nt], *s.* die schräge Richtung, der Winkel (*angle*).
slap [slæp], *v.a.* schlagen. — *s.* der Klaps, Schlag.
slapdash ['slæpdæʃ], *adj.* oberflächlich.
slash [slæʃ], *v.a.* schlitzen, aufschlitzen; (*coll.*) (*Comm.*) herunterbringen (*prices*). — *s.* der Hieb, Schlag.
slate [sleit], *s.* der Schiefer. — *v.a.* mit Schiefer decken; (*fig.*) ankreiden, ausschelten (*scold*).
slattern ['slætǝ:n], *s.* die Schlampe.
slaughter ['slɔ:tǝ], *v.a.* schlachten; niedermetzeln. — *s.* das Schlachten; das Gemetzel.
slave [sleiv], *s.* der Sklave; — *driver*, der Sklavenaufseher. — *v.n.* — (*away*), sich placken, sich rackern.
slavery ['sleivǝri], *s.* die Sklaverei.
slavish ['sleiviʃ], *adj.* sklavisch.
slay [slei], *v.a.* erschlagen, töten.
sled, sledge [sled, sledʒ], *s.* der Schlitten.
sleek [sli:k], *adj.* glatt. — *v.a.* glätten.
sleep [sli:p], *v.n. irr.* schlafen. — *s.* der Schlaf.
sleeper ['sli:pǝ], *s.* der Schläfer; (*Railw.*) die Bahnschwelle; der Schlafwagen (*sleeping car*).
sleepwalker ['sli:pwɔ:kǝ], *s.* der Nachtwandler.
sleet [sli:t], *s.* der Graupelregen.
sleeve [sli:v], *s.* der Ärmel; der Umschlag (*of record*); *have up o.'s —*, eine Überraschung bereithalten; *laugh in o.'s —*, sich ins Fäustchen lachen.
sleigh [slei], *s.* der Schlitten; — *ride*, die Schlittenfahrt.
sleight [slait], *s. — of hand*, der Taschenspielerstreich; der Trick.
slender ['slendǝ], *adj.* schlank, dünn, gering.
slice [slais], *s.* die Schnitte, Scheibe. — *v.a.* in Scheiben schneiden.
slick [slik], *adj.* glatt.
slide [slaid], *v.n. irr.* gleiten, rutschen (*glide*). — *v.a.* einschieben. — *s.* die Rutschbahn; (*Phot.*) das Dia, Diapositiv; — *rule*, der Rechenschieber.

slight [slait], *adj.* leicht (*light*), gering (*small*); (*fig.*) schwach, dünn(*weak*). — *s.* die Geringschätzung, Respektlosigkeit. — *v.a.* mißachten, geringschätzig behandeln.

slim [slim], *adj.* schlank.

slime [slaim], *s.* der Schleim (*phlegm*); der Schlamm (*mud*).

sling [sliŋ], *v.a. irr.* schleudern, werfen. — *s.* die Schleuder; (*Med.*) die Binde; der Wurf (*throw*).

slink [sliŋk], *v.n. irr.* schleichen.

slip [slip], *v.n.* ausgleiten; — *away*, entschlüpfen; — *up*, einen Fehltritt begehen (*err*). — *v.a.* gleiten lassen, schieben. — *s.* das Ausgleiten; (*fig.*) der Fehltritt; der Fehler (*mistake*); der Unterrock (*petticoat*); *give s.o. the* —, einem entgehen, entschlüpfen.

slipper [ˈslipə], *s.* der Pantoffel, Hausschuh.

slippery [ˈslipə], *adj.* schlüpfrig, glatt.

slipshod [ˈslipʃɔd], *adj.* nachlässig.

slit [slit], *v.a.* schlitzen, spalten. — *s.* der Schlitz, Spalt.

slither [ˈsliðə], *v.n.* gleiten, rutschen.

sloe [slou], *s.* (*Bot.*) die Schlehe.

slogan [ˈslougən], *s.* das Schlagwort.

sloop [slu:p], *s.* (*Naut.*) die Schaluppe.

slop [slɔp], *s.* das Spülicht, Spülwasser.

slope [sloup], *s.* der Abhang, die Abdachung. — *v.n.* sich neigen. — *v.a.* abschrägen.

sloppy [ˈslɔpi], *adj.* unordentlich, nachlässig.

slot [slɔt], *s.* der Spalt, Schlitz (*slit*); die Kerbe (*notch*); — *machine*, der Automat.

sloth [slouθ], *s.* die Trägheit; (*Zool.*) das Faultier.

slouch [slautʃ], *v.n.* umherschlendern; sich schlaff halten.

slough [slau], *s.* der Morast, Sumpf.

slovenly [ˈslʌvnli], *adj.* schlampig, schmutzig.

slow [slou], *adj.* langsam; (*Phot.*) — *motion*, die Zeitlupenaufnahme. — *v.n.* — *down*, langsamer fahren *or* laufen.

slow-worm [ˈslouwəːm], *s.* (*Zool.*) die Blindschleiche.

sludge [slʌdʒ], *s.* der Schlamm, Schmutz.

slug [slʌg], *s.* (*Zool.*) die Wegschnecke; (*Am.*) die Kugel.

sluggish [ˈslʌgiʃ], *adj.* träg(e).

sluice [slu:s], *s.* die Schleuse. — *v.a.* ablassen (*drain*); begießen (*water*).

slum [slʌm], *s.* das Elendsviertel; Haus im Elendsviertel.

slumber [ˈslʌmbə], *s.* der Schlummer. — *v.n.* schlummern.

slump [slʌmp], *s.* (*Comm.*) der Tiefstand der Konjunktur; der Preissturz. — *v.n.* stürzen.

slur [sləː], *v.a.* undeutlich sprechen. — *s.* der Schandfleck, die Beleidigung; das Bindezeichen.

slush [slʌʃ], *s.* der Matsch, Schlamm; (*Lit.*) der Kitsch, die Schundliteratur.

slut [slʌt], *s.* die Schlampe.

sly [slai], *adj.* schlau, listig.

smack [smæk], *v.n.* schmecken (*of*, nach, *Dat.*). — *v.a.* schmatzen, lecken. — *s.* der Klaps. — *adv.* (*coll.*) — *in the middle*, gerade in die Mitte.

small [smɔ:l], *adj.* klein; (*fig.*) kleinlich (*petty*); — *talk*, das Geplauder.

smallpox [ˈsmɔ:lpɔks], *s.* (*Med.*) die Blattern, *f. pl.*

smart [sma:t], *adj.* schneidig; elegant, schick (*well-dressed*). — *v.n.* schmerzen. — *s.* der Schmerz.

smash [smæʃ], *v.a.* zertrümmern, in Stücke schlagen. — *v.n.* zerschmettern; (*fig.*) zusammenbrechen. — *s.* der Krach.

smattering [ˈsmætəriŋ], *s.* die oberflächliche Kenntnis.

smear [smiə], *v.a.* beschmieren; (*Am. coll.*) den Charakter angreifen, verleumden. — *s.* die Beschmierung, Befleckung.

smell [smel], *v.a. irr.* riechen. — *v.n.* riechen (nach, *Dat.*). — *s.* der Geruch.

smelt (1) [smelt], *v.a.* (*Metall.*) schmelzen.

smelt (2) [smelt], *s.* (*Zool.*) der Stintfisch.

smile [smail], *v.n.* lächeln. — *s.* das Lächeln.

smirk [sməːk], *v.n.* grinsen. — *s.* das Grinsen, die Grimasse.

smite [smait], *v.a. irr.* treffen, schlagen.

smith [smiθ], *s.* der Schmied.

smitten [smitn], *adj.* verliebt.

smock [smɔk], *s.* der Arbeitskittel.

smoke [smouk], *v.a., v.n.* rauchen; räuchern (*fish etc.*). — *s.* der Rauch.

smoked [smoukd], *adj.* — *ham*, der Räucherschinken.

smooth [smu:ð], *adj.* glatt, sanft (*to touch*); (*fig.*) glatt, geschmeidig, wendig. — *v.a.* glätten, ebnen.

smother [ˈsmʌðə], *v.a.* ersticken.

smoulder [ˈsmouldə], *v.n.* schwelen.

smudge [smʌdʒ], *v.a.* beschmutzen. — *v.n.* schmieren, schmutzen. — *s.* der Schmutzfleck, Schmutz.

smug [smʌg], *adj.* selbstgefällig.

smuggle [ˈsmʌgl], *v.a.* schmuggeln.

smuggler [ˈsmʌglə], *s.* der Schmuggler.

smut [smʌt], *v.a., v.n.* beschmutzen. — *s.* (*fig.*) der Schmutz.

snack [snæk], *s.* der Imbiß.

snaffle [snæfl], *s.* die Trense.

snag [snæg], *s.* die Schwierigkeit; der Haken.

snail [sneil], *s.* (*Zool.*) die Schnecke.

snake [sneik], *s.* (*Zool.*) die Schlange.

snap [snæp], *v.n.* schnappen (*at*, nach, *Dat.*); (*fig.*) einen anfahren (*shout at s.o.*). — *v.a.* (er)schnappen; (*Phot.*) knipsen. — *s.* (*abbr. for* **snapshot** [ˈsnæpʃɔt]) (*Phot.*) das Photo.

snare [snɛə], *s.* die Schlinge. — *v.a. see* **ensnare**.

snarl [sna:l], *v.n.* knurren (*dog*); — *at s.o.*, einen anfahren, anschnauzen.

snatch

snatch [snætʃ], *v.a.* erschnappen, erhaschen.
sneak [sniːk], *v.n.* kriechen, schleichen. — *s.* der Kriecher.
sneer [sniə], *v.n.* höhnen, verhöhnen (*at, Acc.*). — *s.* der Spott.
sneeze [sniːz], *v.n.* niesen. — *s.* das Niesen.
sniff [snif], *v.a., v.n.* schnüffeln.
snigger [ˈsnigə], *v.n.* kichern. — *s.* das Kichern.
snip [snip], *v.a.* schneiden, schnippeln.
snipe (1) [snaip], *s.* (*Orn.*) die Schnepfe.
snipe (2) [snaip], *v.n.* schießen.
snivel [snivl], *v.n.* schluchzen (*from weeping*); verschnupft sein (*with a cold*).
snob [snɔb], *s.* der Snob.
snobbish [ˈsnɔbiʃ], *adj.* vornehm tuend; protzig, snobistisch.
snooze [snuːz], *s.* das Schläfchen. — *v.n.* einschlafen, ein Schläfchen machen.
snore [snɔː], *v.n.* schnarchen. — *s.* das Schnarchen.
snort [snɔːt], *v.n.* schnaufen; schnarchen (*snore*).
snout [snaut], *s.* die Schnauze, der Rüssel.
snow [snou], *s.* der Schnee. — *v.n.* schneien.
snowdrift [ˈsnoudrift], *s.* das Schneegestöber.
snowdrop [ˈsnoudrɔp], *s.* (*Bot.*) das Schneeglöckchen.
snub [snʌb], *v.a.* kurz abfertigen; (*fig.*) schneiden (*ignore*). — *adj.* — *nosed*, stumpfnasig. — *s.* die Geringschätzung, das Ignorieren.
snuff [snʌf], *s.* der Schnupftabak. — *v.a.* ausblasen (*candle*).
snug [snʌg], *adj.* behaglich; geborgen (*protected*).
so [sou], *adv.* so, also; *not — as,* nicht so wie. — *conj.* so.
soak [souk], *v.a.* einweichen, durchtränken. — *v.n.* weichen, durchsickern (*in(to)*), in, *Acc.*). — *s.* der Regenguß.
soap [soup], *s.* die Seife. — *v.a.* einseifen.
soar [sɔː], *v.n.* sich aufschwingen, schweben.
sob [sɔb], *v.n.* schluchzen. — *s.* das Schluchzen.
sober [ˈsoubə], *adj.* nüchtern. — *v.a., v.n. — (down),* (sich) ernüchtern.
sobriety [souˈbraiəti], *s.* die Nüchternheit.
soccer [ˈsɔkə], *s.* (*Sport*) das Fußballspiel.
sociable [ˈsouʃəbl], *adj.* gesellig.
social [ˈsouʃəl], *adj.* sozial, gesellschaftlich. — *s.* die Gesellschaft (*party*).
socialism [ˈsouʃəlizm], *s.* (*Pol.*) der Sozialismus.
socialist [ˈsouʃəlist], *adj.* (*Pol.*) sozialistisch, sozial-. — *s.* der Sozialist.
society [səˈsaiəti], *s.* die Gesellschaft (*human —*); der Verein (*association*); (*Comm.*) die (Handels)gesellschaft.

sock (1) [sɔk], *s.* der Strumpf.
sock (2) [sɔk], *v.a.* (*sl.*) schlagen, boxen.
socket [ˈsɔkit], *s. eye —,* die Augenhöhle; (*Elec.*) die Steckdose.
sod [sɔd], *s.* der Rasen, die Erde.
sodden [sɔdn], *adj.* durchweicht.
sofa [ˈsoufə], *s.* das Sofa.
soft [sɔft], *adj.* weich, sanft; einfältig (*stupid*).
soften [sɔfn], *v.a.* weich machen, erweichen. — *v.n.* weich werden, erweichen.
soil [sɔil], *s.* der Boden, die Erde. — *v.a.* beschmutzen.
sojourn [ˈsɔdʒən *or* ˈsɔdʒən], *s.* der Aufenthalt. — *v.n.* sich aufhalten.
solace [ˈsɔlis], *s.* der Trost.
solar [ˈsoulə], *adj.* Sonnen-.
solder [ˈsɔldə *or* ˈsɔːdə], *v.a.* löten. — *s.* das Lötmittel.
soldier [ˈsouldʒə], *s.* der Soldat. — *v.n.* dienen, Soldat sein.
sole (1) [soul], *s.* (*Zool.*) die Seezunge.
sole (2) [soul], *s.* die Sohle (*foot*).
sole (3) [soul], *adj.* allein, einzig.
solecism [ˈsɔlisizm], *s.* der Sprachschnitzer.
solemn [ˈsɔləm], *adj.* feierlich.
solemnize [ˈsɔləmnaiz], *v.a.* feiern, feierlich begehen.
solicit [səˈlisit], *v.a.* direkt erbitten, angehen, anhalten (*for,* um).
solicitor [səˈlisitə], *s.* (*Law*) der Anwalt, Rechtsanwalt.
solicitous [səˈlisitəs], *adj.* besorgt.
solid [ˈsɔlid], *adj.* fest; solide; (*fig.*) gediegen; massiv (*bulky*).
solidify [səˈlidifai], *v.a.* verdichten, fest machen. — *v.n.* sich verfestigen.
soliloquy [səˈliləkwi], *s.* das Selbstgespräch, der Monolog.
solitaire [sɔliˈtɛə], *s.* der Solitär; (*Am.*) die Patience.
solitary [ˈsɔlitəri], *adj.* einzeln (*single*); einsam (*lonely*).
solitude [ˈsɔlitjuːd], *s.* die Einsamkeit.
solstice [ˈsɔlstis], *s.* die Sonnenwende.
soluble [ˈsɔljubl], *adj.* (*Chem.*) löslich; lösbar.
solution [səˈljuːʃən], *s.* die Lösung.
solvable [ˈsɔlvəbl], *adj.* (auf)lösbar (*problem, puzzle*).
solve [sɔlv], *v.a.* lösen (*problem, puzzle*).
solvent [ˈsɔlvənt], *adj.* (*Chem.*) auflösend; (*Comm.*) zahlungsfähig. — *s.* das Lösungsmittel.
sombre [ˈsɔmbə], *adj.* düster; schwermütig, traurig.
some [sʌm], *adj.* irgend ein, etwas; (*pl.*) einige, manche; etliche.
somebody [ˈsʌmbɔdi], *s.* jemand.
somersault [ˈsʌməsɔːlt], *s.* der Purzelbaum.
sometimes [ˈsʌmtaimz], *adv.* manchmal, zuweilen.
somewhat [ˈsʌmwɔt], *adv.* etwas, ziemlich.
somewhere [ˈsʌmwɛə], *adv.* irgendwo(hin).

somnambulist [sɔm'næmbjulist], *s.* der Nachtwandler.

somnolent ['sɔmnələnt], *adj.* schläfrig, schlafsüchtig.

son [sʌn], *s.* der Sohn; —*-in-law,* der Schwiegersohn.

song [sɔŋ], *s.* (*Mus.*) das Lied; der Gesang; *for a* —, spottbillig.

sonnet ['sɔnit], *s.* (*Poet.*) das Sonett.

sonorous ['sɔnərəs], *adj.* wohlklingend.

soon [su:n], *adv.* bald.

sooner ['su:nə], *comp. adv.* lieber (*rather*); früher, eher (*earlier*), *no* — *said than done,* gesagt, getan.

soot [sut], *s.* der Ruß.

soothe [su:ð], *v.a.* besänftigen.

soothsayer ['su:θseiə], *s.* der Wahrsager.

sop [sɔp], *s.* der eingetunkte Bissen; (*fig.*) die Bestechung (*bribe*).

soporific [sɔpə'rifik], *adj.* einschläfernd.

soprano [sə'prɑ:nou], *s.* (*Mus.*) der Sopran.

sorcerer ['sɔ:sərə], *s.* der Zauberer.

sorceress ['sɔ:sərəs], *s.* die Hexe.

sorcery ['sɔ:səri], *s.* die Zauberei, Hexerei.

sordid ['sɔ:did], *adj.* schmutzig; gemein.

sore [sɔ:], *adj.* wund, schmerzhaft; empfindlich. — *s.* die wunde Stelle.

sorrel (1) ['sɔrəl], *s.* (*Bot.*) der Sauerampfer.

sorrel (2) ['sɔrəl], *s.* (*Zool.*) der Rotfuchs.

sorrow ['sɔrou], *s.* der Kummer, das Leid, der Gram.

sorry ['sɔri], *adj.* traurig; *I am* —, es tut mir leid.

sort [sɔ:t], *s.* die Art, Gattung, Sorte. — *v.a.* aussortieren.

sortie ['sɔ:ti:], *s.* (*Mil.*) der Ausfall.

sot [sɔt], *s.* der Trunkenbold.

soul [soul], *s.* die Seele; *not a* —, niemand, keine Menschenseele.

sound (1) [saund], *v.n., v.a.* tönen, klingen, erklingen lassen. — *s.* der Klang, Ton, Laut.

sound (2) [saund], *adj.* gesund; (*fig.*) vernünftig (*plan etc.*); solide.

soup [su:p], *s.* die Suppe.

sour [sauə], *adj.* sauer; (*fig.*) mürrisch.

source [sɔ:s], *s.* die Quelle; der Ursprung (*origin*).

souse [saus], *v.a.* einpökeln, einsalzen.

south [sauθ], *s.* der Süden.

South African [sauθ 'æfrikən], *adj.* südafrikanisch. — *s.* der Südafrikaner.

southern ['sʌðən], *adj.* südlich, Süd-.

sou(th)-wester [sau(θ)'westə], *s.* (*Naut.*) der Südwester.

souvenir ['su:vəniə], *s.* das Andenken.

sovereign ['sɔvrin], *s.* der Herrscher (*ruler*); das Goldstück (£1 *coin*). — *adj.* allerhöchst, souverän.

Soviet ['souviit], *adj.* sowjetisch. — *s.* der Sowjet.

sow (1) [sau], *s.* (*Zool.*) die Sau.

sow (2) [sou], *v.a. irr.* säen, ausstreuen (*cast*).

spa [spɑ:], *s.* das Bad; der Kurort.

space [speis], *s.* der Zwischenraum (*interval*); der Raum, das Weltall, der Kosmos (*interplanetary*); der Platz (*room*). — *v.a.* sperren, richtig plazieren.

spacious ['speiʃəs], *adj.* geräumig.

spade [speid], *s.* der Spaten; *call a* — *a* —, das Kind beim rechten Namen nennen; (*Cards*) das Pik.

span [spæn], *s.* die Spanne (*time*); die Spannweite. — *v.a.* überspannen (*bridge*); ausmessen.

spangle [spæŋgl], *s.* der Flitter. — *v.a.* beflittern, schmücken.

Spaniard ['spænjəd], *s.* der Spanier.

spaniel ['spænjəl], *s.* (*Zool.*) der Wachtelhund.

Spanish ['spæniʃ], *adj.* spanisch.

spanner ['spænə], *s.* der Schraubenschlüssel.

spar (1) [spɑ:], *s.* (*Naut.*) der Sparren.

spar (2) [spɑ:], *s.* (*Geol.*) der Spat.

spar (3) [spɑ:], *v.n.* boxen.

spare [spɛə], *v.a.* schonen (*save*); sparsam sein; übrig haben. — *v.n.* sparen; sparsam sein. — *adj.* übrig (*extra*); mager, hager (*lean*); Reserve- (*tyre etc.*).

sparing ['spɛəriŋ], *adj.* sparsam, karg.

spark [spɑ:k], *s.* der Funken; (*fig.*) der helle Kopf.

sparkle [spɑ:kl], *v.n.* glänzen, funkeln. — *s.* das Funkeln.

sparrow ['spærou], *s.* (*Orn.*) der Sperling.

sparrowhawk ['spærouhɔ:k], *s.* (*Orn.*) der Sperber.

sparse [spɑ:s], *adj.* spärlich, dünn.

spasm [spæzm], *s.* der Krampf.

spasmodic [spæz'mɔdik], *adj.* krampfhaft; (*fig.*) ab und zu auftretend.

spats [spæts], *s. pl.* die Gamaschen, *f.pl.*

spatter ['spætə], *v.a.* bespritzen, besudeln.

spatula ['spætjulə], *s.* der Spachtel.

spawn [spɔ:n], *s.* der Laich, die Brut.

speak [spi:k], *v.a., v.n. irr.* sprechen, reden; — *out,* frei heraussprechen.

speaker ['spi:kə], *s.* der Sprecher.

spear [spiə], *s.* der Spieß, Speer, die Lanze. — *v.a.* aufspießen.

special [speʃl], *adj.* besonder, speziell, Sonder-.

specific [spi'sifik], *adj.* spezifisch, eigentümlich.

specify ['spesifai], *v.a.* spezifizieren.

specimen ['spesimən], *s.* die Probe; (*Comm.*) das Muster.

specious ['spi:ʃəs], *adj.* bestechend, trügerisch.

speck [spek], *s.* der Fleck.

speckle [spekl], *s.* der Tüpfel, Sprenkel. — *v.a.* sprenkeln.

spectacle ['spektəkl], *s.* das Schauspiel, der Anblick; (*pl.*) die Brille.

spectator [spek'teitə], *s.* der Zuschauer.

spectre ['spektə], *s.* das Gespenst.

speculate ['spekjuleit], *v.n.* nachsinnen, grübeln (*ponder*); spekulieren.

speculative

speculative ['spekjulətiv], *adj.* spekulativ; sinnend.

speech [spi:tʃ], *s.* die Rede, Ansprache; das Sprechen (*articulation*); *figure of* —, die Redewendung; *make a* —, eine Rede halten.

speechify ['spi:tʃifai], *v.n.* viele Worte machen, unermüdlich reden.

speed [spi:d], *s.* die Eile; die Geschwindigkeit (*velocity*); (*Mus.*) das Tempo. — *v.a.* (eilig) fortschicken. — *v.n.* eilen, schnell fahren; — *up*, sich beeilen.

spell (1) [spel], *s.* der Zauber (*enchantment*). — *v.a.* buchstabieren (*verbally*); richtig schreiben (*in writing*).

spell (2) [spel], *s.* die Zeitlang, Zeit (*period*).

spellbound ['spelbaund], *adj.* bezaubert, gebannt.

spend [spend], *v.a. irr.* ausgeben (*money*); verbringen (*time*); aufwenden (*energy*); erschöpfen (*exhaust*).

spendthrift ['spendθrift], *s.* der Verschwender.

spew [spju:], *v.a.* speien; ausspeien.

sphere [sfiə], *s.* die Sphäre (*also fig.*); (*Geom.*) die Kugel.

spice [spais], *s.* die Würze (*seasoning*); das Gewürz (*herb*). — *v.a.* würzen.

spider ['spaidə], *s.* (*Zool.*) die Spinne.

spigot ['spigət], *s.* (*Mech.*) der Zapfen.

spike [spaik], *s.* die Spitze, der lange Nagel; (*fig.*) der Dorn. — *v.a.* durchbohren, spießen; (*Mil.*) vernageln (*a gun*).

spill (1) [spil], *v.a. irr.* ausschütten, vergießen; (*Am. coll.*) — *the beans*, mit der Sprache herausrücken, alles verraten; *it's no good crying over spilt milk*, was geschehen ist, ist geschehen.

spill (2) [spil], *s.* der Fidibus.

spin [spin], *v.a. irr.* spinnen, drehen, wirbeln. — *v.n.* wirbeln, sich schnell drehen; — *dry*, schleudern. — *s.* die schnelle Drehung; — *drier*, die Wäscheschleuder.

spinach ['spinidʒ], *s.* (*Bot.*) der Spinat.

spinal ['spainəl], *adj.* Rückgrats-.

spine [spain], *s.* (*Anat.*) die Wirbelsäule; der Rücken (*of book*).

spinney ['spini], *s.* das Gestrüpp.

spinster ['spinstə], *s.* die (alte) Jungfer; die unverheiratete Dame.

spiral ['spaiərəl], *adj.* Spiral-, gewunden. — *s.* (*Geom.*) die Spirale.

spirant ['spaiərənt], *s.* (*Phonet.*) der Spirant.

spire [spaiə], *s.* (*Archit.*) die Turmspitze.

spirit ['spirit], *s.* der Geist; das Gespenst (*ghost*); der Mut (*courage*); die Stimmung, Verfassung (*mood*); die geistige Getränk (*drink*), (*pl.*) Spirituosen, *pl.*; *in high* —*s*, in guter Stimmung, Laune. — *v.a.* — *away*, entführen, verschwinden lassen.

spiritual ['spiritjuəl], *adj.* geistig (*mental*); (*Rel.*) geistlich. — *s.* (*Mus.*) das Negerlied.

spit (1) [spit], *s.* der Spieß, Bratspieß. — *v.a.* aufspießen.

spit (2) [spit], *v.n. irr.* ausspucken. — *s.* die Spucke.

spite [spait], *s.* der Groll; *in* — *of*, trotz (*Genit.*). — *v.a.* ärgern.

spiteful ['spaitful], *adj.* boshaft.

spittle [spitl], *s.* der Speichel.

spittoon [spi'tu:n], *s.* der Spucknapf.

splash [splæʃ], *s.* der Spritzer; *make a* —, Aufsehen erregen. — *v.a.*, *v.n.* spritzen; (*fig.*) um sich werfen (*money etc.*).

splay [splei], *v.a.* ausrenken, verrenken.

spleen [spli:n], *s.* (*Anat.*) die Milz; (*fig.*) der Spleen, die Laune, Marotte.

splendour ['splendə], *s.* die Pracht, der Glanz.

splice [splais], *v.a.* splissen; (*Naut.*) — *the mainbrace*, das Hauptfaß öffnen!

splint [splint], *s.* (*Med.*) die Schiene.

splinter ['splintə], *s.* der Span; der Splitter (*fragment*).

split [split], *v.a. irr.* spalten; (*fig.*) verteilen, teilen (*divide*). — *v.n.* sich trennen; (*coll.*) — *on s.o.*, einen verraten. — *adj.* — *second timing*, auf den Bruchteil einer Sekunde. — *s.* die Spaltung.

splutter ['splʌtə], *v.n.* sprudeln. — *s.* das Sprudeln.

spoil [spoil], *v.a. irr.* verderben; (*child*) verwöhnen; (*Mil.*) plündern, berauben. — *v.n.* verderben. — *s.* ; [*l.*) die Beute.

spoilsport ['spoilspo:t], *s.* der Spielverderber.

spoke [spouk], *s.* die Speiche; die Sprosse.

spokesman ['spouksmən], *s.* der Wortführer, Sprecher.

sponge [spʌndʒ], *s.* der Schwamm; — *cake*, die Sandtorte. — *v.a.* mit dem Schwamm wischen. — *v.n.* (*coll.*) schmarotzen (*on*, bei, *Dat.*).

sponger ['spʌndʒə], *s.* (*coll.*) der Schmarotzer (*parasite*).

sponsor ['sponsə], *s.* der Bürge (*guarantor*); der Förderer; Pate. — *v.a.* fördern, unterstützen.

spontaneous [spon'teiniəs], *adj.* spontan, freiwillig.

spook [spuk], *s.* der Spuk, Geist, das Gespenst.

spool [spu:l], *s.* die Spule. — *v.a.* aufspulen.

spoon [spu:n], *s.* der Löffel. — *v.a.* mit dem Löffel essen, löffeln.

sport [spo:t], *s.* der Sport; (*fig.*) der Scherz. — *v.a.* tragen (*wear*). — *v.n.* scherzen.

spot [spot], *s.* die Stelle, der Ort, Platz; (*stain*) der Fleck; (*fig.*) der Schandfleck (*on o.'s honour*); *on the* —, sogleich; auf der Stelle; *in a* —, (*Am. coll.*) in Verlegenheit; — *cash*, Barzahlung, *f.* — *v.a.* entdecken, finden.

spotted ['spotid], *adj.* — *dick*, der Korinthenpudding.

spouse [spauz], *s.* der Gatte; die Gattin.

spout [spaut], *v.a.*, *v.n.* ausspeien, sprudeln, sprudeln lassen; (*sl.*) predigen, schwatzen. — *s.* die Tülle (*teapot etc.*); die Abflußröhre.

sprain [sprein], *v.a.* (*Med.*) verrenken. — *s.* die Verrenkung.

sprat [spræt], *s.* (*Zool.*) die Sprotte.

sprawl [sprɔːl], *v.n.* sich spreizen, ausbreiten.

spray [sprei], *v.a.*, *v.n.* sprühen spritzen. — *s.* die Sprühe; der Sprühregen.

spread [spred], *v.a.*, *v.n. irr.* ausbreiten; verbreiten (*get abroad*); streichen (*overlay with*). — *s.* die Ausbreitung; Verbreitung.

spree [spriː], *s.* das Vergnügen, der lustige Abend, Bummel.

sprig [sprig], *s.* der Zweig, Sprößling.

sprightly [ˈspraitli], *adj.* munter, lebhaft.

spring [spriŋ], *s.* die Quelle (*water*); der Ursprung (*origin*); der Frühling (*season*); (*Mech.*) die Feder, Sprungfeder, Spirale. — *v.n. irr.* springen (*jump*); entspringen (*originate*). — *v.a.* — *a surprise*, eine Überraschung bereiten.

springe [sprindʒ], *s.* der Sprenkel.

sprinkle [ˈspriŋkl], *v.a.* (be)sprengen; (*Hort.*) berieseln.

sprint [sprint], *s.* der Kurzstreckenlauf, Wettlauf.

sprite [sprait], *s.* der Geist, Kobold.

sprout [spraut], *s.* (*Bot.*) die Sprosse, der Sprößling; *Brussels —s*, der Rosenkohl.

spruce (1) [spruːs], *adj.* sauber, geputzt; schmuck.

spruce (2) [spruːs], *s.* (*Bot.*) die Fichte, Rottanne.

spume [spjuːm], *s.* der Schaum.

spur [spəː], *s.* der Sporn (*goad*); (*fig.*) der Stachel; der Ansporn, Antrieb; (*Geog.*) der Ausläufer (*of range*). — *v.a.* anspornen.

spurious [ˈspjuəriəs], *adj.* unecht, falsch.

spurn [spəːn], *v.a.* verschmähen, verachten.

spurt [spəːt], *v.a.* spritzen. — *v.n.* sich anstrengen. — *s.* die Anstrengung.

sputter [ˈspʌtə], *v.a.* herausprudeln. — *v.n.* sprühen, sprudeln.

spy [spai], *s.* der Spion. — *v.n.* spionieren (*on*, bei, *Dat.*).

squabble [ˈskwɔbl], *v.n.* zanken. — *s.* der Zank, Streit.

squad [skwɔd], *s.* der Trupp.

squadron [ˈskwɔdrən], *s.* die Schwadron, das Geschwader.

squalid [ˈskwɔlid], *adj.* schmutzig, elend, eklig.

squall [skwɔːl], *s.* der Windstoß.

squalor [ˈskwɔlə], *s.* der Schmutz.

squander [ˈskwɔndə], *v.a.* verschwenden, vergeuden.

square [skwɛə], *s.* das Quadrat; der Platz; (*coll.*) der Philister, Spießer. — *v.a.* ausrichten; (*coll.*) ins Reine bringen. — *adj.* viereckig; quadratisch; redlich (*honest*); quitt (*quits*).

squash (1) [skwɔʃ], *v.a.* zerquetschen, zerdrücken (*press together*). — *s.* das Gedränge (*crowd*); der Fruchtsaft (*drink*).

squash (2) [skwɔʃ], *s.* (*Sport*) eine Art Racketspiel.

squat [skwɔt], *v.n.* kauern; sich niederlassen. — *adj.* stämmig, untersetzt.

squatter [ˈskwɔtə], *s.* der Ansiedler.

squaw [skwɔː], *s.* die Indianerfrau.

squeak [skwiːk], *v.n.* quieken, quietschen. — *s.* das Gequiek.

squeal [skwiːl], *v.n.* quieken; (*Am. coll.*) verraten, preisgeben.

squeamish [ˈskwiːmiʃ], *adj.* empfindlich, zimperlich.

squeeze [skwiːz], *v.a.* drücken, quetschen. — *s.* das Gedränge.

squib [skwib], *s.* der Frosch (*firework*); (*Lit.*) das Spottgedicht.

squint [skwint], *v.n.* schielen. — *s.* das Schielen.

squire [skwaiə], *s.* der Landedelmann, Junker.

squirrel [ˈskwirəl], *s.* (*Zool.*) das Eichhörnchen.

squirt [skwəːt], *v.a.* spritzen. — *s.* der Spritzer, Wasserstrahl; (*sl.*) der Wicht.

stab [stæb], *v.a.* erstechen, erdolchen. — *s.* der Dolchstich, Dolchstoß.

stability [stəˈbiliti], *s.* die Beständigkeit, Stabilität.

stable (1) [steibl], *adj.* fest, beständig; (*Phys.*) stabil.

stable (2) [steibl], *s.* der Stall.

stack [stæk], *s.* der Stoß (*pile*); der Schornstein (*chimneys*). — *v.a.* aufschichten.

staff [staːf], *s.* der Stab, Stock; (*Mil.*) der Stab, Generalstab; (*Sch.*) der Lehrkörper; das Personal. — *v.a.* besetzen.

stag [stæg], *s.* (*Zool.*) der Hirsch; — *party*, die Herrengesellschaft.

stage [steidʒ], *s.* (*Theat.*) die Bühne; die Stufe, das Stadium (*phase*); (*fig.*) der Schauplatz; *fare —*, die Teilstrecke. — *v.a.* (*Theat.*) inszenieren, abhalten (*hold*).

stagecoach [ˈsteidʒkoutʃ], *s.* die Postkutsche.

stagger [ˈstægə], *v.n.* schwanken, wanken, taumeln. — *v.a.* (*coll.*) verblüffen (*astonish*); staffeln (*graduate*).

stagnate [stægˈneit], *v.n.* stocken, stillstehen.

staid [steid], *adj.* gesetzt, gelassen.

stain [stein], *s.* der Fleck, Makel. — *v.a.* beflecken; beizen; färben (*dye*).

stained [steind], *adj.* — *glass window*, buntes Fenster.

stainless [ˈsteinlis], *adj.* rostfrei.

stair [stɛə], *s.* die Stufe, Stiege.

staircase [ˈstɛəkeis], *s.* das Treppenhaus; die Treppe.

stake [steik], *s.* der Pfahl, Pfosten; Scheiterhaufen; (*Gambling*) der Einsatz; *at —*, auf dem Spiel. — *v.a.* aufs Spiel setzen.

stale [steil], *adj.* abgestanden, schal.

stalemate

stalemate ['steilmeit], *s.* (*Chess*) das Patt; der Stillstand.

stalk (1) [stɔ:k], *s.* (*Bot.*) der Stengel, Halm.

stalk (2) [stɔ:k], *v.n.* stolzieren, steif gehen. — *v.a.* pirschen (*hunt*).

stall [stɔ:l], *s.* die Bude (*booth*), der Stand (*stand*); (*Eccl.*) der Chorstuhl; (*Theat.*) der Sperrsitz; Parterresitz. — *v.n.* (*Motor.*) stehenbleiben.

stallion ['stæljən], *s.* (*Zool.*) der Hengst.

stalwart ['stɔ:lwət], *adj.* kräftig, stark, verläßlich.

stamina ['stæminə], *s.* die Ausdauer, Widerstandskraft.

stammer ['stæmə], *v.n.* stammeln, stottern.

stamp [stæmp], *s.* der Stempel (*rubber* —); die Marke (*postage*); die Stampfe, Stanze (*die* —). — *v.a.* stempeln; (*Mech.*) stanzen; frankieren (*letters*). — *v.n.* stampfen.

stampede [stæm'pi:d], *s.* die wilde Flucht. — *v.n.* in wilder Flucht davonlaufen.

stand [stænd], *v.n. irr.* stehen. — *v.a.* aushalten, standhalten (*Dat.*). — *s.* der Ständer (*hats etc.*); der Stand (*stall*); (*fig.*) die Stellung.

standard ['stændəd], *s.* der Standard (*level*); (*Mil.*) die Standarte; der Maßstab (*yardstick*). — *adj.* normal.

standing ['stændiŋ], *s.* der Rang, das Ansehen. — *adj.* — *orders*, die Geschäftsordnung; (*Mil.*) die Vorschriften, *f. pl.*, Dauerbefehle, *m. pl.*

standpoint ['stændpɔint], *s.* der Standpunkt (*point of view*).

standstill ['stændstil], *s.* der Stillstand.

stanza ['stænzə], *s.* (*Poet.*) die Stanze, Strophe.

staple [steipl], *s.* das Haupterzeugnis; der Stapelplatz. — *adj.* Haupt-. — *v.a.* stapeln; heften (*paper*).

stapler ['steiplə], *s.* die Heftmaschine.

star [stɑ:], *s.* der Stern; (*Theat. etc.*) der Star. — *v.n.* (*Theat. etc.*) die Hauptrolle spielen.

starboard ['stɑ:bəd], *s.* das Steuerbord.

starch [stɑ:tʃ], *s.* die Stärke (*laundry*). — *v.a.* stärken.

stare [steə], *v.n.* starren. — *s.* der starre Blick, das Starren.

stark [stɑ:k], *adj.* völlig, ganz.

starling ['stɑ:liŋ], *s.* (*Orn.*) der Star.

start [stɑ:t], *v.n.* anfangen; aufbrechen; auffahren, aufspringen; stutzen (*jerk*); abfahren (*depart*). — *v.a.* starten (*car etc.*), in Gang setzen. — *s.* der Anfang; (*Sport*) der Start, Anlauf; der Aufbruch (*departure*); *by fits and* —*s,* ruckweise.

starter ['stɑ:tə], *s.* (*Sport*) der Starter, Teilnehmer (*participant*); das Rennpferd (*horse*); (*Motor.*) der Anlasser.

startle [stɑ:tl], *v.a.* erschrecken.

starve [stɑ:v], *v.n.* verhungern, hungern. — *v.a.* aushungern.

state [steit], *s.* der Zustand, die Lage; (*Pol.*) der Staat; (*personal*) der Stand (*single etc.*). — *v.a.* erklären, darlegen.

stately ['steitli], *adj.* stattlich, prachtvoll.

statement ['steitmənt], *s.* die Feststellung; *bank* —, der Kontoauszug.

statesman ['steitsmən], *s.* der Staatsmann, Politiker.

statics ['stætiks], *s.* die Statik.

station ['steiʃən], *s.* (*Railw.*) die Station; der Bahnhof; die Stellung, der Rang (*position*); (*Mil.*) die Stationierung. — *v.a.* (*Mil.*) aufstellen, stationieren; (*fig.*) hinstellen.

stationary ['steiʃənri], *adj.* stationär, stillstehend.

stationer ['steiʃənə], *s.* der Papierhändler.

stationery ['steiʃənri], *s.* das Briefpapier, Schreibpapier; die Papierwaren, *f. pl.*

statuary ['stætjuəri], *s.* die Bildhauerkunst.

statue ['stætju:], *s.* das Standbild.

status ['steitəs], *s.* die Stellung (*rank, position*).

statute ['stætju:t], *s.* das Statut; — *law*, das Landesrecht, Gesetzesrecht.

staunch [stɔ:ntʃ], *adj.* zuverlässig.

stave [steiv], *s.* die Faßdaube (*of vat*); (*Poet.*) die Strophe; (*Mus.*) die Linie. — *v.a.* — (*off*), abwehren.

stay [stei], *v.n.* bleiben, verweilen, wohnen. — *v.a.* hindern, aufhalten. — *s.* der Aufenthalt; (*pl.*) das Korsett.

stead [sted], *s.* die Stelle; *in his* —, an seiner Statt.

steadfast ['stedfɑ:st], *adj.* standhaft, fest.

steadiness ['stedinis], *s.* die Beständigkeit.

steady ['stedi], *adj.* fest, sicher; beständig, treu.

steak [steik], *s.* das Steak.

steal [sti:l], *v.a. irr.* stehlen. — *v.n.* sich stehlen, schleichen.

stealth [stelθ], *s.* die Heimlichkeit.

stealthy ['stelθi], *adj.* heimlich, verstohlen.

steam [sti:m], *s.* der Dampf; *get up* —, in Gang bringen *or* kommen; — *boiler*, der Dampfkessel. — *v.n.* dampfen; davondampfen. — *v.a.* dämpfen, (*Cul.*) dünsten.

steed [sti:d], *s.* das Schlachtroß.

steel [sti:l], *s.* der Stahl. — *adj.* stählern. — *v.n.* — *o.s.*, sich stählen.

steep (1) [sti:p], *adj.* steil; (*fig.*) hoch; (*coll.*) gesalzen (*price*).

steep (2) [sti:p], *v.a.* einweichen, sättigen.

steeple [sti:pl], *s.* (*Archit.*) der Kirchturm.

steeplechase ['sti:pltʃeis], *s.* das Hindernisrennen.

steeplejack ['sti:pldʒæk], *s.* der Turmdecker.

steer (1) [stiə], *s.* (*Zool.*) der junge Stier.

steer (2) [stiə], *v.a.* steuern (*guide*).

steerage ['stiəridʒ], *s.* die Steuerung; (*Naut.*) das Zwischendeck.

stellar ['stelə], *adj.* Stern-, Sternen-.

stem (1) [stem], *s.* der Stamm; (*Phonet.*) der Stamm; der Stiel, die Wurzel. — *v.n.* — *from,* kommen von, abstammen.

stem (2) [stem], *v.a.* sich entgegenstemmen (*Dat.*); (*fig.*) eindämmen.

stench [stentʃ], *s.* der Gestank.

stencil ['stensil], *s.* die Schablone, Matrize; *cut a —,* auf Matrize schreiben.

step [step], *s.* der Schritt, Tritt; (*of ladder*) die Sprosse; (*of stairs*) die Stufe. — *v.n.* treten, schreiten (*stride*). — *v.a.* (*coll.*) — *up,* beschleunigen.

step- [step], *pref.* Stief- (*brother, mother etc.*).

stereo- ['stiariou], *pref.* Stereo-.

sterile ['sterail], *adj.* steril.

sterling ['stə:liŋ], *adj.* echt, vollwertig; *pound —,* ein Pfund Sterling.

stern (1) [stə:n], *adj.* streng.

stern (2) [stə:n], *s.* (*Naut.*) das Heck.

stevedore ['sti:vədɔ:], *s.* der Hafenarbeiter.

stew [stju:], *s.* (*Cul.*) das Schmorfleisch, das Gulasch.

steward ['stju:əd], *s.* der Verwalter; der Haushofmeister; (*Naut.*) der Steward.

stick [stik], *s.* der Stock, Stecken. — *v.a.* stecken (*insert*); kleben (*glue*). — *v.n.* stecken, haften bleiben; (*fig., coll.*) — *to s.o.,* zu jemandem halten (*be loyal*).

sticky ['stiki], *adj.* klebrig; (*fig.*) prekär, schwierig (*difficult*); *come to a — end,* ein böses Ende nehmen.

stiff [stif], *adj.* steif; schwer, schwierig (*examination*); formell (*manner*).

stiffen [stifn], *v.a.* steifen, versteifen. — *v.n.* steif werden, sich versteifen.

stifle [staifl], *v.a., v.n.* ersticken; (*fig.*) unterdrücken.

stigmatize ['stigmətaiz], *v.a.* stigmatisieren, brandmarken.

stile [stail], *s.* der Zauntritt, Übergang.

still (1) [stil], *adj.* still, ruhig. — *adv.* immer noch. — *conj.* doch, dennoch. — *v.a.* stillen, beruhigen.

still (2) [stil], *s.* die Destillierflasche, der Destillierkolben.

stilt [stilt], *s.* die Stelze.

stilted ['stiltid], *adj.* auf Stelzen; (*fig.*) hochtrabend, geschraubt.

stimulant ['stimjulənt], *s.* das Reizmittel. — *adj.* anreizend, anregend.

stimulate ['stimjuleit], *v.a.* anreizen, stimulieren, anregen.

stimulus ['stimjuləs], *s.* der Reiz, die Anregung.

sting [stiŋ], *v.a. irr.* stechen; (*fig.*) kränken, verwunden. — *v.n. irr.* stechen, brennen, schmerzen. — *s.* der Stachel (*prick*); der Stich (*stab*).

stink [stiŋk], *v.n. irr.* stinken. — *s.* der Gestank.

stint [stint], *s.* die Einschränkung (*limit*); das Maß, Tagespensum. — *v.a.* beschränken, einschränken.

stipend ['staipend], *s.* die Besoldung, das Gehalt.

stipendiary [stai'pendiəri], *adj.* besoldet, bezahlt.

stipulate ['stipjuleit], *v.a.* festsetzen, ausbedingen.

stir [stə:], *v.a.* rühren, bewegen. — *v.n.* sich rühren. — *s.* die Aufregung; *cause a —,* Aufsehen erregen.

stirrup ['stirəp], *s.* der Steigbügel.

stitch [stitʃ], *v.a.* sticken, nähen. — *s.* der Stich; der stechende Schmerz, der Seitenstich (*pain*).

stoat [stout], *s.* (*Zool.*) das Hermelin.

stock [stɔk], *s.* das Lager; *in —,* auf Lager; vorrätig; der Stamm, die Familie; (*Fin.*) das Kapital; — *exchange,* die Börse; (*pl.*) die Börsenpapiere, *n. pl.;* Aktien, *f. pl.* — *v.a.* halten, führen.

stockade [stɔ'keid], *s.* das Staket.

stockbroker ['stɔkbroukə], *s.* (*Fin.*) der Börsenmakler.

stockholder ['stɔkhouldə], *s.* (*Fin., Am.*) der Aktionär.

stocking ['stɔkiŋ], *s.* der Strumpf.

stocktaking ['stɔkteikiŋ], *s.* die Inventuraufnahme.

stoical ['stouikəl], *adj.* stoisch.

stoke [stouk], *v.a.* schüren.

stoker ['stoukə], *s.* der Heizer.

stole [stoul], *s.* (*Eccl.*) die Stola; der Pelzkragen (*fur*).

stolid ['stɔlid], *adj.* schwerfällig, gleichgültig.

stomach ['stʌmək], *s.* der Magen; (*fig.*) der Appetit.

stone [stoun], *s.* der Stein; der Kern (*fruit*). — *v.a.* steinigen (*throw — at*); entsteinen (*fruit*).

stony ['stouni], *adj.* steinig; (*sl.*) — *broke,* pleite.

stool [stu:l], *s.* der Schemel, Hocker; (*Med.*) der Stuhlgang.

stoop [stu:p], *v.n.* sich bücken; (*fig.*) sich herablassen.

stooping ['stu:piŋ], *adj.* gebückt.

stop [stɔp], *v.a.* halten, stoppen; aufhören; aufhalten (*halt*); — *up,* verstopfen, versperren (*block*); (*tooth*) plombieren. — *v.n.* stehen bleiben (*stand*); sich aufhalten (*stay*). — *s.* der Halt, die Haltestelle (*of bus etc.*); das Aufhalten, Innehalten (*stoppage*); das Register (*organ*); (*Gram.*) der Punkt.

stoppage ['stɔpidʒ], *s.* die Stockung, Hemmung (*hindrance*); die Arbeitseinstellung (*strike*).

stopper ['stɔpə], *s.* der Stöpsel.

storage ['stɔ:ridʒ], *s.* das Lagern.

store [stɔ:], *s.* der Vorrat, das Lagerhaus, Magazin; (*Am.*) das Kaufhaus; (*fig.*) die Menge (*of anecdotes etc.*). — *v.a.* lagern.

storey ['stɔ:ri], *s.* das Stockwerk.

stork [stɔ:k], *s.* (*Orn.*) der Storch.

storm [stɔ:m], *s.* der Sturm, das Gewitter.

story ['stɔ:ri], *s.* die Geschichte, Erzählung (*narrative*).

stout [staut], *adj.* fest; stark, kräftig. — *s.* das starke Bier.

stove [stouv], *s.* der Ofen.

stow [stou], *v.a.* verstauen, packen. — *v.n.* — *away*, als blinder Passagier fahren.

stowaway ['stouəwei], *s.* der blinde Passagier.

straddle [strædl], *v.n.* rittlings sitzen.

straggle [strægl], *v.n.* umherschweifen, streifen; (*Bot.*) wuchern.

straight [streit], *adj.* gerade, offen. — *adv.* — *away*, sofort, sogleich.

straighten [streitn], *v.a.* ausrichten, gerade richten. — *v.n.* sich ausrichten.

strain [strein], *s.* die Anstrengung, Anspannung; (*Mus.*) der Ton, Stil; der Hang. — *v.a.* anstrengen, filtrieren; seihen. — *v.n.* sich anstrengen.

strainer ['streinə], *s.* der Seiher, der Filter, das Sieb.

strait [streit], *adj.* eng. — *s.* (*usually pl.*) die Enge, Meerenge.

strand (1) [strænd], *s.* der Strand.

strand (2) [strænd], *s.* die Litze (*of rope, string*).

strange [streindʒ], *adj.* fremd (*unknown*); seltsam (*queer*).

stranger ['streindʒə], *s.* der Fremdling, Fremde; der Unbekannte.

strangle [stræŋgl], *v.a.* erdrosseln, erwürgen.

strangulation [stræŋgju'leiʃən], *s.* die Erdrosselung, Erwürgung.

strap [stræp], *v.a.* festschnallen, anschnallen. — *s.* der Gurt, Riemen.

strapping ['stræpiŋ], *adj.* stark, stämmig.

strata *see under* **stratum**.

stratagem ['strætədʒəm], *s.* die List, (*Mil.*) der Plan.

strategy ['strætidʒi], *s.* die Strategie.

stratification [strætifi'keiʃən], *s.* die Schichtung; (*Geol.*) die Lagerung.

stratum ['streitəm], *s.* (*pl.* **strata** ['streitə]) die Schicht, Lage.

straw [strɔ:], *s.* das Stroh; *that's the last* —, das ist die Höhe!

strawberry ['strɔ:bəri], *s.* (*Bot.*) die Erdbeere.

stray [strei], *v.n.* irregehen, schweifen; sich verirren. — *adj.* irr, verirrt.

streak [stri:k], *s.* der Strich; der Streifen; (*fig.*) der Anflug.

streaky ['stri:ki], *adj.* gestreift; (*bacon*) durchwachsen.

stream [stri:m], *v.n.* strömen, wehen (*in the wind*). — *s.* die Strömung (*flow*); der Bach (*brook*), der Strom (*river*).

streamer ['stri:mə], *s.* der Wimpel, das Band, die Papierschlange.

street [stri:t], *s.* die Straße; —*s ahead*, weit voraus.

streetcar ['stri:tka:], *s.* (*Am.*) *see* **tram**.

streetlamp ['stri:tlæmp], *s.* die Straßenlaterne.

strength [streŋθ], *s.* die Stärke; die Kraft.

strengthen ['streŋθən], *v.a.* stärken; (*fig.*) bekräftigen (*support*).

strenuous ['strenjuəs], *adj.* anstrengend.

stress [stres], *v.a.* (*Phonet.*) betonen; (*fig.*) hervorheben. — *s.* die Betonung (*emphasis*); der Druck (*pressure*).

stretch [stretʃ], *v.a.* spannen; strecken, ausstrecken; — *a point*, eine Ausnahme machen. — *s.* die Strecke (*distance*); (*coll.*) die Zuchthausstrafe (*penal sentence*).

stretcher ['stretʃə], *s.* die Tragbahre.

strew [stru:], *v.a.* streuen, ausstreuen.

strict [strikt], *adj.* streng (*severe*); genau (*exact*).

stricture ['striktʃə], *s.* der Tadel, die Kritik; (*pl.*) die kritische Rede.

stride [straid], *v.n. irr.* schreiten. — *s.* der Schritt; *take in o.'s* —, leicht bewältigen.

strident ['straidənt], *adj.* laut, lärmend; grell.

strife [straif], *s.* der Streit, Zank.

strike [straik], *v.a., v.n. irr.* schlagen; abmachen (*bargain*); (*Mus.*) — *up*, anstimmen (*song*), aufspielen (*instrument*); beginnen; — *the eye*, auffallen; streiken, in Streik treten. — *s.* der Streik, die Arbeitseinstellung.

striking ['straikiŋ], *adj.* auffallend.

string [striŋ], *s.* die Schnur; (*Mus.*) die Saite; — *quartet*, das Streichquartett; die Reihe (*series*). — *v.a.* anreihen (*beads etc.*); — *together*, verbinden. — *v.n.* — *along*, sich anschließen.

stringency ['strindʒənsi], *s.* die Strenge (*severity*); die Knappheit (*shortage*).

stringent ['strindʒənt], *adj.* streng (*severe*); knapp (*short*).

strip [strip], *s.* der Streifen. — *v.a., v.n.* abstreifen, (sich) entkleiden; (sich) entblößen.

stripe [straip], *s.* der (Farb)streifen; die Strieme (*mark on body*). — *v.a.* streifen, bestreifen.

strive [straiv], *v.n. irr.* sich bemühen (*for*, um, *Acc.*), streben (*for*, nach, *Dat.*).

stroke (1) [strouk], *v.a.* streicheln.

stroke (2) [strouk], *s.* der Strich (*brush*); der Streich (*sword*), der Stoß (*blow*); (*Med.*) der Schlaganfall.

stroll [stroul], *v.n.* schlendern.

strolling ['strouliŋ], *adj.* — *players*, die Wandertruppe.

strong [strɔŋ], *adj.* stark.

strongbox ['strɔŋbɔks], *s.* die Geldkassette.

strongroom ['strɔŋrum], *s.* der Geldtresor.

strop [strɔp], *s.* der Streichriemen.

structure ['strʌktʃə], *s.* der Bau, Aufbau; die Struktur.

struggle [strʌgl], *s.* der Kampf, das Ringen. — *v.n.* kämpfen, ringen.

strut [strʌt], *v.n.* stolzieren.

stub [stʌb], *s.* der Stumpf, Stummel (*cigarette*). — *v.a.* — *out*, ausmachen, auslöschen (*cigarette etc.*).

stubble ['stʌbl], s. die Stoppel, das Stoppelfeld; die (Bart)stoppeln, f. pl. (beard).

stubborn ['stʌbən], adj. eigensinnig, hartnäckig.

stucco ['stʌkou], s. die Stuckarbeit.

stud (1) [stʌd], s. der Hemdenknopf, Kragenknopf (collar —). — v.a. beschlagen (nail); besetzen (bejewel).

stud (2) [stʌd], s. das Gestüt (horses).

student ['stju:dənt], s. der Student.

studied ['stʌdid], adj. geziert, absichtlich (deliberate); gelehrt (learned).

studio ['stju:diou], s. (Phot.) das Atelier; (Film, Rad.) das Studio.

studious ['stju:diəs], adj. beflissen, fleißig; lernbegierig.

study ['stʌdi], v.a., v.n. studieren. — s. das Studium; das Arbeitszimmer (room); (Mus. etc.) die Studie; (Art) der Entwurf; die Untersuchung (investigation).

stuff [stʌf], s. der Stoff, das Material; (coll.) das Zeug (rubbish). — v.a. stopfen, ausstopfen (animals); (Cul.) füllen.

stuffing ['stʌfiŋ], s. die Füllung, das Füllsel.

stultify ['stʌltifai], v.a. dumm machen.

stumble [stʌmbl], v.n. stolpern; — upon, zufällig stoßen (auf, Acc.).

stumbling ['stʌmbliŋ], s. das Stolpern; — block, das Hindernis, der Stein des Anstoßes.

stump [stʌmp], s. der Stumpf. — v.a. verblüffen; abstumpfen. — v.n. schwerfällig gehen.

stun [stʌn], v.a. betäuben, verdutzen.

stunning ['stʌniŋ], adj. betörend, fabelhaft, überwältigend.

stunt (1) [stʌnt], v.a. am Wachstum behindern, klein halten.

stunt (2) [stʌnt], s. der Trick, das Kunststück; (Aviat.) der Kunstflug.

stupefy ['stju:pifai], v.a. betäuben.

stupendous [stju:'pendəs], adj. erstaunlich.

stupid ['stju:pid], adj. dumm.

stupor ['stju:pə], s. die Erstarrung, Lähmung (of mind).

sturdy ['stə:di], adj. derb, stark, stämmig.

sturgeon ['stə:dʒən], s. (Zool.) der Stör.

stutter ['stʌtə], v.n. stottern.

sty [stai], s. der Schweinestall.

sty(e) [stai], s. (Med.) das Gerstenkorn (on eyelid).

style [stail], s. (Lit.) der Stil; der Griffel (stylus); die Mode (fashion); die Anrede (address). — v.a. anreden.

stylish ['stailiʃ], adj. elegant, modern.

suave [sweiv, swa:v], adj. höflich, gewinnend.

sub- [sʌb], pref. Unter-.

subaltern ['sʌbəltən], s. (Mil.) der Leutnant, Oberleutnant.

subject ['sʌbdʒikt], s. (Gram.) das Subjekt; (Pol.) der Untertan; der Gegenstand. — adj. untertan (to,

Dat.); — to, abhängig von. — [səb'dʒekt], v.a. unterwerfen (to, Dat.); aussetzen (Dat.).

subjunctive [səb'dʒʌŋktiv], s. (Gram.) der Konjunktiv.

sublet [sʌb'let], v.a. in Untermiete vermieten, untervermieten.

sublimate ['sʌblimeit], v.a. sublimieren.

submarine ['sʌbməri:n], s. das Unterseeboot.

submission [səb'miʃən], s. die Unterwerfung (subjection); der Vorschlag (suggestion).

submit [səb'mit], v.a. unterwerfen (subjugate); vorlegen. — v.n. sich beugen (to, Dat.).

suborn [sʌ'bɔ:n], v.a. anstiften; bestechen (corrupt).

subpoena [sʌb'pi:nə], s. (Law) die Vorladung.

subscribe [səb'skraib], v.a. unterschreiben. — v.n. zeichnen (to, zu); abonnieren (paper).

subscription [səb'skripʃən], s. das Abonnement (to, Genit.); (club) der Beitrag.

subsequent ['sʌbsikwənt], adj. folgend.

subservient [sʌb'sə:viənt], adj. unterwürfig.

subside [səb'said], v.n. sinken; abnehmen (decrease).

subsidence [sʌb'saidəns, 'sʌbsidəns], s. das Sinken, Sichsetzen.

subsidiary [sʌb'sidjəri], adj. Hilfs-, Neben-.

subsidize ['sʌbsidaiz], v.a. unterstützen (with money), subventionieren.

subsidy ['sʌbsidi], s. die Unterstützung, Subvention.

subsist [səb'sist], v.n. leben, existieren.

subsistence [səb'sistəns], s. das Dasein, Auskommen; der Lebensunterhalt.

substance ['sʌbstəns], s. das Wesen, der Stoff, die Substanz.

substantial [səb'stænʃəl], adj. wesentlich, beträchtlich.

substantiate [səb'stænʃieit], v.a. dartun, nachweisen, bestätigen.

substantive ['sʌbstəntiv], s. (Gram.) das Substantiv, Hauptwort. — adj. (Mil.) effektiv, wirklich.

substitute ['sʌbstitju:t], v.a. ersetzen, an die Stelle setzen. — s. der Ersatzmann, Vertreter.

subterfuge ['sʌbtəfju:dʒ], s. die Ausflucht.

subtle [sʌtl], adj. fein, schlau, subtil.

subtract [səb'trækt], v.a. abziehen; (Maths.) subtrahieren.

suburb ['sʌbə:b], s. die Vorstadt, der Vorort.

subversion [səb'və:ʃən], s. (Pol.) der Umsturz.

subversive [səb'və:siv], adj. umstürzlerisch, umstürzend.

subway ['sʌbwei], s. die Unterführung; (Am.) die Untergrundbahn.

succeed [sək'si:d], v.n. erfolgreich sein, Erfolg haben. — v.a. nachfolgen (Dat.) (follow).

success [sək'ses], s. der Erfolg.
successful [sək'sesful], adj. erfolgreich.
succession [sək'seʃən], s. die Nachfolge.
successive [sək'sesiv], adj. der Reihe nach, aufeinanderfolgend.
succinct [sək'siŋkt], adj. bündig, kurz.
succour ['sʌkə], v.a. beistehen (Dat.), helfen (Dat.).
succulent ['sʌkjulənt], adj. saftig.
succumb [sə'kʌm], v.n. unterliegen (to, Dat.).
such [sʌtʃ], adj. solch, derartig. — pron. ein solcher; — as, diejenigen, alle die.
suchlike ['sʌtʃlaik], pron. (coll.) dergleichen.
suck [sʌk], v.a., v.n. saugen.
suckle [sʌkl], v.a. säugen, stillen.
suction ['sʌkʃən], s. das Saugen; (Engin.) Saug-.
Sudanese [su:də'ni:z], adj. sudanisch, sudanesisch. — s. der Sudan(es)er.
sudden [sʌdn], adj. plötzlich.
suds [sʌdz], s. pl. das Seifenwasser.
sue [sju:], v.a. gerichtlich belangen, verklagen.
suède [sweid], s. das Wildleder.
suet ['su:it], s. das Nierenfett.
suffer ['sʌfə], v.a. ertragen, dulden. — v.n. leiden (from, an).
sufferance ['sʌfərəns], s. die Duldung; on —, nur widerwillig.
suffice [sə'fais], v.n. genügen, langen, (aus)reichen.
sufficient [sə'fiʃənt], adj. genügend, hinreichend.
suffocate ['sʌfəkeit], v.a., v.n. ersticken.
suffragan ['sʌfrəgən], s. (Eccl.) der Weihbischof.
suffrage ['sʌfridʒ], s. das Wahlrecht, Stimmrecht.
suffuse [sə'fju:z], v.a. übergießen, überfließen.
sugar ['ʃugə], s. der Zucker; — basin, die Zuckerdose.
suggest [sə'dʒest], v.a. vorschlagen, anregen.
suggestion [sə'dʒestʃən], s. der Vorschlag.
suggestive [sə'dʒestiv], adj. zweideutig.
suicide ['sju:isaid], s. der Selbstmord, Freitod.
suit [su:t], s. das Gesuch, die Bitte (request); die Farbe (cards); (Law) der Prozeß; der Anzug (clothes). — v.n. passen (Dat.) (be convenient to); passen zu (look well with). — v.a. anpassen (match).
suitcase ['su:tkeis], s. der Handkoffer.
suitable ['su:təbl], adj. passend.
suite [swi:t], s. das Gefolge (following); die Zimmerflucht (rooms); die Reihe (cards).
suitor ['su:tə], s. der Brautwerber, Freier.
sulk [sʌlk], v.n. schmollen.
sullen ['sʌlən], adj. düster, mürrisch.
sully ['sʌli], v.a. beschmutzen.
sulphur ['sʌlfə], s. (Chem.) der Schwefel.

Sultan ['sʌltən], s. der Sultan.
Sultana [sʌl'ta:nə], s. die Sultanin.
sultana [sʌl'ta:nə], s. (Bot.) die Sultanine.
sultry ['sʌltri], adj. schwül.
sum [sʌm], s. die Summe; (fig.) der Inbegriff. — v.a., v.n. — up, zusammenfassen.
summary ['sʌməri], s. die Zusammenfassung, der Auszug. — adj. summarisch.
summer ['sʌmə], s. der Sommer; Indian —, der Spätsommer, Altweibersommer, Nachsommer.
summit ['sʌmit], s. der Gipfel, die Spitze.
summon(s) ['sʌmən(z)], v.a. (Law) vorladen. — s. (summons) die Vorladung.
sump [sʌmp], s. (Motor.) die Ölwanne.
sumptuous ['sʌmptjuəs], adj. prächtig, mit Aufwand, kostbar.
sun [sʌn], s. die Sonne. — v.r. sich sonnen.
sunburn ['sʌnbə:n], s. der Sonnenbrand.
Sunday ['sʌnd(e)i], s. der Sonntag.
sundial ['sʌndaiəl], s. die Sonnenuhr.
sundown ['sʌndaun] see sunset.
sundry ['sʌndri], adj. mehrere, verschiedene. — s. (pl.) Gemischtwaren, f. pl.
sunny ['sʌni], adj. sonnig.
sunrise ['sʌnraiz], s. der Sonnenaufgang.
sunset ['sʌnset], s. der Sonnenuntergang.
sunshade ['sʌnʃeid], s. das Sonnendach, der Sonnenschirm (parasol).
super ['su:pə], s. (Theat.) der Statist. — adj. (coll.) fein, famos.
super- ['su:pə], pref. über-, hinzu-.
superannuation [su:pərænju'eiʃən], s. die Pensionierung.
superb [su'pə:b], adj. hervorragend, herrlich.
supercilious [su:pə'siliəs], adj. hochmütig, anmaßend.
superficial [su:pə'fiʃəl], adj. oberflächlich.
superfluous [su:'pə:fluəs], adj. überflüssig.
superintendent [su:pərin'tendənt], s. der Oberaufseher.
superior [su:'piəriə], adj. ober, höher. — s. der Vorgesetzte.
superiority [su:piəri'oriti], s. die Überlegenheit.
superlative [su:'pə:lətiv], s. (Gram.) der Superlativ. — adj. ausnehmend gut.
supermarket ['su:pəma:kit], s. das Selbstbedienungsgeschäft, SB-Geschäft, der grosse Lebensmittelladen.
supersede [su:pə'si:d], v.a. verdrängen.
superstition [su:pə'stiʃən], s. der Aberglaube.
superstitious [su:pə'stiʃəs], adj. abergläubisch.
supervise ['su:pəvaiz], v.a. beaufsichtigen, überwachen.

supine [su'pain], *adj.* auf dem Rücken liegend. — ['su:pain], *s.* (*Gram.*) das Supinum.

supper ['sʌpə], *s.* das Abendessen; *Last Supper*, das Heilige Abendmahl.

supplant [sə'plɑːnt], *v.a.* verdrängen.

supple [sʌpl], *adj.* geschmeidig, biegsam.

supplement ['sʌplimənt], *s.* die Beilage (*paper*); der Zusatz.

supplementary [sʌpli'mentri], *adj.* zusätzlich.

supplier [sə'plaiə], *s.* der Lieferant.

supply [sə'plai], *v.a.* liefern (*s. th.*); beliefern, versorgen (*s.o.*). — *s.* die Versorgung.

support [sə'pɔːt], *v.a.* unterstützen. — *s.* die Stütze (*prop*); die Unterstützung (*financial etc.*).

suppose [sə'pouz], *v.a.* annehmen, vermuten.

supposition [sʌpə'ziʃən], *s.* die Annahme, Vermutung, Voraussetzung.

suppress [sə'pres], *v.a.* unterdrücken.

suppurate ['sʌpjureit], *v.n.* eitern.

supremacy [su'preməsi], *s.* die Überlegenheit (*pre-eminence*); Obergewalt (*power*).

supreme [su'priːm], *adj.* höchst, oberst.

surcharge ['səːtʃɑːdʒ], *s.* die Sonderzahlung, der Aufschlag, Zuschlag.

sure [ʃuə], *adj.* sicher; *to be —,* sicherlich; *make —,* sich überzeugen.

surety ['ʃuəti], *s.* (*Law*) die Kaution.

surf [səːf], *s.* die Brandung.

surface ['səːfis], *s.* die Oberfläche.

surfeit ['səːfit], *s.* die Übersättigung, das Übermaß. — *v.a.* übersättigen.

surge [səːdʒ], *v.n.* wogen, rauschen. — *s.* die Woge, das Aufwallen.

surgeon ['səːdʒən], *s.* (*Med.*) der Chirurg.

surgery ['səːdʒəri], *s.* (*Med.*) die Chirurgie (*subject*); — *hours,* die Sprechstunde.

surgical ['səːdʒikəl], *adj.* chirurgisch.

surly ['səːli], *adj.* mürrisch.

surmise [səː'maiz], *v.a.* mutmaßen, vermuten. — *s.* die Mutmaßung, Vermutung.

surmount [səː'maunt], *v.a.* übersteigen; überwinden (*overcome*).

surname ['səːneim], *s.* der Zuname.

surpass [səː'pɑːs], *v.a.* übertreffen.

surplice ['səːplis], *s.* das Chorhemd.

surplus ['səːpləs], *s.* der Überfluß.

surprise [sə'praiz], *s.* die Überraschung. — *v.a.* überraschen.

surrender [sə'rendə], *v.a.* übergeben, aufgeben. — *v.n.* sich ergeben. — *s.* die Waffenstreckung, Kapitulation.

surreptitious [sʌrəp'tiʃəs], *adj.* heimlich.

surround [sə'raund], *v.a.* umgeben, einschließen.

surroundings [sə'raundiŋz], *s. pl.* die Umgegend, Umgebung.

survey ['səːvei], *s.* die Übersicht; die Vermessung. — [səː'vei], *v.a.* überblicken; vermessen.

surveyor [sə'veiə], *s.* der Vermesser, Feldmesser.

survival [sə'vaivəl], *s.* das Überleben.

survive [sə'vaiv], *v.a.* überleben, überstehen.

susceptibility [səsepti'biliti], *s.* die Empfänglichkeit.

susceptible [sə'septibl], *adj.* empfänglich, empfindlich.

suspect [səs'pekt], *v.a.* verdächtigen. — ['sʌspekt], *adj.* verdächtig. — *s.* die Verdachtsperson, der Verdächtigte.

suspend [səs'pend], *v.a.* aufhängen; unterbrechen (*procedure*); einstellen (*work*).

suspense [səs'pens], *s.* die Spannung (*tension*); Ungewißheit (*uncertainty*).

suspension [səs'penʃən], *s.* (*Law*) die Suspension; die Einstellung (*stoppage*); die Aufhängung, Suspension; (*Motor.*) die Federung; — *bridge,* die Kettenbrücke, Hängebrücke.

suspicion [səs'piʃən], *s.* der Verdacht, Argwohn.

suspicious [səs'piʃəs], *adj.* verdächtig; argwöhnisch.

sustain [səs'tein], *v.a.* erleiden (*suffer*); ertragen (*bear*); aufrechterhalten (*maintain*).

sustenance ['sʌstinəns], *s.* der Unterhalt (*maintenance*); die Nahrung (*food*).

suture ['sjuːtʃə], *s.* (*Med.*) die Naht.

suzerain ['sjuːzərein], *s.* der Oberherr, Oberlehnsherr.

swab [swɔb], *s.* (*Med.*) die Laborprobe, der Abstrich; der Schrubber (*scrubber*). — *v.a.* (*Med.*) eine Probe entnehmen; schrubben (*scrub*).

swaddle [swɔdl], *s.* die Windel.

swaddling ['swɔdliŋ], *adj.* — *clothes,* die Windeln, *f. pl.*

swagger ['swægə], *v.n.* großtun. — *s.* das Großtun, Renommieren.

swallow (1) ['swɔlou], *s.* (*Orn.*) die Schwalbe.

swallow (2) ['swɔlou], *v.a.* schlucken; verschlingen (*devour*).

swamp [swɔmp], *s.* der Sumpf. — *v.a.* versenken; (*fig.*) überschütten.

swan [swɔn], *s.* (*Orn.*) der Schwan.

swank [swæŋk], *v.n.* großtun, angeben, aufschneiden. — *s.* der Großtuer.

swap, swop [swɔp], *v.a.* eintauschen, tauschen. — *v.n.* tauschen. — *s.* der Tausch.

sward [swɔːd], *s.* (*Poet.*) der Rasen.

swarm [swɔːm], *v.n.* schwärmen. — *s.* der Schwarm.

swarthy ['swɔːði], *adj.* dunkel, dunkelbraun.

swashbuckler ['swɔʃbʌklə], *s.* der Aufschneider, Angeber, Renommist.

swastika ['swɔstikə], *s.* das Hakenkreuz.

swathe [sweið], *v.a.* einhüllen, einwickeln.

sway [swei], *v.a.* schwenken; beeinflußen. — *v.n.* schwanken, sich schwingen. — der Einfluß, die Macht.

swear [sweə], *v.a.*, *v.n.* *irr.* schwören (*an oath*); fluchen (*curse*).

sweat [swet], *v.n.* schwitzen. — *s.* der Schweiß.

Swede [swi:d], *s.* der Schwede.

Swedish ['swi:diʃ], *adj.* schwedisch.

sweep [swi:p], *v.a.*, *v.n.* *irr.* fegen, kehren; *a new broom —s clean*, neue Besen kehren gut. — *s.* der Schornsteinfeger (*chimney —*).

sweet [swi:t], *adj.* süß. — *s.* der Nachtisch; (*pl.*) Süßigkeiten, *f. pl.*

swell [swel], *v.a. irr.* anschwellen lassen. — *v.n.* anschwellen. — *adj.*, *adv.* (*Am. sl.*) ausgezeichnet. — *s.* (*sl.*) der feine Kerl.

swelter ['sweltə], *v.n.* vor Hitze vergehen.

swerve [swə:v], *v.n.* abschweifen, abbiegen.

swift (1) [swift], *adj.* schnell, behende, rasch.

swift (2) [swift], *s.* (*Orn.*) die Turmschwalbe.

swill [swil], *v.a.* spülen (*rinse*); (*sl.*) saufen (*drink heavily*). — *s.* das Spülicht (*dishwater*); (*coll.*) das Gesöff.

swim [swim], *v.n. irr.* schwimmen. — *s.* das Schwimmen.

swindle [swindl], *v.a.* beschwindeln. — *s.* der Schwindel.

swine [swain], *s. pl.* die Schweine; (*sing.*) der Schweinehund, das Schwein.

swing [swiŋ], *v.a.*, *v.n. irr.* schwingen, schaukeln. — *s.* der Schwung; die Schaukel.

swipe [swaip], *v.a.* schlagen; (*fig.*) stehlen. — *s.* der Schlag.

swirl [swə:l], *v.a.*, *v.n.* wirbeln (*in air*). — *s.* der Wirbel.

Swiss [swis], *s.* der Schweizer. — *adj.* schweizerisch, Schweizer-.

switch [switʃ], *v.a.* (*Elec.*) — *on*, andrehen, einschalten; — *off*, abschalten; (*fig.*) wechseln, vertauschen (*change*). — *v.n.* umstellen, umschalten. — *s.* (*Elec.*) der Schalter.

switchboard ['switʃbɔ:d], *s.* die Telephonzentrale, das Schaltbrett.

switchgear ['switʃgiə], *s.* (*Elec.*) das Schaltgerät, die Schaltung.

swivel [swivl], *v.n.* drehen. — *s.* der Drehring; — *chair*, der Drehstuhl.

swoon [swu:n], *v.n.* in Ohnmacht fallen. — *s.* die Ohnmacht.

swoop [swu:p], *s.* der Stoß. — *v.n.* (herab)stoßen; stürzen; (nieder)schießen.

swop see **swap**.

sword [sɔ:d], *s.* das Schwert.

syllable ['siləbl], *s.* die Silbe.

syllabus ['siləbəs], *s.* das Verzeichnis, der Lehrplan.

symbol ['simbəl], *s.* das Symbol, Sinnbild.

sympathetic [simpə'θetik], *adj.* mitfühlend, teilnehmend; sympathisch.

sympathy ['simpəθi], *s.* die Sympathie, das Mitgefühl.

symphony ['simfəni], *s.* (*Mus.*) die Symphonie.

synchronize ['siŋkrənaiz], *v.a.* synchronisieren.

syndicate ['sindikit], *s.* die Arbeitsgruppe, das Syndikat.

synod ['sinəd], *s.* die Synode, Kirchentagung.

synonymous [si'nɔniməs], *adj.* synonym.

synopsis [si'nɔpsis], *s.* die Zusammenfassung, Übersicht.

Syrian ['siriən], *adj.* syrisch. — *s.* der Syrer.

syringe ['sirindʒ], *s.* die Spritze.

syrup ['sirəp], *s.* der Sirup.

system ['sistəm], *s.* das System.

systematize ['sistəmətaiz], *v.a.* ordnen, in ein System bringen.

T

T [ti:]. das T.

tab [tæb], *s.* das Schildchen, der Streifen.

tabard ['tæbəd], *s.* der Wappenrock, Heroldsrock.

tabby ['tæbi], *s.* (*cat*) die getigerte Katze.

table [teibl], *s.* der Tisch; (*Maths.*) die Tabelle, das Einmaleins. — *v.a.* (*Parl.*) einen Entwurf einbringen; (*Am.*) auf die lange Bank schieben.

tablecloth ['teiblklɔθ], *s.* das Tischtuch.

tablemat ['teiblmæt], *s.* der Untersatz.

tablenapkin ['teiblnæpkin], *s.* die Serviette.

tablespoon ['teiblspu:n], *s.* der Eßlöffel.

tablet ['tæblit], *s.* die Tablette (*pill*); die Schreibtafel, der Block (*writing*).

taboo [tə'bu:], *s.* das Verbot, Tabu.

tabular ['tæbjulə], *adj.* tabellarisch; wie eine Tafel.

tacit ['tæsit], *adj.* stillschweigend.

taciturn ['tæsitə:n], *adj.* schweigsam, einsilbig.

tack [tæk], *s.* der Stift; der Stich (*sewing*). — *v.a.* nageln; heften (*sew*).

tackle [tækl], *v.a.* (*Naut.*) takeln; (*Footb.*, *fig.*) angreifen; anpacken. — *s.* (*Naut.*) das Takel; (*fig.*) das Zeug; (*Footb.*) das Angreifen.

tact [tækt], *s.* der Takt; das Zartgefühl.

tactics ['tæktiks], *s. pl.* die Taktik.

tadpole ['tædpoul], *s.* (*Zool.*) die Kaulquappe.

taffeta ['tæfitə], *s.* (*Text.*) der Taft.

tag [tæg], *s.* der Anhängezettel; das Sprichwort (*saying*). — *v.a.* anhängen. — *v.n.* — *on to*, sich anschließen.

tail [teil], *s.* der Schwanz; (*fig.*) das Ende; (*pl.*) der Frack (*tailcoat*). — *v.a.* (*Am.*) folgen (*Dat.*).

tailor [´teilə], *s.* der Schneider; —*made*, geschneidert, nach Maß gemacht. — *v.a.* schneidern.

taint [teint], *v.a.* beflecken; verderben (*corrupt*). — *s.* der Fleck.

take [teik], *v.a. irr.* nehmen; bringen, ergreifen (*seize*); erfordern (*require*); — *up*, aufnehmen, beginnen; ertragen (*suffer, tolerate*); — *breath,* Atem holen; — *care,* sich in acht nehmen; — *offence at,* Anstoß nehmen an; — *place,* stattfinden; — *for,* halten für. — *v.n.* wirken (*be effective*); — *to,* Gefallen finden (an, *Dat.*); — *to flight or o.'s heels,* sich aus dem Staube machen; — *after,* ähnlich sein.

takings [´teikiŋz], *s.* (*pl.*) die Einnahmen, *f. pl.*

tale [teil], *s.* das Märchen, die Geschichte.

talent [´tælənt], *s.* das Talent, die Begabung.

talented [´tæləntid], *adj.* talentiert, begabt.

talk [tɔ:k], *v.a., v.n.* reden, sprechen. — *s.* das Gespräch (*discussion*); der Vortrag (*lecture*); das Reden, Gerede (*speaking*).

talkative [´tɔ:kətiv], *adj.* geschwätzig, redselig, gesprächig.

tall [tɔ:l], *adj.* hoch (*high*); groß (*grown high*); *a — order,* eine schwierige Aufgabe; *a — story,* eine Aufschneiderei, das Seemannsgarn.

tallow [´tælou], *s.* der Talg.

tally [´tæli], *v.n.* passen (*match*); stimmen (*be correct*).

talon [´tælən], *s.* die Klaue, Kralle.

tame [teim], *adj.* zahm. — *v.a.* zähmen.

tamper [´tæmpə], *v.n.* hineinpfuschen (*with,* in, *Acc.*).

tan [tæn], *s.* die Lohe; die braune Farbe; der Sonnenbrand (*sun*). — *v.a.* bräunen; (*leather*) gerben; (*fig.*) verbleuen (*beat*).

tang [tæŋ], *s.* der Seetang; (*fig.*) der Beigeschmack.

tangible [´tændʒibl], *adj.* greifbar.

tangle [´tæŋgl], *v.a.* verwickeln (*entangle*). — *s.* die Verwirrung, Verwicklung.

tank [tæŋk], *s.* der Tank; (*Mil.*) der Panzer; der Wasserspeicher (*cistern*). — *v.a., v.n.* tanken.

tankard [´tæŋkəd], *s.* der Maßkrug, Bierkrug.

tanner (1) [´tænə], *s.* der Gerber.

tanner (2) [´tænə], *s.* (*sl.*) das Sechspencestück.

tantalize [´tæntəlaiz], *v.a.* quälen.

tantamount [´tæntəmaunt], *adj.* gleich, gleichwertig.

tap [tæp], *v.a.* anzapfen (*barrel*); klopfen; tippen (*on shoulder etc.*); (*fig.*) anpumpen (*for money*). — *s.* der Hahn; der Zapfen (*barrel*); der leichte Schlag (*on shoulder etc.*).

tape [teip], *s.* das Band; *red* —, die Bürokratie, der Bürokratismus; — *measure,* das Bandmaß; — *recorder,* das Tonbandgerät.

taper [´teipə], *v.n.* spitz zulaufen. — *v.a.* spitzen. — *s.* die (spitze) Kerze.

tapestry [´tæpistri], *s.* die Tapete, der Wandteppich.

tapeworm [´teipwə:m], *s.* der Bandwurm.

taproot [´tæpru:t], *s.* die Pfahlwurzel, Hauptwurzel.

tar [ta:], *s.* der Teer; (*Naut. sl.*) der Matrose. — *v.a.* teeren.

tardy [´ta:di], *adj.* träge (*sluggish*), langsam.

tare (1) [teə], das Taragewicht, die Tara (*weight*). — *v.a.* auswägen, tarieren.

tare (2) [teə], *s.* (*Bot.*) die Wicke.

target [´ta:git], *s.* das Ziel; die Zielscheibe (*board*).

tariff [´tærif], *s.* der Tarif.

tarnish [´ta:niʃ], *v.a.* trüben. — *v.n.* anlaufen.

tarpaulin [ta:´pɔ:lin], *s.* die Persenning.

tarry (1) [´tæri], *v.n.* zögern (*hesitate*); warten (*wait*).

tarry (2) [´ta:ri], *adj.* teerig.

tart (1) [ta:t], *s.* die Torte.

tart (2) [ta:t], *adj.* herb, sauer.

tart (3) [ta:t], *s.* (*sl.*) die Dirne.

Tartar [´ta:tə], *s.* der Tatar; (*fig.*) der Tyrann.

tartar [´ta:tə], *s.* (*Chem.*) der Weinstein.

task [ta:sk], *s.* die Aufgabe, das Tagewerk; *take to* —, zur Rechenschaft ziehen.

tassel [tæsl], *s.* die Quaste.

taste [teist], *v.a.* schmecken; versuchen, kosten. — *s.* die Probe (*tasting*); der Geschmack (*flavour*).

tasteful [´teistful], *adj.* geschmackvoll.

tasteless [´teistlis], *adj.* geschmacklos.

tasty [´teisti], *adj.* schmackhaft.

tatter [´tætə], *s.* der Lumpen. — *v.a.* in Fetzen reißen, zerfetzen.

tattle [tætl], *v.n.* schwatzen. — *s.* das Geschwätz.

tattoo (1) [tə´tu:], *s.* (*Mil.*) der Zapfenstreich, das militärische Schaustück, die Parade.

tattoo (2) [tə´tu:], *v.a.* tätowieren. — *s.* die Tätowierung.

taunt [tɔ:nt], *v.a.* höhnen, schmähen. — *s.* der Hohn, Spott.

tavern [´tævən], *s.* die Schenke.

tawdry [´tɔ:dri], *adj.* kitschig, flitterhaft.

tawny [´tɔ:ni], *adj.* braungelb, lohfarbig.

tax [tæks], *s.* die Abgabe, Steuer; Besteuerung (*taxation*). — *v.a.* besteuern; (*fig.*) anstrengen, ermüden (*strain*).

taxi [´tæksi], *s.* das Taxi.

tea [ti:], *s.* der Tee.

teach [ti:tʃ], *v.a., v.n. irr.* lehren, unterrichten.

teacher [´ti:tʃə], *s.* der Lehrer, die Lehrerin.

team

team [ti:m], *s.* (*Sport*) die Mannschaft;
das Gespann (*horses*); (*fig.*) der Stab;
— *spirit*, der Korpsgeist.

tear (1) [tɛə], *s.* der Riß (*rent*). — *v.a. irr.*
zerreißen (*rend*).

tear (2) [tiə], *s.* die Träne.

tearing [ˈtɛəriŋ], *adj.* — *hurry*, rasende
Eile.

tease [ti:z], *v.a.* necken (*mock*); auf-
räuhen (*roughen*).

teat [ti:t], *s.* die Brustwarze, Zitze.

technical [ˈtɛknikəl], *adj.* technisch.

technique [tekˈniːk], *s.* die Technik,
Methode.

techy *see* tetchy.

tedious [ˈtiːdiəs], *adj.* langweilig,
lästig.

tedium [ˈtiːdiəm], *s.* der Überdruß, die
Langeweile.

tee [ti:], *s.* (*Sport*) der Golfballhalter.

teem [ti:m], *v.n.* wimmeln.

teenager [ˈtiːneidʒə], *s.* der, die Jugendliche; Teenager.

teeth *see under* tooth.

teethe [ti:ð], *v.n.* Zähne bekommen,
zahnen.

teetotal [tiːˈtoutl], *adj.* abstinent, anti-
alkoholisch.

teetotaller [tiːˈtoutlə], *s.* der Antialkoholiker.

telegram [ˈteligræm], *s.* das Telegramm.

telephone [ˈtelifoun], *s.* (*abbr.* phone)
das Telephon; — *box*, die Fernsprech-
zelle; — *exchange*, das Fernsprechamt.

television [teliˈviʒən], *s.* das Fernsehen; — *set*, der Fernsehapparat.

tell [tel], *v.a. irr.* erzählen, berichten
(*relate*); verraten (*reveal*).

tell-tale [ˈtelteil], *s.* der Angeber,
Zuträger. — *adj.* sprechend; Warn-
nungs-.

teller [ˈtelə], *s.* der Zähler; der Kassier
(*cashier*).

temerity [tiˈmeriti], *s.* die Verwegenheit, Tollkühnheit.

temper [ˈtempə], *v.a.* vermischen
(*mix*); mäßigen (*moderate*); (*Metall.*)
härten. — *s.* die üble Stimmung, Wut,
Laune; (*Metall.*) die Härte.

temperance [ˈtempərəns], *s.* die Mäßigkeit, Enthaltsamkeit.

temperate [ˈtempərit], *adj.* gemäßigt,
temperiert.

temperature [ˈtemprətʃə], *s.* die Temperatur.

tempest [ˈtempist], *s.* der Sturm.

tempestuous [temˈpestjuəs], *adj.* stürmisch.

temple (1) [templ], *s.* der Tempel.

temple (2) [templ], *s.* (*Anat.*) die
Schläfe (*side of brow*).

temporal [ˈtempərəl], *adj.* weltlich,
zeitlich.

temporary [ˈtempərəri], *adj.* zeitweilig,
vorläufig, provisorisch.

temporize [ˈtempəraiz], *v.n.* zögern,
Zeit zu gewinnen suchen.

tempt [tempt], *v.a.* versuchen.

temptation [tempˈteiʃən], *s.* die Versuchung.

ten [ten], *num. adj.* zehn.

tenth [tenθ], *num. adj.* zehnte. — *s.* der
Zehnte.

tenable [ˈtenəbl], *adj.* haltbar.

tenacious [tiˈneiʃəs], *adj.* zähe, festhal-
tend, hartnäckig.

tenacity [tiˈnæsiti], *s.* die Zähigkeit,
Ausdauer.

tenancy [ˈtenənsi], *s.* das Mietver-
hältnis; die Mietdauer.

tenant [ˈtenənt], *s.* der Mieter, Pächter.

tench [tentʃ], *s.* (*Zool.*) die Schleie.

tend (1) [tend], *v.a.*, *v.n.* warten,
pflegen (*nurse*).

tend (2) [tend], *v.n.* neigen, gerichtet
sein (*be inclined*).

tendency [ˈtendənsi], *s.* die Tendenz,
Neigung.

tender (1) [ˈtendə], *s.* das Angebot
(*offer*); *legal* —, das Zahlungsmittel.
— *v.a.* einreichen.

tender (2) [ˈtendə], *adj.* sanft (*affectionate*); zart, zärtlich, weich (*delicate*).

tender (3) [ˈtendə], *s.* (*Railw.*) der
Tender.

tendon [ˈtendən], *s.* (*Anat.*) die Sehne,
Flechse.

tendril [ˈtendril], *s.* (*Bot.*) die Ranke.

tenement [ˈtenimənt], *s.* die Miets-
wohnung, die Mietskaserne.

tenet [ˈtenit], *s.* der Grundsatz (*principle*); die Lehre (*doctrine*).

tenfold [ˈtenfould], *adj.* zehnfach.

tennis [ˈtenis], *s.* das Tennis.

tenor [ˈtenə], *s.* (*Mus.*) der Tenor; der
Sinn, Inhalt (*meaning*).

tense (1) [tens], *adj.* gespannt; straff
(*taut*).

tense (2) [tens], *s.* (*Gram.*) die Zeitform.

tension [ˈtenʃən], *s.* die Spannung.

tent [tent], *s.* das Zelt.

tentacle [ˈtentəkl], *s.* (*Zool.*) das Fühlhorn, der Fühler.

tentative [ˈtentətiv], *adj.* versuchend,
vorsichtig; (*fig.*) vorläufig.

tenterhooks [ˈtentəhuks], *s. pl.* die
Spannhaken, *m. pl.*; *be on* —, in
größter Spannung sein.

tenuous [ˈtenjuəs], *adj.* dünn, fadenscheinig, spärlich.

tenure [ˈtenjuə], *s.* der Mietbesitz, die
Mietvertragslänge, das Mietrecht; —
of office, die Amtsdauer.

tepid [ˈtepid], *adj.* lau, lauwarm.

term [tə:m], *s.* der Ausdruck (*expression*); die Bedingung (*condition*); der
Termin, die Frist (*period*); (*Sch.*) das
Semester, Trimester; *be on good* —*s
with* (*s.o.*), auf gutem Fuß stehen mit.
— *v.a.* benennen, bezeichnen.

terminate [ˈtə:mineit], *v.a.* beenden,
zu Ende bringen. — *v.n.* zu Ende
kommen.

terminus [ˈtə:minəs], *s.* die Endstation.

terrace [ˈteris], *s.* die Terrasse.

terrestrial [təˈrestriəl], *adj.* irdisch.

terrible [ˈteribl], *adj.* schrecklich,
furchtbar.

terrific [təˈrifik], *adj.* fürchterlich;
(*coll.*) ungeheuer.

terrify ['terifai], v.a. erschrecken.
territory ['teritəri], s. das Gebiet.
terror ['terə], s. der Schrecken.
terse [tə:s], adj. bündig, kurz.
tertiary ['tə:ʃəri], adj. tertiär.
test [test], s. die Prüfung; (Chem.) die Probe; — -tube, das Reagensglas or Reagenzglas. — v.a. prüfen.
testament ['testəmənt], s. das Testament.
testator [tes'teitə], s. der Erblasser.
testicle ['testikl], s. (Anat.) die Hode.
testify ['testifai], v.a. bezeugen.
testimonial [testi'mouniəl], s. das Zeugnis.
testimony ['testiməni], s. das Zeugnis, die Zeugenaussage (oral).
testiness ['testinis], s. die Verdrießlichkeit.
testy ['testi], adj. verdrießlich, reizbar.
tetanus ['tetənəs], s. (Med.) der Starrkrampf.
tetchy, techy ['tetʃi], adj. mürrisch, reizbar.
tether ['teðə], s. das Spannseil; (fig.) at the end of o.'s —, am Ende seiner Geduld. — v.a. anbinden.
text ['tekst], s. der Text, Wortlaut.
textile ['tekstail], s. die Textilware, der Webstoff.
textual ['tekstjuəl], adj. textlich, Text-.
texture ['tekstʃə], s. das Gewebe, die Struktur.
Thai [tai], adj. Thai-, siamesisch. — s. pl. die Thaivölker, pl.
than [ðæn], conj. als (after comparatives).
thank [θæŋk], v.a. danken (Dat.). — s. (pl.) der Dank.
that [ðæt], dem. adj. der, die, das, jener. — dem. pron. der, die, das; (absolute, no pl.) das. — rel. pron. der, die, das, welcher, was. — conj. daß; damit (in order —).
thatch [θætʃ], v.a. decken (mit Stroh). — s. das Strohdach.
thaw [θɔ:], v.n. tauen; auftauen. — s. das Tauwetter.
the [ðə, before vowel ði], def. art. der, die, das. — adv. — bigger — better, je grösser desto or umso besser.
theatre [θiətə], s. das Theater; (fig.) der Schauplatz.
theatrical [θi'ætrikəl], adj. bühnenhaft (of the stage); theatralisch; Bühnen-, Theater-.
theft [θeft], s. der Diebstahl.
their [ðeə], poss. adj. ihr.
theirs [ðeəz], poss. pron. der, die, das ihrige, der, die, das ihre.
them [ðem], pers. pron. sie, ihnen.
theme [θi:m], s. das Thema; (Mus.) das Thema, Motiv.
then [ðen], adv. dann, damals; by —, till —, bis dahin. — conj. dann, denn. — adj. damalig.
thence [ðens], adv. von da; daher.
theology [θi'ɔlədʒi], s. die Theologie.
theorem ['θiərəm], s. (Maths.) der Lehrsatz, Grundsatz.
theorize ['θiəraiz], v.n. theoretisieren.

therapeutics [θerə'pju:tiks], s. pl. die Heilkunde.
therapy ['θerəpi], s. die Therapie.
there [ðeə], adv. dort, da; dorthin, dahin (thereto); — is, — are, es gibt; here and —, hier und da.
thereabout(s) [ðeərəbaut(s)], adv. ungefähr, da herum.
thereafter [ðeər'ɑ:ftə], adv. hernach, danach.
thereby [ðeə'bai], adv. dadurch.
therefore ['ðeəfɔ:], adv. darum, deshalb.
thermal, thermic ['θə:məl, 'θə:mik], adj. thermisch; warm; Wärme-.
thermometer [θə'mɔmitə], s. das Thermometer.
these [ði:z], dem. adj. & pron. pl. diese.
thesis ['θi:sis], s. die These; die Dissertation.
they [ðei], pers. pron. pl. sie.
thick [θik], adj. dick; dicht; (fig.) dick befreundet; — as thieves, wie eine Diebsbande.
thicken ['θikən], v.a. verdicken. — v.n. dick werden.
thicket ['θikit], s. das Dickicht.
thickness ['θiknis], s. die Dicke.
thief [θi:f], s. der Dieb.
thieve [θi:v], v.n. stehlen.
thigh [θai], s. (Anat.) der Oberschenkel.
thimble [θimbl], s. der Fingerhut.
thin [θin], adj. dünn. — v.a., v.n. (sich) verdünnen.
thine [ðain], poss. pron. (Poet.) dein, der, die, das deinige.
thing [θiŋ], s. das Ding; die Sache (matter).
think [θiŋk], v.a., v.n. irr. denken; meinen, glauben.
thinker ['θiŋkə], s. der Denker.
third [θə:d], num. adj. der, die, das dritte. — s. das Drittel.
thirdly ['θə:dli], adv. drittens.
thirst [θə:st], s. der Durst (for, nach). — v.n. dürsten.
thirsty ['θə:sti], adj. durstig; be —, Durst haben.
thirteen [θə:'ti:n], num. adj. dreizehn.
thirty ['θə:ti], num. adj. dreißig.
this [ðis], dem. adj. dieser, diese, dieses. — dem. pron. dieser, diese, dieses; dies.
thistle [θisl], s. (Bot.) die Distel.
thither ['ðiðə], adv. dahin, dorthin.
tho' [ðou] see under though.
thong [θɔŋ], s. der Riemen (strap); die Peitschenschnur.
thorn [θɔ:n], s. (Bot.) der Dorn.
thorough ['θʌrə], adj. gründlich; völlig (complete).
thoroughbred ['θʌrəbred], s. das Vollblut, der Vollblüter. — adj. Vollblut-.
thoroughfare ['θʌrəfeə], s. der Durchgang (path); die Durchfahrt.
those [ðouz], dem. adj. pl. die, jene. — dem. pron. pl. jene, diejenigen.
thou [ðau], pers. pron. (Poet.) du.
though [ðou], conj. (abbr. tho') obgleich, obwohl, wenn auch (even if). — adv. doch, zwar.

501

thought

thought [θɔ:t], *s.* der Gedanke; *also past tense and participle of* think *q.v.*

thoughtful ['θɔ:tful], *adj.* rücksichtsvoll, nachdenklich.

thoughtless ['θɔ:tlis], *adj.* gedankenlos.

thousand ['θauzənd], *num. adj.* a —, tausend. — *s.* das Tausend.

thrash [θræʃ], *v.a.* dreschen (*corn*); prügeln (*s.o.*).

thread [θred], *s.* der Faden. — *v.a.* einfädeln. — *v.n.* sich schlängeln, sich winden.

threadbare ['θredbɛə], *adj.* fadenscheinig.

threat [θret], *s.* die Drohung.

threaten [θretn], *v.a.* drohen, androhen (*Dat.*).

three [θri:], *num. adj.* drei.

threescore ['θri:skɔ:], *num. adj.* sechzig.

thresh [θreʃ], *v.a.* dreschen (*corn*). — *See also* **thrash.**

threshold ['θreʃould], *s.* die Schwelle (*of door*).

thrice [θrais], *num. adv.* dreimal.

thrift [θrift], *s.* die Sparsamkeit; (*Bot.*) die Grasnelke, Meernelke.

thrill [θril], *v.a.* packen (*grip*). — *v.n.* erschauern, zittern (vor, *Dat.*). — *s.* der Schauer; die Spannung.

thriller ['θrilə], *s.* der Thriller, der spannende Roman *or* Film etc.

thrive [θraiv], *v.n.* gedeihen (*also fig.*); (*fig.*) gut weiterkommen, Glück haben.

thriving ['θraiviŋ], *adj.* blühend, (*Comm.*) gut gehend.

throat [θrout], *s.* (*Anat.*) der Schlund, die Kehle.

throb [θrɔb], *v.n.* pochen, klopfen.

throes [θrouz], *s. pl.* die Wehen, *f. pl.*; die Schmerzen, *m. pl.*

throne [θroun], *s.* der Thron.

throng [θrɔŋ], *s.* die Menge, das Gedränge. — *v.a., v.n.* (sich) drängen.

throttle [θrɔtl], *s.* die Kehle, Luftröhre; (*Mech.*) das Drosselventil; (*Motor.*) open the —, Gas geben.

through [θru:], *prep.* durch (*Acc.*); mittels (*Genit.*) (*by means of*). — *adv.* (mitten) durch.

throughout [θru:'aut], *prep.* ganz (hin)durch (*space*); während, hindurch (*time*). — *adv.* durchaus, in jeder Beziehung.

throw [θrou], *v.a. irr.* werfen; *open,* eröffnen. — *s.* der Wurf.

thrush [θrʌʃ], *s.* (*Orn.*) die Drossel.

thrust [θrʌst], *v.a.* stoßen, drängen. — *v.n.* stoßen (*at,* nach); sich drängen. — *s.* der Stoß, Angriff; *cut and* —, Hieb und Gegenhieb.

thud [θʌd], *s.* der Schlag, das Dröhnen, der dumpfe Ton. — *v.n.* dröhnen, aufschlagen.

thumb [θʌm], *s.* (*Anat.*) der Daumen; *rule of* —, die Faustregel; (*Am.*) *tack* see **drawing pin.** — *v.a.* durchblättern (*book*); — *a lift,* per Anhalter fahren.

thump [θʌmp], *v.a.* schlagen, puffen. —

v.n. schlagen (*on,* auf; *against,* gegen). — *s.* der Schlag, Stoß.

thunder ['θʌndə], *s.* der Donner. — *v.n.* donnern.

thunderstruck ['θʌndəstrʌk], *adj.* wie vom Donner gerührt.

Thursday ['θə:zdi]. der Donnerstag.

Thuringian [θuə'rindʒiən], *adj.* thüringisch. — *s.* der Thüringer.

thus [ðʌs], *adv.* so, auf diese Weise (*in this way*).

thwart [θwɔ:t], *v.a.* vereiteln, durchkreuzen.

thy [ðai], *poss. adj.* (*Poet.*) dein, deine, dein.

thyme [taim], *s.* (*Bot.*) der Thymian.

tic [tik], *s.* (*Med.*) das Zucken.

tick (1) [tik], *s.* das Ticken (*watch*). — *v.n.* ticken.

tick (2) [tik], *s.* (*coll.*) der Kredit, Borg.

ticket ['tikit], *s.* die Fahrkarte (*travel*); die Eintrittskarte (*entry*); (*Am.*) der Strafzettel (*driving*).

ticking (1) ['tikiŋ], *s.* das Ticken (*of watch*).

ticking (2) ['tikiŋ], *s.* (*Text.*) der Zwillich.

tickle [tikl], *v.a., v.n.* kitzeln. — *s.* das Kitzeln.

ticklish ['tikliʃ], *adj.* kitzlig.

tidal [taidl], *adj.* Gezeiten-, Ebbe-, Flut-.

tide [taid], *s.* die Gezeiten, *f.pl.*, die Ebbe und Flut. — *v.a.* — *over,* hinweghelfen (über, *Acc.*).

tidiness ['taidinis], *s.* die Sauberkeit, Ordnung.

tidings ['taidiŋz], *s. pl.* (*Poet.*) die Nachricht.

tidy ['taidi], *adj.* nett, sauber, ordentlich. — *v.a.* — *up,* sauber machen.

tie [tai], *v.a.* binden, knüpfen. — *v.n.* (*Sport*) unentschieden sein. — *s.* die Binde, Krawatte; (*Sport*) das Unentschieden.

tier [tiə], *s.* der Rang, die Reihe, Sitzreihe.

tiger ['taigə], *s.* (*Zool.*) der Tiger.

tight [tait], *adj.* fest, eng, dicht (*close*); (*coll.*) betrunken (*drunk*); — *fisted,* geizig (*stingy*). — *s. pl.* die Trikothosen, *f.pl.*

tighten [taitn], *v.a.* festziehen.

tile [tail], *s.* der Ziegel (*roof etc.*); die Kachel (*glazed*). — *v.a.* kacheln, ziegeln.

till (1) [til], *prep., conj.* bis.

till (2) [til], *v.a.* aufbauen, beackern (*land*).

till (3) [til], *s.* die Ladenkasse.

tilt [tilt], *v.a.* kippen, neigen, umschlagen (*tip over*). — *v.n.* sich neigen, kippen, kentern. — *s.* die Neigung.

timber ['timbə], *s.* das Holz, Bauholz.

time [taim], *s.* die Zeit; (*Mus.*) das Tempo, Zeitmaß; *in* —, zur rechten Zeit; *every* —, jedesmal; *what is the* —? wieviel Uhr ist es? — *v.a.* zeitlich messen, rechtzeitig einrichten.

timely ['taimli], *adj.* rechtzeitig.

timetable ['taimteibl], *s.* (*Railw.*) der Fahrplan; (*Sch.*) der Stundenplan.

timid ['timid], *adj.* furchtsam.

timpani ['timpəni], *s. pl.* (*Mus.*) die Kesselpauken, *f. pl.*

tin [tin], *s.* das Zinn, Weißblech; die Dose, Büchse (*preserved foods*); — *opener*, der Büchsenöffner.

tincture ['tiŋktʃə], *s.* die Tinktur, das Färbungsmittel.

tinder ['tində], *s.* der Zunder.

tinfoil ['tinfɔil], *s.* das Stanniol.

tinge [tindʒ], *v.a.* färben, anfärben. — *s.* die Färbung, leichte Farbe; (*fig.*) die Spur.

tingle [tiŋgl], *v.n.* klingen (*bells*); (*Anat.*) prickeln. — *s.* das Klingen; Prickeln.

tinker ['tiŋkə], *s.* der Kesselflicker. — *v.n.* basteln.

tinkle [tiŋkl], *v.a.* klingeln.

tinsel ['tinsəl], *s.* das Lametta, Flittergold.

tint [tint], *v.a.* färben. — *s.* die Farbe; der Farbton.

tiny ['taini], *adj.* winzig.

tip (1) [tip], *v.a.* kippen; (*coll.*) ein Trinkgeld geben (*Dat.*). — *s.* (*Sport etc.*) (*coll.*) der Tip; das Trinkgeld (*gratuity*).

tip (2) [tip], *s.* die Spitze; das Mundstück (*cigarette*).

tipple [tipl], *v.n.* (viel) trinken, zechen.

tipsy ['tipsi], *adj.* beschwipst.

tiptoe ['tiptou], *s. on* —, auf Zehenspitzen.

tiptop ['tiptɔp], *adj.* (*coll.*) erstklassig.

tirade [ti'reid *or* tai'reid], *s.* der Wortschwall, die Tirade.

tire (1) [taiə], *v.a., v.n.* ermüden.

tire (2) *see under* tyre.

tired ['taiəd], *adj.* müde.

tiresome ['taiəsəm], *adj.* langweilig (*boring*); auf die Nerven gehend (*annoying*).

tissue ['tiʃju:], *s.* das Gewebe; — *paper*, das Seidenpapier.

titbit ['titbit], *s.* der Leckerbissen.

tithe [taið], *s.* der Zehnte.

title [taitl], *s.* der Titel, die Überschrift; (*fig.*) der Anspruch (*claim*).

titmouse ['titmaus], *s.* (*Orn.*) die Meise.

titter ['titə], *v.n.* kichern. — *s.* das Kichern.

tittle [titl], *s.* das Tüpfelchen; — *tattle*, das Geschwätz.

titular ['titjulə], *adj.* Titular-.

to [tu], *prep.* zu (*Dat.*), gegen (*Acc.*); bis (*until, as far as*), nach, an, auf; *in order* —, um zu. — [tu:], *adv.* zu; — *and fro*, hin und her.

toad [toud], *s.* (*Zool.*) die Kröte.

toadstool ['toudstu:l], *s.* (*Bot.*) der Giftpilz.

toady ['toudi], *v.n.* kriechen. — *s.* der Kriecher.

toast [toust], *s.* der Toast, das Röstbrot; der Trinkspruch. — *v.a.* toasten,

rösten; trinken auf; — *s.o.*, einen Trinkspruch ausbringen auf einen.

tobacco [tə'bækou], *s.* der Tabak.

toboggan [tə'bɔgən], *s.* der Rodel, der Schlitten. — *v.n.* rodeln, Schlitten fahren.

tocsin ['tɔksin], *s.* die Sturmglocke.

today [tə'dei], *adv.* heute.

toddle [tɔdl], *v.n.* watscheln; *abschieben* (— *off*).

toddler ['tɔdlə], *s.* (*coll.*) das kleine Kind (das gehen lernt).

toe [tou], *s.* (*Anat.*) die Zehe.

toffee ['tɔfi], *s.* der Sahnebonbon.

together [tə'geðə], *adv.* zusammen.

toil [tɔil], *v.n.* hart arbeiten. — *s.* die schwere, harte Arbeit.

toilet ['tɔilit], *s.* das Anziehen, Ankleiden; die Toilette, der Abort, das Klosett (*lavatory*).

token ['toukən], *s.* das Zeichen (*sign*); der Beweis (*proof*); das Andenken (*keepsake*).

tolerable ['tɔlərəbl], *adj.* erträglich, leidlich.

tolerance ['tɔlərəns], *s.* die Toleranz, Duldsamkeit; (*Tech.*) die Toleranz.

tolerant ['tɔlərənt], *adj.* tolerant, duldsam.

tolerate ['tɔləreit], *v.a.* ertragen, dulden.

toll [toul], *v.a., v.n.* läuten. — *s.* der Zoll; — *gate*, — *bar*, der Schlagbaum.

tomato [tə'mɑ:tou], *s.* (*Bot.*) die Tomate.

tomb [tu:m], *s.* das Grab, Grabmal.

tomboy ['tɔmbɔi], *s.* der Wildfang.

tomcat ['tɔmkæt], *s.* (*Zool.*) der Kater.

tome [toum], *s.* der große Band, (*coll.*) der Wälzer.

tomfoolery [tɔm'fu:ləri], *s.* die Narretei.

Tommy ['tɔmi], *s.* (*Mil.*) (*coll.*) der englische Soldat.

tomorrow [tə'mɔrou], *adv.* morgen; — *morning*, morgen früh; *the day after* —, übermorgen.

ton [tʌn], *s.* die Tonne.

tone [toun], *s.* der Ton, Klang; (*fig.*) die Stimmung (*mood*). — *v.a.* — *down*, abtönen, abstimmen.

tongs [tɔŋz], *s. pl.* die Zange.

tongue [tʌŋ], *s.* (*Anat.*) die Zunge.

tonic ['tɔnik], *s.* das Stärkungsmittel. — *adj.* tonisch, stärkend.

tonight [tu'nait], *adv.* heute abend, heute nacht.

tonnage ['tʌnidʒ], *s.* die Tonnage, das Tonnengeld.

tonsil ['tɔnsil], *s.* (*Anat.*) die Mandel.

tonsilitis [tɔnsi'laitis], *s.* (*Med.*) die Mandelentzündung.

tonsure ['tɔnʃə], *s.* die Tonsur.

too [tu:], *adv.* allzu, zu, allzusehr; auch (*also*).

tool [tu:l], *s.* das Werkzeug, das Gerät; — *machine* —, die Werkzeugmaschine.

tooth [tu:θ], *s.* (*pl.* teeth [ti:θ]) der Zahn.

toothache ['tu:θeik], *s.* das Zahnweh.

toothbrush ['tu:θbrʌʃ], *s.* die Zahnbürste.

toothpaste ['tu:θpeist], *s.* die Zahnpaste.

top (1) [tɔp], *s.* die Spitze; der Gipfel (*mountain*); der Wipfel (*tree*); der Giebel (*house*); die Oberfläche (*surface*); *big* —, das Zirkuszeltdach; — *hat*, der Zylinder. — *v.a.* übertreffen (*surpass*); bedecken (*cover*).

top (2) [tɔp], *s.* der Kreisel (*spinning* —).

topaz ['toupæz], *s.* der Topas.

tope [toup], *v.n.* zechen, saufen.

toper ['toupə], *s.* der Zecher.

topic ['tɔpik], *s.* das Thema, der Gegenstand.

topical ['tɔpikəl], *adj.* aktuell (*up to date*).

topmost ['tɔpmoust], *adj.* höchst, oberst.

topsy-turvy ['tɔpsi 'tə:vi], *adv.* durcheinander, auf den Kopf gestellt.

torch [tɔ:tʃ], *s.* die Fackel; (*Elec.*) die Taschenlampe.

torment ['tɔ:ment], *s.* die Qual, Marter. — [tɔ:'ment], *v.a.* quälen, martern, peinigen.

tornado [tɔ:'neidou], *s.* der Wirbelsturm.

torpid ['tɔ:pid], *adj.* starr, betäubt; (*fig.*) stumpfsinnig.

torpor ['tɔ:pə], *s.* die Starre; die Stumpfheit, Stumpfsinnigkeit.

torrent ['tɔrənt], *s.* der Gießbach, der (reißende) Strom.

torrid ['tɔrid], *adj.* brennend heiß, verbrannt.

torsion ['tɔ:ʃən], *s.* die Drehung, Windung.

tortoise ['tɔ:təs], *s.* (*Zool.*) die Schildkröte.

tortoiseshell ['tɔ:təsʃel], *s.* das Schildpatt.

tortuous ['tɔ:tjuəs], *adj.* gewunden.

torture ['tɔ:tʃə], *s.* die Folter; (*fig.*) die Folterqualen, *f. pl.* — *v.a.* foltern.

Tory ['tɔ:ri], *s.* (*Pol.*) der englische Konservative.

toss [tɔs], *s.* der Wurf (*of coin, etc.*); *argue the* —, sich streiten. — *v.a.* werfen. — *v.n.* — *up*, losen.

total ['toutl], *adj.* ganz, gänzlich, total. — *s.* die Gesamtsumme. — *v.a.* sich (im ganzen) belaufen auf.

totality [tou'tæliti], *s.* die Gesamtheit.

totter ['tɔtə], *v.n.* wanken, schwanken, torkeln.

touch [tʌtʃ], *v.a.* berühren; anfassen; (*coll.*) anpumpen (*for money*); — *up*, auffrischen. — *s.* die Berührung (*contact*); (*Mus.*) der Anschlag.

touching ['tʌtʃiŋ], *adj.* rührend, ergreifend.

touchline ['tʌtʃlain], *s.* (*Sport*) der Rand des Spielfeldes, die Seitenlinie.

touchy ['tʌtʃi], *adj.* empfindlich.

tough [tʌf], *adj.* zäh, widerstandsfähig (*resistant*); *get* —, grob werden; — *luck!* Pech! — *s.* (*Am. coll.*) der Grobian.

tour [tuə], *s.* die Tour, Reise; (*Theat.*) die Tournee. — *v.a.*, *v.n.* touren, bereisen.

tourist ['tuərist], *s.* der Tourist.

tournament ['tuə- *or* 'tə:nəmənt], *s.* der Wettkampf, das Turnier.

tout [taut], *v.n.* Kunden suchen, anlocken. — *s.* der Kundenfänger.

tow [tou], *s.* das Schlepptau. — *v.a.* ziehen, schleppen.

toward(s) [tu'wɔ:d(z), tɔ:d(z)], *prep.* gegen; gegenüber; zu . . . hin; auf . . . zu; für.

towel ['tauəl], *s.* das Handtuch.

towelling ['tauəliŋ], *s.* der Handtuchdrell; *Turkish* —, das Frottiertuch.

tower [tauə], *s.* der Turm, Zwinger. — *v.n.* emporragen, hervorragen (über).

towing path ['tou(iŋ) pɑ:θ] *see* **towpath**.

town [taun], *s.* die Stadt; — *crier*, der Ausrufer; — *hall*, das Rathaus (*offices*).

townsman ['taunzmən], *s.* der Städter.

towpath ['toupɑ:θ], *s.* der Treidelpfad.

toy [tɔi], *s.* das Spielzeug; (*pl.*) Spielsachen, Spielwaren, *f. pl.*; — *shop*, der Spielwarenladen. — *v.n.* spielen.

trace [treis], *s.* die Spur. — *v.a.* suchen, aufspüren; pausen (*through paper*).

track [træk], *s.* die Spur, Fährte (*path*); (*Railw.*) das Geleis(e).

tract [trækt], *s.* der Traktat (*pamphlet*); die Strecke (*stretch*).

traction ['trækʃən], *s.* das Ziehen (*pulling*); (*Tech.*) der Zug.

tractor ['træktə], *s.* der Traktor.

trade [treid], *s.* der Handel (*commerce*); das Gewerbe (*craft*); — *wind*, der Passatwind; — *union*, die Gewerkschaft. — *v.a.* — *in*, in Zahlung geben. — *v.n.* handeln, Handel treiben; — *in*, eintauschen.

trademark ['treidmɑ:k], *s.* die (Schutz-)marke, das Warenzeichen.

tradesman ['treidzmən], *s.* der Lieferant.

traduce [trə'dju:s], *v.a.* verleumden.

traffic ['træfik], *s.* der Verkehr; (*Comm.*) der Handel; — *light*, die Verkehrsampel.

trafficator ['træfikeitə], *s.* (*Motor.*) der Winker.

tragedy ['trædʒədi], *s.* die Tragödie, das Trauerspiel.

tragic ['trædʒik], *adj.* tragisch.

tradition [trə'diʃən], *s.* die Tradition.

traditional [trə'diʃənəl], *adj.* traditionell.

trail [treil], *s.* die Spur, Fährte; (*Am.*) der Pfad. — *v.a.* nach sich ziehen, schleppen; (*Am.*) nachfolgen (*Dat.*).

trailer ['treilə], *s.* (*Motor.*) der Anhänger; (*Film*) die Voranzeige.

train [trein], *v.a.* ausbilden; (*Sport*) trainieren, abrichten, dressieren (*animal*). — *v.n.* (*Sport*) sich vorbereiten; sich ausbilden (*for profession*). — *s.* (*Railw.*) der Zug; (*Mil.*) der Zug, Transport; die Schleppe (*bridal gown, etc.*); — *of thought*, die Gedankenfolge.

training ['treiniŋ], *s.* die Erziehung; Ausbildung; — *college,* das Lehrerseminar, die pädagogische Hochschule.

trait [trei, treit], *s.* der Zug, Wesenszug.

traitor ['treitə], *s.* der Verräter.

tram(car) ['træm(ka:)], *s.* die Straßenbahn, der Strassenbahnwagen.

trammelled [træmld], *adj.* gebunden, gefesselt.

tramp [træmp], *s.* der Landstreicher, Strolch. — *v.n.* trampeln; (zu Fuß) wandern.

trample [træmpl], *v.a.* niedertrampeln. — *v.n.* trampeln, treten.

tramway ['træmwei], *s.* die Strassenbahn.

trance [tra:ns], *s.* die Verzückung.

tranquil ['træŋkwil], *adj.* ruhig, still, friedlich.

tranquillizer ['træŋkwilaizə], *s.* (*Med.*) das Beruhigungsmittel.

transact [træn'zækt], *v.a.* abmachen; verrichten (*conclude*), erledigen.

transaction [træn'zækʃən], *s.* die Verhandlung, Abmachung, Durchführung.

transcend [træn'send], *v.a.* übersteigen.

transcendental [trænsen'dentl], *adj.* transzendental.

transcribe [træn'skraib], *v.a.* übertragen; umschreiben (*cipher etc.*); abschreiben.

transcription [træn'skripʃən], *s.* die Umschrift; die Abschrift (*copy*).

transept ['trænsept], *s.* (*Archit.*) das Querschiff.

transfer [træns'fə:], *v.a.* versetzen, überführen; übertragen; überweisen (*money*). — *v.n.* verlegt werden. — ['trænsfə:], *s.* der Wechsel, Transfer; die Versetzung; Überweisung.

transfigure [træns'figə], *v.a.* verklären.

transfix [træns'fiks], *v.a.* durchbohren.

transform [træns'fɔ:m], *v.a.* verändern, umwandeln. — *v.r.* sich verwandeln.

transgress [træns'gres], *v.a.* überschreiten (*trespass on*). — *v.n.* sich vergehen.

transient ['trænsiənt], *adj.* vergänglich.

transit ['trænsit, 'trænzit], *s.* der Durchgang; die Durchfahrt, Durchfuhr (*travel*); (*Comm.*) der Transit. — *v.n.* (*Am.*) durchfahren (*of goods*).

transitive ['trænsitiv], *adj.* (*Gram.*) transitiv.

transitory ['trænsitəri], *adj.* vergänglich, flüchtig.

translate [træns'leit], *v.a.* übersetzen; versetzen (*office*).

translation [træns'leiʃən], *s.* die Übersetzung, die Übertragung.

translucent [trænz'lju:sənt], *adj.* durchscheinend.

transmission [trænz'miʃən], *s.* die Übersendung, Übermittlung; (*Rad.*) die Sendung; (*Motor.*) die Transmission.

transmit [trænz'mit], *v.a.* übersenden,

übermitteln; (*Rad., T.V.*) übertragen, senden.

transmutation [trænzmju'teiʃən], *s.* die Verwandlung.

transparent [træns'pɛərənt], *adj.* durchsichtig.

transpire [træns'paiə, trænz–], *v.n.* bekannt werden.

transplant [træns'pla:nt, trænz–], *v.a.* verpflanzen; (*Med.*) übertragen.

transport [træns'pɔ:t], *v.a.* transportieren; (*fig.*) entzücken. — ['trænspɔ:t], *s.* der Transport; die Versendung (*sending*); (*fig.*) die Entzückung.

transpose [træns'pouz], *v.a.* (*Mus.*) transponieren.

transverse [trænz'və:s], *adj.* quer; schräg (*oblique*).

trap [træp], *v.a.* in eine Falle führen; ertappen (*detect*). — *s.* die Falle; der Einspänner (*gig*).

trapeze [trə'pi:z], *s.* das Trapez.

trapper ['træpə], *s.* der Fallensteller.

trappings ['træpiŋz], *s. pl.* der Schmuck; (*fig.*) die Äußerlichkeiten, *f. pl.*

trash [træʃ], *s.* (*Lit.*) der Schund; **der** Kitsch; das wertlose Zeug.

trashy ['træʃi], *adj.* wertlos, kitschig.

travail ['træveil], *s.* die Wehen, Sorgen, die Mühe.

travel [trævl], *v.n.* reisen. — *v.a.* bereisen. — *s.* das Reisen; — *agency,* das Reisebüro.

traveller ['trævələ], *s.* der Reisende; (*Comm.*) der Handelsreisende, Vertreter.

traverse ['trævə:s], *adj.* quer. — *s.* die Traverse, der Querbalken. — [trə'və:s], *v.a.* durchqueren; (*fig.*) durchwandern.

trawl [trɔ:l], *v.n.* (mit Schleppnetz) fischen.

trawler ['trɔ:lə], *s.* das Fischerboot, **der** Fischdampfer.

tray [trei], *s.* das Tablett.

treacherous ['tretʃərəs], *adj.* verräterisch; (*fig.*) gefährlich.

treachery ['tretʃəri], *s.* der Verrat.

treacle [tri:kl], *s.* der Sirup.

tread [tred], *v.a., v.n. irr.* (be)treten, auftreten. — *s.* der Tritt, Schritt; die Lauffläche (*of a tyre*).

treason [tri:zn], *s.* der Verrat.

treasure ['treʒə], *s.* der Schatz.

treasurer ['treʒərə], *s.* der Schatzmeister.

treasury ['treʒəri], *s.* die Schatzkammer; (*U.K.*) *the Treasury,* das Schatzamt, Finanzministerium.

treat [tri:t], *v.a.* behandeln; bewirten (*as host*). — *v.n.* (*Pol.*) unterhandeln (*negotiate*). — *s.* der Genuß (*pleasure*).

treatise ['tri:tis], *s.* die Abhandlung.

treatment ['tri:tmənt], *s.* die Behandlung.

treaty ['tri:ti], *s.* der Vertrag.

treble [trebl], *s.* (*Mus.*) die Sopranstimme, Knabenstimme, der Diskant; (*Maths.*) das Dreifache. — *v.a.* verdreifachen.

tree [tri:], *s.* (*Bot.*) der Baum.
trefoil ['tri:fɔil], *s.* (*Bot.*) der dreiblätt(e)rige Klee; das Dreiblatt.
trellis ['trelis], *s.* das Gitter.
tremble [trembl], *v.n.* zittern. — *s.* das Zittern.
tremendous [tri'mendəs], *adj.* ungeheuer (groß); schrecklich.
tremor ['tremə], *s.* das Zittern; (*Geol.*) das Beben; (*Med.*) das Zucken.
trench [trentʃ], *s.* der Graben.
trenchant ['trentʃənt], *adj.* einschneidend, scharf.
trend [trend], *s.* die Tendenz; (*Comm.*) der Trend.
trepidation [trepi'deiʃən], *s.* die Angst, das Zittern.
trespass ['trespəs], *v.n.* sich vergehen, übertreten (*law*); — *on*, unbefugt betreten. — *s.* die Übertretung.
tress [tres], *s.* die Flechte, Haarlocke.
trestle [tresl], *s.* das Gestell; — *table*, der Klapptisch.
trial ['traiəl], *s.* die Probe, der Versuch; (*Law*) die Verhandlung, der Prozeß, das Verhör.
triangle ['traiæŋgl], *s.* das Dreieck; (*Mus.*) der Triangel.
tribe [traib], *s.* der Stamm.
tribulation [tribju'leiʃən], *s.* die Trübsal, Drangsal.
tribunal [trai'bju:nəl], *s.* das Tribunal, der Gerichtshof.
tributary ['tribjutəri], *adj.* Neben-. — *s.* der Nebenfluß.
tribute ['tribju:t], *s.* der Tribut.
trice [trais], *s. in a* —, im Nu.
trick [trik], *s.* der Kniff, Trick. — *v.a.* betrügen.
trickery ['trikəri], *s.* der Betrug.
trickle [trikl], *v.n.* tröpfeln, sickern. — *s.* das Tröpfeln.
tricky ['triki], *adj.* verwickelt; (*fig.*) bedenklich, heikel.
tricycle ['traisikl], *s.* das Dreirad.
tried [traid], *adj.* erprobt, bewährt.
triennial [trai'eniəl], *adj.* dreijährlich.
trifle [traifl], *v.n.* scherzen, spielen. — *s.* die Kleinigkeit; (*Cul.*) der süße Auflauf.
trigger ['trigə], *s.* der Drücker. — *v.a.* — *off*, auslösen.
trilateral [trai'lætərəl], *adj.* dreiseitig.
trill [tril], *s.* (*Mus.*) der Triller. — *v.a.*, *v.n.* trillern.
trim [trim], *adj.* niedlich, schmuck; nett (*dress*). — *v.a.* beschneiden; (*Naut.*) — *sails*, einziehen. — *s.* die Ausrüstung; (*Naut.*) das Gleichgewicht.
trimmer ['trimə], *s.* die Putzmacherin; (*fig.*) der Opportunist.
trimmings ['triminz], *s. pl.* (*fig.*) der Kleinkram; (*Tail.*) der Besatz.
Trinity ['triniti], *s.* (*Theol.*) die Dreifaltigkeit, Dreieinigkeit.
trinket ['triŋkit], *s.* das Geschmeide; (*pl.*) Schmucksachen, *f. pl.*
trip [trip], *s.* der Ausflug, die Reise. —

v.a. — *up*, ein Bein stellen (*Dat.*). — *v.n.* stolpern.
tripe ['traip], *s.* die Kaldaunen, *f. pl.*; (*fig.*) der Unsinn.
triple [tripl], *adj.* dreifach.
triplet ['triplit], *s.* der Drilling; (*Mus.*) die Triole; (*Poet.*) der Dreireim.
tripod ['traipɔd], *s.* der Dreifuß.
tripos ['traipɔs], *s.* das Schlußexamen (*Cambridge Univ.*).
trite [trait], *adj.* abgedroschen.
triumph ['traiʌmf], *s.* der Triumph. — *v.n.* triumphieren.
triumphant [trai'ʌmfənt], *adj.* triumphierend.
trivial ['triviəl], *adj.* trivial, platt, alltäglich.
troll (1) [troul], *v.n.* trällern (*hum*); fischen. — *s.* der Rundgesang (*song*).
troll (2) [troul], *s.* der Kobold (*gnome*).
trolley ['trɔli], *s.* der Teewagen (*furniture*); (*Tech.*) die Dräsine, der Karren.
trollop ['trɔləp], *s.* die Schlampe.
trombone [trɔm'boun], *s.* (*Mus.*) die Posaune.
troop [tru:p], *s.* der Haufe; (*Mil.*) die Truppe, der Trupp. — *v.n.* sich sammeln. — *v.a. Trooping the Colour*, die Fahnenparade.
trophy ['troufi], *s.* die Trophäe, das Siegeszeichen.
tropic ['trɔpik], *s.* (*Geog.*) der Wendekreis; (*pl.*) die Tropen, *f. pl.*
tropical ['trɔpikəl], *adj.* tropisch.
trot [trɔt], *v.n.* traben. — *s.* der Trab, Trott.
troth [trouθ], *s.* (*obs.*) die Treue; *pledge o.'s* —, Treue geloben.
trouble [trʌbl], *s.* die Mühe, Sorge (*worry*); der Kummer (*sadness*); die Störung (*disturbance*). — *v.a.* bemühen (*ask favour of*); bekümmern (*worry*); stören (*disturb*).
troublesome ['trʌblsəm], *adj.* ärgerlich, schwierig, unangenehm.
trough [trɔf], *s.* der Trog; (*Met.*) das Tief.
trounce [trauns], *v.a.* verprügeln.
trouncing ['traunsiŋ], *s.* die Tracht Prügel.
trousers ['trauzəz], *s. pl.* die Hosen, *f. pl.*
trout [traut], *s.* (*Zool.*) die Forelle.
trowel ['trauəl], *s.* die Kelle.
troy(weight) ['trɔi(weit)], *s.* das Troygewicht.
truant ['tru:ənt], *s.* (*Sch.*) der Schulschwänzer; *play* —, die Schule schwänzen.
truce [tru:s], *s.* der Waffenstillstand.
truck (1) [trʌk], *s.* (*Rail.*) der Güterwagen; (*Am.*) see **lorry**.
truck (2) [trʌk], *s. have no* — *with*, nichts zu tun haben mit.
truculent ['trʌkjulənt], *adj.* streitsüchtig.
trudge [trʌdʒ], *v.n.* sich schleppen.
true [tru:], *adj.* wahr; treu (*faithful*); echt (*genuine*); richtig (*correct*).

truffle [trʌfl], *s.* die Trüffel.
truism ['truːizm], *s.* der Gemeinplatz, die Binsenwahrheit.
truly ['truːli], *adv.* yours —, Ihr ergebener.
trump [trʌmp], *s.* der Trumpf; — *card*, die Trumpfkarte. — *v.a.* — *up*, erfinden, erdichten.
trumpery ['trʌmpəri], *s.* der Plunder, Schund. — *adj.* wertlos, belanglos.
trumpet ['trʌmpit], *s.* (*Mus.*) die Trompete. — *v.a.* stolz austrompeten, ausposaunen. — *v.n.* trompeten.
truncate [trʌŋ'keit], *v.a.* verstümmeln, stutzen.
truncheon ['trʌnʃən], *s.* der Knüppel. — *v.a.* durchprügeln.
trundle [trʌndl], *v.n.* trudeln; sich wälzen. — *v.a.* — *a hoop*, Reifen schlagen.
trunk [trʌŋk], *s.* der Stamm (*tree*); der Rüssel (*of elephant*); der (große) Koffer (*chest*); — *call*, das Ferngespräch.
truss [trʌs], *s.* das Band, Bruchband. — *v.a.* zäumen, stützen; aufschürzen.
trust [trʌst], *v.a.* u. *v.n.* trauen (*Dat.*), vertrauen (*Dat.*); anvertrauen (*Dat., Acc.*). — *s.* das Vertrauen; in —, zu treuen Händen, als Treuhänder; (*Comm.*) der Trust.
trustworthy ['trʌstwəːði], *adj.* zuverlässig.
truth [truːθ], *s.* die Wahrheit.
truthful ['truːθful], *adj.* wahrhaftig.
try [trai], *v.a.* *irr.* versuchen (*s. th.*); (*Law*) verhören; — *on* (*clothes*), anprobieren; — *out*, ausprobieren. — *v.n.* versuchen, sich bemühen. — *s.* der Versuch (*attempt*); (*Rugby*) der Try.
Tsar [zaː], *s.* der Zar.
tub [tʌb], *s.* das Faß; die Wanne (*bath*); (*Naut.*) das Übungsboot.
tube [tjuːb], *s.* die Tube (*paste etc.*); die Röhre (*pipe, also Elec.*); der Schlauch (*tyre*); das Rohr (*tubing*); (*Transport*) die Londoner Untergrundbahn.
tuberous ['tjuːbərəs], *adj.* knollenartig, knollig.
tubular ['tjuːbjulə], *adj.* röhrenförmig.
tuck [tʌk], *s.* (*Tail.*) die Falte; (*Sch. sl.*) der Leckerbissen. — *v.a.* — *up*, zudecken; — *in*, einschlagen. — *v.n.* (*sl.*) — *in*, tüchtig zugreifen.
tucker ['tʌkə], *s.* (*sl.*) das Essen.
tuckshop ['tʌkʃɔp], *s.* der Schulladen.
Tuesday ['tjuːzdi], *s.* der Dienstag.
tuft [tʌft], *s.* der Büschel.
tug [tʌg], *v.a.* ziehen, zerren. — *s.* (*Naut.*) der Schlepper; — *of war*, das Tauziehen.
tuition [tjuː'iʃən], *s.* der Unterricht, Privatunterricht.
tulip ['tjuːlip], *s.* (*Bot.*) die Tulpe.
tumble [tʌmbl], *v.n.* purzeln. — *s.* der Sturz, Fall.
tumbril ['tʌmbril], *s.* der Karren.
tumid ['tjuːmid], *adj.* geschwollen.
tumour ['tjuːmə], *s.* (*Med.*) die Geschwulst, der Tumor.

tumult ['tjuːmʌlt], *s.* der Tumult, Auflauf; der Lärm (*noise*).
tun [tʌn], *s.* die Tonne, das Faß.
tune [tjuːn], *s.* die Melodie. — *v.a.* stimmen; (*Rad.*) — *in* (*to*), einstellen (auf).
tuneful ['tjuːnful], *adj.* melodisch.
tuner ['tjuːnə], *s.* der (Klavier)stimmer.
tunic ['tjuːnik], *s.* der Kittel.
tuning ['tjuːniŋ], *s.* das Stimmen; die Abstimmung (*also Rad.*); — *fork*, die Stimmgabel.
tunnel [tʌnl], *s.* der Tunnel. — *v.n.* graben, einen Tunnel bauen.
turbid ['təːbid], *adj.* trüb, dick.
turbot ['təːbət], *s.* (*Zool.*) der Steinbutt.
turbulence ['təːbjuləns], *s.* der Sturm, das Ungestüm; (*Aviat.*) die Turbulenz.
tureen [tjuə'riːn], *s.* die Suppenterrine, Suppenschüssel.
turf [təːf], *s.* der Rasen; (*Sport*) die Rennbahn, der Turf. — *v.a.* mit Rasen belegen; (*sl.*) — *out*, hinausschmeißen.
turgid ['təːdʒid], *adj.* schwülstig (*style*).
Turk [təːk], *s.* der Türke.
turkey ['təːki], *s.* (*Orn.*) der Truthahn.
Turkish ['təːkiʃ], *adj.* türkisch.
turmoil ['təːmɔil], *s.* die Unruhe, der Aufruhr.
turn [təːn], *v.a.* wenden, drehen, kehren (*to*); — *down*, ablehnen; (*coll.*) — *in*, abgeben (*hand over*); — *on*, andrehen (*tap etc.*); — *off*, ausdrehen; — *out*, produzieren. — *v.n.* sich drehen, sich ändern; werden; — *on s.o.*, jemanden verraten; (*coll.*) — *out*, ausrücken; (*coll.*) — *up*, auftauchen. — *s.* die Drehung, Windung; der Hang; die Reihe; die Nummer (*act*); *it is my* —, ich bin an der Reihe.
turncoat ['təːnkout], *s.* der Überläufer.
turner ['təːnə], *s.* der Drechsler.
turnip ['təːnip], *s.* (*Bot.*) die Rübe.
turnpike ['təːnpaik], *s.* der Schlagbaum.
turnstile ['təːnstail], *s.* das Drehkreuz.
turntable ['təːnteibl], *s.* die Drehscheibe.
turpentine ['təːpəntain], *s.* der *or* das Terpentin.
turquoise ['təːkwɔiz *or* 'təːkɔiz], *s.* der Türkis.
turret ['tʌrit], *s.* (*Archit.*) der Turm, das Türmchen.
turtle [təːtl], *s.* (*Zool.*) die Schildkröte; (*Orn.*) -*dove*, die Turteltaube.
tusk [tʌsk], *s.* (*Zool.*) der Stoßzahn.
tussle [tʌsl], *s.* der Streit, die Rauferei.
tutelage ['tjuːtilidʒ], *s.* die Vormundschaft.
tutor ['tjuːtə], *s.* der Privatlehrer; der Tutor, Studienleiter. — *v.a.* unterrichten.
twaddle [twɔdl], *s.* das Geschwätz. — *v.n.* schwätzen.
twang [twæŋ], *s.* der scharfe Ton. — *v.n.* scharf klingen.
tweed [twiːd], *s.* (*Text.*) der Tweed.
twelfth [twelfθ], *num.adj.* zwölft; *Twelfth Night*, das Fest der Heiligen Drei Könige (*6th January*).

twelve

twelve [twelv], *num. adj.* zwölf.
twenty ['twenti], *num. adj.* zwanzig.
twice [twais], *num. adv.* zweimal, doppelt.
twig [twig], *s.* (*Bot.*) der Zweig, die Rute.
twilight ['twailait], *s.* das Zwielicht, die Dämmerung.
twill [twil], *s.* (*Text.*) der Köper. — *v.a.* köpern.
twin [twin], *s.* der Zwilling.
twine [twain], *s.* der Bindfaden, die Schnur. — *v.a.* drehen, zwirnen. — *v.n.* sich verflechten; sich winden (*plant*).
twinge [twind3], *s.* der Zwick, Stich.
twinkle [twiŋkl], *v.n.* blinzeln, blinken. — *s.* das Zwinkern, der Blick.
twirl [twə:l], *s.* der Wirbel. — *v.a.* schnell drehen, wirbeln.
twist [twist], *v.a.* flechten, drehen; verdrehen. — *s.* die Drehung, Krümmung; das Geflecht; (*fig.*) die Wendung (*sudden change*).
twitch [twitʃ], *v.a.* zupfen, zucken. — *v.n.* zucken. — *s.* das Zucken, der Krampf.
twitter ['twitə], *v.n.* zwitschern; (*fig.*) zittern. — *s.* das Gezwitscher; (*fig.*) die Angst.
two [tu:], *num. adj.* zwei; — *-faced*, falsch.
twofold ['tu:fould], *adj.* zweifach.
tympanum ['timpənəm], *s.* (*Med.*) das Trommelfell.
type [taip], *s.* (*Typ.*) die Type; (*Psych.*) der Typ, Typus. — *v.a., v.n.* tippen; mit der Maschine schreiben.
typewriter ['taipraitə], *s.* die Schreibmaschine.
typhoid ['taifoid], *s.* (*Med.*) der (Unterleibs)typhus. — *adj.* typhusartig.
typist ['taipist], *s.* der (die) Maschinenschreiber(in).
typhoon [tai'fu:n], *s.* der Taifun.
typical ['tipikəl], *adj.* typisch, charakteristisch.
typography [tai'pɔgrəfi], *s.* die Typographie, Buchdruckerkunst.
tyrannical [ti' rænikəl], *adj.* tyrannisch.
tyranny ['tirəni], *s.* die Tyrannei.
tyrant ['taiərənt], *s.* der Tyrann.
tyre, (*Am.*) **tire** [taiə], *s.* der Reifen.
tyro ['taiərou], *s.* der Anfänger.
Tyrolese [tiro'li:z], *adj.* tirolisch, Tiroler-. — *s.* der Tiroler.

U

U [ju:]. das U.
ubiquitous [ju'bikwitəs], *adj.* überall da, überall zu finden.
udder ['ʌdə], *s.* (*Zool.*) das Euter.
ugly ['ʌgli], *adj.* häßlich.

Ukrainian [ju:'kreiniən], *adj.* ukrainisch. — *s.* der Ukrainer.
ulcer ['ʌlsə], *s.* (*Med.*) das Geschwür.
ulcerate ['ʌlsəreit], *v.n.* (*Med.*) schwären.
ulcerous ['ʌlsərəs], *adj.* (*Med.*) geschwürig.
ulterior [ʌl'tiəriə], *adj.* weiter, ferner, weiterliegend.
ultimate ['ʌltimit], *adj.* letzt, endlich, äußerst.
ultimatum [ʌlti'meitəm], *s.* das Ultimatum.
umbrage ['ʌmbrid3], *s.* der Schatten; *take —*, Anstoß nehmen (an, *Dat.*).
umbrella [ʌm'brelə], *s.* der Schirm, Regenschirm.
umpire ['ʌmpaiə], *s.* (*Sport*) der Schiedsrichter.
umpteen ['ʌmpti:n], *adj.* zahlreiche, verschiedene.
un- [ʌn], *negating pref.* un-, nicht-; *with verbs,* auf-, ent-, los-, ver-; *where a word is not given, see the simple form.*
unable [ʌn'eibl], *adj.* unfähig; *be —*, nicht können.
unaccustomed [ʌnə'kʌstəmd], *adj.* ungewohnt.
unaided [ʌn'eidid], *adj.* allein, ohne Hilfe.
unaware [ʌnə'weə], *adj.* unbewußt.
uncertain [ʌn'sə:tin], *adj.* unsicher.
uncle [ʌŋkl], *s.* der Onkel.
unconscious [ʌn'kɔnʃəs], *adj.* bewußtlos; unbewusst.
uncouth [ʌn'ku:θ], *adj.* ungehobelt, roh.
unction ['ʌŋkʃən], *s.* die Salbung (*anointing*); die Salbe; *Extreme Unction*, (*Eccl.*) die Letzte Ölung.
unctuous ['ʌŋktjuəs], *adj.* salbungsvoll.
under ['ʌndə], *prep.* unter. — *adv.* darunter, unten (*underneath*); *pref.* (*compounds*) unter-.
undercarriage ['ʌndəkærid3], *s.* (*Aviat.*) das Fahrwerk.
underfed [ʌndə'fed], *adj.* unterernährt.
undergo [ʌndə'gou], *v.a. irr.* durchmachen, erdulden.
undergraduate [ʌndə'grædjuit], *s.* (*Univ.*) der Student.
underground ['ʌndəgraund], *adj.* unterirdisch; — *railway* die Untergrundbahn. — [ʌndə'graund], *adv.* unterirdisch.
underhand [ʌndə'hænd], *adj.* heimlich, hinterlistig.
underline [ʌndə'lain], *v.a.* unterstreichen.
undermine [ʌndə'main], *v.a.* untergraben.
underneath [ʌndə'ni:θ], *adv.* unten, darunter. — ['ʌndəni:θ], *prep.* unter.
undersigned ['ʌndəsaind], *adj.* unterzeichnet. —*s.* der Unterzeichnete.
understand [ʌndə'stænd], *v.a. irr.* verstehen, begreifen.
understatement ['ʌndəsteitmənt], *s.* die zu bescheidene Festellung, Unterbewertung.

undertaker [ˈʌndəteikə], s. der Leichenbestatter.
undertaking [ʌndəˈteikiŋ], s. das Unternehmen (*business*); das Versprechen (*promise*).
undertone [ˈʌndətoun], s. der Unterton.
underwrite [ʌndəˈrait], v.a. irr. (*Comm.*) versichern.
underwriter [ˈʌndəraitə], s. (*Comm.*) der Assekurant, Versicherer, Mitversicherer.
undeserved [ʌndiˈzəːvd], adj. unverdient.
undeserving [ʌndiˈzəːviŋ], adj. unwürdig.
undignified [ʌnˈdignifaid], adj. würdelos.
undiscerning [ʌndiˈzəːniŋ], adj. geschmacklos.
undiscriminating [ʌndisˈkrimineitiŋ], adj. unterschiedslos, unkritisch.
undisputed [ʌndisˈpjuːtid], adj. unbestritten.
undo [ʌnˈduː], v.a. irr. zerstören (*destroy*); öffnen (*open*).
undoubted [ʌnˈdautid], adj. zweifellos.
undress [ʌnˈdres], v.a., v.n. — (sich)ausziehen. — [ʌnˈdres], s. das Hauskleid.
undue [ʌnˈdjuː], adj. unangemessen.
undulate [ˈʌndjuleit], v.n. wallen, Wellen schlagen.
unduly [ʌnˈdjuːli], adv. ungebührlich, übermäßig.
unearth [ʌnˈəːθ], v.a. ausgraben.
unearthly [ʌnˈəːθli], adj. überirdisch.
uneasy [ʌnˈiːzi], adj. unruhig, unbehaglich.
unemployed [ʌnimˈplɔid], adj. arbeitslos.
unemployment [ʌnimˈplɔimənt], s. die Arbeitslosigkeit.
unending [ʌnˈendiŋ], adj. endlos.
uneven [ʌnˈiːvən], adj. uneben; ungerade.
unexceptionable [ʌnikˈsepʃənəbl], adj. tadellos.
unexpired [ʌniksˈpaiəd], adj. noch nicht abgelaufen, noch gültig.
unfair [ʌnˈfeə], adj. unfair; unehrlich.
unfeeling [ʌnˈfiːliŋ], adj. gefühllos.
unfit [ʌnˈfit], adj. (*Mil., Med.*) untauglich, schwach; (*food etc.*) ungenießbar.
unfold [ʌnˈfould], v.a. entfalten.
unforeseen [ʌnfɔːˈsiːn], adj. unerwartet.
unfounded [ʌnˈfaundid], adj. grundlos.
unfurnished [ʌnˈfəːniʃd], adj. unmöbliert.
ungrudging [ʌnˈgrʌdʒiŋ], adj. bereitwillig.
unhappy [ʌnˈhæpi], adj. unglücklich.
unhinge [ʌnˈhindʒ], v.a. aus den Angeln heben.
unicorn [ˈjuːnikɔːm], s. (*Myth.*) das Einhorn.
uniform [ˈjuːnifɔːm], s. die Uniform. — adj. gleichförmig, einförmig.
union [ˈjuːniən], s. die Vereinigung; trade —, die Gewerkschaft; *Union Jack*, die britische Nationalflagge.

unique [juˈniːk], adj. einzigartig.
unison [ˈjuːnisən], s. (*Mus.*) der Einklang, die Harmonie.
unit [ˈjuːnit], s. die Einheit (*measure etc.*).
unite [juˈnait], v.a. vereinen. — v.n. sich vereinen, verbünden.
unity [ˈjuːniti], s. die Einigkeit.
universal [juːniˈvəːsəl], adj. allgemein.
universe [ˈjuːnivəːs], s. das Weltall.
university [juːniˈvəːsiti], s. die Universität, Hochschule; — degree, der akademische Grad.
unkempt [ʌnˈkempt], adj. ungekämmt, ungepflegt.
unleavened [ʌnˈlevənd], adj. ungesäuert.
unless [ʌnˈles], conj. außer, wenn nicht, es sei denn.
unlettered [ʌnˈletəd], adj. ungebildet.
unlicensed [ʌnˈlaisənsd], adj. nicht (für Alkoholverkauf) lizenziert.
unlike [ʌnˈlaik], adj. ungleich. — [ˈʌnlaik], prep. anders als, verschieden von.
unlikely [ʌnˈlaikli], adj., adv. unwahrscheinlich.
unlock [ʌnˈlɔk], v.a. aufschließen.
unmask [ʌnˈmɑːsk], v.a. entlarven.
unpack [ʌnˈpæk], v.a., v.n. auspacken.
unpleasant [ʌnˈpleznt], adj. unangenehm.
unreliable [ʌnriˈlaiəbl], adj. unzuverlässig.
unremitting [ʌnriˈmitiŋ], adj. unablässig.
unrepentant [ʌnriˈpentənt], adj.reuelos.
unrest [ʌnˈrest], s. die Unruhe.
unsafe [ʌnˈseif], adj. unsicher.
unscathed [ʌnˈskeiðd], adj. unversehrt.
unscrew [ʌnˈskruː], v.a. abschrauben.
unscrupulous [ʌnˈskruːpjuləs], adj. skrupellos, gewissenlos.
unseat [ʌnˈsiːt], v.a. aus dem Sattel heben; absetzen.
unselfish [ʌnˈselfiʃ], adj. selbstlos.
unsettle [ʌnˈsetl], v.a. verwirren; (*fig.*) aus dem Konzept bringen.
unsew [ʌnˈsou], v.a. auftrennen.
unshrinking [ʌnˈʃriŋkiŋ], adj. unverzagt.
unsophisticated [ʌnsəˈfistikeitid], adj. naiv, natürlich.
unsparing [ʌnˈspeəriŋ], adj. schonungslos.
unstable [ʌnˈsteibl], adj. unsicher; labil.
unstitch [ʌnˈstitʃ], v.a. auftrennen.
unstop [ʌnˈstɔp], v.a. aufstöpseln, öffnen (*a bottle*).
unstudied [ʌnˈstʌdid], adj. ungekünstelt.
unsuccessful [ʌnsəkˈsesful], adj. erfolglos.
unsuspecting [ʌnsəˈspektiŋ], adj. arglos.
untie [ʌnˈtai], v.a. losbinden.
until [ʌnˈtil], prep., conj. bis.

untimely

untimely [ʌn'taimli], *adj.* vorzeitig, unzeitig.

untiring [ʌn'taiəriŋ], *adj.* unermüdlich.

unto ['ʌntu], *prep.* (*Poet.*) zu.

untold [ʌn'tould], *adj.* ungezählt, unermeßlich.

untoward [ʌn'tɔːd *or* ʌn'touəd], *adj.* unangenehm; widerspenstig (*recalcitrant*).

untrustworthy [ʌn'trʌstwəːði], *adj.* unzuverlässig.

unveil [ʌn'veil], *v.a.* enthüllen.

unwieldy [ʌn'wiːldi], *adj.* sperrig, schwerfällig.

unwind [ʌn'waind], *v.a.* abwickeln.

unwitting [ʌn'witiŋ], *adj.* unwissentlich, unbewusst.

unwonted [ʌn'wountid], *adj.* ungewohnt.

unwrap [ʌn'ræp], *v.a.* auspacken, auswickeln.

unyielding [ʌn'jiːldiŋ], *adj.* unnachgiebig; hartnäckig.

unyoke [ʌn'jouk], *v.a.* ausspannen.

up [ʌp], *adv.* auf, aufwärts (*upward*); aufgestanden (*out of bed*); — (*there*), oben; *what's up?* was ist los? — *to,* bis zu; *be — to s.th.,* auf etwas aus sein, etwas im Schilde führen; *it's — to you,* es liegt an dir. — *prep.* auf, hinauf. — *s. ups and downs,* das wechselnde Schicksal, Auf und Ab.

upbraid [ʌp'breid], *v.a.* tadeln.

upheaval [ʌp'hiːvl], *s.* das Chaos, Durcheinander, die Umwälzung.

uphill [ʌp'hil], *adv.* bergauf(wärts). — ['ʌphil], *adj.* (an)steigend; (*fig.*) mühsam.

uphold [ʌp'hould], *v.a.* aufrechterhalten.

upholster [ʌp'houlstə], *v.a.* polstern.

upholstery [ʌp'houlstəri], *s.* die Polsterung.

upon [ʌ'pɔn] *see* **on**.

upper ['ʌpə], *adj.* ober, höher; — *hand,* die Oberhand.

uppish ['ʌpiʃ], *adj.* anmaßend.

upright ['ʌprait], *adj.* aufrecht, gerade; (*fig.*) aufrichtig, rechtschaffen.

uproar ['ʌprɔː], *s.* der Lärm, Aufruhr.

uproot [ʌp'ruːt], *v.a.* entwurzeln.

upset [ʌp'set], *v.a.* umwerfen; (*fig.*) aus der Fassung bringen. — ['ʌpset], *s.* das Umwerfen; (*fig.*) die Bestürzung.

upshot ['ʌpʃɔt], *s.* der Ausgang, das Ergebnis.

upside ['ʌpsaid], *s.* die Oberseite; — *down,* auf den Kopf gestellt.

upstairs [ʌp'stɛəz], *adv.* oben, nach oben.

upstart ['ʌpstɑːt], *s.* der Parvenü, Emporkömmling.

upward ['ʌpwəd], *adj.* steigend, aufwärtsgehend. — *adv.* (*also* **upwards**) aufwärts; — *of,* mehr als.

urban ['əːbən], *adj.* städtisch.

urbane [əː'bein], *adj.* zivilisiert.

urbanity [əː'bæniti], *s.* die Bildung, der Schliff.

urchin ['əːtʃin], *s.* der Schelm; (*Zool.*) *sea* —, der Seeigel.

urge [əːdʒ], *v.a.* drängen. — *s.* der Drang.

urgent ['əːdʒənt], *adj.* dringend, drängend, dringlich.

urine ['juərin], *s.* der Urin.

urn [əːn], *s.* die Urne.

Uruguayan [juːruˈgwaiən], *adj.* uruguayisch. — *s.* der Uruguayer.

us [ʌs], *pers. pron.* uns.

usage ['juːsidʒ], *s.* der (Sprach)gebrauch; die Sitte.

use [juːz], *v.a.* gebrauchen, benutzen. — [juːs], *s.* der Gebrauch, die Benutzung; der Nutzen (*usefulness*).

usher ['ʌʃə], *s.* der Türhüter, Platzanweiser. — *v.a.* — *in,* anmelden, einführen.

usherette [ʌʃə'ret], *s.* die Platzanweiserin, Programmverkäuferin.

usual ['juːʒuəl], *adj.* gewöhnlich, üblich.

usurer ['juːʒərə *or* 'juːzjuərə], *s.* der Wucherer.

usurp [juːˈzəːp], *v.a.* an sich reißen, usurpieren.

usury ['juːʒuəri], *s.* der Wucher.

utensil [juːˈtensil], *s.* das Gerät, Werkzeug.

utility [juːˈtiliti], *s.* die Nützlichkeit (*usefulness*); der Nutzen; *public* —, (die) öffentliche Einrichtung.

utilize ['juːtilaiz], *v.a.* nutzbar machen, ausbeuten, ausnützen.

utmost ['ʌtmoust], *adj.* äußerst, weitest, höchst. — *s.* das Höchste, Äußerste.

utter ['ʌtə], *adj.* äußerst, gänzlich. — *v.a.* äußern, aussprechen.

utterly ['ʌtəli], *adv.* äußerst, völlig.

uvula ['juːvjulə], *s.* (*Anat.*) das Zäpfchen.

V

V [viː]. das V.

vacancy ['veikənsi], *s.* die freie Stelle, die Vakanz.

vacant ['veikənt], *adj.* frei; leer.

vacate [və'keit], *v.a.* frei machen.

vacation [vəˈkeiʃən], *s.* die Niederlegung (*of a post*); die Ferien, *pl.* (*school*); der Urlaub (*holiday*).

vaccinate ['væksineit], *v.a.* (*Med.*) impfen.

vaccine ['væksiːn], *s.* (*Med.*) der Impfstoff.

vacillate ['væsileit], *v.n.* schwanken.

vacuity [væ'kjuːiti], *s.* die Leere.

vacuous ['vækjuəs], *adj.* leer.

vacuum ['vækjuəm], *s.* das Vakuum; — *cleaner,* der Staubsauger.

vagabond ['vægəbɔnd], *s.* der Landstreicher.

vagary [vəˈgɛəri], *s.* die Laune, Grille.

vagrant ['veigrənt], *adj.* herumstreichend. — *s.* der Landstreicher.

vague [veig], *adj.* vage, unbestimmt, unklar.

vain [vein], *adj.* nichtig, vergeblich, eitel; *in* —, vergebens, umsonst.

vale [veil], *s.* (*Poet.*) das Tal.

valerian [və'liəriən], *s.* (*Bot.*) der Baldrian.

valet ['vælei, 'vælit], *s.* der Diener.

valiant ['væljənt], *adj.* mutig, tapfer.

valid ['vælid], *adj.* gültig, stichhaltig.

valley ['væli], *s.* das Tal.

valuable ['væljuəbl], *adj.* wertvoll, kostbar.

valuation [vælju'eiʃən], *s.* die Schätzung.

value ['vælju:], *s.* der Wert. — *v.a.* wertschätzen, schätzen.

valve [vælv], *s.* (*Mech.*) das Ventil; (*Rad.*) die Röhre.

vamp (1) [væmp], *s.* das Oberleder.

vamp (2) [væmp], *s.* (*Am. coll.*) der Vamp.

vampire ['væmpaiə], *s.* der Vampir.

van [væn], *s.* der Lieferwagen.

vane [vein], *s.* die Wetterfahne.

vanguard ['vænga:d], *s.* die Vorhut, der Vortrupp.

vanilla [və'nilə], *s.* die Vanille.

vanish ['væniʃ], *v.n.* verschwinden.

vanity ['væniti], *s.* die Nichtigkeit; die Eitelkeit (*conceit*).

vanquish ['væŋkwiʃ], *v.a.* besiegen.

vantage ['vɑːntidʒ], *s.* der Vorteil; — *point*, die günstige Position.

vapid ['væpid], *adj.* leer, schal.

vapour ['veipə], *s.* der Dunst; (*Chem.*) der Dampf.

variable ['vɛəriəbl], *adj.* variabel, veränderlich.

variance ['vɛəriəns], *s.* die Uneinigkeit.

variation [vɛəri'eiʃən], *s.* die Variation; die Veränderung, Abweichung.

varicose ['værikəs], *adj.* Krampf-, krampfaderig.

variegated ['vɛərigeitid], *adj.* bunt, vielfarbig.

variety [və'raiəti], *s.* die Mannigfaltigkeit; (*Bot.*) die Varietät, Abart; (*Theat.*) das Varieté, das Varieté-theater.

various ['vɛəriəs], *adj.* verschieden; mannigfaltig.

varnish ['vɑːniʃ], *s.* der Firnis, der Lack. — *v.a.* mit Firnis anstreichen, lackieren.

vary ['vɛəri], *v.a.* abändern. — *v.n.* sich ändern, variieren.

vase [vɑːz], *s.* die Vase.

vassal ['væsl], *s.* der Vasall, Lehnsmann.

vast [vɑːst], *adj.* ungeheuer, groß.

vat [væt], *s.* die Kufe, das große Faß.

vault [vɔːlt], *s.* das Gewölbe; die Gruft (*grave*); (*Sport*) der Sprung, *pole* —, der Stabhochsprung. — *v.n.* springen.

vaunt [vɔːnt], *v.a.* rühmen. — *v.n.* prahlen, sich rühmen. — *s.* die Prahlerei.

veal [viːl], *s.* das Kalbfleisch.

veer [viə], *v.n.* sich drehen.

vegetable ['vedʒitəbl], *s.* das Gemüse.

vegetarian [vedʒi'tɛəriən], *adj.* vegetarisch. — *s.* der Vegetarier.

vegetate ['vedʒiteit], *v.n.* vegetieren.

vehemence ['viːəməns], *s.* die Vehemenz, Heftigkeit.

vehicle ['viːikl], *s.* das Fahrzeug, Fuhrwerk; (*Motor.*) der Wagen.

veil [veil], *s.* der Schleier. — *v.a.* verschleiern.

vein [vein], *s.* die Ader.

vellum ['veləm], *s.* das feine Pergamentpapier.

velocity [vi'lɔsiti], *s.* die Geschwindigkeit, Schnelligkeit.

velvet ['velvit], *s.* (*Text.*) der Samt.

venal ['viːnəl], *adj.* käuflich.

vend [vend], *v.a.* verkaufen; —*ing machine*, der Automat.

veneer [və'niə], *s.* das Furnier. — *v.a.* furnieren.

venerable ['venərəbl], *adj.* ehrwürdig.

venerate ['venəreit], *v.a.* verehren.

venereal [və'niəriəl], *adj.* Geschlechts-.

Venezuelan [veni'zweilən], *adj.* venezolanisch. — *s.* der Venezolaner.

vengeance ['vendʒəns], *s.* die Rache.

venison ['venizn *or* venzn], *s.* das Wildpret.

venom ['venəm], *s.* das Gift.

vent [vent], *v.a.* Luft machen (*Dat.*). — *s.* das Luftloch, die Öffnung.

ventilate ['ventileit], *v.a.* ventilieren, lüften.

ventricle ['ventrikl], *s.* (*Anat.*) die Herzkammer.

ventriloquist [ven'triləkwist], *s.* der Bauchredner.

venture ['ventʃə], *s.* das Wagnis, Unternehmen. — *v.a.* wagen, riskieren. — *v.n.* sich erlauben, (sich) wagen.

venue ['venju:], *s.* der Treffpunkt, Versammlungsort.

veracity [və'ræsiti], *s.* die Glaubwürdigkeit, Wahrhaftigkeit.

verbose [və:'bous], *adj.* wortreich, weitschweifig.

verdant ['və:dənt], *adj.* grünend, grün.

verdict ['və:dikt], *s.* das Urteil, die Entscheidung.

verdigris ['və:digriːs], *s.* der Grünspan.

verdure ['və:djə], *s.* das Grün.

verge [və:dʒ], *s.* der Rand, die Einfassung. — *v.n.* grenzen (*on*, an, *Acc.*).

verify ['verifai], *v.a.* bestätigen; (*Law*) beglaubigen.

verily ['verili], *adv.* (*Bibl.*) wahrlich.

veritable ['veritəbl], *adj.* wahr, echt.

vermicelli [və:mi'seli], *s.* die Nudeln, *f. pl.*

vermilion [və'miljən], *s.* das Zinnober (*paint*).

vermin ['və:min], *s. pl.* das Ungeziefer.

vermouth ['və:mu:θ, -mu:t], *s.* der Wermut.

vernacular [və'nækjulə], *s.* die Landessprache. — *adj.* einheimisch.

vernal ['və:nəl], *adj.* frühlingsartig, Frühlings-.

versatile ['vɔːsɔtail], *adj.* gewandt; vielseitig.

verse [vɔːs], *s.* der Vers; (*Poet.*) die Strophe.

versed [vɔːsd], *adj.* bewandert.

version ['vɔːʃən], *s.* die Version, Fassung, Lesart; (*fig.*) die Darstellung.

vertebrate ['vɔːtibrət], *s.* (*Zool.*) das Wirbeltier. — *adj.* mit Rückenwirbeln versehen.

vertex ['vɔːteks], *s.* der Zenit.

vertigo ['vɔːtigou], *s.* (*Med.*) der Schwindel, das Schwindelgefühl.

verve [vɔːv], *s.* der Schwung.

very ['veɹi], *adv.* sehr. — *adj.* echt, wirklich, wahrhaftig.

vespers ['vespəz], *s. pl.* (*Eccl.*) der Abendgottesdienst, die Vesper.

vessel [vesl], *s.* das Gefäß (*container*); (*Naut.*) das Fahrzeug, Schiff.

vest [vest], *s.* das Gewand; (*Tail.*) die Weste; das Unterhemd (*undergarment*). — *v.a.* übertragen.

vested ['vestid], *adj.* — *interests,* das Eigeninteresse.

vestige ['vestidʒ], *s.* die Spur.

vestment ['vestmənt], *s.* (*Eccl.*) das Meßgewand.

vestry ['vestri], *s.* (*Eccl.*) die Sakristei.

vetch [vetʃ], *s.* (*Bot.*) die Wicke.

veterinary ['vetərinri], *adj.* tierärztlich; — *surgeon,* der Tierarzt.

veto ['viːtou], *s.* (*Pol.*) der Einspruch, das Veto.

vex [veks], *v.a.* quälen, plagen.

vexation [vek'seiʃən], *s.* die Plage, der Verdruß.

via [vaiə], *prep.* über.

vibrate [vai'breit], *v.n.* schwingen, vibrieren.

vicar ['vikə], *s.* (*Eccl.*) der Pfarrer, Vikar.

vicarious [vi'kɛəriəs], *adj.* stellvertretend.

vice (1) [vais], *s.* das Laster (*immorality*).

vice (2) [vais], *s.* (*Mech.*) der Schraubstock.

vice- [vais], *pref.* Vize-, zweiter (*chairman etc.*).

vicinity [vi'siniti], *s.* die Nachbarschaft, Nähe.

vicious ['viʃəs], *adj.* böse, bösartig.

vicissitude [vi'sisitjuːd], *s.* der Wechsel, Wandel; (*pl.*) Wechselfälle, *m. pl.*

victim ['viktim], *s.* das Opfer.

victuals [vitlz], *s. pl.* die Lebensmittel, *n. pl.*

vie [vai], *v.n.* wetteifern.

Vietnamese [vjetnə'miːz], *adj.* vietnamesisch. — *s.* der Vietnamese.

view [vjuː], *s.* der Anblick, die Aussicht (*panorama*); die Ansicht (*opinion*); die Absicht (*intention*). — *v.a.* betrachten; besichtigen (*inspect*).

vigil ['vidʒil], *s.* die Nachtwache.

vigilance ['vidʒiləns], *s.* die Wachsamkeit.

vigorous ['vigərəs], *adj.* kräftig, rüstig, energisch.

vigour ['vigə], *s.* die Kraft, Energie.

vile [vail], *adj.* schlecht, niedrig.

vilify ['vilifai], *v.a.* beschimpfen, erniedrigen.

villa ['vilə], *s.* das Landhaus, die Villa.

village ['vilidʒ], *s.* das Dorf.

villain ['vilən], *s.* der Schurke.

villainous ['vilənəs], *adj.* niederträchtig.

villainy ['viləni], *s.* die Niedertracht, Schändlichkeit.

vindicate ['vindikeit], *v.a.* behaupten, verteidigen; rechtfertigen (*justify*).

vindictive [vin'diktiv], *adj.* rachsüchtig.

vine [vain], *s.* (*Bot.*) der Weinstock, die Rebe.

vinegar ['vinigə], *s.* der Essig.

vintage ['vintidʒ], *s.* die Weinernte; der Jahrgang (*also fig.*).

vintner ['vintnə], *s.* der Weinbauer, Winzer.

viola [vi'oulə], *s.* (*Mus.*) die Viola, Bratsche.

violate ['vaiəleit], *v.a.* verletzen, schänden.

violence ['vaiələns], *s.* die Gewalt; die Gewalttätigkeit.

violent ['vaiələnt], *adj.* gewalttätig (*brutal*); heftig (*vehement*).

violet ['vaiəlit], *s.* (*Bot.*) das Veilchen. — *adj.* veilchenblau, violett.

violin [vaiə'lin], *s.* (*Mus.*) die Violine, Geige.

viper ['vaipə], *s.* (*Zool.*) die Viper, Natter.

virago [vi'rɑːgou], *s.* das Mannweib.

virgin ['vɔːdʒin], *s.* die Jungfrau.

virile ['virail], *adj.* männlich, kräftig.

virtual ['vɔːtjuəl], *adj.* eigentlich.

virtue ['vɔːtjuː], *s.* die Tugend; *by — of,* kraft (*Genit.*).

virtuoso [vɔːtju'ousou], *s.* der Virtuose.

virtuous ['vɔːtjuəs], *adj.* tugendhaft.

virulent ['virulənt], *adj.* bösartig, giftig.

virus ['vaiərəs], *s.* (*Med.*) das Gift, Virus.

viscosity [vis'kɔsiti], *s.* die Zähigkeit, Zähflüssigkeit.

viscount ['vaikaunt], *s.* der Vicomte.

viscous ['viskəs], *adj.* zähflüssig, klebrig.

visibility [vizi'biliti], *s.* die Sichtbarkeit, Sicht.

visible ['vizibl], *adj.* sichtbar.

vision ['viʒən], *s.* die Sehkraft; (*fig.*) die Vision (*dream*); die Erscheinung (*apparition*).

visionary ['viʒənri], *s.* der Träumer, (*Poet.*) der Seher. — *adj.* visionär, phantastisch, seherisch.

visit ['vizit], *s.* der Besuch. — *v.a.* besuchen.

visitation [vizi'teiʃən], *s.* die Heimsuchung.

visor ['vaizə], *s.* das Visier.

vista ['vistə], *s.* (*Art*) die Aussicht, der Ausblick.

visual ['viʒuəl], *adj.* visuell, Seh-.

vital [vaitl], *adj.* lebenswichtig; (*fig.*) wesentlich.

vitality [vai'tæliti], *s.* die Lebenskraft, Vitalität.

vitiate ['viʃieit], *v.a.* verderben, umstoßen.

vitreous ['vitriəs], *adj.* gläsern, glasartig.

vitrify ['vitrifai], *v.a.* verglasen.

vivacious [vi'veiʃəs], *adj.* lebhaft, munter.

viva (voce) ['vaivə ('vousi)], *s.* die mündliche Prüfung.

vivacity [vi'væsiti], *s.* die Lebhaftigkeit.

vivid ['vivid], *adj.* lebhaft.

vixen ['viksən], *s.* (*Zool.*) die Füchsin; (*fig.*) das zänkische Weib.

vizier [vi'ziə], *s.* der Wesir.

vocabulary [vo'kæbjuləri], *s.* das Vokabular; der Wortschatz.

vocal ['voukəl], *adj.* laut; (*Mus.*) Stimm-, Sing-.

vocation [vo'keiʃən], *s.* die Berufung (*call*); der Beruf (*occupation*).

vociferous [vo'sifərəs], *adj.* schreiend, laut.

vogue [voug], *s.* die Mode.

voice [vɔis], *s.* die Stimme.

void [vɔid], *adj.* leer (*empty*); ungültig, (*invalid*); *null and* —, null und nichtig. — *s.* die Leere.

volatile ['vɔlətail], *adj.* flüchtig.

volcanic [vɔl'kænik], *adj.* vulkanisch.

volcano [vɔl'keinou], *s.* der Vulkan.

volition [vo'liʃən], *s.* der Wille.

volley ['vɔli], *s.* (*Mil.*) die Salve; (*Footb.*) der Volleyschuß; (*Tennis*) der Flugball.

volt [voult], *s.* (*Elec.*) das Volt.

voltage ['voultidʒ], *s.* die Spannung.

voluble ['vɔljubl], *adj.* gesprächig, zungenfertig.

volume ['vɔlju:m], *s.* (*Phys.*) das Volumen; der Band (*book*); (*fig.*) der Umfang.

voluminous [və'lju:minəs], *adj.* umfangreich.

voluntary ['vɔləntri], *adj.* freiwillig. — *s.* (*Mus.*) das Orgelsolo.

volunteer [vɔlən'tiə], *s.* der Freiwillige. — *v.n.* sich freiwillig melden.

voluptuous [və'lʌptjuəs], *adj.* wollüstig, lüstern.

vomit ['vɔmit], *v.a.*, *v.n.* (sich) erbrechen, übergeben.

voracious [vo'reiʃəs], *adj.* gierig, gefräßig.

vortex ['vɔ:teks], *s.* der Wirbel, Strudel.

vote [vout], *v.n.* (*Pol.*) wählen, abstimmen, die Stimme abgeben. — *s.* (*Pol.*) die Stimme.

voter ['voutə], *s.* der Wähler.

votive ['voutiv], *adj.* (*Eccl.*) geweiht, gelobt; Votiv-.

vouch [vautʃ], *v.a.*, *v.n.* (sich) verbürgen, einstehen(für).

voucher ['vautʃə], *s.* der Beleg; (*Comm.*) der Gutschein.

vouchsafe [vautʃ'seif], *v.a.* bewilligen, gewähren; *v.n.* geruhen, sich herablassen.

vow [vau], *s.* das Gelübde. — *v.a.* schwören, geloben.

vowel ['vauəl], *s.* der Vokal.

voyage ['vɔidʒ], *s.* die Seereise. — *v.n.* zur See reisen.

vulcanize ['vʌlkənaiz], *v.a.* vulkanisieren.

vulgar ['vʌlgə], *adj.* gemein, pöbelhaft, ordinär, vulgär.

vulnerable ['vʌlnərəbl], *adj.* verwundbar, verletzbar.

vulture ['vʌltʃə], *s.* (*Orn.*) der Geier.

W

W ['dʌblju:]. das W.

wabble *see* wobble.

wad [wɔd], *s.* das Bündel (*notes*); der Bausch (*cotton wool*).

waddle ['wɔdl], *v.n.* watscheln.

wade [weid], *v.n.* waten, durchwaten.

wafer ['weifə], *s.* die Oblate, die Waffel; (*Eccl.*) die Hostie.

waffle [wɔfl], *s.* (*Cul.*) die Waffel. — *v.n.* (*coll.*) schwafeln.

waft [wæft], *v.a.* wegwehen.

wag (1) [wæg], *v.a.* wedeln, schütteln.

wag (2) [wæg], *s.* der Spaßvogel.

wage (1) [weidʒ], *v.a.* unternehmen; — *war,* Krieg führen.

wage (2) ['weidʒ], *s.* (*often in pl.*) der Lohn.

wager ['weidʒə], *v.a.* wetten. — *s.* die Wette.

waggish ['wægiʃ], *adj.* spaßhaft, mutwillig, schelmisch.

wag(g)on ['wægən], *s.* der Wagen, Güterwagen.

wagtail ['wægteil], *s.* (*Orn.*) die Bachstelze.

waif [weif], *s.* das verwahrloste Kind; das herrenlose Gut.

wail [weil], *v.n.* wehklagen. — *s.* das Wehklagen, die Klage.

waist [weist], *s.* (*Anat.*) die Taille.

waistcoat ['weiskout, 'weskət], *s.* die Weste, das Wams.

wait [weit], *v.n.* warten; — *for,* warten auf; — *upon,* bedienen. — *v.a.* erwarten.

waiter ['weitə], *s.* der Kellner; *head* —, der Oberkellner, (*coll.*) der Ober.

waiting room ['weitiŋ rum], *s.* das Wartezimmer; (*Railw.*) der Wartesaal.

waive [weiv], *v.a.* aufgeben, verzichten (auf, *Acc.*).

wake (1) [weik], *v.n. irr.* wachen, aufwachen, wach sein. — *v.a.* aufwecken.

wake (2) [weik], *s.* (*Naut.*) das Kielwasser; (*fig.*) die Spur; *in the* — *of,* in den Fußstapfen (*Genit.*).

waken ['weikən], *v.a.* aufwecken. — *v.n.* aufwachen.

walk [wɔ:k], *v.n.* (zu Fuß) gehen. — *s.* der Gang (*gait*); der Spaziergang.

wall

wall [wɔːl], s. die Wand, Mauer.

wallet ['wɔlit], s. die Brieftasche.

wallflower ['wɔːlflauə], s. (Bot.) der Goldlack; (fig.) das Mauerblümchen.

wallow ['wɔlou], v.n. schwelgen; sich wälzen.

walnut ['wɔːlnʌt], s. (Bot.) die Walnuß.

walrus ['wɔːlrəs], s. (Zool.) das Walroß.

waltz [wɔːlts], s. der Walzer.

wan [wɔn], adj. blaß, bleich.

wand [wɔnd], s. der Stab.

wander ['wɔndə], v.n. wandern, durchwandern; (fig.) — from the subject, vom Thema abkommen.

wane [wein], v.n. abnehmen, verfallen.

want [wɔnt], v.a. brauchen, wollen, nötig haben, wünschen. — v.n. mangeln, fehlen. — s. die Not.

wanton ['wɔntən], adj. mutwillig, ausgelassen.

war [wɔː], s. der Krieg.

warble ['wɔːbl], v.a., v.n. singen; (Mus.) trillern.

warbler ['wɔːblə], s. (Orn.) der Singvogel.

ward [wɔːd], s. die Verwahrung; das or der Mündel (child in care); (Pol.) der Wahlbezirk; die Station (hospital). — v.a. — off, abwehren.

warden ['wɔːdn], s. der Vorstand, Vorsteher; Rektor.

warder ['wɔːdə], s. der Wächter; (in prison) der Wärter, Gefängniswärter.

wardrobe ['wɔːdroub], s. der Kleiderschrank.

ware [wɛə], s. die Ware.

warehouse ['wɛəhaus], s. das Warenlager.

warfare ['wɔːfɛə], s. der Krieg, die Kriegsführung.

warlike ['wɔːlaik], adj. kriegerisch.

warm [wɔːm], adj. warm.

warn [wɔːn], v.a. warnen, ermahnen.

warning ['wɔːniŋ], s. die Warnung.

warp [wɔːp], v.a. krümmen, verziehen (of wood); (fig.) verderben; verzerren, verdrehen. — v.n. sich werfen, krümmen.

warrant ['wɔrənt], s. (Law) der Haftbefehl; — officer, der Unteroffizier; (Comm.) die Vollmacht, Bürgschaft. — v.a. garantieren (vouch for); versichern (assure).

warranty ['wɔrənti], s. (Law) die Gewähr; Garantie.

warren ['wɔrən], s. das Gehege.

warrior ['wɔriə], s. der Krieger.

wart [wɔːt], s. (Med.) die Warze.

wary ['wɛəri], adj. vorsichtig, achtsam (careful).

wash [wɔʃ], v.a., v.n. (sich) waschen; — up, spülen, abwaschen. — s. die Wäsche (laundry).

wasp [wɔsp], s. (Ent.) die Wespe.

waspish ['wɔspiʃ], adj. reizbar, zänkisch, bissig.

wassail ['wɔsl], s. das Trinkgelage. — v.n. zechen.

waste [weist], v.a. zerstören, verwüsten;

verschwenden. — adj. wüst, öde. — s. die Verschwendung (process); der Abfall (product); — paper, die Makulatur; — paper basket, der Papierkorb.

wasteful ['weistful], adj. verschwenderisch.

watch [wɔtʃ], v.a. bewachen; beobachten (observe); hüten (guard). — s. die Wache (guard); die Uhr, Taschenuhr (time-piece).

watchful ['wɔtʃful], adj. wachsam.

watchman ['wɔtʃmən], s. der Nachtwächter.

water ['wɔːtə], s. das Wasser; (pl.) die Kur; — colour, das Aquarell; — gauge, der Pegel. — v.a. wässern; begießen (flowers).

watercress ['wɔːtəkres], s. (Bot.) die Brunnenkresse.

waterproof ['wɔːtəpruːf], adj. wasserdicht.

watt [wɔt], s. (Elec.) das Watt.

wattle [wɔtl], s. (Bot.) die Hürde.

wave [weiv], s. die Welle; permanent —, die Dauerwelle. — v.n. zuwinken (Dat.); wehen; winken. — v.a. schwenken (handkerchief).

waver ['weivə], v.n. schwanken, unentschlossen sein.

wax [wæks], s. das Wachs, der Siegellack. — v.a. wachsen, bohnern.

waxen [wæksn], adj. aus Wachs, wächsern.

way [wei], s. der Weg (road etc.); die Strecke; Richtung; in no —, keineswegs; (pl.) die Art und Weise; Milky Way, die Milchstraße.

wayward ['weiwəd], adj. eigensinnig.

we [wiː], pers. pron. wir.

weak [wiːk], adj. schwach, kraftlos.

weaken ['wiːkən], v.a. schwächen. — v.n. schwach werden.

weakling ['wiːkliŋ], s. der Schwächling.

wealth [welθ], s. der Wohlstand, Reichtum.

wealthy ['welθi], adj. wohlhabend, reich.

wean [wiːn], v.a. entwöhnen.

weapon ['wepən], s. die Waffe.

wear [wɛə], v.a. irr. tragen (clothes). — v.n. — off, sich abtragen, schäbig werden; — out, sich erschöpfen. — s. die Abnutzung.

weariness ['wiərinis], s. die Müdigkeit, der Überdruß.

weary ['wiəri], adj. müde, überdrüssig.

weasel [wiːzl], s. (Zool.) das Wiesel.

weather ['weðə], s. das Wetter. — v.a. überstehen. — v.n. (Geol.) verwittern.

weatherbeaten ['weðəbiːtn], adj. abgehärtet, wetterhart.

weathercock ['weðəkɔk], s. der Wetterhahn; (fig.) wetterwendischer Mensch.

weave [wiːv], v.a. irr. (Text.) weben, — s. das Gewebe.

web [web], s. das Gewebe.

wed [wed], v.a. heiraten; trauen (a couple). — v.n. (sich ver)heiraten.

wedding ['wediŋ], s. die Hochzeit; Trauung (ceremony).

wedge [wedʒ], *s.* der Keil. — *v.a.* keilen.

wedlock ['wedlɔk], *s.* die Ehe.

Wednesday ['wenzd(e)i]. der Mittwoch.

wee [wi:], *adj.* (*Scot.*) winzig, klein.

weed [wi:d], *s.* das Unkraut. — *v.a.* ausjäten, jäten.

week [wi:k], *s.* die Woche.

weep [wi:p], *v.n. irr.* weinen; —*ing willow*, die Trauerweide.

weigh [wei], *v.a.* wiegen, wägen; (*fig.*) abwägen, beurteilen; (*Naut.*) — *anchor*, den Anker lichten. — *v.n.* wiegen.

weighing machine ['weiiŋ mə'ʃi:n], *s.* die Waage.

weight [weit], *s.* das Gewicht; *gross* —, das Bruttogewicht; *net* —, das Nettogewicht.

weighty ['weiti], *adj.* (ge)wichtig; (*fig.*) schwer.

weir [wiə], *s.* das Wehr.

weird [wiəd], *adj.* unheimlich.

welcome ['welkəm], *adj.* willkommen. — *s.* der *or* das Willkommen. — *v.a.* willkommen heißen, begrüßen.

weld [weld], *v.a.* schweißen.

welfare ['welfɛə], *s.* die Wohlfahrt, soziale Fürsorge.

well (1) [wel], *s.* der Brunnen. — *v.n.* hervorquellen.

well (2) [wel], *adv.* gut, wohl; durchaus; — *bred*, wohlerzogen. — *pred. adj.* gesund, wohl.

Welsh [welʃ], *adj.* walisisch. — *s. pl.* die Waliser, *m.pl.*

Welshman ['welʃmən], *s.* der Waliser.

welt [welt], *s.* der Rand, die Einfassung.

welter ['weltə], *s.* die Masse, das Chaos. — *v.n.* sich wälzen.

wen [wen], *s.* (*Med.*) die Schwellung.

wench [wentʃ], *s.* die Magd, das Mädchen.

west [west], *s.* der Westen. — *adj.* (*also* **westerly, western** ['westəli, 'westən]) westlich.

Westphalian [west'feiliən], *adj.* westfälisch. — *s.* der Westfale.

wet [wet], *adj.* naß, feucht; — *paint*, frisch gestrichen. — *v.a.* anfeuchten, benetzen, naß machen.

whack [hwæk], *v.a.* durchprügeln. — *s.* die Tracht Prügel, der Schlag.

whale [hweil], *s.* (*Zool.*) der Walfisch.

whalebone ['hweilboun], *s.* das Fischbein.

wharf [hwɔ:f], *s.* der Kai.

wharfinger ['hwɔ:findʒə], *s.* der Kaimeister.

what [hwɔt], *rel. & interr. pron.* was; welcher, welche, welches; was für.

what(so)ever [hwɔt(sou)'evə], *rel. pron.* was auch immer. — *adj.* einerlei welche-r, -s, -n.

wheat [hwi:t], *s.* (*Bot.*) der Weizen.

wheedle [hwi:dl], *v.a.* beschwatzen.

wheel [hwi:l], *s.* das Rad; die Umdrehung, Drehung. — *v.a., v.n.* drehen, sich drehen, schieben.

wheelbarrow ['hwi:lbærou], *s.* der Schubkarren.

wheeze [hwi:z], *v.n.* keuchen, schnaufen. — *s.* das Keuchen.

whelp [hwelp], *s.* (*Zool.*) das Junge, der junge Hund. — *v.n.* Junge werfen.

when [hwen], *adv.* (*interr.*) wann? — *conj.* als (*in past*), wenn, während.

whence [hwens], *adv.* woher, von wo.

where [hwɛə], *adv.* wo, wohin; (*interr.*) wo? wohin?

whereabout(s) ['hwɛərəbaut(s)], *adv.* wo, wo etwa. — *s.* (**whereabouts**) der zeitweilige Aufenthalt *or* Wohnort.

whereas [hwɛər'æz], *conj.* wohingegen, während.

whereupon [hwɛərə'pɔn], *conj.* woraufhin.

wherewithal ['hwɛəwiðɔ:l], *s.* die gesamte Habe, das Nötige. — *adv.* (*obs.*) womit.

whet [hwet], *v.a.* wetzen, schleifen.

whether ['hweðə], *conj.* ob.

whey [hwei], *s.* die Molke.

which [hwitʃ], *rel. & interr. pron.* welcher, welche, welches; der, die, das.

whiff [hwif], *s.* der Hauch, Luftzug.

while [hwail], *s.* die Weile, Zeit. — *v.a.* — *away the time*, dahinbringen, vertreiben. — *conj.* (*also* **whilst**) während, so lange als.

whim [hwim], *s.* die Laune, Grille.

whimper ['hwimpə], *v.n.* winseln.

whimsical ['hwimzikəl], *adj.* grillenhaft.

whine [hwain], *v.n.* weinen, wimmern, klagen. — *s.* das Gewimmer, Gejammer.

whinny ['hwini], *v.n.* wiehern.

whip [hwip], *s.* die Peitsche; (*Pol.*) der Einpeitscher. — *v.a.* peitschen.

whir [hwə:], *v.n.* schwirren. — *s.* das Schwirren.

whirl [hwə:l], *s.* der Wirbel, Strudel. — *v.a., v.n.* wirbeln.

whirligig ['hwə:ligig], *s.* der Karussel.

whirlpool ['hwə:lpu:l], *s.* der Strudel.

whirr *see* whir.

whisk [hwisk], *v.a.* fegen; schlagen; —*away or off*, schnell wegtun (*a th.*), schnell fortnehmen (*a p.*). — *v.n.* — *away*, dahinhuschen. — *s.* der Schläger.

whiskers ['hwiskəz], *s.* der Backenbart, Bart.

whisky ['hwiski], *s.* der Whisky.

whisper ['hwispə], *s.* das Geflüster. *v.a., v.n.* flüstern.

whistle [hwisl], *s.* die Pfeife (*instrument*); der Pfiff (*sound*). — *v.a., v.n.* pfeifen.

whit [hwit], *s.* die Kleinigkeit; *not a* —, nicht im geringsten.

white [hwait], *adj.* weiß; — *lead*, das Bleiweiß; — *lie*, die Notlüge.

whitebait ['hwaitbeit], *s.* (*Zool.*) der Breitling.

whiten [hwaitn], *v.a.* weißen, bleichen.

whitewash ['hwaitwɔʃ], *s.* die Tünche. — *v.a.* reinwaschen.

whither ['hwiðə], *adv.* wohin; dahin wo.

whiting ['hwaitiŋ], *s.* (*Zool.*) der Weißfisch; die Schlämmkreide (*chalk*).

whitlow ['hwitlou], *s.* (*Med.*) das Nagelgeschwür.

Whitsun(tide) ['hwitsən(taid)], *s.* (das) Pfingsten; *Whit Sunday*, der Pfingstsonntag.

whittle [hwitl], *v.a.* schnitzen, abschaben.

whiz [hwiz], *v.n.* zischen; (*fig.*) vorbeiflitzen.

who [hu:], *interr. pron.* wer ?, welcher ?, welche ? — *rel. pron.* welcher, welche, welches, der, die, das.

whoever [hu:'evə], *rel. pron.* wer auch immer.

whole [houl], *adj.* ganz, völlig. — *s.* das Ganze.

wholesale ['houlseil], *adv.* im Engros. — *adj.* Engros-, Großhandels-.

wholesome ['houlsəm], *adj.* gesund.

whoop [hu:p], *s.* das Geschrei; — *v.n.* laut keuchen; —*ing cough*, der Keuchhusten.

whortleberry ['hwə:tlbəri], *s.* (*Bot.*) die Heidelbeere.

whose [hu:z], *pron.* wessen, dessen, deren.

whosoever [hu:sou'evə] *see* **whoever.**

why [hwai], *rel. & interr. adv.* warum ?

wick [wik], *s.* der Docht.

wicked ['wikid], *adj.* böse, schlecht.

wicker ['wikə], *adj.* Rohr-, geflochten.

wicket ['wikit], *s.* das Pförtchen.

wide [waid], *adj.* weit, breit; (*fig.*) schlau; (*Am.*) schlau, gerieben. — *adv. far and* —, weit und breit; — *awake*, völlig wach.

widen [waidn], *v.a.* erweitern.

widgeon ['widʒən], *s.* die Pfeifente.

widow ['widou], *s.* die Witwe.

widower ['widouə], *s.* der Witwer.

width [widθ], *s.* die Weite, Breite.

wield [wi:ld], *v.a.* schwingen; — *power*, die Macht ausüben.

wife [waif], *s.* die Frau, Gattin.

wig [wig], *s.* die Perücke.

wild [waild], *adj.* wild.

wilderness ['wildənis], *s.* die Wildnis.

wildfire ['waildfaiə], *s.* das Lauffeuer.

wilful ['wilful], *adj.* absichtlich; vorsätzlich.

wiliness ['wailinis], *s.* die Schlauheit, Arglist.

will [wil], *s.* der Wille; (*Law*) der letzte Wille, das Testament. — *v.n.* wollen. — *v.a.* (*Law*) vermachen, hinterlassen.

willing ['wiliŋ], *adj.* bereitwillig.

will-o'-the-wisp [wiləðə'wisp], *s.* das Irrlicht.

willow ['wilou], *s.* (*Bot.*) die Weide.

wily ['waili], *adj.* schlau, verschmitzt.

wimple [wimpl], *s.* der Schleier.

win [win], *v.a., v.n. irr.* gewinnen, siegen, erringen.

wince [wins], *v.n.* zucken, zusammenzucken.

winch [wintʃ], *s.* die Kurbel, Winde.

wind (1) [wind], *s.* der Wind; der Atem (*breath*); *get* — *of s.th.*, von etwas hören.

wind (2) [waind], *v.a. irr.* winden; wenden, drehen (*turn*); —(*up*), aufziehen (*timepiece*); — *up*, (*business, debate*) beenden. — *v.n.* sich schlängeln, winden.

windfall ['windfɔ:l], *s.* das Fallobst (*fruit*); (*fig.*) der Glücksfall.

windlass ['windləs], *s.* die Winde.

window ['windou], *s.* das Fenster; — *sill*, das Fensterbrett.

windpipe ['windpaip], *s.* (*Anat.*) die Luftröhre.

windscreen ['windskri:n], *s.* (*Motor.*) die Windschutzscheibe.

windshield ['windʃi:ld] (*Am.*) *see* **windscreen.**

windy ['windi], *adj.* windig.

wine [wain], *s.* der Wein; — *merchant*, der Weinhändler.

wing [wiŋ], *s.* der Flügel; (*Poet.*) die Schwinge.

wink [wiŋk], *s.* das Zwinkern; der Augenblick.—*v.n.* blinzeln, zwinkern.

winner ['winə], *s.* der Sieger, Gewinner.

winning ['winiŋ], *adj.* einnehmend.

winsome ['winsəm], *adj.* reizend, einnehmend.

winter ['wintə], *s.* der Winter.

wintry ['wintri], *adj.* winterlich.

wipe [waip], *v.a.* wischen, abwischen.

wire [waiə], *s.* der Draht; (*coll.*) das Telegramm; *barbed* —, (*fig.*) der Stacheldraht. — *v.a.* verbinden; (*fig.*) telegraphieren. — *v.n.* telegraphieren.

wireless ['waiəlis], *s.* das Radio. — *adj.* drahtlos.

wirepuller ['waiəpulə], *s.* der Puppenspieler; (*fig.*) der Intrigant.

wiry ['waiəri], *adj.* zäh, stark.

wisdom ['wizdəm], *s.* die Weisheit.

wise [waiz], *adj.* weise, verständig, klug.

wiseacre ['waizeikə], *s.* der Allzuschlaue, Naseweis.

wish [wiʃ], *v.a., v.n.* wünschen. — *s.* der Wunsch.

wistful ['wistful], *adj.* nachdenklich (*pensive*); wehmütig (*sad*).

wit [wit], *s.* der Witz; Geist; Verstand; der witzige Mensch; der Witzbold.

witch [witʃ], *s.* die Hexe, Zauberin.

witchcraft ['witʃkra:ft], *s.* die Zauberkunst, Hexerei.

with [wið], *prep.* mit, mitsamt, bei, durch, von.

withal [wi'ðɔ:l], *adv.* obendrein.

withdraw [wið'drɔ:], *v.a., v.n. irr.* (sich) zurückziehen; widerrufen; abheben (*money from bank*).

withdrawal [wið'drɔ:əl], *s.* der Rückzug; (*Comm. etc.*) die Widerrufung; Abhebung (*bank*).

wither [wiðə], *v.a.* welk machen. — *v.n.* verwelken; ausdorren, verdorren (*dry up*); (*fig.*) vergehen.

withhold [wið'hould], *v.a. irr.* zurückhalten, vorenthalten.

within [wi'ðin], *prep.* innerhalb; (*time*) binnen (*Genit.*). — *adv.* darin, drinnen.

without [wi'ðaut], *prep.* ohne; (*obs.*) außerhalb (*outside*); do —, entbehren. — *adv.* draußen, außen.

withstand [wið'stænd], *v.a. irr.* widerstehen (*Dat.*).

withy ['wiði], *s.* der Weidenzweig.

witless ['witlis], *adj.* einfältig.

witness ['witnis], *s.* der Zeuge. — *v.a.* bezeugen, Zeuge sein von. — *v.n.* zeugen, Zeuge sein.

witticism ['witisizm], *s.* das Bonmot, die witzige Bemerkung.

witty ['witi], *adj.* witzig, geistreich.

wizard ['wizəd], *s.* der Zauberer.

wizened ['wizənd], *adj.* verwelkt, vertrocknet, runzlig.

wobble ['wɔbl], *v.n.* wackeln.

woe [wou], *s.* (*Poet.*) das Weh, Leid.

wolf [wulf], *s.* (*Zool.*) der Wolf.

woman ['wumən], *s.* die Frau, das Weib.

womanly ['wumənli], *adj.* weiblich.

womb [wu:m], *s.* der Mutterleib, Schoß; (*Anat.*) die Gebärmutter.

wonder ['wʌndə], *s.* das Wunder. — *v.n.* sich wundern (*be amazed*); gern wissen mögen (*like to know*); sich fragen.

wonderful ['wʌndəful], *adj.* wunderbar.

wondrous ['wʌndrəs], *adj.* (*Poet.*) wunderbar.

wont [wount], *s.* die Gewohnheit. — *pred. adj.* gewohnt.

won't [wount], = **will not.**

woo [wu:], *v.a.* freien, werben (um).

wood [wud], *s.* das Holz (*timber*); der Wald (*forest*).

woodbine ['wudbain], *s.* das Geißblatt.

woodcock ['wudkɔk], *s.* (*Orn.*) die Waldschnepfe.

woodcut ['wudkʌt], *s.* (*Art*) der Holzschnitt.

wooded ['wudid], *adj.* bewaldet.

wooden [wudn], *adj.* hölzern, Holz-.

woodlark ['wudla:k], *s.* (*Orn.*) die Heidelerche.

woodpecker ['wudpekə], *s.* (*Orn.*) der Specht.

woodruff ['wudrʌf], *s.* (*Bot.*) der Waldmeister.

woof [wu:f], *s.* (*Text.*) der Einschlag, das Gewebe.

wool [wul], *s.* die Wolle; — *gathering*, zerstreut.

woollen ['wulən], *adj.* wollen, aus Wolle.

woolly ['wuli], *adj.* wollig; (*fig.*) unklar, verschwommen.

word [wə:d], *s.* das Wort; *send* —, Botschaft senden. — *v.a.* ausdrücken.

wording ['wə:diŋ], *s.* die Fassung, der Stil.

work [wə:k], *s.* die Arbeit; *out of* —, arbeitslos; das Werk (*opus*); (*pl.*) die Fabrik. — *v.a., v.n.* arbeiten, bearbeiten; (*engine*) funktionieren.

worker ['wə:kə], *s.* der Arbeiter.

workhouse ['wə:khaus], *s.* das Armenhaus.

workshop ['wə:kʃɔp], *s.* die Werkstatt.

world [wə:ld], *s.* die Welt.

worldly ['wə:ldli], *adj.* weltlich, zeitlich.

worm [wə:m], *s.* (*Zool.*) der Wurm. — *v.a.* — *o.'s way*, sich einschleichen. — *v.n.* sich einschleichen.

wormeaten ['wə:mi:tn], *adj.* wurmstichig.

worry ['wʌri], *v.a., v.n.* plagen, quälen, sorgen, ängstigen; sich beunruhigen; *don't* —, bitte machen Sie sich keine Mühe. — *s.* die Plage, Mühe, Qual, Sorge (*about*, um, *Acc.*).

worse [wə:s], *comp. adj., adv.* schlechter, schlimmer.

worship ['wə:ʃip], *s.* die Verehrung; der Gottesdienst (*divine* —).

worst [wə:st], *superl. adj.* schlechtest, schlimmst. — [*adv.* am schlimmsten *or* schlechtesten. — *s.* das Schlimmste.

worsted ['wustid], *s.* (*Text.*) das Kammgarn.

worth [wə:θ], *adj.* wert. — *s.* der Wert.

worthy ['wə:ði], *adj.* würdig, wert, verdient.

would [wud] *past tense of* **will**, *q.v.*

wound [wu:nd], *s.* die Wunde. — *v.a.* verwunden.

wraith [reiθ], *s.* das Gespenst.

wrangle ['ræŋgl], *v.n.* zanken, streiten. — *s.* der Zank, Streit.

wrap [ræp], *v.a.* einwickeln, einhüllen. — *s.* (*Am.*) der Mantel (*coat*), Pelz (*fur*), Schal (*stole*).

wrapper ['ræpə], *s.* der Umschlag, die Hülle.

wrath [rɔ:θ], *s.* der Zorn, Grimm.

wreak [ri:k], *v.a.* (*Lit.*) auslassen, üben.

wreath [ri:θ], *s.* der Kranz.

wreathe [ri:ð], *v.a.* winden, bekränzen.

wreck [rek], *s.* der Schiffbruch; das Wrack (*debris*). — *v.a.* zerstören, zertrümmern, (*fig.*) verderben.

wren [ren], *s.* (*Orn.*) der Zaunkönig.

wrench [rentʃ], *v.a.* entreißen (*tear from*); verdrehen. — *s.* heftiger Ruck; (*fig.*) der (Trennungs)schmerz.

wrest [rest], *v.a.* zerren.

wrestle [resl], *v.n.* ringen, im Ringkampf kämpfen.

wrestling ['resliŋ], *s.* der Ringkampf.

wretch [retʃ], *s.* der Schuft, Lump (*scoundrel*).

wretched ['retʃid], *adj.* elend.

wriggle [rigl], *v.n.* sich winden, schlängeln.

wring [riŋ], *v.a. irr.* auswinden, ausringen.

wrinkle [riŋkl], *s.* die Hautfalte, Runzel. — *v.a.* runzeln (*brow*); rümpfen (*nose*).

wrist [rist], *s.* (*Anat.*) das Handgelenk.

wristwatch ['ristwɔtʃ], *s.* die Armbanduhr.

writ [rit], *s.* die Schrift; (*Law*) die Vorladung.

write

write [rait], *v.a., v.n. irr.* schreiben, verfassen.
writer ['raitə], *s.* der Schreiber; (*Lit.*) der Schriftsteller.
writhe [raiδ], *v.n.* sich winden.
writing ['raitiŋ], *s.* die Schrift; der Stil (*style*).
wrong [rɔŋ], *adj.* falsch, verkehrt; *to be —,* unrecht haben. *— s.* das Unrecht. *— v.a.* Unrecht *or* Schaden tun (*Dat.*).
wrongful ['rɔŋful], *adj.* unrechtmäßig.
wrongheaded [rɔŋ'hedid], *adj.* querköpfig.
wroth [rouθ], *adj.* (*Lit.*) zornig.
wrought [rɔːt], *adj.* (*work*) gearbeitet; *— iron,* das Schmiedeeisen.
wry [rai], *adj.* verkehrt, krumm, schief, verdreht.

X

X [eks]. das X.
X-ray ['eksrei], *s.* (der) Röntgenstrahl.
xylophone ['zailəfoun], *s.* (*Mus.*) das Xylophon.

Y

Y [wai]. das Y, Ypsilon.
yacht [jɔt], *s.* (*Naut.*) die Jacht.
yachtsman ['jɔtsmən], *s.* (*Naut.*) der Segelsportler.
yap [jæp], *v.n.* kläffen.
yard (1) [jɑːd], *s.* der Hof.
yard (2) [jɑːd], *s.* die englische Elle, der Yard.
yarn [jɑːn], *s.* das Garn; (*coll.*) die Geschichte (*tale*).
yarrow ['jærou], *s.* (*Bot.*) die Schafgarbe.
yawl [jɔːl], *s.* (*Naut.*) die Yawl.
yawn [jɔːn], *v.n.* gähnen. *— s.* das Gähnen.
ye [jiː], *pron.* (*obs.*) *see* you.
year [jəː *or* jiə], *s.* das Jahr; *every other —,* alle zwei Jahre.
yearly ['jiəli], *adj., adv.* jährlich.
yearn [jəːn], *v.n.* sich sehnen (nach, *Dat.*).
yeast [jiːst], *s.* die Hefe.
yell [jel], *v.n.* gellen, schreien. *— s.* der Schrei.
yellow ['jelou], *adj.* gelb; (*sl.*) feige.
yelp [jelp], *v.n.* kläffen, bellen. *— s.* das Gebelle.
yeoman ['joumən], *s.* der Freisasse; (*Mil.*) der Leibgardist (*Yeoman of the Guard*).

yes [jes], *adv.* ja; jawohl.
yesterday ['jestəd(e)i], *adv.* gestern; *the day before —,* vorgestern.
yet [jet], *conj.* doch, dennoch. *— adv.* noch, außerdem; *as —,* bisher; *not —,* noch nicht.
yew [juː], *s.* (*Bot.*) die Eibe.
yield [jiːld], *v.a.* hervorbringen, ergeben; abwerfen (*profit*). *— v.n.* nachgeben (*to, Dat.*). *— s.* der Ertrag.
yoke [jouk], *s.* das Joch (Ochsen). *— v.a.* einspannen, anspannen.
yolk [jouk], *s.* das Eidotter.
yon, yonder [jɔn, 'jɔndə], *dem. adj.* (*obs.*) jener, jene, jenes; der *or* die *or* das da drüben.
yore [jɔː], *adv.* (*obs.*) *of —,* von damals; ehedem.
you [juː], *pers. pron.* du, dich, ihr, euch; (*formal*) sie (*in letters,* Du, Dich *etc.*).
young [jʌŋ], *adj.* jung. *— s.* (*Zool.*) das Junge.
your [juə], *poss. adj.* dein, deine, dein; euer, eure, euer; (*formal*) ihr, ihre, ihr (*in letters* Dein, Euer *etc.*).
yours [jɔːz], *poss. pron.* deinig, eurig; der, die *or* das ihrige (*in letters* Deinig, der Ihrige *etc.*).
yourself [juə'self], *pers. pron.* du selbst, Sie selbst; ihr selbst; dich (selbst), euch (selbst) (*in letters* Du selbst; Dich (selbst) *etc.*).
youth [juːθ], *s.* die Jugend.
youthful ['juːθful], *adj.* jugendlich.
Yugoslav [juːgo'slɑːv], *adj.* jugoslawisch. *— s.* der Jugoslawe.
Yule, Yuletide [juːl, 'juːltaid], *s.* das Julfest, die Weihnachtszeit.

Z

Z [zed, (*Am.*) ziː]. das Z.
zany ['zeini], *s.* der Hanswurst.
zeal [ziːl], *s.* der Eifer.
zealous ['zeləs], *adj.* eifrig.
zebra ['ziːbrə], *s.* (*Zool.*) das Zebra.
zenith ['zeniθ], *s.* der Zenit, Scheitelpunkt.
zero ['ziərou], *s.* der Nullpunkt, die (Ziffer) Null; — *hour,* die festgesetzte Stunde; festgesetzter Zeitpunkt.
zest [zest], *s.* die Lust; der Genuß; die Würze.
zigzag ['zigzæg], *s.* der Zickzack. *— adj.* Zickzack-.
zinc [ziŋk], *s.* das Zink.
zip(per) ['zip(ə)], *s.* der Reißverschluß (*zip fastener*).
zone [zoun], *s.* die Zone.
zoological gardens [zouə'lɔdʒikəl gɑːdnz], *s.* (*abbr.* zoo [zuː]) zoologischer Garten, der Zoo, Tiergarten.

German Irregular Verbs

Note: *Where a compound irregular verb is not given, its forms are identical with those of the simple irregular verb as listed.*

Infin.	Pres. Indic. 3rd Pers. Sing.	Imperf. Indic.	Imperf. Subj.
backen	bäckt	backte (buk)	backte
befehlen	befiehlt	befahl	beföhle
beginnen	beginnt	begann	begönne
beißen	beißt	biß	bisse
bergen	birgt	barg	bürge
bersten	birst	barst	börste
bewegen	bewegt	bewog	bewöge
biegen	biegt	bog	böge
bieten	bietet	bot	böte
binden	bindet	band	bände
bitten	bittet	bat	bäte
blasen	bläst	blies	bliese
bleiben	bleibt	blieb	bliebe
braten	brät	briet	briete
brechen	bricht	brach	bräche
brennen	brennt	brannte	brennte
bringen	bringt	brachte	brächte
denken	denkt	dachte	dächte
dreschen	drischt	drosch	drösche
dringen	dringt	drang	dränge
dürfen	darf	durfte	dürfte
empfangen	empfängt	empfing	empfinge
empfehlen	empfiehlt	empfahl	empföhle
empfinden	empfindet	empfand	empfände
erlöschen	erlischt	erlosch	erlösche

Imper.	Past Participle	English
backe	gebacken	bake
befiehl	befohlen	order, command
beginn(e)	begonnen	begin
beiß(e)	gebissen	bite
birg	geborgen	save, conceal
birst	geborsten	burst
beweg(e)	bewogen	induce
bieg(e)	gebogen	bend
biet(e)	geboten	offer
bind(e)	gebunden	tie, bind
bitte	gebeten	request
blas(e)	geblasen	blow
bleib(e)	geblieben	remain
brat(e)	gebraten	roast
brich	gebrochen	break
brenne	gebrannt	burn
bring(e)	gebracht	bring
denk(e)	gedacht	think
drisch	gedroschen	thrash
dring(e)	gedrungen	press forward
	gedurft	be permitted
empfang(e)	empfangen	receive
empfiehl	empfohlen	(re)commend
empfind(e)	empfunden	feel, perceive
erlisch	erloschen	be extinguished

German Irregular Verbs

Infin.	Pres. Indic. 3rd Pers. Sing.	Imperf. Indic.	Imperf. Subj.
erschrecken (*v.n.*)	erschrickt	erschrak	erschräke
essen	ißt	aß	äße
fahren	fährt	fuhr	führe
fallen	fällt	fiel	fiele
fangen	fängt	fing	finge
fechten	ficht	focht	föchte
finden	findet	fand	fände
flechten	flicht	flocht	flöchte
fliegen	fliegt	flog	flöge
fliehen	flieht	floh	flöhe
fließen	fließt	floß	flösse
fressen	frißt	fraß	fräße
frieren	friert	fror	fröre
gebären	gebiert	gebar	gebäre
geben	gibt	gab	gäbe
gedeihen	gedeiht	gedieh	gediehe
gehen	geht	ging	ginge
gelingen (*impers.*)	(mir) gelingt	gelang	gelänge
gelten	gilt	galt	gälte
genesen	genest	genas	genäse
genießen	genießt	genoß	genösse
geschehen (*impers.*)	(mir) geschieht	geschah	geschähe
gewinnen	gewinnt	gewann	gewönne
gießen	gießt	goß	gösse
gleichen	gleicht	glich	gliche
gleiten	gleitet	glitt	glitte
graben	gräbt	grub	grübe
greifen	greift	griff	griffe

Imper.	Past Participle	English
erschrick	erschrocken	be frightened
iß	gegessen	eat
fahr(e)	gefahren	travel
fall(e)	gefallen	fall
fang(e)	gefangen	catch
ficht	gefochten	fight
find(e)	gefunden	find
flicht	geflochten	twine together
flieg(e)	geflogen	fly
flieh(e)	geflohen	flee
fließ(e)	geflossen	flow
friß	gefressen	eat (of animals)
frier(e)	gefroren	freeze
gebier	geboren	give birth to
gib	gegeben	give
gedeih(e)	gediehen	thrive
geh(e)	gegangen	go
geling(e)	gelungen	succeed
gilt	gegolten	be worth, be valid
genese	genesen	recover
genieß(e)	genossen	enjoy
	geschehen	happen
gewinn(e)	gewonnen	win
gieß(e)	gegossen	pour
gleich(e)	geglichen	equal, resemble
gleit(e)	geglitten	glide
grab(e)	gegraben	dig
greif(e)	gegriffen	grasp

German Irregular Verbs

Infin.	Pres. Indic. 3rd Pers. Sing.	Imperf. Indic.	Imperf. Subj.
haben	hat	hatte	hätte
halten	hält	hielt	hielte
hangen (v.n.)	hängt	hing	hinge
heben	hebt	hob	höbe
heißen	heißt	hieß	hieße
helfen	hilft	half	hülfe
kennen	kennt	kannte	kennte
klimmen	klimmt	klomm	klömme
klingen	klingt	klang	klänge
kneifen	kneift	kniff	kniffe
kommen	kommt	kam	käme
können	kann	konnte	könnte
kriechen	kriecht	kroch	kröche
laden	lädt	lud	lüde
lassen	läßt	ließ	ließe
laufen	läuft	lief	liefe
leiden	leidet	litt	litte
leihen	leiht	lieh	liehe
lesen	liest	las	läse
liegen	liegt	lag	läge
lügen	lügt	log	löge
mahlen	mahlt	mahlte	mahlte
meiden	meidet	mied	miede
messen	mißt	maß	mäße
mißlingen (impers.)	(mir) mißlingt	mißlang	mißlänge
mögen	mag	mochte	möchte
müssen	muß	mußte	müßte
nehmen	nimmt	nahm	nähme

German Irregular Verbs

Imper.	Past Participle	English
habe	gehabt	have
halt(e)	gehalten	hold
häng(e)	gehangen	hang
hebe	gehoben	lift
heiß(e)	geheißen	be called
hilf	geholfen	help
kenn(e)	gekannt	know
klimm(e)	geklommen	climb
kling(e)	geklungen	ring, sound
kneif(e)	gekniffen	pinch
komm(e)	gekommen	come
	gekonnt	be able
kriech(e)	gekrochen	creep
lad(e)	geladen	load
laß	gelassen	let
lauf(e)	gelaufen	run
leid(e)	gelitten	suffer
leih(e)	geliehen	lend
lies	gelesen	read
lieg(e)	gelegen	lie
lüg(e)	gelogen	lie, be untruthful
mahle	gemahlen	grind
meid(e)	gemieden	avoid
miß	gemessen	measure
	mißlungen	fail
	gemocht	wish, be willing
	gemußt	have to
nimm	genommen	take

German Irregular Verbs

Infin.	Pres. Indic. 3rd Pers. Sing.	Imperf. Indic.	Imperf. Subj.
nennen	nennt	nannte	nennte
pfeifen	pfeift	pfiff	pfiffe
preisen	preist	pries	priese
quellen (v.n.)	quillt	quoll	quölle
raten	rät	riet	riete
reiben	reibt	rieb	riebe
reißen	reißt	riß	risse
reiten	reitet	ritt	ritte
rennen	rennt	rannte	rennte
riechen	riecht	roch	röche
ringen	ringt	rang	ränge
rinnen	rinnt	rann	rönne
rufen	ruft	rief	riefe
saufen	säuft	soff	söffe
saugen	saugt	sog	söge
schaffen	schafft	schuf	schüfe
scheiden	scheidet	schied	schiede
scheinen	scheint	schien	schiene
schelten	schilt	schalt	schölte
schieben	schiebt	schob	schöbe
schießen	schießt	schoß	schösse
schinden	schindet	schund	schünde
schlafen	schläft	schlief	schliefe
schlagen	schlägt	schlug	schlüge
schleichen	schleicht	schlich	schliche
schleifen	schleift	schliff	schliffe
schließen	schließt	schloß	schlösse
schlingen	schlingt	schlang	schlänge

Imper.	Past Participle	English
nenne	genannt	name
pfeif(e)	gepfiffen	whistle
preis(e)	gepriesen	praise
quill	gequollen	spring
rat(e)	geraten	counsel
reib(e)	gerieben	rub
reiß(e)	gerissen	tear
reit(e)	geritten	ride
renn(e)	gerannt	run
riech(e)	gerochen	smell
ring(e)	gerungen	struggle
rinn(e)	geronnen	flow
ruf(e)	gerufen	call
sauf(e)	gesoffen	drink (to excess)
saug(e)	gesogen	suck
schaff(e)	geschaffen	create
scheid(e)	geschieden	separate
schein(e)	geschienen	appear
schilt	gescholten	scold
schieb(e)	geschoben	shove
schieß(e)	geschossen	shoot
schind(e)	geschunden	skin
schlaf(e)	geschlafen	sleep
schlag(e)	geschlagen	beat
schleich(e)	geschlichen	slink, creep
schleif(e)	geschliffen	slide, polish
schließ(e)	geschlossen	shut, close
schling(e)	geschlungen	wind, devour

German Irregular Verbs

Infin.	Pres. Indic. 3rd Pers. Sing.	Imperf. Indic.	Imperf. Subj.
schmeißen	schmeißt	schmiß	schmisse
schmelzen (v.n.)	schmilzt	schmolz	schmölze
schneiden	schneidet	schnitt	schnitte
schrecken (v.n.)	schrickt	schrak	schräke
schreiben	schreibt	schrieb	schriebe
schreien	schreit	schrie	schriee
schreiten	schreitet	schritt	schritte
schweigen	schweigt	schwieg	schwiege
schwellen	schwillt	schwoll	schwölle
schwimmen	schwimmt	schwamm	schwömme
schwinden	schwindet	schwand	schwände
schwingen	schwingt	schwang	schwänge
schwören	schwört	schwur	schwüre
sehen	sieht	sah	sähe
sein	ist	war	wäre
senden	sendet	sandte or sendete	sendete
singen	singt	sang	sänge
sinken	sinkt	sank	sänke
sinnen	sinnt	sann	sänne
sitzen	sitzt	saß	säße
sollen	soll	sollte	sollte
speien	speit	spie	spiee
spinnen	spinnt	spann	spönne
sprechen	spricht	sprach	spräche
sprießen	sprießt	sproß	sprösse
springen	springt	sprang	spränge
stechen	sticht	stach	stäche
stehen	steht	stand	stände

German Irregular Verbs

Imper.	Past Participle	English
schmeiß(e)	geschmissen	hurl
schmilz	geschmolzen	melt
schneid(e)	geschnitten	cut
schrick	(erschrocken)	frighten
schreib(e)	geschrieben	write
schrei(e)	geschrien	cry
schreit(e)	geschritten	stride
schweig(e)	geschwiegen	be silent
schwill	geschwollen	swell
schwimm(e)	geschwommen	swim
schwind(e)	geschwunden	vanish
schwing(e)	geschwungen	swing
schwör(e)	geschworen	swear
sieh	gesehen	see
sei	gewesen	be
send(e)	gesandt *or* gesendet	send
sing(e)	gesungen	sing
sink(e)	gesunken	sink
sinn(e)	gesonnen	meditate
sitz(e)	gesessen	sit
	gesollt	be obliged
spei(e)	gespieen	spit
spinn(e)	gesponnen	spin
sprich	gesprochen	speak
sprieß(e)	gesprossen	sprout
spring(e)	gesprungen	leap
stich	gestochen	prick
steh(e)	gestanden	stand

German Irregular Verbs

Infin.	Pres. Indic. 3rd Pers. Sing.	Imperf. Indic.	Imperf. Subj.
stehlen	stiehlt	stahl	stöhle
steigen	steigt	stieg	stiege
sterben	stirbt	starb	stürbe
stinken	stinkt	stank	stänke
stoßen	stößt	stieß	stieße
streichen	streicht	strich	striche
streiten	streitet	stritt	stritte
tragen	trägt	trug	trüge
treffen	trifft	traf	träfe
treiben	treibt	trieb	triebe
treten	tritt	trat	träte
trinken	trinkt	trank	tränke
trügen	trügt	trog	tröge
tun	tut	tat	täte
verderben	verdirbt	verdarb	verdürbe
verdrießen	verdrießt	verdroß	verdrösse
vergessen	vergißt	vergaß	vergäße
verlieren	verliert	verlor	verlöre
wachsen	wächst	wuchs	wüchse
wägen	wägt	wog	wöge
waschen	wäscht	wusch	wüsche
weichen	weicht	wich	wiche
weisen	weist	wies	wiese
werben	wirbt	warb	würbe
werden	wird	wurde	würde
werfen	wirft	warf	würfe
wiegen	wiegt	wog	wöge
winden (v.a.)	windet	wand	wände

German Irregular Verbs

Imper.	Past Participle	English
stiehl	gestohlen	steal
steig(e)	gestiegen	climb
stirb	gestorben	die
stink(e)	gestunken	stink
stoß(e)	gestoßen	push
streich(e)	gestrichen	stroke, touch
streit(e)	gestritten	quarrel, fight
trag(e)	getragen	carry
triff	getroffen	meet
treib(e)	getrieben	drive
tritt	getreten	step
trink(e)	getrunken	drink
trüg(e)	getrogen	deceive
tu(e)	getan	do
verdirb	verdorben (and verderbt)	spoil
verdrieß(e)	verdrossen	grieve
vergiß	vergessen	forget
verlier(e)	verloren	lose
wachs(e)	gewachsen	grow
wäg(e)	gewogen	weigh
wasch(e)	gewaschen	wash
weich(e)	gewichen	yield
weis(e)	gewiesen	show
wirb	geworben	court
werde	geworden	become
wirf	geworfen	throw
wieg(e)	gewogen	weigh
wind(e)	gewunden	wind

German Irregular Verbs

Infin.	Pres. Indic. 3rd. Pers. Sing.	Imperf. Indic.	Imperf. Subj.
wissen	weiß	wußte	wüßte
wollen	will	wollte	wollte
zeihen	zeiht	zieh	ziehe
ziehen	zieht	zog	zöge
zwingen	zwingt	zwang	zwänge

Imper.	Past Participle	English
wisse	gewußt	know
wolle	gewollt	wish, want
zeih(e)	geziehen	accuse
zieh(e)	gezogen	draw, pull
zwing(e)	gezwungen	force, compel

English Irregular Verbs

Infin.	Past Indic.	Past Participle	German
abide	abode	abode	bleiben
arise	arose	arisen	aufstehen
awake	awoke	awoke	aufwecken
be	was; were	been	sein
bear	bore	borne	tragen
beat	beat	beaten	schlagen
become	became	become	werden
beget	begot	begotten	zeugen
begin	began	begun	beginnen
bend	bent	bent	biegen
bereave	bereaved, bereft	bereaved, bereft	berauben
beseech	besought	besought	bitten
bid	bade, bid	bidden, bid	gebieten
bide	bided, bode	bided	verbleiben
bind	bound	bound	binden
bite	bit	bitten	beißen
bleed	bled	bled	bluten
blow	blew	blown	blasen
break	broke	broken	brechen
breed	bred	bred	zeugen
bring	brought	brought	bringen
build	built	built	bauen
burn	burnt, burned	burnt, burned	brennen
burst	burst	burst	bersten
buy	bought	bought	kaufen

Infin.	Past Indic.	Past Participle	German
can (*pres. indic.*)	could	—	können
cast	cast	cast	werfen
catch	caught	caught	fangen
chide	chid	chidden, chid	schelten
choose	chose	chosen	wählen
cleave	cleft, clove	cleft, cloven	spalten
cling	clung	clung	sich anklammern
clothe	clothed, clad	clothed, clad	kleiden
come	came	come	kommen
cost	cost	cost	kosten
creep	crept	crept	kriechen
crow	crowed, crew	crowed	krähen
cut	cut	cut	schneiden
dare	dared, durst	dared	wagen
deal	dealt	dealt	austeilen, handeln
dig	dug	dug	graben
do	did	done	tun
draw	drew	drawn	ziehen
dream	dreamt, dreamed	dreamt, dreamed	träumen
drink	drank	drunk	trinken
drive	drove	driven	treiben
dwell	dwelt	dwelt	wohnen
eat	ate	eaten	essen
fall	fell	fallen	fallen
feed	fed	fed	füttern
feel	felt	felt	fühlen
fight	fought	fought	kämpfen
find	found	found	finden

English Irregular Verbs

Infin.	Past Indic.	Past Participle	German
flee	fled	fled	fliehen
fling	flung	flung	schleudern
fly	flew	flown	fliegen
forbid	forbad(e)	forbidden	verbieten
forget	forgot	forgotten	vergessen
forgive	forgave	forgiven	vergeben
forsake	forsook	forsaken	verlassen
freeze	froze	frozen	frieren
get	got	got	bekommen
gird	girded, girt	girden, girt	gürten
give	gave	given	geben
go	went	gone	gehen
grind	ground	ground	mahlen
grow	grew	grown	wachsen
hang	hung	hung	hängen
have	had	had	haben
hear	heard	heard	hören
heave	heaved, hove	heaved, hove	heben
hew	hewed	hewn, hewed	hauen
hide	hid	hidden, hid	verstecken
hit	hit	hit	schlagen
hold	held	held	halten
hurt	hurt	hurt	verletzen
keep	kept	kept	halten
kneel	knelt	knelt	knien
knit	knitted, knit	knitted, knit	stricken
know	knew	known	kennen, wissen
lay	laid	laid	legen

Infin.	Past Indic.	Past Participle	German
lead	led	led	führen
lean	leant, leaned	leant, leaned	lehnen
leap	leaped, leapt	leaped, leapt	springen
learn	learned, learnt	learned, learnt	lernen
leave	left	left	lassen
lend	lent	lent	leihen
let	let	let	lassen
lie (= recline)	lay	lain	liegen
light	lit, lighted	lit, lighted	beleuchten
lost	lost	lost	verlieren
make	made	made	machen
may (*pres. indic.*)	might	—	mögen
mean	meant	meant	meinen
meet	met	met	treffen, begegnen
melt	melted	melted, molten	schmelzen
mow	mowed	mown	mähen
must (*pres. indic.*)	—	—	müssen
pay	paid	paid	zahlen
put	put	put	stellen
quit	quit(ted)	quit(ted)	verlassen
—	quoth	—	sagte
read	read	read	lesen
rend	rent	rent	reissen
rid	rid	rid	befreien
ride	rode	ridden	reiten, fahren
ring	rang	rung	klingeln
rise	rose	risen	aufstehen
run	ran	run	laufen

English Irregular Verbs

Infin.	Past Indic.	Past Participle	German
saw	sawed	sawn	sägen
say	said	said	sagen
see	saw	seen	sehen
seek	sought	sought	suchen
sell	sold	sold	verkaufen
send	sent	sent	senden
set	set	set	setzen
shake	shook	shaken	schütteln
shall (*pres. indic.*)	should	—	werden, sollen
shape	shaped	shaped, shapen	formen
shear	sheared	shorn	scheren
shed	shed	shed	vergiessen
shine	shone	shone	scheinen
shoe	shod	shod	beschuhen
shoot	shot	shot	schiessen
show	showed	shown	zeigen
shrink	shrank	shrunk	schrumpfen
shut	shut	shut	schliessen
sing	sang	sung	singen
sink	sank	sunk	sinken
sit	sat	sat	sitzen
slay	slew	slain	erschlagen
sleep	slept	slept	schlafen
slide	slid	slid	gleiten
sling	slung	slung	schleudern
slink	slunk	slunk	schleichen
slit	slit	slit	schlitzen
smell	smelt	smelt	riechen

English Irregular Verbs

Infin.	Past Indic.	Past Participle	German
smit	smote	smitten	schlagen
sow	sowed	sown, sowed	säen
speak	spoke	spoken	sprechen
speed	sped, speeded	sped, speeded	eilen
spell	spelt, spelled	spelt, spelled	buchstabieren
spend	spent	spent	ausgeben
spill	spilled, spilt	spilled, spilt	verschütten
spin	spun, span	spun	spinnen
spit	spat	spat	speien
split	split	split	spalten
spread	spread	spread	ausbreiten
spring	sprang	sprung	springen
stand	stood	stood	stehen
steal	stole	stolen	stehlen
stick	stuck	stuck	stecken
sting	stung	stung	stechen
stink	stank, stunk	stunk	stinken
strew	strewed	strewed, strewn	streuen
stride	strode	stridden	schreiten
strike	struck	struck, stricken	schlagen
string	strung	strung	(auf)reihen
strive	strove	striven	streben
swear	swore	sworn	schwören
sweep	swept	swept	kehren
swell	swelled	swollen	schwellen
swim	swam	swum	schwimmen
swing	swung	swung	schwingen
take	took	taken	nehmen

English Irregular Verbs

Infin.	Past Indic.	Past Participle	German
teach	taught	taught	lehren
tear	tore	torn	zerreißen
tell	told	told	erzählen
think	thought	thought	denken
thrive	thrived, throve	thrived, thriven	gedeihen
throw	threw	thrown	werfen
thrust	thrust	thrust	stoßen
tread	trod	trodden	treten
wake	woke, waked	waked, woken woke	wachen
wear	wore	worn	tragen
weave	wove	woven	weben
weep	wept	wept	weinen
will	would	—	wollen
win	won	won	gewinnen
wind	wound	wound	winden
work	worked, wrought	worked, wrought	arbeiten
wring	wrung	wrung	ringen
write	wrote	written	schreiben

Numerical Tables

Cardinal Numbers

0	nought, zero	null
1	one	eins
2	two	zwei
3	three	drei
4	four	vier
5	five	fünf
6	six	sechs
7	seven	sieben
8	eight	acht
9	nine	neun
10	ten	zehn
11	eleven	elf
12	twelve	zwölf
13	thirteen	dreizehn
14	fourteen	vierzehn
15	fifteen	fünfzehn
16	sixteen	sechzehn
17	seventeen	siebzehn
18	eighteen	achtzehn
19	nineteen	neunzehn
20	twenty	zwanzig
21	twenty-one	einundzwanzig
22	twenty-two	zweiundzwanzig
25	twenty-five	fünfundzwanzig
30	thirty	dreißig
36	thirty-six	sechsunddreißig
40	forty	vierzig
50	fifty	fünfzig
60	sixty	sechzig
70	seventy	siebzig
80	eighty	achtzig
90	ninety	neunzig
100	(one)hundred	(one)
101	(a)hundred and one	hundert(und)eins
102	(a)hundred and two	hundert(und)zwei
200	two hundred	zweihundert
300	three hundred	dreihundert
600	six hundred	sechshundert
625	six hundred and twenty-five	sechshundertfünf-undzwanzig
1000	(a)thousand	tausend
1965	nineteen hundred and sixty-five	neunzehnhundert-fünfundsechzig
2000	two thousand	zweitausend
1,000,000	a million	eine Million
2,000,000	two million	zwei Millionen

Various suffixes may be added to German numerals, the commonest of which are cited in the following examples:

zehnfach	tenfold
dreisilbig	trisyllabic
vierstimmig	four-part (*i.e.* for four voices)
sechsteilig	in six parts

Ordinal Numbers

1st	first	erste (abbr. 1.)
2nd	second	zweite (abbr. 2.)
3rd	third	dritte (abbr. 3.)
4th	fourth	vierte
5th	fifth	fünfte
6th	sixth	sechste
7th	seventh	siebte
8th	eighth	achte
9th	ninth	neunte
10th	tenth	zehnte
11th	eleventh	elfte
12th	twelfth	zwölfte
13th	thirteenth	dreizehnte
14th	fourteenth	vierzehnte
15th	fifteenth	fünfzehnte
16th	sixteenth	sechzehnte
17th	seventeenth	siebzehnte
18th	eighteenth	achtzehnte
19th	nineteenth	neunzehnte
20th	twentieth	zwanzigste
21st	twenty-first	einundzwanzigste
22nd	twenty-second	zweiundzwanzigste
25th	twenty-fifth	fünfundzwanzigste
30th	thirtieth	dreißigste
40th	fortieth	vierzigste
50th	fiftieth	fünfzigste
60th	sixtieth	sechzigste
70th	seventieth	siebzigste
80th	eightieth	achtzigste
90th	ninetieth	neunzigste
100th	hundredth	hundertste
102nd	hundred and second	hundert(und)zweite
200th	two hundredth	zweihundertste
300th	three hundredth	dreihundertste
625th	six hundred and twenty-fifth	sechshundertfünf-undzwanzigste
1000th	thousandth	tausendste
2000th	two thousandth	zweitausendste
1,000,000th	millionth	millionste

Fractions etc.

$\frac{1}{4}$	a quarter	ein Viertel
$\frac{1}{3}$	a third	ein Drittel
$\frac{1}{2}$	a half	(ein)halb
$\frac{2}{3}$	two thirds	zwei Drittel
$\frac{3}{4}$	three quarters	drei Viertel
$1\frac{1}{4}$	one and a quarter	ein und ein Viertel
$1\frac{1}{2}$	one and a half	anderthalb
$5\frac{1}{2}$	five and a half	fünfeinhalb
$7\frac{2}{5}$	seven and two-fifths	sieben zwei Fünftel
$\frac{15}{20}$	fifteen-twentieths	fünfzehn Zwanzigstel
.7	point seven	0,7 Null Komma sieben

edited by D. C. Browning
Everyman's Roget's Thesaurus £1.50

Roget's Thesaurus is one of the English-speaking world's most valuable and celebrated works of reference. It is a treasury of synonyms, antonyms, parallel and related words, designed to help you find the right words or phrase to express your ideas with force and clarity.

This edition preserves the original plan of classification and categories (including the vast and ingenious index) and has been completely revised to bring all words and phrases into accordance with current usage. Over ten thousand more of these have been added, including many technical terms, everyday neologisms, Americanisms and slang.

'Among reference books Roget's Thesaurus stands by itself . . . a treasury upon which writers can draw'
THE TIMES LITERARY SUPPLEMENT

Margaret Allen
The Money Book £1.75

Work out your income properly, fill in your tax return; make the best use of your bank; buy a freezer, a house or a car; decide on an allowance for your children; understand a company annual report; make a will; get a divorce; invest in unit trusts or buy by mail order . . .

'The most comprehensive book about money'
MANCHESTER EVENING NEWS

G. H. Vallins
Good English 70p

Words 'have enabled us to rise above the brutes and often sink to the level of the demons' ALDOUS HUXLEY
Can you always write exactly what you mean? Are you sometimes at a loss for the right word? G. H. Vallins states clearly and simply the main principles of current English usage, outlines the basic conventions, and deals entertainingly with jargon, idiom and cliché. It is a perfect guide on how to achieve a good simple style for business and everyday usage.

Better English 80p

This fascinating sequel to *Good English* leaves the world of accidence and syntax for that of idiom, figure, the logical expression of thought and the niceties of language . . . Introducing examples of unsound sentences from a variety of books, magazines and newspapers G. H. Vallins shows how they can be reconstructed far more effectively.

The Best English 60p

Believing that English is a rich and living language. G. H. Vallins takes the reader on an exciting exploration of literature. Dealing with the techniques of composition – in poetry, drama and prose – he shows how words, properly used, can communicate directly with the minds and emotions of others.

Clifford Allen
Passing Examinations 50p

This invaluable book for students of all ages explains the techniques
of study which are afforded by modern psychology and advises how these
can be applied to both written and oral examinations.

'Refreshingly down to earth' BIRMINGHAM POST

C. L. Barber
The Story of Language 80p

In the first half of this book more general topics such as the nature of
language, its origins, the causes of linguistic changes and language
families, are gone into – the second half is, in effect, a history of the
English language.

Robin Hyman
A Dictionary of Famous Quotations £1.25

This collection took over five years to compile. Its exceptionally clear
and attractive presentation makes it a delight to read, and the lively
selection of quotations encourages the browser as well as the seeker
of specific references. The comprehensive index, with over 25,000
entries, enables one to trace a partly-remembered quotation with
maximum speed.